Compact Oxford Italian Dictionary

Italian → English
English → Italian

Editors
Pat Bulhosen
Francesca Logi
Loredana Riu

UNIVERSITY PRESS
Great Clarendon Street, Oxford, OX2 6DP,
United Kingdom

Oxford University Press is a department of the University of Oxford.
It furthers the University's objective of excellence in research, scholarship,
and education by publishing worldwide. Oxford is a registered trade mark of
Oxford University Press in the UK and in certain other countries

First Edition published in 2013

British Library Cataloguing in Publication Data
Data available

ISBN 978–0–19–966313–2

Printed in Great Britain by CPI Group (UK) Ltd, Croydon CR0 4YY

Preface

This dictionary has been designed to meet the needs of students, tourists, and all those who require quick and reliable answers to their translation questions. It provides clear guidance on selecting the most appropriate translation, illustrative examples to help with construction and usage, and precise information on grammar and style.

Focusing on everyday, idiomatic Italian and English, both spoken and written, this easy-to-use dictionary offers up-to-the-minute coverage of a wide range of vocabulary. The most appropriate new English words and senses have been selected from those sourced for recent updates to Oxford's English dictionary range, which draws on the two-billion-word Oxford English Corpus. New Italian words and senses have been drawn from an exciting initiative, the Oxford Languages Tracker, which enables us to track the latest developments in Italian and other modern languages. Approximately 2,000 of the commonest words in each language have been marked with a 'key' symbol.

This dictionary also offers a wide range of supplementary materials such as an A–Z of Italian life and culture, a calendar of festive days in Italy, a practical guide to writing letters and emails in Italian, a guide to text messaging, a section on navigating online services in Italian, and a grammar summary. A *Phrasefinder* section enables you to communicate in commonly encountered situations such as travel, shopping, eating out, and organizing leisure activities.

Visit the Oxford Dictionaries site (www.oxforddictionaries.com) today to find free current English definitions and translations in French, German, Spanish, and Italian, as well as grammar guidance, puzzles and games, and our popular blog about words and language.

Prefazione

Questo dizionario è stato creato per soddisfare le esigenze degli studenti, dei turisti e di tutti coloro che hanno bisogno di risposte rapide e sicure ai problemi di traduzione. Il lettore è guidato con chiarezza nella scelta del termine più appropriato, con esempi di uso della lingua e con indicazioni precise di grammatica e di stile.

Basandosi sull'uso idiomatico dell'inglese e dell'italiano contemporanei, scritto e parlato, questo dizionario di facile consultazione offre una trattazione aggiornata di un'ampia gamma di vocaboli. Neologismi e nuovi significati dei termini inglesi sono stati accuratamente selezionati tra quelli introdotti nei più recenti aggiornamenti dei dizionari inglesi pubblicati da Oxford University Press, che a loro volta attingono ai due miliardi di parole presenti nell'Oxford English Corpus. Neologismi e nuove accezioni di parole italiane sono stati individuate grazie ad un nuovo strumento, l'Oxford Languages Tracker, che permette di monitorare gli sviluppi più recenti dell'italiano e di altre lingue moderne. Circa 2.000 delle parole di uso più frequente in italiano e in inglese sono state segnalate con il simbolo di una 'chiave'.

Questo dizionario contiene anche un vasto repertorio di materiali supplementari: una sezione su aspetti della civiltà britannica e statunitense, le principali festività del Regno Unito e degli Stati Uniti, una guida pratica alla stesura di lettere ed e-mail in inglese, una guida agli SMS, una sezione sulla navigazione nei servizi online in lingua inglese e un compendio di grammatica. Una sezione Phrasefinder consente all'utente di comunicare in situazioni comuni come viaggiare, fare acquisti, mangiare al ristorante e organizzare attività per il tempo libero.

Contents

Introduction / Introduzione

Here is some basic information on the way the entries in this dictionary are organized.

A swung dash ~ is used to replace the headword within the entry.

Compounds are listed in alphabetical order. Remember this when looking for a word. The entry 'password', for example, is entered alphabetically – at some distance from the entry 'pass'. Likewise 'paintbrush' and 'paintpot' will have 'painter', 'pain threshold' and 'painting' entered in between.

Indicators are provided to guide the user to the best translation for a specific sense of a word. Types of indicator are:

field labels (see the list on p x), which indicate a general area of usage (commercial, computing, photography etc);

sense indicators, e.g. **bore** *n* (*of gun*) calibro *m*; (*person*) seccatore, -trice *mf*;

typical subjects of verbs, e.g. **bond** *vt* ‹*glue*› attaccare;

typical objects of verbs, placed after the translation of the verb, e.g. **boost** *vt* stimolare ‹*sales*›; sollevare ‹*morale*›;

nouns that typically go together with certain adjectives, e.g. **rich** *a* ricco; ‹*food*› pesante.

A, **B**, etc mean that the same word is being translated as a different part of speech, e.g. **partition** **A** *n* ... **B** *vt* ...

Ecco le informazioni essenziali su come sono organizzate le voci nel dizionario.

Un trattino ondulato ~ è utilizzato al posto del lemma all'interno della voce.

I vocaboli composti sono in ordine alfabetico. È importante ricordarlo quando si cerca la parola che interessa. La voce 'password', ad esempio, essendo in ordine alfabetico, compare a una certa distanza dopo la voce 'pass'. Per la stessa ragione fra 'paintbrush' and 'paintpot' compaiono 'painter', 'pain threshold' e 'painting'.

Degli indicatori vengono forniti per indirizzare l'utente verso la traduzione corrispondente al senso voluto di una parola. I tipi di indicatori sono:

etichette semantiche (vedi la lista a p x), indicanti l'ambito specifico in cui la parola viene generalmente usata in quel senso (commercio, informatica, fotografia ecc);

indicatori di significato, es.: **redazione** *f* (*ufficio*) editorial office; (*di testi*) editing;

soggetti tipici di verbi, es.: **trovarsi** *vr* ‹*luogo*› be;

complementi oggetti tipici di verbi, collocati dopo la traduzione dello stesso verbo, es: **superare** *vt* overtake ‹*veicolo*›; pass ‹*esame*›;

sostantivi che ricorrono tipicamente con certi aggettivi, es.: **solare** *a* ‹*energia, raggi*› solar; ‹*crema*› sun.

A, **B**, ecc indicano che la stessa parola viene tradotta come una

A solid black square is used to identify phrasal verbs, e.g. ■ **strip down** *vt* ... Phrasal verbs are listed in alphabetical order directly after the main verb. So 'strip down' comes after 'strip' and before 'strip cartoon'.

English pronunciation is given for the Italian user in the International Phonetic Alphabet (see p ix).

Italian stress is shown by a ˈ placed in front of the stressed syllable in a word.

Square brackets are used around parts of an expression which can be omitted without altering the sense.

The ✓ symbol marks a word identified as being among the most frequently used words in English or Italian.

diversa parte del discorso, es. **calcolatore** **A** *a* ... **B** *m* ...

Un quadratino nero viene utilizzato per indicare i phrasal verbs, ad esempio: ■ **strip down** *vt* ... I phrasal verbs si trovano in ordine alfabetico immediatamente dopo il verbo principale. Così 'strip down' viene subito dopo 'strip' e subito prima di 'strip cartoon'.

La pronuncia inglese è data usando l'Alfabetico Fonetico Internazionale (vedi p ix).

L'accento tonico nelle parole italiane è indicato dal segno ˈ collocato davanti alla sillaba accentata.

Delle parentesi quadre racchiudono parti di espressioni che possono essere omesse senza alterazioni di senso.

Il simbolo ✓ contrassegna una parola identificata come una delle parole d'uso più frequente in inglese o in italiano.

Proprietary terms / Marche depositate

This dictionary includes some words which are, or are asserted to be, proprietary names or trademarks. Their inclusion does not imply that they have acquired for legal purposes a non-proprietary or general significance, nor is any other judgment implied concerning their legal status. In cases where the editor has some evidence that a word is used as a proprietary name or trademark this is indicated by the symbol ®, but no judgement concerning the legal status of such words is made or implied thereby.

Questo dizionario include alcune parole che sono o vengono considerate nomi di marche depositate. La loro presenza non implica che abbiano acquisito legalmente un significato generale, né si suggerisce alcun altro giudizio riguardo il loro stato giuridico. Qualora il redattore abbia trovato testimonianza dell'uso di una parola come marca depositata, questa è stata contrassegnata dal simbolo ®, ma nessun giudizio riguardo lo stato giuridico di tale parola viene espresso o suggerito in tal modo.

Pronunciation of Italian

Vowels

a is broad like *a* in *father*: **casa**.
e has two sounds: closed like *ey* in *they*: **sera**; open like *e* in *egg*: **sette**.
i is like *ee* in *feet*: **venire**.
o has two sounds: closed like *o* in *show*: **croma**; open like *o* in *dog*: **bocca**.
u is like *oo* in *moon*: **luna**.

When two or more vowels come together each vowel is pronounced separately: **buono; baia**.

Consonants

b, **d**, **f**, **l**, **m**, **n**, **p**, **t**, **v** are pronounced as in English. When these are double they are sounded distinctly: **bello**.

c before **a**, **o**, or **u** and before consonants is like *k* in *king*: **cane**.
before **e** or **i** is like *ch* in *church*: **cena**.
ch is also like *k* in *king*: **chiesa**.
g before **a**, **o**, or **u** is hard like *g* in *got*: **gufo**.
before **e** or **i** is like *j* in *jelly*: **gentile**.
gh is like *g* in *gun*: **ghiaccio**.
gl when followed by **a**, **e**, **o**, or **u** is like *gl* in *glass*: **gloria**.
gli is like *lli* in *million*: **figlio**.
gn is like *ni* in *onion*: **bagno**.
h is silent.
ng is like *ng* in *finger* (not *singer*): **ringraziare**.
r is pronounced distinctly.
s between two vowels is like *s* in *rose*: **riso**.
at the beginning of a word it is like *s* in *soap*: **sapone**.
sc before *e* or *i* is like *sh* in *shell*: **scienza**.
z sounds like *ts* within a word: **fazione**; like *dz* at the beginning: **zoo**.

The stress is shown by the sign ˈ printed before the stressed syllable.

Pronuncia inglese

Simboli fonetici

Vocali e dittonghi

æ	b*a*d	ʊ	p*u*t	aʊ	n*ow*
ɑ:	*ah*	u:	t*oo*	aʊə	fl*ou*r
e	w*e*t	ə	*a*go	ɔɪ	c*oi*n
ɪ	s*i*t	ɜ:	w*or*k	ɪə	h*ere*
i:	s*ee*	eɪ	m*a*de	eə	h*ai*r
ɒ	g*o*t	əʊ	h*o*me	ʊə	p*oo*r
ɔ:	d*oo*r	aɪ	f*i*ve		
ʌ	c*u*p	aɪə	f*i*re		

Consonanti

b	*b*oy	l	*l*eg	t	*t*en
d	*d*ay	m	*m*an	tʃ	*ch*ip
dʒ	pa*g*e	n	*n*ew	θ	*th*ree
f	*f*oot	ŋ	si*ng*	ð	*th*is
g	*g*o	p	*p*en	v	*v*erb
h	*h*e	r	*r*un	w	*w*et
j	*y*es	s	*s*peak	z	hi*s*
k	*c*oat	ʃ	*sh*ip	ʒ	plea*s*ure

Note:

ˈ precede la sillaba accentata.
La vocale nasale in parole quali *nuance* è indicata nella trascrizione fonetica come ɒ̃: nju:ɒ̃s.

Abbreviations / Abbreviazioni

adjective	**adj**	aggettivo
abbreviation	**abbr**	abbreviazione
administration	**Admin**	amministrazione
adverb	**adv**	avverbio
aeronautics	**Aeron**	aeronautica
American	**AmE**	americano
anatomy	**Anat**	anatomia
archaeology	**Archaeol**	archeologia
architecture	**Archit**	architettura
astrology, astronomy	**Astr**	astrologia, astronomia
attributive	**attrib**	attributo
automobiles	**Auto**	automobile
auxiliary	**aux**	ausiliario
biology	**Biol**	biologia
botany	**Bot**	botanica
British English	**BrE**	inglese britannico
Chemistry	**Chem**	chimica
commerce	**Comm**	commercio
computers	**Comput**	informatica
conjunction	**conj**	congiunzione
cooking	**Culin**	cucina
definite article	**def art**	articolo determinativo
	ecc	eccetera
economics	**Econ**	economia
electricity	**Electr**	elettricità
et cetera	**etc**	
feminine	**f**	femminile
figurative	**fig**	figurato
finance	**Fin**	finanza
formal	**fml**	formale
geography	**Geog**	geografia
geology	**Geol**	geologia
grammar	**Gram**	grammatica
humorous	**hum**	umoristico
indefinite article	**indef art**	articolo indeterminativo
familiar	**infml**	familiare
interjection	**int**	interiezione
interrogative	**inter**	interrogativo
invariable *(no plural form)*	**inv**	invariabile
journalism	**Journ**	giornalismo
law	**Jur**	legge/giuridico
literary	**liter**	letterario
masculine	**m**	maschile
mathematics	**Math**	matematica
mechanics	**Mech**	meccanica
medicine	**Med**	medicina
meteorology	**Metereol**	meteorologia
masculine or feminine	**mf**	maschile o femminile
military	**Mil**	militare
music	**Mus**	musica
noun	**n**	sostantivo
nautical	**Naut**	nautica
old use	**old**	antiquato
pejorative	**pej**	peggiorativo
personal	**pers**	personale
photography	**Phot**	fotografia
physics	**Phys**	fisica
plural	**pl**	plurale
politics	**Pol**	politica
possessive	**poss**	possessivo
past participle	**pp**	participio passato
prefix	**pref**	prefisso
preposition	**prep**	preposizione
present tense	**pres**	presente
pronoun	**pron**	pronome
psychology	**Psych**	psicologia
past tense	**pt**	tempo passato
	qcno	qualcuno
	qcsa	qualcosa
proprietary term	**®**	marca depositata
rail	**Rail**	ferrovia
reflexive	**refl**	riflessivo
religion	**Relig**	religione
relative pronoun	**rel pron**	pronome relativo
somebody	**sb**	
school	**Sch**	scuola
singular	**sg**	singolare
slang	**sl**	gergo
something	**sth**	
suffix	**suff**	suffisso
technical	**Techn**	tecnico
telephone	**Teleph**	telefono
theatrical	**Theat**	teatrale
television	**TV**	televisione
typography	**Typ**	tipografia
university	**Univ**	università
auxiliary verb	**v aux**	verbo ausiliare
intransitive verb	**vi**	verbo intransitivo
reflexive verb	**vr**	verbo riflessivo
transitive verb	**vt**	verbo transitivo
transitive and intransitive	**vt/i**	verbo transitivo e intransitivo
vulgar	**vulg**	volgare
cultural equivalent	**≈**	equivalenza culturale

Aa

a (**ad** *before vowel*) *prep* to; (stato in luogo, tempo, età) at; (con mese, città) in; (mezzo, modo) by; **dire qualcosa a qualcuno** tell somebody something; **alle tre** at three o'clock; **a vent'anni** at the age of twenty; **a Natale** at Christmas; **a dicembre** in December; **ero al cinema** I was at the cinema; **vivo a Londra** I live in London; **a due a due** two by two; **a piedi** on *or* by foot; **maglia a maniche lunghe** long-sleeved sweater; **casa a tre piani** house with three floors; **giocare a tennis** play tennis; **50 km all'ora** 50 km an hour; **2 euro al chilo** 2 euros a kilo; **al mattino/alla sera** in the morning/evening; **a venti chilometri/due ore da qui** twenty kilometres/two hours away

'abaco *m* abacus

a'bate *m* abbot

abbacchia'mento *m* infml dejection

abbacchi'ato *adj* infml dejected, downhearted

ab'bacchio *m* [young] lamb
■ **abbacchio alla romana** spring lamb

abbaci'nare *vt* dazzle, blind; fig deceive

abbagli'ante **A** *adj* dazzling
B *m* headlight, high beam AmE; **mettere gli abbaglianti** put the headlights on full beam

abbagli'are *vt* dazzle

ab'baglio *m* blunder; **prendere un ~** make a blunder

abbaia'mento *m* barking

abbai'are *vi* bark

abba'ino *m* dormer window; (mansarda) loft

abbando'nare *vt* abandon; leave ‹*luogo*›; give up ‹*piani ecc.*›; **~ il campo** Mil desert in the face of the enemy

abbando'narsi *vr* let oneself go; **~ a** give oneself up to ‹*ricordi ecc.*›

abbando'nato *adj* abandoned

abban'dono *m* abandoning; fig abandon; (stato) neglect

abbarbi'carsi *vr* **~ a** cling to

abbassa'mento *m* (di temperatura, acqua, prezzi) drop

abbas'sare *vt* lower; turn down ‹*radio, TV*›; **~ i fari** dip the headlights

abbas'sarsi *vr* stoop; ‹*sole ecc.*› sink; fig demean oneself

ab'basso **A** *adv* below
B *int* down with

abba'stanza *adv* enough; (alquanto) quite; **~ nuovo** newish; **ne ho ~!** I've had enough!, I'm fed up!

ab'battere *vt* demolish; shoot down ‹*aereo*›; put down ‹*animale*›; topple ‹*regime*›; fig (demoralizzare) dishearten

ab'battersi *vr* (cadere) fall; fig be discouraged; **~ a terra/al suolo** fall down

abbatti'mento *m* (morale) despondency

abbat'tuto *adj* despondent, down-in-the-mouth

abba'zia *f* abbey

abbelli'mento *m* embellishment

abbel'lire *vt* embellish

abbel'lirsi *vr* adorn oneself

abbeve'rare *vt* water

abbevera'toio *m* drinking trough

abbicci *m inv* fig rudiments *pl*; **l'~ di** the ABC of

abbi'ente *adj* well-to-do

abbi'etto *adj* despicable, abject

abbiglia'mento *m* clothes *pl*; (industria) clothing industry, rag trade infml
■ **abbigliamento da bambino** children's wear; **abbigliamento da donna** ladies' wear; **abbigliamento per uomo** menswear; **abbigliamento sportivo** sportswear

abbigli'are *vt* dress

abbigli'arsi *vr* dress up

abbina'mento *m* combining

abbi'nare *vt* combine; match ‹*colori*›

abbindo'lare *vt* cheat

abbocca'mento *m* interview; (conversazione) talk

abboc'care *vi* bite; ‹*tubi*› join; fig swallow the bait

abboc'cato *adj* ‹*vino*› fairly sweet

abbof'farsi = **abbuffarsi**

abbona'mento *m* subscription; (ferroviario ecc.) season ticket; **fare l'~** take out a subscription
■ **abbonamento all'autobus** bus pass; **abbonamento mensile** monthly ticket; **abbonamento alla televisione** television licence

abbo'nare *vt* make a subscriber

abbo'narsi *vr* subscribe (**a** to); take out a season ticket (**a** for) ‹*teatro, stadio*›

abbo'nato, -a *mf* subscriber

abbon'dante *adj* abundant; ‹*quantità*› copious; ‹*nevicata*› heavy; ‹*vestiario*› roomy; **~ di** abounding in

abbondante'mente *adv* ‹*mangiare*› copiously

a

abbon'danza *f* abundance

abbon'dare *vi* abound

abbor'dabile *adj* ‹*persona*› approachable; ‹*prezzo*› reasonable

abbor'daggio *m* Mil boarding

abbor'dare *vt* board ‹*nave*›; approach ‹*persona*›; infml (attaccar bottone a) chat up; tackle ‹*compito ecc.*›

abbotto'nare *vt* button up

abbotto'nato *adj* fig tight-lipped

abbottona'tura *f* [row of] buttons; **con ~ da donna/uomo** ‹*giacca*› that buttons on the left/right

abboz'zare **A** *vt* sketch [out] ‹*disegno*›; draft ‹*documento*›; **~ un sorriso** give a little smile
B *vi* infml (rassegnarsi) resign oneself

ab'bozzo *m* (di disegno) sketch; (di documento) draft

⚷ **abbracci'are** *vt* embrace ‹*causa*›; hug, embrace ‹*persona*›; take up ‹*professione*›; fig include

ab'braccio *m* hug

abbrevi'are *vt* shorten; (ridurre) curtail; abbreviate ‹*parola*›

abbreviazi'one *f* abbreviation

abbron'zante *m* suntan lotion

abbron'zare *vt* bronze; tan ‹*pelle*›

abbron'zarsi *vr* get a tan

abbron'zato *adj* tanned

abbronza'tura *f* [sun]tan

abbrusto'lire *vt* toast; roast ‹*caffè ecc.*›

abbruti'mento *m* brutalization

abbru'tire *vt* brutalize; ‹*lavoro*› stultify

abbru'tirsi *vr* become brutalized

abbuf'farsi *vr* infml stuff oneself

abbuf'fata *f* infml blowout

abbuo'nare *vt* reduce; fig overlook ‹*mancanza, errore*›

abbu'ono *m* allowance; Sport handicap

abdi'care *vi* abdicate

abdicazi'one *f* abdication

aber'rante *adj* aberrant

aberrazi'one *f* aberration

abe'taia *f* wood of fir trees

a'bete *m* fir

abi'etto *adj* despicable

abiezi'one *f* degradation

abige'ato *m* Jur cattle stealing, rustling

'abile *adj* able; (idoneo) fit; (astuto) clever

abilità *f inv* ability; (idoneità) fitness; (astuzia) cleverness

abili'tante *adj* **corso ~** [officially recognized] training course

abili'tare *vt* qualify

abili'tato *adj* qualified

abilitazi'one *f* qualification; (titolo) diploma

abil'mente *adv* ably; (con astuzia) cleverly

abis'sale *adj* abysmal

a'bisso *m* abyss

abi'tabile *adj* inhabitable

abitabilità *f inv* fitness for human habitation; **licenza di ~** *document certifying that a building is fit for human habitation*

abi'tacolo *m* Auto passenger compartment

abi'tante *mf* inhabitant

⚷ **abi'tare** *vi* live

abi'tato **A** *adj* inhabited
B *m* built-up area

abitazi'one *f* house; **crisi delle abitazioni** housing problem

abi'tino *m* Relig scapular

⚷ **'abito** *m* (da donna) dress; (da uomo) suit; **abiti** *pl* clothes
■ **abito da ballo** ball dress; **abito da cerimonia** formal dress; **abito da cocktail** cocktail dress; **abito mentale** mentality; **'abito scuro'** (su inviti) 'black tie'; **abito da sera** evening dress; **abito talare** cassock; **abito da uomo** suit

abitu'ale *adj* usual, habitual

abitual'mente *adv* usually

⚷ **abitu'are** *vt* accustom

abitu'arsi *vr* **~ a** get used to

abitu'ato *adj* **~ a** used to

abitudi'nario, -a **A** *adj* of fixed habits
B *mf* person of fixed habits

⚷ **abi'tudine** *f* habit; **d'~** usually; **per ~** out of habit; **avere l'~ di fare qualcosa** be in the habit of doing something; **abitudini** *pl* customs

abiu'rare *vt* renounce

abla'tivo *m* ablative

abluzi'oni *fpl* **fare le ~** wash

abnegazi'one *f* self-sacrifice

ab'norme *adj* abnormal

abo'lire *vt* abolish; repeal ‹*legge*›

abolizi'one *f* abolition; (di legge) repeal

abolizio'nismo *m* abolitionism

abolizio'nista *adj & nmf* abolitionist

abomi'nevole *adj* abominable

abo'rigeno, -a *adj & nmf* aboriginal

abor'rire *vt* abhor

abor'tire *vi* miscarry; (volontariamente) have an abortion; fig fail

abor'tista *adj* pro-choice

abor'tivo *adj* abortive

a'borto *m* miscarriage; (volontario) abortion

abrasi'one *f* abrasion

abra'sivo *adj & nm* abrasive

abro'gare *vt* repeal

abroga'tivo *adj* **referendum ~** referendum to repeal a law

abrogazi'one *f* repeal

abruz'zese **A** *adj* Abruzzi *attrib*
B *mf* person from the Abruzzi
C *m* Abruzzi dialect

⚷ key word

'abside *f* apse

abu'lia *f* apathy

a'bulico *adj* apathetic

abu'sare *vi* ~ **di** abuse; over-indulge in ‹*alcol*›; (approfittare di) take advantage of; (violentare) rape

abusi'vismo *m* large-scale abuse
■ **abusivismo edilizio** building without planning permission

abu'sivo *adj* illegal

a'buso *m* abuse; **'ogni ~ sarà punito'** 'penalty for misuse'
■ **abuso di confidenza** breach of confidence; **abusi** *pl* **sessuali** sexual abuse

a.C. *abbr* (**avanti Cristo**) BC

a'cacia *f* acacia

'acaro *m* Zool mite

'acca *f* infml **non ho capito un'~** I understood damn all

acca'demia *f* academy
■ **Accademia di Belle Arti** Academy of Fine Arts; **accademia militare** military academy

acca'demico, -a **A** *adj* academic
B *mf* academician

acca'dere *vi* happen; **accada quel che accada** come what may

acca'duto *m* event

accalappia'cani *m inv* dog catcher

accalappi'are *vt* catch; fig allure

accal'care *vt* cram together

accal'carsi *vr* crowd

accal'darsi *vr* get overheated; (per fatica) get hot; fig get excited

accal'dato *adj* overheated; (per fatica) hot; fig excited

accalo'rarsi *vr* get excited

accampa'mento *m* camp

accam'pare *vt* fig put forth

accam'parsi *vr* camp

accani'mento *m* tenacity; (odio) rage

acca'nirsi *vr* persist; (infierire) rage

accanita'mente *adv* ‹*odiare*› fiercely; ‹*insistere*› persistently; ‹*lavorare*› assiduously

acca'nito *adj* persistent; ‹*odio*› fierce; ‹*fumatore*› inveterate; ‹*lavoratore*› assiduous

ac'canto *adv* near; ~ **a** *prep* next to; **la ragazza della porta ~** the girl next door

accanto'nare *vt* set aside; Mil billet

accaparra'mento *m* hoarding; Comm cornering

accapar'rare *vt* hoard

accapar'rarsi *vr* grab; corner ‹*mercato*›

accaparra|'tore, -trice *mf* hoarder

accapigli'arsi *vr* scuffle; (litigare) squabble

accappa'toio *m* bathrobe; (per spiaggia) beach robe

accappo'nare *vt* **fare ~ la pelle a qualcuno** make somebody's flesh creep

accarez'zare *vt* caress, stroke; fig cherish

accartocci'are *vt* scrunch up

accartocci'arsi *vr* curl up

acca'sarsi *vr* get married

accasci'arsi *vr* flop down; fig lose heart

accata'stare *vt* pile up

accatti'vante *adj* beguiling

accatti'varsi *vr* ~ **le simpatie/la stima/l'affetto di qualcuno** gain somebody's sympathy/respect/affection

accatto'naggio *m* begging

accat'tone, -a *mf* beggar

accaval'lare *vt* cross ‹*gambe*›

accaval'larsi *vr* pile up; fig overlap

acce'cante *adj* ‹*luce*› blinding

acce'care **A** *vt* blind
B *vi* go blind

ac'cedere *vi* access; ~ **a** enter; (acconsentire) comply with; Comput access

accele'rare **A** *vi* accelerate
B *vt* speed up, accelerate; ~ **il passo** quicken one's pace

accele'rata *f* sudden acceleration

accele'rato *adj* rapid

accelera'tore *m* accelerator
■ **acceleratore grafico** Comput graphics accelerator

accelerazi'one *f* acceleration

ac'cendere *vt* light; turn on, switch on ‹*luce, TV ecc.*›; fig inflame; **ha da ~?** have you got a light?

ac'cendersi *vr* catch fire; (illuminarsi) light up; fig become inflamed; ‹*TV, computer*› turn on, switch on

accendi'gas *m inv* gas lighter; (su cucina) automatic ignition

accen'dino *m* lighter

accendi'sigari *m inv* cigar lighter

accen'nare **A** *vt* indicate; hum ‹*melodia*›; give a hint of ‹*sorriso*›
B *vi* ~ **a** beckon to; fig hint at; (far l'atto di) make as if to; **accenna a piovere** it looks like rain

ac'cenno *m* gesture; (con il capo) nod; fig hint

accensi'one *f* lighting; (di motore) ignition

accen'tare *vt* accent; (con accento tonico) stress

accentazi'one *f* accentuation

ac'cento *m* accent; (tonico) stress
■ **accento acuto** acute [accent]; **accento circonflesso** circumflex [accent]; **accento grave** grave [accent]

accentra'mento *m* centralizing

accen'trare *vt* centralize

accentra'tore *adj* ‹*persona*› who refuses to delegate; ‹*politica*› of centralization

accentu'are *vt* accentuate

accentu'arsi *vr* become more noticeable

accentu'ato *adj* marked

accerchia'mento *m* surrounding

accerchi'are *vt* surround
accerchi'ato *adj* surrounded
accer'tabile *adj* ascertainable
accerta'mento *m* check; **accertamenti** *pl* **[medici]** tests
accer'tare *vt* ascertain; (controllare) check; assess ‹*reddito*›
ac'ceso *adj* lighted; ‹*radio, TV ecc.*› on; ‹*colore*› bright
acces'sibile *adj* accessible; ‹*persona*› approachable; ‹*spesa*› reasonable
ac'cesso *m* access; Med (di rabbia) fit; **'vietato l'~'** 'no entry'; **'~ riservato a ...'** 'access restricted to ...'
■ **accesso diretto** Comput direct access; **accesso disabili** wheelchair access; **accesso a Internet** Comput Internet access; **accesso multiplo** Comput multi-access; **accesso remoto** Comput remote access
accessori'ato *adj* accessorized
acces'sorio **A** *adj* accessory; (secondario) of secondary importance
B *m* accessory; **accessori** *pl* (rifiniture) fittings
■ **accessori** *pl* **per il bagno** bathroom fittings; **accessori** *pl* **moda** fashion accessories
ac'cetta *f* hatchet
accet'tabile *adj* acceptable
accet'tare *vt* accept; (aderire a) agree to
accettazi'one *f* acceptance; (luogo) reception; **[banco] accettazione** check-in [desk]; **accettazione [bagagli]** check-in
ac'cetto *adj* agreeable; **essere bene ~** be very welcome
accezi'one *f* meaning
acchiap'pare *vt* catch
+acchiotto *suff* **lupacchiotto** *nm* wolf cub; (affettuoso) baby wolf; **orsacchiotto** *nm* teddy bear; **fessacchiotto** *nm* nitwit
ac'chito *m* **di primo ~** at first
acciac'care *vt* crush; fig prostrate
acciac'cato, -a *adj* **essere ~** ache all over
acci'acco *m* infirmity; *pl* **acciacchi** (afflizioni) aches and pains
acciaie'ria *f* steelworks
acci'aio *m* steel
■ **acciaio inossidabile** stainless steel
acciambel'larsi *vr* curl up
acciden'tale *adj* accidental
accidental'mente *adv* accidentally
acciden'tato *adj* ‹*terreno*› uneven
acci'dente *m* accident; Med stroke; **non capisce/non vede un ~** infml he doesn't understand/can't see a damn thing; **mandare un ~ a qualcuno** infml tell somebody to go to hell
acci'denti *int* infml damn!; **~ a te!** damn you!, blast you!
ac'cidia *f* sloth
accigli'arsi *vr* frown
accigli'ato *adj* frowning
ac'cingersi *vr* **~ a** be about to
+accio *suff* **erbaccia** *nf* weed; **donnaccia** *nf* tart; **faticaccia** *nf* hard slog; **lavoraccio** *nm* (lavoro faticoso) helluva job infml; (lavoro malfatto) botched job; **fattaccio** *nm* (hum) foul deed; **parolaccia** *nf* swear word; **avaraccio** *nm* skinflint
acciotto'lato *m* cobbled paving, cobblestones *pl*
acci'picchia *int* good Lord!
acciuf'fare *vt* catch
acci'uga *f* anchovy
accla'mare *vt* applaud; (eleggere) acclaim
acclamazi'one *f* applause
acclima'tare *vt* acclimatize
acclima'tarsi *vr* get acclimatized
acclimatazi'one *f* acclimatization
ac'cludere *vt* enclose
ac'cluso *adj* enclosed
accocco'larsi *vr* squat
acco'darsi *vr* tag along
accogli'ente *adj* welcoming; (confortevole) cosy
accogli'enza *f* welcome
ac'cogliere *vt* receive; (con piacere) welcome; (contenere) hold
accol'lare *vt* **~ qualcosa a qualcuno** fig saddle somebody with something
accol'larsi *vr* take on ‹*responsabilità, debiti, doveri*›
accol'lato *adj* ‹*maglia*› high necked
accoltel'lare *vt* knife
accoman'dante *mf* Jur sleeping partner
accomanda'tario, -a *mf* Jur general partner
accoman'dita *f* Jur limited partnership
■ **accomandita per azioni** limited partnership based on shares
accomia'tare *vt* dismiss
accomia'tarsi *vr* take one's leave (**da** of)
accomoda'mento *m* arrangement
accomo'dante *adj* accommodating
accomo'dare *vt* (riparare) mend; (disporre) arrange
accomo'darsi *vr* make oneself at home; **si accomodi!** come in!; (si sieda) take a seat!
accompagna'mento *m* accompaniment; (seguito) retinue
accompa'gnare *vt* accompany; **~ qualcuno a casa** see somebody home; **~ qualcuno alla porta** show somebody to the door; **~ qualcuno con lo sguardo** follow somebody with one's eyes
accompa'gnarsi *vr* ‹*cibi, colori ecc.*› go [well] together; **~ con** *o* **a qualcuno** accompany somebody
accompagna|'tore, -trice *mf* companion; (di comitiva) escort; Mus accompanist

key word

■ **~ turistico** tour guide
accomu'nare *vt* pool
acconci'are *vt* arrange
acconci'arsi *vr* do one's hair
acconcia'tura *f* hairstyle; (ornamento) headdress; **'acconciature'** 'ladies' hairdresser'
accondiscen'dente *adj* too obliging
accondiscen'denza *f excessive desire to please*
accondi'scendere *vi* **~ a** condescend; comply with ‹*desiderio*›; (acconsentire) consent to
acconsen'tire *vi* consent
acconten'tare *vt* satisfy
acconten'tarsi *vr* be content (**di** with)
ac'conto *m* deposit; **in ~** on account; **lasciare un ~** leave a deposit
■ **acconto di dividendo** interim dividend
accop'pare *vt* infml bump off
accoppia'mento *m* coupling; (di animali) mating
accoppi'are *vt* couple; mate ‹*animali*›
accoppi'arsi *vr* pair off; ‹*animali*› mate
accoppi'ata *f* (scommessa) *bet placed on two horses for first and second place*; **sono una strana ~** they make strange bedfellows; **accoppiata vincente** fig winning combination
accoppia'tore *m*
■ **accoppiatore acustico** Comput acoustic coupler
acco'rato *adj* sorrowful
accorci'are *vt* shorten
accorci'arsi *vr* get shorter
accor'dare *vt* concede; match ‹*colori ecc.*›; Mus tune
accor'darsi *vr* agree
accorda|'tore, -trice *mf* Mus tuner
ac'cordo *m* agreement; Mus chord; (armonia) harmony; **andare d'~** get on well; **d'~!** agreed!; **essere d'~** agree; **in ~ con** in collusion with; **prendere accordi con qualcuno** make arrangements with somebody
■ **accordo collettivo** joint agreement
ac'corgersi *vr* **~ di** notice; (capire) realize
accorgi'mento *m* shrewdness; (espediente) device
accorpa'mento *m* amalgamation
accor'pare *vt* amalgamate
ac'correre *vi* hasten
accorta'mente *adv* astutely
accor'tezza *f* (previdenza) forethought
ac'corto *adj* shrewd; **mal ~** incautious
accosta'mento *m* (di colori) combination
acco'stare *vt* draw close to; approach ‹*persona*›; put ajar ‹*porta ecc.*›
acco'starsi *vr* **~ a** come near to
accovacci'arsi *vr* crouch, squat down
accovacci'ato *adj* squatting
accoz'zaglia *f* jumble; (di persone) mob
accoz'zare *vt* **~ colori** mix colours that clash
accredi'tabile *adj* reliable
accredita'mento *m* credit
■ **accreditamento tramite bancogiro** Bank Giro Credit
accredi'tare *vt* confirm ‹*notizia*›; Comm credit
accredi'tato *adj* accredited; ‹*notizia*› reliable
ac'crescere *vt* increase
ac'crescersi *vr* grow larger
accresci'mento *m* increase
accresci'tivo *adj* augmentative
accucci'arsi *vr* ‹*cane*› lie down; ‹*persona*› crouch
accu'dire *vi* **~ a** attend to
accumu'lare *vt* accumulate
accumu'larsi *vr* pile up, accumulate
accumula'tore *m* accumulator; Auto, Comput battery
accumulazi'one *f* accumulation
ac'cumulo *m* (di merce) build-up
accurata'mente *adv* carefully
accura'tezza *f* care
accu'rato *adj* careful
ac'cusa *f* accusation; Jur charge; **essere in stato di ~** Jur have been charged; **mettere qualcuno sotto ~** Jur charge somebody; **la Pubblica Accusa** Jur the public prosecutor
accu'sare *vt* accuse; Jur charge; complain of ‹*dolore*›; **~ ricevuta di** Comm acknowledge receipt of
accusa'tivo *m* Gram accusative
accu'sato, -a *mf* accused
accusa'tore **A** *adj* accusing
B *m* Jur prosecutor
a'cerbo *adj* sharp; (non maturo) unripe
'acero *m* maple
a'cerrimo *adj* implacable
ace'tato *m* acetate
a'ceto *m* vinegar
■ **aceto di vino** wine vinegar
ace'tone *m* nail polish remover
ace'tosa *f* Culin [edible] sorrel
aceto'sella *f* Bot sorrel
A.C.I. *nf abbr* (**Automobile Club d'Italia**) Italian Automobile Association, ≈ AAA AmE, ≈ RAC BrE
acidità *f inv* acidity
■ **acidità di stomaco** acid stomach
'acido **A** *adj* acid; ‹*persona*› sour
B *m* acid
■ **~ cloridrico** hydrochloric acid
a'cidulo *adj* slightly sour
'acino *m* berry; (chicco) grape
'acme *f* acme
'acne *f* acne
'acqua *f* water; **fare ~** Naut leak; **~ in bocca!** fig mum's the word!; **avere l'~ alla gola,**

a

essere con l'~ alla gola fig be pushed for time; **ho fatto un buco nell'~** fig I had no luck whatsoever; **in cattive acque** in deep water; **navigare in cattive acque** be in financial difficulties

■ **acqua calda** hot water; **acqua di Colonia** eau de Cologne; **acqua corrente** running water; **acqua dolce** fresh water; **acqua minerale** mineral water; **acqua minerale gassata** fizzy mineral water; **acqua naturale** still mineral water; **acqua potabile** drinking water; **acqua del rubinetto** tap water; **acqua salata** salt water; **acqua saponata** suds; **acqua tonica** tonic water

acqua'forte *f* etching
acqua'gym *f* aquarobics *sg*
ac'quaio *m* sink
acquama'rina *adj* aquamarine
acquapark *m inv* water park
acqua'plano *m* hydroplane
acqua'ragia *f* white spirit
acqua'rello *m* watercolour
ac'quario *m* aquarium, fish tank; Astr Aquarius
acquartie'rare *vt* Mil billet
acqua'santa *f* holy water
acquasanti'era *f* font
acqua'scivolo *m* water slide
acqua'scooter *m inv* water scooter
ac'quata *f* infml downpour
ac'quatico *adj* aquatic; **sport acquatico** water sport
acquat'tarsi *vr* crouch
acqua'vite *f* brandy
acquaz'zone *m* downpour
acque'dotto *m* aqueduct
'acqueo *adj* **vapore ~** steam, water vapour
acque'rello *m* watercolour
acquicol'tura *f* aquaculture
acquie'scente *adj* acquiescent
acquie'tare *vt* appease; calm ‹*dolore*›
acquie'tarsi *vr* calm down
acqui'rente *mf* purchaser
acqui'sire *vt* acquire
acqui'sito *adj* acquired
acquisizi'one *f* attainment
✓ **acqui'stare** *vt* purchase; (ottenere) acquire; **~ in** ‹*prestigio, bellezza*› gain in
a'cquisto *m* purchase; **uscire per acquisti** go shopping; **fare acquisti** shop; **ufficio acquisti** purchasing department

■ **acquisto rateale** hire purchase, HP, installment plan AmE; **acquisto d'impulso** impulse buy; **acquisto a termine** Fin forward buying

acqui'trino *m* marsh
acquo'lina *f* **far venire l'~ in bocca a qualcuno** make somebody's mouth water; **ho l'~ in bocca** my mouth is watering

✓ key word

a'cquoso *adj* watery
'acre *adj* acrid; (al gusto) sour; fig harsh
a'credine *f* acridity; (al gusto) sourness; fig harshness
acre'mente *adv* acridly
a'crilico *m* acrylic
a'critico *adj* acritical
a'crobata *mf* acrobat
acro'batico *adj* acrobatic
acroba'zia *f* acrobatics *pl* **fare ~** fig do acrobatics
a'cronimo *m* acronym
a'cropoli *f* acropolis
acu'ire *vt* sharpen
acu'irsi *vr* become more intense
a'culeo *m* sting; Bot prickle
a'cume *m* acumen
acumi'nato *adj* pointed
a'custica *f* acoustics *pl*
acustica'mente *adv* acoustically
a'custico *adj* acoustic
acuta'mente *adv* shrewdly
acu'tezza *f* acuteness; fig shrewdness; (di suoni) shrillness
acutiz'zare *vt* aggravate ‹*dolore*›
acutiz'zarsi *vr* become worse
a'cuto **A** *adj* sharp; ‹*suono*› shrill; ‹*freddo, odore*› intense; Gram, Math, Med acute
B *m* Mus high note
ad **A** *prep* (*before vowel*) = **a**
B *m* (*abbr* **amministratore delegato**) managing director
A.D. *abbr* Pol (**Alleanza Democratica**) Democratic Alliance
adagi'are *vt* lay down
adagi'arsi *vr* lie down
a'dagio **A** *adv* slowly
B *m* Mus adagio; (proverbio) adage
ada'mitico *adj* **in costume ~** in one's birthday suit, stark naked
adat'tabile *adj* adaptable
adattabilità *f inv* adaptability
adatta'mento *m* adaptation; **avere spirito di ~** be adaptable

■ **adattamento cinematografico** film adaptation, adaptation for the cinema

adat'tare *vt* adapt; (aggiustare) fit
adat'tarsi *vr* adapt
adatta'tore *m* adaptor
✓ **a'datto** *adj* suitable (**a** for) (giusto) right
addebita'mento *m* debit

■ **addebitamento diretto** direct debit

addebi'tare *vt* debit; fig ascribe ‹*colpa*›
ad'debito *m* charge
addensa'mento *m* thickening; (di persone) gathering
adden'sare *vt* thicken
adden'sarsi *vr* thicken; (affollarsi) gather

adden'tare *vt* bite
adden'trarsi *vr* penetrate
ad'dentro *adv* deeply; **essere ~ in** be in on
addestra'mento *m* training
■ **addestramento iniziale** basic training
adde'strare *vt* train
adde'strarsi *vr* train
addestra|'tore, -trice *mf* trainer
ad'detto, -a **A** *adj* assigned
B *mf* employee; (diplomatico) attaché
■ **addetti** *pl* **ai lavori** persons involved in the work; **'vietato l'ingresso ai non addetti ai lavori'** 'staff only'; **addetto commerciale** salesman; **addetto culturale** cultural attaché; **addetto stampa** information officer, press officer; **addetto ai traslochi** removal man
addì *adv* **~ 15 settembre 2011** on 15th September 2011
addi'accio *m* **dormire all'~** sleep in the open
addi'etro *adv* (indietro) back; (nel passato) before
ad'dio *nm & int* goodbye
■ **addio al celibato** stag night, stag party; **addio al nubilato** hen night; **cena d'addio** farewell dinner
addirit'tura *adv* (perfino) even; (assolutamente) absolutely; **~!** really!
ad'dirsi *vr* **~ a** suit
addi'tare *vt* point at; (per identificare) point out; fig point to
addi'tivo *adj & nm* additive
addizio'nale **A** *adj* additional
B *f* (imposta) surtax
addizional'mente *adv* additionally
addizio'nare *vt* add [up]
addiziona'trice *f* adding machine
addizi'one *f* addition
addob'bare *vt* decorate
ad'dobbo *m* decoration
addol'cire *vt* sweeten; tone down ‹*colore*›; fig soften
addol'cirsi *vr* fig mellow
addolo'rare *vt* grieve
addolo'rarsi *vr* be upset (**per** by)
addolo'rato *adj* pained, distressed
ad'dome *m* abdomen
addomesti'care *vt* tame
addomestica'tore, -trice *mf* tamer
addomi'nale **A** *adj* abdominal
B *mpl* **addominali** abdominals
addormen'tare *vt* put to sleep
addormen'tarsi *vr* go to sleep
addormen'tato *adj* asleep; fig slow
addos'sare *vt* **~ a** (appoggiare) lean against; (attribuire) lay on
addos'sarsi *vr* (ammassarsi) crowd; shoulder ‹*responsabilità ecc.*›
ad'dosso *adv* on; **~ a** *prep* on; (molto vicino) right next to; **andare/venire ~ qualcuno** run into somebody; **mettere gli occhi ~ a qualcuno/qualcosa** hanker after somebody/something; **non mettermi le mani ~!** keep your hands off me!; **stare ~ a qualcuno** fig be on somebody's back; **farsela ~** infml (bisogni corporali) dirty oneself; (pipì) wet oneself
ad'durre *vt* produce ‹*prova, documento*›; give ‹*pretesto, esempio*›
adegua'mento *m* adjustment
adegu'are *vt* adjust
adegu'arsi *vr* conform
adeguata'mente *adv* suitably
adegua'tezza *f* suitability
adegu'ato *adj* suitable; **~ a** suited to, suitable for
a'dempiere *vt* fulfil
adempi'mento *m* fulfilment
adem'pire *vt* fulfil
ade'noidi *fpl* adenoids
a'depto, -a *mf* adherent
ade'rente **A** *adj* adhesive; ‹*vestito*› tight
B *mf* follower
ade'renza *f* adhesion; **aderenze** *pl* connections
ade'rire *vi* **~ a** stick to, adhere to; support ‹*sciopero, petizione*›; agree to ‹*richiesta*›
adesca'mento *m* Jur soliciting
ade'scare *vt* bait; fig entice
adesca'trice *f* fille de joie
adesi'one *f* adhesion; fig agreement
ade'sivo **A** *adj* adhesive
B *m* sticker; Auto bumper sticker
a'desso *adv* now; (poco fa) just now; (tra poco) any moment now; **da ~ in poi** from now on; **per ~** for the moment; **fino ~** up till now
adia'cente *adj* adjacent; **~ a** next to
adia'cenze *fpl* adjacent areas
adi'bire *vt* **~ a** put to use as
'adipe *m* adipose tissue
adi'poso *adj* adipose
adi'rarsi *vr* get irate
adi'rato *adj* irate
a'dire *vt* resort to; **~ le vie legali** take legal proceedings; **~ la successione** Jur take possession of an inheritance
'adito *m* **dare ~ a** give rise to
ADM *fpl abbr* (**Armi di Distruzione di Massa**) WMD
adocchi'are *vt* eye; (con desiderio) covet
adole'scente *adj & nmf* adolescent *attrib*
adole'scenza *f* adolescence
adolescenzi'ale *adj* adolescent
adombra'mento *m* darkening
adom'brare *vt* darken; fig veil
adom'brarsi *vr* (offendersi) take offence
adope'rare *vt* use
adope'rarsi *vr* take trouble
ado'rabile *adj* adorable

a

⚷ **ado'rare** *vt* adore
adorazi'one *f* adoration; **in ~** adoring
ador'nare *vt* adorn
a'dorno *adj* adorned (**di** with)
adot'tare *vt* adopt
adot'tivo *adj* adoptive
adozi'one *f* adoption
adrena'lina *f* adrenalin
adri'atico **A** *adj* Adriatic
B *m* **l'Adriatico** the Adriatic
adu'lare *vt* flatter
adula|'tore, -trice *mf* flatterer
adula'torio *adj* sycophantic
adulazi'one *f* flattery
a'dultera *f* adulteress
adulte'rare *vt* adulterate
adulte'rato *adj* adulterated
adulte'rino *adj* adulterous
adul'terio *m* adultery
a'dultero **A** *adj* adulterous
B *m* adulterer
⚷ **a'dulto, -a** *adj & nmf* adult; (maturo) mature
adu'nanza *f* assembly
adu'nare *vt* gather
adu'nata *f* Mil parade
a'dunco *adj* hooked
adunghi'are *vt* claw
ae'rare *vt* air ‹*stanza*›
aera'tore *m* ventilator
aerazi'one *f* ventilation
a'ereo **A** *adj* aerial; (dell'aviazione) air *attrib*
B *m* aeroplane, plane; **andare in ~** fly
■ **aereo da carico** cargo plane; **aereo da guerra** warplane; **aereo di linea** airliner; **aereo navetta** shuttle; **aereo a reazione** jet [plane]
ae'robica *f* aerobics *sg*
ae'robico *adj* aerobic
aerodi'namica *f* aerodynamics *sg*
aerodi'namico *adj* aerodynamic
aero'grafo *m* airbrush
aero'gramma *m* aerogramme
aero'linea *f* airline
aero'mobile *m* aircraft
aeromo'dello *m* model aircraft
aero'nautica *adj n* aeronautics *sg*; Mil Air Force
aero'nautico *adj* aeronautical
aerona'vale *adj* air and sea *attrib*
⚷ **aero'plano** *m* aeroplane
aero'porto *m* airport
aeroportu'ale *adj* airport *attrib*
aero'scalo *m* cargo and servicing area
aero'sol *m inv* aerosol
■ **apparecchio per aerosol** vaporizer
aerospazi'ale *adj* aerospace *attrib*
aero'statico *adj*
■ **pallone aerostatico** aerostat

⚷ key word

ae'rostato *m* aerostat
aerostazi'one *f* air terminal
aerosti'ere *m* balloonist
aero'via *f* air corridor
A.F. *abbr* (**alta frequenza**) HF
'afa *f* sultriness
af'fabile *adj* affable
affabilità *f inv* affability
affaccen'darsi *vr* busy oneself (**a** with)
⚷ **affacci'arsi** *vr* show oneself; **~ alla finestra** appear at the window
affacen'dato *adj* busy
affa'mare *vt* starve [out]
affa'mato *adj* starving
affan'nare *vt* leave breathless
affan'narsi *vr* busy oneself; (agitarsi) get worked up
affan'nato *adj* breathless; **dal respiro ~** wheezy
af'fanno *m* breathlessness; fig worry; **essere in ~ per** be anxious about
affannosa'mente *adv* breathlessly
affan'noso *adj* exhausting; **respiro ~** heavy breathing
⚷ **af'fare** *m* matter; (occasione) bargain; Comm transaction, deal; **pensa agli affari tuoi** mind your own business; **non sono affari tuoi** infml it's none of your business; **fare affari d'oro** have a field day; **affari** *pl* business; **d'affari** ‹*uomo, cena, viaggio*› business; **affari** *pl* **esteri** foreign affairs; **ministro degli affari esteri** Foreign Secretary BrE, Secretary of State AmE
affa'rismo *m* derog wheeling and dealing
affa'rista *mf* wheeler-dealer
affasci'nante *adj* fascinating; ‹*persona, sorriso*› bewitching
affasci'nare *vt* bewitch; fig charm
affastel'lare *vt* tie up in bundles
affatica'mento *m* fatigue
affati'care *vt* tire; (sfinire) exhaust
affati'carsi *vr* tire oneself out; (affannarsi) strive
affati'cato *adj* fatigued, suffering from fatigue; **~ dal troppo lavoro** overworked
⚷ **af'fatto** *adv* completely; **non ... ~** not ... at all; **niente ~!** not at all!
⚷ **affer'mare** *vt* affirm; (sostenere) assert
affer'marsi *vr* establish oneself
affermativa'mente *adv* in the affirmative
afferma'tivo *adj* affirmative
affer'mato *adj* established
affermazi'one *f* assertion; (successo) achievement
affer'rare *vt* seize; catch ‹*oggetto*›; (capire) grasp; **~ al volo** fig be quick on the uptake
affer'rarsi *vr* **~ a** grasp at, clutch at
affet'tare *vt* slice; (ostentare) affect

affet'tato **A** *adj* sliced; ‹*sorriso, maniere*› affected
B *m* cold meat, sliced meat
affetta'trice *f* bacon slicer
affettazi'one *f* affectation
affet'tivo *adj* affective; **rapporto affettivo** emotional tie
af'fetto¹ *m* affection; **con ~** affectionately; **gli affetti familiari** family ties
af'fetto² *adj* **~ da** suffering from
affettuosa'mente *adv* affectionately
affettuosità *f inv* (gesto) affectionate gesture
affettu'oso *adj* affectionate
affezio'narsi *vr* **~ a** grow fond of
affezio'nato *adj* devoted, attached (**a** to)
affezi'one *f* affection; Med ailment
affian'care *vt* put side by side; Mil flank; fig support
affian'carsi *vr* come side by side; fig stand together, stand shoulder to shoulder; **~ a qualcuno** fig help somebody out
affiata'mento *m* harmony
affia'tarsi *vr* get on well together
affia'tato *adj* close-knit; **una coppia affiatata** a very close couple
affibbi'are *vt* **~ qualcosa a qualcuno** saddle somebody with something; **~ un pugno a qualcuno** let fly at somebody
affi'dabile *adj* reliable, dependable
affidabilità *f inv* reliability, dependability
affida'mento *m* Jur (dei minori) custody; **fare ~ su qualcuno** rely on somebody; **non dare ~ (a qualcuno)** not inspire confidence (in somebody)
affi'dare *vt* entrust
affi'darsi *vr* **~ a** rely on
affida'tario *adj* (famiglia) foster
af'fido *m* **un bambino in ~** a foster child
affievoli'mento *m* weakening
affievo'lirsi *vr* grow weak
af'figgere *vt* affix
affilacol'telli *m inv* knife sharpener
affi'lare *vt* sharpen
affili'are *vt* affiliate
affili'arsi *vt* become affiliated
affiliazi'one *f* affiliation
affi'nare *vt* sharpen; (perfezionare) refine
affinché *conj* so that, in order that
af'fine *adj* similar
affinità *f inv* affinity
affiora'mento *m* emergence; Naut surfacing
affio'rare *vi* emerge; fig come to light
affissi'one *f* bill posting; **'divieto di ~'** 'stick no bills'
af'fisso *m* bill; Gram affix
affitta'camere **A** *m inv* landlord
B *f inv* landlady
affit'tare *vt* (dare in affitto) let; (prendere in affitto) rent
■ **af'fittasi** to let, for rent
af'fitto *m* rent; **contratto d'~** lease; **dare in ~** let; **prendere in ~** rent
affittu'ario, -a *mf* Jur lessee
af'fliggere *vt* torment
af'fliggersi *vr* distress oneself
af'flitto *adj* distressed
afflizi'one *f* distress; fig affliction
afflosci'are *vt* **la pioggia ha afflosciato le foglie** the rain has made the leaves go all limp
afflosci'arsi *vr* become floppy; (accasciarsi) flop down
afflu'ente *adj & nm* tributary
afflu'enza *f* flow; (di gente) crowd
afflu'ire *vi* flow; fig pour in
af'flusso *m* influx
affoga'mento *m* drowning
affo'gare *vt & vi* drown; Culin poach; **~ in** fig be swamped with
affo'garsi *vr* (suicidarsi) drown oneself
affo'gato *adj* ‹*persona*› drowned; ‹*uova*› poached
■ **affogato al caffè** *ice cream with hot espresso poured over it*
affolla'mento *m* crowd
affol'lare *vt* crowd
affol'larsi *vr* crowd
affol'lato *adj* crowded
affonda'mento *m* sinking
affon'dare *vt & vi* sink
affon'darsi *vr* sink
affossa'mento *m* (avvallamento) pothole; fig burial
affran'care *vt* redeem ‹*bene*›; stamp ‹*lettera*›; free ‹*schiavo*›
affran'carsi *vr* free oneself
affran'cato *adj* ‹*lettera*› stamped; ‹*schiavo*› freed; **già ~** ‹*busta*› prepaid
affranca'trice *f* franking machine, franker
affranca'tura *f* stamping; (di spedizione) postage
■ **affrancatura a carico del destinatario** Freepost; **affrancatura per l'estero** postage abroad
af'franto *adj* prostrate with grief, grief-stricken; (esausto) worn out
affre'scare *vt* paint a fresco on
af'fresco *m* fresco
affret'tare *vt* speed up
affret'tarsi *vr* hurry
affrettata'mente *adv* hastily
affret'tato *adj* ‹*passo*› fast; ‹*decisione*› hasty; ‹*lavoro*› rushed
affron'tare *vt* face; confront ‹*nemico*›; meet ‹*spese*›
affron'tarsi *vr* clash

a

af'fronto *m* affront, insult; **fare un ~ a qualcuno** insult somebody
affumi'care *vt* fill with smoke; Culin smoke
affumi'cato *adj ‹prosciutto, formaggio›* smoked; *‹lenti, vetro›* tinted
affuso'lare *vt* taper [off]
affuso'lato *adj* tapering
Af'ganistan *m* Afghanistan
af'gano *adj & nmf* Afghani, Afghan
AFI *nm abbr* (**Alfabeto Fonetico Internazionale**) IPA
aficio'nado, -a *mf* aficionado
'afide *m* aphid
'afono *adj* (rauco) hoarse
afo'risma *m* aphorism
a'foso *adj* sultry
'Africa *f* Africa
■ **Africa orientale** East Africa; **Africa nera** Black Africa; **Africa del Nord** North Africa
afri'cano, -a *adj & nmf* African
afri'kaans *m* Afrikaans
afroameri'cano, -a *adj & nmf* Afro-American
afroasi'atico *adj* Afro-Asian
afroca'ribico *adj* Afro-Caribbean
afrocu'bano *adj* Afro-Cuban
afrodi'siaco *adj & nm* aphrodisiac
a'genda *f* diary
■ **agenda elettronica** personal organizer, electronic organizer; **agenda da tavolo** desk diary
agen'dina *f* pocket diary
🔑 **a'gente** *m* agent; **agenti** *pl* **atmosferici** atmospheric agents
■ **agente di cambio** stockbroker; **agente di custodia** prison warder; **agente del fisco** assessor; **agente immobiliare** estate agent, realtor AmE; **agente marittimo** shipping agent; **agente di polizia** police officer; **agente segreto** secret agent; **agente teatrale** theatrical agent; (di compagnia) impresario; **agente di viaggio** travel agent
agen'zia *f* agency; (filiale) branch office; (di banca) branch
■ **agenzia di collocamento** employment exchange; **agenzia immobiliare** estate agency, realtor AmE; **agenzia matrimoniale** dating agency; **agenzia pubblicitaria** advertising agency; **agenzia di rating** credit rating agency; **agenzia di recupero crediti** debt collection agency; **agenzia di stampa** news agency, press agency; **agenzia di viaggi** travel agency
agevo'lare *vt* facilitate
agevolazi'one *f* facilitation
■ **agevolazioni** *pl* **fiscali** tax breaks
a'gevole *adj* easy; *‹strada›* smooth
agevol'mente *adv* easily
agganci'are *vt* hook up; Rail couple
agganci'arsi *vr ‹vestito›* hook up; **~ a** *‹maglia›* catch on; *‹rimorchio›* hook onto
ag'gancio *m* Aeron docking
ag'geggio *m* gadget
agget'tivo *m* adjective
agghiacci'ante *adj* terrifying
agghiacci'are *vt* fig **~ qualcuno** make somebody's blood run cold
agghiacci'arsi *vr* freeze
agghin'dare *vt* infml dress up
agghin'darsi *vr* infml doll oneself up
agghin'dato *adj* dressed up; *‹sala›* decorated; fig *‹stile›* stilted
aggiornabilità *f inv* Comput upgradability
aggiorna'mento *m* update; (azione) updating; **corso di ~** refresher course
aggior'nare *vt* (rinviare) postpone; (mettere a giorno) bring up to date, update
aggior'narsi *vr* get up to date
aggior'nato *adj* up-to-date; *‹versione›* updated
aggio'taggio *m* Jur manipulation of the market
aggira'mento *m* Mil outflanking
aggi'rare *vt* surround; fig (ingannare) trick
aggi'rarsi *vr* hang about; **~ su** *‹discorso ecc.›* be about; *‹somma›* be around
aggiudi'care *vt* award; (all'asta) knock down
aggiudi'carsi *vr* win
🔑 **aggi'ungere** *vt* add
aggi'unta *f* addition; **in ~** in addition
aggiun'tare *vt* splice
aggiun'tivo *adj* supplementary
aggi'unto **A** *adj* added
B *adj & nm* (assistente) assistant
🔑 **aggiu'stare** *vt* mend; (sistemare) settle; infml (mettere a posto) fix; **ora l'aggiusto io** fig I'll sort him out
aggiu'starsi *vr* adapt; (mettersi in ordine) tidy oneself up; (decidere) sort things out; *‹tempo›* clear up
aggiusta'tina *f* **dare un'~ a** neaten
agglomera'mento *m* conglomeration
agglome'rante *m* binder
agglome'rato *m* built-up area
aggrap'pare *vt* grasp
aggrap'parsi *vr* **~ a** cling to
aggrava'mento *m* worsening; (di pena) increase
aggra'vante Jur **A** *f* aggravation
B *adj* aggravating; **circostanza aggravante** aggravation
aggra'vare *vt* (peggiorare) make worse; increase *‹pena›*; (appesantire) weigh down
aggra'varsi *vr* worsen
ag'gravio *m*
■ **aggravio fiscale** tax burden
aggrazi'ato *adj* graceful

🔑 key word

aggre'dire *vt* attack
aggre'gare *vt* add; (associare a un gruppo ecc.) admit
aggre'garsi *vr* ~ **a** join
aggre'gato **A** *adj* associated
B *m* aggregate; (di case) block
aggregazi'one *f* (di persone) gathering
aggressi'one *f* aggression; (atto) attack
■ **aggressione a mano armata** armed assault
aggressività *f inv* aggressiveness
aggres'sivo *adj* aggressive
aggres'sore *m* aggressor
aggrin'zare, **aggrinzire** *vt* wrinkle
aggrin'zirsi *vr* wrinkle
aggrot'tare *vt* ~ **le ciglia/la fronte** frown
aggrovigli'are *vt* tangle
aggrovigli'arsi *vr* get entangled; fig get complicated
aggrovigli'ato *adj* entangled; fig confused
agguan'tare *vt* catch
agguan'tarsi *vr* ~ **a** grasp
aggu'ato *m* ambush; (tranello) trap; **stare in** ~ lie in wait; **tendere un** ~ **a qualcuno** set an ambush for somebody
agguer'rito *adj* fierce
agiata'mente *adv* comfortably
agia'tezza *f* comfort
agi'ato *adj* ‹*persona*› well off; ‹*vita*› comfortable
a'gibile *adj* ‹*palazzo*› fit for human habitation
agibilità *f inv* fitness for human habitation
'agile *adj* agile
agilità *f inv* agility
agil'mente *adv* agilely
'agio *m* ease; **mettersi a proprio** ~ make oneself at home
a'gire *vi* act; ‹*comportarsi*› behave; (funzionare) work; ~ **su** affect
agi'tare *vt* shake; wave ‹*mano*›; fig (turbare) trouble; **'~ prima dell'uso'** 'shake before using'
agi'tarsi *vr* toss about; (essere inquieto) be restless; ‹*mare*› get rough
agi'tato *adj* restless; ‹*mare*› rough
agita|'tore, **-trice** *mf* (persona) agitator
agitazi'one *f* agitation; **mettere in** ~ **qualcuno** send somebody into a flat spin
'agli = **a** + **gli**
'aglio *m* garlic
a'gnello *m* lamb
agno'lotti *mpl* ravioli *sg*
a'gnostico, **-a** *adj & nmf* agnostic
'ago *m* needle; **a 9 aghi** ‹*stampante*› 9 pin
■ **ago di pino** pine needle
ago'gnare *vt* (liter) yearn for, thirst for
ago'nia *f* agony
ago'nismo *m* competitiveness
ago'nistica *f* competition
ago'nistico *adj* competitive
agoniz'zante *adj* in one's death throes
agoniz'zare *vi* be on one's deathbed
agopun|'tore, **-trice** *mf* acupuncturist
agopun'tura *f* acupuncture
agorafo'bia *f* agoraphobia
ago'rafobo, **-a** *mf* agoraphobic
agostini'ano, **-a** *adj & nmf* Augustinian
a'gosto *m* August
a'graria *f* agriculture
a'grario **A** *adj* agricultural
B *m* landowner
a'greste *adj* rustic
a'gricolo *adj* agricultural
agricol'tore *m* farmer
agricol'tura *f* agriculture
■ **agricoltura biologica** organic farming
agri'foglio *m* holly
agrimen'sore *m* land surveyor
agritu'rismo *m* farm holidays, agrotourism
'agro¹ *adj* sour; **all'**~ Culin pickled
'agro² *m countryside around a town*
agroalimen'tare *adj* food *attrib*
agro'dolce *adj* bitter-sweet; Culin sweet-and-sour; **in** ~ sweet and sour
agrono'mia *f* agronomy
a'gronomo, **-a** *mf* agriculturalist
agropasto'rale *adj* based on farming
a'grume *m* citrus fruit; (pianta) citrus tree
agru'meto *m* citrus plantation
aguz'zare *vt* sharpen; ~ **le orecchie** prick up one's ears; ~ **la vista** look hard
aguz'zino *m* slave-driver; (carceriere) jailer
a'guzzo *adj* pointed
ah *int* ah!; **ah, davvero?** oh really?
ahi *int* ow!
ahimè *int* alas!
'ai = **a** + **i**
'aia *f* threshing floor
'Aia *f* **L'**~ The Hague
Aids *m* Aids
AIE *abbr* (**Associazione Italiana degli Editori**) *association of Italian publishers*
air bag *m inv* Auto air bag
ai'rone *m* heron
air terminal *m inv* air terminal
ai'tante *adj* sturdy
aiu'ola *f* flower bed
aiu'tante **A** *mf* assistant
B *m* Mil adjutant
■ **aiutante di campo** aide-de-camp
aiu'tare *vt* help
ai'uto *m* help, aid; (assistente) assistant; **dare un** ~ lend a hand; **venire in** ~ **a qualcuno** come to somebody's rescue; ~**!** help!; **aiuti** *pl* **alimentari** food aid
■ **aiuti** *pl* **umanitari** relief supplies; **aiuto chirurgo** assistant surgeon; **aiuto domestico**

a

mother's help; **aiuto infermiere** nursing auxiliary; **aiuto in linea** Comput on-line help

aiz'zare *vt* incite; ~ **contro** set on

al = a + il

⚷ **'ala** *f* wing; **fare ~** make way; **avere le ali ai piedi** fig run like the wind; **tarpare le ali a qualcuno** fig clip somebody's wings

■ **ala destra/sinistra** (in calcio) right/left wing

ala'bastro *m* alabaster

a'lacre *adj* brisk

alam'bicco *m* alembic

a'lano *m* Great Dane

a'lare *m* firedog

A'laska *f* Alaska

⚷ **'alba** *f* dawn

alba'nese *adj & nmf* Albanian

Alba'nia *f* Albania

'albatro *m* albatross

albeggi'are *vi* dawn

albe'rare *vi* line with trees ‹*strada*›

albe'rato *adj* wooded; ‹*viale*› tree lined

albera'tura *f* Naut masts *pl*

albe'rello *m* sapling

alber'gare **A** *vt* ‹*edificio*› accommodate **B** *vi* (liter) lodge

alberga|'tore, -trice *mf* hotel-keeper

alberghi'ero *adj* hotel *attrib*

⚷ **al'bergo** *m* hotel

■ **albergo diurno** *hotel where rooms are rented during the daytime*; **albergo a 3 stelle** 3 star hotel

⚷ **'albero** *m* tree; Naut mast; Mech shaft

■ **albero a camme** camshaft; **albero a foglie caduche** deciduous tree; **albero da frutto** fruit tree; **albero genealogico** family tree; **albero a gomiti** crankshaft; **albero della gomma** rubber tree; **albero maestro** Naut mainmast; **albero di Natale** Christmas tree; **albero di trasmissione** Mech transmission shaft, prop shaft

albi'cocca *f* apricot

albi'cocco *m* apricot (tree)

al'bino *m* albino

'albo *m* register; (libro ecc.) album; (per avvisi) notice board

album *m inv* album

■ **album da colorare** colouring book; **album da disegno** sketchbook

al'bume *m* albumen

albu'mina *f* albumin

alca'lino *adj* alkaline

'alce *m* elk

alchi'mia *f* alchemy

alchi'mista *m* alchemist

'alcol *m* alcohol; Med spirit; (liquori forti) spirits *pl*; **darsi all'~** take to drink

■ **alcol denaturato** meths, surgical spirit; **alcol etilico** ethyl alcohol

⚷ key word

alcolicità *f inv* alcohol content

al'colico **A** *adj* alcoholic **B** *m* alcoholic drink

alco'lismo *m* alcoholism

alco'lista *mf* alcoholic

alcoliz'zato, -a *adj & nmf* alcoholic

alcol'test® *m inv* (prova) breath test, breath testing; (apparecchio) Breathalyzer®

al'cova *f* alcove

⚷ **al'cun, al'cuno** *adj & pron* any; **non ha ~ amico** he hasn't any friends, he has no friends; **alcuni** *pl* some, a few; **alcuni suoi amici** some of his friends

aldilà *m inv* next world, hereafter

alea'torio *adj* unpredictable; Jur aleatory

aleggi'are *vi* ‹*brezza*› blow gently; ‹*profumo*› waft

a'letta *f* Mech fin

alet'tone *m* Aeron aileron; Auto stabilizer

'alfa *f inv* alpha

alfa'betico *adj* alphabetical

alfabetizzazi'one *f*:

■ **alfabetizzazione della popolazione** teaching people to read and write; **tasso di alfabetizzazione** literacy rate

alfa'beto *m* alphabet

■ **Alfabeto Fonetico Internazionale** International Phonetic Alphabet; **alfabeto Morse** Morse code

alfanu'merico *adj* alphanumeric

alfi'ere *m* (negli scacchi) bishop

al'fine *adv* eventually, in the end

'alga *f* weed; **alghe** *pl* **marine** seaweed

'algebra *f* algebra

Al'geri *f* Algiers

Alge'ria *f* Algeria

alge'rino, -a *adj & nmf* Algerian

algocol'tura *f* seaweed farming

algo'ritmo *m* algorithm

ali'ante *m* glider

'alibi *m inv* alibi

a'lice *f* anchovy

alie'nabile *adj* Jur alienable

alie'nare *vt* alienate

alie'narsi *vr* become estranged; **~ le simpatie di qualcuno** lose somebody's good will

alie'nato, -a **A** *adj* alienated **B** *mf* lunatic

alienazi'one *f* alienation

ali'eno, -a **A** *mf* alien **B** *adj* **è ~ da invidia** envy is foreign *or* alien to him

alimen'tare **A** *vt* feed; fig foment **B** *adj* food *attrib*; ‹*abitudine*› dietary **C** *m* **alimentari** *pl* foodstuffs

alimenta'tore *m* power unit

■ **alimentatore automatico di documenti** automatic paper feed

alimentazi'one *f* feeding; (cibo) food; (elettrica, a gas ecc.) supply

ali'mento *m* food; **alimenti** *pl* food; Jur alimony

a'liquota *f* share; (di imposta) rate
■ **aliquota minima** basic rate; **ad ~ zero** zero-rated

ali'scafo *m* hydrofoil

'alito *m* breath; **alito cattivo** bad breath

ali'tosi *f inv* halitosis

all. *abbr* (**allegato**) encl

'alla = a + la A, B

allaccia'mento *m* connection

allacci'are *vt* fasten ‹*cintura*›; lace up ‹*scarpe*›; do up ‹*vestito*›; (collegare) connect; form ‹*amicizia*›

allacci'arsi *vr* do up, fasten ‹*vestito, cintura*›

allaga'mento *m* flooding

alla'gare *vt* flood

alla'garsi *vr* to become flooded

allampa'nato *adj* lanky

allarga'mento *m* (di strada, ricerche) widening

allar'gare *vt* widen; open ‹*braccia, gambe*›; let out ‹*vestito ecc.*›; fig extend

allar'garsi *vr* to widen

allar'mante *adj* alarming

allar'mare *vt* alarm

allar'mato *adj* panicky, alarmed

al'larme *m* alarm; **dare l'~** raise the alarm; **mettere in ~ qualcuno** alarm somebody; **far scattare il campanello d'~** set the alarm bells ringing
■ **falso allarme** fig false alarm; **allarme aereo** air-raid siren; (suono) air-raid warning; **allarme antifumo** smoke alarm; **allarme antincendio** fire alarm; **allarme rosso** red alert

allar'mismo *m* alarmism

allar'mista *mf* alarmist

allatta'mento *m* (di animale) suckling; (di neonato) feeding

allat'tare *vt* suckle ‹*animale*›; feed ‹*neonato*›; **~ artificialmente** bottle feed

'alle = a + le

alle'anza *f* alliance
■ **Alleanza Democratica** Pol Democratic Alliance; **Alleanza Nazionale** Pol National Alliance

alle'are *vt* unite

alle'arsi *vr* form an alliance

alle'ato, -a **A** *adj* allied
B *mf* ally

alle'gare[1] *vt* Jur allege

alle'gare[2] *vt* (accludere) enclose; set on edge ‹*denti*›

alle'gato **A** *adj* enclosed; Comput attached
B *m* enclosure; Comput attachment; **in ~** attached, appended

allegazi'one *f* Jur allegation

alleggeri'mento *m* alleviation

allegge'rire *vt* lighten; fig alleviate

allegge'rirsi *vr* become lighter; (vestirsi leggero) put on lighter clothes

allego'ria *f* allegory

alle'gorico *adj* allegorical

allegra'mente *adv* breezily

alle'gria *f* gaiety

al'legro **A** *adj* cheerful; ‹*colore*› bright; (brillo) tipsy
B *m* Mus allegro

alle'luia *int* hallelujah

allena'mento *m* training

alle'nare *vt* train

alle'narsi *vr* train

allena|'tore, -trice *mf* trainer, coach

allen'tare *vt* loosen; fig relax

allen'tarsi *vr* become loose; Mech work loose

aller'gia *f* allergy

al'lergico *adj* allergic

aller'gologo, -a *mf* allergist

al'lerta *f* **stare ~** be alert, be on the alert; **essere in stato di ~** Mil be in a state of alert; **mettere in stato di ~** put on the alert

allesti'mento *m* preparation; **in ~** in preparation
■ **allestimento scenico** Theat set

alle'stire *vt* prepare; stage ‹*spettacolo*›; Naut fit out

allet'tante *adj* alluring; **poco ~** unattractive

allet'tare *vt* entice

allet'tato *adj* bed-bound, laid up

alleva'mento *m* breeding; (processo) bringing up; (luogo) farm; (per piante) nursery; **pollo di allevamento** battery chicken
■ **allevamento in batteria** battery farming; **allevamento a terra** free-range farming; **pollo/uova di allevamento a terra** free-range chicken/eggs

alle'vare *vt* bring up ‹*bambini*›; breed ‹*animali*›; grow ‹*piante*›

alleva|'tore, -trice *mf* breeder

allevia'mento *m* alleviation

allevi'are *vt* alleviate; fig lighten

alli'bito *adj* astounded; **rimanere ~** be astounded

allibra'tore *m* bookmaker

allie'tare *vt* gladden

allie'tarsi *vr* rejoice

alli'evo, -a **A** *mf* pupil
B *m* Mil cadet

alliga'tore *m* alligator

allinea'mento *m* alignment

alline'are *vt* line up; Typ align; Fin adjust

alline'arsi *vr* line up; fig fall into line; **~ con qualcuno** fig align oneself with somebody

alline'ato *adj* lined up; **i paesi non allineati** the non-aligned states

'allo = a + lo

a

allo'care *vt* allocate
al'locco[1] *m* tawny owl
al'locco[2], **-a** *mf* fig idiot
allocuzi'one *f* speech
al'lodola *f* [sky]lark
alloggi'are **A** *vt* ‹*persona*› put up; ‹*casa*› provide accommodation for; Mil billet **B** *vi* put up, stay; Mil be billeted
al'loggio *m* (appartamento) flat, apartment AmE; Mil billet
■ **alloggio popolare** council flat
allontana'mento *m* removal
⚷ **allonta'nare** *vt* move away; (licenziare) dismiss; avert ‹*pericolo*›
allonta'narsi *vr* go away
allopa'tia *f* Med allopathy
⚷ **al'lora** *adv* then; (in quel tempo) at that time; (in tal caso) in that case; **~ ~** just then; **d'~ in poi** from then on; **e ~?** what now?; (e con ciò?) so what?; **fino ~** until then
allorché *conj* when, as soon as
al'loro *m* laurel; Culin bay; **dormire sugli allori** rest on one's laurels
'alluce *m* big toe
alluci'nante *adj* infml incredible; **sostanza allucinante** hallucinogen
alluci'nato, **-a** *mf person who suffers from hallucinations*
allucina'torio *adj* hallucinatory
allucinazi'one *f* hallucination
alluci'nogeno *adj* ‹*sostanza*› hallucinatory
al'ludere *vi* **~ a** allude to
allu'minio *m* aluminium
allu'naggio *m* moon landing
allu'nare *vi* land on the moon
allun'gabile *adj* ‹*tavolo*› extending
⚷ **allun'gare** *vt* lengthen; stretch out ‹*mano*›; stretch ‹*gamba*›; extend ‹*tavolo*›; (diluire) dilute; **~ il collo** crane one's neck; **~ il muso** pull a long face; **~ il passo** quicken one's step; **~ le mani su qualcuno** touch somebody up; (picchiare) start fighting with somebody; **~ uno schiaffo a qualcuno** slap somebody
allun'garsi *vr* grow longer; (crescere) grow taller; (sdraiarsi) lie down, stretch out
allun'gato *adj* ‹*forma*› elongated
al'lungo *m* (nel calcio) pass; (nella corsa) spurt; (nel pugilato) lunge
allusi'one *f* allusion
allu'sivo *adj* allusive
alluvio'nale *adj* alluvial
alluvio'nato *adj* ‹*popolazione*› flooded out; ‹*territorio*› flooded
alluvi'one *f* flood
alma'nacco *m* almanac
■ **almanacco nobiliare** peerage
⚷ **al'meno** *adv* at least; **[se] ~ venisse il sole!** if only the sun would come out!
a'logena *f* halogen lamp
a'logeno **A** *m* halogen **B** *adj* **lampada alogena** halogen lamp
a'lone *m* halo
alo'pecia *f* Med alopecia
'alpaca *m inv* alpaca
al'pestre *adj* Alpine
'Alpi *fpl* **le ~** the Alps
alpi'nismo *m* mountaineering
alpi'nista *mf* mountaineer
alpi'nistico *adj* mountaineering *attrib*
al'pino **A** *adj* Alpine **B** *m* Mil; **gli alpini** the Alpine troops
al'quanto **A** *adj* a certain amount of **B** *adv* rather
Al'sazia *f* Alsace
alt *int* stop; **intimare l'~** give the order to halt
alta'lena *f* swing; (tavola in bilico) see-saw
altale'nare *vi* fig vacillate
alta'mente *adv* highly
al'tare *m* altar
alta'rino *m* **scoprire gli altarini di qualcuno** reveal somebody's guilty secrets
alte'rabile *adj* which can be changed, alterable
alte'rare *vt* alter; adulterate ‹*vino*›; (falsificare) falsify
alte'rarsi *vr* be altered; ‹*cibo*› go bad; ‹*merci*› deteriorate; (arrabbiarsi) get angry
alte'rato *adj* ‹*suono*› distorted; ‹*viso*› careworn; ‹*cibo*› spoilt; ‹*vino*› adulterated; (arrabbiato) angry
alterazi'one *f* alteration; (di vino) adulteration
al'terco *m* altercation
alte'rigia *f* haughtiness
alter'nanza *f* alternation; (in agricoltura) rotation; Pol regular change in government
alter'nare *vt* alternate
alter'narsi *vr* alternate
alterna'tiva *f* alternative
alterna'tivo *adj* alternate; **medicina alternativa** alternative medicine
alter'nato *adj* alternating
alterna'tore *m* Electr alternator
al'terno *adj* alternate; **a giorni alterni** every other day
al'tero *adj* haughty
⚷ **al'tezza** *f* height; (profondità) depth; (suono) pitch; (di tessuto) width; (titolo) Highness; **essere all'~ di** be on a level with; fig be up to
■ **altezza libera di passaggio** headroom
altezzosa'mente *adv* haughtily
altezzosità *f inv* haughtiness
altez'zoso *adj* haughty
al'ticcio *adj* tipsy, merry

⚷ key word

al'timetro *m* altimeter

altipi'ano *m* plateau

altiso'nante *adj* high-sounding

alti'tudine *f* altitude

'alto A *adj* high; (di statura) tall; (profondo) deep; ‹*suono*› high-pitched; ‹*tessuto*› wide; Geog northern; **a notte alta** in the middle of the night; **avere degli alti e bassi** have some ups and downs; **di ~ bordo** high-class; **di ~ rango** high-ranking; **ad alta definizione** high definition; **ad alta fedeltà** high-fidelity; **ad ~ livello** high-level; **a voce alta, ad alta voce** in a loud voice; ‹*leggere*› aloud; **essere in ~ mare** be on the high seas; fig be all at sea

■ **alta borghesia** *nf* gentry; **alta finanza** *nf* high finance; **alta frequenza** *nf* high frequency; **alta moda** *nf* high fashion; **alta pressione** *nf* (meteorologica) high pressure; **alta società** *nf* high society; **alta tensione** *nf* high voltage; **alto commissariato** *nm* High Commission; **alto medioevo** *nm* Dark Ages; **alto tradimento** *nm* high treason

B *adv* high; **in ~** ‹*essere*› at the top; ‹*guardare*› up; **mani in ~!** hands up!; **dall'~** from above; **guardare qualcuno dall'~ in basso** look down on somebody

altoate'sino *adj* South Tyrolean

alto'forno *m* blast furnace

altolà *int* halt there!

altolo'cato *adj* highly placed

altopar'lante *m* loudspeaker

altopi'ano *m* plateau

altret'tanto A *adj & pron* as much (*pl*) as many

B *adv* likewise; **buona fortuna! - grazie, ~** good luck! - thank you, the same to you

altri'menti *adv* otherwise

'altro A *adj* other; **un ~, un'altra** another; **l'altr'anno** last year; **l'~ ieri** the day before yesterday; **domani l'~** the day after tomorrow; **l'ho visto l'~ giorno** I saw him the other day

B *pron* other [one]; **un ~, un'altra** another [one]; **ne vuoi dell'~?** would you like some more?; **l'un l'~** one another; **nessun ~** nobody else; **gli altri** (la gente) other people

C *m* something else; **non fa ~ che lavorare** he does nothing but work; **desidera ~?** (in negozio) anything else?; **più che ~, sono stanco** I'm tired more than anything; **se non ~** at least; **senz'~** certainly; **tra l'~** what's more; **~ che!** absolutely!

altroché *adv* absolutely!

altroi'eri *m* **l'~** the day before yesterday

al'tronde d'~ *adv* on the other hand

al'trove *adv* elsewhere

al'trui A *adj* other people's

B *m* other people's belongings *pl*

altru'ismo *m* altruism

altru'ista *mf* altruist

al'tura *f* high ground; Naut deep sea

a'lunno, -a *mf* pupil

alve'are *m* hive

'alveo *m* bed

alzabandi'era *m inv* flag raising

alzacri'stallo *m* Auto window winder

al'zare *vt* lift, raise; (costruire) build; Naut hoist; **~ le spalle** shrug one's shoulders; **~ i tacchi** fig take to one's heels; **~ la voce** raise one's voice; **~ il volume** turn up the volume

al'zarsi *vr* (in piedi) stand up; (da letto) get up; ‹*vento, temperatura*› rise

al'zata *f* lifting; (aumento) rise; (da letto) getting up; Archit elevation

■ **alzata di spalle** shrug of the shoulders

alza'taccia *f* infml **fare un'~** get up at the crack of dawn

al'zato *adj* up

A.M. *abbr* (**aeronautica militare**) Air Force

a'mabile *adj* lovable; ‹*vino*› sweet

amabilità *f inv* kindness

amabil'mente *adv* kindly

a'maca *f* hammock

a'malgama *m* amalgam

amalga'mare *vt* amalgamate

amalga'marsi *vr* amalgamate

ama'nita *f* Bot Amanita

a'mante A *adj* **~ di** fond of

B *mf* fig lover

■ **amante degli animali** animal lover; **amante della lettura** book lover

C *m* lover

D *f* mistress

amara'mente *adv* bitterly

ama'ranto A *m* Bot Amaranthus; (colore) rich purple

B *adj* rich purple

a'mare *vt* love; be fond of ‹*musica, sport ecc.*›

amareggia'mento *m* bitterness

amareggi'are *vt* embitter

amareggi'arsi *vr* become embittered

amareggi'ato *adj* embittered

ama'rena *f* sour black cherry

ama'retto *m* macaroon

ama'rezza *f* bitterness; (dolore) sorrow

a'maro A *adj* bitter

B *m* bitterness; (liquore) bitters *pl*

ama'rognolo *adj* rather bitter

a'mato, -a A *adj* loved

B *mf* beloved

ama|'tore, -trice *mf* lover

a'mazzone *f* (in mitologia) Amazon; **all'~** side saddle

Amaz'zonia *f* Amazonia

amaz'zonico *adj* Amazonian

ambasce'ria *f* diplomatic mission

ambasci'ata *f* embassy; (messaggio) message

ambascia|'tore, -trice A *m* ambassador

B *f* ambassadress

ambe'due *adj & pron* both

a

ambi'destro *adj* ambidextrous
ambien'tale *adj* environmental
ambienta'lismo *m* environmentalism
ambienta'lista *adj & nmf* environmentalist
ambienta'mento *m* acclimatization
ambien'tare *vt* acclimatize; set ‹*storia, film ecc.*›
ambien'tarsi *vr* get acclimatized
⚷ **ambi'ente** *m* environment; (stanza) room
ambiguità *f inv* ambiguity; (di persona) shadiness
am'biguo *adj* ambiguous; ‹*persona*› shady
am'bire *vi* ~ **a** aspire to
am'bito¹ *adj* ‹*lavoro, incarico*› much sought-after
'ambito² *m* sphere
ambiva'lente *adj* ambivalent
ambiva'lenza *f* ambivalence
ambizi'one *f* ambition
ambizi'oso *adj* ambitious
amblio'pia *f* lazy eye
'ambo **A** *adj inv* both
B *m* (in tombola, lotto) double
'ambra *f* amber
am'brato *adj* amber
ambu'lante *adj* wandering; **venditore ambulante** hawker
ambu'lanza *f* ambulance
ambulatori'ale *adj* **essere trattato con intervento** ~ have day surgery
ambula'torio *m* (di medico) surgery; (di ospedale) out-patients' [department]
■ **ambulatorio dentistico** dental clinic
Am'burgo *f* Hamburg
a'meba *f* amoeba
a'mebico *adj* amoebic
'amen *int* amen; **e allora** ~**!** well, so be it!
amenità *f inv* (facezia) pleasantry
a'meno *adj* pleasant
amenor'rea *f* Med amenorrhoea
A'merica *f* America
■ **America centrale** Central America; **America Latina** Latin America; **America del Nord/Sud** North/South America
america'nata *f* derog (film) American rubbish
america'nismo *m* Americanism; (patriottismo) flag-waving
americaniz'zarsi *vr* become Americanized
⚷ **ameri'cano, -a** *adj & nmf* American
ame'rindio *adj* Native American
ame'tista *f* amethyst
ami'anto *m* asbestos
ami'chevole *adj* friendly
⚷ **ami'cizia** *f* friendship; **fare** ~ **con qualcuno** make friends with somebody; **amicizie** *pl* (amici) friends
⚷ **a'mico, -a** **A** *adj* ‹*parola, persona*› friendly
B *mf* friend
■ **amico del cuore** bosom friend; **amico d'infanzia** childhood friend; **amico intimo** close friend; **amico di penna** penfriend, pen pal
'amido *m* starch
ammac'care *vt* dent ‹*metallo*›; bruise ‹*frutto*›
ammac'carsi *vr* ‹*metallo*› get dented; ‹*frutto*› bruise
ammac'cato *adj* ‹*metallo*› dented; ‹*frutto*› bruised
ammacca'tura *f* dent; (livido) bruise
ammaestra'mento *m* training
ammae'strare *vt* (istruire) teach; train ‹*animale*›
ammae'strato *adj* trained
ammaestra|'tore, -trice *mf* trainer
ammainabandi'era *m inv* flag lowering
ammai'nare *vt* lower ‹*bandiera*›; furl ‹*vele*›
⚷ **amma'larsi** *vr* fall ill
amma'lato, -a **A** *adj* ill
B *mf* sick person; (paziente) patient
ammali'are *vt* bewitch
ammali'ato *adj* bewitched
ammalia|'tore, -trice **A** *adj* bewitching
B *m* enchanter
C *f* enchantress
am'manco *m* deficit
ammanet'tare *vt* handcuff
ammani'carsi *vr* fig acquire connections
ammani'cato *adj* **essere** ~ have connections
ammanigli'arsi *vr* fig = **ammanicarsi**
ammanigli'ato *adj* fig = **ammanicato**
amman'sire *vt* tame, domesticate ‹*animali*›; fig pacify, placate
amman'sirsi *vr* ‹*animali*› become tame; fig calm down
amman'tarsi *vr* ‹*persona*› wrap oneself up in a cloak; ~ **di** fig feign ‹*virtù*›
amma'raggio *m* splashdown
amma'rare *vi* put down on the sea; ‹*navicella spaziale*› splash down
ammassa'mento *m* Mil build-up
ammas'sare *vt* amass
ammas'sarsi *vr* crowd together
am'masso *m* mass; (mucchio) pile
ammat'tire *vi* go mad
ammazzacaffè *m inv* liqueur
ammazza'fame *m inv* stodge
⚷ **ammaz'zare** *vt* kill
ammaz'zarsi *vr* fig (suicidarsi) kill oneself; (rimanere ucciso) be killed
am'menda *f* amends *pl*; (multa) fine; **fare** ~ **di qualcosa** make amends for something
am'messo **A** pp di **ammettere**

⚷ key word

B *conj* ~ **che** supposing that

am'mettere *vt* admit; (riconoscere) acknowledge; (supporre) suppose; **ammettiamo che ...** let's suppose [that]...

ammez'zato *m* (piano ammezzato) mezzanine

ammic'care *vi* wink

ammini'strare *vt* administer; (gestire) run

ammini'strarsi *vr* fig manage one's finances

amministra'tivo *adj* administrative

amministra|'tore, -trice *mf* administrator; (di azienda) manager; (di società) director

▪ **amministratore aggiunto** associate director; **amministratore del condominio** property manager; **amministratore delegato** managing director; **amministratore unico** sole director

amministrazi'one *f* administration; **fatti di ordinaria** ~ fig routine matters

▪ **amministrazione aziendale** (studi) business studies; **amministrazione comunale** local council; **amministrazione controllata** receivership; **amministrazione pubblica** civil service; **amministrazione regionale** regional council

ammino'acido *m* amino acid

ammi'rabile *adj* admirable

ammi'raglia *f* flagship

ammiragli'ato *m* admiralty

ammi'raglio *m* admiral

ammi'rare *vt* admire

ammi'rato *adj* **restare/essere** ~ be full of admiration

ammira|'tore, -trice *mf* admirer

ammirazi'one *f* admiration

ammis'sibile *adj* admissible

ammissibilità *f inv* acceptability

ammissi'one *f* admission; (approvazione) acknowledgement

ammobili'are *vt* furnish

ammobili'ato *adj* furnished; **stanza ammobiliata** furnished room

ammoderna'mento *m* modernization

ammoder'nare *vt* modernize

ammoder'narsi *vr* move with the times

am'modo **A** *adj* proper
B *adv* properly

ammogli'are *vt* marry off

ammogli'arsi *vr* get married

ammogli'ato **A** *adj* married
B *m* married man

am'mollo *m* **in** ~ soaking; **mettere in** ~ pre-soak

ammo'niaca *f* ammonia

ammoni'mento *m* warning; (di rimprovero) admonishment

ammo'nire *vt* warn; (rimproverare) admonish

ammoni'tore *adj* admonishing

ammonizi'one *f* Sport warning; (rimprovero) admonishment

ammon'tare **A** *vi* ~ **a** amount to
B *m* amount

ammonticchi'are *vt* heap up, pile up

ammonticchi'arsi *vr* pile up

ammor'bare *vt* (con odore) pollute; (con malattie) infect

ammorbi'dente *m* (per panni) softener

ammorbi'dire *vt* soften

ammorbi'dirsi *vr* soften

ammorta'mento *m* Comm amortization

ammor'tare *vt* pay off ‹*spesa*›; Comm amortize ‹*debito*›

ammortiz'zare *vt* Comm = **ammortare**; Mech damp

ammortizza'tore *m* shock absorber

ammosci'are *vt* make flabby

ammosci'arsi *vt* get flabby

ammucchi'are *vt* pile up

ammucchi'arsi *vr* pile up

ammucchi'ata *f* sl (orgia) orgy; **un'~ di** infml (ammasso) loads of

ammuf'fire *vi* go mouldy

ammuf'firsi *vr* go mouldy

ammuf'fito *adj* mouldy; fig stuffy

ammutina'mento *m* mutiny

ammuti'narsi *vr* mutiny

ammuti'nato **A** *adj* mutinous
B *m* mutineer

ammuto'lire *vi* be struck dumb

ammuto'lirsi *vr* fall silent

amne'sia *f* amnesia

amni'stia *f* amnesty

amnisti'are *vt* amnesty

'amo *m* hook; fig bait

amo'rale *adj* amoral

amoralità *f inv* amorality

a'more *m* love; **d'**~ ‹*canzone, film*› love; **fare l'**~ make love; **per l'amor di Dio/del cielo!** for heaven's sake!; **andare d'~ e d'accordo** get on like a house on fire; **amor proprio** self-respect; **amor cortese** courtly love; **è un** ~ ‹*persona*› he's/she's a darling; **per ~ di** for the sake of; **amori** *pl* love affairs

amoreggi'are *vi* flirt

amo'revole *adj* loving

amorevol'mente *adv* lovingly

a'morfo *adj* shapeless; ‹*persona*› colourless, grey

amo'rino *m* cherub

amorosa'mente *adv* lovingly

amo'roso *adj* loving; ‹*sguardo ecc.*› amorous; ‹*lettera, relazione*› love *attrib*

am'pere *m inv* ampere; **da 15** ~ 15 amp

ampe'rometro *m* ammeter

ampia'mente *adv* widely

ampi'ezza *f* (di esperienza) breadth; (di stanza) spaciousness; (di gonna) fullness; (importanza) scale

a

■ **ampiezza di vedute** broadmindedness

'**ampio** *adj* ample; ‹*esperienza*› wide; ‹*stanza*› spacious; ‹*vestito*› loose; ‹*gonna, descrizione*› full; ‹*pantaloni*› baggy; **di ampie vedute** broad-minded

am'plesso *m* embrace

amplia'mento *m* (di cosa, porto) enlargement; (di strada, conoscenze) broadening

ampli'are *vt* broaden, widen ‹*strada, conoscenze*›; enlarge ‹*casa*›

ampli'arsi *vr* broaden, grow wider

amplifi'care *vt* amplify; fig magnify

amplifica'tore *m* amplifier

amplificazi'one *f* amplification

am'polla *f* cruet

ampol'loso *adj* pompous

ampu'tare *vt* amputate

amputazi'one *f* amputation

amu'leto *m* amulet

A.N. *abbr* Pol (**Alleanza Nazionale**) National Alliance (*right-wing party*)

anabbagli'ante **A** *adj* Auto dipped **B** *m* **anabbaglianti** *pl* dipped headlights

anaboliz'zante *m* anabolic steroid

ana'cardio *m* (albero) cashew; (noce) cashew nut

ana'conda *f* Zool anaconda

anacro'nismo *m* anachronism

anacro'nistico *adj* anachronistic; **essere ~** be an anachronism

anae'robico *adj* anaerobic

anafi'lassi *f* anaphylaxis

anafi'lattico *adj* **shock ~** Med anaphylactic shock

a'nagrafe *f* (ufficio) registry office; (registro) register of births, marriages and deaths

ana'grafico *adj* **dati** *pl* **anagrafici** personal data

ana'gramma *m* anagram

anal'colico **A** *adj* non-alcoholic **B** *m* soft drink, non-alcoholic drink

a'nale *adj* anal

analfa'beta *adj & nmf* illiterate

analfabe'tismo *m* illiteracy

anal'gesico *m* painkiller

a'nalisi *f inv* analysis; Med test; **in ultima ~** in the final analysis

■ **analisi grammaticale/del periodo/logica** parsing; **analisi di mercato** market research; **analisi del percorso critico** critical path analysis; **analisi del sangue** blood test

ana'lista *mf* analyst

■ **analista economico** economic analyst; **analista finanziario** business analyst

ana'litico *adj* analytical

analiz'zabile *adj* analysable

analiz'zare *vt* analyse; Med test, analyse

anal'lergico *adj* hypoallergenic

analoga'mente *adv* analogously

analo'gia *f* analogy

ana'logico *adj* analogue

analo'gismo *m* reasoning by analogy

a'nalogo *adj* analogous

an'amnesi *f inv* medical history

'**ananas** *m inv* pineapple

anar'chia *f* anarchy

a'narchico, -a **A** *adj* anarchic **B** *mf* anarchist

anar'chismo *m* anarchism

A.N.A.S. *nf abbr* (**Azienda Nazionale Autonoma delle Strade**) *national road maintenance authority*

ana'tema *m* anathema

anato'mia *f* anatomy

ana'tomico *adj* anatomical; ‹*sedia*› contoured, ergonomic

'**anatra** *f* duck

■ **anatra selvatica** mallard

ana'troccolo *m* duckling

'**anca** *f* hip; (di animale) flank

ance'strale *adj* ancestral

'**anche** *conj* also, too, as well; (persino) even; **parla ~ francese** he also speaks French, he speaks French too, he speaks French as well; **~ se** even if

ancheggi'are *vi* wiggle one's hips

anchilo'sarsi *vr* fig stiffen up

anchilo'sato *adj* fig stiff

an'cora[1] *adv* still; (con negazione) yet; (di nuovo) again; (di più) some more; **~ una volta** once more; **non ~** not yet; **~ esistente** extant; **~ più bello** even more beautiful; **~ una birra** another beer, one more beer

'**ancora[2]** *f* anchor; **gettare l'~** drop anchor

■ **ancora di salvezza** fig last hope

anco'raggio *m* anchorage

anco'rare *vt* anchor

anco'rarsi *vr* anchor; drop anchor; **~ a** fig cling to

Andalu'sia *f* Andalusia

anda'luso, -a *adj & nmf* Andalusian

anda'mento *m* (del mercato, degli affari) trend

an'dante **A** *adj* (corrente) current; (di poco valore) cheap **B** *m* Mus andante

an'dare **A** *vi* go; (funzionare) work; (essere di moda) be in; **~ via** (partire) leave; ‹*macchia*› come out; **~ a piedi** walk; **~ a sciare** go skiing; **~ [bene]** (confarsi) suit; ‹*taglia*› fit; **ti va bene alle tre?** does three o'clock suit you?; **non mi va di mangiare** I don't feel like eating; **~ di fretta** be in a hurry; **~ fiero di** be proud of; **~ di moda** be in fashion; **va per i 40 anni** he's nearly 40; **ma va' [là]!** come on!; **come va?** how are things?; **~ a male** go off; **~ a fuoco** go up in flames; **~ perduto** be lost; **va spedito [entro] stamattina** it must be sent this morning; **ne va del mio lavoro** my job is at stake; **come è**

andata a finire? how did it turn out?; **cosa vai dicendo?** what are you talking about?; **andarsene** go away; (morire) pass away
B *m* going; ~ **e venire** (andirivieni) comings and goings *pl*; **a lungo** ~ eventually; **a tutto** ~ at full speed; **con l'**~ **del tempo** with the passing of time

an'data *f* going; (viaggio) outward journey; **biglietto di sola andata/di andata e ritorno** single/return [ticket]

anda'tura *f* walk; (portamento) bearing; Naut tack; Sport pace

an'dazzo *m* infml turn of events; **prendere un brutto** ~ turn nasty

'Ande *fpl* **le** ~ the Andes

an'dino *adj* Andean

andirivi'eni *m inv* comings and goings *pl*

'andito *m* passage

An'dorra *f* Andorra

an'drone *m* entrance

andro'pausa *f* male menopause

a'neddoto *m* anecdote

ane'lare *vt* ~ **a** long for

a'nelito *m* longing

a'nello *m* ring; (di catena) link
■ **anello di fidanzamento** engagement ring; **anello d'oro** gold ring

ane'mia *f* anaemia

a'nemico *adj* anaemic

a'nemone *m* anemone

aneste'sia *f* anaesthesia; (sostanza) anaesthetic
■ **anestesia peridurale** epidural

aneste'sista *mf* anaesthetist

ane'stetico *adj & nm* anaesthetic

anestetiz'zare *vt* anaesthetize

a'neto *m* dill

anfeta'mina *f* amphetamine

an'fibi *mpl* (scarponi) army boots

an'fibio **A** *m* amphibian
B *adj* amphibious

anfite'atro *m* amphitheatre

'anfora *f* amphora

an'fratto *m* ravine

an'gelico *adj* angelic

'angelo *m* angel
■ **angelo custode** guardian angel

anghe'ria *f* harassment

an'gina *f inv*
■ **angina [pectoris]** angina [pectoris]

angi'ologo, -a *mf* Med angiologist

anglica'nesimo *m* Relig Anglicanism

angli'cano, -a *adj & nmf* Relig Anglican

angli'cismo *m* Anglicism

angliciz'zare *vt* anglicize

anglo+ *pref* Anglo+

angloameri'cano, -a *mf* Anglo-American

an'glofilo, -a *adj & nmf* Anglophile

an'glofono, -a *mf* English speaker

anglofran'cese *adj* Anglo-French

anglo'sassone *adj & nmf* Anglo-Saxon

An'gola *f* Angola

ango'lano, -a *adj & nmf* Angolan

ango'lare *adj* angular

angolazi'one *f* angle shot; fig point of view

angoli'era *f* (mobile) corner cupboard

'angolo *m* corner; Math angle; **dietro l'**~ round the corner; **fare** ~ **con** ‹*negozio, casa*› be on the corner of
■ **angolo acuto** acute angle; **angolo [di] cottura** kitchenette; **angolo retto** right angle

ango'loso *adj* angular; ‹*carattere*› difficult to get on with

'angora *f*
■ **[lana d']angora** angora

an'goscia *f* anguish

angosci'are *vt* torment

angosci'arsi *vr* (preoccuparsi) worry oneself sick, torment oneself

angosci'ato *adj* agonized

angosci'oso *adj* (disperato) anguished; (che dà angoscia) distressing

angu'illa *f* eel

an'guria *f* watermelon

an'gustia *f* (ansia) anxiety; (penuria) poverty

angusti'are *vt* distress

angusti'arsi *vr* be distressed (**per** about)

angusti'ato *adj* distressed

an'gusto *adj* narrow

'anice *m* anise; Culin aniseed; (liquore) anisette

ani'cino *m* (biscotto) aniseed biscuit

ani'dride *f*:
■ **anidride carbonica** carbon dioxide; **anidride solforosa** sulphur dioxide

'anima *f* soul; **non c'era** ~ **viva** there was not a soul about; **all'**~ **!** good grief!; **mi fa dannare l'**~ **!** he'll be the death of me!; **l'** ~ **della festa** the life and soul of the party; **un'**~ **in pena** a soul in torment; **volere un bene dell'**~ **a qualcuno** love somebody to death; **la buon'**~ **della zia** my late aunt, God rest her soul
■ **anima gemella** soul mate

ani'male *adj & nm* animal
■ **animali** *pl* **domestici** pets; **animali** *pl* **selvatici** wild animals

anima'lesco *adj* animal

anima'lista *mf* animal rights activist

ani'mare *vt* give life to; (ravvivare) enliven; (incoraggiare) encourage

ani'marsi *vr* come to life; (accalorarsi) become animated

ani'mato *adj* animate; ‹*discussione*› animated; ‹*strada, paese*› lively

anima'tore, -trice *mf* leading spirit; Cinema animator

animazi'one *f* animation; **con** ~ animatedly
■ **animazione elettronica** animatronics *sg*

ani'melle *fpl* (di agnello, vitello) sweet-bread

'animo *m* (mente) mind; (indole) disposition; (cuore) heart; **perdersi d'~** lose heart; **farsi ~** take heart

animosa'mente *adv* with animosity

animosità *f inv* animosity

ani'moso *adj* brave; (ostile) hostile

ani'setta *f* anisette

'anitra *f* duck

annacqua'mento *m* fig watering down, dilution

annac'quare *vt* anche fig water down

annac'quato *adj* watered down; ‹*colore, resoconto*› insipid

annaffi'are *vt* water

annaffia'toio *m* watering can

an'nali *mpl* annals; **restare negli ~** go down in history

anna'spare *vi* flounder

an'nata *f* year; (importo annuale) annual amount; ‹*di vino*› vintage

▪ **vino d'annata** vintage wine

annebbia'mento *m* fog build-up; fig clouding

annebbi'are *vt* cloud ‹*vista, mente*›

annebbi'arsi *vr* get misty; (in città, su autostrada) get foggy; ‹*vista, mente*› grow dim

annega'mento *m* drowning

anne'gare *vt & vi* drown

anne'rire *vt & vi* blacken

anne'rirsi *vr* become black

an'nessi *mpl* (costruzioni) outbuildings; **tutti gli ~ e i connessi** all the appurtenances

annessi'one *f* (di nazione) annexation

an'nesso **A** pp di **annettere**
B *adj* attached; ‹*stato*› annexed

an'nettere *vt* add; (accludere) enclose; annex ‹*stato*›

annichi'lire *vt* annihilate

anni'darsi *vr* nest

annienta'mento *m* annihilation

annien'tare *vt* annihilate

annien'tarsi *vr* abase oneself

anniver'sario *adj & nm* anniversary

▪ **anniversario di matrimonio** *o* **di nozze** wedding anniversary

'anno *m* year; **Buon Anno!** Happy New Year!; **quanti anni ha?** how old are you?; **Tommaso ha dieci anni** Thomas is ten [years old]; **gli anni '30** the '30s

▪ **anno accademico** academic year; **anno bisestile** leap year; **anno civile** calendar year; **anno giudiziario** law year; **anno luce** light year; **anno nuovo** New Year; **anno sabbatico** Univ sabbatical; **anni verdi** *pl* salad days

anno'dare *vt* knot; do up ‹*cintura*›; fig form

anno'darsi *vr* become knotted

annoi'are *vt* bore; (recare fastidio) annoy

annoi'arsi *vr* get bored; (condizione) be bored

annoi'ato *adj* bored

an'noso *adj* ‹*questione*› age-old

anno'tare *vt* note down; annotate ‹*testo*›

annotazi'one *f* note

annove'rare *vt* number

annu'ale *adj* annual, yearly

annual'mente *adv* annually

annu'ario *m* yearbook

annu'ire *vi* nod; (acconsentire) agree

annulla'mento *m* annulment; (di appuntamento) cancellation

annul'lare *vt* annul; cancel ‹*appuntamento*›; (togliere efficacia a) undo; disallow ‹*gol*›; (distruggere) destroy

annul'larsi *vr* cancel each other out

an'nullo *m* (timbro) franking

annunci'are *vt* announce; (preannunciare) foretell

annuncia|'tore, -trice *mf* announcer

annunciazi'one *f* Annunciation

an'nuncio *m* announcement; (pubblicitario) advertisement, ad; (notizia) news

▪ **annunci** *pl* **economici** classified advertisements; **annunci** *pl* **mortuari** obituaries, death notices; **annuncio personale** personal ad; **annuncio pubblicitario** advertisement

'annuo *adj* annual, yearly

annu'sare *vt* sniff

annu'sata *f* **dare un'~ a** have a sniff at

annuvola'mento *m* clouding over

annuvo'lare *vt* cloud

annuvo'larsi *vr* cloud over

'ano *m* anus

ano'dino *adj* anodyne

'anodo *m* anode

anoma'lia *f* anomaly

a'nomalo *adj* anomalous

a'nonima *f*:

▪ **Anonima Alcolisti** Alcoholics Anonymous; **anonima sequestri** *Italian criminal organization specializing in kidnapping*

anoni'mato *m* **mantenere l'~** remain anonymous

anonimità *f inv* anonymity

a'nonimo, -a **A** *adj* anonymous
B *mf* unknown person; (pittore, scrittore) anonymous painter/writer

anores'sia *f* Med anorexia

ano'ressico, -a *mf* anorexic

anor'male **A** *adj* abnormal
B *mf* deviant, abnormal person

anormalità *f inv* abnormality

'ansa *f* handle; (di fiume) bend

ANSA *nf abbr* (**Agenzia Nazionale Stampa Associata**) *Italian press agency*

an'sante *adj* panting

an'sare *vi* pant

'ansia, ansietà *f inv* anxiety; **stare/essere**

key word

in ~ per be anxious about
ansi'mante *adj* breathless
ansi'mare *vi* gasp for breath
ansio'litico *m* tranquillizer
ansi'oso *adj* anxious
'anta *f* (di finestra) shutter; (di armadio) door
antago'nismo *m* antagonism
antago'nista *mf* antagonist
antago'nistico *adj* antagonistic
an'tartico *adj & nm* Antarctic
An'tartide *f* Antarctica
ante'bellico *adj* pre-war
antece'dente **A** *adj* preceding
B *m* precedent
ante'fatto *m* prior event
ante'guerra **A** *adj* pre-war
B *m* pre-war period
ante'nato, -a *mf* ancestor
an'tenna *f* Radio, TV aerial; (di animale) antenna; Naut yard; **rizzare le antenne** fig prick up one's ears
■ **antenna parabolica** satellite dish; **antenna radar** radar scanner
ante'porre *vt* put before
ante'prima *f* preview; **vedere qualcosa in ~** have a sneak preview of something
■ **anteprima di stampa** Comput print preview
anteri'ore *adj* front *attrib*; (nel tempo) previous
anterior'mente *adv* (nel tempo) previously; (nello spazio) in front
antesi'gnano, -a *mf* fig forerunner
anti+ *pref* anti+
antiabor'tista **A** *mf* anti-abortionist
B *adj* anti-abortion *attrib*
anti'acido *m* antacid
antiade'rente *adj* ‹*padella*› non-stick
antia'ereo *adj* anti-aircraft *attrib*
antial'lergico *adj* hypoallergenic
antiapar'theid *adj inv* anti-apartheid
antia'tomico *adj* anti-nuclear; **rifugio antiatomico** fallout shelter
antibat'terico *adj* antibacterial
antibi'otico *adj & nm* antibiotic
antibloc'caggio *adj inv* anti-lock *attrib*
anti'caglia *f* (oggetto) piece of old junk
antical'care *m* softener
antica'mente *adv* in ancient times, long ago
anti'camera *f* ante-room; **fare ~** be kept waiting
antichità *f inv* antiquity; (oggetto) antique
antici'clone *m* anticyclone
antici'clonico *adj* ‹*area*› anti-cyclonic
antici'pare **A** *vt* advance; Comm pay in advance; (prevedere) anticipate; (prevenire) forestall
B *vi* be early
anticipata'mente *adv* in advance
antici'pato *adj* upfront; **pagamento anticipato** advance payment
anticipazi'one *f* anticipation; (notizia) advance news
an'ticipo *m* advance; (caparra) deposit; **in ~** early; (nel lavoro) ahead of schedule; **giocare d'~** Sport fig anticipate the next move
✓ **an'tico** **A** *adj* ancient; ‹*mobile ecc.*› antique; (vecchio) old; **all'antica** old-fashioned
B *m* **gli antichi** the ancients
anticomu'nista *adj & nmf* anti-communist
anticoncezio'nale *adj & nm* contraceptive
anticonfor'mismo *m* unconventionality
anticonfor'mista *mf* nonconformist
anticonfor'mistico *adj* unconventional, nonconformist
anticonge'lante *adj & nm* anti-freeze
anticonsu'mismo *m* anti-consumerism
anti'corpo *m* antibody
anticostituzio'nale *adj* unconstitutional
anti'crimine *adj inv* ‹*squadra*› crime *attrib*
antidemo'cratico *adj* undemocratic
antidepres'sivo *m* antidepressant
antidiluvi'ano *adj* fig antediluvian
antidolo'rifico *m* painkiller
anti'doping *m inv* Sport dope test
an'tidoto *m* antidote
anti'droga *adj inv* ‹*compagna*› anti-drugs; ‹*squadra*› drug *attrib*
antie'stetico *adj* ugly
antie'tà *adj inv* anti-ageing
antifa'scismo *m* anti-fascism
antifa'scista *adj & nmf* anti-fascist
an'tifona *f* fig dull and repetitive speech; **capire l'~** take the hint; **sempre la stessa ~** always the same old story
anti'forfora *adj inv* dandruff *attrib*
anti'fumo *adj inv* anti-smoking
anti'furto **A** *m* anti-theft device; (allarme) alarm
■ **antifurto della macchina** car alarm
B *adj inv* ‹*sistema*› anti-theft
anti'gelo **A** *adj inv* anti-freeze
B *m* antifreeze; (parabrezza) defroster
an'tigene *m* antigen
antigi'enico *adj* unhygienic
anti'graffio *adj* scratch-resistant
anti-inflazi'one *adj inv* anti-inflation
An'tille *fpl* **le ~** the West Indies
an'tilope *f* antelope
anti'mafia *adj inv* anti-Mafia
antimilita'rista **A** *adj inv* anti-militaristic, anti-war
B *mf* anti-militarist
antin'cendio *adj inv* **allarme ~** fire alarm; **porta ~** fire door
anti'nebbia *adj inv* **[faro] ~** Auto fog lamp, fog light
antine'vralgico **A** *adj* pain-killing

a

B *m* pain-killer
antinfiamma'torio *adj & nm* anti-inflammatory
antinflazio'nistico *adj* anti-inflationary
antinquina'mento *adj inv* anti-pollution
antinucle'are *adj* anti-nuclear
antio'rario *adj* anti-clockwise, counter-clockwise AmE
antiparassi'tario *m* insecticide
antiparlamen'tare *adj* unparliamentary
antipasti'era *f* hors d'oeuvre dish
anti'pasto *m* hors d'oeuvre, starter
■ **antipasti** *pl* **caldi** hot starters; **antipasti** *pl* **freddi** cold starters; **antipasti** *pl* **misti** variety of starters
antipa'tia *f* antipathy
anti'patico *adj* unpleasant
an'tipodi *mpl* Antipodes; **essere agli ~** fig be poles apart
anti'polio **A** *f inv* (vaccino) polio vaccine; **fare l'~** have a polio injection
B *adj* ‹*siero, vaccino*› polio *attrib*
antipopo'lare *adj* anti-working-class
antiprobizio'nismo *m* anti-prohibitionism
antiproibizio'nista *adj & nmf* anti-prohibitionist
antiproi'ettile *adj inv* bullet-proof
antiquari'ato *m* antique trade; **pezzo d'antiquariato** antique
anti'quario, -a *mf* antique dealer
anti'quato *adj* antiquated
antiraz'zismo *m* anti-racism
antiraz'zista *adj* anti-racist
antiretrovi'rale *adj* antiretroviral
antireu'matico *adj & nm* anti-rheumatic
antiri'flesso *adj inv* anti-glare
anti'ruggine **A** *m inv* rust-inhibitor
B *adj* anti-rust
anti'rughe *adj inv* anti-wrinkle *attrib*
anti'scasso *adj inv* ‹*porta*› burglar-proof
antisci'opero *adj inv* anti-strike
anti'scippo *adj inv* theft-proof
anti'scivolo *adj inv* non-skid
antise'mita *adj* anti-Semitic
antisemi'tismo *m* anti-Semitism
anti'settico *adj & nm* antiseptic
antisinda'cale *adj* ‹*comportamento*› anti-trade-union
anti'sismico *adj* earthquake-proof
antisoci'ale *adj* anti-social
antiso'lare *adj & nm* suntan
antisommer'gibile **A** *adj inv* anti-submarine
B *m* submarine hunter
antista'minico *m* antihistamine
anti'stante *prep* **~ a** in front of
anti'tarlo *m inv* woodworm treatment

⚷ key word

anti'tarmico *adj* mothproof
antiterro'rismo *m* counter-terrorism
antiterro'rista *adj* antiterrorist
antiterro'ristico *adj* antiterrorist
an'titesi *f inv* antithesis
antite'tanica *f* tetanus injection
antite'tanico *adj* tetanus *attrib*
anti'tetico *adj* antithetical
anti'trust *adj* antitrust
antitumo'rale *adj* which stops the growth of tumours
anti'urto *adj* shockproof
antivaio'losa *f* smallpox injection
anti'vipera *adj* **siero ~** snakebite antidote
antivi'rale *adj* anti-viral
anti'virus *m inv* Comput antivirus software
antolo'gia *f* anthology
an'tonimo *m* antonym
antono'masia *f* **per ~** *adj* ‹*poeta*› quintessential
antra'cite *f* anthracite; (colore) charcoal [grey]
'antro *m* cavern
antro'pofago *adj* man-eating, cannibalistic
antropolo'gia *f* anthropology
antropo'logico *adj* anthropological
antro'pologo, -a *mf* anthropologist
anu'lare *m* ring finger
An'versa *f* Antwerp
⚷ **'anzi** *conj* in fact; (o meglio) or better still; (al contrario) on the contrary
anzianità *f inv* old age; (di servizio) seniority
anzi'ano, -a **A** *adj* old, elderly; (di grado ecc.) senior
B *mf* elderly person
anziché *conj* rather than
anzi'tempo *adv* prematurely
anzi'tutto *adv* first of all
a'orta *f* aorta
A'pache *mf inv* Apache
apar'theid *f* apartheid
apar'titico *adj* unaligned
apa'tia *f* apathy
a'patico *adj* apathetic
'ape *f* bee
■ **ape regina** queen bee
aperi'tivo *m* aperitif
aperta'mente *adv* openly
⚷ **a'perto** *adj* open; **all'aria aperta** in the open air; **all'~** ‹*teatro*› open-air; ‹*piscina*› outdoor; **~ a tutti** open to all comers; **rimanere a bocca aperta** be dumbfounded
aper'tura *f* opening; (inizio) beginning; (ampiezza) spread; (di arco) span; Pol overtures *pl*; Phot aperture
■ **apertura alare** wing span; **apertura di credito** loan agreement; **apertura di credito presso un negozio** charge account; **apertura domenicale**

[dei negozi] Sunday trading; **apertura mentale** openness
api'ario *m* apiary
'apice *m* apex; **l'~ di** the acme of
apicol|'tore, -trice *mf* beekeeper
apicol'tura *f* beekeeping
a'plomb *m inv* (di un abito) hang; fig aplomb, self-assuredness
ap'nea *f*
■ **immersione in apnea** free diving
Apoca'lisse *f* **l'~** the Apocalypse
apoca'littico *adj* apocalyptic
a'pocrifo *adj* apocryphal
apo'geo *m* apogee
a'polide **A** *adj* stateless
B *mf* stateless person
apo'litico *adj* apolitical
A'pollo *m* Apollo
apolo'geta *mf* apologist (**di** for)
apolo'gia *f* apologia; (celebrazione) eulogy
■ **apologia di reato** *condoning of a criminal act*
apoples'sia *f* apoplexy
apo'plettico *adj* apoplectic
a'postolo *m* apostle
apostro'fare *vt* (mettere un apostrofo a) write with an apostrophe; reprimand ‹*persona*›
a'postrofo *m* apostrophe
apote'osi *f* apotheosis
app *f* app; **~ gratuita per iPad** free iPad app
appaga'mento *m* fulfilment
appa'gare *vt* satisfy
appa'garsi *vr* **~ di** be satisfied with
appa'gato *adj* sated
appai'are *vt* pair; mate ‹*animali*›
appallotto'lare *vt* roll into a ball
appallotto'larsi *vr* ‹*gatto*› curl up in a ball; ‹*farina*› become lumpy
appal'tare *vt* contract out; **~ a imprese esterne** outsource
appalta'tore *m* contractor
ap'palto *m* contract; **dare in ~** contract out; **~ a imprese esterne** outsourcing; **gara di ~** call for tenders
appan'naggio *m* (in denaro) annuity; fig prerogative
appan'nare *vt* mist ‹*vetro*›; dim ‹*vista*›
appan'narsi *vr* mist over; ‹*vista*› grow dim
appa'rato *m* apparatus; (apparecchiamento) array; (pompa) display
■ **apparato digerente** digestive system; **apparato scenico** set
apparecchi'are **A** *vt* prepare
B *vi* lay the table BrE, set the table
apparecchia'tura *f* (impianti) equipment
⚷ **appa'recchio** *m* apparatus; (congegno) device; (radio, TV ecc.) set; (aeroplano) aircraft; (telefono) phone
■ **apparecchio acustico** hearing aid
appa'rente *adj* apparent
apparente'mente *adv* apparently
appa'renza *f* appearance; **in ~** apparently
⚷ **appa'rire** *vi* appear; (sembrare) look
appari'scente *adj* striking; derog gaudy
apparizi'one *f* apparition
⚷ **apparta'mento** *m* flat, apartment AmE
■ **appartamento ammobiliato** furnished flat; **appartamento in multiproprietà** timeshare
appar'tarsi *vr* withdraw
appar'tato *adj* secluded
apparte'nente *adj* **~ a** belonging to
apparte'nenza *f* membership
⚷ **apparte'nere** *vi* belong
appassio'nante *adj* (storia, argomento) exciting
appassio'nare *vt* excite; (commuovere) move
appassio'narsi *vr* **~ a** become excited by
appassio'nato *adj* passionate; **~ di** (entusiastico) fond of
appas'sire *vi* wither
appas'sirsi *vr* fade
appas'sito *adj* faded
appel'larsi *vr* **~ a** appeal to
ap'pello *m* appeal; (chiamata per nome) roll call; (esami) exam session; **fare l'~** call the roll
⚷ **ap'pena** **A** *adv* just; (a fatica) hardly
B *conj* **[non] ~** as soon as, no sooner ... than; **~ prima di** just before
ap'pendere *vt* hang [up]
appendi'abiti *m inv* hat-stand, hallstand
appen'dice *f* appendix; **romanzo d'~** *novel serialized in a magazine or newspaper*
appendi'cite *f* appendicitis
Appen'nini *mpl* **gli ~** the Apennines
appen'ninico *adj* Apennine
appesan'tire *vt* weigh down
appesan'tirsi *vr* become heavy
ap'peso **A** pp di **appendere**
B *adj* hanging; (impiccato) hanged
⚷ **appe'tito** *m* appetite; **aver ~** be hungry; **buon ~!** enjoy your meal!
appeti'toso *adj* appetizing; fig tempting
appezza'mento *m* plot of land
appia'nare *vt* level; fig smooth over
appia'narsi *vr* improve
appiat'tire *vt* flatten
appiat'tirsi *vr* flatten oneself; fig level out
appic'care *vt* **~ il fuoco a** set fire to
appicci'care **A** *vt* stick; **~ a** fig (appioppare) palm off on
B *vi* be sticky
appicci'carsi *vr* stick; ‹*cose*› stick together; **~ a qualcuno** fig stick to somebody like glue
appiccica'ticcio *adj* sticky; fig clingy
appicci'cato *adj* **stare ~ a qualcuno** be all over somebody
appicci'coso *adj* sticky; fig clingy

a

appie'dato *adj* **sono ~** I don't have the car; **sono rimasto ~** I was stranded

appi'eno *adv* fully

appigli'arsi *vr* **~ a** get hold of; fig stick to

ap'piglio *m* fingerhold; (per piedi) foothold; fig pretext

appiop'pare *vt* **~ a** palm off on; infml (dare) give; **~ un ceffone a qualcuno** slap somebody

appiso'larsi *vr* doze off

applau'dire *vt & vi* applaud

ap'plauso *m* applause

appli'cabile *adj* applicable

⚷ **appli'care** *vt* apply; enforce ‹*legge ecc.*›

appli'carsi *vr* apply oneself

appli'cato **A** *mf* (impiegato) senior clerk **B** *adj* (nel ricamo) appliqué; **matematica applicata** applied mathematics *sg*

applica'tore *m* applicator

applicazi'one *f* **1** (di vernice, crema, cerotto) application **2** (di legge) enforcement **3** Comput app, application

■ **applicazioni** *pl* **tecniche** handicrafts

⚷ **appoggi'are** *vt* lean (**a** against); (mettere) put; (sostenere) back

appoggi'arsi *vr* **~ a** lean against; fig rely on

appoggi'ato *adj* leaning (**su** on, **contro**, **a** against)

ap'poggio *m* support; **appoggi** *pl* fig influential contacts

appollai'arsi *vr* fig perch

ap'porre *vt* affix

appor'tare *vt* bring; (causare) cause; **~ delle modifiche a qualcosa** modify something

ap'porto *m* contribution

apposita'mente *adv* (specialmente) especially; **fatto ~** purpose-made

ap'posito *adj* proper

apposizi'one *f* apposition

⚷ **ap'posta** *adv* on purpose; (espressamente) specially; **neanche a farlo ~!** what a coincidence!

apposta'mento *m* ambush; (caccia) lying in wait

appo'stare *vt* post ‹*soldati*›

appo'starsi *vr* lie in wait

ap'prendere *vt* understand; (imparare) learn

apprendi'mento *m* learning

■ **apprendimento assistito dal computer** computer-aided learning

appren'dista *mf* apprentice

apprendi'stato *m* apprenticeship

apprensi'one *f* apprehension; **essere in ~ per** be anxious about

appren'sivo *adj* apprehensive

ap'presso *adv & prep* (vicino) near; (dietro) behind; **come ~** as follows

appre'stare *vt* prepare

appre'starsi *vr* get ready

apprez'zabile *adj* appreciable

apprezza'mento *m* appreciation; (giudizio) opinion

apprez'zare *vt* appreciate

apprez'zato *adj* appreciated

ap'proccio *m* approach

appro'dare *vi* land; **~ a** fig come to; **non ~ a nulla** come to nothing

ap'prodo *m* landing; (luogo) landing-stage

⚷ **approfit'tare** *vi* take advantage (**di** of, profit (**di** by)

approfitta|'tore, -trice *mf* chancer

approfondi'mento *m* deepening; **di ~** ‹*corso*› advanced

approfon'dire *vt* broaden, widen ‹*indagine, conoscenze*›

approfon'dirsi *vr* ‹*divario*› widen

approfon'dito *adj* ‹*studio, ricerca*› in-depth

appron'tare *vt* get ready, prepare

appropri'arsi *vr* **~ a** (essere adatto a) suit; **~ di** take possession of; **~ indebitamente di** embezzle, misappropriate

appropri'ato *adj* appropriate

appropriazi'one *f* Jur appropriation

■ **appropriazione indebita** Jur embezzlement

approssi'mare *vt* **~ per eccesso/difetto** round up/down

approssi'marsi *vr* draw near

approssimativa'mente *adv* approximately

approssima'tivo *adj* approximate

approssimazi'one *f* approximation

⚷ **appro'vare** *vt* approve of; approve ‹*legge*›

approvazi'one *f* approval

approvvigiona'mento *m* supplying; **approvvigionamenti** *pl* provisions

approvvigio'nare *vt* supply

approvvigio'narsi *vr* stock up

⚷ **appunta'mento** *m* appointment; infml date; **fissare un ~, prendere un ~** make an appointment; **darsi ~** decide to meet

appun'tare *vt* (annotare) take notes; (fissare) fix; (con spillo) pin; (appuntire) sharpen

appun'tarsi *vr* **~ su** ‹*teoria*› be based on

appun'tato *m* (carabiniere) *lowest rank in the Carabinieri*

appuntel'larsi *vr* (sostenersi) support oneself

appun'tino *adv* meticulously

appun'tire *vt* sharpen

appun'tito *adj* ‹*matita*› sharp; ‹*mento*› pointed

ap'punto¹ *m* note; (piccola critica) niggle

⚷ **ap'punto²** *adv* exactly; **per l'~!** exactly!; **stavo ~ dicendo** ... I was just saying ...

appura'mento *m* verification

appu'rare *vt* verify

a

a'pribile *adj* that can be opened; **tettuccio apribile** Auto sun roof

apribot'tiglie *m inv* bottle opener

a'prile *m* April
■ **primo d'aprile** April Fool's Day

aprio'ristico *adj* a priori

a'prire *vt* open; turn on ‹*luce, acqua ecc.*›; (con chiave) unlock; open up ‹*ferita ecc.*›; **~ le ostilità** Mil commence hostilities; **apriti cielo!** heavens above!

a'prirsi *vr* open; (spaccarsi) split; (confidarsi) confide (**con** in)

apri'scatole *f inv* tin opener BrE, can opener

APT *abbr* (**Azienda di Promozione Turistica**) Tourist Board

aqua'planing *m* **andare in ~** aquaplane

'aquila *f* eagle; **non è un'~!** fig he's no genius!

aqui'lino *adj* aquiline

aqui'lone *m* (giocattolo) kite

aqui'lotto *m* (piccolo dell'aquila) eaglet

AR **1** (*abbr* **andata e ritorno**) return [ticket] **2** (*abbr* **avviso di ricevimento**) return receipt for registered letters

ara'besco *m* arabesque; (hum) scribble

A'rabia *f* Arabia
■ **l'Arabia Saudita** Saudi Arabia

'arabo, -a **A** *adj* Arab; ‹*lingua*› Arabic
B *mf* Arab
C *m* (lingua) Arabic

arabo-israeli'ano *adj* Arab-Israeli

a'rachide *f* peanut

arago'nese *adj* Aragonese

ara'gosta *f* lobster

a'raldica *f* heraldry

a'raldico *m* heraldic

aran'ceto *m* orange grove

a'rancia *f* orange; **succo d'arancia** orange juice

aranci'ata *f* orangeade

a'rancio *m* orange (tree); (colore) orange

aranci'one *adj & nm* orange

a'rare *vt* plough

ara'tore *m* ploughman

a'ratro *m* plough

ara'tura *f* ploughing

a'razzo *m* tapestry

arbi'traggio *m* Comm arbitrage; Sport refereeing; Jur arbitration

arbi'trare *vt* arbitrate in; Sport referee

arbitrarietà *f inv* arbitrariness

arbi'trario *adj* arbitrary

arbi'trato *m* arbitration

ar'bitrio *m* will; **è un ~** it's very high-handed

'arbitro *m* arbiter; Sport (nel calcio, boxe) referee, ref infml; (nel baseball, tennis, cricket) umpire

arboricol'tura *f* arboriculture

ar'busto *m* shrub

'arca *f* ark; (cassa) chest
■ **l'~ di Noè** Noah's Ark

ar'caico *adj* archaic

arca'ismo *m* archaism

ar'cangelo *m* archangel

ar'cano **A** *adj* mysterious
B *m* mystery

ar'cata *f* arch; (serie di archi) arcade

archeolo'gia *f* archaeology

archeo'logico *adj* archaeological

arche'ologo, -a *mf* archaeologist

ar'chetipo *m* archetype

ar'chetto *m* Mus bow

architet'tare *vt* fig devise; **cosa state architettando?** fig what are you plotting?

archi'tetto *m* architect
■ **architetto d'interni** interior designer

architet'tonico *adj* architectural

architet'tura *f* anche Comput architecture

archi'trave *m* lintel

archivi'abile *adj* that can be filed

archivi'are *vt* file, archive; Jur close

archiviazi'one *f* filing; Jur (di caso) closing
■ **archiviazione dati** data storage

ar'chivio *m* archives *pl*; Comput file

archi'vista *mf* filing clerk

archi'vistica *f rules governing the keeping of archives and records*

ARCI *nf abbr* (**Associazione Ricreativa Culturale Italiana**) *Italian cultural and leisure association*

arci'duca *m* archduke

arcidu'chessa *f* archduchess

arci'ere *m* archer

ar'cigno *adj* grim

arci'one *m* saddle

arci'pelago *m* archipelago

arci'vescovo *m* archbishop

'arco *m* arch; Math arc; (arma) Mus bow; **nell'~ di una giornata/due mesi** in the space of a day/two months
■ **arco rampante** flying buttress; **arco temporale** time frame

arcoba'leno *m* rainbow

arcu'are *vt* bend; **~ la schiena** ‹*gatto*› arch its back

arcu'arsi *vr* bend

arcu'ato *adj* bent; ‹*schiena di gatto*› arched

ar'dente *adj* burning; fig ardent
■ **camera ardente** chapel of rest

ardente'mente *adv* ardently

'ardere *vt & vi* burn
■ **legna da ardere** firewood

ar'desia *f* slate

ardi'mento *m* boldness

ar'dire **A** *vi* dare
B *m* (coraggio) daring, boldness; (sfrontatezza) impudence

ar'dito *adj* daring; (coraggioso) bold; (sfacciato) impudent
ar'dore *m* (calore) heat; fig ardour
'arduo *adj* arduous; (ripido) steep
'area *f* area; (superficie) surface
■ **area fabbricabile** building land; **area di rigore** (in calcio) penalty area, penalty box; **area di servizio** service area; **area soggetta a vincoli ambientali** conservation area; **area [di sosta] per roulotte** trailer park AmE, caravan site; **area di sviluppo** growth area
a'rena *f* arena
are'naria *f* sandstone
are'narsi *vr* run aground; fig ‹*trattative*› reach deadlock; **mi sono arenato** I'm stuck
are'nile *m* stretch of sand
areo'plano *m* aeroplane
'argano *m* winch
argen'tato *adj* silver-plated
ar'genteo *adj* silvery
argente'ria *f* silver[ware]
argenti'ere *m* silversmith
argen'tina *f* (maglia) round-necked pullover
Argen'tina *f* Argentina
argen'tino[1] *adj* silvery
argen'tino[2], **-a** *adj & nmf* Argentinian
ar'gento *m* silver; **d'~** silver
■ **argento vivo** Chem quicksilver
ar'gilla *f* clay
argil'loso *adj* ‹*terreno*› clayey; (simile all'argilla) clay-like
argi'nare *vt* embank; fig hold in check, contain
'argine *m* embankment; (diga) dike; **fare ~ a** fig hold in check, contain
argomen'tare *vi* argue
argo'mento *m* argument; (motivo) reason; (soggetto) subject
argu'ire *vt* deduce
arguta'mente *adv* (con astuzia) shrewdly; (con facezia) wittily
ar'guto *adj* witty; (astuto) shrewd
ar'guzia *f* wit; (battuta) witticism; (astuzia) shrewdness
'aria *f* air; (aspetto) appearance; Mus tune; Auto choke; **avere l'~...** look ...; **mandare all'~ qualcosa** fig ruin something; **andare all'~** fig fall through; **a tenuta d'~** draughtproof; **avere la testa per ~** fig be absent-minded, have one's head in the clouds; **che ~ tirava?** fig what was the atmosphere like?; **cambiare ~** fig have a change of scene; **cambia ~ !** (hum) get out of here!
■ **corrente d'aria** draught; **aria-aria** *adj inv* Mil air-to-air; **aria condizionata** air conditioning; **aria-terra** *adj inv* air-to-ground
ari'ano *adj* Aryan
arida'mente *adv* without emotion
aridità *f inv* aridity
'arido *adj* arid
arieggi'are *vt* air; **~ una stanza** give a room an airing
arieggi'ato *adj* airy
ari'ete *m* ram; (strumento) battering ram; **Ariete** Astr Aries
ari'etta *f* (brezza) breeze
a'ringa *f* herring
ari'oso *adj* ‹*locale*› light and airy
'arista *f* chine of pork
aristo'cratico, -a **A** *adj* aristocratic **B** *mf* aristocrat
aristocra'zia *f* aristocracy
arit'metica *f* arithmetic
arit'metico *adj* arithmetical
arlec'chino *m* Harlequin; fig buffoon
'arma *f* weapon; (forze armate) [armed] forces; **armi** *pl* arms; **chiamare alle armi** call up; **sotto le armi** in the army; **alle prime armi** fig inexperienced, fledgling; **prendere/deporre le armi** take up arms/put down one's arms; **passare qualcuno per le armi** execute somebody; **confrontarsi ad armi pari** compete on an equal footing
■ **arma bianca** knife; **arma a doppio taglio** fig double-edged sword; **arma da fuoco** firearm; **arma di distruzione di massa** weapon of mass destruction; **arma impropria** makeshift weapon; **arma segreta** fig secret weapon; **armi** *pl* **nucleari** nuclear weapons
armadi'etto *m* locker, cupboard; (in aereo) overhead locker
■ **armadietto del bagno** bathroom cabinet; **armadietto dei medicinali** medicine cabinet
arma'dillo *m* armadillo
ar'madio *m* cupboard; (guardaroba) wardrobe
■ **armadio a muro** fitted cupboard
armamen'tario *m* tools *pl*; fig paraphernalia
arma'mento *m* armament, weaponry; Naut fitting out
ar'mare *vt* arm; (equipaggiare) fit out; Archit reinforce
ar'marsi *vr* arm oneself (**di** with)
ar'mata *f* army; (flotta) fleet
ar'mato *adj* armed; **rapina a mano armata** armed robbery
arma'tore *m* shipowner
arma'tura *f* framework; (impalcatura) scaffolding; (di guerriero) armour
armeggi'are *vi* fig manoeuvre
Ar'menia *f* Armenia
ar'meno, -a *adj & nmf* Armenian
arme'ria *f* Mil armoury
armi'stizio *m* armistice
armo'nia *f* harmony
ar'monica *f*
■ **armonica [a bocca]** mouth organ
ar'monico *adj* harmonic

---
key word

armoniosa'mente *adv* harmoniously
armoni'oso *adj* harmonious
armoniz'zare **A** *vt* harmonize
B *vi* match
armoniz'zarsi *vr* ‹*colori*› go together, match
ar'nese *m* tool; (oggetto) thing; (congegno) gadget; **male in ~** in bad condition
'arnia *f* beehive
a'roma *m* aroma; **aromi** *pl* herbs; **aromi** *pl* **naturali/artificiali** natural/artificial flavourings
aromatera'pia *f* aromatherapy
aro'matico *adj* aromatic
aromatiz'zare *vt* flavour
'arpa *f* harp
ar'peggio *m* arpeggio
ar'pia *f* harpy
arpi'one *m* hook; (pesca) harpoon
ar'pista *mf* harpist
arrabat'tarsi *vr* do all one can
arrabbi'arsi *vr* get angry
arrabbi'ato *adj* angry
arrabbia'tura *f* rage; **prendersi un'~** fly into a rage
arraf'fare *vt* grab
arraf'fone *mf* infml thief
arrampi'carsi *vr* climb [up]; **~ sugli specchi** fig clutch at straws
arrampi'cata *f* climb
arrampica|'tore, -trice *mf* climber
■ **arrampicatore sociale** social climber
arran'care *vi* limp, hobble; fig struggle, limp along
arrangia'mento *m* arrangement
arrangi'are *vt* arrange
arrangi'arsi *vr* manage; **~ alla meglio** get by; **ar'rangiati!** get on with it!
arrangia|'tore, -trice *mf* Mus arranger
arra'parsi *vr* vulg get randy
arre'care *vt* bring; (causare) cause
arreda'mento *m* interior decoration; (l'arredare) furnishing; (mobili ecc.) furnishings *pl*
arre'dare *vt* furnish
arreda|'tore, -trice *mf* interior designer
ar'redo *m* furnishings *pl*
arrem'baggio *m* **lanciarsi all'~** fig stampede
ar'rendersi *vr* surrender; **~ all'evidenza dei fatti** face facts
arren'devole *adj* ‹*persona*› yielding
arrendevo'lezza *f* softness
arre'stare *vt* arrest; (fermare) stop
arre'starsi *vr* halt
ar'resto *m* stop; Jur arrest; **la dichiaro in [stato d']** ~ you are under arrest
■ **mandato di arresto** warrant; **arresto cardiaco** heart failure, cardiac arrest; **arresti** *pl* **domiciliari** Jur house arrest

arretra'mento *m* withdrawal
arre'trare **A** *vt* withdraw; pull back ‹*giocatore*›
B *vi* withdraw
arre'trato **A** *adj* (paese ecc.) backward; Mil (posizione) rear; **numero arretrato** (di rivista) back number; **del lavoro ~** a backlog of work
B *m* (di stipendio) back pay; **essere in ~** be behind schedule; **arretrati** *pl* arrears
■ **arretrati** *pl* **di paga** back pay
arricchi'mento *m* enrichment
arric'chire *vt* enrich
arric'chirsi *vr* get rich
arric'chito, -a *mf* nouveau riche
arricciaca'pelli *m inv* tongs
arricci'are *vt* curl; **~ il naso** turn up one's nose
ar'ridere *vi* **~ a qualcuno** ‹*sorte*› smile on somebody
ar'ringa *f* Jur closing address
arrin'gare *vt* harangue
arrischi'arsi *vr* dare
arrischi'ato *adj* risky; (imprudente) rash
arri'vare *vi* arrive; **~ a** (raggiungere) reach; (ridursi) be reduced to
arri'vato, -a **A** *adj* successful; **ben ~!** welcome!
B *mf* successful person; **il primo/secondo ~** (in gare) the first/second to finish
arrive'derci *int* goodbye; **~ a domani** see you tomorrow
arri'vismo *m* social climbing; (nel lavoro) careerism
arri'vista *mf* social climber; (nel lavoro) careerist
ar'rivo *m* arrival; Sport finish; **~ previsto per le ore ...** expected time of arrival ...
arro'gante *adj* arrogant
arro'ganza *f* arrogance
arro'garsi *vr* **~ il diritto di fare qualcosa** take it upon oneself to do something; **~ il merito** take the credit
arrossa'mento *m* reddening
arros'sare *vt* make red, redden ‹*occhi*›
arros'sarsi *vr* go red
arros'sire *vi* blush, go red
arro'stire *vt* roast; toast ‹*pane*›; (ai ferri) grill
arro'stirsi *vr* fig broil
ar'rosto *adj & nm* roast; **molto fumo e poco ~** fig all show and no substance
■ **arrosto d'agnello** roast lamb
arro'tare *vt* sharpen; infml (investire) run over
arro'tino *m* knife sharpener
arroto'lare *vt* roll up
arroton'dare *vt* round; Math ecc. round off; **~ lo stipendio** supplement one's income
arroton'darsi *vr* become round; ‹*persona*› get plump

a

arrovel'larsi *vr* ~ **il cervello** rack one's brains
arroven'tare *vt* make red-hot
arroven'tarsi *vr* become red-hot
arroven'tato *adj* red-hot; fig ‹*discorso*› fiery
arruf'fare *vt* ruffle; fig confuse
arruf'farsi *vr* become ruffled
arruf'fato *adj* ‹*capelli*› dishevelled, tousled
arruffia'narsi *vr* ~ **[con] qualcuno** fig butter somebody up
arruggi'nire *vt* rust
arruggi'nirsi *vr* go rusty; fig (fisicamente) stiffen up; ‹*conoscenze*› go rusty
arruggi'nito *adj* rusty
arruola'mento *m* enlistment
arruo'lare *vt & vi* enlist
arruo'larsi *vr* enlist
arse'nale *m* arsenal; (cantiere) [naval] dockyard
ar'senico *m* arsenic
'arso **A** pp di **ardere**
B *adj* burnt; (arido) dry
ar'sura *f* burning heat; (sete) parching thirst
art déco *f* art deco
'arte *f* art; (abilità) craftsmanship; **senza ~ né parte** incapable; **nome d'arte** professional name
■ **arte drammatica** dramatics; **le belle arti** *pl* the fine arts; **arti** *pl* **figurative** figurative arts; **arti** *pl* **dello spettacolo** performing arts
arte'fare *vt* adulterate ‹*vino*›; disguise ‹*voce*›
arte'fatto *adj* fake; ‹*vino*› adulterated
ar'tefice **A** *m* craftsman; fig author
B *f* craftswoman
ar'teria *f* artery
■ **arteria [stradale]** arterial road
arterio'sclerosi *f* arteriosclerosis, hardening of the arteries
arterioscle'rotico *adj* senile
arteri'oso *adj* Anat arterial
'artico *adj* Arctic
'Artico *m* **l'~** the Arctic
artico'lare **A** *adj* articular
B *vt* articulate; (suddividere) divide
artico'larsi *vr* fig ~ **in** consist of
artico'lato *adj* Auto articulated; fig well-constructed
articolazi'one *f* Anat articulation
ar'ticolo *m* article; **articoli** *pl* **per la casa** household goods; **articoli** *pl* **per la cucina** kitchenware; **articoli** *pl* **di marca** brand name goods; **articoli** *pl* **da regalo** gifts; **articoli** *pl* **da spiaggia** beach gear; **articoli** *pl* **sportivi** sports gear; **negozio di articoli sportivi** sports shop; **articoli** *pl* **vari** sundries
■ **articolo civetta** Comm loss leader; **articolo determinativo** Gram definite article; **articolo di fondo** leader, leading article; **articolo indeterminativo** Gram indefinite article; **articolo di prima pagina** Journ cover story; **articolo principale** Journ lead story
'Artide *f* **l'~** the Arctic [region]
artifici'ale *adj* artificial
artifici'ere *m* Mil explosives expert, bomb disposal expert
arti'ficio *m* artifice; (affettazione) affectation
artificiosità *f inv* artificiality
artifici'oso *adj* artful; (affettato) affected
artigi'ana *f* craftswoman
artigia'nale *adj* made by hand; (hum) amateurish
artigianal'mente *adv* with craftsmanship; (hum) amateurishly
artigia'nato *m* craftsmanship; (ceto) craftsmen *pl*
artigi'ano *m* craftsman
artigli'ato *adj* with claws
artigli'ere *m* artilleryman
artiglie'ria *f* artillery
■ **artiglieria antiaerea** flak
ar'tiglio *m* claw; fig clutch; **sfoderare gli artigli** fig show one's claws
ar'tista *mf* artist
artistica'mente *adv* artistically
ar'tistico *adj* artistic
arti'stoide *adj* arty
art nouveau *f* art nouveau
'arto *m* limb
ar'trite *f* arthritis
ar'tritico, -a *mf* arthritic
ar'trosi *f* rheumatism
arzigogo'lato *adj* fantastic, bizarre
ar'zillo *adj* sprightly
a'scella *f* armpit
ascen'dente **A** *adj* ascending
B *m* (antenato) ancestor; (influenza) ascendancy; Astr ascendant
ascen'denza *f* ancestry
a'scendere *vi* ascend
ascensi'one *f* ascent; **l'Ascensione** the Ascension
ascen'sore *m* (in una costruzione) lift, elevator AmE; Comput scroll box
a'scesa *f* ascent; (al trono) accession; (al potere) rise
a'scesi *f* asceticism
a'scesso *m* abscess
a'sceta *mf* ascetic
a'scetico *adj* ascetic
'ascia *f* axe
asciugabianche'ria *m inv* (stenditoio) clothes horse; (macchina) tumble drier
asciugaca'pelli *m inv* hair dryer, hairdrier
asciuga'mano *m* towel

key word

■ **asciugamano di carta** paper towel

asciu'gare *vt* dry; ~ **le stoviglie** do the drying up

asciu'garsi *vr* dry oneself; (diventare asciutto) dry up; ~ **le mani** dry one's hands

asciuga'trice *f* tumble dryer

asci'utto *adj* dry; (magro) wiry; ‹*risposta*› curt; **essere all'~** fig be hard up

ascol'tare **A** *vt* listen to
B *vi* listen

ascolta|'tore, -trice *mf* listener

a'scolto *m* listening; **dare ~ a** listen to; **essere in ~** Radio be listening; **mettersi in ~** Radio tune in; **prestare ~** listen

a'scrivere *vt* (attribuire) ascribe; ~ **a** (annoverare) number among

asessu'ato *adj* asexual

a'settico *adj* aseptic

asfal'tare *vt* asphalt

asfal'tato *adj* tarmac

a'sfalto *m* asphalt

asfis'sia *f* asphyxia

asfissi'ante *adj* ‹*caldo*› oppressive; fig ‹*persona*› annoying

asfissi'are *vt* asphyxiate; fig annoy

'Asia *f* Asia
■ **Asia Minore** Asia Minor

asi'ago *m full-fat white cheese*

asi'atico, -a *adj & nmf* Asian

a'silo *m* shelter; (d'infanzia) nursery school
■ **asilo infantile** day nursery; **asilo nido** day nursery; **asilo politico** political asylum

asim'metrico *adj* asymmetric[al]

a'sincrono *adj* asynchronous

'asino *m* donkey; fig (persona stupida) ass; Sch dunce; **qui casca l'~!** fig that's where it falls down!

'asma *f* asthma

a'smatico *adj* asthmatic

asoci'ale *adj* asocial

'asola *f* buttonhole

a'sparagi *mpl* asparagus *sg*

aspara'gina *f* Bot asparagus fern

a'sparago *m* asparagus

a'spergere *vt* ~ **con/di** sprinkle with

asperità *f inv* harshness; (di terreno) roughness

asper'sorio *m* aspergillum, holy-water sprinkler

aspet'tare **A** *vt* wait for; (prevedere) expect; ~ **un bambino** be expecting [a baby]; **fare ~ qualcuno** keep somebody waiting
B *vi* wait

aspet'tarsi *vr* expect

aspetta'tiva *f* expectation; (nel lavoro) leave of absence; **all'altezza delle aspettative** up to expectations; **inferiore alle aspettative** not up to expectations
■ **aspettativa per malattia** sick leave; **aspettativa per maternità** maternity leave

a'spetto[1] *m* look; (di problema) aspect; **di bell'~** good-looking

a'spetto[2] *m*
■ **sala d'aspetto** waiting room

'aspic *m* aspic

aspi'rante **A** *adj* aspiring; ‹*pompa*› suction *attrib*
B *mf* (a un posto) applicant; (al trono) aspirant; **gli aspiranti al titolo** the contenders for the title

aspira'polvere *m inv* vacuum cleaner; **passare l'~** vacuum, hoover

aspi'rare **A** *vt* inhale; Mech suck in; (con elettrodomestici) vacuum, hoover
B *vi* ~ **a** aspire to

aspi'rato *adj* aspirate

aspira'tore *m* extractor fan

aspirazi'one *f* inhalation; Mech suction; (ambizione) ambition

aspi'rina® *f* aspirin

aspor'tare *vt* take away

a'sporto *m* **da ~** take-away

aspra'mente *adv* (duramente) severely

a'sprezza *f* (al gusto) sourness; (di clima) severity; (di carattere, parole, suono) harshness; (di odore) pungency; (di litigio) bitterness

a'sprigno *adj* slightly sour

'aspro *adj* ‹*al gusto*› sour; ‹*clima*› severe; ‹*suono, parole*› harsh; ‹*odore*› pungent; ‹*litigio*› bitter

assaggi'are *vt* taste

assaggia|'tore, -trice *mf* taster

assag'gini *mpl* Culin samples

as'saggio *m* tasting; (piccola quantità) taste; fig (campione) sample

as'sai *adv* very; (moltissimo) very much; (abbastanza) enough

assa'lire *vt* attack

assali|'tore, -trice *mf* assailant

assal'tare *vt* Mil attack, charge; hold up ‹*banca, treno*›

assalta'tore *m* hold-up man

as'salto *m* attack; **d'~** ‹*giornalismo*› aggressive; **prendere d'~** storm ‹*città*›; fig mob ‹*persona*›; hold up ‹*banca*›

assapo'rare *vt* savour

assas'sina *f* murderess

assassi'nare *vt* murder, assassinate; fig murder

assas'sinio *m* murder, assassination

assas'sino **A** *adj* murderous
B *m* murderer

'asse **A** *f* board
B *m* Techn axle; Math axis
■ **asse da stiro** ironing board

assecon'dare *vt* satisfy; (favorire) support; ~ **i capricci di qualcuno** indulge somebody's every whim; ~ **i desideri di qualcuno** comply with somebody's wishes

assedi'are *vt* besiege

a

assedi'ato *adj* besieged
as'sedio *m* siege
assegna'mento *m* allotment; **fare ~ su** rely on
asse'gnare *vt* allot; award ‹*premio*›
assegna'tario, -a *mf* recipient
assegnazi'one *f* (di alloggio, denaro, borsa di studio) allocation; (di premio) award
as'segno *m* allowance; (bancario) cheque; **contro ~** cash on delivery; **pagare con un ~** pay by cheque
■ **assegno circolare** bank draft; **assegni familiari** *pl* family allowance; **assegno post-datato** post-dated cheque; **assegno sbarrato** crossed cheque; **assegno non trasferibile** cheque made out to "account payee only"; **assegno turistico** traveller's cheque; **assegno a vuoto** bad cheque, dud cheque
assem'blaggio *m* assemblage
assem'blare *vt* assemble
assem'blea *f* assembly; (adunanza) gathering
■ **assemblea generale annuale** Annual General Meeting, AGM
assembra'mento *m* gathering
assem'brare *vt* gather
assen'nato *adj* sensible
as'senso *m* assent
assen'tarsi *vr* go away; (da stanza) leave the room
as'sente **A** *adj* absent; (distratto) absent-minded
B *mf* absentee
assente'ismo *m* absenteeism
assente'ista *mf* frequent absentee
assen'tire *vi* acquiesce (**a** in)
as'senza *f* absence; (mancanza) lack
■ **assenza di gravità** zero gravity; **assenze** *pl* **ingiustificate** (a scuola) truancy
asse'rire *vi* assert
asserragli'arsi *vr* barricade oneself
asser'tivo *adj* assertive
asser|'tore, -trice *mf* supporter
asservi'mento *m* subservience
asser'vire *vt* fig enslave
asser'virsi *vr* fig be subservient
asserzi'one *f* assertion
assesso'rato *m* [council] department
asses'sore *m* councillor
assesta'mento *m* settlement
asse'stare *vt* arrange; **~ un colpo** deal a blow
asse'starsi *vr* settle oneself
asse'stato *adj* **ben ~** well-judged
asse'tato *adj* parched
as'setto *m* order; Naut, Aeron trim; **in ~ di guerra** on a war footing; **cambiare l'~ territoriale dell'Europa** change the map of Europe

assi'cella *f* lath
assicu'rabile *adj* insurable
✓ **assicu'rare** *vt* assure; Comm insure; register ‹*posta*›; (fissare) secure; (accertare) ensure
assicu'rarsi *vr* (con contratto) insure oneself; (legarsi) fasten oneself; **~ che** make sure that
assicu'rata *f* registered letter
assicura'tivo *adj* insurance *attrib*
assicu'rato *adj* insured; **lettera assicurata** registered letter
assicura|'tore, -trice **A** *mf* insurance agent
B *adj* insurance; **società assicuratrice** insurance company
assicurazi'one *f* assurance; (contratto) insurance; **fare un'~** take out insurance
■ **assicurazione multirischi** blanket cover; **assicurazione sanitaria** medical insurance; **assicurazione di viaggio** travel insurance
assidera'mento *m* exposure
asside'rarsi *vr* infml be frozen; Med be suffering from exposure
asside'rato *adj* Med suffering from exposure; infml frozen
assidua'mente *adv* assiduously
assiduità *f inv* assiduity
as'siduo *adj* assiduous; ‹*cliente*› regular
assi'eme *adj* [together] with
assil'lante *adj* ‹*persona, pensiero*› nagging
assil'lare *vt* pester
assil'larsi *vr* torment oneself
as'sillo *m* worry
assimi'lare *vt* assimilate
assimilazi'one *f* assimilation
assi'oma *m* axiom
assio'matico *adj* axiomatic
As'siria *f* Assyria
as'sise *fpl* assizes; **Corte d'Assise** Court of Assize[s]
assi'stente *mf* assistant
■ **assistente sociale** social worker; **assistente sociosanitario** care worker; **assistente universitario** assistant lecturer; **assistente di volo** flight attendant
assi'stenza *f* assistance; (presenza) presence
■ **assistenza alla clientela** customer care; **assistenza medica** medical care; **assistenza ospedaliera** hospital treatment; **assistenza sanitaria** health care; **assistenza sociale** social work
assistenzi'ale *adj* welfare
assistenzia'lismo *m abuse of the welfare state*
✓ **as'sistere** **A** *vt* assist; (curare) nurse
B *vi* **~ a** (essere presente) be present at; watch ‹*spettacolo ecc.*›
assi'stito *adj* **~ da computer** computer-aided
'**asso** *m* ace; **piantare in ~** leave in the lurch
■ **asso nella manica** trump card

✓ key word

associ'are *vt* join; (collegare) associate
associ'arsi *vr* join forces; Comm enter into partnership; **~ a** join; subscribe to ‹*giornale ecc.*›
associ'ato, -a **A** *adj* associate **B** *mf* partner
associazi'one *f* association
▪ **associazione di categoria** trade-union; **associazione per delinquere** criminal organization; **Associazione Europea di Libero Scambio** European Free Trade Association; **associazione in partecipazione** Comm joint venture
associazio'nismo *m* Pol excessive tendency to form associations; Psych associationism
asso'dare *vt* ascertain ‹*verità*›
assogget'tare *vt* subject
assogget'tarsi *vr* submit
asso'lato *adj* sunny
assol'dare *vt* recruit
as'solo *m* Mus solo
as'solto pp di **assolvere**
assoluta'mente *adv* absolutely
assolu'tismo *m* absolutism
assolu'tista *mf* absolutist
assolu'tistico *adj* absolutist
asso'luto *adj* absolute
assolu'torio *adj* **formula assolutoria** acquittal
assoluzi'one *f* acquittal; Relig absolution
as'solvere *vt* perform ‹*compito*›; Jur acquit; Relig absolve
assolvi'mento *m* performance
assomigli'are *vi* **~ a** be like, resemble
assomigli'arsi *vr* resemble each other
assom'marsi *vr* combine; **~ a qualcosa** add to something
asso'nanza *f* assonance
asson'nato *adj* drowsy
asso'pirsi *vr* doze off
assor'bente *adj & nm* absorbent
▪ **assorbente igienico** sanitary towel
assor'bire *vt* absorb
assor'dante *adj* deafening
assor'dare *vt* deafen
assorti'mento *m* assortment
assor'tire *vt* match ‹*colori*›
assor'tito *adj* assorted; ‹*colori, persone*› matched
as'sorto *adj* engrossed
assottiglia'mento *m* thinning; (aguzzamento) sharpening
assottigli'are *vt* make thin; (aguzzare) sharpen; (ridurre) reduce
assottigli'arsi *vr* grow thin; ‹*finanze*› be whittled away
assue'fare *vt* accustom
assue'farsi *vr* **~ a** get used to
assue'fatto *adj* (a caffe, aspirina) immune to the effects; (a droga) addicted
assuefazi'one *f* (a caffè, aspirina) immunity to the effects; (a droga) addiction
as'sumere *vt* assume; take on ‹*impiegato*›; **~ informazioni** make inquiries
as'sunto **A** pp di **assumere** **B** *m* task
assunzi'one *f* (di impiegato) employment; Relig **l'Assunzione** Assumption
assurdità *f inv* absurdity; **dire delle ~** talk nonsense
as'surdo *adj* absurd
'asta *f* pole; Mech bar; Comm auction; **a mezz'~** at half mast
▪ **asta di livello [dell'olio]** Auto dipstick
a'stemio *adj* abstemious
aste'nersi *vr* abstain (**da** from)
astensi'one *f* abstention
astensio'nismo *m* persistent abstention
astensio'nista *mf* persistent abstainer
astensio'nistico *adj* **tendenza astensionistica** tendency to abstain
aste'nuto, -a *mf* abstainer
aste'risco *m* (simbolo) asterisk; (tasto) star key, asterisk key
aste'roide *m* asteroid
'astice *m* crayfish
asti'cella *f* stick; (in salto in alto) bar
astig'matico *adj* astigmatic
astigma'tismo *m* astigmatism
asti'nenza *f* abstinence; **crisi di astinenza** withdrawal symptoms
'astio *m* rancour; **avere ~ contro qualcuno** bear somebody a grudge
asti'oso *adj* resentful
a'stragalo *m* ankle bone
'astrakan *m* astrakhan
astrat'tezza *f* abstractness
astrat'tismo *m* abstractionism
a'stratto *adj* abstract
astrin'gente *adj & nm* astringent
+astro *suff* **giovinastro** *nm* lout; **giallastro** *adj* yellowish; **dolciastro** *adj* sweetish
'astro *m* star
astro'fisica *f* astrophysics *sg*
astro'fisico, -a **A** *adj* astrophysical **B** *mf* astrophysicist
astrolo'gia *f* astrology
astro'logico *adj* astrological
a'strologo, -a *mf* astrologer
astro'nauta *mf* astronaut
astro'nautica *f* astronautics *sg*
astro'nave *f* spaceship
astrono'mia *f* astronomy
astro'nomico *adj* anche fig astronomic, astronomical
a'stronomo *m* astronomer
astrusità *f inv* abstruseness

a

a'struso *adj* abstruse
a'stuccio *m* case
a'stuto *adj* shrewd; (furbo) cunning
a'stuzia *f* shrewdness; (azione) trick
a'tavico *adj* atavistic
ate'ismo *m* atheism
ate'lier *m inv* (di alta moda) atelier; (di artista) [artist's] studio
A'tene *f* Athens
ate'neo *m* university
ateni'ese *adj & nmf* Athenian
'ateo, -a *adj & nmf* atheist
a'tipico *adj* atypical
at'lante *m* atlas; **i monti dell'Atlante** the Atlas Mountains
at'lantico *adj* Atlantic; **l'[Oceano] Atlantico** the Atlantic [Ocean]
at'leta *mf* athlete
a'tletica *f* athletics *sg*
■ **atletica leggera** track and field events; **atletica pesante** *weight-lifting, boxing, wrestling, etc*
a'tletico *adj* athletic
atle'tismo *m* athleticism
⚷ **atmo'sfera** *f* atmosphere
atmo'sferico *adj* atmospheric
a'tollo *m* atoll
a'tomica *f* atom bomb
a'tomico *adj* atomic
atomiz'zare *vt* atomize
atomizza'tore *m* atomizer
'atomo *m* atom
'atono *adj* unstressed
'atrio *m* entrance hall, lobby
a'troce *adj* atrocious; ‹*terrible*› dreadful
atroce'mente *adv* atrociously
atrocità *f inv* atrocity
atro'fia *f* atrophy
atrofiz'zare *vt* atrophy
atrofiz'zarsi *vr* Med fig atrophy
attac'cabile *adj* attachable
attaccabot'toni *mf inv* [crashing] bore
attacca'brighe *mf inv* troublemaker
attacca'mento *m* attachment
attac'cante **A** *adj* attacking
B *m* Sport forward
attacca'panni *m inv* coat hanger; (a muro) clothes hook
⚷ **attac'care** **A** *vt* attach; (legare) tie; (appendere) hang; (cucire) sew on; (contagiare) pass on; (assalire) attack; (iniziare) start
B *vi* stick; (diffondersi) catch on
attac'carsi *vr* cling; (affezionarsi) become attached; (litigare) quarrel
attacca'ticcio *adj* sticky; fig clinging and tiresome
attac'cato *adj* stuck
attacca'tura *f* junction
■ **attaccatura dei capelli** hairline
attac'chino *m* billposter
at'tacco *m* attack; (punto d'unione) junction; (accesso) fit
■ **attacco aereo** air attack; **attacco cardiaco** heart attack; **attacco epilettico** epileptic fit
attanagli'are *vt* fig (tormentare) haunt
attar'darsi *vr* stay late; (indugiare) linger
attec'chire *vi* take; (moda ecc.) catch on
⚷ **atteggia'mento** *m* attitude
atteggi'are *vt* assume
atteggi'arsi *vr* ~ **a** pose as
attem'pato *adj* elderly
atten'darsi *vr* camp, pitch camp
atten'dente *m* Mil batman
⚷ **at'tendere** **A** *vt* wait for
B *vi* ~ **a** attend to
at'tendersi *vr* expect
atten'dibile *adj* reliable
attendibilità *f inv* reliability
atte'nersi *vr* ~ **a** stick to
attenta'mente *adv* attentively
atten'tare *vi* ~ **a** make an attempt on
atten'tato *m* act of violence; (contro politico ecc.) assassination attempt; ~ **alla vita di** attempted murder of
■ **attentato dinamitardo** bombing; **attentato suicida** suicide attack
attenta|'tore, -trice *mf* attacker; (a scopo politico) terrorist
⚷ **at'tento** *adj* attentive; (accurato) careful; ~**!** look out!; **stare** ~ pay attention; **'attenti al cane'** 'beware of the dog'
attenu'ante *f* extenuating circumstance
attenu'are *vt* attenuate; (minimizzare) minimize; subdue ‹*colori ecc.*›; calm ‹*dolore*›; soften ‹*colpo*›
attenu'arsi *vr* diminish
attenuazi'one *f* lessening
⚷ **attenzi'one** *f* attention; (cura) care; **fare** ~ be careful; ~**!** watch out!; ~**, prego** your attention, please; **coprire di attenzioni** lavish attention on
atter'raggio *m* landing
■ **atterraggio di fortuna** emergency landing
atter'rare **A** *vt* knock down
B *vi* land
atter'rire *vt* terrorize
atter'rirsi *vr* be terrified
⚷ **at'tesa** *f* waiting; (aspettativa) expectation; **in** ~ **di** waiting for
at'teso pp di **attendere**
atte'stabile *adj* certifiable
atte'stare *vt* state; (certificare) certify
atte'stato *m* certificate
attestazi'one *f* certificate; (dichiarazione) declaration
'Attica *f* Attica
'attico¹ *m* (lingua) Attic

⚷ key word

'**attico²** *m* (appartamento) penthouse
at'tiguo *adj* adjacent
attil'lato *adj* ‹*vestito*› close-fitting
'attimo *m* second; **un ~!** just a sec!; **in un ~** in double quick time; **non ho avuto un ~ di respiro** I haven't had time to draw breath
atti'nente *adj* **~ a** pertaining to
at'tingere *vt* draw; fig obtain
atti'rare *vt* attract
atti'rarsi *vr* draw ‹*attenzione*›; incur ‹*odio*›
attitudi'nale *m*
■ **test attitudinale** aptitude test
atti'tudine *f* (disposizione) aptitude; (atteggiamento) attitude
atti'vare *vt* activate
attivazi'one *f* setting in motion, turning on; Phys, Chem activation
atti'vismo *m* activism
atti'vista *mf* activist
attività *f inv* activity; Comm assets *pl*
■ **attività fisse** *pl* fixed assets; **attività liquide** *pl* Comm liquid assets
at'tivo **A** *adj* active; Comm productive **B** *m* assets *pl*
attiz'zare *vt* poke; fig stir up
attizza'toio *m* poker
'atto *m* act; (azione) action; Comm, Jur deed; (certificato) certificate; **fare ~ di presenza** put in an appearance; **mettere in ~** put into action; **atti** *pl* (di società ecc.) proceedings; **atti** *pl* **di libidine violenta** indecent assault; **atti** *pl* **osceni** gross indecency
■ **atto di vendita** bill of sale
+attolo *suff* **vermiciattolo** *nm* slimy individual
at'tonito *adj* astonished
attorcigli'are *vt* twist
attorcigli'arsi *vr* get twisted
at'tore *m* actor
attorni'are *vt* surround
attorni'arsi *vr* **~ di** surround oneself with
at'torno **A** *adv* around, about **B** *prep* **~ a** around, about
attrac'care *vt & vi* dock
attra'ente *adj* attractive
at'trarre *vt* attract
at'trarsi *vr* be attracted to each other
attrat'tiva *f* charm, attraction
attraversa'mento *m* (di strada) crossing
■ **attraversamento pedonale** pedestrian crossing, crosswalk AmE
attraver'sare *vt* cross; (passare) go through
attra'verso *prep* through; (obliquamente) across
attrazi'one *f* attraction; **attrazioni** *pl* **turistiche** tourist attractions
attrez'zare *vt* equip; Naut rig
attrez'zarsi *vr* kit oneself out
attrezza'tura *f* equipment; Naut rigging
■ **attrezzatura da campeggio** camping equipment
at'trezzo *m* tool; **attrezzi** *pl* equipment; Sport appliances *pl*
attribu'ibile *adj* attributable
attribu'ire *vt* attribute
attribu'irsi *vr* ascribe to oneself; **~ il merito di** claim credit for
attri'buto *m* attribute
attribuzi'one *f* attribution
at'trice *f* actress
at'trito *m* friction
attrup'pare *vt* assemble
attrup'parsi *vr* gather
attu'abile *adj* feasible
attuabilità *f inv* viability
attu'ale *adj* present; (di attualità) topical; (effettivo) actual
attualità *f inv* topicality; (avvenimento) news; **programma di attualità** current affairs programme
attualiz'zare *vt* update
attual'mente *adv* at present
attu'are *vt* carry out
attu'ario, -a *mf* actuary
attu'arsi *vr* be realized
attua'tore *m* Techn actuator
attuazi'one *f* carrying out
attuti'mento *m* (di colpo) softening; (di suoni) muffling
attu'tire *vt* deaden; **~ il colpo** soften the blow
au'dace *adj* daring, bold; (insolente) audacious
au'dacia *f* daring, boldness; (insolenza) audacity
audiapprendi'mento *m* audio-based learning
'audience *f inv* (telespettatori) audience
'audio *m* audio
audiocas'setta *f* audio cassette
audio'leso *adj* hearing-impaired
audio'libro *m* audiobook, talking book
audio'metrico *adj* Med aural
audiovi'sivo *adj* audiovisual
'auditing *m* auditing
audi'torio *m* auditorium
audizi'one *f* audition; Jur hearing
'auge *m* height; **essere in ~** be popular
augu'rare *vt* wish
augu'rarsi *vr* hope
au'gurio *m* wish; (presagio) omen; **auguri!** all the best!; (a Natale) Happy Christmas!; **tanti auguri** best wishes
au'gusto *adj* august
'aula *f* classroom; Univ lecture hall; (sala) hall; **silenzio in ~!** silence in court!
■ **aula bunker** (in tribunale) secure courtroom; **aula magna** Univ great hall; **aula del tribunale** courtroom

a

aumen'tare *vt & vi* increase; ~ **di peso** gain weight
au'mento *m* increase; (di stipendio) [pay] rise
■ **aumento di prezzo** price increase
'aureo *adj* golden
au'reola *f* halo
au'rora *f* dawn
■ **aurora boreale** aurora borealis, Northern Lights
auscul'tare *vt* Med auscultate
ausili'are *adj & nmf* auxiliary
auspi'cabile *adj* **è ~ che ...** it is to be hoped that ...
auspi'care *vt* hope for
au'spicio *m* omen; **auspici** *pl* (protezione) auspices; **è di buon ~** it is a good omen
austerità *f inv* austerity
au'stero *adj* austere
Austra'lasia *f* Australasia
au'strale *adj* southern
Au'stralia *f* Australia
australi'ano, -a *adj & nmf* Australian
'Austria *f* Austria
au'striaco, -a *adj & nmf* Austrian
austroun'garico *adj* Austro-Hungarian
autar'chia *f* autarchy
au'tarchico *adj* autarchic
aut aut *m inv* either-or (*choice*)
autenti'care *vt* authenticate
autenti'cato *adj* certified
autenticità *f inv* authenticity
au'tentico *adj* authentic; (vero) true
au'tismo *m* autism
au'tista *m* driver
au'tistico *adj* autistic
'auto *f inv* car; **viaggiare in ~** travel by car
■ **auto blindata** armour-plated car; **auto elettrica** electric car; **auto ibrida** hybrid car; **auto a quattro ruote motrici** four-wheel drive car; **auto sportiva** sports car; **auto a trazione anteriore** front-wheel drive car; **auto usata** second-hand car
auto+ *pref* self+
autoabbron'zante **A** *m* self-tan **B** *adj* self-tanning
autoaccesso'rista *mf* car accessory supplier
autoade'sivo **A** *adj* self-adhesive **B** *m* sticker
autoaffermazi'one *f* self-assertion
autoambu'lanza *f* ambulance
autoa'nalisi *f* self-analysis
autoartico'lato *m* articulated lorry
autobiogra'fia *f* autobiography
autobio'grafico *adj* autobiographical
auto'blinda *f* armoured car
auto'bomba *f* car-bomb

auto'botte *f* tanker
'autobus *m inv* bus
auto'carro *m* lorry
autocertificazi'one *f* self-certification
autoci'sterna *f* tanker
auto'clave *f* (contenitore ad alta pressione) autoclave; (idraulica) surge tank
autocombusti'one *f* spontaneous combustion
autocommiserazi'one *f* self-pity
autocompiaci'mento *m* smugness, self-satisfaction
autocompiaci'uto *adj* smug, self-satisfied
autoconcessio'nario *m* car dealer
autocon'trollo *m* self-control
au'tocrate *m* autocrat
auto'cratico *adj* autocratic
auto'critica *f* self-criticism
au'toctono *adj* native, aboriginal
autode'nuncia *f* spontaneous confession
autodeterminazi'one *f* self-determination
autodi'datta **A** *adj* self-taught **B** *mf* self-educated person, autodidact
autodi'fesa *f* self-defence
autodisci'plina *f* self-discipline
autodi'struggersi *vr* self-destruct, auto-destruct
autodistrut'tivo *adj* self-destructive
autodistruzione *f* self-destruction
autoferrotranvi'ario *adj* public transport *attrib*
autoferrotranvi'eri *mpl* public transport workers
autoffi'cina *f* garage
autofinanzia'mento *m* self-financing
autofinanzi'arsi *vr* be self-financing; ‹*persona*› use one's own finance
autogesti'one *f* self-management
autoge'stirsi *vr* ‹*operai, studenti*› be self-managing
autoge'stito *adj* self-managed
auto'gol *m inv* Sport own goal
autogo'verno *m* home rule, self-rule
au'tografo *adj & nm* autograph
auto'grill *m inv* motorway café
autogrù *f inv* breakdown truck, recovery vehicle
autogui'dato *adj* homing *attrib*
autoim'mune *adj* autoimmune
autoiro'nia *f* self-mockery
autola'vaggio *m* car wash
autolesi'one *f* self-inflicted wound
autolesio'nismo *m* self-harm; fig self-destruction
autolesio'nistico *adj* self-destructive
auto'linea *f* bus line
au'toma *m* robot
automatica'mente *adv* automatically

key word

auto'matico **A** *adj* automatic; **auto con cambio ~** automatic
B *m* (bottone) press stud; (fucile) automatic

automatiz'zare *vt* automate

automatizzazi'one *f* automation

automazi'one *f* automation

auto'mezzo *m* motor vehicle; **uscita automezzi** motor vehicles exit

auto'mobile *f* [motor] car
▪ **automobile da corsa** racing car

automobi'lina *f* toy car

automobi'lismo *m* motoring

automobi'lista *mf* motorist

automobi'listico *adj* ‹*industria*› automobile *attrib*

automodel'lismo *m* model car making; (collezione) model car collecting

automu'nito *adj* owning a car

autono'leggio *m* car rental

autonoma'mente *adv* autonomously

autono'mia *f* autonomy; Auto range; (di laptop, cellulare) battery life

au'tonomo *adj* autonomous

auto'parco *m* (insieme di auto) fleet of cars

autopat'tuglia *f* patrol car

auto'pista *f* [fairground] race track

auto'pompa *f* fire engine

auto'psia *f* autopsy

autopunizi'one *f* self-punishment

auto'radio *f inv* car radio; (veicolo) radio car

au|'tore, -trice *mf* author; (di pitture) painter; (di furto ecc.) perpetrator; **quadro d'~** genuine master

autoreg'gente *f* (calza) hold-up, stay-up

autoregolamentazi'one *f* self-regulation

autore'parto *m* Mil mechanized unit

auto'revole *adj* authoritative; (che ha influenza) influential

autorevo'lezza *f* authority

autoriduzi'one *f protest which takes the form of paying less than the requisite amount*

autori'messa *f* garage

autoriparazi'oni *fpl* **'~'** 'car repairs', 'auto repairs'

autorità *f inv* authority

autori'tario *adj* autocratic

autorita'rismo *m* authoritarianism

autori'tratto *m* self-portrait

autoriz'zare *vt* authorize

autorizzazi'one *f* authorization

auto'scatto *m* Phot automatic shutter release

auto'scontro *m inv* bumper car

autoscu'ola *f* driving school

autosno'dato *m* articulated bus

autosoc'corso *m* breakdown service; (veicolo) breakdown van, breakdown truck

auto'starter *m inv* Auto self-starter

auto'stop *m* hitch-hiking, hitching; **fare l'~** hitch-hike, hitch

autostop'pista *mf* hitch-hiker

auto'strada *f* motorway, highway AmE
▪ **autostrada dell'informazione** information superhighway; **autostrada a pedaggio** toll motorway; **Autostrada del Sole** Highway of the Sun (*connecting Milan and Napoli*)

autostra'dale *adj* motorway *attrib*, highway *attrib* AmE

autosuffici'ente *adj* self-sufficient

autosuffici'enza *f* self-sufficiency

autosuggesti'one *f* autosuggestion

autotrasporta|'tore, -trice *mf* haulier, carrier

autotra'sporto *m* road haulage

auto'treno *m* articulated lorry, road train

autove'icolo *m* motor vehicle

auto'velox® *m inv* speed camera

autovet'tura *f* motor vehicle

autun'nale *adj* autumnal; (giornata, vestiti) autumn *attrib*

au'tunno *m* autumn

aval'lare *vt* endorse, back ‹*cambiale*›; fig endorse

a'vallo *m* endorsement

avam'braccio *m* forearm

avam'posto *m* Mil forward position

a'vana **A** *m inv* (sigaro) Havana [cigar]; (colore) tobacco, dark brown
B *adj inv* (colore) tobacco-coloured, dark brown

A'vana *f* Havana

avangu'ardia *f* vanguard; fig avant-garde; **essere all'~** be in the forefront; Techn be at the leading edge; **d'~** avant-garde

avansco'perta *f* reconnaissance; **andare in ~** reconnoitre

avanspet'tacolo *m* **da ~** in poor taste

a'vanti **A** *adv* (in avanti) forward; (davanti) in front; (prima) before; **~!** (entrate) come in!; (suvvia) come on!; **'~'** (su semaforo) 'cross now', 'walk' AmE; **~ diritto** straight ahead; **più ~** further on; **va' ~!** go ahead!; **andare ~** (precedere) go ahead; ‹*orologio*› be fast; **~ e indietro** backwards and forwards
B *adj* (precedente) before
C *prep* **~ a** before; (in presenza di) in the presence of

avanti'eri *adv* the day before yesterday

avan'treno *m* front axle assembly

avanza'mento *m* progress; (promozione) promotion

avan'zare **A** *vi* advance; (progredire) progress; (essere d'avanzo) be left [over]
B *vt* advance; (superare) surpass; (promuovere) promote

avan'zarsi *vr* advance; (avvicinarsi) approach

avan'zata *f* advance

avan'zato *adj* advanced; (nella notte) late; **in età avanzata** elderly

a'vanzo *m* remainder; Comm surplus; **avanzi** *pl* (rovine) remains; (di cibo) left-overs; **ce n'è d'~** there is more than enough
■ **avanzo di galera** jailbird

ava'raccio *m* Scrooge

ava'ria *f* (di motore) engine failure

avari'arsi *vr* spoil

avari'ato *adj* ‹*frutta, verdura*› rotten; ‹*carne*› tainted

ava'rizia *f* avarice

a'varo, -a **A** *adj* stingy
B *mf* miser

a'vena *f* oats *pl*

⚷ **a'vere** **A** *vt* have; (ottenere) get; (indossare) wear; (provare) feel; **ho trent'anni** I'm thirty; **ha avuto il posto** he got the job; **~ fame/freddo** be hungry/cold; **ho mal di denti** I've got toothache; **cos'ha a che fare con lui?** what has it got to do with him?; **~ da fare** be busy; **~ luogo** take place; **che hai?** what's the matter with you?; **nei hai per molto?** will you be long?; **quanti ne abbiamo oggi?** what date is it today?; **avercela con qualcuno** have it in for somebody
B *v aux* have; **non l'ho visto** I haven't seen him; **lo hai visto?** have you seen him?; **l'ho visto ieri** I saw him yesterday
C *m* **averi** *pl* wealth *sg*

avia|'tore, -trice *mf* aviator

aviazi'one *f* aviation; Mil Air Force

avicol'tura *m* poultry farming

avida'mente *adv* avidly

avidità *f inv* avidness

'avido *adj* avid

avi'ere *m* aircraft[s]man

avio'getto *m* jet [plane]

avio'linea *f* airline

aviotraspor'tato *adj* airborne

avitami'nosi *f* vitamin deficiency

a'vito *adj* ancestral

'avo, -a *mf* ancestor

avo'cado *m inv* avocado

a'vorio *m* ivory

a'vulso *adj* **~ dal contesto** fig taken out of context

Avv. *abbr* (**avvocato**) lawyer

avva'lersi *vr* avail oneself (**di** of)

avvalla'mento *m* depression

avvalo'rare *vt* bear out ‹*tesi*›; endorse ‹*documento*›; (accrescere) enhance

avvam'pare *vi* flare up; (arrossire) blush

avvantaggi'are *vt* favour

avvantaggi'arsi *vr* **~ di** benefit from; (approfittare) take advantage of

avve'dersi *vr* (accorgersi) notice; (capire) realize

⚷ key word

avve'duto *adj* shrewd

avvelena'mento *m* poisoning

avvele'nare *vt* poison

avvele'narsi *vr* poison oneself

avvele'nato *adj* poisoned

avve'nente *adj* attractive

avve'nenza *f* attraction, charm

⚷ **avveni'mento** *m* event

⚷ **avve'nire** **A** *vi* happen; (aver luogo) take place
B *m* future

avveni'rismo *m* excessive confidence in the future

avveni'ristico *adj* futuristic

avven'tarsi *vr* fling oneself

avventata'mente *adv* recklessly

avven'tato *adj* ‹*decisione*› rash

avven'tizio *adj* (personale) temporary; (guadagno) casual

av'vento *m* advent; Relig Advent

avven'tore *m* regular customer

⚷ **avven'tura** *f* adventure; (amorosa) affair; **d'~** ‹*film*› adventure *attrib*

avventu'rarsi *vr* venture

avventuri'ero, -a **A** *m* adventurer
B *f* adventuress

avventu'rismo *m* adventurism

avventu'ristico *adj* adventurist

avventu'roso *adj* adventurous

avve'rabile *adj* ‹*previsione*› that may come true

avve'rarsi *vr* come true

av'verbio *m* adverb

avver'sare *vt* oppose

⚷ **avver'sario, -a** **A** *adj* opposing
B *mf* opponent

avversi'one *f* aversion

avversità *f inv inv* adversity

av'verso *adj* (sfavorevole) adverse; (contrario) averse

avver'tenza *f* (cura) care; (avvertimento) warning; (avviso) notice; (premessa) foreword; **avvertenze** *pl* (istruzioni) instructions

avver'tibile *adj* (disagio) perceptible

avverti'mento *m* warning

⚷ **avver'tire** *vt* warn; (informare) inform; (sentire) feel

avvertita'mente *adv* deliberately

avvez'zare *vt* accustom

avvez'zarsi *vr* accustom oneself

av'vezzo *adj* **~ a** used to

avvia'mento *m* starting; Comm goodwill

⚷ **avvi'are** *vt* start

avvi'arsi *vr* set out

avvi'ato *adj* under way; **bene ~** thriving

avvicenda'mento *m* (in agricoltura) rotation; (nel lavoro) replacement; (delle stagioni) change

avvicen'dare *vt* rotate

avvicen'darsi *vr* take turns, alternate

avvicina'mento *m* approach

avvici'nare *vt* bring near; approach ‹*persona*›

avvici'narsi *vr* come nearer, approach; **avvicinarsi a** come nearer to, approach

avvi'lente *adj* demoralizing; (umiliante) humiliating

avvili'mento *m* despondency; (degradazione) degradation

avvi'lire *vt* dishearten; (degradare) degrade

avvi'lirsi *vr* lose heart; (degradarsi) degrade oneself

avvi'lito *adj* disheartened; (degradato) degraded

avvilup'pare *vt* envelop

avvilup'parsi *vr* wrap oneself up; (aggrovigliarsi) get entangled

avvinaz'zato *adj* drunk

avvin'cente *adj* ‹*libro ecc.*› enthralling

av'vincere *vt* enthral

avvinghi'are *vt* clutch

avvinghi'arsi *vr* cling

av'vio *m* start-up; **dare l'~ a qualcosa** get something under way; **prendere l'~** get under way

avvi'saglia *f* (di malattia) first sign

avvi'sare *vt* inform; (mettere in guardia) warn

av'viso *m* notice; (annuncio) announcement; (avvertimento) warning; (pubblicitario) advertisement; **a mio ~** in my opinion

■ **avviso di accreditamento** advice slip; **avviso a cura del ministero della salute** government health warning; **avviso di chiamata in linea** call waiting; **avviso di garanzia** Jur *notification that one is to be the subject of a legal enquiry*

avvista'mento *m* sighting

avvi'stare *vt* catch sight of; **~ terra** make landfall

avvi'tare *vt* screw in; screw down ‹*coperchio*›

avvi'tarsi *vr* ‹*aereo*› go into a spin

avvi'tata *f* (di aereo) spin

avviz'zire *vi* wither

avviz'zito *adj* withered

avvo'cato *m* lawyer; fig advocate

■ **avvocato del diavolo** devil's advocate

avvoca'tura *f* legal profession; (insieme di avvocati) lawyers

av'volgere *vt* wrap [up]

av'volgersi *vr* wrap oneself up

avvol'gibile *m* roller blind

avvolgi'mento *m* winding

av'volto *adj* **~ in** wrapped in

avvol'toio *m* vulture

aza'lea *f* azalea

Azerbaigi'an *m* Azerbaijan

azerbaigi'ano, -a *adj & nmf* Azerbaijani

azi'enda *f* business, firm

■ **azienda agricola** farm; **azienda elettrica** electricity board; **azienda a partecipazioni statali** *enterprise in which the government has a shareholding*; **azienda di soggiorno** tourist bureau

azien'dale *adj* ‹*politica, dirigente*› company *attrib*; ‹*giornale*› in-house

azienda'listico *adj* company *attrib*

azio'nabile *adj* which can be operated

aziona'mento *m* operation

azio'nare *vt* operate

azio'nario *adj* share *attrib*; **mercato ~** share market

azi'one *f* action; Fin share; **d'~** ‹*romanzo, film*› action packed; **ad ~ ritardata** delayed action

■ **azione sindacale** industrial action

azio'nista *mf* shareholder

a'zoto *m* nitrogen

az'teco, -a *adj & nmf* Aztec

azzan'nare *vt* seize with its teeth; sink its teeth into ‹*gamba*›

azzar'dare *vt* risk

azzar'darsi *vr* dare

azzar'dato *adj* risky; (precipitoso) rash

az'zardo *m* hazard

■ **gioco d'azzardo** (singolo gioco) game of chance; (il giocare) gambling

azzec'care *vt* hit; fig (indovinare) guess

azzera'mento *m* setting to zero; fig

■ **corso di azzeramento** remedial classes *pl*

azze'rare *vt* reset

azzi'mato *adj* dapper

'azzimo *adj* unleavened

azzit'tire *vt* silence, hush

azzit'tirsi *vr* go quiet, fall silent

azzop'pare *vt* lame

Az'zorre *fpl* **le ~** the Azores

azzuf'farsi *vr* come to blows

azzur'rato *adj* ‹*lenti*› blue-tinted

az'zurro *adj & nm* blue; **principe azzurro** Prince Charming; **gli azzurri** *the Italian national team*

azzur'rognolo *adj* bluish

b

Bb

babà *m inv* **~ al rum** rum baba
bab'beo **A** *adj* foolish
B *m* idiot
⚷ **'babbo** *m* infml dad, daddy
■ **Babbo Natale** Father Christmas
bab'buccia *f* slipper
babbu'ino *m* baboon
ba'bordo *m* Naut port side
baby boom *m* baby boom
baby'sitter *mf inv* baby-sitter; **fare il/la ~** babysit, do baby-sitting
ba'cato *adj* worm-eaten; **avere il cervello ~** have a slate loose
'bacca *f* berry
baccalà *m inv* dried salted cod
bac'cano *m* din
bac'cello *m* pod
bac'chetta *f* rod; (magica) wand; (di direttore d'orchestra) baton; (di tamburo) drumstick
ba'checa *f* showcase; (in ufficio) notice board
■ **bacheca elettronica** Comput bulletin board
bacia'mano *m* kiss on the hand; **fare il ~ a qualcuno** kiss somebody's hand
⚷ **baci'are** *vt* kiss
baci'arsi *vr* kiss [each other]
ba'cillo *m* bacillus
baci'nella *f* basin; (contenuto) basinful
ba'cino *m* basin; Anat pelvis; (di porto) dock; (di minerali) field
■ **bacino carbonifero** coalfield; **bacino d'utenza** catchment area
⚷ **'bacio** *m* kiss; **bacio sulla bocca** kiss on the lips
backgammon *m* backgammon
'baco *m* worm
■ **baco da seta** silkworm
'bacon *m* bacon
ba'cucco *adj* **un vecchio ~** a senile old man
'bada *f* **tenere qualcuno a ~** keep somebody at bay
⚷ **ba'dare** *vi* take care (**a** of); (fare attenzione) look out; **bada ai fatti tuoi!** mind your own business!
ba'dia *f* abbey
ba'dile *m* shovel
'badminton *m* badminton
'baffi *mpl* moustache *sg*; (di animale) whiskers; **mi fa un baffo** I don't give a damn; **ridere sotto i ~** laugh up one's sleeve
baf'futo *adj* moustached

⚷ key word

ba'gagli *mpl* luggage, baggage; **ritiro ~** baggage claim
bagagli'aio *m* Rail luggage van, baggage car AmE; Auto boot
ba'gaglio *m* luggage, baggage; Mil kit; **un ~** a piece of luggage
■ **bagaglio a mano** hand luggage, hand baggage; **bagaglio in eccesso, bagaglio eccedente** excess baggage
baga'rino *m* ticket tout
baga'tella *f* trifle; Mus bagatelle
baggia'nata *f* piece of nonsense; **non dire baggianate** don't talk nonsense
Bagh'dad *f* Baghdad
bagli'ore *m* glare; (improvviso) flash; fig (di speranza) glimmer
bagna'cauda *f vegetables (especially raw) in an oil, garlic and anchovy sauce, typical of Piedmont*
ba'gnante *mf* bather
⚷ **ba'gnare** *vt* wet; (inzuppare) soak; (immergere) dip; (innaffiare) water; ‹*mare, lago*› wash; ‹*fiume*› flow through
ba'gnarsi *vr* get wet; (al mare ecc.) swim, bathe; **'vietato ~'** 'no bathing'
bagnasci'uga *m inv* edge of the water, waterline
ba'gnato *adj* wet; **~ fradicio** soaked
ba'gnino, -a *mf* life guard
⚷ **'bagno** *m* bath; (stanza) bathroom; (gabinetto) toilet; (al mare) swim, bathe; **bagni** *pl* (stabilimento) lido; **fare il ~** have a bath; (nel mare ecc.) [have a] swim, bathe; **andare in ~** go to the bathroom, go to the toilet; **mettere a ~** soak; **con ~** ‹*camera*› en suite
■ **bagno oculare** eyebath; **bagno rivelatore** Phot developing bath; **bagno di sangue** bloodbath; **bagno di sviluppo** Phot developing bath; **bagno turco** Turkish bath
bagnoma'ria *m* **cuocere a ~** cook in a double saucepan
bagnoschi'uma *m inv* bubble bath, foam bath
ba'guette *f inv* French loaf, baguette
Ba'hamas *fpl* **le ~** the Bahamas
Bah'rain *m* Bahrain
'baia *f* bay
baio'netta *f* bayonet
'baita *f* mountain chalet
bala'ustra, balau'strata *f* balustrade
balbet'tare *vt & vi* stammer; ‹*bambino*› babble

balbet'tio *m* stammering; (di bambino) babble
bal'buzie *f* stutter
balbuzi'ente **A** *adj* stuttering **B** *mf* stutterer
Bal'cani *mpl* Balkans
bal'canico *adj* Balkan
balco'nata *f* Theat balcony, dress circle
balcon'cino *m*
■ **reggiseno a balconcino** underwired bra
bal'cone *m* balcony
baldac'chino *m* canopy; **letto a ~** four-poster bed
bal'danza *f* boldness
baldan'zoso *adj* bold
bal'doria *f* revelry; **far ~** have a riotous time
Bale'ari *fpl* **le [isole] ~** the Balearics, the Balearic Islands
ba'lena *f* whale
bale'nare *vi* lighten; fig flash; **mi è balenata un'idea** I've just had an idea
bale'niera *f* whaler
ba'leno *m* **in un ~** in a flash
balenot'tera *f*
■ **balenottera azzurra** blue whale
ba'lera *f* dance hall
ba'lestra *f* crossbow
ba'lia[1] *f* **in ~ di** at the mercy of
'balia[2] *f* wet nurse
ba'listico *adj* ballistic; **perito balistico** ballistics expert
'balla *f* bale; infml (frottola) tall story
bal'labile *adj* **essere ~** be good for dancing to
bal'lare *vi* dance; **andare a ~** go dancing
bal'lata *f* ballad
balla'toio *m* (nelle scale) landing
balle'rino, -a **A** *mf* dancer; (classico) ballet dancer **B** *f* (classica) ballet dancer, ballerina
bal'letto *m* ballet
bal'lista *mf* infml bullshitter
'ballo *m* dance; (il ballare) dancing; **sala da ballo** ballroom; **essere in ~** ‹*lavoro, vita*› be at stake; ‹*persona*› be committed; **tirare qualcuno in ~** involve somebody
■ **ballo liscio** ballroom dancing; **ballo in maschera** masked ball
ballonzo'lare *vi* skip about
ballot'taggio *m* second count [of votes]
balne'are *adj* bathing *attrib*; **stagione balneare** swimming season; **stazione balneare** seaside resort
balneazi'one *f*
■ **'divieto di balneazione'** 'no bathing'
ba'lordo *adj* foolish; (stordito) stunned; **tempo ~** nasty weather
bal'samico *adj* ‹*aria*› balmy; (aceto) balsamic
'balsamo *m* balsam; (per capelli) conditioner; (lenimento) remedy

'baltico *adj* Baltic; **il [mar] Baltico** the Baltic [Sea]
balu'ardo *m* bulwark
'balza *f* crag; (di abito) flounce
bal'zano *adj* (idea) weird
bal'zare *vi* bounce; (saltare) jump; **~ in piedi** leap to one's feet
'balzo *m* bounce; (salto) jump; **prendere la palla al ~** fig seize an opportunity
bam'bagia *f* cotton wool; **vivere nella ~** fig be in clover
bam'bina *f* little girl; (piccola) baby; **ha avuto una ~** she had a [baby] girl
bambi'naia *f* nursemaid, nanny
bambi'nata *f* childish thing to do/say
bam'bino *m* child; (appena nato) baby; **avere un ~** have a baby; (maschio) have a [baby] boy; **bambini** *pl* children, kids; (piccoli) babies
■ **bambino prodigio** child prodigy
bambi'none, -a *mf* derog big *or* overgrown child
bam'boccio *m* chubby child; (sciocco) simpleton; (fantoccio) rag doll
'bambola *f* doll
bambo'lotto *m* male doll
bambù *m inv* bamboo
ba'nale *adj* banal
banalità *f inv* banality
banaliz'zare *vt* trivialize
ba'nana *f* banana
ba'nano *m* banana (tree)
'banca *f* bank
■ **banca d'affari** merchant bank, investment bank; **banca dati** databank; **banca etica** ethical bank; **Banca Europea per la Ricostruzione e lo Sviluppo** European Bank for Reconstruction and Development; **banca degli occhi** eye bank; **banca del sangue** blood bank; **banca dello sperma** sperm bank
banca'rella *f* stall
bancarel'lista *mf* stallholder
ban'cario, -a **A** *adj* banking *attrib*; **trasferimento ~** bank transfer **B** *mf* bank employee
banca'rotta *f* bankruptcy; **fare ~** go bankrupt
banchet'tare *vi* banquet
ban'chetto *m* banquet
banchi'ere *m* banker
ban'china *f* Naut quay; (in stazione) platform; (di strada) path
■ **banchina spartitraffico** central reservation, median strip AmE; **banchina non transitabile** soft verge
ban'chisa *f* floe
'banco *m* (di scuola) desk; (di negozio) counter; (di officina) bench; (di gioco, banca) bank; (di mercato) stall; (degli imputati) dock; **sotto ~** under the counter; **medicinale da banco** over the counter medicine
■ **banco dei formaggi** (in supermercato) cheese

b

counter; (in mercato) cheese stall; **banco di ghiaccio** ice floe; **banco informazioni** information desk; **banco di nebbia** fog bank; **banco di sabbia** sandbank

'bancomat® *m inv* (sportello) cash dispenser, cash machine, cashpoint; (carta) bank card, cash card

ban'cone *m* counter; (in bar) bar

banco'nota *f* banknote, bill AmE; **banconote** *pl* paper currency

'banda *f* band; (di delinquenti) gang

■ **banda d'atterraggio** Aeron landing strip; **banda larga** Comput broadband; **banda passante** bandwidth; **banda rumorosa** rumble strip

ban'dana *f* bandanna

banderu'ola *f* weathercock; Naut pennant

⚷ **bandi'era** *f* flag; **cambiare ~** change sides, switch allegiances

bandie'rina *f* (nel calcio) corner flag

bandie'rine *fpl* bunting

ban'dire *vt* banish; (pubblicare) publish; fig dispense with ‹*formalità, complimenti*›

ban'dista *mf* bandsman

bandi'tismo *m* banditry

ban'dito *m* bandit

bandi'tore *m* (di aste) auctioneer

'bando *m* proclamation

■ **bando di concorso** job advertisement (*published in an official gazette for a job for which a competitive examination has to be sat*)

bang *m inv* wham

■ **bang sonico** sonic boom

Bangla'desh *m* Bangladesh

⚷ **bar** *m inv* bar

'bara *f* coffin

ba'racca *f* hut; (catapecchia) hovel; **mandare avanti la ~** keep the ship afloat

barac'cato, -a **A** *adj* living in a shanty town **B** *mf* shanty town dweller

barac'chino *m* (di gelati, giornali) kiosk; Radio CB radio

barac'cone *m* (roulotte) circus caravan; (in luna park) booth; fig (organizzazione) lumbering great dinosaur of an organization

barac'copoli *f inv* shanty town

bara'onda *f* chaos; **non fare ~** don't make a mess

ba'rare *vi* cheat

'baratro *m* chasm

barat'tare *vt* barter

ba'ratto *m* barter

ba'rattolo *m* jar; (di latta) tin

⚷ **'barba** *f* beard; infml (noia) bore; **farsi la ~** shave; **in ~ a** in spite of; **è una ~** (noia) it's boring

barbabi'etola *f* beetroot; **barbabietole** *pl* beetroot

■ **barbabietola da zucchero** sugar beet

Bar'bados *fpl* **le ~** Barbados

barbagi'anni *m inv* barn owl

bar'barico *adj* barbaric

bar'barie *f inv* barbarity

barba'rismo *m* barbarism

'barbaro **A** *adj* barbarous **B** *m* barbarian

'barbecue *m inv* barbecue, BBQ

bar'betta *f* Naut painter

barbi'ere *m* barber; (negozio) barber's

bar'biglio *m* barb

barbi'turico *m* barbiturate

bar'bone, -a **A** *m* (vagabondo) vagrant; (cane) poodle **B** *f* bag lady

bar'boso *adj* infml boring

barbu'gliare *vi* mumble

bar'buto *adj* bearded

'barca *f* boat; **una ~ di** fig a lot of

■ **barca a motore** motor boat; **barca da pesca** fishing boat; **barca a remi** rowing boat, rowboat AmE; **barca di salvataggio** lifeboat; **barca a vela** sailing boat, sailboat AmE

barcai'olo *m* boatman

barcame'narsi *vr* manage

barca'rola *f* Mus barcarole

Barcel'lona *f* Barcelona

barcol'lare *vi* stagger

barcol'loni *adv* **camminare ~** stagger

bar'cone *m* barge; (di ponte) pontoon

bar'dare *vt* harness

bar'darsi *vr* (hum) dress up

barda'tura *f* (per cavallo) harness

ba'rella *f* stretcher

barelli'ere *m* stretcher-bearer

'Barents *m*

■ **mare di Barents** Barents Sea

ba'rese *adj* from Bari

bari'centro *m* centre of gravity

ba'rile *m* barrel

bari'lotto *m* fig tub of lard

ba'rista **A** *m* barman **B** *f* barmaid

ba'ritono *m* baritone

bar'lume *m* glimmer; **un ~ di speranza** a glimmer of hope

'barman *m inv* barman

'baro *m* card sharp

ba'rocco *adj & nm* baroque

ba'rometro *m* barometer

baro'nale *adj* baronial

ba'rone *m* baron; **i baroni** fig the top brass

baro'nessa *f* baroness

'barra *f* bar; (lineetta) oblique; Naut tiller

■ **barra delle applicazioni** Comput task bar; **barre** *pl* **laterali antintrusione** Auto side impact bars; **barra dei menu** Comput menu bar; **barra di navigazione** navigation bar; **barra retroversa**

⚷ key word

backslash; **barra di rimorchio** tow bar; **barra di scorrimento** Comput scroll bar; **barra spaziatrice** space bar; **barra di stato** Comput status bar; **barra degli strumenti** Comput tool bar; **barra di titolo** Comput title bar

bar'rage *m inv* Sport jump-off

bar'rare *vt* block off ‹*strada*›

barri'care *vt* barricade

barri'cata *f* barricade

barri'era *f* barrier; (stradale) road block; Geol reef

■ **barriera corallina** coral reef; **barriera linguistica** language barrier; **barriera razziale** colour bar; **barriera del suono** sound barrier

bar'rire *vi* trumpet

bar'rito *m* trumpeting

ba'ruffa *f* scuffle; **far ~** quarrel

barzel'letta *f* joke; **~ sporca** *o* **spinta** dirty joke

basa'mento *m* base; Geol bedrock

ba'sare *vt* base

ba'sarsi *vr* **~ su** be based on; **mi baso su ciò che ho visto** I'm going on [the basis of] what I saw

'basco, -a **A** *adj & mf* Basque
B *m* (copricapo) beret

'base *f* basis; (fondamento) foundation; Mil base; Pol rank and file; **a ~ di** containing; **in ~ a** on the basis of

■ **base di controllo** ground control; **base [di] dati** database; **base d'intesa** common ground; **base logica** logical basis; **base navale** naval base

'baseball *m* baseball

ba'setta *f* sideburn

basi'lare *adj* basic

ba'silica *f* basilica

Basili'cata *f* Basilicata

ba'silico *m* basil

ba'sista *m* grass roots politician; (di un crimine) mastermind

'basket *m* basketball

bas'sezza *f* lowness; (di statura) shortness; (viltà) vileness

bas'sista *mf* bassist

'basso **A** *adj* low; (di statura) short; ‹*acqua*› shallow; ‹*televisione*› quiet; (vile) despicable; **parlare a bassa voce** speak quietly, speak in a low voice; **la bassa Italia** southern Italy
B *m* lower part; Mus bass [guitar]; **guardare in ~** look down

basso'fondo *m* (*pl* **bassifondi**) shallows; **bassifondi** *pl* (quartieri poveri) slums

bassorili'evo *m* bas-relief

bas'sotto *m* dachshund

ba'stardo, -a **A** *adj* bastard; (di animale) mongrel
B *mf* bastard; (animale) mongrel

ba'stare *vi* be enough; (durare) last; **basta!** that's enough!, that'll do!; **basta che** (purché) provided that; **basta così** that's enough; **basta così?** is that enough?, will that do?; (in negozio) will there be anything else?; **basta andare alla posta** you only have to go to the post office; **basta che tu lo faccia bene** make sure you do it well

Basti'an con'trario *m* contrary old so-and-so

basti'mento *m* ship; (carico) cargo

basti'one *m* bastion

basto'nare *vt* beat

basto'nata *f* **dare una ~ a** beat with a stick

baston'cino *m* (da sci) ski pole

■ **bastoncino di pesce** fish finger, fish stick AmE

ba'stone *m* stick; (da golf) club; (da passeggio) walking stick

■ **bastone da hockey** hockey stick

ba'tosta *f* blow

bat'tage *m inv*

■ **battage pubblicitario** media hype

bat'taglia *f* battle; (lotta) fight

battagli'are *vi* battle; fig fight

bat'taglio *m* (di campana) clapper; (di porta) knocker

battagli'one *m* battalion

bat'tello *m* boat; (motonave) steamer

bat'tente *m* (di porta) wing; (di finestra) shutter; (battaglio) knocker

'battere **A** *vt* beat; hit, knock ‹*testa, spalla*›; (percorrere) scour; thresh ‹*grano*›; break ‹*record*›
B *vi* (bussare, urtare) knock; ‹*cuore*› beat; ‹*ali ecc.*› flap; Tennis serve; **~ a macchina** type; **~ gli occhi** blink; **~ il piede** tap one's foot; **~ le mani** clap [one's hands]; **~ le ore** strike the hours

bat'teri *mpl* bacteria

batte'ria *f* battery; Mus drums *pl*; Sport (eliminatoria) heat

■ **batteria a bottone** button battery

bat'terico *adj* bacterial

bat'terio *m* bacterium

batteriolo'gia *f* bacteriology

batterio'logico *adj* bacteriological

batte'rista *mf* drummer

'battersi *vr* fight

bat'tesimo *m* baptism, christening

battez'zare *vt* baptize, christen

battiba'leno *m* **in un ~** in a flash

batti'becco *m* squabble

batticu'ore *m* palpitation; **mi venne il ~** I was scared

bat'tigia *f* water's edge

batti'mano *m* applause

batti'panni *m inv* carpet beater

batti'scopa *m inv* skirting board

batti'stero *m* baptistery

batti'strada *m inv* outrider; (di pneumatico) tread; Sport pacesetter

battitap'peto *m inv* carpet sweeper

b

'battito *m* (alle tempie) throbbing; (di orologio) ticking; (della pioggia) beating
■ **battito cardiaco** heartbeat
batti'tore, -trice *mf* Sport batsman
bat'tuta *f* beat; (colpo) knock; (spiritosaggine) wisecrack; (osservazione) remark; Mus bar; Tennis service; Theat cue; (dattilografia) stroke
■ **battuta d'arresto** setback
ba'tuffolo *m* flock
ba'ule *m* trunk
bau'xite *f* bauxite
'bava *f* dribble; (di cane ecc.) slobber; **aver la ~ alla bocca** foam at the mouth
bava'glino *m* bib
ba'vaglio *m* gag
bava'rese *f ice-cream cake with milk, eggs and cream*
'bavero *m* collar
ba'zar *m inv* bazaar
ba'zooka *m inv* bazooka
baz'zecola *f* trifle
bazzi'care *vt & vi* haunt
baz'zotto *adj* soft-boiled
be'arsi *vr* delight (**di** in)
beata'mente *adv* blissfully
beatifi'care *vt* beatify
beati'tudine *f* bliss
⚷ **be'ato** *adj* blissful; Relig blessed; **~ te!** lucky you!
beauty-'case *m inv* toilet bag
bebè *m inv* baby
bec'caccia *f* woodcock
bec'care *vt* peck; fig catch
bec'carsi *vr* (litigare) quarrel
bec'cata *f* beakful; (colpo) peck
beccheggi'are *vi* pitch
bec'chime *m* birdseed
bec'chino *m* gravedigger
'becco *m* beak; (di caffettiera ecc.) spout; **chiudi il ~** infml shut your trap; **non ha il ~ di un quattrino** infml he's skint; **restare a ~ asciutto** infml end up with nothing
■ **becco Bunsen** Bunsen [burner]; **becco a gas** gas burner
bec'cuccio *m* spout
'beeper *m inv* beeper
be'fana *f legendary old woman who brings presents to children on Twelfth Night*; (giorno) Twelfth Night; (donna brutta) old witch
'beffa *f* hoax; **farsi beffe di qualcuno** mock somebody
bef'fardo *adj* derisory; ‹*persona*› mocking
bef'fare *vt* mock
bef'farsi *vr* **~ di** make fun of
beffeggi'are *vt* taunt
'bega *f* quarrel; **è una bella ~** it's really annoying

⚷ key word

be'gonia *f* begonia
beh *int* well
'beige *adj inv & nm* beige
Bei'rut *f* Beirut
be'lare *vi* bleat
be'lato *m* bleating
'belga *adj & nmf* Belgian
'Belgio *m* Belgium
Bel'grado *f* Belgrade
Be'lize *m* Belize
'bella *f* (in carte, Sport) decider; (innamorata) sweetheart
■ **bella di giorno** Bot morning glory; **bella di notte** fig lady of the night
⚷ **bel'lezza** *f* beauty; **che ~!** how lovely!; **per ~** (per decorazione) for decoration; **chiudere/finire in ~** end on a high note; **la ~ di tre mesi/500 euro** all of three months/500 euros
belli'cismo *m* warmongering
belli'cistico *adj* warmongering
'bellico *adj* war *attrib*; **periodo ~** wartime
bellicosità *f inv* belligerence
belli'coso *adj* warlike
bellige'rante *adj & nmf* belligerent
bellige'ranza *f* belligerence
bellim'busto *m* dandy
⚷ **'bello** **A** *adj* nice; (di aspetto) beautiful; ‹*uomo*› handsome; (moralmente) good; **cosa fai di ~ stasera?** what are you up to tonight?; **oggi fa ~** it's a nice day today; **una bella cifra** a lot; **un bel piatto di pasta** a big plate of pasta; **nel bel mezzo** right in the middle; **un bel niente** absolutely nothing; **bell'e fatto** over and done with; **bell'amico sei!** fine friend you are!; **questa è bella!** that's a good one!; **bel voto** good mark; **il bel mondo** the beautiful people; **le belle arti** the fine arts
B *m* (bellezza) beauty; (innamorato) sweetheart; **sul più ~** at the crucial moment; **il ~ è che ...** the funny thing is that ...
beltà *f inv* (liter) beauty
'belva *f* wild beast
be'molle *m* Mus flat
ben ▸ **bene**
benché *conj* though, although
'benda *f* bandage; (per occhi) blindfold
ben'dare *vt* bandage; blindfold ‹*occhi*›
bendi'sposto *adj* **essere ~ verso** be well-disposed towards
⚷ **'bene** **A** *adv* well; **ben ~** thoroughly; **~!** good!; **star ~** (di salute) be well; ‹*vestito, stile*› suit; (finanziariamente) be well off; **non sta ~** (non è educato) it's not nice; **sta/va ~!** all right!; **ti sta ~!** [it] serves you right!; **ti auguro ~** I wish you well; **voler ~ a** love; **di ~ in meglio** better and better; **fare ~** (aver ragione) do the right thing; **fare ~ a** ‹*cibo*›

be good for; **una persona per ~** a good person; **per ~** (fare) properly; **è ben difficile** it's very difficult; **ben cotto** well done; **come tu ben sai** as you well know; **lo credo ~!** I can well believe it!
B *m* good; **per il tuo ~** for your own good; **beni** *pl* (averi) property *sg*; **un ~ di famiglia** a family heirloom; Fin assets
■ **beni ambientali** *pl* environment; **beni di consumo** *pl* consumer products, consumer goods; **beni culturali** *pl* cultural heritage; **beni immobili** *pl* real estate, realty AmE; **beni mobili** *pl* movables

benedet'tino *adj & nm* Benedictine

bene'detto *adj* blessed

bene'dire *vt* bless; **mandare qualcuno a farsi ~** infml tell somebody to get lost

benedizi'one *f* blessing

benedu'cato *adj* well-mannered

benefat|'tore, -trice *mf* benefactor; benefactress

benefi'care *vt* help

benefi'cenza *f* charity

benefici'are *vi* **~ di** profit by

benefici'ario, -a *adj & nmf* beneficiary

bene'ficio *m* benefit; **con ~ di inventario** with reservations
■ **beneficio accessorio** perquisite

be'nefico *adj* beneficial; (di beneficenza) charitable

'Benelux *m* Benelux

beneme'renza *f* benevolence

bene'merito *adj* worthy

bene'placito *m* consent, approval

be'nessere *m* well-being

bene'stante **A** *adj* well off
B *mf* well-off person

bene'stare *m* consent

benevo'lenza *f* benevolence

be'nevolo *adj* benevolent

ben'fatto *adj* well-made

Ben'gala *m* Bengal

ben'godi *m* **il paese di ~** a land of plenty

benia'mino *m* favourite

be'nigno *adj* kindly; Med benign

Be'nin *m* Benin

beninfor'mato **A** *adj* well-informed
B *npl* **i beninformati** those in the know

benintenzio'nato, -a **A** *adj* well-meaning
B *mf* well-meaning person

benin'teso *adv* needless to say, of course; **~ che** ... of course, ...

be'nissimo *int* fine

benpen'sante *adj & nmf* self-righteous

benser'vito *m* **dare il ~ a qualcuno** give somebody the sack

bensì *conj* but rather

benve'nuto *adj & nm* welcome; **benvenuta!** welcome!

ben'visto *adj* **essere ~ (da qualcuno)** go down well (with somebody)

benvo'lere *vt* **farsi ~ da qualcuno** win somebody's affection; **prendere a ~ qualcuno** take a liking to somebody; **essere benvoluto da tutti** be well-liked by everyone

ben'zene *m* benzene

ben'zina *f* petrol, gas AmE; **far ~** get petrol
■ **benzina avio** aviation fuel; **benzina con piombo** leaded petrol; **benzina senza piombo** *o* **verde** lead-free petrol, unleaded petrol; **benzina super** four-star petrol, premium gas AmE

benzi'naio, -a *mf* petrol station attendant, gas station attendant AmE

be'one, -a *mf* infml boozer

'berbero, -a *adj & nmf* Berber

'bere **A** *vt* drink; (assorbire) absorb; fig swallow; **~ una tazza di tè** have a cup of tea
B *m* drinking; **da ~ e da mangiare** food and drink

berga'motto *m* bergamot

'Bering *m* **il mare di ~** the Bering Sea; **lo stretto di ~** the Bering Straits

ber'lina *f* Auto saloon; **mettere alla ~ qualcuno** ridicule somebody

berli'nese **A** *mf* Berliner
B *adj* Berlin *attrib*

Ber'lino *m* Berlin
■ **Berlino Est** East Berlin

ber'muda *fpl* (pantaloni) Bermuda shorts

Ber'muda *fpl* **le ~** the Bermudas

'Berna *f* Berne

ber'noccolo *m* bump; (disposizione) flair

ber'retto *m* beret, cap
■ **berretto a pompon** bobble hat

bersagli'are *vt* fig bombard

ber'saglio *m* target

bescia'mella *f* béchamel, white sauce

be'stemmia *f* swear word; (maledizione) oath; (sproposito) blasphemy

bestemmi'are *vi* swear

'bestia *f* animal; (persona brutale) beast; (persona sciocca) fool; **andare in ~** infml blow one's top; **lavorare come una ~** slave away
■ **bestia nera** fig pet hate

besti'ale *adj* bestial; ‹*espressione, violenza*› brutal; infml ‹*freddo, fame*› terrible; **fa un caldo/freddo ~** it's dreadfully hot/cold

bestialità *f inv* bestiality; fig nonsense

besti'ame *m* livestock

betabloc'cante *m* beta blocker

Be'tlemme *f* Bethlehem

betoni'era *f* concrete mixer

'bettola *f* fig dive

be'tulla *f* birch
■ **betulla bianca** silver birch

be'vanda *f* drink

b

■ **bevanda alcolica** alcoholic drink
bevi'tore, -trice *mf* drinker
be'vuta *f* drink
be'vuto pp di **bere**
Bhu'tan *m* Bhutan
bi+ *pref* bi+
bi'ada *f* fodder
✓ **bianche'ria** *f* linen
■ **biancheria per la casa** household linen; **biancheria intima** underwear; (da donna) lingerie; **biancheria da letto** bed linen
bian'chetto *m* correction fluid
✓ **bi'anco, -a** **A** *adj* white; ‹*foglio*› blank; **voce bianca** treble voice
B *mf* white
C *m* white; **mangiare in ~** eat bland food; **andare in ~** infml not score; **in ~ e nero** (film, fotografia) black and white, monochrome; **passare una notte in ~** have a sleepless night
■ **bianco sporco** off white; **bianco d'uovo** egg white
biancomangi'are *m* blancmange
bian'core *m* (bianchezza) whiteness
bianco'segno *m* Jur *blank document bearing a signature*
bianco'spino *m* hawthorn
biasci'care *vt* (mangiare) eat noisily; (parlare) mumble
biasi'mare *vt* blame
biasi'mevole *adj* blameworthy
bi'asimo *m* blame
'Bibbia *f* Bible
bibe'ron *m inv* [baby's] bottle
'bibita *f* [soft] drink
■ **bibita alcolica** alcopop; **bibita gasata** fizzy drink
'biblico *adj* biblical
bibliogra'fia *f* bibliography
biblio'grafico *adj* bibliographical
biblio'teca *f* library; (mobile) bookcase
bibliote'cario, -a *mf* librarian
bicame'rale *adj* two-chamber *attrib*, bicameral
bicarbo'nato *m* bicarbonate
■ **bicarbonato di sodio** bicarbonate of soda
bicchie'rata *f* glassful
✓ **bicchi'ere** *m* glass
bicchie'rino *m* infml tipple
bicente'nario *m* bicentenary
'bici *f* infml bike
✓ **bici'cletta** *f* bicycle, bike; **andare in ~** cycle, go by bike; (saper portare la bicicletta) ride a bicycle
■ **bicicletta da corsa** racer
bi'cipite *m* biceps
bi'cocca *f* hovel
bico'lore *adj* two-coloured

✓ key word

bidè *m inv* bidet
bi'dello, -a *mf* janitor, [school] caretaker
bidirezio'nale *adj* bidirectional
bido'nare *vt* con, swindle; **farsi ~** be conned
bido'nata *f* infml swindle
bi'done *m* bin; infml (truffa) swindle; **fare un ~ a qualcuno** infml stand somebody up
■ **bidone dell'immondizia, bidone della spazzatura** rubbish bin, trash can AmE
bidon'ville *f inv* shanty town
bi'eco *adj* callous
bi'ella *f* connecting rod
Bielo'russia *f* Belarus
bielo'russo, -a *adj & nmf* Belorussian
bien'nale *adj* biennial
bi'ennio *m* two-year period
bi'erre *fpl* (Brigate Rosse) Red Brigades
bi'etola *f* beet
bifo'cale *adj* bifocal
bi'folco, -a *mf* fig boor
bifor'carsi *vr* fork
biforcazi'one *f* fork
bifor'cuto *adj* forked
biga'mia *f* bigamy
'bigamo, -a **A** *adj* bigamous
B *mf* bigamist
big bang *m* big bang
bighello'nare *vi* loaf around
bighel'lone *m* loafer
bigiotte'ria *f* costume jewellery; (negozio) jeweller's
bigliet'taio *m* booking clerk; (sui treni) ticket collector
bigliette'ria *f* ticket office; Theat box office
■ **biglietteria automatica** ticket vending machine
✓ **bigli'etto** *m* ticket; (lettera breve) note; (cartoncino) card; (di banca) banknote
■ **biglietto di sola andata** single [ticket]; **biglietto di andata e ritorno** return [ticket]; **biglietto di auguri** card; **biglietto chilometrico** *ticket allowing travel up to a maximum specified distance*; **biglietto collettivo** group ticket; **biglietto elettronico** e-ticket; **biglietto giornaliero** day pass; **biglietto d'ingresso** entrance ticket; **biglietto d'invito** invitation card; **biglietto della lotteria** lottery ticket; **biglietto da visita** business card
bigliet'tone *m* infml (soldi) big one
bignè *m inv* puff
■ **bignè alla crema** cream puff
bigo'dino *m* roller
bi'gotto *m* religionist
bi'kini *m inv* bikini
bi'lancia *f* scales *pl*; (di orologio) Comm balance; **Bilancia** Astr Libra
■ **bilancia commerciale** balance of trade; **bilancia da cucina** kitchen scales; **bilancia dei pagamenti** balance of payments; **bilancia**

pesapersone scales
bilanci'are *vt* balance; fig weigh
bilancia'tura *f*
■ **bilanciatura gomme** wheel balancing
bilanci'ere *m* (in sollevamento pesi) bar bell; (di orologio) balance wheel
bi'lancio *m* budget; Comm balance [sheet]; **fare il ~** balance the books; fig take stock; **chiudere il ~ in attivo/passivo** to end the financial year in profit/with a loss
■ **bilancio patrimoniale** balance sheet; **bilancio preventivo** budget
bilate'rale *adj* bilateral
'bile *f* bile; fig rage
bili'ardo *m* billiards *sg*
'bilico *m* equilibrium; **in ~** in the balance
bi'lingue *adj* bilingual
bilingu'ismo *m* bilingualism
bili'one *m* billion
bili'oso *adj* bilious
bilo'cale **A** *adj* two-room
B *m* two-room flat
'bimbo, -a *mf* child
■ **~ in fasce** babe in arms
bimen'sile *adj* fortnightly BrE, twice monthly
bime'strale *adj* bimonthly
bi'mestre *m* two months
bi'nario *m* track; (piattaforma) platform
bi'nocolo *m* binoculars *pl*
bi'nomio *m* binomial
bio+ *pref* bio+
bioagricol'tore *m* organic farmer
bioagricol'tura *f* organic farming
bio'chimica *f* biochemistry
bio'chimico, -a **A** *mf* biochemist
B *adj* biochemical
biocompa'tibile *adj* biocompatible
biodegra'dabile *adj* biodegradable
biodiversità *f inv* biodiversity
bio'etica *f* bioethics *sg*
bio'fisica *f* biophysics *sg*
bio'gas *m* biogas
biogra'fia *f* biography
bio'grafico *adj* biographical
bi'ografo, -a *mf* biographer
bioingegne'ria *f* bioengineering
biolo'gia *f* biology
biologica'mente *adv* biologically
bio'logico *adj* biological; ‹*agricoltura*› organic
bi'ologo, -a *mf* biologist
bi'onda *f* blonde
■ **bionda ossigenata** peroxide blonde; **bionda platinata** platinum blonde
bi'ondo **A** *adj* blond
B *m* fair colour; (uomo) fair-haired man
■ **biondo cenere** ash blond; **biondo platino** platinum blonde

bi'onico *adj* bionic
bio'psia *f* biopsy
bio'ritmo *m* biorhythm
bio'sfera *f* biosphere
bi'ossido *m* dioxide
■ **biossido di carbonio** carbon dioxide
biotecnolo'gia *f* biotechnology
bioterro'rismo *m* bioterrorism
bip *m inv* blip
bipar'titico *adj* bipartisan
biparti'tismo *m* two-party system
bipar'tito **A** *adj* bipartite, two-party *attrib*
B *m* two-party coalition
bipartizi'one *f* division into two parts
bipo'lare *adj* Electr bipolar; Pol dominated by two large parties
bipola'rismo *m* Pol *system in which the numerous parties line up behind two main parties*
bipolarizazzi'one *f* Pol *tendency towards 'bipolarism'*
bi'posto *adj inv & m inv* two-seater
'birba *f*, **birbante** *m* rascal, rogue
birbo'nata *f* trick
bir'bone *adj* wicked
birdie *m inv* (golf) birdie
biri'chino, -a **A** *adj* naughty
B *mf* little devil
bi'rillo *m* skittle; (di segnaletica stradale) traffic cone
Bir'mania *f* Burma
bir'mano, -a *adj & nmf* Burmese
'birra *f* beer; **a tutta ~** fig flat out
■ **birra chiara** lager; **birra grande** ≈ pint; **birra piccola** ≈ half-pint; **birra scura** dark beer, brown ale BrE
birre'ria *f* beer-house; (fabbrica) brewery
bis *m inv* encore
bi'saccia *f* haversack
bi'sbetica *f* shrew
bi'sbetico *adj* bad-tempered
bisbigli'are *vt & vi* whisper
bi'sboccia *f* **fare ~** make merry
'bisca *f* gambling house
Bi'scaglia *f* **il golfo di ~** the Bay of Biscay
'biscia *f* snake
biscotti'era *f* biscuit barrel, biscuit tin
bi'scotto *m* biscuit
■ **biscotto per cani** dog biscuit
bisessu'ale *adj & nmf* bisexual
bise'stile *adj* **anno ~** leap year
bisettima'nale *adj* twice weekly
biset'trice *f* bisector
bisezi'one *f* bisection
bisil'labico *adj* two syllable *attrib*, bisyllabic
bi'slacco *adj* peculiar
bi'slungo *adj* oblong
bi'snonno, -a **A** *m* great-grandfather

b

B *f* great-grandmother

biso'gnare *vi* **bisogna agire subito** we must act at once; **bisogna farlo** it is necessary to do it; **non bisogna scongelarlo** you don't need to defrost it

bi'sogno *m* need; (povertà) poverty; **aver ~ di** need

biso'gnoso *adj* needy; (povero) poor; **~ di** in need of

bi'sonte *m* bison

bi'stecca *f* steak

■ **bistecca di cavallo** horsemeat steak; **bistecca ai ferri** grilled steak; **bistecca alla fiorentina** large grilled beef steak

bi'sticci *mpl* bickering

bisticci'are *vi* quarrel

bi'sticcio *m* quarrel; (gioco di parole) pun

bistrat'tare *vt* mistreat

bistrò *m inv* bistro

'bisturi *m inv* scalpel

bi'sunto *adj* very greasy

bit *m inv* bit

bito'nale *adj* two-tone

bi'torzolo *m* lump

'bitter *m inv* bitter aperitif

bi'tume *m* bitumen

bivac'care *vi* bivouac

bi'vacco *m* bivouac

'bivio *m* crossroads; (di strada) fork

bizan'tino *adj* Byzantine

'bizza *f* tantrum; **fare le bizze** ‹*bambini*› play up

bizzar'ria *f* eccentricity

biz'zarro *adj* bizarre

biz'zeffe *adv* **a ~** galore

black'jack *m* blackjack

blan'dire *vt* soothe; (allettare) flatter

'blando *adj* mild

bla'sfemo *adj* blasphemous

bla'sone *m* coat of arms

blate'rare *vi* blather; **~ di qualcosa** burble on about something

'blatta *f* cockroach

'bleso *adj* lisping

blin'dare *vt* armour-plate

blin'dato *adj* armoured

'blinker *m inv* blinker

'blister *m inv* blister pack

blitz *m inv* blitz

bloc'care *vt* block; (isolare) cut off; Mil blockade; Comm freeze; stop ‹*assegno*›; **~ l'accesso a** seal off

bloc'carsi *vr* Mech jam

blocca'sterzo *m* steering lock

bloc'cato *adj* blocked

bloc'chetto *m*:

■ **blocchetto per appunti** memo pad; **blocchetto di biglietti** book of tickets

'blocco *m* block; Mil blockade; (dei fitti) restriction; (di carta) pad; (unione) coalition; **in ~** Comm in bulk

■ **blocco chiamate** Teleph call barring; **blocco per appunti** notepad; **blocco psicologico** mental block; **blocco stradale** road block

block-'notes *m inv* memo pad

blog *m inv* blog

blog'gare *vi* blog

'blogger *mf* blogger

blogos'fera *f* blogosphere

blu *adj & nm* blue

blu'astro *adj* bluish

blue chip *f inv* Fin blue chip

blue-'jeans *mpl* jeans

bluff *m inv* (carte, fig) bluff

bluf'fare *vi* (carte, fig) bluff

'blusa *f* blouse

'boa **A** *m* boa [constrictor]; (sciarpa) [feather] boa

B *f* Naut buoy

bo'ato *m* rumbling

bo'bina *f* spool; (di film) reel; Electr coil

bobi'nare *vt* spool

'bocca *f* mouth; **a ~ aperta** fig dumbfounded; **in ~ al lupo!** infml break a leg!; **fare la respirazione ~ a ~ a qualcuno** give somebody mouth to mouth resuscitation, give somebody the kiss of life; **essere di ~ buona** eat anything; fig be easily satisfied; **essere sulla ~ di tutti** be the talk of the town

■ **bocca del camino** chimney breast; **bocca di leone** snapdragon

boccac'cesco *adj* licentious

boc'caccia *f* grimace; **far boccacce** make faces

boc'caglio *m* nozzle

boc'cale *m* jug; (da birra) mug

bocca'porto *m* Naut hatch

bocca'scena *m inv* proscenium

boc'cata *f* (di fumo) puff; **prendere una ~ d'aria** get a breath of fresh air

boc'cetta *f* small bottle

boccheggi'are *vi* gasp

boc'chino *m* cigarette holder; (di pipa) Mus mouthpiece

'boccia *f* (palla) bowl; **bocce** *pl* (gioco) bowls *sg*; **giocare a bocce** play bowls

bocci'are *vt* (agli esami) fail; (respingere) reject; (alle bocce) hit; **essere bocciato** fail; (ripetere) repeat a year

boccia'tura *f* failure

bocci'olo *m* bud

'boccolo *m* ringlet

boccon'cino *m* morsel

boc'cone *m* mouthful; (piccolo pasto) snack

boc'coni *adv* face down[wards]

Bo'emia *f* Bohemia

key word

bo'emo, -a *adj & nmf* Bohemian
bo'ero, -a *mf* Afrikaner
bofonchi'are *vi* grumble
boh *int* dunno
'boia *m* executioner; **fa un freddo ~** infml it's brass monkey weather; **ho un sonno ~** infml I can't keep my eyes open
boi'ata *f* infml rubbish
boicot'taggio *m* boycotting
boicot'tare *vt* boycott
bo'lero *m* bolero
'bolgia *f* (caos) bedlam
'bolide *m* meteor; **passare come un ~** shoot past [like a rocket]
Bo'livia *f* Bolivia
bolivi'ano, -a *adj & nmf* Bolivian
'bolla *f* bubble; (vescica, in tappezzeria) blister; **finire in una ~ di sapone** go up in smoke; **~ immobiliare** property bubble
■ **bolla di accompagnamento** packing list; **bolla d'aria** (in acqua) air bubble; **bolla di consegna** packing list; **bolla speculativa** speculative bubble
bol'lare *vt* stamp; fig brand
bol'lato *adj* fig branded; **carta bollata** *paper with stamp showing payment of duty*
bol'lente *adj* boiling [hot]
bol'letta *f* bill; **essere in ~** be hard up
bollet'tino *m* bulletin; Comm list
■ **bollettino d'informazione** fact sheet; **bollettino meteorologico** weather report; **bollettino ufficiale** gazette
bolli'latte *m* milk pan
bol'lino *m* stamp
bol'lire *vt & vi* boil
bol'lito *m* boiled meat
bolli'tore *m* boiler; (per l'acqua) kettle
bolli'tura *f* boiling
'bollo *m* stamp; Auto tax disc
bol'lore *m* boil; (caldo) intense heat; fig ardour
Bo'logna *f* Bologna
bolo'gnese *mf* person from Bologna; **spaghetti alla ~** spaghetti bolognese
'bomba *f* bomb; **a prova di ~** bomb-proof; **tornare a ~** get back to the point
■ **bomba atomica** nuclear bomb; **bomba intelligente** smart bomb; **bomba a mano** hand grenade; **bomba molotov** petrol bomb; **bomba ad orologeria** time bomb; **bomba sporca** dirty bomb
bombarda'mento *m* shelling; (con aerei) bombing; fig bombardment
■ **bombardamento aereo** air raid
bombar'dare *vt* shell; (con aerei) bomb; fig bombard; **~ a tappeto** carpet-bomb
bombardi'ere *m* bomber
bom'bato *adj* domed
'bomber *m inv* bomber jacket
bom'betta *f* bowler [hat]
'bombo *m* bumblebee
'bombola *f* cylinder
■ **bombola di gas** gas bottle, gas cylinder
bombo'letta *f* spray can
bombo'lone *m* doughnut
bomboni'era *f wedding keepsake*
bo'naccia *f* Naut calm
bonacci'one, -a **A** *mf* good-natured person
B *adj* good-natured
bo'nario *adj* kindly
bo'nifica *f* land reclamation
bonifi'care *vt* reclaim
bo'nifico *m*
■ **bonifico [bancario]** [credit] transfer
bontà *f inv* goodness; (gentilezza) kindness
'bonus-'malus *m inv* Auto *car insurance policy with no claims bonus clause*
'boogie *m* boogie
'book'maker *m inv* bookmaker
'boomerang *m inv* boomerang
boot *m* Comput boot-up; **eseguire il ~** boot up
'bora *f cold north-east wind in the upper Adriatic*
borbot'tare *vi* mumble; (stomaco) rumble
borbot'tio *m* mumbling; (di stomaco) rumbling
'borchia *f* stud
borchi'ato *adj* studded
bor'dare *vt* border
bor'data *f* Naut broadside
borda'tura *f* border
bor'deaux **A** *m inv* (vino) claret, Bordeaux
B *adj inv* (colore) claret
bor'dello *m* brothel; fig bedlam; (disordine) mess
bor'dino *m* narrow border
'bordo *m* border; (estremità) edge; **a ~** Aeron, Naut on board; **d'alto ~** ‹*prostituta*› high-class
■ **bordo d'attacco** Aeron leading edge
bor'dura *f* border
bor'gata *f* hamlet
bor'ghese *adj* bourgeois; ‹*abito*› civilian; **in ~** in civilian dress; ‹*poliziotto*› in plain clothes
borghe'sia *f* middle classes *pl*
'borgo *m* village; (quartiere) district
'boria *f* conceit
bori'oso *adj* conceited
bor'lotto *m*
■ **[fagiolo] borlotto** pinto bean
'Borneo *m* Borneo
boro'talco *m* talcum powder
bor'raccia *f* flask
'borsa *f* bag; (borsetta) handbag
■ **borsa dell'acqua calda** hot-water bottle; **borsa frigo** cool box; **borsa della spesa** shopping

bag; **borsa di studio** scholarship; **borsa termica** cool bag; **borsa da viaggio** travel bag

'Borsa *f*

■ **Borsa [valori]** Stock Exchange

borsai'olo *m* pickpocket

bor'seggio *m* pickpocketing

borsel'lino *m* purse

bor'sello *m* (portamonete) purse; (borsetto) man's handbag

bor'setta *f* handbag

bor'setto *m* man's handbag

bor'sino *m* Fin dealing room

bor'sista *mf* Fin speculator; Sch scholarship holder

bor'sone *m* carryall

bo'scaglia *f* woodlands *pl*

boscai'olo *m* woodman; (guardaboschi) forester

bo'schetto *m* grove

'bosco *m* wood

bo'scoso *adj* wooded

'Bosnia *f* Bosnia

bos'niaco, -a *adj & nmf* Bosnian

Bosnia-Erzego'vina *f* Bosnia-Herzegovina

boss *m inv*

■ **boss mafioso** Mafia boss

'bosso *m* boxwood

'bossolo *m* cartridge case

Bot *nm abbr* (**Buoni Ordinari Del Tesoro**) T-bills

bo'tanica *f* botany

bo'tanico **A** *adj* botanical
B *m* botanist

'botola *f* trapdoor

Bot'swana *m* Botswana

'botta *f* blow; (rumore) bang; **fare a botte** come to blows

■ **botta e risposta** fig thrust and counter-thrust

botta'trice *f* monkfish

'botte *f* barrel

bot'tega *f* shop; (di artigiano) workshop

botte'gaio, -a *mf* shopkeeper

botte'ghino *m* Theatr box office; (del lotto) lottery shop

bot'tiglia *f* bottle; **in ~** bottled

bottiglie'ria *f* wine shop

bot'tino *m* loot; Mil booty

'botto *m* bang; **di ~** all of a sudden

bot'tone *m* button; Bot bud

■ **bottone di carica** winder

botu'lino *m* botulin

botu'lismo *m* botulism

bour'bon *m inv* bourbon

bo'vini *mpl* cattle

bo'vino *adj* bovine

■ **carne bovina** beef

'bowling *m* bowling, tenpin bowling BrE

box *m inv* (per cavalli) loose box; (recinto per bambini) play pen

'boxe *f* boxing

'boxer *mpl* jockey shorts

'bozza *f* draft; Typ proof; (bernoccolo) bump

■ **bozza in colonna** galley [proof]; **bozza definitiva** page proof; **bozza impaginata** page proof; **bozza di stampa** page proof

boz'zetto *m* sketch

'bozzolo *m* cocoon

BR *fpl abbr* (**Brigate Rosse**) Red Brigades

brac'care *vt* hunt

brac'cetto *m* **a ~** arm in arm

bracci'ale *m* bracelet; (fascia) armband

braccia'letto *m* bracelet; (di orologio) watch strap

■ **braccialetto identificativo** identity bracelet

bracci'ante *m* day labourer

bracci'ata *f* (nel nuoto) stroke

'braccio *m* (*pl nf* **braccia**) arm ((di fiume) *pl* **bracci**) arm

■ **braccio di ferro** arm wrestling

bracci'olo *m* (di sedia) arm[rest]; (da nuoto) armband

'bracco *m* hound

bracconi'ere *m* poacher

'brace *f* embers *pl*; **alla ~** char-grilled

'brache *fpl* infml (pantaloni) britches; **calare le ~** fig chicken out

braci'ere *m* brazier

braci'ola *f* chop

■ **braciola di maiale** pork chop

'brado *adj* **allo stato ~** in the wild

braille *m* Braille

brain-'storming *m inv* brainstorming

'brama *f* longing

bra'mare *vt* long for

bra'mino *m* Brahmin

bramo'sia *f* yearning

'branca *f* branch

'branchia *f* gill

'branco *m* (di cani) pack; derog (di persone) gang

branco'lare *vi* grope

'branda *f* camp bed

bran'dello *m* scrap; **a brandelli** in tatters

bran'dina *f* cot

bran'dire *vt* brandish

'brandy *m inv* brandy

'brano *m* piece; (di libro) passage

bran'zino *m* sea bass

bra'sare *vt* braise

bra'sato *m* *braised beef with herbs*

Bra'sile *m* Brazil

brasili'ano, -a *adj & nmf* Brazilian

bra'vata *f* bragging

'bravo *adj* good; (abile) clever; (coraggioso) brave; **~!** well done!

bra'vura *f* skill

key word

'breccia *f* breach; **sulla ~** fig very successful, at the top
brecci'ame *m* loose chipping *pl*
bre'saola *f dried, salted beef sliced thinly and eaten cold*
Bre'tagna *f* Brittany
bre'tella *f* shoulder strap; (strada) link road; Mech brace; **bretelle** *pl* (di calzoni) braces, suspenders AmE
'bretone *adj & nmf* Breton
'breve *adj* brief, short; **in ~** briefly; **tra ~** shortly
brevet'tare *vt* patent
bre'vetto *m* patent; (attestato) licence
brevità *f inv* shortness
'brezza *f* breeze
bricco'nata *f* dirty trick
bric'cone *m* blackguard; (hum) rascal
'briciola *f* crumb; fig grain
'briciolo *m* fragment; **non hai un ~ di cervello!** you don't have an ounce of common sense!
bridge *m inv* (carte) bridge
'briga *f* (fastidio) trouble; (lite) quarrel; **attaccar ~** pick a quarrel; **prendersi la ~ di fare qualcosa** go to the trouble of doing something
brigadi'ere *m* (dei carabinieri) sergeant
brigan'taggio *m* highway robbery
bri'gante *m* bandit; (hum) rogue
bri'gare *vi* to intrigue
bri'gata *f* brigade; (gruppo) group
briga'tista *mf* Pol member of the Red Brigades
'briglia *f* rein; **a ~ sciolta** at full gallop; fig at breakneck speed
bril'lante **A** *adj* brilliant; (scintillante) sparkling
B *m* diamond
brillan'tina *f* brilliantine
bril'lare *vi* shine; ‹*metallo*› glitter; (scintillare) sparkle
'brillo *adj* tipsy
'brina *f* hoar frost
brin'dare *vi* toast; **~ a qualcuno** drink a toast to somebody
'brindisi *m inv* toast
'brio *m* vivacity
bri'oche *f inv* croissant
bri'oso *adj* vivacious
'briscola *f* (seme) trumps
bri'tannico *adj* British
'brivido *m* shiver; (di paura ecc.) shudder; (di emozione) thrill; **avere i brividi** have the shivers; **dare i brividi a qualcuno** give somebody the shivers
brizzo'lato *adj* ‹*capelli, barba*› greying
'brocca *f* jug
broc'cato *m* brocade
'broccoli *mpl* broccoli *sg*
bro'daglia *f* derog dishwater
'brodo *m* broth; (per cucinare) stock
■ **brodo di manzo** beef tea; **brodo di pollo** chicken broth; (per cucinare) chicken stock; **brodo ristretto** consommé; **brodo vegetale** clear broth; (per cucinare) vegetable stock
'broglio *m*
■ **broglio elettorale** gerrymandering
'broker *mf inv* broker
■ **broker d'assicurazioni** insurance broker
'bromo *m* Chem bromine
bro'muro *m* bromide
bronchi'ale *adj* bronchial
bron'chite *f* bronchitis
bron'chitico *adj* chesty
'broncio *m* sulk; **fare il ~** sulk
bronto'lare *vi* grumble; ‹*tuono ecc.*› rumble; **~ contro qualcuno/qualcosa** grumble *or* grouch about somebody/something
bronto'lio *m* grumbling; (di tuono, stomaco) rumbling
bronto'lone, -a *mf* grumbler
'bronzo *m* bronze; **una faccia di ~** infml a brass neck
bros'sura *f*
■ **edizione in brossura** paperback
browser *m* Comput browser
bru'care *vt* ‹*pecora*› graze
bruciacchi'are *vt* scorch
bruci'ante *adj* burning
brucia'pelo *adv* **a ~** point-blank
bruci'are **A** *vt* burn; (scottare) scald; (incendiare) set fire to
B *vi* burn; (scottare) scald
bruci'arsi *vr* burn oneself
bruci'ato *adj* burnt; fig burnt-out
brucia'tore *m* burner
brucia'tura *f* burn
bruci'ore *m* burning sensation
'bruco *m* caterpillar
'brufolo *m* spot, pimple
brufo'loso *adj* spotty, pimply
brughi'era *f* heath
bruli'care *vi* swarm
bruli'chio *m* swarming
'brullo *adj* bare
'bruma *f* mist
Bru'nei *m* Brunei
'bruno *adj* brown; ‹*occhi, capelli*› dark
brusca'mente *adv* (di colpo) suddenly; (in tono brusco) sharply
bru'schetta *f toasted bread rubbed with garlic and sprinkled with olive oil*
'brusco *adj* sharp; (persona) brusque, abrupt; (improvviso) sudden
bru'sio *m* buzzing
bru'tale *adj* brutal

b

brutalità *f inv* brutality
brutaliz'zare *vt* brutalize
'bruto *adj & nm* brute
brut'tezza *f* ugliness
'brutto *adj* ugly; ‹*tempo, tipo, situazione, affare*› nasty; (cattivo) bad
■ **brutta copia** rough copy; **~ tiro** dirty trick
brut'tura *f* ugly thing
bub'bone *m* Med swelling
'buca *f* hole; (avvallamento) hollow
■ **buca delle lettere** letter box
buca'neve *m inv* snowdrop
bucani'ere *m* buccaneer
bu'care **A** *vt* make a hole in; (pungere) prick; punch ‹*biglietti*›
B *vi* have a puncture
'Bucarest *f* Bucharest
bu'carsi *vr* prick oneself; (con droga) shoot up
buca'tini *mpl pasta similar to spaghetti but thicker and hollow*
bu'cato *m* washing; **fare il ~** do the washing
'buccia *f* peel, skin; **bucce** *pl* (di frutta) parings
■ **buccia di banana** banana skin
bucherel'lare *vt* riddle
bucherel'lato *adj* pitted
'buco *m* hole
■ **buco della serratura** keyhole
bu'colica *f* bucolic
bu'colico *m* bucolic
'Budda *m* Buddha
bud'dista *mf* Buddhist
bu'dello *m* (*pl nf* **budella**) bowel
'budget *m inv* budget
■ **budget provvisorio** mini budget
budge'tario *adj* budgetary
bu'dino *m* pudding
'bue *m* (*pl* **buoi**) ox
'bufalo *m* buffalo
bu'fera *f* storm; (di neve) blizzard
bufferiz'zato *adj* Comput buffered
buf'fet *m inv* snack bar; (mobile) sideboard; (pasto) buffet
buf'fetto *m* cuff
'buffo **A** *adj* funny; Theat comic
B *m* funny thing
buffo'nata *f* (scherzo) joke
buf'fone *m* buffoon; **fare il ~** play the fool
bu'gia *f* lie; **~ pietosa** white lie
bugi'ardo, -a **A** *adj* lying
B *mf* liar
bugi'gattolo *m* cubby-hole
'buio **A** *adj* dark
B *m* darkness; **al ~** in the dark; **~ pesto** pitch dark
'bulbo *m* bulb; (dell'occhio) eyeball

Bulga'ria *f* Bulgaria
'bulgaro, -a *adj & nmf* Bulgarian
buli'mia *f* bulimia
bu'limico *mf* bulimic
'bullo *m* bully
bul'lone *m* bolt
'bunker *m inv* bunker
buona'fede *f* good faith
buo'nanima *f* **la ~ di mio zio** my late uncle, God rest his soul
buona'notte *int* good night
buona'sera *int* good evening
buonco'stume *f* Vice Squad
buondì *int* good day!
buon'giorno *int* good morning; (di pomeriggio) good afternoon
buon'grado *m* **di ~** willingly
buongu'staio, -a *mf* gourmet, foodie infml
buon'gusto *m* good taste
bu'ono **A** *adj* good; (momento) right; **dar ~** (convalidare) accept; **alla buona** easy-going; ‹*cena*› informal; **buona fortuna!** good luck!; **buona notte/sera** good night/evening; **buon compleanno/Natale!** happy birthday/merry Christmas!; **buon viaggio!** have a good trip!; **buon appetito!** enjoy your meal!; **~ senso** common sense; **di buon'ora** early; **a buon mercato** cheap; **una buona volta** once and for all; **buona parte di** the best part of; **tre ore buone** three good hours
B *m* good; (in film) goody; (tagliando) voucher; (titolo) bond; **con le buone** gently
■ **buono acquisto** gift token; **buono sconto** money-off coupon
C *mf* **buono, -a a nulla** dead loss
buontem'pone, -a *mf* happy-go-lucky person
buonu'more *m* good temper
buonu'scita *f* retirement bonus; (di dirigente) golden handshake
buratti'naio *m* puppeteer
burat'tino *m* puppet
'burbero *adj* surly; (nei modi) rough
bu'rino, -a *mf* hick
Bur'kina 'Faso *m* Burkina (Faso)
'burla *f* joke; **fare una ~ a** play a trick on; **per ~** for fun
bur'lare *vt* make a fool of
bur'larsi *vr* **~ di** make fun of
bu'rocrate *m* bureaucrat
burocra'tese *m* gobbledygook
buro'cratico *adj* bureaucratic
burocra'zia *f* bureaucracy
bu'rotica *f* office automation
bur'rasca *f* storm
burra'scoso *adj* stormy
'burro *m* butter
■ **burro di arachidi** peanut butter
bur'rone *m* ravine
Bu'rundi *m* Burundi

key word

bus *m inv* Comput bus
■ **bus locale** local bus
bu'scare *vt* catch; **buscarle** infml get a hiding
bu'scarsi *vr* catch
bus'sare *vt* knock
'bussola *f* compass; **perdere la ~** lose one's bearings
'busta *f* envelope; (astuccio) case
■ **busta affrancata** business reply envelope; **busta a finestra** window envelope; **busta imbottita** Jiffy bag®, padded envelope; **busta paga** pay packet
busta'rella *f* bribe
bu'stina *f* (di tè) tea bag; (per medicine) sachet
'busto *m* bust; (indumento) girdle; **a mezzo ~** half-length
bu'tano *m* Calor gas®
buttafu'ori *m inv* bouncer
but'tare *vt* throw; **~ giù** (demolire) knock down; (inghiottire) gulp down; scribble down ‹*scritto*›; infml put on ‹*pasta*›; (scoraggiare) dishearten; **~ via** throw away
but'tarsi *vr* throw oneself; (saltare) jump
butte'rato *adj* pitted
buz'zurro *m* infml yokel
byte *m inv* Comput byte

Cc

c.a. *abbr* (**cortese attenzione**) attn.
caba'ret *m inv* cabaret
cabaret'tistico *adj* cabaret *attrib*
ca'bina *f* Naut Aeron cabin; (al mare) beach hut; (di funivia) [cable] car
■ **cabina elettorale** polling booth; **cabina di pilotaggio** cockpit; (di aereo di linea) flight deck; **cabina di prova** fitting room; **cabina telefonica** telephone box BrE, phone booth
cabi'nato *m* cabin cruiser
ca'blaggio *m* Electr wiring
ca'blato *adj* ‹*messaggio*› cable *attrib*
cablo'gramma *m* cablegram
cabo'taggio *m* Naut coastal navigation
cabrio'let *m inv* Auto convertible
ca'cao *m* cocoa
ca'care *vi* vulg have a crap
caca'tua *m inv* cockatoo
'cacca *f* infml poo, number two
'cacchio *m* infml hell; **ma che ~ fai/dici?** infml what the hell are you doing/saying?
'caccia **A** *f* hunt; (con fucile) shooting; (inseguimento) chase; (selvaggina) game
B *m inv* Aeron fighter; Naut destroyer; **andare a ~** go hunting
■ **caccia alla balena** whaling; **caccia grossa** big game; **caccia all'uomo** manhunt; **caccia alla volpe** fox hunting
cacciabombardi'ere *m* Aeron fighter-bomber
cacciagi'one *f* game
cacci'are **A** *vt* hunt; (mandar via) chase away; (scacciare) drive out; (ficcare) shove; **caccia [fuori] i soldi!** infml out with the money!; **~ un urlo** infml let out a yell
B *vi* go hunting
cacci'arsi *vr* (nascondersi) hide; (andare a finire) get to; **~ nei guai** get into trouble
caccia'tora *f* **alla ~** Culin chasseur
caccia|'tore, -trice *mf* hunter
■ **cacciatore di dote** gold digger; **cacciatore di frodo** poacher; **cacciatore di taglie** bounty hunter; **cacciatore di teste** Comm head-hunter
cacciatorpedini'ere *m inv* destroyer
caccia'vite *m inv* screwdriver
cacci'ucco *m*
■ **cacciucco alla livornese** *soup of seafood, tomato and wine served with bread*
cache-'sexe *m inv* thong
ca'chet *m inv* Med capsule; (colorante) colour rinse; (stile) cachet
'cachi **A** *m inv* persimmon
B *adj inv* (colore) khaki
'cacio *m* (formaggio) cheese
caci'otta *f creamy, fairly soft cheese*
'caco *m* persimmon
cacofo'nia *f* cacophony
'cactus *m inv* cactus
cada'uno *adj* each
ca'davere *m* corpse
cada'verico *adj* fig deathly pale
ca'dente *adj* falling; ‹*casa*› crumbling
ca'denza *f* cadence; (ritmo) rhythm; Mus cadenza
caden'zare *vt* give rhythm to
caden'zato *adj* measured
ca'dere *vi* fall; ‹*capelli ecc.*› fall out; (capitombolare) tumble; ‹*vestito ecc.*› hang; **far ~** (di mano) drop; **~ dal pero** infml be flabbergasted; **~ dal sonno** feel very sleepy; **lasciar ~** drop; **~ dalle nuvole** fig be taken aback; **~ dalla finestra** fall out of

the window
ca'detto *m* cadet
ca'duta *f* fall; fig downfall
■ **caduta dei capelli** hair loss; **caduta libera** free fall; **caduta massi** rockfall; (avviso) falling rocks
ca'duto *m* **i caduti** the dead; **monumento ai caduti** war memorial
caffè *m inv* coffee; (locale) café
■ **caffè corretto** espresso with a dash of liqueur; **caffè lungo** weak black coffee; **caffè macchiato** coffee with a dash of milk; **caffè ristretto** extra strong espresso coffee; **caffè solubile** instant coffee
caffe'ina *f* caffeine
caffel'latte *m inv* white coffee
caffette'ria *f* coffee bar
caffetti'era *f* coffee pot
■ **caffettiera a stantuffo** cafetière
cafo'naggine *f* boorishness
cafo'nata *f* boorishness
ca'fone, -a *mf* boor
cafone'ria *f* (comportamento) boorishness; **è stata una ~** it was boorish
ca'gare *vi* vulg crap; **va' a ~!** go and get stuffed!
cagio'nare *vt* cause
cagio'nevole *adj* delicate
cagli'are *vi* curdle
cagli'arsi *vr* curdle
cagli'ata *f* curd cheese
caglia'tura *f* curdling
'cagna *f* bitch
ca'gnara *f* infml din
ca'gnesco *adj* **guardare qualcuno in ~** scowl at somebody
ca'gnetto *m* lapdog
C.A.I. *nm abbr* (**Club Alpino Italiano**) *Italian mountain sports association*
cai'mano *m* cayman
'caio *m* so-and-so
'Cairo *m* **il ~** Cairo
'cala *f* creek
cala'brese *adj & nmf* Calabrian
Ca'labria *f* Calabria
cala'brone *m* hornet
cala'maio *m* ink pot
calama'retto *m* small squid
cala'mari *mpl* squid *sg*
cala'maro *m* squid
cala'mita *f* magnet
calamità *f inv* calamity; **~ *pl* naturali** natural disasters
calami'tare *vt* draw ‹*attenzione*›
ca'lante *adj* waning
ca'lare **A** *vi* come down; ‹*vento*› drop; (diminuire) fall; (tramontare) set; **~ di peso** lose weight; **~ di tono** fig drag
B *vt* (abbassare) lower; (nei lavori a maglia) decrease
C *m* (di luna) waning
ca'larsi *vr* lower oneself
ca'lata *f* (invasione) invasion
'calca *f* throng
cal'cagno *m* (*pl f* **calcagna**) heel; **stare alle calcagna di qualcuno** fig follow somebody around
cal'care¹ *m* limestone
cal'care² *vt* tread; (premere) press [down]; **~ la mano** fig exaggerate; **~ le orme di qualcuno** fig follow in somebody's footsteps; **~ le scene** fig tread the boards
'calce¹ *f* lime
■ **calce viva** quicklime
'calce² *m* **in ~** at the foot of the page
calce'struzzo *m* concrete
cal'cetto *m* Sport five-a-side [football]; (da tavolo) table football
calci'are *vt* kick
calcia'tore *m* footballer
calcifi'carsi *vr* calcify
calcificazi'one *f* calcification
cal'cina *f* mortar
calci'naccio *m* (pezzo di intonaco) flake of plaster; (pezzo di muro) piece of rubble
'calcio¹ *m* kick; Sport football; (di arma da fuoco) butt; **dare un ~ a** kick; **giocare a ~** play football
■ **calcio d'angolo** corner [kick]; **calcio di punizione** free kick; **calcio di rigore** penalty [kick]
'calcio² *m* Chem calcium
calcio-mer'cato *m inv* transfer market
calcioscom'messe *mpl* **1** (scommesse clandestine) illegal football pools **2** (combine) match fixing
'calco *m* (con carta) tracing; (arte) cast
calco'lare *vt* calculate; (considerare) consider
calco'lato *adj* calculated
calcola'tore **A** *adj* calculating
B *m* calculator; (macchina elettronica) computer
■ **calcolatore digitale** (calcolatrice) calculator
calcola'trice *f* calculating machine
'calcolo *m* calculation; Med stone; **per ~** fig out of self-interest; **mi sono fatto i calcoli** fig I've weighed up the pros and cons
■ **calcolo approssimativo** guesstimate; **calcolo biliare** gallstone; **calcolo renale** kidney stone
cal'daia *f* boiler
■ **caldaia ad accumulo** storage heater
caldar'rosta *f* roast chestnut
caldeggi'are *vt* support
'caldo **A** *adj* warm; (molto caldo) hot; ‹*situazione, zona*› dangerous; ‹*notizie*› latest; **non gli fa né ~ né freddo** fig he doesn't give a damn; **ondata di ~** heatwave; **tavola calda** snack bar
B *m* heat; **avere ~** be warm, be hot; **fa ~**

key word

it's warm, it's hot
caleido'scopio *m* kaleidoscope
calen'dario *m* calendar
■ **calendario sportivo** sporting calendar
ca'lesse *m* gig
cali'brare *vt* calibrate
cali'brato *adj* calibrated; fig balanced; **taglie** *pl* **calibrate** clothes for non-standard sizes
'calibro *m* calibre; (strumento) callipers *pl*; **di grosso ~** ‹*persona*› top *attrib*
'calice *m* goblet; Relig chalice
californi'ano, -a *adj & nmf* Californian
ca'ligine *m* fog; (industriale) smog
call-girl *f inv* call girl
calligra'fia *f* handwriting; (arte) calligraphy
calli'grafico *adj* **perizia calligrafica** handwriting analysis
cal'ligrafo, -a *mf* calligrapher
cal'lista *mf* chiropodist
'callo *m* corn; **fare il ~ a** become hardened to
cal'loso *adj* callous
'calma *f* calm; **mantenere la ~** keep calm; **prendersela con ~** fig take it easy; **fare qualcosa con ~** take one's time doing something
cal'mante **A** *adj* calming
B *m* sedative
cal'mare *vt* calm [down]; (lenire) soothe
cal'marsi *vr* calm down; ‹*vento*› drop; ‹*dolore*› die down
calmie'rare *vt* control the prices of
calmi'ere *m* price control
'calmo *adj* calm
'calo *m* Comm fall; (di volume) shrinkage; (di peso) loss; **in ~** dwindling
ca'lore *m* heat; (moderato) warmth; **in ~** (di animale) on heat
calo'ria *f* calorie
ca'lorico *adj* calorific
calo'rifero *m* radiator
calorosa'mente *adv* warmly
calorosità *f inv* fig warmth
calo'roso *adj* warm
ca'lotta *f*:
■ **calotta cranica** skullcap; **calotta glaciale** ice cap; **calotta polare** polar ice cap
calpe'stare *vt* trample [down]; fig trample on ‹*diritti, sentimenti*›; **'vietato ~ l'erba'** 'keep off the grass'
calpe'stio *m* (passi) footsteps *pl*; (rumore) stamping
ca'lunnia *f* slander
calunni'are *vt* slander
calunni'oso *adj* slanderous
ca'lura *f* heat
cal'vario *m* Calvary; fig trial
calvi'nismo *m* Calvinism
calvi'nista *mf* Calvinist
cal'vizie *f* baldness
'calvo *adj* bald
'calza *f* (da reggicalze) stocking; (da uomo) sock
■ **calza della befana** ≈ Christmas stocking
calza'maglia *f* tights *pl*; (per danza) leotard
cal'zante *adj* fig fitting
cal'zare **A** *vt* (indossare) wear; (mettersi) put on
B *vi* fit; **~ a pennello** ‹*indumenti*› fit like a glove
calza'scarpe *m inv* shoehorn
calza'tura *f* footwear; **calzature** *pl* footwear *sg*
calzaturi'ficio *m* shoe factory
cal'zetta *f* ankle sock; **è una mezza ~** fig he's no use
calzet'tone *m* knee-length woollen sock
cal'zino *m* sock
calzo'laio *m* shoe mender
calzole'ria *f* (negozio) shoe shop
calzon'cini *mpl* shorts
■ **calzoncini da bagno** swimming trunks
cal'zone *m* Culin *folded pizza with tomato, mozzarella etc inside*
cal'zoni *mpl* trousers, pants AmE
■ **calzoni alla cavallerizza** jodhpurs
camale'onte *m* chameleon
cambi'ale *f* Comm bill of exchange
cambia'mento *m* change
■ **cambiamento climatico** climate change
cambi'are **A** *vt* change; move ‹*casa*›; (fare cambio di) exchange; **~ canale** TV switch over; **~ rotta** Naut alter course; **~ l'aria in una stanza** air a room; **~ sesso** have a sex change
B *vi* change; (fare cambio) exchange
cambi'arsi *vr* change
cambiava'lute *m* bureau de change
'cambio *m* change; Comm (scambio) exchange; Mech gear; **dare il ~ a qualcuno** relieve somebody; **in ~ di** in exchange for
■ **cambio della guardia** changeover; **cambio dell'olio** oil change
Cam'bogia *f* Cambodia
cambogi'ano *adj & nmf* Cambodian
cam'busa *f* pantry
ca'melia *f* camellia
'camera *f* room; (mobili) [bedroom] suite; **Camera** Pol, Comm Chamber
■ **camera ammobiliata** bedsit; **camera ardente** chapel of rest; **camera d'aria** inner tube; **camera blindata** strong room; **Camera di Commercio** Chamber of Commerce; **Camera dei Comuni** House of Commons; **Camera dei Deputati** ≈ House of Commons; **Camera dei Lord** House of Lords; **Camera dei Rappresentanti** House of Representatives; **camera doppia** double room; **camera a gas** gas chamber; **camera da letto** bedroom; **camera a due letti** twin room; **camera matrimoniale** double room; **camera oscura** darkroom; **camera degli ospiti** guest room; **camera singola** single room
came'rata[1] *f* (dormitorio) dormitory; Mil barrack room

came'rata² *mf* mate
camera'tesco *adj* comradely
camera'tismo *m* comradeship
cameri'era *f* maid; (di ristorante) waitress; (in albergo) chambermaid
C ✓ **cameri'ere** *m* manservant; (di ristorante) waiter
came'rino *m* dressing room
came'ristico *adj* Mus chamber
'Camerun *m* **il ~** Cameroon
'camice *m* overall
camice'ria *f* shirt shop
cami'cetta *f* blouse
✓ **ca'micia** *f* shirt; **essere nato con la ~** fig be born lucky
■ **uovo in camicia** poached egg; **camicia di forza** strait-jacket; **camicia nera** Blackshirt; **camicia da notte** nightdress; (da uomo) nightshirt
camici'aio *m* (venditore) shirt seller; (sarto) shirt maker
camici'ola *f* vest
cami'netto *m* fireplace
■ **caminetto alimentato a carbone** coal fire
ca'mino *m* chimney; (focolare) fireplace, hearth
'camion *m inv* lorry BrE, truck
■ **camion della nettezza urbana** dust-cart BrE, garbage truck AmE
camion'cino *m* van
camio'netta *f* jeep
camio'nista *mf* lorry driver BrE, truck driver
'camma *f* cam; **albero a camme** Auto camshaft
cam'mello **A** *m* camel; (tessuto) camel-hair **B** *adj inv* (colore) camel
cam'meo *m* cameo
✓ **cammi'nare** *vi* walk; ‹*auto, orologio*› go; **~ avanti e indietro** pace up and down
cammi'nata *f* walk; **fare una ~** go for a walk
✓ **cam'mino** *m* way; **essere in ~** be on the way; **mettersi in ~** set out; **cammin facendo** on the way
camo'milla *f* camomile; (bevanda) camomile tea
camo'millarsi *vr sl* **camomillati!** don't get your knickers in a twist!, cool it!
Ca'morra *f local mafia*
camor'rista *mf member of the 'Camorra'*
ca'moscio *m* chamois; (pelle) suede
✓ **cam'pagna** *f* country; (paesaggio) countryside; Comm, Mil campaign; **in ~** in the country
■ **campagna elettorale** election campaign; **campagna promozionale** promotional campaign, marketing campaign; **campagna pubblicitaria** advertising campaign
campa'gnola *f* Auto cross-country vehicle

✓ key word

campa'gnolo, -a **A** *adj* rustic **B** *m* countryman **C** *f* countrywoman
cam'pale *adj* field *attrib*; **giornata campale** fig strenuous day
cam'pana *f* bell; (di vetro) bell jar; **a ~** bell shaped; **essere sordo come una ~** be as deaf as a doorpost; **sentire anche l'altra ~** fig hear the other side of the story; **vivere sotto una ~ di vetro** fig be mollycoddled; **campane** *pl* **eoliche** wind chimes; **campane** *pl* **a morto** death knell
campa'naccio *m* cowbell
campa'naro *m* bell-ringer
campa'nella *f* (di tenda) curtain ring
campa'nello *m* doorbell; (cicalino) buzzer
Cam'pania *f* Campania
campa'nile *m* bell tower
campani'lismo *m* parochialism
campani'lista *mf* person with a parochial outlook
campani'listico *adj* parochial
cam'panula *f* Bot campanula
cam'pare *vi* live; (a stento) get by; **tirare a ~** fig live from day to day
cam'pato *adj* **~ in aria** unfounded
campeggi'are *vi* camp; (spiccare) stand out; **'vietato ~'** 'no camping'
campeggia|'tore, -trice *mf* camper
cam'peggio *m* camping; (terreno) campsite; **andare in ~** go camping; **fare ~ libero** camp in the wild
■ **campeggio per roulotte** caravan site
'camper *m inv* camper (van)
cam'pestre *adj* rural
Campi'doglio *m* Capitol
'camping *m inv* campsite
campiona'mento *m* sampling
campio'nario **A** *m* [set of] samples **B** *adj* **fiera campionaria** trade fair
campio'nato *m* championship
■ **Campionato Mondiale di Calcio** World Cup
campiona'tura *f* (di merce) range of samples; (in statistica) sampling
■ **campionatura casuale** random sample
✓ **campi'one** *m* champion; Comm sample; (esemplare) specimen; **indagine ~** (in statistica) sample
■ **campione gratuito** free sample; **'campione senza valore'** 'sample, no commercial value'
campio'nessa *f* ladies' champion
✓ **'campo** *m* field; (accampamento) camp; Mil encampment; **abbandonare il ~** Mil desert in the face of the enemy; fig throw in the towel; **a tutto ~** fig wide-ranging; **avere ~ libero** fig have a free hand; **non avere ~** ‹*cellulare*› to be out of range; **giocare a tutto ~** Sport cover the entire pitch
■ **campo d'aviazione** airfield; **campo base** base camp; **campo di battaglia** battlefield; **campo da calcio** football pitch; **campo di**

concentramento concentration camp; **campo in erba** grass court; **campo da golf** golf course; **campo di grano** cornfield; **campo da hockey** hockey field; **campo di mais** cornfield; **campo di prigionia** prison camp; **campo profughi** refugee camp; **campo sportivo** sports ground; **campo di sterminio** death camp; **campo in superficie dura** hard court; **campo da tennis** tennis court

campo'santo *m* cemetery

'campus *m inv* (di università) campus

camuf'fare *vt* disguise

camuf'farsi *vr* disguise oneself

ca'muso *adj* **naso ~** snub nose

'Canada *m* Canada

cana'dese *adj & nmf* Canadian

ca'naglia *f* scoundrel; (plebaglia) rabble

ca'nale *m* channel; (artificiale) canal
■ **Canal Grande** Gran Canal; **canale della Manica** English Channel; **canale di scolo** dyke

canaliz'zare *vt* channel ‹*acque, energie*›

canalizzazi'one *f* channelling; (rete) pipes *pl*

'canapa *f* hemp
■ **canapa indiana** (droga) cannabis

Ca'narie *fpl* **le ~** the Canaries

cana'rino *m* canary

ca'nasta *f* (gioco) canasta

cancel'labile *adj* erasable; ‹*impegno, incontro*› which can be cancelled

cancel'lare *vt* cross out; (con la gomma) rub out; fig wipe out; (annullare) cancel; Comput delete, erase

cancel'larsi *vr* be erased, be wiped out

cancel'lata *f* railings *pl*

cancel'lato *adj* cancelled

cancella'tura *f* erasure

cancellazi'one *f* cancellation; Comput deletion; **~ del debito** (ai paesi poveri) debt relief

cancelle'ria *f* chancellery; (articoli per scrivere) stationery

cancel'letto *m* hash sign

cancelli'ere *m* chancellor; (di tribunale) clerk

cancel'lino *m* duster

can'cello *m* gate

cance'rogeno **A** *m* carcinogen **B** *adj* carcinogenic

cance'roso *adj* cancerous

can'crena *f* gangrene; **andare in ~** become gangrenous

cancre'noso *adj* gangrenous

'cancro *m* cancer; **Cancro** Astr Cancer; **tropico del Cancro** Tropic of Cancer

candeggi'are *vt* bleach

candeg'gina *f* bleach

can'deggio *m* bleaching

can'dela *f* candle; Auto spark plug; **a lume di ~** by candlelight; ‹*cena*› candlelit; **il gioco non vale la ~** the game is not worth the candle
■ **candela magica** sparkler

cande'labro *m* candelabra

cande'letta *f* Med pessary

candeli'ere *m* candlestick

cande'line *fpl* candles

cande'lotto *m* (di dinamite) stick
■ **candelotto lacrimogeno** tear gas grenade

candida'mente *adv* innocently

candi'dare *vt* put forward as a candidate

candi'darsi *vr* stand as a candidate

candi'dato, -a *mf* candidate

candida'tura *f* Pol candidacy; (per lavoro) application

'candido *adj* snow-white; (sincero) candid; (puro) pure

can'dito **A** *adj* candied **B** *m* piece of candied fruit

can'dore *m* whiteness; fig innocence

'cane *m* dog; (di arma da fuoco) cock; **un tempo da cani** foul weather; **fa un freddo ~** it's bitterly cold; **non c'era un ~** fig there wasn't a soul about; **solo come un ~** fig all on one's own; **essere come ~ e gatto** fig fight like cat and dog; **essere un ~** ‹*attore, cantante*› be appalling, be a dog sl; **fatto da cani** fig ‹*lavoro*› botched; **mangiare da cani** fig eat very badly; **figlio di un ~** infml son of a bitch
■ **cane da caccia** hunting dog; **cane per ciechi** guide dog; **cane da corsa** greyhound; **cane da guardia** guard dog; **cane lupo** Alsatian; **cane poliziotto** police dog; **cane da salotto** lapdog; **cane sciolto** fig maverick

ca'nestro *m* basket; **fare ~** score a basket

'canfora *f* camphor

cangi'ante *adj* iridescent; **seta ~** shot silk

can'guro *m* kangaroo

ca'nicola *f* scorching heat

ca'nile *m* kennel; (di allevamento) kennels *pl*
■ **canile municipale** dog pound

ca'nino *adj & nm* canine

ca'nizie *m* white hair

'canna *f* reed; (da zucchero) cane; (di fucile) barrel; (bastone) stick; (di bicicletta) crossbar; (asta) rod; infml (hashish) joint; **povero in ~** destitute
■ **canna fumaria** flue; **canna da pesca** fishing rod; **canna da zucchero** sugar cane

'cannabis *f* cannabis

can'nella *f* cinnamon

cannel'loni *mpl*
■ **cannelloni al forno** *rolls of pasta stuffed with meat and baked in the oven*

can'neto *m* bed of reeds

can'nibale *m* cannibal

canniba'lismo *m* cannibalism

cannocchi'ale *m* telescope

can'nolo *m* pastry roll
■ **cannolo siciliano** *cylindrical pastry filled with ricotta and candied fruit*

C

canno'nata *f* cannon shot; **è una ~** fig it's brilliant
cannon'cino *m* (dolce) cream horn
can'none *m* cannon; fig ace
cannoneggia'mento *m* cannonade
cannoni'era *f* gunboat
cannoni'ere *m* (soldato) gunner; (calciatore) top goal scorer
can'nuccia *f* [drinking] straw; (di pipa) stem
ca'noa *f* canoe
cano'ismo *m* canoeing
'canone *m* canon; (del telefono) standing charge; (affitto) rent; **equo canone** rent set by law
ca'nonica *f* manse
ca'nonico *m* canon
canoniz'zare *vt* canonize
canonizzazi'one *f* canonization
ca'noro *adj* melodious
ca'notta *f* (estiva) vest top, singlet
canot'taggio *m* canoeing; (voga) rowing
canotti'era *f* vest, singlet
canotti'ere *m* oarsman
ca'notto *m* [rubber] dinghy
cano'vaccio *m* (trama) plot; (straccio) duster; (per ricamo) canvas
can'tante *mf* singer
■ **cantante lirico** opera singer
⚷ **can'tare** *vt & vi* sing; **~ vittoria** fig crow; **fare ~ qualcuno** sl make somebody talk; **me le ha cantate** infml he told me off
canta'storie *mf inv* storyteller
can'tata *f* Mus cantata
can'tato *adj* sung
cantau|'tore, -trice *mf* singer-songwriter
canticchi'are *vt* sing softly; (a bocca chiusa) hum
'cantico *m* hymn
canti'ere *m* yard; Naut shipyard; (di edificio) construction site
■ **cantiere navale** naval dockyard; (per piccole imbarcazioni) boatyard
cantie'ristica *f* construction
canti'lena *f* singsong; (ninna-nanna) lullaby
can'tina *f* cellar; (per vini) wine cellar; (osteria) wine shop
⚷ **'canto[1]** *m* singing; (canzone) song; Relig chant; (poesia) poem
■ **canto di Natale** *o* **natalizio** Christmas carol; **canto degli uccelli** birdsong
'canto[2] *m* (angolo) corner; (lato) side; **dal ~ mio** for my part; **d'altro ~** on the other hand
canto'nale *adj* cantonal
canto'nata *f* **prendere una ~** fig drop a clanger
can'tone *m* canton; (angolo) corner
can'tore *m* chorister

⚷ key word

can'tuccio *m* nook; **stare in un ~** fig hold oneself aloof
ca'nuto *adj* (liter) white-haired
canzo'nare *vt* tease
canzona'torio *adj* teasing
canzona'tura *f* teasing
⚷ **can'zone** *f* song
■ **canzone d'amore** love song
canzo'netta *f* infml pop song
canzoni'ere *m* songbook
'caos *m* chaos
ca'otico *adj* chaotic
cap. *abbr* (**capitolo**) chap, chapter
C.A.P. *nm abbr* (**Codice di Avviamento Postale**) post code, zip code AmE
⚷ **ca'pace** *adj* able; (esperto) skilled; ‹*stadio, contenitore*› big; **~ di** (disposto a) capable of; **è ~ di cantare?** can he sing?
capacità *f inv* ability; (attitudine) skill; (capienza) capacity
■ **capacità d'assorbimento** absorbency; **capacità di credito** creditworthiness; **capacità di memorizzazione** retentiveness; **capacità produttiva** production capacity; **capacità di resistenza** staying power
capaci'tarsi *vr* **~ di** (rendersi canto) understand; (accorgersi) realize
ca'panna *f* hut
capan'nello *m* knot of people; **fare ~ intorno a qualcuno/qualcosa** gather round somebody/something
ca'panno *m*:
■ **capanno degli attrezzi** garden shed; **capanno da spiaggia** beach hut, cabana
capan'none *m* shed; Aeron hangar
caparbietà *f inv* obstinacy
ca'parbio *adj* obstinate
ca'parra *f* deposit
capa'tina *f* short visit; **fare una ~ in città/da qualcuno** pop into town/in on somebody
⚷ **ca'pello** *m* hair; **non torcere un ~ a qualcuno** fig not lay a finger on somebody; **capelli** *pl* (capigliatura) hair *sg*; **avere i capelli a spazzola** have a crew cut; **spaccare il ~ in quattro** split hairs; **averne fin sopra i capelli** fig be fed up to the back teeth; **mettersi le mani nei capelli** fig tear one's hair out; **capelli** *pl* **d'angelo** vermicelli
capel'lone *m* long-haired type, hippie
capel'luto *adj* hairy; **cuoio capelluto** scalp
ca'pestro *m* noose; **contratto capestro** strait-jacket of a contract
capez'zale *m* bolster; fig bedside
ca'pezzolo *m* nipple
capi'ente *adj* capacious
capi'enza *f* capacity
capiglia'tura *f* hair
capil'lare *adj* capillary
⚷ **ca'pire** *vt* understand; **non capisco** I don't understand; **~ male** misunderstand;

si capisce! naturally!; sì, ho capito yes, I see

capi'tale **A** *adj* Jur capital; (principale) main **B** *f* (città) capital **C** *m* Comm capital
■ **capitale di avviamento** start-up capital; **capitale azionario** Fin equity capital, share capital; **capitale di investimento** investment capital; **capitale di rischio** venture capital; **capitale sociale** Fin share capital

capita'lismo *m* capitalism

capita'lista *mf* capitalist

capita'listico *adj* capitalist

capitaliz'zare *vt* capitalize

capitalizzazi'one *f* capitalization

capita'nare *vt* lead ‹*rivolta*›; Sport captain

capitane'ria *f*
■ **capitaneria di porto** port authorities *pl*

capi'tano *m* captain
■ **capitano di lungo corso** Naut captain

capi'tare *vi* (giungere per caso) come; (accadere) happen

'capite **pro ~** *adv* per capita

capi'tello *m* Archit *capital*

capito'lare *vi* capitulate

capitolazi'one *f* capitulation

ca'pitolo *m* chapter

capi'tombolo *m* headlong fall; **fare un ~** tumble down

'capo *m* head; (chi comanda) boss infml; (di vestiario) item; Geog cape; (in tribù) chief; (parte estrema) top; **a ~** (in dettato) new paragraph; **da ~** over again; **giramento di ~** dizziness; **mal di ~** headache; **in ~ a un mese** within a month; **non ha né ~ né coda** ‹*discorso, ragionamento*› I can't make head nor tail of it
■ **capo d'abbigliamento** item of clothing; **capo d'accusa** Jur charge, count; **capo di bestiame** head of cattle; **Capo di Buona Speranza** Cape of Good Hope; **capo reparto** head of department; **il Capo Verde** Cape Verde

capo'banda *m* Mus band-master; (di delinquenti) ringleader

capocameri'ere, -a **A** *m* head waiter **B** *f* head waitress

ca'pocchia *f*
■ **capocchia di spillo** pinhead

ca'poccia *m* infml (testa) nut

capocci'one, -a *mf* infml brainbox

capo'classe *mf* ≈ form captain

capocor'data *mf* (alpinista) leader

capocu'oco, -a *mf* head cook

capo'danno *m* New Year's Day

capofa'miglia *m* head of the family

capoffi'cina *m* head mechanic

capo'fitto *m* **a ~** headlong

capo'giro *m* giddiness

capo'gruppo *m* group leader

capola'voro *m* masterpiece

capo'linea *m* terminus

capo'lino *m* **fare ~** peep in

capo'lista *mf* Sport league leaders *pl*; Pol *candidate whose name appears first on the list*

capolu'ogo *m* main town

capo'mafia *m* Mafia boss

capo'mastro *m* master builder

capo'rale *m* lance corporal

capore'parto *mf* department head, head of department

capo'sala *f inv* Med ward sister

capo'saldo *m* stronghold

capo'scalo *m* airline manager

capo'squadra *m inv* foreman; Sport team captain

capostazi'one *m inv* stationmaster

capo'stipite *mf* (di famiglia) progenitor; (di esemplare) archetype

capo'tavola *mf* (persona) head of the table; **sedere a ~** sit at the head of the table

capo'treno *m* guard

ca'potta *f* top

capot'tare *vi* somersault

capouf'ficio *mf* department head

capo'verso *m* first line; Jur paragraph

capo'volgere *vt* overturn; fig reverse

capo'volgersi *vr* overturn; ‹*barca*› capsize; fig be reversed

capovolgi'mento *m* turnaround

capo'volto **A** pp di **capovolgere** **B** *adj* upside down

'cappa *f* cloak; (di camino) cowl; (di cucina) hood

cappa'santa *f* Culin scallop

cap'pella *f* chapel
■ **la Cappella Sistina** the Sistine Chapel

cappel'lano *m* chaplain

cappel'letti *mpl small filled pasta parcels*

cappelli'era *f* (per cappelli) hatbox; (in aereo) overhead locker

cappel'lino *m*
■ **cappellino di carta** party hat

cap'pello *m* hat; **tanto di ~!** I take my hat off to you!
■ **cappello a cilindro** top hat; **cappello da cow boy** Stetson, cowboy hat; **cappello di feltro** homburg; **cappello di paglia** straw hat; **cappello da sole** sun hat

'cappero *m* caper; **capperi!** infml gosh!

'cappio *m* noose; **avere il ~ al collo** fig have a millstone round one's neck; ‹*marito*› be henpecked

cap'pone *m* capon

cap'potto *m* [over] coat

cappuc'cino *m* (frate) Capuchin [friar]; (bevanda) white coffee

cap'puccio *m* hood; (di penna stilografica) cap

'capra *f* goat; **salvare ~ e cavoli** fig run with the hare and hunt with the hounds

ca'pretto *m* kid

ca'priccio *m* whim; (bizzarria) freak; **fare i capricci** have tantrums

capricci'oso *adj* capricious; ‹*bambino*› naughty

Capri'corno *m* Astr Capricorn

capri'foglio *m* honeysuckle

ca'prino *m* goat's cheese

capri'ola *f* somersault

capriolo *m* roe (deer)

'capro *m* (billy) goat
■ **capro espiatorio** scapegoat

ca'prone *m* (billy) goat

'capsula *f* capsule; (di proiettile) cap; (di dente) crown

cap'tare *vt* Radio, TV pick up; catch ‹*attenzione*›

C.A.R. *nm abbr* (**Centro Addestramento Reclute**) basic training camp

cara'bina *f* carbine

⚷ **carabiniere** *m* carabiniere; **carabini'eri** *pl Italian police force (which is a branch of the army)*

ca'raffa *f* carafe

Ca'raibi *mpl* (zona) Caribbean *sg*; (isole) Caribbean Islands; **il mar dei ~** the Caribbean [Sea]

Cara'ibico *adj* Caribbean

cara'mella *f* sweet
■ **caramella alla menta** mint

cara'mello *m* caramel

ca'rato *m* carat

⚷ **ca'rattere** *m* character; (caratteristica) characteristic; **di buon ~** good-natured; **in ~ con** (intonato) in keeping with; **è una persona di ~** (deciso) he's got character
■ **carattere jolly** Comput wild card; **carattere tipografico** typeface

caratte'rino *m* difficult nature

caratte'rista **A** *m* character actor
B *f* character actress

⚷ **caratte'ristico, -a** **A** *adj* characteristic; (pittoresco) quaint
B *f* characteristic

caratteriz'zare *vt* characterize

caratterizzazi'one *f* characterization

cara'tura *f* carats; Comm part ownership

'caravan *m inv* caravan

carboi'drato *m* carbohydrate

car'bonchio *m* anthrax

carbon'cino *m* (per disegno) charcoal

⚷ **car'bone** *m* coal; **stare sui carboni ardenti** fig be on tenterhooks
■ **carbone fossile** anthracite

carbo'nifero *adj* Carboniferous

car'bonio *m* carbon
■ **carbonio 14** carbon-14

carboniz'zare *vt* burn to a cinder, burn to a crisp; **é morto carbonizzato** he was burned to death

carboniz'zato *adj* charred

carbu'rante *m* fuel

carbu'rare **A** *vt* carburize
B *vi* fig be firing on all four cylinders; **il motore carbura male** the mixture is wrong

carbura'tore *m* carburettor

carburazi'one *f* carburation

car'cassa *f* carcass; fig old wreck

carce'rario *adj* prison *attrib*

carce'rato, -a *mf* prisoner

carcerazione *f* imprisonment

⚷ **'carcere** *m* prison; (punizione) imprisonment
■ **carcere di massima sicurezza** maximum security prison

carceri'ere, -a *mf* gaoler

carci'noma *m* carcinoma

carcio'fino *m* baby artichoke

carci'ofo *m* artichoke

cardel'lino *m* goldfinch

car'diaco *adj* cardiac; **disturbo ~** heart disease

'cardigan *m inv* cardigan

cardi'nale *adj & nm* cardinal

'cardine *m* hinge

cardiochi'rurgo *m* heart surgeon

cardiolo'gia *f* cardiology

cardi'ologo *m* heart specialist

cardio'patico *mf* person suffering from a heart complaint

cardio'tonico *m* heart stimulant

cardiovasco'lare *adj* cardiovascular

'cardo *m* thistle

ca'rena *f* Naut bottom

care'naggio *m*
■ **bacino di carenaggio** dry dock

ca'rente *adj* **~ di** lacking in

ca'renza *f* lack; (scarsità) scarcity

care'stia *f* famine; (mancanza) dearth

ca'rezza *f* stroke; (di madre, amante) caress; **fare una ~ a** stroke; (madre, amante) caress

carez'zare *vt* stroke; ‹*madre, amante*› caress

carez'zevole *adj* fig sweet

'cargo *m inv* (nave) cargo boat, freighter; (aereo) cargo plane, freight plane

cari'are *vt* decay

cari'arsi *vi* decay

cari'ato *adj* decayed

⚷ **'carica** *f* office; Mil, Electr charge; fig drive; **dotato di una forte ~ di simpatia** really likeable
■ **carica esplosiva** payload

caricabatte'ria *m inv* battery charger

⚷ **cari'care** *vt* load ‹*camion, software*›; Mil, Electr charge; wind up ‹*orologio*›; Comput upload ‹*programma*›

cari'carsi *vr* Electr charge [up]; **~ di lavoro** take on too much work

⚷ key word

cari'cato *adj* fig affected (esagerato)
carica'tore *m* (per proiettile) magazine; (per diapositive) carousel
carica'tura *f* caricature
caricatu'rale *adj* grotesque
caricatu'rista *mf* caricaturist
'carico **A** *adj* loaded (**di** with); ‹*colore*› strong; ‹*orologio*› wound [up]; ‹*batteria*› charged
B *m* load; (di nave) cargo; (il caricare) loading; **avere un ~ di lavoro** have a heavy workload; **testimone a ~** Jur witness for the prosecution; **a ~ di** Comm to be charged to; ‹*persona*› dependent on
■ **carico utile** payload
'carie *f* [tooth] decay
caril'lon *m inv* musical box
carino *adj* pretty, nice-looking; (piacevole) agreeable
ca'risma *m* charisma
cari'smatico *adj* charismatic
carità *f inv* charity; **per ~!** (come rifiuto) God forbid!
carita'tevole *adj* charitable
car'linga *f* fuselage
car'lino *m* pug
carnagi'one *f* complexion
car'naio *m* fig shambles
car'nale *adj* carnal; **cugino ~** first cousin
'carne *f* flesh; (alimento) meat; **di ~** meaty
■ **carne macinata** mince, ground beef AmE; **carne di maiale** pork; **carne di manzo** beef; **carne di vitella** veal
car'nefice *m* executioner
carnefi'cina *f* slaughter
carne'vale *m* carnival
carneva'lesco *adj* carnival
car'nivoro **A** *m* carnivore
B *adj* carnivorous
car'noso *adj* fleshy
'caro, -a **A** *adj* dear; **cari saluti** kind regards
B *mf* infml darling, dear; **i miei cari** my nearest and dearest
ca'rogna *f* carcass; fig bastard
caro'sello *m* merry-go-round
ca'rota *f* carrot
caro'vana *f* caravan; (di veicoli) convoy
caro'vita *m* high cost of living
'carpa *f* carp
car'paccio *m finely sliced raw beef with oil, lemon and slivers of Parmesan*
Car'pazi *mpl* **i ~** the Carpathians
carpenti'ere *m* carpenter
car'pire *vt* seize; (con difficoltà) extort
car'pone, car'poni *adv* on all fours; **camminare ~** crawl
car'rabile *adj* suitable for vehicles; **passo ~** = **passo carraio**
car'raio *adj* **passo ~** *entrance to driveway, garage etc where parking is forbidden*
carreggi'ata *f* roadway; **doppia carreggiata** dual carriageway, divided highway AmE; **rimettersi in ~** fig straighten oneself out
carrel'lata *f* TV pan; fig (di notizie) round-up
car'rello *m* trolley; (di macchina da scrivere) carriage; Aeron undercarriage; Cinema, TV dolly
■ **carrello d'atterraggio** Aeron landing gear; **carrello dei dolci** dessert trolley; **carrello portabagagli** luggage trolley, baggage cart AmE; **carrello della spesa** shopping trolley
car'retta *f* (veicolo vecchio) old banger; **tirare la ~** fig plod along
car'retto *m* cart
carri'era *f* career; **di gran ~** at full speed; **fare ~** get on
carrie'rismo *m* careerism
carrie'rista *mf* **è un ~** his career is all that matters
carri'ola *f* wheelbarrow
'carro *m* cart
■ **carro armato** tank; **carro attrezzi** breakdown vehicle, tow truck, wrecker AmE; **carro funebre** hearse; **carro merci** truck
car'rozza *f* carriage; Rail coach, car
■ **carrozza bagagliaio** Rail guard's van; **carrozza belvedere** Rail observation car; **carrozza cuccette** sleeping car; **carrozza fumatori** Rail smoker; **carrozza letti** Rail sleeping car; **carrozza ristorante** Rail restaurant car, buffet car
carroz'zella *f* (per bambini) pram; (per invalidi) wheelchair
carrozze'ria *f* bodywork; (officina) body shop
carrozzi'ere *m* panel beater
carroz'zina *f* pram; (pieghevole) pushchair, stroller AmE
carroz'zone *m* (di circo) caravan; fig (organizzazione) slow-moving great monster of an organization
car'ruba *f* carob
car'rubo *m* carob
car'rucola *f* pulley
carta *f* paper; (da gioco) card; (statuto) charter; Geog map
■ **carta di addebito** charge card; **carta d'argento** senior citizens' railcard; **carta assegni** cheque card; **carta assorbente** blotting paper; **carta carbone** carbon paper; **carta di credito** credit card; **carta crespata** crepe paper; **carta di debito** debit card; **carta fedeltà** loyalty card; **carta geografica** map; **carta d'identità** identity card; **carta igienica** toilet paper; **carta d'imbarco** boarding pass, boarding card; **carta intelligente** smart card; **carta da lettere** writing paper; **carta millimetrata** graph paper; **carta da pacchi** wrapping paper; **carta da parati** wallpaper; **carta da regali** gift wrap; **carta di riso** rice paper; **carta SIM** SIM card; **carta smerigliata** emery paper; **carta stagnola**

C

silver paper, silver foil; Culin aluminium foil; **carta straccia** waste paper; **carta stradale** road map; **carta termica** thermal paper; **carta topografica** ≈ Ordnance Survey Map; **carta velina** tissue paper; **carta verde** Auto green card; **carta vetrata** sandpaper; **carta dei vini** wine list

car'taccia *f* waste paper

car'taceo *adj* paper *attrib*

carta'modello *m* pattern

cartamo'neta *f* paper money

carta'pecora *f* vellum

carta'pesta *f* papier mâché

cartave'trare *vt* sand [down]

car'teggio *m* correspondence

car'tella *f* (per documenti ecc.) briefcase; (di cartoncino) folder; (di scolaro) satchel, school bag

■ **cartella clinica** medical record

cartel'lina *f* document wallet, folder

cartel'lino *m* (etichetta) label; (dei prezzi) price tag; (di presenza) time card; **timbrare il ~** clock in; (all'uscita) clock out

car'tello *m* sign; (pubblicitario) poster; (stradale) road sign; (di protesta) placard; Comm (di droga) cartel

cartel'lone *m* poster; Theat bill

■ **cartellone pubblicitario** billboard

cartello'nista *mf* poster designer

cartello'nistica *f* poster designing

carti'era *f* paper mill

carti'lagine *f* cartilage

car'tina *f* (geografica) map; (per sigarette) cigarette paper

■ **cartina di tornasole** litmus paper

car'toccio *m* paper bag; **al ~** Culin baked in foil

cartogra'fia *f* cartography

car'tografo *m* cartographer

carto'laio, -a *mf* stationer

cartole'ria *f* stationer's [shop]

cartolibre'ria *f* stationer's and book shop

⚷ **carto'lina** *f* postcard

■ **cartolina postale** postcard; **cartolina [precetto]** call-up papers

carto'mante *mf* fortune-teller

carton'cino *m* (materiale) card; (biglietto) card

car'tone *m* cardboard; (arte) cartoon

■ **cartone animato** [animated] cartoon; **cartone ondulato** corrugated cardboard; **cartone di uova** egg box

car'tuccia *f* cartridge; **mezza ~** fig weakling

■ **cartuccia d'inchiostro** ink cartridge

⚷ **'casa** *f* house; (abitazione propria) home; (ditta) firm; **amico di ~** family friend; **andare a ~** go home; **uscire di ~** leave the house; **essere di ~** be like one of the family; **fatto in ~** home-made; **~ per ~** house-to-house

■ **casa d'aste** auction house; **casa di correzione** ≈ reform school; **casa di cura** nursing home; **casa del custode** gatehouse; **casa famiglia** care home; **casa madre** Comm parent company; **casa di mode** fashion house; **casa in multiproprietà** timeshare; **casa popolare** council house; **casa rifugio** women's refuge; **casa di riposo** old people's home, retirement home; **casa dello studente** hall of residence; **casa per le vacanze** holiday home

ca'sacca *f* military coat; (giacca) jacket

ca'saccio *adv* **a ~** at random; **sparare a ~ su qualcuno/qualcosa** take a potshot at somebody/something

ca'sale *m* (gruppo di case) hamlet; (casolare) farmhouse

casa'linga *f* housewife

casa'lingo **A** *adj* domestic; (fatto in casa) home-made; (amante della casa) home-loving; (semplice) homely

B *m* **casalinghi** *pl* household goods

casa'nova *m inv* (donnaiolo) Casanova

ca'sata *f* family

ca'sato *m* family name

ca'scante *adj* falling; (floscio) flabby

⚷ **ca'scare** *vi* fall [down]

ca'scata *f* (di acqua) waterfall

casca|'tore, -trice **A** *m* stuntman

B *f* stuntwoman

cas'chetto *m*

■ **[capelli a] caschetto** bob

ca'scina *f* farm building

casci'nale *f* farmhouse

'casco *m* crash helmet; (asciugacapelli) (hair) drier

■ **casco di banane** bunch of bananas; **Caschi blu** *pl* Mil Blue Helmets, Blue Berets

caseggi'ato *m* block of flats BrE, apartment block

casei'ficio *m* dairy

ca'sella *f* pigeon-hole

■ **casella postale** post office box, PO box; (elettronica) mailbox

casel'lante *mf* (per treni) signalman; (in autostrada) toll collector

casel'lario *m* (mobile) filing cabinet; (di documenti) file

■ **casellario giudiziario** record of convictions; **avere il ~ giudiziario vuoto** have no criminal record

ca'sello *m* (di autostrada) [motorway] toll booth

case'reccio *adj* home-made

ca'serma *f* barracks *pl*; **da ~** ‹*linguaggio*› barrack room *attrib*

■ **caserma dei carabinieri** military police station; **caserma dei pompieri, caserma dei vigili del fuoco** fire station

caser'mone *m* derog barracks *pl*

cash and carry *m inv* cash-and-carry

casi'nista *mf* infml muddler

ca'sino *m* infml (bordello) brothel; fig *sl* (confusione) racket; (disordine) mess; **un ~**

⚷ key word

di loads of; **è un** ~ (complicato) it's too complicated

casinò *m inv* casino

ca'sistica *f* (classificazione) record of occurrences

'caso *m* chance; (fatto, circostanza) Med, Gram case; **a** ~ at random; ~ **mai** if need be; **far** ~ **a** pay attention to; **non far** ~ **a** take no account of; **per** ~ by chance

■ **caso [giudiziario]** [legal] case, court case; **caso urgente** Med emergency case

caso'lare *m* farmhouse

'caspita *int* good gracious

'cassa *f* till; (di legno) crate; Comm cash; (luogo di pagamento) cash desk; (mobile) chest; (istituto bancario) bank

■ **cassa automatica prelievi** cash dispenser, automatic teller; **cassa comune** kitty; **cassa continua** cash machine; **cassa da morto** coffin; **cassa di risparmio** savings bank; **cassa toracica** ribcage

cassa'forte *f* safe

cassa'panca *f* linen chest

cas'sata *f* ice-cream cake

cas'sero *m* Naut quarterdeck

casseru'ola *f* saucepan

cas'setta *f* case; (per registratore) cassette; **far buona** ~ Theatr be good box-office

■ **cassetta degli attrezzi** toolbox; **cassetta delle lettere** postbox, letterbox; **cassetta delle offerte** charity box; **cassetta portapane** bread bin; **cassetta portavalori** cash box; **cassetta del pronto soccorso** first-aid kit; **cassetta di sicurezza** strong-box, safe-deposit box

cas'setto *m* drawer; (di fotocopiatrice ecc.) tray

■ **cassetto di inserimento [dei] fogli** paper feed tray

casset'tone *m* chest of drawers

cassi'ere, -a *mf* cashier; (di supermercato) checkout assistant, checkout operator; (di banca) teller

cassinte'grato, -a *mf* person who has been laid off

cas'sone *m* (cassa) chest; (per acqua) cofferdam

casso'netto *m* rubbish bin, wheelie bin, trash can AmE

'casta *f* caste

ca'stagna *f* chestnut; **prendere qualcuno in** ~ fig catch somebody in the act

■ **castagna d'India** horse chestnut

casta'gnaccio *m tart made with chestnut flour*

casta'gneto *m* chestnut grove

ca'stagno *m* chestnut (tree)

casta'gnola *f* (petardo) firecracker

ca'stano *adj* chestnut; ‹*occhi, capelli*› brown

ca'stello *m* castle; (impalcatura) scaffold

■ **castello incantato** enchanted castle; **castello di sabbia** sandcastle

casti'gare *vt* punish

casti'gato *adj* (casto) chaste; ‹*abito, atteggiamento*› prim and proper

ca'stigo *m* punishment

castità *f inv* chastity

'casto *adj* chaste

ca'storo *m* beaver

ca'strante *adj* fig frustrating

ca'strare *vt* castrate

ca'strato *adj* castrated; (inibito) inhibited; (cantante) castrato

castrazi'one *f* gelding

ca'strone *m* gelding

castrone'ria *f* infml rubbish

'casual *m inv* casual wear

casu'ale *adj* chance *attrib*

casual'mente *adv* by chance

ca'supola *f* little house

cata'clisma *m* fig upheaval

cata'comba *f* catacomb

cata'falco *m* catafalque

cata'fascio *m* **andare a** ~ go to rack and ruin

cata'litico *adj* **marmitta catalitica** Auto catalytic converter

cataliz'zare *vt* fig heighten

cataliz'zato *adj* Auto fitted with a catalytic converter

catalizza'tore **A** *adj* Phys catalysing; **centro** ~ fig catalyst
B *m* Auto catalytic converter; fig catalyst

catalo'gabile *adj* which can be listed

catalo'gare *vt* catalogue

catalogazi'one *f* cataloguing

cata'logna *f type of chicory with large leaves*

ca'talogo *m* catalogue

catama'rano *m* (da diporto) catamaran

cata'pecchia *f* hovel; infml dump

cata'pulta *f* catapult

catapul'tare *vt* (scaraventare fuori) eject

catapul'tarsi *vr* (precipitarsi) dive

catarifran'gente *m* reflector

ca'tarro *m* catarrh

catar'roso *adj* ‹*voce*› catarrhal

ca'tarsi *f inv* catharsis

ca'tartico *adj* cathartic

ca'tasta *f* pile

cata'stale *adj* **registro** ~ land registry; **rendita** ~ revenue from landed property

ca'tasto *m* land register

ca'tastrofe *f* catastrophe

cata'strofico *adj* catastrophic

catastro'fismo *m* catastrophe theory

catch *m* all-in wrestling

cate'chismo *m* catechism

catego'ria *f* category

cate'gorico *adj* categorical

C

categoriz'zare *vt* categorize
ca'tena *f* chain
■ **catena montuosa** mountain range; **catene da neve** *pl* [snow] chains
cate'naccio *m* bolt
cate'nella *f* (collana) chain; (di orologio) watch chain; **tirare la ~** (del gabinetto) flush, pull the plug
cate'nina *f* chain
cate'ratta *f* cataract
ca'terva *f* **una ~ di** heaps of, loads of
ca'tetere *m* catheter
'catgut *m inv* catgut
cati'nella *f* basin; **piovere a catinelle** bucket down
ca'tino *m* basin
ca'todico *adj* cathode; **raggi catodici** cathode rays
ca'torcio *m* infml old wreck
catra'mare *vt* tar
ca'trame *m* tar
'cattedra *f* (tavolo di insegnante) desk; (di università) chair
catte'drale *f* cathedral
catte'dratico, -a **A** *mf* professor **B** *adj* ‹*pedante*› pedantic; ‹*insegnamento*› university *attrib*
catti'veria *f* wickedness; (azione) wicked action; **fare una ~ a qualcuno** be nasty to somebody
cattività *f inv* captivity
cat'tivo *adj* bad; ‹*bambino*› naughty
cattocomu'nista *mf* Catholic-communist
cattoli'cesimo *m* Catholicism
cat'tolico, -a *adj & nmf* [Roman] Catholic
cat'tura *f* capture
cattu'rare *vt* capture
cau'casico, -a *mf* Caucasian
'Caucaso *m* **il ~** the Caucasus
caucciù *m inv* rubber
'causa *f* cause; Jur lawsuit; **far ~ a qualcuno** sue somebody
■ **causa di forza maggiore** circumstances beyond one's control; (in assicurazione) act of God
cau'sale *adj* causal
cau'sare *vt* cause
'caustico *adj* caustic
cauta'mente *adv* cautiously
cau'tela *f* caution
caute'lare *vt* protect
caute'larsi *vr* take precautions
cauteriz'zare *vt* cauterize
cauterizzazi'one *f* cauterization
'cauto *adj* cautious
cauzi'one *f* security; (per libertà provvisoria) bail; (deposito) deposit

cav. *abbr* (**cavaliere**) Kt, Knight
'cava *f* quarry; fig mine
caval'care *vt* ride; (stare a cavalcioni) sit astride
caval'cata *f* ride; (corteo) cavalcade
cavalca'via *m* flyover
cavalci'oni **a ~** *adv* astride
cavali'ere *m* rider; (titolo) knight; (accompagnatore) escort; (al ballo) partner
cavalle'resco *adj* chivalrous
cavalle'ria *f* chivalry; Mil cavalry
cavalle'rizzo, -a **A** *m* horseman **B** *f* horsewoman
caval'letta *f* grasshopper
caval'letto *m* trestle; (di macchina fotografica) tripod; (di pittore) easel
caval'lina *f* (ginnastica) horse; (gioco) leapfrog; **correre la ~** fig pursue a life of pleasure
caval'lino *adj* equine
ca'vallo *m* horse; (misura di potenza) horsepower; (scacchi) knight; (dei pantaloni) crotch; **a ~** on horseback; **andare a ~** go horse riding
■ **cavallo di battaglia** war horse; **cavallo a dondolo** rocking horse; **cavallo da tiro** carthorse; **cavallo di Troia** Trojan horse
caval'lona *f* derog ungainly female
caval'lone *m* (ondata) roller
caval'luccio *m*
■ **cavalluccio marino** sea horse
ca'vare *vt* take out; (di dosso) take off; **cavarsela** get away with it; **se la cava bene** he's/she's doing all right
cavasti'vali *m inv* bootjack
cava'tappi *m inv* corkscrew
ca'veau *m inv* (di banca) vault
ca'verna *f* cave
caver'nicolo, -a *mf* cave dweller
caver'noso *adj* ‹*voce*› deep
ca'vetto *m* Electr lead
ca'vezza *f* halter; **mettere la ~ al collo a qualcuno** put somebody on a tight rein
'cavia *f* guinea pig
cavi'ale *m* caviar
ca'viglia *f* ankle
cavil'lare *vi* quibble
ca'villo *m* quibble
cavil'loso *adj* pettifogging
cavità *f inv* cavity
'cavo **A** *adj* hollow **B** *m* cavity; (di metallo) cable; Naut rope
■ **televisione via cavo** cable TV; **cavo di collegamento** [connecting] cable; **cavo seriale** serial cable; **cavo di spiegamento** ripcord
cavo'lata *f* infml rubbish; **non dire cavolate** infml don't talk rubbish; **non fare cavolate** infml don't act like an idiot
cavo'letto *m*
■ **cavoletto di Bruxelles** Brussels sprout

key word

cavolfi'ore *m* cauliflower

'cavolo *m* cabbage; **~!** infml sugar!; **non ho capito un ~** infml I understood bugger all; **che ~ succede?** what the heck is going on?
■ **cavolo cappuccio** spring cabbage

caz'zata *f* vulg shit; **non dire cazzate** don't talk shit; **non fare cazzate** don't fuck things up

'cazzo **A** *vulg nm* prick
B *int* fuck!; **non capisce un ~** he doesn't understand a fucking thing; **non me ne importa un ~!** I don't give a fuck!; **sono cazzi miei!** it's my fucking business!

caz'zotto *m* punch; **prendere qualcuno a cazzotti** beat somebody up

cazzu'ola *f* trowel

CB *nf abbr* (**banda cittadina**) CB

cc *abbr* (**centimetri cubi**) cc

c/c *abbr* (**conto corrente**) c/a

ccn *nf abbr* (**copia carbone nascosta**) bcc

CCT *nm abbr* (**Certificato di Credito del Tesoro**) T-bill

CD *m inv* CD

CD-ROM *m inv* CD-ROM

ce **A** *pers pron* (a noi) us; **ce lo ha dato** he gave it to us
B *adv* there; **ce ne sono molti** there are many; **ce ne vuole!** it takes some doing!

cec'chino *m* sniper; Pol *MP who votes against his own party*

'cece *m* chickpea

Ce'cenia *f* Chechnya

cecità *f inv* blindness

'ceco, -a *adj & nmf* Czech; **la Repubblica Ceca** the Czech Republic

Cecoslo'vacchia *f* Hist Czechoslovakia

'cedere **A** *vi* (arrendersi) surrender; (concedere) yield; (sprofondare) subside
B *vt* give up; make over ‹*proprietà ecc.*›

ce'devole *adj* ‹*terreno ecc.*› soft; fig yielding

ce'diglia *f* cedilla

cedi'mento *m* (di terreno) subsidence

'cedola *f* coupon

cedo'lino *m* (dello stipendio) wage slip

'cedro *m* (albero) cedar; (frutto) citron

C.E.E. *nf abbr* (**Comunità Economica Europea**) EEC, EC

cefa'lea *f* headache

ce'falo *m* mullet

'ceffo *m* (muso) snout; derog (persona) mug

cef'fone *m* slap

ce'lare *vt* conceal

ce'larsi *vr* conceal oneself

ce'lato *adj* concealed

cele'brare *vt* celebrate, observe ‹*festività*›

celebra'tivo *adj* celebratory

celebrazi'one *f* celebration

'celebre *adj* famous

celebrità *f inv* celebrity

'celere **A** *adj* swift; **corso ~** crash course
B *f* (polizia) flying squad

celerità *f inv* speed; **con ~** speedily

ce'leste **A** *adj* (divino) heavenly
B *adj & nm* (colore) pale blue

celesti'ale *adj* celestial

celi'bato *m* state of being single

'celibe **A** *adj* single
B *m* bachelor

'cella *f* cell
■ **cella frigorifera** cold store; **cella di isolamento** solitary confinement

+cello *suff* **monticello** *nm* mound; **praticello** *nm* small meadow

'cellofan *m inv* cellophane; Culin cling film

cellofa'nare *vt* wrap in cling film

'cellula *f* cell
■ **cellula fotoelettrica** electronic eye

cellu'lare *m* (telefono) mobile (phone), cell phone; **furgone ~** police van; **telefono ~** mobile (phone)

cellu'lite *f* cellulite

cellu'litico *adj* full of cellulite

cellu'loide *adj* celluloid; **il mondo della ~** fig the celluloid world

cellu'losa *f* cellulose

'Celsius *adj inv* Celsius

'celta *m* Celt

'celtico *adj* Celtic

'cembalo *m* Mus cembalo, harpsichord

cemen'tare *vt* cement

cementifi'care *vt* turn into a cement jungle

cementificazi'one *f* turning into a cement jungle

cementi'ficio *m* cement factory

ce'mento *m* cement
■ **cemento armato** reinforced concrete

'cena *f* dinner; (leggera) supper; (festa) dinner party

ce'nacolo *m* circle

ce'nare *vi* have dinner; **~ fuori** eat out

'cencio *m* rag; (per spolverare) duster; **bianco come un ~** white as a sheet

cenci'oso *adj* in rags

'cenere *f* ash; (di carbone ecc.) cinders *pl*; **le Ceneri** *pl* Ash Wednesday

Cene'rentola *f* Cinderella

ce'netta *f* (cena semplice) informal dinner; (cena intima) romantic dinner

'cenno *m* sign; (col capo) nod; (con la mano) wave; (allusione) hint; (breve resoconto) mention; **far ~ di sì** nod

ce'none *m* **il ~ di Capodanno/Natale** *special New Year's Eve/Christmas Eve dinner*

ceno'tafio *m* cenotaph

censi'mento *m* census

cen'sire *vt* take a census of

CENSIS *nm abbr* (**Centro Studi Investimenti Sociali**) *national opinion*

c

C

research institute

cen'sore *m* censor

cen'sura *f* censorship

censu'rare *vt* censor

centelli'nare *vt* sip; fig measure out carefully

cente'nario, -a **A** *adj & mf* centenarian **B** *m* (commemorazione) centenary

centen'nale *adj* centennial

centesimo **A** *adj* hundredth **B** *m* hundredth; (di dollaro, euro) cent; **non avere un ~** be penniless

cen'tigrado *adj* centigrade

cen'tilitro *m* centilitre

cen'timetro *m* centimetre

centi'naia *fpl* hundreds

⚷ **centi'naio** *m* hundred

⚷ **'cento** *adj & nm* a *or* one hundred; **per ~** per cent

centodi'eci *m* a *or* one hundred and ten; **~ e lode** Univ ≈ first class honours

centome'trista *mf* Sport one hundred metres runner

cento'mila *m* a *or* one hundred thousand

⚷ **cen'trale** **A** *adj* central **B** *f* (di azienda ecc.) head office

■ **centrale atomica** atomic power station; **centrale elettrica** power station, power plant; **centrale idroelettrica** hydroelectric power station; **centrale nucleare** nuclear power station; **centrale operativa** (di polizia) operations room; **centrale telefonica** [telephone] exchange

centra'lina *f* Teleph switchboard; (apparecchiatura) junction box

centrali'nista *mf* (switchboard/telephone) operator

centra'lino *m* Teleph exchange; (di albergo ecc.) switchboard

centra'lismo *m* centralism

centraliz'zare *vt* centralize

cen'trare *vt* **~ qualcosa** hit something in the centre; (fissare nel centro) centre; fig hit on the head ‹*idea*›

cen'trato *adj* ‹*tiro, colpo*› well aimed; fig ‹*osservazione*› right on target

centrat'tacco *m* Sport centre forward

cen'trifuga *f* spin drier

■ **centrifuga [asciugaverdure]** shaker; **centrifuga elettrica** juice extractor

centrifu'gare *vt* Techn centrifuge; ‹*lavatrice*› spin

cen'trino *m* doily

cen'trismo *m* Pol centrism

cen'trista *adj* Pol centrist

⚷ **'centro** *m* centre; **in ~** ‹*essere*› in town; ‹*andare*› into town

■ **centro di accoglienza** detention centre; **centro di attrazione** focal point; **centro benessere** wellness centre; **centro città** city centre, midtown AmE; **centro commerciale** shopping centre, mall; **centro di costi** Comm cost centre; **centro culturale** arts centre; **centro di gravità** centre of gravity; **centro di identificazione ed espulsione** immigration removal centre; **centro di informazioni turistiche** tourist information office; **centro operativo** Mil operations room; **centro polisportivo** sports centre; **centro di riabilitazione** halfway house; **centro sociale** community centre; **centro sportivo** leisure centre; **centro storico** old town

centrocam'pista *m* Sport midfield player, midfielder

centro'campo *m* midfield

centro'destra *m inv* Pol centre right

centromedi'ano *m* Sport centre half

centrosi'nistra *m inv* Pol centre left

centro'tavola *m inv* centre-piece

centupli'care *vt* fig multiply

'ceppo *m* (di albero) stump; (da ardere) log; fig (gruppo) stock

'cera *f* wax; (aspetto) look

■ **cera d'api** beeswax; **cera per auto** car wax; **cera per il pavimento** floor polish

cera'lacca *f* sealing wax

ce'ramica *f* (arte) ceramics *sg*; (materia) pottery; (oggetto) piece of pottery

cera'mista *mf* ceramicist

ce'rata *f* (giacca) waxed jacket

ce'rato *adj* ‹*tela*› waxed

cerbi'atto *m* fawn

cerbot'tana *f* blowpipe

'cerca *f* **andare in ~ di** look for

cercaper'sone *m inv* beeper; **chiamare con il ~** beep

⚷ **cer'care** **A** *vt* look for **B** *vi* **~ di** try to

cerca|'tore, -trice *mf*

■ **cercatore d'oro** gold seeker

'cerchia *f* circle

■ **cerchia familiare** family circle

cerchi'are *vt* circle, draw a circle around ‹*parola*›

cerchi'ato *adj* ‹*occhi*› black ringed

cerchi'etto *m* (per capelli) hairband

'cerchio *m* circle; (giocattolo) hoop

cerchi'one *m* alloy wheel

cere'ale *m* cereal

cerea'licolo *adj* grain *attrib*, cereal *attrib*

cere'brale *adj* cerebral

'cereo *adj* waxen

ce'retta *f* depilatory wax; **fare la ~** wax

cer'foglio *m* chervil

⚷ **ceri'monia** *f* ceremony

■ **cerimonia inaugurale** induction ceremony; **cerimonia nuziale** marriage ceremony; **cerimonia di premiazione** awards ceremony

cerimoni'ale *m* ceremonial

⚷ key word

cerimoni'ere *m* master of ceremonies
cerimoni'oso *adj* ceremonious
ce'rino *m* [wax] match
cerni'era *f* hinge; (di borsa) clasp
■ **cerniera lampo** zip, zipper AmE
'cernita *f* selection
'cero *m* candle
ce'rone *m* greasepaint
ce'rotto *m* [sticking] plaster
■ **cerotto callifugo** corn plaster; **cerotto [transdermico] alla nicotina** nicotine patch
certa'mente *adv* certainly
cer'tezza *f* certainty
certifi'care *vt* certify
certifi'cato *m* certificate
■ **certificato medico** doctor's note, sick note; **certificato di morte** death certificate
certificazi'one *f* certification
■ **certificazione di bilancio** Fin auditors' report
'certo **A** *adj* certain; ‹*notizia*› definite; (indeterminativo) some; **sono ~ di riuscire** I am certain to succeed; **a una certa età** at a certain age; **certi giorni** some days; **un ~ signor Giardini** a Mr Giardini; **una certa Anna** somebody called Anna; **certa gente** derog some people; **ho certi dolori!** I'm in such pain!; **certi** *pron pl* some; (alcune persone) some people
B *adv* of course; **sapere per ~** know for certain, know for sure; **di ~** surely; **~ che ...** surely ...
cer'tosa *f* Carthusian monastery
certo'sino *m* Carthusian [monk]; **pazienza certosina** exceptional patience
cer'tuni *pron* some
ce'rume *m* earwax
cer'vello *m* brain; **avere un ~ da gallina** be a bird-brain
cervel'lone, -a *mf* (hum) brainbox
cervel'lotico *adj* (macchinoso) over-elaborate
cervi'cale *adj* cervical
cer'vice *f* cervix
'cervo *m* deer
ce'sareo *adj* Med Caesarean; **parto cesareo** Caesarean
cesel'lare *vt* chisel
cesel'lato *adj* chiselled
cesella'tura *f* chiselling
ce'sello *m* chisel
ce'soie *fpl* shears
'cespite *m* source of income
ce'spuglio *m* bush
cespugli'oso *adj* ‹*terreno*› bushy
ces'sare **A** *vi* stop, cease
B *vt* stop
ces'sate *m*
■ **cessate il fuoco** ceasefire
ces'sato *adj* **~ allarme/pericolo** all clear
cessazi'one *f* cessation
■ **cessazione d'esercizio** closing down
cessi'one *f* handover
'cesso *nm sl* (gabinetto) bog, john AmE; fig (locale, luogo) dump
'cesta *f* [large] basket
ce'stello *m* (di lavatrice) drum
cesti'nare *vt* throw away; bin ‹*lettera*›; turn down ‹*proposta*›
ce'stino *m* [small] basket; (per la carta straccia) waste-paper basket; Comput recycle bin, trash can AmE
'cesto *m* basket
■ **cesto della biancheria** linen basket
ce'sura *f* caesura
ce'taceo *m* cetacean
'ceto *m* [social] class
'cetra *f* lyre
cetrio'lino *m* gherkin
cetri'olo *m* cucumber
cfr *abbr* (**confronta**) cf
C.G.I.L. *nf abbr* (**Confederazione Generale Italiana del Lavoro**) *trades union organization*
'Chad *m* Chad
cha'let *m inv* chalet
cham'pagne *m inv* champagne
'chance *f inv* chance
chape'ron *m inv* chaperone
char'lotte *f inv ice-cream cake with fresh cream, biscuits and fruit*
'charter *m inv* charter plane; **volo charter** charter flight
chat'tare *vi* chat
che **A** *rel pron* (persona: soggetto) who; (persona: oggetto) whom; (cosa, animale) which; **questa è la casa ~ ho comprato** this is the house [that] I've bought; **il ~ mi sorprende** which surprises me; **dal ~ deduco ~ ...** from which I gather that ...; **avere di ~ vivere** have enough to live on; **grazie! - non c'è di ~!** thank you - don't mention it; **il giorno ~ ti ho visto** infml the day I saw you
B *inter adj* what; (esclamativo: con aggettivo) how; (con nome) what a; **~ macchina prendiamo, la tua o la mia?** which car are we taking, yours or mine?; **~ bello!** how nice!; **~ idea!** what an idea!; **~ bella giornata!** what a lovely day!
C *inter pron* what; **a ~ pensi?** what are you thinking about?
D *conj* that; (con comparazioni) than; **credo ~ abbia ragione** I think [that] he is right; **era così commosso ~ non riusciva a parlare** he was so moved, [that] he couldn't speak; **aspetto ~ telefoni** I'm waiting for him to phone; **è da un po' ~ non lo vedo** it's been a while since I saw him; **mi piace più Roma ~ Milano** I like Rome better than Milan; **~ ti piaccia o no** whether you like it or not; **~ io sappia** as far as I know
'checca *f* infml queen

checché *pron* whatever
check-'in *m inv* check-in; **fare il ~** check in
check-'up *m inv* Med check-up; **fare un ~** have a check-up
cheese'burger *m inv* cheeseburger
'chef *m inv* chef
'chela *f* nipper
chemiotera'pia *f* chemotherapy, chemo infml
chemisi'er *m inv* chemise
chero'sene *m* paraffin
cheru'bino *m* cherub
che'tare *vt* quieten
che'tarsi *vr* quieten down
cheti'chella **alla ~** *adv* silently
'cheto *adj* quiet
chi **A** *rel pron* whoever; (coloro che) people who; **ho trovato ~ ti può aiutare** I found somebody who can help you; **c'è ~ dice che ...** some people say that ...; **senti ~ parla!** look who's talking!
B *inter pron* (soggetto) who; (oggetto, con preposizione) whom; (possessivo) **di ~** whose; **~ sei?** who are you?; **~ hai incontrato?** who did you meet?, whom did you meet? fml; **di ~ sono questi libri?** whose books are these?; **con ~ parli?** who are you talking to?, to whom are you talking? fml; **a ~ lo dici!** tell me about it!
chi'acchiera *f* chat; (pettegolezzo) gossip; **chiacchiere** *pl* chit-chat; **far quattro chiacchiere** have a chat
chiacchie'rare *vi* chat; (far pettegolezzi) gossip
chiacchie'rato *adj* **essere ~** ‹*persona*› be the subject of gossip
chi'acchiere *fpl* (dolci) *sweet pastries fried and sprinkled with icing sugar*
chiacchie'rone, -a **A** *adj* talkative
B *mf* chatterbox
chia'mare *vt* call; (far venire) send for; **come ti chiami?** what's your name?; **mi chiamo Roberto** my name is Robert; **~ alle armi** call up; **mandare a ~** send for; **~ a rapporto** debrief
chia'marsi *vr* be called
chia'mata *f* call; Mil call-up
■ **chiamata a carico del destinatario** reverse charge call, transferred charge call; **chiamata interurbana** long-distance call; **chiamata in teleselezione** direct dialling, toll call AmE; **chiamata urbana** local call
chi'appa *f* infml buttock, cheek
chiara'mente *adv* clearly
chia'rezza *f* clarity; (limpidezza) clearness
chiarifi'care *vt* clarify
chiarifica'tore *adj* clarificatory
chiarificazi'one *f* clarification
chiari'mento *m* clarification
chia'rire *vt* make clear; (spiegare) clear up

key word

chia'rirsi *vr* become clear
chi'aro *adj* clear; (luminoso) bright; ‹*colore*› light; ‹*capelli*› fair
chia'rore *m* glimmer
chiaro'scuro *m* (tecnica) chiaroscuro
chiaroveg'gente **A** *adj* clear-sighted
B *mf* clairvoyant
chi'asso *m* din
chiassosa'mente *adv* (rumorosamente) rowdily; (vistosamente) gaudily
chias'soso *adj* (rumoroso) rowdy; (vistoso) gaudy
chi'atta *f* canal boat, canal barge
chi'ave *f* key; **chiudere a ~** lock
■ **chiave dell'accensione** ignition key; **chiave di basso** Mus bass clef; **chiave inglese** monkey-wrench; **chiave [inglese] a rullino** adjustable spanner; **chiave USB** ▶ **chiavetta USB**
chia'vetta *f* (in tubi) key
■ **chiavetta USB** USB key
chiavi'stello *m* latch
chi'azza *f* stain
■ **chiazza di petrolio** oil slick
chiaz'zare *vt* stain
chiaz'zato *adj* dappled
chic *adj inv* chic
chicches'sia *pron* anybody
chicchirichì *m inv* cock-a-doodle-doo
'chicco *m* grain; (di caffe) bean; (d'uva) grape
■ **chicco di caffè** coffee bean; **chicco di grandine** hailstone; **chicco d'orzo** barleycorn
chi'edere *vt* ask; (per avere) ask for; (esigere) demand; **~ notizie di** ask after
chi'edersi *vr* wonder
chieri'chetto *m* altar boy
chi'erico *m* cleric
chi'esa *f* church
■ **Chiesa anglicana** Church of England
chi'esto pp di **chiedere**
chif'fon *m* chiffon
'chiglia *f* keel
chi'gnon *m inv* bun
'chilo *m* kilo
chilo'grammo *m* kilogram[me]
chilo'hertz *m inv* kilohertz
chilome'traggio *m* Auto ≈ mileage
chilo'metrico *adj* in kilometres; fig endless
chi'lometro *m* kilometre
'chilowatt *m inv* kilowatt
chilowat'tora *m inv* kilowatt hour
chi'mera *f* fig illusion
'chimica *f* chemistry
■ **chimica organica** organic chemistry
'chimico, -a **A** *adj* chemical
B *mf* chemist
chi'mono *m* kimono
'china *f* (declivio) slope; **inchiostro di ~** Indian ink
chi'nare *vt* lower

chi'narsi *vr* stoop
chincaglie'rie *fpl* knick-knacks
chinesitera'pia *f* physiotherapy
chi'nino *m* quinine
'chino *adj* bent
chi'notto *m sparkling soft drink*
chintz *m* chintz
chi'occia *f* sitting hen
chi'occiola *f* snail; Comput at sign, @
■ **scala a chiocciola** spiral staircase
chio'dato *adj* **pneumatici chiodati** snow tyres; **scarpe chiodate** shoes with crampons
chi'odo *m* nail; (idea fissa) obsession
■ **chiodo di garofano** clove
chi'oma *f* [head of] hair; (fogliame) foliage
chi'osco *m* kiosk; (per giornali) news-stand
chi'ostro *m* cloister
chip *m inv*
■ **chip [di silicio]** chip
'chipset *m inv* chipset
chiro'mante *mf* fortune teller, palmist
chiroman'zia *f* palmistry
chiro'pratico, -a *mf* chiropractor
chirur'gia *f* surgery
■ **chirurgia endoscopica** keyhole surgery; **chirurgia estetica** cosmetic surgery
chirurgica'mente *adv* surgically
chi'rurgico *adj* surgical
chi'rurgo *m* surgeon
chissà *adv* who knows; **~ quando arriverà** I wonder when he will arrive
chi'tarra *f* guitar
■ **chitarra acustica** acoustic guitar; **chitarra basso** bass guitar
chitar'rista *mf* guitarist
chi'udere **A** *vt* shut, close; (con chiave) lock; turn off, switch off ‹*luce ecc.*›; turn off ‹*acqua*›; (per sempre) close down ‹*negozio, fabbrica ecc.*›; (recingere) enclose; **chiudi il becco!** shut up!
B *vi* shut, close; (con chiave) lock up
chi'udersi *vr* shut; ‹*tempo*› cloud over; ‹*ferita*› heal over; fig withdraw into oneself
chi'unque **A** *pron* anyone, anybody
B *rel pron* whoever
chi'usa *f* enclosure; (di canale) lock; (conclusione) close
chi'uso **A** pp di **chiudere**
B *adj* closed, shut; ‹*tempo*› overcast; ‹*persona*› reserved; **'~ per turno'** 'closing day'
chiu'sura *f* closing; (sistema) lock; (allacciatura) fastener; **'~ settimanale il lunedì'** 'closed on Mondays'
■ **chiusura centralizzata** Auto central locking; **chiusura lampo** zip, zipper AmE
ci **A** *pron* (personale) us; (riflessivo) ourselves; (reciproco) each other; (a ciò, di ciò ecc.) about it; **non ci disturbare** don't disturb us; **aspettateci** wait for us; **ci ha detto tutto** he told us everything; **ci consideriamo ...** we consider ourselves ...; **ci laviamo le mani** we wash our hands; **ci odiamo** we hate each other; **non ci penso mai** I never think about it; **pensaci!** think about it!
B *adv* (qui) here; (lì) there; (moto per luogo) through it; **ci siamo** here we are; **ci siete?** are you there?; **ci siamo passati tutti** we all went through it; **c'è** there is; **ci vuole pazienza** it takes patience; **non ci vedo/sento** I can't see/hear
C.ia *abbr* (**compagnia**) Co.
cia'batta *f* slipper
ciabat'tare *vi* shuffle
ciabat'tino *m* cobbler
ci'ac *m inv* Cinema; **~, si gira!** action!
ci'alda *f* wafer
cial'trone *m* (mascalzone) scoundrel; (fannullone) wastrel
ciam'bella *f* Culin ring-shaped cake; (salvagente) lifebelt; (gonfiabile) rubber ring
ci'ance *fpl* yapping
cianci'are *vi* gossip
cianfru'saglie *fpl* knick-knacks
cia'notico *adj* ‹*viso*› puce
cia'nuro *m* cyanide
ci'ao *int* infml (all'arrivo) hello!, hi!; (alla partenza) bye-bye!, cheerio!
ciar'lare *vi* chat
ciarla'tano *m* charlatan
ciarli'ero *adj* (loquace) talkative
cia'scuno **A** *adj* each
B *pron* everyone, everybody; (distributivo) each [one]; **per ~** each
ci'aspole *fpl* snowshoes
ci'bare *vt* feed
ci'barie *fpl* provisions
ci'barsi *vr* eat; **~ di** live on
ciber'netica *f* cybernetics *sg*
ciber'netico *adj* cybernetic
ciber'spazio *m* cyberspace
'cibo *m* food; **non toccare ~** leave one's food untouched; **non ha toccato ~ da ieri** he hasn't had a bite to eat since yesterday
■ **cibo per animali** pet food; **cibi** *pl* **precotti** ready meals
ci'cala *f* cicada
cica'lino *m* buzzer
cica'trice *f* scar
cicatriz'zante *m* ointment
cicatriz'zare *vi* heal [up]
cicatriz'zarsi *vr* heal [up]
cicatrizzazi'one *f* healing
'cicca *f* cigarette end; infml (sigaretta) fag; infml (gomma) [chewing] gum
cic'chetto *m* infml (bicchierino) nip; (rimprovero) telling-off
'ciccia *f* infml fat, flab
cicci'one, -a *mf* infml fatty, fatso
cice'rone *m* guide
cicla'mino *m* cyclamen

C

ciclica'mente *adv* cyclically
'ciclico *adj* cyclical
ci'clismo *m* cycling
ci'clista *mf* cyclist
'ciclo *m* cycle; (di malattia) course
■ **ciclo economico** business cycle
ciclo'cross *m inv* cyclo-cross
ciclomo'tore *m* moped
ci'clone *m* cyclone
ci'clonico *adj* cyclonic
ciclosti'lare *vt* duplicate
ciclosti'lato **A** *m* duplicate [copy] **B** *adj* duplicate
ci'cogna *f* stork
ci'coria *f* chicory
ci'cuta *f* hemlock
C.I.E. *nm abbr* (**centro di identificazione ed espulsione**) immigration removal centre
⚷ **ci'eco, -a** **A** *adj* blind **B** *mf* blind man; blind woman; **i parzialmente ciechi** the partially sighted
ciel'lino *mf* Pol *member of the Comunione e Liberazione movement*
⚷ **ci'elo** *m* sky; Relig heaven; **al settimo ~** in seventh heaven; **santo ~!** good heavens!
⚷ **'cifra** *f* figure; (somma) sum; (monogramma) monogram; (codice) code; **una ~** sl like crazy
ci'frare *vt* embroider with a monogram; (codificare) code
ci'frato *adj* monogrammed; (codificato) coded
'ciglio *m* (bordo) edge; (degli occhi) eyelash; **ciglia** *pl* eyelashes
'cigno *m* swan
cigo'lante *adj* squeaky
cigo'lare *vt* squeak
cigo'lio *m* squeak
'Cile *m* Chile
ci'lecca *f* **far ~** miss
ci'leno, -a *adj & nmf* Chilean
cili'egia *f* cherry
cili'egio *m* cherry (tree)
cilin'drata *f* cubic capacity, c.c.; **macchina di grossa ~** high-powered car
ci'lindro *m* cylinder; (cappello) top hat, topper
⚷ **'cima** *f* top; fig (persona) genius; **in ~ a** at the top of; **da ~ a fondo** from top to bottom
■ **cima alla genovese** *baked veal stuffed with chicken and chopped vegetables, served cold*; **cime di rapa** *pl* turnip greens
ci'melio *m* relic; **cimeli** *pl* memorabilia
cimen'tare *vt* put to the test
cimen'tarsi *vr* (provare) try one's hand; **~ in** (arrischiarsi) venture into
'cimice *f* bug; (puntina) drawing pin, thumbtack AmE; (microspia) bug
cimini'era *f* chimney; Naut funnel

⚷ key word

⚷ **cimi'tero** *m* cemetery
■ **cimitero delle macchine** breaker's yard
ci'mosa *f* selvage, selvedge
ci'murro *m* distemper
'Cina *f* China
cincial'legra *f* great tit
cincia'rella *f* blue tit
cincillà *m inv* chinchilla
cin cin *int* cheers!
cincischi'are *vi* fiddle
cincischi'arsi *vr* mess around
'cine *m* infml cinema
cine'asta *mf* film maker
Cinecittà *f inv* (stabilimento) *film complex in the suburbs of Rome*
cine'club *m inv* film club
ci'nefilo, -a *mf* cinemagoer, film buff
cinegior'nale *m* newsreel
⚷ **'cinema** *m inv* cinema, movie theater AmE
■ **cinema d'essai** arts cinema
cine'matica *f* kinematics *sg*
cinematogra'fare *vt* film
cinematogra'fia *f* cinematography
cinemato'grafico *adj* film *attrib*
cinema'tografo *m* cinema
cine'presa *f* cine camera
ci'nereo *adj* ashen
ci'nese *adj & nmf* Chinese
cinese'rie *fpl* chinoiserie
cine'teca *f* (raccolta) film collection
ci'netica *f* kinetics *sg*
ci'netico *adj* kinetic
'cingere *vt* (circondare) surround
'cinghia *f* strap; (cintura) belt
■ **cinghia del ventilatore** fan belt; **cinghia della ventola** fan belt
cinghi'ale *m* wild boar; **pelle di cinghiale** pigskin
cinghi'ata *f* lash
cingo'lato **A** *adj* (mezzi) caterpillar *attrib* **B** *m* caterpillar
'cingolo *m* Mech belt
cinguet'tare *vi* twitter
cinguet'tio *m* **1** (di uccelli) twittering **2** Comput tweet
cinica'mente *adv* cynically
'cinico *adj* cynical
ci'niglia *f* (tessuto) chenille
ci'nismo *m* cynicism
ci'nofilo *adj* ‹*unità*› dog-loving
⚷ **cin'quanta** *adj & nm* fifty
cinquanten'nale *m* fiftieth anniversary
cinquan'tenne *adj & nmf* fifty year-old
cinquan'tesimo *adj & nm* fiftieth
cinquan'tina *f* **una ~ di** about fifty
⚷ **'cinque** *adj & nm* five
cinquecen'tesco *adj* sixteenth century
cinque'cento **A** *adj* five hundred

B *m* **il Cinquecento** the sixteenth century

cinque'mila *adj & nm* five thousand

cin'quina *f* (in tombola) five in a row

'cinta *f* (di pantaloni) belt; **muro di cinta** [boundary] wall

cin'tare *vt* enclose

'cintola *f* (di pantaloni) belt

cin'tura *f* belt

■ **cintura nera** black belt; **cintura di salvataggio** lifebelt; **cintura di sicurezza** Aeron, Auto seat belt

cintu'rato *m* Auto radial tyre

cintu'rino *m*

■ **cinturino [dell'orologio]** watch strap; (di metallo) bracelet

ciò *pron* this; that; **~ che** what; **~ nondimeno** nevertheless

ci'occa *f* lock

ciocco'lata *f* chocolate; (bevanda) [hot] chocolate

■ **cioccolata in polvere** drinking chocolate

cioccola'tino *m* chocolate

ciocco'lato *m* chocolate

■ **cioccolato fondente** plain chocolate, dark chocolate; **cioccolato al latte** milk chocolate; **cioccolato da pasticceria** cooking chocolate

cioè *adv* that is

ciondo'lare *vi* dangle

ciondo'lio *m* dangling

ci'ondolo *m* pendant

ciondo'loni *adv* fig hanging about

cionono'stante *adv* nonetheless

ci'otola *f* bowl

ci'ottolo *m* pebble; **ciottoli** *pl* (in spiaggia) shingle

ci'piglio *m* frown; **con ~** with a frown

ci'polla *f* onion; (bulbo) bulb

cipol'lotto *m* green onion

ci'presso *m* cypress

'cipria *f* [face] powder

cipri'ota *adj & nmf* Cypriot

'Cipro *m* Cyprus

'circa *adv & prep* about

cir'cense *adj* circus *attrib*

'circo *m* circus

circo'lare **A** *adj* circular
B *f* circular; (di metropolitana) circle line
C *vi* circulate

circola'torio *adj* Med circulatory

circolazi'one *f* circulation; (traffico) traffic

'circolo *m* circle; (società) club

■ **circolo del golf** golf club; **Circolo polare antartico** Antarctic Circle; **Circolo polare artico** Arctic Circle; **circolo sociale** social club; **circolo virtuoso** virtuous circle

circon'cidere *vt* circumcise

circoncisi'one *f* circumcision

circon'dare *vt* surround

circon'dario *m* (amministrativo) administrative district; (vicinato) neighbourhood

circon'darsi *vr* **~ di** surround oneself with

circonfe'renza *f* circumference

■ **circonferenza del collo** collar size; **circonferenza dei fianchi** hip measurement; **circonferenza [della] vita** waist measurement

circon'flesso *adj* **e con l'accento ~** circumflex e

circonvallazi'one *f* ring road

circo'scritto **A** pp di **circoscrivere**
B *adj* limited

circo'scrivere *vt* circumscribe

circoscrizio'nale *adj* area

circoscrizi'one *f* area

■ **circoscrizione elettorale** constituency

circo'spetto *adj* wary

circospezi'one *f* **con ~** warily

circo'stante *adj* surrounding

circo'stanza *f* circumstance; (occasione) occasion

circostanzi'ato *adj* circumstantial

circu'ire *vt* (ingannare) trick

circuite'ria *f* circuitry

cir'cuito *m* circuit

circumnavi'gare *vt* circumnavigate

circumnavigazi'one *f* circumnavigation

ci'rillico *adj* Cyrillic

cir'ripede *m* barnacle

cir'rosi *f* cirrhosis

Cisgior'dania *f* West Bank

C.I.S.L. *nf abbr* (**Confederazione Italiana Sindacati Lavoratori**) *trades union organization*

C.I.S.N.A.L. *nf abbr* (**Confederazione Italiana Sindacati Nazionali dei Lavoratori**) *trades union organization*

'cispa *f* (nell'occhio) sleep

ci'sposo *adj* bleary eyed

'ciste *f inv* cyst

ci'sterna *f* cistern; (serbatoio) tank

'cisti *f inv* cyst

cisti'fellea *f* gall bladder

ci'stite *f* cystitis

C.I.T. *nm abbr* (**Compagnia Italiana Turismo**) *Italian tourist organization*

ci'tare *vt* (riportare brani ecc.) quote; (come esempio) cite; Jur summons

citazi'one *f* quotation; Jur summons *sg*

citofo'nare *vt* buzz

ci'tofono *m* entry phone; (in ufficio, su aereo ecc.) intercom

cito'logico *adj* cytological

'citrico *adj* citric

ci'trullo *mf* infml dimwit

città *f inv* town; (grande) city

■ **Città del Capo** Cape Town; **città dormitorio** dormitory town; **città fantasma** ghost town; **città giardino** garden city; **città stato** city state; **Città del Vaticano** Vatican City

citta'della *f* citadel

citta'dina *f* town

cittadi'nanza *f* citizenship; (popolazione) citizens *pl*

citta'dino, -a *mf* citizen; (abitante di città) city dweller

ciucci'are *vt* infml suck

ci'uccio *m* infml dummy

ci'uco *m* ass

ci'uffo *m* tuft

ci'urma *f* Naut crew

ciur'maglia *f* (gentaglia) rabble

ci'vetta *f* owl; fig (donna) flirt; **[auto] civetta** unmarked police car

civet'tare *vi* flirt

civette'ria *f* flirtatiousness, coquettishness

civettu'olo *adj* flirtatious, coquettish

'civico *adj* civic

ci'vile **A** *adj* civil
B *m* civilian

civi'lista *mf* (avvocato) specialist in civil law

civiliz'zare *vt* civilize

civiliz'zarsi *vr* become civilized

civiliz'zato *adj* ‹*paese*› civilized

civilizzazi'one *f* civilization

civil'mente *adv* civilly

civiltà *f inv* civilization; (cortesia) civility

ci'vismo *m* public spirit

cl *abbr* (**centilitro**) centilitre(s)

CL *nf abbr* (**Comunione e Liberazione**) *young Catholics association*

'clacson *m inv* horn

clacso'nare *vi* beep the horn, hoot

cla'more *m* clamour; **fare ~** cause a sensation

clamorosa'mente *adv* ‹*sbagliare*› sensationally

clamo'roso *adj* noisy; ‹*sbaglio*› sensational

clan *m inv* clan; fig clique

clandestina'mente *adv* secretly

clandestinità *f inv* secrecy; **vivere nella ~** live underground

clande'stino *adj* clandestine; **movimento ~** underground movement; **passeggero ~** stowaway

claque *f inv* claque

clarinet'tista *mf* clarinettist

clari'netto *m* clarinet

'classe *f* class; (aula) classroom; **di prima ~** first-class
■ **classe economica** economy class; **classe operaia** working class; **classe turistica** tourist class

classicheggi'ante *adj* classical

classi'cismo *m* classicism

classi'cista *mf* classicist

'classico **A** *adj* classical; (tipico) classic
B *m* classic

key word

classifica *f* classification; Sport league
■ **classifica dei singoli** singles charts

classifi'cabile *adj* classifiable

classifi'care *vt* classify

classifi'carsi *vr* be placed

classifica'tore *m* (cartella) folder; (mobile) filing cabinet

classificazi'one *f* classification

clas'sista **A** *adj* class-conscious
B *mf* class-conscious person

claudi'cante *adj* lame

'clausola *f* clause
■ **clausola penale** Jur, Comm penalty clause; **clausola di recesso** Jur, Comm escape clause

claustrofo'bia *f* claustrophobia

claustro'fobico *adj* claustrophobic

clau'sura *f* Relig cloistered life; **di ~** ‹*suora*› cloistered; **essere in ~** fig shut oneself up; **vivere in ~** fig live like a hermit

'clava *f* club

clavicemba'lista *mf* harpsichord player

clavi'cembalo *m* harpsichord

cla'vicola *f* collar-bone

clavi'cordo *m* clavichord

cle'mente *adj* merciful; ‹*tempo*› mild

cle'menza *f* mercy, clemency

clep'tomane *mf* kleptomaniac

cleptoma'nia *f* kleptomania

cleri'cale *adj* clerical

'clero *m* clergy

cles'sidra *f* hourglass

clic *m inv* Comput click; **fare ~ su** click on; **fare doppio ~** double-click

clic'care *vi* Comput click; **~ su** click on

cliché *m inv* cliché

click ▸ **clic**

cli'ente *mf* client; (di negozio) customer

clien'tela *f* customers *pl*, clientele; (di avvocato) clientele

cliente'lare *adj* Pol nepotistic

cliente'lismo *m* nepotism

'clima *m* climate

clima'terio *m* climacteric

climatica'mente *adv* climatically

cli'matico *adj* climatic; **stazione climatica** health resort

climatizza'tore *m* air conditioner

climatizzazi'one *f* air conditioning

'clinica *f* clinic
■ **clinica di allergologia** allergy clinic; **clinica odontoiatrica** dental clinic; **clinica ostetrica** maternity hospital; **clinica psichiatrica** mental hospital

'clinico **A** *adj* clinical
B *m* clinician

clip *f inv* paper clip; (di orecchino) clip

cli'stere *m* Med enema

clo'aca *f* sewer

'cloche *f inv* cloche hat
clo'nare *vt* clone
clonazi'one *f* cloning
'clone *m* clone
clo'rato *adj* chlorate
'cloro *m* chlorine
cloro'filla *f* chlorophyll
clorofluorocar'buro *m* chlorofluorocarbon, CFC
cloro'formio *m* chloroform
clou *adj inv* **momenti ~** highlights
club *m inv* club
■ **club per i giovani** youth club; **club sportivo** sports club
club-'sandwich *m inv* club sandwich
cm *abbr* (**centimetro**) cm
CNR *nm abbr* (**Consiglio Nazionale delle Ricerche**) national research council
Co. *abbr* (**compagnia**) Co
coabi'tare *vi* live together
coabitazi'one *f* (di razze) coexistence
coadiu|'tore, -trice *mf* (in ufficio) assistant
coadiu'vare *vt* cooperate with
coagu'lante *m* coagulant
coagu'lare *vt* coagulate
coagu'larsi *vr* coagulate
coagulazi'one *f* coagulation
coalizi'one *f* coalition
coaliz'zare *vt* fig unite
coaliz'zarsi *vr* unite
co'atto *adj* Jur compulsory
co'balto *m* cobalt; (colore) cobalt blue
COBAS *mpl abbr* (**Comitati di Base**) *independent trade unions*
'cobra *m inv* cobra
'Coca® *f* Coke®
Coca 'cola® *f* Coca Cola
coca'ina *f* cocaine
cocai'nomane *mf* cocaine addict
coc'carda *f* rosette
cocchi'ere *m* coachman
'cocchio *m* coach
'coccige *m* coccyx
cocci'nella *f* ladybird
'coccio *m* earthenware; (frammento) fragment
cocciu'taggine *f* stubbornness
cocciuta'mente *adv* stubbornly
cocci'uto *adj* stubborn
'cocco *m* coconut palm; infml love; **noce di ~** coconut
coccodè *m inv* cluck
cocco'drillo *m* crocodile
cocco'lare *vt* cuddle
co'cente *adj* ‹*sole*› burning; ‹*lacrime, delusione*› bitter
'cocker *m inv*
■ **cocker [spaniel]** cocker spaniel
'cocktail *m inv* (ricevimento) cocktail party
co.co.'co. *nmf abbr* **1** (**collaboratore coordinato e continuativo**) freelancer on a fixed-term contract **2** (**collaborazione coordinata e continuativa**) fixed-term freelance contract
co'comero *m* watermelon
co.co.pro. *nf abbr* (**collaborazione coordinata a progetto**) *type of freelance work for a planned activity and a fixed period on a client's behalf*
co'cuzzolo *m* top; (di testa, cappello) crown
⚷ **'coda** *f* tail; (di abito) train; (fila) queue; (di traffico) tailback; **fare la ~** queue [up], stand in line AmE
■ **coda di cavallo** (acconciatura) pony tail; **coda dell'occhio** corner of one's eye; **coda di paglia** guilty conscience
co'dardo, -a **A** *adj* cowardly **B** *mf* coward
co'dazzo *m* train
code'ina *f* codeine
co'desto *adj* that
'codice *m* code; **in ~** ‹*messaggio*› coded, in code; **mettere in ~** encode
■ **codice di avviamento postale** postal code, zip code AmE; **codice a barre** bar-code; **codice civile** civil code; **codice fiscale** National Insurance number BrE, tax code; **codice penale** penal code; **codice PIN** PIN; **codice della strada** highway code
codi'cillo *m* codicil
co'difica *f* coding
codifi'care *vt* encode; codify ‹*legge*›
codifica|'tore, -trice *mf* Comput encoder
codificazi'one *f* encoding; (di legge) codification
co'dini *mpl* bunches
coeffici'ente *m* coefficient
coercizi'one *f* coercion
coe'rente *adj* consistent
coe'renza *f* consistency
coesi'one *f* cohesion
coe'sistere *vi* coexist
coe'sivo *adj* cohesive
coe'taneo, -a *adj & nmf* contemporary
cofa'netto *m* casket
'cofano *m* (forziere) chest; Auto bonnet, hood AmE
cofirma'tario, -a *mf* cosignatory
coge'stire *vt* co-manage
cogi'tare *vi* ponder
⚷ **'cogliere** *vt* pick; (sorprendere) catch; (afferrare) seize; (colpire) hit; **~ la palla al balzo** seize the opportunity; **~ di sorpresa** take by surprise
co'glione *m* vulg ball; (sciocco) dickhead; **rompere i coglioni a qualcuno** get on somebody's tits
'Cognac *m* cognac
co'gnato, -a **A** *m* brother-in-law **B** *f* sister-in-law

C

C

cognizi'one *f* knowledge; **con ~ di causa** on an informed basis

⚷ **co'gnome** *m* surname, second name
■ **cognome da ragazza/da nubile** maiden name

cogu'aro *m* cougar

'coi = con + i

coiben'tare *vt* to insulate

coi'bente *adj* insulating

coinci'denza *f* coincidence; (di treno ecc.) connection

coin'cidere *vi* coincide

coinqui'lino *m* flatmate

cointesta'tario *m* Fin joint account-holder

coin'volgere *vt* involve

coinvolgi'mento *m* involvement

coin'volto *adj* involved

'coito *m* coitus

col = con + il

colà *adv* there

cola'brodo *m inv* strainer; **ridotto a un ~** infml full of holes

cola'pasta *m inv* colander

co'lare **A** *vt* strain; (versare lentamente) drip **B** *vi* (gocciolare) drip; (perdere) leak; **~ a picco** Naut sink

co'lata *f* (di metallo) casting; (di lava) flow

⚷ **colazi'one** *f* (del mattino) breakfast; (di mezzogiorno) lunch; **far ~** have breakfast/lunch
■ **prima colazione** breakfast; **colazione di lavoro** working lunch; **colazione al sacco** packed lunch

col'bacco *m* fur hat

co'lei *pron f* the one

co'lera *m* cholera

coleste'rolo *m* cholesterol

colf *f inv abbr* (**collaboratrice familiare**) home help

colibrì *m inv* humming bird

'colica *f* colic

co'lino *m* [tea] strainer

'colla *f* glue; (di farina) paste
■ **colla di pesce** gelatine

collabo'rare *vi* collaborate; **~ con** ‹*polizia*› co-operate with; **~ a** ‹*rivista*› contribute to

collabora|'tore, -trice *mf* collaborator; (di rivista) contributor
■ **collaboratrice familiare** domestic help

collaborazi'one *f* collaboration; (con polizia) co-operation

collaborazio'nista *mf* collaborator

col'lage *m inv* collage

col'lana *f* necklace; (serie) series
■ **collana di perle** pearl necklace

col'lant *mpl* tights
■ **collant velati** sheer tights

col'lante *adj* adhesive

col'lare *m* collar

⚷ key word

colla'rino *m* dog collar

col'lasso *m* collapse
■ **collasso cardiaco** syncope; **collasso renale** kidney failure

collate'rale *adj* collateral

collau'dare *vt* test

collauda|'tore, -trice *mf* tester

col'laudo *m* test

collazio'nare *vt* collate

'colle *m* hill; (passo) pass

⚷ **col'lega** *mf* colleague

colle'gabile *adj* compatible (**a** with)

collega'mento *m* connection; Mil liaison; Radio ecc. link
■ **collegamento dati** data link; **collegamento ipertestuale** hyperlink; **collegamento in rete** networking

colle'gare *vt* connect

colle'garsi *vr* TV, Radio link up (**a** with); Comput (a una rete ecc.) go on line (**a** to)

collegi'ale **A** *mf* boarder **B** *adj* ‹*responsabilità, decisione*› collective

col'legio *m* (convitto) boarding school
■ **collegio elettorale** constituency

'collera *f* anger; **andare in ~** get angry

col'lerico *adj* irascible

col'letta *f* collection

collettività *f inv* community

collet'tivo **A** *adj* collective; ‹*interesse*› general; **biglietto ~** group ticket **B** *m* (studentesco, femminista) collective

col'letto *m* collar

collet'tore *m* (di fognatura) main sewer

collezio'nare *vt* collect

collezi'one *f* collection
■ **collezione invernale** winter collection

collezio'nismo *m* collecting

collezio'nista *mf* collector
■ **collezionista di francobolli** stamp collector

colli'mare *vi* coincide

⚷ **col'lina** *f* hill

colli'nare *adj* hill *attrib*

colli'netta *f* knoll

colli'noso *adj* ‹*terreno*› hilly

col'lirio *m* eyewash

collisi'one *f* collision

⚷ **'collo** *m* neck; (pacco) package; **a ~ alto** high necked; **a rotta di ~** at breakneck speed
■ **collo del piede** instep

colloca'mento *m* placing; (impiego) employment

collo'care *vt* place

collo'carsi *vr* take one's place

collocazi'one *f* placing

colloqui'ale *adj* ‹*termine*› colloquial; ‹*tono*› informal

col'loquio *m* conversation; (di lavoro, udienza ecc.) interview; (esame) oral [exam]

col'loso *adj* glutinous

col'lottola *f* nape
collusi'one *f* collusion
colluttazi'one *f* scuffle
col'mare *vt* fill; bridge ‹*divario*›; **~ qualcuno di gentilezze** overwhelm somebody with kindness
'colmo **A** *adj* full; **un cucchiaio ~** a heaped spoonful
B *m* top; fig height; **al ~ della disperazione** in the depths of despair; **questo è il ~!** (con indignazione) this is the last straw!; (con stupore) I don't believe it!; **per ~ di sfortuna** to crown it all
+colo *suff* **poetucolo** second rate poet
co'lomba *f* dove
■ **colomba pasquale** *dove-shaped cake with candied fruit eaten at Easter*
colom'baccio *m* wood pigeon
colom'baia *f* dovecote
Co'lombia *f* Colombia
colombi'ano *adj & nmf* Colombian
co'lombo *m* pigeon; **colombi** *pl* (innamorati) lovebirds
co'lonia *f* colony; (per bambini) holiday camp, summer camp
Co'lonia *f* Cologne; **[acqua di] colonia** [eau de] Cologne
coloni'ale *adj* colonial
colonia'lista *mf* colonialist
co'lonico *adj* ‹*terreno, casa*› farm *attrib*
coloniz'zare *vt* colonize
colonizza|'tore, -trice *mf* colonizer
colonizzazi'one *f* colonization
co'lonna *f* column; (di auto) tailback
■ **colonna sonora** soundtrack; **colonna vertebrale** spine
colon'nato *m* colonnade
colon'nello *m* colonel
colon'nina *f* (distributore) petrol pump, gas pump AmE
co'lono *m* tenant farmer
colo'rante *m* colouring
■ **colorante alimentare** food colouring
colo'rare *vt* colour; colour in ‹*disegno*›
co'lore *m* colour; (carte) suit; **a colori** in colour; **di ~** coloured; **farne di tutti i colori** get up to all sorts of mischief; **passarne di tutti i colori** go through hell; **diventare di tutti i colori** fig turn scarlet
■ **colore a olio** oil paint; **colore primario** primary colour
colori'ficio *m* paint and dyes shop
colo'rito **A** *adj* coloured; ‹*viso*› rosy; ‹*racconto, linguaggio*› colourful
B *m* complexion
co'loro *pron pl* the ones
colos'sale *adj* colossal
Colos'seo *m* Coliseum
co'losso *m* colossus
'colpa *f* fault; (biasimo) blame; (colpevolezza) guilt; (peccato) sin; **dare la ~ a** blame; **essere in ~** be at fault; **per ~ di** because of; **è ~ mia** it's my fault
col'pevole **A** *adj* guilty
B *mf* culprit
col'pire *vt* hit, strike; fig strike; **~ nel segno** hit the nail on the head
'colpo *m* blow; (di arma da fuoco) shot; (urto) knock; (emozione) shock; Med, Sport stroke; (furto) robbery; **di ~** suddenly; **far ~** make a strong impression; **far venire un ~ a qualcuno** fig give somebody a fright; **perdere colpi** ‹*motore*› keep missing; **a ~ d'occhio** at a glance; **a ~ sicuro** for certain
■ **colpo d'aria** chill; **colpo basso** blow below the belt; **colpo di frusta** Med whiplash injury; **colpo di grazia** kiss of death; **colpo da maestro** master stroke; **colpo di scena** sensational development; **colpo di sole** sunstroke; **colpi di sole** *pl* (su capelli) highlights; **colpo di Stato** coup [d'état]; **colpo di telefono** ring, call; **dare un ~ di telefono a qualcuno** give somebody a ring *or* call; **colpo di testa** [sudden] impulse; **colpo di vento** gust of wind
col'poso *adj* **omicidio ~** manslaughter
coltel'lata *f* stab
coltelle'ria *f* cutlery shop
col'tello *m* knife; **avere il ~ dalla parte del manico** have the upper hand
■ **coltello per il pane** bread knife; **coltello a serramanico** jackknife
colti'vare *vt* cultivate
coltiva|'tore, -trice *mf* farmer
coltivazi'one *f* farming; (di piante) growing
■ **coltivazione intensiva** intensive farming
'colto **A** pp di **cogliere**
B *adj* cultured
'coltre *f* blanket
col'tura *f* cultivation
■ **coltura alternata** crop rotation
co'lui *pron m* the one
'colza *f* Bot (oilseed) rape
'coma *m inv* coma; **in ~** in a coma; **in ~ irreversibile** brain dead
comanda'mento *m* commandment
coman'dante *m* commander; Naut, Aeron captain
coman'dare **A** *vt* command; Mech control; **~ a qualcuno di fare qualcosa** order somebody to do something
B *vi* be in charge
co'mando *m* command; (di macchina) control
co'mare *f* (pettegola) gossip
coma'toso *adj* Med comatose
combaci'are *vi* fit together; ‹*testimonianze*› concur
combat'tente **A** *adj* fighting
B *m* combatant
■ **ex combattente** ex-serviceman; **combattente per la libertà** freedom fighter

c

✓ **com'battere** *vt & vi* fight
combatti'mento *m* fight; Mil battle; **fuori ~** ‹*pugilato*› knocked out
combat'tuto *adj* ‹*gara*› hard fought; (tormentato) torn; ‹*discussione*› heated

C

✓ **combi'nare** *vt & vi* arrange; (mettere insieme) combine; infml (fare) do; **cosa stai combinando?** what are you up to?
combi'narsi *vr* combine; (mettersi d'accordo) come to an agreement
combinazi'one *f* combination; (caso) coincidence; **per ~** by chance
com'briccola *f* gang
combu'stibile **A** *adj* combustible
B *m* fuel
combusti'one *f* combustion
com'butta *f* gang; **in ~** in league
✓ **'come** **A** *adv* like; (in qualità di) as; (interrogativo, esclamativo) how; **questo vestito è ~ il tuo** this dress is like yours; **~?** pardon?; **~ stai?** how are you?; **~ va?** how are things?; **~ mai?** how come?; **~?** what?; **non sa ~ fare** he doesn't know what to do; **~ sta bene!** how well he looks!; **~ no!** that will be right!; **~ tu sai** as you know; **fa' ~ vuoi** do as you like; **~ se** as if
B *conj* (non appena) as soon as
come'done *m* blackhead
co'meta *f* comet
'comfort *m inv* comfort; **con tutti i ~** with all mod cons
'comico **A** *adj* comical; ‹*teatro, attore*› comic
B *m* funny side; (attore) comic actor, comedian
C *f* comedienne; (attrice) comic actress, comedienne; (a torte in faccia) slapstick sketch
co'mignolo *m* chimney pot
✓ **cominci'are** *vt & vi* begin, start; **a ~ da oggi** from today; **per ~** to begin with; **cominciamo bene!** we're off to a fine start!
comi'tato *m* committee
■ **comitato consultivo** advisory committee; **comitato direttivo** steering committee; **comitato esecutivo** executive committee; **comitato di gestione** management committee
comi'tiva *f* party, group
co'mizio *m* meeting
■ **comizio elettorale** election rally
'comma *m* (capoverso) paragraph
com'mando *m inv* commando
com'media *f* comedy; (opera teatrale) play; fig sham
■ **commedia musicale** musical
commedi'ante **A** *m* comic actor; fig derog phoney
B *f* comic actress; fig derog phoney
commedi'ografo, -a *mf* playwright
commemo'rare *vt* commemorate

✓ key word

commemorazi'one *f* commemoration
■ **commemorazione dei defunti** (2 novembre) All Soul's Day
commenda'tore *m* commander
commen'sale *mf* fellow diner
commen'tare *vt* comment on; (annotare) annotate
commen'tario *m* commentary
commenta|'tore, -trice *mf* commentator
com'mento *m* comment; TV, Radio commentary
■ **commento musicale** music
✓ **commerci'ale** *adj* commercial; ‹*relazioni, trattative*› trade; ‹*attività*›; business; **centro commerciale** shopping centre
commerci'alista *mf* business consultant; (contabile) accountant, certified public accountant AmE
commercializ'zare *vt* market; derog commercialize
commercializzazi'one *f* marketing; derog commercialization
■ **commercializzazione di massa** mass-marketing
commerci'ante *mf* trader, merchant; (negoziante) shopkeeper
■ **commerciante all'ingrosso** wholesaler; **commerciante di oggetti d'arte** art dealer
commerci'are *vi* **~ in** deal in
✓ **com'mercio** *m* commerce; (internazionale) trade; (affari) business; **in ~** (prodotto) on sale
■ **commercio al dettaglio** *o* **al minuto** retail trade; **commercio all'ingrosso** wholesale trade
com'messo, -a **A** *pp di* **commettere**
B *mf* shop assistant; **commessi** *pl* counter staff
■ **commesso viaggiatore** commercial traveller
C *f* (ordine) order
comme'stibile **A** *adj* edible
B *m* **commestibili** *pl* groceries
✓ **com'mettere** *vt* commit; make ‹*sbaglio*›; **~ un reato** commit an offence
commi'ato *m* leave; **prendere ~ da** take leave of
commise'rare *vt* commiserate
commise'rarsi *vr* feel sorry for oneself
commissari'ato *m* (di polizia) police station
commis'sario *m* ≈ [police] superintendent; (membro di commissione) commissioner; Sport steward; Comm commission agent
■ **commissario di bordo** purser; **commissario capo** chief superintendent; **commissario d'esame** examiner; **commissario di gara** race official, steward; **commissario tecnico** (della nazionale) national team manager
commissi'one *f* (incarico) errand; (comitato, percentuale) commission; Comm (di merce) order; **commissioni** *pl* (acquisti) **fare commissioni** go shopping
■ **commissione d'esame** board of examiners; **Commissione Europea** European

Commission; **commissione d'inchiesta** court of inquiry

commit'tente *mf* purchaser

com'mosso **A** pp di **commuovere** **B** *adj* moved

commo'vente *adj* moving

commozi'one *f* emotion
■ **commozione cerebrale** concussion

commu'overe *vt* touch, move

commu'oversi *vr* be touched

commu'tare *vt* change; Jur commute

commuta'tore *m* Electr commutator

commutazi'one *f* (di pena) commutation

comò *m inv* chest of drawers

comoda'mente *adv* comfortably

como'dino *m* bedside table

comodità *f inv* comfort; (convenienza) convenience

'comodo **A** *adj* comfortable; (conveniente) convenient; (spazioso) roomy; (facile) easy; **stia ~!** don't get up!; **far ~** be useful **B** *m* comfort; **fare il proprio ~** do as one pleases; **prendila con ~!** take it easy!

Co'more *fpl* **le (isole) ~** Comoros

'compact disc *m inv* compact disc

compae'sano, -a **A** *m* fellow countryman **B** *f* fellow countrywoman

com'pagine *f* (squadra) team

compa'gnia *f* company; (gruppo) party; **fare ~ a qualcuno** keep somebody company; **essere di ~** be sociable
■ **compagnia aerea** airline; **compagnia di bandiera** (aerea) national airline; **compagnia low cost** budget airline, no frills airline

com'pagno, -a *mf* companion; Comm, Sport (in coppia) partner; Pol comrade
■ **compagno di classe** classmate; **compagno di scuola** schoolmate, school friend; **compagno di squadra** team-mate; **compagno di viaggio** fellow traveller

compa'rabile *adj* comparable

compa'rare *vt* compare

compara'tivo *adj & nm* comparative

comparazi'one *f* comparison

com'pare *m* sidekick

compa'rire *vi* appear; (spiccare) stand out; **~ in giudizio** appear in court

com'parso, -a **A** pp di **comparire** **B** *f* appearance; Cinema extra; Theat walk-on

compartecipazi'one *f* sharing; (quota) share

comparti'mento *m* compartment; (amministrativo) department

compas'sato *adj* calm and collected

compassi'one *f* compassion; **aver ~ per** feel pity for; **far ~** arouse pity

compassio'nevole *adj* compassionate

com'passo *m* [pair of] compasses *pl*

compa'tibile *adj* (conciliabile) compatible; (scusabile) excusable

compatibilità *f inv* compatibility

compatibil'mente *adv* **~ con i miei impegni** if my commitments allow

compati'mento *m* **un'aria di ~** air of condescension

compa'tire *vt* pity; (scusare) make allowances for

compatri'ota *mf* compatriot

compat'tezza *f* (di materia) compactness; fig (di partito) solidarity

com'patto *adj* compact; (denso) dense; (solido) solid; fig united

compendi'are *vt* (fare un sunto) summarize

com'pendio *m* outline; (sunto) synopsis; (libro) compendium

compene'trare *vt* pervade

compen'sare *vt* compensate; (supplire) make up for

compen'sarsi *vr* balance each other out

compen'sato *m* (legno) plywood

compensazi'one *f* compensation

com'penso *m* compensation; (retribuzione) remuneration; **in compenso** (in cambio) in return; (d'altra parte) on the other hand; (invece) instead

'compera *f* purchase; **far compere** do some shopping

compe'rare *vt* buy

compe'tente *adj* competent; ‹*ufficio*› appropriate

compe'tenza *f* competence; (responsabilità) responsibility; **competenze** *pl* (onorari) fees

com'petere *vi* compete; **~ a** ‹*compito*› be the responsibility of

competitività *f inv* competitiveness

competi'tivo *adj* ‹*prezzo, carattere*› competitive

competi|'tore, -trice *mf* competitor

competizi'one *f* competition

compia'cente *adj* obliging

compia'cenza *f* obligingness; **avere la ~ di ...** be so obliging as to ...

compia'cere *vt & vi* please

compia'cersi *vr* (congratularsi) congratulate; **~ di** (degnarsi) condescend to

compiaci'mento *m* satisfaction; derog smugness

compiaci'uto *adj* satisfied; ‹*aria, sorriso*› smug

compi'angere *vt* pity; (per lutto ecc.) sympathize with

'compiere *vt* (concludere) complete; commit ‹*delitto*›; **~ gli anni** have one's birthday

'compiersi *vr* end; (avverarsi) come true

compi'lare *vt* compile; fill in ‹*modulo*›

compila|'tore, -trice *mf* compiler

compilazi'one *f* compilation

compi'mento *m* completion; **portare a ~ qualcosa** conclude something

com'pire *vt* = **compiere**

C

compi'tare *vt* spell
⚷ **'compito¹** *m* task; (dovere) duty; Sch homework; **fare i compiti** do one's homework
com'pito² *adj* polite
compiu'tezza *f* completeness
compi'uto *adj* **avere 30 anni compiuti** be over 30
comple'anno *m* birthday
complemen'tare *adj* complementary; (secondario) subsidiary
comple'mento *m* complement; Mil draft
■ **complemento oggetto** Gram direct object
comples'sato *adj* hung up
complessità *f inv* complexity
complessiva'mente *adv* on the whole; (in totale) altogether
comples'sivo *adj* comprehensive; (totale) total
⚷ **com'plesso** **A** *adj* complex; (difficile) complicated
B *m* complex, hang up infml; Psych complex; (di cantanti ecc.) group; (di circostanze, fattori) combination; **in ~** on the whole; (in totale) altogether
■ **complesso di inferiorità** inferiority complex
completa'mente *adv* completely
completa'mento *m* completion
⚷ **comple'tare** *vt* complete
comple'tezza *f* completeness
⚷ **com'pleto** **A** *adj* complete; (pieno) full [up]; **al ~** ‹*teatro*› sold out; ‹*albergo*› full; **'~ '** 'no vacancies'; **la famiglia al ~** the whole family
B *m* (vestito) suit; (insieme di cose) set
⚷ **compli'care** *vt* complicate
compli'carsi *vr* become complicated
compli'cato *adj* complicated
complicazi'one *f* complication; **salvo complicazioni** all being well
'complice **A** *mf* accomplice
B *adj* ‹*sguardo*› knowing
complicità *f inv* complicity
complimen'tare *vt* compliment
complimen'tarsi *vr* **~ con** congratulate
⚷ **compli'mento** *m* compliment; **complimenti** *pl* (ossequi) regards; (congratulazioni) congratulations; **fare complimenti** stand on ceremony
complot'tare *vi* plot
com'plotto *m* plot
compo'nente **A** *adj & nm* component
B *mf* member
componen'tistica *f* (per auto, elettronica) accessories *pl*
compo'nibile *adj* ‹*cucina*› fitted; ‹*mobili*› modular
componi'mento *m* composition; (letterario) work

⚷ **com'porre** *vt* compose; (sistemare) put in order; Typ set; lay out ‹*salma*›; settle ‹*lite*›
com'porsi *vr* **~ di** be made up of
comportamen'tale *adj* behavioural
comporta'mento *m* behaviour
⚷ **compor'tare** *vt* (implicare) involve
compor'tarsi *vr* behave
com'posito *adj* Chem, Phot composite
composi|'tore, -trice *mf* composer; Typ compositor
composizi'one *f* composition
■ **composizione floreale** flower arrangement
'compost *m inv* compost
com'posta *f* stewed fruit; (concime) compost
compo'stabile *adj* compostable
compo'staggio *m* composting
compo'stezza *f* composure
com'posto **A** pp di **comporre**
B *adj* ‹*parola*› compound; **essere ~ da** consist of, comprise; **stai ~!** sit properly!
C *m* Chem compound; Culin mixture
⚷ **com'prare** *vt* buy; fig (corrompere) buy off, bribe
compra|'tore, -trice *mf* buyer
compra'vendita *f* buying and selling; **atto di ~** deed of sale
⚷ **com'prendere** *vt* understand; (includere) comprise
compren'donio *m* **essere duro di ~** be slow on the uptake
compren'sibile *adj* understandable
comprensibil'mente *adv* understandably
comprensi'one *f* understanding
compren'sivo *adj* understanding; (che include) inclusive
com'preso **A** pp di **comprendere**
B *adj* included; **tutto ~** ‹*prezzo*› all-in; **da lunedì a venerdì ~** Monday to Friday inclusive
com'pressa *f* compress; (pastiglia) tablet
compressi'one *f* compression
■ **compressione dati** Comput data compression
com'presso **A** pp di **comprimere**
B *adj* compressed
compres'sore *m* (rullo) steamroller
compri'mario, -a **A** *m* Theat supporting actor
B *f* supporting actress
com'primere *vt* press; (reprimere) repress; Comput compress
compro'messo **A** pp di **compromettere**
B *m* compromise; (contratto) *preliminary but binding agreement*
compromet'tente *adj* compromising
compro'mettere *vt* compromise
comproprietà *f inv* multiple ownership
comproprie'tario, -a *mf* joint owner
compro'vare *vt* prove
com'punto *adj* contrite
compunzi'one *f* compunction

⚷ key word

compu'tare *vt* calculate; (addebitare) estimate
com'puter *m inv* computer
■ **computer da casa** home computer
computeriz'zare *vt* computerize
computeriz'zato *adj* computerized
computerizzazi'one *f* computerization
computiste'ria *f* book-keeping
'computo *m* calculation
comu'nale *adj* municipal
co'mune **A** *adj* common; ‹*parti*› communal, common; ‹*amico*› mutual; (ordinario) ordinary
B *m* municipality; **in ~** shared; **fuori del ~** out of the ordinary; **avere qualcosa in ~** have something in common
C *f* collective farm; commune
comu'nella *f* **fare ~** form a clique
comune'mente *adv* commonly
comuni'cante *adj* interconnecting
comuni'care *vt* communicate; pass on ‹*malattia*›; Relig administer Communion to
comuni'carsi *vr* receive Communion
comunica'tiva *f* communicativeness
comunica'tivo *adj* communicative
comuni'cato *m* communiqué
■ **comunicato commerciale** Radio commercial; **comunicato stampa** press release
comunicazi'one *f* communication; Teleph [phone] call; **avere la ~** get through; **dare la ~ a qualcuno** put somebody through
■ **comunicazione dati** Comput data communications
comuni'one *f* communion; Relig [Holy] Communion
comu'nismo *m* communism
comu'nista *adj & nmf* communist
comunità *f inv* community
■ **Comunità [Economica] Europea** European [Economic] Community; **Comunità degli Stati Indipendenti** Commonwealth of Independent States; **comunità terapeutica** rehabilitation centre
co'munque **A** *conj* however
B *adv* anyhow
con *prep* with; (mezzo) by; **~ facilità** easily; **~ mia grande gioia** to my great delight; **è gentile ~ tutti** he is kind to everyone; **col treno** by train; **~ questo tempo** in this weather
co'nato *m*
■ **conato di vomito** retching
'conca *f* basin; (valle) dell
concate'nare *vt* link together
concate'narsi *vr* ‹*idee*› be connected
concatenazi'one *f* connection
'concavo *adj* concave
con'cedere *vt* grant; award ‹*premio*›; (ammettere) admit
con'cedersi *vr* allow oneself ‹*pausa*›; treat oneself to ‹*lusso, vacanza*›
concentra'mento *m* concentration
concen'trare *vt* concentrate
concen'trarsi *vr* concentrate
concen'trato **A** *adj* concentrated
B *m* concentrate
■ **concentrato di pomodoro** tomato pureé
concentrazi'one *f* concentration
con'centrico *adj* concentric
concepi'mento *m* conception
conce'pire *vt* conceive ‹*bambino*›; (capire) understand; (figurarsi) conceive of; devise ‹*piano ecc.*›
con'cernere *vt* concern
concer'tare *vt* Mus harmonize; (organizzare) arrange
concer'tarsi *vr* agree
concer'tista *mf* concert performer
con'certo *m* concert; (composizione) concerto
■ **concerto rock** rock concert
concessio'nario *m* agent
concessi'one *f* concession
con'cesso pp di **concedere**
con'cetto *m* concept; (opinione) opinion
concet'toso *adj* cerebral
concezi'one *f* conception; (idea) concept
con'chiglia *f* [sea] shell
■ **conchiglia del pellegrino** scallop shell; **conchiglia di san Giacomo** scallop shell
'concia *f* tanning; (di tabacco) curing
conci'are *vt* tan; cure ‹*tabacco*›; **~ qualcuno per le feste** give somebody a good hiding
conci'arsi *vr* (sporcarsi) get dirty; (vestirsi male) dress badly
conci'ato *adj* ‹*pelle, cuoio*› tanned; **essere ~ come un barbone** look like something the cat dragged in
concili'abile *adj* compatible
concili'abolo *m* private meeting
concili'ante *adj* conciliatory
concili'are *vt* reconcile; pay ‹*contravvenzione*›; (favorire) induce
concili'arsi *vr* go together; (mettersi d'accordo) become reconciled
conciliazi'one *f* reconciliation; Jur settlement
con'cilio *m* Relig council; (riunione) assembly
conci'maia *f* dunghill
conci'mare *vt* feed ‹*pianta*›
con'cime *m* manure; (chimico) fertilizer
concisi'one *f* conciseness
con'ciso *adj* concise
conci'tato *adj* excited
concitta'dino, -a *mf* fellow citizen
concla'mato *adj* Med full blown
con'clave *m* conclave
con'cludere *vt* conclude; (finire con successo) successfully complete
con'cludersi *vr* come to an end
conclusi'one *f* conclusion; **in ~** (insomma) in short

C

C

conclu'sivo *adj* conclusive
con'cluso pp di **concludere**
concomi'tante *adj* contributory
concomi'tanza *f* (di circostanze, fatti) combination; **in ~ con** combined with, in conjunction with
concor'danza *f* agreement
concor'dare **A** *vt* agree [on]; Gram make agree
B *vi* (sul prezzo) agree
concor'dato *m* agreement; Jur, Comm composition
con'corde *adj* in agreement; (unanime) unanimous
con'cordia *f* concord
concor'rente **A** *adj* concurrent; (rivale) competing
B *mf* Comm, Sport competitor; (candidato) candidate; (a quiz, concorso di bellezza) contestant
concor'renza *f* competition
■ **concorrenza sleale** unfair competition
concorrenzi'ale *adj* competitive
con'correre *vi* (contribuire) combine; (andare insieme) go together; (competere) compete
con'corso **A** pp di **concorrere**
B *m* competition; **fuori ~** not in the official competition
■ **concorso di bellezza** beauty contest; **concorso di circostanze** combination of circumstances; **concorso di colpa** contributory negligence; **concorso ippico** showjumping event; **concorso a premi** prize-winning competition; **concorso in reato** Jur complicity; **concorso per titoli** *competition in which exam results are not the sole criterion*
concreta'mente *adv* concretely
concre'tare, concretiz'zare *vt* put into concrete form
con'creto *adj* concrete; **in ~** in concrete terms
concu'bina *f* concubine
concussi'one *f* acceptance of a bribe
con'danna *f* sentence; **pronunziare una ~** hand down a sentence
■ **condanna a morte** death sentence; **condanna penale** prison sentence
✎ **condan'nare** *vt* (disapprovare) condemn; Jur sentence
condan'nato, -a **A** *adj* (destinato) forced
B *mf* prisoner
con'densa *f* condensation
conden'sare *vt* condense
conden'sarsi *vr* condense
condensa'tore *m* Electr condenser
condensazi'one *f* condensation
condi'mento *m* seasoning; (salsa) dressing
■ **condimento per insalata** salad dressing
con'dire *vt* flavour; dress ‹*insalata*›

✎ key word

condiscen'dente *adj* indulgent; derog condescending; (arrendevole) compliant
condiscen'denza *f* indulgence; derog condescension; (arrendevolezza) compliance
con'dito *adj* Culin seasoned
condi'videre *vt* share
condivisi'one *f* sharing; **~ delle risorse** resource sharing
condizio'nale **A** *adj & nm* conditional
B *f* Jur suspended sentence
condiziona'mento *m* Psych conditioning
condizio'nare *vt* condition
condizionata'mente *adv* conditionally
condizio'nato *adj* conditional (**da** on); **aria condizionata** air conditioning
condiziona'tore *m* air conditioner
✎ **condizi'one** *f* condition; **a ~ che** on condition that; **condizioni** *pl* **di credito** credit terms
■ **condizione imprescindibile** precondition
condogli'anze *fpl* condolences; **fare le ~ a** offer one's condolences to
'condom *m inv* condom
condomini'ale *adj* ‹*spese*› common; ‹*riunione*› tenants' *attrib*
con'dominio *m* joint ownership; (edificio) condominium
condo'mino, -a *mf* joint owner
condo'nare *vt* remit
con'dono *m* remission
con'dotta *f* conduct; (circoscrizione di medico) country practice; (di gara ecc.) management; (tubazione) pipe
con'dotto **A** pp di **condurre**
■ **medico condotto** country doctor
B *m* pipe; Anat duct
■ **condotto dell'aria** air duct; **condotto sotterraneo** culvert
condu'cente *m* driver
■ **conducente di autobus** bus driver
✎ **con'durre** *vt* lead; drive ‹*veicoli*›; (accompagnare) take; conduct ‹*gas, elettricità ecc.*›; (gestire) run; **~ a termine** complete; **~ delle indagini** carry out an investigation
con'dursi *vr* behave
condut'tore *adj*
■ **filo conduttore** leitmotif
condut|'tore *adj* **-trice** **A** *mf* TV presenter; (di veicolo) driver
B *m* Electr conductor
condut'tura *f* duct
■ **conduttura del gas** gas main
conduzi'one *f* conduction
confabu'lare *vi* have a confab
confa'cente *adj* suitable
con'farsi *vr* **confarsi a** suit
confederazi'one *f* confederation
■ **Confederazione elvetica** Swiss Confederation
confe'renza *f* (discorso) lecture; (congresso) conference
■ **conferenza stampa** press conference, news

conference

conferenzi'ere, -a *mf* lecturer, speaker

confe'rire **A** *vt* (donare) confer
B *vi* (consultarsi) confer

con'ferma *f* confirmation; **dare ~** confirm

confer'mare *vt* confirm

confes'sare *vt* confess

confes'sarsi *vr* confess

confessio'nale **A** *adj* ‹*segreto*› of the confession
B *m* confessional

confessi'one *f* confession

confes'sore *m* confessor

con'fetto *m* (di mandorla) sugared almond

confet'tura *f* jam

confezionare *vt* tailor ‹*vestito*›; package ‹*prodotto*›; **~ sottovuoto** vacuum-pack

confezio'nato *adj* ‹*vestiti*› off-the-peg; ‹*gelato*› wrapped

confezi'one *f* manufacture; (di abiti) making; (di pacchi) packaging; **di ~** ‹*abiti*› off-the-peg; **confezioni** *pl* clothes
■ **confezione economica** economy pack, economy size; **confezione famiglia** family size; **confezione multipla** multipack; **confezione regalo** gift set; **confezione da sei** (di bottiglie, lattine) six-pack

confic'care *vt* thrust

confic'carsi *vr* lodge

confic'cato *adj* **~ in** lodged in, embedded in

confi'dare **A** *vt* confide
B *vi* **~ in** trust

confi'darsi *vr* **~ con** confide in

confi'dente **A** *adj* confident
B *mf* confidant; (informatore) informer

confi'denza *f* confidence; (familiarità) familiarity; **prendersi delle confidenze** take liberties

confidenzi'ale *adj* confidential; ‹*tono*› familiar; **in via ~** confidentially

configu'rare *vt* Comput configure

configurazi'one *f* configuration

confi'nante *adj* neighbouring

confi'nare **A** *vt* (relegare) confine
B *vi* **~ con** border on

confi'narsi *vr* (ritirarsi) withdraw

confi'nato **A** *adj* confined
B *m* prisoner

CONFIN'DUSTRIA *f abbr* (**Confederazione generale dell'Industria italiana**) ≈ CBI

con'fine *m* border; (tra terreni) boundary

con'fino *m* political exile

con'fisca *f* (di proprietà) confiscation

confi'scare *vt* confiscate

conflagrazi'one *f* conflagration

con'flitto *m* conflict
■ **conflitto aereo** air war

conflittu'ale *adj* adversarial

conflittualità *f inv* adversarial nature

conflu'enza *f* confluence; (di strade) junction

conflu'ire *vi* ‹*fiumi*› flow together; ‹*strade*› meet

con'fondere *vt* confuse; (imbarazzare) embarrass

con'fondersi *vr* (mescolarsi) mingle; (sbagliarsi) be mistaken

confor'mare *vt* standardize (**a** in line with)

confor'marsi *vr* conform

conformazi'one *f* conformity (**a** with); (del terreno) nature

con'forme *adj* standard

conforme'mente *adv* accordingly

confor'mismo *m* conformity

confor'mista *mf* conformist

conformità *f inv* (a norma) conformity (**a** with); **in ~ a** in accordance with, in conformity with

confor'tante *adj* comforting

confor'tare *vt* comfort

confor'tevole *adj* (comodo) comfortable

con'forto *m* comfort; **a ~ di** ‹*una tesi*› in support of; **conforti** *pl* **religiosi** last rites

confra'telli *mpl* brethren

confra'ternita *f* brotherhood

confron'tare *vt* compare

con'fronto *m* comparison; **in ~ a** by comparison with; **nei tuoi confronti** towards you; **senza ~** far and away, by far
■ **confronto diretto** head to head

confusio'nario *adj* ‹*persona*› muddle-headed

confusi'one *f* confusion; (baccano) racket; (disordine) mess; (imbarazzo) embarrassment

con'fuso **A** pp di **confondere**
B *adj* confused; (indistinto) indistinct; (imbarazzato) embarrassed

confu'tare *vt* confute

conge'dare *vt* dismiss; Mil discharge

conge'darsi *vr* take one's leave

con'gedo *m* leave; **essere in ~** be on leave
■ **congedo malattia** sick leave; **congedo [di] maternità** maternity leave; **congedo [di] paternità** paternity leave

conge'gnare *vt* devise; (mettere insieme) assemble

con'gegno *m* device

congela'mento *m* freezing; Med frostbite
■ **congelamento dei prezzi** price freeze

conge'lare *vt* freeze

conge'lato *adj* ‹*cibo*› deep-frozen

congela'tore *m* freezer

congeni'ale *adj* congenial

con'genito *adj* congenital

congestio'nare *vt* congest

congestio'nato *adj* ‹*traffico*› congested; ‹*viso*› flushed

congesti'one *f* congestion

conget'tura *f* conjecture

congi'ungere *vt* join ‹*mani*›; combine ‹*sforzi*›

C

congi'ungersi *vr* join, connect
congiunti'vite *f* conjunctivitis
congiun'tivo *m* subjunctive
congi'unto **A** pp di **congiungere**
B *adj* joined; ‹*azione*› joint; ‹*forze, sforzo*› combined
C *m* relative
congiun'tura *f* junction; (situazione) situation
congiuntu'rale *adj* economic
congiunzi'one *f* Gram conjunction
congi'ura *f* conspiracy
congiu'rare *vi* conspire
conglome'rato *m* conglomerate; fig conglomeration; (da costruzione) concrete
'Congo *m* Congo
congo'lese *adj & nmf* Congolese
congratu'larsi *vr* ~ **con qualcuno per** congratulate somebody on
congratulazi'oni *fpl* congratulations
con'grega *f* band
congre'gare *vt* gather
congre'garsi *vr* congregate
congregazi'one *f* congregation
congres'sista *mf* convention participant
con'gresso *m* congress, convention; (americano) Congress
■ **Congresso Nazionale Africano** African National Congress
'congrua *f* stipend
'congruo *adj* proper; (giusto) fair
conguagli'are *vt* balance
congu'aglio *m* balance
coni'are *vt* coin
conia'tura *f* coinage
coniazi'one *f* coinage
'conico *adj* conical
co'nifera *f* conifer
co'niglia *f* female rabbit, doe
conigli'era *f* rabbit hutch
conigli'etta *f* bunny girl
conigli'etto *m* bunny
co'niglio *m* rabbit
coniu'gale *adj* marital; ‹*vita*› married
coniu'gare *vt* conjugate
coniu'garsi *vr* get married; Gram conjugate
coniu'gato *adj* (sposato) married
coniugazi'one *f* conjugation
'coniuge *mf* spouse
connazio'nale *mf* compatriot
connessi'one *f* connection
■ **connessione a banda larga** broadband connection
con'nesso pp di **connettere**
con'nettere **A** *vt* connect
B *vi* think rationally
con'nettersi *vr* Comput (a Internet) log on (a to)
connet'tore *m* connector
conni'vente *adj* conniving
conno'tare *vt* connote
conno'tato *m* distinguishing feature; **connotati** *pl* description; **rispondere ai connotati** fit the description; **cambiare i connotati a qualcuno** (hum) re-arrange somebody's face
con'nubio *m* fig union
'cono *m* cone
cono'scente *mf* acquaintance
⚷ **cono'scenza** *f* knowledge; (persona) acquaintance; (sensi) consciousness; **perdere** ~ lose consciousness; **riprendere** ~ regain consciousness, come to
■ **conoscenza di lavoro** business contact
⚷ **co'noscere** *vt* know; (essere a conoscenza di) be acquainted with; (fare la conoscenza di) meet; ~ **qualcosa a fondo** know something inside out
conosci|'tore, -trice *mf* connoisseur
conosci'uto **A** pp di **conoscere**
B *adj* well-known
con'quista *f* conquest
⚷ **conqui'stare** *vt* conquer; fig win
conquista'tore *m* conqueror; fig ladykiller
consa'crare *vt* consecrate; ordain ‹*sacerdote*›; (dedicare) dedicate
consa'crarsi *vr* devote oneself
consa'crato *adj* ‹*suolo*› hallowed
consacrazi'one *f* consecration
consangu'ineo, -a *mf* blood relation
consa'pevole *adj* conscious
consapevo'lezza *f* consciousness
consapevol'mente *adv* consciously
conscia'mente *adv* consciously
'conscio *adj* conscious
consecu'tivo *adj* consecutive; (seguente) next
con'segna *f* delivery; (merce) consignment; (custodia) care; (di prigioniero) handover; Mil (ordine) orders *pl*; Mil (punizione) confinement to barracks; **pagamento alla** ~ cash on delivery
■ **consegna della posta** mail delivery
⚷ **conse'gnare** *vt* deliver; Mil confine to barracks; hand over ‹*prigioniero, chiavi*›
consegna'tario *m* consignee
consegu'ente *adj* consequent
⚷ **consegu'enza** *f* consequence; **di** ~ (perciò) consequently; ‹*agire, comportarsi*› accordingly
consegui'mento *m* achievement
consegu'ire **A** *vt* achieve
B *vi* follow
⚷ **con'senso** *m* consent; (della popolazione) consensus
consensu'ale *adj* consensus-based
⚷ **consen'tire** **A** *vi* consent
B *vt* allow

⚷ key word

consenzi'ente *adj* consenting
con'serto *adj* **a braccia conserte** with one's arms folded
con'serva *f* preserve; (di frutta) jam; (di agrumi) marmalade
■ **conserva di pomodoro** tomato sauce
conser'vare *vt* preserve; (mantenere) keep; **~ in frigo** keep refrigerated; **~ in luogo asciutto** keep dry
conser'varsi *vr* keep; **~ in salute** keep well
conserva|'tore, -trice *adj & nmf* Pol conservative; **partito conservatore** Conservative Party, Tory Party BrE
conserva'torio *m* conservatory, school of music
conservato'rismo *m* conservatism
conservazi'one *f* preservation; **a lunga ~** long-life
con'sesso *m* assembly
conside'rare *vt* consider; (stimare) regard
conside'rato *adj* (stimato) esteemed
considerazi'one *f* consideration; (osservazione, riflessione) remark; (stima) respect
conside'revole *adj* considerable
consigli'abile *adj* advisable
consigli'are *vt* advise; (raccomandare) recommend
consigli'arsi *vr* **~ con qualcuno** ask somebody's advice
consigli'ere, -a *mf* adviser; (membro di un consiglio) councillor
■ **consigliere d'amministrazione** board member; **consigliere delegato** managing director
con'siglio *m* advice; (ente) council; **un ~** a piece of advice
■ **consiglio d'amministrazione** board of directors; **consiglio di guerra** war cabinet; **consiglio d'istituto** parent-teacher association; **consiglio dei ministri** Cabinet; **consiglio scolastico** education committee; **Consiglio di Sicurezza** (dell'ONU) Security Council; **Consiglio Superiore della Magistratura** *body responsible for ensuring the independence of the judiciary*
con'simile *adj* similar
consi'stente *adj* substantial; (spesso) thick; fig ‹*argomento*› solid
consi'stenza *f* consistency; (spessore) thickness; fig (di argomento) solidity
con'sistere *vi* **~ in** consist of
consoci'arsi *vr* go into partnership
consoci'ata *f* (azienda) subsidiary
consociati'vismo *m* *excessive tendency to form associations*
consoci'ato *m* associate
con'socio, -a *mf* fellow member
conso'lante *adj* consoling
conso'lare¹ *adj* consular
conso'lare² *vt* console
conso'larsi *vr* console oneself
conso'lato *m* consulate

consolazi'one *f* consolation
'console¹ *m* consul
con'sole² *f inv* (tastiera) console
■ **console per videogiochi** games console
consolida'mento *m* consolidation
consoli'dare *vt* consolidate
consoli'darsi *vr* consolidate
consommé *m inv* consommé
conso'nante *f* consonant
conso'nanza *f* consonance
'consono *adj* appropriate (**a** to, suitable (**a** for)
con'sorte *mf* consort
con'sorzio *m* consortium
con'stare *vi* **~ di** consist of; (risultare) appear; **a quanto mi consta** as far as I know; **mi consta che ...** seemingly ...
consta'tare *vt* ascertain
constatazi'one *f* statement of fact
consu'eto **A** *adj* usual
B *m* **più del ~** more than usual
consuetudi'nario *adj* ‹*diritto*› common; ‹*persona*› set in one's ways
consue'tudine *f* habit; (usanza) custom
consu'lente *mf* consultant
■ **consulente aziendale** management consultant; (azienda) management consultancy; **consulente matrimoniale** marriage guidance counsellor
consu'lenza *f* consultancy
consul'tare *vt* consult
consul'tarsi *vr* **~ con** consult with
consultazi'one *f* consultation
consul'tivo *adj* consultative
con'sulto *m* consultation
consul'torio *m* *free clinic providing treatment for sexual problems and advice*
consu'mare *vt* (usare) consume; wear out ‹*abito, scarpe*›; consummate ‹*matrimonio*›; commit ‹*delitto*›
consu'marsi *vr* consume; ‹*abito, scarpe*› wear out; (struggersi) pine; **'da ~ preferibilmente entro il ...'** best before ...
consu'mato *adj* ‹*politico*› consummate; ‹*scarpe, tappeto*› worn [out]
consuma|'tore, -trice *mf* consumer
consumazi'one *f* consumption; (bibita) drink; (spuntino) snack; (di matrimonio) consummation; (di delitto) commission
consu'mismo *m* consumerism
consu'mista *mf* consumerist
con'sumo *m* consumption; (uso) use; **generi di ~** consumer goods
■ **consumo [di carburante]** [fuel] consumption
consun'tivo *m* **fare il ~ di** fig take stock of
■ **bilancio consuntivo** balance sheet
con'sunto *adj* well-worn
conta'balle *mf* infml storyteller
con'tabile **A** *adj* book-keeping
B *mf* accountant

C

contabilità *f inv* accounting; (ufficio) accounts department; **tenere la ~** keep the accounts
■ **contabilità di gestione** management accounts; **contabilità in partita doppia** double entry book-keeping

contachi'lometri *m inv* mileometer, odometer AmE

conta'dino, -a *mf* farm worker, agricultural labourer; (proprietario) farmer; (medievale) peasant

contagi'are *vt* infect; **la sua allegria contagia tutti** his cheerfulness is very contagious

contagi'ato *adj* infected

con'tagio *m* contagion

contagi'oso *adj* contagious

conta'giri *m inv* rev counter

conta'gocce *m inv* dropper; **dare qualcosa col ~** fig dole something out in dribs and drabs

contami'nare *vt* contaminate

contaminazi'one *f* contamination
■ **contaminazione incrociata** cross-contamination

contami'nuti *m inv* timer

con'tante *m* cash; **pagare in contanti** pay cash

con'tare **A** *vt* count; (tenere conto di) take into account; **devi ~ un'ora per il viaggio** you have to allow an hour for the journey **B** *vi* count; **~ di fare qualcosa** plan to do something

conta'scatti *m inv* Teleph time unit counter

con'tato *adj* ‹*giorni, ore*› numbered

conta'tore *m* meter
■ **contatore del gas** gas meter

contat'tare *vt* contact

con'tatto *m* contact; **essere in ~ con** be in touch *or* contact with; **mettersi in ~ con** contact, get in touch with

'conte *m* count, earl BrE

con'tea *f* county

conteggi'are **A** *vt* count **B** *vi* calculate

con'teggio *m* calculation
■ **conteggio alla rovescia** countdown

con'tegno *m* behaviour; (atteggiamento) attitude; **darsi un ~** pull oneself together

conte'gnoso *adj* dignified

contem'plare *vt* contemplate; (fissare) gaze at

contempla'tivo *adj* contemplative

contemplazi'one *f* contemplation

con'tempo *m* **nel ~** in the meantime

contemporanea'mente *adv* at the same time

contempo'raneo, -a *adj & nmf* contemporary

✓ key word

conten'dente *mf* competitor

con'tendere **A** *vi* compete; (litigare) quarrel **B** *vt* dispute

con'tendersi *vr* **~ qualcosa** compete for something

conte'nere *vt* contain; (reprimere) repress

conte'nersi *vr* contain oneself

conteni'tore *m* container

conten'tabile *adj* **facilmente ~** easy to please

conten'tare *vt* please

conten'tarsi *vr* **~ di** be content with

conten'tezza *f* happiness

conten'tino *m* placebo

con'tento *adj* glad; (soddisfatto) happy

conte'nuto *m* contents *pl*; (di libro, testo) content

contenzi'oso **A** *adj* contentious **B** *m* dispute; (ufficio) legal department

con'tesa *f* disagreement; Sport contest

con'teso **A** *pp* di **contendere** **B** *adj* contested

con'tessa *f* countess

conte'stare *vt* contest; Jur give notification of ‹*contravvenzione*›; **~ un reato a qualcuno** charge somebody with an offence

contesta|'tore, -trice **A** *mf person who is anti authority* **B** *adj* anti-authority

contestazi'one *f* (disputa) dispute; (protesta) protest; (di contravvenzione) notification

con'testo *m* context

con'tiguo *adj* adjacent

continen'tale *adj* continental

conti'nente *m* continent

conti'nenza *f* continence

contin'gente *m* contingent; (quota) quota

contin'genza *f* contingency

continua'mente *adv* (senza interruzione) continuously; (frequentemente) continually

continu'are *vt & vi* continue; (riprendere) resume; **~ gli studi** stay on at school

continua'tivo *adj* on-going, continuous

continuazi'one *f* continuation

continuità *f inv* continuity

con'tinuo *adj* (senza interruzione) continuous; (molto frequente) continual; **di ~** continuously; (frequentemente) continually; **corrente continua** direct current

con'tinuum *m inv* continuum

'conto *m* calculation; (in banca, negozio) account; (di ristorante ecc.) bill, check AmE; (stima) consideration; **a conti fatti** all things considered; **ad ogni buon ~** in any case; **di poco/nessun ~** of little/no importance; **in fin dei conti** when all's said and done; **per ~ di** on behalf of; **per ~ mio** (a mio parere) in my opinion; (da solo) on my own; **per ~ terzi** for a third party; **sul ~ di qualcuno** ‹*voci, informazioni*› about somebody; **far ~ di**

(supporre) suppose; (proporsi) intend; **far ~ su** rely on; **fare i propri conti** do one's accounts; **fare i conti con qualcuno** fig sort somebody out; **fare i conti in tasca a qualcuno** estimate how much somebody is worth; **fare i conti senza l'oste** forget the most important thing; **render ~ a qualcuno di qualcosa** be accountable to somebody for something; **rendersi ~ di qualcosa** realize something; **starsene per ~ proprio** be on one's own; **tener ~ di qualcosa** take something into account; **tenere da ~ qualcosa** look after something

■ **conto in banca** bank account; **conto congiunto** joint account; **conto corrente** current account, checking account AmE; **conto [corrente] comune** joint account; **conto corrente postale** Giro account; **conto profitti e perdite** profit and loss account; **conto alla rovescia** countdown; **conto spese** expense account

con'torcere *vt* twist

con'torcersi *vr* twist about

contor'nare *vt* surround

con'torno *m* contour; Culin vegetables *pl*

contorsi'one *f* contortion

contorsio'nista *mf* contortionist

con'torto **A** pp di **contorcere**
B *adj* twisted

contrabban'dare *vt* smuggle

contrabbandi'ere, -a *mf* smuggler

contrab'bando *m* contraband

contrabbas'sista *mf* double bass player

contrab'basso *m* double bass

contraccambi'are *vt* return

contrac'cambio *m* return

contraccet'tivo *m* contraceptive

contraccezi'one *f* contraception

contrac'colpo *m* rebound; (di arma da fuoco) recoil; fig repercussion

con'trada *f* (rione) district

contrad'detto pp di **contraddire**

contrad'dire *vt* contradict

contraddi'stinguere *vt* differentiate, distinguish

contraddi'stinto **A** pp di **contraddistinguere**
B *adj* **~ da** distinguished by

contraddit'torio *adj* contradictory

contraddizi'one *f* contradiction

contra'ente *mf* contracting party

contra'ereo *adj* anti-aircraft

contraf'fare *vt* disguise

contraf'fatto **A** pp di **contraffare**
B *adj* disguised

contraffazi'one *f* disguising

contraf'forte *m* buttress

con'tralto **A** *m* counter-tenor
B *f* contralto

contrap'peso *m* counterbalance

contrap'porre *vt* (confrontare) compare; **~ A a B** counter B with A

contrap'porsi *vr* be in opposition; **~ a** contrast with; (opporsi a) be opposed to

contrap'punto *m* Mus counterpoint

contraria'mente *adv* **~ a** contrary to; **~ a me** unlike me

contrari'are *vt* oppose; (infastidire) annoy

contrari'arsi *vr* get annoyed

contrarietà *f inv* adversity; (ostacolo) set-back

con'trario **A** *adj* contrary, opposite; ‹*direzione*› opposite; ‹*esito, vento*› unfavourable
B *m* contrary, opposite; **al ~** on the contrary

con'trarre *vt* contract

contrasse'gnare *vt* mark

contras'segno *m* mark; **[in] ~** ‹*spedizione*› cash on delivery, COD

■ **contrassegno IVA** VAT receipt

contra'stante *adj* contrasting

contra'stare **A** *vt* oppose; (contestare) contest
B *vi* contrast; ‹*colori*› clash

con'trasto *m* contrast; (di colori) clash; (litigio) dispute

contrattac'care *vt* counter-attack

contrat'tacco *m* counter-attack

contrat'tare *vt & vi* negotiate; (mercanteggiare) bargain

contrattazi'one *f* contravention; (salariale) bargaining

■ **contrattazione di azioni** share dealing

contrat'tempo *m* hitch

con'tratto **A** pp di **contrarre**
B *m* contract

■ **contratto di lavoro** employment contract; **contratto a termine** fixed-term contract; **contratti a termine** *pl* Fin futures

contrattu'ale *adj* contractual

contravve'nire *vi* contravene a law

contrazi'one *f* contraction; (di prezzi) reduction

contribu'ente *mf* contributor; (del fisco) taxpayer

contribu'ire *vi* contribute

contribu'tivo *adj* contributory

contri'buto *m* contribution; **contributi** *pl* **pensionistici** pension contributions

con'trito *adj* contrite

'contro **A** *prep* against; **~ di me** against me
B *m* **il pro e il ~** the pros and cons *pl*

contro'battere *vt* counter

controbilanci'are *vt* counterbalance

controcor'rente **A** *adj* ‹*idee, persona*› nonconformist
B *adv* upriver; fig upstream; **andare ~** fig swim against the tide

controcul'tura *f* counterculture

contro'curva *f* second bend

contro'esodo *m* *massive return from holiday*

controfa'gotto *m* double bassoon
controffen'siva *f* counter-offensive
controfi'gura *f* stand-in
controfi'letto *m* sirloin
contro'firma *f* countersignature
controfir'mare *vt* countersign
controindicazi'one *f* Med contraindication
controinterroga'torio *m* cross-examination
control'labile *adj* ‹*emozione*› controllable; Tech *which can be monitored*
control'lare *vt* control; (verificare) check
control'larsi *vr* control oneself
control'lato *adj* controlled
con'troller *m inv* Fin controller
con'trollo *m* control; (verifica) check; Med check-up; **perdere il ~ di** lose control of
■ **controllo degli armamenti** arms control; **controllo automatico della velocità** automatic speed check; **controllo bagagli** baggage control; **controllo biglietti** ticket inspection; **controllo dei cambi** exchange control; **controllo del credito** credit control; **controllo medico** check-up; **controllo delle nascite** birth control; **controllo ortografico** Comput spellchecker; **fare il ~ ortografico** spellcheck; **controllo passaporti** passport control; **controllo [di] qualità** quality control
control'lore *m* controller; (sui treni ecc.) [ticket] inspector
■ **controllore di volo** air-traffic controller
contro'luce *f* **in ~** against the light
contro'mano *adv* on the wrong side of the road, in the wrong direction
contromi'sura *f* countermeasure
contropar'tita *f* compensation; **in ~** in return
contropi'ede *m* Sport breakaway; **prendere in ~** fig catch off guard
controprodu'cente *adj* counter-productive
contro'prova *f* cross-check; **fare la ~ di qualcosa** cross-check something
con'trordine *m* counter order; **salvo contrordini** unless I/you hear to the contrary
contro'senso *m* contradiction in terms
controspio'naggio *m* counter-espionage
controten'denza *f* countertrend
controva'lore *m* equivalent
contro'vento *adv* against the wind
contro'versia *f* controversy; Jur dispute
contro'verso *adj* controversial
contro'voglia *adv* unwillingly
contu'mace *adj* Jur in default, absent
contu'macia *f* default; **in ~** in one's absence
contun'dente *adj* ‹*corpo, arma*› blunt
contur'bante *adj* perturbing
contur'bare *vt* perturb
contusi'one *f* bruise
con'tuso *m person suffering from cuts and bruises*
convale'scente *adj & nmf* convalescent
convale'scenza *f* convalescence; **essere in ~** be convalescing
con'valida *f* ratification; (di nomina) confirmation; (di biglietto) validation
convali'dare *vt* ratify; confirm ‹*nomina*›; validate ‹*atto, biglietto*›
con'vegno *m* meeting; (congresso) convention, congress
conve'nevole *adj* suitable
conve'nevoli *mpl* pleasantries
conveni'ente *adj* convenient; (vantaggioso) advantageous; ‹*prezzo*› attractive
conveni'enza *f* convenience; (interesse) advantage; (di prezzo) attractiveness
conve'nire **A** *vi* agree; (riunirsi) gather; (essere opportuno) be convenient; **ci conviene andare** it's better to go; **non mi conviene stancarmi** I'd better not tire myself out
B *vt* agree [on]
conven'ticola *f* clique
con'vento *m* (di suore) convent; (di frati) monastery
conve'nuto *adj* agreed
convenzio'nale *adj* conventional
convenzio'nato *adj* ‹*prezzo*› controlled
convenzi'one *f* convention
conver'gente *adj* converging
conver'genza *f* convergence
con'vergere *vi* converge
con'versa *f* lay sister
conver'sare *vi* converse
conversa|'tore, -trice *mf* conversationalist
conversazi'one *f* conversation
conversi'one *f* conversion
con'verso pp di **convergere**
conver'tibile *f* Auto convertible
conver'tire *vt* convert
conver'tirsi *vr* convert
conver'tito, -a **A** *adj* converted
B *mf* convert
converti'tore *m* converter
con'vesso *adj* convex
convezi'one *f* convection
convin'cente *adj* convincing
con'vincere *vt* convince
con'vinto *adj* convinced
convinzi'one *f* conviction
convi'tato *m* guest
con'vitto *m* boarding school
convi'vente **A** *m* common-law husband
B *f* common-law wife
convi'venza *f* cohabitation
con'vivere *vi* live together

key word

convivi'ale *adj* convivial
convo'care *vt* summon; Jur summons; convene ‹*riunione*›
convocazi'one *f* summoning; Jur summoning; (atto) summons; (riunione) meeting
convogli'are *vt* convey; ‹*navi*› convoy
con'voglio *m* convoy; (ferroviario) train
convo'lare *vi* **~ a giuste nozze** (hum) tie the knot
convulsa'mente *adv* convulsively
convulsi'one *f* convulsion; fig fit
convul'sivo *adj* Med convulsive; ‹*riso*› hysterical
coope'rante *mf* aid worker
coope'rare *vi* co-operate
coopera'tiva *f* co-operative
cooperazi'one *f* co-operation
coordina'mento *m* co-ordination
coordi'nare *vt* co-ordinate
coordi'nata *f* Math co-ordinate; **coordinate** *pl* (su mappa) grid reference; **coordinate** *pl* **bancarie** bank details
coordi'nato **A** *adj* co-ordinated **B** *m* (intimo) lingerie set
coordina|'tore, -trice *mf* co-ordinator
coordinazi'one *f* co-ordination
■ **coordinazione occhio-mano** hand-eye coordination
co'perchio *m* lid; (copertura) cover
co'perta *f* blanket; (copertura) cover; Naut deck
■ **coperta elettrica** electric blanket
coper'tina *f* cover; (foderina di libro) dust jacket
co'perto **A** pp di **coprire** **B** *adj* covered; (vestito) wrapped up; ‹*cielo*› overcast; ‹*piscina*› indoor **C** *m* (a tavola) place; (prezzo del coperto) cover charge; **al ~** under cover
coper'tone *m* tarpaulin; (gomma) tyre
coper'tura *f* cover; (azione) covering; (di strada) surfacing; (di malefatta) cover-up
■ **copertura globale** blanket coverage
'copia *f* copy; **bella/brutta ~** fair/rough copy; **essere la ~ spiccicata di qualcuno** be the spitting image of somebody
■ **copia su carta** hard copy; **copia pirata** pirate copy; **copia di riserva** Comput backup copy
'copia e in'colla *m inv* Comput copy and paste; **fare un ~** copy and paste
copi'are *vt* copy
copia'trice *f* copier
copi'lota *mf* co-pilot; (di auto) co-driver
copi'one *m* Cinema, TV script
copi'oso *adj* copious
'coppa *f* (calice) goblet; (bicchiere) glass; (per gelato ecc.) dish; Sport cup
■ **coppa [di] gelato** ice-cream (*served in a dish*); **coppa del mondo** World Cup
cop'petta *f* (di ceramica, vetro) bowl; (di gelato) small tub
'coppia *f* couple; (in carte, voga) pair; **~ di fatto** de facto couple
co'prente *adj* (cipria, vernice) thick; ‹*collant*› opaque
copri'capo *m* head covering
coprifu'oco *m* curfew
copri'letto *m* bedspread
copri'mozzo *m* hub cap
copriobiet'tivo *m* lens cap
copripiu'mino *m* duvet cover
co'prire *vt* cover; drown [out] ‹*suono*›; hold ‹*carica*›
co'prirsi *vr* (vestirsi) cover oneself up; (vestirsi pesante) dress warmly; fig cover up; (proteggersi) cover oneself; ‹*cielo*› become overcast
copritei'era *m* tea cosy
co-protago'nista *mf* Cinema co-star
'coque alla ~ *adj* ‹*uovo*› soft-boiled
co'raggio *m* bravery, courage; (sfacciataggine) nerve; **~!** chin up!
coraggiosa'mente *adv* bravely, courageously
coraggi'oso *adj* brave, courageous
co'rale *adj* choral
co'rallo *m* coral
co'rano *m* Koran
co'razza *f* armour; (di animali) shell
coraz'zata *f* battleship
coraz'zato *adj* ‹*nave*› armour-plated
corazza'tura *f* armour plating
corazzi'ere *m* cuirassier
corbelle'ria *of* piece of nonsense; **dire corbellerie** talk nonsense
'corda *f* cord; (spago, Mus) string; (fune) rope; (cavo) cable; **essere giù di ~** be down; **dare ~ a qualcuno** encourage somebody; **tagliare la ~** cut and run; **tenere qualcuno sulla ~** keep somebody on tenterhooks; **corde** *pl* **vocali** vocal cords
■ **corda per il bucato** washing line
cor'data *f* roped party
cordi'ale **A** *adj* cordial; **cordiali saluti** best wishes **B** *m* (bevanda) cordial
cordialità *f inv* cordiality; **~** *pl* (saluti) best wishes
'cordless *m inv* Teleph cordless (phone)
cor'doglio *m* grief; (lutto) mourning
cor'done *m* cord; (schieramento) cordon
■ **cordone ombelicale** umbilical cord; **cordone sanitario** cordon sanitaire
Corea *f* Korea
■ **Corea del Nord** North Korea; **Corea del Sud** South Korea
core'ano, -a *adj & nmf* Korean
coreogra'fare *vt* choreograph
coreogra'fia *f* choreography; **fare la ~ di** choreograph
core'ografo, -a *mf* choreographer

Corfù *f inv* Corfu
cori'aceo *adj* tough
cori'andoli *mpl* (di carta) confetti *sg*
cori'andolo *m* (spezia) coriander
cori'care *vt* put to bed
cori'carsi *vr* go to bed
Co'rinto *f* Corinth
co'rista *mf* **1** (in chiesa) choir member **2** (di accompagnamento) backing singer
'corna = **corno**
cor'nacchia *f* crow
corna'musa *f* bagpipes *pl*
'cornea *f* cornea
'corner *m inv* corner; **salvarsi in ~** fig have a lucky escape
cor'netta *f* Mus cornet; (del telefono) receiver
cor'netto *m* (brioche) croissant
■ **cornetto acustico** ear trumpet
cor'nice *f* frame
■ **cornice a giorno** clip frame; **cornice digitale** digital frame
cornici'one *m* cornice
cornifi'care *vt* infml cheat on
'corno *m* (*pl f* **corna**) horn; **fare le corna a qualcuno** infml cheat on somebody; **fare le corna** (per scongiuro) ≈touch wood; **un ~!** you must be joking!; (per niente) nonsense!
■ **corno da caccia** French horn
Corno'vaglia *f* Cornwall
cornu'copia *f* cornucopia
cor'nuto **A** *adj* horned **B** *m* infml (marito tradito) cuckold; (insulto) bastard
'coro *m* chorus; Relig choir
co'rolla *f* corolla
corol'lario *m* corollary
co'rona *f* crown; (di fiori) wreath; (rosario) rosary
corona'mento *m* (di sogno) fulfilment; (di carriera) crowning achievement
coro'nare *vt* fulfil ‹*sogno*›
coro'nario *adj* ‹*arteria*› coronary
cor'petto *m* bodice
'corpo *m* body; Mil (diplomatico) corps *inv*; **[a] ~ a ~** Mil hand to hand; **lottare [a] ~ a ~** have a punch-up, slug it out; **dare ~ a qualcosa** give substance to something; **buttarsi a ~ morto in qualcosa** throw oneself desperately into something; **andare di ~** move one's bowels
■ **corpo di ballo** corps de ballet; **corpo estraneo** foreign body; **corpo insegnante** teaching staff; **corpo del reato** murder weapon
corpo'rale *adj* corporal
corporati'vismo *m* corporatism
corpora'tura *f* build
corporazi'one *f* corporation
cor'poreo *adj* bodily
cor'poso *adj* full-bodied
corpu'lento *adj* stout
'corpus *m inv* corpus
cor'puscolo *m* corpuscle
corre'dare *vt* (di note) supply (**di** with); **corredato di curriculum** accompanied by a CV
corre'dino *m* (per neonato) layette
cor'redo *m* (nuziale) trousseau; (di informazioni ecc.) set
correggere *vt* correct; lace ‹*bevanda*›; **~ le bozze** proof-read
corre'lare *vt* correlate
cor'rente **A** *adj* running; (in vigore) current; (frequente) everyday; ‹*inglese ecc.*› fluent **B** *f* current; (d'aria) draught; **essere al ~ di qualcosa** be aware of something; **tenersi al ~** keep up to date (**di** with)
■ **corrente continua** direct current; **corrente trasversale** cross current
corrente'mente *adv* ‹*parlare*› fluently; (comunemente) commonly
'correre **A** *vi* run; (affrettarsi) hurry; Sport race; ‹*notizie*› circulate; **lascia ~!** let it go!; **~ dietro a** run after; **tra loro non corre buon sangue** there is bad blood between them **B** *vt* run; **~ un pericolo** run a risk; **corre voce che ...** there's a rumour that ...
correspon'sabile *mf* person jointly responsible
corresponsi'one *f* payment
corretta'mente *adv* correctly; ‹*sedersi, mangiare*› properly; ‹*trattare, fare qualcosa*› right
corret'tivo *m* corrective
cor'retto **A** pp di **correggere** **B** *adj* correct; ‹*caffè*› with a drop of alcohol
corret'tore, -trice **A** *mf*
■ **correttore di bozze** proof-reader
B *m*
■ **correttore grammaticale** Comput grammar checker; **correttore ortografico** Comput spellchecker
correzi'one *f* correction
■ **correzione di bozze** proof-reading; **correzione errori** Comput error correction
cor'rida *f* bullfight
corri'doio *m* corridor; Aeron aisle
corri'dore, -trice *mf* (automobilistico) driver; (ciclista) cyclist; (a piedi) runner
corri'era *f* coach, bus
corri'ere *m* courier; (posta) mail; (spedizioniere) carrier
■ **corriere della droga** drug mule
corri'mano *m* hand rail
corrispet'tivo *m* amount due
corrispon'dente **A** *adj* corresponding **B** *mf* correspondent
■ **corrispondente estero** foreign correspondent
corrispon'denza *f* correspondence; **tenersi in ~ con** correspond with; **per ~**

key word

‹*fare un corso*› by correspondence; **corso per corrispondenza** correspondence course; **vendite per corrispondenza** mail-order [shopping]

corri'spondere *vi* correspond; ‹*stanza*›; communicate; ~ **a** (contraccambiare) return

corri'sposto *adj* ‹*amore*› reciprocated

corrobo'rare *vt* strengthen; fig corroborate

cor'rodere *vt* corrode

cor'rodersi *vr* corrode

cor'rompere *vt* corrupt; (con denaro) bribe

corrosi'one *f* corrosion

corro'sivo *adj* corrosive

cor'roso pp di **corrodere**

cor'rotto **A** pp di **corrompere**
B *adj* corrupt

corrucci'arsi *vr* be vexed

corrucci'ato *adj* vexed

corru'gare *vt* wrinkle; ~ **la fronte** knit one's brows

corrut'tela *f* depravity

corruzi'one *f* corruption; (con denaro) bribery

'**corsa** *f* running; (rapida) dash; Sport race; (di treno ecc.) journey; **di** ~ at a run; **di gran** ~ in a great hurry; **fare una** ~ (sbrigarsi) run, hurry
■ **corsa agli armamenti** arms race; **corsa ciclistica** cycle race; **corsa ippica** horse race; **corsa all'oro** gold rush; **corsa a ostacoli** obstacle race; **corsa piana** flat racing; **corsa semplice** one way [ticket]

cor'sia *f* gangway; (di ospedale) ward; Aut lane; (di supermercato) aisle
■ **corsia autobus** bus lane; **corsia d'emergenza** Aut hard shoulder; **corsia a scorrimento veloce** express lane; **corsia di sorpasso** fast lane, outside lane

'**Corsica** *f* Corsica

cor'sivo *m* italics *pl*; **in** ~ in italics

'**corso** **A** pp di **correre**
B *m* course; (strada) main street; Comm circulation; (in borsa) price, quotation; **essere in** ~ be under way; **lavori in** ~ work in progress; **nel** ~ **di** during; **avere** ~ **legale** be legal tender
■ **corso d'acqua** waterway; **corso per corrispondenza** correspondence course; **corso di formazione** training course; **corso di formazione professionale** vocational course; **corso full immersion** immersion course; **corso del giorno** current daily price; **corso di laurea** degree course; **corso serale** evening class; **corsi** *pl* **di studio a distanza** distance learning

'**corte** *f* [court] yard; Jur (regale) court; **fare la** ~ **a qualcuno** court somebody
■ **corte d'appello** court of appeal; **corte d'assise** crown court; **Corte di cassazione** supreme court of appeal; **Corte dei conti** National Audit Office; **Corte europea per i diritti dell'uomo** European Court of Human Rights; **Corte europea di giustizia** European Court of Justice; **corte di giustizia** court of law

cor'teccia *f* bark

corteggia'mento *m* courtship

corteggi'are *vt* court

corteggia'tore *m* admirer

cor'teo *m* procession
■ **corteo di auto** motorcade; **corteo funebre** funeral cortège; **corteo nuziale** bridal party

cor'tese *adj* courteous

corte'sia *f* courtesy; **per** ~ please

cortigi'ano, -a **A** *mf* courtier
B *f* courtesan

cor'tile *m* courtyard

cor'tina *f* curtain; (schermo) screen

'**corto** *adj* short; **per farla corta** to cut a long story short; **a** ~ **di** short of, hard up for
■ **corto circuito** *nm* short [circuit]

cortome'traggio *m* Cinema short

cor'vino *adj* jet-black

'**corvo** *m* raven

'**cosa** **A** *f* thing; (faccenda) matter
B *inter, rel pron* what; **[che]** ~ what; **nessuna** ~ nothing; **ogni** ~ everything; **per prima** ~ first of all; **tante cose** [so] many things; (augurio) all the best; ~? what?; ~ **hai detto?** what did you say?; **le cose le vanno bene** she's doing all right

'**cosca** *f* clan

'**coscia** *f* thigh; Culin leg; **cosce** *pl* **di rana** frogs' legs

cosci'ente *adj* conscious

cosci'enza *f* conscience; (consapevolezza) consciousness; **mettersi la** ~ **a posto** salve one's conscience

coscienziosa'mente *adv* conscientiously

coscienzi'oso *adj* conscientious

cosci'otto *m* leg

co'scritto *m* conscript

coscrizi'one *f* conscription

così **A** *adv* so; (in questo modo) like this, like that; (perciò) therefore; **le cose stanno** ~ that's how things stand; **fermo** ~**!** hold it!; **proprio** ~**!** exactly!; **basta** ~**!** that will do!; **ah, è** ~**?** it's like that, is it?; ~ ~ so-so; **e** ~ **via** and so on; **per** ~ **dire** so to speak; **più di** ~ any more; **una** ~ **cara ragazza!** such a nice girl!; **è stato** ~ **generoso da aiutarti** he was kind enough to help you
B *conj* (allora) so
C *adj inv* (tale) like that, such; **una ragazza** ~ a girl like that, such a girl

cosicché *conj* and so

cosid'detto *adj* so-called

co'smesi *f* beauty treatment

co'smetico **A** *adj* cosmetic
B *m* **cosmetici** *pl* cosmetics; (trucchi) make-up

'**cosmico** *adj* cosmic

'**cosmo** *m* cosmos

cosmo'nauta *mf* cosmonaut

cosmopo'lita *adj* cosmopolitan

C

co'spargere *vt* sprinkle; (disseminare) scatter; ~ **il pavimento di cera** spread wax on the floor
co'spetto *m* **al** ~ **di** in the presence of
co'spicuo *adj* conspicuous; ‹*somma ecc.*› considerable
cospi'rare *vi* conspire, plot
cospira|'tore, -trice *mf* conspirator, plotter
cospirazi'one *f* conspiracy, plot
⚷ **'costa** *f* coast, coastline; Anat rib; **sotto** ~ inshore
■ **Costa d'Avorio** Ivory Coast; **Costa Azzurra** Côte d'Azur; **Costa Smeralda** Emerald coast (*in Sardinia*)
costà *adv* there
co'stante *adj & nf* constant
co'stanza *f* constancy
⚷ **co'stare** *vi* cost; **quanto costa?** how much is it?; **costi quel che costi** whatever the cost
'Costa 'Rica *m* Costa Rica
co'stata *f* chop
■ **costata [di manzo]** rib steak
co'stato *m* ribs *pl*
costeggi'are *vt* (per mare) coast; (per terra) skirt
co'stei *pers pron* (soggetto) she; (complemento) her
costellazi'one *f* constellation
coster'nato *adj* dismayed
costernazi'one *f* consternation
costi'era *f* stretch of coast
costi'ero *adj* coastal
co'stine *fpl* (di maiale) spare ribs
'costing *m inv* costing
costi'pato *adj* (stitico) constipated; **essere** ~ (raffreddato) have a bad cold
costipazi'one *f* (stitichezza) constipation; (raffreddore) bad cold
⚷ **costitu'ire** *vt* constitute; (essere) be; (formare) form; (nominare) appoint
costitu'irsi *vr* ‹*criminale*› give oneself up
costituzio'nale *adj* constitutional
costituzional'mente *adv* Pol constitutionally
costituzi'one *f* constitution; (formazione) formation
⚷ **'costo** *m* cost; **a nessun** ~ on no account; **a** ~ **di perdere la salute** at the cost of one's health; **sotto** ~ at less than cost price; **costi** *pl* **di gestione** administration costs; **costi** *pl* **spedizione** freight charges
■ **costo del denaro** Fin cost of money; **costo unitario** unit cost; **costo della vita** cost of living
'costola *f* rib; (di libro) spine; **stare alle costole di qualcuno** follow somebody around
costo'letta *f* cutlet

⚷ key word

co'storo *pron* (soggetto) they; (complemento) them
co'stoso *adj* costly
co'stretto pp di **costringere**
⚷ **co'stringere** *vt* force, compel
costrit'tivo *adj* coercive
costrizi'one *f* compulsion
⚷ **costru'ire** *vt* build, construct
costrut'tivo *adj* constructive
⚷ **costruzi'one** *f* building, construction; (edificio) building
⚷ **co'stui** *pers pron* (soggetto) he; (complemento) him
co'stume *m* (usanza) custom; (indumento) costume; **costumi** *pl* (morale) morals
■ **costume da bagno** swimsuit; (da uomo) swimming trunks; **costume intero** one-piece; **costume tradizionale** traditional costume
costu'mista *mf* wardrobe assistant
cote'chino *m* spiced pork sausage
co'tenna *f* pigskin; (della pancetta) rind
■ **cotenna arrostita** crackling
co'togna *f* quince
coto'letta *f* cutlet
■ **cotoletta alla milanese** veal cutlet in breadcrumbs
coto'nato *adj* ‹*capelli*› back-combed
co'tone *m* cotton
■ **cotone idrofilo** cotton wool, absorbent cotton AmE
cotoni'ficio *m* cotton mill
'cotta *f* Relig surplice; infml (innamoramento) crush; **prendere una** ~ **per qualcuno** infml have a crush on somebody
'cottimo *m* piece-work
'cotto **A** pp di **cuocere**
B *adj* done; infml (innamorato) in love; (sbronzo) drunk; **ben** ~ well cooked; ‹*carne*› underdone; **troppo** ~ overcooked; ‹*carne*› overdone
cotton fi'oc® *m inv* cotton bud
cot'tura *f* cooking
'country *m inv* country and western
cou'pon *m inv* coupon
cou'scous *m inv* couscous
co'vare *vt* hatch; sicken for ‹*malattia*›; harbour ‹*rancore*›
co'vata *f* brood
'covo *m* den
co'vone *m* sheaf
cow-'boy *m inv* cowboy
'cozza *f* mussel
■ **cozze alla marinara** *pl* moules marinière
coz'zare *vi* ~ **contro** bump into
'cozzo *m* fig clash
C.P. *abbr* (**Casella Postale**) PO Box
crac *m inv* crack; (di tessuto) rip
crack *m* (droga) crack
Cra'covia *f* Cracow
'crafen *m inv* cream doughnut

'crampo *m* cramp
'cranio *m* skull
cra'tere *m* crater
cra'vatta *f* tie; (a farfalla) bow-tie
cre'anza *vt* manners *pl*; **mala ~** bad manners
cre'are *vt* create; **~ assuefazione** be habit-forming
creatività *f inv* creativity
crea'tivo *adj* creative
cre'ato *m* creation
crea|'tore, -trice *mf* creator; **andare al ~** go to meet one's maker
crea'tura *f* creature; (bambino) baby; **povera ~!** poor thing!
creazi'one *f* creation
cre'dente *mf* believer
cre'denza *f* belief; Comm credit; (mobile) sideboard
credenzi'ali *fpl* credentials
'credere **A** *vt* believe; (pensare) think
B *vi* **~ in** believe in; **credo di sì** I think so; **non ti credo** I don't believe you; **non posso crederci!** I can't believe it!
'credersi *vr* think oneself to be; **si crede uno scrittore** he flatters himself he is a writer
cre'dibile *adj* credible, believable
credibilità *f inv* credibility
credi'tizio *adj* credit (*attrib*)
'credito *m* credit; (stima) esteem; **comprare a ~** buy on credit; **dare ~ a qualcosa** give credence to something; **fare ~** give credit
■ **credito all'esportazione** export credit; **credito inesigibile** bad debt
credi|'tore, -trice *mf* creditor
'credo *m inv* credo
credulità *f inv* credulity
'credulo *adj* credulous
credu'lone, -a *mf* simpleton
'crema *f* cream; (di uova e latte) custard
■ **crema base per il trucco** vanishing cream; **crema depilatoria** depilatory [cream]; **crema detergente** cleansing cream; **crema idratante** moisturizer; **crema per le mani** hand cream; **crema pasticciera** confectioner's custard; **crema per la pelle** skin cream; **crema protettiva** barrier cream; **crema solare** suntan lotion; **crema per il viso** face cream
cremagli'era *f* ratchet
cre'mare *vt* cremate
crema'torio *m* crematorium
cremazi'one *f* cremation
crème cara'mel *f* crème caramel
creme'ria *f* dairy (*also selling ice cream and cakes*)
Crem'lino *m* Kremlin
cre'moso *adj* creamy
cren *m* horseradish
'crepa *f* crack
cre'paccio *m* cleft; (di ghiacciaio) crevasse
crepacu'ore *m* heartbreak
crepa'pelle **a ~** *adv* fit to burst
cre'pare *vi* crack; infml (morire) kick the bucket; **~ dal ridere** laugh fit to burst
crepa'tura *f* crevice
crêpe *f inv* pancake
crepi'tare *vi* crackle
crepi'tio *m* crackling
cre'puscolo *m* twilight
cre'scendo *m* crescendo
cre'scenza *f creamy white cheese*
'crescere **A** *vi* grow; (aumentare) increase, grow
B *vt* (allevare) bring up; (aumentare) increase
cresci'one *m* watercress
'crescita *f* growth; (aumento) increase, growth
cresci'uto pp di **crescere**
'cresima *f* confirmation
cresi'mare *vt* confirm
cre'spato *adj* crinkly
cre'spella *f* pancake
'crespo **A** *adj* ‹*capelli*› frizzy
B *m* crêpe
'cresta *f* crest; (cima) peak; **abbassare la ~** become less cocky; **alzare la ~** become cocky; **sulla ~ dell'onda** on the crest of a wave
'creta *f* clay
'Creta *f* Crete
cre'tese *adj & nmf* Cretan
creti'nata *f* something stupid; **dire cretinate** talk nonsense
cre'tino, -a **A** *adj* stupid
B *mf* idiot
C.R.I. *abbr* (**Croce Rossa Italiana**) Italian Red Cross
'cribbio *int* gosh!, golly!
cric *m inv* jack
'cricca *f* gang
'cricco *m* jack
cri'ceto *m* hamster
'cricket *m* cricket
crimi'nale *adj & nmf* criminal
criminalità *f inv* crime
■ **criminalità organizzata** organized crime
'crimine *m* crime
criminolo'gia *f* criminology
crimi'nologo, -a *mf* criminologist
crimi'noso *adj* criminal
'crine *m* horsehair
crini'era *f* mane
crino'lina *f* crinoline
crioge'nia *f* cryogenics *sg*
'cripta *f* crypt
crip'tare *vt* encrypt
crisan'temo *m* chrysanthemum
'crisi *f inv* crisis; Med fit; **essere in ~ di astinenza** be having withdrawal symptoms,

C

be cold turkey infml
■ **crisi di nervi** hysterics; **crisi del settimo anno** seven-year itch
cristal'lino **A** *adj* crystal clear
B *m* crystalline lens
C
cristalliz'zare *vt* crystallize
cristalliz'zarsi *vr* crystallize; fig ‹*parola, espressione*› become part of the language
cri'stallo *m* crystal
cristia'nesimo *m* Christianity
cristianità *f inv* Christendom
⚷ **cristi'ano, -a** *adj & nmf* Christian
⚷ **'Cristo** *m* Christ; **avanti** ~ BC; **dopo** ~ AD; **un povero cristo** a poor beggar
cri'terio *m* criterion; (buon senso) [common] sense
'critica *f* criticism; (recensione) review; **fare la** ~ **di** review ‹*film, libro*›
■ **critica letteraria** literary criticism
criti'care *vt* criticize
'critico **A** *adj* critical
B *m* critic
■ **critico letterario** literary critic
criti'cone, -a *mf* fault finder
crittazi'one *f*
■ **crittazione [dei] dati** Comput data encryption
crivel'lare *vt* riddle (**di** with)
cri'vello *m* sieve
cro'ato, -a *adj & nmf* Croatian, Croat
Cro'azia *f* Croatia
croc'cante **A** *adj* crisp
B *m type of crunchy nut biscuit*
croc'chetta *f* croquette
'crocchia *f* bun
'crocchio *m* cluster
⚷ **'croce** *f* cross; **a occhio e** ~ roughly; **fare testa e** ~ toss a coin; **fare** *o* **mettere una** ~ **sopra qualcosa** fig forget about something; **mettere in** ~ (criticare) crucify; (tormentare) nag non-stop
■ **Croce Rossa** Red Cross
croceros'sina *f* Red Cross nurse
croce'via *m inv* crossroads *sg*
croci'ata *f* crusade
croci'ato **A** *adj* cruciform
B *m* crusader
cro'cicchio *m* crossroads *sg*
croci'era *f* cruise; **velocità di** ~ cruising speed
croci'figgere *vt* crucify
crocifissi'one *f* crucifixion
croci'fisso **A** pp di **crocifiggere**
B *adj* crucified
C *m* crucifix
crogio'larsi *vr* bask
crogi'olo *m* crucible; fig melting pot
crogiu'olo = **crogiolo**
crois'sant *m inv* croissant

⚷ key word

crol'lare *vi* collapse; ‹*prezzi*› slump
'crollo *m* collapse; (dei prezzi) slump
'croma *f* quaver
cro'mato *adj* chromium-plated
'cromo *m* chrome
cromo'soma *m* chromosome
'cronaca *f* chronicle; (di giornale) news; TV, Radio commentary; **fatto di** ~ news item
■ **cronaca mondana** gossip column; **cronaca nera** crime news
'cronico *adj* chronic
cro'nista *mf* reporter; (di partita) commentator
croni'storia *f* chronicle
cro'nografo *m* chronograph
cronolo'gia *f* chronology
cronologica'mente *adv* chronologically
crono'logico *adj* chronological
cronome'traggio *m* timing
cronome'trare *vt* time
cronome'trista *mf* Sport timekeeper
cro'nometro *m* chronometer; Sport stopwatch
cross *m* (corsa campestre) cross-country; (motocross) motocross
cros'sista *mf* scrambler; (a piedi) cross-country runner
'crosta *f* crust; (di formaggio) rind; (di ferita) scab; (quadro) daub
cro'staceo *m* shellfish
cro'stata *f* tart
■ **crostata di frutta** fruit tart; **crostata di mele** apple pie
cro'stino *m* crouton; **crostini** *pl pieces of toasted bread served as a starter*
croupi'er *mf inv* croupier
crucci'are *vt* torment
crucci'arsi *vr* torment oneself
'cruccio *m* torment
cruci'ale *adj* crucial
cruci'verba *m inv* crossword [puzzle]
⚷ **cru'dele** *adj* cruel
crudel'mente *adv* cruelly
crudeltà *f inv* cruelty
'crudo *adj* raw; ‹*linguaggio*› crude
cru'ento *adj* bloody
crumi'raggio *m* strike-breaking
cru'miro *m* blackleg, scab
'crusca *f* bran
cru'scotto *m* dashboard
C.S.I. *nf abbr* (**Comunità degli Stati Indipendenti**) CIS
c.t. *abbr* (**commissario tecnico**) Sport team manager
'Cuba *f* Cuba
cu'bano, -a *adj & nmf* Cuban
cu'betto *m*
■ **cubetto di ghiaccio** ice cube
'cubico *adj* cubic
cu'bismo *m* cubism

cu'bista *adj & nmf* cubist
cubi'tale *adj* **a caratteri cubitali** in enormous letters
'cubo *m* cube
cuc'cagna *f* abundance; (baldoria) merry-making; **paese della ~** land of plenty
cuc'cetta *f* (su un treno) couchette; Naut berth
cucchiai'ata *f* spoonful
cucchia'ino *m* teaspoon; (contenuto) teaspoonful
cucchi'aio *m* spoon; **un ~** a spoonful (di of); **al ~** ‹*dolce*› creamy
■ **cucchiaio di legno** wooden spoon; **cucchiaio da minestra** soup spoon; **cucchiaio da tavola** tablespoon; (contenuto) tablespoonful
cucchiai'one *m* serving spoon
'cuccia *f* basket; (in giardino) kennel; **[fa' la] ~!** down!
cuccio'lata *f* litter
'cucciolo *m* puppy
cu'cina *f* kitchen; (il cucinare) cooking; (cibo) food; (apparecchio) cooker; **far da ~** cook; **libro di ~** cookery book
■ **cucina casalinga** home cooking; **cucina componibile** fitted kitchen; **cucina a gas** gas cooker
cuci'nare *vt* cook
cuci'nino *m* kitchenette
cu'cire *vt* sew; **macchina da ~** sewing machine; **cucilo a macchina** do it on the machine
cu'cito *m* sewing
cuci'tura *f* seam
cucù *m inv* cuckoo; **~!** peekaboo!
'cuculo *m* cuckoo
'cuffia *f* bonnet; (ricevitore) headphones *pl*
■ **cuffia da bagno** bathing cap; **cuffia con microfono** (per telefonino) headset
cu'gino, -a *mf* cousin
'cui *pron rel* (persona: con prep) who[m]; (cose, animali: con prep) which; (tra articolo e nome) whose; **la persona con ~ ho parlato** the person I spoke to, the person to whom I spoke fml; **la ditta per ~ lavoro** the company I work for, the company for which I work; **l'amico il ~ libro è stato pubblicato** the friend whose book was published; **in ~** (dove) where; (quando) that; **per ~** (perciò) so; **la città in ~ vivo** the city I live in, the city where I live; **il giorno in ~ l'ho visto** the day [that] I saw him
cu'latta *f* breech
culi'naria *f* cookery
culi'nario *adj* culinary
'culla *f* cradle
cul'lare *vt* rock; fig cherish ‹*sogno, speranza*›
cul'larsi *vr* **~ nella speranza di** (liter) cherish the fond hope that
culmi'nante *adj* culminating
culmi'nare *vi* culminate
'culmine *m* peak
'culo *m* vulg arse; (fortuna) luck; **prendere qualcuno per il ~** take the piss out of somebody
'culto *m* cult; Relig religion; (adorazione) worship
cul'tura *f* culture
■ **cultura generale** general knowledge; **cultura di massa** mass culture
cultu'rale *adj* cultural
cultu'rismo *m* body-building
cultu'rista *mf* body-builder
cu'mino *m*
■ **cumino nero** cumin
cumula'tivo *adj* cumulative; ‹*prezzo*› all-in, all-inclusive; **biglietto ~** group ticket
'cumulo *m* pile; (mucchio) heap; (nuvola) cumulus
'cuneo *m* wedge
cu'netta *f* gutter
cu'nicolo *m* tunnel
cu'ocere **A** *vt* cook; fire ‹*ceramica*› **B** *vi* cook; ‹*ceramica*› fire
cu'oco, -a *mf* cook
cu'oia *fpl* **tirare le ~** infml kick the bucket
cu'oio *m* leather
■ **cuoio capelluto** scalp
cu'ore *m* heart; **cuori** *pl* (carte) hearts; **di [buon] ~** ‹*persona*› kind-hearted; **di tutto ~** wholeheartedly; **ti ringrazio di tutto ~** many thanks; **nel profondo del ~** in one's heart of hearts; **nel ~ della notte** in the middle of the night; **senza ~** heartless; **mettersi il ~ in pace** come to terms with it; **parlare a ~ aperto** have a heart-to-heart (**con** with); **stare a ~ a qualcuno** be very important to somebody
■ **cuore tenero** (persona) softy
cupa'mente *adv* darkly
cupi'digia *f* greed
Cu'pido *m* Cupid
'cupo *adj* gloomy; ‹*voce*› deep
'cupola *f* dome; **a ~** domed
'cura *f* care; (amministrazione) management; Med treatment; **aver ~ di** look after; **a ~ di** ‹*libro*› edited by; **in ~** under treatment; **fare delle cure termali** take the waters
■ **cura dimagrante** diet; **cura della fertilità** fertility treatment
cu'rabile *adj* curable
cu'rante *adj* **medico ~** GP, doctor
cu'rare *vt* take care of, look after; Med treat; (guarire) cure; edit ‹*testo*›
cu'rarsi *vr* take care of oneself, look after oneself; **~ dei fatti propri** mind one's own business
cu'rato *m* parish priest
cura|'tore, -trice *mf* trustee; (di testo) editor
■ **curatore fallimentare** official receiver
'curcuma *f* turmeric
curcu'mina *f* turmeric

c d

'**curdo**, **-a** **A** *mf* Kurd **B** *adj* Kurdish
'**curia** *f* curia
curio'saggine *f* nosiness
curio'sare *vi* be curious; (mettere il naso) pry (in into); (nei negozi) look around
✓ **curiosità** *f inv* curiosity
✓ **curi'oso** **A** *adj* curious; (strano) odd, curious **B** *m* busybody
'**curling** *m inv* Sport curling
cur'ricolo *m* curriculum
cur'riculum *m inv* curriculum
'**curry** *m inv* curry
■ **curry in polvere** curry powder
cur'sore *m* Comput cursor
✓ '**curva** *f* curve; (stradale) bend
■ **curva a gomito** dog-leg; **curva di apprendimento** learning curve
cur'vare *vt & vi* bend, curve
cur'varsi *vr* bend, curve
✓ '**curvo** *adj* curved; (piegato) bent
cusci'netto *m* pad; Mech bearing
■ **cuscinetto puntaspilli** pincushion; **cuscinetto a sfere** ball bearing
cu'scino *m* cushion; (guanciale) pillow
■ **cuscino gonfiabile** air cushion
cu'scus *m inv* couscous
'**cuspide** *f* spire
✓ **cu'stode** *m* caretaker; (di abitazione) concierge; (di fabbrica) guard; (di museo) custodian
■ **~ giudiziario** official receiver
✓ **cu'stodia** *f* care; Jur custody; (astuccio) case; **ottenere la ~ di** get custody of
■ **custodia cautelare** remand
custo'dire *vt* keep; (badare) look after
cu'taneo *adj* skin *attrib*
'**cute** *f* skin
cu'ticola *f* cuticle
'**cutter** *m inv* cutter
CV *abbr* (**cavallo vapore**) hp
cyber'spazio *m* cyberspace
cyberterro'rismo *m* cyberterrorism
cy'clette® *f inv* exercise bicycle

Dd

✓ **da** *prep* from; (con verbo passivo) by; (moto a luogo) to; (moto per luogo) through; (stato in luogo) at; (temporale) since; (continuativo) for; (causale) with; (in qualità di) as; (con caratteristica) with; (come) like; **da Roma a Milano** from Rome to Milan; **staccare un quadro dalla parete** take a picture off the wall; **i bambini dai 5 ai 10 anni** children between 5 and 10; **vedere qualcosa da vicino/lontano** see something from up close/from a distance; **amato da tutti** loved by everybody; **scritto da** written by; **andare dal panettiere** go to the baker's; **passo da te più tardi** I'll come over to your place later; **passiamo da qui** let's go this way; **un appuntamento dal dentista** an appointment at the dentist's; **il treno passa da Venezia** the train goes through Venice; **dall'anno scorso** since last year; **vivo qui da due anni** I've been living here for two years; **da domani** from tomorrow; **piangere dal dolore** cry with pain; **ho molto da fare** I have a lot to do; **occhiali da sole** sunglasses; **qualcosa da mangiare** something to eat; **un uomo dai capelli scuri** a man with dark hair; **è un oggetto da poco** it's not worth much; **da solo** alone; **l'ho fatto da solo** I did it by myself; **si è fatto da sé** he is a self-made man; **vive da re** he lives like a king; **non è da lui** it's not like him
dab'bene *adj* honest
dac'capo *adv* again; (dall'inizio) from the beginning
dacché *conj* since
dada'ismo *m* (arte) Dadaism
dada'ista *adj & nmf* Dadaist
'**dado** *m* dice; Culin stock cube; Techn nut
■ **dado ad alette** wing nut
daf'fare *m* work
'**dagli** = da + gli
dai[1] = da + i
dai[2] *int* come on!; **~, non fare così!** come on, don't be like that!; **~, sbrigati!** come on, get a move on!
'**daino** *m* deer; (pelle) buckskin
dal = da + il
'**dalia** *f* dahlia
'**dalla** = da + la A, B
'**dalle** = da + le
'**dallo** = da + lo
'**dalmata** *m* (cane) Dalmatian
Dal'mazia *f* Dalmatia
dal'tonico *adj* colour-blind

✓ key word

'dama *f* lady; (nei balli) partner; (gioco) draughts
■ **dama di compagnia** lady's companion; **dama di corte** lady-in-waiting

dama'scato *adj* damask

da'masco *m* (tessuto) damask

dame'rino *m* (bellimbusto) dandy

dami'gella *f* (di sposa) bridesmaid

damigi'ana *f* demijohn

dam'meno *adv* **non essere ~** be no less good (**di** than)

DAMS *nm abbr* (**Discipline delle Arti, della Musica e dello Spettacolo**) (corso di laurea) *degree in fine art, music and drama*

da'naro = **denaro**

dana'roso *adj* infml (ricco) loaded

da'nese **A** *adj* Danish
B *mf* Dane
C *m* (lingua) Danish

Dani'marca *f* Denmark

dan'nare *vt* damn; **far ~ qualcuno** drive somebody mad

dan'narsi *vr* fig wear oneself out; **~ l'anima (a fare qualcosa)** wear oneself out (doing something)

dan'nato, -a **A** *adj* damned, damn infml
B *mf* damned person; **lavorare/studiare come un ~** fig work/study like mad

dannazi'one *f* damnation

danneggia'mento *m* damage

danneggi'are *vt* damage; (nuocere) harm

danneggi'ato *adj* Jur injured

'danno *m* damage; (a persona) harm; **danni** *pl* damage; **danni collaterali** collateral damage; **danni** *pl* **alla struttura portante** structural damage

dan'noso *adj* harmful

dan'tesco *adj* Dantean, Dantesque

danubi'ano *adj* Danubian

Da'nubio *m* Danube

'danza *f* dance; (il danzare) dancing
■ **~ folcloristica** country dancing

dan'zante *adj* **serata ~** dance

dan'zare *vi* dance

danza|'tore, -trice *mf* dancer
■ **danzatrice del ventre** belly dancer

dapper'tutto *adv* everywhere

dap'poco *adj* worthless

dap'prima *adv* at first

Darda'nelli *mpl* **i ~** the Dardanelles

'dardo *m* dart

'dare **A** *vt* give; sit ‹*esame*›; have ‹*festa*›; **~ qualcosa a qualcuno** give somebody something; **~ da mangiare a qualcuno** give somebody something to eat; **~ fuoco a qualcosa** set fire to something; **~ il benvenuto a qualcuno** welcome somebody; **~ la buonanotte a qualcuno** say good night to somebody; **~ del tu/del lei a qualcuno** address somebody as "tu/lei"; **~ del cretino a qualcuno** call somebody an idiot; **~ qualcosa per scontato** take something for granted; **~ fastidio a** annoy; **~ cosa danno alla TV stasera?** what's on TV tonight?; **darle a qualcuno** (picchiare) give somebody a walloping
B *vi* **~ nell'occhio** be conspicuous; **~ alla testa** go to one's head; **~ su** ‹*finestra, casa*› look on to; **~ sui** *o* **ai nervi a qualcuno** get on somebody's nerves
C *m* Comm debit

'darsena *f* dock

'darsi *vr* (scambiarsi) give each other; **~ da fare** get down to it; **si è dato tanto da fare!** he went to so much trouble!; **~ a** (cominciare) take up; **~ al bere** take to drink; **~ per** ‹*malato*› pretend to be; **~ per vinto** give up; **può ~** maybe

darwini'ano *adj* Darwinian

darwi'nista *mf* Darwinist

'data *f* date; **di lunga ~** old established
■ **data di emissione** date of issue; **data di nascita** date of birth; **data di scadenza** expiry date; (su alimenti) best before date

data'base *m inv* database
■ **database relazionale** relational database

da'tabile *adj* datable

da'tare *vt* date; **a ~ da** as from

da'tario *m* (su orologio) calendar

da'tato *adj* dated

da'tivo *m* dative

'dato **A** *adj* given; (dedito) addicted; **~ che** seeing that, given that
B *m* datum; **dati** *pl* data
■ **dato di fatto** well established fact; **dati sensibili** sensitive data

da'tore *m* giver
■ **datore di lavoro** employer

'dattero *m* date

dattilogra'fare *vt & vi* type; **~ a tastiera cieca** touch-type

dattilogra'fia *f* typing
■ **dattilografia a tastiera cieca** touch-typing

datti'lografo, -a *mf* typist

dattilo'scritto *adj* ‹*copia*› typewritten, typed

dat'torno *adv* **togliersi ~** clear off

da'vanti **A** *adv* before; (dirimpetto) opposite; (di fronte) in front
B *adj inv* front
C *m* front; **~ di dietro** ‹*maglia*› back-to-front; **~ a** *prep* before, in front of; **passare ~ a** pass, go past

davan'zale *m* window sill

dav'vero *adv* really; **per ~** in earnest; **dici ~?** honestly?

dazi'ario *adj* excise

'dazio *m* duty; (ufficio) customs *pl*
■ **dazi doganali** *pl* customs duties; **dazio**

d'importazione import duty
d.C. *abbr* (**dopo Cristo**) AD
D.C. *nf abbr* (**Democrazia Cristiana**) Christian Democratic Party
D.D.T. *m* (insetticida) DDT
'dea *f* goddess
deambula'torio *adj* ambulatory
debel'lare *vt* defeat
debili'tante *adj* weakening
debili'tare *vt* weaken
debili'tarsi *vr* become debilitated
debilitazi'one *f* debilitation
debita'mente *adv* duly
🔑 **'debito** **A** *adj* due; **a tempo ~** in due course
B *m* debt
■ **debito pubblico** national debt
debi|'tore, -trice *mf* debtor
🔑 **'debole** **A** *adj* weak; ‹*luce*› dim; ‹*suono*› faint
B *m* weak point; **avere un ~ per qualcuno** have a soft spot for somebody; **avere un ~ per qualcosa** have a weakness for something
debo'lezza *f* weakness
debor'dare *vi* overflow
debosci'ato *adj* debauched
debrai'ata *f* Auto declutching
debut'tante **A** *adj* beginner
B *mf* beginner; (attore) actor/actress making his/her debut
debut'tare *vi* make one's debut
de'butto *m* début
'decade *f* period of ten days
deca'dente *adj* decadent
decaden'tismo *m* decadence
deca'denza *f* decline; Jur loss
deca'dere *vi* lapse
decadi'mento *m* (delle arti) decline
deca'duto *adj* ‹*persona*› impoverished; ‹*decreto, norma*› no longer in force
decaffei'nato **A** *adj* decaffeinated
B *m* decaffeinated coffee, decaf infml
deca'grammo *m* decagram
decal'care *vt* trace
decalcifi'carsi *vr* become brittle
decalcificazi'one *f* (condizione) brittle bones
decalcoma'nia *f* transfer
de'calitro *m* decalitre
de'calogo *m* fig rule book
de'cametro *m* decametre
de'cano *m* dean
decan'tare *vt* (lodare) praise
decapi'tare *vt* decapitate; behead ‹*condannato*›
decapitazi'one *f* decapitation; beheading
decappot'tabile *adj* convertible
decappot'tare *vt* take down the hood of

🔑 key word

'decathlon *m inv* decathlon
de'cedere *vi* (morire) die
dece'duto *adj* deceased
decele'rare *vt & vi* slow down, decelerate
decelerazi'one *f* deceleration
decen'nale **A** *adj* ten-yearly
B *m* (anniversario) tenth anniversary
de'cenne *adj* ‹*bambino*› ten year-old
de'cennio *m* decade
de'cente *adj* decent
decente'mente *adv* decently
decentraliz'zare *vt* decentralize
decentra'mento *m* decentralization
decen'trare *vt* decentralize
de'cenza *f* decency
de'cesso *m* death, decease fml; **atto di ~** death certificate
'decibel *m inv* decibel
🔑 **de'cidere** *vt* decide; settle ‹*questione*›
de'cidersi *vr* make up one's mind
deci'frabile *adj* decipherable
deci'frare *vt* decipher; (documenti cifrati) decode
decifrazi'one *f* deciphering
de'cigrado *m* tenth of a degree
deci'grammo *m* decigram
de'cilitro *m* decilitre
deci'male *adj* decimal
deci'mare *vt* decimate
de'cimetro *m* decimetre
'decimo *adj & nm* tenth
🔑 **de'cina** *f* Math ten; **una ~ di** (circa dieci) about ten
decisa'mente *adv* definitely, decidedly
decisio'nale *adj* decision-making
🔑 **decisi'one** *f* decision; **prendere una ~** make *or* take a decision; **con ~** decisively
decisio'nismo *m tendency to make decisions without consulting others*
decisio'nista *mf person who does not consult others before making decisions*
deci'sivo *adj* decisive
de'ciso **A** pp di **decidere**
B *adj* decided
decla'mare *vt & vi* declaim
declama'torio *adj* ‹*stile*› declamatory
declas'sare *vt* downgrade
decli'nabile *adj* Gram declinable; ‹*offerta*› that can be refused
decli'nare **A** *vt* decline; turn down, refuse ‹*invito*›; **~ ogni responsabilità** disclaim all responsibility
B *vi* go down; (tramontare) set
declinazi'one *f* Gram declension
de'clino *m* decline; **in ~** ‹*popolarità*› on the decline
de'clivio *m* downward slope
dé'co *adj inv* Art Deco
de'coder *m inv* TV set-top box

deco'difica *f* decoding
decodifi'care *vt* decode
decodifica'tore *m* TV descrambler
decodificazi'one *f* decoding
decol'lare *vi* take off
décolle'té **A** *adj inv* low cut
B *m inv* low neckline
de'collo *m* take-off
decolonizzazi'one *f* decolonization
decolo'rante *m* bleach
decolo'rare *vt* bleach
decolorazi'one *f* bleaching
decom'porre *vt* decompose
decom'porsi *vr* decompose
decomposizi'one *f* decomposition
decompressi'one *f* decompression
decom'primere *vt* decompress
deconcen'trarsi *vr* become distracted
deconge'lare *vt* defrost
decongestio'nare *vt* Med fig relieve congestion in
decontami'nare *vt* Techn decontaminate
decontaminazi'one *f* decontamination
decontrazi'one *f* relaxation
deco'rare *vt* decorate
decora'tivo *adj* decorative
deco'rato *adj* (ornato) decorated
decora|'tore, -trice *mf* decorator
decorazi'one *f* decoration
■ **decorazione floreale** flower arranging
de'coro *m* decorum
decorosa'mente *adv* decorously
deco'roso *adj* dignified
decor'renza *f* ~ **dal** ... with effect from ..., effective ...
de'correre *vi* pass; **a ~ da** with effect from
de'corso **A** pp di **decorrere**
B *m* passing; Med course
decre'mento *m* decrease
de'crepito *adj* decrepit
decre'scente *adj* decreasing
de'crescere *vi* decrease; ‹*prezzi*› go down; ‹*acque*› subside
decre'tare *vt* decree; **~ lo stato d'emergenza** declare a state of emergency
de'creto *m* decree
■ **decreto ingiuntivo** decree; **decreto legge** *decree which has the force of law*; **decreto legislativo** *decree requiring the approval of Parliament*
decre'tone *m* Pol portmanteau bill
de'cubito *m*
■ **piaghe da decubito** bedsores
decur'tare *vt* reduce
decurtazi'one *f* reduction
'dedalo *m* maze
'dedica *f* dedication
dedi'care *vt* dedicate
dedi'carsi *vr* dedicate oneself
'dedito *adj* ~ a given to; (assorto) engrossed in; addicted to ‹*vizi*›
dedizi'one *f* dedication
de'dotto **A** pp di **dedurre**
B *adj* deduced
dedu'cibile *adj* ‹*tassa*› allowable
de'durre *vt* deduce; (sottrarre) deduct
dedut'tivo *adj* deductive
deduzi'one *f* deduction
défail'lance *f inv* (cedimento) collapse
defal'care *vt* deduct
defalcazi'one *f* deduction
defe'care *vi* defecate
defecazi'one *f* defecation
defene'strare *vt* fig remove from office
defe'rente *adj* deferential
defe'renza *f* deference
deferi'mento *m* referral
defe'rire *vt* Jur remit
defezio'nare *vi* (abbandonare) defect
defezi'one *f* defection
defezio'nista *mf* defector
defici'ente **A** *adj* (mancante) deficient; Med mentally deficient
B *mf* mental defective; derog half-wit
defici'enza *f* deficiency; (lacuna) gap; Med mental deficiency
'deficit *m inv* deficit, shortfall; **essere in ~** be in deficit
defici'tario *adj* ‹*bilancio*› deficit *attrib*; ‹*sviluppo*› insufficient
defi'larsi *vr* (scomparire) slip away; **~ da qualcosa** sneak away from something
défi'lé *m inv* fashion show
defi'nibile *adj* definable; **~ dall'utente** Comput user-definable
defi'nire *vt* define; (risolvere) settle
definitiva'mente *adv* for good
defini'tivo *adj* definitive
defi'nito *adj* definite
definizi'one *f* definition; (soluzione) settlement
defiscaliz'zare *vt* abolish the tax on
defiscalizzazi'one *f* abolition of tax
defla'grare *vt* (esplodere) explode
deflagrazi'one *f* (esplosione) explosion
deflazio'nare *vt* deflate
deflazi'one *f* deflation
deflazio'nistico *adj* deflationary
deflet'tore *m* Auto quarter light
deflu'ire *vi* ‹*liquidi*› flow away; ‹*persone*› stream out
de'flusso *m* (di marea) ebb
defogli'ante **A** *adj* defoliating
B *m* defoliant
deforestazi'one *f* deforestation
defor'mante *adj* **artrite ~** acute arthritis
defor'mare *vt* deform ‹*arto*›; fig distort
defor'marsi *vr* lose its shape

d

defor'mato *adj* warped
deformazi'one *f* (di fatti) distortion; **è una ~ professionale** put it down to the job
de'forme *adj* deformed
deformità *f inv* deformity
deframmen'tare *vt* defragment; infml defrag
defrau'dare *vt* defraud
de'funto, -a *adj & nmf* deceased
degene'rare *vi* degenerate
degenera'tivo *adj* ‹*processo*› degenerative
degene'rato *adj* degenerate
degenerazi'one *f* degeneration
de'genere *adj* degenerate
de'gente **A** *adj* bedridden
B *mf* patient
de'genza *f* confinement
■ **degenza ospedaliera** stay in hospital
'degli = di + gli
deglu'tire *vt* swallow
deglutizi'one *f* swallowing
de'gnare *vt* **~ qualcuno/qualcosa di uno sguardo** deign *or* condescend to look at somebody/something
de'gnarsi *vr* deign, condescend
'degno *adj* worthy; (meritevole) deserving
■ **degno di lode** praiseworthy; **degno di nota** noteworthy
degrada'mento *m* degradation
degra'dante *adj* demeaning
degra'dare *vt* degrade
degra'darsi *vr* lower oneself; ‹*città*› fall into a state of disrepair
degradazi'one *f* degradation
de'grado *m* deterioration
■ **degrado ambientale** environmental damage; **degrado urbano** urban blight, urban decay
degu'stare *vt* taste
degustazi'one *f* tasting
■ **degustazione di vini** wine tasting
'dei = di + i
deindiciz'zare *vt* de-index
déjà vu *m inv* déjà vu
del = di + il
dela'tore, -trice *mf* [police] informer
delazi'one *f* informing
'delega *f* proxy; **legge ~** *law that does not require Parliamentary approval*
dele'gante *mf* Jur representative
dele'gare *vt* delegate
dele'gato *m* delegate
delegazi'one *f* delegation
delegitti'mare *vt* delegitimize
dele'terio *adj* harmful
del'fino *m* dolphin; (stile di nuoto) butterfly [stroke]; **nuotare a ~** do the butterfly
de'libera *f* by-law

delibe'rante *adj* ‹*organo*› decision making
delibe'rare *vt & vi* deliberate; **~ su/in** rule on/in
deliberata'mente *adv* deliberately
delibe'rato *adj* (intenzionale) deliberate
delicata'mente *adv* delicately
delica'tezza *f* delicacy; (fragilità) frailty; (tatto) tact
deli'cato *adj* delicate; ‹*salute*› frail; ‹*suono, colore*› soft
delimi'tare *vt* define
delimita'tivo *adj* defining
delimitazi'one *f* definition
deline'are *vt* outline
deline'arsi *vr* be outlined; fig take shape
deline'ato *adj* outlined
delineazi'one *f* outline
delinqu'ente *mf* delinquent
■ **delinquente minorile** young offender; **delinquente recidivo** habitual offender
delinqu'enza *f* delinquency
■ **delinquenza minorile** juvenile crime
delinquenzi'ale *adj* criminal
de'linquere *vi* commit a criminal act; **associazione per ~** conspiracy [to commit a crime]; **istigazione a ~** incitement to crime
de'liquio *m* **cadere in ~** swoon
deli'rante *adj* Med delirious; (assurdo) insane; (sfrenato) frenzied
deli'rare *vi* be delirious
de'lirio *m* delirium; fig frenzy; **mandare/andare in ~** fig send/go into a frenzy
de'litto *m* crime
■ **delitto passionale** crime of passion
delittu'oso *adj* criminal
de'lizia *f* delight
delizi'are *vt* delight
delizi'arsi *vr* **~ di** delight in
delizi'oso *adj* delightful; (cibo) delicious
'della = di + la **A, B**
'delle = di + le
'dello = di + lo
'delta *m inv* delta
delta'plano *m* hang-glider; **fare ~** go hang-gliding
deluci'dare *vt* fig clarify
delucidazi'one *f* clarification
delu'dente *adj* disappointing
de'ludere *vt* disappoint
delusi'one *f* disappointment
de'luso *adj* disappointed; **essere ~ di qualcosa/qualcuno** be disillusioned with something/somebody
dema'gogico *adj* popularity-seeking, demagogic
dema'gogo *m* demagogue
deman'dare *vt* entrust

key word

demani'ale *adj* ‹*proprietà*› government *attrib*
de'manio *m* government property
demar'care *vt* demarcate
demarcazi'one *f* demarcation; **linea di ~** demarcation line
de'mente *adj* demented
de'menza *f* dementia
■ **demenza senile** senile dementia
demenzi'ale *adj* (assurdo) zany
de'merito *m* **nota di ~** demerit mark
demilitariz'zare *vt* demilitarize
demilitarizzazi'one *f* demilitarization
demistifi'care *vt* debunk
demistifica|'tore, -trice *mf* debunker
demistifica'torio *adj* debunking
demistificazi'one *f* debunking
demitiz'zare *vt* demythologize
demitizzazi'one *f* demythologization
democratica'mente *adv* democratically
demo'cratico *adj* democratic
democratiz'zare *vt* democratize
democra'zia *f* democracy
democristi'ano, -a *adj & nmf* Christian Democrat
'demodisk *m inv* Comput demo disk
demogra'fia *f* demography
demo'grafico *adj* demographic; **incremento ~** increase in population
demo'lire *vt* demolish
demo'lito *adj* demolished
demolizi'one *f* demolition
'demone *m* demon
demo'niaco *adj* demonic
de'monio *m* demon
demoniz'zare *vt* demonize
demonizzazi'one *f* demonization
demoraliz'zante *adj* demoralizing
demoraliz'zare *vt* demoralize
demoraliz'zarsi *vr* become demoralized
demoraliz'zato *adj* demoralized
de'mordere *vi* give up
demoti'vare *vt* demotivate
demoti'varsi *vr* become demotivated
demoti'vato *adj* demotivated
demotivazi'one *f* demotivation
de'nari *mpl* (nelle carte) diamonds
🔑 **de'naro** *m* money
■ **denaro virtuale** e-cash
denatu'rato *adj* **alcol ~** methylated spirits
denazionaliz'zare *vt* denationalize
deni'grare *vt* denigrate
denigra|'tore, -trice **A** *adj* denigrating **B** *mf* denigrator
denigra'torio *adj* denigratory
denigrazi'one *f* denigration
denomi'nare *vt* name
denomi'narsi *vr* be named
denomina'tivo *adj* denominative
denomina'tore *m* denominator
denominazi'one *f* denomination
■ **denominazione di origine controllata** *mark guaranteeing the quality of a wine*
deno'tare *vt* denote
denotazi'one *f* denotation
densa'mente *adv* densely
densità *f inv* density
■ **ad alta/bassa densità di popolazione** densely/sparsely populated
'denso *adj* thick, dense
den'tale *adj* dental
den'tario *adj* dental
den'tata *f* bite
den'tato *adj* ‹*lama*› serrated
denta'tura *f* teeth *pl*; Techn serration
🔑 **'dente** *m* tooth; (di forchetta) prong; (di montagna) jagged peak; **al ~** Culin just slightly firm; **lavarsi i denti** brush one's teeth
■ **dente del giudizio** wisdom tooth; **dente da latte** milk tooth; **dente di leone** Bot dandelion
'dentice *m* dentex (*type of sea bream*)
denti'era *f* dentures *pl*, false teeth *pl*; **mettersi la ~** put one's false teeth in
denti'fricio *m* toothpaste
den'tista *mf* dentist
🔑 **'dentro** **A** *adv* in, inside; (in casa) indoors; **da ~** from within; **qui ~** in here; **metter ~** infml (in prigione) lock up, put inside **B** *prep* in, inside; (di tempo) within, by **C** *m* inside
denucleariz'zare *vt* denuclearize
denucleariz'zato *adj* nuclear-free, denuclearized
denuclearizzazi'one *f* denuclearization
denu'dare *vt* bare
denu'darsi *vr* strip
de'nuncia *f* denunciation; (alla polizia) reporting; **fare una ~** draw up a report
■ **denuncia dei redditi** income tax return
🔑 **denunci'are** *vt* denounce; (accusare) report
de'nunzia = **denuncia**
denu'trito *adj* underfed
denutrizi'one *f* malnutrition
deodo'rante *adj & nm* deodorant
■ **deodorante antitraspirante** antiperspirant; **deodorante per ambienti** air freshener; **deodorante a sfera** roll-on
deodo'rare *vt* deodorize
deontolo'gia *f* (etica professionale) code of conduct
depenaliz'zare *vt* decriminalize
depenalizzazi'one *f* decriminalization
dépen'dance *f inv* outbuilding
depe'ribile *adj* perishable
deperi'mento *m* wasting away; (di merci) deterioration
depe'rire *vi* waste away

d

depe'rito *adj* wasted
depi'lare *vt* depilate
depi'larsi *vr* shave ‹*gambe*›; pluck ‹*sopracciglia*›
depila'tore **A** *adj* depilatory **B** *m* (apparecchio) hair remover
depila'torio *m* depilatory
depilazi'one *f* hair removal
■ **depilazione diatermica** electrolysis
depi'staggio *m* fig diversionary manoeuvre
depi'stare *vt* fig throw off the track
dépli'ant *m inv* brochure, leaflet
deplo'rabile *adj* deplorable
deplo'rare *vt* deplore; (dolersi di) grieve over
deplo'revole *adj* deplorable
depoliticiz'zare *vt* depoliticize
de'porre *vt* put down; lay down ‹*armi*›; lay ‹*uova*›; (togliere da una carica) depose; (testimoniare) testify
depor'tare *vt* deport
depor'tato, -a *mf* deportee
deportazi'one *f* deportation
deposi'tante *mf* Fin depositor
deposi'tare *vt* Fin deposit; (lasciare in custodia) leave; (in magazzino) store
deposi'tario, -a *mf* (di segreto) repository
deposi'tarsi *vr* settle
de'posito *m* deposit; (luogo) warehouse; Mil depot
■ **deposito d'armi** arms dump; **deposito bagagli** left luggage office, baggage checkroom AmE; **deposito bagagli automatico** left luggage lockers; **deposito bancario** deposit account; **deposito bancario vincolato** fixed term deposit account
deposizi'one *f* deposition; (da una carica) removal
de'posto *adj* deposed
depotenzi'are *vt* weaken
depra'vare *vt* deprave
depra'vato *adj* depraved
depravazi'one *f* depravity
depre'cabile *adj* appalling
depre'care *vt* deprecate
depre'dare *vt* plunder
depressio'nario *adj* **area depressionaria** Metereol area of low pressure
depressi'one *f* depression; **area di depressione** Metereol area of low pressure; Econ depressed area
depres'sivo *adj* depressive
de'presso **A** pp di **deprimere** **B** *adj* depressed
depressuriz'zare *vt* depressurize
depressurizzazi'one *f* depressurization
deprezza'mento *m* depreciation
deprez'zare *vt* depreciate
deprez'zarsi *vr* depreciate
depri'mente *adj* depressing
de'primere *vt* depress
de'primersi *vr* get depressed
deprivazi'one *f* deprivation
depu'rare *vt* purify
depu'rarsi *vr* be purified
depura'tore *m* purifier
depurazi'one *f* purification; (di detriti) effluent
depu'tare *vt* delegate
depu'tato, -a *mf* ≈ Member of Parliament, MP
deputazi'one *f* deputation
dequalifi'care *vt* disqualify
dequalifi'carsi *vr* disqualify oneself
dequalificazi'one *f* disqualification
deraglia'mento *m* derailment
deragli'are *vi* go off the lines; **far ~** derail
deraglia'tore *m* derailleur gears *pl*
dera'pare *vi* Auto skid; ‹*sciatore*› side-slip
derattiz'zare *vt* clear of rats
derattizzazi'one *f* rodent control
'derby *m inv* Sport local derby
deregolamen'tare *vt* Comm deregulate
deregolamentazi'one *f* deregulation
dere'litto *adj* derelict
deresponsabiliz'zare *vt* deprive of responsibility
deresponsabiliz'zarsi *vr* abdicate responsibility
deresponsabilizzazi'one *f* depriving of responsibility
dere'tano *m* backside, bottom
de'ridere *vt* deride
derisi'one *f* derision
deri'sorio *adj* derisory
de'riva *f* drift; **andare alla ~** drift
deri'vabile *adj* derivable
deri'vare **A** *vi* **~ da** (provenire) derive from **B** *vt* derive; (sviare) divert
deri'vata *f* Math derivative
deri'vato **A** *adj* derived **B** *m* by-product
derivazi'one *f* derivation; (di fiume) diversion
derma'tite *f* dermatitis
dermatolo'gia *f* dermatology
dermato'logico *adj* dermatological
derma'tologo, -a *mf* dermatologist
derma'tosi *f* dermatosis
dermoprotet'tivo *adj* ‹*crema*› skin *attrib*; ‹*azione*› protective
'deroga *f* dispensation
dero'gare *vi* **~ a** depart from
deroga'torio *adj* derogatory
der'rata *f* merchandise
■ **derrate alimentari** *pl* foodstuffs
deru'bare *vt* rob
deru'bato *adj* robbed

desaliniz'zare *vt* desalinate
desalinizzazi'one *f* desalination
desapare'cido *mf* (*pl* ~**s**) disappeared man/woman, desaparecido
descolarizzazi'one *f* deschooling
descrit'tivo *adj* descriptive
de'scritto pp di **descrivere**
de'scrivere *vt* describe
descri'vibile *adj* describable
descrizi'one *f* description
desensibiliz'zare *vt* desensitize
desensibilizzazi'one *f* desensitization
de'sertico *adj* desert
de'serto **A** *adj* uninhabited
B *m* desert
deside'rabile *adj* desirable
deside'rare *vt* wish; (volere) want; (intensamente) long for; (bramare) desire; **desidera?** what would you like?, can I help you?; **lasciare a** ~ leave a lot to be desired
deside'rato *adj* intended
desi'derio *m* wish; (brama) desire; (intenso) longing
deside'roso *adj* desirous; (bramoso) longing
desi'gnare *vt* appoint, designate; (fissare) fix
desi'gnato *adj* designate *attrib*
designazi'one *f* appointment
de'signer *mf inv* designer
desi'nare **A** *vi* dine
B *m* dinner
desi'nenza *f* ending
de'sistere *vi* ~ **da** desist from
'desktop 'publishing *m inv* desktop publishing, DTP
deso'lante *adj* distressing
deso'lare *vt* distress
deso'lato *adj* desolate; (spiacente) sorry; **siamo desolati di dovervi comunicare che ...** (in lettere) we are sorry to have to inform you that ...
desolazi'one *f* desolation
'despota *m* despot
desqua'marsi *vr* flake off
desquamazi'one *f* flaking off
destabiliz'zante *adj* destabilizing
destabiliz'zare *vt* destabilize
destabilizzazi'one *f* destabilization
de'stare *vt* waken; fig awaken
de'starsi *vr* waken; fig awaken
desti'nare *vt* destine; (nominare) appoint; (assegnare) assign; (indirizzare) address
destina'tario *m* (di lettera, pacco) addressee
desti'nato *adj* **essere ~ a fare qualcosa** be destined *or* fated to do something
destinazi'one *f* destination; fig purpose; **con ~ Parigi** ‹*aereo, treno*› destined for Paris
de'stino *m* destiny; (fato) fate
destitu'ire *vt* dismiss
destitu'ito *adj* ~ **di** devoid of
destituzi'one *f* dismissal
'desto *adj* (liter) awake
'destra *f* (parte) right; (mano) right hand; **prendere a** ~ turn right; **a** ~ ‹*essere*› on the right; ‹*andare*› to the right; **la prima a** ~ the first on the right; **sulla** ~ on the right-hand side; **di** ~ Pol right wing; **la** ~ Pol the Right
destreggi'are *vi* manoeuvre
destreggi'arsi *vr* manoeuvre
de'strezza *f* dexterity; (abilità) skill
'destro *adj* right; (abile) skilful
de'stroide *adj* Pol right-wing
destruttu'rato *adj* (incoerente) unstructured
desu'eto *adj* obsolete
de'sumere *vt* (congetturare) infer; (ricavare) obtain
desu'mibile *adj* inferable
detas'sare *vt* abolish the tax on
detassazi'one *f* abolition of tax
detei'nato *adj* tannin free
dete'nere *vt* hold; ‹*polizia*› detain
deten'tivo *adj* **pena detentiva** custodial sentence
deten|'tore, -trice *mf* holder
▪ **detentore del titolo** title-holder
dete'nuto, -a *mf* prisoner
detenzi'one *f* detention
deter'gente **A** *adj* cleaning; ‹*latte, crema*› cleansing
B *m* detergent; (per la pelle) cleanser
deteriora'mento *m* deterioration
deterio'rare *vt* cause to deteriorate ‹*cibo, relazione*›
deterio'rarsi *vr* deteriorate
determi'nabile *adj* determinable
determinabilità *f inv* determinability
determi'nante *adj* decisive
determi'nare *vt* determine
determi'narsi *vr* ~ **a** resolve to
determina'tezza *f* determination
determina'tivo *adj* ‹*articolo*› definite; **pronome** ~ determiner
determi'nato *adj* (risoluto) determined; (particolare) specific; (stabilito) certain
determinazi'one *f* determination; (decisione) decision
determi'nismo *m* determinism
deter'rente *adj & nm* deterrent
deter'sivo *m* detergent
▪ **detersivo biologico** biological powder; **detersivo per bucato** washing powder; **detersivo per i piatti** washing-up liquid, dishwashing liquid AmE
dete'stare *vt* detest, hate
dete'starsi *vr* hate oneself
deto'nare *vi* detonate
detona'tore *m* detonator

detonazi'one *f* detonation
detra'ibile *adj* deductible
de'trarre *vt* deduct (**da** from)
de'tratto **A** pp di **detrarre**
B *adj* deducted
detrat|'tore, -trice *mf* detractor
detrazi'one *f* deduction; (da tasse) tax allowance
detri'mento *m* detriment; **a ~ di** to the detriment of
de'trito *m* debris; **detriti** *pl* (di fiume) detritus
▪ **detrito di falda** scree
detroniz'zare *vt* dethrone
'detta *f* **a ~ di** according to
dettagli'ante *mf* Comm retailer
dettagli'are *vt* detail
dettagliata'mente *adv* in detail
det'taglio *m* detail; **al ~** Comm retail
det'tame *m* dictate; **i dettami della moda** the dictates of fashion
det'tare *vt* dictate; **~ legge** fig lay down the law
det'tato *m* Sch dictation
detta'tura *f* dictation
'detto **A** *adj* said; (chiamato) called; (soprannominato) nicknamed; **~ fatto** no sooner said than done
B *m* **~ [popolare]** saying
detur'pare *vt* disfigure
deturpazi'one *f* disfigurement
deumidifi'care *vt* dehumidify
deumidifica'tore *m* dehumidifier
deumidificazi'one *f* dehumidification
devalutazi'one *f* devaluation
deva'stante *adj* devastating
deva'stare *vt* devastate
deva'stato *adj* devastated
devasta|'tore, -trice **A** *adj* destructive; fig devastating
B *mf* destroyer
devastazi'one *f* devastation; fig ravages *pl*
devi'ante *adj* deviant
devi'anza *f* deviance
devi'are **A** *vi* deviate
B *vt* divert
devi'ato *adj* ‹*mente*› warped
deviazi'one *f* deviation; (stradale) diversion; **fare una ~** Auto make a detour
devitaliz'zare *vt* kill the nerve of, devitalize fml
devitalizzazi'one *f* killing of the nerve, devitalization fml
devo'luto **A** pp di **devolvere**
B *adj* devolved
devoluzi'one *f* devolution
de'volvere *vt* devolve; **~ qualcosa in beneficenza** give something to charity
devota'mente *adv* devoutly

⚷ key word

de'voto *adj* devout; (affezionato) devoted
devozi'one *f* devotion
dg *abbr* (**decigrammi**) decigrams
⚷ **di** *prep* of; (partitivo) some; (scritto da) by; ‹*parlare, pensare ecc.*› about; (con causa, mezzo) with; (con provenienza) from; (in comparazioni) than; (con infinito) to; **la casa di mio padre/dei miei genitori** my father's house/my parents' house; **compra del pane** buy some bread; **hai del pane?** do you have any bread?; **un film di guerra** a war film; **piangere di dolore** cry with pain; **coperto di neve** covered with snow; **sono di Genova** I'm from Genoa; **uscire di casa** leave one's house; **mi è uscito di mente** it slipped my mind; **più alto di te** taller than you; **è ora di partire** it's time to go; **crede di aver ragione** he thinks he's right; **dire di sì** say yes; **di domenica** on Sundays; **di sera** in the evening; **una pausa di un'ora** an hour's break; **un corso di due mesi** a two-month course
dia'bete *m* diabetes
dia'betico, -a *adj & nmf* diabetic
diabolica'mente *adv* devilishly
dia'bolico *adj* diabolic[al]
di'acono *m* deacon
dia'critico *adj* diacritic
dia'dema *m* diadem; (di donna) tiara
di'afano *adj* diaphanous
dia'framma *m* diaphragm; (divisione) screen
di'agnosi *f inv* diagnosis
▪ **diagnosi precoce** early detection, early diagnosis
dia'gnostica *f* Med diagnostics *sg*
diagnosti'care *vt* diagnose
dia'gnostici *mpl* Comput diagnostics *sg*
dia'gnostico *adj* diagnostic
diago'nale *adj & nf* diagonal
diagonal'mente *adv* diagonally
dia'gramma *m* diagram
▪ **diagramma a barre** bar chart; **diagramma di flusso** flow chart
dialet'tale *adj* dialect *attrib*; **poesia ~** poetry in dialect
dialettaleggi'ante *adj* dialect *attrib*
dia'lettica *f* dialectics *sg*
dia'lettico *adj* dialectic
dia'letto *m* dialect
di'alisi *f* dialysis
dialo'gante *adj* **unità ~** Comput interactive terminal
dialo'gare **A** *vt* write the dialogue for ‹*scena*›
B *vi* **~ con** converse with
dialo'gato *adj* in dialogue
dialo'ghista *mf* (scrittore) dialogue writer
di'alogo *m* dialogue
dia'mante *m* diamond
diaman'tifero *adj* diamond bearing

diametral'mente *adv* diametrically
di'ametro *m* diameter
di'amine *int* **che ~...** what on earth ...
di'apason *m inv* (per accordatura) tuning fork
diaposi'tiva *f* slide
di'aria *f* daily allowance
di'ario *m* diary
■ **diario di bordo** logbook; **diario di classe** class register
dia'rista *mf* (scrittore) diarist
diar'rea *f* diarrhoea
di'aspora *f* Diaspora
dia'triba *f* diatribe
diavole'ria *f* (azione) devilment; (marchingegno) weird contraption
diavo'letto *m* imp; hum (bambino) little devil
di'avolo *m* devil; **va' al ~!** infml go to hell!; **che ~ fai?** infml what the hell are you doing?
di'battere *vt* debate
di'battersi *vr* struggle
dibattimen'tale *adj* Jur of the hearing
dibatti'mento *m* (discussione) debate; Jur hearing
di'battito *m* debate; (meno formale) discussion
dica'stero *m* office
di'cembre *m* December
dice'ria *f* rumour
dichia'rare *vt* state; (ufficialmente) declare; **~ colpevole** Jur convict; **niente da ~?** anything to declare?
dichia'rarsi *vr* (in amore) declare one's love; **~ soddisfatto** declare oneself satisfied; **si dichiara innocente** he says he's innocent; **~ a favore di qualcosa** declare oneself in favour of something; **si dichiara che ...** (in documenti) it is hereby declared that ...; **~ vinto** acknowledge defeat
dichia'rato *adj* avowed
dichiarazi'one *f* statement; (documento, di guerra, d'amore) declaration; **fare una ~** (ufficialmente) make a statement
■ **dichiarazione dei diritti** Pol bill of rights; **dichiarazione doganale** customs declaration; **dichiarazione dei redditi** [income] tax return
dician'nove *adj & nm* nineteen
dicianno'venne *adj & nmf* nineteen year-old
dicianno'vesimo *adj & nm* nineteenth
dicias'sette *adj & nm* seventeen
diciasset'tenne *adj & nmf* seventeen year-old
diciasset'tesimo *adj & nm* seventeenth
diciot'tenne *adj & nmf* eighteen year-old
diciot'tesimo *adj & nm* eighteenth
dici'otto *adj & nm* eighteen; Univ pass mark
dici'tura *f* wording
dicoto'mia *f* dichotomy
didasca'lia *f* (di film) subtitle; (di illustrazione) caption; Theat stage direction
dida'scalico *adj* <*letteratura*> didactic
di'dattica *f* didactics *sg*
didattica'mente *adv* didactically
di'dattico *adj* didactic; <*televisione*> educational
di'dentro *adv* inside
didi'etro **A** *adv* behind
B *m* (hum) hindquarters *pl*
di'eci *adj & nm* ten
dieci'mila *adj & nm* ten thousand
die'cina = **decina**
di'eresi *f* diaeresis
'diesel *adj & m inv* diesel
di'esis *m inv* sharp
di'eta *f* diet; **a ~** on a diet
■ **dieta mediterranea** Mediterranean diet
die'tetica *f* dietetics *sg*
die'tetico *adj* diet
die'tista *mf* dietician
die'tologo *mf* dietician
di'etro **A** *adv* behind
B *prep* behind; (dopo) after
C *adj* back; <*zampe*> hind
D *m* back; **le stanze di ~** the back rooms; **le zampe di ~** the hind legs
dietro'front *m inv* about-turn; fig U-turn; **~!** about turn!
dietrolo'gia *f obsessive search for supposedly hidden motives behind events or behind people's actions and words*
di'fatti *adv* in fact
di'fendere *vt* defend
di'fendersi *vr* defend oneself; infml (cavarsela) get by
difen'dibile *adj* defendable, defensible
difen'siva *f* **stare sulla ~** be on the defensive
difen'sivo *adj* defensive
difen'sore **A** *adj* **avvocato ~** defence counsel
B *m* defender
■ **difensore civico** ombudsman
di'fesa *f* defence; **prendere le difese di qualcuno** come to somebody's defence
■ **difesa civile** Civil Defence
di'feso **A** pp di **difendere**
B *adj* defended; (luogo) sheltered
difet'tare *vi* be defective; **~ di** lack
difet'tivo *adj* defective
di'fetto *m* defect; (morale) fault, flaw; (mancanza) lack; (in tessuto, abito) flaw; **essere in ~** be at fault; **far ~** be lacking
■ **difetto di pronuncia** speech impediment
difet'toso *adj* defective; <*abito*> flawed
diffa'mare *vt* (con parole) slander; (per iscritto) libel
diffama|'tore, -trice *mf* slanderer; (per iscritto) libeller
diffama'torio *adj* slanderous; (per iscritto) libellous
diffamazi'one *f* slander; (scritta) libel

d

diffe'rente *adj* different
differente'mente *adv* differently
⚷ **diffe'renza** *f* difference; **a ~ di** unlike; **non fare ~** make no distinction (**fra** between)
▪ **differenza di fuso orario** time difference
differenzi'abile *adj* differentiable
differenzi'ale *adj & nm* differential
differenzi'are *vt* differentiate
differenzi'arsi *vr* **~ da** differ from
differenzi'ato *adj* differentiated
differenziazi'one *f* differentiation
diffe'ribile *adj* postponable
diffe'rire [A] *vt* postpone
[B] *vi* be different
diffe'rita *f* **in ~** TV pre-recorded
⚷ **dif'ficile** [A] *adj* difficult; (duro) hard; (improbabile) unlikely
[B] *m* difficulty
difficil'mente *adv* with difficulty
⚷ **difficoltà** *f inv* difficulty; **trovarsi in ~** be in trouble; **mettere qualcuno in ~** put somebody on the spot
▪ **difficoltà d'apprendimento** special needs; **bambini con ~ d'apprendimento** children with special needs
dif'fida *f* warning
diffi'dare [A] *vi* **~ di** distrust
[B] *vt* warn
diffi'dente *adj* mistrustful
diffi'denza *f* mistrust
⚷ **dif'fondere** *vt* spread; diffuse ‹*calore, luce ecc.*›
dif'fondersi *vr* spread
difformità *f inv* deformation; (di opinioni) difference of opinion
diffusa'mente *adv* at length
diffusi'one *f* diffusion; (di giornale) circulation
dif'fuso [A] pp di **diffondere**
[B] *adj* common; ‹*malattia*› widespread; ‹*luce*› diffuse
diffu'sore *m* (per asciugacapelli) diffuser
difi'lato *adv* straight; (subito) straightaway
di'fronte *adj inv & adv* opposite; **~ all'ingresso** in front of the entrance; (dall'altro lato della strada) opposite the entrance
difte'rite *f* diphtheria
'diga *f* dam; (argine) dike
dige'rente *adj* alimentary
dige'ribile *adj* digestible
digeribilità *f inv* digestibility
dige'rire *vt* digest; infml stomach
digesti'one *f* digestion
dige'stivo [A] *adj* digestive
[B] *m* digestive; (dopo cena) liqueur
Digi'one *f* Dijon
digi'tale [A] *adj* digital; (delle dita) finger *attrib*
[B] *f* (fiore) foxglove
digitaliz'zare *vt* digitalize
digitalizzazi'one *f* digitalizing
digi'tare *vt* key in ‹*dati*›
digiu'nare *vi* fast
digi'uno [A] *adj* **essere ~** have an empty stomach
[B] *m* fast; **a ~** ‹*bere ecc.*› on an empty stomach
dignità *f inv* dignity
digni'tario *m* dignitary
dignitosa'mente *adv* with dignity
digni'toso *adj* dignified
DIGOS *nf abbr* (**Divisione Investigazioni Generali e Operazioni Speciali**) ≈ riot police
digressi'one *f* digression
digri'gnare *vi* **~ i denti** grind one's teeth
digros'sare *vt* fig impart basic concepts to
dik'tat *m inv* (trattato) diktat
dila'gare *vi* flood; fig spread
dilani'are *vt* tear to pieces
dilapi'dare *vt* squander
dilapidazi'one *f* squandering
dila'tare *vt* dilate
dila'tarsi *vr* dilate; ‹*legno*› swell; ‹*metallo, gas*› expand
dila'tato *adj* dilated; ‹*legno*› swollen; ‹*metallo, gas*› expanded
dilatazi'one *f* dilation; (di legno) swelling; (di metallo, gas) expansion
dilazio'nabile *adj* postponable
dilazio'nare *vt* delay
dilazi'one *f* delay
dileggi'are *vt* mock
dilegu'are *vt* disperse
dilegu'arsi *vr* disappear
di'lemma *m* dilemma
dilet'tante *mf* amateur
dilettan'tesco *adj* amateurish
dilettan'tismo *m* amateurism
dilettan'tistico *adj* amateurish
dilet'tare *vt* delight
dilet'tarsi *vr* **~ di** delight in
dilet'tevole *adj* delightful
di'letto, -a [A] *adj* beloved
[B] *m* (piacere) delight
[C] *mf* (persona) beloved
dili'gente *adj* diligent; ‹*lavoro*› accurate
dili'genza *f* diligence
dilu'ente *m* Techn diluent; (per vernici) thinner
dilu'ire *vt* dilute
diluizi'one *f* dilution
dilun'gare *vt* prolong
dilun'garsi *vr* **~ su** dwell on ‹*argomento*›
diluvi'are *vi* pour [down]
di'luvio *m* downpour; fig flood
▪ **il ~ universale** the Flood

⚷ key word

dima'grante *adj* slimming, diet
dimagri'mento *m* loss of weight
dima'grire *vi* lose weight
dima'grirsi *vr* lose weight
dime'nare *vt* wave; wag ‹*coda*›
dime'narsi *vr* be agitated
dimensio'nare *vt* fig get into proportion
dimensi'one *f* dimension; (misura) size
dimenti'canza *f* forgetfulness; (svista) oversight; **per ~** accidentally
dimenti'care *vt* forget; **l'ho dimenticato a casa** I left it at home
dimenti'carsi *vr* **~[di]** forget
dimentica'toio *m* **andare/finire nel ~** (hum) fall into oblivion
di'mentico *adj* **~ di** (che non ricorda) forgetful of; (non curante) oblivious of
dimessa'mente *adv* modestly
di'messo **A** pp di **dimettere**
B *adj* humble; (trasandato) shabby; ‹*voce*› low
dimesti'chezza *f* familiarity
di'mettere *vt* dismiss; (da ospedale ecc.) discharge
di'mettersi *vr* resign
dimez'zare *vt* halve
diminu'ire *vt & vi* diminish; (in maglia) decrease
diminu'ito *adj* Mus diminished
diminu'tivo *adj & nm* diminutive
diminuzi'one *f* decrease; (riduzione) reduction; **in ~** dwindling
dimissio'nario **A** *adj* outgoing
B *mf* outgoing chairman/president etc
dimissi'oni *fpl* resignation *sg*; **dare le ~** resign
di'mora *f* residence
dimo'rare *vi* reside
dimo'strabile *adj* demonstrable
dimostrabilità *f inv* demonstrability
dimo'strante *mf* demonstrator
dimo'strare *vt* demonstrate; (provare) prove; (mostrare) show
dimo'strarsi *vr* prove [to be]
dimostra'tivo *adj* demonstrative
dimostrazi'one *f* demonstration; Math proof
di'namica *f* dynamics *sg*; **~ dei fatti** sequence of events
di'namico *adj* dynamic
dina'mismo *m* dynamism
dinami'tardo **A** *adj* **attentato ~** bomb attack
B *mf* bomber
dina'mite *f* dynamite
'dinamo *f inv* dynamo
di'nanzi **A** *adv* in front
B *prep* **~ a** in front of
'dinaro *m* (moneta) dinar
dina'stia *f* dynasty
di'nastico *adj* dynastic
din'don *m inv* ding-dong
'dingo *m* (cane) dingo
dini'ego *m* denial
dinocco'lato *adj* lanky
dino'sauro *m* dinosaur
din'torni *mpl* outskirts; **nei ~ di** in the vicinity of
din'torno *adv* around
'dio *m* (*pl* **dei**) god; **Dio** God; **Dio mio!** my God!
dioce'sano *adj* diocesan
di'ocesi *f inv* diocese
dioni'siaco *adj* Dionysian
dios'sina *f* dioxin
diot'tria *f* dioptre
dipa'nare *vt* wind into a ball; fig unravel
diparti'mento *m* department
dipen'dente **A** *adj* depending
B *mf* employee
dipen'denza *f* dependence; (edificio) annexe
di'pendere *vi* **~ da** depend on; (provenire) derive from; **dipende** it depends
di'pingere *vt* paint; (descrivere) describe
di'pinto **A** pp di **dipingere**
B *adj* painted
C *m* painting
di'ploma *m* diploma
diplo'mare *vt* graduate
diplo'marsi *vr* graduate
diplomatica'mente *adv* diplomatically
diplo'matico **A** *adj* diplomatic
B *m* diplomat; (pasticcino) millefeuille (*with alcohol*)
diplo'mato **A** *mf person with school qualification*
B *adj* qualified
diploma'zia *f* diplomacy
di'porto *m* **imbarcazione da ~** pleasure craft
dirada'mento *f* thinning out
dira'dare *vt* thin out; make less frequent ‹*visite*›
dira'darsi *vr* thin out; ‹*nebbia*› clear
dira'mare *vt* issue
dira'marsi *vr* branch out
diramazi'one *f* (di strada, fiume) fork; (di albero, impresa) branch; (di ordine) issuing
'dire **A** *vt* say; (raccontare, riferire) tell; **~ quello che si pensa** speak one's mind; **voler ~** mean; **volevo ben ~!** I wondered!; **~ di sì/no** say yes/no; **si dice che ...** rumour has it that ...; **come si dice "casa" in inglese?** what's the English for "casa"?; **questo nome mi dice qualcosa** the name rings a bell; **che ne dici di...?** how about...?; **non c'è che ~** there's no disputing that; **e ~ che ...** to think that ...; **a dir poco/tanto** at least/most
B *vi* **~ bene/male di** speak highly/ill of

d

somebody; **dica pure** (in negozio) how can I help you?; **dici sul serio?** are you serious?; **per modo di ~** as it were

di'retta *f* TV live broadcast; **in ~** live

diretta'mente *adv* directly

diret'tissima *f* (strada) main route; **per ~** Jur ‹*processare*› without going through the normal procedures

diret'tissimo *m* fast train

diret'tiva *f* directive; **direttive** *pl* (indicazioni) guidelines

diret'tivo **A** *adj* (dirigente) management *attrib*, managerial
B *m* Pol executive

di'retto **A** *pp di* **dirigere**
B *adj* direct; **il mio ~ superiore** my immediate superior; **~ a** (inteso) meant for; **essere ~ a** be heading for; **in diretta** ‹*trasmissione*› live
C *m* (treno) through train

✓ **diret'tore** *m* manager; (più in alto nella gerarchia) director; (di scuola) headmaster
■ **direttore amministrativo** company secretary; **direttore artistico** artistic director; **direttore del carcere** prison governor; **direttore di filiale** branch manager; **direttore di gara** referee; **direttore generale** managing director, chief executive officer; **direttore di giornale** newspaper editor; **direttore d'istituto** Univ department head; **direttore d'orchestra** conductor; **direttore del personale** personnel manager/director; **direttore di produzione** production manager/director; **direttore spirituale** spiritual advisor; **direttore sportivo** team manager; **direttore tecnico** Sport manager; **direttore di zona** area manager, regional director

diret'trice *f* manageress; (di scuola) headmistress; (indirizzo) guiding principle

direzio'nale *adj* directional

direzio'nare *vt* direct

✓ **direzi'one** *f* direction; (di società) management; Sch headmaster's/headmistress's office (*primary school*); **in ~ nord** (traffico) northbound; **'tutte le direzioni'** Auto 'all routes'

diri'gente **A** *adj* ruling
B *mf* executive
■ **dirigente d'azienda** company director; **dirigente di partito** Pol party leader

diri'genza *f* (gestione) management; (i dirigenti) top management; Pol leadership
■ **dirigenza aziendale** business management

dirigenzi'ale *adj* management *attrib*, managerial

✓ **di'rigere** *vt* direct; conduct ‹*orchestra*›; run ‹*impresa*›

di'rigersi *vr* **~ verso** head for

diri'gibile *m* airship

dirim'petto **A** *adv* opposite
B *prep* **~ a** facing

✓ **di'ritto**[1] **A** *adj* straight; (destro) right
B *adv* straight; **andare ~** go straight on; **sempre ~** straight ahead, straight on
C *m* right side; Tennis forehand; **fare un ~** (a maglia) knit one

✓ **di'ritto**[2] *m* right; Jur law
■ **diritti degli animali** *pl* animal rights; **diritti d'autore** *pl* royalties; **diritti civili** *pl* civil rights; **diritti di prelievo** *pl* Fin drawing rights; **diritti umani** *pl* human rights; **diritto civile** civil law; **diritto commerciale** commercial law; **diritto penale** criminal law; **diritto di voto** right to vote, suffrage

dirit'tura *f* straight line; fig honesty
■ **~ d'arrivo** Sport fig home straight

diroc'cato *adj* tumbledown

dirom'pente *adj* anche fig explosive

dirotta'mento *m* hijacking

dirot'tare **A** *vt* re-route ‹*treno, aereo*›; (illegalmente) hijack; divert ‹*traffico*›
B *vi* alter course

dirotta'tore, -trice *mf* hijacker; (solo di aereo) skyjacker

di'rotto *adj* ‹*pioggia*› pouring; ‹*pianto*› uncontrollable; **piovere a ~** rain heavily

di'rupo *m* precipice

di'sabile **A** *adj* disabled
B *mf* disabled person

disabili'tare *vt* disable

disabi'tato *adj* uninhabited

disabitu'arsi *vr* **~ a** get out of the habit of

disac'cordo *m* disagreement

disadatta'mento *m* maladjustment

disadat'tato, -a **A** *adj* maladjusted
B *mf* misfit

disa'dorno *adj* unadorned

disaffezi'one *f* disaffection

disa'gevole *adj* (scomodo) uncomfortable; (difficile) inconvenient

disagi'ato *adj* poor; ‹*vita*› hard; (scomodo) uncomfortable

di'sagio *m* discomfort; (difficoltà) inconvenience; (imbarazzo) embarrassment, uneasiness; **sentirsi a ~** feel uncomfortable; **disagi** *pl* (privazioni) hardships
■ **disagio sociale** social distress

di'samina *f* close examination

disamora'mento *m* estrangement

disanco'rare *vt* Fin de-link

disappro'vare *vt* disapprove of

disapprovazi'one *f* disapproval

disap'punto *m* disappointment; **con suo grande ~** [much] to his chagrin

disarcio'nare *vt* unseat

disar'mante *adj* fig disarming

disar'mare *vt & vi* disarm

disar'mato *adj* disarmed; fig defenceless

di'sarmo *m* disarmament

disartico'lato *adj* fig disjointed

✓ key word

disa'strato, -a **A** *adj* devastated
B *mf* victim (*of flood, earthquake etc*)

di'sastro *m* disaster; infml (grande confusione) mess; infml (persona) disaster area
■ **disastro aereo** air crash

disastrosa'mente *adv* disastrously

disa'stroso *adj* disastrous

disat'tento *adj* inattentive

disattenzi'one *f* inattention; (svista) oversight

disatti'vare *vt* de-activate

disa'vanzo *m* deficit

disavve'duto *adj* thoughtless

disavven'tura *f* misadventure

disavver'tenza *f* inadvertence

di'sbrigo *m* dispatch

di'scapito *m* **a ~ di** to the detriment of

di'scarica *f* scrap yard

di'scarico *m* (di merce) unloading; **prova a ~** evidence for the defence; **testimone a ~** witness for the defence

discen'dente **A** *adj* descending
B *mf* descendant

discen'denza *f* descent; (discendenti) descendants *pl*

di'scendere **A** *vi* (dal treno) get off; (da cavallo) dismount; (sbarcare) land; **~ da** (trarre origine da) be a descendant of
B *vt* descend

discen'sore *m* (attrezzo) karabiner

di'scepolo, -a *mf* disciple

di'scernere *vt* discern

discerni'mento *m* discernment

di'scesa *f* descent; (pendio) slope; **~ in picchiata** (di aereo) nosedive; **essere in ~** ‹*strada*› go downhill
■ **discesa libera** (in sci) downhill race

disce'sista *mf* (sciatore) downhill skier

di'sceso pp di **discendere**

di'schetto *m* Comput diskette

dischi'udere *vt* open; (svelare) disclose

dischi'udersi *vr* open up

di'scinto *adj* scantily dressed

disci'ogliere *vt* ‹*acido*› dissolve; ‹*neve*› thaw; (fondersi) melt

disci'olto pp di **disciogliere**

disci'plina *f* discipline

discipli'nare **A** *adj* disciplinary
B *vt* discipline

discipli'nato *adj* disciplined

disc-'jockey *m inv* disc jockey, DJ

'disco *m* disc; Sport discus; Mus record; **ernia del disco** slipped disc
■ **disco a 33 giri** LP; **disco a 45 giri** single; **disco fisso** Comput fixed disk, hard disk; **disco dei freni** brake disc; **disco master** Comput master disk; **disco rigido** Comput hard disk; **disco volante** flying saucer

discogra'fia *f* (insieme di incisioni) discography; (industria) record industry

disco'grafico **A** *adj* ‹*industria*› record *attrib*, recording; ‹*mercato, raccolta*› record *attrib*; **casa discografica** record company, recording company
B *mf* record producer

'discolo **A** *mf* rascal
B *adj* unruly

di'scolpa *f* clearing; **a sua ~ si deve dire che ...** in his defence it must be said that ...

discol'pare *vt* clear

discol'parsi *vr* clear oneself

discon'nettere *vt* disconnect

disco'noscere *vt* deny; disown ‹*figlio*›

discontinuità *f inv* (nel lavoro) irregularity; (di stile) unevenness

discon'tinuo *adj* intermittent; fig ‹*impegno, rendimento*› uneven

discopa'tia *f* disc problems *pl*

discor'dante *adj* discordant

discor'danza *f* discordance; **essere in ~** clash

discor'dare *vi* ‹*opinioni*› conflict

di'scorde *adj* clashing

di'scordia *f* discord; (dissenso) dissension

di'scorrere *vi* talk (**di** about)

discor'sivo *adj* colloquial

di'scorso **A** pp di **discorrere**
B *m* speech; (conversazione) talk
■ **discorso indiretto** indirect speech; **discorso di ringraziamento** vote of thanks

di'scosto **A** *adj* distant
B *adv* far away; **stare ~** stand apart

disco'teca *f* disco; (raccolta) record library

discote'caro *mf* derog disco freak

di'scount *m inv* discount store

discredi'tare *vt* discredit

di'scredito *m* discredit

discre'pante *adj* contradictory

discre'panza *f* discrepancy

di'screto *adj* discreet; (moderato) moderate; (abbastanza buono) fairly good

discrezionalità *f inv* discretion

discrezi'one *f* discretion; (giudizio) judgement; **a ~ di** at the discretion of

discrimi'nante **A** *adj* extenuating
B *f* Jur extenuating circumstances *pl*

discrimi'nare *vt* discriminate

discrimina'tivo *adj* ‹*provvedimento*› discriminatory

discrimina'torio *adj* ‹*atteggiamento*› discriminatory

discriminazi'one *f* discrimination
■ **discriminazione in base all'età** age discrimination; **discriminazione sessuale** sexual discrimination

discussi'one *f* discussion; (alterco) argument; **messa in ~** questioning

di'scusso **A** pp di **discutere**
B *adj* controversial

di'scutere **A** *vt* discuss; (formale) debate;

(litigare) argue
B *vi* ~ **su qualcosa** discuss something
discu'tibile *adj* debatable; ‹*gusto*› questionable
disde'gnare *vt* disdain
di'sdegno *m* disdain
disde'gnoso *adj* disdainful
di'sdetta *f* retraction; (sfortuna) bad luck; Comm cancellation
di'sdetto pp di **disdire**
disdi'cevole *adj* unbecoming
di'sdire *vt* retract; (annullare) cancel
disedu'care *vt* have a bad effect on
diseduca'tivo *adj* bad for children
dise'gnare *vt* draw; (progettare) design
disegna|'tore, -trice *mf* designer
■ **disegnatore di moda** fashion designer
⚷ **di'segno** *m* drawing; (progetto, linea) design
■ **disegno di legge** bill; **disegno in scala** scale drawing; **disegno tecnico** technical drawing; **disegno dal vero** life drawing
diser'bante **A** *m* herbicide, weed killer
B *adj* herbicidal, weed-killing
diser'bare *vt* weed
disere'dare *vt* disinherit
disere'dato **A** *adj* dispossessed
B *mf* **i diseredati** the dispossessed
diser'tare *vt & vi* desert; ~ **la scuola** stay away from school
diser'tore *m* deserter
diserzi'one *f* desertion
disfaci'mento *m* decay; fig decline; **in** ~ decaying; fig in decline
di'sfare *vt* undo; strip ‹*letto*›; (smantellare) take down; (annientare) defeat; ~ **le valigie** unpack [one's bags]
di'sfarsi *vr* fall to pieces; (sciogliersi) melt; ~ **di** (liberarsi di) get rid of; ~ **in lacrime** dissolve into tears
di'sfatta *f* defeat
disfat'tismo *m* defeatism
disfat'tista *adj & nmf* defeatist
di'sfatto *adj* fig worn out
disfunzio'nale *adj* dysfunctional
disfunzi'one *f* disorder
disge'lare *vt & vi* thaw
disge'larsi *vr* thaw
di'sgelo *m* thaw
disgi'ungere *vt* disconnect
disgi'unto *adj* ‹*firme*› separate
⚷ **di'sgrazia** *f* misfortune; (incidente) accident; (sfavore) disgrace
disgraziata'mente *adv* unfortunately
⚷ **disgrazi'ato, -a** **A** *adj* unfortunate
B *mf* wretch
disgrega'mento *m* disintegration
disgre'gare *vt* break up
disgre'garsi *vr* disintegrate

⚷ key word

disgrega'tivo *adj* disintegrating
disgrega'tore *adj* disintegrating
disgregazi'one *f* (di società) break-up
disgu'ido *m*
■ **disguido postale** mistake in delivery
disgu'stare *vt* disgust
disgu'starsi *vr* ~ **di** be disgusted by
di'sgusto *m* disgust
disgustosa'mente *adv* disgustingly; ~ **dolce** nauseatingly sweet
disgu'stoso *adj* disgusting
disidra'tante *adj* dehydrating
disidra'tare *vt* dehydrate
disidra'tarsi *vr* become dehydrated
disidra'tato *adj* dehydrated
disidratazi'one *f* dehydration
disil'ludere *vt* disenchant, disillusion
disil'ludersi *vr* become disenchanted, become disillusioned
disillusi'one *f* disenchantment, disillusionment
disil'luso *adj* disenchanted, disillusioned
disimbal'laggio *m* unpacking
disimbal'lare *vt* unpack
disimpa'rare *vt* forget
disimpe'gnare *vt* release; (compiere) fulfil; redeem ‹*oggetto dato in pegno*›
disimpe'gnarsi *vr* disengage oneself; (cavarsela) manage
disim'pegno *m* (locale) vestibule; (disinteresse) lack of interest
disimpi'ego *m* re-allocation; (di truppe) reassignment
disincagli'are *vt* Naut refloat
disincagli'arsi *vr* Naut float off
disincan'tato *adj* (disilluso) disillusioned, disenchanted
disincar'nato *adj* disembodied
disincenti'vante *adj* demotivating
disincenti'vare *vt* demotivate
disincen'tivo *m* disincentive
disincroci'are *vt* uncross
disinfe'stare *vt* disinfest
disinfestazi'one *f* disinfestation
disinfet'tante *adj & nm* disinfectant
disinfet'tare *vt* disinfect
disinfezi'one *f* disinfection
disinfiam'marsi *vr* become less inflamed
disinflazio'nare *vt* disinflate
disinflazi'one *f* disinflation
disinflazio'nistico *adj* disinflationary
disinfor'mato *adj* uninformed
disinformazi'one *f* lack of information; (informazione erronea) misinformation
disingan'nare *vt* disabuse
disin'ganno *m* disillusion
disini'birsi *vr* lose one's inhibitions
disini'bito *adj* uninhibited

disinne'scare *vt* defuse
disin'nesco *m* (di bomba) bomb disposal
disinne'stare *vt* disengage
disinne'starsi *vr* disengage
disin'nesto *m* disengagement
disinquina'mento *m* cleaning up
disinqui'nare *vt* clean up
disinse'rire *vt* disconnect
disinse'rito *adj* disconnected
disinte'grare *vt* disintegrate
disinte'grarsi *vr* disintegrate
disintegrazi'one *f* disintegration
disinteressa'mento *m* lack of interest
disinteres'sarsi *vr* **~ di** take no interest in
disinteressata'mente *adv* without interest; (senza secondo fine) disinterestedly
disinteres'sato *adj* uninterested; (senza secondo fine) disinterested
disinte'resse *m* indifference; (oggettività) disinterestedness
disintossi'care *vt* detoxify
disintossi'carsi *vr* come off drugs; ‹*alcolizzato*› dry out, detox
disintossicazi'one *f* giving up alcohol/drugs, detox; **programma di ~** detox programme
disinvolta'mente *adv* in a relaxed way
disin'volto *adj* relaxed
disinvol'tura *f* confidence
disi'stima *f* lack of respect
disles'sia *f* dyslexia
di'slessico *adj* dyslexic
disli'vello *m* difference in height; fig inequality
disloca'mento *m* Mil posting
dislo'care *vt* Mil post
dismenor'rea *f* dysmenorrhoea
dismi'sura *f* excess; **a ~** excessively
disobbedi'ente *adj* disobedient
disobbe'dire *vt* disobey
disoccu'pato, -a **A** *adj* unemployed
B *mf* unemployed person
disoccupazi'one *f* unemployment
disonestà *f inv* dishonesty
diso'nesto *adj* dishonest
disono'rare *vt* dishonour
disono'rato *adj* dishonoured
diso'nore *m* dishonour
di'sopra **A** *adv* above
B *adj* upper
C *m* top
disordi'nare *vt* disarrange
disordinata'mente *adv* untidily
disordi'nato *adj* untidy; (sregolato) immoderate
🔑 **di'sordine** *m* disorder, untidiness; (sregolatezza) debauchery
disores'sia *f* eating disorder
disor'ganico *adj* inconsistent
disorganiz'zare *vt* disorganize
disorganiz'zato *adj* disorganized
disorganizzazi'one *f* disorganization
disorienta'mento *m* disorientation
disorien'tare *vt* disorientate
disorien'tarsi *vr* lose one's bearings
disorien'tato *adj* fig bewildered
disos'sare *vt* bone
disos'sato *adj* boned
di'sotto **A** *adv* below
B *adj* lower
C *m* bottom
di'spaccio *m* dispatch
dispa'rato *adj* disparate
'dispari *adj* odd, uneven
dispa'rire *vi* disappear
disparità *f inv* disparity
di'sparte *adv* **in ~** apart; **stare in ~** stand aside
di'spendio *m* expenditure; derog waste
dispendiosa'mente *adv* extravagantly
dispendi'oso *adj* expensive
di'spensa *f* pantry; (distribuzione) distribution; (mobile) cupboard; Jur exemption; Relig dispensation; (pubblicazione periodica) number
dispen'sare *vt* distribute; (esentare) exonerate
dispen'sario *m* dispensary
di'spenser *m inv* display rack; (confezione) dispenser
🔑 **dispe'rare** *vi* despair (**di** of)
dispe'rarsi *vr* despair
disperata'mente *adv* ‹*piangere*› desperately; ‹*studiare*› like mad
dispe'rato *adj* desperate; ‹*tentativo*› last-ditch
🔑 **disperazi'one** *f* despair
di'sperdere *vt* scatter; disperse
di'sperdersi *vr* scatter; disperse
dispersi'one *f* dispersion; (di truppe) dispersal
disper'sivo *adj* disorganized
di'sperso **A** pp di **disperdere**
B *adj* scattered; (smarrito) lost
C *m* missing soldier
di'spetto *m* spite; **a ~ di** in spite of; **fare un ~ a qualcuno** spite somebody
dispet'toso *adj* spiteful
🔑 **dispia'cere** **A** *m* upset; (rammarico) regret; (dolore) sorrow; (preoccupazione) worry
B *vi* **mi dispiace** I'm sorry; **non mi dispiace** I don't dislike it; **se non ti dispiace** if you don't mind
dispiaci'uto *adj* sorry
dispie'gare *vt* unfold
dispie'garsi *vr* unfurl
dispo'nibile *adj* available; (gentile) helpful
disponibilità *f inv* availability; (gentilezza) helpfulness

d

■ **disponibilità correnti** *pl* Fin current assets

di'sporre **A** *vt* arrange
B *vi* dispose; (stabilire) order; ~ **di** have at one's disposal

di'sporsi *vr* (in fila) line up

disposi'tivo *m* device
■ **dispositivo di emergenza** emergency button/ handle; **dispositivo di puntamento** Comput pointing device

disposizi'one *f* disposition; (ordine) order; (libera disponibilità) disposal

di'sposto **A** pp di **disporre**
B *adj* ready; (incline) disposed; **essere ben ~ verso** be favourably disposed towards

dispotica'mente *adv* despotically

di'spotico *adj* despotic

dispo'tismo *m* despotism

dispregia'tivo *adj* disparaging

disprez'zabile *adj* despicable

disprez'zare *vt* despise

di'sprezzo *m* contempt

'disputa *f* dispute

dispu'tare *vi* dispute; (gareggiare) compete

dispu'tarsi *vr* ~ **qualcosa** contend for something

disqui'sire *vi* discourse

disquisizi'one *f* disquisition

dissa'crante *adj* debunking

dissa'crare *vt* debunk

dissacra|'tore, -trice *mf* debunker

dissacra'torio *adj* debunking

dissacrazi'one *f* debunking

dissangua'mento *m* loss of blood; fig impoverishment

dissangu'are *vt* bleed; fig bleed dry

dissangu'arsi *vr* bleed; fig become impoverished

dissangu'ato *adj* bloodless; fig impoverished

dissa'pore *m* disagreement

dissec'care *vt* dry up

dissec'carsi *vr* dry up

dissemi'nare *vt* disseminate; (notizie) spread

dissen'nato *adj* ‹*politica*› senseless

dis'senso *m* dissent; (disaccordo) disagreement

dissente'ria *f* dysentery

dissen'tire *vi* disagree (**da** with)

dissepelli'mento *m* exhumation

dissepel'lire *vt* exhume ‹*cadavere*›; disinter ‹*rovine*›; fig unearth

dissertazi'one *f* dissertation

disser'vizio *m* poor service

disse'stare *vt* upset; Comm damage

disse'stato *adj* ‹*strada*› uneven; ‹*azienda*› shaky

dis'sesto *m* ruin

disse'tante *adj* thirst-quenching

disse'tare *vt* ~ **qualcuno** quench somebody's thirst

disse'tarsi *vr* quench one's thirst

dissezio'nare *vr* dissect

dissezi'one *f* dissection

dissi'dente *adj & nmf* dissident

dissi'denza *f* dissidence

dis'sidio *m* disagreement

dis'simile *adj* unlike, dissimilar

dissimu'lare *vt* conceal

dissimu'lato *adj* concealed

dissimula|'tore, -trice *mf* dissembler

dissimulazi'one *f* concealment

dissi'pare *vt* dissipate; (sperperare) squander

dissi'parsi *vr* ‹*nebbia*› clear; ‹*dubbio*› disappear

dissipa'tezza *f* dissipation

dissi'pato *adj* dissipated

dissipa'tore *m*
■ **dissipatore termico** heat sink

dissipazi'one *f* squandering

dissoci'abile *adj* separable

dissoci'are *vt* dissociate

dissoci'arsi *vr* dissociate oneself

dissoci'ato, -a **A** *adj* Pol dissenting
B *mf* Pol dissenter

dissociazi'one *f* Pol dissociation

dissoda'mento *m* tillage

disso'dare *vt* till

dis'solto pp di **dissolvere**

disso'lubile *adj* dissoluble

dissolu'tezza *f* dissoluteness

dissolu'tivo *adj* divisive

disso'luto *adj* dissolute

dissol'venza *f* (di immagine) fade-out, dissolve

dis'solvere *vt* dissolve; (disperdere) dispel

dis'solversi *vr* dissolve; (disperdersi) clear

disso'nante *adj* dissonant

disso'nanza *f* dissonance

dissotterra'mento *m* disinterment

dissotter'rare *vt* disinter ‹*bara*›; fig resurrect ‹*rancore*›

dissua'dere *vt* dissuade

dissuasi'one *f* dissuasion

dissua'sivo *adj* dissuasive

distacca'mento *m* Mil detachment

distac'care *vt* detach; Sport leave behind

distac'carsi *vr* be detached

distac'cato *adj* ‹*tono, voce*› expressionless

di'stacco *m* detachment; (separazione) separation; Sport lead

di'stante **A** *adj* far away; fig ‹*person*› detached
B *adv* far away

di'stanza *f* distance

distanzia'mento *m* spacing [out]; Sport outdistancing

key word

distanzi'are *vt* space out; Sport outdistance
di'stare *vi* be distant; **quanto dista?** how far is it?; **Roma dista 20 chilometri da qui** Rome is 20 kilometres away, Rome is 20 kilometres from here
di'stendere *vt* stretch out ‹*parte del corpo*›; (spiegare) spread; (deporre) lay
di'stendersi *vr* stretch; (sdraiarsi) lie down; (rilassarsi) relax
distensi'one *f* stretching; (rilassamento) relaxation; Pol détente
disten'sivo *adj* relaxing
di'stesa *f* expanse
di'steso pp di **distendere**
distil'lare *vt & vi* distil
distil'lato **A** *adj* distilled
B *m* distillate
distillazi'one *f* distillation
distille'ria *f* distillery
di'stinguersi *vr* (per bravura ecc.) distinguish oneself; **si distingue dagli altri per ...** it is distinguished from the others by ...
distin'guibile *adj* distinguishable
di'stinguo *m inv* distinction
di'stinta *f* Comm list
■ **distinta di pagamento** receipt; **distinta di versamento** paying-in slip
distinta'mente *adv* (separatamente) individually, separately; (chiaramente) clearly; (in modo elegante) in a distinguished way; **vi saluto ~** Yours truly
distin'tivo **A** *adj* distinctive
B *m* badge
di'stinto **A** pp di **distinguersi**
B *adj* distinct; (signorile) distinguished; **distinti saluti** Yours faithfully
distinzi'one *f* distinction
di'stogliere *vt* **~ da** (allontanare) remove from; (dissuadere) dissuade from
di'stolto pp di **distogliere**
di'storcere *vt* twist; distort ‹*suono*›
di'storcersi *vr* sprain ‹*caviglia*›
distorsi'one *f* Med sprain; (alterazione) distortion
di'storto *adj* warped; ‹*suono*› distorted
di'strarre *vt* distract; (divertire) amuse
di'strarsi *vr* (deconcentrarsi) be distracted; (svagarsi) amuse oneself; **non ti distrarre!** pay attention!
distratta'mente *adv* absently
di'stratto **A** pp di **distrarre**
B *adj* absent-minded; (disattento) inattentive
distrazi'one *f* absent-mindedness; (errore) inattention; (svago) amusement; **errore di ~** absent-minded mistake
di'stretto *m* district
distrettu'ale *adj* district *attrib*
distribu'ire *vt* distribute; (disporre) arrange; deal ‹*carte*›
distribu'tore *m* distributor; (di benzina) petrol pump, gas pump AmE; (automatico) slot machine
■ **distributore automatico di biglietti** ticket machine; **distributore di bevande** drinks dispenser; **distributore di monete** change machine
distribuzi'one *f* distribution
distri'care *vt* disentangle
distri'carsi *vr* fig get out of it
distro'fia *f*
■ **distrofia muscolare** muscular dystrophy
di'strofico *adj* dystrophic
di'struggere *vt* destroy
di'struggersi *vr* **si distrugge col bere** he is destroying himself with drink; **la macchina si è distrutta** the car has been written off
distruttività *f inv* destructiveness
distrut'tivo *adj* destructive; ‹*critica*› negative
di'strutto **A** pp di **distruggere**
B *adj* destroyed; **un uomo ~** a broken man
distrut'tore *m*
■ **distruttore di documenti** paper shredder
distruzi'one *f* destruction
distur'bare *vt* disturb; (sconvolgere) upset
distur'barsi *vr* trouble oneself; **non si disturbi** please don't trouble yourself
distur'bato *adj* Med ‹*mente*› disordered; ‹*intestino*› upset
di'sturbo *m* bother; (indisposizione) trouble; Med problem; Radio, TV interference; **disturbi** *pl* Radio, TV static
■ **disturbo da deficit dell'attenzione** attention deficit disorder; **disturbi di stomaco** *pl* stomach trouble
disubbidi'ente *adj* disobedient
disubbidi'enza *f* disobedience
disubbi'dire *vi* **~ a** disobey
disuguagli'anza *f* disparity; (eterogeneità) irregularity
disugu'ale *adj* unequal; (eterogeneo) irregular
disumanità *f inv* inhumanity
disu'mano *adj* inhuman
disuni'one *f* disunity
disu'nire *vt* divide
di'suso *m* **cadere in ~** fall into disuse
di'tale *m* thimble
di'tata *f* poke; (impronta) finger mark
'dito *m* (*pl nf* **dita**) finger; (di vino, acqua) finger
■ **dito del piede** toe
'ditta *f* firm
■ **ditta di vendita per corrispondenza** mail order firm
dit'tafono *m* Dictaphone
ditta'tore *m* dictator
dittatori'ale *adj* dictatorial

ditta'tura *f* dictatorship

dit'tongo *m* diphthong

diu'retico *adj* diuretic

di'urno *adj* daytime; **spettacolo ~** matinée

'diva *f* diva

diva'gare *vi* digress

divagazi'one *f* digression
■ **divagazione sul tema** digression

divam'pare *vi* burst into flames; fig spread like wildfire

di'vano *m* settee, sofa
■ **divano letto** sofa bed

divari'care *vt* open

divari'carsi *vr* splay

divari'cata *f* splits *pl*

divari'cato *adj* ‹*gambe, braccia*› splayed

di'vario *m* discrepancy; **un ~ di opinioni** a difference of opinion

di'vellere *vt* (sradicare) uproot

di'velto pp di **divellere**

🔑 **dive'nire** *vi* = **diventare**

🔑 **diven'tare** *vi* become; (lentamente) grow; (rapidamente) turn

dive'nuto pp di **divenire**

di'verbio *m* squabble

diver'gente *adj* divergent

diver'genza *f* divergence
■ **divergenza di opinioni** difference of opinion

di'vergere *vi* diverge

diversa'mente *adv* (altrimenti) otherwise; (in modo diverso) differently
■ **diversamente abile** differently abled

di'versi *adj & pron* (parecchi) several

diversifi'care *vt* diversify

diversifi'carsi *vr* differ; be different

diversifi'cato *adj* broad-based

diversificazi'one *f* diversification

diversi'one *f* diversion

diversità *f inv* diversity; **ci sono molte ~** there are many differences

diver'sivo **A** *adj* diversionary
B *m* diversion

🔑 **di'verso** *adj* different

diver'tente *adj* amusing

diver'ticolo *m* diverticulum

diverti'mento *m* fun, amusement; **buon ~!** enjoy yourself!, have fun!

🔑 **diver'tire** *vt* amuse

diver'tirsi *vr* enjoy oneself, have fun

diver'tito *adj* amused

divi'dendo *m* dividend

🔑 **di'videre** *vt* divide; (condividere) share

di'vidersi *vr* (separarsi) separate

divi'eto *m* prohibition; **'~ di pesca'** 'fishing prohibited'; **'~ di sosta'** 'no parking'

divina'mente *adv* divinely

divinco'larsi *vr* wriggle

divinità *f inv* divinity

di'vino *adj* divine

di'visa *f* uniform; Fin currency

divi'sibile *adj* divisible

🔑 **divisi'one** *f* division

divisio'nismo *m* (in arte) pointillism

di'vismo *m* worship; (atteggiamento) superstar mentality

di'viso **A** pp di **dividere**
B *adj* divided

divi'sore *m* divisor

divi'sorio *adj* dividing; **muro ~** partition wall

'divo, -a *mf* star

divo'rare *vt* devour

divo'rarsi *vr* **~ da** be consumed with

divorzi'are *vi* divorce

divorzi'ato, -a *mf* divorcee

di'vorzio *m* divorce

divul'gare *vt* divulge; (rendere popolare) popularize

divul'garsi *vr* spread

divulga'tivo *adj* popular

divulgazi'one *f* spread; (di cultura, scienza) popularization

dizio'nario *m* dictionary
■ **dizionario dei sinonimi** thesaurus

dizi'one *f* diction

DJ *m inv* DJ

DNA *m inv* DNA

do *m* Mus (chiave, nota) C

D.O.C. *abbr* (**Denominazione di Origine Controllata**) *mark guaranteeing the quality of a wine*

'doccia *f* shower; (grondaia) gutter; **fare la ~** have a shower, shower

doccia'tura *f* Med douche

do'cente **A** *adj* teaching
B *mf* teacher; (di università) lecturer

do'cenza *f* university teacher's qualification

D.O.C.G. *abbr* (**Denominazione di Origine Controllata e Garantita**) *mark guaranteeing the high quality of a wine*

'docile *adj* docile

docilità *f inv* docility

documen'tare *vt* document

documen'tario *adj & nm* documentary

documen'tarsi *vr* gather information (**su** about)

documen'tato *adj* well documented; ‹*persona*› well-informed

documentazi'one *f* documentation

🔑 **docu'mento** *m* document; **documenti** *pl* papers
■ **documento d'identità** ID

dodeca'fonico *adj* Mus dodecaphonic

🔑 key word

Dodecan'neso *m* **il ~** the Dodecanese
dodi'cenne *adj & nmf* twelve year-old
dodi'cesimo *adj & nm* twelfth
'dodici *adj & nm* twelve
do'gana *f* customs *pl*; (dazio) duty
■ **dogana merci** customs for freight; **dogana passeggeri** passenger customs
doga'nale *adj* customs *attrib*
dogani'ere *m* customs officer
'doglie *fpl* labour pains
'dogma *m* dogma
dog'matico *adj* dogmatic
dogma'tismo *m* dogmatism
'dolce **A** *adj* sweet; ‹*clima*› mild; ‹*voce, consonante*› soft; ‹*acqua*› fresh
B *m* (portata) dessert; (torta) cake; **non mangio dolci** I don't eat sweet things; **dolci** *pl* **della casa** (in menu) home-made cakes
dolce'mente *adv* sweetly
dolce'vita *adj inv* (maglione) roll-neck
dol'cezza *f* sweetness; (di clima) mildness
dolci'ario *adj* confectionery
dolci'astro *adj* sweetish
dolcifi'cante **A** *m* sweetener
B *adj* sweetening
dolcifica'tore *m* (per acqua) softener
dolci'umi *mpl* sweets
do'lente *adj* painful; (spiacente) sorry; **punto ~** sore point
do'lere *vi* ache, hurt; (dispiacere) regret
do'lersi *vr* regret; (protestare) complain; **~ di** be sorry for
'dollaro *m* dollar
'dolly *m inv* Cinema, TV dolly
'dolmen *m inv* dolmen
'dolo *m* Jur malice; (truffa) fraud
Dolo'miti *fpl* **le ~** the Dolomites
dolo'mitico *adj* Dolomite, of the Dolomites
dolo'rante *adj* aching
do'lore *m* pain; (morale) sorrow; **avere dei dolori** be in pain
■ **dolori post-partum** *pl* after-pains
dolorosa'mente *adv* painfully
dolo'roso *adj* painful
do'loso *adj* malicious
do'manda *f* question; (richiesta) request; (scritta) application; Comm demand; **~ e offerta** supply and demand; **fare una ~ (a qualcuno)** ask (somebody) a question
■ **domanda di impiego** job application; **domanda riconvenzionale** counterclaim; **domanda trabocchetto** trick question
doman'dare *vt* ask; (esigere) demand; **~ qualcosa a qualcuno** ask somebody for something
doman'darsi *vr* wonder
do'mani **A** *adv* tomorrow; **~ sera** tomorrow evening; **a ~** see you tomorrow
B *m* **il ~** the future
do'mare *vt* tame; fig control ‹*emozioni*›
doma|'tore, -trice *mf* tamer
■ **domatore di cavalli** horsebreaker
domat'tina *adv* tomorrow morning
doma'tura *f* (di cavallo) breaking
do'menica *f* Sunday; **di ~** on Sundays
■ **Domenica delle Palme** Palm Sunday
domeni'cale *adj* Sunday *attrib*
domeni'cano *adj* Dominican
do'mestico, -a **A** *adj* domestic; **le pareti domestiche** one's own four walls
B *m* servant
C *f* maid
domicili'are *adj* **arresti domiciliari** Jur house arrest; **perquisizione domiciliare** Jur house search
domicili'arsi *vr* settle
domi'cilio *m* domicile; (abitazione) home; **recapitiamo a ~** we do home deliveries
domi'nante *adj* ‹*nazione, colore*› dominant; ‹*caratteri*› chief; ‹*opinione*› prevailing; ‹*motivo*› main
domi'nanza *f* Biol, Zool dominance
domi'nare **A** *vt* dominate; (controllare) control
B *vi* rule over; (prevalere) be dominant
domi'narsi *vr* control oneself
domina|'tore, -trice **A** *adj* domineering
B *mf* ruler
dominazi'one *f* domination
Domi'nica *f* Dominica
domini'cano *adj* **la Repubblica Dominicana** the Dominican Republic
do'minio *m* control; Pol dominion; (ambito) field; **di ~ pubblico** common knowledge
'domino *m* (gioco) dominoes
don *m inv* (ecclesiastico) Father
do'nare **A** *vt* give; donate ‹*sangue, organo*›
B *vi* **~ a** (giovare esteticamente) suit
do'narsi *vr* dedicate oneself
dona|'tore, -trice *mf* donor
■ **donatore di organi** organ donor; **donatore del seme** sperm donor
donazi'one *f* donation
dondo'lare **A** *vt* swing; (cullare) rock
B *vi* sway
dondo'larsi *vr* swing
dondo'lio *m* rocking
'dondolo *m* swing; **cavallo/sedia a ~** rocking horse/chair
dongio'vanni *m inv* Romeo, Don Juan
'donna *f* woman; **fare la prima ~** act like a prima donna; **'donne'** 'ladies'
■ **donna d'affari** businesswoman; **donna delle pulizie** cleaner; **donna di servizio** domestic help; **donna di vita** (prostituta) lady of the night
don'naccia *f* derog hussy
donnai'olo *m* womanizer
donnicci'ola *f* fig old woman

d

'donnola *f* weasel
'dono *m* gift
'doping *m inv* Sport drug-taking; **fa uso di ~** he takes drugs; **essere positivo al ~** test positive for doping
✓ **'dopo** A *prep* after; (a partire da) since
B *adv* after; afterwards; (più tardi) later; (in seguito) later on; **~ di me** after me

d

dopo'barba *m inv* aftershave
dopo'cena *m inv* evening
dopodiché *adv* after which
dopodo'mani *adv* the day after tomorrow
dopogu'erra *m inv* post-war period
dopola'voro *m inv* working man's club
dopo'pranzo *m inv* afternoon
dopo'sci *adj & m inv* après-ski
doposcu'ola *m inv* after-school activities *pl*
dopo-'shampoo A *m inv* conditioner
B *adj inv* conditioning
dopo'sole A *m inv* aftersun cream
B *adj inv* aftersun
✓ **dopo'tutto** *adv* after all
doppi'aggio *m* dubbing
doppia'mente *adv* (in misura doppia) doubly
doppi'are *vt* Naut double; Sport lap; Cinema dub
doppia|'tore, -trice *mf* sound dubber
doppi'etta *f* (fucile) double-barrelled shotgun; Auto double-declutch; (in calcio) two goals; (in pugilato) one-two
doppi'ezza *f* duplicity
✓ **'doppio** A *adj & adv* double
■ **doppia nazionalità** dual nationality; **doppi vetri** double glazing; **doppio clic** Comput double click; **fare un ~ su** double-click on; **doppio fallo** Tennis double fault; **doppio gioco** double-dealing; **doppio mento** double chin; **doppio senso** double entendre
B *m* double, twice the quantity; Tennis doubles *pl*
■ **doppio misto** Tennis mixed doubles
doppio'fondo *m* Naut double hull; (in valigia) false bottom
doppiogio'chista *mf* double-dealer
doppi'one *m* duplicate
doppio'petto *adj* double-breasted
dop'pista *mf* Tennis doubles player
do'rare *vt* gild; Culin brown
do'rato *adj* gilt; (color oro) golden
dora'tura *f* gilding
'dorico *adj* Archit Doric
do'rifora *f* Colorado beetle
dormicchi'are *vi* doze
dormigli'one, -a *mf* sleepyhead; fig lazybones
✓ **dor'mire** *vi* sleep; (essere addormentato) be asleep; fig be asleep; **andare a ~** go to bed; **~ come un ghiro** sleep like a log; **~ in piedi** fig be half asleep; (essere stanco) be dead tired; **dormirci sopra** sleep on it
dor'mita *f* good sleep; **fare una bella ~** have a good sleep
dormi'tina *f* nap
dormi'torio *m* dormitory
■ **dormitorio pubblico** night shelter
dormi'veglia *m* **essere nel ~** be half asleep
dor'sale A *adj* dorsal
B *f* (di monte) ridge
dor'sista *mf* backstroke swimmer
'dorso *m* back; (di libro) spine; (di monte) crest; (nel nuoto) backstroke; **a ~ di cavallo** on horseback
do'saggio *m* dosage; fig weighing; **sbagliare il ~** get the amount wrong
do'sare *vt* dose; fig measure; **~ le parole** weigh one's words
do'sato *adj* measured
dosa'tore *m* measuring jug
'dose *f* dose; **~ eccessiva** overdose; **in buona ~** fig in good measure
dos'sier *m inv* (raccolta di dati, fascicolo) file
'dosso *m* (dorso) back; (su strada) bump; **levarsi di ~ gli abiti** take off one's clothes
■ **dosso di rallentamento** road hump, speed hump
do'tare *vt* endow; (di accessori) equip
do'tato *adj* <*persona*> gifted; (fornito) equipped
dotazi'one *f* (attrezzatura) equipment; (mezzi finanziari) endowment; **avere qualcosa in ~** be equipped with something
✓ **'dote** *f* dowry; (qualità) gift
dott. *abbr* (**dottore**) Dr
'dotto A *adj* learned
B *m* scholar; Anat duct
dotto'rale *adj* doctoral; derog pedantic
dotto'rando, -a *mf* postgraduate student
dotto'rato *m* doctorate
✓ **dot'tor|e, dottor'essa** *mf* doctor
dot'trina *f* doctrine
dott.ssa *abbr* (**dottoressa**) Dr.
double-'face *adj inv* reversible
✓ **'dove** *adv* where; **di ~ sei?** where do you come from; **fin ~?** how far?; **per ~?** which way?
✓ **do'vere** A *vi* (obbligo) have to, must; **devo andare** I have to go, I must go; **devo venire anch'io?** do I have to come too?; **avresti dovuto dirmelo** you should have told me, you ought to have told me; **devo sedermi un attimo** I must sit down for a minute, I need to sit down for a minute; **dev'essere successo qualcosa** something must have happened; **come si deve** properly
B *vt* (essere debitore di, derivare) owe; **essere dovuto a** be due to
C *m* duty; **per ~** out of duty; **rivolgersi a chi di ~** apply to the appropriate authorities
dove'roso *adj* right and proper
do'vizia *f* **con ~ di particolari** in great detail

do'vunque **A** *adv* (dappertutto) everywhere; (in qualsiasi luogo) anywhere
B *conj* wherever

dovuta'mente *adv* duly

do'vuto *adj* due; (debito) proper; **essere ~ a** be attributable to; **ha fatto più del ~** he did more than he had to

Down sindrome di ~ *nf* Med Down's syndrome

doz'zina *f* **una ~ di uova** a dozen eggs; **mezza ~ di uova** half a dozen eggs

dozzi'nale *adj* cheap

'draga *f* (scavatrice) dredger

draga'mine *f* minesweeper

dra'gare *vt* dredge

'drago *m* dragon

'dramma *m* drama; **fare un ~ di qualcosa** fig make a drama out of something

drammatica'mente *adv* dramatically

drammaticità *f inv* dramatic force

dram'matico *adj* dramatic

drammatiz'zare *vt* dramatize

drammatizzazi'one *f* dramatization

drammatur'gia *f* (genere) drama

dramma'turgo *m* playwright

dram'mone *m* (film) tear-jerker, weepy

drappeggi'are *vt* drape

drap'peggio *m* drapery

drap'pello *m* Mil squad; (gruppo) band

'drappo *m* (tessuto) cloth

drastica'mente *adv* drastically

'drastico *adj* drastic

dre'naggio *m* drainage
■ **drenaggio di capitali** transfer of capital; **drenaggio fiscale** fiscal drag

dre'nare *vt* drain

'Dresda *f* Dresden

dres'sage *m inv* (gara) dressage

drib'blare *vt* (in calcio) dribble; fig dodge

'dribbling *m inv* (in calcio) dribble

'dritta *f* (mano destra) right hand; Naut starboard; (informazione) pointer; tip; **a ~ e a manca** (dappertutto) left, right and centre

dritta'mente *adv* (furbescamente) craftily

'dritto, -a **A** *adj* = **diritto**[1]
B *mf* infml crafty so-and-so

drive *m inv* Comput drive

drive-'in *m inv* drive-in

driz'zare *vt* straighten; (rizzare) prick up

driz'zarsi *vr* straighten [up]; (alzarsi) raise; **mi sono drizzati i capelli** fig my hair stood on end

'droga *f* drug
■ **droga leggera** soft drug; **droga di passaggio** gateway drug; **droga pesante** hard drug

dro'gare *vt* drug

dro'garsi *vr* take drugs

drogato, -a **A** *adj* drugged
B *mf* drug addict

droghe'ria *f* grocery

droghi'ere, -a *mf* grocer

drome'dario *m* dromedary

'druso *mf* Druse

dua'lismo *m* dualism; (contrasto) conflict

'dubbio **A** *adj* doubtful; (ambiguo) dubious
B *m* doubt; (sospetto) suspicion; **mettere in ~** doubt; **essere fuori ~** be beyond doubt; **essere in ~** be doubtful

dubbiosa'mente *adv* doubtfully

dubbi'oso, dubi'tante *adj* doubtful

dubi'tare *vi* doubt; **~ di** doubt; (diffidare) mistrust; **dubito che venga** I doubt whether he'll come

dubita'tivo *adj* (ambiguo) ambiguous

Du'blino *f* Dublin

'duca *m* duke

du'cale *adj* ducal

'duce *m* (nel fascismo) Duce

du'chessa *f* duchess

'due *adj & nm* two

duecen'tesco *adj* thirteenth-century

duecen'tesimo *m* two hundredth

due'cento *adj & nm* two hundred

duel'lante *mf* dueller

duel'lare *vi* duel

du'ello *m* duel

due'mila *adj & nm* two thousand

due'pezzi *m inv* (bikini) bikini; (vestito) two-piece suit

du'etto *m* duo; Mus duet

'dumping *m inv* Fin dumping

'duna *f* dune

dune 'buggy *m inv* beach buggy

'dunque *conj* therefore; (allora) well [then]; **arrivare al ~** get down to the nitty-gritty

'duo *m inv* duo; Mus duet

duodeci'male *adj* duodecimal

duode'nale *adj* **ulcera ~** duodenal ulcer

duo'deno *m* duodenum

du'omo *m* cathedral

'duplex *m* Teleph party line

dupli'care *vt* duplicate

dupli'cato *m* duplicate

duplicazi'one *f* duplication

'duplice *adj* double; **in ~** in duplicate

duplicità *f inv* duplicity

dura'mente *adv* ‹*lavorare*› hard; ‹*rimproverare*› harshly

du'rante *prep* during

du'rare **A** *vi* last; ‹*cibo*› keep; (resistere) hold out; **così non può ~** this can't go on any longer; **~ in carica** remain in office; **finché dura** as long as it lasts
B *vt* **~ fatica** sweat blood

du'rata *f* duration
■ **durata del collegamento** on-line time; **durata di conservazione** shelf life; **durata della vita** life span

d

dura'turo *adj* lasting
du'revole *adj* ‹*pace*› lasting, enduring
du'rezza *f* hardness; (di carne) toughness; (di voce, padre) harshness
'duro, -a **A** *adj* hard; ‹*persona, carne*› tough; ‹*voce*› harsh; ‹*pane*› stale; **tieni ~!** (resistere) hang in there!; **~ d'orecchio** hard of hearing
B *mf* (persona) tough person, toughie infml
du'rone *m* hardened skin
'duttile *adj* ‹*materiale*› ductile; ‹*carattere, persona*› malleable
duttilità *f inv* (di materiale) ductility; (di individuo) malleability
'duty free *m inv* duty-free shop
DVD **A** *m inv* (disco) DVD
B *m inv* (lettore) DVD player

Ee

e *conj* and
eba'nista *mf* cabinet-maker
'ebano *m* ebony
eb'bene *conj* well [then]
eb'brezza *f* inebriation; (euforia) elation; **guida in stato di ~** drink-driving; **l'~ della velocità** the thrill of speed
'ebbro *adj* inebriated; **~ di gioia** delirious with joy
'ebete *adj* stupid
ebollizi'one *f* boiling
'ebook *m* e-book
e'braico *adj & nm* Hebrew
ebra'ismo *m* Judaism
e'breo, -a **A** *adj* Jewish
B *m* Jew
C *f* Jewess
'Ebridi *fpl* **le ~** the Hebrides
eca'tombe *f* **fare un'~** wreak havoc
ecc *abbr* (**eccetera**) etc
ecce'dente *adj* ‹*peso, bagaglio*› excess
ecce'denza *f* excess; (d'avanzo) surplus; **avere qualcosa in ~** have an excess of something; **bagagli in ~** excess baggage
■ **eccedenza di cassa** surplus; **eccedenza di peso** excess weight
ec'cedere **A** *vt* exceed
B *vi* go too far; **~ nel bere** drink to excess; **~ nel mangiare** overeat
eccel'lente *adj* excellent
eccel'lenza *f* excellence; (titolo) Excellency; **per ~** par excellence
ec'cellere *vi* excel (**in** at)
eccentricità *f inv* eccentricity
ec'centrico, -a *adj & nmf* eccentric
ecce'pire *vt* object to
eccessiva'mente *adv* excessively
ecces'sivo *adj* excessive
ec'cesso *m* excess; **andare agli eccessi** go to extremes; **dare in eccessi** fly into a temper; **all'~** to excess
■ **eccesso di personale** over-manning; **eccesso di peso** excess weight; **eccesso di velocità** speeding
ec'cetera *adv* et cetera
ec'cetto *prep* except; **~ che** (a meno che) unless
eccettu'are *vt* except
eccezio'nale *adj* exceptional; **in via [del tutto] ~** as an exception
eccezional'mente *adv* exceptionally; (contrariamente alla regola) as an exception
eccezi'one *f* exception; Jur objection; **a ~ di** with the exception of; **d'~** exceptional
ec'chimosi *f inv* bruising
ecci *int* atishoo
ec'cidio *m* massacre
ecci'tabile *adj* ‹*persona, carattere*› excitable
eccita'mento *m* excitement
ecci'tante **A** *adj* exciting; ‹*sostanza*› stimulant
B *m* stimulant
ecci'tare *vt* excite; (sessualmente) excite, arouse
ecci'tarsi *vr* get excited; (sessualmente) become aroused *or* excited
ecci'tato *adj* excited; (sessualmente) excited, aroused; **~ da** flushed with
eccitazi'one *f* excitement; (sessuale) arousal, excitement
ecclesi'astico **A** *adj* ecclesiastical
B *m* priest
'ecco *adv* (qui) here; (là) there; **~!** (con approvazione) that's right!; **~ qua!** (dando qualcosa) here you are!; **~ la tua borsa** here is your bag; **~ mio figlio** there is my son; **eccomi** here I am; **~ fatto** there we are; **~ perché** this is why; **~ tutto** that is all
ec'come *adv & int* and how!

key word

ECG *abbr* (**elettrocardiogramma**) ECG
echeggi'are *vi* echo
e'clettico *adj* eclectic
eclet'tismo *m* eclecticism
eclis'sare *vt* fig eclipse
eclis'sarsi *vr* (sparire) disappear
e'clissi *f inv* eclipse
■ **eclissi di sole** solar eclipse
'eco *mf* (*pl m* **echi**) echo; **ha suscitato una vasta ~** it caused a great stir
eco+ *pref* eco+; **eco-guerrigliero** eco-warrior
ecocompa'tibile *adj* environmental
ecogra'fia *f* scan
ecolo'gia *f* ecology
eco'logico *adj* ecological; ‹*prodotto*› environmentally friendly, eco-friendly
e'cologo, -a *mf* ecologist
e commerci'ale *f* ampersand
econo'mia *f* economy; (scienza) economics *sg*; **fare ~** economize (**di** on); **[fatto] in ~** [done] on the cheap; **senza ~** unstintingly; **fare qualcosa senza ~** spare no expense doing something
■ **economia aziendale** business administration; **economia domestica** Sch home economics; **economia di mercato** market economy; **economia di libero mercato** free market; **economia mista** mixed economy; **economia sommersa** black economy
economicità *f inv* economy
eco'nomico *adj* economic; (a buon prezzo) cheap; (con pochi costi) economical; **difficoltà economiche** financial difficulties; **classe economica** economy class; **edizione economica** paperback
econo'mie *fpl* (risparmi) savings
econo'mista *mf* economist
economiz'zare **A** *vt* save ‹*tempo, denaro*› **B** *vi* economize (**su** on)
economizza'tore *m* Auto fuel economizer
e'conomo, -a **A** *adj* thrifty **B** *mf* (di collegio) bursar
ecosi'stema *m* ecosystem
ecososte'nibile *adj* environmentally-friendly, eco-friendly
eco'tassa *f* carbon tax
ecoterro'rismo *m* ecoterrorism
ecotu'rismo *m* ecotourism
é'cru *adj inv* fawn
Ecua'dor *m* Ecuador
ecuadori'ano, -a *adj & nmf* Ecuadorian
ecu'menico *adj* ecumenical
ec'zema *m* eczema
ed *conj* ▶ **e**
e'dema *m* oedema
'Eden *m* Eden
'edera *f* ivy
e'dicola *f* [newspaper] kiosk
edifi'cabile *adj* ‹*area, terreno*› *classified as suitable for development*
edifi'cante *adj* edifying
edifi'care *vt* build; (indurre al bene) edify
edi'ficio *m* building; fig structure
e'dile **A** *adj* building *attrib* **B** *m* **edili** *pl* construction workers
edi'lizia *f* building trade
edi'lizio *adj* building *attrib*
Edim'burgo *f* Edinburgh
E'dipo *m* Oedipus; **complesso di ~** Oedipus complex
edi'tare *vt* edit
'editing *m* editing
'edito *adj* published
edi|'tore, -trice **A** *adj* publishing **B** *mf* publisher; (curatore) editor
edito'ria *f* publishing
■ **editoria elettronica** desktop publishing, electronic publishing; **editoria telematica** online publishing
editori'ale **A** *adj* publishing **B** *m* (articolo) editorial, leader
e'ditto *m* edict
edizi'one *f* edition; (di manifestazione) performance; **in ~ italiana** ‹*film*› dubbed into Italian
■ **edizione ridotta** abridgement, abridged version; **edizione della sera** (di telegiornale) evening news
edo'nismo *m* hedonism
edo'nistico *adj* hedonistic
educagi'oco *m* edutainment
edu'canda *f* [convent school] boarder; fig prim and proper girl
edu'care *vt* educate; (allevare) bring up
educa'tivo *adj* educational
edu'cato *adj* polite
educa|'tore, -trice *mf* educator
educazione *f* education; (di bambini) upbringing; (buone maniere) [good] manners *pl*; **bella ~!** what manners!
■ **educazione alla cittadinanza** education for citizenship; **educazione fisica** physical education; **educazione sessuale** sex education
edulco'rare *vt* **~ la pillola** sweeten the pill
EED *abbr* (**elaborazione elettronica [dei] dati**) EDP
e'felide *f* freckle
effemi'nato *adj* effeminate
effe'rato *adj* brutal
efferve'scente *adj* effervescent; (frizzante) fizzy; ‹*aspirina*®› soluble
effettiva'mente *adv* **è troppo tardi - ~** it's too late - so it is
effet'tivo **A** *adj* actual; (efficace) effective; ‹*personale*› permanent; Mil regular **B** *m* (somma totale) sum total
ef'fetto *m* effect; (impressione) impression; (cambiale) bill; **fare ~** ‹*medicina*› take effect; **fare ~ su** have an effect on, affect; **in effetti** in fact; (a tutti gli effetti) to all intents and

purposes; **ad effetto** ‹*frase*› catchy; **la vista del sangue mi fa ~** I can't stand the sight of blood; **tiro con ~** spin
■ **effetto boomerang** boomerang effect; **effetto domino** domino effect; **effetto di luce** trick of the light; **effetti personali** *pl* personal belongings, personal effects fml; **effetto ritardato** delayed effect; **effetto serra** greenhouse effect; **effetto sonoro** sound effect; **effetto speciale** Cinema, TV special effect

effettu'are *vt* effect; carry out ‹*controllo, sondaggio*›

effettu'arsi *vr* take place; **'si effettua dal ... al ...'** this service is available from ... till ...

effi'cace *adj* effective

effi'cacia *f* effectiveness

effici'ente *adj* efficient

effici'enza *f* efficiency; **in piena ~** in full swing

ef'figie *f* effigy

ef'fimero *adj* ephemeral

ef'flusso *m* outflow

ef'fluvio *m* stink

ef'fondersi *vr* **~ in ringraziamenti** thank somebody profusely

effrazi'one *f*
■ **effrazione con scasso** Jur breaking and entering

effusi'one *f* effusion

'Egadi *fpl* **le [isole] ~** the Egadi Islands

egemo'nia *f* hegemony

E'geo *m* **l'~** the Aegean [Sea]

e'gida *f* **sotto l'~ di** under the aegis of

E'gitto *m* Egypt

egizi'ano, -a *adj & nmf* Egyptian

e'gizio, -a *adj & nmf* ancient Egyptian

'egli *pers pron* he; **~ stesso** he himself

ego'centrico, -a **A** *adj* egocentric
B *mf* egocentric person

egocen'trismo *m* egocentricity

ego'ismo *m* selfishness

ego'ista **A** *adj* selfish
B *mf* selfish person

egoistica'mente *adv* selfishly

ego'istico *adj* selfish

Egr. *abbr* (**egregio**) **~ Sig.** (su busta) Mr

e'gregio *adj* distinguished; **Egregio Signore** Dear Sir

egualI'tario *adj & nm* egalitarian

eh *int* huh!

'ehi *int* hey!

ehilà *int* hi!

ehm *int* um

eiacu'lare *vi* ejaculate

eiaculazi'one *f* ejaculation

eiet'tabile *adj* ‹*sedile*› ejector

eiezi'one *f* Aeron ejection

key word

'Eire *f* Eire

elabo'rare *vt* elaborate; process ‹*dati*›

elabo'rato **A** *adj* elaborate
B *m* (tabulato) preprinted form

elabora'tore *m*
■ **elaboratore [di testi]** word processor

elaborazione *f* elaboration; (di dati) processing
■ **elaborazione [dei] dati** data processing; **elaborazione elettronica [dei] dati** electronic data processing; **elaborazione sequenziale** Comput batch processing; **elaborazione [di] testi** word processing

elar'gire *vt* lavish

elasticità *f inv* elasticity
■ **elasticità mentale** mental agility; **elasticità di movimento** litheness

elasticiz'zato *adj* ‹*stoffa*› elasticated

e'lastico **A** *adj* elastic; ‹*tessuto*› stretch; ‹*passo*› springy; ‹*orario, mente*› flexible; ‹*persona*› easy-going; ‹*morale*› lax; **collant** *pl* **elastici** support tights
B *m* elastic; (fascia) rubber band

'Elba *f* Elba

eldo'rado *m* eldorado

ele'fante *m* elephant; **avere una memoria da ~** have a memory like an elephant; **fare passi da ~** thump about
■ **~ marino** sea elephant

elefan'tesco *adj* elephantine

elefan'tessa *f* cow[-elephant]

elefan'tiaco *adj* (enorme) elephantine

ele'gante *adj* elegant

elegante'mente *adv* elegantly

ele'ganza *f* elegance

e'leggere *vt* elect

eleg'gibile *adj* eligible

ele'gia *f* elegy

elemen'tare *adj* elementary; **scuola ~** primary school

ele'mento *m* element; (componente) part; **trovarsi nel proprio ~** be in one's element; **elementi** *pl* (fatti) data; (rudimenti) elements

ele'mosina *f* charity; **chiedere l'~** beg; **vivere d'~** live on charity; **fare l'~** give money to beggars

elemosi'nare *vt & vi* beg

elen'care *vt* list

e'lenco *m* list
■ **elenco [degli] abbonati** Teleph telephone directory; **elenco telefonico** telephone directory

elet'tivo *adj* ‹*carica*› elective

e'letto, -a **A** pp di **eleggere**
B *adj* chosen
C *mf* (nominato) elected member; **per pochi eletti** fig for the chosen few

eletto'rale *adj* electoral

elettora'lismo *m* electioneering

eletto'rato *m* electorate

elet|'tore, -trice *mf* voter

elet'trauto *m* electrics garage
elettri'cista *m* electrician
elettricità *f inv* electricity; **togliere l'∼** cut the electricity off; **è mancata l'∼** there was a power cut
e'lettrico *adj* electric
elettriz'zante *adj* ‹*notizia, gara*› electrifying
elettriz'zare *vt* fig electrify
elettriz'zato *adj* fig electrified
elettro+ *pref* electro+
elettrocardio'gramma *m* electrocardiogram, ECG
elettrocuzi'one *f* electrocution
e'lettrodo *m* electrode
elettrodo'mestico *m* [electrical] household appliance
elettroencefalo'gramma *m* electroencephalogram
elettroesecuzi'one *f* electrocution
elet'trogeno *adj* **gruppo ∼** generator
elet'trolisi *f* electrolysis
elettromo'tore *m* electric motor
elettromo'trice *f* electric train
elet'trone *m* electron
elet'tronico, -a **A** *adj* electronic **B** *f* electronics *sg*
elettroshocktera'pia *f* electroshock therapy, electroshock treatment, EST
elettro'tecnica *f* electrical engineering
elettro'tecnico *m* electrical engineer
elettro'treno *m* electric train
ele'vare *vt* raise; (promuovere) promote; (erigere) erect; fig (migliorare) better; **∼ al quadrato/cubo** square/cube
ele'varsi *vr* rise; ‹*edificio*› stand
ele'vato *adj* high; fig (sentimento) lofty; **∼ al cubo/al quadrato** cubed/squared; **∼ a dieci** raised to the power of ten
eleva'tore *m* fork-lift truck
elevazi'one *f* elevation
elezi'one *f* election; **elezioni** *pl* **amministrative** local council elections; **elezioni** *pl* **politiche** general election
eliambu'lanza *f* air ambulance
'elica *f* Naut screw, propeller; Aeron propeller; (del ventilatore) blade
eli'cottero *m* helicopter
elimi'nabile *adj* which can be eliminated
elimi'nare *vt* eliminate
elimina'toria *f* Sport [preliminary] heat
eliminazi'one *f* elimination
'elio *m* (gas) helium
eli'porto *m* heliport
elisabetti'ano *adj & nmf* Elizabethan
é'lite *f inv* élite
eli'tista *adj* élitist
'ella *pers pron* (liter) she; **∼ stessa** she herself
el'lenico *adj* Hellenic
elle'nistico *adj* Hellenistic
ellepì *m inv* LP
+ellino *suff* **campanellino** *nm* [small] bell; **fiorellino** *nm* [little] flower; **gonnellina** *nf* short skirt
el'lisse *f* ellipse
el'lissi *f inv* ellipsis
el'littico *adj* elliptical
+ello *suff* **finestrella** *nf* little window; **pecorella** *nf* woolly sheep; **saltello** *nm* skip
el'metto *m* helmet
elogi'are *vt* praise
elogia'tivo *adj* laudatory
e'logio *m* praise; (discorso, scritto) eulogy; **degno di ∼** laudable, praiseworthy; **ti faccio i miei elogi per** congratulations on
■ **∼ funebre** funeral oration
elo'quente *adj* eloquent; fig tell-tale
elo'quenza *f* eloquence
El Salva'dor *m* El Salvador; **nel Salvador** in El Salvador
e'ludere *vt* elude; evade ‹*sorveglianza, controllo*›
elusi'one *f*
■ **elusione fiscale** tax avoidance
elu'sivo *adj* elusive
el'vetico *adj* Swiss; **Confederazione Elvetica** Swiss Confederation
emaci'ato *adj* emaciated
e-mail *f inv* email; **mandare per ∼** email, send by email; **indirizzo ∼** email address
ema'nare **A** *vt* give off; pass ‹*legge*› **B** *vi* emanate
emanazi'one *f* giving off; (di legge) enactment
emanci'pare *vt* emancipate
emanci'parsi *vr* become emancipated
emanci'pato *adj* emancipated
emancipazi'one *f* emancipation
emargi'nato *m* marginalized person
emarginazi'one *f* marginalization
ema'toma *m* haematoma
em'bargo *m* embargo
■ **embargo sulle armi** arms embargo
em'blema *m* emblem
emble'matico *adj* emblematic
embo'lia *f* embolism
'embolo *m* embolus
embrio'nale *adj* Biol fig embryonic; **allo stato ∼** ‹*progetto, idea*› embryonic
embri'one *m* embryo
emenda'mento *m* amendment
emen'dare *vt* amend
emen'darsi *vr* reform
emer'gente *adj* emergent
emer'genza *f* emergency; **in caso di ∼** in an emergency; **di ∼** (di riserva) stand-by; **uscita d'∼** emergency exit
■ **emergenza sanitaria** ambulance

e

e'mergere *vi* emerge; ‹*sottomarino*› surface; (distinguersi) stand out
e'merito *adj* ‹*professore*› emeritus; **un ~ imbecille** a prize idiot
e'merso pp di **emergere**
e'messo pp di **emettere**
e'metico *adj* emetic
e'mettere *vt* emit; give out ‹*luce, suono*›; let out ‹*grido*›; (mettere in circolazione) issue
emi'crania *f* migraine
emi'grare *vi* emigrate
emi'grato, -a *mf* immigrant
emigrazi'one *f* emigration
emi'nente *adj* eminent
emi'nenza *f* eminence; **Sua Eminenza** His/ Your Eminence
■ **eminenza grigia** éminence grise
emi'rato *m* emirate; **Emirati** *pl* **Arabi Uniti** United Arab Emirates
e'miro *m* emir
emi'sfero *m* hemisphere
emis'sario *m* emissary; (fiume) effluent
emissi'one *f* emission; (di denaro, francobolli) issue; (trasmissione) broadcast; **'~ del biglietto'** 'take your ticket here'; **a emissioni zero** carbon neutral; **a basse emissioni** low carbon; **emissioni di CO2** carbon emissions
emit'tente **A** *adj* issuing; (trasmittente) broadcasting
B *f* Radio transmitter
'emmental *m* Emmenthal
emofi'lia *f* haemophilia
emofi'liaco, -a *mf* haemophiliac
emoglo'bina *f* haemoglobin
emorra'gia *f* haemorrhage; **avere un'~** haemorrhage
emor'roidi *fpl* haemorrhoids, piles
emo'statico *adj* haemostatic
emotiva'mente *adv* emotionally
emotività *f inv* emotional make-up
emo'tivo *adj* emotional; **con turbe emotive** emotionally disturbed
emozio'nante *adj* exciting; (commovente) moving
emozio'nare *vt* excite; (commuovere) move
emozio'narsi *vr* become excited; (commuoversi) be moved
emozio'nato *adj* excited; (commosso) moved
⚷ **emozi'one** *f* emotion; (agitazione) excitement
empietà *f inv* impiety
'empio *adj* impious; (spietato) pitiless; (malvagio) wicked
em'pirico *adj* empirical
empi'rismo *m* empiricism
empi'rista *mf* empiricist
em'porio *m* emporium; (negozio) general store

⚷ key word

emù *m inv* emu
emu'lare *vt* emulate
emulazi'one *f* emulation
■ **emulazione di terminale** terminal emulation
emulsio'nare *vt* emulsify
emulsio'narsi *vr* emulsify
emulsi'one *f* emulsion
ena'lotto *m weekly lottery*
encefa'lite *f*
■ **encefalite spongiforme bovina** Bovine Spongiform Encephalopathy, BSE
encefalo'gramma *m* encephalogram
en'ciclica *f* encyclical
enciclope'dia *f* encyclopaedia
enciclo'pedico *adj* ‹*mente, cultura, dizionario*› encyclopaedic
encomi'are *vt* commend
en'comio *m* commendation
ende'mia *f* (situazione) endemic
en'demico *adj* endemic
endocrinolo'gia *f* endocrinology
endo'vena **A** *f* intravenous injection
B *adv* intravenously
endove'noso *adj* intravenous; **per via endovenosa** intravenously
ener'getico *adj* ‹*risorse, crisi*› energy *attrib*; ‹*alimento*› energy-giving
⚷ **ener'gia** *f* energy; **pieno di ~** full of energy
■ **energia alternativa** alternative energy; **energia atomica** atomic energy; **energia elettrica** electricity; **energia eolica** wind power; **energia idroelettrica** hydroelectricity; **energia nucleare** nuclear energy, nuclear power; **energia rinnovabile** renewable energy; **energia solare** solar energy, solar power
energica'mente *adv* energetically
e'nergico *adj* energetic; (efficace) strong
ener'gumeno *m* Neanderthal
'enfasi *f* emphasis
en'fatico *adj* emphatic
enfatiz'zare *vt* emphasize
enfi'sema *m* emphysema
e'nigma *m* enigma
enig'matico *adj* enigmatic
enig'mistica *f* puzzles *pl*
E.N.I.T. *nm abbr* (**Ente Nazionale Italiano per il Turismo**) Italian State Tourist Office
en'nesimo *adj* Math nth; infml umpteenth; **all'ennesima potenza** Math fig to the nth power/degree
eno'logico *adj* wine (*attrib*)
⚷ **e'norme** *adj* enormous, great big infml; **è un'ingiustizia ~** it's enormously unfair
enorme'mente *adv* massively
enormità *f inv* enormity; (assurdità) absurdity
eno'teca *f* wine-tasting shop
eno'tera *f* evening primrose

en pas'sant *adv* in passing
'ente *m* board; (società) company; (in filosofia) being
ente'rite *f* enteritis
entero'clisma *m* Med enema
entità *f inv* (filosofia) entity; (gravità) seriousness; (dimensione) extent
entomolo'gia *f* entomology
entou'rage *m inv* entourage
en'trambi *adj & pron* both
en'trare *vi* go in, enter; **~ in** go into; (stare in, trovar posto in) fit into; (arruolarsi) join; **entrarci** (avere a che fare) have to do with; **tu che c'entri?** what has it got to do with you?; **da che parte si entra?** how do you get in?; **fallo ~** (in ufficio, dal medico ecc.) show him in; **'vietato ~'** 'no entry'
en'trata *f* entry, entrance; (*pl* **entrate**) Comm takings; (reddito) income *sg*
■ **entrata libera** admission free; **entrata di servizio** tradesman's entrance
entre'côte *f inv* beef entrecôte
'entro *prep* (tempo) within; **~ oggi** by the end of today
entro'bordo *m* (motore) inboard motor; (motoscafo) speedboat
entro'terra *m inv* hinterland
entusia'smante *adj* fascinating, exciting
entusia'smare *vt* arouse enthusiasm in
entusia'smarsi *vr* be enthusiastic (per about)
entusi'asmo *m* enthusiasm
entusi'asta **A** *adj* enthusiastic **B** *mf* enthusiast
entusi'astico *adj* enthusiastic
enucle'are *vt* define
enume'rare *vt* enumerate
enumerazi'one *f* enumeration
enunci'are *vt* enunciate
enunciazi'one *f* enunciation
E'olie *fpl* **le ~** the Aeolian Islands
epa'tite *f* hepatitis
ep'eira *f* garden spider
epi'centro *m* epicentre
'epico *adj* epic
epide'mia *f* epidemic
epi'dermide *f* epidermis
epidu'rale *adj* Med (anestesia) epidural
Epifa'nia *f* Epiphany
epi'gramma *m* epigram
epiles'sia *f* epilepsy
epi'lettico, -a *adj & nmf* epileptic
e'pilogo *m* epilogue
episco'pato *m* episcopacy
epi'sodico *adj* episodic; **caso ~** one-off case
epi'sodio *m* episode
e'pistola *f* epistle
episto'lare *adj* epistolary
episto'lario *m* correspondence, letters *pl*
epi'taffio *m* epitaph
e'piteto *m* epithet
'epoca *f* age; (periodo) period; **a quell'~** in those days; **un avvenimento che ha fatto ~** an epoch-making event; **auto d'epoca** vintage car; **mobile d'epoca** period furniture
e'ponimo *adj* eponymous
epo'pea *f* epic
ep'pure *conj* [and] yet
E.P.T. *abbr* (**Ente Provinciale per il Turismo**) *Italian local tourist board*
epu'rare *vt* purge; purify ‹*acqua*›
epura'tore *m* water purifier
epurazi'one *f* purging; (di acqua) purification
■ **epurazione etnica** ethnic cleansing
equalizza'tore *m* equalizer
e'quanime *adj* level-headed; (imparziale) impartial
equa'tore *m* equator
equatori'ale *adj* equatorial
equazi'one *f* equation
e'questre *adj* equestrian; **circo ~** circus
equidi'stante *adj* equidistant
equi'latero *adj* equilateral
equili'brare *vt* balance
equili'brato *adj* (persona) well-balanced
equi'librio *m* balance; (buon senso) common sense; (di bilancia) equilibrium
equili'brismo *m* **fare ~** do a balancing act
equili'brista *mf* tightrope walker
e'quino *adj* horse *attrib*
equi'nozio *m* equinox
equipaggia'mento *m* equipment
equipaggi'are *vt* equip; (di persone) man
equi'paggio *m* crew; Aeron cabin crew
■ **equipaggio di volo** aircrew
equipa'rare *vt* make equal
equipa'rato *adj* equal
é'quipe *f inv* team
equità *f inv* equity
equitazione *f* riding, horse riding, horseback riding AmE
equiva'lente *adj & nm* equivalent
equiva'lenza *f* equivalence
equiva'lere *vi* **~ a** be equivalent to
equivo'care *vi* misunderstand
e'quivoco **A** *adj* equivocal; (sospetto) suspicious; **un tipo ~** a shady character **B** *m* misunderstanding; **a scanso di equivoci** to avoid any misunderstandings; **giocare sull'~** equivocate
'equo *adj* fair, just
equosoli'dale *adj* fair trade *attrib*
'era *f* era
■ **era glaciale** Ice Age
'erba *f* grass; (medicinale) herb; **in ~** ‹*atleta,*

attore› budding
■ **erba cipollina** chives
er'baccia *f* weed
er'baceo *adj* herbaceous
erbi'cida *m* weedkiller
er'bivoro **A** *adj* herbivorous
B *m* herbivore
erbo'rista *mf* herbalist
erboriste'ria *f* herbalist's shop
er'boso *adj* grassy
Erco'lano *f* Herculaneum
'Ercole *m* Hercules
er'culeo *adj ‹forza›* Herculean
e'rede **A** *m* heir
B *f* heiress
eredità *f inv* inheritance; Biol heredity
eredi'tare *vt* inherit
ereditarietà *f inv* heredity
eredi'tario *adj* hereditary
erediti'era *f* heiress
+erello *suff* **furterello** *nm* petty theft; **pioggerella** *nf* drizzle
ere'mita *m* hermit
'eremo *m* isolated place; fig retreat
ere'sia *f* heresy
e'retico, -a **A** *adj* heretical
B *mf* heretic
e'retto **A** pp di **erigere**
B *adj* erect
erezi'one *f* erection; (costruzione) building
ergasto'lano, -a *mf prisoner serving a life sentence* lifer infml
er'gastolo *m* life sentence; (luogo) prison
ergono'mia *f* ergonomics *sg*
ergo'nomico *adj* ergonomic
ergotera'pia *f* occupational therapy
ergotera'pista *mf* occupational therapist
'erica *f* heather
e'rigere *vt* erect; fig (fondare) found
eri'tema *m* (cutaneo) inflammation; (solare) sunburn
■ **eritema da pannolini** nappy rash
Eri'trea *f* Eritrea
eri'treo, -a *adj & nmf* Eritrean
ermafro'dito *adj & nm* hermaphrodite
ermel'lino *m* ermine
ermetica'mente *adv* hermetically
er'metico *adj* hermetic; (a tenuta d'aria) airtight
'ernia *f* hernia
e'rodere *vi* erode
⚷ **e'roe** *m* hero
ero'gare *vt* distribute; (fornire) supply
erogazi'one *f* supply
e'rogeno *adj* erogenous
eroica'mente *adv* heroically
e'roico *adj* heroic

⚷ key word

ero'ina *f* heroine; (droga) heroin
eroi'nomane *mf* heroin addict
ero'ismo *m* heroism
'eros *m* Eros
erosi'one *f* erosion
e'rotico *adj* erotic
ero'tismo *m* eroticism
'erpice *m* harrow
er'rante *adj* wandering
er'rare *vi* (vagare) wander; (sbagliare) be mistaken
er'rato *adj* (sbagliato) mistaken; **se non vado ~** if I'm not mistaken
'erre *f*
■ **erre moscia** burr
erronea'mente *adv* mistakenly
⚷ **er'rore** *m* error, mistake; (di stampa) misprint; **essere in ~** be wrong
■ **errore giudiziario** miscarriage of justice; **errore di stampa** printing error, typo
'erta *f* **stare all'~** be on the alert
eru'dirsi *vr* get educated
eru'dito *adj* learned
erut'tare **A** *vt ‹vulcano›* erupt
B *vi* (ruttare) belch
eruzi'one *f* eruption; Med rash
Es *m* Psych **l'~** the id
es. *abbr* (**esempio**) eg
esacer'bare *vt* exacerbate
⚷ **esage'rare** **A** *vt* exaggerate; **~ le cose** exaggerate things, go over the top
B *vi* exaggerate; (nel comportamento) go over the top; **~ nel mangiare** eat too much
esagerata'mente *adv* excessively
esage'rato **A** *adj* exaggerated; *‹prezzo›* exorbitant
B *m* **è un ~** he exaggerates
esagerazi'one *f* exaggeration; **è costato un'~** it cost the earth; **senza ~** with no exaggeration
esago'nale *adj* hexagonal
e'sagono *m* hexagon
esa'lare **A** *vt* give off; **~ l'ultimo respiro** breathe one's last
B *vi* emanate
esalazi'one *f* emission; **esalazioni** *pl* fumes
esal'tare *vt* exalt; (entusiasmare) elate
esal'tarsi *vr* (entusiasmarsi) get excited (**per** about)
esal'tato **A** *adj* (fanatico) fanatical
B *m* fanatic
esaltazi'one *f* exaltation; (in discorso) fervour
⚷ **e'same** *m* examination, exam; **dare un ~** take *or* sit an exam; **prendere in ~** examine
■ **esame di ammissione** Sch entrance examination; **esame di coscienza** soul-searching; **esame di guida** driving test; **esami di maturità** ≈ A levels; **esame orale** Sch, Univ viva; **esame del sangue** blood test; **esame**

della vista eye test
esami'nando, -a *mf* examinee
esami'nare *vt* examine
esamina|'tore, -trice *mf* examiner
e'sangue *adj* bloodless
e'sanime *adj* lifeless
esaspe'rante *adj* exasperating
esaspe'rare *vt* exasperate
esaspe'rarsi *vr* get exasperated
esasperazi'one *f* exasperation
esatta'mente *adv* exactly
esat'tezza *f* exactness; (precisione) precision; (di risposta, risultato) accuracy
e'satto *adj* exact; (risposta, risultato) correct; ‹*orologio*› right; **hai l'ora esatta?** do you have the right time?; **sono le due esatte** it's two o'clock exactly
esat'tore *m* collector
■ **esattore dei crediti** Fin debt collector; **esattore delle imposte** tax collector, tax man
esau'dire *vt* grant; fulfil ‹*speranze*›
esauri'ente *adj* exhaustive
esauri'mento *m* exhaustion; **'fino ad ~ delle scorte'** 'subject to availability'
■ **esaurimento nervoso** nervous breakdown
esau'rire *vt* exhaust
esau'rirsi *vr* exhaust oneself; ‹*merci ecc.*› run out
esau'rito *adj* exhausted; ‹*merci*› sold out; ‹*libro*› out of print; **fare il tutto ~** ‹*spettacolo*› play to a full house; **'tutto ~'** 'sold out'
esazi'one *f* collection
■ **esazione crediti** debt collection
'esca *f* bait
escande'scenza *f* outburst; **dare in escandescenze** lose one's temper
escava'tore *m* excavator
escava'trice *f* excavator
escla'mare *vi* exclaim
esclama'tivo *adj* exclamatory
esclamazi'one *f* exclamation
e'scludere *vt* exclude; rule out ‹*possibilità, ipotesi*›
esclusi'one *f* exclusion; **senza ~ di colpi** ‹*attacco*› all-out
esclu'siva *f* exclusive right, sole right; **in ~** exclusive
esclusiva'mente *adv* exclusively
esclusi'vista *mf* exclusive agent
esclu'sivo *adj* exclusive
e'scluso **A** pp di **escludere**
B *adj* **non è ~ che ci sia** it's not out of the question that he'll be there; **esclusi i presenti** with the exception of those present; **esclusi sabati e festivi** except Saturdays and Sundays/holidays
C *m* outcast
escogi'tare *vt* contrive
escoriazi'one *f* graze
'escort *f* high-class call girl
escre'mento *m* excrement; **escrementi** *pl* excrement
escursi'one *f* (gita) excursion; (camminata) hike; (scorreria) raid
■ **escursione termica** temperature range
escursio'nismo *m* hiking
ese'crabile *adj* abominable
ese'crare *vt* abhor
esecu'tivo *adj & nm* executive
esecu|'tore, -trice *mf* executor; Mus performer
esecuzi'one *f* execution; Mis performance
■ **esecuzione capitale** capital punishment
esegu'ibile *m* Comput executable file
esegu'ire *vt* carry out; Jur execute; Mus perform
e'sempio *m* example; **ad** *o* **per ~** for example; **dare l'~ a qualcuno** set somebody an example; **fare un ~** give an example
esem'plare **A** *adj* exemplary
B *m* specimen; (di libro) copy
esemplifi'care *vt* exemplify
esen'tare *vt* exempt
esen'tarsi *vr* free oneself
esen'tasse *adj* tax-free
e'sente *adj* exempt
■ **esente da imposta** duty-free; **esente da IVA** VAT exempt
e'sequie *fpl* funeral rites
eser'cente *mf* shopkeeper
eserci'tare *vt* exercise; (addestrare) train; (fare uso di) exert; (professione) practise
eserci'tarsi *vr* practise; **~ nella danza** practise dancing
eserci'tato *adj* ‹*occhio*› practised; **tenere la memoria esercitata** give one's memory some exercise
esercitazi'one *f* exercise; Mil drill; (di musica, chimica) practical class
e'sercito *m* army
■ **Esercito della Salvezza** Salvation Army
eser'cizio *m* exercise; (pratica) practice; Comm financial year; (azienda) business; **essere fuori ~** be out of practice; **nell'~ delle proprie funzioni** in the line of duty
■ **esercizio finanziario** financial year; **esercizio fiscale** fiscal year, tax year; **esercizi a terra** *pl* floor exercises; **esercizio tributario** fiscal year, tax year
esi'bire *vt* show off; produce ‹*documenti*›
esi'birsi *vr* Theat perform; fig show off
esibizi'one *f* Theat performance; (di documenti) production
■ **esibizione in volo** Aeron air display
esibizio'nismo *m* showing off
esibizio'nista *mf* exhibitionist
esi'gente *adj* exacting; (pignolo) fastidious
esi'genza *f* demand; (bisogno) need

e'sigere *vt* demand; (riscuotere) collect

e'siguo *adj* meagre

esila'rante *adj* exhilarating

esila'rare *vt* exhilarate

'esile *adj* slender; ‹*voce*› thin

esili'are *vt* exile

esili'arsi *vr* go into exile

esili'ato, -a **A** *adj* exiled **B** *mf* exile

e'silio *m* exile

e'simere *vt* release

e'simersi *vr* ~ **da** get out of

e'simio *adj* distinguished

esi'stente *adj* existing

esi'stenza *f* existence

esistenzi'ale *adj* existential

esistenzia'lismo *m* existentialism

e'sistere *vi* exist

esi'tante *adj* hesitating; ‹*voce*› faltering

esi'tare *vi* hesitate

esitazi'one *f* hesitation

'esito *m* result; **avere buon** ~ be a success

'esodo *m* exodus; **l'~ estivo, il grande** ~ (per le vacanze) the summer *or* holiday exodus

e'sofago *m* oesophagus

esone'rare *vt* exempt

e'sonero *m* exemption

esorbi'tante *adj* exorbitant

esorbi'tare *vi* ~ **da** exceed

esor'cismo *m* exorcism

esor'cista *mf* exorcist

esorciz'zare *vt* exorcise

esordi'ente *mf* person making his/her debut

e'sordio *m* opening; (di attore) debut

esor'dire *vi* debut

esor'tare *vt* (pregare) beg; (incitare) urge

eso'terico *adj* esoteric

e'sotico *adj* exotic

espa'drillas *fpl* espadrilles

e'spandere *vt* expand

e'spandersi *vr* expand; (diffondersi) extend

espan'dibile *adj* Comput upgradeable

espandibilità *f inv* Comput upgradeability

espansi'one *f* expansion; **in** ~ expanding

espansio'nista *mf* expansionist

espansio'nistico *adj* expansionist

espan'sivo *adj* expansive; ‹*persona*› friendly

espatri'are *vi* leave one's country

espatri'ato, -a *mf* expatriate, expat infml

e'spatrio *m* expatriation

espedi'ente *m* expedient; **vivere di espedienti** live by one's wits

e'spellere *vt* expel; send off ‹*calciatore*›

esperi'enza *f* experience; **per** ~ ‹*sapere, parlare*› from experience; **non ha** ~ he doesn't have any experience

esperi'mento *m* experiment

e'sperto, -a *adj & nmf* expert

■ **esperto di computer** computer expert

espi'are *vt* atone for

espia'torio *adj* expiatory

espi'rare *vt & vi* breathe out

espirazi'one *f* exhalation; (scadenza) expiry

espli'care *vt* carry on

esplicita'mente *adv* explicitly

e'splicito *adj* explicit

e'splodere **A** *vi* explode **B** *vt* ‹*arma*› fire

esplo'rare *vt* explore

esplora|'tore, -trice *mf* explorer; **giovane** ~ boy scout; **giovane esploratrice** girl guide

esplorazi'one *f* exploration

esplosi'one *f* explosion

esplo'sivo *adj & nm* explosive

espo'nente *m* exponent; **2 all'~** superscript 2

esponenzi'ale *adj* exponential

e'sporre *vt* expose; display ‹*merci*›; (spiegare) expound; exhibit ‹*quadri ecc.*›

e'sporsi *vr* (compromettersi) compromise oneself; (al sole) expose oneself; (alle critiche) lay oneself open

espor'tare *vt* Comm, Comput export

esporta|'tore, -trice *mf* exporter

esportazi'one *f* export

espo'simetro *m* light meter

esposi|'tore, -trice **A** *mf* exhibitor **B** *m* display rack

esposizi'one *f* (mostra) exhibition; (in vetrina) display; (spiegazione ecc.) exposition; (posizione, fotografia) exposure; **con** ~ **a nord/sud** north-/south-facing

■ **esposizione a radiazioni** radiation exposure

e'sposto **A** pp di **esporre** **B** *adj* exposed; ‹*merce*› on show; ‹*spiegato*› set out; ~ **a nord/sud** north-/south-facing **C** *m* submission

espressa'mente *adv* expressly; **non l'ha detto** ~ he didn't put it in so many words

espressi'one *f* expression

espressio'nismo *m* expressionism

espressio'nista *adj & nmf* expressionist

espressio'nistico *adj* expressionistic

espres'sivo *adj* expressive

e'spresso **A** pp di **esprimere** **B** *adj* express **C** *m* (lettera) special delivery; (treno) express train; (caffè) espresso; **per** ~ ‹*spedire*› [by] express [post]; **piatto** ~ meal made to order

e'sprimere *vt* express

e'sprimersi *vr* express oneself

espropri'are *vt* dispossess

espropriazi'one *f* Jur expropriation

key word

e'sproprio *m* expropriation
espulsi'one *f* expulsion
e'spulso pp di **espellere**
esqui'mese *adj & nmf* Eskimo
es'senza *f* essence
essenzi'ale **A** *adj* essential
B *m* important thing; **l'~** (di teoria ecc.) the bare bones; **l'~ è** ... (la cosa più importante) the main thing is ...
essenzial'mente *adj* essentially
'essere **A** *vi* be; **c'è** there is; **ci sono** there are; **ci sono!** (ho capito) I've got it!; **ci siamo!** (siamo arrivati) here we are at last!; **non ce n'è più** there's none left; **c'è di che essere contenti** there's a lot to be happy about; **che ora è? - sono le dieci** what time is it? - it's ten o'clock; **chi è? - sono io** who is it? - it's me; **è stato detto che** it has been said that; **siamo in due** there are two of us; **questa camicia è da lavare** this shirt is to be washed; **non è da te** it's not like you; **~ di** belong to; (provenire da) be from; **~ per** (favorevole) be in favour of; **se fossi in te, ...** if I were you, ...; **sarà!** if you say so!; **come sarebbe a dire?** what are you getting at?
B *v aux* have; (in passivi) be; **siamo arrivati** we have arrived; **ci sono stato ieri** I was there yesterday; **sono nato a Torino** I was born in Turin; **è riconosciuto come...** he is recognized as ...
C *m* being; **~ umano** human being; **~ vivente** living creature
essic'care *vt* dry
essic'cato *adj* dried; ‹*noce di cocco*› desiccated
'esso, -a *pers pron* he, she; (cosa, animale) it
est *m* east; **l'Est europeo** Eastern Europe
'estasi *f* ecstasy; **andare in ~ per** go into raptures over
estasi'are *vt* enrapture
estasi'arsi *vr* go into raptures
e'state *f* summer
e'statico *adj* ecstatic
estempo'raneo *adj* impromptu
e'stendere *vt* extend
e'stendersi *vr* spread; (allungarsi) stretch
estensi'one *f* extension; (ampiezza) expanse; Mus range
■ **estensione del file** Comput file extension
esten'sivo *adj* extensive
estenu'ante *adj* exhausting
estenu'are *vt* exhaust
estenu'arsi *vr* exhaust oneself
'estere *m* ester
esteri'ore *adj & nm* exterior
esteriorità *f inv* outward appearance; **badare all'~** judge by appearances
esterioriz'zare *vt* externalize
esterior'mente *adv* externally; (di persone) outwardly
esterna'mente *adv* on the outside
ester'nare *vt* express, show
e'sterno, -a **A** *adj* external; (scala) outside; **per uso ~** for external use only
B *m* Archit exterior; (in film) location shot
C *mf* day pupil
'estero **A** *adj* foreign
B *m* foreign countries *pl*; **all'~** abroad; **ministero degli esteri** ≈ Foreign Office BrE, State Department AmE
esterofi'lia *f* xenophilia
este'rofilo *adj* xenophile
esterre'fatto *adj* horrified
e'steso **A** pp di **estendere**
B *adj* extensive; (diffuso) widespread; **per ~** ‹*scrivere*› in full
e'steta *mf* aesthete
e'stetica *f* aesthetics *sg*
estetica'mente *adv* aesthetically
esteticità *f inv* aestheticism
e'stetico *adj* aesthetic; ‹*chirurgia, chirurgo*› plastic
este'tismo *m* (dottrina, carattere) aestheticism
este'tista *mf* beautician
estima'tore, -trice *mf* fan
'estimo *m* estimate
e'stinguere *vt* extinguish; close ‹*conto*›
e'stinguersi *vr* die out
e'stinto, -a **A** pp di **estinguere**
B *mf* deceased
estin'tore *m* [fire] extinguisher
estinzi'one *f* extinction; (di incendio) putting out
estir'pare *vt* uproot; extract ‹*dente*›; fig eradicate ‹*crimine, malattia*›
estirpazi'one *f* eradication; (di dente) extraction
e'stivo *adj* summer *attrib*
'estone *adj & nm* Estonian
E'stonia *f* Estonia
e'storcere *vt* extort
estorsi'one *f* extortion
e'storto pp di **estorcere**
estradizi'one *f* extradition
estra'gone *m* tarragon
estra'ibile *adj* removable
e'straneo, -a **A** *adj* extraneous; (straniero) foreign
B *mf* stranger
estrani'are *vt* estrange
estrani'arsi *vr* become estranged
estrapo'lare *vt* extrapolate
e'strarre *vt* extract; (sorteggiare) draw
e'stratto **A** pp di **estrarre**
B *m* extract; (brano) excerpt; (documento) abstract
■ **estratto conto** statement [of account], bank statement
estrazi'one *f* extraction; (a sorte) draw
■ **estrazione a premi** prize draw
estrema'mente *adv* extremely

estre'mismo *m* extremism
estre'mista *mf* extremist
estremità **A** *f inv* extremity; (di una corda) end
B *pl* Anat extremities
e'stremo **A** *adj* extreme; (ultimo) last; **misure estreme** drastic measures; **fare un ~ tentativo** make one last try; **l'Estremo Oriente** the Far East; **~ saluto** Mil military funeral; **l'estrema unzione** last rites
B *m* (limite) extreme; **all'~** in the extreme; **passare da un ~ all'altro** go from one extreme to the other; **estremi** *pl* (di documento) main points; (di reato) essential elements; **essere agli estremi** be at the end of one's tether; **andare agli estremi** go to extremes; **essere all'~ delle forze** have no strength left
'estro *m* (disposizione artistica) talent; (ispirazione) inspiration; (capriccio) whim
e'strogeno *m* oestrogen
estro'mettere *vt* expel
estromissi'one *f* ejection
e'stroso *adj* talented; (capriccioso) unpredictable
estro'verso **A** *adj* extroverted
B *m* extrovert
estu'ario *m* estuary
esube'rante *adj* exuberant
esube'ranza *f* exuberance
e'subero *m*
■ **esubero cassa integrazione** voluntary redundancy
esu'lare *vt* **~ da** be beyond the scope of
'esule *mf* exile
esul'tante *adj* exultant
esul'tanza *f* exultation
esul'tare *vi* rejoice
esu'mare *vt* exhume
età *f inv* age; **raggiungere la maggiore ~** come of age; **un uomo di mezz'~** a middle-aged man; **avere la stessa ~** be the same age; **che ~ gli daresti?** how old would you say he was?; **fin dalla più tenera ~** from his/her etc earliest years; **in ~ avanzata** of advanced years; **è senza ~** it's hard to tell his age
■ **età del bronzo** Bronze Age; **età della pensione** retirement age
e'tano *m* ethane
eta'nolo *m* ethanol
'etere *m* ether
■ **etere etilico** ether
e'tereo *adj* ethereal
eterna'mente *adv* eternally
eternità *f inv* eternity; **è un'~ che non la vedo** I haven't seen her for ages
e'terno *adj* eternal; ‹*questione, problema*› age-old; fig ‹*discorso, conferenza*› never-ending; **in ~** infml for ever; **giurare amore ~** swear undying love; **un ~ bambino** a child
etero'geneo *adj* diverse, heterogeneous
eterosessu'ale *adj & nmf* heterosexual
eterosessualità *f inv* heterosexuality
'etica *f* ethics *sg*
eti'chetta[1] *f* label; (con il prezzo) price tag
eti'chetta[2] *f* (cerimoniale) etiquette
etichet'tare *vt* label
etichetta'trice *f* labelling machine
etichetta'tura *f* (operazione) labelling
'etico *adj* ethical
eti'lometro *m* Breathalyzer®
etimolo'gia *f* etymology
e'tiope *adj & nmf* Ethiopian
Eti'opia *f* Ethiopia
eti'opico *adj* Ethiopian
'Etna *m* Etna
et'nia *f* ethnic group
'etnico *adj* ethnic
etnolo'gia *f* ethnology
e'trusco *adj & nmf* Etruscan
'ettaro *m* hectare
+ettino *suff* **cosettina** *nf* small thing; **è una cosettina da niente** it's nothing
+etto *suff* **cameretta** *nf* little bedroom; **scherzetto** *nf* prank; **piccoletto** *nm* derog shorty
'etto, etto'grammo *m* hundred grams, quarter pound
et'tolitro *m* hectolitre
euca'lipto *m* eucalyptus
eucari'stia *f* Eucharist
eufe'mismo *m* euphemism
eufe'mistico *adj* euphemistic
eufo'ria *f* elation; Med euphoria
eu'forico *adj* elated; Med euphoric
euge'netica *f* eugenics *sg*
eu'nuco *m* eunuch
Eur'asia *f* Eurasia
eurasi'atico *adj* Eurasian
'EURATOM *nf abbr* (**Comunità Europea dell'Energia Atomica**) EURATOM
'euro *m inv* Fin euro
euro+ *pref* Euro+
eurobbligazi'one *f* Eurobond
euro'cheque *m inv* Eurocheque
Euro'city *m inv* Rail international intercity
eurodepu'tato *m* Euro MP, MEP
eurodi'visa *f* Eurocurrency
euro'dollaro *m* Eurodollar
Eu'ropa *f* Europe
europe'ismo *m* Europeanism
euro'peo, -a *adj & nmf* European
euro'scettico *m* Euro-sceptic
Euro'zona *f* Eurozone
eutana'sia *f* euthanasia
evacu'are *vt* evacuate
evacuazi'one *f* evacuation

key word

e'vadere **A** *vt* evade; (sbrigare) deal with **B** *vi* ~ **da** escape from
evane'scente *adj* vanishing
evan'gelico *adj* evangelical
evange'lista *m* evangelist
evan'gelo = **vangelo**
evapo'rare *vi* evaporate
evaporazi'one *f* evaporation
evasi'one *f* escape; (fiscale) evasion; *fig* escapism
evasiva'mente *adv* evasively
eva'sivo *adj* evasive
e'vaso, -a **A** pp di **evadere** **B** *mf* fugitive
eva'sore *m*
■ **evasore fiscale** tax evader
eveni'enza *f* eventuality; **in ogni** ~ if need be
e'vento *m* event
eventu'ale *adj* possible
eventualità *f inv* eventuality; **in ogni** ~ at all events; **nell'**~ **che** in the event that
eventual'mente *adv* if necessary
ever'sivo *adj* subversive
evi'dente *adj* evident
evidente'mente *adv* evidently
evi'denza *f* evidence; **mettere in** ~ emphasize; **mettersi in** ~ make oneself conspicuous; **arrendersi all'**~ face the facts
evidenzi'are *vt* highlight
evidenzia'tore *m* (penna) highlighter
evi'rare *vt* emasculate
evi'tare *vt* avoid; (risparmiare) spare
'evo *m* age
evo'care *vt* evoke
evolu'tivo *adj* evolutionary
evo'luto **A** pp di **evolvere** **B** *adj* evolved; (progredito) progressive; ‹*civiltà, nazione*› advanced; **una donna evoluta** a modern woman
evoluzi'one *f* evolution; (di ginnasta, aereo) circle
e'volvere *vt* develop
e'volversi *vr* evolve
ev'viva *int* hurray; ~ **il Papa!** long live the Pope!; **gridare** ~ cheer; ~ **la modestia!** what modesty!
ex *prep* ex, former; **ex moglie** ex-wife
ex 'aequo *adv* **arrivare** ~ come in joint first
ex-Jugo'slavia *f* ex-Yugoslavia
ex-jugo'slavo *adj & nmf* ex-Yugoslav
ex 'libris *m inv* bookplate
ex'ploit *m inv* feat, exploit
'extra **A** *adj inv* extra; ‹*qualità*› first-class **B** *m inv* extra
extracomuni'tario, -a **A** *adj* non-EC, non-EU **B** *mf immigrant from outside the EU*
extraconiu'gale *adj* extramarital
extraeuro'peo *adj* non-European
extraparlamen'tare *adj* extra-parliamentary
extrasco'lastico *adj* extra-curricular
extrasensori'ale *adj* extrasensory
extrater'restre *mf* extra-terrestrial
extrauniversi'tario *adj* extramural
ex 'voto *m inv* ex-voto

Ff

fa[1] *m inv* Mus (chiave, nota) F
fa[2] *adv* ago; **due mesi** ~ two months ago
fabbi'sogno *m* requirements *pl*, needs *pl*
■ **fabbisogno dello Stato** government spending estimates
'fabbrica *f* factory
fabbri'cabile *adj* ‹*area, terreno*› that can be built on
fabbri'cante *m* manufacturer
■ **fabbricante d'armi** arms manufacturer
fabbri'care *vt* build; (produrre) manufacture; *fig* (inventare) fabricate
fabbri'cato *m* building
fabbricazi'one *f* manufacturing; (costruzione) building
'fabbro *m* blacksmith
fac'cenda *f* matter; **faccende** *pl* **domestiche** housework *sg*
faccendi'ere *m* wheeler-dealer
fac'chino *m* porter
'faccia *f* face; (di foglio) side; ~ **a** ~ face to face; ~ **tosta** cheek; **voltar** ~ change sides; **di** ~ (palazzo) opposite; **alla** ~ **di** infml (a dispetto di) in spite of; **alla** ~**!** (stupore) bloody hell!
facci'ata *f* façade; (di foglio) side; *fig* (esteriorità) outward appearance
fa'cente *mf*

■ **facente funzioni** deputy

fa'ceto *adj* facetious; **tra il serio e il ~** half joking

fa'cezia *f* (battuta) witticism

fa'chiro *m* fakir

🔑 **'facile** *adj* easy; (affabile) easy-going; **essere ~ alle critiche** be quick to criticize; **essere ~ al riso** laugh a lot; **~ a farsi** easy to do; **è ~ che piova** it's likely to rain

facilità *f inv* ease; (disposizione) aptitude; **avere ~ di parola** express oneself well

■ **facilità d'uso** ease of use, user-friendliness

facili'tare *vt* facilitate

facilitazi'one *f* facility; **facilitazioni** *pl* Fin special terms; **facilitazioni** *pl* **di pagamento** easy terms; **facilitazioni** *pl* **creditizie** credit facilities

facil'mente *adv* (con facilità) easily; (probabilmente) probably

faci'lone *adj* slapdash

facilone'ria *f* slapdash attitude

facino'roso *adj* violent

facoltà *f inv* faculty; (potere) power; **essere nel pieno possesso delle proprie ~** be compos mentis

facolta'tivo *adj* optional; **fermata facoltativa** request stop

facol'toso *adj* wealthy

fac'simile *m* facsimile

fac'totum **A** *m inv* man Friday **B** *f inv* girl Friday

'faggio *m* beech

fagi'ano *m* pheasant

fagio'lino *m* French bean

fagi'olo *m* bean; **a ~** ‹*arrivare, capitare*› at the right time

■ **fagiolo borlotto** borlotti bean; **fagiolo bianco di Spagna** runner bean, haricot bean

fagoci'tare *vt* gobble up ‹*società*›

fa'gotto *m* bundle; Mus bassoon

Fahren'heit *adj* Fahrenheit

'faida *f* feud

fai da te *m* do-it-yourself, DIY

fa'ina *f* weasel

fa'lange *f* (dito) Mil phalanx

fal'cata *f* stride

'falce *f* scythe

■ **falce e martello** (simbolo) the hammer and sickle

fal'cetto *m* sickle

falci'are *vt* cut; fig mow down

falci'ata *f* (quantità d'erba) swathe

falcia'trice *f* [lawn]mower

'falco *m* hawk

fal'cone *m* falcon

'falda *f* stratum; (di neve) flake; (di cappello) brim; (di cappotto, frac) coat-tails; (pendio) slope

■ **falda freatica** water table

fale'gname *m* carpenter

falegname'ria *f* carpentry

fa'lena *f* moth

'Falkland *fpl* **le [isole] ~** the Falklands

'falla *f* leak

fal'lace *adj* deceptive

'fallico *adj* phallic

fallimen'tare *adj* disastrous; Jur bankruptcy

falli'mento *m* Comm bankruptcy; fig failure

fal'lire **A** *vi* Comm go bankrupt; fig fail **B** *vt* miss ‹*colpo*›

fal'lito **A** *adj* unsuccessful **B** *adj & nm* bankrupt

'fallo *m* fault; (errore) mistake; Sport foul; (imperfezione) flaw; **senza ~** without fail; **cogliere in ~** catch red-handed; **mettere un piede in ~** slip

■ **fallo di mano** (in calcio) handball

falò *m inv* bonfire

fal'sare *vt* alter; (falsificare) falsify

falsa'riga *f* **sulla ~ di** along the same lines as

fal'sario, -a *mf* forger; (di documenti) counterfeiter

fal'setto *m* falsetto

falsifi'care *vt* fake; (contraffare) forge

falsificazi'one *f* (di documenti) falsification

falsità *f inv* falseness

🔑 **'falso** **A** *adj* false; (sbagliato) wrong; ‹*opera d'arte ecc.*› fake; ‹*gioielli, oro*› imitation; **essere un ~ magro** be fatter than one looks **B** *m* forgery; **giurare il ~** commit perjury

■ **falso in atto pubblico** forgery of a legal document

'fama *f* fame; (reputazione) reputation

🔑 **'fame** *f* hunger; **aver ~** be hungry; **fare la ~** barely scrape a living; **da ~** ‹*stipendio*› miserly; **avere una ~ da lupo** be ravenous

fa'melico *adj* ravenous

famige'rato *adj* infamous

🔑 **fa'miglia** *f* family

■ **famiglia affidataria** foster family, foster home

famili'are **A** *adj* family *attrib*; (ben noto) familiar; (senza cerimonie) informal **B** *m* relative, relation

familiarità *f inv* familiarity; (informalità) informality

familiariz'zarsi *vr* familiarize oneself

🔑 **fa'moso** *adj* famous

fa'nale *m* lamp; Auto ecc. light

■ **fanali posteriori** *pl* Auto rear lights

fana'lino *m*

■ **fanalino di coda** Auto tail light; **essere il ~ di coda** fig bring up the rear, be the back marker

fa'natico, -a **A** *adj* fanatical; **essere ~ di calcio/cinema** be a football/cinema fanatic **B** *mf* fanatic

fana'tismo *m* fanaticism

fanciul'lezza *f* childhood

🔑 key word

fanci'ullo, -a *mf* literary young boy; young girl
fan'donia *f* lie; **fandonie!** nonsense!
fan'fara *f* fanfare; (complesso) brass band
fanfaro'nata *f* brag; **fanfaronate** *pl* bragging
fanfa'rone, -a *mf* braggart
fan'ghiglia *f* mud
'fango *m* mud
fan'goso *adj* muddy
fannul'lone, -a *mf* idler
fantasci'enza *f* science fiction
fanta'sia *f* fantasy; (immaginazione) imagination; (capriccio) fancy; (di tessuto) pattern; **fantasie** *pl* (sciocchezze) moonshine
fantasi'oso *adj* ‹*stilista, ragazzo*› imaginative; ‹*resoconto*› improbable, fanciful
fan'tasma *m* ghost; **essere il ~ di se stesso** be a shadow of one's former self; **città fantasma** ghost town; **governo fantasma** shadow cabinet
fantasti'care *vi* day-dream, fantasize
fantastiche'ria *f* day-dream, fantasy
fan'tastico *adj* fantastic; ‹*racconto*› fantasy *attrib*
'fante *m* infantryman; (nelle carte) jack
fante'ria *m* infantry
fan'tino *m* jockey
fan'toccio *m* puppet
fanto'matico *adj* (inafferrabile) phantom *attrib*; (immaginario) mythical
fara'butto *m* trickster
fara'ona *f* (uccello) guinea fowl
'farcia *f* stuffing; (di torta) filling
far'cire *vt* stuff; fill ‹*torta*›
far'cito *adj* stuffed; ‹*dolce*› filled
fard *m inv* blusher
far'dello *m* bundle; fig burden
'fare **A** *vt* do; make ‹*dolce, letto, ecc.*›; (recitare la parte di) play; (trascorrere) spend; **~ una pausa/un sogno** have a break/a dream; **~ colpo su** impress; **~ paura a** frighten; **~ piacere a** please; **farla finita** put an end to it; **~ l'insegnante** be a teacher; **~ lo scemo** play the idiot; **~ una settimana al mare** spend a week at the seaside; **3 più 3 fa 6** 3 and 3 makes 6; **quanto fa? - fanno 50 euro** how much is it? - it's 50 euros; **far ~ qualcosa a qualcuno** get somebody to do something; (costringere) make somebody do something; **~ vedere** show; **fammi parlare** let me speak; **niente a che ~ con** nothing to do with; **non c'è niente da ~** (per problema) there is nothing we/you etc can do; **fa caldo/buio** it's warm/dark; **non fa niente** it doesn't matter; **strada facendo** on the way; **farcela** (riuscire) manage
B *vi* **fai in modo di venire** try and come; **~ da** act as; **~ per** make as if to; **~ presto** be quick; **non fa per me** it's not for me
C *m* (comportamento) manner; **sul far del giorno** at daybreak
fa'retto *m* spot[light]
far'falla *f* butterfly
farfal'lino *m* (cravatta) bow tie
farfugli'are *vt* mutter
fa'rina *f* flour
■ **farina di ceci** chickpea flour, gram flour; **farina gialla** maize flour; **farina integrale** wholemeal flour; **farina lattea** powdered milk for babies; **farina d'ossa** bonemeal
fari'nacei *mpl* starchy food *sg*
fa'ringe *f* pharynx
farin'gite *f* pharyngitis
fari'noso *adj* ‹*neve*› powdery; ‹*mela*› soft; ‹*patata*› floury
farma'ceutico *adj* pharmaceutical; **industria farmaceutica** pharmaceuticals industry
farma'cia *f* pharmacy; (negozio) chemist's [shop]
■ **farmacia di turno** duty pharmacy
farma'cista *mf* chemist, pharmacist
'farmaco *m* drug; **essere sotto farmaci** be on medication
'faro *m* Auto headlight; Aeron beacon; (costruzione) lighthouse; **abbassare i fari** dip one's headlights; **accendere i fari** switch on one's lights
■ **fari antinebbia** *pl* fog lamps; **fari posteriori** *pl* rear lights
farragi'noso *adj* confused
'farsa *f* farce
far'sesco *adj* farcical
'farsi *vr* (diventare) get; sl (drogarsi) shoot up; **~ avanti** come forward; **~ i fatti propri** mind one's own business; **~ la barba** shave; **~ la villa** infml buy a villa; **~ il ragazzo** infml find a boyfriend; **~ due risate** have a laugh; **~ male** hurt oneself; **~ un nome** make a name for oneself; **farsela sotto** infml wet oneself
Far 'west *m* Wild West
fa'scetta *f* strip; (per capelli) hair band; (di giornale) wrapper
'fascia *f* band; (zona) area; (ufficiale) sash; (benda) bandage; (di smoking) cummerbund; (in statistica) bracket; **le fasce deboli** the underprivileged
■ **fascia per capelli** hair band; **fascia elastica** crepe bandage; (ventriera) girdle; **fascia d'età** age bracket, age group; **fascia d'ozono** ozone layer; **fascia di reddito** income bracket
fasci'are *vt* bandage; cling to ‹*fianchi*›
fasci'arsi *vr* bandage; **~ la testa prima di rompersela** worry about something that might never happen
fascia'tura *f* dressing; (azione) bandaging
fascicola|'tore, -trice *mf* sorter
fa'scicolo *m* file; (di rivista) issue; (libretto) booklet
fa'scina *f* faggot

'fascino *m* fascination
fasci'noso *adj* charming
'fascio *m* bundle; (di fiori) bunch
■ **fascio di luce** beam of light
fa'scismo *m* fascism
fa'scista *adj & nmf* fascist
'fase *f* phase; **il motore è fuori ~** the timing is wrong; **sono fuori ~** I'm not firing on all four cylinders; **essere in ~ di miglioramento** be on the mend, be recovering; **essere in ~ di espansione** be expanding
fast 'food *m inv* fast food; (ristorante) fast food restaurant

f

fa'stidio *m* nuisance; (scomodo) inconvenience; **fastidi** *pl* (preoccupazioni) worries; (disturbi) troubles; **dar ~ a qualcuno** bother somebody
fastidi'oso *adj* tiresome
'fasto *m* pomp
fa'stoso *adj* sumptuous
fa'sullo *adj* bogus
'fata *f* fairy
fa'tale *adj* fatal; (inevitabile) fated; **donna fatale** femme fatale
fata'lismo *m* fatalism
fata'lista **A** *mf* fatalist
B *adj* fatalistic
fatalità *f inv* fate; (caso sfortunato) misfortune
fatal'mente *adv* inevitably
fa'tato *adj* ‹*anello, bacchetta*› magic
fa'tica *f* effort; (lavoro faticoso) hard work; (stanchezza, di metalli) fatigue; **a ~** with great difficulty; **è ~ sprecata** it's a waste of time; **fare ~ a fare qualcosa** find it difficult to do something; **senza [nessuna] ~** without [any] effort; **fare ~ a finire qualcosa** struggle to finish something; **uomo di ~** odd-job man
fati'caccia *f* pain
fati'care *vi* toil; **~ a** (stentare) find it difficult to
fati'cata *f* effort; (sfacchinata) grind
fati'coso *adj* tiring; (difficile) difficult
fati'scente *adj* crumbling
'fato *m* fate
fat'taccio *nm hum* foul deed
fat'tezze *fpl* features
fat'tibile *adj* feasible
fatti'specie *f* **nella ~** in this case
'fatto **A** (pp di **fare**) **ormai è fatta!** what's done is done
B *adj* made; **~ a mano/in casa** handmade/ home-made; **essere ben ~** ‹*persona*› have a nice figure; **un uomo ~** a grown man
C *m* fact; (azione) action; (avvenimento) event; (faccenda) business, matter; **sa il ~ suo** he knows his business; **le ho detto il ~ suo** I told her what I thought of her; **di ~** in fact; **in ~ di** as regards; **~ sta che** the fact remains that; **mettere di fronte al ~ compiuto** present with a fait accompli
fat'tore *m* (causa) Math factor; (di fattoria) farm manager
■ **fattore di protezione solare** protection factor
fatto'ria *f* farm; (casa) farmhouse
fatto'rino *m* messenger [boy]
■ **fattorino d'albergo** bellboy
fattucchi'era *f* witch
fat'tura *f* (stile) cut; (lavorazione) workmanship; Comm invoice
■ **fattura di acquisto** purchase invoice; **fattura pro-forma** pro forma [invoice]; **fattura di vendita** sales invoice
fattu'rare *vt* invoice; (adulterare) adulterate
fattu'rato *m* turnover, sales *pl*
fatturazi'one *f* invoicing, billing
'fatuo *adj* fatuous
'fauci *fpl* (di leone) maw *sg*, jaws *pl*
'fauna *f* fauna
'fausto *adj* propitious
fau'tore *m* supporter
'fava *f* broad bean
fa'vella *f* speech
fa'villa *f* spark
'favo *m* honeycomb
'favola *f* fable; (fiaba) story; (oggetto di pettegolezzi) laughing stock; **è una ~!** (meraviglia) it's divine!
favo'loso *adj* fabulous
fa'vore *m* favour; **essere a ~ di** be in favour of; **per ~** please; **di ~** ‹*condizioni, trattamento*› preferential; **col ~ delle tenebre** under cover of darkness
favoreggia'mento *m* Jur aiding and abetting
favo'revole *adj* favourable
favorevol'mente *adv* favourably
favo'rire *vt* favour; (promuovere) promote; **vuol ~?** (a cena, pranzo) will you have some?; (entrare) will you come in?; **favorisca alla cassa** please pay at the cash desk; **favorisca i documenti** your papers please
favo'rito, -a *adj & nmf* favourite
fax *m inv* fax; **inviare via ~** fax, send by fax
■ **fax a carta comune** plain paper fax
fa'xare *vt* fax
fazi'one *f* faction
faziosità *f inv* bias
fazi'oso *m* sectarian
fazzolet'tino *m*
■ **fazzolettino [di carta]** [paper] tissue
fazzo'letto *m* handkerchief, hanky; (da testa) headscarf
feb'braio *m* February
'febbre *f* fever; **avere la ~** have o run a temperature
■ **febbre da fieno** hay fever
febbrici'tante *adj* fevered

key word

feb'brile *adj* feverish
febbril'mente *adv* feverishly
'feccia *f* dregs *pl*
'fecola *f* potato flour
fecon'dare *vt* fertilize
feconda'tore *m* fertilizer
fecondazi'one *f* fertilization
■ **fecondazione artificiale** artificial insemination; **fecondazione in vitro** in vitro fertilization, IVF
fe'condo *adj* fertile
'fede *f* faith; (fiducia) trust; (anello) wedding ring; **in buona/mala ~** in good/bad faith; **prestar ~ a** believe; **tener ~ alla parola** keep one's word; **aver ~ in qualcuno** have faith in somebody, believe in somebody; **degno di ~** reliable; **in ~** Yours faithfully
fe'dele **A** *adj* faithful
B *mf* believer, worshipper; (seguace) follower; **i fedeli** the faithful
fedel'mente *adv* faithfully
fedeltà *f inv* faithfulness; **alta ~** high fidelity
'federa *f* pillowcase
fede'rale *adj* federal
federa'lismo *m* federalism
federa'lista *adj* federalist
fede'rato *adj* federate
federazi'one *f* federation
fe'difrago, -a **A** *adj* faithless; hum two-timing
B *m* faithless wretch; hum two-timer
fe'dina *f* **avere la ~ penale sporca/pulita** have a/no criminal record
fega'telli *mpl* (di maiale) pork liver
fega'tino *m* **fegatini** *pl* **di pollo** chicken livers
'fegato *m* liver; fig guts *pl*; **mangiarsi il ~, rodersi il ~** be consumed with rage
'felce *f* fern
fe'lice *adj* happy; (fortunato) lucky; **~ come una Pasqua** blissfully happy
felice'mente *adv* happily; (con successo) successfully
felicità *f inv* happiness
felici'tarsi *vr* **~ con** congratulate
felicitazi'oni *fpl* congratulations
fe'lino *adj* feline
'felpa *f* (indumento) sweatshirt; (stoffa) felt
fel'pato *adj* brushed; ‹*passo*› stealthy
'feltro *m* felt; (cappello) felt hat
'femmina *f* female
femmi'nile **A** *adj* feminine; ‹*rivista, abbigliamento*› women's; ‹*sesso*› female
B *m* feminine
femminilità *f inv* femininity
femmi'nismo *m* feminism
'femore *m* femur
'fendere *vt* split
fendi'nebbia *m inv* fog lamp
fendi'tura *f* split; (in roccia) crack
fe'nice *f* phoenix
feni'cottero *m* flamingo
fenome'nale *adj* phenomenal
fe'nomeno *m* phenomenon
'feretro *m* coffin
feri'ale *adj* weekday; **giorno ~** weekday
'ferie *fpl* holidays; (di università, tribunale ecc.) vacation *sg*; **andare in ~** go on holiday; **prendere le ~** go on holiday; **prendere delle ~** take time off; **prendere un giorno di ~** take a day off
feri'mento *m* wounding
fe'rire *vt* wound; (in incidente) injure; fig hurt
fe'rirsi *vr* injure oneself
fe'rita *f* wound
■ **ferita d'arma da fuoco** gunshot wound
fe'rito **A** *adj* wounded
B *m* wounded person; Mil casualty; **~ grave** seriously injured person; **i feriti** the injured
feri'toia *f* loophole; **feritoie** *pl* **per le schede di espansione** Comput expansion slots
'ferma *f* Mil period of service
fermacal'zoni *m inv* cycle clip
fermaca'pelli *m inv* hair slide
ferma'carte *m inv* paperweight
ferma'coda *m inv* (di stoffa) scrunchie
fermacra'vatta *m inv* tiepin
ferma'fogli *m inv* bulldog clip
fer'maglio *m* clasp; (spilla) brooch; (per capelli) hair slide
ferma'mente *adv* firmly
ferma'porta *m inv* doorstop
fer'mare **A** *vt* stop; (fissare) fix; Jur detain
B *vi* stop
fer'marsi *vr* stop
fer'mata *f* stop; **'~ prenotata'** 'bus stopping'; **senza fermate** ‹*tragitto*› non-stop
■ **fermata dell'autobus** bus stop; **fermata obbligatoria** compulsory stop; **fermata a richiesta** request stop
fermen'tare *vi* ferment
fermentazi'one *f* fermentation
fer'mento *m* ferment; (lievito) yeast; **essere in ~** be in/get into a tizzy
fer'mezza *f* firmness
'fermo **A** *adj* still; ‹*veicolo*› stationary; (stabile) steady; ‹*orologio*› not working; **~!** don't move!; **~ restando che ...** it being understood that ...; **'~ per manutenzione'** 'closed for repairs'
B *m* Jur detention; Mech catch; **in stato di ~** in custody
■ **fermo immagine** TV freeze frame; **fermo posta** poste restante, general delivery AmE
fer'net® *m inv bitter digestive liqueur*
fe'roce *adj* fierce, ferocious; ‹*bestia*› wild; ‹*freddo, dolore*› unbearable
feroce'mente *adv* fiercely, ferociously

fe'rocia *f* ferocity
fer'raglia *f* scrap iron
ferra'gosto *m* 15 August (*bank holiday in Italy*); (periodo) August holidays *pl*
ferra'menta *fpl* ironmongery *sg*; **negozio di ~** ironmonger's
fer'rare *vt* shoe ‹*cavallo*›
fer'rato *adj* **~ in** (preparato in) well up in
'ferreo *adj* iron
'ferro *m* iron; (attrezzo) tool; (di chirurgo) instrument; **di ~** ‹*memoria*› excellent; ‹*alibi*› cast-iron; **salute di ~** iron constitution; **ai ferri** ‹*bistecca*› grilled; **essere ai ferri corti** be at daggers drawn; **mettere il paese a ~ e fuoco** put a country to the sword; **i ferri del mestiere** the tools of the trade
■ **ferro battuto** wrought iron; **ferro da calza** knitting needle; **ferro di cavallo** horseshoe; **ferro da stiro** iron; **ferro a vapore** steam iron
fer'roso *adj* ferrous
ferro'vecchio *m* scrap merchant
ferro'via *f* railway, railroad AmE; **Ferrovie** *pl* **dello Stato** Italian State Railways
ferrovi'ario *adj* railway *attrib*, railroad AmE *attrib*
ferrovi'ere *m* railwayman, railroad worker AmE
'fertile *adj* fertile
fertilità *f inv* fertility
fertiliz'zante *m* fertilizer
fertilizzazi'one *f* fertilization
fer'vente *adj* blazing; fig fervent
fervente'mente *adv* fervently
'fervere *vi* ‹*preparativi*›; be well under way
fervida'mente *adv* fervently
'fervido *adj* fervent; **fervidi auguri** best wishes
fer'vore *m* fervour; (di discussione) heat
'fesa *f* (carne) rump
fesse'ria *f* **dire/fare una ~** infml say/do something stupid
'fesso **A** pp di **fendere**
B *adj* cracked; infml (sciocco) foolish
C *m* infml (idiota) fool; **far ~ qualcuno** infml con somebody
fes'sura *f* crack; (per gettone ecc.) slot
■ **fessura [per la scheda] di espansione** Comput expansion slot
'festa *f* feast; (giorno festivo) holiday; (compleanno) birthday; (ricevimento) party; fig joy; **fare ~ a qualcuno** welcome somebody; **essere in ~** be on holiday; **far ~** celebrate; **della ~** ‹*vestito, tovaglia*› best; **conciare qualcuno per le feste** give somebody a sound thrashing; **le feste** (Natale, Capodanno ecc.) the holidays
■ **festa di addio al celibato** stag night, stag party; **festa di addio al nubilato** hen party; **festa di compleanno** birthday party; **festa della mamma** Mother's Day, Mothering Sunday; **festa mascherata** fancy dress party; **festa nazionale** public holiday, legal holiday AmE; **festa del papà** Father's Day
festai'olo, -a **A** *adj* festive
B *mf* party animal
festeggia'mento *m* celebration; (manifestazione) festivity; **festeggiamenti** *pl* celebrations
festeggi'are *vt* celebrate; (accogliere festosamente) give a hearty welcome to
fe'stino *m* party
'festival *m inv* festival
■ **festival cinematografico** film festival
festività *fpl* festivities
fe'stivo *adj* holiday; (lieto) festive; **festivi** *pl* public holidays
fe'stone *m* (nel cucito) scallop, scollop; (di carta) paper chain
fe'stoso *adj* merry
fe'tente **A** *adj* evil smelling; fig revolting
B *mf* infml bastard
fe'ticcio *m* fetish
'feto *m foetus*
fe'tore *m* stench
'fetta *f* slice; **a fette** sliced
■ **fetta biscottata** rusk
fet'tina *f* thin slice
fet'tuccia *f* tape; (con nome) name tape
fettuc'cine *fpl ribbon-shaped pasta*
feu'dale *adj* feudal
'feudo *m* feud
fez *m inv* fez
FFSS *abbr* (**Ferrovie dello Stato**) Italian State Railways
fi'aba *f* fairy-tale
fia'besco *adj* fairy-tale *attrib*
fi'acca *f* weariness; (indolenza) laziness; **battere la ~** be sluggish
fiac'care *vt* weaken
fi'acco *adj* weak; (indolente) slack; (stanco) weary; ‹*partita*› dull
fi'accola *f* torch
fiacco'lata *f* torchlight procession
fi'ala *f* phial
fia'letta *f* phial
■ **fialetta puzzolente** stink bomb
fi'amma *f* flame; Naut pennant; **in fiamme** in flames; **andare in fiamme** go up in flames; **dare alle fiamme** commit to the flames; **alla ~** Culin flambé; **le Fiamme Gialle** *body responsible for border control and investigating fraud*
■ **fiamma ossidrica** blowtorch
fiam'mante *adj* flaming; **nuovo ~** brand new
fiam'mata *f* blaze
fiammeggi'are **A** *vi* blaze
B *vt* singe ‹*pollo*›

key word

fiam'mifero *m* match

fiam'mingo, **-a** **A** *adj & nm* Flemish **B** *mf* Fleming

fian'cata *f* wing

fiancheggi'are *vt* border; fig support

fi'anco *m* side; (di persona) hip; (di animale) flank; Mil wing; **al mio ~** by my side; **~ a ~** ‹*lavorare*› side by side

Fi'andre *fpl* **le ~** Flanders

fia'schetta *f* hip flask

fiaschette'ria *f* wine shop

fi'asco *m* flask; fig fiasco; **fare ~** be a fiasco

fia'tare *vi* breathe; (parlare) breathe a word

fi'ato *m* breath; (vigore) stamina; **strumenti a ~** wind instruments; **avere il ~ corto** be short of breath; **senza ~** breathlessly; **tutto d'un ~** ‹*bere, leggere*› all in one go

'fibbia *f* buckle

'fibra *f* fibre; **fibre** *pl* (alimentari) roughage
■ **fibre artificiali** *pl* man-made fibres; **fibra ottica** optical fibre; **a fibre ottiche** ‹*cavo*› fibre optic; **fibra sintetica** man-made fibre, synthetic fibre; **fibra di vetro** fibreglass

fi'broma *m* fibroid

fi'broso *adj* fibrous

ficca'naso *mf inv* nosey parker

fic'care *vt* thrust; drive ‹*chiodo ecc.*›; infml (mettere) shove

fic'carsi *vr* thrust oneself; (nascondersi) hide; **~ nei guai** get oneself into trouble

'fiche *f inv* (gettone) chip

'fico[1] *m* (albero) fig tree; (frutto) fig; **non me ne importa un ~ [secco]** infml I don't give a damn; **non capisce un ~ [secco]** infml he doesn't understand a bloody thing; **non vale un ~ [secco]** infml it's totally worthless
■ **fico d'India** prickly pear

'fico[2], **-a** **A** *mf* infml cool sort **B** *adj* cool

fidanza'mento *m* engagement; **rompere il ~** break off one's engagement, break it off

fidan'zarsi *vr* get engaged

fidan'zata *f* (ufficiale) fiancée; (innamorata) girlfriend

fidan'zato *m* (ufficiale) fiancé; (innamorato) boyfriend

fi'darsi *vr* **~ di** trust

fi'dato *adj* trustworthy

'fido **A** *adj* ‹*compagno*› loyal **B** *m* devoted follower; Comm credit

fi'ducia *f* confidence; **degno di ~** trustworthy; **persona di ~** reliable person; **di ~** ‹*fornitore, banca*› regular, usual; **avere ~ in se stessi** believe in oneself; **incarico di ~** important job

fiduci'ario, **-a** **A** *adj* ‹*rapporto, transazione*› based on trust **B** *mf* trustee

fiduci'oso *adj* hopeful

fi'ele *m* bile; fig bitterness; **amaro come il ~** bitter as gall

fienagi'one *f* haymaking

fie'nile *m* barn

fi'eno *m* hay

fi'era *f* fair
■ **fiera commerciale** trade fair; **fiera del libro** book fair

fie'rezza *f* (dignità) pride

fi'ero *adj* proud

fi'evole *adj* faint; ‹*luce*› dim

'fifa *f* infml jitters; **aver ~** have the jitters

fi'fone, **-a** *mf* infml chicken, yellow-belly

FIGC *nf abbr* (**Federazione Italiana Gioco Calcio**) Italian Football Association

Figi *fpl* **le isole ~** Fiji

'figli *mpl* children

'figlia *f* daughter
■ **figlia unica** only child

figli'are *vi* ‹*animale*› calve

figli'astra *f* stepdaughter

figli'astro *m* stepson

'figlio *m* son; (generico) child; **è ~ d'arte** he was born in a trunk
■ **figlio adottivo** adopted child; **figlio di papà** spoilt brat; **figlio di puttana** vulg son of a bitch; **figlio unico** only child

figli'occia *f* god-daughter

figli'occio *m* godson

figli'ola *f* girl

figlio'lanza *f* offspring

figli'olo *m* boy; **figlioli** *pl* children

'figo, **-a** *adj* ▸ **fico**[2]

fi'gura *f* figure; (aspetto esteriore) shape; (illustrazione) illustration; (in carte da gioco) picture [card]; **far bella/brutta ~** make a good/bad impression; **mi hai fatto fare una brutta ~** you made me look a fool; **che ~!** how embarrassing!
■ **figura paterna** father figure; **figura retorica** figure of speech

figu'raccia *f* bad impression

figu'rare **A** *vt* represent; (simboleggiare) symbolize; (immaginare) imagine **B** *vi* (far figura) cut a fine figure; (in lista) appear, figure; **~ in testa al cartellone** Theat get top billing

figu'rarsi *vr* (immaginarsi) imagine; **figurati!** imagine that!; **posso? - [ma] figurati!** may I? - of course!; **grazie - figurati!** thank you - don't mention it!

figura'tivo *adj* figurative

figu'rina *f* (da raccolta) cigarette card; (statuetta) figurine

figuri'nista *mf* dress designer

figu'rino *m* fashion sketch

fi'guro *m* **un losco ~** a shady character

figu'rone *m* **fare un ~** make an excellent impression

fil *m*
■ **fil di ferro** wire

'fila *f* line; (di soldati ecc.) file; (di oggetti) row; (coda) queue; **di ~** in succession; **fare la ~**

f

queue [up], stand in line AmE; **in ~ indiana** single file
fila'mento *m* filament
fi'lanca® *f* type of synthetic stretch fabric
fi'lante *adj* ‹*formaggio*› stringy; **stella ~** (di carta) streamer
filantro'pia *f* philanthropy
filan'tropico *adj* philanthropic
fi'lantropo, -a *mf* philanthropist
fi'lare **A** *vt* spin; Naut pay out
B *vi* (andarsene) run away; ‹*liquido*› trickle; ‹*ragionamento*› hang together; **fila!** infml scram!; **~ con** infml (amoreggiare) go out with; **~ dritto** toe the line
C *m* (di viti, alberi) row
filar'monica *f* (orchestra) orchestra
filar'monico *adj* philharmonic
fila'strocca *f* rigmarole; (per bambini) nursery rhyme
filate'lia *f* philately, stamp collecting
fila'telico, -a *mf* philatelist
fi'lato **A** *adj* spun; (ininterrotto) running; (continuato) uninterrupted; **di ~** (subito) immediately; **andare dritto ~ a** go straight to
B *m* yarn
fila|'tore, -trice *mf* spinner
fila'tura *f* spinning; (filanda) spinning mill
file *m inv* Comput file
filetta'tura *f* (di vite) thread
fi'letto *m* (bordo) border; ‹*di vite*› thread; Culin fillet
■ **filetto ai ferri** grilled fillet of beef
fili'ale **A** *adj* filial
B *f* Comm branch
filibusti'ere *m* rascal
fili'forme *adj* stringy
fili'grana *f* filigree; (su carta) watermark
fi'lippica *f* invective
filip'pino, -a *adj & nmf* Filipino
film *m inv* film
■ **film catastrofico** disaster movie; **film comico** comedy; **film drammatico** drama; **film di fantascienza** science fiction film; **film giallo** thriller; **film a lungometraggio** feature film; **film dell'orrore** horror film; **film poliziesco** detective film; **film verità** docudrama
fil'mare *vt* film
fil'mato **A** *adj* filmed
B *m* short film
fil'mina *f* film strip
fil'mino *m* home movie
'filo *m* thread; (tessile) yarn; (metallico) wire; (di lama) edge; (venatura) grain; (di perle) string; (d'erba) blade; (di luce) ray; **un ~ di** (poco) a drop of; **con un ~ di voce** in a whisper; **per ~ e per segno** in detail; **fare il ~ a qualcuno** fancy somebody; **perdere il ~** lose the thread; **essere appeso a un ~** be hanging by a thread; **essere sul ~ del rasoio** be on a knife-edge; **un ~ d'aria** a breath of air; **un ~ di speranza** a glimmer of hope
■ **filo interdentale** dental floss; **filo a piombo** plumb line; **filo spinato** barbed wire
filo+ *pref* philo+
filoameri'cano *adj* pro-American
'filobus *m inv* trolleybus
filocomu'nista *adj* pro-communist
filodiffusi'one *f* rediffusion
filodram'matica *f* amateur dramatic society
filolo'gia *f* philology
filo'logico *adj* philological
fi'lologo, -a *mf* philologist
filon'cino *m* ≈ French stick
fi'lone *m* vein; (di pane) long loaf, Vienna loaf
fi'loso *adj* stringy
filoso'fia *f* philosophy
fi'losofo, -a *mf* philosopher
fil'traggio *m* filtering
fil'trare *vt* filter
'filtro *m* filter
■ **filtro chiamate** Teleph call screening; **filtro dell'olio** oil filter
'filza *f* string
fin ▸ **fino**[1]
fi'nale **A** *adj* final
B *m* end; **~ a sorpresa** surprise ending
C *f* Sport final
fina'lista *mf* finalist
finalità *f inv* finality; (scopo) aim
final'mente *adv* at last; (in ultimo) finally
fi'nanza *f* finance; **Guardia di ~** *body of police officers responsible for border control and for investigating fraud*; **intendenza di ~** inland revenue office
finanzia'mento *m* funding
finanzi'are *vt* fund, finance
finanzi'aria *f* investment company; (holding) holding company; Jur finance bill
finanzi'ario *adj* financial
finanzia|'tore, -trice *mf* backer
finanzi'ere *m* financier; (guardia di finanza) customs officer
finché *conj* until; (per tutto il tempo che) as long as
'fine **A** *adj* fine; (sottile) thin; ‹*udito, vista*› keen; (raffinato) refined
B *f* end; **alla ~** in the end; **alla fin ~** after all; **in fin dei conti** when all's said and done; **che ~ ha fatto Anna?** what became of Anna?; **che ~ hanno fatto le chiavi?** where have the keys got to?; **senza ~** endless
C *m* aim; **andare a buon ~** be successful; **te lo dico a fin di bene** I'm telling you for your own good
■ **fine settimana** weekend
fi'nestra *f* window
■ **finestra a battenti** casement window

key word

fine'strella *f* Comput box
■ **finestrella di aiuto** help window; **finestrella di dialogo** dialog box, dialogue box BrE; **finestrella di messaggio** message box

fine'strino *m* Rail, Auto window

fi'nezza *f* fineness; (sottigliezza) thinness; (raffinatezza) refinement

'fingere *vt* pretend; feign ‹*affetto ecc.*›

'fingersi *vr* pretend to be

fini'menti *mpl* finishing touches; (per cavallo) harness *sg*

fini'mondo *m* end of the world; fig pandemonium

fi'nire *vt* finish, end; (smettere) stop; (diventare, andare a finire) end up; **finiscila!** stop it!

fi'nito *adj* finished; (abile) accomplished

fini'tura *f* finish

finlan'dese **A** *adj* Finnish
B *mf* Finn
C *m* (lingua) Finnish

Fin'landia *f* Finland

'fino[1] *prep* **~ a** till, until; (spazio) as far as; **~ all'ultimo** to the last; **~ alla nausea** ‹*ripetere, leggere*› ad nauseam; **fin da** (tempo) since; (spazio) from; **fin dall'inizio** from the beginning; **fin qui** as far as here; **fin troppo** too much; **~ a che punto** how far

'fino[2] *adj* fine; (acuto) subtle; (puro) pure

fi'nocchio *m* fennel; infml (omosessuale) poof

fi'nora *adv* so far, up till now

'finta *f* pretence, sham; Sport feint; **far ~ di** pretend to; **far ~ di niente** act as if nothing had happened; **per ~** (per scherzo) for a laugh

'finto, -a **A** pp di **fingere**
B *adj* false; (artificiale) artificial; **finta pelle** fake leather; **fare il ~ tonto** act dumb

finzi'one *f* pretence

fi'occo *m* bow; (di neve) flake; (nappa) tassel; Naut jib; **coi fiocchi** fig excellent; **fiocchi** *pl* **di avena** oatmeal; (cotti) porridge; **fiocchi** *pl* **di granoturco** cornflakes; **fiocchi** *pl* **di latte** cottage cheese
■ **fiocco di neve** snowflake

fi'ocina *f* harpoon

fi'oco *adj* weak; ‹*luce*› dim

fi'onda *f* catapult

fio'raio, -a *mf* florist

fiorda'liso *m* cornflower

fi'ordo *m* fiord

fi'ore *m* flower; **a fior d'acqua** on the surface of the water; **a fiori** flowery; **in ~** flowering; **fior di** (abbondanza) a lot of; **il fior ~ di the** cream of; **ha i nervi a fior di pelle** his nerves are on edge; **nel ~ degli anni** in one's prime; **è il suo ~ all'occhiello** that's a feather in his cap; **suo figlio è il suo ~ all'occhiello** his son is his pride and joy
■ **fiori d'arancio** *pl* orange blossom; **fiore di campo** wild flower; **fior di latte** (formaggio) soft cheese; **fiore selvatico** wild flower; **fiori di zucca fritti** *pl* fried pumpkin flowers

fio'rente *adj* ‹*industria*› booming

fioren'tina *f* (bistecca) T-bone steak

fioren'tino *adj* Florentine

fio'retto *m* (scherma) foil; Relig act of mortification

fi'ori *mpl* (nelle carte) clubs

fiori'era *f* container

fio'rino *m*
■ **fiorino olandese** guilder

fio'rire *vi* flower; ‹*albero*› blossom; fig flourish

fio'rista *mf* florist; (nègozio) florist's

fiori'tura *f* flowering; (di albero) blossoming; (insieme di fiori) flowers *pl*

fio'rone *m* (fico) early fig

fi'otto *m* (di sangue) spurt; **scorrere a fiotti** pour out; **piove a fiotti** the rain is pouring down

Fi'renze *f* Florence

'firma *f* signature; (nome) name

firma'mento *m* firmament

fir'mare *vt* sign

firma'tario, -a *mf* signatory

fir'mato *adj* ‹*quadro, lettera*› signed; ‹*abito, borsa*› designer *attrib*

fisar'monica *f* accordion

fi'scale *adj* fiscal

fisca'lista *mf* tax consultant

fiscaliz'zare *vt* finance with government funds

fischi'are **A** *vi* whistle; **mi fischiano le orecchie** I've got a ringing noise in my ears; fig my ears are burning
B *vt* whistle; (in segno di disapprovazione) boo

fischi'ata *f* whistle

fischiet'tare *vt* whistle

fischiet'tio *m* whistling

fischi'etto *m* whistle

'fischio *m* whistle; **fischi** *pl* Theat booing; **prendere fischi per fiaschi** get hold of the wrong end of the stick

'fisco *m* Inland Revenue BrE, IRS AmE; (tasse) taxation; **il ~** the taxman

'fisica *f* physics *sg*
■ **fisica atomica** atomic physics; **fisica nucleare** nuclear physics

fisica'mente *adv* physically

'fisico, -a **A** *adj* physical
B *mf* physicist
■ **fisico nucleare** atomic scientist
C *m* physique

'fisima *f* whim

fisiolo'gia *f* physiology

fisio'logico *adj* physiological

fisi'ologo, -a *mf* physiologist

fisiono'mia *f* features *pl*, face; (di paesaggio) appearance

fisiotera'pia *f* physiotherapy

fisiotera'pista *mf* physiotherapist, physio infml

f

fissa'mente *adv* fixedly; (permanentemente) steadily

fis'sare *vt* fix, fasten; (guardare fissamente) stare at; arrange ‹*appuntamento, ora*›

fis'sarsi *vr* (stabilirsi) settle; (fissare lo sguardo) stare; ~ **su** (ostinarsi) set one's mind on; ~ **di fare qualcosa** become obsessed with doing something

fissa'tivo *m* Phot fixative

fis'sato, -a **A** *adj* (persona) obsessed; (al muro) fixed; (prezzo) agreed
B *m* (persona) person with an obsession

fissa'tore *m* hair spray

fissazi'one *f* fixation; (ossessione) obsession

'fisso **A** *adj* fixed; **un lavoro** ~ a regular job; **senza fissa dimora** of no fixed abode; **avere una ragazza fissa** have a steady girlfriend
B *adv* fixedly; **guardare** ~ **negli occhi qualcuno** stare at somebody; ‹*innamorato*› gaze into somebody's eyes

fitotera'pia *f* herbalism; (per piante) plant health

'fitta *f* sharp pain

fit'tavolo *m* tenant

fit'tizio *adj* fictitious

'fitto[1] **A** *adj* thick; ~ **di** full of
B *m* depth

'fitto[2] *m* (affitto) rent; **dare a** ~ let; **prendere a** ~ rent; (noleggiare) hire

fiu'mana *f* swollen river; fig stream

fi'ume **A** *m* river; fig stream
B *adj inv* ‹*discussione*› endless, never-ending; **romanzo** ~ roman-fleuve

fiu'tare *vt* smell; ‹*animale*› scent; snort ‹*cocaina*›

fi'uto *m* [sense of] smell; fig nose

'flaccido *adj* flabby

fla'cone *m* bottle

flagel'lare *vt* flog

flagellazi'one *f* flagellation

fla'gello *m* scourge

fla'grante *adj* flagrant; **in** ~ in the act

fla'menco *m* flamenco

flan *m inv* baked custard

fla'nella *f* flannel

'flangia *f* (su ruota) flange

flash *m inv* Phot flash; Journ newsflash

flau'tista *mf* flautist

'flauto *m* flute
■ **flauto diritto** recorder; **flauto traverso** flute

'flebile *adj* feeble

fle'bite *f* phlebitis

flebo'clisi *f* drip

'flemma *f* calm; Med phlegm

flem'matico *adj* phlegmatic

fles'sibile *adj* flexible

flessibilità *f inv* flexibility

flessi'one *f* (del busto in avanti) forward bend; (a terra) sit-up; (delle ginocchia) knee bend; (di vendite, produzione) drop, fall

fles'sivo *adj* Gram inflected

'flesso **A** pp di **flettere**
B *adj* Gram inflected

flessu'oso *adj* supple

'flettere *vt* bend

flip-'flop *m inv* flip flop

flir'tare *vi* flirt

F.lli *abbr* (**fratelli**) Bros.

'floppy disk *m inv* floppy disk

'flora *f* flora

'florido *adj* flourishing

floroviva'istica *f* ‹*attività*› growing under glass

'floscio *adj* limp; (flaccido) flabby

'flotta *f* fleet

flot'tiglia *f* flotilla

flu'ente *adj* fluent

fluidità *f inv* fluidity; (nel parlare) fluency

'fluido *m* fluid

flu'ire *vi* flow

fluore'scente *adj* fluorescent

fluore'scenza *f* fluorescence

flu'oro *m* fluorine

fluo'ruro *m* fluoride

'flusso *m* flow; Med flux; (del mare) flood tide
■ **flusso e riflusso** ebb and flow; **flusso di cassa** cash flow

'flutti *mpl* billows

fluttu'ante *adj* fluctuating

fluttu'are *vi* ‹*prezzi*› fluctuate; ‹*moneta*› float

fluttuazi'one *f* fluctuation; (di moneta) floating

fluvi'ale *adj* river *attrib*

fo'bia *f* phobia

'fobico *adj* phobic

'foca *f* seal

fo'caccia *f* (pane) flat bread; (dolce) ≈ raisin bread

fo'cale *adj* ‹*distanza, punto*› focal

focaliz'zare *vt* get into focus ‹*fotografia*›; focus ‹*attenzione*›; define ‹*problema*›

'foce *f* mouth

fo'chista *m* stoker

foco'laio *m* Med focus; fig centre

foco'lare *m* hearth; (caminetto) fireplace; Techn furnace

fo'coso *adj* fiery

'fodera *f* lining; (di libro) dust jacket; (di poltrona ecc.) loose cover

fode'rare *vt* line; cover ‹*libro*›

fode'rato *adj* lined; ‹*libro*› covered

'foga *f* impetuosity

'foggia *f* fashion; ‹*maniera*› manner; (forma) shape

foggi'are *vt* mould

key word

'foglia *f* leaf; (di metallo) foil; **mangiare la ~** catch on
■ **foglia di alloro** bay leaf
fogli'ame *m* foliage
fogliet'tino *m*
■ **foglietino igienico** (per pannolini) nappy liner
fogli'etto *m* (pezzetto di carta) piece of paper
'foglio *m* sheet; (pagina) leaf; (di domanda, iscrizione) form
■ **foglio di carta** sheet of paper; **foglio elettronico** Comput spreadsheet; **foglio illustrativo** instruction leaflet; **foglio protocollo** foolscap; **foglio rosa** provisional driving licence; **foglio di via** expulsion order
'fogna *f* sewer
fogna'tura *f* sewerage
fohn *m inv* hair dryer
fo'lata *f* gust
fol'clore *m* folklore
folclo'ristico *adj* folk; (bizzarro) weird
folgo'rante *adj* ‹*idea*› brilliant
folgo'rare **A** *vi* (splendere) shine
B *vt* (con un fulmine) strike
folgo'rato *adj* fig thunderstruck
folgorazi'one *f* (da fulmine, elettrica) electrocution; fig (idea) brainwave
'folgore *f* thunderbolt
'folio in **~** *adj* folio
'folla *f* crowd
'folle *adj* mad; ‹*velocità*› breakneck; **in ~** Auto in neutral; **andare in ~** Auto coast
folleggi'are *vi* paint the town red
folle'mente *adv* madly
fol'letto *m* elf
fol'lia *f* madness; **alla ~** ‹*amare*› to distraction; **costare una ~** cost the earth; **fare una ~** go mad; **farei follie per lei** I'd do anything for her
'folto *adj* thick
fomen'tare *vt* stir up
fond'ale *m* Theat backcloth
■ **fondale marino** sea bed
fonda'menta *fpl* foundations
fondamen'tale *adj* fundamental
fondamenta'lismo *m* fundamentalism
fondamenta'lista *mf* fundamentalist
fonda'mento *m* (di principio, teoria) foundation; **privo di ~** groundless, without foundation
fon'dant *m inv* fondant
fon'dare *vt* establish; base ‹*ragionamento, accusa*›
fon'darsi *vr* be based (**su** on)
fon'dato *adj* ‹*ragionamento*› well-founded; **~ su** based on
fondazi'one *f* establishment; **fondazioni** *pl* (di edificio) foundations
fon'delli *mpl* **prendere qualcuno per i ~** infml pull somebody's leg
fon'dente *adj* ‹*cioccolato*› dark
'fondere **A** *vt* melt; fuse ‹*metallo*›
B *vi* melt; ‹*metallo*› fuse; ‹*colori*› blend
fonde'ria *f* foundry
'fondersi *vr* melt; Comm merge
'fondo **A** *adj* deep; **è notte fonda** it's the middle of the night
B *m* bottom; (fine) end; (sfondo) background; (indole) nature; (somma di denaro) fund; (feccia) dregs *pl*; (terreno) land; **[sci di] ~** cross-country skiing; **andare a ~** ‹*nave*› sink; **in ~** after all; **in ~ a** at the end/bottom of; **in ~ in ~** deep down; **fino in ~** right to the end; ‹*capire*› thoroughly; **andare fino in ~ a qualcosa** get to the bottom of something; **dar ~ a** use up; **a doppio ~** false bottomed; **toccare il ~** touch bottom; fig hit rock bottom; **senza ~** bottomless; **fondi** *pl* (denaro) funds; (di caffè) grounds; **fondi** *pl* **di magazzino** old stock; **fondi** *pl* **neri** slush fund; **fondi** *pl* **sovrani** sovereign wealth funds
■ **articolo di fondo** (in giornale) editorial; **fondo fiduciario** trust fund; **fondo [comune] di investimento** investment trust; **Fondo Monetario Internazionale** International Monetary Fund; **fondo pensione** pension fund; **fondo per la ricostruzione** disaster fund; **fondo sopravvenienze passive** contingency fund; **fondo stradale** road surface
fondo'tinta *m inv* foundation [cream]
fon'due *f* (di formaggio) fondue
fon'duta *f* fondue
fo'nema *m* phoneme
fo'netica *f* phonetics *sg*
fo'netico *adj* phonetic
fonolo'gia *f* phonology
fon'tana *f* fountain; (di farina) well
fonta'nella *f* drinking fountain; Anat fontanelle
'fonte **A** *f* spring; fig source
B *m* font
fon'tina *f soft mature cheese often used in cooking*
'football *m*
■ **football americano** American football
foraggi'are *vt* fodder
fo'raggio *m* forage
fo'rare **A** *vt* pierce: punch ‹*biglietto*›
B *vi* puncture
fo'rarsi *vr* ‹*gomma, pallone*› go soft
fora'tura *f* puncture
'forbici *fpl* scissors; **un paio di ~** a pair of scissors
■ **forbici da siepe** garden shears; **forbici a zigzag** pinking shears, pinking scissors
forbi'cina *f* earwig; **forbicine** *pl* (per le unghie) nail scissors
for'bito *adj* erudite
'forca *f* fork; (patibolo) gallows *pl*
for'cella *f* fork; (per capelli) hairpin

for'chetta *f* fork; **essere una buona ~** enjoy one's food
forchet'tata *f* (quantità) forkful
forchet'tone *m* carving fork
for'cina *f* hairpin
'forcipe *m* forceps *pl*
for'cone *m* pitchfork
fo'rense *adj* forensic
fo'resta *f* forest
■ **foresta equatoriale** rain forest; **Foresta Nera** Black Forest

f

fore'stale *adj* forest *attrib*; **la Forestale** *branch of the police with responsibility for national forests*
foreste'ria *f* guest rooms *pl*
foresti'ero, -a **A** *adj* foreign
B *mf* foreigner
for'fait *m inv* fixed price; **dare ~** (abbandonare) give up; **prezzo [a] forfait** all-in price; **contratto [a] forfait** lump sum contract
forfe'tario *adj* flat rate
'forfora *f* dandruff
'forgia *f* forge
forgi'are *vt* forge
'forma *f* form; (sagoma) shape; Culin mould; (per scarpe) shoe tree; (di calzolaio) last; **essere in ~** be in good form; **in (gran) ~** (very) fit, on (top) form; **a ~ di** in the shape of; **sotto ~ di** in the form of; **forme** *pl* (del corpo) curves; (convenzioni) appearances
formag'gera *f* [covered] cheese board
formag'gino *m* processed cheese
for'maggio *m* cheese
■ **formaggio erborinato** blue cheese
for'male *adj* formal
forma'lina *f* formalin
forma'lismo *m* formalism
forma'lista *mf* formalist
formalità *f inv* formality
formaliz'zare *vt* formalize
formaliz'zarsi *vr* stand on ceremony, be formal
formal'mente *adv* formally
'forma 'mentis *f inv* way of thinking, mindset
for'mare *vt* form; dial ‹*numero di telefono*›
for'marsi *vr* form; (svilupparsi) develop
for'mato *m* size; (di libro, dischetto) format
■ **formato famiglia** economy pack, economy size; **formato tessera** ‹*fotografia*› passport size
format'tare *vt* format
formattazi'one *f* formatting
formazi'one *f* formation; Sport line-up; **in ~** in the process of being formed
■ **formazione professionale** vocational training; **formazione professionale postlaurea** graduate training scheme
for'mella *f* tile
for'mica¹ *f* ant
'formica®² *f* Formica
formi'caio *m* anthill
formichi'ere *m* anteater
formico'lare *vi* ‹*braccio ecc.*› tingle; **~ di** be swarming with; **mi formicola la mano** I have pins and needles in my hand
formico'lio *m* swarming; (di braccio ecc.) pins and needles *pl*
formi'dabile *adj* (tremendo) formidable; (eccezionale) tremendous
for'mina *f* mould
for'moso *adj* curvy
'formula *f* formula; **assolvere con ~ piena** acquit
■ **formula di cortesia** polite form of address
formu'lare *vt* formulate; (esprimere) express
formulazi'one *f* formulation
for'nace *f* furnace; (per laterizi) kiln
for'naio, -a *mf* baker; (negozio) bakery
fornel'letto *m*:
■ **fornelletto da campeggio** camping stove; **fornelletto a gas** gas stove
for'nello *m* stove; (di pipa) bowl
■ **fornello da campeggio** camping stove
fornicazi'one *f* fornication
for'nire *vt* supply (**di** with); **~ qualcosa a qualcuno** supply somebody with something
for'nirsi *vr* **~ di** provide oneself with
forni'tore *m* supplier
■ **fornitore di servizi [Internet]** [Internet] service provider
forni'tura *f* supply; **forniture** *pl* **per ufficio** office supplies
'forno *m* oven; (panetteria) bakery; **al ~** roast; **da ~** ‹*stoviglie*› ovenproof
■ **forno autopulente** self-cleaning oven; **forno crematorio** cremator; **forno elettrico** electric oven; **forno a gas** gas oven; **forno a microonde** microwave [oven]
'foro *m* hole; (romano) forum; (tribunale) [law] court
'forse *adv* perhaps, maybe; **essere in ~** be in doubt
forsen'nato, -a **A** *adj* mad
B *mf* madman; madwoman
'forte **A** *adj* strong; ‹*colore*› bright; ‹*suono*› loud; (resistente) tough; ‹*spesa*› considerable; ‹*dolore*› severe; ‹*pioggia*› heavy; infml (simpatico) great; ‹*taglia*› large; **essere ~ in qualcosa** be good at something
B *adv* strongly; ‹*parlare*› loudly; (velocemente) fast; ‹*piovere*› heavily
C *m* (fortezza) fort; (specialità) strong point
for'tezza *f* fortress; (forza morale) fortitude
fortifi'care *vt* fortify
fortifi'cato *adj* ‹*città*› walled
for'tino *m* Mil blockhouse
for'tissimo *adj* ‹*caffè, liquore*› extra strong

key word

for'tuito *adj* fortuitous; **incontro ~** chance encounter

for'tuna *f* fortune; (successo) success; (buona sorte) luck; **atterraggio di ~** forced landing; **aver ~** be lucky; **buona ~!** good luck!; **di ~** makeshift; **per ~** luckily; **hai una ~ sfacciata!** infml you lucky blighter!

fortu'nale *m* storm

fortunata'mente *adv* fortunately

fortu'nato *adj* lucky, fortunate; ‹*impresa*› successful

fortu'noso *adj* ‹*giornata*› eventful

fo'runcolo *m* pimple; (grosso) boil

forunco'loso *adj* spotty

'forza *f* strength; (potenza) power; (fisica) force; **di ~** by force; **a ~ di** by dint of; **con ~** hard; **~!** come on!; **in ~ di** under, in accordance with; **~ maggiore** circumstances beyond one's control; **la ~ pubblica** the police; **le forze armate** the armed forces; **per ~** against one's will; (naturalmente) of course; **farsi ~** bear up; **mare ~ 8** force 8 gale; **bella ~!** infml big deal!; **che ~!** (che simpatico, divertente) cool eh?
■ **forza di gravità** [force of] gravity; **forza lavoro** workforce; **forze** *pl* **di mercato** market forces; **forza di volontà** willpower

for'zare *vt* force; (scassare) break open; (sforzare) strain

for'zato **A** *adj* forced; ‹*sorriso*› strained **B** *m* convict

forza'tura *f* (di cassaforte) forcing; **sostenere che ... è una ~** to maintain that ... is forcing things

forzi'ere *m* coffer

for'zuto *adj* strong

fo'schia *f* haze, mist

'fosco *adj* dark

fo'sfato *m* phosphate

'fosforo *m* phosphorus

'fossa *f* pit; (tomba) grave
■ **fossa biologica** cesspool; **fossa comune** mass grave; **fossa dell'orchestra** orchestra pit

fos'sato *m* (di fortificazione) moat

fos'setta *f* (di guancia) dimple

'fossile *m* fossil

'fosso *m* ditch; Mil trench

'foto *f inv* infml photo; **fare delle ~** take some photos

foto'camera *f* camera
■ **fotocamera digitale** digital camera; infml digicam

foto'cellula *f* photocell

fotocomposi|'tore, -trice *mf* filmsetter

fotocomposizi'one *f* filmsetting, photo-composition

foto'copia *f* photocopy

fotocopi'are *vt* photocopy

fotocopia'trice *f* photocopier

foto'finish *m inv* photo finish

foto'gallery *f* photogallery

foto'genico *adj* photogenic

fotogiorna'lista *mf* photojournalist

fotogra'fare *vt* photograph

fotogra'fia *f* (arte) photography; (immagine) photograph; **fare fotografie** take photographs
■ **fotografia aerea** aerial photography

foto'grafico *adj* photographic; **macchina fotografica** camera

fo'tografo, -a *mf* photographer; (negozio) photographer's

foto'gramma *m* frame

fotoincisi'one *f* photo engraving

fotomo'dello, -a *mf* [photographer's] model

fotomon'taggio *m* photomontage

foto'ottica *f* camera shop and optician's

fotorepor'tage *m inv* photo essay

fotore'porter *mf inv* newspaper photographer; (di rivista) magazine photographer

fotori'tocco *m* retouching, image manipulation

fotoro'manzo *m* photo story

foto'sintesi *f* photosynthesis

'fottere *vt* sl (rubare) nick; sl (imbrogliare) screw; vulg fuck, screw

'fottersene *vr* vulg not give a fuck; **va' a farti ~!** vulg fuck off!

fot'tuto *adj* sl (maledetto) bloody

fou'lard *m inv* scarf

'foxhound *m inv* foxhound

fox-'terrier *m inv* fox terrier

fo'yer *m inv* foyer

fra *prep* (in mezzo a due) between; (in un insieme) among; (tempo, distanza) in; **detto ~ noi** between you and me; **~ sé e sé** to oneself; **~ l'altro** what's more; **~ breve** soon; **~ quindici giorni** in two weeks' time; **~ tutti, siamo in venti** there are twenty of us altogether

fracas'sare *vt* smash

fracas'sarsi *vr* shatter

fracas'sato *adj* smashed

fra'casso *m* din; (di cose che cadono) crash

fracas'sone, -a *mf* clumsy person

'fradicio *adj* (bagnato) soaked; **ubriaco ~** blind drunk

'fragile *adj* fragile; fig frail

fragilità *f inv* fragility; fig frailty

'fragola *f* strawberry

fra'gore *m* uproar; (di cose rotte) clatter; (di tuono) rumble

frago'roso *adj* uproarious; ‹*tuono*› rumbling; ‹*suono*› clanging

fra'grante *adj* fragrant

fra'granza *f* fragrance

frain'tendere *vt* misunderstand

frain'tendersi *vr* be at cross purposes

frain'teso pp di **fraintendere**

frammen'tario *adj* fragmentary
fram'mento *m* fragment
fram'misto *adj* ~ **di** interspersed with
'frana *f* landslide; infml (persona) walking disaster area
fra'nare *vi* slide down
franca'mente *adv* frankly
france'scano *adj & nm* Franciscan
fran'cese **A** *adj* French
B *m* Frenchman; (lingua) French
C *f* Frenchwoman
france'sina *f* (scarpa) brogue

f

fran'chezza *f* frankness; **in tutta** ~ in all honesty
fran'chigia *f*
■ **franchigia bagaglio** (per aereo) baggage allowance
'Francia *f* France
'franco¹ *adj* frank; Comm free; **farla franca** get away with something; **parlare** ~ speak frankly
■ **franco a bordo** free on board; **franco domicilio** delivered free of charge; **franco fabbrica** ex-works; **franco di porto** carriage free, carriage paid
'franco² *m* (moneta) franc
franco'bollo *m* stamp
franco-cana'dese *adj & nmf* French Canadian
fran'cofono *adj* Francophone, French-speaking
Franco'forte *f* Frankfurt
fran'gente *m* (onda) breaker; (scoglio) reef; fig (momento difficile) crisis; **in quel** ~ in the circumstances
fran'getta *f* fringe
'frangia *f* fringe
frangi'flutti *m inv* bulwark
frangi'vento *m* windbreak
fra'noso *adj* subject to landslides
fran'toio *m* olive press
frantu'mare *vt* shatter
frantu'marsi *vr* shatter
fran'tumi *mpl* splinters; **in** ~ smashed; **andare in** ~ be smashed to smithereens
frappé *m inv* milkshake
frap'porre *vt* interpose
frap'porsi *vr* intervene
fra'sario *m* vocabulary; (libro) phrase book
'frasca *f* [leafy] branch; **saltare di palo in** ~ jump from subject to subject
'frase *f* sentence; (espressione) phrase
■ **frase fatta** cliché
fraseolo'gia *f* phrases *pl*
'frassino *m* ash [tree]
frastagli'are *vt* make jagged
frastagl'iato *adj* jagged
frastor'nare *vt* daze
frastor'nato *adj* dazed
frastu'ono *m* racket
'frate *m* friar; (monaco) monk
fratel'lanza *f* brotherhood
fratel'lastro *m* step brother, half-brother
fratel'lino *m* little brother
fra'tello *m* brother; **fratelli** *pl* (fratello e sorella) brother and sister; Relig brethren
■ **fratello gemello** twin brother; **fratello di sangue** blood brother
fraternità *f inv* brotherhood
fraterniz'zare *vi* fraternize
fra'terno *adj* brotherly
fratri'cida **A** *adj* fratricidal
B *m* fratricide
frat'taglie *fpl* (di pollo ecc.) giblets
frat'tanto *adv* in the meantime
frat'tura *f* fracture
frattu'rare *vt* break
frattu'rarsi *vr* break
fraudo'lento *adj* fraudulent
frazi'one *f* fraction; (borgata) hamlet; (paese) *administrative division of a municipality*
'freccia *f* arrow; Auto indicator
frecci'ata *f* (osservazione pungente) cutting remark
fredda'mente *adv* coldly
fred'dare *vt* cool; fig (con sguardo, battuta) cut down; (uccidere) kill
fred'dezza *f* coldness
'freddo *adj & nm* cold; **aver** ~ be cold; **fa** ~ it's cold; **a** ~ ‹*sparare*› in cold blood; ‹*lavare*› in cold water
freddo'loso *adj* sensitive to cold, chilly
fred'dura *f* pun
fre'gare *vt* rub; infml (truffare) cheat; infml (rubare) swipe; **fregarsene** infml not give a damn; **me ne frego!** I don't give a damn!; **chi se ne frega!** what the heck!
fre'garsi *vr* rub ‹*occhi, mani*›
fre'gata *f* rub; (nave) frigate
frega'tura *f* infml (truffa) swindle; (delusione) let-down
'fregio *m* Archit frieze; (ornamento) decoration
'fregola *f* rutting; **avere la** ~ **di fare qualcosa** infml have a craze for doing something
fre'mente *adj* quivering
'fremere *vi* quiver
'fremito *m* quiver
fre'nare **A** *vt* brake; fig restrain; hold back ‹*lacrime, impazienza*›
B *vi* brake
fre'narsi *vr* check oneself
fre'nata *f* **fare una** ~ **brusca** hit the brakes
frene'sia *f* frenzy; (desiderio smodato) craze
frenetica'mente *adv* frantically
fre'netico *adj* frantic
'freno *m* brake; fig check; **togliere il** ~ release the brake; **usare il** ~ apply the

---
key word

brake; **tenere a ~** restrain; **tenere a ~ la lingua** hold one's tongue; **porre un ~ a** fig rein in; **freni** *pl* **a disco** disc brakes
■ **freno a mano** handbrake; **freno a pedale** footbrake

frequen'tare *vt* frequent; attend ‹*scuola ecc.*›; mix with ‹*persone*›; **non ci frequentiamo più** we don't see each other any more

fre'quente *adj* frequent; **di ~** frequently

fre'quenza *f* frequency; (assiduità) attendance

'fresa *f* mill

fre'sare *vt* mill

fre'schezza *f* freshness; (di temperatura) coolness

'fresco **A** *adj* fresh; ‹*temperatura*› cool; **~ di studi** fresh out of school; **stai ~!** infml you're for it!; **se ti vede stai ~** infml you're done for if he sees you
B *m* coolness; **far ~** be cool; **mettere/tenere in ~** put/keep in a cool place; **al ~** infml (in prigione) inside

fre'scura *f* cool

'fresia *f* freesia

'fretta *f* hurry, haste; **aver ~** be in a hurry; **mettere ~ a qualcuno** hurry somebody; **in ~ e furia** in a great hurry; **andarsene in ~** rush away; **senza [nessuna] ~** at your/his etc leisure

frettolosa'mente *adv* hurriedly

fretto'loso *adj* ‹*persona*› hasty; ‹*lavoro*› rushed, hurried

fri'abile *adj* crumbly

fricas'sea *f stewed meat served with an egg and lemon sauce*

'friggere **A** *vt* fry; **vai a farti ~!** get lost!
B *vi* sizzle; **~ di impazienza** be on tenterhooks

friggi'trice *f* electric chip pan

frigidità *f inv* frigidity

'frigido *adj* frigid

fri'gnare *vi* whine

fri'gnone, -a *mf* whiner

'frigo *m inv* fridge

frigo'bar *m inv* minibar

frigocongela'tore *m* fridge-freezer

frigo'rifero **A** *adj* refrigerating; ‹*camion*› refrigerated
B *m* refrigerator

fringu'ello *m* chaffinch

'frisbee® *m inv* frisbee

frit'tata *f* omelette

frit'tella *f* fritter; infml (macchia d'unto) grease stain

'fritto **A** pp di **friggere**
B *adj* fried; **essere ~** be done for
C *m* fried food
■ **fritto misto** mixed fried fish/vegetables

frit'tura *f* (pietanza) fried dish
■ **frittura di pesce** variety of fried fish

frivo'lezza *f* frivolity

'frivolo *adj* frivolous

frizio'nare *vt* rub

frizi'one *f* friction; Mech clutch; (di pelle) rub

friz'zante *adj* fizzy; ‹*vino*› sparkling; ‹*aria*› bracing

'frizzo *m* gibe

fro'dare *vt* defraud

'frode *f* fraud; **con la ~** Jur under false pretences
■ **frode fiscale** tax evasion

frol'lino *m* (biscotto) ≈ shortbread biscuit

'frollo *adj* tender; ‹*selvaggina*› high; ‹*persona*› spineless; **pasta frolla** short[crust] pastry

'fronda *f* [leafy] branch; fig rebellion

fron'doso *adj* leafy

fron'tale *adj* frontal; ‹*scontro*› head-on

'fronte **A** *f* forehead; (di edificio) front; **di ~** opposite; **di ~ a** opposite, facing; (a paragone) compared with
B *m* Mil, Pol front; **far ~ a** face

fronteggi'are *vt* face

fronte'spizio *m* title page

fronti'era *f* frontier, border

fron'tone *m* pediment

'fronzolo *m* frill

'frotta *f* swarm; (di animali) flock

'frottola *f* fib; **frottole** *pl* nonsense *sg*

fru'gale *adj* frugal

fru'gare **A** *vi* rummage
B *vt* search

fru'ire *vi* **~ di** make use of, take advantage of

frul'lare **A** *vt* Culin whisk
B *vi* ‹*ali*› whirr

frul'lato *m*
■ **frullato di frutta** *fruit drink with milk and crushed ice*

frulla'tore *m* [electric] mixer

frul'lino *m* whisk

fru'mento *m* wheat

frusci'are *vi* rustle

fru'scio *m* rustle; (radio, giradischi) ground noise; (di acque) murmur

'frusta *f* whip; (frullino) whisk

fru'stare *vt* whip

fru'stata *f* lash

fru'stino *m* riding crop

fru'strare *vt* frustrate

fru'strato *adj* frustrated

frustrazi'one *f* frustration

'frutta *f* fruit; **negozio di ~ e verdura** greengrocer's
■ **frutta esotica** exotic fruit, tropical fruit; **frutta fresca di stagione** seasonal fruit; **frutta secca** nuts *pl*

frut'tare **A** *vi* bear fruit; Comm give a return
B *vt* yield

frut'teto *m* orchard

frutticol'tore *m* fruit farmer

frutticol'tura *f* fruit farming, fruit growing

frutti'era *f* fruit bowl

frut'tifero *adj* ‹*albero*› fruit-bearing; Fin ‹*deposito*› interest-bearing
frutti'vendolo, -a *mf* greengrocer
'frutto *m* anche fig fruit; Fin yield; **frutti di bosco** *pl* mixed berries; **frutti di mare** *pl* seafood *sg*
■ **frutto della passione** passion fruit
fruttu'oso *adj* profitable
FS *abbr* (**Ferrovie dello Stato**) Italian State Railways
f.to *abbr* (**firmato**) signed
fu *adj* (defunto) late; **il fu signor Rossi** the late Mr Rossi
f
fuci'lare *vt* shoot, execute by firing squad
fuci'llata *f* shot
fucilazi'one *f* execution [by firing squad]
fu'cile *m* rifle
■ **fucile ad aria compressa** air rifle; **fucile a canne mozze** sawn-off shotgun
fu'cina *f* forge
'fuco *m* kelp
'fucsia *f* fuchsia
'fuga *f* escape; (perdita) leak; (di ciclisti) breakaway; Mus fugue; **darsi alla ~** take to flight; **mettere qualcuno in ~** put somebody to flight
■ **fuga di cervelli** brain drain; **fuga di gradini** flight of steps; **fuga di notizie** leak; **fuga romantica** elopement
fu'gace *adj* fleeting
fug'gevole *adj* short-lived
fuggi'asco, -a *mf* fugitive
fuggi'fuggi *m* stampede
fug'gire *vi* flee; ‹*innamorati*› elope; fig fly
fuggi'tivo, -a *mf* fugitive
'fulcro *m* fulcrum
ful'gore *m* splendour
fu'liggine *f* soot
fuliggi'noso *adj* sooty
full *m inv* (nel poker) full house
fulmi'nante *adj* (sguardo) withering; **è morto di leucemia ~** he died very soon after contracting leukaemia
fulmi'nare *vt* strike by lightning; (con sguardo) look daggers at; (con scarica elettrica) electrocute
fulmi'narsi *vr* burn out
fulmi'nato *adj* **rimanere ~** electrocute oneself
'fulmine *m* lightning; **colpo di ~** fig love at first sight; **un ~ a ciel sereno** a bolt from the blue
ful'mineo *adj* rapid; ‹*sguardo*› withering
'fulvo *adj* tawny
fumai'olo *m* funnel; (di casa) chimney
fu'mante *adj* ‹*minestra, tazza*› steaming
fu'mare *vt & vi* smoke; (in ebollizione) steam; **'vietato ~'** 'no smoking'
fu'mario *adj* (canna) flue
fu'mata *f* (segnale) smoke signal
fuma|'tore, -trice *mf* smoker; **non fumatori** ‹*scompartimento*› non-smoker, non-smoking
fu'metto *m* comic strip; **fumetti** *pl* comics
'fumo *m* smoke; (vapore) steam; fig hot air; **andare in ~** vanish; **vendere ~** put on an act; **cercava di vendere ~** it was all hot air; **fumi** *pl* (industriali) fumes; **sotto i fumi dell'alcol** under the influence of alcohol
■ **fumo passivo** passive smoking
fu'mogeno *adj* **cortina fumogena** smoke screen
fu'moso *adj* ‹*ambiente*› smoky; ‹*discorso*› vague
funambo'lesco *adj* acrobatic
fu'nambolo, -a *mf* tightrope walker
'fune *f* rope; (cavo) cable
'funebre *adj* funeral; (cupo) gloomy
fune'rale *m* funeral
fu'nereo *adj* ‹*aria*› funereal
fu'nesto *adj* sad
'fungere *vi* **~ da** act as
'fungo *m* mushroom; Bot, Med fungus; **funghi** *pl* Bot fungi
■ **fungo atomico** mushroom cloud; **fungo commestibile** edible mushroom
funico'lare *f* funicular [railway]
funi'via *f* cableway
funzio'nale *adj* functional
funzionalità *f inv* functionality
funziona'mento *m* functioning
funzio'nare *vi* work, function; **~ da** (fungere da) act as
funzio'nario *m* official
■ **funzionario statale** civil servant
funzi'one *f* function; (carica) office; Relig service; **entrare in ~** take up office; **mettere in ~** ‹*motore*› start up; **vivere in ~ di** live for
fu'oco *m* fire; (fisica, fotografia) focus; **far ~** fire; **dar ~ a** set fire to; **andare a ~** go up in flames; **prendere ~** catch fire; **a ~ vivo** ‹*cuocere*› on a high heat; **a ~ lento** ‹*cuocere*› on a low heat; **'vietato accendere fuochi'** 'no campfires'; **fuochi** *pl* **d'artificio** fireworks
■ **fuoco amico** friendly fire; **fuoco di paglia** nine-days' wonder; **fuochi** *pl* **pirotecnici** pyrotechnics
fuorché *prep* except
fu'ori **A** *adv* out; (all'esterno) outside; (all'aperto) outdoors; **~!** infml get out!; **~ i soldi!** fork up!; **andare di ~** (traboccare) spill over; **essere ~ di sé** be beside oneself; **essere in ~** (sporgere) stick out; **far ~** infml get rid of; **~ commercio** not for sale; **~ luogo** (inopportuno) out of place; **~ mano** out of the way; **~ moda** old-fashioned; **~ pasto** between meals; **~ pericolo** out of danger; **~ programma** unscheduled;

key word

~ questione out of the question; **~ uso** out of use
B *m* outside
fuori'bordo *m* speedboat (*with outboard motor*); powerboat
fuori'campo *adj inv* Cinema ‹*voce*› off-screen
fuori'classe *mf inv* champion
fuoricombatti'mento *m* knockout
fuorigi'oco *nm & adv* offside
fuori'legge *mf* outlaw
fuori'pista *m inv* (sci) off-piste skiing
fuori'serie **A** *adj* custom-made
B *f* Auto custom-built model
fuori'strada *m inv* off-road vehicle, off-roader
fuoriu'scita *f* (perdita) leak
fuoriu'scito, -a *mf* exile
fuorvi'are **A** *vt* lead astray
B *vi* go astray
furbacchi'one *m* crafty old devil
fur'bastro, -a *mf* crafty devil
furbe'ria *f* cunning
fur'besco *adj* sly, cunning
fur'bizia *f* cunning
'furbo *adj* sly, cunning; (intelligente) clever; (astuto) shrewd; **bravo ~!** nice one!; **fare il ~** try to be clever
fu'rente *adj* furious
fu'retto *m* ferret
fur'fante *m* scoundrel
furgon'cino *m* delivery van
fur'gone *m* van
■ **furgone postale** mail van
'furia *f* fury; (fretta) haste; **a ~ di** by dint of; **andare su tutte le furie** fly into a rage
furi'bondo *adj* furious
furi'ere *m* Mil quartermaster
furiosa'mente *adv* furiously
furi'oso *adj* furious; ‹*litigio*› violent
fu'rore *m* fury; (veemenza) frenzy; **far ~** be all the rage
furoreggi'are *vi* be a great success
furtiva'mente *adv* covertly, stealthily
fur'tivo *adj* furtive, stealthy
🔑 **'furto** *m* theft; **commettere un ~** steal; **è un ~!** fig it's daylight robbery!
■ **furto d'auto** car theft; **furto di minore entità** petty theft; **furto con scasso** burglary
'fusa *fpl* **fare le ~** purr
fu'scello *m* (di legno) twig; (di paglia) straw; **sei un ~** you're as light as a feather
fu'seaux *mpl* leggings
fu'sibile *m* fuse
fu'silli *mpl* pasta twirls
fusi'one *f* fusion; Comm merger
■ **fusione fredda** Phys cold fusion
'fuso **A** pp di **fondere**
B *adj* melted
C *m* spindle; **a ~** spindle-shaped
■ **fuso orario** time zone
fusoli'era *f* fuselage
fu'stagno *m* corduroy
fu'stella *f* (talloncino) *part of packaging on prescribed medicine returned by the pharmacist to claim a refund*
fusti'gare *vt* flog; fig castigate
fu'stino *m* (di detersivo) box
'fusto *m* stem; (tronco) trunk; (recipiente di metallo) drum; (di legno) barrel
■ **fusto del letto** bedstead
'futile *adj* futile
futilità *f inv* futility
futu'rismo *m* futurism
futu'rista *mf* futurist
🔑 **fu'turo** *adj & nm* future; **predire il ~** tell fortunes, foretell
■ **futuro anteriore** Gram future perfect

Gg

gabardine *f* (tessuto) gabardine
gab'bare *vt* cheat
gab'barsi *vr* **~ di** make fun of
'gabbia *f* cage; (da imballaggio) crate
■ **gabbia dell'ascensore** lift cage; **gabbia degli imputati** dock; **gabbia toracica** rib cage
gabbi'ano *m* [sea]gull
■ **gabbiano comune** common gull
gabi'netto *m* (di medico) consulting room; Pol cabinet; (toilette) toilet; (laboratorio) laboratory; **andare al ~** go to the toilet; **gabinetti** *pl* **pubblici** public convenience
'Gabon *m* Gabon
ga'elico *m* Gaelic
'gaffa *f* boathook
'gaffe *f inv* blunder
gagli'ardo *adj* vigorous

gai'ezza *f* gaiety
'gaio *adj* cheerful
'gala *f* gala
ga'lante *adj* gallant
galante'ria *f* gallantry
galantu'omo *m* (*pl* **galantuomini**) gentleman
ga'lassia *f* galaxy
gala'teo *m* [good] manners *pl*; (trattato) book of etiquette
gale'otto *m* (rematore) galley slave; (condannato) convict
ga'lera *f* (nave) galley; infml slammer
'galla *f* Bot gall; **a** ~ afloat; **venire a** ~ surface

g

galleggi'ante **A** *adj* floating **B** *m* craft; (boa) float
galleggi'are *vi* float
galle'ria *f* (traforo) tunnel; (d'arte) gallery; Theat circle; (arcata) arcade; **prima** ~ dress circle
■ **galleria aerodinamica** wind tunnel; **galleria d'arte** art gallery
'Galles *m* Wales
gal'lese **A** *adj* Welsh **B** *m* Welshman; (lingua) Welsh **C** *f* Welshwoman
gal'letta *f* cracker
gal'letto *m* cockerel; **fare il** ~ show off, impress the girls
'gallico *adj* Gallic
gal'lina *f* hen
galli'nella *f*
■ **gallinella d'acqua** moorhen
gal'lismo *m* machismo
'gallo *m* cock
■ **gallo cedrone** capercaillie
gal'lone *m* stripe; (misura) gallon
galop'pante *adj* galloping
galop'pare *vi* gallop
galop'pino *m* **fare da** ~ **a qualcuno** infml be somebody's gopher
ga'loppo *m* gallop; **al** ~ at a gallop
galvaniz'zare *vt* galvanize
⚷ **'gamba** *f* leg; (di lettera) stem; **darsela a gambe** take to one's heels; **essere in** ~ (essere forte) be strong; (capace) be smart
gam'bale *m* (di stivale) bootleg
gamba'letto *m* pop sock
gambe'retti *mpl* shrimps
■ **gamberetti in salsa rosa** prawn cocktail
'gambero *m* prawn; (di fiume) crayfish
gambe'roni *mpl* king prawns
'Gambia *f* the Gambia
gambiz'zare *vt* kneecap
'gambo *m* stem; (di pianta) stalk
ga'mella *f* billy
game 'point *m inv* game point

⚷ key word

ga'mete *m* gamete
'gamma *f* Mus scale; fig range
■ **gamma d'onda** waveband; **gamma di prezzi** price range; **gamma di prodotti** product range
ga'nascia *f* jaw; **ganasce** *pl* **del freno** brake shoes
'gancio *m* hook
'Gange *m* Ganges
'ganghero *m* **uscire dai gangheri** fig get into a temper
'gangster *m inv* gangster
⚷ **'gara** *f* competition; (di velocità) race; **fare a** ~ compete
■ **gara d'appalto** call for tenders; **gara a cronometro** time trial
ga'rage *m inv* garage
gara'gista *mf* garage owner
ga'rante *mf* guarantor
⚷ **garan'tire** *vt* guarantee; (rendersi garante) vouch for; (assicurare) assure
garan'tirsi *vr* ~ **contro**, ~ **da** guard against, insure against
garan'tismo *m* protection of civil liberties
garan'tito *adj* guaranteed
garan'zia *f* guarantee; **in** ~ under guarantee
■ **garanzia collaterale** collateral; **garanzia di rimborso** money-back guarantee; **garanzia a vita** lifetime guarantee
gar'bare *vi* like; **non mi garba** I don't like it
gar'bato *adj* courteous
'garbo *m* courtesy; (grazia) grace; **con** ~ graciously
gar'buglio *m* muddle
gar'denia *f* gardenia
gareggi'are *vi* compete
garga'nella *f* **a** ~ from the bottle
garga'rismo *m* gargle; **fare i gargarismi** gargle
ga'ritta *f* sentry box
ga'rofano *m* carnation; **chiodo di** ~ clove
gar'retto *m* shank
gar'rire *vi* chirp
gar'rotta *f* garrotte
'garrulo *adj* garrulous
'garza *f* gauze
gar'zone *m* boy
■ **garzone di stalla** stable boy
⚷ **gas** *m inv* gas; **dare** ~ Auto accelerate; **a** ~ gas-fired; **a tutto** ~ flat out
■ **gas asfissiante** poisonous gas; **gas esilarante** laughing gas; **gas lacrimogeno** tear gas; **gas nobile** inert gas; **gas propellente** propellant; **gas di scarico** *pl* exhaust fumes; **gas serra** greenhouse gas
gas'dotto *m* natural gas pipeline
ga'solio *m* diesel oil
■ **gasolio invernale** diesel containing anti-freeze

ga'sometro *m* gasometer
gas'sare *vt* aerate; (uccidere col gas) gas
gas'sato *adj* gassy
gas'soso, -a *adj* gaseous
'gastrico *adj* gastric
ga'strite *f* gastritis
gastroente'rite *f* gastroenteritis
gastrono'mia *f* gastronomy
gastro'nomico *adj* gastronomic[al]
ga'stronomo, -a *mf* gourmet
'gatta *f* **una ~ da pelare** a headache
gatta'buia *nf hum* clink
gatta'iola *f* cat flap
gat'tile *m* cattery
gat'tino, -a *mf* kitten
'gatto, -a *mf* cat; **c'erano solo quattro gatti** there were only a few people
■ **gatto delle nevi** snowmobile; **gatto a nove code** cat-o'-nine-tails; **gatto selvatico** wildcat
gat'toni *adv* on all fours
gat'tuccio *m* dogfish
gau'dente *adj* pleasure-loving
'gaudio *m* joy
ga'vetta *f* mess tin; **fare la ~** rise through the ranks
gay *adj inv* gay
Gaza *f* **la striscia di ~** the Gaza strip
ga'zebo *m inv* gazebo
'gazza *f* magpie
gaz'zarra *f* racket; **fare ~** make a racket
gaz'zella *f* gazelle; Auto police car
gaz'zetta *f* gazette
■ **Gazzetta Ufficiale** official journal
gazzet'tino *m* (titolo) title page; (rubrica) page
gaz'zosa *f* clear lemonade
GB *abbr* (**Gran Bretagna**) GB
'geco *m* gecko
ge'lare *vt & vi* freeze; **far ~ il sangue** make somebody's blood run cold
ge'lata *f* frost
gela'taio, -a **A** *mf* ice-cream seller
B *m* (negozio) ice-cream shop
gelate'ria *f* ice-cream parlour
gelati'era *f* ice-cream maker
gela'tina *f* gelatine; (dolce) jelly
■ **gelatina di frutta** fruit jelly
gelati'noso *adj* gelatinous
ge'lato **A** *adj* frozen
B *m* ice-cream
■ **gelato alla vaniglia** vanilla ice-cream
'gelido *adj* freezing
'gelo *m* (freddo intenso) freezing cold; (brina) frost; fig chill
ge'lone *m* chilblain
gelosa'mente *adv* jealously
gelo'sia *f* jealousy
ge'loso *adj* jealous
'gelso *m* mulberry (tree)
gelso'mino *m* jasmine
gemel'laggio *m* twinning
gemel'lare **A** *vt* twin
B *adj* twin
ge'mello, -a *adj & nmf* twin; **gemelli** *pl* (di polsino) cuff-link; **Gemelli** *pl* Astr Gemini *sg*
■ **gemelli** *pl* **monozigoti** identical twins
'gemere *vi* groan
'gemito *m* groan
'gemma *f* gem; Bot bud
gemmolo'gia *f* gemmology
gen'darme *m* gendarme
'gene *m* gene
genealo'gia *f* genealogy
genea'logico *adj* genealogical
gene'rale[1] *adj* general; **in ~** (tutto sommato) in general, on the whole; **parlando in ~** generally speaking
gene'rale[2] *m* Mil general
■ **generale di divisione** major-general
generalità *f inv* (qualità) generality, general nature; (maggior parte) majority; **~** *pl* (dati) particulars *pl*
generaliz'zare *vt* generalize
generalizzazi'one *f* generalization
general'mente *adv* generally
gene'rare *vt* give birth to; (causare) breed; Techn generate
genera'tore *m* Techn generator
generazio'nale *adj* generation *attrib*
generazi'one *f* generation; **di ~ in ~** from generation to generation
'genere *m* kind; Biol genus; Gram gender; (letterario, artistico) genre; (prodotto) product; **cose del ~** such things; **il ~ umano** mankind; **in ~** generally; **generi** *pl* **alimentari** provisions; **generi** *pl* **di prima necessità** essentials
generica'mente *adv* generically
ge'nerico *adj* generic; **medico ~** general practitioner
'genero *m* son-in-law
generosa'mente *adv* generously
generosità *f inv* generosity
gene'roso *adj* generous
'genesi *f* genesis
genetica'mente *adv* genetically; **~ modificato** genetically modified
ge'netico, -a **A** *adj* genetic
B *f* genetics *sg*
gene'tista *mf* geneticist
gen'giva *f* gum
geni'ale *adj* ingenious; (congeniale) congenial
geni'ere *m* Mil sapper
'genio *m* genius; **andare a ~ a qualcuno** be to one's taste
■ **genio civile** civil engineering; **genio incompreso** misunderstood genius; **genio [militare]** Engineers

geni'tale **A** *adj* genital
B *m* **genitali** *pl* genitals
⚷ **geni'tore** *m* parent
gen'naio *m* January
geno'cidio *m* genocide
ge'noma *m* genome
geno'teca *f* gene library
'Genova *f* Genoa
geno'vese *adj* Genoese
gen'taglia *f* rabble
⚷ **'gente** *f* people *pl*
⚷ **gen'tile** *adj* kind; **Gentile Signore** (in lettere) Dear Sir
genti'lezza *f* kindness; **per ~** (per favore) please
gentil'mente *adv* kindly
gentilu'omo (*pl* **gentiluomini**) *m* gentleman
genu'flettersi *vr* kneel down
genuina'mente *adv* genuinely
genu'ino *adj* genuine; ‹*cibo, prodotto*› natural
genzi'ana *f* gentian
geo'fisica *f* geophysics *sg*
geo'fisico, -a *mf* geophysician
geogra'fia *f* geography
geo'grafico *adj* geographical
ge'ografo, -a *mf* geographer
geolo'gia *f* geology
geo'logico *adj* geological
ge'ologo, -a *mf* geologist
ge'ometra *mf* surveyor
geome'tria *f* geometry
geometrica'mente *adv* geometrically
geo'metrico *adj* geometric[al]
geopo'litico *adj* geopolitical
Ge'orgia *f* Georgia
geo'termico *adj* geothermal, geothermic
ge'ranio *m* geranium
gerar'chia *f* hierarchy
gerarchica'mente *adv* hierarchically
ge'rarchico *adj* hierarchic[al]
ger'billo *m* gerbil
ge'rente **A** *m* manager
B *f* manageress
'gergo *m* jargon; (dei giovani) slang
■ **gergo burocratico** bureaucratic jargon
geri'atra[1] *mf* geriatrician
geria'tria[2] *f* geriatrics *sg*
geri'atrico *adj* geriatric
'gerla *f* wicker basket
Ger'mania *f* Germany
■ **Germania [dell']Est** East Germany; **Germania [dell']Ovest** West Germany
ger'manico *adj* Germanic
'germe *m* germ; fig (principio) seed
■ **germe di grano** wheat germ

⚷ key word

germogli'are *vi* sprout
ger'moglio *m* sprout; **in ~** Bot sprouting; **germogli** *pl* **di soia** bean sprouts
gero'glifico *m* hieroglyph; **geroglifici** *pl* hieroglyphics
geron'tologo, -a *mf* gerontologist
ge'rundio *m* gerund
Gerusa'lemme *f* Jerusalem
ges'setto *m* chalk
'gesso *m* chalk; Med (scultura) plaster
ge'staccio *m* ≈ V-sign
gestazi'one *f* gestation
gestico'lare *vi* gesticulate
gestio'nale *adj* management *attrib*
gesti'one *f* management
■ **gestione aziendale** business management; **gestione dei dati** Comput data management; **gestione disco** Comput disk management; **gestione dell'energia** energy resource management; **gestione del flusso di cassa** cash flow management; **gestione patrimoniale** financial management
ge'stire *vi* manage; **~ male** mishandle
ge'stirsi *vr* budget one's time and money
⚷ **'gesto** *m* gesture (*pl f* **gesta**) (azione) deed
ge'store *m* manager
Gesù *m inv* Jesus
■ **Gesù bambino** baby Jesus
gesu'ita *m* Jesuit
gesu'itico *adj* Jesuit *attrib*
⚷ **get'tare** *vt* throw; (scagliare) fling; (emettere) spout; Techn fig cast; **~ via** throw away
get'tarsi *vr* throw oneself; **~ in** ‹*fiume*› flow into
get'tata *f* throw; Techn casting
'gettito *m*
■ **gettito fiscale** tax revenue
'getto *m* throw; (di liquidi, gas) jet; **a ~ continuo** in a continuous stream; **di ~** straight off
getto'nato *adj* ‹*canzone*› popular
get'tone *m* token; (per giochi) counter; **a ~** coin operated
gettoni'era *f* coin box
'geyser *m inv* geyser
'Ghana *m* Ghana
ghe'pardo *m* cheetah
'gheppio *m* kestrel
gher'mire *vt* grasp
'ghette *fpl* (per neonato) leggings
ghettiz'zare *vt* ghettoize
'ghetto *m* ghetto
ghiacci'aia *f* icebox
ghiacci'aio *m* glacier
ghiacci'are *vt & vi* freeze
ghiacci'ato *adj* frozen; (freddissimo) ice-cold
⚷ **ghi'accio** *m* ice; Auto black ice
■ **ghiaccio secco** dry ice
ghiacci'olo *m* icicle; (gelato) ice lolly

ghi'aia *f* gravel
ghiai'oso *adj* gritty
ghi'anda *f* acorn
ghian'daia *f* jay
ghi'andola *f* gland
■ **ghiandola pituitaria** pituitary gland; **ghiandola sudoripara** sweat gland; **ghiandola surrenale** adrenal gland
ghigliot'tina *f* guillotine
ghi'gnare *vi* sneer
'ghigno *m* sneer
ghi'otto *adj* greedy, gluttonous; (appetitoso) appetizing
ghiot'tone, -a *mf* glutton
ghiottone'ria *f* (caratteristica) gluttony; (cibo) tasty morsel
ghiri'goro *m* flourish
ghir'landa *f* (corona) wreath; (di fiori) garland
'ghiro *m* dormouse; **dormire come un ~** sleep like a log
'ghisa *f* cast iron
🔑 **già** *adv* already; (un tempo) formerly; **~!** indeed!; **~ da ieri** since yesterday
🔑 **gi'acca** *f* jacket
■ **giacca a vento** windcheater
giacché *conj* since
giac'cone *m* jacket
gia'cenza *f* **giacenze** *pl* **di magazzino** unsold stock
gia'cere *vi* lie
giaci'mento *m* deposit
■ **giacimento di petrolio** oil deposit
gia'cinto *m* hyacinth
gi'ada *f* jade
giaggi'olo *m* iris
giagu'aro *m* jaguar
gial'lastro *adj* yellowish
🔑 **gi'allo** *adj & nm* yellow; **[libro] giallo** crime novel; **[film] giallo** thriller
■ **giallo dell'uovo** egg yolk
Gia'maica *f* Jamaica
giamai'cano, -a *adj & nmf* Jamaican
gian'duia *m inv soft hazelnut chocolate typical of Piedmont*
Giap'pone *m* Japan
giappo'nese *adj & nmf* Japanese
gi'ara *f* jar
giardi'naggio *m* gardening
giardini'ere, -a **A** *mf* gardener
■ **giardiniera di verdure** *diced, mixed vegetables, cooked and pickled*
🔑 **giar'dino** *m* garden
■ **giardino d'infanzia** kindergarten; **giardino pensile** roof garden; **giardini** *pl* **pubblici** park; **giardino zoologico** zoo
giarretti'era *f* garter
Gi'ava *f* Java
giavel'lotto *m* javelin
Gi'buti *f* Djibouti
gi'gante *m* giant
gigan'tesco *adj* gigantic
gigantogra'fia *f* blow-up
'giglio *m* lily
gilè *m inv* waistcoat
gin *m inv* gin
gin'cana *f* gymkhana
ginecolo'gia *f* gynaecology
gineco'logico *adj* gynaecological
gine'cologo, -a *mf* gynaecologist
gi'nepro *m* juniper
gi'nestra *f* broom
Gi'nevra *f* Geneva
gingil'larsi *vr* fiddle; (perder tempo) potter
gin'gillo *m* plaything; (ninnolo) knick-knack
gin'nasio *m* (scuola) grammar school
gin'nasta *mf* gymnast
gin'nastica *f* gymnastics *sg*; (esercizi) exercises *pl*
■ **ginnastica ritmica** eurhythmics
ginocchi'ata *f* **prendere una ~** bang one's knee
ginocchi'era *f* knee pad
🔑 **gi'nocchio** *m* (*pl m* **ginocchi** *o f* **ginocchia**) knee; **in ~** on one's knees, kneeling; **mettersi in ~** kneel down; (per supplicare) go down on one's knees; **al ~** ‹*gonna*› knee-length
ginocchi'oni *adv* kneeling
🔑 **gio'care** *vt & vi* play; (giocherellare) toy; (d'azzardo) gamble; (puntare) stake; (ingannare) trick; **~ a calcio/a pallavolo** play football/volleyball; **~ d'astuzia** be crafty; **~ d'azzardo** gamble; **~ in Borsa** speculate on the Stock Exchange; **~ in casa** Sport fig play at home
gio'carsi *vr* **~ la carriera** throw one's career away
gioca|'tore, -trice *mf* player; (d'azzardo) gambler
gio'cattolo *m* toy
giocherel'lare *vi* toy; (nervosamente) fiddle
giocherel'lone *adj* skittish
🔑 **gi'oco** *m* game; (di bambini) Techn play; (d'azzardo) gambling; (scherzo) joke; (insieme di pezzi ecc.) set; **essere in ~** be at stake; **fare il doppio ~ con qualcuno** double-cross somebody; **è un ~ da ragazzi** infml it's a cinch
■ **gioco elettronico** computer game; **giochi** *pl* **della gioventù** nation-wide sports tournament for children; **gioco dell'oca** snakes and ladders; **Giochi** *pl* **Olimpici** Olympic Games; **giochi** *pl* **online** on-line gaming; **gioco di parole** play on words; **gioco di pazienza** game of manual skill; **gioco di prestigio** conjuring trick; **gioco di società** board game
giocoli'ere *m* juggler
gio'coso *adj* playful

g

gi'ogo *m* yoke
gi'oia *f* joy; (gioiello) jewel; (appellativo) sweetie
gioielle'ria *f* jeweller's [shop]
gioi'elli *mpl* jewellery
gioielli'ere, -a *mf* jeweller; (negozio) jeweller's
gioi'ello *m* jewel
gioiosa'mente *adv* joyfully
gioi'oso *adj* joyful
gio'ire *vi* **~ per** rejoice at
Gior'dania *f* Jordan
gior'dano, -a *adj & nmf* Jordanian
giorna'laio, -a *mf* newsagent, news dealer
gior'nale *m* [news]paper; (diario) journal
■ **giornale di bordo** logbook; **giornale gratuito** freebie; **giornale del mattino** morning paper; **giornale radio** radio news; **giornale della sera** evening paper
giornali'ero **A** *adj* daily
B *m* (per sciare) day pass
giorna'lino *m* comic
giorna'lismo *m* journalism
giorna'lista *mf* journalist
giornal'mente *adv* daily
gior'nata *f* day; **buona ~!** have a good day!; **in ~** today; **a ~** ‹*essere pagato*› on a day-to-day basis; **vivere alla ~** live from day to day
■ **giornata lavorativa** working day
gi'orno *m* day; **al ~** per day; **al ~ d'oggi** nowadays; **di ~** by day; **in pieno ~** in broad daylight; **un ~ sì, un ~ no** every other day; **~ per ~** day by day
■ **giorno di chiusura** closing day; **giorno delle elezioni** polling day; **giorno fatidico** (importante) D-Day; **giorno feriale** weekday; **giorno festivo** public holiday; **giorno del giudizio** Judgement Day; **giorno dei morti** All Souls' day; **giorno di paga** pay day
gi'ostra *f* merry-go-round
gio'strarsi *vr* manage
giova'mento *m* **trarre ~ da** derive benefit from
gi'ovane **A** *adj* young; (giovanile) youthful
B *m* youth; young man; **giovani** *pl* young people
C *f* girl, young woman
giova'nile *adj* youthful; ‹*scritto*› early
giova'notto *m* young man
gio'vare *vi* **~ a** be useful to; (far bene a) be good for
gio'varsi *vr* **~ di** avail oneself of
Gi'ove *m* Jupiter, Jove
giovedì *m inv* Thursday; **di ~** on Thursdays
■ **giovedì grasso** *last Thursday before Lent*; **giovedì santo** Maundy Thursday
gioventù *f inv* youth; (i giovani) young people *pl*; **~ bruciata** young drop-outs *pl*

giovi'ale *adj* jovial
giovi'nezza *f* youth
gi'rabile *adj* ‹*assegno*› endorsable
gira'dischi *m inv* record player
gi'raffa *f* giraffe; Cinema boom
gira'mondo *mf inv* globetrotter; **da ~** globetrotting
gi'randola *f* (fuoco d'artificio) Catherine wheel; (giocattolo) windmill; (banderuola) weathercock
gi'rare **A** *vt* turn; (andare intorno, visitare) go round; Comm endorse; Cinema shoot
B *vi* turn; ‹*aerei, uccelli*› circle; (andare in giro) wander; **~ sotto...** Comput run under ...; **mi gira la testa** I feel dizzy; **far ~ la testa a qualcuno** make somebody's head spin; **far ~ le scatole a qualcuno** infml drive somebody round the twist; **~ al largo** steer clear
girar'rosto *m* spit
gi'rarsi *vr* turn [round]
gira'sole *m* sunflower
gi'rata *f* turn; Comm endorsement; (in macchina ecc.) ride; **fare una ~** (a piedi) go for a walk; (in macchina) go for a ride
gira'volta *f* spin; fig U-turn
gi'rello *m* (per bambini) baby walker; Culin topside
gi'revole *adj* revolving; **ponte ~** swing bridge
gi'rino *m* tadpole
'giro *m* turn; (circolo) circle; (percorso) round; (viaggio) tour; (passeggiata) short walk; (in macchina) drive; (in bicicletta) ride; (circolazione di denaro) circulation; **andare a fare un ~** (a piedi) go for a stroll; (in macchina) go for a drive; (in bicicletta) go for a cycle ride; **fare il ~ di** go round; **nel ~ di un mese/anno** within a month/year; **prendere in ~ qualcuno** pull somebody's leg; **sentir dire in ~ qualcosa** hear something on the grapevine; **a ~ di posta** by return mail
■ **giro d'affari** Comm turnover; **giro in barca** boat trip; **giro guidato** guided tour; **giro [della] manica** armhole; **giri** *pl* **al minuto** revs per minute, rpm; **giro d'onore** lap of honour; **giri** *pl* **di parole** beating about the bush; **giro di pista** lap; **giro di prova** trial lap; **giro turistico** sightseeing tour; **giro vita** waist measurement; **giro di vite** fig clampdown
giro'collo *m* choker; **a ~** round-neck
gi'rone *m* round
■ **girone di andata** first half of the season; **girone di ritorno** second half of the season
gironzo'lare *vi* wander about
giro'tondo *m* ring-a-ring o' roses
girova'gare *vi* wander about
gi'rovago *m* wanderer
'gita *f* trip; **andare in ~** go on a trip
■ **gita didattica** field trip; **gita organizzata** package tour; **gita in pullman** coach trip; **gita scolastica** school trip
gi'tano, -a *mf* gipsy

key word

gi'tante *mf* tripper

giù *adv* down; (sotto) below; (dabbasso) downstairs; **a testa in ~** (a capofitto) headlong; **essere ~** (di morale) be down, be depressed; (di salute) be run down; **~ di corda** down; **~ di lì, su per ~** more or less; **non andare ~ a qualcuno** stick in somebody's craw

gi'ubba *f* jacket; Mil tunic

giub'botto *m* bomber jacket, jerkin
■ **giubbotto antiproiettile** bulletproof vest; **giubbotto di pelle** leather jacket; **giubbotto di salvataggio** life jacket

gi'ubilo *m* rejoicing

giudi'care *vt* judge; (ritenere) consider

gi'udice *m* judge
■ **giudice conciliatore** Justice of the Peace, JP; **giudice di gara** umpire; **giudice di linea** linesman; **giudice di pace** Justice of the Peace, JP

giudizi'ario *adj* legal, judicial

giu'dizio *m* judgement; (opinione) opinion; (senno) wisdom; (processo) trial; (sentenza) sentence; **mettere ~** become wise
■ **giudizio universale** Last Judgement

giudizi'oso *adj* sensible

gi'ugno *m* June

giugu'lare *f* jugular

giul'lare *m* jester

giu'menta *f* mare

giun'chiglia *f* jonquil

gi'unco *m* reed

gi'ungere **A** *vi* arrive; **~ a** (riuscire) succeed in; **mi giunge nuovo** it's news to me
B *vt* (unire) join

gi'ungla *f* jungle
■ **giungla d'asfalto** concrete jungle

gi'unta *f* addition; **per ~** in addition
■ **giunta comunale** district council; **giunta [militare]** [military] junta

gi'unto **A** pp di **giungere**
B *m* Mech joint
■ **giunto sferico** ball-and-socket joint

giun'tura *f* joint

giuo'care, **giuoco** = **giocare**, **gioco**

giura'mento *m* oath; **sotto ~** under oath; **prestare ~** take the oath
■ **giuramento d'Ippocrate** Hippocratic oath

giu'rare *vt & vi* swear

giu'rato, **-a** **A** *adj* sworn
B *mf* juror

giu'ria *f* jury

giu'ridico *adj* legal

giurisdizi'one *f* jurisdiction

giurispru'denza *f* jurisprudence

giu'rista *mf* jurist

giu'stezza *f* justness

giustifi'care *vt* justify

giustifi'carsi *vr* justify oneself; **~ di** *o* **per qualcosa** give an explanation for something

giustificazi'one *f* justification

giu'stizia *f* justice; **farsi ~ da sé** take the law into one's own hands

giustizi'are *vt* execute

giustizi'ere *m* executioner

gi'usto **A** *adj* just, fair; (adatto) right; (esatto) exact
B *m* (uomo retto) just man; (cosa giusta) right
C *adv* exactly; **~ ora** just now

glaci'ale *adj* glacial

gladia'tore *m* gladiator

gla'diolo *m* gladiolus

'glassa *f* Culin icing

glau'coma *m* glaucoma

gli **A** (def art) *m pl*, the; ▶ **il**
B *pers pron* (a lui) [to] him; (a esso) [to] it; (a loro) [to] them; **non ~ credo** I don't believe him/them

glice'mia *f* glycaemia

glice'rina *f* glycerine

'glicine *m* wisteria

gli'elo *pron* (a lui) to him; (a lei) to her; (a loro) to them; (a Lei, forma di cortesia) to you; **~ prestai** I lent it to him/her etc; **gliel'ho chiesto** I've asked him/her etc

glie'ne *pron* (di ciò) of it; **~ ho dato un po'** I gave him/her/them/you some [of it]; **~ ho parlato** I've talked to him/her etc about it

glis'sare *vi* avoid the issue; **~ su qualcosa** skate over something

glo'bale *adj* global; fig overall

globalizzazi'one *f* globalization

global'mente *adv* globally

'globo *m* globe
■ **globo oculare** eyeball; **globo terrestre** globe

'globulo *m* globule; Med corpuscle
■ **globulo bianco** white cell, white corpuscle; **globulo rosso** red cell, red corpuscle

'gloria *f* glory

glori'arsi *vr* **~ di** be proud of

glorifi'care *vt* glorify

gloriosa'mente *adv* gloriously

glori'oso *adj* glorious

'glossa *f* gloss

glos'sario *m* glossary

glottolo'gia *f* linguistics *sg*

glu'cosio *m* glucose

glutam'mato *m*
■ **glutammato di sodio** monosodium glutamate

'gluteo *m* buttock

'gnocchi *mpl* (di patate) *small flour and potato dumplings*

'gnomo *m* gnome

'gnorri *m* **fare lo ~** play dumb

'goal *m inv* goal; **fare un ~** score *or* get a goal

'gobba *f* hump

'gobbo, **-a** **A** *adj* hunchbacked
B *mf* hunchback

goc'cetto *m* pick-me-up

'goccia *f* drop; (di sudore) bead; **è stata l'ultima ~** it was the last straw
■ **goccia di pioggia** raindrop; **goccia di rugiada** dewdrop

goccio'lare *vi* drip

goccio'lio *m* dripping

go'dere *vi* sl (sessualmente) come; **~ di qualcosa** enjoy something, make the most of something

go'dersi *vr* **~ qualcosa** enjoy something; **godersela** have a good time

godi'mento *m* enjoyment

gof'faggine *f* awkwardness

goffa'mente *adv* awkwardly

'goffo *adj* awkward

go-'kart *m inv* go-kart

'gola *f* throat; (ingordigia) gluttony; Geog gorge; (di camino) flue; **avere mal di ~** have a sore throat; **far ~ a qualcuno** tempt somebody

go'letta *f* schooner

golf *m inv* jersey; Sport golf

gol'fino *m* jumper

'golfo *m* gulf

goli'ardico *adj* student *attrib*

golosità *f inv* greediness; (cibo) tasty morsel

go'loso *adj* greedy

'golpe *m inv* coup

go'mena *f* painter

gomi'tata *f* nudge; **dare una ~ a qualcuno** elbow somebody

'gomito *m* elbow; **alzare il ~** infml (bere) raise one's elbow; **~ a ~** (lavorare) side by side

go'mitolo *m* ball

'gomma *f* rubber; (colla) gum; (pneumatico) tyre; **avere una ~ a terra** have a flat
■ **gomma arabica** gum arabic; **gomma da masticare** chewing gum; **gomma di scorta** spare tyre

gommapi'uma® *f* foam rubber

gom'mino *m* rubber tip

gom'mista *m* tyre specialist

gom'mone *m* [rubber] dinghy

gom'moso *adj* chewy

'gondola *f* gondola

gondoli'ere *m* gondolier

gonfa'lone *m* banner

gonfi'abile *adj* inflatable

gonfi'are **A** *vi* swell
B *vt* blow up; pump up ‹*pneumatico*›; (esagerare) exaggerate

gonfi'arsi *vr* swell; ‹*acque*› rise

'gonfio *adj* swollen; ‹*pneumatico*› inflated

gonfi'ore *m* swelling

gongo'lante *adj* overjoyed

gongo'lare *vi* be overjoyed

goni'ometro *m* protractor

'gonna *f* skirt
■ **gonna pantalone** culottes *pl*; **gonna a pieghe** pleated skirt; **gonna a portafoglio** wrap-around skirt

gonor'rea *f* gonorrhoea

'gonzo *m* simpleton

gorgheggi'are *vi* warble

gor'gheggio *m* warble

'gorgo *m* whirlpool

gorgogli'ante *adj* burbling, gurgling

gorgogli'are *vi* gurgle

gor'goglio *m* burble

gorgon'zola *f* *strong, soft blue cheese*

go'rilla *m inv* gorilla; (guardia del corpo) bodyguard, minder

'gota *f* cheek

'gotico *adj & nm* Gothic

'gotta *f* gout

gover'nante *f* housekeeper

gover'nare *vt* govern; (dominare) rule; (dirigere) manage; (curare) look after

governa'tivo *adj* government

governa'tore *m* governor

go'verno *m* government; (dominio) rule; **al ~** in power
■ **governo ombra** shadow cabinet

'gozzo *m* (di animale) crop; Med goitre; infml throat

gozzovigli'are *vi* eat, drink and be merry

gr, GR *nm abbr* (**giornale radio**) radio news

gracchi'are *vi* caw; fig ‹*persona*› screech

'gracchio *m* caw

graci'dare *vi* croak

'gracile *adj* delicate

gra'dasso *m* braggart

gradata'mente *adv* gradually

gradazi'one *f* gradation
■ **gradazione alcolica** alcohol content; **a bassa gradazione alcolica** ‹*birra*› low alcohol

gra'devole *adj* agreeable

gradevol'mente *adv* pleasantly, agreeably

gradi'ente *m* gradient

gradi'mento *m* liking; **indice di ~** Radio, TV popularity rating; **non è di mio ~** it's not to my liking

gradi'nata *f* flight of steps; (di stadio, teatro) tiers *pl*

gra'dino *m* step

gra'dire *vt* like; (desiderare) wish

gra'dito *adj* pleasant; (bene accetto) welcome

'grado *m* degree; (rango) rank; **di buon ~** willingly; **essere in ~ di fare qualcosa** be in a position to do something; (essere capace a) be able to do something; **per gradi** ‹*procedere*› by degrees

gradu'ale *adj* gradual

gradual'mente *adv* gradually

gradu'are *vt* graduate

key word

gradu'ato **A** *adj* graded; (provvisto di scala graduata) graduated
B *m* Mil *non-commissioned officer*
gradua'toria *f* list
graduazi'one *f* graduation
'graffa *f* clip; (segno grafico) brace
graf'fetta *f* staple
graffi'are *vt* scratch
graffia'tura *f* scratch
'graffio *m* scratch
gra'fia *f* [hand]writing; (ortografia) spelling
'grafica *f* graphics *sg*; (disciplina) graphics *sg*, graphic design
■ **grafica pubblicitaria** commercial art
grafica'mente *adv* in graphics, graphically
'grafico **A** *adj* graphic
B *m* graph; (persona) graphic designer
■ **grafico a torta** pie chart
gra'fite *f* graphite
gra'fologo, -a *mf* graphologist
gra'migna *f* weed
gram'matica *f* grammar
grammati'cale *adj* grammatical
grammatical'mente *adv* grammatically
gram'matico *m* grammarian
'grammo *m* gram[me]
gram'mofono *m* gramophone
gran ▶ **grande**
gran'turco *m* corn
'grana *f* grain; (formaggio) Parmesan; infml (seccatura) trouble; infml (soldi) readies *pl*
gra'naio *m* barn
gra'nata *f* Mil grenade; (frutto) pomegranate
granati'ere *m* Mil grenadier
gra'nato *m* garnet
Gran Bre'tagna *f* Great Britain
gran'cassa *f* bass drum
gran'cevola *f* spiny spider crab
'granchio *m* crab; fig (errore) blunder; **prendere un ~** make a blunder
grandango'lare *m* wide-angle lens
gran'dangolo *m* wide-angle lens
'grande **A** (*a volte* **gran**) *adj* (ampio) large; (grosso) big; (alto) tall; (largo) wide; fig (senso morale) great; (grandioso) grand; (adulto) grown-up; **~ e grosso** beefy; **ho una gran fame** I'm very hungry; **fa un gran caldo** it's very hot; **in ~** on a large scale; **in gran parte** to a great extent; **non è un gran che** it is nothing much; **di gran carriera** hotfoot; **un gran ballo** a grand ball; **alla ~** sl in a big way
B *mf* (persona adulta) grown-up; (persona eminente) great man/woman
grandeggi'are *vi* **~ su** tower over; (darsi arie) show off
gran'dezza *f* greatness; (ampiezza) largeness; (larghezza) width, breadth; (dimensione) size; (fasto) grandeur; (prodigalità) lavishness; **a ~ naturale** life-size
grandi'nare *vi* hail; **grandina** it's hailing
'grandine *f* hail
grandiosità *f inv* grandeur
grandi'oso *adj* grand
gran'duca *m* grand duke
grandu'cato *m* grand duchy
grandu'chessa *f* grand duchess
gra'nello *m* grain; (di frutta) pip
gra'nita *f crushed ice drink*
gra'nito *m* granite
'grano *m* grain; (frumento) wheat
■ **grano di pepe** peppercorn; **grano saraceno** buckwheat
grano'turco *m* corn
'granulo *m* granule
'grappa *f very strong, clear spirit distilled from grapes*; (morsa) cramp
'grappolo *m* bunch
■ **grappolo d'uva** bunch of grapes
gras'setto *m* bold [type]
gras'sezza *f* fatness; (untuosità) greasiness
'grasso **A** *adj* fat; ‹*cibo*› fatty; (unto) greasy; ‹*terreno*› rich; (grossolano) coarse
B *m* fat; (sostanza) grease; **a basso contenuto di grassi** low-fat; **senza grassi** non-fat, fat-free
gras'soccio *adj* plump
gras'sone, -a *mf* dumpling
'grata *f* grating
gra'tella *f* Culin grill
gra'ticcio *m* (per piante) trellis; (stuoia) rush matting
gra'ticola *f* Culin grill
gra'tifica *f* bonus
gratificazi'one *f* satisfaction
gra'tin *m inv* gratin
■ **gratin di patate** *potatoes with grated cheese*
grati'nare *vt* cook au gratin
grati'nato *adj* au gratin
'gratis *adv* free
grati'tudine *f* gratitude
'grato *adj* grateful; (gradito) pleasant
gratta'capo *m* trouble
grattaci'elo *m* skyscraper
'gratta e 'vinci *m inv* scratch card
grat'tare **A** *vt* scratch; (raschiare) scrape; (grattugiare) grate; infml (rubare) pinch
B *vi* grate
grat'tarsi *vr* scratch oneself
grat'tugia *f* grater
grattugi'are *vt* grate
gratuita'mente *adv* free [of charge]
gra'tuito *adj* free [of charge]; (ingiustificato) gratuitous
gra'vare **A** *vt* burden
B *vi* **~ su** weigh on
'grave *adj* (pesante) heavy; (serio) serious; (difficile) hard; ‹*voce, suono*› low; (fonetica) grave; **essere ~** (gravemente ammalato) be seriously ill
grave'mente *adv* seriously, gravely

g

gravi'danza *f* pregnancy
■ **gravidanza extrauterina** ectopic pregnancy; **gravidanza indesiderata** unwanted pregnancy

'gravido *adj* pregnant

gravità *f inv* seriousness; Phys gravity

gravi'tare *vi* gravitate

gra'voso *adj* onerous

🗝 **'grazia** *f* grace; (favore) favour; Jur pardon; **entrare nelle grazie di qualcuno** get into somebody's good books; **ministero di ~ e giustizia** Ministry of Justice

grazi'are *vt* pardon

'grazie *int* thank you!, thanks!; **~ mille!** many thanks!, thanks a lot!; **~ a Dio/al cielo!** thank God/goodness!; **~ a** thanks to

g

grazi'oso *adj* charming; (carino) pretty

'Grecia *f* Greece

🗝 **'greco, -a** *adj & nmf* Greek
■ **greco antico** (lingua) classical Greek

gre'gario **A** *adj* gregarious
B *m* (ciclismo) supporting rider

'gregge *m* flock

'greggio **A** *adj* raw
B *m* (petrolio) crude [oil]

grembi'ale, grembi'ule *m* apron

'grembo *m* lap; (utero) womb; fig bosom

gre'mire *vt* pack

gre'mirsi *vr* become crowded (**di** with)

gre'mito *adj* packed

'gretto *adj* stingy; (di vedute ristrette) narrow-minded

'greve *adj* heavy

'grezzo *adj* = **greggio**

🗝 **gri'dare** **A** *vi* shout; (di dolore) scream; ‹*animale*› cry
B *vt* shout; **~ qualcosa ai quattro venti** shout something from the rooftops

🗝 **'grido** *m* (*pl m* **gridi** *o pl f* **grida**) shout, cry; (di animale) cry; **all'ultimo ~** the latest fashion; **scrittore di ~** celebrated writer
■ **grido d'aiuto** cry for help; **grido di battaglia** battle cry

🗝 **'grigio** *adj & nm* grey
■ **grigio perla** pearl grey

'griglia *f* grill; **alla ~** grilled; **cuocere alla ~** grill

grigli'ata *f* barbecue
■ **grigliata mista** mixed grill; **grigliata di pesce** grilled fish

gril'letto *m* trigger

'grillo *m* cricket; fig (capriccio) whim

grimal'dello *m* picklock

'grinfia *f* fig clutch

'grinta *f* grit

grin'toso *adj* determined

'grinza *f* wrinkle; (di stoffa) crease; **non fare una ~** fig ‹*ragionamento*› be flawless

grip'pare *vi* Mech seize up

🗝 key word

gri'sou *m* firedamp

gris'sino *m* bread stick

'grizzly *m inv* grizzly

groenlan'dese **A** *adj* of Greenland
B *mf* Greenlander

Groen'landia *f* Greenland

'groggy *adj inv* punch-drunk

'gronda *f* eaves *pl*

gron'daia *f* gutter

gron'dare *vi* pour; (essere bagnato fradicio) be dripping wet

'groppa *f* back

'groppo *m* knot; **avere un ~ alla gola** have a lump in one's throat

gros'sezza *f* size; (spessore) thickness

gros'sista *mf* wholesaler

🗝 **'grosso** **A** *adj* big, large; (spesso) thick; (grossolano) coarse; (grave) serious
B *m* big part; (massa) bulk; **farla grossa** do a stupid thing

grossolanità *f inv* (qualità) coarseness; (di errore) grossness; (gesto) boorishness

grosso'lano *adj* coarse; ‹*errore*› gross; ‹*comportamento*› boorish

grosso'modo *adv* roughly

'grotta *f* cave, grotto

grot'tesco *adj & nm* grotesque

grovi'era *mf* Gruyère

gro'viglio *m* tangle; fig muddle

gru *f inv* (uccello, edilizia) crane

'gruccia *f* (stampella) crutch; (per vestito) hanger
■ **gruccia appendiabiti** clothes hanger

grufo'lare *vi* root

gru'gnire *vi* grunt

gru'gnito *m* grunt

'grugno *m* snout

'grullo *adj* silly

'grumo *m* clot; (di farina ecc.) lump

gru'moso *adj* lumpy

grunge *m inv* grunge

🗝 **'gruppo** *m* group; (comitiva) party
■ **gruppo d'azione** action group; **gruppo pop** pop group; **gruppo sanguigno** blood group; **gruppo di sostegno** support group; **gruppo di utenti** user group

gruvi'era *mf* = **groviera**

'gruzzolo *m* nest egg

🗝 **guada'gnare** *vt* earn; gain ‹*tempo, forza ecc.*›

guada'gnarsi *vr* **~ da vivere** earn a living

gua'dagno *m* gain; (profitto) profit; (entrate) earnings *pl*; **guadagni** *pl* **illeciti** ill-gotten gains

gu'ado *m* ford; **passare a ~** ford

gu'aina *f* sheath; (busto) girdle

🗝 **gu'aio** *m* trouble; **che ~!** that's just brilliant!; **essere nei guai** be in a fix; **guai a te se lo tocchi!** don't you dare touch it!

gua'ire *vi* yelp

gua'ito *m* yelp; **guaiti** *pl* yelping
gu'ancia *f* cheek
guanci'ale *m* pillow
gu'anto *m* glove
■ **guanto da forno** oven glove; **guanto di spugna** face cloth
guan'tone *m* mitt; **guantoni** *pl* **[da boxe]** boxing gloves
guarda'boschi *m inv* forester
guarda'caccia *m inv* gamekeeper
guarda'coste *m inv* coastguard
guarda'linee *m inv* Sport linesman
guarda'macchine *mf* car park attendant
guarda'parco *m inv* park ranger
guar'dare **A** *vt* look at; (osservare) watch; (badare a) look after; ‹*finestra*› look out on; ~ **la televisione** watch television
B *vi* look; (essere orientato verso) face; ~ **in su** look up
guarda'roba *m inv* wardrobe; (di locale pubblico) cloakroom
guardarobi'ere, **-a** *mf* cloakroom attendant
guar'darsi *vr* look at oneself; ~ **da** beware of; (astenersi) refrain from
gu'ardia *f* guard; (poliziotto) policeman; (vigilanza) watch; **essere di** ~ be on guard; ‹*medico*› be on duty; **fare la** ~ **a** keep guard over; **mettere in** ~ **qualcuno** warn somebody; **stare in** ~ be on one's guard
■ **guardia carceraria** prison warder, prison officer; **guardia del corpo** bodyguard, minder; **Guardia di finanza** *body of police officers responsible for border control and for investigating fraud*; **guardia forestale** forest ranger; **guardia medica** duty doctor
guardi'ano, **-a** *mf* caretaker
■ **guardiano notturno** night watchman; **guardiano dello zoo** zoo keeper
guar'dingo *adj* cautious
guardi'ola *f* gatekeeper's lodge
guarigi'one *f* recovery
gua'rire **A** *vt* cure
B *vi* recover; ‹*ferita*› heal [up]
gua'rito *adj* cured
guari|'tore, **-trice** *mf* healer
guarnigi'one *f* garrison
guar'nire *vt* trim; Culin garnish
guarnizi'one *f* trimming; Culin garnish; Mech gasket
■ **guarnizione del freno** brake lining
guasta'feste *mf inv* spoilsport
gua'stare *vt* spoil; (rovinare) ruin; break ‹*meccanismo*›
gua'starsi *vr* spoil; (andare a male) go bad; ‹*tempo*› change for the worse; ‹*meccanismo*› break down
gu'asto **A** *adj* broken; ‹*ascensore, telefono*› out of order; ‹*auto*› broken down; ‹*cibo, dente*› bad
B *m* breakdown; (danno) damage; **ho un** ~ **alla macchina** my car's not working
■ **guasto al motore** engine failure
Guate'mala *m* Guatemala
guazza'buglio *m* muddle
guaz'zare *vi* wallow
gu'ercio *adj* cross-eyed
gu'erra *f* war; (tecnica bellica) warfare; **la grande** ~ the Great War, World War I
■ **guerra batteriologica** germ warfare; **guerra biologica** biological warfare; **guerra civile** civil war; **guerra fredda** Cold War; **guerra del Golfo** Gulf War; **guerra lampo** blitzkrieg; **guerra mondiale** world war; **prima guerra mondiale** World War I, WW1; **seconda guerra mondiale** World War II, WW2; **guerra dei prezzi** price war; **guerra di secessione** American Civil War
guerrafon'daio, **-a** *mf* warmonger
guerreggi'are *vi* wage war
guer'resco *adj* (di guerra) war; (bellicoso) warlike
guerri'ero *m* warrior
guer'riglia *f* guerrilla warfare
guerrigli'ero, **-a** *mf* guerrilla
'gufo *m* owl
'guglia *f* spire
gu'ida *f* guide; (direzione) guidance; (comando) leadership; (elenco) directory; Auto driving; (tappeto) runner; **chi era alla** ~**?** who was driving?; **essere alla** ~ **di** fig be the head of; **fare da** ~ be a guide (**a** to)
■ **guida commerciale** trade directory; **guida a destra** right-hand drive; **guida a sinistra** left-hand drive; **guida telefonica** phone book, telephone directory; **guida turistica** tourist guide
gui'dare *vt* guide; Auto drive; steer ‹*nave*›; ~ **a passo d'uomo** drive at walking speed
guida|'tore, **-trice** *mf* driver
■ **guidatore della domenica** Sunday driver
Gui'nea *f* Guinea
Gui'nea-Bis'sau *f* Guinea-Bissau
Gui'nea Equato'riale *f* Equatorial Guinea
guin'zaglio *m* leash
gu'isa *f* **a** ~ **di** like
guiz'zare *vi* dart; ‹*luce*› flash
gu'izzo *m* dart; (di luce) flash
'gulag *m inv* Gulag
'gulasch *m inv* goulash
'guru *m inv* high priest
'guscio *m* shell; (di cellulare) fascia
gu'stare **A** *vt* taste
B *vi* like
'gusto *m* taste; (piacere) liking; **mangiare di** ~ eat heartily; **prenderci** ~ come to enjoy it, develop a taste for it; **al** ~ **di pistacchio** pistachio flavoured; **buon** ~ good taste
gu'stoso *adj* tasty; fig delightful
guttu'rale *adj* guttural
Gu'yana *f* Guyana

g

Hh

'habitat *m inv* habitat
habitué *mf inv* regular [customer]
'hacker *mf inv* Comput hacker
Ha'iti *f* Haiti
haiti'ano, -a *adj & nmf* Haitian
'halal *adj* halal
hall *f inv* foyer; (di stazione) concourse
ham'burger *m inv* hamburger
■ **hamburger vegetariano** veggie burger
'handicap *m inv* handicap
handicap'pare *vt* handicap
handicap'pato, -a **A** *adj* disabled **B** *mf* disabled person
■ **handicappato mentale** person with learning difficulties
'hangar *m inv* hangar
'hard[-core] *adj* hard core
hard 'disk *m inv* hard disk
hard 'rock *m* hard rock
'hardware *m inv* Comput hardware
'harem *m inv* harem
'hashish *m* hashish
hawa'iano, -a *adj & nmf* Hawaiian
'Hawaii *fpl* **le ~** Hawaii
'heavy metal *m* Mus heavy metal
henné *m* henna
'herpes *m inv* herpes; (su labbra) cold sore
■ **herpes zoster** shingles
'hi-fi *m inv* hi-fi
high 'tech *f* high tech
'Himalaia *m* Himalayas *pl*
'hinterland *m inv* hinterland
'hippy *adj & mf inv* hippy
'hit parade *f* hit parade, charts *pl*
HIV *m* HIV
'hockey *m* hockey
■ **hockey su ghiaccio** ice hockey; **hockey su prato** field hockey
'holding *f inv* holding company
hollywoo'diano *adj* Hollywood
Hong 'Kong *f* Hong Kong
'hostess *f inv* (air) stewardess
hot 'dog *m inv* hot dog
'hotel *m inv* hotel
'humus *m* humus

Ii

i *def art mpl* the; ▶ **il**
i'ato *m* hiatus
i'berico *adj* Iberian
iber'nare *vi* hibernate
ibernazi'one *f* hibernation
i'bisco *m* hibiscus
ibri'dare *vt* interbreed
ibridazi'one *f* interbreeding
'ibrido *adj & nm* hybrid
'iceberg *m inv* iceberg; **la punta dell'~** fig the tip of the iceberg
i'cona *f* icon
iconiz'zare *vt* iconize
icono'clasta *adj & nmf* iconoclast
icono'clastico *adj* iconoclastic
id'dio *m* God
⚷ **i'dea** *f* idea; (opinione) opinion; (ideale) ideal; (indizio) inkling; (piccola quantità) hint; (intenzione) intention; **cambiare ~** change one's mind; **neanche per ~!** not on your life!; **chiarirsi le idee** get one's ideas straight; **dare l'~ di ...** give the impression that ...; **essere dell'~ che ...** be of the opinion that ...; **non ne ho ~!** I've no idea!
■ **idea fissa** obsession
⚷ **ide'ale** *adj & nm* ideal
idea'lista *mf* idealist
idealiz'zare *vt* idealize
ide'are *vt* conceive
idea|'tore, -trice *mf* originator
'idem *adv* the same
identica'mente *adv* identically

⚷ key word

i'dentico *adj* identical
identifi'cabile *adj* identifiable
identifi'care *vt* identify
identifica'tivo *m*
■ **identificativo del chiamante** caller identification
identificazi'one *f* identification
identi'kit® *m inv* identikit
■ **identikit elettronico** e-fit
identità *f inv* identity
ideo'gramma *m* ideogram
ideolo'gia *f* ideology
ideologica'mente *adv* ideologically
ideo'logico *adj* ideological
idillica'mente *adv* idyllically
i'dillico *adj* idyllic
i'dillio *m* idyll
idi'oma *m* language
idio'matico *adj* idiomatic; **espressione idiomatica** idiom, idiomatic expression
idiosincra'sia *f* fig aversion; Med allergy
idi'ota **A** *adj* idiotic
B *mf* idiot
idio'zia *f* idiocy; **dire/fare un'~** do/say something stupid; **dire idiozie** talk nonsense; **non fare idiozie!** don't act daft!
idola'trare *vt* worship
idoleggi'are *vt* idolize
'idolo *m* idol
idoneità *f inv* suitability; Mil fitness; **esame di ~** qualifying examination
i'doneo *adj* **~ a** suitable for; Mil fit for
i'drante *m* hydrant; (tubo) hose; (usato dalla polizia) water cannon
idra'tante *adj* ‹*crema*› moisturizing
idra'tare *vt* hydrate; ‹*cosmetico*› moisturize
idratazi'one *f* moisturizing
i'draulico **A** *adj* hydraulic
B *m* plumber
'idrico *adj* water *attrib*
idrocar'buro *m* hydrocarbon
idroelettricità *f inv* hydroelectricity
idroe'lettrico *adj* hydroelectric
i'drofilo *adj* **cotone ~** cotton wool, absorbent cotton AmE
idrofo'bia *f* rabies *sg*
i'drofobo *adj* rabid; fig furious
i'drofugo *adj* water-repellent
i'drogeno *m* hydrogen
idrogra'fia *f* hydrography
i'drolisi *f* hydrolysis
idromas'saggio *m* (sistema) whirlpool bath; **vasca con ~** jacuzzi®
idro'mele *m* mead
idrorepel'lente *adj & nm* water-repellent
idroso'lubile *adj* water-soluble
idrotera'pia *f* hydrotherapy
idrovo'lante *m* seaplane
i'druro *m* hydride
i'ella *f* infml bad luck; **portare ~** be bad luck
iel'lato *adj* infml jinxed, plagued by bad luck
i'ena *f* hyena
i'eri *adv* yesterday; **~ l'altro, l'altro ~** the day before yesterday; **il giornale di ~** yesterday's paper; **~ mattina** yesterday morning
ietta|'tore, -trice *mf* jinx
ietta'tura *f* (sfortuna) bad luck
igi'ene *f* hygiene; **ufficio d'~** ≈ Public Health Service
■ **igiene mentale** mental health; **igiene personale** personal hygiene; **igiene pubblica** public health
igienica'mente *adv* hygienically
igi'enico *adj* hygienic
igie'nista *mf* hygienist
ig'loo *m inv* igloo
i'gname *m* yam
i'gnaro *adj* unaware
i'gnifugo *adj* flame-retardant, fire-retardant
i'gnobile *adj* despicable
ignobil'mente *adv* despicably
igno'minia *f* disgrace
igno'rante **A** *adj* ignorant
B *mf* ignoramus
igno'ranza *f* ignorance; **~ crassa** crass ignorance
igno'rare *vt* (non sapere) be unaware of; (trascurare) ignore; **essere ignorato** go unheeded
i'gnoto *adj* unknown
igu'ana *f* iguana
il *def art m* the; **il latte fa bene** milk is good for you; **il signor Magnetti** Mr Magnetti; **il dottor Piazza** Doctor Piazza; **ha il naso grosso** he's got a big nose; **ha gli occhi azzurri** he's got blue eyes; **mettiti il cappello** put your hat on; **il lunedì** on Mondays; **il 2010** 2010; **costa 5 euro il chilo** it costs 5 euros a kilo
'ilare *adj* merry
ilarità *f inv* hilarity
i'leo *m* hip bone
illangui'dire *vi* grow weak
illazi'one *f* inference
illecita'mente *adv* illicitly
il'lecito *adj* illicit
ille'gale *adj* illegal
illegalità *f inv* illegality
illegal'mente *adv* illegally
illeg'gibile *adj* illegible; ‹*libro*› unreadable
illegittimità *f inv* illegitimacy
ille'gittimo *adj* illegitimate
il'leso *adj* unhurt, uninjured
illette'rato, -a *adj & nmf* illiterate
illi'bato *adj* chaste
illimitata'mente *adv* indefinitely
illimi'tato *adj* unlimited

i

illivi'dire **A** *vt* bruise
B *vi* (per rabbia) turn livid
illogica'mente *adv* illogically
il'logico *adj* illogical
🔑 **il'ludere** *vt* deceive
il'ludersi *vr* deceive oneself
🔑 **illumi'nare** *vt* light up; fig enlighten; **~ a giorno** floodlight
illumi'narsi *vr* light up
illuminazi'one *f* lighting; fig enlightenment
■ **illuminazione a gas** gas lighting; **illuminazione al neon** strip lighting
Illumi'nismo *m* Enlightenment
🔑 **illusi'one** *f* illusion; **farsi illusioni** delude oneself
■ **illusione ottica** optical illusion
illusio'nismo *m* conjuring
illusio'nista *mf* conjurer
il'luso, -a **A** pp di **illudere**
B *adj* deluded
C *mf* day-dreamer
illu'sorio *adj* illusory
illu'strare *vt* illustrate
illustra'tivo *adj* illustrative
illustra|'tore, -trice *mf* illustrator
illustrazi'one *f* illustration
■ **illustrazione a colori/in bianco e nero** colour/black and white illustration
il'lustre *adj* distinguished
imbacuc'care *vt* wrap up
imbacuc'carsi *vr* wrap up
imbacuc'cato *adj* wrapped up
imbal'laggio *m* packing
imbal'lare *vt* pack; Auto race
imballa|'tore, -trice *mf* packer
imbalsa'mare *vt* embalm; stuff ‹*animale*›
imbalsa'mato *adj* embalmed; ‹*animale*› stuffed
imbambo'lato *adj* vacant
imban'dito *adj* ‹*tavola*› covered with food
imbaraz'zante *adj* embarrassing
imbaraz'zare *vt* embarrass; (ostacolare) encumber
imbaraz'zato *adj* embarrassed
imba'razzo *m* embarrassment; (ostacolo) hindrance; **trarre qualcuno d' ~** help somebody out of a difficulty; **avere l' ~ della scelta** be spoilt for choice
■ **imbarazzo di stomaco** indigestion
imbarba'rire *vt* barbarize
imbarba'rirsi *vr* become barbarized
imbarca'dero *m* landing stage
imbar'care *vt* embark; infml (rimorchiare) score; **~ acqua** ship water
imbar'carsi *vr* go on board; fig embark (**in** on)
imbarcazi'one *f* boat
■ **imbarcazione da pesca** fishing boat; **imbarcazione di salvataggio** lifeboat
im'barco *m* boarding; (banchina) landing stage; **'~ immediato'** 'now boarding'
imbastar'dire *vt* debase
imbastar'dirsi *vr* become debased
imba'stire *vt* tack, baste; fig sketch
imbasti'tura *f* tacking, basting
im'battersi *vr* **~ in** run into
imbat'tibile *adj* unbeatable
imbat'tuto *adj* unbeaten
imbavagli'are *vt* gag
imbec'cata *f* Theat prompt
imbe'cille **A** *adj* stupid
B *mf* Med imbecile
imbellet'tarsi *vr* hum doll oneself up
imbel'lire *vt* embellish
im'berbe *adj* beardless; fig inexperienced
imbestia'lire *vi* fly into a rage; **far ~ qualcuno** drive somebody crazy
imbestia'lirsi *vr* fly into a rage
imbestia'lito *adj* enraged
im'bevere *vt* imbue (**di** with)
im'beversi *vr* absorb
imbe'vibile *adj* undrinkable
imbe'vuto *adj* **~ di** ‹*acqua*› soaked in; ‹*nozioni*› imbued with
imbian'care **A** *vt* whiten
B *vi* turn white
imbian'chino *m* [house] painter
imbion'dire **A** *vt* bleach
B *vi* become bleached
imbion'dirsi *vr* become bleached
imbizzar'rire *vr* become restless; (arrabbiarsi) become angry
imbizzar'rirsi *vi* become restless; (arrabbiarsi) become angry
imboc'care *vt* feed; (entrare) enter; fig prompt
imbocca'tura *f* opening; (ingresso) entrance; Mus (di strumento) mouthpiece
im'bocco *m* entrance
imboni'mento *m* spiel
imboni'tore *m* clever talker
imborghe'sire *vi* become middle class
imborghe'sirsi *vr* become middle class
imbo'scare *vt* hide
imbo'scarsi *vr* Mil shirk military service
imbo'scata *f* ambush
imbo'scato *m* draft dodger
imbottiglia'mento *m* traffic jam
imbottigli'are *vt* bottle
imbottigli'arsi *vr* get snarled up in a traffic jam
imbottigli'ato *adj* (vino, acqua) bottled; ‹*auto*› stuck in a traffic jam, snarled up; **nave imbottigliata** ship in a bottle
imbot'tire *vt* stuff; pad ‹*giacca*›; Culin fill
imbot'tirsi *vr* **~ di** fig (di pasticche) stuff oneself with

🔑 key word

imbot'tita *f* quilt
imbot'tito *adj* ‹*spalle*› padded; ‹*cuscino*› stuffed; ‹*panino*› filled
imbotti'tura *f* stuffing; (di giacca) padding; Culin filling
imbraca'tura *f* harness
imbracci'are *vt* shoulder ‹*fucile*›; grasp ‹*scudo*›
imbra'nato *adj* clumsy
imbrat'tare *vt* mark
imbrat'tarsi *vr* dirty oneself
imbrigli'are *vt* bridle ‹*cavallo*›; dam ‹*acque*›
imbroc'care *vt* hit; **imbroccarla giusta** hit the nail on the head
imbrogli'are *vt* muddle; (raggirare) cheat; **~ le carte** fig confuse the issue
imbrogli'arsi *vr* get tangled; (confondersi) get confused
im'broglio *m* tangle; (pasticcio) mess; (inganno) trick
imbrogli'one, -a *mf* cheat
imbronci'are *vi* sulk
imbronci'arsi *vr* sulk
imbronci'ato *adj* sulky
imbru'nire *vi* get dark; **all'~** at dusk
imbrut'tire **A** *vt* make ugly **B** *vi* become ugly
imbu'care *vt* post, mail; (nel biliardo) pot
imbu'cato *adj* infml **è ~** he only got the job because of who he knows
imbufa'lirsi *vr* hit the roof
imbur'rare *vt* butter
im'buto *m* funnel
i'mene *m* hymen
imi'tare *vt* imitate
imita|'tore, -trice *mf* imitator, impersonator
imitazi'one *f* imitation; **'diffidare delle imitazioni'** 'beware of imitations'
immaco'lato *adj* spotless, immaculate; **l'immacolata Concezione** the Immaculate Conception
immagazzi'nare *vt* store
immagi'nare *vt* imagine; (supporre) suppose; (formula di cortesia) **s'immagini!** don't mention it!
immagi'nario *adj* imaginary
immaginazi'one *f* imagination; **è frutto della tua ~** it's a figment of your imagination
im'magine *f* image; (rappresentazione, idea) picture
■ **immagine aziendale** corporate image; **immagine della marca** brand image; **immagine speculare** mirror image
immagi'noso *adj* full of imagery
immalinco'nire *vt* sadden
immalinco'nirsi *vr* grow melancholy
imman'cabile *adj* unfailing
immancabil'mente *adv* without fail
im'mane *adj* huge; (orribile) terrible
imma'nente *adj* immanent
immangi'abile *adj* inedible
immatrico'lare *vt* register
immatrico'larsi *vr* ‹*studente*› matriculate
immatrico'lato *adj* registered
immatricolazi'one *f* registration; (di studente) matriculation
immaturità *f inv* immaturity
imma'turo *adj* unripe; ‹*persona*› immature; (precoce) premature
immedesi'marsi *vr* **~ in** identify oneself with
immedesimazi'one *f* identification
immediata'mente *adv* immediately
immedia'tezza *f* immediacy
immedi'ato *adj* immediate; **nell'~ futuro** in the immediate future
immemo'rabile *adj* immemorial
im'memore *adj* oblivious
immensa'mente *adv* enormously
immensità *f inv* immensity
im'menso *adj* immense
immensu'rabile *adj* immeasurable
im'mergere *vt* immerse
im'mergersi *vr* plunge; ‹*sommergibile*› dive; **~ in** immerse oneself in
immeritata'mente *adv* undeservedly
immeri'tato *adj* undeserved
immeri'tevole *adj* undeserving
immersi'one *f* immersion; (di sommergibile, palombaro) dive
■ **immersione [subacquea]** skin diving, scuba diving
im'merso pp di **immergere**
im'mettere *vt* introduce
im'mettersi *vr* introduce oneself
immi'grante *adj & nmf* immigrant
immi'grare *vi* immigrate
immi'grato, -a *mf* immigrant
immigrazi'one *f* immigration
■ **immigrazione interna** migration
immi'nente *adj* imminent
immi'nenza *f* imminence
immischi'are *vt* involve
immischi'arsi *vr* **~ in** meddle in
immi'scibile *adj* immiscible
immis'sario *m* tributary
immissi'one *f* insertion; Techn intake; (introduzione) introduction
■ **immissione [di] dati** data entry
im'mobile *adj* motionless
im'mobili *mpl* real estate
immobili'are *adj* **società ~** building society, savings and loan AmE
immobilità *f inv* immobility
immobiliz'zare *vt* immobilize; Comm tie up
immobiliz'zato *adj* immobilized

■ **immobilizzato a letto** confined to bed
immobilizza'tore *m*
■ **immobilizzatore elettronico** Auto immobilizer
immobilizzazi'one *f* immobilization; Fin fixed asset; **spese d'~** capital expenditure
immoderata'mente *adv* immoderately
immode'rato *adj* immoderate
immo'destia *f* immodesty
immo'desto *adj* immodest
immo'lare *vt* sacrifice
immo'larsi *vr* sacrifice oneself
immondez'zaio *m* rubbish tip
immon'dizia *f* filth; (spazzatura) rubbish
im'mondo *adj* filthy
immo'rale *adj* immoral
immoral'mente *adv* immorally
immorta'lare *vt* immortalize
immor'tale *adj* immortal
immortalità *f inv* immortality
immoti'vato *adj* unjustified, unmotivated
im'moto *adj* motionless
im'mune *adj* exempt; Med immune
immunità *f inv* immunity
■ **immunità diplomatica** diplomatic immunity; **immunità parlamentare** parliamentary privilege
immuniz'zare *vt* immunize
immunizzazi'one *f* immunization
immunodefici'enza *f* immunodeficiency
immunodepres'sivo *adj & nm* immunodepressant
immunolo'gia *f* immunology
immuno'logico *adj* immunological
immuso'nirsi *vr* sulk
immuso'nito *adj* sulky
immu'tabile *adj* unchangeable
immu'tato *adj* unchanging
impacchet'tare *vt* wrap up
impacci'are *vt* hamper; (disturbare) inconvenience; (imbarazzare) embarrass
impacciata'mente *adv* awkwardly
impacci'ato *adj* embarrassed; (goffo) awkward
im'paccio *m* embarrassment; (ostacolo) hindrance; (situazione difficile) awkward situation; **trarsi d'~** get out of an awkward situation
im'pacco *m* compress
impadro'nirsi *vr* **~ di** take possession of; fig (imparare) master
impa'gabile *adj* priceless
impagi'nare *vt* paginate
impaginazi'one *f* pagination
impagli'are *vt* stuff ‹*animale*›
impa'lare *vt* impale
impa'lato *adj* fig stiff
impalca'tura *f* scaffolding; fig structure

impal'lare *vt* snooker
impalli'dire *vi* turn pale; fig (perdere d'importanza) pale into insignificance
impalli'nare *vt* riddle with bullets
impal'pabile *adj* impalpable; ‹*tessuto*› gossamer-like
impa'nare *vt* Culin bread
impa'nato *adj* breaded
impanta'narsi *vr* get bogged down
impape'rarsi *vr* falter, stammer
impappi'narsi *vr* falter, stammer
⚷ **impa'rare** *vt* learn; **~ a proprie spese** learn to one's cost
impara'ticcio *m* half-baked
impareggi'abile *adj* incomparable
imparen'tarsi *vr* **~ con** become related to
imparen'tato *adj* related
'impari *adj* unequal; (dispari) odd
impar'tire *vt* impart
imparzi'ale *adj* impartial
imparzialità *f inv* impartiality
im'passe *f inv* impasse
impas'sibile *adj* impassive; **con aria ~** impassively
impa'stare *vt* Culin knead; blend ‹*colori*›
impasta'tura *f* kneading
impastic'carsi *vr* pop pills
impasticci'are *vt* make a mess of
im'pasto *m* Culin dough; (miscuglio) mixture
im'patto *m* impact
■ **impatto ambientale** environmental impact
impau'rire *vt* frighten
impau'rirsi *vr* get frightened
im'pavido *adj* fearless
impazi'ente *adj* impatient; **~ di fare qualcosa** eager to do something
impazien'tirsi *vr* lose patience
impazi'enza *f* impatience
impaz'zata *f* **all'~** at breakneck speed
⚷ **impaz'zire** *vi* go mad; ‹*maionese*› separate; **far ~ qualcuno** drive somebody mad; **~ per** be crazy about; **da ~** ‹*mal di testa*› blinding
impaz'zito *adj* crazed
impec'cabile *adj* impeccable
impeccabil'mente *adv* impeccably
impedi'mento *m* hindrance; (ostacolo) obstacle
⚷ **impe'dire** *vt* (impacciare) hinder; (ostruire) obstruct; **~ di** prevent from; **~ a qualcuno di fare qualcosa** prevent somebody [from] doing something
⚷ **impe'gnare** *vt* (dare in pegno) pawn; (vincolare) bind; (prenotare) reserve; (assorbire) take up
impe'gnarsi *vr* apply oneself; **~ a fare qualcosa** commit oneself to doing something
impegna'tiva *f* referral
impegna'tivo *adj* binding; ‹*lavoro*› demanding

⚷ key word

impe'gnato *adj* committed

✓ **im'pegno** *m* engagement; Comm commitment; (zelo) care; **con ~** with dedication; **ho un ~** I'm doing something

impego'larsi *vr* **~ in** become enmeshed in

impel'lente *adj* pressing

impene'trabile *adj* impenetrable

impen'narsi *vr* ‹*cavallo*› rear; fig bristle

impen'nata *f* (di prezzi) sharp rise; (di cavallo) rearing; (di moto) wheelie; (di aereo) climb

impen'sabile *adj* unthinkable

impen'sato *adj* unexpected

impensie'rire *vt* worry

impensie'rirsi *vr* worry

impe'rante *adj* prevailing

impe'rare *vi* reign

impera'tivo *adj & nm* imperative

impera|'tore, -trice **A** *m* emperor **B** *f* empress

impercet'tibile *adj* imperceptible

impercettibil'mente *adv* imperceptibly

imperdo'nabile *adj* unforgivable

imperfetta'mente *adv* imperfectly

imper'fetto *adj & nm* imperfect

imperfezi'one *f* imperfection

imperi'ale *adj* imperial

imperia'lismo *m* imperialism

imperia'lista *adj & nmf* imperialist

imperia'listico *adj* imperialistic

imperi'oso *adj* imperious; (impellente) urgent

imperi'turo *adj* immortal

impe'rizia *f* lack of skill

imper'lare *vt* bead

imperma'lire *vt* offend

imperma'lirsi *vr* take offence

imperme'abile **A** *adj* ‹*orologio*› waterproof; ‹*terreno*› impermeable **B** *m* raincoat

imperni'are *vt* pivot; (fondare) base

imperni'arsi *vr* **~ su** be based on

im'pero *m* empire; (potere) rule; **stile ~** empire style

imperscru'tabile *adj* inscrutable

imperso'nale *adj* impersonal

imperso'nare *vt* personify; (interpretare) act [the part of]

imper'territo *adj* undaunted, undeterred

imperti'nente *adj* impertinent

imperti'nenza *f* impertinence

impertur'babile *adj* imperturbable

impertur'bato *adj* unperturbed

imperver'sare *vi* rage

im'pervio *adj* inaccessible

'impeto *m* impetus; (impulso) impulse; (slancio) transport

impet'tito *adj* stiff

impetuosa'mente *adv* impetuously

impetu'oso *adj* impetuous; ‹*vento*› blustering

impiallacci'are *vt* veneer

impiallacci'ato *adj* veneered

impian'tare *vt* install; set up ‹*azienda*›

impi'anto *m* plant; (sistema) system; (operazione) installation; Med implant

■ **impianto di amplificazione** public address system, PA system; **impianto audio** sound system; **impianto elettrico** electrical system; **impianti** *pl* **fissi** fixtures and fittings; **impianto radio** Auto car stereo system; **impianto di rilavorazione [di scorie nucleari]** reprocessing plant; **impianto di riscaldamento** heating system; **impianto stereo** hi-fi

impia'strare *vt* plaster; (sporcare) dirty

impia'strarsi *vr* get dirty; **~ le mani** get one's hands dirty

impi'astro *m* poultice; ‹*persona noiosa*› bore; (pasticcione) cack-handed person

impiccagi'one *f* hanging

impic'care *vt* hang

impic'carsi *vr* hang oneself

impic'cato, -a **A** *m* hanged man **B** *f* hanged woman

impicci'arsi *vr* meddle

im'piccio *m* hindrance; (seccatura) bother

impicci'one, -a *mf* nosey parker

impie'gare *vt* employ; (usare) use; spend ‹*tempo, denaro*›; Fin invest; **l'autobus ha impiegato un'ora** it took the bus an hour

impie'garsi *vr* get [oneself] a job

impiega'tizio *adj* clerical

impie'gato, -a *mf* employee; (di ufficio) office worker

■ **impiegato di banca** bank clerk; **impiegato di concetto** administrative employee; **impiegato in prova** probationer; **impiegato statale** civil servant

impi'ego *m* employment; (posto) job; Fin investment; **pubblico impiego** public sector; **impiego fisso** permanent job; **impieghi** *pl* **saltuari** odd jobs, casual employment

■ **impiego temporaneo** temporary job

impieto'sire *vt* move to pity

impieto'sirsi *vr* be moved to pity

impie'toso *adj* pitiless

impie'trito *adj* petrified

impigli'are *vt* entangle

impigli'arsi *vr* get entangled

impi'grire *vt* make lazy

impi'grirsi *vr* get lazy

impi'lare *vt* stack

impingu'are *vt* fig fill

impiom'bare *vt* seal ‹*cassa, porta*›

impla'cabile *adj* implacable

implemen'tare *vt* implement

impli'care *vt* implicate; (sottintendere) imply

impli'carsi *vr* become involved

implicazi'one *f* implication

implicita'mente *adv* implicitly

im'plicito *adj* implicit

implo'rante *adj* imploring

implo'rare *vt* implore

implorazi'one *f* entreaty

implosi'one *f* implosion

impolli'nare *vt* pollinate

impollinazi'one *f* pollination

impoltro'nire *vt* make lazy

impoltro'nirsi *vr* become lazy

impolve'rare *vt* cover with dust

impolve'rarsi *vr* get covered with dust

impolve'rato *adj* dusty

impoma'tare *vt* put brilliantine on ‹*capelli*›

impoma'tarsi *vr* put brilliantine on

imponde'rabile *adj* imponderable; ‹*causa, eveto*› unpredictable

impo'nente *adj* imposing

impo'nenza *f* impressiveness

impo'nibile **A** *adj* taxable **B** *m* taxable income

impopo'lare *adj* unpopular

impopolarità *f inv* unpopularity

imporpo'rarsi *vr* turn red

⚷ **im'porre** *vt* impose; (ordinare) order

im'porsi *vr* assert oneself; (aver successo) be successful; **~ di** (prefiggersi di) set oneself the task of

⚷ **impor'tante** **A** *adj* important **B** *m* important thing

⚷ **impor'tanza** *f* importance; **di vitale ~** crucially important

⚷ **impor'tare** **A** *vt* Comm, Comput import; (comportare) cause **B** *vi* matter; (essere necessario) be necessary; **non importa!** it doesn't matter!; **non me ne importa niente!** I couldn't care less!

importa|'tore, -trice **A** *adj* importing **B** *mf* importer

importazi'one *f* importation; (merce importata) import

import-'export *m inv* import-export

im'porto *m* amount

importu'nare *vt* pester; **~ qualcuno per qualcosa** pester somebody for something

impor'tuno *adj* troublesome; (inopportuno) untimely

imposizi'one *f* imposition; (imposta) tax

imposses'sarsi *vr* **~ di** seize

⚷ **impos'sibile** **A** *adj* impossible **B** *m* **fare l'~** do absolutely all one can

impossibilità *f inv* impossibility

im'posta¹ *f* tax

■ **imposta fondiaria** land tax; **imposta patrimoniale** property tax; **imposta sul reddito** income tax; **imposta sui redditi di capitale** capital gains tax; **imposta sulle società** corporation tax; **imposta supplementare** surtax; **imposta sul valore aggiunto** value added tax

im'posta² *f* (di finestra) shutter

impo'stare *vt* (progettare) plan; (basare) base; Mus pitch; (imbucare) post, mail; set out ‹*domanda, problema*›

impostazi'one *f* planning; (di voce) pitching; **impostazioni** *pl* Comput, Teleph settings

im'posto pp di **imporre**

impo'store, -a *mf* impostor

impo'stura *f* imposture

impo'tente *adj* powerless; Med impotent

impo'tenza *f* powerlessness; Med impotence

impoveri'mento *m* impoverishment

impove'rire *vt* impoverish

impove'rirsi *vr* become poor; ‹*risorse*› become depleted; ‹*linguaggio*› become impoverished

imprati'cabile *adj* impracticable; ‹*strada*› impassable

impraticabilità *f inv* **per ~ del terreno/delle strade** because of the state of the pitch/roads

imprati'chire *vt* train

imprati'chirsi *vr* **~ in, ~ a** get practice in

impre'care *vi* curse

imprecazi'one *f* curse

impreci'sabile *adj* indeterminable

impreci'sato *adj* indeterminate

imprecisi'one *f* inaccuracy

impre'ciso *adj* inaccurate

impre'gnare *vt* impregnate; (imbevere) soak; fig imbue

impre'gnarsi *vr* become impregnated with

imprendi|'tore, -trice *mf* entrepreneur

imprenditori'ale *adj* entrepreneurial

imprepa'rato *adj* unprepared

⚷ **im'presa** *f* undertaking; (gesta) exploit; ‹*azienda*› firm

■ **impresa edile** property developer; **impresa familiare** family business; **impresa di pompe funebri** undertakers, funeral directors; **impresa pubblica** state-owned company; **impresa di traslochi** removals firm BrE

impre'sario *m* impresario; (appaltatore) contractor

■ **impresario di pompe funebri** undertaker, funeral director, mortician AmE; **impresario teatrale** theatre manager

imprescin'dibile *adj* inescapable

impressio'nabile *adj* impressionable

impressio'nante *adj* impressive; (spaventoso) frightening

impressio'nare *vt* impress; (spaventare) frighten; expose ‹*foto*›

impressio'narsi *vr* be affected; (spaventarsi) be frightened

⚷ **impressi'one** *f* impression; (sensazione)

sensation; (impronta) mark; **far ~ a qualcuno** upset somebody; **dare l'~ di essere ...** give the impression of being ...

impressio'nismo *m* Impressionism

impressio'nista *adj & nmf* impressionist

impressio'nistico *adj* impressionistic

im'presso **A** pp di **imprimere** **B** *adj* printed

impre'stare *vt* lend

impreve'dibile *adj* unforeseeable; ‹*persona*› unpredictable

imprevedibil'mente *adv* unexpectedly

imprevi'dente *adj* improvident

impre'visto **A** *adj* unforeseen **B** *m* unforeseen event; **salvo imprevisti** all being well

imprigiona'mento *m* imprisonment

imprigio'nare *vt* imprison

im'primere *vt* impress; (stampare) print; (comunicare) impart; **rimanere impresso a qualcuno** stick in somebody's mind

impro'babile *adj* unlikely, improbable; **è ~ che ci sia** he is unlikely to be there

improbabilità *f inv* improbability

improdut'tivo *adj* unproductive

im'pronta *f* impression; (di dito) print; fig mark
■ **impronta digitale** fingerprint; **impronta ecologica** ecological footprint; **impronte** *pl* **genetiche** genetic fingerprinting; **impronta del piede** footprint

impron'tato *adj* **~ all'ironia** tinged with irony

impronunci'abile *adj* unpronounceable

impro'perio *m* insult; **improperi** *pl* abuse *sg*

impropo'nibile *adj* unrealistic

im'proprio *adj* improper

improro'gabile *adj* which cannot be extended

improvvisa'mente *adv* suddenly

improvvi'sare *vt & vi* improvise

improvvi'sarsi *vr* turn oneself into a

improvvi'sata *f* surprise

improvvi'sato *adj* ‹*discorso*› unrehearsed

improvvisazi'one *f* improvisation

improv'viso *adj* unexpected, sudden; **all'~** unexpectedly, suddenly

impru'dente *adj* imprudent

imprudente'mente *adv* imprudently

impru'denza *f* imprudence

impu'dente *adj* impudent

impudente'mente *adv* impudently

impu'denza *f* impudence

impu'dico *adj* immodest

impu'gnare *vt* grasp; Jur contest

impugna'tura *f* grip; (manico) handle
■ **impugnatura a due mani** two-handed grip

impulsiva'mente *adv* impulsively

impulsività *f inv* impulsiveness

impul'sivo *adj* impulsive

im'pulso *m* impulse; **agire d'~** act on impulse

impune'mente *adv* with impunity

impunità *f inv* impunity

impu'nito *adj* unpunished

impun'tarsi *vr* fig dig one's heels in

impun'tura *f* stitching

impuntu'rare *vt* backstitch

impurità *f inv* impurity

im'puro *adj* impure

impu'tabile *adj* attributable (**a** to); Jur indictable

impu'tare *vt* attribute; Jur charge

impu'tato, -a *mf* accused

imputazi'one *f* charge
■ **imputazione di omicidio** murder charge

imputri'dire *vi* putrefy

imputri'dito *adj* putrefied

in *prep* in; (moto a luogo) to; (su) on; (dentro) within; (mezzo) by; (con materiale) made of; **essere in casa/ufficio** be at home/at the office; **in mano/tasca** in one's hand/pocket; **in fondo alla strada/borsa** at the bottom of the street/bag; **andare in Francia/campagna** go to France/the country; **salire in treno** get on the train; **versa la birra nel bicchiere** pour the beer into the glass; **in alto** up there; **in giornata** within the day; **nel 2011** in 2011; **una borsa in pelle** a bag made of leather, a leather bag; **in macchina** ‹*viaggiare, venire*› by car; **in contanti** [in] cash; **in vacanza** on holiday; **di giorno in giorno** from day to day; **se fossi in te** if I were you; **siamo in sette** there are seven of us

inabbor'dabile *adj* unapproachable

i'nabile *adj* incapable; (fisicamente) unfit

inabilità *f inv* incapacity

inabi'tabile *adj* uninhabitable

inacces'sibile *adj* inaccessible; ‹*persona*› unapproachable

inaccet'tabile *adj* unacceptable

inaccettabilità *f inv* unacceptability

inacer'barsi *vr* grow bitter

inacer'bire *vt* embitter; exacerbate ‹*rapporto*›

inaci'dire *vt* turn sour

inaci'dirsi *vr* go sour; ‹*persona*› become embittered

ina'datto *adj* unsuitable

inadegua'tezza *f* inadequacy

inadegu'ato *adj* inadequate

inadempi'ente *mf* defaulter

inadempi'enza *f* non-fulfilment (**a** of)
■ **inadempienza contrattuale** breach of contract

inadempi'mento *m* non-fulfilment

inaffer'rabile *adj* elusive

inaffi'dabile *adj* untrustworthy

inaffon'dabile *adj* unsinkable

ina'lare *vt* inhale

i

inala'tore *m* inhaler
inalazi'one *f* inhalation
inalbe'rare *vt* hoist
inalbe'rarsi *vr* ‹*cavallo*› rear [up]; (adirarsi) lose one's temper
inalie'nabile *adj* inalienable
inalte'rabile *adj* unchanging; ‹*colore*› fast
inalte'rato *adj* unchanged
inami'dare *vt* starch
inami'dato *adj* starched
inammis'sibile *adj* inadmissible
inamo'vibile *adj* ‹*disco ecc.*› non-removable
inanel'lato *adj* bejewelled
inani'mato *adj* inanimate; (senza vita) lifeless
inappa'gabile *adj* unsatisfiable
inappaga'mento *m* non-fulfilment
inappa'gato *adj* unfulfilled
inappel'labile *adj* final
inappe'tenza *f* lack of appetite
inappli'cabile *adj* inapplicable
inappropri'ato *adj* inapt
inappun'tabile *adj* faultless
inar'care *vt* arch; raise ‹*sopracciglia*›
inar'carsi *vr* ‹*legno*› warp; ‹*ripiano*› sag; (linea) curve
inari'dire *vt* parch; empty of feelings ‹*persona*›
inari'dirsi *vr* dry up; ‹*persona*› become empty of feelings
inarre'stabile *adj* unstoppable
inartico'lato *adj* inarticulate
inascol'tato *adj* unheard
inaspettata'mente *adv* unexpectedly
inaspet'tato *adj* unexpected
inaspri'mento *m* (di carattere) embitterment; (di conflitto) worsening
ina'sprire *vt* embitter
ina'sprirsi *vr* become embittered
inattac'cabile *adj* unassailable; (irreprensibile) irreproachable
inatten'dibile *adj* unreliable
inat'teso *adj* unexpected
inattività *f inv* inactivity
inat'tivo *adj* inactive
inattu'abile *adj* impracticable
inau'dito *adj* unheard of
inaugu'rale *adj* inaugural; **cerimonia ~** official opening; **viaggio ~** maiden voyage
inaugu'rare *vt* inaugurate, open ‹*mostra*›; unveil ‹*statua*›; christen ‹*lavastoviglie ecc.*›
inaugurazi'one *f* inauguration; (di mostra) opening; (di statua) unveiling
inavve'duto *adj* inadvertent; (sbadato) careless
inavver'tenza *f* inadvertence
inavvertita'mente *adv* inadvertently
inavvici'nabile *adj* unapproachable
in'breeding *m inv* inbreeding
'inca *adj & nmf* (*pl* **inca** *o* **incas**) Inca
incagli'are **A** *vi* ground
B *vt* hinder
incagli'arsi *vr* run aground
in'caglio *m* running aground; fig obstacle
incalco'labile *adj* incalculable
incal'lirsi *vr* grow callous; (abituarsi) become hardened
incal'lito *adj* callous; (abituato) hardened
incal'zante *adj* ‹*ritmo*› driving; ‹*richiesta*› urgent; ‹*crisi*› imminent
incal'zare *vt* pursue; fig press
incame'rare *vt* appropriate
incammi'nare *vt* get going; fig (guidare) set off
incammi'narsi *vr* set out
incanala'mento *m* canalization; fig channelling
incana'lare *vt* canalize; fig channel
incana'larsi *vr* converge on
incancel'labile *adj* indelible
incande'scente *adj* incandescent; ‹*discussione*› burning
incande'scenza *f* incandescence
incan'tare *vt* enchant
incan'tarsi *vr* stand spellbound; (incepparsi) jam
incanta|'tore, -trice *mf* enchanter; enchantress
■ **incantatore di serpenti** snake charmer
incan'tesimo *m* spell
incan'tevole *adj* enchanting
in'canto *m* spell; fig delight; (asta) auction; **come per ~** as if by magic
incanu'tire *vt* turn white
incanu'tito *adj* white
inca'pace *adj* incapable; **~ d'intendere e di volere** Jur unfit to plead
incapacità *f inv* incapability
incapo'nirsi *vr* be set
incap'pare *vi* **~ in** run into
incappucci'arsi *vr* wrap up
incapretta'mento *m method of trussing up a victim by the ankles*
incapricci'arsi *vr* **~ di** take a fancy to
incapsu'lare *vt* seal; crown ‹*dente*›
incarce'rare *vt* imprison
incarcerazi'one *f* imprisonment
incari'care *vt* charge
incari'carsi *vr* take upon oneself; **me ne incarico io** I will see to it
incari'cato, -a **A** *adj* in charge
B *mf* representative
■ **incaricato d'affari** chargé d'affaires
in'carico *m* charge; **per ~ di** on behalf of
incar'nare *vt* embody

incar'narsi *vr* become incarnate
incarnazi'one *f* incarnation
incarta'mento *m* documents *pl*
incartapeco'rito *adj* shrivelled up
incar'tare *vt* wrap [in paper]
incasel'lare *vt* pigeonhole
incasi'nato *adj* infml ‹*vita*› screwed up; ‹*stanza*› messed up
incas'sare *vt* pack; Mech embed; (incastonare) set; (riscuotere) cash; take ‹*colpo*›
incas'sato *adj* set; ‹*fiume*› deeply embanked
in'casso *m* collection; (introito) takings *pl*
incasto'nare *vt* set
incasto'nato *adj* embedded; ‹*anello*› inset (di with)
incastona'tura *f* setting
inca'strare *vt* fit in; infml (in situazione) corner
inca'strarsi *vr* fit, interlock
in'castro *m* joint; **a ~** ‹*pezzi*› interlocking
▪ **incastro a coda di rondine** dovetail joint
incate'nare *vt* chain
incatra'mare *vt* tar
incatti'vire *vt* turn nasty
incauta'mente *adv* imprudently
in'cauto *adj* imprudent
inca'vare *vt* hollow out
inca'vato *adj* hollow
incava'tura *f* hollow
'incavo *m* hollow; (scanalatura) groove
incavo'larsi *vr* infml get shirty
incavo'lato *adj* infml shirty
in'cedere fml **A** *vi* advance solemnly
B *m* solemn gait
incendi'are *vt* set fire to; fig inflame
incendi'ario, -a **A** *adj* incendiary; fig ‹*discorso*› inflammatory; fig ‹*bellezza*› sultry
B *mf* arsonist
incendi'arsi *vr* catch fire
in'cendio *m* fire
▪ **incendio doloso** arson; **incendi** *pl* **dolosi** cases of arson
inceneri'mento *m* incineration; (cremazione) cremation
incene'rire *vt* burn to ashes; (cremare) cremate
incene'rirsi *vr* be burnt to ashes
inceneri'tore *m* incinerator
in'censo *m* incense
incensu'rabile *adj* irreproachable
incensu'rato *adj* blameless; **essere ~** Jur have a clean record
incenti'vare *vt* motivate
incen'tivo *m* incentive
▪ **incentivo fiscale** tax incentive
incen'trarsi *vr* **~ su** centre on
incep'pare *vt* block; fig hamper
incep'parsi *vr* jam
ince'rata *f* oilcloth
incerot'tato *adj* with a plaster on
incer'tezza *f* uncertainty
in'certo **A** *adj* uncertain, unsure
B *m* uncertainty; **sono gli incerti del mestiere** that's the way it goes in this business
incespi'care *vi* (inciampare) stumble
inces'sante *adj* unceasing
incessante'mente *adv* incessantly
in'cesto *m* incest
incestu'oso *adj* incestuous
in'cetta *f* buying up; **fare ~ di** stockpile
inchi'esta *f* investigation; **fare un'~** conduct an inquiry
▪ **inchiesta giudiziaria** criminal investigation; **inchiesta parlamentare** parliamentary inquiry
inchi'nare *vt* bow
inchi'narsi *vr* bow
in'chino *m* bow; (di donna) curtsy
inchio'dare *vt* nail; nail down ‹*coperchio*›; **~ a letto** ‹*malattia*› confine to bed
inchi'ostro *m* ink
▪ **inchiostro di china** Indian ink; **inchiostro simpatico** invisible ink; **inchiostro di stampa** newsprint
inciam'pare *vi* stumble; **~ in** trip over; (imbattersi) run into
inci'ampo *m* hindrance
inciden'tale *adj* incidental
inci'dente *m* (episodio) incident; (infortunio) accident
▪ **incidente aereo** plane crash; **incidente d'auto** car accident; **incidente sul lavoro** industrial accident; **incidente stradale** road accident
inci'denza *f* incidence
in'cidere **A** *vt* cut; (arte) engrave; (registrare) record
B *vi* **~ su** (gravare) weigh upon
in'cinta *adj* pregnant
incipi'ente *adj* incipient
incipri'are *vt* powder
incipri'arsi *vr* powder one's face
in'circa *adv* **all'~** more or less
incisi'one *f* incision; (arte) engraving; (acquaforte) etching; (registrazione) recording
inci'sivo **A** *adj* incisive
B *m* (dente) incisor
in'ciso *m* **per ~** incidentally
inci'sore *m* engraver
incita'mento *m* incitement
inci'tare *vt* incite
inci'vile *adj* uncivilized; (maleducato) impolite
inciviltà *f inv* barbarism; (maleducazione) rudeness
inclassifi'cabile *adv* unclassifiable
incle'mente *adj* harsh
incle'menza *f* harshness
incli'nabile *adj* reclining
incli'nare **A** *vt* tilt

B *vi* ~ a be inclined to
incli'narsi *vr* (torre) lean; (aereo) tilt
incli'nato *adj* tilted; ‹*terreno*› sloping
inclinazi'one *f* slope, inclination
in'cline *adj* inclined
in'cludere *vt* include; (allegare) enclose
inclusi'one *f* inclusion
inclu'sivo *adj* inclusive
in'cluso **A** pp di **includere**
B *adj* included; (compreso) inclusive; (allegato) enclosed
incoe'rente *adj* (contraddittorio) inconsistent
incoerente'mente *adv* inconsistently
incoe'renza *f* inconsistency
in'cognita *f* unknown quantity
in'cognito **A** *adj* unknown
B *m* in ~ incognito
incol'lare *vt* stick; (con colla liquida) glue; Comput paste
incol'larsi *vr* stick to; ~ **a qualcuno** stick close to somebody
incolla'tura *f* (nell'ippica) neck
incolle'rirsi *vr* lose one's temper
incolle'rito *adj* enraged
incol'mabile *adj* ‹*differenza*› unbridgeable; ‹*vuoto*› unfillable
incolon'nare *vt* line up
inco'lore *adj* colourless
incol'pare *vt* blame
in'colto *adj* uncultivated; ‹*persona*› uneducated
in'colume *adj* unhurt
incom'bente *adj* impending
incom'benza *f* task
in'combere *vi* ~ **su** hang over; ~ **a** (spettare) be incumbent on
incombu'stibile *adj* non-combustible
incominci'are *vt & vi* begin, start
incommensu'rabile *adj* immeasurable
incomo'dare *vt* inconvenience
incomo'darsi *vr* trouble
in'comodo **A** *adj* uncomfortable; (inopportuno) inconvenient
B *m* inconvenience; **fare il terzo** ~ play gooseberry
incompa'rabile *adj* incomparable
incompa'tibile *adj* incompatible
incompatibilità *f inv* incompatibility
■ **incompatibilità di carattere** incompatibility
incompe'tente *adj* incompetent
incompe'tenza *f* incompetence
incompi'uto *adj* unfinished
incom'pleto *adj* incomplete
incompren'sibile *adj* incomprehensible, unintelligible
incomprensibil'mente *adv* incomprehensibly

key word

incomprensi'one *f* lack of understanding; (malinteso) misunderstanding
incom'preso *adj* misunderstood
inconce'pibile *adj* inconceivable
inconcili'abile *adj* irreconcilable
inconclu'dente *adj* inconclusive; ‹*persona*› ineffectual
incondizionata'mente *adv* unconditionally
incondizio'nato *adj* unconditional
inconfes'sabile *adj* unmentionable
inconfon'dibile *adj* unmistakable
inconfondibil'mente *adv* unmistakably
inconfu'tabile *adj* irrefutable
inconfutabil'mente *adv* irrefutably
incongru'ente *adj* inconsistent
incongru'enza *f* incongruity
in'congruo *adj* inadequate
inconsa'pevole *adj* unaware; (inconscio) unconscious
inconsapevol'mente *adv* unwittingly
inconscia'mente *adv* unconsciously
in'conscio *adj & nm* Psych unconscious
inconsegu'ente *adj* **essere** ~ be a non sequitur
inconside'rabile *adj* negligible
inconside'rato *adj* inconsiderate
inconsi'stente *adj* insubstantial; ‹*notizia ecc.*› unfounded
inconsi'stenza *f* (di ragionamento, prove) flimsiness
inconso'labile *adj* inconsolable
inconsu'eto *adj* unusual
incon'sulto *adj* rash
incontami'nato *adj* uncontaminated
inconte'nibile *adj* irrepressible
inconten'tabile *adj* insatiable; (esigente) hard to please
inconte'stabile *adj* indisputable
inconte'stato *adj* unchallenged
inconti'nente *adj* incontinent
inconti'nenza *f* incontinence
incon'trare *vt* meet; encounter, meet with ‹*difficoltà*›
incon'trario **all'**~ *adv* the other way around; (in modo sbagliato) the wrong way around
incon'trarsi *vr* meet; ~ **con qualcuno** meet somebody
incontra'stabile *adj* incontrovertible
incontra'stato *adj* undisputed
in'contro **A** *m* meeting; (casuale) encounter; (di calcio, rugby) match; (di tennis) game; (di pugilato) fight
■ **incontro al vertice** summit meeting
B *prep* ~ **a** towards; **andare** ~ **a qualcuno** go to meet somebody; fig meet somebody half way
incontrol'labile *adj* uncontrollable
incontrollata'mente *adv* uncontrollably

inconveni'ente *m* drawback
incoraggia'mento *m* encouragement
incoraggi'ante *adj* encouraging
incoraggi'are *vt* encourage
incor'nare *vt* gore
incornici'are *vt* frame
incornicia'tura *f* framing
incoro'nare *vt* crown
incoronazi'one *f* coronation
incorpo'rare *vt* incorporate; (mescolare) blend
incorpo'rarsi *vr* blend; ‹*territori*› merge
incorreg'gibile *adj* incorrigible
in'correre *vt* ~ **in** incur; ~ **nel pericolo di ...** run the risk of ...
incorrut'tibile *adj* incorruptible
incosci'ente **A** *adj* unconscious; (irresponsabile) reckless
B *mf* irresponsible person
incosci'enza *f* unconsciousness; (irresponsabilità) recklessness
inco'stante *adj* changeable; ‹*persona*› fickle
inco'stanza *f* changeableness; (di persona) fickleness
incostituzio'nale *adj* unconstitutional
incostituzionalità *f inv* unconstitutionality
incre'dibile *adj* incredible, unbelievable
incredibil'mente *adv* incredibly, unbelievably
incredulità *f inv* incredulity
in'credulo *adj* incredulous
incremen'tale *adj* Comput, Math incremental
incremen'tare *vt* increase; (intensificare) step up
incre'mento *m* increase
■ **incremento demografico** population growth; **incremento produttivo** increase in production
incresci'oso *adj* regrettable
incre'spare *vt* ruffle; wrinkle ‹*tessuto*›; make frizzy ‹*capelli*›; ~ **la fronte** frown
incre'sparsi *vr* ‹*acqua*› ripple; ‹*tessuto*› wrinkle; ‹*capelli*› go frizzy
incrimi'nabile *adj* indictable
incrimi'nante *adj* incriminating
incrimi'nare *vt* indict; fig incriminate
incriminazi'one *f* indictment
incri'nare *vt* crack; fig affect ‹*amicizia*›
incri'narsi *vr* crack; ‹*amicizia*› be affected
incrina'tura *f* crack
incroci'are **A** *vt* cross
B *vi* Naut, Aeron cruise
incroci'arsi *vr* cross; ‹*razze*› interbreed
incroci'ato *adj* crossover
incrocia'tore *m* cruiser
in'crocio *m* crossing; (di strade) crossroads *sg*
incrol'labile *adj* indestructible
incro'stare *vt* encrust
incrostazi'one *f* encrustation

incuba'trice *f* incubator
incubazi'one *f* incubation
'incubo *m* nightmare; **da** ~ nightmarish
in'cudine *f* anvil
incul'care *vt* inculcate
incune'are *vt* wedge
incune'arsi *vr* slot in
incune'ato *adj* Med impacted
incu'pirsi *vr* fig darken
incu'rabile *adj* incurable
incu'rante *adj* careless
in'curia *f* negligence
incurio'sire *vt* make curious
incurio'sirsi *vr* become curious
incursi'one *f* raid
■ **incursione aerea** air raid, air strike
incurva'mento *m* bending
incur'vare *vt* bend
incur'varsi *vr* bend
incurva'tura *f* bending
in'cusso pp di **incutere**
incusto'dito *adj* unguarded
in'cutere *vt* arouse; ~ **spavento a qualcuno** strike fear into somebody
'indaco *m* indigo
indaffa'rato *adj* busy
inda'gare *vt & vi* investigate
indaga'tore *adj* ‹*sguardo*› enquiring
in'dagine *f* research; (giudiziaria) investigation
■ **indagine demoscopica** public opinion poll; **indagine di mercato** market survey
indebi'tare *vt* get into debt
indebi'tarsi *vr* get into debt
in'debito *adj* undue
indeboli'mento *m* weakening
indebo'lire *vt* weaken
indebo'lirsi *vr* weaken
inde'cente *adj* indecent
indecente'mente *adv* indecently
inde'cenza *f* indecency; (vergogna) disgrace
indeci'frabile *adj* indecipherable
indecisi'one *f* indecision
inde'ciso *adj* undecided
indecli'nabile *adj* indeclinable
indeco'roso *adj* indecorous
inde'fesso *adj* tireless
indefi'nibile *adj* indefinable
indefi'nito *adj* indefinite
indefor'mabile *adj* crush-proof
in'degno *adj* unworthy
inde'lebile *adj* indelible
indelebil'mente *adv* indelibly
indelicata'mente *adv* indiscreetly
indelica'tezza *f* indelicacy; (azione) tactless act
indeli'cato *adj* indiscreet; (grossolano) indelicate
indemagli'abile *adj* ladder-proof

indemoni'ato *adj* possessed

in'denne *adj* uninjured; (da malattia) unaffected

inden'nità *f inv* allowance; (per danni) compensation
■ **indennità di accompagnamento** mobility allowance; **indennità di contingenza** cost-of-living allowance; **indennità di disoccupazione** job seeker's allowance; **indennità di fine rapporto** severance payment; **indennità di malattia** sick pay; **indennità parlamentare** MP's salary; **indennità di trasferimento** relocation allowance; **indennità di trasferta** travel allowance

indenniz'zare *vt* compensate

inden'nizzo *m* compensation

indero'gabile *adj* binding

indescri'vibile *adj* indescribable

indescrivibil'mente *adv* indescribably

indeside'rabile *adj* undesirable

indeside'rato *adj* ‹*figlio, ospite*› unwanted

indetermi'nabile *adj* indeterminable

indetermina'tezza *f* vagueness

indetermina'tivo *adj* indefinite

indetermi'nato *adj* indeterminate

'India *f* India

indi'ano, -a *adj & nmf* Indian; **in fila indiana** in single file
■ **indiano d'America** American Indian

indiavo'lato *adj* possessed; (vivace) wild

🔑 **indi'care** *vt* show, indicate; (col dito) point at; (far notare) point out; (consigliare) advise

indicativa'mente *adv* as an idea; **può dirmi quanto costa ~?** can you give me an idea of the price?

indica'tivo **A** *adj* indicative; ‹*prezzo, cifra*› rough
B *m* Gram indicative

indica'tore *m* indicator; Techn gauge; (prontuario) directory
■ **indicatore di direzione** indicator light; **indicatore economico** economic indicator; **indicatore [del livello] dell'olio** oil gauge; **indicatore di velocità** speedometer

indicazi'one *f* indication; (istruzione) direction
■ **indicazione stradale** road sign

'indice *m* (dito) forefinger; (lancetta) pointer; (di libro, statistica) index; fig (segno) sign
■ **indice di ascolto** audience rating; **indice azionario** share index; **indice di gradimento** popularity rating; **indice di massa corporea** body mass index; **indice di mortalità** death rate; **indice di natalità** birth rate

indi'cibile *adj* inexpressible

indiciz'zare *vt* index-link

indiciz'zato *adj* index-linked

indicizzazi'one *f* indexing

indietreggi'are *vi* draw back; Mil withdraw

🔑 **indi'etro** *adv* back, behind; **all' ~** backwards; **essere ~** be behind; (mentalmente) be backward; (con pagamenti) be in arrears; (di orologio) be slow; **fare marcia ~** reverse; **rimandare ~** send back; **rimanere ~** be left behind; **torna ~!** come back!

indifen'dibile *adj* indefensible

indi'feso *adj* undefended; (inerme) helpless

🔑 **indiffe'rente** *adj* indifferent; **mi è ~** it's all the same to me

indifferente'mente *adv* (senza fare distinzioni) without distinction; (con indifferenza) indifferently; **funziona ~ con i due programmi** it works equally well with either program

indiffe'renza *f* indifference

in'digeno, -a **A** *adj* indigenous
B *mf* native

indi'gente *adj* needy, poverty-stricken

indi'genza *f* poverty

indigesti'one *f* indigestion

indi'gesto *adj* indigestible

indi'gnare *vt* make indignant

indi'gnarsi *vr* be indignant

indi'gnato *adj* indignant

indignazi'one *f* indignation

indimenti'cabile *adj* unforgettable

'indio, -a **A** *adj* Indian
B *mf* (*mpl* **indii** *o* **indios**) Indian

indipen'dente *adj* independent; ‹*economicamente*› self-supporting

indipendente'mente *adv* independently; **~ da** regardless of

🔑 **indipen'denza** *f* independence

in'dire *vt* announce

indiretta'mente *adv* indirectly

indi'retto *adj* indirect

indiriz'zare *vt* address; (mandare) send; (dirigere) direct

indiriz'zario *m* mailing list

indiriz'zarsi *vr* direct one's steps

🔑 **indi'rizzo** *m* address; (direzione) direction
■ **indirizzo di consegna** delivery address; **'indirizzo del destinatario'** 'addressee'; **indirizzo di memoria** Comput memory address; **'indirizzo del mittente'** 'sender's address'; **indirizzo di posta elettronica** email address

indisci'plina *f* lack of discipline

indiscipli'nato *adj* undisciplined

indi'screto *adj* indiscreet; **in modo ~** indiscreetly

indiscrezi'one *f* indiscretion

indiscriminata'mente *adv* indiscriminately

indiscrimi'nato *adj* indiscriminate

indi'scusso *adj* unquestioned

indiscu'tibile *adj* unquestionable

indiscutibil'mente *adv* unquestionably

indispen'sabile *adj* essential; ‹*persona*› indispensable

🔑 key word

indispet'tire *vt* irritate
indispet'tirsi *vr* get irritated
indi'sporre *vt* anger
indisposizi'one *f* indisposition
indi'sposto **A** pp di **indisporre**
B *adj* indisposed
indisso'lubile *adj* indissoluble
indissolubil'mente *adv* indissolubly
indistin'guibile *adj* indiscernible
indistinta'mente *adv* without exception
indi'stinto *adj* indistinct
indistrut'tibile *adj* indestructible
indistur'bato *adj* undisturbed
in'divia *f* endive
individu'abile *adj* detectable
individu'ale *adj* individual
individua'lista *mf* individualist
individua'listico *adj* individualistic
individualità *f inv* individuality
individu'are *vt* individualize; (localizzare) locate; (riconoscere) single out
indi'viduo *m* individual
indivi'sibile *adj* indivisible
indivisibilità *f inv* indivisibility
indi'viso *adj* undivided
indizi'are *vt* throw suspicion on
indizi'ario *adj* circumstantial
indizi'ato, -a **A** *adj* suspected
B *mf* suspect
in'dizio *m* sign; Jur circumstantial evidence
Indo'cina *f* Indo-China
indoeuro'peo *adj* Indo-European
'indole *f* nature
indo'lente *adj* indolent
indo'lenza *f* indolence
indolenzi'mento *m* stiffness, ache
indolen'zire *vt* stiffen up
indolen'zirsi *vr* stiffen up, go stiff
indolen'zito *adj* stiff
indo'lore *adj* painless
indo'mabile *adj* untameable
indo'mani *m* l'~ the following day
in'domito *adj* untamed
Indo'nesia *f* Indonesia
indonesi'ano, -a *adj & nmf* Indonesian
indo'rare *vt* gild; ~ **la pillola** sugar the pill
indos'sare *vt* wear; (mettere addosso) put on
indossa|'tore, -trice **A** *m* [male] model
B *f* model
in'dotto pp di **indurre**
indottri'nare *vt* indoctrinate
indovi'nare *vt* guess; (predire) foretell
indovi'nato *adj* successful; (scelta) well-chosen
indovi'nello *m* riddle
indo'vino, -a *mf* fortune-teller
indù *adj inv & mf inv* Hindu
indubbia'mente *adv* undoubtedly
in'dubbio *adj* undoubted
indubi'tabile *adj* indubitable
indubitabil'mente *adv* indubitably
indugi'are *vi* linger
indugi'arsi *vr* linger
in'dugio *m* delay
indu'ismo *m* Hinduism
indul'gente *adj* indulgent
indul'genza *f* indulgence
in'dulgere *vi* ~ **a** indulge in
in'dulto **A** pp di **indulgere**
B *m* Jur pardon
indu'mento *m* garment; **indumenti** *pl* clothes
■ **indumenti intimi** *pl* underwear
induri'mento *m* hardening
indu'rire *vt* harden
indu'rirsi *vr* harden
in'durre *vt* induce; ~ **qualcuno a fare** induce somebody to do; ~ **in tentazione** lead into temptation
in'dustria *f* industry
■ **industria dell'abbigliamento** clothing industry; infml rag trade; **industria leggera** light industry; **industria pesante** heavy industry; **industria dello spettacolo** show business, entertainment industry; infml showbiz; **industria terziaria** service industry; **industria tessile** textile industry, textiles
industri'ale **A** *adj* industrial; **zona ~** industrial estate
B *mf* industrialist
industrializ'zare *vt* industrialize
industrializ'zato *adj* industrialized
industrializzazi'one *f* industrialization
industrial'mente *adv* industrially
industri'arsi *vr* ~ **per guadagnare qualcosa** set to and earn some money
industriosa'mente *adv* industriously
industri'oso *adj* industrious
indut'tivo *adj* inductive
indut'tore *m* inductor
induzi'one *f* induction
inebe'tire *vt* daze
inebe'tito *adj* stunned
inebri'ante *adj* intoxicating, exciting
inebri'are *vt* intoxicate
inebri'arsi *vr* become inebriated
inecce'pibile *adj* unexceptionable
i'nedia *f* starvation
i'nedito *adj* unpublished
inedu'cato *adj* impolite
inef'fabile *adj* inexpressible
ineffi'cace *adj* ineffective
inefficì'ente *adj* inefficient
inefficì'enza *f* inefficiency
ineguagli'abile *adj* incomparable
ineguagli'anza *f* inequality
ineguagli'ato *adj* unequalled

i

inegu'ale *adj* unequal; ‹*superficie*› uneven
inelut'tabile *adj* inescapable
inenar'rabile *adj* indescribable
inequivo'cabile *adj* unequivocal
inequivocabil'mente *adv* unequivocally
ine'rente *adj* **~ a** inherent in
inerente'mente *adv* **~ a** concerning
i'nerme *adj* unarmed; fig defenceless
inerpi'carsi *vr* **~ su** clamber up
i'nerte *adj* inactive; Phys inert
i'nerzia *f* inactivity; Phys inertia
inesat'tezza *f* inaccuracy
ine'satto *adj* inaccurate; (erroneo) incorrect; (non riscosso) uncollected
inesau'ribile *adj* inexhaustible
inesi'stente *adj* non-existent
inesi'stenza *f* non-existence
ineso'rabile *adj* inexorable
inesorabil'mente *adv* inexorably
inesperi'enza *f* inexperience
ine'sperto *adj* inexperienced
inespli'cabile *adj* inexplicable
inesplicabil'mente *adv* inexplicably
inesplo'rato *adj* undiscovered
ine'sploso *adj* unexploded
inespres'sivo *adj* expressionless
inespri'mibile *adj* inexpressible
inespu'gnabile *adj* impregnable
ineste'tismo *m* blemish
inesti'mabile *adj* inestimable
inestin'guibile *adj* ‹*sete*› insatiable; ‹*odio*› undying
inestir'pabile *adj* impossible to eradicate
inestri'cabile *adj* inextricable
inestricabil'mente *adv* inextricably
inetti'tudine *f* ineptitude
i'netto *adj* inept; **~ a** unsuited to
ine'vaso *adj* ‹*pratiche, corrispondenza*› pending
inevi'tabile *adj* inevitable
inevitabil'mente *adv* inevitably
in ex'tremis *adv* ‹*segnare un gol*› in the nick of time; (prima di morire) in extremis
i'nezia *f* trifle
infagot'tare *vt* wrap up
infagot'tarsi *vr* wrap [oneself] up
infal'libile *adj* infallible
infa'mante *adj* defamatory
infa'mare *vt* defame
infama'torio *adj* defamatory
in'fame *adj* infamous; infml (orrendo) awful, shocking
in'famia *f* infamy
infan'gare *vt* cover with mud; fig sully
infan'garsi *vr* get muddy
infanti'cida *mf* infanticide
infanti'cidio *m* infanticide
infan'tile *adj* ‹*letteratura, abbigliamento*› children's *attrib*; ‹*ingenuità*› childlike; derog childish
🔑 **in'fanzia** *f* childhood; (bambini) children *pl*; **prima ~** infancy
infar'cire *vt* stuff (**di** with)
infari'nare *vt* flour; **~ di** sprinkle with
infarina'tura *f* fig smattering
in'farto *m* heart attack
infasti'dire *vt* irritate
infasti'dirsi *vr* get irritated
infati'cabile *adj* untiring
infaticabil'mente *adv* tirelessly
🔑 **in'fatti** *conj* as a matter of fact; (veramente) indeed
infatu'arsi *vr* **~ di** become infatuated with
infatu'ato *adj* infatuated
infatuazi'one *f* infatuation
in'fausto *adj* ill-omened
infecondità *f inv* infertility
infe'condo *adj* infertile
infe'dele *adj* unfaithful
infedeltà *f inv* unfaithfulness
🔑 **infe'lice** *adj* unhappy; (inappropriato) unfortunate; (cattivo) bad
infelicità *f inv* unhappiness
infel'trire *vi* matt
infel'trirsi *vr* matt
infel'trito *adj* matted
🔑 **inferi'ore** **A** *adj* (più basso) lower; ‹*qualità*› inferior
B *mf* inferior
inferiorità *f inv* inferiority
infe'rire *vt* infer; strike ‹*colpo*›
inferme'ria *f* infirmary; (di nave, scuola) sickbay
infermi'ere, -a **A** *m* [male] nurse
B *f* nurse
infermità *f inv* sickness
▪ **infermità mentale** mental illness
in'fermo, -a **A** *adj* sick
B *mf* invalid
infer'nale *adj* infernal; (spaventoso) hellish
🔑 **in'ferno** *m* hell; **va' all'~!** go to hell!
infero'cirsi *vr* become fierce
inferri'ata *f* grating
infervo'rare *vt* arouse enthusiasm in
infervo'rarsi *vr* get excited
infe'stare *vt* infest
infe'stato *adj* infested; **~ dai fantasmi** haunted
infestazi'one *f* infestation
infet'tare *vt* infect
infet'tarsi *vr* become infected
infet'tivo *adj* infectious
in'fetto *adj* infected
infezi'one *f* infection
infiac'chire *vt & vi* weaken

infiac'chirsi *vr* weaken
infiam'mabile *adj* [in]flammable
infiam'mare *vt* set on fire; Med fig inflame
infiam'marsi *vr* catch fire; Med become inflamed
infiammazi'one *f* Med inflammation
infia'scare *vt* bottle
infici'are *vt* Jur invalidate
in'fido *adj* treacherous
infie'rire *vi* (imperversare) rage; ~ **su** attack furiously
in'figgere *vt* drive
in'figgersi *vr* ~ **in** penetrate
infi'lare *vt* thread; (mettere) insert; (indossare) put on
infi'larsi *vr* slip on ‹*vestito*›; ~ **in** (introdursi) slip into
infil'trarsi *vr* infiltrate
infil'trato, -a *mf* infiltrator
infiltrazi'one *f* infiltration; (d'acqua) seepage; Med (iniezione) injection
infil'zare *vt* pierce; (infilare) string; (conficcare) stick
'infimo *adj* lowest
in'fine *adv* finally; (insomma) in short
infin'gardo *adj* slothful
infinità *f inv* infinity; **un'~ di** masses of
infinita'mente *adv* infinitely
infinitesi'male *adj* infinitesimal
infi'nito **A** *adj* infinite; Gram infinitive **B** *m* infinite; Gram infinitive; Math infinity; **all'~** endlessly
infinocchi'are *vt* infml hoodwink
infiocchet'tare *vt* tie up with ribbons
infiore'scenza *f* inflorescence
infischi'arsi *vr* ~ **di** not care about; **me ne infischio** infml I couldn't care less
in'fisso **A** pp di **infiggere** **B** *m* fixture; (di porta, finestra) frame
infit'tire *vt* & *vi* thicken
infit'tirsi *vr* thicken
inflazi'one *f* inflation
■ **inflazione galoppante** galloping inflation; **inflazione strisciante** creeping inflation
inflazio'nistico *adj* inflationary
infles'sibile *adj* inflexible
inflessibilità *f inv* inflexibility
inflessi'one *f* inflection, inflexion
in'fliggere *vt* inflict
in'flitto pp di **infliggere**
influ'ente *adj* influential
influ'enza *f* influence; Med influenza; **prendere l'~** catch the flu
■ **influenza A** swine flu; **influenza aviaria** *o* **dei polli** bird flu; **influenza gastrointestinale** gastric flu
influen'zabile *adj* ‹*mente, opinione*› impressionable
influen'zare *vt* influence
influen'zato *adj* **essere ~** (con febbre) have the flu
influ'ire *vi* ~ **su** influence
in'flusso *m* influence
info'carsi *vr* catch fire; ‹*viso*› go red; ‹*discussione*› become heated
info'gnarsi *vr* infml get into a mess
infol'tire *vt* & *vi* thicken
infon'dato *adj* unfounded
in'fondere *vt* instil
infor'care *vt* fork ‹*fieno*›; get on ‹*bici*›; put on ‹*occhiali*›
inforca'tura *f* crotch
infor'male *adj* informal
infor'mare *vt* inform
infor'marsi *vr* inquire (**di** about)
infor'matica *f* information technology
infor'matico *adj* computer *attrib*
informa'tivo *adj* informative
infor'mato *adj* informed; **male ~** ill-informed
informa|'tore, -trice *mf* (di polizia) informer
■ **informatore medico scientifico** representative of a pharmaceutical company
informazi'one *f* information; **un'~** a piece of information; **informazioni** *pl* information; **servizio informazioni** enquiries
■ **informazione genetica** genetic code; **informazione riservata** confidential information; **informazioni** *pl* **sbagliate** misinformation; **informazioni** *pl* **sulla viabilità** travel news
in'forme *adj* shapeless
infor'nare *vt* put into the oven
infortu'narsi *vr* have an accident
infortu'nato, -a **A** *adj* injured **B** *mf* injured person; **gli infortunati** the injured
infor'tunio *m* accident
■ **infortunio sul lavoro** industrial accident
infortu'nistica *f* study of industrial accidents
infos'sarsi *vr* sink; ‹*guance, occhi*› become hollow
infos'sato *adj* sunken, hollow
infradici'are *vt* drench
infradici'arsi *vr* get drenched; (diventare marcio) rot
infra'dito *mpl* (scarpe) flip-flops
in'frangere *vt* break; (in mille pezzi) shatter
in'frangersi *vr* break; (in mille pezzi) shatter
infran'gibile *adj* unbreakable
in'franto **A** pp di **infrangere** **B** *adj* shattered; fig ‹*cuore*› broken
infra'rosso *adj* infra-red
infrasettima'nale *adj* midweek
infrastrut'tura *f* infrastructure
infrazi'one *f* offence

i

■ **infrazione al codice della strada** traffic offence

infredda'tura *f* cold

infreddo'lirsi *vr* feel cold

infreddo'lito *adj* cold

infre'quente *adj* infrequent

infruttu'oso *adj* fruitless

infuo'care *vt* make red-hot

infuo'cato *adj* burning

infu'ori *adv* **all'~** outwards; **all'~ di** except; **denti ~** buck teeth

infuri'are *vi* rage

infuri'arsi *vr* fly into a rage

infuri'ato *adj* blustering

infusi'one *f* infusion

in'fuso **A** pp di **infondere**
B *m* infusion

Ing. *abbr* (**ingegnere**)

ingabbi'are *vt* cage; fig (mettere in prigione) jail

ingaggi'are *vt* engage; sign up ‹*calciatori ecc.*›; begin ‹*lotta, battaglia*›

in'gaggio *m* engagement; (di calciatore) signing [up]

ingan'nare *vt* deceive; (essere infedele a) be unfaithful to; **~ l'attesa** kill time

ingan'narsi *vr* deceive oneself; **se non m'inganno** if I am not mistaken

ingan'nevole *adj* deceptive

in'ganno *m* deceit; (frode) fraud; **trarre in ~** deceive

ingarbugli'are *vt* entangle; (confondere) confuse

ingarbugli'arsi *vr* get entangled; (confondersi) become confused

ingarbu'gliato *adj* confused

inge'gnarsi *vr* do one's best; **~ per vivere** try to scrape a living

🔑 **inge'gnere** *m* engineer
■ **ingegnere aeronautico** aeronautical engineer; **ingegnere civile** civil engineer; **ingegnere edile** structural engineer; **ingegnere meccanico** mechanical engineer; **ingegnere minerario** mining engineer; **ingegnere navale** marine engineer

ingegne'ria *f* engineering
■ **ingegneria aeronautica** aeronautical engineering; **ingegneria civile** civil engineering; **ingegneria edile** structural engineering; **ingegneria genetica** genetic engineering; **ingegneria meccanica** mechanical engineering

in'gegno *m* brains *pl*; (genio) genius; (abilità) ingenuity

ingegnosa'mente *adv* ingeniously

ingegnosità *f inv* ingenuity

inge'gnoso *adj* ingenious

ingelo'sire *vt* make jealous

ingelo'sirsi *vr* become jealous

in'gente *adj* huge

ingenua'mente *adv* artlessly

ingenuità *f inv* ingenuousness

in'genuo *adj* ingenuous; (credulone) naïve

inge'renza *f* interference

inge'rire *vt* swallow

inges'sare *vt* put in plaster

inges'sato *adj* in plaster, in a cast; fig (rigidamente formale) stilted, stiff

ingessa'tura *f* plaster, plaster cast

Inghil'terra *f* England

inghiot'tire *vt* swallow

in'ghippo *m* trick

ingial'lire *vi* turn yellow

ingial'lirsi *vr* turn yellow

ingial'lito *adj* yellowed

ingigan'tire **A** *vt* magnify; blow up out of proportion ‹*problema*›
B *vi* take on gigantic proportions

ingigan'tirsi *vr* take on gigantic proportions

inginocchi'arsi *vr* kneel [down]

inginocchi'ato *adj* kneeling

inginocchia'toio *m* prie-dieu

ingioiel'larsi *vr* put on one's jewels

ingioiel'lato *adj* bejewelled

ingiù *adv* down; **all'~** downwards; **a testa ~** head downwards

ingi'ungere *vt* order

ingiunzi'one *f* injunction, court order
■ **~ di pagamento** final demand

ingi'uria *f* insult; (torto) wrong; (danno) damage

ingiuri'are *vt* insult; (fare un torto a) wrong

ingiuri'oso *adj* insulting

ingiusta'mente *adv* unjustly

ingiustifi'cabile *adj* unjustifiable; ‹*comportamento*› indefensible

ingiustifi'cato *adj* unjustified

ingiu'stizia *f* injustice

ingi'usto *adj* unjust

🔑 **in'glese** **A** *adj* English
B *m* Englishman; (lingua) English; **gli inglesi** the English
C *f* Englishwoman

inglori'oso *adj* inglorious

ingob'bire *vi* become stooped

ingoi'are *vt* swallow

ingol'fare *vt* flood ‹*motore*›

ingol'farsi *vr* fig get involved; ‹*motore*› flood

ingol'lare *vt* gulp down

ingom'brante *adj* cumbersome

ingom'brare *vt* clutter up; fig cram ‹*mente*›

in'gombro *m* encumbrance; **essere d'~** be in the way

ingor'digia *f* greed

in'gordo *adj* greedy

ingor'gare *vt* block

ingor'garsi *vr* be blocked [up]

🔑 key word

in'gorgo *m* blockage; (del traffico) jam
ingoz'zare *vt* gobble up; (nutrire eccessivamente) stuff; fatten ‹*animali*›
ingoz'zarsi *vr* stuff oneself (**di** with)
ingra'naggio *m* gear; fig mechanism
ingra'nare **A** *vt* engage
B *vi* be in gear
ingrandi'mento *m* enlargement
ingran'dire *vt* enlarge; (esagerare) magnify
ingran'dirsi *vr* become larger; (aumentare) increase
ingrandi'tore *m* Phot enlarger
ingras'saggio *m* greasing, lubrication
ingras'sare **A** *vt* fatten [up]; Mech lubricate, grease
B *vi* put on weight
ingras'sarsi *vr* put on weight
in'grasso *m* **mettere all'~** force-feed
ingrati'tudine *f* ingratitude
in'grato *adj* ungrateful; (sgradevole) thankless
ingrazi'arsi *vr* ingratiate oneself with
ingredi'ente *m* ingredient
in'gresso *m* entrance; (accesso) admittance; (sala) hall; Comput input
■ **ingresso gratuito** *o* **libero** admission free; **'vietato l'~'** 'no entry', 'no admittance'; **ingresso degli artisti** stage door; **ingresso principale** main entrance; **ingresso di servizio** tradesmen's entrance; **ingresso/uscita** Comput input/output; **ingresso video** Techn video input
ingros'sare **A** *vt* make big; (gonfiare) swell
B *vi* grow big; (gonfiare) swell
ingros'sarsi *vr* grow big; (gonfiare) swell
in'grosso **all'~** *adv* wholesale; (pressappoco) roughly
inguai'arsi *vr* get into trouble
inguai'nare *vt* sheathe
ingual'cibile *adj* crease-resistant
ingua'ribile *adj* incurable
inguaribil'mente *adv* incurably
'inguine *m* groin
ingurgi'tare *vt* gulp down
ini'bire *vt* inhibit; (vietare) forbid
ini'bito *adj* inhibited
inibi'tore *m* suppressant
inibizi'one *f* inhibition; (divieto) prohibition
iniet'tare *vt* inject
iniet'tarsi *vr* **~ di sangue** ‹*occhi*› become bloodshot
iniezi'one *f* injection
■ **iniezione endovenosa** intravenous injection; **iniezione intramuscolare** intramuscular injection
inimic'arsi *vr* **~ qualcuno** make an enemy of somebody
inimi'cizia *f* enmity
inimi'tabile *adj* inimitable
inimmagi'nabile *adj* unimaginable
ininfiam'mabile *adj* non-flammable
inintelli'gibile *adj* unintelligible
ininterrotta'mente *adv* continuously
ininter'rotto *adj* continuous
iniquità *f inv* iniquity
i'niquo *adj* iniquitous
inizi'ale *adj & nf* initial
inizial'mente *adv* initially
inizi'are **A** *vt* begin; (avviare) open; **~ a fare qualcosa** begin doing something; **~ qualcuno a qualcosa** initiate somebody in something
B *vi* begin
inizia'tiva *f* initiative; **prendere l'~** take the initiative
■ **iniziativa privata** private enterprise
inizi'ato, -a *mf* initiated
inizia|'tore, -trice *mf* initiator
iniziazi'one *f* initiation
i'nizio *m* beginning, start; **dare ~ a** start; **avere ~** get under way
innaffi'are *vt* water
innaffia'toio *m* watering can
innal'zare *vt* raise; (erigere) erect
innal'zarsi *vr* rise
innamo'rarsi *vr* fall in love (**di** with)
innamo'rato, -a **A** *adj* in love
B *mf* sweetheart
in'nanzi **A** *adv* (stato in luogo) in front; (di tempo) ahead; (avanti) forward; (prima) before; **d'ora ~** from now on
B *prep* (prima) before; **~ a** in front of; **~ tutto** = **innanzitutto**
innanzi'tutto *adv* (soprattutto) above all; (per prima cosa) first of all
in'nato *adj* innate
innatu'rale *adj* unnatural
inne'gabile *adj* undeniable
innegabil'mente *adv* undeniably
inneggi'are *vi* **~ a** praise
innervo'sire *vt* make nervous
innervo'sirsi *vr* get irritated
inne'scare *vt* prime
in'nesco *m* primer
inne'stare *vt* graft; Mech engage; (inserire) insert
in'nesto *m* graft; Mech clutch; Electr connection
inneva'mento *m* snowfall
■ **innevamento artificiale** snow making
inne'vato *adj* covered in snow
'inno *m* hymn
■ **inno nazionale** national anthem
inno'cente *adj* innocent; Jur not guilty
innocente'mente *adv* innocently
inno'cenza *f* innocence
in'nocuo *adj* innocuous
inno'vare *vt* update
innova'tivo *adj* innovative

innova'tore *adj* trail-blazing
innovazi'one *f* innovation
innume'revole *adj* innumerable
+ino *suff* **fratellino** *nm* little brother; **sorellina** *nf* little sister; **freddino** *adj* (piuttosto freddo) chilly; **bellino** *adj* (abbastanza bello) pretty; **benino** *adv* (così così) not bad; **pochino** *adv* (troppo poco) not enough; **un pochino** a little bit
inocu'lare *vt* inoculate
ino'doro *adj* odourless
inoffen'sivo *adj* inoffensive, harmless; ‹*animale*› harmless
inol'trare *vt* forward
inol'trarsi *vr* advance
inol'trato *adj* late
🔑 **i'noltre** *adv* besides
i'noltro *m* forwarding
inon'dare *vt* flood
inondazi'one *f* flood
inope'roso *adj* idle
inopi'nabile *adj* unimaginable
inoppor'tuno *adj* untimely
inor'ganico *adj* inorganic
inorgo'glire *vt* make proud
inorgo'glirsi *vr* become proud
inorri'dire **A** *vt* horrify **B** *vi* be horrified
inospi'tale *adj* inhospitable
inosser'vato *adj* unobserved; (non rispettato) disregarded; **passare ~** go unnoticed
inossi'dabile *adj* stainless
'inox *adj inv* ‹*acciaio*› stainless; ‹*pentole*› stainless steel *attrib*
'input *m inv*
■ **input dati** data input
inqua'drare *vt* frame; fig set
inqua'drarsi *vr* **~ in** fit into
inquadra'tura *f* framing
inqualifi'cabile *adj* unspeakable
inquie'tante *adj* unnerving
inquie'tare *vt* worry
inquie'tarsi *vr* get worried; (impazientirsi) get cross
inqui'eto *adj* restless; (preoccupato) worried
inquie'tudine *f* anxiety
inqui'lino, -a *mf* tenant
inquina'mento *m* pollution
■ **inquinamento acustico** noise pollution; **inquinamento atmosferico** air pollution; **inquinamento luminoso** light pollution; **inquinamento delle prove** Jur tampering with the evidence
inqui'nare *vt* pollute
inqui'nato *adj* polluted
inqui'rente *adj* Jur ‹*magistrato*› examining; ‹*commissione*› of investigation
inqui'sire *vt & vi* investigate
inqui'sito **A** *adj* under investigation **B** *m* person under investigation
inquisi|'tore, -trice **A** *adj* inquiring **B** *mf* inquisitor
inquisi'torio *adj* questioning
inquisizi'one *f* inquisition
insabbi'are *vt* bury
insabbi'arsi *vr* run aground
insa'lata *f* salad
■ **insalata belga** Belgian endive; **insalata di mare** seafood salad; **insalata mista** mixed salad; **insalata di riso** rice salad; **insalata russa** Russian salad
insalati'era *f* salad bowl
insa'lubre *adj* unhealthy
insa'nabile *adj* incurable
insangui'nare *vt* stain with blood
insangui'nato *adj* blood-stained
insapo'nare *vt* soap
insapo'narsi *vr* soap oneself
insapo'nata *f* soaping
insa'pore *adj* tasteless
insapo'rire *vt* flavour
insa'puta *f* **all'~ di** unknown to
in'saturo *adj* unsaturated
insazi'abile *adj* insatiable
inscato'lare *vt* can
inscatola'trice *f* canning machine
insce'nare *vt* stage
inscin'dibile *adj* inseparable
in'scrivere *vt* Math inscribe
insec'chire *vt & vi* wither
insedia'mento *m* installation
insedi'are *vt* install
insedi'arsi *vr* install oneself
in'segna *f* sign; (bandiera) flag; (decorazione) decoration; (emblema) insignia *pl*; (stemma) symbol
■ **insegna luminosa** neon sign
insegna'mento *m* teaching
inse'gnante **A** *adj* teaching **B** *mf* teacher
■ **insegnante di matematica** maths teacher; **insegnante di sostegno** tutor; **insegnante tirocinante** student teacher
🔑 **inse'gnare** *vt & vi* teach; **~ qualcosa a qualcuno** teach somebody something
insegui'mento *m* pursuit
insegu'ire *vt* pursue
insegui|'tore, -trice *mf* pursuer
inselvati'chire **A** *vt* make wild **B** *vi* grow wild
inselvati'chirsi *vr* grow wild
insemi'nare *vt* inseminate
inseminazi'one *f* insemination
■ **inseminazione artificiale** artificial insemination
insena'tura *f* inlet
insensata'mente *adv* senselessly
insen'sato *adj* senseless; (folle) crazy

🔑 key word

insen'sibile *adj* fig insensitive; **avere le gambe insensibili** have no feeling in one's legs
insensibilità *f inv* lack of feeling; fig insensitivity
insepa'rabile *adj* inseparable
inseri'mento *m* insertion
inse'rire *vt* insert, place ‹*annuncio*›; Electr connect
inse'rirsi *vr* ~ **in** get into
inseri'tore *m*
■ **inseritore fogli (singoli)** (single) sheet feed
in'serto *m* file; (in un giornale) supplement; (in un film ecc.) insert
inservi'ente *mf* attendant
inserzi'one *f* insertion; (avviso) advertisement; **inserzioni** *pl* classified ads
inserzio'nista *mf* advertiser
insetti'cida *m* insecticide
insetti'fugo *m* insect repellent
in'setto *m* insect
insicu'rezza *f* insecurity
insi'curo *adj* insecure
in'sidia *f* trick; (tranello) snare
insidi'are *vt & vi* lay a trap for
insidi'oso *adj* insidious
insi'eme **A** *adv* together; (contemporaneamente) at the same time **B** *prep* ~ **a** [together] with **C** *m* whole; (completo) outfit; Theat ensemble; Math set; **nell'~** as a whole; **tutto ~** (in una volta) at one go
insie'mistica *f* set theory
in'signe *adj* renowned
insignifi'cante *adj* insignificant
insi'gnire *vt* decorate
insin'cero *adj* insincere
insinda'cabile *adj* final
insinu'ante *adj* insinuating
insinu'are *vt* insinuate
insinu'arsi *vr* penetrate; ~ **in** fig creep into
insinuazi'one *f* insinuation
in'sipido *adj* insipid
insi'stente *adj* insistent
insistente'mente *adv* repeatedly
insi'stenza *f* insistence
in'sistere *vi* insist; (perseverare) persevere
'insito *adj* inherent
insoddisfa'cente *adj* unsatisfactory
insoddi'sfatto *adj* unsatisfied; (scontento) dissatisfied
insoddisfazi'one *f* dissatisfaction
insoffe'rente *adj* intolerant
insoffe'renza *f* intolerance
insolazi'one *f* sunstroke
inso'lente *adj* rude, insolent
insolente'mente *adv* insolently
inso'lenza *f* rudeness, insolence; (commento) insolent remark
insolita'mente *adv* unusually
in'solito *adj* unusual
inso'lubile *adj* insoluble
inso'luto *adj* unsolved; (non pagato) unpaid
insol'vente *adj* Jur insolvent
insol'venza *f* insolvency
insol'vibile *adj* insolvent
in'somma *adv* in short; ~! well!
inson'dabile *adj* unfathomable
in'sonne *adj* sleepless
in'sonnia *f* insomnia
insonno'lito *adj* sleepy
insonoriz'zare *vt* soundproof
insonoriz'zato *adj* soundproofed
insoppor'tabile *adj* unbearable
insoppri'mibile *adj* unsuppressible
insor'genza *f* onset
in'sorgere *vi* revolt, rise up; ‹*problema*› arise
insormon'tabile *adj* ‹*ostacolo, difficoltà*› insurmountable
in'sorto **A** pp di **insorgere** **B** *adj* rebellious **C** *m* rebel
insospet'tabile *adj* unsuspected
insospet'tire **A** *vt* make suspicious **B** *vi* become suspicious
insospet'tirsi *vr* becomes suspicious
insoste'nibile *adj* untenable; (insopportabile) unbearable
insostitu'ibile *adj* irreplaceable
insoz'zare *vt* dirty
inspe'rabile *adj* hopeless; (insperato) unhoped-for
inspe'rato *adj* unhoped-for
inspie'gabile *adj* inexplicable
inspiegabil'mente *adv* inexplicably
inspi'rare *vt* breathe in
in'stabile *adj* unstable; (variabile) unsettled
instabilità *f inv* instability; (di tempo) changeability
instal'lare *vt* install
instal'larsi *vr* (in casa, lavoro) settle in
installa|'tore, -trice *mf* fitter
installazi'one *f* installation; **installazioni** *pl* **di bordo** on-board equipment
instan'cabile *adj* untiring
instancabil'mente *adv* tirelessly
instau'rare *vt* found
instau'rarsi *vr* become established
instaurazi'one *f* foundation
instra'dare *vt* direct
insù **all'~** *adv* upwards; **naso all'~** turned-up nose
insubordi'nato *adj* insubordinate
insubordinazi'one *f* insubordination
insuc'cesso *m* failure
insudici'are *vt* dirty

insudici'arsi *vr* get dirty
insuffici'ente **A** *adj* insufficient; (inadeguato) inadequate
B *m* Sch fail
insufficiente'mente *adv* insufficiently
insuffici'enza *f* insufficiency; (inadeguatezza) inadequacy; Sch fail
■ **insufficienza cardiaca** cardiac insufficiency; **insufficienza di prove** lack of evidence
insu'lare *adj* insular
insu'lina *f* insulin
in'sulso *adj* insipid; (sciocco) silly
insul'tare *vt* insult
in'sulto *m* insult; **coprire qualcuno di insulti** heap abuse on somebody
insupe'rabile *adj* insuperable; (eccezionale) incomparable
insurrezi'one *f* insurrection
insussi'stente *adj* groundless
intac'cabile *adj* subject to corrosion; fig open to criticism
intac'care *vt* nick; (corrodere) corrode; draw on ‹*capitale*›; (danneggiare) damage
intagli'are *vt* carve
in'taglio *m* carving
intan'gibile *adj* untouchable
⚷ **in'tanto** *adv* meanwhile; (per ora) for the moment; (avversativo) but; **~ che** while
intarsi'are *vt* inlay
intarsi'ato *adj* **~ di** inset with
in'tarsio *m* inlay
intasa'mento *m* (ostruzione) blockage; (ingorgo) traffic jam
inta'sare *vt* block, clog
inta'sarsi *vr* become blocked
inta'sato *adj* blocked
inta'scare *vt* pocket
in'tatto *adj* intact
intavo'lare *vt* start
inte'gerrimo *adj* of integrity
inte'grale *adj* whole; **edizione ~** unabridged edition; **pane ~** wholemeal bread; **versione ~** (di film) uncut version; (di romanzo) unabridged version
integra'lista *mf* fundamentalist
integral'mente *adv* fully
inte'grante *adj* integral
inte'grare *vt* integrate; (aggiungere) supplement
inte'grarsi *vr* integrate
integra'tivo *adj* supplementary, additional; **esame ~** *test taken by pupil wishing to transfer from arts to a scientific stream etc*
integra'tore *m*
■ **integratore alimentare** dietary supplement
integrazi'one *f* integration

⚷ key word

integrità *f inv* integrity
'integro *adj* complete; (retto) upright
intelaia'tura *f* framework
intellet'tivo *adj* intellectual
intel'letto *m* intellect
intellettu'ale *adj & nmf* intellectual
intellettual'mente *adv* intellectually
⚷ **intelli'gente** *adj* intelligent
intelligente'mente *adv* intelligently
⚷ **intelli'genza** *f* intelligence
■ **intelligenza artificiale** artificial intelligence
intelli'ghenzia *f* intelligentsia
intelli'gibile *adj* intelligible
intelligibil'mente *adv* intelligibly
intempe'rante *adj* intemperate
intempe'ranza *f* intemperance; **intemperanze** *pl* excesses
intem'perie *fpl* bad weather
intempe'stivo *adj* untimely
inten'dente *m* superintendent
inten'denza *f*
■ **intendenza di finanza** inland revenue office
⚷ **in'tendere** *vt* (comprendere) understand; (udire) hear; (avere intenzione) intend; (significare) mean; **[siamo] intesi?** is that clear?
in'tendersi *vr* (capirsi) understand each other; **~ di** (essere esperto in) have a good knowledge of; **intendersela con** infml (avere una relazione con) have it off with
intendi'mento *m* understanding; (intenzione) intention
intendi|'tore, -trice *mf* connoisseur; **intenditori** *pl* cognoscenti
intene'rire *vt* soften; (commuovere) touch
intene'rirsi *vr* be touched
intensa'mente *adv* intensely
intensifi'care *vt* intensify
intensifi'carsi *vr* intensify
intensità *f inv* intensity
intensiva'mente *adv* intensively
inten'sivo *adj* intensive
■ **terapia intensiva** intensive care
in'tenso *adj* intense
inten'tare *vt* start up; **~ causa contro qualcuno** bring *or* institute proceedings against somebody
inten'tato *adj* **non lasciare nulla di ~** try everything
in'tento **A** *adj* engrossed (**a** in)
B *m* purpose
intenzio'nale *adj* intentional
intenzio'nato *adj* **essere ~ a fare qualcosa** have the intention of doing something
⚷ **intenzi'one** *f* intention; **senza ~** unintentionally; **avere ~ di fare qualcosa** intend to do something, have the intention of doing something
intera'gire *vi* interact

intera'mente *adv* completely, entirely
interat'tivo *adj* interactive
interazi'one *f* interaction
interca'lare **A** *m* stock phrase
B *vt* insert ‹*esclamazione*›
intercambi'abile *adj* interchangeable
interca'pedine *f* cavity
inter'cedere *vi* intercede
intercessi'one *f* intercession
intercet'tare *vt* intercept; tap ‹*telefono*›
intercettazi'one *f* interception
■ **intercettazione telefonica** telephone tapping
inter'city *m inv* inter-city
intercomuni'cante *adj* [inter] communicating
interconfessio'nale *adj* interdenominational
intercon'nettere *vt* interconnect
intercontinen'tale *adj* intercontinental
inter'correre *vi* ‹*tempo*› elapse; (esistere) exist
interco'stale *adj* intercostal
interden'tale *adj* between the teeth; **filo** ~ dental floss
inter'detto **A** pp di **interdire**
B *adj* astonished; (proibito) forbidden; **rimanere** ~ be taken aback; **lasciare qualcuno** ~ astonish somebody, dumbfound somebody
C *m* Relig interdict
interdipartimen'tale *adj* interdepartmental
interdipen'dente *adj* interdependent
interdipen'denza *f* interdependence
inter'dire *vt* ban; (nel calcio) intercept; Jur deprive of civil rights; Relig interdict; ~ **a qualcuno di fare qualcosa** forbid somebody to do something
interdiscipli'nare *adj* interdisciplinary
interdizi'one *f* ban; (nel calcio) interception; Relig interdict
■ **interdizione giudiziale** *appointment of a legal guardian to a person of unsound mind*; **interdizione legale** *legally imposed ban*; **interdizione dai pubblici uffici** *ban on taking public office*
interessa'mento *m* interest
interes'sante *adj* interesting; **essere in stato** ~ be pregnant
interes'sare **A** *vt* interest; (riguardare) concern
B *vi* ~ **a** interest; **non mi interessa** I'm not interested; (non mi importa) I don't care, it doesn't matter to me
interes'sarsi *vr* ~ **a** take an interest in; ~ **di** take care of
interes'sato *adj* (attento) interested; derog self-interested; **diretto** ~ person concerned
inte'resse *m* interest; **fare qualcosa per** ~ do something out of self-interest; **essere nell'**~ **di qualcuno** be in somebody's interest; **un** ~ **del 4%** 4% interest
■ **interesse attivo** interest charge; **interesse maturato** accrued interest; **interesse privato in atti di ufficio** abuse of public office; **interesse a tasso variabile** floating rate interest
interes'senza *f* Econ profit-sharing
inter'faccia *f* interface
■ **interfaccia grafica** graphics interface; **interfaccia uomo/macchina** man/machine interface; **interfaccia utente** user interface
interfacci'are *vt* interface
interfacci'arsi *vr* interface
interfe'renza *f* interference
interfe'rire *vi* interfere
inter'fono *m* intercom
interga'lattico *adj* intergalactic
interiet'tivo *adj* interjectory
interiezi'one *f* interjection
'interim *m inv* (incarico) temporary appointment; (periodo) interim; **ad** ~ on a temporary basis; ‹*presidente*› acting
interi'ora *fpl* entrails
interi'ore *adj* inner
interioriz'zare *vt* internalize
interior'mente *adv* (nella parte interiore) internally; (emotivamente) inwardly
inter'linea *f* line spacing; Typ leading
■ **interlinea doppia** double spacing
interline'are **A** *vt* space out
B *adj* line *attrib*
interlocu|'tore, -trice *mf* speaker, interlocutor fml; **il mio** ~ the person I am/was speaking to
inter'ludio *m* interlude
intermedi'ario, -a *adj & nmf* intermediary; Econ middleman
intermediazi'one *f* (intervento) mediation
inter'medio *adj* in-between
inter'mezzo *m* Theat, Mus intermezzo
intermi'nabile *adj* interminable
interministeri'ale *adj* interdepartmental
intermissi'one *f* intermission
intermit'tente *adj* intermittent; ‹*vulcano*› dormant
intermit'tenza *f* **a** ~ intermittent
interna'mente *adv* internally
interna'mento *m* internment; (in manicomio) committal
inter'nare *vt* intern; (in manicomio) commit [to a mental institution]
inter'nato, -a **A** *adj* interned
B *mf* internee
C *m* boarding school
internazio'nale *adj* international
internazional'mente *adv* internationally
'Internet *f* Internet; **in** ~ on the Internet; **via** ~ through the Internet
■ **Internet point** Internet kiosk
inter'nista *mf* internist

✓ **in'terno** **A** *adj* internal; Geog inland; (interiore) inner; ‹*politica*› national; **alunno ~** boarder
B *m* interior; (di condominio) flat; Teleph extension; Cinema interior shot; **all'~** inside; **ministero degli interni** Ministry of the Interior, ≈ Home Office

✓ **in'tero** **A** *adj* whole, entire; Math whole; (intatto) intact; (completo) complete; **per ~** in full
B *m* (totalità) whole

interparlamen'tare *adj* inter-parliamentary

interpar'titico *adj* cross-party

interpel'lanza *f* parliamentary question

interpel'lare *vt* consult

interpel'lato, -a *mf* person being questioned

interperso'nale *adj* interpersonal

i

interplane'tario *adj* interplanetary

interpo'lare *vt* interpolate

inter'porre *vt* interpose; use ‹*influenza*›; **~ ostacoli a** put obstacles in the way of

inter'porsi *vr* intervene; **~ tra** come between

inter'posto *adj* **per interposta persona** through a third party

interpre'tare *vt* interpret; Mus perform; **~ male** misinterpret

interpretari'ato *m* interpreting

interpretazi'one *f* interpretation; Mus performance

in'terprete *mf* interpreter; Mus performer

interpunzi'one *f* punctuation

inter'rare *vt* (seppellire) bury; (riempire) fill in; lay underground ‹*cavo, tubo*›; plant ‹*pianta, seme*›

inter'rato *m* basement

interregio'nale *m* *long-distance train, stopping at most stations*

interro'gante *mf* questioner

interro'gare *vt* question; Sch examine

interrogativa'mente *adv* ‹*guardare*› inquiringly

interroga'tivo **A** *adj* interrogative; (sguardo) questioning; **punto ~** question mark
B *m* question

interro'gato *adj* ‹*studente*› examinee; Jur person questioned

interroga'torio *adj & nm* questioning

interrogazi'one *f* question; Sch oral [test]
■ **interrogazione ciclica** polling; **interrogazione parlamentare** parliamentary question

✓ **inter'rompere** *vt* interrupt; (sospendere) stop; cut off ‹*collegamento*›

inter'rompersi *vr* break off

interrut'tore *m* switch
■ **interruttore a reostato** dimmer

✓ key word

interruzi'one *f* interruption; **senza ~** non-stop
■ **interruzione della corrente** power cut; **interruzione di gravidanza** termination of pregnancy

interscambi'abile *adj* interchangeable

inter'scambio *m* import-export trade

interse'care *vt* intersect

interse'carsi *vr* intersect

intersezi'one *f* intersection

inter'stizio *m* interstice

interur'bana *f* long-distance call

interur'bano *adj* inter-city; **telefonata interurbana** long-distance call

interval'lare *vt* space out

inter'vallo *m* interval; (spazio) space; (in ufficio) tea/coffee break; TV, Sch break; **fare un ~** have a break; **a intervalli regolari** at regular intervals
■ **intervallo del pranzo** lunch hour, lunch break; **intervallo pubblicitario** commercial break

✓ **interve'nire** *vi* intervene; Med (operare) operate; **~ a** take part in

inter'vento *m* intervention; (presenza) presence; (chirurgico) operation; **pronto ~** emergency services; **un ~ a cuore aperto** open-heart surgery

inter'vista *f* interview
■ **intervista esclusiva** exclusive interview

intervi'stare *vt* interview

intervi'stato, -a *mf* interviewee

intervista|'tore, -trice *mf* interviewer

in'tesa *f* understanding; **d'~** ‹*cenno*› of acknowledgement

in'teso, -a **A** pp di **intendere**
B *adj* **resta ~ che ...** needless to say, ...; **~ a** meant to; **[siamo] intesi!** agreed!
C *f* understanding

in'tessere *vt* weave together

inte'stare *vt* head; write one's name and address at the top of ‹*lettera*›; Comm register

inte'starsi *vr* **~ a fare qualcosa** take it into one's head to do something

intesta'tario, -a *mf* holder

intestazi'one *f* heading; (su carta da lettere) letterhead

intesti'nale *adj* intestinal

inte'stino **A** *adj* ‹*lotte*› internal
B *m* intestine
■ **intestino crasso** large intestine; **intestino tenue** small intestine

intiepi'dire *vt* (scaldare) warm; cool ‹*passione, desiderio*›

intiepi'dirsi *vr* cool [down]; (scaldarsi) warm [up]; ‹*fede*› wane

intima'mente *adv* ‹*conoscere*› intimately

inti'mare *vt* order; **~ l'alt** give the order to halt; **~ l'alt a qualcuno** order somebody to stop

intimazi'one *f* order
▪ **intimazione di sfratto** eviction notice
intimida'torio *adj* threatening, intimidating
intimidazi'one *f* intimidation
intimi'dire *vt* intimidate
intimi'dirsi *vr* be overwhelmed with shyness
intimità *f inv* intimacy, togetherness
'intimo **A** *adj* intimate; (interno) innermost; ‹*amico*› close
B *m* (amico) close friend; (dell'animo) heart
intimo'rire *vt* frighten
intimo'rirsi *vr* get frightened
intimo'rito *adj* frightened
in'tingere *vt* dip
in'tingolo *m* sauce; (pietanza) stew
intiriz'zire *vt* numb
intiriz'zirsi *vr* grow numb
intiriz'zito *adj* **essere ~** (dal freddo) be perished
intito'lare *vt* entitle; (dedicare) dedicate
intito'larsi *vr* be called
intolle'rabile *adj* intolerable
intolle'rante *adj* intolerant
intona'care *vt* plaster
intonaca'tore *m* plasterer
in'tonaco *m* plaster
▪ **intonaco a pinocchino** pebble-dash
into'nare *vt* start to sing; tune ‹*strumento*›; (accordare) match ‹*colori*›
into'narsi *vr* match
into'nato *adj* ‹*persona*› able to sing in tune; ‹*voce, strumento*› in tune; ‹*colore*› matching
intonazi'one *f* (inflessione) intonation; ‹*ironica*› tone; (cantando) ability to sing in tune
in'tonso *adj* ‹*libro*› untouched
inton'tire **A** *vt* ‹*botta*› stun, daze; ‹*gas*› make dizzy; fig stun
B *vi* go gaga
inton'tito *adj* dazed; fig stunned; ‹*con l'età*› gaga
intop'pare *vi* **~ in** run into
in'toppo *m* **c'è un ~** something's come up
in'torno **A** *adv* around
B *prep* **~ a** around; (circa) about; **~ al mondo** round-the-world
intorpi'dire *vt* numb
intorpi'dirsi *vr* become numb
intorpi'dito *adj* torpid
intossi'care *vt* poison
intossi'carsi *vr* be poisoned
intossicazi'one *f* poisoning
▪ **intossicazione alimentare** food poisoning
intra-azien'dale *adj* in-house
intradu'cibile *adj* untranslatable
intralci'are *vt* hamper
in'tralcio *m* hitch; **essere d'~ (a qualcuno/qualcosa)** be a hindrance (to somebody/something)
intrallaz'zare *vi* intrigue
intral'lazzo *m* racket
intramon'tabile *adj* timeless
intramusco'lare *adj* intramuscular
'intranet *f inv* intranet
intransi'gente *adj* intransigent, uncompromising
intransi'genza *f* intransigence
intransi'tivo *adj* intransitive
intrappolato *adj* **rimanere ~** be trapped
intrapren'dente *adj* enterprising
intrapren'denza *f* initiative
intra'prendere *vt* undertake
intrat'tabile *adj* very difficult
intratte'nere *vt* entertain
intratte'nersi *vr* linger
intratteni'mento *m* entertainment
intrave'dere *vt* catch a glimpse of; (presagire) foresee
intrecci'are *vt* interweave; plait ‹*capelli, corda*›; **~ le mani** clasp one's hands
intrecci'arsi *vr* intertwine; (aggrovigliarsi) become tangled
in'treccio *m* (trama) plot; (di nastri, strade) tangle
in'trepido *adj* intrepid
intri'cato *adj* tangled
intri'gante **A** *adj* intriguing
B *mf* schemer
intri'gare **A** *vt* entangle; (incuriosire) intrigue
B *vi* be intriguing
intri'garsi *vr* become entangled; (immischiarsi) meddle
in'trigo *m* plot; **intrighi** *pl* plotting; (di corte) intrigues
intrinseca'mente *adv* intrinsically
in'trinseco *adj* intrinsic
in'triso *adj* **~ di** soaked with; fig imbued with
intri'stire *vt* sadden
intri'stirsi *vr* grow sad
intro'durre *vt* introduce; (inserire) insert; **~ a** (iniziare a) introduce to
intro'dursi *vr* get in; **~ in** get into
introdut'tivo *adj* ‹*pagine, discorso*› introductory
introduzi'one *f* introduction
in'troito *m* income, revenue; (incasso) takings *pl*
intro'mettere *vt* introduce
intro'mettersi *vr* interfere; (interporsi) intervene
intromissi'one *f* intervention
introspet'tivo *adj* introspective
intro'vabile *adj* unobtainable

intro'verso, -a **A** *adj* introverted
B *mf* introvert
intrufo'larsi *vr* sneak in
in'truglio *m* concoction
intrusi'one *f* intrusion
in'truso, -a *mf* intruder
intu'ibile *adj* deducible
intu'ire *vt* perceive
intuitiva'mente *adv* intuitively
intui'tivo *adj* intuitive
in'tuito *m* intuition
intuizi'one *f* intuition
inu'mano *adj* inhuman
inu'mare *vt* inter
inumi'dire *vt* dampen; moisten ‹*labbra*›
inumi'dirsi *vr* become damp
i'nutile *adj* useless; (superfluo) unnecessary
inutilità *f inv* uselessness
inutiliz'zabile *adj* unusable
inutiliz'zato *adj* unused
inutil'mente *adv* fruitlessly
inva'dente *adj* intrusive
in'vadere *vt* invade; (affollare) overrun
inva'ghirsi *vr* ~ **di** take a fancy to
invali'cabile *adj* impassable; **'limite ~'** Mil 'no access beyond this point'
invali'dare *vt* invalidate
invalidità *f inv* disability; Jur invalidity
in'valido, -a **A** *adj* invalid; (handicappato) disabled
B *mf* disabled person; **gli invalidi** the disabled
■ **invalido di guerra** disabled ex-serviceman; **invalido del lavoro** industrial accident victim
in'vano *adv* in vain
invari'abile *adj* invariable
invariabil'mente *adv* invariably
invari'ato *adj* unchanged
invasi'one *f* invasion
in'vaso pp di **invadere**
inva'sore **A** *adj* invading
B *m* invader
invecchia'mento *m* (di vino) maturation
invecchi'are *vt & vi* age
in'vece *adv* instead; (anzi) but; ~ **di** instead of
inve'ire *vi* ~ **contro** inveigh against
invele'nito *adj* embittered
inven'dibile *adj* unsaleable
inven'duto *adj* unsold
inven'tare *vt* invent
inventari'are *vt* make an inventory of
inven'tario *m* inventory
inven'tato *adj* made-up
inven'tiva *f* inventiveness
inven'tivo *adj* inventive
inven|'tore, -trice *mf* inventor

key word

invenzi'one *f* invention
inver'nale *adj* wintry; **sport** *pl* **invernali** winter sports
in'verno *m* winter
invero'simile *adj* improbable
inverosimil'mente *adv* incredibly
inversa'mente *adv* inversely; ~ **proporzionale** in inverse proportion
inversi'one *f* inversion; Mech reversal; **fare un'~ a U** do a U-turn
■ **inversione di fondo** Comput reverse video; **inversione di tendenza** turnaround
in'verso **A** *adj* inverse; (opposto) opposite
B *m* opposite
inverte'brato *adj & nm* invertebrate
inver'tire *vt* reverse; (capovolgere) turn upside-down
inver'tito, -a *mf* homosexual
investi'gare *vt* investigate
investiga|'tore, -trice *mf* investigator
■ **investigatore privato** private investigator, private eye
investigazi'one *f* investigation
investi'mento *m* investment; (incidente) crash
inve'stire *vt* invest; (urtare) collide with; (travolgere) run over; ~ **qualcuno di** invest somebody with
investi'tura *f* investiture
invete'rato *adj* inveterate
invet'tiva *f* invective
invi'are *vt* send
invi'ato, -a *mf* envoy; (di giornale) correspondent
■ **inviato di pace** peace envoy
in'vidia *f* envy
invidi'are *vt* envy
invidi'oso *adj* envious
invigo'rire *vt* invigorate
invigo'rirsi *vr* become strong
invin'cibile *adj* invincible
in'vio *m* dispatch; Comput enter
invio'labile *adj* inviolable
invipe'rirsi *vr* get nasty
invipe'rito *adj* furious
invischi'arsi *vr* get involved (**in** in)
invi'sibile *adj* invisible
invisibilità *f* invisibility
invi'tante *adj* ‹*piatto, profumo*› enticing
invi'tare *vt* invite
invi'tato, -a *mf* guest
in'vito *m* invitation
invo'care *vt* invoke; (implorare) beg
invocazi'one *f* invocation
invogli'are *vt* tempt; (indurre) induce
invogli'arsi *vr* ~ **di** take a fancy to
involga'rire *vt* vulgarize
involontaria'mente *adv* involuntarily
involon'tario *adj* involuntary

invol'tini *mpl* stuffed rolls (*of meat, pastry*)
in'volto *m* parcel; (fagotto) bundle
in'volucro *m* wrapping
invo'luto *adj* involved
invulne'rabile *adj* invulnerable
inzacche'rare *vt* splash with mud
inzup'pare *vt* soak; (intingere) dip
inzup'parsi *vr* get soaked
'io **A** *pers pron* I; **sono io** it's me; **l'ho fatto io [stesso]** I did it myself
B *m* **l'io** the ego
i'odio *m* iodine
i'one *m* ion
i'onico *adj* Ionic
I'onio *m* **lo ~** the Ionian [Sea]
iono'sfera *f* ionosphere
i'osa a ~ *adv* in abundance
iperattività *f inv* hyperactivity
iperat'tivo *adj* hyperactive
i'perbole *f* hyperbole
iper'critico *adj* hypercritical
ipermer'cato *m* hypermarket
iper'metrope *adj* long-sighted
ipersen'sibile *adj* hypersensitive
ipertensi'one *f* high blood pressure
iper'testo *m* Comput hypertext
iperte'stuale *adj*
■ **collegamento ipertestuale** hyperlink
iperventi'lare *vi* hyperventilate
ip'nosi *f* hypnosis
ipnotera'pia *f* hypnotherapy
ip'notico *adj* hypnotic
ipno'tismo *m* hypnotism
ipnotiz'zare *vt* hypnotize
ipoaller'genico *adj* hypoallergenic
ipoca'lorico *adj* low calorie
ipo'centro *m* focus
ipocon'dria *f* hypochondria
ipocon'driaco, -a *adj & nmf* hypochondriac
ipocri'sia *f* hypocrisy
i'pocrita **A** *adj* hypocritical
B *mf* hypocrite
ipocrita'mente *adv* hypocritically
ipo'dermico *adj* hypodermic
i'pofisi *f inv* pituitary gland
ipo'teca *f* mortgage
ipote'cabile *adj* mortgageable
ipote'care *vt* mortgage
ipote'cario *adj* mortgage *attrib*
ipote'nusa *f* hypotenuse
ipo'termia *f* hypothermia
i'potesi *f inv* hypothesis; (caso, eventualità) eventuality; **nella migliore delle ~** at best; **nella peggiore delle ~** if the worst comes to the worst
ipo'tetico *adj* hypothetical
ipotiz'zare *vt* hypothesize

'ippico, -a **A** *adj* horse *attrib*
B *f* riding
ippoca'stano *m* horse chestnut
ip'podromo *m* racecourse
ippo'potamo *m* hippopotamus
'ipsilon *f inv* [the letter] y
'ira *f* anger
ira'scibile *adj* irascible
i'rato *adj* irate
'iride *f* Anat iris; (arcobaleno) rainbow
'iris *m inv* Bot iris
Ir'landa *f* Ireland
■ **Irlanda del Nord** Northern Ireland
irlan'dese **A** *adj* Irish
B *m* Irishman; (lingua) Irish
C *f* Irishwoman
iro'nia *f* irony
i'ronico *adj* ironic[al]
irradi'are *vt & vi* radiate
irradiazi'one *f* radiation
irraggiun'gibile *adj* unattainable
irragio'nevole *adj* unreasonable; ‹*speranza, timore*› irrational; (assurdo) absurd
irranci'dire *vi* go rancid
irrazio'nale *adj* irrational
irrazionalità *adj* irrationality
irrazional'mente *adv* irrationally
irre'ale *adj* unreal
irrea'listico *adj* unrealistic
irrealiz'zabile *adj* unattainable
irrealtà *f inv* unreality
irrecupe'rabile *adj* irrecoverable
irrecu'sabile *adj* incontrovertible
irredi'mibile *adj* irredeemable
irrefre'nabile *adj* uncontrollable
irrefu'tabile *adj* irrefutable
irrego'lare *adj* irregular
irregolarità *f inv* irregularity; (di terreno) unevenness; Sport foul
irregolar'mente *adv* ‹*frequentare*› irregularly; ‹*comportarsi*› erratically; ‹*disporre*› unevenly
irremo'vibile *adj* fig adamant
irrepa'rabile *adj* irreparable
irrepe'ribile *adj* ‹*persona*› not to be found; **sarò ~** I'm not going to be contactable
irrepren'sibile *adj* irreproachable
irrepri'mibile *adj* irrepressible
irrequi'eto *adj* restless
irresi'stibile *adj* irresistible
irresistibil'mente *adv* irresistibly
irreso'luto *adj* irresolute
irrespon'sabile *adj* irresponsible
irresponsabilità *f inv* irresponsibility
irrestrin'gibile *adj* pre-shrunk
irre'tire *vt* seduce
irrever'sibile *adj* irreversible

irreversibil'mente *adv* irrevocably
irrevo'cabile *adj* irrevocable
irrevocabil'mente *adv* irreversibly
irricono'scibile *adj* unrecognizable
irridu'cibile *adj* irreducible
irri'gare *vt* irrigate; ‹*fiume*› flow through
✓ **irrigazi'one** *f* irrigation
irrigidi'mento *m* (di muscoli) stiffening; (di disciplina) tightening
irrigi'dire *vt* stiffen up
irrigi'dirsi *vr* stiffen up
irrile'vante *adj* unimportant
irrimedi'abile *adj* irreparable
irrimediabil'mente *adv* irreparably
irripe'tibile *adj* unrepeatable
irri'solto *adj* unresolved
irri'sorio *adj* derisive; (insignificante) derisory
irri'tabile *adj* irritable
irri'tante *adj* aggravating, annoying
irri'tare *vt* irritate, annoy
irri'tarsi *vr* get annoyed
irri'tato *adj* irritated, annoyed; ‹*gola*› sore
irritazi'one *f* irritation
irrive'renza *f* (qualità) irreverence; (azione) irreverent action
irrobu'stire *vt* fortify
irrobu'stirsi *vr* get stronger
ir'rompere *vi* burst (**in** into)
irro'rare *vt* sprinkle
irrorazi'one *f* (di piante) crop spraying
irru'ente *adj* impetuous
irruvi'dire *vt* roughen
irruvi'dirsi *vr* become rough
irruzi'one *f* raid; fig eruption; **fare ~ in** burst into
ir'suto *adj* shaggy
'irto *adj* bristly
i'scritto, -a **A** pp di **iscrivere**
B *adj* registered
C *mf* member; **per ~** in writing
✓ **i'scrivere** *vt* register
i'scriversi *vr* **~ a** register at, enrol at ‹*scuola*›; join ‹*circolo ecc.*›
iscrizi'one *f* registration; (epigrafe) inscription
i'slamico *adj* Islamic
isla'mismo *m* Islam
isla'mista *mf* Islamist
I'slanda *f* Iceland
islan'dese **A** *adj* Icelandic
B *mf* Icelander
'ismi *mpl* isms
i'sobara *f* isobar
✓ **'isola** *f* island; **le isole britanniche** the British Isles; **l'~ di Man** Isle of Man
■ **isola deserta** desert island; **isola ecologica** recycling centre; **isola pedonale** traffic island; **isola spartitraffico** traffic island
iso'lano, -a **A** *adj* insular
B *mf* islander
iso'lante **A** *adj* insulating
B *m* insulator
✓ **iso'lare** *vt* isolate; Mech, Electr insulate; (acusticamente) soundproof
iso'lato **A** *adj* isolated
B *m* (di appartamenti) block
isolazio'nismo *m* isolationism
iso'metrico *adj* isometric
i'soscele *adj* isosceles
is'panico *adj* Hispanic
ispessi'mento *m* thickening
ispes'sire *vt* thicken
ispes'sirsi *vr* thicken
ispetto'rato *m* inspectorate
ispet'tore *m* inspector
■ **ispettore capo** chief inspector; **ispettore di polizia** police inspector; **ispettore scolastico** inspector of schools; **ispettore delle tasse** tax inspector; **ispettore di zona** Comm area manager
ispezio'nare *vt* inspect
ispezi'one *f* inspection; (di nave) boarding
'ispido *adj* bristly
ispi'rare *vt* inspire; suggest ‹*idea, soluzione*›
ispi'rarsi *vr* **~ a** be based on
ispi'rato *adj* inspired
ispirazi'one *f* inspiration; (idea) idea
Isra'ele *m* Israel
israeli'ano, -a *adj & nmf* Israeli
is'sare *vt* hoist
ist. *abbr* (**istituto**) dept.
istan'taneo, -a **A** *adj* instantaneous
B *f* snapshot
✓ **i'stante** *m* instant; **all'~** instantly
i'stanza *f* petition
■ **istanza di divorzio** petition for divorce
isterecto'mia *f* hysterectomy
i'sterico *adj* hysterical; **attacco ~** hysterics *pl*
iste'rismo *m* hysteria
■ **isterismo di massa** mass hysteria
isti'gare *vt* instigate; **~ qualcuno al male** incite somebody to evil
istiga|'tore, -trice *mf* instigator
istigazi'one *f* instigation; **~ a delinquere** incitement to crime
istintiva'mente *adv* instinctively
istin'tivo *adj* instinctive
i'stinto *m* instinct; **d'~** instinctively
■ **istinto di conservazione** instinct of self-preservation; **istinto materno** maternal instinct
istitu'ire *vt* institute; (fondare) found; initiate ‹*manifestazione*›
isti'tuto *m* institute; Sch secondary school; Univ department
■ **istituto di bellezza** beauty salon; **istituto**

✓ key word

commerciale business college; **istituto di credito** bank; **istituto per l'infanzia** children's home; **istituto tecnico professionale** technical college

istitu|'tore, -trice *mf* (insegnante) tutor; (fondatore) founder

istituzio'nale *adj* institutional

istituzionaliz'zare *vt* institutionalize

istituzionaliz'zarsi *vr* become an institution

istituzionalizzazi'one *f* institutionalization

istituzi'one *f* institution; **le istituzioni** state institutions

'istmo *m* isthmus

isto'gramma *m* bar chart

istolo'gia *f* histology

istra'dare *vt* divert; fig guide (**a** towards)

'istrice *m* porcupine

istri'one *m* clown; Theat sl ham

istru'ire *vt* instruct; (addestrare) train; (informare) inform; Jur prepare

istru'ito *adj* well-educated

istrut'tivo *adj* instructive, enlightening

istrut|'tore, -trice *mf* instructor

■ **giudice istruttore** examining magistrate; **istruttore di guida** driving instructor; **istruttore di nuoto** swimming instructor

istrut'toria *f* Jur investigation

istruzi'one *f* instruction; Sch education; **ministero della pubblica istruzione** Department of Education

■ **istruzioni** *pl* **per l'uso** instructions for use

istupi'dire *vt* stupefy

I'talia *f* Italy

itali'ano, -a *adj & nmf* Italian

italoameri'cano *adj* Italian-American

itine'rante *adj* wandering; ‹*mostra*› touring; ‹*spettacolo*› travelling

itine'rario *m* route, itinerary

■ **itinerario turistico** tourist route

itte'rizia *f* jaundice

'ittico *adj* fishing *attrib*

i'uta *f* jute

I.V.A. *nf abbr* (**imposta sul valore aggiunto**) VAT; ~ **compresa** inclusive of VAT, VAT inclusive

'ivi *adv* (linguaggio burocratico) therein

Jj

ja'bot *m inv* jabot

jack *m inv* jack

ja'cquard *adj inv* (nella maglia) jacquard

'jais *m* jet

'jam-session *f inv* jam session

jazz *m* jazz

jaz'zista *mf* jazz player

jeep® *f inv* jeep®

'jersey *m* jersey

jet *m inv* jet

■ **jet privato** private jet

jet-'set *m* jet set

'jingle *m inv* jingle

'jodel *m inv* yodel

'jogging *m* jogging

joint 'venture *f inv* Comm joint venture

'jolly A *m inv* (carta da gioco) joker **B** *adj* Comput

■ **carattere jolly** wild card [character]

'joystick *m inv* joystick

Jugo'slavia *f* Hist Yugoslavia

jugo'slavo, -a *adj & nmf* Hist Yugoslavian

ju'jitsu *m* ju-jitsu

juke'box *m inv* juke box

jumbo-jet *m inv* jumbo jet

junghi'ano, -a *adj & nmf* Jungian

'junior A *adj inv* junior **B** *m* (*pl* **juniores**) junior

'juta *f* jute

Kk

kafki'ano *adj* Kafkaesque
ka'jal *m inv* kohl
'kaki **A** *adj inv* khaki
B *m inv* persimmon
ka'pok *m* kapok
ka'putt *adj inv* kaput
kara'kiri *m* **fare ~** commit hara-kiri
kara'oke *m inv* karaoke; **apparecchio per ~** karaoke machine
kara'te *m* karate
kart *m inv* go-kart
kar'tismo *m* go-karting; **fare del ~** go go-karting
ka'sher *adj inv* kosher
'Kashmir *m* Kashmir
ka'yak *m inv* kayak
Ka'zakistan *m* Kazakhstan
KB Comput *abbr* (**kilobyte**) K, KB
Kbyte Comput *abbr* (**kilobyte**) kbyte
ke'bab *m inv* kebab
'Kenya *m* Kenya
ker'messe *f inv* fair; fig rowdy celebration
kero'sene *m* paraffin
'ketchup *m* ketchup
kg *abbr* (**chilogrammo**) kg
kib'butz *m inv* kibbutz
'killer *mf inv* assassin, hit man
'kilo *m* kilo
kilt *m inv* kilt
ki'mono *m inv* kimono
kinesitera'pia *f* physiotherapy
Kir'ghizistan *m* Kyrgyzstan
kit *m inv*:
■ **kit di aggiornamento** upgrade kit; **kit multimediale** multimedia kit
kitsch *adj inv* kitschy
'kiwi *m inv* kiwi
'kleenex® *m inv* Kleenex
km *abbr* (**chilometro**) km
km/h *abbr* (**chilometri all'ora**) kph
kmq *abbr* (**chilometro quadrato**) km²
ko'ala *m inv* koala
koso'varo, -a *adj & nmf* Kosovan
'Kosovo *m* Kosovo
'krapfen *m inv* doughnut
'kripton *m* krypton
'Kurdistan *m* Kurdistan
kuwaiti'ano *m* Kuwaiti
kW *abbr* (**kilowatt**) kW
K-'way® *m inv* cagoule
kWh *abbr* (**kilowatt all'ora**) kWh

Ll

l' *def art mf* (*before vowel*) the; ▶ **il**
⚷ **la** **A** *def art f* the; ▶ **il**
B *pron* (oggetto, riferito a persona) her; (riferito a cosa, animale) it; (forma di cortesia) you
C *m inv* Mus (chiave, nota) A
⚷ **là** *adv* there; **di là** (in quel luogo) in there; (da quella parte) that way; **eccolo là!** there he is!; **farsi più in là** (far largo) make way; **là dentro** in there; **là fuori** out there; **[ma] va' là!** come off it!; **più in là** (nel tempo) later on; (nello spazio) further on
⚷ **'labbro** *m* (*pl nf* **labbra**) lip; **pendere dalle labbra di qualcuno** hang on somebody's every word
■ **labbro leporino** harelip
labi'ale *adj & nf* labial
'labile *adj* fleeting
labiolet'tura *f* lip-reading
labi'rinto *m* labyrinth; (di sentieri ecc.) maze
⚷ **labora'torio** *m* laboratory; (di negozio, officina ecc.) workshop
■ **laboratorio linguistico** language lab
laboriosa'mente *adv* laboriously
labori'oso *adj* (operoso) industrious; (faticoso) laborious
labra'dor *m inv* Labrador

⚷ key word

k
l

labu'rista **A** *adj* Labour
B *mf* member of the Labour Party

'lacca *f* lacquer; (per capelli) hairspray

lac'care *vt* lacquer

lacchè *m inv* lackey

'laccio *m* noose; (lazo) lasso; (trappola) snare; (stringa) lace
■ **laccio emostatico** tourniquet

lace'rante *adj* ‹*grido*› ear-splitting

lace'rare *vt* tear; lacerate ‹*carne*›

lace'rarsi *vr* tear

lacerazi'one *f* laceration

'lacero *adj* torn; (cencioso) ragged

la'conico *adj* laconic

'lacrima *f* tear; (goccia) drop

lacri'male *adj* ‹*condotto, ghiandola*› tear *attrib*

lacri'mare *vi* weep

lacri'mevole *adj* tear-jerking

lacri'mogeno *adj* **gas ~** tear gas

lacri'moso *adj* tearful

la'cuna *f* gap

lacu'noso *adj* ‹*preparazione, resoconto*› incomplete

la'custre *adj* lake *attrib*

lad'dove *conj* whereas

'ladro, -a **A** *adj* thieving
B *mf* thief; **al ~!** stop thief!

ladro'cinio *m* theft

la'druncolo *m* petty thief

'lager *m inv* concentration camp

laggiù *adv* down there; (lontano) over there

'lagna *f* infml (persona) moaning Minnie; (film) bore

la'gnanza *f* complaint

la'gnarsi *vr* moan, whinge; (protestare) complain (**di** about)

la'gnoso *adj* ‹*persona*› moaning, whining; ‹*film*› weepy

'lago *m* lake
■ **lago di Garda** Lake Garda; **lago di sangue** pool of blood

la'guna *f* lagoon

lagu'nare *adj* lagoon *attrib*

laiciz'zare *vt* laicize

'laico, -a **A** *adj* lay; ‹*vita*› secular
B *m* layman
C *f* laywoman

'lama **A** *f* blade; **a doppia ~** ‹*rasoio*› twin blade
B *m inv* (animale) llama

lambic'carsi *vr* **~ il cervello** rack one's brains

lam'bire *vt* lap

lamé *m inv* lamé

la'mella *f* (di fungo) lamella; (di metallo, plastica) sheet

lamen'tare *vt* lament

lamen'tarsi *vr* moan; **~ di** (lagnarsi) complain about

lamen'tela *f* complaint

lamen'tevole *adj* mournful; (pietoso) pitiful

la'mento *m* moan

la'metta *f*
■ **lametta [da barba]** razor blade

lami'era *f* sheet metal
■ **lamiera ondulata** corrugated iron

'lamina *f* foil
■ **lamina d'oro** gold leaf

lami'nare *vt* laminate

lami'naria *f* kelp

lami'nato **A** *adj* laminated
B *m* laminate; (tessuto) lamé

'lampada *f* lamp
■ **lampada abbronzante** sunlamp; **lampada alogena** halogen lamp; **lampada da comodino** beside lamp; **lampada a gas** gas lamp; **lampada a olio** oil lamp; **lampada a pila** torch; **lampada da soffitto** overhead light; **lampada da tavolo** table lamp

lampa'dario *m* chandelier

lampa'dato *m* sl sun-bed freak

lampa'dina *f* light bulb

lam'pante *adj* clear

lam'para *f light used when fishing at night*

lampeg'giante *adj* flashing

lampeggi'are *vi* flash

lampeggia'tore *m* Auto indicator

lampi'one *m* street lamp

'lampo *m* flash of lightning; (luce) flash; **lampi** *pl* lightning *sg*
■ **cerniera lampo** zip [fastener], zipper AmE; **lampo di genio** stroke of genius; **lampo al magnesio** magnesium flash

lam'pone *m* raspberry

'lana *f* wool; **di ~** woollen
■ **lana d'acciaio** steel wool; **lana grossa** double knitting [wool]; **lana merino** botany wool; **lana vergine** new wool; **lana di vetro** glass wool

lan'cetta *f* pointer; (di orologio) hand
■ **lancetta dei minuti** minute hand; **lancetta delle ore** hour hand; **lancetta dei secondi** second hand

'lancia *f* (arma) spear, lance; Naut launch
■ **lancia di salvataggio** lifeboat

lanciafi'amme *m inv* flame thrower

lancia'missili *m inv* missile launcher

lancia'palle *adj inv* **macchina ~** ball launcher for tennis practice

lancia'razzi **A** *adj inv* **pistola lanciarazzi** Very pistol
B *m inv* rocket launcher

lanci'are *vt* throw; (da un aereo) drop; launch ‹*missile, prodotto, attacco*›; give ‹*grido*›; Comput run ‹*file*›; **~ uno sguardo a** glance at; **~ in alto** throw up

lanci'arsi *vr* fling oneself; (intraprendere) launch out

lanci'nante *adj* piercing

I

'lancio *m* throwing; (da aereo) drop; (di missile, prodotto) launch; Comput (di file) running
■ **lancio del disco** discus [throwing]; **lancio del giavellotto** javelin [throwing]; **lancio col paracadute** (di persona) parachute jump; (di pacco) airdrop, parachute drop; **lancio del peso** putting the shot, shot put

'landa *f* moor

languida'mente *adv* languidly

'languido *adj* languid; (debole) feeble

langu'ore *m* languor; (spossatezza) listlessness
■ **languore di stomaco** hunger pangs *pl*

lani'ero *adj* wool; **industria laniera** wool industry

lani'ficio *m* woollen mill

lano'lina *f* lanolin

la'noso *adj* woolly

lan'terna *f* lantern; (faro) lighthouse

la'nugine *f* down

'Laos *m* Laos

lapalissi'ano *adj* obvious

laparosco'pia *f* laparoscopy

lapi'dare *vt* stone; fig demolish

lapi'dario *adj* (conciso) terse; **arte lapidaria** stone carving

l

'lapide *f* tombstone; (commemorativa) memorial tablet

'lapis *m inv* pencil

lapi'slazzuli *m inv* lapis lazuli

'lappa *f* Bot burr

Lap'ponia *f* Lapland

'lapsus *m inv* lapse, error
■ **lapsus freudiano** Freudian slip

'laptop *m inv* laptop

lardel'lare *vt* Culin lard

'lardo *m* lard

larga'mente *adv* (ampiamente) widely

largheggi'are *vi* ~ **in** be free with

lar'ghezza *f* width; (di spalle) breadth; fig liberality
■ **larghezza di vedute** broad-mindedness

✓ **'largo** **A** *adj* wide; (ampio) broad; ‹*abito*› loose; (liberale) liberal; (abbondante) generous; **stare alla larga** keep away; ~ **di manica** fig generous; ~ **di spalle/vedute** broad-shouldered/-minded; **a gambe larghe** with one's legs wide apart; **di larghe vedute** broad-minded
B *m* width; **andare al** ~ Naut go out to sea; **fare** ~ make room; **farsi** ~ make one's way; **al** ~ **di** off the coast of

'larice *m* larch

la'ringe *f* larynx

larin'gite *f* laryngitis

'larva *f* larva; (persona emaciata) shadow
■ **larva di pidocchio** nit

la'sagne *fpl* lasagne

'lasca *f* roach

lasciapas'sare *m inv* pass

✓ **lasci'are** *vt* leave; (rinunciare) give up; (rimetterci) lose; (smettere di tenere) let go [of]; (concedere) let; ~ **a desiderare** leave a lot to be desired; ~ **di fare qualcosa** (smettere) stop doing something; **lascia perdere!** forget it!; **lascialo venire, lascia che venga** let him come

lasci'arsi *vr* (reciproco) leave each other, split up; ~ **andare** let oneself go

'lascito *m* legacy

la'scivo *adj* lascivious

'laser *adj & m inv* **[raggio]** ~ laser [beam]

lasertera'pia *f* laser treatment

lassa'tivo *adj & nm* laxative

las'sismo *m* laxity

'lasso *m*
■ **lasso di tempo** period of time

✓ **lassù** *adv* up there

'lastra *f* slab; (di ghiaccio) sheet; (di metallo, Phot) plate; (radiografia) X-ray [plate]
■ **lastra di pietra** paving slab, paving stone; **lastra di vetro** plate glass

lastri'care *vt* pave

lastri'cato *m* pavement

'lastrico *m* paving; **sul** ~ on one's beam ends

la'tente *adj* latent

late'rale *adj* side *attrib*; Med, Techn ecc. lateral; **via** ~ side street

lateral'mente *adv* sideways

late'rizi *mpl* bricks

'latice *m* latex

latifon'dista *m* big landowner

lati'fondo *m* large estate

lati'nismo *m* Latinism

✓ **la'tino** *adj & nm* Latin

latino-ameri'cano, -a *adj & nmf* Latin American

lati'tante **A** *adj* in hiding
B *mf* fugitive [from justice]

lati'tanza *f* **darsi alla** ~ go into hiding

lati'tudine *f* latitude

✓ **'lato** **A** *adj* (ampio) broad; **in senso** ~ broadly speaking
B *m* side; (aspetto) aspect; **a** ~ **di** beside; **dal** ~ **mio** (punto di vista) for my part; **d'altro** ~ fig on the other hand
■ **lato B** B side; infml backside, bottom

la'tore, -trice *mf* Comm bearer

la'trare *vi* bark

la'trato *m* barking

la'trina *f* latrine

'latta *f* tin, can

lat'taio, -a **A** *m* milkman
B *f* milkwoman

lat'tante **A** *adj* breast-fed
B *mf* suckling

✓ **'latte** *m* milk
■ **latte acido** sour milk; **latte condensato**

✓ key word

condensed milk, evaporated milk; **latte detergente** cleansing milk; **latte di gallina** eggnog; **latte intero** whole milk, full-cream milk; **latte a lunga conservazione** long-life milk; **latte materno** mother's milk, breast milk; **latte parzialmente scremato** semi-skimmed milk; **latte in polvere** powdered milk; **latte scremato** skimmed milk; **latte di soia** soya milk

lat'teo *adj* milky; **dieta lattea** milk diet; **la Via Lattea** the Milky Way

latte'ria *f* dairy

'lattice *m* latex

latti'cello *m* buttermilk

latti'cini *mpl* dairy products

latti'era *f* milk jug

lattigi'noso *adj* milky

lat'tina *f* can, tin can

lat'tosio *m* lactose

lat'tuga *f* lettuce
■ **lattuga romana** cos lettuce

'laudano *m* laudanum

'laurea *f* degree; **prendere la ~** graduate
■ **laurea breve** *degree that takes less than the standard period of time*; **laurea in Lettere** arts degree; **laurea specialistica** *Italian degree similar to a master's degree*; **laurea triennale** ▶ **laurea breve**

laure'ando, -a *mf* final-year student

laure'are *vt* confer a degree on

laure'arsi *vr* graduate

laure'ato, -a *adj & nmf* graduate

'lauro *m* laurel

'lauto *adj* lavish; **~ guadagno** handsome profit

'lava *f* lava

la'vabile *adj* washable
■ **lavabile in lavastoviglie** dishwasher safe

la'vabo *m* wash-basin

lavacri'stallo *m* windscreen wiper

la'vaggio *m* washing
■ **lavaggio automatico** (per auto) car wash; **lavaggio del cervello** brainwashing; **lavaggio a secco** dry-cleaning

la'vagna *f* slate; Sch blackboard
■ **lavagna a fogli mobili** flip chart; **lavagna luminosa** overhead projector, OHP

lava'macchine *mf inv* car washer

la'vanda *f* wash; Bot lavender; **gli hanno fatto la ~ gastrica** he had his stomach pumped

lavan'daia *f* washerwoman

lavande'ria *f* laundry
■ **lavanderia automatica** launderette

lavan'dino *m* sink; hum (persona) bottomless pit

lavapi'atti *mf inv* dishwasher

la'vare *vt* wash; **~ i piatti** wash up; **~ a secco** dry-clean; **~ a mano** wash by hand; **~ i panni** do the washing

la'varsi *vr* wash, have a wash; **~ i denti** brush one's teeth; **~ le mani/il viso** wash one's hands/face; **~ la testa** *o* **i capelli** wash one's hair

lava'secco *mf inv* dry-cleaner's

lavasto'viglie *f inv* dishwasher

la'vata *f* wash; **darsi una ~** have a wash
■ **lavata di capo** fig scolding

lava'tivo, -a *mf* idler

lava'trice *f* washing machine

lava'vetri *m inv* squeegee

la'vello *m* kitchen sink

'lavico *adj* formed by lava

la'vina *f* snowslide

lavo'rante *mf* worker

lavo'rare **A** *vi* work; **~ di fantasia** (sognare) day-dream
B *vt* work; knead ‹*pasta ecc.*›; till ‹*la terra*›; **~ a maglia** knit; **~ troppo** overwork

lavora'tivo *adj* working; **giorno ~** workday; **settimana lavorativa** working week

lavo'rato *adj* ‹*pietra, legno*› carved; ‹*cuoio*› tooled; ‹*metallo*› wrought; ‹*maglione*› patterned; ‹*terra*› cultivated

lavora|'tore, -trice **A** *mf* worker
■ **lavora|tore a domicilio** outworker, homeworker
B *adj* working

lavorazi'one *f* manufacture; (di terra) working; (del terreno) cultivation
■ **lavorazione [artigianale]** workmanship; **lavorazione del metallo** metalwork; **lavorazione in serie** mass production

lavo'rio *m* intense activity

la'voro *m* work; (faticoso, sociale) labour; (impiego) job; Theat play; **andare al ~** go to work; **essere senza ~** be out of work; **mettersi al ~ (su qualcosa)** set to work (on something); **ministero dei lavori pubblici** Department of Public Works; **lavori** *pl* **di casa** housework; **lavori** *pl* **in corso** roadworks; **lavori** *pl* **forzati** hard labour *sg*; **lavori** *pl* **stradali** roadworks
■ **lavoro atipico** *employment relationship not conforming to the usual model of full-time, continuous employment with a single employer over a long time span*; **lavoro a domicilio** home working; **lavoro di gruppo** Sch working in groups, group work; **lavoro interinale** temping; **lavoro a maglia** knitting; **lavoro nero** moonlighting; **lavoro part time** part-time job; **lavoro straordinario** overtime; **lavoro teatrale** play; **lavoro a tempo pieno** full-time job

lazza'rone *m* rascal

le **A** *def art fpl* the; ▶ **il**
B *pers pron* (oggetto) them; (a lei) her; **le hai parlato?** did you talk to her?; (forma di cortesia) you

'leader **A** *m inv* leader
■ **leader della marca** brand leader
B *adj inv* leading; **prodotto ~** market leader

le'ale *adj* loyal
leal'mente *adv* loyally
lealtà *f inv* loyalty
'leasing *m inv* lease purchase, leasing
'lebbra *f* leprosy
lecca 'lecca *m inv* lollipop
leccapi'edi *mf inv* derog bootlicker
lec'care *vt* lick; fig suck up to
lec'carsi *vr* lick; fig (agghindarsi) doll oneself up; **da ~ i baffi** mouth-watering
lec'cata *f* lick
lec'cato *adj* ‹*persona*› dressed to kill
'leccio *m* holm oak
leccor'nia *f* delicacy
lecita'mente *adv* lawfully
'lecito *adj* lawful; (permesso) permissible
'ledere *vt* damage; Med injure
'lega *f* league; (di metalli) alloy; **far ~ con qualcuno** take up with somebody
■ **lega doganale** customs union; **Lega Nord** Northern League
le'gaccio *m* string; (delle scarpe) shoelace
le'gale **A** *adj* legal
B *m* lawyer
legalità *f inv* legality
legaliz'zare *vt* authenticate; (rendere legale) legalize
legalizzazi'one *f* legalization
legal'mente *adv* legally
Legam'biente *f Italian association for environmental protection*
le'game *m* tie; (amoroso) liaison; (connessione) link
■ **legame di parentela** family relationship; **legame di sangue** blood relationship; **legame sentimentale** emotional relationship
lega'mento *m* Med ligament
le'gare **A** *vt* tie; tie up ‹*persona*›; tie together ‹*due cose*›; (unire, rilegare) bind; alloy ‹*metalli*›; (connettere) connect; **legarsela al dito** fig bear a grudge
B *vi* (far lega) get on well
le'garsi *vr* bind oneself; **~ a qualcuno** become attached to somebody
lega'tario, -a *mf* legatee
le'gato *m* legacy; Relig legate
lega'tura *f* tying; (di libro) binding
legazi'one *f* legation
le'genda *f* legend
'legge *f* law; (parlamentare) act; **a norma di ~** by law
■ **legge marziale** martial law
leg'genda *f* legend; (didascalia) caption
■ **leggenda metropolitana** urban myth
leggen'dario *adj* legendary
'leggere *vt & vi* read; **~ male** (sbagliato) misread
legge'rezza *f* lightness; (frivolezza) frivolity; (incostanza) fickleness

legger'mente *adv* slightly
leg'gero *adj* light; ‹*bevanda*› weak; (lieve) slight; (frivolo) frivolous; (incostante) fickle; **~ come una piuma** [as] light as a feather; **alla leggera** lightly
leggi'adro *adj* (liter) graceful
leg'gibile *adj* ‹*scrittura*› legible; ‹*stile*› readable
leg'gio *m* lectern; Mus music stand
legife'rare *vi* legislate
legio'nario *m* legionary
legi'one *f* legion
legisla'tivo *adj* legislative
legisla'tore *m* legislator
legisla'tura *f* legislature
legislazi'one *f* legislation
legittima'mente *adv* legitimately
legittimità *f inv* legitimacy
le'gittimo *adj* legitimate; (giusto) proper; **legittima difesa** self-defence
'legna *f* firewood
le'gnaia *f* woodshed
le'gname *m* timber
le'gnata *f* blow with a stick
'legno *m* wood; **di ~** wooden; **legni** *pl* Mus woodwind
■ **legno compensato** plywood
le'gnoso *adj* woody; (di legno) wooden; ‹*gambe*› stiff; ‹*movimento*› wooden
le'gume *m* pod
'lei *pers pron* (soggetto) she; (oggetto, con prep) her; (forma di cortesia) you; **lo ha fatto ~ stessa** she did it herself
'lembo *m* edge; (di terra) strip
'lemma *m* headword
'lemming *m inv* lemming
'lena *f* vigour
'lendine *m* nit
le'nire *vt* soothe
lenta'mente *adv* slowly
'lente *f* lens
■ **lente a contatto** contact lens; **mettersi le lenti a contatto** put in one's contact lenses; **lente a contatto morbida** soft lens; **lente a contatto rigida** hard lens; **lente d'ingrandimento** magnifying glass; **lente semi-rigida** gas-permeable lens
len'tezza *f* slowness
len'ticchia *f* lentil
len'tiggine *f* freckle
'lento *adj* slow; (allentato) slack; ‹*abito*› loose
'lenza *f* fishing line
len'zuolo *m* sheet; **le lenzuola** the sheets
■ **lenzuolo con gli angoli** fitted sheet; **lenzuolo funebre** shroud
leon'cino *m* lion cub
le'one *m* lion; Astr Leo
■ **leone marino** sea lion
leo'nessa *f* lioness

key word

leo'pardo *m* leopard
lepo'rino *adj* **labbro ~** harelip
'lepre *f* hare
le'protto *m* leveret
'lercio *adj* filthy
lerci'ume *m* filth
'lesbica *f* lesbian
'lesbico *adj* lesbian
lesi'nare **A** *vt* grudge
B *vi* be stingy
lesio'nare *vt* damage
lesi'one *f* lesion; (danno) damage
■ **lesione cerebrale** brain damage; **lesione interna** internal injury; **lesioni personali** *pl* grievous bodily harm, GBH
'leso **A** pp di **ledere**
B *adj* injured; **lesa maestà** high treason
les'sare *vt* boil
lessi'cale *adj* lexical
'lessico *m* vocabulary
lessicogra'fia *f* lexicography
lessi'cografo, -a *mf* lexicographer
'lesso **A** *adj* boiled
B *m* boiled meat
'lesto *adj* quick; ‹*mente*› sharp
■ **lesto di mano** light-fingered
le'tale *adj* lethal
leta'maio *m* dunghill; fig pigsty
le'tame *m* dung
le'targico *adj* lethargic
le'targo *m* lethargy; (di animali) hibernation
le'tizia *f* joy
'lettera *f* letter; **alla ~** literally; **eseguire qualcosa alla ~** carry out something to the letter; **lettere** *pl* (letteratura) literature *sg*; Univ Arts; **dottore in lettere** BA, Bachelor of Arts
■ **lettera d'accompagnamento** covering letter; **lettera d'amore** love letter; **lettera assicurata** registered letter; **lettera di cambio** bill of exchange; **lettera di credito** letter of credit; **lettera maiuscola** capital [letter]; **lettera minuscola** small letter; **lettera di presentazione** letter of introduction; **lettera raccomandata** recorded delivery letter; **lettera di scuse** letter of apology; **lettera di trasporto aereo** air waybill
lette'rale *adj* literal
letteral'mente *adv* literally
lette'rario *adj* literary
lette'rato **A** *adj* well read
B *m* scholar; **letterati** *pl* literati
lettera'tura *f* literature
■ **letteratura pulp** pulp fiction
letti'era *f* (per gatto) litter
let'tiga *f* stretcher
let'tino *m* cot; Med couch
■ **lettino [pieghevole]** camp bed
'letto *m* bed; **andare a ~** go to bed; **[ri]fare il ~** make the bed
■ **letto a castello** bunk bed; **letto di fiume** river bed; **letti gemelli** *pl* twin beds; **letto matrimoniale** double bed; **letto a una piazza** single bed; **letto a due piazze** double bed; **letto singolo** single bed
Let'tonia *f* Latvia
letto'rato *m* (corso) tutorial
let|'tore, -trice **A** *mf* reader; Univ language assistant
B *m* Comput disk drive
■ **lettore di CD** CD player, CD system; **lettore [di] CD-ROM** CD-ROM drive; **lettore di codice a barre** barcode reader, scanner; **lettore di compact disc** compact disc player; **lettore di disco** disk drive; **lettore di floppy** floppy [disk] drive; **lettore di minidisc** minidisc player; **lettore [di] MP3** MP3 player
let'tura *f* reading
leuce'mia *f* leukaemia
'leva *f* lever; Mil call-up; **nuove leve** *pl* new blood, young blood; **far ~** lever
■ **leva del cambio** gear lever; **leva di comando** control lever
le'vante *m* East; (vento) east wind
leva'punti *m inv* staple remover
le'vare *vt* (alzare) raise; (togliere) take away; (rimuovere) take off; (estrarre) pull out, lift, abolish ‹*divieto, tassa*›; **~ di mezzo qualcosa** get something out of the way
le'varsi *vr* move (**da** away from); ‹*vento*› get up; ‹*sole*› rise; **~ di mezzo** get out of the way
le'vata *f* rising; (di posta) collection
leva'taccia *f* **fare una ~** get up at the crack of dawn
leva'toio *adj* **ponte ~** drawbridge
leva'trice *f* midwife
leva'tura *f* intelligence
levi'gare *vt* smooth; (con carta vetro) rub down
levi'gato *adj* ‹*superficie*› polished; ‹*pelle*› smooth
leviga'trice *f* sander
levi'tare *vi* levitate
levitazi'one *f* levitation
Le'vitico *m* Leviticus
levri'ero *m* greyhound
■ **levriero afgano** Afghan hound
lezi'one *f* lesson; Univ lecture; fig lesson
■ **lezione di guida** driving lesson; **lezione di italiano** Italian lesson, Italian class
lezi'oso *adj* ‹*stile, modi*› affected
'lezzo *m* stench
li *pers pron mpl* them
lì *adv* there; **fin lì** as far as there; **giù di lì** thereabouts; **lì per lì** there and then; **la cosa è finita lì** that was the end of it
li'ana *f* liana
liba'nese *adj & nmf* Lebanese
'Libano *m* Lebanon
'libbra *f* (peso) pound
li'beccio *m* south-west wind

li'bello *m* libel
li'bellula *f* dragonfly
libe'rale **A** *adj* liberal; (generoso) generous **B** *mf* liberal
libera'lismo *m*
■ **liberalismo [economico]** economic liberalism
liberalità *f inv* generosity
liberal'mente *adv* liberally
libe'rare *vt* free, release ‹*prigioniero*›; vacate ‹*stanza*›; (salvare) rescue
libe'rarsi *vr* ‹*stanza*› become vacant; Teleph become free; (da impegno) get out of it; **~ di** get rid of
libera|'tore, -trice **A** *adj* liberating **B** *mf* liberator
libera'torio *adj* liberating
■ **pagamento liberatorio** full and final payment
liberazi'one *f* liberation; **la Liberazione** (ricorrenza) Liberation Day
■ **liberazione della donna** women's liberation, women's lib
Li'beria *f* Liberia
libe'rismo *m* free trade
'libero *adj* free; ‹*strada*› clear; **~ come l'aria** free as a bird
■ **libero arbitrio** *nm* free will; **libero docente** *nm* qualified university lecturer; **libero professionista** *nm* self-employed person
libertà *f inv* freedom; (di prigioniero) release; **~** *pl* (confidenze) liberties; **prendersi la ~ di fare qualcosa** take the liberty of doing something
■ **libertà di espressione** freedom of speech; **libertà di parola** free speech; **libertà di pensiero** freedom of thought; **libertà provvisoria** Jur bail; **libertà di stampa** freedom of the press; **libertà vigilata** probation
liber'tino, -a **A** *adj* dissolute, libertine **B** *mf* libertine
'liberty *nm & adj inv* Art Nouveau
'Libia *f* Libya
'libico, -a *adj & nmf* Libyan
li'bidine *f* lust
libidi'noso *adj* lustful
li'bido *f* libido
li'braio *m* bookseller
libre'ria *f* (negozio) bookshop; (mobile) bookcase; (biblioteca) library
li'bretto *m* booklet; Mus libretto
■ **libretto degli assegni** cheque book; **libretto di circolazione** logbook; **libretto d'istruzioni** instruction booklet; **libretto di risparmio** savings account; (documento) passbook, savings book; **libretto universitario** *book held by students which records details of their exam performances*
'libro *m* book
■ **libro bianco** White Paper; **libro dei canti** hymn book; **libro contabile** account book; **libro di esercizi** workbook; **libro giallo** crime novel; **libro mastro** Comm ledger; **libro paga** payroll; **libro di ricette** cookbook, recipe book; **libri** *pl* **sociali** company's books; **libro tascabile** paperback; **libro di testo** course book
li'cantropo *m* werewolf
lice'ale **A** *mf* secondary school student **B** *adj* secondary school *attrib*
li'cenza *f* licence; (permesso) permission; Mil leave; Sch school-leaving certificate; **essere in ~** be on leave
■ **licenza di caccia** hunting licence; **licenza di esportazione** export licence; **licenza matrimoniale** marriage licence; **licenza di pesca** fishing licence; **licenza poetica** poetic licence; **licenza di porto d'armi** gun licence
licenzia'mento *m* dismissal, lay-off
licenzi'are *vt* dismiss, sack infml; (conferire un diploma) grant a school-leaving certificate to
licenzi'arsi *vr* (da un impiego) resign; (accomiatarsi) take one's leave
licenzi'oso *adj* licentious
li'ceo *m* secondary school, high school
■ **liceo classico** *secondary school with an emphasis on humanities*; **liceo scientifico** *secondary school with an emphasis on sciences*
li'chene *m* lichen
'lido *m* beach
'Liechtenstein *m* Liechtenstein
lieta'mente *adv* happily
li'eto *adj* glad; ‹*evento*› happy; **molto ~!** pleased to meet you!
■ **lieto fine** happy ending
li'eve *adj* light; (debole) faint; (trascurabile) slight
lievi'tare **A** *vi* rise **B** *vt* leaven
li'evito *m* yeast
■ **lievito in polvere** baking powder
lift *m inv* lift boy
'lifting *m inv* face-lift
'ligio *adj* **essere ~ al dovere** have a sense of duty
li'gnaggio *m* lineage
'ligneo *adj* wooden
'lilla *m* (colore) lilac
lillà *m inv* Bot lilac
'lima *f* file
limacci'oso *adj* slimy
li'manda *f* dab
li'mare *vt* file
lima'tura *f* (atto) filing; (residui) filings *pl*
'limbo *m* limbo
li'metta *f* **limetta [da unghie]** nail file; (di carta) emery board
limi'tare **A** *m* threshold **B** *vt* limit
limi'tarsi *vr* **~ a fare qualcosa** restrict oneself to doing something; **~ in qualcosa** cut down on something

key word

limitata'mente *adv* to a limited extent
limita'tivo *adj* limiting
limi'tato *adj* limited
limitazi'one *f* limitation
'limite **A** *adj* ‹*caso*› extreme
B *m* limit; (confine) boundary; **entro certi limiti** within certain limits
■ **limite di credito** credit limit, credit ceiling; **limite di sopportazione** breaking point; **'limite di sosta'** 'restricted parking'; **limite di tempo** time limit; **limite di velocità** speed limit; **rispettare il ~ di velocità** keep to the speed limit
li'mitrofo *adj* neighbouring
'limo *m* slime
limo'nata *f* (bibita) lemonade; (succo) lemon juice
■ **limonata amara** bitter lemon
li'mone *m* lemon; (albero) lemon tree
'limpido *adj* clear; ‹*occhi*› limpid
'lince *f* lynx
linci'are *vt* lynch
'lindo *adj* neat; (pulito) clean
'linea *f* line; (di autobus, aereo) route; (di metropolitana) line; (di abito) cut; (di auto, mobile) design; (fisico) figure; **in ~ d'aria** as the crow flies; **è caduta la ~** I've been cut off; **in ~ di massima** as a rule; **a grandi linee** in outline; **mantenere la ~** keep one's figure; **in ~** Comput on-line; **in prima ~** in the front line; **mettersi in ~** line up
■ **nave di linea** liner; **volo di linea** scheduled flight; **linea aerea** airline; **linea d'arrivo** Sport finishing line; **linea commutata** Teleph switched line; **linea di confine** boundary; **linea continua** unbroken line; **linea dedicata** dedicated line; **linea di demarcazione** border line; **linea ferroviaria** railway line; **linea di fondo** baseline; **linea d'immersione** water line; **linea laterale** Sport touch line; **linee della mano** *pl* lines of the hand; **linea di marea** tidemark; **linea mediana** Sport halfway line; **linea di partenza** Sport starting line; **linea principale** Rail main line; **linea punteggiata** dotted line; **linea secondaria** Rail branch line; **linea di tiro** line of fire; **linea tratteggiata** broken line
linea'menti *mpl* features
line'are *adj* linear; ‹*discorso*› to the point; ‹*ragionamento*› consistent
line'etta *f* (tratto lungo) dash; (d'unione) hyphen
'linfa *f* Anat lymph; Bot sap
■ **linfa vitale** fig life blood
lin'fatico *adj* Anat lymphatic
linfoghi'andola *f* lymph gland
linfo'nodo *m* lymph node
linge'rie *f* lingerie
lin'gotto *m* ingot
'lingua *f* tongue; (linguaggio) language; **avere la ~ lunga** fig have a big mouth
■ **lingua d'arrivo** target language; **lingua moderna** modern language; **lingua morta** dead language; **lingua di partenza** source language; **lingua straniera** foreign language
lingu'accia *f* (persona) backbiter; **fare le linguacce** put one's tongue out (**a** at)
lingu'aggio *m* language
■ **linguaggio infantile** baby talk; **linguaggio per la marcatura di ipertesti** Comput hypertext markup language; **linguaggio dei segni** sign language
lingu'etta *f* (di scarpa) tongue; (di busta) flap; Mus reed; (da tirare) tab
lingu'ista *mf* linguist
lingu'istica *f* linguistics *sg*
lingu'istico *adj* linguistic
link *m* Comput link
lin'kare *vt* Comput link ‹*siti Web*›
'lino *m* Bot flax; (tessuto) linen
li'noleum *m* linoleum
liofiliz'zare *vt* freeze-dry
liofiliz'zato *adj* freeze dried
li'pide *m* lipid
liposuzi'one *f* liposuction
li'quame *m* slurry
lique'fare *vt* liquefy; (sciogliere) melt
lique'farsi *vr* liquefy; (sciogliersi) melt
liqui'dare *vt* liquidate; settle ‹*conto*›; pay off ‹*debiti*›; clear ‹*merce*›; infml (uccidere) get rid of
liquida'tore *m* liquidator
liquidazi'one *f* liquidation; (di conti) settling; (di merce) clearance sale
■ **liquidazione totale [per cessata attività]** closing down sale
'liquido *adj & nm* liquid
■ **liquido dei freni** brake fluid; **liquido scongelante** Auto de-icer; **liquido tergicristallo** screen wash
liqui'gas® *m inv* Calor gas®
liqui'rizia *f* liquorice
li'quore *m* liqueur; **liquori** *pl* (superalcolici) liquors
'lira *f* (ex moneta italiana) lira; (moneta di vari paesi) pound; Mus lyre
■ **lira sterlina** pound sterling
'lirico, -a **A** *adj* lyrical; ‹*poesia*› lyric; ‹*cantante*› (musica) opera *attrib*
B *f* lyric poetry; Mus opera
li'rismo *m* lyricism
'lisca *f* fish bone; **avere la ~** infml (nel parlare) have a lisp
lisci'are *vt* smooth; (accarezzare) stroke
'liscio *adj* smooth; ‹*capelli*› straight; ‹*liquore*› neat, straight; ‹*acqua minerale*› still; **passarla liscia** get away with it
li'seuse *f inv* bed jacket
'liso *adj* worn [out]
'lista *f* list; (striscia) strip; **fare una ~** make out a list
■ **lista di attesa** waiting list; **in ~ di attesa** on the waiting list; Aeron on stand-by; **lista**

elettorale list of candidates; **lista degli invitati** guest list; **lista nera** blacklist; **lista di nozze** wedding list; **lista della spesa** shopping list; **lista dei vini** wine list

li'stare *vt* edge; Comput list

li'stino *m* list

■ **listino di borsa** Stock Exchange list; **listino dei cambi** exchange rates *pl*; **listino [dei] prezzi** price list

Lit. *abbr* (**lire italiane**) Italian lire

lita'nia *f* litany

'litchi *m inv* lychee

'lite *f* quarrel; (baruffa) row; Jur lawsuit

liti'gante *mf* Jur litigant

⚷ **liti'gare** *vi* quarrel; Jur litigate

li'tigio *m* quarrel

litigi'oso *adj* quarrelsome

'litio *m* lithium

litogra'fia *f* (procedimento) lithography; (stampa) lithograph

li'tografo, -a *mf* lithographer

lito'rale **A** *adj* coastal

B *m* coast

lito'raneo *adj* coastal

'litro *m* litre

Litu'ania *f* Lithuania

l

litu'ano, -a *adj & nmf* Lithuanian

litur'gia *f* liturgy

li'turgico *adj* liturgical

li'uto *m* lute

li'vella *f* level

■ **livella a bolla d'aria** spirit level

livella'mento *m* levelling out, levelling off

livel'lare *vt* level

livel'larsi *vr* level out

livella'tore *adj* levelling

livella'trice *f* bulldozer

li'vello *m* level; **passaggio a ~** level crossing; **sotto/sul ~ del mare** below/above sea level; **ad alto ~** ‹*conferenza, trattative*› top-level, high-level; **a più livelli** multilevel

■ **livello di guardia** danger level; **livello di magazzino** stock level; **livello occupazionale** level of employment

'livido **A** *adj* livid; (per il freddo) blue; (per una botta) black and blue

■ **livido di rabbia** livid

B *m* bruise

li'vore *m* spite

Li'vorno *f* Leghorn

li'vrea *f* livery

'lizza *f* lists *pl*; **essere in ~ per qualcosa** be in the running for something

⚷ **lo** **A** *def art m before s + consonant, gn, ps, z,* the; ▸ **il**

B *pron* (riferito a persona) him; (riferito a cosa) it; **non lo so** I don't know

'lobbia *f* Homburg [hat]

⚷ key word

lob'bismo *m* lobbying

lob'bista *mf* lobbyist

'lobby *f inv* lobby

lo'belia *f* lobelia

'lobo *m* lobe

loboto'mia *f* lobotomy

lo'cale **A** *adj* local

B *m* (stanza) room; (treno) local train; **locali** *pl* (edifici) premises

■ **locale notturno** nightclub

⚷ **località** *f inv* locality

■ **località balneare** seaside resort; **località turistica** tourist resort; **località di villeggiatura** holiday resort

localiz'zare *vt* localize; (reperire) locate

localiz'zarsi *vr* **~ in** be located in

localiz'zato *adj* localized

localizzazi'one *f* localization; (reperimento) location

local'mente *adv* locally

lo'canda *f* inn

locandi'ere, -a *mf* innkeeper

locan'dina *f* bill, poster

loca'tario, -a *mf* tenant

■ **locatario residente** sitting tenant

loca'tivo *adj* Gram locative; Jur rental

loca|'tore, -trice **A** *m* landlord

B *f* landlady

locazi'one *f* tenancy

locomo'tiva *f* locomotive

■ **locomotiva a vapore** steam engine

locomo'tore *m* locomotive, engine

locomozi'one *f* locomotion; **mezzi di locomozione** means of transport

'loculo *m* burial niche

lo'custa *f* locust

locuzi'one *f* expression

lo'dare *vt* praise

'lode *f* praise; **degno di ~** praiseworthy; **laurea con ~** first-class degree

'loden *m inv* (cappotto) loden [coat]; (stoffa) loden

lo'devole *adj* praiseworthy

'lodola *f* lark

loga'ritmo *m* logarithm

'loggia *f* loggia; (massonica) lodge

loggi'one *m* gallery, gods *pl*

'logica *f* logic

logica'mente *adv* (in modo logico) logically; (ovviamente) of course

logicità *f inv* logic

'logico *adj* logical

lo'gistica *f* logistics

lo'gistico *adj* logistic[al]

'logo *m inv* logo

logope'dia *f* speech therapy

logope'dista *mf* speech therapist

logo'rante *adj* ‹*attesa, esperienza*› wearing

logo'rare *vt* wear out; (sciupare) waste

logo'rarsi *vr* wear out; ‹*persona*›; wear oneself out
logo'rio *m* wear and tear; (stress) stress
'logoro *adj* worn-out
logor'roico *adj* loquacious
lom'baggine *f* lumbago
Lombar'dia *f* Lombardy
lom'bardo *adj* Lombardy *attrib*
lom'bare *adj* lumbar
lom'bata *f* loin
■ **lombata di manzo** sirloin
'lombo *m* Anat loin
lom'brico *m* earthworm
londi'nese **A** *adj* London *attrib*
B *mf* Londoner
'Londra *f* London
long-'drink *m inv* long drink
longevità *f inv* longevity
lon'gevo *adj* long-lived
longhe'rone *m* strut
longi'lineo *adj* rangy
longitudi'nale *adj* lengthwise
longitudinal'mente *adv* lengthwise
longi'tudine *f* longitude
long 'playing *m inv* LP, long-playing record
lontana'mente *adv* distantly; (vagamente) vaguely; **neanche ~** not for a moment
lonta'nanza *f* distance; (separazione) separation; **in ~** in the distance
lon'tano **A** *adj* far; (distante) distant; (nel tempo) far off, distant; ‹*parente*› distant; (vago) vague; (assente) absent; **più ~** further; **è ~ un paio di chilometri** it is a couple of kilometres away
B *adv* far [away]; **da ~** from a distance; **tenersi ~ da** keep away from; **andare ~** (allontanarsi) go away; (avere successo) go far
'lontra *f* otter
'lonza *f* (lombata) loin
lo'quace *adj* talkative
'lordo *adj* dirty; ‹*somma, peso*› gross; **al ~ di imposte** pre-tax
'loro[1] *pers pron pl* (soggetto) they; (oggetto) them; (forma di cortesia) you; **sta a ~** it is up to them
'loro[2] **A** (**il ~** *m* **la ~** *f* **i ~** *mpl* **le ~** *fpl*) *poss adj* their; (forma de cortesia) your; **un ~ amico** a friend of theirs; (forma di cortesia) a friend of yours
B *poss pron* theirs; (forma di cortesia) yours; **i ~** (famiglia) their folk
lo'sanga *f* lozenge; **a losanghe** diamond shaped
losca'mente *adv* suspiciously
'losco *adj* suspicious
'loto *m* lotus
'lotta *f* fight, struggle; (contrasto) conflict; Sport wrestling
■ **lotta di classe** class struggle; **lotta libera** all-in wrestling
lot'tare *vi* fight, struggle; Sport fig wrestle
lotta|'tore, -trice *mf* wrestler
lotte'ria *f* lottery
■ **Lotteria di Stato** National Lottery
lottiz'zare *vt* divide up ‹*terreno*›; fig parcel out
lottizzazi'one *f* (di terreno) division into lots; fig parcelling out
'lotto *m* [state] lottery; (porzione) lot; (di terreno) plot
lozi'one *f* lotion
■ **lozione idratante** moisturizer; **lozione solare** suntan lotion
lubrifi'cante **A** *adj* lubricating
B *m* lubricant
lubrifi'care *vt* lubricate
luc'chetto *m* padlock
lucci'cante *adj* sparkling
lucci'care *vi* sparkle
lucci'chio *m* sparkle
lucci'cone *m* **far venire i lucciconi** bring tears to the eyes
'luccio *m* pike
'lucciola *f* glow-worm; infml (prostituta) lady of the night
'luce *f* light; **accendere/spegnere la ~** switch the light on/off; **far ~ su** fig shed light on; **dare alla ~** give birth to; **venire alla ~** come to light
■ **luci** *pl* **di arresto** Auto stop lights; **luci** *pl* **d'atterraggio** landing lights; **luci** *pl* **d'emergenza** Auto hazard [warning] lights, hazards; **luce della luna** moonlight; **luci** *pl* **di posizione** Auto sidelights; **luci** *pl* **posteriori** Auto rear lights; **luci** *pl* **di retromarcia** Auto reversing lights; **luce del sole** sunlight; **luce stroboscopica** strobe
lu'cente *adj* shining
lucen'tezza *f* shine
lucer'nario *m* skylight
lu'certola *f* lizard
lucida'labbra *m inv* lip gloss
luci'dare *vt* polish
lucida'trice *f* [floor] polisher
'lucido **A** *adj* shiny; ‹*pavimento, scarpe*› polished; (chiaro) clear; ‹*persona, mente*› lucid; ‹*occhi*› watery
B *m* shine
■ **lucido [da scarpe]** [shoe] polish
lucra'tivo *adj* lucrative
'lucro *m* lucre; **senza fini di ~** non-profit-making, not-for-profit AmE
luculli'ano *adj* ‹*pranzo*› lavish
ludo'teca *f* playroom
'luglio *m* July
'lugubre *adj* gloomy
'lui *pers pron* (soggetto) he; (oggetto, con prep) him; **lo ha fatto ~ stesso** he did it himself
lu'maca *f* (mollusco) snail; fig slowcoach

'lume *m* lamp; (luce) light; **a ~ di candela** by candlelight; **perdere il ~ della ragione** be beside oneself with rage
lumi'nare *mf* luminary
lumi'narie *fpl* illuminations
lumine'scente *adj* luminescent
lumine'scenza *f* luminescence
lu'mino *m* (da cimitero) grave lamp
■ **lumino da notte** night light
luminosa'mente *adv* luminously
luminosità *f inv* brightness
lumi'noso *adj* luminous; ‹*stanza, cielo ecc.*› bright; **idea luminosa** brain wave
✓ **'luna** *f* moon; **chiaro di ~** moonlight; **avere la ~ storta** be in a bad mood
■ **luna di miele** honeymoon; **luna piena** full moon
'luna park *m inv* fairground
lu'nare *adj* lunar
lu'naria *f* moonstone
lu'nario *m* almanac; **sbarcare il ~** make [both] ends meet
lu'natico *adj* moody
lunedì *m inv* Monday; **di ~** on Mondays
lu'netta *f* half-moon [shape]
lun'gaggine *f* slowness
lunga'mente *adv* at great length
lun'ghezza *f* length; **di ~ media** medium length
■ **lunghezza d'onda** wavelength
'lungi *adv* **ero [ben] ~ dall'immaginare che...** I never dreamt for a moment that...
lungimi'rante *adj* far-seeing
lungimi'ranza *f* far-sightedness
✓ **'lungo** **A** *adj* long; (diluito) weak; (lento) slow; **a ~ andare** in the long run; **saperla lunga** be shrewd; **andare per le lunghe** drag on; **di gran lunga** by far; **di lunga data** long-term
B *m* length
C *prep* (durante) throughout; (per la lunghezza di) along
lungofi'ume *m* riverside
lungo'lago *m* lakeside
lungo'mare *m inv* seafront
lungome'traggio *m* feature film

lu'notto *m* rear window
■ **lunotto termico** heated rear window
'lunula *f* half-moon
✓ **lu'ogo** *m* place; (punto preciso) spot; (passo d'autore) passage; **aver ~** take place; **dar ~ a** give rise to; **fuori ~** out of place; **del ~** ‹*usanze*› local
■ **luogo comune** cliché; **luogo di nascita** birthplace; **luogo natale** birthplace; **luogo pubblico** public place; **luogo di villeggiatura** holiday resort
luogote'nente *m* Mil lieutenant
'lupa *f* she-wolf
lu'para *f* sawn-off shotgun
lu'petto *m* Cub [Scout]
✓ **'lupo** *m* wolf
■ **lupo mannaro** werewolf
'luppolo *m* hop
'lurido *adj* filthy
luri'dume *m* filth
lu'singa *f* flattery
lusin'gare *vt* flatter
lusin'garsi *vr* flatter oneself; (illudersi) fool oneself
lusinghi'ero *adj* flattering
lus'sare *vt* dislocate
lus'sarsi *vr* dislocate
lussazi'one *f* dislocation
Lussem'burgo *m* Luxembourg
✓ **'lusso** *m* luxury; **di ~** luxury *attrib*
lussuosa'mente *adv* luxuriously
lussu'oso *adj* luxurious
lussureggi'ante *adj* luxuriant
lus'suria *f* lust
lussuri'oso *adj* dissolute
lu'strare *vt* polish
lu'strino *m* sequin
'lustro **A** *adj* shiny
B *m* sheen; fig prestige; (quinquennio) five-year period
lute'rano *adj & nmf* Lutheran
'lutto *m* mourning; **parato a ~** draped in black
■ **lutto stretto** deep mourning
luttu'oso *adj* mournful

L

✓ key word

Mm

m *abbr* (**metro**) m

ma *conj* but; (eppure) yet; **ma!** (dubbio) I don't know; (indignazione) really!; **ma davvero?** really?; **ma va'?** really?; **ma sì!** why not!; (certo che sì) of course!

'macabro *adj* macabre

macché *int* of course not!

macche'roni *mpl* macaroni *sg*

macche'ronico *adj* ‹*italiano*› broken

'macchia¹ *f* stain; (di diverso colore) spot; (piccola) speck; **senza ~** spotless; **spargersi a ~ d'olio** spread rapidly

■ **macchia di colore** splash of colour; **macchia d'inchiostro** ink stain; **macchia di sangue** bloodstain

'macchia² *f* (boscaglia) scrub; **darsi alla ~** take to the woods

macchi'are *vt* stain

macchi'arsi *vr* stain

macchi'ato **A** *adj* ‹*caffè*› with a dash of milk; ‹*pelo*› spotted; **~ di** (sporco) stained with; **~ d'inchiostro** ink stained, inky **B** *m* (caffè) espresso with a dash of milk

macchi'etta *f* spot; (persona) real character

'macchina *f* machine; (motore) engine; (automobile) car; **in ~** by car; **giro in ~** drive; **cimitero delle macchine** scrapyard

■ **macchina del caffè** coffee maker; **macchina da cucire** sewing machine; **macchina per l'espresso** coffee machine; **macchina fotografica** camera; **macchina fototessere** photo booth; **macchina obliteratrice** ticket-stamping machine; **macchina da presa** cine camera; **macchina da scrivere** typewriter; **macchina sverniciante** paint stripper; **macchina utensile** machine tool; **macchina della verità** lie detector

macchinal'mente *adv* mechanically

macchi'nare *vt* plot

macchi'nario *m* machinery

macchinazi'oni *fpl* machinations, scheming

macchi'netta *f* (per i denti) brace; (per il caffè) espresso coffee maker; (accendino) lighter

macchi'nista *m* Rail engine driver; Naut engineer; Theat stagehand

macchi'noso *adj* complicated

mace'donia *f* fruit salad

Mace'donia *f* Macedonia

macel'laio, -a *mf* butcher

macel'lare *vt* slaughter

macellazi'one *f* slaughtering

macelle'ria *f* butcher's [shop]

ma'cello *m* (mattatoio) slaughterhouse; fig shambles *sg*; **andare al ~** fig go to the slaughter; **mandare al ~** fig send to his/her death

mace'rare *vt* macerate; fig distress

mace'rarsi *vr* be consumed

macerazi'one *f* maceration

ma'cerie *fpl* rubble *sg*; (rottami) debris *sg*

'macero *m* pulping; (stabilimento) pulping mill

Mach *m inv* Mach

ma'chete *m inv* machete

machia'vellico *adj* Machiavellian

ma'chismo *m* machismo

'macho *adj* macho

ma'cigno *m* boulder

maci'lento *adj* emaciated

'macina *f* millstone

macinacaffè *m inv* coffee mill

macina'pepe *m inv* pepper mill

maci'nare *vt* mill

maci'nato **A** *adj* ground **B** *m* (carne) mince

maci'nino *m* mill; hum (macchina) old banger

maciul'lare *vt* (stritolare) crush

'macro *f inv* Comput macro

macrobi'otica *f*

■ **negozio di macrobiotica** health food shop

macrobi'otico *adj* macrobiotic

macro'clima *m* macroclimate

macro'cosmo *m* macrocosm

macrofotogra'fia *f* macrophotography

macro'scopico *adj* macroscopic

macu'lato *adj* spotted

Madaga'scar *m* Madagascar

madami'gella *f* young lady

'madia *f cupboard with a covered trough on top for making bread*

'madido *adj* **~ di** damp with ‹*sudore*›

Ma'donna *f* Our Lady

mador'nale *adj* gross

'madre *f* mother

■ **madre biologica** birth mother; **madre single** single mother

madre'lingua *adj inv* **inglese ~** English native speaker

madre'patria *f* native land

madre'perla *f* mother-of-pearl

ma'drepora *f* madrepore

madri'gale *m* madrigal

ma'drina *f* godmother

maestà *f inv* majesty
maestosa'mente *adv* majestically
maestosità *f inv* majesty
mae'stoso *adj* majestic
ma'estra *f* teacher; Sch primary school teacher
■ **maestra d'asilo** kindergarten teacher; **maestra di canto** singing teacher; **maestra di piano** piano teacher; **maestra di sci** ski instructor
mae'strale *m* north-west wind
mae'stranza *f* workers *pl*
mae'stria *f* mastery
⚷ **ma'estro** **A** *m* teacher; Sch primary school teacher; Mus maestro; (esperto) master; **colpo da ~** master stroke
■ **maestro d'asilo** kindergarten teacher; **maestro di canto** singing teacher; **maestro di cerimonie** master of ceremonies; **maestro di piano** piano teacher; **maestro di sci** ski instructor
B *adj* (principale) main; (di grande abilità) skilful
'mafia *f* Mafia
mafi'oso **A** *adj* of the Mafia
B *m* member of the Mafia, Mafioso
'maga *f* sorceress, magician
ma'gagna *f* fault
⚷ **ma'gari** **A** *adv* (forse) maybe
B *int* I wish!
C *conj* (per esprimere desiderio) if only; (anche se) even if
magazzini'ere *m* storeman, warehouseman
magaz'zino *m* (deposito) warehouse; (in negozio) stockroom; (emporio) shop; **grande ~** department store
■ **magazzini** *pl* **portuali** naval stores
Magg. *abbr* (**maggiore**) Maj
mag'gese *m* field lying fallow
⚷ **'maggio** *m* May
maggio'lino *m* May bug
maggio'rana *f* marjoram
maggio'ranza *f* majority
maggio'rare *vt* increase
maggior'domo *m* butler
⚷ **maggi'ore** **A** *adj* (di dimensioni, numero) bigger, larger; (superlativo) biggest, largest; (di età) older; (superlativo) oldest; (di importanza, Mus) major; (superlativo) greatest; **la maggior parte di** most; **la maggior parte del tempo** most of the time
B *pron* (di dimensioni) the bigger, the larger; (superlativo) the biggest, the largest; (di età) the older; (superlativo) the oldest; (di importanza) the major; (superlativo) the greatest
C *m* Mil major; Aeron squadron leader
maggio'renne **A** *adj* of age
B *mf* adult

maggiori'tario *adj* (della maggioranza) majority; ‹*sistema*› first-past-the-post *attrib*
maggior'mente *adv* [all] the more; (più di tutto) most
'Magi *mpl* **i re ~** the Magi
ma'gia *f* magic; (trucco) magic trick
magica'mente *adv* magically
'magico *adj* magic
magi'stero *m* (insegnamento) teaching; (maestria) skill; **facoltà di ~** arts faculty
magi'strale *adj* masterly; **istituto ~** teacher training college
magistral'mente *adv* in a masterly fashion
magi'strato *m* magistrate
magistra'tura *f* magistrature; **la ~** the Bench
⚷ **'maglia** *f* stitch; (lavoro ai ferri) knitting; (tessuto) jersey; (di rete) mesh; (indumento intimo) vest; (esterno) top; (di calciatore) shirt; **fare la ~** knit
■ **maglia con cappuccio** infml hoody; **maglia diritta** knit; **maglia rosa** (ciclismo) yellow jersey; **maglia rovescia** purl
magli'aia *f* knitter
maglie'ria *f* knitwear
magli'etta *f*
■ **maglietta [a maniche corte]** tee shirt
magli'ficio *m* knitwear factory
ma'glina *f* (tessuto) jersey
'maglio *m* mallet
magli'one *m* sweater, jumper
■ **maglione dolcevita** polo neck [jumper]; **maglione a girocollo** crew neck [sweater]; **maglione a V** V-neck [sweater]
'magma *m* magma
ma'gnaccia *m inv* infml pimp
ma'gnanimo *adj* magnanimous
ma'gnate *m* magnate
ma'gnesia *f* magnesia
ma'gnesio *m* magnesium
ma'gnete *m* magnet
magnetica'mente *adv* magnetically
ma'gnetico *adj* magnetic
magne'tismo *m* magnetism
magne'tofono *m* tape recorder
magnifica'mente *adv* magnificently
magnifi'cenza *f* magnificence; (generosità) munificence
⚷ **ma'gnifico** *adj* magnificent; (generoso) munificent
magni'tudine *f* Astr magnitude
'magno *adj* **aula magna** main hall
ma'gnolia *f* magnolia
'magnum *f inv* (bottiglia, pistola) magnum
'mago *m* magician
ma'gone *m* **avere il ~** be down; **mi è venuto il ~** I've got a lump in my throat

m

⚷ key word

'magra *f* low water

ma'grezza *f* thinness

'magro *adj* thin; ‹*carne*› lean; (scarso) meagre; **magra consolazione** cold comfort

'mai *adv* never; (inter, talvolta) ever; **caso ~** if anything; **caso ~ tornasse** in case he comes back; **come ~?** why?; **cosa ~?** what on earth?; **~ più** never again; **più che ~** more than ever; **quando ~?** whenever?; **quasi ~** hardly ever

mai'ale *m* pig; (carne) pork
■ **maiale arrosto** roast pork

maia'lino *m* piglet

'mailing *m* direct mail, mailing

mai'olica *f* majolica

maio'nese *f* mayonnaise

'mais *m* maize

mai'uscola *f* capital [letter]; **bloc maiusc** (tasto) caps lock

mai'uscolo *adj* capital

mai'zena® *f* cornflour

mal ▸ **male**

'mala *nf sl* **la ~** the underworld

malac'corto *adj* unwise

mala'fede *f* bad faith

malaf'fare *m*
■ **gente di malaffare** shady characters *pl*

mala'lingua *f* backbiter

mala'mente *adv* ‹*ridotto*› badly; ‹*rispondere*› rudely

malan'dato *adj* in bad shape; (di salute) in poor health

ma'lanimo *m* ill will

ma'lanno *m* misfortune; (malattia) illness; **prendersi un ~** catch something

mala'pena *adv* **a ~** hardly

ma'laria *f* malaria

mala'ticcio *adj* sickly

ma'lato, -a **A** *adj* ill, sick; ‹*pianta*› diseased **B** *mf* sick person
■ **malato di Aids** AIDS sufferer; **malato di cancro** cancer patient; **malato di mente** mentally ill person

malat'tia *f* disease, illness; **ho preso due giorni di ~** I had two days off sick; **essere in ~** be on sick leave
■ **malattia nervosa** nervous disease; **malattia venerea** venereal disease, VD

malaugurata'mente *adv* unfortunately

malaugu'rato *adj* ill-omened

malau'gurio *m* bad *or* ill omen

mala'vita *f* underworld

malavi'toso, -a *mf* gangster

mala'voglia *f* unwillingness; **di ~** unwillingly

Ma'lawi *m* Malawi

malcapi'tato *adj* wretched

malce'lato *adj* ill-concealed

mal'concio *adj* battered

malcon'tento *m* discontent

malco'stume *m* immorality

mal'destro *adj* awkward; (inesperto) inexperienced

maldi'cente *adj* slanderous

maldi'cenza *f* slander

maldi'sposto *adj* ill-disposed

Mal'dive *fpl* Maldives

'male **A** *adv* badly; **funzionare ~** not work properly; **star ~** be ill; **star ~ a qualcuno** ‹*vestito ecc.*› not suit somebody; **rimanerci ~** be hurt; **ho dormito ~** I didn't sleep well; **non c'è ~!** not bad at all!
B *m* evil; (dolore) pain, ache; (malattia) illness; (danno) harm; **distinguere il bene dal ~** know right from wrong; **andare a ~** go off; **aver ~ a** have a pain in; **dove hai ~?** where does it hurt?, where is the pain?; **far ~ a qualcuno** (provocare dolore) hurt somebody; ‹*cibo*› be bad for somebody; **le cipolle mi fanno ~** onions don't agree with me; **mi fa ~ la schiena** my back is hurting; **farsi ~ alla schiena** hurt one's back
■ **mal d'aereo** airsickness; **mal d'aria** airsickness; **soffrire il mal d'aria** be airsick; **mal d'auto** carsickness; **mal di denti** toothache; **mal di gola** sore throat; **mal di mare** seasickness; **avere il mal di mare** be seasick; **mal d'orecchi** earache; **mal di pancia** lit stomach ache; fig, fam trouble; **mal di schiena** backache; **mal di testa** headache

maledetta'mente *adv* flipping

male'detto *adj* cursed; (orribile) awful

male'dire *vt* curse

maledizi'one *f* curse; **~!** damn!

maleducata'mente *adv* rudely

maledu'cato *adj* ill-mannered

maleducazi'one *f* rudeness

male'fatta *f* misdeed

male'ficio *m* witchcraft

ma'lefico *adj* ‹*azione*› evil; (nocivo) harmful

maleodo'rante *adj* foul-smelling

ma'lese *adj & nmf* Malaysian

Ma'lesia *f* Malaysia

ma'lessere *m* indisposition; fig uneasiness

ma'levolo *adj* malevolent

malfa'mato *adj* of ill repute

mal'fatto *adj* badly done; (malformato) ill-shaped

malfat'tore *m* wrongdoer

mal'fermo *adj* unsteady; ‹*salute*› poor

malfor'mato *adj* misshapen

malformazi'one *f* malformation

mal'gascio, -a *adj & nmf* Malagasy

malgo'verno *m* misgovernment

mal'grado **A** *prep* in spite of **B** *conj* although

'Mali *m* Mali

ma'lia *f* spell

maligna'mente *adv* maliciously

mali'gnare *vi* malign

malignità *f inv* malice; Med malignancy
ma'ligno *adj* malicious; (perfido) evil; Med malignant
malinco'nia *f* melancholy
malinconica'mente *adv* melancholically
malin'conico *adj* melancholy
malincu'ore **a ~** *adv* unwillingly, reluctantly
malinfor'mato *adj* misinformed
malintenzio'nato, -a *mf* miscreant
malin'teso **A** *adj* mistaken
B *m* misunderstanding
ma'lizia *f* malice; (astuzia) cunning; (espediente) trick
maliziosa'mente *adv* mischievously, naughtily
maliziosità *f inv* naughtiness
malizi'oso *adj* (birichino) mischievous, naughty
malle'abile *adj* malleable
mal'leolo *m* Anat malleolus
malleva'dore *m* guarantor
'mallo *m* husk
mal'loppo *m* infml loot
malme'nare *vt* ill-treat
mal'messo *adj* (vestito male) shabbily dressed; ‹*casa*› poorly furnished; fig (senza soldi) hard up
m
malnu'trito *adj* undernourished
malnutrizi'one *f* malnutrition
'malo *adj* **in ~ modo** badly
ma'locchio *m* evil eye
ma'lora *f* ruin; **della ~** awful; **andare in ~** go to ruin
ma'lore *m* illness; **essere colto da ~** be suddenly taken ill
malri'dotto *adj* ‹*persona*› in a sorry state; (auto, casa) dilapidated, in a sorry state
mal'sano *adj* unhealthy
malsi'curo *adj* unsafe; (incerto) uncertain
'malta *f* mortar
mal'tempo *m* bad weather
mal'tese *adj & nmf* Maltese
'malto *m* malt
mal'tosio *m* maltose
maltratta'mento *m* ill-treatment
maltrat'tare *vt* ill-treat
malu'more *m* bad mood; **di ~** in a bad mood
'malva *adj inv* mauve
mal'vagio *adj* wicked
malvagità *f inv* wickedness
malva'sia *f type of dessert wine*
malversazi'one *f* embezzlement
mal'visto *adj* unpopular (**da** with)
malvi'vente *m* criminal
malvolenti'eri *adv* unwillingly

⚷ key word

malvo'lere *vt* **farsi ~** make oneself unpopular; **prendere qualcuno a ~** take a dislike to somebody
⚷ **'mamma** *f* mummy, mum; **~ mia!** good gracious!
mam'mario *adj* mammary
mam'mella *f* breast
mam'mifero *m* mammal
mam'mismo *m* (del figlio) dependency on the mother figure; (della madre) excessive motherliness
mammogra'fia *f* mammograph
'mammola *f* violet
mammo'letta *f* shrinking violet
mam'mone *m* mummy's boy
mam'mut *m inv* mammoth
ma'nata *f* handful; (colpo) slap
'manca *f* ▶ **manco**
manca'mento *m* **avere un ~** faint
man'cante *adj* missing
⚷ **man'canza** *f* lack; (assenza) absence; (insufficienza) shortage; (fallo) fault; (imperfezione) defect; **in ~ d'altro** failing all else; **sento la sua ~** I miss him
■ **mancanza di tatto** lack of tact, indelicacy
⚷ **man'care** **A** *vi* be lacking; (essere assente) be missing; (venir meno) fail; (morire) pass away; **~ di** be lacking in; **~ a** fail to keep ‹*promessa*›; **mi manca casa** I miss home; **mi manchi** I miss you; **mi è mancato il tempo** I didn't have [the] time; **mi mancano 10 euro** I'm 10 euros short; **quanto manca alla partenza?** how long before we leave?; **~è mancata la corrente** there was a power failure; **sentirsi ~** feel faint; **sentirsi ~ il respiro** be unable to breathe [properly]
B *vt* miss ‹*bersaglio*›; **è mancato poco che cadesse** he nearly fell
man'cato *adj* ‹*appuntamento*› missed; ‹*tentativo*› unsuccessful; ‹*occasione*› wasted
'manche *f inv* heat
man'chevole *adj* defective
'mancia *f* tip
■ **~ competente** reward
manci'ata *f* handful
man'cino *adj* left-handed
'manco, -a **A** *adj* left
B *f* left hand
C *adv* (nemmeno) not even
⚷ **man'dante** *mf* (di delitto) instigator; Jur principal
manda'rancio *m* clementine
man'dare *vt* send; (emettere) give off; utter ‹*suono*›; **~ a chiamare** send for; **~ avanti la casa** run the house; **~ giù** (ingoiare) swallow
manda'rino *m* Bot mandarin
man'data *f* consignment; (di serratura) turn; **chiudere a doppia ~** double lock
manda'tario *m* Jur agent
man'dato *m* (incarico) mandate; Jur warrant

■ **mandato di comparizione [in giudizio]** subpoena; **mandato di pagamento** money order; **mandato di perquisizione** search warrant

man'dibola *f* jaw

mando'lino *m* mandolin

'mandorla *f* almond; **a ~** ‹*occhi*› almond shaped

■ **mandorla amara** bitter almond

mandor'lato *m* nut brittle (*type of nougat*)

'mandorlo *m* almond [tree]

man'dragola *f* mandrake

'mandria *f* herd

mandri'ano *m* cowherd

man'drillo *m* (scimmia) mandrill; (attrezzo) mandrel; fig fam goat

maneg'gevole *adj* easy to handle

maneggi'are *vt* handle

ma'neggio *m* handling; (intrigo) plot; (scuola di equitazione) riding school

ma'nesco *adj* quick to hit out

ma'netta *f* lever; **a tutta ~** flat out; **manette** *pl* handcuffs

man'forte *m* **dare ~ a qualcuno** support somebody

manga'nello *m* truncheon

manga'nese *m* manganese

mange'reccio *adj* edible

mangiacas'sette *m inv* cassette player

mangia'dischi® *m inv* portable record player

mangia'fumo *adj inv* **candela ~** air-purifying candle

mangia'nastri *m inv* cassette player

mangi'are **A** *vt & vi* eat; (consumare) eat up; (corrodere) eat away; take ‹*scacchi, carte ecc.*›; **dar da ~ al gatto/cane** feed the cat/dog
B *m* eating; (cibo) food; (pasto) meal

mangi'arsi *vr* **~ le parole** mumble; **~ le unghie** bite one's nails

mangia'soldi *adj inv* **macchinetta ~** one-armed bandit

mangi'ata *f* big meal; **farsi una bella ~ di...** feast on...

mangia'toia *f* manger

mangia|'tore, -trice *mf* eater

■ **mangiatore di fuoco** fire-eater; **mangiatrice di uomini** maneater

man'gime *m* fodder

■ **mangime per i polli** chicken feed

mangi'one, -a *mf* infml glutton

mangiucchi'are *vt* nibble

'mango *m* mango

man'grovia *f* mangrove

man'gusta *f* mongoose

ma'nia *f* mania

■ **mania di grandezza** delusions of grandeur; **mania di persecuzione** persecution complex

mania'cale *adj* manic

ma'niaco, -a **A** *adj* maniacal
B *mf* maniac

■ **maniaco sessuale** sex maniac

ma'niaco-depres'sivo *adj & nmf* manic-depressive

'manica *f* sleeve; infml (gruppo) band; **a maniche lunghe** long-sleeved; **senza maniche** sleeveless; **essere in maniche di camicia** be in shirt sleeves; **essere di ~ larga** be generous; **essere di ~ stretta** be strict

■ **manica a vento** wind sock

'Manica *f* **la ~** the [English] Channel

manica'retto *m* tasty dish

maniche'ismo *m* Manicheism

mani'chetta *f* hose

mani'chino *m* (da sarto, vetrina) dummy

'manico *m* handle; Mus neck

■ **manico di scopa** broom handle

mani'comio *m* mental home; infml (confusione) tip

mani'cotto *m* muff; Mech sleeve

mani'cure **A** *f* manicure
B *mf inv* (persona) manicurist

mani'era *f* manner; **in ~ che** so that

manie'rato *adj* affected; ‹*stile*› mannered

manie'rismo *m* mannerism

mani'ero *m* manor

manifat'tura *f* manufacture; (fabbrica) factory

manifatturi'ero *adj* manufacturing

manifesta'mente *adv* demonstrably, manifestly

manife'stante *mf* demonstrator

manife'stare **A** *vt* show; (esprimere) express
B *vi* demonstrate

manifes'tarsi *vr* show oneself

manifestazi'one *f* show; (espressione) expression; (sintomo) manifestation; (dimostrazione pubblica) demonstration

mani'festo **A** *adj* evident
B *m* poster; (dichiarazione pubblica) manifesto

ma'niglia *f* handle; (sostegno, in autobus ecc.) strap

manipo'lare *vt* handle; (massaggiare) massage; (alterare) adulterate; fig manipulate

manipola|'tore, '-trice **A** *mf* manipulator
B *adj* manipulative

manipolazi'one *f* handling; (massaggio) massage; (alterazione) adulteration; fig manipulation

mani'scalco *m* smith

'manna *f*

■ **manna dal cielo** manna from heaven

man'naia *f* (scure) axe; (da macellaio) cleaver

man'naro *adj* **lupo ~** werewolf

'mano *f* hand; (strato di vernice ecc.) coat; **alla ~** informal; **fuori ~** out of the way; **man ~** little by little; **man ~ che** as; **sotto ~** to hand; **di seconda ~** second-hand; **a mani vuote** empty-handed; **a ~** ‹*scritto, ricamato, fatto*› by hand; ‹*trapano ecc.*›

hand-held; **dare una ~ a qualcuno** give *or* lend somebody a hand; **ha le mani di pastafrolla** he is a butterfingers

mano'dopera *f* labour

ma'nometro *m* manometer, pressure gauge

mano'mettere *vt* tamper with; (violare) violate

ma'nopola *f* (di apparecchio) knob; (guanto) mitten; (su pullman) handle

mano'scritto **A** *adj* handwritten **B** *m* manuscript

mano'vale *m* labourer

mano'vella *f* handle; Techn crank
■ **manovella alzacristalli** winder

ma'novra *f* manoeuvre; Rail shunting; **fare le manovre** Auto manoeuvre; **manovre** *pl* **di corridoio** lobbying

mano'vrabile *adj* manoeuvrable; fig ‹*persona*› easy to manipulate

mano'vrare **A** *vt* (azionare) operate; fig manipulate ‹*persona*› **B** *vi* manoeuvre

manro'vescio *m* slap

man'sarda *f* attic

mansio'nario *m* job description

mansi'one *f* task; (dovere) duty

mansu'eto *adj* meek; ‹*animale*› docile

'manta *f* Zool manta

mante'cato **A** *m* soft ice cream **B** *adj* creamy

man'tella *f* cape

man'tello *m* cloak; (soprabito, di animale) coat; (di neve) mantle

mante'nere *vt* (conservare) keep; (in buono stato, sostentare) maintain

mante'nersi *vr* **~ in forma** keep fit

manteni'mento *m* maintenance
■ **mantenimento dell'ordine pubblico** policing; **mantenimento della pace** Mil, Pol peacekeeping

mante'nuta *f* kept woman

'mantice *m* bellows *pl*; (di automobile) hood, top

'mantide *f* mantis

man'tiglia *f* mantilla

'manto *m* cloak; (coltre) mantle

'Mantova *f* Mantua

manto'vana *f* (di tende) pelmet

manu'ale *adj & nm* manual
■ **manuale di conversazione** phrase book; **manuale d'uso** user manual

manual'mente *adv* manually

ma'nubrio *m* handle; (di bicicletta) handlebars *pl*; (per ginnastica) dumb-bell

manu'fatto *adj* manufactured

manutenzi'one *f* maintenance; **un giardino che richiede poca ~** a low-maintenance garden

'manzo *m* steer; (carne) beef

maomet'tano *adj & nm* Muslim

Mao'metto *m* Mohammed, Muhammad

ma'ori *adj inv & m inv* Maori

'mappa *f* map

mappa'mondo *m* globe

mar ▸ **mare**

mara'chella *f* prank

maragià *m inv* maharajah

maran'tacea *f* Bot arrowroot

mara'schino *m* maraschino (*sweet liqueur*)

ma'rasma *m* fig decline

mara'tona *f* marathon

marato'neta *mf* marathon runner

'marca *f* mark; Comm brand; (fabbricazione) make; (scontrino) ticket; **di ~** branded
■ **marca da bollo** *stamp showing that the necessary duties have been paid*

mar'care *vt* mark; Sport score

marcata'mente *adv* markedly

mar'cato *adj* ‹*tratto, accento*› strong, marked

marca'tore *m* (chi segna un gol) scorer; (chi marca un avversario) marker; (pennarello) marker pen

'Marche *fpl* Marches

mar'chese, -a **A** *m* marquis **B** *f* marchioness

mar'chetta *f* (assicurativa) National Insurance stamp; **fare marchette** infml be on the game

marchi'are *vt* brand

'marchio *m* brand; (caratteristica) mark
■ **marchio depositato** registered trademark; **marchio di fabbrica** trademark, TM; **marchio registrato** registered trademark

'marcia *f* march; Auto gear; Sport walk; **mettere in ~** put into gear; **mettersi in ~** start off; **cambiare ~** change gear
■ **marcia a senso unico alternato** temporary one way system in operation; **marcia forzata** forced march; **marcia funebre** funeral march; **marcia indietro** reverse gear; **fare ~ indietro** reverse; fig back-pedal; **marcia nuziale** wedding march

marcia'longa *f* (di sci) cross-country skiing race; (a piedi) long-distance race

marciapi'ede *m* pavement, sidewalk AmE; (di stazione) platform

marci'are *vi* march; (funzionare) go, work

marcia|'tore, -trice *mf* walker

'marcio **A** *adj* rotten **B** *m* rotten part; fig corruption

mar'cire *vi* go bad, rot

mar'cita *f* water meadow

'marco *m* (moneta) mark

marco'nista *mf* radio operator

'mare *m* sea; (luogo di mare) seaside; **sul ~** ‹*casa*› at the seaside; ‹*città*› on the sea; **andare al ~** go to the sea; **in alto ~** on the

high seas; **d'alto ~** ocean-going; **essere in alto ~** fig not know which way to turn
■ **mare Adriatico** Adriatic Sea; **mar Cinese** China Sea; **mar Ionio** Ionian Sea; **mare d'Irlanda** Irish Sea; **mar Mediterraneo** Mediterranean; **mar Morto** Dead Sea; **mar Nero** Black Sea; **mare del Nord** North Sea; **mar Tirreno** Tyrrhenian Sea

ma'rea *f* tide; **una ~ di** hundreds of; **alta/bassa marea** high/low tide
■ **marea montante** flood tide

mareggi'ata *f* [sea] storm

mare'moto *m* tidal wave, seaquake

maresci'allo *m* (ufficiale) marshal; (sottufficiale) warrant officer

ma'retta *f* choppiness; fig tension

marga'rina *f* margarine

marghe'rita *f* marguerite
■ **margherita settembrina** Michaelmas daisy

margheri'tina *f* daisy

margi'nale *adj* marginal

marginaliz'zare *vt* marginalize

marginal'mente *adv* marginally

'margine *m* margin; (orlo) brink; (bordo) border
■ **margine di errore** margin of error; **margine di sicurezza** safety margin; **margine di vendita** mark-up

mari'ano *adj* Relig Marian

ma'rina *f* navy; (costa) seashore; (quadro) seascape
■ **marina mercantile** merchant navy; **marina militare** navy

mari'naio *m* sailor
■ **marinaio d'acqua dolce** landlubber

mari'nare *vt* marinate; **~ la scuola** play truant

mari'naro *adj* seafaring

mari'nata *f* marinade

mari'nato *adj* Culin marinated

ma'rino *adj* sea *attrib*, marine

mario'netta *f* puppet

mari'tare *vt* marry

mari'tarsi *vr* get married

ma'rito *m* husband

mari'tozzo *m* currant bun

ma'rittimo *adj* maritime

mar'maglia *f* rabble

marmel'lata *f* jam; (di agrumi) marmalade

mar'mitta *f* pot; Auto silencer
■ **marmitta catalitica** catalytic converter

'marmo *m* marble *attrib*

mar'mocchio *m* infml brat

mar'moreo *adj* marble

marmoriz'zato *adj* marbled

mar'motta *f* marmot

maroc'chino *adj & nmf* Moroccan

Ma'rocco *m* Morocco

ma'roso *m* breaker

mar'rone **A** *adj* brown
B *m* brown; (castagna) chestnut; **marroni** *pl* **canditi** marrons glacés

'Marshall *fpl* **le isole ~** Marshall Islands

mar'sina *f* tails *pl*

marsupi'ale *m* marsupial

mar'supio *m* (borsa) bumbag

'Marte *m* Mars

martedì *m inv* Tuesday; **di ~** on Tuesdays
■ **martedì grasso** Shrove Tuesday

martel'lante *adj* ‹*mal di testa*› pounding, throbbing; **hanno fatto una pubblicità ~** they hyped the product, they bombarded the market with publicity

martel'lare **A** *vt* hammer
B *vi* throb

martel'lata *f* hammer blow

martel'letto *m* (di giudice) gavel; (di pianoforte) hammer; (di medico) percussion hammer

martel'lio *m* hammering

mar'tello *m* hammer; (di battente) knocker
■ **~ pneumatico** pneumatic drill

marti'netto *m* Mech jack

mar'tin pesca'tore *m inv* kingfisher

'martire *mf* martyr

mar'tirio *m* martyrdom

'martora *f* marten

martori'are *vt* torment

mar'xismo *m* Marxism

mar'xista *adj & nmf* Marxist

marza'pane *m* marzipan

marzi'ale *adj* martial

marzi'ano, -a *adj & nmf* Martian

'marzo *m* March

mascal'zone *m* rascal

ma'scara *m inv* mascara

mascar'pone *m full-fat cream cheese often used for desserts*

ma'scella *f* jaw

'maschera *f* mask; (costume) fancy dress; Cinema, Theat usher *m*, usherette *f*; (nella commedia dell'arte) stock character
■ **maschera antigas** gas mask; **maschera di bellezza** face pack; **maschera mortuaria** death mask; **maschera ad ossigeno** oxygen mask

maschera'mento *m* masking; Mil camouflage

masche'rare *vt* mask; fig camouflage

masche'rarsi *vr* put on a mask; **~ da** dress up as

masche'rata *f* masquerade

maschi'accio *m* (ragazza) tomboy

ma'schile **A** *adj* masculine; ‹*sesso*› male
B *m* masculine [gender]

maschilismo *m* male chauvinism

maschi'lista **A** *adj* sexist
B *m* male chauvinist

'maschio **A** *adj* male; (virile) manly
B *m* male; (figlio) son
■ **maschio dominante** alpha male

masco'lino *adj* masculine

m

ma'scotte *f inv* mascot
maso'chismo *m* masochism
maso'chista *adj & nmf* masochist
'massa *f* mass; Electr earth, ground AmE; una ~ **[di gente]** a crowd [of people]
massa'crante *adj* gruelling
massa'crare *vt* massacre
mas'sacro *m* massacre; fig mess
massaggi'are *vt* massage
massaggia|'tore, -trice **A** *m* masseur **B** *f* masseuse
mas'saggio *m* massage
■ **massaggio cardiaco** heart massage
mas'saia *f* housewife
mas'sello **A** *m* (metallo) ingot **B** *adj* ‹*legno*› solid
masse'rizie *fpl* household effects
massiccia'mente *adv* on a big scale
massicci'ata *f* hard core
mas'siccio **A** *adj* massive; ‹*oro ecc.*› solid; ‹*corporatura*› heavy **B** *m* massif
massifi'care *vt* de-individualize ‹*società*›
massificazi'one *f* de-individualization
'massima *f* maxim; (temperatura) maximum
massi'male *m* (assicurazione) limit of indemnity
massimiz'zare *vt* maximize
massimizzazi'one *f* maximization
'massimo **A** *adj* greatest; ‹*quantità*› maximum, greatest **B** *m* **il** ~ the maximum; **al** ~ at [the] most, as a maximum
■ **massimo storico** all-time high
'masso *m* rock
mas'sone *m* [Free]mason
massone'ria *f* Freemasonry
mastecto'mia *f* mastectomy
ma'stello *m wooden box for the grape or olive harvest*
masteriz'zare *vt* ‹*CD, DVD*› burn
masterizza'tore *m*
■ **masterizzatore di CD/DVD** CD/DVD burner
masti'care *vt* chew; (borbottare) mumble
'mastice *m* mastic, filler; (per vetri) putty
ma'stino *m* mastiff
masto'dontico *adj* gigantic
ma'stoide *m* mastoid
'mastro *m* master; **libro** ~ ledger
mastur'barsi *vr* masturbate
masturbazi'one *f* masturbation
ma'tassa *f* skein
match 'point *m inv* Tennis match point
matelassé *m inv* quilting
mate'matica *f* mathematics *sg*, maths *sg*, math AmE
■ **matematica pura** pure mathematics

key word

mate'matico, -a **A** *adj* mathematical **B** *mf* mathematician
materas'sino *m* small mattress
■ **materassino gonfiabile** air bed, lilo®
mate'rasso *m* mattress
■ **materasso ad acqua** water bed; **materasso di gommapiuma** foam mattress; **materasso a molle** spring mattress
ma'teria *f* matter; (materiale) material; (di studio) subject
■ **materia grigia** grey matter; **materia oscura** dark matter; **materia prima** raw material
materi'ale **A** *adj* material; (grossolano) coarse **B** *m* material
■ **materiale da costruzione** building material; **materiale pubblicitario** publicity material; **materiale di scarto** waste material
materia'lismo *m* materialism
materia'lista **A** *adj* materialistic; **non** ~ unworldly **B** *mf* materialist
materializ'zarsi *vr* materialize
material'mente *adv* physically
materna'mente *adv* maternally
maternità *f inv* motherhood; **è alla prima** ~ it's her first baby; **ospedale di maternità** maternity hospital
ma'terno *adj* maternal; **lingua materna** mother tongue
ma'tita *f* pencil; **matite** *pl* **colorate** coloured pencils
■ **matita emostatica** styptic pencil; **matita per gli occhi** eyeliner pencil
matriar'cale *adj* matriarchal
ma'trice *f* matrix; (origini) roots *pl*; Comm counterfoil
■ **matrice attiva** Comput active matrix; **matrice passiva** Comput passive matrix
ma'tricola *f* (registro) register; Univ fresher; **numero di** ~ (di studente) matriculation number
ma'trigna *f* stepmother
matrimoni'ale *adj* matrimonial; **vita** ~ married life
matri'monio *m* marriage; (cerimonia) wedding
■ **matrimonio in bianco** white wedding; **matrimonio civile** civil wedding; **matrimonio di convenienza** marriage of convenience; **matrimonio di fatto** common-law marriage; **matrimonio gay** gay marriage; **matrimonio omosessuale** gay marriage
ma'trona *f* matron
'matta *f* (nelle carte) joker
mattacchi'one, -a *mf* rascal
mat'tanza *f* (di tonni) tuna fishing; fig killings *pl*
matta'toio *m* slaughterhouse
matta'tore *m* (artista) star performer
matte'rello *m* rolling pin

mat'tina *f* morning; **la ~, alla ~** in the morning; **domani ~** tomorrow morning; **ieri ~** yesterday morning

matti'nata *f* morning; Theat matinée

mattini'ero *adj* **essere ~** be an early riser

mat'tino *m* morning

'matto, -a **A** *adj* mad, crazy; Med insane; (falso) false; (opaco) matt; **avere una voglia matta di...** be dying for...
■ **matto da legare** barking mad
B *m* madman
C *f* madwoman

mat'tone *m* brick; (libro) bore

matto'nella *f* tile
■ **mattonella grezza** quarry tile

mattu'tino *adj* morning *attrib*

matu'rare *vt* ripen; Fin mature

maturazi'one *f* ripening; Fin maturity; fig (di idea ecc.) gestation; **arrivare a ~** ‹*frutta*› ripen; ‹*polizza*› mature

maturità *f inv* maturity; Sch school-leaving certificate

ma'turo *adj* mature; ‹*frutto*› ripe

ma'tusa *m* old fogey

Mauri'tania *sf* Mauritania

Mau'rizio *f* **[isola di] ~** Mauritius

mauso'leo *m* mausoleum

maxi'schermo *m* wide screen

'mayday *m inv* Radio Mayday

'mazza *f* club; (martello) hammer; (da baseball, cricket) bat
■ **mazza da golf** golf club

maz'zata *f* blow

maz'zetta *f* (di banconote) bundle; (tangente) bribe

'mazzo *m* bunch; (carte da gioco) pack

Mb *nm abbr* (**megabyte**) Comput Mb

me *pers pron* me; **me lo ha dato** he gave it to me; **secondo me** in my opinion; **fai come me** do as I do; **è più veloce di me** he is faster than me *or* faster than I am

me'andro *m* meander

'Mecca *f* **la ~** Mecca

mec'canica *f* mechanics *sg*
■ **meccanica quantistica** quantum mechanics

meccanica'mente *adv* mechanically

mec'canico **A** *adj* mechanical
B *m* mechanic

mecca'nismo *m* mechanism

meccanizza'zione *f* mechanization

meccanogra'fia *f* data processing

meccano'grafico *adj* data processing *attrib*

mece'nate *mf* patron

mèche *fpl* highlights; **farsi [fare] le ~** have highlights put in, have one's hair streaked

me'daglia *f* medal
■ **medaglia d'oro** (premio) gold medal; (atleta) gold medallist; **medaglia al valore** medal for valour

medagli'ere *m* medal collection

medagli'one *m* medallion; (gioiello) locket; **medaglioni** *pl* **di vitello** Culin medallions of veal

me'desimo *adj* same

'media *f* average; Sch average mark; Math mean; **essere nella ~** be in the mid-range

medi'ano **A** *adj* middle
B *m* (calcio) half-back
■ **mediano di mischia** scrum half

medi'ante *prep* by

medi'are *vt* act as intermediary in

media|'tore, -trice *mf* mediator; Comm middleman
■ **mediatore d'affari** business agent; **mediatore culturale** *voluntary or professional worker who helps immigrants integrate into Italian daily life*

mediazi'one *f* mediation

medica'mento *m* medicine

medi'care *vt* treat; dress ‹*ferita*›

medi'cato *adj* ‹*shampoo*› medicated

medicazi'one *f* medication; (di ferita) dressing

me'diceo *adj* from the period of the Medici, Medicean

medi'cina *f* medicine
■ **medicina alternativa** alternative medicine, complementary medicine; **medicina del lavoro** occupational health; **medicina legale** forensic medicine, forensic science; **medicina popolare** folk medicine

medici'nale **A** *adj* medicinal
B *m* medicine

'medico **A** *adj* medical
B *m* doctor
■ **medico di base** general practitioner, GP; **medico di famiglia** family doctor; **medico generico** general practitioner, GP; **medico legale** forensic scientist; **medico di turno** duty doctor

medie'vale *adj* medieval

'medio **A** *adj* average; ‹*punto*› middle; ‹*statura*› medium; **scuola media** secondary school
B *m* (dito) middle finger
■ **Medio Oriente** Middle East

medi'ocre *adj* mediocre; (scadente) poor

mediocre'mente *adv* indifferently

medio'evo *m* Middle Ages *pl*

mediorien'tale *adj* Middle Eastern

medita'bondo *adj* meditative

medi'tare **A** *vt* meditate; (progettare) plan; (considerare attentamente) think over
B *vi* meditate

medita'tivo *adj* meditative

meditazi'one *f* meditation

mediter'raneo *adj* Mediterranean; **il [mar] Mediterraneo** the Mediterranean [Sea]

me'dusa *f* jellyfish

'megabyte *m inv* Comput megabyte

m

me'gafono *m* megaphone
megaga'lattico *adj* gigantic
mega'lite *m* megalith
mega'lomane *mf* megalomaniac
me'gera *f* hag
'meglio **A** *adv* better; **tanto ~, ~ così** so much the better
B *adj* better; (superlativo) best
C *mf* best
D *f* **avere la ~ su** have the better of; **fare qualcosa alla [bell'e] ~** do something as best one can
E *m* **fare del proprio ~** do one's best; **fare qualcosa il ~ possibile** make an excellent job of something; **al ~** to the best of one's ability; **per il ~** for the best
'mela *f* apple; **succo di ~** apple juice
■ **mela cotogna** quince
mela'grana *f* pomegranate
mé'lange **A** *m inv* flecked wool
B *adj inv* ‹*lana*› flecked
mela'nina *f* melanin
melan'zana *f* aubergine, eggplant AmE; **melanzane** *pl* **alla parmigiana** *baked layers of aubergine, tomato and cheese*
me'lassa *f* molasses *sg*
me'lenso *adj* ‹*persona, film*› dull
me'leto *m* apple orchard
mel'lifluo *adj* ‹*parole*› honeyed; ‹*voce*› sugary
'melma *f* slime
mel'moso *adj* slimy
'melo *m* apple [tree]
melo'dia *f* melody
me'lodico *adj* melodic
melodi'oso *adj* melodious
melo'dramma *m* melodrama
melodrammatica'mente *adv* melodramatically
melodram'matico *adj* melodramatic
melo'grano *m* pomegranate tree
me'lone *m* melon
mem'brana *f* membrane
'membro *m* member (*pl nf* **membra**) Anat limb
memo'rabile *adj* memorable
'memore *adj* mindful; (riconoscente) grateful
me'moria *f* memory; (oggetto ricordo) souvenir; **imparare a ~** learn by heart; **memorie** *pl* (biografiche) memoirs
■ **memoria cache** Comput cache memory; **memoria collettiva** folk memory; **memoria dinamica** Comput RAM; **memoria di massa** Comput mass storage; **memoria permanente** Comput non-volatile memory; **memoria di sola lettura** Comput read-only memory, ROM; **memoria a tampone** Comput buffer [memory]; **memoria volatile** Comput volatile memory
memori'ale *m* memorial

memoriz'zare *vt* memorize; Comput save, store
mena'dito **a ~** *adv* perfectly
me'nare *vt* lead; infml (picchiare) hit; **~ la coda** ‹*cane*› wag its tail; **~ qualcuno per il naso** pull somebody's leg
mendi'cante *mf* beggar, panhandler AmE infml
mendi'care *vt & vi* beg
menefre'ghista *adj* devil-may-care
mene'strello *m* minstrel
me'ningi *fpl* **spremersi le ~** rack one's brains
menin'gite *f* meningitis
me'nisco *m* meniscus
'meno **A** *adv* less; (superlativo) least; (in operazioni, con temperatura) minus; **~ di** less than; **di ~** less; **~ moderno** less modern; **il ~ moderno di tutti** the least modern of all; **far qualcosa alla ~ peggio** do something as best one can; **fare a ~ di qualcosa** do without something; **non posso fare a ~ di ridere** I can't help laughing; **~ male!** thank goodness!; **sempre ~** less and less; **venir ~** (svenire) faint; **venir ~ a qualcuno** ‹*coraggio*› fail somebody; **sono le tre ~ un quarto** it's a quarter to three; **che tu venga o ~** whether you're coming or not; **quanto ~** at least
B *adj inv* less; (con nomi plurali) fewer
C *m* least; Math minus sign; **il ~ possibile** as little as possible; **per lo ~** at least
D *prep* except [for]
E *conj* **a ~ che** unless
meno'mare *vt* ‹*incidente*› maim
meno'mato **A** *adj* disabled
B *mf* disabled person
meno'pausa *f* menopause
'mensa *f* table; Mil mess; Sch, Univ canteen
men'sile **A** *adj* monthly
B *m* (stipendio) [monthly] salary; (rivista) monthly
mensilità *f inv* monthly salary
mensil'mente *adv* monthly
'mensola *f* bracket; (scaffale) shelf
'menta *f* mint; **al gusto di ~** mint flavoured
■ **menta piperita** peppermint; **menta verde** spearmint
men'tale *adj* mental
mentalità *f inv* mentality
■ **mentalità ristretta** bigotry
'mente *f* mind; **a ~ fredda** in cold blood; **cosa ti è saltato in ~?** what possessed you?; **venire in ~ a qualcuno** occur to somebody
men'tina *f* mint
men'tire *vi* lie
'mento *m* chin
men'tolo *m* menthol; **al ~** mentholated
'mentre *conj* (temporale) while; (invece) whereas
me'nu *m inv* menu
■ **menu a discesa** Comput pull-down menu;

key word

menu fisso set menu; **menu a tendina** Comput pull-down menu, drop-down menu; **menu turistico** tourist menu

menzio'nare *vt* mention

menzi'one *f* mention
■ **menzione speciale** special mention

men'zogna *f* lie

mera'viglia *f* wonder; **a ~** marvellously; **che ~!** how wonderful!; **con mia grande ~** much to my amazement; **mi fa ~ che...** I am surprised that...

meravigli'are *vt* surprise

meravigli'arsi *vr* **~ di** be surprised at

meravigliosa'mente *adv* marvellously

meravigli'oso *adj* marvellous, wonderful

mer'cante *m* merchant
■ **mercante d'arte** art dealer; **mercante di schiavi** slave trader

mercanteggi'are *vi* trade; (sul prezzo) bargain

mercan'tile **A** *adj* mercantile **B** *m* merchant ship

mercan'zia *f* merchandise, goods *pl*

merca'tino *m* (di quartiere) local street market; Fin unlisted securities market

mer'cato *m* market; Fin market[place]; **a buon ~** ‹*comprare*› cheaply; ‹*articolo*› cheap
■ **mercato all'aperto** street market; **mercato aperto** Econ open market; **mercato azionario** Fin equity market, share market; **mercato dei cambi** foreign exchange market; **Mercato Comune [Europeo]** [European] Common Market; **mercato coperto** covered market, indoor market; **mercato dell'eurovaluta** Eurocurrency market; **mercato immobiliare** property market; **mercato del lavoro** job market; **mercato libero** free market; **mercato di massa** mass market; **mercato nero** black market; **mercato del pesce** fish market; **mercato di prova** test market; **mercato al rialzo** Fin bull market; **mercato al ribasso** Fin bear market; **mercato specializzato** niche market; **mercato unico** Single Market

'merce *f* goods *pl*, merchandise; **la ~ venduta non si cambia senza lo scontrino** goods will not be exchanged without a receipt
■ **merce in conto vendita** sale or return goods; **merce deperibile** perishable goods

mercé *f* **alla ~ di** at the mercy of

merce'nario *adj & nm* mercenary

merceolo'gia *f* study of commodities

merce'ria *f* haberdashery; (negozio) haberdasher's

mercifi'care *vt* commercialize

mercificazi'one *f* commercialization

mercoledì *m inv* Wednesday; **di ~** on Wednesdays
■ **mercoledì delle Ceneri** Ash Wednesday

mer'curio *m* mercury

me'renda *f* afternoon snack; **far ~** have an afternoon snack

meridi'ana *f* sundial

meridi'ano **A** *adj* midday **B** *m* meridian

meridio'nale **A** *adj* southern **B** *mf* southerner

meridi'one *m* south

me'ringa *f* meringue

merin'gata *f* meringue pie

meri'tare *vt* deserve

meri'tato *adj* deserved

meri'tevole *adj* deserving

'merito *m* merit; (valore) worth; **in ~ a** as to; **per ~ di** thanks to

merito'cratico *adj* meritocratic

meri'torio *adj* meritorious

merla'tura *f* battlements *pl*

merlet'taia *f* lacemaker

mer'letto *m* lace

'merlo *m* blackbird; **bravo ~!** you fool!

mer'luzzo *m* cod

'mero *adj* mere

mesca'lina *f* mescaline

'mescere *vt* pour out

meschine'ria *f* meanness

me'schino **A** *adj* wretched; (gretto) mean **B** *m* wretch

'mescita *f* wine shop

mescola'mento *m* mixing

mesco'lanza *f* mixture

mesco'lare *vt* mix; shuffle ‹*carte*›; (confondere) mix up; blend ‹*tè, tabacco ecc.*›

mesco'larsi *vr* mix; (immischiarsi) meddle

mesco'lata *f* (a carte) shuffle; Culin stir

'mese *m* month
■ **mese civile** calendar month

me'setto *m* **un ~** about a month, a month or so

'messa[1] *f* Mass
■ **messa nera** black mass; **messa da requiem** requiem mass; **messa solenne** High Mass

'messa[2] *f* (il mettere) putting
■ **messa in moto** Auto starting; **messa in piega** (di capelli) set; **farsi fare la ~ in piega** have one's hair set; **messa a punto** adjustment; **messa in scena** production; fig production number; **messa a terra** earthing, grounding AmE

messagge'ria *f*
■ **messaggeria elettronica** Comput messaging

messag'gero *m* messenger

messag'giare *vi* Teleph text

messag'gino *m* text message

mes'saggio *m* message
■ **messaggio di errore** Comput error message; **messaggio di testo** Teleph text message

mes'sale *m* missal

'messe *f* harvest

m

Mes'sia *m* Messiah
messi'cano, -a *adj & nmf* Mexican
'Messico *m* Mexico
messin'scena *f* staging; fig act
'messo **A** pp di **mettere**
B *m* messenger
✔ **mesti'ere** *m* trade; ‹*lavoro*› job; **essere del ~** be an expert, know one's trade
'mesto *adj* sad
'mestola *f* (di cuoco) ladle; (di muratore) trowel
mestru'ale *adj* menstrual
mestruazi'one *f* menstruation; **mestruazioni** *pl* period
'meta *f* destination; fig aim
✔ **metà** *f inv* half; (centro) middle; **a ~ prezzo** half price; **a ~ strada** halfway; **a ~ serata** halfway through the evening; **fare a ~ con qualcuno** go halves with somebody, go fifty-fifty with somebody; **fare [a] ~ e ~** go fifty-fifty, go halves
metabo'lismo *m* metabolism
meta'carpo *m* metacarpus
meta'done *m* methadone
meta'fisica *n* metaphysics *sg*
meta'fisico *adj* metaphysical
me'tafora *f* metaphor
metaforica'mente *adv* metaphorically
meta'forico *adj* metaphorical
me'tallico *adj* metallic
metalliz'zato *adj* ‹*grigio*› metallic
me'tallo *m* metal
■ **metallo vile** base metal
metal'loide *m* metalloid
metallur'gia *f* metallurgy
metal'lurgico *adj* metallurgical
metalmec'canico **A** *adj* engineering
B *m* engineering worker
meta'morfosi *f* metamorphosis
me'tano *m* methane
metano'dotto *m* methane pipeline
meta'nolo *m* methanol
me'tastasi *f inv* metastasis
meta'tarso *m* metatarsus
me'teora *f* meteor
meteo'rite *m* meteorite
meteorolo'gia *f* meteorology
meteoro'logico *adj* meteorological
meteo'rologo *m* meteorologist
me'ticcio, -a *mf* person of mixed race
meticolosa'mente *adv* meticulously
metico'loso *adj* meticulous
me'tile *m* methyl
me'todico *adj* methodical
meto'dista *adj & nmf* Methodist
'metodo *m* method
metodolo'gia *f* methodology
metodo'logico *adj* methodological

me'traggio *m* length (*in metres*); **vendere a ~** sell by the metre
'metrica *f* metrics
'metrico *adj* metric; (in poesia) metrical
✔ **'metro¹** *m* metre; (nastro) tape measure
■ **metro cubo** cubic metre; **metro quadrato** square metre
'metro² *f inv* infml underground, subway AmE
me'tronomo *m* metronome
metro'notte *mf inv* night security guard
me'tropoli *f inv* metropolis
metropoli'tana *f* underground, subway AmE
metropoli'tano *adj* metropolitan
✔ **'mettere** *vt* put; (indossare) put on; infml (installare) put in; **~ al mondo** bring into the world; **~ da parte** set aside; **~ fiducia** inspire trust; **~ qualcosa in chiaro** make something clear; **~ in mostra** display; **~ a posto** tidy up; **~ in vendita** put up for sale; **~ su** set up ‹*casa, azienda*›; **metter su famiglia** start a family; **ci ho messo un'ora** it took me an hour; **mettiamo che...** let's suppose that...
'mettersi *vr* (indossare) put on; (diventare) turn out; **~ a** start to; **~ con qualcuno** infml (formare una coppia) start to go out with somebody; **~ a letto** go to bed; **~ a sedere** sit down; **~ in viaggio** set out
metti'foglio *m* feeder
'mezza *f* **è la ~** it's half past twelve; **sono le quattro e ~** it's half past four
mezza'dria *f* sharecropping
mezza'luna *f* half moon; (simbolo islamico) crescent; (coltello) two-handled chopping knife; **a ~** half-moon *attrib*
mezza'manica *f* **a ~** ‹*maglia*› short-sleeved; **mezzemaniche** *pl* derog lowest grade of clerks, pen-pushers
mezza'nino *m* mezzanine
mez'zano, -a *adj* middle
mezza'notte *f* midnight; **aspettare la ~** see in the New Year
mezz'asta **a ~** *adv* at half mast
mezze'ria *f* centre line
✔ **'mezzo** **A** *adj* half; **di mezza età** middle aged; **~ bicchiere** half a glass; **una mezza idea** a vague idea; **siamo mezzi morti** we're half dead; **sono le quattro e ~** it's half past four
■ **mezza cartuccia** *nf* runt; **mezza dozzina** *nf* half-dozen; **mezza età** *nf* midlife; **mezza giornata** *nf* half day; **mezzo guanto** *nm* mitt; **mezzo litro** *nm* half a litre; **mezz'ora** *nf* half an hour; **mezza pensione** *nf* half board; **mezza stagione** *nf* demi-season; **una giacca di ~ stagione** a spring/autumn jacket; **mezza verità** *nf* half-truth
B *adv* (a metà) half; **~ addormentato** half asleep; **~ morto** half-dead; **~ morto di paura** petrified; **~ e ~** (così così) so so

✔ key word

C *m* (metà) half; (centro) middle; (per raggiungere un fine) means *sg*; **uno e ~** one and a half; **tre anni e ~** three and a half years; **in ~ a** in the middle of; **il giusto ~** the happy medium; **levare di ~** clear away; **per ~ di** by means of; **a ~ posta** by mail; **via di ~** fig halfway house; (soluzione) middle way; **mezzi** *pl* (denaro) means *pl*; **mezzi** *pl* **di comunicazione di massa** mass media; **mezzi** *pl* **pubblici** public transport; **mezzi** *pl* **di trasporto** [means of] transport

mezzo'busto *m* (statua) bust; TV talking head; **a ~** ‹*foto, ritratto*› half-length

mezzo'fondo *m* middle-distance running

mezzogi'orno *m* midday, noon; (sud) South; **il Mezzogiorno** Southern Italy
■ **mezzogiorno in punto** high noon

mezzo'sangue *mf* cross-breed

mezzo'servizio *m* **lavorare a ~** do part-time cleaning work

mi **A** *pers pron* me; *refl*, myself; **mi ha dato un libro** he gave me a book; **non mi parla** he doesn't talk to me; **mi lavo le mani** I wash my hands; **eccomi** here I am
B *m* Mus (chiave, nota) E

'mia ▸ **mio**

miago'lare *vi* miaow

miago'lio *m* miaowing

mi'ao *m* miaow

'mica¹ *f* mica

'mica² *adv* infml (per caso) by any chance; **hai ~ visto Paolo?** have you seen Paul, by any chance?; **non è ~ bello** it is not at all nice; **~ male** not bad

'miccia *f* fuse

micidi'ale *adj* deadly

'micio *m* pussy cat

mi'cosi *f* athlete's foot

mi'cotico *adj* fungal

microbiolo'gia *f* microbiology

'microbo *m* microbe

microchirur'gia *f* microsurgery

micro'clima *m* microclimate

microcom'puter *m inv* microcomputer

micro'cosmo *m* microcosm

micro'fiche *f inv* microfiche

micro'film *m inv* microfilm

micro'fisica *f* microphysics *sg*

mi'crofono *m* microphone
■ **microfono con la clip** clip-on microphone; **microfono spia** bugging device, bug; **microfono a stelo** boom microphone

microfotogra'fia *f* Phot micrograph; (tecnica) micrography

microinfor'matica *f* microcomputing

micro'onda *f* microwave

microorga'nismo *m* microorganism

microproces'sore *m* microprocessor

micro'scheda *f* microfiche

micro'scopico *adj* microscopic

micro'scopio *m* microscope; **passare qualcosa al ~** fig examine something in microscopic detail

microse'condo *m* microsecond

micro'solco *m* (disco) long-playing record

micro'spia *f* bug

mi'dollo Anat *m* (*pl nf* **midolla**) marrow; **fino al ~** ‹*bagnato*› through and through; ‹*corrotto*› to the core
■ **midollo osseo** bone marrow; **midollo spinale** spinal cord

'mie ▸ **mio**

mi'ei ▸ **mio**

mi'ele *m* honey
■ **miele d'acacia** acacia honey

mi'etere *vt* reap

mietitrebbia'trice *f* combine harvester

mieti'trice *f* harvester

mieti'tura *f* harvest

migli'aia *fpl* thousands

migli'aio *m* (*pl nf* **migliaia**) thousand; **a migliaia** in thousands

'miglio *m* Bot millet (misura: *pl f* **miglia**) mile
■ **miglia aeree** *pl* BrE Air Miles AmE, frequent flyer miles; **miglio nautico** nautical mile; **miglia all'ora** *pl* miles per hour, mph; **miglio terrestre** mile

migliora'mento *m* improvement

miglio'rare *vt & vi* improve

migli'ore **A** *adj* better; (superlativo) the best; **~ amico** best friend; **i migliori auguri** best wishes
B *mf* **il/la ~** the best

miglio'ria *f* improvement

mi'gnatta *f* leech

'mignolo *m* little finger, pinkie infml; (del piede) little toe

mi'gnon *adj inv* (bottiglie) miniature

mi'grante *mf* (persona) migrant

mi'grare *vi* migrate

migra'tore *adj* migratory

migra'torio *adj* migratory

migrazi'one *f* migration

'mila ▸ **mille**

mila'nese *adj & nmf* Milanese

Mi'lano *f* Milan

miliar'dario, -a **A** *m* millionaire; (pluri-miliardario) billionaire
B *f* millionairess; billionairess

mili'ardo *m* billion

mili'are *adj* **pietra ~** milestone

milio'nario, -a **A** *m* millionaire
B *f* millionairess

mili'one *m* million

milio'nesimo *adj & nm* millionth

mili'tante *adj & nmf* militant

mili'tanza *f* militancy

mili'tare **A** *vi* **~ in** be a member of ‹*un partito ecc.*›
B *adj* military

m

C *m* soldier; **fare il ~** do one's military service

■ **militare di carriera** regular [soldier]; **militare di leva** National Serviceman

milita'rismo *m* militarism

milita'rista *adj* militaristic

militariz'zare *vt* militarize

militas'solto *adj* having done National Service

'milite *m* soldier

milite'sente *adj* exempt from National Service

mi'lizia *f* militia

millanta|'tore, -trice *mf* boaster

⚷ **'mille** *adj & nm* (*pl* **mila**) a *or* one thousand; **due/tre mila** two/three thousand; **~ grazie!** thanks a lot!; **millenovecentonovantaquattro** *nm* nineteen ninety-four

mille'foglie *m inv* Culin vanilla slice

mil'lennio *m* millennium

millepi'edi *m inv* centipede

mil'lesimo *adj & nm* thousandth

milli'bar *m inv* millibar

milli'grammo *m* milligram

mil'lilitro *m* millilitre

mil'limetro *m* millimetre

'milza *f* spleen

mi'mare **A** *vt* mimic ‹*persona*›

B *vi* mime

mi'metico *adj* **tuta** *f* **mimetica** camouflage; **animale ~** animal which has the ability to camouflage itself; **vernice mimetica** camouflage paint

mime'tismo *m* ability to camouflage itself

■ **mimetismo politico** chameleon-like political traits

mimetiz'zare *vt* camouflage

mimetiz'zarsi *vr* camouflage oneself

'mimica *f* mime

■ **mimica facciale** facial expressions *pl*

'mimico *adj* mimic

'mimo *m* mime

mi'mosa *f* mimosa

'mina *f* mine; (di matita) lead

mi'naccia *f* threat; **avere una ~ di aborto** come close to having a miscarriage

■ **minaccia di morte** death threat

⚷ **minacci'are** *vt* threaten

minacciosa'mente *adv* threateningly, menacingly

minacci'oso *adj* threatening; ‹*onde*› menacing

mi'nare *vt* mine; fig undermine

mina'reto *m* minaret

mina'tore *m* miner

mina'torio *adj* threatening

⚷ **mine'rale** *adj & nm* mineral

mineralo'gia *f* mineralogy

⚷ key word

mine'rario *adj* mining *attrib*

mi'nestra *f* soup

■ **minestra in brodo** noodle soup; **minestra di verdure** vegetable soup

mine'strone *m* minestrone (*vegetable soup*); infml (insieme confuso) hotchpotch

mingher'lino *adj* skinny

'mini **A** *f inv* (gonna) mini

B *adj inv* mini

mini+ *pref* mini+

miniapparta'mento *m* studio flat BrE, studio apartment

minia'tura *f* miniature

miniaturiz'zato *adj* miniaturized

mini'bus *m inv* minibus

mini'disc *m inv* minidisc

mini'disco *m* minidisc

mini'era *f* mine; **una ~ di notizie** a mine of information; **è una ~ di idee** he's full of ideas

■ **miniera a cielo aperto** opencast mine; **miniera d'oro** gold mine

mini'golf *m* minigolf, miniature golf

mini'gonna *f* miniskirt, mini

'minima *f* (atmosferica) minimum temperature; Med diastolic blood-pressure level; Mus minim

minima'lista *mf* minimalist

minima'mente *adv* minimally

mini'market *m inv* minimarket

minimiz'zare *vt* minimize, downplay

⚷ **'minimo** **A** *adj* least, slightest; (il più basso) lowest; ‹*salario, quantità ecc.*› minimum

B *m* minimum; **girare al ~** Auto idle; **toccare il ~ storico** be at an all-time low; **come ~** at least, as a minimum

mini'moto *f inv* pocket bike

'minio *m* red lead

ministeri'ale *adj* (di ministero) ministerial; (di governo) government

mini'stero *m* ministry; (governo) government

■ **ministero dell'Ambiente e della Tutela del Territorio** Department of Natural Resources AmE, Department for Environment, Food, and Rural Affairs BrE; **ministero degli [affari] Esteri** Foreign Office BrE, State Department AmE; **ministero della Difesa** Ministry of Defence BrE, Department of Defense AmE; **ministero di Grazia e Giustizia** Justice Department AmE; **ministero degli Interni** Ministry of the Interior, Home Office; **ministero dell'Istruzione** Department for Education and Skills BrE; **ministero del Lavoro e delle Politiche Sociali** Department for Work and Pensions; **ministero per le Politiche Agricole e Forestali** Department for Environment, Food, and Rural Affairs BrE; **ministero della Salute** Department of Health

⚷ **mi'nistro** *m* minister

■ **ministro della Difesa** Defence Minister BrE,

Defense Secretary AmE; **ministro degli Esteri** Foreign Secretary BrE, Secretary of State AmE, foreign minister; **ministro di Grazia e Giustizia** Attorney General; **ministro dell'Interno** Home Secretary BrE, Secretary of the Interior AmE; **ministro del Lavoro** Secretary of State for Work and Pensions BrE, Secretary of Labor AmE; **ministro del Tesoro** Chancellor of the Exchequer BrE, Secretary of the Treasury AmE

mini'tower *m* Comput minitower

mino'ranza *f* minority
■ **minoranza etnica** ethnic minority

mino'rato, -a **A** *adj* disabled
B *mf* disabled person

Mi'norca *f* Menorca

mi'nore **A** *adj* ‹*gruppo, numero*› smaller; (superlativo) smallest; ‹*distanza*› shorter; (superlativo) shortest; ‹*prezzo*› lower; (superlativo) lowest; (di età) younger; (superlativo) youngest; (di importanza) minor; (superlativo) least important
B *mf* younger; (superlativo) youngest; Jur minor; **il ~ dei mali** the lesser of two evils; **i minori di 14 anni** children under 14

mino'renne **A** *adj* under age
B *mf* minor

minori'tario *adj* minority *attrib*

minu'etto *m* minuet

mi'nuscolo, -a **A** *adj* tiny, minuscule
B *f* small letter

mi'nuta *f* rough copy

minuta'mente *adv* ‹*esaminato*› in minute detail, minutely; ‹*lavorato, tritato*› finely

mi'nuto¹ *adj* minute; (persona) delicate; (ricerca) detailed; ‹*pioggia, neve*› fine; **al ~** Comm retail

mi'nuto² *m* ‹*di timpo*› minute; **spaccare il ~** be dead on time; **minuti** *pl* **di recupero** Sport injury time

mi'nuzia *f* trifle; **minuzie** *pl* minutiae

minuziosa'mente *adv* minutely

minuzi'oso *adj* minute, detailed; ‹*persona*› meticulous

'mio **A** (**il mio** *m* **la mia** *f* **i miei** *mpl* **le mie** *fpl*) *poss adj* my; **questa macchina è mia** this car is mine; **~ padre** my father; **un ~ amico** a friend of mine
B *poss pron* mine; **i miei** (genitori ecc.) my folks

'miope *adj* short-sighted

mio'pia *f* short-sightedness

'mira *f* aim; (bersaglio) target; **prendere la ~** take aim; **prendere di ~ qualcuno** fig have it in for somebody

mi'rabile *adj* admirable

miraco'lato *adj* ‹*malato*› miraculously cured

mi'racolo *m* miracle

miracolosa'mente *adv* miraculously

miraco'loso *adj* miraculous

mi'raggio *m* mirage

mi'rare *vi* [take] aim; **~ alto** aim high

mi'rarsi *vr* (guardarsi) look at oneself

mi'riade *f* myriad

mi'rino *m* sight; Phot viewfinder

'mirra *f* myrrh

mir'tillo *m* blueberry

'mirto *m* myrtle

mi'santropo, -a *mf* misanthropist

mi'scela *f* mixture; ‹*di caffè, tabacco ecc.*› blend

misce'lare *vt* mix

miscela'tore *m* ‹*apparecchio*› blender; (di acqua) mixer tap

miscel'lanea *f* miscellany

'mischia *f* scuffle; (nel rugby) scrum

mischi'are *vt* mix; shuffle ‹*carte da gioco*›

mischi'arsi *vr* mix; (immischiarsi) interfere

misco'noscere *vt* not appreciate

miscre'dente *mf* heretic

mi'scuglio *m* mixture; fig medley

mise'rabile *adj* wretched

misera'mente *adv* ‹*finire*› miserably; ‹*vivere*› in abject poverty; ‹*vestito*› shabbily

mi'seria *f* poverty; (infelicità) misery; **guadagnare una ~** earn a pittance; **miserie** *pl* (disgrazie) misfortunes; **porca ~!** infml hell!

miseri'cordia *f* mercy

misericordi'oso *adj* merciful

'misero *adj* (miserabile) wretched; (povero) poor; (scarso) paltry

mi'sfatto *m* misdeed

mi'sogino *m* misogynist

mis'saggio *m* mixing

'missile *m* missile
■ **missile cruise** cruise missile; **missile terra-aria** surface-to-air missile

missi'listico *adj* missile *attrib*

missio'nario, -a *mf* missionary

missi'one *f* mission
■ **missione di pace** peace mission

misteriosa'mente *adv* mysteriously

misteri'oso *adj* mysterious

mi'stero *m* mystery

'mistica *f* mysticism

misti'cismo *m* mysticism

'mistico **A** *adj* mystic[al]
B *m* mystic

mistifi'care *vt* distort ‹*verità*›

mistificazi'one *f* (della verità) distortion

'misto **A** *adj* mixed; **scuola mista** mixed *or* co-educational school
B *m* mixture; (di oggetti) miscellany
■ **misto lana** wool mixture; **misto lana/cotone** wool/cotton mix

mi'sura *f* measure; (dimensione) measurement; (taglia) size; (limite) limit; **su ~** ‹*abiti*› made to measure; ‹*mobile*› custom-made; **a ~**

‹*andare, calzare*› perfectly; **a ~ che** as; **nella ~ in cui** insofar as
■ **misura di capacità** unit of capacity; **misura di lunghezza** unit of length; **misura profilattica** prophylactic; **misura di sicurezza** safety measure; **misure antidiscriminatorie** *pl* positive discrimination

⚷ **misu'rare** *vt* measure; try on ‹*indumenti*›; (limitare) limit

misu'rarsi *vr* **~ con** (gareggiare) compete with

misu'rato *adj* measured

misu'rino *m* measuring spoon

'mite *adj* mild; ‹*prezzo*› moderate

'mitico *adj* mythical

miti'gare *vt* mitigate

miti'garsi *vr* calm down; ‹*clima*› become mild

'mitilo *m* mussel

mitiz'zare *vt* mythicize

'mito *m* myth

mitolo'gia *f* mythology

mito'logico *adj* mythological

mi'tomane *mf* compulsive liar

'mitra **A** *f* Relig mitre
B *m inv* Mil machine-gun

mitragli'are *vt* machine-gun; **~ di domande** fire questions at

mitraglia'trice *f* machine-gun

m

mitt. *abbr* (**mittente**) sender

mitteleuro'peo *adj* Central European

mit'tente *mf* sender

'mixer *m inv* mixer

mne'monico *adj* mnemonic; **frase mnemonica** mnemonic

mo' *m* **a mo' di** by way of ‹*esempio, consolazione*›

⚷ **'mobile[1]** *adj* mobile; ‹*volubile*› fickle; (che si può muovere) movable; **beni** *pl* **mobili** movable personal estate; **squadra mobile** flying squad

⚷ **'mobile[2]** *m* piece of furniture; **mobili** *pl* furniture *sg*
■ **mobile bar** drinks cabinet; **mobili** *pl* **da giardino** garden furniture; **mobili** *pl* **in stile** reproduction furniture

mo'bilia *f* furniture

mobili'are *adj* ‹*capitale*› movable; ‹*credito*› medium-term; ‹*mercato*› share (*attrib*); **patrimonio mobiliare** non-property assets

mobili'ere *m* furniture dealer

mobili'ficio *m* furniture factory

mo'bilio *m* furniture

mobili'tà *f inv* mobility; **~ sostenibile** sustainable mobility
■ **mobilità del lavoro** labour mobility; **mobilità sociale** social mobility

mobili'tare *vt* mobilize

mobilitazi'one *f* mobilization

'moca *m inv* mocha

mocas'sino *m* moccasin

mocci'coso, -a **A** *adj* snotty
B *mf* snotty nosed kid; brat

'moccolo *m* (di candela) candle end; (moccio) snot

⚷ **'moda** *f* fashion; **di ~** in fashion; **andare di ~** be in fashion; **alla ~** ‹*musica, vestiti*› up to date; **fuori ~** unfashionable

mo'dale *adj* ‹*verbo*› modal

modalità *f inv* formality
■ **modalità d'uso** instruction

modana'tura *f* moulding

mo'della *f* model

model'lante *adj* ‹*gel per capelli*› styling

model'lare *vt* model

model'lino *m* model

model'lismo *m* model-making; (collezionismo) collecting models

model'lista *mf* model maker; (moda) [fashion] designer

⚷ **mo'dello** *m* model; ‹*stampo*› mould; (di carta) pattern; (modulo) form; (moda) male model
■ **modello CUD** P45; **modello in scala** scale model

'modem *m inv* modem; **mandare per ~** modem, send by modem

'modem-fax *m* fax-modem

mode'rare *vt* moderate; (diminuire) reduce

mode'rarsi *vr* control oneself

moderata'mente *adv* moderately

mode'rato *adj* moderate

modera|'tore, -trice **A** *mf* (in tavola rotonda) moderator
B *adj* moderating

moderazi'one *f* moderation

moderna'mente *adv* (in modo moderno) in a modern style

modernari'ato *m collecting 20th century art and products*

moder'nismo *m* modernism

modernità *f inv* modernity

moderniz'zare *vt* modernize

modernizzazi'one *f* modernization

⚷ **mo'derno** *adj* modern

mo'destia *f* modesty

⚷ **mo'desto** *adj* modest

'modico *adj* reasonable

mo'difica *f* modification

modifi'care *vt* modify

modifi'cato *adj* modified
■ **modificato geneticamente** genetically modified

modifica'tore *m* modifier

modificazi'one *f* modification

mo'dista *f* milliner

⚷ **'modo** *m* way; (garbo) manners *pl*; (occasione) chance; Gram mood; **ad ogni ~** anyhow; **di ~ che** so that; **fare in ~ di** try to; **in che**

⚷ key word

~ (inter) how; **in qualche ~** somehow; **in questo ~** like this; **in ~ ottimistico/pessimistico/anormale** optimistically/pessimistically/abnormally
■ **modo di dire** idiom; **per ~ di dire** so to speak

modu'lare *vt* modulate

modula'tore *m* modulator
■ **modulatore di frequenza** frequency modulator

modulazi'one *f* modulation
■ **modulazione di frequenza** frequency modulation

'modulo *m* form; ‹*lunare, di comando*› module
■ **modulo continuo** continuous paper; **modulo di domanda** application form; **modulo di iscrizione** enrolment form; **modulo di ordinazione** order form; **modulo di richiesta** claim form

'modus ope'randi *m inv* modus operandi

'modus vi'vendi *m inv* modus vivendi

mof'fetta *f* skunk

'mogano *m* mahogany

'mogio *adj* dejected

'moglie *f* wife

moi'cano *adj* **taglio [di capelli] alla moicana** Mohican [haircut]

mo'ine *fpl* **fare le ~** behave in an affected way

'mola *f* millstone; Mech grindstone

mo'lare *m* molar

mo'lato *adj* ‹*vetro*› cut

mola'trice *f* Mech grinder

Mol'davia *f* Moldavia

'mole *f* mass; (dimensione) size

mo'lecola *f* molecule

moleco'lare *adj* molecular

mole'stare *vt* bother; (più forte) molest

molesta|'tore, -trice *mf* molester

mo'lestia *f* nuisance; **molestie** *pl* **sessuali** sexual harassment *sg*

mo'lesto *adj* bothersome

Mo'lise *m* Molise

'molla *f* spring; **molle** *pl* tongs; **prendere qualcuno con le molle** handle somebody with kid gloves

mol'lare **A** *vt* let go; infml (lasciare) leave; infml give ‹*ceffone*›; Naut cast off
B *vi* cease; **mollala!** infml stop that!

'molle *adj* soft; (bagnato) wet

molleggi'are **A** *vi* be springy
B *vt* spring

molleggi'arsi *vr* bend at the knees

molleggi'ato *adj* bouncy, springy

mol'leggio *m* (di auto) suspension; (di letto) springs *pl*; (esercizio) knee bends *pl*

mol'letta *f* (per capelli) hairgrip, barrette AmE; **mollette** *pl* (per ghiaccio ecc.) tongs
■ **molletta da bucato** clothes peg

mollet'tone *m* (per tavolo) padded table cloth

mol'lezza *f* softness; **mollezze** *pl* fig luxury

mol'lica *f* crumb

mol'liccio *adj* squidgy

mol'lusco *m* mollusc

'molo *m* pier; (banchina) dock

'molotov *adj inv* **bottiglia ~** Molotov cocktail

mol'teplice *adj* manifold; (numeroso) numerous

molteplicità *f inv* multiplicity

mol'tiplica *f* (di bicicletta) gear ratio, gear wheel

moltipli'care *vt* multiply

moltipli'carsi *vr* multiply

moltiplica'tore *m* multiplier

moltiplica'trice *f* calculating machine

moltiplicazi'one *f* multiplication

molti'tudine *f* multitude

'molto **A** *adj* a lot of; (con negazione e interrogazione) much, a lot of; (con nomi plurali) many, a lot of; **non ~ tempo** not much time, not a lot of time; **molte grazie** thank you very much
B *adv* very; (con verbi) a lot; (con avverbi) much; **~ stupido** very stupid; **~ bene, grazie** very well, thank you; **mangiare ~** eat a lot; **~ più veloce** much faster; **non mangiare ~** not eat a lot, not eat much
C *pron* a lot; (molto tempo) a lot of time; (con negazione e interrogazione) much, a lot; (plurale) many; **non ne ho ~** I don't have much, I don't have a lot; **non ne ho molti** I don't have many, I don't have a lot; **non ci metterò ~** I won't be long; **fra non ~** before long; **molti** (persone) a lot of people; **eravamo in molti** there were a lot of us

momentanea'mente *adv* momentarily; **è ~ assente** he's not here at the moment

momen'taneo *adj* momentary

mo'mento *m* moment; **a momenti** (a volte) sometimes; (fra un momento) in a moment; **dal ~ che** since; **per il ~** for the time being; **al ~** at the moment; **da un ~ all'altro** ‹*cambiare idea ecc.*› from one moment to the next; ‹*aspettare l'arrivo di qualcuno ecc.*› at any moment

'monaca *f* nun

'monaco *m* monk

'Monaco *f* (di Baviera) Munich; **Principato di ~** Monaco

mo'narca *m* monarch

monar'chia *f* monarchy

mo'narchico, -a **A** *adj* monarchic
B *mf* monarchist

mona'stero *m* (di monaci) monastery; (di monache) convent

mo'nastico *adj* monastic

monche'rino *m* stump

'monco *adj* maimed; fig (troncato) truncated; **~ di un braccio** one-armed

m

mon'dana *f* lady of the night

mondanità *f inv* (gente) beau monde; ~ *pl* pleasures of the world

mon'dano *adj* worldly; **vita mondana** social life

mon'dare *vt* (sbucciare) peel; shell ‹*piselli*›; (pulire) clean

mondi'ale *adj* world *attrib*; ‹*scala*› worldwide; infml (fantastico) fantastic; **di fama** ~ world-famous

mondi'ali *mpl* World Cup

mondial'mente *adv* ‹*operare*› worldwide; ~ **noto** world-famous

mon'dina *f* seasonal worker in the rice fields

'mondo *m* world; **il bel** ~ fashionable society; **un** ~ (molto) a lot; **non è la fine del** ~ it's not the end of the world; **è la fine del** ~ infml (fantastico) it's out of this world; ~ **cane!** infml damn!
■ **mondo accademico** academia; **mondo del lavoro** world of work; **mondo dei sogni** never-never land; **mondo dello spettacolo** show biz

mondovisi'one *f* **in** ~ transmitted worldwide

monelle'ria *f* prank

mo'nello, -a *mf* urchin

mo'neta *f* coin; (denaro) money; (denaro spicciolo) [small] change
■ **moneta estera** foreign currency; **moneta [a corso] legale** legal tender; **moneta unica** single currency

mone'tario *adj* monetary

mongolfi'era *f* hot air balloon

Mon'golia *f* Mongolia

'mongolo *adj* Mongol

mo'nile *m* jewel

'monito *m* warning

'monitor *m inv* monitor

monito'raggio *m* monitoring

moni'tore *m* monitor

mono'albero *adj inv* single camshaft *attrib*

mono'blocco **A** *m* Auto cylinder block **B** *adj inv* ‹*cucina*› fitted

mo'nocolo *m* monocle

monoco'lore *adj* Pol one-party

monocro'matico *adj* monochrome

mono'dose *adj inv* individually packaged

monoga'mia *f* monogamy

mo'nogamo *adj* monogamous

monogra'fia *f* monograph

mono'gramma *m* monogram

mono'kini *m inv* monokini

mono'lingue *adj* monolingual

mono'lito *m* monolith

monolo'cale *m* studio flat BrE, studio apartment

mo'nologo *m* monologue

monoma'nia *f* monomania

mononucle'osi *f inv*
■ **mononucleosi infettiva** glandular fever

monoparen'tale *adj* single-parent *attrib*

mono'pattino *m* [child's] scooter

mono'petto *adj* single-breasted

mono'plano *m* monoplane

mono'polio *m* monopoly
■ **monopolio di Stato** state monopoly

monopoliz'zare *vt* monopolize

mono'posto *m* single-seater

mono'reddito *adj* single-income *attrib*

monosac'caride *m* monosaccharide

mono'sci *m inv* monoski

monosil'labico *adj* monosyllabic

mono'sillabo **A** *m* monosyllable **B** *adj* monosyllabic

mo'nossido *m*
■ **monossido di carbonio** carbon monoxide

monote'istico *adj* monotheistic

monotona'mente *adv* monotonously

monoto'nia *f* monotony

mo'notono *adj* monotonous

mono'uso *adj* disposable

monou'tente *adj inv* single-user *attrib*

monovo'lume *f* people carrier, multi-purpose vehicle

monsi'gnore *m* Monsignor

mon'sone *m* monsoon

'monta *f* Zool covering; (modo di cavalcare) riding style; **stallone da** ~ stud horse

monta'carichi *m inv* hoist

mon'taggio *m* Mech assembly; Cinema editing; **scatola di** ~ assembly kit; **catena di** ~ production line

mon'tagna *f* mountain; (zona) mountains *pl*
■ **Montagne** *pl* **Rocciose** Rocky Mountains; **montagne** *pl* **russe** roller coaster, big dipper

monta'gnoso *adj* mountainous

monta'naro, -a *mf* highlander

mon'tano *adj* mountain *attrib*

mon'tante *m* (di finestra, porta) upright; Fin total amount; (nel pugilato) upper cut

mon'tare *vt & vi* mount; get on ‹*veicolo*›; (aumentare) rise; Mech assemble; frame ‹*quadro*›; Culin whip; edit ‹*film*›; (a cavallo) ride; fig blow up

mon'tarsi *vr* ~ **la testa** get big-headed

monta'scale *m inv* stairlift

mon'tato, -a *mf* infml poser

monta|'tore, -trice *mf* assembler

monta'tura *f* Mech assembling; (di occhiali) frame; (di gioiello) mounting; fig exaggeration

'monte *m* mountain; **a** ~ up stream; **andare a** ~ be ruined; **mandare a** ~ **qualcosa** ruin something
■ **Monte Bianco** Mont Blanc; **monte di pietà** pawnshop

key word

Monte'negro *m* Montenegro
monte'premi *m inv* jackpot
mont'gomery *m inv* duffel coat
mon'tone *m* ram; **carne di ~** mutton
montu'oso *adj* mountainous
monumen'tale *adj* monumental
monu'mento *m* monument
■ **monumento ai caduti** war memorial; **monumento commemorativo** memorial; **monumento nazionale** national monument
mo'plen® *m* moulded plastic
mo'quette *f* (tappeto) fitted carpet
'mora *f* (di gelso) mulberry; (di rovo) blackberry
mo'rale **A** *adj* moral
B *f* morals *pl*; (di storia) moral
C *m* morale
mora'lista *mf* moralist
mora'listico *adj* moralistic
moralità *f inv* morality; (condotta) morals *pl*
moraliz'zare *vt & vi* moralize
moral'mente *adv* morally
mora'toria *f* moratorium
morbida'mente *adv* softly
morbi'dezza *f* softness
'morbido *adj* soft
mor'billo *m* measles *sg*
'morbo *m* disease
■ **morbo di Alzheimer** Alzheimer's disease; **morbo di Creutzfeldt Jakob** Creutzfeldt-Jakob disease, CJD; **morbo della mucca pazza** mad cow disease
morbosa'mente *adv* morbidly
morbosità *f inv* (qualità) morbidity
mor'boso *adj* morbid
'morchia *f* sludge
mor'dace *adj* cutting
mor'dente *adj* biting
'mordere *vt* bite; (corrodere) bite into
mordicchi'are *vt* gnaw
'mordi e 'fuggi *adj* ‹*vacanza*› very short
mo'rello **A** *m* black horse
B *adj* blackish
mo'rena *f* moraine
mo'rente *adj* dying
mo'resco *adj* Moorish
mor'fina *f* morphine
morfi'nomane *mf* morphine addict
morfolo'gia *f* morphology
morfo'logico *adj* morphological
mori'bondo *adj* dying; ‹*istituzione*› moribund
morige'rato *adj* moderate
mo'rire *vi* die; fig die out; **fa un freddo da ~** it's freezing cold, it's perishing; **~ di noia** be bored to death; **c'era da ~ dal ridere** it was hilariously funny; **morir di fame** starve to death; fig starve
mor'mone *mf* Mormon
mormo'rare *vt & vi* murmur; ‹*brontolare*› mutter
mormo'rio *m* murmuring; (lamentela) grumbling
'moro **A** *adj* dark
B *m* Moor
morosità *f inv* default
mo'roso *adj* in arrears
'morra *f game for two players where each shouts a number at the same time as showing a number of fingers*
'morsa *f* vice; fig grip
'morse *adj* **alfabeto ~** Morse code
mor'setto *m* clamp; (stringinaso) nose clip
■ **morsetto per batteria** battery lead connection
morsi'care *vt* bite
morsica'tura *f* [snake] bite
'morso *m* bite; (di cibo, briglia) bit; **i morsi della fame** hunger pangs
morta'della *f* mortadella (*type of salted pork*)
mor'taio *m* mortar
mor'tale *adj* mortal; (simile a morte) deadly; **di una noia ~** deadly
mortalità *f inv* mortality
mortal'mente *adv* ‹*ferito*› fatally; ‹*offeso*› mortally; ‹*annoiato*› to death; **~ stanco** infml dead tired
morta'retto *m* firecracker
'morte *f* death; **non è la ~ di nessuno** it's not the end of the world; **lo odia a ~** infml she can't stand the sight of him; **annoiarsi a ~** infml be bored to death
■ **~ cerebrale** brain death
mortifi'cante *adj* mortifying
mortifi'care *vt* mortify
mortifi'carsi *vr* be mortified
mortifi'cato *adj* mortified
mortificazi'one *f* mortification
'morto, -a **A** *pp di* **morire**
B *adj* dead; **~ di freddo** frozen to death; **stanco ~** dead tired
C *m* dead man
D *f* dead woman
mor'torio *m* funeral
mo'saico *m* mosaic
'mosca *f* fly; (barba) goatee; **cadere come le mosche** be dropping like flies; **essere una ~ bianca** be a rarity; **non si sentiva volare una ~** you could have heard a pin drop
■ **mosca cieca** blind man's buff
'Mosca *f* Moscow
mo'scato **A** *adj* muscat; **noce moscata** nutmeg
B *m* muscatel
mosce'rino *m* midge; infml (persona) midget
mo'schea *f* mosque
moschetti'ere *m* musketeer
mo'schetto *m* musket

moschet'tone *m* (in alpinismo) snap link; (gancio) spring clip

moschi'cida **A** *adj inv* **carta ∼** fly paper **B** *m* fly spray

'moscio *adj* limp; **avere l'erre moscia** not be able to say one's r's properly

mo'scone *m* bluebottle; (barca) pedalo

Mosè *m inv* Moses

'mossa *f* movement; (passo) move

'mosso **A** pp di **muovere** **B** *adj* ‹*mere*› rough; ‹*capelli*› wavy; ‹*fotografia*› blurred

mo'starda *f* mustard

■ **mostarda di Cremona** *preserve made from candied fruit in grape must or sugar with mustard*

'mostra *f* show; (d'arte) exhibition; **far ∼ di** pretend; **in ∼** on show; **mettersi in ∼** make oneself conspicuous; **far ∼ di sé** show off; **far bella ∼ di sé** look impressive

■ **mostra dell'artigianato** craft fair

'mostra-mer'cato *f* trade fair

mo'strare *vt* show; (indicare) point out; (spiegare) explain; **∼ di** (sembrare) seem; (fingere) pretend

mo'strarsi *vr* show oneself; (apparire) appear

mo'strina *f* flash

'mostro *m* monster; fig (persona) genius

■ **mostro sacro** fig sacred cow

mostruosa'mente *adv* tremendously

mostru'oso *adj* monstrous; (incredibile) enormous

mo'tel *m inv* motel

moti'vare *vt* cause; Jur justify

moti'vato *adj* ‹*persona*› motivated; ‹*azione*› justified

motivazi'one *f* motivation; (giustificazione) justification

mo'tivo *m* reason; (movente) motive; (in musica, letteratura) theme; (disegno) pattern, motif; **senza ∼** for no reason; (senza giustificazione) unjustifiably

■ **motivo cachemire** paisley; **motivo a scacchi** chequered pattern

'moto **A** *m* motion; (esercizio) exercise; (gesto) movement; (sommossa) rising; **mettere in ∼** start ‹*motore*›

■ **moto ondoso** swell; **moto perpetuo** perpetual motion

B *f inv* (motocicletta) motor bike

moto'carro *m* three-wheeler

motoci'cletta *f* motorcycle, motorbike

■ **motocicletta da corsa** racing motorbike, racer

motoci'clismo *m* motorcycling

motoci'clista *mf* motorcyclist, biker

moto'cross *m* motocross, scrambling

motocros'sista *mf* scrambler

moto'lancia *f* motor launch

moto'nautica *f* speedboat racing

moto'nave *f* motor vessel

mo'tore **A** *adj* motor *attrib* **B** *m* motor, engine; **con ∼ turbo** turbocharged

■ **motore diesel** diesel engine; **motore a iniezione** fuel injection engine; **motore raffreddato ad aria** air-cooled engine; **motore a reazione** jet [engine]; **motore di ricerca** Comput search engine; **motore a scoppio** internal combustion engine

moto'retta *f* motor scooter

moto'rino *m* moped

■ **motorino d'avviamento** starter motor

mo'torio *adj* motor *attrib*

moto'rista *mf*

■ **motorista di bordo** flight engineer

motoriz'zare *vt* motorize

motoriz'zato *adj* Mil motorized

motorizzazi'one *f* (ufficio) vehicle licensing office

moto'scafo *m* motor boat

moto'sega *f* chain saw

motove'detta *f* patrol vessel, patrol boat

mo'trice *f* engine

'motto *m* motto; (facezia) witticism; (massima) saying

'mountain bike *f inv* mountain bike

mouse *m inv* Comput mouse

mousse *f inv* Culin mousse

■ **mousse al cioccolato** chocolate mousse

mo'vente *m* motive

mo'venze *fpl* movements

mo'vida *f* night life

movimen'tare *vt* enliven

movimen'tato *adj* lively

movi'mento *m* movement; **essere sempre in ∼** be always on the go

■ **movimento passeggeri e merci** passenger and freight traffic

Mozam'bico *m* Mozambique

mozi'one *f* motion

■ **mozione d'ordine** point of order

mozzafi'ato *adj inv* nail-biting

moz'zare *vt* cut off; dock ‹*coda*›; **∼ il fiato a qualcuno** take somebody's breath away

mozza'rella *f* mozzarella (*mild, white cheese*)

■ **mozzarella di bufala** buffalo mozzarella

mozzi'cone *m* (di sigaretta) stub

'mozzo **A** *m* Mech hub; Naut ship's boy **B** *adj* ‹*coda*› truncated; ‹*testa*› severed

ms *abbr* (**manoscritto**) MS

'mucca *f* cow; **morbo della ∼ pazza** mad cow disease

'mucchio *m* heap, pile; **un ∼ di** fig lots of

mucil'lagine *f* Bot mucilage

'muco *m* mucus

'muffa *f* mould; **fare la ∼** go mouldy

muf'fire *vi* go mouldy

muf'fola *f* mitt
mu'flone *m* Zool mouflon
mugghi'are *vi* ‹*vento, mare*› roar
mug'gire *vi* ‹*mucca*› moo, low; ‹*toro*› bellow
mug'gito *m* moo; (di toro) bellow; (azione) mooing; bellowing
mu'ghetto *m* lily of the valley
mugo'lare *vi* whine; ‹*persona*› moan
mugo'lio *m* whining
mugu'gnare *vt* infml mumble
mulatti'era *f* mule track
mu'latto, -a *mf* mulatto
mu'leta *f inv* muleta
muli'ebre *adj* (liter) feminine
muli'nare *vi* spin
muli'nello *m* (d'acqua) whirlpool; (di vento) eddy; (giocattolo) windmill
mu'lino *m* mill
■ **mulino a vento** windmill
'mulo *m* mule
'multa *f* fine
■ **multa per divieto di sosta** parking ticket
mul'tare *vt* fine
multico'lore *adj* multicoloured
multicultu'rale *adj* multicultural
multi'etnico *adj* multi-ethnic
multifo'cale *adj* ‹*lente*› varifocal
■ **occhiali multifocali** varifocals
multifunzio'nale *adj* multifunction[al]
multilate'rale *adj* multilateral
multi'lingue *adj* multilingual
multi'media *mpl* multimedia
multimedi'ale *adj* multimedia *attrib*
multimedialità *f inv* multimedia
multimiliar'dario, -a *mf* multimillionaire
multinazio'nale *adj & nf* multinational
'multiplo *adj & nm* multiple
multiproprietà *nf nv* time-share; **una casa in ~** a time-share
multiraz'ziale *adj* multiracial
multi'sala *adj inv* **cinema ~** multiplex [cinema]
multi'tasking *m* Comput multitasking
multi'uso *adj* ‹*utensile*› all-purpose
'mummia *f* mummy; fig (persona) old fogey
mummifi'care *vt* mummify
'mungere *vt* milk
mungi'tura *f* milking
munici'pale *adj* municipal
municipalità *f inv* town council
muni'cipio *m* town hall
munifi'cenza *f* munificence, bounty
mu'nifico *adj* munificent
mu'nire *vt* fortify; **~ di** (provvedere) supply with; **munitevi di un carrello/cestino** please take a trolley/basket
munizi'oni *fpl* ammunition *sg*
'munto pp di **mungere**
mu'overe *vt* move; (suscitare) arouse
mu'oversi *vr* move; **muoviti!** hurry up!, come on!
'mura *fpl* (cinta di città) walls
mu'raglia *f* wall
mu'rale *adj* mural; ‹*pittura*› wall *attrib*
mur'are *vt* wall up
mu'rario *adj* masonry *attrib*; **cinta muraria** walls *pl*; **opera muraria** masonry
mura'tore *m* bricklayer; (con pietre) mason; (operaio edile) builder
mura'tura *f* (di pietra) masonry, stonework; (di mattoni) brickwork
mu'rena *f* moray eel
'muro *m* wall; (di nebbia) bank; **a ~** ‹*armadio*› built-in
■ **muro divisorio** partition wall; **muro di gomma** fig wall of indifference; **fare ~ di gomma** stonewall; **muro a intercapedine** cavity wall; **Muro del pianto** Wailing Wall; **muro portante** load-bearing wall; **muro del suono** sound barrier
'musa *f* anche fig muse
muschi'ato *adj* musky
'muschio *m* musk; Bot moss
musco'lare *adj* muscular
muscola'tura *f* muscles *pl*
'muscolo *m* muscle
musco'loso *adj* muscular
mu'seo *m* museum
museru'ola *f* muzzle
'musica *f* music
■ **musica gospel** gospel music; **musica folk** folk [music]
'musical *m inv* musical
musi'cale *adj* musical
musi'care *vt* set to music
musicas'setta *f* cassette
musi'cista *mf* musician
musicolo'gia *f* musicology
'muso *m* muzzle; derog (di persona) mug; (di aeroplano) nose; **fare il ~** sulk
mu'sone, -a *adj & nmf* sulker
'mussola *f* muslin
mussul'mano, -a *adj & nmf* Muslim, Moslem
'muta *f* (cambio) change; (di penne) moult; (di cani) pack; (per immersione subacquea) wetsuit
muta'mento *m* change
mu'tande *fpl* pants
mutan'dine *fpl* panties
■ **mutandine da bagno** bathing trunks; (da donna) bikini bottom
mutan'doni *mpl* (da uomo) long johns; (da donna) bloomers
mu'tante *mf* mutant
mu'tare *vt* change
mutazi'one *f* mutation

m

mu'tevole *adj* changeable
muti'lare *vt* mutilate
muti'lato, -a **A** *adj* disabled
B *mf* disabled person
■ **mutilato di guerra** disabled ex-serviceman; **mutilato del lavoro** person disabled at work
mutilazi'one *f* mutilation
mu'tismo *m* dumbness; fig obstinate silence
🔑 **'muto** *adj* dumb; (silenzioso) silent; (fonetica) mute offensive
'mutua *f*
■ **[cassa] mutua** sickness benefit fund
mutu'abile *adj* ‹*farmaco*› prescribable on the NHS
mutu'are *vt* borrow ‹*teoria, parola*›
mutua'tario, -a *mf* Fin borrower
mutu'ato, -a *mf* NHS patient
'mutuo¹ *adj* mutual
'mutuo² *m* loan; (per la casa) mortgage; **fare un ~** take out a mortgage; **società di mutuo soccorso** friendly society
■ **mutuo ipotecario** mortgage

Nn

na'babbo *m* nabob; **vivere da ~** live in the lap of luxury
'nacchera *f* castanet
na'dir *m* nadir
'nafta *f* naphtha; (per motori) diesel oil; **a ~** ‹*bruciatore*› oil-burning
'naia *f* cobra; sl (servizio militare) national service
'nailon *m* nylon
Na'mibia *f* Namibia
na'nismo *m* dwarfism
'nanna *f* sl (infantile) bye-byes; **andare a ~** go bye-byes; **fare la ~** sleep
'nano, -a *adj & nmf* dwarf
nanoparti'cella *f* nanoparticle
nanose'condo *m* nanosecond
'napalm *m* napalm
napole'tana *f* (caffettiera) Neapolitan coffee maker
napole'tano, -a *adj & nmf* Neapolitan
'Napoli *f* Naples
'nappa *f* tassel; (pelle) soft leather
narci'sismo *m* narcissism
narci'sista *adj & nmf* narcissist
nar'ciso *m* narcissus
nar'cosi *f* general anaesthesia
nar'cotici *f* Drug Squad
nar'cotico *adj & nm* narcotic
na'rice *f* nostril
nar'rare *vt* tell
narra'tivo, -a **A** *adj* narrative
B *f* fiction
narra|'tore, -trice *mf* narrator
narrazi'one *f* narration; (racconto) story
na'sale *adj* nasal
na'scente *adj* budding
🔑 **'nascere** *vi* (venire al mondo) be born; (germogliare) sprout; (sorgere) rise; **~ da** fig arise from
🔑 **'nascita** *f* birth
nasci'turo *m* unborn child
🔑 **na'scondere** *vt* hide
na'scondersi *vr* hide
nascon'diglio *m* hiding place
nascon'dino *m* hide-and-seek
na'scosto **A** pp di **nascondere**
B *adj* hidden; **di ~** secretly; **ascoltare di ~** listen in on ‹*conversazione*›
na'sello *m* (pesce) hake
🔑 **'naso** *m* nose
na'sone *m* big nose, hooter infml
'nassa *f* lobster pot
'nastro *m* ribbon; (di registratore ecc.) tape
■ **nastro adesivo** adhesive tape, sticky tape; **nastro isolante** insulating tape; **nastro magnetico** magnetic tape, mag tape infml; **nastro trasportatore** conveyor belt
🔑 **na'tale** *adj* ‹*giorno, paese*› of one's birth
🔑 **Na'tale** *m* Christmas
na'tali *mpl* parentage
natalità *f inv* [number of] births, birth rate
nata'lizio *adj* ‹*del Natale*› Christmas *attrib*
na'tante **A** *adj* floating
B *m* craft
'natica *f* buttock
na'tio *adj* native
Natività *f inv* Nativity
na'tivo, -a *adj & nmf* native
'nato **A** pp di **nascere**
B *adj* born; **uno scrittore ~** a born writer; **nata Rossi** née Rossi
'NATO *f* Nato, NATO

na'tura *f* nature; **pagare in ~** pay in kind; **di ~ politica** of a political nature
■ **natura morta** still life

natu'rale *adj* natural; **al ~** ‹*alimento*› plain, natural; **~!** naturally, of course

natura'lezza *f* naturalness

naturaliz'zare *vt* naturalize

natural'mente *adv* (ovviamente) naturally, of course

natu'rista *mf* naturalist

natu'ristico *adj* naturist

naufra'gare *vi* be wrecked; ‹*persona*› be shipwrecked

nau'fragio *m* shipwreck; fig wreck

'naufrago, -a *mf* survivor

'nausea *f* nausea; **avere la ~** feel sick

nausea'bondo *adj* nauseating

nause'are *vt* nauseate

'nautica *f* navigation

'nautico *adj* nautical

na'vale *adj* naval

na'vata *f* (centrale) nave; (laterale) aisle

'nave *f* ship
■ **nave ammiraglia** flagship; **nave da carico** cargo boat; **nave cisterna** tanker; **nave da crociera** cruise liner; **nave fattoria** factory ship; **nave da guerra** warship; **nave di linea** liner; **nave passeggeri** passenger ship; **nave portacontainer** container ship; **nave spaziale** spaceship; **nave traghetto** ferry

na'vetta *f* shuttle

navi'cella *f*
■ **navicella spaziale** spacecraft

navi'gabile *adj* navigable

navi'gare *vi* sail; **~ in Internet** surf the Net, browse

naviga|'tore, -trice *mf* navigator; (in Internet) surfer
■ **navigatore solitario** lone yachtsman; **navigatore spaziale** spaceman

navigazi'one *f* navigation; **della ~** navigational

na'viglio *m* fleet; (canale) canal

nazifa'scismo *m* Nazi fascism

nazifa'scista *mf* Nazi fascist

nazio'nale **A** *adj* national
B *f* Sport national team

naziona'lismo *m* nationalism

naziona'lista *mf* nationalist

nazionalità *f inv* nationality

nazionaliz'zare *vt* nationalize

nazi'one *f* nation; **Nazioni** *pl* **Unite** United Nations

na'zista *adj & nmf* Nazi

N.B. *abbr* (**nota bene**) NB

n.d.r. *abbr* (**nota del redattore**) editor's note

'n'drangheta *f* Calabrian Mafia

n.d.t. *abbr* (**nota del traduttore**) translator's note

ne **A** *pron* (di lui) about him; (di lei) about her; (di loro) about them; (di ciò) about it; (da ciò) from that; (di un insieme) of it; (di un gruppo) of them; **ne sono contento** I'm happy about it; **non ne conosco nessuno** I don't know any of them; **ne ho** I have some; **non ne ho più** I don't have any left
B *adv* from there; **ne vengo ora** I've just come from there; **me ne vado** I'm off; **ne va della mia reputazione** my reputation is at stake

NE *abbr* (**nord-est**) NE

né *conj* **né... né...** neither... nor...; **non ne ho il tempo né la voglia** I don't have either the time or the inclination; **né tu né io vogliamo andare** neither you nor I want to go; **né l'uno né l'altro** neither [of them/us]

ne'anche **A** *adv* (neppure) not even; (senza neppure) without even
B *conj* (e neppure) neither...nor; **io non parlo inglese e lui ~** I don't speak English, neither does he *or* and he doesn't either

'nebbia *f* mist; (in città, autostrada) fog

nebbi'oso *adj* misty; (in città, autostrada) foggy

nebuliz'zare *vt* atomize

nebulizza'tore *m* atomizer; (per il naso) nasal spray

nebulizzazi'one *f* atomizing; **fare delle nebulizzazioni** take nasal sprays

nebulosità *f inv* vagueness

nebu'loso *adj* hazy; ‹*teoria*› nebulous; ‹*discorso*› woolly

necessaria'mente *adv* necessarily

neces'sario **A** *adj* necessary
B *m* **fare il ~** do the necessary, do the needful

necessità *f inv* necessity; (bisogno) need

necessi'tare *vi* **~ di** need; (essere necessario) be necessary

necro'logio *m* obituary

ne'cropoli *f inv* necropolis

ne'crosi *f* necrosis

ne'fando *adj* wicked

ne'fasto *adj* ill-omened

ne'frite *f* nephritis

nefrolo'gia *f* nephrology

ne'frologo, -a *mf* nephrologist

ne'gabile *adj* deniable

ne'gare *vt* deny; (rifiutare) refuse; **essere negato per qualcosa** be no good at something

nega'tiva *f* negative

nega'tivo *adj* negative

negazi'one *f* negation; (diniego) denial; Gram negative

ne'gletto *adj* neglected

'negli = **in + gli**

negli'gente *adj* negligent

negli'genza *f* negligence

negozi'abile *adj* negotiable

negozi'ante *mf* dealer; (bottegaio) shopkeeper

negozi'are **A** *vt* negotiate
B *vi* ~ in trade in, deal in

negozi'ati *mpl* negotiations

ne'gozio *m* shop
■ **negozio di abbigliamento** clothes shop; **negozio di alimentari** grocer's; **negozio di antiquariato** antique shop; **negozio duty free** duty-free shop; **negozio di ferramenta** hardware shop; **negozio giuridico** legal transaction; **negozio di souvenir** gift shop

'negro, -a **A** *adj* offensive Negro, black
B *mf* offensive Negro, black person; (scrittore) ghost writer; **come un ~** offensive ‹*lavorare*› like a slave

negro'mante *mf* necromancer

'nei = in + i

nel = in + il

'nella = in, la A, B

'nelle = in + le

'nello = in + lo

'nembo *m* nimbus

'nemesi *f* nemesis

ne'mico, -a **A** *adj* hostile
B *mf* enemy

nem'meno *conj* not even

'nenia *f* dirge; (per bambini) lullaby; (piagnucolio) wail

'neo *m* mole; (applicato) beauty spot

neo+ *pref* neo+

neo'classico *adj* neoclassical

neocolonia'lismo *m* neocolonialism

neofa'scismo *m* neofascism

neola'tino *adj* Romance

neolaure'ato, -a *mf* recent graduate

neo'litico *adj* Neolithic

neolo'gismo *m* neologism

'neon *m* neon

neo'nato, -a **A** *adj* new born
B *mf* newborn baby

neona'zismo *m* neo-Nazism

neona'zista *adj & nmf* neo-Nazi

neozelan'dese **A** *adj* New Zealand *attrib*
B *mf* New Zealander

'Nepal *m* Nepal

nep'pure *conj* not even

ne'rastro *adj* blackish

'nerbo *m* (forza) strength; fig backbone; **senza ~** effete

nerbo'ruto *adj* brawny

ne'retto *m* Typ bold [type]

'nero **A** *adj* black; infml (arrabbiato) fuming
B *m* black; **l'ho visto ~ su bianco** I've seen it in black and white; **mettere ~ su bianco** put in writing
■ **nero pieno** Typ solid; **nero di seppia** sepia

nerva'tura *f* nerves *pl*; Bot veining; (di libro) band

ner'vetti *mpl chopped beef and veal with onions*

ner'vino *adj* ‹*gas*› nerve *attrib*

'nervo *m* nerve; Bot vein; **avere i nervi** be bad-tempered; **dare ai** *o* **sui nervi a qualcuno** get on somebody's nerves

nervo'sismo *m* nerviness

ner'voso *adj* nervous, edgy; (irritabile) bad-tempered; **avere il ~** be irritable; **esaurimento ~** nervous breakdown

'nespola *f* medlar

'nespolo *m* medlar tree

'nesso *m* link, connection

nes'suno **A** *adj* no, not... any; (qualche) any; **non ho nessun problema** I don't have any problems, I have no problems; **non ha nessun valore** it hasn't any value, it has no value; **da nessuna parte** nowhere; **non lo trovo da nessuna parte** I can't find it anywhere; **in nessun modo** on no account; **per nessun motivo** for no reason; **nessuna notizia?** any news?
B *pron* nobody, no one, not... anybody, not... anyone; (qualcuno) anybody, anyone; **hai delle domande? - nessuna** do you have any questions? - none; **~ di voi** none of you; **~ dei due** (di voi due) neither of you; **non ho visto ~ dei tuoi amici** I haven't seen any of your friends; **c'è ~?** is anybody there?

'nesting *m inv* Comput nesting

net *m inv* Tennis net cord

net'tare *vt* clean

'nettare *m* nectar

netta'rina *f* nectarine

net'tezza *f* cleanliness
■ **nettezza urbana** cleansing department

'netto *adj* clean; (chiaro) clear; Comm net; **di ~** just like that

Net'tuno *m* Neptune

nettur'bino *m* dustman

'network *m inv* network
■ **network televisivo** network television

'neuro *f* neurological clinic

neuro+ *pref* neuro+

neurochirur'gia *f* brain surgery

neurochi'rurgo *m* brain surgeon

neurolo'gia *f* neurology

neuro'logico *adj* neurological

neuropsichi'atra *mf* neuropsychiatrist

neuropsichia'tria *f* neuropsychiatry

neu'trale *adj & nm* neutral

neutralità *f inv* neutrality

neutraliz'zare *vt* neutralize

'neutro **A** *adj* neutral; Gram neuter
B *m* Gram neuter

neu'trone *m* neutron

ne'vaio *m* snow-field

'neve *f* snow

nevi'care *vi* snow; **nevica** it is snowing

nevi'cata *f* snowfall

key word

ne'vischio *m* sleet
ne'voso *adj* snowy
nevral'gia *f* neuralgia
ne'vralgico *adj* neuralgic; **punto nevralgico** nerve centre; (di questione ecc.) crucial point
nevraste'nia *f* neurasthenia
nevra'stenico *adj* neurasthenic; (irritabile) hot tempered
ne'vrite *f* neuritis
ne'vrosi *f inv* neurosis
ne'vrotico *adj* neurotic
'nibbio *m* kite
Nica'ragua *m* Nicaragua
nicara'guense *adj & nmf* Nicaraguan
'nicchia *f* niche
nicchi'are *vi* shilly-shally
'nichel *m* nickel
nichi'lista **A** *mf* nihilist
B *adj* nihilistic
nico'tina *f* nicotine
nidi'ace *m* nestling
nidi'ata *f* brood
nidifi'care *vi* nest
nidifi'cato *adj* Comput nested
nidificazi'one *f* Zool nesting
'nido *m* nest; (giardino d'infanzia) crèche; **a ~ d'ape** ‹*tessuto*› honeycomb *attrib*
■ **nido di uccello** bird's nest; **nido di vipere** fig nest of vipers
ni'ente **A** *pron* nothing, not... anything; (qualcosa) anything; **non ho fatto ~ di male** I didn't do anything wrong, I did nothing wrong; **nient'altro?** anything else?; **grazie! - di ~!** thank you! - don't mention it!; **non serve a ~** it is no use; **vuoi ~?** do you want anything?; **dal ~** ‹*venire su*› from nothing; **da ~** (poco importante) minor; (di poco valore) worthless
B *adj inv* infml **~ pesci oggi** no fish today; **non ho ~ fame** I'm not the slightest bit hungry
C *adv* **non fa ~** (non importa) it doesn't matter; **per ~** at all; ‹*litigare*› over nothing; **~ affatto!** no way!
D *m* **un bel ~** absolutely nothing, damn all infml; **basta un ~ per spaventarlo** it doesn't take much to scare him
E *inter* **"cos'è successo?" – "~... mi hanno rubato l'auto"** infml "what happened?" – "well, er... I had my car stolen"
nientedi'meno, niente'meno **A** *adv* **~ che** no less than
B *int* fancy that!
'Niger *m* Niger
Ni'geria *f* Nigeria
night *m inv* night club
'Nilo *m* Nile
'ninfa *f* nymph
nin'fea *f* water lily
nin'fomane *f* nymphomaniac; **da ~** nymphomaniac
ninna'nanna *f* lullaby
'ninnolo *m* plaything; (fronzolo) knick-knack
ni'pote **A** *m* (di zii) nephew; (di nonni) grandson, grandchild; **nipoti** *pl* (collettivo) grandchildren, nephews and nieces
B *f* (di zii) niece; (di nonni) granddaughter, grandchild
nip'ponico *adj* Japanese
'nisba *pron* sl (niente) zilch
'nitido *adj* neat; (chiaro) clear
ni'trato *m* nitrate
'nitrico *adj* nitric
ni'trire *vi* neigh
ni'trito *m* (di cavallo) neigh; Chem nitrite
nitro+ *pref* nitro+
nitroglice'rina *f* nitroglycerine
'niveo *adj* snow-white
N.N. *abbr* (**numeri**) Nos
no **A** *adv* no; **credo di no** I don't think so; **perché no?** why not?; **io no** not me; **sì o no?** yes or no?; **ha detto così, no?** he said so, didn't he?; **fa freddo, no?** it's cold, isn't it?; **se no** otherwise
B *m* no; (nelle votazioni) nay
NO *abbr* (**nord-ovest**) NW
nobil'donna *f* noblewoman
'nobile **A** *adj* noble; **metallo ~** noble metal; **di animo ~** noble-minded
B *m* noble, nobleman
C *f* noble, noblewoman
nobili'are *adj* noble
nobiltà *f inv* nobility
nobilu'omo *m* nobleman
'nocca *f* knuckle
nocci'ola *f* hazelnut
noccio'line [americane] *fpl* peanuts
'nocciolo *m* stone; Phys core; fig heart; **il ~ della questione** the heart of the matter
nocci'olo *m* (albero) hazel
'noce **A** *f* walnut
■ **noce moscata** nutmeg; **noce pecan** pecan; **noce di vitello** veal with mushrooms
B *m* (legno) walnut; (albero) walnut [tree]
noce'pesca *f* nectarine
no'cino *m* walnut liqueur
no'civo *adj* harmful
no'dino *m* veal chop
'nodo *m* knot; fig lump; Comput node; **fare il ~ della cravatta** do up one's tie
■ **nodo alla gola** lump in the throat; **nodo della questione** crux of the matter; **nodo ferroviario** railway junction; **nodo piano** reef knot; **nodo scorsoio** slip knot
no'doso *adj* knotty
'nodulo *m* nodule
Noè *m inv* Noah
no-'global *adj* anti-globalization
'noi *pers pron* (soggetto) we; (oggetto, con prep)

us; **chi è? - siamo** ~ who is it? - it's us; ~ **due** the two of us

✓ **'noia** *f* boredom; (fastidio) bother; (persona) bore; **dar** ~ annoy

noi'altri *pers pron* we

✓ **noi'oso** *adj* boring; (fastidioso) tiresome

noleggi'are *vt* hire; (dare a noleggio) hire out; charter ‹*nave, aereo*›

no'leggio *m* hire; (di nave, aereo) charter

■ **noleggio barche/biciclette/sci** boat/cycle/ski hire

'nolo *m* hire; Naut freight; **a** ~ for hire

'nomade **A** *adj* nomadic

B *mf* nomad

✓ **'nome** *m* name; Gram noun; **a** ~ **di** ‹*da parte di*› on behalf of; **di** ~ by name; **farsi un** ~ make a name for oneself; **nel** ~ **di...** in the name of....

■ **nome d'arte** professional name; **nome di battaglia** nom de guerre; **nome di battesimo** first name, Christian name, given name; **nome in codice** code name; **nome depositato** trade name; **nome di dominio** Comput domain name; **nome per esteso** full name; **nome di famiglia** surname, family name; **nome del file** filename; **nome proprio** proper name, proper noun; **nome da ragazza** maiden name; **nome da sposata** married name; **nome utente** username

no'mea *f* reputation

nomencla'tura *f* nomenclature

no'mignolo *m* nickname

'nomina *f* appointment; **di prima** ~ newly appointed

nomi'nale *adj* nominal; Gram noun *attrib*

✓ **nomi'nare** *vt* name; (menzionare) mention; (eleggere) appoint

nomina'tivo **A** *adj* nominative; Comm registered

B *m* nominative; (nome) name; **caso** ~ nominative case

✓ **non** *adv* not; ~ **ti amo** I do not *or* don't love you; ~ **c'è di che** not at all; ~ **più** no longer

nonché *conj* (tanto meno) let alone; (e anche) as well as

nonconfor'mista *adj & mf inv* nonconformist

nonconformità *f inv* non-compliance

noncu'rante *adj* nonchalant; (negligente) indifferent

noncu'ranza *f* nonchalance; (negligenza) indifference

nondi'meno *conj* nevertheless

✓ **'nonna** *f* grandmother, grandma infml, gran infml

✓ **'nonno** *m* grandfather, grandpa infml; **nonni** *pl* grandparents

non'nulla *m inv* trifle

'nono *adj & nm* ninth

✓ key word

✓ **nono'stante** **A** *prep* in spite of

B *conj* although

non stop *adj inv & adv* non-stop

nontiscordardimé *m inv* forget-me-not

nonvio'lento *adj* nonviolent

nonvio'lenza *f* non-violence

no 'profit *adj* non profit

nor'cino *m* pig butcher

✓ **nord** *m* north; **del** ~ northern

nord-'est *m* north-east; **a** ~ north-easterly; **del** ~ north-eastern; **vento di** ~ north-easterly [wind]

'nordico *adj* northern

nor'dista *adj & nmf* Yankee

nordocciden'tale *adj* north-western

nordorien'tale *adj* northeastern

nord-'ovest *m* north-west; **a** ~ north-westerly; **del** ~ north-western; **vento di** ~ north-westerly [wind]

'norma *f* norm; (regola) rule; (per l'uso) instruction; **a** ~ **di legge** according to law; **è buona** ~ it's advisable; **di** ~ as a rule, normally

✓ **nor'male** **A** *adj* normal

B *m* **fuori del** ~ out of the ordinary; **superiore al** ~ above average

normalità *f inv* normality; **rientrare nella** ~ be quite normal

normaliz'zare *vt* normalize

normal'mente *adv* normally

Norman'dia *f* Normandy

nor'manno *adj* from Normandy; (storico) Norman

norma'tiva *f* regulations *pl*, laws *pl*

norma'tivo *adj* normative, prescriptive

nor'mografo *m* stencil

nor'reno *adj* Norse

norve'gese *adj & nmf* Norwegian

Nor'vegia *f* Norway

noso'comio *nm fml* hospital

nossi'gnore *adv* (assolutamente no) no way

nostal'gia *f* (di casa, patria) homesickness; (del passato) nostalgia; **aver** ~ be homesick; **aver** ~ **di qualcuno** miss somebody

no'stalgico, -a **A** *adj* nostalgic

B *mf* reactionary

nostra ▸ **nostro**

no'strale *adj* local

no'strano *adj* local; (fatto in casa) home-made

'nostre ▸ **nostro**

'nostri ▸ **nostro**

✓ **'nostro** **A** (**il nostro** *m* **la nostra** *f* **i nostri** *mpl* **le nostre** *fpl*) *poss adj* our; **quella macchina è nostra** that car is ours; ~ **padre** our father; **un** ~ **amico** a friend of ours

B *poss pron* ours

no'stromo *m* bo's'n, boatswain

'nota *f* (segno) sign; (comunicazione, commento, Mus) note; (conto) bill; (lista) list; **degno di**

~ noteworthy; **prendere ~** take note; **una ~ di colore** a touch of colour; **mettere in ~ qualcosa** add something to the list
■ **nota di accredito** Comm credit note; **note** *pl* **caratteristiche** distinguishing marks; **nota spese** expense account

no'tabile *adj & nm* notable

no'taio *m* notary

no'tare *vt* (segnare) mark; (annotare) note down; (osservare) notice; **far ~ qualcosa** point something out; **farsi ~** get oneself noticed; **nota bene che...** please note that...

notazi'one *f* marking; (annotazione) notation

'notebook *m inv* Comput notebook (PC)

'notes *m inv* notepad

no'tevole *adj* (degno di nota) remarkable; (grande) considerable

no'tifica *f* notification

notifi'care *vt* notify; Comm advise; **~ un ordine di comparizione [in giudizio]** subpoena

notificazi'one *f* notification

no'tizia *f* **una ~** a piece of news, some news; (informazione) a piece of information, some information; **le notizie** the news *sg*; **per avere ~ di** ‹*telefonare*› for news of; **non ha più dato notizie di sé** he hasn't been in touch since
■ **notizia di attualità** news item

notizi'ario *m* news *sg*

'noto *adj* well-known; **rendere ~** (far sapere) announce

notorietà *f inv* fame; **raggiungere la ~** become famous

no'torio *adj* well-known; derog notorious

not'tambulo *m* night-bird

not'tata *f* night; **far ~** stay up all night

'notte *f* night; **di ~** at night; **a ~ fatta** when night had fallen; **la ~** (durante la notte) at night; **buona ~** good night; **fermarsi per la ~** stay overnight; **peggio che andar di ~** worse than ever; **prima ~ di nozze** wedding night
■ **notte bianca** (notte insonne) sleepless night; (manifestazione) all-night cultural festival, Light Night BrE

notte'tempo *adv* at night-time

not'turno *adj* nocturnal; ‹*servizio ecc.*› night *attrib*; **in notturna** ‹*partita*› under floodlights

'notula *f* (conto) fee note

no'vanta *adj & nm* ninety

novan'tenne *adj & nmf* ninety year old

novan'tesimo *adj & nm* ninetieth

novan'tina *f* about ninety

'nove *adj & nm* nine; **prova del ~** Math casting out nines

nove'cento *adj & nm* nine hundred; **il Novecento** the twentieth century; **stile ~** twentieth-century

no'vella *f* short story

novelli'ere *m* short-story writer

novel'lino, -a **A** *adj* inexperienced **B** *mf* novice, beginner

no'vello *adj* new
■ **patate novelle** new potatoes

no'vembre *m* November

nove'mila *adj & nm* nine thousand

no'vena *f* novena

novi'lunio *m* new moon

novità *f inv* novelty; (notizie) news *sg*; **l'ultima ~** (moda) the latest fashion

novizi'ato *m* Relig novitiate; (tirocinio) apprenticeship

nozi'one *f* notion; **perdere la ~ del tempo** lose track of time; **non avere la ~ del tempo** have no sense of time; **nozioni** *pl* rudiments; **poche nozioni di inglese** very basic English

nozio'nismo *m* accumulation of facts

'nozze *fpl* marriage *sg*; (cerimonia) wedding *sg*; **andare a ~** (godersela) have a field day
■ **nozze d'argento** silver wedding [anniversary]; **nozze di diamante** diamond wedding [anniversary]; **nozze d'oro** golden wedding [anniversary]

'nube *f* cloud
■ **nube di mistero** shroud of mystery; **nube tossica** toxic cloud

nubi'fragio *m* cloudburst

'nubile **A** *adj* unmarried **B** *f* unmarried woman

'nuca *f* nape

nucle'are *adj* nuclear

'nucleo *m* nucleus; (unità) unit
■ **nucleo familiare** family unit

nu'dismo *m* nudism

nu'dista *mf* nudist

nudità *f inv* nudity, nakedness

'nudo *adj* naked; ‹*spoglio, terra*› bare; **a occhio ~** to the naked eye; **verità nuda e cruda** naked truth; **a piedi nudi** barefoot

'nugolo *m* large number

'nulla **A** *pron* = **niente** **B** *m* **da ~** worthless; **per ~** for nothing

nulla'osta *m inv* permit

nullate'nente *m* **i nullatenenti** the have-nots

nullità *f inv* (persona) nonentity

'nullo *adj* Jur null and void

'nume *m* numen

nume'rabile *adj* countable

nume'rale *adj & nm* numeral

nume'rare *vt* number

numera'tore *m* Math numerator

numerazi'one *f* numbering

nu'merico *adj* numerical

'numero *m* number; (romano, arabo) numeral; (di scarpe ecc.) size; **fare** *o* **comporre il ~** dial [the number]; **dare i numeri** infml be off one's head; **avere tutti i numeri per** have what it takes to; **~ civico** street number
■ **numero arretrato** back issue; **numero**

n

cardinale cardinal [number]; **numero di conto** account number; **numero decimale** decimal; **numero di fax** fax number; **numero intero** whole number; **numero ordinale** ordinal [number]; **numero d'ordine** Comm order number; **numero di previdenza sociale** National Insurance number; **numero di protocollo** reference number; **numero di scarpa** shoe size; **numero di telefono** phone number; **numero uno** number one; **numero verde** ≈ Freephone number®, toll-free number AmE; **numero di volo** flight number

✓ **nume'roso** *adj* numerous
numi'smatico *adj* numismatic
'nunzio *m* nuncio
nu'ocere *vi* ~ **a** harm
nu'ora *f* daughter-in-law
nuo'tare *vi* swim; fig wallow; ~ **come un pesce** swim like a fish; ~ **nell'oro** be stinking rich, be rolling in it
nuo'tata *f* swim; **fare una** ~ have a swim
nuota|'tore, -trice *mf* swimmer
nu'oto *m* swimming; **stili** *mpl* **di** ~ swimming strokes
nu'ova *f* piece of news; **buone nuove** good news; **nessuna** ~, **buona** ~ no news is good news
Nu'ova Cale'donia *f* New Caledonia
Nu'ova Gui'nea *f* New Guinea
nuova'mente *adv* again
Nu'ova Ze'landa *f* New Zealand
✓ **nu'ovo** *adj* new; **di** ~ again; **uscire di** ~ go/come back out, go/come out again; **mi risulta** ~ that's news to me; ~ **di pacca** *o* **zecca** brand new; **rimettere a** ~ give a new lease of life to; ~ **del mestiere** new to the job; **il** ~ **anno** [the] New Year
■ **nuova linfa** *nf* new blood; **nuovo stile** *nm* new look; **Nuovo Testamento** *nm* New Testament
'nursery *f* nursery
nutri'ente *adj* nourishing
nutri'mento *m* nourishment
✓ **nu'trire** **A** *vt* feed ‹*animale, malato, pianta*›; harbour ‹*sentimenti*›; cherish ‹*sogno*› **B** *vi* (essere nutriente) be nourishing
nu'trirsi *vr* eat; ~ **di** fig live on
nutri'tivo *adj* nourishing, nutritional
nutrizi'one *f* nutrition
✓ **'nuvola** *f* cloud; **avere la testa fra le nuvole** have one's head in the clouds; **vivere fra le nuvole** live in cloud cuckoo land; **cadere dalle nuvole** be astounded
nuvo'loso *adj* cloudy
nuzi'ale *adj* nuptial; ‹*vestito, anello ecc.*› wedding *attrib*; **pranzo** ~ wedding breakfast
N° *abbr* (**numero**) No.

Oo

✓ **o** *conj* or; **o l'uno o l'altro** one or the other; either; **o... o...** either...or...
O *abbr* (**ovest**) W
'oasi *f inv* oasis
obbedi'ente = **ubbidiente**
obbedi'enza = **ubbidienza**
obbe'dire = **ubbidire**
✓ **obbli'gare** *vt* force, oblige
obbli'garsi *vr* ~ **a** undertake to
obbli'gato *adj* obliged
obbligatoria'mente *adv* **fare qualcosa** ~ be obliged to do something; **bisogna** ~ **farlo** you absolutely have to do it
obbliga'torio *adj* compulsory
obbligazi'one *f* obligation; Fin bond
■ **obbligazione a premio** premium bond
✓ **'obbligo** *m* obligation; (dovere) duty; **avere obblighi verso** be under an obligation to; **d'**~ obligatory
ob'brobrio *m* disgrace
obbrobri'oso *adj* disgraceful
obe'lisco *m* obelisk
obe'rare *vt* overburden
obesità *f inv* obesity
o'beso *adj* obese
obiet'tare *vt & vi* object; ~ **su** object to
obiettiva'mente *adv* objectively
obiettività *f inv* objectivity
obiet'tivo **A** *adj* objective **B** *m* objective; (scopo) object
obiet'tore *m* objector
■ **obiettore di coscienza** conscientious objector
obiezi'one *f* objection; **fare** ~ **di coscienza** be a conscientious objector
obi'torio *m* mortuary
o'blio *m* oblivion
o'bliquo *adj* oblique; fig underhand
oblite'rare *vt* obliterate

✓ key word

oblò *m inv* porthole
ob'lungo *adj* oblong
'oboe *m* oboe
obsole'scenza *f* obsolescence
obso'leto *adj* obsolete
'oca *f* (*pl* **oche**) goose; (donna) silly girl
occasio'nale *adj* occasional
occasional'mente *adv* occasionally
occasi'one *f* occasion; (buon affare) bargain; (motivo) cause; (opportunità) chance; **d'~** second-hand
occhi'aia *f* eye socket; **occhiaie** *pl* shadows under the eyes
occhi'ali *mpl* glasses, spectacles
■ **occhiali multifocali** varifocals; **occhiali scuri** dark glasses; **occhiali da sole** sunglasses; **occhiali da sole avvolgenti** wraparound sunglasses; **occhiali da vista** glasses, spectacles
occhia'luto *adj* wearing glasses
occhi'ata *f* look; **dare un'~ a** have a look at
occhieggi'are **A** *vt* ogle **B** *vi* (far capolino) peep
occhi'ello *m* buttonhole; (asola) eyelet
'occhio *m* eye; **~!** watch out!; **~ ai falsi** beware of imitations; **a quattr'occhi** in private; **abbassare gli occhi** look down, lower one's eyes; **sollevare gli occhi** look up, raise one's eyes; **tenere d'~ qualcuno** keep an eye on somebody; **perdere d'~** lose sight of; **a ~ [e croce]** roughly; **chiudere un ~ (su qualcosa)** turn a blind eye (to something); **dare nell'~** attract attention; **pagare** *o* **spendere un ~ [della testa]** pay an arm and a leg; **saltare agli occhi** be blindingly obvious
■ **occhio di falco** eagle eye; **occhio nero** (pesto) black eye; **occhio di pernice** (callo) corn
occhio'lino *m* **fare l'~ a qualcuno** wink at somebody, give somebody a wink
occiden'tale **A** *adj* western **B** *mf* westerner
occidentaliz'zare *vt* westernize
occidentaliz'zarsi *vr* become westernized
occi'dente *m* west; (paesi capitalisti) West
oc'cludere *vt* obstruct
occlusi'one *f* occlusion
occor'rente **A** *adj* necessary **B** *m* the necessary
occor'renza *f* need; **all'~** if need be
oc'correre *vi* be necessary; **non occorre farlo** there is no need to do it
occulta'mento *m*
■ **occultamento di prove** concealment of evidence
occul'tare *vt* hide
occul'tismo *m* occult
oc'culto *adj* hidden; (magico) occult
occu'pante *mf* occupier; (abusivo) squatter
occu'pare *vt* occupy; spend ‹*tempo*›; take up ‹*spazio*›; (dar lavoro a) employ
occu'parsi *vr* occupy oneself; (trovare lavoro) find a job; **~ di** (badare) look after; **occupati dei fatti tuoi!** mind your own business!
occu'pato *adj* engaged; ‹*persona*› busy; ‹*posto*› taken; **casa occupata** (alloggio abusivo) squat
occupazi'one *f* occupation; Comm employment; (passatempo) pastime; **trovarsi un'~** (interesse) find oneself something to do
o'ceano *m* ocean
■ **oceano Atlantico** Atlantic [Ocean]; **oceano Indiano** Indian Ocean; **oceano Pacifico** Pacific [Ocean]
'ocra *f* ochre
'OCSE *nf abbr* (**Organizzazione per la Cooperazione e lo Sviluppo Economico**) OECD
ocu'lare *adj* ocular; ‹*testimone, bagno*› eye *attrib*
ocula'tezza *f* care
ocu'lato *adj* ‹*scelta, persona*› prudent
ocu'lista *mf* ophthalmologist
od *conj* (davanti alla vocale o) or
'ode *f* ode
odi'are *vt* hate; **~ a morte** to loathe
odi'erno *adj* of today; (attuale) present
'odio *m* hatred; **avere in ~** hate
odi'oso *adj* hateful
odis'sea *f* odyssey
o'dometro *m* Auto milometer, odometer AmE
odo'rare **A** *vt* smell; (profumare) perfume **B** *vi* **~ di** smell of
odo'rato *m* sense of smell
o'dore *m* smell; (profumo) scent; **c'è ~ di...** there's a smell of...; **avere un buon/cattivo ~** smell nice/awful; **sentire ~ di** smell; **odori** *pl* Culin herbs
odo'roso *adj* fragrant
of'fendere *vt* offend; (ferire) injure
of'fendersi *vr* take offence
offen'siva *f* Mil fig offensive
offen'sivo *adj* offensive
offen'sore *m* offender
offe'rente *mf* offerer; (in aste) bidder; **il miglior ~** the highest bidder
of'ferta *f* offer; (donazione) donation; Comm supply; (nelle aste) bid; (di appalto) tender; **in ~ speciale** on special offer; **"offerte d'impiego"** "situations vacant"
■ **offerta pubblica di acquisto** takeover bid
of'ferto pp di **offrire**
offer'torio *m* offertory
of'fesa *f* offence
of'feso **A** pp di **offendere** **B** *adj* offended
offi'ciare *vt* officiate
offi'cina *f* workshop

O

■ **officina [meccanica]** garage
officinale *adj ‹pianta›* medicinal
of'frire *vt* offer
of'frirsi *vr* offer oneself; *‹occasione›* present itself; ~ **di fare qualcosa** offer to do something
'offset *m inv* offset printing
off'shore *m inv* (motoscafo) speedboat
offu'scare *vt* darken; fig dull *‹memoria, bellezza›*; blur *‹vista›*
offu'scarsi *vr* darken; fig *‹memoria, bellezza›* fade away; *‹vista›* become blurred
of'talmico *adj* ophthalmic
ogget'tistica *f manufacture and selling of household and gift items*; (oggetti) household and gift items; **negozio di** ~ gift shop
oggettività *f inv* objectivity
ogget'tivo *adj* objective
og'getto *m* object; (argomento) subject
■ **oggetto sessuale** sex object; **oggetti** *pl* **smarriti** lost property, lost and found AmE
'oggi *adv & nm* today; (al giorno d'oggi) nowadays; **da** ~ **in poi** from today on; ~ **[a] otto** a week today; **dall'**~ **al domani** overnight; **il giornale di** ~ today's paper; **al giorno d'**~ these days, nowadays
oggigi'orno *adv* nowadays
o'giva *f* Mil warhead
'ogni *adj inv* every; (qualsiasi) any; ~ **tre giorni** every three days; **ad** ~ **costo** at any cost; **ad** ~ **modo** anyway; ~ **ben di Dio** all sorts of good things; ~ **cosa** everything; ~ **tanto** now and then; ~ **volta che** every time, whenever
o'gnuno *pron* everyone, everybody; ~ **di voi** each of you
ohibò *int* oh dear!
ohimè *int* oh dear!
o'kay *m* **dare l'**~ **a qualcuno/qualcosa** give somebody/something the OK
'ola *f inv* Mexican wave
O'landa *f* Holland
olan'dese **A** *adj* Dutch
B *m* Dutchman; (lingua) Dutch; (formaggio) Edam
C *f* Dutchwoman
ole'andro *m* oleander
ole'ato *adj* oiled; **carta oleata** greaseproof paper
oleo'dotto *m* oil pipeline
ole'oso *adj* oily
ol'fatto *m* sense of smell
oli'are *vt* oil
olia'tore *m* oilcan
oli'era *f* cruet
olim'piadi *fpl* Olympic games, Olympics
o'limpico *adj* Olympic

key word

olimpi'onico *adj ‹primato, squadra›* Olympic; **costume** ~ Olympic swimming costume
+olino *suff* **bestiolina** *nf* (affettuoso) little creature; **macchiolina** *nf* spot; **pesciolino** *nm* little fish; **risolino** *nm* giggle; **sassolino** *nm* pebble; **strisciolina** *nf* thin strip; **magrolino** *adj* skinny
'olio *m* oil; **sott'**~ in oil; **colori a** ~ oils; **quadro a** ~ oil painting
■ **olio [di semi] di arachidi** groundnut oil; **olio essenziale** essential oil; **olio extravergine di oliva** extra-virgin olive oil; **olio di fegato di merluzzo** cod-liver oil; **olio di gomito** elbow grease; **olio lubrificante** lubricating oil; **olio di mais** corn oil; **olio minerale** mineral oil; **olio [del] motore** engine oil; **olio d'oliva** olive oil; **olio di semi** vegetable oil; **olio [di semi] di lino** linseed oil; **olio solare** suntan oil; **olio [di semi] di vinaccioli** grapeseed oil
o'liva *f* olive
oli'vastro *adj* olive
oli'veto *m* olive grove
oli'vetta *f* toggle
o'livo *m* olive tree
'olmo *m* elm
olo'causto *m* holocaust; **l'Olocausto** the Holocaust
o'lografo *adj* holograph
olo'gramma *m* hologram
oltraggi'are *vt* offend
ol'traggio *m* offence
■ **oltraggio al pudore** Jur gross indecency
oltraggi'oso *adj* offensive
ol'tranza *f* **ad** ~ to the bitter end
'oltre **A** *adv* (di luogo) further; (di tempo) longer
B *prep* (nello spazio) beyond; (di tempo) later than; (più di) more than; (in aggiunta) besides; ~ **a** (eccetto) except, apart from; **per** ~ **due settimane** for more than two weeks; **una settimana e** ~ a week and more
oltrecon'fine *adj* cross-border
oltre'mare *adv* overseas
oltre'modo *adv* extremely
oltrepas'sare *vt* go beyond; (eccedere) exceed; **oltrepassi il semaforo** go past the traffic lights; ~ **il limite di velocità** break the speed limit; **'non** ~**'** 'no trespassing'
OM *abbr* Radio (**onde medie**) MW
omacci'one *m* bruiser
o'maggi *mpl* (saluti) respects
o'maggio *m* homage; (dono) gift; **in** ~ **con** free with
'Oman *m* Oman
ombeli'cale *adj* umbilical; **cordone** ~ umbilical cord
ombe'lico *m* navel
'ombra *f* (zona) shade; (immagine oscura) shadow; **all'**~ in the shade
ombreggi'are *vt* shade

O

ombreggia'ture *fpl* shading
om'brello *m* umbrella
ombrel'lone *m* beach umbrella
om'bretto *m* eye-shadow
om'broso *adj* shady; ‹*cavallo*› skittish; ‹*persona*› touchy
ome'lette *f inv* omelette
ome'lia *f* Relig sermon
omeopa'tia *f* homeopathy
omeo'patico **A** *adj* homeopathic **B** *m* homeopath
omertà *f inv* conspiracy of silence
o'messo pp di **omettere**
o'mettere *vt* omit
'OMG *nm abbr* (**Organismo Modificato Geneticamente**) GMO
omi'cida **A** *adj* murderous, homicidal **B** *mf* murderer
omi'cidio *m* murder
■ **omicidio colposo** manslaughter; **omicidio di massa** mass murder; **omicidio volontario** Jur culpable homicide
omissi'one *f* omission
'omnibus *m inv* omnibus
omofo'bia *f* homophobia
omogeneiz'zare *vt* homogenize
omogeneiz'zato *adj* homogenized
omo'geneo *adj* homogeneous
o'mografo *m* homograph
omolo'gare *vt* approve; **fare ~ un testamento** prove a will
omologazi'one *f* probate
o'monimo, -a **A** *mf* namesake **B** *m* (parola) homonym **C** *adj* of the same name
omosessu'ale *adj & nmf* homosexual
omosessualità *f inv* homosexuality
'OMS *nf abbr* (**Organizzazione Mondiale della Sanità**) WHO
On. *abbr* (**onorevole**) MP, Hon.
'oncia *f* ounce
■ **oncia fluida** fluid ounce
'onda *f* wave; **andare in ~** TV, Radio go on the air; **seguire l'~** go with the crowd; **onde** *pl* **corte** short wave; **onde** *pl* **lunghe** long wave
■ **onda di maremoto** tidal wave; **onde** *pl* **medie** medium wave; **onde** *pl* **radio** radio waves; **onda d'urto** shock wave
on'data *f* wave; **a ondate** in waves
■ **ondata di freddo** cold snap
'onde *conj fml* so that
ondeggi'are *vi* wave; ‹*barca*› roll
ondu'lato *adj* wavy
ondula'torio *adj* undulating
ondulazi'one *f* undulation; (di capelli) wave
+one *suff* **cucchiaione** *nm* big spoon; **gattone** *nm* fat cat; **bacione** *nm* smacker; **bacioni** *pl* (in lettera) love and kisses; **omone** *nm* big guy; **nasone** *nm* big nose; **nebbione** *nm* dense fog, pea-souper infml; **simpaticone** *nm* very friendly person; **lumacone** *nm* slowcoach; **testone** *nm* mule; **facilone** *nm pej* overly casual sort of person; **grassone** *nm pej* fat slob; **pigrone** *nm* lazy-bones *sg*; **chiacchierone** *nm* chatterbox; **criticone** *nm* nit-picker; **pasticcione** *nm* bungler
'onere *m* burden
oner'oso *adj* onerous
onestà *f inv* honesty; (rettitudine) integrity, honesty
o'nesto *adj* honest; (giusto) just
'ONG *nf abbr* (**organizzazione non governativa**) non-governmental organization, NGO
'onice *f* onyx
o'nirico *adj* dream *attrib*
o'nisco *m* slater
ONLUS *nf abbr* (**organizzazione non lucrativa di utilità sociale**) non-profit organization
onnipo'tente *adj* omnipotent
onnipre'sente *adj* ubiquitous; Rel omnipresent
onnisci'ente *adj* omniscient
ono'mastico *m* name day
onomato'pea *f* onomatopoeia
onomato'peico *adj* onomatopoeic
ono'rabile *adj* honourable
ono'rare *vt* (fare onore a) be a credit to; honour ‹*promessa*›
ono'rario **A** *adj* honorary **B** *m* fee
ono'rarsi *vr* **~ di** be proud of
ono'rato *adj* ‹*famiglia, professione*› respectable; **considerarsi ~ da qualcosa** consider oneself honoured by something; **l'onorata società** *nf* the Mafia
o'nore *m* honour; **in ~ di** ‹*festa, ricevimento*› in honour of; **fare ~ a** do justice to ‹*pranzo*›; **farsi ~ in** excel in; **a onor del vero** to tell the truth; **fare gli onori di casa** do the honours
ono'revole **A** *adj* honourable **B** *mf* Member of Parliament
onorifi'cenza *f* honour; (decerazione) decoration
ono'rifico *adj* honorary
'onta *f* shame
on'tano *m* alder
'O.N.U. *nf abbr* (**Organizzazione delle Nazioni Unite**) UN
opacità *f inv* opaqueness, opacity
o'paco *adj* opaque; ‹*colori ecc.*› dull; ‹*fotografia, rossetto*› matt
o'pale *f* opal
'OPEC *f inv* OPEC
'opera *f* (lavaro) work; (azione) deed; Mus opera; (teatro) opera house; (ente) institution; **mettere in ~** put into effect; **mettersi all'~** get to work
■ **opera d'arte** work of art; **opera lirica** opera;

O

opere *pl* **pubbliche** public works
ope'rabile *adj* operable
ope'raio, -a **A** *adj* working
B *mf* worker
■ **operaio edile** building worker; **operaio specializzato** skilled worker
ope'rare **A** *vt* Med operate on; **~ qualcuno al cuore** operate on somebody's heart; **farsi ~** have an operation
B *vi* operate; (agire) work
opera'tivo, opera'torio *adj* operating *attrib*
opera|'tore, -trice *mf* operator; TV cameraman
■ **operatore ecologico** refuse collector; **operatore sanitario** health worker; **operatore turistico** tour operator
operazi'one *f* operation; Comm transaction
■ **operazione antidroga** anti-drug operation; **operazioni** *pl* **di soccorso** rescue operations; **operazione d'urgenza** emergency operation
ope'retta *f* operetta
ope'roso *adj* industrious
opini'one *f* opinion; **rimanere della propria ~** still feel the same way
■ **opinione pubblica** public opinion, vox pop
oplà *int* oops
o'possum *m inv* possum
'oppio *m* opium
oppo'nente **A** *adj* opposing
B *mf* opponent
op'porre *vt* oppose; (obiettare) object; **~ resistenza** offer resistance
op'porsi *vr* **~ a** oppose
opportu'nismo *m* expediency
opportu'nista *mf* opportunist
opportunità *f inv* opportunity; (l'essere opportuno) timeliness; **avere il senso dell'~** have a sense of what is appropriate
oppor'tuno *adj* opportune; (adeguato) appropriate; **ritenere ~ fare qualcosa** think it appropriate to do something; **il momento ~** the right moment
opposi'tore *m* opposer
opposizi'one *f* opposition; **d'~** ‹*giornale, partito*› opposition *attrib*; **in ~** in opposition
op'posto **A** pp di **opporre**
B *adj* opposite; ‹*opinioni*› opposing
C *m* opposite; **all'~** on the contrary
oppressi'one *f* oppression
oppres'sivo *adj* oppressive
op'presso **A** pp di **opprimere**
B *adj* oppressed
oppres'sore *m* oppressor
oppri'mente *adj* oppressive
op'primere *vt* oppress; (gravare) weigh down
op'pure *conj* otherwise, or [else]; **lunedì ~ martedì** Monday or Tuesday
ops *int* oops
op'tare *vi* **~ per** opt for
'optional *m inv* optional extra
opu'lento *adj* opulent
opu'lenza *f* opulence
o'puscolo *m* booklet; (pubblicitario) brochure
opzio'nale *adj* optional
opzi'one *f* option
'ora[1] *f* time; (unità) hour; **di buon'~** early; **che ~ è?, che ore sono?** what time is it?; **a che ~?** at what time?; **mezz'~** half an hour; **a ore** ‹*lavorare, pagare*› by the hour; **50 km all'~** 50 km an hour; **è ~ di finirla!** that's enough now!; **a un'~ di macchina** one hour by car; **non vedo l'~ di vederti** I can't wait to see you; **fare le ore piccole** stay up until the small hours
■ **~ d'arrivo** arrival time; **~ di cena** dinner time; **l'ora esatta** Teleph speaking clock; **ora legale** daylight saving time; **ora locale** local time; **ora di pranzo** dinner time; **ora di punta, ore di punta** *pl* peak time; (per il traffico) rush hour; **ora solare** Greenwich Mean Time, GMT; **ora zero** Mil fig zero hour
ora[2] **A** *adv* now; (tra poco) presently; **~ come ~** just now, at the moment; **d'~ in poi** from now on; **per ~** for the time being, for now
B *conj* (dunque) now [then]; **~ che ci penso, ...** now that I [come to] think about it...
o'racolo *m* oracle
'orafo *m* goldsmith
o'rale *adj & nm* oral; **per via ~** by mouth
ora'mai = **ormai**
o'rario **A** *adj* ‹*tariffa*› hourly; ‹*segnale*› time *attrib*; ‹*velocità*› per hour; **in senso ~** clockwise
B *m* time; (tabella dell'orario) timetable, schedule AmE; **essere in ~** be on time; **partire in ~** leave on time; **lavorare fuori ~** work outside normal hours
■ **orario di apertura** opening hours *pl*; **orario di chiusura** closing time; **orario estivo** summer timetable; **orario ferroviario** railway timetable, railroad schedule AmE; **orario flessibile** flexitime; **orario invernale** winter timetable; **orario di lavoro** working hours *pl*; **orario degli spettacoli** performance times *pl*; **orario di sportello** banking hours *pl*; **orario d'ufficio** business hours *pl*; **orario di visita** visiting hours *pl*, visiting time; (del medico) consulting hours *pl*; **orario di volo** flight time
o'rata *f* gilt-head
ora|'tore, -trice *mf* orator; (conferenziere) speaker
ora'torio, -a **A** *adj* oratorical
B *m* Mus oratorio
C *mf* oratory
orazi'one *f* Relig prayer
'orbita *f* orbit; Anat eye socket
'Orcadi *fpl* Orkneys
or'chestra *f* orchestra; (parte del teatro) pit

O

key word

■ **orchestra da camera** chamber orchestra; **orchestra sinfonica** symphony orchestra

orche'strale **A** *adj* orchestral
B *mf* member of an/the orchestra

orche'strare *vt* orchestrate

orchi'dea *f* orchid

'orco *m* ogre

'orda *f* horde

or'digno *m* device; (arnese) tool
■ **ordigno esplosivo** explosive device; **ordigno incendiario** incendiary device, firebomb

ordi'nale *adj & nm* ordinal

ordina'mento *m* order; (leggi) rules *pl*

ordi'nanza *f* (del sindaco) bylaw; **d'~** ‹*soldato*› on duty

ordi'nare *vt* (sistemare) arrange; (comandare) order; (prescrivere) prescribe; Relig ordain

ordi'nario **A** *adj* ordinary; ‹*grossolano*› common; (professore) with a permanent position; **di ordinaria amministrazione** routine
B *m* ordinary; Univ professor; **fuori dell'~** out of the ordinary

ordi'nato *adj* (in ordine) tidy

ordinazi'one *f* order; **fare un'~** place an order

'ordine *m* order; (di avvocati, medici) association; **mettere in ~** put in order; tidy up ‹*appartamento ecc.*›; **di prim'~** first-class; **di terz'~** ‹*film, albergo*› third-rate; **di ~ pratico/economico** ‹*problema*› of a practical/economic nature; **fino a nuovo ~** until further notice; **parola d'ordine** password
■ **ordine di acquisto** Comm purchase order; **ordine del giorno** agenda; **ordine di pagamento** banker's order; **ordine permanente** Fin standing order; **ordine pubblico** law and order; **ordini** *pl* **sacri** Holy Orders

or'dire *vt* (tramare) plot

orecchi'ette *fpl* small pasta shells

orec'chino *m* earring; **orecchini** *pl* **con le clip** clip-ons

o'recchio *m* (*pl nf* **orecchie**) ear; **avere ~** have a good ear; **esser duro d'~** be hard of hearing; **mi è giunto all'~ che...** I've heard that...; **parlare all'~ a qualcuno** whisper in somebody's ear; **suonare a ~** play by ear

orecchi'oni *mpl* Med mumps *sg*

o'refice *m* jeweller

orefice'ria *f* (arte) goldsmith's art; (negozio) goldsmith's [shop]

'orfano, -a **A** *adj* orphan
B *mf* orphan

orfano'trofio *m* orphanage

orga'netto *m* barrel organ; (a bocca) mouth organ; (fisarmonica) accordion

or'ganico **A** *adj* organic
B *m* personnel

orga'nino *m* hurdy-gurdy

orga'nismo *m* organism; (corpo umano) body

orga'nista *mf* organist

organiz'zare *vt* organize

organiz'zarsi *vr* get organized

organizza'tivo *adj* organizational

organizza|'tore, -trice *mf* organizer

organizzazi'one *f* organization
■ **organizzazione del servizio d'ordine** policing; **organizzazione studentesca** student union; **organizzazione umanitaria** relief agency, aid agency

'organo *m* organ

or'gasmo *m* orgasm; fig agitation

'orgia *f* orgy

or'goglio *m* pride

orgogli'oso *adj* proud

orien'tale *adj* eastern; (cinese ecc.) oriental

orienta'mento *m* orientation; **perdere l'~** lose one's bearings; **senso dell'~** sense of direction
■ **orientamento professionale** careers guidance; **orientamento scolastico** educational guidance

orien'tare *vt* orientate

orien'tarsi *vr* find one's bearings; (tendere) tend

ori'ente *m* east
■ **l'Estremo Oriente** the Far East; **il Medio Oriente** the Middle East

orien'teering *m inv* orienteering

o'rigano *m* oregano

origi'nale **A** *adj* original; (eccentrico) odd
B *m* original

originalità *f inv* originality

origi'nare *vt & vi* originate

origi'nario *adj* (nativo) native

o'rigine *f* origin; **in ~** originally; **aver ~ da** originate from; **dare ~ a** give rise to

origli'are *vi* eavesdrop

o'rina *f* urine

ori'nale *m* chamber pot

ori'nare *vi* urinate

ori'undo *adj* native

orizzon'tale *adj* horizontal

orizzon'tare = **orientare**

oriz'zonte *m* horizon

or'lare *vt* hem

orla'tura *f* hem

'orlo *m* edge; (di vestito ecc.) hem

'orma *f* track; (di piede) footprint; (impronta) mark

or'mai *adv* by now; (passato) by then; (quasi) almost

ormeggi'are *vt* moor

or'meggio *m* mooring

ormo'nale *adj* hormonal

or'mone *m* hormone

ornamen'tale *adj* ornamental

orna'mento *m* ornament; **d'~** ‹*oggetto*› ornamental

or'nare *vt* decorate

or'narsi *vr* deck oneself

or'nato *adj* ‹*stile*› ornate
ornitolo'gia *f* ornithology
orni'tologo, -a *mf* ornithologist
ornito'rinco *m* platypus
✓ **'oro** *m* gold; **d'~** gold; fig golden; **una persona d'~** a wonderful person
■ **oro nero** black gold
orologe'ria *f* watchmaking
orologi'aio, -a *mf* clockmaker, watchmaker
✓ **oro'logio** *m* (da polso, tasca) watch; (da tavolo, muro ecc.) clock
■ **orologio biologico** biological clock; **orologio a carica automatica** self-winding watch; **orologio a cucù** cuckoo clock; **orologio digitale** digital clock; **orologio a pendolo** grandfather clock; **orologio da polso** wristwatch; **orologio al quarzo** quartz watch; **orologio a sveglia** alarm clock
o'roscopo *m* horoscope
or'rendo *adj* awful, dreadful
or'ribile *adj* horrible
orribil'mente *adv* horribly
orripi'lante *adj* horrifying
✓ **or'rore** *m* horror; **avere qualcosa in ~** hate something; **~!** heck!; **film/romanzo dell'~** horror film/story
orsacchi'otto *m* teddy bear
or'setto *m*
■ **orsetto lavatore** raccoon
'orso *m* bear; (persona scontrosa) hermit
■ **orso bianco** polar bear; **orso bruno** brown bear
orsù *int* come now!
or'taggio *m* vegetable
or'tensia *f* hydrangea
or'tica *f* nettle; **buttare qualcosa alle ortiche** fig fam chuck in
orti'caria *f* nettle rash
orticol'tura *f* horticulture
✓ **'orto** *m* vegetable plot
orto'dontico *adj* orthodontic
ortodon'zia *f* orthodontics *sg*
ortodos'sia *f* conformity
orto'dosso *adj* orthodox
ortofrut'ticolo *adj* **mercato ~** fruit and vegetable market
ortofrutticol'tore *m* market gardener, truck farmer AmE
ortofrutticol'tura *f* market gardening
ortogo'nale *adj* perpendicular
ortogra'fia *f* spelling
orto'grafico *adj* spelling *attrib*
orto'lano *m* market gardener, truck farmer AmE; (negozio) greengrocer's
ortope'dia *f* orthopaedics *sg*
orto'pedico **A** *adj* orthopaedic
B *m* orthopaedic specialist
orzai'olo *m* sty
or'zata *f* barley water

✓ key word

'orzo *m* barley
■ **orzo perlato** pearl barley
osan'nato *adj* (esaltato) praised to the skies
✓ **o'sare** *vt & vi* dare; (avere audacia) be daring
oscenità *f inv* obscenity
o'sceno *adj* obscene
oscil'lare *vi* swing; ‹*prezzi ecc.*› fluctuate; Tech oscillate; fig (essere indeciso) vacillate
oscillazi'one *f* swinging; (di prezzi) fluctuation; Tech oscillation
oscura'mento *m* darkening; fig (di vista, mente) dimming; (totale) black-out
oscu'rare *vt* darken; fig obscure
oscu'rarsi *vr* get dark
oscurità *f inv* darkness; (incomprensibilità) obscurity; **uscire dall'~** fig emerge from obscurity; **morire nell'~** fig die in obscurity
✓ **o'scuro** *adj* dark; (triste) gloomy; (incomprensibile) obscure
o'smosi *f inv* osmosis
✓ **ospe'dale** *m* hospital
■ **ospedale universitario** teaching hospital
ospedali'ero *adj* hospital *attrib*
ospi'tale *adj* hospitable
ospitalità *f inv* hospitality; **non voglio abusare della tua ~** I don't want to outstay my welcome
ospi'tare *vt* give hospitality to
✓ **'ospite** **A** *m* (chi ospita) host; (chi viene ospitato) guest
B *f* hostess; guest
o'spizio *m* (per anziani) [old people's] home
ossa'tura *f* bone structure; (di romanzo) structure, framework
'osseo *adj* bone *attrib*
osse'quente *adj* deferential; **~ alla legge** law-abiding
ossequi'are *vt* pay one's respects to
os'sequio *m* homage; **ossequi** *pl* respects
ossequi'oso *adj* obsequious
osser'vabile *adj* observable
osser'vante *adj* ‹*cattolico*› practising
osser'vanza *f* observance
✓ **osser'vare** *vt* observe; (notare) notice; keep ‹*ordine, silenzio*›
osserva|'tore, -trice *mf* observer
osserva'torio *m* Astr observatory; Mil observation post
osservazi'one *f* observation; (rimprovero) reproach
ossessio'nante *adj* haunting; ‹*persona*› nagging
ossessio'nare *vt* obsess; (infastidire) nag
ossessi'one *f* obsession; (assillo) pain in the neck
osses'sivo *adj* obsessive; ‹*paura*› neurotic
os'sesso *adj* obsessed
✓ **os'sia** *conj* that is
ossi'dabile *adj* liable to tarnish

ossi'dante *adj* tarnishing
ossi'dare *vt* oxidize
ossi'darsi *vr* oxidize
'ossido *m* oxide
■ **ossido di carbonio** carbon monoxide; **ossido di zinco** zinc oxide
os'sidrico *adj* **fiamma ossidrica** blowlamp
ossige'nare *vt* oxygenate; (decolorare) bleach
ossige'narsi *vr* put back on its feet ‹*azienda*›; ~ **i capelli** dye one's hair blonde
os'sigeno *m* oxygen
'osso *m* Anat (*pl nf* **ossa**) bone; (di frutto) stone; **senz'~** boneless
■ **osso mascellare** jawbone
osso'buco *m* marrowbone
os'suto *adj* bony
ostaco'lare *vt* hinder, obstruct
ostaco'lista *mf* hurdler
o'stacolo *m* obstacle; Sport hurdle
o'staggio *m* hostage; **prendere in ~** take hostage
o'stello *m*
■ **ostello della gioventù** youth hostel
osten'tare *vt* show off; ~ **indifferenza** pretend to be indifferent
ostentata'mente *adv* ostentatiously
ostentazi'one *f* ostentation
osteopo'rosi *f inv* osteoporosis
oste'ria *f* inn
oste'tricia *f* obstetrics *sg*
o'stetrico, -a **A** *adj* obstetric **B** *mf* obstetrician
'ostia *f* host; (cialda) wafer
'ostico *adj* tough
o'stile *adj* hostile
ostilità *f inv* hostility
osti'narsi *vr* ~ persist (**a** in)
osti'nato *adj* obstinate
ostinazi'one *f* obstinacy
ostra'cismo *m* ostracism
'ostrica *f* oyster
ostro'goto *m* **parlare ~** talk double Dutch
ostru'ire *vt* obstruct
ostruzi'one *f* obstruction
ostruzio'nismo *m* obstructionism; Sport obstruction
■ **ostruzionismo sindacale** work-to-rule
oto'rino *m* ear, nose and throat *attrib*
otorinolaringoi'atra *mf* ear, nose and throat specialist
'otre *m* leather bottle
ottago'nale *adj* octagonal
ot'tagono *m* octagon
ot'tanta *adj & nm* eighty
ottan'tenne *adj & nmf* eighty year-old
ottan'ttesimo *adj & nm* eightieth
ottan'tina *f* about eighty
ot'tava *f* octave
ot'tavo *adj & nm* eighth
otte'nere *vt* obtain; (più comune) get; (conseguire) achieve
ot'tetto *m* Mus octet
'ottico, -a **A** *adj* optic[al] **B** *mf* optician **C** *f* (scienza) optics *sg*; (di lenti ecc.) optics *pl*
otti'male *adj* optimum
ottima'mente *adv* very well
otti'mismo *m* optimism
otti'mista *mf* optimist
otti'mistico *adj* optimistic
ottimiz'zare *vt* optimize
'ottimo **A** *adj* very good **B** *m* optimum; **essere all'~ della forma** be on top form
+otto *suff* **bassotto** *adj* (piuttosto basso) quite short; **contadinotto** *nm* derog (sempliciotto) country bumpkin; **paesotto** *nm* hamlet; **leprotto** *nm* leveret; (affettuoso) baby hare; **pienotto** *adj* ‹*viso*› chubby
'otto *adj & nm* eight
ot'tobre *m* October
otto'cento *adj & nm* eight hundred; **l'Ottocento** the nineteenth century
ot'tone *m* brass; **gli ottoni** Mus the brass
ottuage'nario, -a *adj & nmf* octogenarian
ot'tundere *vt* blunt
ottu'rare *vt* block; fill ‹*dente*›
ottu'rarsi *vr* clog
ottura'tore *m* Phot shutter
otturazi'one *f* stopping; (di dente) filling
ot'tuso **A** pp di **ottundere** **B** *adj* obtuse
ouver'ture *f inv* overture
o'vaia *f* ovary
o'vale *adj & nm* oval
o'vatta *f* cotton wool, absorbent cotton AmE
ovat'tato *adj* ‹*suono, passi*› muffled
ovazi'one *f* ovation
'ove *adv* (liter) where
over'dose *f inv* overdose
'overdrive *m inv* Auto overdrive
'ovest *m* west
o'vile *m* sheep-fold, pen
o'vino *adj* sheep *attrib*
ovoi'dale *adj* egg-shaped
ovo'via *f two-seater cable car*
ovulazi'one *f* ovulation
o'vunque = **dovunque**
ov'vero *conj* or; (cioè) that is
ovvia'mente *adv* obviously
ovvi'are *vi* ~ **a qualcosa** counter something
'ovvio *adj* obvious
ozi'are *vi* laze around
'ozio *m* idleness; **stare in ~** idle about
ozi'oso *adj* idle; ‹*questione*› pointless
o'zono *m* ozone; **buco nell'~** hole in the ozone layer

O

Pp

pa'care *vt* calm
paca'tezza *f* calm[ness]
pa'cato *adj* calm
'pacca *f* slap
pac'chetto *m* packet; (postale) parcel, package; (di sigarette) pack, packet
■ **pacchetto informativo** information pack; **pacchetto integrato** Comput integrated package; **pacchetto software** software package
'pacchia *f* infml (situazione) bed of roses
pacchia'nata *f* **è una ~** it's so garish
pacchi'ano *adj* garish
✓ **'pacco** *m* parcel; (involto) bundle; **disfare un ~** unwrap a parcel; **fare un ~** make up a parcel; **pacchi postali** *pl* parcels, packages
■ **pacco bomba** parcel bomb; **pacco regalo** gift-wrapped package; **le faccio un ~ regalo?** would you like it gift-wrapped?; **pacco umanitario** aid package
paccot'tiglia *f* (roba scadente) junk, rubbish
✓ **'pace** *f* peace; **darsi ~** forget it; **fare ~ con qualcuno** make it up with somebody; **lasciare in ~ qualcuno** leave somebody in peace; **mettere ~ fra** pacify, make [the] peace between; **andate in ~** Relig peace be with you; **in tempo di ~** in peacetime; **del tempo di ~** peacetime *attrib*; **di ~** ‹*milizia*› peacekeeping; **firmare la ~** sign a peace treaty; **per amor di ~** for a quiet life
pace-'maker *m* (apparecchio) pacemaker
pachi'derma *m* (animale) pachyderm; fig thick-skinned person
pachi'stano, -a *nmf & adj* Pakistani
paci'ere *m* peacemaker
pacifi'care *vt* reconcile; (mettere pace) pacify
pacificazi'one *f* reconciliation
pa'cifico **A** *adj* pacific; (calmo) peaceful; **è ~ che...** (comunemente accettato) it is clear that...
B *m* **il Pacifico** the Pacific
paci'fismo *m* pacifism
paci'fista *adj & nmf* pacifist
pacioc'cone, -a *mf* infml chubby chops
paci'ugo *m* (poltiglia) mush
pa'dano *adj* **pianura padana** Po Valley
pa'della *f* frying pan; (per malati) bedpan; **cuocere in ~** fry; **della ~ alla brace** out of the frying pan into the fire
padel'lata *f* **una ~ di** a frying-panful of

✓ key word

padigli'one *m* pavilion
■ **padiglione auricolare** auricle
'Padova *f* Padua
✓ **'padre** *m* father; **padri** *pl* (antenati) forefathers; **i padri della chiesa** the Church Fathers; **di ~ in figlio** from father to son
■ **padre adottivo** (marito della madre) stepfather; **padre di famiglia** father, paterfamilias; **sono ~ di famiglia** I have a family to look after; **padre spirituale** spiritual father
padre'nostro *m* **il ~** the Lord's Prayer
padre'terno *m* God Almighty
pa'drino *m* godfather; **~ e madrina** godparents
padro'nale *adj* principal
padro'nanza *f* mastery
■ **padronanza di sé** self-control
✓ **pa'drone, -a** *mf* master; mistress; (datore di lavoro) boss; (proprietario) owner
■ **padrone di casa** (di inquilini) landlord; landlady; (in ricevimento) master of the house; lady of the house
padroneggi'are *vt* master
padro'nesco *adj* domineering
padro'nissimo *adj* **essere ~ di fare qualcosa** be quite at liberty to do something
pae'saggio *m* scenery; (pittura) landscape
■ **paesaggio marino** seascape; **paesaggio montano** mountain landscape
paesag'gista *mf* landscape architect
paesag'gistico *adj* landscape *attrib*
pae'sano, -a **A** *adj* country *attrib*
B *mf* villager
✓ **pa'ese** *m* (nazione) country; (territorio) land; (villaggio) village; **il Bel Paese** Italy; **va' a quel ~!** get lost!; **il mio ~ natio** where I was born; **Paesi Bassi** *pl* Netherlands; **paesi dell'est** *pl* Eastern Bloc countries
paf'futo *adj* plump
pag. *abbr* (**pagina**) p.
'paga *f* pay, wages *pl*
pa'gabile *adj* payable
pa'gaia *f* paddle
paga'mento *m* payment; **a ~** (parcheggio) which you have to pay to use.
■ **pagamento anticipato** Comm advance payment; **pagamento alla consegna** cash on delivery, COD; **pagamento pedaggio** toll
paga'nesimo *m* paganism
pa'gano, -a *adj & nmf* pagan

pa'gante *mf* payer

pa'gare *vt & vi* pay; **~ da bere a qualcuno** buy somebody a drink; **pagato in anticipo** prepaid, paid in advance; **te la faccio ~** you'll pay for this; **quanto pagherei per poter venire!** what I wouldn't give to be able to come!

pa'gella *f* [school] report

pagg. *abbr* (**pagine**) pp

pag'gio *m* pageboy

'pagina *f* page; **prima ~** Journ front page; **~ economica** financial news, financial pages; **pagine gialle** *pl* Yellow Pages
■ **pagina mastra** master page; **pagina web** Comput web page

pagi'none *m* centrefold

'paglia *f* straw
■ **paglia e fieno** Culin *mixture of ordinary and green tagliatelle*

pagliac'cesco *adj* farcical

pagliac'cetto *m* (per bambini) rompers *pl*; (da donna) camiknickers

pagliac'ciata *f* farce

pagli'accio *m* clown; **fare il ~** act *or* play the clown

pagli'aio *m* haystack

paglie'riccio *m* straw mattress

pagli'etta *f* (cappello) boater; (per pentole) steel wool

pagli'uzza *f* wisp of straw; (di metallo) particle

pa'gnotta *f* [round] loaf

'pago *adj* satisfied

pa'goda *f* pagoda

pa'guro *m* hermit crab

pail'lard *f inv* slice of grilled veal

pail'lette *f inv* sequin

'paio *m* (*pl nf* **paia**) pair; **un ~** (circa due) a couple; **un ~ di** ‹*scarpe, forbici*› a pair of; **è un altro ~ di maniche** fig that's a different kettle of fish

pai'olo *m* copper pot

'Pakistan *m* Pakistan

paki'stano, -a *adj & nmf* Pakistani

'pala *f* shovel; (di remo, elica) blade; (di ruota) paddle; (di mulino) blade, vane
■ **pala d'altare** altar piece; **pala da fornaio** shovel; **pala meccanica** mechanical digger

pala'dino *m* paladin; fig champion

pala'fitta *f* pile dwelling

palan'drana *f* (abito largo) big long coat

pala'sport *m inv* indoor sports arena

pa'late *fpl* **a ~** ‹*fare soldi*› hand over fist

pa'lato *m* palate

palaz'zetto *m*
■ **palazzetto dello sport** indoor sports arena

palaz'zina *f* villa

pa'lazzo *m* palace; (edificio) building
■ **~ comunale** town hall; **Palazzo Ducale** Doge's Palace; **palazzo delle esposizioni** exhibition centre; **palazzo di giustizia** law courts *pl*, courthouse; **palazzo dello sport** indoor sports arena

'palco *m* (pedana) platform; Theat box; (palcoscenico) stage

palco'scenico *m* stage

paleogra'fia *f* palaeography

paleo'grafico *adj* palaeographical

pale'ografo, -a *mf* palaeographer

paleo'litico *adj* Palaeolithic

pale'sare *vt* disclose

pale'sarsi *vr* reveal oneself

pa'lese *adj* evident

Pale'stina *f* Palestine

palesti'nese *adj & nmf* Palestinian

pa'lestra *f* gymnasium, gym; (ginnastica) gymnastics *pl*

pa'letta *f* spade; (per focolare) shovel
■ **paletta [della spazzatura]** dustpan

palet'tata *f* shovelful

pa'letto *m* peg

palin'sesto *m* (documento) palimpsest; TV programme schedule

'palio *m* (premio) prize; **il Palio** *horse race held at Siena and other towns*

palis'sandro *m* rosewood

paliz'zata *f* fence

'palla *f* ball; (proiettile) bullet; infml (bugia) porky pie; **prendere la ~ al balzo** seize an opportunity; **essere una ~** sl be a drag; **che palle!** vulg this is a pain in the arse!, what a drag!
■ **palla da biliardo** billiard ball; **palla medica** medicine ball; **palla di neve** snowball; **palla al piede** fig millstone round one's neck

pallaca'nestro *f* basketball

palla-'goal *f* **hanno avuto molte palle-goal** they had a lot of goal-scoring opportunities

palla'mano *f* handball

pallanuo'tista *mf* water polo player

pallanu'oto *f* water polo

pallavo'lista *mf* volleyball player

palla'volo *f* volleyball

palleggi'are *vi* (calcio) practise ball control; Tennis knock up

pal'leggio *m* Sport warm-up

'pallet *m inv* pallet

pallet'toni *mpl* buckshot

pallia'tivo *m* palliative

'pallido *adj* pale; **non ne ho la più pallida idea** I don't have the faintest *or* foggiest idea

pal'lina *f* (di vetro) marble

pal'lino *m* **avere il ~ del calcio** be crazy about football, be football crazy

pallon'cino *m* balloon; (lanterna) Chinese lantern; infml (etilometro) Breathalyzer®

pal'lone *m* ball; (calcio) football; (aerostato) balloon; **essere/andare nel ~** be/become confused

P

■ **pallone da calcio** football; **pallone gonfiato: è un ~ gonfiato** he's so puffed-up; **pallone sonda** weather balloon
pallo'netto *m* lob
pal'lore *m* pallor
pal'loso *adj* sl boring
pal'lottola *f* pellet; (proiettile) bullet
■ **pallottola dum-dum** dumdum bullet
pallottoli'ere *m* abacus
'palma *f* Bot palm
■ **palma da cocco** coconut palm; **palma da datteri** date palm
palmarès *m inv* (di festival) award winners *pl*; fig (i migliori) top names *pl*
pal'mato *adj* ‹*piede*› webbed
pal'mento *m* **mangiava a quattro palmenti** he was really tucking in
pal'meto *m* palm grove
palmi'pede *m* web-footed animal
'palmo *m* Anat palm; (misura) hand's breadth; **restare con un ~ di naso** feel disappointed
'palo *m* pole; (di sostegno) stake; (in calcio) goalpost; **fare il ~** ‹*ladro*› keep a lookout
■ **palo d'arrivo** (in ippica) finishing post; **palo della luce** lamp post; **palo di partenza** (in ippica) starting post
palom'baro *m* diver
pa'lombo *m* dogfish
pal'pare *vt* feel
pal'pata *f* **dare una ~ a qualcosa** give something a feel
'palpebra *f* eyelid
palpeggi'are *vt* feel
palpi'tare *vi* throb; (fremere) quiver
palpitazi'one *f* palpitation; **avere le palpitazioni** have palpitations
'palpito *m* throb; (del cuore) beat
paltò *m inv* overcoat
pa'lude *f* marsh, swamp
palu'doso *adj* marshy
pa'lustre *adj* marshy; ‹*piante, uccelli*› marsh *attrib*
'pampas *fpl* pampas
pam'phlet *m inv* pamphlet
pamphlet'tista *mf* pamphleteer
'pampino *m* vine leaf
pan *m* ▸ **pane**
pana'cea *f* panacea
pa'nache *m inv* **far ~** (in ippica) fall
'Panama *m* Panama; **il canale di ~** the Panama Canal
'panca *f* bench; (in chiesa) pew
pancarré *m* sliced bread
pan'cetta *f* Culin bacon; (addome) paunch
■ **pancetta affumicata** smoked bacon
pan'chetto *m* [foot]stool
pan'china *f* garden seat; (in calcio) bench
⚷ **'pancia** *f* belly, tummy infml; (di bottiglia, vaso) body; **di ~** infml gut-level; **mal di ~** stomach ache; **a ~ piena/vuota** on a full/empty stomach; **metter su ~** develop a paunch; **a ~ in giù** lying face down
panci'ata *f* **prendere una ~** (in tuffo) do a belly flop
panci'era *f* corset
panci'olle *adv* **stare in ~** lounge about
panci'one *m* (persona) pot belly
panci'otto *m* waistcoat
panci'uto *adj* pot-bellied
'pancreas *m inv* pancreas
pancre'atico *adj* pancreatic
'panda *m inv* panda
pande'monio *m* pandemonium
pan'dolce *m Christmas cake similar to panettone*
pan'doro *m kind of sponge cake traditionally eaten at Christmas time*
⚷ **'pane** *m* bread; (pagnotta) loaf; (di burro) block
■ **pane casereccio** home-made bread; **pane a cassetta** sliced bread; **pan grattato** breadcrumbs *pl*; **pane integrale** wholemeal bread, granary bread; **pane nero** black bread; **pane di segale** rye bread; **pan di Spagna** sponge cake; **pane tostato** toast
'panel *m inv* (gruppo) panel
panette'ria *f* bakery; (negozio) baker's [shop]
panetti'ere, -a *mf* baker
panet'tone *m dome-shaped cake with sultanas and candied fruit eaten at Christmas*
'panfilo *m* yacht
pan'forte *m nougat-like spicy delicacy from Siena*
'panico *m* panic; **farsi prendere dal ~** panic
pani'ere *m* basket; (cesta) hamper
pani'ficio *m* bakery; (negozio) baker's [shop]
pani'naro, -a *mf* preppie
pa'nino *m* [bread] roll
■ **panino imbottito** filled roll; **panino al prosciutto** ham roll
panino'teca *f* sandwich bar
'panna *f* cream
■ **panna cotta** *kind of creme caramel*; **panna da cucina** [single] cream; **panna montata** whipped cream
'panne *f inv* Mech; **in ~** broken down; **restare in ~** break down
panneggi'ato *adj* draped
pan'neggio *m* drapery
pan'nello *m* panel
■ **pannello di controllo** control panel; **pannello fotovoltaico** solar panel, solar module; **pannello solare** solar panel
'panno *m* cloth; (di tavolo da gioco) baize; **panni** *pl* (abiti) clothes; **mettersi nei panni di qualcuno** fig put oneself in somebody's shoes

⚷ key word

pan'nocchia *f* (di granturco) cob
panno'lenci® *m inv* brightly coloured felt
panno'lino *m* (per bambini) nappy; (da donna) sanitary towel
pano'rama *m* panorama; fig overview
pano'ramica *f* (rassegna) overview
pano'ramico *adj* panoramic
panpe'pato *m type of gingerbread*
pantacol'lant *mpl* leggings
pantagru'elico *adj* ‹*pranzo*› gargantuan
pantalon'cini *mpl* shorts
■ **pantaloncini da ciclista** cycling shorts; **pantaloncini corti** shorts
panta'loni *mpl* trousers, pants AmE
■ **pantaloni da sci** ski pants; **pantaloni della tuta** sweat pants; **pantaloni a tubo** drainpipe trousers; **pantaloni a zampa d'elefante** bell-bottoms, flares
pan'tano *m* bog
panta'noso *adj* marshy
pan'tera *f* panther; (auto della polizia) high-speed police car
■ **pantera nera** black panther
pan'tofola *f* slipper
pantofo'laio, -a *mf* fig stay-at-home
panto'mima *f* pantomime; fig act
pan'zana *f* fib
'panzer *m inv* Mil tank
pao'nazzo *adj* purple
'papa *m* Pope; **a ogni morte di ~** fig once in a blue moon
papà *m inv* dad, daddy
pa'paia *f* pawpaw, papaya
pa'pale *adj* papal
papa'lina *f* skull-cap
papa'razzo *m* paparazzo
pa'pato *m* papacy
pa'pavero *m* poppy
'papera *f* (errore) slip of the tongue
'papero *m* gosling
'papi *m* infml daddy
pa'pilla *f*
■ **papilla gustativa** taste bud
papil'lon *m inv* bow tie
pa'piro *m* papyrus
'pappa *f* (per bambini) baby food; **trovare la ~ pronta** fig have everything ready and waiting
pappagal'lino *m* budgerigar, budgie
pappa'gallo *m* parrot
pappa'gorgia *f* double chin
pappa'molle *mf* wimp
pappar'delle *fpl strips of pasta with a meat sauce*
pap'parsi *vr* infml tuck away
pap'pone *m* sl (mangione) pig; (sfruttatore) pimp
'paprica *f* paprika
Pap test *m inv* smear test, cervical smear
'Papua Nu'ova Gui'nea *f* Papua New Guinea
'para *f* **suole di ~** crepe soles
parà *m inv* para
pa'rabola *f* parable; (curva) parabola
para'bolico *adj* parabolic
para'brezza *m inv* windscreen, windshield AmE
paracadu'tare *vt* parachute
paracadu'tarsi *vr* parachute
paraca'dute *m inv* parachute
paracadu'tismo *m* parachuting
■ **paracadutismo ascensionale** parascending
paracadu'tista *mf* parachutist
para'carro *m* roadside post
para'digma *m* Gram paradigm
paradi'siaco *adj* heavenly
para'diso *m* paradise
■ **paradiso fiscale** tax haven; **paradiso terrestre** Eden, earthly paradise
parados'sale *adj* paradoxical
para'dosso *m* paradox
para'fango *m* mudguard
parafarma'cia *f* over-the-counter products
paraf'fina *f* paraffin
parafra'sare *vt* paraphrase
pa'rafrasi *f inv* paraphrase
para'fulmine *m* lightning conductor
parafu'oco *m inv* fireguard
pa'raggi *mpl* neighbourhood *sg*
parago'nabile *adj* comparable (**a** to)
parago'nare *vt* compare
parago'narsi *vr* compare oneself
para'gone *m* comparison; **a ~ di** in comparison with; **non c'è ~!** there's no comparison!
paragra'fare *vt* paragraph
pa'ragrafo *m* paragraph
paraguai'ano, -a *adj & nmf* Paraguayan
Paragu'ay *m* Paraguay
pa'ralisi *f inv* paralysis
para'litico, -a *adj & nmf* paralytic
paraliz'zante *adj* crippling
paraliz'zare *vt* paralyse
paraliz'zato *adj* (dalla paura) transfixed
paral'lela *f* parallel line; **è una ~ di...** ‹*strada*› it runs parallel to...; **parallele** *pl* parallel bars
parallela'mente *adv* in parallel
paralle'lismo *m* parallelism
paral'lelo *adj & nm* parallel; **fare un ~ tra** draw a parallel between
parallelo'gramma *m* parallelogram
para'lume *m* lampshade
para'medico *m* paramedic
para'mento *m* hangings *pl*
pa'rametro *m* parameter

paramili'tare *adj* paramilitary
pa'ranco *m* block and tackle
para'noia *f* paranoia
para'noico, -a *adj & nmf* paranoid
paranor'male *adj & nm* paranormal
para'occhi *mpl* blinkers
parao'recchie *m* earmuffs
parapen'dio *m* paragliding
para'petto *m* parapet
para'piglia *m* turmoil
para'plegico, -a *adj & nmf* paraplegic
pa'rare **A** *vt* (addobbare) adorn; (riparare) shield; save ‹*tiro, pallone*›; ward off, parry ‹*schiaffo, pugno*›
B *vi* (mirare) lead up to
pa'rarsi *vr* (abbigliarsi) dress up; (da pioggia, pugni) protect oneself; ~ **dinanzi a qualcuno** appear in front of somebody
parasco'lastico *adj* ‹*attività*› extracurricular
para'sole *m inv* parasol
paras'sita **A** *adj* parasitic
B *m* parasite
parassi'tario *adj* anche fig parasitic
parassi'tismo *m* parasitism
parasta'tale *adj* government-controlled
para'stinchi *m inv* shin pad, shin guard
pa'rata *f* parade; (in calcio) save; (in scherma, pugilato) parry
■ **parata aerea** fly-past
para'tia *f* bulkhead
parauniversi'tario *adj* at university level
para'urti *m inv* Auto bumper, fender AmE
■ **paraurti** *pl* **tubolari rigidi** bull bars
para'vento *m* screen
par'boiled *adj* **riso** ~ parboiled rice
par'cella *f* bill
parcheggi'are *vt* anche fig park; ~ **in doppia fila** double-park
parcheggia|'tore, -trice *mf* parking attendant
■ **parcheggiatore abusivo** *person who illegally earns money by looking after parked cars*
par'cheggio *m* parking; (posteggio) car park, parking lot AmE
■ **parcheggio carta** Comput paper park; **parcheggio custodito** car park with attendant; **parcheggio incustodito** unattended car park; **parcheggio a pagamento** paying car park; **parcheggio sotterraneo** underground car park, underground parking garage AmE
par'chimetro *m* parking meter
'parco¹ *adj* sparing; (moderato) moderate; **essere** ~ **nel mangiare** eat sparingly
⚷ **'parco²** *m* park
■ **parco di divertimenti** fun fair; **parco fotovoltaico** solar farm; **parco giochi** playground; **parco macchine** Auto fleet of cars; **parco naturale** wildlife park; **parco nazionale** national park; **parco regionale** [regional] wildlife park
par'cometro *m* (pay-and-display) ticket machine
⚷ **pa'recchio** **A** *adj* quite a lot of; **parecchi** *pl* several, quite a lot of
B *pron* quite a lot; **parecchi** *pl* several, quite a lot
C *adv* rather; (parecchio tempo) quite a time
pareggi'are **A** *vt* level; (eguagliare) equal; Comm balance; ~ **il bilancio** balance the scales
B *vi* draw; **hanno pareggiato nel secondo tempo** they equalized in the second half
pa'reggio *m* Comm balance; Sport draw; **il gol del** ~ the equalizer
paren'tado *m* relatives *pl*; (vincolo di sangue) relationship
⚷ **pa'rente** *mf* relative, relation
■ **parente acquisito** relation by marriage; **parente alla lontana** distant relation; **parente stretto** close relation
paren'tela *f* relatives *pl*; (vincolo di sangue) relationship; **grado di** ~ degree of kinship
pa'rentesi *f inv* parenthesis; (segno grafico) bracket; fig (pausa) break; **aprire una** ~ fig digress; ~ *pl* **graffe** curly brackets; ~ *pl* **quadre** square brackets; **tra** ~ **quadre** in square brackets; ~ *pl* **tonde** round brackets; **fra** ~,... (a proposito) by the way,...
pa'reo *m* (copricostume) sarong; **a** ~ ‹*gonna*› wrap-around
pa'rere¹ *m* opinion; **a mio** ~ in my opinion; **essere del** ~ **che** be of the opinion that
⚷ **pa'rere²** *vi* seem; (pensare) think; **che te ne pare?** what do you think of it?; **pare di sì** it seems so; **mi pare che...** I think that...; **non mi par vero** I can't believe it; **mi pareva bene!** I thought as much!
⚷ **pa'rete** *f* wall; (in alpinismo) face
■ **parete divisoria** partition wall
'pargolo *f* (liter) child
⚷ **'pari** **A** *adj inv* equal; ‹*numero*› even; **andare di** ~ **passo** keep pace; **essere** ~ be even *or* quits; **arrivare** ~ draw; ~ ~ ‹*copiare, ripetere*› word for word; **fare** ~ **o dispari** toss a coin
B *mf inv* equal, peer; **ragazza alla** ~ au pair [girl]; **lavorare alla** ~ work [as an] au pair; **mettersi in** ~ **con qualcosa** catch up with something
C *m* (titolo nobiliare) peer
'paria *m inv* pariah
parifi'cato *adj* ‹*scuola*› state-recognized
Pa'rigi *f* Paris
pari'gino, -a *adj & nmf* Parisian
pa'riglia *f* pair; **rendere la** ~ **a qualcuno** give somebody tit for tat
parità *f inv* equality; Tennis deuce; **a** ~ **di condizioni/voti** if all circumstances/the

⚷ key word

votes are equal; **finire in** ~ ‹*partita*› end in a draw

■ **parità dei diritti** equal rights; **parità monetaria** monetary parity; **parità dei sessi** sexual equality, equality of the sexes

pari'tario *adj* parity *attrib*

'parka *m inv* parka

parlamen'tare **A** *adj* parliamentary **B** *mf* Member of Parliament **C** *vi* negotiate

parla'mento *m* Parliament; **il Parlamento europeo** the European Parliament

par'lante *adj* ‹*bambola, pappagallo*› talking

parlan'tina *f* **avere la** ~ be a chatterbox

par'lare *vt & vi* speak, talk; speak ‹*inglese, italiano*›; (confessare) talk; ~ **bene/male di qualcuno** speak well/ill of somebody; ~ **da solo** speak to oneself; **chi parla?** Teleph who's speaking?; **senti chi parla!** look who's talking!; **non parliamone più** let's forget about it; **non se ne parla memmeno!** don't even mention it!; ~ **a braccio** speak off the top of one's head; **far** ~ **qualcuno** make somebody talk

par'lato *adj* ‹*lingua*› spoken

parla|'tore, -trice *mf* speaker

parla'torio *m* parlour; (in prigione) visiting room

parlot'tare *vi* mutter

parlot'tio *m* muttering

parlucchi'are *vt* speak a little, have a smattering of ‹*lingua*›

parmigi'ano *m* Parmesan

paro'dia *f* parody, send-up; **fare la** ~ **di qualcuno** take somebody off

parodi'are *vt* parody, mimic

paro'distico *adj* ‹*tono*› parodying; **programma** ~ take-off show

pa'rola *f* word; (facoltà) speech; **è una** ~**!** it is easier said than done!; **parole** *pl* (di canzone) words, lyrics; **rivolgere la** ~ **a** address; **passare** ~ spread the word; **non fare** ~ **di qualcosa con nessuno** not breathe a word of something to anybody; **ti credo sulla** ~ I'll take your word for it; **togliere la** ~ **di bocca a qualcuno** take the words [right] out of somebody's mouth; **voler sempre l'ultima** ~ always want to have the last word; **dire due parole a qualcuno** have a word *or* chat with somebody; **di poche parole** ‹*persona*› of few words; **dare a qualcuno la propria** ~ give somebody one's word; ~ **per** ~ word for word; **in parole povere** crudely speaking

■ **parola chiave** *inv* keyword; **parole** *pl* **incrociate** crossword [puzzle]; **parola di moda** buzzword; **parola d'onore** word of honour; **parola d'ordine** password

paro'laccia *f* swear word

paro'liere *m* lyricist

paro'lina *f* **dire due paroline a qualcuno** have a word *or* chat with somebody

paro'loni *mpl* mumbo jumbo

paros'sismo *m* paroxysm

paros'sistico *adj* Med paroxysmal

par'quet *m inv* (pavimento) parquet flooring

parri'cida *mf* parricide

parri'cidio *m* parricide

par'rocchia *f* parish

parrocchi'ale *adj* parish (*attrib*)

parrocchi'ano, -a *mf* parishioner

'parroco *m* parish priest

par'rucca *f* wig

parrucchi'ere, -a *mf* hairdresser

parruc'chino *m* toupée, hairpiece

parsi'monia *f* thrift

parsimoni'oso *adj* thrifty

'parso pp di **parere²**

'parte *f* part; (lato) side; (partito) party; (porzione) share; (fazione) group; **a** ~ apart from; **in** ~ in part; **la maggior** ~ **di** the majority of; **d'altra** ~ on the other hand; **da** ~ aside; (in disparte) to one side; **farsi da** ~ stand aside; **da** ~ **di** from; (per conto di) on behalf of; **è gentile da** ~ **tua** it is kind of you; **fare una brutta** ~ **a qualcuno** behave badly towards somebody; **da che** ~ **è...?** whereabouts is...?; **da una parte..., dall'altra...** on the one hand..., on the other hand...; **dall'altra** ~ **di** on the other side of; **da nessuna** ~ nowhere; **da qualche** ~ somewhere; **da qualche altra** ~ somewhere else, elsewhere; **da tutte le parti** (essere) everywhere; **da questa** ~ (in questa direzione) this way; **da queste parti** hereabouts; **da un anno a questa** ~ for about a year now; **mettere qualcosa da** ~ put something aside; **essere dalla** ~ **di qualcuno** be on somebody's side; **prendere le parti di qualcuno** take somebody's side; **dalla** ~ **della ragione/del torto** in the right/the wrong; **essere** ~ **in causa** be involved; **fare** ~ **di** (appartenere a) be a member of; **fare la propria** ~ do one's share *or* bit; **mettere qualcuno a** ~ **di qualcosa** inform somebody of something; **prendere** ~ **a qualcosa** take part in something

■ **parte civile** plaintiff; **parte del discorso** part of speech

parteci'pante *mf* participant

parteci'pare *vi* ~ **a** participate in, take part in; (condividere) share in

partecipazi'one *f* participation; (annuncio) announcement; Fin shareholding; (presenza) presence; **con la** ~ **[straordinaria] di...** featuring...

■ **partecipazione statale** (quota) state interest

par'tecipe *adj* participating

parteggi'are *vi* ~ **per** side with

par'tenza *f* departure; Sport start; **in** ~ **per** leaving for; **falsa** ~ false start

parti'cella *f* particle

parti'cina *f* bit part

parti'cipio *m* participle

■ **participio passato** past participle; **participio**

P

presente present participle

🔑 **partico'lare** **A** *adj* particular; (privato) private; (speciale) special, particular
B *m* detail, particular; **fin nei minimi particolari** down to the smallest detail; **in ~** (particolarmente) in particular

particolareggi'ato *adj* detailed

particolarità *f inv* particularity; (dettaglio) detail

particolar'mente *adv* particularly

🔑 **partigi'ano, -a** *adj & nmf* partisan

🔑 **par'tire** *vi* leave; (aver inizio) start; infml (rompersi) break; **a ~ da** [beginning] from; **~ molto bene** get off to a flying start; **~ in quarta** go off at half cock; **è partito** infml (ubriaco) he's away

🔑 **par'tita** *f* game; (incontro) match; Comm lot; (contabilità) entry; **dare ~ vinta a qualcuno** fig give in to somebody
■ **partita amichevole** friendly [match]; **partita di calcio** football match; **partita a carte** game of cards; **partita doppia** Comm double-entry book keeping; **partita di ritorno** Sport return match, rematch; **partita semplice** Comm single-entry book keeping

parti'tario *m* Comm ledger
■ **partitario vendite** sales ledger

🔑 **par'tito** *m* party; (scelta) choice; (occasione di matrimonio) match; **per ~ preso** out of sheer pig-headedness
■ **partito di governo** governing party; **partito di maggioranza** majority party; **partito politico** political party

partitocra'zia *f concentration of power in the hands of political parties to the detriment of parliamentary democracy*

partizi'one *f* (divisione) division; Comput (di disco) partition

'partner *mf inv* (in affari, coppia) partner

'parto *m* childbirth; **un ~ facile** an easy birth *or* labour; **dolori del ~** *pl* labour pains; **morire di ~** die in childbirth
■ **parto cesareo** Caesarean; **parto in acqua** water birth; **parto indolore** natural childbirth; **parto pilotato** induction, induced labour; **parto prematuro** premature birth

partori'ente *f* woman in labour

parto'rire *vt* anche fig give birth to

part-'time **A** *adj* part-time
B *m* **chiedere il ~** ask to work part-time

pa'rure *f inv* (di gioielli) set of jewellery; (di biancheria intima) set of matching lingerie

par'venza *f* appearance

parzi'ale *adj* partial

parzialità *f inv* partiality; **fare ~ per qualcuno** be biased towards somebody

parzial'mente *adv* partially; (con parzialità) with bias; **~ cieco** partially sighted; **~ scremato** semi-skimmed

'pascere **A** *vi* ‹*mucche*› graze
B *vt* graze on ‹*erba*›

pasci'uto *adj* **ben ~** plump

pasco'lare *vt* graze

'pascolo *m* pasture

'Pasqua *f* Easter; **l'isola di ~** Easter Island

pa'squale *adj* Easter *attrib*

pa'squetta *f* (lunedì di Pasqua) Easter Monday

'passa *adv* **e ~** (e oltre) plus

pas'sabile *adj* passable

🔑 **pas'saggio** *m* passage; (traversata) crossing; Sport pass; (su veicolo) lift, ride; **essere di ~** be passing through; **è stato un ~ obbligato** fig it was something essential, it had to be done
■ **passaggio a livello** level crossing, grade crossing AmE; **passaggio pedonale** pedestrian crossing, crosswalk AmE; **passaggio di proprietà** transfer of ownership, conveyancy

passamane'ria *f* braid

passamon'tagna *m inv* balaclava

pas'sante **A** *mf* passer-by
B *m* (di cintura) loop
C *adj* Tennis passing

passa'porto *m* anche fig passport
■ **passaporto europeo** European passport, Europassport

🔑 **pas'sare** **A** *vi* pass; (attraversare) pass through; (far visita) call; (andare) go; (essere approvato) be passed; **~ davanti a qualcuno** go in front of somebody; **~ alla storia** go down in history; **~ di moda** go out of fashion; **mi è passato di mente** it slipped my mind; **~ sopra a qualcosa** pass over something; **~ per un genio/idiota** be taken for a genius/an idiot; **farsi ~ per qualcuno** pass oneself off as somebody; **passo!** (nelle carte) pass!; (per radio) over!
B *vt* (far scorrere) pass over; (sopportare) go through; (al telefono) put through; Culin strain; pass ‹*esame, visita*›; **~ in rivista** review; **~ qualcosa a qualcuno** pass something to somebody; **le passo il signor Rossi** Teleph I'll put you through to Mr Rossi; **~ qualcosa su qualcosa** ‹*crema, cera ecc.*› give something a coat of something; **~ il limite** go over the limit; **passarsela bene** be well off; **come te la passi?** how are you doing?
C *m* **col ~ del tempo** with the passing *or* passage of time

pas'sata *f* (di vernice) coat; (spolverata) dusting; (occhiata) look; Culin purée

passa'tempo *m* pastime

🔑 **pas'sato** **A** *adj* past; **l'anno ~** last year; **sono le tre passate** it's past *or* after three o'clock
B *m* past; Culin purée; Gram past tense; **in ~** in the past; **la musica del ~** the music of yesteryear
■ **passato di moda** old-fashioned; **passato prossimo** present perfect; **passato remoto**

🔑 key word

[simple] past; **passato di verdure** cream of vegetable soup

passaver'dure *m inv* food mill

passavi'vande *m inv* serving hatch

passeg'gero, -a **A** *adj* passing **B** *mf* passenger
■ **passeggero in transito** transit passenger

passeggi'are *vi* walk, stroll

passeg'giata *f* walk, stroll; (luogo) public walk; (in bicicletta) ride; **fare una ~** go for a walk

passeggia'trice *f* streetwalker

passeg'gino *m* pushchair, stroller AmE

pas'seggio *m* walk; (luogo) promenade; **andare a ~** go for a walk; **scarpe da ~** walking shoes

passe-par'tout *m inv* master key

passe'rella *f* gangway; Aeron boarding bridge; (per sfilate) catwalk

'passero *m* sparrow

passe'rotto *m* (passero) sparrow

pas'sibile *adj* **~ di** liable to

passio'nale *adj* passionate; **delitto ~** crime of passion

passi'one *f* passion; **avere la ~ del gioco** have a passion for gambling

passiva'mente *adv* passively

passività *f inv* (inerzia) passiveness, passivity; Fin liabilities *pl*; **~ *pl* correnti** current liabilities

pas'sivo **A** *adj* passive **B** *m* passive; Fin liabilities *pl*; **in ~** ‹*azienda*› in deficit; ‹*bilancio*› debit, in deficit

'passo *m* step; (orma) footprint; (andatura) pace, step; (di libro) passage; (valico) pass; **a due passi da qui** a stone's throw away; **a ~ d'uomo** at walking pace; **di buon ~** at a spanking pace, at a cracking pace; **a passi felpati** stealthily; **di questo ~** at this rate; **~ ~** step by step; **fare due passi** go for a stroll; **allungare il ~** quicken one's pace, step out; **tornare sui propri passi** retrace one's steps; **fare un ~ avanti** anche fig take a step forward; **fare un ~ falso** fig make a wrong move; **di pari ~** fig hand in hand; **stare al ~ con i tempi** keep up with the times, keep abreast of the times; **tenere il ~** keep up
■ **passo carrabile, passo carraio** driveway; **passo dell'oca** goose-step

'pasta *f* (impasto per pane ecc.) dough; (per dolci, pasticcino) pastry; (pastasciutta) pasta; (massa molle) paste; fig nature; **sono fatti della stessa ~** they're birds of a feather
■ **pasta e fagioli** *very thick soup with blended borlotti beans and small pasta*; **pasta al forno** *pasta baked in white sauce with grated cheese*; **pasta frolla** shortcrust pastry; **pasta al ragù** pasta with Bolognese sauce

pastasci'utta *f* pasta

pa'stella *f* batter

pa'stello *m* pastel

pa'sticca *f* pastille; infml (pastiglia) pill

pasticce'ria *f* cake shop, patisserie; (pasticcini) pastries *pl*; (arte) confectionery

pasticci'are **A** *vi* make a mess **B** *vt* make a mess of

pasticci'ere, -a *mf* confectioner

pastic'cino *m* little cake

pa'sticcio *m* Culin pie; (lavoro disordinato) mess; **mettersi nei pasticci** get into trouble

pasticci'one, -a **A** *mf* bungler **B** *adj* bungling

pasti'ficio *m* pasta factory

pa'stiglia *f* Med pill, tablet; (di menta) sweet
■ **pastiglia dei freni** Auto brake pad; **pastiglia per la gola** throat pastille; **pastiglia per la tosse** cough sweet

pa'stina *f* small pasta shape
■ **pastina in brodo** noodle soup

'pasto *m* meal; **fuori ~** between meals; **dare qualcosa in ~ a** fig serve something up on a platter to ‹*pubblico, stampa*›
■ **pasto pronto** TV dinner

pa'stora *f* shepherdess

pasto'rale *adj* pastoral

pa'store *m* shepherd; Relig pastor, vicar
■ **pastore scozzese** collie; **pastore tedesco** German shepherd, Alsatian

pasto'rizio *adj* sheep farming *attrib*

pastoriz'zare *vt* pasteurize

pastoriz'zato *adj* pasteurized

pastorizzazi'one *f* pasteurization

pa'stoso *adj* doughy; fig mellow

pa'strocchio *m* mess

pa'stura *f* pasture; (per pesci) bait

pa'tacca *f* (macchia) stain; fig (oggetto senza valore) piece of junk

pa'tata *f* potato
■ **patata americana** sweet potato; **patate *pl* arrosto** roast potatoes; **patate *pl* al cartoccio** jacket potatoes; **patate *pl* fritte** chips BrE, French fries; **patate *pl* in insalata** potato salad; **patate *pl* lesse** boiled potatoes

pata'tine *fpl* [potato] crisps, [potato] chips AmE

pata'trac *m inv* (crollo) crash

'patchwork *m inv* patchwork

pâté *m inv* pâté
■ **pâté di fegato** liver pâté

pa'tella *f* limpet

pa'tema *m* anxiety

pa'tente *f* licence; **prendere la ~** get one's driving licence
■ **patente di guida** driving licence, driver's license AmE

pater'nale *f* scolding

paterna'lismo *m* paternalism

paterna'lista *m* paternalist

paterna'listico *adj* paternalistic

paternità *f inv* paternity

pa'terno *adj* paternal; ‹*affetto ecc.*› fatherly

P

pa'tetico *adj* pathetic; **cadere nel ~** become over-sentimental
'pathos *m* pathos
pa'tibolo *m* gallows *sg*
pati'mento *m* suffering
'patina *f* patina; (sulla lingua) coating
'patio *m* patio garden
✐ **pa'tire** *vt & vi* suffer
pa'tito, -a **A** *adj* suffering
B *mf* fanatic
■ **patito della musica** music lover
patolo'gia *f* pathology
■ **patologia da radiazioni** radiation sickness; **patologia da sforzo ripetuto** repetitive strain injury, RSI
pato'logico *adj* pathological
pa'tologo, -a *mf* pathologist
✐ **'patria** *f* native land; **amor di ~** love of one's country
patri'arca *m* patriarch
patriar'cale *adj* patriarchal
patriar'cato *m* patriarchy
pa'trigno *m* stepfather
patrimoni'ale **A** *adj* property *attrib*
B *f* wealth tax
patri'monio *m* estate
patri'ota *mf* patriot
patri'ottico *adj* patriotic
patriot'tismo *m* patriotism
pa'trizio, -a *adj & nmf* patrician
patroci'nante *adj* sponsoring
patroci'nare *vt* support
patro'cinio *m* support; **sotto il ~ di** under the sponsorship of; Jur defended by
■ **patrocinio gratuito** legal aid
patro'nato *m* patronage
pa'trono *m* Relig patron saint; Jur counsel
'patta[1] *f* (di tasca) flap
'patta[2] *f* (pareggio) draw
patteggia'mento *m* bargaining
patteggi'are *vt & vi* negotiate
patti'naggio *m* skating
■ **pattinaggio artistico** figure skating; **pattinaggio su ghiaccio** ice skating; **pattinaggio a rotelle** roller-skating
patti'nare *vi* skate; (auto) skid
pattina|'tore, -trice *mf* skater
'pattino *m* skate; Aeron skid
■ **pattino da ghiaccio** ice skate; **pattino a rotelle** roller skate
✐ **'patto** *m* deal; Pol pact; **a ~ che** on condition that; **scendere a patti, venire a patti** reach a compromise
pat'tuglia *f* patrol; **essere di ~** be on patrol
■ **pattuglia stradale** highway patrol AmE, ≈ patrol car; police motorbike
pattu'ire *vt* negotiate
pat'tume *m* rubbish
pattumi'era *f* dustbin, trash can AmE

✐ key word

✐ **pa'ura** *f* fear; (spavento) fright; **aver ~** be afraid; **mettere ~ a** frighten; **per ~ di** for fear of; **da ~** sl (libro, film) brilliant
pau'roso *adj* (che fa paura) frightening; (che ha paura) fearful; infml (enorme) awesome
'pausa *f* pause; (nel lavoro) break; **fare una ~** pause; (nel lavoro) have a break
■ **pausa [per il] caffè** coffee break; **pausa [per il] pranzo** lunch break, lunch hour
pavida'mente *adv* timidly
'pavido **A** *adj* cowardly
B *m* coward
pavimen'tare *vt* pave ‹*strada*›
pavimentazi'one *f* paving
pavi'mento *m* floor
pa'vone *m* peacock
pavoneggi'arsi *vr* strut
pay tv *f inv* pay TV
pazien'tare *vi* be patient
pazi'ente *adj & nmf* patient
paziente'mente *adv* patiently
✐ **pazi'enza** *f* patience; **~!** never mind!; **perdere la ~** lose one's patience
'pazza *f* madwoman
pazza'mente *adv* madly
pazzerel'lone, -a *mf* madcap
paz'zesco *adj* foolish; (esagerato) crazy
paz'zia *f* madness; (azione) [act of] folly
✐ **'pazzo** **A** *adj* mad; fig crazy; **sei ~?** you must be crazy!, are you crazy?; **essere ~ di/per** be crazy about; **~ di gioia** mad with joy; **da pazzi** infml crackpot; **darsi alla pazza gioia** live it up
B *m* madman
paz'zoide *adj* infml whacky
P.C.I. *nm abbr* (**Partito Comunista Italiano**) Italian Communist Party
PD, pd *nm abbr* (**Partito Democratico**) Democratic Party
PdL *nm abbr* (**Popolo della Libertà**) *Italian political party*
'pecan *m inv* pecan
'pecca *f* fault; **senza ~** flawless
peccami'noso *adj* sinful
pec'care *vi* sin; **~ di** be guilty of ‹*ingratitudine*›
✐ **pec'cato** *m* sin; **~ che...** it's a pity that...; **[che] ~!** [what a] pity!
■ **peccato di gioventù** youthful folly
pecca|'tore, -trice *mf* sinner
'pece *f* pitch; **nero come la ~** black as pitch
pechi'nese *m* Pekingese
Pe'chino *f* Peking
'pecora *f* sheep
■ **pecora nera** black sheep
peco'raio *m* shepherd
peco'rella *f* **cielo a pecorelle** sky full of fluffy white clouds
■ **pecorella smarrita** lost sheep
peco'rino *m* (formaggio) sheep's milk cheese

peculi'are *adj* ~ **di** peculiar to
peculiarità *f inv* peculiarity
pecuni'ario *adj* money *attrib*
pe'daggio *m* toll
pedago'gia *f* pedagogy
peda'gogico *adj* pedagogical
peda'gogo, -a *mf* pedagogue
peda'lare *vi* pedal
peda'lata *f* push on the pedals
pe'dale *m* pedal
■ **pedale dell'acceleratore** gas pedal; **pedale del freno** brake pedal
pedalò *m inv* pedalo
pe'dana *f* footrest; Sport springboard
pe'dante *adj* pedantic
pedante'ria *f* pedantry
pedan'tesco *adj* pedantic
pe'data *f* (calcio) kick; (impronta) footprint
pede'rasta *m* pederast
pe'destre *adj* pedestrian
pedi'atra *mf* paediatrician
pedia'tria *f* paediatrics *sg*
pedi'atrico *adj* paediatric
pedi'cure **A** *mf inv* chiropodist, podiatrist AmE
B *m* (cura dei piedi) pedicure
pedi'gree *m inv* pedigree
pedi'luvio *m* footbath
pe'dina *f* (alla dama) piece; fig pawn
pedina'mento *m* shadowing
pedi'nare *vt* shadow
pedofi'lia *f* paedophilia
pe'dofilo, -a *mf* paedophile
pedo'nale *adj* pedestrian
pe'done, -a *mf* pedestrian
'pedule *fpl* hiking boots
'peeling *m inv* exfoliation treatment
'peggio **A** *adv* worse; ~ **per te!** too bad!, tough!; **tanto** ~ too bad; ~ **di così** any worse; **la persona** ~ **vestita** the worst dressed person
B *adj* worse; **niente di** ~ nothing worse; **stare** ~ **di** be worse off than
C *m* **il** ~ **è che...** the worst of it is that...; **pensare al** ~ think the worst
D *f* **alla** ~ at worst; **avere la** ~ get the worst of it; **alla meno** ~ as best I can
peggiora'mento *m* worsening
peggio'rare **A** *vt* make worse, worsen
B *vi* get worse, worsen
peggiora'tivo *adj* pejorative
peggi'ore **A** *adj* worse; (superlativo) worst; **nella** ~ **delle ipotesi** if the worst comes to the worst
B *mf* **il/la** ~ the worst
'pegno *m* pledge; (nei giochi di società) forfeit; fig token; **dare qualcosa in** ~ pawn something; **in** ~ **d'amicizia** as a token of friendship
pelan'drone *m* slob
pe'lare *vt* (spennare) pluck; (spellare) skin; (sbucciare) peel; infml (spillare denaro) fleece
pe'larsi *vr* infml lose one's hair
pe'lati *mpl* (pomodori) peeled tomatoes
pe'lato *adj* (calvo) bald
pel'lame *m* skins *pl*
'pelle *f* skin; (cuoio) leather; (buccia) peel; **avere la** ~ **d'oca** have goose-flesh; **non stare più nella** ~ be beside oneself; **salvare la** ~ save one's skin; **lasciarci la** ~ buy it; **essere** ~ **e ossa** be all skin and bones; **avere la** ~ **dura** be tough; **borsa di pelle** leather bag
■ **pelle scamosciata** suede
pellegri'naggio *m* pilgrimage
pelle'grino, -a *mf* pilgrim
pelle'rossa *mf* Red Indian
pellette'ria *f* leather goods *pl*
pelli'cano *m* pelican
pellicce'ria *f* furrier's [shop]
pel'liccia *f* fur; (indumento) fur [coat]
pellicci'aio, -a *mf* furrier
pel'licola *f* Phot, Cinema film
■ **pellicola a colori** colour film; **pellicola trasparente** Culin cling film
'pelo *m* hair; (di animale) coat; (di lana) pile; **per un** ~ by the skin of one's teeth; **cavarsela per un** ~ have a narrow escape; **cercare il** ~ **nell'uovo** nitpick
pe'loso *adj* hairy
'peltro *m* pewter
pe'luche *m*:
■ **giocattolo di peluche** soft toy; **orsetto di peluche** teddy bear
pe'luria *f* down
'pelvico *adj* pelvic
'pena *f* (punizione) punishment; (sofferenza) pain; (dispiacere) sorrow; (disturbo) trouble; **a mala** ~ hardly; **mi fa** ~ I pity him; **vale la** ~ **andare** it is worth [while] going; **pene** *pl* **dell'inferno** hellfire
■ **pena di morte** death sentence
pe'nale *adj* criminal; **diritto** ~ criminal law
pena'lista *mf* criminal lawyer
penalità *f inv* penalty
penaliz'zare *vt* penalize
penalizzazi'one *f* (penalità) penalty
pe'nare *vi* suffer; (faticare) find it difficult
pen'daglio *m* pendant
pen'dant *m inv* **fare** ~ **[con]** match
pen'dente **A** *adj* hanging; Comm outstanding
B *m* (ciondolo) pendant; **pendenti** *pl* drop earrings
pen'denza *f* slope; Comm outstanding account
'pendere *vi* hang; (superficie) slope; (essere inclinato) lean
pen'dio *m* slope; **in** ~ sloping
'pendola *f* grandfather clock

P

pendo'lare **A** *adj* pendulum
B *mf* commuter

pendo'lino *m* (treno) *special, first class only, fast train*

'pendolo *m* pendulum; **orologio a ~** grandfather clock

'pene *m* penis

pene'trante *adj* penetrating; (freddo) biting

pene'trare **A** *vt & vi* penetrate; (trafiggere) pierce
B *vt* (odore) get into
C *vi* (entrare furtivamente) steal in

penetrazi'one *f* penetration

penicil'lina *f* penicillin

pe'nisola *f* peninsula

peni'tente *adj & nmf* penitent

peni'tenza *f* penitence; (punizione) penance; (in gioco) forfeit

penitenzi'ario *m* penitentiary

'penna *f* (da scrivere) pen; (di uccello) feather
■ **penna a feltro** felt-tip pen; **penna ottica** light pen; **penna a sfera** ball-point [pen]; **penna stilografica** fountain pen; **penna USB** pen drive

pen'nacchio *m* plume

penna'rello *m* felt-tip pen

'penne *fpl* pasta quills

pennel'lare *vt* paint

pennel'lata *f* brushstroke

pen'nello *m* brush; **a ~** (a perfezione) perfectly
■ **~ da barba** shaving brush

pen'nino *m* nib

pen'none *m* (di bandiera) flagpole

pen'nuto *adj* feathered

pe'nombra *f* half-light

pe'noso *adj* infml (pessimo) painful

pen'sabile *adj* **non è ~** it's unthinkable

⚷ **pen'sare** **A** *vi* think; **penso di sì** I think so; **~ a** think of; remember to (*fill up with gas etc*); **pensa ai fatti tuoi!** mind your own business!; **ci penso io** I'll take care of it; **~ di fare qualcosa** think of doing something; **a pensarci bene** on second thoughts; **~ tra sé e sé** think to oneself; **pensarci su** think it over
B *vt* think

pen'sata *f* idea

pensa|'tore, -trice *mf* thinker

⚷ **pensi'ero** *m* thought; (mente) mind; (preoccupazione) worry; **stare in ~ per** be anxious about; **levarsi il ~** to get something out of the way

pensie'roso *adj* pensive

'pensile **A** *adj* hanging; **giardino ~** roof garden
B *m* (mobile) wall unit

pensi'lina *f* (di fermata d'autobus) bus shelter

pensio'nante *mf* boarder; (ospite pagante) lodger

⚷ key word

pensio'nato, -a **A** *mf* pensioner
B *m* (per anziani) [old folks'] home; (per studenti) hostel

⚷ **pensi'one** *f* pension; (albergo) boarding house; (vitto e alloggio) board and lodging; (da lavoro) retirement; **andare in ~** retire; **essere in ~** be retired; **mezza ~** half board
■ **pensione di anzianità** old-age pension; **pensione completa** full board; **pensione di invalidità** disability pension

pen'soso *adj* pensive

pen'tagono *m* pentagon; **il Pentagono** the Pentagon

pen'tathlon *m inv* pentathlon

Pente'coste *f* Whitsun, Whit Sunday

penti'mento *m* repentance

pen'tirsi *vr* **~ di** repent of; (rammaricarsi) regret

penti'tismo *m* turning informant

pen'tito *m* terrorist or Mafioso turned informant

'pentola *f* saucepan; (contenuto) potful
■ **pentola a pressione** pressure cooker

pento'lino *f* saucepan

pe'nultimo *adj* last but one, penultimate

pe'nuria *f* shortage

penzo'lare *vi* dangle

penzo'loni *adv* dangling

pe'onia *f* peony

pepai'ola *f* pepper pot

pe'pare *vt* pepper

pe'pato *adj* peppery

'pepe *m* pepper; **grano di ~** peppercorn
■ **pepe di Caienna** cayenne pepper; **pepe in grani** whole peppercorns; **pepe macinato** ground pepper; **pepe nero** black pepper

pepero'nata *f dish of stewed peppers and tomatoes*

peperon'cino *m* chilli pepper

pepe'rone *m* [sweet] pepper; **rosso come un ~** red as a beetroot; **peperoni** *pl* **ripieni** stuffed peppers
■ **peperone rosso** red pepper; **peperone verde** green pepper

pepi'era *f* pepper pot; (macinino) pepper mill

pe'pita *f* nugget

'peptico *adj* peptic

⚷ **'per** *prep* for; (attraverso) through; (stato in luogo) in, on; (distributivo) per; (mezzo, entro) by; (causa) with; (in qualità di) as; **mi è passato ~ la mente** it crossed my mind; **~ strada** on the street; **~ la fine del mese** by the end of the month; **in fila ~ due** in double file; **l'ho sentito ~ telefono** I spoke to him on the phone; **~ iscritto** in writing; **~ caso** by chance; **~ esempio** for example; **ho aspettato ~ ore** I've been waiting for hours; **~ tutta la durata del viaggio** for the entire journey; **~ tempo** in time; **~ sempre** forever; **~ scherzo** as a joke; **gridare ~ il dolore** scream with pain; **vendere ~ 10 milioni** sell for 10 million; **uno ~ volta** one at a time; **uno ~ uno** one by one; **venti ~ cento** twenty per cent; **~ fare qualcosa** [in order to] do something; **stare ~** be about to; **è troppo bello ~ essere vero** it's too good to be true

'pera *f* pear; **farsi una ~** sl (di eroina) shoot up

perbe'nismo *m* prissiness

perbe'nista *adj inv* prissy

per'calle *m* gingham

per'cento *adv* per cent

percentu'ale *f* percentage

perce'pibile *adj* perceivable; (somma) payable

perce'pire *vt* perceive; (riscuotere) cash

percet'tibile *adj* perceptible

percettibil'mente *adv* perceptibly

percezi'one *f* perception

perché **A** *conj* (in interrogazioni) why; (per il fatto che) because; (affinché) so that; **~ non vieni?** why don't you come?; **dimmi ~** tell me why; **~ no/sì!** because!; **è troppo difficile ~ lo possa capire** it's too difficult for him to understand
B *m inv* reason [why]; **senza un ~** without any reason

perciò *conj* so

per'correre *vt* cover ‹*distanza*›; (viaggiare) travel

percor'ribile *adj* (strada) drivable, passable

percorribilità *f inv*
■ **percorribilità delle strade** road conditions *pl*

per'corso **A** pp di **percorrere**
B *m* (tragitto) course, route; (distanza) distance; (viaggio) journey
■ **percorso ecologico** nature trail; **percorso di guerra** assault course; **percorso a ostacoli** obstacle course; **percorso vascolare** cardiovascular circuit

per'cossa *f* blow; **percosse** *pl* Jur assault and battery

per'cosso pp di **percuotere**

percu'otere *vt* strike

percussi'one *f* percussion; **strumenti a ~** percussion instruments

percussio'nista *mf* percussionist

per'dente *mf* loser

'perdere **A** *vt* lose; (sprecare) waste; (non prendere) miss; fig (vizio) ruin; **~ tempo** waste time; **lascia ~!** forget it!; **~ di vista** lose touch [with each other]
B *vi* lose; (recipiente) leak; **a ~** (vuoto) non-returnable; **non avere niente da ~** have nothing to lose

'perdersi *vr* get lost; (reciproco) lose touch

perdifi'ato **a ~** *adv* ‹*gridare*› at the top of one's voice

perdigi'orno *mf inv* idler

'perdita *f* loss; (spreco) waste; (falla) leak; **a ~ d'occhio** as far as the eye can see; **chiudere in ~** (azienda) show a loss
■ **perdita di gas** gas leak; **perdita di sangue** loss of blood, bleeding; **perdita di tempo** waste of time

perdi'tempo *m* time-waster

perdizi'one *f* perdition

perdo'nare **A** *vt* forgive; (scusare) excuse; **mi perdoni se interrompo** sorry to interrupt, excuse me for interrupting; **per farsi ~** as an apology
B *vi* **~ a qualcuno** forgive somebody; **un male che non perdona** an incurable disease

per'dono *m* forgiveness; Jur pardon; **chiedere ~** ask for forgiveness; (scusarsi) apologize

perdu'rare *vi* last; (perseverare) persist

perduta'mente *adv* hopelessly

per'duto **A** pp di **perdere**
B *adj* lost; (rovinato) ruined

pe'renne *adj* everlasting; Bot perennial; **nevi perenni** perpetual snow

perenne'mente *adv* perpetually

peren'torio *adj* peremptory

per'fetto **A** *adj* perfect
B *m* Gram perfect [tense]

perfezio'nare *vt* perfect; (migliorare) improve

perfezio'narsi *vr* improve oneself; (specializzarsi) specialize

perfezi'one *f* perfection; **alla ~** to perfection

perfezio'nismo *m* perfectionism

perfezio'nista *mf* perfectionist

per'fidia *f* wickedness; (atto) wicked act

'perfido *adj* treacherous; (malvagio) perverse

per'fino *adv* even

perfo'rare *vt* pierce; punch ‹*schede*›; Mech drill

perfora'tore *m* (apparecchio) punch
■ **perforatore di schede** card punch

perfora|'tore, -trice *mf* punch-card operator

perforazi'one *f* perforation; (di schede) punching

per'formance *f inv* Theat performance

perga'mena *f* parchment

'pergola *f* pergola

pergo'lato *m* bower

periar'trite *f* periarthritis

perico'lante *adj* precarious; ‹*azienda*› shaky

pe'ricolo *m* danger; (rischio) risk; **mettere in ~** endanger; **essere fuori ~** be out of danger
■ **pericolo pubblico** danger to society; **pericolo di valanghe** danger of avalanches

pericolosa'mente *adv* dangerously

pericolosità *f inv* danger

perico'loso *adj* dangerous

peridu'rale *f* epidural

perife'ria *f* periphery; (di città) outskirts *pl*; fig fringes *pl*

P

peri'ferica *f* peripheral; ‹*strada*› ring road
■ **periferica di input** Comput input device

peri'ferico *adj* peripheral; ‹*quartiere*› outlying

pe'rifrasi *f inv* circumlocution

perime'trale *adj* ‹*muro*› perimeter *attrib*

pe'rimetro *m* perimeter

peri'odico **A** *m* periodical
B *adj* periodical; ‹*vento, mal di testa*› Math recurring

pe'riodo *m* period; Gram sentence
■ **periodo nero** bad patch; **periodo di prova** trial period; **periodo di ripensamento** cooling-off period; **periodo di riposo** breathing space; **periodo di transizione** transitional period, interim; **periodo di validità** period of validity

peripe'zie *fpl* misadventures

pe'rire *vi* perish

peri'scopio *m* periscope

pe'rito, -a **A** *adj* skilled
B *mf* expert
■ **perito agrario** agriculturalist; **perito di assicurazione** Comm loss adjuster; **perito edile** chartered surveyor; **perito elettronico** electronics engineer

perito'nite *f* peritonitis

pe'rizia *f* skill; (valutazione) survey
■ **perizia medico-legale** forensic tests

peri'zoma *m inv* loincloth

'perla *f* pearl
■ **perla coltivata** cultured pearl

per'lina *f* bead

perli'nato *m* matchboard

perlo'meno *adv* at least

perlu'strare *vt* patrol

p

perlustrazi'one *f* patrol; **andare in ~** go on patrol

perma'loso *adj* touchy

perma'nente **A** *adj* permanent
B *f* perm; **farsi [fare] la ~** have a perm

perma'nenza *f* permanence; (soggiorno) stay; **in ~** permanently
■ **permanenza in carica** tenure

perma'nere *vi* remain

perme'are *vt* permeate

perme'ato *adj* **~ di** fig permeated with

per'messo **A** pp di **permettere**
B *m* permission; (autorizzazione) permit, licence; Mil leave; **[è] ~?, con ~** (posso entrare?) may I come in?; (posso passare?) excuse me
■ **permesso di lavoro** work permit; **permesso di soggiorno** residence permit

per'mettere *vt* allow, permit; **potersi ~ qualcosa** (finanziariamente) be able to afford something

per'mettersi *vr* **~ di fare qualcosa** allow oneself to do something; **come si permette?** how dare you?

permis'sivo *adj* permissive

permutazi'one *f* exchange; Math permutation

per'nacchia *f* infml raspberry infml

per'nice *f* partridge

pernici'oso *adj* pernicious

'perno *m* pivot

pernot'tare *vi* stay overnight

'pero *m* pear tree

però *conj* but; (tuttavia) however

'perone *m* Anat fibula

pero'rare *vt* plead

perpendico'lare *adj & nf* perpendicular

perpe'trare *vt* perpetrate

per'petua *f* (di prete) priest's housekeeper

perpetu'are *vt* perpetuate

per'petuo *adj* perpetual

perplessità *f inv* perplexity; (dubbio) doubt

per'plesso *adj* perplexed, puzzled

perqui'sire *vt* search

perquisizi'one *f* search
■ **perquisizione domiciliare** search of the premises

persecu|'tore, -trice *mf* persecutor

persecuzi'one *f* persecution

persegu'ire *vt* pursue

persegui'tare *vt* persecute

persegui'tato, -a *mf* victim of persecution

perseve'rante *adj* persevering

perseve'ranza *f* perseverance

perseve'rare *vi* persevere

'Persia *f* Persia

persi'ana *f* shutter
■ **persiana avvolgibile** roller shutter

persi'ano, -a *adj & nmf* Persian

'persico *adj* Persian

per'sino = **perfino**

persi'stente *adj* persistent; ‹*dubbio*› nagging

persi'stenza *f* persistence

per'sistere *vi* persist; **~ nel fare qualcosa** persist in doing something

'perso **A** pp di **perdere**
B *adj* lost; **a tempo ~** in one's spare time

per'sona *f* person; (un tale) somebody; **di ~, in ~** in person, personally; **per ~** per person, a head; **per interposta ~** through an intermediary; **curare la propria ~** look after oneself, look after number one; **persone** *pl* people
■ **persona a carico** dependant; **persona di colore** black person; **persona giuridica** legal person; **persona di servizio** domestic

perso'naggio *m* (persona di riguardo) personality; Theat ecc. character

perso'nale **A** *adj* personal
B *m* staff; (aspetto) build
■ **personale di terra** ground crew

personalità *f inv* personality

key word

personaliz'zare *vt* customize ‹*auto ecc.*›; personalize ‹*penna ecc.*›
personifi'care *vt* personify
personificazi'one *f* personification
perspi'cace *adj* shrewd
perspi'cacia *f* shrewdness
persua'dere *vt* convince; impress ‹*critici*›; **~ qualcuno a fare qualcosa** persuade somebody to do something
persuasi'one *f* persuasion; **fare opera di ~ su qualcuno** try to persuade somebody
persuasività *f inv* persuasiveness
persua'sivo *adj* persuasive
persu'aso pp di **persuadere**
persua'sore *m* persuader
per'tanto *conj* therefore
'pertica *f* pole
perti'nace *adj* pertinacious
perti'nente *adj* relevant
per'tosse *f* whooping cough
per'tugio *m* opening
pertur'bare *vt* perturb
perturbazi'one *f* disturbance
■ **perturbazione atmosferica** atmospheric disturbance
Perù *m inv* Peru
peruvi'ano, -a *adj & nmf* Peruvian
per'vadere *vt* pervade
perva'sivo *adj* pervasive
per'vaso pp di **pervadere**
perven'ire *vi* reach; **far ~ qualcosa a qualcuno** send something to somebody
perversa'mente *adv* perversely
perversi'one *f* perversion
perversità *f inv* perversity
per'verso *adj* perverse
perver'tire *vt* pervert
perver'tirsi *vr* (gusti, costumi) become debased
perver'tito **A** *adj* perverted
B *m* pervert
pervi'cace *adj* obstinate
pervicace'mente *adv* obstinately
pervi'cacia *f* obstinacy
per'vinca¹ *m* (colore) blue with a touch of purple
per'vinca² *f* Bot periwinkle
p.es. *abbr* (**per esempio**) e.g.
'pesa *f* weighing; (bilancia) weighing machine; (per veicoli) weighbridge
pe'sante **A** *adj* heavy; ‹*stomaco*› overfull; ‹*accusa, ingiuria*› serious; (noioso) boring; **andarci ~ con qualcuno** be heavy-handed with somebody
B *adv* ‹*vestirsi*› warmly
pesante'mente *adv* ‹*cadere*› heavily; ‹*insultare*› seriously
pesan'tezza *f* heaviness
pesaper'sone *m inv* scales
pe'sare **A** *vt* weigh; **~ le parole** weigh one's words
B *vi* weigh; (essere pesante) be heavy; **~ su** fig lie heavy on
pe'sarsi *vr* weigh oneself
'pesca¹ *f* (frutto) peach
'pesca² *f* fishing; **andare a ~** go fishing
■ **pesca di beneficenza** lucky dip; **pesca con la lenza** angling; **pesca subacquea** underwater fishing
pe'scare *vt* (andare a pesca di) fish for; (prendere) catch; infml (trovare) dig up, find; **guai se ti pesco!** there will be trouble if I catch you!
pesca'tore *m* fisherman
■ **pescatore di frodo** poacher; **pescatore di perle** pearl diver
'pesce *m* fish; **non sapere che pesci pigliare** fig not know which way to turn; **prendere qualcuno a pesci in faccia** fig treat somebody like dirt; **sentirsi un ~ fuor d'acqua** feel like a fish out of water
■ **pesce d'aprile!** April Fool!; **pesce in carpione** soused fish; **pesce al cartoccio** fish baked in foil; **pesce gatto** catfish; **pesce grosso** fig big fish; **pesce persico** perch; **pesce piccolo** fig small fry; **pesce rosso** goldfish; **pesce spada** swordfish
pesce'cane *m* shark
pesche'reccio *m* fishing boat
pesche'ria *f* fishmonger's [shop]
peschi'era *f* fish pond
'Pesci *mpl* Astr Pisces
pescio'lino *m*
■ **pesciolino d'acqua dolce** minnow
pesci'vendolo *m* fishmonger
'pesco *m* peach tree
pe'scoso *adj* teeming with fish
pe'seta *f* peseta
pe'sista *m* (in sollevamento pesi) weight-lifter; (in lancio del peso) shot-putter
'peso *m* weight; **essere di ~ per qualcuno** be a burden to somebody; **alzare di ~** lift up in one go; **avere un ~ sullo stomaco** have a lead weight on one's stomach; **di poco ~** (senza importanza) not very important; **non dare ~ a qualcosa** not attach any importance to something
■ **peso massimo** (nel pugilato) heavy weight; **peso medio** (nel pugilato) middleweight; **peso morto** dead weight; **peso netto** net weight; **peso piuma** (nel pugilato) featherweight; **peso specifico** specific gravity; **peso welter** (nel pugilato) welterweight
pessi'mismo *m* pessimism
pessi'mista **A** *mf* pessimist
B *adj* pessimistic
pessimistica'mente *adv* pessimistically
'pessimo *adj* very bad
pe'staggio *m* beating-up
pe'stare *vt* tread on; (picchiare) beat; crush ‹*aglio, prezzemolo, uva*›; **~ i piedi [per terra]**

stamp one's feet [on the ground]; **~ un piede a qualcuno** tread on somebody's foot

pe'stata *f* bash; **dare una ~ a un piede a qualcuno** tread on somebody's foot

'peste *f* plague; (persona) pest; **dire ~ e corna di qualcuno** tear somebody to bits
■ **peste bubbonica** bubonic plague

pe'stello *m* pestle

pesti'cida *m* pesticide

pe'stifero *adj* (fastidioso) pestilential

pesti'lenza *f* pestilence; (fetore) stench, stink

pestilenzi'ale *adj* ‹*odore, aria*› noxious

'pesto **A** *adj* ground; **occhio pesto** black eye **B** *m* basil and garlic sauce

'petalo *m* petal

pe'tardo *m* banger

petizi'one *f* petition; **fare una ~** draw up a petition

petro'dollaro *m* petrodollar

petrol'chimico *adj* petrochemical

petroli'era *f* [oil] tanker

petroli'ere *m* oilman

petro'lifero *adj* oil-bearing

⚷ **pe'trolio** *m* oil

pettego'lare *vi* gossip

pettego'lezzo *m* piece of gossip; **pettegolezzi** *pl* gossip *sg*; **far pettegolezzi** gossip

pet'tegolo, -a **A** *adj* gossipy **B** *mf* gossip

petti'nare *vt* comb

petti'narsi *vr* comb one's hair

pettina'tura *f* combing; (acconciatura) hairstyle; **~ a caschetto** bob

P

'pettine *m* comb

'petting *m* petting

petti'nino *m* (fermaglio) comb

petti'rosso *m* robin [redbreast]

⚷ **'petto** *m* chest; (seno) breast; **a doppio ~** double-breasted; **prendere qualcosa/qualcuno di ~** face up to something/somebody; **petti** *pl* **di pollo** chicken breasts

petto'rale **A** *m* Sport number; **pettorali** pecs **B** *adj* pectoral

petto'rina *f* (di salopette) bib

petto'ruto *adj* ‹*donna*› full-breasted; ‹*uomo*› broad-chested

petu'lante *adj* impertinent

petu'lanza *f* impertinence

pe'tunia *f* petunia

'pezza *f* cloth; (toppa) patch; (rotolo di tessuto) roll; **trattare qualcuno come una ~ da piedi** walk all over somebody
■ **pezza d'appoggio** voucher; **pezza giustificativa** voucher

pez'zato *adj* ‹*cavallo, mucca*› piebald

pez'zente *mf* tramp; (avaro) miser

⚷ key word

⚷ **'pezzo** *m* piece; (parte) part; Mus piece; **un bel ~ d'uomo** a fine figure of a man; **un ~** (di tempo) some time; (di spazio) a long way; **al ~** ‹*costare*› each; **essere a pezzi** (stanco) be shattered; **fare a pezzi** tear to shreds; **andare in mille pezzi** break into a thousand pieces; **cadere a pezzi** fall to pieces, fall to bits
■ **pezzo forte** centre-piece; **pezzi** *pl* **grossi** top brass; **pezzo grosso** bigwig, big shot; **pezzi** *pl* **grossi** top brass; **pezzo di imbecille** stupid idiot; **pezzo di ricambio** spare [part]

pezzu'ola *f* scrap of material

photo'fit® *m inv* Photofit

pia'cente *adj* attractive

⚷ **pia'cere** **A** *m* pleasure; (favore) favour; **a ~** as much as one likes; **per ~!** please!; **~ [di conoscerla]!** (nelle presentazioni) pleased to meet you!; **con ~** with pleasure; **fare un ~ a qualcuno** do somebody a favour **B** *vi* **la Scozia mi piace** I like Scotland; **mi piacciono i dolci** I like sweets; **mi piacerebbe venire** I'd like to come; **faccio come mi pare e piace** I do as I please; **ti piace?** do you like it?; **lo spettacolo è piaciuto** the show was a success

pia'cevole *adj* pleasant

piacevol'mente *adv* agreeably

piaci'mento *m* **a ~** as much as you like

pia'dina *f unleavened focaccia bread*

pi'aga *f* sore; fig scourge; fig (persona noiosa) pain; fig (ricordo doloroso) wound

pia'gato *adj* covered with sores

piagni'steo *m* whining

piagnuco'lare *vi* whimper

piagnuco'lio *m* whimpering

piagnuco'loso *adj* maudlin

pi'alla *f* plane

pial'lare *vt* plane

pialla'tura *f* planing

pi'ana *f* (pianura) plane

pianeggi'ante *adj* level

piane'rottolo *m* landing

pia'neta *m* planet

⚷ **pi'angere** **A** *vi* cry; (disperatamente) weep; **mi piange il cuore** my heart bleeds; **mettersi a ~ come una fontana** turn the waterworks on; **~ sul latte versato** cry over spilt milk **B** *vt* (lamentare) lament; (per un lutto) mourn; **~ la morte di qualcuno** mourn somebody's death

pianifi'care *vt* plan

pianificazi'one *f* planning
■ **pianificazione aziendale** corporate planning; **pianificazione familiare** family planning; **pianificazione territoriale** town and country planning

pia'nista *mf* Mus pianist

⚷ **pi'ano** **A** *adj* flat; (a livello) flush; (regolare) smooth; (facile) easy; **i 400 metri piani** the 400 metres flat race **B** *adv* slowly; (con cautela) gently; (sottovoce)

quietly; **andarci ~** go carefully
C *m* plain; (di edificio) floor, storey; (livello) plane; (progetto) plan; Mus piano; **di primo ~** first-rate; **primo ~** Phot close-up; **in primo ~** in the foreground; **essere/mettersi in primo ~** fig take/occupy centre stage; **secondo ~** middle distance
■ **piano d'azione** action plan; **piano bar** piano bar; **piano d'emergenza** contingency plan; **piano di incentivi** incentive scheme; **piano di lavoro** work surface; (programma) work schedule; **piano di pensionamento** pension plan, pension scheme; **piano regolatore** town plan; **piano di sopra** upstairs; **piano di sotto** downstairs; **piano di studi** syllabus; **piano superiore** upper floor

piano'forte *m* piano
■ **pianoforte a coda** grand [piano]; **pianoforte verticale** upright [piano]

pia'nola® *f* pianola

piano'terra *m inv* ground floor, first floor AmE

pi'anta *f* plant; (del piede) sole; (disegno) plan; (di città) map; **di sana ~** (totalmente) entirely; **in ~ stabile** permanently
■ **pianta da appartamento** house plant; **pianta stradale** road map

piantagi'one *f* plantation

pianta'grane *mf* infml **è un/una ~** he's/she's bolshy

pian'tare *vt* plant; (conficcare) drive; pitch ‹*tenda*›; infml (abbandonare) dump; **piantala!** infml stop it!; **piantato in** ‹*spina, chiodo*› embedded in; **~ baracca e burattini** drop everything; (per sempre) chuck everything in

pian'tarsi *vr* plant oneself; infml (lasciarsi) leave each other

pianta|'tore, -trice *mf* planter

pianter'reno *m* ground floor, first floor AmE

pi'anto **A** pp di **piangere**
B *m* crying; (disperato) weeping; (lacrime) tears *pl*

pianto'nare *vt* guard

pian'tone *m* guard; **stare di ~** stand guard; **mettere di ~** put on guard
■ **piantone dello sterzo** Auto steering column

pia'nura *f* plain
■ **pianura padana** Po valley

pi'astra *f* plate; (lastra) slab; Culin griddle
■ **piastra elettronica** circuit board; **piastra madre** Comput motherboard; **piastra di registrazione** cassette deck

pia'strella *f* tile

pia'strina *f* Mil identity disc; Med platelet; Comput chip
■ **piastrina di riconoscimento** identity tag; **piastrina di silicio** silicon chip

piatta'forma *f* platform
■ **piattaforma di lancio** launch pad; **piattaforma petrolifera** oil platform, offshore rig; **piattaforma rivendicativa** *o* **sindacale** union claims *pl*

piat'tino *m* (di tazzina) saucer; (piatto piccolo) side plate

pi'atto **A** *adj* flat; (monotono) dull
B *m* plate; (da portata, vivanda) dish; (portata) course; (parte piatta) flat; (di giradischi) turntable; (di bilancia) pan; **piatti** *pl* Mus cymbals; **lavare i piatti** do the dishes, do the washing-up; **piatti** *pl* **da asporto** takeaway, carry-out AmE; **piatti** *pl* **caldi** hot dishes; **piatti** *pl* **di carne** meat dishes
■ **piatto fondo** soup plate; **piatto del giorno** dish of the day; **piatto piano** [ordinary] plate; **piatto di portata** serving dish, server; **piatto pronto** ready meal; **piatto unico** complete meal

piaz'z[u]ola *f*:
■ **piazz[u]ola di partenza** (nel golf) tee; **piazz[u]ola di sosta** pull-in

pi'azza *f* square; Comm market; **letto a una ~** single bed; **letto a due piazze** double bed; **far ~ pulita** make a clean sweep; **mettere qualcosa in ~** fig make something public; **scendere in ~** fig take to the streets
■ **piazza d'armi** parade ground; **piazza del mercato** market square; **Piazza San Pietro** St Peter's Square

piazza'forte *f* stronghold

piaz'zale *m* large square

piazza'mento *m* (in classifica) placing

piaz'zare *vt* place

piaz'zarsi *vr* Sport be placed; **~ secondo** come second, be placed second

piaz'zato *adj* ‹*cavallo*› placed; **ben ~** (robusto) well-built

piaz'zista **A** *m* salesman
B *f* saleswoman

pic'cante *adj* hot; (pungente) sharp; (salace) spicy

pic'carsi *vr* (risentirsi) take offence; **~ di** (vantarsi di) claim to

pic'cata *f veal in sour lemon sauce*

'picche *fpl* (in carte) spades

picchet'taggio *m* picketing

picchet'tare *vt* stake; ‹*scioperanti*› picket

pic'chetto *m* picket

picchi'are **A** *vt* hit; **~ la testa (contro qualcosa)** bang *or* hit one's head (against something)
B *vi* (bussare) knock; Aeron nosedive; **~ in testa** (motore) knock

picchi'arsi *vr* **~ il petto** beat one's breast

picchi'ata *f* beating; Aeron nosedive; **scendere in ~** nosedive

picchi'ato *adj* (matto) touched

picchia'tore *m* goon

picchiet'tare *vt* tap; (punteggiare) spot

picchiet'tato *adj* spotted

picchiet'tio *m* tapping

'picchio *m* woodpecker

pic'cino **A** *adj* tiny; (gretto) mean; (di poca importanza) petty

P

B *m* little one, child

piccion'cini *mpl* infml lovebirds; **fare i ~** get all lovey-dovey

picci'one *m* pigeon; **prendere due piccioni con una fava** kill two birds with one stone
■ **piccione viaggiatore** carrier pigeon

'picco *m* peak; **a ~** vertically; **colare a ~** sink

picco'lezza *f* (di persona, ambiente) smallness; (grettezza) meanness; (inezia) trifle

'piccolo, -a **A** *adj* small, little; ‹*vacanza, pausa*› little, short; (di statura) short; (gretto) petty
B *mf* child, little one; **da ~** as a child; **in ~** in miniature; **nel mio ~** in my own small way

pic'cone *m* pickaxe
■ **piccone da ghiaccio** ice pick

pic'cozza *f* ice axe

pic'nic *m inv* picnic

pi'docchio *m* louse

pidocchi'oso **A** *adj* flea-bitten; infml (avaro) stingy
B *m* infml miser

piè *m inv* **a ~ di pagina** at the foot of the page; **saltare a ~ pari** skip; **ad ogni ~ sospinto** all the time, endlessly

pi'ede *m* foot; (di armadio, letto) leg; **a piedi** on foot; **andare a piedi** walk; **a piedi nudi** barefoot; **avere i piedi piatti** have flat feet, be flat-footed; **a ~ libero** free; **in piedi** standing; **alzarsi in piedi** stand up; **in punta di piedi** on tiptoe; **ai piedi di** ‹*montagna*› at the foot of; **avere qualcuno ai propri piedi** have somebody at one's feet; **essere sul ~ di guerra** be ready for action; (nazione) be on a war footing; **prendere ~** fig gain ground; ‹*moda*› catch on; **partire col ~ sbagliato** get off on the wrong foot; **mettere in piedi** (allestire) set up; **togliti dai piedi!** get out of the way!
■ **piede di insalata** head of lettuce; **piede di porco** (strumento) jemmy

pie'dino *m* **fare ~ a qualcuno** infml play footsie with somebody

piedi'stallo *m* pedestal

pi'ega *f* (piegatura) fold; (di gonna) pleat; (di pantaloni) crease; (grinza) wrinkle; (andamento) turn; **a pieghe** with pleats, pleated; **non fare una ~** (ragionamento) be flawless; (persona) not bat an eyelid; **prendere una brutta ~** get into bad ways

pie'gare **A** *vt* fold; (flettere) bend
B *vi* bend

pie'garsi *vr* bend; **~ a** fig yield to

piega'tura *f* folding; (piega) fold

pieghet'tare *vt* pleat

pieghet'tato *adj* pleated

pie'ghevole **A** *adj* pliable; (tavolo) folding
B *m* leaflet

Pie'monte *m* Piedmont

piemon'tese *adj & nmf* Piedmontese

pi'ena *f* (di fiume) flood; (folla) crowd

pi'eno **A** *adj* full; (massiccio) solid; **in piena estate** in the middle of summer; **a pieni voti** (diplomarsi) ≈ with A grades, with first class honours
B *m* (colmo) height; (carico) full load; **in ~** (completamente) fully; **fare il ~** (di benzina) fill up; **nel ~ delle forze** in top physical form

pie'none *m* **c'era il ~** the place was packed

'piercing *m inv* body piercing
■ **piercing all'ombelico** navel ring; **piercing nella lingua** tongue stud

pietà *f inv* pity; (misericordia) mercy; **senza ~** (persona) pitiless; (spietatamente) pitilessly; **avere ~ di qualcuno** take pity on somebody; **far ~** (far pena) be pitiful; infml (essere orrendo) be useless

pie'tanza *f* dish

pie'toso *adj* pitiful, merciful; infml (pessimo) terrible

pi'etra *f* stone
■ **pietra dura** semi-precious stone; **pietra preziosa** precious stone; **pietra dello scandalo** cause of the scandal

pie'traia *f* scree

pie'trame *m* stones *pl*

pietrifi'care *vt* petrify

pie'trina *f* (di accendino) flint

pie'troso *adj* stony

'piffero *m* fife

pigi'ama *m* pyjamas *pl*, pajamas AmE

'pigia 'pigia *m inv* crowd, crush

pigi'are *vt* press

pigia'trice *f* wine press

pigi'one *f* rent; **dare a ~** let, rent out; **prendere a ~** rent

pigli'are *vt* infml (afferrare) catch

'piglio *m* air

pig'mento *m* pigment

pig'meo, -a *adj & nmf* pygmy

'pigna *f* cone
■ **pigna di abete** fir cone

pi'gnolo *adj* pedantic

pignora'mento *m* Jur distraint

pigno'rare *vt* Jur distrain upon

pigo'lare *vi* chirp

pigo'lio *m* chirping

pigra'mente *adv* lazily

pi'grizia *f* laziness

'pigro *adj* lazy; (intelletto) slow

PIL *abbr* (**prodotto interno lordo**) GDP

'pila *f* pile; Electr battery; infml (lampadina tascabile) torch; (vasca) basin; **a pile** battery operated, battery powered

pi'lastro *m* pillar

'pillola *f* pill; **prendere la ~** be on the pill
■ **pillola del giorno dopo** morning-after pill

pi'lone *m* pylon; (di ponte) pier

pi'lota **A** *mf* pilot; Auto driver

key word

■ **pilota automatico** automatic pilot; **pilota di caccia** fighter pilot
B *adj inv* **progetto** ~ pilot project
pilo'taggio *m* flying; **cabina di** ~ flight deck
pilo'tare *vt* pilot; drive ‹*auto*›
pinaco'teca *f* art gallery
'Pinco Pal'lino *m* so-and-so
pi'neta *f* pine-wood
ping-'pong *m* table tennis, ping-pong infml
'pingue *adj* fat
pingu'edine *f* fatness
pingu'ino *m* penguin; (gelato) choc ice on a stick
'pinna *f* fin; (per nuotare) flipper
pin'nacolo *m* pinnacle
'pino *m* pine tree
■ **pino marittimo** cluster pine, maritime pine
pi'nolo *m* pine kernel
'pinta *f* pint
pin-'up *f inv* pin-up [girl]
'pinza *f* pliers *pl*; Med forceps *pl*; **prendere qualcosa con le pinze** fig treat something cautiously
pin'zare *vt* (con pinzatrice) staple
pinza'trice *f* stapler
pin'zette *fpl* tweezers
pinzi'monio *m sauce for crudités*
'pio *adj* pious; (benefico) charitable
piogge'rella *f* drizzle
pi'oggia *f* rain; fig (di pietre, insulti) hail, shower; **sotto la** ~ in the rain
■ **pioggia acida** acid rain; **pioggia radioattiva** radioactive fallout
pi'olo *m* (di scala) rung
piom'bare A *vi* fall heavily; ~ **su** fall upon; ~ **all'improvviso nella stanza** suddenly burst into the room
B *vt* ~ **qualcuno nella disperazione** plunge somebody into despair
piom'bino *m* (sigillo) [lead] seal; (da pesca) sinker; (in tende) weight
pi'ombo *m* lead; (sigillo) [lead] seal; **a** ~ plumb; **senza** ~ (benzina) lead-free; **avere un sonno di** ~ be a very heavy sleeper; **andare con i piedi di** ~ tread carefully; **anni di** ~ *years when terrorism was at its height*
pioni'ere, -a *mf* pioneer
pi'oppo *m* poplar
pior'rea *f* pyorrhoea
pio'vano *adj* **acqua piovana** rainwater
pi'overe *vi* rain; ~ it's raining; ~ **addosso a qualcuno** (guai, debiti) rain down on somebody; **[su questo] non ci piove** infml that's for sure
pioviggi'nare *vi* drizzle
pio'voso *adj* rainy
pi'ovra *f* octopus
pio'vuto *adj* ~ **dal cielo** fallen into one's lap
'pipa *f* pipe
pipe'rito *adj* **menta piperita** peppermint
pipì *f inv* **fare [la]** ~ pee, piddle; **andare a fare [la]** ~ go for a pee
pipi'strello *m* bat
piqué *m inv* piqué
'pira *f* pyre
pi'ramide *f* pyramid
pi'ranha *m inv* piranha
pi'rata A *m* pirate
■ **pirata dell'aria** skyjacker; **pirata della strada** hit-and-run driver; (prepotente) road hog
B *adj inv* pirate
pirate'ria *f* piracy
■ **pirateria informatica** software piracy
pi'rite *f* pyrite
piro'etta *f* pirouette
pi'rofila *f* (tegame) oven-proof dish
pi'rofilo *adj* heat-resistant
pi'romane *mf* pyromaniac
piroma'nia *f* pyromania
pi'roscafo *m* steamer
■ **piroscafo di linea** liner
'piscia *f* vulg piss
pisci'are *vi* vulg piss
pisci'ata *f* vulg piss
pi'scina *f* [swimming] pool
■ **piscina coperta** indoor [swimming] pool; **piscina gonfiabile** [inflatable] paddling pool; **piscina olimpionica** Olympic [swimming] pool; **piscina per il parto** birthing pool; **piscina scoperta** outdoor [swimming] pool, lido
pi'sello *m* pea; infml (pene) willie; **piselli** *pl* **odorosi** sweet peas
piso'lino *m* nap; **fare un** ~ have a nap
'pista *f* track; Aeron runway, tarmac; (orma) footprint; (sci) slope, piste
■ **pista d'atterraggio** runway; **pista da ballo** dance floor; **pista ciclabile** cycle track; **pista da fondo** cross-country ski track; **pista di pattinaggio** ice rink; **pista per principianti** nursery slope; **pista da sci** ski slope, ski run, piste; **pista per slitte** toboggan run
pi'stacchio *m* pistachio
pi'stola *f* pistol; (per spruzzare) spray gun
■ **pistola a capsule** cap gun; **pistola a spruzzo** paint spray; **pistola a tamburo** revolver
pisto'lero *m* gunslinger
pi'stone *m* piston
'pitbull *m inv* pit bull (terrier)
pi'tocco *m* miser
pi'tone *m* python
pitto'gramma *m* pictogram
pit|'tore, -trice *mf* painter
pitto'resco *adj* picturesque
pit'torico *adj* pictorial
pit'tura *f* painting; **pitture** *pl* **di guerra** warpaint
■ **pittura a guazzo** poster paint; **pittura rupestre** cave painting
pittu'rare *vt* paint

P

pitui'tario *adj* pituitary

più **A** *adv* more; (superlativo) most; Math plus; **~ importante** more important; **il ~ importante** the most important; **~ caro/grande** dearer/bigger; **il ~ caro/grande** the dearest/biggest; **di ~** more; **una coperta in ~** an extra blanket; **non ho ~ soldi** I don't have any more money; **non vive ~ a Milano** he no longer lives in Milan; **~ o meno** more or less; **il ~ lentamente possible** as slowly as possible; **al ~ presto** as soon as possible; **per di ~** what's more; **mai ~!** never again!; **~ di** more than; **sempre ~** more and more
B *adj* more; (superlativo) most; **~ tempo** more time; **la classe con ~ alunni** the class with most pupils; **~ volte** several times
C *m* most; Math plus sign; **il ~ è fatto** the worst is over; **parlare del ~ e del meno** make small talk; **i ~** the majority

piuccheper'fetto *m* pluperfect

pi'uma *f* feather

piu'maggio *m* plumage

piu'mato *adj* plumed

piu'mino *m* (di cigni) down; (copriletto) eiderdown; (per cipria) powder-puff; (per spolverare) feather duster; (giacca) down jacket

piu'mone® *m* duvet, continental quilt

piut'tosto *adv* rather; (invece) instead

'piva *f* **con le pive nel sacco** empty-handed

pi'vello *m* infml greenhorn

pi'vot *m inv* (in pallacanestro) centre

'pizza *f* pizza; Cinema reel; infml (noia) bore
■ **pizza margherita** *tomato and mozzarella pizza*; **pizza marinara** *pizza with tomato, oregano, garlic and anchovies*; **pizza napoletana** *pizza with tomato, mozzarella and anchovies*; **pizza quattro stagioni** *pizza with tomato, mozzarella, ham, mushrooms and artichokes*

pizzai'ola alla ~ *adj* with tomatoes, garlic, and oregano

pizze'ria *f* pizza restaurant, pizzeria

piz'zetta *f* small pizza

piz'zetto *m* (barba) goatee

pizzi'care **A** *vt* pinch; (pungere) sting; (di sapore) taste sharp; infml (sorprendere) catch; Mus pluck
B *vi* scratch; ‹*cibo*› be spicy

'pizzico, pizzi'cotto *m* pinch

'pizzo *m* lace; (di montagna) peak

pla'care *vt* placate; assuage ‹*fame, dolore*›

pla'carsi *vr* calm down

'placca *f* plate; (commemorativa, dentale) plaque; Med patch
■ **placca batterica** plaque

plac'care *vt* plate

plac'cato *adj* **~ d'argento** silver-plated; **~ d'oro** gold-plated

placca'tura *f* plating

pla'cebo *m inv* placebo; **effetto ~** placebo effect

pla'centa *f* placenta, afterbirth

'placido *adj* placid

pla'fond *m inv* Comm ceiling

plafoni'era *f* ceiling light

plagi'are *vt* plagiarize; pressure ‹*persona*›

'plagio *m* plagiarism

plaid *m inv* tartan rug

pla'nare *vi* glide

'plancia *f* Naut bridge; (passerella) gangplank

'plancton *m* plankton

plane'tario **A** *adj* planetary
B *m* planetarium

pla'smare *vt* mould

'plastica *f* (materia) plastic; Med plastic surgery; (arte) plastic art; **sacchetto di ~** plastic bag

'plastico **A** *adj* plastic; (rappresentazione) three-dimensional
B *m* plastic model

'platano *m* plane tree

pla'tea *f* stalls *pl* (pubblico) audience

'platino *m* platinum

pla'tonico *adj* platonic

plau'sibile *adj* plausible; **poco ~** implausible

plausibilità *f inv* plausibility

'plauso *m* (consenso) approval

play'back *m* **cantare in ~** mime

play'boy *m inv* playboy

play'maker *m inv* Sport playmaker

p.le *abbr* (**piazzale**) Sq

ple'baglia *f* derog mob

'plebe *f* common people

ple'beo, -a *adj & nmf* plebeian

plebi'scito *m* plebiscite

ple'nario *adj* plenary

pleni'lunio *m* full moon

'plettro *m* plectrum

pleu'rite *f* pleurisy

'plico *m* packet; **in ~ a parte** under separate cover

plissé *adj inv* plissé; (gonna) accordion pleated

plop *m inv* plop; **fare ~** plop

plo'tone *m* platoon; (di ciclisti) group
■ **plotone d'esecuzione** firing squad

'plotter *m inv* Comput plotter
■ **plotter da tavolo** flatbed plotter

'plumbeo *adj* leaden

plum-'cake *m inv* fruit cake

plu'rale *adj & nm* plural; **al ~** in the plural

pluralità *f inv* (maggioranza) majority

pluridisciplì'nare *adj* multidisciplinary

plurien'nale *adj* **~ esperienza** many years' experience

plurigemel'lare *adj* (parto) multiple

plurìpar'titico *adj* Pol multi-party

key word

Plu'tone *m* Pluto
plu'tonio *m* plutonium
pluvi'ale *adj* rain *attrib*
pluvi'ometro *m* rain gauge
pneu'matico **A** *adj* pneumatic
B *m* tyre
■ **pneumatico radiale** radial [tyre]
pneu'monia *f* pneumonia
PNL *abbr* (**prodotto nazionale lordo**) GNP
Po *m* Po
po' ▶ **poco**
po'chette *f inv* clutch bag
po'chino *m* **un ~** a little bit
'poco **A** *adj* little; (tempo) short; (con nomi plurali) few
B *pron* little; (poco tempo) a short time; (plurale) few
C *m* little; **un po'** a little [bit]; **un po' di** a little, some; (con nomi plurali) a few; **a ~ a ~** little by little; **fra ~** soon; **per ~** (a poco prezzo) cheap; (quasi) nearly; **~ fa** a little while ago; **sono arrivato da ~** I have just arrived; **un bel po'** quite a lot; **un bel po' di più/meno** quite a lot more/less; **un ~ di buono** a shady character
D *adv* (con verbi) not much; (con avverbi, aggettivi) not very; **parla ~** he doesn't speak much; **lo conosco ~** I don't know him very well; **~ spesso** not very often
po'dere *m* farm
pode'roso *adj* powerful
'podio *m* dais; Mus podium
po'dismo *m* walking
po'dista *mf* walker
po'ema *m* poem
■ **poema epico** epic [poem]; **poema sinfonico** symphonic poem
poe'sia *f* poetry; (componimento) poem
po'eta *m* poet
poe'tessa *f* poetess
po'etico *adj* poetic
poggiapi'edi *m inv* footrest
poggi'are **A** *vt* lean; (posare) place
B *vi* **~ su** be based on
poggia'testa *m inv* head-rest
'poggio *m* hillock
poggi'olo *m* balcony
'poi **A** *adv* (dopo) then; (più tardi) later [on]; (finalmente) finally; **d'ora in ~** from now on; **questa ~!** well!
B *m* **pensare al ~** think of the future
poiché *conj* since
pois *m inv* **a ~** polka-dot
'poker *m* poker
po'lacco, -a **A** *adj* Polish
B *mf* Pole
C *m* (lingua) Polish
po'lare *adj* polar
polarità *f inv* polarity
polariz'zare *vt* polarize
pola'roid® *f inv* instant camera
'polca *f* polka
po'lemica *f* controversy
polemica'mente *adv* controversially
polemiciz'zare *vi* engage in controversy
po'lemico *adj* controversial
po'lenta *f cornmeal porridge*
poli'clinico *m* general hospital
policro'mia *f* polychromy
po'licromo *adj* polychrome
poli'estere *m* polyester
polieti'lene *m* polyethylene
poliga'mia *f* polygamy
poli'gamico *adj* polygamous
po'ligamo *adj* polygamous
poli'glotta *mf* polyglot
po'ligono *m* polygon; (di tiro) rifle range
po'limero *m* polymer
Poli'nesia *f* Polynesia
polinesi'ano *adj & nmf* Polynesian
'polio[mie'lite] *f* polio[myelitis]
'polipo *m* polyp
polisti'rolo *m* polystyrene
poli'tecnico *m* polytechnic
po'litica *f* politics *sg*; (linea di condotta) policy; **fare ~** be in politics; **darsi alla ~** go into politics
■ **politica energetica** energy policy; **politica estera** foreign policy; **politica monetaria** monetary policy
politica'mente *adv* politically; **~ corretto** politically correct, pc
politi'chese *m* political jargon
politiciz'zare *vt* politicize
po'litico, -a **A** *adj* political
B *mf* politician
poliva'lente *adj* all-purpose
poli'zia *f* police, police force
■ **polizia giudiziaria** Criminal Investigation Department, CID; **polizia scientifica** forensics; **polizia stradale** traffic police
polizi'esco *adj* police *attrib*; (romanzo, film) detective *attrib*
polizi'otto **A** *m* policeman
■ **poliziotto in borghese** plain clothes policeman; **poliziotto privato** private detective
B *adj* police *attrib*
'polizza *f* policy
■ **polizza di assicurazione** insurance policy
pol'laio *m* chicken run; infml (luogo chiassoso) mad house
pol'lame *m* poultry
polla'strella *f* spring chicken; fig fam bird
polla'strello *m* spring chicken
pol'lastro *m* cockerel
polle'ria *f* poultry butcher, poulterer
'pollice *m* thumb; (unità di misura) inch

ˈ**polline** *m* pollen; **allergia al ~** hay fever
polliˈvendolo, -a *mf* poulterer
ˈ**pollo** *m* chicken; infml (semplicione) simpleton; **far ridere i polli** be ridiculous
■ **pollo allevato a terra** free-range chicken; **pollo arrosto** roast chicken; **pollo di batteria** battery chicken; **pollo alla cacciatora** chicken chasseur
polmoˈnare *adj* pulmonary
polˈmone *m* lung
■ **polmone d'acciaio** iron lung
polmoˈnite *f* pneumonia
ˈ**polo** *m* pole; Sport polo; (maglietta) polo top; Pol party; (conservatori) Italian Conservatives
■ **polo magnetico** magnetic pole; **polo nord** North Pole; **polo sud** South Pole
Poˈlonia *f* Poland
ˈ**polpa** *f* pulp
polˈpaccio *m* calf
polpaˈstrello *m* fingertip
polˈpetta *f* meatball
polpetˈtone *m* meat loaf
■ **polpettone sentimentale** infml hokum
ˈ**polpo** *m* octopus
polˈposo *adj* fleshy
polˈsino *m* cuff
ˈ**polso** *m* pulse; Anat wrist; fig authority; **avere ~** be strict; **essere privo di ~** be soft
polˈtiglia *f* mush
polˈtrire *vi* lie around
⚷ **polˈtrona** *f* armchair; Theat seat in the stalls
polˈtrone *adj* lazy
⚷ ˈ**polvere** *f* dust; (sostanza polverizzata) powder; **in ~** powdered; **sapone in ~** soap powder
■ **polvere da sparo** gun powder

p

polveriˈera *f* gunpowder magazine; fig tinderbox
polveˈrina *f* (medicina) powder
polverizˈzare *vt* pulverize; (nebulizzare) atomize; smash, shatter ‹*record*›; **~ qualcuno** pulverize somebody
polveˈrone *m* cloud of dust
polveˈroso *adj* dusty
poˈmata *f* ointment, cream
■ **pomata cicatrizzante** healing cream for cuts
pomelˈlato *adj* dappled
poˈmello *m* knob; (guancia) cheek
pomeridiˈano *adj* afternoon *attrib*; **alle tre pomeridiane** at three in the afternoon, at three p.m.
⚷ **pomeˈriggio** *m* afternoon; **buon ~!** have a good afternoon!; **oggi ~** this afternoon; **questo ~** this afternoon
ˈ**pomice** *f* pumice
pomiciˈare *vi* infml snog, neck
pomiciˈata *f* infml snogging, necking
ˈ**pomo** *m* (oggetto) knob
■ **pomo d'Adamo** Adam's apple
⚷ **pomoˈdoro** *m* tomato
ˈ**pompa** *f* pump; (sfarzo) pomp
■ **pompa della benzina** petrol pump, gas pump AmE; **pompe** *pl* **funebri** (funzione) funeral
pomˈpare *vt* pump; (gonfiare d'aria) pump up; fig (esagerare) exaggerate; **~ fuori** pump out
pompeiˈano, -a *adj & nmf* Pompeian
pomˈpelmo *m* grapefruit
pompiˈere *m* fireman; **i pompieri** the fire brigade
pomˈpon *m inv* pompom
pomˈposo *adj* pompous
ˈ**poncho** *m inv* poncho
pondeˈrare *vt* ponder
pondeˈroso *adj* ponderous
poˈnente *m* west
⚷ ˈ**ponte** *m* bridge; Naut deck; (impalcatura) scaffolding; **fare il ~** fig make a long weekend of it; **governo ~** interim government; **legge ~** interim *or* bridging law
■ **ponte aereo** airlift; **ponte auto** car deck; **ponte di coperta** main deck; **ponte levatoio** drawbridge; **ponte radio** radio link; **ponte dei Sospiri** Bridge of Sighs; **ponte di volo** flight deck
ponˈtefice *m* pontiff
pontifiˈcare *vi* pontificate
pontifiˈcato *m* pontificate
pontiˈficio *adj* papal
ponˈtile *m* jetty
ˈ**pony** *m inv* pony
■ **pony express** express delivery service
pool *m inv* Comm consortium; (di giornalisti) team; (di esperti) pool, team
■ **~ genico** gene pool
popˈcorn *m inv* popcorn
ˈ**popelin** *m* poplin
popò¹ *f inv* infml pooh
popò² *m inv* infml bot, bum
popoˈlano *adj* of the [common] people
popoˈlare **A** *adj* popular; (comune) common **B** *vt* populate; **essere popolato da** (pieno di) be full of
popolarità *f inv* popularity
popoˈlarsi *vr* get crowded
popolaziˈone *f* population
⚷ ˈ**popolo** *m* people
popoˈloso *adj* populous
ˈ**poppa** *f* Naut stern; (mammella) breast; **a ~** astern
popˈpare *vt* suck
popˈpata *f* (pasto) feed
poppaˈtoio *m* feeding bottle
popuˈlista *mf* populist
porˈcaio *f* anche fig pigsty; **fare un ~** infml make a mess
porˈcata *f* load of rubbish; **porcate** *pl* infml (cibo) junk food; **fare una ~ a qualcuno** play

⚷ key word

a dirty trick on somebody
porcel'lana *f* porcelain, china
■ **porcellana fine** bone china
porcel'lino *m* piglet
■ **porcellino d'India** guinea pig
porche'ria *f* dirt; fig (cosa orrenda) piece of filth; infml (robaccia) rubbish
por'chetta *f* roast sucking pig
por'cile *m* pigsty
por'cino **A** *adj* pig *attrib*
B *m* (fungo) cep (*edible mushroom*)
'porco *m* pig; (carne) pork
porco'spino *m* porcupine
'porfido *m* porphyry
'porgere *vt* give; (offrire) offer; ~ **orecchio** lend an ear; **porgo distinti saluti** (in lettera) I remain, yours sincerely
'porno *adj inv* porn
pornogra'fia *f* pornography
porno'grafico *adj* pornographic
'poro *m* pore
po'roso *adj* porous
'porpora *f* purple
'porre *vt* put; (collocare) place; (supporre) suppose; ask ‹*domanda*›; present ‹*candidatura*›; ~ **una domanda a qualcuno** ask somebody a question; **poniamo [il caso] che...** let us suppose that...; ~ **fine** *o* **termine a** put an end to
'porro *m* Bot leek; (verruca) wart
'porsi *vr* put oneself; ~ **a sedere** sit down; ~ **in cammino** set out
'porta *f* door; Sport goal; (di città) gate; Comput port; ~ **a** ~ door-to-door; **mettere alla** ~ show somebody the door; **a porte chiuse** (riunione, processo) behind closed doors, in camera; **essere alle porte** (vicino) be on the doorstep
■ **porta a due battenti** double door[s]; **porta d'ingresso** front door; **porta parallela** Comput parallel port; **porta seriale** Comput serial port; **porta di servizio** tradesman's entrance; **porta di sicurezza** emergency exit; **porta per la stampante** Comput printer port; **porta a vento** swing door
portaba'gagli *m inv* (facchino) porter; (di treno ecc.) luggage rack; Auto boot, trunk AmE; (sul tetto di un'auto) roof rack
portabandi'era *mf inv* standard-bearer
portabici'clette *m inv* cycle rack
portabot'tiglie *m inv* bottle rack, wine rack
porta'burro *m inv* butter dish
porta'cenere *m inv* ashtray
portachi'avi *m inv* key ring
porta'cipria *m inv* compact
portacon'tainer *m inv* container truck
portadocu'menti *m inv* document wallet
porta'erei *f inv* aircraft carrier
portafi'nestra *f* French window
porta'foglio *m* wallet; (per documenti) portfolio; (ministero) ministry; **a** ~ ‹*gonna*› wrap-over
portafor'tuna **A** *m inv* lucky charm
B *adj inv* lucky
portagi'oie *m inv* jewellery box
por'tale *m* door; Comput portal
portama'tite *m inv* pencil case
porta'mento *m* carriage; (condotta) behaviour
porta'mina *m inv* propelling pencil
portamo'nete *m inv* purse
por'tante *adj* bearing *attrib*
portan'tina *f* sedan chair
portaom'brelli *m inv* umbrella stand
porta'pacchi *m inv* roof rack; (su bicicletta) luggage rack
porta'penne *m inv* pencil case
por'tare *vt* (verso chi parla) bring; (lontano da chi parla) take; (sorreggere) Math carry; (condurre) lead; (indossare) wear; (avere) bear; ~ **a spasso il cane** take the dog for a walk; ~ **a termine** bring to a close; ~ **avanti** carry on; ~ **bene/male** bring good/bad luck; ~ **bene/male gli anni** look young/old for one's age; ~ **fortuna** be lucky; ~ **rancore** bear a grudge; ~ **via** take away
portari'viste *m inv* magazine rack
por'tarsi *vr* (trasferirsi) move; (comportarsi) behave
porta'sci *m inv* ski rack
portasciuga'mano *m* towel rail
portasiga'rette *m inv* cigarette case
porta'spilli *m inv* pin-cushion
por'tata *f* (di pranzo) course; Auto carrying capacity; (di arma) range; fig (abilità) capability; **a** ~ **di mano** within reach; **alla** ~ **di tutti** accessible to all; (finanziariamente) within everybody's reach; **di grande** ~ (scoperta) with far-reaching consequences
por'tatile **A** *adj*, portable
B *m* Comput laptop
por'tato *adj* (indumento) worn; (dotato) gifted; **essere** ~ **per qualcosa** have a gift for something; **essere** ~ **a** (tendere a) be inclined to
porta|'tore, -trice *mf* bearer; **al** ~ to the bearer
■ **portatore di handicap** disabled person
portatovagli'olo *m* napkin ring
portau'ovo *m inv* egg cup
porta'voce *mf inv* spokesperson
por'tello *m* hatch
■ **portello di sicurezza** escape hatch
por'tento *m* marvel; (persona dotata) prodigy
porten'toso *adj* wonderful
port'folio *m inv* (di fotografie ecc.) portfolio
porti'cato *m* portico
'portico *m* portico
porti'era *f* door; (tendaggio) door curtain

porti'ere *m* porter, doorman; Sport goalkeeper
■ **portiere di notte** night porter
porti'naio, -a *mf* caretaker, concierge
portine'ria *f* concierge's room; (di ospedale) porter's lodge
⚷ **'porto** **A** pp di **porgere**
B *m* harbour; (complesso) port; (vino) port [wine]; (spesa di trasporto) carriage; **andare in ~** succeed
■ **porto d'armi** gun licence; **porto container** container port; **porto fluviale** river port; **porto franco** free port; **porto marittimo** seaport
Porto'gallo *m* Portugal
porto'ghese *adj & nmf* Portuguese
por'tone *m* main door
portori'cano, -a *adj & nmf* Puerto Rican
Porto'rico *m* Puerto Rico
portu'ale *m* dock worker, docker
porzi'one *f* portion
'posa *f* laying; (riposo) rest; Phot exposure; (atteggiamento) pose; **mettersi in ~** pose; **senza ~** without rest
⚷ **po'sare** **A** *vt* put; (giù) put [down]
B *vi* (poggiare) rest; (per un ritratto) pose
po'sarsi *vr* alight; (sostare) rest; Aeron land
po'sata *f* piece of cutlery; **posate** *pl* cutlery *sg*, flatware *sg* AmE
po'sato *adj* sedate
po'scritto *m* postscript
posi'tivo *adj* positive
posizio'nare *vt* position
⚷ **posizi'one** *f* position; **farsi una ~** get ahead; **prendere ~** take a stand
posolo'gia *f* dosage
po'sporre *vt* place after; (posticipare) postpone
po'sposto pp di **posporre**
⚷ **posse'dere** *vt* possess, own
possedi'mento *m* possession
posses'sivo *adj* possessive
pos'sesso *m* possession, ownership; (bene) possession; **entrare in ~ di** come into possession of; **essere in ~ di** be in possession of; **prendere ~ di** take possession of
posses'sore *m* owner
⚷ **pos'sibile** **A** *adj* possible; **il più presto ~** as soon as possible
B *m* **fare [tutto] il ~** do one's best
⚷ **possibilità** **A** *f inv* possibility; (occasione) chance; **avere la ~ di fare qualcosa** have the chance *or* opportunity to do something
B *fpl* (mezzi) means
possi'dente *mf* land owner
'posso ▸ **potere**
⚷ **'posta** *f* post, mail; (ufficio postale) post office; (al gioco) stake; **spese di ~** postage; **per ~** by post, by mail; **la ~ in gioco è...** fig what's at stake is...; **a bella ~** on purpose; **Poste e Telecomunicazioni** [Italian] Post Office
■ **posta aerea** airmail; **posta centrale** main post office, central post office; **posta del cuore** agony column; **posta elettronica** electronic mail, e-mail; **spedire per ~ elettronica** email; **posta elettronica vocale** voicemail; **posta in arrivo** inbox; **posta prioritaria** first-class mail
posta'giro *m* postal giro
po'stale *adj* postal
po'stare *vt* Comput (in un blog, su un social network) post
postazi'one *f* position; Mil emplacement
post'bellico *adj* post-war
postda'tare *vt* post-date ‹*assegno*›
posteggi'are *vt & vi* park
posteggia|'tore, -trice *mf* parking attendant
po'steggio *m* car park, parking lot AmE; (di taxi) taxi rank
'posteri *mpl* descendants
posteri'ore **A** *adj* back *attrib*, rear *attrib*; (nel tempo) later
B *m* infml posterior; behind
posterità *f inv* posterity
po'sticcio **A** *adj* artificial; (baffi, barba) false
B *m* hair-piece
postici'pare *vt* postpone
po'stilla *f* note; Jur rider
⚷ **po'stino** *m* postman, mailman AmE
postmo'derno *adj* postmodern
'posto **A** pp di **porre**
B *m* place; (spazio) room; (impiego) job; Mil post; (sedile) seat; **a/fuori ~** in/out of place; **prendere ~** take up room; **sul ~** on-site; **essere a ~** ‹*casa, libri*› be tidy; **non grazie, sono a ~** no thanks, I'm all right; **mettere a ~** tidy ‹*stanza*›; **fare ~ a** make room for; **al ~ di** (invece di) in place of, instead of
■ **posto di blocco** checkpoint; **posto di guardia** guard post; **posto di guida** driving seat; **posto di lavoro** job; Comput workstation; **posti** *pl* **in piedi** standing room; **posto di polizia** police station; **posti** *pl* **a sedere** seating, seats
post-'partum *adj* post-natal
'postumo **A** *adj* posthumous
B *m* after-effect; **postumi** *pl* **della sbornia** hangover
po'tabile *adj* drinkable; **acqua ~** drinking water; **non ~** undrinkable
po'tare *vt* prune
po'tassa *f* potash
po'tassio *m* potassium
⚷ **po'tente** *adj* powerful; (efficace) potent
⚷ **po'tenza** *f* power; (efficacia) potency
■ **potenza mondiale** world power; **potenza nucleare** nuclear power
potenzi'ale *adj & nm* potential
⚷ **po'tere** **A** *m* power; **al ~** in power
■ **potere d'acquisto** purchasing power,

⚷ key word

spending power; **il quarto potere** the fourth estate
B *vi* can, be able to; **posso entrare?** can I come in?; (formale) may I come in?; **mi spiace, non posso venire alla festa** I'm sorry, I can't come to the party *or* I won't be able to come to the party; **posso fare qualche cosa?** can I do something?; **che tu possa essere felice!** may you be happy!; **non ne posso più** (sono stanco) I can't go on; (sono stufo) I can't take any more; **può darsi** perhaps; **può darsi che sia vero** perhaps it's true; **potrebbe aver ragione** he could be right, he might be right; **avresti potuto telefonare** you could have phoned, you might have phoned; **spero di poter venire** I hope to be able to come; **senza poter telefonare** without being able to phone; **spero che potremo incontrarci presto** I hope we can meet soon

potestà *f inv* power

pot-pour'ri *m inv* medley

⚷ **'povero, -a** **A** *adj* poor; (semplice) plain; **~ di** (paese, terreno) lacking in; **in parole povere** in a few words
B *f* poor woman
C *m* poor man; **i poveri** the poor

povertà *f inv* poverty

pozi'one *f* potion

'pozza *f* pool

poz'zanghera *f* puddle

⚷ **'pozzo** *m* well; (minerario) pit
■ **pozzo petrolifero** oil well; **pozzo di petrolio** oil well; **pozzo di ventilazione** air shaft

pp. *abbr* (**pagine**) pp

PP.TT. *abbr* (**Poste e Telecomunicazioni**) [Italian] Post Office

PR *fpl abbr* PR

'Praga *f* Prague

prag'matico *adj* pragmatic

prali'nato *adj* (mandorla, gelato) praline-coated

pram'matica *f* **essere di ~** be customary

pranotera'pia *f* laying on of hands

pran'zare *vi* dine; (a mezzogiorno) lunch

⚷ **'pranzo** *m* dinner; (a mezzogiorno) lunch
■ **pranzo di lavoro** business lunch, working lunch; **pranzo della mensa scolastica** school lunch; **pranzo di nozze** wedding breakfast

'prassi *f* standard procedure

prate'ria *f* grassland, prairie

⚷ **'pratica** *f* practice; (esperienza) experience; (documentazione) file; **avere ~ di qualcosa** be familiar with something, have experience of something; **mettere qualcosa in ~** put something into practice; **far ~** gain experience; **fare le pratiche per** gather the necessary papers for

prati'cabile *adj* practicable; (strada) passable

pratica'mente *adv* practically

prati'cante *mf* apprentice; Relig [regular] churchgoer

prati'care *vt* practise; (frequentare) associate with; (fare) make

praticità *f inv* practicality

⚷ **'pratico** *adj* practical; (esperto) experienced, knowledgeable; (comodo) convenient; **essere ~ di qualcosa** know about something; **all'atto ~** in practice

⚷ **'prato** *m* meadow; (di giardino) lawn
■ **prato all'inglese** lawn

preaccensi'one *f* Auto pre-ignition

pre'ambolo *m* preamble

preannunci'are *vt* give advance notice of

prean'nuncio *m* advance notice

preavvi'sare *vt* forewarn

preav'viso *m* warning

precari'cato *adj* preloaded

precarietà *f inv* frailty

pre'cario *adj* precarious

precauzi'one *f* precaution; (cautela) care

⚷ **prece'dente** **A** *adj* previous
B *m* precedent; **avere dei precedenti penali** have a police record; **senza precedenti** (successo) unprecedented

precedente'mente *adv* previously

prece'denza *f* precedence; (di veicoli) right of way; **dare la ~ a** give priority to; Auto give way to; **avere la ~** have priority; Auto have right of way; **~ assoluta** top priority

⚷ **pre'cedere** *vt* precede

pre'cetto *m* precept

precet|'tore, -trice *mf* tutor

⚷ **precipi'tare** **A** *vt* **~ le cose** precipitate events; **~ qualcuno nella disperazione** cast somebody into a state of despair
B *vi* fall headlong; (situazione, eventi) come to a head

precipi'tarsi *vr* (gettarsi) throw oneself; (affrettarsi) rush; **~ a fare qualcosa** rush to do something

precipitazi'one *f* (fretta) haste; (atmosferica) precipitation

precipi'toso *adj* hasty; (avventato) reckless; (caduta) headlong

preci'pizio *m* precipice; **a ~** headlong

preci'sabile *adj* specifiable

precisa'mente *adv* precisely

preci'sare *vt* specify; (spiegare) clarify; **ci tengo a ~ che...** I want to make the point that...

precisazi'one *f* clarification

precisi'one *f* precision

⚷ **pre'ciso** *adj* precise; (calcolo, risposta) accurate; (ore) sharp; (identico) identical

pre'cludere *vt* preclude

pre'cludersi *vr* **~ ogni possibilità** preclude every possibility

pre'cluso pp di **precludere**

pre'coce *adj* precocious; (prematuro) premature

precocità *f inv* precociousness

P

precon'cetto **A** *adj* preconceived
B *m* prejudice
preconfezio'nato *adj* pre-packed
preconfigu'rato *adj* preconfigured
pre'correre *vt* (anticipare) anticipate; **~ i tempi** be ahead of one's time
precorri|'tore, -trice *mf* precursor, forerunner
pre'cotto *adj* ready-cooked
■ **precotto e surgelato** cook-chill
precur'sore *m* forerunner, precursor
'preda *f* prey; (bottino) booty; **essere in ~ al panico** be panic-stricken; **in ~ alle fiamme** engulfed in flames
pre'dare *vt* plunder
preda'tore *m* predator
predeces'sore *mf* predecessor
pre'della *f* platform
predel'lino *m* step
predesti'nare *vt* predestine
predesti'nato *adj* predestined, preordained
predestinazi'one *f* predestination
predetermi'nare *vt* predetermine
predetermi'nato *adj* predetermined, preordained
pre'detto pp di **predire**
'predica *f* sermon; fig lecture
predi'care *vt* preach
predi'cato *m* predicate
predige'rito *adj* predigested
predi'letto, -a **A** pp di **prediligere**
B *adj* favourite
C *mf* pet infml
predilezi'one *f* predilection; **avere una ~ per** have a predilection for, be partial to
predi'ligere *vt* prefer
predisposizi'one *f* predisposition; (al disegno ecc.) bent (a for)
pre'dire *vt* foretell
predi'sporre *vt* arrange; **~ qualcuno a qualcosa** Med predispose somebody to something; (preparare) prepare somebody for something
predi'sporsi *vr* **~ a** prepare oneself for
predi'sposto, -a **A** pp di **predisporre**
B *adj* arranged
■ **predisposto per la TV via cavo** cable-ready
predizi'one *f* prediction
predomi'nante *adj* predominant
predomi'nare *vi* predominate
predo'minio *m* predominance
pre'done *m* robber
prefabbri'cato **A** *adj* prefabricated
B *m* prefabricated building
prefazi'one *f* preface
prefe'renza *f* preference; **di ~** preferably
preferenzi'ale *adj* preferential; **corsia ~** bus and taxi lane

⚷ key word

prefe'ribile *adj* preferable
preferibil'mente *adv* preferably
⚷ **prefe'rire** *vt* prefer
prefe'rito, -a *adj & nmf* favourite
pre'fetto *m* prefect
prefet'tura *f* prefecture
pre'figgere *vt* decide in advance, pre-arrange ‹*termine*›
pre'figgersi *vr* **~ uno scopo** set oneself an objective
prefigu'rare *vt* (anticipare) foreshadow
prefinanzia'mento *m* bridging loan
prefis'sare *vt* pre-arrange ‹*data, appuntamento*›
pre'fisso **A** pp di **prefiggere**
B *m* prefix; Teleph [dialling] code
⚷ **pre'gare** **A** *vi* Relig pray
B *vt* Relig pray to; (supplicare) beg; **farsi ~** need persuading; **~ qualcuno di fare qualcosa** ask somebody to do something; **si prega di...** please...; **si prega di non...** please do not...; **si prega di non fumare** please refrain from smoking
pre'gevole *adj* valuable
preghi'era *f* prayer; (richiesta) request
pregi'arsi *vr* **si pregia di non essere mai in ritardo** he prides himself on never being late
pre'giato *adj* esteemed; (prezioso) valuable
'pregio *m* esteem; (valore) value; (di persona) good point; **di ~** valuable
pregiudi'care *vt* prejudice; (danneggiare) harm
pregiudi'cato **A** *adj* prejudiced
B *m* Jur previous offender
pregiu'dizio *m* prejudice; (danno) detriment
pre'gnante *adj* (parola) pregnant, pregnant with meaning
'pregno *adj* (parola) pregnant; (pieno) full; **~ di** (umidità) saturated with; (significato) pregnant with
'prego *int* (non c'è di che) don't mention it!; (per favore) please; **~?** I beg your pardon?; **posso? - ~** may I? - please do
pregu'stare *vt* look forward to
preinstal'lato *adj* pre-installed
prei'storia *f* prehistory
prei'storico *adj* prehistoric
pre'lato *m* prelate
prela'vaggio *m* pre-wash
preleva'mento *m* withdrawal
prele'vare *vt* withdraw ‹*soldi*›; collect ‹*merci*›; Med take
preli'evo *m* (di soldi) withdrawal
■ **prelievo di sangue** blood sample
prelimi'nare **A** *adj* preliminary
B *m* **preliminari** *pl* preliminaries
pre'ludere *vi* **~ a** herald
pre'ludio *m* prelude
prema'man **A** *m inv* maternity dress
B *adj* maternity *attrib*

prematrimoni'ale *adj* premarital

prematura'mente *adv* prematurely

prema'turo, -a **A** *adj* premature **B** *mf* premature baby

premedi'tare *vt* premeditate

premeditazi'one *f* premeditation; **con ~** (omicidio) premeditated

'premere **A** *vt* press; Comput hit ‹*tasto*› **B** *vi* **~ a** (importare) matter to; **mi preme sapere** I need to know; **~ su** press on; push ‹*pulsante*›; fig (fare pressione su) put pressure on, pressure; **~ per ottenere qualcosa** push for something

pre'messa *f* introduction; **senza tante premesse** without further ado

pre'messo (pp di **premettere**) **~ che** bearing in mind that

pre'mettere *vt* (mettere prima) put before; **premetto che...** I want to make it clear first that...; **~ un'introduzione a un libro** put an introduction at the beginning of a book

premi'are *vt* give a prize to; (ricompensare) reward

premi'ato *adj* award-winning

premiazi'one *f* prize giving

premi'nente *adj* pre-eminent

premi'nenza *f* pre-eminence

'premio *m* prize; (ricompensa) reward; (di produzione ecc.) bonus; Fin premium
■ **premio di assicurazione** insurance premium; **premio di consolazione** consolation prize; (ridicolo) booby prize; **premio di ingaggio** Sport signing fee; **premio di produzione** productivity bonus

premoni'tore *adj* ‹*sogno, segno*› premonitory

premonizi'one *f* premonition

premu'nire *vt* fortify

premu'nirsi *vr* take protective measures; **~ di** provide oneself with; **~ contro** protect oneself against

pre'mura *f* (fretta) hurry; (cura) care; **far ~ a qualcuno** hurry somebody up

premu'roso *adj* thoughtful

prena'tale *adj* antenatal

'prendere **A** *vt* take; (afferrare) seize; catch ‹*treno, malattia, ladro, pesce*›; have ‹*cibo, bevanda*›; (far pagare) charge; ‹*assumere*› take on; (ottenere) get; (occupare) take up; (guadagnare) earn; **~ informazioni** make inquiries; **~ in giro qualcuno** pull somebody's leg; **~ a calci/pugni** kick/punch; **che ti prende?** what's got into you?; **quanto prende?** what do you charge?; **~ una persona per un'altra** mistake a person for somebody else; **passare a ~ qualcuno** collect somebody, pick somebody up **B** *vi* (voltare) turn; (attecchire) take root; (rapprendersi) set; ‹*fuoco*› catch, take; **~ a destra/sinistra** turn right/left; **~ a fare qualcosa** start doing something; **la colla non ha preso** the glue didn't take

'prendersi *vr* **~ a pugni** come to blows; **~ cura di** take care of ‹*ammalato*›; **prendersela** take it to heart; **si prende troppo sul serio** he takes himself too seriously

prendi'sole *m* sundress

preno'tare *vt* book, reserve

preno'tarsi *vr* **~ per** put one's name down for

preno'tato *adj* booked, reserved

prenotazi'one *f* booking, reservation
■ **prenotazione di gruppo** group booking

'prensile *adj* prehensile

preoccu'pante *adj* alarming

preoccu'pare *vt* worry

preoccu'parsi *vr* **~** worry (**di** about); **~ di fare qualcosa** take the trouble to do something

preoccu'pato *adj* worried; (apprensivo) concerned

preoccupazi'one *f* worry; (apprensione) concern

preopera'torio *adj* preoperative

prepa'gato, -a **A** *adj* prepaid **B** *m* Teleph pay-as-you-go

prepa'rare *vt* prepare; study for ‹*esame*›; **~ da mangiare** prepare a meal

prepa'rarsi *vr* get ready

prepara'tivi *mpl* preparations

prepa'rato *m* (prodotto) preparation

prepara'torio *adj* preparatory

preparazi'one *f* preparation; (competenza) knowledge

prepensiona'mento *m* early retirement

preponde'rante *adj* predominant, preponderant

preponde'ranza *f* preponderance, prevalence

pre'porre *vt* place before

preposizi'one *f* preposition

pre'posto **A** pp di **preporre** **B** *adj* **~ a** (addetto a) in charge of

prepo'tente **A** *adj* overbearing **B** *mf* bully; **fare il/la ~ con qualcuno** bully somebody

prepo'tenza *f* high-handedness

preprogram'mato *adj* Comput preprogrammed

pre'puzio *m* foreskin, prepuce

preroga'tiva *f* prerogative

'presa *f* taking; (conquista) capture; (stretta) hold; (di cemento ecc.) setting; Electr socket; (di gas, acqua) inlet, connection; (pizzico) pinch; **essere alle prese con** be struggling *or* grappling with; **a ~ rapida** ‹*cemento, colla*› quick setting; **fare ~ su qualcuno** influence somebody
■ **macchina da presa** cine camera; **presa d'aria** air vent; **presa in giro** leg-pull; **presa multipla** adaptor; **presa scart** Scart connector

pre'sagio *m* omen

p

presa'gire *vt* foretell
presa'lario *m* maintenance grant
'**presbite** *adj* long-sighted
presbiteri'ano, -a *adj & nmf* Presbyterian
presbi'terio *m* presbytery
pre'scelto *adj* selected
pre'scindere *vi* ~ **da** leave aside; **a** ~ **da** apart from
presco'lare *adj* pre-school; **in età** ~ pre-school
pre'scritto pp di **prescrivere**
pre'scrivere *vt* prescribe
prescrizi'one *f* prescription; (norma) rule; **cadere in** ~ cease to be valid as a result of the statute of limitations
preselezi'one *f* preliminary selection; (per il traffico) advance lane markings; Sport [qualifying] heats *pl*
⚷ **presen'tare** *vt* present; (far conoscere) introduce; show ‹*documento*›; (inoltrare) submit
presen'tarsi *vr* present oneself; (farsi conoscere) introduce oneself; (a ufficio) attend; (alla polizia ecc.) report; (come candidato) stand, run (**a** for); ‹*occasione*› occur; ~ **bene/male** ‹*persona*› make a good/ bad impression; ‹*situazione*› look good/bad
presenta|'tore, -trice *mf* presenter; (di notiziario) announcer
■ **presentatore di talk show** chat show host
presentazi'one *f* presentation; (per conoscersi) introduction; **fare le presentazioni** do the introductions; **dietro** ~ **di ricetta medica** on doctor's prescription only
⚷ **pre'sente** **A** *adj* present; (attuale) current; (questo) this; **aver** ~ remember
B *m* present; **i presenti** those present
C *f* **allegato alla** ~ (in lettera) enclosed
presenti'mento *m* foreboding
⚷ **pre'senza** *f* presence; (aspetto) appearance; **in** ~ **di, alla** ~ **di** in the presence of; **di bella** ~ personable
■ **presenza di spirito** presence of mind
presenzi'are *vi* ~ **a** attend
pre'sepe, pre'sepio *m* crib
preser'vare *vt* preserve; (proteggere) protect (**da** from)
preserva'tivo *m* condom
preservazi'one *f* preservation
'**preside** **A** *m* headmaster; Univ dean
B *f* headmistress; Univ dean
⚷ **presi'dente** **A** *m* chairman; Pol president
B *f* chairwoman; Pol president
■ **presidente del consiglio [dei ministri]** Prime Minister; **presidente della repubblica** President of the Republic
presiden'tessa *f* chairwoman
presi'denza *f* presidency; (di assemblea) chairmanship

⚷ key word

presidenzi'ale *adj* presidential
presidi'are *vt* garrison
pre'sidio *m* garrison
presi'edere *vt* preside over
'**preso** pp di **prendere**
'**pressa** *f* Mech press
press-'agent *mf inv* publicist, press agent
pres'sante *adj* urgent
pressap'poco *adv* about
pres'sare *vt* press
pressi'one *f* pressure; **far** ~ **su** put pressure on; **essere sotto** ~ fig be under pressure; **esercitare pressioni su qualcuno** put pressure on somebody; **a/di alta** ~ high pressure
■ **pressione fiscale** tax burden; **pressione [delle] gomme** tyre pressure; **pressione del sangue** blood pressure
⚷ '**presso** **A** *prep* near; (a casa di) with; (negli indirizzi) care of, c/o; ‹*lavorare*› for; **richiedere qualcosa** ~ **una società** request something from a company
B *mpl* **pressi: nei pressi di...** in the neighbourhood *or* vicinity of...
pressoché *adv* almost
pressuriz'zare *vt* pressurize
pressuriz'zato *adj* pressurized
prestabi'lire *vt* arrange in advance
prestabi'lito *adj* agreed, predetermined
prestam'pato **A** *adj* printed
B *m* (modulo) form
pre'stante *adj* good-looking
pre'stanza *f* good looks *pl*
⚷ **pre'stare** *vt* lend; ~ **attenzione** pay attention; ~ **aiuto** lend a hand; ~ **ascolto** lend an ear; ~ **fede a** give credence to; ~ **giuramento** take the oath; **farsi** ~ borrow (**da** from)
pre'starsi *vr* ‹*frase*› lend itself; ‹*persona*› offer
prestazi'one *f* performance; **prestazioni** *pl* (servizi) services
prestigia|'tore, -trice *mf* conjuror, conjurer
pre'stigio *m* prestige; **gioco di** ~ conjuring trick
prestigi'oso *m* prestigious
⚷ '**prestito** *m* loan; **dare in** ~ lend; **prendere in** ~ borrow
■ **prestito bancario** bank loan; **prestito con garanzia collaterale** collateral loan
⚷ '**presto** *adv* soon; (di buon'ora) early; (in fretta) quickly; **a** ~ see you soon; **al più** ~ as soon as possible; ~ **o tardi** sooner or later; **far** ~ be quick
pre'sumere *vt* presume; (credere) think
presu'mibile *adj* **è** ~ **che...** presumably, ...
pre'sunto *adj* ‹*colpevole*› presumed
presuntu'oso **A** *adj* presumptuous
B *mf* presumptuous person
presunzi'one *f* presumption

presup'porre *vt* suppose; (richiedere) presuppose
presupposizi'one *f* presupposition
presup'posto *m* essential requirement
prêt-à-por'ter *m* ready-to-wear clothing
'prete *m* priest
preten'dente **A** *mf* pretender
B *m* (corteggiatore) suitor
pre'tendere **A** *vt* (sostenere) claim; (esigere) demand
B *vi* **~ a** claim to; **~ di** (esigere) demand to
pretensi'one *f* pretension
pretenzi'oso *adj* pretentious
preterintenzio'nale *adj* **omicidio ~** manslaughter
pre'terito *m* preterite
pre'tesa *f* pretension; (esigenza) claim; **senza pretese** unpretentious
pre'teso pp di **pretendere**
pre'testo *m* pretext
pre'tore *m* magistrate
pretta'mente *adv* decidedly
'pretto *adj* pure
pre'tura *f* magistrate's court
preva'lente *adj* prevalent
prevalente'mente *adv* primarily, predominantly
preva'lenza *f* prevalence
preva'lere *vi* prevail
pre'valso pp di **prevalere**
preve'dere *vt* foresee; forecast ‹*tempo*›; (legge ecc.) provide for
preve'nire *vt* precede; (evitare) prevent; (avvertire) forewarn
preventi'vare *vt* estimate; (aspettarsi) budget for
preven'tivo **A** *adj* preventive; **bilancio ~** budget
B *m* Comm estimate
preve'nuto *adj* forewarned; (maldisposto) prejudiced
prevenzi'one *f* prevention; (preconcetto) prejudice
previ'dente *adj* provident
previ'denza *f* foresight
■ **previdenza integrativa** supplementary social security, supplementary welfare AmE; **previdenza sociale** social security, welfare AmE
previdenzi'ale *adj* provident
'previo *adj* **~ pagamento** on payment
previsi'one *f* forecast; **in ~ di** in anticipation of; **previsioni** *pl* **del tempo** weather forecast
pre'visto **A** pp di **prevedere**
B *adj* foreseen
C *m* **più/meno/prima del ~** more/less/ earlier than expected
prezi'oso *adj* precious
prez'zemolo *m* parsley
'prezzo *m* price; **[a] metà ~** half price; **a ~ ribassato** at a reduced price; **non aver ~** fig be priceless
■ **prezzo d'acquisto** purchase price; **prezzo di costo** cost price; **prezzo al dettaglio** retail price; **prezzo di fabbrica** factory price; **prezzo di favore** special price; **prezzo all'ingrosso** wholesale price; **prezzo intero** full price; **prezzo di listino** list price; **prezzo di mercato** market price; **prezzo al minuto** retail price; **prezzo d'offerta** offer price; **prezzo politico** subsidized price; **prezzo di riferimento** benchmark price; **prezzo scontato** sale price; **prezzo sorvegliato** controlled price; **prezzo stracciato** slashed price, drastically reduced price; **prezzo trattabile** price negotiable; **prezzo unitario** unit price; **prezzo di vendita** selling price
prigi'one *f* prison; (pena) imprisonment; **mettere in ~** imprison, put in prison
prigio'nia *f* imprisonment
prigioni'ero, -a **A** *adj* imprisoned
B *mf* prisoner; **tenere ~ qualcuno** keep somebody prisoner
■ **prigioniero di guerra** prisoner of war, POW; **prigioniero politico** political prisoner
'prima **A** *adv* before; (più presto) earlier; (in anticipo) beforehand; (in primo luogo) first; **finiamo questo, ~** let's finish this first; **puoi venire ~?** (di giorni) can't you come any sooner?; (di ore) can't you come any earlier?; **~ o poi** sooner or later; **quanto ~** as soon as possible
B *prep* **~ di** before; **~ di mangiare** before eating; **~ d'ora** before now
C *conj* **~ che** before; **~ che posso** as soon as I can; **~ possibile** ASAP
D *f* first class; Theat first night; Auto first [gear]
■ **prima elementare** first grade
pri'mario *adj* primary; (principale) principal
pri'mate *m* primate
prima'tista *mf* record holder
pri'mato *m* supremacy; Sport record
prima'vera *f* spring
■ **primavera araba** Arab Spring
primave'rile *adj* spring *attrib*
primeggi'are *vi* excel
primi'tivo *adj* primitive; (originario) original
pri'mizie *fpl* early produce *sg*
'primo **A** *adj* first; (fondamentale) principal; (in importanza) main; (precedente di due) former; (iniziale) early; (migliore) best
B *m* first; **il ~ d'aprile** April the first, April Fools' Day; **primi** *pl* **tempi** (i primi giorni) the beginning; **in un ~ tempo** at first
■ **prima colazione** *nf* breakfast; **prima copia** *nf* master copy; **prima linea** *nf* Mil front line; **prima serata** *nf* prime time; **in prima serata trasmetteremo...** in the early evening slot we're bringing you...
primo'genito, -a *adj* & *nmf* first-born
primogeni'tura *f* primogeniture; **vendere la ~** sell one's birthright

primordi'ale *adj* primordial

'primula *f* primrose

🔑 **princi'pale** **A** *adj* main
B *m* head, boss infml

princi'pato *m* principality
■ **il Principato di Monaco** Monaco

🔑 **'principe** *m* prince; **da ~** princely
■ **principe ereditario** crown prince; **principe del foro** *famous lawyer*

princi'pesco *adj* princely

🔑 **princi'pessa** *f* princess

principi'ante *mf* beginner

principi'are *vt & vi* begin, start

🔑 **prin'cipio** *m* beginning; (concetto) principle; (causa) cause; **per ~** on principle; **una questione di ~** a matter of principle
■ **principio attivo** active ingredient

pri'ore *m* prior

pri'ori, a priori **A** *adv* ‹*decidere*› a priori; **farsi a ~ un'opinione di** prejudge
B *adj* a priori

priorità *f inv* priority

priori'tario *adj* having priority; ‹*obiettivo*› priority *attrib*; **la nostra scelta prioritaria** our decision, which must take priority

'prisma *m* prism

'privacy *f* privacy

pri'vare *vt* deprive

pri'varsi *vr* deprive oneself

privatiz'zare *vt* privatize

privatizzazi'one *f* privatization

🔑 **pri'vato, -a** **A** *adj* private
B *mf* private citizen; **in ~** in private; **ritirarsi a vita privata** withdraw from public life

privazi'one *f* deprivation

privilegi'are *vt* privilege; (considerare più importante) favour

privi'legio *m* privilege; **avere il ~ di** have the privilege of; **questo dizionario ha il ~ della chiarezza** this dictionary has the merit of clarity

🔑 **'privo** *adj* **~ di** devoid of; (mancante) lacking in

pro **A** *prep* for
B *m* advantage; **a che ~?** what's the point?; **il ~ e il contro** the pros and cons

pro'babile *adj* probable

probabilità *f inv* probability; **avere buone ~** have a fighting chance; **~ di riuscita** chances of success

probabil'mente *adv* probably

pro'bante *adj* convincing

probi'otico *adj* probiotic

probità *f inv* probity

🔑 **pro'blema** *m* problem; **non c'è ~** no problem

proble'matico *adj* problematic

pro'boscide *f* trunk

procacci'are *vt* obtain

procacci'arsi *vr* obtain

pro'cace *adj* ‹*ragazza*› provocative

🔑 **pro'cedere** *vi* (in percorso, discorso) go on, proceed fml; (iniziare) start; **il lavoro procede bene** the work is going well; **~ contro** Jur start legal proceedings against

procedi'mento *m* process; Jur proceedings *pl*
■ **procedimento giudiziario** legal proceedings

proce'dura *f* procedure
■ **procedura civile** civil proceedings *pl*; **procedura fallimentare** bankruptcy proceedings *pl*

procedu'rale *adj* procedural

proces'sare *vt* Jur try

processi'one *f* procession

🔑 **pro'cesso** *m* process; Jur trial; **essere sotto ~** be on trial; **mettere sotto ~** put on trial
■ **processo di pace** peace process

proces'sore *m* Comput processor

processu'ale *adj* trial *attrib*

pro'cinto *m* **essere in ~ di** be about to

proci'one *m* raccoon

pro'clama *m* proclamation

procla'mare *vt* proclaim

proclamazi'one *f* proclamation

procrasti'nare *vt* (liter) postpone

procre'are *vt* procreate

procreazi'one *f* procreation

pro'cura *f* power of attorney; **per ~** by proxy
■ **Procura [della Repubblica]** Public Prosecutor's office

🔑 **procu'rare** *vt & vi* procure; (causare) cause; (cercare) try

procura'tore *m* attorney
■ **Procuratore Generale** Attorney General; **procuratore legale** lawyer; **procuratore della repubblica** public prosecutor

'prode *adj* brave

pro'dezza *f* bravery

prodi'gare *vt* lavish

prodi'garsi *vr* do one's best

pro'digio *m* prodigy

prodigi'oso *adj* prodigious

'prodigo *adj* prodigal

prodi'torio *adj* treasonable

🔑 **pro'dotto** **A** pp di **produrre**
B *m* product
■ **prodotti** *pl* **agricoli** farm produce *sg*; **prodotto artigianalmente** *adj* made by craftsmen; **prodotti** *pl* **di bellezza** cosmetics; **prodotto derivato** by-product; **prodotto in fabbrica** *adj* factory-made; **prodotto finito** end product, finished product; **prodotto interno lordo** gross domestic product; **prodotto nazionale lordo** gross national product

🔑 **pro'durre** *vt* produce

pro'dursi *vr* ‹*attore*› play; (accadere) happen, occur

🔑 key word

produttività *f inv* productivity
produt'tivo *adj* productive; **poco ~** unproductive
produt|'tore, -trice **A** *adj* producing
■ **produttore di petrolio** oil-producing
B *mf* producer
produzi'one *f* production
■ **produzione in serie** mass production
Prof. *abbr* (**professore**) Prof
profa'nare *vt* desecrate
profanazi'one *f* desecration
pro'fano **A** *adj* profane
B *m* **i profani** *pl* the uninitiated
profe'rire *vt* utter
Prof.essa *abbr* (**Professoressa**) Prof
profes'sare *vt* profess; practise ‹*professione*›
professio'nale *adj* professional; **istituto ~** training college
professionalità *f inv* professionalism
professi'one *f* profession; **libera professione** profession
professio'nismo *m* professionalism
professio'nista *mf* professional
professo'rale *adj* professorial
profes'sor|e, -essa *mf* Sch teacher; Univ lecturer; (titolare di cattedra) professor
pro'feta *m* prophet
pro'fetico *adj* prophetic
profetiz'zare *vt* prophesy
profe'zia *f* prophecy
pro'ficuo *adj* profitable
profi'lare *vt* outline; (ornare) border; Aeron streamline
profi'larsi *vr* stand out
profi'lattico **A** *adj* prophylactic
B *m* condom
pro'filo *m* profile; (breve studio) outline; **di ~** in profile
■ **profilo genetico** genetic profiling
profite'roles *mpl* profiteroles
profit'tare *vi* **~ di** (avvantaggiarsi) profit by; (approfittare) take advantage of
pro'fitto *m* profit; (vantaggio) advantage; **mettere qualcosa a ~** turn something to one's advantage; **trarre ~ da** (vantaggio) derive benefit from
profonda'mente *adv* deeply, profoundly
profondità *f inv* depth; (del pensiero ecc.) depth, profundity; **in ~** in depth; **passaggio in ~** Sport deep pass [down the field]
■ **profondità di campo** Phot depth of field
pro'fondo *adj* deep; ‹*pensiero ecc.*› profound; ‹*cultura*› great
pro 'forma **A** *adj* routine; **fattura ~** pro forma [invoice]
B *adv* as a formality
C *m* formality
'profugo, -a *mf* refugee
profu'mare **A** *vi* smell good; **~ di** smell of
B *vt* perfume
profu'marsi *vr* put on perfume
profumata'mente *adv* **pagare ~** pay through the nose
profu'mato *adj* ‹*fiore*› fragrant; ‹*fazzoletto ecc.*› scented
profume'ria *f* perfumery
pro'fumo *m* perfume, scent
profusi'one *f* profusion; **a ~** in profusion
pro'fuso *adj* profuse
pro'genie *f* progeny
progeni|'tore, -trice *mf* ancestor
proget'tare *vt* plan; plan, design ‹*costruzione*›
progettazione *f* planning, design
■ **progettazione assistita da computer** computer-aided design, CAD
proget'tista *mf* designer
pro'getto *m* plan; (di lavoro importante) project
■ **progetto di legge** bill; **progetto pilota** pilot scheme
'prognosi *f inv* prognosis; **in ~ riservata** on the danger list
pro'gramma *m* programme; Comput program; **avere qualcosa in ~** have something planned, have something on; **programmi** *pl* **televisivi del mattino** breakfast TV
■ **programma antivirus** Comput antivirus program, antivirus software; **programma assemblatore** Comput assembler; **programma aziendale** business plan; **programma per la gestione dei file** Comput file manager; **programma di grafica** Comput graphics program; **programma politico** manifesto; **programma scolastico** syllabus; **programma di setup** Comput set-up program; **programma di utilità** Comput utility
program'mare *vt* programme; Comput program
program'mato *adj* (sviluppo) planned
programma|'tore, -trice *mf* [computer] programmer
programmazi'one *f* programming
progre'dire *vi* [make] progress
progres'sione *f* progression
progres'sista *mf* progressive
progres'sivo *adj* progressive
pro'gresso *m* progress; **fare progressi** make progress
proi'bire *vt* forbid
proibi'tivo *adj* prohibitive
proi'bito *adj* forbidden; **è ~ fumare qui** it's no smoking here
proibizi'one *f* prohibition
proibizio'nismo *m* prohibition
proiet'tare *vt* project; show ‹*film*›
proi'ettile *m* bullet
proiet'tore *m* projector; Auto headlight
■ **proiettore per diapositive** slide projector
proiezi'one *f* projection
■ **proiezione di diapositive** slide show

p

'prole *f* offspring
proletari'ato *m* proletariat
prole'tario *adj & nm* proletarian
prolife'rare *vi* proliferate
pro'lifico *adj* prolific
prolissità *f inv* prolixity, diffuseness
pro'lisso *adj* verbose, prolix
pro 'loco *f* tourist office (*in small towns*)
'prologo *m* prologue
pro'lunga *f* extension
prolunga'mento *m* extension
prolun'gare *vt* extend ‹*contratto, scadenza, strada*›; prolong ‹*vita*›; lengthen ‹*vita, strada*›
prolun'garsi *vr* continue, go on; **~ su** (dilungarsi) dwell upon
prome'moria *m* memo; (per se stessi) reminder; note; (formale) memorandum
pro'messa *f* promise; **era già una ~ del...** he was already a promising new talent in...
pro'messo **A** pp di **promettere**
B *adj* ‹*terra*› promised
■ **promesso sposo, promessa sposa** *nm,f* betrothed
promet'tente *adj* promising
pro'mettere *vt & vi* promise
promi'nente *adj* prominent
promi'nenza *f* prominence
promiscuità *f inv* promiscuity
pro'miscuo *adj* promiscuous
promon'torio *m* promontory
pro'mosso **A** pp di **promuovere**
B *adj* Sch who has gone up a year; Univ who has passed an exam
promo|'tore, -trice *mf* promoter
promozio'nale *adj* promotional; **vendita ~** special offer
promozi'one *f* promotion
promul'gare *vt* promulgate
promulgazi'one *f* promulgation
promu'overe *vt* promote; Sch move up a class; **essere promosso** Sch, Univ pass one's exams
proni'pote **A** *m* (di bisnonno) great-grandson; (di prozio) great-nephew; **pronipoti** *pl* great-grandchildren
B *f* (di bisnonno) great-granddaughter; (di prozio) great-niece
pro'nome *m* pronoun
pronomi'nale *adj* pronominal
pronosti'care *vt* forecast, predict
pronostica|'tore, -trice *mf* forecaster
pro'nostico *m* forecast
pron'tezza *f* readiness; (rapidità) quickness; **con ~ di spirito** quick-wittedly
■ **prontezza di riflessi** quick reflexes *pl*
'pronto *adj* ready; (rapido) quick; **~!** Teleph hello!; **tenersi ~ (per qualcosa)** be ready (for something); **pronti, via!** (in gare) ready! steady! go!; **a pronta cassa** cash on delivery
■ **pronto intervento** *nm* emergency service; **pronto soccorso** *nm* first aid; (in ospedale) accident and emergency, A&E
prontu'ario *m* handbook
pro'nuncia *f* pronunciation
pronunci'are *vt* pronounce; (dire) utter; deliver ‹*discorso*›
pronunci'arsi *vr* (su un argomento) give one's opinion; **~ a favore/contro qualcosa** pronounce oneself in favour of/against something
pronunci'ato *adj* pronounced; (prominente) prominent
pro'nunzia = **pronuncia**
pronunzi'are = **pronunciare**
propa'ganda *f* propaganda
■ **propaganda elettorale** electioneering; **propaganda di partito** party political propaganda
propa'gare *vt* propagate
propa'garsi *vr* spread
propagazi'one *f* propagation
prope'deutico *adj* introductory
propel'lente *m* propellant
pro'pendere *vi* **~ per** be in favour of
propensi'one *f* inclination, propensity
pro'penso **A** pp di **propendere**
B *adj* **essere ~ a fare qualcosa** be inclined to do something
propi'nare *vt* administer
pro'pizio *adj* favourable
proponi'mento *m* resolution
pro'porre *vt* propose; (suggerire) suggest
pro'porsi *vr* set oneself ‹*obiettivo, meta*›; **~ di** intend to
proporzio'nale *adj* proportional
proporzio'nare *vt* proportion
proporzio'nato *adj* proportioned
proporzi'one *f* proportion
pro'posito *m* intention; **ho fatto il ~ di...** I have made the decision to...; **a ~** by the way; **a ~ di** with regard to; **di ~** (apposta) on purpose; **capitare a ~, giungere a ~** come at just the right time; **propositi** *pl* **per l'anno nuovo** New Year's resolutions
proposizi'one *f* clause; (frase) sentence
pro'posta *f* proposal, suggestion
■ **proposta di legge** bill; **proposta di matrimonio** [marriage] proposal
pro'posto pp di **proporre**
propria'mente *adv* **~ detto** in the strict sense of the word
proprietà *f inv* property; (diritto) ownership; (correttezza) propriety; **essere di ~ di qualcuno** be somebody's property
■ **proprietà collettiva** collective ownership; **proprietà immobiliare** property; **proprietà di linguaggio** correct use of language; **proprietà**

key word

P

privata private property

proprie'taria *f* owner; (di casa affittata) landlady

proprie'tario *m* owner; (di casa affittata) landlord

'proprio **A** *adj* one's [own]; (caratteristico) typical; (appropriato) proper
B *adv* just; (veramente) really; **non ~** not really, not exactly; (affatto) not... at all
C *pron* one's own
D *m* one's own; **lavorare in ~** be one's own boss; **mettersi in ~** set up on one's own

propu'gnare *vt* support

propulsi'one *f* propulsion; **a ~ atomica** atomic
■ **propulsione a getto** jet propulsion

propul'sore *m* propeller

'prora *f* Naut prow

'proroga *f* extension

proro'gabile *adj* extendable

proro'gare *vt* extend

pro'rompere *vi* burst out

'prosa *f* prose

pro'saico *adj* prosaic

pro'sciogliere *vt* release; Jur acquit

prosciogli'mento *m* release

pro'sciolto pp di **prosciogliere**

prosciu'gare *vt* dry up; (bonificare) reclaim

prosciu'garsi *vr* dry up

prosci'utto *m* ham
■ **prosciutto cotto** cooked ham; **prosciutto crudo** type of dry-cured ham, Parma ham

pro'scritto, -a **A** pp di **proscrivere**
B *mf* exile

pro'scrivere *vt* exile, banish

proscrizi'one *f* exile, banishment

prosecuzi'one *f* continuation

prosegui'mento *m* continuation; **buon ~!** (viaggio) have a good journey!; (festa) enjoy the rest of the party!

prosegu'ire **A** *vt* continue
B *vi* go on, continue

pro'selito *m* convert

prospe'rare *vi* prosper

prosperità *f inv* prosperity

'prospero *adj* prosperous; (favorevole) favourable

prospe'roso *adj* flourishing; (ragazza) buxom

prospet'tare *vt* show

prospet'tarsi *vr* seem

prospet'tiva *f* perspective; (panorama) view; fig prospect

pro'spetto *m* (vista) view; (facciata) façade; (tabella) table

prospici'ente *adj* facing

prossima'mente *adv* soon

prossimità *f inv* proximity; **in ~ di** near

'prossimo, -a **A** *adj* near; (seguente) next; (molto vicino) close; **l'anno ~** next year; **~ venturo** next; **essere ~ a fare qualcosa** be about to do something
B *mf* neighbour

'prostata *f* prostate

prostitu'irsi *vr* prostitute oneself

prosti'tuta *f* prostitute

prostituzi'one *f* prostitution

pro'strare *vt* prostrate

pro'strarsi *vr* prostrate oneself

pro'strato *adj* prostrate

protago'nista *mf* protagonist; **ruolo/attore non ~** supporting role/actor

pro'teggere *vt* protect; (favorire) favour; **~ da sovrascrittura** write-protect

pro'teico *adj* protein *attrib*; **molto ~** rich in protein

prote'ina *f* protein

pro'tendere *vt* stretch out

pro'tendersi *vr* (in avanti) lean out

pro'teso pp di **protendere**

pro'testa *f* protest; (dichiarazione) protestation

prote'stante *adj & nmf* Protestant

prote'stare *vt & vi* protest

prote'starsi *vr* **~ innocente** protest one's innocence

protet'tivo *adj* protective

pro'tetto, -a **A** pp di **proteggere**
B *adj* protected; **non ~** unprotected
■ **protetto da password** password-protected

protetto'rato *m* protectorate

protet|'tore, -trice **A** *mf* protector; (sostenitore) patron
B *m* (di prostituta) pimp

protezi'one *f* protection
■ **protezione aerea** air cover; **protezione dell'ambiente** environmental protection; **protezione antivirus** virus protection; **protezione civile** civil defence

protocol'lare **A** *adj* (visita) protocol
B *vt* register

proto'collo *m* protocol; (registro) register; **carta ~** official stamped paper
■ **protocollo di gestione remota della posta elettronica** IMAP; **protocollo Internet** Internet protocol; **protocollo per il trasferimento di file** file transfer protocol; **protocollo per il trasferimento di ipertesti** hypertext transfer protocol

pro'totipo *m* prototype

pro'trarre *vt* protract; (differire) postpone

pro'trarsi *vr* go on, continue

pro'tratto pp di **protrarre**

protube'rante *adj* protuberant

protube'ranza *f* protuberance

'prova *f* test; (dimostrazione) proof; (tentativo) try, attempt; (di abito) fitting; Sport heat; Theat rehearsal; (bozza) proof; **prove** *pl* evidence; **fino a ~ contraria** until I'm told otherwise; **in ~** (assumere) for a trial period; **mettere alla ~** put to the test; **a ~ di bomba**

bombproof; **a ~ di ladro** burglar-proof
■ **prova del fuoco** fig acid test; **prova generale** dress rehearsal; **prova medico-legale** forensic evidence

⚷ **pro'vare** *vt* test; (dimostrare) prove; (tentare) try; try on ‹*abiti ecc.*›; (sentire) feel; Theat rehearse; **prova!** just try!

pro'varsi *vr* try

proveni'enza *f* origin

prove'nire *vi* **~ da** come from

pro'vento *m* proceeds *pl*

prove'nuto pp di **provenire**

pro'verbio *m* proverb

pro'vetta *f* test-tube; **bambino in ~** test-tube baby

pro'vetto *adj* skilled

⚷ **pro'vincia** *f* province

⚷ **provinci'ale** *adj* provincial; **strada ~** B road, secondary road

pro'vino *m* specimen; Cinema screen test

provo'cante *adj* provocative

⚷ **provo'care** *vt* provoke; (causare) cause

provoca|'tore, -trice *mf* trouble-maker

provoca'torio *adj* provocative, confrontational

provocazi'one *f* provocation

provo'lone *m type of cheese with a slightly smoked flavour*

⚷ **provve'dere** *vi* **~ a** provide for

provvedi'mento *m* measure; (previdenza) precaution
■ **provvedimento disciplinare** disciplinary measure

provvedito'rato *m*
■ **provveditorato agli studi** education department

provvedi'tore *m*
■ **provveditore agli studi** director of education

provvi'denza *f* providence

provvidenzi'ale *adj* providential

provvigi'one *f* Comm commission; **lavorare a ~** work on commission

provvi'sorio *adj* provisional; **in via provvisoria** provisionally, for the time being

prov'vista *f* supply

pro'zia *f* great-aunt

pro'zio *m* great-uncle

'prua *f* Naut prow

pru'dente *adj* prudent

pru'denza *f* prudence; **per ~** as a precaution

prudenzi'ale *adj* prudential

'prudere *vi* itch

'prugna *f* plum
■ **prugna secca** prune; **prugna selvatica** damson

'prugno *m* plum tree

'prugnolo *m* sloe

prurigi'noso *adj* itchy

⚷ key word

pru'rito *m* itch

P.S. *abbr* (**Pubblica Sicurezza**) police

pseu'donimo *m* pseudonym

psica'nalisi *f* psychoanalysis

psicana'lista *mf* psychoanalyst

psicanaliz'zare *vt* psychoanalyse

'psiche *f* psyche

psiche'delico *adj* psychedelic

psichi'atra *mf* psychiatrist

psichia'tria *f* psychiatry

psichi'atrico *adj* psychiatric

'psichico *adj* mental

psico'farmaco *m* drug that affects the mind

psicolo'gia *f* psychology

psico'logico *adj* psychological

psi'cologo, -a *mf* psychologist

psico'patico, -a **A** *adj* psychopathic
B *mf* psychopath

psicopedago'gia *f* educational psychology

psi'cosi *f inv* psychosis

psicoso'matico *adj* psychosomatic

psicotera'peuta *mf* psychotherapist

psicotera'pista *mf* psychotherapist

psi'cotico, -a *adj & nmf* psychotic

PT *abbr* (**Posta e Telegrafi**) PO

puàh *int* yuck!

pub *m inv* pub

pubbli'care *vt* publish

pubblicazi'one *f* publication; **pubblicazioni** *pl* (di matrimonio) banns
■ **pubblicazione periodica** periodical

pubbli'cista *mf* Journ correspondent

pubblicità *f inv* publicity, advertising; (annuncio) advertisement, advert; **fare ~ a qualcosa** advertise something; **piccola ~** small advertisements

pubblici'tario *adj* advertising

⚷ **'pubblico** **A** *adj* public; **scuola pubblica** state school
B *m* public; (spettatori) audience; **in ~** in public; **grande ~** general public; **Pubblica Sicurezza** police
■ **pubblico ministero** public prosecutor; **pubblico ufficiale** civil servant

'pube *m* pubis

pubertà *f inv* puberty

pu'dico *adj* modest

pu'dore *m* modesty

pue'rile *adj* children's; derog childish

'puerpera *f* new mother

puerpe'rale *adj* of childbirth, puerperal fml; ‹*depressione*› postnatal

puer'perio *m* post-natal period

pugi'lato *m* boxing

'pugile *m* boxer

'Puglia *f* Apulia

pugli'ese *adj & nmf* Apulian

pugna'lare *vt* stab

pugna'lata *f* stab

pu'gnale *m* dagger

'pugno *m* fist; (colpo) punch; (manciata) fistful; fig (numero limitato) handful; **dare un ~ a** punch; **di proprio ~** ‹*scrivere*› in one's own hand; **fare a pugni** ‹*colori*› clash; **tenere in ~** ‹*situazione*› have under control; have in the palm of one's hand ‹*persona*›; **un ~ in un occhio** fig an eyesore

■ **pugno di ferro** iron fist

'pula *f* sl **la ~** the fuzz

'pulce *f* flea; (microfono) bug; **mettere la ~ nell'orecchio a qualcuno** sow a doubt in somebody's mind

pul'cino *m* chick; (nel calcio) junior

pu'ledra *f* filly

pu'ledro *m* foal, colt

pu'leggia *f* pulley

pu'lire *vt* clean; **~ a secco** dry-clean; **far ~ qualcosa** have something cleaned

puliscipi'edi *m inv* boot scraper

pu'lito *adj* clean

puli'tura *f* cleaning

puli'zia *f* (il pulire) cleaning; (l'essere pulito) cleanliness; **pulizie** *pl* housework; **fare le pulizie** do the cleaning

■ **pulizia personale** personal hygiene

'pullman *m inv* coach, bus; (urbano) bus; **gita in ~** coach trip

pull'over *m* pullover

pul'mino *m* minibus

'pulpito *m* pulpit

pul'sante *m* button; Electr push-button

■ **pulsante di accensione** on/off switch; **pulsante di alimentazione** power switch

pul'sare *vi* pulsate

pulsazi'one *f* pulsation

pul'viscolo *m* dust

'puma *m inv* puma

'punching 'bag *f inv* punchbag

pun'gente *adj* prickly; ‹*insetto*› stinging; ‹*odore ecc.*› sharp

'pungere *vt* prick; ‹*insetto*› sting; **~ qualcuno sul vivo** cut somebody to the quick

pungersi *vr* prick oneself; **~ un dito** prick one's finger

pungigli'one *m* sting

pungo'lare *vt* goad

pu'nire *vt* punish

puni'tivo *adj* punitive

punizi'one *f* punishment; Sport penalty; (in calcio) free kick

■ **punizione corporale** corporal punishment

'punta *f* point; (estremità) tip; (di monte) peak, top; (un po) pinch; Sport forward; **doppie punte** (di capelli) split ends; **di ~** ‹*ore*› peak; ‹*personaggio*› leading

pun'tare **A** *vt* point; (spingere con forza) push; (scommettere) bet; infml (appuntare) fasten **B** *vi* **~ su** fig rely on; (scommettere) bet on; **~ verso** (dirigersi) head for; **~ a** aspire to; **punta e clicca** Comput point and click

punta'spilli *m inv* pincushion

pun'tata *f* (di una storia) instalment; (televisiva) episode; (al gioco) stake, bet; (breve visita) flying visit; **a puntate** serialized, in instalments; **fare una ~ a/in** pop over to ‹*luogo*›

punteggia'tura *f* punctuation

pun'teggio *m* score

puntel'lare *vt* prop

pun'tello *m* prop

punteru'olo *m* awl

pun'tiglio *m* spite; (ostinazione) obstinacy

puntigli'oso *adj* punctilious, pernickety derog

pun'tina *f* (da disegno) drawing pin, thumb tack AmE; (di giradischi) stylus

■ **puntina da disegno** drawing pin, thumb tack AmE

pun'tine *fpl* Aut; **~ [platinate]** points

pun'tino *m* dot; **a ~** perfectly; ‹*cotto*› to a T; **puntini** *pl* **[di sospensione]** suspension points

'punto *m* point; (in cucito, Med) stitch; (in punteggiatura) full stop; **in che ~?** where, exactly?; **di ~ in bianco** all of a sudden; **essere sul ~ di fare qualcosa** be on the point of doing something, be about to do something; **in ~** sharp; **mettere a ~** put right; fig fine-tune; tune up ‹*motore*›; **messa a ~** fine tuning; **due punti** colon; **punti** *pl* **cardinali** points of the compass

■ **punto cieco** blind spot; **punto di congelamento** freezing point; **punto croce** cross-stitch; **punto debole** weak spot; **punto di domanda** question mark; **punto di ebollizione** boiling point; **punto esclamativo** exclamation mark; **punto di fuga** vanishing point; **punto di fusione** melting point; **punto d'incontro** meeting point; **punto di infiammabilità** flashpoint; **punto interrogativo** question mark; **punto morto** fig stand-off; **punto nero** (comedone) blackhead; **punto di pareggio** Fin break-even point; **punto di partenza** starting point; **punto di riferimento** landmark; (per la qualità) benchmark; **punto di rottura** breaking point; **punto a smerlo** blanket stitch; **punto [di] vendita** point of sale, outlet; **pubblicità al ~ [di] vendita** point-of-sale publicity; **punto e virgola** semicolon; **punto di vista** point of view

puntu'ale *adj* punctual; **essere ~** be punctual, be on time

puntualità *f inv* punctuality

puntualiz'zare *vt* make clear, clarify

puntual'mente *adv* punctually, on time; (come al solito) as usual

pun'tura *f* (di insetto) sting; (di ago ecc.) prick; Med puncture; (iniezione) injection; (fitta) stabbing pain

▪ **puntura d'ape** bee sting; **puntura d'insetto** insect bite; **puntura di spillo** pinprick; **puntura di zanzara** mosquito bite

punzecchi'are *vt* prick; fig tease

punzo'nare *vt* Techn punch, stamp

pun'zone *m* punch

può ▶ **potere**; ~ **darsi** maybe, perhaps

'pupa *f* doll

pu'pazzo *m* puppet

▪ **pupazzo di neve** snowman

pup'illa *f* Anat pupil

pu'pillo, -a *mf* Jur ward; (di professore) favourite

⚷ **purché** *conj* provided

⚷ **'pure** **A** *adv* too, also; (concessivo) **fate ~!** please do!; **io ~** me too; **è venuto ~ lui** he came too, he also came

B *conj* (tuttavia) yet; (anche se) even if; **pur di** just to

⚷ **purè** *m inv* purée

▪ **purè di patate** mashed potatoes, creamed potatoes

pu'rezza *f* purity

'purga *f* purge

pur'gante *m* laxative

pur'gare *vt* purge

purga'torio *m* purgatory

purifi'care *vt* purify

purificazi'one *f* purification

pu'rista *mf* purist

puri'tano, -a *adj & nmf* Puritan

⚷ **'puro** *adj* pure; ‹*vino ecc.*› undiluted; **per ~ caso** by sheer chance, purely by chance

▪ **puro cotone** *nm* pure cotton, 100% cotton; **pura lana vergine** *nf* pure new wool; **pura seta** *nf* pure silk

puro'sangue *adj & nm* thoroughbred

⚷ **pur'troppo** *adv* unfortunately

'pus *m* pus

'pustola *f* pimple

puti'ferio *m* uproar

putre'fare *vi* putrefy

putre'farsi *vr* putrefy

putre'fatto *adj* rotten

putrefazi'one *f* putrefaction

'putrido *adj* putrid

putt *m inv* putt

put'tana *f* vulg whore

'puzza *f* stink; **avere la ~ sotto il naso** be sniffy

puz'zare *vi* anche fig stink; **~ di bruciato** fig smell fishy; **~ d'imbroglio** stink; **~ di corruzione** stink of corruption; **questa storia mi puzza** the story stinks

⚷ **'puzzo** *m* stink

'puzzola *f* polecat

puzzo'lente *adj* stinking

puz'zone *m* infml bastard

p.zza *abbr* (**piazza**) sq.

p

q

Qq

Qatar *m* Qatar

QI *abbr* (**quoziente di intelligenza**) IQ

⚷ **qua** *adv* here; **da un anno in ~** for the last year; **da quando in ~?** since when?; **di ~** this way; **di ~ di** on this side of; **~ dentro** in here; **~ sotto** under here; **~ vicino** near here; **~ e là** here and there

'quacchero, -a *mf* Quaker

qua'derno *m* exercise book; (per appunti) notebook

▪ **quaderno a quadretti** maths exercise book; **quaderno a righe** lined exercise book

quadrango'lare *adj* ‹*forma*› quadrangular; **incontro ~** Sport four-sided tournament

qua'drangolo *m* quadrangle

qua'drante *m* quadrant; (di orologio) dial

qua'drare **A** *vt* square; (contabilità) balance

B *vi* fit in

qua'drato **A** *adj* square; (equilibrato) level-headed

B *m* square; (nel pugilato) ring; **al ~** squared

quadra'tura *f* Math squaring; (di bilancio) balancing

quadret'tare *vt* divide into small squares

quadret'tato *adj* squared; ‹*carta*› graph (*attrib*); ‹*tessuto*› check, checked

qua'dretto *m* square; (piccolo quadro) small picture; **a quadretti** ‹*tessuto*› check

quadricro'mia *f* four-colour printing

quadrien'nale *adj* (che dura quattro anni) four-year; (ogni quattro anni) four-yearly

quadri'foglio *m* four-leaf clover

⚷ key word

qua'driglia *f* square dance
quadri'latero *m* quadrilateral
quadri'mestre *m* (periodo) four-month period; Sch term
quadrimo'tore *m* four-engined plane
quadri'nomio *m* Math quadrinomial
quadripar'tito **A** *adj* four-party
B *m* (politica) four-party government
quadri'plegico *adj* quadriplegic
'quadro *m* picture, painting; (quadrato) square; fig (scena) sight; (tabella) table; Theat scene; (dirigente) executive; **fare il ~ della situazione** outline the situation; **fuori ~** Cinema, TV out of shot; **quadri** *pl* (carte) diamonds; **a quadri** ‹*tessuto, giacca, motivo*› check, checked
■ **quadro clinico** case history; **quadro di comando** control panel; **quadri** *pl* **direttivi** senior management; **quadro di distribuzione** Electr switchboard; **quadri** *pl* **intermedi** middle management; **quadro degli interruttori** switch panel; **quadro degli strumenti** instrument panel
qua'drupede *m* quadruped
quadrupli'care *vt* quadruple
quadrupli'carsi *vr* quadruple
qua'druplice *adj* quadruple
'quadruplo *adj & nm* quadruple
quaggiù *adv* down here
'quaglia *f* quail
'qualche *adj* (alcuni) a few, some; (un certo) some; (in interrogazioni) any; **ho ~ problema** I have a few problems, I have some problems; **~ tempo fa** some time ago; **hai ~ libro italiano?** have you any Italian books?; **posso prendere ~ libro?** can I take some books?; **in ~ modo** somehow; **in ~ posto** somewhere; **~ volta** sometimes; **~ cosa** = **qualcosa**
qualche'duno *pron* somebody, someone
qual'cosa *pron* something; (in interrogazioni) anything; **qualcos'altro** something else; **vuoi qualcos'altro?** would you like anything else?; **~ di strano** something strange; **vuoi ~ da mangiare?** would you like something to eat?; **vuoi ~ da bere?** would you like a drink?, would you like something to drink?
qual'cuno *pron* someone, somebody; (in interrogazioni) anyone, anybody; (alcuni) some; (in interrogazioni) any; **c'è ~?** is anybody in?; **qualcun altro** someone else, somebody else; **c'è qualcun altro che aspetta?** is anybody else waiting?; **ho letto ~ dei suoi libri** I've read some of his books; **conosci ~ dei suoi amici?** do you know any of his friends?
'quale **A** *adj* which; (indeterminato) what; (come) as, like; **~ macchina è la tua?** which car is yours?; **~ motivo avrà di parlare così?** what reason would he have to speak like that?; **~ onore!** what an honour!; **città quali Venezia** towns like Venice; **~ che sia la tua opinione** whatever you may think
B *pron* (inter) which [one]; **~ preferisci?** which [one] do you prefer?
C *pron rel* **il/la ~** (persona) who; (animale, cosa) that, which; (oggetto: con prep) whom; (oggetto: animale, cosa) which; **ho incontrato tua madre, la ~ mi ha detto...** I met your mother who told me...; **l'ufficio nel ~ lavoro** the office in which I work; **l'uomo con il ~ parlavo** the man to whom I was speaking
D *adv* (come) as
qua'lifica *f* qualification; (titolo) title
qualifi'cabile *adj* qualifiable
qualifi'care *vt* qualify; (definire) define
qualifi'carsi *vr* be placed
qualifica'tivo *adj* qualifying
qualifi'cato *adj* ‹*operaio*› semi-skilled
qualificazi'one *f* qualification
qualità *f inv* quality; (specie) kind; **in ~ di** in one's capacity as; **di prima ~** high quality; **di ottima/cattiva ~** top/poor quality
qualitativa'mente *adv* qualitatively
qualita'tivo *adj* qualitative
qua'lora *conj* in case
qual'siasi, qua'lunque *adj* any; (non importa quale) whatever; (ordinario) ordinary; **dammi una penna ~** give me any pen [whatsoever]; **farei ~ cosa** I would do anything; **~ cosa io faccia** whatever I do; **~ persona** anyone, anybody; **in ~ caso** in any case; **uno ~** any one, whichever; **l'uomo qualunque** the man in the street; **vivo in una casa ~** I live in an ordinary house
qualunqu'ismo *m* lack of political views
qualunqu'ista *mf* (menefreghista) person with no political views
'quando *conj & adv* when; **da ~ ti ho visto** since I saw you; **da ~ esci con lui?** how long have you been going out with him?; **da ~ in qua?** since when?; **~... ~...** sometimes..., sometimes...; **continua ad insistere ~ sa di avere torto** he keeps on insisting even when he knows he's wrong
quantifi'cabile *adj* quantifiable
quantifi'care *vt* quantify
quantità *f inv* quantity, amount; **una ~ di** (gran numero) a great deal of
quantitativa'mente *adv* quantitatively
quantita'tivo **A** *m* amount
B *adj* quantitative
'quanto **A** *adj inter* how much; (con nomi plurali) how many; (in esclamazione) what a lot of; (tempo) how long; **quanti anni hai?** how old are you?
B *adj* (rel) as much...as; (tempo) as long as; (con nomi plurali) as many... as; **prendi ~ denaro ti serve** take as much money as you need; **prendi quanti libri vuoi** take as many books as you like; **e quant'altro** and whatever, and so on
C *pron* (inter) how much; (quanto tempo) how

q

long; (plurale) how many; **quanti ne abbiamo oggi?** what date is it today?
D *pron* (rel) as much as; (quanto tempo) as long as; (plurale) as many as; **prendine ~/ quanti ne vuoi** take as much/as many as you like; **stai ~ vuoi** stay as long as you like; **questo è ~** that's it
E *adv* (inter) how much; (quanto tempo) how long; **~ sei alto?** how tall are you?; **~ hai aspettato?** how long did you wait for?; **~ costa?** how much is it?; **~ mi dispiace!** I'm so sorry!; **quant'è bello!** how nice!
F *adv rel* as much as; **lavoro ~ posso** I work as much as I can; **è tanto intelligente ~ bello** he's as intelligent as he's good-looking; **in ~** (in qualità di) as; (poiché) since; **~ a** as for; **in ~ a me** as far as I'm concerned; **per ~** however; **per ~ ne sappia** as far as I know; **per ~ mi riguarda** as far as I'm concerned; **per ~ mi sia simpatico** much as I like him; **~ prima** (al più presto) as soon as possible

quan'tunque *conj* although

✓ **qua'ranta** *adj & nm* forty

quaran'tena *f* quarantine

quaran'tenne **A** *adj* forty year-old; (sulla quarantina) in his/her forties
B *mf* forty year-old; (sulla quarantina) person in his/her forties

quaran'tennio *m* period of forty years

quaran'tesimo *adj & nm* fortieth

quaran'tina *f* **una ~** about forty

qua'resima *f* Lent

quar'tetto *m* quartet

✓ **quarti'ere** *m* district, area; Mil quarters *pl*; **quartieri** *pl* **alti** smart districts; **quartieri** *pl* **bassi** poor areas
■ **quartiere cinese** Chinatown; **quartiere dormitorio** dormitory town; **quartiere generale** headquarters; **quartiere a luci rosse** red light area; **quartiere residenziale** residential area

q

quar'tino *m* (strumento musicale) *instrument similar to a clarinet*; Typ quarto; (di vino) quarter litre

✓ **'quarto** **A** *adj* fourth
B *m* fourth; (quarta parte) quarter; **le sette e un ~** [a] quarter past seven, [a] quarter after seven AmE; **a tre quarti** (giacca, maniche) three-quarter length; **quarti** *pl* **di finale** quarter-finals
■ **quarto d'ora** quarter of an hour
C *f* (marcia) fourth [gear]

quarto'genito, -a *mf* fourth child

quar'tultimo, -a *adj & nmf* fourth last

'quarzo *m* quartz; **al ~** quartz
■ **quarzo rosa** rose quartz

✓ **'quasi** **A** *adv* almost, nearly; **~ mai** hardly ever
B *conj* (come se) as if; **~ ~ sto a casa** I'm tempted to stay home

quassù *adv* up here

qua'terna *f* (lotto, tombola) set of four winning numbers

quater'nario *m* (era) Quaternary

'quatto *adj* crouching; (silenzioso) silent; **starsene ~ ~** keep very quiet

quattordi'cenne *adj & nmf* fourteen year-old

quattordi'cesimo *adj & nm* fourteenth

quat'tordici *adj & nm* fourteen

quat'trini *mpl* money *sg*, dosh *sg* infml

✓ **'quattro** *adj & nm* four; **dirne ~ a qualcuno** give somebody a piece of one's mind; **farsi in ~ (per qualcuno/per fare qualcosa)** go to a lot of trouble (for somebody/to do something); **in ~ e quattr'otto** in a flash; **a ~ tempi** Auto four-stroke
■ **~ per ~** *f inv* Auto four-wheel drive [vehicle], four-by-four

quat'trocchi *adv* **a ~** in private

quattrocen'tesco *adj* fifteenth-century

quattro'cento *adj & nm* four hundred; **il Quattrocento** the fifteenth century

quattro'mila *adj & nm* four thousand

Qué'bec *m* Quebec

✓ **'quello** **A** *adj* that *pl*, those; **quell'albero** that tree; **quegli alberi** those trees; **quel cane** that dog; **quei cani** those dogs
B *pron* that [one] *pl*, those [ones]; **~ lì** that one over there; **~ che** the one that; (ciò che) what; **quelli che** the ones that, those that; **~ a destra** the one on the right

'quercia *f* oak; **di ~** oak

que'rela *f* [legal] action

quere'lante *mf* plaintiff

quere'lare *vt* bring an action against

quere'lato, -a *mf* defendant

que'sito *m* question

questio'nare *vi* dispute

questio'nario *m* questionnaire

✓ **quest'ione** *f* question; (faccenda) matter; (litigio) quarrel; **in ~** in doubt; **è fuori ~** it's out of the question; **è ~ di vita o di morte** it's a matter of life and death; **mettere qualcosa in ~** cast doubt on something; **una ~ personale** a personal matter

✓ **'questo** **A** *adj* this *pl*, these
B *pron* this [one] *pl*, these [ones]; **~ qui, ~ qua** this one here; **~ è quello che ha detto** that's what he said; **per ~** for this *or* that reason; **quest'oggi** today

que'store *m* chief of police

'questua *f* collection

que'stura *f* police headquarters

✓ **qui** **A** *adv* here; **da ~ in poi, da ~ in avanti** from now on; **di ~ a una settimana** in a week's time; **fin ~** (di tempo) up till now, until now; **~ dentro** in here; **~ sotto** under here; **~ vicino** *adv* near here
B *m* **~ pro quo** misunderstanding

quie'scenza *f* (di vulcano) dormancy; (pensione) retirement; **trattamento di**

✓ key word

quiescenza retirement package
quie'tanza *f* receipt
quie'tare *vt* calm
quie'tarsi *vr* calm down
qui'ete *f* quiet; **disturbo della ~ pubblica** breach of the peace; **stato di ~** Phys state of rest
qui'eto *adj* quiet
'quindi **A** *adv* then
B *conj* therefore
quindi'cenne *adj & nmf* fifteen year-old
quindi'cesimo *adj & nm* fifteenth
'quindici *adj & nm* fifteen; **~ giorni** a fortnight BrE, two weeks *pl*
quindi'cina *f* **una ~** about fifteen; **una ~ di giorni** a fortnight BrE, two weeks *pl*
quindici'nale **A** *adj* fortnightly BrE, twice-monthly
B *m* fortnightly magazine BrE, twice-monthly magazine
quinquen'nale *adj* (che dura cinque anni) five-year; (ogni cinque anni) five-yearly
quin'quennio *m* [period of] five years
'quinta *f* Auto fifth [gear], overdrive
quin'tale *m* a hundred kilograms
'quinte *fpl* Theat wings
quintes'senza *f* quintessence
quin'tetto *m* quintet
'quinto *adj & nm* fifth
quintupli'care *vt* quintuple
'quintuplo *adj* quintuple
qui'squilia *f* trifle; **perdersi in quisquilie** get bogged down in details
quiz *m inv*:
■ **[gioco a] quiz** quiz game; **quiz radiofonico** radio quiz
'quota *f* quota; (rata) instalment; (altitudine) height; Aeron altitude, height; (ippica) odds *pl*; **perdere/prendere ~** lose/gain altitude *or* height; **da alta ~** high-flying
■ **quota fissa** fixed amount; **quota non imponibile** personal allowance; **quota di iscrizione** entry fee; (di club) membership fee; **quota di mercato** market share; **quota zero** sea level
quo'tare *vt* Comm quote
quo'tato *adj* quoted; **essere ~ in Borsa** be quoted on the Stock Exchange
quotazi'one *f* quotation
■ **quotazione d'acquisto** buying rate; **quotazione ufficiale** (in Borsa) official quotation; **quotazione di vendita** selling rate
quotidiana'mente *adv* daily
quotidi'ano **A** *adj* daily; (ordinario) everyday
B *m* daily [paper]
'quoto *m* Math quotient
quozi'ente *m* quotient
■ **quoziente d'intelligenza** intelligence quotient, IQ; **quoziente di purezza** purity

Rr

ra'barbaro *m* rhubarb
'rabbia *f* rage; (ira) anger; Med rabies *sg*; **che ~!** what a nuisance!; **mi fa ~** it makes me angry
'rabbico *adj* ‹*virus*› rabies *attrib*
rab'bino *m* rabbi
rabbiosa'mente *adv* furiously
rabbi'oso *adj* hot-tempered; Med rabid; (violento) violent
rabboc'care *vt* top up ‹*fiasco*›
rabbo'nire *vt* pacify
rabbo'nirsi *vr* calm down
rabbrivi'dire *vi* shudder; (di freddo) shiver
rabbuf'fare *vt* reprimand; ruffle ‹*capelli*›
rab'buffo *m* reprimand
rabbui'arsi *vr* get dark; ‹*viso*› darken
rabdo'mante *mf* water diviner
rabdoman'zia *f* water divining
raccapez'zare *vt* put together
raccapez'zarsi *vr* see one's way ahead
raccapricci'ante *adj* horrifying
raccatta'palle **A** *m inv* ball boy
B *f inv* ball girl
raccat'tare *vt* pick up
rac'chetta *f* racket
■ **racchetta da neve** snowshoe; **racchetta da ping pong** table-tennis bat; **racchetta da sci** ski stick, ski pole; **racchetta da tennis** tennis racket
'racchio *adj* infml ugly
racchi'udere *vt* contain
rac'cogliere *vt* pick; (da terra) pick up; (mietere) harvest; (collezionare) collect; (radunare) gather; win ‹*voti ecc.*›; (dare asilo a) take in
rac'cogliersi *vr* gather; (concentrarsi) collect one's thoughts

q
r

raccogli'mento *m* concentration

raccogli|'tore, -trice *mf* collector
■ **raccoglitore a fogli mobili** ring binder

rac'colta *f* collection; (di scritti) compilation; (del grano ecc.) harvesting; (adunata) gathering; **chiamare a ~** call *or* gather together
■ **raccolta differenziata** separate waste collection; **raccolta di fondi** fund-raising

rac'colto, -a **A** pp di **raccogliere**
B *adj* (rannicchiato) hunched; (intimo) cosy; (concentrato) engrossed
C *m* (mietitura) harvest

raccoman'dabile *adj* advisable; **poco ~** ‹*persona*› shady

⚷ **raccoman'dare** *vt* recommend; (affidare) entrust

raccoman'darsi *vr* (implorare) beg

raccoman'data *f* letter sent by recorded delivery, certified mail AmE; **per ~** by recorded delivery
■ **raccomandata con ricevuta di ritorno** *letter sent by recorded delivery with acknowledgement of receipt*

raccoman'data-e'spresso *f express recorded delivery service*

raccomandazi'one *f* recommendation

raccomo'dare *vt* repair

⚷ **raccon'tare** *vt* tell

rac'conto *m* story
■ **racconto dell'orrore** horror story

raccorci'are *vt* shorten

raccorci'arsi *vr* become shorter; ‹*giorni*› draw in

raccor'dare *vt* join

rac'cordo *m* connection; (stradale) feeder
■ **raccordo anulare** ring road; **raccordo autostradale** motorway junction BrE, intersection; **raccordo ferroviario** siding; **raccordo a gomito** elbow

ra'chitico *adj* rickety; (poco sviluppato) stunted

racimo'lare *vt* scrape together

'racket *m inv* racket

'rada *f* Naut roads *pl*

'radar *m* radar; **uomo ~** air traffic controller

radden'sare *vt* thicken

radden'sarsi *vr* thicken

raddob'bare *vt* refit

rad'dobbo *m* refit

raddol'cire *vt* sweeten; fig soften

raddol'cirsi *vr* become milder; ‹*carattere*› mellow

raddoppia'mento *m* doubling

raddoppi'are *vt* double; increase twofold

rad'doppio *m* doubling, twofold increase; (equitazione) gallop; (biliardo) double

raddriz'zabile *adj* which can be straightened

raddriz'zare *vt* straighten

⚷ key word

raddrizza'tore *m* (di corrente) rectifier

ra'dente *adj* grazing, shaving; **tiro ~** Mil grazing fire; Sport low shot just skimming the surface; **volo ~** Aeron hedge-hopping

'radere *vt* shave; graze ‹*muro*›; **~ al suolo** raze [to the ground]

'radersi *vr* shave

radi'ale *adj* radial

radi'ante **A** *adj* radiant
B *m* Math radian

radi'are *vt* strike off; **~ dall'albo** strike off ‹*medico*›; debar ‹*avvocato*›

radia'tore *m* radiator

radiazi'one *f* radiation
■ **radiazione nucleare** nuclear radiation

'radica *f* briar

radi'cale **A** *adj* radical
B *m* Gram root; Pol radical

radical'mente *adv* radically

radi'carsi *vr* **~ in** be rooted in

radi'cato *adj* deep-seated

ra'dicchio *m* chicory

ra'dice *f* root; **mettere [le] radici** ‹*pianta*› take root; fig put down roots
■ **radice quadrata** square root

⚷ **'radio** **A** *f inv* radio; **via ~** by radio; **contatto ~** radio contact; **ponte ~** radio link
■ **radio pirata** pirate radio; **radio portatile** portable radio; **radio ricevente** receiver; **radio [a] transistor** transistor radio; **radio trasmittente** transmitter
B *m* Chem radium

radioama|'tore, -trice *mf* radio ham

radioascolta|'tore, -trice *mf* listener

radioassi'stito *adj* radio-assisted

radioattività *f inv* radioactivity

radioat'tivo *adj* radioactive

radiobiolo'gia *f* radiobiology

radio'bussola *f* radio compass

radiocoman'dare *vt* operate by remote control

radiocoman'dato *adj* remote-controlled, radio-controlled

radio'cronaca *f* radio commentary; **fare la ~ di** commentate on

radiocro'nista *mf* radio reporter

radiodiffusi'one *f* broadcasting

radio'faro *m* radio beacon

radio'fonico *adj* radio *attrib*

radiofre'quenza *f* radio frequency

radiogoni'ometro *m* direction finder, radiogoniometer

radiogra'fare *vt* X-ray

radiogra'fia *f* X-ray [photograph]; (radiologia) radiography; **fare una ~** ‹*paziente*› have an X-ray; ‹*dottore*› take an X-ray

radio'lina *f* transistor

radiolocaliz'zare *vt* locate by radar

radiolo'gia *f* radiology

radi'ologo, -a *mf* radiologist

radio'onda *f* radio wave

radioregistra'tore *m*
■ **radioregistratore portatile** portable radio cassette recorder

radiosco'pia *f* Med radioscopy

radio'scopico *adj* radioscopic

radi'oso *adj* radiant

radio'spia *f* bug

radio'sveglia *f* radio alarm, clock radio

radio'taxi *m inv* radio taxi

radiote'lefono *m* radio-telephone; (privato) cordless [phone]

radiotelevi'sivo *adj* broadcasting *attrib*

radiotera'pia *f* radiotherapy

radiotra'smettere *vt* radio

radiotrasmetti'tore *m* radio

radiotrasmit'tente *f* radio station

'rado *adj* sparse; (non frequente) rare; **di ~** seldom

radu'nare *vt* gather [together]

radu'narsi *vr* gather [together]

radu'nata *f* gathering
■ **radunata sediziosa** seditious assembly

ra'duno *m* meeting; Sport rally

ra'dura *f* clearing

'rafano *m* horseradish

raffazzo'nato *adj* ‹*discorso, lavoro*› botched

raf'fermo *adj* stale

'raffica *f* gust; (di armi da fuoco) burst; (di domande, insulti) barrage

raffigu'rare *vt* represent

raffigurazi'one *f* representation

raffi'nare *vt* refine

raffinata'mente *adv* elegantly

raffina'tezza *f* refinement

raffi'nato *adj* refined

raffine'ria *f* refinery
■ **raffineria di petrolio** oil refinery

rafforza'mento *m* reinforcement; (di muscolatura, carattere) strengthening

raffor'zare *vt* reinforce

rafforza'tivo **A** *adj* Gram intensifying **B** *m* Gram intensifier

raffredda'mento *m* (processo) cooling; **di ~** cooling
■ **raffreddamento ad acqua** water cooling; **raffreddamento ad aria** air cooling

raffred'dare *vt* cool

raffred'darsi *vr* get cold; (prendere un raffreddore) catch a cold; ‹*sentimento, passione*› cool [off]

raffred'dato *adj* **essere ~** ‹*persona*› have a cold

raffred'dore *m* cold; **avere il ~** have a cold
■ **raffreddore da fieno** hay fever

raf'fronto *m* comparison

'rafia *f* raffia

Rag. *abbr* = **ragioniere**

ra'gazza *f* girl; (fidanzata) girlfriend; **nome da ragazza** maiden name
■ **ragazza copertina** cover girl; **ragazza madre** unmarried mother; **ragazza alla pari** au pair [girl]; **ragazza squillo** call girl

ragaz'zata *f* prank

ra'gazzo *m* boy; (fidanzato) boyfriend; **da ~** (da giovane) as a boy
■ **ragazzo padre** unmarried father; **ragazzo di strada** guttersnipe; **ragazzo di vita** rent boy

ragge'lare *vt* fig freeze

ragge'larsi *vr* fig turn to ice

raggi'ante *adj* radiant

raggi'era *f* (di ruota) spokes *pl*; **a ~** with a pattern like spokes radiating from a centre

'raggio *m* ray; Math radius; (di ruota) spoke; **a raggi infrarossi** infrared
■ **raggio d'azione** range; **raggio laser** laser beam; **raggio di luna** moonbeam; **raggio di sole** ray of sunshine, sunbeam; **raggio di speranza** ray of hope; **raggio ultravioletto** ultraviolet ray; **raggi** *pl* **X** X-rays

raggi'rare *vt* trick, deceive

rag'giro *m* trick, con trick

raggi'ungere *vt* reach; (conseguire) achieve

raggiun'gibile *adj* ‹*luogo*› within reach

raggiungi'mento *m* attainment

raggomito'lare *vt* wind

raggomito'larsi *vr* curl up

raggranel'lare *vt* scrape together

raggrin'zire *vt* wrinkle

raggrin'zirsi *vr* wrinkle

raggru'mare *vt* curdle ‹*latte*›

raggru'marsi *vr* ‹*latte*› curdle

raggruppa'mento *m* (gruppo) group; (azione) grouping; Comm groupage

raggrup'pare *vt* group together

ragguagli'are *vt* compare; (informare) inform

raggu'aglio *m* comparison; (informazione) information

ragguar'devole *adj* considerable

'ragia *f* resin; **acqua ~** turpentine

ragià *m inv* rajah

ragiona'mento *m* reasoning; (discussione) discussion
■ **ragionamento per assurdo** reductio ad absurdum

ragio'nare *vi* reason; (discutere) discuss

ragio'nato *adj* ‹*argomento*› reasoned; ‹*cruciverba*› cryptic

ragi'one *f* reason; (ciò che è giusto) right; **a ~ o a torto** rightly or wrongly; **aver ~** be right; **perdere la ~** go out of one's mind; **a ragion veduta** after due consideration; **prenderle/darle di santa ~** get/give a good walloping
■ **ragion d'essere** raison d'être; **ragione di scambio** terms of trade; **ragione sociale** company name; **ragion di Stato** reasons of State

ragione'ria *f* accountancy; (scuola) *secondary school which provides training in accountancy*
ragio'nevole *adj* reasonable
ragionevol'mente *adv* reasonably
ragioni'ere, -a *mf* accountant
ra'glan *adj inv* ‹*manica*› raglan
ragli'are *vi* bray
'raglio *m* bray
ragna'tela *f* cobweb, web, spider web
'ragno *m* spider
ragù *m inv* meat sauce
RAI *nf abbr* (**Radio Audizioni Italiane**) Italian public broadcasting company
'raid *m inv* raid
'raion® *m* rayon®
ra'lenti *m* **al ~** in slow motion
rallegra'menti *mpl* congratulations
ralle'grare *vt* gladden
ralle'grarsi *vr* rejoice; **~ con qualcuno** congratulate somebody
rallenta'mento *m* slowing down
rallen'tare *vt & vi* slow down; (allentare) slacken
rallen'tarsi *vr* slow down
rallenta'tore *m* (su strada) speed bump; **al ~** in slow motion
'rally *m inv* rally
RAM *f inv* RAM
ramai'olo *m* ladle
raman'zina *f* reprimand
ra'mare *vt* stake ‹*pianta*›
ra'marro *m* (animale) type of lizard
ra'mato *adj* ‹*capelli*› copper-coloured, coppery
'rame *m* copper; **color ~** copper-coloured
ramifi'care *vi* ‹*pianta*› put out branches
ramifi'carsi *vr* ‹*pianta*› put out branches; ‹*strada, fiume ecc.*› branch; ‹*teoria*› ramify, branch
ramificazi'one *f* ramification
ra'mino *m* rummy
rammari'carsi *vr* **~ di** regret; (lamentarsi) complain (**di** about)
ram'marico *m* regret
rammen'dare *vt* darn
ram'mendo *m* darning
rammen'tare *vt* remember; **~ qualcosa a qualcuno** (richiamare alla memoria) remind somebody of something
rammen'tarsi *vr* remember
rammol'lire *vt* soften
rammol'lirsi *vr* go soft
rammol'lito, -a *mf* wimp
⚷ **'ramo** *m* branch
ramo'scello *m* twig
'rampa *f* (di scale) flight
■ **rampa d'accesso** slip road; **rampa di carico** loading ramp; **rampa di lancio** launch pad
ram'pante *adj* ‹*leone, cavallo*› rampant; **giovane ~** yuppie
rampi'cante **A** *adj* climbing
B *m* Bot creeper
ram'pino *m* hook; fig pretext
ram'pollo *m* (hum) brat; (discendente) descendant
ram'pone *m* harpoon; (per scarpe) crampon
'rana *f* frog; (nel nuoto) breaststroke; **uomo ~** frogman
ranch *m inv* ranch
'rancido *adj* rancid
'rancio *m* rations *pl*
⚷ **ran'core** *m* rancour, resentment; **serbare ~ verso qualcuno** bear somebody a grudge
'randa *f* mainsail
ran'dagio *adj* stray
randel'lata *f* blow with a club
ran'dello *m* club
'rango *m* rank
rannicchi'arsi *vr* huddle up
rannuvola'mento *m* clouding over
rannuvo'larsi *vr* cloud over
ra'nocchio *m* frog
ranto'lare *vi* wheeze
'rantolo *m* wheeze; (di moribondo) death rattle
ra'nuncolo *m* buttercup
'rapa *f* turnip
ra'pace *adj* rapacious; ‹*uccello*› predatory
rapa'nello *m* radish
ra'pare *vt* crop
ra'parsi *vr* infml have one's head shaved
'rapida *f* rapids *pl*
rapida'mente *adv* quickly, rapidly
rapidità *f inv* speed
⚷ **'rapido** **A** *adj* fast, quick; ‹*guarigione, sviluppo*› rapid
B *m* (treno) express [train]
rapi'mento *m* (crimine) kidnapping
ra'pina *f* robbery, hold-up infml
■ **rapina a mano armata** armed robbery; **rapina in banca** bank robbery
rapi'nare *vt* rob
rapina'tore *m* robber
■ **rapinatore di banca** bank robber
ra'pire *vt* abduct; (per riscatto) kidnap; fig (estasiare) ravish
ra'pito, -a **A** *adj* abducted; (per riscatto) kidnapped; (estasiato) rapt
B *mf* kidnap victim
rapi|'tore, -trice *mf* kidnapper
rappacifi'care *vt* pacify
rappacifi'carsi *vr* be reconciled, make it up
rappacificazi'one *f* reconciliation
'rapper *mf inv* Mus rapper

r

⚷ key word

rappez'zare *vt* patch up
rappor'tare *vt* reproduce ‹*disegno*›; (confrontare) compare
rap'porto *m* report; (connessione) relation; (legame) relationship; Math, Techn ratio; **rapporti** *pl* relations, relationship; **essere in buoni rapporti** be on good terms
■ **rapporti** *pl* **d'affari** business relations; **rapporto di amicizia** friendship; **avere un ~ di amicizia con qualcuno** be friends with somebody; **rapporto di lavoro** working relationship; **rapporto di parentela** family relationship; **aver un ~ di parentela con qualcuno** be related to somebody; **rapporti** *pl* **prematrimoniali** premarital sex; **rapporto prezzo-prestazioni** price/performance ratio; **rapporto prezzo-qualità** value for money; **rapporti** *pl* **sessuali** sexual intercourse; **rapporto di trasmissione** Auto gear
rap'prendersi *vr* set; ‹*latte*› curdle
rappre'saglia *f* reprisal
rappresen'tante *mf* representative
■ **rappresentante di classe** class representative; **rappresentante di commercio** sales representative, [sales] rep infml; **rappresentante sindacale** trade union representative
rappresen'tanza *f* delegation; Comm agency; **spese di ~** entertainment expenses; **di ~** ‹*appartamento, macchina*› company *attrib*
■ **rappresentanza esclusiva** sole agency; **rappresentanza legale** legal representation; **rappresentanza proporzionale** proportional representation, PR
rappresen'tare *vt* represent; Theat perform
rappresenta'tiva *f* representatives *pl*
rappresenta'tivo *adj* representative
rappresentazi'one *f* representation; (spettacolo) performance
rap'preso pp di **rapprendersi**
rapso'dia *f* rhapsody
'raptus *m inv* fit of madness
rara'mente *adv* rarely, seldom
rare'fare *vt* rarefy
rare'farsi *vr* rarefy
rare'fatto *adj* rarefied
rarità *f inv* rarity
'raro *adj* rare
ra'sare *vt* shave; trim ‹*siepe ecc.*›
ra'sarsi *vr* shave
ra'sato *adj* shaved
rasa'tura *f* shaving
raschia'mento *m* Med curettage
raschi'are *vt* scrape; (togliere) scrape off
raschi'arsi *vr* **~ la gola** clear one's throat
rasen'tare *vt* go close to
ra'sente *prep* very close to
'raso **A** pp di **radere**
B *adj* smooth; (colmo) full to the brim; ‹*barba*› close-cropped; **~ terra** close to the ground; **un cucchiaio ~** a level spoonful
C *m* satin
ra'soio *m* razor
■ **rasoio elettrico** electric shaver; **rasoio a mano libera** cut-throat razor
'raspa *f* rasp
'raspo *m* (di uva) small bunch
ras'segna *f* review; (mostra) exhibition; (musicale, cinematografica) festival; **passare in ~** review; Mil inspect
rasse'gnare *vt* present
rasse'gnarsi *vr* resign oneself
rassegnata'mente *adv* with resignation
rasse'gnato *adj* ‹*persona, aria, tono*› resigned
rassegnazi'one *f* resignation
rassere'nare *vt* clear; fig cheer up
rassere'narsi *vr* become clear; fig cheer up
rasset'tare *vt* tidy up; (riparare) mend
rassicu'rante *adj* ‹*persona, parole, presenza*› reassuring
rassicu'rare *vt* reassure
rassicurazi'one *f* reassurance
rasso'dare *vt* harden; fig strengthen
rassomigli'ante *adj* similar
rassomigli'anza *f* resemblance
rassomigli'are *vi* **~ a** resemble
rastrella'mento *m* (di fieno) raking; (perlustrazione) combing
rastrel'lare *vt* rake; (perlustrare) comb
rastrelli'era *f* rack; (per biciclette) bicycle rack; (scolapiatti) [plate] rack
ra'strello *m* rake
'rata *f* instalment; (di mutuo) mortgage repayment; **pagare a rate** pay by instalments; **comprare qualcosa a rate** buy something on hire purchase, buy something on the installment plan AmE
rate'ale *adj* by instalments; **pagamento rateale** payment by instalments; **vendita rateale** hire purchase
rate'are, **rateiz'zare** *vt* divide into instalments
ra'tifica *f* Jur ratification
ratifi'care *vt* Jur ratify
'ratto[1] *m* (rapimento) abduction
'ratto[2] *m* (raditore) rat
■ **ratto comune** black rat
rattop'pare *vt* patch
rat'toppo *m* patch
rattrap'pire *vt* make stiff
rattrap'pirsi *vr* become stiff
rattri'stare *vt* sadden
rattri'starsi *vr* become sad
rau'cedine *f* hoarseness
'rauco *adj* hoarse
rava'nello *m* radish
ravi'oli *mpl* ravioli *sg*
ravve'dersi *vr* mend one's ways

ravvi'are *vt* tidy ‹*capelli, stanza*›
ravvicina'mento *m* (tra persone) reconciliation; Pol rapprochement
ravvici'nare *vt* bring closer; (riconciliare) reconcile
ravvici'narsi *vr* be reconciled
ravvi'sare *vt* recognize
ravvi'vare *vt* revive; fig brighten up
ravvi'varsi *vr* revive
rav'volgere *vt* roll up
rav'volgersi *vr* wrap oneself up
'rayon® *m* rayon
razio'cinio *m* rational thought; (buon senso) common sense
razio'nale *adj* rational
razionalità *f inv* (raziocinio) rationality; (di ambiente) functional nature
razionaliz'zare *vt* rationalize ‹*programmi, metodi, spazio*›
razional'mente *adv* (con raziocinio) rationally
raziona'mento *m* rationing
razio'nare *vt* ration
razi'one *f* ration
🔑 **'razza** *f* race; (di cani ecc.) breed; (genere) kind; **che ~ di idiota!** infml what an idiot!
raz'zia *f* raid
razzi'ale *adj* racial
raz'zismo *m* racism
raz'zista *adj & nmf* racist
'razzo *m* rocket
■ **razzo da segnalazione** flare
razzo'lare *vi* ‹*polli*› scratch about
🔑 **re** *m inv* king; Mus (chiave, nota) D; **Re** *pl* **Magi** Wise Men
rea'gente *adj & nm* reactant
rea'gire *vi* react
🔑 **re'ale** *adj* real; (di re) royal
rea'lismo *m* realism
rea'lista *mf* realist; (fautore del re) royalist
realistica'mente *adv* realistically
rea'listico *adj* realistic
realiz'zabile *adj* feasible
🔑 **realiz'zare** *vt* (attuare) carry out, realize; Comm make; score ‹*gol, canestro*›; (rendersi conto di) realize
realiz'zarsi *vr* come true; (nel lavoro ecc.) fulfil oneself
realiz'zato *adj* ‹*persona*› fulfilled
realizzazi'one *f* realization; (di sogno, persona) fulfilment
■ **realizzazione scenica** production
rea'lizzo *m* (vendita) proceeds *pl*; (riscossione) yield
real'mente *adv* really
🔑 **realtà** *f inv* reality; **in ~** in reality; (a dire il vero) actually
■ **realtà virtuale** virtual reality

🔑 key word

re'ame *m* realm
re'ato *m* crime, criminal offence; **reati** *pl* **informatici** computer crime
■ **reato minore** minor offence
reattività *f inv* reactivity; (a farmaco) reaction
reat'tivo *adj* reactive
reat'tore *m* reactor; Aeron jet [aircraft]
■ **reattore nucleare** atomic reactor
reazio'nario, -a *adj & nmf* reactionary
reazi'one *f* reaction; **a ~** ‹*motore, aereo*› jet
■ **reazione a catena** chain reaction; **reazione chimica** chemical reaction
'rebus *m inv* rebus; (enigma) puzzle
recapi'tare *vt* deliver
re'capito *m* address; (consegna) delivery; **in caso di mancato ~...** if undelivered...
■ **recapito a domicilio** home delivery; **recapito telefonico** contact telephone number
re'care *vt* bear; (produrre) cause
re'carsi *vr* go
re'cedere *vi* recede; fig give up
recensi'one *f* review
recen'sire *vt* review
recen'sore *m* reviewer
🔑 **re'cente** *adj* recent; **di ~** recently
recente'mente *adv* recently
re'ception *f inv* reception [desk]
re'ceptionist *mf* receptionist
recessi'one *f* recession; **~a w** double-dip recession
reces'sivo *adj* Biol recessive; Econ recessionary
re'cesso *m* recess
re'cidere *vt* cut off
reci'diva *f* Jur recidivism; Med relapse; **furto con ~** repeat offence of theft
recidività *f inv* recidivism
reci'divo, -a **A** *adj* Med recurrent
B *mf* repeat offender, persistent offender, recidivist fml; **è ~** fig he's lapsed back into his old ways
recin'tare *vt* close off
re'cinto *m* enclosure; (per animali) pen; (per bambini) playpen
■ **recinto delle grida** Fin [trading] floor; **recinto del peso** (ippica) weigh-in room
recinzi'one *f* (azione) enclosure; (muro) wall; (rete) wire fence; (cancellata) railings *pl*
recipi'ente *m* container
re'ciproco *adj* reciprocal
re'ciso **A** pp di **recidere**
B *adj* (risoluto) definite
'recita *f* performance
■ **recita scolastica** school play
'recital *m inv* recital
🔑 **reci'tare** **A** *vt* recite; Theat act; play ‹*ruolo*›
B *vi* act; **~ a soggetto** improvise
recitazi'one *f* recitation; Theat acting; **scuola di ~** drama school
recla'mare **A** *vi* protest

B *vt* claim

ré'clame *f inv* advertising; (avviso pubblicitario) advertisement

reclamiz'zare *vt* advertise

re'clamo *m* complaint; **ufficio reclami** complaints department

recli'nabile *adj* reclining; **sedile ~** reclining seat

recli'nare *vt* tilt ‹*sedile*›; lean ‹*capo*›

reclusi'one *f* imprisonment

re'cluso, -a **A** *adj* secluded
B *mf* prisoner

'recluta *f* recruit

recluta'mento *m* recruitment

reclu'tare *vt* recruit

re'condito *adj* secluded; (intimo) secret

'record **A** *m inv* record; **a tempo di ~** in record time
B *adj inv* ‹*cifra*› record *attrib*

recrimi'nare *vi* recriminate

recriminazi'one *f* recrimination

recrude'scenza *f* Med fresh outbreak; fig (di violenza) renewed outbreak; (di criminalità) upsurge

recupe'rare **A** *vt* recover; rehabilitate ‹*tossicodipendente*›; make up ‹*ore di assenza*›; **~ il tempo perduto** make up for lost time
B *vi* catch up

re'cupero *m* recovery; (di tossicodipendenti) rehabilitation; (salvataggio) rescue; **corso di ~** additional classes *pl*; **materiali di ~** recycled material; (che possono essere recuperati) recyclable material; **[minuti di] ~** Sport injury time; **partita di ~** rematch
■ **recupero crediti** debt collection; **recupero [dei] dati** data recovery

redargu'ire *vt* rebuke

re'datto pp di **redigere**

redat|'tore, -trice *mf* editor; (di testo) writer
■ **redattore capo** editor in chief

redazi'one *f* (ufficio) editorial office; (di testi) editing

redditività *f inv* earning power

reddi'tizio *adj* profitable

'reddito *m* income; **a basso ~** ‹*famiglia*› low income
■ **imposta sul reddito** income tax; **reddito complessivo** gross income; **reddito imponibile** taxable income; **reddito non imponibile** non-taxable income; **reddito da lavoro** earned income; **redditi** *pl* **occasionali** casual earnings; **reddito pubblico** government revenue

re'dento pp di **redimere**

reden'tore *m* redeemer

redenzi'one *f* redemption

re'digere *vt* write; draw up ‹*documento*›

re'dimere *vt* redeem

re'dimersi *vr* redeem oneself

redi'mibile *adj* ‹*titoli*› redeemable

'redine *f* rein

redin'gote *f inv* frock coat; **abito a ~** fitted button-through dress

'redini *fpl* reins

redi'vivo *adj* restored to life

'reduce **A** *adj* **~ da** back from
B *mf* survivor

refe'rendum *m inv* referendum

refe'renza *f* reference

referenzi'ato *adj* with references

re'ferto *m* report
■ **referto medico** medical report

refet'torio *m* refectory

reflazio'nare *vt* Econ reflate

reflazi'one *f* Econ reflation

'reflex *m inv* reflex camera

'refluo *m* effluent

refrat'tario *adj* refractory; **essere ~ a** fig be insensitive to ‹*sentimenti*›; **sono ~ alla matematica** maths are a closed book to me

refrige'rante *adj* cooling *attrib*

refrige'rare *vt* refrigerate

refrigerazi'one *f* refrigeration

refur'tiva *f* stolen goods *pl*

re'fuso *m* Typ literal, typo

rega'lare *vt* give

re'gale *adj* regal

re'galo *m* present, gift; **articoli da ~** gifts
■ **confezione regalo** gift set

re'gata *f* regatta

'reggae *m inv* Mus reggae

reg'gente *mf* regent

reg'genza *f* regency

'reggere **A** *vt* (sorreggere) bear; (tenere in mano) hold; (dirigere) run; (governare) govern; Gram take
B *vi* (resistere) hold out; (durare) last; fig stand

'reggersi *vr* stand

'reggia *f* royal palace

reggi'calze *m inv* suspender belt

reggi'mento *m* regiment; fig (molte persone) army

reggi'petto, reggi'seno *m* bra

re'gia *f* Cinema direction; Theat production

re'gime *m* regime; (dieta) diet; (di fiume) rate of flow; **a ~ torrentizio** in spate; **a pieno ~** ‹*funzionare*› at full speed
■ **regime alimentare** diet; **regime fiscale** tax system; **regime di giri** (di motore) revs per minute, rpm; **regime militare** military regime; **regime monetario aureo** gold standard; **regime di vita** lifestyle

re'gina *f* queen; **ape ~** queen bee
■ **regina madre** queen mother

'regio *adj* royal

regio'nale *adj* regional

regiona'lismo *m* (parola) regionalism

regional'mente *adv* regionally
regi'one *f* region
re'gista *mf* Cinema, TV director; Theat producer
regi'strare *vt* register; Comm enter; (incidere su nastro) tape, record; (su disco) record
registra'tore *m* recorder; (magnetofono) tape recorder
■ **registratore di cassa** cash register; **registratore a cassette** tape recorder, cassette recorder; **registratore di volo** flight recorder
registrazi'one *f* registration; Comm entry; (di programma) recording; **sala di ~** recording studio
■ **registrazione [dei] dati** data capture
re'gistro *m* register; (ufficio) registry
■ **registro di bordo** log; **registro di cassa** ledger; **registro di classe** class register; **registro linguistico** register
re'gnare *vi* reign
✓ **'regno** *m* kingdom; (sovranità) reign
■ **regno animale** animal kingdom; **Regno Unito** United Kingdom; **regno vegetale** plant kingdom
✓ **'regola** *f* rule; **essere in ~** be in order; ‹*persona*› have one's papers in order; **a ~ d'arte** in a workmanlike fashion
rego'labile *adj* ‹*velocità. luminosità*› adjustable
regola'mento *m* regulation; Comm settlement
■ **regolamento di conti** settling of scores
✓ **rego'lare** **A** *adj* regular
B *vt* regulate; (ridurre, moderare) limit; (sistemare) settle
regolarità *f inv* regularity
regolariz'zare *vt* settle ‹*debito*›; regularize ‹*situazione*›
rego'larsi *vr* (agire) act; (moderarsi) control oneself
rego'lata *f* **darsi una ~** pull oneself together
regola'tore, -trice **A** *adj* **piano ~** urban development plan
B *mf* regulator
'regolo *m* ruler
■ **regolo calcolatore** slide rule
regre'dire *vi* Biol, Psych regress
regressi'one *f* regression
regres'sivo *adj* regressive
re'gresso *m* decline
reincar'narsi *vr* **~ in...** be reincarnated as...
reincarnazi'one *f* reincarnation
reinseri'mento *m* (di persona) reintegration
reinse'rirsi *vr* (in ambiente) reintegrate
reinstal'lare *vt* reinstall
reinte'grare *vt* restore
reinven'tare *vt* reinvent
reinvesti'mento *m* reinvestment
reinve'stire *vt* reinvest ‹*soldi*›

✓ key word

reite'rare *vt* reiterate
reiterazi'one *f* reiteration
re'lais *m inv* relay
relativa'mente *adv* relatively; **~ a** as regards
relatività *f inv* relativity
rela'tivo *adj* relative
rela|'tore, -trice *mf* (in una conferenza) speaker; (di tesi) supervisor
re'lax *m* relaxation
✓ **relazi'one** *f* relation; (di lavoro ecc.) relationship; (rapporto amoroso) [love] affair; (resoconto) report; **pubbliche relazioni** *pl* public relations
■ **relazione extraconiugale** extramarital relationship; **relazioni** *pl* **industriali** industrial relations
rele'gare *vt* relegate
relegazi'one *f* relegation
religi'one *f* religion
religi'oso, -a **A** *adj* religious
B *m* monk
C *f* nun
re'liquia *f* relic
reliqui'ario *m* reliquary
re'litto *m* wreck
re'mainder *m inv* (libro) remainder
re'make *m inv* remake
re'mare *vi* row
rema|'tore, -trice *mf* rower
remini'scenza *f* reminiscence
remissi'one *f* remission; (sottomissione) submissiveness
■ **remissione del debito** remission of debt; **remissione di querela** withdrawal of an action
remissiva'mente *adv* submissively
remis'sivo *adj* submissive
re'mix *m inv* Mus remix
'remo *m* oar
'remora *f* **senza remore** without hesitation
re'moto *adj* remote
remo'vibile *adj* removable
remune'rare *vt* remunerate
remunera'tivo *adj* remunerative
remunerazi'one *f* remuneration
re'nale *adj* renal, kidney *attrib*
✓ **'rendere** *vt* (restituire) return; (esprimere) render; (fruttare) yield; (far diventare) make
'rendersi *vr* become; **~ conto di qualcosa** realize something; **~ utile** make oneself useful
rendi'conto *m* report
rendi'mento *m* rendering; (produzione) yield
'rendita *f* income; (dello Stato) revenue; **vivere di ~** fig rest on one's laurels
■ **rendita vitalizia** life annuity
'rene *m* kidney
■ **rene artificiale** kidney machine

r

'reni *fpl* (schiena) back

reni'tente **A** *adj* **essere ~ a** ‹*consigli di qualcuno*› be loath to accept; refuse to obey ‹*legge*›

■ **renitente alla leva** *person who fails to report for military service after being called up*

B *m* draft dodger AmE

'renna *f* reindeer (*pl inv*); (pelle) buckskin

'Reno *m* Rhine

'reo, -a **A** *adj* guilty

B *mf* criminal

■ **reo confesso** self-confessed criminal

Rep. *abbr* (**repubblica**) Rep.

re'parto *m* department; Mil unit; **reparti** *pl* **d'assalto** Mil assault troops

■ **reparto d'attacco** Sport attack; **reparto difensivo** Sport defence; **reparto grandi ustionati** Med burns unit; **reparto di massima sicurezza** secure unit; **reparto maternità** obstetrics [department]; **reparto radiologia** X-ray unit

repel'lente *adj* repulsive

repen'taglio *m* **mettere a ~** risk

repentina'mente *adv* suddenly

repen'tino *adj* sudden

repe'ribile *adj* available; **non è ~** (perduto) it's not to be found

reperibilità *f inv* availability

repe'rire *vt* trace ‹*fondi*›

re'perto *m*:

■ **reperto archeologico** find; **reperto giudiziario** exhibit

reper'torio *m* repertory; (elenco) index; **immagini** *pl* **di ~** archive footage

re'play *m inv* [instant] replay

'replica *f* reply; (obiezione) objection; (copia) replica; Theat repeat performance

repli'care *vt* reply; Theat repeat

repor'tage *m inv* report

repressi'one *f* repression

repres'sivo *adj* repressive

re'presso pp di **reprimere**

re'primere *vt* repress

re'pubblica *f* republic

■ **Repubblica Ceca** Czech Republic; **Repubblica Centrafricana** Central African Republic; **Repubblica Dominicana** Dominican Republic; **Repubblica d'Irlanda** Republic of Ireland, Irish Republic; **repubblica parlamentare** parliamentary republic; **Repubblica Popolare cinese** People's Republic of China; **repubblica presidenziale** presidential-style republic; **Repubblica Slovacca** Slovakia

repubbli'cano, -a *adj & nmf* republican

repu'tare *vt* consider

repu'tarsi *vr* consider oneself

reputazi'one *f* reputation

'requiem *m inv* requiem

requi'sire *vt* requisition

requi'sito *m* requirement

■ **requisiti di sistema** Comput system requirements

requisi'toria *f* (arringa) closing speech

requisizi'one *f* requisition

'resa *f* surrender; Comm rendering

■ **resa dei conti** rendering of accounts; **resa incondizionata** unconditional surrender

re'scindere *vt* cancel

'residence *m inv* residential hotel

resi'dente *adj & nmf* resident

resi'denza *f* residence; (soggiorno) stay

■ **residenza protetta** sheltered accommodation

residenzi'ale *adj* residential; **zona ~** residential district

re'siduo **A** *adj* residual

B *m* remainder; **residui** *pl* **industriali** industrial waste

'resina *f* resin

resi'stente *adj* resistant

■ **resistente all'acqua** water resistant

resi'stenza *f* resistance; (fisica) stamina; Electr resistor; **la Resistenza** the Resistance

■ **resistenza passiva** passive resistance; **resistenza a pubblico ufficiale** resisting arrest

re'sistere *vi* **~ [a]** resist; (a colpi, scosse) stand up to; **~ alla pioggia/al vento** be rain/wind-resistant

'reso pp di **rendere**

reso'conto *m* report

■ **resoconto annuale** annual report

respin'gente *m* Rail buffer

re'spingere *vt* repel; (rifiutare) reject; (bocciare) fail

respingi'mento *m* repatriation

re'spinto pp di **respingere**

respi'rare *vt & vi* breathe

respira'tore *m* respirator

■ **respiratore artificiale** life support machine; **respiratore [a tubo]** snorkel

respira'torio *adj* respiratory

respirazi'one *f* breathing; Med respiration

■ **respirazione artificiale** artificial respiration; **respirazione assistita** life support; **respirazione bocca a bocca** mouth-to-mouth resuscitation, kiss of life

re'spiro *m* breath; (il respirare) breathing; fig respite

■ **respiro di sollievo** sigh of relief

respon'sabile **A** *adj* responsible (**di** for); Jur liable

B *mf* person responsible

■ **responsabile della gestione del portafoglio fondi di investimento** investment manager; **responsabile della produzione** production manager; **responsabile delle risorse umane** human resources manager

responsabilità *f inv* responsibility; Jur liability

■ **responsabilità civile** Jur civil liability; **responsabilità limitata** limited liability; **responsabilità penale** criminal liability

responsabiliz'zare *vt* give responsibility to ‹*dipendente*›; give a sense of responsibility to ‹*gente*›

responsabil'mente *adv* responsibly

re'sponso *m* response

'ressa *f* crowd

re'stante **A** *adj* remaining
B *m* remainder

⚷ **re'stare** = **rimanere**

restau'rare *vt* restore

restaura|'tore, -trice *mf* restorer

restaurazi'one *f* restoration

re'stauro *m* (riparazione) repair

re'stio *adj* restive; **~ a** reluctant to

restitu'ibile *adj* returnable

restitu'ire *vt* return; (reintegrare) restore

restituzi'one *f* return; Jur restitution

⚷ **'resto** *m* rest, remainder; (saldo) balance; (denaro) change; **resti** *pl* (avanzi) remains; **del ~** besides

re'stringere *vt* contract; take in ‹*vestiti*›; (limitare) restrict; shrink ‹*stoffa*›

re'stringersi *vr* contract; (farsi più vicini) close up; ‹*stoffa*› shrink

restringi'mento *m* (di tessuto) shrinkage
■ **restringimento del campo visivo** Med tunnel vision

restrit'tivo *adj* restrictive

restrizi'one *f* restriction

resurrezi'one *f* resurrection

resusci'tare **A** *vt* revive; resuscitate ‹*moribondo*›
B *vi* ‹*Cristo*› rise again; fig revive

re'taggio *m* legacy

re'tata *f* round-up

⚷ **'rete** *f* net; (sistema) network; (televisiva) channel; (in calcio, hockey) goal; fig trap; (per la spesa) string bag; **la Rete** (Internet) the net, the web
■ **rete commutata pubblica** Teleph switched public network; **rete di distribuzione** Comm distribution network; **rete fissa** Teleph fixed telephone network; **rete locale** Comput local [area] network, LAN; **rete mobile** Teleph mobile telephone network; **rete di protezione** (per acrobata) safety net; **rete sociale** social network; **rete stradale** road network; **rete telematica** communications network; **rete televisiva** television channel; **rete televisiva satellitare** satellite channel; **rete televisiva via cavo** cable company

reti'cente *adj* reticent

reti'cenza *f* reticence

retico'lato *m* grid; (rete metallica) wire netting

re'ticolo *m* network
■ **reticolo geografico** grid

'retina *f* Anat retina

re'tina *f* (per capelli) hair net

⚷ key word

re'tino *m* net

retorica'mente *adv* rhetorically

re'torico, -a **A** *adj* rhetorical; **domanda retorica** rhetorical question; **figura retorica** figure of speech
B *f* rhetoric

re'trattile *adj* ‹*punta*› retractable

retribu'ire *vt* remunerate

retribu'tivo *adj* salary *attrib*

retribuzi'one *f* remuneration

'retro **A** *adv* behind; **vedi ~** see over
B *m inv* back
■ **retro di copertina** outside back cover

retroat'tivo *adj* retroactive

retrobot'tega *m inv* back shop

retro'cedere **A** *vi* retreat
B *vt* Mil demote; Sport relegate

retrocessi'one *f* Sport relegation

retroda'tare *vt* backdate, predate

retro'fit *m inv* Auto retrofitted catalytic converter

re'trogrado *adj* retrograde; fig old-fashioned; Pol reactionary

retrogu'ardia *f* Mil rearguard

retro'gusto *m* after-taste

retro'marcia *f* reverse [gear]

retro'scena *m inv* Theat backstage; **i ~** fig the real story

retrospettiva'mente *adv* retrospectively

retrospet'tivo *adj* retrospective

retro'stante *adj* **il palazzo ~** the building behind

retro'via *f* Mil area behind the front lines

retro'virus *m inv* retrovirus

retrovi'sore *m* rear-view mirror

'retta[1] *f* Math straight line; (di collegio, pensionato) fee

'retta[2] *f* **dar ~ a qualcuno** take somebody's advice

rettango'lare *adj* rectangular

ret'tangolo **A** *adj* right-angled
B *m* rectangle

ret'tifica *f* rectification

rettifi'care *vt* rectify

'rettile *m* reptile

retti'lineo **A** *adj* rectilinear; (retto) upright
B *m* Sport back straight

retti'tudine *f* rectitude

'retto **A** pp di **reggere**
B *adj* straight; fig upright; (giusto) correct; **angolo ~** right angle
C *m* rectum

ret'tore *m* Relig rector; Univ chancellor

reu'matico *adj* rheumatic

reuma'tismi *mpl* rheumatism

reve'rendo *adj* reverend

rever'sibile *adj* reversible

revisio'nare *vt* revise; Comm audit; Auto overhaul

revisi'one *f* revision; Comm audit; Auto overhaul
revisio'nismo *m* Pol revisionism
revisio'nista *adj* ‹*politica*› revisionist
revi'sore *m* (di conti) auditor; (di bozze) proofreader; (di traduzioni) reviser
re'vival *m inv* revival
'revoca *f* repeal
revo'care *vt* repeal
revolve'rata *f* revolver shot
rhythm and blues *m* rhythm and blues, R & B
riabbas'sare *vt* lower again
riabbas'sarsi *vr* ‹*acque*› recede; ‹*temperatura*› fall again
riabbotto'nare *vt* button up again
riabbracci'are *vt* (abbracciare di nuovo) embrace again; fig (rivedere) see again
riabili'tare *vt* rehabilitate
riabilitazi'one *f* rehabilitation; **centro di ~** rehabilitation centre
riabitu'are *vt* **~ qualcuno a qualcosa** reaccustom somebody to something, get somebody used to something again
riabitu'arsi *vr* **~ a qualcosa** get used to something again, reaccustom oneself to something
riac'cendere *vt* switch on again ‹*luce, TV*›; rekindle, revive ‹*interesse, passione*›; rekindle ‹*fuoco*›
riac'cendersi *vr* ‹*luce*› come back on; ‹*interesse, passione*› rekindle, revive
riaccensi'one *f* **la continua ~** continual switching on and off
riaccer'tare *vt* reassess
riacqui'stare *vt* buy back; regain ‹*libertà, prestigio*›; recover ‹*vista, udito*›
riacutiz'zarsi *vr* get worse again
riadatta'mento *m* readjustment
riadat'tare *vt* convert ‹*stanza*›; alter ‹*indumento*›
riadat'tarsi *vr* readjust
riaddormen'tare *vt* get [back] to sleep again
riaddormen'tarsi *vr* fall asleep again
riadope'rare *vt* reuse
riaffacci'arsi *vr* (alla finestra) appear again; ‹*idea*› surface again
riaffer'mare *vt* reaffirm, reassert
riaffon'dare *vi* sink again
riaffron'tare *vt* deal with again ‹*situazione*›; take up again ‹*argomento*›
riagganci'are **A** *vt* replace ‹*ricevitore*›; **~ la cornetta** hang up
B *vi* hang up
riaggre'garsi *vr* regroup
riallac'ciare *vt* refasten; reconnect ‹*corrente*›; renew ‹*amicizia*›
riallar'gare *vt* widen again ‹*tunnel, strada*›
riallinea'mento *m* realignment
rialline'are *vt* realign
rialloggi'are *vt* rehouse
rial'zare **A** *vt* raise
B *vi* rise
rial'zarsi *vr* get up again
rial'zato *adj* **piano ~** mezzanine
ri'alzo *m* rise; **al ~** Fin bullish
■ **rialzo dei prezzi** price rise
ria'mare *vt* **~ qualcuno** reciprocate somebody's love, love somebody back
riamma'larsi *vr* fall ill again
riam'mettere *vt* readmit ‹*socio, studente*›
rian'dare *vi* return
riani'mare *vt* Med resuscitate; (ridare forza a) revive; (ridare coraggio a) cheer up
riani'marsi *vr* regain consciousness; (riprendere forza) revive; (riprendere coraggio) cheer up
rianimazi'one *f* intensive care [unit]; **sala di rianimazione** intensive care unit
rianno'dare *vt* retie ‹*filo*›; renew ‹*rapporti*›
riaper'tura *f* reopening
riappa'rire *vi* reappear
riap'pendere *vt* replace ‹*cornetta*›; **~ [il telefono]** hang up
riappiso'larsi *vr* doze off again
riappropri'arsi *vr* **~ di** take back
ria'prire *vt* reopen
ria'prirsi *vr* reopen
ri'armo *m* rearmament
ri'arso *adj* parched
riascol'tare *vt* listen to again
riasse'gnare *vt* reallocate
riassicu'rare *vt* reinsure
riassicurazi'one *f* reinsurance
riassorbi'mento *m* reabsorption
riassor'bire *vt* reabsorb
rias'sumere *vt* re-employ, take on again ‹*impiegato*›; ‹*ricapitolare*› resume
riassu'mibile *adj* (riepilogabile) which can be summarized, summarizable
riassun'tivo *adj* summarizing
rias'sunto **A** pp di **riassumere**
B *m* summary
riattac'care **A** *vt* **~ il telefono** hang up
B *vi* (al telefono) hang up
riatti'vare *vt* reactivate ‹*processo*›; reintroduce, bring back ‹*servizio*›; start up again, restart ‹*congegno*›; stimulate ‹*circolazione sanguigna*›
ria'vere *vt* get back; regain ‹*salute, vista*›
ria'versi *vr* recover
riavvicina'mento *m* (tra persone) reconciliation; (tra paesi) rapprochement
riavvici'nare *vt* fig reconcile ‹*paesi, persone*›
riavvici'narsi *vr* (riconciliarsi) be reconciled, make it up infml

riav'volgere *vt* rewind
riba'dire *vt* (confermare) reaffirm
ri'balta *f* flap; Theat footlights *pl*; fig limelight
ribal'tabile *adj* tip-up
ribal'tare *vt & vi* tip over; Naut capsize
ribal'tarsi *vr* tip over; Naut capsize
ribas'sare **A** *vt* lower
B *vi* fall
ribas'sato *adj* reduced
ri'basso *m* fall; (sconto) discount
ri'battere **A** *vt* (a macchina) retype; (controbattere) deny
B *vi* answer back
ribattez'zare *vt* rename
⚷ **ribel'larsi** *vr* rebel
ri'belle **A** *adj* rebellious
B *mf* rebel
ribelli'one *f* rebellion
'ribes *m inv* (rosso) redcurrant; (nero) blackcurrant
ribol'lire *vi* (fermentare) ferment; fig seethe
ri'brezzo *m* disgust; **far ~ a** disgust
ribut'tante *adj* repugnant
ribut'tare *vt* (buttare di nuovo) throw back
rica'dere *vi* fall back; (nel peccato ecc.) lapse; (pendere) hang [down]; **~ su** (riversarsi) fall on
rica'duta *f* relapse; **avere una ~** to have a relapse
rical'care *vt* trace
ricalci'trante *adj* recalcitrant
ricalco'lare *vt* recalculate
rica'mare *vt* embroider
rica'mato *adj* embroidered
ri'cambi *mpl* spare parts
ricambi'are *vt* return; reciprocate ‹*sentimento*›; **~ qualcosa a qualcuno** repay somebody for something
ri'cambio *m* replacement; Biol metabolism; **pezzo di ricambio** spare [part]
ri'camo *m* embroidery
ricandi'dare *vt* (a elezioni) put forward as a candidate again
ricandi'darsi *vr* (a elezioni) stand again
ricapito'lare *vt* sum up; **ricapitoliamo** let's recap
ricapitolazi'one *f* summary, recap infml
ri'carica *f* (di sveglia) winder; (di batteria) recharging; (di penna) refill; (di fucile) reloading; Teleph top-up card
ricari'cabile *adj* rechargeable
ricari'care *vt* reload ‹*macchina fotografica, fucile, camion*›; recharge ‹*batteria*›; Comput reboot; rewind ‹*orologio*›; top up ‹*cellulare*›
ricat'tare *vt* blackmail
ricatta|'tore, -trice *mf* blackmailer
ricatta'torio *adj* blackmail *attrib*
ri'catto *m* blackmail
■ **ricatto morale** moral blackmail, emotional blackmail
rica'vare *vt* get; (ottenere) obtain; (dedurre) draw
rica'vato *m* proceeds *pl*
ri'cavo *m* proceeds *pl*
ricca'mente *adv* lavishly
ric'chezza *f* wealth; fig richness; **ricchezze** *pl* riches
'riccio **A** *adj* curly
B *m* curl; (animale) hedgehog
■ **riccio di mare** sea urchin
'ricciolo *m* curl
riccio'luto *adj* curly
ricci'uto *adj* ‹*barba*› curly; ‹*persona*› curly-haired
⚷ **'ricco, -a** **A** *adj* rich
■ **ricco sfondato** infml filthy rich
B *mf* rich person; **i ricchi** the rich
⚷ **ri'cerca** *f* search; (indagine) investigation; (scientifica) research; Sch project
■ **ricerca avanzata** Comput advanced search; **ricerca sul campo** field work; **ricerca di mercato** market research; **ricerca operativa** operational research
ricer'care *vt* search for; (fare ricerche su) research
ricer'cata *f* wanted woman
ricercata'mente *adv* ‹*vestire*› with refinement; ‹*parlare*› in a refined way
ricerca'tezza *f* refinement
ricer'cato **A** *adj* sought-after; (raffinato) refined
B *m* (dalla polizia) wanted man
ricerca|'tore, -trice *mf* researcher
ricetrasmit'tente *f* transceiver, two-way radio
ri'cetta *f* Culin recipe; Med prescription
ricet'tacolo *m* receptacle
ricet'tario *m* (di cucina) recipe book; (di medico) prescription pad
ricetta|'tore, -trice *mf* receiver of stolen goods, fence infml
ricettazi'one *f* receiving [stolen goods]
rice'vente **A** *adj* ‹*apparecchio, stazione*› receiving
B *mf* receiver
⚷ **ri'cevere** *vt* receive; (dare il benvenuto) welcome; (di albergo) accommodate
ricevi'mento *m* receiving; (accoglienza) welcome; (trattenimento) reception
ricevi'tore *m* receiver
■ **ricevitore delle imposte** tax man; **ricevitore del lotto** lottery ticket agent
ricevito'ria *f*:
■ **ricevitoria delle imposte** ≈ Inland Revenue; **ricevitoria del lotto** *agency authorized to sell lottery tickets*
rice'vuta *f* receipt
■ **ricevuta d'acquisto** proof of purchase; **ricevuta doganale** docket; **ricevuta fiscale** tax receipt;

⚷ key word

ricevuta di ritorno acknowledgement of receipt; **ricevuta di versamento** receipt (*given for bills etc paid at the Post Office*)

rice'vuto *int* roger

ricezi'one *f* Radio, TV reception

richia'mare *vt* (al telefono) call back; (far tornare) recall; (rimproverare) rebuke; (attirare) draw; **~ alla mente** call to mind

richi'amo *m* recall; (attrazione) call

richie'dente *mf* applicant

richi'edere *vt* ask for; (di nuovo) ask again for; **~ a qualcuno di fare qualcosa** ask *or* request somebody to do something

richi'esta *f* request; Comm demand

■ **richiesta di indennizzo** claim for damages

richi'esto *adj* sought-after

ri'chiudere *vt* shut again, close again

ri'chiudersi *vr* ‹*ferita*› heal; ‹*porta*› shut again, close again

rici'clabile *adj* recyclable

rici'claggio *m* recycling; (di denaro) laundering

rici'clare *vt* recycle ‹*carta, vetro*›; launder ‹*denaro sporco*›

rici'clarsi *vr* retrain; (cambiare lavoro) change one's line of work

rici'clato *adj* recycled

'ricino *m*

■ **olio di ricino** castor oil

ricogni'tore *m* reconnaissance plane

ricognizi'one *f* Mil reconnaissance

ricolle'gare *vt* (collegare di nuovo) reconnect

ricolle'garsi *vr* **~ a** ‹*evento, fatto*› relate to, tie up with

ricol'mare *vt* fill to the brim

ri'colmo *adj* full

ricominci'are *vt & vi* start again; **~ da capo** start all over again

ricompa'rire *vi* reappear

ricom'parsa *f* reappearance

ricom'pensa *f* reward

ricompen'sare *vt* reward

ricom'porre *vt* (riscrivere) rewrite; (ricostruire) reform; Teleph redial; Typ reset

ricom'porsi *vr* regain one's composure

ricomposizi'one *f* Teleph

■ **ricomposizione automatica dell'ultimo numero** redial facility

riconcili'are *vt* reconcile

riconcili'arsi *vr* be reconciled

riconciliazi'one *f* reconciliation

riconfer'mare *vt* reappoint

ricongi'ungere *vt* reunite

ricongi'ungersi *vr* become reunited

ricongiungi'mento *m* reunion

ricono'scente *adj* grateful

ricono'scenza *f* gratitude

rico'noscere *vt* recognize; (ammettere) acknowledge

ricono'scibile *adj* recognizable

riconosci'mento *m* recognition; (ammissione) acknowledgement; (per la polizia) identification

■ **riconoscimento vocale** Comput voice recognition

riconosci'uto *adj* recognized

ricon'quista *f* reconquest

riconqui'stare *vt* Mil reconquer

ricon'segna *f* return

riconse'gnare *vt* return

riconside'rare *vt* rethink

ricontrol'lare *vt* double-check

riconversi'one *f* Econ restructuring

ricopi'are *vt* copy again

rico'prire *vt* re-cover; (rivestire) coat; (di insulti) shower (**di** with); hold ‹*carica*›; **~ qualcuno di attenzioni** lavish attention on somebody

ricor'dare *vt* remember; (richiamare alla memoria) recall; (far ricordare) remind; (rassomigliare) look like

ricor'darsi *vr* **~ [di]** remember; **~ di fare qualcosa** remember to do something

ri'cordo *m* memory; (oggetto) memento; (di viaggio) souvenir; **ricordi** *pl* (memorie) memoirs

■ **~ di famiglia** family heirloom

ricor'reggere *vt* correct again

ricor'rente *adj* recurrent

ricor'renza *f* recurrence; (anniversario) anniversary

ri'correre *vi* recur; (accadere) occur; ‹*data*› fall; **~ a** have recourse to; (rivolgersi a) turn to

ri'corso **A** pp di **ricorrere**
B *m* recourse; Jur appeal

ricostitu'ente *m* tonic

ricostitu'ire *vt* re-establish

ricostru'ire *vt* reconstruct

ricostruzi'one *f* reconstruction

ricove'rare *vt* give shelter to; **~ in ospedale** admit to hospital, hospitalize

ricove'rato, -a *mf* hospital patient

ri'covero *m* shelter; (ospizio) home

ricre'are *vt* recreate; (ristorare) restore

ricre'arsi *vr* amuse oneself

ricrea'tivo *adj* recreational

ricreazi'one *f* recreation; Sch break, playtime

ri'credersi *vr* change one's mind

ri'crescere *vi* grow again

ricu'cire *vt* sew up; stitch up ‹*ferita*›

ricupe'rare, **ri'cupero** = **recuperare, recupero**

ri'curvo *adj* bent

ricu'sare *vt* refuse

ridacchi'are *vi* giggle

ri'dare *vt* give back, return

rida'rella *f* giggles *pl*

ridefi'nire *vt* redefine

ri'dente *adj* (piacevole) pleasant

r

✓ **'ridere** *vi* laugh; **~ di** (deridere) laugh at
ride'stare *vt* reawaken ‹*ricordo, sentimento*›
ri'detto pp di **ridire**
ridicoliz'zare *vt* ridicule
✓ **ri'dicolo** *adj* ridiculous
ridimensiona'mento *m* restructuring
ridimensio'nare *vt* restructure ‹*azienda*›; fig get into perspective
ridi'pingere *vt* repaint
ri'dire *vt* repeat; **trova sempre da ~** he's always finding fault; **hai qualcosa da ~?** do you have something to say?; **se non hai niente da ~, ...** if you've no objection...
ridi'scendere *vi* go back down
ridistribu'ire *vt* redistribute
ridistribuzi'one *f* redistribution
ridon'dante *adj* redundant
ri'dosso a ~ di *adv* behind
ri'dotto **A** pp di **ridurre** **B** *adj* reduced; **essere ~ male** be worn out **C** *m* Theat foyer
✓ **ri'durre** *vt* reduce
ri'dursi *vr* diminish; **~ a fare qualcosa** be reduced to doing something; **~ a** ‹*problema*› come down to
ridut'tivo *adj* reductive
ridut'tore *m* Electr adaptor
riduzi'one *f* reduction; (per cinema, teatro) adaptation
■ **riduzione cinematografica** film adaptation; **riduzione della pena** reduced sentence; **riduzione di prezzo** price cut; **riduzione teatrale** adaptation for the theatre
riedifi'care *vt* rebuild
rieducazi'one *f* (di malato) rehabilitation
rie'leggere *vt* re-elect
rielezi'one *f* re-election
rie'mergere *vi* resurface
✓ **riem'pire** *vt* fill [up]; fill in ‹*moduli ecc.*›
riem'pirsi *vr* fill [up]
riempi'tivo **A** *adj* filling **B** *m* filler
rien'tranza *f* recess
✓ **rien'trare** *vi* go/come back in; (tornare) return; (piegare indentro) recede; **~ in** (far parte) fall within
ri'entro *m* return; (di astronave) re-entry; **grande ~** mass return home after the holidays
riepilo'gare *vt* recapitulate
rie'pilogo *m* summing-up
rie'same *m* reassessment
riesami'nare *vt* reappraise
ri'essere *vi* **ci risiamo!** here we go again!
riesu'mare *vt* exhume
rievo'care *vt* (commemorare) commemorate; recall ‹*passato*›

✓ key word

rievocazi'one *f* (commemorazione) commemoration; (ricordo) recollection
rifaci'mento *m* remake
✓ **ri'fare** *vt* do again; (creare) make again; (riparare) repair; (imitare) imitate; make ‹*letto*›
ri'farsi *vr* (rimettersi) recover; (vendicarsi) get even; **~ una vita/carriera** make a new life/career for oneself; **~ il trucco** touch up one's make-up; **~ di** make up for
ri'fatto pp di **rifare**
riferi'mento *m* reference
✓ **rife'rire** **A** *vt* report; **~ a** attribute to **B** *vi* make a report
rife'rirsi *vr* **~ a** refer to
rifi'lare *vt* (tagliare a filo) trim; infml (affibbiare) saddle
rifi'nire *vt* finish off
rifini'tura *f* finish
rifio'rire *vi* blossom again; fig flourish again
✓ **rifiu'tare** *vt* refuse; **~ di fare qualcosa** refuse to do something
rifi'uto *m* refusal; **acque** *pl* **di ~** waste water; **rifiuti** *pl* (immondizie) rubbish; **rifiuti** *pl* **industriali** industrial waste; **rifiuti** *pl* **urbani** urban *or* municipal waste
riflessi'one *f* reflection; (osservazione) remark
rifles'sivo *adj* thoughtful; Gram reflexive
✓ **ri'flesso** **A** pp di **riflettere** **B** *m* (luce) reflection; Med reflex; **per ~** indirectly
✓ **ri'flettere** **A** *vt* reflect **B** *vi* think (**su** about)
ri'flettersi *vr* be reflected
riflet'tore *m* reflector; (proiettore) search light
ri'flusso *m* ebb
rifocil'lare *vt* restore
rifocil'larsi *vr* (liter, hum) take some refreshment
rifondazi'one *f* refounding
■ **Rifondazione Comunista** *diehard Communist party*
ri'fondere *vt* (rimborsare) refund
ri'forma *f* reform; Relig reformation; Mil exemption on medical grounds
rifor'mare *vt* re-form; (migliorare) reform; Mil declare unfit for military service
rifor'mato *adj* ‹*chiesa*› Reformed; ‹*recluta, soldato*› unfit for military service
riforma|'tore, -trice *mf* reformer
riforma'torio *m* reformatory
riformat'tare *vt* Comput reformat
rifor'mista *adj & nmf* reformist
riformu'lare *vt* recast
riforni'mento *m* supply; (scorta) stock; (di combustibile) refuelling; **stazione di ~** petrol station
rifor'nire *vt* restock; **~ di** provide with

rifor'nirsi *vr* restock, stock up (**di** with)
ri'frangere *vt* refract
ri'fratto pp di **rifrangere**
rifrazi'one *f* refraction
rifug'gire **A** *vt* shun ‹*gloria, celebrità*›
B *vi* escape again; ~ **da** fig shun
rifugi'arsi *vr* take refuge
rifugi'ato, -a *mf* refugee
ri'fugio *m* shelter; (nascondiglio) hideaway, safe house
■ **rifugio antiaereo** bomb shelter; **rifugio antiatomico** fallout shelter
'riga *f* line; (fila) row; (striscia) stripe; (scriminatura) parting; (regolo) rule; **a righe** (stoffa) striped; ‹*quaderno*› ruled; **mettersi in ~** line up
ri'gaglie *fpl* (interiora) giblets
ri'gagnolo *m* rivulet
ri'gare **A** *vt* rule ‹*foglio*›
B *vi* ~ **dritto** behave well
riga'toni *mpl small ridged pasta tubes*
rigatti'ere *m* junk dealer
rigene'rante *adj* regenerative
rigene'rare *vt* regenerate
riget'tare *vt* (gettare indietro) throw back; (respingere) reject; (vomitare) throw up
ri'getto *m* rejection
ri'ghello *m* ruler
rigida'mente *adv* rigidly
rigidità *f inv* rigidity; (di clima) severity; (severità) strictness
■ **rigidità cadaverica** rigor mortis
'rigido *adj* rigid; (freddo) severe; (severo) strict
rigi'rare **A** *vt* turn again; (ripercorrere) go round; fig twist ‹*argomentazione*›
B *vi* walk about
rigi'rarsi *vr* turn round; (nel letto) turn over
'rigo *m* line; Mus staff
ri'goglio *m* bloom
rigogliosa'mente *adv* luxuriantly
rigogli'oso *adj* luxuriant
rigonfia'mento *m* swelling
rigonfi'are *vt* reinflate
ri'gonfio *adj* swollen
ri'gore *m* rigours *pl*; **a rigor di logica** strictly speaking; **calcio di ~** penalty [kick]; **area di ~** penalty area; **essere di ~** be compulsory
rigorosa'mente *adv* ‹*giudicare*› severely; (seguire istruzioni) exactly; **vestito ~ in giacca e cravatta** wearing the obligatory jacket and tie
rigo'roso *adj* (severo) strict; (scrupoloso) rigorous
rigover'nare *vt* wash up
riguada'gnare *vt* regain, win back ‹*stima*›; win more ‹*tempo, punti*›
⚷ **riguar'dare** *vt* look at again; (considerare) regard; (concernere) concern; **per quanto riguarda...** with regard to...
riguar'darsi *vr* take care of oneself
⚷ **rigu'ardo** *m* care; (considerazione) consideration; **nei riguardi di** towards; ~ **a** with regard to
rigurgi'tante *adj* ~ **di** swarming with
rigurgi'tare **A** *vt* regurgitate
B *vi* ~ **di** fig be swarming with
ri'gurgito *m* regurgitation; fig (di xenofobia, nazionalismo ecc.) resurgence
rilanci'are **A** *vt* throw back ‹*palla*›; (di nuovo) throw again; increase ‹*offerta*›; revive ‹*moda*›; relaunch ‹*prodotto*›
B *vi* (a carte) raise the stakes; **rilancio di dieci** I'll raise you ten
ri'lancio *m* (di offerta) increase; (di prodotto) re-launch
rilasci'are *vt* (concedere) grant; (liberare) release; issue ‹*documento*›
rilasci'arsi *vr* relax
ri'lascio *m* release; (di documento) issue
rilassa'mento *m* relaxation
■ **rilassamento cutaneo** sagging of the skin
rilas'sare *vt* relax
rilas'sarsi *vr* relax
rilas'sato *adj* relaxed
rile'gare *vt* bind ‹*libro*›
rile'gato *adj* bound
rilega|'tore, -trice *mf* bookbinder
rilega'tura *f* binding
ri'leggere *vt* reread
ri'lento a ~ *adv* slowly
rileva'mento *m* survey; Comm buyout
■ **rilevamento dirigenti** management buyout, MBO
rile'vante *adj* considerable
rile'vanza *f* significance
rile'vare *vt* (trarre) get; (mettere in evidenza) point out; (notare) notice; (topografia) survey; Comm take over; Mil relieve
rilevazi'one *f* (statistica) survey
rili'evo *m* relief; Geog elevation; (topografia) survey; (importanza) importance; (osservazione) remark; **mettere in ~ qualcosa** point something out
rilut'tante *adj* reluctant
rilut'tanza *f* reluctance, unwillingness
'rima *f* rhyme; **far ~ con qualcosa** rhyme with something; **rispondere a qualcuno per le rime** give somebody as good as one gets
■ **rima alternata** alternate rhyme; **rima baciata** rhyming couplet
⚷ **riman'dare** *vt* (posporre) postpone; (mandare indietro) send back; (mandare di nuovo) send again; (far ridare un esame) make resit an examination
ri'mando *m* return; (in un libro) cross-reference
rimaneggia'mento *m* rejig
rimaneggi'are *vt* rejig, recast

r

rima'nente **A** *adj* remaining
B *m* remainder
rima'nenza *f* remainder; **rimanenze** *pl* remnants; **rimanenze** *pl* **di magazzino** unsold stock
rima'nere *vi* stay, remain; (essere d'avanzo) be left; (venirsi a trovare) be; (restare stupito) be astonished; (restare d'accordo) agree; **~ senza parole** be speechless
rimangi'are *vt* (mangiare di nuovo) have again, eat again
rimangi'arsi *vr* **~ la parola** break one's promise
rimar'care *vt* remark
rimar'chevole *adj* remarkable
ri'mare *vt* & *vi* rhyme
rimargi'nare *vt* heal
rimargi'narsi *vr* heal
ri'masto pp di **rimanere**
rima'sugli *mpl* (di cibo) leftovers
rimbal'zare *vi* rebound; (proiettile) ricochet; **far ~** bounce
rim'balzo *m* rebound; (di proiettile) ricochet
rimbam'bire **A** *vi* be in one's dotage
B *vt* stun
rimbam'bito *adj* in one's dotage
rimbec'care *vi* retort
rimbecil'lire *vt* make brain-dead
rimbecil'lito *adj* (stupido) brain-dead; (frastornato) stunned
rimboc'care *vt* turn up; roll up ‹*maniche*›; tuck in ‹*coperte*›; **~ le coperte a qualcuno** tuck somebody into bed
rimboc'carsi *vr* **~ le maniche** roll up one's sleeves
rimbom'bare *vi* boom, resound
rim'bombo *m* boom
rimbor'sabile *adj* reclaimable
rimbor'sare *vt* reimburse, repay
rim'borso *m* reimbursement, repayment
■ **rimborso d'imposta** tax rebate; **rimborso spese** reimbursement of expenses
rimboschi'mento *m* reafforestation BrE, reforestation
rim'brotto *m* reproach
rimedi'abile *adj* ‹*errore*› which can be remedied
rimedi'are *vi* **~ a** remedy; make up for ‹*errore*›; (procurare) scrape up
ri'medio *m* remedy
rimesco'lare *vt* mix [up]; shuffle ‹*carte*›; (rivangare) rake up; **mi fa ~ il sangue** it makes my blood boil
rimesco'lio *m* (turbamento) shock
ri'messa *f* (per veicoli) garage; (per aerei) hangar; (per autobus) depot; (di denaro) remittance; (di merci) consignment
■ **rimessa laterale** Sport throw-in

ri'messo pp di **rimettere**
rime'stare *vt* stir well
ri'mettere *vt* (a posto) put back; (restituire) return; (affidare) entrust; (perdonare) remit; (rimandare) put off; (vomitare) bring up; **~ in gioco** (nel calcio) throw in; **~ in moto** restart; **rimetterci** infml (perdere) lose [out]
ri'mettersi *vr* (ristabilirsi) recover; ‹*tempo*› clear up; **~ a** start again
'rimmel® *m inv* mascara
rimoder'nare *vt* modernize
ri'monta *f* Sport recovery
rimon'tare **A** *vt* (risalire) go up; Mech reassemble
B *vi* remount; **~ a** (risalire) go back to
rimorchi'are *vt* tow; infml pick up ‹*ragazza*›
rimorchia'tore *m* tug[boat]
ri'morchio *m* tow; (veicolo) trailer
ri'mordere *vt* **mi rimorde la coscienza** fig it's preying on my conscience
ri'morso *m* remorse
rimo'stranza *f* complaint
rimo'vibile *adj* removable
rimozi'one *f* removal; (da un incarico) dismissal
■ **rimozione forzata** *illegally parked vehicles removed at owner's expense*
rim'pallo *m* bounce
rim'pasto *m* Pol reshuffle
rimpatri'are **A** *vt* repatriate
B *vi* return home
rimpatri'ata *f* reunion
rim'patrio *m* repatriation
rim'piangere *vt* regret
rimpi'anto **A** pp di **rimpiangere**
B *m* regret
rimpiat'tino *m* hide-and-seek
rimpiaz'zare *vt* replace
rimpi'azzo *m* replacement
rimpiccioli'mento *m* shrinkage
rimpiccio'lire **A** *vt* make smaller
B *vi* become smaller
rimpinz'are *vt* **~ di** stuff with
rimpinz'arsi *vr* stuff oneself
rimpol'pare *vt* (ingrassare) fatten up; fig pad out ‹*scritto*›
rimprove'rare *vt* reproach; **~ qualcosa a qualcuno** reproach somebody for something
rim'provero *m* reproach
rimugi'nare *vt* literary rummage; fig **~ su** brood over
rimune'rare *vt* remunerate
rimunera'tivo *adj* remunerative
rimunerazi'one *f* remuneration
rimu'overe *vt* remove
ri'nascere *vi* be reborn, be born again
rinascimen'tale *adj* Renaissance
Rinasci'mento *m* Renaissance

⚷ key word

ri'nascita *f* rebirth
rincal'zare *vt* (sostenere) support; (rimboccare) tuck in
rin'calzo *m* support; **rincalzi** *pl* Mil reserves
rincantucci'arsi *vr* hide oneself away in a corner
rinca'rare **A** *vt* increase the price of **B** *vi* become more expensive
rin'caro *m* price increase
rincar'tare *vt* rewrap
rinca'sare *vi* return home
rinchi'udere *vt* shut up
rinchi'udersi *vr* shut oneself up
rincon'trare *vt* meet again
rincon'trarsi *vr* meet [each other] again
rin'correre *vt* run after
rin'corsa *f* run-up
rin'corso pp di **rincorrere**
rin'crescere *vi* **mi rincresce di non...** I'm sorry *or* I regret that I can't...; **se non ti rincresce** if you don't mind; **rincresce vedere...** it's sad to see...
rincresci'mento *m* regret
rincresci'uto pp di **rincrescere**
rincreti'nire **A** *vt* make brain-dead **B** *vi* go brain-dead
rincu'lare *vi* ‹*arma*› recoil; ‹*cavallo*› shy
rin'culo *m* recoil
rincuo'rare *vt* encourage
rincuo'rarsi *vr* take heart
rinfacci'are *vt* ~ **qualcosa a qualcuno** throw something in somebody's face
rinfode'rare *vt* sheathe
rinfor'zare *vt* strengthen; (rendere più saldo) reinforce
rinfor'zarsi *vr* become stronger
rin'forzo *m* reinforcement; fig support; **rinforzi** *pl* Mil reinforcements
rinfran'care *vt* reassure
rinfre'scante *adj* cooling
rinfre'scare **A** *vt* cool; (rinnovare) freshen up **B** *vi* get cooler
rinfre'scarsi *vr* freshen [oneself] up
rin'fresco *m* light refreshment; (ricevimento) party
rin'fusa *f* **alla** ~ at random
ringalluz'zire **A** *vt* make cocky **B** *vi* get cocky
ringhi'are *vi* snarl
ringhi'era *f* railing; (di scala) banisters *pl*
ringhi'oso *adj* snarling
ringiova'nire **A** *vt* rejuvenate ‹*pelle, persona*›; ‹*vestito*› make look younger **B** *vi* become young again; (sembrare) look young again
ringrazia'mento *m* thanks *pl*
⚷ **ringrazi'are** *vt* thank
rinne'gare *vt* disown
rinne'gato, -a *mf* renegade
rinno'vabile *adj* renewable; ‹*risorsa, foresta*› sustainable
rinnova'mento *m* renewal; (di edifici) renovation
rinno'vare *vt* renew; renovate ‹*edifici*›
rinno'varsi *vr* be renewed; (ripetersi) recur, happen again
rin'novo *m* renewal
rinoce'ronte *m* rhinoceros
rino'mato *adj* renowned
rinsal'dare *vt* consolidate
rinsa'vire *vi* come to one's senses
rinsec'chire *vi* shrivel up
rinsec'chito *adj* shrivelled up
rinta'narsi *vr* hide oneself away; ‹*animale*› retreat into its den
rintoc'care *vi* ‹*compana*› toll; ‹*orologio*› strike
rin'tocco *m* toll; (di orologio) stroke
rinton'tire *vt* anche fig stun
rinton'tito *adj* (stordito) dazed
rintracci'are *vt* trace
rintro'nare **A** *vt* stun **B** *vi* boom
rintuz'zare *vt* blunt; (ribattere) retort; (reprimere) repress
ri'nuncia *f* renunciation
⚷ **rinunci'are** *vi* ~ **a** renounce, give up
rinuncia'tario *adj* defeatist
ri'nunzia, rinunzi'are = **rinuncia, rinunciare**
rinveni'mento *m* (di reperti) discovery; (di refurtiva) recovery
rinve'nire **A** *vt* find **B** *vi* (riprendere i sensi) come round; (ridiventare fresco) revive
rinvi'are *vt* put off; (mandare indietro) return; (in libro) refer; ~ **a giudizio** indict
rinvigo'rire *vt* strengthen
rin'vio *m* Sport goal kick; (in libro) cross-reference; (di appuntamento) postponement; (di merce) return
■ **rinvio a giudizio** indictment
rioccu'pare *vt* reoccupy
rio'nale *adj* local
ri'one *m* district
riordina'mento *m* reorganization
riordi'nare *vt* tidy [up]; (ordinare di nuovo) reorder
riorganiz'zare *vt* reorganize
riorganizzazi'one *f* reorganization
R.I.P. *abbr* (**riposi in pace**) RIP
ripa'gare *vt* repay
⚷ **ripa'rare** **A** *vt* (proteggere) shelter, protect; (aggiustare) repair; (porre rimedio) remedy **B** *vi* ~ **a** make up for
ripa'rarsi *vr* take shelter
ripa'rato *adj* ‹*luogo*› sheltered
riparazi'one *f* repair; fig reparation

ripar'lare *vi* **ne riparliamo stasera** we'll talk about it again tonight

ri'paro *m* shelter; (rimedio) remedy

ripar'tire **A** *vt* (dividere) divide **B** *vi* leave again

ripartizi'one *f* division

ripas'sare **A** *vt* recross; (rivedere) revise **B** *vi* pass again

ripas'sata *f* (spolverata) quick dust; (stirata) quick iron; (di vernice) second coat; infml (rimprovero) telling-off; **dar una ~ a** (lezione) revise

ri'passo *m* (di lezione) revision

ripensa'mento *m* second thoughts *pl*

🔑 **ripen'sare** *vi* **~ a** think back to; **ripensarci** (cambiare idea) change one's mind; **ripensaci!** think again!

riper'correre *vt* (con la memoria) go back over; trace ‹*storia*›; **~ la strada fatta** go back the way one came

riper'cosso pp di **ripercuotere**

ripercu'otere *vt* strike again

ripercu'otersi *vr* ‹*suono*› reverberate; **~ su qualcosa** fig (avere conseguenze) impact on something

ripercussi'one *f* repercussion

ripe'scare *vt* (recuperare) fish out; (ritrovare) find again

ripe'tente *mf student who is repeating a year*

🔑 **ri'petere** *vt* repeat

ri'petersi *vr* ‹*evento*› recur; ‹*persona*› repeat oneself

ripeti'tore *m* TV relay

ripetizi'one *f* repetition; (di lezione) revision; (lezione privata) private lesson

ripetuta'mente *adv* repeatedly

ri'piano *m* (di scaffale) shelf; (terreno pianeggiante) terrace

ripi'cca *f* spite; **fare qualcosa per ~** do something out of spite

ri'picco = **ripicca**

ripida'mente *adv* steeply

'ripido *adj* steep

ripie'gare **A** *vt* refold; (abbassare) lower **B** *vi* (indietreggiare) retreat

ripie'garsi *vr* bend; ‹*sedile*› fold

ripi'ego *m* expedient; (via d'uscita) way out

ripi'eno **A** *adj* full; Culin stuffed **B** *m* filling; Culin stuffing

ripiom'bare *vi* (per terra) fall down again; **~ nella disperazione** sink back into despair

ripopo'lare *vt* repopulate

ripopo'larsi *vr* be repopulated

ri'porre *vt* put back; (mettere da parte) put away; (collocare) place; repeat ‹*domanda*›

🔑 **ripor'tare** *vt* (restituire) bring/take back; (riferire) report; (subire) suffer; Math carry; win ‹*vittoria*›; transfer ‹*disegno*›

ripor'tarsi *vr* go back; (riferirsi) refer

🔑 **ri'porto** *m* (su abito, scarpa) appliqué; **~ di 4** Math carry 4; **cane da ~** gun dog, retriever; **nascondere la calvizie con un ~** comb one's hair over a bald spot

ripo'sante *adj* restful

ripo'sare **A** *vi* rest **B** *vt* put back

ripo'sarsi *vr* rest

ripo'sato *adj* ‹*mente*› fresh; ‹*viso*› rested

🔑 **ri'poso** *m* rest; **andare a ~** retire; **~!** Mil at ease!; **giorno di ~** day off

ripo'stiglio *m* cupboard

ri'posto pp di **riporre**

rip'pare *vt* ‹*CD, DVD*› to rip

🔑 **ri'prendere** *vt* take again; (prendere indietro) take back; (riconquistare) recapture; (ricuperare) recover; (ricominciare) resume; (rimproverare) reprimand; take in ‹*cucitura*›; Cinema shoot

ri'prendersi *vr* recover; (correggersi) correct oneself

ri'presa *f* resumption; (ricupero) recovery; Theat revival; Cinema shot; Auto acceleration; Mus repeat; **riprese** *pl* Cinema filming
■ **ripresa aerea** bird's-eye view

ripresen'tare *vt* resubmit ‹*domanda, certificato*›; reintroduce ‹*problema, persona*›

ripresen'tarsi *vr* (a ufficio) go/come back again; (come candidato) stand again, run again; ‹*occasione*› arise again; ‹*problema*› come up again, reappear; (a esame) resit

ri'preso pp di **riprendere**

ripristi'nare *vt* restore

ripro'dotto pp di **riprodurre**

ripro'durre *vt* reproduce

ripro'dursi *vr* Biol reproduce; ‹*fenomeno*› happen again, recur

riprodut'tivo *adj* reproductive

riproduzi'one *f* reproduction
■ **'riproduzione vietata'** 'copyright'

ripro'mettersi *vr* (intendere) intend

ripro'porre *vt* put forward again

ripro'porsi *vr* **~ di fare qualcosa** intend to do something; (come candidato) stand again; ‹*problema*› come up again, reappear

ri'prova *f* confirmation; **a ~ di** as confirmation of

ripro'vare *vt & vi* retry

riprovazi'one *f*
■ **riprovazione generale** outcry

ripro'vevole *adj* reprehensible

ripubbli'care *vt* republish

ripudi'are *vt* repudiate

ripu'gnante *adj* repugnant

ripu'gnanza *f* disgust

ripu'gnare *vi* **~ a** disgust

ripu'lire *vt* clean [up]; fig polish

r

🔑 key word

ripu'lita *f* quick clean; **darsi una ~** have a wash and brush-up

ripulsi'one *f* repulsion

ripul'sivo *adj* repulsive

ri'quadro *m* square; (pannello) panel

riqualifi'care *vt* reskill ‹*lavoratori*›

riqualifica'zione *f* retraining

ri'sacca *f* undertow

ri'saia *f* rice field, paddy field

risa'lire **A** *vt* go back up
B *vi* **~ a** (nel tempo) date back to; (individuare) trace ‹*colpevole*›

risa'lita *f* ascent; **impianto di ~** ski lift

risal'tare *vi* (emergere) stand out

ri'salto *m* prominence; (rilievo) relief

risana'mento *m* reclamation, redevelopment

risa'nare *vt* heal; (bonificare) reclaim; redevelop ‹*area, quartiere*›

risa'puto *adj* well-known

risar'cibile *adj* refundable

risarci'mento *m* compensation

risar'cire *vt* indemnify; **mi hanno risarcito i danni** they compensated me for the damage

ri'sata *f* laugh

riscalda'mento *m* heating
■ **riscaldamento autonomo** central heating (*for one flat*); **riscaldamento centralizzato** *central heating system for whole block of flats*

riscal'dare *vt* heat; warm ‹*persona*›

riscal'darsi *vr* warm up

riscat'tabile *adj* redeemable

riscat'tare *vt* ransom

riscat'tarsi *vr* redeem oneself

ri'scatto *m* ransom; (morale) redemption

rischia'rare *vt* light up; brighten ‹*colore*›

rischia'rarsi *vr* light up; ‹*cielo*› clear up

rischi'are **A** *vt* risk
B *vi* run the risk; **~ inutilmente** take needless risks

'rischio *m* risk; **a ~** ‹*soggetti*› at risk; **a basso ~** low risk *attrib*

rischi'oso *adj* risky

risciac'quare *vt* rinse

risci'acquo *m* rinse

risciò *m inv* rickshaw

riscon'trare *vt* (confrontare) compare; (verificare) verify; (rilevare) find

ri'scontro *m* comparison; (verifica) verification; Comm (risposta) reply

risco'prire *vt* rediscover

ri'scossa *f* revolt; (riconquista) recovery

riscossi'one *f* collection

ri'scosso pp di **riscuotere**

ri'scrivere *vt* (scrivere di nuovo) rewrite; (rispondere) write back

riscri'vibile *adj* rewritable

riscu'otere *vt* shake; (percepire) draw; (ottenere) gain; cash ‹*assegno*›

riscu'otersi *vr* rouse oneself

risen'tire **A** *vt* hear again; (provare) feel
B *vi* **~ di** feel the effect of

risen'tirsi *vr* (offendersi) take offence

risentita'mente *adv* resentfully

risen'tito *adj* resentful

ri'serbo *m* reserve; **mantenere il ~** remain tight-lipped

ri'serva *f* reserve; (di caccia, pesca) preserve; Sport substitute, reserve; **di ~** spare; **senza riserve** wholeheartedly ‹*accettare, appoggiare*›
■ **riserva di caccia** game reserve; **riserva indiana** Indian reservation; **riserva naturale** wildlife reserve

riser'vare *vt* reserve; (prenotare) book; (per occasione) keep

riser'varsi *vr* (ripromettersi) plan for oneself ‹*cambiamento*›; **mi riservo la sorpresa** I want it to be a surprise

riserva'tezza *f* reserve

riser'vato *adj* reserved; (confidenziale) classified; **'~ ai clienti dell'albergo'** 'for hotel guests only'; **'~ carico'** 'loading only'

ri'sguardo *m* endpaper

risi'edere *vi* **~ a** reside in

'risma *f* ream; fig kind

'riso¹ **A** pp di **ridere**
B *m* (*pl nf* **risa**) laughter; (singolo) laugh

'riso² *m* (cereale) rice
■ **riso integrale** brown rice

riso'lino *m* giggle

risolle'vare *vt* raise again; raise ‹*il morale*›; raise again, bring up again ‹*problema, questione*›; increase, improve ‹*le sorti*›

risolle'varsi *vr* (da terra) rise again; fig pick up

ri'solto pp di **risolvere**

risoluta'mente *adv* energetically

risolu'tezza *f* determination

risolu'tivo *adj* (determinante) decisive; **scelta risolutiva** solution

riso'luto *adj* resolute, determined

risoluzi'one *f* resolution

ri'solvere *vt* resolve; Math solve

ri'solversi *vr* (decidersi) decide; **~ in** turn into

riso'nanza *f* resonance; **aver ~** fig arouse great interest
■ **risonanza magnetica** magnetic resonance, magnetic resonance imaging

riso'nare *vi* resound; (rimbombare) echo

ri'sorgere *vi* rise again

risorgi'mento *m* revival; **il Risorgimento** the Risorgimento

ri'sorsa *f* resource; (espediente) resort; **risorse** *pl* **energetiche** energy resources; **risorse** *pl* **naturali** natural resources; **risorse** *pl* **umane** human resources

ri'sorto pp di **risorgere**

ri'sotto *m* risotto

■ **risotto alla marinara** seafood risotto; **risotto alla milanese** risotto with saffron
ri'sparmi *mpl* (soldi) savings
risparmi'are *vt* save; (salvare) spare
risparmia|'tore, -trice *mf* saver
ri'sparmio *m* saving
■ **risparmio di carburante** fuel economy; **risparmio energetico** energy saving
rispecchi'are *vt* reflect
rispe'dire *vr* send back, return
rispet'tabile *adj* respectable
rispettabilità *f inv* respectability
rispet'tare *vt* respect; **farsi ~** command respect
rispet'tivo *adj* respective
ri'spetto *m* respect; **~ a** as regards; (a paragone di) compared to
rispettosa'mente *adv* respectfully
rispet'toso *adj* respectful
risplen'dente *adj* shining
ri'splendere *vi* shine
rispon'dente *adj* **~ a** in keeping with
rispon'denza *f* correspondence
ri'spondere *vi* answer; (rimbeccare) answer back; (obbedire) respond; **~ a** reply to; **~ di** (rendersi responsabile) answer for
rispo'sare *vt* remarry
rispo'sarsi *vr* remarry
ri'sposta *f* answer, reply; (reazione) response; **senza ~** unanswered ‹*domanda, lettera*›
ri'sposto pp di **rispondere**
rispun'tare *vi* ‹*persona, sole*› reappear
'rissa *f* brawl
ris'soso *adj* pugnacious
ristabi'lire *vt* re-establish
ristabi'lirsi *vr* (in salute) recover
rista'gnare *vi* stagnate; (sangue) coagulate
ri'stagno *m* stagnation
ri'stampa *f* reprint; (azione) reprinting
ristam'pare *vt* reprint
risto'rante *m* restaurant
risto'rare *vt* refresh
risto'rarsi *vr* literary take some refreshment; (riposarsi) take a rest
ristora|'tore, -trice A *mf* (proprietario di ristorante) restaurateur; (fornitore) caterer
B *adj* refreshing
ri'storo *m* refreshment; (sollievo) relief; **servizio di ~** refreshments *pl*
ristret'tezza *f* narrowness; (povertà) poverty; **vivere in ristrettezze** live in straitened circumstances
ri'stretto A pp di **restringere**
B *adj* narrow; (condensato) condensed; (limitato) restricted; **di idee ristrette** narrow-minded
ristruttu'rante *adj* ‹*cosmetico*› conditioning
ristruttu'rare *vt* Comm restructure; renovate ‹*casa*›; repair ‹*capelli*›
ristrutturazi'one *f* Comm restructuring; (di casa) renovation
risucchi'are *vt* suck in
ri'succhio *m* whirlpool; (di corrente) undertow
risul'tare *vi* result; (riuscire) turn out
risul'tato *m* result; **risultati** *pl* **parziali** (di elezioni) preliminary results; (di partite) half-time results
risuo'nare A *vt* play again ‹*pezzo musicale*›; ring again ‹*campanello*›
B *vi* ‹*grida, parola*› echo; Phys resonate
risurrezi'one, risusci'tare = **resurrezione, resuscitare**
risvegli'are *vt* reawaken ‹*interesse*›
risvegli'arsi *vr* wake up; ‹*natura*› awake; ‹*desiderio*› be aroused
ri'sveglio *m* waking up; (dell'interesse) revival; (del desiderio) arousal
ri'svolto *m* (di giacca) lapel; (di pantaloni) turn-up, cuff AmE; (di manica) cuff; (di tasca) flap; (di libro) inside flap
ritagli'are *vt* cut out
ri'taglio *m* cutting; (di stoffa) scrap
ritar'dare A *vi* be late; ‹*orologio*› be slow
B *vt* delay; slow down ‹*progresso*›; (differire) postpone
ritarda'tario, -a *mf* latecomer
ritar'dato A pp di **ritardare**
B *adj* delayed; **a scoppio ~** delayed action *attrib*; Psych retarded offensive
ri'tardo *m* delay; **essere in ~** be late; ‹*volo*› be delayed
ri'tegno *m* reserve
ritem'prare *vt* restore
rite'nere *vt* retain; deduct ‹*somma*›; (credere) believe
riten'tare *vt* try again
rite'nuta *f* (sul salario) deduction
■ **ritenuta d'acconto** *tax deducted in advance from payments made to self-employed people*; **ritenuta diretta** taxation at source; **ritenuta alla fonte** taxation at source, deduction at source
ritenzi'one *f* Med retention
riti'rare *vt* throw back ‹*palla*›; (prelevare) withdraw; (riscuotere) draw; collect ‹*pacco*›
riti'rarsi *vr* withdraw; ‹*stoffa*› shrink; (da attività) retire; ‹*marea*› recede
riti'rata *f* retreat; (WC) toilet
ri'tiro *m* withdrawal; Relig retreat; (da attività) retirement
■ **ritiro bagagli** baggage reclaim
'ritmica *f* rhythmic gymnastics
ritmica'mente *adv* rhythmically
'ritmico *adj* rhythmic[al]
'ritmo *m* rhythm; **a ~ serrato** at a cracking pace
'rito *m* rite; **di ~** customary
■ **rito funebre** funeral service

key word

ritoc'care *vt* (correggere) touch up
ri'tocco *m* alteration; **ritocchi** *pl* Phot retouching
ri'torcersi *vr* **~ contro qualcuno** boomerang on somebody
ritor'nare *vi* return; (andare/venire indietro) go/come back; (ricorrere) recur; (ridiventare) become again
ritor'nello *m* refrain
ri'torno *m* return
ritorsi'one *f* retaliation
ri'torto *adj* ‹*filo, cavo*› twisted
ritra'durre *vt* (tradurre di nuovo) retranslate
ri'trarre *vt* (ritirare) withdraw; (distogliere) turn away; (rappresentare) portray
ritra'smettere *vt* TV show again, re-broadcast
ritrat'tabile *adj* ‹*accusa*› which can be withdrawn
ritrat'tare *vt* retract, withdraw ‹*dichiarazione*›
ritrattazi'one *f* withdrawal, retraction
ritrat'tista *mf* portrait painter
ri'tratto **A** pp di **ritrarre**
B *m* portrait
ritrazi'one *f* retraction
ritrosa'mente *adv* shyly
ritro'sia *f* shyness
ri'troso *adj* (timido) shy; **a ~** backwards; **~ a** reluctant to
ritrova'mento *m* (azione) finding; (cosa) find
ritro'vare *vt* find [again]; regain ‹*salute*›
ritro'varsi *vr* meet; (di nuovo) meet again; (capitare) find oneself; (raccapezzarsi) see one's way
ritro'vato *m* discovery
ri'trovo *m* meeting place
■ **ritrovo notturno** night club
'ritto *adj* upright; (diritto) straight
ritu'ale *adj & nm* ritual
ritual'mente *adv* ritually
riunifi'care *vt* reunify
riunifi'carsi *vr* be reunited
riunificazi'one *f* reunification
riuni'one *f* meeting; (dopo separazione) reunion
■ **riunione del corpo insegnante** staff meeting; **riunione dei genitori (degli alunni)** parents' evening
riu'nire *vt* (unire) join together; (radunare) gather
riu'nirsi *vr* be reunited; (adunarsi) meet
riu'sare *vt* reuse
riu'scire *vi* (aver successo) succeed; (in matematica ecc.) be good (**in** at); (aver esito) turn out; **le è riuscito simpatico** she found him likeable
riu'scita *f* (esito) result; (successo) success
ri'uso *m* reuse
riutiliz'zare *vt* reuse
'riva *f* (di mare, lago) shore; (di fiume) bank; **in ~ al mare** on the seashore
rivacci'nare *vt* revaccinate
ri'vale *mf* rival
rivaleggi'are *vi* compete (**con** with)
rivalità *f inv* rivalry
ri'valsa *f* revenge; **prendersi una ~ su qualcuno** take revenge on somebody
rivalu'tare *vt* reappraise
rivalutazi'one *f* revaluation
rivan'gare *vt* dig up again
rive'dere *vt* see again; revise ‹*lezione*›; review ‹*accordo*›; ‹*verificare*› check
rive'dibile *adj* ‹*accordo*› reviewable; ‹*recluta*› temporarily unfit
rive'lare *vt* reveal
rive'larsi *vr* (dimostrarsi) turn out
rivela'tore **A** *adj* revealing
B *m* Techn detector
■ **rivelatore di mine** mine detector
rivelazi'one *f* revelation
ri'vendere *vt* resell
rivendi'care *vt* claim
rivendicazi'one *f* claim
ri'vendita *f* (negozio) shop
■ **rivendita autorizzata** authorized retailer
rivendi|'tore, -trice *mf* retailer
■ **rivenditore autorizzato** authorized retailer
riverbe'rare *vt* reflect ‹*luce*›
ri'verbero *m* reverberation; (bagliore) glare
rive'renza *f* reverence; (inchino) curtsy; (di uomo) bow
rive'rire *vt* respect; (ossequiare) pay one's respects to
rivernici'are *vt* repaint; (con smalto) revarnish
river'sare *vt* pour
river'sarsi *vr* ‹*fiume*› flow
rivesti'mento *m* covering
rive'stire *vt* (rifornire di abiti) clothe; (ricoprire) cover; (internamente) line; hold ‹*carica*›
rive'stirsi *vr* get dressed again
rive'stito *adj* **~ di** covered with
rivi'era *f* coast; (in corsa a ostacoli) water jump; **la ~ ligure** the Italian Riviera
ri'vincita *f* Sport return match; (vendetta) revenge
rivis'suto pp di **rivivere**
ri'vista *f* review; (pubblicazione) magazine; Theat revue; **passare in ~** review
■ **rivista patinata** glossy magazine
rivitaliz'zare *vt* revitalize
rivitalizzazi'one *f* revitalization
ri'vivere **A** *vi* come to life again; (riprendere le forze) revive
B *vt* relive
'rivo *m* stream

rivo'lere *vt* (volere di nuovo) want again; (volere indietro) want back

ri'volgere *vt* turn; (indirizzare) address

ri'volgersi *vr* turn round; ~ **a** (indirizzarsi) turn to

rivolgi'mento *m* upheaval

ri'volta *f* revolt

rivol'tante *adj* revolting, disgusting

rivol'tare *vt* turn [over]; (mettendo l'interno verso l'esterno) turn inside out; (sconvolgere) upset

rivol'tarsi *vr* (ribellarsi) revolt

rivol'tella *f* revolver

ri'volto pp di **rivolgere**

rivol'toso, -a *mf* rebel, insurgent

rivoluzio'nare *vt* revolutionize

rivoluzio'nario, -a *adj & nmf* revolutionary

rivoluzi'one *f* revolution; fig (disordine) chaos
■ **rivoluzione francese** French Revolution; **rivoluzione industriale** Industrial Revolution

riz'zare *vt* raise; (innalzare) erect; prick up ‹*orecchie*›

riz'zarsi *vr* stand up; ‹*capelli*› stand on end; ‹*orecchie*› prick up

'roaming *m* Teleph
■ **roaming internazionale** roaming

'roast-beef *m inv* roast beef

'roba *f* stuff; (personale) belongings *pl*, stuff; (faccenda) thing; sl (droga) drugs *pl*; ~ **da matti!** absolute madness!
■ **roba da bere** drink; **roba da lavare** washing; **roba da mangiare** food, things to eat; **roba da stirare** ironing

ro'baccia *f* rubbish

robi'vecchi *m inv* second-hand dealer

ro'bot *m inv* robot; (da cucina) food processor

ro'botica *f* robotics *sg*

ro'botico *adj* robotic

robotiz'zato *adj* robotic, robotized

robu'stezza *f* sturdiness, robustness; (forza) strength

ro'busto *adj* sturdy, robust; (forte) strong

rocambo'lesco *adj* incredible

'rocca *f* fortress

rocca'forte *f* stronghold

rocchetti'era *f* winder

roc'chetto *m* reel

'roccia *f* rock; (sport) rock-climbing

rock *m* rock [music]
■ **rock acrobatico** rock 'n' roll

'roco *adj* throaty

ro'daggio *m* running in

'Rodano *m* Rhone

ro'dare *vt* run in

ro'deo *m* rodeo

'rodere *vt* gnaw; (corrodere) corrode

'rodersi *vr* ~ **da** (logorarsi) be consumed with

rodi'tore *m* rodent

rodo'dendro *m* rhododendron

'rogito *m* Jur deed

'rogna *f* scabies *sg*; fig nuisance

ro'gnone *m* Culin kidney

ro'gnoso *adj* scabby

'rogo *m* (supplizio) stake; (per cadaveri) pyre

rol'lare **A** *vt* roll ‹*sigaretta*›
B *vi* ‹*aereo, nave*› roll

rom *adj inv & mf inv* (zingaro) Roma, Romany

ROM *f inv* Comput ROM

'Roma *f* Rome

Roma'nia *f* Romania

ro'manico *adj* Romanesque

ro'mano, -a *adj & nmf* Roman

romantica'mente *adv* romantically

romanti'cismo *m* romanticism

ro'mantico *adj* romantic

ro'manza *f* romance

roman'zare *vt* fictionalize

roman'zato *adj* romanticized, fictionalized

roman'zesco *adj* fictional; (stravagante) wild, unrealistic

roman'zetto *m*
■ **romanzetto rosa** novelette

romanzi'ere *m* novelist

ro'manzo **A** *adj* Romance
B *m* novel; (storia incredibile romantica) romance
■ **romanzo d'appendice** serial story; **romanzo giallo** thriller; **romanzo sceneggiato** novel adapted for television/radio

rom'bare *vi* rumble

'rombo *m* rumble; Math rhombus; (pesce) turbot

romboi'dale *adj* rhomboid, diamond-shaped

'rompere *vt* break; break off ‹*relazione*›; **non ~ [le scatole]!** infml (seccare) don't be a pain [in the neck]!

'rompersi *vr* break; ~ **una gamba** break one's leg

rompi'capo *m* nuisance; (indovinello) puzzle

rompi'collo *m* daredevil; **a ~** at breakneck speed

rompighi'accio *m* ice-breaker

rompi'mento *m* infml pain

rompi'scatole *mf inv* infml pain

'ronda *f* rounds *pl*

ron'della *f* Mech washer

'rondine *f* swallow

ron'done *m* swift

ron'fare *vi* (russare) snore; (fare le fusa) purr

ron'zare *vi* buzz; ~ **attorno a qualcuno** fig hang about somebody

ron'zino *m* jade
ron'zio *m* buzz
'rosa **A** *f* rose
■ **rosa rampicante** rambler, rambling rose; **rosa selvatica** wild rose; **rosa dei venti** wind rose
B *adj & nm* (colore) pink
ro'saio *m* rose bush
ro'sario *m* rosary
ro'sato **A** *adj* rosy
B *m* (vino) rosé
'rosbif = **roast-beef**
rosé *m inv* rosé
'roseo *adj* pink
ro'seto *m* rose garden
ro'setta *f* (coccarda) rosette; Mech washer
rosicchi'are *vt* nibble; (rodere) gnaw
rosma'rino *m* rosemary
'roso pp di **rodere**
roso'lare *vt* brown
roso'lato *adj* sauté
roso'lia *f* German measles *sg*
ro'sone *m* rosette; (apertura) rose window
'rospo *m* toad
ros'setto *m* lipstick
'rosso *adj & nm* red; **diventare ~** go red; **ha i capelli rossi** she's a redhead; **passare col ~** go through a red light, jump a red light
■ **rosso mattone** *adj* brick red; **rosso sangue** *adj* blood red; **rosso scarlatto** *adj* scarlet; **rosso d'uovo** [egg] yolk; **rosso vermiglio** *adj* vermilion
ros'sore *m* redness; (della pelle) flush
rosticce'ria *f shop selling cooked meat and other prepared food*
'rostro *m* rostrum; (becco) bill
ro'tabile *adj* **strada ~** carriageway
ro'taia *f* rail; (solco) rut
ro'tante *adj* rotating
ro'tare *vt & vi* rotate
rota'tiva *f* rotary press
rota'torio *adj* rotary
rotazi'one *f* rotation; (di personale) turnover
■ **rotazione delle colture** crop rotation
rote'are *vt & vi* roll
ro'tella *f* small wheel; (di mobile) castor
roto'calco *m* (sistema) rotogravure; ‹*rivista*› illustrated magazine
roto'lare *vt & vi* roll
roto'larsi *vr* roll [about]
roto'lio *m* rolling
'rotolo *m* roll; (di pergamena) scroll; **andare a rotoli** go to rack and ruin
■ **rotolo di carta igienica** toilet roll
roto'loni *adv* **cadere ~** tumble
ro'tonda *f* roundabout, traffic circle AmE
rotondità *f inv* (qualità) roundness; **~** *pl* (curve femminili) curves *pl*, curvaceousness
ro'tondo, -a **A** *adj* round
B *f* (spiazzo) terrace

ro'tore *m* rotor
'rotta¹ *f* Naut, Aeron course; **far ~ per** set a course for; **fuori ~** off course; **in ~ di collisione** on a collision course
'rotta² *f* **a ~ di collo** at breakneck speed; **essere in ~ con** be on bad terms with
rotta'maio *m* junkyard
rot'tame *m* scrap; fig wreck
'rotto **A** pp di **rompere**
B *adj* broken; (stracciato) torn
rot'tura *f* break; **che ~ di scatole!** infml what a pain!
'rotula *f* kneecap
rou'lette *f inv* roulette
■ **roulette russa** Russian roulette
rou'lotte *f inv* caravan, trailer AmE
rou'tine *f inv* routine; **di ~** ‹*operazioni, controlli*› routine
ro'vente *adj* scorching
'rovere *m* (legno) oak
rovescia'mento *m* overthrow
rovesci'are *vt* (buttare a terra) knock over; (sottosopra) turn upside down; (rivoltare) turn inside out; spill ‹*liquido*›; overthrow ‹*governo*›; reverse ‹*situazione*›
rovesci'arsi *vr* (capovolgersi) overturn; (riversarsi) pour
ro'vescio **A** *adj* (contrario) reverse; **alla rovescia** (capovolto) upside down; (con l'interno all'esterno) inside out
B *m* reverse; (nella maglia) purl; (di pioggia) downpour; Tennis backhand
ro'vina *f* ruin; (crollo) collapse; **in ~** in ruins
rovi'nare **A** *vt* ruin; (guastare) spoil
B *vi* crash
rovi'narsi *vr* be ruined; ‹*persona*› ruin oneself
rovi'nato *adj* ruined
rovi'noso *adj* ruinous
rovi'stare *vt* ransack
'rovo *m* bramble
rozza'mente *adv* crudely
roz'zezza *f* indelicacy
'rozzo *adj* rough
R.R. *abbr* (**ricevuta di ritorno**) acknowledgement of receipt
R.U. *abbr* (**Regno Unito**) UK
'ruba *f* **andare a ~** sell like hot cakes
rubacchi'are *vt* pilfer
rubacu'ori *m inv* heart-throb
ru'bare *vt* steal
rubi'condo *adj* ruddy
rubi'netto *m* tap, faucet AmE
ru'bino *m* ruby
ru'bizzo *adj* spry
'rublo *m* rouble
ru'brica *f* (in giornale) column; (in programma televisivo) TV report; (quaderno con indice) address book

■ **rubrica degli annunci personali** personal column; **rubrica dei cuori solitari** lonely hearts' column; **rubrica sportiva** sports column; **rubrica degli spettacoli** listings; **rubrica telefonica** telephone and address book

'rucola *f* rocket

'rude *adj* rough

'rudere *m* ruin

ru'dezza *f* bluntness

rudimen'tale *adj* rudimentary

rudi'menti *mpl* rudiments

ruffi'ana *f* procuress

ruffi'ano *m* pimp; (adulatore) bootlicker

'ruga *f* wrinkle

'ruggine *f* rust; **fare la ~** go rusty

ruggi'noso *adj* rusty

rug'gire *vi* roar

rug'gito *m* roar

rugi'ada *f* dew

ru'goso *adj* wrinkled

rul'lare *vi* roll; Aeron taxi

rul'lino *m* film

rul'lio *m* rolling; Aeron taxiing

'rullo *m* roll; Techn roller

rum *m inv* rum

ru'meno, -a *adj & nmf* Romanian

rumi'nante *m* ruminant

rumi'nare *vt* ruminate

⚷ **ru'more** *m* noise; fig rumour

rumoreggi'are *vi* rumble

rumorosa'mente *adv* noisily

rumo'roso *adj* noisy; (sonoro) loud

ru'olo *m* roll; Theat role; **di ~** on the staff

■ **ruolo delle imposte** tax notice; **ruolo primario/secondario** major/minor role

⚷ **ru'ota** *f* wheel; **andare a ~ libera** free-wheel; **fare la ~** do a cartwheel

■ **ruota dentata** cogwheel; **ruota di scorta** spare wheel; **ruota di stampa** (di stampante) print wheel; **ruota del timone** helm

'rupe *f* cliff

ru'pestre *adj* ‹*pittura*› rock *attrib*

ru'pia *f* rupee

ru'rale *adj* rural

ru'scello *m* stream

'ruspa *f* bulldozer

ru'spante *adj* free-range

rus'sare *vi* snore

'Russia *f* Russia

⚷ **'russo, -a** **A** *adj & mf* Russian
B *m* (lingua) Russian

'rustico *adj* rural; ‹*carattere*› rough

'ruta *f* Bot rue

rut'tare *vi* belch, burp

rut'tino *m* (di bambino) burp

'rutto *m* belch, burp

'ruvido *adj* coarse

ruzzo'lare *vi* tumble down

ruzzo'lone *m* tumble; **cadere ruzzoloni** tumble down, tumble [helter-skelter]

'Rwanda *f* Rwanda

Ss

S. 1 *abbr* (**santo, santa**) St. **2** *abbr* (**sud**) south

⚷ **'sabato** *m* Saturday; **di ~** on Saturdays

sab'batico *adj* sabbatical; **anno ~** sabbatical [year]

⚷ **'sabbia** *f* sand; **sabbie** *pl* **mobili** quicksand

sabbi'are *vt* sandblast

sabbia'tura *f* (di vetro, metallo) sandblasting; (terapeutica) sand bath

sabbi'oso *adj* sandy

sabo'taggio *m* sabotage

sabo'tare *vt* sabotage

sabota|'tore, -trice *mf* saboteur

'sacca *f* bag

■ **sacca di resistenza** pocket of resistance; **sacca da viaggio** travelling-bag, duffel bag

sacca'rina *f* saccharin

sac'cente **A** *adj* conceited
B *mf* know-all, know-it-all AmE

saccente'ria *f* conceit

saccheggi'are *vt* sack; (hum) plunder ‹*frigo*›

saccheggia|'tore, -trice *mf* plunderer

sac'cheggio *m* sack

sac'chetto *m* bag

■ **sacchetto di plastica** plastic bag; **sacchetto per la spazzatura** bin liner, bin bag

⚷ **'sacco** *m* sack; Anat sac; (contenuto) sackful; **mettere nel ~** fig swindle; **un ~** (moltissimo) a lot; **un ~ di** (gran quantità) lots of; **un ~ di soldi** shedloads of money infml

■ **sacco a pelo** sleeping bag; **sacco postale** mailbag

⚷ key word

saccope'lista *mf* backpacker
sacer'dote *m* priest
sacer'dozio *m* priesthood
sacra'mento *m* sacrament
sacrifi'cale *adj* sacrificial
sacrifi'care *vt* sacrifice
sacrifi'carsi *vr* sacrifice oneself
sacrifi'cato *adj* sacrificed; (non valorizzato) wasted
sacri'ficio *m* sacrifice
sacri'legio *m* sacrilege
sa'crilego *adj* sacrilegious
'sacro **A** *adj* sacred; **la Sacra Bibbia** the Holy Bible
B *m* Anat sacrum
sacro'santo *adj* sacrosanct; (verità) gospel *attrib*; (diritto) sacred
'sadico, -a **A** *adj* sadistic
B *mf* sadist
sa'dismo *m* sadism
sa'etta *f* arrow; (fulmine) thunderbolt; **correre come una ~** run like the wind
sa'fari *m inv* safari
'saga *f* saga
sa'gace *adj* shrewd
sa'gacia *f* sagacity
sag'gezza *f* wisdom
saggia'mente *adv* sagely
saggi'are *vt* test
'saggio[1] *m* (scritto) essay; (prova) proof; (di metallo) assay; (campione) sample; (esempio) example
'saggio[2] **A** *adj* wise
B *m* (persona) sage
sag'gista *mf* essayist
sag'gistica *f* non-fiction
Sagit'tario *m* Astr Sagittarius
'sago = **sagù**
'sagoma *f* shape; (profilo) outline; (in falegnameria) template; **che ~!** infml what a character!
sago'mare *vt* make according to a template
'sagra *f* festival
sa'grato *m* churchyard
sagre'stano *m* sacristan
sagre'stia *f* sacristy
sagù *m inv* sago
Sa'hara *m* Sahara
'sala *f* hall; (salotto) living room; (per riunioni ecc.) room; (di cinema) cinema
■ **sala arrivi** arrivals lounge; **sala d'aspetto** waiting room; **sala d'attesa** waiting room; **sala da ballo** ballroom; **sala di comando** control room; **sala conferenze** conference hall; **sala giochi** amusement arcade, games room; **sala d'imbarco** departure lounge; **sala di lettura** reading room; **sala macchine** engine room; **sala operatoria** operating theatre BrE, operating room AmE; **sala parto** delivery room; **sala da pranzo** dining room; **sala professori** staff room, common room; **sala di regia** Radio, TV control room; **sala di ricevimento** function room; **sala riunioni** conference room; **sala da tè** tea shop
sa'lace *adj* salacious
sa'lame *m* salami
salame'lecchi *mpl* **fare ~** bow and scrape; **prendi quello che vuoi senza tanti ~** don't stand on ceremony, take what you want
sala'moia *f* brine
sa'lare *vt* salt
salari'ato *m* wage earner
sa'lario *m* wages *pl*
salas'sare *vt* Med bleed; fig bleed dry
sa'lasso *m* bleeding; **essere un ~** fig cost a fortune
sala'tini *mpl* savouries (*eaten with aperitifs*)
sa'lato *adj* salty; (costoso) dear; **acqua salata** salt water
sal'ciccia = **salsiccia**
sal'dare *vt* weld; set ‹*osso*›; pay off ‹*debito*›; settle ‹*conto*›; **~ a stagno** solder
sal'darsi *vr* ‹*osso*› knit; ‹*ferita*› heal
saldat'rice *f* soldering iron
salda'tura *f* soldering; (giunzione) join
'saldo **A** *adj* firm, unshaken; (resistente) strong; **~ come una roccia** solid as a rock; **essere ~ nei propri principi** stick to one's principles
B *m* (pagamento) settlement; Comm balance; ‹*di conto corrente*› bank balance; **saldi** *pl* sale; **i saldi di fine stagione** the end of season sales; **in ~** ‹*essere*› on sale; ‹*comprato*› in a sale
■ **saldo iniziale** opening balance
'sale *m* salt; **non ha ~ in zucca** infml he hasn't got an ounce of common sense; **restare di ~** be struck dumb [with astonishment]; **sali** *pl* Med smelling salts; **sali da bagno** *pl* bath salts
■ **sale da cucina** cooking salt; **sale fino** table salt; **sale grosso** cooking salt; **sale marino** sea salt; **sali e tabacchi** *pl* (negozio) tobacconist's shop
'salice *m* willow
■ **salice piangente** weeping willow
sali'ente *adj* outstanding; **i punti salienti** the main points, the highlights
sali'era *f* salt cellar
sa'lina *f* salt works *sg*
salinità *f inv* saltiness
sa'lino *adj* saline
sa'lire **A** *vi* go/come up; (levarsi) rise; (su treno ecc.) get on; (in macchina) get in
B *vt* go/come up ‹*scale*›
sa'lita *f* climb; (aumento) rise; **in ~** uphill
sa'liva *f* saliva
sali'vare **A** *vt* salivate
B *adj* ‹*ghiandola*› salivary
'salma *f* corpse

sal'mastro **A** *adj* brackish
B *m* salt air
salmì *m inv* **in ~** *marinated and slowly cooked in the marinade*
salmi'strare *vt* Culin cure
'salmo *m* psalm
sal'mone *nm & adj inv* salmon
■ **salmone affumicato** smoked salmon
salmo'nella *f* salmonella
sa'lone *m* (salotto) living room; (di parrucchiere) salon
■ **salone dell'automobile** motor show; **salone di bellezza** beauty parlour; **salone del libro** book fair
salo'pette *f inv* dungarees *pl*
salotti'ero *adj* derog mundane; **discorso ~** small talk
salot'tino *m* bower
sa'lotto *m* drawing room; (soggiorno) sitting room; (mobili) [three-piece] suite; **fare ~** chat
■ **salotto letterario** literary salon
sal'pare **A** *vi* sail
B *vt* **~ l'ancora** weigh anchor
'salsa *f* sauce; Mus salsa
■ **salsa di pomodoro** tomato sauce; **salsa di rafano** horseradish sauce; **salsa di soia** soy sauce; **salsa tartara** tartar sauce
sal'sedine *f* saltiness
sal'siccia *f* sausage
salsi'era *f* sauce boat, gravy boat
⚷ **sal'tare** **A** *vi* jump; (venir via) come off; (balzare) leap; (esplodere) blow up; **saltar fuori** spring from nowhere; ‹*oggetto cercato*› turn up; **è saltato fuori che ...** it emerged that ...; **~ fuori con ...** come out with ...; **salta agli occhi** (è evidente) it hits you; **~ in aria** blow up; **~ in mente** spring to mind
B *vt* jump [over]; skip ‹*pasti, lezioni*›; Culin sauté
sal'tato *adj* Culin sautéed
saltel'lare *vi* hop; (di gioia) skip
saltim'banco *m* acrobat
saltim'bocca *m inv slice of veal rolled with ham and sage and shallow-fried*
S
⚷ **'salto** *m* jump; (balzo) leap; (dislivello) drop; fig (omissione, lacuna) gap; **fare un ~ da** (visitare) drop in on; **in un ~** fig in a jiffy; **fare i salti mortali** fig go to great lengths; **fare quattro salti** infml go dancing; **fare un ~ nel buio** fig take a leap in the dark
■ **salto in alto** high jump; **salto con l'asta** pole-vault; **salto con l'elastico** bungee jump; **salto con la corda** skipping; **salto in lungo** long jump; **salto pagina** Comput page down; **salto di qualità** quality leap
saltuaria'mente *adv* occasionally, from time to time
saltu'ario *adj* desultory
■ **lavoro saltuario** casual work
sa'lubre *adj* healthy

⚷ key word

salume'ria *f* delicatessen
sa'lumi *mpl* cold cuts
salumi'ere *m person who sells cold meat*
⚷ **salu'tare** **A** *vt* greet; (congedandosi) say goodbye to; (portare i saluti a) give one's regards to; Mil salute; **ti saluto!** infml cheerio!
B *adj* healthy
salu'tarsi *vr* (all'arrivo) greet each other; (in partenza) say goodbye to each other
⚷ **sa'lute** *f* health; **godere di ottima ~** be in the best of health, enjoy excellent health; **in ~** in good health; **~!** (dopo uno starnuto) bless you!; (a un brindisi) cheers!
■ **salute di ferro** iron constitution
salu'tista *mf* health fanatic; (dell'Esercito della Salvezza) Salvationist
⚷ **sa'luto** *m* greeting; (di addio) goodbye; Mil salute; **saluti** *pl* (ossequi) regards
'salva *f* salvo; **sparare a salve** shoot blanks; **a salve** ‹*pistola*› loaded with blank cartridges
salvacon'dotto *m* safe conduct
salvada'naio *m* money box
salva'gente *m* lifebelt; (a giubbotto) life jacket; (ciambella) rubber ring; (spartitraffico) traffic island
salvaguar'dare *vt* protect, safeguard
salvaguar'darsi *vr* protect oneself
salvagu'ardia *f* safeguard
⚷ **sal'vare** *vt* save; (proteggere) protect; **~ la faccia** save face; **~ la pelle** save one's skin
sal'varsi *vr* save oneself
salva'schermo *m* Comput screen saver
salva'slip *m inv* panty liner
salva'taggio *m* **1** rescue; Naut salvage; Comput saving; **battello di salvataggio** lifeboat **2** Econ bailout
salva|'tore, -trice *mf* saviour
salva'vita *m inv* Electr circuit breaker
'salve ▶ **salva**
sal'vezza *f* safety; Relig salvation
■ **ancora di salvezza** fig salvation
'salvia *f* sage
salvi'etta *f* serviette
⚷ **'salvo** **A** *adj* safe
B *m* **trarre in ~** rescue
C *prep* except [for]
D *conj* **~ che** (a meno che) unless; (eccetto che) except that
samari'tano, -a *adj & nmf* Samaritan; **un buon ~** a good Samaritan
'samba *f* samba
sam'buca *f* sambuca
sam'buco *m* elder
Sa'moa *fpl*
■ **Samoa Occidentali** Western Samoa
san *m* (*before proper names starting with a consonant*) saint; ▶ **santo**
sa'nabile *adj* curable
sa'nare *vt* heal; (bonificare) reclaim; **~ il bilancio** balance the books

sana'toria *f decree legitimizing a situation which is in principle illegal*
sana'torio *m* sanatorium
san'cire *vt* sanction
'sandalo *m* sandal; Bot sandalwood
sandi'nista *adj & nmf* Sandinista
'sandwich *m inv* sandwich
■ **uomo sandwich** sandwich man
san'gallo *m* (tessuto) broderie anglaise
san'gria *f* sangria
'sangue *m* blood; **a ~ freddo** in cold blood; **al ~** Culin rare; **appena al ~** Culin medium-rare; **farsi cattivo ~ per** worry about; **iniettato di ~** ‹*occhio*› bloodshot; **all'ultimo ~** ‹*lotta*› to the death; **di ~ blu** blue-blooded; **perdere ~ dal naso** have a nose bleed; **sudare ~** sweat blood
■ **sangue freddo** composure
sangue'misto *m* mixed-race
sangu'igno *adj* blood *attrib*
sangui'naccio *m* Culin black pudding
sangui'nante *adj* bleeding
sangui'nare *vi* bleed
sangui'nario *adj* bloodthirsty
sangui'noso *adj* bloody
sangui'suga *f* leech
sanità *f inv* soundness; (salute) health; **ministero della ~** Department of Health
■ **sanità di costumi** morality; **sanità mentale** sanity, mental health
sani'tario **A** *adj* sanitary; **servizio ~** health service
B *m* doctor
San Ma'rino *m* San Marino
'sano *adj* sound; (salutare) healthy; **~ come un pesce** as fit as a fiddle
■ **sano di mente** sane
'sansa *f* husk
San Sil'vestro *m* New Year's Eve
santifi'care *vt* sanctify
santità *f inv* sainthood
'santo, -a **A** *adj* holy; (con nome proprio) saint; **Sant'Antonio** St Anthony; **San Francesco d'Assisi** St Francis of Assisi; **di santa ragione** badly
B *mf* saint
■ **santo patrono, santa patrona** patron saint
san'tone *m* guru
santo'reggia *f* Bot savory
santu'ario *m* sanctuary
san Valen'tino *m* St Valentine's Day; **giorno di ~** Valentine's Day
sanzio'nare *vt* sanction
sanzi'one *f* sanction
■ **sanzione amministrativa** administrative sanction; **sanzione penale** legal sanction
sa'pere **A** *vt* know; (essere capace di) be able to; (venire a sapere) hear; **saperla lunga** know a thing or two; **non lo so** I don't know; **non so che farci** there's nothing I can do about it; **~ a memoria** know by heart; **~ il fatto proprio** know what one is talking about; **per quanto ne sappia** insofar as I know
B *vi* **~ di** know about; (aver sapore di) taste of; (aver odore di) smell of; **saperci fare** know how to go about it; **saperci fare con i bambini** be good with children
C *m* knowledge
sapi'ente **A** *adj* wise; (esperto) expert
B *m* sage
sapiente'mente *adv* wisely; (abilmente) skilfully
sapien'tone *m* smart alec[k]
sapi'enza *f* wisdom
sa'pone *m* soap; **bolla di ~** soap bubble; **finire in una bolla di ~** fig come to nothing
■ **sapone da barba** shaving soap; **sapone da bucato** washing soap
sapo'netta *f* bar of soap
sapo'noso *adj* soapy
sa'pore *m* taste; **sentire ~ di** detect a hint of
saporita'mente *adv* ‹*condire*› skilfully; ‹*mangiare*› appreciatively; ‹*dormire*› soundly
sapo'rito *adj* tasty
sapu'tello, -a *adj & nm* sl know-all, know-it-all AmE
sara'banda *f* fig uproar
sara'ceno, -a *adj & nmf* Saracen; **grano ~** buckwheat
saraci'nesca *f* roller shutter; (di chiusa) sluice gate
'sarago *m* white bream
sar'casmo *m* sarcasm
sarcastica'mente *adv* sarcastically
sar'castico *adj* sarcastic
sar'cofago *m* sarcophagus
Sar'degna *f* Sardinia
sar'dina *f* sardine
'sardo, -a *adj & nmf* Sardinian
sar'donico *adj* sardonic
SARS *f* SARS
sarti'ame *m* rigging
'sarto, -a **A** *m* tailor
B *f* dressmaker
sarto'ria *f* (da uomo) tailor's; (da donna) dressmaker's; (arte) couture
s.a.s. *abbr* (**società in accomandita semplice**) limited partnership
sas'saia *f* stony ground
sassai'ola *f* hail of stones
sas'sata *f* blow with a stone; **una ~ ha rotto il vetro** a stone broke the window; **prendere a sassate** throw stones at, stone
'sasso *m* stone; (ciottolo) pebble; **sono rimasto di ~** I was struck dumb [with astonishment]
sassofo'nista *mf* saxophonist
sas'sofono *m* saxophone
'sassone *mf* Saxon; **genitivo ~** Saxon genitive

sas'soso *adj* stony
'Satana *m* Satan
sa'tanico *adj* satanic
sa'tellite *adj inv & nm* satellite; **città ~** satellite town
sati'nare *vt* glaze; polish ‹*metallo*›
sati'nato *adj* glazed; ‹*metallo*› polished
'satira *f* satire
sa'tirico *adj* satirical
satol'lare *vt* (hum) stuff
sa'tollo *adj* (hum) replete, full
satu'rare *vt* saturate
saturazi'one *f* saturation
satur'nismo *m* lead poisoning
Sa'turno *m* Saturn
'saturo *adj* saturated; (pieno) full
S.A.U.B. *nf abbr* (**Struttura Amministrativa Unificata di Base**) *Italian national health service*
'sauna *f* sauna
sa'vana *f* savannah
savoi'ardo *m* (biscotto) sponge finger
savoir-'faire *m inv* expertise, know-how
sazi'are *vt* satiate
sazi'arsi *vr* **~ di** fig weary of, grow tired of
sazietà *f inv* **mangiare a ~** eat one's fill
'sazio *adj* satiated
sbaciucchi'are *vt* smother with kisses
sbaciucchi'arsi *vr* kiss and cuddle
sbada'taggine *f* carelessness; **è stata una ~** it was careless
sbadata'mente *adv* carelessly
sba'dato *adj* careless
sbadigli'are *vi* yawn
sba'diglio *m* yawn
sba'fare *vt* sponge
sba'fata *f* infml nosh; **farsi una ~** infml have a nosh-up
'sbaffo *m* smear
'sbafo *m* sponging; **a ~** (gratis) without paying
S ⚷ **sbagli'are** **A** *vi* make a mistake; (aver torto) be wrong
B *vt* make a mistake in; **~ strada** go the wrong way; **~ numero** get the number wrong; Teleph dial a wrong number; **sbagliando s'impara** practice makes perfect
sbagli'arsi *vr* make a mistake; **ti sbagli** you're mistaken, you're wrong; **~ di grosso** be totally wrong
sbagli'ato *adj* wrong
'sbaglio *m* mistake; **per ~** by mistake
sbale'strare *vt* fig disconcert
sbale'strato *adj* disconcerted
sbal'lare **A** *vt* unpack; infml screw up ‹*conti*›
B *vi* infml go crazy
sbal'lato *adj* (squilibrato) unbalanced

⚷ key word

'sballo *m* infml scream; (per droga) trip; **da ~** sl terrific
sballot'tare *vt* toss about
sbalordi'mento *m* amazement
sbalor'dire **A** *vt* stun
B *vi* be stunned
sbalordi'tivo *adj* amazing
sbalor'dito *adj* stunned; **restare ~** be stunned
sbal'zare **A** *vt* throw; (da una carica) dismiss
B *vi* bounce; (saltare) leap
'sbalzo *m* bounce; (sussulto) jolt; (di temperatura) sudden change; **a sbalzi** in spurts; **a ~** (a rilievo) embossed
sban'care *vt* bankrupt; excavate ‹*terreno*›; **~ il banco** break the bank
sbanda'mento *m* Auto skid; Naut list; fig going off the rails
sban'dare *vi* Auto skid; Naut list
sban'darsi *vr* (disperdersi) disperse
sban'data *f* skid; Naut list; **prendere una ~ per** get a crush on
sban'dato, -a **A** *adj* mixed-up
B *mf* mixed-up person
sbandie'rare *vt* wave; fig display
sbarac'care *vt & vi* clear up
sbaragli'are *vt* rout
sba'raglio *m* rout; **mettere allo ~** rout
sbaraz'zare *vt* clear
sbaraz'zarsi *vr* **~ di** get rid of
sbaraz'zino, -a **A** *adj* mischievous
B *mf* scamp
sbar'bare *vt* shave
sbar'barsi *vr* shave
sbarba'tello, -a *adj & nmf* novice
sbar'care *vt & vi* disembark; **~ il lunario** make ends meet
'sbarco *m* landing; (di merci) unloading
'sbarra *f* bar; (di passaggio a livello) barrier
■ **sbarra spaziatrice** space bar
sbarra'mento *m* barricade
sbar'rare *vt* bar; (ostruire) block; cross ‹*assegno*›; (spalancare) open wide
sbar'retta *f* oblique
sbatacchi'are *vt/i sl* bang, slam
⚷ **'sbattere** **A** *vt* bang; slam, bang ‹*porta*›; (urtare) knock; Culin beat; flap ‹*ali*›; shake ‹*tappeto*›; **~ le palpebre** blink
B *vi* bang; ‹*porta*› slam, bang; **~ contro** knock against; **andare a ~ contro** run into
sbat'tersi *vr* sl rush around; **sbattersene di qualcosa** not give a toss about something
sbat'tuto *adj* tossed; Culin beaten; fig run down
sba'vare *vi* dribble; ‹*colore*› smear
sbava'tura *f* smear; **senza sbavature** fig faultless
sbec'care *vt* chip
sbec'cato *adj* chipped
sbeffeggi'are *vt* mock

sbelli'carsi *vr* ~ **dalle risa** split one's sides [with laughter]
sben'dare *vt* unbandage
'sberla *f* slap
sbevaz'zare *vi* infml tipple
sbia'dire *vt & vi* fade
sbia'dirsi *vr* fade
sbia'dito *adj* faded; fig colourless
sbianca'mento *m* whitening; ~ **denti** teeth whitening
sbian'cante *m* whitener
sbian'care *vt & vi* whiten
sbian'carsi *vr* whiten
sbi'eco *adj* slanting; **di** ~ on the slant; ‹*guardare*› sidelong; **guardare qualcuno di** ~ look askance at somebody; **tagliare di** ~ cut on the bias
sbigot'tire **A** *vt* dismay **B** *vi* be dismayed
sbigot'tirsi *vr* be dismayed
sbigot'tito *adj* dismayed
sbilanci'are **A** *vt* unbalance **B** *vi* (perdere l'equilibrio) overbalance
sbilanci'arsi *vr* lose one's balance
sbi'lancio *m* lack of balance; Comm deficit
sbirci'are *vt* cast sidelong glances at
sbirci'ata *f* furtive glance
sbircia'tina *f* **dare una** ~ **a** sneak a glance at
'sbirro *m* derog cop
sbizzar'rirsi *vr* satisfy one's whims
sbloc'care *vt* unblock; Mech release; decontrol ‹*prezzi*›
'sbobba *f* infml pigswill
sboc'care *vi* ~ **in** ‹*fiume*› flow into; ‹*strada*› lead to; ‹*folla*› pour into
sboc'cato *adj* foul-mouthed
sbocci'are *vi* blossom
'sbocco *m* flowing; (foce) mouth; Comm outlet
sbolo'gnare *vt* infml get rid of
'sbornia *f* **prendere una** ~ get drunk; **smaltire la** ~ sober up
sbor'sare *vt* pay out
sbot'tare *vi* burst out
sbotto'nare *vt* unbutton
sbotto'narsi *vr* infml (confidarsi) open up; ~ **la camicia** unbutton one's shirt
sboz'zare *vt* draft; sketch out ‹*dipinto*›
sbra'carsi *vr* put on something more comfortable; ~ **dalle risate** infml kill oneself laughing
sbracci'arsi *vr* wave one's arms
sbracci'ato *adj* bare-armed; ‹*abito*› sleeveless
sbrai'tare *vi* bawl
sbra'nare *vt* tear to shreds *or* pieces
sbra'narsi *vr* tear each other to shreds
sbrat'tare *vt* clean up
sbrec'cato *adj* chipped
sbricio'lare *vt* crumble
sbricio'larsi *vr* crumble
sbri'gare *vt* expedite; (occuparsi di) attend to
sbri'garsi *vr* hurry up, be quick
sbriga'tivo *adj* hurried, quick
sbrigli'ato *adj* ‹*fantasia*› unbridled
sbri'nare *vt* defrost; Auto de-ice
sbrina'tore *m* Auto de-icer; (di frigo) defrost button
sbrindel'lare *vt* tear to shreds
sbrindel'lato *adj* in rags
sbrodo'lare *vt* stain
sbrodo'lone, -a *mf* messy eater
sbrogli'are *vt* disentangle
'sbronza *f* infml **prendersi una** ~ get drunk, get hammered infml
sbron'zarsi *vr* get drunk, get hammered infml
'sbronzo *adj* (ubriaco) drunk, hammered infml
sbruffo'nata *f* boast
sbruf'fone, -a *mf* boaster
sbu'care *vi* come out
sbucci'are *vt* peel; shell ‹*piselli*›
sbucci'arsi *vr* graze oneself
sbuccia'tore *m* parer
sbuccia'tura *f* graze
sbudel'lare *vt* gut ‹*pesce*›; draw ‹*pollo*›; disembowel ‹*persona*›
sbudel'larsi *vr* ~ **dal ridere** die laughing
sbuf'fare *vi* snort; (per impazienza) fume
'sbuffo *m* puff; **a** ~ ‹*maniche*› puff *attrib*
sbugiar'dare *vt* show to be a liar
sbuz'zare *vt* infml gut ‹*pesce*›; draw ‹*pollo*›; disembowel ‹*persona*›
'scabbia *f* scabies *sg*
'scabro *adj* rough; ‹*terreno*› uneven; ‹*stile*› bald
sca'broso *adj* rough; ‹*terreno*› uneven; fig ‹*questione*› difficult; ‹*scena*› offensive
scacchi'era *f* chessboard
scacciapensi'eri *m inv* Mus Jew's harp
scacci'are *vt* chase away
'scacco *m* check; **scacchi** *pl* (gioco) chess; (pezzi) chessmen; **dare** ~ **matto a** checkmate; **a scacchi** ‹*tessuto*› checked; **subire uno** ~ fig suffer a humiliating defeat
sca'dente *adj* shoddy, low quality
sca'denza *f* (di contratto) expiry; (di progetto, candidatura) deadline; Comm maturity; **a breve/lunga** ~ short/long term
scaden'zario *m* schedule
sca'dere *vi* expire; ‹*valore*› decline; ‹*debito*› be due
sca'duto *adj* ‹*biglietto*› out-of-date
sca'fandro *m* diving suit
scaffala'tura *f* shelves *pl*, shelving
scaf'fale *m* shelf; (libreria) bookshelf
sca'fista *mf person who ferries illegal immigrants to Italy by boat for a high fee*
'scafo *m* hull

scagio'nare *vt* exonerate
'scaglia *f* scale; (di sapone) flake; (scheggia) chip
scagli'are *vt* fling
scagli'arsi *vr* fling oneself; ~ **contro** fig rail against
scaglio'nare *vt* space out
scagli'one *m* group; **a scaglioni** in groups
■ **scaglione di reddito** tax bracket
sca'gnozzo *m* henchman
🔑 **'scala** *f* staircase; (portatile) ladder; Mus (misura) scale; **scale** *pl* stairs; **in** ~ to scale; **su larga** ~ large-scale *attrib*
■ **scala allungabile** extension ladder; **scala antincendio** fire escape; **scala Beaufort** Beaufort scale; **scala a chiocciola** spiral staircase; **scala mobile** escalator; (dei salari) cost of living index; **scala Richter** Richter scale; **scala di servizio** backstairs; **scala di sicurezza** fire escape
sca'lare **A** *adj* scalar
B *vt* climb; layer ‹*capelli*›; (detrarre) deduct
sca'lata *f* climb; (dell'Everest ecc.) ascent; **fare delle scalate** go climbing
scala|'tore, -trice *mf* climber
scalca'gnato *adj* down at heel
scalci'are *vi* kick
scalci'nato *adj* shabby
scalda'acqua *m inv* water heater
scalda'bagno *m* water heater
scalda'muscoli *m inv* leg warmer
scal'dare *vt* heat
scal'darsi *vr* warm up; (eccitarsi) get excited
sca'leno *adj* scalene
sca'leo *m* step-ladder
scal'fire *vt* scratch
scalfit'tura *f* scratch
scali'nata *f* flight of steps
■ **scalinata di piazza di Spagna** Spanish Steps
sca'lino *m* step; (di scala a pioli) rung
scalma'narsi *vr* rush about; (nel parlare) get worked up
scalma'nato *adj* worked up; **è** ~ (vivace) he can't sit still
'scalmo *m* rowlock
'scalo *m* slipway; Naut port of call; **fare** ~ **a** call at; Aeron land at; **senza** ~ non-stop
■ **scalo merci** freight depot, goods yard; **scalo passeggeri** stopover
sca'logna *f* infml bad luck
scalo'gnato *adj* infml unlucky
sca'logno *m* Bot scallion
scalop'pina *f* escalope
scal'pare *vt* scalp
scalpel'lare *vt* chisel
scalpel'lino *m* stone-cutter
scal'pello *m* chisel
scalpi'tare *vi* paw the ground; fig champ at the bit
scalpi'tio *m* pawing of the ground
'scalpo *m* scalp
scal'pore *m* noise; **far** ~ fig cause a sensation
scal'trezza *f* shrewdness
scal'trirsi *vr* get shrewder
'scaltro *adj* shrewd
scal'zare *vt* bare the roots of ‹*albero*›; fig undermine; (da una carica) oust
'scalzo *adj & adv* barefoot
scambi'are *vt* exchange; ~ **qualcuno per qualcun altro** mistake somebody for somebody else
scambi'arsi *vr* exchange; ~ **i saluti** exchange greetings
scambi'evole *adj* reciprocal
🔑 **'scambio** *m* exchange; Comm trade
■ **libero scambio** free trade; **scambio di persona** mistaken identity
scamici'ato *f* pinafore [dress]
sca'morza *f* soft cheese
scamosci'ato *adj* suede *attrib*
scampa'gnata *f* trip to the country
scampa'nato *adj* ‹*gonna*› flared
scampanel'lata *f* [loud] ring
scampanel'lio *m* ringing
scampa'nio *m* peal, pealing
scam'pare *vt* save; (evitare) escape; **scamparla bella** have a lucky escape
scam'pato **A** *adj* **lo** ~ **pericolo** the escape from danger
B *mf* survivor
'scampo *m* escape; (crostaceo) scampi; **non c'è** ~ there's no way out
'scampolo *m* remnant
scanala'tura *f* groove
scandagli'are *vt* sound
scanda'lismo *m* muckraking
scanda'listico *adj* sensational; ‹*giornale*› sensationalist
scandaliz'zare *vt* scandalize
scandaliz'zarsi *vr* be scandalized
'scandalo *m* scandal
scanda'loso *adj* scandalous; ‹*somma ecc.*› scandalous; ‹*fortuna*› outrageous
Scandi'navia *f* Scandinavia
scan'dinavo, -a *adj & nmf* Scandinavian
scan'dire *vt* scan ‹*verso*›; pronounce clearly ‹*parole*›; ~ **il tempo** beat time
scandi'tore *m* scanner
scan'nare *vt* slaughter
scan'nello *m* lectern
'scanner *m inv* scanner
■ **scanner manuale** Comput handheld scanner; **scanner piatto** flatbed scanner
scanneriz'zare *vt* Comput scan
scansafa'tiche *mf inv* lazybones *sg*

🔑 key word

scan'sare *vt* shift; (evitare) avoid
scan'sarsi *vr* get out of the way
scan'sia *f* shelves *pl*
scansi'one *f* Comput scanning
'scanso *m* **a ~ di** in order to avoid; **a ~ di equivoci** to avoid any misunderstanding
scanti'nato *m* basement
scanto'nare *vi* turn the corner; (svignarsela) sneak off
scanzo'nato *adj* easy-going
scapacci'one *m* smack
scape'strato *adj* dissolute
scapigli'ato *adj* dishevelled
'scapito *m* loss; **a ~ di** to the detriment of
'scapola *f* shoulder blade
'scapolo *m* bachelor
scappa'mento *m* Auto exhaust
scap'pare *vi* escape; (andarsene) dash [off]; (sfuggire) slip; **mi scappa da ridere!** I want to burst out laughing; **mi scappa la pipì** I'm bursting, I need a pee; **mi ha fatto ~ la pazienza** he tried my patience a bit too far; **lasciarsi ~ l'occasione** let the opportunity slip; **scappar via** run off *or* away
scap'pata *f* infml short visit
scappa'tella *f* escapade; (infedeltà) fling
scappa'toia *f* way out
scappel'lotto *m* cuff
scara'beo¹ *m* scarab beetle
scara'beo®² *m* Scrabble®
scarabocchi'are *vt* scribble
scara'bocchio *m* scribble
scara'faggio *m* cockroach
scara'mantico *adj* ‹*gesto*› to ward off the evil eye
scaraman'zia *f* superstition
scara'mazzo *adj* ‹*perla*› baroque
scara'muccia *f* skirmish
scaraven'tare *vt* hurl
scarcas'sato *adj* infml (macchina) beat-up
scarce'rare *vt* release [from prison]
scardi'nare *vt* unhinge
'scarica *f* discharge; (di arma da fuoco) volley; fig shower; **una ~ di botte** a hail of blows
scaricaba'rili *m* **fare a ~** blame each other
scari'care *vt* discharge; Comput download; unload ‹*arma, merci, auto*›; fig unburden
scari'carsi *vr* ‹*fiume*› flow; ‹*orologio, batteria*› run down; fig unwind
scarica'tore *m* loader; (di porto) docker
'scarico **A** *adj* unloaded; (vuoto) empty; ‹*orologio*› run-down; ‹*batteria*› flat; fig untroubled
B *m* unloading; (di rifiuti) dumping; (di acqua) draining; (di sostanze inquinanti) discharge; (luogo) [rubbish] dump; Auto exhaust; (idraulico) drain; (tubo) waste pipe
■ **'divieto di scarico'** 'no dumping'; **tubo di scarico** waste pipe

scarlat'tina *f* scarlet fever
scar'latto *adj* scarlet
scarmigli'ato *adj* ruffled
sca'rnire *vt* fig simplify
'scarno *adj* thin; fig ‹*stile*› bare
scaro'gna, scarognato = **scalogna, scalognato**
sca'rola *f* curly endive
'scarpa *f* shoe; infml (persona) dead loss; **fare le scarpe a qualcuno** fig double-cross somebody; **scarpe** *pl* **basse** flat shoes, flats; **scarpe** *pl* **da danza** ballet shoes; **scarpe** *pl* **da ginnastica** trainers, gym shoes; **scarpe** *pl* **col tacco** high heels; **scarpe** *pl* **col tacco a spillo** stilettos; **scarpe** *pl* **con la zeppa** platform shoes
scar'pata *f* slope; (burrone) escarpment
scarpi'era *f* shoe rack
scarpi'nare *vi* hike
scarpon'cino *m* ankle boot
■ **scarponcino Clark®** desert boot
scar'pone *m* boot
■ **scarpone da alpinismo** climbing boot; **scarponi da sci** *pl* ski boots; **scarponi da trekking** *pl* walking boots
scarroz'zare *vt & vi* drive around
scarroz'zata *f* infml trip
scarruf'fato *adj* ruffled
scarseggi'are *vi* be scarce; **~ di** (mancare) be short of
scar'sezza *f* scarcity, shortage
scarsità *f inv* shortage
'scarso *adj* scarce; (manchevole) short
scartabel'lare *vt* skim through
scarta'mento *m* Rail gauge
■ **scartamento ridotto** narrow gauge
scar'tare **A** *vt* discard; unwrap ‹*pacco*›; (respingere) reject
B *vi* (deviare) swerve
scartave'trare *vt* sand
'scarto *m* scrap; (in carte) discard; (deviazione) swerve; (distacco) gap
scartocci'are *vt* unwrap
scar'toffie *fpl* bumf, bumph
scas'sare *vt* break
scas'sato *adj* infml clapped out
scassi'nare *vt* force open; pick ‹*serratura*›
scassina|'tore, -trice *mf* burglar
'scasso *m* (furto) house-breaking
scata'fascio = **catafascio**
scate'nare *vt* fig stir up ‹*folla*›; arouse ‹*sentimenti*›
scate'narsi *vr* break out; fig ‹*temporale*› break; infml (darsi alla pazza gioia) go crazy, go wild; infml (infiammarsi) get excited
scate'nato *adj* crazy, wild; **pazzo ~** infml off his head
'scatola *f* box; (di latta) can, tin BrE; **in ~** ‹*cibo*› canned, tinned BrE; **rompere le scatole a qualcuno** infml get on somebody's nerves;

S

a ~ **chiusa** ‹*comprare*› sight unseen
■ **scatola del cambio** gearbox; **scatola nera** Aeron black box

scato'lame *m* (cibo) canned food

scato'letta *f* small box; (di cibo) tin

scato'logico *adj* scatological

scat'tante *adj* zippy

🔑 **scat'tare** *vi* go off; (balzare) spring up; (adirarsi) lose one's temper; take ‹*foto*›

'scatto *m* (balzo) spring; (d'ira) outburst; (di telefono) unit; (dispositivo) release; **a scatti** jerkily; **di ~** suddenly

scatu'rire *vi* spring

scaval'care *vt* jump over ‹*muretto*›; climb over ‹*muro*›; fig (superare) overtake

sca'vare *vt* dig ‹*buca*›; dig up ‹*tesoro*›; excavate ‹*città sepolta*›

scava'trice *f* excavator

scavezza'collo *m* daredevil

'scavo *m* excavation

scazzot'tare *vt* infml beat up

scazzot'tata *f* infml punch-up; **prendersi una ~** get beaten up

🔑 **'scegliere** *vt* choose, select

sce'icco *m* sheikh

scelle'rato *adj* wicked

🔑 **'scelta** *f* choice; (di articoli) range; **... a ~** (in menù) choice of ...; **prendine uno a ~** take your choice *or* pick; **di prima ~** top grade, choice; ‹*albergo*› first-rate; **di seconda ~** second grade; derog second-rate
■ **scelta multipla** multiple choice

'scelto **A** pp di **scegliere**
B *adj* select; ‹*merce ecc.*› choice
■ **tiratore scelto** marksman

sce'mare *vt & vi* diminish

sce'menza *f* silliness; (azione) silly thing to do/say; **non diciamo scemenze!** let's not be silly!

🔑 **'scemo** **A** *adj* idiotic
B *m* idiot

scempi'aggine *f* foolish thing to do/say

'scempio *m* havoc; fig (di paesaggio) ruination; **fare ~ di** play havoc with

🔑 **'scena** *f* scene; (palcoscenico) stage; **entrare in ~** Theat go/come on [stage]; fig come on the scene; **fare ~** make an impression; **fare una ~** make a scene; **fare scene** make a fuss; **andare in ~** ‹*Theat: spettacolo*› be staged, be put on; **fare ~ muta** not open one's mouth; **scomparire dalla ~** fig vanish from the scene; **mettere in ~** produce, stage; **messa in ~** production, staging; fig set-up

sce'nario *m* scenery

sce'nata *f* row, scene

🔑 **'scendere** **A** *vi* go/come down; (da treno, autobus) get off; (da macchina) get out; ‹*strada*› slope; ‹*notte, prezzi*› fall
B *vt* go/come down ‹*scale*›

🔑 key word

scendi'letto *m* bedside rug

sceneggi'are *vt* dramatize

sceneggi'ato *m* television serial

sceneggia'tura *f* screenplay

'scenico *adj* scenic

scenogra'fia *f* set design

sce'nografo, -a *mf* set designer

sce'riffo *m* sheriff

scervel'larsi *vr* rack one's brains

scervel'lato *adj* brainless

'sceso pp di **scendere**

scespi'riano *adj* Shakespearean

scetti'cismo *m* scepticism

'scettico, -a **A** *adj* sceptical
B *mf* sceptic

'scettro *m* sceptre

'scheda *f* card
■ **scheda audio** Comput sound card; **scheda elettorale** ballot paper; **scheda di espansione** Comput expansion card; **scheda grafica** Comput graphics card; **scheda madre** Comput motherboard; **scheda magnetica** card key; **scheda perforata** punch card; **scheda di rete** Comput network card; **scheda sonora** Comput sound card; **scheda telefonica** phonecard; **scheda di valutazione scolastica** report card, school report; **scheda video** Comput video card

sche'dare *vt* file

sche'dario *m* file; (mobile) filing cabinet

sche'dato, -a **A** *adj* with a police record
B *mf* person with a police record

sche'dina *f* pools coupon; **giocare la ~** do the pools

'scheggia *f* fragment; (di legno) splinter

scheggi'are *vt* splinter

scheggi'arsi *vr* chip; ‹*legno*› splinter

sche'letrico *adj* skeletal

'scheletro *m* skeleton; **essere ridotto ad uno ~** be all skin and bones

'schema *m* diagram; (abbozzo) outline; **uscire dagli schemi** break with tradition

schematica'mente *adv* schematically

sche'matico *adj* schematic

schematiz'zare *vt* present schematically

'scherma *f* fencing

scher'maglia *f* skirmish

scher'mirsi *vr* protect oneself

'schermo *m* screen; **sul grande ~** on the big screen; **farsi ~ con** shield oneself with
■ **schermo panoramico** wide screen; **schermo al plasma** plasma screen; **schermo a sfioramento** Comput touch screen

scher'nire *vt* mock

'scherno *m* mockery

🔑 **scher'zare** *vi* joke; (giocare) play; **c'è poco da ~!** it's nothing to laugh about!

🔑 **'scherzo** *m* joke; (trucco) trick; (effetto) play; Mus scherzo; **fare uno ~ a qualcuno** play a joke on somebody; **giocare brutti scherzi**

(a qualcuno) ‹*memoria, vista*› play tricks (on somebody); **per ~** for fun; **scherzi a parte** joking apart, seriously; **stare allo ~** take a joke
■ **scherzo di natura** freak of nature

scher'zoso *adj* playful

schiaccia'noci *m inv* nutcrackers *pl*

schiacci'ante *adj* damning; ‹*vittoria*› crushing

schiacci'are *vt* crush; (in tennis ecc.) smash; press ‹*pulsante*›; crack ‹*noce*›; **~ un pisolino** grab forty winks

schiacci'arsi *vr* get crushed

schiaccia'sassi *f inv* steamroller

schiaf'fare *vt* infml shove

schiaffeggi'are *vt* slap

schi'affo *m* slap; **dare uno ~** a slap; **avere una faccia da schiaffi** have the kind of face you'd love to take a swipe at
■ **schiaffo morale** slap in the face

schiamaz'zare *vi* make a racket; ‹*galline*› cackle

schia'mazzo *m* din; **schiamazzi** *pl* **notturni** disturbing the peace

schian'tare **A** *vt* break
B *vi* **schianto dalla fatica** I'm wiped out

schian'tarsi *vr* crash

schi'anto *m* crash; infml knock-out; (divertente) scream

schia'rire **A** *vt* clear; (sbiadire) fade
B *vi* brighten up

schia'rirsi *vr* brighten up; **~ la gola** clear one's throat; **~ le idee** get things clear in one's head; (dopo aver bevuto) clear one's head

schia'rita *f* sunny interval

schiat'tare *vi* burst; **~ di invidia** be green with envy

schia'vista *mf* slave-driver

schiavitù *f inv* slavery

schi'avo, -a *mf* slave

schi'ena *f* back
■ **mal di schiena** backache

schie'nale *m* (di sedia) back

schi'era *f* Mil rank; (moltitudine) crowd

schiera'mento *m* lining up; Mil battle line
■ **schieramento di forze** rallying of the troops

schie'rare *vt* draw up; rally ‹*forze*›

schie'rarsi *vr* draw up; ‹*forze*› rally; **~ dalla parte di qualcuno, ~ con qualcuno** rally [in support] to somebody; **~ contro qualcuno** rally in opposition to somebody

schiet'tezza *f* frankness

schi'etto *adj* frank; (puro) pure

schi'fezza *f* **è una ~** it's disgusting; ‹*film, libro*› it's rubbish

schifil'toso *adj* fussy

'schifo *m* disgust; **fare ~** be disgusting; **è uno ~!** it's disgusting!

schi'foso *adj* disgusting, yucky infml; (di cattiva qualità) rubbishy

schioc'care **A** *vt* crack ‹*frusta*›; snap, click ‹*dita*›; click ‹*lingua*›
B *vi* crack

schi'occo *m* (di frusta) crack; (di bacio) smack; (di dita, lingua) click

schioppet'tata *f* shot

schi'oppo *m* infml rifle; **a un tiro di ~** fig a stone's throw away

schiri'bizzo *m* infml fancy; **se mi salta lo ~** ... if it takes my fancy ...

schi'udere *vt* open

schi'udersi *vr* open

schi'uma *f* foam; (di sapone) lather; (di bucato) suds; (feccia) scum
■ **schiuma da barba** shaving foam

schiu'mare **A** *vt* skim
B *vi* foam

schiuma'rola *f* Culin skimmer

schiu'mogeno *adj* foaming

schiu'moso *adj* ‹*birra, crema*› frothy, foamy; ‹*liquido*› scummy

schi'uso pp di **schiudere**

schi'vare *vt* avoid

'schivo *adj* bashful

schizofre'nia *f* schizophrenia

schizo'frenico, -a *adj & nmf* schizophrenic

schiz'zare **A** *vt* squirt; (inzaccherare) splash; (abbozzare) sketch; **~ qualcuno/qualcosa di qualcosa** splatter somebody/something with something
B *vi* spurt; **~ via** fig scurry away

schiz'zato, -a *adj & nmf* infml loony

schizzi'noso *adj* squeamish

'schizzo *m* squirt; (di fango) splash; (abbozzo) sketch

sci *m inv* ski; (sport) skiing
■ **sci d'acqua, sci acquatico** water-skiing; **sci acrobatico** hot dogging; **sci di fondo** cross-country skiing

'scia *f* wake; (di fumo ecc.) trail; **sulla ~ di qualcuno** following in somebody's footsteps

sci'abola *f* sabre

sciabor'dare *vt & vi* lap

sciabor'dio *m* lapping

sciacal'laggio *m* profiteering

scia'callo *m* jackal; fig profiteer

sciac'quare *vt* rinse

sciac'quarsi *vr* rinse oneself

sci'acquo *m* mouthwash

scia'gura *f* disaster

sciagu'rato *adj* unfortunate; (scellerato) wicked

scialac'quare *vt* squander

scialacqua|'tore, -trice *mf* squanderer

scia'lare *vi* spend money like water

sci'albo *adj* pale; fig dull

sci'alle *m* shawl

scia'luppa *f* dinghy
■ **scialuppa di salvataggio** lifeboat

sciaman'nato *adj* good-for-nothing
scia'mano *n* shaman
scia'mare *vi* swarm
sci'ame *m* swarm; **a sciami** in swarms
sci'ampo *m* shampoo
scian'cato *adj* lame
sci'are *vi* ski; **andare a ~** go skiing
sci'arpa *f* scarf
sci'atica *f* Med sciatica
scia|'tore, -trice *mf* skier
sciatte'ria *f* slovenliness
sci'atto *adj* slovenly; ‹*stile*› careless
sciat'tone, -a *mf* slovenly person
'scibile *m* knowledge; **lo ~ umano** the sum of human knowledge
scic'coso *adj* infml snazzy
scienti'fico *adj* scientific
✓ **sci'enza** *f* science; (sapere) knowledge; **avere la ~ infusa** be naturally talented; **scienze** *pl* **sociali** social science
scienzi'ato, -a *mf* scientist
sci'ita *adj & nmf* Shiite
scilingu'agnolo *m* fig; **avere lo ~** be a chatterbox
'scimmia *f* monkey
scimmiot'tare *vt* ape
scimpanzé *m inv* chimpanzee, chimp
scimu'nito *adj* idiotic
'scindere *vt* separate; **~ in** break down into
'scindersi *vr* divide; **~ in** divide into
scin'tilla *f* spark
scintil'lante *adj* sparkling
scintil'lare *vi* sparkle
scintil'lio *m* sparkle
sciò *int* shoo!
scioc'cante *adj* shocking
scioc'care *vt* shock
✓ **scioc'chezza** *f* foolishness; (assurdità) foolish thing; **sciocchezze!** nonsense!
sci'occo *adj* foolish
✓ **sci'ogliere** *vt* untie; undo, untie ‹*nodo*›; (liberare) release; (liquefare) melt; dissolve ‹*contratto, qualcosa nell'acqua*›; loosen up ‹*muscoli*›
sci'ogliersi *vr* ‹*nodo*› come undone; (liquefarsi) melt; ‹*contratto*› be dissolved; ‹*pastiglia*› dissolve
sciogli'lingua *m inv* tongue-twister
scio'lina *f* ski wax
sciol'tezza *f* agility; (disinvoltura) ease
sci'olto **A** pp di **sciogliere**
B *adj* loose; (agile) agile; (disinvolto) easy; **versi** *pl* **sciolti** blank verse
sciope'rante *mf* striker
sciope'rare *vi* go on strike, strike
sci'opero *m* strike, industrial action; **in ~** on strike
■ **sciopero bianco** work-to-rule; **sciopero generale** general strike; **sciopero a singhiozzo** on-off strike
sciori'nare *vt* fig show off
sciovi'nismo *m* chauvinism
sciovi'nista *mf* Pol chauvinist
sciovi'nistico *adj* Pol chauvinistic
sci'pito *adj* insipid
scip'pare *vt* infml snatch; **~ qualcuno** snatch somebody's bag/bracelet etc
scippa|'tore, -trice *mf* bag-snatcher
'scippo *m* bag snatching
sci'rocco *m* sirocco
scirop'pato *adj* ‹*frutta*› in syrup
sci'roppo *m* syrup
scirop'poso *adj* syrupy
'scisma *m* schism
scissi'one *f* division
scissio'nista *adj* breakaway *attrib*
'scisso pp di **scindere**
sciupacchi'are *vt* spoil
sciupacchi'ato *adj* spoilt
sciu'pare *vt* spoil; (sperperare) waste
sciu'parsi *vr* get spoiled; (deperire) wear oneself out
sciu'pio *m* waste
✓ **scivo'lare** *vi* slide; (involontariamente) slip
'scivolo *m* slide; Techn chute
scivo'lone *m* fall; fig (errore) blunder
scivo'loso *adj* slippery
scle'rosi *f* sclerosis
■ **sclerosi multipla, sclerosi a placche** multiple sclerosis, MS
scoc'care **A** *vt* fire ‹*freccia*›; strike ‹*ore*›
B *vi* ‹*scintilla*› shoot out; **sono scoccate le cinque** five o'clock has just struck
scocci'are *vt* infml (dare noia a) bother
scocci'arsi *vr* infml be bored; **mi sono scocciato di aspettare** I'm fed up with waiting
scocci'ato *adj* infml fed up
scoccia|'tore, -trice *mf* nuisance
scoccia'tura *f* infml nuisance
sco'della *f* bowl
scodel'lare *vt* dish out, dish up
scodinzo'lare *vi* wag its tail
scogli'era *f* cliff; (a fior d'acqua) reef
'scoglio *m* rock; fig (ostacolo) stumbling block
scoglio'nato *adj* vulg pissed off
scoi'attolo *m* squirrel
scola'pasta *m inv* colander
scolapi'atti *m inv* dish drainer
sco'lara *f* schoolgirl
sco'lare[1] **A** *vt* drain; strain ‹*pasta, verdura*›
B *vi* drip
sco'lare[2] *adj* school *attrib*; **in età ~** ‹*bambino*› school-age
scola'resca *f* pupils *pl*

✓ key word

sco'laro *m* schoolboy
sco'lastico *adj* school *attrib*; **gita scolastica** school trip
scoli'osi *f* curvature of the spine
scollacci'ato *adj* low-cut
scol'lare *vt* cut away the neck of ‹*abito*›; (staccare) unstick
scol'lato *adj* ‹*abito*› low-necked
scolla'tura *f* neckline; ~ **profonda** plunging neckline
scolle'gare *vt* disconnect
'scollo *m* neckline
■ **scollo a V** V-neck
'scolo *m* drainage
scolo'rare *vt* fade
scolori'mento *m* fading
scolo'rire *vt* fade
scolo'rirsi *vr* fade
scolo'rito *adj* faded
scol'pire *vt* carve; (imprimere) engrave
scombi'nare *vt* upset
scombusso'lare *vt* muddle up
scom'messa *f* bet
scom'messo pp di **scommettere**
scom'mettere *vt* bet; **ci puoi ~!** you bet!
scomo'dare *vt* trouble
scomo'darsi *vr* trouble
scomodità *f inv* discomfort
'scomodo **A** *adj* uncomfortable
B *m* **essere di ~ a qualcuno** be a trouble to somebody
scompagi'nare *vt* mess up
scompa'gnare *vt* split
scompa'gnato *adj* odd
scompa'rire *vi* disappear; (morire) pass away
scom'parsa *f* disappearance; (morte) death, passing
scom'parso, -a **A** pp di **scomparire**
B *adj* missing; (morto) departed
C *mf* missing person; (morto) departed
scomparti'mento *m* compartment
scom'parto *f* compartment
■ **scomparto freezer** freezer compartment
scompen'sare *vt* throw off balance
scom'penso *m* imbalance
■ **scompenso cardiaco** cardiac insufficiency
scompigli'are *vt* disarrange
scom'piglio *m* confusion
scompisci'arsi *vr* infml ~ **[dalle risa]** split one's sides laughing, wet oneself infml
scom'porre *vt* break down; ruffle ‹*capelli*›; fig (turbare) upset
scom'porsi *vr* lose one's composure
scomposizi'one *f* breaking down
scom'posto **A** pp di **scomporre**
B *adj* (sguaiato) unseemly; (disordinato) untidy
sco'munica *f* excommunication
scomuni'care *vt* excommunicate

sconcer'tante *adj* disconcerting; (che rende perplesso) bewildering, baffling
sconcer'tare *vt* disconcert; (rendere perplesso) bewilder; baffle
sconcer'tato *adj* disconcerted; (perplesso) bewildered, baffled
scon'cezza *f* indecency
'sconcio **A** *adj* indecent
B *m* **è uno ~ che ...** it's a disgrace that ...
sconclusio'nato *adj* incoherent
scon'dito *adj* unseasoned; (insalata) with no dressing
sconfes'sare *vt* disown
scon'figgere *vt* defeat
sconfi'nare *vi* cross the border; (in proprietà privata) trespass
sconfi'nato *adj* unlimited
scon'fitta *f* defeat; **subire una ~** be defeated, suffer defeat
scon'fitto pp di **sconfiggere**
sconfor'tante *adj* disheartening, discouraging
scon'forto *m* discouragement; **farsi prendere dallo ~** get discouraged, get disheartened
sconge'lare *vt* thaw out ‹*cibo*›; defrost ‹*frigo*›
scongiu'rare *vt* beseech; (evitare) avert
scongi'uro *m* **fare gli scongiuri** ≈ touch wood, knock on wood AmE
scon'nesso **A** pp di **sconnettere**
B *adj* fig incoherent
scon'nettere *vt* disconnect
sconosci'uto, -a **A** *adj* unknown
B *mf* stranger
sconquas'sare *vt* smash; (sconvolgere) upset
sconsa'crare *vt* deconsecrate
sconsiderata'mente *adv* inconsiderately
sconsidera'tezza *f* lack of consideration, thoughtlessness
sconside'rato *adj* inconsiderate, thoughtless
sconsigli'abile *adj* not advisable
sconsigli'are *vt* advise against
sconso'lato *adj* disconsolate
scon'tare *vt* discount; (dedurre) deduct; (pagare) pay off; serve ‹*pena*›; **~ la propria colpa** pay for one's sins
scon'tato *adj* discounted; (ovvio) expected; **~ del 10%** with 10% discount; **era ~** it was to be expected; **dare qualcosa per ~** take something for granted
scon'tento **A** *adj* displeased
B *m* discontent
'sconto *m* discount; **fare uno ~** give a discount
■ **sconto commerciale** trade discount
scon'trarsi *vr* clash; (urtare) collide
scon'trino *m* ticket; (di cassa) receipt; **'munirsi dello ~ alla cassa'** *sign reminding*

S

customers that payment must be made at the cash desk beforehand

'scontro *m* clash; (urto) collision
■ **scontro automobilistico** car crash; **scontro di civiltà** clash of civilizations; **scontro frontale** head-on collision; **scontro a fuoco** shoot-out

scontrosità *f inv* surliness

scon'troso *adj* surly

sconveni'ente *adj* unprofitable; (scorretto) unseemly

sconvol'gente *adj* (sorpendente) mind-blowing; (inquietante) upsetting

scon'volgere *vt* upset; (mettere in disordine) disarrange

sconvolgi'mento *m* upheaval

scon'volto **A** pp di **sconvolgere**
B *adj* distraught, upset

'scooter *m inv* scooter

'scopa *f* broom; (gioco di carte) *type of card game*

sco'pare *vt* sweep; vulg shag

sco'pata *f* sweep; vulg shag; **dare una ~ per terra** give the floor a sweep

scoperchi'are *vt* take the lid off ‹*pentola*›; take the roof off ‹*casa*›

sco'perta *f* discovery

sco'perto **A** pp di **scoprire**
B *adj* uncovered; (senza riparo) exposed; (conto) overdrawn; (spoglio) bare

⚷ **'scopo** *m* aim; **a ~ di** for the sake of; **allo ~ di** in order to

sco'pone *m* (gioco di carte) *type of card game*

⚷ **scoppi'are** *vi* burst; fig break out

scoppiet'tare *vi* crackle

⚷ **'scoppio** *m* burst; (di guerra) outbreak; (esplosione) explosion; **a ~ ritardato** ‹*bomba*› delayed action; **ha reagito a ~ ritardato** he did a double take

⚷ **sco'prire** *vt* discover; (togliere la copertura a) uncover; unveil ‹*statua*›; **~ gli altarini** infml reveal his/her etc guilty secrets

scoraggia'mento *m* discouragement

scoraggi'ante *adj* discouraging

scoraggi'are *vt* discourage

scoraggi'arsi *vr* lose heart

scor'butico *adj* Med suffering from scurvy; fig (scontroso) disagreeable

scor'buto *m* Med scurvy

scorci'are *vt* shorten

scorcia'toia *f* short cut

'scorcio *m* (di cielo) patch; (in arte) foreshortening; **di ~** (vedere) from an angle
■ **scorcio panoramico** panoramic view; **scorcio del secolo** end of the century

scor'dare *vt* forget; **~ qualcosa a casa** leave something at home

scor'darsi *vr* forget; **~ di qualcosa** forget something

scor'dato *adj* Mus out of tune

⚷ key word

scorda'tura *f* Mus going out of tune

sco'reggia *f* infml fart

scoreggi'are *vi* infml fart

'scorfano *m* scorpion fish

'scorgere *vt* make out; (notare) notice

'scoria *f* waste; (di carbone) slag; **scorie** *pl* **nucleari** nuclear waste

scor'nare *vt* fig humiliate

scor'narsi *vr* fig come a cropper

scor'nato *adj* fig hangdog

'scorno *m* humiliation

scorpacci'ata *f* bellyful; **fare una ~ di** stuff oneself with

scorpi'one *m* scorpion; Astr Scorpio

scorraz'zare *vi* run about

⚷ **'scorrere** **A** *vt* (dare un'occhiata) glance through
B *vi* run; (scivolare) slide; (fluire) flow; Comput scroll; (attorno a un oggetto) wrap

scorre'ria *f* raid

scorret'tezza *f* (mancanza di educazione) bad manners *pl*

scor'retto *adj* incorrect; (sconveniente) improper

scor'revole *adj* **porta ~** sliding door

scorri'banda *f* raid; fig excursion

scorri'mento *m* Comput scrolling; (attorno a un oggetto) wrapping

'scorsa *f* glance; **dare una ~ a** glance through

'scorso **A** pp di **scorrere**
B *adj* last; **l'anno ~** last year

scor'soio *adj* **nodo ~** noose

'scorta *f* escort; (provvista) supply

scor'tare *vt* escort

scortecci'are *vt* debark ‹*albero*›; strip ‹*muro*›

scor'tese *adj* rude

scorte'sia *f* rudeness

scorti'care *vt* skin

scortica'tura *f* graze

'scorto pp di **scorgere**

'scorza *f* peel; (crosta) crust; (corteccia) bark; fig exterior
■ **scorza d'arancia** orange peel

scorzo'nera *f* salsify

sco'sceso *adj* steep

'scossa *f* shake; Electr fig shock; **prendere la ~** get an electric shock
■ **scossa elettrica** electric shock; **scossa sismica** earth tremor

'scosso **A** pp di **scuotere**
B *adj* shaken; (sconvolto) upset

scos'sone *m* jolt

sco'stante *adj* off-putting

sco'stare *vt* push away

sco'starsi *vr* stand aside

scostu'mato *adj* dissolute; (maleducato) ill-mannered

scotch® *m* Scotch tape

scoten'nare *vt* skin ‹*maiale*›; scalp ‹*persona*›

scot'tante *adj* ‹*argomento*› burning; fig ‹*notizia*› sensational

scot'tare **A** *vt* burn; (con liquido, vapore) scald; Culin blanch
B *vi* ‹*bevanda, cibo*› be too hot; ‹*sole, pentola*› be very hot

scot'tarsi *vr* burn oneself; (con liquido, vapore) scald oneself; (al sole) get sunburnt; fig get one's fingers burnt

scot'tato *adj* Culin blanched

scotta'tura *f* burn; (da liquido) scald; fig painful experience
■ **scottatura solare** sunburn

'Scottex® *m* paper towel

'scotto¹ *adj* overcooked

'scotto² *m* score; **pagare lo ~ di qualcosa** pay for something

scout **A** *adj inv* scout *attrib*
B *mf inv* scout

scou'tismo *m* scout movement

sco'vare *vt* (scoprire) discover

scovo'lino *m* bottle brush; (per pipa) pipe cleaner

'Scozia *f* Scotland

scoz'zese **A** *adj* Scottish
B *mf* Scot

'scrambler *m inv* Radio, Teleph scrambler

screan'zato *adj* rude

scredi'tare *vt* discredit

scre'mare *vt* skim

screpo'lare *vt* chap

screpo'larsi *vr* get chapped; ‹*intonaco*› crack

screpo'lato *adj* chapped; ‹*intonaco*› cracked

screpola'tura *f* crack

screzi'ato *adj* speckled

'screzio *m* disagreement

scribacchi'are *vt* scribble

scribac'chino, -a *mf* scribbler; ‹*impiegato*› pen pusher

scricchio'lante *adj* creaky

scricchio'lare *vi* creak

scricchio'lio *m* creaking

'scricciolo *m* wren; fig delicate-looking creature

'scrigno *m* casket

scrimina'tura *f* parting

scriteri'ato *adj* empty-headed

'scritta *f* writing; (su muro) graffiti

'scritto **A** *pp di* **scrivere**
B *adj* written; **~ col computer** word-processed; **~ a macchina** typed; **~ a mano** handwritten
C *m* writing; (lettera) letter

scrit'toio *m* writing desk

scrit|'tore, -trice *mf* writer

scrit'tura *f* writing; Relig scripture; (calligrafia) handwriting; **scritture** *pl* **contabili** account books
■ **scrittura privata** Jur *legal document drawn up by an individual*

scrittu'rare *vt* engage

scriva'nia *f* desk

scri'vente *mf* writer

'scrivere *vt* write; (descrivere) write about; **~ a macchina** type

scroc'care *vt* infml

scrocchi'are *vi* crack

'scrocco¹ *m* infml **a ~** without paying; **vivere a ~** sponge off other people

'scrocco² *m*:
■ **coltello a scrocco** pocket knife; **serratura a scrocco** spring lock

scroc'cone, -a *mf* infml sponger

'scrofa *f* sow

scrol'lare *vt* shake; **~ le spalle** shrug one's shoulders; **~ la testa** shake one's head

scrol'larsi *vr* shake oneself; **~ qualcosa di dosso** shake something off

'scrolling *m* Comput scrolling

scrosci'ante *adj* pouring; ‹*applauso*› thunderous

scrosci'are *vi* roar; ‹*pioggia*›; pelt down

'scroscio *m* roar; (di pioggia) pelting; **uno ~ di applausi** thunderous applause; **piovere a ~** lash down

scro'stare *vt* scrape

scro'starsi *vr* flake

scro'stato *adj* flaky

'scroto *m* scrotum

'scrupolo *m* scruple; (diligenza) care; **senza scrupoli** unscrupulous, without scruples; **farsi scrupoli per qualcosa** have scruples about something

scrupo'loso *adj* scrupulous

scru'tare *vt* scan; (indagare) search

scruta'tore *m* (di voti) returning officer

scruti'nare *vt* scrutinize

scru'tinio *m* (di voti) poll; Sch assessment of progress; **scrutini** *pl* Sch *meeting of teachers to discuss pupils' work and assign marks*
■ **scrutinio segreto** secret ballot

scu'cire *vt* unstitch; **scuci i soldi!** fig fam cough up [the money]!

scu'cirsi *vr* come unstitched; fig (parlare) talk; **non si scuce** he won't talk

scuci'tura *f* unstitching

scude'ria *f* stable; **scuderie** *pl* mews

scu'detto *m* Sport championship shield; (campionato) national championship

scudi'ero *m* squire

scudisci'ata *f* whipping

'scudo *m* shield; **farsi ~ con qualcosa** shield oneself with something

scuffi'are *vi* capsize

scu'gnizzo *m* street urchin

sculacci'are *vt* spank
sculacci'ata *f* spanking; **prendere a sculacciate** spank
sculacci'one *m* spanking
sculet'tare *vi* wiggle one's hips
scul|'tore, -trice **A** *m* sculptor
B *f* sculptress
scul'tura *f* sculpture
scu'ola *f* school
■ **scuola allievi ufficiali** cadet school; **scuola per bambini con difficoltà d'apprendimento** special school; **scuola elementare** primary school, grade school AmE; **scuola guida** driving school; **scuola materna** day nursery; **scuola media** secondary school; **scuola media inferiore** secondary school (10-13); junior high school AmE; **scuola media superiore** secondary school (13-18); **scuola dell'obbligo** compulsory education; **scuola privata** private school, public school BrE; **scuola di sci** ski school; **scuola serale** evening school; **scuola statale** state school; **scuola superiore** high school
scu'otere *vt* shake
scu'otersi *vr* (destarsi) rouse oneself; **~ qualcosa di dosso** fig shake something off
'scure *f* axe
scu'rire *vt & vi* darken
'scuro **A** *adj* dark
B *m* darkness; (imposta) shutter
scur'rile *adj* scurrilous
'scusa *f* excuse; (giustificazione) apology; (pretesto) pretext; **chiedere ~** apologize; **chiedo ~!** [I'm] sorry!
scu'sare *vt* excuse
scu'sarsi *vr* apologize (**di** for); **[mi] scusi!** excuse me!; (chiedendo perdono) [I'm] sorry!
sdebi'tarsi *vr* repay the kindness
sde'gnare *vt* despise; (fare arrabbiare) enrage
sde'gnarsi *vr* become angry
sde'gnato *adj* indignant
'sdegno *m* disdain; (ira) indignation
sde'gnoso *adj* disdainful
sden'tato *adj* toothless
sdipa'nare *vt* wind
sdogana'mento *m* customs clearance
sdoga'nare *vt* clear through customs
sdolci'nato *adj* sentimental, schmaltzy
sdoppia'mento *m* splitting
■ **sdoppiamento della personalità** split personality
sdoppi'are *vt* halve
sdrai'arsi *vr* lie down
'sdraio *f* **[sedia a] ~** deckchair
sdrammatiz'zare **A** *vt* take the heat out of
B *vi* take the heat out of the situation
sdruccio'lare *vi* slither
sdruccio'levole *adj* slippery
sdruccio'lone *m* slip
se **A** *conj* if; (interrogativo) whether, if; **se mai** (caso mai) if need be; **se mai telefonasse,...** should he call,..., if he calls,...; **se no** otherwise, or else; **se non altro** at least, if nothing else; **se pure** (sebbene) even though; (anche se) even if; **non so se sia vero** I don't know whether it's true, I don't know if it's true; **come se** as if; **se lo avessi saputo prima!** if only I had known before!; **e se andassimo fuori a cena?** how about going out for dinner?
B *m inv* if; **non voglio né se né ma** I don't want any ifs or buts
SE *abbr* (**sud-est**) SE
sé *pers pron* oneself; (lui) himself; (lei) herself; (esso, essa) itself; (loro) themselves; **l'ha fatto da sé** he did it himself; **ha preso i soldi con sé** he took the money with him; **si sono tenuti le notizie per sé** they kept the news to themselves
se'baceo *adj* sebaceous
seb'bene *conj* although
'sebo *m* sebum
sec. *abbr* (**secolo**) c.
'secca *f* shallows *pl*; **in ~** (nave) grounded
sec'cante *adj* annoying
sec'care **A** *vt* dry; (importunare) annoy
B *vi* dry up
sec'carsi *vr* dry up; (irritarsi) get annoyed
secca|'tore, -trice *mf* nuisance
secca'tura *f* bother; **dare una ~ a qualcuno** trouble somebody, bother somebody; **non voglio seccature!** I don't want the bother!
secchi'ata *f* bucketful
secchi'ello *m* bucket
■ **secchiello del ghiaccio** ice bucket
'secchio *m* bucket
■ **secchio della spazzatura** rubbish bin, trash can AmE
sec'chione, -a *mf* infml dweeb
'secco, -a **A** *adj* dry; (disseccato) dried; (magro) thin; (brusco) curt; (preciso) sharp; **restare a ~** be left penniless; **restarci ~** infml (morire di colpo) be killed on the spot; **frutta secca** dried fruit; (in guscio) nuts *pl*
B *m* (siccità) drought; **lavare a ~** dry-clean
secessi'one *f* secession
■ **guerra di secessione** War of Secession
seco'lare *adj* age-old; (laico) secular
'secolo *m* century; (epoca) age; **è un ~ che non lo vedo** infml I haven't seen him for ages *o* yonks
se'conda **A** *f* Sch, Rail second class; Auto second [gear]
B *prep* **a ~ di** according to
secon'dario *adj* Jur collateral; **effetto ~** side effect
se'condo **A** *adj* second
B *m* second, sec infml; (secondo piatto) main

key word

course; **un ~!** just a second!
C *prep* according to; **~ me** in my opinion
secondo'genito, **-a** *adj & nm* second-born
secrezi'one *f* secretion
'sedano *m* celery
■ **sedano rapa** celeriac
se'dare *vt* put down, suppress ‹*rivolta*›; fig soothe
seda'tivo *adj & nm* sedative; **somministrare sedativi a** sedate
'sede *f* seat; (centro) centre; Relig see; Comm head office; **in ~ di esami** during the exams; **in separata ~** in private
■ **sede centrale** head office; **sede sociale** registered office
seden'tario *adj* sedentary
se'dere **A** *vi* sit
B *m* (deretano) bottom
se'dersi *vr* sit down
'sedia *f* chair
■ **sedia a dondolo** rocking chair; **sedia elettrica** electric chair; **sedia da giardino** garden seat; **sedia girevole** swivel chair; **sedia a rotelle** wheelchair; **sedia a sdraio** deckchair
sedi'cenne *adj & nmf* sixteen year-old
sedi'cente *adj* self-styled
sedi'cesimo, **-a** *adj & nm* sixteenth
'sedici *adj & nm* sixteen
se'dile *m* seat
sedimen'tare *vi* leave a sediment
sedi'mento *m* sediment
sedizi'one *f* sedition
sedizi'oso *adj* seditious
se'dotto pp di **sedurre**
sedu'cente *adj* seductive; (allettante) enticing
se'durre *vt* seduce
se'duta *f* session; (di posa) sitting; **~ stante** *adv* here and now
se'duto *adj* sitting
sedut|'tore, **-trice** **A** *m* charmer
B *f* temptress
seduzi'one *f* seduction
seg. *abbr* (**seguente**) foll.
'sega *f* saw; vulg wank; **mezza ~** vulg tosser; **non capire una ~** understand damn all
■ **sega circolare** circular saw; **sega a mano** handsaw; **sega a nastro** band saw
'segale *f* rye
■ **pane di segale** rye bread
sega'ligno *adj* wiry
se'gare *vt* saw
sega'trice *f* saw
■ **segatrice a nastro** band saw
sega'tura *f* sawdust
'seggio *m* seat
■ **seggio elettorale** polling station
seg'giola *f* chair
seggio'lino *m* seat; (da bambino) child seat
■ **seggiolino per auto** car seat; **seggiolino regolabile** adjustable seat
seggio'lone *m* (per bambini) high chair
seggio'via *f* chair lift
seghe'ria *f* sawmill
se'ghetto *m* hacksaw
segmen'tare *vt* segment
seg'mento *m* segment
segna'carte *m* bookmark
segna'lare *vt* signal; (annunciare) announce; (indicare) point out
segna'larsi *vr* distinguish oneself
segnalazi'one *f* signals *pl*; (di candidato) recommendation
■ **segnalazione stradale** road signs *pl*
se'gnale *m* signal; (stradale) sign
■ **segnale acustico** beep; **segnale d'allarme** alarm; (in treno) communication cord BrE, emergency brake; fig warning sign; **segnale digitale** Comput digital signal; **segnale di libero** Teleph dialling tone; **segnale orario** time signal, speaking clock
segna'letica *f* signals *pl*; **'~ in rifacimento'** 'road signs being repainted'
■ **segnaletica orizzontale** painted road markings *pl*; **segnaletica stradale** road signs *pl*
segna'letico *adj* **dati segnaletici** description; **foto segnaletica** *photograph used for identification purposes*
segna'libro *m* bookmark
segna'punti *m inv* pegboard
se'gnare *vt* mark; (prendere nota) note; (indicare) indicate; Sport score; **~ la fine di qualcosa** sound the death knell for something; **~ il passo** mark time
se'gnarsi *vr* cross oneself
se'gnato *adj* marked
'segno *m* sign; (traccia, limite) mark; (bersaglio) target; **far ~** (col capo) nod; (con la mano) beckon; **fare ~ di no** (con la testa) shake one's head; **fare ~ di sì** (con la testa) nod [one's head]; **lasciare il ~** leave a mark; **non dare segni di vita** give no sign of life; **oltrepassare il ~** fig overstep the mark
■ **segno della croce** sign of the cross; **segno premonitore** early warning; **segno di sottolineatura** underscore; **segno più** plus sign; **segno zodiacale** sign of the Zodiac, birth sign, star sign
segre'gare *vt* segregate
segre'garsi *vr* cut oneself off
segre'gato *adj* in isolation
segregazi'one *f* segregation
segregazio'nistico *adj* segregated
segretari'ato *m* secretariat
segre'tario, **-a** *mf* secretary; **fare da ~ a qualcuno** be somebody's secretary; **segretaria tuttofare** girl Friday
■ **segretario bilingue** bilingual secretary; **segretario comunale** town clerk; **segretario di direzione** executive secretary; **segretario personale** personal assistant, PA; **Segretario di Stato** Secretary of State

segrete'ria *f* (ufficio) administrative office; (segretariato) secretariat
■ **segreteria studenti** Univ admissions office; **segreteria telefonica** answering machine, answerphone

segre'tezza *f* secrecy

⚷ **se'greto** *adj & nm* secret; **in ~** in secret

segu'ace *mf* follower; **avere molti seguaci** have a large following

segu'ente *adj* following, next

se'gugio *m* bloodhound

⚷ **segu'ire** *vt & vi* follow; (continuare) continue; **~ con lo sguardo** follow with one's eyes; **~ le orme di qualcuno** follow in somebody's footsteps; **~ un corso** take a course; **~ on Twitter** follow on Twitter

segui'tare *vt & vi* continue

⚷ **'seguito** *m* retinue; (sequela) series; (continuazione) continuation; **di ~** in succession; **in ~** later on; **in ~ a** following; (a causa di) owing to; **al ~** in his/her wake; **fare ~ a** Comm follow up

⚷ **'sei** *adj & nm* six

sei'cento *adj & nm* six hundred; **il Seicento** the seventeenth century

sei'mila *adj & nm* six thousand

'selce *f* flint

sel'ciato *m* paving

se'lenio *m* selenium

selettività *f inv* selectivity

selet'tivo *adj* selective; **memoria selettiva** selective memory

selet'tore *m* selector

selezio'nare *vt* select; **'~ il numero'** 'dial [the number]'

selezi'one *f* selection
■ **selezione naturale** natural selection

self-con'trol *m* self-control

self-'service *adj & m inv* self-service

'sella *f* saddle

sel'lare *vt* saddle

seltz *m inv* soda water

'selva *f* forest; fig (di errori, capelli) mass; (di ammiratori) horde

selvag'gina *f* game

sel'vaggio, -a **A** *adj* wild; (primitivo) savage **B** *mf* savage

sel'vatico *adj* wild

selvicol'tura *f* forestry

se'maforo *m* traffic lights *pl*

se'mantica *f* semantics *sg*

se'mantico *adj* semantic

sembi'anza *f* semblance; **sembianze** *pl* (di persona) appearance

⚷ **sem'brare** *vi* seem; (assomigliare) look like; **che te ne sembra?** what do you think?; **mi sembra che ...** I think ...; **sembra che vada bene** it's fine, seemingly *or* apparently

'seme *m* seed; (di mela) pip; (di carte) suit; (sperma) semen
■ **seme della discordia** seeds *pl* of discord

se'mente *f* seed

seme'strale *adj* ‹*corso*› six-month; ‹*pagamento*› six-monthly, half-yearly

se'mestre *m* six months; Univ term, semester AmE

semia'perto *adj* half open

semi'asse *m* axle

semiauto'matico *adj* semi-automatic

semi'breve *f* Mus semibreve

semi'cerchio *m* semicircle

semicirco'lare *adj* semicircular

semicirconfe'renza *f* semicircle

semicondut'tore *adj & nm* semiconductor

semicon'vitto *m*
■ **scuola a semiconvitto** *school for day boarders*

semicosci'ente *adj* semi-conscious; half-conscious

semi'croma *f* Mus semiquaver

semifi'nale *f* semi-final

semifina'lista *mf* semifinalist

semi'freddo *m cold dessert resembling ice cream*

semilavo'rato **A** *adj* semi-finished **B** *m* **semilavorati** *pl* semi-finished goods

semi'minima *f* Mus crotchet

'semina *f* sowing

⚷ **semi'nare** *vt* sow; infml shake off ‹*inseguitori*›; **~ zizzania** cause trouble

semi'nario *m* seminar; Relig seminary

semina'rista *m* seminarist

seminfermità *f inv* partial disability
■ **seminfermità mentale** diminished responsibility

seminter'rato *m* basement

semi'nudo *adj* half-naked

semioscurità *f inv* semi-darkness

semiprezi'oso *adj* semi-precious

semi'secco *adj* medium-dry

semi'serio *adj* semi-serious

se'mitico *adj* Semitic

semi'tono *m* Mus semitone

sem'mai **A** *conj* in case **B** *adv* **è lui, ~, che ...** if anyone, it's him who...

'semola *f* bran

semo'lato *adj* ‹*zucchero*› caster *attrib*

semo'lino *m* semolina

⚷ **'semplice** *adj* simple; **in parole semplici** in plain words

semplice'mente *adv* simply

semplici'otto, -a *mf* simpleton

sempli'cistico *adj* simplistic

semplicità *f inv* simplicity

semplifi'care *vt* simplify

⚷ **'sempre** *adv* always; (ancora) still; **di ~** ever;

S

⚷ key word

per ~ for ever; ~ **più** more and more; **pur** ~ still, nevertheless

sempre'verde *adj & nm* evergreen

'senape *f* mustard

se'nato *m* senate

sena|'tore, -trice *mf* senator

'Senegal *m* Senegal

se'nile *adj* senile

senilità *f inv* senility

'senior **A** *adj* senior **B** *mf* (*pl* **seniores**); Sport senior

'senno *m* sense; **giudicare col ~ del poi** use hindsight

sennò *adv* otherwise, or else

sennonché *conj* but, except that; (fuorché) but, except

'seno *m* (petto) breast; Math sine; **in ~ a** in the bosom of

sen'sale *m* broker

sen'sato *adj* sensible

sensazio'nale *adj* sensational

sensaziona'listico *adj* sensationalist

sensazi'one *f* sensation; **fare ~** ‹*notizia, scoperta*› cause a sensation

sen'sibile *adj* sensitive; (percepibile) perceptible; (notevole) considerable; **mondo ~** tangible world

sensibilità *f inv* sensitivity

sensibiliz'zare *vt* make more aware (**a**

sensibil'mente *adv* appreciably

sensi'tivo **A** *adj* sensory **B** *mf* sensitive person; (medium) medium

'senso *m* sense; (significato) meaning; (direzione) direction; **far ~ a qualcuno** make somebody shudder; **in ~ orario/antiorario** clockwise/anticlockwise; **ai sensi della legge** in accordance with the law; **non ha ~** it doesn't make sense; **avere il ~ degli affari** have good business sense; **di buon ~** ‹*persona*› sensible; **senza ~** meaningless; **in un certo ~ ...** in a sense *o* way ...; **perdere i sensi** lose consciousness; **a ~** ‹*ripetere, tradurre*› in general terms; **in ~ opposto** in the opposite direction; **a ~ unico** ‹*strada*› one-way; **a doppio ~ [di marcia]** ‹*strada*› two-way; **a doppio ~** ‹*parola, espressione*› with a double meaning

■ **senso dell'umorismo** sense of humour; **'senso vietato'** 'no entry'

sen'sore *m* sensor

sensu'ale *adj* sensual

sensualità *f inv* sensuality

sen'tenza *f* sentence; (massima) saying; **pronunciare una ~** hand down a sentence; **pronunciare la ~** pronounce sentence

sentenzi'are *vi* pass judgement

senti'ero *m* path

■ **sentiero luminoso di avvicinamento** Aeron approach lights

sentimen'tale *adj* sentimental

sentimenta'lista *mf* sentimentalist

sentimental'mente *adv* sentimentally

senti'mento *m* feeling; **essere fuori di ~** be out of one's mind

sen'tina *f* Naut bilge

senti'nella *f* sentry; **essere di ~** be on guard

sen'tire **A** *vt* feel; (udire) hear; (ascoltare) listen to; (gustare) taste; (odorare) smell **B** *vi* feel; (udire) hear; **~ caldo/freddo** feel hot/cold

sen'tirsi *vr* feel; **~ di fare qualcosa** feel like doing something; **~ bene/male** feel well/ill; **sentirsela di fare qualcosa** feel up to doing something

sen'tito *adj* (sincero) sincere; **per ~ dire** by hearsay

sen'tore *m* inkling

'senza *prep* without; **~ ombrello** without an umbrella; **~ correre** without running; **senz'altro** certainly; **~ un soldo** penniless; **'~ conservanti'** 'no preservatives'; **fare ~** do without

senza'tetto *m inv* **i ~** the homeless

'sepalo *m* sepal

sepa'rare *vt* separate

sepa'rarsi *vr* separate; ‹*prendere commiato*› part; **~ da** be separated from

separata'mente *adv* separately

separa'tista *mf* separatist

sepa'rato *adj* separate

separazi'one *f* separation

■ **separazione consensuale** separation by mutual consent; **separazione legale** legal separation

sepol'crale *adj* (liter) sepulchral

se'polcro *m* sepulchre

se'polto **A** pp di **seppellire** **B** *adj* buried; **morto e ~** fig dead and buried

sepol'tura *f* burial; **dare ~ a qualcuno** bury somebody

seppel'lire *vt* bury

seppel'lirsi *vr* fig cut oneself off

'seppia **A** *f* cuttle fish **B** *adj inv* sepia

sep'pure *conj* even if

se'quela *f* series, succession; (di insulti) string

se'quenza *f* sequence

sequenzi'ale *adj* sequential

seque'strare *vt* (rapire) kidnap; (confiscare) confiscate; Jur impound

sequestra|'tore, -trice *mf* kidnapper

se'questro *m* Jur impounding; (di persona) kidnap[ping]

se'quoia *f* sequoia

'sera *f* evening, night; **di ~, la ~** in the evening; **da ~** ‹*abito*› evening *attrib*; **alle 8 di ~** at 8 o'clock in the evening, at 8 o'clock at night; **buona ~!** good evening!; **dalla mattina alla ~** from morning to night; **ieri ~** yesterday evening, last night; **questa ~**

S

this evening, tonight

se'rale *adj* evening *attrib*

seral'mente *adv* every evening, every night

se'rata *f* evening; (ricevimento) party

■ **serata danzante** dance; **serata di gala** gala night

ser'bare *vt* keep; harbour ‹*odio*›; cherish ‹*speranza*›

serba'toio *m* tank

■ **serbatoio d'acqua** water tank; **serbatoio della benzina** petrol tank, gas tank AmE

'Serbia *f* Serbia

'serbo[1], **-a** **A** *adj & mf* Serbian **B** *m* (lingua) Serbian

'serbo[2] *m* **mettere in ~** put aside

serbo-cro'ato *mf* Serbo-Croat

sere'nata *f* serenade

serenità *f inv* serenity

⚷ **se'reno** *adj* serene; ‹*cielo*› clear; **un fulmine a ciel ~** infml a bolt from the blue

ser'gente *m* sergeant

'serial *m inv*

■ **serial [televisivo]** television serial

seri'ale *adj* serial

seria'mente *adv* seriously

'serico *adj* silk

⚷ **'serie** *f inv* series; (complesso) set; Sport division; **fuori ~** custom-built; **produzione in ~** mass production

■ **serie A** (di calcio) Premier League; **serie B** (di calcio) First Division; **di ~ B** fig second-rate; **serie numerica** numerical series

serietà *f inv* seriousness

⚷ **'serio** *adj* serious; (degno di fiducia) reliable; **sul ~** seriously; (davvero) really

ser'mone *m* sermon

seroto'nina *f* serotonin

'serpe *f* (liter) viper

serpeggi'ante *adj* ‹*strada*› twisting, winding

serpeggi'are *vi* ‹*strada*› twist, wind; fig (diffondersi) spread

ser'pente *m* snake

■ **serpente a sonagli** rattlesnake; **serpente velenoso** poisonous snake

serpen'tina *f* **a ~** twisting and turning, winding; **fare una ~** weave

'serra *f* greenhouse

■ **effetto serra** greenhouse effect

ser'raglio *m* harem

ser'randa *f* shutter

ser'rare *vt* shut; (stringere) tighten; (incalzare) press on

ser'rata *f* lockout

serra'tura *f* lock

'server *m inv* server

■ **server di posta** mail server; **server web** web server

ser'vibile *adj* usable

ser'vile *adj* servile

servi'lismo *m* servility

⚷ **ser'vire** **A** *vt* serve; (al ristorante) wait on **B** *vi* serve; (essere utile) be of use; **non serve** it's no good; **'~ freddo'** 'serve chilled'

ser'virsi *vr* (di cibo) help oneself; **~ da** buy from; **~ di** use

servi|'tore, -trice *mf* retainer

servitù *f inv* servitude; (personale di servizio) servants *pl*

servizi'evole *adj* obliging

⚷ **ser'vizio** *m* service; (da caffè ecc.) set; (di cronaca, sportivo) report; (in tennis) serve; **servizi** *pl* bathroom; **essere di ~** be on duty; **fare ~** ‹*autobus ecc.*› run; **fuori ~** ‹*bus*› not in service; ‹*ascensore*› out of order; **servizi** *pl* (terziario) services; **servizi** *pl* **bancari a domicilio** home banking; **servizi** *pl* **bancari via telefono** telephone banking; **servizi** *pl* **igienici** toilet block; **servizi** *pl* **di pronto intervento** emergency services; **servizi** *pl* **pubblici** (bagni) public toilets; **servizi** *pl* **sociali** welfare services

■ **donna di servizio** maid; **servizio bus navetta** courtesy bus; **servizio compreso** service charge included; **servizio escluso** not including service charge; **area di servizio** service station; **servizio in camera** room service; **servizio civile** *civilian duties done instead of national service*; **servizio filmato** film report; **servizio di linea** passenger service; **servizio militare** military service; **servizio pubblico** utility company; **servizio al tavolo** waiter service; **servizio da tavola** dinnerware; **servizio traghetto** passenger ferry

⚷ **'servo, -a** *mf* servant

servo'freno *m* servo brake

servo'sterzo *m* power steering

'sesamo *m* sesame

ses'santa *adj & nm* sixty

sessan'tenne *adj & nmf* sixty year-old

sessan'tesimo *adj & nm* sixtieth

sessan'tina *f* **una ~ di** about sixty

Sessan'totto *m protest movement of 1968*

sessi'one *f* session

ses'sista *adj* sexist

⚷ **'sesso** *m* sex; **fare ~** have sex

■ **sesso forte** stronger sex; **gentil sesso** fair sex; **sesso sicuro** safe sex

sessu'ale *adj* sexual

sessualità *f inv* sexuality

'sesto[1] *adj & nm* sixth

sesto[2] *m* **rimettere in ~** put back on its feet ‹*azienda*›; restore ‹*vestito*›; recondition ‹*motore, auto*›

set *m inv* set

'seta *f* silk; **di ~** silk *attrib*

setacci'are *vt* sieve

se'taccio *m* sieve; **passare qualcosa al ~** fig go through something with a fine-tooth comb

S

⚷ key word

'sete *f* thirst; **avere ~** be thirsty
■ **sete di sangue** blood lust

'setola *f* bristle

'setta *f* sect

set'tanta *adj & nm* seventy

settan'tenne *adj & nmf* seventy year-old

settan'tesimo *adj & nm* seventieth

settan'tina *f* **una ~ di** about seventy

set'tario *adj* sectarian

'sette *adj & nm* seven

sette'cento *adj & nm* seven hundred; **il Settecento** the eighteenth century

set'tembre *m* September

settentrio'nale **A** *adj* northern
B *mf* northerner

settentri'one *m* north

'setter *m inv* setter

'settico *adj* septic

setti'mana *f* week; **alla ~** per week; **a metà ~** midweek, half-way through the week
■ **settimana corta** five-day week; **settimana lavorativa** working week

settima'nale *adj & nm* weekly

setti'mino, -a **A** *adj born two months premature*
B *mf baby born two months premature*

'settimo *adj & nm* seventh

set'tore *m* sector

settori'ale *adj* sector-based

severità *f inv* severity

se'vero *adj* severe; (rigoroso) strict

se'vizia *f* torture; **sevizie** *pl* torture *sg*

sevizi'are *vt* torture

Sey'chelles *fpl* Seychelles

sezio'nare *vt* divide; Med dissect

sezi'one *f* section; (reparto) department; Med dissection

sfaccen'dare *vi* bustle about

sfaccen'dato *adj* idle

sfaccet'tare *vt* cut

sfaccet'tato *adj* cut; fig many-sided, multifaceted

sfaccetta'tura *f* cutting; fig facet

sfacchi'nare *vi* toil

sfacchi'nata *f* drudgery

sfaccia'taggine *f* cheek

sfacciata'mente *adv* cheekily

sfacci'ato *adj* cheeky, fresh AmE

sfa'celo *m* ruin; **in ~** in ruins

sfagio'lare *vi* infml **non mi sfagiola** it's/he's/she's not my cup of tea

sfal'darsi *vr* flake off

sfal'sare *vt* stagger; **~ il tiro** shoot wide

sfa'mare *vt* feed

sfa'marsi *vt* satisfy one's hunger, eat one's fill

sfarfal'lio *m* (di schermo, luce) flicker

'sfarzo *m* pomp

sfar'zoso *adj* sumptuous

sfa'sato *adj* infml confused; ‹*motore*› which needs tuning; **sentirsi ~** infml be out of sync[h]

sfasci'are *vt* unbandage; (fracassare) smash

sfasci'arsi *vr* fall to pieces

sfasci'ato *adj* beat-up

'sfascio *m* ruin; **andare allo ~** go to rack and ruin

sfa'tare *vt* explode

sfati'cato *adj* lazy

'sfatto *adj* unmade

sfavil'lante *adj* sparkling

sfavil'lare *vi* sparkle

sfavo'revole *adj* unfavourable

sfavo'rire *vt* disadvantage, put at a disadvantage

sfeb'brare *vi* **comincia a ~** his temperature is starting to come down

'sfera *f* sphere
■ **sfera affettiva** area of feelings and emotions; **sfera celeste** celestial sphere; **sfera di cristallo** crystal ball; **sfera di influenza** sphere of influence

'sferico *adj* spherical

sfer'rare *vt* unshoe ‹*cavallo*›; give ‹*calcio, pugno*›

sferruz'zare *vi* knit

sfer'zare *vt* whip

sfer'zata *f* whip; fig telling-off

sfian'cante *adj* wearing

sfian'care *vt* wear out

sfian'carsi *vr* wear oneself out

sfiata'toio *m* blowhole

sfi'brare *vt* exhaust

sfi'brato *adj* exhausted

'sfida *f* challenge

sfi'dare *vt* challenge

sfi'ducia *f* mistrust

sfiduci'ato *adj* discouraged

'sfiga *f* sl bloody bad luck; **avere ~** be bloody unlucky

sfi'gato, -a sl **A** *adj* bloody unlucky
B *mf* unlucky beggar

sfigu'rare **A** *vt* disfigure
B *vi* (far cattiva figura) look out of place

sfilacci'are *vt* fray

sfilacci'arsi *vr* fray

sfi'lare **A** *vt* unthread; (togliere di dosso) take off
B *vi* ‹*truppe*› march past; (in parata) parade

sfi'larsi *vr* come unthreaded; ‹*collant*› ladder; take off ‹*pantaloni*›

sfi'lata *f* parade; (sfilza) series
■ **sfilata di moda** fashion show

sfila'tino *m long, thin loaf*

'sfilza *f* string

'sfinge *f* sphinx

sfi'nire *vt* wear out

sfi'nito *adj* worn out

S

sfio'rare *vt* skim; touch on ‹*argomento*›
sfio'rire *vi* wither; ‹*bellezza*› fade
sfis'sare *vt* cancel
'sfitto *adj* vacant
'sfizio *m* whim, fancy; **togliersi uno ~** satisfy a whim
sfizi'oso *adj* nifty
sfo'cato *adj* out of focus
sfoci'are *vi* **~ in** flow into
sfode'rare *vt* draw ‹*pistola, spada*›; fig show off ‹*cultura*›; **~ un sorriso** smile insincerely
sfode'rato *adj* ‹*giacca*› unlined
sfo'gare *vt* vent
sfo'garsi *vr* give vent to one's feelings
sfoggi'are *vt & vi* show off
'sfoggio *m* show, display; **fare ~ di** show off
'sfoglia *f* sheet of pastry
■ **pasta sfoglia** puff pastry
sfogli'are *vt* leaf through
sfogli'ata[1] *f flaky pastry with filling*
sfogli'ata[2] *f* **dare una ~ a** ‹*libro, giornale*› flick through
'sfogo *m* outlet; fig outburst; Med rash; **dare ~ a** give vent to
sfolgo'rante *adj* blazing
sfolgo'rare *vi* blaze
sfolla'gente *m* truncheon, billy AmE
sfol'lare **A** *vt* clear
B *vi* Mil be evacuated
sfol'lato, -a *mf* evacuee
sfol'tire *vt* thin [out]; **farsi ~ i capelli** have one's hair thinned
sfon'dare **A** *vt* break down
B *vi* (aver successo) make a name for oneself
'sfondo *m* background; **un'aggressione a ~ politico/razziale** a politically/racially motivated attack
sfon'done *m* infml blunder
sfor'mare *vt* pull out of shape ‹*tasche*›
sfor'marsi *vi* lose its shape; ‹*persona*› lose one's figure
sfor'mato *m* Culin flan
sfor'nito *adj* **~ di** ‹*negozio*› out of
sfor'tuna *f* bad luck
sfortunata'mente *adv* unfortunately, unluckily
sfortu'nato *adj* unlucky
sfor'zare *vt* force
sfor'zarsi *vr* try hard
sfor'zato *adj* forced
⚷ **'sforzo** *m* effort; (tensione) stress
'sfottere *vt* sl tease
sfracel'larsi *vr* smash; **~ al suolo** crash to the ground
sfrangi'ato *adj* fringed
sfrat'tare *vt* evict
'sfratto *m* eviction

⚷ key word

sfrecci'are *vi* flash past
sfrega'mento *m* crackling
sfre'gare *vt* rub
sfregi'are *vt* slash
sfregi'ato, -a **A** *adj* scarred
B *mf* scarface
'sfregio *m* slash
sfre'narsi *vr* run wild
sfre'nato *adj* wild
sfrigo'lio *m* crackling
sfron'dare *vt* prune
sfron'tato *adj* shameless, brazen
sfrutta'mento *m* exploitation
⚷ **sfrut'tare** *vt* exploit; take advantage of, make the most of ‹*occasione*›
sfug'gente *adj* elusive; ‹*mento*› receding
⚷ **sfug'gire** **A** *vi* escape; **~ a** escape [from]; **mi sfugge** it escapes me; **mi è sfuggito [di mente]** it [completely] slipped my mind; **mi è sfuggito di mano** I lost hold of it; **lasciarsi ~ un'occasione** let an opportunity slip; **mi è sfuggito un rutto** I just came out with a belch; **gli è sfuggito un colpo dal fucile** the rifle just went off in his hands
B *vt* avoid
sfug'gita *f* **di ~** in passing
sfu'mare **A** *vi* (svanire) vanish; ‹*colore*› shade off
B *vt* soften ‹*colore*›
sfuma'tura *f* shade
sfuri'ata *f* outburst [of anger]
sga'bello *m* stool
sgabuz'zino *m* cupboard
sgam'bato *adj* ‹*costume da bagno*› high-cut
sgambet'tare *vi* kick one's legs; (camminare) trot
sgam'betto *m* **fare lo ~ a qualcuno** trip somebody up
sganasci'arsi *vr* **~ dalle risa** roar with laughter
sganci'are *vt* unhook; Rail uncouple; drop ‹*bombe*›; infml cough up ‹*denaro*›
sganci'arsi *vr* become unhooked; fig get away
sganghe'rato *adj* ramshackle
sgar'bato *adj* rude
'sgarbo *m* discourtesy; **fare uno ~ a qualcuno** be rude to somebody; **ricevere uno ~** be treated rudely
sgargi'ante *adj* garish
sgar'rare *vi* be wrong; (da regola) stray from the straight and narrow
'sgarro *m* mistake, slip
sga'sato *adj* flat
sgattaio'lare *vi* sneak away; **~ via** decamp
sge'lare *vt & vi* thaw
'sghembo *adj* slanting; **a ~** obliquely
sghiacci'are *vt* defrost; thaw out ‹*carne*›
sghignaz'zare *vi* laugh scornfully
sghiri'bizzo *m* whim, fancy

sgob'bare *vi* slog; ‹*fam: studente*› swot
sgob'bone, -a *mf* slogger; infml (studente) swot
sgoccio'lare *vi* drip
'sgocciolo *m* dripping
sgo'larsi *vr* shout oneself hoarse
sgombe[e]'rare *vt* clear [out]
'sgombro **A** *adj* clear
B *m* (trasloco) removal; (pesce) mackerel
sgomen'tare *vt* dismay
sgomen'tarsi *vr* be dismayed
sgo'mento *m* dismay
sgomi'nare *vt* defeat
sgom'mare *vi* make the tyres screech
sgom'mata *f* screech of tyres
sgonfi'are *vt* deflate
sgonfi'arsi *vr* go down
'sgonfio *adj* flat
'sgorbio *m* scrawl; fig (vista sgradevole) sight
sgor'gare **A** *vi* gush [out]
B *vt* flush out, unblock ‹*lavandino*›
sgoz'zare *vt* ~ **qualcuno** cut somebody's throat
sgra'devole *adj* disagreeable
sgra'dito *adj* unwelcome
sgraffi'are *vt* scratch
'sgraffio *m* scratch
sgrammaticata'mente *adv* ungrammatically
sgrammati'cato *adj* ungrammatical
sgra'nare *vt* shell ‹*piselli*›; open wide ‹*occhi*›
sgra'nato *adj* grainy; ‹*fagioli*› shelled; ‹*occhi*› wide open
sgran'chire *vt* stretch
sgran'chirsi *vr* stretch
sgranocchi'are *vt* munch
sgras'sare *vt* remove the grease from
'sgravio *m* relief
■ **sgravio fiscale** tax relief
sgrazi'ato *adj* ungainly
sgreto'lare *vt* crumble
sgreto'larsi *vr* crumble
sgri'dare *vt* scold
sgri'data *f* scolding
sgron'dare *vt* drain
sgros'sare *vt* rough-hew ‹*marmo*›; fig polish
sguai'ato *adj* coarse
sgual'cire *vt* crumple
sgual'drina *f* slut
sgu'ardo *m* look; (breve) glance; **dare uno** ~ a glance at ‹*giornale, testo*›
■ **sguardo di insieme** overview
sguar'nito *adj* unadorned; (privo di difesa) undefended
'sguattero, -a *mf* skivvy
sguaz'zare *vi* splash; (nel fango) wallow
'sguincio *m* sidelong glance
sguinzagli'are *vt* unleash
sgusci'are **A** *vt* shell
B *vi* (sfuggire) slip away; ~ **fuori** slip out
'shaker *m inv* shaker
shake'rare *vt* shake
'shampoo *m inv* shampoo; ~ **e messa in piega** shampoo and set
'shopper *m inv* carrier bag
'shuttle *m inv* [space] shuttle
si[1] *pers pron* (riflessivo) oneself; (lui) himself; (lei) herself; (esso, essa) itself; (loro) themselves; (reciproco) each other; (tra più di due) one another; (impersonale) you, one fml; **lavarsi** wash [oneself]; **si è lavata** she washed [herself]; **lavarsi le mani** wash one's hands; **si è lavata le mani** she washed her hands; **si è mangiato un pollo intero** he ate an entire chicken by himself; **incontrarsi** meet each other; **la gente si aiuta a vicenda** people help one another; **si potrebbe pensare che** ... you might think that ..., one might think that ... fml; **non si sa mai** you never know, one never knows; **queste cose si dimenticano facilmente** these things are easily forgotten
si[2] *m* Mus (chiave, nota) B
sì *adv* yes; **credo di sì** I believe so; **penso di sì** I think so; **ha detto di sì** she said yes; **sì?** really?; **sì che mi piace!** yes I do like it!
sia[1] ▶ **essere**
sia[2] *conj* ~... ~... (entrambi) both...and...; (o l'uno o l'altro) either...or...; ~ **che venga,** ~ **che non venga** whether he comes or not; **scegli** ~ **questo** ~ **quello** choose either this one or that one; **voglio** ~ **questo che quello** I want both this one and that one; **verranno** ~ **Giuseppe** ~ **Giacomo** both Giuseppe and Giacomo are coming
sia'mese *adj* Siamese
Si'beria *f* Siberia
sibi'lare *vi* hiss
sibil'lino *adj* sibylline
'sibilo *m* hiss
si'cario *m* hired killer
sicché *conj* (perciò) so [that]; (allora) then
siccità *f inv* drought
sic'come *conj* as
Si'cilia *f* Sicily
sicili'ano, -a *adj & nmf* Sicilian
sico'moro *m* sycamore
si'cura *f* safety catch; (di portiera) childproof lock
sicura'mente *adv* definitely; ~ **sarà arrivato** he must have arrived by now
sicu'rezza *f* (certezza) certainty; (salvezza) safety; (personale di sorveglianza e protezione) security, security guards; **chiamare la** ~ call security; **di** ~ ‹*dispositivo*› safety *attrib*; **di massima** ~ top security
■ **uscita di sicurezza** emergency exit
si'curo **A** *adj* (non pericoloso) safe; (certo) sure;

S

‹*saldo*› steady; Comm sound
B *adv* certainly
C *m* safety; **al ~** safe; **andare sul ~** play [it] safe; **di ~** definitely; **di ~ sarà arrivato** he must have arrived; **~!** sure!

'sidecar *m inv* sidecar
siderur'gia *f* iron and steel industry
side'rurgico *adj* iron and steel *attrib*
'sidro *m* cider
si'epe *f* hedge
si'ero *m* serum
sieronega'tivo, -a **A** *adj* HIV negative
B *mf* person who is HIV negative
sieroposi'tivo, -a **A** *adj* HIV positive
B *mf* person who is HIV positive
Si'erra Le'one *f* Sierra Leone
si'esta *f* afternoon nap, siesta; **fare la ~** have an afternoon nap
si'fone *m* siphon
Sig. *abbr* (**signore**) Mr
Sig.a *abbr* (**signora**) Mrs, Ms
⚷ **siga'retta** *f* cigarette; **pantaloni** *pl* **a ~** drainpipes
'sigaro *m* cigar
Sigg. *abbr* (**signori**) Messrs
sigil'lare *vt* seal
si'gillo *m* seal
'sigla *f* initials *pl*
■ **sigla musicale** signature tune
si'glare *vt* initial
Sig.na *abbr* (**signorina**) Miss, Ms
⚷ **signifi'care** *vt* mean
significa'tivo *adj* significant
signifi'cato *m* meaning
⚷ **si'gnora** *f* lady; (davanti a nome proprio) Mrs; (non sposata) Miss; (in lettere ufficiali) Dear Madam; **la ~ Rossi** Mrs Rossi; **il signor Vené e ~** Mr and Mrs Vené
⚷ **si'gnore** *m* gentleman; Relig lord; (davanti a nome proprio) Mr; **il signor Rossi** Mr Rossi
signo'rile *adj* gentlemanly; (di lusso) luxury
signo'rina *f* young lady; (seguito da nome proprio) Miss; **la ~ Rossi** Miss Rossi
silenzia'tore *m* silencer
⚷ **si'lenzio** *m* silence
■ **silenzio di tomba** deathly hush
silenzi'oso *adj* silent
'silfide *f* sylph
silhou'ette *f inv* silhouette, outline; **che ~!** you're so slim!
si'licio *m*
■ **piastrina di silicio** silicon chip
sili'cone *m* silicone
'sillaba *f* syllable
silla'bario *m* primer
sillaba'tore *m* Comput hyphenation program
sillo'gismo *m* syllogism
silu'rare *vt* torpedo

⚷ key word

si'luro *m* torpedo
simbi'osi *f* symbiosis; **vivere in ~** need each other, have a symbiotic relationship
simboleggi'are *vt* symbolize
sim'bolico *adj* symbolic[al]
simbo'lismo *m* symbolism
simbo'lista *mf* symbolist
'simbolo *m* symbol
similarità *f inv* similarity
⚷ **'simile** **A** *adj* similar; (tale) such; **è ~ a...** it's like..., it's similar to...; **qualcosa di ~** something similar
B *m* (il prossimo) fellow human being, fellow man
simili'tudine *f* Gram simile
simil'mente *adv* similarly
simil'pelle *f* Leatherette®
simme'tria *f* symmetry
sim'metrico *adj* symmetric[al]
⚷ **simpa'tia** *f* liking; (compenetrazione) sympathy; **prendere qualcuno in ~** take a liking to somebody; **provare ~ per** like
⚷ **sim'patico** *adj* nice
■ **inchiostro simpatico** invisible ink
simpatiz'zante *mf* well-wisher
simpatiz'zare *vt* **~ con** take a liking to; **~ per qualcosa/qualcuno** lean towards something/somebody
sim'posio *m* symposium
simu'lare *vt* simulate; feign ‹*amicizia, interesse*›
simula'tore *m* simulator
simulazi'one *f* simulation
■ **simulazione di reato** Jur *making of false accusations*
simul'tanea *f* **in ~** simultaneously
simul'taneo *adj* simultaneous
sina'goga *f* synagogue
sincera'mente *adv* sincerely; (a dire il vero) honestly
since'rarsi *vr* make sure
sincerità *f inv* sincerity
⚷ **sin'cero** *adj* sincere
'sincope *f* syncopation; Med fainting fit
sincron'ia *f* sync[h]
sincro'nismo *m* synchronism
sincroniz'zare *vt* synchronize
sincroniz'zato *adj* synchronized; **essere ben ~ con** be in sync[h] with
sincronizzazi'one *f* synchronization
'sincrono *adj* synchronous
sinda'cabile *adj* arguable
sinda'cale *adj* [trade] union *attrib*, [labour] union AmE
sindaca'lista *mf* trade unionist, labor union member AmE
sinda'care *vt* inspect
sinda'cato *m* [trade] union, [labour] union AmE; (associazione) syndicate

■ **sindacato di categoria** trade union
'sindaco *m* mayor
'sindrome *f* syndrome
■ **sindrome da colon irritabile** irritable bowel syndrome; **sindrome di Down** Down's syndrome; **sindrome da edifici malsani** sick building syndrome; **sindrome premestruale** premenstrual syndrome, PMS; **sindrome respiratoria acuta severa** severe acute respiratory syndrome, SARS
sinfo'nia *f* symphony
sin'fonico *adj* symphonic
Singa'pore *f* Singapore
singhioz'zare *vi* (di pianto) sob
singhi'ozzo *m* hiccup; (di pianto) sob; **avere il ~** have the hiccups
'single *mf inv* single
singo'lare **A** *adj* singular; (strano) peculiar
B *m* Gram singular
singolar'mente *adv* individually; (stranamente) peculiarly
'singolo **A** *adj* single
B *m* individual; Mus single; Tennis singles *pl*; **un ~ di successo** a hit single
si'nistra *f* left; **a ~** on the left; **girare a ~** turn to the left; **la seconda a ~** the second on the left; **con la guida a ~** ‹*auto*› with left-hand drive; **la ~** Pol the left; **di ~** Pol left wing
sini'strare *vt* injure; damage ‹*casa*›
sini'strato *adj* injured; ‹*casa*› damaged
si'nistro **A** *adj* left, left-hand; (avverso) sinister
B *m* accident
sini'strorso, -a *mf* derog leftie
'sino *prep* = **fino**[1]
si'nonimo **A** *adj* synonymous
B *m* synonym
sin'tassi *f* syntax
sin'tattico *adj* syntactic[al]
'sintesi *f* synthesis; (riassunto) summary
sin'tetico *adj* synthetic; (conciso) summary
sintetiz'zare *vt* summarize
sintetizza'tore *m* synthesizer
sinto'matico *adj* symptomatic
'sintomo *m* symptom
sinto'nia *f* tuning; **in ~** on the same wavelength; **in ~ con** in harmony with, in tune with
sintonizza'tore *m* tuner
sinu'oso *adj* ‹*strada*› winding
sinu'site *f* sinusitis
sio'nismo *m* Zionism
sio'nista *adj & nmf* Zionist
si'pario *m* curtain
si'rena *f* siren; (di nave) hooter
'Siria *f* Syria
siri'ano, -a *adj & nmf* Syrian
si'ringa *f* syringe
'sismico *adj* seismic
si'smografo *m* seismograph
sismolo'gia *f* seismology
si'stema *m* system; **non è ~!** that's no way to behave!
■ **sistema di amplificazione sonora** induction loop; **sistema di gestione banca dati** database management system, DBMS; **sistema immunitario** immune system; **Sistema Monetario Europeo** European Monetary System; **sistema nervoso** nervous system; **sistema operativo** Comput operating system; **sistema solare** solar system; **sistema di vita** way of life
siste'mare *vt* (mettere) put; tidy up ‹*casa, camera*›; (risolvere) sort out; (procurare lavoro a) fix up with a job; (trovare alloggio a) find accommodation for; (sposare) marry off; infml (punire) sort out
siste'marsi *vr* settle down; (trovare un lavoro) find a job; (trovare alloggio) find accommodation; (sposarsi) marry
sistematica'mente *adv* systematically
siste'matico *adj* systematic
sistemazi'one *f* arrangement; (di questione) settlement; ‹*lavoro*› job; (alloggio) accommodation; (matrimonio) marriage
siste'mista *mf* Comput systems engineer
'sistole *f* systole
'sit-in *m inv* sit-in
'sito *m* site
■ **sito web** Comput web site
situ'are *vt* place
situazi'one *f* situation; **essere all'altezza della ~** be equal to the situation, be up to the situation
'skai *m* Leatherette®
'skateboard *m inv* skateboard
sketch *m inv* sketch
ski-'lift *m* ski tow
'skipper *mf inv* skipper
slab'brare *vt* stretch out of shape ‹*maglia, tasca*›
slab'brato *adj* ‹*maglia, tasca*› shapeless
slacci'are *vt* unfasten; unlace ‹*scarpe*›
'slalom *m inv* slalom; **a ~** slalom *attrib*
slanci'arsi *vr* hurl oneself
slanci'ato *adj* slender
'slancio *m* impetus; (impulso) impulse; **agire di ~** act on impulse
sla'vato *adj* ‹*carnagione, capelli*› fair
'slavo *adj* Slav
sle'ale *adj* disloyal; **concorrenza ~** unfair competition
slealtà *f inv* disloyalty
sle'gare *vt* untie
sle'garsi *vr* untie oneself
slip *mpl* underpants
'slitta *f* sledge; (trainata) sleigh
slitta'mento *m* (di macchina) skid; fig (di riunione) postponement

slit'tare *vi* Auto skid; ‹*riunione*› be put off
slit'tata *f* skid
slit'tino *m* toboggan
'slogan *m inv* slogan, rallying cry
slo'gare *vt* dislocate
slo'garsi *vr* ~ **una caviglia** sprain one's ankle
slo'gato *adj* sprained
sloga'tura *f* sprain
sloggi'are **A** *vt* dislodge **B** *vi* move out
slot *m*
▪ **slot di espansione** Comput expansion slot
slot-ma'chine *f inv* slot machine, one-armed bandit
Slo'vacchia *f* Slovakia
slo'vacco, -a *adj & nmf* Slovak
Slo'venia *f* Slovenia
smacchi'are *vt* clean
smacchia'tore *m* stain remover
'smacco *m* humiliating defeat
smagli'ante *adj* dazzling
smagli'arsi *vr* ‹*calza*› ladder BrE, run
smaglia'tura *f* ladder BrE, run
smagnetiz'zare *vt* demagnetize
smagnetiz'zatore *m* demagnetizer
sma'grito *adj* thinner
smalizi'ato *adj* cunning
smal'tare *vt* enamel; glaze ‹*ceramica*›; varnish ‹*unghie*›
smal'tato *adj* enamelled; ‹*ceramica*› glazed; ‹*unghie*› varnished
smalta'tura *f* enamelling; (di ceramica) glazing
smalti'mento *m* disposal; (di merce) selling off; (di grassi) burning off
▪ **smaltimento [dei] rifiuti** waste disposal
smal'tire *vt* burn off; (rifiuti) dispose of, treat; (merce) sell off; fig get through ‹*corrispondenza*›; ~ **la sbornia** sober up
'smalto *m* enamel; (di ceramica) glaze; (per le unghie) nail varnish, nail polish
smance'ria *f* **fare smancerie** be overly polite
smance'roso *adj* simpering
'smania *f* fidgets *pl*; (desiderio) longing; **avere la ~ di** have a craving for
smani'are *vi* have the fidgets; ~ **per** long for
smani'oso *adj* restless
smantella'mento *m* dismantling
smantel'lare *vt* dismantle
smarri'mento *m* loss; (psicologico) bewilderment
smar'rire *vt* lose; (temporaneamente) mislay
smar'rirsi *vr* get lost; (turbarsi) be bewildered
smar'rito *adj* lost; ‹*sguardo*› bewildered, lost
'smartphone *m* smartphone

smasche'rare *vt* unmask
smasche'rarsi *vr* fig reveal oneself
SME *nm abbr* (**Sistema Monetario Europeo**) EMS
smem'brare *vt* dismember
smemo'rato, -a **A** *adj* forgetful **B** *mf* scatterbrain
smen'tire *vt* deny
smen'tita *f* denial
sme'raldo *nm & adj inv* emerald
smerci'are *vt* sell off
'smercio *m* sale
smerigli'ato *adj* emery
▪ **vetro smerigliato** frosted glass
sme'riglio *m* emery
smer'lare *vt* scallop
'smerlo *m* scallop
'smesso **A** pp di **smettere** **B** *adj* ‹*abiti*› cast-off
'smettere *vt* stop; stop wearing ‹*abiti*›; **smettila!** stop it!
smidol'lato *adj* spineless
smilitariz'zare *vt* demilitarize
'smilzo *adj* thin
sminu'ire *vt* diminish
sminu'irsi *vr* fig belittle oneself
sminuz'zare *vt* crumble; fig (analizzare) analyse in detail
smista'mento *m* clearing; (postale) sorting; **stazione di ~** shunting yard, marshalling yard
▪ **smistamento rifiuti** sorting of waste
smi'stare *vt* sort; Mil post; Rail marshal
smisu'rato *adj* boundless; (esorbitante) excessive
smitiz'zare *vt* demythologize
smobili'tare *vt* demobilize
smobilitazi'one *f* demobilization
smo'dato *adj* immoderate
smog *m* smog
'smoking *m inv* dinner jacket, tuxedo AmE
smon'tabile *adj* jointed
smon'taggio *m* disassembly
smon'tare **A** *vt* take to pieces; (scoraggiare) dishearten; take down ‹*tenda*› **B** *vi* (da veicolo) get off; (da cavallo) dismount; (dal servizio) go off duty
smon'tarsi *vr* lose heart
'smorfia *f* grimace; (moina) simper; **fare smorfie** make faces
smorfi'oso *adj* affected
'smorto *adj* pale; ‹*colore*› dull
smor'zare *vt* dim ‹*luce*›; tone down ‹*colori*›; deaden ‹*suoni*›; quench ‹*sete*›
smor'zata *f* Sport drop shot
'smosso pp di **smuovere**
smotta'mento *m* landslide
SMS *nm abbr* SMS message, text message; **mandare un ~ a qualcuno** text somebody

S

key word

'smunto *adj* emaciated
smu'overe *vt* shift; (commuovere) move
smu'oversi *vr* move; (commuoversi) be moved
smus'sare *vt* round off; fig (attenuare) tone down
smus'sarsi *vr* go blunt
smussa'tura *f* bevel
snack bar *m inv* snack bar
snatu'rato *adj* inhuman
snazionaliz'zare *vt* denationalize
S.N.C. *abbr* (**società in nome collettivo**)
snel'lire *vt* slim down
snel'lirsi *vr* slim [down]
'snello *adj* slim
sner'vante *adj* enervating
sner'vare *vt* enervate
sner'varsi *vr* get exhausted
sni'dare *vt* drive out
snif'fare *vt* snort
snob'bare *vt* snub
sno'bismo *m* snobbery
snoccio'lare *vt* stone; fig blurt out
snoccio'lato *adj* ‹*olive*› pitted, with the stones removed
sno'dabile *adj* jointed
sno'dare *vt* untie; (sciogliere) loosen
sno'darsi *vr* come untied; ‹*strada*› wind
sno'dato *adj* ‹*persona*› double-jointed; ‹*dita*› flexible
'snodo *m* coupling
■ **snodo ferroviario** coupling
'snowboard *m inv* snowboard; **fare ~** snowboard
SO *abbr* (**sud-ovest**) SW
soap 'opera *f inv* soap [opera]
so'ave *adj* gentle
sobbal'zare *vi* jerk; (trasalire) start
sob'balzo *m* jerk; (trasalimento) start
sobbar'carsi *vr* **~ a** undertake
sobbol'lire *vi* simmer
sob'borgo *m* suburb
sobil'lare *vt* stir up
sobilla|'tore, -trice *m* instigator
sobrietà *f inv* sobriety
'sobrio *adj* sober
soc'chiudere *vt* half-close
socchi'uso **A** pp di **socchiudere**
B *adj* ‹*occhi*› half-closed; ‹*porta*› ajar
soc'combere *vi* succumb
soc'correre *vt* assist
soccorri'tore, -trice *mf* rescue worker
soc'corso **A** pp di **soccorrere**
B *m* assistance, help; **venire in ~** come to help, come to the rescue; **venire in ~ a qualcuno** come to somebody's rescue; **soccorsi** *pl* help; (persone) rescuers; (dopo disastro) relief workers
■ **soccorso alpino** mountain rescue; **soccorso disastri** disaster relief; **soccorso stradale** breakdown service, wrecking service AmE
socialdemo'cratico, -a **A** *adj* Social Democratic
B *mf* Social Democrat
socialdemocra'zia *f* Social Democracy
soci'ale *adj* social
socia'lismo *m* Socialism
socia'lista *adj & nmf* Socialist
socializ'zare *vi* socialize
società *f inv* society; Comm company
■ **società in accomandita semplice** limited partnership; **società per azioni** public limited company, plc; **società dei consumi** consumer society; **società in nome collettivo** commercial partnership; **società fiduciaria** trust company; **società a responsabilità limitata** limited liability company; **società di telecomunicazioni** communications company
soci'evole *adj* sociable
'socio, -a *mf* member; Comm partner
socioeco'nomico *adj* socio-economic
soci'ologa *f* sociologist
sociolo'gia *f* sociology
socio'logico *adj* sociological
soci'ologo *m* sociologist
'soda *f* soda
■ **soda da bucato** washing soda
soda'lizio *m* association, society
soddisfa'cente *adj* satisfactory
soddi'sfare *vt & vi* satisfy; meet ‹*richiesta*›; make amends for ‹*offesa*›
soddi'sfatto **A** pp di **soddisfare**
B *adj* satisfied
soddisfazi'one *f* satisfaction
'sodo **A** *adj* hard; fig firm; ‹*uovo*› hard-boiled
B *adv* hard; **dormire ~** sleep soundly
C *m* **venire al ~** get to the point
sofà *m inv* sofa
soffe'rente *adj* (malato) ill
soffe'renza *f* suffering
soffer'marsi *vr* pause; **~ su** dwell on
sof'ferto pp di **soffrire**
soffi'are **A** *vt* blow; reveal ‹*segreto*›; (rubare) pinch infml
B *vi* blow
soffi'ata *f* **datti una ~ al naso** blow your nose; **fare una ~ a qualcuno** fig sl tip somebody off, give somebody a tip-off
'soffice *adj* soft
soffi'etto *m* bellows; **a ~** ‹*borsa*› expanding
■ **soffietto editoriale** blurb
'soffio *m* puff; Med murmur
sof'fitta *f* attic
sof'fitto *m* ceiling
soffoca'mento *m* suffocation
soffo'cante *adj* suffocating

S

soffo'care *vt & vi* choke; fig stifle

sof'friggere *vt* fry lightly

sof'frire *vt & vi* suffer; (sopportare) bear; **~ di** suffer from; **~ di [mal di] cuore** suffer from *or* have a heart condition; **~ la fame/il freddo** be hungry/cold

sof'fritto **A** pp di **soffriggere**
B *m* fried ingredients *pl*

sof'fuso *adj* ‹*luce*› soft, suffused

sofisti'care **A** *vt* (adulterare) adulterate
B *vi* (sottilizzare) quibble

sofisti'cato *adj* sophisticated

soft *adj* soft

'softcopy *f* Comput soft copy

'soft-core **A** *m* soft-core, soft porn
B *adj* **pornografia ~** soft porn

'software *m inv* software; **dei ~** software packages
■ **software di accesso** access software; **software applicativo** application software; **software di autoapprendimento** tutorial package, tutorial software; **software di comunicazione** communications software, comms software; **software didattico** educational software; **software di gestione errori** error correction software; **software di OCR** OCR software; **software di sistema** system software

softwa'rista *m* Comput software engineer

soggettiva'mente *adv* subjectively

sogget'tivo *adj* subjective

sog'getto **A** *m* subject; **cattivo ~** bad sort
B *adj* subject; **essere ~ a** be subject to

soggezi'one *f* subjection; (rispetto) awe

sogghi'gnare *vi* sneer

sog'ghigno *m* sneer

soggio'gare *vt* subdue

soggior'nare *vi* stay

soggi'orno *m* stay; (stanza) living room
■ **permesso di soggiorno** residence permit

soggi'ungere *vt* add

'soglia *f* threshold; **alle soglie di qualcosa** on the threshold of something
■ **soglia del dolore** pain threshold; **soglia di povertà** poverty line

'sogliola *f* sole
■ **sogliola limanda** lemon sole

so'gnare *vt & vi* dream; **~ a occhi aperti** daydream

so'gnarsi *vr* dream; **non te lo sogni neppure!** forget it!, don't even think of it!

sogna|'tore, -trice *mf* dreamer

'sogno *m* dream; **fare un ~** have a dream; **neanche per ~!** not on your life!; **essere un ~** (bellissimo) be a dream; **una casa da ~** a dream house; **il mio ~ nel cassetto** my secret dream

'soia *f* soya

sol *m* Mus (chiave, nota) G

key word

so'laio *m* attic

sola'mente *adv* only

so'lare *adj* ‹*energia, raggi*› solar; ‹*crema*› sun *attrib*

so'larium *m inv* solarium

sol'care *vt* plough

'solco *m* furrow; (di ruota) track; (di nave) wake; (di disco) groove

solda'tessa *f* servicewoman

sol'dato *m* soldier
■ **soldato semplice** private

'soldo *m* **non ha un ~** he hasn't got a penny to his name; **senza un ~** penniless; **al ~ di** in the pay of; **soldi** *pl* (denaro) money *sg*; **fare [i] soldi** make money; **prelevare dei soldi** withdraw money; **da quattro soldi** cheapo, nickel-and-dime AmE

'sole *m* sun; (luce del sole) sun[light]; **al ~** in the sun; **prendere il ~** sunbathe

sole'cismo *m* solecism

soleggi'ato *adj* sunny

so'lenne *adj* solemn

solennità *f inv* solemnity

so'lere *vi* be in the habit of; **come si suol dire** as they say

so'letta *f* insole

sol'fato *m* sulphate

sol'feggio *m* sol-fa

sol'furo *m* sulphide

soli'dale *adj* in agreement

solidarietà *f inv* solidarity

solidifi'care *vt & vi* solidify

solidifi'carsi *vr* solidify

solidità *f inv* solidity; (di colori) fastness

'solido **A** *adj* solid; (robusto) sturdy; ‹*colore*› fast; **in ~** *Jur* jointly and severally
B *m* solid

soli'loquio *m* soliloquy

so'lista **A** *adj* solo
B *mf* soloist

solita'mente *adv* usually

soli'tario **A** *adj* solitary; (isolato) lonely
B *m* (brillante) solitaire; (gioco di carte) patience, solitaire

'solito **A** *adj* usual; **essere ~ fare qualcosa** be in the habit of doing something
B *m* the usual; **di ~** usually

soli'tudine *f* solitude

solleci'tare *vt* speed up; urge ‹*persona*›

sollecitazi'one *f* (richiesta) request; (preghiera) entreaty

sol'lecito **A** *adj* prompt
B *m* reminder

solleci'tudine *f* promptness; (interessamento) concern; **con la massima ~** Comm as soon as possible

solle'one *m* noonday sun; (periodo) dog days of summer

solleti'care *vt* tickle

sol'letico *m* tickling; **fare il ~ a qualcuno** tickle somebody; **soffrire il ~** be ticklish

solleva'mento *m*
■ **sollevamento pesi** weightlifting

solle'vare *vt* lift; (elevare) raise; (confortare) comfort; **~ una questione** raise a question; **~ qualcuno da un incarico** relieve somebody of a responsibility

solle'varsi *vr* rise; (riaversi) recover

solle'vato *adj* relieved

solli'evo *m* relief; **che ~!** what a relief!

'**solo, -a** **A** *adj* alone; (isolato) lonely; (unico) only; Mus solo; **da ~** by myself/yourself/himself etc
B *mf* **il ~, la sola** the only one
C *m* Mus solo
D *adv* only; **~ il sabato/la domenica** Saturdays/Sundays only, only on Saturdays/Sundays

sol'stizio *m* solstice

sol'tanto *adv* only

so'lubile *adj* soluble; ‹*caffè*› instant

soluzi'one *f* solution; Comm payment; **senza ~ di continuità** without interruption; **in un'unica ~** Comm as a lump sum
■ **soluzione salina per lenti** soaking solution

sol'vente **A** *m* solvent
■ **solvente per lo smalto** nail varnish remover; **solvente per unghie** nail polish remover
B *adj* solvent
■ **reparto solvente** pay ward

solvibilità *f inv* Fin solvency

'**soma** *f* load
■ **bestia da soma** beast of burden

'**somalo, -a** *adj & nmf* Somali

so'maro *m* ass, donkey; Sch dunce

so'matico *adj* somatic; **tratti somatici** physical features

somatiz'zare *vt* react psychosomatically to

som'brero *m* sombrero

somigli'ante *adj* similar

somigli'anza *f* resemblance

somigli'are *vi* **~ a** look like, resemble

somigli'arsi *vr* be alike; **chi si somiglia si piglia** birds of a feather flock together

'**somma** *f* sum; Math addition

som'mare *vt* add; (totalizzare) add up

sommaria'mente *adv* summarily

som'mario *adj & nm* summary

som'mato *adj* **tutto ~** all things considered

somme'lier *m inv* wine waiter

som'mergere *vt* submerge

sommer'gibile *m* submarine

som'merso **A** pp di **sommergere**
B *m* Econ black economy

som'messo *adj* soft

sommini'strare *vt* administer

somministrazi'one *f* administration; **~ per via orale** to be taken orally

sommità *f inv* summit

'**sommo** **A** *adj* highest; fig supreme
B *m* summit

som'mossa *f* rising

sommozza'tore *m* frogman

so'naglio *m* bell

'**sonar** *m* sonar

so'nata *f* sonata; fig fam beating

'**sonda** *f* Mech drill; (spaziale) Med probe

son'daggio *m* drilling; (spaziale) Med probe; (indagine) survey
■ **sondaggio d'opinione** opinion poll

son'dare *vt* sound; (investigare) probe

so'netto *m* sonnet

sonnambu'lismo *m* sleepwalking

son'nambulo, -a *mf* sleepwalker

sonnecchi'are *vi* doze

son'nifero *m* sleeping pill

'**sonno** *m* sleep; **aver ~** be sleepy; **morire di ~** be dead tired, be dead on one's feet; **morto di ~** infml (stupido) zombie; **perdere il ~** anche fig lose sleep
■ **sonno eterno** Relig eternal rest

sonno'lenza *f* sleepiness

'**sono** ▸ **essere**

sonoriz'zare *vt* add a soundtrack to

so'noro **A** *adj* resonant; (rumoroso) loud; ‹*onde, scheda*› sound *attrib*
B *m* Tech (di film) soundtrack

sontu'oso *adj* sumptuous

sopo'rifero *adj* soporific

sop'palco *m* platform
■ **soppalco abitabile** loft conversion

soppe'rire *vi* **~ a qualcosa** provide for something

soppe'sare *vt* weigh up ‹*situazione*›

soppi'atto di ~ *adv* furtively

soppor'tare *vt* support; (tollerare) stand; bear ‹*dolore*›

sopportazi'one *f* patience

soppressi'one *f* removal; (di legge) abolition; ‹*di diritti, pubblicazione*› suppression; (annullamento) cancellation

sop'presso pp di **sopprimere**

sop'primere *vt* get rid of: abolish ‹*legge*›; suppress ‹*diritti, pubblicazione*›; (annullare) cancel

'**sopra** **A** *adv* on top; (più in alto) higher [up]; (al piano superiore) upstairs; (in testo) above; **mettilo lì ~** put it up there; **di ~** upstairs; **dormirci ~** fig sleep on it; **pensarci ~** think about it; **vedi ~** see above
B *prep* **~ [a]** on; (senza contatto, oltre) over; (riguardo a) about; **è ~ al tavolo, è ~ il tavolo** it's on the table; **il quadro è appeso ~ al camino** the picture is hanging over the fireplace; **il ponte passa ~ all'autostrada** the bridge crosses over the motorway; **è caduto ~ il tetto** it fell on the roof; **l'uno ~ l'altro** one on top of the other; (senza contatto) one above the other; **abita ~ di me** he lives upstairs from me; **i bambini ~ i**

S

dieci anni children over ten; **20° ~ lo zero** 20 above zero; **~ il livello del mare** above sea level; **rifletti ~ quello che è successo** think about what happened; **prendere ~ di sé la responsabilità di qualcosa** assume responsibility for something; **scaricare la colpa ~ qualcuno** put the blame on somebody; **non ha nessuno ~ di sé** he has nobody above him; **al di ~ di** over; **al di ~ di ogni sospetto** beyond suspicion
C *m* **il [di] ~** the top

so'prabito *m* overcoat

soprac'ciglio *m* (*pl nf* **sopracciglia**) eyebrow

sopracco'perta *f* (di letto) bedspread

sopraccoper'tina *f* book jacket, dust jacket

soprad'detto *adj* above-mentioned

sopraele'vare *vt* raise

sopraele'vata *f* elevated railway

sopraele'vato *adj* raised

sopraf'fare *vt* overwhelm

sopraf'fatto pp di **sopraffare**

sopraffazi'one *f* abuse of power

sopraf'fino *adj* excellent; ‹*gusto, udito*› highly refined

sopraggi'ungere *vi* ‹*persona*› turn up; (accadere) happen; **è sopraggiunta la pioggia** and then it started to rain

soprallu'ogo *m* inspection

sopram'mobile *m* ornament

soprannatu'rale *adj & nm* supernatural

sopran'nome *m* nickname

soprannomi'nare *vt* nickname

sopran'numero *adv* **sono in ~** there are too many of them; **ce ne sono 15 in ~** there are 15 too many of them, there are 15 of them too many

so'prano *mf* soprano

soprappensi'ero *adv* lost in thought

sopras'salto *m* **di ~** with a start

soprasse'dere *vi* **~ a** postpone

soprat'tassa *f* surtax
■ **soprattassa postale** excess postage

soprat'tetto *m* fly sheet

soprat'tutto *adv* above all

sopravvalu'tare *vt* overvalue; overestimate ‹*forze*›

sopravvalutazi'one *f* overvaluation; (di forze) overestimation

sopravve'nire *vi* turn up; (accadere) happen

soprav'vento *m* fig upper hand; **prendere il ~** take the upper hand

sopravvis'suto, -a **A** pp di **sopravvivere**
B *adj* surviving
C *mf* survivor

sopravvi'venza *f* survival

soprav'vivere *vi* survive; **~ a** outlive

‹*persona*›

soprinten'dente *mf* supervisor; (di museo ecc.) keeper

soprinten'denza *f* supervision; (ente) board

so'pruso *m* abuse of power

soq'quadro *m* **mettere a ~** turn upside down

sor'betto *m* sorbet

sor'bire *vt* sip; fig put up with

'sorcio *m* mouse; **far vedere i sorci verdi a qualcuno** give somebody a rough time

'sordido *adj* sordid; (avaro) stingy

sor'dina *f* mute; **in ~** fig on the quiet

sordità *f inv* deafness

'sordo, -a **A** *adj* deaf; ‹*rumore, dolore*› dull
B *mf* deaf person

sordo'muto, -a **A** *adj* deaf and dumb
B *mf* deaf mute dated or offensive

so'rella *f* sister
■ **sorella gemella** twin sister

sorel'lastra *f* stepsister, half-sister

sor'gente *f* spring; (fonte) source
■ **programma sorgente** Comput source program

'sorgere *vi* rise; fig arise

sormon'tare *vt* surmount

sorni'one *adj* sly

sorpas'sare *vt* surpass; (eccedere) exceed; overtake, pass AmE ‹*veicolo*›

sorpas'sato *adj* old-fashioned

sor'passo *m* overtaking, passing AmE

sorpren'dente *adj* surprising; (straordinario) remarkable

sorprendente'mente *adv* surprisingly

sor'prendere *vt* surprise; (cogliere in flagrante) catch

sor'prendersi *vr* be surprised; **~ a fare qualcosa** catch oneself doing something; **non c'è da ~** it's hardly surprising

sor'presa *f* surprise; **di ~** by surprise; **provare ~** feel surprised

sor'preso pp di **sorprendere**

sor'reggere *vt* support; (tenere) hold up

sor'reggersi *vr* support oneself

sor'retto pp di **sorreggere**

sorri'dente *adj* smiling

sor'ridere *vi* smile; **la fortuna mi ha sorriso** fortune smiled on me

sor'riso **A** pp di **sorridere**
B *m* smile

sorseggi'are *vt* sip

'sorso *m* sip; (piccola quantità) drop

'sorta *f* sort; **di ~** whatever; **ogni ~ di** all sorts of

'sorte *f* fate; (caso imprevisto) chance; **tirare a ~** draw lots; **per buona ~** (liter) by good fortune

sorteggi'are *vt* draw lots for

sor'teggio *m* draw

sorti'legio *m* witchcraft

---

key word

sor'tire **A** *vi* come out
B *vt* bring about ‹*effetto*›
sor'tita *f* Mil sortie; (battuta) witticism
'sorto pp di **sorgere**
sorvegli'ante *mf* keeper; (controllore) overseer
sorvegli'anza *f* watch; Mil ecc. surveillance
■ **sorveglianza tramite braccialetto elettronico** electronic tagging
sorvegli'are *vt* watch over; (controllare) oversee; ‹*polizia*› watch, keep under surveillance
sorvegli'ato, -a **A** *adj* under surveillance
B *mf* ~ **speciale** person kept under special surveillance
sorvo'lare *vt* fly over; fig skip
SOS *m* SOS
'sosia *m inv* double
⚷ **so'spendere** *vt* hang; (interrompere) stop; (privare di una carica) suspend
sospensi'one *f* suspension
■ **sospensione condizionale [della pena]** suspended sentence
sospen'sorio *m* Sport jockstrap
so'speso **A** pp di **sospendere**
B *adj* ‹*impiegato, alunno*› suspended; ~ **a** hanging from; ~ **a un filo** fig hanging by a thread
C *m* **in** ~ pending; (emozionato) in suspense
⚷ **sospet'tare** *vt* suspect
⚷ **so'spetto** **A** *adj* suspicious
B *m* suspicion; (persona) suspect; **al di sopra di ogni** ~ above suspicion
sospet'toso *adj* suspicious
so'spingere *vt* drive
so'spinto pp di **sospingere**
sospi'rare **A** *vi* sigh
B *vt* long for
so'spiro *m* sigh
'sosta *f* stop, stop-off; (pausa) pause; **senza** ~ non-stop; **'~ autorizzata ...'** 'parking permitted for ...'
■ **'divieto di sosta'** 'no parking'
sostan'tivo *m* noun
⚷ **so'stanza** *f* substance; **sostanze** *pl* (patrimonio) property *sg*; **in** ~ to sum up; **la** ~ **della questione** the nub of the matter
sostanzi'oso *adj* substantial; ‹*cibo*› nourishing; **poco** ~ insubstantial
so'stare *vi* stop; (fare una pausa) pause
so'stegno *m* support
■ **sostegno morale** moral support
⚷ **soste'nere** *vt* support; (sopportare) bear; (resistere) withstand; (affermare) maintain; (nutrire) sustain: sit ‹*esame*›; ~ **le spese** meet the costs; ~ **delle spese** incur expenditure; ~ **una carica** hold a position; ~ **una parte** play a role
soste'nersi *vr* support oneself
soste'nibile *adj* ‹*sviluppo, crescita*› sustainable
sosteni|'tore, -trice *mf* supporter
sostenta'mento *m* maintenance
soste'nuto **A** *adj* ‹*stile*› formal; ‹*velocità*› high; ‹*mercato, prezzi*› steady
B *m* **fare il** ~ be stand-offish
⚷ **sostitu'ire** *vt* substitute (**a** for, replace (**con** with)
sostitu'irsi *vr* ~ **a** replace
sosti'tuto, -a **A** *mf* replacement, stand-in
B *m* (surrogato) substitute
sostituzi'one *f* substitution
sotta'ceto *adj* pickled; **sottaceti** *pl* pickles
sot'tacqua *adv* underwater
sot'tana *f* petticoat; (di prete) cassock
sotter'fugio *m* subterfuge; **di** ~ secretly
sotter'raneo **A** *adj* underground
B *m* cellar
sotter'rare *vt* bury
sottigli'ezza *f* slimness; fig subtlety
⚷ **sot'tile** *adj* thin; ‹*udito, odorato*› keen; ‹*osservazione, distinzione*› subtle
sotti'letta® *f* cheese slice
sottiliz'zare *vi* split hairs
sottin'tendere *vt* imply
sottin'teso **A** pp di **sottintendere**
B *m* allusion; **senza sottintesi** openly
C *adj* implied
⚷ **'sotto** **A** *adv* below; (più in basso) lower [down]; (al di sotto) underneath; (al piano di sotto) downstairs; **è lì** ~ it's underneath; ~ ~ deep down; (di nascosto) on the quiet; **di** ~ downstairs; **mettersi** ~ fig get down to it; **mettere** ~ infml (investire) knock down; **fatti** ~**!** infml get stuck in!
B *prep* ~ **[a]** under; (al di sotto di) under[neath]; **il fiume passa** ~ **un ponte** the river passes under[neath] a bridge; **è** ~ **il tavolo, è** ~ **al tavolo** it's under[neath] the table; **abita** ~ **di me** he lives downstairs from me; **i bambini** ~ **i dieci anni** children under ten; **20°** ~ **zero** 20 below zero; ~ **il livello del mare** below sea level; ~ **la pioggia** in the rain; ~ **Elisabetta I** under Elizabeth I; ~ **calmante** under sedation; ~ **chiave** under lock and key; ~ **condizione che ...** on condition that ...; ~ **giuramento** under oath; ~ **sorveglianza** under surveillance; ~ **Natale/gli esami** around Christmas/exam time; **al di** ~ **di** under; **andare** ~ **i 50 all'ora** do less than 50km an hour
C *m* **il [di]** ~ the bottom
sotto'banco *adv* ‹*vendere, comprare*› under the counter
sottobicchi'ere *m* coaster
sotto'bosco *m* undergrowth
sotto'braccio *adv* arm in arm
sottoccu'pato *adj* underemployed
sottochi'ave *adv* under lock and key
sotto'costo *adj & adv* at less than cost price

sottodi'rectory *f* Comput subdirectory
sottoe'sporre *vt* underexpose
sotto'fondo *m* background
sotto'gamba *adv* **prendere qualcosa ~** take something lightly
sotto'gonna *f* underskirt
sottoindi'cato *adj* undermentioned
sottoinsi'eme *m* Math subset
sottoline'are *vt* underline; fig underline ‹*importanza*›; emphasize ‹*forma degli occhi ecc.*›
sot'tolio *adv* in oil
sotto'mano *adv* within reach
sottoma'rino *adj & nm* submarine
sotto'messo **A** pp di **sottomettere** **B** *adj* (remissivo) submissive
sotto'mettere *vt* submit; subdue ‹*popolo*›
sotto'mettersi *vr* submit
sottomissi'one *f* submission
sottopa'gare *vt* underpay
sottopas'saggio *m* underpass; (pedonale) subway
sottopi'atto *m* place mat, table mat
sotto'porre *vt* submit; (costringere) subject
sotto'porsi *vr* submit oneself; **~ a** undergo
sotto'posto pp di **sottoporre**
sottoproletari'ato *m* underclass
sotto'scala *m* cupboard under the stairs
sotto'scritto **A** pp di **sottoscrivere** **B** *m* undersigned
sotto'scrivere *vt* sign; (approvare) sanction, subscribe to
sottoscrizi'one *f* (petizione) petition; (approvazione) sanction; (raccolta di denaro) appeal
sottosegre'tario *m* undersecretary
sotto'sopra *adv* upside-down
sotto'stante *adj* **la strada ~** the road below
sottosu'olo *m* subsoil
sottosvilup'pato *adj* underdeveloped
sottosvi'luppo *m* underdevelopment
sottote'nente *m* second lieutenant; Naut sub lieutenant
sotto'terra *adv* underground
sottotito'lato *adj* subtitled
sotto'titolo *m* (di film, programma) subtitle; (in libro, giornale) subheading
sottovalu'tare *vt* underestimate
sotto'vento *adv* downwind
sotto'veste *f* slip
sotto'voce *adv* in a low voice
sottovu'oto *adj* vacuum-packed
sotto'zero *adj inv* sub-zero
sot'trarre *vt* remove; embezzle ‹*fondi*›; Math subtract
sot'trarsi *vr* **~ a** escape from; avoid ‹*responsabilità*›

sot'tratto pp di **sottrarre**
sottrazi'one *f* removal; (di fondi) embezzlement; Math subtraction
sottuffici'ale *m* non-commissioned officer; Naut petty officer
sou'brette *f* showgirl
soufflé *m inv* soufflé
souve'nir *m inv* souvenir
■ **negozio di souvenir** souvenir shop
so'vente *adv* (liter) often
soverchie'ria *f* bullying; **fare soverchierie a** bully
so'vietico, -a *adj & nmf* Soviet
sovrabbon'danza *f* overabundance
sovraccari'care *vt* overload
sovrac'carico **A** *adj* overloaded (**di** with) **B** *m* overload
sovraffati'carsi *vr* overexert oneself
sovraffolla'mento *m* overcrowding
sovralimen'tare *vt* overfeed
sovrannatu'rale *adj & nm* = **soprannaturale**
sovrannazio'nale *adj* supranational
so'vrano, -a **A** *adj* sovereign; fig supreme **B** *mf* sovereign
sovrappopo'lato *adj* overpopulated
sovrap'porre *vt* superimpose
sovrap'porsi *vr* overlap
sovrapposizi'one *f* superimposition
sovrapro'fitto *m* excess profits
sovra'stare *vt* dominate; fig ‹*pericolo*› hang over
sovrastrut'tura *f* superstructure
sovratensi'one *f* Electr overload, over-voltage
sovrecci'tarsi *vr* get overexcited
sovrecci'tato *adj* overexcited
sovresposizi'one *f* Phot overexposure
sovrimpressi'one *f* Phot double exposure
sovrinten'dente, sovrinten'denza = **soprintendente, soprintendenza**
sovru'mano *adj* superhuman
sovvenzio'nare *vt* subsidize
sovvenzio'nato **A** (pp di **sovvenzionare**) subsidized **B** *adj* **~ dallo Stato** state-funded
sovvenzi'one *f* subsidy
sovver'sivo, -a *adj & nmf* subversive
sovver'tire *vt* subvert
'sozzo *adj* filthy
SP *nf abbr* (**strada provinciale**) secondary road
S.p.A. *abbr* (**società per azioni**) plc
spac'care *vt* split; chop ‹*legna*›; **~ il minuto** keep perfect time; **~ il muso a qualcuno** *sl* smash somebody's face in; **o la va o la spacca** it's all or nothing; **un sole che spacca le pietre** a sun hot enough to fry an egg
spac'carsi *vr* split

🔑 key word

spacca'tura *f* split

spacci'are *vt* deal in, push ‹*droga*›; ~ **qualcosa per qualcosa** pass something off as something; **essere spacciato** be done for, be a goner

spacci'arsi *vr* ~ **per** pass oneself off as

spaccia|'tore, -trice *mf* (di droga) dealer, pusher; (di denaro falso) distributor of forged bank notes

'spaccio *m* (di droga) dealing; (negozio) shop

'spacco *m* split

spacco'nate *fpl* blustering

spac'cone, -a *mf* boaster

'spada *f* sword

spadac'cino *m* swordsman

spadroneggi'are *vi* act the boss

spae'sato *adj* disorientated

spa'ghetti *mpl* spaghetti *sg*
■ **spaghetti in bianco** *spaghetti with butter, oil and cheese*; **spaghetti alla carbonara** *spaghetti with egg, cheese and diced bacon*; **spaghetti al sugo** *spaghetti with a sauce*

spa'ghetto *m* infml (spavento) fright

'Spagna *f* Spain

spagno'letta *f* spool

spa'gnolo, -a **A** *adj* Spanish
B *mf* Spaniard
C *m* (lingua) Spanish

'spago *m* string; infml (spavento) fright; **dare ~ a qualcuno** encourage somebody

spai'ato *adj* odd

spalan'care *vt* open wide

spalan'carsi *vr* open wide

spalan'cato *adj* wide open

spa'lare *vt* shovel

'spalla *f* shoulder; (di comico) straight man; **spalle** *pl* (schiena) back; **alzata di spalle** shrug [of the shoulders]; **alle spalle di** behind; **alle spalle di qualcuno** ‹*ridere*› behind somebody's back; **avere qualcuno/qualcosa alle spalle** have somebody/something behind one; **di ~** ‹*violino ecc.*› second; **vivere alle spalle di qualcuno** live off somebody; **con le spalle al muro** anche fig with one's back to the wall; **voltare le spalle** turn one's back

spal'lata *f* push with the shoulder; (alzata di spalle) shrug [of the shoulders]

spalleggi'are *vt* back up

spal'letta *f* parapet

spalli'era *f* back; (di letto) headboard; (ginnastica) wall bars *pl*

spal'lina *f* strap; (imbottitura) shoulder pad; **senza spalline** strapless

spal'mare *vt* spread

spal'marsi *vr* cover oneself

spa'nato *adj* ‹*vite*› threadless

spanci'ata *f* belly flop

'spandere *vt* spread; (versare) spill; **spendere e ~** spend and spend

'spandersi *vr* spread

spandighi'aia *m inv* gritter

'spaniel *m inv* spaniel

spappo'lare *vt* crush

spa'rare *vt & vi* shoot; **spararle grosse** talk big; ~ **fandonie** talk nonsense

spa'rarsi *vr* shoot oneself; **si è sparato un colpo alla tempia** he shot himself in the temple

spa'rata *f* infml tall story

spa'rato *m* (della camicia) dicky

spara'toria *f* shooting
■ **sparatoria da auto in corsa** drive-by shooting

sparecchi'are *vt* clear

spa'reggio *m* Comm deficit; Sport play-off

'spargere *vt* scatter; (diffondere) spread; shed ‹*lacrime, sangue*›

'spargersi *vr* spread

spargi'mento *m* scattering; (di lacrime, sangue) shedding
■ **spargimento di sangue** bloodshed

spa'rire *vi* disappear; **sparisci!** get lost!, scram!

sparizi'one *f* disappearance

spar'lare *vi* ~ **di** run down

'sparo *m* shot
■ **sparo d'avvertimento** warning shot

sparpagli'are *vt* scatter

sparpagli'arsi *vr* scatter

sparpagli'ato *adj* far-flung

'sparso **A** pp di **spargere**
B *adj* scattered; (sciolto) loose

sparti'neve *m inv* snowplough

spar'tire *vt* share out; (separare) separate

spar'tirsi *vr* share

spar'tito *m* Mus score

sparti'traffico *m inv* traffic island; (di autostrada) central reservation, median strip AmE

spartizi'one *f* division

spa'ruto *adj* gaunt; ‹*gruppo*› small; ‹*peli, capelli*› sparse

sparvi'ero *m* sparrow-hawk

spasi'mante *m* (hum) admirer

spasi'mare *vi* suffer agonies; ~ **per** be madly in love with

'spasimo *m* spasm

spa'smodico *adj* spasmodic

spas'sarsi *vr* amuse oneself; **spas'sarsela** have a good time

spassio'nato *adj* ‹*osservatore*› dispassionate, impartial

'spasso *m* fun; **essere uno ~** be hilarious; **andare a ~** go for a walk; **essere a ~** be out of work

spas'soso *adj* hilarious

'spastico *adj* spastic offensive

'spatola *f* spatula

spau'racchio *m* scarecrow; fig bugbear

spau'rire *vt* frighten

spa'valdo *adj* defiant

spaventa'passeri *m inv* scarecrow

⚷ **spaven'tare** *vt* frighten, scare

spaven'tarsi *vr* be frightened, be scared

spa'vento *m* fright; **brutto da fare ~** incredibly ugly

spaven'toso *adj* frightening; infml (enorme) incredible

spazi'ale *adj* spatial; (cosmico) space *attrib*

spazi'are **A** *vt* space out **B** *vi* range

spazien'tirsi *vr* lose [one's] patience

⚷ **'spazio** *m* space
■ **spazio aereo** airspace; **spazio indietro** Comput backspace; **spazio di tempo** period of time; **spazio vitale** elbow room; **spazio web** web space

spazi'oso *adj* spacious

spazio-tempo'rale *adj* spatio-temporal

spazzaca'mino *m* chimney sweep

spazza'neve *m inv* (anche sci) snowplough

spaz'zare *vt* sweep; **~ via** sweep away; infml (mangiare) devour

spazza'trice *f* sweeper

spazza'tura *f* (immondizia) rubbish

spaz'zino *m* road sweeper; (netturbino) dustman, refuse collector

'spazzola *f* brush; (di tergicristallo) blade; **capelli a ~** crew cut

spazzo'lare *vt* brush

spazzo'larsi *vr* **~ i capelli** brush one's hair

spazzo'lino *m* small brush
■ **spazzolino da denti** toothbrush; **spazzolino per le unghie** nail brush

spazzo'lone *m* scrubbing brush

'speaker *m inv* Radio, TV announcer

specchi'arsi *vr* look at oneself in a/the mirror; (riflettersi) be mirrored; **~ in qualcuno** model oneself on somebody

specchi'ato *adj* **di specchiata onestà** of spotless integrity

specchi'etto *m* small mirror
■ **specchietto laterale** wing mirror; **specchietto retrovisore** driving mirror; rear-view mirror

S

⚷ **'specchio** *m* mirror
■ **specchio unilaterale** two-way mirror

⚷ **speci'ale** **A** *adj* special **B** *m* TV special [programme]

specia'lista *mf* specialist

specialità *f inv* speciality, specialty

specializ'zare *vt* specialize

specializ'zarsi *vr* specialize

specializ'zato *adj* ‹*operaio*› skilled; **siamo specializzati in ...** we specialize in ...

special'mente... *adv* especially

⚷ **'specie** *f* (scientifico) species; (tipo) kind; **fare ~ a** surprise; **in ~** especially
■ **specie a rischio** endangered species

specifi'care *vt* specify

⚷ key word

specificata'mente *adv* specifically

spe'cifico *adj* specific

speci'oso *adj* specious

specu'lare[1] *vi* speculate; **~ su** (indagare) speculate on; Fin speculate in

specu'lare[2] *adj* mirror *attrib*

specula'tivo *adj* speculative

specula'tore *m* speculator

speculazi'one *f* speculation

⚷ **spe'dire** *vt* send; **~ per posta** mail, post BrE; **~ qualcuno all'altro mondo** send somebody to meet his/her maker

spe'dito **A** pp di **spedire** **B** *adj* quick; ‹*parlata*› fluent

spedizi'one *f* (di lettere ecc.) dispatch; Comm consignment, shipment; ‹*scientifica*› expedition

spedizioni'ere *m* Comm freight forwarder

⚷ **'spegnere** *vt* put out; turn off, switch off ‹*motore, luce, televisione*›; turn off ‹*gas*›; quench, slake ‹*sete*›

'spegnersi *vr* go out; (morire) pass away

spegni'mento *m* standby

spelacchi'ato *adj* ‹*tappeto*› threadbare; ‹*cane*› mangy

spe'lare *vt* remove the fur of ‹*coniglio*›

spe'larsi *vr* ‹*cane, tappeto*› moult

speleolo'gia *f* potholing, speleology

spel'lare *vt* skin; fig fleece

spel'larsi *vr* ‹*serpente*› shed its skin; (per il sole) peel; **mi sono spellato un ginocchio** I grazed *or* skinned my knee

spe'lonca *f* cave; fig dingy hole

spendacci'one, -a *mf* spendthrift

⚷ **'spendere** *vt* spend; **~ fiato** waste one's breath

spen'nare *vt* pluck; infml fleece ‹*cliente*›

spennel'lare **A** *vt* brush **B** *vi* paint

spensierata'mente *adv* blithely

spensiera'tezza *f* light-heartedness

spensie'rato *adj* light-hearted, carefree

'spento **A** pp di **spegnere** **B** *adj* off; ‹*gas*› out; (smorto) dull; ‹*vulcano*› extinct

spenzo'lare *vt* dangle

⚷ **spe'ranza** *f* hope; **pieno di ~** hopeful; **senza ~** hopeless

⚷ **spe'rare** **A** *vt* hope for; (aspettarsi) expect **B** *vi* **~ in** trust in; **spero di sì** I hope so

'sperdersi *vr* get lost

sper'duto *adj* lost; (isolato) secluded

spergiu'rare *vi* commit perjury

spergi'uro, -a **A** *mf* perjurer **B** *m* perjury

sperico'lato *adj* swashbuckling

sperimen'tale *adj* experimental

sperimen'tare *vt* experiment with; test ‹*resistenza, capacità, teoria*›

sperimen'tato *adj ‹metodo›* tried and tested

sperimentazi'one *f* experimentation; ~ **sugli animali** animal testing

'sperma *m* sperm

spermi'cida **A** *adj* spermicidal **B** *m* spermicide

spero'nare *vt* ram

spe'rone *m* spur

sperpe'rare *vt* squander

'sperpero *m* waste, squandering

spersonaliz'zare *vt* depersonalize

spersonaliz'zarsi *vr* become depersonalized

spersonalizzazi'one *f* depersonalization

'spesa *f* expense; (acquisto) purchase; **andare a far spese** go shopping; **darsi a spese folli** go on a shopping spree; **fare la** ~ do the shopping; **fare le spese di** pay for; **a proprie spese** at one's own expense; **spese** *pl* **di amministrazione** handling charge; **spese** *pl* **bancarie** bank charges; **spese** *pl* **di capitale** capital expenditure; **spese** *pl* **a carico del destinatario** carriage forward; **spese** *pl* **di esercizio** business expenses; **spese** *pl* **extra** out-of-pocket expenses; **spese** *pl* **di gestione** operating costs; **spese** *pl* **di movimentazione** handling charge; **spese** *pl* **di spedizione** shipping costs; **spese** *pl* **di viaggio** travel expenses

spe'sare *vt* pay expenses for

spe'sato *adj* all expenses paid; ~ **dalla ditta** paid for by the company, on the company

'speso pp di **spendere**

'spesso¹ *adj* thick

'spesso² *adv* often

spes'sore *m* thickness; fig (consistenza) substance

spet'tabile *adj* (*comm abbr* **Spett.**) **Spettabile ditta Rossi** Messrs Rossi

spettaco'lare *adj* spectacular

spet'tacolo *m* spectacle; (rappresentazione) show; **dare** ~ **di sé** make a spectacle *or* an exhibition of oneself; **il mondo dello** ~ show business

■ **spettacolo di burattini** Punch and Judy show; **spettacolo di varietà** variety show

spettaco'loso *adj* spectacular

spet'tanza *f* concern

spet'tare *vi* ~ **a** be up to; *‹diritto›* be due to

spetta|'tore, -trice *mf* spectator; **spettatori** *pl* (di cinema ecc.) audience *sg*

spettego'lare *vi* gossip

spetti'nare *vt* ~ **qualcuno** ruffle somebody's hair

spetti'narsi *vr* ruffle one's hair

spet'trale *adj* ghostly

'spettro *m* ghost; fig (della fame) spectre; Phys spectrum; **ad ampio** ~ *‹medicina›* broad-spectrum

spezi'are *vt* add spices to, spice

spezi'ato *adj* spicy

'spezie *fpl* spices

spez'zare *vt* break

spez'zarsi *vr* break

spezza'tino *m* stew

spez'zato **A** *adj* broken **B** *m* coordinated jacket and trousers

spezzet'tare *vt* break into small pieces

spez'zone *m* Cinema clip, footage *no pl*; (bomba) cluster bomb

'spia *f* spy; (della polizia) informer; (di porta) peep-hole; **fare la** ~ sneak

■ **spia di accensione** power-on light; **spia di attività dell'hard disk** Comput hard disk activity light; **spia della benzina** petrol gauge; **spia luminosa** warning light; **spia dell'olio** oil [warning] light

spiacci'care *vt* squash

spia'cente *adj* sorry

spia'cevole *adj* unpleasant

spi'aggia *f* beach

spiag'giare *vi ‹balena›* strand, beach

spiag'giarsi *vr* strand oneself, beach oneself

spia'nare *vt* level; (rendere liscio) smooth; roll out *‹pasta›*; raze to the ground *‹edificio›*

spia'nata *f* flat ground

spi'ano *m* **a tutto** ~ flat out

spian'tato *adj* fig penniless

spi'are *vt* spy on; wait for *‹occasione ecc.›*

spiattel'lare *vt* blurt out; shove *‹oggetto›*

spiaz'zare *vt* wrong-foot

spi'azzo *m* (radura) clearing

spic'care **A** *vt* ~ **un salto** jump; ~ **il volo** take flight **B** *vi* stand out

spic'cato *adj* marked

'spicchio *m* (di agrumi) segment; (di aglio) clove

spicci'arsi *vr* hurry up

spiccia'tivo *adj* speedy

'spiccio *adj* no-nonsense

'spiccioli *mpl* change

'spicciolo *adj* (comune) banal; *‹denaro›* in change

'spicco *m* relief; **fare** ~ stand out; **di** ~ high-profile

'spider *mf inv* open-top sports car

spie'dino *m* kebab

spi'edo *m* spit; **allo** ~ on a spit, spit-roasted

spiega'mento *m* deployment

spie'gare *vt* explain; open out *‹cartina›*; unfurl *‹vele›*

spie'garsi *vr* explain oneself; *‹vele, bandiere›* unfurl; **non so se mi spiego** need I say more?; **mi sono spiegato?** (minaccia) do I make myself clear?; **non riesco a spiegarmi come …** I can't understand how …

S

spie'gato *adj ‹ali›* outspread; **a sirene spiegate** with sirens blaring; **a voce spiegata** at the top of one's voice; **a vele spiegate** under full sail, with all sails in the wind

⚷ **spiegazi'one** *f* explanation; **venire a una ~ con qualcuno** sort things out with somebody

spiegaz'zare *vt* crumple

spiegaz'zato *adj* crumpled

spieta'tezza *f* ruthlessness

spie'tato *adj* ruthless

spiffe'rare **A** *vt* blurt out
B *vi ‹vento›* whistle

'spiffero *m* (corrente d'aria) draught

'spiga *f* spike; Bot ear

spi'gato *adj* herringbone

spigli'ato *adj* self-possessed

'spigola *f* sea bass

spigo'lare *vt* glean

'spigolo *m* edge; (angolo) corner

'spilla *f* (gioiello) brooch
■ **spilla da balia** safety pin; **spilla di sicurezza** safety pin

spil'lare *vt* tap

'spillo *m* pin
■ **spillo di sicurezza** safety pin

spil'lone *m* hatpin

spilluzzi'care *vt* pick at

spi'lorcio, -a **A** *adj* stingy
B *m* miser, skinflint

spilun'gone, -a *mf* beanpole

'spina *f* thorn; (di pesce) bone; Electr plug; **a ~ di pesce** *‹tessuto, disegno›* herringbone; *‹parcheggio›* in two angled rows; **stare sulle spine** be on tenterhooks; **una ~ nel fianco** a thorn in one's side
■ **spina dorsale** spine

spi'naci *mpl* spinach

spi'nale *adj* spinal

spi'nato **A** *adj ‹filo›* barbed
B *m* (tessuto) herringbone

spi'nello *m* infml (droga) joint

S

⚷ **'spingere** *vt* push; fig drive

'spingersi *vr* (andare) proceed

spin'naker *m* spinnaker

spi'noso *adj* thorny

spi'notto *m* Electr plug

'spinta *f* push; (violenta) thrust; fig spur; **dare una ~ a qualcosa/qualcuno** give somebody/something a push; **farsi largo a spinte** push one's way through

spinta'rella *f* infml (raccomandazione) **ha ottenuto il lavoro grazie alla ~ dello zio** his uncle got him the job by pulling a few strings

'spinto **A** pp di **spingere**
B *adj ‹barzelletta, spettacolo›* risqué

spin'tone *m* shove

spio'naggio *m* espionage, spying

spi'one, -a *mf* tell-tale

spio'vente **A** *adj ‹tetto›* sloping
B *m* slope

spi'overe *vi* (liter) stop raining; (ricadere) fall; (scorrere) flow down

'spira *f* coil

spi'raglio *m* small opening; (soffio d'aria) breath of air; (raggio di luce) gleam of light

spi'rale **A** *adj* spiral
B *m* spiral; (negli orologi) hairspring; (anticoncezionale) coil; **a ~** spiral-shaped

spi'rare *vi* (soffiare) blow; (morire) pass away

spiri'tato *adj* possessed; *‹espressione›* wild

spiri'tismo *m* spiritualism

spiri'tista *mf* spiritualist

spiri'tistico *adj* spiritualist

⚷ **'spirito** *m* spirit; (arguzia) wit; (intelletto) mind; **fare dello ~** be witty; **persona di ~** witty person; **sotto ~** in brandy
■ **spirito civico** community spirit; **spirito di contraddizione** contrariness; **Spirito Santo** Holy Spirit, Holy Ghost

spirito'saggine *f* witticism

spiri'toso *adj* witty

spiritu'ale *adj* spiritual

spiritual'mente *adv* spiritually

splen'dente *adj* shining; **denti bianchi splendenti** gleaming white teeth

'splendere *vi* shine

⚷ **'splendido** *adj* splendid

splen'dore *m* splendour

'spocchia *f* conceit

spocchi'oso *adj* conceited

spode'stare *vt* dispossess; depose *‹re›*

spoetiz'zare *vt* disenchant

'spoglia *f* (di animale) skin; **spoglie** *pl* (salma) mortal remains; (bottino) spoils; **sotto false spoglie** under false pretences

⚷ **spogli'are** *vt* strip; (svestire) undress; (fare lo spoglio di) go through; **~ qualcuno di un diritto** divest somebody of a right

spogliarel'lista *f* strip-tease artist, stripper

spoglia'rello *m* strip-tease

spogli'arsi *vr* strip, undress

spoglia'toio *m* (in piscina, palestra) locker room; Sport changing room; (guardaroba) cloakroom, checkroom AmE

'spoglio **A** *adj* undressed; *‹albero, muro›* bare; **~ di** (privo) stripped of
B *m* (scrutinio) perusal

'spoiler *m inv* Auto spoiler

'spola *f* shuttle; **fare la ~** shuttle

spo'letta *f* spool

spolmo'narsi *vr* shout oneself hoarse

spol'pare *vt* take the flesh off; fig fleece

spolve'rare *vt* dust; infml devour *‹cibo›*

'sponda *f* (di mare, lago) shore; (di fiume) bank; (bordo) edge

⚷ key word

■ **sponda posteriore ribaltabile** Auto tailgate
sponsoriz'zare *vt* sponsor
sponsorizzazi'one *f* sponsorship
spontaneità *f inv* spontaneity
spon'taneo *adj* spontaneous
'spooling *m inv* Comput spooling
spopola'mento *m* depopulation
spopo'lare **A** *vt* depopulate
B *vi* (avere successo) draw the crowds
spopo'larsi *vr* become depopulated
'spora *f* spore
sporadica'mente *adv* sporadically
spo'radico *adj* sporadic
sporcacci'one, -a *mf* dirty pig
spor'care *vt* dirty; (macchiare) soil
spor'carsi *vr* get dirty
spor'cizia *f* dirt
'sporco **A** *adj* dirty; (macchiato) soiled; **avere la coscienza sporca** have a guilty conscience
B *m* dirt
spor'gente *adj* jutting, protruding; **ha i denti sporgenti** infml she has goofy teeth
spor'genza *f* projection
'sporgere **A** *vt* stretch out; **~ querela contro** take legal action against
B *vi* jut out
'sporgersi *vr* lean out
sport *m inv* sport; **fare qualcosa per ~** do something for fun
■ **sport estremi** *pl* extreme sports; **sport invernali** *pl* winter sports
'sporta *f* shopping bag
spor'tello *m* door; (di banca ecc.) window
■ **sportello automatico** cash dispenser, cash point, cash machine, hole in the wall; **sportello della biglietteria** ticket window; **sportello pacchi** parcels counter
spor'tivo, -a **A** *adj* sports *attrib*; ‹*persona*› sporty
B *m* sportsman
C *f* sportswoman
'sporto pp di **sporgere**
'sposa *f* bride; **dare in ~** give in marriage, give away; **prendere in ~** marry
sposa'lizio *m* wedding
spo'sare *vt* marry; fig espouse
spo'sarsi *vr* get married; ‹*vino*› go (**con** with)
spo'sato *adj* married
spo'sini *mpl* newly-weds
'sposo *m* bridegroom; **sposi** *pl* **[novelli]** newly-weds
spossa'tezza *f* exhaustion
spos'sato *adj* exhausted, worn out
sposses'sato *adj* dispossessed
sposta'mento *m* displacement
■ **spostamento d'aria** airflow
spo'stare *vt* move; (differire) postpone; (cambiare) change
spo'starsi *vr* move

spo'stato, -a **A** *adj* ill-adjusted
B *mf* (disadattato) misfit
spot *m inv*
■ **spot [pubblicitario]** commercial
S.P.R. *abbr* (**si prega rispondere**) RSVP
'spranga *f* bar
spran'gare *vt* bar
'sprazzo *m* (di colore) splash; (di luce) flash; fig glimmer
spre'care *vt* waste
'spreco *m* waste
spre'cone *adj* spendthrift
spre'gevole *adj* despicable
spregia'tivo *adj* pejorative
'spregio *m* contempt; **fare uno ~ a qualcuno** offend somebody
spregiudi'cato *adj* unprejudiced; derog unscrupulous
'spremere *vt* squeeze
'spremersi *vr* **~ le meningi** rack one's brains
spremi'aglio *m inv* garlic press
spremia'grumi *m inv* lemon squeezer
spremili'moni *m inv* lemon squeezer
spre'muta *f* juice
■ **spremuta d'arancia** fresh orange [juice], freshly squeezed orange juice
spre'tato *m* former priest
sprez'zante *adj* contemptuous
sprigio'nare *vt* emit
sprigio'narsi *vr* burst out
sprint *m* sprint; **fare uno ~** put on a spurt
spriz'zare *vt & vi* spurt; be bursting with ‹*salute, gioia*›
sprofon'dare *vi* sink; (crollare) collapse
sprofon'darsi *vr* **~ in** sink into; fig be engrossed in
spron *m* ▸ **sprone**
spro'nare *vt* spur on
'sprone *m* spur; (sartoria) yoke; **a spron battuto** instantly; **andare a spron battuto** go hell for leather
sproporzio'nato *adj* disproportionate
sproporzi'one *f* disproportion
sproposi'tato *adj* full of blunders; (enorme) huge
spro'posito *m* blunder; (eccesso) excessive amount; **a ~** inopportunely
sprovve'duto *adj* unprepared; **~ di** lacking in
sprov'visto *adj* **~ di** out of; lacking in ‹*fantasia, pazienza*›; **alla sprovvista** unexpectedly
spruz'zare *vt* sprinkle; (vaporizzare) spray; (inzaccherare) spatter
spruzza'tore *m* spray
'spruzzo *m* spray; (di fango) splash
spudorata'mente *adv* shamelessly
spudora'tezza *f* shamelessness

spudo'rato *adj* shameless
'spugna *f* sponge; (tessuto) towelling
spu'gnoso *adj* spongy
'spuma *f* foam; (schiuma) froth; Culin mousse
spu'mante *m* sparkling wine, spumante
spumeggi'ante *adj* bubbly; ‹*mare*› foaming
spumeggi'are *vi* ‹*champagne*› bubble; ‹*birra*› foam
'spunta *f*
■ **segno di spunta** tick
⚷ **spun'tare** **A** *vt* (rompere la punta di) break the point of; trim ‹*capelli*›; ‹*lista, elenco*› check off; **spuntarla** fig win
B *vi* ‹*pianta*› sprout; ‹*capelli*› begin to grow; (sorgere) rise; (apparire) appear
spun'tarsi *vr* get blunt
spun'tata *f* trim
spun'tino *m* snack
'spunto *m* cue; fig starting point; **dare ~ a** give rise to
spur'gare *vt* purge
spur'garsi *vr* Med expectorate
'spurio *adj* spurious
spu'tacchio *m* spittle
spu'tare *vt & vi* spit; spit out ‹*cibo*›; **~ sentenze** pass judgement; **~ l'osso** *sl* spit it out
'sputo *m* spit
⚷ **'squadra** *f* (gruppo) team, squad; (di polizia ecc.) squad; (da disegno) square; **lavoro di squadra** teamwork
■ **squadra del buoncostume** Vice Squad; **squadra mobile** Flying Squad; **squadra narcotici** Drug Squad; **squadra di soccorso** rescue team
squa'drare *vt* square; (guardare) look up and down
squa'driglia *f*, **squadriglione** *m* squadron
squa'drone *m* squadron
squagli'are *vt* melt
squagli'arsi *vr* melt; **squagliarsela** infml (svignarsela) steal out
squa'lifica *f* disqualification
squalifi'care *vt* disqualify
'squallido *adj* squalid
squal'lore *m* squalor
'squalo *m* shark
'squama *f* scale; (di pelle) flake
squa'mare *vt* scale
squa'marsi *vr* ‹*pelle*› flake off
squa'moso *adj* scaly; ‹*pelle*› flaky
squarcia'gola **a ~** *adv* at the top of one's voice
squarci'are *vt* rip
'squarcio *m* rip; (di ferita, in nave) gash; (di cielo) patch
squar'tare *vt* quarter; dismember ‹*animale*›
squarta'tore *m* **Jack lo ~** Jack the Ripper
squash *m inv* squash
squas'sare *vt* shake
squattri'nato *adj* penniless
squaw *f inv* offensive squaw
squili'brare *vt* unbalance
squili'brato, -a **A** *adj* unbalanced
B *mf* lunatic
squi'librio *m* imbalance
squil'lante *adj* shrill
squil'lare *vi* ‹*campana*› peal; ‹*tromba*› blare; ‹*telefono*› ring
'squillo *m* blare; Teleph ring
squinter'nato *adj* anche fig crazy
squisi'tezza *f* refinement
squi'sito *adj* exquisite; infml (pietanza) yummy
squit'tire *vi* fig ‹*pappagallo*› squawk; ‹*topo*› squeak
sradi'care *vt* uproot; eradicate ‹*vizio, male*›
sragio'nare *vi* rave
sregola'tezza *f* dissipation
srego'lato *adj* inordinate; (dissoluto) dissolute
s.r.l. *abbr* (**società a responsabilità limitata**) Ltd
sroto'lare *vt* uncoil
ss *abbr* (**seguenti**) following
SS **1** *abbr* (**strada statale**) national road
2 *abbr* (**Santissimo**) Most Holy
sst *int* sh!
'stabile **A** *adj* stable; (permanente) lasting; ‹*saldo*› steady
■ **compagnia stabile** Theat repertory company
B *m* (edificio) building
stabili'mento *m* factory; (industriale) plant; (edificio) establishment
■ **stabilimento balneare** lido
⚷ **stabi'lire** *vt* establish; (decidere) decide
stabi'lirsi *vr* settle
stabilità *f inv* stability
stabi'lito *adj* established
stabiliz'zare *vt* stabilize
stabiliz'zarsi *vr* stabilize
stabilizza'tore *m* stabilizer
stacano'vista *mf* workaholic
⚷ **stac'care** **A** *vt* detach; pronounce clearly ‹*parole*›; (separare) separate; turn off ‹*corrente*›; **~ gli occhi da** take one's eyes off
B *vi* infml (finire di lavorare) knock off
stac'carsi *vr* come off; **~ da** break away from ‹*partito, famiglia*›; **si stacca alle cinque** knocking off time is five o'clock
staccata'mente *adv* staccato
stac'cato *adj* Mus staccato
staccio'nata *f* fence
'stacco *m* gap

S

⚷ key word

'stadio *m* stadium, sports ground

'staffa *f* stirrup; **perdere le staffe** fig fly off the handle

staf'fetta *f* Sport relay [race]; Mil dispatch rider

staffet'tista *mf* Sport relay runner

stagio'nale *adj* seasonal

stagio'nare *vt* season ‹*legno*›; mature ‹*formaggio*›

stagio'nato *adj* ‹*legno*› seasoned; ‹*formaggio*› matured

stagiona'tura *f* (di legno) seasoning; (di formaggio) maturation, maturing

stagi'one *f* season; **di ~** in season; **fuori ~** out of season
■ **alta/bassa stagione** high/ low season; **stagione lirica** opera season; **stagione delle piogge** rainy season

stagli'arsi *vr* stand out

sta'gnante *adj* stagnant

sta'gnare **A** *vt* (saldare) solder; (chiudere ermeticamente) seal
B *vi* ‹*acqua*› stagnate

'stagno **A** *adj* (a tenuta d'acqua) watertight
B *m* (acqua ferma) pond; (metallo) tin

sta'gnola *f* tinfoil

stalag'mite *f* stalagmite

stalat'tite *f* stalactite

'stalla *f* stable; (per buoi) cowshed

stalli'ere *m* groom

stal'lone *m* stallion

sta'mani, stamat'tina *adv* this morning

stam'becco *m* ibex

stam'berga *f* hovel

'stampa *f* Typ printing; (giornali, giornalisti) press; (riproduzione) print; **stampe** (postale) printed matter
■ **stampa fronte retro** two-sided printing, duplex printing; **stampa scandalistica** gutter press, tabloid press

stam'pante *f* printer
■ **stampante ad aghi** dot matrix printer; **stampante a getto d'inchiostro** inkjet printer; **stampante laser** laser printer; **stampante a matrice di punti** dot matrix printer; **stampante seriale** serial printer; **stampante termica** thermal printer

stam'pare *vt* print

stampa'tello *m* block letters *pl*, block capitals *pl*

stam'pato **A** *adj* printed
B *m* leaflet; Comput hard copy, printout; (modulo) print; **stampati** (pubblicità) promotional literature

stam'pella *f* crutch

stampigli'are *vt* stamp

stampiglia'tura *f* stamping; (dicitura) stamp

stam'pino *m* stencil

'stampo *m* mould; **di vecchio ~** ‹*persona*› of the old school

sta'nare *vt* drive out

stan'care *vt* tire; (annoiare) bore

stan'carsi *vr* get tired

stan'chezza *f* tiredness

'stanco *adj* tired; **~ di** (stufo) fed up with; **~ morto** dead tired, knackered infml

stand *m inv* stand

'standard *adj & m inv* standard

standardiz'zare *vt* standardize

standardizzazi'one *f* standardization

'stand-by *adj inv* stand-by

'stanga *f* bar; (persona) beanpole

stan'gare *vt* infml fail ‹*studente*›; (con le tasse ecc.) clobber

stan'gata *f* fig blow; infml (nel calcio) big kick; **prendere una ~** infml (agli esami, economica) come a cropper

stan'ghetta *f* (di occhiali) leg

sta'notte *f* tonight; (la notte scorsa) last night

'stante *prep* on account of; **a sé ~** separate

stan'tio *adj* stale

stan'tuffo *m* piston

'stanza *f* room; (metrica) stanza
■ **stanza dei giochi** games room; **stanza da pranzo** dining room

stanzia'mento *m* allocation

stanzi'are *vt* allocate

stan'zino *m* walk-in cupboard

stap'pare *vt* uncork

star *f inv* (del cinema, dello sport) star

'stare *vi* (rimanere) stay; (abitare) live; (con gerundio) be; **sto solo cinque minuti** I'll stay only five minutes; **sto in piazza Peyron** I live in Peyron Square; **sta dormendo** he's sleeping; **~ a** (attenersi) keep to; (spettare) be up to; **~ bene** (economicamente) be well off; (di salute) be well; (addirsi) suit; **sta bene!** that's fine!; **~ dietro a** (seguire) follow; (sorvegliare) keep an eye on; (corteggiare) run after; **~ in piedi** stand; **~ per** be about to; **~ sempre a fare qualcosa** be always doing something; **ben ti sta!** it serves you right!; **come stai/sta?** how are you?; **lasciar ~** leave alone; **starci** (essere contenuto) go into; (essere d'accordo) agree; **il 3 nel 12 ci sta 4 volte** 3 into 12 goes 4; **non sa ~ agli scherzi** he can't take a joke; **~ su** (con la schiena) sit up straight; **~ sulle proprie** keep oneself to oneself

'starna *f* partridge

starnaz'zare *vi* quack; fig shriek

starnu'tire *vi* sneeze

star'nuto *m* sneeze

'starsene *vr* (rimanere) stay

'starter *m inv* choke

sta'sera *adv* this evening, tonight

'stasi *f* stasis

sta'tale **A** *adj* state *attrib*
B *mf* state employee, civil servant
C *f* (strada) main road, trunk road

S

'statico *adj* static
sta'tista *m* statesman
sta'tistica *f* statistics *sg*
sta'tistico *adj* statistical
'Stati U'niti [d'America] *mpl* **gli ~ ~** the United States [of America]
'stato **A** pp di **essere, stare**
B *m* state; (posizione sociale) position; Jur status; **lo Stato** Pol the state
■ **stato d'animo** frame of mind; **stato di attesa** Comput wait state; **stato canaglia** rogue state; **stato civile** marital status; **stato cuscinetto** buffer state; **Stato Maggiore** Mil General Staff; **stato di salute** state of health
stato-nazi'one *m* nation-state
'statua *f* statue
■ **statua di cera** waxwork
statu'ario *adj* statuesque
statuni'tense **A** *adj* United States *attrib*, US *attrib*
B *mf* citizen of the United States, US citizen
sta'tura *f* height; **di alta ~** tall; **di bassa ~** short; **di media ~** of average height
■ **statura morale** moral stature
sta'tuto *m* statute
sta'volta *adv* this time
stazio'nario *adj* stationary
stazi'one *f* station; (città) resort
■ **stazione degli autobus** bus station; **stazione balneare** seaside resort; **stazione climatica** health resort; **stazione ferroviaria** railway station BrE, train station; **stazione marittima** ferry terminal; **stazione master** Comput master station; **stazione multimediale** Comput multimedia station; **stazione dei pullman** coach station BrE, bus station; **stazione radiofonica** radio station; **stazione di servizio** petrol station BrE, service station; **stazione slave** Comput slave station; **stazione spaziale** space station; **stazione termale** spa, health resort
'stecca *f* stick; (di ombrello) rib; (da biliardo) cue; Med splint; (di sigarette) carton; (di reggiseno) stiffener; **fare una ~** Mus fluff a note
stec'cato *m* fence
stec'chino *m* cocktail stick
stec'chito *adj* skinny; (rigido) stiff; (morto) stone cold dead
'stele *f* stele
'stella *f* star; **salire alle stelle** ‹*prezzi*› rise sky-high, rocket
■ **stella alpina** edelweiss; **stella cadente** shooting star; **stella del cinema** movie star; **stella cometa** comet; **stella filante** streamer; **stella di mare** starfish; **stella polare** Pole Star, North Star
stel'lare *adj* star *attrib*; ‹*grandezza*› stellar
stel'lato *adj* starry

key word

stel'lina *f* starlet
'stelo *m* stem
■ **lampada a stelo** standard lamp BrE, floor lamp
'stemma *m* coat of arms
stempe'rare *vt* dilute
stempi'ato *adj* bald at the temples
sten'dardo *m* standard
'stendere *vt* spread out; (appendere) hang out; (distendere) stretch [out]; (scrivere) write down
'stendersi *vr* stretch out
stendibianche'ria *m inv* clothes horse
stendi'toio *m* clothes horse
stenodattilogra'fia *f* shorthand typing
stenodatti'lografo, -a *mf* shorthand typist
stenogra'fare *vt* take down in shorthand
stenogra'fia *f* shorthand
sten'tare *vi* **~ a** find it hard to
sten'tato *adj* laboured
'stento *m* (fatica) effort; **a ~** with difficulty; **stenti** *pl* hardships, privations
'step *m inv* step aerobics *sg*
'steppa *f* steppe
'sterco *m* dung
stereo, stereo'fonico *adj* stereo[phonic]
stereo'scopico *adj* stereoscopic
stereoti'pato *adj* stereotyped; ‹*sorriso*› insincere
stere'otipo *m* stereotype
'sterile *adj* sterile; ‹*terreno*› barren
sterilità *f inv* sterility
steriliz'zare *vt* sterilize
sterilizzazi'one *f* sterilization
ster'lina *f* pound
■ **lira sterlina** [pound] sterling
stermi'nare *vt* exterminate
stermi'nato *adj* immense
ster'minio *m* extermination
'sterno *m* breastbone
sternu'tire, ster'nuto = **starnutire, starnuto**
ste'roide *m* steroid
ster'paglia *f* brushwood
ster'rare *vt* excavate; dig up ‹*strada*›
ster'rato **A** *adj* ‹*strada*› dug up
B *m* excavation; (di strada) digging up
ster'zare *vi* steer
'sterzo *m* steering; (volante) steering wheel
'steso pp di **stendere**
'stesso **A** *adj* same; **io ~** myself; **tu ~** yourself; **me ~** myself; **se ~** himself; **in quel momento ~** at that very moment; **è stato ricevuto dalla stessa regina** (in persona) he was received by the Queen herself; **tuo fratello ~ dice che hai torto** even your brother says you're wrong; **l'ho visto coi miei stessi occhi** I saw it with my own eyes; **con le mie stesse mani** with my own hands;

è venuto il giorno ~ he came the same day, he came that very day; **lo farò oggi ~** I'll do it straight away today
B *pron* **lo ~** the same one; (la stessa cosa) the same; **fa lo ~** it's all the same; **ci vado lo ~** I'll go just the same

ste'sura *f* drawing up; (documento) draft

steto'scopio *m* stethoscope

'steward *m inv* steward, air steward

stick *m inv*:
■ **colla a stick** glue stick; **deodorante in stick** stick deodorant

stiepi'dire *vt* warm

'stigma *m* stigma

'stigmate *fpl* stigmata

sti'lare *vt* draw up

'stile *m* style; **in grande ~** in style; **essere nello ~ di qualcuno** be typical of somebody, be just like somebody
■ **stile libero** (nel nuoto) freestyle, crawl; **stile di vita** life style

sti'lista *mf* [fashion] designer; (parrucchiere) stylist

stiliz'zato *adj* stylized

'stilla *f* drop

stil'lare *vi* ooze

stilo'grafica *f* fountain pen

stilo'grafico *adj* **penna stilografica** fountain pen

'stima *f* esteem; (valutazione) estimate

sti'mare *vt* esteem; (valutare) estimate; (ritenere) consider

sti'marsi *vr* consider oneself

sti'mato *adj* well thought of

stimo'lante **A** *adj* stimulating
B *m* stimulant

stimo'lare *vt* stimulate; (incitare) incite

'stimolo *m* stimulus; (fitta) pang

'stinco *m* shin; **non è uno ~ di santo** infml he's no saint

'stingere *vt & vi* fade

'stingersi *vr* fade

'stinto pp di **stingere**

sti'pare *vt* cram

sti'parsi *vr* crowd together

stipendi'are *vt* pay a salary to

stipendi'ato **A** *adj* salaried
B *m* salaried worker

sti'pendio *m* salary
■ **stipendio base** basic salary; **stipendio iniziale** starting salary

'stipite *m* doorpost

stipu'lare *vt* stipulate

stipulazi'one *f* stipulation; (accordo) agreement

stira'mento *m* sprain

sti'rare *vt* iron; (distendere) stretch

sti'rarsi *vr* (distendersi) stretch; pull ‹*muscolo*›

stira'tura *f* ironing

'stiro *m*
■ **ferro da stiro** iron

'stirpe *f* stock

stiti'chezza *f* constipation

'stitico *adj* constipated

'stiva *f* Naut hold

sti'vale *m* boot; **lo Stivale** (Italia) Italy; **stivali** *pl* **di gomma** Wellington boots, Wellingtons; **poeta dei miei stivali!** infml poet my eye!, poet my foot!

stiva'letto *m* ankle boot

stiva'lone *m* high boot; **stivaloni** *pl* **da caccia** hunting boots; **stivaloni** *pl* **di gomma** waders

sti'vare *vt* load

'stizza *f* anger

stiz'zire *vt* irritate

stiz'zirsi *vr* become irritated

stiz'zito *adj* irritated

stiz'zoso *adj* peevish

stocca'fisso *m* stockfish

stoc'cata *f* stab; (battuta pungente) gibe

Stoc'colma *f* Stockholm

stock *m inv* Comm stock

'stock-car *m inv* stock car

⚷ **'stoffa** *f* material; fig stuff; **avere ~** have what it takes

stoi'cismo *m* stoicism

'stoico *adj & nm* stoic

sto'ino *m* doormat

'stola *f* stole

'stolido *adj* stolid

'stolto *adj* foolish

stoma'chevole *adj* revolting

⚷ **'stomaco** *m* stomach
■ **mal di stomaco** stomach ache

stoma'tite *f* stomatitis

sto'nare **A** *vt & vi* sing/play out of tune
B *vi* (non intonarsi) clash

sto'nato *adj* out of tune; (discordante) clashing; (confuso) bewildered

stona'tura *f* false note; (discordanza) clash

stop *m inv* (segnale stadale) stop sign; (in telegramma) stop

stop'pare *vt* stop

'stopper *m* Sport full back

'stoppia *f* stubble

stop'pino *m* wick

stop'poso *adj* tough

'storcere *vt* twist

'storcersi *vr* twist

stor'dire *vt* stun; (intontire) daze

stor'dirsi *vr* dull one's senses

stor'dito *adj* stunned; (intontito) dazed; (sventato) heedless

⚷ **'storia** *f* history; (racconto, bugia) story; (pretesto) excuse; **senza storie!** no fuss!; **fare [delle] storie** make a fuss
■ **storia d'amore** love story; **storia di vita vissuta**

human interest story

🔑 **'storico** **A** *adj* historical; (di importanza storica) historic

B *m* historian

stori'ella *f* infml little story

storiogra'fia *f* historiography

stori'ografo *m* historiographer

stori'one *m* sturgeon

'stormo *m* flock

stor'nare *vt* avert; transfer ‹*somma*›

'storno *m* starling

storpi'are *vt* cripple; mangle ‹*parole*›

storpia'tura *f* deformation

'storpio, -a offensive **A** *adj* crippled offensive

B *mf* cripple offensive

'storta *f* (distorsione) sprain; **prendere una ~ alla caviglia** sprain one's ankle

'storto **A** pp di **storcere**

B *adj* crooked; (ritorto) twisted; ‹*gambe*› bandy; fig wrong

stor'tura *f* deformity; **~ mentale** twisted way of thinking

sto'viglie *fpl* crockery *sg*, flatware AmE

'strabico *adj* cross-eyed; **essere ~** be cross-eyed, [have a] squint

strabili'ante *adj* astonishing

strabili'are *vt* astonish

stra'bismo *m* squint

straboc'care *vi* overflow

strabuz'zare *vt* **~ gli occhi** goggle; **ha strabuzzato gli occhi** his eyes popped out of his head

straca'narsi *vr* infml work like a slave, slave away

stra'carico *adj* overloaded

strac'chino *m soft cheese from Lombardy*

stracci'are *vt* tear; infml (vincere) thrash

straccia'tella *f* vanilla ice cream with chocolate chips

stracci'ato *adj* torn; ‹*persona*› in rags; ‹*prezzi*› slashed; **a un prezzo ~** at a knock-down price, dirt cheap

'straccio **A** *adj* torn

B *m* rag; (strofinaccio) cloth; **essere ridotto ad uno ~** feel like a wet rag

stracci'one *m* tramp

stracci'vendolo *m* ragman

stracol'larsi *vr* sprain

stra'cotto **A** *adj* overdone; infml (innamorato) head over heels

B *m* stew

🔑 **'strada** *f* road; (di città) street; fig (cammino) way; **essere fuori ~** be on the wrong track; **fare ~** lead the way; **tener la macchina in ~** keep the car on the road; (parcheggiare) keep the car on the street; **su ~** ‹*trasportare*› by road; **farsi ~** (aver successo) make one's way [in the world]

■ **strada d'accesso** approach road; **strada camionabile** road for heavy vehicles; **strada maestra** main road; **strada pedonale** pedestrianized street; **strada principale** main road; **strada privata** private road; **strada secondaria** secondary road; **strada a senso unico** one-way street; **strada senza uscita** dead end, cul-de-sac; **strada di terra battuta** dirt track

🔑 **stra'dale** **A** *adj* road *attrib*

B *f* **la Stradale** infml traffic police

stra'dario *m* street plan

stra'dina *f* little street; (in campagna) little road

strafalci'one *m* blunder

stra'fare *vi* overdo it, overdo things

stra'foro di ~ *adv* on the sly

strafot'tente *adj* arrogant

strafot'tenza *f* arrogance

'strage *f* slaughter

stra'grande *adj* vast

stralci'are *vt* remove

'stralcio *m* removal; (parte) extract

stralu'nare *vt* **~ gli occhi** open one's eyes wide

stralu'nato *adj* ‹*occhi*› staring; ‹*persona*› distraught

stramaz'zare *vi* fall heavily; **~ al suolo** crash to the ground

strambe'ria *f* oddity

'strambo *adj* strange

strampa'lato *adj* odd

stra'nezza *f* strangeness

strango'lare *vt* strangle

🔑 **strani'ero, -a** **A** *adj* foreign

B *mf* foreigner

🔑 **'strano** *adj* strange; **~ ma vero** surprisingly enough, funnily enough

straordinaria'mente *adv* extraordinarily

🔑 **straordi'nario** *adj* extraordinary; (notevole) remarkable; ‹*edizione*› special

■ **lavoro straordinario** overtime; **treno straordinario** special [train]

strapaz'zare *vt* ill-treat; scramble ‹*uova*›

strapaz'zarsi *vr* tire oneself out

stra'pazzo *m* strain; **da ~** fig worthless

strapi'eno *adj* overflowing

strapi'ombo *m* projection; **a ~** sheer

strapo'tere *m* overwhelming power

strappa'lacrime *adj inv* weepy

🔑 **strap'pare** *vt* tear; (per distruggere) tear up; pull out ‹*dente, capelli*›; (sradicare) pull up; (estorcere) wring

strap'parsi *vr* get torn; (allontanarsi) tear oneself away; **~ i capelli** fig be tearing one's hair out

'strappo *m* tear; (strattone) jerk; infml (passaggio) lift; **fare uno ~ alla regola** make an exception to the rule

■ **strappo muscolare** muscle strain

strapun'tino *m* folding seat

🔑 key word

strari'pare *vi* flood
strasci'care *vt* trail; shuffle ‹*piedi*›; drawl ‹*parole*›
'strascico *m* train; fig after-effect
strasci'coni a ~ *adv* dragging one's feet
straseco'lare *vi* be amazed
strass *m inv* rhinestone
strata'gemma *m* stratagem
stra'tega *mf* strategist
strate'gia *f* strategy
stra'tegico *adj* strategic; **mossa strategica** strategic move
stratifi'care *vt* stratify
stratigra'fia *f* Geol stratigraphy
'strato *m* layer; (di vernice ecc.) coat, layer; (roccioso, sociale) stratum
■ **strato di nuvole** cloud layer
strato'sfera *f* stratosphere
strato'sferico *adj* stratospheric; fig sky-high
stravac'carsi *vr* infml slouch
stravac'cato *adj* infml slouching
strava'gante *adj* extravagant; (eccentrico) eccentric
strava'ganza *f* extravagance; (eccentricità) eccentricity
stra'vecchio *adj* ancient
strave'dere *vt* **~ per** worship
stravizi'are *vi* indulge oneself
stra'vizio *m* excess
stra'volgere *vt* twist; (turbare) upset
stravolgi'mento *m* twisting
stra'volto *adj* distraught; infml (stanco) done in
strazi'ante *adj* heart-rending; ‹*dolore*› agonizing
strazi'are *vt* grate on ‹*orecchie*›; break ‹*cuore*›
'strazio *m* agony; **essere uno ~** be agony; **che ~!** infml it's awful!; **fare ~ di qualcosa** ‹*fam: attore, cantante*› murder something
'streamer *m inv* Comput streamer
'strega *f* witch
stre'gare *vt* bewitch
stre'gone *m* wizard
stregone'ria *f* witchcraft
'stregua *f* **alla ~ di** in the same way as; **alla stessa ~** ‹*giudicare*› by the same yardstick; **a questa ~** at this rate
stre'mare *vt* exhaust
stre'mato *adj* exhausted
'stremo **A** *adj* extreme
B *m* **ridotto allo ~** at the end of one's tether
'strenna *f* present
'strenuo *adj* strenuous
strepi'tare *vi* make a din
strepi'tio *m* din, uproar
strepi'toso *adj* noisy; fig resounding
strepto'cocco *m* Med streptococcus
streptomi'cina *f* Med streptomycin
stress *m* stress
stres'sante *adj* ‹*lavoro, situazione*› stressful
stres'sare *vt* put under stress, be stressful for
stres'sarsi *vr* get stressed
stres'sato *adj* stressed [out]
'stretta *f* grasp, squeeze; (dolore) pang; **essere alle strette** be in dire straits; **mettere alle strette qualcuno** have somebody's back up against the wall; **provare una ~ al cuore** feel a pang
■ **stretta creditizia** credit crunch; **stretta di mano** handshake
stret'tezza *f* narrowness; **stret'tezze** *pl* (difficoltà finanziarie) financial difficulties
'stretto **A** pp di **stringere**
B *adj* narrow; (serrato) tight; (vicino) close; ‹*dialetto*› broad; (rigoroso) strict; **lo ~ necessario** the bare minimum
C *m* Geog strait
■ **stretto di Messina** Straits of Messina
stret'toia *f* bottleneck; infml (difficoltà) tight spot
stri'ato *adj* striped
stria'tura *f* streak
stri'dente *adj* strident
'stridere *vi* squeak; fig clash
stri'dore *m* screech
'stridulo *adj* shrill
strigli'are *vt* groom
strigli'ata *f* grooming; fig dressing down
stril'lare *vi & vt* scream
'strillo *m* scream
stril'lone *m* newspaper seller
strimin'zito *adj* skimpy; (magro) skinny
strimpel'lare *vt* strum
stri'nare *vt* singe, scorch
'stringa *f* lace; Comput string
strin'gato *adj* fig terse
'stringere **A** *vt* press; (serrare) squeeze; (tenere stretto) hold tight; take in ‹*abito*›; (comprimere) be tight; (restringere) tighten; **~ la mano a** shake hands with
B *vi* (premere) press
'stringersi *vr* (accostarsi) draw close (**a** to); (avvicinarsi) squeeze up
strip'pata *f* infml nosh-up; **farsi una ~** have a nosh-up
strip-'tease *m* striptease
'striscia *f* strip; (riga) stripe; **a strisce** striped; **strisce** *pl* **di mezzeria** Auto lane markings; **strisce** *pl* **[pedonali]** zebra crossing *sg*, crosswalk AmE
strisci'are **A** *vi* crawl; (sfiorare) graze
B *vt* drag ‹*piedi*›
strisci'arsi *vr* **~ a** rub against
strisci'ata *f* scratch

'striscio *m* graze; Med smear; **colpire di ~** graze
strisci'one *m* banner
strito'lare *vt* grind
strizzacer'velli *mf* sl shrink
striz'zare *vt* squeeze; (torcere) wring [out]; **~ l'occhio** wink
'strofa *f* strophe
strofi'naccio *m* cloth; (per spolverare) duster ▪ **strofinaccio da cucina** tea towel; **strofinaccio per i piatti** dish towel
strofi'nare *vt* rub
strofi'nio *m* rubbing
strom'bare *vt* splay
strombaz'zare **A** *vt* boast about **B** *vi* hoot
strombaz'zata *f* (di clacson) hoot
stron'care *vt* cut off; (reprimere) crush; (criticare) tear to shreds
stron'zate *fpl* vulg crap
'stronzo *m* vulg shit
stropicci'are *vt* rub; crumple ‹*vestito*›
stropicci'ata *f* rub
stro'piccio *m* rubbing
stroppi'are *vt* **il troppo stroppia** enough is as good as a feast
stroz'zare *vt* strangle
strozza'tura *f* strangling; (di strada) narrowing
strozzi'naggio *m* loan sharking
stroz'zino *m* derog usurer; (truffatore) shark
struc'cante *m* make-up remover
struc'carsi *vr* remove one's make-up
strug'gente *adj* all-consuming
'struggersi *vr* (liter) pine [away]; **~ di invidia/desiderio** be consumed with envy/desire
struggi'mento *m* yearning
strumen'tale *adj* instrumental
strumentaliz'zare *vt* make use of
strumen'tario *m* instruments *pl*
strumentazi'one *f* instrumentation
strumen'tista *m* instrumentalist
stru'mento *m* instrument; (arnese) tool ▪ **strumento a corda/fiato** string/wind instrument; **strumento musicale** musical instrument; **strumento a percussione** percussion instrument
strusci'are *vt* rub
strusci'arsi *vr* ‹*gatto*› rub itself; ‹*due innamorati*› caress each other; **~ intorno a qualcuno** infml suck up to somebody
'strutto *m* lard
strut'tura *f* structure
struttu'rale *adj* structural
struttura'lismo *m* structuralism
struttural'mente *adv* structurally
struttu'rare *vt* structure
strutturazi'one *f* structuring
'struzzo *m* ostrich
stuc'care *vt* plaster; (per decorazione) stucco; put putty in ‹*vetri*›
stucca'tore *m* plasterer; (decorativo) stucco worker
stucca'tura *f* plastering; (decorativo) stucco work
stuc'chevole *adj* nauseating
'stucco *m* plaster; (decorativo) stucco; (per vetro) putty; **rimanere di ~** be thunderstruck
⚷ **stu'dente, studen'tessa** *mf* student; (di scuola) schoolboy; schoolgirl
studen'tesco *adj* student; (di scolaro) school *attrib*
⚷ **studi'are** *vt* study
studi'arsi *vr* **~ di** try to
⚷ **'studio** *m* studying; (stanza, ricerca) study; (di artista, TV ecc.) studio; (di professionista) office ▪ **studio cinematografico** film studio; **studio dentistico** dental surgery
studi'oso, -a **A** *adj* studious **B** *mf* scholar
'stufa *f* stove ▪ **stufa elettrica** electric fire; **stufa a gas** gas fire; **stufa a legna** wood-burning stove; **stufa a pellet** pellet stove
stu'fare *vt* Culin stew; (dare fastidio) bore
stu'farsi *vr* get bored
stu'fato *m* stew
'stufo *adj* bored; **essere ~ di** be bored with, be fed up with
stu'oia *f* mat
stu'olo *m* crowd
stupefa'cente **A** *adj* amazing **B** *m* drug
stupe'fare *vt* stun
⚷ **stu'pendo** *adj* stupendous; **~ !** brilliant!
stupi'daggine *f* (azione) stupid thing; (cosa da poco) nothing; **non dire stupidaggini!** don't talk stupid!
stupi'data *f* stupid thing
stupidità *f inv* stupidity
⚷ **'stupido** *adj* stupid
stu'pire **A** *vt* astonish **B** *vi* be astonished
stu'pirsi *vr* be astonished
stu'pore *m* amazement
stu'prare *vt* rape
stupra'tore *m* rapist
'stupro *m* rape
sturabot'tiglie *m inv* corkscrew
sturalavan'dini *m inv* plunger
stu'rare *vt* uncork; unblock ‹*lavandino*›
stuzzica'denti *m inv* toothpick
stuzzi'care *vt* prod [at]; pick ‹*denti*›; poke ‹*fuoco*›; (molestare) tease; whet ‹*appetito*›
stuzzi'chino *m* Culin appetizer

S

⚷ key word

su **A** *prep* on; (senza contatto) over; (riguardo a) about; (circa, intorno a) about, around; **le chiavi sono sul tavolo** the keys are on the table; **il quadro è appeso sul camino** the picture is hanging over the fireplace; **un libro sull'antico Egitto** a book on *or* about Ancient Egypt; **sarò lì sulle cinque** I'll be there about five, I'll be there around five; **è durato sulle tre ore** it lasted for about three hours; **costa sui 75 euro** it costs about 75 euros; **decidere sul momento** decide at the time; **su commissione** on commission; **su due piedi** on the spot; **su misura** made to measure; **uno su dieci** one out of ten; **stare sulle proprie** keep oneself to oneself; **sul mare** ‹*casa*› by the sea
B *adv* (sopra) up; (al piano di sopra) upstairs; (addosso) on; **andare su** go up; (al piano di sopra) go upstairs; **ho su il cappotto** I've got my coat on; **in su** ‹*guardare*› up; **dalla vita in su** from the waist up; **su!** come on!

sua'dente *adj* persuasive

sub *mf inv* skin-diver

sub+ *pref* sub+

su'bacqueo, -a **A** *adj* underwater **B** *mf* skin-diver

subaffit'tare *vt* sublet

subaf'fitto *m* sublet; **in ~** sublet

suba'gente *m* subagent

subal'terno *adj & nm* subordinate

subappal'tare *vt* subcontract

subappalta|'tore, -trice *mf* subcontractor

subap'palto *m* subcontract; **in ~** subcontracted; **dare in ~** subcontract; **prendere in ~** take on a subcontract basis

sub'buglio *m* turmoil

sub'conscio *adj & nm* subconscious

subconti'nente *m* subcontinent

subcosci'ente *adj & nm* subconscious

subdi'rectory *f* Comput subdirectory

subdola'mente *adv* deviously

'subdolo *adj* devious, underhand

suben'trare *vi* ‹*circostanze*› come up; **~ a** take the place of

su'bentro *m* changeover

subequatori'ale *adj* subequatorial

su'bire *vt* undergo; (patire) suffer

subis'sare *vt* fig **~ di** overwhelm with

subi'taneo *adj* sudden

'subito *adv* at once, immediately, right away; **~ dopo** straight after; **vengo ~** I'll be right there

subli'mare *vt* sublimate

su'blime *adj* sublime

sublimi'nale *adj* subliminal

sublingu'ale *adj* sublingual

sublo'care *vt* sublease

subloca'tario *m* sub-lessor

sublocazi'one *f* sublease

subnor'male *adj* subnormal

subodo'rare *vt* suspect

subordi'nare *vt* subordinate

subordi'nato, -a *adj & nmf* subordinate

su'bordine *m* **in ~** second in order of importance

subrou'tine *f* Comput subroutine

subsi'denza *f* Geol subsidence

sub'strato *m* substratum, substrate

subto'tale *m* subtotal

subtropi'cale *adj* subtropical

subu'mano *adj* subhuman

subur'bano *adj* suburban

suc'cedere *vi* (accadere) happen; **~ a** (in carica) succeed; (venire dopo) follow; **~ al trono** succeed to the throne

suc'cedersi *vr* happen one after the other; **si sono succeduti molti ...** there was a series of ...

successi'one *f* succession; **in ~** in succession

successiva'mente *adv* subsequently

succes'sivo *adj* successive; ‹*mese, giorno*› following

suc'cesso **A** pp di **succedere** **B** *m* success; (esito) outcome; (disco ecc.) hit

succes'sone *m* huge success

succes'sore *m* successor

succhi'are *vt* suck [up]; **~ il sangue a qualcuno** fig bleed somebody dry

succhi'ello *m* gimlet

succinta'mente *adv* succinctly

suc'cinto *adj* (conciso) concise; ‹*abito*› scanty

'succo *m* juice; fig essence
■ **succo d'arancia** orange juice; **succo di frutta** fruit juice; **succo di limone** lemon juice

suc'coso *adj* juicy

'succube *m* **essere ~ di qualcuno** be totally dominated by somebody

succu'lento *adj* succulent

succur'sale *f* branch [office]

sud *m* south; **del ~** southern; **a ~ di** [to the] south of

Sud'africa *m* South Africa

sudafri'cano *adj & nmf* South African

Suda'merica *f* South America

sudameri'cano, -a *adj & nmf* South American

Su'dan *m* **il ~** the Sudan

suda'nese *adj & nmf* Sudanese

su'dare *vi* sweat, perspire; (faticare) sweat blood; **~ freddo** be in a cold sweat; **~ sangue** sweat blood; **mi fa ~ freddo** it brings me out in a cold sweat; **~ sette camicie** sweat blood

su'data *f* anche fig sweat

suda'ticcio *adj* sweaty

su'dato *adj* sweaty; ‹*vittoria*› hard-won; ‹*pane*› hard-earned

sud'detto *adj* above-mentioned

'suddito, -a *mf* subject
suddi'videre *vt* subdivide
suddivisi'one *f* subdivision
su'd-est *m* south-east
'sudicio *adj* dirty, filthy
sudici'ume *m* dirt, filth
sudocciden'tale *adj* south-western
su'doku *m inv* sudoku, sudoku puzzle
sudorazi'one *f* perspiring
su'dore *m* sweat, perspiration; fig sweat; **in un bagno di ~** bathed in sweat; **con il ~ della fronte** fig by the sweat of one's brow
■ **sudore freddo** cold sweat
sudo'riparo *adj* sweat *attrib*
su'd-ovest *m* south-west
'sue ▸ **suo**
⚷ **suffici'ente** **A** *adj* sufficient; (presuntuoso) conceited
B *m* bare essentials *pl*; Sch pass mark
suffici'enza *f* sufficiency; (presunzione) conceit; Sch pass; **a ~** enough; **prendere la ~** get the pass mark
suf'fisso *m* suffix
sufflè *m inv* Culin soufflé
suffra'getta *f* suffragette
suf'fragio *m* (voto) vote; **in ~ di qualcuno** in homage to
■ **suffragio universale** universal suffrage
suffu'migio *m* inhalation
suggel'lare *vt* seal
suggeri'mento *m* suggestion
sugge'rire *vt* suggest; Theat prompt
suggeri|'tore, -trice *mf* Theat prompter
suggestio'nabile *adj* suggestible
suggestio'nare *vt* influence
suggestio'nato *adj* influenced
suggesti'one *f* influence
sugge'stivo *adj* charming; ‹*musica ecc.*› evocative
'sughero *m* cork
'sugli = **su + gli**
S **'sugo** *m* (di frutta) juice; (di carne) gravy; (salsa) sauce; (sostanza) substance
'sui = **su + i**
sui'cida **A** *adj* suicidal
B *mf* suicide
suici'darsi *vr* commit suicide
sui'cidio *m* anche fig suicide; **commettere ~** commit suicide; **tentato ~** attempted suicide
su'ino **A** *adj* **carne suina** pork
B *m* swine
su'ite *f inv* suite
sul = **su + il**
sulfa'midico *m* sulphonamide, sulpha drug
sul'fureo *adj* sulphuric
'sulla = **su + la A, B**
'sulle = **su + le**
'sullo = **su + lo**
sul'tana *f* (persona) sultana
sulta'nina *adj* **uva ~** sultana
sul'tano *m* sultan
'sunto *m* summary
⚷ **'suo, -a** **A** *poss adj* **il ~, i suoi, la sua, le sue** (di lui) his; (di lei) her; (di cosa o animale) its; (forma di cortesia) your; **questa macchina è sua** this car is his/hers; **~ padre** his/her/your father; **un ~ amico** a friend of his/hers/yours
B *poss pron* **il ~, i suoi, la sua, le sue** (di lui) his; (di lei) hers; (di cosa o animale) its; (forma di cortesia) yours; **i suoi** his/her folk[s]
su'ocera *f* mother-in-law
su'ocero *m* father-in-law
su'oi ▸ **suo**
su'ola *f* sole; **suole *pl* di para** crepe soles
su'olo *m* ground; (terreno) soil
■ **suolo pubblico** public land
⚷ **suo'nare** **A** *vt* Mus play; ring ‹*campanello*›; sound ‹*allarme, clacson*›; ‹*orologio*› strike ‹*ore*›; **~ il clacson** sound the horn, hoot the horn; infml (imbrogliare) do
B *vi* ‹*campanello, telefono, sveglia*› ring; ‹*clacson*› hoot; ‹*sirena*› go [off]; ‹*giradischi*› play
suo'nato *adj* infml bonkers
suona|'tore, -trice *mf* player
suone'ria *f* alarm; (di cellulare) ringtone
⚷ **su'ono** *m* sound
su'ora *f* nun; **Suor Maria** Sister Maria
'super *f* 4-star [petrol], premium [gas] AmE
super+ *pref* super+
supe'rabile *adj* surmountable
superal'colico **A** *m* spirit
B *adj* **bevande superalcoliche** spirits
supera'mento *m* (di timidezza) overcoming; (di esame) success **(di** in)
⚷ **supe'rare** *vt* surpass; (eccedere) exceed; (vincere) overcome; overtake, pass AmE ‹*veicolo*›; pass ‹*esame*›; **~ la barriera del suono** break the sound barrier; **~ se stessi** surpass oneself; **ha superato la trentina** he's over thirty
su'perbia *f* haughtiness
su'perbo *adj* haughty; (magnifico) superb
super'donna *f* superwoman
superdo'tato *adj* highly gifted, super-talented
superfici'ale **A** *adj* superficial
B *mf* superficial person
superficialità *f inv* superficiality
⚷ **super'ficie** *f* surface; (area) area; **in ~** on the surface; fig ‹*esaminare*› superficially
su'perfluo *adj* superfluous
Super-'Io *m* Psych superego
superi'ora *f* superior; Relig mother superior
⚷ **superi'ore** **A** *adj* superior; (di grado) senior;

⚷ key word

(più elevato) higher; (sovrastante) upper; (al di sopra) above
B *m* superior
superiorità *f inv* superiority
superla'tivo *adj & nm* superlative
supermer'cato *m* supermarket
supermo'della *f* supermodel
super'nova *f* Astr supernova
superpetroli'era *f* Naut supertanker
superpo'tenza *f* superpower
super'sonico *adj* supersonic
su'perstite **A** *adj* surviving
B *mf* survivor
superstizi'one *f* superstition
superstizi'oso *adj* superstitious
super'strada *f* toll-free motorway
■ **superstrada informatica** information superhighway
superu'omo *m* superman
superu'tente *m* Comput superuser
supervalu'tare *vt* overvalue
supervalutazi'one *f* overvaluation
supervisi'one *f* supervision
supervi'sore *m* supervisor
su'pino *adj* supine
suppel'lettili *fpl* furnishings
suppergiù *adv* about
supplemen'tare *adj* additional, supplementary
supple'mento *m* supplement
■ **supplemento illustrato** colour supplement; **supplemento rapido** express train supplement
sup'plente **A** *adj* temporary
B *mf* Sch supply teacher
sup'plenza *f* temporary post
'supplica *f* plea; (domanda) petition
suppli'care *vt* beg
suppli'chevole *adj* imploring
sup'plire **A** *vt* replace
B *vi* ~ **a** (compensare) make up for
sup'plizio *m* torture
sup'porre *vt* suppose
suppor'tare *vt* Comput support
sup'porto *m* support
■ **supporto di sistema** Comput system support
supposizi'one *f* supposition
sup'posta *f* suppository
sup'posto pp di **supporre**
suppu'rare *vi* fester
suppurazi'one *f* suppuration; **andare in ~** fester
suprema'zia *f* supremacy
su'premo *adj* supreme
surclas'sare *vt* outclass
surf *m inv* surfboard; (sport) surfboarding
sur'fista *mf* surfer
surge'lare *vt* deep-freeze
surge'lato **A** *adj* frozen
B *m* **surgelati** *pl* frozen food *sg*

Suri'name *m* Surinam
'surplus *m* sur'plus
surre'ale *adj* surreal
surrea'lismo *m* surrealism
surrea'lista *mf* surrealist
surrea'listico *adj* surrealist
surre'nale *adj* adrenal
surriscal'dare *vt* overheat
surriscal'darsi *vr* overheat
surro'gato *m* substitute
suscet'tibile *adj* touchy
suscettibilità *f inv* touchiness
susci'tare *vt* stir up; arouse ‹*ammirazione ecc.*›
su'sina *f* plum
■ **susina selvatica** damson
su'sino *m* plum tree
su'spense *f* suspense
sussegu'ente *adj* subsequent
sussegu'irsi *vr* follow one after the other
sussidi'are *vt* subsidize
sussidi'ario *adj* subsidiary
sus'sidio *m* subsidy; (aiuto) aid
■ **sussidio didattico** study aid; **sussidio di disoccupazione** unemployment benefit; **sussidio di malattia** sickness benefit
sussi'ego *m* haughtiness; **con ~** haughtily
sussi'stenza *f* subsistence
sus'sistere *vi* subsist; (essere valido) hold good
sussul'tare *vi* start; **far ~ qualcuno** give somebody a start
sus'sulto *m* start
sussur'rare *vt & vi* whisper; **si sussurra che ...** it is rumoured that ...
sussur'rio *m* murmur
sus'surro *m* whisper
su'tura *f* suture
sutu'rare *vt* suture
suv, SUV *m inv* SUV
suv'via *int* come on!
sva'gare *vt* amuse
sva'garsi *vr* amuse oneself
'svago *m* relaxation; (divertimento) amusement; **prendersi un po' di ~** have a break
svaligi'are *vt* rob; burgle ‹*casa*›
svalu'tare *vt* devalue; fig underestimate
svalu'tarsi *vr* lose value
svalutazi'one *f* devaluation
svam'pito, -a *mf* airhead
sva'nire *vi* vanish
sva'nito, -a **A** *adj* ‹*persona*› absent-minded; ‹*sapore, sogno*› faded
B *mf* absent-minded person
svantaggi'ato *adj* at a disadvantage; ‹*bambino, paese*› disadvantaged
svan'taggio *m* disadvantage; **essere in ~** Sport be losing; **in ~ di tre punti** three points down; **in ~ rispetto a qualcuno** at a disadvantage compared with somebody

svantaggi'oso *adj* disadvantageous
svapo'rare *vi* evaporate
svari'ato *adj* varied
svari'one *m* blunder
sva'sare *vt* splay; flare ‹*gonna*›
sva'sato *adj* ‹*gonna*› flared
svasa'tura *f* flare
'svastica *f* swastika
sve'dese **A** *adj & nm* (lingua) Swedish **B** *mf* Swede
'sveglia *f* ‹*orologio*› alarm [clock]; **~!** get up!; **mettere la ~** set the alarm [clock]
■ **sveglia automatica** alarm call; **sveglia telefonica** wake-up call
✓ **svegli'are** *vt* wake up; fig awaken; **~ l'appetito a qualcuno** whet somebody's appetite
svegli'arsi *vr* wake up
'sveglio *adj* awake; (di mente) alert, sharp
sve'lare *vt* reveal
svel'tezza *f* speed; fig quick-wittedness
svel'tire *vt* quicken
svel'tirsi *vr* ‹*persona*› liven up
✓ **'svelto** *adj* quick; (slanciato) svelte; **alla svelta** quickly; **a passo ~** quickly
sve'narsi *vr* slash one's wrists; fig reduce oneself to poverty
'svendere *vt* undersell
'svendita *f* [clearance] sale
sve'nevole *adj* sentimental
sveni'mento *m* fainting fit
sve'nire *vi* faint; **da ~** incredibly
sven'tare *vt* foil
sven'tato **A** *adj* thoughtless **B** *mf* thoughtless person
'sventola *f* slap
■ **orecchie a sventola** protruding ears, jug handle ears infml
svento'lare *vt & vi* wave
svento'larsi *vr* fan oneself
svento'lio *m* flutter
sventra'mento *m* disembowelment; (di pollo) gutting; fig (di edificio) demolition ‹*edificio*›
sven'trare *vt* disembowel; gut ‹*pollo*›; fig demolish ‹*edificio*›
sven'tura *f* misfortune
sventu'rato *adj* unfortunate
sve'nuto pp di **svenire**
svergi'nare *vt* deflower
svergo'gnato *adj* shameless
sver'nare *vi* winter
svernici'ante *m* paint stripper
svernici'are *vt* strip
sve'stire *vt* undress
sve'stirsi *vr* undress, get undressed
svet'tare *vi* ‹*albero, torre*› stand out; **~ verso il cielo** stretch skywards

✓ key word

'Svezia *f* Sweden
svezza'mento *m* weaning
svez'zare *vt* wean
svi'are *vt* divert; (corrompere) lead astray
svi'arsi *vr* fig go astray
svico'lare *vi* turn down a side street; fig (dalla questione ecc.) evade the issue; fig (da una persona) dodge out of the way
svi'gnarsela *vr* slip away
svigo'rire *vt* emasculate
svili'mento *m* debasement
svi'lire *vt* debase
✓ **svilup'pare** *vt* develop
svilup'parsi *vr* develop
sviluppa|'tore, -trice *mf* developer
■ **sviluppatore web** web developer
✓ **svi'luppo** *m* development
■ **paese in via di sviluppo** developing country
svinco'lare *vt* release; clear ‹*merce*›; redeem ‹*deposito*›
svinco'larsi *vr* free oneself
'svincolo *m* clearance; (di autostrada) exit; **~ di un deposito cauzionale** redemption of a deposit
svioli'nata *f* fawning
svisce'rare *vt* gut; fig dissect
svisce'rato *adj* ‹*amore*› passionate; (ossequioso) obsequious
'svista *f* oversight
svi'tare *vt* unscrew
svi'tato *adj* infml (matto) cracked, nutty
'svizzera *f* hamburger
'Svizzera *f* Switzerland
✓ **'svizzero, -a** *adj & nmf* Swiss
svoglia'taggine *f* laziness; (riluttanza) unwillingness
svogli'atamente *adv* half-heartedly; (senza energia) listlessly
svoglia'tezza *f* half-heartedness; (mancanza di energia) listlessness
svogli'ato *adj* half-hearted; (senza energic) listless
svolaz'zante *adj* ‹*capelli*› wind-swept
svolaz'zare *vi* flutter
svolaz'zio *m* flutter
✓ **'svolgere** *vt* unwind; unwrap ‹*pacco*›; (risolvere) solve; (portare a termine) carry out; (sviluppare) develop
'svolgersi *vr* (accadere) take place
svolgi'mento *m* course; (sviluppo) development
'svolta *f* turning; fig turning point
svol'tare *vi* turn
'svolto pp di **svolgere**
svuo'tare *vt* empty [out]; fig (di significato) deprive
'Swaziland *m* Swaziland
swing *m* Mus swing
switch *m* Comput switch

Tt

T *abbr* (**tabaccheria**) tobacconist's
tabac'caio, **-a** *mf* tobacconist
tabacche'ria *f* tobacconist's (*which also sells stamps, postcards etc*)
ta'bacco *m* tobacco; **tabacchi** *pl* cigarettes and tobacco
taba'gismo *m* nicotine addiction
ta'bella *f* table; (lista) list
■ **tabella di conversione** conversion table; **tabella di marcia** fig schedule; **tabella dei prezzi** price list; **tabella retributiva** salary scale
tabel'lina *f* Math multiplication table
tabel'lone *m* wall chart
■ **tabellone degli arrivi** arrivals board; **tabellone del canestro** backboard; **tabellone delle partenze** departures board; **tabellone segnapunti** scoreboard
taber'nacolo *m* tabernacle
'tablet *m* tablet, tablet PC
tabù *adj & m inv* taboo
tabu'lare *vt* tabulate
tabu'lato *m* Comput [data] printout
tabula'tore *m* tabulator
tabulazi'one *f* tabulation
TAC *nf abbr* (**tomografia assiale computerizzata**) CAT scan
'tacca *f* notch; **di mezza ∼** ‹*attore*› (giornalista) second-rate
taccagne'ria *f* penny-pinching
tac'cagno *adj* infml stingy
taccheggia|'tore, **-trice** *mf* shoplifter
tac'cheggio *m* shoplifting
tac'chetto *m* Sport stud
tac'chino *m* turkey
tacci'are *vt* **∼ qualcuno di qualcosa** accuse somebody of something
'tacco *m* heel; **alzare i tacchi** take to one's heels; **scarpe senza ∼** flat shoes, flats; **colpo di ∼** back-heel
■ **tacchi a spillo** *pl* stiletto heels, stilettos
taccu'ino *m* notebook
ta'cere **A** *vi* be silent
B *vt* say nothing about; **mettere a ∼ qualcosa** ‹*scandalo*› hush something up; **mettere a ∼ qualcuno** silence somebody
tachicar'dia *f* tachycardia
ta'chigrafo *m* tachograph
ta'chimetro *m* speedometer
tacita'mente *adv* tacitly; (in silenzio) silently
'tacito *adj* tacit, unspoken; (silenzioso) silent
taci'turno *adj* taciturn
ta'fano *m* horsefly
taffe'ruglio *m* scuffle
taffettà *m inv* taffeta
tag *m inv* Comput tag
tag'gare *vt* Comput to tag
'taglia *f* (riscatto) ransom; (ricompensa) reward; (statura) height; (di abiti) size; **per taglie forti** outsize, OS
■ **taglia unica** one size
taglia'carte *m inv* paperknife
'taglia e in'colla *m inv* cut and paste; **fare un ∼** cut and paste
taglia'erba *m inv* lawnmower
tagliafu'oco **A** *adj inv* **porta ∼** fire door; **striscia ∼** fire break
B *m* (in bosco) fire break
tagli'ando *m* coupon; **fare il ∼** put one's car in for its MOT
■ **tagliando di controllo** manufacturer's sticker; (da raccogliere) token; **tagliando controllo bagaglio** baggage claim sticker; **tagliando di garanzia** warranty
taglia'pasta **A** *adj inv* **rotella ∼** pastry cutter
B *m inv* pastry cutter
tagliapa'tate *m inv* potato cutter
tagli'are **A** *vt* cut; (attraversare) cut across; cut off ‹*telefono, elettricità*›; carve ‹*carne*›; mow ‹*erba*›; **farsi ∼ i capelli** have a haircut, have one's hair cut; **∼ i viveri a qualcuno** stop somebody's allowance
B *vi* cut
tagli'arsi *vr* cut oneself; **∼ il dito** cut one's finger; **∼ i capelli** have a haircut, have one's hair cut
taglia'sigari *m inv* cigar cutter
tagli'ata *f* finely-cut beef fillet; **dare una ∼ a qualcosa** give something a cut, cut something
tagli'ato *adj* (a pezzi) jointed; **essere ∼ per qualcosa** fig be cut out for something
taglia'unghie *m inv* nail clippers *pl*
taglieggi'are *vt* extort money from
tagli'ente **A** *adj* sharp
B *m* cutting edge
tagli'ere *m* chopping board
■ **∼ per il pane** breadboard
taglie'rina *f* (per carta) guillotine; (per foto) trimmer; (per metallo, vetro) cutter
'taglio *m* cut; (di stoffa) length; (di capelli) hair cut; (parte tagliente) cutting edge; **di ∼** edgeways; **a doppio ∼** fig double-edged;

t

dacci un ~! infml put a sock in it!
■ **taglio e cucito** dressmaking; **taglio di carne** cut of meat; **taglio cesareo** Caesarean section; **taglio di personale** personnel cut; **taglio dei prezzi** price cutting; **taglio alla spesa** spending cut

tagli'ola *f* trap

taglio'lini *mpl thin soup noodles*

tagli'one *m*
■ **legge del taglione** an eye for an eye and a tooth for a tooth

tagliuz'zare *vt* cut into small pieces

tail'leur *m inv* [lady's] suit

Tai'wan *f* Taiwan

ta'lare *adj* **prendere la veste ~** take holy orders

talassotera'pia *f therapy based on seawater*

'talco *m* talcum powder, talc

✓ **'tale** **A** *adj* such a; (con nomi plurali) such; **c'è un ~ disordine** there is such a mess; **non accetto tali scuse** I won't accept such excuses; **è un ~ bugiardo!** he's such a liar!; **il rumore era ~ che non si sentiva nulla** there was so much noise you couldn't hear yourself think; **il ~ giorno** on such and such a day; **vai il tal giorno alla tal ora** go on such a day at such a time; **quel tal signore** that gentleman; **~ padre ~ figlio** like father like son; **~ quale** just like
B *pron* **un ~** someone; **quel ~** that man; **il tal dei tali** such and such a person

ta'lea *f* cutting

tale'bano *adj & nm* Taliban

ta'lento *m* talent

'talent scout *mf inv* talent scout

tali'smano *m* talisman

tallo'nare *vt* be hot on the heels of

tallon'cino *m* coupon
■ **talloncino del prezzo** price tag

tal'lone *m* heel
■ **tallone di Achille** fig Achilles' heel; **tallone aureo** Econ gold standard

✓ **tal'mente** *adv* so

ta'lora *adj* = **talvolta**

'talpa *f* mole

tal'volta *adv* sometimes

tamburel'lare *vi* (con le dita) drum; (pioggia) beat, drum

tambu'rello *m* tambourine

tambu'rino *m* drummer

tam'buro *m* drum
■ **tamburo del freno** brake drum

tame'rice *f* tamarisk

'tamia *m inv* chipmunk

Ta'migi *m* Thames

tampona'mento *m* Auto collision; (di ferita) dressing; (di falla) plugging
■ **tamponamento a catena** pile-up

✓ key word

tampo'nare *vt* (urtare) crash into; plug ‹*falla*›; dress ‹*ferita*›

tam'pone *m* swab; (per timbri) pad; (per mestruazioni) tampon; (per treni) Comput buffer

tam'tam *m inv* bush telegraph

TAN *abbr* (**tasso annuale nominale**) Fin nominal interest rate

'tana *f* den

'tandem *m inv* tandem; **in ~** (lavorare) in tandem

'tanfo *m* stench

'tanga *m inv* tanga

tan'gente **A** *adj* tangent
B *f* tangent; (somma) bribe

tangen'topoli *f widespread corruption in Italy in the early 90s*

tangenzi'ale *f* orbital road

tan'gibile *adj* tangible

tangibil'mente *adv* tangibly

'tango *m inv* tango

'tanica *f* (contenitore) jerry can; (serbatoio di nave) tank
■ **tanica di benzina** petrol can

tan'nino *m* tannin

tan'tino **un ~** *adv* a little [bit]

✓ **'tanto** **A** *adj* [so] much; (con nomi plurali) [so] many, [such] a lot of; **~ tempo** [such] a long time; **non ha tanta pazienza** he doesn't have much patience; **~ tempo quanto ti serve** as much time as you need; **tanti amici quanti parenti** as many friends as relatives
B *pron* much; (plurale) many; (tanto tempo) much time; **è un uomo come tanti** he's just an ordinary man; **tanti** (molte persone) many people; **non ci vuole così ~** it doesn't take that long; **~ quanto** as much as; **tanti quanti** as many as
C *conj* (comunque) anyway, in any case
D *adv* (così) so; (con verbi) so much; **è ~ debole che non sta in piedi** he's so weak that he can't stand; **è ~ ingenuo da crederle** he's naive enough to believe her; **di ~ in ~** every now and then; **~ l'uno come l'altro** both; **~ quanto** as much as; **non è ~ intelligente quanto suo padre** he's not as intelligent as his father; **tre volte ~** three times as much; **una volta ~** once in a while; **~ meglio così!** so much the better!; **tant'è** so much so; **~ vale che andiamo a casa** we might as well go home; **~ per cambiare** for a change

Tan'zania *f* Tanzania

tapi'oca *f* tapioca

ta'piro *m* tapir

ta'pis rou'lant *m inv* conveyor belt

'tappa *f* (parte di viaggio) stage; **fare ~ a** break one's journey in

tappa'buchi *m inv* stopgap

tap'pare *vt* plug; cork ‹*bottiglia*›; **~ la bocca a qualcuno** infml shut somebody up

tappa'rella *f* infml roller blind; **tirar su la ~** pull the blind up

tap'parsi *vr* ~ **gli occhi** cover one's eyes; ~ **il naso** hold one's nose; ~ **le orecchie** put one's fingers in one's ears

tappe'tino *m* mat; Comput mouse mat
■ **tappetino antiscivolo** [anti-slip] safety bath mat; **tappetino da bagno** bath mat

tap'peto *m* carpet; (piccolo) rug; **andare al** ~ (pugilato) hit the canvas; **mandare qualcuno al** ~ knock somebody down; **bombardamento a** ~ carpet bombing
■ **tappeto erboso** lawn; **tappeto persiano** Persian carpet; **tappeto stradale** road surface; **tappeto verde** (tavolo) card table; **tappeto volante** magic carpet

tappez'zare *vt* paper ‹*pareti*›; (con manifesti) cover

tappezze'ria *f* tapestry; (di carta) wallpaper; (arte) upholstery; **fare da** ~ fig be a wallflower

tappezzi'ere *m* upholsterer; (imbianchino) decorator

'tappo *m* plug; (di sughero) cork; (di metallo, per penna) top; infml (persona piccola) dwarf
■ **tappo di bottiglia** bottle top; **tappo a corona** crown cap; **tappi per le orecchie** *pl* earplugs; **tappo salvagocce** anti-drip top; **tappo di scarico [della coppa]** sump drain plug; **tappo a strappo** ring pull; **tappo di sughero** cork; **tappo a vite** screw top

'tara *f* (difetto) flaw; (ereditaria) hereditary defect; (peso) tare

taran'tella *f* tarantella

ta'rantola *f* tarantula

ta'rare *vt* Techn calibrate; Comm discount

ta'rato *adj* Comm discounted; Techn calibrated; Med with a hereditary defect; infml crazy

tarchi'ato *adj* stocky

tar'dare **A** *vi* be late
B *vt* delay

'tardi *adv* late; **al più** ~ at the latest; **più** ~ later [on]; **sul** ~ late in the day; **far** ~ (essere in ritardo) be late; (con gli amici) stay up late; **a più** ~ see you later; **svegliarsi troppo** ~ oversleep

tardiva'mente *adv* late

tar'divo *adj* late; (bambino) intellectually challenged

'tardo *adj* slow; (pomeriggio, mattinata) late

'targa *f* plate; Auto number plate

tar'gato *adj* **un'auto targata...** a car with the registration number...

targ'hetta *f* (su porta) nameplate; (sulla valigia) name tag
■ **targhetta di circolazione** number plate; **targhetta commemorativa** memorial plaque; **targhetta stradale** street sign

ta'riffa *f* rate, tariff; **a** ~ **ridotta** Teleph off-peak
■ **tariffa aerea** airfare; **tariffa doganale** customs tariff; **tariffa ferroviaria** [rail] fares; **tariffa interna** inland postage; **tariffa ore di punta** peak rate; **tariffa professionale** [professional] fee; **tariffa telefonica** telephone charges; **tariffa unica** flat rate

tarif'fario **A** *adj* tariff (*adv*)
B *m* price list

tar'larsi *vr* get worm-eaten

tar'lato *adj* worm-eaten

'tarlo *m* woodworm

'tarma *f* moth

tar'marsi *vr* get moth-eaten

tarmi'cida *m* moth-repellent

ta'rocco *m* tarot; **tarocchi** *pl* tarot

tar'pare *vt* clip

tartagli'are *vi* stutter

'tartaro *adj & nm* tartar; **salsa tartara** tartar[e] sauce

tarta'ruga *f* **1** Zool tortoise; (di mare) turtle; (per pettine ecc.) tortoiseshell **2** infml (addominali) six pack

tartas'sare *vt* (angariare) harass

tar'tina *f* canapé

tar'tufo *m* truffle

'tasca *f* pocket; (in borsa) compartment; **da** ~ pocket *attrib*; **avere le tasche piene di qualcosa** infml have had a bellyful of something; **se ne è stato con le mani in** ~ fig he didn't lift a finger [to help]
■ **tasca a battente** flap pocket; **tasca del nero** (di polpo, seppia) ink sac; **tasca da pasticciere** icing bag; **tasca tagliata** slit pocket; **tasca a toppa** patch pocket

ta'scabile **A** *adj* pocket *attrib*
B *m* paperback

tasca'pane *m inv* haversack

ta'schino *m* breast pocket

'tassa *f* tax; (d'iscrizione ecc.) fee; (doganale) duty
■ **tassa di circolazione** road tax; **tassa di esportazione** export duty; **tassa d'iscrizione** registration fee; **tassa di soggiorno** tourist tax, visitors' tax; **tasse** *pl* **scholastiche** school fees; **tasse** *pl* **universitarie** tuition fees

tas'sabile *adj* taxable

tas'sametro *m* meter

tas'sare *vt* tax

tassativa'mente *adv* without fail

tassa'tivo *adj* strict

tassazi'one *f* taxation

tas'sello *m* wedge; (di stoffa) gusset; (per legno, parete) Rawlplug

tassì *m inv* taxi

tas'sista *mf* taxi driver

'tasso[1] *m* Bot yew; (animale) badger

'tasso[2] *Comm* rate
■ **tasso agevolato** cut rate; **prestito a** ~ **agevolato** soft loan; **tasso base** base rate; **tasso base di interesse** base lending rate; **tasso di cambio** exchange rate; **tasso di crescita** growth rate; **tasso di disoccupazione** unemployment rate; **tasso d'inquinamento** pollution level; **tasso di interesse** interest

rate; **tasso di mortalità** death rate; **tasso di sconto** discount rate

ta'stare *vt* feel; ~ **il terreno** fig test the water *or* ground

tasti'era *f* keyboard

■ **tastiera numerica** Comput numeric keypad; **telefono a tastiera** touch-tone telephone

tastie'rino *m*

■ **tastierino numerico** numeric keypad

tastie'rista *mf* keyboarder

'tasto *m* key; (tatto) touch

■ **tasto Alt** Alt key; **tasto di cancellazione** delete key; **tasto control** Comput control key; **tasto cursore** Comput cursor key; **tasto delicato** fig touchy subject; **tasto eject** eject button; **tasto escape** escape key; **tasto funzione** Comput function key; **tasto numerico** Comput numeric[al] key; **tasto di ritorno a margine** return key; **tasto tabulatore** tab [key]

ta'stoni *adv* **a** ~ gropingly; **camminare a** ~ grope around; **cercare qualcosa a** ~ grope for something

'tattica *f* tactics *pl*

'tattico *adj* tactical

'tattile *adj* tactile

'tatto *m* (senso) touch; (accortezza) tact; **aver** ~ be tactful

tatu'aggio *m* tattoo

tatu'are *vt* tattoo

tautolo'gia *f* tautology

tauto'logico *adj* tautological

⚷ **'tavola** *f* table; (illustrazione) plate; (asse) plank; **saper stare a** ~ have good table manners; **calmo come una** ~ (mare) like a mill pond

■ **tavola calda** snack bar; **tavola fredda** salad bar; **tavola periodica degli elementi** periodic table; **tavola pitagorica** multiplication table; **tavola rotonda** fig round table; **tavola a vela** sailboard; **fare** ~ **a vela** sailboard, windsurf

tavo'lato *m* (pavimento) wooden flooring

tavo'letta *f* bar; (medicinale) tablet; **andare a** ~ Auto drive flat out

■ **tavoletta di cioccolata** chocolate bar; **tavoletta grafica** Comput digitizing tablet

tavo'lino *m* [small] table; (da salotto) coffee table

⚷ **'tavolo** *m* table

■ **tavolo anatomico** mortuary table, slab infml; **tavolo da biliardo** pool table; **tavolo da cucina** kitchen table; **tavolo da gioco** card table; **tavolo operatorio** Med operating table; **tavolo da pranzo** dining table

tavo'lozza *f* palette

'taxi *m inv* taxi

'tazza *f* cup; (del water) bowl

■ **tazza da caffè/tè** coffee cup/teacup

taz'zina *f*

■ **tazzina da caffè** espresso coffee cup

TBC *nf abbr* (**tubercolosi**) TB

⚷ key word

T.C.I. *abbr* (**Touring Club Italiano**) *association promoting tourism nationally and internationally*

⚷ **te** *pers pron* you; **te l'ho dato** I gave it to you

⚷ **tè** *m inv* tea

■ **tè al latte** tea with milk; **tè al limone** lemon tea

TEAM *nf abbr* (**Tessera Europea di Assicurazione Malattia**) EHIC

tea'trale *adj* theatre *attrib*; (affettato) theatrical

⚷ **te'atro** *m* theatre

■ **teatro all'aperto** open-air theatre; **teatro lirico** opera [house]; **teatro neorealista** kitchen sink drama; **teatro di posa** Cinema set; **teatro tenda** *marquee for fashions shows, concerts etc.*

'techno *f inv* techno (music)

⚷ **'tecnico, -a** **A** *adj* technical

B *mf* technician

■ **tecnico elettronico** electronics engineer; **tecnico informatico** computer engineer; **tecnico delle luci** Cinema, TV gaffer; **tecnico delle riparazioni** repairman; **tecnico del suono** sound technician

C *f* technique

tec'nigrafo *m* drawing board

tec'nocrate *mf* technocrat

tec'nofobo *adj* technophobe

tecnolo'gia *f* technology

tecno'logico *adj* technological

⚷ **te'desco, -a** *adj & nmf* German

'tedio *m* tedium

tedi'oso *adj* tedious

'TEE *nm abbr* (**treno espresso transeuropeo**) Trans Europe Express [train]

te'game *m* saucepan; **uova al** ~ fried eggs

'teglia *f* baking tin

'tegola *f* tile; fig blow

tei'era *f* teapot

te'ina *f* theine

tek *m* teak

tel. *abbr* (**telefono**) tel.

'tela *f* cloth; (per quadri, vele) canvas; Theat curtain

■ **tela cerata** oilcloth; **tela indiana** cheesecloth; **tela di iuta** hessian; **tela di lino** linen; **tela rigida** buckram

te'laio *m* (di bicicletta, finestra) frame; Auto chassis; (per tessere) loom

'tele *f* infml telly, TV

tele'camera *f* television camera

telecoman'dato *adj* remote-controlled, remote control *attrib*

teleco'mando *m* remote control

'Telecom I'talia *f* Italian State telephone company

telecomunicazi'oni *fpl* telecommunications, telecomms

teleconfe'renza *f* teleconference

tele'cronaca *f* [television] commentary; **fare la ~ di** commentate on
■ **telecronaca diretta** live [television] coverage; **telecronaca registrata** recording

telecro'nista *mf* television commentator

tele'ferica *f* cableway

tele'film *m inv* film [made] for television
■ **telefilm a episodi** series

✓ **telefo'nare** *vt & vi* [tele]phone, ring

telefo'nata *f* call, [tele]phone call; **fare una ~** make a phone call
■ **telefonata anonima** nuisance call; **telefonata a carico del destinatario** reverse charge [phone] call; **fare una ~ a carico [del destinatario]** reverse the charges; **telefonata interurbana** long-distance call; **telefonata di lavoro** business call; **telefonata in teleselezione** ≈ STD call; **telefonata urbana** local call

telefonica'mente *adv* by [tele]phone

tele'fonico *adj* [tele]phone *attrib*

telefo'nino *m* mobile [phone]

telefo'nista *mf* operator

✓ **te'lefono** *m* telephone, phone; **numero di ~** telephone number
■ **telefono amico** the Samaritans; **telefono azzurro** children in need help line; **telefono cellulare** cell [tele]phone, mobile; **telefono cordless** cordless [phone]; **telefono interno** intercom; **telefono a monete** pay phone; **telefono pubblico** public telephone; **telefono rosso** Mil, Pol hotline; **telefono satellitare** satellite phone; **telefono a scatti** *telephone with call charges based on time units*; **telefono a scheda** cardphone; **telefono a tastiera** push-button phone

tele'genico *adj* telegenic

telegior'nale *m* television news

telegra'fare *vt* telegraph

telegra'fia *f* telegraphy

telegrafica'mente *adv* (con telegrafo) by telegram

tele'grafico *adj* telegraphic; (risposta) monosyllabic; **sii ~** keep it brief

te'legrafo *m* telegraph

tele'gramma *m* telegram

telela'voro *m* teleworking

tele'matica *f* data communications, telematics *sg*

teleno'vela *f* soap opera

teleobiet'tivo *m* telephoto lens

telepa'tia *f* telepathy

tele'patico *adj* telepathic

tele'quiz *m inv* TV quiz programme

teleradiotra'smettere *vt* simulcast

telero'manzo *m* television serial

tele'schermo *m* television screen

tele'scopio *m* telescope

telescri'vente *f* telex [machine]

teleselet'tivo *adj* direct dialling

teleselezi'one *f* subscriber trunk dialling, STD; **chiamare in ~** call direct, dial direct
■ **teleselezione internazionale** international direct dialling

telespetta'tore, -trice *mf* viewer; **i telespettatori** the viewing public

tele'text *m* Teletext

'telethon *m inv* telethon

Tele'video *m* Teletext, Ceefax

televisi'one *f* television; **guardare la ~** watch television; **alla ~** on television
■ **televisione ad alta definizione** high-definition television; **televisione in bianco e nero** black and white television; **televisione via cavo** cable TV; **televisione a circuito chiuso** closed-circuit television, CCTV; **televisione a colori** colour television; **televisione satellitare** satellite television

televi'sivo *adj* television, TV *attrib*; **apparecchio ~** television set; **operatore ~** television cameraman

televi'sore *m* television [set], TV [set]
■ **televisore portatile** portable [TV], portable [television set]; **televisore con schermo panoramico** wide-screen TV

tele'voto *m* phone voting, phone vote

'telex **A** *m inv* telex
B *adj inv* telex *attrib*

tel'lurico *adj* telluric

'telo *m* [piece of] cloth
■ **telo da bagno** beach towel; **telo di salvataggio** rescue blanket

'tema *m* theme; Sch essay

te'matica *f* main theme

teme'rario *adj* reckless

✓ **te'mere** **A** *vt* be afraid of
B *vi* be afraid

tem'paccio *m* filthy weather

'tempera *f* tempera; (pittura) painting in tempera

temperama'tite *m inv* pencil sharpener

tempera'mento *m* temperament

tempe'rare *vt* temper; sharpen ‹*matita*›

tempe'rato *adj* temperate

✓ **tempera'tura** *f* temperature
■ **temperatura ambiente** room temperature

tempe'rino *m* penknife

tem'pesta *f* storm
■ **tempesta magnetica** magnetic storm; **tempesta di neve** snowstorm; **tempesta di sabbia** sandstorm

tempe'stare *vt* **~ qualcuno di colpi** rain blows on somebody; **~ qualcuno di domande** bombard somebody with questions

tempe'stato *adj* (anello, diadema) encrusted (**di** with)

tempestiva'mente *adv* quickly, in a short space of time

tempe'stivo *adj* timely, well-timed

tempe'stoso *adj* stormy

'tempia *f* Anat temple
'tempio *m* Relig temple
tem'pismo *m* timing
'tempo *m* time; (atmosferico) weather; Mus tempo; Gram tense; (di film) part; (di partita) half; **a suo ~** in due course; **~ fa** some time ago; **per molto ~, per tanto ~** for a long time; **tanto ~ fa** a long time ago; **un ~** once; **ha fatto il suo ~** it's out of date; **a ~ indeterminato** (contratto) permanent; **primo tempo** (di film, partita) first half
■ **tempo di accesso** Comput access time; **tempo di cottura** cooking time; **tempo di esposizione** Phot exposure time; **tempo libero** free time, leisure time; **tempo limite di accettazione** latest check-in time; **tempo di pace** peacetime; **tempo reale** Comput real time; **in tempo reale** real-time *attrib*; **tempo supplementare** extra time; Sport extra time, overtime AmE; **andare ai tempi supplementari** Sport go into extra time
tempo'rale **A** *adj* temporal
B *m* [thunder]storm
temporanea'mente *adv* temporarily
tempo'raneo *adj* temporary
temporeggi'are *vi* play for time
tem'prare *vt* form
te'nace *adj* tenacious, strong-willed
tenace'mente *adv* tenaciously
te'nacia *f* tenacity
te'naglia *f* pincers *pl*
'tenda *f* curtain; (per campeggio) tent; (tendone) awning; **tirare le tende** draw the curtains
■ **tenda della doccia** shower curtain; **tenda a igloo** dome tent; **tenda a ossigeno** oxygen tent
ten'denza *f* tendency
■ **tendenza al rialzo/ribasso** Fin bull/bear market
tendenzial'mente *adv* by nature
tendenzi'oso *adj* tendentious
'tendere **A** *vt* (allargare) stretch [out]; (tirare) tighten; (porgere) hold out; fig lay ‹*trappola*›
B *vi* **~ a** aim at; (essere portato a) tend to
'tendersi *vr* tauten
'tendine *m* tendon
■ **tendine d'Achille** Achilles tendon; **tendine del garretto** hamstring; **tendine del ginocchio** hamstring
ten'done *m* awning; (di circo) tent
■ **tendone del circo** big top
ten'dopoli *f inv* tent city
'tenebre *fpl* darkness
tene'broso **A** *adj* gloomy
B *m* **bel ~** dark and handsome man
te'nente *m* lieutenant
■ **tenente colonnello** wing commander
tenera'mente *adv* tenderly
te'nere **A** *vt* hold; (mantenere) keep; (gestire) run; (prendere) take; (seguire) follow; (considerare) consider
B *vi* hold; **~ stretto** hold tight; **~ a qualcosa** (oggetto) be fond of something; **tengo alla sua presenza** I very much want him to be there; **~ per** (squadra) support
tene'rezza *f* tenderness
'tenero *adj* tender
tene'rone, -a *mf* softie
te'nersi *vr* hold on (**a** to); (in una condizione) keep oneself; **~ indietro** stand back
'tenia *f* tapeworm
'tennis *m* tennis
■ **tennis da tavolo** table tennis
ten'nista *mf* tennis player
te'nore *m* standard; Mus tenor; **a ~ di legge** by law
■ **tenore di vita** standard of living
tensi'one *f* tension; Electr voltage; **mettere sotto ~** energize; **in ~** under stress
■ **alta tensione** high voltage; **tensione premestruale** premenstrual tension, PMT
ten'tacolo *m* tentacle
ten'tare *vt* attempt; (sperimentare) try; (indurre in tentazione) tempt; **~ la strada di** make a foray *or* venture into
tenta'tivo *m* attempt
ten'tato *adj* **~ suicidio** suicide attempt
tentazi'one *f* temptation
tentenna'mento *m* wavering; **ha avuto dei tentennamenti** he wavered a bit
tenten'nare *vi* waver
ten'toni *adv* **cercare qualcosa a ~** grope for something
'tenue *adj* fine; (debole) weak; (esiguo) small; (leggero) slight
te'nuta *f* (capacità) capacity; Sport; (resistenza) stamina; (possedimento) estate; (divisa) uniform; (abbigliamento) clothes *pl*; **a ~ d'aria** airtight
■ **tenuta di strada** road holding
teolo'gia *f* theology
teo'logico *adj* theological
te'ologo *m* theologian
teo'rema *m* theorem
teo'ria *f* theory
■ **teoria del complotto** conspiracy theory
teorica'mente *adv* theoretically
te'orico *adj* theoretical
te'pore *m* warmth
'teppa *f* mob
tep'pismo *m* hooliganism
tep'pista *m* hooligan, yob infml
te'quila *f inv* tequila
tera'peutico *adj* therapeutic
tera'pia *f* therapy; **in ~** in therapy
■ **terapia genica** gene therapy; **terapia di gruppo** group therapy; **terapia intensiva** critical care; **terapia ormonale sostitutiva** hormone replacement therapy, HRT; **terapia**

key word

t

d'urto shock treatment

tergicri'stallo *m* windscreen wiper, windshield wiper AmE

tergilu'notto *m* rear windscreen wiper

tergiver'sante *adj* equivocating, pussyfooting infml

tergiver'sare *vi* equivocate, pussyfoot around infml

'tergo *m* **a ~** behind; **segue a ~** please turn over, PTO

teri'lene® *m* Terylene®

'terital® *m* Terylene®

ter'male *adj* thermal; **stazione ~** spa

'terme *fpl* thermal baths

'termico *adj* thermal; **borsa termica** cool bag

'terminal *m inv* air terminal

termi'nale *adj & nm* terminal; **malato ~** terminally ill person

termina'lista *mf* computer operator

termi'nare *vt & vi* end, finish

terminazi'one *f* (fine) termination; Gram ending

■ **terminazione nervosa** nerve ending

'termine *m* (limite) limit; (fine) end; (condizione, parola) term; (scadenza) deadline; **ai termini della legge...** under the terms of act...; **contratto a ~** fixed-term contract

■ **termine di paragone** Gram term of comparison; **termine ultimo** final deadline

terminolo'gia *f* terminology

'termite *f* termite

termoco'perta *f* electric blanket

termogra'fia *f* thermal imaging

ter'mometro *m* thermometer

'termos *m inv* thermos®

termosi'fone *m* radiator; (sistema) central heating

ter'mostato *m* thermostat

termotera'pia *f* Med heat treatment

termovalorizza'tore *m* waste-to-energy plant

termoventila'tore *m* fan heater

'terra *f* earth; (regione) land; (terreno) ground; (argilla) clay; (cosmetico) bronzing powder; **a ~** (sulla costa) ashore; (installazioni) onshore; **essere a ~** (gomma) be flat; fig be at rock bottom; **per ~** on the ground; (su pavimento) on the floor; **sotto ~** underground; **far ~ bruciata** carry out a scorched earth policy

■ **terra promessa** Promised Land; **Terra Santa** Holy Land; **terra di Siena** sienna

terra'cotta *f* terracotta; **vasellame di ~** earthenware

terra'ferma *f* dry land

Terra'nova *f* Newfoundland

terrapi'eno *m* embankment

ter'razza *f*, **ter'razzo** *m* balcony

terremo'tato, -a **A** *adj* (zona) affected by an earthquake

B *mf* earthquake victim

terre'moto *m* earthquake

ter'reno **A** *adj* earthly

B *m* ground; (suolo) soil; (proprietà terriera) land; **perdere/guadagnare ~** lose/gain ground

■ **terreno alluvionale** alluvial soil; **terreno di bonifica** reclaimed land; **terreno boschivo** woodland; **terreno edificabile** building land; **terreno di gioco** playing field; **terreno di scontro** battlefield

ter'restre *adj* terrestrial; (superficie, diametro) of the earth; **esercito ~** land forces *pl*

ter'ribile *adj* terrible

terribil'mente *adv* terribly

ter'riccio *m* potting compost

'terrier *m inv* terrier

terri'ero *adj* (proprietario) land *attrib*; (aristocrazia) landed; **proprietà** *pl* **terriere** landed property

terrifi'cante *adj* terrifying

territori'ale *adj* territorial; **acque territoriali** territorial waters

terri'torio *m* territory

ter'rone, -a *mf* derog bloody Southerner

ter'rore *m* terror

terro'rismo *m* terrorism

terro'rista *mf* terrorist

terroriz'zare *vt* terrorize

'terso *adj* clear

'terza *f* (marcia) third [gear]

ter'zetto *m* trio

terzi'ario **A** *adj* tertiary

B *m* service sector, tertiary sector

'terzo **A** *adj* third; **di terz'ordine** (locale, servizio) third-rate; **fare il ~ grado a qualcuno** give somebody the third degree; **la terza età** the third age; **il ~ mondo** the Third World

■ **terzo settore** voluntary sector

B *m* third; **terzi** *pl* Jur third party

terzo'genito, -a *mf* third-born

ter'zultimo, -a *adj & n* third from last

'tesa *f* brim

'teschio *m* skull

'tesi *f inv* thesis

'teso **A** pp di **tendere**

B *adj* taut; fig tense

tesore'ria *f* treasury

tesori'ere *m* treasurer

te'soro *m* treasure; (tesoreria) treasury; **ministro del Tesoro** Finance Minister; Chancellor of the Exchequer BrE

'tessera *f* card; (abbonamento all'autobus) season ticket; (di club) membership card

■ **tessera magnetica** swipe card; **tessera dei trasporti pubblici** travel card; **tessera di sconto** discount card

'tessere *vt* weave; hatch ‹*complotto*›; **~ le lodi di qualcosa** sing the praises of something

tesse'rino *m* travel card
'tessile **A** *adj* textile
B *m* **tessili** *pl* textiles; (operai) textile workers
tessi|'tore, -trice *mf* weaver
tessi'tura *f* weaving
tes'suto **A** pp di **tessere**
B *adj* woven; **~ a mano** hand-woven
C *m* fabric, material; Anat tissue
■ **tessuto sintetico** synthetic material; **tessuto di spugna** terry towelling
'test *m inv* test; **test genetici** *pl* genetic testing
■ **test alcolimetrico** alcohol test; **test del DNA** DNA test
⚷ **'testa** *f* head; (cervello) brain; **essere in ~ a** be ahead of; **in ~** Sport in the lead; **~ o croce?** heads or tails?; **fare a ~ o croce** spin a coin, toss a coin; **andare a ~ alta** hold one's head up
■ **testa di rapa** infml pinhead; **testa di sbarco** beachhead; **testa di serie** (squadra) seeded team; **testa del treno** front of the train
testa-'coda *m inv* **fare un ~** spin right round
testa'mento *m* will
■ **testamento biologico** living will; **Antico Testamento** Relig Old Testament; **Nuovo Testamento** Relig New Testament
testar'daggine *f* stubbornness
testarda'mente *adv* stubbornly
te'stardo *adj* stubborn
te'stare *vt* test
te'stata *f* head; (intestazione) heading; (colpo) [head]butt
■ **testata nucleare** nuclear warhead
'teste *mf* witness
'tester *m inv* tester
te'sticolo *m* testicle
testi'mone *mf* witness; **essere ~ di qualcosa** witness something
■ **testimone di Geova** Jehovah's Witness; **testimone oculare** eye witness
testi'monial *mf inv celebrity who endorses a product*
testimoni'anza *f* testimony; **falsa ~** Jur perjury
testimoni'are **A** *vt* testify to
B *vi* testify, give evidence
te'stina *f* head; (di stampante) printhead
■ **testina di cancellazione** Comput erase head; **testina di lettura** Comput read head; **testina rotante** (di macchina da scrivere) golf ball; **testina di vitello** Culin calf's head
'testo *m* text; **far ~** be authoritative; **con ~ a fronte** (traduzione) with the original text on the opposite page
te'stone, -a *mf* blockhead
testoste'rone *m* testosterone
testu'ale *adj* textual

⚷ key word

'tetano *m* tetanus
te'traggine *f* bleakness
tetra'pak® *m inv* tetrapak
'tetro *adj* bleak
tetta'rella *f* teat
⚷ **'tetto** *m* roof; **abbandono del ~ coniugale** Jur desertion
■ **tetto apribile** (di auto) sun[shine] roof; **tetto a terrazza** flat roof
tet'toia *f* roofing
tet'tuccio *m*
■ **tettuccio apribile** sun-roof
teu'tonico *adj* Teutonic
'Tevere *m* Tiber
TFR *nm abbr* (**trattamento di fine rapporto**) severance pay
tg, TG *nm abbr* (**telegiornale**) (television) news
⚷ **ti** *pers pron* you; (riflessivo) yourself; **ti ha dato un libro** he gave you a book; **lavati le mani** wash your hands; **eccoti!** here you are!; **sbrigati!** hurry up!
ti'ara *f* tiara
'Tibet *m* Tibet
tic *m inv* tic
ticchet'tare *vi* tick
ticchet'tio *m* ticking
'ticchio *m* tic; (ghiribizzo) whim
'ticket *m inv* (per farmaco, analisi) prescription charges (*amount paid by National Health patients*)
tie-break *m inv* tie break[er]
tiepida'mente *adv* half-heartedly
ti'epido *adj* lukewarm; fig half-hearted
ti'fare *vi* **~ per** be a fan of
'tifo *m* Med typhus; **fare il ~ per** (appoggiare) be a fan of
tifoi'dea *f* typhoid
ti'fone *m* typhoon
ti'foso, -a *mf* fan
tight *m inv* morning dress
'tiglio *m* lime
'tigna *f* ringworm
ti'grato *adj* **gatto ~** tabby [cat]
'tigre *f* tiger
'tilde *mf* tilde
tim'ballo *m* Culin pie
tim'brare *vt* stamp; **~ il cartellino** (all'entrata) clock in; (all'uscita) clock out
'timbro *m* stamp; (di voce) tone
■ **timbro a secco** embossing stamp
time out *m inv* Sport time out
'timer *m inv* timer
timida'mente *adv* timidly, shyly
timi'dezza *f* timidity, shyness
'timido *adj* timid, shy
'timo *m* thyme
ti'mone *m* rudder
■ **timone di direzione** (di aereo) rudder; **timone**

di quota (di aereo) elevator

timoni'ere *m* helmsman

timo'rato *adj* ~ **di Dio** God-fearing

ti'more *m* fear; (soggezione) awe

'Timor 'Est *m* East Timor

timo'roso *adj* timorous

'timpano *m* eardrum; Mus kettledrum; **timpani** *pl* Mus timpani, kettledrums; **rompere i timpani a qualcuno** fig shatter somebody's eardrums

ti'nello *m* dining room

'tingere *vt* dye; (macchiare) stain

'tingersi *vr* (viso, cielo) be tinged (**di** with); ~ **i capelli** have one's hair dyed; (da solo) dye one's hair

'tino *m*, **ti'nozza** *f* tub

'tinta *f* dye; (colore) colour; **in** ~ **unita** plain, self-coloured

tinta'rella *f* infml suntan

tintin'nare *vi* tinkle

'tinto pp di **tingere**

tinto'ria *f* (negozio) cleaner's

tin'tura *f* dyeing; (colorante) dye

■ **tintura di iodio** iodine

tipica'mente *adv* typically

'tipico *adj* typical

'tipo *m* type; infml (individuo) chap, guy

tipogra'fia *f* printer's; (arte) typography

tipo'grafico *adj* typographic[al]

ti'pografo *m* printer

tip tap *m* tap dancing

ti'raggio *m* draught

tiranneggi'are *vt* tyrannize

tiran'nia *f* tyranny

ti'ranno, -a **A** *adj* tyrannical
B *mf* tyrant

tiranno'sauro *m* tyrannosaurus

ti'rante *m* rope

tirapi'edi *m inv* derog hanger-on

tira'pugni *m inv* knuckle-duster

ti'rare **A** *vt* pull; (gettare) throw; (nel calcio) kick; (tracciare) draw; (stampare) print; infml land ‹*calci, pugni*›
B *vi* pull; (vento) blow; (abito) be tight; (sparare) fire; ~ **avanti** fig get by; ~ **su** bring up ‹*figli*›; (da terra) pick up; **tirar su [col naso]** sniffle

ti'rarsi *vr* ~ **indietro** fig back out, pull out

tiras'segno *m* target shooting; (alla fiera) rifle range

ti'rata *f* (strattone) pull, tug; **in una** ~ in one go; **dare a qualcuno una** ~ **d'orecchi** fig give somebody a telling off

tira'tore *m* shot

■ **tiratore scelto** marksman

tira'tura *f* printing; (di giornali) circulation; (di libri) [print] run

tirchie'ria *f* meanness

'tirchio *adj* mean

tiri'tera *f* spiel

'tiro *m* (lancio) throw; (azione) throwing; (sparo) shot; (azione) shooting; (scherzo) trick; **cavallo da** ~ draught horse

■ **tiro con l'arco** archery; **tiro al bersaglio** target practice; **tiro alla fune** tug of war; **tiro al piattello** clay pigeon shooting; **tiro in porta** shot at goal; **tiro a segno** rifle range

tiroci'nante *mf* trainee

tiro'cinio *m* training

ti'roide *f* thyroid

Tir'reno *m* **il [mar]** ~ the Tyrrhenian Sea

ti'sana *f* herb[al] tea

'tisi *f* consumption

ti'tanio *m* titanium

tito'lare **A** *adj* permanent
B *mf* (proprietario) owner; (calcio) regular player; Jur (di diritto) holder

'titolo *m* title; (accademico) qualification; Comm security; **a** ~ **di** as; **a** ~ **di favore** as a favour; **titoli** *pl* (di giornale, telegiornale) headlines

■ **titoli di coda** closing credits; **titolo di credito** credit instrument; **titolo mondiale** world title; **titolo obbligazionario** bond; **titoli delle principali notizie** *pl* news headlines; **titolo in sovrimpressione** superimposed title; **titolo di Stato** government security; **titoli di studio** *pl* qualifications; **titoli di testa** *pl* Cinema, TV opening credits; **titolo a tutta pagina** banner headline

titu'bante *adj* hesitant

titu'banza *f* hesitation

titu'bare *vi* hesitate

tivù *f inv* infml TV, telly

'tizio, -a **A** *m* so-and-so; **un** ~ some man
B *f* **una tizia** some woman

tiz'zone *m* brand

toc'cante *adj* touching

toc'care **A** *vt* touch; touch on ‹*argomento*›; (tastare) feel; (riguardare) concern
B *vi* ~ **a** (capitare) happen to; **mi tocca aspettare** I'll have to wait; **tocca a te** it's your turn; (a pagare da bere) it's your round; **'non** ~**'** 'please do not touch'

tocca'sana *m inv* panacea

toc'cato *adj* infml (matto) touched

'tocco **A** *m* touch; (di pennello, orologio) stroke; (di pane ecc.) chunk; **il** ~ **finale** the finishing touches
B *adj* infml crazy, touched

toc 'toc *m inv* knock, knock

'toga *f* toga; (accademica, di magistrato) gown

'togliere *vt* take off ‹*coperta*›; Math (da scuola) take away; quench ‹*sete*›; take out, remove ‹*tonsille, dente ecc.*›; ~ **qualcosa di mano a qualcuno** take something away from somebody; ~ **qualcuno dai guai** get somebody out of trouble; **ciò non toglie che...** nevertheless..., the fact remains that...; **farsi** ~ **le tonsille** have one's tonsils

t

[taken] out

'togliersi *vr* take off ‹*abito*›; ~ **la vita** take one's [own] life; ~ **di mezzo** get out of the way; **togliti dai piedi!** get out of the way!

'Togo *m* Togo

toi'lette *f inv* toilet; (mobile) dressing table

to'letta *f* toilet; (mobile) dressing table

tolle'rante *adj* tolerant

tolle'ranza *f* tolerance; **casa di** ~ brothel

tolle'rare *vt* tolerate

'tolto pp di **togliere**

to'maia *f* upper

'tomba *f* grave

tom'bino *m* manhole cover

'tombola *f* bingo; (caduta) tumble

to'mino *m* goat cheese

'tomo *m* tome

tomogra'fia *f* Med tomography
■ **tomografia assiale computerizzata** computerized axial tomography, CAT

'tonaca *f* habit

to'nale *adj* tonal

tonalità *f inv* Mus tonality

to'nante *adj* booming

'tondo **A** *adj* (cifra) round
B *m* circle

'toner *m inv* toner

'tonfo *m* thud; (in acqua) splash

'Tonga *f* Tonga

'tonica *f* Mus keynote

'tonico **A** *adj* (sillaba) stressed; (muscoli) well toned
B *m* tonic

tonifi'care *vt* tone up ‹*muscoli*›

ton'nara *f* tuna-fishing net

ton'nato *adj* **vitello** ~ *veal with a tuna and mayonnaise sauce*

tonnel'laggio *m* tonnage

tonnel'lata *f* ton
■ **tonnellata corta americana** short ton, net ton

'tonno *m* tuna [fish]

'tono *m* tone

ton'sille *fpl* tonsils

tonsil'lite *f* tonsillitis

'tonto *adj* infml thick

top *m inv* (indumento) sun-top

to'pazio *m* topaz

'topless *m inv* **in** ~ topless

top 'model *f inv* supermodel, top model

'topo *m* mouse
■ **topo di albergo/appartamento** *thief in a hotel/block of flats*; **topo di biblioteca** bookworm; **topo domestico** domestic mouse

topogra'fia *f* topography

topo'grafico *adj* topographic[al]

to'ponimo *m* place name

topo'ragno *m* shrew

'toppa *f* (rattoppo) patch; (serratura) keyhole

to'race *m* chest

to'racico *adj* thoracic; **gabbia toracica** rib cage

'torba *f* peat

'torbido *adj* cloudy; fig troubled

'torcere *vt* twist; wring [out] ‹*biancheria*›

'torcersi *vr* twist

'torchio *m* press

'torcia *f* torch
■ **torcia elettrica** torch

torci'collo *m* stiff neck

'tordo *m* thrush

to'rero *m* bullfighter

To'rino *f* Turin

tor'menta *f* snowstorm

tormen'tare *vt* torment

tormen'tato *adj* tormented

tor'mento *m* torment

tormen'tone *m* (frase) catchphrase; (argomento) *constantly repeated topic*; (canzone) *catchy song that is constantly played on the radio*

torna'conto *m* benefit

tor'nado *m* tornado

tor'nante *m* hairpin bend

tor'nare *vi* return, go/come back; (ridiventare) become again; ‹*conto*› add up; ~ **a sorridere** smile again; ~ **su** go back up

tor'neo *m* tournament

'tornio *m* lathe

'torno *m* **togliersi di** ~ get out of the way

'toro *m* bull; Astr Taurus

tor'pedine *f* torpedo

torpedini'era *f* torpedo boat

tor'pore *m* torpor

'torre *f* tower; (scacchi) castle
■ **torre d'avorio** ivory tower; **torre di controllo** control tower; **torre di osservazione** observation tower; **torre pendente, torre di Pisa** Leaning Tower of Pisa

torrefazi'one *f* roasting; (negozio) coffee retailer

tor'rente *m* torrent, mountain stream; fig (di lacrime) flood; fig (di parole) torrent

torrenzi'ale *adj* torrential; **in regime** ~ in spate

tor'retta *f* turret

'torrido *adj* torrid, sweltering

torri'one *m* keep

tor'rone *m* nougat

torsi'one *f* twisting; (in ginnastica) twist

'torso *m* torso; (di mela, pera) core; **a** ~ **nudo** bare chested

'torsolo *m* core

'torta *f* cake; (crostata) tart
■ **torta di compleanno** birthday cake; **torta di mele** apple tart; **torta nuziale** wedding cake;

key word

torta pasqualina spinach pie
torti'era *f* cake tin
tor'tino *m* pie
'torto **A** pp di **torcere**
B *adj* twisted
C *m* wrong; (colpa) fault; **aver ~** be wrong; **a ~** wrongly; **far ~ a qualcuno** wrong somebody; fig not do somebody justice; **non hai tutti i torti** you're not altogether wrong
'tortora *f* turtle dove
tortuosa'mente *adv* tortuously
tortu'oso *adj* winding; (ambiguo) tortuous
tor'tura *f* torture
tortu'rare *vt* torture
'torvo *adj* (sguardo) menacing
tosa'erba *m inv* lawnmower
to'sare *vt* shear
tosasi'epi *m inv* hedge trimmer
tosa'tura *f* shearing
To'scana *f* Tuscany
to'scano, **-a** *adj & nmf* Tuscan
'tosse *f* cough
'tossico **A** *adj* toxic
B *m* poison
tossicodipen'denza *f* drug addiction, drug habit
tossi'comane *mf* drug addict, drug user
tos'sire *vi* cough
tosta'pane *m inv* toaster
■ **tostapane a espulsione automatica** pop-up toaster
to'stare *vt* toast ‹*pane*›; roast ‹*caffe*›
'tosto **A** *adv* (subito) soon
B *adj* infml cool; **faccia tosta** cheek
tot **A** *adj inv* **una cifra ~** such and such a figure
B *m* **un ~** so much
to'tale *adj & nm* total
■ **totale complessivo** grand total; **totale parziale** subtotal
totalità *f inv* entirety; **la ~ dei presenti** all those present
totali'tario *adj* totalitarian
totaliz'zare *vt* total; score ‹*punti*›
totalizza'tore *m* (per scommesse) totalizer, tote
total'mente *adv* totally
'totano *m* squid
'totem *m inv* totem pole
toto'calcio *m* [football] pools *pl*
'touche *f inv* touch line
tou'pet *m inv* toupee
tournée *f inv* tour
to'vaglia *f* tablecloth
tovagli'etta *f*
■ **tovaglietta [all'americana]** place mat
tovagli'olo *m* napkin
■ **tovagliolo di carta** paper napkin
'tozzo *adj* squat
■ **tozzo di pane** stale piece of bread

tra = **fra**
trabal'lante *adj* staggering; (sedia) rickety, wonky
trabal'lare *vi* stagger; (veicolo) jolt
tra'biccolo *m* infml contraption; (auto) jalopy
traboc'care *vi* overflow
traboc'chetto *m* trap
traca'gnotto *adj* dumpy
tracan'nare *vt* gulp down
'traccia *f* track; (orma) footstep; (striscia) trail; (residuo) trace; fig sign
tracci'are *vt* trace; sketch out ‹*schema*›; draw ‹*linea*›
tracci'ato *m* (schema) layout
■ **tracciato di gara** circuit
tra'chea *f* windpipe, trachea
tra'colla *f* shoulder strap; **borsa a ~** shoulder bag
tra'collo *m* collapse
tradi'mento *m* betrayal; Pol treason; **alto ~** high treason
tra'dire *vt* betray; be unfaithful to ‹*moglie, marito*›
tradi|'tore, **-trice** *mf* traitor
tradizio'nale *adj* traditional
tradiziona'lista *mf* traditionalist
tradizional'mente *adv* traditionally
tradizi'one *f* tradition
tra'dotto pp di **tradurre**
tra'durre *vt* translate
tradut|'tore, **-trice** *mf* translator
■ **traduttore elettronico** electronic phrase book
traduzi'one *f* translation
■ **traduzione consecutiva** consecutive interpreting; **traduzione simultanea** simultaneous interpreting
tra'ente *mf* Comm drawer
trafe'lato *adj* breathless
traffi'cante *mf* dealer, trafficker
■ **trafficante d'armi** arms dealer; **trafficante di droga** drug dealer
traffi'care *vi* (affaccendarsi) busy oneself; **~ in** derog traffic in
'traffico *m* traffic; Comm trade
■ **traffico aereo** air traffic; **traffico della droga** drug trafficking; **traffico ferroviario** rail traffic; **traffico di stupefacenti** drug trafficking
traffi'cone, **-a** *mf* infml wheeler dealer
tra'figgere *vt* penetrate, pierce; fig pierce
tra'fila *f* fig rigmarole
trafi'letto *m* minor news item
trafo'rare *vt* bore, drill
tra'foro *m* boring, drilling; (galleria) tunnel; **lavoro di ~** fretwork
trafu'gare *vt* steal
tra'gedia *f* tragedy
traghet'tare *vt* ferry
tra'ghetto *m* ferrying; (nave) ferry

tragica'mente *adv* tragically
'tragico **A** *adj* tragic
B *m* (autore) tragedian
tra'gitto *m* journey; (per mare) crossing
tragu'ardo *m* finishing post; (meta) goal
traiet'toria *f* trajectory
trai'nare *vt* drag; (rimorchiare) tow
tralasci'are *vt* interrupt; (omettere) leave out; ~ **di fare qualcosa** fail to do something, omit to do something
'tralcio *m* Bot shoot
tra'liccio *m* (tela) ticking; (graticcio) trellis
tra'lice **in** ~ *adv* (tagliare) on the slant; (guardare) sideways
tralu'cente *adj* shining
tram *m inv* tram, streetcar AmE
'trama *f* weft; (di film ecc.) plot
traman'dare *vt* hand down
tra'mare *vt* weave; (macchinare) plot
tram'busto *m* turmoil
trame'stio *m* bustle
tramez'zino *m* sandwich
tra'mezzo *m* partition
'tramite **A** *prep* through
B *m* link; **con il** ~ **di** by means of; **fare da** ~ act as go-between
tramon'tana *f* north wind
tramon'tare *vi* set; (declinare) decline
⚷ **tra'monto** *m* sunset; (declino) decline
tramor'tire **A** *vt* stun
B *vi* faint
trampoli'ere *m* wader
trampo'lino *m* springboard; (per lo sci) ski jump
■ **trampolino di lancio** fig launch pad
'trampolo *m* stilt
tramu'tare *vt* transform
trance *f inv* trance; **essere in** ~ be in a trance
'trancia *f* shears *pl*; (fetta) slice
tra'nello *m* trap
trangugi'are *vt* gulp down
'tranne *prep* except
tranquilla'mente *adv* peacefully
tranquil'lante *m* tranquillizer
tranquillità *f inv* calm; (di spirito) tranquillity
tranquilliz'zare *vt* reassure
⚷ **tran'quillo** *adj* quiet; (pacifico) peaceful; (coscienza) easy; **stai** ~ **!** (non preoccuparti) don't worry!
transa'tlantico **A** *adj* transatlantic
B *m* ocean liner
tran'satto pp di **transigere**
transazi'one *f* Comm transaction; Jur settlement
tran'senna *f* (barriera) barrier
transessu'ale *mf* transsexual

⚷ key word

tran'setto *m* transept
'transfert *m inv* Psych transference
tran'sigere *vi* Jur reach a settlement; (cedere) compromise
tran'sistor *m inv* infml transistor [radio]
transi'tabile *adj* passable
transi'tare *vi* pass
transi'tivo *adj* transitive
'transito *m* transit; **'divieto di** ~**'** 'no thoroughfare'; **diritto di** ~ right of way
■ **'transito alterno'** 'temporary one-way system'
transi'torio *adj* transitory
transizi'one *f* transition; **di** ~ transitional
tran'tran *m* infml routine
tranvi'ere *m* tram driver, streetcar driver AmE
'trapano *m* drill
■ **trapano elettrico** electric drill
trapas'sare **A** *vt* pierce, penetrate
B *vi* (morire) pass away
trapas'sato *m* pluperfect
tra'passo *m* passage
trape'lare *vi anche* fig leak out
tra'pezio *m* trapeze; Math trapezium
trapian'tare *vt* transplant
trapi'anto *m* transplant
■ **trapianto di cuore** heart transplant
'trappola *f* trap
tra'punta *f* quilt
'trarre *vt* draw; (ricavare) obtain; ~ **in inganno** deceive
trasa'lire *vi* start
trasan'dato *adj* shabby
trasbor'dare **A** *vt* transfer; Naut trans-ship
B *vi* change
tra'sbordo *m* trans-shipment
trascenden'tale *adj* transcendental
tra'scendere **A** *vt* transcend
B *vi* (eccedere) go too far
⚷ **trasci'nare** *vt* drag; fig (entusiasmo) carry away; ~ **e rilasciare** Comput drag and drop
trasci'narsi *vr* drag oneself; (camminare piano) dawdle
⚷ **tra'scorrere** **A** *vt* spend
B *vi* pass
tra'scritto pp di **trascrivere**
tra'scrivere *vt* transcribe
trascrizi'one *f* transcription
trascu'rabile *adj* negligible
trascu'rare *vt* neglect; (non tenere conto di) disregard
trascurata'mente *adv* carelessly
trascura'tezza *f* negligence
trascu'rato *adj* negligent; (curato male) neglected; (nel vestire) slovenly
traseco'lato *adj* amazed
trasferi'mento *m* transfer; (trasloco) move
■ **trasferimento automatico** direct debit;

t

trasferimento bancario bank transfer
trasfe'rire *vt* transfer
trasfe'rirsi *vr* move
tra'sferta *f* transfer; (indennità) subsistence allowance; Sport away match; **in ~** (impiegato) on secondment; **giocare in ~** play away
trasfigu'rare *vt* transfigure
trasfor'mare *vt* transform; (in rugby) convert
trasfor'marsi *vr* be transformed; **~ in** turn into
trasforma'tore *m* transformer
trasformazi'one *f* transformation; (in rugby) conversion
trasfor'mista *mf* (artista) quick-change artist
trasfusi'one *f* transfusion
trasgre'dire *vt* disobey; Jur infringe
trasgredi'trice *f* transgressor
trasgressi'one *f* infringement; (di ordine) failure to obey
trasgres'sivo *adj* intended to shock
trasgres'sore *m* transgressor
tra'slato *adj* metaphorical
traslitte'rare *vt* transliterate
traslo'care **A** *vt* move
B *vi* move [house]
traslo'carsi *vr* move [house]
tra'sloco *m* move; **compagnia di ~** removal company
tra'smesso pp di **trasmettere**
tra'smettere *vt* pass on; TV, Radio broadcast; Techn, Med transmit
trasmetti'tore *m* transmitter
trasmis'sibile *adj* transmissible
trasmissi'one *f* transmission; TV, Radio programme
■ **trasmissione dati** data transmission; **trasmissione via fax** fax transmission; **trasmissione radiofonica** radio programme; **trasmissione remota** remote transmission; **trasmissione televisiva** television programme
trasmit'tente **A** *m* transmitter
B *f* broadcasting station
traso'gnare *vi* day-dream
traso'gnato *adj* dreamy
traspa'rente *adj* transparent
traspa'renza *f* transparency; **in ~** against the light
traspa'rire *vi* show [through]
traspi'rare *vi* perspire; fig transpire
traspirazi'one *f* perspiration
tra'sporre *vt* transpose
traspor'tare *vt* transport; **lasciarsi ~ da** get carried away by; **~ con ponte aereo** airlift
traspor'tato *adj* transported; **~ dall'aria** airborne
trasporta'tore *m* conveyor; (società) transport company, road haulier
tra'sporto *m* transport; fig (passione) passion; **ministro dei trasporti** Ministry of Transport
■ **trasporto aereo** air freight; **trasporto ferroviario** rail transport; **trasporto pesante** heavy goods transport; **trasporti pubblici** *pl* public transport; **trasporto stradale** road transport, road haulage
trastul'lare *vt* amuse
trastul'larsi *vr* amuse oneself; (perdere tempo) fool around
trasu'dare **A** *vt* ooze [with]
B *vi* ooze
trasver'sale *adj* transverse; **strada ~** cross street
trasversal'mente *adv* widthways
trasvo'lare **A** *vt* fly over
B *vi* **~ su** fig skim over
trasvo'lata *f* crossing [by air]
'tratta *f* (traffico illegale) trade; Comm draft
■ **tratta bancaria** Fin banker's draft; **tratta delle bianche** white slave trade; **tratta documentaria** documentary bill
trat'tabile *adj* or nearest offer, o.n.o.
tratta'mento *m* treatment
■ **trattamento automatico delle informazioni** electronic data processing, EDP; **trattamento di bellezza** beauty treatment; **trattamento di fine rapporto** severance pay; **trattamento dell'immagine** image processing; **trattamento di riguardo** special treatment
trat'tante *adj* conditioning
trat'tare **A** *vt* treat; (commerciare in) deal in; (negoziare) negotiate
B *vi* **~ di** deal with
trat'tario *m* Comm drawee
trat'tarsi *vr* **di che si tratta?** what's it about?; **si tratta di...** it's about...
tratta'tive *fpl* negotiations; **il tavolo delle ~** the negotiating table
trat'tato *m* treaty; (opera scritta) treatise
■ **trattato di pace** peace treaty
tratteggi'are *vt* outline; (descrivere) sketch
tratte'nere *vt* (far restare) keep; hold ‹*respiro, in questura*›; hold back ‹*lacrime, riso*›; (frenare) restrain; (da paga) withhold; **sono stato trattenuto** (ritardato) I got held up
tratte'nersi *vr* restrain oneself; (fermarsi) stay; **~ su** (indugiare) dwell on
tratteni'mento *m* entertainment; (ricevimento) party
tratte'nuta *f* deduction
trat'tino *m* dash; (in parole composte) hyphen
'tratto **A** pp di **trarre**
B *m* (di spazio, tempo) stretch; (di penna) stroke; (linea) line; (brano) passage; **tratti** *pl* (lineamenti) features; **a tratti** at intervals; **ad un ~** suddenly
trat'tore *m* tractor
tratto'ria *f* restaurant

'trauma *m* trauma
trau'matico *adj* traumatic
traumatiz'zante *adj* traumatic
traumatiz'zare *vt* traumatize
tra'vaglio *m* labour; (angoscia) anguish
trava'sare *vt* decant
tra'vaso *m* decanting
trava'tura *f* beams *pl*
'trave *f* beam
■ **trave a sbalzo** cantilever
tra'veggole *fpl* **avere le ~** be seeing things
'travellers cheque *m inv* traveller's cheque
tra'versa *f* (nel calcio) crossbar; **è una ~ di via Roma** it's off via Roma, it crosses via Roma
traver'sare *vt* cross
traver'sata *f* crossing
traver'sie *fpl* misfortunes
traver'sina *f* Rail sleeper
tra'verso **A** *adj* crosswise
B *adv* **di ~** crossways; **andare di ~** (cibo) go down the wrong way; **camminare di ~** not walk in a straight line; **guardare qualcuno di ~** look askance at somebody; **sapere per vie traverse** infml find out indirectly
traver'sone *m* (in calcio) cross
travesti'mento *m* disguise
trave'stire *vt* disguise
trave'stirsi *vr* disguise oneself
travesti'tismo *m* transvestism, cross-dressing
trave'stito **A** *adj* disguised
B *m* transvestite
travi'are *vt* lead astray
travisa'mento *m* distortion
travi'sare *vt* distort
travol'gente *adj* overwhelming
tra'volgere *vt* sweep away; (sopraffare) overwhelm
tra'volto pp di **travolgere**
trazi'one *f* traction
■ **trazione anteriore/posteriore** front-/rear-wheel drive
⚷ **tre** *adj & nm* three
tre'alberi *m inv* three-masted ship, three master
trebbi'are *vt* thresh
trebbia'trice *f* threshing machine
'treccia *f* plait, braid; (in maglia) cable; **a trecce** cable *attrib*
tre'cento *adj & nm* three hundred; **il Trecento** the fourteenth century
tredi'cesima *f extra month's salary paid as a Christmas bonus*
tredi'cesimo, -a *adj & nm* thirteenth

⚷ **'tredici** *adj & nm* thirteen
'tregua *f* truce; fig respite
'trekking *m* trekking
tre'mante *adj* trembling, quivering; (per il freddo) shivering
⚷ **tre'mare** *vi* tremble, quiver; (di freddo) shiver
trema'rella *f* infml jitters *pl*
tremenda'mente *adv* terribly, tremendously
tre'mendo *adj* terrible, tremendous; **ho una fame tremenda** I'm terribly hungry
tremen'tina *f* turpentine
tre'mila *adj & nm* three thousand
'tremito *m* tremble, quiver; (per il freddo) shiver
tremo'lare *vi* shake; (luce) flicker
tre'more *m* trembling
'tremulo *adj* tremulous
tre'nino *m* miniature railway
⚷ **'treno** *m* train
■ **treno merci** freight train, goods train; **treno navetta** shuttle; **treno passeggeri** passenger train; **treno postale** mail train; **treno straordinario** special train
⚷ **'trenta** *adj & nm* thirty
■ **trenta e lode** Univ first-class honours
trentatré 'giri *m inv* LP
tren'tenne *adj & nmf* thirty year-old
tren'tesimo *adj & nm* thirtieth
tren'tina *f* **una ~ di** about thirty
trepi'dare *vi* be anxious
'trepido *adj* anxious
treppi'ede *m* tripod
'tresca *f* intrigue; (amorosa) affair
'trespolo *m* perch
triango'lare *adj* triangular
tri'angolo *m* triangle
■ **triangolo delle Bermude** Bermuda Triangle; **triangolo equilatero** equilateral triangle; **triangolo isoscele** isosceles triangle; **triangolo rettangolo** right-angled triangle; **triangolo di segnalazione** warning triangle
tri'bale *adj* tribal
tribo'lare *vi* (soffrire) suffer; (fare fatica) go to a lot of trouble
tribolazi'one *f* suffering
tri'bordo *m* starboard
tribù *f inv* tribe
tri'buna *f* podium, dais; (per uditori) gallery; Sport stand
■ **tribuna coperta** stand; **tribuna riservata al pubblico** public gallery; **tribuna della stampa** press gallery
tribu'nale *m* court
■ **tribunale fallimentare** bankruptcy court; **tribunale minorile** juvenile court; **tribunale penale internazionale** international criminal court, ICC
tribu'tare *vt* bestow, confer

⚷ key word

tribu'tario *adj* tax *attrib*
tri'buto *m* tribute; (tassa) tax
tri'checo *m* walrus
tri'ciclo *m* tricycle
trico'lore **A** *adj* three-coloured
B *m* (bandiera) Italian flag
tri'dente *m* trident
tridimensio'nale *adj* three-dimensional
trien'nale *adj* (ogni tre anni) three-yearly; (lungo tre anni) three-year
tri'ennio *m* three-year period
tri'fase *adj* three-phase
tri'foglio *m* clover
trifo'lato *adj sliced thinly and cooked with olive oil, parsley and garlic*
tri'gemino *adj* **parto ~** birth of triplets
'triglia *f* mullet
trigonome'tria *f* trigonometry, trig infml
tri'lingue *adj* trilingual
tril'lare *vi* trill
'trillo *m* trill
trilo'gia *f* trilogy
trime'strale *adj* quarterly
tri'mestre *m* quarter
'trina *f* lace
trin'cea *f* trench
trince'rare *vt* entrench
trincia'pollo *m inv* poultry shears *pl*
trinci'are *vt* cut up
trincia'trice *f*
■ **trinciatrice di documenti** document shredder
Trini'dad e To'bago *m* Trinidad and Tobago
Trinità *f inv* Trinity
'trio *m* trio
trion'fale *adj* triumphal
trionfal'mente *adv* triumphantly
trion'fante *adj* triumphant
trion'fare *vi* triumph (**su** over)
tri'onfo *m* triumph
tri'pletta *f* Sport hat trick
tripli'care *vt* triple
'triplice *adj* triple; **in ~ [copia]** in triplicate
'triplo **A** *adj* treble, triple; **una somma tripla del previsto** an amount three times as much as forecast
B *m* **il ~ (di)** three times as much (as)
'trippa *f* tripe; infml (pancia) belly
tripudi'are *vi* rejoice
tri'pudio *m* jubilation
tris *m* (gioco) noughts and crosses, tick-tack-toe AmE
'triste *adj* sad; (luogo) gloomy
tri'stezza *f* sadness; (di luogo) gloominess
'tristo *adj* nasty
trita'carne *m inv* mincer
tritaghi'accio *m inv* ice crusher
tri'tare *vt* mince
trita'tutto *m inv* (elettrico) [food] processor
'trito *adj* **~ e ritrito** well-worn, trite
tri'tolo *m* TNT
tri'tone *m* (mitologia) Triton; Zool newt
'trittico *m* triptych
trit'tongo *m* triphthong
tritu'rare *vt* chop finely
triumvi'rato *m* triumvirate
tri'vella *f* drill
trivel'lare *vt* drill
trivi'ale *adj* vulgar
tro'feo *m* trophy
troglo'dita *mf* (preistoria) cave-dweller; fig Neanderthal
'trogolo *m* (per maiali) trough
'troia *f* sow; vulg bitch; (sessuale) whore
'tromba *f* trumpet; Auto horn; (delle scale) well; **partire in ~** dive in head first
■ **tromba d'aria** whirlwind; **tromba di Eustachio** Eustachian tube; **tromba di Falloppio** Fallopian tube; **tromba delle scale** stairwell
trom'bare **A** *vt* vulg bonk; infml (in esame) fail
B *vi* vulg bonk
trom'betta *m* toy trumpet
trombetti'ere *m* bugler
trombet'tista *mf* trumpet player
trom'bone *m* trombone
trom'bosi *f* thrombosis
■ **trombosi coronarica** coronary thrombosis; **trombosi venosa profonda** deep-vein thrombosis, DVT
tron'care *vt* sever; truncate ‹*parola*›
tron'chese *m* wire cutters *pl*
tronche'sino *m* (per le unghie) nail clippers *pl*
tron'chetto *m*
■ **tronchetto natalizio** Yule log
'tronco **A** *adj* truncated; **licenziare in ~** fire on the spot
B *m* trunk; (di strada) section
■ **tronco d'albero** tree trunk; **tronco di cono** truncated cone
tron'cone *m* stump
troneggi'are *vi* **~ su** tower over
'trono *m* throne
tropi'cale *adj* tropical
'tropici *mpl* Tropics
'tropico *m* tropic
■ **tropico del Cancro** Tropic of Cancer; **tropico del Capricorno** Tropic of Capricorn
'troppo **A** *adj* too much; (con nomi plurali) too many
B *pron* too much; (plurale) too many; (troppo tempo) too long; **troppi** (troppa gente) too many people; **me ne hai dato ~** you gave me too much
C *adv* too; (con verbi) too much; **~ stanco** too tired; **ho mangiato ~** I ate too much; **hai fame? - non ~** are you hungry? - not very; **sentirsi di ~** feel unwanted

t

'trota *f* trout
■ **trota di mare** sea trout; **trota salmonata** salmon trout

trot'tare *vi* trot

trotterel'lare *vi* trot along; (bambino) toddle

'trotto *m* trot; **andare al ~** trot

'trottola *f* [spinning] top; (movimento) spin

troupe *f inv*
■ **troupe televisiva** camera crew

trousse *f inv* (per trucco) make-up bag

⚷ **tro'vare** *vt* find; (scoprire) find out; (incontrare) meet; (ritenere) think; **andare a ~** go to see

trova'robe *mf* (persona) props *sg*

tro'varsi *vr* find oneself; (luogo) be; (sentirsi) feel

tro'vata *f* bright idea
■ **trovata pubblicitaria** advertising gimmick, publicity stunt

trova'tello, -a *mf* foundling

truc'care *vt* make up; cook ‹*libri contabili*›; soup up ‹*motore*›; rig ‹*partita, elezioni*›

truc'carsi *vr* put one's make-up on

truc'cato *adj* made-up; (libri contabili) cooked; (partita, elezioni) rigged; (motore) souped up

trucca|'tore, -trice *mf* make-up artist

⚷ **'trucco** *m* (cosmetici) make-up; (imbroglio) trick; **trucchi** *pl* **del mestiere** tricks of the trade

'truce *adj* fierce; (delitto) savage

truci'dare *vt* slay

trucio'lato *m* chipboard

'truciolo *m* shaving

trucu'lento *adj* (delitto) savage; (film) violent

'truffa *f* fraud

truf'fare *vt* defraud

truffa|'tore, -trice *mf* fraudster

'trullo *m traditional house with a conical roof found in Apulia*

⚷ **'truppa** *f* troops *pl* (gruppo) group; **truppe** *pl* **d'assalto** assault troops; **truppe** *pl* **di terra** ground troops

T-shirt *f inv* tee shirt, T-shirt

tsu'nami *m* tsunami

⚷ **tu** *pers pron* you; **sei tu?** is that you?; **l'hai fatto tu?** did you do it yourself?; **a tu per tu** in private; **darsi del tu** use the familiar **tu** to each other

'tua ▶ tuo

'tuba *f* Mus tuba; (cappello) top hat

tu'bare *vi* coo; (innamorati) bill and coo

tuba'tura *f* piping

tubazi'one *f* piping; **tubazioni** *pl* piping *sg*, pipes

tuberco'lina *f* tuberculin

tuberco'losi *f* tuberculosis

'tubero *m* tuber

tube'rosa *f* tuberose

tu'betto *m* tube
■ **tubetto di colore** tube of paint

tu'bino *m* (vestito) shift; (cappello) bowler; derby AmE

'tubo *m* pipe; Anat canal; **non ho capito un ~** infml I understood zilch
■ **tubo digerente** alimentary canal; **tubo a raggi catodici** cathode ray tube; **tubo di scappamento** exhaust [pipe]; **tubo di scarico** waste pipe

tubo'lare *adj* tubular

'tue ▶ tuo

tuf'fare *vt* plunge

tuf'farsi *vr* dive; **'vietato ~'** 'no diving'

tuffa|'tore, -trice *mf* diver

'tuffo *m* dive; (bagno) dip; **ho avuto un ~ al cuore** my heart leapt into my mouth
■ **tuffo di testa** dive

'tufo *m* tufa

tu'gurio *m* hovel

tuli'pano *m* tulip

'tulle *m* tulle

tume'fatto *adj* swollen

tumefazi'one *f* swelling

'tumido *adj* swollen

tu'more *m* tumour
■ **tumore benigno** benign tumour; **tumore del collo dell'utero** cervical cancer; **tumore maligno** malignant tumour

tumulazi'one *f* burial

'tumulo *m* (di pietre) cairn

tu'multo *m* turmoil; (sommossa) riot

tumultu'oso *adj* tumultuous

tung'steno *m* tungsten

'tunica *f* tunic

Tuni'sia *f* Tunisia

tuni'sino *adj & nmf* Tunisian

'tunnel *m inv* tunnel
■ **tunnel sotto la Manica** Channel Tunnel

⚷ **'tuo** **A** (**il ~** *m* **la tua** *f* **i tuoi** *mpl* **le tue** *fpl*) *poss adj* your; **è tua questa macchina?** is this car yours?; **un ~ amico** a friend of yours; **~ padre** your father
B *poss pron* yours; **i tuoi** your folk

tu'oi ▶ tuo

tuo'nare *vi* thunder

tu'ono *m* thunder

tu'orlo *m* yolk

tu'racciolo *m* stopper; (di sughero) cork

tu'rare *vt* block; cork ‹*bottiglia*›

tu'rarsi *vr* become blocked; **~ le orecchie** stick one's fingers in one's ears; **~ il naso** hold one's nose

'turba *f* (folla) rabble
■ **turba psichica** mental illness

turba'mento *m* disturbance; (sconvolgimento) upsetting
■ **turbamento della quiete pubblica** breach of the peace

tur'bante *m* turban

tur'bare *vt* upset

⚷ key word

t

tur'barsi *vr* get upset
tur'bato *adj* upset
tur'bina *f* turbine
turbi'nare *vi* whirl
'turbine *m* whirl
■ **turbine di polvere** dust storm; **turbine di vento** whirlwind
'turbo *m inv* turbo
turbocompres'sore *m* Tech turbocharger
turbo'lento *adj* turbulent
turbo'lenza *f* turbulence
turboreat'tore *m* turbo-jet
tur'chese *adj & nmf* turquoise
Tur'chia *f* Turkey
tur'chino *adj & nm* deep blue
'turco, -a A *adj* Turkish
B *mf* Turk; **fumare come un ~** smoke like a chimney; **bestemmiare come un ~** swear like a trooper
C *m* (lingua) Turkish; fig double Dutch
'turgido *adj* turgid
tu'rismo *m* tourism
tu'rista *mf* tourist
tu'ristico *adj* tourist *attrib*
tur'nista *mf* shift worker
'turno *m* turn; **a ~** in turn; **fare a ~** take turns; **fare i turni** work shifts; **di ~** on duty
■ **turno eliminatorio** heat; **turno di giorno** day shift; **turno di guardia** guard duty; **turno di lavoro** shift; **turno di notte** night shift; **del turno di notte** night shift *attrib*; **fare il turno di notte** be on night shift
'turpe *adj* base
turpi'loquio *m* foul language
'tuta *f* overalls *pl*; Sport tracksuit
■ **tuta da ginnastica** tracksuit; **tuta da lavoro** overalls *pl*; **tuta mimetica** camouflage; **tuta da sci** ski suit; **tuta spaziale** spacesuit; **tuta subacquea** wetsuit
tu'tela *f* Jur guardianship; (protezione) protection
■ **tutela dell'ambiente** environmental protection
tute'lare *vt* protect
tu'tina *f* sleepsuit; (da danza) leotard
tu|'tore, -trice *mf* guardian
'tutta *f* **mettercela ~ per fare qualcosa** go flat out for something
tutta'via *conj* nevertheless, still
'tutto A *adj* whole; (con nomi plurali) all; (ogni) every; **tutta la classe** the whole class, all the class; **tutti gli alunni** all the pupils; **a tutta velocità** at full speed; **ho aspettato ~ il giorno** I waited all day [long]; **vestito di ~ punto** all kitted out; **in ~ il mondo** all over the world; **noi tutti** all of us; **era tutta contenta** she was delighted; **tutti e due** both; **tutti e tre** all three
B *pron* all; (tutta la gente) everybody; (tutte le cose) everything; (qualunque cosa) anything; **c'è ancora del dolce? - no, l'ho mangiato ~** is there still some cake? - no, I ate it all; **le finestre sono pulite, le ho lavate tutte** the windows are clean, I washed them all; **raccontami ~** tell me everything; **lo sanno tutti** everybody knows; **è capace di ~** he's capable of anything; **~ compreso** all in; **del ~** quite; **in ~** altogether
C *adv* completely; **tutt'a un tratto** all at once; **tutt'altro** not at all; **tutt'altro che** anything but
D *m* whole; **tentare il ~ per ~** go for broke; **~ compreso** all-inclusive; **~ esaurito** Theat full house
tutto'fare *adj inv & mf inv* **[impiegato] ~** general handyman
tut'tora *adv* still
tutù *m inv* tutu; (lungo) ballet dress
tv *f inv* TV
■ **tv via cavo** cable TV; **tv digitale** digital (television); **tv interattiva** interactive TV
tweed *m inv* tweed
tweet *m* (su Twitter) tweet
twittare *vt & vi* (postare su Twitter) to tweet

Uu

ubbidi'ente *adj* obedient
ubbidiente'mente *adv* obediently
ubbidi'enza *f* obedience
ubbi'dire *vi* **~ (a)** obey
ubi'cato *adj* located
ubicazi'one *f* location
ubiquità *f inv* **non ho il dono dell'~** I can't be in two places at once
ubria'care *vt* get drunk
ubria'carsi *vr* get drunk; **~ di** fig become intoxicated with
ubria'chezza *f* drunkenness; **in stato di ~** inebriated; **in stato di ~ molesta** drunk and disorderly
ubri'aco, -a A *adj* drunk
■ **ubriaco fradicio** dead *or* blind drunk

B *mf* drunk

ubria'cone **A** *m* drunkard

B *adj* **un marito ~** a drunkard of a husband

uccelli'era *f* aviary

uccel'lino *m* baby bird

⚷ **uc'cello** *m* bird; vulg (pene) cock

■ **uccello acquatico** water fowl; **uccello da cacciagione** game bird; **uccello del malaugurio** bird of ill omen; **uccello notturno** night *or* nocturnal bird; **uccello del paradiso** bird of paradise; **uccello di passo** bird of passage; **uccello rapace** bird of prey

⚷ **uc'cidere** *vt* kill

uc'cidersi *vr* kill oneself; (morire) be killed

+uccio *suff* **boccuccia** *nf* pretty little mouth; **calduccio** *nm* cosy warmth; **c'è un bel calduccio** it's nice and cosy; **tesoruccio** *nm* sweetie; **avvocatuccio** *nm* derog small town lawyer; **cosuccia** *nf* trifle; **è una cosuccia da niente** it's nothing; **doloruccio** *nm* twinge; **vestituccio** *nm* derog skimpy little dress

uccisi'one *f* killing

uc'ciso pp di **uccidere**

ucci'sore *m* killer

U'craina *f* **l' ~** the Ukraine

u'craino, -a *adj & nmf* Ukrainian

u'dente *adj* **i non udenti** the hearing-impaired

u'dibile *adj* audible

udi'enza *f* audience; (colloquio) interview; Jur hearing

■ **udienza a porte chiuse** hearing in camera

⚷ **u'dire** *vt* hear

udi'tivo *adj* auditory

u'dito *m* hearing

udi|'tore, -trice *mf* listener; Sch unregistered student (*allowed to sit in on lectures*)

udi'torio *m* audience

UE *abbr* (**Unione Europea**) EU

uff *int* phew!

'uffa *int* (con impazienza) come on!; (con tono seccato) damn!

⚷ **uffici'ale** **A** *adj* official

B *m* officer; (funzionario) official; **pubblico ~** public official

■ **ufficiale dell'esercito** army officer; **ufficiale giudiziario** clerk of the court; **ufficiale sanitario** health officer; **ufficiale dello Stato civile** registrar

ufficialità *f inv* official status

ufficializ'zare *vt* make official, officialize

ufficial'mente *adv* officially

⚷ **uf'ficio** *m* office; (dovere) duty; (reparto) department; **andare in ~** go to the office

■ **ufficio acquisti** purchasing department; **ufficio cambi** bureau de change, exchange bureau; **ufficio di collocamento** employment office, jobcentre BrE; **Ufficio Dazi e Dogana** Customs and Excise; **ufficio funebre** Relig funeral service; **ufficio delle imposte** tax office; **ufficio informazioni** information office; **ufficio di informazioni turistiche** tourist information office *or* centre; **ufficio oggetti smarriti** lost property office, lost and found AmE; **ufficio del personale** personnel department; **ufficio postale** post office; **ufficio prenotazioni** advance booking office; **ufficio della redazione** newspaper office; **ufficio del turismo** tourist office; **ufficio turistico** tourist office

ufficiosa'mente *adv* unofficially

uffici'oso *adj* unofficial, off the record

'ufo[1] *m inv* UFO

'ufo[2] **a ~** *adv* without paying

ufolo'gia *f* ufology

U'ganda *f* Uganda

ugan'dese *adj & nmf* Ugandan

uggiosità *f inv* dullness

uggi'oso *adj* boring

uguagli'anza *f* equality

uguagli'are *vt* make equal; (essere uguale) equal; (livellare) level

uguagli'arsi *vr* **~ a** compare oneself to

⚷ **ugu'ale** **A** *adj* equal; (lo stesso) the same; (simile) like; **due più due è ~ a quattro** two plus two equals four

B *m* Math equals sign; **che non ha ~** unequalled

ugual'mente *adv* equally; (malgrado tutto) all the same

'ulcera *f* ulcer

■ **ulcera gastrica** gastric ulcer; **ulcera peptica** peptic ulcer

uli'veto *m* olive grove

u'livo *m* olive [tree]

'ulna *f* Anat ulna

ulteri'ore *adj* further

ulterior'mente *adv* further

ultima'mente *adv* lately

ulti'mare *vt* complete

ulti'matum *m inv* ultimatum

ulti'missime *fpl* Journ stop press, latest news *sg*

⚷ **'ultimo** **A** *adj* last; (notizie ecc.) latest; (più lontano) farthest; fig ultimate; ‹*prezzo*› rock-bottom; **l' ~ piano** the top floor

B *m* last; **fino all' ~** to the last; **per ~** at the end

ultimo'genito, -a *mf* last-born

ultrà *mf inv* Sport fanatical supporter

ultraleg'gero *m* (aereo) microlight

ultrapi'atto *adj* ultra-thin

ultrapo'tente *adj* extra-strong

ultra'rapido *adj* extra-fast

ultraresi'stente *adj* extra-strong

ultrasen'sibile *adj* ultra-sensitive

ultrasessan'tenne *m* **gli ultrasessantenni** the over 60s

u

⚷ key word

ultra'sonico *adj* ultrasonic
ultrasu'ono *m* ultrasound
ultrater'reno *adj* ‹*vita*› after death
ultravio'letto *adj* ultraviolet
ulu'lare *vi* howl
ulu'lato *m* howling; **gli ululati** the howls, the howling
umana'mente *adv* ‹*trattare*› humanely; ~ **impossibile** not humanly possible
uma'nesimo *m* humanism
uma'nista *mf* humanist
umanità *f inv* humanity
umani'tario *adj* humanitarian
u'mano *adj* human; (benevolo) humane
'Umbria *f* Umbria
'umbro, -a *adj & nmf* Umbrian
umet'tare *vt* moisten
umidifica'tore *m* humidifier
umidità *f inv* dampness; (di clima) humidity
'umido **A** *adj* damp; ‹*clima*› humid; ‹*mani, occhi*› moist
B *m* **1** (clima) dampness; **in** ~ Culin stewed **2** Ecol organic waste
'umile *adj* humble
umili'ante *adj* humiliating
umili'are *vt* humiliate
umili'arsi *vr* humble oneself
umiliazi'one *f* humiliation
umil'mente *adv* humbly
umiltà *f inv* humility
u'more *m* humour; (stato d'animo) mood; **di cattivo/buon** ~ in a bad/good mood
umo'rismo *m* humour
umo'rista *mf* humorist
umoristica'mente *adv* humorously
umo'ristico *adj* humorous
un ▸ uno
un' ▸ uno
'una ▸ uno
u'nanime *adj* unanimous
unanime'mente *adv* unanimously
unanimità *f inv* unanimity; **all'** ~ unanimously
unci'nare *vt* hook
unci'nato *adj* hooked; ‹*parentesi*› angle *attrib*
unci'netto *m* crochet hook
un'cino *m* hook
undi'cenne *adj & nmf* eleven year-old
undi'cesimo *adj & nm* eleventh
'undici *adj & nm* eleven
'ungere *vt* grease; (sporcare) get greasy; Relig anoint; (blandire) flatter
'ungersi *vr* (con olio solare) oil oneself; ~ **le mani** get one's hands greasy
unghe'rese **A** *adj & mf* Hungarian
B *m* (lingua) Hungarian
Unghe'ria *f* Hungary
'unghia *f* nail; (di animale) claw; **cadere sotto le unghie di qualcuno** fall into somebody's clutches
■ **unghia fessa** cloven hoof
unghi'ata *f* (graffio) scratch
ungu'ento *m* ointment
unica'mente *adv* only
unicellu'lare *adj* single-cell, unicellular
unicità *f inv* uniqueness
'unico *adj* only; (singolo) single; (incomparabile) unique
uni'corno *m* unicorn
unidimensio'nale *adj* one-dimensional
unidirezio'nale *adj* unidirectional
unifamili'are *adj* one-family
unifi'care *vt* unify
unificazi'one *f* unification
unifor'mare *vt* level
unifor'marsi *vr* conform (**a** to)
uni'forme **A** *adj* uniform
B *f* uniform
■ **uniforme di gala** Mil mess dress
uniformità *f inv* uniformity
unilate'rale *adj* unilateral
unilateral'mente *adv* unilaterally
uninomi'nale *adj* Pol single-candidate
uni'one *f* union; (armonia) unity; **Unione economica e monetaria** Economic and Monetary Union
■ **unione di fatto** registered partnership; **Unione Europea** European Union; **Unione Monetaria Europea** European Monetary Union; **unione sindacale** trade union, labour union AmE; **Unione Sovietica** Soviet Union
unio'nista *mf* Pol Unionist
u'nire *vt* unite; (collegare) join; blend ‹*colori ecc.*›
u'nirsi *vr* unite; (collegarsi) join
'unisex *adj inv* unisex
u'nisono *m* **all'**~ in unison
unità *f inv* unity; Math, Mil (reparto ecc.) unit; Comput drive
■ **unità di archivio dati** data storage device; **unità di backup a nastro** Comput tape backup drive; **unità centrale di elaborazione** Comput central processing unit, CPU; **unità floppy disk** Comput floppy disk drive; **unità di inizializzazione** Comput boot drive; **unità di memoria di massa** Comput mass storage device; **unità di misura** unit of measurement; **unità a nastro magnetico** Comput tape drive; **unità periferica** Comput peripheral; **unità di produzione** factory unit; **unità socio-sanitaria locale** local health centre; **unità di visualizzazione** Comput visual display unit, VDU
uni'tario *adj* unitary; **prezzo** ~ unit price
u'nito *adj* united; ‹*tinta*› plain; ‹*comunità*› tight-knit
univer'sale *adj* universal
universaliz'zare *vt* universalize

universal'mente *adv* universally

università *f inv* university

universi'tario, -a **A** *adj* university *attrib* **B** *mf* (docente) university lecturer; (studente) undergraduate

uni'verso *m* universe

u'nivoco *adj* unambiguous

'uno, -a **A** *art indef* a; (davanti a vocale o h muta) an; **un esempio** an example **B** *pron* one; **a ~ a ~** one by one; **~ alla volta** one at a time; **l'~ e l'altro** both [of them]; **né l'~ né l'altro** neither [of them]; **~ di noi** one of us; **~ fa quello che può** you do what you can **C** *adj* a, one **D** *m* (numerale) one; (un tale) some man **E** *f* some woman

'unto **A** pp di **ungere** **B** *adj* greasy **C** *m* grease

untu'oso *adj* greasy

unzi'one *f*
■ **l'Estrema Unzione** Extreme Unction, last rites

u'omo *m* (*pl* **uomini**) man; **'uomini'** (bagni) 'gents', 'men's room'
■ **uomo d'affari** business man; **uomo di colore** black man; **uomo di fiducia** right-hand man; **uomo di mondo** man of the world; **uomo-oggetto** toy boy; **uomo delle pulizie** cleaner; **uomo sandwich** sandwich man; **uomo di Stato** statesman; **uomo della strada** man on the street

u'ovo *m* (*pl f* **uova**) egg; **uova** *pl* **al bacon** bacon and eggs
■ **uovo barzotto** *o* **bazzotto** soft-boiled egg; **uovo in camicia** poached egg; **uovo di Colombo** obvious simple solution; **uovo all'occhio di bue** fried egg; **uovo all'ostrica** raw egg; **uovo di Pasqua** Easter egg; **uova al prosciutto** *pl* ham and eggs; **uovo sodo** hard-boiled egg; **uovo strapazzato** scrambled egg; **uovo al tegamino** fried egg

upgra'dabile *adj* upgradeable

'upupa *f* hoopoe

ura'gano *m* hurricane

u'ranio *m* uranium

U'rano *m* Uranus

urba'nesimo *m* urbanization

urba'nista *mf* town planner

urba'nistica *f* town planning

urba'nistico *adj* urban

urbaniz'zare *vt* urbanize

urbanizzazi'one *f* urbanization

ur'bano *adj* urban; (cortese) urbane

u'rea *f* urea

u'retra *f* Anat urethra

ur'gente *adj* urgent

urgente'mente *adv* urgently

ur'genza *f* urgency; **in caso d'~** in an emergency; **d'~** ‹*misura, chiamata*› emergency *attrib*; **operare d'~** perform an emergency operation on

'urgere *vi* be urgent

u'rina *f* urine

uri'nare *vi* urinate

ur'lare *vi* shout, yell; ‹*cane, vento*› howl

'urlo *m* (*pl m* **urli** *o pl f* **urla**) shout; (di cane, vento) howling

'urna *f* urn; (elettorale) ballot box; **andare alle urne** go to the polls

urrà *int* hurrah!

URSS *nf abbr* (**Unione delle Repubbliche Socialiste Sovietiche**) USSR

ur'tare *vt* knock against; (scontrarsi) bump into; fig irritate

ur'tarsi *vr* collide; fig clash

'urto *m* knock; (scontro) crash; (contrasto) conflict; fig clash; **d'~** ‹*misure, terapia*› shock

Uru'guay *m* Uruguay

U.S.A. *mpl* US[A] *sg*

usa e getta *adj inv* ‹*rasoio, siringa*› throw-away, disposable

u'sanza *f* custom; (moda) fashion

u'sare **A** *vt* use; (impiegare) employ; (esercitare) exercise; **~ fare qualcosa** be in the habit of doing something **B** *vi* (essere di moda) be fashionable; **non si usa più** it is out of fashion; ‹*attrezzatura, espressione*› it's not used any more

u'sato **A** *adj* used; (non nuovo) second-hand **B** *m* second-hand goods *pl*; **dell'~** second-hand; **fuori dell'~** unusual

u'sbeco, -a *adj & nmf* Uzbek

u'scente *adj* ‹*presidente*› outgoing

usci'ere *m* usher

'uscio *m* door

u'scire *vi* come out; (andare fuori) go out; (sfuggire) get out; (essere sorteggiato) come up; ‹*giornale*› come out; **~ da** Comput exit from, quit; **~ di strada** leave the road

u'scita *f* exit, way out; (spesa) outlay; (di autostrada) junction; (battuta) witty remark; (in ginnastica artistica) dismount; **uscite** *pl* Fin outgoings; **essere in libera ~** be off duty
■ **uscita di servizio** back door; **uscita di sicurezza** emergency exit, fire exit

usi'gnolo *m* nightingale

'uso *m* use; (abitudine) custom; (usanza) usage; **fuori ~** out of use; **per ~ esterno** ‹*medicina*› for external use only
■ **uso e dosi** use and dosage

us'saro *m* hussar

U.S.S.L. *nf abbr* (**Unità Socio-Sanitaria Locale**) local health centre

ustio'narsi *vr* burn oneself

ustio'nato, -a **A** *mf* burns case **B** *adj* burnt

key word

usti'one *f* burn; **ustioni di primo grado** first-degree burns
usu'ale *adj* usual
usual'mente *adv* usually
usucapi'one *f* Jur usucaption
usufru'ire *vi* ~ **di** take advantage of, make use of
usu'frutto *m* Jur use, usufruct fml
usufruttu'ario, -a *mf* user, usufructuary fml
u'sura *f* usury
usu'raio *m* usurer
usur'pare *vt* usurp
usurpa|'tore, -trice *mf* usurper
u'tensile *m* tool; Culin utensil; **cassetta degli utensili** tool box; **utensili** *pl* **da cucina** kitchen utensils
u'tente *mf* user
■ **utente finale** end user; **utenti della strada** *pl* road users
u'tenza *f* use; (utenti) users *pl*
■ **utenza finale** end users *pl*
ute'rino *adj* uterine
'utero *m* womb
'utile **A** *adj* useful
B *m* Comm profit; **unire l'~ al dilettevole** combine business with pleasure
■ **utile su cambi** foreign exchange gain; **utile sul capitale investito** return on investment
utilità *f inv* usefulness, utility; Comput utility
utili'tario, -a **A** *adj* utilitarian
B *f* Auto small car
utilita'ristico *adj* utilitarian
u'tility *m* utility
utiliz'zare *vt* utilize
utilizzazi'one *f* utilization
uti'lizzo *m* use
util'mente *adv* usefully
Uto'pia *f* Utopia
uto'pista *mf* Utopian
uto'pistico *adj* Utopian
'uva *f* grapes *pl*; **chicco d'uva** grape
■ **uva bianca** white grapes; **uva nera** black grapes; **uva passa** raisins *pl*; **uva sultanina** currants *pl*; **uva da tavola** [eating] grapes; **uva da vino** wine grapes
UVA *mpl abbr* (**ultravioletto prossimo**) UV
u'vetta *f* raisins *pl*
uxori'cida **A** *m* wife killer, uxoricide fml
B *f* husband killer
Uzbeki'stan *m* Uzbekistan

Vv

va' ▸ **andare**
va'cante *adj* vacant
va'canza *f* holiday, vacation AmE; **[giorno di] ~** holiday; (posto vacante) vacancy; **vacanze** *pl* holidays, vacation AmE; Univ vacation, vac infml; **essere in ~** be on holiday/vacation; **prendersi una ~** take a holiday/vacation; **andare in ~** go on holiday/vacation; **è ~** it's a holiday
■ **vacanza avventura** adventure holiday; **vacanze** *pl* **estive** summer holidays/vacation; **vacanze** *pl* **di Natale** Christmas holidays/vacation; **vacanze** *pl* **di Pasqua** Easter holidays/vacation; **vacanze** *pl* **scolastiche** school holidays/vacation
vacan'ziere, -a *mf* vacationer AmE, holidaymaker BrE
'vacca *f* cow
■ **vacca da latte** dairy cow
vac'caro, -a *f* cowherd
vacci'nare *vt* vaccinate; **farsi ~** get vaccinated
vaccinazi'one *f* vaccination
vac'cino *m* vaccine
vacil'lante *adj* tottering; ‹*oggetto*› wobbly; ‹*luce*› flickering; fig wavering, faltering
vacil'lare *vi* totter; ‹*oggetto*› wobble; ‹*luce*› flicker; fig waver
'vacuo **A** *adj* (vano) vain; fig empty
B *m* vacuum
'vado ▸ **andare**
vaffan'culo *int* vulg fuck off!
vagabon'daggio *m* Jur vagrancy
vagabon'dare *vi* wander
vaga'bondo **A** *adj* ‹*cane*› stray
B *mf* tramp
vaga'mente *adv* vaguely
va'gante *adj* wandering; **mina ~** floating mine; **proiettile ~** stray bullet
va'gare *vi* wander
vagheggi'are *vt* long for
va'ghezza *f* vagueness
va'gina *f* vagina
vagi'nale *adj* vaginal

va'gire *vi* whimper
va'gito *m* whimper
'vaglia *m inv* money order
■ **vaglia bancario** bank draft; **vaglia cambiario** promissory note; **vaglia internazionale** international money order; **vaglia postale** postal order
vagli'are *vt* sift; fig weigh
'vaglio *m* sieve
'vago *adj* vague
vagon'cino *m* (di funivia) car
■ **vagoncino a piattaforma** flat[bed] wagon
va'gone *m* (per passeggeri) carriage, car; (per merci) truck, wagon
■ **vagone bagagliaio** luggage van, baggage car AmE; **vagone ferroviario** railway carriage BrE, railroad car AmE; **vagone frigorifero** refrigerator van; **vagone letto** sleeper; **vagone postale** mail coach; **vagone ristorante** restaurant car, dining car
vai'olo *m* smallpox
va'langa *f* avalanche
val'chiria *f* Valkyrie
val'dese *adj & nmf* Waldensian
va'lente *adj* skilful
va'lenza *f* Chem valency; fig (valore) value
⚷ **va'lere** **A** *vi* be worth; (contare) count; ‹*regola*› apply (**per** to); (essere valido) be valid; **far ~ i propri diritti** assert one's rights; **farsi ~** assert oneself; **non vale!** that's not fair!; **tanto vale che me ne vada** I might as well go
B *vt* **~ qualcosa a qualcuno** (procurare) earn somebody something; **valerne la pena** be worth it; **vale la pena di vederlo** it's worth seeing; **valersi di** avail oneself of
valeri'ana *f* valerian
va'levole *adj* valid
'valgo *adj* **ginocchia** *pl* **valghe** knock knees
■ **alluce valgo** hallux valgus
vali'care *vt* cross
'valico *m* pass
valida'mente *adv* validly; (efficacemente) efficiently; ‹*contribuire*› effectively
validità *f inv* validity; **con ~ illimitata** valid indefinitely
'valido *adj* valid; (efficace) efficient; ‹*contributo*› valuable
valige'ria *f* (fabbrica) leather factory; (negozio) leather goods shop
vali'getta *f* small case; (per attrezzi) box
■ **valigetta del pronto soccorso** first aid kit; **valigetta ventiquattrore** overnight bag
⚷ **va'ligia** *f* suitcase; **fare le valigie** pack; fig pack one's bags
■ **valigia diplomatica** diplomatic bag
val'lata *f* valley
⚷ **'valle** *f* valley; **a ~** downstream
val'letta *f* TV assistant

val'letto *m* valet; TV assistant
'vallo *m* wall; **il ~ Adriano** Hadrian's Wall
val'lone¹ *m* (valle) deep valley
val'lone², **-a** *adj & nmf* Walloon
⚷ **va'lore** *m* value, worth; (merito) merit; (coraggio) valour; **valori** *pl* Comm securities; **di ~** (oggetto) valuable; **oggetti di ~** valuables; **di grande ~** of great value; ‹*medico, scienziato*› top *attrib*; **senza ~** worthless; **a ~ aggiunto** value-added
■ **valore bollato** revenue stamp; **valore contabile** book value; **valore effettivo** real value; **valore di mercato** market value, street value; **valore mobiliare** security; **valore nominale** nominal value; **valore di realizzo** break-up value; **valore di riscatto** surrender value
valoriz'zare *vt* (mettere in valore) use to advantage; (aumentare di valore) increase the value of; (migliorare l'aspetto di) enhance
valoriz'zarsi *vr* **il paese ha bisogno di ~ migliorando...** the country needs to enhance the value of its assets by improving...
valorosa'mente *adv* courageously
valo'roso *adj* courageous
'valso pp di **valere**
va'luta *f* currency
■ **valuta a corso legale** legal tender; **valuta estera** foreign currency
valu'tare *vt* value; weigh up ‹*situazione*›
valu'tario *adj* ‹*mercato, norme*› currency *attrib*
valuta'tivo *adj* for evaluation, evaluative
valutazi'one *f* valuation
'valva *f* valve
'valvola *f* valve; Electr fuse
■ **valvola a farfalla** butterfly valve; **valvola pneumatica** air valve; **valvola di sicurezza** anche fig safety valve
'valzer *m inv* waltz
vamp *f inv* vamp
vam'pata *f* blaze; (di calore) blast; (al viso) flush
vam'piro *m* vampire; fig bloodsucker
va'nadio *m* vanadium
vanaglori'oso *adj* vainglorious
vana'mente *adv* (inutilmente) in vain; (con vanità) vainly
van'dalico *adj* **atto ~** act of vandalism
vanda'lismo *m* vandalism
vandaliz'zare *vt* vandalize
vandalizzazi'one *f* vandalizing
'vandalo, **-a** *mf* vandal
vaneggia'mento *m* delirium
vaneggi'are *vi* rave
va'nesio *adj* conceited
'vanga *f* spade
van'gare *vt* dig
van'gata *f* (quantità) spadeful; (azione) blow with a spade

⚷ key word

van'gelo *m* Gospel; infml; (verità) gospel [truth]
vanifi'care *vt* nullify
va'niglia *f* vanilla
vanigli'ato *adj* ‹*zucchero*› vanilla *attrib*
vanil'lina *f* vanillin
vanità *f inv* vanity
vanitosa'mente *adv* vainly
vani'toso *adj* vain
'vano **A** *adj* vain
B *m* (stanza) room; (spazio vuoto) hollow
■ **vano doccia** shower room; **vano portabagagli** Auto boot, trunk AmE
van'taggio *m* advantage; Sport lead; Tennis advantage; **trarre ~ da qualcosa** derive benefit from something
vantaggiosa'mente *adv* advantageously
vantaggi'oso *adj* advantageous
van'tare *vt* praise; (possedere) boast
van'tarsi *vr* boast
vante'ria *f* boasting; **vanterie** *pl* boasting
'vanto *m* boast
'vanvera *f* **a ~** at random; **parlare a ~** talk nonsense
va'pore *m* steam; (di benzina, cascata) vapour; **a ~** steam *attrib*; **al ~** Culin steamed; **battello a ~** steamboat
■ **vapore acqueo** steam, water vapour
vapo'retto *m* ferry
vapori'era *f* steam engine
vaporiz'zare *vt* vaporize
vaporizza'tore *m* spray
vapo'roso *adj* ‹*vestito*› filmy; **capelli vaporosi** *pl* big hair
va'rano *m* monitor [lizard]
va'rare *vt* launch
var'care *vt* cross
'varco *m* passage; **aspettare al ~** lie in wait
vare'china *f* bleach
vari'abile **A** *adj* changeable, variable
B *f* Math variable
variabilità *f inv* changeableness, variability
varia'mente *adu* variously
vari'ante *f* variant
vari'are *vt & vi* vary; **~ di umore** change one's mood
vari'ato *adj* varied
variazi'one *f* variation
va'rice *f* varicose vein
vari'cella *f* chickenpox
vari'coso *adj* varicose
varie'gato *adj* variegated
varietà **A** *f inv* variety
B *m inv* variety show
'vario *adj* varied; (al pl, parecchi) various; **varie** *pl* (molti) several; **varie ed eventuali** any other business
vario'pinto *adj* multicoloured
'varo *m* launch
Var'savia *f* Warsaw
va'saio *m* potter
'vasca *f* tub; (piscina) pool; (lunghezza) length
■ **vasca da bagno** bath; **vasca con idromassaggio** whirlpool bath; **vasca di sviluppo** Phot developing tank
va'scello *m* vessel; **capitano di ~** captain
va'schetta *f* tub; Phot tray
■ **vaschetta per il ghiaccio** ice tray
vasco'lare *adj* Anat, Bot vascular
vasecto'mia *f* vasectomy
vase'lina *f* Vaseline®
vasel'lame *m* china
■ **vasellame d'oro/d'argento** gold/silver plate
va'setto *m* small pot; (per marmellata) jam jar
'vaso *m* pot; (da fiori) vase; Anat vessel; (per cibi) jar
■ **vaso da notte** chamber pot; **vaso sanguigno** blood vessel
vasocostrit'tore *adj* vasoconstrictor
vasodilata'tore *adj* vasodilator
vas'sallo *m* vassal
vas'soio *m* tray
vastità *f inv* vastness
'vasto *adj* vast; **di vaste vedute** broad-minded
Vati'cano *m* Vatican
vati'cinio *m* prophecy
vattela'pesca *adv* infml God knows
'vattene! go away!; ▶ **andare**
VCR *abbr* (**videoregistratore**) VCR
ve *pers pron* you; **ve l'ho dato** I gave it to you
'vecchia *f* old woman
vecchi'aia *f* old age
'vecchio, -a **A** *adj* old
B *mf* old man; old woman; **i vecchi** old people; **~ mio** old man
'veccia *f* vetch
'vece *f* **in ~ di** in place of; **fare le veci di qualcuno** take somebody's place
ve'dente *adj* **i non vedenti** the visually impaired
ve'dere **A** *vt* see; see, watch ‹*film, partita*›; **farsi ~** show one's face; **non si vede** ‹*macchia, imperfezione*› it doesn't show; **non veder l'ora di andare** be raring to go; **non poter ~ qualcuno** not be able to stand the sight of somebody; **vederci doppio** have double vision; **ne ho viste di tutti i colori** fig I've really seen life; **da ~** ‹*film, spettacolo*› not to be missed; **questo è da ~!** that remains to be seen!; **chi si vede!** infml look who it is!
B *vi* see
ve'dersi *vr* see oneself; (reciproco) see each other; **vedersela brutta** have a narrow escape
ve'detta *f* (luogo) lookout; Naut patrol vessel
'vedova *f* widow
■ **vedova nera** Zool black widow [spider]
'vedovo *m* widower

V

ve'duta *f* view
vee'mente *adj* vehement
ve'gano *adj & nmf* vegan
vege'tale *adj & nm* vegetable
vegeta'lismo *m* veganism
vege'tare *vi* vegetate
vegetaria'nismo *m* vegetarianism
vegetari'ano, -a *adj & nmf* vegetarian
vegeta'tivo *adj* vegetative
vegetazi'one *f* vegetation
'vegeto *adj* ▶ **vivo**
veg'gente *mf* clairvoyant
'veglia *f* watch; **fare la ~** keep watch
■ **veglia funebre** vigil
vegli'are *vi* be awake; **~ su** watch over
vegli'one *m*
■ **veglione di capodanno** New Year's Eve celebration
veico'lare **A** *vt* carry ‹*malattia*› **B** *adj* ‹*traffico*› vehicular
ve'icolo *m* vehicle
■ **veicolo pesante** heavy goods vehicle, HGV; **veicolo spaziale** spacecraft
'vela *f* sail; Sport sailing; **andare a gonfie vele** fig go beautifully; ‹*affari*› be booming; **far ~** set sail
■ **vela di taglio** mainsail
ve'lare *vt* veil; fig (nascondere) hide
ve'larsi *vr* ‹*vista*› mist over; ‹*voce*› go husky
velata'mente *adv* indirectly
ve'lato *adj* veiled; ‹*occhi*› misty; ‹*collant*› sheer
vela'tura *f* sails *pl*
'velcro® *m* Velcro®
veleggi'are *vi* sail
ve'leno *m* poison
velenosa'mente *adv* ‹*rispondere*› venomously
vele'noso *adj* poisonous; ‹*frase*› venomous
ve'letta *f* (di cappello) veil
'velico *adj* ‹*circolo*› sailing *attrib*; **superficie velica** sail area
veli'ero *m* sailing ship
ve'lina *f young female assistant on some entertainment programmes who dances around and looks pretty*
■ **(carta) velina** tissue paper; (copia) carbon copy
ve'lista **A** *m* yachtsman **B** *f* yachtswoman
ve'livolo *m* aircraft
velleità *f inv* foolish ambition
vellei'tario *adj* unrealistic
'vello *m* fleece
vellu'tato *adj* velvety
vel'luto *m* velvet
■ **velluto a coste** corduroy
'velo *m* veil; (di zucchero, cipria) dusting; (tessuto) voile

♂ key word

♂ **ve'loce** *adj* fast
veloce'mente *adv* quickly
velo'cipede *m* penny-farthing
velo'cista *mf* Sport sprinter
velocità *f inv* speed; Auto (marcia) gear; **a due ~** fig two-tier
■ **velocità di clock** Comput clock speed; **velocità di crociera** cruising speed; **velocità di stampa** print speed
velociz'zare *vt* speed up
ve'lodromo *m* cycle track
'vena *f* vein; **essere in ~ di** be in the mood for
■ **vena poetica** poetic mood
ve'nale *adj* venal; ‹*persona*› mercenary, venal
ve'nato *adj* grainy
vena'torio *adj* hunting *attrib*
vena'tura *f* (di legno) grain; (di foglia, marmo) vein
ven'demmia *f* grape harvest
vendemmi'are *vt* harvest
vendemmia|'tore, -trice *mf* grape picker
♂ **'vendere** *vt* sell; **'vendesi'** 'for sale'
'vendersi *vr* sell oneself
♂ **ven'detta** *f* revenge
■ **vendetta trasversale** vendetta
vendi'care *vt* avenge
vendi'carsi *vr* take revenge, get one's revenge; **~ di qualcuno** take one's vengeance on somebody; **~ di qualcosa** take revenge for something
vendicativa'mente *adv* vindictively
vendica'tivo *adj* vindictive
vendica|'tore, -trice *mf* avenger
'vendita *f* sale; **in ~** on sale
■ **vendita all'asta** sale by auction; **vendita di beneficenza** bring and buy sale; **vendita per corrispondenza** mail-order; **azienda di ~ per corrispondenza** mail-order company; **catalogo di ~ per corrispondenza** mail-order catalogue; **vendita al dettaglio** retailing; **vendite** *pl* **al dettaglio** retail sales; **vendita all'ingrosso** wholesaling; **vendita al minuto** retailing; **vendita porta a porta** door-to-door selling; **vendita a rate** hire purchase, installment plan AmE
vendi|'tore, -trice *mf* seller
■ **venditore ambulante** hawker, pedlar; **venditore al dettaglio** retailer; **venditore all'ingrosso** wholesaler; **venditore al mercato** market trader; **venditore al minuto** retailer
ven'duto *adj* ‹*merce*› sold; fig ‹*arbitro*› bent; **arbitro ~!** whose side are you on, ref!
vene'rabile, vene'rando *adj* venerable
vene'rare *vt* revere
venerazi'one *f* reverence
venerdì *m inv* Friday; **di ~** on Fridays
■ **Venerdì Santo** Good Friday
'Venere *f* Venus
ve'nereo *adj* venereal
'veneto *adj* from the Veneto

'Veneto *m* Veneto
Ve'nezia *f* Venice
venezi'ano, -a **A** *adj & mf* Venetian
B *f* (persiana) Venetian blind; Culin sweet bun
Venezu'ela *m* Venezuela
venezue'lano, -a *adj & nmf* Venezuelan
'vengo ▶ **venire**
veni'ale *adj* venial
ve'nire *vi* come; (riuscire) turn out; (costare) cost; (in passivi) be; **quanto viene?** how much is it?; **viene prodotto in serie** it's mass-produced; **~ a sapere** learn; **~ in mente** occur; **mi è venuto un dubbio** I've just had a doubt; **gli è venuta la febbre** he's got a temperature; **~ meno** (svenire) faint; **~ meno a un contratto** go back on a contract, renege on a contract; **~ via** come away; (staccarsi) come off; **mi viene da piangere** I feel like crying; **vieni a prendermi** come and pick me up; **vieni a trovarmi** come and see me; **nei giorni a ~** in [the] days to come
ve'noso *adj* venous
ven'taglio *m* fan
ven'tata *f* gust [of wind]; fig breath
ven'tenne *adj & nmf* twenty year-old
ven'tesimo *adj & nm* twentieth
'venti *adj & nm* twenty
venti'lare *vt* ventilate, air; **~ un'idea** give an idea an airing; **poco ventilato** ‹*stanza*› airless
ventila'tore *m* fan
ventilazi'one *f* ventilation
ven'tina *f* **una ~** (circa venti) about twenty
ventiquat'trore **A** *f inv* (valigetta) overnight bag
B *adv* **~ su ventiquattro** ‹*lavorare*› round-the-clock; ‹*aperto*› 24 hours
'vento *m* wind; **c'è molto ~** it's very windy; **farsi ~** fan oneself
■ **vento contrario** headwind; **vento di prua** headwind; **vento di traverso** crosswind
'ventola *f* fan
vento'lina *f* fan
■ **ventolina di raffreddamento** Comput cooling fan
ven'tosa *f* sucker, suction pad
ven'toso *adj* windy
'ventre *m* stomach; fig (di terra) bowels *pl*; **basso ~** lower abdomen
ventrico'lare *adj* Med ventricular
ven'tricolo *m* ventricle
ven'triloquo *m* ventriloquist
ventu'nesimo *adj & nm* twenty-first
ven'tuno *adj & nm* twenty-one
ven'tura *f* fortune; **andare alla ~** trust to luck
ven'turo *adj* next
ve'nuta *f* coming; **~ meno** a breaking
'vera *f* (anello) wedding ring
vera'mente *adv* really
ve'randa *f* veranda
ver'bale **A** *adj* verbal
B *m* (di riunione) minutes *pl*
■ **verbale di contravvenzione** fine
verbal'mente *adv* verbally
ver'bena *f* verbena
'verbo *m* verb; **il Verbo** Relig the Word
■ **verbo ausiliare** auxiliary [verb]; **verbo modale** modal auxiliary; **verbo riflessivo** reflexive verb
ver'boso *adj* verbose
ver'dastro *adj* greenish
'verde **A** *adj* green; **~ d'invidia** green with envy
B *m* green; (vegetazione) greenery; (semaforo) green light; **essere al ~** be broke
■ **verde bottiglia** bottle green; **verde oliva** olive green; **verde pisello** pea green; **verde pubblico** public parks *pl*
verdeggi'ante *adj* (liter) verdant
verde'mare *adj & m inv* sea-green
verde'rame *m* verdigris
ver'detto *m* verdict
■ **verdetto di assoluzione** not guilty verdict; **verdetto di condanna** guilty verdict
ver'done *m* greenfinch
ver'dura *f* vegetables *pl*; **una ~** a vegetable; **verdure** *pl* **miste** mixed vegetables
'verga *f* rod
ver'gato *adj* lined
vergi'nale *adj* virginal
'vergine **A** *f* virgin; Astr Virgo
B *adj* virgin; ‹*cassetta*› blank
verginità *f inv* virginity
ver'gogna *f* shame; (timidezza) shyness
vergo'gnarsi *vr* feel ashamed; (essere timido) feel shy
vergognosa'mente *adv* shamefully
vergo'gnoso *adj* ashamed; (timido) shy; (disonorevole) shameful
veridicità *f inv* veracity
ve'rifica *f* check
■ **verifica dei bilanci** audit; **verifica di cassa** cash check
verifi'cabile *adj* verifiable
verifi'care *vt* check; verify ‹*teoria*›
verifi'carsi *vr* come true
verifica'tore, -trice *mf* checker
ve'rismo *m* realism
verità *f inv* truth
veriti'ero *adj* truthful
'verme *m* worm
■ **verme solitario** tapeworm
vermi'celli *mpl* vermicelli *sg* (*pasta thinner than spaghetti*)
ver'mifugo **A** *adj* vermifugal
B *m* vermifuge
ver'miglio *adj & nm* vermilion
'vermut *m inv* vermouth

ver'nacolo *m* vernacular

ver'nice *f* paint; (trasparente) varnish; (pelle) patent leather; fig veneer; **'~ fresca'** 'wet paint'

■ **vernice a spirito** spirit varnish

vernici'are *vt* paint; (con vernice trasparente) varnish

vernicia'tura *f* painting; (con vernice trasparente) varnishing; (strato) paintwork; fig veneer

vernis'sage *m inv* vernissage

🗝 **'vero** **A** *adj* true; (autentico) real; (perfetto) perfect; **è ~?** is that so?; **~ e proprio** full-blown; **sei stanca, ~?** you're tired, aren't you; **non ti piace, ~?** you don't like it, do you?

■ **vero cuoio** real leather

B *m* truth; (realtà) life

verosimigli'anza *f* plausibility

vero'simile *adj* probable, likely

verosimil'mente *adv* probably

ver'ruca *f* wart; (sotto la pianta del piede) verruca

versa'mento *m* (pagamento) payment; (in banca) deposit

ver'sante *m* slope

🗝 **ver'sare** **A** *vt* pour; (spargere) shed; (rovesciare) spill; pay ‹*denaro*›; (in banca) pay in

B *vi* (trovarsi) be

ver'sarsi *vr* spill; (sfociare) flow

ver'satile *adj* versatile

versatilità *f inv* versatility

ver'sato *adj* (pratico) versed

ver'setto *m* verse

versifica|'tore, -trice *mf* versifier

versi'one *f* version; (traduzione) translation

■ **'versione integrale'** (libro) 'unabridged version'; (film) 'uncut'; **versione originale** original version; **'versione ridotta'** 'abridged version'; **versione teatrale** dramatization

'verso¹ *m* verse; (grido) cry; (gesto) gesture; (senso) direction; (modo) manner; **fare il ~ a qualcuno** ape somebody; **non c'è ~ di** there is no way of; **versi** *pl* **sciolti** blank verse

🗝 **'verso²** *prep* towards; (nei pressi di) round about; **~ dove?** which way?

'vertebra *f* vertebra

verte'brale *adj* vertebral

V

verte'brato *m* vertebrate

ver'tenza *f* dispute

■ **vertenza sindacale** industrial dispute

'vertere *vi* **~ su** focus on

verti'cale **A** *adj* vertical; (in parole crociate) down

B *m* vertical

C *f* handstand; **fare la ~** do a handstand

vertical'mente *adv* vertically

🗝 key word

'vertice *m* summit; Math vertex; **conferenza al ~** summit conference; **incontro al ~** summit meeting

ver'tigine *f* dizziness; Med vertigo; **vertigini** *pl* giddy spells; **avere le vertigini** feel dizzy

vertiginosa'mente *adv* dizzily

vertigi'noso *adj* dizzy; ‹*velocità*› breakneck; ‹*prezzi*› sky-high; ‹*scollatura*› plunging

'vescia *f* puffball

ve'scica *f* bladder; (sulla pelle) blister

'vescovo *m* bishop

'vespa *f* wasp

Vespa® *f* scooter, Vespa®

vespasi'ano *m* urinal

'vespro *m* vespers *pl*

ves'sare *vt fml* oppress

ves'sillo *m* standard

ve'staglia *f* dressing gown, robe AmE

'veste *f* dress; (rivestimento) covering; **in ~ di** in the capacity of; **in ~ ufficiale** in an official capacity

■ **veste da camera** dressing gown, robe AmE; **veste editoriale** layout; **veste tipografica** typographical design

vesti'ario *m* clothing

ve'stibolo *m* hall

ve'stigio *m* (*pl m* **vestigi**, *pl f* **vestigia**) trace

🗝 **ve'stire** *vt* dress

ve'stirsi *vr* get dressed; **~ da** dress up as a

🗝 **ve'stito** **A** *adj* dressed

B *m* (da uomo) suit; (da donna) dress; **vestiti** *pl* clothes

■ **vestito da sposa** wedding dress; **vestito da uomo** suit

vete'rano, -a *adj & nmf* veteran

veteri'nario, -a **A** *adj* veterinary

B *m* veterinary surgeon

C *f* veterinary science

'veto *m inv* veto

ve'traio *m* glazier

ve'trato, -a **A** *adj* glazed

B *f* big window; (in chiesa) stained-glass window; (porta) glass door

vetre'ria *f* glass works

ve'trina *f* [shop] window; (mobile) display cabinet

vetri'nista *mf* window dresser

ve'trino *m* (di microscopio) slide

vetri'olo *m* vitriol

🗝 **'vetro** *m* glass; (di finestra, porta) pane

■ **~ di sicurezza** safety glass

vetro'resina *f* fibreglass

ve'troso *adj* vitreous

'vetta *f* peak

vet'tore *m* vector

vetto'vaglie *fpl* provisions

vet'tura *f* coach; (ferroviaria) coach, carriage; Auto car

■ **vettura di cortesia** courtesy car; **vettura d'epoca** vintage car

vettu'rino *m* coachman

vezzeggi'are *vt* fondle

vezzeggia'tivo *m* pet name

'vezzo *m* habit; (attrattiva) charm; **vezzi** *pl* (moine) affectation

vez'zoso *adj* charming; derog affected

VF *abbr* (**Vigili del Fuoco**) fire brigade, fire department AmE

vi **A** *pers pron* you; (riflessivo) yourselves; (reciproco) each other; (tra più persone) one another; **vi ho dato un libro** I gave you a book; **lavatevi le mani** wash your hands; **eccovi!** here you are!

B *adv* = **ci**

via¹ *f* street, road; fig way; Anat tract; **in ~ di** in the course of; **per ~ di** on account of; **per ~ aerea** by airmail

■ **Via Lattea** Astr Milky Way; **via di mezzo** halfway house; **via respiratoria** Anat airway; **via d'uscita** let-out

via² **A** *adv* away; (fuori) out; **andar ~** go away; ‹*macchia*› come off, come out; **e così ~** and so on; **e ~ dicendo** and whatnot; **~ ~ che** as

B *int* **~!** go away!; Sport go!; (andiamo) come on!; **~, non ci credo** come off it *or* come on, I don't believe it

C *m* starting signal

viabilità *f inv* road conditions *pl*; (rete) road network; (norme) road and traffic laws *pl*

via'card *f inv* motorway card

vi'ado *m* (*pl* **viados**) rent boy

via'dotto *m* viaduct

viaggi'are *vi* travel; **il treno viaggia con 20 minuti di ritardo** the train is 20 minutes late

viaggia|'tore, trice *mf* traveller

vi'aggio *m* journey; (breve) trip; **buon ~!** safe journey!, have a good trip!; **fare un ~** go on a journey; **essere in ~** be under way; **mettersi in ~** get under way

■ **viaggio d'affari** business trip; **viaggio di lavoro** working trip; **viaggio di nozze** honeymoon; **viaggio organizzato** package tour

vi'ale *m* avenue; (privato) drive

via'letto *m* path

via'vai *m* coming and going

vi'brante *adj* vibrant

vi'brare *vi* vibrate; (fremere) quiver

vibra'tore *m* vibrator

vibra'torio *adj* vibratory

vibrazi'one *f* vibration

vi'cario *m* vicar

'vice *mf* deputy

vice+ *pref* vice+

vicecoman'dante *m* Mil second in command

vicediret|'tore, -trice **A** *m* assistant manager

B *f* assistant manageress

vi'cenda *f* event; **a ~** (fra due) each other; (a turno) in turn[s]

vicendevol'mente *adv* each other

vice'preside *mf* vice-principal

vicepresi'dente *m* vice-president; Comm vice-chairman, vice-president AmE

vicepresi'denza *f* vice-presidency; Sch deputy head's office

vicerè *m inv* viceroy

viceret'tore *m* vice-chancellor

vice'versa *adv* vice versa

vi'chingo, -a *adj & nmf* Viking

vi'cina *f* neighbour

vici'nanza *f* nearness; *pl* **vicinanze** (paraggi) neighbourhood

vici'nato *m* neighbourhood; (vicini) neighbours *pl*

vi'cino, -a **A** *adj* near; (accanto) next

B *adv* near, close

C *prep* **~ a** near [to]

D *mf* neighbour

■ **vicino di casa** next-door neighbour

vicissi'tudine *f* vicissitude

'vicolo *m* alley

■ **vicolo cieco** anche fig blind alley

'video *m* (musicale) video; (schermo) screen

■ **video interattivo** interactive video

video'camera *f* camcorder

videocas'setta *f* video, video cassette

videoci'tofono *m* video entry phone, videophone

video'clip *m inv* video clip

videoconfe'renza *f* videoconference

video'disco *m* videodisc

videofo'nino® *n* videophone, camera phone

videogi'oco *m* video game

video'leso, -a **A** *adj* visually impaired

B *mf* visually impaired person

videoregistra'tore *m* video recorder

videoscrit'tura *f* word processing

videosorvegli'anza *f* video surveillance

video'teca *f* video library

video'tel® *m* Videotex®

videote'lefono *m* view phone

videotermi'nale *m* visual display unit, VDU

vidi'mare *vt* authenticate

vi'eni ▶ **venire**

Vi'enna *f* Vienna

vien'nese *adj & nmf* Viennese

vie'tare *vt* forbid; **~ qualcosa a qualcuno** forbid somebody something

vie'tato *adj* forbidden; **sosta vietata** no parking; **~ fumare** no smoking; **~ ai minori di 18 anni** ‹*film*› for over 18s only, X-rated

Vi'etnam *m* Vietnam

vietna'mita *adj & nmf* Vietnamese

V

vi'gente *adj* in force
'vigere *vi* be in force
vigi'lante *adj* vigilant
vigi'lanza *f* vigilance; (sorveglianza, a scuola) supervision; (di polizia) surveillance
■ **vigilanza notturna** night security guards *pl*; **vigilanza urbana** traffic police (*in towns*)
vigi'lare **A** *vt* keep an eye on
B *vi* keep watch
vigi'lato, -a **A** *adj* under surveillance
B *mf* person under police surveillance
■ **vigilato speciale** person under special police surveillance
'vigile **A** *adj* watchful
B *m* ~ **[urbano]** traffic policeman
■ **vigile del fuoco** fireman, firefighter; **vigili del fuoco** *pl* firemen, fire brigade, fire service; **vigili urbani** *pl* traffic police (*in towns*)
vi'gilia *f* eve; Relig fast
■ **vigilia di Natale** Christmas Eve
vigliacca'mente *adv* in a cowardly way
vigliacche'ria *f* cowardice
⚷ **vigli'acco, -a** **A** *adj* cowardly
B *mf* coward
'vigna *f*, **vi'gneto** *m* vineyard
vi'gnetta *f* cartoon
vignet'tista *m* cartoonist
vi'gogna *f* (tessuto) vicuña
vi'gore *m* vigour; **entrare in** ~ come into force; **essere in** ~ be in force
vigorosa'mente *adv* energetically
vigo'roso *adj* vigorous
'vile *adj* cowardly; (abietto) vile
vili'pendio *m* scorn, contempt
⚷ **'villa** *f* villa
vil'laggio *m* village
■ **villaggio olimpico** Olympic village; **villaggio residenziale** commuter town; **villaggio satellite** satellite village; **villaggio turistico** holiday village
villa'nia *f* rudeness
vil'lano **A** *adj* rude
B *m* boor; (contadino) peasant
villeggi'ante *mf* holidaymaker
villeggi'are *vi* spend one's holidays
villeggia'tura *f* holiday[s] *pl*
vil'letta *f* small detached house
■ **villetta bifamiliare** semi-detached house; **villette a schiera** *pl* terraced houses
vil'lino *m* detached house
vil'loso *adj* hairy
vil'mente *adv* in a cowardly way; (in modo spregevole) contemptibly
viltà *f inv* cowardice
'vimine *m* wicker; **sedia di vimini** wicker chair
vi'naio, -a *mf* wine merchant
⚷ **'vincere** *vt* win; (sconfiggere) beat; (superare) overcome
'vincita *f* win; (somma vinta) winnings *pl*
vinci|'tore, -trice **A** *mf* winner; (di battaglia) victor, winner
B *adj* winning, victorious
vinco'lante *adj* binding
vinco'lare *vt* bind; Comm tie up
vinco'lato *adj* non-redeemable; **deposito** ~ fixed deposit, term deposit
'vincolo *m* bond
vi'nicolo *adj* wine *attrib*
vi'nile *m* vinyl
vi'nilico *adj* vinyl
vinil'pelle® *m* Leatherette®
⚷ **'vino** *m* wine
■ **vino d'annata** vintage wine; **vino bianco** white wine; **vino della casa** house wine; **vino da dessert** dessert wine; **vino nuovo** new wine; **vino rosato** rosé [wine]; **vino rosé** rosé [wine]; **vino rosso** red wine; **vino spumante** sparkling wine; **vino da taglio** blending wine; **vino da tavola** table wine
vin'santo *m dessert wine from Tuscany*
'vintage *adj* vintage; **moda** ~ vintage fashion
'vinto pp di **vincere**
vi'ola *f* Bot violet; Mus viola
■ **viola del pensiero** Bot pansy
vio'laceo *adj* purplish; ‹*labbra*› blue
vio'lare *vt* violate
violazi'one *f* violation
■ **violazione di contratto** breach of contract; **violazione di domicilio** breaking and entering
violen'tare *vt* rape
violente'mente *adv* violently
⚷ **vio'lento** *adj* violent
⚷ **vio'lenza** *f* violence
■ **violenza carnale** rape
vio'letto, -a **A** *adj & nm* (colore) violet
B *f* violet
violi'nista *mf* violinist
vio'lino *m* violin
violon'cello *m* cello
vi'ottolo *m* path
'vipera *f* viper
vi'raggio *m* Phot toning; Naut, Aeron turn
vi'rale *adj* viral; **video** ~ viral video
vi'rare *vi* turn; ‹*nave*› put about; **virare di bordo** change course
vi'rata *f* (di aereo) turning; (di nave) coming about; (nel nuoto) turn; fig change of direction
'virgola *f* comma; Math [decimal] point; **punto e virgola** semicolon; **quattro** ~ **due (4,2)** (decimali) four point two (4.2)
virgo'lette *fpl* inverted commas, quotation marks
vi'rile *adj* virile; (da uomo) manly
virilità *f inv* virility; manliness
viril'mente *adv* in a manly way

⚷ key word

V

vi'rologo *m* virologist
virtù *f inv* virtue; **in ~ di** ‹*legge*› under
virtu'ale *adj* virtual
virtual'mente *adv* virtually
virtuo'sismo *m* bravura
virtu'oso **A** *adj* virtuous
B *m* virtuoso
viru'lento *adj* virulent
'virus *m* virus
visa'gista *mf* beautician
visce'rale *adj* visceral; ‹*odio*› deep-seated; ‹*reazione*› gut
'viscere **A** *m* internal organ
B *fpl* guts
'vischio *m* mistletoe
vischi'oso *adj* viscous; (appiccicoso) sticky
'viscido *adj* slimy
vi'sconte *m* viscount
viscon'tessa *f* viscountess
vi'scoso *adj* viscous
vi'sibile *adj* visible
visi'bilio *m* profusion; **andare in ~** go into ecstasies
visibilità *f inv* visibility; **scarsa ~** poor visibility
visi'era *f* (di elmo) visor; (di berretto) peak
visio'nare *vt* examine; Cinema screen
visio'nario, -a *adj & nmf* visionary
visi'one *f* vision; **prima visione** Cinema first showing; **seconda ~** re-release, second showing
■ **visione notturna** night vision
'visita *f* visit; (breve) call; Med examination; **fare ~ a qualcuno** pay somebody a visit
■ **visita di controllo** Med check-up; **visita di cortesia** courtesy visit; **visita doganale** customs inspection; **visita a domicilio** home visit, call-out, house call; **visita fiscale** tax inspection; **visita guidata** guided tour; **visita lampo** flying visit; **visita di leva** medical examination (*for military service*)
visi'tare *vt* visit; (brevemente) call on; Med examine
visita|'tore, -trice *mf* visitor
visiva'mente *adv* visually
vi'sivo *adj* visual
'viso *m* face
■ **viso pallido** paleface
vi'sone *m* mink
'vispo *adj* lively
vis'suto **A** pp di **vivere**
B *adj* experienced
'vista *f* sight; (veduta) view; **a ~ d'occhio** ‹*crescere*› visibly; ‹*estendersi*› as far as the eye can see; **in ~ di** in view of; **perdere di ~ qualcuno** lose sight of somebody; fig lose touch with somebody; **a prima ~** at first sight
■ **vista sul mare** sea view
'visto **A** pp di **vedere**
B *m* visa
■ **visto di entrata** *o* **di ingresso** entry visa, entry permit; **visto d'uscita** exit visa
C *conj* **~ che...** seeing that...
vistosa'mente *adv* conspicuously
vi'stoso *adj* showy; (notevole) considerable
visu'ale *adj* visual
visualiz'zare *vt* visualize; Comput display
visualizza'tore *m* Comput display, VDU
■ **visualizzatore a cristalli liquidi** Comput liquid crystal display
visualizzazi'one *f* Comput display
'vita *f* life; (durata della vita) lifetime; Anat waist; **a ~** for life; **essere in fin di ~** be at death's door; **essere in ~** be alive; **fare la bella ~** lead the good life; **costo della ~** cost of living
■ **vita eterna** eternal life; **vita media** Biol life expectancy; **vita mondana** high life; **fare ~ mondana** lead the high life; **vita notturna** night life; **vita terrena** Relig life on earth
vi'taccia *f* slog
vi'tale *adj* vital
vitalità *f inv* vitality
vita'lizio **A** *adj* life *attrib*
B *m* [life] annuity
vita'mina *f* vitamin
vita'minico *adj* vitamin-enriched
vitaminiz'zato *adj* vitamin-enriched
'vite *f* Mech screw; Bot vine; **giro di ~** fig clampdown
■ **vite canadese** Virginia creeper; **vite di coda** Aeron tailspin; **vite perpetua** endless screw
vi'tella *f* (animale) calf; (carne) veal
vi'tello *m* calf; (carne) veal; (pelle) calfskin
■ **vitello di latte** milk-fed veal; **vitello tonnato** *sliced veal with tuna, anchovy, oil and lemon sauce*
vi'ticcio *m* tendril
viticol'tore *m* wine grower
viticol'tura *f* wine growing
vi'tino *m* narrow waist
■ **vitino di vespa** slender little waist
'vitreo *adj* vitreous; ‹*sguardo*› glassy
'vittima *f* victim
'vitto *m* food; (pasti) board
■ **vitto e alloggio** board and lodging
vit'toria *f* victory
vittori'ano *adj* Victorian
vittoriosa'mente *adv* victoriously, triumphantly
vittori'oso *adj* victorious
vitupe'rare *vt* vituperate
vitu'perio *m* insult
vi'uzza *f* narrow lane
'viva *int* hurrah!; **~ la Regina!** long live the Queen!
vi'vace *adj* vivacious; ‹*mente*› lively; ‹*colore*› bright
vivace'mente *adv* vivaciously

vivacità *f inv* vivacity; (di mente) liveliness; (di colore) brightness
vivaciz'zare *vt* liven up
vi'vaio *m* nursery; (per pesci) pond; fig breeding ground
viva'mente *adv* ‹*ringraziare*› warmly
vi'vanda *f* food; (piatto) dish
vi'vente **A** *adj* living
B *mpl* **i viventi** the living
⚷ **'vivere** **A** *vi* live; ~ **di** live on; **vive** Typ stet
B *vt* (passare) go through
C *m* life; **modo di vivere** way of life
'viveri *mpl* provisions
vivida'mente *adv* vividly
'vivido *adj* vivid
vi'viparo *adj* viviparous
vivisezio'nare *vt* vivisect
vivisezi'one *f* vivisection
⚷ **'vivo** **A** *adj* alive; (vivente) living; (vivace) lively; ‹*colore*› bright; **farsi ~** keep in touch; (arrivare) turn up
B *m* **colpire qualcuno sul ~** cut somebody to the quick; **dal ~** (trasmissione) live; ‹*disegnare*› from life; **i vivi** the living
■ **vivo e vegeto** alive and kicking
vizi'are *vt* spoil ‹*bambino ecc.*›; (guastare) vitiate
vizi'ato *adj* spoilt; ‹*aria*› stale
'vizio *m* vice; (cattiva abitudine) bad habit; (difetto) flaw
■ **vizio capitale** deadly sin; **vizio di forma** legal technicality; **vizio procedurale** procedural error
vizi'oso *adj* dissolute; (difettoso) faulty; **circolo ~** vicious circle
'vizzo *adj* ‹*pelle*› wrinkled; ‹*pianta*› withered
V.le *abbr* (**viale**) Ave
vocabo'lario *m* dictionary; (lessico) vocabulary
vo'cabolo *m* word
vo'cale **A** *adj* vocal
B *f* vowel
vo'calico *adj* ‹*corde*› vocal; ‹*suono*› vowel *attrib*
vocazi'one *f* vocation
⚷ **'voce** *f* voice; (diceria) rumour; (di bilancio, dizionario) entry
■ **voce bianca** Mus treble voice; **voce fuori campo** voice-over
voci'are **A** *vi* (spettegolare) gossip
B *m* buzz of conversation
vocife'rare *vi* shout; **si vocifera che...** it is rumoured that...
'vodka *f inv* vodka
'voga *f* rowing; (lena) enthusiasm; (moda) vogue; **essere in ~** be in vogue
vo'gare *vi* row; **~ a bratto** scull; **~ di coppia** scull

voga'tore *m* oarsman; (attrezzo) rowing machine
⚷ **'voglia** *f* desire; (volontà) will; (della pelle) birthmark; **aver ~ di fare qualcosa** feel like doing something; **morire dalla ~ di qualcosa** be dying for something; **di buona ~** willingly
'voglio ▸ **volere**
vogli'oso *adj* ‹*occhi, persona*› covetous; **essere ~ di qualcosa** want something
⚷ **'voi** *pers pron* you; **siete ~?** is that you?; **l'avete fatto ~?** did you do it yourselves?
voia'ltri *pers pron* you
vo'lano *m* shuttlecock; Mech flywheel
vo'lant *m inv* valance
vo'lante **A** *adj* flying; ‹*foglio*› loose
B *m* steering wheel
volanti'nare *vi* hand out leaflets
volan'tino *m* leaflet
⚷ **vo'lare** *vi* fly
vo'lata *f* Sport final sprint; **di ~** in a rush
vo'latile **A** *adj* ‹*liquido*› volatile
B *m* bird
volatiliz'zarsi *vr* vanish
vol-au-'vent *m inv* vol-au-vent
vo'lée *f inv* Tennis volley
vo'lente *adj* **~ o nolente** whether you like it or not
volente'roso *adj* willing
⚷ **volenti'eri** *adv* willingly; **~!** with pleasure!
⚷ **vo'lere** **A** *vt* want; (chiedere di) ask for; (aver bisogno di) need; **non voglio** I don't want to; **vuole che lo faccia io** he wants me to do it; **fai come vuoi** do as you like; **se tuo padre vuole, ti porto al cinema** if your father agrees, I'll take you to the cinema; **questa pianta vuole molte cure** this plant needs a lot of care; **vorrei un caffè** I'd like a coffee; **la leggenda vuole che...** legend has it that...; **la vuoi smettere?** will you stop that!; **senza ~** without meaning to; **voler bene/male a qualcuno** love/have something against somebody; **voler dire** mean; **ci vuole il latte** we need milk; **ci vuole tempo/pazienza** it takes time/patience; **volerne a** have a grudge against; **vuoi... vuoi...** either... or...
B *m* will; **voleri** *pl* wishes
⚷ **vol'gare** *adj* vulgar; (popolare) common
volgarità *f inv* vulgarity; **dire ~** use vulgar language, be vulgar
volgariz'zare *vt* popularize
volgarizzazi'one *f* popularization
volgar'mente *adv* (grossolanamente) vulgarly; (comunemente) commonly, popularly
⚷ **'volgere** *vt & vi* turn
'volgersi *vr* turn [round]; **~ a** (dedicarsi) take up
'volgo *m* common people
voli'era *f* aviary
voli'tivo *adj* strong-minded

⚷ key word

'volo *m* flight; **al ~** ‹*fare qualcosa*› quickly; ‹*prendere qualcosa*› in mid-air; **alzarsi in ~** ‹*uccello*› take off; **in ~** airborne
■ **volo di andata** outward flight; **volo charter** charter flight; **volo diretto** direct flight; **volo di linea** scheduled flight; **volo nazionale** domestic flight; **volo di ritorno** return flight; **volo strumentale** flying on instruments; **volo a vela** gliding

volontà *f inv* will; (desiderio) wish; **a ~** ‹*mangiare*› as much as you like

volontaria'mente *adv* voluntarily

volon'tario **A** *adj* voluntary
B *m* volunteer

volonte'roso *adj* willing

'volpe *f* fox

vol'pino **A** *adj* ‹*astuzia*› fox-like
B *m* (cane) Pomeranian

volt *m inv* volt

'volta *f* time; (turno) turn; (curva) bend; Archit vault; **4 volte 4** 4 times 4; **a volte, qualche ~** sometimes; **c'era una ~...** once upon a time there was...; **una ~** once; **due volte** twice; **tre/quattro volte** three/four times; **una ~ per tutte** once and for all; **una ~ ogni tanto** every so often; **uno alla ~** one at a time; **alla ~ di** in the direction of
■ **volta a botte** barrel vault; **volta celeste** vault of heaven; **volta cranica** cranial vault; **volta a crociera** groin vault; **volta a vela** ribbed vault; **volta a ventaglio** fan vault

volta'faccia *m inv* volte-face

voltagab'bana *mf inv* turncoat

vol'taggio *m* voltage

vol'tare *vt & vi* turn; (rigirare) turn round; (rivoltare) turn over; **~ pagina** fig turn over a new leaf

vol'tarsi *vr* turn [round]

volta'stomaco *m* nausea; fig disgust

volteggi'are *vi* circle; (ginnastica) vault

'volto **A** pp di **volgere**
B *m* face; **ha mostrato il suo vero ~** he revealed his true colours

vol'tura *f* (catastale) transfer of property
■ **~ di contratto** transfer of contract

vo'lubile *adj* fickle

volubil'mente *adv* in a fickle way, inconstantly

vo'lume *m* volume
■ **volume di gioco** Sport possession

volumi'noso *adj* voluminous

vo'luta *f* (spirale) spiral; (di capitello) volute

voluta'mente *adv* deliberately

vo'luto *adj* deliberate, intended

voluttà *f inv* voluptuousness

voluttu'ario *adj* non-essential; **beni** *pl* **voluttuari** non-essentials

voluttu'oso *adj* voluptuous

vomi'tare *vt* vomit, be sick

vomi'tevole *adj* nauseating

'vomito *m* vomit

'vongola *f* clam

vo'race *adj* voracious

vorace'mente *adv* voraciously

vo'ragine *f* abyss

vor'rei ▸ **volere**

'vortice *m* whirl; (gorgo) whirlpool; (di vento) whirlwind

vorticosa'mente *adv* in whirls

'vostro **A** (**il ~** *m* **la vostra** *f* **i vostri** *mpl* **le vostre** *fpl*) *poss adj* your; **è vostra questa macchina?** is this car yours?; **un ~ amico** a friend of yours; **~ padre** your father
B *poss pron* yours; **i vostri** your folks

vo'tante *mf* voter

vo'tare *vi* vote

votazi'one *f* voting; Sch marks *pl*
■ **votazione di fiducia** Pol fig vote of confidence; **votazione per alzata di mano** show of hands; **votazione a scrutinio segreto** secret ballot

'voto *m* vote; Sch mark; Relig vow
■ **voto decisivo** casting vote; **voto per alzata di mano** show of hands

vs. *abbr* Comm (**vostro**) yours

vudù *m inv* voodoo

vul'canico *adj* volcanic

vul'cano *m* volcano
■ **vulcano intermittente** dormant volcano; **vulcano spento** extinct volcano

vulne'rabile *adj* vulnerable

vulnerabilità *f inv* vulnerability

'vulva *f* vulva

vuo'tare *vt* empty

vuo'tarsi *vr* empty

vu'oto **A** *adj* empty; (non occupato) vacant; **~ di** (sprovvisto) devoid of
B *m* empty space; Phys vacuum; fig void; **assegno a ~** dud cheque; **sotto ~** ‹*prodotto*› vacuum-packed
■ **vuoto d'aria** air pocket; **vuoto a perdere** no deposit; **vuoto a rendere** ‹*bottiglia*› returnable

Ww

W *abbr* (**viva**) long live
'wafer *m inv* (biscotto) wafer
wagon-'lit *m inv* sleeping car
walkie-'talkie *m inv* walkie-talkie
'water *m inv* toilet, loo infml
watt *m inv* watt
wat'tora *m inv* Phys watt-hour
WC *m* WC
'web *m inv* Web
'webcam *f inv* webcam
web'master *m inv* webmaster
wee'kend *m inv* weekend
'welter *adj & m inv* (in pugilato) welterweight
'western A *adj inv* cowboy *attrib*
B *m inv* Cinema western
'whisky *m inv* whisky
■ **whisky di malto** malt [whisky]
wi-'fi *m* wi-fi; **rete ~** wi-fi network
wind'surf *m inv* (tavola) windsurf; (sport) windsurfing; **fare ~** windsurf
windsur'fista *mf* sailboarder, windsurfer
'würstel *m inv* frankfurter

Xx

xenofo'bia *f* xenophobia
xe'nofobo, -a A *adj* xenophobic
B *mf* xenophobe
'xeres *m inv* sherry
xero'copia *f* xerox
xeroco'piare *vt* photocopy
xerocopia'trice *f* photocopier
xilofo'nista *mf* xylophone player
xi'lofono *m* xylophone

Yy

yacht *m inv* yacht
yak *m inv* Zool yak
'yankee *mf inv* Yank
'Yemen *m* Yemen
yeme'nita *mf* Yemeni
yen *m inv* yen
'yeti *m* yeti
'yiddish *adj inv & nm* Yiddish
'yoga A *m* yoga
B *adj inv* yoga *attrib*
'yogurt *m inv* yoghurt
yogurti'era *f* yoghurt maker
'yorkshire *m inv* (cane) Yorkshire terrier
yo-'yo® *m inv* yo-yo®
yup'pismo *m* yuppiedom

Zz

zaba[gl]ione *m* zabaglione (*dessert made from eggs, wine or marsala and sugar*)
'zacchera *f* (schizzo) splash of mud
zaf'fata *f* whiff; (di fumo) cloud
zaffe'rano *m* saffron
zaf'firo *m* sapphire
'zagara *f* orange blossom
'zaino *m* rucksack
Za'ire *m* Zaire
'Zambia *m* Zambia
'zampa *f* leg; **a quattro zampe** (animale) four-legged; (carponi) on all fours; **zampe** *pl* **di gallina** fig crow's feet; **zampe** *pl* **posteriori** hind legs
zam'pata *f* paw; **dare una ~** a hit with its paw
zampet'tare *vi* scamper
zam'petto *m* Culin knuckle
zampil'lante *adj* spurting
zampil'lare *vi* spurt
zam'pillo *m* spurt
zam'pino *m* paw; **mettere lo ~ in** fig have a hand in
zam'pogna *f* bagpipe
zampo'gnaro *m* piper
zam'pone *fpl stuffed pigs trotter with lentils*
'zangola *f* churn
'zanna *f* fang; (di elefante) tusk
zan'zara *f* mosquito
zanzari'era *f* (velo) mosquito net; (su finestra) insect screen
'zappa *f* hoe; **darsi la ~ sui piedi** fig shoot oneself in the foot
zap'pare *vt* hoe
zap'pata *f* **dare una ~** a hit with a hoe
zappet'tare *vt* hoe
'zapping *m inv* channel-hopping BrE, channel-surfing AmE; **fare lo ~** channel-hop BrE, channel-surf AmE
zar *m inv* tzar
za'rina *f* tzarina
za'rista *adj & nmf* tzarist
'zattera *f* raft
zatte'roni *mpl* (scarpe) wedge shoes
za'vorra *f* ballast; fig dead wood
zavor'rare *vt* load with ballast
'zazzera *f* mop of hair
'zebra *f* zebra; **zebre** *pl* (passaggio pedonale) zebra crossing, crosswalk AmE
ze'brato *adj* ‹*tessuto*› with black and white stripes
'zecca¹ *f* mint; **nuovo di ~** brand new
'zecca² *f* (parassita) tick
zec'chino *m* sequin; **oro ~** pure gold
ze'lante *adj* zealous
'zelo *m* zeal
'zenit *m* zenith
'zenzero *m* ginger
'zeppa *f* wedge
'zeppo *adj* packed full; **pieno ~ di** crammed *or* packed with
zer'bino *m* doormat
'zero *m* zero, nought; (in calcio) nil; Tennis love; **due a ~** (in partite) two nil; **ricominciare da ~** fig start again from scratch; **sparare a ~ su qualcuno** fig lay into somebody; **avere il morale sotto ~** fig be down in the dumps
'zeta *f* zed, zee AmE
🔑 **'zia** *f* aunt
zibel'lino *m* sable
zi'gano, -a *adj & nmf* gypsy
'zigolo *m* Zool bunting
'zigomo *m* cheekbone
zigri'nato *adj* ‹*pelle*› grained; ‹*metallo*› milled
zig'zag *m inv* zigzag; **andare a ~** zigzag
Zim'babwe *m* Zimbabwe
zim'bello *m* decoy; (oggetto di scherno) laughing stock
'zinco *m* zinc
zinga'resco *adj* gypsy *attrib*
'zingaro, -a *mf* gypsy
🔑 **'zio** *m* uncle
'zippo *m* sl lighter
zi'tella *f* spinster; derog old maid
zitel'lona *f* derog old maid
zit'tire **A** *vi* fall silent **B** *vt* silence
🔑 **'zitto** *adj* silent; **sta' ~!** keep quiet!
ziz'zania *f* (discordia) discord; **seminare ~** cause trouble
'zoccola *f* vulg whore
'zoccolo *m* clog; (di cavallo) hoof; (di terra) clump; (di parete) skirting board, baseboard AmE; (di colonna) base
■ **zoccolo duro** Pol hard core; **zoccolo fesso** cloven foot, cloven hoof
zodia'cale *adj* of the zodiac; **segno ~** sign of the zodiac, birth sign
zo'diaco *m* zodiac
zolfa'nello *m* match
'zolfo *m* sulphur

'zolla *f* clod
zol'letta *f* sugar cube, sugar lump
'zombi *mf inv* fig zombie
zom'pare *vi* sl bonk
🔑 **'zona** *f* zone; (area) area
■ **zona calda** fig hot spot; **zona denuclearizzata** nuclear-free zone; **zona di depressione** area of low pressure; **zona disastrata** disaster area; **zona disco** area for parking discs only; **zona erogena** erogenous zone; **zona di esclusione aerea** air exclusion zone; **zona euro** Eurozone; **zona giorno** living area; **zona industriale** industrial estate; **zona notte** sleeping area; **zona d'ombra** fig twilight zone; **zona pedonale** pedestrian precinct; **zona a traffico limitato** restricted traffic area; **zona verde** green belt
zonizzazi'one *f* zoning
'zonzo *adv* **andare a ~** stroll about
'zoo *m inv* zoo
zoolo'gia *f* zoology
zoo'logico *adj* zoological
zo'ologo, -a *mf* zoologist
zoosa'fari *m inv* safari park
zootec'nia *f* animal husbandry
zoo'tecnico *adj* ‹*progresso*› in animal husbandry; **patrimonio ~** livestock
zoppi'cante *adj* limping; fig shaky
zoppi'care *vi* limp; (essere debole) be shaky
'zoppo, -a **A** *adj* lame
B *mf* cripple offensive
'zotico *adj* uncouth
zoti'cone *m* boor
zu'ava *f* **calzoni** *pl* **alla ~** plus fours
'zucca *f* marrow; infml (testa) head; infml (persona) thickie; **cos'hai in quella ~?** haven't you got anything between your ears?
zuc'cata *f* **prendere una ~** infml hit one's head
zucche'rare *vt* sugar
zucche'rato *adj* sugared; **non ~** ‹*succo d'arancia ecc.*› unsweetened
zuccheri'era *f* sugar bowl
zuccheri'ficio *m* sugar refinery
zucche'rino **A** *adj* sugary
B *m* sugar cube, sugar lump; fig sweetener; **essere uno ~** fig ‹*persona*› be a softy; ‹*cosa*› be a cinch
'zucchero *m* sugar
■ **zucchero di canna** cane sugar; **zucchero filato** candyfloss; **zucchero greggio** brown sugar; **zucchero vanigliato** vanilla sugar; **zucchero a velo** icing sugar, confectioners' sugar AmE
zucche'roso *adj* fig honeyed
zuc'chetto *m* (cappello) beanie
zuc'china *f* courgette, zucchini AmE
zuc'chino *m* courgette, zucchini AmE
zuc'cone *m* infml blockhead
zuc'cotto *m* *dessert made with sponge, cream, chocolate and candied fruit*
'zuffa *f* scuffle
zufo'lare *vt & vi* whistle
'zufolo *m* penny whistle
zu'mare *vi* zoom
zu'mata *f* zoom
'zuppa *f* soup
■ **zuppa inglese** trifle
zup'petta *f* **fare ~ [con]** dunk
zuppi'era *f* soup tureen
'zuppo *adj* soaked

Contents

Italian traditions, festivals, and holidays

1 January

Capodanno (New Year's Day).
A public holiday often spent getting over the excesses of New Year's Eve.

6 January

Epifania (Twelfth Night).
A public holiday and religious festival celebrating the adoration of Jesus by the three kings. By popular tradition it is also the day when Befana, a legendary old woman on a broomstick, brings children gifts: they are supposed to hang up their stockings the night before and in the morning should find them full of sweets, cakes, and little presents or, if they have been naughty, coal (though nowadays it is usually a sugary substitute).

14 February

San Valentino (St Valentine's Day).
As in other countries, this day is for lovers, marked by flowers, chocolates, and candlelit dinners.

8 March

Festa delle donne (Women's Day).
Since the 1970s, Women's Day has been celebrated with sprays of mimosa and discussions on women's issues.

19 March

Festa del papà (Father's Day).
St Joseph's Day is the day on which Italian fathers are celebrated.

1 April

Pesce d'aprile.
This is April Fool's Day, when it is traditional to play jokes and tricks on people. Children have fun trying to stick a little paper fish (*pesciolino*) onto people's backs without their noticing, and then calling, '*Il pesce d'aprile!*' (literally, 'April fish').

25 April

Anniversario della Liberazione (Anniversary of the Liberation).
A public holiday, this is a day of official ceremonies. It commemorates the day in 1945 when Italy was liberated from Nazi German occupation by invading Allied forces.

1 May

Festa del lavoro (International Labour Day) is a public holiday. This is a civil festival celebrating the workers of the world.

2 June

Festa della Repubblica is a public holiday, a civil festival to commemorate the referendum of 2 June 1946 which led to the proclamation of the Italian Republic.

15 August

L'Assunzione (Feast of the Assumption) is a public holiday – a religious festival that celebrates the Assumption of the Virgin Mary to heaven. Also known as *ferragosto*, it marks the peak of the summer holidays. The factories in the north are closed, as are many shops, except for those in tourist areas.

1 November

I Santi/Ognissanti (All Saints' Day).
Public holiday and religious festival celebrating all the saints. Typically, cakes made with nuts and raisins, which vary from region to region, are eaten during this festival. People go to the cemetery to take flowers for their dead loved ones, although the Festival of the Dead (I Morti) is the following day, 2 November, which is not a public holiday.

8 December

L'immacolata Concezione (Feast of the Immaculate Conception).
Public holiday and religious festival that celebrates the purity of the Virgin Mary.

24 December

La vigilia di Natale (Christmas Eve) is not a public holiday, although the schools are usually closed. Families get together, and often a large dinner is prepared. Afterwards people open their Christmas presents from under the tree. The faithful go to midnight Mass.

25 December

Natale (Christmas Day) is a public holiday and one of the most important religious festivals for Italians. Families who did not open their presents the night before do so on Christmas morning. Children who believe in Father Christmas think that he has come down the chimney to bring their presents during the night. Families get together to eat a big dinner, typically including a capon and ending with *panettone* (a dome-shaped cake with sultanas and candied fruit) and a glass of spumante, Italian sparkling wine.

26 December

Santo Stefano (St Stephen's Day).
A public and religious holiday during which Christmas celebrations continue.

31 December

San Silvestro (New Year's Eve).
The celebration of the end of the old year and beginning of the new. It is a working day for many people, although students are on holiday, but in the evening there is usually a big meal and a party, either at home or in a restaurant. Typical dishes are lentils (which are said to bring wealth) and *cotechino* (a large pork sausage), and a great deal of champagne and spumante is drunk. On the stroke of midnight, fireworks are set off. In days gone by, it was traditional to throw crockery and other belongings out of the window to mark the rejection of the old in readiness for the New Year, but this no longer happens, to avoid damage to cars and injury to passers-by.

Movable holidays

Giovedì grasso (the Thursday before Lent).
Fancy dress parties are held and people traditionally eat pancakes and fried pastries.

Martedì grasso (Shrove Tuesday).
In some regions schools are closed.

Mercoledì delle ceneri (Ash Wednesday) is a religious occasion that marks the beginning of Lent. Some people fast on this day.

Venerdì santo (Good Friday).
A religious occasion. It is not a public holiday, though some schools are closed.

Pasqua (Easter) is the most important Catholic festival, celebrating the resurrection of Christ. A popular saying goes: *'Natale con i tuoi, Pasqua con chi vuoi'* (Christmas with your family, Easter with whoever you want), and in fact Italians often take the opportunity of the holiday period to go away on holiday. Those who stay at home cook a big meal, usually of lamb because of its symbolic meaning. A *colomba* (dove-shaped cake) is the traditional Easter cake.

Pasquetta (Easter Monday) is a public holiday when people often go out for the day, to the sea, the mountains, or the countryside.

L'Ascensione (Ascension).
A religious festival celebrating the ascension of Christ to heaven. It falls on the Thursday forty days after Easter.

Pentecoste (Whitsun) is a religious festival celebrating the descent of the holy spirit to the apostles. It falls fifty days after Easter.

Festa della Mamma (Mothers' Day) is on the second Sunday in May. Cards are sent and sometimes a present: perfume, chocolates, or flowers, especially roses.

Festival dei Due Mondi or Festival di Spoleto (in the province of Perugia) takes place each year from late June to mid-July. It hosts dance, theatre, opera, and music events, to which the biggest world names are invited.

Festival di Sanremo This Ligurian tourist resort has hosted the festival of Italian music every year since 1951. After a period of decline in the 1970s, the festival has recently regained its popularity. Established singers take part, but it is also often the launch pad for new talent.

Giorni festivi nei paesi anglofoni

1 gennaio

New Year's Day (Capodanno).
Giorno festivo, generalmente trascorso a riprendersi dai festeggiamenti della notte precedente.

2 gennaio

Giorno festivo in Scozia.

6 gennaio

Epiphany o **Twelfth Night** (Epifania).
Non ci sono particolari tradizioni legate a questa giornata, ma molti in questo giorno disfano l'albero di Natale e mettono via le decorazioni natalizie.

25 gennaio

Burns Night.
Ricorrenza della nascita del poeta scozzese Robert Burns (XVIII secolo).
Gli scozzesi festeggiano con una cena detta *Burns Supper* il cui piatto forte si chiama *haggis* (intestino di pecora farcito con una miscela di avena, frattaglie, cipolle e spezie). Tradizionalmente, durante la cena accompagnata dal suono delle cornamuse, si beve whisky e si leggono ad alta voce brani delle poesie di Robert Burns.

2 febbraio

Groundhog Day.
Giorno in cui, secondo la tradizione statunitense, la marmotta (*groundhog*) esce dalla sua tana sotterranea alla fine del letargo. Se c'è il sole e la marmotta vede la propria ombra si nasconderà nella tana e ci saranno altre sei settimane di cattivo tempo. Se non vede la propria ombra, si crede che la primavera comincerà presto.

14 febbraio

St Valentine's Day (San Valentino).
Nel giorno di San Valentino gli innamorati si scambiano fiori e regali. Esiste inoltre la tradizione di inviare un biglietto anonimo alla persona per cui si prova una tenera simpatia.

1 marzo

St David's Day.
Giorno di festa nazionale in Galles, di cui San Davide è il santo protettore.

17 marzo

St Patrick's Day.
La festa di San Patrizio, patrono d'Irlanda, viene celebrata dagli irlandesi in tutto il mondo con musica, canti e grandi bevute.

1 aprile

April Fools' Day (Pesce d'Aprile).
Giornata in cui si fanno numerosi scherzi: le vittime di tali scherzi sono dette *April Fools*.

23 aprile

St George's Day.
San Giorgio è il patrono d'Inghilterra.

1 luglio

Canada Day.
Festa nazionale che commemora l'unificazione delle colonie britanniche nordamericane del 1° luglio 1867.

4 luglio

Independence Day.
In questo giorno di festa nazionale negli Stati Uniti si celebra l'approvazione della Dichiarazione d'Indipendenza (1776) con parate, spettacoli di fuochi artificiali e picnic. In moltissime case viene esposta la bandiera americana.

12 ottobre

Columbus Day.
Giorno festivo negli Stati Uniti, ricorrenza della scoperta dell'America da parte di Cristoforo Colombo nel 1492.

31 ottobre

Hallowe'en (vigilia d'Ognissanti).
La notte della vigilia d'Ognissanti in cui, secondo un'antica credenza anglosassone,

è possibile vedere i fantasmi. Oggi è festeggiata per lo più dai bambini, che ricavano lanterne dalle zucche svuotate, si mascherano e fanno il giro del vicinato per chiedere dolci e regalini con il *trick or treat* ('dolcetto o scherzetto').

5 novembre

Bonfire Night/Guy Fawkes Night.
In Gran Bretagna si festeggia il fallimento della Congiura delle Polveri per far saltare in aria il Parlamento nel 1605. Ovunque si organizzano spettacoli di fuochi d'artificio e falò in cui viene bruciato un pupazzo rudimentale detto *guy* che rappresenta Guy Fawkes, uno dei cospiratori.

11 novembre

Remembrance Day,
Veteran's Day negli USA.
Giornata in cui si commemorano i caduti di tutte le guerre e la firma dell'armistizio (1918) che mise fine alla prima guerra mondiale.

In Gran Bretagna la ricorrenza è anche nota come Poppy Day (giorno del papavero), per l'usanza di portare un papavero rosso di stoffa o carta sul petto (dai campi di papaveri in cui morirono migliaia di soldati sui fronti francese e belga).

30 novembre

St Andrew's Day.
Sant'Andrea è il patrono della Scozia.

25 dicembre

Christmas Day (giorno di Natale).
Giorno festivo. Per tradizione i familiari si scambiano i doni intorno all'albero la mattina di Natale e i bambini spesso trovano, al risveglio, una calza (*Christmas stocking*) piena di dolci e regalini lasciata da Father Christmas, anche chiamato Santa Claus.

26 dicembre

Boxing Day in Gran Bretagna,
St Stephen's Day in Irlanda.
Giorno festivo.

31 dicembre

New Year's Eve (la notte di San Silvestro).
In Scozia si chiama **Hogmanay** ed è tradizione andare a trovare amici e vicini di casa per augurare loro pace e prosperità portando in dono un pezzo di carbone o del whisky o qualcosa da mangiare.

A–Z of Italian life and culture

Accademia della Crusca An academy for the study of the Italian language, founded in Florence in 1583, with the original aim of establishing the supremacy of the literary dialect in Florence – or of separating the 'flour' of pure language from the 'bran' (*crusca* – hence its name) of vulgarity. From 1612 it published the *Vocabolario degli accademici della Crusca* (Dictionary of the Members of the Accademia della Crusca), which became a model for similar works on the major European languages, and was printed in various editions until 1923. With only one interruption, from 1783 to 1811, the Academy has continued its work down to the present day. Currently based in the Villa di Castello near Florence, it is a centre for linguistic, philological, and lexicographical research. Unlike the French Académie Française or the Spanish Real Academia, however, it does not have the last word on what is correct or incorrect in Italian.

acqua alta An exceptionally high tide that sometimes affects the lagoon of Venice during the winter months. It is caused by particular wind conditions, but exacerbated by human interference with the environment. When the level of the lagoon rises, peaking sometimes at 1.4 metres (4.6 feet) and over, many of the streets and piazzas of Venice disappear under centimetres of water. Sirens are sounded three or four hours before the *acqua alta* reaches full height, and footbridges are put up to allow pedestrians to continue to use the busiest routes.

agriturismo A holiday based on a farm. It was originally intended that the holiday-makers would help with work on the farm in some capacity, but nowadays this virtually never happens. The word *agriturismo* is also used for the venue – the farmhouse, often renovated and refurbished specially for tourists. This type of holiday offers activities such as walking, horse-riding, etc. Locally-produced food and the open-air lifestyle are the main attractions. It is becoming much more popular and more expensive than it was at first.

Alto Adige The northern part of the Trentino-Alto Adige region, consisting of the province of Bolzano (called Südtirol [South Tirol] in German), ceded to Italy after the First World War. The majority of the population are German-speaking and of German descent. Since 1948 it has had a degree of autonomy, reinforced in 1972; place names are shown in Italian and German and holders of public offices have to pass an exam to show they are bilingual. Teaching in schools, however, is in German only for those of German descent, or Italian only for those of Italian descent. In future, this system is to be replaced by genuine bilingualism.

anno scolastico The Italian school year usually begins in mid-September and ends at the beginning of June (except for students who are taking exams). As well as a few days' holiday for the various civil and religious festivals, there are about ten days' holiday over Christmas, New Year, and Twelfth Night, plus a few days at Easter. *See also* SCUOLA.

aperitivo It is an Italian tradition to have an aperitif, which may or may not be alcoholic and is served with a few peanuts, olives, or other appetizers, before lunch or dinner. Many bars have their own, homemade *aperitivo*, based on liqueurs and fruit juices. Taking time for a pre-meal drink also provides a chance to catch up with friends.

ASL – Azienda Sanitaria Locale The Servizio Nazionale di Assistenza Sanitaria (or National Health Service) provides care for citizens through these local health authorities.

autoricarica A mobile phone scheme available in Italy where customers are rewarded by having their accounts re-credited according to either how long they have spent on incoming (or outgoing) calls, or how many text messages they have received (or sent).

autostrade Italy has a network of motorways – toll roads with two or more lanes on each carriageway. The tolls paid for using motorways finance their construction, management, and maintenance. The tariff depends on the vehicle in which you are travelling and the stretch of motorway concerned, the relative costs of construction and maintenance being taken into account (e.g. mountain stretches can be more expensive). Usually you take a ticket from the booth when joining the motorway and hand it in for payment at the other end. Alternatively you use an electronic toll collection (Telepass). The maximum speed limit for cars is 130 km/h (80 mph), or up to 150 km/h (94 mph) on some stretches.

Azzurri A popular name for the Italian national team in sports such as football, rugby, and hockey, from the blue shirts worn by the players.

Banca d'Italia The Italian central bank, founded in 1893. Since 1926 it has had a monopoly on the issue of currency, and supervisory jurisdiction over the Italian banking system. It also acts as the state treasury. Its central offices are located in the Via Nazionale in Rome. In the media, Via Nazionale is often used to mean the Bank of Italy.

Bancomat This is the name of the system of automatic cash withdrawal, of the actual cash machine, and of the card itself. The same card is often used as both a credit card and a bancomat card, so when you pay with the card in a shop you can use it as a credit card, or – by keying in your PIN on a special keypad – as a debit card.

bandiera arancione The orange flag is the mark of environmental quality awarded by the Italian Touring Club in inland areas. The criteria for the awarding of the orange flag are the development of cultural heritage, protection of the environment, standards of hospitality, and quality both of restoration and of local products.

bandiera blu The blue flag is an award given to beaches and ports in the member countries of the FEE (Federation for Environmental Education). The criteria that have to be met are, for beaches, the quality of the water and the coast, safety measures and services, and the promotion of environmental education. For ports, it is the quality of the water in the harbour, safety and disposal services, and environmental information.

bar A real institution of Italian life and culture, the bar is the place where you can have snacks, sandwiches, coffees, soft and alcoholic drinks, etc. Usually drinks are taken standing at the bar. In many bars there are also tables where you can sit and read the newspapers. Bars also play an important role in the lives of sports fans, as they meet there to watch football matches or other events on the television.

bel canto A style of singing, still practised today, that combines a light, bright quality of voice with the ability to sustain a beautifully clear and even tone through complicated passages. It emerged in Italy in the 15th and 16th centuries and was at its height in the early 19th century, when the composers Rossini, Bellini, and Donizetti exploited it to the full in their operas.

Biennale di Venezia An international show for the visual arts, cinema, architecture, dance, music, and theatre. The visual arts section still takes place every two years and often welcomes avant-garde artists. *See also* MOSTRA INTERNAZIONALE D'ARTE CINEMATOGRAFICA.

Bocconi With its headquarters in Milan, the Bocconi commercial university is an extremely prestigious private university, with only one faculty – economics.

caffè Coffee is a favourite Italian drink. Outside the home it can be drunk quickly standing at a bar counter, or in a more leisurely fashion while chatting at a table. In bars or restaurants you can order *un caffè* (normal), *ristretto* or *lungo* (weaker or stronger), *macchiato* (hot or cold, with a drop of milk), or *corretto* (with a drop of spirits). Also on offer are decaff and hot malt drinks (*caffè d'orzo*).

calcio Football is the sport that Italians love most, and of course it is a sport in which Italian teams have always excelled. The national league is divided into Serie A, Serie B, and Serie C. Some of the most famous Italian teams are Juventus, Milan, Inter (also based in Milan), Roma, and Lazio. *See also* AZZURRI.

Camera dei Deputati The legislative assembly that, along with the SENATO, makes up the Italian Parliament. It is composed of 630 deputies, elected by universal direct suffrage by citizens over 18 years of age.

Camicie rosse ▸ I MILLE

Camorra An organized-crime network operating in Naples and the Campania. The Camorra is not a single organization but made up of groups (families) who often fight for control of criminal activities. Emerging in the 1500s, it has for centuries practised blackmail and extortion on small businesses in Naples. After the Second World War, and particularly from the 1980s, it began to control drugs and arms trafficking, prostitution, and the allocation of public contracts, developing political links and assuming ever greater control of the Naples area.

Canton Ticino This is the only canton of the Swiss Confederation which has Italian as its official language. It is also the only Swiss region located south of the Alps. The history, culture, and language of this area are intermingled with those of the neighbouring Italian regions.

Capitoline One of the SEVEN HILLS OF ROME, the Capitoline was the acropolis and religious centre of the ancient city, and is now the headquarters of the City of Rome. The Piazza del Campidoglio at its top was designed by Michelangelo; the square is flanked by three palazzi now housing the Capitoline Museums. In the centre of the piazza stands a statue of Roman emperor, Marcus Aurelius, on horseback.

Caporetto A First World War battle in which Italian troops were heavily defeated. On 24 October 1917, Austrian and German troops launched a major offensive on the Italian front, breaking through near the small town of Caporetto (now Kobarid in Slovenia). The Italians retreated in disorder with very heavy losses. The name Caporetto entered the language as a byword for a total defeat or failure.

Capri An island close to the southern entrance to the Bay of Naples, and favourite tourist destination. Capri is chiefly famous for its romantic setting, for the Blue Grotto – a sea cave with a low entrance, which gets its name from the colour of the light filtered through the water, and for the remains of Roman villas built by the Emperor Tiberius, who made Capri his headquarters from AD 27–37.

carabinieri A corps of the Italian army that has the task of guaranteeing the safety of citizens and their property and ensuring that state laws are observed. As well as being a military police force and responsible for public safety, the *carabinieri* also function as judiciary police. *See also* POLIZIA DI STATO.

Carnevale This is the period before Lent running from Twelfth Night to Ash Wednesday. It is celebrated with fancy dress parties, confetti, and streamers, especially during the weekend running from '*giovedì grasso*' (the last Thursday) to '*martedì grasso*' (Shrove Tuesday), which is the final day. The Venice Carnival is one of the most famous, with its open-air shows and fancy-dress balls, and the Viareggio Carnival, with its parade of gigantic paper-pulp floats depicting caricatures of popular characters, is also well known.

carta d'identità An identity document issued to all citizens aged 15 and over. It is valid for foreign travel within the countries of the European Union, and for trips to some other countries with which there is an agreement. It is renewed every ten years at the town hall. An electronic card, the same size as a credit card, is gradually substituting the old paper identity cards.

Cassa integrazione or Cassa integrazione guadagni The benefit system for employees who are temporarily laid off because of a crisis in the company they work for. It is run by the INPS, which undertakes to pay a maximum of 80 per cent of normal salary for a period of one or two years.

Cattolica The 'Catholic university' is a prestigious private institute with humanities and science faculties, spread over five different campuses in Milan, Rome, Brescia, Cremona, and Piacenza.

Cavaliere – short for *Cavaliere al merito del lavoro* (Knight for services to industry) – is an official title, conferred since 1901 on those who make a major contribution to economic development. However, it is not uncommon for successful entrepreneurs to give their surnames the prefix *cavaliere* unofficially. Another frequently encountered title is that of *commendatore*, in common use over the past few decades as an honorific for any wealthy person.

Cavallino rampante The 'prancing horse' symbol of Ferrari. Enzo Ferrari adopted the symbol from a coat of arms belonging to a First World War flying ace. He first used it on the Alfa Romeo cars in his racing stable, then on the cars he began to produce himself in 1947 in Maranello (near Modena). Today it is synonymous with Ferrari both as a car-maker and as a Formula 1 team.

Cinecittà A complex of all of the different cinematographic studios set up on the outskirts of Rome in 1937. It includes a large number of film studios as well as studios for soundtracking.

CNR The Consiglio Nazionale delle Ricerche (National Research Council) is a national public body which carries out and promotes research activities for the scientific, technological, economic, and social development of the country.

codice civile e penale The civil and penal codes. The Italian codes, like those of other continental European countries, were modelled on the Code Napoléon, the French civil code first introduced in 1804. These superseded the common law, restructuring it on the enlightened principles of the French Revolution. The unified Italian state, founded in 1861, brought together the codes of the various states that made it up to constitute the civil code, the code of civil procedure, and the code of criminal procedure (on the French model) in 1865, and the criminal code in 1889. The new codes drawn up in the 20th century followed the same lines, with some modifications.

codice fiscale A combination of letters and numbers, based on the holder's particulars, which identifies every citizen or resident of Italy for tax purposes and other dealings with the authorities. It is indispensable if a person wishes to work, open a bank account, use the health service, etc. In current usage the term *codice fiscale* (tax code) also refers to the plastic card, similar in size to a credit card, issued to everybody by the Ministry of the Economy and Finance and bearing the holder's code and personal details.

Colosseo The name given in the Middle Ages to the 'colossal' Flavian Amphitheatre, the most famous monument of Ancient Rome, which was begun by Vespasian in about 75 AD and inaugurated by Titus in 80 AD. It is oval in shape and up to 50,000 spectators could attend the bloody battles between gladiators and beasts that were staged there.

comuni Each province is subdivided into municipalities (*comuni*), each of which is run by a council and municipal committee headed by a *sindaco* (mayor). The functions of the *comuni* are mainly administrative.

confederazioni sindacali The three large Italian trade union organizations that represent workers in all categories and sectors: the formerly Communist-oriented CGIL (Confederazione generale italiana del lavoro); the Christian-oriented CISL (Confederazione italiana sindacati lavoratori) and the social-democrat-oriented UIL (Unione italiana del lavoro). During the 1970s and 1980s they formed an alliance and collaborated to play a central role in politics and in the Italian economy. However, recent transformations in the economy and the labour market have reduced their unity of action, and their role has been partly reshaped by the rise of autonomous sectoral unions.

Consiglio dei ministri A body composed of ministers and headed by the PRESIDENTE DEL CONSIGLIO: it forms the government.

consultorio familiare Social-health service set up in the mid-1970s. It provides health education (including preventive medicine) in the fields of gynaecology and paediatrics, as well as advice and support for people with mental health or legal problems.

Corte Costituzionale The constitutional court, in operation since 1955, which has the duty of ensuring that laws passed by parliament do not conflict with the *costituzione* and of ruling on conflicts between the powers of the state and those of the regions. It is made up partly of magistrates and partly of jurists chosen by the parliament and the PRESIDENTE DELLA REPUBBLICA. It is based in Rome, in the Palazzo della Consulta (the Consulta being a former papal institution) next door to the QUIRINALE, and is often referred to as La Consulta.

costituzione The constitution of the Italian Republic, which came into force on 1 January 1948. It was drawn up by a constituent assembly, elected by the people, and based on the principles of liberty, equality, and democracy. A constitutional court (*corte costituzionale*) ensures that any individual laws passed by parliament conform to the constitution.

denominazione di origine controllata (*DOC*) The state-certified mark of quality awarded to Italian wines that possess certain verified characteristics, such as origin within a defined zone of production, derivation from particular types of vines and soils, ratio between the quantity of grapes used and quantity of wine obtained, and methods used in production. *DOC* wines that have become particularly famous for their special qualities are now certified as *DOCG* (*denominazione di origine controllata e garantita*), a mark based on even stricter standards of verification. *See also* VINO.

Divina Commedia The most celebrated and important work in Italian literature, written by Dante Alighieri between 1306 and 1321. *The Divine Comedy* is divided into three parts, *Inferno* (Hell), *Purgatorio* (Purgatory), and *Paradiso* (Heaven), each containing thirty-three cantos (plus one introductory canto to make 100). It describes a journey through the Christian afterlife and is probably best known and loved for its retelling of the stories of the characters Dante discovers in the three realms. Part of Dante's purpose was to prove that the Italian language could be used for serious works of literature. In his writing, he blended the language of court with the most expressive elements of his native Tuscan and other dialects, helping to lay the foundations of modern Italian.

Dolce Vita, La A film, whose title literally means 'The Sweet Life', made by the director Federico Fellini and released in 1960. It depicted the emptiness and squalor of high society in Rome. Its title very quickly became a cliché for a worldly Italian lifestyle that perhaps never even existed, and it ended up as banal slogan for a lazy life of pleasure.

dottore Traditionally, the legally recognized title in Italy for a person who receives a degree after completing a university course lasting at least four years. Today this is also the name for a specialist degree. It is widely used both in writing (on letters or on business cards) or as a form of address to refer formally to all graduates, not simply graduates in medicine. There is a saying in Italy that 'no one ever denies being doctor', meaning that anyone – with or without a degree – is happy to accept *dottore* as a term of deference from waiters, parking attendants, and so on. *See also* LAUREA.

enoteca A place where good local wines are offered for sale and often for tasting. In many *enoteche* you can also eat while tasting the wines.

extracomunitari The Italian term used to refer to immigrants from Third World countries (black Africa, the Arab countries of North Africa, the Philippines, Sri Lanka, and China) or European countries that are not yet members of the European Union (such as Albania). Though the term may seem purely bureaucratic, *extracomunitario* (literally, 'outside the community') is a discriminatory word in common speech reflecting deep-seated prejudices; it is used with mistrust or fear, sometimes with scorn or hostility, as a label for poor immigrants, exploited as underpaid labour, often staying illegally without a residence permit, and involved in illegal trafficking or criminal activities.

FAI The Fondo per l'Ambiente Italiano (Fund for the Italian Environment), set up in 1975 with the aim of contributing to the protection, conservation, and use of Italy's artistic and environmental heritage. It has acquired, mostly through donations, many important buildings and sites (villas, palaces, castles, parks, and gardens) that it has subsequently restored and opened to the public.

farmaci Following a change in the law, it is now possible to buy over-the-counter medicines in the "health corner" of supermarkets, where a pharmacist must be present by law. They can also be bought from the so-called *parafarmacie*, which are similar to traditional pharmacies except that a doctor's prescription is not necessary.

Farnesina A term used in the media to refer to the Italian Ministry of Foreign Affairs which, since 1959, has been housed in the Palazzo della Farnesina, a vast building constructed in a functional style between 1938 and the 1950s outside the historic centre of Rome.

Fascism A movement, based on an ultra-conservative, anti-socialist, nationalist, racist, and authoritarian ideology, which controlled Italy from 1922 to 1943. The name comes from the *fasces*, an axe with its handle encased in a bundle of rods, which was a symbol of power and unity in Roman times. The Fascists, led by Benito Mussolini (known as *il duce*, the leader), were both a political party and a paramilitary organization. They ruled dictatorially, intimidating, imprisoning, and sometimes murdering, their political opponents. Under the Fascist regime Italian armies conquered Abyssinia, Lybia and Albania, but military failures during World War II, in which Italy was initially allied with Germany and Japan, led to the Fascists' downfall.

Fiamme Gialle The nickname (literally meaning 'Yellow Flames') for the *Guardia di finanza*, an Italian police force organized along military lines, which specializes in combating economic, financial, and fiscal crime (fraud, tax evasion, and money laundering) and guarding Italy's land and sea borders (against smuggling, drug trafficking, and illegal immigration). It was set up in 1881 and its members wear uniforms with yellow insignia, hence the nickname.

foglio rosa This is the provisional driving licence, which can be applied for before passing the theory test and is valid for six months.

Fratelli d'Italia The name by which Italy's national anthem is commonly known. Its official name is the *Inno di Mameli* (Mameli's hymn), after its author, the poet and patriot Goffredo Mameli, who died in 1849, aged 22, fighting with Garibaldi for the defence of the Roman Republic (*see* I MILLE). It was adopted as the national anthem in 1946. The common name comes from the opening lines of the first verse: *Fratelli d'Italia, l'Italia s'è desta, / dell'elmo di Scipio s'è cinta la testa* (Brothers of Italy, Italy has awoken / It has circled its head with the helmet of Scipio). All Italians know the tune (composed by Mameli's friend, the choirmaster Michele Novaro), but very few know the rest of the words (it has five verses) by heart.

Gazzetta dello Sport This is the sports daily, printed on its characteristic pink paper. It was founded in Milan in 1896 and is the most widely read sports newspaper in Italy. It organizes the GIRO D'ITALIA.

Gazzetta Ufficiale The official newspaper of the Italian state, which publishes approved laws, decrees, and various official announcements.

gelato Made with milk, sugar, eggs, and various other ingredients, this is an Italian speciality. The hand-made variety, bought in *gelaterie*, can be served in a dish or in a cone. There are dozens of flavours to choose from.

giornali Among the main Italian dailies are *Repubblica* and *Corriere della Sera*. The daily financial paper is *il Sole 24 ore*. The weekly magazines *L'Espresso* and *Panorama* deal with current affairs, politics, and culture. As well as Italian versions of international titles, the weekly magazines *Grazia*, *A*, and *Donna Moderna* cater for women. *Famiglia Cristiana* is the Catholic weekly. Of the gossip magazines, *Novella 2000* and *Chi* are the most popular.

Giro d'Italia Like the Tour de France, one of the most famous cycling races in the world. It takes place from mid-May to the beginning of June. The route changes every year, but the last stage always ends in Milan. The winner is awarded the pink jersey. *See also* GAZZETTA DELLO SPORT.

gondola A low narrow boat with a raised curved prow, used on the canals of Venice. The gondola is propelled by a *gondoliere* (gondolier) using a single oar that pivots on a small post attached to the starboard side. The gondoliers usually dress in traditional striped tops and a straw hat. A 17th-century *doge* (*see* VENETIAN REPUBLIC) ordered that all gondolas should be painted black, so as not to glorify worldly wealth. They remain black, but are now used almost exclusively for tourists.

Herculaneum ▸ VESUVIUS

Informagiovani As the name suggests, this is a service of information and guidance for young people. Promoted by local bodies, the various centres (and their web sites) provide information about all areas of interest to young people: courses and training, jobs, culture, politics, voluntary work, travel, etc. The first centres opened in Turin and Milan in the early 1980s; now there are about 600 centres throughout Italy. In addition to supplying information, they carry out a role of 'listening' to young people and also promote projects created by young people for young people.

INPS – Istituto Nazionale per la Previdenza Sociale (National Institute of Social Security). This is the major public body in Italy that pays workers' old-age pensions after receiving contributions from them during their working lives. It also manages the various kinds of assistance provided by the welfare state, such as the *cassa integrazione*, sickness, maternity, unemployment, and invalidity benefit.

Internet The World Wide Web is much used in Italy, as elsewhere. All major Italian newspapers and television stations have their own websites, as do councils, museums, etc. The suffix for Italian sites is '.it'.

laghi The north of Italy is the area with the highest concentration of lakes, which includes the three largest and most famous: Lake Garda (the largest of all), Lake Maggiore, and Lake Como. The area's mild climate and abundant greenery have always held a great attraction for both Italians and foreigners. Some lakes are equipped for water sports; others offer luxurious hotels and health farms.

laurea The title, meaning 'graduate', was traditionally awarded in Italy to people who completed a course of study at a university, usually lasting four years. Recently a *laurea triennale* (or *breve*) was introduced; this 'three-year' or 'short degree' gives immediate access to the labour market. In contrast the *laurea specialistica*, 'specialist degree', requires a further two years of study and entitles the holder to be known as *dottore*.

Leaning Tower of Pisa The eight-storey bell tower of the cathedral of Pisa. Building work began in 1183, but the tower started to lean noticeably to the north, as the ground beneath it was unstable. Work continued on and off on the tower for the next 200 years, and by 1360 it was complete – it was now leaning to the south, however. Over the centuries, the problem worsened. Finally, in the late 1990s, engineers removed rock and soil from under the north side of the tower and succeeded in reducing the angle of tilt from 10 per cent to 5 per cent. The tower is now said to be safe for the next 300 years.

Liberazione The effective end of the Second World War in Italy in late April 1945, when a general uprising staged by the *Resistenza* in the northern cities (Turin, Milan, and Genoa) led to the surrender or retreat of German troops before the arrival of the victorious Anglo-American forces. It is celebrated by the *Festa della Liberazione* (Liberation Day holiday) on 25 April each year.

liceo A type of secondary school, similar to a grammar school, which aims to form students' characters, pass on theoretical rather than applied knowledge, and develop the capacity for independent judgement and criticism. These aims are fully embodied in the more traditional type of *liceo*, the *liceo classico*, focused on the study of ancient languages (Latin and Greek). In the *liceo scientifico*, a more recent type, mathematics and the sciences are strongly represented in the curriculum along with Latin and philosophy, the latter being trademark subjects of *liceo* teaching whatever the school's specialism, whether science, modern languages, or art, etc.

Lotto The lottery game first appeared in Italy in Genoa during the 16th century, and during the following century spread to the other Italian states. From the 19th century it has been run directly by the state, and since 1871 there have been weekly draws in ten cities (known as *ruote*). Over the centuries a popular myth has grown up that the interpretation of dreams can help in the selection of winning numbers. The principles, a mixture of esotericism and cabbalism, are set out in the book of *Smorfia* (a corruption of Morpheus, the name of the Greek and Roman god of sleep and dreams). This ancient game still has great potential, as the development of recent variants such as the hugely popular Superenalotto has shown.

Mafia Since the Second World War, the Sicilian Mafia (also called *Cosa Nostra*) has expanded and developed substantially, creating an alternative power that is partly complementary to that of the state. Starting from illegal activities such as extortion and usury, it then assumed control of the building trade and the award of public contracts, and finally took over the traffic in illegal drugs, which brought in enormous profits. The Mafia has a vertical structure (a strict hierarchy of 'families'), but it is distinguished from other criminal organizations above all by its close relationships and complicity with political authorities.

Mani pulite The name (meaning 'clean hands') given to the landmark judicial inquiry, which, beginning in 1992 in Milan, brought to light the system of *tangenti* (payments on the side) and corruption in which the governing parties were involved. It resulted in their dissolution and the end of the so-called 'first republic' (*prima repubblica*).

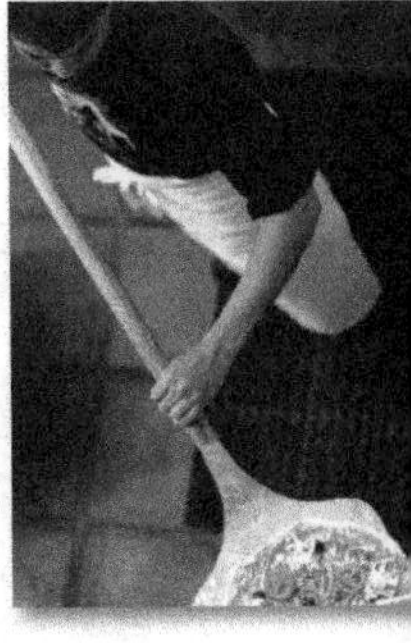

manifesti funebri Small posters printed by the family of someone who has died, announcing the death, saying a few words about the deceased, and giving the date and time of the funeral. These are put up on special boards – or indeed on any available surface – to inform local people of what has happened and to ensure a large attendance at the funeral.

maturità Traditional and colloquial term for "*esame di stato*". This is the exam that students take at the end of the five years of secondary school, between the ages of 18 and 19. It consists of three written tests (one of which is Italian language) and one oral. Marks (the minimum is 60 out of 100) depend on both the result of the tests and the number of credits gained by the student over the previous three years. The diploma is a requirement for university entrance and, depending on the type of secondary school attended, it can be in science, classics, arts, or technology, etc.

mercato Every Italian town and city has its own market, either open-air or covered, where fruit, vegetables, cheeses, cooked meats, and a range of other produce is sold. There is also a weekly market where it is possible to buy clothes, bags, household goods, and other items. The prices are cheaper than in the shops, and people often haggle over the goods displayed on the stalls.

Mezzogiorno A term referring to southern Italy, including Sicily and Sardinia, which is less economically developed than the north. The name literally means 'midday', i.e. the southern part of the country where the sun shines at noon.

I Mille In 1860, soldier Giuseppe Garibaldi (1807–82) set sail from Genoa with two ships and just over 1,000 volunteers, known as the *Camicie rosse* (Red Shirts). Garibaldi and his followers managed to wrest Sicily and Naples from Bourbon hands, territory which he then handed over to King Victor Emmanuel II of Sardinia-Piedmont. In the following year, Victor Emmanuel was declared king of the newly unified Italy. The original 1,000 volunteers remained a symbol of the most notable event of the Italian RISORGIMENTO, and are commemorated in street names in many Italian cities.

Mole Antonelliana The Mole Antonelliana, an extremely unusual monument (167 m – 548 ft – high), is the symbol of Turin. Destined to be a synagogue, the building was begun in 1863 but, following financial problems and arguments about its stability, it was not finished until 1889. Subsequently acquired by the city, it is now the home of the New Museum of the Cinema. A glass lift provides access to the steeple.

Montecitorio A palace, built between 1650 and 1697, to house papal courts. It is situated in a piazza of the same name in the centre of Rome. Since 1871 it has been home to the lower house of the Italian parliament, the *Camera dei deputati* (Chamber of Deputies). The term Montecitorio is used in the media to refer to the Chamber itself.

Monza A small city north of Milan, best known as the site of Autodromo nazionale, the motor-racing circuit where the Italian Grand Prix is held.

Mostra Internazionale d'Arte Cinematografica Also known as the Venice Film Festival, this is the film section of the BIENNALE DI VENEZIA. It was started in the 1930s and takes place every year at the end of August at the Palazzo del Cinema on the Venice Lido. One of the largest film festivals in Europe (and indeed the world), it attracts films, actors, directors, and other technicians from around the world. The festival winners are awarded the Golden Lion.

negozi The hours of opening for shops vary according to the type of shop and where it is located. In general, food shops open at about 8 a.m. and close at 7.30 p.m. with a lunch break from 12.30 to 3.30 p.m. Clothes shops, bookshops, etc. open from 9 a.m. until 12.30 or 1 p.m. and then again from 3.30 to 7.30 p.m. In summer the lunch break is longer and shops stay open until 8.00 p.m. Some supermarkets and department stores in the big cities are open all day. Weekly closing also varies according to the type of shop. Some shops close for two to three weeks in August, after the summer sales, then reopen with the new autumn-season stock.

Nordest The northeast, the area comprising the regions Veneto, Trentino, and Friuli, where a highly successful model of industrial development was applied during the 1990s. This led to the rapid emergence of many small and medium-sized companies, producing mainly textiles, footwear, and mechanical goods, and to strong export growth. Since then, however, the 'northeastern model' has been discussed mainly in terms of its downsides (damage to the environment, absence of general social development, lack of professional training for workers).

Normale The Scuola Normale Superiore di Pisa was set up in the early 1800s as a branch of the Paris Ecole Normale. Today, it is an extremely prestigious institute offering first degree courses and research doctorates in science and the humanities.

onomastico This is the feast day of the saint whose name a person bears. Although less important than his or her birthday, a saint's day is sometimes celebrated with a card or a small gift.

oratorio In Italy there are thousand of *oratorios* (usually buildings with courtyards and playing fields attached to Catholic parishes), which are used by pupils – on afternoons when they are not in school – as meeting places and for recreation (typically for ball games, but also for many other sporting or theatrical activities, etc.) and educational purposes. They are supervised by priests or their lay assistants. Created in the 19th century to rescue poor boys from immorality and crime, they have become a typical feature of young people's lives at all social levels in Italy.

Padania A term used by the political party Lega Nord (the Northern League) to refer to the whole of northern Italy, roughly the area falling within the basin of the River Po and the Venetian regions, supposed to be inhabited by a population of Celtic rather than Latin origin. According to its more extreme proponents, Padania should aim to secede from the rest of Italy (dominated by a 'corrupt' Rome), and especially from the uncivilized and backward south. But, for critics and opponents of the League, Padania is a meaningless term, because it does not correspond to a unified area that can be defined geographically, historically, or linguistically – and because the idea that the Padanians are direct descendants of the ancient Celts is mythical nonsense.

Palazzo Chigi The seat of the Italian government since 1961. The Palazzo Chigi, built in the 16th and 17th centuries, is situated in Piazza Colonna in the heart of Rome near the MONTECITORIO palace. In the media, the term Palazzo Chigi means the Italian government or PRESIDENTE DELLA REPUBBLICA.

Palio di Siena A popular event that takes place every year in Siena on 2 July and 16 August. The *contrade*, or districts of the city, fight for the *palio*, a banner, in a frantic race on horseback around the medieval Piazza del Campo. It has deep historical roots but is still passionately followed by the Sienese and is a huge attraction for tourists from all over the world. There is a spectacular historical procession in brightly coloured Renaissance costumes before the race.

Papal States Areas of central Italy owned and governed by the Pope from the early Middle Ages until the 19th century, including Latium, Umbria, Marche, and the city of Rome itself. The process of transferring these areas to secular government began with the conquest of Italy by Napoleon Bonaparte, but was not completed until 1870, when the Pope was forced to relinquish control of Rome, enabling it to become the capital of a united Italy.

parchi nazionali In Italy there are about twenty national parks covering 5 per cent of the territory. Controlled by the Ministry of the Environment, their objective is the protection and development of large areas that are of particular importance in terms of environment and landscape. The best-known are 'Gran Paradiso', the national parks in Abruzzi, Lazio, and Molise, and the National Park of the Maddalena Archipelago. The marine parks, which aim to protect stretches of sea, coast, and sometimes whole islands and archipelagos, are becoming increasingly important.

partiti politici While political parties have always been numerous in Italy, particularly at a local level, nationally there has been a gradual polarization between the centreright – whose main party is the Popolo della Libertà (PdL, formed by a merger of Forza Italia and Alleanza Nazionale) – and the centreleft, dominated by the Partito Democratico (PD, the result of a merger between the Unione dei Democratici di Sinistra and la Margherita). The other three most important political parties in Italy are Italia dei Valori (IdV, founded by Antonio di Pietro, the judge who led the *mani pulite* inquiry), the Lega Nord (sometimes known as just Lega), and the Unione di Centro (UDC).

pasta The basic ingredient of many Italian dishes, which is made by mixing flour from durum (hard) wheat with water, and sometimes adding other ingredients such as beaten egg or cooked spinach. Fresh pasta is soft and can be moulded into a variety of different forms, such as flat sheets (lasagne), long thin sticks (spaghetti), tubes (macaroni, cannelloni), or small square pillow shapes (ravioli). Commercially made pasta is dried after shaping until hard. In this form it will keep for a long time. Pasta is also a healthy food as it contains very little fat.

patente a punti Following reform of the Italian highway code, each driving licence is now given an initial value of twenty points, which are reduced if traffic offences are committed. For example, for the more serious offences (overtaking on a bend, drink driving, or driving while under the effect of drugs), ten points are deducted; passing a red light costs you six points, while parking in an area reserved for public transport costs two points. Once the number of infringements committed has reduced the initial number of points to zero, the licence is withdrawn and the driving test has to be retaken. Drivers with the worst records are required to undergo courses of 're-education'. The points system is also applied to foreign citizens who are passing though Italy: the penalties are totted up and filed in a special register.

permesso di soggiorno Foreigners who enter Italy with a passport and visa, especially for work or study, have to apply for this residence permit from the state police – that is from a *questura* or a *commissariato* (police headquarters or local police station) – within eight days of arrival. The permit is valid for between three months and two years, depending on the circumstances, and is renewable. It entitles the holder to be issued with an identity card (*carta d'identità*) and a tax code (*codice fiscale*). *See also* POLIZIA DI STATO.

Piazza Affari A term commonly used in the media to refer to the Milan stock exchange. The stock exchange came into existence in 1808 and is now housed in the Palazzo della Borsa (built between 1928 and 1931), situated in the centre of the city in the Piazza degli Affari.

Pinocchio The hero of the children's book, *Le Avventure di Pinocchio* (The Adventures of Pinocchio) by Carlo Collodi (1826–90), Pinocchio is a wooden puppet whose nose grows whenever he tells a lie. After various tribulations, accompanied by such famous characters as Geppetto (the puppetmaker), the Blue Fairy, the Fire-Eater, Lucignolo, and the whale, etc., Pinocchio is turned into a real boy. Adapted over and over for television, the cinema, and as a cartoon, the story has also been reinterpreted from a sociological and psychoanalytical point of view.

pizza Now a 'global food', pizza was for centuries a speciality of the city of Naples, and many people still think that it cannot be properly appreciated elsewhere. Pizze (flattened pieces of bread dough) were eaten in Naples in the late Middle Ages with garlic and lard, cheese and basil, or small fish. The modern pizza, with tomato, appeared in the late 1700s. The first pizzeria was opened in Naples in 1830 (before that, pizza was sold and eaten in the street). In 1889 the *pizzaiolo* (pizza-maker) Raffaele Esposito made a pizza topped with tomato, ricotta, and some leaves of basil (thus red, white, and green, the colours of the Italian flag) for Queen Margherita, the wife of Umberto I. Since then, this, the most widespread type of pizza, has been known as *pizza margherita*.

politecnico A scientific and technological university that includes faculties of engineering and architecture among its specializations. There are three in Italy. The oldest and most famous are those of Turin (1859) and Milan (1863); the latest is in Bari.

polizia di stato The name, meaning 'state police', of the Italian civil police force. The force was organized along military lines from 1919 to 1981 and called the Corpo delle Guardie di Pubblica Sicurezza (PS), Guards of Public Safety. It had headquarters (*questure*) in the capital city of each province, and police stations (*commissariati*) in city districts and minor centres. The reform of 1981 demilitarized and democratized it, and many of its officers and staff are now women. It continues to assist the CARABINIERI (who cover a wider area) in the task of maintaining law and order.

Pompeii ▸VESUVIUS

Ponte Vecchio The ancient bridge in Florence that spans the River Arno. It carries a roadway lined with goldsmiths' and jewellers' shops.

popular music In Italy the popular and classical traditions of vocal music tend to merge. The repertoires of star singers such as Luciano Pavarotti and Andrea Bocelli include popular Italian, especially Neapolitan songs, alongside operatic arias. Italian pop singers are less well known abroad. Singers such as Mina, Laura Pausini and Eros Ramazzotti tend to specialize in romantic songs. Italy does, however, have its share of rock, hip-hop, etc, artists and groups.

Premio Strega The most famous literary prize in Italy, instituted in 1947 and sponsored by a wealthy liquor manufacturer (producer of the Strega liqueur). Previous winners have included Edoardo De Filippo, Pierpaolo Pasolini, and Umberto Eco. The prize is awarded annually, in July, in the 16th-century Ninfeo (a garden with monumental fountain) of the Villa Giulia in Rome.

presepio (or *presepe*) A 'crib', a representation of the Nativity and the Adoration of the Magi in the form of wood or terracotta statues against a painted landscape. Cribs first appeared in Tuscany in the 13th and 14th centuries, but it was in Naples in the 17th and 18th centuries, during the baroque and rococo periods, that churches began to display magnificent examples. Scenes of everyday life were reproduced down to the smallest detail. During the 19th century, families began to build their own cribs for the Christmas season, with terracotta, plaster, or papier-mâché figurines. In recent decades this custom has become a little less common with the introduction of the Christmas tree from northern Europe.

Presidente del Consiglio This is the title of the Italian prime minister, the head of the government and of the CONSIGLIO DEI MINISTRI. Nominated by the PRESIDENTE DELLA REPUBBLICA, he proposes the ministers. He controls and is responsible for government policy.

Presidente della Repubblica The head of state who represents the nation. He/she is elected by parliament and remains in office for seven years. As Italy is a parliamentary republic, the duties of the president are: to enact laws, to dissolve parliament and call new elections when necessary, to nominate the prime minister and ratify his choice of the ministers, and to grant pardons. He/she also chairs the body which oversees the appointment of judges.

Prima repubblica The name (meaning 'first republic') given to the political system that collapsed in 1992–93 in the wake of scandals revealed by the *mani pulite* (Clean Hands) inquiry and the weakening of the opposing ideological positions associated with the Cold War. The big governing parties of those days – especially the Christian Democrats and the Socialist Party – disbanded, and new parties emerged; these are still active today (*see also* PARTITI POLITICI).

provincia In Italy's system of local government, each province is made up of neighbouring municipalities, the most important of which acts as the provincial capital. Each province is served by a provincial council, a committee, and a president.

quadrilatero della moda The 'fashion quadrilateral' is an area in the centre of Milan defined by the Via Montenapoleone, Via della Spiga, Via Manzoni, and Via Sant'Andrea, where the biggest names in Italian fashion, such as Armani, Trussardi, Coveri, Versace, Prada, Missoni, and Dolce & Gabbana, have their boutiques and showrooms.

questura Provincial headquarters of the police force. Thefts are reported to the *questura* and passports renewed there.

Quirinale A 16th-century building on the hill of the same name in Rome, now the residence of the PRESIDENTE DELLA REPUBBLICA. It was formerly the summer residence of the popes and then of the kings of Italy.

RAI The state radio and television company. There are three television channels, RAI 1, RAI 2, and RAI 3, and three radio stations, Radio 1, Radio 2, and Radio 3, which tend to be supportive of the government. More RAI theme channels have been introduced with digital terrestrial television.

reality Reality television has become as popular in Italy as in other countries. Most Italian shows follow the same formats used elsewhere. Italy has its own version of 'Big Brother' (*Il Grande Fratello*), of 'Survivor' (*L'isola dei Famosi*) and various talent shows such as *X Factor* and *Ballando con le stelle* (*Strictly Come Dancing*).

regione Italy is subdivided into twenty regions, five of which have a certain amount of political autonomy. Each region is subdivided in its turn into provinces (*see* PROVINCIA) and municipalities. The regions can issue legislative standards. They also have administrative duties which can be delegated to the provinces and the municipalities. Each region is served by a council, a committee, and a regional president.

repubblica The Italian republic was founded after the Second World War, based on the results of the referendum of 2 June 1946, which abolished the monarchy in favour of a republican form of government. The COSTITUZIONE published in 1948 established its parliamentary character.

Resistenza On 8 September 1943, Italy, which had been allied to Hitler's Germany, surrendered to British and US forces. The Germans reacted immediately by invading the greater part of the peninsula, which was not yet occupied by allied forces, and by imposing a harshly oppressive regime on their former ally. Soldiers from the disbanded army and antifascist civilians organized themselves into groups of partisans to fight the Germans and their Fascist collaborators behind the lines, leading to the Liberation in 1945. The ideals of liberty and democracy that inspired the partisans and their unity of action in spite of differing political views were the foundation of the new post-war Italian republic. For this reason, the Resistance still carries considerable political weight in present-day Italy.

Risorgimento The name, meaning 'the Resurgence', given to the historical period marked by the struggles for Italian independence and unification. After its beginnings in 1820–21 and 1831 and the uprisings of 1848–49, its principal events were the three wars of independence against Austria-Hungary (1848–49, 1859, and 1866) and the expedition of Garibaldi and I MILLE (the 1,000) in 1860. The moderate monarchical movement prevailed against the republican and revolutionary tendency of Giuseppe Mazzini, so that the House of Savoy (under Victor Emmanuel II) obtained the Italian crown in 1861. Rome became the capital city in 1871 (*see also* PAPAL STATES).

riviera The Italian word *riviera* means a 'coastal region'. It has been borrowed by many other languages and come to mean an area with a warm climate, fashionable resorts, and beaches for holidaymakers. The Italian, or Ligurian, Riviera is the stretch of coastline that begins at the French border and extends as far as the border with Tuscany. The main city and port in the region is Genoa – popular holiday towns include San Remo, Alassio, Portofino, and Rapallo.

sagra A popular festival with a fair and market, which takes place in many villages once a year, sometimes more frequently. *Sagre* usually have a theme such as wine, sausages, fish, or truffles – depending on what the local speciality is.

St Peter's The largest Christian church in the world, situated in the VATICANO in Rome. The Basilica of St Peter's is not a cathedral; its importance lies in its closeness to the papal residence and its use for most papal ceremonies, as well as in its size and architectural magnificence. The present building was designed by Bramante – various other famous artists participated, including Michelangelo, who designed the dome – and it was constructed between 1506 and 1615.

San Marino The republic of San Marino forms an enclave within Italian territory, but is an independent sovereign state completely surrounded by Italian soil, lying between Emilia-Romagna and the Marche, not far from the Adriatic coast. At just over 60 sq. km (23 sq. miles) in area, it is one of the smallest states in the world.

santo patrono In Italy the worship of saints is widespread. The patron saint of a town or community is considered to be its protector. His or her saint's day is a religious holiday on which schools, offices, and most shops are closed. It is celebrated with a special mass and processions. In towns and cities, illuminations are put up and there are stalls and sometimes a fair, in a mixture of the sacred and the secular.

Scala, La The Teatro alla Scala, the Milan opera house, is one of the most famous opera houses in the world. Built in 1776–78, it has recently undergone a programme of restoration, during which the Teatro degli Arcimboldi, outside the city, staged its productions.

scuola The Italian system provides for primary schools, middle schools, and secondary schools. Primary school lasts for five years from the age of six, middle school lasts for three years, and secondary school for five. Primary and middle schools all follow the same curriculum but there are a number of different types of secondary schools: scientific, classical, linguistic, and artistic grammar schools, various technical and commercial institutes, and schools for training nursery school teachers (*see also* LICEO).

Senato The upper house of the Italian Parliament. Three hundred and fifteen senators are elected by universal suffrage by citizens over 25 years of age. Senators must be at least 40 years old. These 315 seats are elected on a regional basis, i.e. they are split between the regions in proportion to population. The elected senators are joined by ex-heads of state and life senators (*senatori a vita*). These are nominated by the PRESIDENTE DELLA REPUBBLICA from people who have given exceptional service to the country in the scientific, social, artistic, or literary fields.

settimana bianca A winter holiday spent with family or schoolfriends in a ski resort.

Seven Hills of Rome A group of seven small hills lying east of the River Tiber. According to tradition, the ancient city of Rome was founded by Romulus on the Palatine hill. The city gradually spread to cover the other six, the CAPITOLINE, Quirinal (QUIRINALE), Viminal (VIMINALE), Esquiline, Caelian, and Aventine hills. The hills are no longer a prominent geographical feature in modern Rome, but some are still associated with districts that have a distinctive character. The Capitoline hill, for instance, remains a seat of government, just as it was in Roman times.

sindaco The mayor is the head of local government and holds power for five years. He chairs and represents the council and municipal committee.

Sistine Chapel A chapel in the Vatican, built by Pope Sixtus IV. In 1505, Pope Julius II commissioned Michelangelo to decorate the ceiling with a series of scenes from the book of Genesis. Michelangelo also painted his vision of the *Last Judgement* on the east wall.

spaghetti western A low-budget western made in Europe by an Italian director or production company, often in English and with an American star, usually featuring lots of explicit violence. The best and most famous of these films are *A Fistful of Dollars*, *For a Few Dollars More*, and *The Good, the Bad and the Ugly*, directed by Sergio Leone.

spumante A sparkling white wine, sometimes seen as the poor relation of French champagne but also often greatly prized. It can be dry or sweet and always features on Italian Christmas, New Year, and party menus.

stabilimento balneare A stretch of beach equipped with parasols, loungers, showers, huts, perhaps a swimming-pool, and a bar. There is a charge for using it. These beach clubs vary from large and crowded to very chic and exclusive, and from fairly basic to luxurious. Many of them organize sports tournaments, card games, beauty contests, and dances.

stellone A big star, *stellone d'Italia* or *stellone italico* (star of Italy) which, since the RISORGIMENTO, has been associated with the personification of Italy (a woman with a star on her forehead or in her crown). Representing a beacon of hope in times of difficulty, it became part of the coat of arms of the unified kingdom and was then incorporated into the emblem of the

Republic. Today it is mainly used ironically or polemically to criticize the tendency of Italians – a sign both of their vitality and of their happy-go-lucky attitude and fatalism – to trust to good luck rather than to hard work to get them through times of national crisis.

tabaccaio The tobacconist sells cigarettes and tobacco and is also the only shop apart from the post office where you can buy revenue stamps and postage stamps. It also sells bus tickets and other products. Sometimes there is also a bar. Its sign features a white 'T' on a black background.

Tangentopoli A name ('kick-back city') widely used in the Italian media to refer first to Milan, where the judiciary investigated a series of episodes of corruption, and then extended to mean the whole system of illicit financing used by the governing parties, unmasked by the famous *mani pulite* inquiry in 1992–93.

Telecom Italia One of the largest telephone companies supplying both land lines and mobile phones.

terrone A pejorative, racist term typically applied by northern Italians to southern Italians, and usually accompanied by equally disparaging adjectives such as 'ignorant', 'filthy', and 'uncivilized'. The word derives from *terra* (earth, land), depicting the typical southerner as an agricultural labourer. It became widespread in the 1960s and 1970s when large-scale immigration from the south to the industrial northwest took place. In present-day Italy, racist insults are mainly reserved for despised foreign immigrants (*extracomunitari*), while the term *terrone* is less widely used and has even acquired a jocular tone (the more so since it is used by southerners themselves). The pejorative sense has, however, been given a new lease of life in the anti-southern polemics of the Northern League (*see* PARTITI POLITICI).

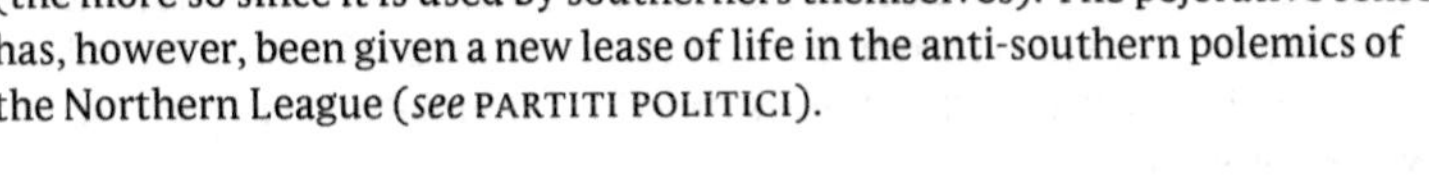

trattoria A trattoria used to be distinguishable from a restaurant because it was simpler, often family-run, and less expensive. Nowadays it is merely a 'typical' local restaurant, serving traditional local dishes in a country-style setting. It can also be very sophisticated, and sometimes quite expensive.

triangolo industriale A name for the industrial zone of northwestern Italy, a triangle with the cities of Milan, Turin, and Genoa at its corners, where modern industry began to develop at the end of the 19th century. It has been the major productive centre in Italy, attracting large-scale internal immigration from the south, especially between the 1950s and 1970s. The subsequent decline of heavy industry has transformed the industrial triangle into an area where small and medium-sized enterprises and the tertiary sector now predominate. Other models of strong development have emerged elsewhere, particularly in the areas around Venice (*see* NORDEST).

Tricolore The Italian national flag: green, white, and red in vertical bands of equal width. It was designed at the end of 1700s and adopted as the flag of the republic after the Second World War.

Uffizi A vast art gallery in Florence, famous for its collection of works by Italian Renaissance painters such as Botticelli, Piero della Francesca, Leonardo, and Raphael. The building containing the gallery was built in the late 15th century to house government administration – hence its name, which means 'offices'.

Ultima cena *The Last Supper*, one of Leonardo da Vinci's most famous works, painted on the wall of the refectory of the monastery of St Maria delle Grazie in Milan. Leonardo was experimenting with a new technique for fresco (painting directly onto fresh plaster), which was not altogether successful. As a result, the painting has deteriorated badly over the centuries and been restored several times.

Valle dei Templi An archaeological zone in the province of Agrigento that provides the most glorious evidence of Ancient Greek civilization in Sicily. The remains of many temples are to be found on a ridge (not a valley as the name suggests), among the almond trees. Built in the Doric style in the 5th century BC, the temples were burnt down by the Carthaginians, restored by the Romans in the 1st century AD, then half-destroyed by earthquakes and plundered over the following centuries, so that the only one that now remains intact is the magnificent Tempio della Concordia.

Vaticano The Vatican (also called Vatican City) has been an independent state within the city of Rome and the seat of the Pope since 1929. The Vatican Palace, which surrounds ST PETER'S, is the Pope's residence and houses artistic treasures such as the SISTINE CHAPEL and Raphael's frescos, as well as museums.

Venetian Republic For over a thousand years, from 697 to 1797, the island city of Venice and the mainland territory surrounding it formed an independent republic ruled by an elected chief magistrate (the *doge*) and a council of ten (the *dieci*). From the time of the Crusades to the late 15th century, Venice was the major power in the eastern Mediterranean and became enormously wealthy thanks to its trade with the Muslim world and Asia. From the 16th century, however, its power began to wane. It lost its independence when conquered by Napoleon, and eventually became part of Italy in 1866.

Vespa A motor scooter designed by aeronautical engineer, Corradino D'Ascanio, for the Piaggio company just after World War II. D'Ascanio's brief was to design a vehicle that would be affordable, easy to drive, carry a passenger, and not get the driver's clothes dirty – hence the trademark upswept mudguard behind the handlebars. The Vespa is particularly associated with the 1950s and 1960s in Italy, but it remains a popular means of transport to this day.

Vesuvius An active volcano, near Naples, that has erupted many times, most notably in AD 79, when it overwhelmed the ancient Roman cities of Pompeii and Herculaneum. The explosion buried the area under volcanic ash, preserving many of the buildings, as well as the bodies of those who did not flee, virtually intact. The towns were only rediscovered in the 18th century; excavations have revealed a stunning record of daily life in Roman times.

vigile urbano This policeman is responsible for controlling traffic and levying fines for traffic offences, for environmental protection, and for ensuring that municipal regulations and town laws are observed. He also deals with social problems, such as abandoned children, and the monitoring of refugees' and travellers' camps.

Viminale A media name for the Italian Ministry of Internal Affairs (or Home Office), which since 1961 has been housed in the Palazzo del Viminale, a vast Renaissance-style building erected in the early 20th century on the Viminal hill in Rome (*see* SEVEN HILLS OF ROME).

vino Wine is produced in every region of Italy, and the Italian wine-making tradition dates back 4,000 years to prehistoric times. Italy produces some white wine, but is mainly renowned for its red wines. The most internationally famous of these is Chianti, produced in Tuscany. Other famous varieties include Valpolicella, Barolo, Marsala, and Soave. High-quality Italian wines are labelled *DOC* (*denominazione di origine controllata*) or *DOCG* (*denominazione di origine controllata e garantita*).

Vita e cultura nel mondo anglofono dalla A alla Z

ABC 1. American Broadcasting Company Una delle principali reti televisive statunitensi, attualmente di proprietà della Walt Disney. **2. Australian Broadcasting Corporation** Rete radiotelevisiva statale australiana.

ACT – American College Test Esame che gli studenti nordamericani devono superare per l'ammissione all'università. Generalmente ha luogo al termine della HIGH SCHOOL e copre alcune delle principali materie, come ad es. inglese e matematica.

Advance Australia Fair Inno nazionale australiano.

A level ▸EXAMINATIONS

Alliance Party ▸NORTHERN IRELAND

American Dream Il sogno americano è la convinzione che negli Stati Uniti chiunque sia disposto a lavorare sodo possa migliorare la propria posizione economica e sociale. Per gli immigrati e le minoranze il concetto significa anche libertà e uguaglianza di diritti.

American Football Il football americano è un gioco simile al rugby. Si gioca con una palla ovale e le due squadre in campo sono composte da undici giocatori ciascuna. È uno sport spettacolare ma molto violento e i giocatori indossano pertanto caschi e imbottiture protettive. L'evento principale della stagione è il Super Bowl, la finale di campionato della National Football League.

American Indian ▸NATIVE AMERICAN

Anglican Church ▸CHURCH OF ENGLAND

Anzac Soldato dell'Australian and New Zealand Army Corps. Questo contingente partecipò alla prima e alla seconda guerra mondiale e viene ricordato in particolare per l'eroismo con cui si distinse durante la disastrosa campagna di Gallipoli (in Turchia), nel 1915–16. Il valore degli *Anzacs* giocò un ruolo importante nel consolidare il sentimento di coscienza nazionale in Australia e Nuova Zelanda; viene commemorato annualmente il 25 aprile, l'Anzac Day.

April Fool's Day ▸GIORNI FESTIVI NEI PAESI ANGLOFONI

Armistice Day ▸POPPY DAY

A/S Level ▸EXAMINATIONS

Australia Day Festa nazionale australiana celebrata il primo lunedì dopo il 26 gennaio. Commemora l'arrivo dei primi coloni britannici nell'allora Port Jackson, oggi la baia di Sydney, nel 1788.

Australian Rules Gioco australiano simile al rugby, giocato in un campo ovale da squadre di 18 giocatori che si disputano un pallone ovale. È lo sport invernale più popolare in gran parte dell'Australia.

Authorized Version Traduzione inglese della Bibbia pubblicata per la prima volta nel 1611. Realizzata da un gruppo di eruditi e commissionata da Giacomo I d'Inghilterra, per cui è anche chiamata la Bibbia di re Giacomo (*King James Bible*). Dal XVII al XX secolo è stata l'unica versione della Bibbia autorizzata per l'uso nell'ambito della Chiesa Anglicana (CHURCH OF ENGLAND). Il testo ha profondamente influenzato la letteratura e la lingua inglese.

bank holiday Termine che nel Regno Unito indica alcuni giorni festivi, nei quali si ha la chiusura di banche, poste, uffici e scuole. Cade sempre di lunedì.

barrister ▸LAWYER

baseball È lo sport nazionale degli Stati Uniti. Il torneo annuale più importante è la *World Series*.

B & B ▸BED AND BREAKFAST

BBC – British Broadcasting Corporation Uno dei principali enti radiotelevisivi britannici. Non è finanziato dalla pubblicità commerciale ma attraverso un canone di abbonamento che chiunque abbia la televisione deve pagare. Ha l'obbligo di fornire un servizio di informazione imparziale.

bed and breakfast I *bed & breakfast* o *B&B* sono piccole pensioni o case di privati che offrono camera e colazione a prezzi generalmente abbastanza convenienti.

Big Apple Significa letteralmente 'la grande mela' ed è l'appellativo di New York.

Bill of Rights I primi dieci emendamenti alla Costituzione degli Stati Uniti d'America. Tra i diritti che essi garantiscono ai cittadini statunitensi ci sono la libertà di culto, di parola, di stampa e vari diritti nel caso una persona venga accusata di un qualche reato. Il celebre Quinto Emendamento (*Fifth Amendment*) stabilisce tra l'altro che nessuno è obbligato a deporre contro se stesso. Il Secondo Emendamento tutela invece il diritto di portare armi.

Bonfire Night ▸ GIORNI FESTIVI NEI PAESI ANGLOFONI

Boxing Day ▸ GIORNI FESTIVI NEI PAESI ANGLOFONI

British Isles Le Isole Britanniche comprendono la Gran Bretagna (GREAT BRITAIN), l'Irlanda – sia l'Irlanda del Nord (NORTHERN IRELAND) che la Repubblica d'Irlanda (Republic of Ireland) – e le isole più piccole quali le Shetlands, l'Isola di Man (Isle of Man), e le Isole Anglo-Normanne o del Canale (CHANNEL ISLANDS).

Broadway Strada nel quartiere newyorkese di Manhattan, celebre per i numerosi teatri. Il termine Broadway si usa infatti anche per indicare il teatro e il mondo dello spettacolo americano in generale. Prima della nascita dell'industria cinematografica era il luogo principale dove attori e artisti potevano esibirsi e diventare famosi.

Buckingham Palace Residenza ufficiale del sovrano britannico a Londra. Il cambio della guardia, accompagnato dalla banda del reggimento, ha luogo quasi tutte le mattine davanti al palazzo reale.

Burns Night ▸ GIORNI FESTIVI NEI PAESI ANGLOFONI

Cabinet È il Gabinetto del governo britannico, equivalente al nostro Consiglio dei Ministri. Formato da una ventina di ministri nominati dal Primo Ministro, ciascuno dei quali è responsabile di un settore specifico. Il Cabinet al completo si riunisce regolarmente per discutere e decidere la politica del governo. Il leader del principale partito all'opposizione nomina lo Shadow Cabinet, un Gabinetto ombra omologo al governo.

Canada Situato a nord degli Stati Uniti e secondo al mondo per superficie, il Canada è uno stato federale costituito da dieci province e tre territori. Storicamente legato alla Gran Bretagna ed appartenente al Commonwealth, è una monarchia costituzionale (il capo dello stato è la regina Elisabetta II) e democrazia parlamentare, con Parlamento a Ottawa, la capitale. Le lingue ufficiali sono l'inglese e il francese; quanto alla religione circa il 42% della popolazione canadese è cattolica, mentre il 23% è protestante. Florida nazione industriale, il Canada è molto ricco di risorse naturali; possiede oltre il 60% dei laghi mondiali: i Grandi Laghi (Superiore, Michigan, Huron, Erie e Ontario) si trovano al confine con gli Stati Uniti, come pure le spettacolari Cascate del Niagara; vanta inoltre ampie foreste da legname e catene montuose (tra cui le Montagne Rocciose canadesi). Una istituzione tipica del paese è infine la Royal Canadian Mounted Police, le leggendarie Giubbe Rosse che vantano la reputazione di acciuffare immancabilmente il loro uomo.

Capitol Il Campidoglio è la sede del Congresso degli Stati Uniti d'America (CONGRESS) situata sul Capitol Hill, nella città di Washington. The Capitol indica anche il Congresso stesso.

CBS – Columbia Broadcasting System Uno dei tre principali enti radiotelevisivi nazionali degli Stati Uniti.

Central Park Vasto parco nel quartiere di Manhattan a New York, caro ai newyorkesi in quanto costituisce un'oasi di verde in una zona fortemente urbanizzata.

Channel Islands Le Isole Anglo-Normanne (o Isole del Canale) sono un arcipelago situato nella Manica, vicino alla costa francese. Non fanno parte del Regno Unito ma sono dipendenze autonome della corona britannica. Jersey e Guernsey sono le isole più grandi.

Christmas Day ▸GIORNI FESTIVI NEI PAESI ANGLOFONI

Church of England Il termine Chiesa d'Inghilterra indica la Chiesa Anglicana, chiesa protestante ufficiale in Inghilterra. Fu creata nel 1534 da Enrico VIII, il quale con l'Atto di supremazia (Act of Supremacy) si sostituì al Papa come capo della chiesa in Inghilterra. Ancora oggi il sovrano è il governatore supremo della Chiesa Anglicana; i vescovi e gli arcivescovi sono nominati dalla Corona su proposta del Primo Ministro. Il capo spirituale è invece l'Arcivescovo di Canterbury. L'Inghilterra è suddivisa in 44 diocesi e da 13.000 parrocchie (*parishes*), ciascuna con a capo un parroco (*vicar*). Nel 1992, il Sinodo Generale (General Synod) ha approvato l'ordinazione di sacerdoti donna. Fuori dall'Inghilterra si hanno altre comunioni anglicane: la Chiesa Episcopale in Scozia e negli Stati Uniti (Episcopalian Church), la Chiesa d'Irlanda (Church of Ireland), la Chiesa gallese (Church of Wales).

City Zona nel centro di Londra dove un tempo si trovava l'antica città. Oggi la City è il centro finanziario della capitale britannica e qui hanno la propria sede centrale banche e istituti finanziari; molto spesso il termine indica proprio tali istituzioni finanziarie.

Civil War 1. (negli Stati Uniti) La Guerra di Secessione (1861–65), combattuta tra gli stati del nord e quelli del sud, scoppiata principalmente per la questione della schiavitù. Gli stati del sud, la cui economia agricola dipendeva dalla manodopera fornita dagli schiavi neri, nel 1861 costituirono la Confederazione degli Stati d'America separandosi così dall'Unione. Il conflitto tra sudisti e nordisti ebbe inizio il 12 aprile 1861 e il 9 aprile 1865 gli stati della Confederazione si arresero. La conclusione della guerra segnò l'abolizione della schiavitù; il 13° emendamento della Costituzione e successivamente il 14° (del 1868) e il 15° (del 1870) garantirono ai neri gli stessi diritti dei cittadini bianchi, almeno sulla carta. **2. (in Inghilterra)** Conflitto tra la Corona e il Parlamento (1642–51). Da un lato erano schierati i Royalists o Cavaliers (i monarchici sostenitori di Carlo I Stuart) e dall'altro le forze parlamentari, le cosiddette Teste rotonde (Roundheads) per il taglio corto dei capelli, capeggiate da Oliver Cromwell. Molti dei fattori all'origine della guerra civile avevano a che vedere con i problemi religiosi ed economici dell'epoca. Il Parlamento si opponeva a concedere fondi a Carlo I per finanziare il suo assolutismo; il tentativo del sovrano di arrestare alcuni parlamentari portò infine allo scoppio della guerra. Sconfitto nelle battaglie di Marston Moor (1644) e di Naseby (1645), il re si arrese all'esercito scozzese un anno più tardi. Processato e condannato a morte da una commissione parlamentare sotto Cromwell, fu decapitato nel 1649. L'Inghilterra si dette un ordinamento repubblicano e Cromwell la governò per anni con pieni poteri, sciogliendo in varie occasioni il Parlamento. La monarchia fu restaurata nel 1660, due anni dopo la morte di Cromwell, quando il figlio di Carlo I, Carlo II, salì al trono.

CNN – Cable News Network Emittente televisiva statunitense che trasmette programmi di informazione via satellite 24 ore su 24.

Cockney Una persona nata e cresciuta nei quartieri popolari della zona est (EAST END) londinese. È anche il nome del dialetto tipico della zona, caratterizzato dalla sostituzione di parole con altre che vi fanno rima, ad esempio '*apples and pears*' significa '*stairs*' e '*trouble and strife*' sta per '*wife*'.

common law Sistema giuridico anglosassone basato sulla consuetudine e sulle sentenze delle corti di giustizia (rispettivamente diritto consuetudinario e giurisprudenza) e non sulle leggi create dal Parlamento e quindi sulla codificazione del diritto. Si ricorre alla *common law* soltanto per quelle questioni su cui il diritto scritto (*statute law*) non si pronuncia.

Commonwealth Il Commonwealth, fondato nel 1931, è l'insieme delle ex colonie e possedimenti dell'ex impero britannico. I paesi membri, oggi per lo più stati indipendenti (a parte alcuni quali Gibilterra, Bermuda e le Isole Falkland o Malvine), sono legati da rapporti economici e culturali. I vari capi di stato si incontrano con scadenza biennale (the Commonwealth Conference) e progetti educativi internazionali vengono promossi regolarmente. Ogni quattro anni, inoltre, si tengono i Commonwealth Games, manifestazioni sportive cui partecipano atleti dei vari paesi.

community college Istituto statunitense che offre corsi biennali indirizzati alla comunità locale, per lo più di carattere pratico.

comprehensive school Tipo di scuola secondaria britannica per studenti dagli 11 ai 18 anni, di tutti i livelli di rendimento. Le *comprehensive schools* vennero istituite negli anni Sessanta allo scopo di creare un sistema educativo più ugualitario, contrapposto al sistema selettivo operante all'epoca. *Vedi anche* GRAMMAR SCHOOL.

Congress L'organo legislativo nazionale degli Stati Uniti. Si riunisce al Campidoglio (CAPITOL) ed è formato da due Camere: il Senato (SENATE) e la Camera dei Rappresentanti (HOUSE OF REPRESENTATIVES). Si rinnova ogni due anni e ha il compito di redigere e approvare le leggi. Ogni nuova legge deve essere approvata prima dalle due Camere e poi dal Presidente (PRESIDENT).

Conservative Party Uno dei maggiori partiti politici britannici. È un partito di centrodestra che appoggia il sistema capitalista, la libera impresa e la privatizzazione dell'industria e dei servizi pubblici. Il Partito Conservatore nacque intorno al 1830–40 dall'evoluzione del Partito Tory, nome col quale ancora oggi viene spesso indicato.

constituency Una delle ripartizioni in cui sono suddivisi Regno Unito, Canada, e Australia a fini elettorali.

Constitution La Costituzione americana, redatta dopo l'indipendenza dalla Gran Bretagna e ratificata nel 1789 dai rappresentanti di ciascuna delle tredici ex colonie che formavano gli Stati Uniti d'America, inclusi alcuni dei padri fondatori della nazione (FOUNDING FATHERS). La Costituzione stabiliva la suddivisione dei tre poteri dello stato: quello legislativo affidato al Congresso (CONGRESS), quello esecutivo al Presidente (PRESIDENT) e quello giudiziario alle Corti federali con al vertice la Corte Suprema di giustizia (SUPREME COURT). La spartizione dei poteri tra diversi organi dello Stato si ispirava alle idee degli Illuministi francesi e aveva lo scopo di garantire maggiore democrazia. Il testo della Costituzione resta essenzialmente in vigore ancora oggi. Dal 1789 ci sono stati tuttavia 27 emendamenti, di cui i primi dieci prendono il nome di BILL OF RIGHTS.

council Ai fini amministrativi la Gran Bretagna è suddivisa in varie aree. Le più grandi sono le COUNTIES, e in Scozia le *regions*, ripartite a loro volta in *districts*. I *parish councils*, e i *community councils* in Scozia e Galles, rappresentano le ripartizioni amministrative più piccole. A capo delle varie unità vi sono i consigli (*councils*). Tali autorità locali hanno poteri conferiti dal governo centrale e sono formate da consiglieri (*councillors*) eletti dai cittadini nelle elezioni amministrative (*local elections*). I *councils* sono responsabili dell'educazione, dei servizi sociali, di polizia e vigili del fuoco, degli alloggi popolari, delle biblioteche, e di altri servizi a livello locale.

county Principale unità amministrativa in Inghilterra, suddivisa a sua volta in *districts*. I confini delle contee hanno spesso radici storiche e risalgono a molti anni fa. Tuttavia, negli ultimi decenni sia l'estensione che i nomi delle *counties* sono cambiati, e il termine stesso è meno usato. Anche negli Stati Uniti la maggior parte degli stati è suddivisa in contee, per un totale di circa 3.000.

courts Negli Stati Uniti la giustizia è amministrata nei vari stati tramite organi giudiziari indipendenti, ma esistono anche tribunali federali che si occupano tra le altre cose di controversie tra stati e tra cittadini di stati diversi. La Corte Suprema (SUPREME COURT) è un tribunale federale. Nella maggior parte degli stati esistono sia tribunali civili che penali e anche una sorta di corti d'appello. Un tipico procedimento penale viene giudicato in un tribunale distrettuale, dove il procuratore distrettuale (*district attorney*) sostiene l'accusa. Il giudice indossa la toga nera mentre gli avvocati (*counsels*) indossano abbigliamento normale. In Inghilterra e in Galles i tribunali locali sono detti *magistrates' courts* e si occupano di cause civili e reati minori. I reati più gravi competono alle *crown courts*, dove i *barristers* (avvocati abilitati ad esercitare in corti di livello superiore) sostengono l'accusa e la difesa. Il tribunale di ultima istanza è la Camera dei Lords (HOUSE OF LORDS). In Scozia, dove esiste un sistema giuridico diverso, le cause per reati minori sono giudicate dalle *magistrates' courts* o da tribunali di polizia. I reati più gravi vengono giudicati dallo *sheriff* (il giudice di grado più alto in un distretto). I tribunali di massimo livello sono la High Court of Justiciary e la Court of Session, rispettivamente per le cause penali e civili. Nelle aule dei tribunali d'Inghilterra, Galles e Scozia sia giudici che avvocati portano toga e parrucca.

Cup final ▸ FOOTBALL

degree Diploma di laurea assegnato alla fine di un corso universitario. Esistono due livelli di laurea e due qualifiche corrispondenti: *bachelor's degree* e *master's degree*; il livello ancora superiore è il *doctorate*, che equivale al dottorato di ricerca. Una laurea di primo livello in lettere e filosofia o altre discipline umanistiche si chiama *Bachelor of Arts* (*BA* e negli Stati Uniti anche *AB*); una laurea di secondo livello in discipline scientifiche è un *Master of Sciences* (*MSc*, in America detto anche *ScM*); il *doctorate* è il *PhD*. *BA*, *MSc*, ecc. indicano il titolo ma anche il titolare della qualifica, ad es. Patricia Ramsay, *MA* (*Master of Arts*).

Democratic Party Fondato nel 1792, è uno dei due principali partiti politici statunitensi. L'altro è il Partito Repubblicano (REPUBLICAN PARTY). Il Partito Democratico è considerato fautore di una politica più liberale, particolarmente rispetto alle questioni sociali. Per questo motivo ha l'appoggio dei sindacati e delle minoranze.

devolution Nel Regno Unito il termine *devolution* indica il trasferimento di alcune competenze del governo centrale a enti regionali della Scozia, del Galles, dell'Irlanda del Nord e di altre regioni periferiche dello stato britannico. Dopo la vittoria del partito laburista nelle elezioni del 1997, il processo di decentramento fu attuato con il riconoscimento del Parlamento Scozzese, dell'Assemblea dell'Irlanda del Nord e di quella gallese. *Vedi anche* SCOTLAND, NORTHERN IRELAND, WALES.

District Attorney ▸COURTS

Dow Jones Averages Detto anche Dow Jones Index (indice Dow Jones), indica il prezzo medio espresso in punti delle trenta azioni industriali principali quotate alla Borsa di New York ogni giorno di transazioni. Viene utilizzato per prevedere le tendenze generali del mercato azionario statunitense.

Downing Street Strada nel centro di Londra, nel quartiere di Westminster. Al numero 10 si trova la residenza ufficiale del Primo Ministro (Prime Minister) britannico e al numero 11 quella del Chancellor of the Exchequer (il Cancelliere dello Scacchiere, equivalente del Ministro delle Finanze e del Tesoro). Le espressioni 'Downing Street' e 'Number 10' sono spesso usate dalla stampa per indicare il Primo Ministro.

driving Nel Regno Unito, in Australia, in Nuova Zelanda e in Sudafrica si ha la guida a sinistra, ossia i veicoli procedono sul lato sinistro della strada. Negli Stati Uniti e in Canada si ha invece la guida a destra, come in Italia e nel resto d'Europa.

East End Quartieri nella zona est di Londra, tradizionalmente abitati dalla classe operaia e sede della zona del porto londinese (Docklands), oggi quasi completamente chiuso alle navi. La zona portuale dei Docklands negli ultimi anni è stata profondamente riurbanizzata e adesso ospita complessi residenziali di lusso e numerose strutture commerciali, quali l'imponente grattacielo di Canary Wharf, sedi di quotidiani e istituti finanziari. La zona è collegata al resto di Londra tramite il servizio ferroviario dei DLR (Docklands Light Railway).

East Side A New York, è la zona a est di Central Park, tradizionalmente più ricca e moderna del West Side, la parte ovest della città.

Edinburgh Festival La più importante manifestazione culturale britannica, istituita nel 1947. Si tiene annualmente nella capitale scozzese ad agosto, per tre settimane. Il festival offre spettacoli di musica, teatro, danza, cabaret e attira ogni anno moltissimi visitatori. Un settore sempre molto interessante è quello del cosiddetto the Edinburgh Fringe, ossia degli eventi fuori dal programma ufficiale.

education Negli Stati Uniti l'insegnamento primario e secondario è fornito gratuitamente dal governo federale. A cinque anni i bambini iniziano a frequentare il *kindergarten* che insieme ai successivi cinque o sei anni di scuola costituisce le elementari (ELEMENTARY SCHOOL). Seguono poi due anni di *junior high school* o tre anni di *middle school* e infine gli ultimi anni di educazione superiore nella HIGH SCHOOL che termina intorno ai 18 anni. Dopodiché l'educazione non è più gratuita, ma i vari stati in qualche modo la sussidiano. Circa il 45% degli americani continua gli studi dopo le superiori e oltre il 20% consegue un diploma presso istituti o università. Nel Regno Unito la scuola obbligatoria va dai 5 ai 16 anni. I bambini iniziano frequentando l'*infant school* e poi la *primary school* (educazione elementare). A partire dagli 11 anni ha inizio la scuola secondaria, e si tratta nella maggioranza dei casi di una COMPREHENSIVE SCHOOL. Un numero ridotto di ragazzi frequenta le più selettive GRAMMAR SCHOOLS. Dopo i 16 anni alcuni alunni lasciano la scuola, mentre altri proseguono gli studi in istituti a carattere più professionale quali i *colleges of further education* o per preparare gli *A levels*. Se desiderano accedere all'università gli studenti devono pagarsi sia le tasse universitarie che le spese di vitto e alloggio, per cui molti devono chiedere prestiti in banca. Nel complesso la maggioranza dei ragazzi frequenta la scuola pubblica e soltanto una minoranza è iscritta alle INDEPENDENT SCHOOLS che sono a pagamento.

elections Negli Stati Uniti si indicono elezioni per la carica di Presidente (PRESIDENT), per i seggi nelle due Camere del Congresso (CONGRESS) e per cariche a livello statale e locale. I candidati si presentano per il Partito Repubblicano (REPUBLICAN PARTY) o per il Partito Democratico (DEMOCRATIC PARTY). I candidati indipendenti possono presentarsi avendo fatto una petizione con le firme dei propri sostenitori. Le elezioni presidenziali hanno luogo ogni quattro anni. I partiti selezionano i propri candidati nelle elezioni primarie (PRIMARY) indette nei singoli stati. La selezione finale dei candidati alla presidenza e vicepresidenza si effettua in occasione della *party convention*, il congresso che ciascun partito tiene nei mesi di luglio e agosto. Il presidente viene eletto a novembre col sistema dell'ELECTORAL COLLEGES. Nel Regno Unito, le elezioni politiche (*general elections*) vengono indette per legge ogni cinque anni. Tuttavia il Primo Ministro può indire elezioni anticipate se ritiene di avere buone probabilità di vittoria. Nel Regno Unito ci sono 659 CONSTITUENCIES, ciascuna delle quali elegge un rappresentante in Parlamento (MP). Il sistema elettorale è il *first-past-the-post system*, vale a dire quello della maggioranza relativa. Il leader del partito che ottiene il maggior numero di seggi diventa Primo Ministro e forma il nuovo governo.

electoral college Sistema adottato negli Stati Uniti per l'elezione del Presidente e del Vicepresidente. In ciascuno stato gli elettori eleggono dei delegati (*electors*), i quali formano l'assemblea dell'*electoral college* e a loro volta si impegnano a votare per un determinato candidato. Tutti i voti di uno stato vanno a un candidato. Bastano 270 voti (*electoral college votes*) per vincere le elezioni, il che significa che il Presidente può essere eletto anche senza ottenere la maggioranza del voto popolare.

elementary school Negli Stati Uniti è una scuola elementare per bambini tra i 6 e i 12 anni. Detta anche *grade school*.

England L'Inghilterra è il più esteso e popolato dei paesi che costituiscono il Regno Unito. Nel corso dei secoli affermò il predominio militare, politico ed economico sulla Scozia, il Galles e gli altri paesi che formano le Isole Britanniche (BRITISH ISLES). Tale processo è oggi parzialmente invertito (*vedi* DEVOLUTION) e Scozia, Galles e Irlanda del Nord hanno organi legislativi distinti con poteri più o meno autonomi. L'Inghilterra è invece governata esclusivamente dal Parlamento Britannico.

examinations In Inghilterra, Galles e Irlanda del Nord al termine del quinto anno di scuola secondaria si sostengono gli esami del *General Certificate of Secondary Education* (*GCSE*), in varie combinazioni di materie. I ragazzi che proseguono gli studi sostengono, in un numero minore di materie, gli esami dell'*Advanced Supplementary* (*A/S*) *Level* alla fine del sesto anno, e poi gli esami dell'*Advanced Level* (*A Level*) l'ultimo anno delle superiori. Per l'accesso all'università è necessario passare almeno due *A levels*. I ragazzi che invece preferiscono compiere studi presso scuole professionali e istituti tecnici sostengono gli esami per le *General National Vocational Qualifications* (*GNVQs*). In Scozia, invece, si sostengono gli esami dello *Standard Grade* al termine del quarto anno di superiori e gli *Higher* e *Advanced Higher* per accedere all'università. Negli Stati Uniti il sistema scolastico non prevede esami ufficiali. Gli alunni conseguono un diploma di scuola secondaria al termine della HIGH SCHOOL, per cui ci si basa principalmente sui voti assegnati dai professori delle varie materie. Per l'accesso ad alcuni istituti universitari è richiesto il *College Test* (*vedi* ACT), un esame in inglese, matematica o scienze. *Vedi anche* EDUCATION.

Fifth Amendment ▶ BILL OF RIGHTS

Flower of Scotland Inno nazionale scozzese.

football Il calcio è lo sport più popolare del Regno Unito. Molte delle squadre più celebri sono a Londra (Arsenal, Chelsea, Tottenham Hotspur) e in città dell'Inghilterra centrale e del nord (Manchester United, Newcastle United, Aston Villa). Le squadre scozzesi giocano in campionati separati; le squadre principali (Celtic e Rangers) hanno sede a Glasgow. Negli Stati Uniti il calcio si chiama *soccer* in quanto per football si intende football americano.

Founding Fathers I padri fondatori che nel 1787 contribuirono a fondare gli Stati Uniti d'America in occasione della *Federal Constitution Convention*, durante la quale venne redatta la costituzione americana (CONSTITUTION). I più noti sono George Washington, Thomas Jefferson e Benjamin Franklin.

fraternity Associazione studentesca maschile presso molte università americane. Il nome delle varie *fraternities* è formato da due o tre lettere dell'alfabeto greco, ad es. '*Lambda Delta Chi*'. Di solito i soci di una *fraternity* dividono gli alloggi della *fraternity house*. Alcune confraternite si occupano di opere di beneficenza, mentre altre approfondiscono argomenti di carattere accademico. Le *fraternities* sono state spesso criticate perché considerate istituzioni elitarie e discriminatorie, ma attualmente sono più accettate: oggi che l'istruzione è sempre più cara, il loro carattere comunitario aiuta a ridurre il costo della vita degli studenti. *Vedi anche* SORORITY.

FTSE-100 (pronunciato *Footsie one hundred*) La media del valore dei 100 principali titoli che compaiono nel listino della Borsa di Londra, pubblicato giornalmente sul quotidiano finanziario, *the Financial Times*. Fornisce importanti indicazioni sulla situazione economica in Gran Bretagna.

further education In Gran Bretagna il termine indica qualunque tipo di istruzione per studenti oltre i 16 anni di età (la fine della scuola dell'obbligo) ad esclusione dell'educazione universitaria, nel qual caso si parla di *higher education*. Negli Stati Uniti, invece, *further education* si usa spesso anche per riferirsi all'istruzione universitaria.

gap year In Gran Bretagna il *gap year* è l'anno di intervallo che molti studenti si prendono tra la fine delle superiori e l'università. Molti studenti utilizzano questo periodo sabbatico per fare esperienza nel mondo del lavoro e mettere da parte qualche risparmio, altri invece ne approfittano per viaggiare all'estero e conoscere il mondo.

GCSE ▸ EXAMINATIONS

Gettysburg Address Il discorso tenuto da Abraham Lincoln nel 1863, per l'inaugurazione del cimitero per i caduti nella battaglia di Gettysburg durante la Guerra di Secessione (CIVIL WAR). Contiene la storica definizione di democrazia come 'governo di popolo, dal popolo e per il popolo'.

GNVQ ▸ EXAMINATIONS

God Save the Queen Inno nazionale britannico. Non si sa chi ne compose il testo o la musica, ma si cantava già nel XVIII secolo.

grade school ▸ ELEMENTARY SCHOOL

grammar school In alcune zone dell'Inghilterra e del Galles è un tipo di scuola secondaria (*secondary school*) a cui accedono alunni che hanno superato una prova d'ammissione. Dal 1965 la maggior parte delle le *grammar schools* sono state sostituite dalle COMPREHENSIVE SCHOOLS.

Grand National In Gran Bretagna, la corsa di cavalli a ostacoli più importante, tenuta annualmente a Aintree, presso Liverpool. È un evento di portata nazionale che attira puntualmente un forte interesse. Sono molte le persone che puntano sui cavalli solo in occasione di questa corsa.

Great Britain La Gran Bretagna è la più grande delle Isole Britanniche (BRITISH ISLES). Include l'Inghilterra, la Scozia e il Galles. Spesso si usa erroneamente il termine '*Britain*' per indicare il Regno Unito (UNITED KINGDOM) o l'Inghilterra.

green card Negli Stati Uniti è un documento ufficiale che concede a qualsiasi persona priva della cittadinanza americana il permesso di risiedere e lavorare a tempo indeterminato negli Stati Uniti. Nel Regno Unito, invece, è un documento che i conducenti o proprietari di autoveicoli devono richiedere alla propria compagnia di assicurazione per convalidare la polizza in occasione di viaggi all'estero.

Greyhound bus Veicolo della più grande compagnia di pulmann statunitense (The Greyhound Lines Company) che collegando le maggiori città copre tutto il paese. È il mezzo di trasporto più usato dai giovani e dai turisti con budget limitato per percorrere grandi distanze.

Groundhog Day ▸GIORNI FESTIVI NEI PAESI ANGLOFONI

gun control Il controllo sulle armi da fuoco è al momento un tema molto controverso negli Stati Uniti. Molti ritengono che il porto d'armi dovrebbe essere vietato ai comuni cittadini, dato il gran numero di omicidi e altri reati commessi. Altri sostengono invece che l'abolizione del porto d'armi contravverrebbe alla Costituzione (CONSTITUTION), la quale con il '*right to bear arms*' ne sancisce il diritto. La NATIONAL RIFLE ASSOCIATION si oppone a ogni legge al riguardo. Nel 1993 il congresso ha tuttavia approvato la Brady Bill che limita la vendita e l'uso di alcuni tipi di arma.

Gunpowder Plot ▸BONFIRE NIGHT

Guy Fawkes' Night ▸BONFIRE NIGHT

haka Il rituale urlo di guerra dei Maori neozelandesi, cantato battendo energicamente i piedi per terra e muovendo le braccia. La nazionale neozelandese di rugby esegue l'*haka* prima di ogni partita.

Halloween ▸GIORNI FESTIVI NEI PAESI ANGLOFONI

high school Negli Stati Uniti indica la scuola secondaria, generalmente per alunni di età compresa tra i 14 e i 18 anni. In Gran Bretagna, il termine si ritrova solo nel nome di alcune scuole.

holidays ▸GIORNI FESTIVI NEI PAESI ANGLOFONI

homecoming Incontro annuale degli ex studenti di istituti universitari o HIGH SCHOOLS statunitensi. In genere ha luogo in autunno quando i vecchi studenti fanno una rimpatriata e partecipano a varie attività, tra cui una partita

Cultura

di football americano, la *homecoming parade* e la *homecoming dance*. In questa occasione viene anche eletta la *homecoming queen*.

House of Commons La Camera dei Comuni è la camera bassa del Parlamento britannico HOUSES OF PARLIAMENT. I deputati eletti si chiamano MPs (*members of Parliament*). La Camera dei Comuni è anche la camera bassa del Parlamento canadese, con 308 membri, eletti per cinque anni a suffragio diretto.

House of Lords La Camera dei Lord è la camera alta del Parlamento britannico (HOUSES OF PARLIAMENT). La sua funzione è discutere e poi approvare alcuni disegni di legge della HOUSE OF COMMONS o suggerire dei cambiamenti. La Camera dei Lord ha anche la funzione nel sistema giudiziario come corte di ultima istanza. I Lord sono per la maggioranza nominati (non eletti), e fino al 1999 un certo numero di cariche erano ereditarie. Sono state proposte alcune riforme per far sì che una percentuale di loro siano eletti direttamente dal popolo.

House of Representatives La camera bassa del Congresso degli Stati Uniti (CONGRESS). È costituita da 435 rappresentanti (REPRESENTATIVES) eletti ogni due anni; a ciascuno stato spetta un numero di rappresentanti proporzionale alla propria popolazione. La House of Representatives è incaricata dell'approvazione di ogni nuova legge.

Houses of Parliament Sono le due camere del Parlamento britannico, la Camera dei Comuni (HOUSE OF COMMONS) e la Camera dei Lord (HOUSE OF LORDS). Il termine indica anche la sede del Parlamento, il Palazzo di Westminster situato in riva al Tamigi nel centro di Londra.

Inauguration Day Negli Stati Uniti è il giorno in cui il neoeletto Presidente assume ufficialmente il potere. La cerimonia di insediamento ha sempre luogo il 20 gennaio, a Washington DC.

Independence Day ▸ GIORNI FESTIVI NEI PAESI ANGLOFONI

independent school Tipo di scuola britannica privata che si autofinanzia tramite il pagamento di quote da parte dei genitori degli alunni, anziché ricevere finanziamenti statali. Le PUBLIC SCHOOLS e le PREPARATORY SCHOOLS rientrano in questa categoria.

infant school ▸ EDUCATION

IRA (Irish Republican Army) L'IRA (Esercito Repubblicano Irlandese) è un'organizzazione paramilitare clandestina il cui obiettivo è l'unificazione della Repubblica d'Irlanda e dell'Irlanda del Nord. Nel 1970, come reazione a una politica considerata repressiva nei confronti delle minoranze cattoliche dell'Irlanda del Nord, una fazione dell'IRA (Provisional IRA) portò avanti atti terroristici in Irlanda del Nord e in Inghilterra. Nel 1998, l'accordo del Venerdì Santo (Good Friday Agreement) ha dato inizio a un periodo di relativa pace tra le comunità contrapposte dell'Irlanda del Nord. *Vedi anche* SINN FEIN.

ITV – Independent Television Gruppo di enti televisivi privati che offrono una programmazione diversificata in 15 diverse zone del Regno Unito.

Ivy League Il gruppo delle più antiche e rinomate università statunitensi, situate nel nordest del paese: Harvard, Yale, Columbia University, Cornell University, Dartmouth College, Brown University, Princeton University e la University of Pennsylvania. Il nome deriva dall'edera che cresce sugli antichi edifici universitari.

junior high school ▸ EDUCATION

junior school Scuola statale britannica per alunni di età compresa tra i 7 e gli 11 anni.

King James Bible ▸ AUTHORIZED VERSION

kirk In scozzese significa chiesa. 'The Kirk' indica the Church of Scotland (la Chiesa Episcopale scozzese).

kiwi Uccello privo di ali e coda originario della Nuova Zelanda. Il termine Kiwis viene anche usato per indicare i neozelandesi e le squadre sportive di questo paese.

Labor Day Festa del Lavoro. Negli Stati Uniti questa festività in onore dei lavoratori viene celebrata a livello nazionale il primo lunedì di settembre.

Labor Party In Australia è uno dei principali partiti politici. Rappresenta il centro-sinistra moderato.

Labour Party In Gran Bretagna il Partito Laburista è uno dei maggiori partiti politici. Andò per la prima volta al potere nel 1924, con l'obiettivo di farsi portavoce degli interessi dei lavoratori e dei sindacati. Negli ultimi anni il partito ha abbandonato alcune posizioni della sinistra storica, ad es. riguardo alla privatizzazione dell'industria e dei servizi pubblici. I suoi leader preferiscono oggi il termine 'New Labour'.

lawyer Termine generico per avvocato. Nel Regno Unito esistono il *solicitor* e il *barrister*. Il primo offre consulenza legale ai cittadini riguardo a questioni minori (è una figura tra l'avvocato e il notaio). Il secondo rappresenta i clienti davanti a corti di livello più alto; quando un *barrister* è ammesso ad esercitare l'avvocatura si dice che '*has been called to the Bar*'. Negli Stati Uniti non esiste questa distinzione. Sia nel Regno Unito che negli Stati Uniti si usa il termine *counsel* per indicare un avvocato o un gruppo di avvocati che presentano una causa in tribunale.

Liberal Democratic Party Il Partito Liberaldemocratico, familiarmente abbreviato in 'Lib Dems'. È per importanza il terzo partito della Gran Bretagna. Si è costituito nel 1988 dalla fusione del Partito Liberale (Liberal Party) e del Partito Socialdemocratico (Social Democratic Party).

Liberal Party Importante partito australiano, fautore di una politica essenzialmente conservatrice.

L-plates Nel Regno Unito è un cartello di plastica bianco, con la lettera 'L' in rosso. Va applicato sul davanti e sul retro di un veicolo per segnalare che il conducente si sta preparando all'esame di guida.

mayor Negli Stati Uniti il sindaco di una città viene eletto dagli abitanti. In Inghilterra e Galles è il capo del consiglio comunale (*council*), tradizionalmente eletto dagli altri consiglieri (*councillors*), ma ha prevalentemente incarichi di rappresentanza nelle cerimonie ufficiali, senza reale autorità politica. Talvolta ha il titolo di *lord mayor* (in Scozia *provost* o *lord provost*). Recentemente in alcune grandi città è stata creata la figura di un *mayor* eletto dal popolo.

member of Parliament ▸ MP

Memorial Day Festività statunitense che commemora gli americani caduti in guerra. Generalmente ricorre l'ultimo lunedì di maggio.

middle school ▸ EDUCATION

midterms (*midterm elections*) Negli Stati Uniti sono le elezioni per la Camera dei Rappresentanti (HOUSE OF REPRESENTATIVES) indette a metà del mandato presidenziale.

Mormon La Chiesa di Gesù Cristo dei Santi degli Ultimi Giorni (Church of Jesus Christ of Latter-Day Saints) conta oggi circa 10 milioni di fedeli, meglio conosciuti come Mormoni. Fu fondata negli Stati Uniti nel 1830 da Joseph Smith. Successivamente, sotto la guida di Brigham Young, i membri si spostarono nella parte ovest del paese, dove fondarono Salt Lake City nello stato dello Utah, i cui abitanti sono ancora oggi Mormoni. Hanno regole morali molto rigide e non bevono né alcolici né caffè.

Morris dancing Una danza folkloristica originaria del Regno Unito, eseguita solitamente da gruppi di soli uomini (*Morris men*) disposti in file. I danzatori, che indossano una camicia bianca, un cappello di paglia e pantaloni con campanelli applicati, agitano bastoni o fazzoletti.

Mother's Day (Mothering Sunday) ▸ GIORNI FESTIVI NEI PAESI ANGLOFONI

motorways La Gran Bretagna ha un'ampia rete di autostrade a tre corsie, segnalate dalla lettera 'M' seguita da un numero. Il limite di velocità sulla motorway è di 70 miglia all'ora, che equivale a 112 km/h. A differenza dell'Italia non si deve in genere pagare il pedaggio. Attualmente una sola *motorway* è a pagamento.

MP (*member of Parliament*) Un membro della Camera dei Comuni che rappresenta una delle 659 'CONSTITUENCIES' in cui è suddiviso il Regno Unito. *Vedi anche* HOUSE OF COMMONS.

National Guard Un corpo militare statunitense la cui origine risale all'epoca coloniale, composto di volontari reclutati in ciascuno stato. In caso di catastrofi naturali o di emergenze civili può passare sotto il comando federale. Oggi la National Guard è considerata parte dell'esercito nazionale.

National Health Service (NHS) È il servizio di assistenza sanitaria britannico, finanziato in gran parte dal governo, per cui l'assistenza è per lo più gratuita. I medicinali prescritti e le cure dentistiche sono a pagamento, eccetto per alcune categorie di persone, quali i bambini e i pensionati.

National Insurance È il servizio di previdenza sociale in Gran Bretagna. Lavoratori e datori di lavoro versano dei contributi fiscali (*National Insurance contributions*) da cui dipendono i diversi servizi che offre lo stato, quali la pensione, l'assistenza sanitaria, i sussidi di disoccupazione. Chiunque lavori o faccia domanda per i sussidi deve richiedere un numero di identificazione (*National Insurance number*).

National Lottery È regolata dalla National Lottery Commission, ente pubblico non governativo che dipende dal Ministero della Cultura, Media e Spettacolo. Parte dei proventi viene destinata a iniziative culturali e sportive, alla conservazione del patrimonio culturale e ambientale e a organizzazioni no-profit.

National Party Importante partito politico neozelandese, fautore di una politica fondamentalmente conservatrice.

National Rifle Association (NRA) Una organizzazione statunitense favorevole al possesso di armi da fuoco da usare nella caccia, gli sport e la legittima difesa. Secondo i suoi 3,4 milioni di iscritti il diritto di ogni cittadino a possedere armi è garantito dalla Costituzione americana (CONSTITUTION).

National Trust Una fondazione britannica senza scopo di lucro finalizzata alla conservazione dei luoghi di interesse storico e del patrimonio ambientale. Finanziato da donazioni e sovvenzioni private, il National Trust è il maggiore proprietario terriero del Regno Unito. Nel corso degli anni ha acquisito enormi estensioni di terreni (circa 248.000 ettari) e di coste (circa 960 km), come pure edifici, borghi e giardini, molti dei quali vengono aperti al pubblico in certi periodi dell'anno. In Scozia esiste una fondazione analoga ma indipendente, il National Trust for Scotland.

Native American È il termine più ampiamente accettato per indicare i popoli indigeni di tutto il continente americano. Secondo il Bureau of Indian Affairs, l'organizzazione governativa statunitense che si occupa delle questioni indiane, esistono circa 562 tribù per un totale di 1,9 milioni di persone. Circa un milione di indiani vive nelle riserve e di questi il 49% è disoccupato. Molte riserve aprono case da gioco grazie all'autonomia di cui godono.

NBC – National Broadcasting Company Il primo ente radiofonico istituito negli Stati Uniti (1926). Il primo canale televisivo della NBC cominciò a trasmettere nel 1940.

Newspapers Negli Stati Uniti il 95% della popolazione legge la stampa locale. Esiste un unico quotidiano nazionale, *USA Today*, gli altri sono locali. I quotidiani di alcune grandi città, quali il *New York Times*, il *Los Angeles Times*, e il *Washington Post*, sono comunque diffusi in tutto il paese. Anche l'*International Herald Tribune*, pubblicato fuori dagli Stati Uniti, viene letto da molti americani all'estero. Il *Wall Street Journal*, che pubblica il DOW JONES AVERAGE, è il quotidiano di economia e finanza più importante degli Stati Uniti. La stampa americana è nel complesso piuttosto conservatrice, in modo da garantirsi una più alta distribuzione. Nel Regno Unito i quotidiani escono in due formati: quello grande dei *broadsheets* e quello più piccolo e compatto dei *tabloids*. Fino a poco tempo fa i quotidiani nazionali più seri erano tutti *broadsheets*. Il *Daily Telegraph* e il *Financial Times* (stampato sull'inconfondibile carta color salmone) hanno conservato questo formato, ma recentemente il *Times*, l'*Independent* e il *Guardian* hanno ridotto il formato. Del gruppo dei popolarissimi quotidiani più sensazionalistici (tutti in formato tabloid), fanno parte il *Sun*, il *Mirror*, l'*Express* e il *Mail*. Questi giornali sono notti per labitudine di dare risalto all'aspeto umano e spesso puramente scandalistico delle notizie. Sia negli Stati Uniti che nel Regno Unito i quotidiani che escono il sabato o la domenica hanno un gran numero di supplementi di sport, viaggi, cultura ecc.

Northern Ireland È una provincia del Regno Unito, situata nella parte nordorientale dell'Irlanda. Rimase a far parte del Regno Unito, con autonomia limitata, quando, nel 1920, il resto dell'isola divenne indipendente. La vita in Irlanda del Nord è stata a lungo dominata dal conflitto tra la maggioranza protestante che vuole restare vincolata al Regno Unito e la minoranza cattolica che vorrebbe unirsi alla Repubblica d'Irlanda. Gli anni dal 1969 al 1998 sono stati anni di sanguinosa violenza, sia in Irlanda nel Nord sia nei territori della Gran Bretagna; mentre i cattolici erano impegnati nella campagna per i diritti civili, organizzazioni paramilitari di ambo le parti hanno portato avanti assassinii, rapresaglie e atti terroristici. Durante gran parte di questo periodo la provincia è tornata sotto il diretto governo britannico e truppe britanniche vi erano stanziate stabilmente. L'accordo del Venerdì Santo (Good Friday Agreement)

del 1998 ha messo fine alla violenza e la semiautonomia è stata restaurata sulla base di un accordo sulla spartizione del potere. Il Parlamento dell'Irlanda del Nord è stato tuttavia sospeso più volte, in quanto la cooperazione tra i partiti non è sempre attuabile. I singoli partiti sono spesso divisi in fazioni. Il Partito Democratico Unionista (Democratic Unionist Party) e il più moderato Partito Unionista dell'Ulster (Ulster Unionist Party) rappresentano la comunità protestante, mentre SINN FEIN e i più moderati Partito Social-democratico e laburista (SDLP, Social Democratic and Labour Party) rappresentano i cattolici. Il piccolo Partito dell'Alleanza (Alliance Party) si oppone invece alla divisione religiosa. *Vedi anche* IRA.

Number Ten ▶ DOWNING STREET

NVQ ▶ EXAMINATIONS

Old Glory ▶ STARS AND STRIPES

Open University (OU) Università a distanza britannica fondata nel 1969.

Oxbridge Termine che indica nel loro insieme le università più antiche e prestigiose del Regno Unito: Oxford e Cambridge.

Pancake Day ▶ SHROVE TUESDAY

Parliament Il Parlamento britannico è l'organo legislativo del Regno Unito ed è suddiviso in due Camere: la Camera dei Comuni (HOUSE OF COMMONS) e la Camera dei Lord (HOUSE OF LORDS). Il Parlamento canadese è costituito dal Senato (SENATE) e dalla Camera dei Comuni. *Vedi anche* MP.

PBS – Public Broadcasting Service Servizio radiotelevisivo statunitense, finanziato dal governo e rinomato per i programmi di qualità. È costituito dall'associazione di emittenti locali che trasmettono senza scopo di lucro e senza pubblicità.

Peace Corps Agenzia federale statunitense fondata nel 1961. I Corpi di Pace, composti da volontari, operano principalmente nei paesi in via di sviluppo in settori quali l'insegnamento, la sanità, l'agricoltura e l'ambiente.

Pentagon L'edificio a pianta ottagonale situato a Washington dove hanno sede gli uffici centrali del ministero della Difesa e delle forze armate americani. Talvolta la stampa utilizza il termine per riferirsi allo Stato Maggiore.

Pledge of Allegiance Giuramento di fedeltà che i cittadini degli Stati Uniti prestano alla bandiera e alla patria. In molte scuole gli studenti lo ripetono tutte le mattine davanti alla bandiera tenendo una mano sul petto.

Poppy Day ▶ GIORNI FESTIVI NEI PAESI ANGLOFONI

preparatory school Negli Stati Uniti è un tipo di scuola secondaria in cui viene offerta una speciale preparazione preuniversitaria. In Gran Bretagna, dov'è anche detta *prep school*, è una scuola privata per alunni dai 7 ai 13 anni. Generalmente non è un istituto misto e in molte *preparatory schools* parte degli alunni stanno a convitto. La maggioranza degli alunni prosegue poi gli studi in una scuola privata (PUBLIC SCHOOL).

President Negli Stati Uniti il Presidente può restare in carica per un massimo di due mandati (*terms*) ciascuno di durata quadriennale. Poiché il paese è una repubblica federale di tipo presidenziale, egli è il capo dello stato e allo stesso tempo il capo del governo. È responsabile della politica estera e il comandante in capo delle forze armate.

President's Day ▸ GIORNI FESTIVI NEI PAESI ANGLOFONI

primary (primary election) Negli Stati Uniti le elezioni primarie (*primaries*) vengono indette per selezionare i candidati prima delle elezioni principali, specialmente nel caso delle presidenziali. I candidati alla carica di presidente (PRESIDENT) vengono eletti dopo una serie di primarie a livello statale. *Vedi anche* ELECTIONS.

primary school ▸ EDUCATION

Provost ▸ MAYOR

pub (*public house*) Letteralmente 'casa aperta al pubblico', il *pub* è il tipico locale dove in Gran Bretagna e Irlanda si va per bere birra e altre bevande, alcoliche e non. Le origini dei *pub* risalgono all'epoca dei Romani. Alla fine del XIV secolo chiunque producesse e vendesse birra (*ale*) doveva esporre un cartello e le caratteristiche insegne colorate contraddistinguono i *pub* ancora oggi. Il *pub* è spesso al centro della vita sociale e culturale del quartiere o del paese.

public access channel Negli Stati Uniti è un canale televisivo riservato a programmi di persone e organizzazioni che operano senza fini di lucro.

public house ▸ PUB

public school In Gran Bretagna sono, al contrario di quanto farebbe pensare il nome, scuole private a pagamento, per alunni tra i 13 e i 18 anni. Spesso si tratta di scuole miste e nella maggior parte di esse gli allievi sono a convitto. In Scozia e negli Stati Uniti il termine *public school* indica invece una scuola statale. *Vedi anche* PREPARATORY SCHOOL.

Remembrance Sunday ▸ POPPY DAY

Representative Un membro della Camera dei Rappresentanti (HOUSE OF REPRESENTATIVES) americana.

Republican Party Uno dei maggiori partiti politici statunitensi. Sebbene sia stato fondato nel 1854 da chi appoggiava l'abolizione della schiavitù, viene considerato più conservatore del Partito Democratico (DEMOCRATIC PARTY), l'altro principale partito americano.

rugby Il gioco della palla ovale, originario della Gran Bretagna. Esistono due varianti di questo sport, il rugby a 13 (*rugby league*) con squadre composte di 13 giocatori e il rugby a 15 (*rugby union*) con 15 giocatori. Il *rugby league* è stato fin dagli inizi giocato a livello professionale, mentre il *rugby union* lo è divenuto nel 1995.

SAT Negli Stati Uniti indica lo *Scholastic Aptitude Test*, una prova attitudinale sostenuta generalmente l'ultimo anno della HIGH SCHOOL. È necessario superare il *SAT* per accedere alla maggior parte delle università. In Inghilterra e Galles indica invece lo *Standard Assessment Test* o *Task*, una prova sostenuta a 7, 11 e 14 anni dagli alunni di tutte le scuole allo scopo di valutarne i progressi.

Scotland La parte più settentrionale del Regno Unito, la cui popolazione è concentrata in una cintura centrale intorno alle due città principali, Glasgow e Edimburgo, la capitale. La Scozia è particolarmente rinomata per la bellezza delle montagne, dei laghi (in scozzese '*loch*') e delle Highlands, la zona a nordest di Edimburgo. Fino al secolo XVI la Scozia era frequentemente in guerra con l'Inghilterra. Nel 1603, re Giacomo IV (James) di Scozia diventò anche re d'Inghilterra (regnandovi come James I) e l'unione dei due paesi venne portata a termine nel 1707 quando il Parlamento scozzese si sciolse. La Scozia tuttavia conserva molte delle proprie istituzioni. Il sistema scolastico, ad esempio, è diverso dal resto del Regno Unito. Tra gli scozzesi ci sono sempre stati coloro che pensano che la Scozia dovrebbe essere completamente indipendente. Reinstaurato nel 1999 (*vedi* DEVOLUTION), lo Scottish Parliament ha sede a Edimburgo. A differenza dell'Assemblea gallese, esso ha pieni poteri sul piano legislativo e esecutivo riguardo alle questioni scozzesi, mentre ha autorità limitata relativamente al sistema fiscale. *Vedi anche* WALES.

SDLP ▸NORTHERN IRELAND

Senate Negli Stati Uniti il Senato è la camera alta del Congresso (CONGRESS). È formato da 100 senatori (*senators*), due per ciascuno stato, eletti con mandato di sei anni. Le nuove leggi devono essere approvate sia dal Senato che dalla Camera dei Rappresentanti (HOUSE OF REPRESENTATIVES). Il Parlamento canadese è costituito dal Senato e dalla Camera dei Comuni (HOUSE OF COMMONS).

Shadow Cabinet ▸CABINET

Shrove Tuesday ▸GIORNI FESTIVI NEI PAESI ANGLOFONI

Sinn Fein Partito politico irlandese fondato nel 1905 con l'obiettivo di unificare le 32 contee dell'Irlanda nella Repubblica d'Irlanda creata nel 1949. Viene considerato l'ala politica dell'IRA, anche se nega qualunque legame con l'organizzazione paramilitare.

Smithsonian Institution Rinomato istituto statunitense che raccoglie vari musei e centri di ricerca. Situato a Washington DC, è familiarmente soprannominato '*the nation's attic*', la soffitta della nazione.

social security number Un numero di identificazione che negli Stati Uniti tutti devono avere. Inizialmente veniva richiesto per poter lavorare ed essere coperti dalla sicurezza sociale. Tuttavia nel 1987 il governo ha deciso di assegnarlo anche ai bambini. Attualmente viene usato in molte occasioni diverse: compare sugli assegni, sulla patente, ed è il numero con cui vengono identificati gli alunni degli istituti superiori.

sorority Una delle associazioni studentesche femminili presenti in molti istituti universitari. *Vedi anche* FRATERNITY.

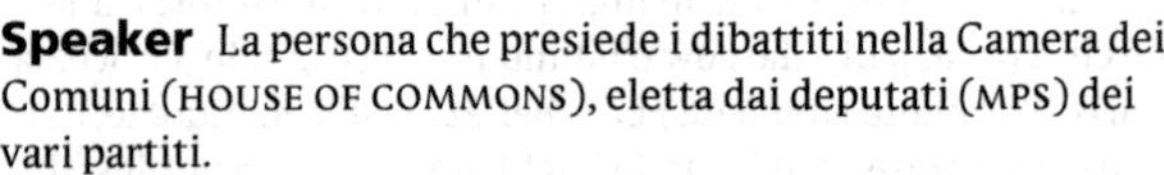

Speaker La persona che presiede i dibattiti nella Camera dei Comuni (HOUSE OF COMMONS), eletta dai deputati (MPS) dei vari partiti.

Speaker of the House Negli Stati Uniti è la persona incaricata di presiedere la maggior parte delle attività della Camera dei Rappresentanti (HOUSE OF REPRESENTATIVES). È responsabile di mantenere l'ordine durante i dibattiti, di nominare i comitati e di presentar loro le proposte di legge. È un rappresentante del partito di maggioranza alla Camera dal quale viene eletto. È la persona che segue al vicepresidente nella successione per la presidenza.

Stars and Stripes La bandiera degli Stati Uniti. Le cinquanta stelle (*stars*) rappresentano i cinquanta stati e le tredici strisce (*stripes*) orizzontali rappresentano le prime tredici colonie che formarono gli Stati Uniti all'epoca dell'indipendenza. Viene anche chiamata Old Glory o STAR-SPANGLED BANNER.

Star-Spangled Banner Uno dei nomi con cui si indica la bandiera degli Stati Uniti. È anche il titolo dell'inno nazionale statunitense, composto nel 1814 ma adottato come tale soltanto nel 1931.

state school In Gran Bretagna indica una scuola statale che è finanziata direttamente o indirettamente dallo stato e offre istruzione gratuita. La maggior parte dei ragazzi frequenta questo tipo di scuole.

State of the Union Address Tradizionale discorso che il Presidente degli Stati Uniti (PRESIDENT) tiene annualmente al Congresso (CONGRESS) per metterlo al corrente della 'situazione dell'Unione', come previsto dalla

Costituzione (CONSTITUTION). Il discorso è l'occasione per parlare dei progressi del governo, dei suoi progetti e della politica per il futuro. Viene trasmesso in diretta alla televisione.

Statue of Liberty La celebre statua situata sulla Liberty Island nella baia di New York. Donata dal popolo francese come omaggio al popolo americano, raffigura una donna che innalza la fiaccola della libertà. È ormai l'inconfondibile simbolo di New York e dell'America.

summer camp Negli Stati Uniti indica il campeggio estivo cui moltissimi ragazzi si recano per socializzare e praticare attività ricreative e sportive all'aria aperta; tra queste il nuoto, il canottaggio, l'arrampicata e i corsi di sopravvivenza.

Super Bowl ▸AMERICAN FOOTBALL

Supreme Court È l'organo più importante del sistema giudiziario statunitense, composto da nove giudici, nominati a vita dal Presidente (PRESIDENT) con l'approvazione del Congresso (CONGRESS). La Corte Suprema decide riguardo alla costituzionalità delle leggi e ha inoltre la facoltà di impedire l'approvazione delle leggi, tanto federali quanto statali o locali. È anche la corte di ultima istanza, che riesamina i casi già passati davanti ai tribunali di grado inferiore. Le sentenze della Corte Suprema costituiscono giurisprudenza, vale a dire possono essere usate come precedenti in altri processi.

tabloid ▸NEWSPAPERS

Teamsters Teamsters Union è il più grosso sindacato degli Stati Uniti, con circa 1 milione e mezzo di iscritti. Sebbene inizialmente rappresentasse i camionisti (*teamsters*), oggi ne fanno parte lavoratori di molti altri settori.

Thanksgiving ▸GIORNI FESTIVI NEI PAESI ANGLOFONI

TOEFL (*Test of English as a Foreign Language*) Un esame che valuta il livello di conoscenza dell'inglese degli studenti che fanno domanda d'iscrizione in un'università americana ma non sono di madrelingua inglese.

Tory ▸CONSERVATIVE PARTY

trick or treat ▸HALLOWEEN

Uncle Sam Personaggio immaginario che rappresenta gli Stati Uniti, il suo governo e i suoi cittadini. Nell'iconografia è tradizionalmente rappresentato con la barba bianca, vestito dei colori nazionali bianco, rosso e azzurro, con un gran cappello a cilindro con le stelle della bandiera statunitense. Spesso utilizzato quando si fa appello al patriottismo americano.

Union Jack o Union Flag Il nome della bandiera del Regno Unito. È formata da tre croci: quella di San Giorgio (St George), patrono d'Inghilterra, quella di Sant'Andrea (St Andrew), patrono di Scozia, e quella di San Patrizio (St Patrick), patrono d'Irlanda. Il Galles e San David suo patrono non vi sono rappresentati.

United Kingdom Il Regno Unito di Gran Bretagna e Irlanda del Nord (United Kingdom of Great Britain and Northern Ireland) comprende l'Inghilterra, la Scozia, il Galles e l'Irlanda del Nord. Fa parte del COMMONWEALTH e dell'Unione Europea.

Veterans Day ▸GIORNI FESTIVI NEI PAESI ANGLOFONI

Wales Parte del Regno Unito confinante con l'Inghilterra centro-occidentale. La maggior parte dei centri abitati sono situati sulla costa (l'interno del paese è montuoso e poco popolato), in particolare lungo la costa meridionale, intorno alle due maggiori città, Cardiff, la capitale, e Swansea. Nel nord del Galles il sentimento nazionalistico è più sentito e la lingua gallese (WELSH) è maggiormente diffusa. L'occupazione inglese del Galles ebbe inizio poco dopo la conquista normanna del 1066. Nel XVI secolo il Galles fu integrato all'Inghilterra ai fini legali, amministrativi e parlamentari. Nel 1999, in seguito al processo di decentramento (DEVOLUTION) è stata istituita l'Assemblea Nazionale del Galles, anche detta Assemblea Gallese (Welsh Assembly). Relativamente agli affari gallesi ha poteri legislativi secondari limitati.

Wall Street Via di Manhattan, a New York, dove hanno sede la Borsa e molti altri istituti finanziari. Quando si parla di Wall Street ci si riferisce spesso a tali istituti.

Weddings Nei paesi anglosassoni il matrimonio tradizionale si svolge in chiesa. La sposa (*bride*) indossa l'abito bianco ed ha al seguito una o più damigelle d'onore (*bridesmaids*). Il padre accompagna la sposa all'altare, mentre lo sposo (*bridegroom*) è affiancato dal *best man*, un parente o amico. Gli sposi si scambiano gli anelli (*wedding rings* o *bands*). Nel caso di matrimonio civile la cerimonia si svolge in comune. Dopo la cerimonia ha luogo il rinfresco nuziale (*wedding reception*) durante il quale il padre della sposa e il *best man* tengono un discorso. Alla fine del rinfresco gli sposi vanno in luna di miele (*honeymoon*). La sera prima del matrimonio, religioso o civile, è tradizione che il promesso sposo esca con gli amici per dare l'addio al celibato (la serata è detta *stag night* o negli Stati Uniti *bachelor party*). Oggi anche la sposa festeggia con le amiche l'addio al nubilato (*hen night*, e negli Stati Uniti *bachelorette party*). Negli Stati Uniti un'amica o una parente della sposa (di solito la damigella d'onore) organizza anche la cosiddetta *shower*, una festicciola in occasione della quale si danno alla sposa dei regali.

Welfare Negli Stati Uniti il termine *welfare* e *welfare programs* indicano le diverse misure di sicurezza sociale prese dal governo per garantire il benessere dei cittadini, in particolare in caso di povertà, malattia, disoccupazione. Fanno parte di questo sistema Medicare, Medicaid e i buoni per l'acquisto di viveri (*food stamps*).

Welsh È il gallese (*Cymraeg*), lingua di origine celtica, come il bretone e il cornico. È la lingua madre del 20% della popolazione gallese e negli ultimi quarant'anni ha vissuto una certa rinascita. In Galles oggi è usata insieme all'inglese in certi contesti ufficiali ed è materia obbligatoria nella maggior parte delle scuole.

Westminster Un quartiere del centro di Londra dove sono situati alcuni dei principali edifici governativi, quali il Parlamento (HOUSES OF PARLIAMENT) e la residenza del Primo Ministro in DOWNING STREET, ed anche l'Abbazia di Westminster (Westminster Abbey). Oggi la stampa usa il termine 'Westminster' per indicare il Parlamento britannico.

West Side ▸EAST SIDE

whip Nella Camera dei Comuni britannica (HOUSE OF COMMONS), *whips* sono i deputati (MPS) incaricati di far rispettare la disciplina parlamentare ai colleghi del proprio partito, di assicurarsi che siano presenti alle sessioni e che votino. Negli Stati Uniti sono membri del Congresso (CONGRESS) con simili responsabilità.

Whitehall Una via nel centro di Londra dove hanno sede vari uffici governativi. La stampa usa il termine per indicare il governo e l'amministrazione statale.

White House La Casa Bianca, situata a Washington, è la residenza ufficiale del Presidente degli Stati Uniti. La stampa usa il termine per indicare il Presidente e i suoi collaboratori.

World Series ▸BASEBALL

Yankee Termine spregiativo con cui durante la Guerra di Secessione i sudisti chiamavano i nordisti. Oggi è usato in tutto il mondo per indicare gli americani in generale. Negli Stati Uniti del sud ha ancora il significato originario, mentre in quelli del nord è utilizzato per indicare gli oriundi del New England.

yearbook Negli Stati Uniti è l'album che annualmente viene pubblicato per gli studenti dell'ultimo anno della HIGH SCHOOL. Contiene un profilo di ciascuno studente con notizie sulle sue attività accademiche, sportive e ricreative, accompagnato da una fotografie e da una dedica.

►54

Letter-writing / Redazione di lettere

Invito (informale)

- *La data si può anche scrivere nei modi seguenti:* April 10, 10 April, 10th April. *Il nome del mese è in maiuscolo.*
- *In alto a destra si indica il nome e l'indirizzo del mittente, e sotto si scrive la data.*

35 Winchester Drive
Stoke Gifford
Bristol
BS34 8PD

April 22nd 2013

Dear Luca,

Is there any chance of your coming to stay with us in the summer holidays? Roy and Debbie would be delighted if you could (as well as David and me, of course). We hope to go to North Wales at the end of July/beginning of August, and you'd be very welcome to come too. It's really beautiful up there. We'll probably take tents - I hope that's OK by you.

Let me know as soon as possible if you can manage it.

All best wishes

Rachel Hemmings

Invito (formale)

Invito a un matrimonio e al rinfresco

Mr and Mrs Peter Thompson
request the pleasure of your company
at the marriage of their daughter
Hannah Louise
to
Steven David Warner
at St Mary's Church, Little Bourton
on Saturday 22nd July 2013 at 2 p.m.
And afterwards at the Golden Cross Hotel, Billing

23 Santers Lane
Little Bourton
Northampton
NN6 1AZ

R.S.V.P

Accepting an invitation (formal)

CARLO E BEATRICE BUOZZI

ringraziano calorosamente per il gentile invito e sono lieti di poter partecipare.

Invitation (informal)

Cara Claudia

È un po' che non ci sentiamo ma spero che tutto vada bene, sia con Andrea che con l'università. Il 7 agosto è il mio compleanno e pensavo di fare una festa. Che ne dici ❶ *di venire qui a Napoli? Naturalmente sei invitata a casa mia per qualche giorno e ne approfitteremo per fare un po' di chiacchiere e un po' di mare. Fammi sapere al più presto! Spero tanto che tu venga, da sola o accompagnata, se tu e Andrea state ancora insieme. Il mio indirizzo email è grazia@hotmail.com.*

Un bacione ❷ *e a prestissimo,*

Grazia

- *Invitations to parties are usually made in person or on the phone, unless it's a really formal occasion.*

❶ *For a letter to a friend you use the 'tu' form.*

❷ *This affectionate ending is used with close friends or relatives. Other informal endings are* Baci *or* Un abbraccio.

Accepting an invitation (informal)

24 aprile 2013

Cara Grazia

Quanto tempo! Scusa se non mi sono fatta più viva ma tra gli esami e altre storie il tempo è volato. Certo che vengo giù a Napoli. L'ultimo esame lo dovrei avere a fine luglio e non ho ancora programmato niente per le vacanze, tanto più che adesso sono sola (mollata da Andrea due mesi fa, ma senza troppi drammi). Ora che ci siamo rimesse in contatto prometto di non sparire e non vedo l'ora di rivederti di persona. Torno a studiare.

Un abbraccio,

Claudia

- *In informal letters you write the date at the top but not your address.*
- *In replies to informal invitations you also use only the Christian name, the 'tu' form and an affectionate ending.*

Writing e-mails and SMS / Scrivere e-mail ed SMS

Sending an e-mail

The illustration shows a typical interface for sending e-mail.

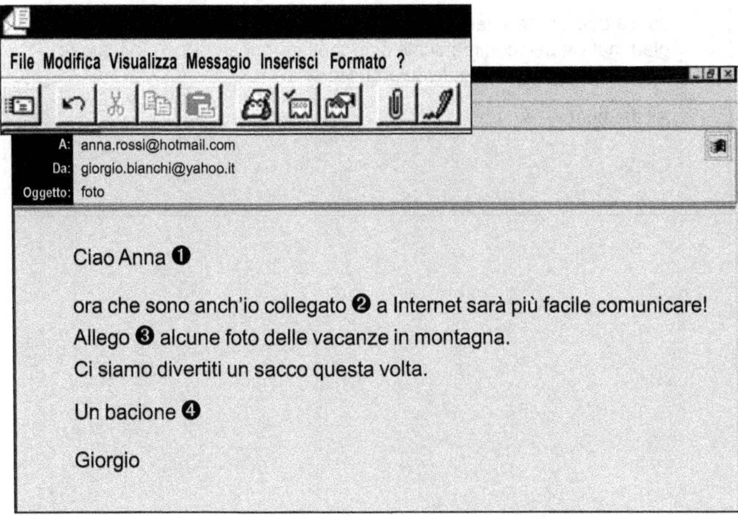

❶ *The beginning changes according to how formal it is. You can use* caro/cara *or leave it out.*

❷ Collegata *if the person writing is a girl or woman.*

❸ Allegare *means to enclose and also to attach in e-mails.*

❹ *In more formal e-mails you can end with* 'Distinti saluti' *like in letters.*

E-mail

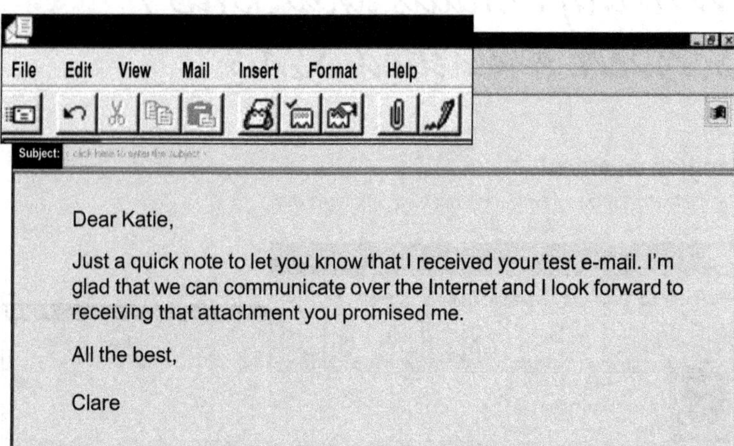
File
Edit
View
Mail
Insert
Format
Help
Subject:
Dear Katie,
Just a quick note to let you know that I received your test e-mail. I'm glad that we can communicate over the Internet and I look forward to receiving that attachment you promised me.
All the best,
Clare

Booking train tickets online

Acquista il tuo biglietto online con ***Europtrains***

Biglietti | Orari | Mappe, destinazioni e itinerari

Partenza
Seleziona la stazione ▼ **Tutte le stazioni**

Arrivo
Seleziona la stazione ▼ **Tutte le stazioni**

Andata
Giu ▼ 17 ▼ 2013 ▼
Ore Qualunque ▼
calendario

Ritorno
(non selezionare per viaggio di sola andata)
Giu ▼ 18 ▼ 2013 ▼
Ore Qualunque ▼
calendario

Le date del mio viaggio sono flessibili ☐

Numero di passeggeri **Adulti** ▼ **Bambini** ▼ **Studenti** ▼ **Ultrasessantenni** ▼

Prima classe ☐
Seconda classe ☐

RICERCA

Offerte speciali

Risparmia il 25%
quando prenoti online
a partire dal 1 luglio 2010

•

Milano-Bruxelles solo andata a metà prezzo

Clicca qui per saperne di più

•

Milano–Londra andata e ritorno a soli € 50,00

Clicca qui per maggiori dettagli

•

Studenti: come risparmiare viaggiando con la pass card

Telefona per scoprire tutti i vantaggi e le condizioni.

Area clienti

Nome utente
Password

Ricorda la mia password ☐
Hai scordato la password?
Registrati ora!

Altre opzioni

In viaggio per lavoro
Viaggiare in gruppo
Assistenza per disabili
Treno e bici

Cambiare una prenotazione
Cancellare una prenotazione
Ricevere i biglietti a domicilio

Altre offerte speciali
Abbonamenti
Hotels
Assicurazione

mappa del sito | chi siamo | FAQ | contatti

Comprare i biglietti su Internet

Buy tickets online with ***Europtrains***

Tickets | Timetables | Maps, destinations & route planner

From
Select station ▼ **See all stations**

To
Select station ▼ **See all stations**

Departure date
June ▼ 17 ▼ 2013 ▼
Time
Anytime ▼
Calendar

Return date
(leave blank for one-way travel)
June ▼ 18 ▼ 2013 ▼
Time
Anytime ▼
Calendar

Flexible dates? ☐

Number of passengers
Adults ▼ Children ▼ Students ▼ Seniors ▼

First class ☐
Second classe ☐

SEARCH

Special offer

Save 25%
when you book online
from 1st July 2010 onwards

•

London to Brussels one way
half-price

To find out more, click here

•

London to Milan round trip
from just €50

Click here for details

•

Students: buy your pass card and
save money on travel

Call for details.

Conditions apply

My account

Username
Password

Remember my password ☐

Forgotten your password?

Register here

More options

Business travellers

Group travellers

Travelling with a wheelchair

Travelling with a bicycle

Changing a reservation

Cancelling a reservation

Receiving your tickets

More special offers

Rail passes

Hotels

Travel Insurance

site map | about us | FAQ | contact us

SMS (electronic text-messaging)

The basic principles governing Italian SMS abbreviations are similar to those governing English SMS. Certain words or syllables can be represented by letters or numbers that sound the same but take up less space. The word 'sei', for example, can be replaced by '6', and the word 'che' shortened to 'ke'. Another way of shortening words and phrases is simply to omit certain letters, especially vowels. For example, 'comunque' becomes 'cmq' and 'ci vediamo dopo' becomes 'cvd'.

As in English, 'faccine' (emoticons) are very popular, and some of the more established ones are included in the table below.

Glossary of Italian SMS abbreviations

Abbreviation	*Full word*
"xxx"	tanti baci
+o-	più o meno
6 la +	sei la migliore
6 sxme	sei speciale per me
amò	amore
ap	a presto
axitivo	aperitivo
ba	bacio
cel	cellulare
cmq	comunque
cvd	ci vediamo dopo
dom	domani
dx	destra
ke	che
-male	meno male
midi	mi dispiace
MMT+	mi manchi tantissimo
msg	messaggio
Nm	numero
Nn	non
qlc	qualcuno
qls	qualcosa
risp	rispondimi
sx	sinistra
t tel + trd	ti telefono + tardi
tat	ti amo tanto
tel	telefono
tipe	ti penso
to	ti odio
ttp	torno tra un pò
tu6	tu sei

Abbreviation	*Full word*
tvb	ti voglio bene
tvtb	ti voglio tanto bene
vng dp	vengo dopo
x	per
x fv	per favore
x me	per me
xdere	perdere
xh	per ora
xké	perché

*Emoticons**	
:-)	sorriso
:-(	tristezza
:-D	risata
;-)	strizzare l'occhio
:-*	baciare
!(	occhio nero
:-/	scettico
:'(	piangere
#:-o	traumatizzato
:-i	penso
:-o	sorpreso
:-q	nauseato
:-P	linguaccia
$)	felice di aver vinto la lotteria
:*)	pagliaccio
***<:-)**	Babbo Natale

*NB: the '-' which depicts the nose is often omitted or replaced by an '**o**' e.g. **:)** or **:o)**

SMS (messaggi elettronici)

Poiché lo spazio per gli SMS è limitato (solitamente 160 caratteri al massimo), anche in inglese quando si scrive un messaggino si ricorre a molte abbreviazioni. Spesso si accorciano le parole eliminando alcune lettere, ad esempio 'please' è in genere abbreviato con 'pls'. Un altro metodo consiste nel sostituire alcune parole o suoni con numeri o lettere. Un tipico esempio è l'uso di '2' invece della parola 'to' e della lettera 'U' al posto di 'you'.

Anche gli 'emoticons' (le faccine) sono popolari e alcuni dei più usati si trovano nel glossario qui sotto.

Glossario di abbreviazioni SMS inglesi

Abbreviazione	*Senso*
afaik	as far as I know
atb	all the best
b4	before
bbl	be back late(r)
brb	be right back
btw	by the way
cu	see you
cul8r	see you later
f2f	face to face
fwiw	for what it's worth
fyi	for your information
gr8	great
h8	hate
hand	have a nice day
hth	hope this helps
ic	I see
imho	in my humble opinion
imo	in my opinion
iow	in other words
jk	just kidding
lol	laughing out loud/lots of luck
msg	message
myob	mind your own business
ne1	anyone
no1	no one
oic	oh I see
otoh	on the other hand
pls	please
ppl	people
r	are
rofl	rolling on the floor, laughing
ruok	are you OK?
som1	someone
thkq	thank you
tx	thanks
ur	you are
wan2	want to
wot	what
xlnt	excellent
2moro	tomorrow

*Faccina**	
:-)	happy face
:-(	sad face
:-D	laughing
;-)	winking
:-*	big kiss!
!(	black eye
:-/	sceptical
:'(	crying
#:-o	traumatized
:-i	I'm thinking
:-o	surprised
:-q	feeling sick
:-P	tongue sticking out
$)	I've just won the lottery
:*)	clown
@}-,-'--	a rose

*NB: il '-' che rappresenta il naso è spesso sostituito con **'o'** ad es. **:)** o **:o)**

Phrasefinder / Frasi utili

Key phrases / Frasi chiave

yes, please	sì, grazie
no, thank you	no, grazie
sorry!	scusa
excuse me	mi scusi
you're welcome	prego
I'm sorry, I don't understand	scusi, non capisco
Meeting people	**Incontri**
hello/goodbye	ciao/arrivederci
how do you do?	come sta?
how are you?	come stai?
nice to meet you	piacere
Asking questions	**Fare domande**
do you speak English/Italian?	parli inglese/italiano?
what's your name?	come ti chiami?
where are you from?	di dove sei?
where is...?	dov'è...?
can I have...?	posso avere...?
would you like...?	vuoi...?
do you mind if...?	le dispiace se...?

About you	**Presentarsi**
my name is...	mi chiamo...
I'm English/Italian/American	sono inglese/italiano/-a/americano/-a
I don't speak Italian/English very well	non parlo molto bene l'italiano/l'inglese
I'm here on holiday	sono qui in vacanza
I live near York/Pisa	abito vicino a York/Pisa

Emergencies	**Emergenze**
can you help me, please?	mi può aiutare, per favore?
I'm lost	mi sono perso/-a
I'm ill	sto male
call an ambulance	chiami un'ambulanza
watch out!	attenzione!

Reading signs	**Segnali e cartelli**
no entry	vietato l'ingresso
no smoking	vietato fumare
fire exit	uscita di sicurezza
for sale	in vendita/vendesi
push	spingere
pull	tirare
press	premere

Going Places / In viaggio

By rail and underground	In treno e sul metrò
where can I buy a ticket?	dove si fanno i biglietti?
what time is the next train to Milan/ New York?	a che ora è il prossimo treno per Milano/ New York?
do I have to change?	devo cambiare?
can I take my bike on the train?	posso portare la bicicletta sul treno?
which platform for the train to Bath/Florence?	da quale binario parte il treno per Bath/Firenze?
a single/return, (*Amer*) round trip to Baltimore/Turin, please	un biglietto di sola andata/di andata e ritorno per Baltimora/Torino, per favore
I'd like an all-day ticket	vorrei un biglietto giornaliero
I'd like to reserve a seat	vorrei prenotare un posto
is there a student/senior citizen discount?	c'è uno sconto per studenti/anziani?
is this the train for Rome/Manchester?	è questo il treno per Roma/Manchester?

what time does the train arrive in Naples/London?	a che ora arriva il treno a Napoli/Londra?
have I missed the train?	ho perso il treno?
which line do I need to take for the Colosseum/London Eye?	che linea si prende per il Colosseo/ London Eye?

YOU WILL HEAR:	**SENTIRAI:**
il treno è in arrivo sul binario 2	the train is arriving at platform 2
c'è un treno per Roma alle 10	there's a train to Rome at 10 o'clock
il treno è in ritardo/orario	the train is delayed/on time
la prossima fermata è…	the next stop is…
il suo biglietto non è valido	your ticket isn't valid

MORE USEFUL WORDS:	**ALTRE PAROLE UTILI:**
underground station, (*Amer*) subway station	stazione di metropolitana
timetable	orario
connection	coincidenza
express train	treno espresso
local train	treno locale
high-speed train	treno ad alta velocità

DID YOU KNOW...?	**LO SAPEVI...?**
In an Italian train station, before you get on the train you must validate your ticket, i.e. have it stamped in the special yellow machine on the platform to make it valid for your journey. You risk a fine if you forget to do this.	Dall'aeroporto di Heathrow è possibile raggiungere il centro di Londra in meno di venti minuti grazie all'Heathrow Express.

At the airport / All'aeroporto

when's the next flight to Paris/Rome?	quand'è il prossimo volo per Parigi/Roma?
what time do I have to check in?	a che ora si fa il check-in?
where do I check in?	dov'è il check-in?
I'd like to confirm my flight	vorrei confermare il mio volo
I'd like a window seat/an aisle seat	vorrei un posto accanto al finestrino/di corridoio
I want to change/cancel my reservation	vorrei cambiare/annullare la mia prenotazione
can I carry this in my hand luggage, (*Amer*) carry-on luggage?	posso portare questo nel bagaglio a mano?
my luggage hasn't arrived	il mio bagaglio non è arrivato

YOU WILL HEAR:	**SENTIRAI:**
il volo BA7057 è in ritardo/cancellato	**flight BA7057 is delayed/cancelled**
presentarsi all'uscita 29	**please go to gate 29**
la sua carta d'imbarco, per favore	**your boarding card, please**

MORE USEFUL WORDS:	**ALTRE PAROLE UTILI:**
arrivals	**arrivi**
departures	**partenze**
baggage claim	**ritiro bagagli**

Asking how to get there / Chiedere e dare indicazioni

how do I get to the airport?	come si arriva all'aeroporto?
how long will it take to get there?	quanto ci vuole per arrivarci?
how far is it from here?	quanto dista da qui?
which bus do I take for the cathedral?	quale autobus devo prendere per andare al duomo?
where does this bus go?	dove va questo autobus?
does this bus/train go to...?	questo autobus/treno va a...?
where should I get off?	pùo dirmi dove devo scendere?
how much is it to the town centre?	quant'è la tariffa per il centro?
what time is the last bus?	che ora è l'ultimo autobus?
where's the nearest underground station, (*Amer*) subway station?	dov'è la metropolitana più vicina?
is this the turning for...?	si svolta qui per...?
can you call me a taxi?	può chiamarmi un taxi, per favore?

YOU WILL HEAR:	SENTIRAI:
prenda la prima a destra	take the first turning on the right
dopo il semaforo/la chiesa svolti a sinistra	turn left at the traffic lights/just past the church

Disabled travellers — Viaggiatori disabili

I'm disabled	sono disabile
is there wheelchair access?	c'è l'accesso per sedia a rotelle?
are guide dogs permitted?	sono ammessi i cani guida per non vedenti?

On the road — Sulla strada

where's the nearest petrol station, (*Amer*) gas station?	dov'è la stazione di servizio più vicina?
what's the best way to get there?	qual è la strada migliore per arrivarci?
I've got a puncture, (*Amer*) flat tire	ho bucato
I'd like to hire, (*Amer*) rent a bike/car	vorrei noleggiare una bicicletta/ una macchina
where can I park around here?	c'è un parcheggio qui vicino?
there's been an accident	c'è stato un incidente
my car's broken down	ho la macchina in panne
the car won't start	la macchina non parte
where's the nearest garage?	dov'è l'officina più vicina?
pump number six, please	pompa numero sei, grazie
fill it up, please	il pieno, per favore
can I wash my car here?	c'è l'autolavaggio?
can I park here?	posso parcheggiare qui?
there's a problem with the brakes/lights	i freni/fari hanno qualcosa che non va
the clutch/gearstick isn't working	la frizione/leva del cambio non funziona
take the third exit off the roundabout, (*Amer*) traffic circle	alla rotatoria prenda la terza uscita
turn right at the next junction	al prossimo incrocio svolti a destra
slow down	rallenta
I can't drink – I'm driving	non posso bere, devo guidare
can I buy a road map here?	vendete cartine stradali?

YOU WILL HEAR:	SENTIRAI:
favorisca la patente	can I see your driving licence?
deve compilare la denuncia di sinistro	you need to fill out an accident report
questa strada è a senso unico	this road is one-way
qui non si può parcheggiare	you can't park here

MORE USEFUL WORDS:	ALTRE PAROLE UTILI:
diesel	gasolio
unleaded	senza piombo/verde
motorway, (*Amer*) expressway	autostrada
toll	pedaggio
satnav, (*Amer*) GPS	navigatore satellitare
speed camera	autovelox
roundabout	rotatoria
crossroads	crocevia
dual carriageway, (*Amer*) divided highway	strada a due carreggiate
exit	uscita
traffic lights	semaforo
driver	conducente

DID YOU KNOW...?	LO SAPEVI...?
In Italy, all drivers are required to wear a reflective vest and to use a reflective triangle warning sign if they need to stop at the roadside.	Il pedaggio per circolare e sostare in auto nel centro di Londra, nei giorni lavorativi, si può pagare presso le stazioni di servizio o le edicole.

COMMON ITALIAN ROAD SIGNS

Alt polizia	Stop for police check
Consentito ai soli mezzi autorizzati	Authorized vehicles only
Passo carrabile	No blocking of passageway
Lavori in corso	Roadworks ahead
Zona pedonale	Pedestrian zone
Rallentare	Slow down
Zona rimozione	Tow-away zone
ZTL (Zona traffico limitato)	Traffic restricted area
Postazione fissa di misuratore della velocità	Speed cameras ahead
Passaggio a livello	Train crossing

SEGNALI STRADALI COMUNI NEI PAESI ANGLOFONI

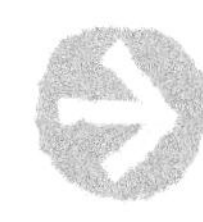

Cattle	Animali domestici vaganti
Contraflow	Doppio senso di circolazione
Ford	Guado
Get in lane	Immettersi in corsia
Give way	Dare precedenza
Keep clear	Lasciare libero il passaggio
No overtaking, (*Amer*) Do not pass	Divieto di sorpasso
Pedestrians crossing	Attraversamento pedonale
Red route – no stopping	Divieto di sosta e fermata
Reduce speed now	Rallentare
Stop	Stop

Keeping in touch / Comunicazioni

On the phone / Al telefono

where can I buy a phone card?	dove si comprano le schede telefoniche?
may I use your phone?	posso usare il telefono?
do you have a mobile, (*Amer*) cell phone?	hai il cellulare?
what is your phone number?	qual è il tuo numero di telefono?
what is the area code for Venice/Sheffield?	qual è il prefisso di Venezia/Sheffield?
I want to make a phone call	vorrei fare una telefonata
I'd like to reverse the charges, (*Amer*) call collect	vorrei fare una telefonata a carico del destinatario
the line's engaged/busy	è occupato
there's no answer	non risponde nessuno
hello, this is Natalie	pronto, sono Natalie
is Riccardo there, please?	c'è Riccardo, per favore?
who's calling?	chi parla?
sorry, wrong number	ha sbagliato numero
just a moment, please	un attimo, prego
would you like to hold?	vuole attendere in linea?
it's a business/personal call	è una chiamata di lavoro/personale
I'll put you through to him/her	le passo la comunicazione
s/he cannot come to the phone at the moment	in questo momento non può venire al telefono
please tell him/her I called	gli/le dica che ho chiamato
I'd like to leave a message for him/her	vorrei lasciare un messaggio

I'll try again later	riproverò più tardi
please tell him/her that Maria called	gli/le dica che ha chiamato Maria
can he/she ring me back?	mi può richiamare?
my home number is...	il mio numero è...
my business number is...	il mio numero al lavoro è...
my fax number is...	il mio numero di fax è...
we were cut off	è caduta la linea
I'll call you later	ti chiamo più tardi
I need to top up my phone	mi serve una ricarica per il cellulare
the battery's run out	ho la batteria scarica
I'm running low on credit	sto esaurendo il credito
send me a text	mandami un sms/messaggino
there's no signal here	non c'è campo
you're breaking up	la linea è molto disturbata
could you speak a little louder?	puoi parlare più forte?

YOU WILL HEAR:	**SENTIRAI:**
pronto?	**hello**
chiamami sul cellulare	**call me on my mobile, (*Amer*) cell phone**
vuole lasciare un messaggio?	**would you like to leave a message?**

MORE USEFUL WORDS:	**ALTRE PAROLE UTILI:**
text message	**SMS/messaggino**
top-up card	**ricarica**
phone box, (*Amer*) phone booth	**cabina telefonica**
dial	**comporre il numero**
directory enquiries	**elenco abbonati**

Writing / Corrispondenza

what's your address?	qual è il tuo indirizzo?
where is the nearest post office?	dov'è l'ufficio postale più vicino?
could I have a stamp for the UK/Italy, please?	mi dà un francobollo per la Gran Bretagna/l'Italia, per favore?
I'd like to send a parcel	vorrei spedire un pacco
where is the nearest postbox, (*Amer*) mailbox?	dov'è la buca delle lettere più vicina?
dear Isabella/Fred	cara Isabella/caro Fred

dear Sir or Madam	gentili Signori
yours sincerely	distinti saluti
yours faithfully	cordialmente
best wishes	cari saluti

YOU WILL HEAR:	**SENTIRAI:**
vuole spedirla per posta prioritaria?	would you like to send it first class?
c'è qualcosa di valore?	is it valuable?

MORE USEFUL WORDS:	**ALTRE PAROLE UTILI:**
letter	lettera
postcode, (*Amer*) ZIP code	codice di avviamento postale/CAP
airmail	posta aerea
postcard	cartolina
fragile	fragile
urgent	urgente
registered post, (*Amer*) mail	raccomandata

On line Internet

are you on the Internet?	siete su Internet?
what's your e-mail address?	qual è il tuo indirizzo email?
I'll e-mail it to you on Tuesday	te lo mando per email martedì
I looked it up on the Internet	l'ho cercato su Internet
the information is on their website	le informazioni si trovano sul sito web
my e-mail address is anna dot rossi at rapido dot com	il mio indirizzo email è: anna punto rossi chiocciola rapido punto com
can I check my e-mail here?	posso controllare l'email qui?
I have broadband/dial-up	ho la linea veloce/connessione dial-up
do you have wireless internet access?	avete accesso internet wireless?
I'll send you the file as an attachment	ti mando il file in allegato

YOU WILL SEE:	**VEDRAI:**
ricerca	search
fare doppio click sull'icona	double-click on the icon
apri l'applicazione	open (up) the application
scarica il file	download file

MORE USEFUL WORDS:	ALTRE PAROLE UTILI:
subject (*of an email*)	oggetto
password	password
social networking site	sito di social network
search engine	motore di ricerca
mouse	mouse
keyboard	tastiera

Meeting up / Appuntamenti

what shall we do this evening?	cosa facciamo stasera?
do you want to go out tonight?	ti va di uscire stasera?
where shall we meet?	dove ci diamo appuntamento?
I'll see you outside the café at 6 o'clock	ci vediamo davanti al bar alle 6
see you later	a più tardi
I can't today, I'm busy	oggi non posso, sono impegnato
I'm sorry, I've got something planned	mi dispiace, ho già altri programmi
let's meet for a coffee in town	troviamoci al centro per un caffè
would you like to see a show/film, (*Amer*) movie?	ti va di andare a teatro/al cinema?
what about next week instead?	che ne dici se facciamo la prossima settimana?
shall we go for something to eat?	andiamo a mangiare qualcosa?

YOU WILL HEAR:	SENTIRAI:
piacere	nice to meet you
posso offrirti qualcosa da bere?	can I buy you a drink?

MORE USEFUL WORDS:	ALTRE PAROLE UTILI:
bar	bar
bar (*serving counter in a bar/pub*)	banco
meal	pasto
snack	spuntino
date	appuntamento
cigarette	sigaretta

Food and Drink / Mangiare e bere

Booking a table	Prenotare un ristorante
can you recommend a good restaurant?	può consigliarmi un buon ristorante?
I'd like to reserve a table for four	vorrei prenotare un tavolo per quattro
a reservation for tomorrow evening at eight o'clock	una prenotazione per domani sera alle otto
I booked a table for two	ho prenotato un tavolo per due

Ordering	Per Ordinare
could we see the menu/wine list, please?	possiamo avere il menù/la carta dei vini, per favore?
do you have a vegetarian menu?	avete un menù vegetariano?
could we have some more bread?	possiamo avere dell'altro pane?
could I have the bill, (*Amer*) check?	il conto, per favore
what would you recommend?	che cosa consiglia?
I'd like a black/white coffee	vorrei un caffè/un caffè macchiato

YOU WILL HEAR:	IL CAMERIERE CHIEDE...
Volete ordinare?	Are you ready to order?
Prendete un antipasto?	Would you like a starter?
Che cosa prendete come secondo?	What will you have for the main course?
Posso consigliare...	I can recommend...
Altro?	Anything else?
Buon appetito!	Enjoy your meal!
Il servizio non è compreso	Service is not included.

The menu Il menu

starters	antipasti
melon	melone
omelette	frittata
soup	zuppa
salad	insalata

fish	pesce
cod	merluzzo
hake	nasello
halibut	ippoglosso
herring	aringa
monk fish	squadro
mussels	cozze
oysters	ostriche
plaice	platessa
prawns	gamberi
red mullet	triglie
salmon	salmone
seafood	frutti di mare
sea bass	spigola
shrimp	gamberetti
sole	sogliola
squid	calamari
trout	trota
tuna	tonno
turbot	rombo

meat	carne
beef	manzo
chicken	pollo
duck	anatra
goose	oca
hare	lepre
lamb	agnello
liver	fegato
pork	maiale
rabbit	coniglio
steak	bistecca
veal	vitello
wild boar	cinghiale

antipasti	starters
antipasto di mare	seafood starter
antipasto di terra	assorted hams etc
prosciutto crudo	cured ham
zuppa	soup

pesce	fish
acciughe	anchovies
calamari	squid
cozze	mussels
dentice	sea bream
frutti di mare	seafood
gamberetti	shrimp
gamberi	prawns
merluzzo	cod
nasello	hake
ostriche	oysters
pesce spada	swordfish
platessa	plaice
rombo	turbot
salmone	salmon
sogliola	sole
spigola	sea bass
tonno	tuna
triglie	red mullet
trota	trout

carne	meat
agnello	lamb
anatra	duck
bistecca	steak
cinghiale	wild boar
coniglio	rabbit
fegato	liver
lepre	hare
maiale	pork
manzo	beef
oca	goose
pollo	chicken
vitello	veal

vegetables	verdure
artichokes	carciofi
asparagus	asparagi
aubergines	melanzane
beans	fagioli
cabbage	cavolo
carrots	carote
cauliflower	cavolfiore
celery	sedano
courgettes	zucchini
green beans	fagiolini
mushrooms	funghi
onions	cipolle
peas	piselli
peppers	peperoni
potatoes	patate
salad	insalata

the way it's cooked	cottura
boiled	lesso
fried	fritto
grilled	alla griglia
griddled	alla piastra
puree	purè
roast	arrosto
stewed	in umido
rare	al sangue
medium	cotta al punto giusto
well done	ben cotta

desserts	dolci
cream	panna
fruit	frutta
ice cream	gelato
pie	torta
tart	crostata

verdure	vegetables
asparagi	asparagus
carciofi	artichokes
carote	carrots
cavolfiore	cauliflower
cavolo	cabbage
cipolle	onions
fagioli	beans
fagiolini	green beans
funghi	mushrooms
insalata	salad
melanzane	aubergines
patate	potatoes
peperoni	peppers
piselli	peas
sedano	celery
zucchini	courgettes

cottura	the way it's cooked
al forno	cooked in the oven
al pomodoro	in tomato sauce
al ragù	in a meat sauce
al sangue	rare
alla griglia	grilled
arrosto	roast
ben cotta	well done
cotta al punto giusto	medium
fritto	fried
in umido	stewed
lesso	boiled

dolci	desserts
crostata	tart
frutta	fruit
gelato	ice cream
panna	cream
torta	pie

sundries	contorni, salse, ecc.
bread	pane
butter	burro
cheese	formaggio
herbs	erbe
mayonnaise	maionese
mustard	senape
olive oil	olio d'oliva
pepper	pepe
rice	riso
salt	sale
sauce	salsa
seasoning	condimento
vinegar	aceto

contorni, salse, ecc.	sundries
aceto	vinegar
burro	butter
condimento	seasoning
erbe	herbs
formaggio	cheese
maionese	mayonnaise
olio d'oliva	olive oil
pane	bread
pepe	pepper
riso	rice
sale	salt
salsa	sauce
senape	mustard

drinks	bevande
beer	birra
bottle	bottiglia
carbonated	gassato
coffee	caffè
decaffeinated coffee	decaffeinato
espresso	espresso
half-bottle	mezza bottiglia
liqueur	liquore
mineral water	acqua minerale
red wine	vino rosso
soft drinks	bibite analcoliche
sparkling wine	spumante
still	naturale
table wine	vino da tavola
white wine	vino bianco
wine	vino

bevande	drinks
acqua minerale	mineral water
bibite analcoliche	soft drinks
birra	beer
bottiglia	bottle
caffè	coffee
decaffeinato	decaffeinated coffee
espresso	espresso
gassato	carbonated
liquore	liqueur
mezza bottiglia	half-bottle
naturale	still
spumante	sparkling wine
vino	wine
vino bianco	white wine
vino da tavola	table wine
vino rosso	red wine

Places to stay / Dove alloggiare

Camping — In campeggio

Camping	In campeggio
can we pitch our tent here?	possiamo montare la tenda qui?
can we park our caravan here?	possiamo parcheggiare la roulotte qui?
what are the facilities like?	che attrezzature ci sono?
how much is it per night?	quant'è a notte?
where do we park the car?	dov'è il parcheggio?
we're looking for a campsite	stiamo cercando un campeggio
this is a list of local campsites	questo è l'elenco dei campeggi della zona
we go on a camping holiday every year	andiamo in campeggio tutti gli anni

At the hotel — In albergo

At the hotel	In albergo
I'd like a double/single room with bath	vorrei una camera doppia/singola con bagno
we have a reservation in the name of Morris	abbiamo prenotato a nome Morris
we'll be staying three nights, from Friday to Sunday	ci fermiamo tre notti, da venerdì a domenica
how much does the room cost?	quant'è la camera?
I'd like to see the room, please	vorrei vedere la camera, per favore
what time is breakfast?	a che ora è la colazione?
can I leave this in your safe?	posso lasciare questo nella cassaforte?
bed and breakfast	camera e prima colazione
we'd like to stay another night	vorremmo fermarci un'altra notte
please call me at 7:30	mi chiami alle 7:30, per favore
are there any messages for me?	ci sono messaggi per me?

Hostels — Ostelli

Hostels	Ostelli
could you tell me where the youth hostel is?	mi sa dire dov'è l'ostello della gioventù?
what time does the hostel close?	a che ora chiude l'ostello?
I'm staying in a hostel	alloggio in un ostello
the hostel we're staying in is great value	l'ostello in cui alloggiamo è molto conveniente
I know a really good hostel in Dublin	conosco un ottimo ostello a Dublino
I'd like to go backpacking in Australia	mi piacerebbe girare l'Australia con zaino e sacco a pelo

Rooms to let	In affitto
I'm looking for a room with a reasonable rent	vorrei affittare una camera a prezzo modico
I'd like to rent an apartment for a few weeks	vorrei affittare un appartamento per qualche settimana
where do I find out about rooms to let?	dove posso informarmi su camere in affitto?
what's the weekly rent?	quant'è l'affitto alla settimana?
I'm staying with friends at the moment	al momento alloggio presso amici
I rent an apartment on the outskirts of town	affitto un appartamento in periferia
the room's fine—I'll take it	la camera mi piace, la prendo
the deposit is one month's rent in advance	la caparra è di un mese d'affitto

Shopping / Spese

At the bank	In banca
I'd like to change some money	vorrei cambiare dei soldi
I want to change some euros into pounds	vorrei cambiare degli euro in sterline
do you take Eurocheques?	accettate Eurochèque?
what's the exchange rate today?	quant'è il tasso di cambio oggi?
I prefer traveller's cheques, (*Amer*) traveler's checks to cash	preferisco i traveller's cheque al contante
I'd like to transfer some money from my account	vorrei fare un bonifico
I'll get some money from the cash machine	prenderò dei soldi dal bancomat®
I'm with another bank	ho il conto in un'altra banca

Finding the right shop	Il negozio giusto
where's the main shopping district?	dov'è la zona commerciale principale?
where's a good place to buy sunglasses/shoes?	qual è il posto migliore per comprare occhiali da sole/scarpe?
where can I buy batteries/postcards?	dove posso comprare pile/cartoline?
where's the nearest chemist/bookshop?	dov'è la farmacia/libreria più vicina?
is there a good food shop around here?	c'è un buon negozio di generi alimentari qui vicino?

what time do the shops open/close?	a che ora aprono/chiudono i negozi?
where can I hire a car?	dove posso noleggiare una macchina?
where did you get those?	dove le/li hai comprate/-i?
I'm looking for presents for my family	sto cercando dei regalini per la mia famiglia
we'll do all our shopping on Saturday	faremo la spesa sabato
I love shopping	adoro fare spese

Are you being served? Nei negozi

how much does that cost?	quanto costa quello?
can I try it on?	posso provarlo?
can you keep it for me?	me lo mette da parte?
could you wrap it for me, please?	me lo incarta, per favore?
can I pay by credit card/cheque, (*Amer*) check?	posso pagare con la carta di credito/ un assegno?
do you have this in another colour, (*Amer*) color?	c'è in altri colori?
could I have a bag, please?	mi dà un sacchetto, per favore?
I'm just looking	sto solo dando un'occhiata
I'll think about it	ci devo pensare
I'd like a receipt, please	mi dà lo scontrino, per favore?
I need a bigger/smaller size	mi serve la taglia più grande/piccola
I take a size 10/a medium	porto la 42/la media
it doesn't suit me	non mi sta bene
I'm sorry, I don't have any change/ anything smaller	mi dispiace, non ho spiccioli/biglietti più piccoli
that's all, thank you	nient'altro, grazie

Changing things Cambiare un acquisto

can I have a refund?	rimborsate i soldi?
can you mend it for me?	può ripararlo?
can I speak to the manager?	posso parlare con il direttore?
it doesn't work	non funziona
I'd like to change it, please	vorrei cambiarlo, per favore
I bought this here yesterday	l'ho comprato qui ieri

Sport and leisure / Sport e tempo libero

Keeping fit	Tenersi in forma
where can we play tennis/badminton?	dove si può giocare a tennis/ badminton?
I'm looking for a swimming pool/ golf course	sto cercando una piscina/un campo da golf
is there a hotel gym?	c'è una palestra in albergo?
are there any yoga/pilates classes here?	ci sono corsi di yoga/pilates?
I would like to go cycling/riding	mi piacerebbe andare in bici/a cavallo
I love swimming/football	mi piace nuotare/il calcio
where can I get tickets for the match, (*Amer*) game on Saturday?	dove si comprano i biglietti per la partita di sabato?

Going out	Uscire
what's on at the theatre/cinema?	cosa danno a teatro/al cinema?
how much are the tickets?	quanto costano i biglietti?
what time does the concert/ performance start?	a che ora inizia il concerto/lo spettacolo?
I'd like to book tickets for tonight	vorrei prenotare dei biglietti per stasera
we'd like to go to a club	vorremmo andare in qualche locale

Good timing / L'Ora giusta

Telling the time	Dire l'ora
could you tell me the time?	mi dica che ore sono?
what time is it?	che ora è?
it's 2 o'clock	sono le due
at about 8 o'clock	verso le otto
at 9 o'clock tomorrow	domani mattina alle nove
from 10 o'clock onwards	dalle dieci in poi
at 8 a.m./p.m.	alle otto di mattina/di sera
at 5 o'clock in the morning/afternoon	alle cinque del mattino/di sera
it's five past/quarter past/half past one	è l'una e cinque/e un quarto/e mezza
it's twenty-five to/quarter to/five to one	è l'una meno venticinque/meno un quarto/meno cinque
a quarter/three quarters of an hour	un quarto/tre quarti d'ora

Public holidays and special days	Festività
Bank holiday	festa civile
Bank holiday Monday	festa civile che cade di lunedì
long weekend	ponte
New Year's Day (Jan 1)	Capodanno (1 gennaio)
Epiphany (Jan 6)	Epifania (la Befana: 6 gennaio)
St Valentine's Day (Feb 14)	San Valentino (14 febbraio)
Shrove Tuesday/Pancake Day	martedì grasso
Ash Wednesday	mercoledì delle Ceneri
St Joseph's Day (Mar 19)	San Giuseppe (19 marzo)
Mother's Day	Festa della mamma
Palm Sunday	domenica delle Palme
Maundy Thursday	giovedì grasso
Good Friday	venerdì santo
Easter Day	Pasqua
Easter Monday	lunedì dell'Angelo (pasquetta)
Anniversary of the liberation of Italy in 1945	anniversario della Liberazione (25 aprile)
May Day (May 1)	Festa del lavoro (1 maggio)
Father's Day	Festa del papà
Independence Day (Jul 4)	anniversario dell'Indipendenza (4 luglio)
Assumption (Aug 15)	Assunzione (ferragosto: 15 agosto)
Halloween (Oct 31)	vigilia d'Ognissanti
All Saints' Day (Nov 1)	Ognissanti (1 novembre)
Thanksgiving	giorno del Ringraziamento
Christmas Eve (Dec 24)	vigilia di Natale (24 dicembre)
Christmas Day (Dec 25)	Natale (25 dicembre)
Boxing Day (Dec 26)	Santo Stefano (26 dicembre)
New Year's Eve (Dec 31)	San Silvestro (31 dicembre)

Health and Beauty / Salute e bellezza

At the doctor's	Dal medico
can I see a doctor?	potrei vedere un medico?
I don't feel well	non mi sento bene
it hurts here	mi fa male qui
I have a migraine/stomachache	ho l'emicrania/il mal di stomaco
are there any side effects?	ci sono effetti collaterali?
I have a sore ankle/wrist/knee	mi fa male la caviglia/il polso/il ginocchio

YOU WILL HEAR:	SENTIRAI:
deve prendere un appuntamento	you need to make an appointment
si accomodi	please take a seat
ha la Tessera Europea di Assicurazione Malattia (TEAM)?	do you have a European Health Insurance Card (EHIC)?
ha l'assistenza medica?	do you have Health Insurance?
devo misurarle la pressione	I need to take your blood pressure

MORE USEFUL WORDS:	ALTRE PAROLE UTILI:
nurse	infermiere/a
antibiotics	antibiotici
medicine	medicina
infection	infezione
treatment	cura
rest	riposo

At the pharmacy / In farmacia

can I have some painkillers?	mi dà un antidolorifico/analgesico?
I have asthma/hay fever/eczema	soffro d'asma/di rinite allergica/d'eczema
I've been stung by a wasp/bee	mi ha punto una vespa/un'ape
I've got a cold/cough/the flu	ho il raffreddore/la tosse/l'influenza
I need something for diarrhoea/ stomachache	vorrei qualcosa per la diarrea/il mal di stomaco
I'm pregnant	sono incinta

YOU WILL HEAR:	SENTIRAI
ha già preso questo farmaco?	have you taken this medicine before?
le sue medicine sono pronte tra dieci minuti	your prescription will be ready in ten minutes
da assumere durante i pasti/tre volte al giorno?	take at mealtimes/three times a day?
è allergico/-a a qualcosa?	are you allergic to anything?
sta prendendo qualche altro farmaco?	are you taking any other medication?

MORE USEFUL WORDS:	ALTRE PAROLE UTILI:
plasters, (*Amer*) Band-Aid™	cerotti
insect repellent	insettifugo
contraception	anticoncezionali
sun cream	solare
aftersun	doposole
dosage	dosi

At the hairdresser's/ beauty salon — Dal parrucchiere/ dall'estetista

I'd like a cut and blow dry	taglio e asciugatura spazzola e phon
just a trim please	solo una spuntatina, per favore
a grade 3 back and sides	9 mm sia sui lati che dietro
I'd like my hair washed first please	mi faccia lo shampoo prima, per favore
can I have a manicure/pedicure/facial?	fate la manicure/pedicure/pulizia del viso?
how much is a head/back massage?	quant'è il massaggio alla testa/schiena?
can I see a price list?	potrei vedere il listino prezzi?
do you offer reflexology/aromatherapy treatments?	fate riflessologia/aromaterapia?

YOU WILL HEAR:	SENTIRAI:
vuole l'asciugatura a spazzola e phon?	would you like your hair blow-dried?
da che lato porta la riga?	where is your parting?
le faccio un taglio scalato?	would you like your hair layered?

MORE USEFUL WORDS:	ALTRE PAROLE UTILI:
dry/greasy/fine/flyaway/frizzy hair	capelli secchi/grassi/sottili/sfibrati/ crespi
highlights	colpi di sole
extensions	allungamento capelli/extensions
sunbed	lettino solare
leg/arm/bikini wax	ceretta gambe/braccia/inguine

Phrasefinder

Weights & measures / Pesi e misure

Length/Lunghezza

inches/pollici	0.39	3.9	7.8	11.7	15.6	19.7	39
cm/centimetri	1	10	20	30	40	50	100

Distance/Distanze

miles/miglia	0.62	6.2	12.4	18.6	24.9	31	62
km/chilometri	1	10	20	30	40	50	100

Weight/Pesi

pounds/libbre	2.2	22	44	66	88	110	220
kg/chilogrammi	1	10	20	30	40	50	100

Capacity/Capacità

gallons/galloni	0.22	2.2	4.4	6.6	8.8	11	22
litres/litri	1	10	20	30	40	50	100

Temperature/Temperatura

°C	0	5	10	15	20	25	30	37	38	40
°F	32	41	50	59	68	77	86	98.4	100	104

Clothing and shoe sizes/Taglie e numeri di scarpe

Women's clothing sizes/Abbigliamento femminile

UK	8	10	12	14	16	18
US	6	8	10	12	14	16
Continent	36	38	40	42	44	46

Men's clothing sizes/Abbigliamento maschile

UK/US	36	38	40	42	44	46
Continent	46	48	50	52	54	56

Men's and women's shoes/Scarpe da uomo e da donna

UK women	4	5	6	7	7.5	8			
UK men			6	7	8	9	10	11	
US	6.5	7.5	8.5	9.5	10.5	11.5	12.5	13.5	14.5
Continent	37	38	39	40	41	42	43	44	45

Aa

a¹, **A** /eɪ/ (letter) a, A *f inv*; Mus la *m inv*

a² /ə/; *accentato* /eɪ/, (*before a vowel* **an**) *indef art* un *m*, una *f*; (before s + consonant, *gn*, *ps*, z) uno; (before *nf* starting with vowel) un'; (each) a; **I am a lawyer** sono avvocato; **a tiger is a feline** la tigre è un felino; **a knife and fork** un coltello e una forchetta; **a Mr Smith is looking for you** un certo signor Smith ti sta cercando; **£2 a kilo/a head** due sterline al chilo/a testa

A & E *n abbr* BrE (**Accident and Emergency**) pronto soccorso *m*

A2 *n ‹exam/course› esame (m) sostenuto al termine del secondo anno del biennio di preparazione agli A-Level*

A4 *adj* A4

AA *n abbr* **1** BrE (**Automobile Association**) ≈ A.C.I. *m* **2** (**Alcoholics Anonymous**)

AAA *n abbr* AmE (**American Automobile Association**) ≈ A.C.I. *m*

aback /əˈbæk/ *adv* **be taken ~** essere preso in contropiede

abacus /ˈæbəkəs/ *n* (*pl* **-cuses**) abaco *m*

abandon /əˈbændən/ **A** *vt* abbandonare; (give up) rinunciare a
B *n* abbandono *m*

abandoned /əˈbændnd/ *adj* abbandonato; *‹behaviour›* dissoluto

abandonment /əˈbændnmənt/ *n* (of strike, plan etc) rinuncia *f*

abashed /əˈbæʃt/ *adj* imbarazzato

abate /əˈbeɪt/ *vi* calmarsi

abattoir /ˈæbətwɑː(r)/ *n* mattatoio *m*

abbess /ˈæbes/ *n* badessa *f*

abbey /ˈæbɪ/ *n* abbazia *f*

abbot /ˈæbət/ *n* abate *m*

abbreviate /əˈbriːvɪeɪt/ *vt* abbreviare

abbreviation /əbriːvɪˈeɪʃn/ *n* abbreviazione *f*

ABC **A** *n* (alphabet) alfabeto *m*; **the ~ of** (basics) l'ABC *m inv* di
B *n abbr* (**American Broadcasting Company**) *rete (f) televisiva americana*

abdicate /ˈæbdɪkeɪt/ **A** *vi* abdicare
B *vt* rinunciare a

abdication /æbdɪˈkeɪʃn/ *n* abdicazione *f*

abdomen /ˈæbdəmən/ *n* addome *m*

abdominal /əbˈdɒmɪnl/ *adj* addominale

abduct /əbˈdʌkt/ *vt* rapire

abduction /əbˈdʌkʃn/ *n* rapimento *m*

abductor /əbˈdʌktə(r)/ *n* rapitore, -trice *mf*

aberrant /əˈberənt/ *adj ‹behaviour, nature›* aberrante

aberration /æbəˈreɪʃn/ *n* aberrazione *f*

abet /əˈbet/ *vt* (*pt/pp* **abetted**) **aid and ~** Jur *essere complice di*

abeyance /əˈbeɪəns/ *n* **in ~** in sospeso; **fall into ~** cadere in disuso

abhor /əbˈhɔː(r)/ *vt* (*pt/pp* **abhorred**) aborrire

abhorrence /əbˈhɒrəns/ *n* orrore *m*

abhorrent /əbˈhɒrənt/ *adj* ripugnante

abide /əˈbaɪd/ **A** *vt* (*pt/pp* **abided**) (tolerate) sopportare
B *vi* **abide by** rispettare

abiding /əˈbaɪdɪŋ/ *adj* perpetuo

ability /əˈbɪlətɪ/ *n* capacità *f*

abject /ˈæbdʒekt/ *adj ‹poverty›* degradante; *‹apology›* umile; *‹coward›* abietto

ablative /ˈæblətɪv/ *n* ablativo *m*

ablaze /əˈbleɪz/ *adj* in fiamme; **be ~ with light** risplendere di luci

able /ˈeɪbl/ *adj* capace, abile; **be ~ to do something** poter fare qualcosa; **were you ~ to...?** sei riuscito a...?

able-bodied /-ˈbɒdɪd/ *adj* robusto; Mil abile

able seaman *n* marinaio *m* scelto

ably /ˈeɪblɪ/ *adv* abilmente

abnegation /æbnɪˈgeɪʃn/ *n* (of rights, privileges) rinuncia *f*; (self-abnegation) abnegazione *f*

abnormal /æbˈnɔːml/ *adj* anormale

abnormality /æbnɔːˈmælətɪ/ *n* anormalità *f*

abnormally /æbˈnɔːməlɪ/ *adv* in modo anormale

aboard /əˈbɔːd/ *adv & prep* a bordo

abode /əˈbəʊd/ *n* dimora *f*

abolish /əˈbɒlɪʃ/ *vt* abolire

abolition /æbəˈlɪʃn/ *n* abolizione *f*

abominable /əˈbɒmɪnəbl/ *adj* abominevole

abominably /əˈbɒmɪnəblɪ/ *adv* disgustosamente

abominate /əˈbɒmɪneɪt/ *vt* abominare

aboriginal /æbəˈrɪdʒɪnl/ *adj & n* (native) aborigeno, -a *mf*, indigeno, -a *mf*

Aborigine /æbəˈrɪdʒəniː/ *n* aborigeno, -a *mf* d'Australia

abort /əˈbɔːt/ *vt* fare abortire; fig annullare

abortion /əˈbɔːʃn/ *n* aborto *m*; **have an ~** abortire

abortionist /əˈbɔːʃnɪst/ *n persona (f) che pratica aborti, specialmente clandestini*

abortive /əˈbɔːtɪv/ *adj ‹attempt›* infruttuoso

a

abound /əˈbaʊnd/ *vi* abbondare (**in** di)

about /əˈbaʊt/ **A** *adv* (here and there) [di] qua e [di] là; (approximately) circa; **be ~** ‹*illness, tourists*› essere in giro; **be up and ~** essere alzato; **leave something lying ~** lasciare in giro qualcosa
B *prep* (concerning) su; (in the region of) intorno a; (here and there in) per; **what is the book/the film ~?** di cosa parla il libro/il film?; **he wants to see you — what ~?** ti vuole vedere — a che proposito?; **talk/know ~** parlare/sapere di; **I know nothing ~ it** non ne so niente; **~ 5 o'clock** intorno alle 5; **travel ~ the world** viaggiare per il mondo; **be ~ to do something** stare per fare qualcosa; **how ~ going to the cinema?** e se andassimo al cinema?

about-face, **about-turn** *n* dietro front *m inv*

above /əˈbʌv/ *adv & prep* sopra; **~ all** soprattutto

above-board *adj* onesto

above-ground *adv* in superficie

above-mentioned /-menʃnd/ *adj* suddetto

above-named /-neɪmd/ *adj* suddetto

abrasion /əˈbreɪʒn/ *n* (injury) abrasione *f*

abrasive /əˈbreɪsɪv/ **A** *adj* abrasivo; ‹*remark*› caustico
B *n* abrasivo *m*

abreast /əˈbrest/ *adv* fianco a fianco; **come ~ of** allinearsi con; **keep ~ of** tenersi al corrente di

abridged /əˈbrɪdʒd/ *adj* ridotto

abridgement /əˈbrɪdʒmnt/ *n* (version) edizione *f* ridotta

abroad /əˈbrɔːd/ *adv* all'estero

abrupt /əˈbrʌpt/ *adj* brusco

abruptly /əˈbrʌptlɪ/ *adv* bruscamente

ABS *n abbr* (**anti-lock braking system**) ABS *m inv*

abscess /ˈæbsɪs/ *n* ascesso *m*

abscond /əbˈskɒnd/ *vi* fuggire

abseiling /ˈæbseɪlɪŋ/ *n* BrE discesa *f* a corda doppia; **to go ~** fare discesa a corda doppia

absence /ˈæbsəns/ *n* assenza *f*; (lack) mancanza *f*

absent[1] /ˈæbsənt/ *adj* assente

absent[2] /æbˈsent/ *vt* **~ oneself** essere assente

absentee /æbsənˈtiː/ *n* assente *mf*

absenteeism /æbsənˈtiːɪzm/ *n* assenteismo *m*

absentee landlord *n proprietario* (*m*) *che affitta una casa in cui non abita*

absently /ˈæbsəntlɪ/ *adv* ‹*say, look*› distrattamente

absent-minded /-ˈmaɪndɪd/ *adj* distratto

absent-mindedly /-ˈmaɪndɪdlɪ/ *adv* distrattamente

absent-mindedness /-ˈmaɪndɪdnɪs/ *n* distrazione *f*

absolute /ˈæbsəluːt/ *adj* assoluto; **an ~ idiot** un perfetto idiota

absolutely /ˈæbsəluːtlɪ/ *adv* assolutamente; infml (indicating agreement) esattamente; **~ not** assolutamente no

absolution /æbsəˈluːʃn/ *n* assoluzione *f*

absolve /əbˈzɒlv/ *vt* assolvere

absorb /əbˈsɔːb/ *vt* assorbire; **~ed in** assorto in

absorbency /əbˈsɔːbənsɪ/ *n* capacità *f* d'assorbimento

absorbent /əbˈsɔːbənt/ *adj* assorbente

absorbent cotton *n* AmE cotone *m* idrofilo, ovatta *f*

absorbing /əbˈsɔːbɪŋ/ *adj* avvincente

absorption /əbˈsɔːpʃn/ *n* assorbimento *m*; (in activity) concentrazione *f*

abstain /əbˈsteɪn/ *vi* astenersi (**from** da)

abstemious /əbˈstiːmɪəs/ *adj* moderato

abstention /əbˈstenʃn/ *n* Pol astensione *f*

abstinence /ˈæbstɪnəns/ *n* astinenza *f*

abstract /ˈæbstrækt/ **A** *adj* astratto
B *n* astratto *m*; (summary) estratto *m*

abstraction /əbˈstrækʃn/ *n* **an air of ~** un'aria distratta

absurd /əbˈsɜːd/ *adj* assurdo

absurdity /əbˈsɜːdətɪ/ *n* assurdità *f*

absurdly /əbˈsɜːdlɪ/ *adv* assurdamente

abundance /əˈbʌndəns/ *n* abbondanza *f*

abundant /əˈbʌndənt/ *adj* abbondante

abundantly /əˈbʌndəntlɪ/ *adv* **~ clear** più che chiaro

abuse[1] /əˈbjuːz/ *vt* (misuse) abusare di; (insult) insultare; (ill-treat) maltrattare

abuse[2] /əˈbjuːs/ *n* abuso *m*; (verbal) insulti *mpl*; (ill-treatment) maltrattamento *m*; **~ of power** sopraffazione *f*

abusive /əˈbjuːsɪv/ *adj* offensivo

abut /əˈbʌt/ *vi* (*pt/pp* **abutted**) confinare (**onto** con)

abysmal /əˈbɪzml/ *adj* infml pessimo; ‹*ignorance*› abissale

abyss /əˈbɪs/ *n* abisso *m*

a/c *abbr* (**account**) c/c

academia /ækəˈdiːmɪə/ *n* mondo *m* accademico

academic /ækəˈdemɪk/ **A** *adj* teorico; ‹*qualifications, system*› scolastico; **be ~** ‹*person*› avere predisposizione allo studio
B *n* docente *mf* universitario, -a

academically /ækəˈdemɪklɪ/ *adv* ‹*gifted*› accademicamente

academician /əkædəˈmɪʃn/ *n* accademico, -a *mf*

academy /əˈkædəmɪ/ *n* accademia *f*; (of music) conservatorio *m*

ACAS /ˈeɪkæs/ *n abbr* BrE (**Advisory Conciliation and Arbitration**

Service) *organismo (m) pubblico di mediazione tra i lavoratori e i datori di lavoro*

accede /ək'si:d/ *vi* ~ **to** accedere a ‹*request*›; salire a ‹*throne*›

accelerate /ək'seləreɪt/ *vt & vi* accelerare

acceleration /əkselə'reɪʃn/ *n* accelerazione *f*

accelerator /ək'seləreɪtə(r)/ *n* Auto, Comput acceleratore *m*

accent¹ /'æksənt/ *n* accento *m*

accent² /æk'sent/ *vt* accentare

accented /'æksəntɪd/ *adj* ‹*speech*› con accento marcato

accentuate /ək'sentjʊeɪt/ *vt* accentuare

accept /ək'sept/ *vt* accettare

acceptability /əkseptə'bɪlɪtɪ/ *n* ammissibilità *f*

acceptable /ək'septəbl/ *adj* accettabile

acceptance /ək'septəns/ *n* accettazione *f*

access /'ækses/ **A** *n* accesso *m*
B *vt* Comput accedere a

accessible /ək'sesəbl/ *adj* accessibile

accession /ək'seʃn/ *n* ‹*to throne*› ascesa *f* al trono

accessory /ək'sesərɪ/ *n* accessorio *m*; Jur complice *mf*

accident /'æksɪdənt/ *n* incidente *m*; (chance) caso *m*; **by** ~ per caso; (unintentionally) senza volere; **I'm sorry, it was an** ~ mi dispiace, non l'ho fatto apposta

accidental /æksɪ'dentl/ *adj* ‹*meeting*› casuale; ‹*death*› incidentale; (unintentional) involontario

accidentally /æksɪ'dentəlɪ/ *adv* per caso; (unintentionally) inavvertitamente

accident-prone /ˌæksɪdənt'prəʊn/ *adj* soggetto a incidenti

acclaim /ə'kleɪm/ **A** *n* acclamazione *f*
B *vt* acclamare (**as** come)

acclimatization /əklaɪmətaɪ'zeɪʃn/ *n* acclimatazione *f*

acclimatize /ə'klaɪmətaɪz/ *vt* **become** ~**d** acclimatarsi

accolade /'ækəleɪd/ *n* riconoscimento *m*

accommodate /ə'kɒmədeɪt/ *vt* ospitare; (oblige) favorire

accommodating /ə'kɒmədeɪtɪŋ/ *adj* accomodante

accommodation BrE **accommodations** AmE /əkɒmə'deɪʃn(z)/ *n* (place to stay) sistemazione *f*; **look for** ~ cercare una sistemazione

accompaniment /ə'kʌmpənɪmənt/ *n* accompagnamento *m*

accompanist /ə'kʌmpənɪst/ *n* Mus accompagnatore, -trice *mf*

accompany /ə'kʌmpənɪ/ *vt* (*pt/pp* **-ied**) accompagnare

accomplice /ə'kʌmplɪs/ *n* complice *mf*

accomplish /ə'kʌmplɪʃ/ *vt* (achieve) concludere; realizzare ‹*aim*›

accomplished /ə'kʌmplɪʃt/ *adj* dotato; ‹*fact*› compiuto

accomplishment /ə'kʌmplɪʃmənt/ *n* realizzazione *f*; (achievement) risultato *m*; (talent) talento *m*

accord /ə'kɔ:d/ **A** *n* (treaty) accordo *m*; **with one** ~ tutti d'accordo; **of his own** ~ di sua spontanea volontà
B *vt* accordare

accordance /ə'kɔ:dəns/ *n* **in** ~ **with** in conformità di *o* a

according /ə'kɔ:dɪŋ/ *adv* ~ **to** secondo

accordingly /ə'kɔ:dɪŋlɪ/ *adv* di conseguenza

accordion /ə'kɔ:dɪən/ *n* fisarmonica *f*

accost /ə'kɒst/ *vt* abbordare

account /ə'kaʊnt/ *n* conto *m*; (report) descrizione *f*; (of eyewitness) resoconto *m*; ~**s** *pl* Comm conti *mpl*; **on** ~ **of** a causa di; **on no** ~ per nessun motivo; **on this** ~ per questo motivo; **on my** ~ per causa mia; **of no** ~ di nessuna importanza; **take into** ~ tener conto di

■ **account for** *vt* (explain) spiegare; ‹*person*› render conto di; (constitute) costituire; (destroy) distruggere

accountability /əkaʊntə'bɪlətɪ/ *n* responsabilità *f*

accountable /ə'kaʊntəbl/ *adj* responsabile (**for** di)

accountancy /ə'kaʊntənsɪ/ *n* ragioneria *f*, contabilità *f*

accountant /ə'kaʊntənt/ *n* (bookkeeper) contabile *mf*; ragioniere, -a *mf*; (consultant) commercialista *mf*

account book *n* libro *m* contabile

account director *n* account director *mf inv*

account holder /ə'kaʊnthəʊldə(r)/ *n* (with bank, credit company) titolare *mf* del conto

accounting /ə'kaʊntɪŋ/ *n* (field) ragioneria *f*; (auditing) contabilità *f*

accounting period *n* periodo *m* contabile

account manager *n* account manager *mf*

account number *n* numero *m* di conto

accounts department *n* [ufficio *m*] contabilità *f*

accounts payable *npl* conto *m* creditori diversi

accounts receivable *npl* conto *m* creditori diversi

accoutrements /ə'ku:trəmənts/ *npl* equipaggiamento *msg*

accredited /ə'kredɪtɪd/ *adj* accreditato

accretion /ə'kri:ʃn/ *n* accrescimento *m*

accrue /ə'kru:/ *vi* ‹*interest*› maturare

accumulate /ə'kju:mjʊleɪt/ **A** *vt* accumulare
B *vi* accumularsi

accumulation /əkju:mjʊ'leɪʃn/ *n* accumulazione *f*

accumulator /ə'kju:mjʊleɪtə(r)/ *n* Electr accumulatore *m*

a

accuracy /ˈækjʊrəsɪ/ *n* precisione *f*
accurate /ˈækjʊrət/ *adj* preciso
accurately /ˈækjʊrətlɪ/ *adv* con precisione
accusation /ækjʊˈzeɪʃn/ *n* accusa *f*
accusative /əˈkjuːzətɪv/ *adj & n* **~ [case]** Gram accusativo *m*
⚷ **accuse** /əˈkjuːz/ *vt* accusare; **~ somebody of doing something** accusare qualcuno di fare qualcosa
accused /əˈkjuːzd/ *n* **the ~** l'accusato *m*, l'accusata *f*
accuser /əˈkjuːzə(r)/ *n* accusatore, trice *mf*
accusing /əˈkjuːzɪŋ/ *adj* accusatore
accusingly /əˈkjuːzɪŋlɪ/ *adv* ‹*say, point*› in modo accusatorio
accustom /əˈkʌstəm/ *vt* abituare (**to** a)
accustomed /əˈkʌstəmd/ *adj* abituato; **grow** *or* **get ~ to** abituarsi a
ace /eɪs/ *n* (in cards) asso *m*; Tennis ace *m inv*
acerbic /əˈsɜːbɪk/ *adj* acido
acetate /ˈæsɪteɪt/ *n* acetato *m*
ache /eɪk/ **A** *n* dolore *m*
B *vi* dolere, far male; **~ all over** essere tutto indolenzito
⚷ **achieve** /əˈtʃiːv/ *vt* ottenere ‹*success*›; realizzare ‹*goal, ambition*›
⚷ **achievement** /əˈtʃiːvmənt/ *n* (feat) successo *m*
achiever /əˈtʃiːvə(r)/ *n* persona *f* di successo
Achilles' heel /əkɪliːzˈhiːl/ *n* tallone *m* di Achille
aching /ˈeɪkɪŋ/ *adj* ‹*body, limbs*› dolorante; **an ~ void** un vuoto incolmabile
acid /ˈæsɪd/ **A** *adj* acido
B *n* acido *m*
acid drop *n* caramella *f* agli agrumi
acidic /əˈsɪdɪk/ *adj* acido
acidity /əˈsɪdətɪ/ *n* acidità *f*
acid rain *n* pioggia *f* acida
acid stomach *n* Med acidità *f* di stomaco
acid test *n* fig prova *f* del fuoco
⚷ **acknowledge** /əkˈnɒlɪdʒ/ *vt* riconoscere; rispondere a ‹*greeting*›; far cenno di aver notato ‹*sb's presence*›; **~ receipt of** accusare ricevuta di; **~ defeat** dichiararsi vinto
acknowledgement /əkˈnɒlɪdʒmənt/ *n* riconoscimento *m*; **send an ~ of a letter** confermare il ricevimento di una lettera
acme /ˈækmɪ/ *n* **the ~ of** l'apice *m* di
acne /ˈæknɪ/ *n* acne *f*
acorn /ˈeɪkɔːn/ *n* ghianda *f*
acoustic /əˈkuːstɪk/ *adj* acustico
acoustically /əˈkuːstɪklɪ/ *adv* acusticamente
acoustic guitar *n* chitarra *f* acustica
acoustics /əˈkuːstɪks/ *npl* acustica *fsg*
acquaint /əˈkweɪnt/ *vt* **~ somebody with** metter qualcuno al corrente di

⚷ parola chiave

acquaintance /əˈkweɪntəns/ *n* (person) conoscente *mf*; **make sb's ~** fare la conoscenza di qualcuno
acquainted *adj* **be ~ with** conoscere ‹*person*›; essere a conoscenza di ‹*fact*›; **get** *or* **become ~ with somebody** fare conoscenza con qualcuno; **get** *or* **become ~ with something** familiarizzare con qualcosa
acquiesce /ækwɪˈes/ *vi* acconsentire (**to, in** a)
acquiescence /ækwɪˈesəns/ *n* acquiescenza *f*
acquiescent /ækwɪˈesənt/ *adj* arrendevole
⚷ **acquire** /əˈkwaɪə(r)/ *vt* acquisire
acquired /əˈkwaɪəd/ *adj* ‹*characteristic*› acquisito; **it's an ~ taste** una cosa che si impara ad apprezzare
acquisition /ækwɪˈzɪʃn/ *n* acquisizione *f*
acquisitive /əˈkwɪzətɪv/ *adj* avido
acquit /əˈkwɪt/ *vt* (*pt/pp* **acquitted**) assolvere; **~ oneself well** cavarsela bene
acquittal /əˈkwɪtəl/ *n* assoluzione *f*
acre /ˈeɪkə(r)/ *n* acro *m* (= 4047 m²)
acreage /ˈeɪkərɪdʒ/ *n* superficie *f* in acri
acrid /ˈækrɪd/ *adj* acre
acrimonious /ækrɪˈməʊnɪəs/ *adj* aspro
acrimony /ˈækrɪmənɪ/ *n* asprezza *f*
acrobat /ˈækrəbæt/ *n* acrobata *mf*
acrobatic /ækrəˈbætɪk/ *adj* acrobatico
acrobatics /ækrəˈbætɪks/ *nsg* acrobazie *fpl*
acronym /ˈækrənɪm/ *n* acronimo *m*
⚷ **across** /əˈkrɒs/ **A** *adv* dall'altra parte; (wide) in larghezza; (not lengthwise) attraverso; (in crossword) orizzontale; **come ~ something** imbattersi in qualcosa; **go ~** attraversare
B *prep* (crosswise) di traverso su; (on the other side of) dall'altra parte di
across-the-board A *adj* generale
B *adv* in generale
acrylic /əˈkrɪlɪk/ **A** *n* acrilico *m*
B *attrib* ‹*garment*› acrilico
⚷ **act** /ækt/ **A** *n* atto *m*; (in variety show) numero *m*; **put on an ~** infml fare scena
B *vi* agire; (behave) comportarsi; Theat recitare; (pretend) fingere; **~ as** fare da
C *vt* recitare ‹*role*›
■ **act for** *vi* agire per conto di
■ **act out** *vt* ‹*part*› recitare; ‹*fantasy*› mettere in atto
■ **act up** *vi* ‹*child, photocopier*› fare i capricci
acting /ˈæktɪŋ/ **A** *adj* ‹*deputy*› provvisorio
B *n* Theat recitazione *f*; (profession) teatro *m*; **~ profession** professione *f* dell'attore
⚷ **action** /ˈækʃn/ *n* azione *f*; Mil combattimento *m*; Jur azione *f* legale; **out of ~** ‹*machine*› fuori uso; **take ~** agire; **~!** Cinema ciac si gira!
action group *n* gruppo *m* d'azione
action-packed *adj* ‹*film*› d'azione
action painting *n* pittura *f* d'azione
action plan *n* piano *m* d'azione
action replay *n* replay *m inv*

activate /ˈæktɪveɪt/ *vt* attivare; Chem, Phys rendere attivo

active /ˈæktɪv/ *adj* attivo

active duty, active service *n* Mil **be on ~** prestare servizio in zona di operazioni

actively /ˈæktɪvlɪ/ *adv* attivamente

activist /ˈæktɪvɪst/ *n* attivista *mf*

activity /ækˈtɪvətɪ/ *n* attività *f*

activity holiday *n* BrE vacanza *f* con attività ricreative

act of God *n* causa *f* di forza maggiore

actor /ˈæktə(r)/ *n* attore *m*

actress /ˈæktrəs/ *n* attrice *f*

actual /ˈæktʃʊəl/ *adj* (real) reale

actually /ˈæktʃʊəlɪ/ *adv* in realtà

actuary /ˈæktʃʊərɪ/ *n* attuario, -a *mf*

acumen /ˈækjʊmən/ *n* acume *m*

acupuncture /ˈækjʊpʌŋktʃə(r)/ *n* agopuntura *f*

acupuncturist /ækjʊˈpʌŋktʃərɪst/ *n* agopuntore, -trice *mf*

acute /əˈkjuːt/ *adj* acuto; ‹*shortage, hardship*› estremo

acute accent *n* accento *m* acuto

acute angle *n* angolo *m* acuto

acutely /əˈkjuːtlɪ/ *adv* acutamente; ‹*embarrassed, aware*› estremamente

ad /æd/ *n* pubblicità *f*; (in paper) inserzione *f*, annuncio *m*

AD *abbr* (**Anno Domini**) d.C.

adage /ˈædɪdʒ/ *n* detto *m*, adagio *m*

adamant /ˈædəmənt/ *adj* categorico (**that** sul fatto che)

Adam's apple /ˈædəmz/ *n* pomo *m* di Adamo

adapt /əˈdæpt/ **A** *vt* adattare ‹*play*› **B** *vi* adattarsi

adaptability /ədæptəˈbɪlətɪ/ *n* adattabilità *f*

adaptable /əˈdæptəbl/ *adj* adattabile

adaptation /ædæpˈteɪʃn/ *n* Theat adattamento *m*

adapter, adaptor /əˈdæptə(r)/ *n* adattatore *m*; (two-way) presa *f* multipla

add /æd/ **A** *vt* aggiungere; Math addizionare **B** *vi* addizionare
- **add in** *vt* (include) includere
- **add on** *vt* aggiungere
- **add to** *vi* fig aggravare
- **add up** **A** *vt* addizionare ‹*figures*› **B** *vi* addizionare; **it doesn't ~ up** fig non quadra; **~ up to** ammontare a

added /ˈædɪd/ *adj* maggiore

adder /ˈædə(r)/ *n* vipera *f*

addict /ˈædɪkt/ *n* tossicodipendente *mf*; fig fanatico, -a *mf*

addicted /əˈdɪktɪd/ *adj* assuefatto (**to** a); **~ to drugs** tossicodipendente; **he's ~ to television** è videodipendente

addiction /əˈdɪkʃn/ *n* dipendenza *f*; (to drugs) tossicodipendenza *f*

addictive /əˈdɪktɪv/ *adj* **be ~** dare assuefazione

addition /əˈdɪʃn/ *adj* Math addizione *f*; (thing added) aggiunta *f*; **in ~** in aggiunta

additional /əˈdɪʃənəl/ *adj* supplementare

additionally /əˈdɪʃnəlɪ/ *adv* in più

additive /ˈædɪtɪv/ *n* additivo *m*

addled /ˈædld/ *adj* ‹*thinking*› confuso

add-on *adj* accessorio

address /əˈdres/ **A** *n* indirizzo *m*; (speech) discorso *m*; **form of ~** formula *f* di cortesia **B** *vt* indirizzare; (speak to) rivolgersi a ‹*person*›; tenere un discorso a ‹*meeting*›

address book *n* rubrica *f*

addressee /ædreˈsiː/ *n* destinatario, -a *mf*

adenoids /ˈædənɔɪdz/ *npl* adenoidi *fpl*

adept /ˈædept/ *adj* esperto, -a *mf* (**at** in)

adequate /ˈædɪkwət/ *adj* adeguato

adequately /ˈædɪkwətlɪ/ *adv* adeguatamente

ADHD *abbr* (**Attention Deficit and Hyperactivity Disorder**) disturbo *m* da deficit dell'attenzione con iperattività

adhere /ədˈhɪə(r)/ *vi* aderire; **~ to** attenersi a ‹*principles, rules*›

adherence /ədˈhɪərəns/ *n* fedeltà *f*

adherent /ədˈhɪərənt/ *n* (of doctrine) adepto, -a *mf*; (of policy) sostenitore, -trice *mf*; (of cult) seguace *mf*

adhesion /ədˈhiːʒn/ *n* adesione *f*

adhesive /ədˈhiːsɪv/ **A** *adj* adesivo **B** *n* adesivo *m*

ad hoc /ædˈhɒk/ *adj* ‹*alliance, arrangement*› ad hoc; ‹*committee, legislation*› apposito; **on an ~ basis** secondo le esigenze del momento

adieu /əˈdjuː/ *n* **bid somebody ~** dire addio a qualcuno

ad infinitum /ædɪnfɪˈnaɪtəm/ *adv* ‹*continue*› all'infinito

adjacent /əˈdʒeɪsənt/ *adj* adiacente

adjective /ˈædʒɪktɪv/ *n* aggettivo *m*

adjoin /əˈdʒɔɪn/ *vt* essere adiacente a

adjoining /əˈdʒɔɪnɪŋ/ *adj* adiacente

adjourn /əˈdʒɜːn/ *vt* aggiornare (**until** a)

adjournment /əˈdʒɜːnmənt/ *n* aggiornamento *m*

adjudge /əˈdʒʌdʒ/ *vt* Jur (decree) giudicare; aggiudicare ‹*costs, damages*›

adjudicate /əˈdʒuːdɪkeɪt/ *vi* decidere; (in competition) giudicare

adjudicator /əˈdʒuːdɪkeɪtə(r)/ *n* giudice *m*, arbitro *m*

adjunct /ˈædʒʌnkt/ *n* aggiunta *f*; hum (person) appendice *f*

adjust /əˈdʒʌst/ **A** *vt* modificare; regolare ‹*focus, sound etc*› **B** *vi* adattarsi

adjustable /əˈdʒʌstəbl/ *adj* regolabile

adjustable spanner *n* chiave *f* [inglese] a rullino

adjustment /ə'dʒʌstmənt/ *n* adattamento *m*; Techn regolamento *m*
adjutant /'ædʒʊtənt/ *n* Mil aiutante *mf*
ad lib /æd'lɪb/ **A** *adj* improvvisato
B *adv* a piacere
C *vi* (**ad-lib**, *pt/pp* **ad-libbed**) infml improvvisare
adman /'ædmæn/ *n* infml pubblicitario *m*
admin /'ædmɪn/ *n* BrE infml amministrazione *f*
administer /əd'mɪnɪstə(r)/ *vt* amministrare; somministrare ‹*medicine*›
🔑 **administration** /ədmɪnɪ'streɪʃn/ *n* amministrazione *f*; Pol governo *m*
administration costs *n* costi *mpl* di gestione
administrative /əd'mɪnɪstrətɪv/ *adj* amministrativo
administrator /əd'mɪnɪstreɪtə(r)/ *n* amministratore, -trice *mf*
admirable /'ædmərəbl/ *adj* ammirevole
admiral /'ædmərəl/ *n* ammiraglio *m*
admiralty /'ædmɪrəltɪ/ *n Br ministero* (*m*) *della marina militare britannica*
admiration /ædmə'reɪʃn/ *n* ammirazione *f*
admire /əd'maɪə(r)/ *vt* ammirare
admirer /əd'maɪrə(r)/ *n* ammiratore, -trice *mf*
admiring /əd'maɪrɪŋ/ *adj* ‹*person*› pieno d'ammirazione; ‹*look*› ammirativo
admiringly /əd'maɪrɪŋlɪ/ *adv* ‹*look, say*› con ammirazione
admissible /əd'mɪsəbl/ *adj* ammissibile
admission /əd'mɪʃn/ *n* ammissione *f*; (to hospital) ricovero *m*; (entry) ingresso *m*
admissions office *n* Univ segreteria *f* studenti
🔑 **admit** /əd'mɪt/ **A** *vt* (*pt/pp* **admitted**) (let in) far entrare; (to hospital) ricoverare; (acknowledge) ammettere
B *vi* ~ **to something** ammettere qualcosa
admittance /əd'mɪtəns/ *n* ammissione *f*; **'no ~'** 'vietato l'ingresso'
admittedly /əd'mɪtɪdlɪ/ *adv* bisogna riconoscerlo
admonish /əd'mɒnɪʃ/ *vt* ammonire
admonition /ædmə'nɪʃn/ *n* ammonimento *m*
ad nauseam /æd'nɔːzɪæm/ *adv* ‹*discuss, repeat*› fino alla nausea
ado /ə'duː/ *n* **without more ~** senza ulteriori indugi
adolescence /ædə'lesns/ *n* adolescenza *f*
adolescent /ædə'lesnt/ *adj & n* adolescente *mf*
🔑 **adopt** /ə'dɒpt/ *vt* adottare; Pol scegliere ‹*candidate*›
adopted /ə'dɒptɪd/ *adj* ‹*son, daughter*› adottivo
adoption /ə'dɒpʃn/ *n* adozione *f*
adoption agency *n* agenzia *f* di adozioni

adoptive /ə'dɒptɪv/ *adj* adottivo
adorable /ə'dɔːrəbl/ *adj* adorabile
adoration /ædə'reɪʃn/ *n* adorazione *f*
adore /ə'dɔː(r)/ *vt* adorare
adoring /ə'dɔːrɪŋ/ *adj* ‹*fan*› in adorazione; **she has an ~ husband** ha un marito che la adora
adoringly /ə'dɔːrɪŋlɪ/ *adv* con adorazione
adorn /ə'dɔːn/ *vt* adornare
adornment /ə'dɔːnmənt/ *n* ornamento *m*
adrenalin /ə'drenəlɪn/ *n* adrenalina *f*
Adriatic /eɪdrɪ'ætɪk/ *adj & n* **the ~ [Sea]** il mare Adriatico, l'Adriatico *m*
adrift /ə'drɪft/ *adj* alla deriva; **be ~** andare alla deriva; **come ~** staccarsi
adroit /ə'drɔɪt/ *adj* abile
adroitly /ə'drɔɪtlɪ/ *adv* abilmente
ADSL *abbr* (**Asymmetric Digital Subscriber Line**) ADSL *f*
adulation /ædjʊ'leɪʃn/ *n* adulazione *f*
🔑 **adult** /'ædʌlt/ *n* adulto, -a *mf*
Adult Education *n* BrE ≈ corsi *mpl* serali
adulterate /ə'dʌltəreɪt/ *vt* adulterare ‹*wine*›
adulterated /ə'dʌltəreɪtɪd/ *adj* ‹*wine*› adulterato
adulterous /ə'dʌltərəs/ *adj* ‹*relationship*› adulterino; ‹*person*› adultero
adultery /ə'dʌltərɪ/ *n* adulterio *m*
adulthood /'ædʌlthʊd/ *n* età *f* adulta
adult literacy classes *n* BrE corso *m* di alfabetizzazione per adulti
advance /əd'vɑːns/ **A** *n* avanzamento *m*; Mil avanzata *f*; (payment) anticipo *m*; **in ~** in anticipo
B *vi* avanzare; (make progress) fare progressi
C *vt* promuovere ‹*cause*›; avanzare ‹*theory*›; anticipare ‹*money*›
advance booking *n* prenotazione *f* [in anticipo]
advance booking office *n* ufficio *m* prenotazioni
advanced /əd'vɑːnst/ *adj* avanzato
Advanced Level *n* BrE Sch = **A level**
advanced search *n* Comput ricerca *f* avanzata; **~ option** opzione *f* ricerca avanzata
advancement /əd'vɑːnsmənt/ *n* promozione *f*
advance notice *n* preannuncio *m*
advance party *n* Mil avanguardia *f*
advance payment *n* Comm pagamento *m* anticipato
advance warning *n* preavviso *m*
🔑 **advantage** /əd'vɑːntɪdʒ/ *n* vantaggio *m*; **take ~ of** approfittare di
advantageous /ædvən'teɪdʒəs/ *adj* vantaggioso
advent /'ædvent/ *n* avvento *m*; **A~** Relig Avvento *m*
adventure /əd'ventʃə(r)/ *n* avventura *f*

🔑 parola chiave

adventure holiday *n* vacanza *f* avventura
adventure playground *n* BrE parco *m* giochi
adventurer /əd'ventʃərə(r)/ *n* avventuriero, -a *mf*
adventuress /əd'ventʃərɪs/ *n* avventuriera *f*
adventurous /əd'ventʃərəs/ *adj* avventuroso
adverb /'ædvɜːb/ *n* avverbio *m*
adversary /'ædvəsərɪ/ *n* avversario, -a *mf*
adverse /'ædvɜːs/ *adj* avverso
adversity /əd'vɜːsətɪ/ *n* avversità *f*
advert /'ædvɜːt/ *n* infml = **advertisement**
advertise /'ædvətaɪz/ **A** *vt* reclamizzare; mettere un annuncio per ‹*job, flat*› **B** *vi* fare pubblicità; (for job, flat) mettere un annuncio
advertisement /əd'vɜːtɪsmənt/ *n* pubblicità *f*; (in paper) inserzione *f*, annuncio *m*
advertiser /'ædvətaɪzə(r)/ *n* (in newspaper) inserzionista *mf*
advertising /'ædvətaɪzɪŋ/ **A** *n* pubblicità *f* **B** *attrib* pubblicitario
advertising agency *n* agenzia *f* pubblicitaria
advertising campaign *n* campagna *f* pubblicitaria
advertising executive *n* dirigente *mf* pubblicitario, -a
advertising industry *n* settore *m* pubblicitario
Advertising Standards Authority *n* BrE *organo (m) di controllo sulla pubblicità*
⚷ **advice** /əd'vaɪs/ *n* consigli *mpl*; **piece of ~** consiglio *m*
advice centre *n* centro *m* di consulenza
advice note *n* avviso *m*
advice slip *n* avviso *m* di accreditamento
advisability /ədvaɪzə'bɪlətɪ/ *n* opportunità *f*
advisable /əd'vaɪzəbl/ *adj* consigliabile
⚷ **advise** /əd'vaɪz/ *vt* consigliare; (inform) avvisare; **~ somebody to do something** consigliare a qualcuno di fare qualcosa; **~ somebody against something** sconsigliare qualcosa a qualcuno
advisedly /əd'vaɪzɪdlɪ/ *adv* ‹*say*› deliberatamente
adviser /əd'vaɪzə(r)/ *n* consulente *mf*
advisory /əd'vaɪzərɪ/ *adj* consultivo
advisory committee *n* comitato *m* consultivo
advisory service *n* servizio *m* di consulenza; **pensions/immigration/pregnancy ~** servizio di consulenza in materia di pensioni/immigrazione/gravidanza
advocacy /'ædvəkəsɪ/ *n* appoggio *m*
advocate¹ /'ædvəkət/ *n* (supporter) fautore, -trice *mf*
advocate² /'ædvəkeɪt/ *vt* propugnare
Aegean /ɪ'dʒɪən/ *n* **the ~** l'Egeo *m*
aegis /'iːdʒɪs/ *n* **under the ~ of** sotto l'egida di
aeon /'iːən/ *n* **~s ago** milioni *mpl* e milioni di anni fa
AER *n abbr* (**Annual Equivalence Rate**) TAN *m*
aerate /'eəreɪt/ *vt* aerare; addizionare anidride carbonica a ‹*water*›
aerial /'eərɪəl/ **A** *adj* aereo **B** *n* antenna *f*
aerial camera *n* macchina *f* fotografica per fotografie aeree
aerial photography *n* fotografia *f* aerea
aerial warfare *n* guerra *f* aerea
aerie /'eərɪ/ *n* AmE **eyrie**
aerobatics /eərə'bætɪks/ *npl* (manoeuvres) acrobazie *fpl* aeree
aerobics /eə'rəʊbɪks/ *n* aerobica *fsg*
aerodrome /'eərədrəʊm/ *n* aerodromo *m*
aerodynamic /eərəʊdaɪ'næmɪk/ *adj* aerodinamico
aerodynamics /eərəʊdaɪ'næmɪks/ *nsg* aerodinamica *fsg*
aerogramme /'eərəʊgræm/ *n* aerogramma *m*
aeronautic /eərə'nɔːtɪk/, **aeronautical** /eərə'nɔːtɪkəl/ *adj* aeronautico
aeronautic engineer, **aeronautical engineer** *n* ingegnere *m* aeronautico
aeronautic engineering, **aeronautical engineering** *n* ingegneria *f* aeronautica
aeronautics /eərə'nɔːtɪks/ *nsg* aeronautica *fsg*
aeroplane /'eərəpleɪn/ *n* aeroplano *m*
aerosol /'eərəsɒl/ *n* bomboletta *f* spray
aerospace /'eərəspeɪs/ **A** *n* (industry) industria *f* aerospaziale **B** *attrib* ‹*engineer, company*› aerospaziale
aesthete /'iːsθiːt/ *n* esteta *mf*
aesthetic /iːs'θetɪk/ *adj* estetico
aesthetically /iːs'θetɪklɪ/ *adv* ‹*restore*› con gusto; ‹*satisfying*› esteticamente
aestheticism /iːs'θetɪsɪzm/ *n* (taste) estetica *f*; (doctrine, quality) estetismo *m*
aesthetics /iːs'θetɪks/ *nsg* estetica *fsg*
afar /ə'fɑː(r)/ *adv* **from ~** da lontano
affable /'æfəbl/ *adj* affabile
affably /'æfəblɪ/ *adv* affabilmente
⚷ **affair** /ə'feə(r)/ *n* affare *m*; (scandal) caso *m*; (sexual) relazione *f*
⚷ **affect** /ə'fekt/ *vt* influire su; (emotionally) colpire; (concern) riguardare; (pretend) affettare
affectation /æfek'teɪʃn/ *n* affettazione *f*
affected /ə'fektɪd/ *adj* affettato
affectedly /ə'fektɪdlɪ/ *adv* ‹*talk*› con affettazione
affection /ə'fekʃn/ *n* affetto *m*
affectionate /ə'fekʃnət/ *adj* affettuoso
affectionately /ə'fekʃnətlɪ/ *adv* affettuosamente

a

affidavit /æfɪ'deɪvɪt/ *n* affidavit *m inv* (*dichiarazione scritta e giurata davanti a un pubblico ufficiale*)
affiliated /ə'fɪlɪeɪtɪd/ *adj* affiliato
affiliation /ə'fɪlɪ'eɪʃn/ *n* (process, state) affiliazione *f*; (link) legame *m*
affinity /ə'fɪnətɪ/ *n* affinità *f*
affinity card *n carta (f) di credito destinata ad una causa sociale*
affirm /ə'fɜːm/ *vt* affermare; Jur dichiarare solennemente
affirmative /ə'fɜːmətɪv/ **A** *adj* affermativo **B** *n* **in the ~** affermativamente
affix /ə'fɪks/ *vt* affiggere; apporre ‹*signature*›
afflict /ə'flɪkt/ *vt* affliggere
affliction /ə'flɪkʃn/ *n* afflizione *f*
affluence /'æflʊəns/ *n* agiatezza *f*
affluent /'æflʊənt/ *adj* agiato
⚷ **afford** /ə'fɔːd/ *vt* (provide) fornire; **be able to ~ something** potersi permettere qualcosa
affordable /ə'fɔːdəbl/ *adj* abbordabile
affray /ə'freɪ/ *n* rissa *f*
affront /ə'frʌnt/ **A** *n* affronto *m* **B** *vt* fare un affronto a
Afghan /'æfgæn/ *n* (person) afgano, -a *mf*; (language) afgano *m*; (coat) pellicciotto *m* afgano
Afghan hound *n* levriero *m* afgano
Afghanistan /æf'gænɪstæn/ *n* Afganistan *m*
aficionado /æfɪsjə'nɑːdəʊ/ *n* aficionado, -a *mf*
afield /ə'fiːld/ *adv* **further ~** più lontano
aflame /ə'fleɪm/ *adj & adv* literary in fiamme, sfolgorante; **be ~** ‹*cheek*› essere in fiamme; **be ~ with desire** ardere dal desiderio
afloat /ə'fləʊt/ *adj* a galla
afoot /ə'fʊt/ *adj* **there's something ~** si sta preparando qualcosa
aforesaid /ə'fɔːsed/ *adj* Jur suddetto
⚷ **afraid** /ə'freɪd/ *adj* **be ~** aver paura; **I'm ~ not** purtroppo no; **I'm ~ so** temo di sì; **I'm ~ I can't help you** mi dispiace ma non posso esserle d'aiuto
afresh /ə'freʃ/ *adv* da capo
Africa /'æfrɪkə/ *n* Africa *f*
⚷ **African** /'æfrɪkən/ *adj & n* africano, -a *mf*
African-American *n* afroamericano, -a *mf*
Afrikaans /æfrɪ'kɑːns/ *n* afrikaans *m*
Afrikaner /æfrɪ'kɑːnə(r)/ *n* boero, -a *mf*
Afro-American /æfrəʊə'merɪkən/ *adj & n* afroamericano, -a *mf*
Afro-Caribbean /æfrəʊkærə'bɪən/ *adj & n* afrocaraibico, -a *mf*
aft /ɑːft/ *adv* Naut a poppa; (towards the stern) verso poppa
⚷ **after** /'ɑːftə(r)/ **A** *adv* dopo; **the day ~** il giorno dopo; **be ~** cercare **B** *prep* dopo; **~ all** dopotutto; **the day ~ tomorrow** dopodomani **C** *conj* dopo che
afterbirth *n* residui *mpl* di placenta
aftercare *n* Med ospedalizzazione *f* domiciliare
after-dinner speaker *n persona (f) invitata a tenere un discorso dopo una cena o un ricevimento*
after-effect *n* conseguenza *f*
afterlife *n* vita *f* nell'aldilà
aftermath /'ɑːftəmɑːθ/ *n* conseguenze *fpl*; **the ~ of war** il dopoguerra; **in the ~ of** nel periodo successivo a
afternoon *n* pomeriggio *m*; **good ~!** buon giorno!
afternoon tea *n* merenda *f*
afterpains *npl* dolori *mpl* post-parto
after-sales service *n* servizio *m* assistenza clienti
after-school *adj* doposcuola; **~ club/activities** club/attività doposcuola
aftershave *n* dopobarba *m inv*
aftershock *n* fig effetti *mpl*
aftersun *n & adj* doposole *m inv*
aftertaste *n* retrogusto *m*
after-tax *adj* ‹*profits, earnings*› al netto
afterthought *n* **added as an ~** aggiunto in un secondo momento; **as an ~, why not...?** ripensandoci bene, perché non...?
afterwards /'ɑːftəwədz/ *adv* in seguito
⚷ **again** /ə'geɪn/ *adv* di nuovo; **[then] ~** (besides) inoltre; (on the other hand) d'altra parte; **~ and ~** continuamente
⚷ **against** /ə'geɪnst/ *prep* contro
⚷ **age** /eɪdʒ/ **A** *n* età *f*; (era) era *f*; **~s** infml secoli; **~s ago** infml secoli fa; **what ~ are you?** quanti anni hai?; **be under ~** non avere l'età richiesta; **he's two years of ~** ha due anni **B** *vt & vi* (*pres p* **ageing**) invecchiare
age bracket, **age group** *n* fascia *f* d'età
aged¹ /eɪdʒd/ *adj* **~ two** di due anni
aged² /'eɪdʒɪd/ **A** *adj* anziano **B** *n* **the ~** *pl* gli anziani
aged debt *n* Fin somma *f* in scadenza
age discrimination *n* discriminazione *f* in base all'età
ageing /'eɪdʒɪŋ/ **A** *n* invecchiamento *m* **B** *adj* ‹*person, population*› che sta invecchiando
ageism /'eɪdʒɪzm/ *n* discriminazione *f* contro chi non è più giovane
ageless /'eɪdʒlɪs/ *adj* senza età
⚷ **agency** /'eɪdʒənsɪ/ *n* agenzia *f*; **have the ~ for** essere un concessionario di
agency fee *n* commissione *f*
agency nurse *n* infermiere, -a *mf* privato, -a
⚷ **agenda** /ə'dʒendə/ *n* ordine *m* del giorno; **on the ~** all'ordine del giorno; fig in

⚷ parola chiave

programma

agent /ˈeɪdʒənt/ *n* agente *mf*

age-old *adj* secolare

age range *n* fascia *f* d'età

aggravate /ˈægrəveɪt/ *vt* aggravare; (annoy) esasperare

aggravating /ˈægrəveɪtɪŋ/ *adj* Jur aggravante; infml (irritating) irritante

aggravation /ægrəˈveɪʃn/ *n* aggravamento *m*; (annoyance) esasperazione *f*

aggregate /ˈægrɪgət/ **A** *adj* totale **B** *n* totale *m*; **on ~** nel complesso

aggression /əˈgreʃn/ *n* aggressione *f*

aggressive /əˈgresɪv/ *adj* aggressivo

aggressively /əˈgresɪvlɪ/ *adv* aggressivamente

aggressiveness /əˈgresɪvnɪs/ *n* aggressività *f*

aggressor /əˈgresə(r)/ *n* aggressore *m*

aggrieved /əˈgriːvd/ *adj* risentito

aggro /ˈægrəʊ/ *n* infml aggressività *f*; (problems) grane *fpl*

aghast /əˈgɑːst/ *adj* inorridito

agile /ˈædʒaɪl/ *adj* agile

agility /əˈdʒɪlətɪ/ *n* agilità *f*

agitate /ˈædʒɪteɪt/ **A** *vt* mettere in agitazione; (shake) agitare **B** *vi* fig **~ for** creare delle agitazioni per

agitated /ˈædʒɪteɪtɪd/ *adj* agitato

agitation /ædʒɪˈteɪʃn/ *n* agitazione *f*

agitator /ˈædʒɪteɪtə(r)/ *n* agitatore, -trice *mf*

AGM *n abbr* (**annual general meeting**) assemblea *f* generale annuale

agnostic /ægˈnɒstɪk/ *adj & n* agnostico, -a *mf*

ago /əˈgəʊ/ *adv* fa; **a long time/a month ~** molto tempo/un mese fa; **how long ~ was it?** quanto tempo fa è successo?

agog /əˈgɒg/ *adj* eccitato

agonize /ˈægənaɪz/ *vi* angosciarsi (**over** per)

agonized /ˈægənaɪzd/ *adj* ‹*expression, cry*› angosciato

agonizing /ˈægənaɪzɪŋ/ *adj* angosciante

agony /ˈægənɪ/ *n* agonia *f*; (mental) angoscia *f*; **be in ~** avere dei dolori atroci

agony aunt *n persona* (*f*) *che tiene la posta del cuore in una rivista*

agoraphobia /ægərəˈfəʊbɪə/ *n* agorafobia *f*

agoraphobic /ægərəˈfəʊbɪk/ *adj* agorafobo, -a *mf*

agree /əˈgriː/ **A** *vt* accordarsi su; **~ to do something** accettare di fare qualcosa; **~ that** essere d'accordo [sul fatto] che **B** *vi* essere d'accordo; ‹*figures*› concordare; (reach agreement) mettersi d'accordo; (get on) andare d'accordo; (consent) acconsentire (**to** a); **it doesn't ~ with me** mi fa male; **~ with something** (approve of) approvare qualcosa

agreeable /əˈgriːəbl/ *adj* gradevole; (willing) d'accordo

agreeably /əˈgriːəblɪ/ *adv* (pleasantly) piacevolmente; (amicably) in modo amichevole

agreed /əˈgriːd/ *adj* convenuto

agreement /əˈgriːmənt/ *n* accordo *m*; **in ~** d'accordo; **reach ~** arrivare ad un accordo

agricultural /ægrɪˈkʌltʃərəl/ *adj* agricolo

agriculturalist /ægrɪˈkʌltʃərəlɪst/ *n* agronomo, -a *mf*

agricultural show *n* fiera *f* agricola

agriculture /ˈægrɪkʌltʃə(r)/ *n* agricoltura *f*

agritourism /ægrɪˈtʊərɪzəm/ *n* agriturismo *m*

agronomy /əˈgrɒnəmɪ/ *n* agronomia *f*

aground /əˈgraʊnd/ *adv* **run ~** ‹*ship*› arenarsi

ah /ɑː/ *int* **~ well!** (resignedly) va bene!

ahead /əˈhed/ *adv* avanti; **be ~ of** essere davanti a; fig essere avanti rispetto a; **draw ~** passare davanti (**of** a); **go on ~** cominciare ad andare; **get ~** ‹*in life*› riuscire; **go ~!** fai pure!; **look ~** pensare all'avvenire; **plan ~** fare progetti per l'avvenire

aid /eɪd/ **A** *n* aiuto *m*; **in ~ of** a favore di **B** *vt* aiutare

aid agency *n* organizzazione *f* umanitaria

aide *n* assistente *mf*

aid package *n* pacco *m* umanitario

Aids /eɪdz/ *n* AIDS *m*

Aids awareness *n* sensibilizzazione *f* all'AIDS

aid worker *n* cooperante *mf*

ailing /ˈeɪlɪŋ/ *adj* malato

ailment /ˈeɪlmənt/ *n* disturbo *m*

aim /eɪm/ **A** *n* mira *f*; fig scopo *m*; **take ~** prendere la mira **B** *vt* puntare ‹*gun*› (**at** su) **C** *vi* mirare; **~ to do something** aspirare a fare qualcosa

aimless /ˈeɪmlɪs/ *adj* senza scopo

aimlessly /ˈeɪmlɪslɪ/ *adv* senza scopo

ain't /eɪnt/ infml *am not; are not; have not; has not*

air /eə(r)/ **A** *n* aria *f*; **be on the ~** ‹*programme*› essere in onda; **put on ~s** darsi delle arie; **by ~** in aereo; (airmail) per via aerea **B** *vt* arieggiare; far conoscere ‹*views*›; derog sfoggiare ‹*knowledge*›

air ambulance *n* aereo *m* ambulanza; (helicopter) eliambulanza *f*

air attack *n* attacco *m* aereo

air bag *n* Auto air bag *m inv*

air bed *n* materassino *m* [gonfiabile]

airborne /ˈeəbɔːn/ *adj* (plane) in volo; ‹*troops*› aerotrasportato

airbrush *n* aerografo *m*

air bubble *n* (in liquid, plastic, wallpaper) bolla *f* d'aria

air-conditioned *adj* con aria condizionata

air conditioner *n* condizionatore *m*

air-conditioning *n* aria *f* condizionata

air-cooled *adj* ‹*engine*› raffreddato ad aria
air cover *n* protezione *f* aerea
🔑 **aircraft** *n* aereo *m*
aircraft carrier *n* portaerei *f inv*
aircraftman, aircraftsman *n* BrE aviere *m*
air crash *n* disastro *m* aereo
aircrew *n* equipaggio *m* di volo
air cushion *n* (inflatable cushion) cuscino *m* gonfiabile; (of hovercraft) cuscino *m* d'aria
air disaster *n* disastro *m* aereo
air display *n* esibizione *f* in volo
airdrop *n* lancio *m* con paracadute
air duct *n* condotto *m* dell'aria
air exclusion zone *n* zona *f* di esclusione aerea
airfare *n* tariffa *f* aerea
airfield *n* campo *m* d'aviazione
airflow *n* spostamento *m* d'aria
air force *n* aviazione *f*
airfreight *n* (goods) merce *f* spedita via aerea; (method of transport) trasporto *m* aereo; (charge) costo *m* per trasporto aereo
air freshener *n* deodorante *m* per ambienti
air gun *n* fucile *m* ad aria compressa
airhead *n* infml svampito, -a *mf*
air hole *n* sfiatatoio *m*
air hostess *n* hostess *f inv*
airing /'eərɪŋ/ *n* **give a room an ~** arieggiare una stanza; **give an idea an ~** fig ventilare un'idea
airing cupboard *n* BrE *sgabuzzino (m) del boiler dove viene riposta la biancheria ad asciugare*
airless /'eəlɪs/ *adj* ‹*evening*› senza vento; ‹*room*› poco ventilato
air letter *n* aerogramma *m*
airlift **A** *vt* trasportare con ponte aereo **B** *n* ponte *m* aereo
airline *n* compagnia *f* aerea
airliner *n* aereo *m* di linea
airlock *n* bolla *f* d'aria
airmail *n* posta *f* aerea
air marshal *n* BrE maresciallo *m* d'aviazione
Air Miles® *npl* BrE miglia *fpl* aeree
airplane *n* AmE aereo *m*
air pocket *n* vuoto *m* d'aria
🔑 **airport** *n* aeroporto *m*
air power *n* potenza *f* aerea
air raid *n* incursione *f* aerea
air-raid shelter *n* rifugio *m* antiaereo
air-raid siren *n* allarme *m* aereo
air-raid warning *n* allarme *m* aereo
air rifle *n* fucile *m* ad aria compressa
air-sea rescue *n salvataggio (m) dal mare con impiego di mezzi aerei*

🔑 parola chiave

air shaft *n* (in mine) pozzo *m* di ventilazione
airship *n* dirigibile *m*
air show *n* (trade exhibition) salone *m* dell'aviazione; (flying show) manifestazione *f* aerea
airsickness *n* mal *m* d'aereo
air sock *n* manica *f* a vento
airspeed *n* velocità *f* relativa all'aria
airspeed indicator *n* indicatore *m* di velocità (*su un aereo*)
air steward *n* steward *m inv*
air stewardess *n* hostess *f inv*
airstream *n* corrente *f* d'aria
air strike *n* incursione *f* aerea
airstrip *n* pista *f* d'atterraggio
air terminal *n* (in town, terminus) [air-]terminal *m inv*
airtight *adj* ermetico
airtime *n* Radio, TV spazio *m* radiofonico/televisivo
air-to-air *adj* ‹*missile*› aria-aria; ‹*refuelling*› in volo
air traffic *n* traffico *m* aereo
air traffic controller *n* controllore *m* di volo
air travel *n* viaggi *mpl* in aereo
air valve *n* valvola *f* pneumatica
air vent *n* presa *f* d'aria
air vice-marshal *n* BrE vice-maresciallo *m* dell'aviazione
air war *n* conflitto *m* aereo
airwaves *npl* Radio, TV onde *fpl* radio
airway *n* (route) rotta *f* aerea; (airline) compagnia *f* aerea; Anat via *f* respiratoria; (ventilating passage) pozzo *m* di ventilazione
air waybill *n* polizza *f* di carico aerea
airworthiness *n* idoneità *f* di volo
airworthy *adj* idoneo al volo
airy /'eərɪ/ *adj* (**-ier**, **-iest**) arieggiato; ‹*manner*› noncurante
airy-fairy /eərɪ'feərɪ/ *adj* BrE infml ‹*plan, person*› fuori dalla realtà
aisle /aɪl/ *n* corridoio *m*; (in supermarket) corsia *f*; (in church) navata *f*
ajar /ə'dʒɑː(r)/ *adj* socchiuso
aka *abbr* (**also known as**) alias
akin /ə'kɪn/ *adj* **~ to** simile a
AI *n abbr* (**artificial intelligence**) I.A. *f*
alabaster /'æləbɑːstə(r)/ *n* alabastro *m*
alacrity /ə'lækrətɪ/ *n* alacrità *f*
alarm /ə'lɑːm/ **A** *n* allarme *m*; **set the ~** (of alarm clock) mettere la sveglia; **in ~** in stato di allarme
B *vt* allarmare; **don't be ~ed!** non si allarmi!
alarm bell *n* campanello *m* d'allarme; **set the ~s ringing** *n* BrE fig far scattare il campanello d'allarme
alarm call *n* Teleph sveglia *f* automatica

alarm clock *n* sveglia *f*

alarmed /əˈlɑːmd/ *adj* allarmato

alarming /əˈlɑːmɪŋ/ *adj* allarmante, preoccupante

alarmist /əˈlɑːmɪst/ *adj & n* allarmista *mf*

alas /əˈlæs/ *int* ahimè

Albania /ælˈbeɪnɪə/ *n* Albania *f*

Albanian /ælˈbeɪnɪən/ **A** *n* (person) albanese *mf*; (language) albanese *m*
B *adj* albanese

albatross /ˈælbətrɒs/ *n* (also in golf) albatro *m*

albeit /ɔːlˈbiːɪt/ *adv & conj* benché

albino /ælˈbiːnəʊ/ *adj & n* albino, -a *mf*

album /ˈælbəm/ *n* album *m inv*

albumen /ˈælbjʊmɪn/ *n* Biol, Bot albume *m*

alchemist /ˈælkɪmɪʃt/ *n* alchimista *m*

alchemy /ˈælkɪmɪ/ *n* Chem, fig alchimia *f*

alcohol /ˈælkəhɒl/ *n* alcol *m*

alcoholic /ælkəˈhɒlɪk/ **A** *adj* alcolico
B *n* alcolizzato, -a *mf*

Alcoholics Anonymous *n* Anonima *f* Alcolisti

alcoholism /ˈælkəhɒlɪzm/ *n* alcolismo *m*

alcohol-related *adj* ‹*illness, disease*› legato al consumo di alcol

alcopop /ˈælkəʊpɒp/ *n* bibita *f* alcolica

alcove /ˈælkəʊv/ *n* alcova *f*

alder /ɔːldə(r)/ *n* (tree, wood) ontano *m*

ale /eɪl/ *n* birra *f*

alert /əˈlɜːt/ **A** *adj* attento; (watchful) vigile
B *n* segnale *m* d'allarme; **be on the ~** stare allerta
C *vt* allertare

alertness /əˈlɜːtnɪs/ *n* (attentiveness) attenzione *f*; (liveliness) vivacità *f*

A level *n* BrE Sch **~s** ≈ esami *mpl* di maturità; **he got an ~ in history** ha portato storia alla maturità

Alexandria /ælɪgˈzændrɪə/ *n* Alessandria *f* [d'Egitto]

alfalfa /ælˈfælfə/ *n* erba *f* medicinale

alfresco /ælˈfreskəʊ/ *adj & adv* all'aperto

algae /ˈældʒiː/ *npl* alghe *fpl*

algebra /ˈældʒɪbrə/ *n* algebra *f*

Algeria /ælˈdʒɪərɪə/ *n* Algeria *f*

Algerian /ælˈdʒɪərɪən/ *adj & n* algerino, -a *mf*

Algiers /ælˈdʒɪəz/ *n* Algeri *f*

algorithm /ˈælgərɪðm/ *n* algoritmo *m*

alias /ˈeɪlɪəs/ **A** *n* pseudonimo *m*
B *adv* alias

alibi /ˈælɪbaɪ/ *n* alibi *m inv*

alien /ˈeɪlɪən/ **A** *adj* straniero; fig estraneo
B *n* straniero, -a *mf*; (from space) alieno, -a *mf*

alienate /ˈeɪlɪəneɪt/ *vt* alienare

alienation /eɪlɪəˈneɪʃn/ *n* alienazione *f*

alight¹ /əˈlaɪt/ *vi* scendere; ‹*bird*› posarsi

alight² *adj* **be ~** essere in fiamme; **set ~** dar fuoco a

align /əˈlaɪn/ *vt* allineare

alignment /əˈlaɪnmənt/ *n* allineamento *m*; **out of ~** non allineato

alike /əˈlaɪk/ **A** *adj* simile; **be ~** rassomigliarsi
B *adv* in modo simile; **look ~** rassomigliarsi; **summer and winter ~** sia d'estate che d'inverno

alimentary /ælɪˈmentərɪ/ *adj* ‹*system*› digerente; ‹*process*› digestivo

alimentary canal *n* tubo *m* digerente

alimony /ˈælɪmənɪ/ *n* alimenti *mpl*

alive /əˈlaɪv/ *adj* vivo; **~ with** brulicante di; **~ to** sensibile a; **~ and kicking** vivo e vegeto

alkali /ˈælkəlaɪ/ *n* alcali *m*

alkaline /ˈælkəlaɪn/ *adj* alcalino

all /ɔːl/ **A** *adj* tutto; **~ the children, ~ children** tutti i bambini; **~ day** tutto il giorno; **he refused ~ help** ha rifiutato qualsiasi aiuto; **for ~ that** (nevertheless) perciò; **in ~ sincerity** in tutta sincerità; **be ~ for** essere favorevole a
B *pron* tutto; **~ of you/them** tutti voi/loro; **~ of it** tutto; **~ of the town** tutta la città; **~ but one** tutti tranne uno; **in ~** in tutto; **~ in ~** tutto sommato; **most of ~** più di ogni altra cosa; **once and for ~** una volta per tutte; **~ being well** salvo complicazioni
C *adv* completamente; **~ but** quasi; **~ at once** (at the same time) tutto in una volta; **~ at once, ~ of a sudden** all'improvviso; **~ too soon** troppo presto; **~ the same** (nevertheless) ciononostante; **~ the better** meglio ancora; **she's not ~ that good an actress** non è poi così brava come attrice; **~ in** in tutto; infml esausto; **thirty/three ~** (in sport) trenta/tre pari; **~ over** (finished) tutto finito; (everywhere) dappertutto; **it's ~ right** (I don't mind) non fa niente; **I'm ~ right** (not hurt) non ho niente; **~ right!** va bene!; **be ~ that** infml esp Am essere in gamba

all-American *adj* ‹*record, champion*› americano; ‹*girl, boy, hero*› tipicamente americano

all-around *adj* AmE ‹*improvement*› generale

allay /əˈleɪ/ *vt* placare ‹*suspicions, anger*›

all-clear *n* Mil cessato *m* allarme/pericolo; (from doctor) autorizzazione *f*; **give somebody the ~** fig dare il via libera a qualcuno

all-consuming *adj* ‹*passion*› sfrenato; ‹*ambition*› smisurato

all-day *adj* ‹*event*› che dura tutto il giorno

allegation /ælɪˈgeɪʃn/ *n* accusa *f*

allege /əˈledʒ/ *vt* dichiarare

alleged /əˈledʒd/ *adj* presunto

allegedly /əˈledʒɪdlɪ/ *adv* a quanto si dice

allegiance /əˈliːdʒəns/ *n* fedeltà *f*

allegorical /ælɪˈgɒrɪkl/ *adj* allegorico

allegory /ˈælɪgəri/ *n* allegoria *f*

all-embracing /-əmˈbreɪsɪŋ/ *adj* globale

allergic /əˈlɜːdʒɪk/ *adj* allergico

allergist /ˈælədʒɪst/ *n* allergologo, -a *mf*

allergy /ˈælədʒɪ/ *n* allergia *f*

allergy clinic *n* clinica *f* di allergologia

alleviate /əˈliːvɪeɪt/ *vt* alleviare

alleviation /əliːvɪˈeɪʃn/ *n* alleviamento *m*, alleggerimento *m*

alley /ˈælɪ/ *n* vicolo *m*; (for bowling) corsia *f*

alleyway /ˈælɪweɪ/ *n* vicolo *m*

all found *adj* **£200 ~** 200 sterline inclusi vitto e alloggio

alliance /əˈlaɪəns/ *n* alleanza *f*

allied /ˈælaɪd/ *adj* alleato; fig (related) connesso (**to** a)

alligator /ˈælɪgeɪtə(r)/ *n* alligatore *m*

all-important *adj* essenziale

all in *adj* BrE infml (exhausted) distrutto; ‹*fee, price*› tutto compreso

all-inclusive *adj* (fee, price) tutto compreso

all-in-one *adj* ‹*garment*› in un pezzo solo

all-in wresting *n* Sport catch *m*

all-night *adj* ‹*party, meeting*› che dura tutta la notte; ‹*radio station*› che trasmette tutta la notte; ‹*service*› notturno

allocate /ˈæləkeɪt/ *vt* assegnare; distribuire ‹*resources*›

allocation /æləˈkeɪʃn/ *n* assegnazione *f*; (of resources) distribuzione *f*

all-or-nothing *adj* ‹*approach, policy*› senza vie di mezzo

allot /əˈlɒt/ *vt* (*pt/pp* **allotted**) distribuire

allotment /əˈlɒtmənt/ *n* distribuzione *f*; (share) parte *f*; (land) piccolo lotto *m* di terreno

all-out **A** *adj* ‹*effort*› estremo; ‹*attack*› senza esclusione di colpi
B *adv* **go all out to do something/for something** mettercela tutta per fare qualcosa/per qualcosa

all over **A** *prep* **~ China** in/per tutta la Cina; **the news is ~ the village** lo sanno tutti in paese; **be ~ somebody** (fawning over) stare appiccicato a qualcuno
B *adv* **be trembling ~** tremare tutto; **that's Mary ~!** è proprio da Mary!
C *adj* **when it's ~** (finished) quando è tutto finito

all-over *adj* ‹*tan*› integrale

⚷ **allow** /əˈlaʊ/ *vt* permettere; (grant) accordare; (reckon on) contare; (agree) ammettere; **~ somebody to do something** permettere a qualcuno di fare qualcosa; **you are not ~ed to...** è vietato...; **how much are you ~ed?** qual è il limite?
▪ **allow for** *vt* tener conto di

allowable /əˈlaʊəbl/ *adj* permissibile; Jur lecito; ‹*tax*› deducibile

allowance /əˈlaʊəns/ *n* sussidio *m*; AmE (pocket money) paghetta *f*; (for petrol etc) indennità *f*; (of luggage, duty free) limite *m*; (for tax purposes) deduzione *f*; **make ~s for** essere indulgente verso ‹*somebody*›; tener conto di ‹*something*›

alloy /ˈælɔɪ/ *n* lega *f*

alloy steel *n* lega *f* d'acciaio

alloy wheel *n* cerchione *m* in lega d'acciaio

all points bulletin *n* AmE allarme *m* generale

all-powerful *adj* onnipotente

all-purpose *adj* ‹*building*› polivalente; ‹*utensil*› multiuso

all right **A** *adj* **is it ~ if...?** va bene se...?; **is that ~ with you?** ti va bene?; **sounds ~ to me** per me va bene; **that's [quite] ~** (it doesn't matter) non c'è problema; **is my hair ~?** sono a posto i miei capelli?; **it's ~ for you!** è facile per te!; **she's ~** (competent) è abbastanza brava; (attractive) non è niente male; (pleasant) è piuttosto simpatica; **will you be ~?** (able to manage) te la caverai?; **feel ~** (well) sentirsi bene
B *adv* ‹*function, see*› bene; (not brilliantly) così così; **can I? - ~** posso? - d'accordo; **she's doing ~** (in life) le cose le vanno bene; (in health) sta bene; (in activity) se la cava bene; **she knows ~!** (without doubt) lei lo sa di sicuro!; **~, ~!** va bene! va bene!

all risk *adj* ‹*policy, cover*› multirischi

all-round BrE **all-around** AmE *adj* ‹*improvement*› generale; ‹*athlete*› completo

all-rounder /-ˈraʊndə(r)/ *n* **be a good ~** essere versatile

allspice /ˈɔːlspaɪs/ *n* pepe *m* della Giamaica

all square *adj* **be ~** ‹*people*› essere pari; ‹*accounts*› quadrare

all-time *adj* ‹*record*› assoluto, senza precedenti; **the ~ greats** (people) i grandi; **~ high** massimo *m* storico; **be at an ~ low** ‹*person, morale*› essere a terra; ‹*figures, shares*› toccare il minimo storico

all told *adv* tutto sommato

allude /əˈluːd/ *vi* alludere

allure /æˈljʊə(r)/ *n* attrattiva *f*

alluring /əˈljʊrɪŋ/ *adj* allettante, affascinante

allusion /əˈluːʒn/ *n* allusione *f*

ally[1] /ˈælaɪ/ *n* alleato, -a *mf*

ally[2] /əˈlaɪ/ *vt* (*pt/pp* **-ied**) alleare; **~ oneself with** allearsi con

almighty /ɔːlˈmaɪtɪ/ **A** *adj* infml (big) mega *inv*
B *n* **the A~** l'Onnipotente *m*

almond /ˈɑːmənd/ *n* mandorla *f*; (tree) mandorlo *m*

⚷ **almost** /ˈɔːlməʊst/ *adv* quasi

alms /ɑːmz/ *npl* literary elemosina *fsg*

aloft /əˈlɒft/ *adv* in alto; Naut sull'alberatura; **from ~** dall'alto

⚷ **alone** /əˈləʊn/ **A** *adj* solo; **leave me ~!**

⚷ parola chiave

lasciami in pace!; **let ~** (not to mention) figurarsi
B *adv* da solo

⚷ **along** /ə'lɒŋ/ **A** *prep* lungo
B *adv* **~ with** assieme a; **all ~** tutto il tempo; **come ~!** (hurry up) vieni qui!; **I'll bring it ~** lo porto lì; **I'll be ~ in a minute** arrivo tra un attimo; **move ~** spostarsi; **move ~!** circolare!

alongside /əlɒŋ'saɪd/ **A** *adv* lungo bordo
B *prep* lungo; **work ~ somebody** lavorare fianco a fianco con qualcuno

aloof /ə'lu:f/ *adj* distante

aloud /ə'laʊd/ *adv* ad alta voce

alpaca /æl'pækə/ *n* alpaca *m inv*

alpha /'ælfə/ *n* (letter) alfa *f inv*; BrE Univ ≈ trenta *m inv* e lode

alphabet /'ælfəbet/ *n* alfabeto *m*

alphabetical /ælfə'betɪkl/ *adj* alfabetico

alphabetically /ælfə'betɪklɪ/ *adv* in ordine alfabetico

alpha male *n* maschio *m* dominante

alpine /'ælpaɪn/ *adj* alpino

Alps /ælps/ *npl* Alpi *fpl*

⚷ **already** /ɔ:l'redɪ/ *adv* già

alright /ɔ:l'raɪt/ = **all right**

Alsace /æl'zæs/ *n* Alsazia *f*

Alsatian /æl'seɪʃn/ *n* (dog) pastore *m* tedesco

⚷ **also** /'ɔ:lsəʊ/ *adv* anche; **~, I need...** inoltre, ho bisogno di...

altar /'ɔ:ltə(r)/ *n* altare *m*

altar boy *n* chierichetto *m*

altar cloth *n* tovaglia *f* da altare

altar piece *n* pala *f* d'altare

alter /'ɔ:ltə(r)/ **A** *vt* cambiare; aggiustare ‹*clothes*›
B *vi* cambiare

alteration /ɔ:ltə'reɪʃn/ *n* modifica *f*

altercation /ɔ:ltə'keɪʃn/ *n* alterco *m*

alternate¹ /'ɔ:ltəneɪt/ **A** *vi* alternarsi
B *vt* alternare

alternate² /ɔ:l'tɜ:nət/ *adj* alterno; **on ~ days** a giorni alterni

alternately /ɔ:l'tɜ:nətlɪ/ *adv* in modo alterno; AmE (alternatively) alternativamente

alternating current /'ɔ:ltəneɪtɪŋ/ *n* corrente *f* alternata

alternation /ɔ:ltə'neɪʃn/ *n* alternanza *f*

⚷ **alternative** /ɔ:l'tɜ:nətɪv/ **A** *adj* alternativo
B *n* alternativa *f*

alternative energy *n* energia *f* alternativa

alternatively /ɔ:l'tɜ:nətɪvlɪ/ *adv* alternativamente

alternative medicine *n* medicina *f* alternativa

alternative technology *n* tecnologia *f* alternativa

alternative vote *n* voto *m* alternativo

alternator /'ɔ:ltəneɪtə(r)/ *n* Electr alternatore *m*

⚷ **although** /ɔ:l'ðəʊ/ *conj* benché, sebbene

altimeter /'æltɪmi:tə(r)/ *n* altimetro *m*

altitude /'æltɪtju:d/ *n* altitudine *f*

Alt key *n* Comput tasto *m* Alt

alto /'æltəʊ/ *n* contralto *m*

altogether /ɔ:ltə'geðə(r)/ *adv* (in all) in tutto; (completely) completamente; **I'm not ~ sure** non sono del tutto sicuro

altruism /'æltrʊɪzm/ *n* altruismo *m*

altruistic /æltrʊ'ɪstɪk/ *adj* altruistico

aluminium /æljʊ'mɪnɪəm/ BrE, **aluminum** AmE /ə'lu:mɪnəm/ *n* alluminio *m*

aluminium foil *n* carta *f* stagnola

alumna /ə'lʌmnə/ *n* AmE Sch, Univ ex allieva *f*

alumnus /ə'lʌmnəs/ *n* AmE Sch, Univ ex allievo *m*

⚷ **always** /'ɔ:lweɪz/ *adv* sempre

Alzheimer's disease /'æltshaɪməz/ *n* morbo *m* di Alzheimer

am /æm/ ▶ **be**

a.m. *abbr* (**ante meridiem**) del mattino

amalgam /ə'mælgəm/ *n* amalgama *m*

amalgamate /ə'mælgəmeɪt/ **A** *vt* fondere
B *vi* fondersi

amalgamation /əmælgə'meɪʃn/ *n* fusione *f*; (of styles) amalgama *m*

amass /ə'mæs/ *vt* accumulare

amateur /'æmətə(r)/ **A** *n* non professionista *mf*; derog dilettante *mf*
B *attrib* dilettante; **~ dramatics** filodrammatica *f*

amateurish /'æmətərɪʃ/ *adj* dilettantesco

amaze /ə'meɪz/ *vt* stupire

amazed /ə'meɪzd/ *adj* stupito

amazement /ə'meɪzmənt/ *n* stupore *m*; **to her ~** con suo grande stupore; **in ~** stupito

⚷ **amazing** /ə'meɪzɪŋ/ *adj* incredibile

amazingly /ə'meɪzɪŋlɪ/ *adv* incredibilmente

Amazon /'æməzən/ **A** *n* (in myths) Amazzone *f*; fig (strong woman) amazzone *f*; (river) Rio *m* delle Amazzoni
B *attrib* ‹*basin, forest, tribe*› amazzonico

ambassador /æm'bæsədə(r)/ *n* ambasciatore, -trice *mf*

ambassador-at-large *n* AmE ambasciatore, -trice *mf* a disposizione

amber /'æmbə(r)/ **A** *n* ambra *f*
B *adj* (colour) ambra *inv*

ambidextrous /æmbɪ'dekstrəs/ *adj* ambidestro

ambience /'æmbɪəns/ *n* atmosfera *f*

ambient /'æmbɪənt/ *adj* ‹*temperature*› ambiente *inv*; ‹*noise*› circostante

ambiguity /æmbɪ'gju:ətɪ/ *n* ambiguità *f*

ambiguous /æm'bɪgjʊəs/ *adj* ambiguo

ambiguously /æm'bɪgjʊəslɪ/ *adv* in modo ambiguo

a

ambition /æm'bɪʃn/ *n* ambizione *f*; (aim) aspirazione *f*
ambitious /æm'bɪʃəs/ *adj* ambizioso
ambivalence /æm'bɪvələns/ *n* ambivalenza *f*
ambivalent /æm'bɪvələnt/ *adj* ambivalente
amble /'æmb(ə)l/ *vi* camminare senza fretta
ambulance /æmbjʊləns/ *n* ambulanza *f*
ambulance man *n* guidatore *m* di ambulanze
ambush /'æmbʊʃ/ **A** *n* imboscata *f*
B *vt* tendere un'imboscata a
ameba /ə'mi:bə/ *n* AmE **amoeba**
amen /ɑ:'men/ *int* amen
amenability /əmi:nə'bɪlɪtɪ/ *n* arrendevolezza *f*
amenable /ə'mi:nəbl/ *adj* conciliante; ~ **to** sensibile a
amend /ə'mend/ **A** *vt* modificare
B *npl* **make ~s** fare ammenda (**for** di, per)
amendment /ə'mendmənt/ *n* modifica *f*
amenities /ə'mi:nətɪz/ *npl* comodità *fpl*
America /ə'merɪkə/ *n* America *f*
🔑 **American** /ə'merɪkən/ *adj & n* americano, -a *mf*
American Civil War *n* guerra *f* di secessione [americana]
American English *n* inglese *m* americano
American Indian *n* indiano, -a *mf* d'America
Americanism /ə'merɪkənɪzm/ *n* americanismo *m*
amethyst /'æməθɪst/ *n* (gem) ametista *f*
Amex /'æmeks/ *n abbr* **1** (**American Stock Exchange**) Borsa *f* valori americana **2** (**American Express**)
amiable /'eɪmɪəbl/ *adj* amabile
amicable /'æmɪkəbl/ *adj* amichevole
amicably /'æmɪkəblɪ/ *adv* amichevolmente
amid /ə'mɪd/, **amidst** /ə'mɪd[st]/ *prep* in mezzo a
amino acid /ə'mi:nəʊ/ *n* amminoacido *m*
amiss /ə'mɪs/ **A** *adj* **there's something ~** c'è qualcosa che non va
B *adv* **take something ~** prendersela [a male]; **it won't come ~** non sarebbe sgradito
ammo /'æməʊ/ *n abbr* (**ammunition**) munizioni *fpl*
ammonia /ə'məʊnɪə/ *n* ammoniaca *f*
ammunition /æmjʊ'nɪʃn/ *n* munizioni *fpl*
amnesia /æm'ni:zɪə/ *n* amnesia *f*
amnesty /'æmnəstɪ/ *n* amnistia *f*
amoeba /ə'mi:bə/ *n* ameba *f*
amoebic /ə'mi:bɪk/ *adj* ‹*dysentery*› amebico
amok /ə'mɒk/ *adv* **run ~** essere in preda a furore; ‹*imagination*› scatenarsi
among /ə'mʌŋ/, **amongst** /ə'mʌŋst/ *prep* tra, fra; **talk ~ yourselves** parlate tra [di] voi
amoral /eɪ'mɒrəl/ *adj* amorale
amorality /eɪmə'rælətɪ/ *n* amoralità *f*
amorous /'æmərəs/ *adj* amoroso
amorphous /ə'mɔ:fəs/ *adj* Chem amorfo; ‹*ideas, plans*› confuso; ‹*shape, collection*› informe
🔑 **amount** /ə'maʊnt/ **A** *n* quantità *f*; (sum of money) ammontare *m*
B *v*
■ **amount to** *vt* ammontare a; fig equivalere a
amp /æmp/ *n* ampere *m inv*
ampere /'æmpeə(r)/ *n* ampere *m inv*
ampersand /'æmpəsænd/ *n* e *f inv* commerciale
amphetamine /æm'fetəmi:n/ *n* anfetamina *f*
amphibian /æm'fɪbɪən/ *n* anfibio *m*
amphibious /æm'fɪbɪəs/ *adj* anfibio
amphitheatre /'æmfɪθɪ:ətə(r)/ *n* anfiteatro *m*
ample /'æmpl/ *adj* (large) grande; ‹*proportions*› ampio; (enough) largamente sufficiente
amplifier /'æmplɪfaɪə(r)/ *n* amplificatore *m*
amplify /'æmplɪfaɪ/ *vt* (*pt/pp* **-ied**) amplificare ‹*sound*›
amply /'æmplɪ/ *adv* largamente
amputate /'æmpjʊteɪt/ *vt* amputare
amputation /æmpjʊ'teɪʃn/ *n* amputazione *f*
amputee /æmpjʊ'ti:/ *n* mutilato, -a *mf* (*in seguito ad amputazione*)
amuse /ə'mju:z/ *vt* divertire
amused /ə'mju:zd/ *adj* divertito
amusement /ə'mju:zmənt/ *n* divertimento *m*
amusement arcade *n* sala *f* giochi
amusement park *n* luna park *m inv*
amusing /ə'mju:zɪŋ/ *adj* divertente
an /ən/, *accentato*/æn/ ▶ **a¹**
anabolic steroid /ænə'bɒlɪk/ *n* anabolizzante *m*
anachronism /ə'nækrənɪzm/ *n* **be an ~** ‹*object, custom etc*› essere anacronistico
anaemia /ə'ni:mɪə/ *n* anemia *f*
anaemic /ə'ni:mɪk/ *adj* anemico
anaerobic /æneə'rəʊbɪk/ *adj* anerobico
anaesthesia /ænəs'θi:zɪə/ *n* anestesia *f*
anaesthetic /ænəs'θetɪk/ *n* anestesia *f*; **give somebody an ~** somministrare a qualcuno l'anestesia
anaesthetist /ə'ni:sθətɪst/ *n* anestesista *mf*
anaesthetize /ə'ni:sθətaɪz/ *vt* anestetizzare
anagram /'ænəgræm/ *n* anagramma *m*
analgesic /ænəl'dʒi:zɪk/ *adj & n* analgesico *m*
analogous /ə'næləgəs/ *adj* analogo
analogue /'ænəlɒg/ *adj* analogico
analogy /ə'nælədʒɪ/ *n* analogia *f*
🔑 **analyse** /'ænəlaɪz/ *vt* analizzare
🔑 **analysis** /ə'næləsɪs/ *n* analisi *f inv*
analyst /'ænəlɪst/ *n* analista *mf*
analytical /ænə'lɪtɪkl/ *adj* analitico

🔑 parola chiave

anaphylaxis, anaphylactic shock /ˌænəfɪˈlæksɪs/ *n* anafilassi *f*, shock *m* anafilattico
anarchic /əˈnɑːkɪk/, **anarchical** /əˈnɑːkɪkl/ *adj* anarchico
anarchist /ˈænəkɪst/ *n* anarchico, -a *mf*
anarchy /ˈænəkɪ/ *n* anarchia *f*
anathema /əˈnæθəmə/ *n* eresia *f*
anatomical /ænəˈtɒmɪkl/ *adj* anatomico
anatomically /ænəˈtɒmɪklɪ/ *adv* anatomicamente
anatomy /əˈnætəmɪ/ *n* anatomia *f*
ANC *n abbr* (**African National Congress**) Congresso *m* Nazionale Africano
ancestor /ˈænsestə(r)/ *n* antenato, -a *mf*
ancestral /ænˈsestrəl/ *adj* ancestrale; ‹*home*› avito
ancestry /ˈænsestrɪ/ *n* antenati *mpl*
anchor /ˈæŋkə(r)/ **A** *n* ancora *f* **B** *vi* gettare l'ancora **C** *vt* ancorare
anchorage /ˈæŋkərɪdʒ/ *n* ancoraggio *m*
anchorman /ˈæŋkəmæn/ *n* Radio, TV anchor man *m inv*; Sport staffettista *m* dell'ultima frazione
anchorwoman /ˈæŋkəwʊmən/ *n* Radio, TV anchor woman *f inv*
anchovy /ˈæntʃəvɪ/ *n* acciuga *f*
ancient /ˈeɪnʃənt/ *adj* antico; infml vecchio; **~ Rome** l'antica Roma *f*
ancillary /ænˈsɪlərɪ/ *adj* ausiliario
and /ənd/, *accentato* /ænd/ *conj* e; **~ so on** e così via; **two ~ two** due più due; **six hundred ~ two** seicentodue; **more ~ more** sempre più; **nice ~ warm** bello caldo; **try ~ come** cerca di venire; **go ~ get** vai a prendere
Andean /ˈændɪən/ *adj* andino
Andes /ˈændiːz/ *npl* **the ~** le Ande
Andorra /ænˈdɔːrə/ *n* Andorra *f*
anecdote /ˈænɪkdəʊt/ *n* aneddoto *m*
anemone /əˈnemənɪ/ *n* Bot anemone *m*
anew /əˈnjuː/ *adv* di nuovo
angel /ˈeɪndʒl/ *n* angelo *m*
angel cake *n* dolce *m* di pan di Spagna
angelfish /ˈeɪndʒlfɪʃ/ *n* angelo *m* di mare
angelic /ænˈdʒelɪk/ *adj* angelico
anger /ˈæŋgə(r)/ **A** *n* rabbia *f* **B** *vt* far arrabbiare
angina /ænˈdʒaɪnə/, **angina pectoris** /ænˈdʒaɪnəˈpektərɪs/ *n* angina *f* pectoris
angle¹ /ˈæŋgl/ *n* angolo *m*; fig angolazione *f*; **at an ~** storto
angle² *vi* pescare con la lenza; **~ for** fig cercare di ottenere
angle bracket *n* Techn parentesi *f inv* uncinata
Anglepoise /ˈæŋglpɔɪz/, **Anglepoise lamp** *n* lampada *f* a braccio estensibile
angler /ˈæŋglə(r)/ *n* pescatore, -trice *mf*
Anglican /ˈæŋglɪkən/ *adj & n* anglicano, -a *mf*
Anglicism /ˈæŋglɪsɪzm/ *n* anglicismo *m*
anglicize /ˈæŋglɪsaɪz/ *vt* anglicizzare
angling /ˈæŋglɪŋ/ *n* pesca *f* con la lenza
Anglo+ /ˈæŋgləʊ/ *pref* anglo+
Anglo-American *adj & n* angloamericano, -a *mf*
Anglophone /ˈæŋgləfəʊn/ *adj & n* anglofono, -a *mf*
Anglo-Saxon /æŋgləʊˈsæksn/ *adj & n* anglosassone *mf*
Angola /æŋˈgəʊlə/ *n* Angola *f*
angora /ænˈgɔːrə/ *n* lana *f* d'angora
angrily /ˈæŋgrɪlɪ/ *adv* rabbiosamente
angry /ˈæŋgrɪ/ *adj* (**-ier, -iest**) arrabbiato; **get ~** arrabbiarsi; **~ with** *or* **at somebody** arrabbiato con qualcuno; **~ at** *or* **about something** arrabbiato per qualcosa
anguish /ˈæŋgwɪʃ/ *n* angoscia *f*; **in ~** in preda all'angoscia
anguished /ˈæŋgwɪʃt/ *adj* (suffering) straziante; ‹*person*› angosciato
angular /ˈæŋgjʊlə(r)/ *adj* angolare
animal /ˈænɪm(ə)l/ *adj & n* animale *m*
animal experiment *n* esperimento *m* sugli animali
animal husbandry /ˈhʌzbəndrɪ/ *n* allevamento *m*
animal kingdom *n* regno *m* animale
animal lover *n* amante *mf* degli animali
animal product *n* prodotto *m* di origine animale
animal rights *npl* diritti *mpl* degli animali
animal rights activist *n* animalista *mf*
animal sanctuary *n* rifugio *m* per animali
animal testing *n* sperimentazione *f* sugli animali
animate¹ /ˈænɪmət/ *adj* animato
animate² /ˈænɪmeɪt/ *vt* animare
animated /ˈænɪmeɪtɪd/ *adj* animato; ‹*person*› vivace
animation /ænɪˈmeɪʃn/ *n* animazione *f*
animator /ˈænɪmeɪtə(r)/ *n* (film cartoonist) animatore, -trice *mf*; (director) regista *mf* di film d'animazione
animatronics /ænɪməˈtrɒnɪks/ *nsg* animazione *fsg* elettronica
animosity /ænɪˈmɒsətɪ/ *n* animosità *f*
aniseed /ˈænɪsiːd/ *n* anice *f*
ankle /ˈæŋk(ə)l/ *n* caviglia *f*
anklebone *n* astragalo *m*
ankle-deep *adj* **be ~ in mud** *adj* essere nel fango fino alle caviglie
ankle-length *adj* (dress) alla caviglia
ankle sock *n* calzino *m*
annals /ˈænəlz/ *npl* **go down in the ~ [of history]** passare agli annali
annex /əˈneks/ **A** *vt* annettere

B **annexe** *n* annesso *m*
annex[e] /'æneks/ *n* annesso *m*
annexation /ænek'seɪʃn/ *n* (action) annessione *f*; (land annexed) territorio *m* annesso
annihilate /ə'naɪəleɪt/ *vt* annientare
annihilation /ənaɪə'leɪʃn/ *n* annientamento *m*
anniversary /ænɪ'vɜːsərɪ/ *n* anniversario *m*
Anno Domini /ænəʊ'dɒmɪnaɪ/ *adv* dopo Cristo
annotate /'ænəteɪt/ *vt* annotare
⚷ **announce** /ə'naʊns/ *vt* annunciare
announcement /ə'naʊnsmənt/ *n* annuncio *m*
announcer /ə'naʊnsə(r)/ *n* annunciatore, -trice *mf*
annoy /ə'nɔɪ/ *vt* dare fastidio a
annoyance /ə'nɔɪəns/ *n* seccatura *f*; (anger) irritazione *f*
annoyed /ə'nɔɪd/ *adj* irritato; **get ~** irritarsi; **~ with somebody** irritato con qualcuno; **~ at/about something** irritato per qualcosa; **~ that** irritato che
annoying /ə'nɔɪɪŋ/ *adj* fastidioso
⚷ **annual** /'ænjʊəl/ **A** *adj* annuale; ‹*income*› annuo
B *n* Bot pianta *f* annua; (children's book) almanacco *m*
Annual General Meeting *n* assemblea *f* generale annuale
annually /'ænjʊəlɪ/ *adv* annualmente; **she earns £50,000~** guadagna 50.000 sterline all'anno
annual report *n* resoconto *m* annuale
annuity /ə'njuːətɪ/ *n* annualità *f*
annul /ə'nʌl/ *vt* (*pt/pp* **annulled**) annullare
Annunciation /ənʌnsɪ'eɪʃn/ *n* Annunciazione *f*
anode /'ænəʊd/ *n* anodo *m*
anodyne /'ænədaɪn/ *adj* literary (bland) anodino; (inoffensive) innocuo
anoint /ə'nɔɪnt/ *vt* ungere
anomalous /ə'nɒmələs/ *adj* anomalo
anomaly /ə'nɒməlɪ/ *n* anomalia *f*
anon /ə'nɒn/ *abbr* (**anonymous**) anonimo
anonymity /ænə'nɪmətɪ/ *n* anonimità *f*
anonymous /ə'nɒnɪməs/ *adj* anonimo; **remain ~** mantenere l'anonimato
anonymously /ə'nɒnɪməslɪ/ *adv* anonimamente
anorak /'ænəræk/ *n* giacca *f* a vento
anorexia /ænə'reksɪə/ *n* anoressia *f*
anorexic /ænə'reksɪk/ *adj & n* anoressico, -a *mf*
⚷ **another** /ə'nʌðə(r)/ *adj & pron* **~ [one]** un altro, un'altra; **~ day** un altro giorno; **in ~ way** diversamente; **~ time** un'altra volta; **one ~** l'un l'altro
⚷ **answer** /'ɑːnsə(r)/ **A** *n* risposta *f*; (solution) soluzione *f*
B *vt* rispondere a ‹*person, question, letter*›; esaudire ‹*prayer*›; **~ the door** aprire la porta; **~ the telephone** rispondere al telefono
C *vi* rispondere
▪ **answer back** *vi* ribattere
▪ **answer for** *vt* rispondere di
answerable /'ɑːnsərəbl/ *adj* responsabile; **be ~ to somebody** rispondere a qualcuno
answering machine *n* Teleph segreteria *f* telefonica
answering service *n* servizio *m* di segreteria telefonica
answerphone /'ɑːnsəfəʊn/ *n* segreteria *f* telefonica
ant /ænt/ *n* formica *f*
antacid /ænt'æsɪd/ *adj & n* antiacido *m*
antagonism /æn'tægənɪzm/ *n* antagonismo *m*
antagonistic /æntægə'nɪstɪk/ *adj* antagonistico
antagonize /æn'tægənaɪz/ *vt* provocare l'ostilità di
Antarctic /æn'tɑːktɪk/ **A** *n* Antartico *m*
B *adj* antartico
Antarctica /æn'tɑːktɪkə/ *n* Antartide *f*
Antarctic Circle *n* Circolo *m* polare antartico
Antarctic Ocean *n* mare *m* antartico
anteater /'æntiːtə(r)/ *n* formichiere *m*
antecedent /æntɪ'siːdənt/ *n* (precedent) antecedente *m*; (ancestor) antenato, -a *mf*
antedate /æntɪ'deɪt/ *vt* (put earlier date on) retrodatare; (predate) precedere
antediluvian /æntɪdɪ'luːvɪən/ *adj* antidiluviano
antelope /'æntɪləʊp/ *n* antilope *m*
antenatal /æntɪ'neɪtl/ *adj* prenatale
antenatal class *n* corso *m* di preparazione al parto
antenatal clinic *n* BrE assistenza *f* medica prenatale
antenna /æn'tenə/ *n* antenna *f*
anterior /æn'tɪərɪə/ *adj* anteriore
anteroom /'æntɪ-/ *n* anticamera *f*
ant heap = **anthill**
anthem /'ænθəm/ *n* inno *m*
anthill /'ænthɪl/ *n* formicaio *m*
anthology /æn'θɒlədʒɪ/ *n* antologia *f*
anthracite /'ænθrəsaɪt/ *n* antracite *f*
anthrax /'ænθræks/ *n* (disease) carbonchio *m*; (pustule) pustola *f* di carbonchio
anthropological /ænθrəpə'lɒdʒɪkl/ *adj* antropologico
anthropologist /ænθrə'pɒlədʒɪst/ *n* antropologo, -a *mf*
anthropology /ænθrə'pɒlədʒɪ/ *n* antropologia *f*
anti /'æntɪ/ **A** *pref* anti
B *prep* **be ~** essere contro

⚷ parola chiave

a

anti-abortion *adj* antiabortista
anti-abortionist *n* antiabortista *mf*
anti-aircraft *adj* antiaereo
anti-apartheid *adj* antiapartheid *inv*
antibacterial /æntɪbæk'tɪərɪəl/ *adj* antibatterico
anti-ballistic missile /æntɪbəlɪstɪk'mɪsaɪl/ *n* missile *m* antimissile
antibiotic /æntɪbaɪ'ɒtɪk/ *n* antibiotico *m*
antibody /'æntɪbɒdɪ/ *n* anticorpo *m*
anticipate /æn'tɪsɪpeɪt/ *vt* prevedere; (forestall) anticipare
anticipation /æntɪsɪ'peɪʃn/ *n* anticipo *m*; (excitement) attesa *f*; **in ~ of** in previsione di
anticlimax /æntɪ'klaɪmæks/ *n* delusione *f*
anticlockwise /æntɪ'klɒkwaɪz/ *adj & adv* in senso antiorario
antics /'æntɪks/ *npl* gesti *mpl* buffi
anticyclone /æntɪ'saɪkləʊn/ *n* anticiclone *m*
antidepressant /æntɪdɪ'pres(ə)nt/ *adj & n* antidepressivo *m*
antidote /'æntɪdəʊt/ *n* antidoto *m*
anti-establishment *adj* contestatario
antifreeze /'æntɪfriːz/ *n* antigelo *m*
anti-glare *adj* ‹*screen*› antiriflesso *inv*
antihistamine /æntɪ'hɪstəmiːn/ *n* antistaminico *m*
anti-inflammatory /-ɪn'flæmətrɪ/ *adj & n* antinfiammatorio *m*
anti-inflation *adj* anti-inflazione *inv*
anti-inflationary /-ɪn'fleɪʃnəri/ *adj* antinflazionistico
anti-lock *adj* antibloccaggio *inv*
antipathy /æn'tɪpəθɪ/ *n* antipatia *f*
antiperspirant /æntɪ'pɜːspɪrənt/ *n* deodorante *m* antitraspirante
Antipodean /æntɪpə'diːən/ *adj & n* australiano, -a, e/o neozelandese *mf*
Antipodes /æn'tɪpədiːz/ *npl* BrE **the ~** gli antipodi
antiquarian /æntɪ'kweərɪən/ *adj* antiquario; **~ bookshop** negozio *m* di libri antichi
antiquated /'æntɪkweɪtɪd/ *adj* antiquato
antique /æn'tiːk/ **A** *adj* antico
B *n* antichità *f*
antique dealer *n* antiquario, -a *mf*
antiques fair *n* fiera *f* dell'antiquariato
antique shop *n* negozio *m* d'antiquariato
antiques trade *n* antiquariato *m*
antiquity /æn'tɪkwətɪ/ *n* antichità *f*
anti-racism *n* antirazzismo *m*
anti-racist *adj* antirazzista
antiretroviral /æntiretrʊˌvaɪrəl/ *adj* antiretrovirale
anti-riot *adj* ‹*police*› antisommossa *inv*
anti-rust *adj* antiruggine *inv*
anti-Semitic /æntɪsɪ'mɪtɪk/ *adj* antisemita
anti-Semitism /æntɪ'semɪtɪzm/ *n* antisemitismo *m*
antiseptic /æntɪ'septɪk/ *adj & n* antisettico *m*
anti-skid *adj* antiscivolo *inv*
anti-smoking *adj* contro il fumo, antifumo
antisocial /æntɪ'səʊʃəl/ *adj* ‹*behaviour*› antisociale; ‹*person*› asociale
antiterrorism /æntɪ'terərɪzm/ *n* antiterrorismo *m*
anti-terrorist *adj* antiterrorista
anti-theft *adj* ‹*lock, device*› antifurto *inv*; ‹*camera*› di sorveglianza; **~ steering lock** bloccasterzo *m*
antithesis /æn'tɪθəsɪs/ *n* antitesi *f*
antitrust /æntɪ'trʌst/ *adj* antitrust *inv*
antivirus program /æntɪ'vaɪrəs/ *n* Comput programma *m* antivirus
antivirus software *n* Comput programma *m* antivirus
antivivisectionist /æntɪvɪvɪ'sekʃənɪst/ **A** *n* antivivisezionista *mf*
B *adj* antivivisezionistico
anti-war *adj* antimilitarista
antlers /'æntləz/ *npl* corna *fpl*
antonym /'æntənɪm/ *n* antonimo *m*
Antwerp /'æntwɜːp/ *n* Anversa *f*
anus /'eɪnəs/ *n* ano *m*
anvil /'ænvɪl/ *n* incudine *f*
anxiety /æŋ'zaɪətɪ/ *n* ansia *f*
anxious /'æŋkʃəs/ *adj* ansioso
anxiously /'æŋkʃəslɪ/ *adv* con ansia
⚷ **any** /'enɪ/ **A** *adj* (no matter which) qualsiasi, qualunque; **have we ~ wine/biscuits?** abbiamo del vino/dei biscotti?; **have we ~ jam/apples?** abbiamo della marmellata/delle mele?; **~ colour/number you like** qualsiasi colore/numero ti piaccia; **we don't have ~ wine/biscuits** non abbiamo vino/biscotti; **I don't have ~ reason to lie** non ho nessun motivo per mentire; **for ~ reason** per qualsiasi ragione
B *pron* (some) ne; (no matter which) uno qualsiasi; **I don't want ~ [of it]** non ne voglio [nessuno]; **there aren't ~** non ce ne sono; **have we ~?** ne abbiamo?; **have you read ~ of her books?** hai letto qualcuno dei suoi libri?
C *adv* **I can't go ~ quicker** non posso andare più in fretta; **is it ~ better?** va un po' meglio?; **would you like ~ more?** ne vuoi ancora?; **I can't eat ~ more** non posso mangiare più niente
anybody /'enɪbʌdɪ/ *pron* chiunque; (after negative) nessuno; **~ can do that** chiunque può farlo; **I haven't seen ~** non ho visto nessuno
anyhow /'enɪhaʊ/ *adv* ad ogni modo, comunque; (badly) non importa come
⚷ **anyone** /'enɪwʌn/ *pron* = **anybody**
anyplace /'enɪpleɪs/ *adv* AmE = **anywhere**
⚷ **anything** /'enɪθɪŋ/ *pron* qualche cosa, qualcosa; (no matter what) qualsiasi cosa;

(after negative) niente; **take/buy ~ you like** prendi/compra quello che vuoi; **I don't remember ~** non mi ricordo niente; **he's ~ but stupid** è tutto fuorché stupido; **I'll do ~ but that** farò qualsiasi cosa, tranne quello

anytime /ˈenɪtaɪm/ *adv* **if at ~ you feel lonely...** se mai ti dovessi sentire solo...; **he could arrive ~ now** potrebbe arrivare da un momento all'altro; **~ after 2 pm** a qualsiasi ora dopo le due; **at ~ of the day or night** a qualsiasi ora del giorno o della notte; **~ you like** quando vuoi

anyway /ˈenɪweɪ/ *adv* ad ogni modo, comunque

anywhere /ˈenɪweə(r)/ *adv* dovunque; (after negative) da nessuna parte; **put it ~** mettilo dove vuoi; **I can't find it ~** non lo trovo da nessuna parte; **~ else** da qualche altra parte; **I don't want to go ~ else** non voglio andare da nessun'altra parte

aorta /eɪˈɔːtə/ *n* aorta *f*

Aosta /æˈɒstə/ *n* Aosta *f*

apace /əˈpeɪs/ *adv* literary liter rapidamente

apart /əˈpɑːt/ *adv* lontano; **live ~** vivere separati; **100 miles ~** lontani 100 miglia; **born 20 minutes ~** nati a distanza di 20 minuti; **~ from** a parte; **you can't tell them ~** non si possono distinguere; **joking ~** scherzi a parte

apartheid /əˈpɑːthaɪt/ *n* apartheid *f*

apartment /əˈpɑːtmənt/ *n* AmE (flat) appartamento *m*; **in my ~** a casa mia

apartment block *n* stabile *m*

apartment house *n* stabile *m*

apathetic /æpəˈθetɪk/ *adj* (by nature) apatico; **~ about something/towards somebody** (from illness, depression) indifferente a qualcosa/nei confronti di qualcuno

apathy /ˈæpəθɪ/ *n* apatia *f*

ape /eɪp/ **A** *n* scimmia *f*
B *vt* scimmiottare

Apennines /ˈæpənaɪnz/ *npl* **the ~** gli Appennini

aperitif /əˈperətiːf/ *n* aperitivo *m*

aperture /ˈæpətʃə(r)/ *n* apertura *f*

apex /ˈeɪpeks/ *n* vertice *m*

aphid /ˈeɪfɪd/ *n* afide *m*

aphrodisiac /æfrəˈdɪzɪæk/ *adj & n* afrodisiaco *m*

apiary /ˈeɪpɪərɪ/ *n* apiario *m*

apiece /əˈpiːs/ *adv* ciascuno

aplenty /əˈplentɪ/ *adv* **there were goals ~** c'è stata una valanga di gol

apocalypse /əˈpɒkəlɪps/ *n* Apocalisse *f*; (disaster, destruction) apocalisse *f*

apocalyptic /əpɒkəˈlɪptɪk/ *adj* apocalittico

apocryphal /əˈpɒkrɪfəl/ *adj* apocrifo

apogee /ˈæpədʒiː/ *n* apogeo *m*

apolitical /eɪpəˈlɪtɪkl/ *adj* apolitico

Apollo /əˈpɒləʊ/ *n* also fig Apollo *m*

apologetic /əpɒləˈdʒetɪk/ *adj* ‹*air, remark*› di scusa; **be ~** essere spiacente

apologetically /əpɒləˈdʒetɪklɪ/ *adv* per scusarsi

apologist /əˈpɒlədʒɪst/ *n* apologeta *mf* (**for** di)

apologize /əˈpɒlədʒaɪz/ *vi* scusarsi (**for** per)

apology /əˈpɒlədʒɪ/ *n* scusa *f*; fig **an ~ for a dinner** una sottospecie di cena

apoplectic /æpəˈplektɪk/ *adj* (furious) furibondo; ‹*fit, attack*› apoplettico

apoplexy /ˈæpəpleksɪ/ *n* Med apoplessia *f*; (rage) rabbia *f*

apostle /əˈpɒsl/ *n* apostolo *m*

apostrophe /əˈpɒstrəfɪ/ *n* apostrofo *m*

apotheosis /əpɒθɪˈəʊsɪs/ *n* apoteosi *f inv*

app *n abbr* (**application**) Comput infml applicazione *f*

appal /əˈpɔːl/ *vt* (*pt/pp* **appalled**) sconvolgere

Appalachians /æpəˈleɪtʃnz/ *npl* **the ~** gli Appalachi

appalling /əˈpɔːlɪŋ/ *adj* sconvolgente; **he's an ~ teacher** fig è un disastro come professore

appallingly /əˈpɔːlɪŋlɪ/ *adv* ‹*behave, treat*› orribilmente; **unemployment figures are ~ high** il tasso di disoccupazione è spaventosamente alto; **furnished in ~ bad taste** arredato con pessimo gusto

apparatus /æpəˈreɪtəs/ *n* apparato *m*

apparel /əˈpærəl/ *n* abbigliamento *m*

apparent /əˈpærənt/ *adj* evidente; (seeming) apparente

apparently /əˈpærəntlɪ/ *adv* apparentemente

apparition /æpəˈrɪʃn/ *n* apparizione *f*

appeal /əˈpiːl/ **A** *n* appello *m*; (attraction) attrattiva *f*
B *vi* fare appello; **~ to** (be attractive to) attrarre

appeal court, **appeals court** *n* corte *f* d'appello

appeal fund *n* raccolta *f* di fondi

appealing /əˈpiːlɪŋ/ *adj* attraente

appealingly /əˈpiːlɪŋlɪ/ *adv* (beseechingly) in modo supplichevole; (attractively) in modo attraente

appear /əˈpɪə(r)/ *vi* apparire; (seem) sembrare; ‹*publication*› uscire; Theat esibirsi; **he finally ~ed at...** infml si è fatto finalmente vedere alle...; **~ in court** comparire in giudizio

appearance /əˈpɪərəns/ *n* apparizione *f*; (look) aspetto *m*; **to all ~s** a giudicare dalle apparenze; **keep up ~s** salvare le apparenze

appease /əˈpiːz/ *vt* placare

appeasement /əˈpiːzmənt/ *n* **a policy of ~** una politica troppo conciliante

append /əˈpend/ *vt* apporre ‹*signature*› (**to** a)

parola chiave

appendage /əˈpendɪdʒ/ *n* appendice *f*
appendicitis /əpendɪˈsaɪtɪs/ *n* appendicite *f*
appendix /əˈpendɪks/ *n* (of book) (*pl* **-ices**) /-əsiːz/ appendice *f* (*pl* **-es**) Anat appendice *f*
appertain /æpəˈteɪn/ *vi* **~ to** essere pertinente a
appetite /ˈæpɪtaɪt/ *n* appetito *m*
appetite suppressant *n* pillola *f* antifame
appetizer /ˈæpɪtaɪzə(r)/ *n* (drink) aperitivo *m*; (starter) antipasto *m*; (biscuit, olive etc) stuzzichino *m*
appetizing /ˈæpɪtaɪzɪŋ/ *adj* appetitoso
applaud /əˈplɔːd/ *vt & vi* applaudire
applause /əˈplɔːz/ *n* applauso *m*
apple /ˈæpl/ *n* mela *f*; **she's the ~ of his eye** è la luce dei suoi occhi
apple core *n* torsolo *m* di mela
apple orchard *n* meleto *m*
applet /ˈæplɪt/ *n* Comput applet *f*
apple tree *n* melo *m*
appliance /əˈplaɪəns/ *n* attrezzo *m*; **[electrical] ~** elettrodomestico *m*
applicable /ˈæplɪkəbl/ *adj* **be ~ to** essere valido per; **not ~** (on form) non applicabile
applicant /ˈæplɪkənt/ *n* candidato, -a *mf*
application /æplɪˈkeɪʃn/ *n* Comput (general) applicazione *f*; (request) domanda *f*; (for job) candidatura *f*; **on ~** su richiesta
application form *n* modulo *m* di domanda
applicator /ˈæplɪkeɪtə(r)/ *n* applicatore *m*
applied /əˈplaɪd/ *adj* applicato
appliqué /əˈpliːkeɪ/ **A** *n* applicazione *f*
B *attrib ‹motif, decoration›* applicato
apply /əˈplaɪ/ **A** *vt* (*pt/pp* **-ied**) applicare; **~ oneself** applicarsi; **~ the brakes** frenare
B *vi* applicarsi; *‹law›* essere applicabile; **~ to** (ask) rivolgersi a; **~ for** fare domanda per *‹job etc›*
appoint /əˈpɔɪnt/ *vt* nominare; fissare *‹time›*; **well ~ed** ben equipaggiato
appointee /əpɔɪnˈtiː/ *n* incaricato, -a *mf*
appointment /əˈpɔɪntmənt/ *n* appuntamento *m*; (to job) nomina *f*; (job) posto *m*
apportion /əˈpɔːʃn/ *vt* ripartire, attribuire
apposite /ˈæpəzɪt/ *adj* appropriato
apposition /æpəˈzɪʃn/ *n* apposizione *f*
appraisal /əˈpreɪzəl/ *n* valutazione *f*; **make an ~ of something** valutare qualcosa
appraise /əˈpreɪz/ *vt* valutare
appreciable /əˈpriːʃəbl/ *adj* sensibile
appreciably /əˈpriːʃəblɪ/ *adv* sensibilmente
appreciate /əˈpriːʃieɪt/ **A** *vt* apprezzare; (understand) comprendere
B *vi* (increase in value) aumentare di valore
appreciation /əpriːsɪˈeɪʃn/ *n* (gratitude) riconoscenza *f*; (enjoyment) apprezzamento *m*; (understanding) comprensione *f*; (in value) aumento *m*; **in ~** come segno di riconoscenza (**of** per)
appreciative /əˈpriːʃətɪv/ *adj* riconoscente
apprehend /æprɪˈhend/ *vt* arrestare
apprehension /æprɪˈhenʃn/ *n* arresto *m*; (fear) apprensione *f*
apprehensive /æprɪˈhensɪv/ *adj* apprensivo
apprehensively /æprɪˈhensɪvlɪ/ *adv* con apprensione
apprentice /əˈprentɪs/ *n* apprendista *mf*
apprenticeship /əˈprentɪsʃɪp/ *n* apprendistato *m*
apprise /əˈpraɪz/ *vt* fml informare (**of** di)
approach /əˈprəʊtʃ/ **A** *n* avvicinamento *m*; (to problem) approccio *m*; (access) accesso *m*; **make ~es to** fare degli approcci con
B *vi* avvicinarsi
C *vt* avvicinarsi a; (with request) rivolgersi a; affrontare *‹problem›*
approachable /əˈprəʊtʃəbl/ *adj* accessibile
approach lights *npl* Aeron sentiero *m* luminoso di avvicinamento
approach path *n* Aeron rotta *f* di avvicinamento
approach road *n* strada *f* d'accesso
approbation /æprəˈbeɪʃn/ *n* approvazione *f*
appropriate¹ /əˈprəʊprɪət/ *adj* appropriato
appropriate² /əˈprəʊprɪeɪt/ *vt* appropriarsi di
appropriately /əˈprəʊprɪətlɪ/ *adv* (suitably) in modo appropriato; *‹sited›* convenientemente; *‹designed, chosen, behave›* adeguatamente
appropriation /əprəʊprɪˈeɪʃn/ *n* AmE Comm stanziamento *m*; Jur (removal) appropriazione *f*
approval /əˈpruːvl/ *n* approvazione *f*; **on ~** in prova
approve /əˈpruːv/ **A** *vt* approvare
B *vi* **~ of** approvare *‹something›*; avere una buona opinione di *‹somebody›*
approving /əˈpruːvɪŋ/ *adj ‹smile, nod›* d'approvazione
approvingly /əˈpruːvɪŋlɪ/ *adv* con approvazione
approximate¹ /əˈprɒksɪmeɪt/ *vi* **~ to** avvicinarsi a
approximate² /əˈprɒksɪmət/ *adj* approssimativo
approximately /əˈprɒksɪmətlɪ/ *adv* approssimativamente
approximation /əprɒksɪˈmeɪʃn/ *n* approssimazione *f*
APR *n* (**annual percentage rate**) tasso *m* percentuale annuo
apricot /ˈeɪprɪkɒt/ *n* albicocca *f*; **~ tree** albicocco *m*
April /ˈeɪprəl/ *n* aprile *m*; **make an ~ Fool of somebody** fare un pesce d'aprile a qualcuno
April Fools' Day *n* il primo d'aprile *m*
apron /ˈeɪprən/ *n* grembiule *m*
apropos /ˈæprəpəʊ/ *adv* **~ [of]** a proposito [di]

apse /æps/ *n* abside *f*
apt /æpt/ *adj* appropriato; ‹*pupil*› dotato; **be ~ to do something** avere tendenza a fare qualcosa
aptitude /'æptɪtju:d/ *n* disposizione *f*
aptitude test *n* test *m inv* attitudinale
aptly /æptlɪ/ *adv* appropriatamente
Apulia /ə'pju:lɪə/ *n* Puglia *f*
aqualung /'ækwəlʌŋ/ *n* autorespiratore *m*
aquamarine /ækwəmə'ri:n/ *adj & n* acquamarina *f*
aquaplane /'ækwəpleɪn/ *vi* Sport praticare l'acquaplano; BrE Auto andare in aquaplaning
aquarium /ə'kweərɪəm/ *n* acquario *m*
Aquarius /ə'kweərɪəs/ *n* Astr Acquario *m*; **be ~** essere dell' Acquario
aquarobics /,ækwə'rɒbɪks/ *nsg* acquagym *fsg inv*
aquatic /ə'kwætɪk/ *adj* acquatico
aqueduct /'ækwədʌkt/ *n* acquedotto *m*
aquiline /'ækwɪlaɪn/ *adj* ‹*nose, features*› aquilino
Arab /'ærəb/ *adj & n* arabo, -a *mf*
Arabia /ə'reɪbɪə/ *n* Arabia *f*
Arabian /ə'reɪbɪən/ *adj* arabo
Arabic /'ærəbɪk/ **A** *adj* arabo; **~ numerals** numeri *mpl* arabi
B *n* arabo *m*
Arab-Israeli *adj* arabo-israeliano
arable /'ærəbl/ *adj* coltivabile
Arab Spring *n* primavera *f* araba
arbiter /'ɑ:bɪtə(r)/ *n* arbitro *m*
arbitrarily /ɑ:bɪ'trerɪlɪ/ *adv* arbitrariamente
arbitrary /'ɑ:bɪtrərɪ/ *adj* arbitrario
arbitrate /'ɑ:bɪtreɪt/ *vi* arbitrare
arbitration /ɑ:bɪ'treɪʃn/ *n* arbitraggio *m*
arbitrator /'ɑ:bɪtreɪtə(r)/ *n* arbitro *m*
arbour /'ɑ:bə(r)/ *n* pergolato *m*
arc /ɑ:k/ *n* arco *m*
arcade /ɑ:'keɪd/ *n* portico *m*; (shops) galleria *f*
arcane /ɑ:'keɪn/ *adj* arcano
arch /ɑ:tʃ/ **A** *n* arco *m*; (of foot) dorso *m* del piede
B *vt* **the cat ~ed its back** il gatto ha arcuato la schiena
archaeological /ɑ:kɪə'lɒdʒɪkl/ *adj* archeologico
archaeologist /ɑ:kɪ'ɒlədʒɪst/ *n* archeologo, -a *mf*
archaeology /ɑ:kɪ'ɒlədʒɪ/ *n* archeologia *f*
archaic /ɑ:'keɪɪk/ *adj* arcaico
archbishop /ɑ:tʃ'bɪʃəp/ *n* arcivescovo *m*
arched /ɑ:tʃt/ *adj* ‹*eyebrows*› arcuato
arch-enemy *n* acerrimo nemico *m*
archer /'ɑ:tʃə(r)/ *n* arciere *m*
archery /'ɑ:tʃərɪ/ *n* tiro *m* con l'arco
archetypal /ɑ:kɪ'taɪpl/ *adj* **the ~ hero** il prototipo dell'eroe

archetype /'ɑ:kɪtaɪp/ *n* archetipo *m*
archipelago /ɑ:kɪ'peləgəʊ/ *n* arcipelago *m*
architect /'ɑ:kɪtekt/ *n* architetto *m*
architectural /ɑ:kɪ'tektʃərəl/ *adj* architettonico
architecturally /ɑ:kɪ'tektʃərəlɪ/ *adv* architettonicamente
architecture /ɑ:kɪ'tektʃə(r)/ *n* architettura *f*
archive /'ɑ:kaɪv/ *vt* also Comput archiviare
archives /'ɑ:kaɪvz/ *npl* archivi *mpl*
archiving /'ɑ:kaɪvɪŋ/ *n* Comput archiviazione *f*
archway /'ɑ:tʃweɪ/ *n* arco *m*
Arctic /'ɑ:ktɪk/ **A** *adj* artico
B *n* **the ~** l'Artico
Arctic Circle *n* Circolo *m* polare artico
Arctic Ocean *n* mare *m* artico
ardent /'ɑ:dənt/ *adj* ardente
ardently /'ɑ:dəntlɪ/ *adv* ardentemente
ardour /'ɑ:də(r)/ *n* ardore *m*
arduous /'ɑ:djʊəs/ *adj* arduo
arduously /'ɑ:djʊəslɪ/ *adv* con fatica, con difficoltà
are /ɑ:(r)/ ▶ **be**
⚷ **area** /'eərɪə/ *n* area *f*; (region) zona *f*; fig (field) campo *m*
area code *n* prefisso *m* [telefonico]
area manager *n* direttore, -trice *mf* di zona
arena /ə'ri:nə/ *n* arena *f*
aren't /ɑ:nt/ *are not* ▶ **be**
Argentina /ɑ:dʒən'ti:nə/ *n* Argentina *f*
Argentine /'ɑ:dʒəntaɪn/ *adj* argentino
Argentinian /ɑ:dʒən'tɪnɪən/ *adj & n* argentino, -a *mf*
arguable /'ɑ:gjʊəbl/ *adj* **it's ~ that...** si può sostenere che...
arguably /'ɑ:gjʊəblɪ/ *adv* **he is ~...** è probabilmente...
⚷ **argue** /'ɑ:gju:/ **A** *vi* litigare (**about** su); (debate) dibattere; **don't ~!** non discutere!
B *vt* (debate) dibattere; (reason) **~ that** sostenere che
⚷ **argument** /'ɑ:gjʊmənt/ *n* argomento *m*; (reasoning) ragionamento *m*; **have an ~** litigare
argumentative /ɑ:gjʊ'mentətɪv/ *adj* polemico
aria /'ɑ:rɪə/ *n* aria *f*
arid /'ærɪd/ *adj* arido
aridity /ə'rɪdətɪ/ *n* also fig aridità *f*
Aries /'eəri:z/ *n* Astr Ariete *m*; **be ~** essere dell'Ariete
⚷ **arise** /ə'raɪz/ *vi* (*pt* **arose**, *pp* **arisen**) ‹*opportunity, need, problem*› presentarsi; (result) derivare
aristocracy /ærɪ'stɒkrəsɪ/ *n* aristocrazia *f*
aristocrat /'ærɪstəkræt/ *n* aristocratico, -a *mf*
aristocratic /ærɪstə'krætɪk/ *adj* aristocratico
arithmetic /ə'rɪθmətɪk/ *n* aritmetica *f*

⚷ parola chiave

a

arithmetical /ærɪθ'metɪkl/ *adj* aritmetico

ark /ɑːk/ *n* **Noah's Ark** l'Arca *f* di Noè

arm /ɑːm/ **A** *n* braccio *m*; (of chair) bracciolo *m*; **~s** *pl* (weapons) armi *fpl*; **~ in ~** a braccetto; **up in ~s** infml furioso (**about** per); fig **with open ~s** a braccia aperte
B *vt* armare

armadillo /ɑːmə'dɪləʊ/ *n* armadillo *m*

armaments /'ɑːməmənts/ *npl* armamenti *mpl*

armband /'ɑːmbænd/ *n* (for swimmer) bracciolo *m* (*per nuotare*) (for mourner) fascia *f* al braccio

armchair /'ɑːmtʃeə(r)/ *n* poltrona *f*

armchair traveller *n persona* (*f*) *che si interessa di viaggi senza viaggiare*

armed /ɑːmd/ *adj* armato

armed forces /'fɔːsɪz/ *npl* forze *fpl* armate

armed robbery *n* rapina *f* a mano armata

Armenia /ɑː'miːnɪə/ *n* Armenia *f*

Armenian /ɑː'miːnɪən/ *adj & n* (person) armeno, -a *mf*; (language) armeno *m*

armful /'ɑːmfʊl/ *n* bracciata *f*

armhole /'ɑːmhəʊl/ *n* giro *m* manica *inv*

armistice /'ɑːmɪstɪs/ *n* armistizio *m*

Armistice Day *n* l'Anniversario *m* dell'Armistizio (*11 nov. 1918*)

armour /'ɑːmə(r)/ *n* armatura *f*

armour-clad /-'klæd/ *adj* ‹*vehicle*› blindato; ‹*ship*› corazzato

armoured /'ɑːməd/ *adj* ‹*vehicle*› blindato

armoured car *n* autoblinda[ta] *f*

armour plate, **armour plating** /'pleɪtɪŋ/ *n* corazzatura *f*

armour-plated /-'pleɪtɪd/ *adj* corazzato

armoury /'ɑːmərɪ/ *n* (factory) fabbrica *f* d'armi; (store) arsenale *m*, armeria *f*

armpit /'ɑːmpɪt/ *n* ascella *f*

armrest /'ɑːmrest/ *n* bracciolo *m* (*di sedia*)

arms control *n* controllo *m* degli armamenti

arms dealer *n* trafficante *mf* d'armi

arms dump *n* deposito *m* d'armi

arms embargo *n* embargo *m* sulle armi

arms limitation *n* controllo *m* degli armamenti

arms manufacturer *n* fabbricante *mf* d'armi

arms race *n* corsa *f* agli armamenti

arms treaty *n* trattato *m* sul controllo degli armamenti

arm-twisting /'ɑːmtwɪstɪŋ/ *n* pressioni *fpl*

arm-wrestling *n* braccio *m* di ferro

army /'ɑːmɪ/ *n* esercito *m*; **join the ~** arruolarsi

A road *n* BrE [strada *f*] statale *f*

aroma /ə'rəʊmə/ *n* aroma *f*

aromatherapist /əˌrəʊmə'θerəpɪst/ *n* aromaterapeuta *mf*

aromatherapy /ərəʊmə'θerəpɪ/ *n* aromaterapia *f*

aromatic /ærə'mætɪk/ *adj* aromatico

arose /ə'rəʊz/ ▶ **arise**

around /ə'raʊnd/ **A** *adv* intorno; **all ~** tutt'intorno; **I'm not from ~ here** non sono di qui; **he's not ~** non c'è
B *prep* intorno a; in giro per ‹*room, shops, world*›

arousal /ə'raʊzl/ *n* eccitazione *f*

arouse /ə'raʊz/ *vt* svegliare; (sexually) eccitare

arpeggio /ɑː'pedʒɪəʊ/ *n* arpeggio *m*

arrange /ə'reɪndʒ/ *vt* sistemare ‹*furniture, books*›; organizzare ‹*meeting*›; fissare ‹*date, time*›; **~ to do something** combinare di fare qualcosa

arrangement /ə'reɪndʒmənt/ *n* (of furniture) sistemazione *f*; Mus arrangiamento *m*; (agreement) accordo; (of flowers) composizione *f*; **make ~s** prendere disposizioni; **I've made other ~s** ho preso altri impegni

array /ə'reɪ/ **A** *n* (clothes) abbigliamento *m*; (of troops, people) schieramento *m*; (of numbers) tabella *f*; (of weaponry) apparato *m*; (of goods, products) assortimento *m*; Comput matrice *f*
B *vt* **~ed in ceremonial robes** abbigliato da gran cerimonia

arrears /ə'rɪəz/ *npl* arretrati *mpl*; **be in ~** essere in arretrato; **paid in ~** pagato a lavoro eseguito

arrest /ə'rest/ **A** *n* arresto *m*; **under ~** in stato d'arresto
B *vt* arrestare

arresting /ə'restɪŋ/ *adj* (striking) che colpisce

arrival /ə'raɪvl/ *n* arrivo *m*; **new ~s** *pl* nuovi arrivati *mpl*

arrival(s) lounge *n* sala *f* arrivi

arrivals board *n* tabellone *m* degli arrivi

arrival time *n* ora *f* d'arrivo

arrive /ə'raɪv/ *vi* arrivare; **~ at** fig raggiungere

arrogance /'ærəg(ə)ns/ *n* arroganza *f*

arrogant /'ærəg(ə)nt/ *adj* arrogante

arrogantly /'ærəg(ə)ntlɪ/ *adv* con arroganza

arrow /'ærəʊ/ *n* freccia *f*

arrowhead /'ærəʊhed/ *n* punta *f* di freccia

arse /ɑːs/ *n* BrE vulg culo *m*

■ **arse about**, **arse around** *vi* vulg coglioneggiare

arsenal /'ɑːsən(ə)l/ *n* arsenale *m*

arsenic /'ɑːsənɪk/ *n* arsenico *m*

arson /'ɑːsən/ *n* incendio *m* doloso

arsonist /'ɑːsənɪst/ *n* incendiario, -a *mf*

art /ɑːt/ *n* arte *f*; **work of ~** opera *f* d'arte; **~s and crafts** *pl* artigianato *m*; **the A~s** *pl* l'arte *f*; **A~s degree** Univ laurea *f* in Lettere

art collection *n* collezione *f* d'arte

art collector *n* collezionista *mf* d'arte

art college *n* ≈ accademia *f* di belle arti

a

art dealer *n* commerciante *mf* di oggetti d'arte
art deco *n* art déco *f*
artefact /ˈɑːtɪfækt/ *n* manufatto *m*
arterial /ɑːˈtɪərɪəl/ *adj* Anat arterioso
arterial road *n* arteria *f* [stradale]
artery /ˈɑːtərɪ/ *n* arteria *f*
art exhibition *n* mostra *f* d'arte
art form *n* forma *f* d'arte
artful /ˈɑːtfl/ *adj* scaltro
artfully /ˈɑːtfʊlɪ/ *adv* astutamente
art gallery *n* galleria *f* d'arte
arthritic /ɑːˈθrɪtɪk/ *adj & n* artritico, -a *mf*
arthritis /ɑːˈθraɪtɪs/ *n* artrite *f*
artichoke /ˈɑːtɪtʃəʊk/ *n* carciofo *m*
⚷ **article** /ˈɑːtɪkl/ *n* articolo *m*; ~ **of clothing** capo *m* d'abbigliamento
articulate¹ /ɑːˈtɪkjʊlət/ *adj* ‹*speech*› chiaro; **be** ~ esprimersi bene
articulate² /ɑːˈtɪkjʊleɪt/ *vt* scandire ‹*words*›
articulated lorry /ɑːˈtɪkjʊleɪtɪd/ *n* autotreno *m*
articulately /ɑːˈtɪkjʊlətlɪ/ *adv* chiaramente
articulation /ɑːtɪkjʊˈleɪʃn/ *n* (pronunciation) Anat articolazione *f*; (expression) espressione *f*
artifice /ˈɑːtɪfɪs/ *n* artificio *m*
artificial /ɑːtɪˈfɪʃl/ *adj* artificiale
artificial insemination *n* inseminazione *f* artificiale
artificial intelligence *n* intelligenza *f* artificiale
artificiality /ɑːtɪfɪʃɪˈælətɪ/ *n* artificiosità *f*
artificial limb *n* arto *m* artificiale
artificially /ɑːtɪˈfɪʃəlɪ/ *adv* artificialmente; ‹*smile*› artificiosamente
artificial respiration *n* respirazione *f* artificiale
artillery /ɑːˈtɪlərɪ/ *n* artiglieria *f*
artisan /ɑːtɪˈzæn/ *n* artigiano, -a *mf*
⚷ **artist** /ˈɑːtɪst/ *n* artista *mf*
artiste /ɑːˈtiːst/ *n* Theat artista *mf*
artistic /ɑːˈtɪstɪk/ *adj* artistico
artistically /ɑːˈtɪstɪklɪ/ *adv* artisticamente
artistry /ˈɑːtɪstrɪ/ *n* arte *f*, talento *m*
artless /ˈɑːtlɪs/ *adj* spontaneo
artlessly /ˈɑːtlɪslɪ/ *adv* ‹*smile*› ingenuamente
art nouveau /ɑːnuːˈvəʊ/ *adj & n* liberty *m*
art school *n* ≈ accademia *f* di belle arti
arts degree *n* laurea *f* in Lettere
arts funding *n* sovvenzioni *fpl* alle arti
arts student *n* studente, -essa *mf* di Lettere
art student *n* studente, -essa *mf* di belle arti
artwork /ˈɑːtwɜːk/ *n* illustrazioni *fpl*
arty /ˈɑːtɪ/ *adj* infml ‹*person*› intellettualoide; ‹*district*› degli intellettuali

⚷ **as** /æz/ **A** *conj* come; (since) siccome; (while) mentre; **as he grew older** diventando vecchio; **as you get to know her** conoscendola meglio; **young as she is** per quanto sia giovane
B *prep* come; **as a friend** come amico; **as a child** da bambino; **as a foreigner** in quanto straniero; **disguised as** travestito da
C *adv* **as well** *also* anche; **as soon as I get home** [non] appena arrivo a casa; **as quick as you** veloce quanto te; **as quick as you can** più veloce che puoi; **as far as** (distance) fino a; **as far as I'm concerned** per quanto mi riguarda; **as long as** finché; (provided that) purché
AS *n esame (m) sostenuto al termine del primo anno del biennio di preparazione agli A-Level*
ASAP /ˈeɪsæp/ *adv abbr* (**as quickly as possible**) prima possibile
asbestos /æzˈbestɒs/ *n* amianto *m*
ASBO /ˈæzbəʊ/ *n abbr* BrE (**Antisocial Behaviour Order**) *ordinanza (f) giudiziaria emessa contro chi ha comportamenti contrari all'ordine pubblico*
ascend /əˈsend/ **A** *vi* salire
B *vi* salire a ‹*throne*›
ascendancy /əˈsend(ə)nsɪ/ *n* **gain the ~ over somebody** acquisire una posizione dominante su qualcuno
ascendant /əˈsend(ə)nt/ *n* **be in the ~** Astr essere in ascendente; fig ‹*person*› essere in auge
Ascension /əˈsenʃn/ *n* Relig Ascensione *f*
ascent /əˈsent/ *n* ascesa *f*
ascertain /æsəˈteɪn/ *vt* accertare
ascetic /əˈsetɪk/ *adj & n* ascetico, -a *mf*
asceticism /əˈsetɪsɪzm/ *n* ascesi *f*
ascribable /əˈskraɪbəbl/ *adj* attribuibile
ascribe /əˈskraɪb/ *vt* attribuire
aseptic /eɪˈseptɪk/ *adj* asettico
asexual /eɪˈseksjʊəl/ *adj* asessuale, asessuato
ash¹ /æʃ/ *n* (tree) frassino *m*
ash² *n* cenere *f*
ashamed /əˈʃeɪmd/ *adj* **be/feel ~** vergognarsi
ash blond *adj* biondo cenere
ashen /ˈæʃ(ə)n/ *adj* (complexion) cinereo
ashore /əˈʃɔː(r)/ *adv* a terra; **go ~** sbarcare
ashtray *n* portacenere *m*
ash tree *n* frassino *m*
Ash Wednesday *n* mercoledì *m* delle Ceneri
Asia /ˈeɪʒə/ *n* Asia *f*
Asia Minor *n* Asia *f* Minore
Asian /ˈeɪʒ(ə)n/ *adj & n* asiatico, -a *mf*; BrE (Indian, Pakistani) indiano, -a *mf*
Asiatic /eɪʒɪˈætɪk/ *adj* asiatico
⚷ **aside** /əˈsaɪd/ **A** *adv* **take somebody ~** prendere qualcuno a parte; **put something ~** mettere qualcosa da parte; **~ from you**

⚷ parola chiave

AmE a parte te; ~ **from his injuries** AmE a parte le sue ferite
B *n* **in an ~** tra parentesi

asinine /ˈæsɪnaɪn/ *adj* sciocco

ask /ɑːsk/ **A** *vt* fare ‹*question*›; (invite) invitare; ~ **somebody something** domandare *or* chiedere qualcosa a qualcuno; ~ **somebody to do something** domandare *or* chiedere a qualcuno di fare qualcosa
B *vi* ~ **about something** informarsi su qualcosa
- **ask after** *vt* chiedere [notizie] di ‹*somebody*›
- **ask for** *vt* chiedere ‹*something*›; chiedere di ‹*somebody*›; ~ **for trouble** infml andare in cerca di guai
- **ask in**: *vt* ~ **somebody in** invitare qualcuno ad entrare
- **ask out**: *vt* ~ **somebody out** chiedere a qualcuno di uscire

askance /əˈskɑːns/ *adv* **look ~ at somebody/something** guardare qualcuno/qualcosa di traverso

askew /əˈskjuː/ *adj & adv* di traverso

asking price /ˈɑːskɪŋ/ *n* prezzo *m* trattabile

asleep /əˈsliːp/ *adj* **be ~** dormire; **fall ~** addormentarsi

asparagus /əˈspærəgəs/ *n* asparagi *mpl*

aspect /ˈæspekt/ *n* aspetto *m*

aspen /ˈæspən/ *n* pioppo *m* tremulo

aspersions /əˈspɜːʃnz/ *npl* **cast ~ on** diffamare

asphalt /ˈæsfælt/ *n* asfalto *m*

asphyxia /əsˈfɪksɪə/ *n* asfissia *f*

asphyxiate /əsˈfɪksɪeɪt/ *vt* asfissiare

asphyxiation /əsfɪksɪˈeɪʃn/ *n* asfissia *f*

aspic /ˈæspɪk/ *n* aspic *m inv*

aspirate[1] /ˈæspəreɪt/ *vt* aspirare

aspirate[2] /ˈæspɪrət/ *adj* aspirato

aspirations /æspəˈreɪʃnz/ *npl* aspirazioni *fpl*

aspire /əˈspaɪə(r)/ *vi* ~ **to** aspirare a

aspirin /ˈæspərɪn/ *n* aspirina *f*

aspiring /əˈspaɪərɪŋ/ *adj* ~ **authors/journalists** aspiranti scrittori/giornalisti

ass /æs/ *n* (animal) asino *m*; AmE vulg (part of body) culo *m*

assailant /əˈseɪlənt/ *n* assalitore, -trice *mf*

assassin /əˈsæsɪn/ *n* assassino, -a *mf*

assassinate /əˈsæsɪneɪt/ *vt* assassinare

assassination /əsæsɪˈneɪʃn/ *n* assassinio *m*

assault /əˈsɔːlt/ **A** *n* Mil assalto *m*; Jur aggressione *f*
B *vt* aggredire

assault and battery *n* Jur lesioni *fpl* personali

assault course *n* Mil percorso *m* di guerra

assemblage /əˈsemblɪdʒ/ assemblaggio *m*

assemble /əˈsembl/ **A** *vi* radunarsi
B *vi* radunare; Techn montare

assembler /əˈsemblə(r)/ *n* (in factory) montatore, -trice *mf*; Comput [programma] *m*, assemblatore *m*

assembly /əˈsemblɪ/ *n* assemblea *f*; Sch assemblea *f* giornaliera di alunni e professori di una scuola; Techn montaggio *m*

assembly line *n* catena *f* di montaggio

assent /əˈsent/ **A** *n* assenso *m*
B *vi* acconsentire

assert /əˈsɜːt/ *vt* asserire; far valere ‹*one's rights*›; ~ **oneself** farsi valere

assertion /əˈsɜːʃn/ *n* asserzione *f*

assertive /əˈsɜːtɪv/ *adj* **be ~** farsi valere

assertiveness /əˈsɜːtɪvnɪs/ *n* capacità *f* di farsi valere; **lack of ~** scarsa sicurezza *f* di sé

assess /əˈses/ *vt* valutare; (for tax purposes) stabilire l'imponibile di

assessment /əˈsesmənt/ *n* valutazione *f*; (of tax) accertamento *m*

assessor /əˈsesə(r)/ *n* Jur (in insurance) perito *m*; (tax) agente *m* del fisco

asset /ˈæset/ *n* (advantage) vantaggio *m*; (person) elemento *m* prezioso; **~s** *pl* beni *mpl*; (on balance sheet) attivo *msg*

asset stripping /ˈæsetstrɪpɪŋ/ *n* *rilevamento (m) di un'azienda per rivenderne le singole attività*

assiduity /æsɪˈdjuːətɪ/ *n* assiduità *f*

assiduous /əˈsɪdjʊəs/ *adj* assiduo

assign /əˈsaɪn/ *vt* assegnare

assignation /æsɪgˈneɪʃn/ *n* hum appuntamento *m* galante

assignment /əˈsaɪnmənt/ *n* (task) incarico *m*

assimilate /əˈsɪmɪleɪt/ *vt* assimilare; integrare ‹*person*›

assimilation /əsɪmɪˈleɪʃn/ *n* assimilazione *f*

assist /əˈsɪst/ *vt & vi* assistere; ~ **somebody to do something** assistere qualcuno nel fare qualcosa

assistance /əˈsɪstəns/ *n* assistenza *f*

assistant /əˈsɪstənt/ *n* assistente *mf*; (in shop) commesso, -a *mf*

assistant manager *n* vicedirettore, -trice *mf*

assistant professor *n* AmE Univ docente *mf* universitario, -a del grado più basso

assisted suicide /əˈsɪstɪd ˈsuːɪsaɪd/ *n* suicidio *m* assistito, eutanasia *f*

associate[1] /əˈsəʊʃɪeɪt/ **A** *vt* associare (with a); **be ~d with something** (involved in) essere coinvolto in qualcosa
B *vi* ~ **with** frequentare

associate[2] /əˈsəʊʃɪət/ **A** *adj* associato
B *n* collega *mf*; (member) socio, -a *mf*

associate company *n* consociata *f*

associate director *n* Comm amministratore *m* aggiunto

associate editor *n* co-redattore, -trice *mf*

associate member *n* membro *m* associato

association /əsəʊsɪ'eɪʃn/ *n* associazione *f*
Association Football *n* [gioco *m* del] calcio *m*
assorted /ə'sɔːtɪd/ *adj* assortito
assortment /ə'sɔːtmənt/ *n* assortimento *m*
assuage /ə'sweɪdʒ/ *vt* literary alleviare
⚷ **assume** /ə'sjuːm/ *vt* presumere; assumere ‹*control*›; ~ **office** entrare in carica; **assuming that you're right,...** ammettendo che tu abbia ragione, ...
assumption /ə'sʌmpʃn/ *n* supposizione *f*; **on the ~ that** partendo dal presupposto che; **the A~** Relig l'Assunzione *f*
assurance /ə'ʃʊərəns/ *n* assicurazione *f*; (confidence) sicurezza *f*
assure /ə'ʃʊə(r)/ *vt* assicurare; **he ~d me of his innocence** mi ha assicurato di essere innocente
assured /ə'ʃʊəd/ *adj* sicuro
Assyria /ə'sɪrɪə/ *n* Assiria *f*
asterisk /'æstərɪsk/ *n* asterisco *m*
astern /ə'stɜːn/ *adv* a poppa
asteroid /'æstərɔɪd/ *n* asteroide *m*
asthma /'æsmə/ *n* asma *f*
asthmatic /æs'mætɪk/ *adj* asmatico
astigmatism /ə'stɪgmətɪzm/ *n* astigmatismo *m*
astonish /ə'stɒnɪʃ/ *vt* stupire
astonished /ə'stɒnɪʃt/ *adj* sorpreso
astonishing /ə'stɒnɪʃɪŋ/ *adj* stupefacente
astonishingly /ə'stɒnɪʃɪŋlɪ/ *adv* sorprendentemente
astonishment /ə'stɒnɪʃmənt/ *n* stupore *m*
astound /ə'staʊnd/ *vt* stupire
astounding /ə'staʊndɪŋ/ *adj* incredible
astrakhan /æstrə'kæn/ *n* astrakan *m*
astray /ə'streɪ/ *adv* **go ~** smarrirsi; (morally) uscire dalla retta via; **lead ~** traviare
astride /ə'straɪd/ **A** *adv* [a] cavalcioni
B *prep* a cavalcioni di
astringent /ə'strɪndʒənt/ **A** *adj* astringente; fig austero
B *n* astringente *m*
astrologer /ə'strɒlədʒə(r)/ *n* astrologo, -a *mf*
astrological /æstrə'lɒdʒɪkl/ *adj* astrologico
astrology /ə'strɒlədʒɪ/ *n* astrologia *f*
astronaut /'æstrənɔːt/ *n* astronauta *mf*
astronomer /ə'strɒnəmə(r)/ *n* astronomo, -a *mf*
astronomic /æstrə'nɒmɪk/ *adj* fig astronomico
astronomical /æstrə'nɒmɪkl/ *adj* also fig astronomico
astronomically /æstrə'nɒmɪklɪ/ *adv* ~ **expensive** dal prezzo astronomico; **prices are ~ high** i prezzi sono astronomici
astronomy /ə'strɒnəmɪ/ *n* astronomia *f*

⚷ parola chiave

astrophysicist /æstrəʊ'fɪzɪsɪst/ *n* astrofisico, -a *mf*
astrophysics /æstrəʊ'fɪzɪks/ *nsg* astrofisica *fsg*
astute /ə'stjuːt/ *adj* astuto
astutely /ə'stjuːtlɪ/ *adv* con astuzia
astuteness /ə'stjuːtnɪs/ *n* astuzia *f*
asylum /ə'saɪləm/ *n* **[political] ~** asilo *m* politico; **[lunatic] ~** manicomio *m*
asylum seeker /ə'saɪləmsiːkə(r)/ *n* persona *f* che chiede asilo politico
asymmetric /æsɪ'metrɪk/, **asymmetrical** /æsɪ'metrɪkl/ *adj* asimmetrico
⚷ **at** /ət/, *accentato* /æt/ *prep* **at the station/the market** alla stazione/al mercato; **at the office/the bank** in ufficio/banca; **at the beginning** all'inizio; **at John's** da John; **at the hairdresser's** dal parrucchiere; **at home** a casa; **at work** al lavoro; **at school** a scuola; **at a party/wedding** a una festa/un matrimonio; **at one o'clock** all'una; **at 50 km an hour** ai 50 all'ora; **at Christmas/Easter** a Natale/Pasqua; **at times** talvolta; **two at a time** due alla volta; **good at languages** bravo nelle lingue; **at sb's request** su richiesta di qualcuno; **are you at all worried?** sei preoccupato?
atavistic /ætə'vɪstɪk/ *adj* atavico
ate /et/ ▶ **eat**
atheism /'eɪθɪɪzm/ *n* ateismo *m*
atheist /'eɪθɪɪst/ *n* ateo, -a *mf*
atheistic /eɪθɪ'ɪstɪk/ *adj* ‹*principle*› ateistico; ‹*person*› ateo
Athenian /ə'θiːnɪən/ *adj & n* ateniese *mf*
Athens /'æθənz/ *n* Atene *f*
athlete /'æθliːt/ *n* atleta *mf*
athlete's foot *n* micosi *f*
athletic /æθ'letɪk/ *adj* atletico
athletics /æθ'letɪks/ *nsg* atletica *fsg*
Atlantic /ət'læntɪk/ *adj & n* **the ~ [Ocean]** l'[Oceano *m*] Atlantico *m*
atlas /'ætləs/ *n* atlante *m*
Atlas Mountains *npl* Monti *mpl* dell'Atlante
ATM *n abbr* (**automatic teller machine**) cassa *f* continua di prelevamento
atmosphere /'ætməsfɪə(r)/ *n* atmosfera *f*
atmospheric /ætməs'ferɪk/ *adj* atmosferico
atom /'ætəm/ *n* atomo *m*
atom bomb *n* bomba *f* atomica
atomic /ə'tɒmɪk/ *adj* atomico
atomic physics *nsg* fisica *fsg* atomica
atomic power station *n* centrale *f* atomica
atomic reactor *n* reattore *m* nucleare
atomic scientist *n* fisico, -a *mf* nucleare
atomize /'ætəmaɪz/ *vt* atomizzare
atomizer /'ætəmaɪzə(r)/ *n* atomizzatore *m*
atone /ə'təʊn/ *vi* ~ **for** pagare per
atonement /ə'təʊnmənt/ *n* espiazione *f*

a

at risk *adj* a rischio; the ~ register l'elenco dei soggetti a rischio

atrocious /ə'trəʊʃəs/ *adj* atroce; infml ‹*meal, weather*› abominevole

atrociously /ə'trəʊʃəslɪ/ *adv* atrocemente; ‹*rude etc*› terribilmente

atrocity /ə'trɒsətɪ/ *n* atrocità *f*

atrophy /'ætrəfɪ/ **A** *n* Med atrofia *f*
B *vi* Med fig atrofizzarsi

at sign *n* Comput chiocciola *f*

attach /ə'tætʃ/ *vt* attaccare; attribuire ‹*importance*›; **be ~ed to** fig essere attaccato a

attaché /ə'tæʃeɪ/ *n* addetto *m*

attaché case *n* ventiquattrore *f inv*

attached /ə'tætʃt/ *adj* ‹*document*› allegato; (fond) ~ **to** affezionato a

attachment /ə'tætʃmənt/ *n* (affection) attaccamento *m*; (accessory) accessorio *m*; Comput allegato *m*

attack /ə'tæk/ **A** *n* attacco *m*; (physical) aggressione *f*
B *vt* attaccare; (physically) aggredire

attacker /ə'tækə(r)/ *n* assalitore, -trice *mf*; (critic) detrattore, -trice *mf*

attain /ə'teɪn/ *vt* realizzare ‹*ambition*›; raggiungere ‹*success, age, goal*›

attainable /ə'teɪnəbl/ *adj* ‹*ambition*› realizzabile; ‹*success*› raggiungibile

attainment /ə'teɪnmənt/ *n* (of knowledge) acquisizione *f*; (of goal) realizzazione *f*, raggiungimento *m*; (success) risultato *m*

attempt /ə'tempt/ **A** *n* tentativo *m*
B *vt* tentare

attend /ə'tend/ **A** *vt* essere presente a; (go regularly to) frequentare; (accompany) accompagnare; ‹*doctor*› avere in cura
B *vi* essere presente; (pay attention) prestare attenzione
■ **attend to** *vt* occuparsi di; (in shop) servire

attendance /ə'tendəns/ *n* presenza *f*

attendance record *n* (of MP, committee member, schoolchild) tasso *m* di presenza

attendance register *n* Sch registro *m*

attendant /ə'tendənt/ *n* guardiano, -a *mf*

attendee /ˌæten'diː/ *n* partecipante *mf*

attention /ə'tenʃn/ *n* attenzione *f*; Mil ~! attenti!; **pay** ~ prestare attenzione; **need** ~ aver bisogno di attenzioni; ‹*skin, hair, plant*› dover essere curato; ‹*car, tyres*› dover essere riparato; **for the** ~ **of** all'attenzione di

attention deficit disorder *n* Med disturbo *m* da deficit dell'attenzione

attention-seeking /ə'tenʃnsiːkɪŋ/ **A** *n* bisogno *m* di attirare l'attenzione
B *adj* ‹*person*› che cerca di attirare l'attenzione

attention span *n* **he has a very short** ~ non è capace di mantenere a lungo la concentrazione

attentive /ə'tentɪv/ *adj* ‹*pupil, audience*› attento; ‹*son*› premuroso

attentively /ə'tentɪvlɪ/ *adv* attentamente

attentiveness /ə'tentɪvnɪs/ *n* (concentration) attenzione *f*; (solicitude) sollecitudine *f*

attenuate /ə'tenjʊeɪt/ *vt* attenuare

attest /ə'test/ *vt & vi* attestare

attic /'ætɪk/ *n* soffitta *f*

attic room *n* mansarda *f*

attic window *n* lucernario *m*

attire /ə'taɪə(r)/ **A** *n* abiti *mpl*
B *vt* vestire (**in** con)

attitude /'ætɪtjuːd/ *n* atteggiamento *m*

attn. *abbr* (**attention**) c.a.

attorney /ə'tɜːnɪ/ *n* AmE (lawyer) avvocato *m*; **power of** ~ delega *f*

Attorney General *n* BrE ≈ Procuratore *m* Generale; AmE ≈ Ministro *m* di Grazia e Giustizia

attract /ə'trækt/ *vt* attirare

attraction /ə'trækʃn/ *n* attrazione *f*; (feature) attrattiva *f*

attractive /ə'træktɪv/ *adj* ‹*person*› attraente; ‹*proposal, price*› allettante

attractiveness /ə'træktɪvnɪs/ *n* (of person, place) fascino *m*; (of proposal) carattere *m* allettante; (of investment) convenienza *f*

attributable /ə'trɪbjʊtəbl/ *adj* (error, fall, loss etc) attribuibile; **be** ~ **to** ‹*change, profit, success etc*› essere dovuto a

attribute¹ /'ætrɪbjuːt/ *n* attributo *m*

attribute² /ə'trɪbjuːt/ *vt* attribuire

attribution /ætrɪ'bjuːʃn/ *n* attribuzione *f*

attributive /ə'trɪbjʊtɪv/ *adj* attributivo

attrition /ə'trɪʃn/ *n* **war of** ~ guerra *f* di logoramento

attune /ə'tjuːn/ *vt* **be ~d to** (in harmony with) essere sintonizzato con; (accustomed to) essere abituato a

aubergine /'əʊbəʒiːn/ *n* melanzana *f*

auburn /'ɔːbən/ *adj* castano ramato

auction /'ɔːkʃn/ **A** *n* asta *f*
B *vt* vendere all'asta

auctioneer /ɔːkʃə'nɪə(r)/ *n* banditore *m*

auction house *n* casa *f* d'aste

auction rooms *npl* sala *f* d'aste

auction sale *n* vendita *f* all'asta

audacious /ɔː'deɪʃəs/ *adj* sfacciato; (daring) audace

audaciously /ɔː'deɪʃəslɪ/ *adv* sfacciatamente; (daringly) con audacia

audacity /ɔː'dæsətɪ/ *n* sfacciataggine *f*; (daring) audacia *f*

audible /'ɔːdəbl/ *adj* udibile

audience /'ɔːdɪəns/ *n* Theat pubblico *m*; TV telespettatori *mpl*; Radio ascoltatori *mpl*; (meeting) udienza *f*

audience participation *n* partecipazione *f* del pubblico

audience ratings *npl* indici *mpl* di ascolto
audience research *n* sondaggio *m* tra il pubblico
audio /ˈɔːdɪəʊ/ *pref* audio
audiobook *n* audiolibro *m*
audio cassette *n* audiocassetta *f*
audio system *n* impianto *m* stereo
audiotape *n* audiocassetta *f*
audio typing *n* trascrizione *f* da audiocassetta
audio typist *n* dattilografo, -a *mf* (*che trascrive registrazioni*)
audiovisual *adj* audiovisivo
audit /ˈɔːdɪt/ **A** *n* verifica *f* del bilancio **B** *vt* verificare
auditing /ˈɔːdɪtɪŋ/ *n* auditing *m inv*
audition /ɔːˈdɪʃn/ **A** *n* audizione *f* **B** *vi* fare un'audizione
auditor /ˈɔːdɪtə(r)/ *n* revisore *m* di conti
auditorium /ɔːdɪˈtɔːrɪəm/ *n* sala *f*
auditory /ˈɔːdɪt(ə)rɪ/ *adj* acustico, uditivo
augment /ɔːgˈment/ *vt* aumentare
augur /ˈɔːgə(r)/ *vi* ~ **well/ill** essere di buon/cattivo augurio
august /ɔːˈgʌst/ *adj* augusto
🔑 **August** /ˈɔːgəst/ *n* agosto *m*
Augustinian /ɔːgəˈstɪnɪən/ *adj* agostiniano
aunt /ɑːnt/ *n* zia *f*
auntie, aunty /ˈɑːntɪ/ *n* infml zietta *f*
au pair /əʊˈpeə(r)/ *n* ~ **[girl]** ragazza *f* alla pari
aura /ˈɔːrə/ *n* aura *f*
aural /ˈɔːrəl/ **A** *adj* uditivo; Sch ‹*comprehension, test*› orale; Med ‹*test*› audiometrico **B** *n* Sch esercizio *m* di comprensione ed espressione orale; Mus ≈ dettato *m* musicale
aurora australis/borealis /ɔːrɔːrəɒˈstrɑːlɪs/bɔːrɪˈɑːlɪs/ *n* aurora *f* australe/boreale
auspices /ˈɔːspɪsɪz/ *npl* **under the** ~ **of** sotto l'egida di
auspicious /ɔːˈspɪʃəs/ *adj* di buon augurio
Aussie /ˈɒzɪ/ *adj & n* infml australiano, -a *mf*
austere /ɒˈstɪə(r)/ *adj* austero
austerity /ɒˈsterətɪ/ *n* austerità *f*
Australasia /ɒstrəˈleɪʒə/ *n* Australasia *f*
Australia /ɒˈstreɪlɪə/ *n* Australia *f*
🔑 **Australian** /ɒˈstreɪlɪən/ *adj & n* australiano, -a *mf*
Austria /ˈɒstrɪə/ *n* Austria *f*
Austrian /ˈɒstrɪən/ *adj & n* austriaco, -a *mf*
Austro-Hungarian /ɒstrəʊhʌŋˈgeərɪən/ *adj* austroungarico
autarchy /ˈɔːtɑːkɪ/ *n* autarchia *f*
authentic /ɔːˈθentɪk/ *adj* autentico
authenticate /ɔːˈθentɪkeɪt/ *vt* autenticare
authenticity /ɔːθenˈtɪsətɪ/ *n* autenticità *f*
🔑 **author** /ˈɔːθə(r)/ *n* autore *m*
authoritarian /ɔːθɒrɪˈteərɪən/ *adj* autoritario
authoritative /ɔːˈθɒrɪtətɪv/ *adj* autorevole; ‹*manner*› autoritario
🔑 **authority** /ɔːˈθɒrətɪ/ *n* autorità *f*; (permission) autorizzazione *f*; **who's in** ~ **here?** chi è il responsabile qui?; **be in** ~ **over** avere autorità su; **be an** ~ **on** essere un'autorità in materia di
authorization /ɔːθəraɪˈzeɪʃn/ *n* autorizzazione *f*
authorize /ˈɔːθəraɪz/ *vt* autorizzare
authorized dealer /ˈɔːθəraɪzd/ rivenditore *m* autorizzato
autism /ˈɔːtɪzm/ *n* autismo *m*
autistic /ɔːˈtɪstɪk/ *adj* autistico
autistic spectrum disorder *n* disordine *m* dello spettro autistico
auto /ˈɔːtəʊ/ **A** *n* AmE infml auto *f* **B** *attrib* ‹*industry*› automobilistico; ‹*workers*› dell'industria autombilistica
autobiographical /ɔːtəbaɪəˈgræfɪkl/ *adj* autobiografico
autobiography /ɔːtəbaɪˈɒgrəfɪ/ *n* autobiografia *f*
autocrat /ˈɔːtəkræt/ *n* autocrate *m*
autocratic /ɔːtəˈkrætɪk/ *adj* autocratico
autocue /ˈɔːtəʊkjuː/ *n* TV gobbo *m*
auto-destruct *vi* ‹*spacecraft, missile*› autodistruggersi
autograph /ˈɔːtəgrɑːf/ **A** *n* autografo *m* **B** *vt* autografare
autoimmune /ɔːtəʊɪˈmjuːn/ *adj* ‹*disease, system*› autoimmune
automate /ˈɔːtəmeɪt/ *vt* automatizzare
automatic /ɔːtəˈmætɪk/ **A** *adj* automatico **B** *n* (car) macchina *f* col cambio automatico; (washing machine) lavatrice *f* automatica
automatically /ɔːtəˈmætɪklɪ/ *adv* automaticamente
automatic pilot *n* (device) pilota *m* automatico; **be on** ~ also fig viaggiare con il pilota automatico inserito
automatic teller machine /ˈtelə/ *n* cassa *f* continua di prelevamento
automation /ɔːtəˈmeɪʃn/ *n* automazione *f*
automaton /ɔːˈtɒmətən/ *n* automa *m*
automobile /ˈɔːtəməbiːl/ *n* AmE automobile *f*
automotive /ɔːtəˈməʊtɪv/ *adj* (self-propelling) autopropulso; ‹*design, industry*› automobilistico
autonomous /ɔːˈtɒnəməs/ *adj* autonomo
autonomously /ɔːˈtɒnəməslɪ/ *adv* autonomamente
autonomy /ɔːˈtɒnəmɪ/ *n* autonomia *f*
autopilot /ˈɔːtəʊpaɪlət/ *n* Aeron fig pilota *m* automatico

🔑 parola chiave

autopsy /'ɔːtɒpsɪ/ *n* autopsia *f*

auto-suggestion /ɔːtəʊsə'dʒestʃən/ *n* autosuggestione *f*

autumn /'ɔːtəm/ *n* autunno *m*

autumnal /ɔː'tʌmnl/ *adj* autunnale

auxiliary /ɔːg'zɪlɪərɪ/ **A** *adj* ausiliario
B *n* ausiliare *m*

auxiliary nurse *n* infermiere, -a *mf* ausiliario

auxiliary verb *n* ausiliare *m*

avail /ə'veɪl/ **A** *n* **to no ~** invano
B *vi* **~ oneself of** approfittare di

availability /əveɪlə'bɪlətɪ/ *n* (option, service) disponibilità *f*; (of drugs) reperibilità *f*, disponibilità *f*; **subject to ~** fino ad esaurimento

available /ə'veɪləbl/ *adj* disponibile; ‹*book, record etc*› in vendita

avalanche /'ævəlɑːnʃ/ *n* valanga *f*

avant-garde /ævɒ̃'gɑːd/ **A** *n* avanguardia *f*
B *adj* d'avanguardia

avarice /'ævərɪs/ *n* avidità *f*

avaricious /ævə'rɪʃəs/ *adj* avido

Ave *abbr* (**Avenue**) V.le

avenge /ə'vendʒ/ *vt* vendicare

avenger /ə'vendʒə(r)/ *n* vendicatore, -trice *mf*

avenging /ə'vendʒɪŋ/ *adj* vendicatore

avenue /'ævənjuː/ *n* viale *m*; fig strada *f*

average /'ævərɪdʒ/ **A** *adj* medio; (mediocre) mediocre
B *n* media *f*; **on ~** in media; **above ~** superiore al normale
C *vt* ‹*sales, attendance etc*› raggiungere una media di
■ **average out at** *vt* risultare in media

averse /ə'vɜːs/ *adj* **not be ~ to something** non essere contro qualcosa

aversion /ə'vɜːʃn/ *n* avversione *f* (**to** per)

avert /ə'vɜːt/ *vt* evitare ‹*crisis*›; distogliere ‹*eyes*›

avian flu /'eɪvɪən fluː/ *n* influenza *f* aviaria

aviary /'eɪvɪərɪ/ *n* uccelliera *f*

aviation /eɪvɪ'eɪʃn/ *n* aviazione *f*

aviation fuel *n* benzina *f* avio

aviation industry *n* industria *f* aeronautica

aviator /'eɪvɪeɪtə(r)/ *n* aviatore, -trice *mf*

avid /'ævɪd/ *adj* avido (**for** di); ‹*reader*› appassionato

avidity /ə'vɪdətɪ/ *n* avidità

avidly /'ævɪdlɪ/ *adv* ‹*read, collect*› avidamente; ‹*support*› con entusiasmo

avocado /ævə'kɑːdəʊ/ *n* avocado *m*

avoid /ə'vɔɪd/ *vt* evitare

avoidable /ə'vɔɪdəbl/ *adj* evitabile

avoidance /ə'vɔɪdəns/ *n* **~ of one's duty** astensione *f* dal proprio dovere

avowed /ə'vaʊd/ *adj* dichiarato

avuncular /ə'vʌŋkʊlə(r)/ *adj* benevolo

await /ə'weɪt/ *vt* attendere

awake /ə'weɪk/ **A** *adj* sveglio; **wide ~** completamente sveglio
B *vi* (*pt* **awoke**, *pp* **awoken**) svegliarsi

awaken /ə'weɪkn/ **A** *vt* svegliare
B *vi* svegliarsi

awakening /ə'weɪknɪŋ/ *n* risveglio *m*

award /ə'wɔːd/ **A** *n* premio *m*; (medal) riconoscimento *m*; (of prize) assegnazione *f*
B *vt* assegnare; ‹*hand over*› consegnare

award ceremony *n* cerimonia *f* di premiazione

award winner *n* vincitore, -trice *mf* di un premio

award-winning *adj* ‹*book, film, design*› premiato

aware /ə'weə(r)/ *adj* **be ~ of** (sense) percepire; (know) essere conscio di; **become ~ of** accorgersi di; (learn) venire a sapere di; **be ~ that** rendersi conto che

awareness /ə'weənɪs/ *n* percezione *f*; (knowledge) consapevolezza *f*

awash /ə'wɒʃ/ *adj* inondato (**with** di)

away /ə'weɪ/ *adv* via; **go/stay ~** andare/stare via; **he's ~ from his desk/the office** non è alla sua scrivania/in ufficio; **far ~** lontano; **four kilometres ~** a quattro chilometri; **play ~** Sport giocare fuori casa

away game *n* partita *f* fuori casa

awe /ɔː/ *n* soggezione *f*; **stand in ~ of somebody** avere soggezione di qualcuno

awe-inspiring *adj* maestoso

awesome /'ɔːsəm/ *adj* imponente

awful /'ɔːf(ə)l/ **A** *adj* terribile; **that's an ~ pity** è un gran peccato
B *adv* infml estremamente

awfully /'ɔːf(ʊ)lɪ/ *adv* terribilmente; ‹*pretty*› estremamente; **that's ~ nice of you** è veramente gentile da parte tua; **thanks ~** grazie mille

awhile /ə'waɪl/ *adv* per un po'

awkward /'ɔːkwəd/ *adj* ‹*movement*› goffo; ‹*moment, situation*› imbarazzante; ‹*time*› scomodo

awkwardly /'ɔːkwədlɪ/ *adv* ‹*move*› goffamente; ‹*say*› con imbarazzo; **the meeting is ~ timed** la riunione è ad un orario scomodo

awkwardness /'ɔːkwədnɪs/ *n* (clumsiness) goffaggine *f*; (inconvenience) scomodità *f*; (embarrassment) imbarazzo *m*; (delicacy of situation) delicatezza *f*

awl /ɔːl/ *n* (for wood etc) punteruolo *m*

awning /'ɔːnɪŋ/ *n* tendone *m*

awoke(n) /ə'wəʊk(ən)/ ▶ **awake**

AWOL /'eɪwɒl/ *adj & adv abbr* (**absent without leave**) **be/go ~** Mil assentarsi senza permesso; hum volatilizzarsi

awry /ə'raɪ/ *adv* storto

axe /æks/ **A** *n* scure *f*; **have an ~ to grind** fig avere il proprio tornaconto

B *vt* (*pres p* **axing**) fare dei tagli a ‹*budget*›; sopprimere ‹*jobs*›; annullare ‹*project*›
axiom /'æksɪəm/ *n* assioma *m*
axiomatic /æksɪə'mætɪk/ *adj* **it is ~ that...** è indiscutibile che...
axis /'æksɪs/ *n* (*pl* **axes** /-si:z/) asse *m*
axle /'æksl/ *n* Techn asse *m*
ay, aye /aɪ/ **A** *adv* sì
B *n* sì *m*
Azerbaijan /æzəbaɪ'dʒɑ:n/ *n* Azerbaigiano *m*
Azerbaijani /æzəbaɪ'dʒɑ:nɪ/ *adj & n* (person) azerbaigiano, -a *mf*; (language) azerbaigiano *m*
Azores /ə'zɔ:z/ *npl* **the ~** le Azzorre
Aztec /'æztek/ *adj & n* (person) azteco, -a *mf*; (language) azteco *m*
azure /'eɪʒə(r)/ *adj & n* azzurro *m*

Bb

b¹, B /bi:/ *n* (letter) b, B *f inv*; Mus si *m inv*
b² *abbr* (**born**) nato (n.)
b. & b. *abbr* (**bed and breakfast**)
B2B /bi:tə'bi:/ *abbr* (**business to business**) ‹*trade, directory*› B2B
BA *abbr* (**Bachelor of Arts**) *(diploma (m) di) dottore in discipline umanistiche*
baa /bɑ:/ **A** *vi* belare
B *int* bee
BAA *n abbr* (**British Airports Authority**) *ente (m) che gestisce gli aeroporti britannici*
babble /'bæbl/ *vi* farfugliare; ‹*stream*› gorgogliare
babe /beɪb/ *n* literary bimbo, -a *mf*; infml (woman) ragazza *f*; infml (form of address) bella *f*; **a ~ in arms** un bimbo in fasce; fig uno sprovveduto
baboon /bə'bu:n/ *n* babbuino *m*
baby /'beɪbɪ/ *n* bambino, -a *mf*; infml (darling) tesoro *m*
baby bird *n* uccellino *m*
baby boom *n* baby boom *m inv*
baby boomer *n persona (f) nata durante il baby boom*
baby buggy *n* BrE carrozzina *f*
baby carriage *n* AmE carrozzina *f*
baby carrier *n* zaino *m* portabimbo *inv*
baby-faced *adj* ‹*person*› con la faccia da bambino
babyish /'beɪbɪɪʃ/ *adj* bambinesco
baby shower *n* AmE *festa (f) in cui si portano regali a una mamma in attesa*
baby-sit *vi* fare da baby-sitter
baby-sitter *n* baby-sitter *mf*
baby-sitting *n* **do ~** fare il/la baby-sitter
baby talk *n* linguaggio *m* infantile
baby tooth *n* dente *m* di latte
baby walker *n* girello *m*
bachelor /'bætʃələ(r)/ *n* scapolo *m*; **B~ of Arts/Science** laureato, -a *mf* in lettere/in scienze
bachelor apartment, bachelor flat BrE *n* appartamento *m* da scapolo
bachelorhood /'bætʃələhʊd/ *n* celibato *m*
bacillus /bə'sɪləs/ *n* (*pl* **-lli**) bacillo *m*
back /bæk/ **A** *n* schiena *f*; (of horse, hand) dorso *m*; (of chair) schienale *m*; (of house, cheque, page) retro *m*; (in football) difesa *f*; **at the ~** in fondo; **in the ~** Auto dietro; **stand ~ to ~** stare in piedi schiena contro schiena; **~ to front** ‹*sweater*› il davanti di dietro; **you've got it all ~ to front** fig hai capito tutto all'incontrario; **at the ~ of beyond** in un posto sperduto
B *adj* posteriore; ‹*taxes, payments*› arretrato
C *adv* indietro; (returned) di ritorno; **turn/move ~** tornare/spostarsi indietro; **put it ~ here/there** rimettilo qui/là; **~ at home** di ritorno a casa; **I'll be ~ in five minutes** torno fra cinque minuti; **I'm just ~** sono appena tornato; **when do you want the book ~?** quando rivuoi il libro?; **pay ~** ripagare ‹*somebody*›; restituire ‹*money*›; **~ in power** di nuovo al potere
D *vt* (support) sostenere; (with money) finanziare; puntare su ‹*horse*›; (cover the back of) rivestire il retro di
E *vi* Auto fare retromarcia
■ **back away** *vi* tirarsi indietro
■ **back down** *vi* battere in ritirata
■ **back in** *vi* Auto entrare in retromarcia; ‹*person*› entrare camminando all'indietro
■ **back out** *vi* Auto uscire in retromarcia; ‹*person*› uscire camminando all'indietro; fig tirarsi indietro (**of** da)
■ **back up** **A** *vt* sostenere; confermare ‹*person's alibi*›; Comput fare una copia di salvataggio di; **be ~ed up** ‹*traffic*› essere congestionato
B *vi* Auto fare retromarcia

parola chiave

backache *n* mal *m* di schiena
backbench *n* BrE Pol *scanni (mpl) del Parlamento dove siedono i parlamentari ordinari*
backbencher *n* BrE Pol parlamentare *mf* ordinario, -a
backbiting *n* maldicenza *f*
backboard *n* (in basketball) tabellone *m*
back boiler *n* caldaia *f* (*posta dietro un caminetto*)
backbone *n* spina *f* dorsale
back-breaking *adj* massacrante
back burner *n* **put something on the ~** rimandare qualcosa
backchat *n* risposta *f* impertinente
backcloth *n* Theat fondale *m*; fig sfondo *m*
back comb *vt* cotonare
back copy *n* numero *m* arretrato
back cover *n* retro *m* di copertina
backdate *vt* retrodatare ‹*cheque*›; **~d to** valido a partire da
back door *n* porta *f* di servizio
backdrop *n* Theat fondale *m*; fig sfondo *m*
back-end *n* (rear) fondo *m*
backer /'bækə(r)/ *n* sostenitore, -trice *mf*; (with money) finanziatore, -trice *mf*
backfire *vi* Auto avere un ritorno di fiamma; fig ‹*plan*› fallire; **the joke ~d on him** lo scherzo si è ritorto contro di lui
backgammon *n* backgammon *m*
background *n* sfondo *m*; (environment) ambiente *m*
background noise *n* rumore *m* di sottofondo
background reading *n* letture *fpl* generali
backhand *n* Tennis rovescio *m*
backhanded *adj* ‹*compliment*› implicito
backhander *n* infml (bribe) bustarella *f*
backing /'bækɪŋ/ *n* (support) supporto *m*; (material used) fondo *m*; Mus accompagnamento *m*; **~ singer/vocals/group** cantante/voci/ gruppo d'accompagnamento
back issue *n* numero *m* arretrato
backlash /'bæklæʃ/ *n* fig reazione *f* opposta
backless /'bæklɪs/ *adj* ‹*dress*› scollato dietro
backlist *n* opere *fpl* pubblicate
backlog *n* **~ of work** lavoro *m* arretrato
back marker *n* Sport ultimo, -a *mf*
back number *n* numero *m* arretrato
backpack *n* zaino *m*
backpacker *n* saccopelista *mf*
backpacking *n* **go ~** viaggiare con zaino e sacco a pelo
back passage *n* Anat retto *m*
back pay *n* arretrato *m* di stipendio
back-pedal *vi* pedalare all'indietro; fig fare marcia indietro
back pocket *n* tasca *f* di dietro
backrest *n* schienale *m*
back room *n* stanza *f* sul retro
back room boys *npl esperti (mpl) che lavorano dietro le quinte*
back-scratcher *n* manina *f* grattaschiena *inv*
back seat *n* sedile *m* posteriore
back-seat driver *n persona (f) che dà consigli non richiesti*
backside *n* infml fondoschiena *m inv*
backslash *n* Typ backslash *nm inv*
backspace *n* Comput backspace *m*
backstage *adj & adv* dietro le quinte
backstairs *npl* scale *f* di servizio
backstitch **A** *n* impuntura *f* **B** *vi* impunturare
backstop *n* Sport ricevitore *m*
backstory *n* vicende *fpl* passate
back straight *n* Sport rettilineo *m*
backstreet **A** *n* vicolo *m* **B** *attrib* ‹*abortionist*› clandestino
backstroke *n* dorso *m*
backtalk *n* AmE *backchat*
backtrack *vi* tornare indietro; fig fare marcia indietro
back translation *n* traduzione *f* di una traduzione
backup *n* rinforzi *mpl*; Comput riserva *f*, backup *m inv*; **do a ~** realizzare un backup
backup copy *n* copia *f* di riserva
backup light *n* AmE luce *f* di retromarcia
backward /'bækwəd/ *adj* ‹*step*› indietro; ‹*child*› lento nell'apprendimento; ‹*country*› arretrato
backward-looking /'bækwədlʊkɪŋ/ *adj* retrogrado
backwards BrE, **backward** AmE /'bækwəd[z]/ *adv* indietro; ‹*fall, walk*› all'indietro; **~ and forwards** avanti e indietro
backwater /'bækwɔːtə(r)/ *n* fig luogo *m* arretrato
backyard /bæk'jɑːd/ *n* cortile *m*; **not in my ~ yard** infml non a casa mia
bacon /'beɪk(ə)n/ *n* ≈ pancetta *f*
bacon-slicer /'beɪkənslaɪsə(r)/ *n* affettarice *f*
bacteria /bæk'tɪərɪə/ *npl* batteri *mpl*
bacterial /bæk'tɪərɪəl/ *adj* batterico
bacteriology /bæktɪərɪ'ɒlədʒɪ/ *n* batteriologia *f*
bad /bæd/ *adj* (**worse**, **worst**) cattivo; ‹*weather, habit, news, accident*› brutto; ‹*apple etc*› marcio; **the light is ~** non c'è una buona luce; **my eyesight is ~** non ho una buona vista; **use ~ language** dire delle parolacce; **she's going through a ~ patch** sta attraversando un brutto periodo; **feel ~** sentirsi male; (feel guilty) sentirsi in colpa; **have a ~ back** avere dei problemi alla schiena; **smoking is ~ for you** fumare fa male; **go ~** andare a male; **that's just too ~!**

b

pazienza!; **not ~** niente male; **things have gone from ~ to worse** le cose sono andate di male in peggio

b

bad blood *n* **there is ~ between them** tra loro non corre buon sangue

bad boy *n* ragazzaccio *m*

bad breath *n* alito *m* cattivo

bad cheque *n* assegno *m* a vuoto

bad debt *n* credito *m* inesigibile

baddie, baddy /ˈbædɪ/ *n* infml cattivo, -a *mf*

bade /bæd/ ▶ **bid**[1]

bad faith *n* malafede *f*

badge /bædʒ/ *n* distintivo *m*

badger /ˈbædʒə(r)/ **A** *n* tasso *m*
B *vt* tormentare

badly /ˈbædlɪ/ *adv* male; ‹*hurt*› gravemente; **~ off** povero; **~ behaved** maleducato; **need ~** aver estremamente bisogno di

bad-mannered /-ˈmænəd/ *adj* maleducato

badminton /ˈbædmɪntən/ *n* badminton *m*

bad-tempered /-ˈtempəd/ *adj* irascibile

baffle /ˈbæfl/ *vt* confondere

baffled /ˈbæfld/ *adj* sconcertato

baffling /ˈbæflɪŋ/ *adj* sconcertante

BAFTA, Bafta /ˈbæftə/ *n abbr* (**British Academy of Film and Television Arts**) *società* (*m*) *britannica delle arti cinematografiche e televisive*

⚷ **bag** /bæg/ **A** *n* borsa *f*; (of paper) sacchetto *m*; **old ~** sl megera *f*; **~s under the eyes** occhiaie *fpl*; **~s of** infml un sacco di; **it's in the ~** fig è fatta
B *vt* (*pt/pp* **bagged**) infml (take) accaparrarsi; **~ somebody a seat** tenere un posto a qualcuno

bagel /ˈbeɪgəl/ *n panino* (*m*) *a forma di ciambella*

baggage /ˈbægɪdʒ/ *n* bagagli *mpl*

baggage allowance *n* franchigia *f* bagaglio

baggage car *n* Rail bagagliaio *m*

baggage carousel *n* nastro *m* trasportatore per ritiro bagagli

baggage check *n* controllo *m* bagagli

baggage handler *n* addetto, -a *mf* ai bagagli

baggage locker *n* armadietto *m* per deposito bagagli

baggage reclaim *n* ritiro *m* bagagli

baggy /ˈbægɪ/ *adj* ‹*clothes*› ampio

Baghdad /bægˈdæd/ *n* Baghdad *f*

bag lady *n* infml barbona *f*

bag person *n* infml barbone, -a *mf*

bagpipes *npl* cornamusa *fsg*

bag snatcher *n* scippatore, -trice *mf*

baguette /bægˈet/ *n* baguette *f inv*

Bahamas /bəˈhɑːməz/ *npl* **the ~** le Bahamas

Bahrain, Bahrein /bɑːˈreɪn/ *n* Bahrein *m*

⚷ parola chiave

bail /beɪl/ *n* cauzione *f*; **on ~** su cauzione
■ **bail out** **A** *vt* Naut aggottare; **~ somebody out** Jur pagare la cauzione per qualcuno; fig trarre qualcuno d'impaccio
B *vi* Aeron paracadutarsi

bail bond *n* AmE Jur cauzione *f*

bailiff /ˈbeɪlɪf/ *n* ufficiale *m* giudiziario; (of estate) fattore *m*

bailout /ˈbeɪlaʊt/ *n* Fin salvataggio *m* (dal fallimento)

bait /beɪt/ **A** *n* esca *f*; **rise to the ~** abboccare [all'amo]
B *vt* innescare; fig (torment) tormentare

baize /beɪz/ *n* panno *m* (*di tavolo da gioco e da biliardo*)

bake /beɪk/ **A** *vt* cuocere al forno; (make) fare
B *vi* cuocersi al forno

baked beans /beɪktˈbiːnz/ *n* Culin fagioli *mpl* al pomodoro

baked potato *n patata* (*f*) *cotta al forno* (*con la buccia*)

baker /ˈbeɪkə(r)/ *n* fornaio, -a *mf*, panettiere, -a *mf*

baker's BrE /ˈbeɪkəz/, **baker's shop, bakeshop** AmE *n* panetteria

bakery /ˈbeɪkərɪ/ *n* panificio *m*, forno *m*

baking /ˈbeɪkɪŋ/ *n* cottura *f* al forno

baking powder *n* lievito *m* in polvere

baking soda *n* Culin bicarbonato *m* di sodio

baking tin *n* teglia *f*

balaclava /bæləˈklɑːvə/ *n* passamontagna *m inv*

⚷ **balance** /ˈbæləns/ **A** *n* (equilibrium) equilibrio *m*; Comm bilancio *m*; (outstanding sum) saldo *m*; **[bank] ~** saldo *m*; **be** *or* **hang in the ~** fig essere in sospeso; **on ~** tutto sommato
B *vt* bilanciare; equilibrare ‹*budget*›; Comm fare il bilancio di ‹*books*›
C *vi* bilanciarsi; Comm essere in pareggio

balanced /ˈbælənst/ *adj* equilibrato

balance of payments *n* bilancia *f* dei pagamenti

balance of power *n* Pol equilibrio *m* delle forze

balance of trade *n* bilancia *f* commerciale

balance sheet *n* bilancio *m* patrimoniale

balancing act /ˈbælənsɪŋ/ *n* fig **do a ~** fare equilibrismo

balcony /ˈbælkənɪ/ *n* balcone *m*

bald /bɔːld/ *adj* ‹*person*› calvo; ‹*tyre*› liscio; ‹*statement*› nudo e crudo; **go ~** perdere i capelli

balderdash /ˈbɔːldədæʃ/ *n* sciocchezze *fpl*

balding /ˈbɔːldɪŋ/ *adj* **be ~** stare perdendo i capelli

baldly /ˈbɔːldlɪ/ *adv* ‹*state*› in modo nudo e crudo

baldness /ˈbɔːldnɪs/ *n* calvizie *f*

bale /beɪl/ *n* balla *f*

Balearic Islands /bælerˈærɪk/ *npl* isole *fpl* Baleari

baleful /ˈbeɪlfl/ *adj* malvagio; (sad) triste

balefully /ˈbeɪlfʊlɪ/ *adv* con malvagità

Bali /ˈbɑːlɪ/ *n* Bali *f*

balk /bɔːlk/ **A** *vt* ostacolare
B *vi* ~ **at** ‹*horse*› impennarsi davanti a; fig tirarsi indietro davanti a

Balkan /ˈbɔːlkən/ *adj* dei Balcani

Balkans /ˈbɔːlknz/ *npl* Balcani *mpl*

ball¹ /bɔːl/ *n* palla *f*; (football) pallone *m*; (of yarn) gomitolo *m*; **on the** ~ infml sveglio

ball² *n* (dance) ballo *m*

ballad /ˈbæləd/ *n* ballata *f*

ball and chain *n* palla *f* al piede

ball-and-socket joint *n* giunto *m* sferico

ballast /ˈbæləst/ *n* zavorra *f*

ball bearing *n* cuscinetto *m* a sfera

ballboy *n* Tennis raccattapalle *m inv*

ballcock *n* Techn galleggiante *m* (*in serbatoio*)

ball control *n* controllo *m* della palla

ball dress *n* abito *m* da sera

ballerina /bæləˈriːnə/ *n* ballerina *f* [classica]

ballet /ˈbæleɪ/ *n* balletto *m*; (art form) danza *f*

ballet dancer *n* ballerino, -a *mf* [classico, -a]

ballet dress *n* tutù *m*

ballet shoes *npl* scarpe *fpl* da danza

ball game *n* gioco *m* con la palla; AmE partita *f* di baseball; **that's a whole different** ~ fig è tutto un altro paio di maniche

ballgirl *n* Tennis raccattapalle *f inv*

ball gown *n* abito *m* da sera

ballistic /bəˈlɪstɪk/ *adj* balistico

ballistics *nsg* balistica *fsg*

balloon /bəˈluːn/ *n* pallone *m*; Aeron mongolfiera *f*

balloonist /bəˈluːnɪst/ *n* aeronauta *mf*

ballot /ˈbælət/ *n* votazione *f*

ballot box *n* urna *f*

ballot paper *n* scheda *f* di votazione

ballpark *n* AmE stadio *m* di baseball

ballpark figure *n* infml cifra *f* approssimativa

ball-point, **ball-point pen** *n* penna *f* a sfera

ballroom *n* sala *f* da ballo

ballroom dancing *n* ballo *m* liscio

balls up vulg **A** *vi* incasinarsi
B *vt* incasinare

ballyhoo /bælɪˈhuː/ *n* (publicity) battage *m inv* pubblicitario; (uproar) baccano *m*

balm /bɑːm/ *n* balsamo *m*

balmy /ˈbɑːmɪ/ *adj* (**-ier**, **-iest**) mite; infml (crazy) strampalato

balsam /ˈbɒlsəm/ *n* (oily) balsamo *m*

Baltic /ˈbɔːltɪk/ *adj* & *n* **the** ~ **[Sea]** il [mar] Baltico

balustrade /bæləˈstreɪd/ *n* balaustra *f*

bamboo /bæmˈbuː/ *n* bambù *m*

bamboozle /bæmˈbuːzl/ *vt* infml (mystify) confondere

ban /bæn/ **A** *n* proibizione *f*
B *vt* (*pt/pp* **banned**) proibire; ~ **from** espellere da ‹*club*›; **she was** ~**ned from driving** le hanno ritirato la patente

banal /bəˈnɑːl/ *adj* banale

banality /bəˈnælətɪ/ *n* banalità *f*

banana /bəˈnɑːnə/ *n* banana *f*

banana republic *n* derog repubblica *f* delle banane

banana skin *n* buccia *f* di banana

band /bænd/ *n* banda *f*; (stripe) nastro *m*; Mus (pop group) complesso *m*; Mus (brass ~) banda *f*; Mil fanfara *f*

▪ **band together** *vi* riunirsi

bandage /ˈbændɪdʒ/ **A** *n* benda *f*
B *vt* fasciare

▪ **bandage up** *vt* fasciare

Band-Aid *n* Med cerotto *m*

bandanna, **bandana** /bænˈdænə/ *n* bandana *f*

bandit /ˈbændɪt/ *n* bandito *m*

band leader *n* leader *mf* di un complesso

bandmaster *n* capobanda *m* (*di banda musicale*)

band saw *n* segatrice *f* a nastro

bandsman *n* bandista *m*

bandstand *n* palco *m* coperto [dell'orchestra].

bandwagon *n* **jump on the** ~ fig seguire la corrente

bandy¹ /ˈbændɪ/ *vt* (*pt/pp* **-ied**) scambiarsi ‹*words*›

▪ **bandy about** *vt* far circolare

bandy² *adj* (**-ier**, **-iest**) **be** ~ avere le gambe storte

bandy-legged /-ˈlegd/ *adj* con le gambe storte

bane /beɪn/ *n* **she/it is the** ~ **of my life!** è la mia rovina!

bang /bæŋ/ **A** *n* (noise) fragore *m*; (of gun, firework) scoppio *m*; (blow) colpo *m*; **go with a** ~ infml essere una cannonata
B *adv* ~ **in the middle of** infml proprio nel mezzo di; **go** ~ ‹*gun*› sparare; ‹*balloon*› esplodere
C *int* bum!
D *vt* battere ‹*fist*›; battere su ‹*table*›; sbattere ‹*door, head*›
E *vi* scoppiare; ‹*door*› sbattere

▪ **bang about**, **bang around** *vi* far rumore

▪ **bang into** *vt* sbattere contro

banger /ˈbæŋə(r)/ *n* (firework) petardo *m*; infml (sausage) salsiccia *f*; **old** ~ infml (car) macinino *m*

Bangladesh /bæŋgləˈdeʃ/ *n* Bangladesh *m*

Bangladeshi /ˌbæŋgləˈdeʃɪ/ **A** *adj* del Bangladesh
B *n* persona *f* del Bangladesh

b

bangle /ˈbæŋgl/ *n* braccialetto *m*
banish /ˈbænɪʃ/ *vt* bandire
banishment /ˈbænɪʃmənt/ *n* bando *m*
banister /ˈbænɪstə/ *n* ringhiera *f*
banjo /ˈbændʒəʊ/ *n* banjo *m inv*
bank¹ /bæŋk/ **A** *n* (of river) sponda *f*; (slope) scarpata *f*
B *vi* Aeron inclinarsi in virata
🔑 **bank²** **A** *n* banca *f*
B *vt* depositare in banca
C *vi* ~ **with** avere un conto [bancario] presso
▪ **bank on** *vt* contare su
bank account *n* conto *m* in banca
bank balance *n* saldo *m*
bank book *n* libretto *m* di risparmio
bank borrowings *npl* prestiti *mpl* bancari
bank card *n* carta *f* assegni
bank charges *npl* spese *fpl* bancarie, commissioni *fpl*
bank clerk *n* bancario, -a *mf*
bank details *npl* coordinate *fpl* bancarie
banker /ˈbæŋkə(r)/ *n* banchiere *m*
banker's draft *n* tratta *f* bancaria
banker's order *n* ordine *m* di pagamento
Bank Giro Credit *n* BrE accreditamento *m* tramite bancogiro
bank holiday *n* giorno *m* festivo
banking /ˈbæŋkɪŋ/ *n* bancario *m*
banking hours *npl* orario *m* di sportello (*in banca*)
bank manager *n* direttore, -trice *mf* di banca
banknote *n* banconota *f*
bank raid *n* rapina *f* in banca
bank robber *n* rapinatore, -trice *mf* di banca
bank robbery *n* rapina *f* in banca
bankroll **A** *n* finanziamento *m*
B *vt* finanziare ‹*person, party*›
bankrupt /ˈbæŋkrʌpt/ **A** *adj* fallito; **go ~** fallire
B *n* persona *f* che ha fatto fallimento
C *vt* far fallire
bankruptcy /ˈbæŋkrʌptsɪ/ *n* bancarotta *f*
bankruptcy court *n* tribunale *m* fallimentare
bankruptcy proceedings *npl* procedura *f* fallimentare
bank statement *n* estratto *m* conto
bank transfer *n* bonifico *m* bancario
banner /ˈbænə(r)/ *n* stendardo *m*; (of demonstrators) striscione *m*
banner headline *n* titolo *m* a tutta pagina
banns /bænz/ *npl* Relig pubblicazioni *fpl* [di matrimonio]

🔑 parola chiave

banquet /ˈbæŋkwɪt/ *n* banchetto *m*
bantam /ˈbæntəm/ *n* gallo *m* bantam
banter /ˈbæntə(r)/ *n* battute *fpl* di spirito
baptism /ˈbæptɪzm/ *n* battesimo *m*; **~ of fire** fig battesimo *m* del fuoco
Baptist /ˈbæptɪst/ *adj & n* battista *mf*
baptize /bæpˈtaɪz/ *vt* battezzare
🔑 **bar** /bɑː(r)/ **A** *n* sbarra *f*; Jur ordine *m* degli avvocati; (of chocolate) tavoletta *f*; (café) bar *m inv*; (counter) banco *m*; Mus battuta *f*; fig (obstacle) ostacolo *m*; **~ of soap/gold** saponetta *f* /lingotto *m*; **be called to the ~** Jur entrare a far parte dell'ordine degli avvocati; **behind ~s** infml dietro le sbarre
B *vt* (*pt/pp* **barred**) sbarrare ‹*way*›; sprangare ‹*door*›; escludere ‹*person*›
C *prep* tranne; **~ none** in assoluto
barb /bɑːb/ *n* barbiglio *m*; fig (remark) frecciata *f*
Barbados /bɑːˈbeɪdɒs/ *n* Barbados *fsg*
barbarian /bɑːˈbeərɪən/ *n* barbaro, -a *mf*
barbaric /bɑːˈbærɪk/ *adj* barbarico
barbarism /ˈbɑːbərɪzm/ *n* (brutality, primitiveness) barbarie *f inv*; (error of style) barbarismo *m*
barbarity /bɑːˈbærətɪ/ *n* barbarie *f inv*
barbarous /ˈbɑːbərəs/ *adj* barbaro
barbecue /ˈbɑːbɪkjuː/ **A** *n* barbecue *m inv*; (party) grigliata *f*, barbecue *m inv*
B *vt* arrostire sul barbecue
barbed /bɑːbd/ *adj* **~ wire** filo *m* spinato
barber /ˈbɑːbə(r)/ *n* barbiere *m*
barber's shop *n* barbiere *m*
barbiturate /bɑːˈbɪtjʊrət/ *n* barbiturico *m*
bar chart *n* istogramma *m*
bar code *n* codice *m* a barre
bar-coded *adj* con codice a barre
bar code reader *n* lettore *m* di codice a barre
bard /bɑːd/ *n* literary bardo *m*
bare /beə(r)/ **A** *adj* nudo; ‹*tree, room*› spoglio; ‹*floor*› senza moquette; **the ~ bones** l'essenziale *m*
B *vt* scoprire; mostrare ‹*teeth*›
bareback *adv* senza sella
barefaced *adj* sfacciato
barefoot *adv* scalzo
bare-headed *adj* a capo scoperto
🔑 **barely** /ˈbeəlɪ/ *adv* appena
bareness /ˈbeənɪs/ *n* nudità *f*
bargain /ˈbɑːgɪn/ **A** *n* (agreement) patto *m*; (good buy) affare *m*; **into the ~** per di più
B *vi* contrattare; (haggle) trattare
▪ **bargain for** *vt* (expect) aspettarsi
bargain basement *n* reparto *m* occasioni
bargaining /ˈbɑːgɪnɪŋ/ **A** *n* (over pay) contrattazione *f*
B *attrib* ‹*power, rights*› contrattuale; ‹*position*› di negoziato
barge /bɑːdʒ/ *n* barcone *m*

■ **barge in** *vi* infml (to room) piombare dentro; (into conversation) interrompere bruscamente; **~ into** piombare dentro a ‹*room*›; venire addosso a ‹*person*›; venire addosso a ‹*person*›

bargepole /ˈbɑːdʒpəʊl/ *n* **I wouldn't touch him/it with a ~** non lo toccherei nemmeno con un dito

barista /bəˈrɪstə/ *n* esp Am barista *mf*

baritone /ˈbærɪtəʊn/ *n* baritono *m*

bark¹ /bɑːk/ *n* (of tree) corteccia *f*

bark² **A** *n* abbaio *m*
B *vi* abbaiare

barking /ˈbɑːkɪŋ/ **A** *n* abbaio *m*
B *adj* ‹*dog*› che abbaia; ‹*cough, laugh*› convulso
C *adv* **be ~ mad** BrE infml essere matto da legare

barley /ˈbɑːlɪ/ *n* orzo *m*

barleycorn *n* orzo *m*; (grain) chicco *m* d'orzo

barley sugar *n* caramella *f* d'orzo

barley water *n* BrE orzata *f*

barley wine *n* BrE birra *f* molto forte

barmaid /ˈbɑːmeɪd/ *n* barista *f*

barman /ˈbɑːmən/ *n* barista *m*

barmy /ˈbɑːmɪ/ *adj* infml strampalato

barn /bɑːn/ *n* granaio *m*

barnacle /ˈbɑːnəkl/ *n* cirripede *m*

barn dance *n ballo (m) tradizionale statunitense*; (social gathering) *festa (f) negli USA in cui si fanno balli tradizionali*

barn owl *n* barbagianni *m inv*

barnstorming *adj* sensazionale

barnyard *n* aia *f*

barometer /bəˈrɒmɪtə(r)/ *n* barometro *m*

baron /ˈbærən/ *n* barone *m*

baroness /ˈbærənɪs/ *n* baronessa *f*

baronial /bəˈrəʊnɪəl/ *adj* baronale

baroque /bəˈrɒk/ *adj & n* barocco *m*

barracking /ˈbærəkɪŋ/ *n* fischi *mpl* e insulti *mpl*

barrack room **A** *n* camerata *f*
B *attrib* derog ‹*language*› da caserma

barracks /ˈbærəks/ *npl* caserma *fsg*

barrage /ˈbærɑːʒ/ *n* (in river) [opera *f* di] sbarramento *m*; Mil sbarramento *m*; fig (of criticism, abuse) sfilza *f*

barrage balloon *n* pallone *m* di sbarramento

barrel /ˈbærəl/ *n* barile *m*, botte *f*; (of gun) canna *f*

barrel organ *n* organetto *m* [a cilindro]

barren /ˈbærən/ *adj* sterile; ‹*landscape*› brullo

barrette /bæˈret/ *n* AmE (for hair) molletta *f*

barricade /bærɪˈkeɪd/ **A** *n* barricata *f*
B *vt* barricare

barrier /ˈbærɪə(r)/ *n* barriera *f*; Rail cancello *m*; fig ostacolo *m*

barrier cream *n* crema *f* protettiva

barrier method *n* Med metodo *m* anticoncezionale meccanico

barrier reef *n* barriera *f* corallina

barring /ˈbɑːrɪŋ/ *prep* **~ accidents** salvo imprevisti

barrister /ˈbærɪstə(r)/ *n* avvocato *m*

barrow /ˈbærəʊ/ *n* carretto *m*; (wheel ~) carriola *f*

bar stool *n* sgabello *m* da bar

bartender /ˈbɑːtendə(r)/ *n* barista *mf*

barter /ˈbɑːtə(r)/ *vi* barattare (**for** con)

base /beɪs/ **A** *n* base *f*
B *adj* vile
C *vt* basare; **be ~d on** basarsi su

baseball /ˈbeɪsbɔːl/ *n* baseball *m*

baseball cap *n* berretto *m* da baseball

base camp *n* campo *m* base *inv*

base form *n* (of verb) forma *f* non coniugata di un verbo

base lending rate *n* tasso *m* base *inv* di interesse

baseless /ˈbeɪslɪs/ *adj* infondato

baseline /ˈbeɪslaɪn/ *n* Tennis linea *f* di fondo; fig riferimento *m*

basement /ˈbeɪsmənt/ *n* seminterrato *m*

basement flat *n* appartamento *m* nel seminterrato

base metal *n* metallo *m* vile *inv*

base rate *n* tasso *m* base *inv*

bash /bæʃ/ **A** *n* colpo *m* violento; **have a ~!** infml provaci!
B *vt* colpire [violentemente]; (dent) ammaccare; **~ed in** ammaccato

■ **bash down** *vt* sfondare ‹*door*›

■ **bash into** *vt* imbattersi in ‹*person*›; sbattere contro ‹*wall, tree*›

bashful /ˈbæʃfl/ *adj* timido

bashfully /ˈbæʃfʊlɪ/ *adv* timidamente

bashing /ˈbæʃɪŋ/ *n* infml (beating) pestaggio *m*; (criticism) critica *f* feroce; (defeat) batosta *f*; **take a ~** prendere una batosta

basic /ˈbeɪsɪk/ *adj* di base; ‹*condition, requirement*› basilare; ‹*living conditions*› povero; **my Italian is pretty ~** il mio italiano è abbastanza rudimentale; **the ~s** (of language, science) i rudimenti; (essentials) l'essenziale *m*

basically /ˈbeɪsɪklɪ/ *adv* fondamentalmente

basic rate *n* tariffa *f* minima; (in tax) aliquota *f* minima

basil /ˈbæzɪl/ *n* basilico *m*

basilica /bəˈzɪlɪkə/ *n* basilica *f*

basin /ˈbeɪsn/ *n* bacinella *f*; (wash-hand ~) lavabo *m*; (for food) recipiente *m*; Geog bacino *m*

basinful /ˈbeɪsɪnfʊl/ *n* bacinella *f* (*contenuto*)

basis /ˈbeɪsɪs/ *n* (*pl* **-ses** /ˈbeɪsiːz/) base *f*

bask /bɑːsk/ *vi* crogiolarsi

basket /ˈbɑːskɪt/ *n* cestino *m*

basketball *n* pallacanestro *f*
basket chair *n* sedia *m* di vimini
basketwork *n* (objects) oggetti *mpl* in vimini; (craft) lavoro *m* artigianale di oggetti in vimini
Basle /bɑːl/ *n* Basilea *f*
Basque /bæsk/ *adj & n* (person) basco, -a *mf*; (language) basco *m*
bass /beɪs/ **A** *adj* basso; ~ **voice** voce *f* di basso
B *n* basso *m*
bass-baritone *n* baritono *m* basso
bass clef *n* chiave *f* di basso
bass drum *n* grancassa *f*
basset hound /ˈbæsɪt/ *n* basset hound *m inv*
bass guitar *n* (chitarra *f*) basso *m*
bassist /ˈbeɪsɪst/ *n* bassista *mf*
bassoon /bəˈsuːn/ *n* fagotto *m*
bastard /ˈbɑːstəd/ *n* (illegitimate child) bastardo, -a *mf*; sl figlio *m* di puttana
baste¹ /beɪst/ *vt* (sew) imbastire
baste² *vt* Culin ungere con grasso
bastion /ˈbæstɪən/ *n* bastione *m*
bat¹ /bæt/ **A** *n* mazza *f*; (for table tennis) racchetta *f*; **off one's own** ~ infml tutto da solo
B *vt* (*pt/pp* **batted**) battere; **she didn't** ~ **an eyelid** fig non ha battuto ciglio
bat² *n* Zool pipistrello *m*
batch /bætʃ/ *n* gruppo *m*; (of goods) partita *f*; (of bread) infornata *f*
batch file *n* Comput batch file *m inv*
batch processing /ˈprəʊsesɪŋ/ *n* Comput elaborazione *f* a gruppi
bated /ˈbeɪtɪd/ *adj* **with** ~ **breath** col fiato sospeso
bath /bɑːθ/ **A** *n* (*pl* ~**s** /bɑːðz/) bagno *m*; (tub) vasca *f* da bagno; ~**s** *pl* piscina *f*; **have a** ~ fare un bagno
B *vt* fare il bagno a
C *vi* fare il bagno
bathe /beɪð/ **A** *n* bagno *m*
B *vi* fare il bagno
C *vt* lavare ‹*wound*›
bather /ˈbeɪðə(r)/ *n* bagnante *mf*
bathing /ˈbeɪðɪŋ/ *n* bagni *mpl*
bathing cap *n* cuffia *f*
bathing costume *n* costume *m* da bagno
bathing hut *n* cabina *f* (*al mare*)
bathing suit *n* costume *m* da bagno
bathing trunks *n* calzoncini *mpl* da bagno
bath mat *n* tappetino *m* da bagno
bathrobe /ˈbæθrəʊb/ *n* accappatoio *m*
bathroom /ˈbæθruːm/ *n also* (toilet) bagno *m*
bathroom cabinet *n* armadietto *m* del bagno
bathroom fittings *npl* accessori *mpl* per il bagno
bathroom scales *npl* bilancia *f* pesapersone
bath salts *npl* sali *mpl* da bagno
bath towel *n* asciugamano *m* da bagno
bathtub *n* vasca *f* da bagno
baton /ˈbæt(ə)n/ *n* Mus bacchetta *f*
baton charge *n* BrE carica *f* con lo sfollagente
baton round *n* BrE proiettile *m* di gomma
batsman /ˈbætsmən/ *n* Sport battitore *m*
battalion /bəˈtælɪən/ *n* battaglione *m*
batten /ˈbætn/ *n* assicella *f*
batter /ˈbætə(r)/ *n* Culin pastella *f*
battered /ˈbætəd/ *adj* ‹*car*› malandato; ‹*wife, baby*› maltrattato
battering /ˈbæt(ə)rɪŋ/ *n* **take a** ~ (from bombs, storm, waves) essere colpito; (from other team) prendersi una batosta; (from other boxer) prenderle
battering ram *n* ariete *m*
battery /ˈbætərɪ/ *n* batteria *f*; (of torch, radio) pila *f*
battery charger *n* caricabatterie *m inv*
battery chicken *n* pollo *m* di allevamento in batteria
battery controlled *adj* a pile
battery farming *n* allevamento *m* in batteria
battery hen *n* gallina *f* d'allevamento in batteria
battery life *n* autonomia *f*
battery operated, **battery powered** *adj* a pile
battery pack *n* battery pack *m inv*
⚷ **battle** /ˈbæt(ə)l/ **A** *n* battaglia *f*; fig lotta *f*
B *vi* fig lottare
battleaxe *n* infml virago *f inv*
battle cry *n* also fig grido *m* di battaglia
battle dress *n* uniforme *f* da combattimento
battlefield, **battleground** *n* campo *m* di battaglia; fig terreno *m* di scontro
battle lines *npl* Mil schieramenti *mpl*
battlements /ˈbætlmənts/ *npl* bordo *m* merlato; (crenellations) merlatura *f*
battle order *n* also fig ordine *m* di battaglia
battle-scarred *adj* agguerrito; fig segnato dalla vita
battleship *n* corazzata *f*
batty /ˈbætɪ/ *adj* infml strampalato
bauble /ˈbɔːb(ə)l/ *n* (ornament) gingillo *m*; (jewellery) ninnolo *m*
bawdiness /ˈbɔːdɪnɪs/ *n* oscenità *f*
bawdy /ˈbɔːdɪ/ *adj* (**-ier**, **-iest**) piccante
bawl /bɔːl/ *vt & vi* urlare
■ **bawl out** *vt* infml urlare ‹*name, order*›; fare una sfuriata a ‹*somebody*›
bay¹ /beɪ/ *n* Geog baia *f*
bay² *n* **keep at** ~ tenere a bada

⚷ parola chiave

bay³ *n* Bot alloro *m*

bay⁴ *n* (horse) baio *m*

bay leaf *n* foglia *f* d'alloro

bayonet /ˈberənet/ *n* baionetta *f*

bay window *n* bay window *f inv* (*grande finestra sporgente*)

bazaar /bəˈzɑː(r)/ *n* bazar *m inv*

bazooka /bəˈzuːkə/ *n* bazooka *m inv*

BBC *n abbr* (**British Broadcasting Corporation**) BBC *f*

BBQ *abbr* (**barbecue**) barbecue *m inv*

BC *abbr* (**before Christ**) a.C.

Bcc *n abbr* (**blind carbon copy**) ccn *f*

be /biː/ **A** *vi* (*pres* **am**, **are**, **is**, **are**, *pt* **was**, **were**, *pp* **been**) essere; **he is a teacher** è insegnante, fa l'insegnante; **what do you want to be?** cosa vuoi fare?; **be quiet!** sta' zitto!; **I am cold/hot** ho freddo/caldo; **it's cold/hot, isn't it?** fa freddo/caldo, vero?; **how are you?** come stai?; **I am well** sto bene; **there is** c'è; **there are** ci sono; **I have been to Venice** sono stato a Venezia; **has the postman been?** è passato il postino?; **you're coming too, aren't you?** vieni anche tu, no?; **it's yours, is it?** è tuo, vero?; **was John there? - yes, he was** c'era John? - sì; **John wasn't there - yes he was!** John non c'era - sì che c'era!; **three and three are six** tre più tre fanno sei; **he is five** ha cinque anni; **that will be £10, please** fanno 10 sterline, per favore; **how much is it?** quanto costa?; **that's £5 you owe me** mi devi 5 sterline
B *v aux* **I am coming/reading** sto venendo/leggendo; **I'm staying** (not leaving) resto; **I am being lazy** sono pigro; **I was thinking of you** stavo pensando a te; **you are not to tell him** non devi dirglielo; **you are to do that immediately** devi farlo subito
C *passive* essere; **I have been robbed** sono stato derubato

BE *abbr* (**bill of exchange**) cambiale *f*

beach /biːtʃ/ *n* spiaggia *f*

beach ball *n* pallone *m* da spiaggia

beach buggy *n* dune buggy *f inv*

beach-comber /-kəʊmə(r)/ *n persona (f) che vive rivendendo gli oggetti trovati sulla spiaggia*

beachhead *n* testa *f* di sbarco

beach hut *n* cabina *f* [da spiaggia]

beach robe *n* accappatoio *m*

beachwear *n* abbigliamento *m* da spiaggia

beacon /ˈbiːk(ə)n/ *n* faro *m*; Naut, Aeron fanale *m*

bead /biːd/ *n* perlina *f*

beady-eyed /biːdɪˈaɪd/ *adj* (sharp-eyed) a cui non sfugge niente

beagle /ˈbiːg(ə)l/ *n* beagle *m inv*, bracchetto *m*

beak /biːk/ *n* becco *m*

beaker /ˈbiːkə(r)/ *n* coppa *f*; (in laboratory) becher *m inv*

beam /biːm/ **A** *n* trave *f*; (of light) raggio *m*
B *vi* irradiare; ‹*person*› essere raggiante; **~at somebody** fare un gran sorriso a qualcuno

beaming /ˈbiːmɪŋ/ *adj* raggiante

bean /biːn/ *n* fagiolo *m*; (of coffee) chicco *m*; **spill the ~s** infml spiattellare tutto

bean bag *n* (seat) *poltrona (f) imbottita di pallini di polistirolo*

beanfeast *n* infml festa *f*

beanie /ˈbiːnɪ/ *n* zucchetto *m*

beanpole *n* fig infml (tall thin person) spilungone, -a *mf*

bean sprout *n* germoglio *m* di soia

bear¹ /beə(r)/ *n* orso *m*

bear² *v* (*pt* **bore**, *pp* **borne**) **A** *vt* (endure) sopportare; mettere al mondo ‹*child*›; (carry) portare; **~ in mind** tenere presente; **~ fruit** ‹*tree*› produrre; fig dare frutto
B *vi* **~left/right** andare a sinistra/a destra

▪ **bear out** *vt* confermare ‹*story, statement*›

▪ **bear with** *vt* aver pazienza con

▪ **bear up** *vi* tirare avanti

bearable /ˈbeərəbl/ *adj* sopportabile

bear cub *n* cucciolo *m* di orso

beard /bɪəd/ *n* barba *f*; **have a ~** avere la barba

bearded /ˈbɪədɪd/ *adj* barbuto

bearer /ˈbeərə(r)/ *n* portatore, -trice *mf*; (of passport) titolare *mf*

bearing /ˈbeərɪŋ/ *n* portamento *m*; Techn cuscinetto *m* [a sfera]; **have a ~ on** avere attinenza con; **get one's ~s** orientarsi; **lose one's ~s** perdere l'orientamento

bear market *n* Fin mercato *m* al ribasso

bearskin *n* (pelt) pelle *f* d'orso; (hat) colbacco *m* militare

beast /biːst/ *n* bestia *f*; infml (person) animale *m*

beastly /ˈbiːstlɪ/ *adj* (**-ier**, **-iest**) infml orribile

beat /biːt/ **A** *n* battito *m*; (rhythm) battuta *f*; (of policeman) giro *m* d'ispezione
B *vt* (*pt* **beat**, *pp* **beaten**) battere; picchiare ‹*person*›; **~ a retreat** Mil battere in ritirata; **~ it!** infml dattela a gambe!; **it ~s me why...** infml non capisco proprio perché...

▪ **beat back** *vt* respingere ‹*flames, crowd*›

▪ **beat down** **A** *vt* buttare giù ‹*door*›
B *vi* ‹*sun*› battere a picco

▪ **beat off** *vt* respingere ‹*attacker*›

▪ **beat out** *vt* domare ‹*flames*›

▪ **beat up** *vt* picchiare

beaten /ˈbiːtn/ *adj* **off the ~ track** fuori mano

beatify /bɪˈætɪfaɪ/ *vt* beatificare

beating /ˈbiːtɪŋ/ *n* bastonata *f*; **get a ~** (with fists) essere preso a pugni; ‹*team, player*› prendere una batosta

beating-up *n* infml pestaggio *m*

beat-up *adj* infml ‹*car*› sfasciato

beau /bəʊ/ *n* literary hum spasimante *m*

Beaufort scale /ˈbəʊfət/ *n* scala *f* Beaufort

b

beautician /bjuːˈtɪʃn/ *n* estetista *mf*

🗝 **beautiful** /ˈbjuːtɪfl/ *adj* bello; **the ~ people** il bel mondo

beautifully /ˈbjuːtɪfʊlɪ/ *adv* splendidamente

beautify /ˈbjuːtɪfaɪ/ *vt* (*pt/pp* **-ied**) abbellire

🗝 **beauty** /ˈbjuːtɪ/ *n* bellezza *f*

beauty contest *n* concorso *m* di bellezza

beauty editor *n* redattore, -trice *mf* di articoli di bellezza

beauty parlour *n* istituto *m* di bellezza

beauty queen *n* reginetta *f* di bellezza

beauty salon *n* istituto *m* di bellezza

beauty sleep *n* hum **need one's ~** aver bisogno delle proprie ore di sonno

beauty spot *n* neo *m*; (place) luogo *m* pittoresco

beaver /ˈbiːvə(r)/ *n* castoro *m*

■ **beaver away** *vi* infml (work hard) sgobbare

becalmed /bɪˈkɑːmd/ *adj* in bonaccia

became /bɪˈkeɪm/ ▶ **become**

🗝 **because** /bɪˈkɒz/ **A** *conj* perché; (at start of sentence) poiché

B *adv* **~ of** a causa di

beck /bek/ *n* **be at sb's ~ and call** dover essere a completa disposizione di qualcuno

beckon /ˈbekn/ *vt & vi* **~ [to]** chiamare con un cenno

🗝 **become** /bɪˈkʌm/ *v* (*pt* **became**, *pp* **become**) **A** *vt* diventare

B *vi* diventare; **what has ~ of her?** che ne è di lei?

becoming /bɪˈkʌmɪŋ/ *adj* <*clothes*> bello

🗝 **bed** /bed/ *n* letto *m*; (of sea, lake) fondo *m*; (layer) strato *m*; (of flowers) aiuola *f*; **in ~** a letto; **go to ~** andare a letto

BEd *n abbr* (**Bachelor of Education**) ≈ laurea *f* in magistero

bed and board *n* vitto e alloggio *m*

bed and breakfast *n* bed and breakfast *m*

bed base *n* fondo *m* del letto

bed bath *n* **give somebody a ~** lavare qualcuno a letto

bedbug *n* cimice *f*

bedchamber *n* camera *f* da letto

bedclothes *npl* lenzuola e coperte *fpl*

bedding /ˈbedɪŋ/ *n biancheria (f) per il letto, materasso e guanciali*

bed down *vi* coricarsi

bedeck /bɪˈdek/ *vt* ornare

bedevil /bɪˈdevəl/ *vt* tormentare <*person*>; intralciare <*plans*>

bedfellow *n* **make strange ~s** fig fare una strana coppia

bedhead *n* testata *f* del letto

bed jacket *n* liseuse *f inv*

bedlam /ˈbedləm/ *n* baraonda *f*

bed linen *n* biancheria *f* per il letto

bedpan /ˈbedpæn/ *n* padella *f*

🗝 parola chiave

bedraggled /bɪˈdrægld/ *adj* inzaccherato

bedridden /ˈbedrɪdən/ *adj* allettato

bedrock /ˈbedrɒk/ *n* basamento *m*; fig fondamento *m*

bedroom /ˈbedruːm/ *n* camera *f* da letto

bedroom farce *n* Theat pochade *f inv*

bedroom slipper *n* pantofola *f*

bedroom suburb *n* AmE città *f* dormitorio

bedside /ˈbedsaɪd/ *n* **at his ~** al suo capezzale

bedside lamp *n* abat-jour *m inv*

bedside manner *n* modo *m* di trattare i pazienti; **have a good ~** saperci fare con i pazienti

bedside rug *n* scendiletto *m*

bedside table *n* comodino *m*

bedsit, **bedsitter**, **bed-sitting room** *n* camera *f* ammobiliata [fornita di cucina]

bedsock *n* calzino *m* da notte

bedsore *n* piaga *f* da decubito

bedspread *n* copriletto *m*

bedstead *n* fusto *m* del letto

bedtime *n* l'ora *f* di andare a letto

bed-wetting *n* il bagnare il letto

bee /biː/ *n* ape *f*

beech /biːtʃ/ *n* faggio *m*

beef /biːf/ *n* manzo *m*

beefburger *n* hamburger *m inv*

beefeater *n guardia (f) della Torre di Londra*

beefsteak *n* bistecca *f*

beefsteak tomato *n* grosso pomodoro *m*

beef stew *n* stufato *m* di manzo

beef tea *n* brodo *m* di manzo

beefy /ˈbiːfɪ/ *adj* <*flavour*> di manzo; infml <*man*> grande e grosso

beehive /ˈbiːhaɪv/ *n* alveare *m*

bee-keeper *n* apicoltore, -trice *mf*

bee-keeping *n* apicoltura *f*

bee-line *n* **make a ~ for** infml precipitarsi verso

been /biːn/ ▶ **be**

beep /biːp/ **A** *n* (of car) suono *m* di clacson; (of telephone) segnale *m* acustico; (of electronic device, radio) bip *m inv*

B *vi* <*car, driver*> clacsonare; <*device*> fare bip

C *vt* (with beeper) chiamare con il cercapersone; **~ the horn** clacsonare

beeper /ˈbiːpə(r)/ *n* cercapersone *m inv*

beer /bɪə(r)/ *n* birra *f*

beer belly *n* pancia *f* da beone

beer bottle *n* bottiglia *f* da birra

beer garden *n* giardino *m* di un pub

beer mat *n* sottobicchiere *m*

beer money *n* infml quattro soldi *mpl*

beer-swilling *adj* derog ubriacone

beer tent *n spazio (m) per incontri con mescita di birra*

bee sting *n* puntura *f* d'ape

beeswax /ˈbiːzwæks/ *n* cera *f* d'api

beet /biːt/ *n* AmE (beetroot) barbabietola *f*; **[sugar]** ~ barbabietola *f* da zucchero

beetle /ˈbiːtl/ *n* scarafaggio *m*

■ **beetle off** *vi* infml (hurry away) scappare

beetroot /ˈbiːtruːt/ *n* barbabietola *f*

befall /bɪˈfɔːl/ *vt* literary accadere a

befit /bɪˈfɪt/ *vt* literary addirsi a

befitting /bɪˈfɪtɪŋ/ *adj* ‹*modesty, honesty*› opportuno

before /bɪˈfɔː(r)/ **A** *prep* prima di; **the day ~ yesterday** ieri l'altro; **~ long** fra poco
B *adv* prima; **never ~ have I seen…** non ho mai visto prima…; **~ that** prima; **~ going** prima di andare
C *conj* (time) prima che; **~ you go** prima che tu vada

beforehand /bɪˈfɔːhænd/ *adv* in anticipo

before tax *adj* ‹*profit, income*› lordo, al lordo di imposte

befriend /bɪˈfrend/ *vt* trattare da amico

befuddle /bɪˈfʌdl/ *vt* confondere ‹*mind*›

beg /beg/ *v* (*pt/pp* **begged**) **A** *vi* mendicare
B *vt* pregare; chiedere ‹*favour, forgiveness*›

began /bɪˈgæn/ ▶ **begin**

beggar /ˈbegə(r)/ *n* mendicante *mf*; **you lucky ~!** che fortuna sfacciata!; **poor ~!** povero cristo!; **you little ~!** monellaccio!

beggarly /ˈbegəlɪ/ *adj* ‹*existence, meal*› miserabile; ‹*wage*› da fame

begging bowl /ˈbegɪŋ/ *n* ciotola *f* del mendicante

begging letter *n lettera (f) che sollecita offerte in denaro*

begin /bɪˈgɪn/ *vt & vi* (*pt* **began**, *pp* **begun**, *pres p* **beginning**) cominciare; **well, to ~ with** dunque, per cominciare

beginner /bɪˈgɪnə(r)/ *n* principiante *mf*

beginning /bɪˈgɪnɪŋ/ *n* principio *m*

begonia /bɪˈgəʊnɪə/ *n* begonia *f*

begrudge /bɪˈgrʌdʒ/ *vt* (envy) essere invidioso di; dare malvolentieri ‹*money*›

beguile /bɪˈgaɪl/ *vt* (charm) affascinare; (cheat) ingannare

beguiling /bɪˈgaɪlɪŋ/ *adj* accattivante

begun /bɪˈgʌn/ ▶ **begin**

behalf /bɪˈhɑːf/ *n* **on ~ of** a nome di; **on my ~** a nome mio; **say hello on my ~** salutalo da parte mia

behave /bɪˈheɪv/ *vi* comportarsi; **~ [oneself]** comportarsi bene

behaviour /bɪˈheɪvjə(r)/ *n* comportamento *m*; (of prisoner, soldier) condotta *f*

behavioural /bɪˈheɪvjərəl/ *adj* comportamentale

behaviourist /bɪˈheɪvjərɪst/ *adj & n* comportamentista *mf*

behaviour pattern *n* modello *m* comportamentale

behead /bɪˈhed/ *vt* decapitare

beheld /bɪˈheld/ ▶ **behold**

behind /bɪˈhaɪnd/ **A** *prep* dietro; (with pronoun) dietro di; **be ~ something** fig stare dietro qualcosa
B *adv* dietro, indietro; (late) in ritardo; **a long way ~** molto indietro; **in the car ~** nella macchina dietro
C *n* infml didietro *m*

b

behindhand /bɪˈhaɪndhænd/ *adv* indietro

behold /bɪˈhəʊld/ *vt* (*pt/pp* **beheld**) literary vedere

beholden /bɪˈhəʊldn/ *adj* obbligato (**to** verso)

beholder /bɪˈhəʊldə(r)/ *n* **beauty is in the eye of the ~** è bello ciò che piace

beige /beɪʒ/ *adj & n* beige *m inv*

Beijing /beɪˈdʒɪŋ/ *n* Pechino *f*

being /ˈbiːɪŋ/ *n* essere *m*; **come into ~** nascere

Beirut /beɪˈruːt/ *n* Beirut *f*

bejewelled /bɪˈdʒuːəld/ *adj* ingioiellato

Belarus /ˌbjeləʊˈrus/ *n* Bielorussia *f*

belated /bɪˈleɪtɪd/ *adj* tardivo

belatedly /bɪˈleɪtɪdlɪ/ *adv* tardi

belch /beltʃ/ **A** *vi* ruttare
B *vt* **~[out]** eruttare ‹*smoke*›

beleaguered /bɪˈliːgəd/ *adj* ‹*city*› assediato; ‹*troops*› accerchiato; fig ‹*person*› tormentato; fig ‹*company*› in difficoltà

Belfast /belˈfɑːst/ *n* Belfast *f*

belfry /ˈbelfrɪ/ *n* campanile *m*

Belgian /ˈbeldʒən/ *adj & n* belga *mf*

Belgium /ˈbeldʒəm/ *n* Belgio *m*

Belgrade /belˈgreɪd/ *n* Belgrado *f*

belie /bɪˈlaɪ/ *vt* (give false impression of) dissimulare; (disprove) smentire

belief /bɪˈliːf/ *n* fede *f*; (opinion) convinzione *f*

believable /bɪˈliːvəbl/ *adj* credibile

believe /bɪˈliːv/ *vt & vi* credere

■ **believe in** *vt* avere fiducia in ‹*person*›; credere a ‹*ghosts*›

believer /bɪˈliːvə(r)/ *n* Relig credente *mf*; **be a great ~ in** credere fermamente in

belittle /bɪˈlɪtl/ *vt* sminuire ‹*person, achievements*›

belittling /bɪˈlɪtlɪŋ/ *adj* ‹*comment*› che sminuisce

Belize /beˈliːz/ *n* Belize *m*

bell /bel/ *n* campana *f*; (on door) campanello *m*; **that rings a ~** fig mi dice qualcosa

bell-bottoms *npl* pantaloni *mpl* a zampa d'elefante

bellboy /ˈbelbɔɪ/ *n* AmE fattorino *m* d'albergo

belle /bel/ *n* bella *f*

bellhop /ˈbelhɒp/ *n* AmE fattorino *m* d'albergo

belligerence /bɪˈlɪdʒərəns/ *n* bellicosità *f*; (pol) belligeranza *f*

b

belligerent /bɪ'lɪdʒərənt/ *adj* belligerante; (aggressive) bellicoso
bell jar *n* campana *f* di vetro
bellow /'beləʊ/ *vi* gridare a squarciagola; ‹*animal*› muggire
■ **bellow out** *vt* urlare ‹*name, order*›
bellows /'beləʊz/ *npl* (for fire) soffietto *m*
bell pull *n* (rope) cordone *m* di campanello
bell push *n* pulsante *m* di campanello
bell-ringer *n* campanaro *m*
bell-shaped *adj* a campana
bell tower *n* campanile *m*
belly /'belɪ/ *n* pancia *f*
bellyache **A** *n* infml mal *m* di pancia
B *vi* infml lamentarsi
belly button *n* infml ombelico *m*
belly dancer *n* danzatrice *f* del ventre
belly flop *n* (in swimming) spanciata *f*
bellyful /'belɪfʊl/ *n* infml **have had a ~ of something** avere le tasche piene di qualcosa
⚷ **belong** /bɪ'lɒŋ/ *vi* appartenere (**to** a); (be member) essere socio (**to** di)
belongings /bɪ'lɒŋɪŋz/ *npl* cose *fpl*
beloved /bɪ'lʌvɪd/ *adj* & *n* amato, -a *mf*
⚷ **below** /bɪ'ləʊ/ **A** *prep* sotto; (with numbers) al di sotto di
B *adv* sotto, di sotto; Naut sotto coperta; **see ~** vedi qui di seguito
belt /belt/ **A** *n* cintura *f*; (area) zona *f*; Techn cinghia *f*
B *vi* infml (rush) **~ along** filare velocemente
C *vt* infml (hit) picchiare
■ **belt out** *vt* cantare a squarciagola ‹*song*›
■ **belt up** *vi* (in car) mettersi la cintura [di sicurezza]; **~ up!** sl (be quiet) stai zitto!
bemoan /bɪ'məʊn/ *vt* lamentare
bemused /bɪ'mju:zd/ *adj* confuso
bench /bentʃ/ *n* panchina *f*; (work ~) piano *m* da lavoro; **the B~** Jur la magistratura
benchmark /'bentʃmɑ:k/ *n* punto *m* di riferimento; Comput paragone *m* con un campione; Fin (price) prezzo *m* di riferimento
bench-test *vt* Comput testare
bend /bend/ **A** *n* curva *f*; (of river) ansa *f*; **round the ~** infml fuori di testa
B *vt* (*pt/pp* **bent**) piegare
C *vi* piegarsi; ‹*road*› curvare; **~ [down]** chinarsi
■ **bend over** *vi* inchinarsi
beneath /bɪ'ni:θ/ **A** *prep* sotto, al di sotto di; **he thinks it's ~ him** fig pensa che sia sotto al suo livello; **~ contempt** indegno
B *adv* giù
Benedictine /benɪ'dɪkti:n/ *adj* & *n* Relig benedettino *m*
benediction /benɪ'dɪkʃn/ *n* Relig benedizione *f*
benefactor /'benɪfæktə(r)/ *n* benefattore, -trice *mf*

⚷ parola chiave

beneficial /benɪ'fɪʃl/ *adj* benefico
beneficiary /benɪ'fɪʃərɪ/ *n* beneficiario, -a *mf*
⚷ **benefit** /'benɪfɪt/ **A** *n* vantaggio *m*; (allowance) indennità *f*
B *vt* (*pt/pp* **-fited**, *pres p* **-fiting**) giovare a
C *vi* trarre vantaggio (**from** da)
Benelux /'benɪlʌks/ **A** *n* Benelux *m*
B *attrib* ‹*countries, organization*› del Benelux
benevolence /bɪ'nevələns/ *n* benevolenza *f*
benevolent /bɪ'nevələnt/ *adj* benevolo
benevolently /bɪ'nevələntlɪ/ *adv* con benevolenza
Bengal /beŋ'gɔ:l/ *n* Bengala *m*
benign /bɪ'naɪn/ *adj* benevolo; Med benigno
benignly /bɪ'naɪnlɪ/ *adv* con benevolenza
Benin /be'ni:n/ *n* Benin *m*
bent /bent/ **A** ▶ **bend**
B *adj* ‹*person*› ricurvo; (distorted) curvato; infml (dishonest) corrotto; **be ~ on doing something** essere ben deciso a fare qualcosa
C *n* predisposizione *f*
benzene /'benzi:n/ *n* benzene *m*
benzine /'benzi:n/ *n* benzina *f*
bequeath /bɪ'kwi:ð/ *vt* lasciare in eredità
bequest /bɪ'kwest/ *n* lascito *m*
berate /bɪ'reɪt/ *vt* fml redarguire
bereaved /bɪ'ri:vd/ *n* **the ~** *pl* i familiari del defunto
bereavement /bɪ'ri:vmənt/ *n* lutto *m*
bereft /bɪ'reft/ *adj* **~ of** privo di
beret /'bereɪ/ *n* berretto *m*
Berlin /bɜ:'lɪn/ *n* Berlino *f*
Berliner /bɜ:'lɪnə(r)/ *n* berlinese *mf*
Bermuda /bə'mju:də/ *n* le Bermuda
Bermuda shorts *npl* bermuda *mpl*
Berne /bɜ:n/ *n* Berna *f*
berry /'berɪ/ *n* bacca *f*
berserk /bə'sɜ:k/ *adj* **go ~** diventare una belva
berth /bɜ:θ/ **A** *n* (bed) cuccetta *f*; (anchorage) ormeggio *m*; **give a wide ~ to** infml stare alla larga da
B *vi* ormeggiare
beseech /bɪ'si:tʃ/ *vt* (*pt/pp* **beseeched** *or* **besought**) supplicare
beseeching /bɪ'si:tʃɪŋ/ *adj* implorante
beset /bɪ'set/ *adj* **a country ~ by strikes** un paese vessato dagli scioperi
⚷ **beside** /bɪ'saɪd/ *prep* accanto a; **~ oneself** fuori di sé
besides /bɪ'saɪdz/ **A** *prep* oltre a
B *adv* inoltre
besiege /bɪ'si:dʒ/ *vt* assediare
besotted /bɪ'sɒtɪd/ *adj* infatuato (**with** di)
besought /bɪ'sɔ:t/ ▶ **beseech**
bespatter /bɪ'spætə(r)/ *vt* schizzare
bespectacled /bɪ'spektək(ə)ld/ *adj* con gli occhiali

bespoke /bɪ'spəʊk/ *adj* ‹*suit*› su misura; ‹*tailor*› che lavora su ordinazione

best /best/ **A** *adj* migliore; **the ~ part of a year** la maggior parte dell'anno; **~ before** Comm preferibilmente prima di; **~ wishes** migliori auguri
B *n* **the ~** il meglio; (person) il/la migliore; **at ~** tutt'al più; **all the ~!** tanti auguri!; **do one's ~** fare del proprio meglio; **to the ~ of my knowledge** per quel che ne so; **make the ~ of it** cogliere il lato buono della cosa
C *adv* meglio, nel modo migliore; **as ~ I could** come meglio ho potuto; **like ~** preferire

best before date *n* data *f* di scadenza

best friend *n* migliore amico, -a *mf*

bestial /'bestɪəl/ *adj also* fig bestiale

bestiality /bestɪ'ælətɪ/ *n* bestialità *f*

best man *n* testimone *m*

bestow /bɪ'stəʊ/ *vt* conferire (**on** a)

best-seller /-'selə(r)/ *n* bestseller *m inv*

best-selling /-'selɪŋ/ *adj* ‹*novelist*› più venduto

bet /bet/ **A** *n* scommessa *f*
B *vt & vi* (*pt/pp* **bet** *or* **betted**) scommettere

beta blocker /'bi:təblɒkə(r)/ *n* betabloccante *m*

beta-test /'bi:tətest/ *vt* Comput testare la versione beta di

Bethlehem /'beθlɪhem/ *n* Betlemme *f*

betray /bɪ'treɪ/ *vt* tradire

betrayal /bɪ'treɪəl/ *n* tradimento *m*

betrothal /bɪ'trəʊðl/ *n* fidanzamento *m*

betrothed /bɪ'trəʊðd/ *n* literary hum promesso sposo *m*; promessa sposa *f*; **be ~** essere fidanzato

better /'betə(r)/ **A** *adj* migliore, meglio; **get ~** migliorare; (after illness) rimettersi; **I waited the ~ part of a week** ho aspettato buona parte della settimana
B *adv* meglio; **~ off** meglio; (wealthier) più ricco; **all the ~** tanto meglio; **the sooner the ~** prima è meglio è; **I've thought ~ of it** ci ho ripensato; **you'd ~ stay** faresti meglio a restare; **I'd ~ not** è meglio che non lo faccia
C *vt* migliorare; **~ oneself** migliorare le proprie condizioni

betting /'betɪŋ/ *n* (activity) scommesse *fpl*; **what's the ~ that...?** quanto scommettiamo che...?

betting shop *n* ricevitoria *f* (*dell'allibratore*)

between /bɪ'twi:n/ **A** *prep* fra, tra; **~ you and me** detto fra di noi; **~ us** (together) tra me e te
B *adv* **[in] ~** in mezzo; (time) frattempo

betwixt /bɪ'twɪkst/ *adv* **be ~ and between** essere una via di mezzo

bevel /'bevl/ **A** *n* (edge) spigolo *m* smussato; (tool) squadra *f* falsa
B *vt* smussare ‹*mirror, edge*›

beverage /'bevərɪdʒ/ *n* bevanda *f*

bevy /'bevɪ/ *n* frotta *f*

beware /bɪ'weə(r)/ *vi* guardarsi (**of** da); **~ of the dog!** attenti al cane!

bewilder /bɪ'wɪldə(r)/ *vt* disorientare

bewildered /bɪ'wɪldəd/ *adj* ‹*look, person*› perplesso, sconcertato

bewildering /bɪ'wɪldərɪŋ/ *adj* sconcertante

bewilderment /bɪ'wɪldəmənt/ *n* perplessità *f*

bewitch /bɪ'wɪtʃ/ *vt* stregare; fig affascinare completamente

beyond /bɪ'jɒnd/ **A** *prep* oltre; **~ reach** irraggiungibile; **~ doubt** senza alcun dubbio; **~ belief** da non credere; **it's ~ me** infml non riesco proprio a capire
B *adv* più in là

B film *n* film *m inv* di serie B

Bhutan /bu:'tɑ:n/ *n* Bhutan *m*

bias /'baɪəs/ **A** *n* (preference) preferenza *f*; derog pregiudizio *m*
B *vt* (*pt/pp* **biased**) (influence) influenzare

bias binding, **bias tape** /'baɪndɪŋ/ *n* (in sewing) fettuccia *f* in sbieco

biased /'baɪəst/ *adj* parziale

bib /bɪb/ *n* bavaglino *m*

Bible /'baɪbl/ *n* Bibbia *f*

Bible Belt *n zona (f) del sud degli USA, dove predomina il fondamentalismo protestante*

biblical /'bɪblɪkl/ *adj* biblico

bibliographic /bɪblɪə'græfɪk/, **bibliographical** /bɪblɪə'græfɪkl/ *adj* bibliografico

bibliography /bɪblɪ'ɒgrəfɪ/ *n* bibliografia *f*

bicarbonate /baɪ'kɑ:bəneɪt/ *n* **~ of soda** bicarbonato *m* di sodio

bicentenary /baɪsen'ti:nərɪ/ **A** *n* bicentenario *m*
B *attrib* ‹*celebration, year*› del bicentenario

biceps /'baɪseps/ *n* bicipite *m*

bicker /'bɪkə(r)/ *vi* litigare

bickering /'bɪkərɪŋ/ *n* bisticci *mpl*

bicycle /'baɪsɪkl/ **A** *n* bicicletta *f*
B *vi* andare in bicicletta

bicycle clip *n* molletta *f* (*per pantaloni*)

bicycle lane *n* pista *f* ciclabile

bicycle rack *n* (in yard) rastrelliera *f* per biciclette; (on car) portabiciclette *m inv*

bid¹ /bɪd/ **A** *n* offerta *f*; (attempt) tentativo *m*
B *vt & vi* (*pt/pp* **bid**, *pres p* **bidding**) offrire; (in cards) dichiarare

bid² *vt* (*pt* **bade** *or* **bid**, *pp* **bidden** *or* **bid**, *pres p* **bidding**) literary (command) comandare; **~ somebody welcome** dare il benvenuto a qualcuno

bidder /'bɪdə(r)/ *n* offerente *mf*

bidding /'bɪdɪŋ/ *n* offerte *fpl* (*durante un'asta*)

bide /baɪd/ *vt* **~ one's time** aspettare il momento buono

b

bidet /ˈbiːdeɪ/ *n* bidè *m*
biennial /baɪˈenɪəl/ *adj* biennale
bier /bɪə(r)/ *n* catafalco *m*
bifocals /baɪˈfəʊklz/ *npl* occhiali *mpl* bifocali
⚷ **big** /bɪɡ/ **A** *adj* (**bigger, biggest**) grande; ‹*brother, sister*› più grande; infml (generous) generoso; **make ~ money** fare i soldi
B *adv* **talk ~** infml spararle grosse
bigamist /ˈbɪɡəmɪst/ *n* bigamo, -a *mf*
bigamous /ˈbɪɡəməs/ *adj* bigamo
bigamy /ˈbɪɡəmɪ/ *n* bigamia *f*
big bang *n* (in astronomy) big bang *m*
big business *n* le grandi imprese; **be ~** essere un grosso affare
big cat *n* grosso felino *m*
big deal *n* infml **~!** bella forza!
big dipper *n* BrE (at fair) montagne *fpl* russe
big game hunting *n* caccia *f* grossa
big-head *n* infml montato, -a *mf*, gasato, -a *mf*
big-headed *adj* infml montato, gasato
big-hearted *adj* generoso
bigmouth *n* infml derog chiacchierone, -a *mf*; **he's such a ~!** (indiscreet) ha una lingua lunga!
big name *n* (in film, art) grosso nome *m*
big noise *n* infml pezzo *m* grosso
bigot /ˈbɪɡət/ *n* fanatico, -a *mf*
bigoted /ˈbɪɡətɪd/ *adj* di mentalità ristretta
bigotry /ˈbɪɡətrɪ/ *n* mentalità *f* ristretta
big screen *n* grande schermo *m*
big shot *n* infml pezzo *m* grosso
Big Smoke *n* BrE hum Londra *f*
big time **A** *n* **make** *or* **hit the ~** infml raggiungere il successo
B *attrib* **big-time** ‹*crook*› di alto livello
big toe *n* alluce *m*
big top *n* ‹*tent*› tendone *m* del circo; fig (circus) circo *m*
bigwig *n* infml pezzo *m* grosso
bike /baɪk/ **A** *n* infml bici *f inv*
B *vi* andare in bici
C *vt* mandare per corriere
biker /ˈbaɪkə(r)/ *n* motociclista *mf*
biker jacket /ˈbaɪkədʒækɪt/, **biker's jacket** /ˈbaɪkəzdʒækɪt/ *n* infml giubbotto *m* di pelle
bikini /bɪˈkiːnɪ/ *n* bikini *m inv*
bilateral /baɪˈlætrəl/ *adj* bilaterale
bilberry /ˈbɪlbərɪ/ *n* mirtillo *m*
bile /baɪl/ *n* bile *f*
bilge /bɪldʒ/ *n* Naut (place) carena *f*; (substance) sentina *f*; infml (nonsense) idiozie *fpl*
bilingual /baɪˈlɪŋɡwəl/ *adj* bilingue
bilingual secretary *n* segretario, -a *mf* bilingue
bilious /ˈbɪljəs/ *adj* Med **~ attack** attacco *m* di bile

⚷ parola chiave

⚷ **bill¹** /bɪl/ **A** *n* fattura *f*; (in restaurant etc) conto *m*; (poster) manifesto *m*; Pol progetto *m* di legge; AmE (note) biglietto *m* di banca; Theat **be top of the ~** essere in testa al cartellone
B *vt* fatturare
bill² *n* (beak) becco *m*
billboard /ˈbɪlbɔːd/ *n* cartellone *m* pubblicitario
billet /ˈbɪlɪt/ **A** *n* Mil alloggio *m*
B *vt* (*pt/pp* **billeted**) alloggiare (**on** presso)
billfold *n* AmE portafoglio *m*
billiard ball *n* palla *f* da biliardo
billiards /ˈbɪljədz/ *n* biliardo *m*
billiard table /ˈbɪljəd/ tavolo *m* da biliardo
billing /ˈbɪlɪŋ/ *n* Comm fatturazione *f*; **get top ~** Theat comparire in testa al cartellone
⚷ **billion** /ˈbɪljən/ *n* (thousand million) miliardo *m*; old-fashioned Br (million million) mille miliardi *mpl*
billionaire /bɪljəˈneə(r)/ *n* miliardario, -a *mf*
bill of exchange *n* cambiale *f*
bill of fare *n* menù *m*
bill of rights *n* dichiarazione *f* dei diritti
bill of sale *n* atto *m* di vendita
billow /ˈbɪləʊ/ **A** *n* (of smoke) nube *f*
B *vi* alzarsi in volute
■ **billow out** *vi* (skirt, sail) gonfiarsi; (smoke, cloud) levarsi in volute
billposter /ˈbɪlpəʊstə(r)/ *n* attacchino *m*
billy /ˈbɪlɪ/ *n* AmE (truncheon) sfollagente *m inv*
billycan /ˈbɪlɪkæn/ *n* gamella *f*
billy goat *n* caprone *m*
bimbo /ˈbɪmbəʊ/ *n* derog infml bambolona *f*; **his latest ~** la sua ultima amichetta
bin /bɪn/ *n* bidone *m*
binary /ˈbaɪnərɪ/ *adj* binario
bin bag *n* sacco *m* per l'immondizia
bind /baɪnd/ *vt* (*pt/pp* **bound**) legare (**to** a); (bandage) fasciare; Jur obbligare
binder /ˈbaɪndə(r)/ *n* (for papers) raccoglitore *m*; (for cement, paint) agglomerante *m*
binding /ˈbaɪndɪŋ/ **A** *adj* ‹*promise, contract*› vincolante
B *n* (of book) rilegatura *f*; (on ski) attacco *m*
binge /bɪndʒ/ **A** *n* infml **have a ~** fare baldoria; (eat a lot) abbuffarsi
B *vi* abbuffarsi (**on** di)
binge-drinking /ˌbɪndʒˈdrɪŋkɪŋ/ *n il bere smodatamente in particolari occasioni, specialmente nelle sere del week-end*
bingo /ˈbɪŋɡəʊ/ *n* ≈ tombola *f*
bin liner *n* BrE sacchetto *m* per la spazzatura
binoculars /bɪˈnɒkjʊləz/ *npl* **[pair of] ~** binocolo *msg*
biochemist /baɪəʊˈkemɪst/ *n* biochimico, -a *mf*
biochemistry /baɪəʊˈkemɪstrɪ/ *n* biochimica *f*

biocompatible /ˌbaɪəʊkəmˈpætəbl/ *adj* biocompatibile

biodegradable /baɪəʊdɪˈgreɪdəbl/ *adj* biodegradabile

biodiesel /ˈbaɪəʊdiːzl/ *n* biodiesel *m*

biodiversity /baɪəʊdaɪˈvɜːsətɪ/ *n* biodiversità *f*

bioengineering /baɪəʊendʒɪˈnɪərɪŋ/ *n* bioingegneria *f*

biographer /baɪˈɒgrəfə(r)/ *n* biografo, -a *mf*

biographical /baɪəˈgræafɪkl/ *adj* biografico

biography /baɪˈɒgrəfɪ/ *n* biografia *f*

biological /baɪəˈlɒdʒɪkl/ *adj* biologico

biological clock *n* orologio *m* biologico

biologically /baɪəˈlɒdʒɪklɪ/ *adv* biologicamente

biological powder *n* detersivo *m* biologico

biological warfare *n* guerra *f* biologica

biologist /baɪˈɒlədʒɪst/ *n* biologo, -a *mf*

biology /baɪˈɒlədʒɪ/ *n* biologia *f*

biometric /ˌbaɪəʊˈmetrɪk/ *adj* biometrico

bionic /baɪˈɒnɪk/ *adj* bionico

biopic /ˈbaɪəʊpɪk/ *n* Cin *film* (*m*) *basato su una biografia*

biopsy /ˈbaɪɒpsɪ/ *n* biopsia *f*

biorhythm /ˈbaɪəʊrɪðəm/ *n* bioritmo *m*

biosphere /ˈbaɪəʊsfɪə(r)/ *n* biosfera *f*

biotechnology /baɪəʊtekˈnɒlədʒɪ/ *n* biotecnologia *f*

bioterrorism /baɪəʊˌterərizəm/ *n* bioterrorismo *m*

bipartisan /baɪpɑːtɪˈzæn/ *adj* Pol bipartitico

bipartite /baɪˈpɑːtaɪt/ *adj* bipartito

bipolar disorder /baɪˈpəʊlədɪsˌɔːdə(r)/ *n* disturbo *m* bipolare

birch /bɜːtʃ/ *n* (tree) betulla *f*

bird /bɜːd/ *n* uccello *m*; infml (girl) ragazza *f*; **kill two ~s with one stone** prendere due piccioni con una fava

birdbrain /ˈbɜːdbreɪn/ *n* infml **he's such a ~** ha un cervello da gallina

bird call *n* cinguettio *m*

bird flu *n* influenza *f* aviaria, influenza *f* dei polli

birdie /ˈbɜːdɪ/ *n* (in golf) birdie *m*

bird-like /ˈbɜːdlaɪk/ *adj* come un uccello

bird of paradise *n* uccello *m* del paradiso

bird of prey *n* [uccello *m*] rapace *m*

bird sanctuary *n* riserva *f* per uccelli

birdseed *n* becchime *m*

bird's eye view *n* veduta *f* panoramica dall'alto

bird's nest *n* nido *m* di uccello

bird's nest soup *n* zuppa *f* di nido di rondine

birdsong *n* canto *m* degli uccelli

birdwatcher *n persona* (*f*) *che pratica il bird-watching*

bird-watching *n* **go ~** fare del bird-watching

Biro® /ˈbaɪrəʊ/ *n* biro® *f inv*

birth /bɜːθ/ *n* nascita *f*; **give ~** partorire; **give ~ to** partorire

birth certificate *n* certificato *m* di nascita

birth control *n* controllo *m* delle nascite

birthday *n* compleanno *m*

birthday party *n* festa *f* di compleanno

birthing pool *n* piccola piscina *f* per il parto

birthmark *n* voglia *f*

birth mother *n* madre *f* biologica

birthplace *n* luogo *m* di nascita

birth rate *n* natalità *f*

birthright *n* diritto *m* di nascita

births column *n* annunci *mpl* delle nascite (*sul giornale*)

birth sign *n* segno *m* zodiacale

births, marriages, and deaths *npl* annunci *mpl* di nascite, di matrimonio, mortuari (*sul giornale*)

biscuit /ˈbɪskɪt/ *n* biscotto *m*

biscuit barrel, **biscuit tin** *n* biscottiera *f*

bisect /baɪˈsekt/ *vt* dividere in due [parti]

bisexual /baɪˈseksjʊəl/ *adj* & *n* bisessuale *mf*

bishop /ˈbɪʃəp/ *n* vescovo *m*; Chess alfiere *m*

bistro /ˈbiːstrəʊ/ *n* bistrò *m*

bit¹ /bɪt/ *n* pezzo *m*; (smaller) pezzetto *m*; (for horse) morso *m*; Comput bit *m inv*; **a ~ of** un pezzo di ‹*cheese, paper*›; un po' di ‹*time, rain, silence*›; **~ by ~** poco a poco; **do one's ~** fare la propria parte

bit² ▶ **bite**

bitch /bɪtʃ/ *n* cagna *f*; sl arpia *f*

bitchy /ˈbɪtʃɪ/ *adj* velenoso

bite /baɪt/ **A** *n* morso *m*; (insect ~) puntura *f*; (mouthful) boccone *m*
B *vt* (*pt* **bit**, *pp* **bitten**) mordere; ‹*insect*› pungere; **~ one's nails** mangiarsi le unghie
C *vi* mordere; ‹*insect*› pungere
▪ **bite off** *vt* staccare (*con un morso*)

biting /ˈbaɪtɪŋ/ *adj* ‹*wind, criticism*› pungente; ‹*remark*› mordace

bit part *n* Theat particina *f*

bitter /ˈbɪtə(r)/ **A** *adj* amaro
B *n* BrE birra *f* amara

bitter almond *n* mandorla *f* amara

bitter lemon *n* limonata *f* amara

bitterly /ˈbɪtəlɪ/ *adv* amaramente; **it's ~ cold** c'è un freddo pungente

bitterness /ˈbɪtənɪs/ *n* amarezza *f*

bittersweet /bɪtəˈswiːt/ *adj* literary agrodolce

bitty /ˈbɪtɪ/ *adj* BrE infml frammentario

bitumen /ˈbɪtjʊmɪn/ *n* bitume *m*

bivouac /ˈbɪvʊæk/ **A** *n* bivacco *m*
B *vi* bivaccare

bizarre /bɪˈzɑː(r)/ *adj* bizzarro

blab /blæb/ *vi* (*pt/pp* **blabbed**) cianciare

b

✐ **black** /blæk/ **A** *adj* nero; **be ~ and blue** essere coperto di lividi
B *n* nero *m*
C *vt* boicottare <*goods*>
■ **black out A** *vt* cancellare
B *vi* (lose consciousness) perdere coscienza
Black Africa *n* Africa *f* nera
Black American *n* nero, -a, americano, -a *mf*
black and white *n* bianco e nero
blackball *vt* dare voto contrario a
black belt *n* cintura *f* nera
blackberry *n* mora *f*
blackberry bush *n* rovo *m*
blackbird *n* merlo *m*
blackboard *n* Sch lavagna *f*
black box *n* Aeron scatola *f* nera
black bread *n* pane *m* nero
blackcurrant *n* ribes *m inv* nero
blacken /ˈblækən/ *vt* annerire
black eye *n* occhio *m* nero
Black Forest gateau *n dolce (m) a base di cioccolato, panna e ciliegie*
black gold *n* infml oro *m* nero
blackguard /ˈblægəd/ *n* hum brigante *m*
blackhead *n* Med punto *m* nero
black-headed gull *n* gabbiano *m* comune
black humour umorismo *m* nero
black ice *n* ghiaccio *m (sulla strada)*
blacking /ˈblækɪŋ/ BrE (boycotting) boicottaggio *m*; (polish) lucido *m* nero *(per scarpe)*
blackish /ˈblækɪʃ/ *adj* nerastro
blackjack *n* blackjack *m*
blackleg *n* BrE crumiro *m*
blacklist *vt* mettere sulla lista nera
blackmail A *n* ricatto *m*
B *vt* ricattare
blackmailer *n* ricattatore, -trice *mf*
black mark *n* fig neo *m*
black market *n* borsa *f* nera
black marketeer *n* borsanerista *mf*
black mass *n* messa *f* nera
blackness /ˈblæknɪs/ *n* nero *m*; (evilness) cattiveria *f*; (of moods) scontrosità *f*
black-out *n* blackout *m inv*; **have a ~** Med perdere coscienza
black pepper *n* pepe *m* nero
black pudding *n* ≈ sanguinaccio *m*
Black Sea *n* Mar *m* Nero
black sheep *n* fig pecora *f* nera
Blackshirt *n* camicia *f* nera
blacksmith *n* fabbro *m*
black spot *n* fig *luogo (m) conosciuto per gli incidenti stradali*
black swan *n* cigno *m* nero
black tie *n* (on invitation) abito *m* scuro

✐ parola chiave

black widow, black widow spider *n* vedova *f* nera
bladder /ˈblædə(r)/ *n* Anat vescica *f*
blade /bleɪd/ *n* lama *f*; (of grass) filo *m*
✐ **blame** /bleɪm/ **A** *n* colpa *f*
B *vt* dare la colpa a; **~ somebody for doing something** dare la colpa a qualcuno per aver fatto qualcosa; **no one is to ~** non è colpa di nessuno
blameless /ˈbleɪmlɪs/ *adj* innocente
blameworthy /ˈbleɪmwɜːðɪ/ *adj* biasimevole
blanch /blɑːntʃ/ **A** *vi* sbiancare
B *vt* Culin sbollentare
blancmange /bləˈmɒnʒ/ *n* biancomangiare *m*
bland /blænd/ *adj* <*food*> insipido; <*person*> insulso
blandly /ˈblændlɪ/ *adv* <*say*> in modo piatto
blank /blæŋk/ **A** *adj* bianco; <*look*> vuoto
B *n* spazio *m* vuoto; (cartridge) cartuccia *f* a salve
C *vt* ignorare; **she completely ~ed me** mi ha completamente ignorato
■ **blank out** *vt* (memory) cancellare dalla memoria
blank cheque *n* assegno *m* in bianco
blanket /ˈblæŋkɪt/ *n* coperta *f*; **wet ~** infml guastafeste *mf inv*
blanket box, blanket chest *n* BrE cassapanca *f*
blanket cover *n* (in insurance) assicurazione *f* che copre tutti i rischi
blanket stitch *n* punto *m* di rinforzo
blankly /ˈblæŋklɪ/ *adv* (uncomprehendingly) con espressione attonita; (without expression) senza espressione
blank verse *n* versi *mpl* sciolti
blare /bleə(r)/ *vi* suonare a tutto volume
■ **blare out** *vt* strombazzare rumorosamente
blarney /ˈblɑːnɪ/ *n* infml lusinga *f*
blasé /ˈblɑːzeɪ/ *adj* blasé *inv*
blaspheme /blæsˈfiːm/ *vi* bestemmiare
blasphemous /ˈblæsfəməs/ *adj* blasfemo
blasphemy /ˈblæsfəmɪ/ *n* bestemmia *f*
blast /blɑːst/ **A** *n* (gust) raffica *f*; (sound) scoppio *m*
B *vt* (with explosive) far saltare
C *int* sl maledizione!
■ **blast off** *vi* (rocket) decollare
blasted /ˈblɑːstɪd/ *adj* sl maledetto
blast furnace *n* altoforno *m*
blasting /ˈblɑːstɪŋ/ *n* brillamento *m*
blast-off *n* (of missile) lancio *m*
blatant /ˈbleɪtənt/ *adj* sfacciato
blatantly /ˈbleɪtəntlɪ/ *adv* <*copy, disregard*> sfacciatamente; **it's ~ obvious** è lampante
blather /ˈblæðə(r)/ *vi* infml blaterare
blaze /bleɪz/ **A** *n* incendio *m*; **a ~ of colour** un'esplosione *f* di colori
B *vi* ardere
■ **blaze down** *vi* <*sun*> essere cocente

blazer /ˈbleɪzə(r)/ *n* blazer *m inv*

blazing /ˈbleɪzɪŋ/ *adj* ‹*row*› acceso; ‹*fire*› violento; ‹*building*› in fiamme

bleach /bliːtʃ/ **A** *n* decolorante *m*; (for cleaning) candeggina *f*, varecchina *f*
B *vt* sbiancare; ossigenare ‹*hair*›

bleak /bliːk/ *adj* desolato; fig ‹*prospects, future*› tetro

bleakly /ˈbliːklɪ/ *adv* ‹*stare, say*› in modo tetro

bleakness /ˈbliːknɪs/ *n* (of weather) tetraggine *f*; (of surroundings, future) desolazione *f*

bleary-eyed /blɪərɪˈaɪd/ *adj* **be ~** avere gli occhi gonfi

bleat /bliːt/ **A** *vi* belare
B *n* belato *m*

bleed /bliːd/ *v* (*pt/pp* **bled**) **A** *vi* sanguinare
B *vt* spurgare ‹*brakes, radiator*›

bleeding /ˈbliːdɪŋ/ **A** *n* perdita di sangue *f*; (heavy) emorragia *f*; (deliberate) salasso *m*
B *adj* ‹*wound, hand*› sanguinante; sl = **bloody**

bleeding heart *n* fig derog cuore *m* troppo tenero

bleep /bliːp/ **A** *n* bip *m*
B *vi* suonare
C *vt* chiamare col cercapersone

bleeper /ˈbliːpə(r)/ *n* cercapersone *m inv*

blemish /ˈblemɪʃ/ *n* macchia *f*

blend /blend/ **A** *n* (of tea, coffee, whisky) miscela *f*; (of colours) insieme *m*
B *vt* mescolare
C *vi* ‹*colours, sounds*› fondersi (**with** con)

■ **blend in A** *vi* ‹*person*› passare inosservato; **~ in with** mescolarsi con
B *vt* **~ something in** mescolare qualcosa

blender /ˈblendə(r)/ *n* Culin frullatore *m*

blending /ˈblendɪŋ/ *n* (of coffees, whiskies) miscela *f*

bless /bles/ *vt* benedire

blessed /ˈblesɪd/ *adj also* sl benedetto

blessing /ˈblesɪŋ/ *n* benedizione *f*

blew /bluː/ ▶ **blow²**

blight /blaɪt/ **A** *n* Bot ruggine *f*
B *vt* far avvizzire ‹*plants*›

blighter /ˈblaɪtə(r)/ BrE infml (annoying person) idiota *mf*; **you lucky ~** hai una fortuna sfacciata!; **poor ~** povero diavolo *m*

blimey /ˈblaɪmɪ/ *int* BrE infml accidenti!

blind /blaɪnd/ **A** *adj* cieco; **~ man/woman** cieco/cieca
B *npl* **the ~** i ciechi
C *vt* accecare
D *n* **[roller] ~** avvolgibile *m*; **[Venetian] ~** veneziana *f*

blind alley *n* vicolo *m* cieco

blind date *n appuntamento* (*m*) *galante con una persona sconosciuta*

blind drunk *adj* ubriaco fradicio

blindfold A *adv* con gli occhi bendati
B *adj* **be ~** avere gli occhi bendati
C *n* benda *f*
D *vt* bendare gli occhi a

blinding /ˈblaɪndɪŋ/ *adj* ‹*light*› acceccante; ‹*headache*› da impazzire, tremendo

blindingly /ˈblaɪndɪŋlɪ/ *adv* ‹*shine*› in modo acceccante; **be ~ obvious** essere così lampante

blindly /ˈblaɪndlɪ/ *adv* ciecamente

blind man's buff *n* moscacieca *f*

blindness /ˈblaɪndnɪs/ *n* cecità *f*

blind spot *n* (in car, on hill) punto *m* privo di visibilità; (in eye) punto *m* cieco; fig (point of ignorance) punto *m* debole

blind trust *n* blind trust *m*

bling bling /blɪŋ ˈblɪŋ/ *n* sl *gioielli e abiti molto appariscenti, specialmente con riferimento a quelli indossati dai rapper americani*

blink /blɪŋk/ *vi* sbattere le palpebre; ‹*light*› tremolare

blinkered /ˈblɪŋkəd/ *adj* ‹*attitude, approach*› ottuso; **be ~** avere i paraocchi

blinkers /ˈblɪŋkəz/ *npl* paraocchi *mpl*

blinking /ˈblɪnkɪŋ/ *n* (of light) intermittenza *f*; (of eye) battere *m*

blip /blɪp/ *n* (on screen) segnale *m* luminoso a intermittenza; (on graph, line) piccola irregolarità *f*; (sound) ticchettio *m*; (hitch) intoppo *m*

bliss /blɪs/ *n* Rel beatitudine *f*; (happiness) felicità *f*

blissful /ˈblɪsfʊl/ *adj* beato; (happy) meraviglioso

blissfully /ˈblɪsfəlɪ/ *adv* beatamente; **~ ignorant** beatamente ignaro

blister /ˈblɪstə(r)/ **A** *n* Med vescica *f*; (in paint) bolla *f*
B *vi* ‹*paint*› formare una bolla/delle bolle

blistering /ˈblɪst(ə)rɪŋ/ **A** *n* (of skin) vescica *f*; (of paint) bolle *fpl*
B *adj* ‹*sun*› scottante; ‹*heat*› soffocante; ‹*attack, criticism*› feroce

blister pack *n* blister *m inv*

blithe /blaɪð/ *adj* (cheerful) gioioso; (nonchalant) spensierato

blithely /ˈblaɪðlɪ/ *adv* (nonchalantly) spensieratamente

blitz /blɪts/ *n* bombardamento *m* aereo; **have a ~ on something** fig darci sotto con qualcosa

blitzkrieg /ˈblɪtskriːg/ *n* guerra *f* lampo

blizzard /ˈblɪzəd/ *n* tormenta *f*

bloated /ˈbləʊtɪd/ *adj* gonfio

blob /blɒb/ *n* goccia *f*

bloc /blɒk/ *n* Pol blocco *m*

block /blɒk/ **A** *n* blocco *m*; (building) isolato *m*; (building **~**) cubo *m* (*per giochi di costruzione*); **~ of flats** palazzo *m*
B *vt* bloccare

■ **block out** *vt* coprire ‹*light, sun*›

■ **block up** *vt* bloccare
blockade /blɒ'keɪd/ **A** *n* blocco *m*
B *vt* bloccare
blockage /'blɒkɪdʒ/ *n* ostruzione *f*
block and tackle *n* paranco *m*
block book *vt* prenotare in blocco
block booking *n* prenotazione *f* in blocco
blockbuster *n* infml (book, film) successone *m*; Mil bomba *f* potente
block capital *n* **in ~s** in stampatello
blockhead *n* infml testone, -a *mf*
blockhouse *n* Mil fortino *m*
block letters *npl* stampatello *m*
block vote *n* voto *m* per delega
block voting *n* votazione *f* per delega
blog /blɒg/ Comput **A** *n* blog *m*
B *vi* bloggare
blogger /'blɒgə(r)/ *n* Comput blogger *m*
blogosphere /'blɒgəʊsfɪə(r)/ *n* blogosfera *f*
bloke /bləʊk/ *n* infml tizio *m*
blonde /blɒnd/ **A** *adj* biondo
B *n* bionda *f*
⚷ **blood** /blʌd/ *n* sangue *m*
blood-and-thunder *adj* ‹*novel, film*› pieno di sangue
blood bank *n* banca *f* del sangue
blood bath *n* bagno *m* di sangue
blood blister *n* vescica *f* di sangue
blood brother *n* fratello *m* di sangue
blood cell, **blood corpuscle** *n* globulo *m*
blood count *n* esame *m* emocromocitometrico
blood-curdling *adj* raccapricciante
blood donor *n* donatore, -trice *mf* di sangue
blood group *n* gruppo *m* sanguigno
bloodhound *n* segugio *m*
bloodless /'blʌdlɪs/ *adj* (pale) esangue; (revolution, coup) senza spargimento di sangue
blood-letting *n* Med salasso *m*; (killing) spargimento *m* di sangue
blood lust *n* sete *f* di sangue
blood money *n compenso* (*m*) *versato ad un killer o delatore*
blood orange *n* arancia *f* sanguigna
blood poisoning *n* setticemia *f*
blood pressure *n* pressione *f* del sangue
blood-red *adj* rosso sangue *inv*
blood relative *n* parente *mf* consanguineo, -a
bloodshed *n* spargimento *m* di sangue
bloodshot *adj* iniettato di sangue
blood sports *npl* sport *mpl* cruenti
bloodstained *adj* macchiato di sangue
bloodstream *n* sangue *m*
bloodsucker *n* also fig sanguisuga *f*
blood test *n* analisi *f inv* del sangue
bloodthirsty *adj* assetato di sangue
blood transfusion *n* trasfusione *f* di sangue
blood type *n* gruppo *m* sanguigno
blood vessel *n* vaso *m* sanguigno
bloody /'blʌdɪ/ **A** *adj* (**-ier**, **-iest**) insanguinato; sl maledetto
B *adv* sl **~ easy/difficult** facile/difficile da matti; **~ tired/funny** stanco/divertente da morire; **you ~ well will!** e, accidenti, lo farai!
bloody-minded /blʌdɪ'maɪndɪd/ *adj* scorbutico
bloom /blu:m/ **A** *n* fiore *m*; **in ~** (of flower) sbocciato; (of tree) in fiore
B *vi* fiorire; fig essere in forma smagliante
bloomer /'blu:mə(r)/ *n* infml papera *f*
bloomers /'blu:məz/ *npl* mutandoni *mpl* da donna
blooming /'blu:mɪŋ/ *adj* infml maledetto
blossom /'blɒsəm/ **A** *n* fiori *mpl* (*d'albero*); (single one) fiore *m*
B *vi* sbocciare
■ **blossom out** *vi* fig trasformarsi
blot /blɒt/ *n also* fig macchia *f*
■ **blot out**: *vt* **blotted** fig cancellare
blotch /blɒtʃ/ *n* macchia *f*
blotchy /'blɒtʃɪ/ *adj* chiazzato
blotter /'blɒtə(r)/ *n* tampone *m* di carta assorbente; AmE (police) registro *m* di polizia
blotting paper /'blɒtɪŋ/ *n* carta *f* assorbente
blotto /'blɒtəʊ/ *adj* infml ubriaco fradicio
blouse /blaʊz/ *n* camicetta *f*
blow¹ /bləʊ/ *n* colpo *m*
⚷ **blow²** *v* (*pt* **blew**, *pp* **blown**) **A** *vi* ‹*wind*› soffiare; ‹*fuse*› saltare
B *vt* infml (squander) sperperare; **~ one's nose** soffiarsi il naso; **~ one's top** fam andare in bestia
■ **blow away** **A** *vt* far volar via ‹*papers*›
B *vi* ‹*papers*› volare via
■ **blow down** **A** *vt* abbattere
B *vi* abbattersi al suolo
■ **blow off** **A** *vt* ‹*wind*› portar via
B *vi* ‹*hat, roof*› volare via
■ **blow out** **A** *vt* (extinguish) soffiare
B *vi* ‹*candle*› spegnersi
■ **blow over** **A** *vt* ‹*wind*› buttare giù
B *vi* ‹*storm*› passare; fig ‹*fuss, trouble*› dissiparsi
■ **blow up** **A** *vt* (inflate) gonfiare; (enlarge) ingrandire ‹*photograph*›; (shatter by explosion) far esplodere
B *vi* esplodere
blow-by-blow *adj* ‹*account*› particolareggiato
blow-dry *vt* asciugare con l'asciugacapelli
blowfly *n* moscone *m* (*della carne*)
blowhole *n* (of whale) sfiatatoio *m*

⚷ parola chiave

blowlamp *n* fiamma *f* ossidrica
blown /bləʊn/ ▶ **blow²**
blowout *n* Elec corto circuito *m*; (in oil or gas well) fuga *f*; (of tyre) scoppio *m*; infml (meal) abbuffata *f*
blowpipe *n* cerbottana *f*
blowtorch *n* cannello *m* ossidrico
blow-up **A** *n* Phot ingrandimento *m*
B *adj* ‹*doll, toy, dinghy*› gonfiabile
blowy /ˈbləʊɪ/ *adj* ventoso
blowzy /ˈblaʊzɪ/ *adj* derog ‹*woman*› volgarmente appariscente
BLT *n abbr* (**bacon, lettuce, and tomato**) sandwich *m* con bacon, lattuga e pomodoro
blubber /ˈblʌbə(r)/ **A** *n* (of whale) grasso *m* di balena; infml (of person) ciccia *f*
B *vi* AmE (to cry) infml piagnucolare
bludgeon /ˈblʌdʒən/ *vt* manganellare
blue /bluː/ **A** *adj* (pale) celeste; (navy) blu; (royal) azzurro; **feel ~** essere giù di corda; **~ with cold** livido per il freddo; **once in a ~ moon** una volta ogni morte di papa
B *n* blu *m inv*; **the ~s** Music il blues; **have the ~s** essere giù di corda; **out of the ~** inaspettatamente; **a bolt from the ~** un fulmine a ciel sereno
bluebell *n* giacinto *m* di bosco
Blue Berets *npl* Mil Caschi *mpl* blu
blueberry *n* mirtillo *m*
blue blood *n* sangue *m* blu
blue-blooded *adj* di sangue blu
bluebottle *n* moscone *m*
blue cheese *n* formaggio *m* erborinato
blue chip *adj* ‹*company*› di altissimo livello; ‹*investment*› sicuro
blue-collar job *n* lavoro *m* manuale
blue-collar worker *n* operaio *m*
blue-eyed *adj* con gli occhi azzurri
blue-eyed boy *n* BrE fig infml prediletto *m*
blue film *n* film *m* a luci rosse
blue jeans *npl* blue jeans *mpl inv*
blue light *n* (on emergency vehicles) *luce* (*f*) *delle auto della polizia*
blueness /ˈbluːnɪs/ *n* azzurro *m*
blue pencil *n* **go through something with the ~** (censor) censurare qualcosa; (edit) fare una revisione di qualcosa
blueprint *n* fig progetto *m*
blue rinse *n* **she's had a ~** si è tinta i capelli color grigio argentato
blue-stocking *n* derog [donna] intellettualoide *f*
blue tit *n* cinciarella *f*
Bluetooth® *n* Bluetooth® *m*
blue whale *n* balenottera *f* azzurra
bluff /blʌf/ **A** *n* bluff *m inv*
B *vi* bluffare
bluish /ˈbluːɪʃ/ *adj* bluastro, azzurrognolo
blunder /ˈblʌndə(r)/ **A** *n* gaffe *f inv*
B *vi* fare una/delle gaffe
blundering /ˈblʌnd(ə)rɪŋ/ *adj* **~ idiot** rimbecillito *m*
blunt /blʌnt/ *adj* spuntato; ‹*person*› reciso
bluntly /ˈblʌntlɪ/ *adv* schiettamente
bluntness /ˈblʌntnɪs/ *n* (of manner) rudezza *f*; (of person) brutale schiettezza *f*
blur /blɜː(r)/ **A** *n* **it's all a ~** fig è tutto confuso
B *vt* (*pt/pp* **blurred**) rendere confuso
blurb /blɜːb/ *n* soffietto *m* editoriale
blurred /blɜːd/ *adj* ‹*vision, photo*› sfocato
blurt /blɜːt/ *v*
▪ **blurt out** *vt* spifferare
blush /blʌʃ/ **A** *n* rossore *m*
B *vi* arrossire
blusher /ˈblʌʃə(r)/ *n* fard *m inv*
bluster /ˈblʌstə(r)/ *n* (showing off) sbruffonata *f*
blustering /ˈblʌst(ə)rɪŋ/ **A** *n* (rage) sfuriata *f*; (boasting) spacconata *f*
B *adj* (angry) infuriato; (boastful) sbruffone
blustery /ˈblʌst(ə)rɪ/ *adj* ‹*wind*› furioso; ‹*day, weather*› molto ventoso
Blu-tack® /ˈbluːtæk/ *n* Blu-tack® *m*
BMI *n abbr* (**body mass index**) IMC *m*
B movie *n* film *m inv* di serie B
BO *n* infml puzza *f* di sudore
boa /ˈbəʊə/ *n* boa *m inv*
boa constrictor /kənˈstrɪktə(r)/ boa *m inv*
boar /bɔː(r)/ *n* cinghiale *m*
board /bɔːd/ **A** *n* tavola *f*; (for notices) tabellone *m*; (committee) assemblea *f*; (of directors) consiglio *m*; **~ of directors** consiglio *m* di amministrazione; **full ~** BrE pensione *f* completa; **half ~** BrE mezza pensione *f*; **~ and lodging** vitto e alloggio *m*; **go by the ~** infml andare a monte
B *vt* Naut, Aeron salire a bordo di
C *vi* ‹*passengers*› salire a bordo; **~ with** stare a pensione da
▪ **board up** *vt* sbarrare con delle assi
boarder /ˈbɔːdə(r)/ *n* pensionante *mf*; Sch convittore, -trice *mf*
board game *n* gioco *m* da tavolo
boarding /ˈbɔːdɪŋ/ *n* Aeron, Naut imbarco *m*; (by customs officer) ispezione *f*; Mil abbordaggio *m*
boarding card *n* carta *f* di imbarco
boarding house *n* pensione *f*
boarding party *n* squadra *f* d'ispezione
boarding school *n* collegio *m*
board meeting *n* riunione *f* del consiglio di amministrazione
boardroom *n* sala *f* consiglio, sala *f* riunioni del consiglio di amministrazione
boardwalk *n* AmE (by sea) lungomare *m*
boast /bəʊst/ **A** *vi* vantarsi (**about** di)
B *vt* vantare
boaster /ˈbəʊstə(r)/ *n* sbruffone, -a *mf*
boastful /ˈbəʊstfʊl/ *adj* vanaglorioso

b

⚷ **boat** /bəʊt/ *n* barca *f*; (ship) nave *f*

boater /ˈbəʊtə(r)/ *n* (hat) paglietta *f*

boat-hook *n* gaffa *f*

boathouse /ˈbəʊthaʊs/ *n* rimessa *f* [per imbarcazioni]

boating /ˈbəʊtɪŋ/ **A** *n* canottaggio *m* **B** *adj* ‹*accident*› di navigazione

boating trip *n* traversata *f* per mare

boatload *n* carico *m*; **~s of tourists** navi *fpl* cariche di turisti

boatswain /ˈbəʊs(ə)n/ *n* nostromo *m*

boatyard *n* cantiere *m* per imbarcazioni

bob /bɒb/ **A** *n* (hairstyle) caschetto *m* **B** *vi* (*pt/pp* **bobbed**); (*also* **~ up and down**) andare su e giù

bobbin /ˈbɒbɪn/ *n* bobina *f*

bobble hat /ˈbɒblhæt/ *n* berretto *m* a pompon

bobby /ˈbɒbɪ/ *n* BrE infml poliziotto *m*

bobcat /ˈbɒbkæt/ *n* lince *f*

bobsleigh /ˈbɒbsleɪ/, **bobsled** /ˈbɒbsleɪ/ **A** *n* bob *m inv* **B** *vi* andare sul bob

bode /bəʊd/ *vi* **~ well/ill** essere di buono/cattivo augurio

bodge /bɒdʒ/ BrE = **botch**

bodice /ˈbɒdɪs/ *n* corpetto *m*

bodily /ˈbɒdɪlɪ/ **A** *adj* fisico **B** *adv* (forcibly) fisicamente

⚷ **body** /ˈbɒdɪ/ *n* corpo *m*; (organization) ente *m*; (amount: of poems etc) quantità *f*; **over my dead ~!** infml devi passare prima sul mio corpo!

body blow *n* **deal a ~ to** fig assestare un duro colpo a

bodyboarding *n* bodyboarding *m inv*

bodybuilder *n* culturista *mf*

body-building *n* culturismo *m*

bodyguard *n* guardia *f* del corpo

body heat *n* calore *m* del corpo

body language *n* linguaggio *m* del corpo

body mass index *n* indice *m* di massa corporea

body odour *n* infml puzza *f* di sudore

body piercing *n* piercing *m inv*

body politic *n* corpo *m* sociale

body shop *n* autocarrozzeria *f*

body snatching *n* furto *m* dei cadaveri

body stocking, **body suit** *n* body *m inv*

body warmer *n* gilet *m inv* imbottito

bodywork *n* Auto carrozzeria *f*

boffin /ˈbɒfɪn/ *n* BrE infml scienziato *m*

bog /bɒg/ *n* palude *f*

▪ **bog down**: *vt* (*pt/pp* **bogged**) **get ~ged down** impantanarsi

bogey /ˈbəʊgɪ/ *n* (evil spirit) spirito *m* malvagio; (to frighten people) spauracchio *m*

boggle /ˈbɒg(ə)l/ *vi* **the mind ~s** non posso neanche immaginarlo

boggy /ˈbɒgɪ/ *adj* (swampy) paludoso; (muddy) fangoso

bog-standard /bɒgˌstændəd/ *adj* infml ordinario

bogus /ˈbəʊgəs/ *adj* falso

bohemian /bəʊˈhiːmɪən/ *adj* ‹*lifestyle, person*› bohémien

boil[1] /bɔɪl/ *n* Med foruncolo *m*

boil[2] **A** *n* **bring/come to the ~** portare/arrivare ad ebollizione **B** *vt* [far] bollire **C** *vi* bollire; fig (with anger) ribollire; **the water** *or* **kettle's ~ing** l'acqua bolle

▪ **boil away** *vi* ‹*water*› evaporare

▪ **boil down to** *vi* fig ridursi a

▪ **boil over** *vi* straboccare (*bollendo*)

▪ **boil up** *vt* far bollire

boiler /ˈbɔɪlə(r)/ *n* caldaia *f*

boiler house *n* caldaia *f*

boiler room *n* locale *m* per la caldaia

boiler suit *n* tuta *f*

boiling /ˈbɔɪlɪŋ/ *adj* ‹*water*› bollente; **it's ~ in here!** qui si bolle!

boiling hot *adj* infml ‹*liquid*› bollente; ‹*day*› torrido

boiling point *n* punto *m* di ebollizione

boisterous /ˈbɔɪstərəs/ *adj* chiassoso

bold /bəʊld/ **A** *adj* audace **B** *n* Typ neretto *m*

boldly /ˈbəʊldlɪ/ *adv* audacemente

boldness /ˈbəʊldnɪs/ *n* audacia *f*

Bolivia /bəˈlɪvɪə/ *n* Bolivia *f*

bollard /ˈbɒlɑːd/ *n* colonnina *m* di sbarramento al traffico

Bolognese /bɒləˈneɪz/ *n* ragù *m*

boloney /bəˈləʊnɪ/ *n* infml idiozie *fpl*

bolshy /ˈbɒlʃɪ/ *adj* BrE infml (on one occasion) brontolone; **he's/she's ~** (by temperament) è un/una piantagrane; **get ~** fare [delle] storie

bolster /ˈbəʊlstə(r)/ **A** *n* cuscino *m* (*cilindrico*) **B** *vt* **~ [up]** sostenere

bolt /bəʊlt/ **A** *n* (for door) catenaccio *m*; (for fixing) bullone *m* **B** *vt* fissare [con bulloni] (**to** a); chiudere col chiavistello ‹*door*›; ingurgitare ‹*food*› **C** *vi* svignarsela; ‹*horse*› scappar via **D** *adv* **~ upright** diritto come un fuso

bolt-hole *n* BrE rifugio *m*

⚷ **bomb** /bɒm/ **A** *n* bomba *f* **B** *vt* bombardare

▪ **bomb along** *vi* infml (move quickly) sfrecciare

bombard /bɒmˈbɑːd/ *vt also* fig bombardare

bombardment /bɒmˈbɑːdmənt/ *n* bombardamento *m*

bombastic /bɒmˈbæstɪk/ *adj* ampolloso

bomb attack *n* bombardamento *m*

bomb blast *n* esplosione *f*

bomb disposal *n* disinnesco *m*

bomb disposal expert *n* artificiere *m*

⚷ parola chiave

bomb disposal squad *n* squadra *f* artificieri

bomber /ˈbɒmə(r)/ *n* Aviat bombardiere *m*; (person) dinamitardo *m*

bomber jacket *n* bomber *m inv*

bombing /ˈbɒmɪŋ/ *n* Mil bombardamento *m*; (by terrorists) attentato *m* dinamitardo

bombproof *adj* a prova di bomba

bomb scare *n stato (m) di allarme per la presunta presenza di una bomba*

bombshell *n* fig (news) bomba *f*; **blonde ~** bionda *f* esplosiva

bomb shelter *n* rifugio *m* antiaereo

bomb site *n* zona *f* bombardata; fig (mess) campo *f* di battaglia

Bomb Squad *n* squadra *f* artificieri

bona fide /bəʊnəˈfaɪdɪ/ *adj* ‹*member, refugee*› autentico; ‹*attempt*› genuino; ‹*offer*› serio

bonanza /bəˈnænzə/ *n* (windfall) momento *m* di prosperità; (in mining) filone *m* d'oro/d'argento

bond /bɒnd/ **A** *n* fig legame *m*; Comm obbligazione *f*
B *vt* ‹*glue*› attaccare

bondage /ˈbɒndɪdʒ/ *n* schiavitù *f*

bonded warehouse /ˈbɒndɪd/ *n* magazzino *m* doganale

bonding /ˈbɒndɪŋ/ *n* (between mother and baby) legame *m* madre-figlio; **male ~** solidarietà *f* maschile

bone /bəʊn/ **A** *n* osso *m*; (of fish) spina *f*
B *vt* disossare ‹*meat*›; togliere le spine da ‹*fish*›

bone china *n* porcellana *f* fine

boned /bəʊnd/ *adj* ‹*joint, leg, chicken*› disossato; ‹*fish*› senza lische; ‹*corset, bodice*› con le stecche

bone dry *adj* secco

bonehead *n* infml cretino, -a *mf*

bone idle *adj* infml fannullone

boneless /ˈbəʊnlɪs/ *adj* ‹*chicken*› disossato; ‹*chicken breast*› senz'osso; ‹*fish*› senza lische

bone marrow *n* midollo *m* osseo

bone marrow transplant *n* trapianto *m* di midollo osseo

bonemeal *n* farina *f* d'ossa

bonfire /ˈbɒnfaɪə(r)/ *n* falò *m*

Bonfire Night *n* BrE *sera (f) del 5 novembre festeggiata con falò e fuochi d'artificio*

bonk /bɒŋk/ *vt* sl scopare

bonkers /ˈbɒŋkəz/ *adj* infml suonato

bonnet /ˈbɒnɪt/ *n* cuffia *f*; (of car) cofano *m*

bonus /ˈbəʊnəs/ *n* (individual) gratifica *f*; (production) premio *m*; (life insurance) dividendo *m*; **a ~** fig qualcosa in più

bonus point *n* **five ~s** un bonus di cinque punti

bony /ˈbəʊnɪ/ *adj* (**-ier**, **-iest**) ossuto; ‹*fish*› pieno di spine

boo /buː/ **A** *interj* (to surprise or frighten) bu!
B *vt & vi* fischiare

boob /buːb/ **A** *n* infml (mistake) gaffe *f inv*; (breast) tetta *f*
B *vi* infml fare una gaffe

booboo /ˈbuːbuː/ *n* infml gaffe *f inv*

booby prize /ˈbuːbɪ/ *n premio (m) di consolazione per il peggior contendente*

booby trap **A** *n* Mil *ordigno (m) che esplode al contatto*; (joke) trabocchetto *m*
B *vt* Mil mettere un ordigno esplosivo in

boogie /ˈbuːgɪ/ *n* infml boogie *m*

booing /ˈbuːɪŋ/ *n* fischi *mpl*

book /bʊk/ **A** *n* libro *m*; (of tickets) blocchetto *m*; **keep the ~s** Comm tenere la contabilità; **be in sb's bad/good ~s** essere nel libro nero/nelle grazie di qualcuno; **do something by the ~** seguire strettamente le regole
B *vt* (reserve) prenotare; (for offence) multare
C *vi* (reserve) prenotare

bookable /ˈbʊkəbl/ *adj* ‹*event, ticket*› che si può prenotare; ‹*offence*› che può essere multato

bookbinder *n* rilegatore, -trice *mf*

bookbinding *n* rilegatura *f*

bookcase *n* libreria *f*

book club *n* club *m inv* del libro

book-ends *npl* reggilibri *mpl*

book fair *n* fiera *f* del libro

bookie /ˈbʊkɪ/ *n* infml bookmaker *m inv*, allibratore *m*

booking /ˈbʊkɪŋ/ *n* BrE (reservation) prenotazione *f*; **make a ~** fare una prenotazione; **get a ~** BrE (from referee) ricevere un'ammonizione

booking clerk *n* BrE impiegato, -a *mf* in un ufficio prenotazioni

booking form *n* BrE modulo *m* di prenotazione

booking office *n* biglietteria *f*

bookish /ˈbʊkɪʃ/ *adj* ‹*person*› secchione

book jacket *n* sopraccoperta *f*

bookkeeper *n* contabile *mf*

bookkeeping *n* contabilità *f*

booklet /ˈbʊklɪt/ *n* opuscolo *m*

book lover *n* amante *mf* della lettura

bookmaker *n* allibratore *m*

bookmark *n* segnalibro *m*

bookplate *n* ex libris *m inv*

bookrest *n* leggio *m*

bookseller *n* libraio, -a *mf*

bookshelf *n* (single) scaffale *f*; (bookcase) libreria *f*

bookshop *n* libreria *f*

bookstall *n* edicola *f*

bookstore *n* AmE libreria *f*

book token *n* BrE buono *m* acquisto per libri

bookworm *n* topo *m* di biblioteca

boom /buːm/ **A** *n* Comm boom *m inv*; (upturn) impennata *f*; (of thunder, gun) rimbombo *m*
B *vi* ‹*thunder, gun*› rimbombare; fig prosperare

boomerang /ˈbuːməræŋ/ **A** *n* boomerang *m inv*
B *vi* ~ **on somebody** ‹*plan*› ritorcersi contro qualcuno

boomerang effect *n* effetto *m* boomerang

booming /ˈbuːmɪŋ/ *adj* ‹*sound*› sonoro; ‹*voice*› tonante; ‹*economy*› fiorente; ‹*demand, exports, sales*› in crescita

boom microphone *n* microfono *m* a stelo

boon /buːn/ *n* benedizione *f*

boor /bʊə(r)/ *n* zoticone *m*

boorish /ˈbʊərɪʃ/ *adj* maleducato

boost /buːst/ **A** *n* spinta *f*
B *vt* stimolare ‹*sales*›; sollevare ‹*morale*›; far crescere ‹*hopes*›

booster /ˈbuːstə(r)/ *n* Med dose *f* supplementare

boot /buːt/ **A** *n* stivale *m*; (up to ankle) stivaletto *m*; (football) scarpetta *f*; (climbing) scarpone *m*; Auto portabagagli *m inv*
B *vt* Comput mettere in funzione
▪ **boot out** *vt* infml cacciare
▪ **boot up** Comput **A** *vi* caricarsi
B *vt* caricare

boot black *n* lustrascarpe *mf inv*

boot camp *n* **1** Mil campo *m* di addestramento reclute **2** (intensive training) *corso (m) di addestramento breve, severo e intensivo*

boot drive *n* Comput unità *f* di inizializzazione

bootee /buːˈtiː/ *n* (knitted) babbuccia *f* di lana; (leather) stivaletto *m*

booth /buːð/ *n* (for phoning, voting) cabina *f*; (at market) bancarella *f*

bootlace *n* laccio *m*, stringa *f*

bootlegger *n* AmE contrabbandiere *m* di alcolici

bootlicker *n* leccapiedi *mf inv*

bootmaker *n* calzolaio *m*

boot polish *n* lucido *m* da scarpe

boot scraper *n* puliscipiedi *m inv*

bootstrap *n* (on boot) linguetta *f* calzastivali; Comput lancio *m*; **pull oneself up by one's ~s** riuscire con le proprie forze

boot-up *n* Comput boot *m inv*

booty /ˈbuːtɪ/ *n* bottino *m*

booze /buːz/ *n* infml alcolici *mpl*

boozer /ˈbuːzə(r)/ *n* infml (person) beone, -a *mf*; BrE (pub) bar *m inv*

booze-up *n* bella bevuta *f*

boozy /ˈbuːzɪ/ *adj* infml ‹*laughter*› da ubriaco; ‹*meal*› in cui si beve molto

bop /bɒp/ infml **A** *n* (blow) colpo *m*
B *vt* dare un colpo a
C *vi* BrE (dance) ballare

🔑 **border** /ˈbɔːdə(r)/ **A** *n* bordo *m*; (frontier) frontiera *f*; (in garden) bordura *f*
B *vt* confinare con; fig essere ai confini di
▪ **border on** *vt* ‹*country, land*› confinare con; ‹*madness, hysteria*› essere al limite di

border dispute *n* (fight) conflitto *m* al confine; (disagreement) contesa *f* sul confine

border guard *n* guardia *f* di frontiera

borderline *n* linea *f* di demarcazione; **~ case** caso *m* dubbio

border raid *n* incursione *f*

bore[1] /bɔː(r)/ ▶ **bear**[2]

bore[2] *vt* Techn forare

bore[3] **A** *n* (of gun) calibro *m*; (person) seccatore, -trice *mf*; (thing) seccatura *f*
B *vt* annoiare

bored /bɔːd/ *adj* annoiato, stufo; **be ~ to tears** *or* **to death** annoiarsi (da morire)

boredom /ˈbɔːdəm/ *n* noia *f*

boring /ˈbɔːrɪŋ/ *adj* noioso

🔑 **born** /bɔːn/ **A** *pp* **be ~** nascere; **I was ~ in 1963** sono nato nel 1963
B *adj* nato; **a ~ liar/actor** un bugiardo/un attore nato

born-again *adj* convertito alla chiesa evangelica

borne /bɔːn/ ▶ **bear**[2]

Borneo /ˈbɔːnɪəʊ/ *n* Borneo *m*

borough /ˈbʌrə/ *n* municipalità *f*

borough council *n* BrE ≈ comune *m*

borrow /ˈbɒrəʊ/ *vt* prendere in prestito (from da); **can I ~ your pen?** mi presti la tua penna?

borrower /ˈbɒrəʊə(r)/ *n* debitore, -trice *mf*

borrowing /ˈbɒrəʊɪŋ/ *n* prestito *m*; **increase in ~** Fin aumento *m* dell'indebitamento

borrowing costs *n* Fin costo *m* del denaro

borstal /ˈbɔːstəl/ *n* BrE riformatorio *m*

Bosnia /ˈbɒznɪə/ *n* Bosnia *f*

Bosnia-Herzegovina /-hɜːtsəgəʊˈviːnə/ *n* Bosnia-Erzegovina *f*

Bosnian /ˈbɒznɪən/ *adj & n* bosniaco, -a *mf*

bosom /ˈbʊzm/ *n* seno *m*

bosom buddy, bosom friend *n* infml amico, -a *mf* del cuore

🔑 **boss** /bɒs/ **A** *n* direttore, -trice *mf*
B *vt* (*also* ~ **about**) comandare a bacchetta

bossy /ˈbɒsɪ/ *adj* autoritario

bosun /ˈbəʊsən/ *n* nostromo *m*

botanical /bəˈtænɪkl/ *adj* botanico

botanist /ˈbɒtənɪst/ *n* botanico, -a *mf*

botany /ˈbɒtənɪ/ *n* botanica *f*

botch /bɒtʃ/ *vt* fare un pasticcio con

🔑 **both** /bəʊθ/ **A** *adj & pron* tutti e due, entrambi
B *adv* ~ **men and women** sia uomini

🔑 parola chiave

che donne; **~ [of] the children** tutti e due i bambini; **they are ~ dead** sono morti entrambi; **~ of them** tutti e due

bother /ˈbɒðə(r)/ **A** *n* preoccupazione *f*; (minor trouble) fastidio *m*; **it's no ~** non c'è problema
B *int* infml che seccatura!
C *vt* (annoy) dare fastidio a; (disturb) disturbare
D *vi* preoccuparsi (**about** di); **don't ~** lascia perdere

Botswana /bɒtˈswɑːnə/ *n* Botswana *m*

bottle /ˈbɒt(ə)l/ **A** *n* bottiglia *f*; (baby's) biberon *m inv*
B *vt* imbottigliare
■ **bottle up** *vt* fig reprimere

bottle bank *n* contenitore *m* per la raccolta del vetro

bottle-feed *vt* allattare col biberon

bottle-feeding *n* allattamento *m* col biberon

bottle green *adj & n* verde *m* bottiglia *inv*

bottleneck *n* fig ingorgo *m*

bottle opener *n* apribottiglie *m inv*

bottle top *n* tappo *m* di bottiglia

bottle washer *n* hum **chief cook and ~** tuttofare *mf inv*

bottom /ˈbɒtm/ **A** *adj* ultimo; **the ~ shelf** l'ultimo scaffale in basso
B *n* (of container) fondo *m*; (of river) fondale *m*; (of hill) piedi *mpl*; (buttocks) sedere *m*; **at the ~** in fondo; **at the ~ of the page** in fondo alla pagina; **get to the ~ of** fig vedere cosa c'è sotto
■ **bottom out** *vi* ‹*inflation, unemployment etc*› assestarsi

bottom drawer *n* fig corredo *m*

bottom gear *n* BrE Auto prima *f*

bottomless /ˈbɒtəmlɪs/ *adj* senza fondo

bottom line *n* Fin utile *m*; **that's the ~** (decisive factor) la questione è tutta qui

botulism /ˈbɒtjʊlɪzm/ *n* botulismo *m*

bouffant /ˈbuːfɒ̃/ *adj* ‹*hair, hairstyle*› cotonato; ‹*sleeve*› a sbuffo

bough /baʊ/ *n* ramoscello *m*

bought /bɔːt/ ▶ **buy**

boulder /ˈbəʊldə(r)/ *n* masso *m*

bounce /baʊns/ **A** *vi* rimbalzare; infml ‹*cheque*› essere respinto
B *vt* far rimbalzare ‹*ball*›
■ **bounce back** *vi* fig riprendersi; ‹*email*› tornare indietro

bouncer /ˈbaʊnsə(r)/ *n* infml buttafuori *m inv*

bouncy /ˈbaʊnsɪ/ *adj* ‹*ball*› che rimbalza bene; ‹*mattress, walk*› molleggiato; fig ‹*person*› esuberante

bound¹ /baʊnd/ **A** *n* balzo *m*
B *vi* balzare

bound² **A** ▶ **bind**
B *adj* **~ for** ‹*ship*› diretto a; **be ~ to do** (likely) dovere fare per forza; (obliged) essere costretto a fare

boundary /ˈbaʊndərɪ/ *n* limite *m*

boundless /ˈbaʊndlɪs/ *adj* illimitato

bounds /baʊndz/ *npl* fig limiti *mpl*; **out of ~** fuori dai limiti

bounty /ˈbaʊntɪ/ *n* (gift) dono *m*; (generosity) munificenza *f*

bounty hunter *n* cacciatore *m* di taglie

bouquet /bʊˈkeɪ/ *n* mazzo *m* di fiori; (of wine) bouquet *m*

bourbon /ˈbʊəbən/ *n* bourbon *m inv*

bourgeois /ˈbʊəʒwɑː/ *adj* derog borghese

bourgeoisie /bʊəʒwɑːˈziː/ *n* borghesia *f*

bout /baʊt/ *n* Med attacco *m*; Sport incontro *m*

boutique /buːˈtiːk/ *n* negozio *m*; **fashion ~** negozio *m* di abbigliamento

bovine /ˈbəʊvaɪn/ *adj* bovino

bow¹ /bəʊ/ *n* (weapon) arco *m*; Mus archetto *m*; (knot) nodo *m*

bow² /baʊ/ **A** *n* inchino *m*
B *vi* inchinarsi
C *vt* piegare ‹*head*›

bow³ /baʊ/ *n* Naut prua *f*
■ **bow out** *vi* (withdraw) ritirarsi (**of** da)

bowel /ˈbaʊəl/ *n* intestino *m*; **have a ~ movement** andare di corpo; **~s** *pl* intestini *mpl*

bower /ˈbaʊə(r)/ *n* (in garden) pergolato *m*; literary (chamber) salottino *m*

bowl¹ /bəʊl/ *n* (for soup, cereal) scodella *f*; (of pipe) fornello *m*

bowl² **A** *n* (ball) boccia *f*
B *vt* lanciare
C *vi* Cricket servire; (in bowls) lanciare
■ **bowl along** *vi* (in car etc) andare spedito
■ **bowl over** *vt* buttar giù; fig (leave speechless) lasciare senza parole

bow-legged /bəʊˈlegd/ *adj* dalle gambe storte

bowler¹ /ˈbəʊlə(r)/ *n* Cricket lanciatore *m*; Bowls giocatore *m* di bocce

bowler² *n* **~ [hat]** bombetta *f*

bowling /ˈbəʊlɪŋ/ *n* gioco *m* delle bocce

bowling alley /ˈbəʊlɪŋælɪ/ *n* pista *f* da bowling

bowling green *n* prato *m* da bocce

bowls /bəʊlz/ *n* gioco *m* delle bocce

bowstring *n* corda *f* d'arco

bow tie *n* cravatta *f* a farfalla

bow window *n* bow window *f inv*

box¹ /bɒks/ *n* scatola *f*; Theat palco *m*

box² **A** *vi* Sport fare il pugile
B *vt* **~ sb's ears** dare uno scapaccione a qualcuno

boxer /ˈbɒksə(r)/ *n* pugile *m*

boxer shorts *npl* boxer *mpl*

boxing /ˈbɒksɪŋ/ *n* pugilato *m*

Boxing Day *n* BrE [giorno *m* di] Santo Stefano *m*

box number *n* casella *f*

b

box office *n* Theat botteghino *m*
box room *n* BrE sgabuzzino *m*
boxwood *n* bosso *m*
⚷ **boy** /bɔɪ/ *n* ragazzo *m*; (younger) bambino *m*
boy band *n* boy band *f inv*
boycott /ˈbɔɪkɒt/ **A** *n* boicottaggio *m*
B *vt* boicottare
boyfriend /ˈbɔɪfrend/ *n* ragazzo *m*
boyhood /ˈbɔɪhʊd/ *n* (childhood) infanzia *f*; (adolescence) adolescenza *f*
boyish /ˈbɔɪɪʃ/ *adj* da ragazzino
boy scout *n* boy scout *m inv*
bpm *abbr* (**beats per minute**) bpm *mpl*
bps *abbr* (**bits per second**) Comput bps *mpl*
BR *abbr* (**British Rail**) *ente* (*m*) *ferroviario britannico* ≈ FS
bra /brɑː/ *n* reggiseno *m*
brace /breɪs/ **A** *n* sostegno *m*; (dental) apparecchio *m*
B *vt* ~ **oneself** fig farsi forza (**for** per affrontare)
bracelet /ˈbreɪslɪt/ *n* braccialetto *m*
braces /ˈbreɪsɪz/ *npl* bretelle *fpl*
bracing /ˈbreɪsɪŋ/ *adj* tonificante
bracken /ˈbrækn/ *n* felce *f*
bracket /ˈbrækɪt/ **A** *n* mensola *f*; (group) categoria *f*; Typ parentesi *f inv*
B *vt* mettere fra parentesi
brackish /ˈbrækɪʃ/ *adj* salmastro
bradawl /ˈbrædɔːl/ *n* punteruolo *m*
brag /bræg/ *vi* (*pt/pp* **bragged**) vantarsi (**about** di)
bragging /ˈbrægɪŋ/ *n* vanterie *fpl*
Brahmin /ˈbrɑːmɪn/ *n* Relig bramino *m*
braid /breɪd/ *n* (edging) passamano *m*
Braille /breɪl/ *n* braille *m*
⚷ **brain** /breɪn/ *n* cervello *m*; ~**s** *pl* fig testa *fsg*
brainbox *n* infml capoccione *m*
brainchild *n* invenzione *f* personale
brain damage *n* lesione *f* cerebrale
brain-dead *adj* Med cerebralmente morto; fig senza cervello
brain death *n* morte *f* cerebrale
brain drain *n* fuga *f* di cervelli
brainless /ˈbreɪnlɪs/ *adj* senza cervello
brain scan *n* scansione *f* del cervello
brain scanner *n* scanner *m inv* (*per il cervello*)
brainstorm *n* Med fig eccesso *m* di pazzia; AmE (brainwave) lampo *m* di genio
brainstorming session *n* brainstorming *m inv*
brains trust *n* brain trust *m inv*, gruppo *m* di esperti
brain surgeon *n* neurochirurgo *m*
brain surgery *n* neurochirurgia *f*
brain teaser *n* infml rompicapo *m*

brainwash *vt* fare il lavaggio del cervello a
brainwashing *n* lavaggio *m* del cervello
brainwave *n* lampo *m* di genio
brainy /ˈbreɪnɪ/ *adj* (**-ier**, **-iest**) intelligente
braise /breɪz/ *vt* brasare
brake /breɪk/ **A** *n* freno *m*
B *vi* frenare
brake block *n* pastiglia *f*
brake disc *n* disco *m* dei freni
brake drum *n* tamburo *m* del freno
brake fluid *n* liquido *m* dei freni
brake light *n* stop *m inv*
brake lining *n* guarnizione *f* del freno
brake pad *n* ganascia *f* del freno
brake pedal *n* pedale *m* del freno
bramble /ˈbræmb(ə)l/ *n* rovo *m*; (fruit) mora *f*
bran /bræn/ *n* crusca *f*
⚷ **branch** /brɑːntʃ/ **A** *n also* fig ramo *m*; Comm succursale *f*; filiale *f*; (of bank) agenzia *f*; **our Oxford St** ~ (of store) il negozio di Oxford St
B *vi* ‹*road*› biforcarsi
▪ **branch off** *vi* biforcarsi
▪ **branch out**: *vi* ~ **out into** allargare le proprie attività nel ramo di
branch line *n* linea *f* secondaria
branch manager *n* (of bank) direttore, -trice *mf* di agenzia; (of company) direttore, -trice *mf* di filiale; (of shop) direttore, -trice *mf* di succursale
branch office *n* filiale *f*; (of bank) agenzia *f*
⚷ **brand** /brænd/ **A** *n* marca *f*; (on animal) marchio *m*
B *vt* marcare ‹*animal*›; fig tacciare (**as** di)
branded /ˈbrændɪd/ *adj* ‹*goods*› di marca
brand image *n* brand image *f*
brandish /ˈbrændɪʃ/ *vt* brandire
brand leader *n* marca *f* leader *inv*
brand name *n* marca *f*
brand new *adj* nuovo fiammante
brandy /ˈbrændɪ/ *n* brandy *m inv*
brash /bræʃ/ *adj* sfrontato
brass /brɑːs/ *n* ottone *m*; **the** ~ Mus gli ottoni *mpl*; **top** ~ infml pezzi *mpl* grossi
brass band *n* banda *f* (*di soli ottoni*)
brassiere /ˈbræzɪə(r)/ AmE *n* fml reggiseno *m*
brass instrument *n* Mus ottone *m*
brass neck *n* BrE infml faccia *f* tosta
brass rubbing *n ricalco* (*m*) *di iscrizione tombale o commemorativa*
brassy /ˈbrɑːsɪ/ *adj* (**-ier**, **-iest**) infml volgare
brat /bræt/ *n* derog marmocchio, -a *mf*
bravado /brəˈvɑːdəʊ/ *n* bravata *f*
brave /breɪv/ **A** *adj* coraggioso
B *vt* affrontare
bravely /ˈbreɪvlɪ/ *adv* con coraggio
bravery /ˈbreɪvərɪ/ *n* coraggio *m*
bravo /brɑːˈvəʊ/ *int* bravo!
bravura /brəˈvjʊərə/ *n* virtuosismo *m*
brawl /brɔːl/ **A** *n* rissa *f*

⚷ parola chiave

B *vi* azzuffarsi
brawn /brɔːn/ *n* Culin ≈ soppressata *f*
brawny /ˈbrɔːnɪ/ *adj* muscoloso
bray /breɪ/ *vi* ‹*donkey*› ragliare
brazen /ˈbreɪzn/ *adj* sfrontato
▪ **brazen out** *vt* affrontare con piglio sicuro
brazier /ˈbreɪzɪə(r)/ *n* braciere *m*
Brazil /brəˈzɪl/ *n* Brasile *m*
Brazilian /brəˈzɪlɪən/ *adj & n* brasiliano, -a *mf*
Brazil nut *n* noce *f* del Brasile
breach /briːtʃ/ **A** *n* (of law) violazione *f*; (gap) breccia *f*; fig (in party) frattura *f*
B *vt* recedere ‹*contract*›
breach of contract *n* Jur inadempienza *f* contrattuale
breach of promise *n* Jur inadempienza *f* a una promessa di matrimonio
breach of the peace *n* Jur violazione *f* dell'ordine pubblico
breach of trust *n* Jur abuso *m* di fiducia
bread /bred/ *n* pane *m*; **a slice of ~ and butter** una fetta di pane imburrato
bread and butter *n* fig fonte *f* di guadagno principale
breadbasket *n* cestino *m* per il pane; fig granaio *m*
bread bin *n* BrE cassetta *f* portapane *inv*
breadboard *n* tagliere *m* per il pane
breadcrumbs *npl* briciole *fpl*; Culin pangrattato *m*
breadfruit *n* frutto *m* dell'albero del pane
bread knife *n* coltello *m* per il pane
breadline *n* **be on the ~** essere povero in canna
bread roll *n* panino *m*
breadstick *n* filoncino *m*
breadth /bredθ/ *n* larghezza *f*
breadwinner /ˈbredwɪnə(r)/ *n* quello, -a *mf* che porta i soldi a casa
⚷ **break** /breɪk/ **A** *n* rottura *f*; (interval) intervallo *m*; (interruption) interruzione *f*; infml (chance) opportunità *f*
B *vt* (*pt* **broke**, *pp* **broken**) rompere; (interrupt) interrompere; **~ one's arm** rompersi un braccio
C *vi* rompersi; ‹*day*› spuntare; ‹*storm*› scoppiare; ‹*news*› diffondersi; ‹*boy's voice*› cambiare
▪ **break away** *vi* scappare; fig chiudere (**from** con)
▪ **break down A** *vi* ‹*machine, car*› guastarsi; ‹*negotiations*› interrompersi; (in tears) scoppiare in lacrime
B *vt* sfondare ‹*door*›; ripartire ‹*figures*›
▪ **break in** *vi* ‹*burglar*› introdursi
▪ **break into** *vt* introdursi con la forza in; forzare ‹*car*›
▪ **break off A** *vt* rompere ‹*engagement*›
B *vi* ‹*part of whole*› rompersi; (when speaking) interrompersi
▪ **break out** *vi* ‹*argument, war*› scoppiare
▪ **break through** *vi* ‹*sun*› spuntare
▪ **break up A** *vt* far cessare ‹*fight*›; disperdere ‹*crowd*›
B *vi* ‹*crowd*› disperdersi; ‹*marriage*› naufragare; ‹*couple*› separarsi; Sch iniziare le vacanze
breakable /ˈbreɪkəbl/ *adj* fragile
breakage /ˈbreɪkɪdʒ/ *n* rottura *f*
breakaway /ˈbreɪkəweɪ/ **A** *n* (from person) separazione *f*, allontanamento *m*; (from organization) scissione *f*; Sport contropiede *m*
B *attrib* ‹*faction, group, state*› separatista
breakdown /ˈbreɪkdaʊn/ *n* (of car, machine) guasto *m*; Med esaurimento *m* nervoso; (of figures) analisi *f inv*
breaker /ˈbreɪkə(r)/ *n* (wave) frangente *m*
breaker's yard *n* Auto cimitero *m* delle macchine
break even *vi* andare in pareggio
break-even point *n* punto *m* di pareggio, punto *m* di equilibrio
breakfast /ˈbrekfəst/ *n* [prima] colazione *f*
breakfast bar *n* tavolo *m* a penisola
breakfast bowl *n* scodella *f* per i cereali
breakfast cereals *npl* cereali *mpl* per la colazione
breakfast television, **breakfast TV** *n* programmi *mpl* televisivi del mattino
breakfast TV *n* programmi *mpl* televisivi del mattino
break free *vi* fuggire
break-in *n* irruzione *f*
breaking /ˈbreɪkɪŋ/ *n* (of glass, seal, contract) rottura *f*; (of bone) frattura *f*; (of law, treaty) violazione *f*; (of voice) cambiamento *m*; (of promise) venuta *f* meno; (of horse) domatura *f*; (of link, sequence, tie) interruzione *f*
breaking and entering /breɪkɪŋənd ˈentərɪŋ/ *n* Jur effrazione *f* con scasso
breaking point *n* Techn punto *m* di rottura; fig limite *m* di sopportazione
breakneck *adj* ‹*pace, speed*› a rotta di collo
break-out *n* (from prison) evasione *f*
breakpoint *n* Tennis breakpoint *m inv*
breakthrough *n* (discovery) scoperta *f*; (in negotiations) passo *m* avanti
break-up *n* (of family, company) disgregazione *f*; (of alliance, relationship) rottura *f*; (of marriage) dissoluzione *f*
breakwater *n* frangiflutti *m inv*
breast /brest/ *n* seno *m*
breastbone *n* sterno *m*
breastfeed *vt* allattare al seno
breast pocket *n* taschino *m*
breaststroke *n* nuoto *m* a rana
⚷ **breath** /breθ/ *n* respiro *m*, fiato *m*; **out of ~** senza fiato; **under one's ~** sottovoce; **a ~ of air** un filo d'aria
breathalyse /ˈbreθəlaɪz/ *vt* sottoporre alla prova del palloncino

breathalyser BrE, **Breathalyzer**® /ˈbreθəlaɪzə(r)/ *n* alcoltest *m inv*

breathe /briːð/ *vt & vi* respirare; ~ **a sigh of relief** tirare un sospiro di sollievo

▪ **breath in** **A** *vi* inspirare
B *vt* respirare ‹*scent, air*›

▪ **breathe out** *vt & vi* espirare

breather /ˈbriːðə(r)/ *n* pausa *f*

breathing /ˈbriːðɪŋ/ *n* respirazione *f*

breathing apparatus *n* respiratore *m*

breathing space *n* (respite) tregua *f*; **give oneself a** ~ riprendere fiato

breathless /ˈbreθlɪs/ *adj* senza fiato

breathlessly /ˈbreθlɪslɪ/ *adv* senza fiato

breathtaking /ˈbreθteɪkɪŋ/ *adj* mozzafiato

breathtakingly /ˈbreθteɪkɪŋlɪ/ *adv* ~ **audacious** di un'audacia stupefacente; ~ **beautiful** di una bellezza mozzafiato

breath test *n* prova *f* del palloncino

bred /bred/ ▶ **breed**

breech /briːtʃ/ *n* Med natiche *fpl*; (of gun) culatta *f*

breed /briːd/ **A** *n* razza *f*
B *vt* (*pt/pp* **bred**) allevare; (give rise to) generare
C *vi* riprodursi

breeder /ˈbriːdə(r)/ *n* allevatore, -trice *mf*

breeding /ˈbriːdɪŋ/ *n* allevamento *m*; fig educazione *f*

breeding ground *n* zona *f* di riproduzione; fig terreno *m* fertile

breeding period, **breeding season** *n* stagione *f* di riproduzione

breeze /briːz/ *n* brezza *f*

breeze block *n* BrE *mattone* (*m*) *fatto con scorie di coke*

breezily /ˈbriːzɪlɪ/ *adv* (confidently) con sicurezza; (casually) con disinvoltura; (cheerfully) allegramente

breezy /ˈbriːzɪ/ *adj* ventoso

brevity /ˈbrevətɪ/ *n* brevità *f*

brew /bruː/ **A** *n* infuso *m*
B *vt* mettere in infusione ‹*tea*›; produrre ‹*beer*›
C *vi* fig ‹*trouble*› essere nell'aria

brewer /ˈbrʊə(r)/ *n* birraio *m*

brewery /ˈbrʊərɪ/ *n* fabbrica *f* di birra

brew-up *n* BrE infml tè *m*

briar /ˈbraɪə(r)/ *n* rosa *f* selvatica; (heather) erica *f*; (thorns) rovo *m*; (pipe) pipa *f* in radica

bribe /braɪb/ **A** *n* (money) bustarella *f*; (large sum of money) tangente *f*
B *vt* corrompere

bribery /ˈbraɪbərɪ/ *n* corruzione *f*

brick /brɪk/ *n* mattone *m*

▪ **brick up** *vt* murare

brickbat *n* fig critica *f* spietata

brick-built *adj* di mattoni

bricklayer *n* muratore *m*

bricklaying *n* muratura *f*

brick red *adj* rosso mattone *inv*

bricks-and-mortar *adj* ‹*company, business*› di tipo tradizionale

brickwork *n* muratura *f* di mattoni

brickworks *n* fabbrica *f* di mattoni

bridal /ˈbraɪdl/ *adj* nuziale

bridal party *n* corteo *m* nuziale

bridal suite *n* camera *f* nuziale

bridal wear *n* confezioni *fpl* da sposa

bride /braɪd/ *n* sposa *f*

bridegroom /ˈbraɪdgruːm/ *n* sposo *m*

bridesmaid /ˈbraɪdzmeɪd/ *n* damigella *f* d'onore

bridge[1] /brɪdʒ/ **A** *n* ponte *m*; (of nose) setto *m* nasale; (of spectacles) ponticello *m*
B *vt* fig colmare ‹*gap*›

bridge[2] *n* Cards bridge *m*

bridge-building *n* costruzione *f* di ponti provvisori; fig mediazione *f*

bridging loan /ˈbrɪdʒɪŋ/ *n* BrE Fin prefinanziamento *m*, credito *m* provvisorio

bridle /ˈbraɪd(ə)l/ *n* briglia *f*

bridle path, **bridleway** /ˈbraɪd(ə)lweɪ/ *n* sentiero *m* per cavalli

🔑 **brief[1]** /briːf/ *adj* breve; **in** ~ in breve

brief[2] **A** *n* istruzioni *fpl*; Jur (case) causa *f*
B *vt* dare istruzioni a; Jur affidare la causa a

briefcase /ˈbriːfkeɪs/ *n* cartella *f*

briefing /ˈbriːfɪŋ/ *n* briefing *m inv*

briefly /ˈbriːflɪ/ *adv* brevemente; **briefly,...** in breve,...

briefness /ˈbriːfnɪs/ *n* brevità *f*

briefs /briːfs/ *npl* slip *m inv*

brigade /brɪˈgeɪd/ *n* brigata *f*

brigadier /brɪgəˈdɪə(r)/ *n* generale *m* di brigata

🔑 **bright** /braɪt/ *adj* ‹*metal, idea*› brillante; ‹*day, room, future*› luminoso; (clever) intelligente; ~ **red** rosso *m* acceso

brighten /ˈbraɪt(ə)n/ *v* ~ **[up]** **A** *vt* ravvivare; rallegrare ‹*person*›
B *vi* ‹*weather*› schiarirsi; ‹*face*› illuminarsi; ‹*person*› rallegrarsi

brightly /ˈbraɪtlɪ/ *adv* ‹*shine*› intensamente; ‹*smile*› allegramente

brightness /ˈbraɪtnɪs/ *n* luminosità *f*; (intelligence) intelligenza *f*

bright spark *n* BrE infml genio *m*

bright young things *npl* BrE i giovani di belle speranze

brill /brɪl/ **A** *n* Zool rombo *m* liscio
B *adj* BrE infml fantastico

brilliance /ˈbrɪljəns/ *n* luminosità *f*; (of person) genialità *f*

brilliant /ˈbrɪljənt/ *adj* (very good) eccezionale; (very intelligent) brillante; ‹*sunshine*› splendente

---

🔑 parola chiave

brilliantly /ˈbrɪljəntlɪ/ *adv ‹shine›* intensamente; *‹perform›* in modo eccezionale

Brillo pad® /ˈbriləʊ/ *n* paglietta *f* d'acciaio

brim /brɪm/ *n* bordo *m*; (of hat) tesa *f*

■ **brim over** *vi* (*pt/pp* **brimmed**) traboccare

brine /braɪn/ *n* salamoia *f*

bring /brɪŋ/ *vt* (*pt/pp* **brought**) portare *‹person, object›*

■ **bring about** *vt* causare

■ **bring along** *vt* portare [con sé]

■ **bring back** *vt* restituire *‹something borrowed›*; reintrodurre *‹hanging›*; fare ritornare in mente *‹memories›*

■ **bring down** *vt* portare giù; fare cadere *‹government›*; fare abbassare *‹price›*

■ **bring forward** *vt* anticipare *‹meeting, date›*; **the meeting has been brought forward to this afternoon** la riunione è stata anticipata al pomeriggio

■ **bring in** *vt* introdurre *‹legislation›*; **his job ~s in £30,000 a year** guadagna 30.000 sterline all'anno

■ **bring off**: *vt* **~ something off** riuscire a fare qualcosa

■ **bring on** *vt* (cause) provocare

■ **bring out** *vt* (emphasize) mettere in evidenza; pubblicare *‹book›*

■ **bring round** *vt* portare; (persuade) convincere; far rinvenire *‹unconscious person›*

■ **bring up** *vt* (vomit) rimettere; allevare *‹children›*; tirare fuori *‹question, subject›*

bring and buy sale *n* BrE vendita *f* di beneficenza

brink /brɪŋk/ *n* orlo *m*; **on the ~ of disaster** sull'orlo del disastro

brinkmanship /ˈbrɪŋkmənʃɪp/ *n* strategia *f* del rischio calcolato

brisk /brɪsk/ *adj* svelto; *‹person›* sbrigativo; *‹trade, business›* redditizio; *‹walk›* a passo spedito

brisket /ˈbrɪskɪt/ *n* Culin punta *f* di petto

briskly /ˈbrɪsklɪ/ *adv* velocemente; *‹say›* frettolosamente; *‹walk›* di buon passo

bristle /ˈbrɪsl/ **A** *n* setola *f*
B *vi* **bristling with** pieno di

bristly /ˈbrɪslɪ/ *adj ‹chin›* ispido

Britain /ˈbrɪtn/ *n* Gran Bretagna *f*

British /ˈbrɪtɪʃ/ **A** *adj* britannico; *‹ambassador›* della Gran Bretagna
B *npl* **the ~** il popolo britannico

British Airports Authority *n ente (m) che gestisce gli aeroporti britannici*

British Broadcasting Corporation *n ente (m) radio-televisivo nazionale britannico*

British Columbia *n* Columbia *f* Britannica

Britisher /ˈbrɪtɪʃə(r)/ *n* AmE britannico, -a *mf*

British Gas *n* BrE *società (f) del gas britannica*

British Isles *npl* Isole *fpl* Britanniche

British Rail *n ente (m) ferroviario britannico*

British Telecom *n* BrE *società (f) britannica di telecomunicazioni*

Briton /ˈbrɪtən/ *n* cittadino, -a, britannico, -a *mf*

Brittany /ˈbrɪtənɪ/ *n* Bretagna *f*

brittle /ˈbrɪtl/ *adj* fragile

brittle bone disease *n* decalcificazione *f* ossea, osteoporosi *f*

broach /brəʊtʃ/ *vt* toccare *‹subject›*

broad /brɔːd/ *adj* ampio; *‹hint›* chiaro; *‹accent›* marcato; **two metres ~** largo due metri; **in ~ daylight** in pieno giorno

B road *n* BrE ≈ strada *f* provinciale

broadband /ˈbrɔːdbænd/ *n* Comput banda *f* larga; **on ~** a banda larga; **~ connection** connessione *f* a banda larga

broad-based /ˈbeɪst/ *adj ‹coalition, education›* diversificato; *‹approach, campaign›* su larga scala; *‹consensus›* generale

broad bean *n* fava *f*

broadcast /ˈbrɔːdkæst/ **A** *n* trasmissione *f*
B *vt & vi* (*pt/pp* **-cast**) trasmettere

broadcaster /ˈbrɔːdkæstə(r)/ *n* giornalista *mf* radiotelevisivo, -a

broadcasting /ˈbrɔːdkæstɪŋ/ *n* diffusione *f* radiotelevisiva; **be in ~** lavorare per la televisione/radio

broad-chested *adj* con il torace robusto

broaden /ˈbrɔːdn/ **A** *vt* allargare; **~ one's horizons** allargare i propri orizzonti
B *vi* allargarsi

broadly /ˈbrɔːdlɪ/ *adv* largamente; **~ [speaking]** generalmente

broad-minded /-ˈmaɪndɪd/ *adj* di larghe vedute

broadness /ˈbrɔːdnɪs/ *n* larghezza *f*

broadsheet *n* quotidiano *m* di grande formato

broad-shouldered *adj* con le spalle larghe

broadside **A** *n* Naut (of ship) fiancata *f*; (enemy fire) bordata *f*; *n* (criticism) attacco *m*; **deliver a ~** lanciare un attacco
B *adv* di fianco

brocade /brəˈkeɪd/ *n* broccato *m*

broccoli /ˈbrɒkəlɪ/ *n inv* broccoli *mpl*

brochure /ˈbrəʊʃə(r)/ *n* opuscolo *m*; (travel) dépliant *m inv*

brogue /brəʊg/ *n* (shoe) scarpa *m* da passeggio; (accent) cadenza *f* dialettale

broil /brɔɪl/ AmE **A** *vt* Culin cuocere alla griglia *‹meat›*
B *vi* cuocere alla griglia; fig arrostire

broiler /ˈbrɔɪlə(r)/ *n* (chicken) pollastro *m*; AmE (grill) griglia *f*

broke /brəʊk/ **A** ▶ **break**
B *adj* infml al verde

b

broken /ˈbrəʊk(ə)n/ **A** ▶ **break**
B *adj* rotto; ~ **English** inglese *m* stentato

broken-down *adj* ‹*machine*› guasto; ‹*wall*› pericolante

broken heart *n* cuore *m* infranto; **die of a ~** essere distrutto da una delusione amorosa

broken-hearted /-ˈhɑːtɪd/ *adj* affranto

broken home *n* **he comes from a ~** i suoi sono divisi

broken marriage *n* matrimonio *m* fallito

broker /ˈbrəʊkə(r)/ *n* broker *m inv*

brokerage /ˈbrəʊkərɪdʒ/ *n* (fee, business) intermediazione *f*

broking /ˈbrəʊkɪŋ/ *n* attività *f* di intermediazione

brolly /ˈbrɒlɪ/ *n* infml ombrello *m*

bromide /ˈbrəʊmaɪd/ *n* (in pharmacy printing) bromuro *m*; fig (comment) banalità *f*

bronchial /ˈbrɒŋkɪəl/ *adj* ‹*infection*› bronchiale; ‹*wheeze, cough*› di petto

bronchitis /brɒŋˈkaɪtɪs/ *n* bronchite *f*

bronze /brɒnz/ **A** *n* bronzo *m*
B *attrib* di bronzo

Bronze Age *n* età *f* del Bronzo

brooch /brəʊtʃ/ *n* spilla *f*

brood /bruːd/ **A** *n* covata *f*; hum (children) prole *f*
B *vi* covare; fig rimuginare

brooding /ˈbruːdɪŋ/ *adj* ‹*person, face*› pensieroso; ‹*landscape*› sinistro

broody /ˈbruːdɪ/ *adj* (depressed) pensieroso; **feel ~** BrE infml ‹*woman*› desiderare un figlio

broody hen *n* chioccia *f*

brook¹ /brʊk/ *n* ruscello *m*

brook² *vt* sopportare

broom /bruːm/ *n* scopa *f*; Bot ginestra *f*

broom cupboard *n* ripostiglio *m*

broom handle *n* BrE manico *m* di scopa

broomstick *n* manico *m* di scopa

Bros. *abbr* (**brothers**) F.lli

broth /brɒθ/ *n* brodo *m*

brothel /ˈbrɒθ(ə)l/ *n* bordello *m*

🔑 **brother** /ˈbrʌðə(r)/ *n* fratello *m*

brotherhood /ˈbrʌðəhʊd/ *n* (bond) fratellanza *f*; (of monks) confraternita *f*

brother-in-law *n* (*pl* **brothers-in-law**) cognato *m*

brotherly /ˈbrʌðəlɪ/ *adj* fraterno

brought /brɔːt/ ▶ **bring**

brow /braʊ/ *n* fronte *f*; (eyebrow) sopracciglio *m*; (of hill) cima *f*

browbeat /ˈbraʊbiːt/ *vt* (*pt* **-beat**, *pp* **-beaten**) intimidire

🔑 **brown** /braʊn/ **A** *adj* marrone; ‹*hair*› castano
B *n* marrone *m*
C *vt* rosolare ‹*meat*›
D *vi* ‹*meat*› rosolarsi

brown ale *n* BrE birra *f* scura

brown bear *n* orso *m* bruno

brown bread *n* pane *m* integrale

browned off /braʊndˈɒf/ *adj* BrE infml stufo (**with** di)

brown envelope *n* busta *f* di carta da pacchi

Brownie /ˈbraʊnɪ/ *n* coccinella *f* (*negli scout*)

brownie point *n* infml punto *m* di merito

brownish /ˈbraʊnɪʃ/ *adj* sul marrone

brown-out *n* AmE oscuramento *m* parziale

brown owl *n* allocco *m*

brown paper *n* carta *f* da pacchi

brown rice *n* riso *m* integrale

brown skinned /-ˈskɪnd/ *adj* scuro di pelle

brownstone *n* AmE (house) palazzo *m* in arenaria

brown sugar *n* Culin zucchero *m* greggio

browse /braʊz/ **A** *vi* (read) leggicchiare; (in shop) curiosare; (on Internet) navigare
B *vt* visitare ‹*Internet, web site*›

browser /ˈbraʊzə(r)/ *n* Comput (program) browser *m inv*; (in shop) persona *f* che curiosa

bruise /bruːz/ **A** *n* livido *m*; (on fruit) ammaccatura *f*
B *vt* ammaccare ‹*fruit*›; **~ one's arm** farsi un livido sul braccio

bruised /bruːzd/ *adj* (physically) contuso; ‹*eye*› pesto; ‹*fruit*› ammaccato; ‹*ego, spirit*› ferito

bruiser /ˈbruːzə(r)/ *n* infml omaccione *m*

bruising /ˈbruːzɪŋ/ **A** *n* livido *m*, contusione *f*
B *adj* ‹*game*› violento; (emotionally) ‹*remark*› pesante; ‹*campaign, encounter*› traumatizzante; ‹*defeat*› cocente

brunch /brʌntʃ/ *n* brunch *m inv*

Brunei /bruːˈnaɪ/ *n* Brunei *m*

brunette /bruːˈnet/ *n* bruna *f*

brunt /brʌnt/ *n* **bear the ~ of something** subire maggiormente qualcosa

brush /brʌʃ/ **A** *n* spazzola *f*; (with long handle) spazzolone *m*; (for paint) pennello *m*; (bushes) boscaglia *f*; fig (conflict) breve scontro *m*
B *vt* spazzolare ‹*hair*›; lavarsi ‹*teeth*›; scopare ‹*stairs, floor*›

■ **brush against** *vt* sfiorare

■ **brush aside** *vt* fig ignorare

■ **brush off** *vt* spazzolare; (with hands) togliere; ignorare ‹*criticism*›

■ **brush up**: *vt & vi* fig **~ up [on]** rinfrescare

brush-off *n* infml **give somebody the ~** mandare qualcuno a quel paese

brushstroke *n* pennellata *f*

brush-up *n* BrE **have a [wash and] brush-up** darsi una ripulita

brushwood /ˈbrʌʃwʊd/ *n* sterpaglie *fpl*

brushwork *n* tocco *m*

brusque /brʊsk/ *adj* brusco

🔑 parola chiave

brusquely /ˈbrʊsklɪ/ *adv* bruscamente

Brussels /ˈbrʌsəlz/ *n* Bruxelles *f*

Brussels sprouts *npl* cavolini *mpl* di Bruxelles

brutal /ˈbru:t(ə)l/ *adj* brutale

brutality /bru:ˈtælətɪ/ *n* brutalità *f*

brutalize /ˈbru:təlaɪz/ *vt* brutalizzare

brutally /ˈbru:təlɪ/ *adv* brutalmente

brute /bru:t/ *n* bruto *m*; ~ **force** forza *f* bruta

brutish /ˈbru:tɪʃ/ *adj* da bruto

BSc BrE **BS** AmE *abbr* (**Bachelor of Science**) (*diploma (m) di) discipline scientifiche*

BSE *n abbr* (**bovine spongiform encephalitis**) encefalite *f* bovina spongiforme

B side *n* (of record) lato *m* B

BST *abbr* (**British Summer Time**) ora *f* legale in Gran Bretagna

BTW *n abbr* (**by the way**) a proposito

bubble /ˈbʌbl/ *n* bolla *f*; (in drink) bollicina *f*

bubble bath *n* bagnoschiuma *m inv*

bubble car *n* BrE infml *auto (f) monoposto a tre ruote*

bubblegum *n* gomma *f* da masticare

bubble pack *n* BrE (for pills) blister *m inv*; (for small item) involucro *m* di plastica

bubble wrap *n* plastica *f* a bolle

bubbling /ˈbʌblɪŋ/ **A** *n* (sound) gorgoglio *m*
B *adj* che ribolle

bubbly /ˈbʌblɪ/ **A** *n* infml champagne *m inv*, spumante *m*
B *adj* ‹*liquid*› effervescente; ‹*personality*› spumeggiante

bubonic plague /bjʊbɒnɪkˈpleɪg/ *n* peste *f* bubbonica

buccaneer /bʌkəˈnɪə(r)/ *n* bucaniere *m*

Bucharest /bju:kəˈrest/ *n* Bucarest *f*

buck[1] /bʌk/ **A** *n* maschio *m* del cervo; (rabbit) maschio *m* del coniglio
B *vi* ‹*horse*› saltare a quattro zampe

buck[2] *n* AmE infml dollaro *m*

buck[3] *n* **pass the** ~ scaricare la responsabilità

▪ **buck up** **A** *vi* infml tirarsi su; (hurry) sbrigarsi
B *vt* **you'll have to ~ your ideas up** infml dovresti darti una regolata

bucket /ˈbʌkɪt/ **A** *n* secchio *m*; **kick the** ~ infml (die) crepare
B *vi* **it's ~ing down** infml piove a catinelle

bucketful /ˈbʌkɪtfʊl/ *n* secchio *m*

bucket seat *n* Auto, Aeron sedile *m* anatomico

bucket shop *n* BrE infml *agenzia (f) di viaggi che vende biglietti a prezzi scontati*

bucking bronco /bʌkɪŋˈbrɒŋkəʊ/ *n* cavallo *m* da rodeo

buckle /ˈbʌkl/ **A** *n* fibbia *f*
B *vt* allacciare
C *vi* ‹*shelf*› piegarsi; ‹*wheel*› storcersi

▪ **buckle down** *vi* (to work) mettersi sotto

▪ **buckle in** *vt* legare

buckram *n* tela *f* rigida

buckshot *n* pallettoni *mpl*

buckskin *n* pelle *f* di daino

buck teeth *npl* denti *mpl* da coniglio

buckwheat *n* grano *m* saraceno

bucolic /bjʊˈkɒlɪk/ *adj & n* bucolico *m*

bud /bʌd/ *n* bocciolo *m*

Buddha /ˈbʊdə/ *n* Budda *m inv*

Buddhism /ˈbʊdɪzm/ *n* buddismo *m*

Buddhist /ˈbʊdɪst/ *adj & n* buddista *mf*

budding /ˈbʌdɪŋ/ *adj* Bot (into leaf) in germoglio; (into flower) in boccio; ‹*athlete, champion, artist*› in erba; ‹*talent, romance*› nascente; ‹*career*› promettente

buddy /ˈbʌdɪ/ *n* infml amico, -a *mf*

budge /bʌdʒ/ **A** *vt* spostare
B *vi* spostarsi

▪ **budge over**, **budge up** *vi* infml farsi più in là

budgerigar /ˈbʌdʒərɪgɑ:(r)/ *n* cocorita *f*

budget /ˈbʌdʒɪt/ **A** *n* bilancio *m*; (allotted to specific activity) budget *m inv*; **I'm on a** ~ cerco di limitare le spese
B *vi* (*pt/pp* **budgeted**) prevedere le spese; ~ **for something** includere qualcosa nelle spese previste

budgetary /ˈbʌdʒɪt(ə)rɪ/ *adj* budgetario; ~ **year** esercizio *m* finanziario

budget day *n* BrE Pol *giorno (m) della presentazione del bilancio dello Stato*

budgie /ˈbʌdʒɪ/ *n* infml = **budgerigar**

buff /bʌf/ **A** *adj* (colour) [color] camoscio
B *n* [color *m*] camoscio *m*; infml fanatico, -a *mf*
C *vt* lucidare

buffalo /ˈbʌfələʊ/ *n* (*inv or pl* **-es**) bufalo *m*

buffer /ˈbʌfə(r)/ *n* Rail respingente *m*; Comput buffer *m inv*; **old** ~ infml vecchio bacucco *m*

buffer state *n* stato *m* cuscinetto *inv*

buffer zone *n* zona *f* cuscinetto *inv*

buffet[1] /ˈbʊfeɪ/ *n* (meal, in station) buffet *m inv*

buffet[2] /ˈbʌfɪt/ *vt* (*pt/pp* **buffeted**) sferzare

buffet car *n* BrE Rail carrozza *f* ristorante

buffoon /bəˈfu:n/ *n* buffone, -a *mf*

bug /bʌg/ **A** *n* (insect) insetto *m*; Comput bug *m inv*; infml (device) cimice *f*
B *vt* (*pt/pp* **bugged**) infml installare delle microspie in ‹*room*›; mettere sotto controllo ‹*telephone*›; infml (annoy) scocciare

bugbear /ˈbʌgbeə(r)/ *n* (problem, annoyance) spauracchio *m*

bugger /ˈbʌgə(r)/ infml **A** *n* bastardo *m*
B *int* merda!

▪ **bugger about**, **bugger around** infml
A *vi* (behave stupidly) fare il cretino
B *vt* ~ **somebody about** creare problemi a qualcuno

▪ **bugger off** *vi* infml (go away) andarsene; ~ **off!** vai a farti friggere!

b

bugging device /ˈbʌgɪŋ/ *n* microfono *m* spia

buggy /ˈbʌgɪ/ *n* **[baby]** ~ passeggino *m*

bugle /ˈbjuːg(ə)l/ *n* tromba *f*

bugler /ˈbjuːglə(r)/ *n* trombettiere *m*

🔑 **build** /bɪld/ **A** *n* (of person) corporatura *f*
B *vt & vi* (*pt/pp* **built**) costruire

■ **build on** *vt* aggiungere ‹*extra storey*›; sviluppare ‹*previous work*›

■ **build up**: **A** *vt* ~ **up one's strength** rimettersi in forza
B *vi* ‹*pressure, traffic*› aumentare; ‹*excitement, tension*› crescere

builder /ˈbɪldə(r)/ *n* (company) costruttore *m*; (worker) muratore *m*

builder's labourer *n* muratore *m*

builder's merchant *n* fornitore *m* di materiale da costruzione

🔑 **building** /ˈbɪldɪŋ/ *n* edificio *m*

building block *n* (child's toy) pezzo *m* delle costruzioni; (basic element) componente *m*

building contractor *n* imprenditore *m* edile

building land *n* terreno *m* edificabile

building materials *npl* materiali *mpl* da costruzione

building permit *n* licenza *f* edilizia

building plot *n* terreno *m* edificabile

building site *n* cantiere *m* [di costruzione]

building society *n* istituto *m* di credito immobiliare

building trade *n* edilizia *f*

building worker *n* BrE muratore *m*

build-up *n* (increase) aumento *m*; (in tension, of gas, in weapons) accumulo *m*; (publicity) battage *m inv* pubblicitario; **give something a good** ~ (publicity) fare buona pubblicità a qualcosa

built /bɪlt/ ▶ **build**

built-in *adj* ‹*unit*› a muro; fig ‹*feature*› incorporato

built-up *adj* (region) urbanizzato; ~ **area** centro *m* abitato

bulb /bʌlb/ *n* bulbo *m*; Electr lampadina *f*

bulbous /ˈbʌlbəs/ *adj* grassoccio

Bulgaria /bʌlˈgeərɪə/ *n* Bulgaria *f*

Bulgarian /bʌlˈgeərɪən/ *adj & n* bulgaro, -a *mf*

bulge /bʌldʒ/ **A** *n* rigonfiamento *m*; **it shows all my** ~**s** mette in evidenza tutti i miei cuscinetti [di grasso]
B *vi* esser gonfio (**with** di); ‹*stomach, wall*› sporgere; ‹*eyes: with surprise*› uscire dalle orbite

bulging /ˈbʌldʒɪŋ/ *adj* gonfio; ‹*eyes*› sporgente

bulimia /bʊˈlɪmɪə/, **bulimia nervosa** /bʊˈlɪmɪənɜːˈvəʊsə/ *n* bulimia *f*

bulimic /bʊˈlɪmɪk/ *adj & n* bulimico, -a *mf*

bulk /bʌlk/ *n* volume *m*; (greater part) grosso *m*; **in** ~ in grande quantità; (loose) sfuso

bulk-buy *vt & vi* comprare in grandi quantità

bulk-buying *n* acquisto *m* in grande quantità

bulk carrier *n* nave *f* per il trasporto di rinfuse

bulkhead *n* Naut, Aeron paratia *f*

bulky /ˈbʌlkɪ/ *adj* voluminoso

bull /bʊl/ *n* toro *m*; **take the** ~ **by the horns** fig prendere il toro per le corna

bull bars *npl* Auto paraurti *mpl* tubolari rigidi

bulldog *n* bulldog *m inv*

bulldog clip *n* fermafogli *m inv*

bulldoze *vt* (knock down) demolire [con bulldozer]; (clear) spianare [con bulldozer]; fig (force) costringere

bulldozer /ˈbʊldəʊzə(r)/ *n* bulldozer *m inv*

bullet /ˈbʊlɪt/ *n* pallottola *f*

bulletin /ˈbʊlɪtɪn/ *n* bollettino *m*

bulletin board *n* Comput bacheca *f* elettronica

bulletproof /ˈbʊlɪtpruːf/ *adj* antiproiettile *inv*; ‹*vehicle*› blindato

bulletproof vest giubbotto *m* antiproiettile

bullfight /ˈbʊlfaɪt/ *n* corrida *f*

bullfighter /ˈbʊlfaɪtə(r)/ *n* torero *m*

bullfighting /ˈbʊlfaɪtɪŋ/ *n* corride *fpl*

bullion /ˈbʊlɪən/ *n* **gold** ~ oro *m* in lingotti

bullish /ˈbʊlɪʃ/ *adj* (optimistic) ottimistico; ‹*market, shares, stocks*› al rialzo

bull market *n* Fin mercato *m* al rialzo

bullock /ˈbʊlək/ *n* manzo *m*

bullring /ˈbʊlrɪŋ/ *n* arena *f*

bullseye /ˈbʊlzaɪ/ *n* centro *m* del bersaglio; **score a** ~ fare centro

bully /ˈbʊlɪ/ **A** *n* prepotente *mf*
B *vt* fare il/la prepotente con

bullying /ˈbʊlɪɪŋ/ *n* prepotenze *fpl*

bulrush /ˈbʊlrʌʃ/ *n* giunco *m* di palude

bulwark /ˈbʊlwək/ *n* Mil fig baluardo *m*; Naut parapetto *m*; (breakwater) frangiflutti *m inv*

bum[1] /bʌm/ *n* sl sedere *m*

bum[2] *n* AmE infml vagabondo, -a *mf*

■ **bum around** *vi* infml vagabondare

bumbag /ˈbʌmbæg/ *n* BrE infml marsupio *m*

bumble-bee /ˈbʌmblbiː/ *n* calabrone *m*

bumbling /ˈbʌmblɪŋ/ *adj* ‹*attempt*› maldestro; ‹*person*› inconcludente

bumf /bʌmf/ *n* BrE (toilet paper) carta *f* igienica; infml (documents) scartoffie *f pl*

bump /bʌmp/ **A** *n* botta *f*; (swelling) bozzo *m*, gonfiore *m*; (in road) protuberanza *f*
B *vt* sbattere

■ **bump into** *vt* sbattere contro; (meet) imbattersi in

■ **bump off** *vt* infml far fuori

🔑 parola chiave

■ **bump up** *vt* infml [far] aumentare ‹*prices, salaries*›

bumper /ˈbʌmpə(r)/ **A** *n* Auto paraurti *m inv*
B *adj* abbondante

bumper car *n* autoscontro *m*

bumph /bʌmf/ *n* = **bumf**

bumpkin /ˈbʌmpkɪn/ *n* **country ~** zoticone, -a *mf*

bumptious /ˈbʌmpʃəs/ *adj* presuntuoso

bumpy /ˈbʌmpɪ/ *adj* ‹*road*› accidentato; ‹*flight*› turbolento

bun /bʌn/ *n* focaccina *f* [dolce]; (hair) chignon *m inv*

bunch /bʌntʃ/ *n* (of flowers, keys) mazzo *m*; (of bananas) casco *m*; (of people) gruppo *m*; **~ of grapes** grappolo *m* d'uva

bundle /ˈbʌndl/ **A** *n* fascio *m*; (of money) mazzetta *f*; **a ~ of nerves** infml un fascio di nervi
B *vt* **~ [up]** affastellare

bundled software /ˈbʌndld-/ *n* Comput software *m inv* in bundle

bung /bʌŋ/ *vt* infml (throw) buttare

■ **bung up** *vt* (block) otturare

bungalow /ˈbʌŋgələʊ/ *n* bungalow *m inv*

bungee jump /ˈbʌndʒɪdʒʌmp/ *n* salto *m* con l'elastico

bungee jumping /ˈbʌndʒɪdʒʌmpɪŋ/ *n* *salto* (*m*) *da ponti, grattacieli, ecc. con un cavo elastico attaccato alla caviglia*

bungle /ˈbʌŋgl/ *vt* fare un pasticcio di

bunion /ˈbʌnjən/ *n* Med callo *m* all'alluce

bunk /bʌŋk/ **A** *n* cuccetta *f*; **do a ~** infml svignarsela
B *vi* **~ off/~ off school** infml marinare la scuola

bunk beds *npl* letti *mpl* a castello

bunker /ˈbʌŋkə(r)/ *n* (for coal) carbonaia *f*; (golf) ostacolo *m*; Mil bunker *m inv*

bunkum /ˈbʌŋkəm/ *n* fandonie *fpl*

bunny /ˈbʌnɪ/ *n* infml coniglietto *m*

Bunsen /ˈbʌnsən/, **Bunsen burner** /ˈbʌnsənbɜːnə(r)/ *n* becco *m* Bunsen

bunting /ˈbʌntɪŋ/ *n* (flags on ship) gran pavese *m*; Zool zigolo *m*

buoy /bɔɪ/ *n* boa *f*

■ **buoy up** *vt* fig sostenere ‹*prices*›; tirare su ‹*person*›

buoyancy /ˈbɔɪənsɪ/ *n* galleggiabilità *f*

buoyancy aid *n* salvagente *m*

buoyant /ˈbɔɪənt/ *adj* ‹*boat*› galleggiante; ‹*water*› che aiuta a galleggiare; fig ‹*person*› allegro; ‹*prices*› in aumento

burble /ˈbɜːb(ə)l/ **A** *n* (of stream) gorgoglio *m*; (of voices) borbottio *m*
B *vi* ‹*stream*› gorgogliare; **~ on about something** ‹*person*› blaterare di qualcosa

burbling /ˈbɜːblɪŋ/ **A** *n* (of stream) gorgoglio *m*; (rambling talk) borbottio *m*
B *adj* ‹*stream*› gorgogliante; ‹*voice*› che borbotta

burden /ˈbɜːdn/ **A** *n* carico *m*
B *vt* caricare

burdensome /ˈbɜːdnsəm/ *adj* gravoso

bureau /ˈbjʊərəʊ/ *n* (*pl* **-x** /ˈbjʊərəʊz/ *or* **~s**) (desk) scrivania *f*; (office) ufficio *m*

bureaucracy /bjʊəˈrɒkrəsɪ/ *n* burocrazia *f*

bureaucrat /ˈbjʊərəkræt/ *n* burocrate *mf*

bureaucratic /bjʊrəˈkrætɪk/ *adj* burocratico

burgeon /ˈbɜːdʒən/ *vi* ‹*plant*› germogliare; fig (flourish) fiorire; fig (multiply) moltiplicarsi rapidamente, crescere rapidamente

burgeoning /ˈbɜːdʒənɪŋ/ *adj* fiorente

burger /ˈbɜːgə(r)/ *n* hamburger *m inv*

burger bar *n* fast-food *m inv*

burglar /ˈbɜːglə(r)/ *n* svaligiatore, -trice *mf*

burglar alarm *n* antifurto *m inv*

burglarize /ˈbɜːgləraɪz/ *vt* AmE svaligiare

burglar-proof *adj* a prova di ladro

burglary /ˈbɜːglərɪ/ *n* furto *m* con scasso

burgle /ˈbɜːgl/ *vt* svaligiare; **they have been ~d** sono stati svaligiati

Burgundy /ˈbɜːgəndɪ/ **A** *n* Borgogna *f*; **burgundy** (wine) borgogna *m inv*
B *adj* (colour) rosso scuro

burial /ˈberɪəl/ *n* sepoltura *f*

burial ground *n* cimitero *m*

burka /ˈbɜːkə/ *n* burka *m*

Burkina /bɜːkinə/, **Burkina Faso** /bɜːkinə ˈfæsəʊ/ *n* Burkina Faso *m*

burlesque /bɜːˈlesk/ *n* parodia *f*

burly /ˈbɜːlɪ/ *adj* (**-ier**, **-iest**) corpulento

Burma /ˈbɜːmə/ *n* Birmania *f*

Burmese /bɜːˈmiːz/ *adj* & *n* birmano, -a *mf*

burn /bɜːn/ **A** *n* bruciatura *f*
B *vt* (*pt/pp* **burnt** *or* **burned**) bruciare; **~ one's boats** *or* **bridges** fig tagliarsi i ponti alle spalle; Comput masterizzare ‹*CD, DVD*›
C *vi* bruciare

■ **burn down** *vt* & *vi* bruciare

■ **burn out** *vi* fig esaurirsi

■ **burn up** *vt* fig bruciare ‹*calories, energy*›

burned-out *adj* = **burnt-out**

burner /ˈbɜːnə(r)/ *n* (on stove) bruciatore *m*

burning /ˈbɜːnɪŋ/ **A** *n* (setting on fire) incendio *m*; **I can smell ~!** sento odore di bruciato!
B *adj* ‹*ember, coal*› acceso; (on fire) in fiamme; fig ‹*fever, desire*› bruciante; **a ~ sensation** una sensazione di bruciore; **a ~ question** una questione scottante

burnish /ˈbɜːnɪʃ/ *vt* lucidare

burns unit *n* Med reparto *m* grandi ustionati

burnt /bɜːnt/ ▶ **burn**

burnt-out *adj* ‹*building, car*› distrutto dalle fiamme; fig ‹*person*› sfinito

burp /bɜːp/ **A** *n* infml rutto *m*
B *vi* infml ruttare

burr /bɜː(r)/ *n* Bot lappa *f*; (in language) erre *f* moscia

b

burrow /ˈbʌrəʊ/ **A** *n* tana *f*
B *vt* scavare ‹*hole*›

bursar /ˈbɜːsə(r)/ *n* economo, -a *mf*

bursary /ˈbɜːsərɪ/ *n* borsa *f* di studio

burst /bɜːst/ **A** *n* (of gunfire, energy, laughter) scoppio *m*; (of speed) scatto *m*
B *vt* (*pt/pp* **burst**) far scoppiare; ~ **its banks** ‹*river*› rompere gli argini
C *vi* scoppiare; ~ **into tears** scoppiare in lacrime; ~ **into flames** andare in fiamme; **she** ~ **into the room** ha fatto irruzione nella stanza; **be** ~**ing at the seams** ‹*room*› scoppiare
▪ **burst in** *vi* (enter suddenly) fare irruzione
▪ **burst out**: *vi* ~ **out laughing/crying** scoppiare a ridere/piangere

Burundi /bʊˈrʊndɪ/ *n* Burundi *m*

bury /ˈberɪ/ *vt* (*pt/pp* **-ied**) seppellire; (hide) nascondere

🔑 **bus** /bʌs/ **A** *n* autobus *m inv*, pullman *m inv*; (long distance) pullman *m inv*, corriera *f*
B *vt* (*pt/pp* **bussed**) trasportare in autobus

busby /ˈbʌzbɪ/ *n* colbacco *m* militare

bus conductor *n* ≈ bigliettaio *m*

bus conductress *n* ≈ bigliettaia *f*

bus driver *n* conducente *mf* di autobus

bush /bʊʃ/ *n* cespuglio *m*; (land) boscaglia *f*

bushed /bʊʃt/ *adj* infml (tired) distrutto

bushel /ˈbʊʃ(ə)l/ *n* **hide one's light under a** ~ essere troppo modesto; AmE infml ~**s of** un sacco di

bush fighting *n* Mil guerriglia *f*

bush fire *n* incendio *m* in aperta campagna

bush telegraph *n* fig hum tamtam *m inv*

bushy /ˈbʊʃɪ/ *adj* (**-ier**, **-iest**) folto

busily /ˈbɪzɪlɪ/ *adv* con grande impegno

🔑 **business** /ˈbɪznɪs/ *n* affare *m*; Comm affari *mpl*; (establishment) attività *f* di commercio; **on** ~ per affari; **he has no** ~ **to** non ha alcun diritto di; **mind one's own** ~ farsi gli affari propri; **that's none of your** ~ non sono affari tuoi

business activity *n* attività *f* economica; (of single company) attività *f* aziendale

business analyst *n* analista *mf* finanziario, -a

business associate *n* socio, -a *mf*

business call *n* (phone call) telefonata *f* di lavoro; (visit) appuntamento *m* di lavoro

business card *n* biglietto *m* da visita

business centre *n* centro *m* affari

business class *n* Aeron business class *f inv*

business college *n* scuola *f* di amministrazione aziendale

business contact *n* contatto *m* di lavoro

business cycle *n* ciclo *m* economico

business deal *n* operazione *f* commerciale

business expenses *npl* spese *fpl* di lavoro

business failures *npl* chiusura *f* di aziende

business hours *npl* (in office) orario *m* d'ufficio; (of shop) orario *m* d'apertura

business-like *adj* efficiente

business lunch *n* pranzo *m* di lavoro *or* d'affari

businessman /ˈbɪznɪsmən/ *n* uomo *m* d'affari

business management *n* amministrazione *f* aziendale

business park *n* centro *m* affari

business plan *n* piano *m* economico; (of single company) programma *m* aziendale

business premises *npl* sede *f* di un'azienda

business proposition *n* proposta *f* d'affari

business reply envelope *n* busta *f* affrancata

business school *n* scuola *f* di amministrazione aziendale

business software *n* software *m inv* per l'ufficio

business studies *npl* economia *f* e commercio

business suit *n* (for man) abito *m* scuro

business trip *n* viaggio *m* di lavoro

businesswoman /ˈbɪznɪswʊmən/ *n* donna *f* d'affari

busk /bʌsk/ *vi* BrE ‹*singer*› cantare per strada; ‹*musician*› suonare per strada

busker /ˈbʌskə(r)/ *n* suonatore, -trice *mf* ambulante

bus lane *n* corsia *f* autobus

busload /ˈbʌsləʊd/ *n* **a** ~ **of tourists** una comitiva di turisti; **by the** ~ in massa

busman's holiday /bʌsmənzˈhɒlɪdeɪ/ *n* BrE *vacanze (fpl) passate a fare quello che si fa normalmente*

bus pass *n* abbonamento *m* all'autobus

bus route *n* percorso *m* dell'autobus

bus shelter *n* pensilina *f* alla fermata dell'autobus

bus station *n* stazione *f* degli autobus

bus stop *n* fermata *f* d'autobus

bust[1] /bʌst/ *n* busto *m*; (chest) petto *m*

bust[2] **A** *adj* infml rotto; **go** ~ fallire
B *vt* (*pt/pp* **busted** *or* **bust**) infml far scoppiare
C *vi* scoppiare

bustle /ˈbʌsl/ *n* (activity) trambusto *m*
▪ **bustle about** *vi* affannarsi

bustling /ˈbʌslɪŋ/ *adj* animato

bust size *n* circonferenza *f* del torace

bust-up *n* infml lite *f*

🔑 **busy** /ˈbɪzɪ/ **A** *adj* (**-ier**, **-iest**) occupato; ‹*day, time*› intenso; ‹*street*› affollato;

🔑 parola chiave

(with traffic) pieno di traffico; **be ~ doing** essere occupato a fare
B *vt* **~ oneself** darsi da fare

busybody /ˈbɪzɪbɒdɪ/ *n* ficcanaso *mf inv*

but /bʌt/ *atono* /bət/ **A** *conj* ma
B *prep* eccetto, tranne; **nobody ~ you** nessuno tranne te; **~ for** (without) se non fosse stato per; **the last ~ one** il penultimo; **the next ~ one** il secondo
C *adv* soltanto; **there were ~ two** ce n'erano soltanto due

butane /ˈbjuːteɪn/ *n* butano *m*

butch /bʊtʃ/ *adj* infml ‹*man*› macho *inv*; ‹*woman*› mascolino

butcher /ˈbʊtʃə(r)/ **A** *n* macellaio *m*
B *vt* macellare; fig massacrare

butcher's /ˈbʊtʃəz/, **butcher's shop** /ˈbʊtʃəzʃɒp/ *n* macelleria *f*

butchery /ˈbʊtʃərɪ/ *n* (trade) macelleria *f*; (slaughter) massacro *m*

butler /ˈbʌtlə(r)/ *n* maggiordomo *m*

butt /bʌt/ **A** *n* (of gun) calcio *m*; (of cigarette) mozzicone *m*; (for water) barile *m*; fig (target) bersaglio *m*
B *vt* dare una testata a; ‹*goat*› dare un'incornata a

■ **butt in** *vi* interrompere

butter /ˈbʌtə(r)/ **A** *n* burro *m*
B *vt* imburrare

■ **butter up** *vt* infml arruffianarsi

butter bean *n* fagiolo *m* bianco

buttercup *n* ranuncolo *m*

butter dish *n* portaburro *m inv*

butter-fingered *adj* con le mani di pasta frolla

butter fingers *n* infml mani *fpl* di pasta frolla

butterfly /ˈbʌtəflaɪ/ *n* farfalla *f*

butterfly net *n* retino *m* per farfalle

butterfly nut *n* dado *m* ad alette

butterfly stroke *n* nuoto *m* a farfalla

buttermilk /ˈbʌtəmɪlk/ *n* latticello *m*

butterscotch /ˈbʌtəskɒtʃ/ *n caramella (f) dura a base di burro e zucchero*

buttocks /ˈbʌtəks/ *npl* natiche *fpl*

button /ˈbʌtn/ **A** *n* bottone *m*; (on mouse, of status bar) pulsante *m*
B *vt* **~ [up]** abbottonare
C *vi* **~ [up]** abbottonarsi

button battery *n* batteria *f* a bottone

button-down *adj* ‹*collar*› button down, coi bottoni; ‹*shirt*› con il colletto coi bottoni, button down

buttonhole *n* occhiello *m*, asola *f*

buttonhook *n* asola *f*, occhiello *m*

button mushroom *n* piccolo champignon *m inv*

buttress /ˈbʌtrɪs/ **A** *n* contrafforte *m*
B *vt* fig sostenere

buxom /ˈbʌksəm/ *adj* formosa

buy /baɪ/ **A** *n* **good/bad ~** buon/cattivo acquisto *m*
B *vt* (*pt/pp* **bought**) comprare; **~ somebody a drink** pagare da bere a qualcuno; **I'll ~ this one** (drink) questo lo offro io

■ **buy into** *vt* (accept) accettare

■ **buy off** *vt* (bribe) comprare

■ **buy out** *vt* rilevare la quota di ‹*one's partner*›

■ **buy up** *vt* (buy all of) accaparrarsi

buyer /ˈbaɪə(r)/ *n* compratore, -trice *mf*

buyout /ˈbaɪaʊt/ *n* Comm rilevamento *m*

buzz /bʌz/ **A** *n* ronzio *m*; **give somebody a ~** infml (on phone) dare un colpo di telefono a qualcuno; (excite) mettere in fermento qualcuno
B *vi* ronzare
C *vt* **~ somebody** chiamare qualcuno col cicalino

■ **buzz off** *vi* infml levarsi di torno

buzzard /ˈbʌzəd/ *n* poiana *f*

buzzer /ˈbʌzə(r)/ *n* cicalino *m*

buzzing /ˈbʌzɪŋ/ **A** *n* (of buzzer) trillo *m*; (of insects) ronzio *m*
B *adj* ‹*party, atmosphere, town*› molto animato

buzzword /ˈbʌzwɜːd/ *n* infml parola *f* di moda

by /baɪ/ **A** *prep* (near, next to) vicino a; (at the latest) per; **by Mozart** di Mozart; **he was run over by a bus** è stato investito da un autobus; **by oneself** da solo; **by the sea** al mare; **by sea** via mare; **by car/bus** in macchina/autobus; **by day/night** di giorno/notte; **by the hour/metre** a ore/metri; **six metres by four** sei metri per quattro; **he won by six metres** ha vinto di sei metri; **I missed the train by a minute** ho perso il treno per un minuto; **I'll be home by six** sarò a casa per le sei; **by this time next week** a quest'ora tra una settimana; **he rushed by me** mi è passato accanto di corsa
B *adv* **she'll be here by and by** sarà qui fra poco; **by and by the police arrived** poco dopo è arrivata la polizia; **by and large** nel complesso; **put by** mettere da parte; **go/pass by** passare

bye /baɪ/ *int* infml ciao!

bye-bye /baɪˈbaɪ/ *int* infml ciao, arrivederci; **go ~s** BrE (baby talk) andare a fare la nanna

by-election *n elezione (f) straordinaria indetta per coprire una carica rimasta vacante in Parlamento*

Byelorussia /bjeləʊˈrʌʃə/ *n* Bielorussia *f*

Byelorussian /bjeləʊˈrʌʃn/ *adj & n* bielorusso

bygone *adj* passato

by-law *n* legge *f* locale

by-line *n* (in newspaper) nome *m* dell'autore; Sport linea *f* laterale

BYO, **BYOB** *adj abbr* (**bring your own bottle**) *di ristorante o festa, in cui ciascuno si porta le proprie bevande, specialmente alcoliche*

bypass **A** *n* circonvallazione *f*; Med by-pass *m inv*
B *vt* evitare

b

by-product *n* sottoprodotto *m*
by-road *n* strada *f* secondaria

c

bystander *n* spettatore, -trice *mf*
byte /baɪt/ *n* Comput byte *m inv*
byway *n* strada *f* secondaria
byword *n* **be a ~ for** essere sinonimo di
by your leave *n* **without so much as a ~** senza neanche chiedere il permesso
Byzantine /bɪˈzæntaɪn/ *adj* bizantino

Cc

c¹, C /siː/ *n* (letter) c, C *f inv*; BrE Sch (grade) *voto (m) scolastico corrispondente alla sufficienza*; Mus do *m inv*
c², C *abbr* **1** (**Celsius, centigrade**) C **2** (**cent(s)**) c **3** (**circa**) ca
C2C *abbr* (**consumer to consumer**) C2C
C4 *abbr* BrE (**channel four**) *rete (f) televisiva britannica*
CA *abbr* **1** BrE (**Chartered Accountant**) [dottore *m*] commercialista *m* **2** AmE (**California**) Cal **3** (**Central America**) America *f* centrale
CAA *n abbr* BrE (**Civil Aviation Authority**) *organismo (m) di controllo dell'aviazione civile*
cab /kæb/ *n* taxi *m inv*; (of lorry, train) cabina *f*
CAB *n abbr* BrE (**Citizens' Advice Bureau**) *ufficio (m) di consulenza legale gratuita per i cittadini*
cabana /kəˈbɑːnə/ *n* AmE (hut) cabina *f* da spiaggia
cabaret /ˈkæbəreɪ/ *n* cabaret *m inv*
cabbage /ˈkæbɪdʒ/ *n* cavolo *m*
cabby /ˈkæbɪ/ *n* infml tassista *mf*
cab driver *n* tassista *mf*
cabin /ˈkæbɪn/ *n* (of plane, ship) cabina *f*; (hut) capanna *f*
cabin boy *n* mozzo *m*
cabin crew *n* Aeron equipaggio *m*
cabin cruiser *n* cabinato *m*
cabinet /ˈkæbɪnɪt/ *n* armadietto *m*; **[display] ~** vetrina *f*; **C~** Pol consiglio *m* dei ministri
cabinet-maker *n* ebanista *mf*
cabinet meeting *n* BrE riunione *f* del governo
cabinet minister *n* BrE ministro *m*
cabinet reshuffle *n* BrE rimpasto *m* ministeriale
cable /ˈkeɪb(ə)l/ *n* cavo *m*; TV TV *f* via cavo; **this channel is only available on ~** questo canale è disponibile solo sulla TV via cavo
cable car *n* cabina *f* (*della funivia*)
cable company *n* rete *f* televisiva via cavo
cablegram *n* cablogramma *m*
cable-knit *adj* ‹*sweater*› a trecce
cable railway *n* funicolare *f*
cable-ready *adj* predisposto per la TV via cavo
cable television *n* televisione *f* via cavo
cable TV *n* TV *f inv* via cavo
cableway *n* (for people) funivia *f*
caboodle /kəˈbuːdl/ *n* infml **the whole ~** baracca e burattini
cab rank, cab stand *n* posteggio *m* dei taxi
cache /kæʃ/ *n* nascondiglio *m*; **~ of arms** deposito *m* segreto di armi
cache memory *n* Comput memoria *f* (*cache*)
cachet /ˈkæʃeɪ/ *n* prestigio *m*
cackle /ˈkækl/ *vi* ridacchiare
cacophony /kəˈkɒfənɪ/ *n* cacofonia *f*
cactus /ˈkæktəs/ *n* (*pl* **-ti** /ˈkæktaɪ/ *or* **-tuses**) cactus *m inv*
CAD /kæd/ *n abbr* (**computer-aided design**) CAD *m inv*
cadaver /kəˈdɑːvə(r)/ *n* cadavere *m*
cadaverous /kəˈdævərəs/ *adj* cadaverico
CADCAM /ˈkædkæm/ *n abbr* (**computer-aided design and computer-aided manufacture**) CADCAM *m inv*
caddie /ˈkædɪ/ *n* portabastoni *m inv*
caddy /ˈkædɪ/ *n* **[tea] ~** barattolo *m* del tè
cadence /ˈkeɪdəns/ *n* cadenza *f*
cadet /kəˈdet/ *n* cadetto *m*
cadet corps *n* Mil corpo *m* dei cadetti
cadet school *n* scuola *f* allievi ufficiali
cadge /kædʒ/ *vt & vi* infml scroccare
cadre /ˈkɑːdr(ə)/ *n* Admin, Pol quadri *mpl*
CAE *n abbr* (**computer-aided engineering**) CAE *m inv*
Caesarean, Caesarian /sɪˈzeərɪən/ *n* parto *m* cesareo

⚷ parola chiave

café /ˈkæfeɪ/ *n* caffè *m*
cafeteria /kæfəˈtɪərɪə/ *n* tavola *f* calda
cafetière /ˈkæfəˌtjeə(r)/ *n* caffettiera *f* a stantuffo
caffeine /ˈkæfiːn/ *n* caffeina *f*
cage /keɪdʒ/ *n* gabbia *f*
cage bird *n* uccello *m* da gabbia
cagey /ˈkeɪdʒɪ/ *adj* infml riservato (**about** su)
cagoule /kəˈguːl/ *n* BrE K-way® *m inv*
cahoots /kəˈhuːts/ *npl* infml **be in ~** essere in combutta
cairn /keən/ *n* (of stones) tumulo *m* di pietre
Cairo /ˈkaɪrəʊ/ *n* il Cairo
cajole /kəˈdʒəʊl/ *vt* persuadere con le lusinghe
cake /keɪk/ *n* torta *f*; (small) pasticcino *m*; **~ of soap** saponetta *f*; **it was a piece of ~** infml è stato un gioco da ragazzi; **you can't have your ~ and eat it** fig non si può avere la botte piena e la moglie ubriaca; **sell like hot ~s** andare a ruba
caked /keɪkt/ *adj* incrostato (**with** di)
cake mix *n* miscela *f* per torte
cake shop *n* pasticceria *f*
cake tin *n* (for baking) tortiera *f*; (for storing) scatola *f* di latta (*per torte*)
CAL *abbr* (**computer-assisted learning**) CAL *m*
Calabria /kəˈlæbrɪə/ *n* Calabria *f*
Calabrian /kəˈlæbrɪən/ *adj & n* calabrese
calamine lotion /ˈkæləmaɪn/ *n* lozione *f* alla calamina
calamitous /kəˈlæmɪtəs/ *adj* disastroso
calamity /kəˈlæmətɪ/ *n* calamità *f*
calcify /ˈkælsɪfaɪ/ *vi* calcificarsi
calcium /ˈkælsɪəm/ *n* calcio *m*
calculate /ˈkælkjʊleɪt/ *vt* calcolare
calculated /ˈkælkjʊleɪtɪd/ *adj* ‹*risk, insult, decision*› calcolato; ‹*crime*› premeditato
calculating /ˈkælkjʊleɪtɪŋ/ *adj* fig calcolatore
calculating machine *n* calcolatrice *f*
calculation /kælkjʊˈleɪʃn/ *n* calcolo *m*
calculator /ˈkælkjʊleɪtə(r)/ *n* calcolatrice *f*
calculus /ˈkælkjʊləs/ *n* Math, Med calcolo *m*
calendar /ˈkælɪndə(r)/ *n* calendario *m*
calendar month *n* mese *m* civile
calendar year *n* anno *m* civile
calf¹ /kɑːf/ *n* (*pl* **calves**) vitello *m*
calf² *n* (*pl* **calves**) Anat polpaccio *m*
calfskin /ˈkɑːfskɪn/ *n* [pelle *f* di] vitello *m*
calibrate /ˈkælɪbreɪt/ *vt* calibrare ‹*instrument*›; tarare ‹*scales*›
calibre /ˈkælɪbə(r)/ *n* calibro *m*
calico /ˈkælɪkəʊ/ *n* cotone *m* grezzo
California /kælɪˈfɔːnɪə/ *n* California *f*
Californian /kælɪˈfɔːnɪən/ *adj & n* californiano, -a *mf*
call /kɔːl/ **A** *n* grido *m*; Teleph telefonata *f*; (visit) visita *f*; **be on ~** ‹*doctor*› essere di guardia; **good/bad ~** infml buona/pessima idea
B *vt* chiamare; indire ‹*strike*›; **be ~ed** chiamarsi
C *vi* chiamare; **~ [in or round]** passare
■ **call back** *vt & vi* richiamare
■ **call by** *vi* (make brief visit) passare
■ **call for** *vt* (ask for) chiedere; (require) richiedere; (fetch) passare a prendere
■ **call in A** *vi* (make brief visit) passare
B *vt* chiamare ‹*patient, client*›; interpellare ‹*expert*›
■ **call off** *vt* richiamare ‹*dog*›; disdire ‹*meeting*›; revocare ‹*strike*›
■ **call on** *vt* chiamare; (appeal to) fare un appello a; (visit) visitare
■ **call out** *vt & vi* chiamare ad alta voce
■ **call together** *vt* riunire
■ **call up** *vt* Mil chiamare alle armi; Teleph chiamare
CALL *n abbr* (**computer-assisted language learning**) CALL *m inv*
callback facility /ˈkɔːlbæk/ *n* Teleph *servizio (m) telefonico che permette di individuare il numero che ha chiamato*
call barring *n* blocco *m* chiamate
call box *n* cabina *f* telefonica
call centre BrE, **call center** AmE *n* call center *m inv*
caller /ˈkɔːlə(r)/ *n* visitatore, -trice *mf*; Teleph *persona (f) che telefona*
caller identification *n* identificativo *m* del chiamante
call girl *n* call-girl *f inv*, [ragazza *f*] squillo *f inv*
calligrapher /kəˈlɪgrəfə(r)/ *n* calligrafo, -a *mf*
calligraphy /kəˈlɪgrəfɪ/ *n* calligrafia *f*
calling /ˈkɔːlɪŋ/ *n* vocazione *f*
calliper /ˈkælɪpə(r)/ (for measuring) calibro *m*; (leg support) tutore *m*
callisthenics /kælɪsˈθenɪks/ *nsg* ginnastica *fsg*
callous /ˈkæləs/ *adj* insensibile
callousness /ˈkæləsnɪs/ *n* insensibilità *f*
call-out *n* (doctor) visita *f* a domicilio; (plumber, electrician) chiamata *f*
call-out charge *n* costo *m* della chiamata
callow /ˈkæləʊ/ *adj* immaturo
call screening *n* filtro *m* chiamate
call sign *n* Radio segnale *m* di chiamata
call-up *n* Mil chiamata *f* alle armi
call-up papers *npl* cartolina *f* precetto
call waiting *n* avviso *m* di chiamata in linea
calm /kɑːm/ **A** *adj* calmo
B *n* calma *f*
■ **calm down A** *vt* calmare
B *vi* calmarsi
calmly /ˈkɑːmlɪ/ *adv* con calma
calmness /ˈkɑːmnɪs/ *n* calma *f*
Calor gas® /ˈkælə/ *n* BrE liquigas® *m inv*

C

calorie /'kælərɪ/ *n* caloria *f*
calorific /kælə'rɪfɪk/ *adj* calorico
calve /kɑːv/ *vi* figliare
cam /kæm/ *n* Techn camma *f*
camaraderie /kæmə'rædərɪ/ *n* cameratismo *m*
camber /'kæmbə(r)/ *n* curvatura *f*
Cambodia /kæm'bəʊdɪə/ *n* Cambogia *f*
Cambodian /kæm'bəʊdɪən/ *adj & n* cambogiano, -a *mf*
camcorder /'kæmkɔːdə(r)/ *n* videocamera *f*
came /keɪm/ ▶ **come**
camel /'kæml/ *n* cammello *m*
camel hair *n* cammello *m*
camellia /kə'miːlɪə/ *n* camelia *f*
cameo /'kæmɪəʊ/ *n* cammeo *m*
cameo role *n* Theat, Cinema breve apparizione *f*
camera /'kæmərə/ *n* macchina *f* fotografica; TV telecamera *f*
camera crew *n* troupe *f inv* televisiva
cameraman /'kæmərəmæn/ *n* operatore *m* [televisivo], cameraman *m inv*
camera phone *n* telefono *m* con fotocamera, telefono *m* con videocamera
Cameroon /'kæməruːn/ *n* il Camerun
camisole /'kæmɪsəʊl/ *n* canotta *f*
camomile /'kæməmaɪl/ *n* camomilla *f*
camouflage /'kæməflɑːʒ/ **A** *n* mimetizzazione *f*
B *vt* mimetizzare
camp¹ /kæmp/ **A** *n* campeggio *f*; Mil campo *m*
B *vi* campeggiare; Mil accamparsi
camp² *adj* (affected) affettato
campaign /kæm'peɪn/ **A** *n* campagna *f*
B *vi* fare una campagna
campaigner /kæm'peɪnə(r)/ *n* partecipante *mf* a una campagna
campaign trail *n* **be on the ~** fare la campagna elettorale
campaign worker *n* BrE Pol membro *m* dello staff di una campagna elettorale
camp bed *n* letto *m* da campo
camper /'kæmpə(r)/ *n* campeggiatore, -trice *mf*; Auto camper *m inv*
campfire /'kæmpfaɪə(r)/ *n* fuoco *m* di bivacco
camphor /'kæmfə(r)/ *n* canfora *f*
camping /'kæmpɪŋ/ *n* campeggio *m*
camping equipment *n* attrezzatura *f* da campeggio
camping gas *n* gas *m inv* da campeggio
camping holiday *n* vacanza *f* in tenda
camping site *n* campeggio *m*
camping stool *n* BrE sgabello *m* pieghevole
camping stove *n* fornello *m* da campeggio
campsite /'kæmpsaɪt/ *n* campeggio *m*
campus /'kæmpəs/ *n* (*pl* **-puses**) Univ città *f* universitaria, campus *m inv*
camshaft /'kæmʃɑːft/ *n* albero *m* a camme
can¹ /kæn/ **A** *n* (for petrol) latta *f*; (tin) scatola *f*; **~ of beer** lattina *f* di birra
B *vt* mettere in scatola
can² /kæn/, *atono*/kən/ *v aux* (*pres* **can**, *pt* **could**) (be able to) potere; (know how to) sapere; **I cannot** *or* **can't go** non posso andare; **he could not** *or* **couldn't go** non poteva andare; **she can't swim** non sa nuotare; **I ~ smell something burning** sento odor di bruciato
Canada /'kænədə/ *n* Canada *m*
Canadian /kə'neɪdɪən/ *adj & n* canadese *mf*
canal /kə'næl/ *n* canale *m*
canal boat, canal barge *n* chiatta *f*
canapé /'kænəpeɪ/ *n* canapè *m*
Canaries /kə'neərɪz/ *npl* Canarie *fpl*
canary /kə'neərɪ/ *n* canarino *m*
cancel /'kænsl/ *v* (*pt/pp* **cancelled**) **A** *vt* disdire ‹*meeting, newspaper*›; revocare ‹*contract, order*›; annullare ‹*reservation, appointment, stamp*›
B *vi* ‹*guest, host*› annullare
cancellation /kænsə'leɪʃn/ *n* (of meeting, contract) revoca *f*; (in hotel, restaurant, for flight) cancellazione *f*
cancer /'kænsə(r)/ *n* cancro *m*; **C~** Astr Cancro *m*
cancerous /'kænsərəs/ *adj* canceroso
cancer patient *n* malato, -a *mf* di cancro
cancer research *n* ricerca *f* sul cancro
candelabra /kændə'lɑːbrə/ *n* candelabro *m*
candid /'kændɪd/ *adj* franco
candidacy /'kændɪdəsɪ/ *n* Pol candidatura *f*
candidate /'kændɪdət/ *n* candidato, -a *mf*
candidly /'kændɪdlɪ/ *adv* francamente
candied /'kændɪd/ *adj* candito
candle /'kænd(ə)l/ *n* candela *f*
candlelight /'kænd(ə)llaɪt/ *n* **by ~** a lume di candela
candlelit dinner /'kænd(ə)llɪt/ *n* cena *f* a lume di candela
candlestick /'kænd(ə)lstɪk/ *n* portacandele *m inv*
candlewick bedspread /'kænd(ə)lwɪk/ *n* copriletto *m inv* di ciniglia
candour /'kændə(r)/ *n* franchezza *f*
candy /'kændɪ/ *n* AmE caramella *f*; **a [piece of] ~** una caramella
candyfloss /'kændɪflɒs/ *n* zucchero *m* filato
candy-striped /straɪpt/ *adj* (blue) a righe bianche e celesti; (pink) a righe bianche e rosa
cane /keɪn/ **A** *n* (stick) bastone *m*; Sch bacchetta *f*
B *vt* prendere a bacchettate ‹*pupil*›
cane sugar *n* zucchero *m* di canna

parola chiave

canine /ˈkeɪnaɪn/ *adj* canino
canine tooth *n* canino *m*
canister /ˈkænɪstə(r)/ *n* barattolo *m*
cannabis /ˈkænəbɪs/ *n* cannabis *f*
canned /kænd/ *adj* in scatola; **~ music** infml musica *f* registrata
cannibal /ˈkænɪbl/ *n* cannibale *mf*
cannibalism /ˈkænɪbəlɪzm/ *n* cannibalismo *m*
cannibalize /ˈkænɪbəlaɪz/ *vt* riciclare parti di
cannon /ˈkænən/ *n inv* cannone *m*
cannon ball *n* palla *f* di cannone
cannon fodder *n* carne *f* da cannone, carne *f* da macello
cannot /ˈkænɒt/ ▶ **can²**
canny /ˈkænɪ/ *adj* astuto
canoe /kəˈnuː/ **A** *n* canoa *f*
B *vi* andare in canoa
canoeing /kəˈnuːɪŋ/ *n* canoismo *m*
canon /ˈkænən/ *n* (rule) canone *m*; (person) canonico *m*
canonization /kænənaɪzˈzeɪʃn/ *n* canonizzazione *f*
canonize /ˈkænənaɪz/ *vt* canonizzare
canoodle /kəˈnuːdl/ *vi* infml sbaciucchiarsi
can opener *n* apriscatole *m inv*
canopy /ˈkænəpɪ/ *n* baldacchino *f*; (of parachute) calotta *f*
cant /kænt/ *n* (hypocrisy) ipocrisia *f*; (jargon) gergo *m*
can't /kɑːnt/ = **cannot**, ▶ **can²**
cantankerous /kænˈtæŋkərəs/ *adj* stizzoso
cantata /kænˈtɑːtə/ *n* Mus cantata *f*
canteen /kænˈtiːn/ *n* mensa *f*; **~ of cutlery** servizio *m* di posate
canter /ˈkæntə(r)/ **A** *n* piccolo galoppo *m*
B *vi* andare a piccolo galoppo
cantilever /ˈkæntɪliːvə(r)/ *n* cantilever *m inv*, trave *f* a sbalzo
cantonal /ˈkæntənəl/ *adj* cantonale
canvas /ˈkænvəs/ *n* tela *f*; (painting) dipinto *m* su tela
canvass /ˈkænvəs/ *vi* Pol fare propaganda elettorale
canvasser /ˈkænvəsə(r)/ *n* propagandista *mf* elettorale (porta a porta)
canvassing /ˈkænvəsɪŋ/ *n* (door to door for votes) propaganda *f* porta a porta; (door to door for sales) vendita *f* porta a porta
canyon /ˈkænjən/ *n* canyon *m inv*
canyoning /ˈkænjənɪŋ/ *n* canyoning *m inv*
cap /kæp/ **A** *n* berretto *m*; (nurse's) cuffia *f*; (top, lid) tappo *m*
B *vt* (*pt/pp* **capped**) fig (do better than) superare
capability /keɪpəˈbɪlətɪ/ *n* capacità *f*
capable /ˈkeɪpəbl/ *adj* capace; (skilful) abile; **be ~ of doing something** essere capace di fare qualcosa
capably /ˈkeɪpəblɪ/ *adv* con abilità
capacious /kəˈpeɪʃəs/ *adj* ‹*pocket, car boot*› capace
capacity /kəˈpæsətɪ/ *n* capacità *f*; (function) qualità *f*; **in my ~ as** in qualità di
cape¹ /keɪp/ *n* (cloak) cappa *f*
cape² *n* Geog capo *m*
Cape of Good Hope *n* Capo *m* di Buona Speranza
caper¹ /ˈkeɪpə(r)/ **A** *vi* saltellare
B *n* infml birichinata *f*
caper² *n* Culin cappero *m*
Cape Town *n* Città *f* del Capo
Cape Verde /vɜːd/ *n* Capo Verde *m*
capful /ˈkæpfʊl/ *n* tappo *m*
cap gun *n* pistola *f* a capsule
capillary /kəˈpɪlərɪ/ *adj & n* capillare *m*
capital /ˈkæpɪtl/ *n* (town) capitale *f*; (money) capitale *m*; (letter) lettera *f* maiuscola
capital allowances *npl* detrazioni *mpl* per ammortamento
capital city *n* capitale *f*
capital expenditure *n* spese *fpl* in conto capitale; (personal) spese *fpl* di capitale
capital gains tax *n* imposta *f* sui redditi di capitale
capital goods *npl* beni *mpl* strumentali
capital-intensive *adj* ad uso intensivo di capitale
capital investment *n* investimento *m* di capitale
capitalism /ˈkæpɪtəlɪzm/ *n* capitalismo *m*
capitalist /ˈkæpɪtəlɪst/ *adj & n* capitalista *mf*
capitalize /ˈkæpɪtəlaɪz/ *vi* **~ on** fig trarre vantaggio da
capital letter *n* lettera *f* maiuscola
capital punishment *n* pena *f* capitale
capital spending *n* spese *fpl* in conto capitale
capital transfer tax *n* imposta *f* sui trasferimenti di capitale
capitulate /kəˈpɪtjʊleɪt/ *vi* capitolare
capitulation /kəpɪtjʊˈleɪʃn/ *n* capitolazione *f*
capon /ˈkeɪpɒn/ *n* cappone *m*
caprice /kəˈpriːs/ *n* (whim) capriccio *m*
capricious /kəˈprɪʃəs/ *adj* capriccioso
Capricorn /ˈkæprɪkɔːn/ *n* Astr Capricorno *m*
caps /kæps/ *npl abbr* (**capital letters**) maius. *fpl*
capsicum /ˈkæpsɪkəm/ *n* peperone *m*
capsize /kæpˈsaɪz/ **A** *vi* capovolgersi
B *vt* capovolgere
caps lock *n* Comput bloccamaiuscole *m inv*
capstan /ˈkæpstən/ *n* argano *m*
capsule /ˈkæpsjuːl/ *n* capsula *f*
captain /ˈkæptɪn/ **A** *n* capitano *m*
B *vt* comandare ‹*team*›
caption /ˈkæpʃn/ *n* intestazione *f*; (of illustration) didascalia *f*
captious /ˈkæpʃəs/ *adj* ‹*remark*› ipercritico

C

captivate /ˈkæptɪveɪt/ *vt* incantare

captive /ˈkæptɪv/ **A** *adj* prigioniero; **hold/take ~** tenere/fare prigioniero **B** *n* prigioniero, -a *mf*

captivity /kæpˈtɪvətɪ/ *n* prigionia *f*; (animals) cattività *f*

captor /ˈkæptə(r)/ *n* (of person) *persona (f) che tiene prigioniero qualcuno*; (of person for ransom) rapitore, -trice *mf*

⚷ **capture** /ˈkæptʃə(r)/ **A** *n* cattura *f* **B** *vt* catturare; attirare ‹*attention*›

⚷ **car** /kɑː(r)/ *n* macchina *f*; **by ~** in macchina

carafe /kəˈræf/ *n* caraffa *f*

car alarm *n* antifurto *m* della macchina

caramel /ˈkærəməl/ *n* (sweet) caramella *f* al mou; Culin caramello *m*

carat /ˈkærət/ *n* carato *m*

caravan /ˈkærəvæn/ *n* roulotte *f inv*; (horse-drawn) carovana *f*

caravan site *n* area *f* per roulotte

caraway /ˈkærəweɪ/ *n* (plant) cumino *m* dei prati

carbohydrate /kɑːbəˈhaɪdreɪt/ *n* carboidrato *m*

carbolic /kɑːˈbɒlɪk/ *adj* (soap) al fenolo

car bomb *n* autobomba *f*

carbon /ˈkɑːbən/ *n* carbonio *m*; (paper) carta *f* carbone; (copy) copia *f* in carta carbone

carbon copy *n* copia *f* in carta carbone; fig (person) ritratto *m*

carbon-date *vt* datare con il carbonio 14

carbon dating *n* datazione *f* con il carbonio 14

carbon dioxide *n* anidride *f* carbonica

carbon fibre *n* fibra *f* di carbonio

carbon filter *n* filtro *m* al carbone

carbon footprint *n* impronta *f* ecologica

carbon monoxide *n* monossido *m* di carbonio

carbon neutral *adj* a emissioni zero, a zero emissioni

carbon offsetting /ˌkɑːbən ˈɒfsetɪŋ/ *n* compensazione *f* delle emissioni

carbon paper *n* carta *f* carbone

carbon trading *n* carbon trading *m inv*, mercato *m* delle emissioni

car boot sale *n* BrE *mercatino (m) di oggetti usati, esposti nei bagagliai delle macchine*

carbuncle /ˈkɑːbʌŋk(ə)l/ *n* Med foruncolo *m*

carburettor /kɑːbjʊˈretə(r)/ *n* carburatore *m*

carcass /ˈkɑːkəs/ *n* carcassa *f*

carcinogen /kɑːˈsɪnədʒən/ *n* cancerogeno *m*

carcinogenic /kɑːsɪnəˈdʒenɪk/ *adj* cancerogeno

car crash *n* scontro *m* automobilistico

⚷ **card** /kɑːd/ *n* (for birthday, Christmas etc) biglietto *m* di auguri; (playing ~) carta *f* [da gioco]; (membership ~) tessera *f*; (business ~) biglietto *m* da visita; (credit ~) carta *f* di credito; Comput scheda *f*

cardboard /ˈkɑːdbɔːd/ *n* cartone *m*

cardboard box *n* scatola *f* di cartone; (large) scatolone *m*

cardboard city *n* infml *zona (f) in cui vivono i senzatetto*

car deck *n* (on ferry) ponte *m* auto

card game *n* gioco *m* di carte

cardiac /ˈkɑːdɪæk/ *adj* cardiaco

cardiac arrest *n* arresto *m* cardiaco

cardigan /ˈkɑːdɪgən/ *n* cardigan *m inv*

cardinal /ˈkɑːdɪnl/ **A** *adj* cardinale; **~ number** numero *m* cardinale **B** *n* Relig cardinale *m*

card index *n* schedario *m*

cardiologist /kɑːdɪˈɒlədʒɪst/ *n* cardiologo, -a *mf*

cardiology /kɑːdɪˈɒlədʒɪ/ *n* cardiologia *f*

cardiovascular /kɑːdɪəˈvæskjʊlə(r)/ *adj* cardiovascolare

card key *n* scheda *f* magnetica

cardphone *n* telefono *m* a scheda

card table *n* tappeto *m* verde

card trick *n* trucco *m* con le carte

⚷ **care** /keə(r)/ **A** *n* cura *f*; (caution) attenzione *f*; (worry) preoccupazione *f*; **~ of** (on letter, abbr: c/o) presso; **take ~** (be cautious) fare attenzione; **bye, take ~** ciao, stammi bene; **take ~ of** occuparsi di; **be taken into ~** essere preso in custodia da un ente assistenziale; **'[handle] with ~'** 'fragile' **B** *vi* **~ about** interessarsi di; **~ for** (feel affection for) volere bene a; (look after) aver cura di; **I don't ~ for chocolate** non mi piace il cioccolato; **I don't ~** non me ne importa; **I couldn't ~ less** BrE *or* **I could care less** AmE; non potrebbe importarmene di meno; **who ~s?** chi se ne frega?; **for all I ~** per quello che me ne importa

care assistant *n* BrE Med assistente *mf* a domicilio

⚷ **career** /kəˈrɪə(r)/ **A** *n* carriera *f*; (profession) professione *f*; **~ woman** *n* donna in carriera **B** *vi* andare a tutta velocità

career break *n* pausa *f* nella carriera

career move *n* passo *m* utile per un avanzamento di carriera

careers adviser *n* consulente *mf* di orientamento professionale

careers office *n* centro *m* di orientamento professionale

careers service *n* servizio *m* di orientamento professionale

carefree /ˈkeəfriː/ *adj* spensierato

careful /ˈkeəfʊl/ *adj* attento; ‹*driver*› prudente

⚷ **carefully** /ˈkeəfʊlɪ/ *adv* con attenzione

caregiver *n* AmE familiare *m* che assiste un anziano o un disabile

---

⚷ parola chiave

care home *n* casa *f* famiglia *inv*

careless /ˈkeəlɪs/ *adj* irresponsabile; (in work) trascurato; ‹*work*› fatto con poca cura; ‹*driver*› distratto

carelessly /ˈkeəlɪslɪ/ *adv* negligentemente

carelessness /ˈkeəlɪsnɪs/ *n* trascuratezza *f*

carer /ˈkeərə(r)/ *n* BrE (relative) *familiare (m) che assiste un anziano o un disabile*; (professional) badante *mf*, assistente *mf* a domicilio

caress /kəˈres/ **A** *n* carezza *f*
B *vt* accarezzare

caretaker /ˈkeəteɪkə(r)/ *n* custode *mf*; (in school) bidello *m*

care worker *n* assistente *mf* sociosanitario

careworn /ˈkeəwɔːn/ *adj* ‹*face*› segnato dalle preoccupazioni

car ferry *n* traghetto *m* (*per il trasporto di auto*)

car free *adj* ‹*environment*› senza macchine

cargo /ˈkɑːgəʊ/ *n* (*pl* **-es**) carico *m*

cargo plane *n* aereo *m* da carico

cargo ship *n* nave *f* da carico

car hire *n* autonoleggio *m*

Caribbean /kærɪˈbiːən/ **A** *n* **the ~** (sea) il Mar *m* dei Caraibi
B *adj* caraibico

caricature /ˈkærɪkətjʊə(r)/ **A** *n* caricatura *f*
B *vt* fare una caricatura di

caricaturist /ˈkærɪkətjʊərɪst/ *n* caricaturista *mf*

caring /ˈkeərɪŋ/ *adj* ‹*parent*› premuroso; ‹*attitude*› altruista; **the ~ professions** le attività assistenziali

carjack /ˈkɑːdʒæk/ *vt furto (m) d'auto con minaccia o violenza al conducente*

carjacker /ˈkɑːdʒækə(r)/ *n chi effettua un furto d'auto con minaccia o violenza al conducente*

carjacking /ˈkɑːdʒækɪŋ/ *n furto (m) d'auto con aggressione al conducente*

carload /ˈkɑːləʊd/ *n* **a ~ of people** un'automobile *f* piena di persone

carnage /ˈkɑːnɪdʒ/ *n* carneficina *f*

carnal /ˈkɑːn(ə)l/ *adj* carnale

carnation /kɑːˈneɪʃn/ *n* garofano *m*

carnival /ˈkɑːnɪvl/ *n* carnevale *m*

carnivore /ˈkɑːnɪvɔː(r)/ *n* carnivoro *m*

carnivorous /kɑːˈnɪvərəs/ *adj* carnivoro

carob /ˈkærəb/ *n* (pod) carruba *f*; (tree) carrubo *m*

carol /ˈkærəl/ *n* **[Christmas] ~** canto *m* natalizio; **~ concert** concerto *m* natalizio; **go ~ singing** andare a cantare le canzoni natalizie per le strade

carousel /kærʊˈsel/ *n* (merry-go-round) giostra *f*; (for luggage) nastro *m* trasportatore; (for slides) caricatore *m* circolare

carp¹ /kɑːp/ *n inv* carpa *f*

carp² *vi* lamentarsi; **~ at** trovare da ridire su

car park *n* parcheggio *m*

carpenter /ˈkɑːpəntə(r)/ *n* falegname *m*

carpentry /ˈkɑːpəntrɪ/ *n* falegnameria *f*

carpet /ˈkɑːpɪt/ **A** *n* tappeto *m*; (wall-to-wall) moquette *f inv*; **be on the ~** fig essere ammonito
B *vt* mettere la moquette in ‹*room*›

C

carpet-bomb *vt* bombardare a tappeto

carpet fitter *n* artigiano *m* che mette in opera la moquette

carpet slipper *n* pantofola *f*

carpet sweeper *n* battitappeto *m inv*

carpet tile *n* riquadro *m* di moquette

car phone *n* telefono *m* in macchina

car radio *n* autoradio *f inv*

carriage /ˈkærɪdʒ/ *n* carrozza *f*; (of typewriter) carrello *m*; (of goods) trasporto *m*; (cost) spese *fpl* di trasporto; (bearing) portamento *m*; **~ paid** Comm franco di porto

carriage clock *n* orologio *m* da tavolo

carriageway /ˈkærɪdʒweɪ/ *n* strada *f* carrozzabile; **north-bound ~** carreggiata *f* nord

carrier /ˈkærɪə(r)/ *n* (company) impresa *f* di trasporti; Aeron compagnia *f* di trasporto aereo; (of disease) portatore *m*

carrier bag *n* borsa *f* [per la spesa]

carrier pigeon *n* piccione *m* viaggiatore

carrot /ˈkærət/ *n* carota *f*

carry /ˈkærɪ/ *v* (*pt/pp* **-ied**) **A** *vt* portare; (transport) trasportare; Math riportare; **get carried away** infml lasciarsi prender la mano
B *vi* ‹*sound*› trasmettersi

■ **carry forward** *vt* riportare ‹*balance, figure*›

■ **carry off** *vt* portare via; vincere ‹*prize*›

■ **carry on** **A** *vi* continuare; fam (make scene) fare delle storie; **~ on with something** continuare qualcosa; **~ on with somebody** fam intendersela con qualcuno
B *vt* mantenere ‹*business*›; **~ on doing something** continuare a fare qualcosa

■ **carry out** *vt* portare fuori; eseguire ‹*instructions, task*›; mettere in atto ‹*threat*›; effettuare ‹*experiment, survey*›

carryall *n* AmE borsone *m*

carrycot /ˈkærɪkɒt/ *n* porte-enfant *m inv*

carry-on *n* infml (complicated procedure) impresa *f*; (bad behaviour) storie *fpl*

carry-out /ˈkærɪaʊt/ *n* AmE piatti *mpl* da asporto

car seat *n* (for baby or child) seggiolino *m* per auto

carsick /ˈkɑːsɪk/ *adj* **be ~** avere il mal d'auto

cart /kɑːt/ **A** *n* carretto *m*; **put the ~ before the horse** fig mettere il carro davanti ai buoi
B *vt* infml (carry) portare

cartel /kɑːˈtel/ *n* cartello *m*

car theft *n* furto *m* d'auto

carthorse /ˈkɑːthɔːs/ *n* cavallo *m* da tiro

cartilage /ˈkɑːtɪlɪdʒ/ *n* Anat cartilagine *f*

cartographer /kɑːˈtɒɡrəfə(r)/ *n* cartografo, -a *mf*

cartography /kɑːˈtɒɡrəfɪ/ *n* cartografia *f*

carton /ˈkɑːt(ə)n/ *n* scatola *f* di cartone; (for drink) cartone *m*; (of cream, yoghurt) vasetto *m*; (of cigarettes) stecca *f*

cartoon /kɑːˈtuːn/ *n* vignetta *f*; (strip) vignette *fpl*; (film) cartone *m* animato; (in art) bozzetto *m*

cartoonist /kɑːˈtuːnɪst/ *n* vignettista *mf*; (for films) disegnatore, -trice *mf* di cartoni animati

cartridge /ˈkɑːtrɪdʒ/ *n* cartuccia *f*; (for film) bobina *f*; (of record player) testina *f*

cartwheel /ˈkɑːtwiːl/ *n* (of cart) ruota *f* di carro; (in gymnastics) ruota *f*; **do a ~** (in gymnastics) fare la ruota

carve /kɑːv/ *vt* scolpire; tagliare ‹*meat*›

▪ **carve out** *vt* crearsi ‹*name, reputation, market*›

▪ **carve up** *vt* spartire ‹*estate, territory, proceeds*›

carving /ˈkɑːvɪŋ/ *n* scultura *f*

carving knife *n* trinciante *m*

car wash *n* autolavaggio *m inv*

car worker *n* operaio, -a *mf* dell'industria automobilistica

Casanova /ˈkæsənəʊvə/ *n* Casanova *m inv*

cascade /kæsˈkeɪd/ **A** *vi* scendere a cascata **B** *n* cascata *f*

🔑 **case¹** /keɪs/ *n* caso *m*; **in any ~** in ogni caso; **in that ~** in questo caso; **just in ~** per sicurezza; **in ~ he comes** nel caso in cui venisse; **in ~ of emergency** in caso d'emergenza

case² *n* (container) scatola *f*; (crate) cassa *f*; (for spectacles) astuccio *m*; (suitcase) valigia *f*; (for display) vetrina *f*

case history *n* Med cartella *f* clinica

casement window /ˈkeɪsmənt/ *n* finestra *f* a battenti

case notes *npl* pratica *f*

case study *n* analisi *f inv*

casework *n* **do ~** occuparsi di assistenza sociale

🔑 **cash** /kæʃ/ **A** *n* denaro *m* contante; infml (money) contanti *mpl*; **pay [in] ~** pagare in contanti; **~ on delivery** pagamento alla consegna **B** *vt* incassare (cheque)

▪ **cash in** *vt* riscuotere ‹*bond, policy*›; AmE incassare ‹*check*›

▪ **cash in on** *vt* infml approfittarsi di

cash-and-carry *n* cash and carry *m inv*

cashback *n contanti* (*mpl*) *che si possono richiedere alla cassa di un negozio quando si effettua un pagamento con carta di debito*

cash box *n* cassetta *f* portavalori

cash card *n* bancomat® *m inv*

cash desk *n* cassa *f*

cash dispenser *n* sportello *m* automatico, cassa *f* automatica

cashew /kəˈʃuː/, **cashew nut** *n* anacardio *m*

cash flow *n* flusso *m* di cassa; **~ difficulties** difficoltà *fpl* di flusso di cassa; **~ management** gestione *f* del flusso di cassa

cashier /kæˈʃɪə(r)/ *n* cassiere, -a *mf*

cashless /ˈkæʃlɪs/ *adj* ‹*society, transaction*› *basato sull'uso di carte di credito, assegni ecc. anziché sul contante*

cash machine *n* (sportello) bancomat® *m inv*

cashmere /ˈkæʃmɪə(r)/ *n* cachemire *m inv*

cash on delivery *n* pagamento *m* alla consegna

cashpoint *n* (sportello) bancomat® *m inv*

cash register *n* registratore *m* di cassa

casing /ˈkeɪsɪŋ/ *n* (of machinery) rivestimento *m*; (of gearbox) scatola *f*; (of tyre) copertone *m*

casino /kəˈsiːnəʊ/ *n* casinò *m*

cask /kɑːsk/ *n* barile *m*

casket /ˈkɑːskɪt/ *n* scrigno *m*; AmE (coffin) bara *f*

casserole /ˈkæsərəʊl/ *n* casseruola *f*; (stew) stufato *m*

cassette /kəˈset/ *n* cassetta *f*

cassette deck *n* piastra *f* di registrazione

cassette player *n* mangiacassette *m inv*

cassette recorder *n* registratore *m* (*a cassette*)

cassette tape *n* cassetta *f*

cassock /ˈkæsək/ *n* tonaca *f*

cast /kɑːst/ **A** *n* (throw) lancio *m*; (mould) forma *f*; Theat cast *m inv*; **[plaster] ~** Med ingessatura *f* **B** *vt* (*pt/pp* **cast**) dare ‹*vote*›; Theat assegnare le parti di ‹*play*›; fondere ‹*metal*›; (throw) gettare; (shed) sbarazzarsi di; **~ an actor as** dare ad un attore il ruolo di; **~ a glance at** lanciare uno sguardo a

▪ **cast off** **A** *vi* Naut sganciare gli ormeggi **B** *vt* (in knitting) diminuire

▪ **cast on** *vt* (in knitting) avviare

castanets /kæstəˈnets/ *npl* nacchere *fpl*

castaway /ˈkɑːstəweɪ/ *n* naufrago, -a *mf*

caste /kɑːst/ *n* casta *f*

caster /ˈkɑːstə(r)/ *n* (wheel) rotella *f*

caster sugar *n* zucchero *m* raffinato

casting /ˈkɑːstɪŋ, AmE ˈkæst-/ *n* casting *m inv*

casting director /ˈkɑːstɪŋ/ *n* direttore *m* del casting

casting vote *n* voto *m* decisivo

cast iron **A** *n* ghisa *f* **B** *adj* **cast-iron** di ghisa; fig solido

castle /ˈkɑːsl/ *n* castello *m*; (in chess) torre *f*

cast-offs *npl* abiti *mpl* smessi

castor /ˈkɑːstə(r)/ *n* (wheel) rotella *f*

castor oil *n* olio *m* di ricino

castor sugar *n* zucchero *m* raffinato

🔑 parola chiave

castrate /kæˈstreɪt/ *vt* castrare

castration /kæˈstreɪʃn/ *n* castrazione *f*

castrato /kæsˈtrɑːtəʊ/ *n* castrato *m*

casual /ˈkæʒʊəl/ *adj* (chance) casuale; ‹*remark*› senza importanza; ‹*glance*› di sfuggita; ‹*attitude, approach*› disinvolto; ‹*chat*› informale; ‹*clothes*› casual *inv*; ‹*work*› saltuario; ~ **wear** abbigliamento *m* casual

casualize /ˈkæʒʊəlaɪz/ *vt* impiegare con contratto a termine ‹*labour*›

casually /ˈkæʒʊəlɪ/ *adv* ‹*dress*› casual; ‹*meet*› casualmente

casualty /ˈkæʒʊəltɪ/ *n* (injured person) ferito *m*; (killed) vittima *f*

casualty department *n* pronto soccorso *m*

cat /kæt/ *n* gatto *m*; derog arpia *f*

catacombs /ˈkætəkuːmz/ *npl* catacombe *fpl*

catalogue /ˈkætəlɒg/ **A** *n* catalogo *m*
B *vt* catalogare

catalyst /ˈkætəlɪst/ *n* Chem, fig catalizzatore *m*

catalytic converter /kætəˈlɪtɪk/ *n* Auto marmitta *f* catalitica

catamaran /kætəməˈræn/ *n* catamarano *m*

catapult /ˈkætəpʌlt/ **A** *n* catapulta *f*; (child's) fionda *f*
B *vt* fig catapultare

cataract /ˈkætərækt/ *n* Med cataratta *f*

catarrh /kəˈtɑː(r)/ *n* catarro *m*

catastrophe /kəˈtæstrəfɪ/ *n* catastrofe *f*

catastrophic /kætəˈstrɒfɪk/ *adj* catastrofico

cat burglar *n* BrE scassinatore, -trice *mf* acrobata

catch /kætʃ/ **A** *n* (of fish) pesca *f*; (fastener) fermaglio *m*; (on door) fermo *m*; (on window) gancio *m*; infml (snag) tranello *m*
B *vt* (*pt/pp* **caught**) acchiappare ‹*ball*›; (grab) afferrare; prendere ‹*illness, fugitive, train*›; ~ **a cold** prendersi un raffreddore; ~ **sight of** scorgere; **I caught him stealing** l'ho sorpreso mentre rubava; ~ **one's finger in the door** chiudersi il dito nella porta; ~ **sb's eye** *or* **attention** attirare l'attenzione di qualcuno
C *vi* ‹*fire*› prendere; (get stuck) impigliarsi
■ **catch on** *vi* infml (understand) afferrare; (become popular) diventare popolare
■ **catch out** *vt* (show to be wrong) prendere in castagna
■ **catch up** **A** *vt* raggiungere
B *vi* recuperare; ‹*runner*› riguadagnare terreno; ~ **up with** raggiungere ‹*somebody*›; mettersi in pari con ‹*work*›

catch-22 situation /kætʃtwentɪˈtuː/ *n* situazione *f* senza uscita

catch-all *adj* ‹*term*› polivalente; ‹*clause*› che comprende tutte le possibilità

catching /ˈkætʃɪŋ/ *adj* contagioso

catchment area /ˈkætʃmənt/ *n* bacino *m* d'utenza

catchphrase /ˈkætʃfreɪz/ *n* tormentone *m*

catchword /ˈkætʃwɜːd/ *n* slogan *m inv*

catchy /ˈkætʃɪ/ *adj* (**-ier, -iest**) orecchiabile

catechism /ˈkætɪkɪzm/ *n* catechismo *m*

categorical /kætɪˈgɒrɪkl/ *adj* categorico

categorically /kætəˈgɒrɪlkɪ/ *adv* categoricamente

categorize /ˈkætəgəraɪz/ *vt* categorizzare

category /ˈkætɪgərɪ/ *n* categoria *f*

cater /ˈkeɪtə(r)/ **A** *vi* ~ **for** provvedere a ‹*needs*›; fig venire incontro alle esigenze di
B *vt* occuparsi del rinfresco di ‹*party*›

caterer /ˈkeɪtərə(r)/ *n* persona *f* che si occupa di ristorazione

catering /ˈkeɪtərɪŋ/ *n* (trade) ristorazione *f*; (food) rinfresco *m*

caterpillar /ˈkætəpɪlə(r)/ *n* bruco *m*

caterwaul /ˈkætəwɔːl/ *vi* miagolare

catfish *n* pesce *m* gatto

cat flap *n* gattaiola *f*

catgut *n* catgut *m inv*

cathedral /kəˈθiːdrl/ *n* cattedrale *f*

Catherine wheel /ˈkæθ(ə)rɪn/ *n* girandola *f*

catheter /ˈkæθɪtə(r)/ *n* catetere *m*

cathode ray tube /kæθeʊdˈreɪ/ *n* tubo *m* a raggi catodici

Catholic /ˈkæθəlɪk/ *adj & n* cattolico, -a *mf*

Catholicism /kəˈθɒlɪsɪzm/ *n* cattolicesimo *m*

catkin /ˈkætkɪn/ *n* Bot amento *m*

cat litter *n* lettiera *f* del gatto

catnap *vi* fare un pisolino

cat-o'-nine-tails *n* gatto *m* a nove code

CAT scan *n* TAC *f*

cat's eye *n* BrE catarifrangente *m* (*inserito nell'asfalto*)

catsuit *n* tuta *f*

cattery /ˈkætərɪ/ *n* pensione *f* per gatti

cattle /ˈkæt(ə)l/ *npl* bestiame *msg*

cattle grid *n recinto* (*m*) *metallico che impedisce al bestiame di accedere a una strada*

cattle market *n* mercato *m* del bestiame; fig infml ‹*for sexual encounters*› *locale* (*m*) *dove la gente va per rimorchiare*

cattle shed *n* stalla *f*

catty /ˈkætɪ/ *adj* (**-ier, -iest**) dispettoso

catwalk /ˈkætwɔːk/ *n* passerella *f*

Caucasian /kɔːˈkeɪʒ(ə)n/ **A** *n* Geog (inhabitant) caucasico, -a *mf*; (white person) bianco, -a *mf*
B Geog caucasico; ‹*race, man*› bianco

caught /kɔːt/ ▸ **catch**

cauldron /ˈkɔːldrən/ *n* calderone *m*

cauliflower /ˈkɒlɪflaʊə(r)/ *n* cavolfiore *m*

cauliflower cheese *n* cavolfiori *mpl* gratinati

causal /ˈkɔːzəl/ *adj* causale

cause /kɔːz/ **A** *n* causa *f*; (reason) motivo *m*; **good** ~ buona causa
B *vt* causare; ~ **somebody to do something** far fare qualcosa a qualcuno

causeway /ˈkɔːzweɪ/ *n* strada *f* sopraelevata
caustic /ˈkɔːstɪk/ *adj* caustico
cauterize /ˈkɔːtəraɪz/ *vt* cauterizzare
caution /ˈkɔːʃn/ **A** *n* cautela *f*; (warning) ammonizione *f*
B *vt* mettere in guardia; Jur ammonire
cautionary /ˈkɔːʃənərɪ, AmE -nerɪ/ *adj* ‹*tale*› di ammonimento
cautious /ˈkɔːʃəs/ *adj* cauto
cautiously /ˈkɔːʃəslɪ/ *adv* cautamente
cavalcade /kævəlˈkeɪd/ *n* sfilata *f*
cavalier /kævəˈlɪə(r)/ **A** *adj* noncurante
B *n* **C~** sostenitore, -trice *mf* di Carlo I durante la guerra civile inglese
cavalry /ˈkævəlrɪ/ *n* cavalleria *f*
cave /keɪv/ *n* caverna *f*
▪ **cave in** *vi* ‹*roof*› crollare; fig (give in) capitolare
caveat /ˈkævɪæt/ *n* avvertimento *m*
cave dweller *n* cavernicolo, -a *mf*
caveman *n* cavernicolo *m*
cave painting *n* pittura *f* rupestre
caver /ˈkeɪvə(r)/ *n* speleologo, -a *mf*
cavern /ˈkævən/ *n* caverna *f*
caviare /ˈkævɪɑː(r)/ *n* caviale *m*
caving /ˈkeɪvɪŋ/ *n* speleologia *f*
cavity /ˈkævətɪ/ *n* cavità *f*; (in tooth) carie *f inv*
cavity wall insulation *n* isolamento *m* per muri a intercapedine
cavort /kəˈvɔːt/ *vi* saltellare
caw /kɔː/ **A** *n* (noise) gracchio *m*
B *vi* gracchiare
cayenne pepper /ˈkaɪen/ *n* pepe *m* di Caienna
cayman /ˈkeɪmən/ *n* caimano *m*
CB **A** *n abbr* (**Citizens' Band**) CB *f inv*
B *attrib* ‹*equipment, radio, wavelength*› CB
CBI *n abbr* BrE (**Confederation of British Industry**) ≈ Confindustria *f*
cc *abbr* **1** (**cubic centimetre**) cc *m*
2 (**carbon copy**) cc
CCJ *n abbr* BrE (**County Court Judgement**) sentenza *f* del tribunale di contea
CCTV *abbr* (**closed-circuit television**) televisione *f* a circuito chiuso
CD *n abbr* **1** (**Civil Defence**) difesa *f* civile **2** (**compact disc**) CD *m inv* **3** AmE (**Congressional District**) circoscrizione *f* del Congresso **4** (**corps diplomatique**) CD *m inv*
CD burner, **CD writer** *n* masterizzatore *m* di CD
CD-I *abbr* (**compact disc interactive**) CD-I *m*
CD player *n* lettore *m* [di] compact, lettore *m* di CD
CD-R *abbr* (**compact disc recordable**) CD-R *m*

CD-ROM /siːdiːˈrɒm/ *n* CD-Rom *m inv*
CD-ROM drive *n* lettore *m* CD-Rom
CD-RW *abbr* (**compact disc rewritable**) CD-RW *m*
cease /siːs/ **A** *n* **without ~** incessantemente
B *vt & vi* cessare
ceasefire /ˈsiːsfaɪə(r)/ *n* cessate il fuoco *m inv*
ceaseless /ˈsiːslɪs/ *adj* incessante
ceaselessly /ˈsiːslɪslɪ/ *adv* incessantemente
cedar /ˈsiːdə(r)/ *n* cedro *m*
cede /siːd/ *vt* cedere
cedilla /sɪˈdɪlə/ *n* cedilla *f*
ceiling /ˈsiːlɪŋ/ *n* soffitto *m*; fig tetto *m* [massimo]
🗝 **celebrate** /ˈselɪbreɪt/ **A** *vt* festeggiare ‹*birthday, victory*›
B *vi* far festa
celebrated /ˈselɪbreɪtɪd/ *adj* celebre (**for** per)
celebration /selɪˈbreɪʃn/ *n* celebrazione *f*
celebrity /sɪˈlebrətɪ/ *n* celebrità *f*
celeriac /sɪˈlerɪæk/ *n* sedano *m* rapa
celery /ˈselərɪ/ *n* sedano *m*
celestial /sɪˈlestɪəl/ *adj* celestiale
celibacy /ˈselɪbəsɪ/ *n* celibato *m*
celibate /ˈselɪbət/ *adj* ‹*man*› celibe; ‹*woman*› nubile
🗝 **cell** /sel/ *n* cella *f*; Biol cellula *f*
cellar /ˈselə(r)/ *n* scantinato *m*; (for wine) cantina *f*
cellist /ˈtʃelɪst/ *n* violoncellista *mf*
cello /ˈtʃeləʊ/ *n* violoncello *m*
Cellophane® /ˈseləfeɪn/ *n* cellophane® *m inv*
cell phone /ˈselfəʊn/ *n* [telefono *m*] cellulare *m*
cellular phone /seljʊləˈfəʊn/ *n* [telefono *m*] cellulare *m*
cellulite /ˈseljʊlaɪt/ *n* cellulite *f*
celluloid /ˈseljʊlɔɪd/ *n* celluloide *f*
Celsius /ˈselsɪəs/ *adj* Celsius
Celt /kelt/ *n* celta *mf*
Celtic /ˈkeltɪk/ *adj* celtico
cement /sɪˈment/ **A** *n* cemento *m*; (adhesive) mastice *m*
B *vt* cementare; (stick) attaccare col mastice; fig consolidare
cement mixer *n* betoniera *f*
cemetery /ˈsemətrɪ/ *n* cimitero *m*
cenotaph /ˈsenətæf/ *n* cenotafio *m*
censor /ˈsensə(r)/ **A** *n* censore *m*
B *vt* censurare
censorship /ˈsensəʃɪp/ *n* censura *f*
censure /ˈsenʃə(r)/ **A** *n* biasimo *m*
B *vt* biasimare
census /ˈsensəs/ *n* censimento *m*
cent /sent/ *n* (coin) centesimo *m*
centenary /senˈtiːnərɪ/ AmE **centennial** /senˈtenɪəl/ *n* centenario *m*
center /ˈsentə(r)/ *n* AmE = **centre**

🗝 parola chiave

centigrade /ˈsentɪgreɪd/ *adj* centigrado
centilitre /ˈsentɪliːtə(r)/ *n* centilitro *m*
centimetre /ˈsentɪmiːtə(r)/ *n* centimetro *m*
centipede /ˈsentɪpiːd/ *n* centopiedi *m inv*
central /ˈsentrəl/ *adj* centrale
Central African Republic *n* Repubblica *f* Centrafricana
Central America *n* America *f* centrale
central heating *n* riscaldamento *m* autonomo
centralize /ˈsentrəlaɪz/ *vt* centralizzare
central locking *n* Auto chiusura *f* centralizzata
centrally /ˈsentrəlɪ/ *adv* al centro; ~ **heated** con riscaldamento autonomo
central nervous system *n* sistema *m* nervoso centrale
central processing unit *n* Comput unità *f* centrale di elaborazione
central reservation *n* Auto banchina *f* spartitraffico *inv*
centre BrE, **center** AmE /ˈsentə(r)/ **A** *n* centro *m*
B *vt* (*pt/pp* **centred**) centrare
■ **centre on, centre around** *vt* ‹*activities, life*› imperniarsi su; ‹*industry, people*› incentrarsi su; ‹*thoughts*› concentrarsi su
centrefold *n* (pin-up picture) paginone *m*; (model) pin-up *f inv*
centre forward *n* centravanti *m inv*
centre ground BrE, **center ground** AmE *n* fig centro *m*
centre half *n* Sport centromediano *m*
centre of gravity *n* centro *m* di gravità
centrepiece *n* (of table) centrotavola *m*; fig (of exhibition) pezzo *m* forte
centre spread *n* paginone *m*
centre stage *n* Theat centro *m* della scena; **stand** ~ tenersi al centro della scena; **take/occupy** ~ fig essere/mettersi in primo piano
centrifugal /sentrɪˈfjʊgl/ *adj* ~ **force** forza *f* centrifuga
century /ˈsentʃərɪ/ *n* secolo *m*
CEO *n abbr* (**Chief Executive Officer**) direttore, -trice *mf* generale
ceramic /sɪˈræmɪk/ *adj* ceramico
ceramics /sɪˈræmɪks/ *n* (art) ceramica *fsg*; (objects) ceramiche *fpl*
cereal /ˈsɪərɪəl/ *n* cereale *m*
cerebral /ˈserɪbrl/ *adj* cerebrale
cerebral palsy /ˈpɔːlzɪ/ *n* paralisi *f* cerebrale
ceremonial /serɪˈməʊnɪəl/ **A** *adj* da cerimonia
B *n* cerimoniale *m*
ceremonially /serɪˈməʊnɪəlɪ/ *adv* secondo il rituale
ceremonious /serɪˈməʊnɪəs/ *adj* cerimonioso
ceremoniously /serɪˈməʊnɪəslɪ/ *adv* in modo cerimonioso
ceremony /ˈserɪmənɪ/ *n* cerimonia *f*; **without** ~ senza cerimonie
cert /sɜːt/ *n* BrE infml **it's a [dead]** ~**!** ci puoi scommettere!
certain /ˈsɜːtn/ *adj* certo; **for** ~ di sicuro; **make** ~ accertarsi; **he is** ~ **to win** è certo di vincere; **it's not** ~ **whether he'll come** non è sicuro che venga
certainly /ˈsɜːtnlɪ/ *adv* certamente; ~ **not!** no di certo!
certainty /ˈsɜːtntɪ/ *n* certezza *f*; **it's a** ~ è una cosa certa
certifiable /ˈsɜːtɪfaɪəbl/ *adj* ‹*verifiable statement, evidence*› dimostrabile; (mad) pazzo
certificate /səˈtɪfɪkət/ *n* certificato *m*
certified /ˈsɜːtɪfaɪd/ *adj* autenticato
certified mail *n* AmE (lettera) raccomandata *f*
certified public accountant *n* AmE ≈ commercialista *mf*
certify /ˈsɜːtɪfaɪ/ *vt* (*pt/pp* **-ied**) certificare; (declare insane) dichiarare malato di mente
certitude /ˈsɜːtɪtjuːd/ *n* certezza *f*
cervical /ˈsɜvɪkl/ *adj* cervicale
cervical cancer *n* tumore *m* del collo dell'utero
cervical smear *n* Pap test *m inv*, striscio *m*
cervix /ˈsɜːvɪks/ *n* cervice *f* uterina, collo *m* dell'utero
cessation /seˈseɪʃn/ *n* cessazione *f*
cesspool /ˈsespuːl/ *n* pozzo *m* nero
cf. *abbr* (**compare**) cf, cfr
CFC *n abbr* (**chlorofluorocarbon**) CFC *m inv*
CFC-free *adj* ‹*product, spray*› senza CFC
CFE *abbr* (**College of Further Education**) *istituto* (*m*) *di istruzione superiore*
CGI *abbr* Comput (**common graphical interface**) CGI *f*
Chad /tʃæd/ *n* Chad *m*
chafe /tʃeɪf/ *vt* irritare
chaff /tʃɑːf/ *n* pula *f*
chaffinch /ˈtʃæfɪntʃ/ *n* fringuello *m*
chagrin /ˈʃægrɪn/ *n* **much to his** ~ con suo grande dispiacere
chain /tʃeɪn/ **A** *n* catena *f*
B *vt* incatenare ‹*prisoner*›; attaccare con la catena ‹*dog*› (**to** a)
■ **chain up** *vt* legare alla catena ‹*dog*›
chain gang *n* gruppo *m* di prigionieri incatenati
chain letter *n* lettera *f* della catena di Sant'Antonio
chain mail *n* cotta *f* di maglia
chain reaction *n* reazione *f* a catena
chain saw *n* motosega *f*
chain-smoke *vi* fumare una sigaretta dopo l'altra

C

C

chain-smoker *n* fumatore, -trice *mf* accanito, -a

chain store *n* negozio *m* appartenente ad una catena

⚷ **chair** /tʃeə(r)/ **A** *n* sedia *f*; Univ cattedra *f* **B** *vt* presiedere

chairlift /ˈtʃeəlɪft/ *n* seggiovia *f*

⚷ **chairman** /ˈtʃeəmən/ *n* presidente *m*; **~ and managing director** presidente *m* direttore generale

chairperson /ˈtʃeəpɜːs(ə)n/ *n* presidente *m*, -essa *f*

chairwoman /ˈtʃeəwʊmən/ *n* presidentessa *f*

chalet /ˈʃæleɪ/ *n* chalet *m inv*; (in holiday camp) bungalow *m inv*

chalice /ˈtʃælɪs/ *n* Relig calice *m*

chalk /tʃɔːk/ *n* gesso *m*

chalky /ˈtʃɔːkɪ/ *adj* gessoso

⚷ **challenge** /ˈtʃælɪndʒ/ **A** *n* sfida *f*; Mil intimazione *f* **B** *vt* sfidare; Mil intimare il chi va là a; fig mettere in dubbio ‹*statement*›

challenger /ˈtʃælɪndʒə(r)/ *n* sfidante *mf*

challenging /ˈtʃælɪndʒɪŋ/ *adj* ‹*job*› impegnativo

chamber /ˈtʃeɪmbə(r)/ *n* camera *f*

chambermaid *n* cameriera *f* ai piani

chamber music *n* musica *f* da camera

Chamber of Commerce *n* Camera *f* di Commercio

chamber orchestra *n* orchestra *f* da camera

chamber pot *n* vaso *m* da notte

chambers /ˈtʃeɪmbəz/ *npl* Jur studio *m* [legale]

chameleon /kəˈmiːlɪən/ *n* also fig camaleonte *m*

chamois[1] /ˈʃæmwɑː/ *n inv* (animal) camoscio *m*

chamois[2] /ˈʃæmɪ/ *n* **~ [leather]** [pelle *f* di] camoscio *m*

champagne /ʃæmˈpeɪn/ *n* champagne *m inv*

⚷ **champion** /ˈtʃæmpɪən/ **A** *n* Sport campione *m*; (of cause) difensore *m*, difenditrice *f* **B** *vt* (defend) difendere; (fight for) lottare per

championship /ˈtʃæmpɪənʃɪp/ *n* Sport campionato *m*

⚷ **chance** /tʃɑːns/ **A** *n* caso *m*; (possibility) possibilità *f*; (opportunity) occasione *f*; **by ~** per caso; **take a ~** provarci; **give somebody a second ~** dare un'altra possibilità a qualcuno **B** *attrib* fortuito **C** *vt* **if you ~ to see him** se ti capita di vederlo; **I'll ~ it** infml corro il rischio

chancel /ˈtʃɑːnsəl/ *n* Archit coro *m*

chancellor /ˈtʃɑːnsələ(r)/ *n* cancelliere *m*; Univ rettore *m*; **C~ of the Exchequer** ≈ ministro *m* del tesoro

chancy /ˈtʃɑːnsɪ/ *adj* rischioso

⚷ parola chiave

chandelier /ʃændəˈlɪə(r)/ *n* lampadario *m*

chandler /ˈtʃɑːndlə(r)/ *n* fornitore *m* navale

⚷ **change** /tʃeɪndʒ/ **A** *n* cambiamento *m*; (money) resto *m*; (small coins) spiccioli *mpl*; **for a ~** tanto per cambiare; **have a ~ of heart** cambiare idea; **a ~ of clothes** un cambio di vestiti; **~ of address** cambiamento *m* d'indirizzo; **a ~ of scene** also fig un cambiamento di scena; **the ~ [of life]** la menopausa **B** *vt* cambiare; (substitute) scambiare, for con; **~ one's clothes** cambiarsi [i vestiti]; **~ trains** cambiare treno **C** *vi* cambiare; (**~** clothes) cambiarsi; **all ~!** stazione terminale!

■ **change down** *vi* Auto passare alla marcia inferiore

■ **change up** *vi* Auto passare alla marcia superiore

changeability /tʃeɪndʒəˈbɪlɪtɪ/ *n* (of weather) instabilità *f*

changeable /ˈtʃeɪndʒəbl/ *adj* mutevole; ‹*weather*› variable

changeless /ˈtʃeɪndʒlɪs/ *adj* ‹*appearance*› inalterabile; ‹*character*› costante; ‹*law, routine*› immutabile

change machine *n* distributore *m* di monete

changeover /ˈtʃeɪndʒəʊvə(r)/ *n* (time period) periodo *m* di transizione; (transition) passaggio *m*; (of leaders) subentro *m*; (of employees, guards) cambio *m*; Sport (in relay) passaggio *m* del testimone; Sport (of ends) cambiamento *m*

changing /ˈtʃeɪndʒɪŋ/ *adj* in mutamento

changing room *n* camerino *m*; (for sports) spogliatoio *m*

⚷ **channel** /ˈtʃænl/ **A** *n* canale *m*; **the [English] C~** la Manica **B** *vt* (*pt/pp* **channelled**) **~ one's energies into something** convogliare le proprie energie in qualcosa

channel ferry *n* traghetto *m* attraverso la Manica

channel-hop *vi* BrE fare lo zapping

channel-hopping *n* BrE zapping *m inv*

Channel Islands *npl* Isole *fpl* del Canale

channel-surf *vi* AmE fare lo zapping

channel-surfing *n* AmE zapping *m inv*

Channel Tunnel *n* tunnel *m inv* sotto la Manica

chant /tʃɑːnt/ **A** *n* cantilena *f*; (of demonstrators) slogan *m inv* di protesta **B** *vt* cantare; ‹*demonstrators*› gridare **C** *vi* ‹*demonstrators*› gridare slogan di protesta

chaos /ˈkeɪɒs/ *n* caos *m*

chaotic /keɪˈɒtɪk/ *adj* caotico

chap /tʃæp/ *n* infml tipo *m*

chapel /ˈtʃæpl/ *n* cappella *f*

chaperone, chaperon /ˈʃæpərəʊn/ **A** *n* chaperon *m inv*

B *vt* fare da chaperon a ‹*person*›
chaplain /ˈtʃæplɪn/ *n* cappellano *m*
chapped /tʃæpt/ *adj* ‹*skin, lips*› screpolato
chapter /ˈtʃæptə(r)/ *n* capitolo *m*
char¹ /tʃɑː(r)/ *n* infml donna *f* delle pulizie
char² *vt* (*pt/pp* **charred**) (burn) carbonizzare
character /ˈkærɪktə(r)/ *n* carattere *m*; (in novel, play) personaggio *m*; **that's out of ~** non è da te/lui; **quite a ~** infml un tipo particolare
character actor *n* caratterista *mf*
character assassination *n* denigrazione *f*
characteristic /kærəktəˈrɪstɪk/ **A** *adj* caratteristico
B *n* caratteristica *f*
characteristically /kærəktəˈrɪstɪklɪ/ *adv* tipicamente
characterization /kærɪktəraɪˈzeɪʃn/ *n* caratterizzazione *f*
characterize /ˈkærɪktəraɪz/ *vt* caratterizzare
character reference *n* referenze *fpl* (*relative al carattere*)
charade /ʃəˈrɑːd/ *n* farsa *f*; **~s** sciarada *fsg*
charcoal /ˈtʃɑːkəʊl/ *n* carbonella *f*
charge /tʃɑːdʒ/ **A** *n* (cost) prezzo *m*; Electr, Mil carica *f*; Jur accusa *f*; **free of ~** gratuito; **be in ~** essere responsabile (**of** di); **take ~** assumersi la responsibilità; **take ~ of** occuparsi di
B *vt* far pagare ‹*fee*›; far pagare a ‹*person*›; Electr, Mil caricare; Jur accusare (**with** di); **~ somebody for something** far pagare qualcosa a qualcuno; **what do you ~?** quanto prende?; **~ it to my account** lo addebiti sul mio conto
C *vi* (attack) caricare
charge account *n* (in store) apertura *m* di credito presso un negozio
charge card *n* (credit card) carta *f* di addebito; (store card) carta *f* di credito [di un negozio]
charged /tʃɑːdʒd/ *adj* Phys carico; **emotionally ~** ‹*atmosphere*› carico di emozione
chargé d'affaires /ʃɑːʒeɪdæˈfeə(r)/ *n* incaricato *m* d'affari
charge hand *n* caposquadra *mf*
charge nurse *n* caposala *mf*
char-grilled /-ˈgrɪld/ *adj* alla brace
chariot /ˈtʃærɪət/ *n* cocchio *m*
charisma /kəˈrɪzmə/ *n* carisma *m*
charismatic /kærɪzˈmætɪk/ *adj* carismatico
charitable /ˈtʃærɪtəbl/ *adj* caritatevole; (kind) indulgente
charity /ˈtʃærətɪ/ *n* carità *f*; (organization) associazione *f* di beneficenza; **concert given for ~** concerto *m* di beneficenza; **live on ~** vivere di elemosina
charity box *n* (in church) cassetta *f* delle offerte
charity shop *n negozio* (*m*) *dell'usato a scopo di beneficenza*
charity work *n* lavoro *m* volontario (*per beneficenza*)
charlady /ˈtʃɑːleɪdɪ/ *n* BrE donna *f* delle pulizie
charlatan /ˈʃɑːlətən/ *n* ciarlatano, -a *mf*
charm /tʃɑːm/ **A** *n* fascino *m*; (object) ciondolo *m*
B *vt* affascinare
charmer /ˈtʃɑːmə(r)/ *n* **he's a real ~** è un vero seduttore
charming /ˈtʃɑːmɪŋ/ *adj* affascinante
charmingly /ˈtʃɑːmɪŋlɪ/ *adv* in modo affascinante
charred /tʃɑːd/ *adj* carbonizzato
chart /tʃɑːt/ *n* carta *f* nautica; (table) tabella *f*
charter /ˈtʃɑːtə(r)/ **A** *n* **~ [flight]** [volo *m*] charter *m inv*
B *vt* noleggiare
chartered accountant *n* commercialista *mf*
chartered flight *n* BrE volo *m* charter *inv*
chartered surveyor *n* BrE perito *m* edile
charter plane *n* BrE charter *m inv*
charwoman /ˈtʃɑːwʊmən/ *n* donna *f* delle pulizie
chase /tʃeɪs/ **A** *n* inseguimento *m*; **give ~** mettersi all'inseguimento
B *vt* inseguire
■ **chase away, chase off** *vt* cacciare via
■ **chase up** *vt* infml cercare
chaser /ˈtʃeɪsə(r)/ *n* infml (drink) *liquore* (*m*) *bevuto dopo la birra*
chasm /ˈkæz(ə)m/ *n* abisso *m*
chassis /ˈʃæsɪ/ (*pl* **chassis** /ˈʃæsɪz/) *n* telaio *m*
chaste /tʃeɪst/ *adj* casto
chasten /ˈtʃeɪs(ə)n/ *vt* castigare; **they looked suitably ~ed** avevano l'aria mortificata
chastise /tʃæˈstaɪz/ *vt* castigare
chastity /ˈtʃæstətɪ/ *n* castità *f*
chat /tʃæt/ **A** *n* chiacchierata *f*; **have a ~ with** fare quattro chiacchiere con; Comput chat *f inv*
B *vi* (*pt/pp* **chatted**) chiacchierare; Comput chattare
■ **chat up** *vt* abbordare
chatline *n* Teleph chat line *f inv*
chat room *n* Comput chat room *f inv*
chat show *n* talk show *m inv*
chat show host *n* presentatore, -trice *mf* di talk show
chattel /ˈtʃæt(ə)l/ *n* Jur **goods and ~s** beni *mpl* mobili
chatter /ˈtʃætə(r)/ **A** *n* chiacchiere *fpl*
B *vi* chiacchierare; ‹*teeth*› battere
chatterbox /ˈtʃætəbɒks/ *n* infml chiacchierone, -a *mf*
chatty /ˈtʃætɪ/ *adj* (**-ier, -iest**) chiacchierone; ‹*style*› familiare

C

chauffeur /ˈʃəʊfə(r)/ *n* autista *mf*
chauvinism /ˈʃəʊvɪnɪzm/ *n* sciovinismo *m*
chauvinist /ˈʃəʊvɪnɪst/ *n* sciovinista *mf*; **male ~** infml maschilista *m*
⚷ **cheap** /tʃiːp/ **A** *adj* a buon mercato; ‹*rate*› economico; (vulgar) grossolano; (of poor quality) scadente
B *adv* a buon mercato
cheapen /ˈtʃiːp(ə)n/ *vt* **~ oneself** screditarsi
cheaply /ˈtʃiːplɪ/ *adv* a buon mercato
cheap rate *adj & adv* Teleph a tariffa ridotta
cheat /tʃiːt/ **A** *n* imbroglione, -a *mf*; (at cards) baro *m*
B *vt* imbrogliare; **~ somebody out of something** sottrarre qualcosa a qualcuno con l'inganno
C *vi* imbrogliare; (at cards) barare
▪ **cheat on** *vt* infml tradire ‹*wife*›
Chechnya /ˌtʃetʃˈnjɑː/ *n* Cecenia *f*
check¹ /tʃek/ **A** *adj* ‹*pattern*› a quadri
B *n* disegno *m* a quadri
⚷ **check²** **A** *n* verifica *f*; (of tickets) controllo *m*; (in chess) scacco *m*; AmE (bill) conto *m*; AmE (cheque) assegno *m*; AmE (tick) segnetto *m*; **keep a ~ on** controllare; **keep in ~** tenere sotto controllo
B *vt* verificare; controllare ‹*tickets*›; (restrain) contenere; (stop) bloccare
C *vi* controllare; **~ on something** controllare qualcosa
▪ **check in** **A** *vi* registrarsi all'arrivo (*in albergo*); Aeron fare il check-in
B *vt* registrare all'arrivo (*in albergo*)
▪ **check off** *vt* spuntare ‹*item on list*›
▪ **check out** **A** *vi* (of hotel) saldare il conto
B *vt* infml (investigate) controllare
▪ **check up** *vi* accertarsi
▪ **check up on** *vt* prendere informazioni su
checkbook *n* AmE libretto *m* d'assegni
checked /tʃekt/ *adj* a quadri
checkered /ˈtʃekəd/ *adj* AmE ‹*cloth, pattern*› a quadretti; ‹*career*› con alti e bassi
checkers /ˈtʃekəz/ *n* AmE dama *f*
check-in *n* accettazione *f*, check-in *m inv*
check-in desk *n* banco *m* dell'accettazione, banco *m* del check-in
checking account /ˈtʃekɪŋ/ *n* AmE conto *m* corrente
check-in time *n* check-in *m inv*
checklist *n* lista *f* di controllo
check mark *n* AmE segnetto *m*
checkmate *int* scacco matto
checkout *n* (in supermarket) cassa *f*
checkout assistant, checkout operator *n* BrE cassiere, -a *mf*
checkpoint *n* posto *m* di blocco
checkroom *n* AmE deposito *m* bagagli
check-up *n* Med visita *f* di controllo, check-up *m inv*

⚷ parola chiave

Cheddar /ˈtʃedə(r)/ *n formaggio (m) semi-stagionato*
cheek /tʃiːk/ *n* guancia *f*; (impudence) sfacciataggine *f*
cheekbone /ˈtʃiːkbəʊn/ *n* zigomo *m*
cheekily /ˈtʃiːkɪlɪ/ *adv* sfacciatamente
cheeky /ˈtʃiːkɪ/ *adj* sfacciato
cheep /tʃiːp/ *vi* pigolare
cheer /tʃɪə(r)/ **A** *n* evviva *m inv*; **three ~s** tre urrà; **~s!** salute!; (goodbye) arrivederci!; (thanks) grazie!
B *vt & vi* acclamare
▪ **cheer up** **A** *vt* tirare su [di morale]
B *vi* tirarsi su [di morale]; **~ up!** su con la vita!
cheerful /ˈtʃɪəfʊl/ *adj* allegro
cheerfully /ˈtʃɪəfʊlɪ/ *adv* allegramente; **I could ~ strangle him!** lo strangolerei volentieri!
cheerfulness /ˈtʃɪəfʊlnɪs/ *n* allegria *f*
cheerily /ˈtʃɪərɪlɪ/ *adv* allegramente
cheering /ˈtʃɪərɪŋ/ *n* acclamazione *f*
cheerio /tʃɪərɪˈəʊ/ *int* infml arrivederci
cheerleader /ˈtʃɪəliːdə(r)/ *n* leader *mf* dei tifosi
cheerless /ˈtʃɪəlɪs/ *adj* triste, tetro
cheery /ˈtʃɪərɪ/ *adj* allegro
cheese /tʃiːz/ *n* formaggio *m*
▪ **cheese off**: *vt* infml **be ~d off with one's job** essere stufo del proprio lavoro; **I'm really ~d off about it** ne ho le scatole piene
cheeseboard *n* (object) vassoio *m* dei formaggi; (selection) piatto *m* di formaggi
cheeseburger *n* cheeseburger *m inv*
cheesecake *n* dolce *m* al formaggio
cheesecloth *n* mussola *f*, tela *f* indiana
cheese counter *n* banco *m* dei formaggi
cheesy /ˈtʃiːzɪ/ *adj* ‹*smell*› di formaggio; ‹*grin*› smagliante
cheetah /ˈtʃiːtə/ *n* ghepardo *m*
chef /ʃef/ **A** *n* cuoco, -a *mf*, chef *m inv*
B *vi* (*pt/pp* **cheffed**) infml fare lo chef
chemical /ˈkemɪkl/ **A** *adj* chimico
B *n* prodotto *m* chimico
chemically /ˈkemɪklɪ/ *adv* chimicamente
chemise /ʃəˈmiːz/ *n* (undergarment) sottoveste *f inv*; (dress) chemisier *m inv*
chemist /ˈkemɪst/ *n* (pharmacist) farmacista *mf*; (scientist) chimico, -a *mf*
chemistry /ˈkemɪstrɪ/ *n* chimica *f*
chemist's, chemist's shop *n* farmacia *f*
chemotherapy /kiːməʊˈθerəpɪ/ *n* chemioterapia *f*
cheque /tʃek/ *n* assegno *m*
chequebook /ˈtʃekbʊk/ *n* libretto *m* degli assegni
cheque card *n* carta *f* assegni
chequer /ˈtʃekə(r)/ *n* (square) scacco *m*; (pattern) motivo *m* a scacchi; (in game) pedina *f*

chequered /'tʃekəd/ *adj* (patterned) a scacchi; fig ‹*career, history*› movimentato
chequers /'tʃekəz/ *n* dama *f*
cherish /'tʃerɪʃ/ *vt* curare teneramente; (love) avere caro; nutrire ‹*hope*›
cherry /'tʃerɪ/ *n* ciliegia *f*; (tree) ciliegio *m*
cherry brandy *n* cherry-brandy *m inv*
cherry-pick *vt* scegliere accuratamente
cherry tree *n* ciliegio *m*
cherub /'tʃerəb/ *n* cherubino *m*
chervil /'tʃɜːvɪl/ *n* cerfoglio *m*
chess /tʃes/ *n* scacchi *mpl*
chessboard *n* scacchiera *f*
chessman *n* pezzo *m* degli scacchi
chess player *n* scacchista *mf*
chess set *n* scacchi *mpl*
chest /tʃest/ *n* petto *m*; (box) cassapanca *f*; **get something off one's ~** fig levarsi un peso [dallo stomaco]
chest freezer *n* freezer *m inv* orizzontale, congelatore *m* orizzontale
chestnut /'tʃesnʌt/ *n* castagna *f*; (tree) castagno *m*
chest of drawers *n* cassettone *m*, comò *m*
chesty /'tʃestɪ/ *adj* ‹*person*› che soffre di bronchite; ‹*cough*› bronchitico
chew /tʃuː/ *vt* masticare
■ **chew over** *vt* infml (think about carefully) rimuginare su
chewing gum /'tʃuːɪŋ/ *n* gomma *f* da masticare
chewy /'tʃuːɪ/ *adj* ‹*meat*› legnoso; ‹*toffee*› gommoso
chic /ʃiːk/ *adj* chic *inv*
chick /tʃɪk/ *n* pulcino *m*; infml (girl) ragazza *f*
chicken /'tʃɪkn/ **A** *n* pollo *m*
B *attrib* ‹*soup, casserole*› di pollo
C *adj* infml fifone
■ **chicken out**: *vi* infml **he ~ed out** gli è venuta fifa
chicken breast *n* petto *m* di pollo
chicken curry *n* pollo *m* al curry
chicken feed *n* mangime *m* per i polli; infml (paltry sum) miseria *f*
chicken livers *npl* fegatini *mpl* di pollo
chicken noodle soup *n* vermicelli *mpl* in brodo di pollo
chickenpox *n* varicella *f*
chicken wire *n* rete *f* metallica (*a maglia esagonale*)
chick flick *n* infml *film* (*m inv*) *mirato ad un pubblico femminile*
chick lit *n* infml *romanzi* (*mpl*) *mirati ad un pubblico femminile*
chickpea /'tʃɪkpiː/ *n* cece *m*
chicory /'tʃɪkərɪ/ *n* cicoria *f*
chief /tʃiːf/ **A** *adj* principale
B *n* capo *m*
chief executive *n* direttore, -trice *mf* generale
chief executive officer *n* direttore, -trice *mf* generale
chief inspector *n* BrE (of police) ispettore *m* capo
chiefly /'tʃiːflɪ/ *adv* principalmente
chief of police *n* capo *m* della polizia
Chief of Staff *n* Mil capo *m* di stato maggiore; (of the White House) segretario *m* generale
chief superintendent *n* BrE (of police) commissario *m* capo
chiffon /'ʃɪfɒn/ **A** *n* chiffon *m*
B *adj* ‹*dress, scarf*› di chiffon
chilblain /'tʃɪlbleɪn/ *n* gelone *m*
child /tʃaɪld/ *n* (*pl* **~ren**) bambino, -a *mf*; (son/daughter) figlio, -a *mf*
child abuse *n* violenza *f* sui minori; (sexual) violenza *f* sessuale sui minori
childbearing *n* gravidanza *f*; **of ~ age** in età feconda
child benefit *n* BrE assegni *mpl* familiari
childbirth *n* parto *m*
childcare *n* (bringing up children) educazione *f* dei bambini; (nurseries etc) strutture *fpl* di assistenza ai bambini
childhood /'tʃaɪldhʊd/ *n* infanzia *f*
childish /'tʃaɪldɪʃ/ *adj* infantile
childishness /'tʃaɪldɪʃnɪs/ *n* puerilità *f*
childless /'tʃaɪldlɪs/ *adj* senza figli
childlike /'tʃaɪldlaɪk/ *adj* ingenuo
child-minder *n* baby-sitter *mf inv*
child molester *n* molestatore, -trice *mf* di bambini
child pornography *n* pedopornografia *f*
child prodigy *n* bambino, -a *mf* prodigio *inv*
child-proof *adj* ‹*container*› a prova di bambino; **~ lock** sicura *f* a prova di bambino
children /'tʃɪldrən/ *npl* ▶ **child**
children's home *n* istituto *m* per l'infanzia
child seat *n* seggiolino *m* per bambini
Chile /'tʃɪlɪ/ *n* Cile *m*
Chilean /'tʃɪlɪən/ *adj & n* cileno, -a *mf*
chill /tʃɪl/ **A** *n* freddo *m*; (illness) infreddatura *f*
B *vt* raffreddare
■ **chill out** *vi* (relax) rilassarsi
chilli /'tʃɪlɪ/ *n* (*pl* **-es**) **~ [pepper]** peperoncino *m*
chilly /'tʃɪlɪ/ *adj* freddo
chime /tʃaɪm/ *vi* suonare
chimera /kɪ'mɪərə/ *n* (beast, idea) chimera *f*
chimney /'tʃɪmnɪ/ *n* camino *m*
chimney breast *n* bocca *f* del camino
chimney pot *n* comignolo *m*
chimney sweep *n* spazzacamino *m*
chimp /tʃɪmp/ *n* infml scimpanzé *m*

C

chimpanzee /tʃɪmpæn'ziː/ *n* scimpanzé *m inv*
chin /tʃɪn/ *n* mento *m*
china *n* porcellana *f*
China /'tʃaɪnə/ *n* Cina *f*
China Sea *n* Mar *m* Cinese
China tea *n* tè *m* cinese
Chinatown *n* quartiere *m* cinese
🔑 **Chinese** /tʃaɪ'niːz/ *adj & n* cinese *mf*; (language) cinese *m*; **the ~** *pl* i cinesi
Chinese lantern *n* lanterna *f* cinese
chink[1] /tʃɪŋk/ *n* (slit) fessura *f*
chink[2] **A** *n* (noise) tintinnio *m*
B *vi* tintinnare
chinos /'tʃiːnəʊz/ *npl* pantaloni *mpl* cachi di cotone
chintz /tʃɪnts/ *n* chintz *m inv*
chip /tʃɪp/ **A** *n* (fragment) scheggia *f*; (in china, paintwork) scheggiatura *f*; Comput chip *m inv*; (in gambling) fiche *f inv*; **~s** *pl* BrE Culin patatine *fpl* fritte; AmE Culin patatine *fpl*; **have a ~ on one's shoulder** avere un complesso di inferiorità
B *vt* (*pt/pp* **chipped**) (damage) scheggiare
■ **chip in** infml *vi* intromettersi; (with money) contribuire
chip and PIN *n sistema (m) di pagamento con carta di credito in cui il possessore della carta deve digitare il proprio PIN invece che apporre una firma*
chipboard /'tʃɪpbɔːd/ *n* truciolato *m*
chipmunk /'tʃɪpmʌŋk/ *n* tamia *m inv*
chip pan *n* friggitrice *f*
chipped /tʃɪpt/ *adj* (damaged) scheggiato
chippings /'tʃɪpɪŋz/ *npl* (on road) breccia *f*; **'loose ~'** 'attenzione: breccia'
chippy /'tʃɪpɪ/ *n* BrE infml (chip shop) negozio *m* di fish and chips
chip shop *n* BrE negozio *m* di fish and chips
chiropodist /kɪ'rɒpədɪst/ *n* podiatra *mf inv*
chiropody /kɪ'rɒpədɪ/ *n* podiatria *f*
chiropractor /'kaɪərəʊpræktə(r)/ *n* chiropratico, -a *mf*
chirp /tʃɜːp/ *vi* cinguettare; ‹*cricket*› fare cri cri
chirpy /'tʃɜːpɪ/ *adj* infml pimpante
chisel /'tʃɪzl/ **A** *n* scalpello *m*
B *vt* (*pt/pp* **chiselled**) scalpellare
chit /tʃɪt/ *n* bigliettino *m*
chit-chat /'tʃɪ(t)tʃæt/ *n* infml chiacchiere *fpl*; **spend one's time in idle ~** infml perdere tempo in chiacchiere
chivalrous /'ʃɪvlrəs/ *adj* cavalleresco
chivalrously /'ʃɪvlrəslɪ/ *adv* con cavalleria
chivalry /'ʃɪvlrɪ/ *n* cavalleria *f*
chives /tʃaɪvz/ *npl* erba *f* cipollina
chlorine /'klɔːriːn/ *n* cloro *m*
chlorofluorocarbon /klɔːrəʊfluərəʊ'kɑːb(ə)n/ *n* clorofluorocarburo *m*
chloroform /'klɒrəfɔːm/ *n* cloroformio *m*
chlorophyll /'klɒrəfɪl/ *n* clorofilla *f*
choc ice *n* BrE gelato *m* ricoperto di cioccolato
chock /tʃɒk/ *n* zeppa *f*
chock-a-block /tʃɒkə'blɒk/, **chock-full** /tʃɒk'fʊl/ *adj* pieno zeppo
chocolate /'tʃɒkələt/ *n* cioccolato *m*; (drink) cioccolata *f*; **a ~** un cioccolatino
🔑 **choice** /tʃɔɪs/ **A** *n* scelta *f*
B *adj* scelto
choir /'kwaɪə(r)/ *n* coro *m*
choirboy /'kwaɪəbɔɪ/ *n* corista *m*
choirgirl /'kwaɪəgɜːl/ *n* corista *f*
choke /tʃəʊk/ **A** *n* Auto aria *f*
B *vt & vi* soffocare; **I ~d on a fish bone** mi è rimasta in gola una lisca
■ **choke back** *vt* soffocare ‹*tears, sob*›
choker /'tʃəʊkə(r)/ *n* girocollo *m*
cholera /'kɒlərə/ *n* colera *m*
cholesterol /kə'lestərɒl/ *n* colesterolo *m*
chomp /tʃɒmp/
■ **chomp on** *vt* infml masticare rumorosamente
🔑 **choose** /tʃuːz/ *vt & vi* (*pt* **chose**, *pp* **chosen**) scegliere; **~ to do something** scegliere di fare qualcosa; **as you ~** come vuoi
choosy /'tʃuːzɪ/ *adj* infml difficile
chop /tʃɒp/ **A** *n* (blow) colpo *m* (*d'ascia*); Culin costata *f*; **get the ~** infml ‹*employee*› essere licenziato; ‹*project*› essere bocciato
B *vt* (*pt/pp* **chopped**) tagliare
■ **chop down** *vt* abbattere ‹*tree*›
■ **chop off** *vt* spaccare
chopper /'tʃɒpə(r)/ *n* accetta *f*; infml elicottero *m*
chopping block *n* ceppo *m*; **put one's head on the ~** fig esporsi a rischi
chopping board *n* tagliere *m*
chopping knife *n* coltello *m*
choppy /'tʃɒpɪ/ *adj* increspato
chopsticks /'tʃɒpstɪks/ *npl* bastoncini *mpl* cinesi
choral /'kɔːrəl/ *adj* corale; **~ society** coro *m*
chord /kɔːd/ *n* Mus corda *f*
chore /tʃɔː(r)/ *n* corvè *f*; **[household] ~s** faccende *fpl* domestiche
choreograph /'kɒrɪəgrɑːf, AmE -græf/ *vt* coreografare
choreographer /kɒrɪ'ɒgrəfə(r)/ *n* coreografo, -a *mf*
choreography /kɒrɪ'ɒgrəfɪ/ *n* coreografia *f*
chorister /'kɒrɪstə(r)/ *n* corista *mf*
chortle /'tʃɔːtl/ *vi* ridacchiare
chorus /'kɔːrəs/ *n* coro *m*; (of song) ritornello *m*
chorus girl *n* ballerina *f* di varietà
chose, chosen /tʃəʊz, 'tʃəʊzn/ ▶ **choose**
chowder /'tʃaʊdə(r)/ *n* zuppa *m* di pesce

🔑 parola chiave

chow mein /tʃaʊˈmeɪn/ *n piatto (m) cinese di spaghettini fritti con gamberetti, ecc. e verdure*
Christ /kraɪst/ *n* Cristo *m*; ~ **Almighty!** infml porca miseria!
christen /ˈkrɪs(ə)n/ *vt* battezzare
christening /ˈkrɪsnɪŋ/ *n* battesimo *m*
Christian /ˈkrɪstʃən/ *adj & n* cristiano, -a *mf*
Christianity /krɪstɪˈænətɪ/ *n* cristianesimo *m*
Christian name *n* nome *m* di battesimo
Christmas /ˈkrɪsməs/ **A** *n* Natale *m* **B** *attrib* di Natale
Christmas box *n* BrE mancia *f* natalizia
Christmas card *n* biglietto *m* d'auguri di Natale
Christmas carol *n* canto *m* natalizio, canto *m* di Natale
Christmas cracker *n tubo (m) di cartone colorato contente una sorpresa*
Christmas Day *n* il giorno di Natale
Christmas Eve *n* la vigilia di Natale
Christmas present *n* regalo *m* di Natale
Christmas stocking *n* calza *f* (*per i doni di Babbo Natale*)
Christmas tree *n* albero *m* di Natale
chrome /krəʊm/ **chromium** /ˈkrəʊmɪəm/ *n* cromo *m*
chromium-plated /-ˈpleɪtɪd/ *adj* cromato
chromosome /ˈkrəʊməsəʊm/ *n* cromosoma *m*
chronic /ˈkrɒnɪk/ *adj* cronico
chronicle /ˈkrɒnɪkl/ *n* cronaca *f*
chronological /krɒnəˈlɒdʒɪkl/ *adj* cronologico
chronologically /krɒnəˈlɒdʒɪklɪ/ *adv* ‹*ordered*› in ordine cronologico
chrysalis /ˈkrɪsəlɪs/ *n* crisalide *f*
chrysanthemum /krɪˈsænθəməm/ *n* crisantemo *m*
chubby /ˈtʃʌbɪ/ *adj* (**-ier**, **-iest**) paffuto
chuck /tʃʌk/ *vt* infml buttare
■ **chuck in** *vt* infml mollare ‹*job, boyfriend*›
■ **chuck out** *vt* infml buttare via ‹*object*›; buttare fuori ‹*person*›
■ **chuck up** *vt* infml vomitare
chuckle /ˈtʃʌk(ə)l/ *vi* ridacchiare
chuffed /tʃʌft/ *adj* infml felice come una Pasqua
chug /tʃʌg/ *vi* **the train ~ged into/out of the station** il treno è entrato nella/uscito dalla stazione sbuffando
chum /tʃʌm/ *n* infml amico, -a *mf*
chummy /ˈtʃʌmɪ/ *adj* infml **be ~ with** essere amico di
chump /tʃʌmp/ *n* infml zuccone, -a *mf*; Culin braciola *f*
chunk /tʃʌŋk/ *n* grosso pezzo *m*
chunky /ˈtʃʌŋkɪ/ *adj* ‹*sweater*› di lana grossa; ‹*jewellery*› massiccio; infml ‹*person*› tarchiato
Chunnel /ˈtʃʌnl/ *n* BrE infml tunnel *m inv* sotto la Manica
church /tʃɜːtʃ/ *n* chiesa *f*
churchgoer *n* praticante *mf*
church hall *n* sala *f* parrocchiale
churchyard /ˈtʃɜːtʃjɑːd/ *n* cimitero *m*
churlish /ˈtʃɜːlɪʃ/ *adj* sgarbato
churn /tʃɜːn/ **A** *n* zangola *f*; (for milk) bidone *m* **B** *vt* fare ‹*butter*›; far rivoltare ‹*stomach*›
■ **churn out** *vt* sfornare ‹*novels, products*›
■ **churn up** *vt* agitare ‹*water*›
chute /ʃuːt/ *n* scivolo *m*; (for rubbish) canale *m* di scarico
chutney /ˈtʃʌtnɪ/ *n salsa (f) piccante a base di frutti e spezie*
CIA *n abbr* AmE (**Central Intelligence Agency**) CIA *f*
cicada /sɪˈkɑːdə, AmE -ˈkeɪdə/ *n* cicala *f*
CID *abbr* (**Criminal Investigation Department**) *dipartimento (m) di investigazione criminale*
cider /ˈsaɪdə(r)/ *n* sidro *m*
cigar /sɪˈgɑː(r)/ *n* sigaro *m*
cigarette /sɪgəˈret/ *n* sigaretta *f*
cigarette butt, **cigarette end** *n* cicca *f*, mozzicone *m* di sigaretta
cigarette lighter *n* accendino *m*
cinch /sɪntʃ/ *n* infml **it's a ~** è un gioco da ragazzi
cinder /ˈsɪndə(r)/ *n* (glowing) brace *f*; **burn something to a ~** carbonizzare qualcosa
Cinderella /sɪndəˈrelə/ *n* Cenerentola *f*
cinder track *n* pista *f* di cenere
cine camera /ˈsɪnɪ-/ *n* cinepresa *f*
cine film *n* filmino *m* a passo ridotto
cinema /ˈsɪnɪmə/ *n* cinema *m inv*
cinema complex *n* cinema *m inv* multisale
cinemagoer /ˈsɪnɪməgəʊə(r)/ *n* (spectator) spettatore, -trice *mf*; (regular) cinefilo, -a *mf*
cinematography /sɪnəməˈtɒgrəfɪ/ *n* cinematografia *f*
cinnamon /ˈsɪnəmən/ *n* cannella *f*
cipher /ˈsaɪfə(r)/ *n* (code) cifre *fpl*; fig nullità *f*
circa /ˈsɜːkə/ *prep* circa
circle /ˈsɜːkl/ **A** *n* cerchio *m*; Theat galleria *f*; **in a ~** in cerchio **B** *vt* girare intorno a; cerchiare ‹*mistake*› **C** *vi* descrivere dei cerchi
circuit /ˈsɜːkɪt/ *n* circuito *m*; (lap) giro *m*
circuit board *n* circuito *m* stampato
circuit breaker *n* salvavita *m*
circuitous /səˈkjuːɪtəs/ *adj* **~ route** percorso *m* lungo e indiretto
circular /ˈsɜːkjʊlə(r)/ *adj & n* circolare *f*; **~ letter** *n* circolare *f*
circular saw *n* sega *f* circolare
circulate /ˈsɜːkjʊleɪt/ **A** *vt* far circolare

C

B *vi* circolare
circulation /sɜːkjʊˈleɪʃn/ *n* circolazione *f*; (of newspaper) tiratura *f*
circulatory /sɜːkjʊˈleɪtərɪ/ *adj* Med circolatorio
circumcise /ˈsɜːkəmsaɪz/ *vt* circoncidere
circumcision /sɜːkəmˈsɪʒn/ *n* circoncisione *f*
circumference /ʃəˈkʌmfərəns/ *n* circonferenza *f*
circumflex /ˈsɜːkəmfleks/ *n* accento *m* circonflesso
circumnavigate /sɜːkəmˈnævɪgeɪt/ *vt* doppiare ‹*cape*›; circumnavigare ‹*world*›
circumnavigation /sɜːkəmnævɪˈgeɪʃn/ *n* circumnavigazione *f*
circumspect /ˈsɜːkəmspekt/ *adj* circospetto
circumspectly /ˈsɜːkəmspektlɪ/ *adv* in modo circospetto
circumstance /ˈsɜːkəmstəns/ *n* circostanza *f*; **~s** *pl* (financial) condizioni *fpl* finanziarie
circumstantial /sɜːkəmˈstænʃl/ *adj* Jur ‹*evidence*› indiziario; (detailed) circostanziato
circus /ˈsɜːkəs/ *n* circo *m*
cirrhosis /sɪˈrəʊsɪs/ *n* cirrosi *f inv*
CIS *abbr* (**Commonwealth of Independent States**) CSI *f*
cistern /ˈsɪstən/ *n* (tank) cisterna *f*; (of WC) serbatoio *m*
citadel /ˈsɪtədel/ *n* cittadella *f*
cite /saɪt/ *vt* citare
citizen /ˈsɪtɪzn/ *n* cittadino, -a *mf*; (of town) abitante *mf*
Citizens' Advice Bureau *n ufficio* (*m*) *di consulenza legale gratuita per i cittadini*
citizen's arrest *n* arresto *m* effettuato da un privato cittadino
citizens' band *n* Radio banda *f* cittadina
citizenship /ˈsɪtɪznʃɪp/ *n* cittadinanza *f*
citric acid /sɪtrɪkˈæsɪd/ acido *m* citrico
citrus /ˈsɪtrəs/ *n* **~ [fruit]** agrume *m*
city /ˈsɪtɪ/ *n* città *f*; **the C~** la City [di Londra]
city centre *n* BrE centro *m* [della città]
city slicker *n* infml cittadino *m* sofisticato
civic /ˈsɪvɪk/ **A** *adj* civico
B *npl* **~s** *npl* educazione *fsg* civica
civic centre *n* centro *m* municipale
civil /ˈʃɪvl/ *adj* civile
civil engineer *n* ingegnere *m* civile
civil engineering *n* ingegneria *f* civile
civilian /sɪˈvɪljən/ **A** *adj* civile; **in ~ clothes** in borghese
B *n* civile *mf*
civility /sɪˈvɪlətɪ/ *n* cortesia *f*
civilization /sɪvɪlaɪˈzeɪʃn/ *n* civiltà *f*
civilize /ˈsɪvɪlaɪz/ *vt* civilizzare
civilized /ˈsɪvɪlaɪzd/ *adj* ‹*country*› civilizzato; ‹*person, behaviour*› civile; **become ~** civilizzarsi
civil law *n* diritto *m* civile
civil liability *n* Jur responsabilità *f* civile
civil liberty *n* libertà *f* civile
civilly /ˈsɪvɪlɪ/ *adv* civilmente
civil partner *n* partner *mf* civile
civil rights **A** *npl* diritti *mpl* civili
B *attrib* ‹*march, activist*› per i diritti civili
civil servant *n* impiegato, -a *mf* statale
Civil Service *n* pubblica amministrazione *f*
civil war *n* guerra *f* civile
civil wedding *n* matrimonio *m* civile
civvies /ˈsɪvɪz/ *npl* infml **in ~** in borghese
CJD *n abbr* (**Creutzfeldt-Jakob disease**) morbo *m* di Creutzfeldt Jakob
cl *abbr* (**centilitre(s)**) cl
clad /klæd/ *adj* vestito (**in** di)
cladding /ˈklædɪŋ/ *n* rivestimento *m*
claim /kleɪm/ **A** *n* richiesta *f*; (right) diritto *m*; (assertion) dichiarazione *f*; **lay ~ to something** rivendicare qualcosa
B *vt* richiedere; reclamare ‹*lost property*›; rivendicare ‹*ownership*›; **~ that** sostenere che
■ **claim back** *vt* reclamare ‹*money*›
claimant /ˈkleɪmənt/ *n* richiedente *mf*; (to throne) pretendente *mf*
claim form *n* modulo *m* di richiesta
clairvoyant /kleəˈvɔɪənt/ *n* chiaroveggente *mf*
clam /klæm/ *n* Culin vongola *f*
■ **clam up** *vi* zittirsi
clamber /ˈklæmbə(r)/ *vi* arrampicarsi
clammy /ˈklæmɪ/ *adj* (**-ier, -iest**) appiccicaticcio
clamour /ˈklæmə(r)/ **A** *n* (noise) clamore *m*; (protest) rimostranza *f*
B *vi* **~ for** chiedere a gran voce
clamp /klæmp/ **A** *n* morsa *f*
B *vt* ammorsare; Auto mettere i ceppi bloccaruote a
■ **clamp down** *vi* infml essere duro
■ **clamp down on** *vt* reprimere
clampdown *n* fig giro *m* di vite
clan /klæn/ *n* clan *m inv*
clandestine /klænˈdestɪn/ *adj* clandestino
clang /klæŋ/ *n* suono *m* metallico
clanger /ˈklæŋə(r)/ *n* infml gaffe *f inv*
clank /klæŋk/ **A** *n* rumore *m* metallico
B *vi* fare un rumore metallico
clannish /ˈklænɪʃ/ *adj* derog ‹*family, profession*› chiuso
clap /klæp/ **A** *n* **give somebody a ~** applaudire qualcuno; **~ of thunder** tuono *m*
B *vt & vi* (*pt/pp* **clapped**) applaudire; **~ one's hands** applaudire
clapboard /ˈklæpbɔːd/ **A** *n* AmE rivestimento *m* di legno
B *attrib* AmE rivestito di legno

parola chiave

clapped out /klæpt/ *adj* infml (past it) sfinito; (exhausted) stanco morto; ‹*car, machine*› scassato
clapping /ˈklæpɪŋ/ *n* applausi *mpl*
claptrap /ˈklæptræp/ *n* infml sciocchezze *fpl*
claret /ˈklærət/ *n* claret *m inv*
clarification /klærɪfɪˈkeɪʃn/ *n* chiarimento *m*
clarify /ˈklærɪfaɪ/ *vt & vi* (*pt/pp* **-ied**) chiarire
clarinet /klærɪˈnet/ *n* clarinetto *m*
clarinettist /klærɪˈnetɪst/ *n* clarinettista *mf*
clarity /ˈklærətɪ/ *n* chiarezza *f*
clash /klæʃ/ **A** *n* scontro *m*; (noise) fragore *m* **B** *vi* scontrarsi; ‹*colours*› stonare; ‹*events*› coincidere
clasp /klɑːsp/ **A** *n* chiusura *f* **B** *vt* agganciare; (hold) stringere
class /klɑːs/ **A** *n* classe *f*; (lesson) corso *m* **B** *vt* classificare
class-conscious *adj* classista
class consciousness *n* classismo *m*
classic /ˈklæsɪk/ **A** *adj* classico **B** *n* classico *m*; **~s** *pl* Univ lettere *fpl* classiche
classical /ˈklæsɪk(ə)l/ *adj* classico
classification /klæsɪfɪˈkeɪʃn/ *n* classificazione *f*
classified /ˈklæsɪfaɪd/ *adj* (secret) riservato
classified ad /klæsɪfaɪdˈæd/ *n* annuncio *m*
classified section *n* pagina *f* degli annunci
classify /ˈklæsɪfaɪ/ *vt* (*pt/pp* **-ied**) classificare
classmate *n* compagno, -a *mf* di classe
classroom *n* aula *f*
class system *n* sistema *m* classista
classy /ˈklɑːsɪ/ *adj* (**-ier, -iest**) infml d'alta classe
clatter /ˈklætə(r)/ **A** *n* fracasso *m* **B** *vi* far fracasso
clause /klɔːz/ *n* clausola *f*; Gram preposizione *f*
claustrophobia /klɒstrəˈfəʊbɪə/ *n* claustrofobia *f*
claustrophobic /klɒstrəˈfəʊbɪk/ *adj* claustrofobico
clavichord /ˈklævɪkɔːd/ *n* clavicordo *m*
clavicle /ˈklævɪkl/ *n* clavicola *f*
claw /klɔː/ **A** *n* artiglio *m*; (of crab, lobster & tool) tenaglia *f* **B** *vt* ‹*cat*› graffiare
clay /kleɪ/ *n* argilla *f*
clayey /ˈkleɪɪ/ *adj* ‹*soil*› argilloso
clay pigeon shooting *n* tiro *m* al piattello
clean /kliːn/ **A** *adj* pulito, lindo **B** *adv* completamente **C** *vt* pulire ‹*shoes, windows*›; **~ one's teeth** lavarsi i denti; **have a coat ~ed** portare un cappotto in lavanderia
■ **clean out** *vt* ripulire ‹*room*›; **be ~ed out** fig (have no money) essere senza un soldo
■ **clean up** **A** *vt* pulire **B** *vi* (far) pulizia
clean-cut *adj* ‹*image, person*› rispettabile
cleaner /ˈkliːnə(r)/ *n* uomo *m* donna *f* delle pulizie; (substance) detersivo *m*; **[dry] ~'s** lavanderia *f*, tintoria *f*
cleaning /ˈkliːnɪŋ/ *n* pulizia *f*; **do the ~** fare le pulizie
cleaning lady *n* donna *f* delle pulizie
cleaning product *n* detergente *m*
cleanliness /ˈklenlɪnɪs/ *n* pulizia *f*
clean-living /-ˈlɪvɪŋ/ **A** *n* vita *f* integra **B** *adj* ‹*person*› integro
cleanse /klenz/ *vt* pulire
cleanser /ˈklenzə(r)/ *n* detergente *m*
clean-shaven /-ˈʃeɪvən/ *adj* sbarbato
clean sheet *n* **start with a ~** fig voltare pagina
cleansing cream /ˈklenzɪŋ/ *n* latte *m* detergente
clear /klɪə(r)/ **A** *adj* chiaro; ‹*conscience*› pulito; ‹*road*› libero; ‹*profit, advantage, majority*› netto; ‹*sky*› sereno; ‹*water*› limpido; ‹*glass*› trasparente; **make something ~** mettere qualcosa in chiaro; **have I made myself ~?** mi sono fatto capire?; **I'm not ~ about what I have to do** non mi è ben chiaro quello che devo fare; **five ~ days** cinque giorni buoni; **be in the ~** essere a posto **B** *adv* **stand ~ of** allontanarsi da; **keep ~ of** tenersi alla larga da **C** *vt* sgombrare ‹*room, street*›; sparecchiare ‹*table*›; (acquit) scagionare; (authorize) autorizzare; scavalcare senza toccare ‹*fence, wall*›; guadagnare ‹*sum of money*›; passare ‹*Customs*›; **~ one's throat** schiarirsi la gola **D** *vi* ‹*face, sky*› rasserenarsi; ‹*fog*› dissiparsi
■ **clear away** *vt* metter via
■ **clear off** *vi* infml filar via
■ **clear out** **A** *vt* sgombrare **B** *vi* infml filar via
■ **clear up** **A** *vt* (tidy) mettere a posto; chiarire ‹*mystery*› **B** *vi* ‹*weather*› schiarirsi
clearance /ˈklɪərəns/ *n* (space) spazio *m* libero; (authorization) autorizzazione *f*; Customs sdoganamento *m*
clearance sale *n* liquidazione *f*
clear-cut *adj* ‹*plan, division*› ben definito; ‹*problem, rule*› chiaro; ‹*difference, outline*› netto; **the matter is not so ~** la faccenda non è così semplice
clear-headed /-ˈhedɪd/ *adj* lucido
clearing /ˈklɪərɪŋ/ *n* radura *f*
clearly /ˈklɪəlɪ/ *adv* chiaramente
clear-out /ˈklɪəraʊt/ *n* ripulita *f*
clear-sighted /-ˈsaɪtɪd/ *adj* perspicace
clearway /ˈklɪəweɪ/ *n* Auto strada *f* con divieto di sosta

C

cleavage /ˈkliːvɪdʒ/ *n* (woman's) décolleté *m inv*
cleave /kliːv/ *vt* spaccare
cleaver /ˈkliːvə(r)/ *n* mannaia *f*
clef /klef/ *n* Mus chiave *f*
cleft /kleft/ *n* fenditura *f*
clemency /ˈklemənsɪ/ *n* clemenza *f*
clement /ˈklemənt/ *adj* clemente
clench /klentʃ/ *vt* serrare
clergy /ˈklɜːdʒɪ/ *npl* clero *m*
clergyman /ˈklɜːdʒɪmən/ *n* ecclesiastico *m*
cleric /ˈklerɪk/ *n* ecclesiastico *m*
clerical /ˈklerɪkl/ *adj* impiegatizio; Relig clericale
clerical assistant *n* impiegato, -a *mf*
clerk /klɑːk/ AmE /klɜːk/ *n* impiegato, -a *mf*; AmE (shop assistant) commesso, -a *mf*
clever /ˈklevə(r)/ *adj* intelligente; (skilful) abile
cleverly /ˈklevəlɪ/ *adv* intelligentemente; (skilfully) abilmente
cliché /ˈkliːʃeɪ/ *n* cliché *m inv*
clichéd /ˈkliːʃeɪd/ *adj* ‹*idea, technique*› convenzionale; ‹*art, music*› stereotipato; ~ **expression** frase *f* fatta
click /klɪk/ **A** *vi* scattare; Comput (with mouse) cliccare
B *n* Comput (with mouse) clic *m inv*
▪ **click on** *vt* Comput cliccare su
🔑 **client** /ˈklaɪənt/ *n* cliente *mf*
clientele /kliːɒnˈtel/ *n* clientela *f*
cliff /klɪf/ *n* scogliera *f*
cliffhanger /ˈklɪfhæŋə(r)/ *n* **it was a real ~** ci ha lasciato in sospeso
climate /ˈklaɪmət/ *n* clima *m*
climate change *n* cambiamento *m* climatico
climatic /klaɪˈmætɪk/ *adj* climatico
climatologist /ˌklaɪməˈtɒlədʒɪst/ *n* climatologo, -a *mf*
climatology /ˌklaɪməˈtɒlədʒɪ/ *n* climatologia *f*
climax /ˈklaɪmæks/ *n* punto *m* culminante
🔑 **climb** /klaɪm/ **A** *n* salita *f*
B *vt* scalare ‹*mountain*›; arrampicarsi su ‹*ladder, tree*›
C *vi* arrampicarsi; (rise) salire; ‹*road*› salire
▪ **climb down** *vi* scendere; (from ladder, tree) scendere; fig tornare sui propri passi
▪ **climb over** *vt* scavalcare ‹*fence, wall*›
▪ **climb up** *vt* salire su ‹*hill*›
climber /ˈklaɪmə(r)/ *n* alpinista *mf*; (plant) rampicante *m*
climbing /ˈklaɪmɪŋ/ *adj* rampicante
climbing boot *n* scarpone *m* da alpinismo
climbing expedition *n* scalata *f*
climbing frame *n* *struttura (f) su cui possono arrampicarsi i bambini*

🔑 parola chiave

clinch /klɪntʃ/ **A** *vt* infml concludere ‹*deal*›
B *n* (in boxing) clinch *m inv*
clincher /ˈklɪntʃə(r)/ *n* infml (act, remark) fattore *m* decisivo; (argument) argomento *m* decisivo
cling /klɪŋ/ *vi* (*pt/pp* **clung**) aggrapparsi; (stick) aderire
cling film *n* pellicola *f* trasparente
clingy /ˈklɪŋɪ/ *adj* ‹*dress*› attillato; ‹*person*› appiccicoso
clinic /ˈklɪnɪk/ *n* ambulatorio *m*
🔑 **clinical** /ˈklɪnɪkl/ *adj* clinico
clinically /ˈklɪnɪklɪ/ *adv* clinicamente
clink /klɪŋk/ **A** *n* tintinnio *m*; infml (prison) galera *f*
B *vi* tintinnare
clip¹ /klɪp/ **A** *n* fermaglio *m*; (jewellery) spilla *f*
B *vt* (*pt/pp* **clipped**) attaccare
clip² **A** *n* (extract) taglio *m*
B *vt* obliterare ‹*ticket*›
clip art *n* clip art *f inv*
clipboard *n* fermablocco *m*
clip-clop *n rumore (m) fatto dagli zoccoli dei cavalli*
clip frame *n* cornice *f* a giorno
clip-on *adj* ‹*bow tie*› con la clip
clip-on microphone *n* microfono *m* con la clip
clip-ons *npl* (earrings) orecchini *mpl* con le clip
clippers /ˈklɪpəz/ *npl* (for hair) rasoio *m*; (for hedge) tosasiepi *m inv*; (for nails) tronchesina *f*
clipping /ˈklɪpɪŋ/ *n* (from newspaper) ritaglio *m*
clique /kliːk/ *n* cricca *f*
cliquey, cliquish /ˈkliːkɪ, ˈkliːkɪʃ/ *adj* ‹*atmosphere*› esclusivo; ‹*profession, group*› chiuso
cloak /kləʊk/ *n* mantello *m*
cloak-and-dagger *adj* ‹*film*› d'avventura; (surreptitious) clandestino
cloakroom *n* guardaroba *m inv*; (toilet) bagno *m*
cloakroom attendant *n* BrE (at toilets) addetto, -a *mf* ai bagni; (in hotel) guardarobiere, -a *mf*
cloakroom ticket *n* scontrino *m* del guardaroba
clobber /ˈklɒbə(r)/ **A** *n* infml armamentario *m*
B *vt* infml (hit) colpire; (defeat) stracciare
cloche /klɒʃ/ *n* (in garden) campana *f* di vetro
cloche hat *n* cloche *f inv*
clock /klɒk/ *n* orologio *m*; infml (speedometer) tachimetro *m*
▪ **clock in, clock on** *vi* attaccare
▪ **clock out, clock off** *vi* staccare
clock face *n* quadrante *m*
clockmaker *n* orologiaio, -a *mf*
clock radio *n* radiosveglia *f*
clock speed *n* Comput velocità *f* di clock

clock tower *n* torre *f* dell'orologio
clock-watch *vi* guardare continuamente l'orologio
clockwise *adj & adv* in senso orario
clockwork **A** *n* meccanismo *m*; **like ~** infml alla perfezione
B *attrib* a molla
clod /klɒd/ *n* zolla *f*
clog /klɒg/ **A** *n* zoccolo *m*
B *vt* (*pt/pp* **clogged**) **~ [up]** intasare ‹*drain*›; inceppare ‹*mechanism*›
C *vi* ‹*drain*› intasarsi
cloister /ˈklɔɪstə(r)/ *n* chiostro *m*
clone /kləʊn/ **A** *n* Biol, Comput, fig clone *m*
B *vt* clonare
cloning /ˈkləʊnɪŋ/ *n* clonazione *f*
close¹ /kləʊs/ **A** *adj* vicino; ‹*friend*› intimo; ‹*weather*› afoso; **have a ~ shave** infml scamparla bella; **be ~ to somebody** essere unito a qualcuno
B *adv* vicino; **~ by** vicino; **it's ~ on five o'clock** sono quasi le cinque
close² /kləʊz/ **A** *n* fine *f*; **draw to a ~** concludere
B *vt* chiudere
C *vi* chiudersi; ‹*shop*› chiudere
▪ **close down** **A** *vt* chiudere
B *vi* ‹*TV station*› interrompere la trasmissione; ‹*factory*› chiudere
▪ **close in** *vi* ‹*mist*› calare; ‹*enemy*› avvicinarsi da ogni lato
▪ **close up** **A** *vi* (come closer together) stringersi; ‹*shop*› chiudere
B *vt* (bring closer together) avvicinare; chiudere ‹*shop*›
close combat *n* corpo a corpo *m inv*
close-cropped /-ˈkrɒpt/ *adj* ‹*hair*› rasato
closed-circuit television /kləʊzdsɜːkɪt-telɪˈvɪʒən/ *n* televisione *f* a circuito chiuso
closed shop /kləʊzdˈʃɒp/ *n azienda (f) che assume solo personale aderente ad un dato sindacato*
close-fitting /kləʊsˈfɪtɪŋ/ *adj* ‹*garment*› attillato
close-knit /kləʊsˈnɪt/ *adj* fig ‹*family, group*› affiatato
closely /ˈkləʊslɪ/ *adv* da vicino; ‹*watch, listen*› attentamente
close-run *adj* ‹*race, competition*› combattutissimo
close season /kləʊs/ *n stagione (f) di chiusura della caccia e della pesca*
closet /ˈklɒzɪt/ *n* AmE armadio *m*
close-up /ˈkləʊs-/ *n* primo piano *m*
closing /ˈkləʊzɪŋ/ *adj* ‹*stages, minutes, words, scene*› ultimo
closing date *n* data *f* di scadenza
closing down sale *n* liquidazione *f* totale [per cessata attività]
closing time *n* orario *m* di chiusura
closure /ˈkləʊʒə(r)/ *n* chiusura *f*
clot /klɒt/ **A** *n* grumo *m*; infml (idiot) tonto, -a *mf*
B *vi* (*pt/pp* **clotted**) ‹*blood*› coagularsi
cloth /klɒθ/ *n* (fabric) tessuto *m*; (duster etc) straccio *m*
clothe /kləʊð/ *vt* vestire
clothes /kləʊðz/ *npl* vestiti *mpl*, abiti *mpl*
clothes brush *n* spazzola *f* per abiti
clothes hanger *n* gruccia *f* appendiabiti
clothes horse *n* stendibiancheria *m inv*
clothes line *n* corda *f* stendibiancheria
clothes peg *n* molletta *f* per bucato
clothes shop *n* negozio *m* di abbigliamento
clothing /ˈkləʊðɪŋ/ *n* abbigliamento *m*
clotted cream *n* BrE panna *f* rappresa (*ottenuta scaldando il latte*)
cloud /klaʊd/ *n* nuvola *f*
▪ **cloud over** *vi* rannuvolarsi
cloudburst /ˈklaʊdbɜːst/ *n* acquazzone *m*
cloudy /ˈklaʊdɪ/ *adj* (**-ier**, **-iest**) nuvoloso; ‹*liquid*› torbido
clout /klaʊt/ **A** *n* infml colpo *m*; (influence) impatto *m* (**with** su)
B *vt* infml colpire
clove /kləʊv/ *n* chiodo *m* di garofano; **~ of garlic** spicchio *m* d'aglio
cloven foot, **cloven hoof** /ˈkləʊvən/ *n* (of animal) zoccolo *m* fesso; (of devil) piede *m* biforcuto
clover /ˈkləʊvə(r)/ *n* trifoglio *m*
clover leaf *n* raccordo *m* di due autostrade
clown /klaʊn/ **A** *n* pagliaccio *m*
B *vi* **~ [about/around]** fare il pagliaccio
club /klʌb/ **A** *n* club *m inv*; (weapon) clava *f*; Sport mazza *f*; **~s** *pl* Cards fiori *mpl*
B *vt* (*pt/pp* **clubbed**) bastonare
▪ **club together** *vi* unirsi
club car *n* AmE *carrozza (f) ferroviaria con sala bar*
club class *n* business class *f inv*
club foot *n* piede *m* deformato
clubhouse *n* (for socializing) circolo *m*; AmE (for changing) spogliatoio *m*
club sandwich *n* club-sandwich *m inv*
cluck /klʌk/ *vi* chiocciare
clue /kluː/ *n* indizio *m*; (in crossword) definizione *f*; **I haven't a ~** infml non ne ho idea
clued-up /kluːdˈʌp/ *adj* BrE infml ben informato
clueless /ˈkluːlɪs/ *adj* BrE infml incapace
clump /klʌmp/ *n* gruppo *m*
clump about, **clump around** *vi* (walk noisily) camminare con passo pesante
clumsily /ˈklʌmzɪlɪ/ *adv* in modo maldestro; ‹*remark*› senza tatto
clumsiness /ˈklʌmzɪnɪs/ *n* goffaggine *f*
clumsy /ˈklʌmzɪ/ *adj* (**-ier**, **-iest**) maldestro; ‹*tool*› scomodo; ‹*remark*› senza tatto
clung /klʌŋ/ ▶ **cling**

cluster /ˈklʌstə(r)/ **A** *n* gruppo *m*
B *vi* raggrupparsi (**round** intorno a)

clutch /klʌtʃ/ **A** *n* stretta *f*; Auto frizione *f*; **be in sb's ~es** essere in balia di qualcuno
B *vt* stringere; (grab) afferrare
C *vi* **~ at** afferrare

clutch bag *n* pochette *f inv*

clutch cable *n* cavo *m* della frizione

clutter /ˈklʌtə(r)/ **A** *n* caos *m*
B *vt* **~ [up]** ingombrare

cm *abbr* (**centimetre(s)**) cm

CND *n abbr* (**Campaign for Nuclear Disarmament**) campagna *f* per il disarmo nucleare

Co. *abbr* **1** (**company**) C., C.ia; **and ~** hum e compagnia **2** (**county**) contea *f*

c/o *abbr* (**care of**) c/o, presso

⚷ **coach** /kəʊtʃ/ **A** *n* pullman *m inv*; Rail vagone *m*; (horse-drawn) carrozza *f*; Sport allenatore, -trice *mf*
B *vt* far esercitare; Sport allenare

coach party *n* BrE gruppo *m* di gitanti (*in pullman*)

coach station *n* BrE stazione *f* dei pullman

coach trip *n* viaggio *m* in pullman

coachwork *n* BrE carrozzeria *f*

coagulate /kəʊˈægjʊleɪt/ *vi* coagularsi

coagulation /kəʊægjʊˈleɪʃn/ *n* coagulazione *f*

coal /kəʊl/ *n* carbone *m*

coalfield *n* bacino *m* carbonifero

coal fire *n* caminetto *m* alimentato a carbone

coalition /kəʊəˈlɪʃn/ *n* coalizione *f*

coal mine *n* miniera *f* di carbone

coal miner *n* minatore *m*

coal scuttle *n* secchio *m* del carbone

coal seam *n* giacimento *m* di carbone

coarse /kɔːs/ *adj* grossolano; ‹*joke*› spinto

coarse-grained /-ˈgreɪnd/ *adj* ‹*texture*› a grana grossa

coarsely /ˈkɔːslɪ/ *adv* ‹*ground*› grossolanamente; ‹*joke*› in modo spinto

coast /kəʊst/ **A** *n* costa *f*
B *vi* (freewheel) scendere a ruota libera; Auto scendere in folle

coastal /ˈkəʊstəl/ *adj* costiero

coaster /ˈkəʊstə(r)/ *n* (mat) sottobicchiere *m inv*

coastguard /ˈkəʊs(t)gɑːd/ *n* guardia *f* costiera

coastline /ˈkəʊstlaɪn/ *n* litorale *m*

coat /kəʊt/ **A** *n* cappotto *m*; (of animal) manto *m*; (of paint) mano *f*; **~ of arms** stemma *m*
B *vt* coprire; (with paint) ricoprire

coat hanger *n* gruccia *f*

coat hook *n* gancio *m* [appendiabiti]

⚷ parola chiave

coating /ˈkəʊtɪŋ/ *n* rivestimento *m*; (of paint) stato *m*

coat rack *n* attaccapanni *m* a muro

coat-tails *npl* falde *fpl*; **be always hanging on sb's ~** attaccarsi sempre alle falde di qualcuno

coax /kəʊks/ *vt* convincere con le moine

cob /kɒb/ *n* (of corn) pannocchia *f*

cobble /ˈkɒbl/ *vt* **~ together** raffazzonare

cobbler /ˈkɒblə(r)/ *n* ciabattino *m*

cobblestones /ˈkɒbəlstəʊnz/ *npl* acciottolato *msg*

cobra /ˈkəʊbrə/ *n* cobra *m inv*

cobweb /ˈkɒbweb/ *n* ragnatela *f*

cocaine /kəˈkeɪn/ *n* cocaina *f*

coccyx /ˈkɒksɪks/ *n* coccige *m*

cock /kɒk/ **A** *n* gallo *m*; (any male bird) maschio *m*; vulg cazzo *m*
B *vt* sollevare il grilletto di ‹*gun*›; **~ its ears** ‹*animal*› drizzare le orecchie
■ **cock up** infml **A** *vt* incasinare
B *vi* incasinarsi

cock-a-doodle-doo /kɒkəduːd(ə)lˈduː/ *int* chicchirichì

cock-a-hoop *adj* infml al settimo cielo

cock and bull story *n* infml panzana *f*

cockatoo /kɒkəˈtuː/ *n* cacatoa *m inv*

cockcrow /ˈkɒkkrəʊ/ *n* **at ~** al primo canto del gallo

cocked hat /kɒktˈhæt/ *n* infml **knock somebody/something into a ~** schiacciare qualcuno/qualcosa

cockerel /ˈkɒkərəl/ *n* galletto *m*

cocker spaniel /ˈkɒkə(r)/ *n* cocker *m inv* [spaniel]

cock-eyed /-ˈaɪd/ *adj* infml storto; (absurd) assurdo

cockfighting /ˈkɒkfaɪtɪŋ/ *n* combattimenti *mpl* di galli

cockle /ˈkɒkl/ *n* cardio *m*

cockney /ˈkɒknɪ/ *n* (dialect) dialetto *m* londinese; (person) abitante *mf* dell'est di Londra

cockpit /ˈkɒkpɪt/ *n* Aeron cabina *f*

cockroach /ˈkɒkrəʊtʃ/ *n* scarafaggio *m*

cocksure /kɒkˈʃʊə(r)/ *adj* ‹*person, manner, attitude*› presuntuoso

cocktail /ˈkɒkteɪl/ *n* cocktail *m inv*

cocktail bar *n* [cocktail] bar *m inv*

cocktail dress *n* abito *m* da cocktail *m inv*

cocktail party *n* cocktail-party *m inv*

cocktail shaker *n* shaker *m inv*

cocktail stick *n* stecchino *m*

cock-up *n* sl **make a ~** fare un casino (**of** con)

cocky /ˈkɒkɪ/ *adj* (**-ier, -iest**) infml presuntuoso

cocoa /ˈkəʊkəʊ/ *n* cacao *m*

coconut /ˈkəʊkənʌt/ *n* noce *f* di cocco

coconut palm *n* palma *f* da cocco

coconut shy *n* BrE *tiro (m) al bersaglio in cui si devono abbattere noci di cocco*
cocoon /kəˈkuːn/ *n* bozzolo *m*
cod /kɒd/ *n inv* merluzzo *m*
COD *abbr* (**cash on delivery**) pagamento *m* alla consegna
coddle /ˈkɒd(ə)l/ *vt* coccolare
code /kəʊd/ *n* codice *m*
coded /ˈkəʊdɪd/ *adj* codificato
codeine /ˈkəʊdiːn/ *n* codeina *f*
code name *n* nome *m* in codice
code word *n* parola *f* d'ordine
coding /ˈkəʊdɪŋ/ *n* Comput codifica *f*
cod liver oil *n* olio *m* di fegato di merluzzo
co-educational /kəʊedjʊˈkeɪʃənəl/ *adj* misto
coefficient /kəʊɪˈfɪʃənt/ *n* coefficiente *m*
coeliac BrE, **celiac** AmE /ˈsiːlɪæk/ *adj* celiaco
coerce /kəʊˈɜːs/ *vt* costringere
coercion /kəʊˈɜːʃn/ *n* coercizione *f*
coexist /kəʊɪgˈzɪst/ *vi* coesistere
coexistence /kəʊɪgˈzɪstəns/ *n* coesistenza *f*
C of E *abbr* (**Church of England**) Chiesa *f* anglicana
coffee /ˈkɒfɪ/ *n* caffè *m*
coffee bar *n* caffè *m*, bar *m inv*
coffee bean *n* chicco *m* di caffè
coffee break *n* pausa *f* per il caffè
coffee grinder *n* macinacaffè *m*
coffee machine *n* (in café) macchina *f* per l'espresso
coffee maker *n* (on stove) caffettiera *f*; (electric) macchina *f* per il caffè (*con il filtro*)
coffee morning *n* BrE *riunione (m) mattutina in cui viene servito il caffè*
coffee percolator *n* (on stove) caffettiera *f*; (electric) macchina *f* per il caffè (*con il filtro*)
coffee pot *n* caffettiera *f*
coffee shop *n* torrefazione *f*; (café) caffè *m*, bar *m inv*
coffee table *n* tavolino *m*
coffer /ˈkɒfə(r)/ *n* forziere *m*
coffin /ˈkɒfɪn/ *n* bara *f*
cog /kɒg/ *n* Techn dente *m*
cogent /ˈkəʊdʒənt/ *adj* convincente
cogitate /ˈkɒdʒɪteɪt/ *vi* cogitare
cognac /ˈkɒnjæk/ *n* Cognac *m*
cognoscenti /kɒnəˈʃentɪ/ *npl* intenditori *mpl*
cogwheel /ˈkɒgwiːl/ *n* ruota *f* dentata
cohabit /kəʊˈhæbɪt/ *vi* Jur convivere
coherent /kəʊˈhɪərənt/ *adj* coerente; (when speaking) logico
cohesion /kəʊˈhiːʒən/ *n* coesione *f*
cohort /ˈkəʊhɔːt/ *n* fig seguito *m*
coil /kɔɪl/ **A** *n* rotolo *m*; Electr bobina *f*; **~s** *pl* spire *fpl*
B *vt* **~ [up]** avvolgere
coin /kɔɪn/ **A** *n* moneta *f*
B *vt* coniare <*word*>
coinage /ˈkɔɪnɪdʒ/ *n* (of coins, currency) coniatura *f*; (word, phrase) neologismo *m*
coin box *n* (pay phone) telefono *m* a monete; (on pay phone, in laundromat) gettoniera *f*
coincide /kəʊɪnˈsaɪd/ *vi* coincidere
coincidence /kəʊˈɪnsɪdəns/ *n* coincidenza *f*
coincidental /kəʊɪnsɪˈdentl/ *adj* casuale
coincidentally /kəʊɪnsɪˈdentlɪ/ *adv* casualmente
coin operated *adj* a gettone
coke *n* carbone *m*, coke *m*
Coke® /kəʊk/ *n* Coca® *f*
Col. *abbr* (**Colonel**) Col. *m*
colander /ˈkʌləndə(r)/ *n* Culin colapasta *m inv*
cold /kəʊld/ **A** *adj* freddo; **I'm ~** ho freddo; **get ~ feet** farsi prendere dalla fifa; **give somebody the ~ shoulder** trattare qualcuno freddamente
B *n* freddo *m*; Med raffreddore *m*
cold-blooded /-ˈblʌdɪd/ *adj* spietato
cold calling *n* Comm visita *f* senza preavviso
cold comfort *n* magra consolazione *f*
cold frame *n telaio (m) coperto di vetro per proteggere le piante dal gelo*
cold-hearted /-ˈhɑːtɪd/ *adj* insensibile
coldly /ˈkəʊldlɪ/ *adv* fig freddamente
cold meat *n* salumi *mpl*
coldness /ˈkəʊldnɪs/ *n* freddezza *f*
cold snap *n* ondata *f* di freddo
cold sore *n* herpes *m inv*
cold store *n* cella *f* frigorifera
cold sweat *n* sudore *m* freddo; **bring somebody out in a ~** far sudare freddo qualcuno
cold turkey *n* (reaction) crisi *f inv* di astinenza; **be ~** avere una crisi di astinenza; **quit ~** smettere di colpo
Cold War *n* guerra *f* fredda
coleslaw /ˈkəʊlslɔː/ *n insalata (f) di cavolo crudo, cipolle e carote in maionese*
colic /ˈkɒlɪk/ *n* colica *f*
collaborate /kəˈlæbəreɪt/ *vi* collaborare; **~ on something** collaborare a qualcosa
collaboration /kəlæbəˈreɪʃn/ *n* collaborazione *f*; (with enemy) collaborazionismo *m*
collaborator /kəˈlæbəreɪtə(r)/ *n* collaboratore, -trice *mf*; (with enemy) collaborazionista *mf*
collage /kɒˈlɑːʒ/ *n* collage *m inv*; (film) montaggio *m*
collapse /kəˈlæps/ **A** *n* crollo *m*
B *vi* <*person*> svenire; <*roof, building*> crollare
collapsible /kəˈlæpsəbl/ *adj* pieghevole
collar /ˈkɒlə(r)/ *n* colletto *m*; (for animal) collare *m*
collarbone /ˈkɒləbəʊn/ *n* clavicola *f*

C

C

collar size *n* taglia *f* di camicia
collate /kəˈleɪt/ *vt* collazionare
collateral /kəˈlætərəl/ *n* garanzia *f* collaterale; **put up ~** offrire una garanzia collaterale
collateral damage *n* danni *mpl* collaterali
collateral loan *adj* Fin prestito *m* con garanzia collaterale
✓ **colleague** /ˈkɒliːg/ *n* collega *mf*
✓ **collect** /kəˈlekt/ **A** *vt* andare a prendere ‹*person*›; ritirare ‹*parcel, tickets*›; riscuotere ‹*taxes*›; raccogliere ‹*rubbish*›; (as hobby) collezionare
B *vi* riunirsi
C *adv* **call ~** AmE telefonare a carico del destinatario
collected /kəˈlektɪd/ *adj* controllato
✓ **collection** /kəˈlekʃn/ *n* collezione *f*; (in church) questua *f*; (of rubbish) raccolta *f*; (of post) levata *f*
collective /kəˈlektɪv/ *adj* collettivo
collective bargaining *n* contrattazione *f* collettiva
collective farm *n* comune *f*
collective noun *n* nome *m* collettivo
collective ownership *n* comproprietà *f*
collector /kəˈlektə(r)/ *n* (of stamps etc) collezionista *mf*
collector's item *n* pezzo *m* da collezionista
✓ **college** /ˈkɒlɪdʒ/ *n* istituto *m* parauniversitario; **C~ of** ... Scuola *f* di ...
college of education *n* BrE ≈ facoltà *f* di magistero
college of further education *n* BrE istituto *m* parauniversitario
collide /kəˈlaɪd/ *vi* scontrarsi
collie /ˈkɒlɪ/ *n* pastore *m* scozzese, collie *m inv*
colliery /ˈkɒlɪərɪ/ *n* miniera *f* di carbone
collision /kəˈlɪʒn/ *n* scontro *m*; **be on a ~ course** essere in rotta di collisione
colloquial /kəˈləʊkwɪəl/ *adj* colloquiale
colloquialism /kəˈləʊkwɪəlɪzm/ *n* espressione *f* colloquiale
colloquially /kəˈləʊkwɪəlɪ/ *adv* colloquialmente
colloquium /kəˈləʊkwɪəm/ *n* colloquio *m*
collude /kəˈl(j)uːd/ *vi* complottare
collusion /kəˈl(j)uːʒn/ *n* collusione *f*; **in ~ with** in accordo con
cologne /kəˈləʊn/ *n* colonia *f*
Colombia /kəˈlɒmbɪə/ *n* Colombia *f*
Colombian /kəˈlɒmbɪən/ *adj & n* colombiano, -a *mf*
colon /ˈkəʊlən/ *n* due punti *mpl*; Anat colon *m inv*
colonel /ˈkɜːnl/ *n* colonnello *m*

✓ parola chiave

colonial /kəˈləʊnɪəl/ *adj* coloniale
colonialist /kəˈləʊnɪəlɪst/ *adj & n* colonialista *mf*
colonization /ˌkɒlənaɪˈzeɪʃn, AmE -nɪˈz-/ *n* colonizzazione *f*
colonize /ˈkɒlənaɪz/ *vt* colonizzare
colonizer /ˈkɒlənaɪzə(r)/ *n* colonizzatore, -trice *mf*
colonnade /kɒləˈneɪd/ *n* colonnato *m*
colony /ˈkɒlənɪ/ *n* colonia *f*
Colorado beetle /kɒləˈrɑːdəʊ/ *n* dorifora *f*
colossal /kəˈlɒsl/ *adj* colossale
✓ **colour** /ˈkʌlə(r)/ **A** *n* colore *m*; (complexion) colorito *m*; **~s** *pl* (flag) bandiera *fsg*; **show one's true ~s** fig buttare giù la maschera; **in ~** a colori; **off ~** infml giù di tono
B *vt* colorare; **~ [in]** colorare
C *vi* (blush) arrossire
colour bar *n* discriminazione *f* razziale
colour-blind *adj* daltonico
colour code *vt* distinguere per mezzo di colori diversi
coloured /ˈkʌləd/ **A** *adj* colorato; offensive ‹*person*› di colore
B *n* offensive (person) persona *f* di colore
colour fast *adj* dai colori resistenti
colour film *n* film *m inv* a colori
colourful /ˈkʌləfʊl/ *adj* pieno di colore
colouring /ˈkʌlərɪŋ/ *n* (of plant, animal) colorazione *f*; (complexion) colorito *m*; (dye: for hair) tinta *f*; (for food) colorante *m*
colouring book *n* album *m inv* da colorare
colourless /ˈkʌləlɪs/ *adj* incolore
colour photograph *n* fotografia *f* a colori
colour scheme *n* [combinazione *f* di] colori *mpl*
colour sense *n* senso *m* del colore
colour supplement *n* supplemento *m* illustrato a colori
colour television *n* televisione *f* a colori
colt /kəʊlt/ *n* puledro *m*
✓ **column** /ˈkɒləm/ *n* colonna *f*
columnist /ˈkɒləmnɪst/ *n giornalista (mf) che cura una rubrica*
coma /ˈkəʊmə/ *n* coma *m inv*
comatose /ˈkəʊmətəʊz/ *adj* Med in stato comatoso
comb /kəʊm/ **A** *n* pettine *m*; (for wearing) pettinino *m*
B *vt* pettinare; fig (search) setacciare; **~ one's hair** pettinarsi i capelli
▪ **comb through** *vt* setacciare ‹*files, desk*›
combat /ˈkɒmbæt/ **A** *n* combattimento *m*
B *vt* (*pt/pp* **combated**) combattere
combat jacket *n* giubba *f* da combattimento
✓ **combination** /kɒmbɪˈneɪʃn/ *n* combinazione *f*
combine, combine harvester *n* mietitrebbia *f*

combine[1] /kəmˈbaɪn/ **A** *vt* unire; **~ a job with being a mother** conciliare il lavoro con il ruolo di madre
B *vi* ‹*chemical elements*› combinarsi

combine[2] /ˈkɒmbaɪn/ *n* Comm associazione *f*

combined /kəmˈbaɪnd/ *adj* combinato

combustible /kəmˈbʌstəbl/ *adj* combustibile

combustion /kəmˈbʌstʃn/ *n* combustione *f*

come /kʌm/ *vi* (*pt* **came**, *pp* **come**) venire; **after coming all this way** dopo tutta questa strada; **where do you ~ from?** da dove vieni?; **~ to** (reach) arrivare a; **that ~s to £10** fanno 10 sterline; **I've ~ to appreciate her** ho finito per apprezzarla; **I don't know what the world is coming to** mi chiedo dove andremo a finire; **~ into money** ricevere dei soldi; **that's what comes of being ...** ecco cosa significa essere...; **~ true/open** verificarsi/aprirsi; **~ first** arrivare primo; fig venire prima di tutto; **~ in two sizes** esistere in due misure; **the years to ~** gli anni a venire; **how ~?** infml come mai?

- **come about** *vi* succedere
- **come across**: **A** *vi* **~ across as being** infml dare l'impressione di essere
  B *vt* (find) imbattersi in
- **come after** *vt* (follow) venire dopo; (chase, pursue) inseguire
- **come along** *vi* venire; ‹*job, opportunity*› presentarsi; (progress) andare bene
- **come apart** *vi* smontarsi; (break) rompersi
- **come at** *vt* (attack) avventarsi su
- **come away** *vi* venir via; ‹*button, fastener*› staccarsi
- **come back** *vi* ritornare
- **come before** *vt* (precede) precedere; (be more important than) venire prima di
- **come by** **A** *vi* passare
  B *vt* (obtain) avere
- **come down** *vi* scendere; **~ down to** (reach) arrivare a; **the situation ~s down to ...** la situazione si riduce a...; **don't ~ down too hard on her** vacci piano con lei; **~ down with flu** prendersi l'influenza
- **come forward** *vi* farsi avanti
- **come in** *vi* entrare; (in race) arrivare; ‹*tide*› salire; **~ in with somebody** (in an undertaking) associarsi a qualcuno
- **come in for**: *vt* **~ in for criticism** essere criticato
- **come into** *vt* (inherit) ereditare ‹*money, inheritance*›
- **come off** *vi* staccarsi; (take place) esserci; (succeed) riuscire; **~ off it!** non farmi ridere!
- **come on** *vi* (make progress) migliorare; **~ on!** (hurry) dai!; (indicating disbelief) ma va là!
- **come out** *vi* venir fuori; ‹*book, sun*› uscire; ‹*stain*› andar via; ‹*homosexual*› rivelare la propria omosessualità; **~ out [on strike]** scioperare
- **come out with** *vt* venir fuori con ‹*joke, suggestion*›
- **come over** *vi* venire; **what's ~ over you?** cosa ti prende?
- **come round**, **come around** *vi* venire; (after fainting) riaversi; (change one's mind) farsi convincere
- **come through** **A** *vi* ‹*news*› arrivare
  B *vt* attraversare ‹*operation*›
- **come to** *vi* (after fainting) riaversi
- **come under** *vi* trovarsi sotto
- **come up** *vi* salire; ‹*sun*› sorgere; ‹*plant*› crescere; ‹*name, subject*› venir fuori; ‹*job, opportunity*› presentarsi; **something came up** (I was prevented) ho avuto un imprevisto
- **come up against** *vt* incontrare
- **come up to** *vt* (reach) arrivare a; essere all'altezza di ‹*expectations*›
- **come up with** *vt* tirar fuori

come-back *n* ritorno *m*

comedian /kəˈmiːdɪən/ *n* [attore *m*], comico *m*

comedienne /kəmiːdɪˈen/ *n* attrice *f* comica

come-down *n* passo *m* indietro

comedy /ˈkɒmədɪ/ *n* commedia *f*

comer /ˈkʌmə(r)/ *n* **open to all ~s** aperto a tutti; **take on all ~s** battersi contro tutti gli sfidanti

comet /ˈkɒmɪt/ *n* cometa *f*

comeuppance /kʌmˈʌpəns/ *n* **get one's ~** infml avere quel che si merita

comfort /ˈkʌmfət/ **A** *n* benessere *m*; (consolation) conforto *m*; **all the ~s** tutti i comfort
B *vt* confortare

comfortable /ˈkʌmfətəbl/ *adj* comodo; **be ~** ‹*person*› stare comodo; fig ‹*in situation*› essere a proprio agio; (financially) star bene

comfortably /ˈkʌmfətəblɪ/ *adv* comodamente

comforting /ˈkʌmfətɪŋ/ *adj* confortante

comfort station *n* AmE bagno *m* pubblico

comfy /ˈkʌmfɪ/ *adj* infml comodo

comic /ˈkɒmɪk/ **A** *adj* comico
B *n* comico, -a *mf*; (periodical) fumetto *m*

comical /ˈkɒmɪk(ə)l/ *adj* comico

comically /ˈkɒmɪk(ə)lɪ/ *adv* comicamente

comic book *n* giornalino *m* [a fumetti]

comic relief *n* Theat **provide some ~** fare una parentesi comica; fig sdrammatizzare

comic strip *n* striscia *f* di fumetti

coming /ˈkʌmɪŋ/ **A** *adj* promettente
B *n* venuta *f*; **~s and goings** viavai *m*

comma /ˈkɒmə/ *n* virgola *f*

command /kəˈmɑːnd/ **A** *n* (gen, Comput) comando *m*; (order) ordine *m*; (mastery) padronanza *f*; **in ~** al comando
B *vt* ordinare; comandare ‹*army*›

commandant /ˈkɒməndænt/ *n* Mil comandante *m*

command centre BrE, **command center** AmE *n* centro *m* di comando

commandeer /kɒmənˈdɪə(r)/ *vt* requisire

commander /kəˈmɑːndə(r)/ *n* comandante *m*

commanding /kəˈmɑːndɪŋ/ *adj* ‹*view*› imponente; ‹*lead*› dominante

commanding officer *n* comandante *m*

commandment /kəˈmɑːndmənt/ *n* comandamento *m*

C

commando /kəˈmɑːndəʊ/ *n* commando *m inv*

command performance *n* BrE Theat *serata (f) di gala (su richiesta del capo di stato)*

commemorate /kəˈmeməreɪt/ *vt* commemorare

commemoration /kəmeməˈreɪʃn/ *n* commemorazione *f*

commemorative /kəˈmemərətɪv/ *adj* commemorativo

commence /kəˈmens/ *vt & vi* cominciare

commencement /kəˈmensmənt/ *n* inizio *m*

commend /kəˈmend/ *vt* complimentarsi con (**on** per); (recommend) raccomandare (**to** a)

commendable /kəˈmendəbl/ *adj* lodevole

commendation /kɒmenˈdeɪʃn/ *n* elogio *m*; (for bravery) riconoscimento *m*

commensurate /kəˈmenʃərət/ *adj* proporzionato (**with** a)

✓ **comment** /ˈkɒment/ **A** *n* commento *m*; **no ~!** no comment!
B *vi* fare commenti (**on** su)

commentary /ˈkɒməntrɪ/ *n* commento *m*; **[running] ~** (on radio, TV) cronaca *f* diretta

commentate /ˈkɒmənteɪt/ *vt* **~ on** TV, Radio fare la cronaca di
■ **commentate on** *vt* fare la radiocronaca/telecronaca di ‹*sporting event*›

commentator /ˈkɒmənteɪtə(r)/ *n* cronista *mf*

commerce /ˈkɒmɜːs/ *n* commercio *m*

✓ **commercial** /kəˈmɜːʃl/ **A** *adj* commerciale
B *n* TV pubblicità *f*

commercial break *n* spot *m inv* [pubblicitario], interruzione *f* pubblicitaria

commercialism /kəˈmɜːʃ(ə)lɪzm/ *n* derog affarismo *m*

commercialize /kəˈmɜːʃ(ə)laɪz/ *vt* commercializzare

commercial law *n* diritto *m* commerciale

commercially /kəˈmɜːʃ(ə)lɪ/ *adv* commercialmente

commercial traveller commesso *m* viaggiatore

commiserate /kəˈmɪzəreɪt/ *vi* esprimere il proprio rincrescimento (**with** a)

commissar /kɒmɪˈsɑː(r)/ *n* commissario *m*

✓ **commission** /kəˈmɪʃn/ **A** *n* commissione *f*; **receive one's ~** Mil essere promosso ufficiale; **out of ~** fuori uso
B *vt* commissionare; Mil promuovere ufficiale; **~ a painting from somebody, ~ somebody to do a painting** commissionare un dipinto a qualcuno

commissionaire /kəmɪʃəˈneə(r)/ *n* portiere *m*

commissioner /kəˈmɪʃənə(r)/ *n* commissario *m*; **C~ for Oaths** ≈ notaio *m*

✓ **commit** /kəˈmɪt/ *vt* (*pt/pp* **committed**) commettere; (to prison, hospital) affidare (**to** a); impegnare ‹*funds*›; **~ oneself** impegnarsi; **~ something to memory** imparare qualcosa a memoria

✓ **commitment** /kəˈmɪtmənt/ *n* impegno *m*; (involvement) compromissione *f*

committed /kəˈmɪtɪd/ *adj* impegnato

✓ **committee** /kəˈmɪtɪ/ *n* comitato *m*

commodity /kəˈmɒdətɪ/ *n* prodotto *m*

commodore /ˈkɒmədɔː(r)/ *n* commodoro *m*

✓ **common** /ˈkɒmən/ **A** *adj* comune; (vulgar) volgare
B *n* prato *m* pubblico; **have in ~** avere in comune; **House of C~s** Camera *f* dei Comuni

common cold *n* raffreddore *m*

commoner /ˈkɒmənə(r)/ *n persona (f) non nobile*

common ground *n* fig terreno *m* d'intesa

common-law *n* diritto *m* consuetudinario

common-law husband *n* convivente *m* (*more uxorio*)

common-law marriage *n* matrimonio *m* di fatto

common-law wife *n* convivente *f* (*more uxorio*)

commonly /ˈkɒmənlɪ/ *adv* comunemente

Common Market *n* Mercato *m* Comune

common-or-garden *adj* ordinario

commonplace *adj* banale

common-room *n* sala *f* dei professori/degli studenti

common sense *n* buon senso *m*

Commonwealth **A** *n* BrE Commonwealth *m inv*
B *attrib* ‹*country, Games*› del Commonwealth

Commonwealth of Independent States *n* Comunità *f* degli stati indipendenti

commotion /kəˈməʊʃŋ/ *n* confusione *f*

communal /ˈkɒmjʊnəl/ *adj* comune

commune /ˈkɒmjuːn/ **A** *n* comune *f*
B /kəˈmjuːn/ *vi* **~ with** essere in comunione con ‹*nature*›; comunicare con (person)

communicable /kəˈmjuːnɪkəbl/ *adj* ‹*disease*› trasmissibile

communicate /kəˈmjuːnɪkeɪt/ *vt & vi* comunicare

✓ **communication** /kəmjuːnɪˈkeɪʃn/ *n* comunicazione *f*; (of disease) trasmissione *f*; **be in ~ with somebody** essere in contatto con qualcuno; **~s** *pl* (technology)

✓ parola chiave

telecomunicazioni *fpl*
communication cord *n* fermata *f* d'emergenza
communications company *n* società *f* di telecomunicazioni
communications satellite *n* satellite *m* per telecomunicazioni
communications software *n* software *m* di comunicazione
communication studies /'stʌdɪz/ *n* studi *mpl* di comunicazione
communicative /kə'mju:nɪkətɪv/ *adj* comunicativo
Communion /kə'mju:nɪən/ *n* **[Holy] ~** comunione *f*
communiqué /kə'mju:nɪkeɪ/ *n* comunicato *m* stampa
Communism /'kɒmjʊnɪzm/ *n* comunismo *m*
Communist /'kɒmjʊnɪst/ *adj & n* comunista *mf*
Communist Party *n* partito *m* communista
community /kə'mju:nətɪ/ *n* comunità *f*
community care *n cura (f) fuori dell'ambito ospedaliero*
community centre *n* centro *m* sociale
community policing *n* polizia *f* di quartiere
community service *n* servizio *m* civile (*in sostituzione di pene per reati minori*)
community spirit *n* spirito *m* civico
commute /kə'mju:t/ **A** *vi* fare il pendolare **B** *vt* Jur commutare
commuter /kə'mju:tə(r)/ *n* pendolare *mf*
commuter belt *n* zona *f* suburbana abitata dai pendolari
commuter train *n* treno *m* dei pendolari
Comoros /'kɒmərəʊz/ *npl* **the ~ (Islands)** le (isole) Comore *fpl*
compact¹ /kəm'pækt/ *adj* compatto
compact² /'kɒmpækt/ *n* portacipria *m inv*
compact disc *n* compact disc *m inv*
compact disc player *n* lettore *m* di compact disc
companion /kəm'pænjən/ *n* compagno, -a *mf*
companionable /kəm'pænjənəbl/ *adj* ‹*person*› socievole; ‹*silence*› non pesante
companionship /kəm'pænjənʃɪp/ *n* compagnia *f*
company /'kʌmpənɪ/ *n* compagnia *f*; (guests) ospiti *mpl*; **I didn't know you had ~** pensavo che fossi solo
company brochure *n* opuscolo *m* dell'azienda
company car *n* macchina *f* della ditta
company director *n* dirigente *mf* d'azienda
company letterhead *n* carta *f* intestata dell'azienda
company pension scheme *n* piano *m* di pensionamento aziendale
company policy *n* politica *f* aziendale
company secretary *n* direttore, -trice *mf* amministrativo, -a
comparable /'kɒmpərəbl/ *adj* paragonabile
comparative /kəm'pærətɪv/ **A** *adj* comparativo; (relative) relativo **B** *n* Gram comparativo *m*
comparatively /kəm'pærətɪvlɪ/ *adv* relativamente
compare /kəm'peə(r)/ **A** *vt* paragonare (**with/to** a) **B** *vi* **it can't ~** non ha paragoni
comparison /kəm'pærɪsn/ *n* paragone *m*
compartment /kəm'pɑ:tmənt/ *n* compartimento *m*; Rail scompartimento *m*
compass /'kʌmpəs/ *n* bussola *f*
compasses /'kʌmpəsɪz/ *npl* **pair of ~** compasso *msg*
compassion /kəm'pæʃn/ *n* compassione *f*
compassionate /kəm'pæʃənət/ *adj* compassionevole
compatible /kəm'pætəbl/ *adj* compatibile; **be ~** ‹*people*› avere caratteri compatibili
compatriot /kəm'pætrɪət/ *n* compatriota *mf*
compel /kəm'pel/ *vt* (*pt/pp* **compelled**) costringere
compelling /kəm'pelɪŋ/ *adj* ‹*reason, argument*› convincente; ‹*performance, film, speaker*› avvincente
compendium /kəm'pendɪəm/ *n* (handbook) compendio *m*; BrE (box of games) scatola *f* di giochi
compensate /'kɒmpənseɪt/ **A** *vt* risarcire **B** *vi* **~ for** fig compensare di
compensation /kɒmpən'seɪʃn/ *n* risarcimento *m*; fig (comfort) consolazione *f*
compère /'kɒmpeə(r)/ *n* presentatore, -trice *mf*
compete /kəm'pi:t/ *vi* competere; (take part) gareggiare
competence /'kɒmpɪtəns/ *n* competenza *f*
competent /'kɒmpɪtənt/ *adj* competente
competition /kɒmpə'tɪʃn/ *n* concorrenza *f*; (contest) gara *f*
competitive /kəm'petɪtɪv/ *adj* competitivo; **~ prices** prezzi *mpl* concorrenziali
competitor /kəm'petɪtə(r)/ *n* concorrente *mf*
compilation /kɒmpɪ'leɪʃn/ *n* compilazione *f*; (collection) raccolta *f*
compile /kəm'paɪl/ *vt* compilare
complacency /kəm'pleɪsənsɪ/ *n* compiacimento *m*
complacent /kəm'pleɪsənt/ *adj* compiaciuto
complacently /kəm'pleɪsəntlɪ/ *adv* con compiacimento
complain /kəm'pleɪn/ *vi* lamentarsi (**about**

di); (formally) reclamare; **~ of** Med accusare

⚷ **complaint** /kəm'pleɪnt/ *n* lamentela *f*; (formal) reclamo *m*; Med disturbo *m*

complement¹ /'kɒmplɪmənt/ *n* complemento *m*; **with a full ~ of 25** con un effettivo al completo di 25

complement² /'kɒmplɪment/ *vt* complementare; **~ each other** complementarsi a vicenda

complementary /kɒmplɪ'mentərɪ/ *adj* complementare

complementary medicine *n* medicina *f* alternativa

⚷ **complete** /kəm'pli:t/ **A** *adj* completo; (utter) finito
B *vt* completare; compilare ‹*form*›

⚷ **completely** /kəm'pli:tlɪ/ *adv* completamente

completion /kəm'pli:ʃn/ *n* fine *f*

⚷ **complex** /'kɒmpleks/ *adj & n* complesso *m*

complexion /kəm'plekʃn/ *n* carnagione *f*; **that puts a different ~ on the matter** questo mette la questione in una luce nuova

complexity /kəm'pleksətɪ/ *n* complessità *f*

compliance /kəm'plaɪəns/ *n* accettazione *f*; (with rules) osservanza *f*; **in ~ with** in osservanza a ‹*law*›; conformemente a ‹*request*›

compliant /kəm'plaɪənt/ *adj* accondiscendente; Comput conforme; **~ with** conforme a

complicate /'kɒmplɪkeɪt/ *vt* complicare

complicated /'kɒmplɪkeɪtɪd/ *adj* complicato

complication /kɒmplɪ'keɪʃn/ *n* complicazione *f*

complicity /kəm'plɪsətɪ/ *n* complicità *f*

compliment /'kɒmplɪmənt/ **A** *n* complimento *m*; **~s** *pl* omaggi *mpl*
B *vt* complimentare

complimentary /kɒmplɪ'mentərɪ/ *adj* complimentoso; (given free) in omaggio

comply /kəm'plaɪ/ *vi* (*pt/pp* **-ied**) **~ with** conformarsi a

⚷ **component** /kəm'pəʊnənt/ *adj & n* **~ [part]** componente *m*

compose /kəm'pəʊz/ *vt* comporre; **~ oneself** ricomporsi; **be ~d of** essere composto da

composed /kəm'pəʊzd/ *adj* (calm) composto

composer /kəm'pəʊzə(r)/ *n* compositore, -trice *mf*

composite /'kɒmpəzɪt/ *adj* composto; ‹*style*› composito

composition /kɒmpə'zɪʃn/ *n* composizione *f*; (essay) tema *m*

compos mentis /kɒmpɒs'mentɪs/ *adj* nel pieno possesso delle proprie facoltà

compost /'kɒmpɒst/ *n* composta *f*

composting /'kɒmpɒstɪŋ/ *n* compostaggio *m*

composure /kəm'pəʊʒə(r)/ *n* calma *f*

compound¹ /kəm'paʊnd/ *vt* (make worse) aggravare

compound² /'kɒmpaʊnd/ **A** *adj* composto
B *n* Chem composto *m*; Gram parola *f* composta; (enclosure) recinto *m*

compound fracture *n* frattura *f* esposta

compound interest *n* interesse *m* composto

comprehend /kɒmprɪ'hend/ *vt* comprendere

comprehensible /kɒmprɪ'hensəbl/ *adj* comprensible

comprehensibly /kɒmprɪ'hensəblɪ/ *adv* comprensibilmente

comprehension /kɒmprɪ'henʃn/ *n* comprensione *f*

comprehensive /kɒmprɪ'hensɪv/ *adj & n* comprensivo; **~ [school]** *scuola (f) media in cui gli allievi hanno capacità d'apprendimento diverse*

comprehensive insurance *n* Auto polizza *f* casco

compress¹ /'kɒmpres/ *n* compressa *f*

compress² /kəm'pres/ *vt* (also Comput) comprimere

compressed air /kəm'prest/ *n* aria *f* compressa

compression /kəm'preʃn/ *n* compressione *f*

comprise /kəm'praɪz/ *vt* comprendere; (form) costituire

compromise /'kɒmprəmaɪz/ **A** *n* compromesso
B *vt* compromettere
C *vi* fare un compromesso

compromising /'kɒmprəmaɪzɪŋ/ *adj* ‹*situation*› compromettente

compulsion /kəm'pʌlʃn/ *n* desiderio *m* irresistibile

compulsive /kəm'pʌlsɪv/ *adj* Psych patologico; **~ eating** voglia *f* ossessiva di mangiare

compulsory /kəm'pʌlsərɪ/ *adj* obbligatorio; **~ subject** materia *f* obbligatoria

compulsory purchase *n* BrE espropriazione *f* (*per pubblica utilità*)

compunction /kəm'pʌŋkʃn/ *n* literary scrupolo *m*

computation /kɒmpjʊ'teɪʃn/ *n* calcolo *m*

⚷ **computer** /kəm'pju:tə(r)/ *n* computer *m inv*

computer-aided *adj* assistito da computer

computer-aided design *n* progettazione *f* assistita da computer

computer-aided learning *n* apprendimento *m* assistito da computer

computer-assisted language learning *n* apprendimento *m* della lingua assistito da computer

computer crime *n* reati *mpl* informatici

⚷ parola chiave

computer dating *n possibilità (f) di incontrare l'anima gemella tramite agenzie in rete*

computer dating service *n* servizio *m* di ricerca dell'anima gemella in rete

computer engineer *n* tecnico *m* informatico

computer error *n* errore *m* informatico

computer game *n* gioco *m* su computer; **~s** intelligiochi *mpl*

computer graphics *nsg* grafica *fsg* computerizzata

computer hacker *n* pirata *m* informatico

computerization /kəmpju:tərar'zeɪʃn/ *n* computerizzazione *f*

computerize /kəm'pju:təraɪz/ *vt* computerizzare

computer-literate *adj* che sa usare il computer

computer operator *n* terminalista *mf*

computer program *n* programma *m* [informatico]

computer programmer *n* programmatore, -trice *mf* di computer

computer science *n* informatica *f*

computer scientist *n* esperto, -a *mf* di informatica

computer virus *n* virus *m inv* [su computer]

computing /kəm'pju:tɪŋ/ *n* informatica *f*

comrade /'kɒmreɪd/ *n* camerata *m*; Pol compagno, -a *mf*

comradeship /'kɒmreɪdʃɪp/ *n* cameratismo *m*

con¹ /kɒn/ ▶ **pro**

con² **A** *n* infml fregatura *f*
B *vt* (*pt/pp* **conned**) infml fregare

concave /'kɒnkeɪv/ *adj* concavo

conceal /kən'si:l/ *vt* nascondere

concealment /kən'si:lmənt/ *n* dissimulazione *f*

concede /kən'si:d/ *vt* (admit) ammettere; (give up) rinunciare a; lasciar fare ‹*goal*›

conceit /kən'si:t/ *n* presunzione *f*

conceited /kən'si:tɪd/ *adj* presuntuoso

conceivable /kən'si:vəbl/ *adj* concepibile

conceive /kən'si:v/ **A** *vt* Biol concepire
B *vi* aver figli; **~ of** fig concepire

⚷ **concentrate** /'kɒnsəntreɪt/ **A** *vt* concentrare
B *vi* concentrarsi
C *n* concentrato *m*

⚷ **concentration** /kɒnsən'treɪʃn/ *n* concentrazione *f*

concentration camp *n* campo *m* di concentramento

concentric /kən'sentrɪk/ *adj* concentrico

⚷ **concept** /'kɒnsept/ *n* concetto *m*

conception /kən'sepʃn/ *n* concezione *f*; (idea) idea *f*

conceptual /kən'septjʊəl/ *adj* concettuale

⚷ **concern** /kən'sɜ:n/ **A** *n* preoccupazione *f*; Comm attività *f*
B *vt* (be about, affect) riguardare; (worry) preoccupare; **~ oneself with** preoccuparsi di; **as far as I am ~ed** per quanto mi riguarda

concerned /kən'sɜ:nd/ *adj* (worried) preoccupato; **be ~ about** essere preoccupato per; (involved) interessato; **all (those) ~** tutti gli interessati

concerning /kən'sɜ:nɪŋ/ *prep* riguardo a

concert /'kɒnsət/ *n* concerto *m*

concerted /kən'sɜ:tɪd/ *adj* collettivo

concert hall *n* sala *f* da concerti

concertina /kɒnsə'ti:nə/ *n* piccola fisarmonica *f*

concert master *n* AmE primo violino *m*

concerto /kən'tʃeətəʊ/ *n* concerto *m*

concession /kən'seʃn/ *n* concessione *f*; (reduction) sconto *m*

concessionary /kən'seʃənrɪ/ *adj* (reduced) scontato

conciliate /kən'sɪlɪeɪt/ *vt* blandire

conciliation /kənsɪlɪ'eɪʃn/ *n* conciliazione *f*

conciliator /kən'sɪlɪeɪtə(r)/ *n* mediatore, -trice *mf*

conciliatory /kən'sɪlɪətərɪ, AmE -tɔ:rɪ/ *adj* conciliatorio

concise /kən'saɪs/ *adj* conciso

concisely /kən'saɪslɪ/ *adv* in modo conciso

conciseness /kən'saɪsnɪs/ *n* concisione *f*

⚷ **conclude** /kən'klu:d/ **A** *vt* concludere
B *vi* concludersi

concluding /kən'klu:dɪŋ/ *adj* finale, conclusivo

⚷ **conclusion** /kən'klu:ʒn/ *n* conclusione *f*; **in ~** per concludere

conclusive /kən'klu:sɪv/ *adj* definitivo

conclusively /kən'klu:sɪvlɪ/ *adv* in modo definitivo

concoct /kən'kɒkt/ *vt* confezionare; fig inventare

concoction /kən'kɒkʃn/ *n* mistura *f*; (drink) intruglio *m*

concord /'kɒŋkɔ:d/ *n* concordia *f*

concordance /kən'kɔ:dəns/ *n* accordo *m*; (index) concordanze *fpl*; **be in ~ with** essere in accordo con

concourse /'kɒŋkɔ:s/ *n* atrio *m*

concrete /'kɒŋkri:t/ **A** *adj* concreto
B *n* calcestruzzo *m*
C *vt* ricoprire di calcestruzzo

concrete jungle *n* giungla *f* d'asfalto

concrete mixer *n* betoniera *f*

concur /kən'kɜ:(r)/ *vi* (*pt/pp* **concurred**) essere d'accordo

concurrently /kən'kʌrəntlɪ/ *adv* contemporaneamente

concuss /kən'kʌs/ *vt* **be ~ed** avere una commozione cerebrale

c

C

concussion /kən'kʌʃn/ *n* commozione *f* cerebrale

condemn /kən'dem/ *vt* condannare; dichiarare inagibile ‹*building*›

condemnation /kɒndem'neɪʃn/ *n* condanna *f*

condensation /kɒnden'seɪʃn/ *n* condensazione *f*

condense /kən'dens/ **A** *vt* condensare; Phys condensare
B *vi* condensarsi

condensed milk /kəndenst'mɪlk/ *n* latte *m* condensato

condescend /kɒndɪ'send/ *vi* degnarsi

condescending /kɒndɪ'sendɪŋ/ *adj* condiscendente

condescendingly /kɒndɪ'sendɪŋlɪ/ *adv* in modo condiscendente

condiment /'kɒndɪmənt/ *n* condimento *m*

⚷ **condition** /kən'dɪʃn/ **A** *n* condizione *f*; **on ~ that** a condizione che
B *vt* Psych condizionare

conditional /kən'dɪʃənəl/ **A** *adj* ‹*acceptance*› condizionato; Gram condizionale; **be ~ on** essere condizionato da
B *n* Gram condizionale

conditionally /kən'dɪʃənəlɪ/ *adv* condizionatamente

conditioner /kən'dɪʃənə(r)/ *n* balsamo *m*; (for fabrics) ammorbidente *m*

conditioning /kən'dɪʃənɪŋ/ **A** *n* (of hair) balsamo *m*; Psych condizionamento *m*
B *adj* ‹*shampoo, lotion etc*› trattante

condo /'kɒndəʊ/ *n* AmE **condominium**

condole /kən'dəʊl/ *vi* fare le condoglianze (**with** a)

condolences /kən'dəʊlənsɪz/ *npl* condoglianze *fpl*

condom /'kɒndəm/ *n* preservativo *m*

condominium /kɒndə'mɪnɪəm/ *n* AmE condominio *m*

condone /kən'dəʊn/ *vt* passare sopra a

conducive /kən'dju:sɪv/ *adj* **be ~ to** contribuire a

conduct[1] /'kɒndʌkt/ *n* condotta *f*

⚷ **conduct**[2] /kən'dʌkt/ *vt* condurre; dirigere ‹*orchestra*›

conduction /kən'dʌkʃn/ *n* conduzione *f*

conductor /kən'dʌktə(r)/ *n* direttore *m* d'orchestra; (of bus) bigliettaio *m*; Phys conduttore *m*

conductress /kən'dʌktrɪs/ *n* bigliettaia *f*

cone /kəʊn/ *n* cono *m*; Bot pigna *f*; Auto birillo *m*
■ **cone off**: *vt* **be ~d off** Auto essere chiuso da birilli

confection /kən'fekʃn/ *n* (cake, dessert) dolce *m*; **a ~ of** (combination) una combinazione di

confectioner /kən'fekʃənə(r)/ *n* pasticciere, -a *mf*

confectionery /kən'fekʃənərɪ/ *n* pasticceria *f*

confederation /kənfedə'reɪʃn/ *n* confederazione *f*

confer /kən'fɜ:(r)/ *v* (*pt/pp* **conferred**)
A *vt* conferire (**on** a)
B *vi* (discuss) conferire

⚷ **conference** /'kɒnfərəns/ *n* conferenza *f*

conference room *n* sala *f* riunioni

confess /kən'fes/ **A** *vt* confessare
B *vi* confessare; Relig confessarsi

confession /kən'feʃn/ *n* confessione *f*

confessional /kən'feʃənəl/ *n* confessionale *m*

confessor /kən'fesə(r)/ *n* confessore *m*

confetti /kən'fetɪ/ *n* coriandoli *mpl*

confide /kən'faɪd/ *vt* confidare
■ **confide in**: *vt* **~ in somebody** fidarsi di

⚷ **confidence** /'kɒnfɪdəns/ *n* (trust) fiducia *f*; (self-assurance) sicurezza *f* di sé; (secret) confidenza *f*; **in ~** in confidenza

confidence trick *n* truffa *f*

confidence trickster /'kɒnfɪdənstrɪkstə(r)/ *n* imbroglione, -a *mf*

confident /'kɒnfɪdənt/ *adj* fiducioso; (self-assured) sicuro di sé

confidential /kɒnfɪ'denʃl/ *adj* confidenziale

confidentiality /kɒnfɪdenʃɪ'ælətɪ/ *n* riservatezza *f*

confidentially /kɒnfɪ'denʃəlɪ/ *adv* confidenzialmente

confidently /'kɒnfɪdəntlɪ/ *adv* con aria fiduciosa; **we ~ expect to win** siamo fiduciosi nella vittoria

confine /kən'faɪn/ *vt* rinchiudere; (limit) limitare; **be ~d to bed** essere confinato a letto

confined /kən'faɪnd/ *adj* ‹*space*› limitato

confinement /kən'faɪnmənt/ *n* detenzione *f*; Med parto *m*

confines /'kɒnfaɪnz/ *npl* confini *mpl*

⚷ **confirm** /kən'fɜ:m/ *vt* confermare; Relig cresimare

confirmation /kɒnfə'meɪʃn/ *n* conferma *f*; Relig cresima *f*

confirmed /kən'fɜ:md/ *adj* incallito; **~ bachelor** scapolo *m* impenitente

confiscate /'kɒnfɪskeɪt/ *vt* confiscare

confiscation /'kɒnfɪs'keɪʃn/ *n* confisca *f*

conflagration /kɒnflə'greɪʃn/ *n* conflagrazione *f*

conflate /kən'fleɪt/ *vt* fondere

⚷ **conflict**[1] /'kɒnflɪkt/ *n* conflitto *m*

conflict[2] /kən'flɪkt/ *vi* essere in contraddizione

conflicting /kən'flɪktɪŋ/ *adj* contraddittorio

confluence /'kɒnflʊəns/ *n* (of rivers) confluenza *f*; fig convergenza *f*

conform /kən'fɔ:m/ *vi* ‹*person*› conformarsi; ‹*thing*› essere conforme (**to** a)

⚷ parola chiave

conformist /kən'fɔːmɪst/ *n* conformista *mf*
conformity /kən'fɔːmɪtɪ/ *n* conformità *f*; Relig ortodossia *f*; **in ~ with** in conformità a
confound /kən'faʊnd/ *vt* (perplex) confondere; (show to be wrong) confutare
confounded /kən'faʊndɪd/ *adj* infml maledetto
confront /kən'frʌnt/ *vt* affrontare; **the problems ~ing us** i problemi che dobbiamo affrontare
confrontation /kɒnfrʌn'teɪʃn/ *n* confronto *m*
confrontational /ˌkɒnfrən'teɪʃənəl/ *adj* provocatorio
confuse /kən'fjuːz/ *vt* confondere
confused /kən'fjuːzd/ *adj* ‹*presentation, idea*› ingarbugliato
confusing /kən'fjuːzɪŋ/ *adj* che confonde
confusion /kən'fjuːʒn/ *n* confusione *f*
congeal /kən'dʒiːl/ *vi* ‹*blood*› coagularsi
congenial /kən'dʒiːnɪəl/ *adj* congeniale
congenital /kən'dʒenɪtl/ *adj* congenito
congested /kən'dʒestɪd/ *adj* congestionato
congestion /kən'dʒestʃn/ *n* congestione *f*
congestion charge *n pedaggio (m) per circolare nelle strade del centro di Londra*
conglomerate /kən'glɒmərət/ *n* conglomerato *m*
Congo /'kɒŋgəʊ/ *n* Congo *m*
Congolese /kɒŋgə'liːz/ *adj & n* congolese *mf*
congratulate /kən'grætjʊleɪt/ *vt* congratularsi con (**on** per)
congratulations /kəngrætjʊ'leɪʃnz/ *npl* congratulazioni *fpl*
congregate /'kɒŋgrɪgeɪt/ *vi* radunarsi
congregation /kɒngrɪ'geɪʃn/ *n* Relig assemblea *f*
congress /'kɒŋgres/ *n* congresso *m*
congressman /'kɒŋgresmən/ *n* AmE Pol membro *m* del congresso
conical /'kɒnɪkl/ *adj* conico
conifer /'kɒnɪfə(r)/ *n* conifera *f*
conjecture /kən'dʒektʃə(r)/ **A** *n* congettura *f*
B *vt* congetturare
C *vi* fare congetture
conjugal /'kɒndʒʊgl/ *adj* coniugale
conjugate /'kɒndʒʊgeɪt/ *vt* coniugare
conjugation /kɒndʒʊ'geɪʃn/ *n* coniugazione *f*
conjunction /kən'dʒʌŋkʃn/ *n* congiunzione *f*; **in ~ with** insieme a
conjunctivitis /kəndʒʌŋktɪ'vaɪtɪs/ *n* congiuntivite *f*
conjure up /'kʌndʒə(r)/ *vt* evocare ‹*image*›; tirar fuori dal nulla ‹*meal*›
conjuring /'kʌndʒərɪŋ/ *n* giochi *mpl* di prestigio
conjuring trick /'kʌndʒərɪŋ/ *n* gioco *m* di prestigio
conjuror, conjurer /'kʌndʒərə(r)/ *n* prestigiatore, -trice *mf*
conk /kɒŋk/ *vi* **~ out** infml ‹*machine*› guastarsi; ‹*person*› crollare
conker /'kɒŋkə(r)/ *n* infml castagna *f* (*d'ippocastano*)
conman /'kɒnmæn/ *n* infml truffatore *m*
connect /kə'nekt/ **A** *vt* collegare; **be ~ed with** avere legami con; (be related to) essere imparentato con; **be well ~ed** aver conoscenze influenti
B *vi* essere collegato (**with** a); ‹*train*› fare coincidenza
connecting /kə'nektɪŋ/ *adj* ‹*room*› di comunicazione
connecting flight *n* coincidenza *f*
connection /kə'nekʃn/ *n* (between ideas) nesso *m*; (in travel) coincidenza *f*; Electr, Comput collegamento *m*; **in ~ with** con riferimento a; **~s** *p* (people) conoscenze *fpl*
connectivity /ˌkɒnek'tɪvɪti/ *n* Comput connettività *f*
connector /kə'nektə(r)/ *n* Comput connettore *m*
connivance /kə'naɪvəns/ *n* connivenza *f*
connive /kə'naɪv/ *vi* **~ at** essere connivente in
connoisseur /kɒnə'sɜː(r)/ *n* intenditore, -trice *mf*
connotation /kɒnə'teɪʃn/ *n* connotazione *f*
connote /kə'nəʊt/ *vt* evocare; (in linguistics) connotare
conquer /'kɒŋkə(r)/ *vt* conquistare; fig superare ‹*fear*›
conqueror /'kɒnkərə(r)/ *n* conquistatore *m*
conquest /'kɒnkwest/ *n* conquista *f*
conscience /'kɒnʃəns/ *n* coscienza *f*
conscientious /kɒnʃɪ'enʃəs/ *adj* coscienzioso
conscientiously /kɒnsɪ'enʃəslɪ/ *adv* coscienziosamente
conscientious objector /əb'dʒektə(r)/ *n* obiettore *m* di coscienza
conscious /'kɒnʃəs/ *adj* conscio; ‹*decision*› meditato; **[fully] ~** cosciente; **be/become ~ of something** rendersi conto di qualcosa
consciously /'kɒnʃəslɪ/ *adv* consapevolmente
consciousness /'kɒnʃəsnɪs/ *n* consapevolezza *f*; Med conoscenza *f*
conscript[1] /'kɒnskrɪpt/ *n* coscritto *m*
conscript[2] /kən'skrɪpt/ *vt* Mil chiamare alle armi; **~ somebody to do something** fig reclutare qualcuno per fare qualcosa
conscription /kən'skrɪpʃn/ *n* coscrizione *f*, leva *f*
consecrate /'kɒnsɪkreɪt/ *vt* consacrare
consecration /kɒnsɪ'kreɪʃn/ *n* consacrazione *f*
consecutive /kən'sekjʊtɪv/ *adj* consecutivo

consecutively /kən'sekjʊtɪvlɪ/ *adv* consecutivamente

consensus /kən'sensəs/ *n* consenso *m*

consent /kən'sent/ **A** *n* consenso *m* **B** *vi* acconsentire

⚷ **consequence** /'kɒnsɪkwəns/ *n* conseguenza *f*; (importance) importanza *f*

consequent /'kɒnsɪkwənt/ *adj* conseguente

consequently /'kɒnsɪkwəntlɪ/ *adv* di conseguenza

conservation /kɒnsə'veɪʃn/ *n* conservazione *f*

conservation area *n* area *f* soggetta a vincoli ambientali

conservationist /kɒnsə'veɪʃənɪst/ *n* fautore, -trice *mf* della tutela ambientale

conservatism /kən'sɜːvətɪzm/ *n* conservatorismo *m*

conservative /kən'sɜːvətɪv/ **A** *adj* conservativo; ‹*estimate*› ottimistico; **C**～ Pol *adj* conservatore **B** *n* conservatore, -trice *mf*

Conservative Party *n* partito *m* conservatore

conservatory /kən'sɜːvətrɪ/ *n spazio (m) chiuso da vetrate adiacente alla casa*

conserve /kən'sɜːv/ *vt* conservare

⚷ **consider** /kən'sɪdə(r)/ *vt* considerare; ～ **doing something** considerare la possibilità di fare qualcosa

considerable /kən'sɪdərəbl/ *adj* considerevole

considerably /kən'sɪdərəblɪ/ *adv* considerevolmente

considerate /kən'sɪdərət/ *adj* pieno di riguardo

considerately /kən'sɪdərətlɪ/ *adv* con riguardo

⚷ **consideration** /kənsɪdə'reɪʃn/ *n* considerazione *f*; (thoughtfulness) attenzione *f*; (respect) riguardo *m*; (payment) compenso *m*; **take into** ～ prendere in considerazione

considering /kən'sɪdərɪŋ/ *prep* considerando; ～ **that** considerando che

consign /kən'saɪn/ *vt* affidare

consignment /kən'saɪnmənt/ *n* consegna *f*

⚷ **consist** /kən'sɪst/ *vi* ～ **of** consistere di

consistency /kən'sɪstənsɪ/ *n* coerenza *f*; (density) consistenza *f*

⚷ **consistent** /kən'sɪstənt/ *adj* coerente; ‹*loyalty*› costante; **be** ～ **with** far pensare a

consistently /kən'sɪstəntlɪ/ *adv* coerentemente; ‹*late, loyal*› costantemente

consolation /kɒnsə'leɪʃn/ *n* consolazione *f*

consolation prize *n* premio *m* di consolazione

console /kən'səʊl/ *vt* consolare

consolidate /kən'sɒlɪdeɪt/ *vt* consolidare

consolidation /kənsɒlɪ'deɪʃn/ *n* (of knowledge, position) consolidamento *m*

consoling /kən'səʊlɪŋ/ *adj* consolante

consonant /'kɒnsənənt/ *n* consonante *f*

consort[1] /'kɒnsɔːt/ *n* consorte *mf*

consort[2] /kən'sɔːt/ *vi* ～ **with** frequentare

consortium /kən'sɔːtɪəm/ *n* consorzio *m*

conspicuous /kən'spɪkjʊəs/ *adj* facilmente distinguibile; **be** ～ **by one's absence** brillare per la propria assenza

conspicuously /kən'spɪkjʊəslɪ/ *adv* ‹*dressed*› vistosamente; ‹*placed*› in evidenza; (silent, empty) in modo evidente

conspiracy /kən'spɪrəsɪ/ *n* cospirazione *f*

conspiracy theory *n* teoria *f* del complotto

conspirator /kən'spɪrətə(r)/ *n* cospiratore, -trice *mf*

conspire /kən'spaɪə(r)/ *vi* cospirare

constable /'kʌnstəbl/ *n* agente *m* [di polizia]

constabulary /kən'stæbjʊlərɪ/ *n* BrE polizia *f*

constancy /'kɒnstənsɪ/ *n* costanza *f*

⚷ **constant** /'kɒnstənt/ *adj* costante

constantly /'kɒnstəntlɪ/ *adv* costantemente

constellation /kɒnstə'leɪʃn/ *n* costellazione *f*

consternation /kɒnstə'neɪʃn/ *n* costernazione *f*

constipated /'kɒnstɪpeɪtɪd/ *adj* stitico

constipation /kɒnstɪ'peɪʃn/ *n* stitichezza *f*

constituency /kən'stɪtjʊənsɪ/ *n collegio (m) elettorale di un deputato nel Regno Unito*

constituent /kən'stɪtjʊənt/ *n* costituente *m*; Pol elettore, -trice *mf*

constitute /'kɒnstɪtjuːt/ *vt* costituire

constitution /kɒnstɪ'tjuːʃn/ *n* costituzione *f*

constitutional /kɒnstɪ'tjuːʃənl/ **A** *adj* costituzionale **B** *n* passeggiata *f* salutare

constitutionally /kɒnstɪ'tjuːʃənəlɪ/ *adv* Pol costituzionalmente; (innately) di costituzione

constrain /kən'streɪn/ *vt* costringere

constraint /kən'streɪnt/ *n* costrizione *f*; (restriction) restrizione *f*; (strained manner) disagio *m*

constrict /kən'strɪkt/ *vt* ‹*tight jacket*› stringere

constriction /kən'strɪkʃn/ *n* (of chest, throat) senso *m* di oppressione; (constraint) costrizione *f*; (of blood vessel) restrizione *f*

⚷ **construct** /kən'strʌkt/ *vt* costruire

⚷ **construction** /kən'strʌkʃn/ *n* costruzione *f*; (interpretation) interpretazione *f*; **under** ～ in costruzione

construction engineer *n* ingegnere *m* edile

construction paper *n* AmE cartoncino *m*

construction site *n* cantiere *m*

construction worker *n* [operaio *m*] edile *m*

⚷ parola chiave

constructive /kən'strʌktɪv/ *adj* costruttivo

constructively /kən'strʌktɪvlɪ/ *adv* in modo costruttivo

construe /kən'stru:/ *vt* interpretare

consul /'kɒnsl/ *n* console *m*

consular /'kɒnsjʊlə(r)/ *adj* consolare

consulate /'kɒnsjʊlət/ *n* consolato *m*

consult /kən'sʌlt/ *vt* consultare

consultancy /kən'sʌltənsɪ/ **A** *n* (advice) consulenza *f*; (firm) ufficio *m* di consulenza; BrE Med posto *m* di specialista; **do ~** fare il/la consulente
B *attrib* <*fees, service, work*> di consulenza

consultant /kən'sʌltənt/ *n* consulente *mf*; Med specialista *mf*

consultation /kɒnsl'teɪʃn/ *n* consultazione *f*; Med consulto *m*

consultative /kən'sʌltətɪv/ *adj* di consulenza

consulting hours /kən'sʌltɪŋ/ *npl* Med orario *m* di visita

consulting room *n* Med ambulatorio *m*

consumable /kən'sju:məbl/ *n* bene *m* di consumo

consume /kən'sju:m/ *vt* consumare

consumer /kən'sju:mə(r)/ *n* consumatore, -trice *mf*

consumer advice *n* consigli *mpl* ai consumatori

consumer confidence *n* fiducia *f* del consumatore

consumer goods *npl* beni *mpl* di consumo

consumerism /kən'sju:mərɪzm/ *n* consumismo *m*

consumer organization *n* organizzazione *f* per la tutela dei consumatori

consumer products *npl* beni *mpl* di consumo

consumer protection *n* tutela *f* dei consumatori

consumer society *n* società *f* consumista, società *f* dei consumi

consuming /kən'sju:mɪŋ/ *adj* <*passion*> struggente; <*urge*> pressante; <*hatred*> insaziabile

consummate /'kɒnsjʊmeɪt/ *vt* consumare

consummation /kɒnsjʊ'meɪʃn/ *n* consumazione *f*

consumption /kən'sʌmpʃn/ *n* consumo *m*

cont. /kɒnt/ *abbr* (**continued**) segue

contact /'kɒntækt/ **A** *n* contatto *m*; (person) conoscenza *f*
B *vt* mettersi in contatto con

contactable /'kɒntæktəbl/ *adj* <*person*> reperibile

contact lenses *npl* lenti *fpl* a contatto

contactless /'kɒntæktləs/ *adj* senza contatti

contagious /kən'teɪdʒəs/ *adj* contagioso

contain /kən'teɪn/ *vt* contenere; **~ oneself** controllarsi

container /kən'teɪnə(r)/ *n* recipiente *m*; (for transport) container *m inv*

container port *n* porto *m* container

container ship *n* [nave *f*] porta-container *f inv*

container truck *n* [autocarro *m*] portacontainer *m inv*

contaminate /kən'tæmɪneɪt/ *vt* contaminare

contamination /kəntæmɪ'neɪʃn/ *n* contaminazione *f*

contemplate /'kɒntəmpleɪt/ *vt* contemplare; (consider) considerare; **~ doing something** considerare di fare qualcosa

contemplation /kɒntəm'pleɪʃn/ *n* contemplazione *f*

contemplative /kən'templətɪv/ *adj* contemplativo

contemporaneous /kəntempə'reɪnɪəs/ *adj* contemporaneo (**with** a)

contemporaneously /kəntempə'reɪnɪəslɪ/ *adv* contemporaneamente (**with** a)

contemporary /kən'tempərərɪ/ *adj & n* contemporaneo, -a *mf*

contempt /kən'tempt/ *n* disprezzo *m*; **beneath ~** più che vergognoso; **~ of court** oltraggio *m* alla Corte

contemptible /kən'tem(p)təbl/ *adj* spregevole

contemptuous /kən'tem(p)tjʊəs/ *adj* sprezzante

contemptuously /kən'tem(p)tjʊəslɪ/ *adv* sprezzantemente

contend /kən'tend/ **A** *vi* **~ with** occuparsi di
B *vt* (assert) sostenere

contender /kən'tendə(r)/ *n* concorrente *mf*

content[1] /'kɒntent/ *n* contenuto *m*

content[2] /kən'tent/ **A** *adj* soddisfatto
B *n* **to one's heart's ~** finché se ne ha voglia
C *vt* **~ oneself** accontentarsi (**with** di)

contented /kən'tentɪd/ *adj* soddisfatto

contentedly /kən'tentɪdlɪ/ *adv* con aria soddisfatta

contention /kən'tenʃn/ *n* (assertion) opinione *f*

contentious /kən'tenʃəs/ *adj* <*subject*> controverso; <*view*> discutibile; <*person, group*> polemico

contentment /kən'tentmənt/ *n* soddisfazione *f*

contents /'kɒntents/ *npl* contenuto *m*

contest[1] /'kɒntest/ *n* gara *f*

contest[2] /kɒn'test/ *vt* contestare <*statement*>; impugnare <*will*>; Pol <*candidates*> contendersi; <*one candidate*> aspirare a

contestant /kən'testənt/ *n* concorrente *mf*

context /'kɒntekst/ *n* contesto *m*

continent /'kɒntɪnənt/ *n* continente *m*; **the Continent** l'Europa *f* continentale

continental /kɒntɪ'nentl/ *adj* continentale

continental breakfast *n prima colazione (f) a base di pane, burro, marmellata, croissant ecc.*

continental quilt *n* piumone *m*

contingency /kən'tɪndʒənsɪ/ *n* eventualità *f*

contingency fund *n* fondo *m* sopravvenienze passive

contingency plan *n* piano *m* d'emergenza

contingent /kən'tɪndʒənt/ **A** *adj* **be ~ on** dipendere da
B *n* Mil contingente *m*

continual /kən'tɪnjʊəl/ *adj* continuo

continually /kən'tɪnjʊəlɪ/ *adv* continuamente

continuation /kəntɪnjʊ'eɪʃn/ *n* continuazione *f*

🔑 **continue** /kən'tɪnju:/ **A** *vt* continuare; **~ doing** *or* **to do something** continuare a fare qualcosa; **to be ~d** continua
B *vi* continuare

continued /kən'tɪnju:d/ *adj* continuo

continuity /kɒntɪ'nju:ətɪ/ *n* continuità *f*

continuity announcer *n* annunciatore, -trice *mf*

continuity girl *n* segretaria *f* di produzione

continuous /kən'tɪnjʊəs/ *adj* continuo

continuously /kən'tɪnjʊəslɪ/ *adv* continuamente

continuum /kən'tɪnjʊəm/ *n* continuum *m inv*

contort /kən'tɔ:t/ *vt* contorcere

contortion /kən'tɔ:ʃn/ *n* contorsione *f*

contortionist /kən'tɔ:ʃənɪst/ *n* contorsionista *mf*

contour /'kɒntʊə(r)/ *n* contorno *m*; (line) curva *f* di livello

contraband /'kɒntrəbænd/ *n* contrabbando *m*

contraception /kɒntrə'sepʃn/ *n* contraccezione *f*; **use ~** ricorrere alla contraccezione

contraceptive /kɒntrə'septɪv/ *adj & n* contraccettivo *m*

🔑 **contract¹** /'kɒntrækt/ *n* contratto *m*

contract² /kən'trækt/ **A** *vi* (get smaller) contrarsi
B *vt* contrarre ‹*illness*›

contraction /kən'trækʃn/ *n* contrazione *f*

contract killer *n* sicario *m*

contractor /kən'træktə(r)/ *n* imprenditore, -trice *mf*

contractual /kən'træktjʊəl/ *adj* contrattuale

contract work *n* lavoro *m* su commissione

contract worker *n* lavoratore, -trice *mf* con contratto a termine

contradict /kɒntrə'dɪkt/ *vt* contraddire

contradiction /kɒntrə'dɪkʃn/ *n* contraddizione *f*

contradictory /kɒntrə'dɪktərɪ/ *adj* contraddittorio

contraflow /'kɒntrəfləʊ/ *n utilizzazione (f) di una corsia nei due sensi di marcia durante lavori stradali*

contraindication /kɒntrəɪndɪ'keɪʃn/ *n* controindicazione *f*

contralto /kən'træltəʊ/ *n* contralto *m*

contraption /kən'træpʃn/ *n* infml aggeggio *m*

contrariness /kən'treərɪnɪs/ *n* spirito *m* di contraddizione

contrariwise /kən'treərɪwaɪz/ *adv* (conversely) d'altra parte, d'altro canto; (in the opposite direction) in direzione opposta

contrary¹ /'kɒntrərɪ/ **A** *adj* contrario
B *adv* **~ to** contrariamente a
C *n* contrario *m*; **on the ~** al contrario

contrary² /kən'treərɪ/ *adj* disobbediente

🔑 **contrast¹** /'kɒntrɑ:st/ *n* contrasto *m*

contrast² /kən'trɑ:st/ **A** *vt* confrontare
B *vi* contrastare

contrasting /kən'trɑ:stɪŋ/ *adj* contrastante

contravene /kɒntrə'vi:n/ *vt* trasgredire

contravention /kɒntrə'venʃn/ *n* trasgressione *f*

🔑 **contribute** /kən'trɪbju:t/ *vt & vi* contribuire

🔑 **contribution** /kɒntrɪ'bju:ʃn/ *n* contribuzione *f*; (what is contributed) contributo *m*

contributor /kən'trɪbjʊtə(r)/ *n* contributore, -trice *mf*

contributory /kən'trɪbjʊtərɪ/ *adj* ‹*factor*› concomitante; **be ~ to** contribuire a

con trick *n* raggiro *m*, truffa *f*

contrite /kən'traɪt/ *adj* contrito

contrive /kən'traɪv/ *vt* escogitare; **~ to do something** riuscire a fare qualcosa

contrived /kən'traɪvd/ *adj* ‹*style, effect*› artificioso; ‹*plot, ending*› forzato; ‹*incident, meeting*› non fortuito

🔑 **control** /kən'trəʊl/ **A** *n* controllo *m*; **~s** *pl* (of car, plane) comandi *mpl*; **get out of ~** sfuggire al controllo
B *vt* (*pt/pp* **controlled**) controllare; **~ oneself** controllarsi

control column *n* Aeron cloche *f inv*

control key *n* Comput tasto *m* control

controlled /kən'trəʊld/ *adj* ‹*explosion, performance, person*› controllato; **Labour-~** dominato dai laburisti

controller /kən'trəʊlə(r)/ *n* controllore *m*; Fin controllore *m* [della gestione]; Radio, TV direttore, -trice *mf*

control panel *n* (on machine) quadro *m* dei comandi; (for plane) quadro *m* di comando

control room *n* sala *f* di comando; Radio, TV sala *f* di regia

control tower *n* torre *f* di controllo

🔑 parola chiave

controversial /kɒntrəˈvɜːʃl/ *adj* controverso
controversy /ˈkɒntrəvɜːsɪ/ *n* controversia *f*
conundrum /kəˈnʌndrəm/ *n* enigma *m*
conurbation /kɒnɜːˈbeɪʃn/ *n* conturbazione *f*
convalesce /kɒnvəˈles/ *vi* essere in convalescenza
convalescence /kɒnvəˈlesəns/ *n* convalescenza *f*
convalescent /kɒnvəˈlesənt/ *adj* convalescente
convalescent home *n* convalescenziario *m*
convection /kənˈvekʃn/ *n* convezione *f*
convector /kənˈvektə(r)/ *n* ~ **[heater]** convettore *m*
convene /kənˈviːn/ **A** *vt* convocare **B** *vi* riunirsi
convener /kənˈviːnə(r)/ *n* (organizer) organizzatore, -trice *mf*; (chair) presidente *m*
convenience /kənˈviːnɪəns/ *n* convenienza *f*; **[public]** ~ gabinetti *mpl* pubblici; **with all modern ~s** con tutti i comfort
convenience foods *npl* cibi *mpl* precotti
convenience store *n* negozio *m* aperto fino a tardi
convenient /kənˈviːnɪənt/ *adj* comodo; **be ~ for somebody** andar bene per qualcuno; **if it is ~ [for you]** se ti va bene
conveniently /kənˈviːnɪəntlɪ/ *adv* comodamente; ~ **located** in una posizione comoda
convent /ˈkɒnvənt/ *n* convento *m*
convention /kənˈvenʃn/ *n* convenzione *f*; (assembly) convegno *m*
conventional /kənˈvenʃnəl/ *adj* convenzionale
conventionally /kənˈvenʃnəlɪ/ *adv* convenzionalmente
convention centre *n* palazzo *m* dei congressi
convent school *n* scuola *f* retta da religiose
converge /kənˈvɜːdʒ/ *vi* convergere
conversant /kənˈvɜːsənt/ *adj* ~ **with** pratico di
⚷ **conversation** /kɒnvəˈseɪʃn/ *n* conversazione *f*
conversational /kɒnvəˈseɪʃnəl/ *adj* di conversazione
conversationalist /kɒnvəˈseɪʃnəlɪst/ *n* conversatore, -trice *mf*
converse¹ /kənˈvɜːs/ *vi* conversare
converse² /ˈkɒnvɜːs/ *n* inverso *m*
conversely /ˈkɒnvɜːslɪ/ *adv* viceversa
conversion /kənˈvɜːʃn/ *n* conversione *f*
conversion rate *n* [tasso *m* di] cambio *m*
conversion table *n* tabella *f* di conversione
convert¹ /ˈkɒnvɜːt/ *n* convertito, -a *mf*
convert² /kənˈvɜːt/ *vt* convertire (**into** in); sconsacrare ‹*church*›
converter /kənˈvɜːtə(r)/ *n* Electr convertitore *m*
convertible /kənˈvɜːtəbl/ **A** *adj* convertibile **B** *n* Auto macchina *f* decappottabile
convex /ˈkɒnveks/ *adj* convesso
convey /kənˈveɪ/ *vt* portare; trasmettere ‹*idea, message*›
conveyance /kənˈveɪəns/ *n* trasporto *m*; (vehicle) mezzo *m* di trasporto
conveyancing /kənˈveɪənsɪŋ/ *n* Jur passaggio *m* di proprietà
conveyor /kənˈveɪə(r)/ *n* (of goods, persons) trasportatore *m*
conveyor belt *n* nastro *m* trasportatore
convict¹ /ˈkɒnvɪkt/ *n* condannato, -a *mf*
convict² /kənˈvɪkt/ *vt* giudicare colpevole
conviction /kənˈvɪkʃn/ *n* condanna *f*; (belief) convinzione *f*; **previous ~** precedente *m* penale
convince /kənˈvɪns/ *vt* convincere
convincing /kənˈvɪnsɪŋ/ *adj* convincente
convincingly /kənˈvɪnsɪŋlɪ/ *adv* in modo convincente
convivial /kənˈvɪvɪəl/ *adj* conviviale
convoluted /ˈkɒnvəluːtɪd/ *adj* contorto
convoy /ˈkɒnvɔɪ/ *n* convoglio *m*
convulse /kənˈvʌls/ *vt* sconvolgere; **be ~d with laughter** contorcersi dalle risa
convulsion /kənˈvʌlʃn/ *n* convulsione *f*
convulsive /kənˈvʌlsɪv/ *adj* convulso; Med convulsivo
convulsively /kənˈvʌlsɪvlɪ/ *adv* convulsamente
coo /kuː/ *vi* tubare
cooing /ˈkuːɪŋ/ *n* (of bird, lovers) tubare *m inv*
cook /kʊk/ **A** *n* cuoco, -a *mf* **B** *vt* cucinare; **is it ~ed?** è cotto?; **~ the books** infml truccare i libri contabili **C** *vi* ‹*food*› cuocere; ‹*person*› cucinare
■ **cook up** *vt* infml inventare ‹*excuse, story etc*›
cookbook /ˈkʊkbʊk/ *n* libro *m* di cucina
cook-chill *adj* ‹*foods, products*› precotto e surgelato
cooked meats /kʊktˈmiːts/ *npl* salumi *mpl*
cooker /ˈkʊkə(r)/ *n* cucina *f*; (apple) mela *f* da cuocere
cookery /ˈkʊkərɪ/ *n* cucina *f*
cookery book *n* libro *m* di cucina
cookie /ˈkʊkɪ/ *n* AmE biscotto *m*
cooking /ˈkʊkɪŋ/ *n* cucina *f*; **be good at ~** saper cucinare bene; **do the ~** cucinare
cooking apple *n* mela *f* da cuocere
cooking chocolate *n* cioccolato *m* da pasticceria
cooking foil *n* carta *f* stagnola
cooking salt *n* sale *m* da cucina
cooking time *n* tempo *m* di cottura

⚷ **cool** /kuːl/ **A** *adj* fresco; (calm) calmo; (unfriendly) freddo; infml (excellent or attractive) fantastico; **a ~ T-shirt** una maglietta fantastica; **'I won!' '~!'** 'ho vinto!' 'fantastico!'
B *n* fresco *m*; **keep/lose one's ~** mantenere/perdere la calma
C *vt* rinfrescare
D *vi* rinfrescarsi
■ **cool down A** *vi* ‹*soup, tea etc*› raffreddarsi; fig (become calm) calmarsi
B *vt* raffreddare ‹*soup, tea etc*›; fig calmare

cool bag *n* BrE borsa *f* frigo
cool box *n* borsa *f* termica
cool-headed *adj* equilibrato
cooling /'kuːlɪŋ/ **A** *n* raffreddamento *m*
B *adj* ‹*agent*› refrigerante; ‹*system, tower*› di raffreddamento; ‹*drink, swim*› rinfrescante
cooling-off period *n* (in industrial relations) periodo *m* di tregua [sindacale]; Comm fase *f* di riflessione
coolly /'kuːllɪ/ *adv* freddamente
coolness /'kuːlnɪs/ *n* freddezza *f*
coop /kuːp/ **A** *n* stia *f*
B *vt* **~ up** rinchiudere
co-op /'kəʊɒp/ *n abbr* (**cooperative**) cooperativa *f*
cooperate /kəʊ'ɒpəreɪt/ *vi* cooperare
cooperation /kəʊɒpə'reɪʃn/ *n* cooperazione *f*
cooperative /kəʊ'ɒpərətɪv/ *adj & n* cooperativa *f*
co-opt /kəʊ'ɒpt/ *vt* eleggere
coordinate /kəʊ'ɔːdɪneɪt/ *vt* coordinare
coordinated /kəʊ'ɔːdɪneɪtɪd/ *adj* coordinato
coordinates /kəʊ'ɔːdɪnəts/ *npl* (clothes) coordinato *m sg*
coordination /kəʊɔːdɪ'neɪʃn/ *n* coordinazione *f*
coordinator /kəʊ'ɔːdɪneɪtə(r)/ *n* coordinatore, -trice *mf*
co-owner /kəʊ'əʊnə(r)/ *n* comproprietario, -a *mf*
cop /kɒp/ *n* infml poliziotto *m*
co-parent /kəʊ'peərənt/ *vt condividere la responsabilità dell'educazione dei figli*
co-parenting /'kəʊˌpeərəntɪŋ/ *n condivisione (f) della responsabilità dell'educazione dei figli*
cope /kəʊp/ *vi* infml farcela; **can she ~ by herself?** ce la fa da sola?; **~ with** farcela con; **I couldn't ~ with five kids** non ce la farei con cinque bambini
Copenhagen /kəʊpən'heɪgən/ *n* Copenaghen *f*
copier /'kɒpɪə(r)/ *n* fotocopiatrice *f*
co-pilot /'kəʊpaɪlət/ *n* copilota *m*
copious /'kəʊpɪəs/ *adj* abbondante
copiously /'kəʊpɪəslɪ/ *adv* abbondantemente

cop-out *n* infml (evasive act) bidone *m*; (excuse) scappatoia *f*
copper¹ /'kɒpə(r)/ **A** *n* rame *m*; **~s** *pl* monete *fpl* da uno o due penny
B *attrib* di rame
copper² *n* infml poliziotto *m*
copper beech *n* faggio *m* rosso
copper-coloured *adj* [color] rame *inv*; ‹*hair*› ramato
copperplate *n* calligrafia *f* ornata
coppice /'kɒpɪs/, **copse** /kɒps/ *n* boschetto *m*
co-property /'kəʊprɒpətɪ/ *n* comproprietà *f*
copulate /'kɒpjʊleɪt/ *vi* accoppiarsi
copulation /kɒpjʊ'leɪʃn/ *n* copulazione *f*
⚷ **copy** /'kɒpɪ/ **A** *n* copia *f*
B *vt* (*pt/pp* **-ied**) copiare
■ **copy down** *vt* = **copy**
■ **copy out** *vt* = **copy**

copybook *n* **blot one's ~** rovinarsi la reputazione
copycat A *n* derog fam copione, -a *mf*
B *adj* ‹*crime, murder*› ispirato da un altro
copy editor *n* segretario, -a *mf* di redazione
copyright *n* diritti *mpl* d'autore
copy typist *n* dattilografo, -a *mf*
copywriter *n* copywriter *mf inv*
coquetry /'kɒkɪtrɪ/ *n* civetteria *f*
coquettish /kɒ'ketɪʃ/ *adj* civettuolo
coral /'kɒrəl/ *n* corallo *m*
coral island *n* isola *f* di corallo
coral pink *adj & n* rosa *m inv* corallo
coral reef *n* barriera *f* corallina
cord /kɔːd/ *n* corda *f*; (thinner) cordoncino *m*; (fabric) velluto *m* a coste; **~s** *pl* pantaloni *mpl* di velluto a coste
cordial /'kɔːdɪəl/ **A** *adj* cordiale
B *n* analcolico *m*
cordially /'kɔːdɪəlɪ/ *adv* con tutto il cuore
cordless /'kɔːdlɪs/ *adj* ‹*phone, kettle*› cordless
cordless telephone /'kɔːdlɪs/ *adj* telefono *m* cordless
cordon /'kɔːdn/ *n* cordone *m* (*di persone*)
■ **cordon off** *vt* bloccare

corduroy /'kɔːdərɔɪ/ *n* velluto *m* a coste
⚷ **core** /kɔː(r)/ *n* (of apple, pear) torsolo *m*; fig (of organization) cuore *m*; (of problem, theory) nocciolo *m*
core curriculum *n* materie *fpl* fondamentali (del programma scolastico)
co-respondent /kəʊrɪ'spɒndənt/ *n* Jur correo, -a *mf* in adulterio
Corfu /kɔː'fuː/ *n* Corfù *f*
coriander /kɒrɪ'ændə(r)/ *n* coriandolo *m*
cork /kɔːk/ *n* sughero *m*; (for bottle) turacciolo *m*
corkage /'kɔːkɪdʒ/ *n somma (f) pagata a un ristorante per servire una bottiglia di vino portata da fuori*

⚷ parola chiave

corker /ˈkɔːkə(r)/ *n* BrE infml (story) storia *f* strabiliante; (stroke, shot) tiro *m* da maestro
corkscrew /ˈkɔːkskruː/ *n* cavatappi *m inv*
corkscrew curls *npl* boccoli *mpl*
corn¹ /kɔːn/ *n* grano *m*; AmE (maize) granturco *m*
corn² *n* Med callo *m*
corncob /ˈkɔːnkɒb/ *n* pannocchia *f* [di mais]
cornea /ˈkɔːnɪə/ *n* cornea *f*
corned beef /kɔːndˈbiːf/ *n* manzo *m* sotto sale
corner /ˈkɔːnə(r)/ **A** *n* angolo *m*; (football) calcio *m* d'angolo, corner *m inv* **B** *vt* fig bloccare; Comm accaparrarsi ‹*market*›
corner shop *n* negozio *m* di quartiere
cornerstone /ˈkɔːnəstəʊn/ *n* pietra *f* angolare
cornet /ˈkɔːnɪt/ *n* Mus cornetta *f*; (for ice-cream) cono *m*
cornfield /ˈkɔːnfiːld/ *n* campo *m* di grano; (sweetcorn) campo *m* di mais
cornflour /ˈkɔːnflaʊə(r)/ *n* farina *f* finissima di mais
cornflower /ˈkɔːnflaʊə(r)/ *n* fiordaliso *m*
cornice /ˈkɔːnɪs/ *n* (inside) cornice *f*; (outside) cornicione *m*
Cornish pasty /kɔːnɪʃˈpæstɪ/ *n fagottino (m) di pasta sfoglia ripieno di carne e verdura*
corn oil *n* olio *m* di mais
corn on the cob *n* pannocchia *f* cotta
corn plaster *n* [cerotto *m*] callifugo *m*
cornstarch *n* AmE fecola *f* di mais
cornucopia /kɔːnjʊˈkəʊpɪə/ *n* cornucopia *f*; fig abbondanza *f*
Cornwall /ˈkɔːnwɔːl/ *n* Cornovaglia *f*
corny /ˈkɔːnɪ/ *adj* (**-ier**, **-iest**) infml ‹*joke, film*› scontato; ‹*person*› banale; (sentimental) sdolcinato
corollary /kəˈrɒlərɪ/ *n* corollario *m*
coronary /ˈkɒrənərɪ/ **A** *adj* coronario **B** *n* ~ **[thrombosis]** trombosi *f* coronarica
coronation /kɒrəˈneɪʃn/ *n* incoronazione *f*
coroner /ˈkɒrənə(r)/ *n* coroner *m inv* (*nel diritto britannico, ufficiale incaricato delle indagini su morti sospette*)
coronet /ˈkɒrənet/ *n* coroncina *f*
corporal¹ /ˈkɔːpərəl/ *n* Mil caporale *m*
corporal² *adj* corporale; ~ **punishment** punizione *f* corporale
corporate /ˈkɔːpərət/ *adj* ‹*decision, policy, image*› aziendale; ~ **life** la vita in un'azienda
corporate hospitality *n omaggi (mpl) offerti dalla ditta ai clienti importanti*
corporate identity *n* logo *m* dell'azienda
corporate image *n* immagine *f* aziendale
corporate lawyer *n* legale *mf* specializzato, -a in diritto aziendale
corporate planning *n* pianificazione *f* aziendale
corporate raider *n* finanziere *m* d'assalto
corporation /kɔːpəˈreɪʃn/ *n* ente *m*; (of town) ≈ consiglio *m* comunale
corporation tax *n* BrE imposta *f* sul reddito delle aziende
corps /kɔː(r)/ *n* (*pl* **corps** /kɔːz/) corpo *m*
corps de ballet /kɔːdəˈbæleɪ/ *n* corpo *m* di ballo
corpse /kɔːps/ *n* cadavere *m*
corpulent /ˈkɔːpjʊlənt/ *adj* corpulento
corpus /ˈkɔːpəs/ *n* (of words) corpus *m inv*
corpuscle /ˈkɔːpʌsl/ *n* globulo *m*
correct /kəˈrekt/ **A** *adj* corretto; **be ~** ‹*person*› aver ragione; **~!** esatto! **B** *vt* correggere
correcting fluid *n* bianchetto *m*
correction /kəˈrekʃn/ *n* correzione *f*
corrective /kəˈrektɪv/ *n* correttivo *m*
correctly /kəˈrektlɪ/ *adv* correttamente
correlate /ˈkɒrəleɪt/ **A** *vt* correlare **B** *vi* essere correlato
correlation /kɒrəˈleɪʃn/ *n* correlazione *f*
correspond /kɒrɪˈspɒnd/ *vi* corrispondere (**to** a); ‹*two things*› corrispondere; (write) scriversi
correspondence /kɒrɪˈspɒndəns/ *n* corrispondenza *f*
correspondence course *n* corso *m* per corrispondenza
correspondent /kɒrɪˈspɒndənt/ *n* corrispondente *mf*
corresponding /kɒrɪˈspɒndɪŋ/ *adj* corrispondente
correspondingly /kɒrɪˈspɒndɪŋlɪ/ *adv* in modo corrispondente
corridor /ˈkɒrɪdɔː(r)/ *n* corridoio *m*
corroborate /kəˈrɒbəreɪt/ *vt* corroborare
corrode /kəˈrəʊd/ **A** *vt* corrodere **B** *vi* corrodersi
corrosion /kəˈrəʊʒn/ *n* corrosione *f*
corrugated /ˈkɒrəgeɪtɪd/ *adj* ondulato
corrugated iron *n* lamiera *f* ondulata
corrupt /kəˈrʌpt/ **A** *adj* corrotto **B** *vt* corrompere
corruption /kəˈrʌpʃn/ *n* corruzione *f*
corset /ˈkɔːsɪt/ *n* busto *m*
Corsica /ˈkɔːsɪkə/ *n* Corsica *f*
Corsican /ˈkɔːsɪkən/ *adj & n* corso, -a *mf*
cortège /kɔːˈteɪʒ/ *n* **[funeral]** ~ corteo *m* funebre
cosh /kɒʃ/ *n* randello *m*
co-signatory /kəʊˈsɪgnətrɪ/ *n* cofirmatario, -a *mf*
cosily /ˈkəʊzɪlɪ/ *adv* ‹*sit, lie*› in modo confortevole
cosiness /ˈkəʊzɪnɪs/ *n* (of room) comodità *f*; (intimacy) intimità *f*
cos lettuce /kɒs/ *n* lattuga *f* romana

C

C

cosmetic /kɒz'metɪk/ **A** *adj* cosmetico
B *n* ~s *pl* cosmetici *mpl*
cosmetic surgery *n* chirurgia *f* estetica
cosmic /'kɒzmɪk/ *adj* cosmico
cosmonaut /'kɒzmənɔːt/ *n* cosmonauta *mf*
cosmopolitan /kɒzmə'pɒlɪtən/ *adj* cosmopolita
cosmos /'kɒzmɒs/ *n* cosmo *m*
Cossack /'kɒsæk/ *adj & n* cosacco, -a *mf*
cosset /'kɒsɪt/ *vt* coccolare
✓ **cost** /kɒst/ **A** *n* costo *m*; **~s** *pl* Jur spese *fpl* processuali; **at all ~s** a tutti i costi; **I learnt to my ~** ho imparato a mie spese
B *vt* (*pt/pp* **cost**) costare; **it ~ me £20** mi è costato 20 sterline
C *vt* (*pt/pp* **costed**) **~ [out]** stabilire il prezzo di
co-star /'kəʊstɑː/ **A** *n* Cinema, Theat co-protagonista *mf*
B *vi & vt* **film ~ring X and Y** un film con X e Y come protagonisti
Costa Rica *n* Costa Rica *m*
cost centre *n* centro *m* di costi
cost-cutting *n* tagli *mpl* sulle spese; **as a ~ exercise** [come misura] per ridurre le spese
cost-effective *adj* conveniente
cost-effectiveness *n* convenienza *f*
costing /'kɒstɪŋ/ *n* (process) determinazione *f* dei costi; (discipline) costing *m inv*
costly /'kɒstlɪ/ *adj* **-ier, -iest** costoso
cost of living *n* costo *m* della vita
cost-of-living index *n* indice *m* del costo della vita
cost price *n* prezzo *m* di costo
costume /'kɒstjuːm/ *n* costume *m*
costume drama *n* dramma *m* storico
costume jewellery *n* bigiotteria *f*
cosy /'kəʊzɪ/ **A** *adj* **-ier, -iest** ‹*pub, chat*› intimo; **it's nice and ~ in here** si sta bene qui
B *n* **tea ~** copriteiera *m inv*
cot /kɒt/ *n* lettino *m*; AmE (camp bed) branda *f*
cot death *n* BrE *morte (f) inspiegabile di un neonato nel sonno*
Côte d'Azur /kəʊtdæ'zʊə(r)/ *n* Costa *f* Azzurra
cottage /'kɒtɪdʒ/ *n* casetta *f*
cottage cheese *n* fiocchi *mpl* di latte
cottage hospital *n* BrE piccolo ospedale *m* (*in zona rurale*)
cottage industry *n attività (f inv) artigianale basata sul lavoro a domicilio*
cottage loaf *n* pagnotta *f* casereccia
cottage pie *n* BrE *pasticcio (m) di patate e carne macinata*
cotton /'kɒtn/ **A** *n* cotone *m*
B *attrib* di cotone
■ **cotton on** *vi* infml capire

cotton bud *n* cotton fioc® *m inv*
cotton mill *n* cotonificio *m*
cotton reel *n* rocchetto *m*, spagnoletta *f*
cotton wool *n* BrE cotone *m* idrofilo
couch /kaʊtʃ/ *n* divano *m*
couchette /kuː'ʃet/ *n* cuccetta *f*
couch potato *n* pantofolaio, -a *mf*
cougar /'kuːgə(r)/ *n* coguaro *m*
cough /kɒf/ **A** *n* tosse *f*
B *vi* tossire
■ **cough up** *vt & vi* sputare; infml (pay) sborsare
cough mixture *n* sciroppo *m* per la tosse
✓ **could** /kʊd/, *atono*/kəd/ *v aux* (▶ *also* **can²**) **~ I have a glass of water?** potrei aver un bicchier d'acqua?; **I ~n't do it even if I wanted to** non potrei farlo nemmeno se lo volessi; **I ~n't care less** non potrebbe importarmene di meno; **he ~n't have done it without help** non avrebbe potuto farlo senza aiuto; **you ~ have phoned** avresti potuto telefonare
✓ **council** /'kaʊnsl/ *n* consiglio *m*
council estate *n* BrE complesso *m* di case popolari
council house *n* casa *f* popolare
council housing *n* BrE case *fpl* popolari
councillor /'kaʊnsələ(r)/ *n* consigliere, -a *mf*
council scheme *n* ▶ **council estate**
council tax *n* imposta *f* locale sugli immobili
counsel /'kaʊnsl/ **A** *n* consigli *mpl*; Jur avvocato *m*
B *vt* (*pt/pp* **counselled**) consigliare a ‹*person*›
counselling, AmE **counseling** /'kaʊnsəlɪŋ/ **A** *n* (psychological) terapia *f* [psichiatrica]; Sch orientamento *m* scolastico; **careers ~** orientamento *m* professionale
B *attrib* ‹*group, centre, service*› di assistenza
counsellor /'kaʊnsələ(r)/ *n* consigliere, -a *mf*
count¹ /kaʊnt/ *n* (nobleman) conte *m*
✓ **count²** **A** *n* conto *m*; **keep ~** tenere il conto
B *vt & vi* contare
■ **count against** *vt* ‹*inexperience, police record*› deporre a sfavore di
■ **count among**: *vt* **~ somebody among one's friends** annoverare qualcuno tra i propri amici
■ **count in** *vt* (include) includere; **~ me in!** io ci sto!
■ **count on** *vt* contare su
■ **count out** *vt* contare ‹*money*›; **~ me out!** fate senza di me!
■ **count up** **A** *vt* contare
B *vi* **~ to ten** contare fino a dieci
countable /'kaʊntəbl/ *adj* ‹*noun*› numerabile
countdown /'kaʊntdaʊn/ *n* conto *m* alla rovescia

countenance /ˈkaʊntənəns/ **A** *n* espressione *f*
B *vt* approvare

counter¹ /ˈkaʊntə(r)/ *n* banco *m*; (in games) gettone *m*

counter² **A** *adv* ~ **to** contro, in contrasto a; **go ~ to something** andare contro qualcosa
B *vt & vi* opporre ‹*measure, effect*›; parare ‹*blow*›

counteract /kaʊntərˈækt/ *vt* neutralizzare

counter-attack *n* contrattacco *m*

counterbalance /ˈkaʊntəbæləns/ **A** *n* contrappeso *m*
B *vt* controbilanciare

counter-claim *n* replica *f*

counter-clockwise /ˌkaʊntəˈklɒkwaɪz/ AmE
A *adj* antiorario
B *adv* in senso antiorario

counter-culture /ˈkaʊntəkʌltʃə(r)/ *n* controcultura *f*

counter-espionage *n* controspionaggio *m*

counterfeit /ˈkaʊntəfɪt/ **A** *adj* contraffatto
B *n* contraffazione *f*
C *vt* contraffare

counterfoil /ˈkaʊntəfɔɪl/ *n* matrice *f*

counter-inflationary /-ɪnˈfleɪʃənərɪ/ *adj* antinflazionistico

counter-insurgency /-ɪnˈsɜːdʒənsɪ/ *attrib* per reprimere un'insurrezione

counter-intelligence *n* controspionaggio *m*

countermeasure /ˈkaʊntəmeʒə(r)/ *n* contromisura *f*

counter-offensive *n* controffensiva *f*

counterpane /ˈkaʊntəpeɪn/ *n* copriletto *m*

counterpart /ˈkaʊntəpɑːt/ *n* equivalente *mf*

counterpoint /ˈkaʊntəpɔɪnt/ *n* contrappunto *mf*

counter-productive *adj* controproduttivo

countersign /ˈkaʊntəsaɪn/ *vt* controfirmare

countersignature *n* controfirma *f*

counter staff *n* commessi *mpl*

counter-terrorism *n* antiterrorismo *m*

countertop *n* AmE piano *m* di lavoro

countess /ˈkaʊntɪs/ *n* contessa *f*

countless /ˈkaʊntlɪs/ *adj* innumerevole

countrified /ˈkʌntrɪfaɪd/ *adj* ‹*person*› campagnolo

country /ˈkʌntrɪ/ *n* nazione *f*, paese *m*; (native land) patria *f*; (countryside) campagna *f*; **in the ~** in campagna; **go to the ~** andare in campagna; Pol indire le elezioni politiche

country and western *n* country *m inv*

country bumpkin *n* derog buzzurro, -a *mf*

country club *n club* (*m inv*) *sportivo e ricreativo in campagna*

country cousin *n* derog provinciale *mf*

country dancing *n* danza *f* folcloristica

country house *n* villa *f* di campagna

countryman *n* uomo *m* di campagna; (fellow ~man) compatriota *m*

country music *n* country *m inv*

countryside *n* campagna *f*

countrywide *adj & adv* in tutto il paese

county /ˈkaʊntɪ/ *n* contea *f* (*unità amministrativa britannica*)

county council *n* BrE Pol consiglio *m* di contea

county court *n* BrE Jur tribunale *m* di contea

coup /kuː/ *n* Pol colpo *m* di stato

couple /ˈkʌpl/ *n* coppia *f*; **a ~ of** un paio di

coupon /ˈkuːpɒn/ *n* tagliando *m*; (for discount) buono *m* sconto

courage /ˈkʌrɪdʒ/ *n* coraggio *m*

courageous /kəˈreɪdʒəs/ *adj* coraggioso

courageously /kəˈreɪdʒəslɪ/ *adv* coraggiosamente

courgette /kʊəˈʒet/ *n* BrE zucchino *m*

courier /ˈkʊrɪə(r)/ *n* corriere *m*; (for tourists) guida *f*

course /kɔːs/ *n* Sch corso *m*; Naut rotta *f*; Culin portata *f*; (for golf) campo *m*; **~ of treatment** Med serie *f inv* di cure; **of ~** naturalmente; **in the ~ of** durante; **in due ~** a tempo debito; **~ of action** linea *f* d'azione

course book *n* libro *m* di testo

coursework /kɔːswɜːk/ *n* Sch, Univ esercitazioni *fpl* scritte che contano per la media

court /kɔːt/ **A** *n* tribunale *m*; Sport campo *m*; **take somebody to ~** citare qualcuno in giudizio
B *vt* fare la corte a ‹*woman*›; sfidare ‹*danger*›; **~ing couples** coppiette *fpl*

court case *n* caso *m* giudiziario

court circular *n* bollettino *m* quotidiano di corte

courteous /ˈkɜːtɪəs/ *adj* cortese

courteously /ˈkɜːtɪəslɪ/ *adv* cortesemente

courtesy /ˈkɜːtəsɪ/ *n* cortesia *f*

courtesy bus *n* servizio *m* bus navetta

courtesy car *n* vettura *f* di cortesia

courthouse /ˈkɔːthaʊs/ *n* Jur palazzo *m* di giustizia, tribunale *m*

courtier /ˈkɔːtɪə(r)/ *n* cortigiano, -a *mf*

court martial **A** *n* (*pl* **~s martial**) corte *f* marziale
B *vt* (*pt* **~led**) portare davanti alla corte marziale

court of inquiry *n* commissione *f* d'inchiesta

court of law *n* Jur corte *f* di giustizia

court order *n* Jur ingiunzione *f*

courtroom *n* Jur aula *f* [di tribunale]

courtship /ˈkɔːtʃɪp/ *n* corteggiamento *m*

courtyard /ˈkɔːtjɑːd/ *n* cortile *m*

cousin /ˈkʌzn/ *n* cugino, -a *mf*

cove /kəʊv/ *n* insenatura *f*

covenant /ˈkʌvənənt/ *n* (agreement) accordo *m*; (payment agreement) impegno *m* scritto a pagare

⚷ **cover** /ˈkʌvə(r)/ **A** *n* copertura *f*; (of cushion, to protect something) fodera *f*; (of book, magazine) copertina *f*; **take ~** mettersi al riparo; **under separate ~** a parte
B *vt* coprire; foderare ‹*cushion*›; Journ fare un servizio su

■ **cover for** *vt* (replace) sostituire ‹*somebody*›

■ **cover up** *vt* coprire; fig soffocare ‹*scandal*›

■ **cover up for** *vt* fare da copertura a ‹*somebody*›

⚷ **coverage** /ˈkʌvərɪdʒ/ *n* Journ **it got a lot of ~** i media gli hanno dedicato molto spazio

cover charge *n* coperto *m*

covered market *n* mercato *m* coperto

covered wagon *n* carro *m* coperto

cover girl *n* ragazza *f* copertina

covering /ˈkʌv(ə)rɪŋ/ *n* copertura *f*; (for floor) rivestimento *m*; **~ of snow** strato *m* di neve

covering fire *n* fuoco *m* di copertura

covering letter *n* lettera *f* d'accompagnamento

cover note *n* (from insurance company) polizza *f* provvisoria

cover story *n* (in paper) articolo *m* di prima pagina

covert /ˈkəʊvɜːt/ *adj* ‹*threat*› velato; ‹*operation*› segreto; ‹*glance*› furtivo

covertly /ˈkəʊvɜːtlɪ/ *adv* furtivamente; ‹*operate*› in segreto

cover-up *n* messa *f* a tacere

cover version *n* Mus versione *f* non originale

covet /ˈkʌvɪt/ *vt* bramare

covetous /ˈkʌvətəs/ *adj* avido

covetously /ˈkʌvətəslɪ/ *adv* avidamente

cow /kaʊ/ *n* vacca *f*, mucca *f*

coward /ˈkaʊəd/ *n* vigliacco, -a *mf*

cowardice /ˈkaʊədɪs/ *n* vigliaccheria *f*

cowardly /ˈkaʊədlɪ/ *adj* da vigliacco

cowbell /ˈkaʊbel/ *n* campanaccio *m*

cowboy /ˈkaʊbɔɪ/ *n* cowboy *m inv*; fig infml buffone *m*

cower /ˈkaʊə(r)/ *vi* acquattarsi

cowherd /ˈkaʊhɜːd/ *n* vaccaro *m*

cowhide /ˈkaʊhaɪd/ *n* (leather) vacchetta *f*

cowl /kaʊl/ *n* cappuccio *m*

cowlick /ˈkaʊlɪk/ *n* infml ciocca *f* ribelle

cowl neck *n* collo *m* ad anello

cowpat /ˈkaʊpæt/ *n* sterco *m* di vacca

cowshed /ˈkaʊʃed/ *n* stalla *f*

cox /kɒks/, **coxswain** /ˈkɒks(ə)n/ *n* timoniere, -a *mf*

coy /kɔɪ/ *adj* falsamente timido; (flirtatiously) civettuolo; **be ~ about something** essere evasivo su qualcosa

coyly /ˈkɔɪlɪ/ *adv* con falsa modestia; ‹*flirtatiously*› con civetteria

cozy /ˈkəʊzɪ/ *adj* AmE = **cosy**

CPU *n abbr* (**central processing unit**) CPU *f inv*

crab /kræb/ *n* granchio *m*

crab apple *n* mela *f* selvatica

crack /kræk/ **A** *n* (in wall) crepa *f*; (in china, glass, bone) incrinatura *f*; (noise) scoppio *m*; infml (joke) battuta *f*; **have a ~** (try) fare un tentativo
B *adj* infml (best) di prim'ordine
C *vt* incrinare ‹*china, glass*›; schiacciare ‹*nut*›; decifrare ‹*code*›; infml risolvere ‹*problem*›; **~ a joke** infml fare una battuta
D *vt* ‹*china, glass*› incrinarsi; ‹*whip*› schioccare

■ **crack down** *vi* infml prendere seri provvedimenti

■ **crack down on** *vt* infml prendere seri provvedimenti contro

■ **crack up** *vi* crollare

crackdown /ˈkrækdaʊn/ *n* misure *fpl* (**on** contro)

cracked /krækt/ *adj* ‹*plaster*› crepato; ‹*skin*› screpolato; ‹*rib*› incrinato; infml (crazy) svitato

cracker /ˈkrækə(r)/ *n* (biscuit) cracker *m inv*; (firework) petardo *m*; **[Christmas] ~** *cilindro (m) di cartone contenente una sorpresa che produce una piccola esplosione quando viene aperto*

crackers /ˈkrækəz/ *adj* infml matto

cracking /ˈkrækɪŋ/ *adj* BrE infml eccellente; **at a ~ pace** a ritmo incalzante

crackle /ˈkrækl/ *vi* crepitare

crackling /ˈkræklɪŋ/ *n* (on radio) disturbo *m*; (of foil, cellophane) sfregamento *m*; (of fire) crepitio *m*; (crisp pork) cotenna *f* arrostita

crackpot /ˈkrækpɒt/ infml **A** *n* pazzo, -a *mf*
B *adj* da pazzi

cradle /ˈkreɪdl/ *n* culla *f*

cradle-snatcher *n* infml **he's/she's a ~** se la intende con i ragazzini/le ragazzine

craft¹ /krɑːft/ *n inv* (boat) imbarcazione *f*

craft² *n* mestiere *m*; (technique) arte *f*

craft fair *n* mostra *f* dell'artigianato

craftily /ˈkrɑːftɪlɪ/ *adv* con astuzia

craftsman /ˈkrɑːftsmən/ *n* artigiano *m*

craftsmanship /ˈkrɑːftsmənʃɪp/ *n* maestria *f*

crafty /ˈkrɑːftɪ/ *adj* (**-ier**, **-iest**) astuto

crag /kræg/ *n* rupe *f*

craggy /ˈkrægɪ/ *adj* scosceso; ‹*face*› dai lineamenti marcati

cram /kræm/ *v* (*pt/pp* **crammed**) **A** *vt* stipare (**into** in)
B *vi* (for exams) sgobbare

crammer /ˈkræmə(r)/ *n* BrE infml (school) ≈ istituto *m* di recupero

cramp /kræmp/ *n* crampo *m*

cramped /kræmpt/ *adj* ‹*room*› stretto; ‹*handwriting*› appiccicato; **it's a bit ~ed in**

⚷ parola chiave

here si sta un po' stretti qui
crampon /'kræmpən/ *n* rampone *m*
cranberry /'krænbərı/ *n* Culin mirtillo *m* rosso
crane /kreıŋ/ **A** *n* (at docks, bird) gru *f inv*
B *vt* ~ **one's neck** allungare il collo
cranium /'kreınıəm/ *n* cranio *m*
crank¹ /kræŋk/ *n* tipo, -a *mf* strampalato
crank² *n* Techn manovella *f*
crankshaft /'kræŋkʃɑ:ft/ *n* albero *m* a gomiti
cranky /'kræŋkı/ *adj* strampalato; AmE (irritable) irritabile
cranny /'krænı/ *n* fessura *f*
crap /kræp/ *n* sl (faeces) merda *f*; (film, book etc) schifezza *f*; (nonsense) stronzate *fpl*; **have a ~** cacare
crappy /'kræpı/ *adj* sl di merda
crash /kræʃ/ **A** *n* (noise) fragore *m*; Auto, Aeron incidente *m*; Comm crollo *m*; Comput crash *m inv*
B *vi* schiantarsi (**into** contro); ‹*plane*› precipitare
C *vt* schiantare ‹*car*›
■ **crash out** *vi* sl (go to sleep) crollare; (on sofa etc) dormire
crash barrier *n* guardrail *m inv*
crash course *n* corso *m* intensivo
crash diet *n* dieta *f* drastica
crash helmet *n* casco *m*
crash-land *vi* fare un atterraggio di fortuna
crash-landing *n* atterraggio *m* di fortuna
crass /kræs/ *adj* ‹*ignorance*› crasso
crate /kreıt/ *n* (for packing) cassa *f*
crater /'kreıtə(r)/ *n* cratere *m*
cravat /krə'væt/ *n* foulard *m inv*
crave /kreıv/ *vt* morire dalla voglia di
craving /'kreıvıŋ/ *n* voglia *f* smodata
crawl /krɔ:l/ **A** *n* (swimming) stile *m* libero; **do the ~** nuotare a stile libero; **at a ~** a passo di lumaca
B *vi* andare carponi; ~ **with** brulicare di
crawler lane /'krɔ:lə/ *n* Auto corsia *f* riservata al traffico lento
crayfish /'kreıfıʃ/ *n* gambero *m* d'acqua dolce
crayon /'kreıən/ *n* pastello *m* a cera; (pencil) matita *f* colorata
craze /kreız/ *n* mania *f*
crazed /kreızd/ *adj* ‹*china, glaze*› screpolato; ‹*animal, person*› impazzito; **power-~** ubriaco di potere
crazy /'kreızı/ *adj* (**-ier**, **-iest**) matto; **be ~ about** andar matto per
crazy golf *n* BrE minigolf *m inv*
crazy paving *n* BrE pavimentazione *f* a mosaico irregolare
creak /kri:k/ **A** *n* scricchiolio *m*
B *vi* scricchiolare
creaky /'kri:kı/ *adj* ‹*leather*› che cigola; ‹*door, hinge*› cigolante; ‹*joint, bone, floorboard*› scricchiolante; fig infml ‹*alibi, policy*› traballante
cream /kri:m/ **A** *n* crema *f*; (fresh) panna *f*
B *adj* ‹*colour*› [bianco] panna *inv*
C *vt* Culin sbattere
■ **cream off** *vt* accaparrarsi ‹*top pupils, scientists etc*›
cream cheese *n* formaggio *m* cremoso
cream cracker *n* BrE cracker *m inv*
cream puff *n* sfogliatina *f* alla panna
cream soda *n* soda *f* aromatizzata alla vaniglia
cream tea *n* BrE *tè* (*m inv*) *servito con pasticcini da mangiare con marmellata e panna*
creamy /'kri:mı/ *adj* (**-ier**, **-iest**) cremoso
crease /kri:s/ **A** *n* piega *f*
B *vt* stropicciare
C *vi* stropicciarsi
crease-resistant *adj* che non si stropiccia
⚷ **create** /kri:'eıt/ *vt* creare
⚷ **creation** /kri:'eıʃn/ *n* creazione *f*
⚷ **creative** /kri:'eıtıv/ *adj* creativo
creative director *n* direttore, -trice *mf* creativo
creative writing *n* (school subject) composizione *f*
creativity /kri:eı'tıvətı/ *n* creatività *f*
creator /kri:'eıtə(r)/ *n* creatore, -trice *mf*
creature /'kri:tʃə(r)/ *n* creatura *f*
creature comforts *npl* comodità *fpl*; **like one's ~** amare le proprie comodità
crèche /kreʃ/ *n* asilo *m* nido *inv*
credence /'kri:dəns/ *n* credito *m*; **give ~ to something** (believe) dare credito a qualcosa
credentials /krı'denʃlz/ *npl* credenziali *fpl*
credibility /kredə'bılətı/ *n* credibilità *f*
credible /'kredəbl/ *adj* credibile
⚷ **credit** /'kredıt/ **A** *n* credito *m*; (honour) merito *m*; **take the ~ for** prendersi il merito di
B *vt* accreditare; ~ **somebody with something** Comm accreditare qualcosa a qualcuno; fig attribuire qualcosa a qualcuno
creditable /'kredıtəbl/ *adj* lodevole
credit balance *n* saldo *m* attivo
credit card *n* carta *f* di credito
credit control *n* controllo *m* del credito
credit crunch *n* stretta *f* creditizia, stretta *f* del credito
credit facilities *npl* facilitazioni *fpl* creditizie
credit limit *n* limite *m* di credito
credit note *n* Comm nota *f* di accredito
creditor /'kredıtə(r)/ *n* creditore, -trice *mf*
credits /'kredıts/ *npl* titoli *mpl* di coda
credit side *n* **on the ~** tra i lati positivi
credit squeeze *n* stretta *f* creditizia

C

credit terms *npl* condizioni *fpl* di credito
credit transfer *n* bonifico *m*
creditworthiness /ˈkredɪ(t)wɜːðɪnɪs/ *n* capacità *f* di credito
creditworthy /ˈkredɪ(t)wɜːðɪ/ *adj* meritevole di credito
credulity /krɪˈdjuːlətɪ/ *n* credulità *f*; **strain sb's ~** essere ai limiti della credibilità
credulous /ˈkredjʊləs/ *adj* credulo
creed /kriːd/ *n* credo *m inv*
creek /kriːk/ *n* insenatura *f*; AmE (stream) torrente *m*; **up the ~** infml (in trouble) nei guai
creep /kriːp/ **A** *vi* (*pt/pp* **crept**) muoversi furtivamente
B *n* infml tipo *m* viscido; **it gives me the ~s** mi fa venire i brividi
creeper /ˈkriːpə(r)/ *n* pianta *f* rampicante
creepy /ˈkriːpɪ/ *adj* che fa venire i brividi
creepy-crawly /-ˈkrɔːlɪ/ *n* infml insetto
cremate /krɪˈmeɪt/ *vt* cremare
cremation /krɪˈmeɪʃn/ *n* cremazione *f*
crematorium /kreməˈtɔːrɪəm/ *n* crematorio *m*
crepe /kreɪp/ *n* (fabric) crespo *m*
crepe bandage *n* fascia *f* elastica
crepe paper *n* carta *f* crespata
crepe soles *npl* suole *fpl* di para
crept /krept/ ▶ **creep**
crescendo /krɪˈʃendəʊ/ *n* Mus crescendo *m*; **reach a ~** fig ‹*noise, protests*› raggiungere il picco; ‹*campaign*› raggiungere il culmine
crescent /ˈkresənt/ *n* mezzaluna *f*
crescent moon *n* mezzaluna *f*
cress /kres/ *n* crescione *m*
crest /krest/ *n* cresta *f*; (coat of arms) cimiero *m*; **be on the ~ of a wave** essere sulla cresta dell'onda
crestfallen /ˈkrestfɔːlən/ *adj* mogio
Crete /kriːt/ *n* Creta *f*
Creutzfeldt-Jakob disease /krɔɪtsfeldˈjækɒb/ *n* morbo *m* di Creutzfeldt Jakob
crevasse /krɪˈvæs/ *n* crepaccio *m*
crevice /ˈkrevɪs/ *n* crepa *f*
⚷ **crew** /kruː/ *n* equipaggio *m*; (gang) équipe *f inv*
crew cut *n* capelli *mpl* a spazzola
crew neck *n* girocollo *m*
crew neck sweater *n* maglione *m* a girocollo
crib[1] /krɪb/ *n* (for baby) culla *f*
crib[2] *vt & vi* (*pt/pp* **cribbed**) infml copiare
cribbage /ˈkrɪbɪdʒ/ *n gioco* (*m*) *di carte*
crick /krɪk/ *n* **~ in the neck** torcicollo *m*
cricket[1] /ˈkrɪkɪt/ *n* (insect) grillo *m*
cricket[2] *n* cricket *m*
cricketer /ˈkrɪkɪtə(r)/ *n* giocatore *m* di cricket

⚷ parola chiave

⚷ **crime** /kraɪm/ *n* crimine *m*; (criminality) criminalità *f*; **it's a ~** fig è un delitto
crime of passion *n* delitto *m* passionale
crime prevention *n* prevenzione *f* della criminalità
⚷ **criminal** /ˈkrɪmɪnl/ **A** *adj* criminale; ‹*law, court*› penale
B *n* criminale *mf*
criminal charges *npl* **face ~** essere imputato
criminal investigation *n* inchiesta *f* giudiziaria
Criminal Investigation Department *n* BrE ≈ polizia *f* giudiziaria
criminal justice *n* sistema *m* penale
criminal law *n* diritto *m* penale
criminally insane /ˈkrɪmɪnəlɪ/ *adj* pazzo criminale
criminal offence *n* reato *m*
criminal record *n* **have a/no ~** avere la fedina penale sporca/pulita
criminology /krɪmɪˈnɒlədʒɪ/ *n* criminologia *f*
crimp /krɪmp/ *vt* pieghettare ‹*fabric*›; increspare ‹*pastry*›; arricciare ‹*hair*›
crimson /ˈkrɪmz(ə)n/ *adj* cremisi *inv*
cringe /krɪndʒ/ *vi* (cower) acquattarsi; (at bad joke etc) fare una smorfia
crinkle /ˈkrɪŋk(ə)l/ **A** *vt* spiegazzare
B *vi* spiegazzarsi
crinkly /ˈkrɪŋklɪ/ *adj* ‹*paper, material*› crespato; ‹*hair*› crespo
cripple /ˈkrɪpl/ **A** *n* offensive storpio, -a *mf*
B *vt* storpiare; fig danneggiare
crippled /ˈkrɪpld/ *adj* offensive ‹*person*› storpio; ‹*ship*› danneggiato
crippling /ˈkrɪplɪŋ/ *adj* ‹*taxes, debts*› esorbitante; ‹*disease*› devastante; ‹*strike, effect*› paralizzante
⚷ **crisis** /ˈkraɪsɪs/ (*pl* **-ses** /ˈkraɪsiːz/) *n* crisi *f inv*
crisp /krɪsp/ *adj* croccante; ‹*air*› frizzante; ‹*style*› incisivo
crispbread /ˈkrɪs(p)bred/ *n* crostini *mpl* di pane
crisps /krɪsps/ *npl* patatine *fpl*
crispy /ˈkrɪspɪ/ *adj* croccante
criss-cross /ˈkrɪs-/ *adj* a linee incrociate
criterion /kraɪˈtɪərɪən/ (*pl* **-ria** /kraɪˈtɪərɪə/) *n* criterio *m*
⚷ **critic** /ˈkrɪtɪk/ *n* critico, -a *mf*
⚷ **critical** /ˈkrɪtɪkl/ *adj* critico
critically /ˈkrɪtɪklɪ/ *adv* in modo critico; **~ ill** gravemente malato
critical path analysis *n* analisi *f inv* del percorso critico
⚷ **criticism** /ˈkrɪtɪsɪzm/ *n* critica *f*; **he doesn't like ~** non ama le critiche
criticize /ˈkrɪtɪsaɪz/ *vt* criticare
croak /krəʊk/ *vi* gracchiare; ‹*frog*› gracidare
Croatia /krəʊˈeɪʃə/ *n* Croazia *f*

crochet /ˈkrəʊʃeɪ/ **A** *n* lavoro *m* all'uncinetto **B** *vt* fare all'uncinetto
crochet hook *n* uncinetto *m*
crock /krɒk/ *n* infml **old ~** (person) rudere *m*; (car) macinino *m*
crockery /ˈkrɒkərɪ/ *n* terrecotte *fpl*
crocodile /ˈkrɒkədaɪl/ *n* coccodrillo *m*
crocodile tears *npl* lacrime *fpl* di coccodrillo
crocus /ˈkrəʊkəs/ *n* (*pl* **-es**) croco *m*
croft /krɒft/ *n* piccola fattoria *f*
croissant /ˈkrwæsɑ̃/ *n* cornetto *m*, croissant *m inv*
crone /krəʊn/ *n* derog vecchiaccia *f*
crony /ˈkrəʊnɪ/ *n* compare *m*
crook /krʊk/ *n* infml (criminal) truffatore, -trice *mf*
crooked /ˈkrʊkɪd/ *adj* storto; ‹*limb*› storpiato; infml (dishonest) disonesto; **~ deal** fregatura *f*
croon /kruːn/ *vt & vi* canticchiare
crop /krɒp/ **A** *n* raccolto *m*; fig quantità *f* **B** *vt* (*pt/pp* **cropped**) coltivare
■ **crop up** *vi* infml presentarsi
crop rotation *n* rotazione *f* delle colture
crop spraying /ˈkrɒpspreɪɪŋ/ *n* irrorazione *f*
croquet /ˈkrəʊkeɪ/ *n* croquet *m*
croquette /krəʊˈket/ *n* crocchetta *f*
cross /krɒs/ **A** *adj* (annoyed) arrabbiato; **talk at ~ purposes** fraintendersi
B *n* croce *f*; Bot, Zool incrocio *m*
C *vt* sbarrare ‹*cheque*›; incrociare ‹*road, animals*›; **~ oneself** farsi il segno della croce; **~ one's arms** incrociare le braccia; **~ one's legs** accavallare le gambe; **keep one's fingers ~ed for somebody** tenere le dita incrociate per qualcuno; **it ~ed my mind** mi è venuto in mente
D *vi* (go across) attraversare; ‹*lines*› incrociarsi
■ **cross off** *vt* (from list) depennare
■ **cross out** *vt* sbarrare; (from list) depennare
crossbar *n* (of goal) traversa *f*; (on bicycle) canna *f*
cross-border *adj* oltreconfine
crossbow *n* balestra *f*
cross-bred *adj* ibrido
cross-breed **A** *vt* ibridare, incrociare ‹*animals, plants*›
B *n* (animal) incrocio *m*, ibrido *m*
cross-Channel *adj* attraverso la Manica; ‹*ferry*› che attraversa la Manica
cross-check **A** *n* controprova *f* **B** *vt* fare la controprova di
cross-contamination *n* contaminazione *f* incrociata
cross-country *n* Sport corsa *f* campestre
cross-country skiing *n* sci *m* di fondo
cross-court *adj* ‹*shot, volley*› diagonale
cross-cultural *adj* multiculturale
cross-current *n* corrente *f* trasversale
cross-dressing *n* travestitismo *m*
cross-examination *n* controinterrogatorio *m*
cross-examine *vt* sottoporre a controinterrogatorio
cross-eyed /ˈkrɒsaɪd/ *adj* strabico
crossfire *n* fuoco *m* incrociato
crossing /ˈkrɒsɪŋ/ *n* (for pedestrians) passaggio *m* pedonale; (sea journey) traversata *f*
cross-legged /krɒsˈlegd/ *adj & adv* con le gambe incrociate
crossly /ˈkrɒslɪ/ *adv* con rabbia
crossover *adj* ‹*straps*› incrociato
cross-party *adj* ‹*talks, committee*› interpartitico
cross purposes *npl* **we are at ~** non ci siamo capiti
cross-question *vt* interrogare ‹*person*›
cross-reference *n* rimando *m*
crossroads *n* incrocio *m*; **reach a ~** fig arrivare a un bivio
cross-section *n* sezione *f*; (of community) campione *m*
cross-stitch *n* punto *m* croce
crosswalk *n* AmE attraversamento *m* pedonale
crosswind *n* vento *m* di traverso
crosswise *adv* in diagonale
crossword *n* **~ [puzzle]** parole *fpl* crociate
crotch /krɒtʃ/ *n* Anat inforcatura *f*; (in trousers) cavallo *m*
crotchet /ˈkrɒtʃɪt/ *n* Mus semiminima *f*
crotchety /ˈkrɒtʃətɪ/ *adj* irritabile
crouch /kraʊtʃ/ *vi* accovacciarsi
croupier /ˈkruːpɪə(r)/ *n* croupier *m inv*
crouton /ˈkruːtɒn/ *n* crostino *m*
crow /krəʊ/ **A** *n* corvo *m*; **as the ~ flies** in linea d'aria
B *vi* cantare
crowbar /ˈkrəʊbɑː/ *n* piede *m* di porco
crowd /kraʊd/ **A** *n* folla *f*
B *vt* affollare
C *vi* affollarsi
crowd control *n* controllo *m* della folla
crowded /ˈkraʊdɪd/ *adj* affollato
crowd-puller /ˈkraʊdpʊlə(r)/ *n* (event) grande attrazione *f*
crowd scene *n* Cinema, Theat scena *f* di massa
crown /kraʊn/ **A** *n* corona *f*
B *vt* incoronare; incapsulare ‹*tooth*›
Crown court *n* BrE Jur ≈ corte *f* d'Assise
crowning glory /ˈkraʊnɪŋ/ *n* culmine *m*; **her hair is her ~** i capelli sono il suo punto forte
crown jewels *npl* gioielli *mpl* della corona
crown prince *n* principe *m* ereditario
crow's feet /krəʊzˈfiːt/ *npl* (on face) zampe *fpl* di gallina
crow's nest /krəʊzˈnest/ *n* coffa *f*

C

✓ **crucial** /ˈkruːʃl/ *adj* cruciale
crucially /ˈkruːʃəlɪ/ *adv* ~ **important** di vitale importanza
crucifix /ˈkruːsɪfɪks/ *n* crocifisso *m*
crucifixion /kruːsɪˈfɪkʃn/ *n* crocifissione *f*
crucify /ˈkruːsɪfaɪ/ *vt* (*pt/pp* **-ied**) crocifiggere
crude /kruːd/ *adj* ‹*oil*› greggio; ‹*language*› crudo; ‹*person*› rozzo
crudely /ˈkruːdlɪ/ *adv* (vulgarly) in modo crudo; (simply) schematicamente; (roughly: assembled) sommariamente; ‹*painted, made*› rozzamente; ~ **speaking** in parole povere
crudity /ˈkruːdətɪ/ *n* (vulgarity) volgarità *f*
cruel /ˈkruːəl/ *adj* (**-ler, -lest**) crudele (**to** verso)
cruelly /ˈkruːəlɪ/ *adv* con crudeltà
cruelty /ˈkruːəltɪ/ *n* crudeltà *f*
cruelty-free *adj* ‹*cosmetics*› non testato sugli animali
cruise /kruːz/ **A** *n* crociera *f*
B *vi* fare una crociera; ‹*car*› andare a velocità di crociera
cruise liner *n* nave *f* da crociera
cruise missile *n* missile *m* cruise *inv*
cruiser /ˈkruːzə(r)/ *n* Mil incrociatore *m*; (motor boat) motoscafo *m*
cruising speed /ˈkruːzɪŋ/ *n* velocità *m* di crociera
crumb /krʌm/ *n* briciola *f*
crumble /ˈkrʌmbl/ **A** *vt* sbriciolare
B *vi* sbriciolarsi; ‹*building, society*› sgretolarsi
crumbling /ˈkrʌmblɪŋ/ *adj* fatiscente
crumbly /ˈkrʌmblɪ/ *adj* friabile
crummy /ˈkrʌmɪ/ *adj* infml (substandard) scadente; AmE (unwell) malato
crumpet /ˈkrʌmpɪt/ *n* Culin *focaccina (f) da tostare e mangiare con burro e marmellata*
crumple /ˈkrʌmpl/ **A** *vt* spiegazzare
B *vi* spiegazzarsi
crunch /krʌntʃ/ **A** *n* infml **when it comes to the** ~ quando si viene al dunque
B *vt* sgranocchiare
C *vi* ‹*snow*› scricchiolare
crunchy /ˈkrʌntʃɪ/ *adj* ‹*vegetables, biscuits*› croccante
crusade /kruːˈseɪd/ *n* crociata *f*
crusader /kruːˈseɪdə(r)/ *n* crociato *m*
crush /krʌʃ/ **A** *n* (crowd) calca *f*; **have a ~ on somebody** essersi preso una cotta per qualcuno
B *vt* schiacciare; sgualcire ‹*clothes*›
crushed ice /krʌʃtˈaɪs/ *n* ghiaccio *m* tritato
crushed velvet *n* velluto *m* stazzonato
crushing /ˈkrʌʃɪŋ/ *adj* ‹*defeat, weight, blow*› schiacciante; ‹*blow*› tremendo
crust /krʌst/ *n* crosta *f*
crustacean /krʌˈsteɪʃn/ *n* crostaceo *m*

✓ parola chiave

crusty /ˈkrʌstɪ/ *adj* ‹*bread*› croccante; (irritable) scontroso
crutch /krʌtʃ/ *n* gruccia *f*; Anat inforcatura *f*
crux /krʌks/ *n* fig punto *m* cruciale; ~ **of the matter** nodo *m* della questione
✓ **cry** /kraɪ/ **A** *n* grido *m*; ~ **for help** grido d'aiuto; **have a** ~ farsi un pianto; **a far ~ from** fig tutta un'altra cosa rispetto a
B *vi* (*pt/pp* **cried**) (weep) piangere; (call) gridare
■ **cry off** *vi* BrE (cancel) disdire
■ **cry out** *vi* (shout) urlare
cryogenics /ˌkraɪəˈdʒenɪks/ *n* criogenia *fsg*
crypt /krɪpt/ *n* cripta *f*
cryptic /ˈkrɪptɪk/ *adj* criptico
cryptically /ˈkrɪptɪklɪ/ *adv* ‹*say, speak*› in modo enigmatico; ~ **worded** espresso in maniera sibillina
crystal /ˈkrɪstl/ *n* cristallo *m*; (glassware) cristalli *mpl*
crystal ball *n* sfera *f* di cristallo
crystal clear *adj* ‹*water, sound*› cristallino; **let me make it** ~ lasciatemelo spiegare chiaramente
crystal-gazing /ˈkrɪstlgeɪzɪŋ/ *n* predizione *f* del futuro (*con la sfera di cristallo*)
crystallize /ˈkrɪstəlaɪz/ *vi* (become clear) concretizzarsi
CS gas *n* BrE gas *m inv* lacrimogeno
CST *abbr* AmE (**Central Standard Time**) *ora (f) solare della zona centrale dell'America settentrionale*
cub /kʌb/ *n* (animal) cucciolo *m*; **C~ [Scout]** lupetto *m*
Cuba /ˈkjuːbə/ *n* Cuba *f*
Cuban /ˈkjuːbən/ *adj & n* cubano, -a *mf*
cubby-hole /ˈkʌbɪ-/ *n* (compartment) scomparto *m*; (room) ripostiglio *m*
cube /kjuːb/ *n* cubo *m*
cubic /ˈkjuːbɪk/ *adj* cubico
cubicle /ˈkjuːbɪkl/ *n* cabina *f*
cubism /ˈkjuːbɪzm/ *n* cubismo *m*
cubist /ˈkjuːbɪst/ *adj & n* cubista *mf*
cub reporter *n* cronista *mf* alle prime armi
cuckoo /ˈkʊkuː/ *n* cuculo *m*
cuckoo clock *n* orologio *m* a cucù
cucumber /ˈkjuːkʌmbə(r)/ *n* cetriolo *m*
cud /kʌd/ *n* also fig **chew the** ~ ruminare
cuddle /ˈkʌd(ə)l/ **A** *vt* coccolare
B *vi* ~ **up to** starsene accoccolato insieme a
C *n* **have a** ~ ‹*child*› farsi coccolare; ‹*lovers*› abbracciarsi
cuddly /ˈkʌd(ə)lɪ/ *adj* tenerone; (wanting cuddles) coccolone
cuddly toy *n* peluche *m inv*
cudgel /ˈkʌdʒl/ *n* randello *m*
cue¹ /kjuː/ *n* segnale *m*; Theat battuta *f* d'entrata

cue² *n* (in billiards) stecca *f*
cue ball *n* pallino *m*
cuff /kʌf/ **A** *n* polsino *m*; AmE (turn-up) orlo *m*; (blow) scapaccione *m*; **off the ~** improvvisando
B *vt* dare una pacca a
cuff link *n* gemello *m*
cuisine /kwɪˈziːn/ *n* cucina *f*; **haute ~** /əʊt/ haute cuisine *f*
cul-de-sac /ˈkʌldəsæk/ *n* vicolo *m* cieco
culinary /ˈkʌlɪnərɪ/ *adj* culinario
cull /kʌl/ *vt* (farming) selezionare ‹*livestock*›; (hunting) uccidere, massacrare ‹*seal, whale*›; abbattere ‹*fox*›
culminate /ˈkʌlmɪneɪt/ *vi* culminare
culmination /kʌlmɪˈneɪʃn/ *n* culmine *m*
culottes /kjuːˈlɒts/ *npl* gonna *fsg* pantalone
culpable /ˈkʌlpəbl/ *adj* colpevole
culpable homicide *n* Jur omicidio *m* colposo
culprit /ˈkʌlprɪt/ *n* colpevole *mf*
cult /kʌlt/ *n* culto *m*
cultivate /ˈkʌltɪveɪt/ *vt* coltivare; fig coltivarsi ‹*person*›
cultivated /ˈkʌltɪveɪtɪd/ *adj* ‹*soil*› lavorato; ‹*person*› colto
cultural /ˈkʌltʃərəl/ *adj* culturale
cultural attaché *n* addetto *m* culturale
culture /ˈkʌltʃə(r)/ *n* cultura *f*
cultured /ˈkʌltʃəd/ *adj* colto
cultured pearl *n* perla *f* coltivata
culture shock *n* shock *m inv* culturale
culture vulture *n* infml fanatico, -a *mf* di cultura
culvert /ˈkʌlvət/ *n* condotto *m* sotterraneo
cumbersome /ˈkʌmbəsəm/ *adj* ingombrante
cumin /ˈkjuːmɪn/ *n* cumino *m* nero
cummerbund /ˈkʌməbʌnd/ *n* fascia *f* (*dello smoking*)
cumulative /ˈkjuːmjʊlətɪv/ *adj* cumulativo
cunning /ˈkʌnɪŋ/ **A** *adj* astuto
B *n* astuzia *f*
cup /kʌp/ *n* tazza *f*; (prize, of bra) coppa *f*
cupboard /ˈkʌbəd/ *n* armadio *m*
cupboard love *n* BrE hum amore *m* interessato
cupboard space *n* spazio *m* negli armadi
Cup Final *n* finale *f* di coppa
cupful /ˈkʌpfʊl/ *n* tazza *f* (*contenuto*)
Cupid /ˈkjuːpɪd/ *n* Cupido *m*
cupola /ˈkjuːpələ/ *n* Archit cupola *f*
cup tie *n* BrE partita *f* eliminatoria
cur /kɜː(r)/ *n* derog (dog) cagnaccio *m*
curable /ˈkjʊərəbl/ *adj* curabile
curate /ˈkjʊərət/ *n* curato *m*
curator /kjʊəˈreɪtə(r)/ *n* direttore, -trice *mf* (*di museo*)
curb /kɜːb/ *vt* tenere a freno
curd cheese /kɜːd/ *n* cagliata *f*
curdle /ˈkɜːdl/ *vi* coagularsi
cure /kjʊə(r)/ **A** *n* cura *f*
B *vt* curare; (salt) mettere sotto sale; (smoke) affumicare
cure-all *n* toccasana *m inv*, panacea *f*
curfew /ˈkɜːfjuː/ *n* coprifuoco *m*
curio /ˈkjʊərɪəʊ/ *n* curiosità *f*
curiosity /kjʊərɪˈɒsətɪ/ *n* curiosità *f*
curious /ˈkjʊərɪəs/ *adj* curioso
curiously /ˈkjʊərɪəslɪ/ *adv* curiosamente
curl /kɜːl/ **A** *n* ricciolo *m*
B *vt* arricciare
C *vi* arricciarsi
■ **curl up** *vi* raggomitolarsi
curler /ˈkɜːlə(r)/ *n* bigodino *m*
curling /ˈkɜːlɪŋ/ *n* Sport curling *m*
curly /ˈkɜːlɪ/ *adj* (**-ier**, **-iest**) riccio
curly-haired, **curly-headed** /-ˈheəd, -ˈhedɪd/ *adj* (tight curls) dai capelli crespi; (loose curls) riccio
currant /ˈkʌrənt/ *n* (dried) uvetta *f*
currency /ˈkʌrənsɪ/ *n* valuta *f*; (of word) ricorrenza *f*; **foreign ~** valuta *f* estera
current /ˈkʌrənt/ **A** *adj* corrente
B *n* corrente *f*
current account *n* BrE conto *m* corrente
current affairs *npl* attualità *fsg*
current assets *npl* Fin disponibilità *fpl* correnti
current liabilities *npl* Fin passività *fpl* correnti
currently /ˈkʌrəntlɪ/ *adv* attualmente
curriculum /kəˈrɪkjʊləm/ *n* programma *m* di studi
curriculum vitae /ˈviːtaɪ/ *n* curriculum vitae *m inv*
curry /ˈkʌrɪ/ **A** *n* curry *m inv*; (meal) piatto *m* al curry
B *vt* (*pt/pp* **-ied**) **~ favour with somebody** cercare d'ingraziarsi qualcuno
curry powder *n* curry *m* in polvere
curse /kɜːs/ **A** *n* maledizione *f*; (oath) imprecazione *f*
B *vt* maledire
C *vi* imprecare
cursor /ˈkɜːsə(r)/ *n* cursore *m*
cursor keys *npl* tasti *mpl* cursore
cursory /ˈkɜːsərɪ/ *adj* sbrigativo
curt /kɜːt/ *adj* brusco
curtail /kəˈteɪl/ *vt* ridurre
curtailment /kəˈteɪlmənt/ *n* (of rights, freedom) limitazione *f*; (of expenditure, service) riduzione *f*; (of holiday) interruzione *f*
curtain /ˈkɜːtn/ *n* tenda *f*; Theat sipario *m*
■ **curtain off** *vt* separare con una tenda
curtain call *n* Theat chiamata *f* alla ribalta
curtly /ˈkɜːtlɪ/ *adv* bruscamente
curtsy, **curtsey** /ˈkɜːtsɪ/ **A** *n* inchino *m*
B *vi* (*pt/pp* **-ied**) fare l'inchino

curvaceous /kɜːˈveɪʃəs/ *adj* formoso

curve /kɜːv/ **A** *n* curva *f*
B *vi* curvare; ~ **to the right/left** curvare a destra/sinistra

curved /kɜːvd/ *adj* curvo

curvy /ˈkɜːvɪ/ *adj* (**-ier, -iest**) ‹*woman*› formoso

cushion /ˈkʊʃn/ **A** *n* cuscino *m*
B *vt* attutire; (protect) proteggere

cushy /ˈkʊʃɪ/ *adj* (**-ier, -iest**) infml facile

custard /ˈkʌstəd/ *n* (liquid) crema *f* pasticcera

custard cream *n* BrE biscotto *m* farcito alla crema

custard pie *n* torta *f* alla crema (*nei film comici*)

custard tart *n* torta *f* alla crema

custodial sentence /kʌˈstəʊdɪəl/ *n* condanna *f* ad una pena detentiva

custodian /kʌˈstəʊdɪən/ *n* custode *mf*

custody /ˈkʌstədɪ/ *n* (of child) custodia *f*; (imprisonment) detenzione *f* preventiva

custom /ˈkʌstəm/ *n* usanza *f*; Jur consuetudine *f*; Comm clientela *f*

customary /ˈkʌstəmərɪ/ *adj* (habitual) abituale; **it's ~ to...** è consuetudine...

custom-built /-ˈbɪlt/ *adj* ‹*house*› ad hoc

custom car *n* vettura *f* personalizzata

🔑 **customer** /ˈkʌstəmə(r)/ *n* cliente *mf*

customer care *n* assistenza *f* alla clientela

customer feedback *n* feedback *m inv* dai clienti

customer relations *npl* rapporto *m* con i clienti

customer service *n* assistenza *f* ai clienti

customize /ˈkʌstəmaɪz/ *vt* personalizzare

custom-made /-ˈmeɪd/ *adj* su misura

customs /ˈkʌstəmz/ *npl* dogana *f*

Customs and Excise *n* BrE ufficio *m* Dazi e Dogana

customs clearance *n* sdoganamento *m*

customs declaration *n* dichiarazione *f* doganale

customs duties *npl* dazi *mpl* doganali

customs hall *n* dogana *f*

customs officer *n* doganiere *m*, guardia *f* di finanza

🔑 **cut** /kʌt/ **A** *n* (with knife etc, of clothes) taglio *m*; (reduction) riduzione *f*; (in public spending) taglio *m*
B *vt & vi* (*pt/pp* **cut**, *pres p* **cutting**) tagliare; (reduce) ridurre; ~ **one's finger** tagliarsi il dito; ~ **sb's hair** tagliare i capelli a qualcuno
C *vi* (with cards) alzare

■ **cut away** *vt* tagliar via

■ **cut back** *vt* tagliare ‹*hair*›; potare ‹*hedge*›; (reduce) ridurre

■ **cut back on** *vt* (reduce) ridurre

■ **cut down** *vt* abbattere ‹*tree*›; (reduce) ridurre

■ **cut in** **A** *vi* Auto tagliare la strada; (into conversation) interrompere
B *vt* ~ **somebody in on a deal** dare una percentuale a qualcuno

■ **cut off** *vt* tagliar via; (disconnect) interrompere; fig isolare; **I was ~ off** Teleph la linea è caduta

■ **cut out** *vt* ritagliare; (delete) eliminare; **be ~ out for** infml essere tagliato per; ~ **it out!** infml dacci un taglio!

■ **cut short** *vt* interrompere ‹*holiday, discussion*›

■ **cut up** *vt* (slice) tagliare a pezzi

cut and dried *adj* ‹*answer, solution*› ovvio; **I like everything to be ~** mi piace che tutto sia ben chiaro e definito

cut and paste **A** *n* taglia e incolla *m*
B *vt* tagliare e incollare

cut and thrust *n* **the ~ of debate** gli scambi *mpl* animati del dibattito

cutback /ˈkʌtbæk/ *n* riduzione *f*; (in government spending) taglio *m*

cute /kjuːt/ *adj* infml (in appearance) carino; (clever) acuto

cut glass *n* vetro *m* intagliato

cuticle /ˈkjuːtɪkl/ *n* cuticola *f*

cutlery /ˈkʌtlərɪ/ *n* posate *fpl*

cutlet /ˈkʌtlɪt/ *n* cotoletta *f*

cut-off *n* (upper limit) limite *m* [massimo]

cut-off date *n* data *f* di scadenza

cut-off point *n* limite *m*; Comm data *f* di scadenza

cut-offs *npl* (jeans) jeans *mpl* tagliati

cut-out *n* (outline) ritaglio *m*

cut-price *adj* a prezzo ridotto; ‹*shop*› che fa prezzi ridotti

cutter /ˈkʌtə(r)/ *n* (ship) cutter *m inv*; (on ship) lancia *f*; (for metal, glass) taglierina *f*

cut-throat **A** *n* assassino, -a *mf*
B *adj* ‹*competition*› spietato

cut-throat razor *n* BrE rasoio *m* da barbiere

cutting /ˈkʌtɪŋ/ **A** *adj* ‹*remark*› tagliente
B *n* (from newspaper) ritaglio *m*; (of plant) talea *f*

cutting edge *n* (blade) filo *m*; **be at the ~** fig essere all'avanguardia

cuttingly /ˈkʌtɪŋlɪ/ *adv* ‹*speak*› in maniera tagliente

cutting room *n* Cinema **end up on the ~ floor** essere tagliato in fase di montaggio

CV *n abbr* (**Curriculum Vitae**) CV *m*

cwt *abbr* (**hundredweight**) BrE ≈ 50 kg; AmE ≈ 45 kg

cyanide /ˈsaɪənaɪd/ *n* cianuro *m*

cyber attack /ˈsaɪbər əˌtæk/ *n* cyber-attacco *m*

cyberbullying /ˈsaɪbəˌbʊlɪɪŋ/ *n* ciberbullismo *m*, cyberbullismo *m*

cybercafe /ˈsaɪbəkæfeɪ/ *n* caffè *m inv* Internet

cyberculture /ˈsaɪbəkʌltʃə(r)/ *n* cybercultura *f*

cybernetics /saɪbəˈnetɪks/ *nsg* cibernetica *fsg*
cyberspace /ˈsaɪbəspeɪs/ *n* ciberspazio *m*
cyclamen /ˈsɪkləmən/ *n* ciclamino *m*
cycle /ˈsaɪk(ə)l/ **A** *n* ciclo *m*; (bicycle) bicicletta *f*; infml bici *f inv*
B *vi* andare in bicicletta
cycle clip *n* fermacalzoni *m inv*
cycle lane *n* pista *f* ciclabile
cycle race *n* corsa *f* ciclistica
cycle rack *n* portabiciclette *m inv*
cycle track, **cycle path** *n* pista *f* ciclabile
cyclical /ˈsaɪklɪkl/ *adj* ciclico
cycling /ˈsaɪklɪŋ/ *n* ciclismo *m*
cycling holiday *n* BrE vacanza *f* in bicicletta; **go on a ~** fare una vacanza in bicicletta
cycling shorts *npl* pantaloncini *mpl* da ciclista
cyclist /ˈsaɪklɪst/ *n* ciclista *mf*
cyclo-cross /ˈsaɪkləʊ-/ *n* ciclocross *m inv*
cyclone /ˈsaɪkləʊn/ *n* ciclone *m*
cygnet /ˈsɪgnɪt/ *n* cigno *m* giovane
cylinder /ˈsɪlɪndə(r)/ *n* cilindro *m*
cylindrical /sɪˈlɪndrɪkl/ *adj* cilindrico
cymbals /ˈsɪmblz/ *npl* Mus piatti *mpl*
cynic /ˈsɪnɪk/ *n* cinico, -a *mf*
cynical /ˈsɪnɪk(ə)l/ *adj* cinico
cynically /ˈsɪnɪklɪ/ *adv* cinicamente
cynicism /ˈsɪnɪsɪzm/ *n* cinismo *m*
cypress /ˈsaɪprəs/ *n* cipresso *m*
Cypriot /ˈsɪprɪət/ *adj & n* cipriota *mf*
Cyprus /ˈsaɪprəs/ *n* Cipro *m*
Cyrillic /sɪˈrɪlɪk/ *adj* cirillico
cyst /sɪst/ *n* ciste *f*
cystitis /sɪˈstaɪtɪs/ *n* cistite *f*
Czar, **czar** /zɑː(r)/ *n* zar *m inv*
Czech /tʃek/ *adj & n* ceco, -a *mf*
Czechoslovak /tʃekəˈsləʊvæk/ *adj* cecoslovacco
Czechoslovakia /tʃekəsləˈvækɪə/ *n* Cecoslovacchia *f*
Czech Republic *n* Repubblica *f* Ceca

c
d

Dd

d¹, **D** /diː/ *n* (letter) d, D *f inv*; Mus re *m inv*
d² *abbr* (**died**) morto
dab /dæb/ **A** *n* colpetto *m*; **a ~ of** un pochino di
B *vt* (*pt/pp* **dabbed**) toccare leggermente ‹*eyes*›
■ **dab on** *vt* mettere un po' di ‹*paint etc*›
dabble /ˈdæbl/ *vi* **~ in something** fig occuparsi di qualcosa a tempo perso
dachshund /ˈdækshʊnd/ *n* bassotto *m*
dad /ˈdæd/, **daddy** /ˈdædɪ/ *n* infml papà *m*, babbo *m*
daddy-long-legs *n* zanzarone *m* [dei boschi]; AmE (spider) ragno *m*
daffodil /ˈdæfədɪl/ *n* giunchiglia *f*
daft /dɑːft/ *adj* sciocco
dagger /ˈdægə(r)/ *n* stiletto *m*; Typ croce *f*; **be at ~s drawn** infml essere ai ferri corti
dahlia /ˈdeɪlɪə/ *n* dalia *f*
daily /ˈdeɪlɪ/ **A** *adj* giornaliero
B *adv* giornalmente
C *n* (newspaper) quotidiano *m*; infml (cleaner) donna *f* delle pulizie
daintily /ˈdeɪntɪlɪ/ *adv* delicatamente
dainty /ˈdeɪntɪ/ *adj* (**-ier**, **-iest**) grazioso; ‹*movement*› delicato
dairy /ˈdeərɪ/ *n* caseificio *m*; (shop) latteria *f*
dairy cow *n* mucca *f* da latte
dairyman /ˈdeərɪmən/ *n* (on farm) operaio *m* addetto all'allevamento di mucche [da latte]; AmE (farmer) allevatore *m*
dairy products *npl* latticini *mpl*
dais /ˈdeɪɪs/ *n* pedana *f*
daisy /ˈdeɪzɪ/ *n* margheritina *f*; (larger) margherita *f*
dale /deɪl/ *n* literary valle *f*
dally /ˈdælɪ/ *vi* (*pt/pp* **-ied**) stare a gingillarsi
dam /dæm/ **A** *n* diga *f*
B *vt* (*pt/pp* **dammed**) costruire una diga su
damage /ˈdæmɪdʒ/ **A** *n* danno *m* (**to** a); **~s** *pl* Jur risarcimento *msg*
B *vt* danneggiare; fig nuocere a
damage limitation exercise *n* manovra *f* per contenere i danni
damaging /ˈdæmɪdʒɪŋ/ *adj* dannoso
damask /ˈdæməsk/ *n* damasco *m*
dame /deɪm/ *n* literary dama *f*; AmE sl donna *f*
dammit /ˈdæmɪt/ *int* BrE infml accidenti!
damn /dæm/ **A** *adj* infml maledetto
B *adv* ‹*lucky, late*› maledettamente
C *n* **I don't care** *or* **give a ~** infml non me ne frega un accidente
D *vt* dannare

d

damnation /dæm'neɪʃn/ **A** *n* dannazione *f*
B *int* infml accidenti!
damnedest /'dæmdɪst/ **A** *n* **do one's ~ (to do)** infml (hardest) fare del proprio meglio (per fare)
B *adj* **it was the ~ thing** (surprising) era la cosa più straordinaria
damning /'dæmɪŋ/ *adj* schiacciante
damp /dæmp/ **A** *adj* umido
B *n* umidità *f*
C *vt* = **dampen**
dampen /'dæmpən/ *vt* inumidire; fig raffreddare ‹*enthusiasm*›
damper /'dæmpə(r)/ *n* **the news put a ~ on the evening** infml la notizia ha raggelato l'atmosfera della serata
dampness /'dæmpnɪs/ *n* umidità *f*
damson /'dæmzən/ *n* (fruit) susina *f* selvatica, prugna *f* selvatica
⚷ **dance** /dɑːns/ **A** *n* ballo *m*
B *vt & vi* ballare
▪ **dance about, dance up and down** *vi* saltellare qua e là
dance hall *n* sala *f* da ballo
dance music *n* musica *f* da ballo
dancer /'dɑːnsə(r)/ *n* ballerino, -a *mf*
dancing /'dɑːnsɪŋ, AmE 'dænsɪŋ/ *n* ballo *m*
dandelion /'dændɪlaɪən/ *n* dente *m* di leone
dandruff /'dændrʌf/ *n* forfora *f*
Dane /deɪn/ *n* danese *mf*; **Great ~** danese *m*
⚷ **danger** /'deɪndʒə(r)/ *n* pericolo *m*; **in/out of ~** in/fuori pericolo
danger level *n* livello *m* di guardia
danger list *n* **on the ~** in prognosi riservata; **off the ~** fuori pericolo
danger money *n* indennità *f* di rischio
⚷ **dangerous** /'deɪndʒərəs/ *adj* pericoloso
dangerously /'deɪndʒərəslɪ/ *adv* pericolosamente; **~ ill** in pericolo di vita
danger signal *n also* fig segnale *m* di pericolo
dangle /'dæŋgl/ **A** *vi* penzolare; fig **leave somebody dangling** lasciare qualcuno in sospeso
B *vt* far penzolare
Danish /'deɪnɪʃ/ **A** *adj* danese
B *n* (language) danese *m*
Danish pastry *n dolce (m) di pasta sfoglia contenente pasta di mandorle, mele ecc.*
dank /dæŋk/ *adj* umido e freddo
Danube /'dænjuːb/ *n* Danubio *m*
dapper /'dæpə(r)/ *adj* azzimato
dappled /'dæp(ə)ld/ *adj* ‹*grey, horse*› pomellato; ‹*sky*› screziato; ‹*shade, surface*› chiazzato
dare /deə(r)/ **A** *vt & vi* osare; (challenge) sfidare (**to** a); **~ [to] do something** osare fare qualcosa; **I ~ say!** molto probabilmente!
B *n* sfida *f*
daredevil /'deədevl/ *n* spericolato, -a *mf*
daring /'deərɪŋ/ **A** *adj* audace
B *n* audacia *f*
⚷ **dark** /dɑːk/ **A** *adj* buio; **~ blue/brown** blu/marrone scuro; **It's getting ~** sta cominciando a fare buio; **~ horse** fig (in race, contest) vincitore *m* imprevisto; (not much known about) misterioso *m*; **keep something ~** fig tenere qualcosa nascosto
B *n* **after ~** col buio; **in the ~** al buio; **keep somebody in the ~** fig tenere qualcuno all'oscuro
Dark Ages *n* alto Medioevo *m*
dark chocolate *n* cioccolato *m* fondente
darken /'dɑːkn/ **A** *vt* oscurare
B *vi* oscurarsi
dark-eyed /-'aɪd/ *adj* ‹*person*› dagli occhi scuri
dark glasses *npl* occhiali *mpl* scuri
darkly /'dɑːklɪ/ *adv* ‹*mutter, hint*› cupamente
dark matter *n* materia *f* oscura
darkness /'dɑːknɪs/ *n* buio *m*
darkroom /'dɑːkruːm/ *n* camera *f* oscura
dark skinned *adj* ‹*person*› dalla pelle scura
darling /'dɑːlɪŋ/ **A** *adj* adorabile; **my ~ Joan** carissima Joan
B *n* tesoro *m*; **be a ~ and...** sii gentile e...
darn /dɑːn/ *vt* rammendare
darning needle /'dɑːnɪŋ/ *n* ago *m* da rammendo
dart /dɑːt/ **A** *n* dardo *m*; (in sewing) pince *f inv*; **~s** *sg* (game) freccette *fpl*
B *vi* lanciarsi
dartboard /'dɑːtbɔːd/ *n* bersaglio *m* [per freccette]
dash /dæʃ/ **A** *n* Typ trattino *m*; (in Morse) linea *f*; **a ~ of milk** un goccio di latte; **make a ~ for** lanciarsi verso
B *vi* **I must ~** devo scappare
C *vt* far svanire ‹*hopes*›; (hurl) gettare
▪ **dash off** **A** *vi* scappar via
B *vt* (write quickly) buttare giù
▪ **dash out** *vi* uscire di corsa
dashboard /'dæʃbɔːd/ *n* cruscotto *m*
dashing /'dæʃɪŋ/ *adj* (bold) ardito; (in appearance) affascinante
DAT *abbr* (**digital audio tape**) DAT *f inv*
⚷ **data** /'deɪtə/ *npl & sg* dati *mpl*
databank *n* banca *f* di dati
database *n* banca *f* dati, database *m inv*
database management system *n* sistema *m* di gestione di data base
data capture *n* registrazione *f* di dati
data communications *npl* comunicazione *f* dati, telematica *f*
data compression *n* compressione *f* dati
data disk *n* dischetto *m* di dati
data entry *n* immissione *f* [di] dati

data file *n* file *m inv* dati
data handling *n* manipolazione *f* [di] dati
data input *n* input *m* dati
data link *n* collegamento *m* dati
data processing *n* elaborazione *f* [di] dati
data protection *n* protezione *f* dati
data protection act *n* Jur *legge (f) britannica per la salvaguardia delle informazioni personali*
data retrieval *n* recupero *m* dati
data security *n* sicurezza *f* dei dati
data storage *n* archiviazione *f* dati
data storage device *n* unità *f* archivio dati
data transmission *n* trasmissione *f* dati
date[1] /deɪt/ *n* (fruit) dattero *m*
date[2] **A** *n* data *f*; (meeting) appuntamento *m*; **to ~** fino ad oggi; **out of ~** (not fashionable) fuori moda; (expired) scaduto; ‹*information*› non aggiornato; **make a ~ with somebody** dare un appuntamento a qualcuno; **be up to ~** essere aggiornato
B *vt & vi* datare; (go out with) uscire con
■ **date back to** *vi* risalire a
dated /ˈdeɪtɪd/ *adj* fuori moda; ‹*language*› antiquato
date line *n* linea *f* [del cambiamento] di data
date of issue *n* data *f* di emissione
date rape *n stupro (m) perpetrato da persona nota alla vittima*
date stamp *n* (mark) timbro *m* con la data
dating agency /ˈdeɪtɪŋ/ *n* agenzia *f* matrimoniale
dative /ˈdeɪtɪv/ *n* dativo *m*
daub /dɔːb/ *vt* imbrattare ‹*walls*›
daughter /ˈdɔːtə(r)/ *n* figlia *f*
daughter-in-law *n* (*pl* **~s-in-law**) nuora *f*
daunt /dɔːnt/ *vt* scoraggiare; **nothing ~ed** per niente scoraggiato
daunting /ˈdɔːntɪŋ/ *adj* ‹*task, prospect*› poco allettante; ‹*person*› che intimidisce; **I'm faced with a ~ amount of work** mi aspetta una quantità di lavoro preoccupante; **it can be (quite) ~** può essere (piuttosto) allarmante
dauntless /ˈdɔːntlɪs/ *adj* intrepido
dawdle /ˈdɔːdl/ *vi* bighellonare; (over work) cincischiarsi
dawn /dɔːn/ **A** *n* alba *f*; **at ~** all'alba
B *vi* albeggiare; **it ~ed on me** fig mi è apparso chiaro
dawn raid *n* (police) raid *m* della polizia all'alba; (stock market) dawn raid *m inv*
day /deɪ/ *n* giorno *m*; (whole day) giornata *f*; (period) epoca *f*; **~ by ~** giorno per giorno; **~ after ~** giorno dopo giorno; **these ~s** oggigiorno; **in those ~s** a quei tempi; **it's had its ~** infml ha fatto il suo tempo
day boy *n* BrE Sch alunno *m* esterno
daybreak *n* **at ~** allo spuntar del giorno
day-care *n* (for young children) scuola *f* materna
day centre *n* centro *m* di accoglienza
day-dream **A** *n* sogno *m* ad occhi aperti
B *vi* sognare ad occhi aperti
day girl *n* Sch alunna *f* esterna
daylight *n* luce *f* del giorno
daylight robbery *n* infml **it's ~** è un furto!
daylight saving time *n* ora *f* legale
day nursery *n* (0–3 years) asilo *m* nido; (3–6 years) scuola *f* materna
day off *n* giorno *m* di riposo
day pass *n* biglietto *m* giornaliero
day release *n giorno (m) di congedo settimanale dal lavoro da dedicare a corsi di formazione*
day return *n* (ticket) *biglietto (m) di andata e ritorno con validità giornaliera*
day school *n scuola (f) che non fornisce alloggio*
daytime *n* giorno *m*; **in the ~** di giorno
daytime TV *n programmi (mpl) televisivi trasmessi durante il giorno*
day-to-day *adj* quotidiano; **on a ~ basis** giorno per giorno
day trader *n* day trader *m inv*
day trading *n* day trading *m inv*
day trip *n* gita *f* (*di un giorno*)
day tripper *n* gitante *mf*
daze /deɪz/ *n* **in a ~** stordito; fig sbalordito
dazed /deɪzd/ *adj* stordito; fig sbalordito
dazzle /ˈdæzl/ *vt* abbagliare
dazzling /ˈdæzlɪŋ/ *adj* abbagliante
DBMS *n abbr* (**database management system**) DBMS *m*
D-Day *n* Mil D-day *m inv*; (important day) giorno *m* fatidico
deacon /ˈdiːk(ə)n/ *n* diacono *m*
dead /ded/ **A** *adj* morto; (numb) intorpidito; **~ and buried** morto e sepolto; **~ body** morto *m*; **~ centre** pieno centro *m*
B *adv* **~ tired** stanco morto; **~ slow/easy** lentissimo/facilissimo; **you're ~ right** hai perfettamente ragione; **stop ~** fermarsi di colpo; **be ~ on time** essere in perfetto orario
C *n* **the ~** *pl* i morti; **in the ~ of night** nel cuore della notte
deaden /ˈded(ə)n/ *vt* attutire ‹*sound*›; calmare ‹*pain*›
dead end **A** *n* vicolo *m* cieco
B *attrib* **dead-end** ‹*job*› senza prospettive
dead heat *n* **it was a ~** è finita a pari merito
deadline *n* scadenza *f*
deadlock *n* **reach ~** fig giungere ad un punto morto
dead loss *n* infml (person) buono, -a *mf* a nulla; (thing) oggetto *m* inutile

deadly /ˈdedlɪ/ *adj* (**-ier**, **-iest**) mortale; infml (dreary) barboso; ~ **sins** peccati *mpl* capitali
dead on arrival *adj* Med deceduto durante il trasporto
deadpan *adj* impassibile; ‹*humour*› all'inglese
dead ringer *n* infml **be a ~ for somebody** essere la copia spiccicata di qualcuno
Dead Sea *n* Mar *m* Morto
dead weight *n* fig (burden) peso *m* morto
dead wood *n* BrE fig zavorra *f*
deaf /def/ *adj* sordo; ~ **and dumb** sordomuto
deaf aid *n* apparecchio *m* acustico
deafen /ˈdef(ə)n/ *vt* assordare; (permanently) render sordo
deafening /ˈdefənɪŋ/ *adj* assordante
deaf mute *adj* & *n* offensive sordomuto, -a *mf*
deafness /ˈdefnɪs/ *n* sordità *f*
deaf without speech *adj* sordomuto, -a *mf*
deal /diːl/ **A** *n* (agreement) patto *m*; (in business) accordo *m*; **who's ~?** Cards a chi tocca dare le carte?; **a good** *or* **great ~** molto; **get a raw ~** infml ricevere un trattamento ingiusto
B *vt* (*pt/pp* **dealt** /delt/) (in cards) dare; **~ somebody a blow** dare un colpo a qualcuno
▪ **deal in** *vt* trattare in
▪ **deal out** *vt* ‹*hand out*› distribuire
▪ **deal with** *vt* (handle) occuparsi di; trattare con ‹*company*›; (be about) trattare di; **that's been ~t with** è stato risolto
dealer /ˈdiːlə(r)/ *n* commerciante *mf*; (in drugs) spacciatore, -trice *mf*
dealership /ˈdiːləʃɪp/ *n* Comm concessione *f*
dealing /ˈdiːlɪŋ/ *n* (in drugs) traffico *m*, spaccio *m*
dealing room /ˈdiːlɪŋ/ *n* Fin borsino *m*
dealings /ˈdiːlɪŋz/ *npl* **have ~ with** avere a che fare con
dean /diːn/ *n* decano *m*; Univ preside *mf* di facoltà
dear /dɪə(r)/ **A** *adj* caro; (in letter) Caro; (formal) Gentile
B *n* caro, -a *mf*
C *int* **oh ~!** Dio mio!
dearly /ˈdɪəlɪ/ *adv* ‹*love*› profondamente; ‹*pay*› profumatamente
dearth /dɜːθ/ *n* penuria *f*
death /deθ/ *n* morte *f*
deathbed *n* letto *m* di morte
death camp *n* campo *m* di sterminio
death certificate *n* certificato *m* di morte
death duty *n* tassa *f* di successione
death knell *n* campane *fpl* a morto; fig tramonto *m*
death list *n* lista *f* dei bersagli (*di un assassino*)

✓ parola chiave

deathly /ˈdeθlɪ/ **A** *adj* ~ **silence** silenzio *m* di tomba
B *adv* ~ **pale** di un pallore cadaverico
death mask *n* maschera *f* mortuaria
death penalty *n* pena *f* di morte
death rate *n* tasso *m* di mortalità
death ray *n* raggio *m* mortale
death row /rəʊ/ *n* AmE braccio *m* della morte
death sentence *n* also fig condanna *f* a morte
death's head *n* teschio *m*
death threat *n* minaccia *f* di morte
death throes *npl* also fig agonia *f*
death toll *n* bilancio *m* delle vittime
death trap *n* trappola *f* mortale
death warrant *n* ordine *m* di esecuzione di una condanna a morte
death wish *n* desiderio *m* di morire
debacle /deɪˈbɑːk(ə)l/ *n* sfacelo *m*
debar /dɪˈbɑː(r)/ *vt* (*pt/pp* **debarred**) escludere
debase /dɪˈbeɪs/ *vt* degradare
debatable /dɪˈbeɪtəbl/ *adj* discutibile
debate /dɪˈbeɪt/ **A** *n* dibattito *m*
B *vt* discutere; (in formal debate) dibattere
C *vi* **~ whether to...** considerare se
debauchery /dɪˈbɔːtʃərɪ/ *n* dissolutezza *f*
debenture bond /dɪˈbentʃə(r)/ *n* obbligazione *f* non garantita
debilitating /dɪˈbɪlɪteɪtɪŋ/ *adj* ‹*disease*› debilitante
debility /dɪˈbɪlətɪ/ *n* debilitazione *f*
debit /ˈdebɪt/ **A** *n* debito *m*
B *vt* (*pt/pp* **debited**) Comm addebitare ‹*sum, account*›
debit card *n* carta *f* di debito
debonair /debəˈneə(r)/ *adj* ‹*person*› elegante e cortese
debrief /diːˈbriːf/ *vt* chiamare a rapporto; **be ~ed** ‹*defector, freed hostage*› essere interrogato; ‹*diplomat, agent*› essere chiamato a rapporto
debriefing /diːˈbriːfɪŋ/ *n* (of hostage, defector) interrogatorio *m*
debris /ˈdebriː/ *n* macerie *fpl*
debt /det/ *n* debito *m*; **be in ~** avere dei debiti
debt collection *n* esazione *f* crediti
debt collection agency *n* agenzia *f* di recupero crediti
debt collector *n* esattore *m* dei crediti
debtor /ˈdetə(r)/ *n* debitore, -trice *mf*
debt relief *n* cancellazione *f* del debito
debug /diːˈbʌg/ *vt* (*pt/pp* **debugged**) Comput correggere gli errori di; togliere i microfoni spia da ‹*room*›
debunk /dɪˈbʌŋk/ *vt* ridicolizzare ‹*theory, myth*›
debut /ˈdeɪbuː/ *n* debutto *m*

decade /ˈdekeɪd/ *n* decennio *m*
decadence /ˈdekədəns/ *n* decadenza *f*
decadent /ˈdekədənt/ *adj* decadente
decaffeinated /diːˈkæfɪneɪtɪd/ *adj* decaffeinato
decalitre /ˈdekəliːtə(r)/ *n* decalitro *m*
decametre /ˈdekəmiːtə(r)/ *n* decametro *m*
decamp /dɪˈkæmp/ *vi* sgattaiolare via; **~ with something** (steal) squagliarsela con qualcosa
decant /dɪˈkænt/ *vt* travasare
decanter /dɪˈkæntə(r)/ *n* caraffa *f (di cristallo)*
decapitate /dɪˈkæpɪteɪt/ *vt* decapitare
decathlon /dɪˈkæθlɒn/ *n* decathlon *m inv*
decay /dɪˈkeɪ/ **A** *n* also fig decadenza *f*; (rot) decomposizione *f*; (of tooth) carie *f inv* **B** *vi* imputridire; (rot) decomporsi; ‹*tooth*› cariarsi
deceased /dɪˈsiːst/ **A** *adj* defunto **B** *n* **the ~** il defunto; la defunta
deceit /dɪˈsiːt/ *n* inganno *m*
deceitful /dɪˈsiːtfʊl/ *adj* falso
deceitfully /dɪˈsiːtfʊlɪ/ *adv* falsamente
deceive /dɪˈsiːv/ *vt* ingannare
decelerate /diːˈseləreɪt/ *vi* decelerare
deceleration /diːseləˈreɪʃn/ *n* decelerazione *f*
December /dɪˈsembə(r)/ *n* Dicembre *m*
decency /ˈdiːsənsɪ/ *n* decenza *f*
decent /ˈdiːsənt/ *adj* decente; (respectable) rispettabile; **very ~ of you** molto gentile da parte tua
decently /ˈdiːsəntlɪ/ *adv* decentemente; (kindly) gentilmente
decentralization /diːsentrəlaɪˈzeɪʃn/ *n* decentramento *m*
decentralize /diːˈsentrəlaɪz/ *vt* decentrare
deception /dɪˈsepʃn/ *n* inganno *m*
deceptive /dɪˈseptɪv/ *adj* ingannevole
deceptively /dɪˈseptɪvlɪ/ *adv* ingannevolmente; **it looks ~ easy** sembra facile ma non lo è
decibel /ˈdesɪbel/ *n* decibel *m inv*
decide /dɪˈsaɪd/ **A** *vt* decidere; **that's ~d then** siamo d'accordo, allora **B** *vi* decidere (**on** di)
▪ **decide on** *vt* scegliere ‹*date, outfit, course of action*›
decided /dɪˈsaɪdɪd/ *adj* risoluto
decidedly /dɪˈsaɪdɪdlɪ/ *adv* risolutamente; (without doubt) senza dubbio
decider /dɪˈsaɪdə(r)/ *n* (point) punto *m* decisivo; (goal) goal *m inv* decisivo; (game) spareggio *m*
deciduous /dɪˈsɪdjʊəs/ *adj* a foglie decidue
decigram, decigramme /ˈdesɪgræm/ *n* decigrammo *m*
decilitre /ˈdesɪliːtə(r)/ *n* decilitro *m*
decimal /ˈdesɪml/ **A** *adj* decimale **B** *n* numero *m* decimale
decimal point *n* virgola *f*
decimal system *n* sistema *m* decimale
decimate /ˈdesɪmeɪt/ *vt* decimare
decimetre /ˈdesɪmiːtə(r)/ *n* decimetro *m*
decipher /dɪˈsaɪfə(r)/ *vt* decifrare
decision /dɪˈsɪʒn/ *n* decisione *f*
decision-maker /dɪˈsɪʒnmeɪkə(r)/ *n persona (f) che ama o ha il potere di prendere decisioni*
decision-making /dɪˈsɪʒnmeɪkɪŋ/ *n* **be good/bad at ~** saper/non saper prendere decisioni; **~ process** *n* processo *m* decisionale
decisive /dɪˈsaɪsɪv/ *adj* decisivo
decisively /dɪˈsaɪsɪvlɪ/ *adv* con decisione
deck¹ /dek/ *vt* abbigliare
deck² *n* Naut ponte *m*; **on ~** in coperta; **top ~** (of bus) piano *m* di sopra; **~ of cards** mazzo *m*
deckchair /ˈdektʃeə(r)/ *n* [sedia *f* a] sdraio *f inv*
declaration /dekləˈreɪʃn/ *n* dichiarazione *f*
declare /dɪˈkleə(r)/ *vt* dichiarare; **anything to ~?** niente da dichiarare?; **~ one's love** dichiararsi
declassify /diːˈklæsɪfaɪ/ *vt* rimuovere dai vincoli di segretezza ‹*document, information*›
declension /dɪˈklenʃn/ *n* declinazione *f*
decline /dɪˈklaɪn/ **A** *n* declino *m* **B** *vt* (also Gram) declinare **C** *vi* (decrease) diminuire; ‹*health*› deperire; (say no) rifiutare
declutch /diːˈklʌtʃ/ *vi* BrE lasciare la frizione
decode /diːˈkəʊd/ *vt* decifrare; Comput decodificare
decoding /diːˈkəʊdɪŋ/ *n* decodifica *f*, decodificazione *f*
décolleté /deɪˈkɒlteɪ/ *adj* décolleté *inv*, scollato
decompose /diːkəmˈpəʊz/ *vi* decomporsi
decomposition /diːkɒmpəˈzɪʃn/ *n* scomposizione *f*
decompress /ˌdiːkəmˈpres/ *vt* decomprimere
decompression /diːkəmˈpreʃn/ *n* decompressione *f*
decontaminate /diːkənˈtæmɪneɪt/ *vt* decontaminare
décor /ˈdeɪkɔː(r)/ *n* decorazione *f*; (including furniture) arredamento *m*
decorate /ˈdekəreɪt/ *vt* decorare; (paint) pitturare; (wallpaper) tappezzare
decoration /dekəˈreɪʃn/ *n* decorazione *f*
decorative /ˈdekərətɪv/ *adj* decorativo
decorator /ˈdekəreɪtə(r)/ *n* **painter and ~** imbianchino *m*
decorous /ˈdekərəs/ *adj* decoroso
decorously /ˈdekərəslɪ/ *adv* decorosamente

decorum /dɪˈkɔːrəm/ *n* decoro *m*
decoy¹ /ˈdiːkɔɪ/ *n* esca *f*
decoy² /dɪˈkɔɪ/ *vt* adescare
decrease¹ /ˈdiːkriːs/ *n* diminuzione *f*; **be on the ~** essere in diminuzione
decrease² /dɪˈkriːs/ *vt & vi* diminuire
decreasing /dɪˈkriːsɪŋ/ *adj* in diminuzione
decreasingly /dɪˈkriːsɪŋlɪ/ *adv* sempre meno
decree /dɪˈkriː/ **A** *n* decreto *m*
B *vt* decretare
decrepit /dɪˈkrepɪt/ *adj* decrepito
decriminalization /diːkrɪmɪnəlaɪˈzeɪʃn/ *n* depenalizzazione *f*
decriminalize /diːˈkrɪmɪnəlaɪz/ *vt* depenalizzare
dedicate /ˈdedɪkeɪt/ *vt* dedicare
dedicated /ˈdedɪkeɪtɪd/ *adj* ‹*person*› scrupoloso
dedication /dedɪˈkeɪʃn/ *n* dedizione *f*; (in book) dedica *f*
deduce /dɪˈdjuːs/ *vt* dedurre (**from** da)
deduct /dɪˈdʌkt/ *vt* dedurre
deduction /dɪˈdʌkʃn/ *n* deduzione *f*
deed /diːd/ *n* azione *f*; Jur atto *m* di proprietà
deed of covenant *n* Jur *accordo* (*m*) *accessorio ad un contratto immobiliare*
deed poll *n* **change one's name by ~** cambiare nome con un atto unilaterale
deem /diːm/ *vt* ritenere
deep /diːp/ *adj* profondo; **go off the ~ end** infml arrabbiarsi
deepen /ˈdiːpn/ **A** *vt* approfondire; scavare più profondamente ‹*trench*›
B *vi* approfondirsi; fig ‹*mystery*› infittirsi
deep-fat fryer *n* friggitrice *f*
deep-felt *adj* profondo
deep-freeze *n* congelatore *m*
deep-fried *adj* fritto (in molto olio)
deep-frozen *adj* surgelato
deep-fry *vt* friggere (in molto olio)
deeply *adv* profondamente
deep-rooted *adj* ‹*habit, prejudice*› radicato
deep-sea *adj* ‹*exploration, diving*› in profondità; ‹*fisherman, fishing*› d'alto mare
deep-sea diver *n* palombaro *m*
deep-seated *adj* radicato
deep-set *adj* ‹*eyes*› infossato
deep South *n* AmE il profondo Sud
deep-vein thrombosis *n* trombosi *f* venosa profonda
deer /dɪə(r)/ *n inv* cervo *m*
de-escalate /ˌdiːˈeskəleɪt/ *vt* ridurre ‹*crisis, violence*›
deface /dɪˈfeɪs/ *vt* sfigurare ‹*picture*›; deturpare ‹*monument*›
defamation /defəˈmeɪʃn/ *n* diffamazione *f*
defamatory /dɪˈfæmətərɪ/ *adj* diffamatorio

parola chiave

default /dɪˈfɔːlt/ **A** *n* Jur (non-payment) morosità *f*; (failure to appear) contumacia *f*; Comput default *m inv*; **win by ~** Sport vincere per abbandono dell'avversario; **in ~ of** per mancanza di
B *adj* **~ drive** Comput lettore *m* di default
C *vi* (not pay) venir meno ad un pagamento; Comput **~ to something** ritornare all'impostazione di default
defeat /dɪˈfiːt/ **A** *n* sconfitta *f*
B *vt* sconfiggere; (frustrate) vanificare ‹*attempts*›; **that ~s the object** questo fa fallire l'obiettivo
defeatist /dɪˈfiːtɪst/ *adj & n* disfattista *mf*
defecate /ˈdefəkeɪt/ *vi* defecare
defect¹ /dɪˈfekt/ *vi* Pol fare defezione
defect² /ˈdiːfekt/ *n* difetto *m*
defective /dɪˈfektɪv/ *adj* difettoso
defector /dɪˈfektə(r)/ *n* (from party) defezionista *mf*; (from country) fuor[i]uscito, -a *mf*
defence /dɪˈfens/ *n* difesa *f*
defenceless /dɪˈfenslɪs/ *adj* indifeso
Defence Minister *n* ministro *m* della difesa
defend /dɪˈfend/ *vt* difendere; (justify) giustificare
defendant /dɪˈfendənt/ *n* Jur imputato, -a *mf*
defender /dɪˈfendə(r)/ *n* difensore *m*, -ditrice *f*
defensive /dɪˈfensɪv/ **A** *adj* difensivo
B *n* difensiva *f*; **on the ~** sulla difensiva
defer /dɪˈfɜː(r)/ **A** *vt* (*pt/pp* **deferred**) (postpone) rinviare
B *vi* **~ to somebody** rimettersi a qualcuno
deference /ˈdefərəns/ *n* deferenza *f*
deferential /defəˈrenʃl/ *adj* deferente
deferentially /defəˈrenʃəlɪ/ *adv* con deferenza
deferment, **deferral** /dɪˈfɜːmənt, dɪˈfɜːrəl/ *n* (postponement) rinvio *m*
defiance /dɪˈfaɪəns/ *n* sfida *f*; **in ~ of** sfidando
defiant /dɪˈfaɪənt/ *adj* ‹*person*› ribelle; ‹*gesture, attitude*› di sfida
defiantly /dɪˈfaɪəntlɪ/ *adv* con aria di sfida
deficiency /dɪˈfɪʃənsɪ/ *n* insufficienza *f*
deficient /dɪˈfɪʃənt/ *adj* insufficiente; **be ~ in** mancare di
deficit /ˈdefɪsɪt/ *n* deficit *m inv*
defile /dɪˈfaɪl/ *vt* fig contaminare
define /dɪˈfaɪn/ *vt* definire
defined *adj* ‹*role*› definito
definite /ˈdefɪnɪt/ *adj* definito; (certain) ‹*answer, yes*› definitivo; ‹*improvement, difference*› netto; **he was ~ about it** è stato chiaro in proposito
definite article *n* (grammatical) articolo *m* determinativo

definitely /'defɪnɪtlɪ/ *adv* sicuramente

definition /defɪ'nɪʃn/ *n* definizione *f*

definitive /dɪ'fɪnətɪv/ *adj* definitivo

deflate /dɪ'fleɪt/ *vt* sgonfiare

deflation /dɪ'fleɪʃn/ *n* Comm deflazione *f*

deflationary /dɪ'fleɪʃənrɪ/ *adj* deflazionistico

deflect /dɪ'flekt/ *vt* deflettere

deformed /dɪ'fɔːmd/ *adj* deforme

deformity /dɪ'fɔːmətɪ/ *n* deformità *f*

DEFRA /'defrə/ *abbr* BrE (**Department for Environment, Food, and Rural Affairs**) ≈ Ministero *m* per le Politiche Agricole e Forestali

defrag /'diːfræg/ *vt* infml deframmentare

defragment /'diːfræg'ment/ *vt* Comput deframmentare

defragmentation /ˌdiːfrægmen'teɪʃn/ *n* Comput deframmentazione *f*

defraud /dɪ'frɔːd/ *vt* defraudare

defray /dɪ'freɪ/ *vt* fml sostenere

defrost /diː'frɒst/ *vt* sbrinare ‹*fridge*›; scongelare ‹*food*›

deft /deft/ *adj* abile

deftly /'deftlɪ/ *adv* con destrezza

deftness /'deftnɪs/ *n* destrezza *f*

defunct /dɪ'fʌŋkt/ *adj* morto e sepolto; ‹*law*› caduto in disuso

defuse /diː'fjuːz/ *vt* disinnescare; calmare ‹*situation*›

defy /dɪ'faɪ/ *vt* (*pt/pp* **-ied**) (challenge) sfidare; resistere a ‹*attempt*›; (not obey) disobbedire a

degenerate¹ /dɪ'dʒenəreɪt/ *vi* degenerare; **~ into** fig degenerare in

degenerate² /dɪ'dʒenərət/ *adj* degenerato

degeneration /dɪdʒenə'reɪʃn/ *n* degenerazione *f*

degenerative /dɪ'dʒenərətɪv/ *adj* degenerativo

degradation /degrə'deɪʃn/ *n* (debasement) degradazione *f*; (of culture) deterioramento *m*; (squalor) desolazione *f*

degrade /dɪ'greɪd/ *vt* (humiliate) degradare ‹*person*›; (damage) deteriorare ‹*environment*›

degrading /dɪ'greɪdɪŋ/ *adj* degradante

degree /dɪ'griː/ *n* grado *m*; Univ laurea *f*; **20 ~s** 20 gradi; **not to the same ~** non allo stesso livello

degree ceremony *n* BrE Univ cerimonia *f* di consegna delle lauree

degree course *n* BrE Univ corso *m* di laurea

dehydrate /diːhaɪ'dreɪt/ *vt* disidratare

dehydrated /diːhaɪ'dreɪtɪd/ *adj* disidratato

dehydration /diːhaɪ'dreɪʃn/ *n* disidratazione *f*

de-ice /diː'aɪs/ *vt* togliere il ghiaccio da

de-icer /diː'aɪsə(r)/ *n* (mechanical) sbrinatore *m*; (chemical) liquido *m* scongelante

deign /deɪn/ *vi* **~ to do something** degnarsi di fare qualcosa

deity /'diːətɪ/ *n* divinità *f*

déjà vu /deɪʒɑː'vuː/ *n* déjà vu *m inv*

dejected /dɪ'dʒektɪd/ *adj* demoralizzato

dejectedly /dɪ'dʒektɪdlɪ/ *adv* con aria demoralizzata

dejection /dɪ'dʒekʃn/ *n* abbacchiamento *m*

delay /dɪ'leɪ/ **A** *n* ritardo *m*; **without ~** senza indugio
B *vt* ritardare; **be ~ed** ‹*person*› essere trattenuto; ‹*train, aircraft*› essere in ritardo
C *vi* indugiare

delayed action /dɪ'leɪd/ *adj* ad azione ritardata; ‹*bomb*› a scoppio ritardato

delegate¹ /'delɪgət/ *n* delegato, -a *mf*

delegate² /'delɪgeɪt/ *vt* delegare

delegation /delɪ'geɪʃn/ *n* delegazione *f*

delete /dɪ'liːt/ *vt* cancellare

delete key *n* tasto *m* di cancellazione

deletion /dɪ'liːʃn/ *n* cancellatura *f*

deli /'delɪ/ *n* infml (**delicatessen**) gastronomia *f*

deliberate¹ /dɪ'lɪbərət/ *adj* deliberato; (slow) posato

deliberate² /dɪ'lɪbəreɪt/ *vi/i* deliberare

deliberately /dɪ'lɪbərətlɪ/ *adv* deliberatamente; (slowly) in modo posato

deliberation /dɪlɪbə'reɪʃn/ *n* deliberazione *f*; **with ~** in modo posato

delicacy /'delɪkəsɪ/ *n* delicatezza *f*; (food) prelibatezza *f*

delicate /'delɪkət/ *adj* delicato

delicately /'delɪkətlɪ/ *adv* ‹*handle, phrase*› con delicatezza; ‹*crafted, flavoured*› con raffinatezza

delicatessen /delɪkə'tesn/ *n* negozio *m* di specialità gastronomiche

delicious /dɪ'lɪʃəs/ *adj* delizioso

delight /dɪ'laɪt/ **A** *n* piacere *m*
B *vt* deliziare
C *vi* **~ in** dilettarsi con

delighted /dɪ'laɪtɪd/ *adj* lieto

delightful /dɪ'laɪtfʊl/ *adj* delizioso

delineate /dɪ'lɪnɪeɪt/ *vt also* fig delineare

delineation /dɪlɪnɪ'eɪʃn/ *n* delineazione *f*

delinquency /dɪ'lɪŋkwənsɪ/ *n* delinquenza *f*

delinquent /dɪ'lɪŋkwənt/ **A** *adj* delinquente
B *n* delinquente *mf*

delirious /dɪ'lɪrɪəs/ *adj* **be ~** delirare; fig (very happy) essere pazzo di gioia

delirium /dɪ'lɪrɪəm/ *n* delirio *m*

deliver /dɪ'lɪvə(r)/ *vt* consegnare; recapitare ‹*post, newspaper*›; tenere ‹*speech*›; dare ‹*message*›; tirare ‹*blow*›; (set free) liberare; **~ a baby** far nascere un bambino

deliverance /dɪ'lɪv(ə)rəns/ *n* liberazione *f*

delivery /dɪ'lɪvərɪ/ *n* consegna *f*; (of post) distribuzione *f*; Med parto *m*; **cash on ~** pagamento *m* alla consegna

delivery address *n* indirizzo *m* del destinatario

d

delivery man *n* fattorino *m*

delivery room *n* Med sala *f* parto

delta /ˈdeltə/ *n* delta *m inv*

delude /dɪˈlu:d/ *vt* ingannare; ~ **oneself** illudersi

deluge /ˈdelju:dʒ/ **A** *n* diluvio *m* **B** *vt* fig (with requests etc) inondare

delusion /dɪˈlu:ʒn/ *n* illusione; ~**s of grandeur** mania *f* di grandezza

de luxe /dəˈlʌks/ *adj* di lusso

delve /delv/ *vi* ~ **into** (into pocket etc) frugare in; (into notes, the past) fare ricerche in

demagnetize /di:ˈmægnətaɪz/ *vt* smagnetizzare

🔑 **demand** /dɪˈmɑ:nd/ **A** *n* richiesta *f*; Comm domanda *f*; **in** ~ richiesto; **on** ~ a richiesta **B** *vt* esigere (**of/from** da)

demanding /dɪˈmɑ:ndɪŋ/ *adj* esigente

de-manning /di:ˈmænɪŋ/ *n* BrE taglio *m* di personale

demarcation /di:mɑ:ˈkeɪʃn/ *n* demarcazione *f*

demean /dɪˈmi:n/ *vt* ~ **oneself** abbassarsi (to a)

demeaning /dɪˈmi:nɪŋ/ *adj* degradante

demeanour /dɪˈmi:nə(r)/ *n* comportamento *m*

demented /dɪˈmentɪd/ *adj* demente

dementia /dɪˈmenʃə/ *n* demenza *f*

demerara /deməˈreərə/, **demerara sugar** *n* zucchero *m* grezzo di canna

demilitarization /di:mɪlɪtəraɪˈzeɪʃn/ *n* demilitarizzazione *f*

demilitarize /di:ˈmɪlɪtəraɪz/ *vt* smilitarizzare

demise /dɪˈmaɪz/ *n* decesso *m*

demister /di:ˈmɪstə(r)/ *n* Auto sbrinatore *m*

demo /ˈdeməʊ/ *n* (*pl* ~**s**) infml manifestazione *f*

demobilize /di:ˈməʊbəlaɪz/ *vt* Mil smobilitare

🔑 **democracy** /dɪˈmɒkrəsɪ/ *n* democrazia *f*

democrat /ˈdeməkræt/ *n* democratico, -a *mf*

democratic /deməˈkrætɪk/ *adj* democratico

democratically /deməˈkrætɪklɪ/ *adv* democraticamente

demo disk *n* Comput demo disk *m inv*

demographic /deməˈgræfɪk/ *adj* demografico

demolish /dɪˈmɒlɪʃ/ *vt* demolire

demolition /deməˈlɪʃn/ *n* demolizione *f*

demon /ˈdi:mən/ *n* demonio *m*

demonic /dɪˈmɒnɪk/ *adj* ‹*aspect, power*› demoniaco

demonize /ˈdi:mənaɪz/ *vt* demonizzare

demonstrable /ˈdemənstrəbl/ *adj* dimostrabile

demonstrably /ˈdemənstrəblɪ/ *adv* ‹*false, untrue*› manifestamente

🔑 **demonstrate** /ˈdemənstreɪt/ **A** *vt* dimostrare; dare una dimostrazione dell'uso di ‹*appliance*› **B** *vi* Pol manifestare

demonstration /demənˈstreɪʃn/ *n* dimostrazione *f*; Pol manifestazione *f*

demonstrative /dɪˈmɒnstrətɪv/ *adj* Gram dimostrativo; **be** ~ essere espansivo

demonstrator /ˈdemənstreɪtə(r)/ *n* Pol manifestante *mf*; (for product) dimostratore, -trice *mf*

demoralize /dɪˈmɒrəlaɪz/ *vt* demoralizzare

demoralizing /dɪˈmɒrəlaɪzɪŋ/ *adj* demoralizzante, avvilente

demote /dɪˈməʊt/ *vt* retrocedere di grado; Mil degradare

demur /dɪˈmɜ:/ **A** *vi* (*pt/pp* **demurred**) (complain) protestare; (disagree) obiettare **B** *n* **without** ~ senza obiezioni

demure /dɪˈmjʊə(r)/ *adj* schivo

demurely /dɪˈmjʊəlɪ/ *adv* in modo schivo

den /den/ *n* tana *f*; (room) rifugio *m*

denationalize /di:ˈnæʃ(ə)nəlaɪz/ *vt* denazionalizzare

denial /dɪˈnaɪəl/ *n* smentita *f*

denier /ˈdenɪə(r)/ *n* denaro *m*

denigrate /ˈdenɪgreɪt/ *vt* denigrare

denigrating /ˈdenɪgreɪtɪŋ/ *adj* denigratore

denim /ˈdenɪm/ *n* [tessuto *m*] jeans *m*; ~**s** *pl* [blue-]jeans *mpl*

Denmark /ˈdenmɑ:k/ *n* Danimarca *f*

denomination /dɪnɒmɪˈneɪʃn/ *n* Relig confessione *f*; (money) valore *m*

denote /dɪˈnəʊt/ *vt* denotare

denounce /dɪˈnaʊns/ *vt* denunciare

dense /dens/ *adj* denso; ‹*crowd, forest*› fitto; (stupid) ottuso

densely /ˈdenslɪ/ *adv* ‹*populated*› densamente; ~ **wooded** fittamente ricoperto di alberi

density /ˈdensətɪ/ *n* densità *f*; (of forest) fittezza *f*

dent /dent/ **A** *n* ammaccatura *f* **B** *vt* ammaccare

dental /ˈdentl/ *adj* dei denti; ‹*treatment*› dentistico; ‹*hygiene*› dentale

dental appointment *n* appuntamento *m* dal dentista

dental clinic *n* (hospital) clinica *f* odontoiatrica; (part of hospital) reparto *m* odontoiatrico

dental floss *n* filo *m* interdentale

dental plate *n* dentiera *f*

dental surgeon *n* odontoiatra *mf*, medico *m* dentista

dental surgery *n* BrE (premises) studio *m* dentistico; (treatment) visita *f* dentistica

dented /ˈdentɪd/ *adj* ammaccato; ~ **pride** orgoglio *m* ferito

dentist /ˈdentɪst/ *n* dentista *mf*

🔑 parola chiave

dentistry /ˈdentɪstrɪ/ *n* odontoiatria *f*

dentures /ˈdentʃəz/ *npl* dentiera *fsg*

denude /dɪˈnjuːd/ *vt* denudare

denunciation /dɪnʌnsɪˈeɪʃn/ *n* denuncia *f*

Denver boot /ˈdenvə/ *n* AmE = **wheel clamp**

deny /dɪˈnaɪ/ *vt* (*pt/pp* **-ied**) negare; (officially) smentire; ~ **somebody something** negare qualcosa a qualcuno; **I can't ~ it** non posso negarlo

deodorant /diːˈəʊdərənt/ *n* deodorante *m*

deodorize /diːˈəʊdəraɪz/ *vt* deodorare

depart /dɪˈpɑːt/ *vi* ‹*plane, train*› partire; literary ‹*person*› andare via; (deviate) allontanarsi (**from** da)

departed /dɪˈpɑːtɪd/ *adj* euph (dead) scomparso

department /dɪˈpɑːtmənt/ *n* reparto *m*; Pol ministero *m*; (of company) sezione *f*; Univ dipartimento *m*

departmental /diːpɑːtˈmentl/ *adj* Pol ‹*colleague, meeting*› di sezione; (in business) di reparto

department head *n* caporeparto *mf*; Univ direttore, -trice *mf* d'istituto

department manager *n* (of business) direttore, -trice *mf* di reparto; (of store) caporeparto *mf inv*

Department of Defense *n* AmE ministero *m* della Difesa

Department of Energy *n* AmE ≈ ministero *m* dell'Industria

Department of Health *n* ministero *m* della Sanità

Department of Homeland Security *n* AmE ≈ Dipartimento *m* per la sicurezza nazionale

Department of Social Security *n* BrE ≈ Istituto *m* Nazionale della Previdenza Sociale

Department of the Environment *n* BrE ministero *m* dell'Ambiente

Department of Trade and Industry *n* BrE ministero *m* del Commercio e dell'Industria

department store *n* grande magazzino *m*

departure /dɪˈpɑːtʃə(r)/ *n* partenza *f*; (from rule) allontanamento *m*; **new ~** svolta *f*

departure gate *n* (at airport) uscita *f*

departure lounge *n* (at airport) sala *f* d'attesta

departure platform *n* Rail binario *m*

departures board *n* tabellone *m* delle partenze

depend /dɪˈpend/ *vi* dipendere (**on** da); (rely) contare (**on** su); **it all ~s** dipende; **~ing on what he says** a seconda di quello che dice

dependability /dɪpendəˈbɪlətɪ/ *n* affidabilità *f*

dependable /dɪˈpendəbl/ *adj* fidato

dependant /dɪˈpendənt/ *n* persona *f* a carico

dependence /dɪˈpendəns/ *n* dipendenza *f*

dependent /dɪˈpendənt/ *adj* dipendente (**on** da)

depict /dɪˈpɪkt/ *vt* (in writing) dipingere; (with picture) rappresentare

depiction /dɪˈpɪkʃn/ *n* rappresentazione *f*

depilatory /dɪˈpɪlətərɪ/ *n* (cream) crema *f* depilatoria

deplete /dɪˈpliːt/ *vt* ridurre; **totally ~d** completamente esaurito

depletion /dɪˈpliːʃn/ *n* (of resources, funds) impoverimento *m*

deplorable /dɪˈplɔːrəbl/ *adj* deplorevole

deplore /dɪˈplɔː(r)/ *vt* deplorare

deploy /dɪˈplɔɪ/ **A** *vt* Mil spiegare **B** *vi* schierarsi

deployment /dɪˈplɔɪmənt/ *n* schieramento *m*

depoliticize /diːpəˈlɪtɪsaɪz/ *vt* depoliticizzare

depopulate /diːˈpɒpjʊleɪt/ *vt* spopolare

depopulation /diːˌpɒpjʊˈleɪʃn/ *n* spopolamento *m*

deport /dɪˈpɔːt/ *vt* deportare

deportation /diːpɔːˈteɪʃn/ *n* deportazione *f*

deportee /diːpɔːˈtiː/ *n* deportato, -a *mf*

deportment /dɪˈpɔːtmənt/ *n* portamento *m*

depose /dɪˈpəʊz/ *vt* deporre

deposit /dɪˈpɒzɪt/ **A** *n* deposito *m*; (against damage) cauzione *f*; (first instalment) acconto *m* **B** *vt* depositare

deposit account *n* libretto *m* di risparmio; (without instant access) conto *m* vincolato

depositor /dɪˈpɒzɪtə(r)/ *n* Fin depositante *mf*

deposit slip *n* (in bank) distinta *f* di versamento

depot /ˈdepəʊ/ *n* deposito *m*; AmE Rail stazione *f* ferroviaria

deprave /dɪˈpreɪv/ *vt* depravare

depraved /dɪˈpreɪvd/ *adj* depravato

depravity /dɪˈprævətɪ/ *n* depravazione *f*

deprecate /ˈdeprəkeɪt/ *vt* disapprovare

deprecatory /deprɪˈkeɪtərɪ/ *adj* (disapproving) di disapprovazione; (apologetic) di scusa

depreciate /dɪˈpriːʃɪeɪt/ *vi* deprezzarsi

depreciation /dɪpriːsɪˈeɪʃn/ *n* deprezzamento *m*

depress /dɪˈpres/ *vt* deprimere; (press down) premere

depressed /dɪˈprest/ *adj* depresso; **~ area** zona *f* depressa

depressing /dɪˈpresɪŋ/ *adj* deprimente

depression /dɪˈpreʃn/ *n* depressione *f*

depressive /dɪˈpresɪv/ **A** *adj* depressivo **B** *n* depresso, -a *mf*

depressurize /diːˈpreʃəraɪz/ *vi* depressurizzare

deprivation /deprɪˈveɪʃn/ *n* privazione *f*

deprive /dɪˈpraɪv/ *vt* **~ somebody of something** privare qualcuno di qualcosa

deprived /dɪ'praɪvd/ *adj* ‹*area, childhood*› disagiato

Dept *abbr* (**Department**) dipartimento *m* (dip.)

depth /depθ/ *n* profondità *f*; **in ~** ‹*study, analyse*› in modo approfondito; **in the ~s of winter** in pieno inverno; **in the ~s of despair** nella più profonda disperazione; **be out of one's ~** (in water) non toccare il fondo; fig sentirsi in alto mare

deputation /depjʊ'teɪʃn/ *n* deputazione *f*

deputize /'depjʊtaɪz/ *vi* **~ for** fare le veci di

deputy /'depjʊtɪ/ *n* vice *mf*; (temporary) sostituto, -a *mf*

deputy chairman *n* vicepresidente *m*

deputy leader *n* BrE Pol sottosegretario *m*

deputy premier, deputy prime minister *n* Pol vice primo ministro *m*

deputy president *n* vicepresidente *mf*

derail /dɪ'reɪl/ *vt* **be ~ed** ‹*train*› essere deragliato

derailleur gears /dɪ'reɪljə/ *npl* deragliatore *msg*

derailment /dɪ'reɪlmənt/ *n* deragliamento *m*

deranged /dɪ'reɪndʒd/ *adj* squilibrato

deregulate /diː'regjʊleɪt/ *vt* deregolamentare ‹*market*›

deregulation /diːregjʊ'leɪʃn/ *n* deregolamentazione *f*

derelict /'derəlɪkt/ *adj* abbandonato

deride /dɪ'raɪd/ *vt* deridere

derision /dɪ'rɪʒn/ *n* derisione *f*

derisive /dɪ'raɪsɪv/ *adj* derisorio

derisory /dɪ'raɪsərɪ/ *adj* ‹*laughter*› derisorio; ‹*offer*› irrisorio

derivation /derɪ'veɪʃn/ *n* derivazione *f*

derivative /dɪ'rɪvətɪv/ **A** *adj* derivato
B *n* derivato *m*

derive /dɪ'raɪv/ **A** *vt* (obtain) derivare; **be ~d from** ‹*word*› derivare da
B *vi* **~ from** derivare da

dermatitis /dɜːmə'taɪtɪs/ *n* dermatite *f*

dermatologist /dɜːmə'tɒlədʒɪst/ *n* dermatologo, -a *mf*

derogatory /dɪ'rɒgətrɪ/ *adj* ‹*comments*› peggiorativo

derrick /'derɪk/ *n* derrick *m inv*

derv /dɜːv/ *n* BrE gasolio *m*

descaler /diː'skeɪlə(r)/ *n* BrE disincrostante *m*

descend /dɪ'send/ **A** *vi* scendere; **be ~ed from** discendere da
B *vt* scendere da

■ **descend on** *vt* (attack) piombare su; (visit) capitare [all'improvviso]

descendant /dɪ'sendənt/ *n* discendente *mf*

descent /dɪ'sent/ *n* discesa *f*; (lineage) origine *f*

descrambler /diː'skræmblə(r)/ *n* Teleph, TV decodificatore *m*

🔑 parola chiave

🔑 **describe** /dɪ'skraɪb/ *vt* descrivere

🔑 **description** /dɪ'skrɪpʃn/ *n* descrizione *f*; **they had no help of any ~** non hanno avuto proprio nessun aiuto

descriptive /dɪ'skrɪptɪv/ *adj* descrittivo; (vivid) vivido

desecrate /'desɪkreɪt/ *vt* profanare

desecration /desɪ'kreɪʃn/ *n* profanazione *f*

desegregate /diː'segrɪgeɪt/ *vt* abolire la segregazione razziale in ‹*school*›

deselect /diːsɪ'lekt/ *vt* BrE **be ~ed** *non avere riconferma della candidatura alle elezioni da parte del proprio partito*

desensitize /diː'sensɪtaɪz/ *vt* desensibilizzare

desert¹ /'dezət/ **A** *n* deserto *m*
B *adj* deserto; **~ island** isola *f* deserta

desert² /dɪ'zɜːt/ **A** *vt* abbandonare
B *vi* disertare

desert boot *n* scarponcino *m* Clark®

deserted /dɪ'zɜːtɪd/ *adj* deserto

deserter /dɪ'zɜːtə(r)/ *n* Mil disertore *m*

desertion /dɪ'zɜːʃn/ *n* Mil diserzione *f*; (of family) abbandono *m*

deserts /dɪ'zɜːts/ *npl* **get one's just ~** ottenere ciò che ci si merita

🔑 **deserve** /dɪ'zɜːv/ *vt* meritare

deservedly /dɪ'zɜːvədlɪ/ *adv* meritatamente

deserving /dɪ'zɜːvɪŋ/ *adj* meritevole; **~ cause** opera *f* meritoria

desiccated /'desɪkeɪtɪd/ *adj* essiccato; derog (dried up) secco

🔑 **design** /dɪ'zaɪn/ **A** *n* progettazione *f*; (fashion ~, appearance) design *m inv*; (pattern) modello *m*; (aim) proposito *m*; **have ~s on** aver mire su
B *vt* progettare; disegnare ‹*clothes, furniture, model*›; **be ~ed for** essere fatto per

designate /'dezɪgneɪt/ *vt* designare

designation /dezɪg'neɪʃn/ *n* designazione *f*

design consultant *n* progettista *mf*

designer /dɪ'zaɪnə(r)/ *n* progettista *mf*; (of clothes) stilista *mf*; Theat (of set) scenografo, -a *mf*

design fault *n* difetto *m* di concezione

design feature *n* prestazione *f*

designing /dɪ'zaɪnɪŋ/ *adj* derog calcolatore

desirable /dɪ'zaɪərəbl/ *adj* desiderabile

🔑 **desire** /dɪ'zaɪə(r)/ **A** *n* desiderio *m*
B *vt* desiderare

desist /dɪ'zɪst/ *vi* desistere (**from** da)

🔑 **desk** /desk/ *n* scrivania *f*; (in school) banco *m*; (in hotel) reception *f inv*; **cash ~** cassa *f*; **check-in ~** check-in *m inv*

desk-bound *adj* ‹*job*› sedentario

desk diary *n* agenda da tavolo

desk pad *n* (blotter) tampone *m*; (notebook) block-notes *m inv*

desktop *n* piano *m* della scrivania; (computer) [computer *m inv*] desktop *m inv*

desktop publishing *n* desktop publishing *m inv*, editoria *f* da tavolo
desolate /'desələt/ *adj* desolato
desolation /desə'leɪʃn/ *n* desolazione *f*
despair /dɪ'speə(r)/ **A** *n* disperazione *f*; **in ~** disperato; ‹*say*› per disperazione **B** *vi* **I ~ of that boy** quel ragazzo mi fa disperare
desperate /'despərət/ *adj* disperato; **be ~** ‹*criminal*› essere un disperato; **be ~ for something** morire dalla voglia di
desperately /'despərətlɪ/ *adv* disperatamente; **he said ~** ha detto, disperato
desperation /despə'reɪʃn/ *n* disperazione *f*; **in ~** per disperazione
despicable /dɪ'spɪkəbl/ *adj* disprezzevole
despise /dɪ'spaɪz/ *vt* disprezzare
despite /dɪ'spaɪt/ *prep* malgrado
despondency /dɪ'spɒndənsɪ/ *n* abbattimento *m*
despondent /dɪ'spɒndənt/ *adj* abbattuto
despot /'despɒt/ *n* despota *m*
despotism /'despətɪzm/ *n* dispotismo *m*
des res /dez'rez/ *n abbr* infml (**desirable residence**) abitazione *f* desiderabile
dessert /dɪ'zɜːt/ *n* dolce *m*
dessert spoon *n* cucchiaio *m* da dolce
dessert wine *n* vino *m* da dessert
destabilize /diː'steɪbɪlaɪz/ *vt* destabilizzare
destination /destɪ'neɪʃn/ *n* destinazione *f*
destine /'destɪn/ *vt* destinare; **be ~d for something** essere destinato a qualcosa; **~d for each other** fatti l'uno per l'altra
destined /'destɪnd/ *adj* **~ for Paris** ‹*train, package*› con destinazione Parigi; **it was ~ to happen** era destino che succedesse
destiny /'destɪnɪ/ *n* destino *m*
destitute /'destɪtjuːt/ *adj* bisognoso
destitution /destɪ'tjuːʃn/ *n* indigenza *f*
destroy /dɪ'strɔɪ/ *vt* distruggere
destroyer /dɪ'strɔɪə(r)/ *n* Naut cacciatorpediniere *m*
destruct /dɪ'strʌkt/ *vi* distruggersi
destruction /dɪ'strʌkʃn/ *n* distruzione *f*
destructive /dɪ'strʌktɪv/ *adj* distruttivo; fig ‹*criticism*› negativo
destructiveness /dɪ'strʌktɪvnɪs/ *n* distruttività *f*
desultory /'desəltrɪ/ *adj* ‹*conversation*› sconnesso; ‹*friendship*› incostante; ‹*attempt*› poco convinto
detach /dɪ'tætʃ/ *vt* staccare
detachable /dɪ'tætʃəbl/ *adj* separabile
detached /dɪ'tætʃt/ *adj* fig distaccato; **~ house** villetta *f*
detached retina *n* Med retina *f* distaccata
detachment /dɪ'tætʃmənt/ *n* distacco *m*; Mil distaccamento *m*
detail /'diːteɪl/ **A** *n* particolare *m*, dettaglio *m*; **in ~** particolareggiatamente **B** *vt* esporre con tutti i particolari; Mil assegnare
detail drawing *n* disegno *m* dettagliato
detailed /'diːteɪld/ *adj* particolareggiato, dettagliato
detain /dɪ'teɪn/ *vt* ‹*police*› trattenere; (delay) far ritardare
detainee /dɪteɪ'niː/ *n* detenuto, -a *mf*
detect /dɪ'tekt/ *vt* individuare; (perceive) percepire
detectable /dɪ'tektəbl/ *adj* individuabile
detection /dɪ'tekʃn/ *n* scoperta *f*
detective /dɪ'tektɪv/ *n* investigatore, -trice *mf*
detective constable *n* BrE agente *mf* della polizia giudiziaria
detective inspector *n* BrE ispettore, -trice *mf* della polizia giudiziaria
detective story *n* racconto *m* poliziesco
detective work *n* indagini *fpl*
detector /dɪ'tektə(r)/ *n* (for metal) cercametalli *m inv*, metal detector *m inv*
detention /dɪ'tenʃn/ *n* detenzione *f*; Sch punizione *f*
detention centre *n* centro *m* di accoglienza
deter /dɪ'tɜː(r)/ *vt* (*pt/pp* **deterred**) impedire; **~ somebody from doing something** impedire a qualcuno di fare qualcosa
detergent /dɪ'tɜːdʒənt/ *n* detersivo *m*
deteriorate /dɪ'tɪərɪəreɪt/ *vi* deteriorarsi
deterioration /dɪtɪərɪə'reɪʃn/ *n* deterioramento *m*
determination /dɪtɜːmɪ'neɪʃn/ *n* determinazione *f*
determine /dɪ'tɜːmɪn/ *vt* (ascertain) determinare; **~ to** (resolve) decidere di
determined /dɪ'tɜːmɪnd/ *adj* deciso
determining /dɪ'tɜːmɪnɪŋ/ *adj* determinante
deterrent /dɪ'terənt/ *n* deterrente *m*
detest /dɪ'test/ *vt* detestare
detestable /dɪ'testəbl/ *adj* detestabile
detonate /'detəneɪt/ **A** *vt* far detonare **B** *vi* detonare
detonation /detə'neɪʃn/ *n* detonazione *f*
detonator /'detəneɪtə(r)/ *n* detonatore *m*
detour /'diːtʊə(r)/ *n* deviazione *f*
detox /ˌdiː'tɒks/ **A** *n* disintossicazione *f* **B** *vi* disintossicarsi
detoxify /diː'tɒksɪfaɪ/ *vt* disintossicare
detract /dɪ'trækt/ *vi* **~ from** sminuire ‹*merit*›; rovinare ‹*pleasure, beauty*›
detractor /dɪ'træktə(r)/ *n* detrattore, -trice *mf*
detriment /'detrɪmənt/ *n* **to the ~ of** a danno di
detrimental /detrɪ'mentl/ *adj* dannoso

d

d

detritus /dɪˈtraɪtəs/ *n* detriti *mpl*
deuce /djuːs/ *n* Tennis deuce *m inv*
devaluation /diːvæljuˈeɪʃn/ *n* svalutazione *f*
devalue /diːˈvæljuː/ *vt* svalutare ‹*currency*›
devastate /ˈdevəsteɪt/ *vt* devastare
devastated /ˈdevəsteɪtɪd/ *adj* infml sconvolto
devastating /ˈdevəsteɪtɪŋ/ *adj* devastante; ‹*news*› sconvolgente
devastation /devəˈsteɪʃn/ *n* devastazione *f*
⚷ **develop** /dɪˈveləp/ **A** *vt* sviluppare; contrarre ‹*illness*›; (add to value of) valorizzare ‹*area*› **B** *vi* svilupparsi; ~ **into** divenire
developer /dɪˈveləpə(r)/ *n* **[property]** ~ imprenditore, -trice *mf* edile
developing bath *n* Phot bagno *m* di sviluppo, bagno *m* rivelatore
developing country *n* paese *m* in via di sviluppo
developing tank *n* Phot vasca *f* di sviluppo
⚷ **development** /dɪˈveləpmənt/ *n* sviluppo *m*; (of vaccine etc) messa *f* a punto
development company *n* (for property) impresa *f* edile
deviant /ˈdiːvɪənt/ *adj* deviato
deviate /ˈdiːvɪeɪt/ *vi* deviare
deviation /diːvɪˈeɪʃn/ *n* deviazione *f*
⚷ **device** /dɪˈvaɪs/ *n* dispositivo *m*; **leave somebody to his own ~s** lasciare qualcuno per conto suo
devil /ˈdevl/ *n* diavolo *m*
devilish /ˈdev(ə)lɪʃ/ *adj* diabolico
devilishly /ˈdev(ə)lɪʃlɪ/ *adv* fig infml terribilmente
devil-may-care *adj* menefreghista
devilment /ˈdev(ə)lmənt/ *n* BrE cattiveria *f*
devil's advocate *n* avvocato *m* del diavolo
devil worship *n* culto *m* satanico
devious /ˈdiːvɪəs/ *adj* ‹*person*› subdolo; ‹*route*› tortuoso
deviously /ˈdiːvɪəslɪ/ *adv* subdolamente
devise /dɪˈvaɪz/ *vt* escogitare
devoid /dɪˈvɔɪd/ *adj* ~ **of** privo di
devolution /diːvəˈluːʃn/ *n* (of power) decentramento *m*
devote /dɪˈvəʊt/ *vt* dedicare
devoted /dɪˈvəʊtɪd/ *adj* ‹*daughter etc*› affezionato; **be ~ to something** consacrarsi a qualcosa
devotedly /dɪˈvəʊtɪdlɪ/ *adv* con dedizione
devotee /devəˈtiː/ *n* appassionato, -a *mf*
devotion /dɪˈvəʊʃn/ *n* dedizione *f*; **~s** *pl* Relig preghiere *fpl*
devour /dɪˈvaʊə(r)/ *vt* divorare
devout /dɪˈvaʊt/ *adj* devoto
devoutly /dɪˈvaʊtlɪ/ *adv* Relig devotamente; (sincerely) fervidamente

⚷ parola chiave

dew /djuː/ *n* rugiada *f*
dewy /ˈdjuːɪ/ *adj* rugiadoso
dewy-eyed /-ˈaɪd/ *adj* (moved) con gli occhi lucidi; (naive) ingenuo
dexterity /dekˈsterətɪ/ *n* destrezza *f*
dexterous /ˈdekstrəs/ *adj* ‹*person, movement*› agile, destro; ‹*hand*› abile; ‹*mind*› acuto
dexterously /ˈdekstrəslɪ/ *adv* ‹*move*› agilmente; ‹*manage*› abilmente
DfES *abbr* BrE (**Department for Education and Skills**) ≈ Ministero *m* dell'Istruzione
dg *abbr* (**decigram**) dg *m*
diabetes /daɪəˈbiːtiːz/ *n* diabete *m*
diabetic /daɪəˈbetɪk/ *adj & n* diabetico, -a *mf*
diabolical /daɪəˈbɒlɪkl/ *adj* diabolico
diabolically /daɪəˈbɒlɪklɪ/ *adv* (wickedly) diabolicamente; infml (badly) orribilmente
diacritic /daɪəˈkrɪtɪk/ *adj* (accent, mark) diacritico
diaeresis /daɪˈerɪsɪs/ *n* dieresi *f inv*
diagnose /ˈdaɪəgnəʊz/ *vt* diagnosticare
diagnosis /daɪəgˈnəʊsɪs/ *n* (*pl* **-oses** /daɪəgˈnəʊsiːz/) diagnosi *f inv*
diagnostic /daɪəgˈnɒstɪk/ *adj* diagnostico
diagnostics /daɪəgˈnɒstɪks/ *nsg* Med diagnostica *fsg*
diagonal /daɪˈægənl/ *adj & n* diagonale *f*
diagonally /daɪˈægənlɪ/ *adv* diagonalmente
diagram /ˈdaɪəgræm/ *n* diagramma *m*
dial /ˈdaɪəl/ **A** *n* (of clock, machine) quadrante *m*; Teleph disco *m* combinatore **B** *vi* (*pt/pp* **dialled**) Teleph fare il numero; ~ **direct** chiamare in teleselezione **C** *vt* fare ‹*number*›
dialect /ˈdaɪəlekt/ *n* dialetto *m*
dialectic /daɪəˈlektɪk/ **A** *n* dialettica *f* **B** *adj* dialettico
dialectics /daɪəˈlektɪks/ *nsg* dialettica *fsg*
dialling code /ˈdaɪəlɪŋ/ *n* prefisso *m*
dialling tone *n* segnale *m* di linea libera
dialogue /ˈdaɪəlɒg/ *n* dialogo *m*
dialogue box *n* Comput finestra *f* di dialogo
dial tone *n* AmE Teleph segnale *m* di linea libera
dial-up *adj* ‹*connection, access*› dial-up
dialysis /daɪˈælɪsɪs/ *n* dialisi *f*
dialysis machine *n* rene *m* artificiale
diameter /daɪˈæmɪtə(r)/ *n* diametro *m*
diametrically /daɪəˈmetrɪklɪ/ *adv* ~ **opposed** diametralmente opposto
diamond /ˈdaɪəmənd/ *n* diamante *m*, brillante *m*; (shape) losanga *f*; **~s** *pl* (in cards) quadri *mpl*
diamond jubilee *n* sessantesimo anniversario *m*
diamond-shaped *adj* romboidale
diamond wedding, diamond wedding anniversary *n* nozze *fpl* di diamante

diaper /ˈdaɪəpə(r)/ *n* AmE pannolino *m*
diaphanous /daɪˈæfənəs/ *adj* diafano
diaphragm /ˈdaɪəfræm/ *n* diaframma *m*
diarist /ˈdaɪərɪst/ *n* (author) diarista *mf*; (journalist) giornalista *mf* di piccola cronaca
diarrhoea /daɪəˈriːə/ *n* diarrea *f*
diary /ˈdaɪərɪ/ *n* (for appointments) agenda *f*; (for writing in) diario *m*
diatribe /ˈdaɪətraɪb/ *n* diatriba *f*
dice /daɪs/ **A** *n inv* dadi *mpl*
B *vt* Culin tagliare a dadini
dicey /ˈdaɪsɪ/ *adj* infml rischioso
dichotomy /daɪˈkɒtəmɪ/ *n* dicotomia *f*
dicky /ˈdɪkɪ/ **A** *n* (shirt front) pettino *m*, sparato *m*
B *adj* BrE infml ‹*heart*› malandato
dictate /dɪkˈteɪt/ *vt & vi* dettare
dictation /dɪkˈteɪʃn/ *n* dettato *m*
dictator /dɪkˈteɪtə(r)/ *n* dittatore *m*
dictatorial /dɪktəˈtɔːrɪəl/ *adj* dittatoriale
dictatorship /dɪkˈteɪtəʃɪp/ *n* dittatura *f*
diction /ˈdɪkʃn/ *n* dizione *f*
dictionary /ˈdɪkʃənrɪ/ *n* dizionario *m*
dictum /ˈdɪktəm/ *n* (maxim) massima *f*; (statement) affermazione *f*
did /dɪd/ ▶ **do**
didactic /dɪˈdæktɪk/ *adj* didattico
diddle /ˈdɪdl/ *vt* infml gabbare
die¹ /daɪ/ *n* Techn (metal mould) stampo *m*; (for cutting) matrice *f*
die² *vi* (*pres p* **dying**) morire (**of** di); **be dying to do something** infml morire dalla voglia di fare qualcosa; **be dying for a drink** infml morire dalla voglia di bere qualcosa
▪ **die away** *vi* ‹*noise, applause*› smorzarsi
▪ **die down** *vi* calmarsi; ‹*fire, flames*› spegnersi
▪ **die off** *vi* morire uno dopo l'altro
▪ **die out** *vi* estinguersi; ‹*custom*› morire
diehard /ˈdaɪhɑːd/ *n* Pol (in party) fanatico, -a *mf*; (stubborn person) ultraconservatore *mf*
diesel /ˈdiːzl/ *n* diesel *m*
diesel engine *n* motore *m* diesel
diesel train *n* treno *m* con locomotiva diesel
diet /ˈdaɪət/ **A** *n* regime *m* alimentare; (restricted) dieta *f*; **be on a ~** essere a dieta
B *vi* essere a dieta
dietary /ˈdaɪətrɪ/ *adj* ‹*habit*› alimentare
dietary fibre *n* fibre *fpl* alimentari
dietary supplement *n* integratore *m* dietetico
dietician /daɪəˈtɪʃn/ *n* dietologo, -a *mf*
differ /ˈdɪfə(r)/ *vi* differire; (disagree) non essere d'accordo
difference /ˈdɪfrəns/ *n* differenza *f*; (disagreement) divergenza *f*
different /ˈdɪfrənt/ *adj* diverso, differente; (various) diversi; **be ~ from** essere diverso da
differential /dɪfəˈrenʃl/ **A** *adj* differenziale
B *n* differenziale *m*
differentiate /dɪfəˈrenʃɪeɪt/ *vt* distinguere (**between** fra); (discriminate) discriminare (**between** fra); (make different) differenziare
differentiation /dɪfərenʃɪˈeɪʃn/ *n* differenziazione *f*
differently /ˈdɪfrəntlɪ/ *adv* in modo diverso; **~ from** diversamente da
differently abled /ˈeɪbld/ *adj* diversamente abile
difficult /ˈdɪfɪkəlt/ *adj* difficile
difficulty /ˈdɪfɪkəltɪ/ *n* difficoltà *f*; **with ~** con difficoltà
diffidence /ˈdɪfɪdəns/ *n* mancanza *f* di sicurezza
diffident /ˈdɪfɪdənt/ *adj* senza fiducia in se stesso
diffidently /ˈdɪfɪdəntlɪ/ *adv* senza fiducia in se stesso
diffuse¹ /dɪˈfjuːs/ *adj* diffuso; (wordy) prolisso
diffuse² /dɪˈfjuːz/ *vt* Phys diffondere
diffuseness /dɪˈfjuːsnɪs/ *n* (of organization) estensione *f*; (of argument) prolissità *f*
dig /dɪg/ **A** *n* (poke) spinta *f*; (remark) frecciata *f*; Archaeol scavo *m*; **~s** *pl* infml camera *fsg* ammobiliata
B *vt & vi* (*pp/pp* **dug**, *pres p* **digging**) scavare ‹*hole*›; vangare ‹*garden*›; (thrust) conficcare; **~ somebody in the ribs** dare una gomitata a qualcuno
▪ **dig out** *vt* fig tirar fuori
▪ **dig up** *vt* scavare ‹*garden, street, object*›; sradicare ‹*tree, plant*›; fig (find) scovare
digest¹ /ˈdaɪdʒest/ *n* compendio *m*
digest² /daɪˈdʒest/ *vt* digerire
digestible /daɪˈdʒestəbl/ *adj* digeribile
digestion /daɪˈdʒestʃn/ *n* digestione *f*
digestive /daɪˈdʒestɪv/ *adj* digestivo
digestive biscuit *n* BrE *biscotto* (*m*) *di farina integrale*
digestive system *n* apparato *m* digerente
digestive tract *n* apparato *m* digerente
digger /ˈdɪgə(r)/ *n* Techn scavatrice *f*
diggings /ˈdɪgɪŋz/ *npl* (in archaeology) scavi *mpl*
digicam /ˈdɪdʒɪkæm/ *n* infml fotocamera *f* digitale
digit /ˈdɪdʒɪt/ *n* cifra *f*; (finger) dito *m*
digital /ˈdɪdʒɪtl/ *adj* digitale
digital [television] *n* TV *f* digitale
digital audio tape *n* audiocassetta *f* digitale
digital camera *n* fotocamera *f* digitale
digital clock *n* orologio *m* digitale
digital computer *n* computer *m* digitale
digital fingerprinting *n* (identificazione *f* con) impronte *fpl* digitali
digitalize /ˈdɪdʒɪtəlaɪz/ *vt* digitalizzare
digital television *n* televisione *f* digitale

digitization /ˌdɪdʒɪtaɪˈzeɪʃn/ *n* digitalizzazione *f*

digitizer /ˈdɪdʒɪtaɪzə(r)/ *n* Comput tavoletta *f* grafica

dignified /ˈdɪɡnɪfaɪd/ *adj* dignitoso

dignify /ˈdɪɡnɪfaɪ/ *vt* nobilitare ‹*occasion, building*›

dignitary /ˈdɪɡnɪtərɪ/ *n* dignitario *m*

dignity /ˈdɪɡnətɪ/ *n* dignità *f*

digress /daɪˈɡres/ *vi* divagare

digression /daɪˈɡreʃn/ *n* digressione *f*

dike /daɪk/ *n* diga *f*

dilapidated /dɪˈlæpɪdeɪtɪd/ *adj* cadente

dilapidation /dɪlæpɪˈdeɪʃn/ *n* rovina *f*

dilate /daɪˈleɪt/ **A** *vt* dilatare
B *vi* dilatarsi

dilation /daɪˈleɪʃn/ *n* dilatazione *f*

dilatory /ˈdɪlətərɪ/ *adj* dilatorio

dilemma /dɪˈlemə/ *n* dilemma *m*

dilettante /dɪlɪˈtæntɪ/ *n* dilettante *mf*

diligence /ˈdɪlɪdʒəns/ *n* diligenza *f*

diligent /ˈdɪlɪdʒənt/ *adj* diligente

dill /dɪl/ *n* aneto *m*

dilly-dally /ˈdɪlɪdælɪ/ *vi* (*pt/pp* **-ied**) infml tentennare

dilute /daɪˈljuːt/ *vt* diluire

dilution /daɪˈljuːʃn/ *n also* fig diluizione *f*

dim /dɪm/ **A** *adj* (**dimmer**, **dimmest**) ‹*light*› debole; (dark) scuro; ‹*prospect, chance*› scarso; (indistinct) impreciso; infml (stupid) tonto
B *vt & vi* (*pt/pp* **dimmed**) affievolire

dime /daɪm/ *n* AmE moneta *f* da dieci centesimi

dimension /daɪˈmenʃn/ *n* dimensione *f*

dime store *n* AmE *grande magazzino* (*m*) *con prezzi molto bassi*

diminish /dɪˈmɪnɪʃ/ *vt & vi* diminuire

diminished /dɪˈmɪnɪʃt/ *adj* ridotto; Mus diminuito; **on grounds of ~ responsibility** Jur per seminfermità mentale

diminutive /dɪˈmɪnjʊtɪv/ *adj & n* diminutivo *m*

dimly /ˈdɪmlɪ/ *adv* ‹*see, remember*› indistintamente; ‹*shine*› debolmente

dimmer /ˈdɪmə(r)/ *n* interruttore *m* a reostato

dimple /ˈdɪmpl/ *n* fossetta *f*

dimwit /ˈdɪmwɪt/ *n* infml stupido *m*

dim-witted /-ˈwɪtɪd/ *adj* infml stupido

din /dɪn/ *n* baccano *m*

■ **din into**: *vt* **~ something into somebody** ficcare qualcosa in testa a qualcuno

dine /daɪn/ *vi* pranzare

diner /ˈdaɪnə(r)/ *n* AmE (restaurant) tavola *f* calda; **the last ~ in the restaurant** l'ultimo cliente nel ristorante

ding-dong /ˈdɪŋdɒŋ/ *n* dindon *m*

ding-dong battle *n* BrE battibecco *m*

dinghy /ˈdɪŋɡɪ/ *n* dinghy *m*; (inflatable) canotto *m* pneumatico

dingy /ˈdɪndʒɪ/ *adj* (**-ier**, **-iest**) squallido e tetro

dining car *n* carrozza *f* ristorante

dining hall *n* refettorio *m*

dining room *n* sala *f* da pranzo

dining table *n* tavolo *m* da pranzo

dinky /ˈdɪŋkɪ/ *adj* BrE infml carino

🔑 **dinner** /ˈdɪnə(r)/ *n* cena *f*; (at midday) pranzo *m*

dinner dance *n* cena *f* danzante

dinner fork *n* forchetta *f*

dinner hour *n* BrE Sch pausa *f* del pranzo

dinner jacket *n* smoking *m inv*

dinner knife *n* coltello *m*

dinner money *n* BrE Sch *soldi* (*mpl*) *dati dai genitori agli scolari per il pranzo*

dinner party *n* cena *f* (*con invitati*)

dinner plate *n* piatto *m* piano

dinner service, **dinner set** *n* servizio *m* da tavola

dinner time *n* (evening) ora *f* di cena; (midday) ora *f* di pranzo

dinnerware /ˈdɪnəweə(r)/ *n* AmE servizio *m* da tavola

dinosaur /ˈdaɪnəsɔː(r)/ *n* dinosauro *m*

dint /dɪnt/ *n* **by ~ of** a forza di

diocese /ˈdaɪəsɪs/ *n* diocesi *f inv*

diode /ˈdaɪəʊd/ *n* diodo *m*

dioxide /daɪˈɒksaɪd/ *n* biossido *m*

dip /dɪp/ **A** *n* (in ground) inclinazione *f*; Culin salsina *f*; **go for a ~** andare a fare una nuotata
B *vt* (*pt/pp* **dipped**) (in liquid) immergere; abbassare ‹*head, headlights*›
C *vi* ‹*land*› formare un avvallamento

■ **dip into** *vt* scorrere ‹*book*›

diphtheria /dɪfˈθɪərɪə/ *n* difterite *f*

diphthong /ˈdɪfθɒŋ/ *n* dittongo *m*

diploma /dɪˈpləʊmə/ *n* diploma *m*

diplomacy /dɪˈpləʊməsɪ/ *n* diplomazia *f*

diplomat /ˈdɪpləmæt/ *n* diplomatico, -a *mf*

diplomatic /dɪpləˈmætɪk/ *adj* diplomatico

diplomatically /dɪpləˈmætɪklɪ/ *adv* con diplomazia

diplomatic bag *n* valigia *f* diplomatica

diplomatic immunity *n* immunità *f* diplomatica

dippy /ˈdɪpɪ/ *adj* infml (crazy, weird) pazzo

dipstick /ˈdɪpstɪk/ *n* Auto astina *f* dell'olio

dire /ˈdaɪə(r)/ *adj* ‹*situation, consequences*› terribile

🔑 **direct** /daɪˈrekt/ **A** *adj* diretto
B *adv* direttamente
C *vt* (aim) rivolgere ‹*attention, criticism*›; (control) dirigere; fare la regia di ‹*film, play*›; **~ somebody** (show the way) indicare la strada a qualcuno; **~ somebody to do something** ordinare a qualcuno di fare

---

🔑 parola chiave

qualcosa

direct access *n* Comput accesso *m* diretto

direct current *n* corrente *m* continua

direct debit *n* addebitamento *m* diretto

direct dialling *n* teleselezione *f*

direct hit *n* Mil colpo *m* diretto

⚷ **direction** /dɪ'rekʃn/ *n* direzione *f*; (of play, film) regia *f*; **~s** *pl* indicazioni *fpl*; **~s for use** istruzioni *fpl* per l'uso

directional /daɪ'rekʃənəl/ *adj* direzionale

directive /daɪ'rektɪv/ *n* direttiva *f*

direct line *n* linea *f* diretta

⚷ **directly** /daɪ'rektlɪ/ **A** *adv* direttamente; (at once) immediatamente
B *conj* [non] appena

direct mail *n* mailing *m inv*

directness /daɪ'rektnɪs/ *n* (of person, attitude) franchezza *f*; (of play, work, writing) chiarezza *f*

direct object *n* complemento *m* oggetto

⚷ **director** /dɪ'rektə(r)/ *n* Comm direttore, -trice *mf*; (of play, film) regista *mf*

directorate /daɪ'rektərət/ *n* (board) consiglio *m* d'amministrazione

director general *n* presidente *mf*

Director of Public Prosecutions *n* BrE ≈ Procuratore *m* della Repubblica

directorship /dɪ'rektəʃɪp/ *n* posto *m* di direttore

directory /dɪ'rektərɪ/ *n* elenco *m*; Teleph elenco *m* [telefonico]; (of streets) stradario *m*

directory assistance *n* AmE servizio *m* informazioni abbonati

directory enquiries *npl* BrE servizio *m* informazioni abbonati

direct rule *n* Pol sottomissione *f* al governo centrale

direct speech *n* discorso *m* diretto

direct transfer *n* trasferimento *m* automatico

dirt /dɜːt/ *n* sporco *m*; **~ cheap** infml a [un] prezzo stracciato

dirtiness /'dɜːtɪnɪs/ *n* (of person etc) sporcizia *f*

dirt track *n* (road) strada *f* sterrata; Sport pista *f* sterrata

dirty /'dɜːtɪ/ **A** *adj* (**-ier**, **-iest**) sporco
B *vt* sporcare

dirty bomb *n* bomba *f* sporca

dirty-minded /-'maɪndɪd/ *adj* fissato sul sesso

dirty trick *n* brutto scherzo *m*

dirty tricks *npl* Pol faccende *fpl* sporche

dirty weekend *n* infml weekend *m inv* clandestino con l'amante

dirty word *n* parolaccia *f*

disability /dɪsə'bɪlətɪ/ *n* infermità *f*

disable /dɪ'seɪbl/ *vt* (make useless) mettere fuori uso ‹*machine*›; (in accident) rendere invalido; Comput disabilitare; **be ~d by arthritis** essere menomato dall'artrite

disabled /dɪ'seɪbld/ *adj* disabile

disabled access *n* (to public building etc) accesso *m* per disabili

disabled driver *n* automobilista *mf* disabile

disabled person *n* disabile *mf*

disabuse /dɪsə'bjuːz/ *vt* disingannare

disadvantage /dɪsəd'vɑːntɪdʒ/ *n* svantaggio *m*; **at a ~** in una posizione di svantaggio

disadvantaged /dɪsəd'vɑːntɪdʒd/ *adj* svantaggiato

disadvantageous /dɪsædvən'teɪdʒəs/ *adj* svantaggioso

disaffected /dɪsə'fektɪd/ *adj* disilluso

disagree /dɪsə'griː/ *vi* non essere d'accordo; **~ with** ‹*food*› far male a

disagreeable /dɪsə'griːəbl/ *adj* sgradevole

disagreement /dɪsə'griːmənt/ *n* disaccordo *m*; (quarrel) dissidio *m*

disallow /dɪsə'laʊ/ *vt* respingere; Sport annullare

⚷ **disappear** /dɪsə'pɪə(r)/ *vi* scomparire

disappearance /dɪsə'pɪərəns/ *n* scomparsa *f*

disappoint /dɪsə'pɔɪnt/ *vt* deludere

disappointed /dɪsə'pɔɪntɪd/ *adj* deluso; **I am ~ in you** mi hai deluso

disappointing /dɪsə'pɔɪntɪŋ/ *adj* deludente

disappointment /dɪsə'pɔɪntmənt/ *n* delusione *f*

disapproval /dɪsə'pruːvəl/ *n* disapprovazione *f*

disapprove /dɪsə'pruːv/ *vi* disapprovare; **~ of somebody/something** disapprovare qualcuno/qualcosa

disapproving /dɪsə'pruːvɪŋ/ *adj* ‹*look, gesture*› di disapprovazione

disarm /dɪs'ɑːm/ **A** *vt* disarmare
B *vi* Mil disarmarsi

disarmament /dɪs'ɑːməmənt/ *n* disarmo *m*

disarming /dɪs'ɑːmɪŋ/ *adj* ‹*frankness etc*› disarmante

disarrange /dɪsə'reɪndʒ/ *vt* scompigliare

disarray /dɪsə'reɪ/ *n* **in ~** in disordine

disaster /dɪ'zɑːstə(r)/ *n* disastro *m*

disaster area *n* zona *f* disastrata; fig (person) disastro *m*

disaster fund *n* fondi *mpl* a favore dei disastrati

disaster movie *n* film *m inv* catastrofico

disaster relief *n* soccorso *m* disastri

disaster victim *n* disastrato, -a *mf*

disastrous /dɪ'zɑːstrəs/ *adj* disastroso

disastrously /dɪ'zɑːstrəslɪ/ *adv* ‹*fail*› disastrosamente; ‹*end, turn out*› in modo catastrofico; **go ~ wrong** essere un disastro

disband /dɪs'bænd/ **A** *vt* sciogliere; smobilitare ‹*troops*›
B *vi* sciogliersi; ‹*regiment*› essere smobilitato

disbelief /dɪsbɪ'liːf/ *n* incredulità *f*; **in ~** con incredulità

d

disbelieve /dɪsbɪ'li:v/ *vt* non credere
disc /dɪsk/ *n* disco *m*; (CD) compact disc *m inv*
discard /dɪ'skɑ:d/ *vt* scartare; (throw away) eliminare; scaricare ‹*boyfriend*›
disc brakes *npl* Auto freni *mpl* a disco
discern /dɪ'sɜ:n/ *vt* discernere
discernible /dɪ'sɜ:nəbl/ *adj* discernibile
discerning /dɪ'sɜ:nɪŋ/ *adj* perspicace
discharge¹ /'dɪstʃɑ:dʒ/ *n* Electr scarica *f*; (dismissal) licenziamento *m*; Mil congedo *m*; Med (of blood) emissione *f*; (of cargo) scarico *m*
discharge² /dɪs'tʃɑ:dʒ/ **A** *vt* scaricare ‹*battery, cargo*›; (dismiss) licenziare; Mil congedare; Jur assolvere ‹*accused*›; dimettere ‹*patient*›; ~ **one's duty** esaurire il proprio compito
B *vi* Electr scaricarsi
disciple /dɪ'saɪpl/ *n* discepolo *m*
disciplinarian /dɪsɪplɪ'neərɪən/ *n* persona *f* autoritaria
disciplinary /'dɪsɪplɪnərɪ/ *adj* disciplinare
discipline /'dɪsɪplɪn/ **A** *n* disciplina *f*
B *vt* disciplinare; (punish) punire
disciplined /'dɪsɪplɪnd/ *adj* ‹*person, approach*› sistematico
disc jockey *n* disc jockey *m inv*
disclaim /dɪs'kleɪm/ *vt* negare
disclaimer /dɪs'kleɪmə(r)/ *n* rifiuto *m*
disclose /dɪs'kləʊz/ *vt* svelare
disclosure /dɪs'kləʊʒə(r)/ *n* rivelazione *f*
disco /'dɪskəʊ/ *n* discoteca *f*
discoloration /dɪskʌlə'reɪʃn/ *n* (process) scolorimento *m*; (spot) macchia *f* scolorita
discolour /dɪs'kʌlə(r)/ **A** *vt* scolorire
B *vi* scolorirsi
discomfort /dɪs'kʌmfət/ *n* scomodità *f*; fig disagio *m*
disconcert /dɪskən'sɜ:t/ *vt* sconcertare
disconcerting /dɪskən'sɜ:tɪŋ/ *adj* sconcertante
disconnect /dɪskə'nekt/ *vt* disconnettere
disconsolate /dɪs'kɒnsələt/ *adj* sconsolato
discontent /dɪskən'tent/ *n* scontentezza *f*
discontented /dɪskən'tentɪd/ *adj* scontento
discontinue /dɪskən'tɪnju:/ *vt* cessare, smettere; Comm sospendere la produzione di; ~**d line** fine *f* serie
discontinuity /dɪskɒntɪ'nju:ɪtɪ/ *n* discontinuità *f*
discord /'dɪskɔ:d/ *n* discordia *f*; Mus dissonanza *f*
discordant /dɪ'skɔ:dənt/ *adj* ~ **note** nota *f* discordante
discotheque /'dɪskətek/ *n* discoteca *f*
discount¹ /'dɪskaʊnt/ *n* sconto *m*
discount² /dɪs'kaʊnt/ *vt* (not believe) non credere a; (leave out of consideration) non tener conto di
discount card *n* tessera *f* di sconto
discount flight *n* volo *m* a prezzo ridotto
discount store *n* discount *m inv*
discourage /dɪs'kʌrɪdʒ/ *vt* scoraggiare; (dissuade) dissuadere
discouragement /dɪs'kʌrɪdʒmənt/ *n* (despondency) scoraggiamento *m*; (disincentive) disincentivo *m*
discourse /'dɪskɔ:s/ *n* discorso *m*
discourteous /dɪs'kɜ:tɪəs/ *adj* scortese
discourteously /dɪs'kɜ:tɪəslɪ/ *adv* scortesemente
discover /dɪ'skʌvə(r)/ *vt* scoprire
discovery /dɪs'kʌvərɪ/ *n* scoperta *f*
discredit /dɪs'kredɪt/ **A** *n* discredito *m*
B *vt* screditare
discreet /dɪ'skri:t/ *adj* discreto
discreetly /dɪ'skri:tlɪ/ *adv* discretamente
discrepancy /dɪ'skrepənsɪ/ *n* discrepanza *f*
discretion /dɪ'skreʃn/ *n* discrezione *f*
discriminate /dɪ'skrɪmɪneɪt/ *vi* discriminare (**against** contro); ~ **between** distinguere tra
discriminating /dɪ'skrɪmɪneɪtɪŋ/ *adj* esigente
discrimination /dɪskrɪmɪ'neɪʃn/ *n* discriminazione *f*; (quality) discernimento *m*
discriminatory /dɪs'krɪmɪnətərɪ/ *adj* discriminatorio, discriminativo
discus /'dɪskəs/ *n* disco *m*
discuss /dɪ'skʌs/ *vt* discutere; (examine critically) esaminare
discussion /dɪ'skʌʃn/ *n* discussione *f*
discussion board *n* Comput gruppo *m* di discussione, forum *m* inv di discussione
discussion document, **discussion paper** *n* documento *m* in abbozzo
disdain /dɪs'deɪn/ **A** *n* sdegno *f*
B *vt* sdegnare
disdainful /dɪs'deɪnfʊl/ *adj* sdegnoso
disease /dɪ'zi:z/ *n* malattia *f*
diseased /dɪ'zi:zd/ *adj* malato
disembark /dɪsem'bɑ:k/ *vi* sbarcare
disembodied /dɪsem'bɒdɪd/ *adj* ‹*voices*› evanescente; ‹*head*› senza corpo; ‹*soul*› disincarnato
disenchant /dɪsen'tʃɑ:nt/ *vt* disincantare
disenchanted /ˌdɪsɪn'tʃɑ:ntɪd, AmE -'tʃænt-/ *adj* disincantato
disenchantment /dɪsen'tʃɑ:ntmənt/ *n* disincanto *m*
disenfranchise /dɪsen'fræntʃaɪz/ *vt* privare del diritto di voto
disengage /dɪsen'geɪdʒ/ *vt* disimpegnare; disinnestare ‹*clutch*›
disentangle /dɪsen'tæŋgəl/ *vt* districare
disfavour /dɪs'feɪvə(r)/ *n* sfavore *m*; **fall into** ~ perdere il favore
disfigure /dɪs'fɪgə(r)/ *vt* deformare
disgorge /dɪs'gɔ:dʒ/ *vt* rigettare

parola chiave

disgrace /dɪzˈgreɪs/ **A** *n* vergogna *f*; **fail into ~** cadere in disgrazia; **I am in ~** sono caduto in disgrazia; **it's a ~** è una vergogna
B *vt* disonorare

disgraceful /dɪzˈgreɪsfʊl/ *adj* vergognoso

disgruntled /dɪsˈgrʌntld/ *adj* malcontento

disguise /dɪsˈgaɪz/ **A** *n* travestimento *m*; **in ~** travestito
B *vt* contraffare ‹*voice*›; dissimulare ‹*emotions*›; **~d as** travestito da

disgust /dɪsˈgʌst/ **A** *n* disgusto *m*; **in ~** con aria disgustata
B *vt* disgustare

disgusting /dɪsˈgʌstɪŋ/ *adj* disgustoso

dish /dɪʃ/ *n* piatto *m*; **do the ~es** lavare i piatti

▪ **dish out** *vt* (serve) servire; (distribute) distribuire

▪ **dish up** *vt* servire

dishcloth /ˈdɪʃklɒθ/ *n* strofinaccio *m*

dishearten /dɪsˈhɑːt(ə)n/ *vt* scoraggiare

disheartening /dɪsˈhɑːt(ə)nɪŋ/ *adj* scoraggiante

dishevelled /dɪˈʃevld/ *adj* scompigliato

dishonest /dɪsˈɒnɪst/ *adj* disonesto

dishonestly /dɪsˈɒnɪstlɪ/ *adv* disonestamente

dishonesty /dɪsˈɒnɪstɪ/ *n* disonestà *f*

dishonour /dɪsˈɒnə(r)/ **A** *n* disonore *m*
B *vt* disonorare ‹*family*›; non onorare ‹*cheque*›

dishonourable /dɪsˈɒnərəbl/ *adj* disonorevole

dishonourably /dɪsˈɒnərəblɪ/ *adv* in modo disonorevole

dish towel *n* strofinaccio *m* per i piatti

dishwasher /ˈdɪʃwɒʃə(r)/ *n* lavapiatti *f inv*

dishwasher-safe *adj* lavabile in lavastoviglie

dishy /ˈdɪʃɪ/ *adj* (**-ier**, **est**) BrE infml ‹*man, woman*› fico, figo

disillusion /dɪsɪˈluːʒn/ *vt* disilludere

disillusioned /dɪsɪˈluːʒnd/ *adj* deluso (**with** di)

disillusionment /dɪsɪˈluːʒnmənt/ *n* disillusione *f*

disincentive /dɪsɪnˈsentɪv/ *n* disincentivo *m*

disinclined /dɪsɪnˈklaɪnd/ *adj* riluttante

disinfect /dɪsɪnˈfekt/ *vt* disinfettare

disinfectant /dɪsɪnˈfektənt/ *n* disinfettante *m*

disingenuous /dɪsɪnˈdʒenjʊəs/ *adj* ‹*comment*› insincero; ‹*smile*› falso

disinherit /dɪsɪnˈherɪt/ *vt* diseredare

disintegrate /dɪsˈɪntəgreɪt/ *vi* disintegrarsi

disintegration /dɪsɪntɪˈgreɪʃn/ *n* disgregazione *f*

disinterested /dɪsˈɪntərestɪd/ *adj* disinteressato

disjointed /dɪsˈdʒɔɪntɪd/ *adj* sconnesso

disk /dɪsk/ *n* Comput disco *m*; (diskette) dischetto *m*

disk drive *n* lettore *m* [di disco]

disk operating system /ˈdɪskɒpəreɪtɪŋ/ *n* sistema *m* operativo su disco

dislike /dɪsˈlaɪk/ **A** *n* avversione *f*; **your likes and ~s** i tuoi gusti
B *vt* **I ~ him/it** non mi piace; **I don't ~ him/it** non mi dispiace

dislocate /ˈdɪsləkeɪt/ *vt* slogare; **~ one's shoulder** slogarsi una spalla

dislocation /dɪsləˈkeɪʃn/ *n* (of hip, knee) lussazione *f*

dislodge /dɪsˈlɒdʒ/ *vt* sloggiare

disloyal /dɪsˈlɔɪəl/ *adj* sleale

disloyally /dɪsˈlɔɪəlɪ/ *adv* slealmente

disloyalty /dɪsˈlɔɪəltɪ/ *n* slealtà *f*

dismal /ˈdɪzməl/ *adj* ‹*person*› abbacchiato; ‹*news, weather*› deprimente; ‹*performance*› mediocre

dismantle /dɪsˈmæntl/ *vt* smontare ‹*tent, machine*›; fig smantellare

dismay /dɪsˈmeɪ/ *n* sgomento *m*; **much to my ~** con mio grande sgomento

dismayed /dɪsˈmeɪd/ *adj* sgomento

dismember /dɪsˈmembə(r)/ *vt also* fig smembrare

🔑 **dismiss** /dɪsˈmɪs/ *vt* licenziare ‹*employee*›; (reject) scartare ‹*idea, suggestion*›

dismissal /dɪsˈmɪsəl/ *n* licenziamento *m*

dismissive /dɪsˈmɪsɪv/ *adj* ‹*person, attitude*› sprezzante; **be ~ of** essere sprezzante verso

dismount /dɪsˈmaʊnt/ *vi* smontare

disobedience /dɪsəˈbiːdɪəns/ *n* disubbidienza *f*

disobedient /dɪsəˈbiːdɪənt/ *adj* disubbidiente

disobey /dɪsəˈbeɪ/ **A** *vt* disubbidire a ‹*rule*›
B *vi* disubbidire

disorder /dɪsˈɔːdə(r)/ *n* disordine *m*; Med disturbo *m*

disordered /dɪsˈɔːdəd/ *adj* ‹*life*› disordinato; ‹*mind*› disturbato

disorderly /dɪsˈɔːdəlɪ/ *adj* disordinato; ‹*crowd*› turbolento; **~ conduct** turbamento *m* della quiete pubblica

disorganization /dɪsɔːgənaɪˈzeɪʃn/ *n* disorganizzazione *f*

disorganized /dɪsˈɔːgənaɪzd/ *adj* disorganizzato

disorientate /dɪsˈɔːrɪənteɪt/ *vt* disorientare

disorientation /dɪsɔːrɪenˈteɪʃn/ *n* disorientamento *m*

disown /dɪsˈəʊn/ *vt* disconoscere; **I'll ~ you** infml faccio finta di non conoscerti

disparaging /dɪˈspærɪdʒɪŋ/ *adj* sprezzante

disparagingly /dɪˈspærɪdʒɪŋlɪ/ *adv* sprezzantemente

disparate /ˈdɪspərət/ *adj* (different) eterogeneo; ‹*incompatible*› disparato

disparity /dɪˈspærətɪ/ *n* disparità *f*

d

dispassionate /dɪ'spæʃənət/ *adj* spassionato

dispassionately /dɪs'pæʃənətlɪ/ *adv* spassionatamente

dispatch /dɪ'spætʃ/ **A** *n* Comm spedizione *f*; Mil (report) dispaccio *m*; **with ~** con prontezza
B *vt* spedire; (kill) spedire al creatore

dispatch box *n* valigia *f* diplomatica

Dispatch Box *n* BrE Pol *postazione (f) da cui parlano i ministri nel Parlamento britannico*

dispatch rider *n* staffetta *f*

dispel /dɪ'spel/ *vt* (*pt/pp* **dispelled**) dissipare

dispensable /dɪ'spensəbl/ *adj* dispensabile

dispensary /dɪ'spensərɪ/ *n* farmacia *f*

dispense /dɪ'spens/ *vt* distribuire; **~ with** fare a meno di

dispenser /dɪ'spensə(r)/ *n* (device) distributore *m*

dispensing chemist /dɪ'spensɪŋ/ *n* farmacista *mf*; (shop) farmacia *f*

dispensing optician *n* BrE ottico *m*

dispersal /dɪ'spɜːsl/ *n* dispersione *f*

disperse /dɪ'spɜːs/ **A** *vt* disperdere
B *vi* disperdersi

dispersion /dɪ'spɜːʃn/ *n* dispersione *f*

dispirited /dɪ'spɪrɪtɪd/ *adj* scoraggiato

displace /dɪs'pleɪs/ *vt* spostare

displaced person *n* profugo, -a *mf*

displacement /dɪs'pleɪsmənt/ *n* spostamento *m*

⚷ **display** /dɪ'spleɪ/ **A** *n* mostra *f*; Comm esposizione *f*; (of feelings) manifestazione *f*; derog ostentazione *f*; Comput display *m inv*
B *vt* mostrare; esporre ‹*goods*›; manifestare ‹*feelings*›; Comput visualizzare

display advertisement *n* annuncio *m* pubblicitario di grande formato

display cabinet, **display case** *n* vetrina *f*

display rack *n* espositore *m*

display window *n* vetrina *f*

displease /dɪs'pliːz/ *vt* non piacere a; **be ~d with** essere scontento di

displeasure /dɪs'pleʒə(r)/ *n* malcontento *m*; **incur sb's ~** scontentare qualcuno

disposable /dɪ'spəʊzəbl/ *adj* (throwaway) usa e getta; ‹*income*› disponibile

disposal /dɪ'spəʊzl/ *n* (getting rid of) eliminazione *f*; **be at sb's ~** essere a disposizione di qualcuno

dispose /dɪ'spəʊz/ *vi* **~ of** (get rid of) disfarsi di; **be well ~d** essere ben disposto (**to** verso)

disposition /dɪspə'zɪʃn/ *n* disposizione *f*; (nature) indole *f*

dispossessed /dɪspə'zest/ *adj* ‹*family*› spossessato; ‹*son*› diseredato

disproportionate /dɪsprə'pɔːʃənət/ *adj* sproporzionato

disproportionately /dɪsprə'pɔːʃənətlɪ/ *adv* in modo sproporzionato

disprove /dɪs'pruːv/ *vt* confutare

dispute /dɪ'spjuːt/ **A** *n* disputa *f*; (industrial) contestazione *f*
B *vt* contestare ‹*statement*›

disqualification /dɪskwɒlɪfɪ'keɪʃn/ *n* squalifica *f*; (from driving) ritiro *m* della patente

disqualify /dɪs'kwɒlɪfaɪ/ *vt* escludere; Sport squalificare; **~ somebody from driving** ritirare la patente a qualcuno

disquiet /dɪs'kwaɪət/ *n* inquietudine *f*

disquieting /dɪs'kwaɪətɪŋ/ *adj* allarmante

disregard /dɪsrɪ'gɑːd/ **A** *n* mancanza *f* di considerazione
B *vt* ignorare

disrepair /dɪsrɪ'peə(r)/ *n* **fall into ~** deteriorarsi; **in a state of ~** in cattivo stato

disreputable /dɪs'repjʊtəbl/ *adj* malfamato

disrepute /dɪsrɪ'pjuːt/ *n* discredito *m*; **bring somebody into ~** rovinare la reputazione a qualcuno

disrespect /dɪsrɪ'spekt/ *n* mancanza *f* di rispetto

disrespectful /dɪsrɪ'spektfʊl/ *adj* irrispettoso

disrespectfully /dɪsrɪ'spektfʊlɪ/ *adv* irrispettosamente

disrupt /dɪs'rʌpt/ *vt* creare scompiglio in; sconvolgere ‹*plans*›

disruption /dɪs'rʌpʃn/ *n* scompiglio *m*; (of plans) sconvolgimento *m*

disruptive /dɪs'rʌptɪv/ *adj* ‹*person, behaviour*› indisciplinato

dissatisfaction /dɪ(s)sætɪs'fækʃn/ *n* malcontento *m*

dissatisfied /dɪ(s)'sætɪsfaɪd/ *adj* scontento

dissect /dɪ'sekt/ *vt* sezionare

dissection /dɪ'sekʃn/ *n* dissezione *f*

disseminate /dɪ'semɪneɪt/ *vt* divulgare

dissemination /dɪsemɪ'neɪʃn/ *n* divulgazione *f*

dissension /dɪ'senʃn/ *n* (discord) dissenso *m*

dissent /dɪ'sent/ **A** *n* dissenso *m*
B *vi* dissentire

dissertation /dɪsə'teɪʃn/ *n* tesi *f inv*

disservice /dɪ(s)'sɜːvɪs/ *n* **do somebody/oneself a ~** rendere un cattivo servizio a qualcuno/se stesso

dissidence /'dɪsɪdəns/ *n* dissidenza *f*

dissident /'dɪsɪdənt/ *n* dissidente *mf*

dissimilar /dɪ(s)'sɪmɪlə(r)/ *adj* dissimile (**to** da)

dissimilarity /dɪs(s)ɪmɪ'lærətɪ/ *n* diversità *f*

dissipate /'dɪsɪpeɪt/ *vt* dissipare ‹*hope, enthusiasm*›

⚷ parola chiave

dissipated /ˈdɪsɪpeɪtɪd/ *adj* dissipato

dissipation *n* dissipatezza *f*, sregolatezza *f*

dissociate /dɪˈsəʊʃɪeɪt/ *vt* dissociare; ~ **oneself from** dissociarsi da

dissolute /ˈdɪsəluːt/ *adj* dissoluto

dissolution /dɪsəˈluːʃn/ *n* scioglimento *m*

dissolve /dɪˈzɒlv/ **A** *vt* dissolvere
B *vi* dissolversi

dissonance /ˈdɪsənəns/ *n* dissonanza *f*

dissonant /ˈdɪsənənt/ *adj* Mus dissonante

dissuade /dɪˈsweɪd/ *vt* dissuadere

🔑 **distance** /ˈdɪstəns/ *n* distanza *f*; **it's a short ~ from here to the station** la stazione non è lontana da qui; **in the ~** in lontananza; **from a ~** da lontano

distance learning *n* corsi *mpl* di studio a distanza

distant /ˈdɪstənt/ *adj* distante; ‹*relative*› lontano

distantly /ˈdɪstəntlɪ/ *adv* ‹*reply*› con distacco

distaste /dɪsˈteɪst/ *n* avversione *f*

distasteful /dɪsˈteɪstfʊl/ *adj* spiacevole

distemper /dɪˈstempə(r)/ *n* (paint) tempera *f*; (in horses, dogs) cimurro *m*

distend /dɪˈstend/ *vi* dilatarsi

distil /dɪˈstɪl/ *vt* (*pt/pp* **distilled**) distillare

distillation /dɪstɪˈleɪʃn/ *n* distillazione *f*

distillery /dɪˈstɪlərɪ/ *n* distilleria *f*

distinct /dɪˈstɪŋkt/ *adj* chiaro; (different) distinto

distinction /dɪˈstɪŋkʃn/ *n* distinzione *f*; Sch massimo *m* dei voti

distinctive /dɪˈstɪŋktɪv/ *adj* caratteristico

distinctly /dɪˈstɪŋktlɪ/ *adv* chiaramente

distinguish /dɪˈstɪŋgwɪʃ/ *vt & vi* distinguere; ~ **oneself** distinguersi

distinguishable /dɪˈstɪŋgwɪʃəbl/ *adj* distinguibile

distinguished /dɪˈstɪŋgwɪʃt/ *adj* rinomato; ‹*appearance*› distinto; ‹*career*› brillante

distinguishing /dɪˈstɪŋgwɪʃɪŋ/ *adj* ‹*feature*› distintivo

distort /dɪˈstɔːt/ *vt* distorcere

distortion /dɪˈstɔːʃn/ *n* distorsione *f*

distract /dɪˈstrækt/ *vt* distrarre

distracted /dɪˈstræktɪd/ *adj* assente; infml (worried) preoccupato

distracting /dɪˈstræktɪŋ/ *adj* che distrae; **I found the noise too ~** il rumore mi disturbava troppo

distraction /dɪˈstrækʃn/ *n* distrazione *f*; (despair) disperazione *f*; **drive somebody to ~** portare qualcuno alla disperazione

distraught /dɪˈstrɔːt/ *adj* sconvolto

distress /dɪˈstres/ **A** *n* angoscia *f*; (pain) sofferenza *f*; (danger) difficoltà *f*
B *vt* sconvolgere; (sadden) affliggere

distressed /dɪˈstrest/ *adj* (upset) turbato; (stronger) afflitto

distressing /dɪˈstresɪŋ/ *adj* penoso; (shocking) sconvolgente

distress signal *n* segnale *m* di richiesta di soccorso

distribute /dɪˈstrɪbjuːt/ *vt* distribuire

🔑 **distribution** /dɪstrɪˈbjuːʃn/ *n* distribuzione *f*

distribution network *n* rete *f* di distribuzione

distributor /dɪˈstrɪbjʊtə(r)/ *n* distributore *m*

🔑 **district** /ˈdɪstrɪkt/ *n* regione *f*; Admin distretto *m*

district attorney *n* AmE procuratore *m* distrettuale

district council *n* BrE consiglio *m* distrettuale

district court *n* AmE corte *f* distrettuale federale

district manager *n* direttore, -trice *mf* di zona

district nurse *n* infermiere, -a *mf* che fa visite a domicilio

distrust /dɪsˈtrʌst/ **A** *n* sfiducia *f*
B *vt* non fidarsi di

distrustful /dɪsˈtrʌstfʊl/ *adj* diffidente

disturb /dɪˈstɜːb/ *vt* disturbare; (emotionally) turbare; spostare ‹*papers*›

disturbance /dɪˈstɜːbəns/ *n* disturbo *m*; **~s** *pl* (rioting etc) disordini *mpl*

disturbed /dɪˈstɜːbd/ *adj* turbato; **[mentally] ~** malato di mente

disturbing /dɪˈstɜːbɪŋ/ *adj* inquietante

disuse /dɪsˈjuːs/ *n* **fall into ~** cadere in disuso

disused /dɪsˈjuːzd/ *adj* non utilizzato

ditch /dɪtʃ/ **A** *n* fosso *m*
B *vt* infml (abandon) abbandonare ‹*plan, car*›; piantare ‹*lover*›

ditchwater /ˈdɪtʃwɔːtə(r)/ *n* **as dull as ~** una barba

dither /ˈdɪðə(r)/ *vi* titubare

ditto /ˈdɪtəʊ/ *adv* idem; (in list) idem come sopra

ditto marks *npl* virgolette *fpl*

divan /dɪˈvæn/ *n* divano *m*

dive /daɪv/ **A** *n* tuffo *m*; Aeron picchiata *f*; infml (place) bettola *f*
B *vi* tuffarsi; (when in water) immergersi; Aeron scendere in picchiata; infml (rush) precipitarsi

dive-bomb *vt* Mil bombardare in picchiata

diver /ˈdaɪvə(r)/ *n* (from board) tuffatore, -trice *mf*; (scuba) sommozzatore, -trice *mf*; (deep sea) palombaro *m*

diverge /daɪˈvɜːdʒ/ *vi* divergere

divergent /daɪˈvɜːdʒənt/ *adj* divergente

diverse /daɪˈvɜːs/ *adj* vario

diversify /daɪˈvɜːsɪfaɪ/ *vt & vi* (*pt/pp* **-ied**) Comm diversificare

diversion /daɪˈvɜːʃn/ *n* deviazione *f*; (distraction) diversivo *m*

diversionary /daɪˈvɜːʃənərɪ/ *adj* ‹*tactic, attack*› diversivo

diversity /daɪˈvɜːsətɪ/ *n* varietà *f*

divert /daɪˈvɜːt/ *vt* deviare ‹*traffic*›; distogliere ‹*attention*›

divest /daɪˈvest/ *vt* privare (**of** di)

divide /dɪˈvaɪd/ **A** *vt* dividere (**by** per); **six ~d by two** sei diviso due
B *vi* dividersi

■ **divide out** *vt* = **divide**

■ **divide up** *vt* = **divide**

dividend /ˈdɪvɪdend/ *n* dividendo *m*; **pay ~s** fig ripagare

divider /dɪˈvaɪdə(r)/ *n* (in room) divisorio *m*; (in file) cartoncino *m* separatore

dividers /dɪˈvaɪdəz/ *npl* compasso *m* a punte fisse

dividing /dɪˈvaɪdɪŋ/ *adj* ‹*wall, fence*› divisorio

dividing line *n* linea *f* di demarcazione

divine /dɪˈvaɪn/ *adj* divino

divinely /dɪˈvaɪnlɪ/ *adv also* infml divinamente

diving /ˈdaɪvɪŋ/ *n* (from board) tuffi *mpl*; (scuba) immersione *f*

diving board *n* trampolino *m*

diving mask *n* maschera *f* [subacquea]

diving suit *n* muta *f*; (deep sea) scafandro *m*

divinity /dɪˈvɪnətɪ/ *n* divinità *f*; (subject) teologia *f*; (at school) religione *f*

divisible /dɪˈvɪzəbl/ *adj* divisibile (**by** per)

division /dɪˈvɪʒn/ *n* divisione *f*; (in sports league) serie *f*

divisional /dɪˈvɪʃənəl/ *adj* ‹*commander, officer*› di divisione

divisive /dɪˈvaɪsɪv/ *adj* ‹*policy*› che crea discordia; **be socially ~** creare delle divisioni sociali

divorce /dɪˈvɔːs/ **A** *n* divorzio *m*
B *vt* divorziare da

divorced /dɪˈvɔːst/ *adj* divorziato; **get ~** divorziare

divorcee /dɪvɔːˈsiː/ *n* divorziato, -a *mf*

divulge /daɪˈvʌldʒ/ *vt* rendere pubblico

■ **divvy up** *vt* infml = **divide up**

DIY *abbr* (**do-it-yourself**) *fai da te, bricolage*

dizziness /ˈdɪzɪnɪs/ *n* giramenti *mpl* di testa

dizzy /ˈdɪzɪ/ *adj* (**-ier**, **-iest**) vertiginoso; **I feel ~** mi gira la testa

DJ *n abbr* **1** (**disc jockey**) DJ *m inv* **2** BrE (**dinner jacket**) smoking *m inv*

Djibouti /dʒɪˈbuːtɪ/ *n* Gibuti *f*

DNA **A** *n abbr* (**deoxyribonucleic acid**) DNA *m inv*
B *attrib* ‹*testing*› del DNA

DNR *abbr* AmE **1** (**Department of Natural Resources**) ≈ Ministero *m* dell'Ambiente e della Tutela del Territorio **2** (**do not resuscitate**) non rianimare

do /duː/ **A** *n* (*pl* **dos** *or* **do's**) infml festa *f*
B *vt* (3 *sg pres tense* **does**, *pt* **did**, *pp* **done**) fare; infml (cheat) fregare; **do somebody out of something** (money) fregare qualcosa a qualcuno; (opportunity) defraudare qualcuno di qualcosa; **be done** Culin essere cotto; **well done** bravo; Culin ben cotto; **do the flowers** sistemare i fiori; **do the washing up** lavare i piatti; **do one's hair** farsi i capelli
C *vi* (be suitable) andare; (be enough) bastare; **this will do** questo va bene; **that will do!** basta così!; **do well/badly** cavarsela bene/male; **how is he doing?** come sta?
D *v aux* **do you speak Italian?** parli italiano?; **you don't like him, do you?** non ti piace, vero?; (expressing astonishment) non dirmi che ti piace!; **yes, I do** sì; (emphatic) invece sì; **no, I don't** no; **I don't smoke** non fumo; **don't you/doesn't he?** vero?; **so do I** anch'io; **do come in, John** entra, John; **how do you do?** piacere

■ **do away with** *vt* abolire ‹*rule*›

■ **do for** *vt* (ruin) rovinare

■ **do in** *vt* infml (kill) uccidere; farsi male a ‹*back*›; **done in** infml esausto

■ **do up** *vt* (fasten) abbottonare; (renovate) rimettere a nuovo; (wrap) avvolgere

■ **do with**: *vt* **I could do with a spanner** mi ci vorrebbe una chiave inglese

■ **do without** *vt* fare a meno di

d.o.b. *abbr* (**date of birth**) data *f* di nascita

docile /ˈdəʊsaɪl/ *adj* docile

dock[1] /dɒk/ *n* Jur banco *m* degli imputati

dock[2] **A** *n* Naut bacino *m*
B *vi* entrare in porto; ‹*spaceship*› congiungersi

docker /ˈdɒkə(r)/ *n* portuale *m*

docket /ˈdɒkɪt/ **A** *n* Comm (label) etichetta *f*; (customs certificate) ricevuta *f* doganale
B *vt* Comm etichettare ‹*parcel, package*›

docking /ˈdɒkɪŋ/ *n* Naut ormeggio *m*; (of space shuttle) aggancio *m*

docks /dɒks/ *npl* porto *m*

dock worker /ˈdɒkwɜːkə(r)/ *n* portuale *m*

dockyard /ˈdɒkjɑːd/ *n* cantiere *m* navale

doctor /ˈdɒktə(r)/ **A** *n* dottore *m*, dottoressa *f*
B *vt* alterare ‹*drink*›; castrare ‹*cat*›

doctorate /ˈdɒktərət/ *n* dottorato *m*

Doctor of Philosophy *n* titolare *mf* di un dottorato di ricerca

doctor's note /ˈdɒktəz/ *n* certificato *m* medico

doctrine /ˈdɒktrɪn/ *n* dottrina *f*

docudrama /ˈdɒkjʊdrɑːmə/ *n* film *m inv* verità

document /ˈdɒkjʊmənt/ *n* documento *m*

documentary /dɒkjʊˈmentərɪ/ *adj & n* documentario *m*

documentation /dɒkjʊmenˈteɪʃn/ *n* documentazione *f*

parola chiave

document holder *n* (for keyboarder) leggio *m*
document wallet *n* (folder) cartellina *f*
doddery /ˈdɒdərɪ/ *adj* infml barcollante
doddle /ˈdɒd(ə)l/ *n* BrE infml **it's a ~** è un gioco da ragazzi
dodge /dɒdʒ/ **A** *n* infml trucco *m* **B** *vt* schivare ‹*blow*›; evitare ‹*person*› **C** *vi* scansarsi; **~ out of the way** scansarsi
dodgems /ˈdɒdʒəmz/ *npl* autoscontro *msg*
dodgy /ˈdɒdʒɪ/ *adj* (**-ier**, **-iest**) infml (dubious) sospetto
doe /dəʊ/ *n* femmina *f* (*di daino, renna, lepre*); (rabbit) coniglia *f*
DOE *n abbr* **1** BrE (**Department of the Environment**) ministero *m* dell'Ambiente **2** AmE (**Department of Energy**) ≈ ministero *m* dell'Industria
does /dʌz/ ▶ **do**
dog /dɒg/ **A** *n* cane *m* **B** *vt* (*pt/pp* **dogged**) ‹*illness, bad luck*› perseguitare
dog biscuit *n* biscotto *m* per cani
dog breeder *n* allevatore, -trice *mf* di cani
dog collar *n* collare *m* (*per cani*)
dog-eared /-ɪəd/ *adj* con le orecchie
dog-end *n* infml cicca *f*
dogfight *n* combattimento *m* di cani; Aeron combattimento *m* aereo
dogged /ˈdɒgɪd/ *adj* ostinato
doggedly /ˈdɒgɪdlɪ/ *adv* ostinatamente
doggy bag /ˈdɒgɪ/ *n sacchetto* (*m*) *per portarsi a casa gli avanzi di un pasto al ristorante*
doggy-paddle *n* infml nuoto *m* a cagnolino
dog handler *n* addestratore, -trice *mf* di cani
doghouse /ˈdɒghaʊs/ *n* AmE canile *m*; **in the ~** infml in disgrazia
dogma /ˈdɒgmə/ *n* dogma *m*
dogmatic /dɒgˈmætɪk/ *adj* dogmatico
do-gooder /duːˈgʊdə(r)/ *n* derog pseudo benefattore, -trice *mf*
dog-paddle *n* nuoto *m* a cagnolino
dogsbody *n* infml tirapiedi *mf inv*
dog tag *n* AmE Mil infml piastrina *f* di riconoscimento
doh /dəʊ/ *n* Mus do *m*
doily /ˈdɔɪlɪ/ *n* centrino *m*
doing /ˈduːɪŋ/ *n* **it's none of my ~** non sono stato io; **this is her ~** questa è opera sua; **it takes some ~!** ce ne vuole!
do-it-yourself /duːɪtjəˈself/ *n* fai da te *m*, bricolage *m*
do-it-yourself shop *n* negozio *m* di bricolage
doldrums /ˈdɒldrəmz/ *npl* **be in the ~** essere giù di corda; ‹*business*› essere in fase di stasi
dole /dəʊl/ *n* sussidio *m* di disoccupazione; **be on the ~** essere disoccupato
■ **dole out** *vt* distribuire
doleful /ˈdəʊlfl/ *adj* triste
dolefully /ˈdəʊlfʊlɪ/ *adv* tristemente
dole queue *n* BrE *coda* (*f*) *per riscuotere il sussidio di disoccupazione*; fig (number of unemployed) numero *m* dei disoccupati
doll /dɒl/ *n* bambola *f*
■ **doll up**: *vt* infml **~ oneself up** mettersi in ghingheri
dollar /ˈdɒlə(r)/ *n* dollaro *m*
dollar bill *n* banconota *f* da un dollaro
dollar diplomacy *n politica* (*f*) *di investimenti all'estero*
dollar sign *n* simbolo *m* del dollaro
dollop /ˈdɒləp/ *n* infml cucchiaiata *f*
dolly /ˈdɒlɪ/ *n* infml (doll) bambola *f*; Cinema, TV dolly *m inv*
Dolomites /ˈdɒləmaɪts/ *npl* Dolomiti *fpl*
dolphin /ˈdɒlfɪn/ *n* delfino *m*
domain /dəˈmeɪn/ *n* dominio *m*
domain name *n* Comput nome *m* di dominio
dome /dəʊm/ *n* cupola *f*
domed /dəʊmd/ *adj* ‹*skyline, city*› ricco di cupole; ‹*roof, ceiling*› a cupola; ‹*forehead, helmet*› bombato
domestic /dəˈmestɪk/ *adj* domestico; Pol interno; Comm nazionale
domestic animal *n* animale *m* domestico
domestic appliance *n* elettrodomestico *m*
domesticate /dəˈmestɪkeɪt/ *vt* addomesticare
domesticated /dəˈmestɪkeɪtɪd/ *adj* ‹*animal*› addomesticato
domestic flight *n* volo *m* nazionale
domestic help *n* collaboratore, -trice *mf* familiare
domesticity /dɒmeˈstɪsətɪ/ *n* ‹*home life*› vita *f* di famiglia; ‹*household duties*› faccende *fpl* domestiche
domestic servant *n* domestico, -a *mf*
domiciliary /dɒmɪˈsɪlɪərɪ/ *adj* ‹*visit, care*› a domicilio
dominance /ˈdɒmɪnəns/ *n* Biol, Zool dominanza *f*; (domination) predominio *m*; (numerical strength) preponderanza *f*
dominant /ˈdɒmɪnənt/ *adj* dominante
dominate /ˈdɒmɪneɪt/ *vt & vi* dominare
domination /dɒmɪˈneɪʃn/ *n* dominio *m*
domineering /dɒmɪˈnɪərɪŋ/ *adj* autoritario
Dominica /dəˈmɪnɪkə/ *n* Dominica *f*
Dominican Republic /dəˈmɪnɪkən/ *n* Repubblica *f* Dominicana
dominion /dəˈmɪnjən/ *n* BrE Pol dominio *m inv*
domino /ˈdɒmɪnəʊ/ *n* (*pl* **-es**) tessera *f* del domino; **~es** *sg* (game) domino *m*
don¹ /dɒn/ *vt* (*pt/pp* **donned**) literary indossare
don² *n* docente *mf* universitario, -a
donate /dəʊˈneɪt/ *vt* donare

donation /dəʊ'neɪʃn/ *n* donazione *f*
done /dʌn/ ▶ **do**
donkey /'dɒŋkɪ/ *n* asino *m*
donkey jacket *n* giacca *f* pesante
donkey's years: infml **not for ~** non da secoli
donkey work *n* sgobbata *f*
d
donor /'dəʊnə(r)/ *n* donatore, -trice *mf*
donor card *n* tessera *f* del donatore di organi
doodle /'du:dl/ *vi* scarabocchiare
doom /du:m/ **A** *n* fato *m*; (ruin) rovina *f*
B *vt* **be ~ed to failure** essere destinato al fallimento
doomed /du:md/ *adj* ‹*vessel*› destinato ad affondare
doomsday /'du:mzdeɪ/ *n* giorno *m* del giudizio
doomwatch /'du:mwɒtʃ/ *n* catastrofismo *m*
⚷ **door** /dɔ:(r)/ *n* porta *f*; (of car) portiera *f*; **out of ~s** all'aperto
door bell *n* campanello *m*
doorman *n* portiere *m*
doormat *n* zerbino *m*
door plate *n* (of doctor etc) targa *f*
doorstep *n* gradino *m* della porta
doorstop *n* fermaporta *m inv*
door-to-door **A** *adj* ‹*canvassing, selling*› porta a porta
B *adv* ‹*sell*› porta a porta
doorway *n* vano *m* della porta
dope /dəʊp/ **A** *n* infml (drug) droga *f* leggera; (information) indiscrezioni *fpl*; (idiot) idiota *mf*
B *vt* drogare; Sport dopare
dope test *n* Sport antidoping *m inv*
dopey /'dəʊpɪ/ *adj* infml addormentato
dormant /'dɔ:mənt/ *adj* latente; ‹*volcano*› inattivo
dormer /'dɔ:mə(r)/ *n* **~ [window]** abbaino *m*
dormitory /'dɔ:mɪtərɪ/ *n* dormitorio *m*
dormitory town *n* città *f* dormitorio
dormouse /'dɔ:maʊs/ *n* (*pl* **dormice** /'dɔ:maɪs/) ghiro *m*
dosage /'dəʊsɪdʒ/ *n* dosaggio *m*
dose /dəʊs/ *n* dose *f*
doss /dɒs/ *vi* sl accamparsi
▪ **doss down** *vi* sistemarsi [a dormire]
dosser /'dɒsə(r)/ *n* barbone, -a *mf*
doss-house *n* dormitorio *m* pubblico
dot /dɒt/ *n* punto *m*; **at 8 o'clock on the ~** alle 8 in punto
dotage /'dəʊtɪdʒ/ *n* **be in one's ~** essere un vecchio rimbambito
dot-com /dɒt'kɒm/ **A** *adj* ‹*company*› che opera in Internet; ‹*millionaire*› arricchito grazie a Internet
B *n* azienda *f* che opera in Internet
dot-com bubble *n* bolla *f* delle dot-com

⚷ parola chiave

dote /dəʊt/ *vi* **~ on** stravedere per
dot matrix, dot matrix printer *n* stampante *f* a matrice di punti
dotted /'dɒtɪd/ *adj* **~ line** linea *f* punteggiata; **sign on the ~ line** firmare nell'apposito spazio; **be ~ with** essere punteggiato di
dotty /'dɒtɪ/ *adj* (**-ier**, **-iest**) infml tocco; ‹*idea*› folle
⚷ **double** /'dʌbl/ **A** *adj* doppio
B *adv* **cost ~** costare il doppio; **see ~** vedere doppio; **~ the amount** la quantità doppia
C *n* doppio *m*; (person) sosia *m inv*; **~s** *pl* Tennis doppio *m*; **at the ~** di corsa
D *vt* raddoppiare; (fold) piegare in due
E *vi* raddoppiare
▪ **double back** *vi* (go back) fare dietro front
▪ **double up** *vi* (bend over) piegarsi in due (**with** per); (share) dividere una stanza
double act *n* Theat, fig numero *m* eseguito da due attori
double-barrelled /-'bærəld/ *adj* ‹*gun*› a doppia canna
double-barrelled surname *n* cognome *m* doppio
double bass *n* contrabbasso *m*
double bed *n* letto *m* matrimoniale
double bend *n* Auto doppia curva *f*
double bill *n* Theat rappresentazione *f* di due spettacoli
double bluff *n atto (m) del dire la verità facendola sembrare una menzogna*
double-book **A** *vi* ‹*hotel, airline, company*› fare prenotazioni doppie
B *vt* **~ a room/seat etc** riservare la stessa camera/lo stesso posto a due persone
double-breasted *adj* a doppio petto
double-check **A** *vt & vi* ricontrollare
B *n* **double check** ulteriore controllo *m*
double chin *n* doppio mento *m*
double-click /dʌbl'klɪk/ *vi* Comput fare doppio click; **~ on** fare doppio click su
double cream *n* BrE ≈ panna *f* densa
double-cross *vt* ingannare
double cuff *n* polsino *m* con risvolto
double-dealing **A** *n* doppio gioco *m*
B *adj* doppio
double-decker *n* autobus *m inv* a due piani
double-dip *adj* double dip; **~ recession** recessione double dip, recessione a w
double door, double doors *n* porta *f* a due battenti
double Dutch *n* infml ostrogoto *m*
double-edged /-'edʒd/ *adj* also fig a doppio taglio
double entendre /du:blɒ̃'tɒ̃dr(ə)/ *n* doppio senso *m*
double entry book-keeping *n* contabilità *f* in partita doppia
double exposure *n* Phot sovrimpressione *f*

double fault *n* Tennis doppio fallo *m*

double feature *n* Cinema *proiezione (f) di due film con biglietto unico*

double-fronted /-ˈfrʌntɪd/ *adj* ‹*house*› con due finestre ai lati della porta principale

double glazing *n* doppio vetro *m*

double-jointed *adj* ‹*person, limb*› snodato

double knitting, double knitting wool *n* lana *f* grossa

double lock *vt* chiudere a doppia mandata

double-park *vt & vi* parcheggiare in doppia fila

double quick **A** *adv* rapidissimamente
B *adj* **in ~ time** in un baleno

double room *n* camera *f* doppia

double saucepan *n* BrE bagnomaria *m inv*

double spacing *n* Typ interlinea *f* doppia

double spread *n* Journ articolo *m*; pubblicità *f* su due pagine

double standard *n* **have ~s** usare metri diversi

double take *n* **do a ~** reagire a scoppio ritardato

double talk *n* derog discorso *m* ambiguo

double time *n* AmE Mil marcia *f* forzata; **be paid ~** ricevere doppia paga per lo straordinario

double vision *n* **have ~** vederci doppio

double whammy *n* infml (two bits of bad luck) sfortuna *f* doppia

double yellow line, double yellow lines *n[pl]* BrE Aut *due linee (fpl) gialle continue indicanti divieto di fermata e di sosta*

doubly /ˈdʌblɪ/ *adv* doppiamente

doubt /daʊt/ **A** *n* dubbio *m*
B *vt* dubitare di

doubtful /ˈdaʊtfʊl/ *adj* dubbio; (having doubts) in dubbio

doubtfully /ˈdaʊtfʊlɪ/ *adv* con aria dubbiosa

doubtless /ˈdaʊtlɪs/ *adv* indubbiamente

douche /duːʃ/ *n* Med (vaginal) irrigazione *f*

dough /dəʊ/ *n* pasta *f*; (for bread) impasto *m*; infml (money) quattrini *mpl*

doughnut /ˈdəʊnʌt/ *n* bombolone *m*, krapfen *m inv*

dour /dʊə(r)/ *adj* ‹*mood, landscape*› cupo; ‹*person, expression*› arcigno; ‹*building*› austero

douse /daʊs/ *vt* spegnere

dove /dʌv/ *n* colomba *f*

dovecot, dovecote /ˈdʌvkɒt/ *n* colombaia *f*

dovetail /ˈdʌvteɪl/ *n* Techn incastro *m* a coda di rondine

dowdy /ˈdaʊdɪ/ *adj* (**-ier, -iest**) trasandato

down¹ /daʊn/ *n* (feathers) piumino *m*

down² **A** *adv* giù; **go/come ~** scendere; **~ there** laggiù; **sales are ~** le vendite sono diminuite; **£50 ~** 50 sterline d'acconto; **~ 10%** ridotto del 10%; **~ with...!** abbasso...!
B *prep* **walk ~ the road** comminare per strada; **~ the stairs** giù per le scale; **fall ~ the stairs** cadere giù dalle scale; **get that ~ you!** infml butta giù!; **be ~ the pub** infml essere al pub
C *vt* bere tutto d'un fiato ‹*drink*›; **~ tools** staccare; (in protest) interrompere il lavoro per protesta

down-and-out *n* spiantato, -a *mf*

down-beat *adj* (pessimistic) pessimistico; (laid-back) distaccato

downcast *adj* abbattuto

downfall *n* caduta *f*; (of person) rovina *f*

downgrade *vt* (in seniority) degradare

downhearted /-ˈhɑːtɪd/ *adj* scoraggiato

downhill *adv* in discesa; **go ~** fig essere in declino

downhill skiing *n* sci *m* di fondo

down-in-the-mouth *adj* infml abbattuto

download *vt* Comput scaricare

down-market *adj* ‹*newspaper, programme*› rivolto al pubblico delle fasce basse; ‹*products*› dozzinale; ‹*area*› popolare; ‹*hotel, restaurant*› economico

down payment *n* deposito *m*

downpipe *n* BrE tubo *m* di scolo

downplay *vt* minimizzare

downpour *n* acquazzone *m*

downright **A** *adj* (absolute) totale; ‹*lie*› bell'e buono; (idiot) perfetto
B *adv* (completely) completamente

downs /daʊnz/ *npl* BrE (hills) *colline (fpl) di gesso nell'Inghilterra meridionale*

downside /ˈdaʊnsaɪd/ *n* svantaggio *m*

downside up *adj & adv* AmE sottosopra

downsize /ˈdaʊnsaɪz/ **A** *vt* ‹*company*› ridurre l'organico di
B *vi* ridurre l'organico

Down's syndrome /ˈdaʊnz/ *n* sindrome *f* di Down

downstairs **A** *adv* al piano di sotto
B *adj* del piano di sotto

downstream *adv* a valle

down-to-earth *adj* (person) con i piedi per terra

downtown *adv* AmE in centro

downtrodden /ˈdaʊntrɒd(ə)n/ *adj* oppresso

downturn *n* (in economy) fase *f* discendente; (in career) svolta *f* negativa

down under *adv* infml in Australia e/o Nuova Zelanda

downward /ˈdaʊnwəd/, **downwards** /ˈdaʊnwədz/ **A** *adj* verso il basso; ‹*slope*› in discesa
B *adv* verso il basso

downwind /daʊnˈwɪnd/ *adv* sottovento

downy /ˈdaʊnɪ/ *adj* (**-ier, -iest**) coperto di peluria

dowry /ˈdaʊrɪ/ *n* dote *f*

doz. *abbr* (**dozen**) dozzina *f*
doze /dəʊz/ **A** *n* sonnellino *m*
B *vi* sonnecchiare
■ **doze off** *vi* assopirsi
dozen /ˈdʌzn/ *n* dozzina *f*; **~s of books** libri a dozzine
DPhil *n abbr* (**Doctor of Philosophy**) titolare *mf* di un dottorato di ricerca
DPP *n abbr* BrE (**Director of Public Prosecutions**) ≈ Procuratore *m* della Repubblica
Dr *abbr* **1** (**doctor**) Dott. *m*, Dott.essa *f* **2** (**drive**) ≈ via *f*
drab /dræb/ *adj* ‹*colour*› spento; ‹*building*› tetro; ‹*life*› scialbo
draft¹ /drɑːft/ **A** *n* abbozzo *m*; Comm cambiale *f*; AmE Mil leva *f*
B *vt* abbozzare; AmE Mil arruolare
■ **draft in** *vt* chiamare ‹*reinforcements, police*›
draft² *n* AmE = **draught**
draft dodger *n* renitente *mf* alla leva
draftsman /ˈdrɑːftsmən/ *n* AmE = **draughtsman**
drag /dræg/ **A** *n* infml scocciatura *f*; **in ~** infml ‹*man*› travestito da donna
B *vt* (*pt/pp* **dragged**) trascinare; dragare ‹*river*›
■ **drag on** *vi* ‹*time, meeting*› trascinarsi
■ **drag out** *vt* tirare per le lunghe ‹*discussion*›; **~ something out of somebody** tirar fuori qualcosa a qualcuno con le pinze
■ **drag up** *vt* (mention unnecessarily) tirare in ballo
drag and drop *vt* Comput trascinare e rilasciare
dragon /ˈdrægən/ *n* drago *m*
dragonfly /ˈdrægənflaɪ/ *n* libellula *f*
drag show *n* spettacolo *m* di travestiti
drain /dreɪn/ **A** *n* tubo *m* di scarico; (grid) tombino *m*; **the ~s** le fognature; **be a ~ on sb's finances** prosciugare le finanze di qualcuno
B *vt* drenare ‹*land, wound*›; scolare ‹*liquid, vegetables*›; svuotare ‹*tank glass, person*›
C *vi* **~ [away]** andar via; **leave something to ~** lasciare qualcosa a scolare
drainage /ˈdreɪnɪdʒ/ *n* (system) drenaggio *m*; (of land) scolo *m*
draining board /ˈdreɪnɪŋ/ *n* scolapiatti *m inv*
drainpipe /ˈdreɪnpaɪp/ *n* tubo *m* di scarico
drainpipe trousers *npl* pantaloni *mpl* a tubo
drake /dreɪk/ *n* maschio *m* dell'anatra
drama /ˈdrɑːmə/ *n* arte *f* drammatica; (play) opera *f* teatrale; (event) dramma *m*
dramatic /drəˈmætɪk/ *adj* drammatico
dramatically /drəˈmætɪklɪ/ *adv* in modo drammatico
dramatics /drəˈmætɪks/ *npl* arte *fpl* drammatica; derog atteggiamento *msg* teatrale
dramatist /ˈdræmətɪst/ *n* drammaturgo, -a *mf*
dramatization /dræmətaɪˈzeɪʃn/ *n* (for cinema) adattamento *m* cinematografico; (for stage) adattamento *m* teatrale; (for TV) adattamento *m* televisivo; (exaggeration) drammatizzazione *f*
dramatize /ˈdræmətaɪz/ *vt* adattare per il teatro; fig drammatizzare
drank /dræŋk/ ▶ **drink**
drape /dreɪp/ **A** *n* AmE tenda *f*
B *vt* appoggiare (**over** su)
drastic /ˈdræstɪk/ *adj* drastico
drastically /ˈdræstɪklɪ/ *adv* drasticamente
draught /drɑːft/ *n* corrente *f* [d'aria]
draught beer *n* birra *f* alla spina
draught-proof **A** *adj* a tenuta d'aria
B *vt* tappare le fessure di
draughts /drɑːfts/ *n sg* (game) [gioco *m* della] dama *fsg*
draughtsman /ˈdrɑːftsmən/ *n* disegnatore, -trice *mf*
draughty /ˈdrɑːftɪ/ *adj* pieno di correnti d'aria; **it's ~** c'è corrente
⚷ **draw** /drɔː/ **A** *n* (attraction) attrazione *f*; Sport pareggio *m*; (in lottery) sorteggio *m*
B *vt* (*pt* **drew**, *pp* **drawn**) tirare; (attract) attirare; disegnare ‹*picture*›; tracciare ‹*line*›; ritirare ‹*money*›; attingere ‹*water*›; **~ lots** tirare a sorte
C *vi* ‹*tea*› essere in infusione; Sport pareggiare; **~ near** avvicinarsi
■ **draw away** *vi* (go ahead) distanziarsi; (move off) allontanarsi
■ **draw back** **A** *vt* tirare indietro; ritirare ‹*hand*›; tirare ‹*curtains*›
B *vi* (recoil) tirarsi indietro
■ **draw in** **A** *vt* ritrarre ‹*claws etc*›
B *vi* ‹*train*› arrivare; ‹*days*› accorciarsi
■ **draw on** *vt* attingere a ‹*savings, sb's experience*›
■ **draw out** **A** *vt* (pull out) tirar fuori; ritirare ‹*money*›
B *vi* ‹*train*› partire; ‹*days*› allungarsi
■ **draw up** **A** *vt* redigere ‹*document*›; accostare ‹*chair*›; **~ oneself up [to one's full height]** drizzarsi
B *vi* (stop) fermarsi
drawback /ˈdrɔːbæk/ *n* inconveniente *m*
drawbridge /ˈdrɔːbrɪdʒ/ *n* ponte *m* levatoio
drawee *n* trattario *m*
drawer /drɔː(r)/ *n* cassetto *m*; Fin traente *mf*
drawing /ˈdrɔːɪŋ/ *n* disegno *m*
drawing board *n* tavolo *m* da disegno; fig **go back to the ~** ricominciare da capo
drawing pin *n* puntina *f*
drawing rights *npl* Fin diritti *mf* di prelievo
drawing room *n* salotto *m*
drawl /drɔːl/ *n* pronuncia *f* strascicata

⚷ parola chiave

drawn /drɔːn/ ▶ **draw**

dread /dred/ **A** *n* terrore *m*
B *vt* aver il terrore di

dreadful /ˈdredfʊl/ *adj* terribile

dreadfully /ˈdredfʊlɪ/ *adv* terribilmente

dream /driːm/ **A** *n* sogno *m*
B *attrib* di sogno
C *vt & vi* (*pt/pp* **dreamt** /dremt/ *or* **dreamed**) sognare (**about/of** di)

▪ **dream up** *vt* escogitare ‹*plan, idea*›

dreamer /ˈdriːmə(r)/ *n* (idealist) sognatore, -trice *mf*; (inattentive) persona *f* con la testa fra le nuvole

dream-world *n* **live in a ~** vivere tra le nuvole

dreamy /ˈdriːmɪ/ *adj* infml ‹*house etc*› di sogno; ‹*person*› che è un sogno; (distracted) distratto; ‹*sound, music*› dolce

dreary /ˈdrɪərɪ/ *adj* (**-ier**, **-iest**) tetro; (boring) monotono

dredge /dredʒ/ *vt & vi* dragare

▪ **dredge up** *vt* riesumare ‹*the past*›

dredger /ˈdredʒə(r)/ *n* draga *f*

dregs /dregz/ *npl* feccia *fsg*

drench /drentʃ/ *vt* **get ~ed** inzupparsi

drenched /drentʃt/ *adj* zuppo

dress /dres/ **A** *n* (woman's) vestito *m*; (clothing) abbigliamento *m*
B *vt* vestire; (decorate) adornare; Culin condire; Med fasciare; **~ oneself**, **get ~ed** vestirsi
C *vi* vestirsi

▪ **dress up** *vi* mettersi elegante; (in disguise) travestirsi (**as** da)

dress circle *n* Theat prima galleria *f*

dress designer *n* stilista *mf*

dresser /ˈdresə(r)/ *n* (furniture) credenza *f*; AmE (dressing table) toilette *f inv*

dressing /ˈdresɪŋ/ *n* Culin condimento *m*; Med fasciatura *f*

dressing down *n* infml sgridata *f*

dressing gown *n* vestaglia *f*

dressing room *n* (in gym) spogliatoio *m*; Theat camerino *m*

dressing table *n* toilette *f inv*

dressmaker *n* sarta *f*

dressmaking *n* confezioni *fpl* (per donna)

dress rehearsal *n* prova *f* generale

dress sense *n* **have ~** saper abbinare i capi d'abbigliamento

dressy /ˈdresɪ/ *adj* (**-ier**, **-iest**) elegante

drew /druː/ ▶ **draw**

dribble /ˈdrɪbl/ *vi* gocciolare; ‹*baby*› sbavare; Sport dribblare

dribs and drabs /ˈdrɪbzənˈdræbz/ *npl* **in ~** alla spicciolata

dried /draɪd/ *adj* ‹*food*› essiccato

drier /ˈdraɪə(r)/ *n* asciugabiancheria *m inv*

drift /drɪft/ **A** *n* movimento *m* lento; ‹*of snow*› cumulo *m*; (meaning) senso *m*
B *vi* (off course) andare alla deriva; ‹*snow*› accumularsi; fig ‹*person*› procedere senza meta

▪ **drift apart** *vi* ‹*people*› allontanarsi l'uno dall'altro

drifter /ˈdrɪftə(r)/ *n* persona *f* senza meta

driftwood /ˈdrɪftwʊd/ *n* pezzi *mpl* di legno galleggianti

drill /drɪl/ **A** *n* trapano *m*; Mil esercitazione *f*
B *vt* trapanare; Mil fare esercitare
C *vi* Mil esercitarsi; **~ for oil** trivellare in cerca di petrolio

drily /ˈdraɪlɪ/ *adv* seccamente

drink /drɪŋk/ **A** *n* bevanda *f*; (alcoholic) bicchierino *m*; **have a ~** bere qualcosa; **a ~ of water** un po' d'acqua
B *vt & vi* (*pt* **drank**, *pp* **drunk**) bere

▪ **drink to** *vt* (toast) brindare a

▪ **drink up** *vt* finire

drinkable /ˈdrɪŋkəbl/ *adj* potabile

drink-driving *n* BrE guida *f* in stato di ebbrezza

drinker /ˈdrɪnkə(r)/ *n* bevitore, -trice *mf*

drinking chocolate /ˈdrɪnkɪŋ/ *n* BrE cioccolata *f* in polvere

drinking water *n* acqua *f* potabile

drink problem *n* BrE **he has a ~** beve

drinks cupboard *n* BrE mobile *m* bar

drinks dispenser *n* BrE distributore *m* di bevande

drinks machine *n* BrE distributore *m* di bevande

drinks party *n* BrE cocktail *m inv*

drip /drɪp/ **A** *n* gocciolamento *m*; (drop) goccia *f*; Med flebo *f inv*; infml (person) mollaccione, -a *mf*
B *vi* (*pt/pp* **dripped**) gocciolare

drip-dry *adj* che non si stira

drip-feed *n* flebo[clisi] *f inv*

dripping /ˈdrɪpɪŋ/ **A** *n* (from meat) grasso *m* d'arrosto
B *adj* **~ [wet]** fradicio

drive /draɪv/ **A** *n* (in car) giro *m*; (entrance) viale *m*; (energy) grinta *f*; Psych pulsione *f*; (organized effort) operazione *f*; Techn motore *m*; Comput lettore *m*, unità *f*
B *vt* (*pt* **drove**, *pp* **driven**) portare ‹*person by car*›; guidare ‹*car*›; Sport (hit) mandare; Techn far funzionare; **~ somebody mad** far diventare matto qualcuno
C *vi* guidare

▪ **drive at**: *vt* **what are you driving at?** dove vuoi arrivare?

▪ **drive away** **A** *vt* portare via in macchina; (chase) cacciare
B *vi* andare via in macchina

▪ **drive back** **A** *vt* respingere ‹*people, animals*›; (in car) riportare
B *vi* ritornare in macchina

▪ **drive in** **A** *vt* piantare ‹*nail*›
B *vi* arrivare [in macchina]

▪ **drive off** **A** *vt* portare via in macchina;

(chase) cacciare
B *vi* andare via in macchina
■ **drive on** *vi* proseguire; ~ **on!** avanti!
■ **drive up** *vi* arrivare (*in macchina*)
drive-by shooting *n* sparatoria *f* da auto in corsa
drive-in *adj* ~ **cinema** cinema *m inv* drive-in
drivel /'drɪvl/ *n* infml sciocchezze *fpl*
driven /'drɪvn/ ▸ **drive**
driver /'draɪvə(r)/ *n* guidatore, -trice *mf*; (of train) conducente *mf*
driver's license *n* AmE patente *f* di guida
drive-through *n* AmE drive-in *m inv*
driveway /'draɪvweɪ/ *n* strada *f* d'accesso
driving /'draɪvɪŋ/ **A** *adj* ‹*rain*› violento; ‹*force*› motore
B *n* guida *f*
driving force *n* spinta *f*; (person behind) forza *f* trainante
driving instructor *n* istruttore, -trice *mf* di guida
driving lesson *n* lezione *f* di guida
driving licence *n* patente *f* di guida
driving mirror *n* (rear-view) specchietto *m* retrovisore
driving school *n* scuola *f* guida
driving seat *n* **be in the** ~ essere alla guida
driving test *n* esame *m* di guida; **take one's** ~ fare l'esame di guida
drizzle /'drɪzl/ **A** *n* pioggerella *f*
B *vi* piovigginare
droll /drəʊl/ *adj* divertente
drone /drəʊn/ *n* (bee) fuco *m*; (sound) ronzio *m*
■ **drone on** *vi* (talk boringly) tirarla per le lunghe
drool /druːl/ *vi* sbavare; ~ **over something/somebody** fig infml sbavare per qualcosa/qualcuno
droop /druːp/ *vi* abbassarsi; ‹*flowers*› afflosciarsi
drop /drɒp/ **A** *n* (of liquid) goccia *f*; (fall) caduta *f*; (in price, temperature) calo *m*
B *vt* (*pt/pp* **dropped**) far cadere; sganciare ‹*bomb*›; (omit) omettere; (give up) abbandonare; ~ **the subject** cambiare discorso
C *vi* cadere; ‹*price, temperature, wind*› calare; ‹*ground*› essere in pendenza
■ **drop behind** *vi* rimanere indietro
■ **drop by** *vi* = **drop in**
■ **drop in** *vi* passare
■ **drop off** **A** *vt* depositare ‹*person*›
B *vi* cadere; (fall asleep) assopirsi
■ **drop out** *vi* cadere; (from race, society) ritirarsi; ~ **out of school** lasciare la scuola
drop-dead /'drɒpded/ *adv* infml ~ **gorgeous** stupendo

drop-down menu *n* Comput menu *m inv* a tendina
drop handlebars *npl* manubrio *m* ricurvo
drop-out *n* persona *f* contro il sistema sociale
droppings /'drɒpɪŋz/ *npl* sterco *m*
drop shot *n* Sport drop shot *m inv*, smorzata *f*
drop zone *n* (for supplies etc) zona *f* di lancio
drought /draʊt/ *n* siccità *f*
drove /drəʊv/ ▸ **drive**
droves /drəʊvz/ *npl* **in** ~ in massa
drown /draʊn/ **A** *vi* annegare
B *vt* annegare; coprire ‹*noise*›; **he was** ~**ed** è annegato
drowning /'draʊnɪŋ/ *n* annegamento *m*
drowse /draʊz/ *vi* sonnecchiare; (be very sleepy) essere sonnolento
drowsiness /'draʊzɪnɪs/ *n* sonnolenza *f*
drowsy /'draʊzɪ/ *adj* sonnolento
drudgery /'drʌdʒərɪ/ *n* lavoro *m* pesante e noioso
drug /drʌg/ **A** *n* droga *f*; Med farmaco *m*; **take** ~**s** drogarsi
B *vt* (*pt/pp* **drugged**) drogare
drug abuse *n* abuso *m* di stupefacenti
drug addict *n* tossicomane, -a *mf*
drug addiction *n* tossicodipendenza *f*
drug dealer *n* spacciatore, -trice *mf* [di droga]
drugged /drʌgd/ *adj* drogato
druggist /'drʌgɪst/ *n* AmE farmacista *mf*
drug habit *n* tossicodipendenza *f*
drug mule *n* corriere *m* della droga
Drug Squad *n* BrE [squadra *f*] narcotici *f*
drugs raid *n* operazione *f* antidroga
drugs ring *n* rete *f* di narcotrafficanti
drugstore /'drʌgstɔː(r)/ *n* AmE *negozio* (*m*) *di generi vari, inclusi medicinali, che funge anche da bar*; (dispensing) farmacia *f*
drug taking *n* consumo *m* di stupefacenti; Sport doping *m inv*
drug test *n* Sport antidoping *m inv*
drug user *n* tossicomane, -a *mf*
drum /drʌm/ **A** *n* tamburo *m*; (for oil) barile *m*; ~**s** *pl* (in pop group) batteria *f*
B *vi* (*pt/pp* **drummed**) suonare il tamburo; (in pop group) suonare la batteria
C *vt* ~ **something into somebody** infml ripetere qualcosa a qualcuno cento volte; ~ **one's fingers on the table** tamburellare con le dita sul tavolo
■ **drum up** *vt* ottenere ‹*business, customers, support*›
drum kit *n* batteria *f*
drummer /'drʌmə(r)/ *n* percussionista *mf*; (in pop group) batterista *mf*
drumstick /'drʌmstɪk/ *n* bacchetta *f*; (of chicken, turkey) coscia *f*
drunk /drʌŋk/ **A** ▸ **drink**

B *adj* ubriaco; **get ~** ubriacarsi
C *n* ubriaco, -a *mf*

drunkard /ˈdrʌŋkəd/ *n* ubriacone, -a *mf*

drunken /ˈdrʌŋkən/ *adj* ubriaco

drunken driving *n* guida *f* in stato di ebbrezza

⚷ **dry** /draɪ/ **A** *adj* (**drier, driest**) asciutto; ‹*climate, country*› secco
B *vt & vi* asciugare; **~ one's eyes** asciugarsi le lacrime

■ **dry out** *vi* ‹*clothes*› asciugarsi; ‹*alcoholic*› disintossicarsi

■ **dry up** *vi* seccarsi; fig ‹*source*› prosciugarsi; infml (be quiet) stare zitto; (do dishes) asciugare i piatti

dry cell *n* cella *f* a secco

dry-clean *vt* pulire a secco

dry-cleaner's *n* (shop) tintoria *f*

dryer /ˈdraɪə/ *n* = **drier**

dry ice *n* ghiaccio *m* secco

drying up /draɪɪŋ-/ *n* BrE **do the ~** asciugare i piatti

dryness /ˈdraɪnɪs/ *n* secchezza *f*

dry rot *n* carie *f* del legno

DSS *n abbr* BrE (**Department of Social Security**) (local office) ≈ Ufficio *m* della Previdenza Sociale; (ministry) ≈ Istituto *m* Nazionale della Previdenza Sociale

DTI *n abbr* BrE (**Department of Trade and Industry**) ≈ ministero *m* del Commercio e dell'Industria

DTP *n abbr* (**desktop publishing**) DTP *m*

dual /ˈdjuːəl/ *adj* doppio

dual carriageway *n* strada *f* a due carreggiate

dual nationality *n* doppia nazionalità *f*

dual-purpose *adj* a doppio uso

dub /dʌb/ *vt* (*pt/pp* **dubbed**) doppiare ‹*film*›; (name) soprannominare

dubbing /ˈdʌbɪŋ/ *n* doppiaggio *m*

dubious /ˈdjuːbɪəs/ *adj* dubbio; **be ~ about** avere dei dubbi riguardo

dubiously /ˈdjuːbɪəslɪ/ *adv* ‹*look at*› con aria dubbiosa; (say) con esitazione

Dublin /ˈdʌblɪn/ *n* Dublino *f*

duchess /ˈdʌtʃɪs/ *n* duchessa *f*

duck /dʌk/ **A** *n* anatra *f*
B *vt* (in water) immergere; **~ one's head** abbassare la testa
C *vi* abbassarsi

■ **duck out of** *vt* sottrarsi a ‹*task*›

duckling /ˈdʌklɪŋ/ *n* anatroccolo *m*

duct /dʌkt/ *n* condotto *m*; Anat dotto *m*

dud /dʌd/ **A** *adj* Mil infml disattivato; ‹*coin*› falso; ‹*cheque*› a vuoto
B *n* infml (banknote) banconota *f* falsa; Mil (shell) granata *f* disattivata

⚷ **due** /djuː/ **A** *adj* dovuto; **be ~** ‹*train*› essere previsto; **the baby is ~ next week** il bambino dovrebbe nascere la settimana prossima; **~ to** (owing to) a causa di; **be ~ to** (causally) essere dovuto a; **I'm ~ to...** dovrei...; **in ~ course** a tempo debito
B *adv* **~ north** direttamente a nord

duel /ˈdjuːəl/ *n* duello *m*

dues /djuːz/ *npl* quota *f* [di iscrizione]

duet /djuːˈet/ *n* duetto *m*

duffel bag *n* sacca *f* da viaggio

duffel coat /ˈdʌf(ə)l/ *n* montgomery *m inv*

dug /dʌg/ ▶ **dig**

duke /djuːk/ *n* duca *m*

dull /dʌl/ **A** *adj* (overcast, not bright) cupo; (not shiny) opaco; ‹*sound*› soffocato; (boring) monotono; (stupid) ottuso
B *vt* intorpidire ‹*mind*›; attenuare ‹*pain*›

dullness /ˈdʌlnɪs/ *n* (of life) monotonia *f*; (of company, conversation) noia *f*; (no shine) opacità *f*

dully /ˈdʌllɪ/ *adv* ‹*say, repeat*› monotonamente

duly /ˈdjuːlɪ/ *adv* debitamente

dumb /dʌm/ *adj* muto; infml (stupid) ottuso

■ **dumb down** *vt* abbassare il livello intellettuale di ‹*course, programme*›

dumbfounded /dʌmˈfaʊndɪd/ *adj* sbigottito

dummy /ˈdʌmɪ/ *n* (tailor's) manichino *m*; (for baby) succhiotto *m*; (model) riproduzione *f*

dummy run *n* (trial) prova *f*

dump /dʌmp/ **A** *n* (for refuse) scarico *m*; infml (town) mortorio *m*; **be down in the ~s** infml essere depresso
B *vt* scaricare; infml (put down) lasciare; infml (get rid of) liberarsi di

dumping /ˈdʌmpɪŋ/ *n* Fin dumping *m inv*, esportazione *f* sottocosto; **no ~** divieto *m* di scarico

dumpling /ˈdʌmplɪŋ/ *n* gnocco *m*

dumpy /ˈdʌmpɪ/ *adj* (plump) tracagnotto

dunce /dʌns/ *n* zuccone, -a *mf*

dune /djuːn/ *n* duna *f*

dung /dʌŋ/ *n* sterco *m*

dungarees /dʌŋgəˈriːz/ *npl* tuta *fsg*

dungeon /ˈdʌndʒən/ *n* prigione *f* sotterranea

dunk /dʌŋk/ *vt* inzuppare

dunno /dəˈnəʊ/ infml (I don't know) boh

duo /ˈdjuːəʊ/ *n* duo *m inv*; Mus duetto *m*

dupe /djuːp/ **A** *n* zimbello *m*
B *vt* gabbare

duplicate¹ /ˈdjuːplɪkət/ **A** *adj* doppio
B *n* duplicato *m*; (document) copia *f*; **in ~** in duplicato

duplicate² /ˈdjuːplɪkeɪt/ *vt* fare un duplicato di; ‹*research*› essere una ripetizione di ‹*work*›

duplicator /ˈdjuːplɪkeɪtə(r)/ *n* duplicatore *m*

duplicity /djʊˈplɪsətɪ/ *n* duplicità *f*, doppiezza *f*

durable /ˈdjʊərəbl/ *adj* resistente; ‹*basis, institution*› durevole

duration /djʊəˈreɪʃn/ *n* durata *f*

d

duress /djʊəˈres/ *n* costrizione *f*; **under ~** sotto minaccia

⚷ **during** /ˈdjʊərɪŋ/ *prep* durante

dusk /dʌsk/ *n* crepuscolo *m*

dusky /ˈdʌskɪ/ *adj* ‹*complexion*› scuro

dust /dʌst/ **A** *n* polvere *f*
B *vt* spolverare; (sprinkle) cospargere ‹*cake*› (with di)
C *vi* spolverare

dustbin *n* pattumiera *f*

dustbin man *n* BrE netturbino *m*

dust-cart *n* camion *m* della nettezza urbana

dust cover *n* (on book) sopraccoperta *f*; (on furniture) telo *m* di protezione

duster /ˈdʌstə(r)/ *n* strofinaccio *m*

dust jacket *n* sopraccoperta *f*

dustman *n* spazzino *m*

dustpan *n* paletta *f* per la spazzatura

dust sheet *n* (on furniture) telo *m* di protezione

dusty /ˈdʌstɪ/ *adj* (**-ier**, **-iest**) polveroso

Dutch /dʌtʃ/ **A** *adj* olandese; **go ~** infml fare alla romana
B *n* (language) olandese *m*; **the ~** *pl* gli olandesi

Dutch courage *n* spavalderia *f* ispirata dall'alcool

Dutchman /ˈdʌtʃmən/ *n* olandese *m*

dutiable /ˈdju:tɪəbl/ *adj* soggetto a imposta

dutiful /ˈdju:tɪfl/ *adj* rispettoso

dutifully /ˈdju:tɪfʊlɪ/ *adv* a dovere

⚷ **duty** /ˈdju:tɪ/ *n* dovere *m*; (task) compito *m*; (tax) dogana *f*; **be on ~** essere di servizio

duty chemist *n* farmacia *f* di turno

duty-free **A** *adj* esente da dogana
B *n* duty-free *m inv*

duty-free allowance *n limite (m) d'acquisto di merci esenti da dogana*

duty roster, **duty rota** *n* tabella *f* dei turni

duvet /ˈdu:veɪ/ *n* piumone *m*

duvet cover *n* BrE copripiumone *m*

DVD *n abbr* (**digital video disc**) DVD *m*

DVD player *n* lettore *m* DVD

DVT *abbr* (**deep-vein thrombosis**) TVP *f*

dwarf /dwɔ:f/ **A** *n* (*pl* **-s** *or* **dwarves**) nano, -a *mf*
B *vt* rimpicciolire

dweeb /dwi:b/ *n* esp Am infml secchione, -a *mf*

dwell /dwel/ *vi* (*pt/pp* **dwelt**) literary dimorare

■ **dwell on** *vt* fig soffermarsi su

dweller /ˈdwelə(r)/ *n* **city/town ~** cittadino, -a *mf*

dwelling /ˈdwelɪŋ/ *n* abitazione *f*

dwindle /ˈdwɪndl/ *vi* diminuire

dwindling /ˈdwɪndlɪŋ/ *adj* (strength, health) in calo; ‹*resources, audience, interest*› in diminuzione

DWP *abbr* BrE (**Department for Work and Pensions**) ≈ Ministero *m* del Lavoro e delle Politiche Sociali

dye /daɪ/ **A** *n* tintura *f*
B *vt* (*pres p* **dyeing**) tingere

dyed-in-the-wool /daɪdɪnðəˈwʊl/ *adj* inveterato

dying /ˈdaɪɪŋ/ ▶ **die²**

dyke /daɪk/ *n* (to prevent flooding) diga *f*; (beside ditch) argine *m*; BrE (ditch) canale *m* di scolo

dynamic /daɪˈnæmɪk/ *adj* dinamico

dynamics /daɪˈnæmɪks/ *nsg* dinamica *fsg*

dynamism /ˈdaɪnəˈmɪzm/ *n* dinamismo *m*

dynamite /ˈdaɪnəmaɪt/ *n* dinamite *f*

dynamo /ˈdaɪnəməʊ/ *n* dinamo *f inv*

dynasty /ˈdɪnəstɪ/ *n* dinastia *f*

dysentery /ˈdɪsəntrɪ/ *n* dissenteria *f*

dysfunctional /dɪsˈfʌŋkʃənl/ *adj* disfunzionale

dyslexia /dɪsˈleksɪə/ *n* dislessia *f*

dyslexic /dɪsˈleksɪk/ *adj* dislessico

Ee

e¹, **E** /i:/ *n* (letter) e, E *f inv*; Mus mi *m*

e² *abbr* (**euro**) EUR *m*

E *abbr* (**east**) E

⚷ **each** /i:tʃ/ **A** *adj* ogni
B *pron* ognuno; **£1 ~** una sterlina ciascuno; **they love/hate ~ other** si amano/odiano; **we lend ~ other money** ci prestiamo i soldi; **bet on a horse ~ way** puntare su un cavallo piazzato e vincente

eager /ˈi:gə(r)/ *adj* ansioso (**to do** di fare); ‹*pupil*› avido di sapere

eager beaver *n* infml **be an ~** essere pieno di zelo

eagerly /ˈi:gəlɪ/ *adv* ‹*wait*› ansiosamente; ‹*offer*› premurosamente

eagerness /ˈi:gənɪsˈ/ *n* premura *f*

⚷ parola chiave

eagle /ˈiːgl/ *n* aquila *f*
eagle-eyed /ˈ-aɪd/ *adj* (sharp-eyed) che ha un occhio di falco
ear /ɪə(r)/ *n* orecchio *m*; (of corn) spiga *f*
earache /ˈɪəreɪk/ *n* mal *m* d'orecchi
eardrum /ˈɪədrʌm/ *n* timpano *m*
earl /ɜːl/ *n* conte *m*
ear lobe *n* lobo *m* dell'orecchio
early /ˈɜːlɪ/ **A** *adj* (**-ier**, **-iest**) (before expected time) in anticipo; ‹*spring*› prematuro; ‹*reply*› pronto; ‹*works, writings*› primo; **be here ~!** sii puntuale!; **you're ~!** sei in anticipo!; **~ morning walk** passeggiata *f* mattutina; **in the ~ morning** la mattina presto; **in the ~ spring** all'inizio della primavera
B *adv* presto; (ahead of time) in anticipo; **~ in the morning** la mattina presto
early retirement *n* prepensionamento *m*; **take ~** andare in prepensionamento
early warning *n* **come as an ~ of something** essere il segno premonitore di qualcosa
early warning system *n* Mil sistema *m* d'allarme avanzato
earmark /ˈɪəmɑːk/ *vt* riservare (**for** a)
earmuffs /ˈɪəmʌfs/ *npl* paraorecchie *m inv*
earn /ɜːn/ *vt* guadagnare; (deserve) meritare
earned income /ɜːnd/ *n* reddito *m* da lavoro
earner /ˈɜːnə(r)/ *n* (person) *persona (f) che guadagna*; **the main [revenue] ~** la principale fonte di sostentamento; **a nice little ~** infml un'ottima fonte di guadagno
earnest /ˈɜːnɪst/ **A** *adj* serio
B *n* **in ~** sul serio
earnestly /ˈɜːnɪstlɪ/ *adv* con aria seria
earning power /ˈɜːnɪŋ/ *n* (of person) capacità *f* di guadagno; (of company) redditività *f*
earnings /ˈɜːnɪŋz/ *npl* guadagni *mpl*; (salary) stipendio *m*
ear nose and throat department *n* reparto *m* otorinolaringoiatrico
earphones *npl* cuffia *fsg*
earplug *n* (for noise) tappo *m* per le orecchie
earring *n* orecchino *m*
earshot *n* **within ~** a portata d'orecchio; **he is out of ~** non può sentire
ear-splitting /ˈɪəsplɪtɪŋ/ *adj* ‹*scream, shout*› lacerante
earth /ɜːθ/ **A** *n* terra *f*; (of fox) tana *f*; **where/what on ~?** dove/che diavolo?
B *vt* Electr mettere a terra
earthenware /ˈɜːθnweə/ *n* terraglia *f*
earthly /ˈɜːθlɪ/ *adj* terrestre; **be no ~ use** infml essere perfettamente inutile
earthquake *n* terremoto *m*
earth sciences *npl* scienze *fpl* della terra
earth-shaking *adj* infml ‹*news*› sconvolgente; ‹*experience*› travolgente
earth tremor *n* scossa *f* sismica
earthwork *n* (embankment) terrapieno *m*; (excavation work) lavori *mpl* di scavo
earthworm *n* lombrico *m*
earthy /ˈɜːθɪ/ *adj* terroso; (coarse) grossolano
earwax /ˈɪəwæks/ *n* cerume *m*
earwig /ˈɪəwɪg/ *n* forbicina *f*
ease /iːz/ **A** *n* **at ~** a proprio agio; **at ~!** Mil riposo!; **ill at ~** a disagio; **with ~** con facilità
B *vt* calmare ‹*pain*›; alleviare ‹*tension, shortage*›; (slow down) rallentare; (loosen) allentare
C *vi* ‹*pain, situation, wind*› calmarsi
■ **ease off** **A** *vi* ‹*pain, pressure, tension*› attenuarsi
B *vt* (remove gently) togliere con delicatezza
■ **ease up** *vi* = **ease off**
easel /ˈiːzl/ *n* cavalletto *m*
easily /ˈiːzɪlɪ/ *adv* con facilità; **~ the best** certamente il meglio
east /iːst/ **A** *n* est *m*; **to the ~ of** a est di
B *adj* dell'est
C *adv* verso est
East Africa *n* Africa *f* orientale
East Berlin *n* Berlino *f* Est
eastbound *adj* ‹*carriageway, traffic*› diretto a est
East End *n quartiere (m) nella zona est di Londra*
Easter /ˈiːstə(r)/ *n* Pasqua *f*
Easter egg *n* uovo *m* di Pasqua
easterly /ˈiːstəlɪ/ *adj* da levante
Easter Monday *n* lunedì *m* dell'Angelo, Pasquetta *f*
eastern /ˈiːstən/ *adj* orientale
Eastern block *n* paesi *mpl* dell'est
Easter Sunday *n* [domenica *f* di] Pasqua *f*
East German *n* Pol tedesco, -a *mf* dell'est
East Germany *n* Pol Germania *f* est
East Indies *npl* Indie *fpl* orientali
East Timor *n* Timor *m* Est
eastwards BrE **eastward** AmE /ˈiːstwəd[z]/ *adv* verso est
easy /ˈiːzɪ/ *adj* (**-ier**, **-iest**) facile; **take it** *or* **things ~** prendersela con calma; **take it ~!** (don't get excited) calma!; **go ~ with** andarci piano con
easy-care *adj* facilmente lavabile
easy chair *n* poltrona *f*
easy-going *adj* conciliante; **too ~** troppo accomodante
easy money *n* facili guadagni *mpl*
easy terms *npl* facilitazioni *fpl* di pagamento
eat /iːt/ *vt* & *vi* (*pt* **ate**, *pp* **eaten**) mangiare
■ **eat into** *vt* intaccare
■ **eat out** *vi* mangiar fuori
■ **eat up** *vt* mangiare tutto ‹*food*›; fig inghiottire ‹*profits*›

e

eatable /ˈiːtəbl/ *adj* mangiabile
eater /ˈiːtə(r)/ *n* (apple) mela *f* da tavola; **be a big ~** ‹*person*› essere una buona forchetta; **he's a fast ~** mangia sempre in fretta
eatery /ˈiːtərɪ/ *n* infml tavola *f* calda
eating apple *n mela (f) non da cuocere*
eating disorder *n* disoressia *f*
eating habits *npl* abitudini *fpl* alimentari
eau de cologne /əʊdəkəˈləʊn/ *n* acqua *f* di colonia

eaves /iːvz/ *npl* cornicione *msg*
eavesdrop /ˈiːvzdrɒp/ *vi* (*pt/pp* **-dropped**) origliare; **~ on** ascoltare di nascosto
e-banking /ˈiːbæŋkɪŋ/ *n* e-banking *m*
ebb /eb/ **A** *n* (tide) riflusso *m*; **at a low ~** fig a terra
B *vi* rifluire; fig declinare
ebony /ˈebənɪ/ *n* ebano *m*
EBRD *n abbr* (**European Bank for Reconstruction and Development**) BERS *f*
ebullient /ɪˈbʌlɪənt/ *adj* esuberante
e-business /ˈiːbɪznɪs/ *n* e-business *m inv*
EC *n abbr* (**European Community**) CE *f*
e-cash /ˈiːkæʃ/ *n* denaro *m* virtuale
eccentric /ekˈsentrɪk/ *adj & n* eccentrico, -a *mf*
eccentricity /eksenˈtrɪsətɪ/ *n* eccentricità *f*
ecclesiastical /ɪkliːzɪˈæstɪkl/ *adj* ecclesiastico
ECG *n abbr* (**electrocardiogram**) ECG *m*
echo /ˈekəʊ/ **A** *n* (*pl* **-es**) eco *f or m*
B *vt* (*pt/pp* **echoed**, *pres p* **echoing**) echeggiare; ripetere ‹*words*›
C *vi* risuonare (**with** di)
eclectic /ɪˈklektɪk/ *n* eclettico
eclipse /ɪˈklɪps/ **A** *n* Astr eclissi *f inv*
B *vt* fig eclissare
eco+ /ˈiːkəʊ/ *pref* eco+
eco-friendly *adj* che rispetta l'ambiente
eco-labelling /ˈiːkəʊleɪbəlɪŋ/ *n* ecolabelling *m* inv, etichettatura *f* ecologica
ecological /iːkəˈlɒdʒɪkl/ *adj* ecologico
ecological footprint *n* impronta *f* ecologica
ecologist /ɪˈkɒlədʒɪst/ **A** *n* ecologo, -a *mf*
B *adj* ecologico
ecology /ɪˈkɒlədʒɪ/ *n* ecologia *f*
e-commerce /ˈiːkɒmɜːs/ *n* e-commerce *m inv*
⚷ **economic** /iːkəˈnɒmɪk/ *adj* economico
economical /iːkəˈnɒmɪkl/ *adj* economico
economically /iːkəˈnɒmɪklɪ/ *adv* economicamente; ‹*thriftily*› in economia; **~ priced** a prezzo economico
economic analyst *n* analista *mf* economico, -a

⚷ parola chiave

economic migrant *n chi emigra per motivi esclusivamente economici, in contrapposizione a chi cerca asilo politico*
economics /iːkəˈnɒmɪks/ *nsg* economia *fsg*
economist /ɪˈkɒnəmɪst/ *n* economista *mf*
economize /ɪˈkɒnəmaɪz/ *vi* economizzare (**on** su)
⚷ **economy** /ɪˈkɒnəmɪ/ *n* economia *f*
economy class *n* Aeron classe *f* turistica
economy drive *n* campagna *f* di risparmio
economy pack, **economy size** *n* confezione *f* economica *inv*
ecosphere /ˈiːkəʊsfɪə(r)/ *n* ecosfera *f*
ecosystem /ˈiːkəʊsɪstəm/ *n* ecosistema *m*
ecoterrorism *n* ecoterrorismo *m*
ecotourism /ˈiːkəʊtʊərɪzm/ *n* ecoturismo *m*
ecotourist /iːkəʊˈtʊərɪst/ *n* ecoturista *mf*
eco-warrior /ˈiːkəʊwɒrɪə(r), AmE -wɔːr-/ *n* eco-guerrigliero, -a *mf*
ecstasy /ˈekstəsɪ/ *n* estasi *f inv*; (drug) ecstasy *f*
ecstatic /ɪkˈstætɪk/ *adj* estatico
ecstatically /ɪkˈstætɪklɪ/ *adv* estaticamente
ectopic pregnancy /ekˈtɒpɪk/ *n* gravidanza *f* extrauterina
Ecuador /ˈekwədɔː(r)/ *n* Ecuador *m*
ecumenical /iːkjʊˈmenɪkl/ *adj* ecumenico
eczema /ˈeksɪmə/ *n* eczema *m*
eddy /ˈedɪ/ *n* vortice *m*
Eden /ˈiːd(ə)n/ *n* eden *m*, paradiso *m* terrestre
⚷ **edge** /edʒ/ **A** *n* bordo *m*; (of knife) filo *m*; (of road) ciglio *m*; **on ~** con i nervi tesi; **have the ~ on** infml avere un vantaggio su
B *vt* bordare
■ **edge forward** *vi* avanzare lentamente
edgeways /ˈedʒweɪz/ *adv* di fianco; **I couldn't get a word in ~** non ho potuto infilare neanche mezza parola nel discorso
edging /ˈedʒɪŋ/ *n* bordo *m*
edgy /ˈedʒɪ/ *adj* (nervous) nervoso; infml (modern) all'avanguardia
edible /ˈedəbl/ *adj* commestibile; **this pizza's not ~** questa pizza è immangiabile
edict /ˈiːdɪkt/ *n* editto *m*
edifice /ˈedɪfɪs/ *n* edificio *m*
edify /ˈedɪfaɪ/ *vt* (*pt/pp* **-ied**) edificare
edifying /ˈedɪfaɪɪŋ/ *adj* edificante
Edinburgh /ˈedɪmb(ə)rə/ *n* Edimburgo *f*
edit /ˈedɪt/ *vt* (*pt/pp* **edited**) far la revisione di ‹*text*›; curare l'edizione di ‹*anthology, dictionary*›; dirigere ‹*newspaper*›; montare ‹*film*›; editare ‹*tape*›; **~ed by** ‹*book*› a cura di
■ **edit out** *vt* tagliare
edition /ɪˈdɪʃn/ *n* edizione *f*
⚷ **editor** /ˈedɪtə(r)/ *n* (of anthology, dictionary) curatore, -trice *mf*; (of newspaper) redattore, -trice *mf*; (of film) responsabile *mf* del

montaggio

editorial /edɪ'tɔ:rɪəl/ **A** *adj* redazionale
B *n* Journ editoriale *m*

EDP *n abbr* (**electronic data processing**) EDP *m*, EED *f*

EDT *abbr* AmE (**Eastern Daylight Time**) *ora (f) legale degli stati orientali dell'America settentrionale*

educate /'edjʊkeɪt/ *vt* istruire; educare ‹*public, mind*›; **be ~d at Eton** essere educato a Eton

educated /'edjʊkeɪtɪd/ *adj* istruito

education /edjɪ'keɪʃn/ *n* istruzione *f*; (culture) cultura *f*, educazione *f*

educational /edjʊ'keɪʃnəl/ *adj* istruttivo; ‹*visit*› educativo; ‹*publishing*› didattico

educationalist /edjʊ'keɪʃnəlɪst/ *n* studioso, -a *mf* di pedagogia

educationally /edjʊ'keɪʃnəlɪ/ *adv* ‹*disadvantaged, privileged*› dal punto di vista degli studi; ‹*useless, useful*› dal punto di vista didattico

educational psychology *n* psicopedagogia *f*, psicologia *f* dell'educazione

educational television *n* televisione *f* scolastica

education authority *n* BrE autorità *fpl* scolastiche

education committee *n* BrE consiglio *m* scolastico

education department *n* BrE ministero *m* della pubblica istruzione; (in local government) provveditorato *m* agli studi; (in university) istituto *m* di pedagogia

educative /'edjʊkətɪv/ *adj* educativo, istruttivo

educator /'edjʊkeɪtə(r)/ *n* educatore, -trice *mf*

Edwardian /ed'wɔ:dɪən/ *n* del regno di Edoardo VII

EEA *abbr* (**European Economic Area**) EEA *f*

EEC **A** *n abbr* (**European Economic Community**) CEE *f*
B *attrib* ‹*policy, directive*› della CEE

eel /i:l/ *n* anguilla *f*

eerie /'ɪərɪ/ *adj* (**-ier**, **-iest**) inquietante

efface /ɪ'feɪs/ *vt* cancellare

effect /ɪ'fekt/ **A** *n* effetto *m*; **in ~** in effetti; **take ~** ‹*law*› entrare in vigore; ‹*medicine*› fare effetto
B *vt* effettuare

effective /ɪ'fektɪv/ *adj* efficace; (striking) che colpisce; (actual) di fatto; **~ from** in vigore a partire da

effectively /ɪ'fektɪvlɪ/ *adv* efficacemente; (actually) di fatto

effectiveness /ɪ'fektɪvnɪs/ *n* efficacia *f*

effeminate /ɪ'femɪnət/ *adj* effeminato

effervescent /efə'vesnt/ *adj* effervescente

effete /ɪ'fi:t/ *adj* ‹*person*› senza nerbo; ‹*civilization*› che ha fatto il suo tempo

efficacious /efɪ'keɪʃəs/ *adj* efficace

efficacy /'efɪkəsɪ/ *n* efficacia *f*

efficiency /ɪ'fɪʃənsɪ/ *n* efficienza *f*; (of machine) rendimento *m*

efficient /ɪ'fɪʃənt/ *adj* efficiente

efficiently /ɪ'fɪʃəntlɪ/ *adv* efficientemente

effigy /'efɪdʒɪ/ *n* effigie *f*

effluent /'eflʊənt/ **A** *n* (waste) refluo *m*; (river) emissario *m*
B *attrib* ‹*treatment, management*› dei reflui

effort /'efət/ *n* sforzo *m*; **make an ~** sforzarsi

effortless /'efətlɪs/ *adj* facile

effortlessly /'efətlɪslɪ/ *adv* con facilità

effrontery /ɪ'frʌntərɪ/ *n* sfrontatezza *f*

effusion /ɪ'fju:ʒn/ *n* (emotional) effusione *f*

effusive /ɪ'fju:sɪv/ *adj* espansivo; ‹*speech*› caloroso

e-fit /'i:fɪt/ *n* identikit *m inv* elettronico

EFL **A** *n abbr* (**English as a Foreign Language**) EFL *m*
B *attrib* ‹*teacher, course*› di inglese come lingua straniera

EFT *n abbr* (**electronic funds transfer**) *trasferimento (m) fondi elettronico*

EFTA /'eftə/ *n abbr* (**European Free Trade Association**) EFTA *f*

e.g. *abbr* (**exempli gratia**) per es.

egalitarian /ɪgælɪ'teərɪən/ *adj* egalitario

egg /eg/ *n* uovo *m*
■ **egg on** *vt* infml incitare

egg box *n* cartone *m* di uova

egg cup *n* portauovo *m inv*

egg custard *n* crema *f* pasticciera

egghead *n* derog fam intellettuale *mf*

eggplant *n* AmE melanzana *f*

egg-shaped /'egʃeɪpt/ *adj* ovale

eggshell *n* guscio *m* d'uovo

egg timer *n clessidra (f) per misurare il tempo di cottura delle uova*

egg whisk *n* frusta *f*

egg white *n* albume *m*, bianco *m* d'uovo

egg yolk *n* tuorlo *m*, rosso *m*

ego /'i:gəʊ/ *n* ego *m*

egocentric /i:gəʊ'sentrɪk/ *adj* egocentrico

egoism /'egəʊɪzm/ *n* egoismo *m*

egoist /'egəʊɪst/ *n* egoista *mf*

egotism /'egəʊtɪzm/ *n* egotismo *m*

egotist /'egəʊtɪst/ *n* egotista *mf*

Egypt /'i:dʒɪpt/ *n* Egitto *m*

Egyptian /ɪ'dʒɪpʃn/ *adj & n* egiziano, -a *mf*

EHIC *n abbr* (**European Health Insurance Card**) TEAM *f*

Eid al-Adha /ˌi:dʊl'ɑ:də/ *n* Aid al-adha *f*

eiderdown /'aɪdədaʊn/ *n* (quilt) piumino *m*

eight /eɪt/ *adj & n* otto *m*

eighteen /eɪ'ti:n/ *adj & n* diciotto *m*

e

eighteenth /eɪ'ti:nθ/ *adj & n* diciottesimo, -a *mf*

eighth /eɪtθ/ *adj & n* ottavo, -a *mf*

eighties /'eɪtɪz/ *npl* (period) **the ~** gli anni Ottanta *mpl*; (age) ottant'anni *mpl*

eightieth /'eɪtɪɪθ/ *adj & n* ottantesimo, -a *mf*

eighty /'eɪtɪ/ *adj & n* ottanta *m*

Eire /'eərə/ *n* Repubblica *f* d'Irlanda

⚷ **either** /'aɪðə(r)/ **A** *adj & pron* **~ [of them]** l'uno o l'altro; **I don't like ~ [of them]** non mi piace né l'uno né l'altro; **on ~ side** da tutte e due le parti
B *adv* **I don't ~** nemmeno io; **I don't like John or his brother ~** non mi piace John e nemmeno suo fratello
C *conj* **~ John or his brother will be there** ci saranno o John o suo fratello; **I don't like ~ John or his brother** non mi piacciono né John né suo fratello; **~ you go to bed or [else]...** o vai a letto o [altrimenti]...

ejaculate /ɪ'dʒækjʊleɪt/ **A** *vi* eiaculare
B *vt* (exclaim) prorompere

ejaculation /ɪdʒækjʊ'leɪʃn/ *n* eiaculazione *f*; (exclamation) esclamazione *f*

eject /ɪ'dʒekt/ *vt* eiettare ‹*pilot*›; espellere ‹*tape, drunk*›

eject button *n* tasto *m* eject

ejection /ɪ'dʒekʃn/ *n* (of gases, waste, troublemaker) espulsione *f*; (of lava) emissione *f*; Aeron eiezione *f*

eke /i:k/ *vt* **~ out** far bastare; (increase) arrotondare; **~ out a living** arrangiarsi

elaborate¹ /ɪ'læbərət/ *adj* elaborato

elaborate² /ɪ'læbəreɪt/ *vi* entrare nei particolari (**on** di)

elaborately /ɪ'læbərətlɪ/ *adv* in modo elaborato

elaboration /ɪlæbə'reɪʃn/ *n* (of plan, theory) elaborazione *f*

elapse /ɪ'læps/ *vi* trascorrere

elastic /ɪ'læstɪk/ **A** *adj* elastico
B *n* elastico *m*

elasticated /ɪ'læstɪkeɪtɪd/ *adj* ‹*waistband, bandage*› elastico; ‹*material*› elasticizzato

elastic band *n* elastico *m*

elasticity /ɪlæs'tɪsətɪ/ *n* elasticità

elated /ɪ'leɪtɪd/ *adj* esultante

elation /ɪ'leɪʃn/ *n* euforia *f*

elbow /'elbəʊ/ *n* gomito *m*

elbow grease *n* infml olio *m* di gomito

elbow room *n* (room to move) spazio *m* vitale; **there isn't much ~ in this kitchen** si è un po' allo stretto in questa cucina

elder¹ /'eldə(r)/ *n* (tree) sambuco *m*

elder² **A** *adj* maggiore
B *n* **the ~** il/la maggiore

elderberry /'eldəbərɪ/ *n* bacca *f* di sambuco

elderly /'eldəlɪ/ *adj* anziano

elder statesman *n* decano *m* della politica

eldest /'eldɪst/ **A** *adj* maggiore
B *n* **the ~** il/la maggiore

e-learning /'i:lɜ:nɪŋ/ *n* Comput formazione *f* in rete

⚷ **elect** /ɪ'lekt/ **A** *adj* **the president ~** il futuro presidente
B *vt* eleggere; **~ to do something** decidere di fare qualcosa

⚷ **election** /ɪ'lekʃn/ *n* elezione *f*

election campaign *n* campagna *f* elettorale

electioneering /ɪlekʃə'nɪərɪŋ/ *n* (campaigning) propaganda *f* elettorale; derog elettoralismo *m*

elective /ɪ'lektɪv/ *adj* ‹*office, official*› elettivo, eletto; (empowered to elect) elettorale; Sch, Univ facoltativo; **~ surgery** interventi *mpl* chirurgici facoltativi

elector /ɪ'lektə(r)/ *n* elettore, -trice *mf*

electoral /ɪ'lektərəl/ *adj* elettorale

electoral roll *n* liste *fpl* elettorali

electorate /ɪ'lektərət/ *n* elettorato *m*

electric /ɪ'lektrɪk/ *adj* elettrico

electrical /ɪ'lektrɪkl/ *adj* elettrico

electrical engineer *n* elettrotecnico *m*

electrical engineering *n* elettrotecnica *f*

electrically /ɪ'lektrɪk(ə)lɪ/ *adv* **~ driven [a motore] elettrico**

electric blanket *n* termocoperta *f*

electric fire *n* stufa *f* elettrica

electrician /ɪlek'trɪʃn/ *n* elettricista *m*

electricity /ɪlek'trɪsətɪ/ *n* elettricità

electricity board *n* BrE azienda *f* elettrica

electricity supply *n* alimentazione *f* elettrica

electric shock *n* **get an ~** prendere la scossa

electric storm *n* temporale *m*

electrify /ɪ'lektrɪfaɪ/ *vt* (*pt/pp* **-ied**) elettrificare; fig elettrizzare

electrifying /ɪ'lektrɪfaɪɪŋ/ *adj* fig elettrizzante

electrocute /ɪ'lektrəkju:t/ *vt* fulminare; (execute) giustiziare sulla sedia elettrica

electrocution /ɪlektrə'kju:ʃn/ *n* elettrocuzione *f*

electrode /ɪ'lektrəʊd/ *n* elettrodo *m*

electrolysis /ɪlek'trɒlɪsɪs/ *n* Chem elettrolisi *f*; (hair removal) depilazione *f* diatermica

electromagnetic /ɪlektrəʊmæg'netɪk/ *adj* elettromagnetico

electron /ɪ'lektrɒn/ *n* elettrone *m*

electronic /ɪlek'trɒnɪk/ *adj* elettronico

electronic banking *n* servizi *mpl* bancari telematici

electronic engineer *n* tecnico *m* elettronico; (with diploma) perito *m* elettronico; (with degree) ingegnere *m* elettronico

⚷ parola chiave

electronic engineering *n* ingegneria *f* elettronica
electronic eye *n* cellula *f* fotoelettrica
electronic funds transfer *n* sistemi *mpl* telematici di trasferimento fondi
electronic mail *n* posta *f* elettronica
electronic organizer *n* Comput agenda *f* elettronica
electronic publishing *n* editoria *f* elettronica
electronics /ɪlekˈtrɒnɪks/ *nsg* elettronica *fsg*
electronic tagging *n* sorveglianza *f* tramite braccialetto elettronico
electro-shock therapy, **electroshock treatment** /ɪˈlektrəʊ-/ *n* terapia *f* elettroshock
elegance /ˈelɪgəns/ *n* eleganza *f*
elegant /ˈelɪgənt/ *adj* elegante
elegantly /ˈelɪgəntlɪ/ *adv* elegantemente
elegy /ˈelədʒɪ/ *n* elegia *f*
⚷ **element** /ˈelɪmənt/ *n* elemento *m*
elementary /elɪˈmentərɪ/ *adj* elementare
elephant /ˈelɪfənt/ *n* elefante *m*
elephantine /elɪˈfæntaɪn/ *adj* ‹*person*› mastodontico
elevate /ˈelɪveɪt/ *vt* elevare
elevated /ˈelɪveɪtɪd/ *adj* ‹*language, rank*› elevato; ‹*walkway, railway*› soprelevato
elevation /elɪˈveɪʃn/ *n* elevazione *f*; (height) altitudine *f*; (angle) alzo *m*
elevator /ˈelɪveɪtə(r)/ *n* AmE ascensore *m*
eleven /ɪˈlevn/ *adj & n* undici *m*
eleven plus *n* (formerly) *esame (m) di ammissione alla scuola secondaria inglese*
elevenses /ɪˈlevənzɪz/ *n* BrE infml pausa *f* per il caffè (*a metà mattina*)
eleventh /ɪˈlevənθ/ *adj & n* undicesimo, -a *mf*; **at the ~ hour** infml all'ultimo momento
elf /elf/ *n* (*pl* **elves**) elfo *m*
elicit /ɪˈlɪsɪt/ *vt* ottenere
eligible /ˈelɪdʒəbl/ *adj* eleggibile; **~ young man** buon partito; **be ~ for** aver diritto a
eliminate /ɪˈlɪmɪneɪt/ *vt* eliminare
elimination /ɪlɪmɪˈneɪʃn/ *n* eliminazione *f*; **by a process of ~** procedendo per eliminazione
elite /eɪˈliːt/ *n* fior fiore *m*
elitist /ɪˈliːtɪst/ *adj* elitista
ellipse /ɪˈlɪps/ *n* ellisse *f*
elliptical /ɪˈlɪptɪk(ə)l/ *adj* also fig ellittico
elm /elm/ *n* olmo *m*
elocution /eləˈkjuːʃn/ *n* elocuzione *f*
elongate /ˈiːlɒŋgeɪt/ *vt* allungare
elongated /ˈiːlɒŋgeɪtɪd, AmE ɪˈlɔːŋ-/ *adj* allungato
elope /ɪˈləʊp/ *vi* fuggire [per sposarsi]
elopement /ɪˈləʊpmənt/ *n* fuga *f* romantica
eloquence /ˈeləkwəns/ *n* eloquenza *f*
eloquent /ˈeləkwənt/ *adj* eloquente
eloquently /ˈeləkwəntlɪ/ *adv* con eloquenza
El Salvador /elˈsælvədɔː(r)/ *n* El Salvador *m*; **in ~** nel Salvador
⚷ **else** /els/ *adv* altro; **who ~?** e chi altro?; **he did of course, who ~?** l'ha fatto lui e chi, se no?; **nothing ~** nient'altro; **or ~** altrimenti; **someone ~** qualcun altro; **somewhere ~** da qualche altra parte; **anyone ~** chiunque altro; (as question) nessun'altro?; **anything ~** qualunque altra cosa; (as question) altro?
⚷ **elsewhere** /elsˈweə(r)/ *adv* altrove
elucidate /ɪˈluːsɪdeɪt/ *vt* delucidare
elude /ɪˈluːd/ *vt* eludere; (avoid) evitare; **the name ~s me** il nome mi sfugge
elusive /ɪˈluːsɪv/ *adj* elusivo
emaciated /ɪˈmeɪsɪeɪtɪd/ *adj* emaciato
⚷ **email** **A** *n* e-mail *f*, posta *f* elettronica **B** *vt* spedire per e-mail
email account *n* account *m inv* di posta elettronica
email address *n* indirizzo *m* di posta elettronica
emanate /ˈeməneɪt/ *vi* emanare
emancipate /ɪˈmænsɪpeɪt/ *vt* emancipare
emancipated /ɪˈmænsɪpeɪtɪd/ *adj* emancipato
emancipation /ɪmænsɪˈpeɪʃn/ *n* emancipazione *f*; (of slaves) liberazione *f*
e-marketing /ˈiːmɑːkɪtɪŋ/ *n* e-marketing *m inv*
emasculate /ɪˈmæskjʊleɪt/ *vt* evirare; fig svigorire
embalm /ɪmˈbɑːm/ *vt* imbalsamare
embankment /ɪmˈbæŋkmənt/ *n* argine *m*; Rail massicciata *f*
embargo /emˈbɑːgəʊ/ *n* (*pl* **-es**) embargo *m*
embark /ɪmˈbɑːk/ *vi* imbarcarsi; **~ on** intraprendere
embarkation /embɑːˈkeɪʃn/ *n* imbarco *m*
embarrass /emˈbærəs/ *vt* imbarazzare
embarrassed /emˈbærəst/ *adj* imbarazzato
embarrassing /emˈbærəsɪŋ/ *adj* imbarazzante
embarrassment /emˈbærəsmənt/ *n* imbarazzo *m*
embassy /ˈembəsɪ/ *n* ambasciata *f*
embed /ɪmˈbed/ *vt* Comput integrare ‹*command*›; **~ded in** ‹*gem*› incastonato in; ‹*plant*› piantato in; ‹*sharp object*› conficcato in; ‹*rock*› incluso in; **~ded** ‹*traditions, feelings*› radicato; **be ~ded in** fig radicarsi in
embellish /ɪmˈbelɪʃ/ *vt* abbellire
embers /ˈembəz/ *npl* braci *fpl*
embezzle /ɪmˈbezl/ *vt* appropriarsi indebitamente di
embezzlement /ɪmˈbez(ə)lmənt/ *n* appropriazione *f* indebita
embitter /ɪmˈbɪtə(r)/ *vt* amareggiare
emblem /ˈembləm/ *n* emblema *m*

emblematic /emblə'mætɪk/ *adj* emblematico

embodiment /ɪm'bɒdɪmənt/ *n* incarnazione *f*

embody /ɪm'bɒdɪ/ *vt* (*pt/pp* **-ied**) incorporare; **~ what is best in...** rappresentare quanto c'è di meglio di...

embolism /'embəlɪzm/ *n* Med embolia *f*

emboss /ɪm'bɒs/ *vt* sbalzare ‹*metal*›; stampare in rilievo ‹*paper*›

embossed /ɪm'bɒst/ *adj* in rilievo

embrace /ɪm'breɪs/ **A** *n* abbraccio *m*
B *vt* abbracciare
C *vi* abbracciarsi

embroider /ɪm'brɔɪdə(r)/ *vt* ricamare ‹*design*›; fig abbellire

embroidery /ɪm'brɔɪdərɪ/ *n* ricamo *m*

embroil /ɪm'brɔɪl/ *vt* **become ~ed in something** rimanere invischiato in qualcosa

embryo /'embrɪəʊ/ *n* embrione *m*

embryonic /'embrɪ'ɒnɪk/ *adj* Biol, fig embrionale

emend /ɪ'mend/ *vt* emendare

emerald /'emərəld/ *n* smeraldo *m*

🔑 **emerge** /ɪ'mɜːdʒ/ *vi* emergere; (come into being: nation) nascere; ‹*sun, flowers*› spuntare fuori

emergence /ɪ'mɜːdʒəns/ *n* emergere *m*; (of new country) nascita *f*

🔑 **emergency** /ɪ'mɜːdʒənsɪ/ *n* emergenza *f*; **in an ~** in caso di emergenza

emergency ambulance service *n* pronto soccorso *m* autoambulanze

emergency case *n* Med caso *m* di emergenza

emergency centre *n* (for refugees etc) centro *m* di accoglienza; Med centro *m* di soccorso mobile

emergency exit *n* uscita *f* di sicurezza

emergency landing *n* Aeron atterraggio *m* di fortuna

emergency laws *npl* Pol leggi *fpl* straordinarie

emergency number *n* numero *m* di emergenza

emergency powers *npl* Pol poteri *mpl* straordinari

emergency rations *npl* viveri *mpl* di sopravvivenza

emergency service *n* Med servizio *m* di pronto soccorso

emergency services *npl* servizi *mpl* di pronto intervento

emergency surgery *n* **undergo ~** essere operato d'urgenza

emergency ward *n* [reparto *m* di] pronto soccorso *m*

emergency worker *n* addetto *m* a operazioni di soccorso

emergent /ɪ'mɜːdʒənt/ *adj* ‹*industry, nation*› emergente

emery board /'emərɪ/ *n* limetta *f* per le unghie (*di carta*)

emery paper *n* carta *f* vetrata

emigrant /'emɪgrənt/ *n* emigrante *mf*

emigrate /'emɪgreɪt/ *vi* emigrare

emigration /emɪ'greɪʃn/ *n* emigrazione *f*

eminence /'emɪnəns/ *n* (fame) eminenza *f*, gloria *f*; (honour) distinzione *f*; (hill) altura *f*

eminent /'emɪnənt/ *adj* eminente

eminently /'emɪnəntlɪ/ *adv* eminentemente

emirate /'emɪərət/ *n* emirato *m*

emissary /'emɪsərɪ/ *n* emissario *m* (**to** di)

emission /ɪ'mɪʃn/ *n* emissione *f*; (of fumes) esalazione *f*

emit /ɪ'mɪt/ *vt* (*pt/pp* **emitted**) emettere; esalare ‹*fumes*›

Emmy /'emɪ/ *n* Emmy *m* (*Oscar* (*m inv*) *televisivo americano*)

emoticon /ɪ'məʊtɪkɒn, -'mɒtɪ-/ *n* Comput emoticon *m inv*

🔑 **emotion** /ɪ'məʊʃn/ *n* emozione *f*

🔑 **emotional** /ɪ'məʊʃənəl/ *adj* denso di emozione; ‹*person, reaction*› emotivo; **become ~** avere una reazione emotiva; **don't get so ~** non lasciarti prendere dalle emozioni

emotionally /ɪ'məʊʃənəlɪ/ *adv* ‹*speak*› emotivamente; **~ disturbed** con turbe emotive

emotionless /ɪ'məʊʃənlɪs/ *adj* impassibile

emotive /ɪ'məʊtɪv/ *adj* emotivo

empathize /'empəθaɪz/ *vi* **~ with somebody** immedesimarsi nei problemi di qualcuno

empathy /'empəθɪ/ *n* comprensione *f*

emperor /'empərə(r)/ *n* imperatore *m*

emphasis /'emfəsɪs/ *n* enfasi *f*; **put the ~ on something** accentuare qualcosa

🔑 **emphasize** /'emfəsaɪz/ *vt* accentuare ‹*word, syllable*›; sottolineare ‹*need*›

emphatic /ɪm'fætɪk/ *adj* categorico

emphatically /ɪm'fætɪklɪ/ *adv* categoricamente

empire /'empaɪə(r)/ *n* impero *m*

empirical /em'pɪrɪkl/ *adj* empirico

empiricism /em'pɪrɪsɪzm/ *n* empirismo *m*

🔑 **employ** /em'plɔɪ/ *vt* impiegare; fig usare ‹*tact*›

employable /em'plɔɪəbl/ *adj* ‹*person*› che ha i requisiti per svolgere un lavoro

🔑 **employee** /emplɔɪ'iː/ *n* impiegato, -a *mf*

employee buyout *n* rilevamento *m* dipendenti

🔑 **employer** /em'plɔɪə(r)/ *n* datore *m* di lavoro

🔑 **employment** /em'plɔɪmənt/ *n* occupazione *f*; (work) lavoro *m*

employment agency *n* ufficio *m* di collocamento

employment contract *n* contratto *m* di lavoro

🔑 parola chiave

employment exchange *n* agenzia *f* di collocamento

employment figures *npl* dati *mpl* sull'occupazione

Employment Minister, **Employment Secretary** *n* ministro *m* del lavoro

emporium /em'pɔːrɪəm/ *n* hum emporio *m*

empower /ɪm'paʊə(r)/ *vt* autorizzare; (enable) mettere in grado

empowerment /ɪm'paʊəmənt/ *n* empowerment *m inv*

empress /'emprɪs/ *n* imperatrice *f*

empties /'emptɪz/ *npl* vuoti *mpl*

emptiness /'emptɪnɪs/ *n* vuoto *m*

🔑 **empty** /'emptɪ/ **A** *adj* vuoto; ‹*promise, threat*› vano
B *vt* (*pt/pp* **-ied**) vuotare ‹*container*›
C *vi* vuotarsi
▪ **empty out** *vt & vi* = **empty**

empty-handed /-'hændɪd/ *adj* ‹*arrive, leave*› a mani vuote

empty-headed /-'hedɪd/ *adj* scriteriato

EMS *n abbr* (**European Monetary System**) SME *m*

EMU *abbr* (**European Monetary Union**) UME *f*

emulate /'emjʊleɪt/ *vt* emulare

emulsify /ɪ'mʌlsɪfaɪ/ *v* (*pt/pp* **-ied**) **A** *vt* emulsionare
B *vi* emulsionarsi

emulsion /ɪ'mʌlʃn/ *n* emulsione *f*

🔑 **enable** /ɪ'neɪbl/ *vt* ~ **somebody to** mettere qualcuno in grado di

enact /ɪ'nækt/ *vt* Theat rappresentare; decretare ‹*law*›

enamel /ɪ'næml/ **A** *n* smalto *m*
B *vt* (*pt/pp* **enamelled**) smaltare

enamelling /ɪ'næməlɪŋ/ *n* (process) smaltatura *f*; (art) decorazione *f* a smalto

enamoured /ɪ'næməd/ *adj* **be ~ of** essere innamorato di

enc. *abbr* (**enclosures**) all.

encampment /ɪn'kæmpmənt/ *n* accampamento *m*

encapsulate /en'kæpsjʊleɪt/ *vt* (include) incapsulare; (summarize) sintetizzare

encase /en'keɪs/ *vt* rivestire (**in** di)

encash /en'kæʃ/ *vt* BrE incassare

encephalogram /en'kefələgræm/ *n* encefalogramma *m*

enchant /ɪn'tʃɑːnt/ *vt* incantare

enchanting /ɪn'tʃɑːntɪŋ/ *adj* incantevole

enchantment /ɪn'tʃɑːntmənt/ *n* incanto *m*

encircle /ɪn'sɜːkl/ *vt* circondare

encl. *abbr* (**enclosed**, **enclosure**) all.

enclave /'enkleɪv/ *n* enclave *f inv*; fig territorio *m*

enclose /ɪn'kləʊz/ *vt* circondare ‹*land*›; (in letter) allegare (**with** a)

enclosed /ɪn'kləʊzd/ *adj* ‹*space*› chiuso; (in letter) allegato

enclosure /ɪn'kləʊʒə(r)/ *n* (at zoo) recinto *m*; (in letter) allegato *m*

encode /ɪn'kəʊd/ *vt* codificare

encoder /ɪn'kəʊdə(r)/ *n* codificatore, -trice *mf*

encompass /ɪn'kʌmpəs/ *vt* (include) comprendere

encore /'ɒŋkɔː(r)/ *n & int* bis *m inv*

encounter /ɪn'kaʊntə(r)/ **A** *n* incontro *m*; (battle) scontro *m*
B *vt* incontrare

🔑 **encourage** /ɪn'kʌrɪdʒ/ *vt* incoraggiare; promuovere ‹*the arts, independence*›

encouragement /ɪn'kʌrɪdʒmənt/ *n* incoraggiamento *m*; (of the arts) promozione *f*

encouraging /ɪn'kʌrɪdʒɪŋ/ *adj* incoraggiante; ‹*smile*› di incoraggiamento

encroach /ɪn'krəʊtʃ/ *vt* ~ **on** invadere ‹*land, privacy*›; abusare di ‹*time*›; interferire con ‹*rights*›

encrust /en'krʌst/ *vt* **be ~ed with** ‹*ice*› essere incrostato di; ‹*jewels*› essere tempestato di

encrypt /en'krɪpt/ *vt* criptare

encumber /ɪn'kʌmbə(r)/ *vt* **be ~ed with** essere carico di ‹*children, suitcases*›; ingombro di ‹*furniture*›

encumbrance /ɪn'kʌmbrəns/ *n* peso *m*

encyclopaedia /ɪnsaɪklə'piːdɪə/ *n* enciclopedia *f*

encyclopaedic /ɪnsaɪklə'piːdɪk/ *adj* enciclopedico

🔑 **end** /end/ **A** *n* fine *f*; (of box, table, piece of string) estremità *f*; (of town, room) parte *f*; (purpose) fine *m*; **in the ~** alla fine; **at the ~ of May** alla fine di maggio; **at the ~ of the street/garden** in fondo alla strada/ al giardino; **on ~** (upright) in piedi; **for days on ~** per giorni e giorni; **for six days on ~** per sei giorni di fila; **put an ~ to something** mettere fine a qualcosa; **make ~s meet** infml sbarcare il lunario; **no ~ of** infml un sacco di
B *vt & vi* finire
▪ **end in** *vt* ‹*word*› terminare in; finire in ‹*failure, argument*›
▪ **end off** *vt* concludere ‹*meal, speech*›
▪ **end up** *vi* finire; **~ up doing something** finire col fare qualcosa

endanger /ɪn'deɪndʒə(r)/ *vt* rischiare ‹*one's life*›; mettere a repentaglio ‹*somebody else, success of something*›

endangered species /ɪn'deɪndʒəd/ *n* specie *f* a rischio

endear /ɪn'dɪə(r)/ *vt* ~ **oneself to somebody** conquistarsi la simpatia di qualcuno; ~ **somebody to** conquistare a qualcuno la simpatia di

endearing /ɪn'dɪərɪŋ/ *adj* accattivante

endearingly /ɪn'dɪərɪŋlɪ/ *adv* ‹*smile*› in modo accattivante; ~ **honest** di un'onestà disarmante

endearment /ɪn'dɪəmənt/ *n* **term of ~** vezzeggiativo *m*
endeavour /ɪn'devə(r)/ **A** *n* tentativo *m*
B *vi* sforzarsi (**to** di)
endemic /en'demɪk/ **A** *adj* endemico
B *n* (situation) endemia *f*
ending /'endɪŋ/ *n* fine *f*; Gram desinenza *f*
endive /'endaɪv/ *n* indivia *f*
endless /'endlɪs/ *adj* interminabile; ‹*patience*› infinito
endlessly /'endlɪslɪ/ *adv* continuamente; ‹*patient*› infinitamente
endocrinology /endəʊkrɪ'nɒlədʒɪ/ *n* endocrinologia *f*
endorse /en'dɔːs/ *vt* girare ‹*cheque*›; ‹*sports personality*› fare pubblicità a ‹*product*›; approvare ‹*plan*›
endorsement /en'dɔːsmənt/ *n* (of cheque) girata *f*; (of plan) conferma *f*; (on driving licence) registrazione *f* su patente di un'infrazione
endow /ɪn'daʊ/ *vt* dotare
endowment insurance /ɪn'daʊmənt/ *n* *assicurazione (f) sulla vita che fornisce un reddito in caso di sopravvivenza*
endpaper *n* risguardo *m*
end product *n* prodotto *m* finito
end result *n* risultato *m* finale
endurable /ɪn'djʊərəbl/ *adj* sopportabile
endurance /ɪn'djʊrəns/ *n* resistenza *f*; **it is beyond ~** è insopportabile
endurance test *n* prova *f* di resistenza
endure /ɪn'djʊə(r)/ **A** *vt* sopportare
B *vi* durare
enduring /ɪn'djʊərɪŋ/ *adj* duraturo
end user *n* utente *m* finale
enema /'enɪmə/ *n* Med clistere *m*
⚷ **enemy** /'enəmɪ/ **A** *n* nemico, -a *mf*
B *attrib* nemico
energetic /enə'dʒetɪk/ *adj* energico
energetically /enə'dʒetɪklɪ/ *adv* ‹*speak, promote, publicize*› vigorosamente; ‹*work, exercise*› con energia; ‹*deny*› risolutamente
energize /'enədʒaɪz/ *vt* stimolare; Electr alimentare [elettricamente]
energizing /'enədʒaɪzɪŋ/ *adj* ‹*influence*› stimolante
⚷ **energy** /'enədʒɪ/ *n* energia *f*
energy drink *n* energy drink *m*, bevanda *f* energetica
energy efficiency *n* razionalizzazione *f* del consumo energetico
energy-efficient *adj* a consumo ottimale di energia
energy policy *n* politica *f* energetica
energy resources *npl* risorse *fpl* energetiche
energy saving *n* risparmio *m* energetico
energy-saving *adj* ‹*device*› che fa risparmiare energia; ‹*measure*› per risparmiare energia
enervate /'enəveɪt/ *vt* snervare
enfold /en'fəʊld/ *vt* avvolgere
enforce /ɪn'fɔːs/ *vt* far rispettare ‹*law*›
enforced /ɪn'fɔːst/ *adj* forzato
enforcement /ɪn'fɔːsmənt/ *n* applicazione *f*; (of discipline) imposizione *f*
ENG *abbr* (**electronic news gathering**) ENG *m*
⚷ **engage** /ɪn'geɪdʒ/ **A** *vt* assumere ‹*staff*›; Theat ingaggiare; Auto ingranare ‹*gear*›; **~ somebody in conversation** fare conversazione con qualcuno
B *vi* Techn ingranare; **~ in** impegnarsi in
engaged /ɪn'geɪdʒd/ *adj* (in use, busy) occupato; ‹*person*› impegnato; (to be married) fidanzato; **get ~** fidanzarsi (**to** con)
engaged tone *n* BrE segnale *m* di occupato
engagement /ɪn'geɪdʒmənt/ *n* fidanzamento *m*; (appointment) appuntamento *m*; Mil combattimento *m*
engagement ring *n* anello *m* di fidanzamento
engagements book *n* agenda *f*
engaging /ɪn'geɪdʒɪŋ/ *adj* attraente
engender /ɪn'dʒendə(r)/ *vt* fig generare
⚷ **engine** /'endʒɪn/ *n* motore *m*; Rail locomotrice *f*
engine drive *n* macchinista *m*
engineer /endʒɪ'nɪə(r)/ **A** *n* ingegnere *m*; (service, installation) tecnico *m*; Naut, AmE Rail macchinista *m*
B *vt* fig architettare
engineering /endʒɪ'nɪərɪŋ/ *n* ingegneria *f*
engine failure *n* guasto *m* [al motore]; (in jet) avaria *f*
engine oil *n* olio *m* [del] motore
engine room *n* sala *f* macchine
engine shed *n* Rail deposito *m*
England /'ɪŋglənd/ *n* Inghilterra *f*
⚷ **English** /'ɪŋglɪʃ/ **A** *adj* inglese; **the ~ Channel** la Manica
B *n* (language) inglese *m*; **the ~** *pl* gli inglesi
English as a Foreign Language *n* inglese *m* come lingua straniera
English as a Second Language *n* inglese *m* come seconda lingua
English breakfast *n* colazione *f* all'inglese
Englishman *n* inglese *m*
English rose *n* *donna (f) dalla bellezza tipicamente inglese*
English speaker *n* anglofono, -a *mf*
English-speaking *adj* anglofono
Englishwoman *n* inglese *f*
engrave /ɪn'greɪv/ *vt* incidere
engraving /ɪn'greɪvɪŋ/ *n* incisione *f*
engross /ɪn'grəʊs/ *vt* **~ed in** assorto in

⚷ parola chiave

engrossing /ɪnˈgrəʊsɪŋ/ *adj* avvincente

engulf /ɪnˈgʌlf/ *vt* ‹*fire, waves*› inghiottire

enhance /ɪnˈhɑːns/ *vt* accrescere ‹*beauty, reputation*›; migliorare ‹*performance*›

enigma /ɪˈnɪgmə/ *n* enigma *m*

enigmatic /enɪgˈmætɪk/ *adj* enigmatico

enjoy /ɪnˈdʒɔɪ/ *vt* godere di ‹*good health*›; **~ oneself** divertirsi; **I ~ cooking/painting** mi piace cucinare/dipingere; **I ~ed the meal/film** mi è piaciuto il pranzo/il film; **~ your meal** buon appetito

enjoyable /ɪnˈdʒɔɪəbl/ *adj* piacevole

enjoyment /ɪnˈdʒɔɪmənt/ *n* piacere *m*

enlarge /ɪnˈlɑːdʒ/ **A** *vt* ingrandire
B *vi* **~ upon** dilungarsi su

enlargement /ɪnˈlɑːdʒmənt/ *n* ingrandimento *m*

enlarger /ɪnˈlɑːdʒə(r)/ *n* Phot ingranditore *m*

enlighten /ɪnˈlaɪtn/ *vt* illuminare

enlightened /ɪnˈlaɪtənd/ *adj* progressista

enlightening /ɪnˈlaɪtnɪŋ/ *adj* istruttivo

enlightenment /ɪnˈlaɪtənmənt/ *n* **The E~** l'Illuminismo *m*

enlist /ɪnˈlɪst/ **A** *vt* Mil reclutare; **~ sb's help** farsi aiutare da qualcuno
B *vi* Mil arruolarsi

enliven /ɪnˈlaɪvn/ *vt* animare

enmesh /enˈmeʃ/ *vt* **become ~ed in** fig impegolarsi in

enmity /ˈenmətɪ/ *n* inimicizia *f*

ennoble /enˈnəʊbl/ *vt* nobilitare

enormity /ɪˈnɔːmətɪ/ *n* enormità *f*

enormous /ɪˈnɔːməs/ *adj* enorme

enormously /ɪˈnɔːməslɪ/ *adv* estremamente; ‹*grateful*› infinitamente

enough /ɪˈnʌf/ **A** *adj & n* abbastanza; **I didn't bring ~ clothes** non ho portato abbastanza vestiti; **have you had ~?** (to eat/drink) hai mangiato/bevuto abbastanza?; **I've had ~!** infml ne ho abbastanza!; **is that ~?** basta?; **that's ~!** basta così!; **£50 isn't ~** 50 sterline non sono sufficienti
B *adv* abbastanza; **you're not working fast ~** non lavori abbastanza in fretta; **funnily ~** stranamente

enquire /ɪnˈkwaɪə(r)/ *vi* domandare; **~ about** chiedere informazioni su

enquiring /ɪnˈkwaɪərɪŋ/ *adj* ‹*look*› indagatore; ‹*mind*› avido di sapere

enquiry /ɪnˈkwaɪərɪ/ *n* domanda *f*; (investigation) inchiesta *f*

enrage /ɪnˈreɪdʒ/ *vt* fare arrabbiare

enrich /ɪnˈrɪtʃ/ *vt* arricchire; (improve) migliorare ‹*vocabulary*›

enrol /ɪnˈrəʊl/ *vt* (*pt/pp* **-rolled**) (for exam, in club) iscriversi (**for, in** a)

enrolment /ɪnˈrəʊlmənt/ *n* iscrizione *f*

ensconced /ɪnˈskɒnst/ *adj* comodamente sistemato (**in** in)

ensemble /ɒnˈsɒmbl/ *n* (clothing & Mus) complesso *m*

ensign /ˈensaɪn/ *n* insegna *f*

enslave /ɪnˈsleɪv/ *vt* render schiavo

ensue /ɪnˈsjuː/ *vi* seguire; **~ from** sorgere da; **the ensuing discussion** la discussione che ne è seguita

en suite /ɒ̃ˈswiːt/ **A** *n* (bathroom) camera *f* con bagno annesso
B *adj* ‹*bathroom*› annesso; ‹*room*› con bagno

ensure /ɪnˈʃʊə(r)/ *vt* assicurare; **~ that** ‹*person*› assicurarsi che; ‹*measure*› garantire che

ENT *n abbr* (**Ear Nose and Throat**) otorino *m*

entail /ɪnˈteɪl/ *vt* comportare; **what does it ~?** in che cosa consiste?

entangle /ɪnˈtæŋgl/ *vt* **get ~d in** rimanere impigliato in; fig rimanere coinvolto in

entanglement /ɪnˈtæŋg(ə)lmənt/ *n* (emotional) legame *m* sentimentale; (complicated situation) pasticcio *m*

enter /ˈentə(r)/ **A** *vt* entrare in; iscrivere ‹*horse, runner in race*›; cominciare ‹*university*›; partecipare a ‹*competition*›; Comput immettere ‹*data*›; (write down) scrivere
B *vi* entrare; Theat entrare in scena; (register as competitor) iscriversi; (take part) partecipare (**in** a)
C *n* Comput invio *m*

■ **enter into** *vt* (begin) intavolare ‹*negotiations, an argument*›

enteritis /entəˈraɪtɪs/ *n* enterite *f*

enterprise /ˈentəpraɪz/ *n* impresa *f*; (quality) iniziativa *f*

enterprising /ˈentəpraɪzɪŋ/ *adj* intraprendente

entertain /entəˈteɪn/ **A** *vt* intrattenere; (invite) ricevere; nutrire ‹*ideas, hopes*›; prendere in considerazione ‹*possibility*›
B *vi* intrattenersi; (have guests) ricevere

entertainer /entəˈteɪnə(r)/ *n* artista *mf*

entertaining /entəˈteɪnɪŋ/ *adj* ‹*person*› di gradevole compagnia; ‹*evening, film, play*› divertente

entertainment /entəˈteɪnmənt/ *n* (amusement) intrattenimento *m*

entertainment industry *n* l'industria *f* dello spettacolo

enthral /ɪnˈθrɔːl/ *vt* (*pt/pp* **enthralled**) **be ~led** essere affascinato (**by** da)

enthralling /ɪnˈθrɔːlɪŋ/ *adj* ‹*novel, performance*› affascinante

enthuse /ɪnˈθjuːz/ *vi* **~ over** entusiasmarsi per

enthusiasm /ɪnˈθjuːzɪæzm/ *n* entusiasmo *m*

enthusiast /ɪnˈθjuːzɪæst/ *n* entusiasta *mf*

enthusiastic /ɪnθjuːzɪˈæstɪk/ *adj* entusiastico

enthusiastically /ɪnθjuːzɪˈæstɪklɪ/ *adv* entusiasticamente

entice /ɪn'taɪs/ *vt* attirare
enticement /ɪn'taɪsmənt/ *n* (incentive) incentivo *m*
enticing /ɪn'taɪsɪŋ/ *adj* ‹*prospect, offer*› allettante; ‹*person*› seducente; ‹*food, smell*› invitante
entire /ɪn'taɪə(r)/ *adj* intero
entirely /ɪn'taɪəlɪ/ *adv* del tutto; **I'm not ~ satisfied** non sono completamente soddisfatto
entirety /ɪn'taɪərətɪ/ *n* **in its ~** nell'insieme
entitle /ɪn'taɪtl/ *vt* dare diritto a; **~ somebody to something** dare a qualcuno il diritto di qualcosa
entitled /ɪn'taɪtld/ *adj* ‹*book*› intitolato; **be ~ to something** aver diritto a qualcosa
entitlement /ɪn'taɪtlmənt/ *n* diritto *m*
entity /'entətɪ/ *n* entità *f*
entomology /entə'mɒlədʒɪ/ *n* entomologia *f*
entourage /'ɒntʊrɑ:ʒ/ *n* entourage *m inv*
entrails /'entreɪlz/ *npl* intestini *mpl*
entrance¹ /'entrəns/ *n* entrata *f*; Theat entrata *f* in scena; (right to enter) ammissione *f*; **'no ~'** 'ingresso vietato'
entrance² /ɪn'trɑ:ns/ *vt* estasiare
entrance examination *n* esame *m* di ammissione
entrance fee *n* **how much is the ~?** quanto costa il biglietto di ingresso?
entrance hall *n* (in house) ingresso *m*
entrance requirements *npl* requisiti *mpl* di ammissione
entrance ticket *n* biglietto *m* d'ingresso
entrancing /ɪn'trɑ:nsɪŋ/ *adj* incantevole
entrant /'entrənt/ *n* concorrente *mf*
entreat /ɪn'tri:t/ *vt* supplicare
entreatingly /ɪn'tri:tɪŋlɪ/ *adv* ‹*beg, ask*› in tono implorante
entreaty /ɪn'tri:tɪ/ *n* supplica *f*
entrée /'ɒ̃treɪ/ *n* BrE (starter) primo *m*; AmE (main course) secondo *m*; **her wealth gave her an ~ into high society** il denaro le ha aperto le porte dell'alta società
entrenched /ɪn'trentʃt/ *adj* ‹*ideas, views*› radicato
entrepreneur /ɒntrəprə'nɜ:(r)/ *n* imprenditore, -trice *mf*
entrepreneurial /ɒntrəprə'nɜ:rɪəl/ *adj* imprenditoriale; **have ~ skills** avere il senso degli affari
entrust /ɪn'trʌst/ *vt* **~ somebody with something, ~ something to somebody** affidare qualcosa a qualcuno
entry /'entrɪ/ *n* ingresso *m*; (way in) entrata *f*; (in directory etc) voce *f*; (in appointment diary) appuntamento *m*; **no ~** ingresso vietato; Auto accesso vietato
entry fee *n* quota *f* di iscrizione
entry form *n* modulo *m* di ammissione

parola chiave

entry permit *n* visto *m* di entrata
entryphone *n* citofono *m*
entry requirements *npl* requisiti *mpl* di ammissione
entry visa *n* visto *m* di ingresso
entwine /ɪn'twaɪn/ *vt* also fig intrecciare
E-number *n* BrE sigla *f* degli additivi
enumerate /ɪ'nju:məreɪt/ *vt* enumerare
enumeration /ɪnju:mə'reɪʃn/ *n* (list) enumerazione *f*; (counting) conto *m*
enunciate /ɪ'nʌnsɪeɪt/ *vt* enunciare
enunciation /ɪnʌnsɪ'eɪʃn/ *n* (of principle, facts) enunciazione *f*; (of word) articolazione *f*
envelop /ɪn'veləp/ *vt* (*pt/pp* **enveloped**) avviluppare
envelope /'envələʊp/ *n* busta *f*
enviable /'envɪəbl/ *adj* invidiabile
envious /'envɪəs/ *adj* invidioso
enviously /'envɪəslɪ/ *adv* con invidia
environment /ɪn'vaɪrənmənt/ *n* ambiente *m*
environmental /ɪnvaɪrən'mentl/ *adj* ambientale
environmental health *n* salute *f* pubblica
environmentalism /ɪn,vaɪərən'mentəlɪzəm/ *n* ambientalismo *m*
environmentalist /ɪnvaɪrən'mentəlɪst/ *n* ambientalista *mf*
environmentally /ɪnvaɪrən'mentəlɪ/ *adv* **~ friendly** che rispetta l'ambiente
environmental scientist *n* studioso, -a *mf* di ecologia applicata
Environmental Studies *npl* BrE Sch ecogeografia *f* e ecobiologia *f*
envisage /ɪn'vɪzɪdʒ/ *vt* prevedere
envoy /'envɔɪ/ *n* inviato, -a *mf*
envy /'envɪ/ **A** *n* invidia *f*
B *vt* (*pt/pp* **-ied**) **~ somebody something** invidiare qualcuno per qualcosa
enzyme /'enzaɪm/ *n* enzima *m*
EOF *abbr* Comput (**end of file**) EOF *m*
ephemeral /ɪ'femərəl/ *adj* effimero
epic /'epɪk/ **A** *adj* epico
B *n* epopea *f*
epicentre /'epɪsentə(r)/ *n* epicentro *m*
epidemic /epɪ'demɪk/ *n* epidemia *f*
epidermis /epɪ'dɜ:mɪs/ *n* epidermide *f*
epidural /epɪ'djʊərəl/ *n* Med anestesia *f* epidurale
epigram /'epɪgræm/ *n* epigramma *m*
epilepsy /'epɪlepsɪ/ *n* epilessia *f*
epileptic /epɪ'leptɪk/ *adj & n* epilettico, -a *mf*
epilogue /'epɪlɒg/ *n* epilogo *m*
Epiphany /ɪ'pɪfənɪ/ *n* Epifania *f*
episode /'epɪsəʊd/ *n* episodio *m*
episodic /epɪ'sɒdɪk/ *adj* episodico
epistle /ɪ'pɪsl/ *n* literary epistola *f*
epitaph /'epɪtɑ:f/ *n* epitaffio *m*
epithet /'epɪθet/ *n* epiteto *m*

epitome /ɪ'pɪtəmɪ/ *n* epitome *f*
epitomize /ɪ'pɪtəmaɪz/ *vt* essere il classico esempio di
epoch /'i:pɒk/ *n* epoca *f*
epoch-making *adj* che fa epoca
eponymous /ɪ'pɒnɪməs/ *adj* eponimo
EQ *abbr* (**graphic equalizer**) EQ *m*
equable /'ekwəbl/ *adj* ‹*climate*› temperato; ‹*temperament*› equilibrato
equably /'ekwəblɪ/ *adv* con serenità
equal /'i:kwl/ **A** *adj* ‹*parts, amounts*› uguale; **of ~ height** della stessa altezza; **be ~ to the task** essere all'altezza del compito **B** *n* pari *m inv*; **treat somebody as an ~** trattare qualcuno da pari a pari **C** *vt* (*pt/pp* **equalled**) (be same in quantity as) essere pari a; (rival) uguagliare; **5 plus 5 ~s 10** 5 più 5 [è] uguale a 10
equality /ɪ'kwɒlətɪ/ *n* uguaglianza *f*
equalize /'i:kwəlaɪz/ *vi* Sport pareggiare
equalizer /'i:kwəlaɪzə(r)/ *n* Sport pareggio *m*; **get the ~** pareggiare
equally /'i:kwəlɪ/ *adv* ‹*divide*› in parti uguali; **~ intelligent** della stessa intelligenza; **~,...** allo stesso tempo ...
equal opportunities *npl* uguaglianza *f* dei diritti
Equal Opportunities Commission *n* BrE *commissione (f) per l'uguaglianza dei diritti nei rapporti di lavoro*
equal opportunity *attrib* ‹*legislation*› per l'uguaglianza dei diritti nei rapporti di lavoro; ‹*employer*› che applica l'uguaglianza dei diritti
equal rights *npl* parità *f* dei diritti
equals sign *n* segno *m* uguale
equanimity /ekwə'nɪmətɪ/ *n* equanimità *f*
equate /ɪ'kweɪt/ *vt* **~ something with something** equiparare qualcosa a qualcosa
equation /ɪ'kweɪʒn/ *n* Math equazione *f*
equator /ɪ'kweɪtə(r)/ *n* equatore *m*
equatorial /ekwə'tɔ:rɪəl/ *adj* equatoriale
Equatorial Guinea *n* Guinea *f* Equatoriale
equestrian /ɪ'kwestrɪən/ *adj* equestre
equidistant /i:kwɪ'dɪstənt/ *adj* equidistante
equilateral /i:kwɪ'lætərəl/ *adj* equilatero
equilibrium /i:kwɪ'lɪbrɪəm/ *n* equilibrio *m*
equine /'ekwaɪn/ *adj* ‹*disease, species*› equino; ‹*features*› cavallino
equinox /'i:kwɪnɒks/ *n* equinozio *m*
equip /ɪ'kwɪp/ *vt* (*pt/pp* **equipped**) equipaggiare; attrezzare ‹*kitchen, office*›
equipment /ɪ'kwɪpmənt/ *n* attrezzatura *f*
equitable /'ekwɪtəbl/ *adj* giusto
equity /'ekwətɪ/ *n* (justness) equità *f*; Comm azioni *fpl*
equity capital *n* Fin capitale *m* azionario
equity financing *n* Fin finanziamento *m* attraverso l'emissione di azioni
equity market *n* Fin mercato *m* azionario
equivalent /ɪ'kwɪvələnt/ **A** *adj* equivalente; **be ~ to** equivalere a **B** *n* equivalente *m*
equivocal /ɪ'kwɪvəkl/ *adj* equivoco
equivocate /ɪ'kwɪvəkeɪt/ *vi* parlare in modo equivoco, giocare sull'equivoco
equivocation /ɪkwɪvə'keɪʃn/ *n* affermazione *f* equivoca; **too much ~** troppi equivoci
era /'ɪərə/ *n* età *f*; (geological) era *f*
eradicate /ɪ'rædɪkeɪt/ *vt* eradicare
erase /ɪ'reɪz/ *vt* cancellare
erase head *n* Comput testina *f* di cancellazione
eraser /ɪ'reɪzə(r)/ *n* gomma *f* [da cancellare]; (for blackboard) cancellino *m*
erasure /ɪ'reɪʒə(r)/ *n* (act) cancellazione *f*; (on paper) cancellatura *f*
erect /ɪ'rekt/ **A** *adj* eretto **B** *vt* erigere
erection /ɪ'rekʃn/ *n* erezione *f*
ergonomic /3:gə'nɒmɪk/ *adj* ergonomico; ‹*seat*› anatomico
ergonomics /3:gə'nɒmɪks/ *nsg* ergonomia *fsg*
Erie /'ɪərɪ/ *n* **Lake ~** il lago Erie
Eritrea /erɪ'treɪə/ *n* Eritrea *f*
ERM *n abbr* (**Exchange Rate Mechanism**) *sistema (m) di cambio dello SME*
ermine /'3:mɪn/ *n* ermellino *m*
erode /ɪ'rəʊd/ *vt* ‹*water*› erodere; ‹*acid*› corrodere
erogenous /ɪ'rɒdʒɪnəs/ *adj* erogeno
erosion /ɪ'rəʊʒn/ *n* erosione *f*; (by acid) corrosione *f*
erotic /ɪ'rɒtɪk/ *adj* erotico
erotica /ɪ'rɒtɪkə/ *npl* (art) arte *f* erotica; (literature) letteratura *f* erotica; Cinema film *mpl* erotici
eroticism /ɪ'rɒtɪsɪzm/ *n* erotismo *m*
err /3:(r)/ *vi* errare; (sin) peccare
errand /'erənd/ *n* commissione *f*
errant /'erənt/ *adj* ‹*husband, wife*› infedele
erratic /ɪ'rætɪk/ *adj* irregolare; ‹*person, moods*› imprevedibile; ‹*exchange rate*› incostante
erroneous /ɪ'rəʊnɪəs/ *adj* erroneo
erroneously /ɪ'rəʊnɪəslɪ/ *adv* erroneamente
error /'erə(r)/ *n* errore *m*; **in ~** per errore
error message *n* Comput messaggio *m* di errore
ersatz /'3:sæts/ *n* surrogato *m*; **~ tobacco** surrogato del tabacco
erudite /'erʊdaɪt/ *adj* erudito
erudition /erʊ'dɪʃn/ *n* erudizione *f*
erupt /ɪ'rʌpt/ *vi* eruttare; ‹*spots*› spuntare; fig (in anger) dare in escandescenze
eruption /ɪ'rʌpʃn/ *n* eruzione *f*; fig scoppio *m*
escalate /'eskəleɪt/ **A** *vi* intensificarsi **B** *vt* intensificare
escalation /eskə'leɪʃn/ *n* escalation *f inv*

escalator /ˈeskəleɪtə(r)/ *n* scala *f* mobile
escapade /ˈeskəpeɪd/ *n* scappatella *f*
🔑 **escape** /ɪˈskeɪp/ **A** *n* fuga *f*; (from prison) evasione *f*; **have a narrow ~** cavarsela per un pelo
B *vi* ‹*prisoner*› evadere (**from** da); sfuggire (**from somebody** alla sorveglianza di qualcuno); ‹*animal*› scappare; ‹*gas*› fuoriuscire
C *vt* **~ notice** passare inosservato; **the name ~s me** mi sfugge il nome
escape chute *n* Aeron scivolo *m*
escape clause *n* clausola *f* di recesso
escapee /ɪskeɪˈpiː/ *n* evaso *m*
escape hatch *n* Naut portello *m* di sicurezza
escape key *n* tasto *m* escape
escape route *n* (for fugitives) itinerario *m* di fuga; (in case of fire etc) percorso *m* di emergenza
escapism /ɪˈskeɪpɪzm/ *n* evasione *f* dalla realtà
escapologist /eskəˈpɒlədʒɪst/ *n illusionista (mf) capace di liberarsi dalle catene*
escarpment /esˈkɑːpmənt/ *n* scarpata *f*
eschew /ɪsˈtʃuː/ *vt* evitare ‹*discussion*›; rifuggire ‹*temptation*›; rifuggire da ‹*violence*›
escort¹ /ˈeskɔːt/ *n* (of person) accompagnatore, -trice *mf*; Mil etc scorta *f*
escort² /ɪˈskɔːt/ *vt* accompagnare; Mil etc scortare
Eskimo /ˈeskɪməʊ/ *n* esquimese *mf*
esophagus /ɪˈsɒfəgəs/ *n* AmE **oesophagus**
esoteric /esəˈterɪk/ *adj* esoterico
ESP *n abbr* **1** (**extrasensory perception**) ESP *f* **2** (**English for Special Purposes**)
esp. *abbr* (**especially**) specialmente
especial /ɪˈspeʃl/ *adj* speciale
🔑 **especially** /ɪˈspeʃəlɪ/ *adv* specialmente; ‹*kind*› particolarmente
espionage /ˈespɪənɑːʒ/ *n* spionaggio *m*
espouse /ɪˈspaʊz/ *vt* abbracciare ‹*cause*›
espresso /eˈspresəʊ/ *n* (coffee) espresso *m*
Esq. *abbr* BrE (**Esquire**) **James McBride, ~** Egr. Sig. James McBride
essay /ˈeseɪ/ *n* saggio *m*; Sch tema *f*
essence /ˈesns/ *n* essenza *f*; **in ~** in sostanza
🔑 **essential** /ɪˈsenʃl/ **A** *adj* essenziale
B *n* **the ~s** *pl* l'essenziale *msg*
essentially /ɪˈsenʃəlɪ/ *adv* essenzialmente
essential oil *n* olio *m* essenziale
est *abbr* (**established**) fondato nel
EST *abbr* AmE (**Eastern Standard Time**) *ora (f) solare degli stati orientali dell'America settentrionale*
🔑 **establish** /ɪˈstæblɪʃ/ *vt* stabilire ‹*contact, lead*›; fondare ‹*firm*›; (prove) accertare; **~ oneself as** affermarsi come
established /ɪˈstæblɪʃt/ *adj* ‹*way of doing something, view*› generalmente accettato; ‹*company*› affidabile; ‹*brand*› riconosciuto; **a well ~ fact** un dato di fatto; **the ~ church** la religione di Stato
establishment /ɪˈstæblɪʃmənt/ *n* (firm) azienda *f*; **the E~** l'establishment *m*
🔑 **estate** /ɪˈsteɪt/ *n* tenuta *f*; (possessions) patrimonio *m*; (housing) quartiere *m* residenziale
estate agency *n* agenzia *f* immobiliare
estate agent *n* agente *mf* immobiliare
estate car *n* giardiniera *f*
estate duty *n* BrE imposta *f* di successione
esteem /ɪˈstiːm/ **A** *n* stima *f*
B *vt* stimare; (consider) giudicare
ester /ˈestə(r)/ *n* estere *m*
estimate¹ /ˈestɪmət/ *n* valutazione *f*; Comm preventivo *m*; **at a rough ~** a occhio e croce
🔑 **estimate²** /ˈestɪmeɪt/ *vt* stimare
estimated time of arrival /ˈestɪmeɪtɪd/ *n* ora *f* prevista di arrivo
estimation /estɪˈmeɪʃn/ *n* (esteem) stima *f*; **in my ~** (judgement) a mio giudizio
estimator /ˈestɪmeɪtə(r)/ *n* AmE *geometra (mf) che calcola quantità e costo di materiali da costruzione*
Estonia /ɪˈstəʊnɪə/ *n* Estonia *f*
estrange /ɪˈstreɪndʒ/ *vt* estraniare; **~d from somebody** separato da qualcuno; **her ~d husband** il marito da cui è separata
estrangement /ɪˈstreɪndʒmənt/ *n* disamoramento *m*
estuary /ˈestjʊərɪ/ *n* estuario *m*
ETA *n abbr* (**estimated time of arrival**) *ora (f) prevista di arrivo*
et al. /etˈæl/ *abbr* (**et alii**) e altri
🔑 **etc.** /etˈsetərə/ *abbr* (**et cetera**) ecc.
et cetera, etcetera /etˈsetərə/ *adv* eccetera
etch /etʃ/ *vt* incidere all'acquaforte; **~ed on her memory** fig impresso nella sua memoria
etching /ˈetʃɪŋ/ *n* acquaforte *f*
eternal /ɪˈtɜːnl/ *adj* eterno
eternal life *n* vita *f* eterna
eternally /ɪˈtɜːnəlɪ/ *adv* eternamente
eternal triangle *n* eterno triangolo *m*
eternity /ɪˈtɜːnətɪ/ *n* eternità
ether /ˈiːθə(r)/ *n* etere *m*
ethereal /ɪˈθɪərɪəl/ *adj* etereo
ethic /ˈeθɪk/ *n* etica *f*
ethical /ˈeθɪkl/ *adj* etico
ethical bank *n* banca *f* etica
ethics /ˈeθɪks/ *nsg* etica *fsg*
Ethiopia /iːθɪˈəʊpɪə/ *n* Etiopia *f*
ethnic /ˈeθnɪk/ *adj* etnico
ethnically /ˈeθnɪklɪ/ *adv* etnicamente
ethnic cleansing *n* epurazione *f* etnica
ethnic minority *n* minoranza *f* etnica

🔑 parola chiave

ethnology /eθ'nɒlədʒɪ/ *n* etnologia *f*
ethos /'iːθɒs/ *n* **company ~** filosofia *f* dell'azienda
e-ticket /'iːtɪkɪt/ *n* Comput biglietto *m* elettronico
etiquette /'etɪket/ *n* etichetta *f*
etymology /etɪ'mɒlədʒɪ/ *n* etimologia *f*
EU *n abbr* (**European Union**) UE *f*
eucalyptus /juːkə'lɪptəs/ *n* eucalipto *m*
eugenics /juː'dʒenɪks/ *nsg* eugenetica *fsg*
eulogize /'juːlədʒaɪz/ **A** *vt* fare il panegirico di
B *vi* **~ over something** tessere le lodi di qualcosa
eulogy /'juːlədʒɪ/ *n* elogio *m*
eunuch /'juːnək/ *n* eunuco *m*
euphemism /'juːfəmɪzm/ *n* eufemismo *m*
euphemistic /juːfə'mɪstɪk/ *adj* eufemistico
euphemistically /juːfə'mɪstɪklɪ/ *adv* eufemisticamente
euphoria /juː'fɔːrɪə/ *n* euforia *f*
euphoric /juː'fɒrɪk/ *adj* euforico
Eurasian /jʊ'reɪʒ(ə)n/ *adj* ‹*people, region*› eurasiatico
Euratom /jʊr'ætəm/ *n abbr* (**European Atomic Energy Community**) Euratom *f*
eurhythmics /jʊ'rɪðmɪks/ *nsg* ginnastica *fsg* ritmica
euro /'jʊərəʊ/ *n* euro *m inv*
Eurobond *n* eurobbligazione *f*
Eurocheque *n* eurochèque *m*
Eurocrat /'jʊərəʊkræt/ *n* eurocrate *mf*
Eurocurrency *n* eurovaluta *f*
Eurodollar *n* eurodollaro *m*
Euromarket *n* euromercato *m*
Euro-MP *n* eurodeputato, -a *mf*
Europe /'jʊərəp/ *n* Europa *f*
European /jʊərə'pɪən/ *adj & n* europeo, -a *mf*
European Bank for Reconstruction and Development *n* Banca *f* Europea per la Ricostruzione e lo Sviluppo
European Commission *n* Commissione *f* Europea
European Community *n* Comunità *f* Europea
European Court of Human Rights *n* Corte *f* europea per i diritti dell'uomo
European Court of Justice *n* Corte *f* europea di giustizia
European Economic Community *n* Comunità *f* Economica Europea
European Free Trade Association *n* Associazione *f* Europea di Libero Scambio
European Health Insurance Card *n* Tessera *f* Europea Assicurazione Malattia
European Monetary System *n* Sistema *m* Monetario Europeo
European Monetary Union *n* Unione *f* Monetaria Europea
European Parliament *n* Parlamento *m* Europeo
European Union *n* Unione *f* Europea
Euro-sceptic *n* BrE euroscettico, -a *mf*
euthanasia /jʊθə'neɪzɪə/ *n* eutanasia *f*
evacuate /ɪ'vækjʊeɪt/ *vt* evacuare ‹*building, area*›
evacuation /ɪvækjʊ'eɪʃn/ *n* evacuazione *f*
evacuee /ɪvæjʊ'iː/ *n* sfollato *m*
evade /ɪ'veɪd/ *vt* evadere ‹*taxes*›; evitare ‹*the enemy, authorities*›; **~ the issue** evitare l'argomento
evaluate /ɪ'væljʊeɪt/ *vt* valutare
evaluation /ɪvæljʊ'eɪʃn/ *n* valutazione *f*, stima *f*
evangelical /iːvæn'dʒelɪkl/ *adj* evangelico
evangelist /ɪ'vændʒəlɪst/ *n* evangelista *mf*
evaporate /ɪ'væpəreɪt/ *vi* evaporare; fig svanire
evaporated milk *n* latte *m* condensato
evaporation /ɪvæpə'reɪʃn/ *n* evaporazione *f*
evasion /ɪ'veɪʒn/ *n* evasione *f*
evasive /ɪ'veɪsɪv/ *adj* evasivo
evasively /ɪ'veɪsɪvlɪ/ *adv* in modo evasivo
eve /iːv/ *n* literary vigilia *f*
even /'iːvn/ **A** *adj* (level) piatto; (same, equal) uguale; (regular) regolare; ‹*number*› pari; **get ~ with** vendicarsi di; **now we're ~** adesso siamo pari
B *adv* anche, ancora; **~ if** anche se; **~ so** con tutto ciò; **not ~** nemmeno; **~ bigger/hotter** ancora più grande/caldo
C *vt* **~ the score** Sport pareggiare
■ **even out** *vi* livellarsi
■ **even up** *vt* livellare
even-handed /-'hændɪd/ *adj* imparziale
evening /'iːvnɪŋ/ *n* sera *f*; (whole evening) serata *f*; **this ~** stasera; **in the ~** la sera
evening class *n* corso *m* serale
evening dress *n* (man's) abito *m* scuro; (woman's) abito *m* da sera
evening performance *n* spettacolo *m* serale
evening primrose *n* enotera *f*
evening star *n* Venere *f*
evenly /'iːvnlɪ/ *adv* ‹*distributed*› uniformemente; ‹*breathe*› regolarmente; ‹*divided*› in uguali parti
event /ɪ'vent/ *n* avvenimento *m*; (function) manifestazione *f*; Sport gara *f*; **in the ~ of** nell'eventualità di; **in the ~** alla fine
even-tempered /-'tempəd/ *adj* pacato
eventful /ɪ'ventfʊl/ *adj* movimentato
eventing /ɪ'ventɪŋ/ *n* BrE concorso *m* ippico completo
eventual /ɪ'ventjʊəl/ *adj* **the ~ winner was...** alla fine il vincitore è stato ...
eventuality /ɪventjʊ'ælətɪ/ *n* eventualità
eventually /ɪ'ventjʊəlɪ/ *adv* alla fine; **~!**

finalmente!

ever /'evə(r)/ *adv* mai; **I haven't ~...** non ho mai ...; **for ~** per sempre; **hardly ~** quasi mai; **~ since** da quando; (since that time) da allora; **~ so** infml veramente

evergreen /'evəgriːn/ *n* sempreverde *m*

everlasting /evə'læstɪŋ/ *adj* eterno

every /'evrɪ/ *adj* ogni; **~ one** ciascuno; **~ other day** un giorno sì un giorno no

everybody /'evrɪbɒdɪ/ *pron* tutti *pl*

everyday /'evrɪdeɪ/ *adj* quotidiano, di ogni giorno

everyone /'evrɪwʌn/ *pron* tutti *pl*; **~ else** tutti gli altri

everyplace /'evrɪpleɪs/ *adv* AmE infml = **everywhere**

everything /'evrɪθɪŋ/ *pron* tutto; **~ else** tutto il resto

everywhere /'evrɪweə(r)/ *adv* dappertutto; (wherever) dovunque

evict /ɪ'vɪkt/ *vt* sfrattare

eviction /ɪ'vɪkʃn/ *n* sfratto *m*

evidence /'evɪdəns/ *n* evidenza *f*; Jur testimonianza *f*; **give ~** testimoniare

evident /'evɪdənt/ *adj* evidente

evidently /'evɪdəntlɪ/ *adv* evidentemente

evil /'iːvl/ **A** *adj* cattivo
B *n* male *m*

evil-smelling /-'smelɪŋ/ *adj* puzzolente

evocative /ɪ'vɒkətɪv/ *adj* evocativo; **be ~ of** evocare

evoke /ɪ'vəʊk/ *vt* evocare

evolution /iːvə'luːʃn/ *n* evoluzione *f*

evolutionary /iːvə'luːʃn(ə)rɪ/ *adj* evolutivo

evolve /ɪ'vɒlv/ **A** *vt* evolvere
B *vi* evolversi

ewe /juː/ *n* pecora *f*

ex /eks/ *n* infml (former partner) ex *mf*

ex+ *pref* ex+

exacerbate /ɪg'sæsəbeɪt/ *vt* esacerbare ‹*situation*›

exact /ɪg'zækt/ **A** *adj* esatto
B *vt* esigere

exacting /ɪg'zæktɪŋ/ *adj* esigente

exactitude /ɪg'zæktɪtjuːd/ *n* esattezza *f*

exactly /ɪg'zæktlɪ/ *adv* esattamente; **not ~** non proprio

exactness /ɪg'zæktnɪs/ *n* precisione *f*

exaggerate /ɪg'zædʒəreɪt/ *vt & vi* esagerare

exaggerated /ɪg'zædʒəreɪtɪd/ *adj* esagerato; **he has an ~ sense of his own importance** si crede chissà chi

exaggeration /ɪgzædʒə'reɪʃn/ *n* esagerazione *f*

exalt /ɪg'zɔːlt/ *vt* elevare; (praise) vantare

exam /ɪg'zæm/ *n* esame *m*

examination /ɪgzæmɪ'neɪʃn/ *n* esame *m*; (of patient) visita *f*; (of wreckage) ispezione *f*

examination paper *n* testo *m* d'esame

examine /ɪg'zæmɪn/ *vt* esaminare; visitare ‹*patient*›

examinee /ɪgzæmɪ'niː/ *n* esaminando *m*

examiner /ɪg'zæmɪnə(r)/ *n* Sch esaminatore, -trice *mf*

example /ɪg'zɑːmpl/ *n* esempio *m*; **for ~** per esempio; **make an ~ of somebody** punire qualcuno per dare un esempio; **be an ~ to somebody** dare il buon esempio a qualcuno

exasperate /ɪg'zæspəreɪt/ *vt* esasperare

exasperation /ɪgzæspə'reɪʃn/ *n* esasperazione *f*

excavate /'ekskəveɪt/ *vt* scavare; Archaeol fare gli scavi di

excavation /ekskə'veɪʃn/ *n* scavo *m*

excavator /'ekskəveɪtə(r)/ *n* (machine) escavatrice *f*, escavatore *m*

exceed /ɪk'siːd/ *vt* eccedere

exceedingly /ɪk'siːdɪŋlɪ/ *adv* estremamente

excel /ɪk'sel/ *v* (*pt/pp* **excelled**) **A** *vi* eccellere
B *vt* **~ oneself** superare se stessi

excellence /'eksələns/ *n* eccellenza *f*

Excellency /'eksələnsɪ/ *n* (title) Eccellenza *f*

excellent /'eksələnt/ *adj* eccellente

excellently /'eksələntlɪ/ *adv* in modo eccellente

except /ɪk'sept/ **A** *prep* eccetto, tranne; **~ for** eccetto, tranne; **~ that ...** eccetto che ...
B *vt* eccettuare

excepting /ɪk'septɪŋ/ *prep* eccetto, tranne

exception /ɪk'sepʃn/ *n* eccezione *f*; **take ~ to** fare obiezioni a

exceptional /ɪk'sepʃənəl/ *adj* eccezionale

exceptionally /ɪk'sepʃənəlɪ/ *adv* eccezionalmente

excerpt /'eksɜːpt/ *n* estratto *m*

excess /ɪk'ses/ *n* eccesso *m*; **in ~ of** oltre

excess baggage *n* bagaglio *m* eccedente

excess fare *n* supplemento *m*

excessive /ɪk'sesɪv/ *adj* eccessivo

excessively /ɪk'sesɪvlɪ/ *adv* eccessivamente

excess postage *n* soprattassa *f* postale

excess profits *npl* sovraprofitto *m*

exchange /ɪks'tʃeɪndʒ/ **A** *n* scambio *m*; Teleph centrale *f*; Comm cambio *m*; **[stock] ~** borsa *f* valori; **in ~** in cambio (**for** di)
B *vt* scambiare (**for** con), cambiare ‹*money*›; **~ views** scambiarsi i punti di vista; **~ contracts** fare il rogito
C *vi* (on house purchase) fare il rogito

exchange control *n* controllo *m* dei cambi

exchange controls *npl* misure *fpl* di controllo dei cambi

exchange rate *n* tasso *m* di cambio

Exchange Rate Mechanism *n* meccanismo *m* di cambio dello Sme

exchequer /ɪks'tʃekə(r)/ *n* Pol tesoro *m*

excise¹ /'eksaɪz/ *n* dazio *m*
excise² /ek'saɪz/ *vt* recidere
excise duty *n* dazio *m*
excitable /ɪk'saɪtəbl/ *adj* eccitabile
excite /ɪk'saɪt/ *vt* eccitare
excited /ɪk'saɪtɪd/ *adj* eccitato; **get ~** eccitarsi
excitedly /ɪk'saɪtɪdlɪ/ *adv* tutto eccitato
excitement /ɪk'saɪtmənt/ *n* eccitazione *f*
exciting /ɪk'saɪtɪŋ/ *adj* eccitante; ‹*story, film*› appassionante; ‹*holiday*› entusiasmante
excl. *abbr* (**excluding**) escluso
exclaim /ɪk'skleɪm/ *vt & vi* esclamare
exclamation /ekskla'meɪʃn/ *n* esclamazione *f*
exclamation mark, AmE **exclamation point** *n* punto *m* esclamativo
exclude /ɪk'sklu:d/ *vt* escludere
excluding /ɪk'sklu:dɪŋ/ *pron* escluso
exclusion /ɪk'sklu:ʒn/ *n* esclusione *f*
exclusion zone *n* zona *f* proibita
exclusive /ɪk'sklu:sɪv/ *adj* ‹*rights, club*› esclusivo; ‹*interview*› in esclusiva; **~ of...** ...escluso
exclusively /ɪk'sklu:sɪvlɪ/ *adv* esclusivamente
excommunicate /ekskə'mjun:nɪkeɪt/ *vt* scomunicare
excrement /'ekskrɪmənt/ *n* escremento *m*
excreta /ɪk'skri:tə/ *npl* escrementi *mpl*
excrete /ɪk'skri:t/ *vt* espellere; secernere ‹*liquid*›
excretion /ɪk'skri:ʃn/ *n* (of animal, human) escremento *m*
excruciating /ɪk'skru:ʃɪeɪtɪŋ/ *adj* ‹*pain*› atroce; infml (very bad) spaventoso
excursion /ɪk'skɜ:ʃn/ *n* escursione *f*
excusable /ɪk'skju:zəbl/ *adj* perdonabile
excuse¹ /ɪk'skju:s/ *n* scusa *f*
excuse² /ɪk'skju:z/ *vt* scusare; **~ from** esonerare da; **~ me!** (to get attention) scusi!; (to get past) permesso!, scusi!; (indignant) come ha detto?
ex-directory *adj* **be ~** non figurare sull'elenco telefonico
exec /ɪg'zek/ *n abbr* AmE infml (**executive**) executive *mf*, dirigente *mf*
execrable /'eksɪkrəbl/ *adj* esecrabile
executable file /'eksɪkju:təbl/ *n* Comput eseguibile *m*
execute /'eksɪkju:t/ *vt* eseguire; (put to death) giustiziare; attuare ‹*plan*›
execution /eksɪ'kju:ʃn/ *n* esecuzione *f*; (of plan) attuazione *f*
executioner /eksɪ'kju:ʃənə(r)/ *n* boia *m inv*
executive /ɪg'zekjʊtɪv/ **A** *adj* esecutivo **B** *n* dirigente *mf*; Pol esecutivo *m*
executive committee *n* comitato *m* esecutivo
executive director *n* direttore, -trice *mf* [esecutivo, -a]
executive jet *n* jet *m inv* privato
executive producer *n* Cinema direttore, -trice *mf* di produzione
executive secretary *n* segretario, -a *mf* di direzione
executor /ɪg'zekjʊtə(r)/ *n* Jur esecutore, -trice *mf*
exemplary /ɪg'zemplərɪ/ *adj* esemplare
exemplify /ɪg'zemplɪfaɪ/ *vt* (*pt/pp* **-ied**) esemplificare
exempt /ɪg'zempt/ **A** *adj* esente **B** *vt* esentare (**from** da)
exemption /ɪg'zempʃn/ *n* esenzione *f*
exercise /'eksəsaɪz/ **A** *n* esercizio *m*; Mil esercitazione *f*; **physical ~s** ginnastica *f*; **take ~** fare del moto; **you need more ~** devi muoverti di più **B** *vt* esercitare ‹*muscles, horse*›; portare a spasso ‹*dog*›; usare ‹*patience*›; mettere in pratica ‹*skills*› **C** *vi* esercitarsi; **~ more** fare più moto
exercise bike *n* cyclette® *f inv*
exercise book *n* quaderno *m*
exert /ɪg'zɜ:t/ *vt* esercitare; **~ oneself** sforzarsi
exertion /ɪg'zɜ:ʃn/ *n* sforzo *m*
ex gratia /eks'greɪʃə/ *adj* ‹*award, payment*› a titolo di favore
exhale /eks'heɪl/ *vt & vi* esalare
exhaust /ɪg'zɔ:st/ *n* Auto scappamento *m*; (pipe) tubo *m* di scappamento
exhausted /ɪg'zɔ:stɪd/ *adj* esausto
exhaust fumes **A** *npl* fumi *mpl* di scarico *m* **B** *vt* esaurire
exhausting /ɪg'zɔ:stɪŋ/ *adj* estenuante; ‹*climate, person*› sfibrante
exhaustion /ɪg'zɔ:stʃn/ *n* esaurimento *m*
exhaustive /ɪg'zɔ:stɪv/ *adj* fig esauriente
exhibit /ɪg'zɪbɪt/ **A** *n* oggetto *m* esposto; Jur reperto *m* **B** *vt* esporre; fig dimostrare
exhibition /eksɪ'bɪʃn/ *n* mostra *f*; (of strength, skill) dimostrazione *f*
exhibition centre *n* palazzo *m* delle esposizioni
exhibitionist /eksɪ'bɪʃənɪst/ *n* esibizionista *mf*
exhibitor /ɪg'zɪbɪtə(r)/ *n* espositore, -trice *mf*
exhilarated /ɪg'zɪləreɪtɪd/ *adj* rallegrato
exhilarating /ɪg'zɪləreɪtɪŋ/ *adj* stimolante; ‹*mountain air*› tonificante
exhilaration /ɪgzɪlə'reɪʃn/ *n* allegria *f*
exhort /ɪg'zɔ:t/ *vt* esortare
exhume /ɪg'zju:m/ *vt* esumare
exile /'eksaɪl/ **A** *n* esilio *m*; (person) esule *mf* **B** *vt* esiliare
exist /ɪg'zɪst/ *vi* esistere
existence /ɪg'zɪstəns/ *n* esistenza *f*; **in ~**

esistente; **be in ~** esistere
existential /egzɪ'stenʃ(ə)l/ *adj* esistenziale
existentialism /egzɪ'stenʃəlɪzm/ *n* esistenzialismo *m*
existing /ɪg'zɪstɪŋ/ *adj* ‹*policy, management, leadership*› attuale; ‹*laws, order*› vigente
exit /'eksɪt/ **A** *n* uscita *f*; Theat uscita *f* di scena **B** *vi* Theat uscire di scena; Comput uscire (**from** da)
exit sign *n* cartello *m* di uscita
exodus /'eksədəs/ *n* esodo *m*
ex officio /eksə'fɪʃɪəʊ/ *adj* ‹*member*› di diritto
exonerate /ɪg'zɒnəreɪt/ *vt* esonerare
exorbitant /ɪg'zɔːbɪtənt/ *adj* esorbitante
exorcise /'eksɔːsaɪz/ *vt* esorcizzare
exorcism /'eksɔːsɪzm/ *n* esorcismo *m*
exorcist /'eksɔːsɪst/ *n* esorcista *mf*
exotic /ɪg'zɒtɪk/ *adj* esotico
exotica /ɪg'zɒtɪkə/ *npl* oggetti *mpl* esotici
⚷ **expand** /ɪk'spænd/ **A** *vt* espandere; sviluppare ‹*economy*›
B *vi* espandersi; Comm svilupparsi; ‹*metal*› dilatarsi
■ **expand on** *vt* (explain better) approfondire
expandable /ɪk'spændəbl/ *adj* Comput ‹*memory*› espandibile
expanding /ɪk'spændɪŋ/ *adj* ‹*file*› a soffietto *inv*; ‹*population, sector*› in espansione; ‹*bracelet*› allungabile
expanse /ɪk'spæns/ *n* estensione *f*
expansion /ɪk'spænʃn/ *n* espansione *f*; Comm sviluppo *m*; (of metal) dilatazione *f*
expansion board, **expansion card** *n* Comput scheda *f* di espansione
expansionist /ɪk'spænʃənɪst/ *n & adj* espansionista *mf*
expansion slot *n* Comput fessura *f* [per la scheda] di espansione, slot *m* di espansione
expansive /ɪk'spænsɪv/ *adj* espansivo
expatriate /eks'pætrɪət/ *n* espatriato, -a *mf*
⚷ **expect** /ɪk'spekt/ *vt* aspettare ‹*letter, baby*›; (suppose) pensare; (demand) esigere; **I ~ so** penso di sì; **we ~ to arrive on Monday** contiamo di arrivare lunedì; **I didn't ~ that** questo non me lo aspettavo; **she ~s too much from him** pretende troppo da lui; **be ~ing** essere in stato interessante
expectancy /ɪk'spektənsɪ/ *n* aspettativa *f*
expectant /ɪk'spektənt/ *adj* in attesa; **~ mother** donna *f* incinta
expectantly /ɪk'spektəntlɪ/ *adv* con impazienza
⚷ **expectation** /ekspek'teɪʃn/ *n* aspettativa *f*, speranza *f*
expediency /ɪk'spiːdɪənsɪ/ *n* (appropriateness) opportunità *f*; (self-interest) opportunismo *m*
expedient /ɪk'spiːdɪənt/ **A** *adj* conveniente **B** *n* espediente *m*
expedite /'ekspɪdaɪt/ *vt* fml accelerare
expedition /ekspɪ'dɪʃn/ *n* spedizione *f*
expeditionary /ekspɪ'dɪʃənərɪ/ *adj* Mil di spedizione
expeditionary force *n* corpo *m* di spedizione
expel /ɪk'spel/ *vt* (*pt/pp* **expelled**) espellere
expend /ɪk'spend/ *vt* consumare
expendable /ɪk'spendəbl/ *adj* sacrificabile
expenditure /ɪk'spendɪtʃə(r)/ *n* spesa *f*
⚷ **expense** /ɪk'spens/ *n* spesa *f*; **business ~s** *pl* spese *fpl*; **at my ~** a mie spese; **at the ~ of** fig a spese di
expense account *n* conto *m* spese
⚷ **expensive** /ɪk'spensɪv/ *adj* caro, costoso
expensively /ɪk'spensɪvlɪ/ *adv* costosamente
⚷ **experience** /ɪk'spɪərɪəns/ **A** *n* esperienza *f* **B** *vt* provare ‹*sensation*›; avere ‹*problem*›
experienced /ɪk'spɪərɪənst/ *adj* esperto
⚷ **experiment** /ɪk'sperɪmənt/ **A** *n* esperimento **B** /ɪk'sperɪment/ *vi* sperimentare
experimental /ɪksperɪ'mentl/ *adj* sperimentale
experimentation /ɪksperɪmen'teɪʃn/ *n* sperimentazione *f*; **~ with drugs** esperienza *f* della droga
⚷ **expert** /'ekspɜːt/ *adj & n* esperto, -a *mf*
expertise /ekspɜː'tiːz/ *n* competenza *f*
expertly /'ekspɜːtlɪ/ *adv* abilmente
expiate /'ekspɪeɪt/ *vt* espiare ‹*crime, sin*›; fare ammenda per ‹*guilt*›
expiration /ekspɪ'reɪʃn/ *n* (end, exhalation) espirazione *f*
expire /ɪk'spaɪə(r)/ *vi* scadere
expiry /ɪk'spaɪərɪ/ *n* scadenza *f*
expiry date *n* data *f* di scadenza
⚷ **explain** /ɪk'spleɪn/ *vt* spiegare
■ **explain away** *vt* (give reasons for) trovare delle giustificazioni per
⚷ **explanation** /eksplə'neɪʃn/ *n* spiegazione *f*
explanatory /ɪk'splænətərɪ/ *adj* esplicativo
expletive /ɪk'spliːtɪv/ *n* imprecazione *f*
explicit /ɪk'splɪsɪt/ *adj* esplicito
explicitly /ɪk'splɪsɪtlɪ/ *adv* esplicitamente
explode /ɪk'spləʊd/ **A** *vi* esplodere **B** *vt* fare esplodere
exploit¹ /'eksplɔɪt/ *n* impresa *f*
exploit² /ɪk'splɔɪt/ *vt* sfruttare
exploitation /eksplɔɪ'teɪʃn/ *n* sfruttamento *m*
exploitative /ɪk'splɔɪtətɪv/ *adj* inteso a sfruttare gli individui; ‹*attitude, system*› a carattere di sfruttamento
exploration /eksplə'reɪʃn/ *n* esplorazione *f*
exploratory /ɪk'splɒrətərɪ/ *adj* esplorativo
⚷ **explore** /ɪk'splɔː(r)/ *vt* esplorare; fig studiare ‹*implications*›
explorer /ɪk'splɔːrə(r)/ *n* esploratore, -trice *mf*
explosion /ɪk'spləʊʒn/ *n* esplosione *f*

⚷ parola chiave

explosive /ɪk'spləʊsɪv/ *adj & n* esplosivo *m*
exponent /ɪk'spəʊnənt/ *n* esponente *mf*
exponential /ekspə'nenʃəl/ *adj* esponenziale
export¹ /'ekspɔːt/ *n* esportazione *f*
export² /ek'spɔːt/ *vt* esportare
export agent *n* esportatore, -trice *mf*
export control *n* controllo *m* delle esportazioni
export credit *n* credito *m* all'esportazione
export drive *n* campagna *f* di esportazione
export duty *n* tassa *f* di esportazione
export earnings *npl* ricavato *m* delle esportazioni
exporter /ek'spɔːtə(r)/ *n* esportatore, -trice *mf*
export finance *n* finanziamento *m* delle esportazioni
export-import company *n* azienda di import-export
export licence *n* licenza *f* di esportazione
export market *n* mercato *m* delle esportazioni
export trade *n* commercio *m* di esportazione
expose /ɪk'spəʊz/ *vt* esporre; ‹*reveal*› svelare; smascherare ‹*traitor etc*›
exposé /ɪk'spəʊzeɪ/ *n* (of scandal) rivelazioni *fpl*
exposition /ekspə'zɪʃn/ *n* (of facts) esposizione *f*
exposure /ɪk'spəʊʒə(r)/ *n* esposizione *f*; Med espozione *f* prolungata al freddo/caldo; (of crimes) smascheramento *m*; **24 ~s** Phot 24 pose
exposure meter *n* Phot esposimetro *m*
exposure time *n* Phot tempo *m* di esposizione
expound /ɪk'spaʊnd/ *vt* esporre
express /ɪk'spres/ **A** *adj* espresso
B *adv* ‹*send*› per espresso
C *n* (train) espresso *m*
D *vt* esprimere; **~ oneself** esprimersi
expression /ɪk'spreʃn/ *n* espressione *f*
expressionless /ɪk'spreʃənlɪs/ *adj* ‹*tone, voice*› distaccato; ‹*playing*› piatto; ‹*eyes, face*› inespressivo
expressive /ɪk'spresɪv/ *adj* espressivo
expressively /ɪk'spresɪvlɪ/ *adv* espressamente
express lane *n* corsia *f* a scorrimento veloce
expulsion /ɪk'spʌlʃn/ *n* espulsione *f*
expurgate /'ekspəgeɪt/ *vt* espurgare
exquisite /ek'skwɪzɪt/ *adj* squisito
exquisitely /ek'skwɪzɪtlɪ/ *adv* ‹*dressed, written*› in modo elegante e raffinato; **~ beautiful** di una bellezza fine
ex-serviceman /'sɜːvɪsmən/ *n* ex-combattente *m*
ex-servicewoman /'sɜːvɪswʊmən/ *n* ex-combattente *f*
extant /ɪk'stænt/ *adj* ancora esistente
extempore /ɪk'stempərɪ/ *adv* ‹*speak*› senza preparazione
extend /ɪk'stend/ **A** *vt* prolungare ‹*visit, road*›; prorogare ‹*visa, contract*›; ampliare ‹*building, knowledge*›; (stretch out) allungare; tendere ‹*hand*›
B *vi* ‹*garden, knowledge*› estendersi
extendable /ɪk'stendəbl/ *adj* (cable) allungabile; ‹*contract*› prorogabile
extension /ɪk'stenʃn/ *n* prolungamento *m*; (of visa, contract) proroga *f*; (of treaty) ampliamento *m*; (part of building) annesso *m*; (length of cable) prolunga *f*; Teleph interno *m*; **~ 226** interno 226; (hair) **~s** le extension
extension ladder *n* scala *f* allungabile
extension lead *n* Electr prolunga *f*
extensive /ɪk'stensɪv/ *adj* ampio, vasto
extensively /ɪk'stensɪvlɪ/ *adv* ampiamente
extent /ɪk'stent/ *n* (scope) portata *f*; **to a certain ~** fino a un certo punto; **to such an ~ that …** fino al punto che …
extenuating /ɪk'stenjʊeɪtɪŋ/ *adj* **~ circumstances** attenuanti *fpl*
exterior /ɪk'stɪərɪə(r)/ *adj & n* esterno *m*
exterminate /ɪk'stɜːmɪneɪt/ *vt* sterminare
extermination /ɪkstɜːmɪ'neɪʃn/ *n* sterminio *m*
external /ɪk'stɜːnl/ *adj* esterno; **for ~ use only** Med per uso esterno
externalize /ɪk'stɜːnəlaɪz/ *vt* esteriorizzare
externally /ɪk'stɜːnəlɪ/ *adv* esternamente
externals /ɪk'stɜːn(ə)lz/ *npl* apparenze *fpl*
extinct /ɪk'stɪŋkt/ *adj* estinto
extinction /ɪk'stɪŋkʃn/ *n* estinzione *f*
extinguish /ɪk'stɪŋgwɪʃ/ *vt* estinguere
extinguisher /ɪk'stɪŋgwɪʃə(r)/ *n* estintore *m*
extol /ɪk'stəʊl/ *vt* (*pt/pp* **extolled**) lodare
extort /ɪk'stɔːt/ *vt* estorcere
extortion /ɪk'stɔːʃn/ *n* estorsione *f*
extortionate /ɪk'stɔːʃənət/ *adj* esorbitante
extra /'ekstrə/ **A** *adj* in più; ‹*train*› straordinario; **an ~ £10** 10 sterline extra, 10 sterline in più
B *adv* in più; (especially) più; **pay ~** pagare in più, pagare extra; **~ strong/busy** fortissimo/occupatissimo
C *n* Theat comparsa *f*; **~s** *pl* extra *mpl*
extra charge *n* supplemento *m*; **at no ~** senza ulteriori spese
extract¹ /'ekstrækt/ *n* estratto *m*
extract² /ɪk'strækt/ *vt* estrarre ‹*tooth, oil*›; strappare ‹*secret*›; ricavare ‹*truth*›
extraction /ɪk'strækʃn/ *n* (process) estrazione *f*; **of French ~** di origine francese
extractor /ɪk'stræktə(r)/, **extractor fan** *n* aspiratore *m*
extra-curricular /-kə'rɪkjʊlə(r)/ *adj* extrascolastico
extradite /'ekstrədaɪt/ *vt* Jur estradare

extradition /ekstrə'dɪʃn/ *n* estradizione *f*
extra-dry *adj* ‹*sherry, wine*› extra dry *inv*
extra-fast *adj* ultrarapido
extra-large *adj* ‹*pullover, shirt*› extra large *inv*
extramarital /ekstrə'mærɪtəl/ *adj* extraconiugale
extramural /ekstrə'mjʊərəl/ *adj* BrE Univ ‹*course, lecture*› organizzato dall'università e aperto a tutti

e

extraneous /ɪk'streɪnɪəs/ *adj* (not essential) inessenziale; ‹*issue, detail*› superfluo
extraordinarily /ɪk'strɔːdɪnərɪlɪ/ *adv* straordinariamente
extraordinary /ɪk'strɔːdɪnərɪ/ *adj* straordinario
extrapolate /ɪk'stræpəleɪt/ *vt* arguire; Math estrapolare
extrasensory perception /ekstrə'sensərɪ/ *n* percezione *f* extrasensoriale
extra-special *adj* eccezionale
extra-strong *adj* ‹*thread*› robustissimo; ‹*coffee*› fortissimo; ‹*disinfectant, weed killer*› potentissimo; ‹*paper*› ultraresistente *inv*
extraterrestrial /ekstrətɪ'restrɪəl/ *n & adj* extraterrestre *mf*
extra time *n* tempo *m* supplementare; **play ~** giocare i tempi supplementari
extravagance /ɪk'strævəgəns/ *n* (with money) prodigalità *f*; (of behaviour) stravaganza *f*
extravagant /ɪk'strævəgənt/ *adj* spendaccione; (bizarre) stravagante; ‹*claim*› esagerato
extravagantly /ɪk'strævəgəntlɪ/ *adv* dispendiosamente
extravaganza /ɪkstrævə'gænzə/ *n* rappresentazione *f* spettacolare
extra virgin olive oil *n* olio *m* extravergine d'oliva
extreme /ɪk'striːm/ **A** *adj* estremo
B *n* estremo *m*; **in the ~** al massimo
🔑 **extremely** /ɪk'striːmlɪ/ *adv* estremamente
extreme sports *npl* sport *mpl* estremi
extremism /ɪk'striːmɪzm/ *n* estremismo *m*
extremist /ɪk'striːmɪst/ *n* estremista *mf*
extremity /ɪk'stremətɪ/ *n* (end) estremità *f*
extricate /'ekstrɪkeɪt/ *vt* districare
extrovert /'ekstrəvɜːt/ *n* estroverso, -a *mf*
exuberance /ɪg'zjuːbərəns/ *n* esuberanza *f*
exuberant /ɪg'zjuːbərənt/ *adj* esuberante
exude /ɪg'zjuːd/ *vt* also fig trasudare
exult /ɪg'zʌlt/ *vi* esultare
exultant /ɪg'zʌltənt/ *adj* esultante; ‹*cry*› di esultanza
exultantly /ɪg'zʌltəntlɪ/ *adv* con esultanza
ex-works *adj* ‹*price, value*› franco fabbrica
🔑 **eye** /aɪ/ **A** *n* occhio *m*; (of needle) cruna *f*; **keep an ~ on** tener d'occhio; **see ~ to ~** aver le stesse idee
B *vt* (*pt/pp* **eyed**, *pres p* **ey[e]ing**) guardare
■ **eye up** *vt* adocchiare ‹*somebody*›
eyeball *n* bulbo *m* oculare
eyebath *n* bagno *m* oculare
eyebrow *n* sopracciglio *m* (*pl* sopracciglia *f*)
eyebrow pencil *n* matita *f* per le sopracciglia
eye-catching /'aɪkætʃɪŋ/ *adj* che attira l'attenzione
eye contact *n* **avoid ~ with somebody** evitare di incrociare lo sguardo di qualcuno; **try to make ~ with somebody** tentare di incrociare lo sguardo di qualcuno
eye drops *npl* collirio *m*
eyeful /'aɪfʊl/ *n* **get an ~ (of something)** avere gli occhi pieni (di qualcosa); infml (good look) lustrarsi la vista
eyeglass *n* (monocle) monocolo *m*
eyeglasses *npl* AmE occhiali *mpl* [da vista]
eyelash *n* ciglio *m* (*pl* ciglia *f*)
eyelet /'aɪlɪt/ *n* occhiello *m*
eye-level *adj* ‹*grill, shelf*› all'altezza degli occhi
eyelid *n* palpebra *f*
eye liner *n* eye liner *m inv*
eye make-up *n* trucco *m* per gli occhi
eye-opener *n* rivelazione *f*
eyepatch *n* benda *f* per gli occhi
eye-shade *n* visiera *f*
eyeshadow *n* ombretto *m*
eyesight *n* vista *f*
eyesore *n* infml pugno *m* nell'occhio
eye strain *n* affaticamento *m* degli occhi
eye test *n* esame *m* della vista
eyewash *n* bagno *m* oculare; fig (nonsense) fumo *m* negli occhi
eyewitness testimone *mf* oculare
eyrie /'ɪərɪ/ *n* nido *m* [d'aquila]
e-zine /'iːziːn/ *n* Comput e-zine *f inv*

🔑 parola chiave

Ff

f, **F** /ef/ *n* (letter) f, F *f inv*; Mus fa *m inv*

F *abbr* (**Fahrenheit**) F

FA *n abbr* BrE (**Football Association**) associazione *f* calcistica britannica, ≈ FIGC *f*

fable /ˈfeɪbl/ *n* favola *f*

fabric /ˈfæbrɪk/ *n* also fig tessuto *m*

fabricate /ˈfæbrɪkeɪt/ *vt* fabbricare; inventare ‹*story*›

fabrication /fæbrɪkeɪʃn/ *n* invenzione *f*; (manufacture) fabbricazione *f*

fabric softener /sɒfnə(r)/ *n* ammorbidente *m*

fabulous /ˈfæbjʊləs/ *adj* infml favoloso

façade /fəˈsɑːd/ *n* (of building, person) facciata *f*

face /feɪs/ **[A]** *n* faccia *f*, viso *m*; (grimace) smorfia *f*; (surface) faccia *f*; (of clock) quadrante *m*; **pull ~s** far boccacce; **in the ~ of** di fronte a; **on the ~ of it** in apparenza **[B]** *vt* essere di fronte a; (confront) affrontare; **~ north** ‹*house*› dare a nord; **~ the fact that** arrendersi al fatto che

▪ **face up to** *vt* accettare ‹*facts*›; affrontare ‹*person*›

face flannel *n* ≈ guanto *m* di spugna

faceless /ˈfeɪslɪs/ *adj* anonimo

facelift /ˈfeɪslɪft/ *n* plastica *f* facciale

face mask *n* (cosmetic) maschera *f* viso

face pack *n* maschera *f* di bellezza

face powder *n* cipria *f*

face saving *adj* ‹*plan, solution*› per salvare la faccia

facet /ˈfæsɪt/ *n* sfaccettatura *f*; fig aspetto *m*

facetious /fəˈsiːʃəs/ *adj* spiritoso; **~ remarks** spiritosaggini *mpl*

face to face **[A]** *adj* ‹*meeting*› a quattr'occhi **[B]** *adv* ‹*be seated*› faccia a faccia; **meet somebody ~ to ~** avere un incontro a quattr'occhi con qualcuno; **come ~ to ~ with** trovarsi di fronte a

face value *n* (of money) valore *m* nominale; **take someone/something at ~** fermarsi alle apparenze

facial /ˈfeɪʃl/ **[A]** *adj* facciale **[B]** *n* trattamento *m* di bellezza al viso

facile /ˈfæsaɪl/ *adj* semplicistico

facilitate /fəˈsɪlɪteɪt/ *vt* rendere possibile; (make easier) facilitare

facilitator /fəˈsɪlɪteɪtə(r)/ *n* mediatore *m*

facility /fəˈsɪlətɪ/ *n* facilità *f*; **facilities** *pl* (of area, in hotel etc) attrezzature *fpl*; **credit facilities** *pl* facilitazioni *fpl* di pagamento

facing /ˈfeɪsɪŋ/ *prep* **~ the sea** ‹*house*› che dà sul mare; **the person ~ me** la persona di fronte a me

facsimile /fækˈsɪməlɪ/ *n* facsimile *m*

fact /fækt/ *n* fatto *m*; **in ~** infatti

fact finding *adj* ‹*mission, tour, trip*› di inchiesta

faction /ˈfækʃn/ *n* fazione *f*

factional /ˈfækʃnəl/ *adj* ‹*leader, activity*› di una fazione; ‹*fighting, arguments*› tra fazioni

factor /ˈfæktə(r)/ *n* fattore *m*

factory /ˈfæktərɪ/ *n* fabbrica *f*

factory farming *n* allevamento *m* su scala industriale

factory floor *n* (place) reparto *m* produzione; (workers) operai *mpl*

factory inspector *n* verificatore, -trice *mf*

factory made *adj* prodotto in fabbrica

factory shop *n negozio (m) di vendita diretta dalla fabbrica al consumatore*

factory unit *n* unità *f* di produzione

factory worker *n* operaio, -a *mf*

fact sheet *n* (one issue) prospetto *m* illustrativo; (periodical) bollettino *m* d'informazione

factual /ˈfæktʃʊəl/ *adj* **be ~** attenersi ai fatti

factually /ˈfæktʃʊəlɪ/ *adv* ‹*inaccurate*› dal punto di vista dei fatti

faculty /ˈfækəltɪ/ *n* facoltà *f*

fad /fæd/ *n* capriccio *m*

faddish /ˈfædɪʃ/ *adj* ‹*person*› sempre in preda a una nuova mania

fade /feɪd/ *vi* sbiadire; ‹*sound, light*› affievolirsi; ‹*flower*› appassire

▪ **fade away** *vi* ‹*sound*› affievolirsi; (dying person) spegnersi

▪ **fade in** *vt* cominciare in dissolvenza ‹*picture*›

▪ **fade out** *vt* finire in dissolvenza ‹*picture*›

faded /ˈfeɪdɪd/ *adj* ‹*clothing, carpet, colour*› sbiadito; ‹*flower, beauty*› appassito; ‹*glory*› svanito

faeces /ˈfiːsiːz/ *npl* feci *fpl*

fag /fæg/ *n* (chore) fatica *f*; infml (cigarette) sigaretta *f*; AmE sl (homosexual) frocio *m*

fag end *n* infml mozzicone *m* di sigaretta, cicca *f*; (of day, decade, conversation) fine *f*; (of material) scampolo *m*

fagged /fægd/ *adj* **~ out** infml stanco morto

faggot /ˈfægət/ *n* (meatball) polpetta *f* di carne; (firewood) fascina *f*

Fahrenheit /'færənhaɪt/ *adj* Fahrenheit

✓ **fail** /feɪl/ **A** *n* **without ~** senz'altro
B *vi* ‹*attempt*› fallire; ‹*eyesight, memory*› indebolirsi; ‹*engine, machine*› guastarsi; ‹*marriage*› andare a rotoli; (in exam) essere bocciato; **~ to do something** non fare qualcosa; **I tried but I ~ed** ho provato ma non ci sono riuscito; **a ~ed politician** un politico fallito
C *vt* non superare ‹*exam*›; bocciare ‹*candidate*›; (disappoint) deludere; **words ~ me** mi mancano le parole; **unless my memory ~s me** se la memoria non mi tradisce

f

failing /'feɪlɪŋ/ **A** *n* difetto *m*
B *prep* **~ that** altrimenti

fail-safe *adj* ‹*device, system*› di sicurezza

✓ **failure** /'feɪljə(r)/ *n* fallimento *m*; (mechanical) guasto *m*; (person) incapace *mf*

faint /feɪnt/ **A** *adj* leggero; ‹*memory*› vago; **feel ~** sentirsi mancare
B *n* svenimento *m*
C *vi* svenire

faint-hearted /-'hɑːtɪd/ *adj* timido

fainting fit /'feɪntɪŋ/ *n* svenimento *m*

faintly /'feɪntlɪ/ *adv* (slightly) leggermente

faintness /'feɪntnɪs/ *n* (physical) debolezza *f*

fair¹ /feə(r)/ *n* fiera *f*

✓ **fair²** **A** *adj* ‹*hair, person*› biondo; ‹*skin*› chiaro; ‹*weather*› bello; (just) giusto; (quite good) discreto; Sch abbastanza bene; **a ~ amount** abbastanza
B *adv* **play ~** fare un gioco pulito

fair copy *n* bella copia *f*

fairground /'feəgraʊnd/ *n* luna park *m inv*

fair-haired *adj* dai capelli chiari

✓ **fairly** /'feəlɪ/ *adv* con giustizia; (rather) discretamente, abbastanza

fair-minded /feə'maɪndɪd/ *adj* equo

fairness /'feənɪs/ *n* giustizia *f*

fair play *n* fair play *m inv*

fair skinned /-'skɪnd/ *adj* di carnagione chiara

fair trade *n* commercio *m* equo e solidale, commercio *m* equosolidale

fairway *n* Naut via *f* d'acqua navigabile; (in golf) fairway *m inv*

fair weather friend *n* derog amico *m* finché tutto va bene

fairy /'feərɪ/ *n* fata *f*; **good ~** fata [buona]; **wicked ~** strega *f*

fairy godmother *n* fata *f* buona

fairy lights *npl* BrE lampadine *fpl* colorate

fairy story, fairy-tale *n* fiaba *f*

✓ **faith** /feɪθ/ *n* fede *f*; (trust) fiducia *f*; **in good/bad ~** in buona/mala fede

faithful /'feɪθfl/ *adj* fedele

faithfully /'feɪθfʊlɪ/ *adv* fedelmente; **yours ~** distinti saluti

✓ parola chiave

faithfulness /'feɪθfʊlnɪs/ *n* fedeltà *f*

faith healer /-hiːlə(r)/ *n* guaritore, -trice *mf*

faith healing *n* guarigione *f* per fede

faithless /'feɪθlɪs/ *adj* ‹*friend, servant*› sleale; ‹*husband*› infedele

faith school *n* insegnamento *m* religioso

fake /feɪk/ **A** *adj* falso
B *n* falsificazione *f*; (person) impostore *m*
C *vt* falsificare; (pretend) fingere

falcon /'fɔːlkən/ *n* falcone *m*

Falklands /'fɔːlkləndz/ *npl* le isole Falkland, le isole Malvine

✓ **fall** /fɔːl/ **A** *n* caduta *f*; (in prices) ribasso *m*; AmE (autumn) autunno *m*; **have a ~** fare una caduta
B *vi* (*pt* **fell**, *pp* **fallen**) cadere; ‹*night*› scendere; **~ in love** innamorarsi
■ **fall about** *vi* (with laughter) morire dal ridere
■ **fall apart** *vi* ‹*table, car, house*› cadere a pezzi; ‹*shoes*› rompersi; fig ‹*person*› crollare
■ **fall back** *vi* indietreggiare; ‹*army*› ritirarsi
■ **fall back on** *vt* ritornare su
■ **fall behind** *vi* rimanere indietro; **~ behind with** BrE *or* **in** AmE essere indietro con ‹*work, project, payments*›
■ **fall down** *vi* cadere; ‹*building*› crollare
■ **fall for** *vt* infml innamorarsi di ‹*person*›; cascarci ‹*something, trick*›
■ **fall in** *vi* caderci dentro; (collapse) crollare; Mil mettersi in riga; **~ in with** concordare con ‹*suggestion, plan*›
■ **fall off** *vi* cadere; (diminish) diminuire
■ **fall open** *vi* ‹*book*› aprirsi (cadendo); ‹*robe*› aprirsi
■ **fall out** *vi* (quarrel) litigare; **his hair is ~ing out** perde i capelli
■ **fall over** *vi* cadere
■ **fall through** *vi* ‹*plan*› andare a monte

fallacious /fə'leɪʃəs/ *adj* fallace

fallacy /'fæləsɪ/ *n* errore *m*

fallible /'fæləbl/ *adj* fallibile

Fallopian tube /fə'ləʊpɪən/ *n* tromba *f* di Falloppio

fallout /'fɔːlaʊt/ *n* pioggia *f* radioattiva

fallout shelter *n* rifugio *m* antiatomico

fallow /'fæləʊ/ *adj* **lie ~** essere a maggese

false /fɔːls/ *adj* falso

false alarm *n* falso allarme *m*

false bottom *n* doppio fondo *m*

falsehood /'fɔːlshʊd/ *n* menzogna *f*

falsely /'fɔːlslɪ/ *adv* falsamente

falseness /'fɔːlsnɪs/ *n* falsità *f*

false pretences *npl* **under ~** sotto false spoglie; Jur con la frode

false start *n* Sport falsa partenza *f*

false teeth *npl* dentiera *f*

falsetto /fɔːl'setəʊ/ **A** *n* (voice) falsetto *m inv*
B *adj* in falsetto

falsification /fɔːlsɪfɪ'keɪʃn/ *n* (of document, figures) falsificazione *f*; (of truth, facts) deformazione *f*

falsify /ˈfɔːlsɪfaɪ/ *vt* (*pt/pp* **-ied**) falsificare
falsity /ˈfɔːlsətɪ/ *n* falsità *f*
falter /ˈfɔːltə(r)/ *vi* vacillare; (making speech) esitare
faltering /ˈfɔːltərɪŋ/ *adj* ‹*economy*› vacillante; ‹*voice*› esitante
fame /feɪm/ *n* fama *f*
famed /feɪmd/ *adj* rinomato
familiar /fəˈmɪljə(r)/ *adj* familiare; **be ~ with** (know) conoscere; **become too ~** prendersi troppe confidenze
familiarity /fəmɪlɪˈærətɪ/ *n* familiarità *f*
familiarize /fəˈmɪlɪəraɪz/ *vt* familiarizzare; **~ oneself with something** familiarizzarsi con qualcosa
family /ˈfæməlɪ/ *n* famiglia *f*
family allowance *n* assegni *mpl* familiari
family circle *n* (group) cerchia *f* familiare; AmE Theat seconda galleria *f*
family doctor *n* medico *m* di famiglia
family life *n* vita *f* familiare
family name *n* cognome *m*
family planning *n* pianificazione *f* familiare
family tree *n* albero *m* genealogico
family unit *n* nucleo *m* familiare
famine /ˈfæmɪn/ *n* carestia *f*
famished /ˈfæmɪʃt/ *adj* **be ~** infml avere una fame da lupo
famous /ˈfeɪməs/ *adj* famoso
fan¹ /fæn/ **A** *n* ventilatore *m*; (handheld) ventaglio *m*
B *vt* (*pt/pp* **fanned**) far vento a; **~ oneself** sventagliarsi; fig **~ the flames** soffiare sul fuoco
■ **fan out** *vi* spiegarsi a ventaglio
fan² *n* (admirer) ammiratore, -trice *mf*, fan *mf*; Sport tifoso, -a *mf*; (of Verdi etc) appassionato, -a *mf*
fanatic /fəˈnætɪk/ *n* fanatico, -a *mf*
fanatical /fəˈnætɪkl/ *adj* fanatico
fanatically /fəˈnætɪklɪ/ *adv* con fanatismo
fanaticism /fəˈnætɪsɪzm/ *n* fanatismo *m*
fan belt *n* cinghia *f* della ventola
fanciful /ˈfænsɪfl/ *adj* fantasioso
fancy /ˈfænsɪ/ **A** *n* fantasia *f*; **I've taken a real ~ to him** mi è molto simpatico; **as the ~ takes you** come ti pare
B *adj* fantasia *inv*
C *vt* (believe) credere; infml (want) aver voglia di; **he fancies you** infml gli piaci; **~ that!** ma guarda un po'!
fancy dress *n* costume *m*
fancy dress party *n* festa *f* mascherata
fanfare /ˈfænfeə(r)/ *n* fanfara *f*
fang /fæŋ/ *n* zanna *f*; (of snake) dente *m*
fan heater *n* termoventilatore *m*
fanlight *n* lunetta *f*
fan mail *n* posta *f* dei fan
fantasize /ˈfæntəsaɪz/ *vi* fantasticare
fantastic /fænˈtæstɪk/ *adj* fantastico
fantasy /ˈfæntəsɪ/ *n* fantasia *f*
fanzine /ˈfænziːn/ *n* fanzine *f inv*
FAQ *abbr* (**frequently asked questions**) FAQ *fpl*
far /fɑː(r)/ **A** *adv* lontano; (much) molto; **by ~** di gran lunga; **~ away** lontano; **as ~ as the church** fino alla chiesa; **how ~ is it from here?** quanto dista da qui?; **as ~ as I know** per quanto io sappia
B *adj* ‹*end, side*› altro; **the F~ East** l'Estremo Oriente *m*; **in the ~ distance** in lontananza
faraway /ˈfɑːrəweɪ/ *adj* ‹*land*› lontano; ‹*look*› assente
farce /fɑːs/ *n* farsa *f*
farcical /ˈfɑːsɪkl/ *adj* ridicolo
fare /feə(r)/ *n* tariffa *f*; (food) vitto *m*
fare dodger /-dɒdʒə(r)/ *n* passeggero, -a *mf* senza biglietto
farewell /feəˈwel/ **A** *int* literary addio!
B *n* addio *m*; **~ dinner** cena *f* d'addio
far-fetched /-ˈfetʃt/ *adj* improbabile
far flung /-ˈflʌŋ/ *adj* (remote) remoto; (widely distributed) sparpagliato; ‹*network*› esteso
farm /fɑːm/ **A** *n* fattoria *f*, azienda *f* agricola
B *vi* fare l'agricoltore
C *vt* coltivare ‹*land*›
■ **farm out** *vt* dare in appalto ‹*work*›
farmer /ˈfɑːmə(r)/ *n* agricoltore *m*
farmers' market *n vendita (f) diretta dal produttore agricolo al consumatore*
farmhand /ˈfɑːmhænd/ *n* bracciante *m*
farmhouse /ˈfɑːmhaʊs/ *n* casa *f* colonica
farming /ˈfɑːmɪŋ/ *n* agricoltura *f*
farm produce *n* prodotto *m* agricolo
farmyard /ˈfɑːmjɑːd/ *n* aia *f*
far off *adj* lontano
far-reaching /-ˈriːtʃɪŋ/ *adj* ‹*programme, plan, proposal*› di larga portata; ‹*effect, implication, change*› notevole
far-sighted /-ˈsaɪtɪd/ *adj* ‹*policy*› lungimirante; AmE (long-sighted) presbite
fart /fɑːt/ infml **A** *n* scoreggia *f*
B *vi* scoreggiare
farther /ˈfɑːðə(r)/ **A** *adv* più lontano
B *adj* **at the ~ end of** all'altra estremità di
farthest /ˈfɑːðɪst/ *adj & adv* = **furthest**
fascia /ˈfeɪʃɪə/ *n* BrE (dashboard) cruscotto *m*; (for mobile phone) guscio *m*
fascinate /ˈfæsɪneɪt/ *vt* affascinare
fascinating /ˈfæsɪneɪtɪŋ/ *adj* affascinante
fascination /fæsɪˈneɪʃn/ *n* fascino *m*
fascism /ˈfæʃɪzm/ *n* fascismo *m*
fascist /ˈfæʃɪst/ *adj & n* fascista *mf*
fashion /ˈfæʃn/ **A** *n* moda *f*; (manner) maniera *f*; **in ~** di moda; **out of ~** non più di moda
B *vt* modellare

fashionable /ˈfæʃ(ə)nəbl/ *adj* di moda; **be ~** essere alla moda
fashionably /ˈfæʃ(ə)nəblɪ/ *adv* alla moda
fashion designer *n* stilista *mf*
fashion house *n* casa *f* di moda
fashion model *n* indossatore, -trice *mf*, modello, -a *mf*
fashion show *n* sfilata *f* di moda
🔑 **fast¹** /fɑːst/ **A** *adj* veloce; ‹*colour*› indelebile; **be ~** ‹*clock*› andare avanti
B *adv* velocemente; (firmly) saldamente; **~er!** più in fretta!; **be ~ asleep** dormire profondamente

f

fast² **A** *n* digiuno *m*
B *vi* digiunare
fasten /ˈfɑːsn/ **A** *vt* allacciare; chiudere ‹*window*›; (stop flapping) mettere un fermo a
B *vi* allacciarsi
fastener /ˈfɑːsnə(r)/, **fastening** /ˈfɑːsnɪŋ/ *n* chiusura *f*
fast food **A** *n* fast food *m inv*
B *attrib* ‹*chain*› di fast food; **~ restaurant** *n* fast food *m inv*
fast forward **A** *n* avanzamento *m* veloce
B *vt* far avanzare velocemente ‹*tape*›
C *attrib* ‹*key, button*› di avanzamento veloce
fast growing *adj* in rapida espansione
fastidious /fəˈstɪdɪəs/ *adj* esigente
fast lane *n* Auto corsia *f* di sorpasso; **life in the ~** fig vita *f* frenetica
fast-talking *adj* ‹*salesperson*› che raggira con la sua parlantina
fast track *n* corsia *f* preferenziale
fast-track /ˈfɑːsttræk, AmE ˈfæst-/ *vt* accelerare la carriera di ‹*somebody*›
fat /fæt/ **A** *adj* (**fatter**, **fattest**) ‹*person, cheque*› grasso; infml **that's a ~ lot of use** non serve a un accidente
B *n* grasso *m*
fatal /ˈfeɪtl/ *adj* mortale; ‹*error*› fatale
fatalism /ˈfeɪtəlɪzm/ *n* fatalismo *m*
fatalist /ˈfeɪtəlɪst/ *n* fatalista *mf*
fatality /fəˈtælətɪ/ *n* morte *f*
fatally /ˈfeɪtəlɪ/ *adv* mortalmente
fate /feɪt/ *n* destino *m*
fated /ˈfeɪtɪd/ *adj* destinato; **it was ~** era destino
fateful /ˈfeɪtfʊl/ *adj* fatidico
fat free *adj* magro
fat-head *n* infml zuccone, -a *mf*
🔑 **father** /ˈfɑːðə(r)/ **A** *n* padre *m*
B *vt* generare ‹*child*›
Father Christmas Babbo *m* Natale
father confessor *n* Relig confessore *m*
father figure *n* figura *f* paterna
fatherhood *n* paternità *f*
father-in-law *n* (*pl* **~s-in-law**) suocero *m*

🔑 parola chiave

fatherland *n* patria *f*
fatherly /ˈfɑːðəlɪ/ *adj* paterno
Father's Day /ˈfɑːðəz/ *n* la festa del papà
fathom /ˈfæðəm/ **A** *n* Naut braccio *m*
B *vt* **~ [out]** comprendere
fatigue /fəˈtiːg/ **A** *n* fatica *f*
B *vt* affaticare
fatness /ˈfætnɪs/ *n* grassezza *f*
fatten /ˈfætn/ *vt* ingrassare ‹*animal*›
fattening /ˈfætnɪŋ/ *adj* **cream is ~** la panna fa ingrassare
fatty /ˈfætɪ/ **A** *adj* grasso
B *n* infml ciccione, -a *mf*
fatuous /ˈfætjʊəs/ *adj* fatuo
faucet /ˈfɔːsɪt/ *n* AmE rubinetto *m*
🔑 **fault** /fɔːlt/ **A** *n* difetto *m*; Geol faglia *f*; Tennis fallo *m*; **be at ~** avere torto; **find ~ with** trovare da ridire su; **it's your ~** è colpa tua
B *vt* criticare
fault-finding /ˈfɔːltfaɪndɪŋ/ **A** *n* (of person) atteggiamento *m* ipercritico; Techn localizzazione *f* del guasto
B *adj* ‹*attitude*› da criticone; ‹*person*› ipercritico
faultless /ˈfɔːltlɪs/ *adj* impeccabile
faultlessly /ˈfɔːltlɪslɪ/ *adv* impeccabilmente
faulty /ˈfɔːltɪ/ *adj* difettoso
fauna /ˈfɔːnə/ *n* fauna *f*
faux pas /fəʊˈpɑː/ *n* gaffe *f inv*
🔑 **favour** /ˈfeɪvə(r)/ **A** *n* favore *m*; **be in ~ of something** essere a favore di qualcosa; **do somebody a ~** fare un piacere a qualcuno
B *vt* (prefer) preferire
favourable /ˈfeɪv(ə)rəbl/ *adj* favorevole
favourably /ˈfeɪv(ə)rəblɪ/ *adv* favorevolmente
🔑 **favourite** /ˈfeɪv(ə)rɪt/ **A** *adj* preferito
B *n* preferito, -a *mf*; Sport favorito, -a *mf*
favouritism /ˈfeɪv(ə)rɪtɪzm/ *n* favoritismo *m*
fawn /fɔːn/ **A** *adj* fulvo
B *n* (animal) cerbiatto *m*
fax /fæks/ **A** *n* (document, machine) fax *m inv*; **by ~** per fax
B *vt* faxare
fax machine *n* fax *m inv*
fax-modem *n* fax-modem *m inv*
fax number *n* numero *m* di fax
faze /feɪz/ *vt* infml scompaginare
FBI *n abbr* AmE (**Federal Bureau of Investigation**) FBI *m*
FC *abbr* (**football club**) FC
🔑 **fear** /fɪə(r)/ **A** *n* paura *f*; **no ~!** infml vai tranquillo!
B *vt* temere
C *vi* **~ for something** temere per qualcosa
fearful /ˈfɪəfl/ *adj* pauroso; (awful) terribile
fearless /ˈfɪəlɪs/ *adj* impavido
fearlessly /ˈfɪəlɪslɪ/ *adv* senza paura
fearsome /ˈfɪəsəm/ *adj* spaventoso

feasibility /fiːzɪ'bɪlətɪ/ *n* praticabilità *f*

feasible /'fiːzəbl/ *adj* fattibile; (possible) probabile

feast /fiːst/ **A** *n* festa *f*; (banquet) banchetto *m* **B** *vi* banchettare

▪ **feast on** *vt* godersi

feat /fiːt/ *n* impresa *f*

feather /'feðə(r)/ *n* piuma *f*; **you could have knocked me down with a ~** sono rimasto di sasso

feather-brained /-breɪnd/ *adj* che non ha un briciolo di cervello

feather duster *n* piumino *m* (*per spolverare*)

featherweight *n* peso *m* piuma *inv*

feature /'fiːtʃə(r)/ **A** *n* (quality) caratteristica *f*; Journ articolo *m*; **~s** *pl* (of face) lineamenti *mpl* **B** *vt* <*film*> avere come protagonista **C** *vi* (on a list etc) comparire

feature film *n* lungometraggio *m*

feature length film *n* lungometraggio *m*

February /'febrʊərɪ/ *n* febbraio *m*

feckless /'feklɪs/ *adj* inetto

fecund /'fekənd/ *adj* fecondo

fed /fed/ **A** ▸ **feed** **B** *adj* **be ~ up** infml essere stufo (**with** di)

federal /'fed(ə)rəl/ *adj* federale

federalist /'fed(ə)rəlɪst/ *n & adj* federalista *mf*

Federal Republic of Germany *n* Repubblica *f* Federale Tedesca

federate /'fed(ə)rət/ *adj* federato

federation /fedə'reɪʃn/ *n* federazione *f*

fee /fiː/ *n* tariffa *f*; (lawyer's, doctor's) onorario m; (for membership, school) quota *f*

feeble /'fiːbl/ *adj* debole; <*excuse*> fiacco

feeble minded /-'maɪndɪd/ *adj* deficiente

feebleness /'fiːblnɪs/ *n* debolezza *f*

feed /fiːd/ **A** *n* mangiare *m*; (for baby) pappa *f*; **five ~s a day** cinque pasti al giorno **B** *vt* (*pt/pp* **fed**) dar da mangiare a <*animal*>; (support) nutrire; **~ something into something** inserire qualcosa in qualcosa; **~ paper into the printer** alimentare la stampante con fogli **C** *vi* mangiare

▪ **feed up** *vt* ingrassare <*somebody*>

feedback /'fiːdbæk/ *n* controreazione *f*; (of information) reazione *f*, feedback *m*

feeder /'fiːdə(r)/ *n* (for printer, photocopier) mettifoglio *m inv*; BrE (bib) bavaglino *m*; (road) raccordo *m*

feeding bottle /'fiːdɪŋ/ *n* BrE biberon *m inv*

feeding time *n* (in zoo) l'ora *f* del pasto degli animali

feel /fiːl/ *v* (*pt/pp* **felt**) **A** *vt* sentire; (experience) provare; (think) pensare; (touch: searching) tastare; (touch: for texture) toccare **B** *vi* **~ soft/hard** essere duro/morbido al tatto; **~ hot/hungry** aver caldo/fame; **~ ill** sentirsi male; **I don't ~ like it** non ne ho voglia; **how do you ~ about it?** (opinion) che te ne pare?; **it doesn't ~ right** non mi sembra giusto

▪ **feel for** *vt* (feel sympathy for) dispiacersi per

▪ **feel up to**: *vt* **~ up to doing something** sentirsi in grado di fare qualcosa; **I don't ~ up to it** non me la sento

feeler /'fiːlə(r)/ *n* (of animal) antenna *f*; **put out ~s** fig tastare il terreno

feel-good factor *n* sensazione *f* di benessere

feeling /'fiːlɪŋ/ *n* sentimento *m*; (awareness) sensazione *f*

fee paying *adj* <*school*> a pagamento, privato; <*parent, pupil*> che paga l'iscrizione (*a una scuola privata*)

feet /fiːt/ ▸ **foot**

feign /feɪn/ *vt* simulare

feint /feɪnt/ *n* finta *f*

feisty /'faɪstɪ/ *adj* AmE (quarrelsome) stizzoso; infml (lively) esuberante

felicitous /fə'lɪsɪtəs/ *adj* felice

feline /'fiːlaɪn/ *adj* felino

fell[1] /fel/ *vt* (knock down) abbattere

fell[2] ▸ **fall**

fellow /'feləʊ/ *n* (of society) socio *m*; infml (man) tipo *m*

fellow citizen *n* concittadino, -a *mf*

fellow countryman *n* compatriota *m*

fellow men *npl* prossimi *mpl*

fellowship /'feləʊʃɪp/ *n* cameratismo *m*; (group) associazione *f*; Univ incarico *m* di ricercatore, -trice *mf*

fellow traveller *n* compagno, -a *mf* di viaggio; Pol fig compagno, -a *mf* di strada

felon /'felən/ *n* Jur criminale *mf*

felony /'felənɪ/ *n* delitto *m*

felt[1] /felt/ ▸ **feel**

felt[2] *n* feltro *m*

felt-tipped pen /-tɪpt'pen/ *n* pennarello *m*

female /'fiːmeɪl/ **A** *adj* femminile; **the ~ antelope** l'antilope femmina **B** *n* femmina *f*

feminine /'femɪnɪn/ **A** *adj* femminile **B** *n* Gram femminile *m*

femininity /femɪ'nɪnətɪ/ *n* femminilità *f*

feminist /'femɪnɪst/ *adj & n* femminista *mf*

fen /fen/ *n* zona *f* paludosa

fence /fens/ **A** *n* recinto *m*; infml (person) ricettatore *m* **B** *vi* Sport tirar di scherma

▪ **fence in** *vt* chiudere in un recinto

fencer /'fensə(r)/ *n* schermidore *m*

fencing /'fensɪŋ/ *n* steccato *m*; Sport scherma *f*

fend /fend/ *vi* **~ for oneself** badare a se stesso

▪ **fend off** *vt* parare; difendersi da <*criticisms*>

f

fender /'fendə(r)/ *n* parafuoco *m inv*; Naut parabordo *m*; AmE (on car) parafango *m*
fennel /'fenl/ *n* finocchio *m*
ferment¹ /'fɜːment/ *n* fermento *m*
ferment² /fə'ment/ **A** *vi* fermentare **B** *vt* far fermentare
fermentation /fɜːmen'teɪʃn/ *n* fermentazione *f*
fern /fɜːn/ *n* felce *f*
ferocious /fə'rəʊʃəs/ *adj* feroce
ferocity /fə'rɒsətɪ/ *n* ferocia *f*
ferret /'ferɪt/ *n* furetto *m*
■ **ferret about** *vi* curiosare; ~ **about in** curiosare in
■ **ferret out** *vt* scovare
ferrous /'ferəs/ *adj* ferroso
ferry /'ferɪ/ **A** *n* traghetto *m* **B** *vt* (*pt/pp* **-ied**) traghettare
ferryman /'ferɪmən/ *n* traghettatore *m*
fertile /'fɜːtaɪl/ *adj* fertile
fertility /fɜː'tɪlətɪ/ *n* fertilità *f*
fertility drug *n* farmaco *m* contro la sterilità
fertility treatment *n* cura *f* della fertilità
fertilize /'fɜːtɪlaɪz/ *vt* fertilizzare ‹*land, ovum*›
fertilizer /'fɜːtɪlaɪzə(r)/ *n* fertilizzante *m*
fervent /'fɜːvənt/ *adj* fervente
fervour /'fɜːvə(r)/ *n* fervore *m*
fester /'festə(r)/ *vi* suppurare
⚷ **festival** /'festɪvl/ *n* Mus, Theat festival *m*; Relig festa *f*
festive /'festɪv/ *adj* festivo; ~ **season** periodo *m* delle feste natalizie
festivities /fe'stɪvətɪz/ *npl* festeggiamenti *mpl*
festoon /fe'stuːn/ *vt* ~ **with** ornare di
fetch /fetʃ/ *vt* andare/venire a prendere; (be sold for) raggiungere [il prezzo di]
fetching /'fetʃɪŋ/ *adj* attraente
fête /feɪt/ **A** *n* festa *f* **B** *vt* festeggiare
fetid /'fetɪd/ *adj* fetido
fetish /'fetɪʃ/ *n* feticcio *m*
fetter /'fetə(r)/ *vt* incatenare
fettle /'fetl/ *n* **in fine** ~ in buona forma
fetus /'fiːtəs/ *n* (*pl* **-tuses**) feto *m*
feud /fjuːd/ *n* faida *f*
feudal /'fjuːdl/ *adj* feudale
fever /'fiːvə(r)/ *n* febbre *f*
fevered /'fiːvəd/ *adj* ‹*brow*› febbricitante; ‹*imagination*› febbrile
feverish /'fiːvərɪʃ/ *adj* febbricitante; fig febbrile
fever pitch *n* **bring a crowd to** ~ esaltare la folla
⚷ **few** /fjuː/ **A** *adj* pochi; **every** ~ **days** ogni due o tre giorni; **a** ~ **people** alcuni; ~ **people know that** poche persone lo sanno; ~**er reservations** meno prenotazioni; **the** ~**est number** il numero più basso **B** *pron* pochi; ~ **of us** pochi di noi; **a** ~ alcuni; **quite a** ~ parecchi; ~**er than last year** meno dell'anno scorso
fez /fez/ *n* fez *m inv*
fiancé /fɪ'ɒnseɪ/ *n* fidanzato *m*
fiancée /fɪ'ɒnseɪ/ *n* fidanzata *f*
fiasco /fɪ'æskəʊ/ *n* fiasco *m*
fib /fɪb/ *n* storia *f*; **tell a** ~ raccontare una storia
fibber /'fɪbə(r)/ *n* infml contaballe *mf inv*
fibre /'faɪbə(r)/ *n* fibra *f*
fibreglass A *n* fibra *f* di vetro **B** *attrib* in fibra di vetro
fibre optic *adj* ‹*cable*› a fibre ottiche
fibre optics *nsg* fibra *fsg* ottica
fibroid /'faɪbrɔɪd/ **A** *n* fibroma *m* **B** *adj* fibroso
fibula /'fɪbjʊlə/ *n* Anat perone *m*
fiche /fiːʃ/ *n* microscheda *f*
fickle /'fɪkl/ *adj* incostante
fiction /'fɪkʃn/ *n* **[works of]** ~ narrativa *f*; (fabrication) finzione *f*
fictional /'fɪkʃənəl/ *adj* immaginario
fictionalize /'fɪkʃənəlaɪz/ *vt* romanzare
fictitious /fɪk'tɪʃəs/ *adj* fittizio
fiddle /'fɪdl/ **A** *n* infml violino *m*; (cheating) imbroglio *m* **B** *vi* gingillarsi (**with** con) **C** *vt* infml truccare ‹*accounts*›
fiddly /'fɪdlɪ/ *adj* intricato
fidelity /fɪ'delətɪ/ *n* fedeltà *f*
fidget /'fɪdʒɪt/ *vi* agitarsi
fidgety /'fɪdʒətɪ/ *adj* agitato
⚷ **field** /fiːld/ *n* campo *m*
field day *n* **have a** ~ ‹*press, critics*› godersela; (make money) fare affari d'oro
fielder /'fiːldə(r)/ *n* Sport esterno *m*
field events *npl* atletica *fsg* leggera
field glasses *npl* binocolo *msg*
Field Marshal *n* feldmaresciallo *m*
field mouse *n* topo *m* campagnolo
field trip *n* gita *f* didattica
fieldwork *n* ricerche *fpl* sul terreno
fiend /fiːnd/ *n* demonio *m*
fiendish /'fiːndɪʃ/ *adj* diabolico
fierce /fɪəs/ *adj* feroce
fiercely /'fɪəslɪ/ *adv* ferocemente
fierceness /'fɪəsnɪs/ *n* ferocia *f*
fiery /'faɪərɪ/ *adj* (**-ier, -iest**) focoso
fiesta /fɪ'estə/ *n* sagra *f*
fife /faɪf/ *n* piffero *m*
fifteen /fɪf'tiːn/ *adj & n* quindici *m*
fifteenth /fɪf'tiːnθ/ *adj & n* quindicesimo, -a *mf*
fifth /fɪfθ/ *adj & n* quinto, -a *mf*

⚷ parola chiave

fifties /'fɪftɪz/ *npl* (period) **the ~** gli anni Cinquanta *mpl*; (age) cinquant'anni *mpl*

fiftieth /'fɪftɪɪθ/ *adj & n* cinquantesimo, -a *mf*

fifty /'fɪftɪ/ *adj & n* cinquanta *m*

fifty-fifty **A** *adj* **have a ~ chance** avere una probabilità su due **B** *adv* **go ~** fare [a] metà e metà; **split something ~** dividersi qualcosa a metà

fig /fɪg/ *n* fico *m*

fig. *abbr* (**figure**) fig.

fight /faɪt/ **A** *n* lotta *f*; (brawl) zuffa *f*; (argument) litigio *m*; (boxing) incontro *m* **B** *vt* (*pt/pp* **fought**) also fig combattere **C** *vi* combattere; (brawl) azzuffarsi; (argue) litigare

■ **fight back** **A** *vi* reagire **B** *vt* frenare ‹*tears*›

■ **fight for** *vt* lottare per ‹*freedom, independence*›

■ **fight off** *vt* combattere ‹*cold*›

fighter /'faɪtə(r)/ *n* combattente *mf*; Aeron caccia *m inv*; **he's a ~** ha uno spirito combattivo

fighter-bomber *n* cacciabombardiere *m*

fighter pilot *n* pilota *m* di cacciabombardiere

fighting /'faɪtɪŋ/ *n* combattimento *m*

fighting chance *n* **have a ~** avere buone probabilità

fighting fit *adj* in piena forma

figment /'fɪgmənt/ *n* **it's a ~ of your imagination** questo è tutta una tua invenzione

fig tree *n* fico *m*

figurative /'fɪgərətɪv/ *adj* ‹*sense*› figurato; ‹*art*› figurativo

figuratively /'fɪgərətɪvlɪ/ *adv* ‹*use*› in senso figurato

figure /'fɪgə(r)/ **A** *n* (digit) cifra *f*; (carving, sculpture, illustration, form) figura *f*; (body shape) linea *f*; **~ of speech** modo *m* di dire **B** *vi* (appear) figurare **C** *vt* AmE (think) pensare

■ **figure out** *vt* dedurre; capire ‹*person*›

figurehead *n* figura *f* simbolica

figure of speech *n* modo *m* di dire; (literary device) figura *f* retorica

figure skating *n* pattinaggio *m* artistico

figurine /'fɪgəri:n/ *n* statuetta *f*

Fiji /ˌfi:'dʒi:/ *n* Figi *fpl*

filament /'fɪləmənt/ *n* filamento *m*

filch /fɪltʃ/ *vt* infml rubacchiare

file[1] /faɪl/ **A** *n* scheda *f*; (set of documents) incartamento *m*; (folder) cartellina *f*; Comput file *m inv* **B** *vt* archiviare ‹*documents*›

file[2] *n* (line) fila *f*; **in single ~** in fila

file[3] **A** *n* Techn lima *f* **B** *vt* limare

file cabinet *n* AmE = **filing cabinet**

file extension *n* Comput estensione *f* del file

file manager *n* Comput file manager *m inv*

filename *n* Comput nome *m* del file

file sharing *n* file sharing *m inv*

file-sharing *n* file-sharing *m inv*, condivisione *f* di file

file transfer protocol *n* Comput protocollo *m* per il trasferimento di file

filial /'fɪlɪəl/ *adj* filiale

filibuster /'fɪlɪbʌstə(r)/ *n* ostruzionismo *m* parlamentare

filigree /'fɪlɪgri:/ *n* filigrana *f*

filing /'faɪlɪŋ/ *n* archiviazione *f*

filing cabinet *n* schedario *m*, classificatore *m*

filing card *n* scheda *f*

filing clerk *n* archivista *mf*

filings /'faɪlɪŋz/ *npl* limatura *fsg*

filing system *n* sistema *m* di classificazione, sistema *m* di archivio

fill /fɪl/ **A** *n* **eat one's ~** mangiare a sazietà **B** *vt* riempire; otturare ‹*tooth*› **C** *vi* riempirsi

■ **fill in** *vt* compilare ‹*form*›

■ **fill in for sb** *vt* rimpiazzare qualcuno

■ **fill in on**: *vt* **~ somebody in on something** mettere qualcuno al corrente di qualcosa

■ **fill out** *vt* compilare ‹*form*›

■ **fill up** **A** *vi* ‹*room, tank*› riempirsi; Auto far il pieno **B** *vt* riempire

filler /'fɪlə(r)/ *n* mastice *m*

fillet /'fɪlɪt/ **A** *n* filetto *m* **B** *vt* (*pt/pp* **filleted**) disossare

fillet steak *n* bistecca *f* di filetto

fill in *n* infml (replacement) rimpiazzo *m*

filling /'fɪlɪŋ/ *n* Culin ripieno *m*; (of tooth) otturazione *f*

filling station *n* stazione *f* di rifornimento

filly /'fɪlɪ/ *n* puledra *f*

film /fɪlm/ **A** *n* Cinema film *m inv*; Phot pellicola *f*; **[cling] ~** pellicola *f* per alimenti **B** *vt & vi* filmare

film buff *n* cinefilo, -a *mf*

film festival *n* festival *m inv* cinematografico

film-goer /'fɪlmgəʊə(r)/ *n* BrE frequentatore, -trice *mf* di cinema

film industry *n* industria *f* cinematografica

filming /'fɪlmɪŋ/ *n* riprese *fpl*

filmset *n* allestimento *m* scenico

film star *n* star *f inv*, divo, -a *mf*

film studio *n* studio *m* cinematografico

filmy /'fɪlmɪ/ *adj* (thin) ‹*fabric, screen*› trasparente; (thin) sottilissimo

filter /'fɪltə(r)/ **A** *n* filtro *m* **B** *vt* filtrare

■ **filter through** *vi* ‹*news*› trapelare

filter cigarette *n* sigaretta *f* con filtro

filter coffee *n* (ground coffee) caffè *m* macinato per filtro; (cup of coffee) caffè *m*

fatto con il filtro
filter paper *n* carta *f* da filtro
filter tip *n* filtro *m*; (cigarette) sigaretta *f* col filtro
filth /fɪlθ/ *n* sudiciume *m*
filthy /ˈfɪlθɪ/ *adj* (**-ier**, **-iest**) sudicio; ‹*language*› sconcio
filthy rich *adj* infml ricco sfondato
fin /fɪn/ *n* pinna *f*
🔑 **final** /ˈfaɪnl/ **A** *adj* finale; (conclusive) decisivo
B *n* Sport finale *f*; **~s** *pl* Univ esami *mpl* finali
finale /fɪˈnɑːlɪ/ *n* finale *m*
finalist /ˈfaɪnəlɪst/ *n* finalista *mf*
finality /faɪˈnælətɪ/ *n* finalità *f*
finalize /ˈfaɪnəlaɪz/ *vt* mettere a punto ‹*text*›; definire ‹*agreement*›
🔑 **finally** /ˈfaɪnəlɪ/ *adv* (at last) finalmente; (at the end) alla fine; (to conclude) per finire
finance /ˈfaɪnæns/ **A** *n* finanza *f*
B *vt* finanziare
finance company, **finance house** *n* società *f* finanziaria
finance director *n* direttore, -trice *mf* finanziario, -a
finances *npl* finanze *fpl*
🔑 **financial** /faɪˈnænʃl/ *adj* finanziario
financially /faɪˈnænʃəlɪ/ *adv* finanziariamente
financial year *n* BrE esercizio *m* [finanziario]
finch /fɪntʃ/ *n* fringuello *m*
🔑 **find** /faɪnd/ **A** *n* scoperta *f*
B *vt* (*pt/pp* **found**) trovare; (establish) scoprire; **~ somebody guilty** Jur dichiarare qualcuno colpevole
■ **find out** **A** *vt* scoprire
B *vi* (enquire) informarsi
🔑 **findings** /ˈfaɪndɪŋz/ *npl* conclusioni *fpl*
fine¹ /faɪn/ **A** *n* (penalty) multa *f*
B *vt* multare
🔑 **fine²** **A** *adj* bello; (slender) fine; **he's ~** (in health) sta bene
B *adv* bene; **that's cutting it ~** non ci lascia molto tempo
C *int* [va] bene
fine art *n* belle arti *fpl*
fine arts *npl* belle arti *fpl*
finely /ˈfaɪnlɪ/ *adv* ‹*cut*› finemente
finery /ˈfaɪnərɪ/ *n* splendore *m*
finesse /fɪˈnes/ *n* finezza *f*
fine-tooth comb /-tuːθ[t]/ *n* **go over something with a ~** passare qualcosa al setaccio
fine-tune *vt* mettere a punto
fine tuning *n* messa *f* a punto
🔑 **finger** /ˈfɪŋgə(r)/ **A** *n* dito *m* (*pl* dita *f*)
B *vt* tastare
finger bowl *n* lavadita *m inv*
finger hole *n* Mus foro *m*
fingermark *n* ditata *f*
fingernail *n* unghia *f*
finger-paint *vi* dipingere con le dita
fingerprint *n* impronta *f* digitale
fingertip *n* punta *f* del dito; **have something at one's ~s** sapere qualcosa a menadito; (close at hand) avere qualcosa a portata di mano
finicky /ˈfɪnɪkɪ/ *adj* (person) pignolo; ‹*task*› intricato
🔑 **finish** /ˈfɪnɪʃ/ **A** *n* fine *f*; (finishing line) traguardo *m*; (of product) finitura *f*; **have a good ~** ‹*runner*› avere un buon finale
B *vt* finire; **~ reading** finire di leggere
C *vi* finire
■ **finish off** *vt* finire ‹*something*›; infml (exhaust) sfinire
■ **finish with** *vt* (no longer be using) finire (*di adoperare*); (end relationship with) lasciare
■ **finish up** *vt* finire ‹*drink, meal*›
finishing line /ˈfɪnɪʃɪŋlaɪn/ *n* traguardo *m*
finishing touches /ˈtʌtʃɪz/ *npl* ritocchi *mpl*
finite /ˈfaɪnaɪt/ *adj* limitato
Finland /ˈfɪnlənd/ *n* Finlandia *f*
Finn /fɪn/ *n* finlandese *mf*
Finnish /ˈfɪnɪʃ/ **A** *adj* finlandese
B *n* (language) finnico *m*
fiord /fjɔːd/ *n* fiordo *m*
fir /fɜː(r)/ *n* abete *m*
fir cone *n* pigna *f* (*di abete*)
🔑 **fire** /ˈfaɪə(r)/ **A** *n* fuoco *m*; (forest, house) incendio *m*; **be on ~** bruciare; **catch ~** prendere fuoco; **set ~ to** dar fuoco a; **under ~** sotto il fuoco
B *vt* cuocere ‹*pottery*›; sparare ‹*shot*›; tirare ‹*gun*›; infml (dismiss) buttar fuori
C *vi* sparare (**at** a)
fire alarm *n* allarme *m* antincendio *inv*
firearm *n* arma *f* da fuoco
firebomb /ˈfaɪəbɒm/ **A** *n* ordigno *m* incendiario
B *vt* lanciare ordigni incendiari contro ‹*building*›
fire brigade *n* vigili *mpl* del fuoco
fire door *n* porta *f* antincendio
fire drill *n* esercitazione *f* per l'evacuazione in caso di incendio
fire engine *n* autopompa *f*
fire escape *n* uscita *f* di sicurezza
fire exit *n* uscita *f* di sicurezza
fire extinguisher *n* estintore *m*
firefighter *n* vigile *m* del fuoco
fireguard *n* parafuoco *m inv*
fireman *n* pompiere *m*, vigile *m* del fuoco
fireplace *n* caminetto *m*
fireproof /ˈfaɪəpruːf/ *adj* ‹*door*› antincendio; ‹*clothing*› ignifugo
fire-retardant /rɪˈtɑːdənt/ *adj* ‹*material*› ignifugo
fire service *n* vigili *mpl* del fuoco

🔑 parola chiave

fireside *n* **by** *or* **at the ~** accanto al fuoco
fire station *n* caserma *f* dei pompieri
firewall /ˈfaɪəwɔːl/ *n* Comput firewall *m inv*
firewood *n* legna *f* (*da ardere*)
firework *n* fuoco *m* d'artificio; **~s** *pl* (display) fuochi *mpl* d'artificio
firing line *n* **be in the ~** essere sulla linea di tiro
firing squad /ˈfaɪərɪŋ/ *n* plotone *m* d'esecuzione
firm[1] /fɜːm/ *n* ditta *f*, azienda *f*
firm[2] *adj* fermo; ‹*soil*› compatto; (stable, properly fixed) solido; (resolute) risoluto
firmly /ˈfɜːmlɪ/ *adv* ‹*hold*› stretto; ‹*say*› con fermezza
first /fɜːst/ **A** *adj & n* primo, -a *mf*; **at ~** all'inizio; **who's ~?** chi è il primo?; **from the ~** [fin] dall'inizio
B *adv* ‹*arrive, leave*› per primo; (beforehand) prima; (in listing) prima di tutto, innanzitutto
first aid *n* pronto soccorso *m*
first-aid kit *n* cassetta *f* di pronto soccorso
first-class **A** *adj* di prim'ordine; Rail di prima classe
B *adv* ‹*travel*› in prima classe
first cousin *n* cugino, -a *mf* di primo grado
first edition *n* prima edizione *f*
first floor *n* primo piano *m*; AmE (ground floor) pianterreno *m*
first grade *n* AmE prima *f* elementare
first-hand /ˌfɜːstˈhænd/ *adj & adv* di prima mano
firstly /ˈfɜːstlɪ/ *adv* in primo luogo
first name *n* nome *m* di battesimo
first night *n* Theat prima *f*
first-rate *adj* ottimo
first time buyer *n* acquirente *mf* della prima casa
firth /fɜːθ/ *n* foce *f*
fiscal /ˈfɪskəl/ *adj* fiscale
fiscal year *n* AmE esercizio *m* finanziario
fish /fɪʃ/ **A** *n* pesce *m*
B *vt & vi* pescare
■ **fish out** *vt* tirar fuori
fish and chips *n pesce* (*m*) *fritto e patatine*
fish and chip shop *n friggitoria* (*f*) *dove si vende pesce fritto e patatine*
fish bone *n* lisca *f*
fishbowl *n* boccia *f* dei pesci rossi
fisherman /ˈfɪʃəmən/ *n* pescatore *m*
fish farm *n* vivaio *m*
fish finger *n* BrE bastoncino *m* di pesce
fishing /ˈfɪʃɪŋ/ *n* pesca *f*
fishing boat *n* peschereccio *m*
fishing rod *n* canna *f* da pesca
fish market *n* mercato *m* del pesce
fishmonger /ˈfɪʃmʌŋgə(r)/ *n* pescivendolo *m*
fishnet /ˈfɪʃnet/ *adj* ‹*stockings*› a rete
fish slice *n* paletta *f* per fritti
fish stick *n* AmE bastoncino *m* di pesce
fish tank *n* acquario *m*
fishy /ˈfɪʃɪ/ *adj* infml (suspicious) sospetto
fission /ˈfɪʃn/ *n* Phys fissione *f*
fist /fɪst/ *n* pugno *m*
fistful /ˈfɪstfʊl/ *n* manciata *f*, pugno *m*
fit[1] /fɪt/ *n* (attack) attacco *m*; (of rage) accesso *m*; (of generosity) slancio *m*
fit[2] *adj* (**fitter**, **fittest**) (suitable) adatto; (healthy) in buona salute; Sport in forma; **be ~ to do something** essere in grado di fare qualcosa; **~ to eat** buono da mangiare; **keep ~** tenersi in forma; **do as you see ~** fai come ritieni meglio
fit[3] **A** *n* (of clothes) taglio *m*; **it's a good ~** ‹*coat etc*› ti/le sta bene
B *vi* (*pt/pp* **fitted**) (be the right size) andare bene; **it won't ~** (no room) non ci sta
C *vt* (fix) applicare (**to** a); (install) installare; **it doesn't ~ me** ‹*coat etc*› non mi va bene; **~ with** fornire di
■ **fit in** **A** *vi* ‹*person*› adattarsi; **it won't ~ in** (no room) non ci sta
B *vt* (in schedule, vehicle) trovare un buco per
fitful /ˈfɪtfl/ *adj* irregolare
fitfully /ˈfɪtfʊlɪ/ *adv* ‹*sleep*› a sprazzi
fitment /ˈfɪtmənt/ *n* **~s** (in house) impianti *mpl* fissi
fitness /ˈfɪtnɪs/ *n* (suitability) capacità *f*; **[physical] ~** forma *f*, fitness *m inv*
fitness programme *n* programma *m* di fitness
fitness video *n* video *m* di fitness
fitted /ˈfɪtɪd/ *adj* ‹*wardrobe*› a muro; ‹*kitchen, bedroom*› componibile; ‹*jacket*› attillato
fitted carpet *n* moquette *f inv*
fitted cupboard *n* armadio *m* a muro; (smaller) armadietto *m* a muro
fitted kitchen *n* cucina *f* componibile
fitted sheet *n* lenzuolo *m* con angoli
fitter /ˈfɪtə(r)/ *n* installatore, -trice *mf*
fitting /ˈfɪtɪŋ/ **A** *adj* appropriato
B *n* (of clothes) prova *f*; Techn montaggio *m*; **~s** *pl* accessori *mpl*
fitting room *n* camerino *m*
five /faɪv/ *adj & n* cinque *m*
five-a-side *n* BrE (football) calcio *m* a cinque
fiver /ˈfaɪvə(r)/ *n* infml biglietto *m* da cinque sterline
fix /fɪks/ **A** *n* sl (drugs) pera *f*; **be in a ~** infml essere nei guai
B *vt* fissare; (repair) aggiustare; preparare ‹*meal*›
■ **fix up** *vt* fissare ‹*meeting*›
fixation /fɪkˈseɪʃn/ *n* fissazione *f*
fixative /ˈfɪksətɪv/ *n* fissativo *m*
fixed /fɪkst/ *adj* fisso

fixed assets *npl* attività *fpl* fisse, immobilizzazioni *fpl*
fixed price *n* prezzo *m* a forfait
fixed-term contract *n* contratto *m* a tempo determinato
fixer /ˈfɪksə(r)/ *n* Phot fissatore *m*; infml (person) trafficone, -a *mf*
fixture /ˈfɪkstʃə(r)/ *n* Sport incontro *m*; **~s and fittings** impianti *mpl* fissi
fizz /fɪz/ *vi* frizzare
fizzle /ˈfɪzl/ *vi* **~ out** finire in nulla
fizzy /ˈfɪzɪ/ *adj* gassoso

fizzy drink *n* bibita *f* gassata
fjord /fjɔːd/ *n* fiordo *m*
flab /flæb/ *n* infml ciccia *f* cascante
flabbergasted /ˈflæbəgɑːstɪd/ *adj* **be ~** rimanere a bocca aperta
flabby /ˈflæbɪ/ *adj* floscio
flag[1] /flæg/ *n* bandiera *f*
flag[2] *vi* (*pt/pp* **flagged**) cedere
▪ **flag down** *vt* (*pt/pp* **flagged**) far segno di fermarsi a ‹*taxi*›
flagellation /flædʒəˈleɪʃn/ *n* flagellazione *f*
flagon /ˈflægən/ *n* bottiglione *m*
flagpole /ˈflægpəʊl/ *n* asta *f* della bandiera
flagrant /ˈfleɪgrənt/ *adj* flagrante
flagship /ˈflægʃɪp/ *n* Naut nave *f* ammiraglia; fig fiore *m* all'occhiello
flagstone /ˈflægstəʊn/ *n* pietra *f* per lastricato
flail /fleɪl/ **A** *n* (for threshing corn etc) correggiato *m*
B *vt* battere ‹*corn*›
▪ **flail about**, **flail around** *vi* ‹*arms, legs*› agitare
flair /fleə(r)/ *n* (skill) talento *m*; (style) stile *m*
flak /flæk/ *n* Mil artiglieria *f* antiaerea; fig infml (criticism) valanga *f* di critiche; **take a lot of ~** subire molte critiche
flake /fleɪk/ **A** *n* fiocco *m*
B *vi* **~ [off]** cadere in fiocchi
flaky /ˈfleɪkɪ/ *adj* a scaglie
flaky pastry *n* pasta *f* sfoglia
flamboyant /flæmˈbɔɪənt/ *adj* ‹*personality*› brillante; ‹*tie*› sgargiante
flame /fleɪm/ *n* fiamma *f*
flamenco /fləˈmeŋkəʊ/ *n* flamenco *m*
flamer /ˈfleɪmə(r)/ *n* Comput flamer *m* (*utente* (*mf*) *email che manda messaggi offensivi*)
flame retardant /rɪtɑːdənt/ *adj* ‹*substance, chemical*› ignifugo; ‹*furniture, fabric*› ignifugato
flame-thrower /-θrəʊə(r)/ *n* Mil lanciafiamme *m inv*
flaming /ˈfleɪmɪŋ/ **A** *adj* ‹*row*› acceso; ‹*building*› in fiamme
B *n* Comput flaming *m inv* (*invio* (*m*) *di messaggi offensivi*)
flamingo /fləˈmɪŋgəʊ/ *n* fenicottero *m*
flammable /ˈflæməbl/ *adj* infiammabile
flan /flæn/ *n* **[fruit] ~** crostata *f*
flange /flændʒ/ *n* (on pipe etc) flangia *f*
flank /flæŋk/ **A** *n* fianco *m*
B *vt* fiancheggiare
flannel /ˈflæn(ə)l/ *n* flanella *f*; (for washing) ≈ guanto *m* di spugna
flannelette /flænəˈlet/ *n* flanella *f* di cotone
flannels /ˈflæn(ə)lz/ *npl* (trousers) pantaloni *mpl* di flanella
flap /flæp/ **A** *n* (of pocket, envelope) risvolto *m*; (of table) ribalta *f*; **in a ~** infml in grande agitazione
B *vi* (*pt/pp* **flapped**) sbattere; infml agitarsi
C *vt* **~ its wings** battere le ali
flapjack /ˈflæpdʒæk/ *n* BrE *dolcetto* (*m*) *di fiocchi d'avena*; AmE frittella *f*
flare /fleə(r)/ *n* fiammata *f*; (device) razzo *m*
▪ **flare up** *vi* ‹*rash*› venire fuori; ‹*fire*› fare una fiammata; ‹*person, situation*› esplodere
flared /fleəd/ *adj* ‹*garment*› svasato
flares /fleəz/ *npl* (trousers) pantaloni *mpl* a zampa d'elefante
flash /flæʃ/ **A** *n* lampo *m*; **in a ~** infml in un attimo
B *vi* lampeggiare; **~ past** passare come un bolide
C *vt* lanciare ‹*smile*›; **~ one's headlights** lampeggiare; **~ a torch at** puntare una torcia su
▪ **flash by** *vi* ‹*person, years, landscape*› passare come un lampo
flashback *n* scena *f* retrospettiva
flashbulb *n* Phot flash *m inv*
flashcard *n* Sch scheda *f* didattica
flasher /ˈflæʃə(r)/ *n* Auto lampeggiatore *m*
flash flood *n* alluvione *f* improvvisa
flashgun *n* Phot flash *m inv*
flashing /ˈflæʃɪŋ/ *adj* ‹*light*› lampeggiante
flashlight *n* Phot flash *m inv*; AmE (torch) torcia *f* [elettrica]
flashpoint *n* (trouble spot) punto *m* caldo; Chem punto *m* di infiammabilità
flashy /ˈflæʃɪ/ *adj* vistoso
flask /flɑːsk/ *n* fiasco *m*; (vacuum ~) termos *m inv*
flat /flæt/ **A** *adj* (**flatter**, **flattest**) piatto; ‹*refusal*› reciso; ‹*beer*› sgassato; ‹*battery*› scarico; ‹*tyre*› a terra; **A ~** Mus la bemolle
B *n* appartamento *m*; Mus bemolle *m*; (puncture) gomma *f* a terra
flat broke *adj* infml completamente al verde
flat feet *npl* piedi *mpl* piatti
flatfish *n* pesce *m* piatto
flat-footed /-ˈfʊtɪd/ *adj* **be ~** avere i piedi piatti
flat hunting *n* BrE **go ~** andare in cerca di un appartamento
flatly /ˈflætlɪ/ *adv* ‹*refuse*› categoricamente

flatmate *n* BrE *persona (f) con cui si divide un appartamento*

flat out *adv ‹drive, work›* a tutto gas; **it only does 120 kph ~** arriva a 120 km all'ora andando a tutta manetta; **go ~ for something** mettercela tutta per fare qualcosa

flat racing *n* corse *fpl* piane

flat rate **A** *n* forfait *m inv*; (unitary rate) tariffa *f* unica
B *attrib ‹fee, tax›* forfettario

flat spin *n* Aeron virata *f* piatta; **be in a ~** infml essere in fibrillazione

flatten /ˈflætn/ *vt* appiattire

flatter /ˈflætə(r)/ *vt* adulare

flattering /ˈflætərɪŋ/ *adj ‹comments›* lusinghiero; *‹colour, dress›* che fa sembrare più bello

flattery /ˈflætərɪ/ *n* adulazione *f*

flat tyre *n* gomma *f* a terra

flatulence /ˈflætjʊləns/ *n* flatulenza *f*

flaunt /flɔːnt/ *vt* ostentare

flautist /ˈflɔːtɪst/ *n* flautista *mf*

flavour /ˈfleɪvə(r)/ **A** *n* sapore *m*
B *vt* condire; **chocolate ~ed** al sapore di cioccolato

flavour enhancer /-ɪnhɑːnsə(r)/ *n* esaltatore *m* dell'aroma

flavouring /ˈfleɪvərɪŋ/ *n* condimento *m*

flavourless /ˈfleɪvəlɪs/ *adj* insipido

flaw /flɔː/ *n* difetto *m*

flawed /flɔːd/ *adj* difettoso

flawless /ˈflɔːlɪs/ *adj* perfetto

flax /flæks/ *n* lino *m*

flaxen /ˈflæksən/ *adj ‹hair›* biondo platino

flea /fliː/ *n* pulce *f*

flea-bitten /ˈfliːbɪtən/ *adj* infestato dalle pulci; fig pidocchioso

flea market *n* mercato *m* delle pulci

fleapit *n* BrE infml derog pidocchietto *m*

fleck /flek/ *n* macchiolina *f*

fled /fled/ ▶ **flee**

fledgling /ˈfledʒlɪŋ/ **A** *n* uccellino *m* *(che ha appena messo le ali)*
B *attrib* fig *‹democracy, enterprise›* giovane; *‹party, group›* alle prime armi

flee /fliː/ *vt & vi* (*pt/pp* **fled**) fuggire (from da)

fleece /fliːs/ **A** *n* pelliccia *f*
B *vt* infml spennare

fleecy /ˈfliːsɪ/ *adj ‹lining›* felpato

fleet /fliːt/ *n* flotta *f*; (of cars) parco *m*

fleeting /ˈfliːtɪŋ/ *adj* **catch a ~ glance of something** intravedere qualcosa; **for a ~ moment** per un attimo

Flemish /ˈflemɪʃ/ *adj* fiammingo

flesh /fleʃ/ *n* carne *f*; **in the ~** in persona; **one's own ~ and blood** il proprio sangue
■ **flesh out** *vt* dare più consistenza a *‹essay etc›*

flesh eating /-iːtɪŋ/ *adj* carnivoro

flesh wound *n* ferita *f* superficiale

fleshy /ˈfleʃɪ/ *adj* carnoso

flew /fluː/ ▶ **fly²**

flex¹ /fleks/ *vt* flettere *‹muscle›*

flex² *n* Electr filo *m*

flexibility /fleksəˈbɪlətɪ/ *n* flessibilità *f*

flexible /ˈfleksəbl/ *adj* flessibile

flexitime BrE, **flextime** AmE /ˈfleks(ɪ)taɪm/ *n* orario *m* flessibile

flick /flɪk/ *vt* dare un buffetto a; **~ something off something** togliere qualcosa da qualcosa con un colpetto
■ **flick through** *vt* sfogliare

flicker /ˈflɪkə(r)/ *vi* tremolare

flick knife *n* BrE coltello *m* a scatto

flier /ˈflaɪə(r)/ *n* = **flyer**

flight¹ /flaɪt/ *n* (fleeing) fuga *f*; **take ~** darsi alla fuga

flight² *n* (flying) volo *m*; **~ of stairs** rampa *f*

flight attendant *n* assistente *mf* di volo

flight bag *n* bagaglio *m* a mano

flight deck *n* Aeron cabina *f* di pilotaggio; Naut ponte *m* di volo

flight engineer *n* motorista *mf* di bordo

flight lieutenant *n* Mil capitano *m*

flight path *n* traiettoria *f* di volo

flight recorder *n* registratore *m* di volo

flighty /ˈflaɪtɪ/ *adj* (**-ier**, **-iest**) frivolo

flimsy /ˈflɪmzɪ/ *adj* (**-ier**, **-iest**) *‹material›* leggero; *‹shelves›* poco robusto; *‹excuse›* debole

flinch /flɪntʃ/ *vi* (wince) sussultare; (draw back) ritirarsi; **~ from a task** fig sottrarsi a un compito

fling /flɪŋ/ **A** *n* **have a ~** infml (affair) avere un'avventura
B *vt* (*pt/pp* **flung**) gettare
■ **fling away** *vt* gettar via
■ **fling open** *vt* spalancare *‹door, window›*

flint /flɪnt/ *n* pietra *f* focaia; (for lighter) pietrina *f*

flip /flɪp/ *v* (*pt/pp* **flipped**) **A** *vt* dare un colpetto a; buttare in aria *‹coin›*
B *vi* infml uscire dai gangheri; (go mad) impazzire
■ **flip through** *vt* sfogliare

flip chart *n* lavagna *f* a fogli mobili

flip-flop *n* (sandal) infradito *m inv*; Comput (device) flip-flop *m inv*, multivibratore *m* bistabile; AmE (about face) voltafaccia *m inv*

flippant /ˈflɪpənt/ *adj* irriverente

flipper /ˈflɪpə(r)/ *n* pinna *f*

flipping /ˈflɪpɪŋ/ BrE infml **A** *adj* maledetto
B *adv ‹stupid, painful, cold›* maledettamente

flip side *n* (of record) retro *m*; fig (other side) rovescio *m*

flirt /flɜːt/ **A** *n* civetta *f*
B *vi* flirtare

f

flirtation /flɜːˈteɪʃn/ *n* flirt *m inv*

flirtatious /flɜːˈteɪʃəs/ *adj* civettuolo

flit /flɪt/ *vi* (*pt/pp* **flitted**) volteggiare

float /fləʊt/ **A** *n* galleggiante *m*; (in procession) carro *m*; (money) riserva *f* di cassa
B *vi* galleggiare; Fin fluttuare
■ **float off** *vi* ‹*boat*› andare alla deriva; ‹*balloon*› volare via

floating /ˈfləʊtɪŋ/ *adj* ‹*bridge*› galleggiante; ‹*population*› fluttuante

floating rate interest /ˈfləʊtɪŋ/ *n* Fin interesse *m* a tasso variabile

floating voter *n* Pol elettore, -trice *mf* indeciso, -a

flock /flɒk/ **A** *n* gregge *m*; (of birds) stormo *m*
B *vi* affollarsi

floe /fləʊ/ *n* banchisa *f*

flog /flɒg/ *vt* (*pt/pp* **flogged**) bastonare; infml (sell) vendere

flood /flʌd/ **A** *n* alluvione *f*; (of river) straripamento *m*; fig (of replies, letters, tears) diluvio *m*; **be in ~** ‹*river*› essere straripato
B *vt* allagare
C *vi* ‹*river*› straripare

flood control *n* prevenzione *f* delle inondazioni

flood damage *n* danno *m* provocato da un'inondazione

floodgate *n* chiusa *f*; **open the ~s** fig spalancare le porte

floodlight **A** *n* riflettore *m*
B *vt* (*pt/pp* **floodlit**) illuminare con riflettori

floodplain *n* pianura *f* alluvionale

flood tide *n* marea *f* montante

flood waters *npl* acque *fpl* alluvionali

⚷ **floor** /flɔː(r)/ **A** *n* pavimento *m*; (storey) piano *m*; (for dancing) pista *f*
B *vt* (baffle) confondere; (knock down) stendere ‹*person*›

floorboard *n* asse *f* del pavimento

floorcloth *n* straccio *m* per lavare il pavimento

floor exercises *npl* esercizi *mpl* a terra

floor manager *n* TV direttore, -trice *mf* di studio; Comm gerente *mf* di un negozio

floor polish *n* cera *f* per il pavimento

floor show *n* spettacolo *m* di varietà

floor space *n* superficie *f*; **we don't have the ~** non abbiamo lo spazio

flop /flɒp/ **A** *n* infml (failure) tonfo *m*; Theat fiasco *m*
B *vi* (*pt/pp* **flopped**) infml (fail) far fiasco
■ **flop down** *vi* accasciarsi

floppy /ˈflɒpɪ/ *adj* floscio

floppy disk *n* floppy disk *m inv*

floppy drive, **floppy disk drive** *n* lettore *m* di floppy

flora /ˈflɔːrə/ *n* flora *f*

⚷ parola chiave

floral /ˈflɔːrəl/ *adj* floreale

Florence /ˈflɒrəns/ *n* Firenze *f*

Florentine /ˈflɒrəntaɪn/ *adj* fiorentino

florid /ˈflɒrɪd/ *adj* ‹*complexion*› florido; ‹*style*› troppo ricercato

florist /ˈflɒrɪst/ *n* fioraio, -a *mf*

floss /flɒs, AmE flɔːs/ **A** *n* filo *m* interdentale
B *vt* **~ one's teeth** usare il filo interdentale
C *vi* usare il filo interdentale

flotsam /ˈflɒtsəm/ *n* relitti *mpl* alla deriva

flounce /flaʊns/ **A** *n* balza *f*
B *vi* **~ out** uscire con aria melodrammatica

flounder¹ /ˈflaʊndə(r)/ *vi* dibattersi; ‹*speaker*› impappinarsi

flounder² *n* (fish) passera *f* di mare

flour /ˈflaʊə(r)/ *n* farina *f*

flourish /ˈflʌrɪʃ/ **A** *n* gesto *m* drammatico; (scroll) ghirigoro *m*
B *vi* prosperare
C *vt* brandire

flourishing /ˈflʌrɪʃɪŋ/ *adj* ‹*industry, business*› fiorente; ‹*garden*› rigoglioso

floury /ˈflaʊərɪ/ *adj* farinoso

flout /flaʊt/ *vt* fregarsene di ‹*rules*›

⚷ **flow** /fləʊ/ **A** *n* flusso *m*
B *vi* scorrere; (hang loosely) ricadere

flow chart *n* diagramma *m* di flusso

⚷ **flower** /ˈflaʊə(r)/ **A** *n* fiore *m*
B *vi* fiorire

flower arrangement *n* composizione *f* floreale

flower arranging *n* composizione *f* floreale

flower bed *n* aiuola *f*

flowered /ˈflaʊəd/ *adj* a fiori

flower garden *n* giardino *m* fiorito

flowering /ˈflaʊərɪŋ/ **A** *n* Bot fioritura *f*; fig (development) espansione *f*
B *adj* ‹*shrub, tree*› in fiore; **early/late ~** a fioritura precoce/tardiva

flowerpot *n* vaso *m* [per i fiori]

flower shop *n* fiorista *m*

flower show *n* mostra *f* floreale

flowery /ˈflaʊərɪ/ *adj* fiorito

flown /fləʊn/ ▶ **fly²**

fl oz *abbr* (**fluid ounce(s)**) oncia *f* fluida

flu /fluː/ *n* influenza *f*

fluctuate /ˈflʌktjʊeɪt/ *vi* fluttuare

fluctuation /flʌktjʊˈeɪʃn/ *n* fluttuazione *f*

flue /fluː/ *n* (of chimney, stove) canna *f* fumaria

fluency /ˈfluːənsɪ/ *n* (in speaking) competenza *f*; (in writing) speditezza *f*

fluent /ˈfluːənt/ *adj* spedito; **speak ~ Italian** parlare correntemente l'italiano

fluently /ˈfluːəntlɪ/ *adv* speditamente

fluff /flʌf/ *n* peluria *f*

fluffy /ˈflʌfɪ/ *adj* (**-ier**, **-iest**) vaporoso; ‹*toy*› di peluche

fluid /ˈfluːɪd/ **A** *adj* fluido
B *n* fluido *m*

fluid ounce *n* oncia *f* fluida
fluke /flu:k/ *n* colpo *m* di fortuna
flummox /ˈflʌməks/ *vt* infml sbalestrare
flung /flʌŋ/ ▸ **fling**
flunk /flʌŋk/ *vt* AmE infml essere bocciato in
fluorescent /flʊəˈresnt/ *adj* fluorescente
fluorescent lighting *n* luce *f* fluorescente
fluoride /ˈflʊəraɪd/ *n* fluoruro *m*
flurry /ˈflʌrɪ/ *n* (snow) raffica *f*; fig agitazione *f*
flush /flʌʃ/ **A** *n* (blush) [vampata *f* di] rossore *m*
B *vi* arrossire
C *vt* lavare con un getto d'acqua; ~ **the toilet** tirare l'acqua
D *adj* a livello (**with** di); infml (affluent) pieno di soldi
▪ **flush out** *vt* snidare ‹*spy*›
flushed /flʌʃt/ *adj* (cheeks) rosso; ~ **with** eccitato da ‹*success*›; raggiante di ‹*pride*›
fluster /ˈflʌstə(r)/ *vt* agitare
flustered /ˈflʌstəd/ *adj* in agitazione; **get** ~ mettersi in agitazione
flute /flu:t/ *n* flauto *m*
flutter /ˈflʌtə(r)/ **A** *n* battito *m*
B *vi* svolazzare
flux /flʌks/ *n* **in a state of** ~ in uno stato di flusso
fly[1] /flaɪ/ *n* (*pl* **flies**) mosca *f*
fly[2] **A** *vi* (*pt* **flew**, *pp* **flown**) volare; (go by plane) andare in aereo; ‹*flag*› sventolare; (rush) precipitarsi; ~ **open** spalancarsi
B *vt* pilotare ‹*plane*›; trasportare [in aereo] ‹*troops, supplies*›; volare con ‹*Alitalia etc*›
▪ **fly away** *vi* volare via
fly[3] *n* **flies** *pl* (on trousers) patta *f*
flyaway /ˈflaɪəweɪ/ *adj* ‹*hair*› che non stanno a posto
fly-by-night *adj* ‹*person*› irresponsabile; ‹*company*› non affidabile
flycatcher /ˈflaɪkætʃə(r)/ *n* pigliamosche *m inv*
fly-drive *adj* con la formula aereo più auto
flyer /ˈflaɪə(r)/ *n* aviatore *m*; (leaflet) volantino *m*
fly-fishing *n* pesca *f* con la mosca
flying /ˈflaɪɪŋ/ *n* aviazione *f*
flying buttress *n* arco *m* rampante
flying colours: **with** ~ a pieni voti
flying saucer *n* disco *m* volante
flying start *n* ottima partenza *f*; **get off to a flying start** partire benissimo
flying visit *n* visita *f* lampo *inv*
flyleaf *n* risguardo *m*
fly on the wall *adj* ‹*documentary*› con telecamera nascosta
flyover *n* cavalcavia *m inv*
fly-past *n* BrE Aeron parata *f* aerea
flysheet *n* (handbill) volantino *m*; (of tent) soprattenda *m inv*
fly spray *n* moschicida *m*
FM *abbr* (**Frequency Modulation**) FM
foal /fəʊl/ *n* puledro *m*
foam /fəʊm/ **A** *n* schiuma *f*; (synthetic) gommapiuma *f*
B *vi* spumare; ~ **at the mouth** far la bava alla bocca
foam bath *n* bagnoschiuma *m*
foam rubber *n* gommapiuma *f*
fob /fɒb/ *vt* (*pt/pp* **fobbed**) ~ **something off** affibbiare qualcosa (**on somebody** a qualcuno); ~ **somebody off** liquidare qualcuno
focal /ˈfəʊkl/ *adj* focale
focal point *n* (of village, building) centro *m* di attrazione; (main concern) punto *m* centrale; (in optics) fuoco *m*; **the room lacks a** ~ nella stanza manca un punto che focalizzi l'attenzione
focus /ˈfəʊkəs/ **A** *n* fuoco *m*; **in** ~ a fuoco; **out of** ~ sfocato
B *vt* (*pt/pp* **focused** *or* **focussed**) fig concentrare (**on** su)
C *vi* ~ **on something** Phot mettere a fuoco qualcosa; fig concentrarsi su qualcosa
fodder /ˈfɒdə(r)/ *n* foraggio *m*
foe /fəʊ/ *n* nemico, -a *mf*
foetal /ˈfi:tl/ *adj* fetale
foetid /ˈfetɪd/ *adj* fetido
foetus /ˈfi:təs/ *n* (*pl* **-tuses**) feto *m*
fog /fɒg/ *n* nebbia *f*
fog bank *n* banco *m* di nebbia
fogey /ˈfəʊgɪ/ *n* **old** ~ persona *f* antiquata
foggy /ˈfɒgɪ/ *adj* (**foggier**, **foggiest**) nebbioso; **it's** ~ c'è nebbia; **I haven't got the foggiest [idea]** infml hon ne ho la più pallida idea
foghorn /ˈfɒghɔ:n/ *n* sirena *f* da nebbia
fog lamp, **fog light** *n* Auto [faro *m*] antinebbia *m inv*
foible /ˈfɔɪbl/ *n* punto *m* debole
foil[1] /fɔɪl/ *n* lamina *f* di metallo
foil[2] *vt* (thwart) frustrare
foil[3] *n* (sword) fioretto *m*
foist /fɔɪst/ *vt* appioppare (**on somebody** a qualcuno)
fold[1] /fəʊld/ *n* (for sheep) ovile *m*
fold[2] **A** *n* piega *f*
B *vt* piegare; ~ **one's arms** incrociare le braccia
C *vi* piegarsi; (fail) crollare
▪ **fold back** *vt* ripiegare ‹*sheets*›; aprire ‹*shutters*›
▪ **fold in** *vt* incorporare ‹*flour, eggs*›
▪ **fold up** **A** *vt* ripiegare ‹*chair*›
B *vi* essere pieghevole; infml ‹*business*› collassare
foldaway /ˈfəʊldəweɪ/ *adj* ‹*bed*› pieghevole; ‹*table*› estraibile
folder /ˈfəʊldə(r)/ *n* cartella *f*
folding /ˈfəʊldɪŋ/ *adj* pieghevole

folding seat *n* strapuntino *m*, sedile *m* pieghevole
folding stool *n* sgabello *m* pieghevole
fold-out *n* (in magazine) pieghevole *m*
foliage /'fəʊlɪɪdʒ/ *n* fogliame *m*
🔑 **folk** /fəʊk/ *npl* gente *f*; **my ~s** (family) i miei; **hello there ~s** ciao a tutti
folk dance *n* danza *f* popolare
folklore *n* folclore *m*
folk medicine *n* rimedio *m* della nonna
folk memory *n* memoria *f* collettiva
folk music *n* musica *f* folk
folk song *n* canto *m* popolare
folk wisdom *n* saggezza *f* popolare
🔑 **follow** /'fɒləʊ/ *vt & vi* seguire; **it doesn't ~** non è necessariamente così; **~ suit** fig fare lo stesso; **as ~s** come segue
■ **follow through** *vt* portare avanti ‹*project, idea*›
■ **follow up** *vt* fare seguito a ‹*letter*›
follower /'fɒləʊə(r)/ *n* seguace *mf*
following /'fɒləʊɪŋ/ **A** *adj* seguente **B** *n* seguito *m*; (supporters) seguaci *mpl* **C** *prep* in seguito a
follow-on *n* seguito *m*
follow-up **A** *n* (of social work case) controllo *m*; (of patient, ex inmate) visita *f* di controllo; (film, record, single, programme) seguito *m* **B** *attrib* ‹*survey, work, interview*› successivo; **~ letter** lettera *f* che fa seguito
folly /'fɒlɪ/ *n* follia *f*
foment /fə'ment/ *vt* fig fomentare
fond /fɒnd/ *adj* affezionato; ‹*hope*› vivo; **be ~ of** essere appassionato di ‹*music*›; **I'm ~ of...** ‹*food, person*› mi piace moltissimo...
fondle /'fɒndl/ *vt* coccolare
fondly /'fɒndlɪ/ *adv* ‹*hope*› ingenuamente
fondness /'fɒndnɪs/ *n* affetto *m*; (for things) amore *m*
font /fɒnt/ *n* fonte *m* battesimale; Typ carattere *m* di stampa
🔑 **food** /fu:d/ *n* cibo *m*; (for animals, groceries) mangiare *m*; **let's buy some ~** compriamo qualcosa da mangiare
food aid *n* aiuti *mpl* alimentari
foodie /'fu:dɪ/ *n* infml buongustaio, -a *mf*
food mixer *n* frullatore *m*
food poisoning *n* intossicazione *f* alimentare
food processor *n* tritatutto *m inv* elettrico
foodstuffs *npl* generi *mpl* alimentari
fool[1] /fu:l/ **A** *n* sciocco, -a *mf*; **she's no ~** non è una stupida; **make a ~ of oneself** rendersi ridicolo **B** *vt* prendere in giro **C** *vi* **~ around** giocare; ‹*husband, wife*› avere l'amante
fool[2] *n* Culin crema *f*

foolhardy /'fu:lhɑ:dɪ/ *adj* temerario
foolish /'fu:lɪʃ/ *adj* stolto
foolishly /'fu:lɪʃlɪ/ *adv* scioccamente
foolishness /'fu:lɪʃnɪs/ *n* sciocchezza *f*
foolproof /'fu:lpru:f/ *adj* facilissimo
foolscap /'fu:lskæp/ *n* BrE (paper) carta *f* protocollo
🔑 **foot** /fʊt/ *n* (*pl* **feet**) piede *m*; (of animal) zampa *f*; (measure) piede (=*30,48 cm*); **on ~** a piedi; **on one's feet** in piedi; **put one's ~ in it** infml fare una gaffe
footage /'fʊtɪdʒ/ *n* (piece of film) spezzone *m*; **news ~** servizio *m* [filmato]
foot-and-mouth disease *n* afta *f* epizootica
🔑 **football** *n* calcio *m*; (ball) pallone *m*
footballer *n* giocatore *m* di calcio
football pools *npl* totocalcio *m*
footbrake *n* freno *m* a pedale
footbridge *n* passerella *f*
foothills *npl* colline *fpl* pedemontane
foothold *n* punto *m* d'appoggio
footing *n* **lose one's ~** perdere l'appiglio; **on an equal ~** in condizioni di parità
footlights *npl* luci *npl* della ribalta
footloose and fancy-free *adj* libero come l'aria
footman *n* valletto *m*
footnote *n* nota *f* a piè di pagina
foot passenger *n* (on boat) passeggero, -a *mf*
footpath *n* sentiero *m*
footprint *n* orma *f*; (of machine) ingombro *m*
footrest *n* poggiapiedi *m inv*
footsore *adj* **be ~** avere male ai piedi
footstep *n* passo *m*; **follow in somebody's ~s** fig seguire l'esempio di qualcuno
footstool *n* sgabellino *m*
footwear *n* calzature *fpl*
🔑 **for** /fə(r)/, *accentato*/fɔ:(r)/ **A** *prep* per; **~ this reason** per questa ragione; **I have lived here ~ ten years** vivo qui da dieci anni; **~ supper** per cena; **~ all that** nonostante questo; **what ~?** a che scopo?; **send ~ a doctor** chiamare un dottore; **fight ~ a cause** lottare per una causa; **go ~ a walk** andare a fare una passeggiata; **there's no need ~ you to go** non c'è bisogno che tu vada; **it's not ~ me to say** non sta a me dirlo; **now you're ~ it** ora sei nei pasticci **B** *conj* poiché, perché
forage /'fɒrɪdʒ/ **A** *n* foraggio *m* **B** *vi* **~ for** cercare
foray /'fɒreɪ/ *n* Mil incursione *f*; **make a ~ into** ‹*politics, acting*› tentare la strada di
forbade /fə'bæd/ ▶ **forbid**
forbearance /fɔ:'beərəns/ *n* pazienza *f*
forbearing /fɔ:'beərɪŋ/ *adj* tollerante
forbid /fə'bɪd/ *vt* (*pt* **forbade**, *pp* **forbidden**) proibire

🔑 parola chiave

forbidden /fəˈbɪdn/ *adj* ‹*fruit, place*› proibito

forbidding /fəˈbɪdɪŋ/ *adj* ‹*prospect*› che spaventa; (stern) severo

force /fɔːs/ **A** *n* forza *f*; **in ~** in vigore; (in large numbers) in massa; **come into ~** entrare in vigore; **the [armed] ~s** *pl* le forze armate **B** *vt* forzare; **~ something on somebody** ‹*decision*› imporre qualcosa a qualcuno; ‹*drink*› costringere qualcuno a fare qualcosa

▪ **force back** *vt* trattenere ‹*tears*›

▪ **force down** *vt* buttar giù (*controvoglia*) ‹*food, drink*›

forced /fɔːst/ *adj* forzato

forced landing *n* atterraggio *m* forzato

force-feed *vt* (*pt/pp* **-fed**) nutrire a forza

forceful /ˈfɔːsfʊl/ *adj* energico

forcefully /ˈfɔːsfʊlɪ/ *adv* ‹*say, argue*› con forza

forceps /ˈfɔːseps/ *npl* forcipe *msg*

forcible /ˈfɔːsəbl/ *adj* forzato

forcibly /ˈfɔːsəblɪ/ *adv* forzatamente

ford /fɔːd/ **A** *n* guado *m*
B *vt* guadare

fore /fɔː(r)/ *n* **to the ~** in vista; **come to the ~** salire alla ribalta

forearm /ˈfɔːrɑːm/ *n* avambraccio *m*

forebears /ˈfɔːbeəz/ *npl* antenati *mpl*

foreboding /fɔːˈbəʊdɪŋ/ *n* presentimento *m*

forecast /ˈfɔːkɑːst/ **A** *n* previsione *f*
B *vt* (*pt/pp* **forecast**) prevedere

forecaster /ˈfɔːkɑːstə(r)/ *n* pronosticatore, -trice *mf*; (economic) analista *mf* della congiuntura; (of weather) meteorologo, -a *mf*

forecourt *n* (of garage) spiazzo *m* [antistante]

forefathers *npl* antenati *mpl*

forefinger *n* [dito *m*] indice *m*

forefront *n* **be in the ~** essere all'avanguardia

foregone *adj* **be a ~ conclusion** essere una cosa scontata

foreground *n* primo piano *m*

forehand *n* Tennis diritto *m*

forehead /ˈfɔːhed, ˈfɒrɪd/ *n* fronte *f*

foreign /ˈfɒrən/ *adj* straniero; ‹*trade*› estero; (not belonging) estraneo; **he is ~** è uno straniero

foreign affairs *npl* affari *mpl* esteri

foreign body *n* corpo *m* estraneo

foreign correspondent *n* corrispondente *mf* estero

foreign currency *n* valuta *f* estera

foreigner /ˈfɒrənə(r)/ *n* straniero, -a *mf*

foreign exchange *n* (currency) valuta *f* estera

foreign exchange market *n* mercato *m* dei cambi

foreign language *n* lingua *f* straniera

foreign minister *n* ministro *m* degli Esteri

Foreign Office *n* ministero *m* degli [affari] Esteri

Foreign Secretary *n* Ministro *m* degli Esteri

foreleg /ˈfɔːleg/ *n* zampa *f* anteriore

foreman /ˈfɔːmən/ *n* caporeparto *m*

foremost /ˈfɔːməʊst/ **A** *adj* principale
B *adv* **first and ~** in primo luogo

forename /ˈfɔːneɪm/ *n* nome *m* di battesimo

forensic /fəˈrensɪk/ *adj* **~ medicine** medicina legale

forensic evidence *n* prova *f* medico-legale

forensic science *n* medicina *f* legale

forensic scientist *n* medico *m* legale

forensic tests *npl* perizia *f sg* medico-legale

forerunner /ˈfɔːrʌnə(r)/ *n* precursore *m*

foresee /fɔːˈsiː/ *vt* (*pt* **-saw**, *pp* **-seen**) prevedere

foreseeable /fɔːˈsiːəbl/ *adj* **in the ~ future** nel futuro immediato

foreshadow /fɔːˈʃædəʊ/ *vt* prevedere

foresight /ˈfɔːsaɪt/ *n* previdenza *f*

foreskin /ˈfɔːskɪn/ *n* Anat prepuzio *m*

forest /ˈfɒrɪst/ *n* foresta *f*

forestall /fɔːˈstɔːl/ *vt* prevenire

forester /ˈfɒrɪstə(r)/ *n* guardia *f* forestale

forest fire *n* incendio *m* nei boschi

forest ranger /ˈreɪndʒə(r)/ *n* AmE guardia *f* forestale

forestry /ˈfɒrɪstrɪ/ *n* silvicoltura *f*

foretaste /ˈfɔːteɪst/ *n* pregustazione *f*

foretell /fɔːˈtel/ *vt* (*pt/pp* **-told**) predire

forethought /ˈfɔːθɔːt/ *n* accortezza *f*, previdenza *f*

forever /fəˈrevə(r)/ *adv* per sempre; **he's ~ complaining** si lamenta sempre

forewarn /fɔːˈwɔːn/ *vt* avvertire

foreword /ˈfɔːwɜːd/ *n* prefazione *f*

forfeit /ˈfɔːfɪt/ **A** *n* (in game) pegno *m*; Jur penalità *f*
B *vt* perdere

forfeiture /ˈfɔːfɪtʃə(r)/ *n* (of right) perdita *f*; (of property) confisca *f*

forgave /fəˈgeɪv/ ▸ **forgive**

forge[1] /fɔːdʒ/ *vi* **~ ahead** ‹*runner*› lasciarsi indietro gli altri; fig farsi strada

forge[2] **A** *n* fucina *f*
B *vt* fucinare; (counterfeit) contraffare

forger /ˈfɔːdʒə(r)/ *n* contraffattore *m*

forgery /ˈfɔːdʒərɪ/ *n* contraffazione *f*

forget /fəˈget/ *vt & vi* (*pt* **-got**, *pp* **-gotten**) dimenticare; dimenticarsi di ‹*language, skill*›; **~ oneself** perdere la padronanza di sé

▪ **forget about** *vt* dimenticarsi di

forgetful /fə'getfʊl/ *adj* smemorato
forgetfulness /fə'getfʊlnɪs/ *n* smemoratezza *f*
forget-me-not *n* non-ti-scordar-di-mé *m inv*
forgettable /fə'getəbl/ *adj* ‹*day, fact, film*› da dimenticare
forgive /fə'gɪv/ *vt* (*pt* **-gave**, *pp* **-given**) **~ somebody for something** perdonare qualcuno per qualcosa
forgiveness /fə'gɪvnɪs/ *n* perdono *m*
forgiving /fə'gɪvɪŋ/ *adj* ‹*person*› indulgente

f

forgo /fɔː'gəʊ/ *vt* (*pt* **-went**, *pp* **-gone**) rinunciare a
forgot(ten) /fə'gɒt(n)/ ▸ **forget**
fork /fɔːk/ **A** *n* forchetta *f*; (for digging) forca *f*; (in road) bivio *m*
B *vi* ‹*road*› biforcarsi; **~ right** prendere a destra
▪ **fork out A** *vt* infml sborsare
B *vi* sborsare soldi
forked lightning /fɔːkt/ *n* fulmine *m* ramificato
fork-lift truck *n* elevatore *m*
forlorn /fə'lɔːn/ *adj* ‹*look*› perduto; ‹*place*› derelitto; **~ hope** speranza *f* vana
✓ **form** /fɔːm/ **A** *n* forma *f*; (document) modulo *m*; Sch classe *f*
B *vt* formare; formulare ‹*opinion*›
C *vi* formarsi
formal /'fɔːml/ *adj* formale
formal dress *n* abito *m* da cerimonia
formalin /'fɔːməlɪn/ *n* formalina *f*
formality /fɔː'mælətɪ/ *n* formalità *f*
formally /'fɔːməlɪ/ *adv* in modo formale; (officially) ufficialmente
format /'fɔːmæt/ **A** *n* formato *m*
B *vt* formattare ‹*disk, page*›
✓ **formation** /fɔː'meɪʃn/ *n* formazione *f*
formative /'fɔːmətɪv/ *adj* **~ years** anni formativi
✓ **former** /'fɔːmə(r)/ *adj* precedente; ‹*PM, colleague*› ex; **the ~, the latter** il primo, l'ultimo
formerly /'fɔːməlɪ/ *adv* precedentemente; (in olden times) in altri tempi
formidable /'fɔːmɪdəbl/ *adj* formidabile
formless /'fɔːmlɪs/ *adj* ‹*mass*› informe; ‹*novel*› che manca di struttura
form teacher *n* BrE Sch ≈ coordinatore, -trice *mf* del consiglio di classe
formula /'fɔːjʊlə/ *n* (*pl* **-ae** /'fɔːmjʊliː/ *or* **-s**) formula *f*
formulate /'fɔːmjʊleɪt/ *vt* formulare
formulation /fɔːmjʊ'leɪʃn/ *n* formulazione *f*
fornication /fɔːnɪ'keɪʃn/ *n* fornicazione *f*
forsake /fə'seɪk/ *vt* (*pt* **-sook** /fə'sʊk/; *pp* **-saken**) abbandonare
forswear /fɔː'sweə(r)/ *vt* (renounce) abiurare

✓ parola chiave

fort /fɔːt/ *n* Mil forte *m*
forte /'fɔːteɪ/ *n* [pezzo *m*] forte *m*
forth /fɔːθ/ *adv* **back and ~** avanti e indietro; **and so ~** e così via
forthcoming /fɔːθ'kʌmɪŋ/ *adj* prossimo; (communicative) communicativo; **no response was ~** non arrivava nessuna risposta
forthright /'fɔːθraɪt/ *adj* schietto
forthwith /fɔːθ'wɪð/ *adv* immediatamente
forties /'fɔːtɪz/ *npl* (period) **the ~** gli anni Quaranta *mpl*; (age) quarant'anni *mpl*; **a man in his ~** un quarantenne
fortieth /'fɔːtɪɪθ/ *adj & n* quarantesimo, -a *mf*
fortification /fɔːtɪfɪ'keɪʃn/ *n* fortificazione *f*
fortified /'fɔːtɪfaɪd/ *adj* fortificato; **~ wine** vino liquoroso; **~ with vitamins** arricchito con vitamine
fortify /'fɔːtɪfaɪ/ *vt* (*pt/pp* **-ied**) fortificare; fig rendere forte
fortitude /'fɔːtɪtjuːd/ *n* coraggio *m*
fortnight /'fɔːtnaɪt/ *n* BrE quindicina *f*
fortnightly /'fɔːtnaɪtlɪ/ **A** *adj* bimensile
B *adv* ogni due settimane
fortress /'fɔːtrɪs/ *n* fortezza *f*
fortuitous /fɔː'tjuːɪtəs/ *adj* fortuito
fortunate /'fɔːtʃənət/ *adj* fortunato; **that's ~!** meno male!
fortunately /'fɔːtʃənətlɪ/ *adv* fortunatamente
fortune /'fɔːtʃuːn/ *n* fortuna *f*
fortune cookie *n* AmE *biscottino (m) che racchiude un foglietto con una predizione*
fortune-teller *n* indovino, -a *mf*
forty /'fɔːtɪ/ *adj & n* quaranta *m*; **have ~ winks** infml fare un pisolino
forum /'fɔːrəm/ *n* foro *m*
✓ **forward** /'fɔːwəd/ **A** *adv* avanti; (towards the front) in avanti; **move ~** andare avanti
B *adj* in avanti; (presumptuous) sfacciato
C *n* Sport attaccante *m*
D *vt* inoltrare ‹*letter*›; spedire ‹*goods*›
forward buying *n* Fin acquisto *m* a termine
forwarding address *n indirizzo (m) a cui inoltrare la corrispondenza*
forward-looking *adj* ‹*company, person*› lungimirante
forward planning *n* pianificazione *f* a lungo termine
forwards /'fɔːwədz/ *adv* avanti
forward slash *n* slash *m inv*
fossil /'fɒs(ə)l/ *n* fossile *m*
fossil fuel *n* combustibile *m* fossile
fossilized /'fɒsɪlaɪzd/ *adj* fossile; ‹*ideas*› fossilizzato
foster /'fɒstə(r)/ *vt* allevare ‹*child*›
foster child *n* figlio, -a *mf* in affidamento
foster family *n* famiglia *f* affidataria
foster home *n* famiglia *f* affidataria
foster mother *n* madre *f* affidataria

fought /fɔːt/ ▶ **fight**

foul /faʊl/ **A** *adj* ‹*smell, taste*› cattivo; ‹*air*› viziato; ‹*language*› osceno; ‹*mood, weather*› orrendo
B *vt* inquinare ‹*water*›; Sport commettere un fallo contro; ‹*nets, rope*› impigliarsi in

▪ **foul up A** *vt* infml (spoil) mandare in malora
B *n* infml intoppo *m*

foul-mouthed /-ˈmaʊðd/ *adj* sboccato

foul play A *n* Jur delitto *m*
B *n* Sport fallo *m*

foul-smelling /-ˈsmelɪŋ/ *adj* puzzolente

foul-up *n* pasticcio *m*

found[1] /faʊnd/ ▶ **find**

found[2] *vt* fondare

foundation /faʊnˈdeɪʃn/ *n* (basis) fondamento *m*; (charitable) fondazione *f*; ~**s** *pl* (of building) fondamenta *fpl*; **lay the ~ stone** porre la prima pietra

foundation course *n* BrE Univ corso *m* propedeutico

founder[1] /ˈfaʊndə(r)/ *n* fondatore, -trice *mf*

founder[2] *vi* ‹*ship*› affondare

foundry /ˈfaʊndrɪ/ *n* fonderia *f*

fount /faʊnt/ *n* Typ carattere *m* [stampa]

fountain /ˈfaʊntɪn/ *n* fontana *f*

fountain pen *n* penna *f* stilografica

four /fɔː(r)/ *adj & n* quattro *m*

four-by-four /ˌfɔːbaɪˈfɔː(r)/ *n* (vehicle) quattro per quattro *f inv*

four four time *n* Mus quattro quarti

four-letter word *n* parolaccia *f*

four-poster, **four-poster bed** *n* letto *m* a baldacchino

foursome /ˈfɔːsəm/ *n* quartetto *m*

four-star /ˈfɔːstɑː(r)/ **A** *adj* ‹*hotel, restaurant*› a quattro stelle
B *n* (petrol) super *f*

four-stroke *adj* ‹*engine*› a quattro tempi

fourteen /fɔːtiːn/ *adj & n* quattordici *m*

fourteenth /fɔːˈtiːnθ/ *adj & n* quattordicesimo, -a *mf*

fourth /fɔːθ/ *adj & n* quarto, -a *mf*

fourthly /ˈfɔːθlɪ/ *adv* in quarto luogo

fourth rate *adj* ‹*job, hotel, film*› di terz'ordine

four-wheel drive, **four-wheel drive vehicle** *n* quattro per quattro *f inv*

fowl /faʊl/ *n* pollame *m*

fox /fɒks/ **A** *n* volpe *f*
B *vt* (puzzle) ingannare

fox cub *n* volpacchiotto *m*

fox fur *n* pelliccia *f* di volpe

foxglove *n* digitale *f*

foxhound *n* foxhound *m inv*

fox hunt *n* caccia *f* alla volpe

fox hunting *n* caccia *f* alla volpe

fox terrier *n* fox-terrier *m inv*

foxtrot *n* fox-trot *m inv*

foxy /ˈfɒksɪ/ *adj* (**-ier**, **-iest**) infml (sexy) sexy *inv*; (crafty) scaltro

foyer /ˈfɔɪeɪ/ *n* Theat ridotto *m*; (in hotel) salone *m* d'ingresso

fracas /ˈfrækɑː/ *n* baruffa *f*

fracking /ˈfrækɪŋ/ *n* fratturazione *f* idraulica, fracking *m*

fraction /ˈfrækʃn/ *n* frazione *f*

fractionally /ˈfrækʃənəlɪ/ *adv* (slightly) leggermente

fracture /ˈfræktʃə(r)/ **A** *n* frattura *f*
B *vt* fratturare
C *vi* fratturarsi

fragile /ˈfrædʒaɪl/ *adj* fragile

fragment /ˈfrægmənt/ *n* frammento *m*

fragmentary /ˈfrægm(ə)ntərɪ/ *adj* frammentario

fragrance /ˈfreɪgrəns/ *n* fragranza *f*

fragrant /ˈfreɪgrənt/ *adj* fragrante

frail /freɪl/ *adj* gracile

frailty /ˈfreɪltɪ/ *n* (imperfection) debolezza *f*; (of person: moral) fragilità *f*; (of person: physical) gracilità *f*; (of health, state) precarietà *f*

frame /freɪm/ **A** *n* (of picture, door, window) cornice *f*; (of spectacles) montatura *f*; Anat ossatura *f*; (structure, of bike) telaio *m*; **~ of mind** stato *m* d'animo
B *vt* incorniciare ‹*picture*›; fig formulare; sl (incriminate) montare

frame of mind *n* stato *m* d'animo

framework /ˈfreɪmwɜːk/ *n* struttura *f*; **within the ~ of the law** nell'ambito della legge

franc /fræŋk/ *n* franco *m*

France /frɑːns/ *n* Francia *f*

franchise /ˈfræntʃaɪz/ *n* Pol diritto *m* di voto; Comm franchigia *f*

Franciscan /frænˈsɪskən/ *n* francescano *m*

frank[1] /fræŋk/ *vt* affrancare ‹*letter*›

frank[2] *adj* franco

Frankfurt /ˈfræŋkfɜːt/ *n* Francoforte *f*

frankfurter /ˈfræŋkfɜːtə(r)/ *n* würstel *m inv*

frankincense /ˈfræŋkɪnsens/ *n* incenso *m*

franking machine /ˈfræŋkɪŋ/ *n* affrancatrice *f*

frankly /ˈfræŋklɪ/ *adv* francamente

frantic /ˈfræntɪk/ *adj* frenetico; **be ~ with worry** essere agitatissimo

frantically /ˈfræntɪklɪ/ *adv* freneticamente

fraternal /frəˈtɜːnl/ *adj* fraterno

fraternity /frəˈtɜːnətɪ/ *n* (club) associazione *f*; (spirit, brotherhood) fratellanza *f*

fraud /frɔːd/ *n* frode *f*; (person) impostore *m*

fraudulent /ˈfrɔːdjʊlənt/ *adj* fraudolento

fraught /frɔːt/ *adj* **~ with** pieno di

fray[1] /freɪ/ *n* mischia *f*

fray[2] *vi* sfilacciarsi

frayed /freɪd/ *adj* ‹*cuffs*› sfilacciato; ‹*nerves*› a pezzi

frazzle /'fræz(ə)l/ *n* **be worn to a ~** essere ridotto uno straccio; **burn something to a ~** carbonizzare qualcosa

freak /fri:k/ **A** *n* fenomeno *m*; (person) scherzo *m* di natura; infml (weird person) tipo *m* strambo
B *adj* anormale
■ **freak out** *vi* infml (lose control, go crazy) andar fuori di testa

freakish /'fri:kɪʃ/ *adj* strambo

freckle /'frekl/ *n* lentiggine *f*

freckled /'frekld/ *adj* lentigginoso

⚷ **free** /fri:/ **A** *adj* (**freer**, **freest**) libero; ‹*ticket, copy*› gratuito; (lavish) generoso; **~ of charge** gratuito; **set ~** liberare; **~ with...** Comm in omaggio con...
B *vt* (*pt/pp* **freed**) liberare

free agent *n* persona *f* libera di agire come vuole

free and easy *adj* disinvolto

freebie, **freebee** /'fri:bɪ/ *n* infml (free gift) omaggio *m*; (trip) viaggio *m* gratuito; (newspaper) giornale *m* gratuito

⚷ **freedom** /'fri:dəm/ *n* libertà *f*

freedom fighter *n* combattente *mf* per la libertà

free enterprise *n* liberalismo *m* economico

free fall *n* caduta *f* libera

Freefone® /'fri:fəʊn/ *n* = **Freephone**

free-for-all *n* (disorganized situation, fight) baraonda *f*

free gift *n* omaggio *m*

freehand *adv* a mano libera

freehold *n* proprietà *f* [fondiaria] assoluta

free house *n* BrE *pub* (*m inv*) *che non è legato a nessun produttore di birra*

free kick *n* calcio *m* di punizione

freelance *adj & adv* indipendente

freeloader *n* infml scroccone *m*

freely /'fri:lɪ/ *adv* liberamente; (generously) generosamente; **I ~ admit that...** devo ammettere che...

free market *n* economia *f* di libero mercato

Freemason *n* massone *m*

Freemasonry *n* massoneria *f*

Freephone, **Freefone**® /'fri:fəʊn/ *n* numero *m* verde

Freephone number *n* numero *m* verde

Freepost /'fri:pəʊst/ *n* BrE affrancatura *f* a carico del destinatario

free-range *adj* ‹*eggs*› di allevamento a terra; ‹*hens*› allevato a terra

free-range egg *n* uovo *m* di gallina ruspante

free sample *n* campione *m* gratuito

free speech *n* libertà *f* di parola

free spirit *n* persona *f* che ama la sua indipendenza

⚷ parola chiave

free-standing *adj* ‹*heater*› non incassato; ‹*statue*› a tutto tondo; ‹*lamp*› a stelo

freestyle *n* stile *m* libero

free-to-air *adj* BrE ‹*TV programme, channel*› non a pagamento, in chiaro

free trade *n* libero scambio *m*

free trial period *n* periodo *m* di prova gratuito

freeware /'fri:weə(r)/ *n* Comput freeware *m inv*

freeway *n* AmE autostrada *f*

freewheel *vi* ‹*car*› (in neutral) andare in folle; (with engine switched off) andare a motore spento; ‹*bicycle*› andare a ruota libera

free will *n* **of one's own ~** di spontanea volontà

freeze /fri:z/ **A** *vt* (*pt* **froze**, *pp* **frozen**) gelare; bloccare ‹*wages*›
B *vi* ‹*water*› gelare; **it's freezing** si gela; **my hands are freezing** ho le mani congelate

freeze-dried *adj* liofilizzato

freeze-frame *n* (video) fermo *m* immagine

freezer /'fri:zə(r)/ *n* freezer *m inv*, congelatore *m*

freezer compartment *n* scomparto *m* freezer

freezing /'fri:zɪŋ/ **A** *adj* gelido
B *n* **below ~** sotto zero

freezing cold *adj* gelido

freezing fog *n* nebbia *f* ghiacciata

freezing point *n* punto *m* di congelamento

freight /freɪt/ *n* carico *m*

freight charges *npl* costi *mpl* di spedizione

freighter /'freɪtə(r)/ *n* nave *f* da carico

freight forwarder *n* spedizioniere *m*

freight train *n* AmE treno *m* merci

⚷ **French** /frentʃ/ **A** *adj* francese
B *n* (language) francese *m*; **the ~** *pl* i francesi

French beans *npl* fagiolini *mpl* [verdi]

French bread *n* filone *m* (*di pane*)

French Canadian **A** *n* canadese *mf* francofono, -a
B *adj* del Canada francofono

French doors *npl* porta-finestra *f inv*

French dressing *n* BrE vinaigrette *f inv*

French fries *npl* patate *fpl* fritte

French horn *n* corno *m* da caccia

French kiss *n* bacio *m* profondo

French knickers *npl* culottes *fpl*

Frenchman *n* francese *m*

French polish *n* vernice *f* a olio e gommalacca

French-speaking *adj* francofono

French toast *n* *pane* (*m*) *immerso nell'uovo sbattuto e fritto*

French window *n* porta-finestra *f*

Frenchwoman *n* francese *f*
frenetic /frəˈnetɪk/ *adj* ‹*activity*› frenetico
frenzied /ˈfrenzɪd/ *adj* frenetico
frenzy /ˈfrenzɪ/ *n* frenesia *f*
frequency /ˈfriːkwənsɪ/ *n* frequenza *f*
frequent¹ /ˈfriːkwənt/ *adj* frequente
frequent² /frɪˈkwent/ *vt* frequentare
frequent-flyer miles *npl* AmE miglia *fpl* aeree
frequently /ˈfriːkwəntlɪ/ *adv* frequentemente
fresco /ˈfreskəʊ/ *n* affresco *m*
fresh /freʃ/ *adj* fresco; (new) nuovo; AmE (cheeky) sfacciato
fresh air *n* aria *f* fresca; **get some ~** prendere una boccata d'aria
freshen /ˈfreʃn/ *vi* ‹*wind*› rinfrescare
■ **freshen up** **A** *vt* dare una rinfrescata a **B** *vi* rinfrescarsi
fresh-faced /-ˈfeɪst/ *adj* dalla faccia giovanile
freshly /ˈfreʃlɪ/ *adv* di recente
freshman /ˈfreʃmən/ *n* AmE matricola *f*; fig (in congress, in firm) nuovo arrivato *m*
freshness /ˈfreʃnɪs/ *n* freschezza *f*
freshwater /ˈfreʃwɔːtə(r)/ *adj* di acqua dolce
fret /fret/ *vi* (*pt/pp* **fretted**) inquietarsi
fretful /fretfʊl/ *adj* irritabile
fretsaw /ˈfretsɔː/ *n* seghetto *m* da traforo
fretwork /ˈfretwɜːk/ *n* [lavoro *m* di] traforo *m*
Freudian slip /ˈfrɔɪdɪən/ *n* lapsus *m inv* freudiano
friar /ˈfraɪə(r)/ *n* frate *m*
friction /ˈfrɪkʃn/ *n* frizione *f*
Friday /ˈfraɪdeɪ/ *n* venerdì *m*
fridge /frɪdʒ/ *n* frigo *m*
fridge-freezer /ˌfrɪdʒˈfriːzə(r)/ *n* frigocongelatore *m*
fried /fraɪd/ **A** ▶ **fry¹** **B** *adj* fritto; **~ egg** uovo *m* fritto
friend /frend/ *n* amico, -a *mf*
friendly /ˈfrendlɪ/ *adj* (**-ier**, **-iest**) ‹*relations, meeting, match*› amichevole; ‹*neighbourhood, smile*› piacevole; ‹*software*› di facile uso; **be ~ with** essere amico di
friendly fire *n* fuoco *m* amico
friendship /ˈfrendʃɪp/ *n* amicizia *f*
fries /fraɪz/ *npl* AmE infml patatine *fpl* fritte
frieze /friːz/ *n* fregio *m*
frigate /ˈfrɪgət/ *n* fregata *f*
fright /fraɪt/ *n* paura *f*; **take ~** spaventarsi
frighten /ˈfraɪt(ə)n/ *vt* spaventare
■ **frighten away** *vt* far scappare ‹*bird, intruder*›
frightened /ˈfraɪtənd/ *adj* spaventato; **be ~** aver paura (**of** di)
frightening /ˈfraɪt(ə)nɪŋ/ *adj* spaventoso
frightful /ˈfraɪtfl/ *adj* terribile
frightfully /ˈfraɪtfʊlɪ/ *adv* terribilmente
frigid /ˈfrɪdʒɪd/ *adj* frigido
frigidity /frɪˈdʒɪdətɪ/ *n* freddezza *f*; Psych frigidità *f*
frill /frɪl/ *n* volant *m inv*
frilly /ˈfrɪlɪ/ *adj* ‹*dress*› con tanti volant
fringe /frɪndʒ/ *n* frangia *f*; (of hair) frangetta *f*; fig (edge) margine *m*
fringe benefits *npl* benefici *mpl* supplementari
frisk /frɪsk/ *vt* (search) perquisire
frisky /ˈfrɪskɪ/ *adj* (**-ier**, **-iest**) vispo
fritter /ˈfrɪtə(r)/ *n* frittella *f*
■ **fritter away** *vt* sprecare
frivolity /frɪˈvɒlətɪ/ *n* frivolezza *f*
frivolous /ˈfrɪvələs/ *adj* frivolo
frizzy /ˈfrɪzɪ/ *adj* (**-ier**, **-iest**) crespo
fro /frəʊ/ ▶ **to**
frock /frɒk/ *n* abito *m*
frog /frɒg/ *n* rana *f*
frogman *n* uomo *m* rana *inv*
frogmarch *vt* BrE portare via a forza
frogs' legs *npl* cosce *fpl* di rana
frogspawn *n* uova *fpl* di rana
frolic /ˈfrɒlɪk/ *vi* (*pt/pp* **frolicked**) ‹*lambs*› sgambettare; infml ‹*people*› folleggiare
from /frɒm/ *prep* da; **~ Monday** da lunedì; **~ that day** da quel giorno; **he's ~ London** è di Londra; **this is a letter ~ my brother** questa è una lettera di mio fratello; **documents ~ the 16th century** documenti del XVI secolo; **made ~** fatto con; **she felt ill ~ fatigue** si sentiva male dalla stanchezza; **~ now on** d'ora in poi
front /frʌnt/ **A** *n* parte *f* anteriore; fig (organization etc) facciata *f*; (of garment) davanti *m*; **sea ~** lungomare *m*; Mil, Pol, Meteorol fronte *m*; **in ~ of** davanti a; **in** *or* **at the ~** davanti; **to the ~** avanti **B** *adj* davanti; ‹*page, row, wheel*› anteriore
frontage /ˈfrʌntɪdʒ/ *n* (of house) facciata *f*; **with ocean/river ~** (access) prospiciente l'oceano/il fiume
frontal /ˈfrʌntl/ *adj* frontale
front bench *n* BrE Pol parlamentari *mpl* di maggiore importanza
front door *n* porta *f* d'entrata
front garden *n* giardino *m* sul davanti
frontier /ˈfrʌntɪə(r)/ *n* frontiera *f*
front line *n* Mil prima linea *f*; **be in the ~** fig essere in prima linea
front of house *n* BrE Theat foyer *m inv*
front page **A** *n* prima pagina *f* **B** *adj* ‹*picture, spread*› in prima pagina
front runner *n* Sport concorrente *mf* in testa; (favourite) favorito, -a *mf*
front-wheel drive *n* trazione *f* anteriore
frost /frɒst/ *n* gelo *m*; **hoar ~** brina *f*
frostbite /ˈfrɒs(t)baɪt/ *n* congelamento *m*

frostbitten /ˈfrɒs(t)bɪtən/ *adj* congelato
frosted /ˈfrɒstɪd/ *adj* ~ **glass** vetro *m* smerigliato
frostily /ˈfrɒstɪlɪ/ *adv* gelidamente
frosting /ˈfrɒstɪŋ/ *n* AmE Culin glassa *f*
frosty /ˈfrɒstɪ/ *adj* (**-ier**, **-iest**) also fig gelido
froth /frɒθ/ **A** *n* schiuma *f*
B *vi* far schiuma
frothy /ˈfrɒθɪ/ *adj* (**-ier**, **-iest**) schiumoso
frown /fraʊn/ **A** *n* cipiglio *m*
B *vi* aggrottare le sopracciglia
▪ **frown on** *vt* disapprovare

f

froze /frəʊz/ ▶ **freeze**
frozen /ˈfrəʊzn/ **A** ▶ **freeze**
B *adj* ‹*corpse, hand*› congelato; ‹*wastes*› gelido; Culin surgelato; **I'm** ~ sono gelato
frozen food *n* surgelati *mpl*
frugal /ˈfruːgl/ *adj* frugale
frugally /ˈfruːgəlɪ/ *adv* frugalmente
🔑 **fruit** /fruːt/ *n* frutto *m*; (collectively) frutta *f*; **eat more** ~ mangia più frutta
fruit bowl *n* fruttiera *f*
fruit cake *n dolce (m) con frutta candita*
fruit cocktail *n* macedonia *f* [di frutta]
fruit drop *n* drop *m inv* alla frutta
fruiterer /ˈfruːtərə(r)/ *n* fruttivendolo, -a *mf*
fruit farmer *n* frutticoltore *m*
fruit fly *n* moscerino *m* della frutta
fruitful /ˈfruːtfʊl/ *adj* fig fruttuoso
fruit gum *n* caramella *f* alla frutta
fruition /fruːˈɪʃn/ *n* **come to** ~ dare dei frutti
fruit juice *n* succo *m* di frutta
fruitless /ˈfruːtlɪs/ *adj* infruttuoso
fruitlessly /ˈfruːtlɪslɪ/ *adv* senza risultato
fruit machine *n* macchinetta *f* mangiasoldi
fruit salad *n* macedonia *f* [di frutta]
fruity /ˈfruːtɪ/ *adj* ‹*wine*› fruttato
frump /frʌmp/ *n* donna *f* scialba
frumpy /ˈfrʌmpɪ/ *adj* scialbo
frustrate /frʌˈstreɪt/ *vt* frustrare; rovinare ‹*plans*›
frustrated /frʌˈstreɪtɪd, AmE ˈfrʌst-/ *adj* frustrato
frustrating /frʌˈstreɪtɪŋ/ *adj* frustrante
frustration /frʌˈstreɪʃn/ *n* frustrazione *f*
fry[1] /fraɪ/ *n inv* **small** ~ fig pesce *m* piccolo
fry[2] *vt & vi* (*pt/pp* **fried**) friggere
frying pan /ˈfraɪɪŋ/ *n* padella *f*
ft. *abbr* (**foot** *or* **feet**) piede, piedi
FTP *abbr* (**file transfer protocol**) Comput FTP *m*
fuchsia /ˈfjuːʃə/ *n* fucsia *f*
fuck /fʌk/ vulg **A** *vt & vi* scopare
B *n* **I don't give a** ~ me ne sbatto; **what the** ~ **are you doing?** che cazzo fai?
C *int* cazzo!
▪ **fuck off**: *vi* vulg ~ **off!** vaffanculo!
▪ **fuck up** *vt* vulg (ruin) mandare a puttane
fucking /ˈfʌkɪŋ/ *adj* vulg del cazzo
fuddled /ˈfʌd(ə)ld/ *adj* (confused) confuso; (slightly drunk) brillo
fuddy-duddy /ˈfʌdɪdʌdɪ/ *n* infml matusa *mf inv*
fudge /fʌdʒ/ *n caramella (f) a base di zucchero, burro e latte*
🔑 **fuel** /ˈfjuːəl/ **A** *n* carburante *m*; fig nutrimento *m*
B *vt* fig alimentare
fuel consumption *n* consumo *m* di carburante
fuel economy *n* risparmio *m* di carburante
fuel efficient *adj* economico
fuel injection *n* iniezione *f*
fuel injection engine *n* motore *m* a iniezione
fuel oil *n* nafta *f*
fuel pump *n* pompa *f* della benzina
fuel tank *n* serbatoio *m*
fuggy /ˈfʌgɪ/ *adj* BrE (smoky) fumoso
fugitive /ˈfjuːdʒɪtɪv/ *n* fuggiasco, -a *mf*
fugue /fjuːg/ *n* Mus fuga *f*
fulcrum /ˈfʊlkrəm/ *n* fulcro *m*
fulfil /fʊlˈfɪl/ *vt* (*pt/pp* **-filled**) soddisfare ‹*conditions, need*›; adempiere a ‹*promise*›; realizzare ‹*dream, desire*›; ~ **oneself** realizzarsi
fulfilling /fʊlˈfɪlɪŋ/ *adj* soddisfacente
fulfilment /fʊlˈfɪlmənt/ *n* **sense of** ~ senso *m* di appagamento
🔑 **full** /fʊl/ **A** *adj* pieno (**of** di); (detailed) esauriente; ‹*bus, hotel*› completo; ‹*skirt*› ampio; **at** ~ **speed** a tutta velocità; **in** ~ **swing** in pieno fervore
B *adv* in pieno; **you known** ~ **well that** sai benissimo che
C *n* **in** ~ per intero
full-back *n* difensore *m*
full beam *n* Auto [fari *mpl*] abbaglianti *mpl*
full blast *adv* infml **the TV was on** ~ c'era la TV a manetta
full-blown /-ˈblaʊn/ *adj* ‹*epidemic*› vero e proprio; ‹*disease*› conclamato
full board *n* pensione *f* completa
full-bodied /-ˈbɒdɪd/ *adj* ‹*wine*› corposo
full-cream milk *n* latte *m* intero
full-frontal *adj* ‹*photograph*› di nudo frontale
full house *n* Theat tutto esaurito *m inv*; (in poker) full *m inv*
full-length *adj* ‹*dress*› lungo; ‹*curtain*› lungo fino a terra; ‹*portrait*› intero; ~ **film** lungometraggio *m*
full moon *n* luna *f* piena
full name *n* nome *m* per esteso

full price *n* prezzo *m* intero

full-scale *adj* ‹*model*› in scala reale; ‹*alert*› di massima gravità

full stop *n* punto *m*

full-time *adj & adv* a tempo pieno

⚷ **fully** /'fʊlɪ/ *adv* completamente; (in detail) dettagliatamente; ~ **booked** ‹*hotel, restaurant*› tutto prenotato

fully fledged /-'fledʒd/ *adj* ‹*bird*› che ha messo tutte le penne; ‹*lawyer*› con tutte le qualifiche; ‹*member*› a tutti gli effetti

fulsome /'fʊlsəm/ *adj* esagerato

fumble /'fʌmbl/ *vi* ~ **in** rovistare in; ~ **with** armeggiare con; ~ **for one's keys** rovistare alla ricerca delle chiavi

■ **fumble about** *vi* (in dark) andare a tentoni; ~ **in** rovistare in ‹*bag*›

fume /fju:m/ *vi* (be angry) essere furioso

fumes /fju:mz/ *npl* fumi *mpl*; (from car) gas *mpl* di scarico

fumigate /'fju:mɪgeɪt/ *vt* suffumicare

⚷ **fun** /fʌn/ *n* divertimento *m*; **for** ~ per ridere; **make** ~ **of** prendere in giro; **have** ~ divertirsi

⚷ **function** /'fʌŋkʃn/ **A** *n* funzione *f*; (event) cerimonia *f*
B *vi* funzionare; ~ **as** (serve as) funzionare da

functional /'fʌnkʃ(ə)nəl/ *adj* funzionale

function key *n* Comput tasto *m* [di] funzioni

function room *n* sala *f* di ricevimento

⚷ **fund** /fʌnd/ **A** *n* fondo *m*; fig pozzo *m*; ~**s** *pl* fondi *mpl*
B *vt* finanziare

fundamental /fʌndə'mentl/ *adj* fondamentale

fundamentalist /fʌndə'mentəlɪst/ *n* fondamentalista *mf*

⚷ **funding** /'fʌndɪŋ/ *n* (financial aid) finanziamento *m*; (of debt) consolidamento *m*

fund-raiser /-reɪzə(r)/ *n* (person) promotore, -trice *mf* di raccolte di fondi; (event) manifestazione *f* per la raccolta di fondi

fund-raising /-reɪzɪŋ/ *n* raccolta *f* di fondi

funeral /'fju:nərəl/ *n* funerale *m*

funeral directors *n* impresa *f* di pompe funebri

funeral home, funeral parlour AmE *n* camera *f* ardente

funeral march *n* marcia *f* funebre

funeral service *n* rito *m* funebre

funereal /fju:'nɪərɪəl/ *adj* lugubre

funfair /'fʌnfeə(r)/ *n* luna park *m inv*

fungal /'fʌŋgəl/ *adj* ‹*infection*› micotico

fungus /'fʌŋgəs/ *n* (*pl* **-gi** /-gaɪ/) fungo *m*

funicular /fju:'nɪkjʊlə(r)/ *n* funicolare *f*

fun loving /'fʌnlʌvɪŋ/ *adj* ‹*person*› amante del divertimento

funnel /'fʌnl/ *n* imbuto *m*; (on ship) ciminiera *f*

funnily /'fʌnɪlɪ/ *adv* comicamente; (oddly) stranamente; ~ **enough** strano a dirsi

⚷ **funny** /'fʌnɪ/ *adj* (**-ier**, **-iest**) buffo; (odd) strano

funny bone *n* osso *m* del gomito

funny business *n* infml affare *m* losco

fur /fɜ:(r)/ *n* pelo *m*; (for clothing) pelliccia *f*; (in kettle) deposito *m*

fur coat *n* pelliccia *f*

furious /'fjʊərɪəs/ *adj* furioso

furiously /'fjʊərɪəslɪ/ *adv* furiosamente

furl /fɜ:l/ *vt* serrare ‹*sail*›

furnace /'fɜ:nɪs/ *n* fornace *f*

furnish /'fɜnɪʃ/ *vt* ammobiliare ‹*flat*›; fornire ‹*supplies*›

furnished /'fɜ:nɪʃt/ *adj* ~ **room** stanza *f* ammobiliata

furnishings /'fɜ:nɪʃɪŋz/ *npl* mobili *mpl*

furniture /'fɜ:nɪtʃə(r)/ *n* mobili *mpl*

furniture remover /rɪmu:və(r)/ *n* BrE impresa *f* di traslochi

furniture van *n* furgone *m* per i traslochi

furore /fjʊ'rɔ:rɪ/ *n* (outrage, criticism) scalpore *m*; (acclaim) entusiasmo *m*

furred /fɜ:d/ *adj* ‹*tongue*› impastato

furrow /'fʌrəʊ/ *n* solco *m*

furry /'fɜ:rɪ/ *adj* ‹*animal*› peloso; ‹*toy*› di peluche

⚷ **further** /'fɜ:ðə(r)/ **A** *adj* (additional) ulteriore; **at the** ~ **end** all'altra estremità; **until** ~ **notice** fino a nuovo avviso
B *adv* più lontano; ~,... inoltre,...; ~ **off** più lontano
C *vt* promuovere

further education *n* istruzione *f* parauniversitaria

furthermore /fɜ:ðə'mɔ:(r)/ *adv* per di più

furthest /'fɜ:ðɪst/ **A** *adj* più lontano
B *adv* più lontano; **the** ~ **advanced of the students** lo studente più avanti

furtive /'fɜ:tɪv/ *adj* furtivo

furtively /'fɜ:tɪvlɪ/ *adv* furtivamente

fury /'fjʊərɪ/ *n* furore *m*

fuse¹ /fju:z/ *n* (of bomb) detonatore *m*; (cord) miccia *f*

fuse² **A** *n* Electr fusibile *m*
B *vt* fondere; Electr far saltare
C *vi* fondersi; Electr saltare; **the lights have**~**d** sono saltate le luci

fuse box *n* scatola *f* dei fusibili

fuselage /'fju:zəlɑ:ʒ/ *n* Aeron fusoliera *f*

fuse wire *n* [filo *m* di] fusibile *m*

fusillade /fju:zɪl'ɑ:d/ *n* Mil scarica *f*; fig raffica *f*

fusion /'fju:ʒn/ *n* fusione *f*

fuss /fʌs/ **A** *n* storie *fpl*; **make a** ~ fare storie; **make a** ~ **of** colmare di attenzioni
B *vi* fare storie

fussy /'fʌsɪ/ *adj* (**-ier**, **-iest**) ‹*person*› difficile da accontentare; ‹*clothes etc*›

f

pieno di fronzoli

fusty /ˈfʌstɪ/ *adj* che odora di stantio; ‹*smell*› di stantio

futile /ˈfjuːtaɪl/ *adj* inutile

futility /fjʊˈtɪlətɪ/ *n* futilità *f*

future /ˈfjuːtʃə(r)/ *adj & n* futuro; **in ~** in futuro

future perfect *n* futuro *m* anteriore

futures *npl* Fin contratti *mpl* a termine

futuristic /fjuːtʃəˈrɪstɪk/ *adj* futuristico

fuze /fjuːz/ *n & v* AmE = **fuse**[1], **fuse**[2]

fuzz /fʌz/ *n* **the ~** sl (police) la pula

fuzzy /ˈfʌzɪ/ *adj* (**-ier**, **-iest**) ‹*hair*› crespo; ‹*photo*› sfuocato

FYI *abbr* (**for your information**) per vostra informazione

f

g

Gg

g[1], **G** /dʒiː/ *n* (letter) g, G *f inv*; Mus sol *m inv*

g[2] *abbr* (**gram(s)**) g

G8 *n abbr* (**group of 8**) G8 *mpl*

gab /gæb/ *n* infml **have the gift of the ~** avere la parlantina

gabardine /gæbəˈdiːn/ *n* gabardine *f*

gabble /ˈgæb(ə)l/ *vi* parlare troppo in fretta

gable /ˈgeɪb(ə)l/ *n* frontone *m*

Gabon /gəˈbɒn/ *n* Gabon *m*

gad /gæd/ *vi* (*pt/pp* **gadded**) **~ about** andarsene in giro

gadget /ˈgædʒɪt/ *n* aggeggio *m*

Gaelic /ˈgeɪlɪk/ *adj & n* gaelico *m*

gaff /gæf/ *n* BrE infml **blow the ~** spifferare un segreto; **blow the ~ on something** svelare la verità su qualcosa

gaffe /gæf/ *n* gaffe *f inv*

gaffer /ˈgæfə(r)/ *n* BrE (foreman) caposquadra *m*; BrE (boss) capo *m*; Cinema, TV tecnico *m* delle luci

gag /gæg/ **A** *n* bavaglio *m*; (joke) battuta *f*
B *vt* (*pt/pp* **gagged**) imbavagliare

gaga /ˈgɑːgɑː/ *adj* infml rimbambito

gage /geɪdʒ/ *n & vt* AmE = **gauge**

gaiety /ˈgeɪətɪ/ *n* allegria *f*

gaily /ˈgeɪlɪ/ *adv* allegramente

gain /geɪn/ **A** *n* guadagno *m*; (increase) aumento *m*
B *vt* acquisire; **~ weight** aumentare di peso; **~ access** accedere
C *vi* ‹*clock*› andare avanti
▪ **gain on** *vt* guadagnare terreno su ‹*runner, car*›

gainful /ˈgeɪnfʊl/ *adj* **~ employment** lavoro *m* remunerativo

gainsay /geɪnˈseɪ/ *vt* contraddire ‹*person*›; contestare ‹*argument*›

gait /geɪt/ *n* andatura *f*

gala /ˈgɑːlə/ **A** *n* gala *f*; **swimming ~** manifestazione *f* di nuoto
B *attrib* di gala

galaxy /ˈgæləksɪ/ *n* galassia *f*

gale /geɪl/ *n* bufera *f*

gale warning *n* avviso *m* di imminente bufera

gall /gɔːl/ *n* (impudence) impudenza *f*

gallant /ˈgælənt/ *adj* coraggioso; (chivalrous) galante

gallantly /ˈgæləntlɪ/ *adv* galantemente

gallantry /ˈgæləntrɪ/ *n* coraggio *m*

gall bladder *n* cistifellea *f*

gallery /ˈgælərɪ/ *n* galleria *f*

galley /ˈgælɪ/ *n* (ship's kitchen) cambusa *f*

galley proof *n* bozza *f* in colonna

Gallic /ˈgælɪk/ *adj* francese

galling /ˈgɔːlɪŋ/ *adj* irritante

gallivant /ˈgælɪvænt/ *vi* infml andare in giro

gallon /ˈgælən/ *n* gallone *m* (BrE = *4,5 l*; AmE = *3,7 l*)

gallop /ˈgæləp/ **A** *n* galoppo *m*
B *vi* galoppare

gallows /ˈgæləʊz/ *n* forca *f*

gallstone /ˈgɔːlstəʊn/ *n* calcolo *m* biliare

galore /gəˈlɔː(r)/ *adv* a bizzeffe

galvanize /ˈgælvənaɪz/ *vt* Techn galvanizzare; fig stimolare (**into** a)

Gambia /ˈgæmbɪə/ *n* Gambia *m*

gambit /ˈgæmbɪt/ *n* prima mossa *f*

gamble /ˈgæmbl/ **A** *n* (risk) azzardo *m*
B *vi* giocare; (on Stock Exchange) speculare; **~ on** (rely) contare su

gambler /ˈgæmblə(r)/ *n* giocatore, -trice *mf* [d'azzardo]

gambling /ˈgæmblɪŋ/ *n* gioco *m* [d'azzardo]

gambol /ˈgæmb(ə)l/ *vi* saltellare

game /geɪm/ **A** *n* gioco *m*; (match) partita *f*; (animals, birds) selvaggina *f*; **~s** *pl* Sch ≈

ginnastica *f*
B *adj* (brave) coraggioso; **are you ~?** ti va?; **be ~ for** essere pronto per
game bird *n* uccello *m* da cacciagione
gamekeeper *n* guardacaccia *m inv*
game park *n game reserve*
game plan *n* tattica *f*
game point *n* Tennis game point *m inv*
game reserve *n* (for hunting) riserva *f* di caccia; (for preservation) parco *m* naturale [faunistico]
games console *n* console *f* per videogiochi
game show *n* ≈ quiz *m inv* televisivo
gamesmanship /ˈgeɪmzmənʃɪp/ *n* stratagemmi *mpl*
games room *n* sala *f* giochi
games software *n* computer game *m inv*
game warden *n* guardacaccia *m inv*
gaming /ˈgeɪmɪŋ/ *n* **online ~** giochi *mpl* online
gaming laws /ˈgeɪmɪŋ/ *npl* leggi *fpl* che regolano il gioco d'azzardo
gaming machine *n* slot machine *f inv*
gaming zone *n sito (m) su cui giocare online*
gammon /ˈgæmən/ *n coscia (f) di maiale affumicata*
gamut /ˈgæmət/ *n* fig gamma *f*
gander /ˈgændə(r)/ *n* oca *f* maschio; **take a ~ at something** infml dare un'occhiata a qualcosa
gang /gæŋ/ *n* banda *f*; (of workmen) squadra *f*
▪ **gang up** *vi* far comunella (**on** contro)
gangland /ˈgæŋlænd/ *n* malavita *f*
gang leader /ˈgæŋliːdə(r)/ *n* capobanda *mf inv*
gangling /ˈgæŋglɪŋ/ *adj* spilungone
gangplank /ˈgæŋplæŋk/ *n* passerella *f*
gang rape *n* stupro *m* collettivo
gangrene /ˈgæŋgriːn/ *n* cancrena *f*
gangrenous /ˈgæŋgrɪnəs/ *adj* cancrenoso
gangster /ˈgæŋstə(r)/ *n* gangster *m inv*
gangway /ˈgæŋweɪ/ *n* passaggio *m*; Naut, Aeron passerella *f*
gaol /dʒeɪl/ **A** *n* carcere *m*
B *vt* incarcerare
gaoler /ˈdʒeɪlə(r)/ *n* carceriere *m*
⚷ **gap** /gæp/ *n* spazio *m*; (in ages) scarto *m*; (in memory) vuoto *m*; (in story) punto *m* oscuro
gape /geɪp/ *vi* stare a bocca aperta; (be wide open) spalancarsi; **~ at** guardare a bocca aperta
gaping /ˈgeɪpɪŋ/ *adj* aperto
gap year *n anno (m) sabbatico tra la fine della scuola superiore e l'inizio dell'università*
garage /ˈgærɑːʒ/ *n* garage *m inv*; (for repairs) officina *f*; (for petrol) stazione *f* di servizio
garage mechanic *n* meccanico *m*
garage sale *n vendita (f) di articoli usati a casa propria*
garb /gɑːb/ *n* tenuta *f*
garbage /ˈgɑːbɪdʒ/ *n* immondizia *f*; (nonsense) idiozie *fpl*
garbage can *n* AmE bidone *m* dell'immondizia
garbage truck *n* AmE camion *m* della nettezza urbana
garbled /ˈgɑːbld/ *adj* confuso
⚷ **garden** /ˈgɑːdn/ **A** *n* giardino *m*; **[public] ~s** *pl* giardini *mpl* pubblici
B *vi* fare giardinaggio
garden centre *n* BrE vivaio *m* (*che vende anche articoli da giardinaggio*)
garden city *n* città *f* giardino
gardener /ˈgɑːdnə(r)/ *n* giardiniere, -a *mf*
garden flat *n appartamento (m) al pianterreno o seminterrato che dà sul giardino*
gardening /ˈgɑːdnɪŋ/ *n* giardinaggio *m*
garden shears *npl* cesoie *fpl*
garden spider *n* epeira *f*
garden suburb *n* periferia *f* verde
garden-variety *adj* AmE ‹*writer; book*› insignificante
gargle /ˈgɑːgl/ **A** *n* gargarismo *m*
B *vi* fare gargarismi
gargoyle /ˈgɑːgɔɪl/ *n* gargouille *f inv*
garish /ˈgeərɪʃ/ *adj* sgargiante
garland /ˈgɑːlənd/ *n* ghirlanda *f*
garlic /ˈgɑːlɪk/ *n* aglio *m*
garlic bread *n* pane *m* condito con aglio
garlic press *n* spremiaglio *m inv*
garment /ˈgɑːmənt/ *n* indumento *m*
garnet /ˈgɑːnɪt/ *n* granato *m*
garnish /ˈgɑːnɪʃ/ **A** *n* guarnizione *f*
B *vt* guarnire
garret /ˈgærɪt/ *n* soffitta *f*
garrison /ˈgærɪsn/ *n* guarnigione *f*
garrotte /gəˈrɒt/ **A** *n* BrE garrotta *f*
B *vt* (strangle) strangolare
garrulous /ˈgærʊləs/ *adj* chiacchierone
garter /ˈgɑːtə(r)/ *n* giarrettiera *f*; AmE (for man's socks) reggicalze *m inv* da uomo
⚷ **gas** /gæs/ **A** *n* gas *m inv*; AmE infml (petrol) benzina *f*
B *vt* (*pt/pp* **gassed**) asfissiare
C *vi* infml blaterare
gas burner *n* becco *m* a gas
gas chamber *n* camera *f* a gas
gas cooker *n* cucina *f* a gas
gaseous /ˈgæsɪəs/ *adj* gassoso
gas fire *n* stufa *f* a gas
gas-fired /-faɪəd/ *adj* ‹*boiler, water heater*› a gas
gash /gæʃ/ **A** *n* taglio *m*
B *vt* tagliare; **~ one's arm** farsi un taglio nel braccio
gasket /ˈgæskɪt/ *n* Techn guarnizione *f*

g

gas main *n* conduttura *f* del gas
gas mask *n* maschera *f* antigas
gas meter *n* contatore *m* del gas
gasoline /'gæsəli:n/ *n* AmE benzina *f*
gas oven *n* forno *m* a gas
gasp /gɑ:sp/ *vi* avere il fiato mozzato
gas pedal *n* AmE pedale *m* dell'acceleratore
gas ring *n* BrE (fixed) bruciatore *m*; (portable) fornelletto *m* [portatile]
gas station *n* AmE distributore *m* di benzina
gassy /'gæsɪ/ *adj* ‹*drink*› gassato
gastric /'gæstrɪk/ *adj* gastrico
gastric flu *n* influenza *f* gastro-intestinale
g
gastric ulcer *n* ulcera *f* gastrica
gastritis /gæ'straɪtɪs/ *n* gastrite *f*
gastroenteritis /gæstrəʊentə'raɪtɪs/ *n* gastroenterite *f*
gastronomy /gæ'strɒnəmɪ/ *n* gastronomia *f*
gate /geɪt/ *n* cancello *m*; (at airport) uscita *f*
gateau /'gætəʊ/ *n* torta *f*
gatecrash **A** *vt* entrare senza invito a
B *vi* entrare senza invito
gatecrasher *n* intruso, -a *mf*
gatehouse *n* (to castle) corpo *m* di guardia; (to park) casa *f* del custode
gatekeeper *n* custode *mf*
gatepost *n* palo *m* del cancello
gateway *n* ingresso *m*
gateway drug *n* droga *f* di passaggio
✓ **gather** /'gæðə(r)/ **A** *vt* raccogliere; (conclude) dedurre; (in sewing) arricciare; **~ speed** acquistare velocità; **~ together** radunare ‹*people, belongings*›; (obtain gradually) acquistare
B *vi* ‹*people*› radunarsi; **a storm is ~ing** si sta preparando un acquazzone
gathering /'gæðərɪŋ/ *n* **family ~** ritrovo *m* di famiglia
GATT /gæt/ *abbr* (**General Agreement on Tariffs and Trade**) GATT *m*
gauche /gəʊʃ/ *adj* ‹*person, attitude*› impacciato; ‹*remark*› inopportuno
gaudy /'gɔ:dɪ/ *adj* (**-ier**, **-iest**) pacchiano
gauge /geɪdʒ/ **A** *n* calibro *m*; Rail scartamento *m*; (device) indicatore *m*
B *vt* misurare; fig stimare
gaunt /gɔ:nt/ *adj* (thin) smunto
gauntlet /'gɔ:ntlɪt/ *n* **throw down the ~** lanciare il guanto della sfida
gauze /gɔ:z/ *n* garza *f*
gave /geɪv/ ▶ **give**
gawky /'gɔ:kɪ/ *adj* (**-ier**, **-iest**) sgraziato
gawp /gɔ:p/ *vi* **~ (at)** infml guardare con aria da ebete
✓ **gay** /geɪ/ *adj* gaio; (homosexual) omosessuale; ‹*bar, club*› gay
gay marriage *n* matrimonio *m* gay

✓ parola chiave

Gaza strip /'gɑ:zə/ *n* la striscia *f* di Gaza
gaze /geɪz/ **A** *n* sguardo *m* fisso
B *vi* guardare; **~ at** fissare; **~ into space** avere lo sguardo perso nel vuoto
gazelle /gə'zel/ *n* gazzella *f*
gazette /gə'zet/ *n* (official journal) bollettino *m* ufficiale; (newspaper title) gazzetta *f*
gazetteer /gæzɪ'tɪə(r)/ *n* (book) dizionario *m* geografico; (part of book) indice *m* dei nomi geografici
gazump /gə'zʌmp/ *vt* Comm sl **we've been ~ed** il proprietario della casa ha optato per un'offerta migliore dopo avere accettato la nostra
gazunder /gə'zʌndə(r)/ *vt* BrE *cercare di indurre qualcuno a cedere un immobile a un prezzo inferiore a quello pattuito*
GB *abbr* (**Great Britain**) GB
GBH *n abbr* (**grievous bodily harm**) lesioni *fpl* personali gravi
GCSE *n abbr* BrE (**General Certificate of Secondary Education**) *esami* (*mpl*) *conclusivi della scuola dell'obbligo*
GDP *n abbr* (**gross domestic product**) PIL *m*
gear /gɪə(r)/ **A** *n* equipaggiamento *m*; Techn ingranaggio *m*; Auto marcia *f*; **in ~** con la marcia innestata; **change ~** cambiare marcia
B *vt* finalizzare (**to** a)
C *vi* **~ up for** prepararsi per ‹*election*›; **~ up to do something** prepararsi per fare qualcosa
gearbox /'gɪəbɒks/ *n* Auto scatola *f* del cambio
gear lever, **gearstick** AmE, **gear shift** *n* leva *f* del cambio
gear wheel *n* moltiplica *f*
geese /gi:s/ ▶ **goose**
geezer /'gi:zə(r)/ *n* sl tipo *m*
gel /dʒel/ *n* gel *m inv*
gelatine /'dʒelətɪn/ *n* gelatina *f*
gelatinous /dʒɪ'lætɪnəs/ *adj* gelatinoso
gelding /'geldɪŋ/ *n* (horse) castrone *m*; (castration) castrazione *f*
gelignite /'dʒelɪgnaɪt/ *n* gelatina *f* esplosiva
gem /dʒem/ *n* gemma *f*
Gemini /'dʒemɪnaɪ/ *n* Astr Gemelli *mpl*
gen /dʒen/ *n* BrE infml informazioni *fpl*; **what's the ~ on this?** cosa c'è da sapere su questo?
gender /'dʒendə(r)/ *n* Gram genere *m*
gene /dʒi:n/ *n* gene *m*
genealogy /dʒi:nɪ'ælədʒɪ/ *n* genealogia *f*
gene library *n* genoteca *f*
gene pool *n* pool *m* genetico
✓ **general** /'dʒenrəl/ **A** *adj* generale
B *n* generale *m*; **in ~** in generale
general election *n* elezioni *fpl* politiche
generalization /dʒenrəlaɪ'zeɪʃn/ *n* generalizzazione *f*

generalize /ˈdʒenrəlaɪz/ *vi* generalizzare
general knowledge *n* cultura *f* generale
generally /ˈdʒenrəlɪ/ *adv* generalmente
general practitioner *n* medico *m* generico
general public *n* [grande] pubblico *m*
general-purpose *adj* multiuso *inv*
general strike *n* sciopero *m* generale
generate /ˈdʒenəreɪt/ *vt* generare
generation /dʒenəˈreɪʃn/ *n* generazione *f*
generation gap *n* gap *m inv* generazionale
generator /ˈdʒenəreɪtə(r)/ *n* generatore *m*
generic /dʒɪˈnerɪk/ *adj* ~ **term** termine *m* generico
generosity /dʒenərɒsətɪ/ *n* generosità *f*
generous /ˈdʒenərəs/ *adj* generoso
generously /ˈdʒenərəslɪ/ *adv* generosamente
genesis /ˈdʒenəsɪs/ *n* fig genesi *f inv*
gene therapy *n* terapia *f* genica
genetic /dʒɪˈnetɪk/ *adj* genetico
genetically modified /dʒɪnetɪklɪ ˈmɒdɪfaɪd/ *adj* ‹*crops*› modificato geneticamente
genetic engineering *n* ingegneria *f* genetica
genetic fingerprinting /ˈfɪŋgəprɪntɪŋ/ *n* impronte *fpl* genetiche
geneticist /dʒɪˈnetɪsɪst/ *n* genetista *mf*
genetics /dʒɪˈnetɪks/ *nsg* genetica *fsg*
genetic testing *n* test *mpl* genetici
Geneva /dʒɪˈniːvə/ *n* Ginevra *f*
genial /ˈdʒiːnɪəl/ *adj* gioviale
genially /ˈdʒiːnɪəlɪ/ *adv* con giovialità
genie /ˈdʒiːnɪ/ *n* genio *m*
genitals /ˈdʒenɪtlz/ *npl* genitali *mpl*
genitive /ˈdʒenɪtɪv/ *adj* & *n* ~ **[case]** genitivo *m*
genius /ˈdʒiːnɪəs/ *n* (*pl* **-uses**) genio *m*
Genoa /ˈdʒenəʊə/ *n* Genova *f*
genocide /ˈdʒenəsaɪd/ *n* genocidio *m*
genome /ˈdʒiːnəʊm/ *n* genoma *m*
genre /ˈʒɒ̃rə/ *n* genere *m* [letterario]
gent /dʒent/ *n* infml signore *m*; **the ~s** *sg* il bagno per uomini
genteel /dʒenˈtiːl/ *adj* raffinato
gentle /ˈdʒentl/ *adj* delicato; ‹*breeze, tap, slope*› leggero
gentleman /ˈdʒentlmən/ *n* signore *m*; (well-mannered) gentiluomo *m*
gentleness /ˈdʒentlnɪs/ *n* delicatezza *f*
gently /ˈdʒentlɪ/ *adv* delicatamente
gentry /ˈdʒentrɪ/ *n* alta borghesia *f*
genuine /ˈdʒenjʊɪn/ *adj* genuino
genuinely /ˈdʒenjʊɪnlɪ/ *adv* ‹*sorry*› sinceramente
genus /ˈdʒiːnəs/ *n* Biol genere *m*
geoengineering /ˌdʒiəʊˌendʒɪˈnɪərɪŋ/ *n* geoingegneria *f*
geographer /dʒɪˈɒgrəfə(r)/ *n* geografo *m*
geographical /dʒɪəˈgræfɪkl/ *adj* geografico
geographically /dʒɪəˈgræfɪklɪ/ *adv* geograficamente
geography /dʒɪˈɒgrəfɪ/ *n* geografia *f*
geological /dʒɪəˈlɒdʒɪkl/ *adj* geologico
geologist /dʒɪˈɒlədʒɪst/ *n* geologo, -a *mf*
geology /dʒɪˈɒlədʒɪ/ *n* geologia *f*
geometric /dʒɪəˈmetrɪk/, **geometrical** /dʒɪəˈmetrɪk[l]/ *adj* geometrico
geometry /dʒɪˈɒmətrɪ/ *n* geometria *f*
geophysics /dʒɪəʊˈfɪzɪks/ *nsg* geofisica *fsg*
geopolitical /dʒiːəʊpəˈlɪtɪkl/ *adj* geopolitico
Georgia /ˈdʒɔːdʒjə/ *n* Georgia *f*
Georgian /ˈdʒɔːdʒən/ *n* & *adj* georgiano, -a *mf*; (language) georgiano *m*
geothermal /dʒiːəʊˈθɜːml/ *adj* geotermico
geranium /dʒəˈreɪnɪəm/ *n* geranio *m*
gerbil /ˈdʒɜːbəl/ *n* gerbillo *m*
geriatric /dʒerɪˈætrɪk/ *adj* geriatrico
geriatrics /dʒerɪˈætrɪks/ *nsg* geriatria *fsg*
geriatric ward *n* reparto *m* geriatria
germ /dʒɜːm/ *n* germe *m*; **~s** *pl* microbi *mpl*
German /ˈdʒɜːmən/ *n* & *adj* tedesco, -a *mf*; (language) tedesco *m*
germane /dʒəˈmeɪn/ *adj* ‹*point, remark*› pertinente
Germanic /dʒəˈmænɪk/ *adj* germanico *f*
German measles *n* rosolia *f*
German shepherd *n* pastore *m* tedesco
Germany /ˈdʒɜːmənɪ/ *n* Germania *f*
germinate /ˈdʒɜːmɪneɪt/ *vi* germogliare
germ warfare *n* guerra *f* batteriologica
gerrymandering /ˈdʒerɪmænd(ə)rɪŋ/ *n manipolazione (f) dei confini di una circoscrizione elettorale*
gerund /ˈdʒerənd/ *n* gerundio *m*
gestate /dʒeˈsteɪt/ *vi* Biol essere incinta; fig maturare
gestation /dʒeˈsteɪʃən/ *n* gestazione *f*
gesticulate /dʒeˈstɪkjʊleɪt/ *vi* gesticolare
gesture /ˈdʒestʃə(r)/ *n* gesto *m*
get /get/ **A** *vt* (*pt/pp* **got**, *pp Am also* **gotten**, *pres p* **getting**) (receive) ricevere; (obtain) ottenere; trovare ‹*job*›; (buy, catch, fetch) prendere; (transport, deliver to airport etc) portare; (reach on telephone) trovare; infml (understand) comprendere; preparare ‹*meal*›; **~ somebody to do something** far fare qualcosa a qualcuno
B *vi* (become) **~ tired/bored/angry** stancarsi/annoiarsi/arrabbiarsi; **I'm ~ting hungry** mi sta venendo fame; **~ real!** fatti furbo!; **~ dressed/married** vestirsi/sposarsi; **~ something ready** preparare qualcosa; **~ nowhere** non concludere nulla; **this is ~ting us nowhere** questo non ci è di nessun aiuto; **~ to** (reach) arrivare a
■ **get about** *vi* ‹*person*› muoversi; ‹*rumour*› circolare
■ **get across** *vt* far capire ‹*message,*

meaning›; ~ **something across to somebody** far capire qualcosa a qualcuno
- **get ahead** *vi* (progress) fare progressi
- **get along** *vi* **get on**
- **get along with** *vt* andare d'accordo con ‹*somebody*›
- **get around** *vi* **get about**
- **get at** *vi* (criticize) criticare; **I see what you're ~ting at** ho capito cosa vuoi dire; **what are you ~ting at?** dove vuoi andare a parare?
- **get away** *vi* (leave) andarsene; (escape) scappare
- **get away with** *vt* restare impunito per
- **get behind with** *vt* rimanere indietro con
- **get by** *vi* passare; (manage) cavarsela
- **get down** **A** *vi* scendere; ~ **down to work** mettersi al lavoro
  B *vt* (depress) buttare giù
- **get in** **A** *vi* entrare
  B *vt* mettere dentro ‹*washing*›; far venire ‹*plumber*›
- **get into** *vt* penetrare in ‹*building*›; mettersi in ‹*trouble*›; (squeeze into) entrare in ‹*dress*›
- **get off** **A** *vi* scendere; (from work) andarsene; Jur essere assolto; ~ **off the bus/one's bike** scendere dal pullman/dalla bici
  B *vt* (remove) togliere
- **get on** *vi* salire; (be on good terms) andare d'accordo; (make progress) andare avanti; (in life) riuscire; **on the bus/one's bike** salire sul pullman/sulla bici; **how are you ~ting on?** come va?
- **get on with** *vt* andare d'accordo con ‹*person*›; andare avanti in ‹*work*›
- **get out** **A** *vi* uscire; (of car) scendere; ~ **out!** fuori!
  B *vt* togliere ‹*cork, stain*›
- **get out of** *vt* (avoid doing) evitare
- **get over** **A** *vi* andare al di là
  B *vt* fig riprendersi da ‹*illness*›
- **get round** **A** *vt* aggirare ‹*rule*›; rigirare ‹*person*›
  B *vi* **I never ~ round to it** non mi sono mai deciso a farlo
- **get through** *vi* (on telephone) prendere la linea
- **get together** **A** *vi* (meet) incontrarsi
  B *vt* mettere insieme ‹*people, money, report*›
- **get up** **A** *vi* alzarsi; (climb) salire
  B *vt* salire su; ~ **up a hill** salire su una collina
- **get up to** *vt* combinare ‹*mischief*›

getaway *n* fuga *f*
get-together *n* incontro *m* fra amici
get-up *n* tenuta *f*
get-up-and-go *n* dinamismo *m*
geyser /'giːzə(r)/ *n* scaldabagno *m*; Geol geyser *m inv*
g-force *n* forza *f* di gravità
Ghana /'gɑːnə/ *n* Ghana *m*
ghastly /'gɑːstlɪ/ *adj* (**-ier**, **-iest**) terribile; **feel ~** sentirsi da cani
gherkin /'gɜːkɪn/ *n* cetriolino *m*
ghetto /'getəʊ/ *n* ghetto *m*
ghetto blaster /blɑːstə(r)/ *n* infml radio-registratore *m* stereo portatile
ghost /gəʊst/ *n* fantasma *m*
ghostly /'gəʊstlɪ/ *adj* spettrale
ghost town *n* città *f* fantasma
ghost writer *n* ghost-writer *m inv*
ghoulish /'guːlɪʃ/ *adj* macabro
giant /'dʒaɪənt/ **A** *n* gigante *m*
  B *adj* gigante
gibberish /'dʒɪbərɪʃ/ *n* stupidaggini *fpl*
gibe /dʒaɪb/ **A** *n* malignità *f*
  B *vi* beffarsi (**at** di)
giblets /'dʒɪblɪts/ *npl* frattaglie *fpl*
giddiness /'gɪdɪnɪs/ *n* vertigini *fpl*
giddy /'gɪdɪ/ *adj* (**-ier**, **-iest**) vertiginoso; **feel ~** avere le vertigini
giddy spell *n* giramento *m* di testa
✓ **gift** /gɪft/ *n* dono *m*; (made to charity) donazione *f*
gifted /'gɪftɪd/ *adj* dotato
gift shop *n* negozio *m* di souvenir
gift token *n* BrE buono *m* acquisto
gift voucher *n* BrE buono *m* acquisto
gift-wrap *vt* impacchettare in carta da regalo
gig /gɪg/ *n* Mus infml concerto *m*
gigantic /dʒaɪ'gæntɪk/ *adj* gigantesco
giggle /'gɪg(ə)l/ **A** *n* risatina *f*
  B *vi* ridacchiare
giggly /'gɪglɪ/ *adj* ‹*person*› che ha la ridarella
gild /gɪld/ *vt* dorare
gilding /'gɪldɪŋ/ *n* doratura *f*
gill /dʒɪl/ *n* (measure) quarto *m* di pinta
gills /gɪlz/ *npl* branchia *fsg*
gilt /gɪlt/ **A** *adj* dorato
  B *n* doratura *f*
gilt-edged stock /-edʒd/ *n* Fin investimento *m* sicuro
gimlet /'gɪmlɪt/ *n* succhiello *m*
gimmick /'gɪmɪk/ *n* trovata *f*
gimmicky /'gɪmɪkɪ/ *adj* ‹*production*› pieno di trovate a effetto
gin /dʒɪn/ *n* gin *m inv*
ginger /'dʒɪndʒə(r)/ **A** *adj* rosso fuoco *inv*; ‹*cat*› rosso
  B *n* zenzero *m*
ginger ale *n* bibita *f* gassata allo zenzero
ginger beer *n* bibita *f* allo zenzero
gingerbread *n* panpepato *m*
ginger-haired /-'heəd/ *adj* con i capelli rossi
gingerly /'dʒɪndʒəlɪ/ *adv* con precauzione
ginger nut, **ginger snap** *n* biscotto *m* allo zenzero

✓ parola chiave

gingham /ˈgɪŋəm/ *n* tessuto *m* vichy
gin rummy *n variante (f) del gioco del ramino*
gipsy /ˈdʒɪpsɪ/ *n* = **gypsy**
giraffe /dʒɪˈrɑːf/ *n* giraffa *f*
girder /ˈgɜːdə(r)/ *n* Techn trave *f*
girdle /ˈgɜːdl/ *n* cintura *f*; (corset) busto *m*
girl /gɜːl/ *n* ragazza *f*; (female child) femmina *f*
girl Friday *n* segretaria *f* tuttofare *inv*
girlfriend *n* amica *f*; (of boy) ragazza *f*
girl guide *n* BrE giovane esploratrice *f*
girlish /ˈgɜːlɪʃ/ *adj* da ragazza
giro /ˈdʒaɪərəʊ/ *n* bancogiro *m*; (cheque) sussidio *m* di disoccupazione
girth /gɜːθ/ *n* circonferenza *f*
gist /dʒɪst/ *n* **the ~** la sostanza
give /gɪv/ **A** *n* elasticità *f*
B *vt* (*pt* **gave**, *pp* **given**) dare; (as present) regalare (**to** a); fare ‹*lecture, present, shriek*›; donare ‹*blood*›; **~ birth** partorire
C *vi* (to charity) fare delle donazioni; (yield) cedere
■ **give away** *vt* dar via; (betray) tradire; (distribute) assegnare; **~ away the bride** portare la sposa all'altare
■ **give back** *vt* restituire
■ **give in** **A** *vt* consegnare
B *vi* (yield) arrendersi
■ **give off** *vt* emanare
■ **give out** **A** *vi* ‹*supplies, patience*› esaurirsi; ‹*engine, heart*› fermarsi
B *vt* (distribute) distribuire; diffondere ‹*heat*›
■ **give over**: *vi* **~ over!** piantala!
■ **give up** **A** *vt* rinunciare a; **~ oneself up** arrendersi
B *vt* rinunciare
■ **give way** *vi* cedere; Auto dare la precedenza; (collapse) crollare
give and take *n* concessioni *fpl* reciproche
giveaway /ˈgɪvəweɪ/ *n* **to be a dead ~** essere un indizio ovvio
given /ˈgɪvn/ ▶ **give**
given name *n* nome *m* di battesimo
GLA *n abbr* BrE (**Greater London Authority**) *organismo (m) di governo di Londra*
glacier /ˈglæsɪə(r)/ *n* ghiacciaio *m*
glad /glæd/ *adj* contento (**of** di)
gladden /ˈglædn/ *vt* rallegrare
glade /gleɪd/ *n* radura *f*
gladiator /ˈglædɪeɪtə(r)/ *n* gladiatore *m*
gladiolus /glædɪˈəʊləs/ *n* gladiolo *m*
gladly /ˈglædlɪ/ *adv* volentieri
glamorize /ˈglæməraɪz/ *vt* rendere affascinante
glamorous /ˈglæmərəs/ *adj* affascinante
glamour /ˈglæmə(r)/ *n* fascino *m*
glance /glɑːns/ **A** *n* sguardo *m*
B *vi* **~ at** dare un'occhiata a
■ **glance off** *vt* ‹*bullet, stone*› rimbalzare contro
■ **glance up** *vi* alzare gli occhi
gland /glænd/ *n* ghiandola *f*
glandular /ˈglændjʊlə(r)/ *adj* ghiandolare
glandular fever *n* mononucleosi *f*
glare /gleə(r)/ **A** *n* bagliore *m*; (look) occhiataccia *f*
B *vi* **~ at** dare un'occhiataccia a
glaring /ˈgleərɪŋ/ *adj* sfolgorante; ‹*mistake*› madornale
glass /glɑːs/ *n* vetro *m*; (for drinking) bicchiere *m*
glass ceiling *n barriera (f) invisibile che impedisce alle donne di avanzare nella carriera*
glasses /ˈglɑːsɪz/ *npl* (spectacles) occhiali *mpl*
glasshouse /ˈglɑːshaʊs/ *n* serra *f*
glassy /ˈglɑːsɪ/ *adj* vitreo
glassy-eyed /-ˈaɪd/ *adj* (from drink, illness) che ha gli occhi vitrei
glaucoma /glɔːˈkəʊmə/ *n* glaucoma *m*
glaze /gleɪz/ **A** *n* smalto *m*
B *vt* mettere i vetri a ‹*door, window*›; smaltare ‹*pottery*›; Culin spennellare
glazed /gleɪzd/ *adj* ‹*eyes*› vitreo
glazier /ˈgleɪzɪə(r)/ *n* vetraio *m*
gleam /gliːm/ **A** *n* luccichio *m*
B *vi* luccicare
gleaming /ˈgliːmɪŋ/ *adj* (clean) splendente; **~ white teeth** denti bianchi splendenti
glean /gliːn/ *vt* racimolare ‹*information*›
glee /gliː/ *n* gioia *f*
gleeful /ˈgliːfʊl/ *adj* gioioso
gleefully /ˈgliːfʊlɪ/ *adv* gioiosamente
glen /glen/ *n* vallone *m*
glib /glɪb/ *adj* derog insincero
glibly /ˈglɪblɪ/ *adv* derog senza sincerità
glide /glaɪd/ *vi* scorrere; (through the air) planare
glider /ˈglaɪdə(r)/ *n* aliante *m*
gliding /ˈglaɪdɪŋ/ *n* volo *m* a vela
glimmer /ˈglɪmə(r)/ **A** *n* barlume *m*
B *vi* emettere un barlume
glimpse /glɪmps/ **A** *n* occhiata *f*; **catch a ~ of** intravedere
B *vt* intravedere
glint /glɪnt/ **A** *n* luccichio *m*
B *vi* luccicare
glisten /ˈglɪsn/ *vi* luccicare
glitch /glɪtʃ/ *n* Comput problema *m* tecnico
glitter /ˈglɪtə(r)/ *vi* brillare
gloat /gləʊt/ *vi* gongolare (**over** su)
global /ˈgləʊbl/ *adj* mondiale
globalization /ˌgləʊbəlaɪˈzeɪʃən/ *n* globalizzazione *f*
global warming *n* riscaldamento *m* dell'atmosfera terrestre
globe /gləʊb/ *n* globo *m*; (as a map) mappamondo *m*
globe-trotting /-trɒtɪŋ/ **A** *n* viaggi *mpl* intorno al mondo

B *adj* ‹*life*› da giramondo; ‹*person*› giramondo

globule /'glɒbju:l/ *n* globulo *m*

gloom /glu:m/ *n* oscurità *f*; (sadness) tristezza *f*

gloomily /'glu:mɪlɪ/ *adv* (sadly) con aria cupa

gloomy /'glu:mɪ/ *adj* (**-ier**, **-iest**) cupo

glorify /'glɔ:rɪfaɪ/ *vt* (*pt/pp* **-ied**) glorificare; **a glorified waitress** niente più che una cameriera

glorious /'glɔ:rɪəs/ *adj* splendido; ‹*deed, hero*› glorioso

glory /'glɔ:rɪ/ **A** *n* gloria *f*; (splendour) splendore *m*; (cause for pride) vanto *m*
B *vi* ~ **in** vantarsi di

glory hole *n* infml ripostiglio *m*

gloss /glɒs/ *n* lucentezza *f*

■ **gloss over** *vt* sorvolare su

glossary /'glɒsərɪ/ *n* glossario *m*

gloss paint *n* vernice *f* lucida

glossy /'glɒsɪ/ *adj* (**-ier**, **-iest**) lucido; ‹*paper*› patinato; ~ **[magazine]** rivista *f* patinata

glossy magazine *n* rivista *f* patinata

glottal stop /'glɒt(ə)l/ *n* occlusiva *f* glottale

glove /glʌv/ *n* guanto *m*

glove compartment *n* Auto cruscotto *m*

glove puppet *n* burattino *m*

glow /gləʊ/ **A** *n* splendore *m*; (in cheeks) rossore *m*; (of candle) luce *f* soffusa
B *vi* risplendere; ‹*candle*› brillare; ‹*person*› avvampare

glower /'glaʊə(r)/ *vi* ~ **(at)** guardare in cagnesco

glowing /'gləʊɪŋ/ *adj* ardente; ‹*account*› entusiastico

glow-worm *n* lucciola *f*

glucose /'glu:kəʊs/ *n* glucosio *m*

glue /glu:/ **A** *n* colla *f*
B *vt* incollare

glue sniffer *n* persona *f* che sniffa colla

glue-sniffing /-snɪfɪŋ/ *n* sniffare *m* la colla

glum /glʌm/ *adj* (**glummer**, **glummest**) tetro

glumly /'glʌmlɪ/ *adv* con aria tetra

glut /glʌt/ *n* eccesso *m*

glutinous /'glu:tɪnəs/ *adj* colloso

glutton /'glʌtən/ *n* ghiottone, -a *mf*

gluttonous /'glʌtənəs/ *adj* ghiotto

gluttony /'glʌtənɪ/ *n* ghiottoneria *f*

glycerine /'glɪsəri:n/ *n* glicerina *f*

gm *abbr* (**gram**) g

GM *abbr* (**genetically modified**) MG

GMO *abbr* (**genetically modified organism**) OGM *m inv*

GMT *abbr* (**Greenwich mean time**) GMT

gnarled /nɑ:ld/ *adj* nodoso

🔑 parola chiave

gnash /næʃ/ *vt* ~ **one's teeth** digrignare i denti

gnat /næt/ *n* moscerino *m*

gnaw /nɔ:/ *vt* rosicchiare

gnome /nəʊm/ *n* gnomo *m*

GNP *abbr* (**gross national product**) PNL *m*

GNVQ *n abbr* BrE (**General National Vocational Qualification**) *diploma* (*m*) *di istituto tecnico*

🔑 **go** /gəʊ/ **A** *n* (*pl* **goes**) energia *f*; (attempt) tentativo *m*; **on the go** in movimento; **at one go** in una sola volta; **it's your go** tocca a te; **make a go of it** riuscire
B *vi* (*pt* **went**, *pp* **gone**) andare; (leave) andar via; (vanish) sparire; (become) diventare; (be sold) vendersi; **go and see** andare a vedere; **go swimming/shopping** andare a nuotare/fare spese; **where's the time gone?** come ha fatto il tempo a volare così?; **it's all gone** è finito; **be going to do** stare per fare; **I'm not going to** non ne ho nessuna intenzione; **to go** AmE ‹*hamburgers etc*› da asporto; **a coffee to go** un caffè da portar via

■ **go about A** *vi* andare in giro
B *vt* affrontare ‹*task*›

■ **go after** *vt* (chase, pursue) correr dietro a

■ **go ahead** *vi* (event) aver luogo; **go ahead with** mandare avanti ‹*plans, wedding*›

■ **go along**: *vi* **make something up as you go along** inventare qualcosa mentre si va avanti

■ **go along with** *vt* concordare con ‹*person, view, plan*›

■ **go around** *vi* ‹*rumour*› girare; **go around with** (person) andare in giro con

■ **go around together** *vi* ‹*people*› andare in giro insieme

■ **go away** *vi* andarsene

■ **go back** *vi* ritornare

■ **go back on** *vt* rimangiarsi ‹*promise*›; tornare su ‹*decision*›

■ **go by** *vi* passare

■ **go down** *vi* scendere; ‹*sun*› tramontare; ‹*ship*› affondare; ‹*swelling*› diminuire

■ **go for** *vt* andare a prendere; andare a cercare ‹*doctor*›; (choose) optare per; infml (attack) aggredire; **he's not the kind I go for** non è il genere che mi attira

■ **go in** *vi* entrare

■ **go in for** *vt* partecipare a ‹*competition*›; darsi a ‹*tennis*›

■ **go into** *vt* entrare in ‹*building*›; (discuss) discutere

■ **go off** *vi* andarsene; ‹*alarm*› scattare; ‹*gun, bomb*› esplodere; ‹*food, milk*› andare a male; **go off well** riuscire

■ **go on** *vi* andare avanti; **what's going on?** cosa succede?

■ **go on at** *vt* infml scocciare

■ **go on with** *vt* (continue) andare avanti con

■ **go out** *vi* uscire; ‹*light, fire*› spegnersi

■ **go out with** *vt* uscire con (somebody)

■ **go over A** *vi* andare

B *vt* (check) controllare
▪ **go round** *vi* andare in giro; (visit) andare; (turn) girare; **is there enough to go round?** ce n'è abbastanza per tutti?
▪ **go through A** *vi* ‹*bill, proposal*› passare
B *vt* (suffer) subire; (check) controllare; (read) leggere
▪ **go through with** *vt* portare a termine ‹*plan*›
▪ **go under** *vi* passare sotto; ‹*ship, swimmer*› andare sott'acqua; (fail) fallire
▪ **go up** *vi* salire; Theat ‹*curtain*› aprirsi
▪ **go with** *vt* accompagnare
▪ **go without A** *vt* fare a meno di ‹*supper; sleep*›
B *vi* fare senza

goad /gəʊd/ *vt* spingere (**into** a); (taunt) spronare

go-ahead A *adj* ‹*person, company*› intraprendente
B *n* okay *m*

goal /gəʊl/ *n* porta *f*; (point scored) gol *m inv*; (in life) obiettivo *m*; **score a ~** segnare

goalie /ˈgəʊlɪ/ infml **goalkeeper** /ˈgəʊlkiːpə(r)/ *n* portiere *m*

goalpost /ˈgəʊlpəʊst/ *n* palo *m*

goat /gəʊt/ *n* capra *f*

goatee /gəʊˈtiː/ *n* pizzetto *m*

gobble /ˈgɒbl/ *vi* ‹*turkey*› fare glu glu
▪ **gobble up** *vt* trangugiare

gobbledygook /ˈgɒb(ə)ldɪguːk/ *n* ostrogoto *m*

go-between *n* intermediario, -a *mf*

goblet /ˈgɒblɪt/ *n* calice *m*

goblin /ˈgɒblɪn/ *n* folletto *m*

gobsmacked /ˈgɒbsmækt/ *adj* BrE infml **I was ~** sono rimasto a bocca aperta

God, god /gɒd/ *n* Dio *m*, dio *m*

godchild *n* figlioccio, -a *mf*

goddamn *adj* maledetto

god-daughter *n* figlioccia *f*

goddess /ˈgɒdes/ *n* dea *f*

godfather *n* padrino *m*

god-fearing /-fɪərɪŋ/ *adj* timorato di Dio

god-forsaken /-fəseɪkən/ *adj* dimenticato da Dio

godless /ˈgɒdlɪs/ *adj* empio

godlike /ˈgɒdlaɪk/ *adj* divino

godly /ˈgɒdlɪ/ *adj* (**-ier**, **-iest**) pio

godmother *n* madrina *f*

godparents *npl* padrino *m* e madrina *f*

godsend *n* manna *f*

godson *n* figlioccio *m*

goer /ˈgəʊə(r)/ *n* BrE **be a ~** ‹*car*› essere una bomba

go-getter /ˈgəʊgetə(r)/ *n* persona *f* intraprendente

go-getting /-getɪŋ/ *adj* intraprendente

goggle /ˈgɒgl/ *vi* infml **~ at** fissare con gli occhi sgranati

goggles *npl* occhiali *mpl*; (of swimmer) occhialini *mpl* [da piscina]; (of worker) occhiali *mpl* protettivi

going /ˈgəʊɪŋ/ **A** *adj* ‹*price, rate*› corrente; **~ concern** azienda *f* florida
B *n* **it's hard ~** è una faticaccia; **while the ~ is good** finché si può

going-over *n* (cleaning) pulizia *f* da cima a fondo; (examination) revisione *f*; **the doctor gave me a thorough ~** il dottore mi ha fatto una visita completa; **give somebody a ~** (beat up) dare una manica di botte a qualcuno

goings-on *npl* avvenimenti *mpl*

go-kart /-kɑːt/ *n* go-kart *m inv*

go-karting /-kɑːtɪŋ/ *n* kartismo *m*; **go ~** fare del kartismo

gold /gəʊld/ **A** *n* oro *m*
B *adj* d'oro

gold-digger *n* fig cacciatore, -trice *mf* di dote

gold dust *n* polvere *f* d'oro; fig cosa *f* rara

golden /ˈgəʊldn/ *adj* dorato

golden handshake *n* BrE buonuscita *f* (*al termine di un rapporto di lavoro*)

golden rule *n* regola *f* fondamentale

golden wedding *n* nozze *fpl* d'oro

goldfish *n inv* pesce *m* rosso

gold medal *n* medaglia *f* d'oro

gold medallist *n* (vincitore, -trice *mf* della) medaglia *f* d'oro

gold mine *n* miniera *f* d'oro

gold-plated /ˈpleɪtɪd/ *adj* placcato d'oro

gold rush *n* corsa *f* all'oro

goldsmith *n* orefice *m*

golf /gɒlf/ *n* golf *m*

golf club *n* circolo *m* di golf; (implement) mazza *f* da golf

golf course *n* campo *m* di golf

golfer /ˈgɒlfə(r)/ *n* giocatore, -trice *mf* di golf

gondola /ˈgɒndələ/ *n* gondola *f*

gondolier /gɒndəˈlɪə(r)/ *n* gondoliere *m*

gone /gɒn/ ▶ **go**

goner /ˈgɒnə(r)/ *n* infml **be a ~** essere spacciato

gong /gɒŋ/ *n* gong *m inv*

gonorrhoea /gɒnəˈrɪə/ *n* gonorrea *f*

good /gʊd/ **A** *adj* (**better**, **best**) buono; ‹*child, footballer, singer*› bravo; ‹*holiday, film*› bello; **~ at** bravo in; **a ~ deal of anger** molta rabbia; **as ~ as** (almost) quasi; **~ morning, ~ afternoon** buon giorno; **~ evening** buona sera; **~ night** buona notte; **have a ~ time** divertirsi
B *n* bene *m*; **for ~** per sempre; **do ~** far del bene; **do somebody ~** far bene a qualcuno; **it's no ~** è inutile; **be up to no ~** combinare qualcosa

goodbye /gʊdˈbaɪ/ *int* arrivederci

g

good-for-nothing **A** *n* buono, -a *mf* a nulla
B *adj* **her ~ son** quel buono a nulla di suo figlio

Good Friday *n* Venerdì *m* Santo

good-humoured /-ˈhjuːməd/ *adj* amichevole; ‹*remark, smile*› bonario

goodies /ˈgʊdɪz/ *npl* infml (to eat) bontà *fpl*

good-looking /-ˈlʊkɪŋ/ *adj* bello

good-natured /-ˈneɪtʃəd/ *adj* **be ~** avere un buon carattere

goodness /ˈgʊdnɪs/ *n* bontà *f*; **my ~!** santo cielo!; **thank ~!** grazie al cielo!

goods /gʊdz/ *npl* prodotti *mpl*

goods train *n* treno *m* merci

good-time girl *n* (fun-loving) ragazza *f* allegra; euph (prostitute) donnina *f* allegra

goodwill /gʊdˈwɪl/ *n* buona *f* volontà; Comm avviamento *m*

goody /ˈgʊdɪ/ *n* infml (person) buono *m*

goody bag *n omaggi (mpl) consegnati ai visitatori di una fiera dalle aziende espositrici*

goody-goody *n* santarellino, -a *mf*

gooey /ˈguːɪ/ *adj* infml appiccicaticcio; fig sdolcinato

goof /guːf/ *vi* infml cannare

goofy /ˈguːfɪ/ *adj* infml sciocco

google /guːgl/ *vi* usare Google

goon /guːn/ *n* (clown) svitato *m*; (thug) picchiatore *m*

goose /guːs/ *n* (*pl* **geese**) oca *f*

gooseberry /ˈgʊzbərɪ/ *n* uva *f* spina

gooseflesh *n*, **goose pimples** *npl* pelle *fsg* d'oca

goose-step *n* passo *m* dell'oca

gore¹ /gɔː(r)/ *n* sangue *m*

gore² *vt* incornare

gorge /gɔːdʒ/ **A** *n* Geog gola *f*
B *vt* **~ oneself** ingozzarsi

gorgeous /ˈgɔːdʒəs/ *adj* stupendo

gorilla /gəˈrɪlə/ *n* gorilla *m inv*

gormless /ˈgɔːmlɪs/ *adj* infml stupido

gorse /gɔːs/ *n* ginestrone *m*

gory /ˈgɔːrɪ/ *adj* (**-ier**, **-iest**) cruento

gosh /gɒʃ/ *int* infml caspita

gosling /ˈgɒzlɪŋ/ *n* ochetta *f*

go-slow *n forma (f) di protesta che consiste in un rallentamento del ritmo di lavoro*

gospel /ˈgɒspl/ *n* vangelo *m*

gospel music *n* musica *f* gospel

gospel truth *n* sacrosanta verità *f*

gossamer /ˈgɒsəmə(r)/ *n* (fabric) mussola *f*; (cobweb) fili *mpl* di ragnatela

gossip /ˈgɒsɪp/ **A** *n* pettegolezzi *mpl*; (person) pettegolo, -a *mf*
B *vi* pettegolare

gossip column *n* cronaca *f* mondana

gossipy /ˈgɒsɪpɪ/ *adj* pettegolo

got /gɒt/ ▶ **get**; **have ~** avere; **have ~ to do something** dover fare qualcosa

Gothic /ˈgɒθɪk/ *adj* gotico

gotten /ˈgɒtn/ AmE ▶ **get**

gouge /gaʊdʒ/ *vt* **~ out** cavare

goulash /ˈguːlæʃ/ *n* gulash *m inv*

gourd /gʊəd/ *n* (fruit) zucca *f*

gourmet /ˈgʊəmeɪ/ *n* buongustaio, -a *mf*

gout /gaʊt/ *n* gotta *f*

govern /ˈgʌv(ə)n/ *vt & vi* governare; (determine) determinare

governess /ˈgʌvənɪs/ *n* istitutrice *f*

governing /ˈgʌvənɪŋ/ *adj* ‹*party*› al potere; ‹*class*› dirigente; **the ~ body** (school governors) il consiglio d'istituto

government /ˈgʌvnmənt/ *n* governo *m*

governmental /gʌvnˈmentl/ *adj* governativo

government health warning *n* avviso *m* a cura del ministero della salute

government stocks *npl* titoli *mpl* di stato

governor /ˈgʌvənə(r)/ *n* governatore *m*; (of school) amministratore, -trice *mf*; (of prison) direttore, -trice *mf*; infml (boss) capo *m*

gown /gaʊn/ *n* vestito *m*; Univ, Jur toga *f*

GP *abbr* (**general practitioner**) medico *m* generico

GPA *n abbr* AmE (**grade point average**) media *f* scolastica

grab /græb/ *vt* (*pt/pp* **grabbed**) **~ [hold of]** afferrare

grace /greɪs/ *n* grazia *f*; (before meal) benedicite *m inv*; **with good ~** volentieri; **say ~** dire il benedicite; **three days' ~** tre giorni di proroga

Grace *n* **his/your ~** (duke) il signor duca; (archbishop) Sua Eccellenza; **her/your ~**, (duchess) la signora duchessa

graceful /ˈgreɪsfʊl/ *adj* aggraziato

gracefully /ˈgreɪsfʊlɪ/ *adv* con grazia

gracious /ˈgreɪʃəs/ *adj* cortese; (elegant) lussuoso

gradation /grəˈdeɪʃn/ *n* gradazione *f*

grade /greɪd/ **A** *n* livello *m*; Comm qualità *f*; Sch voto *m*; AmE Sch (class) classe *f*; AmE = **gradient**
B *vt* Comm classificare; Sch dare il voto a

grade crossing *n* AmE passaggio *m* a livello

grade school *n* AmE scuola *f* elementare

gradient /ˈgreɪdɪənt/ *n* pendenza *f*

gradual /ˈgrædʒʊəl/ *adj* graduale

gradually /ˈgrædʒʊəlɪ/ *adv* gradualmente

graduate¹ /ˈgrædʒʊət/ *n* laureato, -a *mf*

graduate² /ˈgrædʒʊeɪt/ *vi* Univ laurearsi

graduated /ˈgrædʒʊeɪtɪd/ *adj* ‹*container*› graduato

graduate training scheme *n* formazione *f* professionale postlaurea

parola chiave

graduation /grædʒʊ'eɪʃn/ *n* laurea *f*; (calibration) graduazione *f*
graduation ceremony *n* cerimonia *f* di consegna dei diplomi di laurea
graffiti /grə'fiːtɪ/ *npl* graffiti *mpl*
graffiti artist *n* pittore, -trice *mf* di graffiti
graft /grɑːft/ **A** *n* Bot, Med innesto *m*; Med (organ) trapianto *m*; infml (hard work) duro lavoro *m*; infml (corruption) corruzione *f* **B** *vt* innestare; trapiantare ‹*organ*›
grain /greɪn/ *n* (of sand, salt) granello *m*; (of rice) chicco *m*; (cereals) cereali *mpl*; (in wood) venatura *f*; **it goes against the ~** fig è contro la mia/sua natura
grainy /'greɪnɪ/ *adj* ‹*photograph*› sgranato; ‹*paintwork*› granulato
gram /græm/ *n* grammo *m*
grammar /'græmə(r)/ *n* grammatica *f*
grammarian /grə'meərɪən/ *n* grammatico, -a *mf*
grammar school *n* ≈ liceo *m*
grammatical /grə'mætɪkl/ *adj* grammaticale
grammatically /grə'mætɪklɪ/ *adv* grammaticalmente
gran /græn/ *n* infml nonna *f*
granary /'grænərɪ/ *n* granaio *m*
granary bread *n* pane *m* integrale
grand /grænd/ *adj* grandioso; infml eccellente
grandad /'grændæd/ *n* infml nonno *m*
grandchild *n* nipote *mf*
granddaughter *n* nipote *f*
grandeur /'grændʒə(r)/ *n* grandiosità *f*
grandfather *n* nonno *m*
grandfather clock *n* pendolo *m* (*che poggia a terra*)
grandiose /'grændɪəʊs/ *adj* grandioso
grandma /'grænmɑː/ *n* nonna *f*
grandmother *n* nonna *f*
grandpa /'grændpɑː/ *n* nonno *m*
grandparents *npl* nonni *mpl*
grand piano *n* pianoforte *m* a coda
grand slam® *n vittoria* (*f*) *di tutte le fasi di una gara*
grandson *n* nipote *m*
grandstand *n* tribuna *f*
grand total *n* totale *m* complessivo
granite /'grænɪt/ *n* granito *m*
granny /'grænɪ/ *n* infml nonna *f*
granny flat *n* BrE *appartamentino* (*m*) *indipendente per genitori anziani annesso all'abitazione principale*
⚷ **grant** /grɑːnt/ **A** *n* (money) sussidio *m*; Univ borsa *f* di studio **B** *vt* accordare; (admit) ammettere; **take something for ~ed** dare per scontato qualcosa; **take somebody for ~ed** considerare quello che qualcuno fa come dovuto
granular /'grænjʊlə(r)/ *adj* granulare
granulated /'grænjʊleɪtɪd/ *adj* **~ sugar** zucchero *m* semolato
granule /'grænjuːl/ *n* granello *m*
grape /greɪp/ *n* acino *m*; **~s** *pl* uva *fsg*
grapefruit /'greɪpfruːt/ *n inv* pompelmo *m*
grapeseed oil *n* olio *m* di vinaccioli
grapevine /'greɪpvaɪn/ *n* vite *f*; **hear something on the ~** sentir dire in giro qualcosa
graph /grɑːf/ *n* grafico *m*
graphic /'græfɪk/ *adj* grafico; (vivid) vivido
graphically /'græfɪklɪ/ *adv* graficamente; (vividly) vividamente
graphic design *n* grafica *f*
graphic designer *n* grafico, -a *mf*
graphics /'græfɪks/ *nsg* grafica *fsg*
graphics card *n* Comput scheda *f* grafica
graphics interface *n* Comput interfaccia *f* grafica
graphite /'græfaɪt/ *n* grafite *f*
graphologist /græ'fɒlədʒɪst/ *n* grafologo, -a *mf*
graph paper *n* carta *f* millimetrata
grapple /'græpl/ *vi* **~ with** also fig essere alle prese con
grasp /grɑːsp/ **A** *n* stretta *f*; (understanding) comprensione *f* **B** *vt* afferrare
grasping /'grɑːspɪŋ/ *adj* avido
grass /grɑːs/ *n* erba *f*
grass court *n* campo *m* in erba
grasshopper *n* cavalletta *f*
grassland *n* prateria *f*
grass roots *npl* base *f*; **at the ~** alla base
grass snake *n* biscia *f*
grassy /'grɑːsɪ/ *adj* erboso
grate¹ /greɪt/ *n* grata *f*
grate² **A** *vt* Culin grattugiare; **~ one's teeth** far stridere i denti **B** *vi* stridere
grateful /'greɪtfl/ *adj* grato
gratefully /'greɪtfʊlɪ/ *adv* con gratitudine
grater /'greɪtə(r)/ *n* Culin grattugia *f*
gratification /grætɪfɪ'keɪʃn/ *n* soddisfazione *f*
gratified /'grætɪfaɪd/ *adj* appagato
gratify /'grætɪfaɪ/ *vt* (*pt/pp* **-ied**) appagare
gratifying /'grætɪfaɪɪŋ/ *adj* appagante
grating /'greɪtɪŋ/ *n* grata *f*
gratis /'grɑːtɪs/ *adv* gratis
gratitude /'grætɪtjuːd/ *n* gratitudine *f*
gratuitous /grə'tjuːɪtəs/ *adj* gratuito
gratuity /grə'tjuːətɪ/ *n* gratifica *f*
grave¹ /greɪv/ *adj* grave
grave² *n* tomba *f*
gravedigger /'greɪvdɪgə(r)/ *n* becchino *m*
gravel /'grævl/ *n* ghiaia *f*
gravelly /'grævəlɪ/ *adj* ‹*voice*› rauco
gravely /'greɪvlɪ/ *adv* gravemente

graven image /'greɪvən/ *n* idolo *m*
gravestone /'greɪvstəʊn/ *n* lapide *f*
graveyard /'greɪvjɑːd/ *n* cimitero *m*
gravitate /'grævɪteɪt/ *vi* gravitare
gravity /'grævətɪ/ *n* gravità *f*
gravy /'greɪvɪ/ *n* sugo *m* della carne
gravy boat *n* salsiera *f*
gray /greɪ/ *adj* AmE = **grey**
graze¹ /greɪz/ *vi* ‹*animal*› pascolare
graze² **A** *n* escoriazione *f*
B *vt* (touch lightly) sfiorare; (scrape) escoriare; sbucciarsi ‹*knee*›
grease /griːs/ **A** *n* grasso *m*
B *vt* ungere
greasepaint /'griːspeɪnt/ *n* cerone *m*
greaseproof paper /griːspruːf'peɪpə(r)/ *n* carta *f* oleata
greaser /'griːsə(r)/ *n* (motorcyclist) *componente (m) di una banda giovanile di motociclisti*
greasy /'griːsɪ/ *adj* (**-ier**, **-iest**) untuoso; ‹*hair, skin*› grasso
⚷ **great** /greɪt/ *adj* grande; infml (marvellous) eccezionale
great-aunt *n* prozia *f*
great big *adj* enorme
Great Britain *n* Gran Bretagna *f*
Great Dane *n* danese *m*
great-grandchildren *npl* pronipoti *mpl*
great-grandfather *n* bisnonno *m*
great-grandmother *n* bisnonna *f*
great-great-grandchildren *npl* pronipoti *mpl*
greatly /'greɪtlɪ/ *adv* enormemente
greatness /'greɪtnɪs/ *n* grandezza *f*
great-uncle *n* prozio *m*
Grecian /'griːʃ(ə)n/ *adj* greco
Greece /griːs/ *n* Grecia *f*
greed /griːd/ *n* avidità *f*; (for food) ingordigia *f*
greedily /'griːdɪlɪ/ *adv* avidamente; ‹*eat*› con ingordigia
greedy /'griːdɪ/ *adj* (**-ier**, **-iest**) avido; (for food) ingordo
Greek /griːk/ *adj & n* greco, -a *mf*; (language) greco *m*
⚷ **green** /griːn/ **A** *adj* verde; fig (inexperienced) immaturo
B *n* verde *m*; (grass) prato *m*; (in golf) green *m inv*; **~s** *pl* verdura *f*; **the G~s** *pl* Pol i verdi
green beans *n* fagiolini *mpl*
green belt *n zona (f) verde intorno a una città*
green card *n* carta *f* verde; AmE permesso *m* di soggiorno
greenery /'griːnərɪ/ *n* verde *m*
green-eyed monster /-aɪd'mɒnstə(r)/ *n* gelosia *f*
greenfield site /'griːnfiːld/ *n terreno (m) su cui non sono mai esistiti insediamenti urbani*

⚷ parola chiave

greenfinch *n* verdone *m*
green fingers *npl* **have ~** avere il pollice verde
greenfly *n* afide *m*
greengage *n* susina *f* verde
greengrocer BrE, **greengrocery** AmE *n* fruttivendolo, -a *mf*
greenhorn *n* (new) novellino *m*; (gullible) pivello *m*
greenhouse *n* serra *f*
greenhouse effect *n* effetto *m* serra
greenhouse gas *n* gas *m* serra
Greenland *n* Groenlandia *f*
green light *n* infml verde *m*
green onion *n* AmE cipollotto *m*
green salad *n* insalata *f* verde
greet /griːt/ *vt* salutare; (welcome) accogliere
greeting /'griːtɪŋ/ *n* saluto *m*; (welcome) accoglienza *f*
greetings card /'griːtɪŋz/ *n* biglietto *m* d'auguri
gregarious /grɪ'geərɪəs/ *adj* gregario; (person) socievole
gremlin /'gremlɪn/ *n* hum spirito *m* maligno
Grenada /grə'neɪdə/ *n* Grenada *f*
grenade /grɪ'neɪd/ *n* granata *f*
grenadier /grenə'dɪə(r)/ *n* Mil *guardia (f) reale inglese*
grew /gruː/ ▸ **grow**
grey BrE, **gray** AmE /greɪ/ **A** *adj* grigio; ‹*hair*› bianco
B *n* grigio *m*
C *vi* diventare bianco
■ **grey out** *vt* Comput visualizzare con sfondo azzurro ombreggiato
grey area *n* zona *f* oscura
grey-haired /heəd/ *adj* dai capelli grigi
greyhound *n* levriero *m*
grey matter *n* (brain) materia *f* grigia
grey squirrel *n* scoiattolo *m* grigio
grid /grɪd/ *n* griglia *f*; (on map) reticolato *m*; Electr rete *f*
griddle /'grɪd(ə)l/ *n* (for meat) piastra *f*
gridiron *n* griglia *f*; AmE campo *m* di football americano
gridlock *n* fig (deadlock) situazione *f* di stallo; (in traffic) imbottigliamento *m*
grid reference *n* coordinate *fpl*
grief /griːf/ *n* dolore *m*; **come to ~** ‹*plans*› naufragare
grief-stricken /-strɪkən/ *adj* affranto dal dolore
grievance /'griːvəns/ *n* lamentela *f*
grieve /griːv/ **A** *vt* addolorare
B *vi* essere addolorato
grievous /'griːvəs/ *adj* doloroso
grievous bodily harm *n* lesioni *fpl* personali gravi
grievously /'griːvəslɪ/ *adv* tristemente

grill /grɪl/ **A** *n* graticola *f*; (for grilling) griglia *f*; **mixed ~** grigliata *f* mista
B *vt & vi* cuocere alla griglia; (interrogate) sottoporre al terzo grado

grille /grɪl/ *n* grata *f*

grim /grɪm/ *adj* (**grimmer**, **grimmest**) arcigno; ‹*determination*› accanito

grimace /'grɪməs/ **A** *n* smorfia *f*
B *vi* fare una smorfia

grime /graɪm/ *n* sudiciume *m*

grimly /'grɪmlɪ/ *adv* accanitamente

Grim Reaper *n* Morte *f*

grimy /'graɪmɪ/ *adj* (**-ier**, **-iest**) sudicio

grin /grɪn/ **A** *n* sorriso *m*
B *vi* (*pt/pp* **grinned**) fare un gran sorriso

grind /graɪnd/ **A** *n* infml (hard work) sfacchinata *f*
B *vt* (*pt/pp* **ground**) macinare; affilare ‹*knife*›; AmE (mince) tritare; **~ one's teeth** digrignare i denti

grindstone /'graɪndstəʊn/ *n* mola *f*; **keep one's nose to the ~** lavorare indefessamente

grip /grɪp/ **A** *n* presa *f*; fig controllo *m*; (bag) borsone *m*; **be in the ~ of** essere in preda a; **get a ~ of oneself** controllarsi
B *vt* (*pt/pp* **gripped**) afferrare; ‹*tyres*› far presa su; tenere avvinto ‹*attention*›

gripe /graɪp/ *vi* infml (grumble) lagnarsi

gripping /'grɪpɪŋ/ *adj* avvincente

grisly /'grɪzlɪ/ *adj* (**-ier**, **-iest**) raccapricciante

gristle /'grɪsl/ *n* cartilagine *f*

grit /grɪt/ **A** *n* graniglia *f*; (for roads) sabbia *f*; (courage) coraggio *m*
B *vt* (*pt/pp* **gritted**) spargere sabbia su ‹*road*›; **~ one's teeth** serrare i denti

gritter /'grɪtə(r)/ *n* BrE Auto spandighiaia *m inv*

gritty /'grɪtɪ/ *adj* (sandy) pieno di terra; (gravelly) ghiaioso; (hard, determined) grintoso; (novel, film) crudo

grizzle /'grɪzl/ *vi* piagnucolare

grizzly /'grɪzlɪ/ *n* (bear) grizzly *m inv*

groan /grəʊn/ **A** *n* gemito *m*
B *vi* gemere

grocer /'grəʊsə(r)/ *n* droghiere, -a *mf*

groceries /'grəʊsərɪz/ *npl* generi *mpl* alimentari

grocer's, **grocer's shop** BrE **grocery** AmE *n* drogheria *f*

groggy /'grɒgɪ/ *adj* (**-ier**, **-iest**) stordito; (unsteady) barcollante

groin /grɔɪn/ *n* Anat inguine *m*

groom /gru:m/ **A** *n* sposo *m*; (for horse) stalliere *m*
B *vt* strigliare ‹*horse*›; fig preparare; **well-~ed** ben curato

groove /gru:v/ *n* scanalatura *f*

grope /grəʊp/ *vi* brancolare; **~ for** cercare a tastoni

gross /grəʊs/ **A** *adj* obeso; (coarse) volgare; (glaring) grossolano; ‹*salary, weight*› lordo
B *n inv* grossa *f*

gross domestic product *n* prodotto *m* interno lordo

gross indecency *n* Jur oltraggio *m* al pudore

grossly /'grəʊslɪ/ *adv* (very) enormemente

gross national product *n* prodotto *m* nazionale lordo

grotesque /grəʊ'tesk/ *adj* grottesco

grotesquely /grəʊ'tesklɪ/ *adv* in modo grottesco

grotto /'grɒtəʊ/ *n* (*pl* **-es**) grotta *f*

grotty /'grɒtɪ/ *adj* (**-ier**, **-iest**) infml ‹*flat, street*› squallido

grouch /graʊtʃ/ *vi* brontolare (**about** contro)

grouchy /'graʊtʃɪ/ *adj* brontolone

ground¹ /graʊnd/ ▶ **grind**

ground² **A** *n* terra *f*; Sport terreno *m*; (reason) ragione *f*; **~s** *pl* (park) giardini *mpl*; (of coffee) fondi *mpl*
B *vi* ‹*ship*› arenarsi
C *vt* bloccare a terra ‹*aircraft*›; AmE Electr mettere a terra

ground control *n* base *f* di controllo

ground crew *n* personale *m* di terra

ground floor *n* pianterreno *m*

grounding /'graʊndɪŋ/ *n* base *f*

groundless /'graʊndlɪs/ *adj* infondato

groundnut oil *n* olio *m* d'arachidi

ground rules *npl* principi *mpl* fondamentali

groundsheet *n* telone *m* impermeabile

ground troops *npl* truppe *fpl* di terra

groundwork *n* lavoro *m* di preparazione

group /gru:p/ **A** *n* gruppo *m*
B *vt* raggruppare
C *vi* raggrupparsi

groupage /'gru:pɪdʒ/ *n* Comm raggruppamento *m*

group booking *n* prenotazione *f* di gruppo

group leader *n* capogruppo *m*

group therapy *n* terapia *f* di gruppo

group work *n* lavoro *m* di gruppo

grouse¹ /graʊs/ *n inv* gallo *m* cedrone

grouse² *vi* infml brontolare

grove /grəʊv/ *n* boschetto *m*

grovel /'grɒvl/ *vi* (*pt/pp* **grovelled**) strisciare

grovelling /'grɒv(ə)lɪŋ/ *adj* leccapiedi *inv*

grow /grəʊ/ **A** *vi* (*pt* **grew**, *pp* **grown**) crescere; (become) diventare; ‹*unemployment, fear*› aumentare; ‹*town*› ingrandirsi
B *vt* coltivare; **~ one's hair** farsi crescere i capelli

■ **grow apart** *vi* ‹*friends, couple*› disamorarsi

■ **grow on**: *vt* infml (become pleasing to) **it'll ~ on**

you finirà per piacerti
■ **grow out of**: *vt* **he's ~n out of his jumper** il golf gli è diventato troppo piccolo
■ **grow up** *vi* crescere; ‹*town*› svilupparsi
growbag /ˈgrəʊbæg/ *n sacco (m) di terriccio dentro cui si coltivano piante*
grower /ˈgrəʊə(r)/ *n* coltivatore, -trice *mf*
growing pains /ˈgrəʊɪŋ/ *npl* (of child) dolori *mpl* della crescita; fig (of firm, project) difficoltà *fpl* iniziali nello sviluppo
growl /graʊl/ **A** *n* grugnito *m*
B *vi* ringhiare
grown /grəʊn/ **A** ▸ **grow**
B *adj* adulto
grown-up *adj & n* adulto, -a *mf*
g ✓ **growth** /grəʊθ/ *n* crescita *f*; (increase) aumento *m*; Med tumore *m*
growth area *n* area *f* di sviluppo
growth industry *n* industria *f* in rapida crescita
growth rate *n* tasso *m* di crescita
groyne /grɔɪn/ *n* BrE pennello *m* (*per difendere le spiagge dall'erosione*)
grub /grʌb/ *n* larva *f*; infml (food) mangiare *m*
grubby /ˈgrʌbɪ/ *adj* (**-ier**, **-iest**) sporco
grudge /grʌdʒ/ **A** *n* rancore *m*; **bear somebody a ~** portare rancore a qualcuno
B *vt* dare a malincuore
grudging /ˈgrʌdʒɪŋ/ *adj* riluttante
grudgingly /ˈgrʌdʒɪŋlɪ/ *adv* a malincuore
gruelling /ˈgruːəlɪŋ/ *adj* estenuante
gruesome /ˈgruːsəm/ *adj* macabro
gruff /grʌf/ *adj* burbero
gruffly /ˈgrʌflɪ/ *adv* in modo burbero
grumble /ˈgrʌmbl/ *vi* brontolare (**at** contro)
grumpy /ˈgrʌmpɪ/ *adj* (**-ier**, **-iest**) scorbutico
grunge /grʌndʒ/ *n* (dirt) lerciume *m*; (style) grunge *m inv*
grunt /grʌnt/ **A** *n* grugnito *m*
B *vi* fare un grugnito
G-string *n* (garment) tanga *m inv*
guarantee /gærənˈtiː/ **A** *n* garanzia *f*
B *vt* garantire
guarantor /gærənˈtɔː(r)/ *n* garante *mf*
✓ **guard** /gɑːd/ **A** *n* guardia *f*; (security) guardiano *m*; (on train) capotreno *m*; AmE (in prison) guardia *f* carceraria; Techn schermo *m* protettivo; **be on ~** essere di guardia; **on one's ~** in guardia
B *vt* sorvegliare; (protect) proteggere
■ **guard against** *vt* guardarsi da
guard dog *n* cane *m* da guardia
guarded /ˈgɑːdɪd/ *adj* guardingo
guardian /ˈgɑːdɪən/ *n* (of minor) tutore, -trice *mf*
guardian angel *n also* fig angelo *m* custode
guard of honour *n* guardia *f* d'onore

✓ parola chiave

guardroom *n* corpo *m* di guardia
guard's van *n* BrE Rail carrozza *f* bagagliaio
Guatemala /ˌgwɑːtəˈmɑːlə/ *n* Guatemala *m*
guava /ˈgwɑːvə/ *n* (fruit) guava *f*; (tree) albero *m* di guava
Guernsey /ˈgɜːnzɪ/ *n* Guernsey *f*
guerrilla /gəˈrɪlə/ *n* guerrigliero, -a *mf*
guerrilla warfare *n* guerriglia *f*
✓ **guess** /ges/ **A** *n* supposizione *f*
B *vt* indovinare
C *vi* indovinare; AmE (suppose) supporre
guesstimate /ˈgestɪmət/ *n* calcolo *m* approssimativo
guesswork /ˈgeswɜːk/ *n* supposizione *f*
✓ **guest** /gest/ *n* ospite *mf*; (in hotel) cliente *mf*
guest house *n* pensione *f*
guest room *n* camera *f* degli ospiti
guest worker *n* lavoratore *m* immigrato; lavoratrice *f* immigrata
guff /gʌf/ *n* (nonsense) stupidaggini *fpl*
guffaw /gʌˈfɔː/ **A** *n* sghignazzata *f*
B *vi* sghignazzare
guidance /ˈgaɪdəns/ *n* guida *f*; (advice) consigli *mpl*
guide /gaɪd/ **A** *n* guida *f*; **[Girl] G~** giovane esploratrice *f*
B *vt* guidare
guidebook /ˈgaɪdbʊk/ *n* guida *f* turistica
guided missile /ˈgaɪdɪd/ *n* missile *m* teleguidato
guide dog *n* cane *m* per ciechi
guided tour *n* giro *m* guidato
guidelines /ˈgaɪdlaɪnz/ *npl* direttive *fpl*
guiding principle /gaɪdɪŋˈprɪnsɪp(ə)l/ *n* direttrice *f*
guild /gɪld/ *n* corporazione *f*
guile /gaɪl/ *n* astuzia *f*
guileless /ˈgaɪllɪs/ *adj* senza malizia
guillotine /ˈgɪlətiːn/ *n* ghigliottina *f*; (for paper) taglierina *f*
guilt /gɪlt/ *n* colpa *f*
guiltily /ˈgɪltɪlɪ/ *adv* con aria colpevole
✓ **guilty** /ˈgɪltɪ/ *adj* (**-ier**, **-iest**) colpevole; **have a ~ conscience** avere la coscienza sporca
guinea /ˈgɪnɪ/ *n* ghinea *f*
Guinea /ˈgɪnɪ/ *n* Guinea *f*
Guinea-Bissau /-bɪˈsaʊ/ *n* Guinea-Bissau *f*
guinea fowl faraona *f*
guinea pig *n* porcellino *m* d'India; (in experiments) cavia *f*
guise /gaɪz/ *n* **in the ~ of** sotto le spoglie di
guitar /gɪˈtɑː(r)/ *n* chitarra *f*
guitarist /gɪˈtɑːrɪst/ *n* chitarrista *mf*
Gulag /ˈguːlæg/ *n* gulag *m inv*
gulch /gʌltʃ/ *n* AmE burrone *m*
gulf /gʌlf/ *n* Geog golfo *m*; fig abisso *m*
Gulf States *npl* gli stati *mpl* del Golfo
Gulf War *n* la guerra *f* del Golfo
gull /gʌl/ *n* gabbiano *m*

gullet /ˈɡʌlɪt/ *n* esofago *m*; (throat) gola *f*
gullible /ˈɡʌləbl/ *adj* credulone
gully /ˈɡʌlɪ/ *n* burrone *m*; (drain) canale *m* di scolo
gulp /ɡʌlp/ **A** *n* azione *f* di deglutire; (of food) boccone *m*; (of liquid) sorso *m* **B** *vi* deglutire
■ **gulp down** *vt* trangugiare ‹*food*›; scolarsi ‹*liquid*›
gum¹ /ɡʌm/ *n* Anat gengiva *f*
gum² **A** *n* gomma *f*; (chewing gum) gomma *f* da masticare, chewing-gum *m inv* **B** *vt* (*pt/pp* **gummed**) ingommare (**to** a)
gumboot /ˈɡʌmbuːt/ *n* stivale *m* di gomma
gummed /ɡʌmd/ **A** ▶ **gum²** **B** *adj* ‹*label*› adesivo
gumption /ˈɡʌmpʃn/ *n* infml buon senso *m*
gumshoe /ˈɡʌmʃuː/ *n* infml (private investigator) investigatore *m* privato
gum tree *n* infml **be up a ~** essere in difficoltà
gun /ɡʌn/ *n* pistola *f*; (rifle) fucile *m*; (cannon) cannone *m*; **he had a ~** era armato
■ **gun down** *vt* (*pt/pp* **gunned**) freddare
gun barrel *n* canna *f* di fucile
gunboat *n* cannoniera *f*
gun dog *n* cane *m* da caccia
gunfire *n* spari *mpl*; (of cannon) colpi *mpl* [di cannone]
gunge /ɡʌndʒ/ *n* BrE poltiglia *f* [disgustosa]
gung-ho /ɡʌŋˈhəʊ/ *adj* hum (eager for war) guerrafondaio; (overzealous) esaltato
gun laws *npl* leggi *fpl* sulle armi
gun licence *n* porto *m* d'armi
gunman /ˈɡʌnmən/ *n* uomo *m* armato
gunner /ˈɡʌnə(r)/ *n* artigliere *m*
gunpoint *n* **hold somebody up at ~** assalire qualcuno a mano armata
gunpowder *n* polvere *f* da sparo
gunshot *n* colpo *m* [di pistola]
gunshot wound *n* ferita *f* d'arma da fuoco
gunslinger *n* pistolero *m*
gurgle /ˈɡɜːɡl/ *vi* gorgogliare; ‹*baby*› fare degli urletti
guru /ˈɡʊruː/ *n* guru *m inv*
gush /ɡʌʃ/ *vi* sgorgare; (enthuse) parlare con troppo entusiasmo (**over** di)
■ **gush out** *vi* sgorgare
gushing /ˈɡʌʃɪŋ/ *adj* eccessivamente entusiastico
gusset /ˈɡʌsɪt/ *n* gherone *m*
gust /ɡʌst/ *n* (of wind) raffica *f*
gusto /ˈɡʌstəʊ/ *n* **with ~** con trasporto
gusty /ˈɡʌstɪ/ *adj* ventoso
gut /ɡʌt/ **A** *n* intestino *m*; **~s** *pl* pancia *f*; infml (courage) fegato *m* **B** *vt* (*pt/pp* **gutted**) Culin svuotare delle interiora; **~ted by fire** sventrato da un incendio
gutsy /ˈɡʌtsɪ/ *adj* (brave) coraggioso; (spirited) gagliardo
gutter /ˈɡʌtə(r)/ *n* canale *m* di scolo; (on roof) grondaia *f*; fig bassifondi *mpl*
guttering /ˈɡʌtərɪŋ/ *n* grondaie *fpl*
gutter press *n* stampa *f* scandalistica
guttersnipe /ˈɡʌtəsnaɪp/ *n* ragazzo, -a *mf* di strada
guttural /ˈɡʌtərəl/ *adj* gutturale
guv, **guvnor** /ɡʌv, ˈɡʌvnə(r)/ *n* BrE infml (boss) capo *m*
guy /ɡaɪ/ *n* infml tipo *m*, tizio *m*
Guyana /ɡaɪˈænə/ *n* Guyana *f*
Guy Fawkes Day /fɔːks/ *n* BrE *anniversario (m) del fallimento della Congiura delle Polveri (5 novembre)*
guzzle /ˈɡʌzl/ *vt* ingozzarsi con ‹*food*›; **he's ~d the lot** si è sbafato tutto
gym /dʒɪm/ *n* infml palestra *f*; (gymnastics) ginnastica *f*
gymkhana /dʒɪmˈkɑːnə/ *n* manifestazione *f* equestre
gymnasium /dʒɪmˈneɪzɪəm/ *n* palestra *f*
gymnast /ˈdʒɪmnæst/ *n* ginnasta *mf*
gymnastics /dʒɪmˈnæstɪks/ *nsg* ginnastica *fsg*
gym shoes *npl* scarpe *fpl* da ginnastica
gymslip *n* Sch ≈ grembiule *m* (*da bambina*)
gynaecologist /ɡaɪnɪˈkɒlədʒɪst/ *n* ginecologo, -a *mf*
gynaecology /ɡaɪnɪˈkɒlədʒɪ/ *n* ginecologia *f*
gyp /dʒɪp/ *n* BrE **my back is giving me ~** ho un terribile mal di schiena
gypsum /ˈdʒɪpsəm/ *n* gesso *m*
gypsy /ˈdʒɪpsɪ/ *n* zingaro, -a *mf*
gyrate /dʒaɪˈreɪt/ *vi* roteare

Hh

h, **H** /eɪtʃ/ *n* h, H *f inv*
ha! ha! /hɑːˈhɑː/ *int* ah! ah!
haberdashery /hæbəˈdæʃərɪ/ *n* merceria *f*; AmE negozio *m* d'abbigliamento da uomo
habit /ˈhæbɪt/ *n* abitudine *f*; Relig (costume) tonaca *f*; **be in the ~ of doing something** avere l'abitudine di fare qualcosa
habitable /ˈhæbɪtəbl/ *adj* abitabile
habitat /ˈhæbɪtæt/ *n* habitat *m inv*
h
habitation /hæbɪˈteɪʃn/ *n* **unfit for human ~** inagibile
habit-forming /-fɔːmɪŋ/ *adj* **be ~** creare assuefazione
habitual /həˈbɪtjʊəl/ *adj* abituale; ‹*smoker, liar*› inveterato
habitually /həˈbɪtjʊəlɪ/ *adv* regolarmente
habitual offender *n* delinquente *mf* recidivo
hack¹ /hæk/ *n* (writer) scribacchino, -a *mf*
hack² *vt* tagliare; **~ to pieces** tagliare a pezzi
hacker /ˈhækə(r)/ *n* Comput pirata *m* informatico
hacking /ˈhækɪŋ/ *n* Comput pirateria *f* informatica
hacking cough *n* brutta tosse *f*
hackles /ˈhæk(ə)lz/ *npl* (on animal) pelo *m* del collo; (on bird) piumaggio *m* del collo; **make sb's ~ rise** fig far imbestialire qualcuno
hackney cab /ˈhæknɪ/ *n* fml taxi *m inv*
hackneyed /ˈhæknɪd/ *adj* trito [e ritrito]
hacksaw /ˈhæksɔː/ *n* seghetto *m*
had /hæd/ ▸ **have**
haddock /ˈhædək/ *n inv* eglefino *m*
haematoma /hiːməˈtəʊmə/ *n* ematoma *m*
haemoglobin /hiːməˈgləʊbɪn/ *n* emoglobina *f*
haemophilia /hiːməˈfɪlɪə/ *n* emofilia *f*
haemophiliac /hiːməˈfɪlɪæk/ *n* emofiliaco, -a *mf*
haemorrhage /ˈhemərɪdʒ/ *n* emorragia *f*
haemorrhoids /ˈhemərɔɪdz/ *npl* emorroidi *fpl*
hag /hæg/ *n* **old ~** vecchia befana *f*
haggard /ˈhægəd/ *adj* sfatto
haggis /ˈhægɪs/ *n piatto* (*m*) *scozzese a base di frattaglie di pecora e avena*
haggle /ˈhægl/ *vi* contrattare (**over** per)
Hague /heɪg/ *n* **the ~** l'Aia *f*
hail¹ /heɪl/ **A** *vt* salutare; far segno a ‹*taxi*› **B** *vi* **~ from** provenire da

⚷ parola chiave

hail² **A** *n* grandine *f* **B** *vi* grandinare
hailstone /ˈheɪlstəʊn/ *n* chicco *m* di grandine
hailstorm /ˈheɪlstɔːm/ *n* grandinata *f*
⚷ **hair** /heə(r)/ *n* capelli *mpl*; (on body, of animal) pelo *m*; **wash one's ~** lavarsi i capelli
hairband *n* (rigid) cerchietto *m*; (elastic) fascia *f* [per capelli]
hairbrush *n* spazzola *f* per capelli
hair curler *n* arricciacapelli *m inv*
haircut *n* taglio *m* di capelli; **have a ~** farsi tagliare i capelli
hairdo *n* infml pettinatura *f*
hairdresser *n* parrucchiere, -a *mf*
hairdryer, **hairdrier** *n* fon *m inv*; (with hood) casco *m* (asciugacapelli)
hair gel *n* gel *m inv* [per capelli]
hairgrip *n* molletta *f*
hairless /ˈheəlɪs/ *adj* ‹*animal*› senza peli; ‹*body*› (chin) glabro
hairline *n* (on head) attaccatura *f* dei capelli
hairline crack *n* incrinatura *f* sottilissima
hairline fracture *n* Med frattura *f* capillare
hairnet *n* retina *f* per capelli
hairpiece *n* toupet *m inv*
hairpin *n* forcina *f*
hairpin bend *n* tornante *m*, curva *f* a gomito
hair-raising /heəreɪzɪŋ/ *adj* terrificante
hair remover *n* crema *f* depilatoria
hairslide *n* BrE fermacapelli *m inv*
hair-splitting /ˈheəsplɪtɪŋ/ *n* pedanteria *f*
hairspray *n* lacca *f* [per capelli]
hair straighteners /ˈheə(r) ˌstreɪtnəz/ *n pl* piastra *f* stirante
hairstyle *n* acconciatura *f*
hairstylist *n* parrucchiere, -a *mf*
hair transplant *n* trapianto *m* di capelli
hairy /ˈheərɪ/ *adj* (**-ier**, **-iest**) peloso; infml (frightening) spaventoso
Haiti /ˈheɪtɪ/ *n* Haiti *f*
Haitian /ˈheɪʃ(ə)n/ *n & adj* haitiano, -a *mf*; (language) haitiano *m*
hake /heɪk/ *n inv* nasello *m*
halal /hɑːˈlɑːl/ *adj* ‹*meat, butcher*› halal
halcyon days /ˈhælsɪən/ *npl* bei tempi *mpl* andati
hale /heɪl/ *adj* **~ and hearty** in piena forma
⚷ **half** /hɑːf/ **A** *n* (*pl* **halves**) metà *f*; **cut in ~** tagliare a metà; **one and a ~** uno e mezzo;

~ **a dozen** mezza dozzina; ~ **an hour** mezz'ora
B *adj* mezzo; **[at]** ~ **price** [a] metà prezzo
C *adv* a metà; ~ **past two** le due e mezza

half-and-half **A** *adj* mezzo e mezzo
B *adv* a metà; **go** ~ fare a metà

half-back *n* mediano *m*

half-baked *adj* infml che non sta in piedi

half board *n* mezza pensione *f*

half-breed *n & adj* offensive mezzosangue *mf inv*

half-brother *n* fratellastro *m*

half-century *n* mezzo secolo *m*

half cock *n* **go off at** ~ partire col piede sbagliato

half-conscious *adj* semicosciente

half-crown, half a crown *n* BrE mezza corona *f*

half-cut *adj* infml (drunk) ciucco

half day *n* mezza giornata *f*

half-dead *adj* also fig mezzo morto

half-dozen *n* mezza dozzina *f*

half fare *n* metà tariffa *f*

half-hearted /-'hɑːtɪd/ *adj* esitante

half-heartedly /-'hɑːtɪdlɪ/ *adv* senza entusiasmo

half hour *n* mezz'ora *f*

half-hourly *adj & adv* ogni mezz'ora

half-length *adj* ‹*portrait*› a mezzo busto

half-light *n* penombra *f*

half mast *n* **at** ~ a mezz'asta

half measures *npl* mezze misure *fpl*

half-moon **A** *n* mezzaluna *f*; (of fingernail) lunula *f*
B *attrib* ‹*spectacles*› a mezzaluna

half pay *n* metà stipendio *m*

halfpenny /'heɪpnɪ/ *n* BrE mezzo penny *m inv*

half-pint *n* mezza pinta *f* (*Br* = *0,28 l, Am* = *0,24 l*); (beer) piccola *f*; fig mezza calzetta *f*

half price **A** *adj* a metà prezzo
B *adv* [a] metà prezzo

half-sister *n* sorellastra *f*

half size **A** *n* (of shoe) mezzo numero *m*
B *adj* ‹*copy*› ridotto della metà

half smile *n* mezzo sorriso *m*

half-starved *adj* mezzo morto di fame

half-term *n* vacanza *f* di metà trimestre

half-time *n* Sport intervallo *m*

half-truth *n* mezza verità *f*

halfway **A** *adj* **the** ~ **mark/stage** il livello intermedio
B *adv* a metà strada; **get** ~ fig arrivare a metà

halfway house *n* (compromise) via *f* di mezzo; (rehabilitation centre) centro *m* di riabilitazione per ex detenuti

halfway line *n* Sport linea *f* mediana

halfwit *n* idiota *mf*

half-year **A** *n* Fin, Comm semestre *m*
B *attrib* ‹*profit, results*› semestrale

half-yearly *adj* ‹*meeting, payment*› semestrale

halibut /'hælɪbət/ *n inv* ippoglosso *m*

halitosis /hælɪ'təʊsɪs/ *n* alitosi *f inv*

🗝 **hall** /hɔːl/ *n* (entrance) ingresso *m*; (room) sala *f*; (mansion) residenza *f* di campagna; ~ **of residence** Univ casa *f* dello studente

hallelujah /(h)ælɪ'luːjə/ *int* alleluia!

hallmark /'hɔːlmɑːk/ *n* marchio *m* di garanzia; fig marchio *m*

hallo /hə'ləʊ/ *int* ciao!; (on telephone) pronto!; **say** ~ **to** salutare

hall of residence *n* casa *f* dello studente

hallowed /'hæləʊd/ *adj* ‹*ground*› consacrato; ‹*tradition*› sacro

Halloween /hæləʊ'iːn/ *n vigilia (f) d'Ognissanti e notte delle streghe, celebrata soprattutto dai bambini*

hallucinate /hə'luːsɪneɪt/ *vi* avere le allucinazioni

hallucination /həluːsɪ'neɪʃn/ *n* allucinazione *f*

hallucinatory /hə'luːsɪnət(ə)rɪ/ *adj* ‹*drug*› allucinogeno

hallucinogen /hə'luːsɪnədʒən/ *n* sostanza *f* allucinante

hallucinogenic /həluːsɪnə'dʒenɪk/ *adj* allucinogeno

hallway /'hɔːlweɪ/ *n* ingresso *m*

halo /'heɪləʊ/ *n* (*pl* **-es**) aureola *f*; Astr alone *m*

halogen /'hælədʒən/ *n* alogeno *m*

halt /hɔːlt/ **A** *n* alt *m inv*; **come to a** ~ fermarsi; ‹*traffic*› bloccarsi
B *vi* fermarsi; ~**!** alt!
C *vt* fermare

halter /'hɔːltə(r)/ *n* (for horse) cavezza *f*

halter-neck *n modello (m) con allacciatura dietro il collo che lascia la schiena scoperta*

halting /'hɔːltɪŋ/ *adj* esitante

haltingly /'hɔːltɪŋlɪ/ *adv* con esitazione

halve /hɑːv/ *vt* dividere a metà; (reduce) dimezzare

ham /hæm/ *n* prosciutto *m*; Theat attore, -trice *mf* da strapazzo

hamburger /'hæmbɜːgə(r)/ *n* hamburger *m inv*

ham-fisted /-'fɪstɪd/ *adj* BrE infml maldestro

hamlet /'hæmlɪt/ *n* paesino *m*

hammer /'hæmə(r)/ **A** *n* martello *m*
B *vt* martellare
C *vi* ~ **at/on** picchiare a

▪ **hammer in** *vt* piantare ‹*nail*›

▪ **hammer out** *vt* definire con grandi sforzi ‹*agreement, policy*›

hammer and sickle *n* falce *f* e martello *m*

hammered /'hæməd/ *adj* infml (drunk) sbronzo

hammock /'hæmək/ *n* amaca *f*

hamper[1] /'hæmpə(r)/ *n* cesto *m*; **[gift]** ~ cestino *m*

h

hamper² *vt* ostacolare

hamster /ˈhæmstə(r)/ *n* criceto *m*

hamstring /ˈhæmstrɪŋ/ **A** *n* (of horse) tendine *m* del garretto; (of human) tendine *m* del ginocchio
B *vt* fig rendere impotente

⚷ **hand** /hænd/ **A** *n* mano *f*; (of clock) lancetta *f*; (writing) scrittura *f*; (worker) manovale *m*; **all ~s** Naut l'equipaggio al completo; **at ~, to ~** a portata di mano; **by ~** a mano; **on the one ~** da un lato; **on the other ~** d'altra parte; **out of ~** incontrollabile; (summarily) su due piedi; **in ~** in corso; ‹*situation*› sotto controllo; (available) disponibile; **give somebody a ~** dare una mano a qualcuno; **~ in ~** ‹*run, walk*› mano nella mano; **go ~ in ~** fig andare di pari passo (**with** con)
B *vt* porgere

■ **hand back** *vt* restituire ‹*something*›

■ **hand down** *vt* tramandare

■ **hand in** *vt* consegnare

■ **hand on** *vt* passare

■ **hand out** *vt* distribuire

■ **hand over** *vt* passare; (to police) consegnare

handbag *n* borsa *f* (*da signora*)

hand baggage *n* bagaglio *m* a mano

handball *n* pallamano *f*; (fault in football) fallo *m* di mano; **~!** mano!

handbasin *n* lavandino *m*

handbook *n* manuale *m*

handbrake *n* freno *m* a mano

handcart *n* carretto *m*

hand cream *n* crema *f* per le mani

handcuffs *npl* manette *fpl*

hand dryer, hand drier *n* asciugamani *m inv* ad aria

hand-eye coordination *n* coordinazione *f* occhio-mano

handful /ˈhændfʊl/ *n* manciata *f*; **be [quite] a ~** infml essere difficile da tenere a freno

hand grenade *n* bomba *f* a mano

handgun *n* pistola *f*

hand-held *adj* a mano

handicap /ˈhændɪkæp/ *n* handicap *m inv*

handicapped /ˈhændɪkæpt/ *adj* **mentally/physically ~** mentalmente/fisicamente handicappato

handicraft /ˈhændɪkrɑːft/ *n* artigianato *m*

handiwork /ˈhændɪwɜːk/ *n* opera *f*

handkerchief /ˈhæŋkətʃɪf/ *n* (*pl* **-s** & **-chieves**) fazzoletto *m*

⚷ **handle** /ˈhændl/ **A** *n* manico *m*; (of door) maniglia *f*; **fly off the ~** infml perdere le staffe
B *vt* maneggiare; occuparsi di ‹*problem, customer*›; prendere ‹*difficult person*›; trattare ‹*subject*›; **be good at handling somebody** saperci fare con qualcuno

handlebar moustache /hændlbɑːməˈstɑːʃ/ *n* baffi *mpl* a manubrio

handlebars /ˈhændlbɑːz/ *npl* manubrio *m*

handler /ˈhændlə(r)/ *n* (of dog) addestratore, -trice *mf*

handling /ˈhændlɪŋ/ *n* (touching, holding) manipolazione *f*; (of weapon) maneggio *m*; (dealing with) gestione *f*

handling charge *n* (for goods) spese *fpl* di movimentazione; (administrative) spese *fpl* di amministrazione

hand lotion *n* lozione *f* per le mani

hand luggage *n* bagaglio *m* a mano

handmade *adj* fatto a mano

handout *n* (at lecture) foglio *m* informativo; infml (money) elemosina *f*

handover *n* (of prisoner, ransom) consegna *f*; (of property, territory) cessione *f*; **~ of power** passaggio *m* delle consegne

hand-pick *vt* scegliere ‹*produce*›; selezionare con cura ‹*staff*›

handrail *n* corrimano *m*

hand-reared /-ˈrɪəd/ *adj* ‹*animal*› allattato con il biberon

handset *n* Teleph ricevitore *m*

handshake *n* stretta *f* di mano

hand signal *n* Auto segnalazione *f* con la mano

hands-off *adj* ‹*policy*› di non intervento; ‹*manager*› che delega le responsabilità

handsome /ˈhænsəm/ *adj* bello; fig (generous) generoso; ‹*salary*› considerevole

hands-on *adj* ‹*experience*› pratico; ‹*approach*› pragmatico; ‹*control*› diretto; ‹*manager*› che segue direttamente le varie attività

handspring *n* salto *m* sulle mani

handstand *n* verticale *f*

hand-to-hand *adj & adv* ‹*fight*› corpo a corpo

hand-to-mouth *adj* ‹*existence*› precario

hand towel *n* asciugamano *m*

hand-woven /-ˈwəʊvən/ *adj* tessuto a mano

handwriting *n* calligrafia *f*

handwritten *adj* scritto a mano

handy /ˈhændɪ/ *adj* (**-ier**, **-iest**) pratico; ‹*person*› abile; **have/keep ~** avere/tenere a portata di mano

handyman /ˈhændɪmæn/ *n* tuttofare *m inv*

⚷ **hang** /hæŋ/ **A** *vt* (*pt/pp* **hung**) appendere ‹*picture*› (*pt/pp* **hanged**) impiccare ‹*criminal*›; **~ oneself** impiccarsi; **~ wallpaper** tappezzare
B *vi* (*pt/pp* **hung**) pendere; ‹*hair*› scendere
C *n* **get the ~ of it** infml afferrare

■ **hang about** *vi* gironzolare

■ **hang around** *vi* = **hang about**

■ **hang back** *vi* (hesitate) esitare

■ **hang down** *vi* ‹*hem*› pendere

■ **hang on** *vi* tenersi stretto; infml (wait) aspettare; Teleph restare in linea

■ **hang on to** *vt* tenersi stretto a; (keep) tenere

⚷ parola chiave

■ **hang out** **A** *vi* spuntare; **where does he usually ~ out?** infml dove bazzica di solito? **B** *vt* stendere ‹*washing*›

■ **hang up** **A** *vt* appendere; Teleph riattaccare **B** *vi* essere appeso; Teleph riattaccare

hangar /ˈhæŋə(r)/ *n* hangar *m inv*

hanger /ˈhæŋə(r)/ *n* gruccia *f*

hanger-on *n* leccapiedi *mf inv*

hang-glider *n* deltaplano *m*

hang-gliding *n* deltaplano *m*

hanging /ˈhæŋɪŋ/ *n* (of person) impiccagione *f*; (curtain) tendaggio *m*; (on wall) arazzo *m*

hangman *n* boia *m*

hangover *n* postumi *mpl* della sbornia

hang-up *n* infml complesso *m*

hank /hæŋk/ *n* (of hair) ciocca *f*; (of wool etc) matassa *f*

hanker /ˈhæŋkə(r)/ *vi* **~ after something** smaniare per qualcosa

hanky, hankie /ˈhæŋkɪ/ *n* infml fazzoletto *m*

hanky-panky /hæŋkɪˈpæŋkɪ/ *n* infml qualcosa *m* di losco

ha'penny /ˈheɪpnɪ/ *n abbr* BrE (**halfpenny**) mezzo penny *m inv*

haphazard /hæpˈhæzəd/ *adj* a casaccio; **in a ~ fashion** a casaccio

haphazardly /hæpˈhæzədlɪ/ *adv* a casaccio

hapless /ˈhæplɪs/ *adj* sventurato

happen /ˈhæpn/ *vi* capitare, succedere; **as it ~s** per caso; **I ~ed to meet him** mi è capitato di incontrarlo; **what has ~ed to him?** cosa gli è capitato?; (become of) che fine ha fatto?

happening /ˈhæp(ə)nɪŋ/ *n* avvenimento *m*

happily /ˈhæpɪlɪ/ *adv* felicemente; (fortunately) fortunatamente

happiness /ˈhæpɪnɪs/ *n* felicità *f*

happy /ˈhæpɪ/ *adj* (**-ier**, **-iest**) contento, felice

happy ending *n* lieto fine *m*

happy-go-lucky *adj* spensierato

happy hour *n ora (f) in cui nei pub le bevande vengono vendute a prezzi scontati*

happy medium *n* giusto mezzo *m*

harangue /həˈræŋ/ *vt* ‹*morally*› fare un sermone a; ‹*politically*› arringare

harass /ˈhærəs/ *vt* perseguitare

harassed /ˈhærəst/ *adj* stressato

harassment /ˈhærəsmənt/ *n* persecuzione *f*; **sexual ~** molestie *fpl* sessuali

harbinger /ˈhɑːbɪndʒə(r)/ *n* literary segnale *m*; (person) precursore *m*; precorritrice *f*

harbour /ˈhɑːbə(r)/ **A** *n* porto *m* **B** *vt* dare asilo a; nutrire ‹*grudge*›

hard /hɑːd/ **A** *adj* duro; ‹*question, problem*› difficile; **~ of hearing** duro d'orecchi; **be ~ on somebody** ‹*person*› essere duro con qualcuno **B** *adv* ‹*work*› duramente; ‹*pull, hit, rain, snow*› forte; **~ hit by unemployment** duramente colpito dalla disoccupazione; **take something ~** non accettare qualcosa; **think ~!** pensaci bene!; **try ~** mettercela tutta; **try ~er** metterci più impegno; **~ done by** infml trattato ingiustamente

hard and fast *adj* ‹*rule, distinction*› preciso

hardback *n* edizione *f* rilegata

hardboard *n* truciolato *m*

hard-boiled /-ˈbɔɪld/ *adj* ‹*egg*› sodo

hard cash *n* contante *m*

hard copy *n* copia *f* stampata

hard core **A** *n* (in construction) massicciata *f*; (of group, demonstrators) zoccolo *m* duro **B** *adj* ‹*pornography, video*› hard-core; ‹*supporter, opponent*› irriducibile

hard court *n* campo *m* in superficie dura

hard disk *n* hard disk *m inv*; disco *m* rigido

hard drive *n* Comput hard drive *m*

hard drug *n* droga *f* pesante

hard-earned /-ˈɜːnd/ *adj* ‹*cash*› sudato

harden /ˈhɑːdn/ *vi* indurirsi

hardened /ˈhɑːdnd/ *adj* ‹*criminal*› inveterato; ‹*drinker*› cronico

hard-faced /-ˈfeɪst/ *adj* ‹*person*› dai tratti duri

hard-fought *adj* ‹*battle*› accanito

hard hat *n* casco *m*

hard-headed /-ˈhedɪd/ *adj* pratico; ‹*businessman*› dal sangue freddo

hard-hearted /-ˈhɑːtɪd/ *adj* dal cuore duro

hard-hitting /-ˈhɪtɪŋ/ *adj* ‹*report, speech*› incisivo

hard labour *n* BrE lavori *mpl* forzati

hard lens *n* lente *f* a contatto rigida

hard-line **A** *adj* ‹*policy, regime*› duro **B** *n* linea *f* dura; **~ lines!** che sfortuna!

hardliner *n* Pol fautore, -trice *mf* della linea dura

hard luck *n* sfortuna *f*

hard-luck story *n* **give somebody a ~** raccontare a qualcuno le proprie disgrazie

hardly /ˈhɑːdlɪ/ *adv* appena; **~ ever** quasi mai

hardness /ˈhɑːdnɪs/ *n* durezza *f*

hard-nosed /-ˈnəʊzd/ *adj* ‹*attitude, businessman, government*› duro

hard of hearing *adj* duro d'orecchio

hard-on *n* infml erezione *f*

hard porn *n* pornografia *f* hard-core

hard-pressed /-ˈprest/ *adj* in difficoltà; (for time) a corto di tempo

hard-pushed /-ˈpʊʃt/ *adj* (having problems) in difficoltà

hard rock *n* Mus hard rock *m*

hard sell *n* tecnica *f* di vendita aggressiva

hardship /ˈhɑːdʃɪp/ *n* avversità *f*

hard shoulder *n* Auto corsia *f* d'emergenza

hard up *adj* infml a corto di soldi; **~ up for something** a corto di qualcosa

hardware *n* ferramenta *fpl*; Comput hardware *m inv*

hardware shop *n* negozio *m* di ferramenta

hard-wearing /-ˈweərɪŋ/ *adj* resistente

hardwood *n* legno *m* duro

hard-working /-ˈwɜːkɪŋ/ *adj* **be ~** essere un gran lavoratore

hardy /ˈhɑːdɪ/ *adj* (**-ier**, **-iest**) dal fisico resistente; ‹*plant*› che sopporta il gelo

hare /heə(r)/ *n* lepre *f*

hare-brained /ˈheəbreɪnd/ *adj* ‹*scheme*› da scervellati; ‹*person*› scervellato

harelip /heəˈlɪp/ *n* labbro *m* leporino

harem /ˈhɑːriːm/ *n* harem *m*

haricot /ˈhærɪkəʊ/, **haricot bean** *n* fagiolo *m* bianco

hark /hɑːk/ *v*

▪ **hark back** *vt* fig **~ back to** ritornare su

harm /hɑːm/ **A** *n* male *m*; (damage) danni *mpl*; **out of ~'s way** in un posto sicuro; **it won't do any ~** non farà certo male
B *vt* far male a; (damage) danneggiare

harmful /ˈhɑːmfʊl/ *adj* dannoso

harmless /ˈhɑːmlɪs/ *adj* innocuo

harmonica /hɑːˈmɒnɪkə/ *n* armonica *f* [a bocca]

harmonious /hɑːˈməʊnɪəs/ *adj* armonioso

harmoniously /hɑːˈməʊnɪəslɪ/ *adv* in armonia

harmonize /ˈhɑːmənaɪz/ *vi* fig armonizzare

harmony /ˈhɑːmənɪ/ *n* armonia *f*

harness /ˈhɑːnɪs/ **A** *n* finimenti *mpl*; (of parachute) imbracatura *f*
B *vt* bardare ‹*horse*›; sfruttare ‹*resources*›

harp /hɑːp/ *n* arpa *f*

▪ **harp on** *vi* infml insistere (**about** su)

harpist /ˈhɑːpɪst/ *n* arpista *mf*

harpoon /hɑːˈpuːn/ *n* arpione *m*

harpsichord /ˈhɑːpsɪkɔːd/ *n* clavicembalo *m*

harrow /ˈhærəʊ/ *n* erpice *m*

harrowing /ˈhærəʊɪŋ/ *adj* straziante

harry /ˈhærɪ/ *vt* (pursue, harass) assillare

harsh /hɑːʃ/ *adj* duro; ‹*light*› abbagliante

harshly /ˈhɑːʃlɪ/ *adv* duramente

harshness /ˈhɑːʃnɪs/ *n* durezza *f*

harvest /ˈhɑːvɪst/ **A** *n* raccolta *f*; (of grapes) vendemmia *f*; (crop) raccolto *m*
B *vt* raccogliere

harvester /ˈhɑːvɪstə(r)/ *n* (person) mietitore, -trice *mf*; (machine) mietitrice *f*

harvest festival *n* festa *f* del raccolto

has /hæz/ ▶ **have**

has-been /-biːn/ *n* infml (person) persona *f* che ha fatto il suo tempo; (thing) anticaglia *f*

hash /hæʃ/ *n* **make a ~ of** infml fare un casino con

hashish /ˈhæʃɪʃ/ *n* hashish *m*

hash sign *n* cancelletto *m*

hashtag *n* hashtag *m inv*

hassle /ˈhæsl/ **A** *n* infml rottura *f*
B *vt* rompere le scatole a

hassock /ˈhæsək/ *n* cuscino *m* di inginocchiatoio

haste /heɪst/ *n* fretta *f*; **make ~** affrettarsi

hasten /ˈheɪsn/ **A** *vi* affrettarsi
B *vt* affrettare

hastily /ˈheɪstɪlɪ/ *adv* frettolosamente

hasty /ˈheɪstɪ/ *adj* (**-ier**, **-iest**) frettoloso; ‹*decision*› affrettato

hat /hæt/ *n* cappello *m*

hatbox /ˈhætbɒks/ *n* cappelliera *f*

hatch¹ /hætʃ/ *n* (for food) sportello *m* passavivande *inv*; Naut boccaporto *m*

hatch² **A** *vi* **~ [out]** rompere il guscio; ‹*egg*› schiudersi
B *vt* covare; tramare ‹*plot*›

▪ **hatch up** *vt* tramare ‹*plot*›

hatchback /ˈhætʃbæk/ *n* Auto tre/cinque porte *f inv*; (door) porta *f* del bagagliaio

hatchet /ˈhætʃɪt/ *n* ascia *f*

hate /heɪt/ **A** *n* odio *m*
B *vt* odiare

hateful /ˈheɪtfʊl/ *adj* odioso

hate mail *n* lettere *fpl* offensive o minatorie

hatpin /ˈhætpɪn/ *n* spillone *m*

hatred /ˈheɪtrɪd/ *n* odio *m*

hat-trick *n* tripletta *f*

haughtily /ˈhɔːtɪlɪ/ *adv* altezzosamente

haughty /ˈhɔːtɪ/ *adj* (**-ier**, **-iest**) altezzoso

haul /hɔːl/ **A** *n* (fish) pescata *f*; (loot) bottino *m*; (pull) tirata *f*
B *vt* tirare; trasportare ‹*goods*›
C *vi* **~ on** tirare

haulage /ˈhɔːlɪdʒ/ *n* trasporto *m*

haulier /ˈhɔːlɪə(r)/ *n* autotrasportatore *m*

haunch /hɔːntʃ/ *n* anca *f*

haunt /hɔːnt/ **A** *n* ritrovo *m*
B *vt* frequentare; (linger in the mind) perseguitare; **this house is ~ed** questa casa è abitata da fantasmi

haunted /ˈhɔːntɪd/ *adj* ‹*house*› infestato dai fantasmi; ‹*look*› tormentato

haunting /ˈhɔːntɪŋ/ *adj* ‹*memory, melody*› ossessionante

have /hæv/ **A** *vt* (*3 sg pres tense* **has**, *pt/pp* **had**) avere; fare ‹*breakfast, bath, walk etc*›; **~ a drink** bere qualcosa; **~ lunch/dinner** pranzare/cenare; **~ a rest** riposarsi; **I had my hair cut** mi sono tagliata i capelli; **we had the flat painted** abbiamo fatto tinteggiare la casa; **I had it made** l'ho fatto fare; **~ to do something** dover fare qualcosa; **~ him telephone me tomorrow** digli di telefonarmi domani; **he has** *or* **he's got two houses** ha due case; **you've got the money, ~n't you?** hai i soldi, no?
B *v aux* avere; (*with verbs of motion &*

some others) essere; **I ~ seen him** l'ho visto; **he has never been there** non ci è mai stato **C** *npl* **the ~s and the ~-nots** i ricchi e i poveri

■ **have in** *vt* avere in casa/ufficio etc ‹*builders etc*›

■ **have off**: *vt* infml **he's having it off with his secretary** si fa la segretaria

■ **have on** *vt* (be wearing) portare; (dupe) prendere in giro; **I've got something on tonight** ho un impegno stasera; **you're having me on!** tu mi stai prendendo in giro!

■ **have out**: *vt* **~ it out with somebody** chiarire le cose con qualcuno; **~ a tooth out** farsi togliere un dente

haven /'heɪvn/ *n* fig rifugio *m*

haver /'heɪvə(r)/ *vi* (dither) titubare

haversack /'hævəsæk/ *n* zaino *m*

havoc /'hævək/ *n* strage *f*; **play ~ with** fig scombussolare

haw /hɔː/ ▶ **hum**

Hawaii /hə'waɪː/ *n* le Hawaii

Hawaiian /hə'waɪən/ *n & adj* hawaiano, -a *mf*; (language) hawaiano *m*

hawk¹ /hɔːk/ *n* falco *m*

hawk² *vt* vendere in giro

hawker /'hɔːkə(r)/ *n* venditore, -trice *mf* ambulante

hawkish /'hɔːkɪʃ/ *adj* Pol intransigente

hawthorn /'hɔːθɔːn/ *n* biancospino *m*

hay /heɪ/ *n* fieno *m*

hay fever *n* raffreddore *m* da fieno

hayloft *n* fienile *m*

haymaking *n* fienagione *f*

haystack *n* pagliaio *m*

haywire *adj* infml **go ~** dare i numeri; ‹*plans*› andare all'aria

hazard /'hæzəd/ **A** *n* (risk) rischio *m* **B** *vt* rischiare; **~ a guess** azzardare un'ipotesi

hazard lights, hazard warning lights *npl* Auto luci *fpl* d'emergenza

hazardous /'hæzədəs/ *adj* rischioso

haze /heɪz/ *n* foschia *f*

hazel /'heɪz(ə)l/ *n* nocciolo *m*; (colour) [color *m*] nocciola *m*

hazelnut /'heɪz(ə)lnʌt/ *n* nocciola *f*

hazy /'heɪzɪ/ *adj* (**-ier, -iest**) nebbioso; fig ‹*person*› confuso; ‹*memories*› vago

HD *abbr* (**high-definition**) HD, ad alta definizione

HDTV *abbr* (**high-definition television**) HDTV *f*

he /hiː/ *pron* lui; **he's tired** è stanco; **I'm going but he's not** io vengo, ma lui no

head /hed/ **A** *n* testa *f*; (of firm) capo *m*; (of primary school) direttore, -trice *mf*; (of secondary school) preside *mf*; (on beer) schiuma *f*; **use your ~!** usa la testa!; **be off one's ~** essere fuori di testa; **have a good ~ for business** avere il senso degli affari; **have a good ~ for heights** non soffrire di vertigini; **10 pounds a ~** 10 sterline a testa; **20 ~ of cattle** 20 capi di bestiame; **~ first** a capofitto; **~ over heels in love** innamorato pazzo; **~s or tails?** testa o croce? **B** *vt* essere a capo di; essere in testa a ‹*list*›; colpire di testa ‹*ball*› **C** *vi* **~ for** dirigersi verso

headache *n* mal *m* di testa

headband *n* fascia *f* per capelli

head boy *n* BrE Sch *alunno (m) che rappresenta la scuola nelle manifestazioni ufficiali e che ha responsabilità speciali*

head-butt *vt* dare una testata a

head case *n* infml **be a ~** essere matto da legare

head cold *n* raffreddore *m* di testa

headcount *n* **do a ~** contare i presenti

headdress *n* acconciatura *f*

header /'hedə(r)/ *n* colpo *m* di testa; (dive) tuffo *m* di testa; (on document) intestazione *f*

head first *adv* ‹*dive, fall*› di testa; ‹*rush into*› a testa bassa

headgear *n* copricapo *m*

head girl *n* BrE Sch *alunna (f) che rappresenta la scuola nelle manifestazioni ufficiali e che ha responsabilità speciali*

headhunt *vt* cercare per assumere

headhunter *n* (also Comm) cacciatore, -trice *mf* di teste

headhunting *n* Comm ricerca *f* ad hoc di personale

heading *n* (in list etc) titolo *m*

headlamp *n* Auto fanale *m*

headland *n* promontorio *m*

headlight *n* Auto fanale *m*

headline *n* titolo *m*

headlong *adj & adv* a capofitto

head louse *n* pidocchio *m*

headmaster *n* (of primary school) direttore *m*; (of secondary school) preside *m*

headmistress *n* (of primary school) direttrice *f*; (of secondary school) preside *f*

head of department *n* capo *mf* reparto

head office *n* sede *f* centrale

head-on **A** *adj* ‹*collision*› frontale **B** *adv* frontalmente

headphones *npl* cuffie *fpl*

headquarters *npl* sede *fsg*; Mil quartier *msg* generale

headrest *n* poggiatesta *m inv*

headroom *n* sottotetto *m*; (of bridge) altezza *f* libera di passaggio

headscarf *n* foulard *m inv*, fazzoletto *m*

headset *n* cuffia *f* con microfono

headstand *n* **do a ~** fare la verticale

head start *n* **have a ~** partire avvantaggiato

headstone *n* (of grave) lapide *f*

headstrong *adj* testardo

h

head teacher *n* (of primary school) direttore, -trice *mf*; (of secondary school) preside *mf*
head-to-head **A** *n* confronto *m* diretto **B** *adj* diretto
head waiter *n* capocameriere *m*
headway *n* progresso *m*
headwind *n* vento *m* di prua
heady /'hedɪ/ *adj* che dà alla testa
heal /hi:l/ *vt & vi* guarire
healer /'hi:lə(r)/ *n* guaritore, -trice *mf*; **time is a great ~** il tempo guarisce tutti i mali
healing /'hi:lɪŋ/ *adj* <*power, effect*> curativo; **the ~ process** il processo di guarigione
✓ **health** /helθ/ *n* salute *f*
health care *n* assistenza *f* sanitaria
health centre *n* BrE ambulatorio *m*
health check *n* controllo *m*
health club *n* club *m* ginnico
health farm *n* centro *m* di rimessa in forma
health foods *npl* alimenti *mpl* macrobiotici
health food shop *n* negozio *m* di macrobiotica
health hazard *n* pericolo *m* per la salute
healthily /'helθɪlɪ/ *adv* in modo sano
health insurance *n* assicurazione *f* contro malattie
health officer *n* ufficiale *m* sanitario
health resort *n* (in mountains, by sea) stazione *f* climatica; (spa town) stazione *f* termale
Health Service *n* BrE (for public) servizio *m* sanitario; AmE Univ infermeria *f*
health visitor *n* BrE *infermiere -a (mf) che fa visite a domicilio*
health warning *n* avviso *m* del ministero della sanità
✓ **healthy** /'helθɪ/ *adj* (**-ier**, **-iest**) sano
heap /hi:p/ **A** *n* mucchio *m*; **~s of** infml un sacco di
B *vt* **~ [up]** ammucchiare; **~ed teaspoon** un cucchiaino colmo
heaped /hi:pt/ *adj* **a ~ spoonful** un cucchiaio colmo
✓ **hear** /hɪə(r)/ *vt & vi* (*pt/pp* **heard**) sentire; **~, ~!** bravo!
▪ **hear about** *vt* (learn of) sentir parlare di
▪ **hear from** *vi* aver notizie di
▪ **hear of** *vi* sentir parlare di; **he would not ~ of it** non ne ha voluto sentir parlare
✓ **hearing** /'hɪərɪŋ/ *n* udito *m*; Jur udienza *f*
hearing aid *n* apparecchio *m* acustico
hearing-impaired /-ɪm'peəd/ *adj* audioleso
hearsay /'hɪəseɪ/ *n* **from ~** per sentito dire
hearse /hɜ:s/ *n* carro *m* funebre
✓ **heart** /hɑ:t/ *n* cuore *m*; **~s** *pl* Cards cuori *mpl*; **at ~** di natura; **by ~** a memoria
heartache *n* pena *f*
heart attack *n* infarto *m*
heartbeat *n* battito *m* cardiaco
heartbreak *n* afflizione *f*
heartbreaking *adj* straziante
heart-broken *adj* **be ~** avere il cuore spezzato
heartburn *n* bruciore *m* di stomaco
heart disease *n* malattia *f* cardiaca
hearten /'hɑ:t(ə)n/ *vt* rincuorare
heartening /'hɑ:tnɪŋ/ *adj* rincuorante
heart failure *n* arresto *m* cardiaco
heartfelt /'hɑ:tfelt/ *adj* di cuore
hearth /hɑ:θ/ *n* focolare *m*
hearthrug /'hɑ:θrʌg/ *n tappeto (m) davanti al camino*
heartily /'hɑ:tɪlɪ/ *adv* di cuore; <*eat*> con appetito; **be ~ sick of something** non poterne più di qualcosa
heartland /'hɑ:tlænd/ *n* (industrial, rural) cuore *m*; Pol roccaforte *f*
heartless /'hɑ:tlɪs/ *adj* spietato
heartlessly /'hɑ:tlɪslɪ/ *adv* in modo spietato
heart-lung machine *n* polmone *m* artificiale
heart rate *n* battito *m* cardiaco
heart-rending /-rendɪŋ/ *adj* <*sigh, story*> straziante
heart-searching *n* esame *m* di coscienza
heart surgeon *n* cardiochirurgo, -a *mf*
heart-throb *n* infml rubacuori *m inv*
heart-to-heart **A** *n* conversazione *f* a cuore aperto
B *adj* a cuore aperto
heart transplant *n* trapianto *m* di cuore
heart-warming *adj* toccante
hearty /'hɑ:tɪ/ *adj* caloroso; <*meal*> copioso; <*person*> gioviale
✓ **heat** /hi:t/ **A** *n* calore *m*; Sport prova *f* eliminatoria
B *vt* scaldare
C *vi* scaldarsi
▪ **heat up** *vt* scaldare <*food, drink*>; riscaldare <*room*>
heated /'hi:tɪd/ *adj* <*swimming pool*> riscaldato; <*discussion*> animato
heater /'hi:tə(r)/ *n* (for room) stufa *f*; (for water) boiler *m inv*; Auto riscaldamento *m*
heath /hi:θ/ *n* brughiera *f*
heat haze *n* foschia *f (dovuta all'afa)*
heathen /'hi:ðn/ *adj & n* pagano, -a *mf*
heather /'heðə(r)/ *n* erica *f*
heating /'hi:tɪŋ/ *n* riscaldamento *m*
heat loss *n* perdita *f* di calore
heat-resistant *adj* resistente al calore
heat sink *n* dissipatore *m* termico
heatstroke *n* colpo *m* di sole
heat treatment *n* Med termoterapia *f*

✓ parola chiave

heatwave *n* ondata *f* di calore

heave /hiːv/ **A** *vt* tirare; (lift) tirare su; infml (throw) gettare; emettere ‹*sigh*›
B *vi* tirare; **my stomach ~d** avevo la nausea

heaven /ˈhev(ə)n/ *n* paradiso *m*; **~ help you if...** Dio vi scampi se...; **raise one's eyes to ~** alzare gli occhi al cielo; **H~s!** santo cielo!

heavenly /ˈhev(ə)nlɪ/ *adj* celeste; infml delizioso

heaven-sent /-ˈsent/ *adj* ‹*opportunity*› provvidenziale

heavily /ˈhevɪlɪ/ *adv* pesantemente; ‹*smoke, drink etc*› molto

heaviness /ˈhevɪnɪs/ *n* pesantezza *f*

heavy /ˈhevɪ/ *adj* (**-ier**, **-iest**) pesante; ‹*traffic*› intenso; ‹*rain, cold*› forte; **be a ~ smoker/drinker** essere un gran fumatore/bevitore

heavy-duty *adj* ‹*equipment, shoes*› molto resistente

heavy goods vehicle *n* veicolo *m* per carichi pesanti

heavy-handed /-ˈhændɪd/ *adj* (severe) severo; (clumsy) maldestro

heavy industry *n* industria *f* pesante

heavy metal *n* Mus heavy metal *m*

heavyweight *n* peso *m* massimo

Hebrew /ˈhiːbruː/ *adj & n* ebreo

heck /hek/ infml **A** *int* cavolo
B *n* **a ~ of a lot of** un sacco di; **what the ~!** chi se ne frega!; **what the ~ is going on?** che cavolo succede?

heckle /ˈhekl/ *vt* interrompere di continuo

heckler /ˈheklə(r)/ *n* disturbatore, -trice *mf*

hectare /ˈhekteə(r)/ *n* ettaro *m*

hectic /ˈhektɪk/ *adj* frenetico

hectoring /ˈhektərɪŋ/ *adj* prepotente

hedge /hedʒ/ **A** *n* siepe *f*
B *vi* fig essere evasivo

hedge clippers *npl* cesoie *fpl*

hedge fund *n* hedge fund *m inv*

hedgehog *n* riccio *m*

hedgerow *n* siepe *f*

hedonism /ˈhiːdənɪzm/ *n* edonismo *m*

hedonistic /hiːdəˈnɪstɪk/ *adj* edonistico

heebie-jeebies /hiːbɪˈdʒiːbɪz/ *npl* infml **give somebody the ~** far venire i brividi a qualcuno

heed /hiːd/ **A** *n* **pay ~ to** prestare ascolto a
B *vt* prestare ascolto a

heedless /ˈhiːdlɪs/ *adj* noncurante

heel¹ /hiːl/ *n* tallone *m*; (of shoe) tacco *m*; **down at ~** fig trasandato; **take to one's ~s** infml darsela a gambe

heel² *vi* **~ over** Naut inclinarsi

heel bar *n* calzolaio *m*

hefty /ˈheftɪ/ *adj* (**-ier**, **-iest**) massiccio

heifer /ˈhefə(r)/ *n* giovenca *f*

height /haɪt/ *n* altezza *f*; (of plane) altitudine *f*; (of season, fame) culmine *m*

heighten /ˈhaɪt(ə)n/ *vt* fig accrescere

heinous /ˈhiːnəs/ *adj* abominevole

heir /eə(r)/ *n* erede *mf*

heiress /eəˈres/ *n* ereditiera *f*

heirloom /ˈeəluːm/ *n* cimelio *m* di famiglia

heist /haɪst/ *adj* AmE infml furto *m*; (armed) rapina *f*

held /held/ ▶ **hold²**

helicopter /ˈhelɪkɒptə(r)/ *n* elicottero *m*

heliport /ˈhelɪpɔːt/ *n* eliporto *m*

helium /ˈhiːlɪəm/ *n* elio *m*

helix /ˈhiːlɪks/ *n* elica *f*

hell /hel/ **A** *n* inferno *m*; **go to ~!** sl va' al diavolo!; **make sb's life ~** rendere la vita infernale a qualcuno
B *int* porca miseria!

hell-bent *adj* **~ on doing something** deciso a tutti i costi a fare qualcosa

Hellenic /hɪˈlenɪk/ *adj* ellenico

hellfire /ˈhelfaɪə(r)/ *n* pene *fpl* dell' inferno

hell for leather *adv* infml **go ~** andare a spron battuto

hello /həˈləʊ/ *int & n* = **hallo**

Hell's angel *n* Hell's angel *m inv*

helm /helm/ *n* timone *m*; **at the ~** fig al timone

helmet /ˈhelmɪt/ *n* casco *m*

help /help/ **A** *n* aiuto *m*; (employee) aiuto *m* domestico; **that's no ~** non è d'aiuto
B *vt* aiutare; **~ oneself to something** servirsi di qualcosa; **~ yourself** (at table) serviti pure; **I could not ~ laughing** non ho potuto trattenermi dal ridere; **it cannot be ~ed** non c'è niente da fare; **I can't ~ it** non ci posso far niente
C *vi* aiutare

■ **help out** **A** *vt* dare una mano a
B *vi* dare una mano

help desk *n* help desk *m inv*

helper /ˈhelpə(r)/ *n* aiutante *mf*

helpful /ˈhelpfʊl/ *adj* ‹*person*› di aiuto; ‹*advice*› utile

helping /ˈhelpɪŋ/ *n* porzione *f*

helping hand *n* **give somebody a ~** dare una mano a qualcuno

helpless /ˈhelplɪs/ *adj* (unable to manage) incapace; (powerless) impotente

helplessly /ˈhelplɪslɪ/ *adv* con impotenza; ‹*laugh*› incontrollatamente

helpline *n* assistenza *f* telefonica

help window *n* Comput finestrella *f* di aiuto

helter-skelter /heltəˈskeltə(r)/ **A** *adv* in fretta e furia
B *n scivolo (m) a spirale nei luna park*

hem /hem/ **A** *n* orlo *m*
B *vt* (*pt/pp* **hemmed**) orlare

■ **hem in** *vt* intrappolare

hemisphere /ˈhemɪsfɪə(r)/ *n* emisfero *m*

hemline /ˈhemlaɪn/ *n* orlo *m*

h

hemlock /ˈhemlɒk/ *n* cicuta *f*

hemophilia *n* AmE = **haemophilia**

hemp /hemp/ *n* canapa *f*

hen /hen/ *n* gallina *f*; (any female bird) femmina *f*

hence /hens/ *adv* (for this reason) quindi; (from now on) a partire da ora; (from here) da qui

henceforth /hensˈfɔːθ/ *adv* fml (from that time on) da allora in poi; (from now on) d'ora in poi

henchman /ˈhentʃmən/ *n* derog tirapiedi *m inv*

hen coop *n* stia *f*

hen house *n* pollaio *m*

henna /ˈhenə/ *n* hennè *m*

hen night *n* infml addio *m* al nubilato

hen party *n* infml festa *f* di addio al nubilato

henpecked /ˈhenpekt/ *adj* tiranneggiato dalla moglie

hepatitis /hepəˈtaɪtɪs/ *n* epatite *f*

heptathlete /hepˈtæθliːt/ *n* eptatleta *mf*

heptathlon /hepˈtæθlən, -lɒn/ *n* eptathlon *m*

🔑 **her** /hɜː(r)/ **A** *poss adj* suo *m*, sua *f*, suoi *mpl*, sue *fpl*; ~ **job/house** il suo lavoro/la sua casa; ~ **mother/father** sua madre/suo padre
B *pers pron* (direct object) la; (indirect object) le; (after prep) lei; **I know** ~ la conosco; **give** ~ **the money** dalle i soldi; **give it to** ~ daglielo; **I came with** ~ sono venuto con lei; **it's** ~ è lei; **I've seen** ~ l'ho vista; **I've seen** ~**, but not him** ho visto lei, ma non lui

herald /ˈherəld/ *vt* annunciare

heraldic /heˈrældɪk/ *adj* araldico

heraldry /ˈherəldrɪ/ *n* araldica *f*

herb /hɜːb/ *n* erba *f*

herbaceous /hɜːˈbeɪʃəs/ *adj* erbaceo; ~ **border** aiuola *f*

herbal /ˈhɜːb(ə)l/ *adj* alle erbe

herbalist /ˈhɜːbəlɪst/ *n* erborista *mf*

herbal tea *n* tisana *f*

herb garden *n* aromatario *m*

herbs /hɜːbz/ *npl* (for cooking) aromi *mpl* [da cucina]; (medicinal) erbe *fpl*

herb tea *n* tisana *f*

Herculean /hɜːkjʊˈliːən/ *adj* ‹*task*› erculeo

herd /hɜːd/ **A** *n* gregge *m*
B *vt* (tend) sorvegliare; (drive) far muovere; fig ammassare
■ **herd together A** *vi* raggrupparsi
B *vt* raggruppare

🔑 **here** /hɪə(r)/ *adv* (qui) qua; **in** ~ qui dentro; **come/bring** ~ vieni/porta qui; ~ **is...**, ~ **are...** ecco...; ~ **you are!** ecco qua!

hereabouts /hɪərəˈbaʊts/ BrE, **hereabout** AmE *adv* da queste parti

hereafter *adv* in futuro

here and now A *adv* seduta stante
B *n* **the** ~ il presente

hereby *adv* con la presente

hereditary /hɪˈredɪtərɪ/ *adj* ereditario

heredity /hɪˈredətɪ/ *n* ereditarietà *f*

heresy /ˈherəsɪ/ *n* eresia *f*

heretic /ˈherətɪk/ *n* eretico, -a *mf*

herewith /hɪəˈwɪð/ *adv* Comm con la presente

heritage /ˈherɪtɪdʒ/ *n* eredità *f*

hermetic /hɜːˈmetɪk/ *adj* ermetico

hermetically /hɜːˈmetɪklɪ/ *adv* ermeticamente

hermit /ˈhɜːmɪt/ *n* eremita *mf*

hernia /ˈhɜːnɪə/ *n* ernia *f*

🔑 **hero** /ˈhɪərəʊ/ *n* (*pl* **-es**) eroe *m*

heroic /hɪˈrəʊɪk/ *adj* eroico

heroically /hɪˈrəʊɪklɪ/ *adv* eroicamente

heroin /ˈherəʊɪn/ *n* eroina *f* (*droga*)

heroin addict *n* eroinomane *mf*

heroine /ˈherəʊɪn/ *n* eroina *f*

heroism /ˈherəʊɪzm/ *n* eroismo *m*

heron /ˈherən/ *n* airone *m*

hero-worship A *n* culto *m* degli eroi
B *vt* venerare

herpes /ˈhɜːpiːz/ *n* herpes *m*

herring /ˈherɪŋ/ *n* aringa *f*

herringbone /ˈherɪŋbəʊn/ *adj* ‹*pattern*› spigato

hers /hɜːz/ *poss pron* il suo *m*, la sua *f*, i suoi *mpl*, le sue *fpl*; **a friend of** ~ un suo amico; **friends of** ~ dei suoi amici; **that is** ~ quello è suo; (as opposed to mine) quello è il suo

🔑 **herself** /həˈself/ *pers pron (reflexive)* si; (emphatic) lei stessa; (after prep) sé, se stessa; **she poured** ~ **a drink** si è versata da bere; **she told me so** ~ me lo ha detto lei stessa; **she's proud of** ~ è fiera di sé; **by** ~ da sola

hesitant /ˈhezɪtənt/ *adj* esitante

hesitantly /ˈhezɪtəntlɪ/ *adv* con esitazione

hesitate /ˈhezɪteɪt/ *vi* esitare

hesitation /hezɪˈteɪʃn/ *n* esitazione *f*

hessian /ˈhesɪən/ *n* tela *f* di iuta

heterogeneous /hetərəˈdʒiːnɪəs/ *adj* eterogeneo

heterosexual /hetərəʊˈsekʃʊəl/ *adj* eterosessuale

het up /het/ *adj* infml agitato

hew /hjuː/ *vt* (*pt* **hewed**, *pp* **hewed** *or* **hewn**) spaccare

hexagon /ˈheksəgən/ *n* esagono *m*

hexagonal /hekˈsægənl/ *adj* esagonale

🔑 **hey** /heɪ/ *int* ehi!

heyday /ˈheɪdeɪ/ *n* tempi *mpl* d'oro

hey presto /heɪˈprestəʊ/ *int* (magic) e voilà!

HGV *abbr* (**heavy goods vehicle**) TIR *m*

hi /haɪ/ *int* ciao!

hiatus /haɪˈeɪtəs/ *n* (*pl* **-tuses**) iato *m*

hibernate /ˈhaɪbəneɪt/ *vi* andare in letargo

hibernation /haɪbəˈneɪʃn/ *n* letargo *m*

🔑 parola chiave

hiccup /ˈhɪkʌp/ **A** *n* singhiozzo *m*; infml (hitch) intoppo *m*; **have the ~s** avere il singhiozzo
B *vi* fare un singhiozzo

hick /hɪk/ *n* AmE infml buzzurro, -a *mf*

hick town *n* AmE infml città *f* provinciale

hid /hɪd/, **hidden** /ˈhɪdn/ ▶ **hide²**

hide¹ /haɪd/ *n* (leather) pelle *f* (*di animale*)

hide² **A** *vt* (*pt* **hid**, *pp* **hidden**) nascondere
B *vi* nascondersi

hide-and-seek *n* **play ~** giocare a nascondino

hideaway /ˈhaɪdəweɪ/ *n* (secluded place) rifugio *m*; (hiding place) nascondiglio *m*

hidebound /ˈhaɪdbaʊnd/ *adj* (conventional) limitato

hideous /ˈhɪdɪəs/ *adj* orribile

hideously /ˈhɪdɪəslɪ/ *adv* orribilmente

hideout /ˈhaɪdaʊt/ *n* nascondiglio *m*

hiding¹ /ˈhaɪdɪŋ/ *n* infml (beating) bastonata; (defeat) batosta *f*

hiding² *n* **go into ~** sparire dalla circolazione

hiding place *n* nascondiglio *m*

hierarchic /haɪəˈrɑːkɪk/, **hierarchical** /haɪəˈrɑːkɪkl/ *adj* gerarchico

hierarchy /ˈhaɪərɑːkɪ/ *n* gerarchia *f*

hieroglyphics /haɪərəˈglɪfɪks/, **hieroglyphs** *npl* geroglifici *mpl*

hi-fi /ˈhaɪfaɪ/ *n abbr* (**high fidelity**) hi-fi *m inv*; (set of equipment) impianto *m* hi-fi, stereo *m inv*

higgledy-piggledy /hɪgldɪˈpɪgldɪ/ *adv* alla rinfusa

high /haɪ/ **A** *adj* alto; ‹*meat*› che comincia ad andare a male; ‹*wind*› forte; (on drugs) fatto; **it's ~ time we did something about it** è ora di fare qualcosa in proposito
B *adv* in alto; **~ and low** in lungo e in largo
C *n* massimo *m*; (temperature) massima *f*; **from on ~** dall'alto; **be on a ~** infml essere fatto

high and dry *adj* fig **leave somebody ~** piantare in asso qualcuno

high beam *n* AmE abbagliante *m*

high-born *adj* nobile

highbrow *adj & n* intellettuale *mf*

high chair *n* seggiolone *m*

high-class *adj* ‹*hotel, shop, car*› d'alta classe; ‹*prostitute*› di alto bordo

high command *n* stato *m* maggiore

High Commission *n* alto commissariato *m*

High Commissioner *n* alto commissario *m*

High Court *n* ≈ Corte *f* Suprema

high-definition *adj* ad alta definizione

high-definition television *n* televisione *f* ad alta definizione

high diving *n* tuffo *m*

high-end *adj* ‹*product, model*› della fascia più alta

higher education /haɪəredjʊˈkeɪʃn/ *n* istruzione *f* universitaria

higher mathematics *nsg* matematica *fsg* avanzata

highfaluting /haɪfəˈluːtɪŋ/ *adj* infml ‹*ideas*› pretenzioso; ‹*language*› pomposo

high fashion *n* alta moda *f*

high-fibre *adj* ‹*diet*› ricco di fibre

high-fidelity **A** *n* alta fedeltà *f*
B *adj* ad alta fedeltà

high finance *n* alta finanza *f*

high-flier *n* (person) persona *f* che mira alto

high-flown *adj* ‹*phrases*› ampolloso

high-flying *adj* ‹*aircraft*› da alta quota; ‹*career*› ambizioso; ‹*person*› che mira alto

high-frequency *adj* alta frequenza *f*

High German *n* alto tedesco *m*

high-grade *adj* ‹*oil, mineral, product*› di prima qualità

high ground *n* collina *f*; **take the moral ~** assumere un atteggiamento moralistico

high-handed /-ˈhændɪd/ *adj* dispotico

high-handedly /-ˈhændɪdlɪ/ *adv* dispoticamente

high-heeled *adj* coi tacchi alti

high heels *npl* tacchi *mpl* alti

high jinks /dʒɪŋks/ *npl* baldoria *f*

high jump *n* salto *m* in alto

Highland games /haɪlənd/ *n* *manifestazione (f) tradizionale scozzese con gare sportive e musicali*

Highlands /ˈhaɪləndz/ *npl* Highlands *fpl* (*regione della Scozia del nord*)

high-level *adj* ‹*talks*› ad alto livello; ‹*official*› di alto livello

high life *n* bella vita *f*

highlight /ˈhaɪlaɪt/ **A** *vt* (emphasize, with pen) evidenziare
B *n* (in art) luce *f*; (in hair) riflesso *m*, colpo *m* di sole; (of exhibition) parte *f* saliente; (of week, year) avvenimento *m* saliente; (of match, show) momento *m* clou

highlighter /ˈhaɪlaɪtə(r)/ *n* (marker) evidenziatore *m*

highly /ˈhaɪlɪ/ *adv* molto; **speak ~ of** lodare; **think ~ of** avere un'alta opinione di

highly-paid /-ˈpeɪd/ *adj* ben pagato

highly strung *adj* nervoso

High Mass *n* messa *f* solenne

high-minded /-ˈmaɪndɪd/ *adj* ‹*person*› di animo nobile

high-necked /-ˈnekt/ *adj* a collo alto

Highness /ˈhaɪnɪs/ *n* altezza *f*; **Your ~** Sua Altezza

high noon *n* mezzogiorno *m* in punto

high-performance *adj* ad alta prestazione

high-pitched /-ˈpɪtʃt/ *adj* ‹*voice, sound*› acuto

high point *n* momento *m* culminante

high-powered *adj ‹car, engine›* molto potente; *‹job›* di alta responsabilità; *‹person›* dinamico
high pressure **A** *n* Meteorol alta pressione *f*
B *attrib* Techn ad alta pressione; *‹job›* stressante
high priest *n* Relig gran sacerdote *m*; fig guru *m inv*
high priestess *n* Relig fig gran sacerdotessa *f*
high-principled *adj ‹person›* di alti principi
high-profile *adj ‹politician, group›* di spicco; *‹visit›* di grande risonanza
high-ranking *adj* di alto rango
high-rise **A** *adj ‹building›* molto alto
B *n* edificio *m* molto alto
high road *n* strada *f* principale
high school *n* AmE ≈ scuola *f* superiore; BrE ≈ scuola *f* media e superiore
high sea *n* **on the ~s** in alto mare
high season *n* alta stagione *f*
high society *n* alta società *f*
high-sounding /-ˈsaʊndɪŋ/ *adj ‹title›* altisonante
high-speed *adj ‹train, film›* rapido
high-spirited *adj* pieno di brio
high spirits *npl* brio *m*
high spot *n* momento *m* culminante
high street *n* strada *f* principale
high-street shop *n* negozio *m* popolare
high-street spending *n* acquisto *m* di beni di consumo
high tea *n pasto (m) pomeridiano servito insieme al tè*
high tech /ˈtek/ *n* high tech *f*
high tide *n* alta marea *f*
high treason *n* alto tradimento *m*
high voltage *n* alta tensione *f*
highway /ˈhaɪweɪ/ *n* AmE (motorway) superstrada *f*; **public ~** strada *f* pubblica
Highway Code *n* BrE Codice *m* stradale
highwayman *n* brigante *m*
highway robbery *n* brigantaggio *m*
high wire *n* filo *m* (*per acrobati*)
hijack /ˈhaɪdʒæk/ **A** *vt* dirottare
B *n* dirottamento *m*
hijacker /ˈhaɪdʒækə(r)/ *n* dirottatore, -trice *mf*
hijacking /ˈhaɪdʒækɪŋ/ *n* dirottamento *m*
hike /haɪk/ **A** *n* escursione *f* a piedi; (in price) aumento *m*
B *vi* fare un'escursione a piedi
hiker /ˈhaɪkə(r)/ *n* escursionista *mf*
hiking /ˈhaɪkɪŋ/ *n* escursionismo *m*
hiking boots *npl* pedule *fpl*
hilarious /hɪˈleərɪəs/ *adj* da morir dal ridere
hilarity /hɪˈlærətɪ/ *n* ilarità *f*
hill /hɪl/ *n* collina *f*; (mound) collinetta *f*; (slope) altura *f*
hillbilly /-bɪlɪ/ *n* AmE montanaro *m* degli Stati Uniti sudorientali
hillock /ˈhɪlək/ *n* poggio *m*
hillside /ˈhɪlsaɪd/ *n* pendio *m*
hilltop /ˈhɪltɒp/ *n* sommità *f* di una collina
hilly /ˈhɪlɪ/ *adj* collinoso
hilt /hɪlt/ *n* impugnatura *f*; **to the ~** infml *‹support›* fino in fondo; *‹mortgaged›* fino al collo
⚷ **him** /hɪm/ *pers pron* (direct object) lo; (indirect object) gli; (with prep) lui; **I know ~** lo conosco; **give ~ the money** dagli i soldi; **give it to ~** daglielo; **I spoke to ~** gli ho parlato; **it's ~** è lui; **she loves ~** lo ama; **she loves ~, not you** ama lui, non te
Himalayas /hɪməˈleɪəz/ *npl* Himalaia *msg*
⚷ **himself** /hɪmˈself/ *pers pron (reflexive)* si; (emphatic) lui stesso; (after prep) sé, se stesso; **he poured ~ out a drink** si è versato da bere; **he told me so ~** me lo ha detto lui stesso; **he's proud of ~** è fiero di sé; **by ~** da solo
hind /haɪnd/ *adj* posteriore
hinder /ˈhɪndə(r)/ *vt* intralciare
hind legs *npl* zampe *fpl* posteriori
hindquarters /ˈhaɪn(d)kwɔːtəz/ *npl* didietro *m*
hindrance /ˈhɪndrəns/ *n* intralcio *m*
hindsight /ˈhaɪndsaɪt/ *n* **with ~** con il senno del poi
Hindu /ˈhɪnduː/ *adj & n* indù *mf inv*
Hinduism /ˈhɪndʊɪzm/ *n* induismo *m*
hinge /hɪndʒ/ **A** *n* cardine *m*
B *vi* **~ on** fig dipendere da
hint /hɪnt/ **A** *n* (clue) accenno *m*; (advice) suggerimento *m*; (indirect suggestion) allusione *f*; (trace) tocco *m*
B *vt* **~ that ...** far capire che...
C *vi* **~ at** alludere a
hinterland /ˈhɪntəlænd/ *n* entroterra *m inv*, hinterland *m inv*
hip /hɪp/ *n* fianco *m*
hip bone *n* ileo *m*
hip flask *n* fiaschetta *f*
hippie /ˈhɪpɪ/ *n* hippy *mf inv*
hippo /ˈhɪpəʊ/ *n* infml ippopotamo *m*
hip pocket *n* tasca *f* posteriore
Hippocratic oath /hɪpəˈkrætɪk/ *adj* giuramento *m* d'Ippocrate
hippopotamus /hɪpəˈpɒtəməs/ *n* (*pl* **-muses** *or* **-mi** /hɪpəˈpɒtəmaɪ/) ippopotamo *m*
hip replacement *n* protesi *f inv* all'anca
⚷ **hire** /ˈhaɪə(r)/ **A** *vt* affittare; assumere *‹person›*; **~ [out]** affittare
B *n* noleggio *m*; **'for ~'** 'affittasi'
hire car *n* macchina *f* a noleggio

hire purchase *n* BrE acquisto *m* rateale; **on ~** a rate

his /hɪz/ **A** *poss adj* suo *m*, sua *f*, suoi *mpl*, sue *fpl*; **~ job/house** il suo lavoro/la sua casa; **~ mother/father** sua madre/suo padre **B** *poss pron* il suo *m*, la sua *f*, i suoi *mpl*, le sue *fpl*; **a friend of ~** un suo amico; **friends of ~** dei suoi amici; **that is ~** questo è suo; (as opposed to mine) questo è il suo

Hispanic /hɪ'spænɪk/ *adj* ispanico

hiss /hɪs/ **A** *n* sibilo *m*; (of disapproval) fischio *m* **B** *vt* fischiare **C** *vi* sibilare; (in disapproval) fischiare

historian /hɪ'stɔːrɪən/ *n* storico, -a *mf*

historic /hɪ'stɒrɪk/ *adj* storico

historical /hɪ'stɒrɪkl/ *adj* storico

historically /hɪ'stɒrɪklɪ/ *adv* storicamente

history /'hɪstərɪ/ *n* storia *f*; **make ~** passare alla storia

histrionic /hɪstrɪ'ɒnɪk/ *adj* istrionico

histrionics /hɪstrɪ'ɒnɪks/ *npl* scene *fpl*

hit /hɪt/ **A** *n* (blow) colpo *m*; infml (success) successo *m*; **score a direct ~** ‹*missile*› colpire in pieno **B** *vt* (*pt/pp* **hit**, *pres p* **hitting**) colpire; **~ one's head on the table** battere la testa contro il tavolo; **the car ~ the wall** la macchina ha sbattuto contro il muro; **~ the target** colpire il bersaglio; **~ the nail on the head** fare centro; **~ the roof** infml perdere le staffe

■ **hit back** *vi* ‹*retaliate*› ribattere

■ **hit off**: *vt* **~ it off** andare d'accordo

■ **hit on** *vt* fig trovare

hit-and-miss *adj* ‹*affair, undertaking*› imprevedibile; ‹*method*› a casaccio

hit-and-run *adj* ‹*raid, attack*› lampo *inv*; ‹*accident*› causato da un pirata della strada

hit-and-run driver *n* pirata *m* della strada

hitch /hɪtʃ/ **A** *n* intoppo *m*; **technical ~** problema *m* tecnico **B** *vt* attaccare; **~ a lift** chiedere un passaggio

■ **hitch up** *vt* tirarsi su ‹*trousers*›

hitch-hike *vi* fare l'autostop

hitch-hiker *n* autostoppista *mf*

hitch-hiking *n* autostop *m*

hi-tech *adj* **high tech**

hither /'hɪðə(r)/ *adv* **~ and thither** di qua e di là

hitherto /hɪðə'tuː/ *adv* finora

hit list *n* lista *f* degli obiettivi

hit man *n* sicario *m*

hit-or-miss *adj* **on a very ~ basis** all'improvvisata

hit parade *n* hit parade *f inv*, classifica *f*

hit single *n* singolo *m* di successo

HIV *n abbr* (**human immunodeficiency virus**) HIV; **~ positive** sieropositivo; **~ negative** sieronegativo

hive /haɪv/ *n* alveare *m*; **~ of industry** fucina *f* di lavoro

■ **hive off** *vt* Comm separare

HIV positive *adj* sieropositivo

HM *abbr* (**Her Majesty** *or* **His Majesty**) SM

HMS *abbr* (**His/Her Majesty's Ship**) *nave (f) di Sua Maestà*

hoard /hɔːd/ **A** *n* provvista *f*; (of money) gruzzolo *m* **B** *vt* accumulare

hoarding /'hɔːdɪŋ/ *n* palizzata *f*; (with advertisements) tabellone *m* per manifesti pubblicitari

hoar frost /'hɔː(r)/ *n* brina *f*

hoarse /hɔːs/ *adj* rauco

hoarsely /'hɔːslɪ/ *adv* con voce rauca

hoarseness /'hɔːsnɪs/ *n* raucedine *f*

hoary /'hɔːrɪ/ *adj* ‹*person*› con i capelli bianchi; **~ old joke** barzelletta *f* vecchia

hoax /həʊks/ *n* scherzo *m*; (false alarm) falso allarme *m*

hoaxer /'həʊksə(r)/ *n* burlone, -a *mf*

hob /hɒb/ *n* BrE piano *m* di cottura

hobble /'hɒbl/ *vi* zoppicare

hobby /'hɒbɪ/ *n* hobby *m inv*

hobby horse *n* fig fissazione *f*

hobnailed /'hɒbneɪld/ *adj* **~ boots** *pl* scarponi *mpl* chiodati

hobnob /'hɒbnɒb/ *v*

■ **hobnob with** *vt* (*pt/pp* **hobnobbed**) frequentare

hobo /'həʊbəʊ/ *n* AmE vagabondo, -a *mf*

hock /hɒk/ *n* vino *m* bianco del Reno

hockey /'hɒkɪ/ *n* hockey *m*

hocus-pocus /həʊkəs'pəʊkəs/ *n* (trickery) trucco *m*

hod /hɒd/ *n* (for coal) secchio *m* del carbone; (for bricks) cassetta *f* (*per trasportare mattoni*)

hoe /həʊ/ **A** *n* zappa *f* **B** *vt* (*pres p* **hoeing**) zappare

hog /hɒg/ **A** *n* maiale *m* **B** *vt* (*pt/pp* **hogged**) infml monopolizzare

hog-tie /'hɒgtaɪ/ *vt* legare le quattro zampe di ‹*pig, cow*›; AmE fig ostacolare ‹*person*›

hogwash /'hɒgwɒʃ/ *n* infml cretinate *fpl*

hoi polloi /hɔɪpɒ'lɔɪ/ *npl* plebaglia *fsg*

hoist /hɔɪst/ **A** *n* montacarichi *m inv*; infml (push) spinta *f* in su **B** *vt* sollevare; innalzare ‹*flag*›; levare ‹*anchor*›

hoity-toity /hɔɪtɪ'tɔɪtɪ/ *adj* infml altezzoso

hokum /'həʊkəm/ *n* AmE infml (sentimentality) polpettone *m* sentimentale; (nonsense) cretinate *fpl*

hold[1] /həʊld/ *n* Naut, Aeron stiva *f*

hold[2] **A** *n* presa *f*; fig (influence) ascendente *m*; **get ~ of** trovare; procurarsi ‹*information*› **B** *vt* (*pt/pp* **held**) tenere; ‹*container*› contenere; essere titolare di ‹*licence, passport*›; trattenere ‹*breath, suspect*›; mantenere vivo ‹*interest*›; ‹*civil servant etc*› occupare ‹*position*›; (retain) mantenere; ~ **sb' hand** tenere qualcuno per mano; ~ **one's tongue** tenere la bocca chiusa; ~ **somebody responsible** considerare qualcuno responsabile; ~ **that** (believe) ritenere che

C *vi* tenere; ‹*weather, luck*› durare; ‹*offer*› essere valido; Teleph restare in linea; **I don't ~ with the idea that...** infml non sono d'accordo sul fatto che...

▪ **hold against**: *vt* ~ **something against somebody** avercela con qualcuno per qualcosa

▪ **hold back** **A** *vt* rallentare
B *vi* esitare

▪ **hold down** *vt* tenere a bada ‹*somebody*›

▪ **hold on** *vi* (wait) attendere; Teleph restare in linea

▪ **hold on to** *vt* aggrapparsi a; (keep) tenersi

▪ **hold out** **A** *vt* porgere ‹*hand*›; fig offrire ‹*possibility*›
B *vi* (resist) resistere

▪ **hold to**: *vt* ~ **somebody to something** far mantenere qualcosa a qualcuno

▪ **hold up** *vt* tenere su; (delay) rallentare; (rob) assalire; ~ **one's head up** fig tenere la testa alta

holdall /'həʊldɔːl/ *n* borsone *m*

holder /'həʊldə(r)/ *n* titolare *mf*; (of record) detentore, -trice *mf*; (container) astuccio *m*

holding /'həʊldɪŋ/ *n* (land) terreno *m* in affitto; Comm azioni *fpl*

holding company *n* società *f* finanziaria

hold-up *n* ritardo *m*; (attack) rapina *f* a mano armata

⚷ **hole** /həʊl/ *n* buco *m*

hole in the wall *n* infml sportello *m* del Bancomat®

⚷ **holiday** /'hɒlɪdeɪ/ **A** *n* vacanza *f*; (public) giorno *m* festivo; (day off) giorno *m* di ferie; **go on ~** andare in vacanza
B *vi* andare in vacanza

holiday home *n* casa *f* per le vacanze

holiday job *n* BrE (in summer) lavoretto *m* estivo

holiday-maker *n* vacanziere *mf*

holiday resort *n* luogo *m* di villeggiatura

holier-than-thou /həʊlɪəðən'ðaʊ/ *adj* ‹*attitude*› da santerellino

holiness /'həʊlɪnɪs/ *n* santità *f*; **Your H~** Sua Santità

Holland /'hɒlənd/ *n* Olanda *f*

holler /'hɒlə(r)/ *vi* urlare (**at** contro)

hollow /'hɒləʊ/ **A** *adj* cavo; ‹*promise*› a vuoto; ‹*voice*› assente; ‹*cheeks*› infossato
B *n* cavità *f*; (in ground) affossamento *m*

▪ **hollow out** *vt* scavare

holly /'hɒlɪ/ *n* agrifoglio *m*

hollyhock /'hɒlɪhɒk/ *n* malvone *m*

holocaust /'hɒləkɔːst/ *n* olocausto *m*

hologram /'hɒləgræm/ *n* ologramma *m*

holograph /'hɒləgrɑːf/ *n* documento *m* olografo

hols /hɒlz/ *n* BrE infml (**holidays**) vacanze *fpl*

holster /'həʊlstə(r)/ *n* fondina *f*

holy /'həʊlɪ/ *adj* (**-ier**, **-est**) santo; ‹*water*› benedetto

Holy Bible *n* Sacra Bibbia *f*

Holy Ghost, **Holy Spirit** *n* Spirito *m* Santo

Holy Land *n* Terra *f* Santa

Holy Scriptures sacre scritture *fpl*

Holy Week *n* settimana *f* santa

homage /'hɒmɪdʒ/ *n* omaggio *m*; **pay ~ to** rendere omaggio a

homburg /'hɒmbɜːg/ *n* cappello *m* di feltro

⚷ **home** /həʊm/ **A** *n* casa *f*; (for children) istituto *m*; (for old people) casa *f* di riposo; (native land) patria *f*
B *adv* **at ~** a casa; (football) in casa; **feel at ~** sentirsi a casa propria; **come/go ~** venire/andare a casa; **drive a nail ~** piantare un chiodo a fondo
C *adj* domestico; ‹*movie, video*› casalingo; ‹*team*› ospitante; Pol nazionale

home address *n* indirizzo *m* di casa

home brew *n* (beer) birra *f* fatta in casa

home cinema, **home cinema system**, **home entertainment system** *n* (sistema di) home cinema *m*

homecoming *n* (return home) ritorno *m* a casa

home computer *n* computer *m inv* da casa

home cooking *n* cucina *f* casalinga

Home Counties *npl contee* (*fpl*) *intorno a Londra*

home economics *nsg* Sch economia *fsg* domestica

home front *n* (during war) fronte *m* interno; (in politics) politica *f* interna

home game *n* partita *f* in casa

home ground *n* **play on one's ~** giocare in casa

home-grown /-'grəʊn/ *adj* ‹*produce*› del proprio orto; fig nostrano

home help *n* aiuto *m* domestico (*per persone non autosufficienti*)

homeland *n* patria *f*

homeless /'həʊmlɪs/ *adj* senza tetto

home loan *n* mutuo *m* per la casa

home-loving *adj* casalingo

homely /'həʊmlɪ/ *adj* (**-ier**, **-iest**) *adj* semplice; ‹*atmosphere*› familiare; AmE (ugly) bruttino

home-made *adj* fatto in casa

home market *n* mercato *m* interno

⚷ parola chiave

Home Office *n* BrE ministero *m* degli interni
homeopathic /həʊmɪə'pæθɪk/ *adj* omeopatico
homeopathy /həʊmɪ'ɒpəθɪ/ *n* omeopatia *f*
homeowner *n* proprietario, -a *mf* immobiliare
home page *n* Comput home page *f inv*
home rule *n* autogoverno *m*
Home Secretary *n* BrE ≈ ministro *m* degli interni
home shopping *n* acquisti *mpl* attraverso la televisione
homesick *adj* **be ~** avere nostalgia (**for** di)
homesickness *n* nostalgia *f* di casa
homestead *n* fattoria *f*
home town *n* città *f* natia
home truth *n* **tell somebody a few ~s** dirne quattro a qualcuno
home video *n* filmato *m* di videoamatore
homeward /'həʊmwəd/ **A** *adj* di ritorno **B** *adv* **~[s]** verso casa; **~ bound** sulla strada del ritorno; **travel ~[s]** tornare a casa
homework /'həʊmwɜːk/ *n* Sch compiti *mpl*
homeworker /'həʊmwɜːkə(r)/ *n* lavoratore, -trice *mf* a domicilio
home working /'həʊmwɜːkɪŋ/ *n* lavoro *m* a domicilio
homey /'həʊmɪ/ *adj* (home-loving) casalingo; (cosy) accogliente
homicidal /ˌhɒmɪ'saɪdl/ *adj* omicida
homicide /'hɒmɪsaɪd/ *n* (crime) omicidio *m*
homily /'hɒmɪlɪ/ *n* omelia *f*
homing /'həʊmɪŋ/ *adj* ‹*missile, device*› autoguidato
homing pigeon piccione *m* viaggiatore
homoeopathic /həʊmɪə'pæθɪk/ *adj* omeopatico
homoeopathy /həʊmɪ'ɒpəθɪ/ *n* omeopatia *f*
homogeneous /hɒmə'dʒiːnɪəs/ *adj* omogeneo
homogenize /hə'mɒdʒənaɪz/ *vt* omogeneizzare
homogenous /hə'mɒdʒənəs/ *adj* omogeneo
homograph /'hɒməgrɑːf/ *n* omografo *m*
homonym /'hɒmənɪm/ *n* omonimo *m*
homophobia /həʊmə'fəʊbɪə/ *n* omofobia *f*
homosexual /həʊmə'sekʃʊəl/ *adj & n* omosessuale *mf*
homosexuality /ˌhɒməˌsekʃʊ'ælətɪ/ *n* omosessualità *f*
Hon. *abbr* (**Honourable**) On.
Honduras /hɒn'djʊərəs/ *n* Honduras *m*
hone /həʊn/ *vt* (sharpen) affilare; (perfect) affinare
honest /'ɒnɪst/ *adj* onesto; ‹*frank*› sincero
honestly /'ɒnɪstlɪ/ *adv* onestamente; (frankly) sinceramente; **~!** ma insomma!
honesty /'ɒnɪstɪ/ *n* onestà *f*; (frankness) sincerità *f*
honey /'hʌnɪ/ *n* miele *m*; infml (darling) tesoro *m*
honeycomb /'hʌnɪkəʊm/ *n* favo *m*
honeydew melon /'hʌnɪdjuː/ *n* melone *m* (*dalla buccia gialla*)
honeymoon /'hʌnɪmuːn/ *n* luna *f* di miele
honeysuckle /'hʌnɪsʌkl/ *n* caprifoglio *m*
honey trap *n trappola* (*f*) *tesa a qualcuno servendosi di una collaboratrice graziosa*
Hong Kong /hɒŋ'kɒŋ/ *n* Hong Kong *f*
honk /hɒŋk/ *vi* Auto clacsonare
honky-tonk /'hɒŋkɪtɒŋk/ *adj* ‹*piano*› honkytonky *inv*
honor /'ɒnə(r)/ *n* AmE = **honour**
honorary /'ɒnərərɪ/ *adj* onorario
honorific /ɒnə'rɪfɪk/ *adj* onorifico
honour /'ɒnə(r)/ **A** *n* onore *m* **B** *vt* onorare
honourable /'ɒnərəbl/ *adj* onorevole
honourably /'ɒnərəblɪ/ *adv* con onore
honours degree /'ɒnəz/ *n* ≈ diploma *m* di laurea
hood /hʊd/ *n* cappuccio *m*; (of pram) tettuccio *m*; (over cooker) cappa *f*; AmE Auto cofano *m*
hoodlum /'huːdləm/ *n* teppista *m*
hoodwink /'hʊdwɪŋk/ *vt* infml infinocchiare
hoody, **hoodie** /'hʊdɪ/ *n* infml maglia *f* con cappuccio
hoof /huːf/ *n* (*pl* **~s** *or* **hooves**) zoccolo *m*
hoo-ha /'huːhɑː/ *n* infml **cause a ~** fare scalpore
hook /hʊk/ **A** *n* gancio *m*; (for crochet) uncinetto *m*; (for fishing) amo *m*; **off the ~** Teleph staccato; fig fuori pericolo; **by ~ or by crook** in un modo o nell' altro **B** *vt* agganciare **C** *vi* agganciarsi
hookah /'hʊkə/ *n* narghilè *m*
hook and eye *n* gancino *m*
hooked /hʊkt/ *adj* ‹*nose*› adunco; **~ on** infml (drugs) dedito a; **be ~ on skiing** essere un fanatico dello sci
hooker /'hʊkə(r)/ *n* AmE sl battona *f*
hookey /'hʊkɪ/ *n* **play ~** AmE infml marinare la scuola
hooligan /'huːlɪgən/ *n* teppista *mf*
hooliganism /'huːlɪgənɪzm/ *n* teppismo *m*
hoop /huːp/ *n* cerchio *m*
hoopla /'huːplɑː/ *n* BrE (at fair) lancio *m* degli anelli (*nei luna park*); AmE (fuss) trambusto *m*
hooray /hʊ'reɪ/ *int & n* = **hurrah**
hoot /huːt/ **A** *n* colpo *m* di clacson; (of siren) ululato *m*; (of owl) grido *m*; **~s of laughter** risate *fpl* **B** *vi* ‹*owl*› gridare; ‹*car*› clacsonare; ‹*siren*› ululare; (jeer) fischiare
hooter /'huːtə(r)/ *n* (siren) sirena *f*; Auto clacson *m inv*; BrE infml (nose) nasone *m*
hoover® /'huːvə(r)/ **A** *n* aspirapolvere *m inv*

h

B *vt* passare l'aspirapolvere su ‹*carpet*›; passare l'aspirapolvere in ‹*room*›
C *vi* passare l'aspirapolvere

hop[1] /hɒp/ *n* luppolo *m*

hop[2] **A** *n* saltello *m*; **catch somebody on the ~** infml prendere qualcuno alla sprovvista
B *vi* (*pt/pp* **hopped**) saltellare; **~ it!** infml tela!

▪ **hop in** *vi* infml saltar su

▪ **hop out** *vi* infml saltar giù; **~ to the shops** fare un salto ai negozi

⚷ **hope** /həʊp/ **A** *n* speranza *f*; **there's no ~ of that happening** non c'è nessuna speranza che succeda
B *vi* sperare (**for** in); **I ~ so/not** spero di sì/no
C *vt* **~ that** sperare che

hopeful /ˈhəʊpfʊl/ *adj* pieno di speranza; (promising) promettente; **be ~ that** avere buone speranze che

hopefully /ˈhəʊpfʊlɪ/ *adv* con speranza; (it is hoped) se tutto va bene

hopeless /ˈhəʊplɪs/ *adj* senza speranze; (useless) impossible; (incompetent) incapace

hopelessly /ˈhəʊplɪslɪ/ *adv* disperatamente; ‹*inefficient, lost*› completamente

hopelessness /ˈhəʊplɪsnɪs/ *n* disperazione *f*

hopscotch /ˈhɒpskɒtʃ/ *n* campana *f* (*gioco*)

horde /hɔːd/ *n* orda *f*

horizon /həˈraɪzn/ *n* orizzonte *m*; **on the ~** all'orizzonte

horizontal /hɒrɪˈzɒntl/ *adj* orizzontale

horizontal bar *n* sbarra *f* orizzontale

horizontally /hɒrɪˈzɒntəlɪ/ *adv* orizzontalmente

hormonal /hɔːˈməʊnəl/ *adj* ormonale; (moody) lunatico

hormone /ˈhɔːməʊn/ *n* ormone *m*

hormone replacement therapy *n* terapia *f* ormonale sostitutiva

horn /hɔːn/ *n* corno *m*; Auto clacson *m inv*

hornet /ˈhɔːnɪt/ *n* calabrone *m*

horn-rimmed /-rɪmd/ *adj* ‹*spectacles*› con la montatura di tartaruga

horny /ˈhɔːnɪ/ *adj* calloso; infml (sexually) arrapato

horoscope /ˈhɒrəskəʊp/ *n* oroscopo *m*

horrendous /həˈrendəs/ *adj* spaventoso

horrible /ˈhɒrəbl/ *adj* orribile

horribly /ˈhɒrəblɪ/ *adv* orribilmente

horrid /ˈhɒrɪd/ *adj* orrendo

horrific /həˈrɪfɪk/ *adj* raccapricciante; infml ‹*accident, prices, story*› terrificante

horrify /ˈhɒrɪfaɪ/ *vt* (*pt/pp* **-ied**) far inorridire; **I was horrified** ero inorridito

horrifying /ˈhɒrɪfaɪɪŋ/ *adj* terrificante

horror /ˈhɒrə(r)/ *n* orrore *m*

horror film *n* film *m inv* dell'orrore

horror story *n* racconto *m* dell'orrore

hors d'oeuvre /ɔːˈdɜːvr/ *n* antipasto *m*

⚷ **horse** /hɔːs/ *n* cavallo *m*

▪ **horse around** *vi* fare il pagliaccio

horseback *n* **on ~** a cavallo

horseback riding *n* AmE equitazione *f*

horsebox *n* furgone *m* per il trasporto dei cavalli

horse chestnut *n* ippocastano *m*

horsefly *n* tafano *m*

horsehair *n* crine *m* di cavallo

horseman *n* cavaliere *m*

horse manure *n* concime *m*

horseplay *n* gioco *m* pesante

horsepower *n* cavallo *m* [vapore]

horse race *n* corsa *f* ippica

horse racing *n* corse *fpl* di cavalli

horseradish *n* rafano *m*

horseradish sauce *n* salsa *f* di rafano

horse riding *n* equitazione *f*

horseshoe *n* ferro *m* di cavallo

horse show *n* concorso *m* ippico

horsy, horsey /ˈhɔːsɪ/ *adj* ‹*person*› che adora i cavalli; ‹*face*› cavallino

horticultural /hɔːtɪˈkʌltʃʊrəl/ *adj* di orticoltura

horticulture /ˈhɔːtɪkʌltʃə(r)/ *n* orticoltura *f*

hose /həʊz/ *n* (pipe) manichetta *f*

▪ **hose down** *vt* lavare con la manichetta

hosepipe /ˈhəʊzpaɪp/ *n* manichetta *f*

hosiery /ˈhəʊʒərɪ/ *n* maglieria *f*

hospice /ˈhɒspɪs/ *n* (for the terminally ill) ospedale *m* per i malati in fase terminale

hospitable /hɒˈspɪtəbl/ *adj* ospitale

hospitably /hɒˈspɪtəblɪ/ *adv* con ospitalità

⚷ **hospital** /ˈhɒspɪtl/ *n* ospedale *m*

hospitality /hɒspɪˈtælətɪ/ *n* ospitalità *f*

hospitalize /ˈhɒspɪtəlaɪz/ *vt* ricoverare [in ospedale]

host[1] /həʊst/ *n* **a ~ of** una moltitudine di

⚷ **host**[2] *n* ospite *m*

host[3] *n* Relig ostia *f*

hostage /ˈhɒstɪdʒ/ *n* ostaggio *m*; **hold somebody ~** tenere qualcuno in ostaggio

host country *n* paese *m* ospitante

hostel /ˈhɒstl/ *n* ostello *m*

hostess /ˈhəʊstɪs/ *n* padrona *f* di casa; Aeron hostess *f inv*

hostile /ˈhɒstaɪl/ *adj* ostile

hostility /hɒˈstɪlətɪ/ *n* ostilità *f*; **hostilities** *pl* ostilità *fpl*

⚷ **hot** /hɒt/ *adj* (**hotter, hottest**) caldo; (spicy) piccante; **I am** *or* **feel ~** ho caldo; **it is ~** fa caldo; **in ~ water** fig nei guai

hot-air balloon *n* mongolfiera *f*

hotbed *n* fig focolaio *m*

hot-blooded /-ˈblʌdɪd/ *adj* ‹*person*› focoso; ‹*reaction*› passionale

hot cake *n* **sell like ~s** andare a ruba

hotchpotch /ˈhɒtʃpɒtʃ/ *n* miscuglio *m*

⚷ parola chiave

hot cross bun *n panino (m) dolce con spezie e uvette, tipicamente pasquale*
hot dog *n* hot dog *m inv*
hotdogging *n* sci *m* acrobatico
hotel /həʊˈtel/ *n* hotel *m inv*, albergo *m*
hotelier /həʊˈtelɪə(r)/ *n* albergatore, -trice *mf*
hotfoot *adv* hum ‹*go*› di gran carriera
hothead *n* persona *f* impetuosa
hot-headed /-ˈhedɪd/ *adj* impetuoso
hothouse *n* serra *f*
hotline *n* linea *f* diretta; Mil, Pol telefono *m* rosso
hotly /ˈhɒtlɪ/ *adv* fig accanitamente
hotplate *n* piastra *f* riscaldante
hot seat *n* **be in the ~** essere in una posizione difficile
hotshot *n* infml persona di successo; derog carrierista *mf*
hot spot *n* (trouble zone) zona *f* calda; (sunny place) luogo *m* assolato
hot tap *n* rubinetto *m* dell'acqua calda
hot-tempered /-ˈtempəd/ *adj* irascibile
hot-water bottle *n* borsa *f* dell'acqua calda
hound /haʊnd/ **A** *n* cane da caccia *m*
B *vt* fig perseguire
hour /ˈaʊə(r)/ *n* ora *f*
hourglass /ˈaʊəglɑːs/ *n* clessidra *f*
hourly /ˈaʊəlɪ/ **A** *adj* ad ogni ora; ‹*pay, rate*› a ora
B *adv* ogni ora
house¹ /haʊs/ *n* casa *f*; Pol Camera *f*; Theat sala *f*; **at my ~** a casa mia, da me
house² /haʊz/ *vt* alloggiare ‹*person*›; incastrare ‹*machine*›
houseboat *n* casa *f* galleggiante
housebound /ˈhaʊsbaʊnd/ *adj* costretto in casa
housebreaking *n* furto *m* con scasso
house call *n* visita *f* a domicilio
household *n* casa *f*, famiglia *f*
household appliance *n* elettrodomestico *m*
householder *n* capo *m* famiglia
household name *n* noto *m*
house husband *n* casalingo *m*
housekeeper *n* governante *f* di casa
housekeeping *n* governo *m* della casa; (money) soldi *mpl* per le spese di casa
House of Commons *n* Camera *f* dei Comuni
House of Lords *n* Camera *f* dei Lord
House of Representatives *n* Camera *f* dei Rappresentanti
house plant *n* pianta *f* da appartamento
house-proud *adj* orgoglioso della propria casa
Houses of Parliament *npl* Parlamento *m*
house-to-house *adj* ‹*search*› casa per casa
house-trained /-treɪnd/ *adj* che non sporca in casa
house-warming, house-warming party *n* festa *f* di inaugurazione della nuova casa
housewife *n* casalinga *f*
housework *n* lavori *mpl* domestici
housing /ˈhaʊzɪŋ/ *n* alloggio *m*; Techn alloggiamento *m*
housing estate *n* zona *f* residenziale
hovel /ˈhɒvl/ *n* tugurio *m*
hover /ˈhɒvə(r)/ *vi* librarsi; (linger) indugiare; **~ on the brink of doing something** essere sul punto di fare qualcosa
hovercraft /ˈhɒvəkrɑːft/ *n* hovercraft *m inv*
how /haʊ/ *adv* come; **~ are you?** come stai?; **~ about a coffee/going on holiday?** che ne diresti di un caffè/di andare in vacanza?; **~ do you do?** molto lieto!; **~ old are you?** quanti anni hai?; **~ long** quanto tempo; **~ many** quanti; **~ much** quanto; **~ often** ogni quanto; **and ~!** eccome!; **~ odd!** che strano!
however /haʊˈevə(r)/ *adv* (nevertheless) comunque; **~ small** per quanto piccolo
howl /haʊl/ **A** *n* ululato *m*
B *vi* ululare; (cry with laughter) singhiozzare
howler /ˈhaʊlə(r)/ *n* infml strafalcione *m*
HP *abbr* **1** (**hire purchase**) **2** (**horse power**) C. V.
HQ *n abbr* Mil (**headquarters**) Q.G.
HR *abbr* (**human resources**) RU
HRT *abbr* (**hormone replacement therapy**) TOS *f*
HTML *abbr* (**hypertext markup language**) Comput HTML *m*
HTTP *abbr* (**hypertext transfer protocol**) Comput HTTP *m*
hub /hʌb/ *n* mozzo *m*; fig centro *m*
hubbub /ˈhʌbʌb/ *n* baccano *m*
hubcap /ˈhʌbkæp/ *n* coprimozzo *m*
huckleberry /ˈhʌklbərɪ/ *n* AmE mirtillo *m* americano
huddle /ˈhʌdl/ *vi* **~ together** rannicchiarsi l'uno contro l'altro
hue¹ /hjuː/ *n* colore *m*
hue² *n* **~ and cry** clamore *m*
huff /hʌf/ *n* **be in a/go into a ~** fare il broncio
hug /hʌg/ **A** *n* abbraccio *m*; **give somebody a ~** abbracciare qualcuno
B *vt* (*pt/pp* **hugged**) abbracciare; (keep close to) tenersi vicino a; aggrapparsi a ‹*wall*›
huge /hjuːdʒ/ *adj* enorme
hugely /ˈhjuːdʒlɪ/ *adv* enormemente
huh /hʌ/ *int* (inquiry) eh?; (in surprise) oh!
hulk /hʌlk/ *n* (of ship, tank etc) carcassa *f*
hulking /ˈhʌlkɪŋ/ *adj* infml grosso
hull /hʌl/ *n* Naut scafo *m*
hullabaloo /hʌləbəˈluː/ *n* infml (noise) trambusto *m*; (outcry) fracasso *m*

hullo /həˈləʊ/ *int* = hallo

hum /hʌm/ **A** *n* ronzio *m*
B *vt* (*pt/pp* **hummed**) canticchiare
C *vi* ‹*motor*› ronzare; fig fervere di attività; **~ and haw** esitare

human /ˈhjuːmən/ **A** *adj* umano
B *n* essere *m* umano

human being *n* essere *m* umano

humane /hjuːˈmeɪn/ *adj* umano

humanely /hjuːˈmeɪnlɪ/ *adv* umanamente

human interest story *n* storia *f* di vita vissuta

humanitarian /hjuːmænɪˈteərɪən/ *adj & n* umanitario, -a *mf*

humanities /hjuːˈmænɪtɪz/ *pl* Univ dottrine *fpl* umanistiche

humanity /hjuːˈmænətɪ/ *n* umanità *f*

h

human nature *n* natura *f* umana

human resources *npl* risorse *fpl* umane

human resources manager *n* responsabile *mf* delle risorse umane

human shield *n* scudo *m* umano

humble /ˈhʌmbl/ **A** *adj* umile
B *vt* umiliare

humbly /ˈhʌmblɪ/ *adv* umilmente

humbug /ˈhʌmbʌg/ *n* (nonsense) sciocchezze *fpl*; (dishonesty) falsità *f*; BrE (sweet) caramella *f* alla menta

humdrum /ˈhʌmdrʌm/ *adj* noioso

humid /ˈhjuːmɪd/ *adj* umido

humidifier /hjuːˈmɪdɪfaɪə(r)/ *n* umidificatore *m*

humidity /hjuːˈmɪdətɪ/ *n* umidità *f*

humiliate /hjuːˈmɪlɪeɪt/ *vt* umiliare

humiliating /hjuːˈmɪlɪeɪtɪŋ/ *adj* avvilente

humiliation /hjuːmɪlɪˈeɪʃn/ *n* umiliazione *f*

humility /hjuːˈmɪlətɪ/ *n* umiltà *f*

hummingbird /ˈhʌmɪŋbɜːd/ *n* colibrì *m*

hummock /ˈhʌmək/ *n* (of earth) poggio *m*

hummus /ˈhʊməs/ *n* hummus *m*, purè *m* di ceci

humorist /ˈhjuːmərɪst/ *n* umorista *mf*

humorous /ˈhjuːmərəs/ *adj* umoristico

humorously /ˈhjuːmərəslɪ/ *adv* con spirito

humour /ˈhjuːmə(r)/ **A** *n* umorismo *m*; (mood) umore *m*; **have a sense of ~** avere il senso dell' umorismo
B *vt* compiacere

hump /hʌmp/ *n* protuberanza *f*; (of camel, hunchback) gobba *f*; **he's got the ~** sl è di malumore

humpback bridge /ˈhʌm(p)bæk/, **humpbacked bridge** /ˈhʌm(p)bækt/ *n* ponte *m* a schiena d'asino

humus /ˈhjuːməs/ *n* humus *m*

hunch /hʌntʃ/ *n* (idea) intuizione *f*

hunchback /ˈhʌntʃbæk/ *n* gobbo, -a *mf*

hunched /hʌntʃt/ *adj* **~ up** incurvato

hundred /ˈhʌndrəd/ **A** *adj* **one/a ~** cento
B *n* cento *m inv*; **~s of** centinaia di

hundredfold /ˈhʌndrədfəʊld/ *adv* **increase a ~** centuplicare

hundredth /ˈhʌndrədθ/ *adj & n* centesimo *m*

hundredweight /ˈhʌndrədweɪt/ *n* cinquanta chili *m*

hung /hʌŋ/ ▶ **hang**

Hungarian /hʌŋˈgeərɪən/ *n & adj* ungherese *mf*; (language) ungherese *m*

Hungary /ˈhʌŋgərɪ/ *n* Ungheria *f*

hunger /ˈhʌŋgə(r)/ *n* fame *f*
▪ **hunger for** *vt* aver fame di

hunger strike *n* sciopero *m* della fame

hung-over *adj* **be ~** avere i postumi della sbornia

hungrily /ˈhʌŋgrɪlɪ/ *adv* con appetito

hungry /ˈhʌŋgrɪ/ *adj* (**-ier**, **-iest**) affamato; **be ~** aver fame

hung up *adj* infml (tense) complessato; **be ~ on somebody/something** (obsessed) essere fissato con qualcuno/qualcosa

hunk /hʌŋk/ *n* grosso pezzo *m*; infml (man) figo *m*

hunky-dory /hʌŋkɪˈdɔːrɪ/ *adj* infml perfetto

hunt /hʌnt/ **A** *n* caccia *f*
B *vt* andare a caccia di ‹*animal*›; dare la caccia a ‹*criminal*›
C *vi* andare a caccia; **~ for** cercare

hunter /ˈhʌntə(r)/ *n* cacciatore *m*

hunting /ˈhʌntɪŋ/ *n* caccia *f*

hunt saboteur *n* BrE sabotatore, -trice *mf* della caccia

huntsman /ˈhʌntsmən/ *n* (hunter) cacciatore *m*; (fox-hunter) cacciatore *m* di volpe

hurdle /ˈhɜːdl/ *n* Sport fig ostacolo *m*

hurdler /ˈhɜːdlə(r)/ *n* ostacolista *mf*

hurdy-gurdy /hɜːdɪˈgɜːdɪ/ *n* organino *m*

hurl /hɜːl/ *vt* scagliare

hurly-burly /hɜːlɪˈbɜːlɪ/ *n* chiasso *m*

hurrah /hʊˈrɑː/, **hurray** /hʊˈreɪ/ **A** *int* urrà!
B *n* urrà *m*

hurricane /ˈhʌrɪkən/ *n* uragano *m*

hurried /ˈhʌrɪd/ *adj* affrettato; ‹*job*› fatto in fretta

hurriedly /ˈhʌrɪdlɪ/ *adv* in fretta

hurry /ˈhʌrɪ/ **A** *n* fretta *f*; **be in a ~** aver fretta
B *vi* (*pt/pp* **-ied**) affrettarsi
▪ **hurry up** **A** *vi* sbrigarsi
B *vt* mettere fretta a ‹*person*›; accelerare ‹*things*›

hurt /hɜːt/ **A** *n* male *m*
B *vt* (*pt/pp* **hurt**) far male a; (offend) ferire
C *vi* far male; **my leg ~s** mi fa male la gamba

hurtful /ˈhɜːtfʊl/ *adj* fig offensivo

hurtle /ˈhɜːtl/ *vi* **~ along** andare a tutta velocità

husband /ˈhʌzbənd/ *n* marito *m*

hush /hʌʃ/ *n* silenzio *m*

■ **hush up** *vt* mettere a tacere
hushed /hʌʃt/ *adj* ‹*voice*› sommesso
hush-hush *adj* infml segretissimo
husky /ˈhʌskɪ/ *adj* (**-ier**, **-iest**) ‹*voice*› rauco
hussar /hʊˈzɑː(r)/ *n* ussaro *m*
hustings /ˈhʌstɪŋz/ *n* **on the ~** in campagna elettorale
hustle /ˈhʌsl/ **A** *vt* affrettare **B** *n* attività *f* incessante; **~ and bustle** trambusto *m*
hut /hʌt/ *n* capanna *f*
hutch /hʌtʃ/ *n* conigliera *f*
hyacinth /ˈhaɪəsɪnθ/ *n* giacinto *m*
hybrid /ˈhaɪbrɪd/ **A** *adj* ibrido **B** *n* ibrido *m*
hydrangea /haɪˈdreɪndʒə/ *n* ortensia *f*
hydrant /ˈhaɪdrənt/ *n* **[fire] ~** idrante *m*
hydraulic /haɪˈdrɔːlɪk/ *adj* idraulico
hydrocarbon /haɪdrəʊˈkɑːbən/ *n* idrocarburo *m*
hydrochloric /haɪdrəˈklɔːrɪk/ *adj* **~ acid** acido *m* cloridrico
hydroelectric /haɪdrəʊɪˈlektrɪk/ *adj* idroelettrico
hydroelectricity /ˌhaɪdrəʊɪlekˈtrɪsətɪ/ *n* energia *f* idroelettrica
hydroelectric power station *n* centrale *f* idroelettrica
hydrofoil /ˈhaɪdrəfɔɪl/ *n* aliscafo *m*
hydrogen /ˈhaɪdrədʒən/ *n* idrogeno *m*
hydrolysis /haɪˈdrɒləsɪs/ *n* idrolisi *f*
hydrophobia /haɪdrəˈfəʊbɪə/ *n* idrofobia *f*
hydroplane /ˈhaɪdrəpleɪn/ *n* (boat) aliscafo *m*; AmE (seaplane) idrovolante *m*
hydrotherapy /haɪdrəʊˈθerəpɪ/ *n* idroterapia *f*
hyena /haɪˈiːnə/ *n* iena *f*
hygiene /ˈhaɪdʒiːn/ *n* igiene *m*
hygienic /haɪˈdʒiːnɪk/ *adj* igienico
hygienically /haɪˈdʒiːnɪklɪ/ *adv* igienicamente
hymn /hɪm/ *n* inno *m*
hymn book *n* libro *m* dei canti
hype /haɪp/ *n* infml grande pubblicità *f*; **media ~** battage *m* pubblicitario
■ **hype up** *vt* infml fare grande pubblicità a ‹*film, star, book*›; (exaggerate) gonfiare
hyper /ˈhaɪpə(r)/ *adj* infml eccitato
hyperactive /haɪpərˈæktɪv/ *adj* iperattivo
hyperactivity /haɪpərækˈtɪvɪtɪ/ *n* iperattività *f*
hyperbole /haɪˈpɜːbəlɪ/ *n* iperbole *f*
hypercritical /haɪpəˈkrɪtɪkl/ *adj* ipercritico
hyperlink /ˈhaɪpəlɪŋk/ *n* Comput hyperlink *m inv*, collegamento *m* ipertestuale
hypermarket /ˈhaɪpəmɑːkɪt/ *n* ipermercato *m*
hypersensitive /haɪpəˈsensɪtɪv/ *adj* derog permaloso; (physically) ipersensibile
hypertension /haɪpəˈtenʃn/ *n* ipertensione *f*
hypertext /ˈhaɪpətekst/ *n* Comput ipertesto *m*
hypertext markup language *n* Comput linguaggio *m* per la marcatura di ipertesti
hypertext transfer protocol *n* Comput protocollo *m* per il trasferimento di ipertesti
hyperventilate /haɪpəˈventɪleɪt/ *vi* iperventilare
hyphen /ˈhaɪfn/ *n* trattino *m*
hyphenate /ˈhaɪfəneɪt/ *vt* unire con trattino
hypnosis /hɪpˈnəʊsɪs/ *n* ipnosi *f*
hypnotherapy /hɪpnəʊˈθerəpɪ/ *n* ipnoterapia *f*
hypnotic /hɪpˈnɒtɪk/ *adj* ipnotico
hypnotism /ˈhɪpnətɪzm/ *n* ipnotismo *m*
hypnotist /ˈhɪpnətɪst/ *n* ipnotizzatore, -trice *mf*
hypnotize /ˈhɪpnətaɪz/ *vt* ipnotizzare
hypoallergenic /haɪpəʊæləˈdʒenɪk/ *adj* anallergico
hypochondria /haɪpəˈkɒndrɪə/ *n* ipocondria *f*
hypochondriac /haɪpəˈkɒndrɪæk/ *adj & n* ipocondriaco, -a *mf*
hypocrisy /hɪˈpɒkrəsɪ/ *n* ipocrisia *f*
hypocrite /ˈhɪpəkrɪt/ *n* ipocrita *mf*
hypocritical /hɪpəˈkrɪtɪkl/ *adj* ipocrita
hypocritically /hɪpəˈkrɪtɪklɪ/ *adv* ipocriticamente
hypodermic /haɪpəˈdɜːmɪk/ *adj & n* **~ [syringe]** siringa *f* ipodermica
hypotenuse /haɪˈpɒtənjuːz/ *n* ipotenusa *f*
hypothermia /haɪpəʊˈθɜːmɪə/ *n* ipotermia *f*
hypothesis /haɪˈpɒθəsɪs/ *n* ipotesi *f inv*
hypothetical /haɪpəˈθetɪkl/ *adj* ipotetico
hypothetically /haɪpəˈθetɪklɪ/ *adv* in teoria; ‹*speak*› per ipotesi
hysterectomy /hɪstəˈrektəmɪ/ *n* isterectomia *f*
hysteria /hɪˈstɪərɪə/ *n* isterismo *m*
hysterical /hɪˈsterɪkl/ *adj* isterico
hysterically /hɪˈsterɪklɪ/ *adv* istericamente; **~ funny** da morir dal ridere
hysterics /hɪˈsterɪks/ *npl* attacco *mpl* isterico

Ii

i, I /aɪ/ *n* (letter) i, I *f inv*

✓ **I** /aɪ/ *pron* io; **I'm tired** sono stanco; **he's going, but I'm not** lui va, ma io no

IAP *n abbr* (**Internet access provider**) Comput IAP *m*

IBA *n abbr* (**Independent Broadcasting Authority**) *organismo (m) indipendente di vigilanza sulla radiotelevisione*

IBAN *n abbr* (**International Bank Account Number**) IBAN *m*

ibex /ˈaɪbeks/ *n* stambecco *m*

ICC *n abbr* (**International Criminal Court**) TPI *m*

✓ **ice** /aɪs/ **A** *n* ghiaccio *m*
B *vt* glassare <*cake*>
■ **ice over**, **ice up** *vi* ghiacciarsi

ice age *n* era *f* glaciale

ice axe *n* piccozza *f* per il ghiaccio

iceberg *n* iceberg *m inv*

icebox *n* AmE frigorifero *m*

ice-breaker *n* Naut rompighiaccio *m inv*

ice bucket *n* secchiello *m* del ghiaccio

ice cap *n* calotta *f* glaciale

ice-cold *adj* ghiacciato

ice cream *n* gelato *m*

ice-cream parlour *n* gelateria *f*

ice-cream sundae *n* coppa *f* [di] gelato guarnita

ice cube *n* cubetto *m* di ghiaccio

ice dancer *n* ballerino, -a *mf* sul ghiaccio

ice floe *n* banco *m* di ghiaccio

ice hockey hockey *m* su ghiaccio

Iceland /ˈaɪslənd/ *n* Islanda *f*

Icelander /ˈaɪsləndə(r)/ *n* islandese *mf*

Icelandic /aɪsˈlændɪk/ *adj* & *n* islandese *m*

ice lolly *n* ghiacciolo *m*

ice pack *n* impacco *m* di ghiaccio

ice pick *n* piccone *m* da ghiaccio

ice rink *n* pista *f* di pattinaggio

ice-skate *n* pattino *m* da ghiaccio

ice skater pattinatore, -trice *mf* sul ghiaccio

ice-skating pattinaggio *m* sul ghiaccio

ice tray *n* vaschetta *f* per il ghiaccio

icicle /ˈaɪsɪkl/ *n* ghiacciolo *m*

icily /ˈaɪsɪlɪ/ *adv* gelidamente

icing /ˈaɪsɪŋ/ *n* glassa *f*

icing sugar *n* zucchero *m* a velo

icon /ˈaɪkɒn/ *n* icona *f*

✓ parola chiave

iconize /ˈaɪkənaɪz/ *vt* Comput iconizzare

ICT *n abbr* (**information and communication technology**) ICT *f*

icy /ˈaɪsɪ/ *adj* (**-ier**, **-iest**) ghiacciato; fig gelido

id /ɪd/ *n* **the ~** l'Es *m*

ID *n abbr* (**identification**, **identity**) documento *m* d'identità; **ID card** *n* carta *f* d'identità

✓ **idea** /aɪˈdɪə/ *n* idea *f*; **I've no ~!** non ne ho idea!

ideal /aɪˈdɪəl/ **A** *adj* ideale
B *n* ideale *m*

idealism /aɪˈdɪəlɪzm/ *n* idealismo *m*

idealist /aɪˈdɪəlɪst/ *n* idealista *mf*

idealistic /aɪdɪəˈlɪstɪk/ *adj* idealistico

idealize /aɪˈdɪəlaɪz/ *vt* idealizzare

ideally /aɪˈdɪəlɪ/ *adv* idealmente

identical /aɪˈdentɪkl/ *adj* identico

identical twin *n* gemello, -a *mf* monozigote

identifiable /aɪdentɪˈfaɪəbl/ *adj* identificabile

identification /aɪdentɪfɪˈkeɪʃn/ *n* identificazione *f*; (proof of identity) documento *m* di riconoscimento

identify /aɪˈdentɪfaɪ/ **A** *vt* (*pt/pp* **-ied**) identificare
B *vi* **~ with** identificarsi con

identikit® /aɪˈdentɪkɪt/ *n* identikit *m inv*

identikit picture® *n* identikit *m inv*

✓ **identity** /aɪˈdentətɪ/ *n* identità *f*

identity bracelet *n* braccialetto *m* identificativo

identity card *n* carta *f* d'identità

identity parade *n* confronto *m* all'americana

identity theft *n l'utilizzare il nome e i dati personali di qualcuno allo scopo di ottenere carte di credito, prelevare denaro da conti bancari ecc.*

ideological /aɪdɪəˈlɒdʒɪkl/ *adj* ideologico

ideology /aɪdɪˈɒlədʒɪ/ *n* ideologia *f*

idiocy /ˈɪdɪəsɪ/ *n* idiozia *f*

idiom /ˈɪdɪəm/ *n* idioma *m*

idiomatic /ɪdɪəˈmætɪk/ *adj* idiomatico

idiomatically /ɪdɪəˈmætɪklɪ/ *adv* in modo idiomatico

idiosyncrasy /ɪdɪəˈsɪŋkrəsɪ/ *n* idiosincrasia *f*

idiosyncratic /ˌɪdɪəsɪŋˈkrætɪk/ *adj* particolare

idiot /ˈɪdɪət/ *n* idiota *mf*

idiotic /ɪdɪ'ɒtɪk/ *adj* idiota
idle /'aɪd(ə)l/ **A** *adj* (lazy) pigro, ozioso; (empty) vano; ‹*machine*› fermo
B *vi* oziare; ‹*engine*› girare a vuoto
▪ **idle away** *vt* passare nell'ozio ‹*day, time*›
idleness /'aɪd(ə)lnɪs/ *n* ozio *m*
idly /'aɪdlɪ/ *adv* oziosamente
idol /'aɪd(ə)l/ *n* idolo *m*
idolize /'aɪdəlaɪz/ *vt* idolatrare
idyll /'ɪdɪl/ *n* idillio *m*
idyllic /ɪ'dɪlɪk/ *adj* idillico
i.e. *abbr* (**id est**) cioè
if /ɪf/ *conj* se; **as if** come se
iffy /'ɪfɪ/ *adj* incerto
igloo /'ɪgluː/ *n* igloo *m inv*
ignite /ɪg'naɪt/ **A** *vt* dar fuoco a
B *vi* prender fuoco
ignition /ɪg'nɪʃn/ *n* Auto accensione *f*
ignition key *n* chiave *f* d'accensione
ignoramus /ɪgnə'reɪməs/ *n* ignorante *mf*
ignorance /'ɪgnərəns/ *n* ignoranza *f*
ignorant /'ɪgnərənt/ *adj* (lacking knowledge) ignaro; (rude) ignorante
ignore /ɪg'nɔː(r)/ *vt* ignorare
ill /ɪl/ **A** *adj* ammalato; **feel ~ at ease** sentirsi a disagio
B *adv* male
C *n* male *m*
ill-advised /-əd'vaɪzd/ *adj* avventato
ill-bred /-'bred/ *adj* maleducato
ill-considered /-kən'sɪdəd/ *adj* ‹*measure, remark*› avventato
ill effect *n* effetto *m* negativo
illegal /ɪ'liːgl/ *adj* illegale
illegality /ɪlɪ'gælətɪ/ *n* illegalità *f*
illegally /ɪ'liːgəlɪ/ *adv* illegalmente
illegible /ɪ'ledʒəbl/ *adj* illeggibile
illegibly /ɪ'ledgəblɪ/ *adv* in modo illeggibile
illegitimacy /ɪlɪ'dʒɪtɪməsɪ/ *n* illegittimità *f*
illegitimate /ɪlɪ'dʒɪtɪmət/ *adj* illegittimo
ill-equipped /-ɪ'kwɪpt/ *adj* mal equipaggiato
ill-fated /-'feɪtɪd/ *adj* sfortunato
ill feeling *n* rancore *m*
ill-fitting *adj* ‹*garment, shoe*› che non va bene
ill-founded /-'faʊndɪd/ *adj* ‹*argument, gossip*› infondato
ill-gotten gains /ɪlgɒ(t)n'geɪnz/ *adj* guadagni *mpl* illeciti
ill health *n* problemi *mpl* di salute
illicit /ɪ'lɪsɪt/ *adj* illecito
illicitly /ɪ'lɪsɪtlɪ/ *adv* illecitamente
ill-informed /-ɪn'fɔːmd/ *adj* ‹*person*› male informato
illiteracy /ɪ'lɪtərəsɪ/ *n* analfabetismo *m*
illiterate /ɪ'lɪtərət/ *adj & n* analfabeta *mf*
ill-mannered /-'mænəd/ *adj* maleducato
illness /'ɪlnɪs/ *n* malattia *f*
illogical /ɪ'lɒdʒɪkl/ *adj* illogico
illogically /ɪ'lɒdʒɪklɪ/ *adv* illogicamente
ill-prepared /-prɪ'peəd/ *adj* impreparato
ill-timed /-'taɪmd/ *adj* ‹*arrival*› inopportuno; ‹*campaign*› fatto al momento sbagliato
ill-treat *vt* maltrattare
ill-treatment *n* maltrattamento *m*
illuminate /ɪ'luːmɪneɪt/ *vt* illuminare
illuminated /ɪ'luːmɪneɪtɪd/ *adj* ‹*sign*› luminoso
illuminating /ɪ'luːmɪneɪtɪŋ/ *adj* chiarificatore
illumination /ɪluːmɪ'neɪʃn/ *n* illuminazione *f*
illuminations *npl* BrE luminarie *fpl*
illusion /ɪ'luːʒn/ *n* illusione *f*; **be under the ~ that** avere l'illusione che
illusory /ɪ'luːsərɪ/ *adj* illusorio
illustrate /'ɪləstreɪt/ *vt* illustrare
illustration /ɪlə'streɪʃn/ *n* illustrazione *f*
illustrative /'ɪləstrətɪv/ *adj* illustrativo
illustrator /'ɪləstreɪtə(r)/ *n* illustratore, -trice *mf*
illustrious /ɪ'lʌstrɪəs/ *adj* illustre
ill will *n* malanimo *m*
image /'ɪmɪdʒ/ *n* immagine *f*; (exact likeness) ritratto *m*
image-conscious *adj* attento all'immagine
image maker *n* persona *f* che cura l'immagine
image processing *n* trattamento *m* dell'immagine
imagery /'ɪmɪdʒərɪ/ *n* immagini *fpl*
imaginable /ɪ'mædʒɪnəbl/ *adj* immaginabile
imaginary /ɪ'mædʒɪnərɪ/ *adj* immaginario
imagination /ɪmædʒɪ'neɪʃn/ *n* immaginazione *f*, fantasia *f*; **it's your ~** è solo una tua idea
imaginative /ɪ'mædʒɪnətɪv/ *adj* fantasioso
imaginatively /ɪ'mædʒɪnətɪvlɪ/ *adv* con fantasia *or* immaginazione
imagine /ɪ'mædʒɪn/ *vt* immaginare; (wrongly) inventare
IMAP *abbr* (**Internet mail access protocol**) Comput protocollo *m* di gestione remota della posta elettronica
imbalance /ɪm'bæləns/ *n* squilibrio *m*
imbecile /'ɪmbəsiːl/ *n* imbecille *mf*
imbibe /ɪm'baɪb/ **A** *vt* ingerire; fig assorbire
B *vi* hum bere
imbue /ɪm'bjuː/ *vt* **~d with** impregnato di
IMF *n abbr* (**International Monetary Fund**) FMI *m*
imitate /'ɪmɪteɪt/ *vt* imitare
imitation /ɪmɪ'teɪʃn/ *n* imitazione *f*
imitative /'ɪmɪtətɪv/ *adj* imitativo
imitator /'ɪmɪteɪtə(r)/ *n* imitatore, -trice *mf*
immaculate /ɪ'mækjʊlət/ *adj* immacolato
immaculately /ɪ'mækjʊlətlɪ/ *adv* immacolatamente
immaterial /ɪmə'tɪərɪəl/ *adj* (unimportant) irrilevante

immature /ɪmə'tʃʊə(r)/ *adj* immaturo
immeasurable /ɪ'meʒərəbl/ *adj* incommensurabile
immediacy /ɪ'mi:dɪəsɪ/ *n* immediatezza *f*
⚷ **immediate** /ɪ'mi:dɪət/ *adj* immediato; ‹*relative*› stretto; **in the ~ vicinity** nelle immediate vicinanze
⚷ **immediately** /ɪ'mi:dɪətlɪ/ **A** *adv* immediatamente; **~ next to** subito accanto a
B *conj* [non] appena
immemorial /ɪmɪ'mɔ:rɪəl/ *adj* **from time ~** da tempo immemorabile
immense /ɪ'mens/ *adj* immenso
immensely /ɪ'menslɪ/ *adv* immensamente
immensity /ɪ'mensətɪ/ *n* immensità *f*
immerse /ɪ'mɜ:s/ *vt* immergere; **be ~d in** fig essere immerso in
immersion /ɪ'mɜ:ʃn/ *n* immersione *f*
immersion course *n* BrE corso *m* full immersion
immersion heater *n* scaldabagno *m* elettrico
immigrant /'ɪmɪgrənt/ *n* immigrante *mf*
immigrate /'ɪmɪgreɪt/ *vi* immigrare
immigration /ɪmɪ'greɪʃn/ *n* immigrazione *f*
immigration control *n* controllo *m* dell'immigrazione
imminence /'ɪmɪnəns/ *n* imminenza *f*
imminent /'ɪmɪnənt/ *adj* imminente
immobile /ɪ'məʊbaɪl/ *adj* immobile
immobilize /ɪ'məʊbɪlaɪz/ *vt* immobilizzare
immobilizer /ɪ'məʊbɪlaɪzə(r)/ *n* Auto immobilizzatore *m* elettronico
immoderate /ɪ'mɒdərət/ *adj* smodato
immodest /ɪ'mɒdɪst/ *adj* immodesto
immoral /ɪ'mɒrəl/ *adj* immorale
immorality /ɪmə'rælətɪ/ *n* immoralità *f*
immortal /ɪ'mɔ:tl/ *adj* immortale
immortality /ɪmɔ:'tælətɪ/ *n* immortalità *f*
immortalize /ɪ'mɔ:təlaɪz/ *vt* immortalare
immovable /ɪ'mu:vəbl/ *adj* fig irremovibile
immune /ɪ'mju:n/ *adj* immune (**to/from** da)
immune system *n* sistema *m* immunitario
immunity /ɪ'mju:nətɪ/ *n* immunità *f*
immunization /ɪmjʊnaɪ'zeɪʃn/ *n* immunizzazione *f*
immunize /'ɪmjʊnaɪz/ *vt* immunizzare
immunodeficiency /ɪmjʊnəʊdɪ'fɪʃənsɪ/ *n* immunodeficienza *f*
immunology /ɪmjʊ'nɒlədʒɪ/ *n* immunologia *f*
immunosuppressant /ɪmjʊnəʊsə'pres(ə)nt/ **A** *adj* immunodepressivo
B *n* immunodepressivo *m*
immutable /ɪ'mju:təbl/ *adj* immutabile
imp /ɪmp/ *n* diavoletto *m*

⚷ parola chiave

⚷ **impact** /'ɪmpækt/ *n* impatto *m*
impacted /ɪm'pæktɪd/ *adj* ‹*tooth*› incluso; ‹*fracture*› composto
impair /ɪm'peə(r)/ *vt* danneggiare
impaired /ɪm'peəd/ *adj* **hearing ~** audioleso; **visually ~** videoleso
impale /ɪm'peɪl/ *vt* impalare
impalpable /ɪm'pælpəbl/ *adj* (intangible) impalpabile
impart /ɪm'pɑ:t/ *vt* impartire
impartial /ɪm'pɑ:ʃəl/ *adj* imparziale
impartiality /ɪmpɑ:ʃɪ'ælətɪ/ *n* imparzialità *f*
impassable /ɪm'pɑ:səbl/ *adj* impraticabile
impasse /æm'pɑ:s/ *n* fig impasse *f inv*
impassioned /ɪm'pæʃnd/ *adj* appassionato
impassive /ɪm'pæsɪv/ *adj* impassibile
impassively /ɪm'pæsɪvlɪ/ *adv* impassibilmente
impatience /ɪm'peɪʃns/ *n* impazienza *f*
impatient /ɪm'peɪʃnt/ *adj* impaziente
impatiently /ɪm'peɪʃntlɪ/ *adv* impazientemente
impeach /ɪm'pi:tʃ/ *vt* accusare
impeccable /ɪm'pekəbl/ *adj* impeccabile
impeccably /ɪm'pekəblɪ/ *adv* in modo impeccabile
impede /ɪm'pi:d/ *vt* impedire
impediment /ɪm'pedɪmənt/ *n* impedimento *m*; (in speech) difetto *m*
impel /ɪm'pel/ *vt* (*pt/pp* **impelled**) costringere; **feel ~led to** sentire l'obbligo di
impending /ɪm'pendɪŋ/ *adj* imminente
impenetrable /ɪm'penɪtrəbl/ *adj* impenetrabile
imperative /ɪm'perətɪv/ **A** *adj* imperativo
B *n* Gram imperativo *m*
imperceptible /ɪmpə'septəbl/ *adj* impercettibile
imperfect /ɪm'pɜ:fɪkt/ **A** *adj* imperfetto; (faulty) difettoso
B *n* Gram imperfetto *m*
imperfection /ɪmpə'fekʃn/ *n* imperfezione *f*
imperial /ɪm'pɪərɪəl/ *adj* imperiale
imperialism /ɪm'pɪərɪəlɪzm/ *n* imperialismo *m*
imperialist /ɪm'pɪərɪəlɪst/ *n* imperialista *mf*
imperil /ɪm'perəl/ *vt* (*pt/pp* **imperilled**) mettere in pericolo
imperious /ɪm'pɪərɪəs/ *adj* imperioso
imperiously /ɪm'pɪərɪəslɪ/ *adv* in modo imperioso
impermeable /ɪm'pɜ:mɪəbl/ *adj* impermeabile
impersonal /ɪm'pɜ:sənəl/ *adj* impersonale
impersonate /ɪm'pɜ:səneɪt/ *vt* impersonare
impersonation /ɪmpɜ:sə'neɪʃn/ *n* imitazione *f*
impersonator /ɪm'pɜ:səneɪtə(r)/ *n* imitatore, -trice *mf*

impertinence /ɪmˈpɜːtɪnəns/ *n* impertinenza *f*
impertinent /ɪmˈpɜːtɪnənt/ *adj* impertinente
imperturbable /ɪmpəˈtɜːbəbl/ *adj* imperturbabile
impervious /ɪmˈpɜːvɪəs/ *adj* ~ **to** fig indifferente a
impetuous /ɪmˈpetjʊəs/ *adj* impetuoso
impetuously /ɪmˈpetjʊəslɪ/ *adv* impetuosamente
impetus /ˈɪmpɪtəs/ *n* impeto *m*
impiety /ɪmˈpaɪətɪ/ *n* Relig empietà *f*
impinge /ɪmˈpɪndʒ/ *v*
■ **impinge on** *vt* (affect) influire su; (restrict) condizionare
impious /ˈɪmpɪəs/ *adj* Relig empio
impish /ˈɪmpɪʃ/ *adj* birichino
implacable /ɪmˈplækəbl/ *adj* implacabile
implant¹ /ɪmˈplɑːnt/ *vt* trapiantare; fig inculcare
implant² /ˈɪmplɑːnt/ *n* trapianto *m*
implausible /ɪmˈplɔːzəbl/ *adj* poco plausibile
implement¹ /ˈɪmplɪmənt/ *n* attrezzo *m*
⚷ **implement²** /ˈɪmplɪment/ *vt* mettere in atto
implementation /ˌɪmplɪmenˈteɪʃn/ *n* (of law, policy, idea) attuazione *f*; Comput implementazione *f*
implicate /ˈɪmplɪkeɪt/ *vt* implicare
implication /ɪmplɪˈkeɪʃn/ *n* implicazione *f*; **by** ~ implicitamente
implicit /ɪmˈplɪsɪt/ *adj* implicito; (absolute) assoluto
implicitly /ɪmˈplɪsɪtlɪ/ *adv* implicitamente; (absolutely) completamente
implied /ɪmˈplaɪd/ *adj* implicito, sottinteso
implore /ɪmˈplɔː(r)/ *vt* implorare
imploring /ɪmˈplɔːrɪŋ/ *adj* implorante
implosion /ɪmˈpləʊʒn/ *n* implosione *f*
imply /ɪmˈplaɪ/ *vt* (*pt/pp* **-ied**) implicare; **what are you** ~**ing?** che cosa vorresti insinuare?
impolite /ɪmpəˈlaɪt/ *adj* sgarbato
impolitely /ɪmpəˈlaɪtlɪ/ *adv* sgarbatamente
import¹ /ˈɪmpɔːt/ *n* Comm importazione *f*; (importance) importanza *f*; (meaning) rilevanza *f*
import² /ɪmˈpɔːt/ *vt* importare
⚷ **importance** /ɪmˈpɔːtəns/ *n* importanza *f*
⚷ **important** /ɪmˈpɔːtənt/ *adj* importante
importation /ɪmpɔːˈteɪʃn/ *n* Comm importazione *f*
import duty /ˈɪmpɔːt/ *n* dazio *m* d'importazione
importer /ɪmˈpɔːtə(r)/ *n* importatore, -trice *mf*
import-export /ˈɪmpɔːtˈekspɔːt/ *n* import-export *m inv*
importing country /ɪmˈpɔːtɪŋ/ *n* paese *m* di importazione
⚷ **impose** /ɪmˈpəʊz/ **A** *vt* imporre (**on** a) **B** *vi* imporsi; ~ **on** abusare di
imposing /ɪmˈpəʊzɪŋ/ *adj* imponente
imposition /ɪmpəˈzɪʃn/ *n* imposizione *f*
impossibility /ɪmˈpɒsɪbɪlətɪ/ *n* impossibilità *f*
⚷ **impossible** /ɪmˈpɒsəbl/ *adj* impossibile
impossibly /ɪmˈpɒsəblɪ/ *adv* impossibilmente
impostor /ɪmˈpɒstə(r)/ *n* impostore, -a *mf*
impotence /ˈɪmpətəns/ *n* impotenza *f*
impotent /ˈɪmpətənt/ *adj* impotente
impound /ɪmˈpaʊnd/ *vt* confiscare
impoverished /ɪmˈpɒvərɪʃt/ *adj* impoverito
impracticable /ɪmˈpræktɪkəbl/ *adj* impraticabile
impractical /ɪmˈpræktɪkl/ *adj* non pratico
imprecise /ɪmprɪˈsaɪs/ *adj* impreciso
impregnable /ɪmˈpregnəbl/ *adj* imprendibile
impregnate /ˈɪmpregneɪt/ *vt* impregnare (**with** di); Biol fecondare
impresario /ɪmprɪˈsɑːrɪəʊ/ *n* (*pl* **-os**) impresario *m* (*di spettacoli*)
impress /ɪmˈpres/ *vt* imprimere; fig colpire (*positivamente*); ~ **something [up]on somebody** fare capire qualcosa a qualcuno
impression /ɪmˈpreʃn/ *n* impressione *f*; (imitation) imitazione *f*
impressionable /ɪmˈpreʃənəbl/ *adj* ‹*child, mind*› influenzabile
Impressionism /ɪmˈpreʃənɪzm/ *n* impressionismo *m*
impressionist /ɪmˈpreʃənɪst/ *n* **1** (mimic) imitatore, -trice *mf* **2** (artist) impressionista *mf*
impressionistic /ɪmpreʃəˈnɪstɪk/ *adj* impressionista; ‹*account*› approssimativo
⚷ **impressive** /ɪmˈpresɪv/ *adj* imponente
imprint¹ /ˈɪmprɪnt/ *n* impressione *f*
imprint² /ɪmˈprɪnt/ *vt* imprimere; ~**ed on my mind** impresso nella mia memoria
imprison /ɪmˈprɪzən/ *vt* incarcerare
imprisonment /ɪmˈprɪzənmənt/ *n* reclusione *f*
improbable /ɪmˈprɒbəbl/ *adj* improbabile
impromptu /ɪmˈprɒmptjuː/ **A** *adj* improvvisato **B** *adv* in modo improvvisato
improper /ɪmˈprɒpə(r)/ *adj* ‹*use*› improprio; ‹*behaviour*› scorretto
improperly /ɪmˈprɒpəlɪ/ *adv* scorrettamente
impropriety /ɪmprəˈpraɪətɪ/ *n* scorrettezza *f*
⚷ **improve** /ɪmˈpruːv/ *vt & vi* migliorare
■ **improve [up]on** *vt* perfezionare
⚷ **improvement** /ɪmˈpruːvmənt/ *n* miglioramento *m*
improvident /ɪmˈprɒvɪdənt/ *adj* (heedless of the future) imprevidente
improvisation /ɪmprəvaɪˈzeɪʃn/ *n* improvvisazione *f*
improvise /ˈɪmprəvaɪz/ *vt & vi* improvvisare
imprudent /ɪmˈpruːdənt/ *adj* imprudente
impudence /ˈɪmpjʊdəns/ *n* sfrontatezza *f*

impudent /ˈɪmpjʊdənt/ *adj* sfrontato
impudently /ˈɪmpjʊdəntlɪ/ *adv* sfrontatamente
impulse /ˈɪmpʌls/ *n* impulso *m*; **on [an] ~** impulsivamente
impulse buy *n* acquisto *m* d'impulso
impulse buying *n* acquisti *mpl* fatti d'impulso
impulsive /ɪmˈpʌlsɪv/ *adj* impulsivo
impulsively /ɪmˈpʌlsɪvlɪ/ *adv* impulsivamente
impunity /ɪmˈpjuːnətɪ/ *n* **with ~** impunemente
impure /ɪmˈpjʊə(r)/ *adj* impuro
impurity /ɪmˈpjʊərətɪ/ *n* impurità *f*; **impurities** *pl* impurità *fpl*
impute /ɪmˈpjuːt/ *vt* imputare (**to** a)
in /ɪn/ **A** *prep* in; (with names of towns) a; **in the garden** in giardino; **in the street** in *or* per strada; **in bed/hospital** a letto/all'ospedale; **in the world** nel mondo; **in the rain** sotto la pioggia; **in the sun** al sole; **in this heat** con questo caldo; **in summer/winter** in estate/inverno; **in 1995** nel 1995; **in the evening** la sera; **he's arriving in two hours' time** arriva fra due ore; **deaf in one ear** sordo da un orecchio; **in the army** nell'esercito; **in English/Italian** in inglese/italiano; **in ink/pencil** a penna/matita; **in red** ‹*dressed, circled*› di rosso; **the man in the raincoat** l'uomo con l'impermeabile; **in a soft/loud voice** a voce bassa/alta; **one in ten people** una persona su dieci; **in doing this, he...** nel far questo, ...; **in itself** in sé; **in that** in quanto
B *adv* (at home) a casa; (indoors) dentro; **he's not in yet** non è ancora arrivato; **in there/here** lì/qui dentro; **ten in all** dieci in tutto; **day in, day out** giorno dopo giorno; **have it in for somebody** infml avercela con qualcuno; **send him in** fallo entrare; **come in** entrare; **bring in the washing** portare dentro i panni
C *adj* infml (in fashion) di moda
D *n* **the ins and outs** i dettagli
in. *abbr* (**inch**) pollice *m*
inability /ɪnəˈbɪlətɪ/ *n* incapacità *f*
inaccessible /ɪnækˈsesəbl/ *adj* inaccessibile
inaccuracy /ɪnˈækjʊrəsɪ/ *n* inesattezza *f*
inaccurate /ɪnˈækjʊrət/ *adj* inesatto
inaccurately /ɪnˈækjʊrətlɪ/ *adv* in modo inesatto
inaction /ɪnˈækʃn/ *n* (not being active) inazione *f*; (failure to act) inerzia *f*
inactive /ɪnˈæktɪv/ *adj* inattivo
inactivity /ɪnækˈtɪvətɪ/ *n* inattività *f*
inadequacy /ɪnˈædɪkwəsɪ/ *n* inadeguatezza *f*
inadequate /ɪnˈædɪkwət/ *adj* inadeguato
inadequately /ɪnˈædɪkwətlɪ/ *adv* inadeguatamente
inadmissible /ɪnædˈmɪsəbl/ *adj* inammissibile
inadvertent /ɪnədˈvɜːtənt/ *adj* involontario
inadvertently /ɪnədˈvɜːtəntlɪ/ *adv* inavvertitamente
inadvisable /ɪnædˈvaɪzəbl/ *adj* sconsigliabile
inalienable /ɪnˈeɪlɪənəbl/ *adj* inalienabile
inane /ɪˈneɪn/ *adj* futile
inanely /ɪˈneɪnlɪ/ *adv* in modo vacuo
inanimate /ɪnˈænɪmət/ *adj* esanime
inanity /ɪˈnænətɪ/ *n* stupidità *f*
inapplicable /ɪnəˈplɪkəbl/ *adj* inapplicabile
inappropriate /ɪnəˈprəʊprɪət/ *adj* inadatto
inapt /ɪnˈæpt/ *adj* (inappropriate) inappropriato
inarticulate /ɪnɑːˈtɪkjʊlət/ *adj* inarticolato
inasmuch /ɪnəzˈmʌtʃ/ *conj* **~ as** (insofar as) in quanto; (seeing that) poiché
inattention /ɪnəˈtenʃn/ *n* disattenzione *f*
inattentive /ɪnəˈtentɪv/ *adj* disattento
inaudible /ɪnˈɔːdəbl/ *adj* impercettibile
inaudibly /ɪnˈɔːdəblɪ/ *adv* in modo impercettibile
inaugural /ɪˈnɔːgjʊrəl/ *adj* inaugurale
inaugurate /ɪˈnɔːgjʊreɪt/ *vt* inaugurare
inauguration /ɪnɔːgjʊˈreɪʃn/ *n* inaugurazione *f*
inauspicious /ɪnɔːˈspɪʃəs/ *adj* infausto
in-between *adj* intermedio
inborn /ˈɪnbɔːn/ *adj* innato
inbox /ˈɪnbɒks/ *n* posta *f* in arrivo
inbred /ɪnˈbred/ *adj* congenito
inbreeding /ɪnˈbriːdɪŋ/ *n* (in animals) inbreeding *m*; (in humans) unioni *mpl* fra consanguinei
inbuilt /ɪnˈbɪlt/ *adj* ‹*feeling*› innato
Inc. *abbr* (**Incorporated**) Spa *f*
incalculable /ɪnˈkælkjʊləbl/ *adj* incalcolabile
incandescence /ɪnkænˈdesəns/ *n* literary incandescenza *f*
incandescent /ɪnkænˈdesənt/ *adj* literary incandescente
incapable /ɪnˈkeɪpəbl/ *adj* incapace
incapacitate /ɪnkəˈpæsɪteɪt/ *vt* rendere incapace
incapacity /ɪnkəˈpæsətɪ/ *n* incapacità *f*
incarcerate /ɪnˈkɑːsəreɪt/ *vt* incarcerare
incarnate /ɪnˈkɑːnət/ *adj* **the devil ~** il diavolo in carne e ossa
incarnation /ɪnkɑːˈneɪʃn/ *n* incarnazione *f*
incendiary /ɪnˈsendɪərɪ/ **A** *adj* incendiario
B *n* **~ [bomb]** bomba *f* incendiaria
incendiary device *n* ordigno *m* incendiario
incense¹ /ˈɪnsens/ *n* incenso *m*
incense² /ɪnˈsens/ *vt* esasperare
incensed /ɪnˈsenst/ *adj* furibondo
incentive /ɪnˈsentɪv/ *n* incentivo *m*
incentive scheme *n* piano *m* di incentivi
inception /ɪnˈsepʃn/ *n* inizio *m*

incessant /ɪn'sesənt/ *adj* incessante
incessantly /ɪn'sesəntlɪ/ *adv* incessantemente
incest /'ɪnsest/ *n* incesto *m*
incestuous /ɪn'sestjʊəs/ *adj* incestuoso
inch /ɪntʃ/ **A** *n* pollice *m* (= 2,54 cm)
B *vi* ~ **forward** avanzare gradatamente
incidence /'ɪnsɪdəns/ *n* incidenza *f*
incident /'ɪnsɪdənt/ *n* incidente *m*
incidental /ɪnsɪ'dentl/ *adj* incidentale; ~ **expenses** spese *fpl* accessorie
incidentally /ɪnsɪ'dent(ə)lɪ/ *adv* incidentalmente; (by the way) a proposito
incident room *n* (for criminal investigation) centrale *f* operativa
incinerate /ɪn'sɪnəreɪt/ *vt* incenerire
incinerator /ɪn'sɪnəreɪtə(r)/ *n* inceneritore *m*
incipient /ɪn'sɪpɪənt/ *adj* incipiente
incision /ɪn'sɪʒn/ *n* incisione *f*
incisive /ɪn'saɪsɪv/ *adj* incisivo
incisor /ɪn'saɪzə(r)/ *n* incisivo *m*
incite /ɪn'saɪt/ *vt* incitare
incitement /ɪn'saɪtmənt/ *n* incitamento *m*
incivility /ɪnsɪ'vɪlətɪ/ *n* scortesia *f*
incl. *abbr* **1** (**inclusive**) comprensivo **2** (**including**) incluso
inclement /ɪn'klemənt/ *adj* inclemente
inclination /ɪnklɪ'neɪʃn/ *n* inclinazione *f*
incline[1] /ɪn'klaɪn/ **A** *vt* inclinare; **be ~d to do something** essere propenso a fare qualcosa
B *vi* inclinarsi
incline[2] /'ɪnklaɪn/ *n* pendio *m*
include /ɪn'klu:d/ *vt* includere
including /ɪn'klu:dɪŋ/ *prep* incluso
inclusion /ɪn'klu:ʒn/ *n* inclusione *f*
inclusive /ɪn'klu:sɪv/ **A** *adj* incluso; ~ **of** comprendente; **be ~ of** comprendere
B *adv* incluso
incognito /ɪnkɒg'ni:təʊ/ *adv* in incognito
incoherent /ɪnkə'hɪərənt/ *adj* incoerente; (because drunk etc) incomprensibile
incoherently /ɪnkə'hɪərəntlɪ/ *adv* incoerentemente; (because drunk etc) incomprensibilmente
income /'ɪnkəm/ *n* reddito *m*
income bracket *n* fascia *f* di reddito
income tax *n* imposta *f* sul reddito
income tax return *n* dichiarazione *f* dei redditi
incoming /'ɪnkʌmɪŋ/ *adj* in arrivo; ~ **tide** marea *f* montante
incommunicado /ɪnkəmju:nɪ'kɑ:dəʊ/ *adj* (involuntarily) segregato; **he's ~** (in meeting) non vuole essere disturbato
incomparable /ɪn'kɒmp(ə)rəbl/ *adj* incomparabile
incompatibility /ɪnkəmpætɪ'bɪlətɪ/ *n* incompatibilità *f*
incompatible /ɪnkəm'pætəbl/ *adj* incompatibile
incompetence /ɪn'kɒmpɪtəns/ *n* incompetenza *f*
incompetent /ɪn'kɒmpɪtənt/ *adj* incompetente
incomplete /ɪnkəm'pli:t/ *adj* incompleto
incomprehensible /ɪnkɒmprɪ'hensəbl/ *adj* incomprensibile
inconceivable /ɪnkən'si:vəbl/ *adj* inconcepibile
inconclusive /ɪnkən'klu:sɪv/ *adj* inconcludente
incongruity /ɪnkɒŋ'gru:ətɪ/ *n* (of appearance) contrasto *m*; (of situation) assurdità *f*
incongruous /ɪn'kɒŋgrʊəs/ *adj* contrastante
inconsequential /ɪnkɒnsɪ'kwenʃl/ *adj* senza importanza
inconsiderate /ɪnkən'sɪdərət/ *adj* trascurabile
inconsistency /ɪnkən'sɪstənsɪ/ *n* incoerenza *f*
inconsistent /ɪnkən'sɪstənt/ *adj* incoerente; **be ~ with** non essere coerente con
inconsistently /ɪnkən'sɪstəntlɪ/ *adv* in modo incoerente
inconsolable /ɪnkən'səʊləbl/ *adj* inconsolabile
inconspicuous /ɪnkən'spɪkjʊəs/ *adj* non appariscente
inconspicuously /ɪnkən'spɪkjʊəslɪ/ *adv* modestamente
inconstancy /ɪn'kɒnstənsɪ/ *n* incostanza *f*
inconstant /ɪn'kɒnstənt/ *adj* ‹*conditions*› variabile; ‹*lover*› volubile
incontestable /ɪnkən'testəbl/ *adj* incontestabile
incontinence /ɪn'kɒntɪnəns/ *n* incontinenza *f*
incontinent /ɪn'kɒntɪnənt/ *adj* incontinente
inconvenience /ɪnkən'vi:nɪəns/ *n* scomodità *f*; (drawback) inconveniente *m*; **put somebody to ~** dare disturbo a qualcuno
inconvenient /ɪnkən'vi:nɪənt/ *adj* scomodo; ‹*time, place*› inopportuno
inconveniently /ɪnkən'vi:nɪəntlɪ/ *adv* in modo inopportuno
incorporate /ɪn'kɔ:pəreɪt/ *vt* incorporare; (contain) comprendere
incorrect /ɪnkə'rekt/ *adj* incorretto
incorrectly /ɪnkə'rektlɪ/ *adv* scorrettamente
incorrigible /ɪn'kɒrɪdʒəbl/ *adj* incorreggibile
incorruptible /ɪnkə'rʌptəbl/ *adj* incorruttibile
increase[1] /'ɪnkri:s/ *n* aumento *m*; **on the ~** in aumento
increase[2] /ɪn'kri:s/ *vt & vi* aumentare
increased *adj* ‹*demand, risk*› maggiore
increasing /ɪn'kri:sɪŋ/ *adj* ‹*impatience etc*› crescente; ‹*numbers*› in aumento
increasingly /ɪn'kri:sɪŋlɪ/ *adv* sempre più
incredible /ɪn'kredəbl/ *adj* incredibile

i

incredibly /ɪn'kredəblɪ/ *adv* incredibilmente

incredulity /ɪnkrə'dju:lətɪ/ *n* incredulità *f*

incredulous /ɪn'kredjʊləs/ *adj* incredulo

increment /'ɪnkrɪmənt/ *n* incremento *m*

incremental /ɪnkrɪ'mentəl/ *adj* Comput, Math incrementale; ‹*effect, measures*› progressivo

incriminate /ɪn'krɪmɪneɪt/ *vt* Jur incriminare

incriminating /ɪn'krɪmɪneɪtɪŋ/ *adj* ‹*evidence*› incriminante

in-crowd *n* **be in with the ~** frequentare gente alla moda

incubate /'ɪŋkjʊbeɪt/ *vt* incubare

incubation /ɪŋkjʊ'beɪʃn/ *n* incubazione *f*

incubation period *n* Med periodo *m* di incubazione

incubator /'ɪnkjʊbeɪtə(r)/ *n* (for baby) incubatrice *f*

inculcate /'ɪnkʌlkeɪt/ *vt* inculcare

incumbent /ɪn'kʌmbənt/ *adj* **be ~ on somebody** incombere a qualcuno

incur /ɪn'kɜ:(r)/ *vt* (*pt/pp* **incurred**) incorrere; contrarre ‹*debts*›

incurable /ɪn'kjʊərəbl/ *adj* incurabile

incurably /ɪn'kjʊərəblɪ/ *adv* incurabilmente

incursion /ɪn'kɜ:ʃn/ *n* incursione *f*

indebted /ɪn'detɪd/ *adj* obbligato (**to** verso)

indecency /ɪn'di:sənsɪ/ *n* oscenità *f*; (offence) atti *mpl* osceni; **gross ~** atti *mpl* osceni

indecent /ɪn'di:sənt/ *adj* indecente

indecent assault *n* atti *mpl* di libidine violenta

indecent exposure *n* esibizionismo *m* (*dei genitali*)

indecipherable /ɪndɪ'saɪfərəbl/ *adj* indecifrabile

indecision /ɪndɪ'sɪʒn/ *n* indecisione *f*

indecisive /ɪndɪ'saɪsɪv/ *adj* indeciso

indecisiveness /ɪndɪ'saɪsɪvnɪs/ *n* indecisione *f*

⚷ **indeed** /ɪn'di:d/ *adv* (in fact) difatti; **yes ~!** sì, certamente!; **~ I am/do** veramente!; **very much ~** moltissimo; **thank you very much ~** grazie infinite; **~?** davvero?

indefatigable /ɪndɪ'fætɪgəbl/ *adj* instancabile

indefensible /ɪndɪ'fensəbl/ *adj* Mil indifendibile; (morally) ingiustificabile; (logically) insostenibile

indefinable /ɪndɪ'faɪnəbl/ *adj* indefinibile

indefinite /ɪn'defɪnɪt/ *adj* indefinito

indefinitely /ɪn'defɪnɪtlɪ/ *adv* indefinitamente; ‹*postpone*› a tempo indeterminato

indelible /ɪn'deləbl/ *adj* indelebile

indelibly /ɪn'deləblɪ/ *adv* in modo indelebile

indelicacy /ɪn'delɪkəsɪ/ *n* (tactlessness) mancanza *f* di tatto; (coarseness) rozzezza *f*

⚷ parola chiave

indelicate /ɪn'delɪkət/ *adj* (tactless) privo di tatto; (coarse) rozzo

indemnity /ɪn'demnətɪ/ *n* indennità *f*

indent¹ /'ɪndent/ *n* Typ rientro *m* dal margine

indent² /ɪn'dent/ *vt* Typ fare rientrare dal margine

indentation /ɪnden'teɪʃn/ *n* (notch) intaccatura *f*

independence /ɪndɪ'pendəns/ *n* indipendenza *f*

Independence Day *n* AmE = *anniversario* (*m*) *dell'Indipendenza degli USA (4 luglio)*

⚷ **independent** /ɪndɪ'pendənt/ *adj* indipendente

independently /ɪndɪ'pendəntlɪ/ *adv* indipendentemente

in-depth *adj* ‹*analysis, study, knowledge*› approfondito

indescribable /ɪndɪ'skraɪbəbl/ *adj* indescrivibile

indescribably /ɪndɪ'skraɪbəblɪ/ *adv* indescrivibilmente

indestructible /ɪndɪ'strʌktəbl/ *adj* indistruttibile

indeterminate /ɪndɪ'tɜ:mɪnət/ *adj* indeterminato

index /'ɪndeks/ *n* indice *m*

indexation /ɪndek'seɪʃn/ *n* indicizzazione *f*

index card *n* scheda *f*

index finger *n* dito *m* indice

index-linked *adj* ‹*pension*› legato al costo della vita

India /'ɪndɪə/ *n* India *f*

⚷ **Indian** /'ɪndɪən/ **A** *adj* indiano; (American) degli indiani [d'America]
B *n* indiano, -a *mf*; (American) indiano [d'America], pellerossa *mf inv*

Indian elephant *n* elefante *m* indiano

Indian ink *n* inchiostro *m* di china

Indian Ocean *n* oceano *m* Indiano

Indian summer *n* estate *f* di San Martino

⚷ **indicate** /'ɪndɪkeɪt/ **A** *vt* indicare; (register) segnare
B *vi* Auto mettere la freccia; **~ left** mettere la freccia a sinistra

indication /ɪndɪ'keɪʃn/ *n* indicazione *f*

indicative /ɪn'dɪkətɪv/ **A** *adj* **be ~ of** essere indicativo di
B *n* Gram indicativo *m*

indicator /'ɪndɪkeɪtə(r)/ *n* Auto freccia *f*

indict /ɪn'daɪt/ *vt* accusare

indictment /ɪn'daɪtmənt/ *n* Jur imputazione *f*

indie /'ɪndɪ/ **A** *adj* infml Cinema, Mus indipendente
B *n* (band) *gruppo* (*m*) *musicale legato a una casa discografica indipendente*; (film) *film* (*m*) *prodotto da una casa di produzione indipendente*

indifference /ɪn'dɪf(ə)rəns/ *n* indifferenza *f*

indifferent /ɪn'dɪf(ə)rənt/ *adj* indifferente; (not good) mediocre
indifferently /ɪn'dɪf(ə)rəntlɪ/ *adv* in modo indifferente; (not well) in modo mediocre
indigenous /ɪn'dɪdʒɪnəs/ *adj* indigeno
indigestible /ɪndɪ'dʒestəbl/ *adj* indigesto
indigestion /ɪndɪ'dʒestʃn/ *n* indigestione *f*
indignant /ɪn'dɪgnənt/ *adj* indignato
indignantly /ɪn'dɪgnəntlɪ/ *adv* con indignazione
indignation /ɪndɪg'neɪʃn/ *n* indignazione *f*
indignity /ɪn'dɪgnətɪ/ *n* umiliazione *f*
indigo /'ɪndɪgəʊ/ *n* indaco *m*
indirect /ɪndaɪ'rekt/ *adj* indiretto
indirectly /ɪndaɪ'rektlɪ/ *adv* indirettamente
indirect speech *n* discorso *m* indiretto
indiscernible /ɪndɪ'sɜːnəbl/ *adj* indistinguibile
indiscreet /ɪndɪ'skriːt/ *adj* indiscreto
indiscretion /ɪndɪ'skreʃn/ *n* indiscrezione *f*
indiscriminate /ɪndɪ'skrɪmɪnət/ *adj* indiscriminato
indiscriminately /ɪndɪ'skrɪmɪnətlɪ/ *adv* senza distinzione
indispensable /ɪndɪ'spensəbl/ *adj* indispensabile
indisposed /ɪndɪ'spəʊzd/ *adj* indisposto
indisputable /ɪndɪ'spjuːtəbl/ *adj* indisputabile
indisputably /ɪndɪ'spjuːtəblɪ/ *adv* indisputabilmente
indistinct /ɪndɪ'stɪŋkt/ *adj* indistinto
indistinctly /ɪndɪ'stɪŋktlɪ/ *adv* indistintamente
indistinguishable /ɪndɪ'stɪŋgwɪʃəbl/ *adj* indistinguibile
⚷ **individual** /ɪndɪ'vɪdjʊəl/ **A** *adj* individuale **B** *n* individuo *m*
individualist /ɪndɪ'vɪdjʊəlɪst/ *n* individualista *mf*
individualistic /ɪndɪvɪdjʊə'lɪstɪk/ *adj* individualistico
individuality /ɪndɪvɪdjʊ'ælətɪ/ *n* individualità *f*
individually /ɪndɪ'vɪdjʊəlɪ/ *adv* individualmente
indivisible /ɪndɪ'vɪzəbl/ *adj* indivisibile
Indo-China /ɪndəʊ'tʃaɪnə/ *n* Indocina *f*
indoctrinate /ɪn'dɒktrɪneɪt/ *vt* indottrinare
Indo-European /ɪndəʊjʊərə'pɪən/ *adj* indoeuropeo
indolence /'ɪndələns/ *n* indolenza *f*
indolent /'ɪndələnt/ *adj* indolente
indomitable /ɪn'dɒmɪtəbl/ *adj* indomito
Indonesia /ɪndə'niːzjə/ *n* Indonesia *f*
Indonesian /ɪndə'niːzjən/ *adj & n* (person) indonesiano, -a *mf*; (language) indonesiano *m*
indoor /'ɪndɔː(r)/ *adj* interno; ‹*shoes*› per casa; ‹*plant*› da appartamento; ‹*swimming pool etc*› coperto
indoors /ɪn'dɔːz/ *adv* dentro; **go ~** andare dentro
indubitable /ɪn'djuːbɪtəbl/ *adj* indubitabile
indubitably /ɪn'djuːbɪtəblɪ/ *adv* indubitabilmente
induce /ɪn'djuːs/ *vt* indurre (**to** a); (produce) causare
inducement /ɪn'djuːsmənt/ *n* (incentive) incentivo *m*
induction /ɪn'dʌkʃn/ *n* (inauguration) introduzione *f*; (of labour) parto *m* indotto; Electr induzione *f*
induction ceremony *n* cerimonia *f* inaugurale
induction course *n* corso *m* introduttivo
induction loop *n* sistema *m* di amplificazione sonora
indulge /ɪn'dʌldʒ/ **A** *vt* soddisfare; viziare ‹*child*›
B *vi* **~ in** concedersi
indulgence /ɪn'dʌldʒəns/ *n* lusso *m*; (leniency) indulgenza *f*
indulgent /ɪn'dʌldʒənt/ *adj* indulgente
⚷ **industrial** /ɪn'dʌstrɪəl/ *adj* industriale
industrial accident *n* infortunio *m* sul lavoro
industrial action *n* sciopero *m*; **take ~** scioperare
industrial dispute *n* vertenza *f* sindacale
industrial espionage *n* spionaggio *m* industriale
industrial estate *n* zona *f* industriale
industrialist /ɪn'dʌstrɪəlɪst/ *n* industriale *mf*
industrialized /ɪn'dʌstrɪəlaɪzd/ *adj* industrializzato
industrial relations *npl* relazioni *fpl* industriali
industrial tribunal *n tribunale* (*m*) *competente per i conflitti di lavoro*
industrial waste *n* rifiuti *mpl* industriali
industrious /ɪn'dʌstrɪəs/ *adj* industrioso
industriously /ɪn'dʌstrɪəslɪ/ *adv* in modo industrioso
⚷ **industry** /'ɪndəstrɪ/ *n* industria *f*; (zeal) operosità *f*
inebriated /ɪ'niːbrɪeɪtɪd/ *adj* ebbro
inedible /ɪn'edəbl/ *adj* immangiabile
ineffective /ɪnɪ'fektɪv/ *adj* inefficace
ineffectively /ɪnɪ'fektɪvlɪ/ *adv* inutilmente, invano
ineffectual /ɪnɪ'fektʃʊəl/ *adj* inutile; ‹*person*› inconcludente
inefficiency /ɪnɪ'fɪʃənsɪ/ *n* inefficienza *f*
inefficient /ɪnɪ'fɪʃnt/ *adj* inefficiente
ineligible /ɪn'elɪdʒəbl/ *adj* inadatto
inept /ɪ'nept/ *adj* inetto
ineptitude /ɪ'neptɪtjuːd/ *n* inettitudine *f*
inequality /ɪnɪ'kwɒlətɪ/ *n* ineguaglianza *f*
inert /ɪ'nɜːt/ *adj* inerte
inertia /ɪ'nɜːʃə/ *n* inerzia *f*

inescapable /mɪ'skeɪpəbl/ *adj* inevitabile
inestimable /ɪn'estɪməbl/ *adj* inestimabile
inevitable /ɪn'evɪtəbl/ *adj* inevitabile
inevitably /ɪn'evɪtəblɪ/ *adv* inevitabilmente
inexact /ɪnɪg'zækt/ *adj* inesatto
inexcusable /ɪnɪk'skju:zəbl/ *adj* imperdonabile
inexhaustible /ɪnɪg'zɔ:stəbl/ *adj* inesauribile
inexorable /ɪn'eksərəbl/ *adj* inesorabile
inexorably /ɪn'egzərəblɪ/ *adv* inesorabilmente
inexpensive /ɪnɪk'spensɪv/ *adj* poco costoso
inexpensively /ɪnɪk'spensɪvlɪ/ *adv* a buon mercato
inexperience /ɪnɪk'spɪərɪəns/ *n* inesperienza *f*
inexperienced /ɪnɪk'spɪərɪənst/ *adj* inesperto
inexplicable /ɪnɪk'splɪkəbl/ *adj* inesplicabile
inexplicably /ɪnɪk'splɪkəblɪ/ *adv* inesplicabilmente, inspiegabilmente
inextricable /ɪnɪk'strɪkəbl/ *adj* inestricabile
inextricably /ɪnɪk'strɪkəblɪ/ *adv* inestricabilmente
infallibility /ɪnfælɪ'bɪlətɪ/ *n* infallibilità *f*
infallible /ɪn'fæləbl/ *adj* infallibile
infamous /'ɪnfəməs/ *adj* infame; ‹*person*› famigerato
infamy /'ɪnfəmɪ/ *n* infamia *f*
infancy /'ɪnfənsɪ/ *n* infanzia *f*; **in its ~** fig agli inizi
infant /'ɪnfənt/ *n* bambino, -a *mf* piccolo
infanticide /ɪn'fæntɪsaɪd/ *n* infanticidio *m*
infantile /'ɪnfəntaɪl/ *adj* infantile
infantry /'ɪnfəntrɪ/ *n* fanteria *f*
infant school *n scuola (f) elementare per bambini dai 5 ai 7 anni*
infatuated /ɪn'fætʃʊeɪtɪd/ *adj* infatuato (**with** di)
infatuation /ɪnfætʃʊ'eɪʃn/ *n* infatuazione *f*
infect /ɪn'fekt/ *vt* infettare; **become ~ed** ‹*wound*› infettarsi
infection /ɪn'fekʃn/ infezione *f*
infectious /ɪn'fekʃəs/ *adj* infettivo
infer /ɪn'fɜ:(r)/ *vt* (*pt/pp* **inferred**) dedurre (**from** da); (imply) implicare
inference /'ɪnfərəns/ *n* deduzione *f*
inferior /ɪn'fɪərɪə(r)/ **A** *adj* inferiore; ‹*goods*› scadente; (in rank) subalterno **B** *n* inferiore *mf*; (in rank) subalterno, -a *mf*
inferiority /ɪnfɪərɪ'ɒrətɪ/ *n* inferiorità *f*
inferiority complex *n* complesso *m* di inferiorità
infernal /ɪn'fɜ:nl/ *adj* infernale
inferno /ɪn'fɜ:nəʊ/ *n* inferno *m*
infertile /ɪn'fɜ:taɪl/ *adj* sterile
infertility /ɪnfə'tɪlətɪ/ *n* sterilità *f*
infest /ɪn'fest/ *vt* **be ~ed with** essere infestato di
infestation /ɪnfe'steɪʃn/ *n* infestazione *f*
infidelity /ɪnfɪ'delətɪ/ *n* infedeltà *f*
infighting /'ɪnfaɪtɪŋ/ *n* fig lotta *f* per il potere
infiltrate /'ɪnfɪltreɪt/ *vt* infiltrare; Pol infiltrarsi in
infiltration /ɪnfɪl'treɪʃn/ *n* infiltrazione *f*
infinite /'ɪnfɪnɪt/ *adj* infinito
infinitely /'ɪnfɪnɪtlɪ/ *adv* infinitamente
infinitesimal /ɪnfɪnɪ'tesɪml/ *adj* infinitesimo
infinitive /ɪn'fɪnətɪv/ *n* Gram infinito *m*
infinity /ɪn'fɪnətɪ/ *n* infinità *f*
infinity pool *n* infinity pool *f inv*, piscina *f* a sfioro
infirm /ɪn'fɜ:m/ *adj* debole
infirmary /ɪn'fɜ:m(ə)rɪ/ *n* infermeria *f*
infirmity /ɪn'fɜ:mətɪ/ *n* debolezza *f*
in flagrante delicto /ɪnfləgræntɪdɪ'lɪktəʊ/ *adv* in flagrante
inflame /ɪn'fleɪm/ *vt* infiammare
inflamed /ɪn'fleɪmd/ *adj* infiammato; **become ~** infiammarsi
inflammable /ɪn'flæməbl/ *adj* infiammabile
inflammation /ɪnflə'meɪʃn/ *n* infiammazione *f*
inflammatory /ɪn'flæmətrɪ/ *adj* incendiario
inflatable /ɪn'fleɪtəbl/ *adj* gonfiabile
inflate /ɪn'fleɪt/ *vt* gonfiare
inflated /ɪn'fleɪtɪd/ *adj* ‹*price, fee, claim*› eccessivo; ‹*style*› ampolloso; ‹*tyre*› gonfio; **an ~ ego** un'alta opinione di sé
inflation /ɪn'fleɪʃn/ *n* inflazione *f*
inflationary /ɪn'fleɪʃənərɪ/ *adj* inflazionario
inflect /ɪn'flekt/ *vt* flettere ‹*noun, adjective*›; modulare ‹*voice*›
inflected /ɪn'flektɪd/ *adj* ‹*language*› flessivo; ‹*form*› flesso
inflection /ɪn'flekʃn/ *n* (of voice) modulazione *f*
inflexible /ɪn'fleksəbl/ *adj* inflessibile
inflexion /ɪn'flekʃn/ *n* inflessione *f*
inflict /ɪn'flɪkt/ *vt* infliggere (**on** a)
in-flight *adj* a bordo
influence /'ɪnflʊəns/ **A** *n* influenza *f*; **use one's ~** esercitare la propria influenza **B** *vt* influenzare
influential /ɪnflʊ'enʃl/ *adj* influente
influenza /ɪnflʊ'enzə/ *n* influenza *f*
influx /'ɪnflʌks/ *n* affluenza *f*
info /'ɪnfəʊ/ *n* infml informazione *f*
inform /ɪn'fɔ:m/ **A** *vt* informare; **keep somebody ~ed** tenere qualcuno al corrente **B** *vi* **~ against** denunziare
informal /ɪn'fɔ:məl/ *adj* informale; ‹*agreement*› ufficioso
informality /ɪnfə'mælətɪ/ *n* informalità *f*
informally /ɪn'fɔ:məlɪ/ *adv* in modo informale
informant /ɪn'fɔ:mənt/ *n* informatore, -trice *mf*

parola chiave

information /ɪnfəˈmeɪʃn/ *n* informazioni *fpl*; **a piece of ~** un'informazione

information and communication technology *n* tecnologia *f* dell'informazione e della comunicazione

information desk *n* banco *m* informazioni

information highway *n* autostrada *f* telematica

information officer *n* addetto, -a *mf* stampa

information pack *n* pacchetto *m* informativo

information processing *n* elaborazione *f* dati

information superhighway *n* Comput autostrada *f* dell'informazione

information system *n* sistema *m* informativo

information technology *n* informatica *f*

informative /ɪnˈfɔːmətɪv/ *adj* informativo; ‹*film, book*› istruttivo

informer /ɪnˈfɔːmə(r)/ *n* informatore, -trice *mf*; Pol delatore, -trice *mf*

infra-red /ɪnfrə-ˈred/ *adj* infrarosso

infrastructure /ˈɪnfrəstrʌktʃə(r)/ *n* infrastruttura *f*

infrequent /ɪnˈfriːkwənt/ *adj* infrequente

infrequently /ɪnˈfriːkwəntlɪ/ *adv* raramente

infringe /ɪnˈfrɪndʒ/ *vt* **~ on** usurpare

infringement /ɪnˈfrɪndʒmənt/ *n* violazione *f*

infuriate /ɪnˈfjʊərɪeɪt/ *vt* infuriare

infuriating /ɪnˈfjʊərɪeɪtɪŋ/ *adj* esasperante

infuse /ɪnˈfjuːz/ *vi* ‹*tea*› restare in infusione

infusion /ɪnˈfjuːʒn/ *n* (drink) infusione *f*; (of capital, new blood) afflusso *m*

ingenious /ɪnˈdʒiːnɪəs/ *adj* ingegnoso

ingenuity /ɪndʒɪˈnjuːətɪ/ *n* ingegnosità *f*

ingenuous /ɪnˈdʒenjʊəs/ *adj* ingenuo

ingest /ɪnˈdʒest/ *vt* ingerire ‹*food*›; assimilare ‹*fact*›

ingot /ˈɪŋgət/ *n* lingotto *m*

ingrained /ɪnˈgreɪnd/ *adj* (in person) radicato; ‹*dirt*› incrostato

ingratiate /ɪnˈgreɪʃɪeɪt/ *vt* **~ oneself with somebody** ingraziarsi qualcuno

ingratitude /ɪnˈgrætɪtjuːd/ *n* ingratitudine *f*

ingredient /ɪnˈgriːdɪənt/ *n* ingrediente *m*

ingrowing /ˈɪngrəʊɪŋ/ *adj* ‹*nail*› incarnito

inhabit /ɪnˈhæbɪt/ *vt* abitare

inhabitable /ɪnˈhæbɪtəbl/ *adj* abitabile

inhabitant /ɪnˈhæbɪtənt/ *n* abitante *mf*

inhale /ɪnˈheɪl/ **A** *vt* aspirare; Med inalare
B *vi* inspirare; (when smoking) aspirare

inhaler /ɪnˈheɪlə(r)/ *n* (device) inalatore *m*

inherent /ɪnˈhɪərənt/ *adj* inerente

inherit /ɪnˈherɪt/ *vt* ereditare

inheritance /ɪnˈherɪtəns/ *n* eredità *f*

inhibit /ɪnˈhɪbɪt/ *vt* inibire

inhibited /ɪnˈhɪbɪtɪd/ *adj* inibito

inhibition /ɪnhɪˈbɪʃn/ *n* inibizione *f*

inhospitable /ɪnhɒˈspɪtəbl/ *adj* inospitale

in-house *adj* ‹*training*› interno all'azienda; ‹*magazine*› aziendale

inhuman /ɪnˈhjuːmən/ *adj* disumano

inhumanity /ˌɪnhjuːˈmænətɪ/ *n* disumanità *f*

inimitable /ɪˈnɪmɪtəbl/ *adj* inimitabile

iniquitous /ɪˈnɪkwɪtəs/ *adj* iniquo

initial /ɪˈnɪʃl/ **A** *adj* iniziale
B *n* iniziale *f*
C *vt* (*pt/pp* **initialled**) siglare

initially /ɪˈnɪʃəlɪ/ *adv* all'inizio

initiate /ɪˈnɪʃɪeɪt/ *vt* iniziare

initiation /ɪnɪʃɪˈeɪʃn/ *n* iniziazione *f*

initiative /ɪˈnɪʃətɪv/ *n* iniziativa *f*; **take the ~** prendere l'iniziativa

inject /ɪnˈdʒekt/ *vt* iniettare

injection /ɪnˈdʒekʃn/ *n* iniezione *f*

in-joke *n* **it's an ~** è una battuta tra di noi/loro

injunction /ɪnˈdʒʌŋkʃn/ *n* ingiunzione *f*

injure /ˈɪndʒə(r)/ *vt* ferire; (wrong) nuocere

injured /ˈɪndʒəd/ **A** *adj* ferito; Jur **the ~ party** la parte lesa
B *npl* **the ~** i feriti

injury /ˈɪndʒərɪ/ *n* ferita *f*; (wrong) torto *m*

injury time *n* Sport recupero *m*

injustice /ɪnˈdʒʌstɪs/ *n* ingiustizia *f*; **do somebody an ~** giudicare qualcuno in modo sbagliato

ink /ɪŋk/ *n* inchiostro *m*

ink-jet printer *n* stampante *f* a getto d'inchiostro

inkling /ˈɪŋklɪŋ/ *n* sentore *m*

inky /ˈɪŋkɪ/ *adj* macchiato d'inchiostro

inlaid /ɪnˈleɪd/ *adj* intarsiato

inland /ˈɪnlənd/ **A** *adj* interno
B *adv* all'interno

Inland Revenue *n* fisco *m*

in-laws /ˈɪnlɔːz/ *npl* infml parenti *mpl* acquisiti

inlay /ˈɪnleɪ/ *n* intarsio *m*

inlet /ˈɪnlet/ *n* insenatura *f*; Techn entrata *f*

inmate /ˈɪnmeɪt/ *n* (of hospital) degente *mf*; (of prison) detenuto, -a *mf*

inn /ɪn/ *n* locanda *f*

innards /ˈɪnədz/ *npl* infml frattaglie *fpl*

innate /ɪˈneɪt/ *adj* innato

inner /ˈɪnə(r)/ *adj* interno

inner city **A** *n quartieri (mpl) nel centro di una città caratterizzati da problemi sociali*
B *attrib* ‹*problems*› dell'area urbana con problemi sociali

inner ear *n* orecchio *m* interno

innermost /ˈɪnəməʊst/ *adj* il più profondo

inner tube *n* camera *f* d'aria

innings /ˈɪnɪŋz/ *nsg* (in cricket) turno *m* di battuta; **have had a good ~** BrE fig (when leaving job etc) aver avuto una carriera lunga e gratificante; (when dead) aver avuto una vita lunga e piena di soddisfazioni

innkeeper /ˈɪnkiːpə(r)/ *n* locandiere, -a *mf*

innocence /ˈɪnəsəns/ *n* innocenza *f*

innocent /ˈɪnəsənt/ *adj* innocente

innocently /ˈɪnəsəntlɪ/ *adv* innocentemente

innocuous /ɪˈnɒkjʊəs/ *adj* innocuo

innovate /ˈɪnəveɪt/ *vi* innovare

innovation /ɪnəˈveɪʃn/ *n* innovazione *f*

innovative /ˈɪnəvətɪv/ *adj* innovativo

innovator /ˈɪnəveɪtə(r)/ *n* innovatore, -trice *mf*

innuendo /ɪnjʊˈendəʊ/ *n* (*pl* **-es**) insinuazione *f*

innumerable /ɪˈnjuːmərəbl/ *adj* innumerevole

inoculate /ɪˈnɒkjʊleɪt/ *vt* vaccinare

inoculation /ɪnɒkjʊˈleɪʃn/ *n* vaccinazione *f*

inoffensive /ɪnəˈfensɪv/ *adj* inoffensivo

inoperable /ɪnˈɒpərəbl/ *adj* inoperabile

inopportune /ɪnˈɒpətjuːn/ *adj* inopportuno

inordinate /ɪˈnɔːdɪnət/ *adj* smodato

inordinately /ɪˈnɔːdɪnətlɪ/ *adv* smodatamente

inorganic /ɪnɔːˈgænɪk/ *adj* inorganico

in-patient *n* degente *mf*

input /ˈɪnpʊt/ *n* input *m inv*, ingresso *m*

inquest /ˈɪnkwest/ *n* inchiesta *f*

inquire /ɪnˈkwaɪə(r)/ **A** *vi* informarsi (**about** su); ~ **into** far indagini su
B *vt* domandare

inquiring /ɪnˈkwaɪərɪŋ/ *adj* ‹*mind*› curioso; ‹*look, voice*› interrogativo

🔑 **inquiry** /ɪnˈkwaɪərɪ/ *n* domanda *f*; (investigation) inchiesta *f*

inquisitive /ɪnˈkwɪzətɪv/ *adj* curioso

inquisitively /ɪnˈkwɪzɪtɪvlɪ/ *adv* con molta curiosità

inroad /ˈɪnrəʊd/ *n* **make ~s into** intaccare ‹*savings*›; cominciare a risolvere ‹*problem*›

INS *n abbr* AmE (**Immigration and Naturalization Service**) *ufficio* (*m*) *immigrazione e naturalizzazione*

insalubrious /ɪnsəˈluːbrɪəs/ *adj* (dirty) insalubre; (sleazy) sordido

insane /ɪnˈseɪn/ *adj* pazzo; fig insensato

insanitary /ɪnˈsænɪt(ə)rɪ/ *adj* malsano

insanity /ɪnˈsænətɪ/ *n* pazzia *f*

insatiable /ɪnˈseɪʃəbl/ *adj* insaziabile

inscribe /ɪnˈskraɪb/ *vt* iscrivere

inscription /ɪnˈskrɪpʃn/ *n* iscrizione *f*

inscrutable /ɪnˈskruːtəbl/ *adj* impenetrabile

insect /ˈɪnsekt/ *n* insetto *m*

insecticide /ɪnˈsektɪsaɪd/ *n* insetticida *m*

insect repellent *n* insettifugo *m*

insecure /ɪnsɪˈkjʊə(r)/ *adj* malsicuro; fig ‹*person*› insicuro

insecurity /ɪnsɪˈkjʊərətɪ/ *n* mancanza *f* di sicurezza

insemination /ɪnsemɪˈneɪʃn/ *n* inseminazione *f*

insensitive /ɪnˈsensɪtɪv/ *adj* insensibile

inseparable /ɪnˈsep(ə)rəbl/ *adj* inseparabile

insert¹ /ˈɪnsɜːt/ *n* inserto *m*

insert² /ɪnˈsɜːt/ *vt* inserire

insertion /ɪnˈsɜːʃn/ *n* inserzione *f*

inset /ˈɪnset/ **A** *n* (map, photo) dettaglio *m*
B *adj* ~ **with** ‹*necklace*› incastonato di; ‹*table*› intarsiato di

inshore /ɪnʃɔː(r)/ **A** *adj* ‹*current*› diretto a riva; ‹*fishing, waters, current*› costiero; ‹*wind*› dal mare
B *adv* ‹*fish*› sotto costa

🔑 **inside** /ɪnˈsaɪd/ **A** *n* interno *m*; **~s** *pl* infml pancia *f*
B *adv* dentro; ~ **out** a rovescio; (thoroughly) a fondo
C *prep* dentro; (of time) entro

inside lane *n* Auto corsia *f* interna

inside leg *n* interno *m* della gamba

insider /ɪnˈsaɪdə(r)/ *n* persona *f* all'interno

insider dealer, **insider trader** *n* Fin *persona* (*f*) *che pratica l'insider trading*

insider dealing, **insider trading** /ˈdiːlɪŋ/, /ˈtreɪdɪŋ/ *n* Fin insider trading *m*

insidious /ɪnˈsɪdɪəs/ *adj* insidioso

insidiously /ɪnˈsɪdɪəslɪ/ *adv* insidiosamente

insight /ˈɪnsaɪt/ *n* intuito *m* (**into** per); **an ~ into** un quadro di

insignia /ɪnˈsɪgnɪə/ *npl* insegne *fpl*

insignificant /ɪnsɪgˈnɪfɪkənt/ *adj* insignificante

insincere /ɪnsɪnˈsɪə(r)/ *adj* poco sincero

insincerity /ɪnsɪnˈserətɪ/ *n* mancanza *f* di sincerità

insinuate /ɪnˈsɪnjʊeɪt/ *vt* insinuare

insinuation /ɪnsɪnjʊˈeɪʃn/ *n* insinuazione *f*

insipid /ɪnˈsɪpɪd/ *adj* insipido

🔑 **insist** /ɪnˈsɪst/ **A** *vi* insistere (**on** per)
B *vt* ~ **that** insistere che

insistence /ɪnˈsɪstəns/ *n* insistenza *f*

insistent /ɪnˈsɪstənt/ *adj* insistente

insistently /ɪnˈsɪstəntlɪ/ *adv* insistentemente

insofar /ɪnsəˈfɑː(r)/ *conj* ~ **as** (to the extent that) nella misura in cui; (seeing that) in quanto; ~ **as I know** per quanto ne sappia

insole /ˈɪnsəʊl/ *n* soletta *f*

insolence /ˈɪnsələns/ *n* insolenza *f*

insolent /ˈɪnsələnt/ *adj* insolente

insolently /ˈɪnsələntlɪ/ *adv* con insolenza

insoluble /ɪnˈsɒljʊbl/ *adj* insolubile

insolvency /ɪnˈsɒlvənsɪ/ *n* insolvenza *f*

insolvent /ɪnˈsɒlvənt/ *adj* insolvente

insomnia /ɪnˈsɒmnɪə/ *n* insonnia *f*

insomniac /ɪnˈsɒmnɪæk/ *n persona* (*f*) *che soffre di insonnia*

insomuch /ɪnsəˈmʌtʃ/ *conj* **~ as** (to the extent that) nella misura in cui; (seeing that) in quanto

inspect /ɪnˈspekt/ *vt* ispezionare; controllare ‹*ticket*›

inspection /ɪnˈspekʃn/ *n* ispezione *f*; (of ticket) controllo *m*

inspector /ɪnˈspektə(r)/ *n* ispettore, -trice *mf*; (of tickets) controllore *m*

inspiration /ɪnspəˈreɪʃn/ *n* ispirazione *f*

inspire /ɪnˈspaɪə(r)/ *vt* ispirare

inspired /ɪnˈspaɪəd/ *adj* ‹*person, performance*› ispirato; ‹*idea*› luminosa

inspiring /ɪnˈspaɪərɪŋ/ *adj* ‹*person, speech*› entusiasmante

instability /ɪnstəˈbɪlətɪ/ *n* instabilità *f*

install /ɪnˈstɔːl/ *vt* installare; insediare ‹*person*›

installation /ɪnstəˈleɪʃn/ *n* installazione *f*

instalment /ɪnˈstɔːlmənt/ *n* Comm rata *f*; (of serial) puntata *f*; (of publication) fascicolo *m*

instance /ˈɪnstəns/ *n* (case) caso *m*; (example) esempio *m*; **in the first ~** in primo luogo; **for ~** per esempio

instant /ˈɪnstənt/ **A** *adj* immediato; Culin espresso
B *n* istante *m*

instantaneous /ɪnstənˈteɪnɪəs/ *adj* istantaneo

instant camera *n* polaroid® *f inv*

instant coffee *n* caffè *m* solubile

instantly /ˈɪnstəntlɪ/ *adv* immediatamente

instant messaging *n* instant messaging *m*, messaggistica *f* istantanea

instant replay *n* Sport replay *m inv*

instead /ɪnˈsted/ *adv* invece; **~ of doing** anziché fare; **~ of me** al mio posto; **~ of going** invece di andare

instep /ˈɪnstep/ *n* collo *m* del piede

instigate /ˈɪnstɪgeɪt/ *vt* istigare

instigation /ɪnstɪˈgeɪʃn/ *n* istigazione *f*; **at his ~** dietro suo suggerimento

instigator /ˈɪnstɪgeɪtə(r)/ *n* istigatore, -trice *mf*

instil /ɪnˈstɪl/ *vt* (*pt/pp* **instilled**) inculcare (into in)

instinct /ˈɪnstɪŋkt/ *n* istinto *m*

instinctive /ɪnˈstɪŋktɪv/ *adj* istintivo

instinctively /ɪnˈstɪŋktɪvlɪ/ *adv* istintivamente

institute /ˈɪnstɪtjuːt/ **A** *n* istituto *m*
B *vt* istituire ‹*scheme*›; iniziare ‹*search*›; intentare ‹*legal action*›

institution /ɪnstɪˈtjuːʃn/ *n* istituzione *f*; (home for elderly) istituto *m* per anziani; (for mentally ill) istituto *m* per malati di mente

institutionalize /ɪnstɪˈtjuːʃənəlaɪz/ *vt* istituzionalizzare

institutionalized /ɪnstɪˈtjuːʃənəlaɪzd/ *adj* ‹*racism, violence*› istituzionalizzato; **become ~** (officially established) essere istituzionalizzato; **be ~d** ‹*person*› non essere autonomo a causa di un lungo soggiorno in ospedale psichiatrico

instruct /ɪnˈstrʌkt/ *vt* istruire; (order) ordinare

instruction /ɪnˈstrʌkʃn/ *n* istruzione *f*; **~s** *pl* (orders) ordini *mpl*

instruction book *n* libretto *m* di istruzioni

instructive /ɪnˈstrʌktɪv/ *adj* istruttivo

instructor /ɪnˈstrʌktə(r)/ *n* istruttore, -trice *mf*

instrument /ˈɪnstrʊmənt/ *n* strumento *m*

instrumental /ɪnstrʊˈment(ə)l/ *adj* strumentale; **be ~ in** contribuire a

instrumentalist /ɪnstrʊˈmentəlɪst/ *n* strumentista *mf*

instrument panel *n* quadro *m* degli strumenti

insubordinate /ɪnsəˈbɔːdɪnət/ *adj* insubordinato

insubordination /ɪnsəbɔːdɪˈneɪʃn/ *n* insubordinazione *f*

insubstantial /ɪnsəbˈstænʃəl/ *adj* (unreal) irreale; ‹*evidence*› inconsistente; ‹*flimsy, building*› poco solido; ‹*meal*› poco sostanzioso

insufferable /ɪnˈsʌf(ə)rəbl/ *adj* insopportabile

insufficient /ɪnsəˈfɪʃənt/ *adj* insufficiente

insufficiently /ɪnsəˈfɪʃəntlɪ/ *adv* insufficientemente

insular /ˈɪnsjʊlə(r)/ *adj* fig gretto

insulate /ˈɪnsjʊleɪt/ *vt* isolare

insulating tape /ˈɪnsjʊleɪtɪŋ/ *n* nastro *m* isolante

insulation /ɪnsjʊˈleɪʃn/ *n* isolamento *m*

insulator /ˈɪnsjʊleɪtə(r)/ *n* isolante *m*

insulin /ˈɪnsjʊlɪn/ *n* insulina *f*

insult¹ /ˈɪnsʌlt/ *n* insulto *m*

insult² /ɪnˈsʌlt/ *vt* insultare

insuperable /ɪnˈsuːpərəbl/ *adj* insuperabile

insurable value /ɪnˈʃʊərəbl/ *n* valore *m* assicurabile

insurance /ɪnˈʃʊərəns/ *n* assicurazione *f*

insurance broker *n* broker *mf inv* d'assicurazioni

insurance claim *n* richiesta *f* di indennizzo (*ad assicurazione*)

insurance policy *n* polizza *f* d'assicurazione

insurance premium *n* premio *m* assicurativo

insure /ɪnˈʃʊə(r)/ *vt* assicurare

insurgent /ɪnˈsɜːdʒənt/ *n* rivoltoso, -a *mf*

insurmountable /ɪnsəˈmaʊntəbl/ *adj* insormontabile

insurrection /ɪnsəˈrekʃn/ *n* insurrezione *f*

intact /ɪnˈtækt/ *adj* intatto

intake /ˈɪnteɪk/ *n* immissione *f*; (of food) consumo *m*

intangible /ɪn'tændʒəbl/ *adj* intangibile

integral /'ɪntɪgrəl/ *adj* integrale

integrate /'ɪntɪgreɪt/ **A** *vt* integrare
B *vi* integrarsi

integration /ɪntɪ'greɪʃn/ *n* integrazione *f*

integrity /ɪn'tegrətɪ/ *n* integrità *f*

intellect /'ɪntəlekt/ *n* intelletto *m*

intellectual /ɪntə'lektjʊəl/ *adj & n* intellettuale *mf*

🔑 **intelligence** /ɪn'telɪdʒəns/ *n* intelligenza *f*; Mil informazioni *fpl*

intelligent /ɪn'telɪdʒənt/ *adj* intelligente

intelligently /ɪn'telɪdʒəntlɪ/ *adv* intelligentemente

intelligentsia /ɪntelɪ'dʒentsɪə/ *n* intellighenzia *f*

intelligible /ɪn'telɪdʒəbl/ *adj* intelligibile

intemperate /ɪn'temp(ə)rət/ *adj* ‹*language, person*› intemperante; ‹*weather*› rigido; ‹*attack*› violento

🔑 **intend** /ɪn'tend/ *vt* destinare; (have in mind) aver intenzione di; **be ~ed for** essere destinato a

intended /ɪn'tendɪd/ **A** *adj* ‹*visit, purchase*› programmato; ‹*result*› voluto, desiderato
B *n* **her ~** hum il suo fidanzato; **his ~** hum la sua fidanzata

intense /ɪn'tens/ *adj* intenso; ‹*person*› dai sentimenti intensi

intensely /ɪn'tenslɪ/ *adv* intensamente; (very) estremamente

intensification /ɪntensɪfɪ'keɪʃn/ *n* intensificazione *f*

intensify /ɪn'tensɪfaɪ/ *v* (*pt/pp* **-ied**) **A** *vt* intensificare
B *vi* intensificarsi

intensity /ɪn'tensətɪ/ *n* intensità *f*

intensive /ɪn'tensɪv/ *adj* intensivo; **~ care** terapia *f* intensiva

intensive care, **intensive care unit** *n* [reparto *m*] rianimazione *f*

intensively /ɪn'tensɪvlɪ/ *adv* intensivamente

intent /ɪn'tent/ **A** *adj* intento; **~ on** (absorbed in) preso da; **be ~ on doing something** essere intento a fare qualcosa
B *n* intenzione *f*; **to all ~s and purposes** a tutti gli effetti

🔑 **intention** /ɪn'tenʃn/ *n* intenzione *f*

intentional /ɪn'tenʃənəl/ *adj* intenzionale

intentionally /ɪn'tenʃənəlɪ/ *adv* intenzionalmente

intently /ɪn'tentlɪ/ *adv* attentamente

inter /ɪn'tɜː(r)/ *vt* (*pt/pp* **interred**) fml interrare

interact /ˌɪntər'ækt/ *vi* ‹*two factors, people*› interagire; Comput dialogare

interaction /ɪntər'ækʃn/ *n* cooperazione *f*

interactive /ɪntər'æktɪv/ *adj* interattivo

interactive television *n* televisione *f* interattiva

interactive video *n* video *m* interattivo

interactive whiteboard /ˌɪntəræktɪv'waɪtbɔːd/ *n* lavagna *f* interattiva

interbreed /ɪntə'briːd/ **A** *vt* ibridare
B *vi* incrociarsi

interbreeding /ɪntə'briːdɪŋ/ *n* ibridazione *f*

intercede /ɪntə'siːd/ *vi* intercedere (**on behalf of** a favore di)

intercept /ɪntə'sept/ *vt* intercettare

interchange /'ɪntətʃeɪndʒ/ *n* scambio *m*; Auto raccordo *m* [autostradale]

interchangeable /ɪntə'tʃeɪndʒəbl/ *adj* interscambiabile

intercity /ɪntə'sɪtɪ/ **A** *n* BrE (train) intercity *m inv*
B *adj* intercity

intercom /'ɪntəkɒm/ *n* citofono *m*

interconnecting /ɪntəkə'nektɪŋ/ *adj* ‹*rooms*› comunicante

intercontinental /ɪntəkɒntɪ'nentəl/ *adj* intercontinentale

intercourse /'ɪntəkɔːs/ *n* (sexual) rapporti *mpl* [sessuali]

interdepartmental /ɪntədiːpɑːt'ment(ə)l/ *adj* Univ, Comm interdipartimentale; Pol interministeriale

interdependent /ɪntədɪ'pendənt/ *adj* interdipendente

interdisciplinary /ɪntədɪsɪ'plɪnərɪ/ *adj* interdisciplinare

🔑 **interest** /'ɪntrəst/ **A** *n* interesse *m*; **have an ~ in** Comm essere cointeressato in; **be of ~** essere interessante
B *vt* interessare
C *adj* interessato

interest-bearing *adj* fruttifero

interested /'ɪntrəstɪd/ *adj* interessato

interest-free *adj* senza interessi

interest-free loan *n* prestito *m* senza interessi

🔑 **interesting** /'ɪnt(ə)rəstɪŋ/ *adj* interessante

interest rate *n* tasso *m* di interesse

interface /'ɪntəfeɪs/ **A** *n* Comput fig interfaccia *f*
B *vi* interfacciarsi
C *vt* interfacciare

interfere /ɪntə'fɪə(r)/ *vi* interferire; **~ with** interferire con

interference /ɪntə'fɪərəns/ *n* interferenza *f*

interfering /ˌɪntə'fɪərɪŋ/ *adj* ‹*person*› impiccione

interim /'ɪntərɪm/ **A** *adj* temporaneo; **~ payment** acconto *m*
B *n* **in the ~** nel frattempo

interior /ɪn'tɪərɪə(r)/ **A** *adj* interiore
B *n* interno *m*

interior decorator *n* arredatore, -trice *mf*

interior designer *n* (of colours, fabrics etc) arredatore, -trice *mf*; (of walls, space)

🔑 parola chiave

architetto *m* d'interni
interject /ɪntəˈdʒekt/ *vt* intervenire
interjection /ɪntəˈdʒekʃn/ *n* Gram interiezione *f*; (remark) intervento *m*
interlink /ɪntəˈlɪŋk/ *vt* connettere; **be ~ed with** essere connesso con
interlock /ɪntəˈlɒk/ *vi* ‹*parts*› incastrarsi
interlocking /ˈɪntəlɒkɪŋ/ *adj* a incastro
interloper /ˈɪntələʊpə(r)/ *n* intruso, -a *mf*
interlude /ˈɪntəluːd/ *n* intervallo *m*
intermarry /ɪntəˈmærɪ/ *vi* sposarsi tra parenti; ‹*different groups*› contrarre matrimoni misti
intermediary /ɪntəˈmiːdɪərɪ/ *n* intermediario, -a *mf*
intermediate /ɪntəˈmiːdɪət/ *adj* intermedio
interminable /ɪnˈtɜːmɪnəbl/ *adj* interminabile
intermission /ɪntəˈmɪʃn/ *n* intervallo *m*
intermittent /ɪntəˈmɪtənt/ *adj* intermittente
intermittently /ɪntəˈmɪtəntlɪ/ *adv* a intermittenza
intern /ɪnˈtɜːn/ *vt* internare
internal /ɪnˈtɜːnl/ *adj* interno
internal combustion engine *n* motore *m* a scoppio
internally /ɪnˈtɜːnəlɪ/ *adv* internamente; ‹*deal with*› all'interno
international /ɪntəˈnæʃ(ə)nəl/ **A** *adj* internazionale
B *n* (game) incontro *m* internazionale; (player) competitore, -trice *mf* in gare internazionali
internationally /ɪntəˈnæʃ(ə)nəlɪ/ *adv* internazionalmente; **it applies ~** ha validità internazionale
international money order *n* vaglia *m inv* postale internazionale
International Phonetic Alphabet *n* Alfabeto *m* Fonetico Internazionale
international reply coupon *n* tagliando *m* di risposta internazionale
internee /ˌɪntɜːˈniː/ *n* internato, -a *mf*
Internet /ˈɪntənet/ *n* Internet *f*
Internet access *n* Comput accesso *m* Internet
Internet access provider *n* Comput fornitore *m* di accesso ai servizi Internet
Internet café *n* caffè *m* Internet
Internet kiosk *n* Internet point *m inv*
Internet protocol *n* Comput protocollo *m* Internet
Internet service provider *n* Comput fornitore *m* di servizi Internet
Internet user *n* utente *mf* di Internet
internist /ɪnˈtɜːnɪst/ *n* AmE internista *mf*
internment /ɪnˈtɜːnmənt/ *n* internamento *m*
interplay /ˈɪntəpleɪ/ *n* azione *f* reciproca
interpolate /ɪnˈtɜːpəleɪt/ *vt* interpolare
interpose /ɪntəˈpəʊz/ *vt* (insert) frapporre; interrompere con ‹*comment, remark*›
interpret /ɪnˈtɜːprɪt/ **A** *vt* interpretare
B *vi* fare l'interprete
interpretation /ɪntɜːprɪˈteɪʃn/ *n* interpretazione *f*
interpreter /ɪnˈtɜːprɪtə(r)/ *n* interprete *mf*
interpreting /ɪnˈtɜːprɪtɪŋ/ *n* interpretariato *m*
interrelated /ɪntərɪˈleɪtɪd/ *adj* ‹*facts*› in correlazione
interrogate /ɪnˈterəgeɪt/ *vt* interrogare
interrogation /ɪnterəˈgeɪʃn/ *n* interrogazione *f*; (by police) interrogatorio *m*
interrogative /ɪntəˈrɒgətɪv/ *adj* & *n* ~ **[pronoun]** interrogativo *m*
interrupt /ɪntəˈrʌpt/ *vt* & *vi* interrompere
interruption /ɪntəˈrʌpʃn/ *n* interruzione *f*
intersect /ɪntəˈsekt/ **A** *vi* intersecarsi
B *vt* intersecare
intersection /ɪntəˈsekʃn/ *n* intersezione *f*; (of street) incrocio *m*
interspersed /ɪntəˈspɜːst/ *adj* **~ with** inframmezzato di
interstate /ˈɪntəsteɪt/ AmE **A** *n* superstrada *f* fra stati
B *adj* ‹*commerce, links*› fra stati
intertwine /ɪntəˈtwaɪn/ *vi* attorcigliarsi
interval /ˈɪntəvl/ *n* intervallo *m*; **bright ~s** *pl* schiarite *fpl*
intervene /ɪntəˈviːn/ *vi* intervenire
intervention /ɪntəˈvenʃn/ *n* intervento *m*
interview /ˈɪntəvjuː/ **A** *n* Journ intervista *f*; (for job) colloquio *m* [di lavoro]
B *vt* intervistare
interviewee /ɪntəvjuːˈiː/ *n* (on TV, radio, in survey) intervistato, -a *mf*; (for job) persona *f* sottoposta a un colloquio di lavoro
interviewer /ˈɪntəvjuːə(r)/ *n* intervistatore, -trice *mf*
interwar /ˌɪntəˈwɔː(r)/ *adj* **the ~ years** gli anni tra le due guerre
interweave /ɪntəˈwiːv/ *vt* intrecciare ‹*themes, threads*›; mischiare ‹*rhythms*›
intestinal /ɪnteˈstaɪnəl/ *adj* intestinale
intestine /ɪnˈtestɪn/ *n* intestino *m*
intimacy /ˈɪntɪməsɪ/ *n* intimità *f*
intimate[1] /ˈɪntɪmət/ *adj* intimo; **be ~ with** (sexually) avere relazioni intime con
intimate[2] /ˈɪntɪmeɪt/ *vt* far capire; (imply) suggerire
intimately /ˈɪntɪmətlɪ/ *adv* intimamente
intimidate /ɪnˈtɪmɪdeɪt/ *vt* intimidire
intimidating /ɪnˈtɪmɪdeɪtɪŋ/ *adj* ‹*behaviour, person*› intimidatorio; ‹*prospect*› impressionante
intimidation /ɪntɪmɪˈdeɪʃn/ *n* intimidazione *f*
into /ˈɪntə/, *di fronte a una vocale* /ˈɪntʊ/ *prep* dentro, in; **go ~ the house** andare dentro [casa] *or* in casa; **be ~** infml (like) essere

appassionato di; **I'm not ~ that** questo non mi piace; **7 ~ 21 goes 3** il 7 nel 21 ci sta 3 volte; **translate ~ French** tradurre in francese; **get ~ trouble** mettersi nei guai
intolerable /ɪnˈtɒlərəbl/ *adj* intollerabile
intolerance /ɪnˈtɒlərəns/ *n* intolleranza *f*
intolerant /ɪnˈtɒlərənt/ *adj* intollerante
intonation /ɪntəˈneɪʃn/ *n* intonazione *f*
intone /ɪnˈtəʊn/ *vt* recitare ‹*prayer*›
intoxicated /ɪnˈtɒksɪkeɪtɪd/ *adj* inebriato
intoxicating /ɪnˈtɒksɪkeɪtɪŋ/ *adj* ‹*drink*› alcolico; ‹*smell, sight*› inebriante
intoxication /ɪntɒksɪˈkeɪʃn/ *n* ebbrezza *f*
intractable /ɪnˈtræktəbl/ *adj* intrattabile; ‹*problem*› insolubile
intramural /ɪntrəˈmjʊərəl/ *adj* ‹*studies*› tenuto in sede
intranet /ˈɪntrənet/ *n* Comput intranet *f*
intransigence /ɪnˈtrænzɪdʒəns/ *n* intransigenza *f*
intransigent /ɪnˈtrænzɪdʒənt/ *adj* intransigente
intransitive /ɪnˈtrænzɪtɪv/ *adj* intransitivo
intransitively /ɪnˈtrænzɪtɪvlɪ/ *adv* intransitivamente
intrauterine device /ɪntrəjuːtəraɪndɪˈvaɪs/ *n* Med spirale *f*, dispositivo *m* anticoncezionale intrauterino
intravenous /ɪntrəˈviːnəs/ *adj* endovenoso
intravenous drip *n* flebo[clisi] *f inv*
intravenous drug user *n* tossicomane *mf* che si inietta in vena
intravenously /ɪntrəˈviːnəslɪ/ *adv* per via endovenosa
in-tray *n* vassoio *m* per pratiche e corrispondenza da evadere
intrepid /ɪnˈtrepɪd/ *adj* intrepido
intricacy /ˈɪntrɪkəsɪ/ *n* complessità *f*
intricate /ˈɪntrɪkət/ *adj* complesso
intrigue /ɪnˈtriːg/ **A** *n* intrigo *m*
B *vt* intrigare
C *vi* tramare
intriguing /ɪnˈtriːgɪŋ/ *adj* intrigante
intrinsic /ɪnˈtrɪnsɪk/ *adj* intrinseco
introduce /ɪntrəˈdjuːs/ *vt* presentare; (bring in, insert) introdurre
introduction /ɪntrəˈdʌkʃn/ *n* introduzione *f*; (to person) presentazione *f*; (to book) prefazione *f*
introductory /ɪntrəˈdʌktərɪ/ *adj* introduttivo
introspective /ɪntrəˈspektɪv/ *adj* introspettivo
introvert /ˈɪntrəvɜːt/ *n* introverso, -a *mf*
introverted /ˈɪntrəvɜːtɪd/ *adj* introverso
intrude /ɪnˈtruːd/ *vi* intromettersi
intruder /ɪnˈtruːdə(r)/ *n* intruso, -a *mf*
intrusion /ɪnˈtruːʒn/ *n* intrusione *f*

parola chiave

intrusive /ɪnˈtruːsɪv/ *adj* ‹*camera, question*› indiscreto
intuition /ɪntjʊˈɪʃn/ *n* intuito *m*
intuitive /ɪnˈtjuːɪtɪv/ *adj* intuitivo
intuitively /ɪnˈtjuːɪtɪvlɪ/ *adv* intuitivamente
inundate /ˈɪnəndeɪt/ *vt* fig inondare (**with** di)
inure /ɪnˈjʊə(r)/ *vt* **become ~d to something** assuefarsi a qualcosa
invade /ɪnˈveɪd/ *vt* invadere
invader /ɪnˈveɪdə(r)/ *n* invasore *m*
invalid¹ /ˈɪnvəlɪd/ *n* invalido, -a *mf*
invalid² /ɪnˈvælɪd/ *adj* non valido
invalidate /ɪnˈvælɪdeɪt/ *vt* invalidare
invaluable /ɪnˈvæljʊ(ə)bl/ *adj* prezioso; (priceless) inestimabile
invariable /ɪnˈveərɪəbl/ *adj* invariabile
invariably /ɪnˈveərɪəblɪ/ *adv* invariabilmente
invasion /ɪnˈveɪʒn/ *n* invasione *f*
invective /ɪnˈvektɪv/ *n* invettiva *f*
invent /ɪnˈvent/ *vt* inventare
invention /ɪnˈvenʃn/ *n* invenzione *f*
inventive /ɪnˈventɪv/ *adj* inventivo
inventor /ɪnˈventə(r)/ *n* inventore, -trice *mf*
inventory /ˈɪnvəntrɪ/ *n* inventario *m*
inverse /ɪnˈvɜːs/ **A** *adj* inverso
B *n* inverso *m*
inversely /ɪnˈvɜːslɪ/ *adv* inversamente
invert /ɪnˈvɜːt/ *vt* invertire; **in ~ed commas** tra virgolette
invertebrate /ɪnˈvɜːtɪbrət/ *adj & n* invertebrato *m*
invest /ɪnˈvest/ **A** *vt* investire
B *vi* fare investimenti; **~ in** infml (buy) comprarsi
investigate /ɪnˈvestɪgeɪt/ *vt* investigare
investigation /ɪnvestɪˈgeɪʃn/ *n* investigazione *f*
investigative journalism /ɪnˈvestɪgətɪv/ *n* dietrologia *f*
investiture /ɪnˈvestɪtjə(r)/ *n* investitura *f*
investment /ɪnˈvestmənt/ *n* investimento *m*
investment capital *n* capitale *m* di investimento
investment income *n* reddito *m* di investimento
investment manager *n* responsabile *mf* della gestione del portafoglio fondi di investimento
investment trust *n* fondo *m* comune di investimento
investor /ɪnˈvestə(r)/ *n* investitore, -trice *mf*
inveterate /ɪnˈvetərət/ *adj* inveterato
invidious /ɪnˈvɪdɪəs/ *adj* ingiusto; ‹*position*› antipatico
invigilate /ɪnˈvɪdʒɪleɪt/ *vi* Sch sorvegliare lo svolgimento di un esame
invigilator /ɪnˈvɪdʒɪleɪtə(r)/ *n persona (f) che sorveglia lo svolgimento di un esame*
invigorate /ɪnˈvɪgəreɪt/ *vt* rinvigorire

invigorating /ɪnˈvɪɡəreɪtɪŋ/ *adj* tonificante

invincible /ɪnˈvɪnsəbl/ *adj* invincibile

inviolable /ɪnˈvaɪələbl/ *adj* inviolabile

invisible /ɪnˈvɪzəbl/ *adj* invisibile

invisible ink *n* inchiostro *m* simpatico

invitation /ɪnvɪˈteɪʃn/ *n* invito *m*

invitation card *n* biglietto *m* d'invito

invite /ɪnˈvaɪt/ *vt* invitare; (attract) attirare

■ **invite in** *vt* invitare a entrare

■ **invite round** *vt* invitare a casa

inviting /ɪnˈvaɪtɪŋ/ *adj* invitante

in vitro fertilization /ɪnviːtrəʊfɜːtɪlaɪˈzeɪʃn/ *n* fecondazione *f* in vitro

invoice /ˈɪnvɔɪs/ **A** *n* fattura *f*
B *vt* ~ **somebody** emettere una fattura a qualcuno

invoke /ɪnˈvəʊk/ *vt* invocare

involuntarily /ɪnˈvɒlʌntərɪlɪ/ *adv* involontariamente

involuntary /ɪnˈvɒləntrɪ/ *adj* involontario

involve /ɪnˈvɒlv/ *vt* comportare; (affect, include) coinvolgere; (entail) implicare; **get ~d with somebody** legarsi a qualcuno; (romantically) legarsi sentimentalmente a qualcuno

involved /ɪnˈvɒlvd/ *adj* complesso

involvement /ɪnˈvɒlvmənt/ *n* coinvolgimento *m*

invulnerable /ɪnˈvʌln(ə)rəbl/ *adj* invulnerabile; ‹*position*› inattaccabile

inward /ˈɪnwəd/ **A** *adj* interno; ‹*thoughts etc*› interiore
B *adv* **inwards**

inward investment *n* Comm investimento *m* di capitali stranieri

inward-looking /ˈɪnwədlʊkɪŋ/ *adj* ‹*person*› egocentrico; ‹*society, policy*› chiuso

inwardly /ˈɪnwədlɪ/ *adv* interiormente

inwards /ˈɪnwədz/ *adv* verso l'interno

in-your-face *adj* infml aggressivo

iodine /ˈaɪədiːn/ *n* iodio *m*

Ionian Sea /aɪəʊnɪən/ *n* mar *m* Ionio

iota /aɪˈəʊtə/ *n* briciolo *m*

IOU *abbr* (**I owe you**) pagherò *m*

IPA *n abbr* (**International Phonetic Alphabet**) AFI *m*

IQ *abbr* (**intelligence quotient**) Q.I. *m*

IRA *abbr* (**Irish Republican Army**) I.R.A. *f*

Iran /ɪˈrɑːn/ *n* Iran *m*

Iranian /ɪˈreɪnɪən/ *adj & n* iraniano, -a *mf*

Iraq /ɪˈrɑːk/ *n* Iraq *m*

Iraqi /ɪˈrɑːkɪ/ *adj & n* iracheno, -a *mf*

irascible /ɪˈræsəbl/ *adj* irascibile

irate /aɪˈreɪt/ *adj* adirato

Ireland /ˈaɪələnd/ *n* Irlanda *f*

iris /ˈaɪrɪs/ *n* Anat iride *f*; Bot iris *f inv*

Irish /ˈaɪrɪʃ/ **A** *adj* irlandese
B *n* **the** ~ *pl* gli irlandesi

Irishman /ˈaɪrɪʃmən/ *n* irlandese *m*

Irish Republic *n* Repubblica *f* d'Irlanda

Irish sea *n* mare *m* d'Irlanda

Irishwoman /ˈaɪrɪʃwʊmən/ *n* irlandese *f*

irk /ɜːk/ *vt* infastidire

irksome /ˈɜːksəm/ *adj* fastidioso

iron /ˈaɪən/ **A** *adj* di ferro
B *n* ferro *m*; (appliance) ferro *m* [da stiro]
C *vt & vi* stirare

■ **iron out** *vt* eliminare stirando; fig appianare

Iron Curtain *n* cortina *f* di ferro

iron fist *n* fig pugno *m* di ferro

ironic /aɪˈrɒnɪk/, **ironical** /aɪˈrɒnɪkl/ *adj* ironico

ironing /ˈaɪənɪŋ/ *n* stirare *m*; (articles) roba *f* da stirare; **do the ~** stirare

ironing board *n* asse *f* da stiro

iron lung *n* polmone *m* d'acciaio

ironmonger /ˈaɪənmʌŋɡə(r)/ *n* **~'s [shop]** negozio *m* di ferramenta

irony /ˈaɪərənɪ/ *n* ironia *f*

irradiate /ɪˈreɪdɪeɪt/ *vt* irradiare

irrational /ɪˈræʃənl/ *adj* irrazionale

irreconcilable /ɪˈrekənsaɪləbl/ *adj* irreconciliabile

irrecoverable /ɪrɪˈkʌv(ə)rəbl/ *adj* ‹*debt, object*› irrecuperabile; ‹*loss*› irreparabile

irredeemable /ɪrɪˈdiːməbl/ *adj* Fin ‹*shares, loan*› irredimibile; ‹*loss*› irreparabile; Relig ‹*sinner*› che non è redimibile

irrefutable /ɪrɪˈfjuːtəbl/ *adj* irrefutabile

irregular /ɪˈreɡʊlə(r)/ *adj* irregolare

irregularity /ɪreɡjʊˈlærətɪ/ *n* irregolarità *f*

irregularly /ɪˈreɡjʊləlɪ/ *adv* in modo irregolare

irrelevant /ɪˈreləvənt/ *adj* non pertinente

irreligious /ˌɪrɪˈlɪdʒəs/ *adj* irreligioso

irreparable /ɪˈrepərəbl/ *adj* irreparabile

irreparably /ɪˈrep(ə)rəblɪ/ *adv* irreparabilmente

irreplaceable /ɪrɪˈpleɪsəbl/ *adj* insostituibile

irrepressible /ɪrɪˈpresəbl/ *adj* irrefrenabile; ‹*person*› incontenibile

irreproachable /ɪrɪˈprəʊtʃəbl/ *adj* irreprensibile

irresistible /ɪrɪˈzɪstəbl/ *adj* irresistibile

irresolute /ɪˈrezəluːt/ *adj* irresoluto

irrespective /ɪrɪˈspektɪv/ *adj* ~ **of** senza riguardo per

irresponsible /ɪrɪˈspɒnsəbl/ *adj* irresponsabile

irresponsibly /ɪrɪˈspɒnsəblɪ/ *adv* irresponsabilmente

irretrievable /ɪrɪˈtriːvəbl/ *adj* ‹*loss, harm*› irreparabile

irreverence /ɪˈrevərəns/ *n* irriverenza *f*

irreverent /ɪˈrevərənt/ *adj* irriverente

irreverently /ɪˈrevərəntlɪ/ *adv* in modo irriverente

irreversible /ɪrɪˈvɜːsəbl/ *adj* irreversibile

irreversibly /ɪrɪ'vɜːsɪblɪ/ *adv* irreversibilmente

irrevocable /ɪ'revəkəbl/ *adj* irrevocabile

irrevocably /ɪ'revəkəblɪ/ *adv* irrevocabilmente

irrigate /'ɪrɪgeɪt/ *vt* irrigare

irrigation /ɪrɪ'geɪʃn/ *n* irrigazione *f*

irritability /ɪrɪtə'bɪlətɪ/ *n* irritabilità *f*

irritable /'ɪrɪtəbl/ *adj* irritabile

irritable bowel syndrome *n* sindrome *f* da colon irritabile

irritant /'ɪrɪtənt/ *n* sostanza *f* irritante; fig (person) persona *f* irritante

irritate /'ɪrɪteɪt/ *vt* irritare

irritated /'ɪrɪteɪtɪd/ *adj* irritato, stizzito

irritating /'ɪrɪteɪtɪŋ/ *adj* irritante

irritation /ɪrɪ'teɪʃn/ *n* irritazione *f*

IRS *n abbr* AmE (**Internal Revenue Service**) fisco *m*

is /ɪz/ ▶ **be**

Islam /'ɪzlɑːm/ *n* Islam *m*

Islamic /ɪz'læmɪk/ *adj* islamico

Islamist /'ɪzləmɪst/ *n* (fundamentalist) estremista *mf* islamico, (-a); (scholar) islamista *mf*

⚷ **island** /'aɪlənd/ *n* isola *f*; (in road) isola *f* spartitraffico

islander /'aɪləndə(r)/ *n* isolano, -a *mf*

island hopping /'aɪləndhɒpɪŋ/ *n* **go ~** andare di isola in isola

isle /aɪl/ *n* literary isola *f*

Isle of Man *n* l'isola *f* di Man

isms /'ɪz(ə)mz/ *npl* derog ismi *mpl*

isobar /'aɪsəbɑː(r)/ *n* isobara *f*

isolate /'aɪsəleɪt/ *vt* isolare

isolated /'aɪsəleɪtɪd/ *adj* isolato

isolation /aɪsə'leɪʃn/ *n* isolamento *m*

isosceles /aɪ'sɒsəliːz/ *adj* isoscele

ISP *n abbr* (**Internet service provider**) Comput ISP *m*

Israel /'ɪzreɪl/ *n* Israele *m*

Israeli /ɪz'reɪlɪ/ *adj & n* israeliano, -a *mf*

⚷ **issue** /'ɪʃuː/ **A** *n* (outcome) risultato *m*; (of magazine) numero *m*; (of stamps etc) emissione *f*; (offspring) figli *mpl*; (matter, question) questione *f*; **at ~** in questione; **take ~ with somebody** prendere posizione contro qualcuno
B *vt* distribuire ‹*supplies*›; rilasciare ‹*passport*›; emettere ‹*stamps, order*›; pubblicare ‹*book*›; **be ~d with something** ricevere qualcosa
C *vi* **~ from** uscire da

isthmus /'ɪsməs/ *n* (*pl* **-muses**) istmo *m*

⚷ **it** /ɪt/ *pron* (direct object) lo *m*, la *f*; (indirect object) gli *m*, le *f*; **it's broken** è rotto/rotta; **will it be enough?** basterà?; **it's hot** fa caldo; **it's raining** piove; **it's me** sono io; **who is it?** chi è?; **it's two o'clock** sono le due; **I doubt it** ne dubito; **take it with you** prendilo con te; **give it a wipe** dagli una pulita

IT *n abbr* (**information technology**) informatica *f*

Italian /ɪ'tæljən/ *adj & n* italiano, -a *mf*; (language) italiano *m*

Italian-American *adj & n* italoamericano, -a *mf*

italic /ɪ'tælɪk/ *adj* in corsivo

italics /ɪ'tælɪks/ *npl* corsivo *msg*; **in ~** in corsivo

Italy /'ɪtəlɪ/ *n* Italia *f*

itch /ɪtʃ/ **A** *n* prurito *m*
B *vi* avere prurito, prudere; **be ~ing to** infml avere una voglia matta di

itching powder /'ɪtʃɪŋ/ *n* polverina *f* che dà prurito

itchy /'ɪtʃɪ/ *adj* che prude; **my foot is ~** ho prurito al piede; **have ~ feet** fig avere la terra che scotta sotto i piedi

⚷ **item** /'aɪtəm/ *n* articolo *m*; (on agenda, programme) punto *m*; (on invoice) voce *f*; **~ [of news]** notizia *f*

itemize /'aɪtəmaɪz/ *vt* dettagliare ‹*bill*›

itinerant /aɪ'tɪnərənt/ *adj* itinerante

itinerary /aɪ'tɪnərərɪ/ *n* itinerario *m*

ITN *n abbr* BrE (**independent television**) *rete (f) televisiva britannica*

⚷ **its** /ɪts/ *poss pron* suo *m*, sua *f*, suoi *mpl*, sue *fpl*; **~ mother/cage** sua madre/la sua gabbia

it's = it is, it has

⚷ **itself** /ɪt'self/ *pron* (reflexive) si; (emphatic) stesso, -a; **the baby looked at ~ in the mirror** il bambino si è guardato nello specchio; **by ~** da solo; **the machine in ~ is simple** la macchina di per sé è semplice

ITV *abbr* (**Independent Television**) *stazione (f) televisiva privata*

IUD *n abbr* (**intrauterine device**) spirale *f*

IVF *n abbr* (**in vitro fertilization**) FIV *f*

ivory /'aɪvərɪ/ **A** *n* avorio *m*
B *attrib* d'avorio

Ivory Coast *n* Costa *f* d'Avorio

ivory tower *n* fig torre *f* d'avorio

ivy /'aɪvɪ/ *n* edera *f*

⚷ parola chiave

Jj

j, J /dʒeɪ/ *n* (letter) j, J *f inv*
jab /dʒæb/ **A** *n* colpo *m* secco; infml (injection) puntura *f*
B *vt* (*pt/pp* **jabbed**) punzecchiare
jabber /ˈdʒæbə(r)/ *vi* borbottare
jack /dʒæk/ *n* Auto cric *m inv*; Teleph jack *m inv*; (in cards) fante *m*, jack *m inv*
■ **jack in** *vt* sl piantare ‹*job*›
■ **jack up** *vt* Auto sollevare [con il cric]; infml aumentare di molto ‹*salary etc*›
jackal /ˈdʒæk(ə)l/ *n* sciacallo *m*
jackboot /ˈdʒækbuːt/ *n* stivale *m* militare
jackdaw /ˈdʒækdɔː/ *n* taccola *f*
jacket /ˈdʒækɪt/ *n* giacca *f*; (of book) sopraccopertina *f*
jacket potato *n patata (f) cotta al forno con la buccia*
jack-in-the-box *n scatola (f) a sorpresa contenente un pupazzo a molla*
jackknife /ˈdʒæknaɪf/ **A** *n* coltello *m* a serramanico
B *vi sbandare finendo di traverso rispetto al rimorchio*
jackpot /ˈdʒækpɒt/ *n* premio *m* (*di una lotteria*); **win the ~** vincere alla lotteria; **hit the ~** fig fare un colpo grosso
jackrabbit /ˈdʒækræbɪt/ *n* lepre *f* americana
jade /dʒeɪd/ **A** *n* giada *f*
B *attrib* di giada
jaded /ˈdʒeɪdɪd/ *adj* spossato
jagged /ˈdʒægɪd/ *adj* dentellato
jail /dʒeɪl/ = **gaol**
jailbird *n* avanzo *m* di galera
jailbreak *n* evasione *f*
jail sentence *n* condanna *f* al carcere
jalopy /dʒəˈlɒpɪ/ *n* infml vecchia carretta *f*
jam¹ /dʒæm/ *n* marmellata *f*
jam² **A** *n* Auto ingorgo *m*; infml (difficulty) guaio *m*
B *vt* (*pt/pp* **jammed**) (cram) pigiare; disturbare ‹*broadcast*›; inceppare ‹*mechanism, drawer etc.*›; **be ~med** ‹*roads*› essere congestionato
C *vi* ‹*mechanism*› incepparsi; ‹*window, drawer*› incastrarsi
■ **jam on**: *vt* **~ on the brakes** inchiodare
Jamaica /dʒəˈmeɪkə/ *n* Giamaica *f*
Jamaican /dʒəˈmeɪkən/ *adj & n* giamaicano, -a *mf*
jam jar *n* barattolo *m* per la marmellata
jam-packed *adj* infml pieno zeppo
jam pot *n* vasetto *m* per la marmellata
jangle /ˈdʒæŋgl/ **A** *vt* far squillare
B *vi* squillare
janitor /ˈdʒænɪtə(r)/ *n* (caretaker) custode *m*; (in school) bidello, -a *mf*
⚷ **January** /ˈdʒænjʊərɪ/ *n* gennaio *m*
Japan /dʒəˈpæn/ *n* Giappone *m*
⚷ **Japanese** /dʒæpəˈniːz/ *adj & n* giapponese *mf*; (language) giapponese *m*
jar¹ /dʒɑː(r)/ *n* (glass) barattolo *m*
jar² *vi* (*pt/pp* **jarred**) ‹*sound*› stridere
jargon /ˈdʒɑːgən/ *n* gergo *m*
jarring /ˈdʒɑːrɪŋ/ *adj* stridente
jasmine /ˈdʒæsmɪn/ *n* gelsomino *m*
jaundice /ˈdʒɔːndɪs/ *n* itterizia *f*
jaundiced /ˈdʒɔːndɪst/ *adj* fig inacidito
jaunt /dʒɔːnt/ *n* gita *f*
jaunty /ˈdʒɔːntɪ/ *adj* (**-ier**, **-iest**) sbarazzino
javelin /ˈdʒævlɪn/ *n* giavellotto *m*
jaw /dʒɔː/ **A** *n* mascella *f*; (bone) mandibola *f*
B *vi* infml ciarlare
jawbone /ˈdʒɔːbəʊn/ *n* Anat osso *m* mascellare
jawline *n* mento *m*
jay /dʒeɪ/ *n* ghiandaia *f*
jaywalker /ˈdʒeɪwɔːkə(r)/ *n* pedone *m* indisciplinato
jazz /dʒæz/ *n* jazz *m*
■ **jazz up** *vt* ravvivare
jazz band *n* complesso *m* di jazz
jazzy /ˈdʒæzɪ/ *adj* vistoso
jealous /ˈdʒeləs/ *adj* geloso
jealously /ˈdʒeləslɪ/ *adv* gelosamente
jealousy /ˈdʒeləsɪ/ *n* gelosia *f*
jeans /dʒiːnz/ *npl* [blue] jeans *mpl*
jeep /dʒiːp/ *n* jeep *f inv*
jeer /dʒɪə(r)/ **A** *n* scherno *m*
B *vi* schernire; **~ at** prendersi gioco di
C *vt* (boo) fischiare
jeering /ˈdʒɪərɪŋ/ *n* fischi *mpl*
jell /dʒel/ *vi* concretarsi
jellied /ˈdʒelɪd/ *adj* ‹*eels*› in gelatina
jello /ˈdʒeləʊ/ *n* (*also* **Jell-O**®) AmE *dolce (m) di gelatina di frutta*
jelly /ˈdʒelɪ/ *n* gelatina *f*
jelly baby *n caramella (f) gommosa a forma di pupazzetto*
jelly bean *n caramella (f) di gelatina di frutta*
jellyfish *n* medusa *f*

jemmy /'dʒemɪ/ *n* piede *m* di porco
jeopardize /'dʒepədaɪz/ *vt* mettere in pericolo
jeopardy /'dʒepədɪ/ *n* **in ~** in pericolo
jerk /dʒɜːk/ **A** *n* scatto *m*, scossa *f*
B *vt* scattare
C *vi* sobbalzare; ‹*limb, muscle*› muoversi a scatti
jerkily /'dʒɜːkɪlɪ/ *adv* a scatti
jerkin /'dʒɜːkɪn/ *n* gilè *m*
jerky /'dʒɜːkɪ/ *adj* traballante
jerry-built /'dʒerɪbɪlt/ *adj* derog costruito alla bell'e meglio
jersey /'dʒɜːzɪ/ *n* maglia *f*; Sport maglietta *f*; (fabric) jersey *m*
Jerusalem /dʒə'ruːsələm/ *n* Gerusalemme *f*
jest /dʒest/ **A** *n* scherzo *m*; **in ~** per scherzo
B *vi* scherzare
jester /'dʒestə(r)/ *n* buffone *m*
Jesuit /'dʒezjʊɪt/ **A** *n* gesuita *m*
B *adj* gesuitico
Jesus /'dʒiːzəs/ *n* Gesù *m*
jet¹ /dʒet/ *n* (stone) giaietto *m*
jet² *n* (of water) getto *m*; (nozzle) becco *m*; (plane) aviogetto *m*, jet *m inv*
jet-black *adj* nero ebano
jet engine *n* motore *m* a reazione
jet fighter *n* caccia *m inv* a reazione
jetfoil *n* aliscafo *m*
jet lag *n* scombussolamento *m* da fuso orario; jet lag *m inv*
jet-lagged *adj* **be ~** soffrire di jet lag
jet-propelled *adj* a reazione
jet propulsion *n* propulsione *f* a getto
jet setter *n* **be a ~** appartenere al jet set
jet ski *n* moto *f* d'acqua
jet-skier *n* persona *m* che fa moto d'acqua
jet-skiing *n* moto *f* d'acqua
jettison /'dʒetɪsn/ *vt* gettare a mare; fig abbandonare
jetty /'dʒetɪ/ *n* molo *m*
Jew /dʒuː/ *n* ebreo *m*
jewel /'dʒuːəl/ *n* gioiello *m*
jewelled /'dʒuːəld/ *adj* ornato di pietre preziose
jeweller /'dʒuːələ(r)/ *n* gioielliere *m*; **~'s [shop]** gioielleria *f*
jewellery /'dʒuːəlrɪ/ *n* gioielli *mpl*
Jewess /'dʒuːɪs/ *n* ebrea *f*
Jewish /'dʒjuːɪʃ/ *adj* ebreo
Jew's harp *n* Mus scacciapensieri *m inv*
jib /dʒɪb/ *vi* (*pt/pp* **jibbed**) fig mostrarsi riluttante (**at** a)
jibe /dʒaɪb/ *n* ▶ **gibe**
jiffy /'dʒɪfɪ/ *n* infml **in a ~** in un batter d'occhio
Jiffy bag® *n* busta *f* imbottita

jig /dʒɪg/ *n* Mus giga *f* (*danza popolare*)
jiggle /'dʒɪg(ə)l/ *vt* scuotere
jigsaw /'dʒɪgsɔː/ *n* **~ [puzzle]** puzzle *m inv*
jilt /dʒɪlt/ *vt* piantare
jingle /'dʒɪŋgl/ **A** *n* (rhyme) canzoncina *f* pubblicitaria
B *vi* tintinnare
C *vt* far tintinnare
jingoist /'dʒɪŋgəʊɪst/ *n* Pol sciovinista *mf*
jingoistic /dʒɪŋgəʊ'ɪstɪk/ *adj* Pol sciovinistico
jinx /dʒɪŋks/ *n* infml (person) iettatore, -trice *mf*; **it's got a ~ on it** è iellato
jinxed /dʒɪŋkst/ *adj* **be ~** essere iellato
jitters /'dʒɪtəz/ *npl* infml **have the ~** aver una gran fifa
jittery /'dʒɪtərɪ/ *adj* infml in preda alla fifa
jive /dʒaɪv/ *n* AmE infml (talk) storie *fpl*
Jnr *abbr* (**junior**) junior (jr)
✎ **job** /dʒɒb/ *n* lavoro *m*; **this is going to be quite a ~** infml [questa] non sarà un'impresa facile; **it's a good ~ that ...** meno male che ...
jobcentre *n* ufficio *m* statale di collocamento
job creation scheme *n* BrE programma *m* di creazione di posti di lavoro
job description *n* mansionario *m*
job-hunting *n* ricerca *f* impiego
jobless /'dʒɒblɪs/ *adj* senza lavoro
job lot *n* (at auction) *insieme* (*m*) *di oggetti disparati*
job market *n* mercato *m* del lavoro
job satisfaction *n* soddisfazione *f* nel lavoro
job security *n* sicurezza *f* di impiego
job seeker *n* persona *f* che cerca lavoro
job seeker's allowance *n* BrE indennità *f* di disoccupazione
job-share **A** *n* (position) posto *m* condiviso
B *attrib* ‹*scheme*› di condivisione del posto di lavoro
job-sharing /-'ʃeərɪŋ/ *n* job sharing *m inv*
jockey /'dʒɒkɪ/ *n* fantino *m*
jockey shorts *npl* boxer *mpl*
jockstrap *n* sospensorio *m*
jocular /'dʒɒkjʊlə(r)/ *adj* scherzoso
jocularly /'dʒɒkjʊləlɪ/ *adv* scherzosamente
jodhpurs /'dʒɒdpəz/ *npl* calzoni *mpl* alla cavallerizza
Joe Bloggs /dʒəʊ'blɒgz/ *n* l'uomo qualunque
jog /'dʒɒg/ **A** *n* colpetto *m*; **at a ~** in un balzo; Sport **go for a ~** andare a fare jogging
B *vt* (*pt/pp* **jogged**) (hit) urtare; **~ sb's memory** far ritornare in mente a qualcuno
C *vi* Sport fare jogging
■ **jog along** *vi* fig tirare avanti
jogger /'dʒɒgə(r)/ *n* persona *f* che fa jogging
jogging /'dʒɒgɪŋ/ *n* jogging *m*
john /dʒɒn/ *n* AmE infml (toilet) gabinetto *m*

✎ parola chiave

John Bull *n* il tipico inglese

John Doe *n* AmE uomo *m* non identificato

join /dʒɔɪn/ **A** *n* giuntura *f*
B *vt* raggiungere, unire; raggiungere ‹*person*›; (become member of) iscriversi a; entrare in ‹*firm*›
C *vi* ‹*roads*› congiungersi
▪ **join in** *vi* partecipare
▪ **join up** **A** *vi* Mil arruolarsi
B *vt* unire
▪ **join up with** *vt* (meet) raggiungere ‹*friends*›; congiungersi a ‹*road; river*›

joiner /ˈdʒɔɪnə(r)/ *n* falegname *m*

joint /dʒɔɪnt/ **A** *adj* comune
B *n* articolazione *f*; (in wood, brickwork) giuntura *f*; Culin arrosto *m*; infml (bar) bettola *f*; sl (drug) spinello *m*

joint account *n* conto *m* [corrente] comune

joint agreement *n* accordo *m* collettivo

jointed /ˈdʒɔɪntɪd/ *adj* Culin ‹*chicken*› tagliato a pezzi; ‹*doll, puppet*› snodabile; ‹*rod, pole*› smontabile

joint effort *n* collaborazione *f*

joint honours *npl* BrE Univ *laurea (f) in due discipline*

jointly /ˈdʒɔɪntlɪ/ *adv* unitamente

joint owner *n* comproprietario, -a *mf*

joint venture *n* joint venture *f inv*

joist /dʒɔɪst/ *n* travetto *m*

joke /dʒəʊk/ **A** *n* (trick) scherzo *m*; (funny story) barzelletta *f*
B *vi* scherzare

joker /ˈdʒəʊkə(r)/ *n* burlone, -a *mf*; (in cards) jolly *m inv*

joking /ˈdʒəʊkɪŋ/ *n* ~ **apart** scherzi a parte

jokingly /ˈdʒəʊkɪŋlɪ/ *adv* per scherzo

jollity /ˈdʒɒlətɪ/ *n* allegria *f*

jolly /ˈdʒɒlɪ/ **A** *adj* (**-ier**, **-iest**) allegro
B *adv* infml molto

Jolly Roger /ˈrɒdʒə(r)/ *n* bandiera *f* dei pirati

jolt /dʒəʊlt/ **A** *n* scossa *f*, sobbalzo *m*
B *vt* far sobbalzare
C *vi* sobbalzare

Jordan /ˈdʒɔːdn/ *n* Giordania *f*; (river) Giordano *m*

Jordanian /dʒɔːˈdeɪnɪən/ *adj & n* giordano, -a *mf*

joss stick /ˈdʒɒs/ *n* bastoncino *m* d'incenso

jostle /ˈdʒɒsl/ *vt* spingere

jot /dʒɒt/ *n* nulla *f*
▪ **jot down** *vt* (*pt/pp* **jotted**) annotare

jotter /ˈdʒɒtə(r)/ *n* taccuino *m*; (with a spine) quaderno *m*

jottings /ˈdʒɒtɪŋz/ *npl* annotazioni *fpl*

journal /ˈdʒɜːnl/ *n* giornale *m*; (diary) diario *m*

journalese /dʒɜːnəˈliːz/ *n* gergo *m* giornalistico

journalism /ˈdʒɜːnəlɪzm/ *n* giornalismo *m*

journalist /ˈdʒɜːnəlɪst/ *n* giornalista *mf*

journey /ˈdʒɜːnɪ/ **A** *n* viaggio *m*
B *vi* viaggiare

jovial /ˈdʒəʊvɪəl/ *adj* gioviale

jowl /dʒaʊl/ *n* (jaw) mascella *f*; (fleshy fold) guancia *f*; **cheek by ~ with somebody** fianco a fianco con qualcuno

joy /dʒɔɪ/ *n* gioia *f*

joyful /ˈdʒɔɪfʊl/ *adj* gioioso

joyfully /ˈdʒɔɪfʊlɪ/ *adv* con gioia

joyless /ˈdʒɔɪlɪs/ *adj* ‹*occasion*› triste; ‹*marriage*› infelice

joypad *n* Comput joypad *m inv*

joyride *n* infml *giro (m) con una macchina rubata*

joyrider *n* infml *persona (f) che ruba una macchina per andare a fare un giro*

joyriding /ˈdʒɔɪraɪdɪŋ/ *n* giri *mpl* su una macchina rubata

joystick *n* Comput joystick *m inv*

JP *n abbr* BrE (**Justice of the Peace**) giudice *m* di pace

Jr *abbr* (**junior**)

jubilant /ˈdʒuːbɪlənt/ *adj* giubilante

jubilation /dʒuːbɪˈleɪʃn/ *n* giubilo *m*

jubilee /ˈdʒuːbɪliː/ *n* giubileo *m*

Judaism /ˈdʒuːdeɪɪzm/ *n* giudaismo *m*

judder /ˈdʒʌdə(r)/ *vi* vibrare violentemente

judge /dʒʌdʒ/ **A** *n* giudice *m*
B *vt* giudicare; (estimate) valutare; (consider) ritenere
C *vi* giudicare (**by** da)

judgement, **judgment** /ˈdʒʌdʒmənt/ *n* giudizio *m*; Jur sentenza *f*

judicial /dʒuːˈdɪʃl/ *adj* giudiziario

judiciary /dʒuːˈdɪʃərɪ/ *n* magistratura *f*

judicious /dʒuːˈdɪʃəs/ *adj* giudizioso

judo /ˈdʒuːdəʊ/ *n* judo *m*

jug /dʒʌg/ *n* brocca *f*; (small) bricco *m*

juggernaut /ˈdʒʌgənɔːt/ *n* infml grosso autotreno *m*

juggle /ˈdʒʌgl/ *vi* fare giochi di destrezza

juggler /ˈdʒʌglə(r)/ *n* giocoliere, -a *mf*

jugular /ˈdʒʌgjʊlə(r)/ *n* giugulare *f*; **go straight for the ~** fig colpire nel punto debole

juice /dʒuːs/ *n* succo *m*; ~ **extractor** *n* spremiagrumi *m inv* elettrico

juicy /ˈdʒuːsɪ/ *adj* (**-ier**, **-iest**) succoso; infml ‹*story*› piccante

ju-jitsu /dʒjuːˈdʒɪtsuː/ *n* jujitsu *m*

jukebox /ˈdʒuːkbɒks/ *n* juke-box *m inv*

July /dʒʊˈlaɪ/ *n* luglio *m*

jumble /ˈdʒʌmbl/ **A** *n* accozzaglia *f*
B *vt* ~ **[up]** mischiare

jumble sale *n* vendita *f* di beneficenza

jumbo /ˈdʒʌmbəʊ/ *n* ~ **[jet]** jumbo jet *m inv*

jump /dʒʌmp/ **A** *n* salto *m*; (in prices) balzo *m*; (in horse racing) ostacolo *m*
B *vi* saltare; (with fright) sussultare; ‹*prices*›

salire rapidamente; ~ **to conclusions** saltare alle conclusioni
C *vt* saltare; ~ **the gun** fig precipitarsi; ~ **the queue** non rispettare la fila
▪ **jump at** *vt* fig accettare con entusiasmo ‹*offer*›
▪ **jump back** *vi* fare un salto indietro
▪ **jump down**: *vt* ~ **down sb's throat** saltare addosso a qualcuno
▪ **jump in** *vi* (to vehicle) saltar su
▪ **jump on** *vt* saltare su ‹*bus, train, bike, horse*›; (attack) aggredire ‹*somebody*›
▪ **jump out** *vi* saltare fuori; ~ **out of something** saltare giù da qualcosa ‹*window, train, bed*›
▪ **jump up** *vi* rizzarsi in piedi
jumped-up /dʒʌmpt'ʌp/ *adj* montato
jumper /'dʒʌmpə(r)/ *n* (sweater) golf *m inv*
jump jet *n* aeroplano *m* a decollo e atterraggio verticali
jump leads *npl* cavi *mpl* per batteria
jump-start *vt far partire con i cavi da batteria*

j

jumpsuit *n* tuta *f*
jumpy /'dʒʌmpɪ/ *adj* nervoso
junction /'dʒʌŋkʃn/ *n* (of roads) incrocio *m*; Rail nodo *m* ferroviario
juncture /'dʒʌŋktʃə(r)/ *n* **at this** ~ a questo punto
✔ **June** /dʒu:n/ *n* giugno *m*
Jungian /'jʊŋɪən/ *adj* junghiano
jungle /'dʒʌŋgl/ *n* giungla *f*
junior /'dʒu:nɪə(r)/ **A** *adj* giovane; (in rank) subalterno; Sport junior *inv*
B *n* **the** ~**s** *pl* Sch i più giovani
junior doctor *n* assistente *mf* ospedaliero, -a
junior high school *n* AmE scuola *f* media inferiore
junior minister *n* sottosegretario *m*
junior school *n* scuola *f* elementare
juniper /'dʒu:nɪpə(r)/ *n* ginepro *m*
junk /dʒʌŋk/ *n* cianfrusaglie *fpl*
junk food *n* infml cibo *m* poco sano, porcherie *fpl*
junkie /'dʒʌŋkɪ/ *n* sl tossico, -a *mf*
junk mail *n* posta *f* spazzatura
junk shop *n* negozio *m* di rigattiere
junkyard *n* (for scrap) rottamaio *m*; (for old cars) cimitero *m* delle macchine
junta /'dʒʌntə/ *n* giunta *f* militare
Jupiter /'dʒu:pɪtə(r)/ *n* Giove *m*
jurisdiction /dʒʊərɪs'dɪkʃn/ *n* giurisdizione *f*
jurisprudence /dʒʊrɪs'pru:dəns/ *n* giurisprudenza *f*
jurist /'dʒʊərɪst/ *n* giurista *mf*
juror /'dʒʊərə(r)/ *n* giurato, -a *mf*
jury /'dʒʊərɪ/ *n* giuria *f*
jury box *n* banco *m* dei giurati
jury duty *n* esp Am = **jury service**
jury service *n* **do** ~ far parte di una giuria popolare
✔ **just** /dʒʌst/ **A** *adj* giusto
B *adv* (barely) appena; (simply) solo; (exactly) esattamente; ~ **as tall** altrettanto alto; ~ **as I was leaving** proprio quando stavo andando via; **I've** ~ **seen her** l'ho appena vista; **it's** ~ **as well** meno male; ~ **at that moment** proprio in quel momento; ~ **listen!** almeno ascolta!; **I'm** ~ **going** sto andando proprio ora
✔ **justice** /'dʒʌstɪs/ *n* giustizia *f*; **do** ~ **to** rendere giustizia a
Justice Department *n* AmE ministero *m* di Grazia e Giustizia
Justice of the Peace *n* giudice *m* di pace
justifiable /dʒʌstɪ'faɪəbl/ *adj* giustificabile
justifiably /dʒʌstɪ'faɪəblɪ/ *adv* in modo giustificato
justification /dʒʌstɪfɪ'keɪʃn/ *n* giustificazione *f*
justified /'dʒʌstɪfaɪd/ *adj* ‹*action*› motivato
✔ **justify** /'dʒʌstɪfaɪ/ *vt* (*pt/pp* **-ied**) giustificare
justly /'dʒʌstlɪ/ *adv* giustamente
justness /'dʒʌstnɪs/ *n* (of decision) giustezza *f*; (of claim, request) legittimità *f*
jut /dʒʌt/ *vi* (*pt/pp* **jutted**) ~ **out** sporgere
jute /dʒu:t/ *n* iuta *f*
juvenile /'dʒu:vənaɪl/ **A** *adj* giovanile; (childish) infantile; (for the young) per i giovani
B *n* giovane *mf*
juvenile crime *n* delinquenza *f* minorile
juvenile delinquency *n* delinquenza *f* minorile
juvenile delinquent *n* delinquente *mf* minorile
juvenile offender *n* Jur imputato, -a *mf* minorenne
juxtapose /dʒʌkstə'pəʊz/ *vt* giustapporre

Kk

k¹, **K** /keɪ/ *n* (letter) k, K *f inv*
K² *abbr* **1** (**kilo**) k **2** (**kilobyte**) KB, Kbyte *m inv* **3** (**thousand pounds**) **he earns £50 K** guadagna 50 mila sterline
kale /keɪl/, **curly kale** *n* cavolo *m* riccio
kaleidoscope /kəˈlaɪdəskəʊp/ *n* caleidoscopio *m*
kangaroo /kæŋgəˈruː/ *n* canguro *m*
kaput /kəˈpʊt/ *adj* infml kaputt *inv*
karaoke /kærɪˈəʊkɪ/ *n* karaoke *m inv*
karaoke machine *n* apparecchio *m* per il karaoke
karate /kəˈrɑːtɪ/ *n* karatè *m*
kart /kɑːt/ *n* kart *m inv*
Kashmir /kæʃˈmɪə(r)/ *n* Kashmir *m*
Kashmiri /kæʃˈmɪərɪ/ **A** *adj* del Kashmir **B** *n* nativo, -a *mf* del Kashmir
kayak /ˈkaɪæk/ *n* kayak *m inv*
Kazakhstan /ˌkɑːzɑːkˈstɑːn, ˌkæz-/ *n* Kazakistan *m*
KB *n abbr* (**kilobyte**) KB, Kbyte *m inv*
kebab /kɪˈbæb/ *n* Culin spiedino *m* di carne
kedgeree /ˈkedʒəriː/ *n* BrE *piatto (m) indiano a base di pesce, riso e uova*
keel /kiːl/ *n* chiglia *f*
■ **keel over** *vi* capovolgersi
keen /kiːn/ *adj* (intense) acuto; ‹*interest*› vivo; ‹*eager*› entusiastico; ‹*competition*› feroce; ‹*wind, knife*› tagliente; **~ on** entusiasta di; **she's ~ on him** le piace molto; **be ~ to do something** avere voglia di fare qualcosa
keenly /ˈkiːnlɪ/ *adv* intensamente
keenness /ˈkiːnnɪs/ *n* entusiasmo *m*
keep /kiːp/ **A** *n* (maintenance) mantenimento *m*; (of castle) maschio *m*; **for ~s** per sempre **B** *vt* (*pt/pp* **kept**) tenere; (not throw away) conservare; (detain) trattenere; mantenere ‹*family, promise*›; tenere ‹*shop*›; allevare ‹*animals*›; rispettare ‹*law, rules*›; **~ something hot** tenere qualcosa in caldo; **~ somebody waiting** far aspettare qualcuno; **~ something to oneself** tenere qualcosa per sé **C** *vi* (remain) rimanere; ‹*food*› conservarsi; **~ calm** rimanere calmo; **~ left/right** tenere la sinistra/la destra; **~ [on] doing something** continuare a fare qualcosa
■ **keep at**: *vt* (persevere with) **~ at it!** non mollare!
■ **keep away A** *vi* non avvicinarsi, stare alla larga **B** *vt* tenere lontano
■ **keep away from** *vt* non avvicinarsi a ‹*fire*›; stare alla larga da ‹*somebody*›; **~ somebody away from something** tener qualcuno lontano da qualcosa
■ **keep back A** *vt* trattenere ‹*person*›; **~ something back from somebody** tenere nascosto qualcosa a qualcuno **B** *vi* tenersi indietro
■ **keep down A** *vi* star giù **B** *vt* mandar giù ‹*food*›; mantenere basso ‹*prices, inflation etc*›; **~ one's voice down** non alzare la voce
■ **keep from**: *vt* **~ somebody from doing something** impedire a qualcuno di fare qualcosa; **~ somebody from** impedire a qualcuno di ‹*falling*›; **~ somebody from their work** distogliere qualcuno dal lavoro; **~ something from somebody** tenere nascosto qualcosa a qualcuno; **~ the truth from somebody** nascondere la verità a qualcuno
■ **keep in** *vt* (in school) trattenere oltre l'orario per punizione; reprimere ‹*indignation, anger etc*›
■ **keep in with** *vt* mantenersi in buoni rapporti con
■ **keep off** *vt* (avoid) astenersi da ‹*cigarettes, chocolate etc*›; evitare ‹*delicate subject*›
■ **keep on A** *vi* (continue one's journey) proseguire; infml assillare (**at somebody** qualcuno) **B** *vt* non togliersi ‹*coat, hat*›; tenere ‹*employee*›
■ **keep out A** *vt* tenere fuori; **~ out!** alla larga! **B** *vt* non far entrare ‹*person, animal*›
■ **keep out of** *vt* ‹*person*› non entrare in ‹*place*›; tenersi fuori da ‹*argument*›; **~ somebody out of** tenere qualcuno alla larga da ‹*place*›; **~ me out of this!** lasciamene fuori!
■ **keep to** *vt* non deviare da ‹*path, subject*›; **~ something to oneself** tenere qualcosa per sé
■ **keep up A** *vi* ‹*remain level*› stare al passo; ‹*rain, good weather*› mantenersi **B** *vt* (continue) continuare; (prevent from going to bed) tenere alzato; mantenere alto ‹*prices*›; tener su ‹*trousers*›
■ **keep up with** *vt* (in race) stare al passo con ‹*person, fashion*›; ‹*wages*› seguire il corso di ‹*inflation*›
keeper /ˈkiːpə(r)/ *n* custode *mf*
keep-fit *n* ginnastica *f*
keeping /ˈkiːpɪŋ/ *n* custodia *f*; **be in ~ with** essere in armonia con
keepsake /ˈkiːpseɪk/ *n* ricordo *m*
keg /keg/ *n* barilotto *m*

k

kelp /kelp/ *n* laminaria *f*, fuco *m*
kennel /'kenl/ *n* canile *m*; **~s** *pl* (boarding) canile *m*; (breeding) allevamento *m* di cani
Kenya /'kenjə/ *n* Kenya *m*
Kenyan /'kenjən/ *adj & n* keniota *mf*
kept /kept/ ▶ **keep**
kerb /kɜːb/ *n* bordo *m* del marciapiede
kernel /'kɜːnl/ *n* nocciolo *m*
kerosene /'kerəsiːn/ *n* AmE cherosene *m*
kestrel /'kestrəl/ *n* gheppio *m*
ketchup /'ketʃʌp/ *n* ketchup *m*
kettle /'ket(ə)l/ *n* bollitore *m*; **put the ~ on** mettere l'acqua a bollire
kettledrum /'ket(ə)ldrʌm/ *n* timpano *m*
key /kiː/ **A** *n* (also Mus) chiave *f*; (of piano, typewriter) tasto *m*
B *vt* **~ [in]** digitare <*character*>; **could you ~ this?** puoi battere questo?
keyboard *n* Comput, Mus tastiera *f*
keyboarder *n* tastierista *mf*
keyboard player *n* tastierista *mf*
keyboards *npl* Mus tastiere *fpl*
keyed-up /kiːd'ʌp/ *adj* (excited) teso; (anxious) estremamente agitato; (ready to act) psicologicamente preparato
keyhole *n* buco *m* della serratura
keyhole surgery *n* chirurgia *f* endoscopica
key money *n* (for apartment) *somma (f) richiesta ad un affittuario quando si trasferisce nell'abitazione*
keynote *n* Mus tonica *f*; (main theme) tema *m* principale
keynote speech *n* discorso *m* programmatico
keypad *n* Comput tastierino *m* numerico
key ring *n* portachiavi *m inv*
key signature *n* Mus armatura *f* di chiave
keystroke *n* Comput keystroke *m inv*
keyword *n* parola *f* chiave
key worker *n chi lavora in settori, come l'insegnamento, la sanità, la sicurezza, ritenuti essenziali per la vita di una comunità*
kg *abbr* (**kilogram**) kg
khaki /'kɑːkɪ/ **A** *adj* cachi *inv*
B *n* cachi *m*
kibbutz /kɪ'bʊts/ *n* (*pl* **-es** *or* **-im**) kibbutz *m inv*
kibosh /'kaɪbɒʃ/ *n* infml **put the ~ on something** mandare all'aria qualcosa
kick /kɪk/ **A** *n* calcio *m*; infml (thrill) piacere *m*; **for ~s** infml per spasso; **get a ~ out of something** trovare un piacere incredibile in qualcosa
B *vt* dar calci a; **~ the bucket** infml crepare
C *vi* <*animal*> scalciare; <*person*> dare calci
■ **kick around** **A** *vi* infml essere in giro
B *vt* buttar giù <*idea*>
■ **kick in** *vt* sfondare a calci <*door*>
■ **kick off** *vi* Sport dare il calcio d'inizio; infml iniziare
■ **kick out** *vt* infml (of school, club etc) sbatter fuori
■ **kick up**: *vt* **~ up a row** fare una scenata
kickback /'kɪkbæk/ *n* infml tangente *f*
kick-off *n* Sport calcio *m* d'inizio; **for a ~** infml tanto per cominciare
kick-start /'kɪkstɑːt/ *vt* mettere in moto <*motorbike*>; rilanciare <*economy*>
kid /kɪd/ **A** *n* capretto *m*; infml (child) ragazzino, -a *mf*
B *vt* (*pt/pp* **kidded**) infml prendere in giro
C *vi* infml scherzare
kid gloves *npl* guanti *mpl* di capretto; **handle somebody with ~** trattare qualcuno con i guanti
kidnap /'kɪdnæp/ *vt* (*pt/pp* **kidnapped**) rapire, sequestrare
kidnapper /'kɪdnæpə(r)/ *n* sequestratore, -trice *mf*, rapitore, -trice *mf*
kidnapping /'kɪdnæpɪŋ/ *n* rapimento *m*, sequestro *m* [di persona]
kidney /'kɪdnɪ/ *n* rene *m*; Culin rognone *m*
kidney bean *n* fagiolo *m* comune
kidney dialysis *n* dialisi *f*
kidney failure *n* collasso *m* renale
kidney machine *n* rene *m* artificiale
kidney-shaped /'kɪdnɪʃeɪpt/ *adj* a forma di fagiolo
kidney stone *n* calcolo *m* renale
kill /kɪl/ *vt* uccidere; fig metter fine a; ammazzare <*time*>
■ **kill off** *vt* eliminare <*people*>; distruggere <*plants, insects*>
killer /'kɪlə(r)/ *n* assassino, -a *mf*; **it was a real ~** fig è stato micidiale
killer instinct *n* istinto *m* di uccidere; fig spietatezza *f*
killer whale *n* orca *f*
killing /'kɪlɪŋ/ *n* uccisione *f*; (murder) omicidio *m*
killjoy /'kɪldʒɔɪ/ *n* guastafeste *mf inv*
kiln /kɪln/ *n* fornace *f*
kilo /'kiːləʊ/ *n* chilo *m*
kilobyte *n* kilobyte *m inv*
kilogram *n* chilogrammo *m*
kilohertz *n* chilohertz *m inv*
kilometre *n* chilometro *m*
kilowatt *n* chilowatt *m inv*
kilt /kɪlt/ *n* kilt *m inv* (*gonnellino degli scozzesi*)
kimono /kɪ'məʊnəʊ/ *n* kimono *m inv*
kin /kɪn/ *n* congiunti *mpl*; **next of ~** parente *m* stretto
kind[1] /kaɪnd/ *n* genere *m*, specie *f*; (brand, type) tipo *m*; **what ~ of car?** che tipo di macchina?; **~ of** infml alquanto; **two of a ~**

parola chiave

due della stessa specie
kind² *adj* gentile, buono; ~ **to animals** amante degli animali; ~ **regards** cordiali saluti
kindergarten /ˈkɪndəɡɑːtn/ *n* asilo *m* infantile
kind-hearted /-ˈhɑːtɪd/ *adj* ‹*person*› di [buon] cuore
kindle /ˈkɪndl/ *vt* accendere
kindly /ˈkaɪndlɪ/ **A** *adj* (**-ier**, **-iest**) benevolo **B** *adv* gentilmente; (if you please) per favore
kindness /ˈkaɪndnɪs/ *n* gentilezza *f*
kindred /ˈkɪndrɪd/ *adj* **she's a ~ spirit** è la mia/sua/tua anima gemella
kinetic /kɪˈnetɪk/ *adj* cinetico
kinetics /kɪˈnetɪks/ *nsg* cinetica *fsg*
king /kɪŋ/ *n* re *m inv*
kingdom /ˈkɪŋdəm/ *n* regno *m*
kingfisher /ˈkɪŋfɪʃə(r)/ *n* martin *m inv* pescatore
kingly /ˈkɪŋlɪ/ *adj* also fig regale
king-sized /ˈkɪŋsaɪzd/ *adj* ‹*cigarette*› king-size *inv*, lungo; ‹*bed*› matrimoniale grande
kink /kɪŋk/ *n* attorcigliamento *m*
kinky /ˈkɪŋkɪ/ *adj* infml bizzarro
kinship /ˈkɪnʃɪp/ *n* (blood relationship) parentela *f*; (empathy) affinità *f*
kiosk /ˈkiːɒsk/ *n* chiosco *m*; Teleph cabina *f* telefonica
kip /kɪp/ **A** *n* infml pisolino *m*; **have a ~** schiacciare un pisolino
B *vi* (*pt/pp* **kipped**) infml dormire
kipper /ˈkɪpə(r)/ *n* aringa *f* affumicata
kirk /kɜːk/ *n* Scottish chiesa *f*
kiss /kɪs/ **A** *n* bacio *m*
B *vt* baciare
C *vi* baciarsi
kiss of death *n* colpo *m* di grazia
kiss of life *n* respirazione *f* bocca a bocca; **give somebody the ~** fare la respirazione bocca a bocca a qualcuno
kissogram /ˈkɪsəɡræm/ *n servizio (m) commerciale in cui un messaggio di auguri viene scherzosamente recapitato con un bacio da una ragazza in abiti succinti*
kit /kɪt/ **A** *n* equipaggiamento *m*, kit *m inv*; (tools) attrezzi *mpl*; (construction kit) pezzi *mpl* da montare, kit *m inv*
B *vt* (*pt/pp* **kitted**) ~ **out** equipaggiare
kitbag /ˈkɪtbæɡ/ *n* sacco *m* a spalla
kitchen /ˈkɪtʃɪn/ **A** *n* cucina *f*
B *attrib* di cucina
kitchenette /kɪtʃɪˈnet/ *n* cucinino *m*
kitchen foil *n* carta *f* di alluminio
kitchen garden *n* orto *m*
kitchen paper *n* carta *f* da cucina
kitchen roll *n* Scottex® *m inv*
kitchen scales *npl* bilancia *f* da cucina
kitchen sink *n* lavello *m*; **everything bar the ~** fig proprio tutto quanto
kitchen-sink drama *n* teatro *m* neorealista
kitchen towel *n* Scottex® *m inv*
kitchen unit *n* elemento *m* componibile da cucina
kitchenware *n* (crockery) stoviglie *fpl*; (implements) utensili *mpl* da cucina
kite /kaɪt/ *n* aquilone *m*
Kitemark /ˈkaɪtmɑːk/ *n* BrE marchio *m* di conformità alle norme britanniche
kith /kɪθ/ *n* ~ **and kin** amici e parenti *mpl*
kitsch /kɪtʃ/ *n* kitsch *m inv*
kitten /ˈkɪtn/ *n* gattino *m*
kitty /ˈkɪtɪ/ *n* (money) cassa *f* comune
kiwi /ˈkiːwiː/ *n* Zool kiwi *m inv*
kiwi fruit *n* kiwi *m inv*
kleptomania /kleptəˈmeɪnɪə/ *n* cleptomania *f*
kleptomaniac /kleptəˈmeɪnɪæk/ *n* cleptomane *mf*
km *abbr* (**kilometre**) km
kmh *abbr* (**kilometres per hour**) km/h
knack /næk/ *n* tecnica *f*; **have the ~ for doing something** avere la capacità di fare qualcosa
knapsack /ˈnæpsæk/ *n* sacco *m* da montagna
knave /neɪv/ *n* (in cards) fante *m*; (rogue) furfante *m*
knead /niːd/ *vt* impastare
knee /niː/ *n* ginocchio *m*; **go down on one's ~s to somebody** inginocchiarsi davanti a qualcuno
kneecap /ˈniːkæp/ *n* rotula *f*
knee-deep /ˌniːˈdiːp/ *adj* **the water was ~** l'acqua arrivava alle ginocchia
kneel /niːl/ *vi* (*pt/pp* **knelt**) ~ **[down]** inginocchiarsi; **be ~ing** essere inginocchiato
knee-length *adj* ‹*boots*› alto; ‹*skirt*› al ginocchio; ‹*socks*› lungo
knee-pad *n* ginocchiera *f*
knees-up /ˈniːzʌp/ *n* BrE infml festa *f*
knell /nel/ *n* campana *f* a morto; **sound the death ~ for something** segnare la fine di qualcosa
knelt /nelt/ ▸ **kneel**
knew /njuː/ ▸ **know**
knickerbocker glory /nɪkəbɒkəˈɡlɔːrɪ/ *n* coppa *f* [gelato] gigante
knickers /ˈnɪkəz/ *npl* mutandine *fpl*
knick-knacks /ˈnɪknæks/ *npl* ninnoli *mpl*
knife /naɪf/ **A** *n* (*pl* **knives**) coltello *m*
B *vt* infml accoltellare
knife-edge *n* **be on a ~** ‹*person*› trovarsi sul filo del rasoio; ‹*negotiations*› essere appeso a un filo
knifepoint *n* **at ~** sotto la minaccia di un coltello
knife sharpener *n* affilacoltelli *m inv*

knight /naɪt/ **A** *n* cavaliere *m*; (in chess) cavallo *m*
B *vt* nominare cavaliere

knighthood /ˈnaɪthʊd/ *n* **receive a ~** ricevere il titolo di cavaliere

knit /nɪt/ *vt & vi* (*pt/pp* **knitted**) lavorare a maglia; **~ one, purl one** un diritto, un rovescio; **~ one's brow** aggrottare le sopracciglia

knitted /ˈnɪtɪd/ *adj* lavorato a maglia

knitting /ˈnɪtɪŋ/ *n* lavorare *m a* maglia; (product) lavoro *m* a maglia

knitting needle *n* ferro *m* da calza

knitwear /ˈnɪtweə(r)/ *n* maglieria *f*

knives /naɪvz/ *npl* ▸ **knife**

knob /nɒb/ *n* pomello *m*; (of stick) pomo *m*; (of butter) noce *f*

knobbly /ˈnɒblɪ/ *adj* nodoso; (bony) spigoloso

⚷ **knock** /nɒk/ **A** *n* colpo *m*; **there was a ~ at the door** hanno bussato alla porta
B *vt* bussare a ‹*door*›; infml (criticize) denigrare; **~ a hole in something** fare un buco in qualcosa; **~ one's head** battere la testa (**on** contro)
C *vi* (at door) bussare

▪ **knock about** **A** *vt* malmenare
B *vi* infml girovagare

▪ **knock back** *vt* infml (drink quickly) buttar giù tutto d'un fiato

▪ **knock down** *vt* far cadere; (with fist) stendere con un pugno; (in car) investire; (demolish) abbattere; infml (reduce) ribassare ‹*price*›

▪ **knock off** **A** *vt* infml (steal) fregare; infml (complete quickly) fare alla bell'e meglio
B *vi* infml (cease work) staccare

▪ **knock out** *vt* eliminare; (make unconscious) mettere K.O.; infml (anaesthetize) addormentare

▪ **knock over** *vt* rovesciare; (in car) investire

▪ **knock up** *vt* infml (prepare quickly) buttare giù; sl (make pregnant) mettere incinta

knockabout *n* Sport **have a ~** palleggiare

knock-down furniture *n* mobili *mpl* scomponibili

knock-down price *n* prezzo *m* stracciato

knocker /ˈnɒkə(r)/ *n* battente *m*; (critic) denigratore, -trice *mf*

knocking /ˈnɒkɪŋ/ *n* (on door) colpi *mpl*; Auto battito *m* in testa

knocking off time /nɒkɪŋˈɒf/ *n* **~ is five o'clock** si stacca alle cinque

knock-kneed /-ˈniːd/ *adj* con gambe storte

knock-on effect *n* implicazioni *fpl*

knock-out *n* knock-out *m inv*; **be a ~** fig essere uno schianto

k

knoll /nəʊl/ *n* collinetta *f*

knot /nɒt/ **A** *n* nodo *m*; **to tie the ~** infml convolare a giuste nozze
B *vt* (*pt/pp* **knotted**) annodare; BrE infml **get ~ted!** vai a farti friggere!

knotty /ˈnɒtɪ/ *adj* (**-ier**, **-iest**) infml spinoso

⚷ **know** /nəʊ/ **A** *vt* (*pt* **knew**, *pp* **known**) sapere; conoscere ‹*person, place*›; (recognize) riconoscere; **get to ~ somebody** conoscere qualcuno; **~ how to swim** sapere nuotare; **~ right from wrong** saper distinguere il bene dal male
B *vi* sapere; **did you ~ about this?** lo sapevi?
C *n* **in the ~** infml al corrente

▪ **know of** *vt* conoscere; **not that I ~ of** non che io sappia

know-all *n* infml sapientone, -a *mf*

know-how *n* know-how *m inv*

knowing /ˈnəʊɪŋ/ *adj* d'intesa

knowingly /ˈnəʊɪŋlɪ/ *adv* (intentionally) consapevolmente; ‹*smile etc*› con aria d'intesa

⚷ **knowledge** /ˈnɒlɪdʒ/ *n* conoscenza *f*

knowledgeable, **knowledgable** /ˈnɒlɪdʒəbl/ *adj* ben informato

known /nəʊn/ **A** ▸ **know**
B *adj* noto

knuckle /ˈnʌkl/ *n* nocca *f*

▪ **knuckle down** *vi* darci sotto (**to** con)

▪ **knuckle under** *vi* sottomettersi

knuckle-duster *n* tirapugni *m inv*

koala, **koala bear** /kəʊˈɑːlə/ *n* koala *m inv*

Koran /kəˈrɑːn/ *n* Corano *m*

Korea /kəˈrɪə/ *n* Corea *f*

Korean /kəˈrɪən/ *adj & n* coreano, -a *mf*; (language) coreano *m*

kosher /ˈkəʊʃə(r)/ *adj* kasher *inv*

Kosovan /ˈkɒsəvn/ **A** *adj* kosovaro
B *n* kosovaro, -a *mf*

Kosovo /ˈkɒsəvəʊ/ *n* Kosovo *m*

kowtow /kaʊˈtaʊ/ *vi* piegarsi

kph *abbr* (**kilometres per hour**) km/h

kudos /ˈkjuːdɒs/ *n* infml gloria *f*

Kurd /kɜːd/ **A** *n* curdo, -a *mf*
B *adj* curdo

Kurdish /ˈkɜːdɪʃ/ *adj & n* (language) curdo *m*

Kurdistan /kɜːdɪˈstɑːn/ *n* Kurdistan *m*

Kuwait /kʊˈweɪt/ *n* Kuwait *m*

Kuwaiti /kʊˈweɪtɪ/ *adj & n* kuwaitiano, -a *mf*

kW *abbr* (**kilowatt**) kW

kWh *abbr* (**kilowatt-hour**) kWh

Kyrgyzstan /ˌkɪəgɪˈstɑːn, kɜːgɪ-, -ˈstæn/ *n* Kirghizistan *m*

⚷ parola chiave

Ll

l, **L** /el/ *n* (letter) l, L *f inv*

L *abbr* **1** (**lake**) L **2** (**large**) L **3** (**learner**) P **4** (**left**) sinistra *f* **5** (**line**) v **6** (**litre(s)**) l

lab /læb/ *n* infml laboratorio *m*

lab assistant *n* assistente *mf* di laboratorio

lab coat *n* camice *m*

label /ˈleɪbl/ **A** *n* etichetta *f*
B *vt* (*pt/pp* **labelled**) mettere un'etichetta a; fig etichettare ‹*person*›

labelling /ˈleɪbəlɪŋ/ *n* (act) etichettatura *f*

labor /ˈleɪbə(r)/ *n & v* AmE = **labour**

laboratory /ləˈbɒrətrɪ/ *n* laboratorio *m*

laborer /ˈleɪbərə(r)/ *n* AmE = **labourer**

laborious /ləˈbɔːrɪəs/ *adj* laborioso

laboriously /ləˈbɔːrɪəslɪ/ *adv* in modo laborioso

labour /ˈleɪbə(r)/ **A** *n* lavoro *m*; (workers) manodopera *f*; Med doglie *fpl*; **be in ~** avere le doglie; **L~** Pol partito *m* laburista
B *attrib* Pol laburista
C *vi* lavorare
D *vt* **~ the point** fig ribadire il concetto

labour camp *n* campo *m* di lavoro

laboured /ˈleɪbəd/ *adj* ‹*breathing*› affannato

labourer /ˈleɪbərə(r)/ *n* manovale *m*

labour exchange *n* (old) ufficio *m* di collocamento

labour force *n* manodopera *f*

labouring /ˈleɪbərɪŋ/ *n* lavoro *m* manuale

labour-intensive *adj* ad uso intensivo di lavoro; **be ~** richiedere molta manodopera

labour market *n* mercato *m* del lavoro

Labour Party *n* Partito *m* laburista

labour relations *npl* relazioni *fpl* industriali

labour-saving /ˈleɪbəseɪvɪŋ/ *adj* che fa risparmiare lavoro e fatica

labour union /ˈleɪbə/ *n* AmE sindacato *m*

labour ward *n* reparto *m* maternità

Labrador /ˈlæbrədɔː(r)/ *n* (dog) labrador *m inv*

lab technician *n* tecnico, -a *mf* di laboratorio

laburnum /ləˈbɜːnəm/ *n* maggiociondolo *m*

labyrinth /ˈlæbərɪnθ/ *n* labirinto *m*

lace /leɪs/ **A** *n* pizzo *m*; (of shoe) laccio *m*
B *attrib* di pizzo
C *vt* allacciare ‹*shoes*›; correggere ‹*drink*›

lacerate /ˈlæsəreɪt/ *vt* lacerare

laceration /læsəˈreɪʃn/ *n* lacerazione *f*

lace-up, **lace-up shoe** *n* scarpa *f* stringata

lack /læk/ **A** *n* mancanza *f*; **~ of interest** disinteressamento *m*; **~ of evidence** insufficienza *f* di prove
B *vt* **the programme ~s originality** il programma manca di originalità; **I ~ the time** mi manca il tempo
C *vi* **be ~ing** mancare; **be ~ing in something** mancare di qualcosa

lackadaisical /lækəˈdeɪzɪkl/ *adj* senza entusiasmo

lackey /ˈlækɪ/ *n* lacchè *m*

lackluster /ˈlæklʌstə(r)/ *adj* AmE = **lacklustre**

lacklustre /ˈlæklʌstə(r)/ *adj* scialbo

laconic /ləˈkɒnɪk/ *adj* laconico

laconically /ləˈkɒnɪklɪ/ *adv* laconicamente

lacquer /ˈlækə(r)/ *n* lacca *f*

lactate /lækˈteɪt/ *vi* produrre latte

lactation /lækˈteɪʃn/ *n* lattazione *f*

lacy /ˈleɪsɪ/ *adj* di pizzo

lad /læd/ *n* ragazzo *m*

ladder /ˈlædə(r)/ **A** *n* scala *f*; (in tights) smagliatura *f*
B *vi* smagliarsi

ladder-proof /ˈlædəpruːf/ *adj* ‹*stockings*› indemagliabile

laddish /ˈlædɪʃ/ *adj* infml da ragazzacci

laden /ˈleɪdn/ *adj* carico (**with** di)

la-di-da /lɑːdɪˈdɑː/ *adj* affettato

ladle /ˈleɪdl/ **A** *n* mestolo *m*
B *vt* **~ [out]** versare (*col mestolo*)

lady /ˈleɪdɪ/ *n* signora *f*; (title) Lady *f*; **ladies [room]** *n* bagno *m* per donne

ladybird, AmE **ladybug** *n* coccinella *f*

lady-in-waiting /-weɪtɪŋ/ *n* dama *f* di corte

ladykiller *n* infml dongiovanni *m inv*

ladylike /ˈleɪdɪlaɪk/ *adj* signorile

lady mayoress *n* moglie *f* del Lord Mayor

Ladyship *n* **her/your ~** (to aristocrat) ≈ Signora Contessa

lady's maid *n* cameriera *f* personale

lag[1] /læg/ *vi* (*pt/pp* **lagged**) **~ behind** restare indietro

lag[2] *vt* (*pt/pp* **lagged**) isolare ‹*pipes*›

lager /ˈlɑːgə(r)/ *n* birra *f* chiara

lager lout *n* BrE derog giovinastro *m* ubriaco

lagging /ˈlægɪn/ *n* (for pipes) materiale *m* isolante

lagoon /ləˈguːn/ *n* laguna *f*

laid /leɪd/ ▶ **lay**[3]

laid-back *adj* infml rilassato

laid up *adj* **be ~** essere allettato

lain /leɪn/ ▶ **lie**[2]

lair /leə(r)/ *n* tana *f*
laird /leəd/ *n* (in Scotland) proprietario *m* terriero
laity /'leɪətɪ/ *n* laicato *m*
lake /leɪk/ *n* lago *m*; **L~ Garda** lago di Garda
lakeside /'leɪksaɪd/ **A** *n* riva *f* del lago
B *attrib* ‹*café, scenery*› della/sulla riva del lago
lama /'læmə/ *n* lama *m inv*
lamb /læm/ *n* agnello *m*
lambast, **lambaste** /læm'beɪst/ *vt* biasimare ‹*person, organization*›
lamb chop *n* cotoletta *f* d'agnello
lambskin *n* pelle *f* d'agnello
lambswool *n* lana *f* d'agnello, lambswool *m inv*
lame /leɪm/ *adj* zoppo; fig ‹*argument*› zoppicante; ‹*excuse*› traballante
lamé /'lɑːmeɪ/ *n* lamé *m*
lame duck *n* (person) inetto, -a *mf*; (firm) azienda *f* in cattive acque
lament /lə'ment/ **A** *n* lamento *m*
B *vt* lamentare
C *vi* lamentarsi
lamentable /'læməntəbl/ *adj* deplorevole
laminated /'læmɪneɪtɪd/ *adj* laminato
lamp /læmp/ *n* lampada *f*; (in street) lampione *m*
lampoon /læm'puːn/ **A** *n* satira *f*
B *vt* fare oggetto di satira
lamp post *n* lampione *m*
lampshade /'læmpʃeɪd/ *n* paralume *m*
lance /lɑːns/ **A** *n* lancia *f*
B *vt* Med incidere
lance corporal *n* appuntato *m*
lancet /'lɑːnsɪt/ *n* Med bisturi *m inv*
⚷ **land** /lænd/ **A** *n* terreno *m*; (country) paese *m*; (as opposed to sea) terra *f*; **plot of ~** pezzo *m* di terreno
B *vt* Naut sbarcare; infml ‹*obtain*› assicurarsi; **be ~ed with something** infml ritrovarsi fra capo e collo qualcosa
C *vi* Aeron atterrare; (fall) cadere; **~ on one's feet** fig cadere in piedi
■ **land up** *vi* infml finire
land agent *n* (on estate) fattore *m*
land army *n gruppo (m) di lavoratrici agricole durante la seconda guerra mondiale*
landfall *n* Naut approdo *m*; **make ~** (reach) approdare; (sight) avvistare terra
landfill site *n discarica (f) in cui i rifiuti vengono interrati*
landing /'lændɪŋ/ *n* Naut sbarco *m*; Aeron atterraggio *m*; (top of stairs) pianerottolo *m*
landing card *n* Aeron, Naut carta *f* di sbarco
landing craft *n* mezzo *m* da sbarco
landing gear *n* Aeron carrello *m* d'atterraggio
landing lights *npl* luci *fpl* d'atterraggio
landing party *n* Mil reparto *m* da sbarco
landing stage *n* pontile *m* da sbarco
landing strip *n* pista *f* d'atterraggio
landlady *n* proprietaria *f*; (of flat) padrona *f* di casa
landlocked *adj* privo di sbocco sul mare
landlord *n* proprietario *m*; (of flat) padrone *m* di casa
landlubber *n* marinaio *m* d'acqua dolce
landmark *n* punto *m* di riferimento; fig pietra *f* miliare
land mass *n* continente *m*
landmine *n* Mil mina *f* terrestre
landowner *n* proprietario, -a *mf* terriero, -a
landscape *n* paesaggio *m*
landscape architect *n* paesaggista *mf*
landscape gardener *n* paesaggista *mf*
landslide *n* frana *f*; Pol valanga *f* di voti
landslip *n* smottamento *m*
lane /leɪn/ *n* sentiero *m*; Auto, Sport corsia *f*
lane closure *n* (on motorway) chiusura *f* di corsia
lane markings *n* (on road) [strisce *fpl* di] mezzeria *f*
langoustine /'lɒŋgʊstiːn/ *n* scampo *m*
⚷ **language** /'læŋgwɪdʒ/ *n* lingua *f*; (speech, style) Comput linguaggio *m*
language barrier *n* barriera *f* linguistica
language laboratory *n* laboratorio *m* linguistico
languid /'læŋgwɪd/ *adj* languido
languidly /'læŋgwɪdlɪ/ *adv* languidamente
languish /'læŋgwɪʃ/ *vi* languire
languor /'længə(r)/ *n* languore *m*
lank /læŋk/ *adj* ‹*hair*› liscio
lanky /'læŋkɪ/ *adj* (**-ier**, **-iest**) allampanato
lanolin /'lænəlɪn/ *n* lanolina *f*
lantern /'læntən/ *n* lanterna *f*
lanyard /'lænjəd/ *n* Naut (rope) cima *f*
Laos /lɑːɒs, laʊs/ *n* Laos *m*
lap¹ /læp/ *n* grembo *m*
lap² **A** *n* Sport (of journey) tappa *f*; **~ of honour** giro *m* d'onore
B *vi* (*pt/pp* **lapped**) ‹*water*› **~ against** lambire
C *vt* Sport doppiare
lap³ *vt* (*pt/pp* **lapped**) **~ up** bere avidamente; bersi completamente ‹*lies*›; credere ciecamente a ‹*praise*›
lap and shoulder belt *n* Auto, Aeron cintura *f* di sicurezza
laparoscope /'læpərəskəʊp/ *n* laparoscopio *m*
laparoscopy /læpə'rɒskəpɪ/ *n* laparoscopia *f*
lap belt *n* Auto, Aeron cintura *f* di sicurezza addominale
lapdog /'læpdɒg/ *n* cane *m* da salotto; **he's her ~** è il suo cagnolino
lapel /lə'pel/ *n* bavero *m*

Lapland /ˈlæplænd/ *n* Lapponia *f*

lapse /læps/ **A** *n* sbaglio *m*; (moral) sbandamento *m* [morale]; (of time) intervallo *m*
B *vi* (expire) scadere; (morally) scivolare; **~ into** cadere in

laptop /ˈlæptɒp/ *n* **~ [computer]** computer *m inv* portatile, laptop *m inv*

larceny /ˈlɑːsənɪ/ *n* furto *m*

larch /lɑːtʃ/ *n* larice *m*

lard /lɑːd/ *n* strutto *m*

larder /ˈlɑːdə(r)/ *n* dispensa *f*

large /lɑːdʒ/ *adj & adv* grande; ‹*number, amount*› grande, grosso; **by and ~** in complesso; **at ~** in libertà; (in general) ampiamente

large intestine *n* intestino *m* crasso

largely /ˈlɑːdʒlɪ/ *adv* **~ because of** in gran parte a causa di

largeness /ˈlɑːdʒnɪs/ *n* grandezza *f*

large-scale *adj* ‹*map*› a grande scala; ‹*operation*› su larga scala

largesse /lɑːˈʒes/ *n* generosità *f*

lark[1] /lɑːk/ *n* (bird) allodola *f*

lark[2] *n* (joke) burla *f*

▪ **lark about** *vi* giocherellare

larva /ˈlɑːvə/ *n* (*pl* **-vae** /ˈlɑːviː/) larva *f*

laryngitis /lærɪnˈdʒaɪtɪs/ *n* laringite *f*

larynx /ˈlærɪŋks/ *n* laringe *f*

lasagne /ləˈzænjə/ *n* lasagne *fpl*

lascivious /ləˈsɪvɪəs/ *adj* lascivo

laser /ˈleɪzə(r)/ *n* laser *m inv*

laser disc *n* disco *m* laser

laser printer *n* stampante *f* laser

laser treatment *n* laserterapia *f*

lash /læʃ/ **A** *n* frustata *f*; (eyelash) ciglio *m*
B *vt* (whip) frustare; (tie) legare fermamente

▪ **lash out** *vi* attaccare; (spend) sperperare (**on** in)

lashings /ˈlæʃɪŋz/ *npl* **~ of** infml una marea di

lass /læs/ *n* ragazzina *f*

lasso /ləˈsuː/ *n* lazo *m inv*

last /lɑːst/ **A** *adj* (final) ultimo; (recent) scorso; **~ year** l'anno scorso; **~ night** ieri sera; **at ~** alla fine; **at ~!** finalmente!; **that's the ~ straw** infml questa è l'ultima goccia
B *n* ultimo, -a *mf*; **the ~ but one** il penultimo
C *adv* per ultimo; (last time) l'ultima volta; **~ but not least** per ultimo ma non il meno importante
D *vi* durare

last-ditch *adj* ‹*attempt*› disperato

lasting /ˈlɑːstɪŋ/ *adj* durevole

lastly /ˈlɑːstlɪ/ *adv* infine

last-minute *adj* all'ultimo minuto

last name *n* (surname) cognome *m*

last rites *npl* Relig estrema unzione *f*

Last Supper *n* Ultima Cena *f*

latch /lætʃ/ *n* chiavistello *m*; (on gate) saliscendi *m inv*; **leave the door on the ~** chiudere la porta senza far scattare la serratura

▪ **latch on to** *vt* fissarsi con ‹*person, idea*›

latchkey /ˈlætʃkiː/ *n* chiave *f* di casa

latchkey child *n bambino (m) che ha le chiavi di casa in quanto i genitori lavorano*

late /leɪt/ **A** *adj* (delayed) in ritardo; (at a late hour) tardo; (deceased) defunto; **it's ~** (at night) è tardi; **in ~ November** alla fine di novembre; **of ~** recentemente; **be a ~ developer** ‹*child*› essere lento nell'apprendimento
B *adv* tardi; **stay up ~** stare alzati fino a tardi

latecomer /ˈleɪtkʌmə(r)/ *n* ritardatario, -a *mf*; (to political party etc) nuovo, -a arrivato, -a *mf*

late developer *n* (child) **be a ~** essere tardivo

lately /ˈleɪtlɪ/ *adv* recentemente

lateness /ˈleɪtnɪs/ *n* ora *f* tarda; (delay) ritardo *m*

late-night *adj* ‹*film*› ultimo; **it's ~ shopping on Thursdays** i negozi rimangono aperti fino a tardi il giovedì

latent /ˈleɪtnt/ *adj* latente

later /ˈleɪtə(r)/ **A** *adj* ‹*train*› che parte più tardi; ‹*edition*› più recente
B *adv* più tardi; **~ on** più tardi, dopo

lateral /ˈlætərəl/ *adj* laterale

late riser /ˈraɪzə(r)/ *n* dormiglione, -a *mf*

latest /ˈleɪtɪst/ **A** *adj* ultimo; (most recent) più recente; **the ~ [news]** le ultime notizie
B *n* **six o'clock at the ~** alle sei al più tardi

latex /ˈleɪteks/ *n* la[t]tice *m*

lath /læθ/ *n* assicella *f*

lathe /leɪð/ *n* tornio *m*

lather /ˈlɑːðə(r)/ **A** *n* schiuma *f*
B *vt* insaponare
C *vi* far schiuma

Latin /ˈlætɪn/ **A** *adj* latino
B *n* latino *m*

Latin America *n* America *f* Latina

Latin American *adj & n* latino-americano, -a *mf*

Latino /ləˈtiːnəʊ/ *n* AmE latino-americano, -a *mf*

latitude /ˈlætɪtjuːd/ *n* Geog latitudine *f*; fig libertà *f* d'azione

latrine /ləˈtriːn/ *n* latrina *f*

latter /ˈlætə(r)/ **A** *adj* ultimo
B *n* **the ~** quest'ultimo

latter-day *adj* moderno

latterly /ˈlætəlɪ/ *adv* ultimamente

lattice /ˈlætɪs/ *n* traliccio *m*

lattice window *n* finestra *f* con vetri a losanghe

lattice-work *n* intelaiatura *f* a traliccio

Latvia /ˈlætvɪə/ *n* Lettonia *f*

Latvian /ˈlætvɪən/ *adj & n* lettone *mf*; (language) lettone *m*
laudable /ˈlɔːdəbl/ *adj* lodevole
laudatory /ˈlɔːdətrɪ/ *adj* elogiativo
⚷ **laugh** /lɑːf/ **A** *n* risata *f*
B *vi* ridere (**at/about** di); ~ **at somebody** (mock) prendere in giro qualcuno
▪ **laugh off** *vt* ridere di ‹*criticism*›
laughable /ˈlɑːfəbɪ/ *adj* ridicolo
laughing gas /ˈlɑːfɪŋ/ *n* gas *m inv* esilarante
laughing stock *n* zimbello *m*
laughter /ˈlɑːftə(r)/ *n* risata *f*
launch[1] /lɔːntʃ/ *n* (boat) lancia *f*
⚷ **launch**[2] **A** *n* lancio *m*; (of ship) varo *m*
B *vt* lanciare ‹*rocket, product*›; varare ‹*ship*›; sferrare ‹*attack*›
▪ **launch into** *vt* intraprendere ‹*career*›; imbarcarsi in ‹*speech*›
launcher /ˈlɔːntʃə(r)/ *n* lanciamissili *m inv*
launch pad /ˈlɔːntʃ/, **launching pad** /ˈlɔːntʃ[ɪŋ]/ *n* piattaforma *f* di lancio; fig trampolino *m* di lancio
launder /ˈlɔːndə(r)/ *vt* lavare e stirare; ~ **money** fig riciclare denaro sporco
launderette /lɔːndəˈret/ *n* lavanderia *f* automatica
laundry /ˈlɔːndrɪ/ *n* lavanderia *f*; (clothes) bucato *m*
laureate /ˈlɒrɪət/ *adj* **poet** ~ poeta *m* di corte; **Nobel** ~ vincitore, -trice *mf* del Nobel
laurel /ˈlɒrəl/ *n* alloro *m*; **rest on one's** ~**s** fig dormire sugli allori
lav /læv/ *n* BrE infml gabinetto *m*
lava /ˈlɑːvə/ *n* lava *f*
lavatorial /lævəˈtɔːrɪəl/ *adj* ‹*humour*› scatologico
lavatory /ˈlævətrɪ/ *n* gabinetto *m*
lavender /ˈlævəndə(r)/ *n* lavanda *f*
lavender blue *adj* color lavanda
lavish /ˈlævɪʃ/ **A** *adj* copioso; (wasteful) prodigo; **on a** ~ **scale** su vasta scala
B *vt* ~ **something on somebody** ricoprire qualcuno di qualcosa
lavishly /ˈlævɪʃlɪ/ *adv* copiosamente
⚷ **law** /lɔː/ *n* legge *f*; **study** ~ studiare giurisprudenza, studiare legge; ~ **and order** ordine *m* pubblico; **take the** ~ **into one's own hands** farsi giustizia da sé; ~ **of the jungle** legge della giungla
law-abiding /ˈlɔːəbaɪdɪŋ/ *adj* che rispetta la legge
law and order *n* ordine *m* pubblico
lawbreaker /ˈlɔːbreɪkə(r)/ *n* persona *f* che infrange la legge
law court *n* tribunale *m*
lawful /ˈlɔːfʊl/ *adj* legittimo
lawfully /ˈlɔːfʊlɪ/ *adv* legittimamente
lawfulness /ˈlɔːfʊlnɪs/ *n* legalità *f*
lawless /ˈlɔːlɪs/ *adj* senza legge
lawmaker /ˈlɔːmeɪkə(r)/ *n* legislatore *m*
lawn /lɔːn/ *n* prato *m* [all'inglese]
lawnmower /ˈlɔːnməʊə(r)/ *n* tosaerba *m inv*
law school *n* facoltà *f* di giurisprudenza
lawsuit /ˈlɔːsuːt/ *n* causa *f*
⚷ **lawyer** /ˈlɔːjə(r)/ *n* avvocato *m*
lax /læks/ *adj* negligente; ‹*morals etc*› lassista
laxative /ˈlæksətɪv/ *n* lassativo *m*
laxity /ˈlæksətɪ/ *n* lassismo *m*
lay[1] /leɪ/ *adj* laico
lay[2] ▸ **lie**[2]
⚷ **lay**[3] **A** *vt* (*pt/pp* **laid**) porre, mettere; apparecchiare ‹*table*›
B *vi* ‹*hen*› fare le uova
▪ **lay aside** *vt* mettere da parte
▪ **lay down** *vt* posare; stabilire ‹*rules, conditions*›
▪ **lay in** *vt* farsi una scorta di ‹*coal, supplies etc*›
▪ **lay into** *vt* sl picchiare
▪ **lay off** **A** *vt* licenziare ‹*workers*›
B *vi* infml (stop) ~ **off!** smettila!
▪ **lay on** *vt* (organize) organizzare
▪ **lay out** *vt* (display, set forth) esporre; (plan) pianificare ‹*garden*›; (spend) sborsare; Typ impaginare
▪ **lay up**: *vt* **I was laid up in bed for a week** sono stato costretto a letto per una settimana
layabout /ˈleɪəbaʊt/ *n* fannullone, -a *mf*
lay-by *n* piazzola *f* di sosta
⚷ **layer** /ˈleɪə(r)/ *n* strato *m*
layette /leɪˈet/ *n* corredino *m*
layman /ˈleɪmən/ *n* profano *m*
lay-off /ˈleɪɒf/ *n* (permanent) licenziamento *m*; (temporary) sospensione *f*
layout /ˈleɪaʊt/ *n* disposizione *f*; Typ impaginazione *f*, layout *m inv*
lay preacher *n* predicatore *m* laico
laze /leɪz/ *vi* ~ **[about]** oziare
lazily /ˈleɪzɪlɪ/ *adv* ‹*move, wander etc*› pigramente
laziness /ˈleɪzɪnɪs/ *n* pigrizia *f*
lazy /ˈleɪzɪ/ *adj* (**-ier, -iest**) pigro
lazybones /ˈleɪzɪbəʊnz/ *n* poltrone, -a *mf*
lazy eye *n* ambliopia *f*
lb *abbr* (**pound**) libbra
LCD *n abbr* (**liquid crystal display**) LCD *m*
lead[1] /led/ *n* piombo *m*; (of pencil) mina *f*
⚷ **lead**[2] /liːd/ **A** *n* guida *f*; (leash) guinzaglio *m*; (flex) filo *m*; (clue) indizio *m*; Theat parte *f* principale; (distance ahead) distanza *f* (**over** su); **in the** ~ in testa; **follow sb's** ~ seguire l'esempio di qualcuno
B *vt* (*pt/pp* **led**) condurre; dirigere ‹*expedition, party etc*›; (induce) indurre; ~ **the way** mettersi in testa; ~ **into temptation** indurre in tentazione
C *vi* (be in front) condurre; (in race, competition) essere in testa

⚷ parola chiave

■ **lead astray** *vt* sviare
■ **lead away** *vt* portar via
■ **lead on** *vt* ingannare
■ **lead off** **A** *vi* (begin) cominciare
B *vt* (take away) portare via
■ **lead to** *vt* portare a
■ **lead up to** *vt* preludere; **the period ~ing up to the election** il periodo precedente le elezioni; **what's this ~ing up to?** dove porta questo?

leaded /'ledɪd/ *adj* con piombo

leaded petrol BrE, **leaded gasoline** AmE *n* benzina *f* con piombo

leaden /'ledən/ *adj* di piombo

leader /'liːdə(r)/ *n* capo *m*; (of orchestra) primo violino *m*; (in newspaper) articolo *m* di fondo

leadership /'liːdəʃɪp/ *n* direzione *f*, leadership *f inv*; **show ~** mostrare capacità di comando

leadership contest *n* elezione *f* alla direzione del partito

lead-free /'ledfriː/ *adj* senza piombo

lead-in /'liːdɪn/ *n* presentazione *f*

leading¹ /'liːdɪŋ/ *adj* principale

leading² /'ledɪŋ/ *n* Typ interlinea *f*

leading article *n* articolo *m* di fondo

leading edge *n* Aeron bordo *m* d'attacco; **at the ~ of** (technology) all'avanguardia in

leading lady attrice *f* principale

leading light *n* personaggio *m* di spicco

leading man attore *m* principale

leading question *n* domanda *f* che influenza la risposta

lead poisoning *n* saturnismo *m*

lead story *n* articolo *f* principale

leaf /liːf/ *n* (*pl* **leaves**) foglia *f*; (of table) asse *f*; fig **take a ~ out of sb's book** imparare la lezione di qualcuno; **turn over a new ~** voltare pagina
■ **leaf through** *vt* sfogliare

leaflet /'liːflɪt/ *n* dépliant *m inv*; (advertising) dépliant *m inv* pubblicitario; (political) manifestino *m*

leafy /'liːfɪ/ *adj* ‹*tree*› ricco di foglie; ‹*wood*› molto verde; ‹*suburb, area*› ricco di verde

league /liːg/ *n* lega *f*; Sport campionato *m*; **be in ~ with** essere in combutta con

league table *n* classifica *f* del campionato

leak /liːk/ **A** *n* (hole) fessura *f*; Naut falla *f*; (of gas & fig) fuga *f*
B *vi* colare; ‹*ship*› fare acqua; ‹*liquid, gas*› fuoriuscire
C *vt* **~ something to somebody** fig far trapelare qualcosa a qualcuno

leakage /'liːkɪdʒ/ *n* perdita *f*; (of gas & fig) fuga *f*

leaky /'liːkɪ/ *adj* che perde; Naut che fa acqua

lean¹ /liːn/ *adj* magro

lean² **A** *vt* (*pt/pp* **leaned** *or* **leant** /lent/) appoggiare (**against/on** contro/su); **~ one's elbows on the table** appoggiare i gomiti sul tavolo
B *vi* appoggiarsi (**against/on** contro/su); (not be straight) pendere; **be ~ing against** essere appoggiato contro; **~ on somebody** (depend on) appoggiarsi a qualcuno; infml (exert pressure on) stare alle calcagna di qualcuno
■ **lean back** *vi* sporgersi indietro
■ **lean forward** *vi* piegarsi in avanti
■ **lean out** *vi* sporgersi
■ **lean over** *vi* piegarsi
■ **lean towards** *vt* (favour) propendere per

leaning /'liːnɪŋ/ **A** *adj* pendente; **the L~ Tower of Pisa** la torre di Pisa, la torre pendente
B *n* tendenza *f*

leanness /'liːnnɪs/ *n* magrezza *f*

lean-to *n garage* (*m inv*) *adiacente alla casa*

leap /liːp/ **A** *n* salto *m*
B *vi* (*pt/pp* **leapt** /lept/ *or* **leaped**) saltare; **he leapt at it** infml l'ha preso al volo

leapfrog /'liːpfrɒg/ *n* cavallina *f*

leap year *n* anno *m* bisestile

learn /lɜːn/ **A** *vt* (*pt/pp* **learnt** BrE *or* **learned**) imparare; **~ to swim** imparare a nuotare; **I have ~ed that...** (heard) sono venuto a sapere che...; fig **he's ~t his lesson** ha imparato la lezione
B *vi* imparare; **as I've ~t to my cost** come ho imparato a mie spese

learned /'lɜːnɪd/ *adj* colto

learner /'lɜːnə(r)/ *n* also Auto principiante *mf*

learning /'lɜːnɪŋ/ *n* cultura *f*

learning curve *n* curva *f* di apprendimento

learning difficulties *npl* (of schoolchildren) difficoltà *fpl* d'apprendimento

learning disability *n* difficoltà *fpl* d'apprendimento

lease /liːs/ **A** *n* contratto *m* d'affitto; (rental) affitto *m*; **the job has given him a new ~ of life** grazie al lavoro ha ripreso gusto alla vita
B *vt* affittare

leasehold /'liːshəʊld/ *n* proprietà *f* in affitto

leaseholder /'liːshəʊldə(r)/ *n titolare* (*mf*) *di un contratto d'affitto*

leash /liːʃ/ *n* guinzaglio *m*

leasing /'liːsɪŋ/ *n* (by company) leasing *m*; **~ scheme** piano di leasing

least /liːst/ **A** *adj* più piccolo; (smallest amount) meno; **you've got ~ luggage** hai meno bagagli di tutti
B *n* **the ~** il meno; **that's the ~ of my worries** questa è la cosa che mi preoccupa di meno; **at ~** almeno; **not in the ~** niente affatto
C *adv* meno; **the ~ expensive wine** il vino meno caro

leather /'leðə(r)/ **A** *n* pelle *f*; (of soles) cuoio *m*
B *attrib* di pelle/cuoio; **~ jacket** giubbotto

m di pelle

leathery /ˈleðərɪ/ *adj* (meat, skin) duro

🔑 **leave** /liːv/ **A** *n* (holiday) congedo *m*; Mil licenza *f*; **on ~** in congedo/licenza; **take one's ~** accomiatarsi; **~ of absence** aspettativa *f*
B *vt* (*pt/pp* **left**) lasciare; uscire da ‹*house, office*›; (forget) dimenticare; **there is nothing left** non è rimasto niente; **~ somebody in peace** lasciare in pace qualcuno
C *vi* andare via; ‹*train, bus*› partire
■ **leave aside** *vt* (disregard) lasciare da parte
■ **leave behind** *vt* lasciare; (forget) dimenticare
■ **leave out** *vt* omettere; (not put away) lasciare fuori

leaves /liːvz/ ▶ **leaf**

leaving /ˈliːvɪŋ/ *adj* ‹*party, present*› d'addio

Lebanese /lebəˈniːz/ *adj & n* libanese *mf*

Lebanon /ˈlebənən/ *n* Libano *m*

lecher /ˈletʃə(r)/ *n* libertino *m*

lecherous /ˈletʃərəs/ *adj* lascivo

lechery /ˈletʃərɪ/ *n* lascivia *f*

lectern /ˈlektɜːn/ *n* leggio *m*, scannello *m*

lecture /ˈlektʃə(r)/ **A** *n* conferenza *f*; Univ lezione *f*; (reproof) ramanzina *f*
B *vi* fare una conferenza (**on** su); Univ insegnare (**on something** qualcosa)
C *vt* **~ somebody** rimproverare qualcuno

lecturer /ˈlektʃərə(r)/ *n* conferenziere, -a *mf*; Univ docente *mf* universitario, -a

lecture room *n* BrE Univ aula *f* magna

lectureship /ˈlektʃəʃɪp/ *n* BrE Univ docenza *f* universitaria

lecture theatre *n* BrE Univ aula *f* magna

led /led/ ▶ **lead²**

LED *abbr* (**light-emitting diode**) LED *m inv*

ledge /ledʒ/ *n* cornice *f*; (of window) davanzale *m*

ledger /ˈledʒə(r)/ *n* libro *m* mastro

leech /liːtʃ/ *n* sanguisuga *f*

leek /liːk/ *n* porro *m*

leer /lɪə(r)/ **A** *n* sguardo *m* libidinoso
B *vi* **~ (at)** guardare in modo libidinoso

lees /liːz/ *npl* (wine sediment) fondi *mpl*

leeway /ˈliːweɪ/ *n* fig libertà *f* di azione

left¹ /left/ ▶ **leave**

🔑 **left²** **A** *adj* sinistro
B *adv* a sinistra
C *n* (also Pol) sinistra *f*; **on the ~** a sinistra

left-hand /ˌleftˈhænd/ *adj* di sinistra; **on the ~ side** sulla sinistra

left-hand drive *adj* ‹*car*› con la guida a sinistra

left-handed /-ˈhændɪd/ *adj* mancino; ‹*scissors etc*› per mancini

leftie /ˈleftɪ/ *n* sinistrorso, -a *mf*

leftist /ˈleftɪst/ *adj & n* sinistrorso, -a *mf*

left luggage, left luggage office *n* deposito *m* bagagli

left-luggage lockers *npl* deposito *m* bagagli automatico

leftovers *npl* rimasugli *mpl*

left wing *n* Pol sinistra *f*; Sport ala *f* sinistra

left-wing *adj* Pol di sinistra

left-winger *n* Pol persona *f* di sinistra; Sport ala *f* sinistra

🔑 **leg** /leg/ **A** *n* gamba *f*; ((of animal)) zampa *f*; (of journey) tappa *f*; Culin (of chicken) coscia *f*; (of lamb) cosciotto *m*; **be on one's last ~s** ‹*machine*› funzionare per miracolo; **not have a ~ to stand on** non avere una ragione che regga
B *vi* **~ it** infml darsela a gambe

legacy /ˈlegəsɪ/ *n* lascito *m*

🔑 **legal** /ˈliːgl/ *adj* legale; **take ~ action** intentare un'azione legale

legal adviser *n* consulente *mf* legale

legal aid *n* patrocinio *m* gratuito

legal eagle *n* hum principe *m* del foro

legal holiday *n* AmE festa *f* nazionale

legality /lɪˈgælətɪ/ *n* legalità *f*

legalization /liːgəlaɪˈzeɪʃn/ *n* legalizzazione *f*

legalize /ˈliːgəlaɪz/ *vt* legalizzare

legally /ˈliːgəlɪ/ *adv* legalmente

legal proceedings *npl* procedimento *m sg* giudiziario

legal tender *n* valuta *f* a corso legale

legend /ˈledʒənd/ *n* leggenda *f*

legendary /ˈledʒəndərɪ/ *adj* leggendario

leggings /ˈlegɪŋz/ *npl* (for baby) ghette *fpl*; (for woman) pantacollant *mpl*; (for man) gambali *mpl*

leggy /ˈlegɪ/ *adj* ‹*person*› con le gambe lunghe

Leghorn /ˈleghɔːn/ *n* Livorno *f*

legibility /ledʒəˈbɪlətɪ/ *n* leggibilità *f*

legible /ˈledʒəbl/ *adj* leggibile

legibly /ˈledʒəblɪ/ *adv* in modo leggibile

legion /ˈliːdʒn/ *n* legione *f*

legionnaire /liːdʒəˈneə(r)/ *n* Mil legionario *m*

legionnaire's disease *n* legionellosi *f*

legislate /ˈledʒɪsleɪt/ *vi* legiferare

🔑 **legislation** /ledʒɪsˈleɪʃn/ *n* legislazione *f*

legislative /ˈledʒɪslətɪv/ *adj* legislativo

legislator /ˈledʒɪsleɪtə(r)/ *n* legislatore *m*

legislature /ˈledʒɪsleɪtʃə(r)/ *n* legislatura *f*

legitimacy /lɪˈdʒɪtɪməsɪ/ *n* (lawfulness) legittimità *f*; (of argument) validità *f*

legitimate /lɪˈdʒɪtɪmət/ *adj* legittimo; ‹*excuse*› valido

legitimately /lɪˈdʒɪtɪmətlɪ/ *adv* legittimamente

legitimize /lɪdʒɪtɪˈmaɪz/ *vt* rendere legittimo

legless /ˈleglɪs/ *adj* senza gambe; BrE (drunk) ubriaco fradicio

🔑 parola chiave

leg-pulling *n* presa *f* in giro
legroom *n* spazio *m* per le gambe
leg warmer *n* scaldamuscoli *m inv*
legwork *n* fatica *f*; **do the ∼** fare da galoppino
leisure /ˈleʒə(r)/ *n* tempo *m* libero; **at your ∼** con comodo
leisure centre *n* centro *m* sportivo e ricreativo
leisurely /ˈleʒəlɪ/ *adj* senza fretta
leisure time *n* tempo *m* libero
leisurewear /ˈleʒəweə(r)/ *n* abbigliamento *m* per il tempo libero
lemming /ˈlemɪŋ/ *n* lemming *m inv*
lemon /ˈlemən/ *n* limone *m*
lemonade /leməˈneɪd/ *n* limonata *f*
lemon curd *n* crema *f* al limone
lemon juice *n* (drink) succo *m* di limone
lemon sole *n* sogliola *f* limanda
lemon squash *n* sciroppo *m* di limone
lemon tea *n* tè *m* al limone
lemon tree *n* limone *m*
lemon yellow **A** *n* giallo *m* limone
B *adj* giallo limone
lend /lend/ *vt* (*pt/pp* **lent**) prestare; **∼ a hand** fig dare una mano; **∼ an ear** prestare ascolto; **∼ itself to** prestarsi a
lender /ˈlendə(r)/ *n* prestatore, -trice *mf*
lending library /ˈlendɪn/ *n* biblioteca *f* per il prestito
length /leŋθ/ *n* lunghezza *f*; (piece) pezzo *m*; (of wallpaper) parte *f*; (of visit) durata *f*; **at ∼** a lungo; (at last) alla fine
lengthen /ˈleŋθən/ **A** *vt* allungare
B *vi* allungarsi
lengthways /ˈleŋθweɪz/ *adv* per lungo
lengthwise /ˈleŋθwaɪz/ *adv* longitudinale
lengthy /ˈleŋθɪ/ *adj* (**-ier**, **-iest**) lungo
lenience /ˈliːnɪəns/ *n* indulgenza *f*
lenient /ˈliːnɪənt/ *adj* indulgente
leniently /ˈliːnɪəntlɪ/ *adv* con indulgenza
lens /lenz/ *n* lente *f*; Phot obiettivo *m*; (of eye) cristallino *m*
lens cap *n* copriobiettivo *m*
lent ▸ **lend**
Lent /lent/ *n* Quaresima *f*
lentil /ˈlentl/ *n* Bot lenticchia *f*
Leo /ˈliːəʊ/ *n* Astr Leone *m*
leopard /ˈlepəd/ *n* leopardo *m*
leopard-skin /ˈlepədskɪn/ **A** *n* pelle *f* di leopardo
B *attrib* di [pelle di] leopardo
leotard /ˈliːətɑːd/ *n* body *m inv*
leper /ˈlepə(r)/ *n* lebbroso, -a *mf*; fig appestato, -a *mf*
leprosy /ˈleprəsɪ/ *n* lebbra *f*
lesbian /ˈlezbɪən/ **A** *adj* lesbico
B *n* lesbica *f*
lesbianism /ˈlezbɪənɪzm/ *n* lesbismo *m*
lesion /ˈliːʒn/ *n* lesione *f*
Lesotho /lɪˈsuːtʊ, ləˈsəʊtʊ/ *n* Lesotho *m*
less /les/ **A** *adj* meno di; **∼ and ∼** sempre meno
B *adv & prep* meno
C *n* meno *m*
lessee /leˈsiː/ *n* Jur affittuario, -a *mf*
lessen /ˈlesn/ *vt & vi* diminuire
lesser /ˈlesə(r)/ *adj* minore; **the ∼ of two evils** il minore fra i due mali
lesson /ˈlesn/ *n* lezione *f*; **teach somebody a ∼** fig dare una lezione a qualcuno
lessor /leˈsɔː/ *n* Jur locatore, -trice *mf*
lest /lest/ *conj* literary per timore che
let /let/ **A** *vt* (*pt/pp* **let**, *pres p* **letting**) lasciare, permettere; (rent) affittare; **∼ alone** (not to mention) tanto meno; **'to ∼'** 'affittasi'; **∼ us go** andiamo; **∼ somebody do something** lasciare fare qualcosa a qualcuno, permettere a qualcuno di fare qualcosa; **∼ me know** fammi sapere; **just ∼ him try!** che ci provi solamente!; **∼ oneself in for something** infml impelagarsi in qualcosa
B *n* Tennis colpo *m* nullo; BrE (lease) contratto *m* d'affitto
C *vi* **∼ fly at somebody** aggredire qualcuno
■ **let down** *vt* sciogliersi ‹*hair*›; abbassare ‹*blinds*›; (lengthen) allungare; (disappoint) deludere; **don't ∼ me down** conto su di te
■ **let go** **A** *vi* mollare; **∼ go of** lasciare andare
B *vt* mollare ‹*rope, person*›; **∼ somebody go** rilasciare ‹*prisoner*›; licenziare ‹*employee*›; **∼ oneself go** lasciarsi andare
■ **let in** *vt* far entrare
■ **let off** *vt* far partire; (not punish) perdonare; **∼ somebody off doing something** abbonare qualcosa a qualcuno; **∼ off steam** fig scaricarsi
■ **let on**: *vi sl* **don't ∼ on** non spifferare niente
■ **let out** *vt* far uscire; (make larger) allargare; emettere ‹*scream, groan*›
■ **let through** *vt* far passare
■ **let up** *vi* infml diminuire
let-down *n* delusione *f*
lethal /ˈliːθl/ *adj* letale; **∼ dose** *n* dose *f* letale
lethargic /lɪˈθɑːdʒɪk/ *adj* apatico
lethargy /ˈleθədʒɪ/ *n* apatia *f*
let-out *n* infml via *f* d'uscita
letter /ˈletə(r)/ *n* lettera *f*
letter bomb *n* lettera *f* esplosiva
letter box *n* buca *f* per le lettere
letterhead *n* (heading) intestazione *f*; (paper) carta *f* intestata
lettering /ˈletərɪŋ/ *n* caratteri *mpl*
letter of apology *n* lettera *f* di scuse
letter of credit *n* Comm lettera *f* di credito
letter of introduction *n* lettera *f* di presentazione

lettuce /ˈletɪs/ *n* lattuga *f*
let-up *n* infml pausa *f*
leukaemia /luːˈkiːmɪə/ *n* leucemia *f*
✓ **level** /ˈlevl/ **A** *adj* piano; (in height, competition) allo stesso livello; ‹*spoonful*› raso; **draw ~ with somebody** affiancare qualcuno; **do one's ~ best** fare del proprio meglio
B *n* livello *m*; **on the ~** infml giusto
C *vt* (*pt/pp* **levelled**) livellare; (aim) puntare (**at** su)
▪ **level off** *vi* ‹*inflation, unemployment*› stabilizzarsi
▪ **level out** *vi* ‹*surface*› diventare pianeggiante; ‹*aircraft*› mettersi in orizzontale
▪ **level with** *vt* infml (be honest with) essere franco con
level crossing *n* passaggio *m* a livello
level-headed /-ˈhedɪd/ *adj* posato
level pegging *n* **it's ~ so far** finora sono alla pari
lever /ˈliːvə(r)/ *n* leva *f*
▪ **lever off**, **lever up** *vt* sollevare (*con una leva*)
leverage /ˈliːvərɪdʒ/ *n* azione *f* di una leva; fig influenza *f*
leveret /ˈlevərət/ *n* leprotto *m*
levitate /ˈlevɪteɪt/ *vi* levitare
levity /ˈlevətɪ/ *n* leggerezza *f*
levy /ˈlevɪ/ *vt* (*pt/pp* **levied**) imporre ‹*tax*›
lewd /ljuːd/ *adj* osceno
lexical /ˈleksɪkəl/ *adj* lessicale
lexicographer /leksɪˈkɒgrəfə(r)/ *n* lessicografo, -a *mf*
lexicographic /leksɪkəˈgræfɪk/ *adj* lessicografico
lexicography /leksɪˈkɒgrəfɪ/ *n* lessicografia *f*
lexicon /ˈleksɪkən/ *n* lessico *m*
liability /laɪəˈbɪlətɪ/ *n* responsabilità *f*; infml (burden) peso *m*; **liabilities** *pl* passività *fpl*
liable /ˈlaɪəbl/ *adj* responsabile (**for** di); **be ~ to** ‹*rain, break etc*› rischiare di; (tend to) tendere a
liaise /lɪˈeɪz/ *vi* infml essere in contatto
liaison /lɪˈeɪzɒn/ *n* contatti *mpl*; Mil collegamento *m*; (affair) relazione *f*
liar /ˈlaɪə(r)/ *n* bugiardo, -a *mf*
Lib Dem /lɪbˈdem/ *abbr* BrE Pol (**Liberal Democrat**) liberaldemocratico
libel /ˈlaɪbl/ **A** *n* diffamazione *f*
B *vt* (*pt/pp* **libelled**) diffamare
libellous BrE, **libelous** AmE *adj* diffamatorio
liberal /ˈlɪb(ə)rəl/ **A** *adj* (tolerant) di larghe vedute; (generous) generoso; **L~** *adj* Pol liberale
B *n* liberale *mf*
Liberal Democrat *n* BrE Pol liberal-democratico, -a *mf*
liberalism /ˈlɪbərəlɪzəm/ *n* liberalismo *m*
liberalization /lɪbərəlaɪˈzeɪʃn/ *n* (of trade) liberalizzazione *f*
liberalize /ˈlɪbərəlaɪz/ *vt* liberalizzare
liberally /ˈlɪbrəlɪ/ *adv* liberalmente
liberate /ˈlɪbəreɪt/ *vt* liberare
liberated /ˈlɪbəreɪtɪd/ *adj* ‹*woman*› emancipato
liberating /ˈlɪbəreɪtɪŋ/ *adj* liberatorio
liberation /lɪbəˈreɪʃn/ *n* liberazione *f*; (of women) emancipazione *f*
liberator /ˈlɪbəreɪtə(r)/ *n* liberatore, -trice *mf*
Liberia /laɪˈbɪərɪə/ *n* Liberia *f*
libertarian /lɪbəˈteərɪən/ *adj & n* liberale *mf*
libertarianism /lɪbəˈteərɪənɪzm/ *n* liberalismo *m*
liberty /ˈlɪbətɪ/ *n* libertà *f*; **take the ~ of doing something** prendersi la libertà di fare qualcosa; **take liberties** prendersi delle libertà; **be at ~ to do something** essere libero di fare qualcosa
libido /lɪˈbiːdəʊ/ *n* libido *f inv*
Libra /ˈliːbrə/ *n* Astr Bilancia *f*
librarian /laɪˈbreərɪən/ *n* bibliotecario, -a *mf*
✓ **library** /ˈlaɪbrərɪ/ *n* biblioteca *f*
libretto /lɪˈbretəʊ/ *n* (*pl* **-tti** *or* **-ttos**) libretto *m* di opera
Libya /ˈlɪbɪə/ *n* Libia *f*
Libyan /ˈlɪbɪən/ *adj & n* libico, -a *mf*
lice /laɪs/ ▶ **louse**
✓ **licence** /ˈlaɪsns/ *n* licenza *f*; (for TV) canone *m* televisivo; (for driving) patente *f*; (freedom) sregolatezza *f*
licence number *n* numero *m* di targa
licence plate *n* targa *f*
license /ˈlaɪsns/ *vt* autorizzare; **be ~d** ‹*car*› avere il bollo; ‹*restaurant*› essere autorizzato alla vendita di alcolici
licensee /laɪsənˈsiː/ *n* titolare *mf* di licenza (*per la vendita di alcolici*)
licensing hours /ˈlaɪsənsɪŋ/ *npl* BrE *orario (m) in cui è permessa la vendita di alcolici*
licensing laws *npl* BrE normativa *f sg* sulla vendita di alcolici
licentious /laɪˈsenʃəs/ *adj* licenzioso
licentiousness /laɪˈsenʃəsnɪs/ *n* licenziosità *f*
lichen /ˈlaɪkən/ *n* Bot lichene *m*
lick /lɪk/ **A** *n* leccata *f*; **a ~ of paint** una passata leggera di pittura
B *vt* leccare; infml (defeat) battere; leccarsi ‹*lips*›; infml **~ somebody into shape** rendere qualcuno efficiente
licorice /ˈlɪkərɪs/ *n* AmE = **liquorice**
lid /lɪd/ *n* coperchio *m*; (of eye) palpebra *f*; **keep the ~ on something** infml non lasciare trapelare qualcosa
lido /ˈliːdəʊ/ *n* (beach) lido *m*; BrE ‹*pool*› piscina *f* scoperta
lie¹ /laɪ/ **A** *n* bugia *f*; **tell a ~** mentire
B *vi* (*pt/pp* **lied**, *pres p* **lying**) mentire

✓ parola chiave

lie² *vi* (*pt* **lay**, *pp* **lain**, *pres p* **lying**) ‹*person*› sdraiarsi; ‹*object*› stare; (remain) rimanere; **leave something lying about** *or* **around** lasciare qualcosa in giro; **here ~s...** qui giace...; **~ low** tenersi nascosto

■ **lie around** **A** *vi* ‹*person*› girellare
B *vt* girellare in ‹*house*›

■ **lie back** *vi* (relax) rilassarsi

■ **lie down** *vi* sdraiarsi

■ **lie in** *vi* (stay in bed) rimanere a letto

Liechtenstein /ˈlɪktənstaɪn/ *n* Liechtenstein *m*

lie detector *n* macchina *f* della verità

lie-down *n* **have a ~** fare un riposino

lie-in *n* infml **have a ~** restare a letto fino a tardi

lieu /ljuː/ *n* **in ~ of** in luogo di

lieutenant /lefˈtenənt/ *n* tenente *m*

life /laɪf/ *n* (*pl* **lives**) vita *f*; **give one's ~ for somebody/one's country** dare la vita per qualcuno/la patria; **give one's ~ to** (devote oneself to) dedicare la propria vita a; **lose one's ~** perdere la vita; **for dear ~** per salvare la pelle; **not on your ~!** infml neanche morto!

life-and-death *adj* ‹*struggle*› disperato

lifebelt *n* salvagente *m*

lifeblood *n* fig linfa *f* vitale

lifeboat *n* lancia *f* di salvataggio; (on ship) scialuppa *f* di salvataggio

lifebuoy *n* salvagente *m*

life coach *n* life coach *mf inv*

life drawing *n* disegno *m* dal vero

life expectancy *n* vita *f* media

life form *n* forma *f* di vita

lifeguard *n* (on beach etc) bagnino, -a *mf*

life imprisonment *n* ergastolo *m*

life insurance *n* assicurazione *f* sulla vita

life jacket *n* giubbotto *m* di salvataggio

lifeless /ˈlaɪflɪs/ *adj* inanimato

lifelike *adj* realistico

lifeline *n* sagola *f* di salvataggio

lifelong *adj* di tutta la vita

lifer /ˈlaɪfə(r)/ *n* infml ergastolano, -a *mf*

life saving /ˈlaɪfseɪvɪŋ/ *n* salvataggio *m*

life sentence *n* condanna *f* all'ergastolo

life-size /ˈlaɪfsaɪz/, **life-sized** /ˈlaɪfsaɪzd/ *adj* a grandezza naturale

lifespan *n* durata *f* della vita

life story *n* biografia *f*

lifestyle *n* stile *m* di vita

lifestyle drug *n medicinale* (*m*) *che migliora la qualità della vita*

life support *n* Med respirazione *f* assistita; **on ~** attaccato al respiratore artificiale; **~ machine** respiratore artificiale

lifetime *n* vita *f*; **the chance of a ~** un'occasione unica; **~ guarantee** garanzia *f* a vita

lift /lɪft/ **A** *n* ascensore *m*; Auto passaggio *m*; **give somebody a ~** dare un passaggio a qualcuno; **I got a ~** mi hanno dato un passaggio
B *vt* sollevare; revocare ‹*restrictions*›; infml (steal) rubare
C *vi* ‹*fog*› alzarsi

■ **lift off** *vi* ‹*rocket*› partire

■ **lift up** *vt* sollevare

lift boy *n* BrE lift *m inv*

lift-off *n* decollo *m* (*di razzo*)

ligament /ˈlɪgəmənt/ *n* Anat legamento *m*

light¹ /laɪt/ **A** *adj* (not dark) luminoso; **~ green** verde chiaro
B *n* luce *f*; (lamp) lampada *f*; **in the ~ of** fig alla luce di; **have you got a ~?** ha da accendere?; **come to ~** essere rivelato
C *vt* (*pt/pp* **lit** *or* **lighted**) accendere; (illuminate) illuminare

■ **light up** **A** *vt* accendere ‹*pipe, cigarette*›; illuminare ‹*face*›; rischiarare ‹*sky*›
B *vi* ‹*face*› illuminarsi

light² **A** *adj* (not heavy) leggero; **make ~ of** non dare peso a
B *adv* **travel ~** viaggiare con poco bagaglio

light bulb *n* lampadina *f*

lighten¹ /ˈlaɪtn/ *vt* illuminare

lighten² *vt* alleggerire ‹*load*›

light entertainment *n* varietà *m*

lighter /ˈlaɪtə(r)/ *n* accendino *m*

lighter fuel *n* (liquid) gas *m inv* da accendino

light-fingered /-ˈfɪŋgəd/ *adj* svelto di mano

light-headed /-ˈhedɪd/ *adj* sventato

light-hearted /-ˈhɑːtɪd/ *adj* spensierato

lighthouse *n* faro *m*

light industry *n* industria *f* leggera

lighting /ˈlaɪtɪŋ/ *n* illuminazione *f*

lightly /ˈlaɪtlɪ/ *adv* leggermente; ‹*accuse*› con leggerezza; ‹*take something*› alla leggera; (without concern) senza dare importanza alla cosa; **get off ~** cavarsela a buon mercato

lightness /ˈlaɪtnɪs/ *n* leggerezza *f*

lightning /ˈlaɪtnɪŋ/ *n* lampo *m*, fulmine *m*

lightning conductor *n* parafulmine *m*

lightning strike *n* sciopero *m* a sorpresa

light pen *n* (for computer screen) penna *f* ottica

light pollution *n* inquinamento *m* luminoso

lightweight **A** *adj* leggero
B *n* (in boxing) peso *m* leggero

light year *n* anno *m* luce; **it was ~s ago** è stato secoli fa

like¹ /laɪk/ **A** *adj* simile
B *prep* come; **~ this/that** così; **what's he ~?** com'è?
C *conj* infml (as) come; AmE (as if) come se

like² **A** *vt* piacere, gradire; **I should** *or* **would ~** vorrei, gradirei; **I ~ him** mi piace; **I ~ this**

car mi piace questa macchina; **I ~ dancing** mi piace ballare; **I ~ that!** infml questa mi è piaciuta!; **~ it or lump it!** abbozzala!
B *n* **~s and dislikes** *pl* gusti *mpl*

likeable /'laɪkəbl/ *adj* simpatico

likelihood /'laɪklɪhʊd/ *n* probabilità *f*

likely /'laɪklɪ/ **A** *adj* (**-ier, -iest**) probabile
B *adv* probabilmente; **not ~!** infml neanche per sogno!

like-minded /laɪk'maɪndɪd/ *adj* con gusti affini

liken /'laɪkən/ *vt* paragonare (**to** a)

likeness /'laɪknɪs/ *n* somiglianza *f*

likewise /'laɪkwaɪz/ *adv* lo stesso

liking /'laɪkɪŋ/ *n* gusto *m*; **is it to your ~?** è di suo gusto?; **take a ~ to somebody** prendere qualcuno in simpatia

lilac /'laɪlək/ **A** *n* lillà *m*
B *adj* lilla

Lilo® /'laɪləʊ/ *n* materassino *m* gonfiabile

lilting /'lɪltɪŋ/ *adj* cadenzato

lily /'lɪlɪ/ *n* giglio *m*

lily of the valley *n* mughetto *m*

lily pond *n* stagno *m* con ninfee

limb /lɪm/ *n* arto *m*

limber /'lɪmbə(r)/ *vi* **~ up** sciogliersi i muscoli

limbo /'lɪmbəʊ/ *n* Relig fig (dance) limbo *m*; **be in ~** ‹*person*› essere nel limbo del dubbio; ‹*future of something*› essere in sospeso

lime¹ /laɪm/ *n* (fruit) limetta *f*; (tree) tiglio *m*

lime² *n* calce *f*

lime-green *adj & n* verde *m* limone

limelight /'laɪmlaɪt/ *n* **be in the ~** essere molto in vista

limestone /'laɪmstəʊn/ *n* calcare *m*

limit /'lɪmɪt/ **A** *n* limite *m*; **be the ~** essere il colmo; **that's the ~!** infml questo è troppo!
B *vt* limitare (**to** a)

limitation /lɪmɪ'teɪʃn/ *n* limite *m*

limited /'lɪmɪtɪd/ *adj* ristretto

limited company *n* società *f* a responsabilità limitata

limited edition *n* (book, lithograph) edizione *f* limitata

limited liability *n* responsabilità *f* limitata

limitless /'lɪmɪtlɪs/ *adj* infinito

limousine /'lɪməzi:n/ *n* limousine *f inv*

limp¹ /lɪmp/ **A** *n* andatura *f* zoppicante; **have a ~** zoppicare
B *vi* zoppicare

limp² *adj* floscio

limpet /'lɪmpɪt/ *n* **be like a ~** fig essere attaccaticcio

limpid /'lɪmpɪd/ *adj* limpido

limp-wristed /-'rɪstɪd/ *adj* derog effeminato

linchpin /'lɪntʃpɪn/ *n* fig (essential element) perno *m*

line¹ /laɪn/ **A** *n* linea *f*; (length of rope, cord) filo *m*; (of writing) riga *f*; (of poem) verso *m*; (row) fila *f*; (wrinkle) ruga *f*; (of business) settore *m*; AmE (queue) coda *f*; **in ~ with** in conformità con; **bring into ~** mettere al passo ‹*structure, law*›; **in the ~ of duty** (of policeman) nell'esercizio delle proprie funzioni; **~ of fire** linea *f* di tiro; **stand in ~** AmE (queue) fare la coda; **in ~ for** ‹*promotion etc*› in lista per; **on the ~** ‹*job, career*› in serio pericolo; **read between the ~s** fig leggere tra le righe
B *vt* segnare; fiancheggiare ‹*street*›; foderare ‹*garment*›

■ **line up** **A** *vi* allinearsi
B *vt* allineare

lineage /'lɪnɪɪdʒ/ *n* lignaggio *m*

linear /'lɪnɪə(r)/ *adj* lineare

lined¹ /laɪnd/ *adj* ‹*face*› rugoso; ‹*paper*› a righe

lined² *adj* ‹*garment*› foderato

line manager *n* line manager *m inv*

linen /'lɪnɪn/ **A** *n* lino *m*; (articles) biancheria *f*
B *attrib* di lino

linen basket *n* cesto *m* della biancheria

liner /'laɪnə(r)/ *n* nave *f* di linea

linesman /'laɪnzmən/ *n* Sport guardalinee *m inv*

line-up *n* (personnel) Sport formazione *f*; (identification) confronto *m* all'americana

linger /'lɪŋgə(r)/ *vi* indugiare

lingerie /'lõʒərɪ/ *n* biancheria *f* intima (*da donna*)

lingering /'lɪŋgərɪŋ/ *adj* ‹*illness*› lento; ‹*look*› prolungato; ‹*doubt*› persistente

linguist /'lɪŋgwɪst/ *n* linguista *mf*

linguistic /lɪŋ'gwɪstɪk/ *adj* linguistico

linguistically /lɪŋ'gwɪstɪklɪ/ *adv* linguisticamente

linguistics /lɪŋ'gwɪstɪks/ *nsg* linguistica *fsg*

lining /'laɪnɪŋ/ *n* (of garment) fodera *f*; (of brakes) guarnizione *f*

link /lɪŋk/ **A** *n* (of chain) anello *m*; fig legame *m*
B *vt* collegare; **~ arms** prendersi sottobraccio; Comput ‹*web pages*› linkare

■ **link up** TV *vi* unirsi (**with** a); TV collegarsi

linkage /'lɪŋkɪdʒ/ *n* (connection) connessione *f*; (in genetics) associazione *f*

link road *n* bretella *f*

links /lɪŋks/ *n or npl* campo *msg* da golf

link-up *n* collegamento *m*

lino /'laɪnəʊ/, **linoleum** /lɪ'nəʊlɪəm/ *n* linoleum *m*

linseed oil /'lɪnsi:dɔɪl/ *n* olio *m* [di semi] di lino

lint /lɪnt/ *n* garza *f*

lintel /'lɪntəl/ *n* architrave *m*

lion /'laɪən/ *n* leone *m*; **get the ~'s share** fig prendersi la fetta più grossa

lion cub *n* leoncino *m*

lioness /'laɪənɪs/ *n* leonessa *f*

parola chiave

lip /lɪp/ *n* labbro *m* (*pl* labbra *f*); (edge) bordo *m*
lip gloss *n* lucidalabbra *m inv*
liposuction /ˈlaɪpəʊsʌkʃn/ *n* liposuzione *f*
lip-read *vi* leggere le labbra
lip-reading *n* lettura *f* delle labbra
lipsalve *n* burro *m* [di] cacao
lip service *n* **pay ~ to** approvare soltanto a parole
lipstick *n* rossetto *m*
liquefy /ˈlɪkwɪfaɪ/ *v* (*pt/pp* **-ied**) **A** *vt* liquefare
B *vi* liquefarsi
liqueur /lɪˈkjʊə(r)/ *n* liquore *m*
liquid /ˈlɪkwɪd/ **A** *n* liquido *m*
B *adj* liquido
liquidate /ˈlɪkwɪdeɪt/ *vt* liquidare
liquidation /lɪkwɪˈdeɪʃn/ *n* liquidazione *f*; **go into ~** Comm andare in liquidazione
liquidator /ˈlɪkwɪdeɪtə(r)/ *n* liquidatore, -trice *mf*
liquid crystal display *n* visualizzatore *m* a cristalli liquidi
liquidize /ˈlɪkwɪdaɪz/ *vt* rendere liquido
liquidizer /ˈlɪkwɪdaɪzə(r)/ *n* Culin frullatore *m*
liquor /ˈlɪkə(r)/ *n* bevanda *f* alcolica
liquorice /ˈlɪkərɪs/ *n* liquirizia *f*
liquor store *n* AmE negozio *m* di alcolici
lira /ˈlɪərə/ *n* (old) lira *f*; **50,000 lire** 50.000 lire
lisp /lɪsp/ **A** *n* pronuncia *f* con la lisca; **have a ~** parlare con la lisca
B *vi* parlare con la lisca
list¹ /lɪst/ **A** *n* lista *f*
B *vt* elencare
list² *vi* ‹*ship*› inclinarsi
listen /ˈlɪsn/ *vi* ascoltare; **~ to** ascoltare
▪ **listen in** *vi* (secretly) origliare; **~ in on** ascoltare di nascosto ‹*conversation*›
listener /ˈlɪs(ə)nə(r)/ *n* ascoltatore, -trice *mf*
listeria /lɪˈstɪərɪə/ *n* (illness) listeriosi *f*; (bacteria) listeria *f*
listings /ˈlɪstɪŋz/ *npl* rubrica *f* degli spettacoli
listless /ˈlɪstlɪs/ *adj* svogliato
listlessly /ˈlɪstlɪslɪ/ *adv* in modo svogliato
list price *n* prezzo *m* di listino
lit /lɪt/ ▸ **light¹**
litany /ˈlɪtənɪ/ *n* litania *f*
literacy /ˈlɪtərəsɪ/ *n* alfabetizzazione *f*
literal /ˈlɪtərəl/ *adj* letterale
literally /ˈlɪt(ə)rəlɪ/ *adv* letteralmente
literary /ˈlɪtərərɪ/ *adj* letterario
literary critic *n* critico, -a *mf* letterario
literary criticism *n* critica *f* letteraria
literate /ˈlɪtərət/ *adj* **be ~** saper leggere e scrivere
literati /lɪtəˈrɑːtiː/ *npl* letterati *mpl*
literature /ˈlɪtrətʃə(r)/ *n* letteratura *f*
lithe /laɪð/ *adj* flessuoso
lithographer /lɪˈθɒgrəfə(r)/ *n* litografo, -a *mf*
lithography /lɪˈθɒgrəfɪ/ *n* litografia *f*
Lithuania /lɪθjʊˈeɪnɪə/ *n* Lituania *f*
Lithuanian /lɪθjʊˈeɪnɪən/ *adj & n* lituano, -a *mf*; (language) lituano *m*
litigation /lɪtɪˈgeɪʃn/ *n* causa *f* [giudiziaria]
litmus paper /ˈlɪtməs/ *n* cartina *f* di tornasole
litmus test *n* Chem test *m inv* con cartina di tornasole; fig prova *f* del nove
litre /ˈliːtə(r)/ *n* litro *m*
litter /ˈlɪtə(r)/ **A** *n* immondizie *fpl*; Zool figliata *f*
B *vt* **be ~ed with something** essere ingombrato di qualcosa
litter bin *n* bidone *m* della spazzatura
litterbug /ˈlɪtəbʌg/ *n persona (f) che butta per terra cartacce e rifiuti*
little /ˈlɪtl/ **A** *adj* piccolo; (not much) poco
B *adv & n* poco *m*; **a ~** un po'; **a ~ water** un po' d'acqua; **a ~ better** un po' meglio; **~ by ~** a poco a poco
little finger *n* mignolo *m* (*della mano*)
little-known *adj* poco noto
liturgical /lɪˈtɜːdʒɪkl/ *adj* liturgico
liturgy /ˈlɪtədʒɪ/ *n* liturgia *f*
live¹ /laɪv/ **A** *adj* vivo; ‹*ammunition*› carico; **~ broadcast** trasmissione *f* in diretta; **be ~** Electr essere sotto tensione; **~ wire** *n* fig persona *f* dinamica
B *adv* ‹*broadcast*› in diretta
live² /lɪv/ *vi* vivere; (reside) abitare; **~ with** convivere con
▪ **live down** *vt* far dimenticare
▪ **live for** *vt* vivere solo per ‹*one's work, family*›
▪ **live in** *vi* ‹*nanny, au pair*› abitare sul posto di lavoro
▪ **live off** *vt* vivere alle spalle di
▪ **live on A** *vt* vivere di
B *vi* sopravvivere
▪ **live through** *vt* vivere
▪ **live together** *vi* ‹*friends*› vivere insieme; ‹*lovers*› convivere
▪ **live up**: *vt* **~ it up** far la bella vita
▪ **live up to** *vt* essere all'altezza di
▪ **live with** *vt* convivere con ‹*lover, situation*›; vivere con ‹*mother etc*›
lived-in /ˈlɪvdɪn/ *adj* **have that ~ look** ‹*room, flat*› avere un'aria vissuta
live-in *adj* ‹*maid, nanny*› che vive in casa
livelihood /ˈlaɪvlɪhʊd/ *n* mezzi *mpl* di sostentamento
liveliness /ˈlaɪvlɪnɪs/ *n* vivacità *f*
lively /ˈlaɪvlɪ/ *adj* (**-ier**, **-iest**) vivace
▪ **liven up A** *vt* vivacizzare
B *vi* vivacizzarsi
liver /ˈlɪvə(r)/ *n* fegato *m*
liver pâté *n* pâté *m inv* di fegato
Liverpudlian /lɪvəˈpʌdlɪən/ *n* ‹*born there*› originario, -a *mf* di Liverpool; ‹*living there*›

abitante *mf* di Liverpool
livery /'lɪvərɪ/ *n* (uniform) livrea *f*
lives /laɪvz/ ▶ **life**
livestock /'laɪvstɒk/ *n* bestiame *m*
live wire *n* fig **be a ~** essere superdinamico
livid /'lɪvɪd/ *adj* infml livido
living /'lɪvɪŋ/ **A** *adj* vivo
B *n* **earn one's ~** guadagnarsi da vivere; **the ~** *pl* i vivi
living room *n* soggiorno *m*
living will *n* testamento *m* biologico
lizard /'lɪzəd/ *n* lucertola *f*
llama /'lɑːmə/ *n* lama *m inv*
LLB *abbr* (**Bachelor of Laws**) laureato, -a *mf* in legge
load /ləʊd/ **A** *n* carico *m*; **~s of** infml un sacco di; **that's a ~ off my mind** mi sono tolto un peso [dallo stomaco]
B *vt* **~ [up]** caricare
loaded /'ləʊdɪd/ *adj* carico; infml (rich) ricchissimo; **~ question** domanda *f* esplosiva
loading bay /'ləʊdɪŋ/ *n* piazzola *f* di carico e scarico
loaf[1] /ləʊf/ *n* (*pl* **loaves**) pane *m*; (round) pagnotta *f*; **use one's ~** infml pensare con il proprio cervello
loaf[2], **~ about** *or* **around** *vi* oziare
loafer /'ləʊfə(r)/ *n* (idler) scansafatiche *mf inv*; (shoe) mocassino *m*
loan /ləʊn/ **A** *n* prestito *m*; **on ~** in prestito
B *vt* prestare
loan shark *n* infml strozzino, -a *mf*
loath /ləʊθ/ *adj* **be ~ to do something** essere restio a fare qualcosa
loathe /ləʊð/ *vt* detestare
loathing /'ləʊðɪŋ/ *n* disgusto *m*
loathsome /'ləʊðsəm/ *adj* disgustoso
loaves /ləʊvz/ ▶ **loaf**[1]
lob /lɒb/ **A** *vt* (*pres p etc* **-bb-**) lanciare in alto; Sport respingere a pallonetto
B *n* Sport pallonetto *m*
lobby /'lɒbɪ/ *n* atrio *m*; Pol gruppo *m* di pressione, lobby *f inv*
lobbying /'lɒbɪɪŋ/ *n* lobbismo *m*; **~ for something** fare pressioni per qualcosa
lobbyist /'lɒbɪɪst/ *n* lobbista *mf*
lobe /ləʊb/ *n* (of ear) lobo *m*
lobelia /lə'biːlɪə/ *n* lobelia *f*
lobster /'lɒbstə(r)/ *n* aragosta *f*
lobster pot *n* nassa *f* per aragoste
local /'ləʊkl/ **A** *adj* locale; **under ~ anaesthetic** sotto anestesia locale; **I'm not ~** non sono del posto
B *n* abitante *mf* del luogo; infml (public house) pub *m inv* locale
local authority *n* autorità *f* locale
local bus *n* bus *m* locale
local call *n* Teleph telefonata *f* urbana
local election *n* elezioni *fpl* amministrative
local government *n* autorità *f* locale
locality /ləʊ'kælətɪ/ *n* zona *f*
localized /'ləʊkəlaɪzd/ *adj* localizzato
locally /'ləʊkəlɪ/ *adv* localmente; ‹*live, work*› nei paraggi
local network *n* Comput rete *f* locale
locate /ləʊ'keɪt/ *vt* situare; trovare ‹*person*›; **be ~d** essere situato
location /ləʊ'keɪʃn/ *n* posizione *f*; **filmed on ~** girato in esterni
loch /lɒx/ *n* lago *m*
lock[1] /lɒk/ *n* (of hair) ciocca *f*
lock[2] **A** *n* (on door) serratura *f*; (on canal) chiusa *f*
B *vt* chiudere a chiave; bloccare ‹*wheels*›
C *vi* chiudersi
▪ **lock in** *vt* chiudere dentro
▪ **lock out** *vt* chiudere fuori
▪ **lock together** *vi* ‹*pieces*› incastrarsi
▪ **lock up** **A** *vt* (in prison) mettere dentro
B *vi* chiudere
locker /'lɒkə(r)/ *n* armadietto *m*
locker room *n* spogliatoio *m*
locket /'lɒkɪt/ *n* medaglione *m*
lockout *n* serrata *f*
locksmith *n* fabbro *m*
lock-up *n* (prison) guardina *f*
loco /'ləʊkəʊ/ *adj* BrE (crazy) toccato
locomotion /ləʊkə'məʊʃn/ *n* locomozione *f*
locomotive /ləʊkə'məʊtɪv/ *n* locomotiva *f*
locum /'ləʊkəm/ *n* sostituto, -a *mf*
locust /'ləʊkəst/ *n* locusta *f*
lodge /lɒdʒ/ **A** *n* (porter's) portineria *f*; (Masonic) loggia *f*
B *vt* presentare ‹*claim, complaint*›; (with bank, solicitor) depositare; **be ~d** essersi conficcato
C *vi* essere a pensione (**with** da); (become fixed) conficcarsi
lodger /'lɒdʒə(r)/ *n* inquilino, -a *mf*
lodgings /'lɒdʒɪŋ/ *npl* camere *fpl* in affitto
loft /lɒft/ *n* soffitta *f*
loft conversion *n* soppalco *f* abitabile
lofty /'lɒftɪ/ *adj* (**-ier**, **-iest**) alto; (haughty) altezzoso
log /lɒg/ **A** *n* ceppo *m*; Auto libretto *m* di circolazione; Naut giornale *m* di bordo; **sleep like a ~** infml dormire come un ghiro
B *vt* (*pt/pp* **logged**) registrare
▪ **log in** *vi* aprire una sessione
▪ **log off** *vi* disconnettersi
▪ **log on** *vi* connettersi (**to** a)
▪ **log out** *vi* chiudere una sessione
logarithm /'lɒgərɪðm/ *n* logaritmo *m*
logbook /'lɒgbʊk/ *n* Naut giornale *m* di bordo; Auto libretto *m* di circolazione
log cabin *n* capanna *f* di tronchi
logger /'lɒgə(r)/ *n* boscaiolo *m*

parola chiave

loggerheads /'lɒgəhedz/ *npl* **be at ~** infml essere in totale disaccordo
logic /'lɒdʒɪk/ *n* logica *f*
logical /'lɒdʒɪkl/ *adj* logico
logically /'lɒdʒɪklɪ/ *adv* logicamente
logistics /lə'dʒɪstɪks/ *npl* logistica *fsg*
logo /'ləʊgəʊ/ *n* logo *m inv*
loin /lɔɪn/ *n* Culin lombata *f*
loin chop *n* lombatina *f*
loincloth /'lɔɪnklɒθ/ *n* perizoma *m*
loiter /'lɔɪtə(r)/ *vi* gironzolare
loll /lɒl/ *vi* **~ about** (posture) stravaccarsi; (do nothing) starsene in panciolle
lollipop /'lɒlɪpɒp/ *n* lecca-lecca *m inv*
lollop /'lɒləp/ *vi* ‹*rabbit, person*› avanzare a balzi
lolly /'lɒlɪ/ *n* lecca-lecca *m inv*; infml (money) quattrini *mpl*
Lombardy /'lɒmbədɪ/ *n* Lombardia *f*
London /'lʌndən/ **A** *n* Londra *f*
B *attrib* londinese, di Londra
Londoner /'lʌndənə(r)/ *n* londinese *mf*
lone /ləʊn/ *adj* solitario
loneliness /'ləʊnlɪnɪs/ *n* solitudine *f*
lonely /'ləʊnlɪ/ *adj* (**-ier**, **-iest**) solitario; ‹*person*› solo
lonely hearts' column *n* rubrica *f* dei cuori solitari
loner /'ləʊnə(r)/ *n* persona *f* solitaria
lonesome /'ləʊnsəm/ *adj* solo
long¹ /lɒŋ/ **A** *adj* (**-er** /'lɒŋgə(r)/ **-est** /'lɒŋgɪst/) lungo; **a ~ time** molto tempo; **a ~ way** distante; **in the ~ run** a lungo andare; (in the end) alla fin fine
B *adv* a lungo, lungamente; **how ~ is it** quanto è lungo?; ‹*in time*› quanto dura?; **all day ~** tutto il giorno; **not ~ ago** non molto tempo fa; **before ~** fra breve; **he's no ~er here** non è più qui; **as** *or* **so ~ as** finché; (provided that) purché; **so ~** infml ciao!; **will you be ~?** ti ci vuole molto?
long² *vi* **~ for** desiderare ardentemente
long-awaited *adj* tanto atteso
long-distance *adj* a grande distanza; Sport di fondo; ‹*call*› interurbano
long division *n* divisione *f*
longevity /lɒn'dʒevətɪ/ *n* longevità *f*
long face *n* muso *m* lungo
longhand /'lɒŋhænd/ *n* **in ~** in scrittura ordinaria
long-haul *attrib* su lunga distanza; ‹*plane*› per lunghi tragitti
longing /'lɒŋɪŋ/ **A** *adj* desideroso
B *n* brama *f*
longingly /'lɒŋɪŋlɪ/ *adv* con desiderio
longitude /'lɒŋgɪtju:d/ *n* Geog longitudine *f*
long jump *n* salto *m* in lungo
long-life milk *n* latte *m* a lunga conservazione
long-lived /-'lɪvd/ *adj* longevo
long-playing record *n* 33 giri *m inv*
long-range *adj* Mil, Aeron a lunga portata; ‹*forecast*› a lungo termine
long-sighted /-saɪtɪd/ *adj* presbite
long-sleeved /-'sli:vd/ *adj* a maniche lunghe
long-standing *adj* di vecchia data
long-suffering *adj* infinitamente paziente
long-term *adj* a lunga scadenza
long-time *adj* ‹*partner*› di lunga data
long wave *n* onde *fpl* lunghe
long-winded /-'wɪndɪd/ *adj* prolisso
loo /lu:/ *n* infml gabinetto *m*
look /lʊk/ **A** *n* occhiata*f*; (appearance) aspetto *m*; **[good] ~s** *pl* bellezza*f*; **have a ~ at** dare un'occhiata a
B *vi* guardare; **~ here!** mi ascolti bene!; **~ at** guardare; **~ for** cercare; **~ somebody in the eye** guardare negli occhi qualcuno; **~ somebody up and down** guardare qualcuno dall'alto in basso; **~ a fool** fare la figura del cretino; **~ young/old for one's age** portarsi bene/male gli anni; **~ like** (resemble) assomigliare a; **it ~s as if it's going to rain** sembra che stia per piovere; **~ sharp** infml (hurry up) darsi una mossa
■ **look after** *vt* badare a
■ **look ahead** *vi* (think of the future) guardare al futuro
■ **look back** *vi* girarsi; (think of the past) guardare indietro
■ **look down** *vi* guardare in basso; **~ down on somebody** fig guardare dall'alto in basso qualcuno
■ **look forward to** *vt* essere impaziente di
■ **look in on** *vt* passare da
■ **look into** *vt* (examine) esaminare
■ **look on A** *vi* (watch) guardare
B *vt* **~ somebody/something as** (consider to be) considerare qualcuno/qualcosa come
■ **look on to** *vt* ‹*room*› dare su
■ **look out A** *vi* guardare fuori; (take care) fare attenzione; **~ out!** attento!
B *vt* cercare ‹*something for somebody*›
■ **look out for** *vt* cercare
■ **look over** *vt* riguardare ‹*notes*›; ispezionare ‹*house*›
■ **look round** *vi* girarsi; (in shop, town etc) dare un'occhiata
■ **look through** *vt* dare un'occhiata a ‹*script, notes*›
■ **look to** *vt* (rely on) contare su
■ **look up A** *vi* guardare in alto
B *vt* cercare [nel dizionario] ‹*word*›; (visit) andare a trovare
■ **look up to** *vt* fig rispettare
look-alike *n* sosia *mf inv*
looker-on /lʊkər'ɒn/ *n* (*pl* **lookers-on**) spettatore, -trice *mf*
look-in *n* BrE infml **give somebody a ~** dare una chance a qualcuno; **get a ~** avere una chance
lookout /'lʊkaʊt/ *n* guardia *f*; (prospect) prospettiva *f*; **be on the ~ for** tenere gli

occhi aperti per
loom¹ /luːm/ *n* telaio *m*
loom² *vi* apparire; fig profilarsi
loony /ˈluːnɪ/ *adj & n* infml matto, -a *mf*; **~ bin** manicomio *m*
loop /luːp/ *n* cappio *m*; (on garment) passante *m*; **be in/out of the ~** essere/non essere tra quelli che contano *o* nella stanza dei bottoni
loophole /ˈluːphəʊl/ *n* (in the law) scappatoia *f*
loopy /ˈluːpɪ/ *adj* infml matto
loose /luːs/ *adj* libero; ‹*knot*› allentato; ‹*page*› staccato; ‹*clothes*› largo; ‹*morals*› dissoluto; (inexact) vago; **be at a ~ end** non sapere cosa fare; **come ~** ‹*knot*› sciogliersi; **set ~** liberare
loose change *n* spiccioli *mpl*
loose chippings *npl* ghiaino *m*
loose-leaf notebook *n* raccoglitore *m* di fogli
loosely /ˈluːslɪ/ *adv* scorrevolmente; ‹*defined*› vagamente
loosely knit *adj* ‹*group*› poco unito
loosen /ˈluːsn/ *vt* sciogliere
▪ **loosen up** **A** *vt* sciogliere ‹*muscles*›
B *vi* infml (relax) rilassarsi
loot /luːt/ **A** *n* bottino *m*
B *vt & vi* depredare
looter /ˈluːtə(r)/ *n* saccheggiatore, -trice *mf*
looting /ˈluːtɪŋ/ *n* saccheggio *m*
lop *vt* (*pt/pp* **lopped**) **~ off** potare
lope *vi* **~ off** andarsene a passi lunghi
lop-eared /lɒpɪəd/ *adj* con le orecchie [a] penzoloni
lopsided /lɒpˈsaɪdɪd/ *adj* sbilenco
loquacious /ləˈkweɪʃəs/ *adj* loquace
🔑 **lord** /lɔːd/ *n* signore *m*; (title) Lord *m*; **House of L~s** Camera *f* dei Lord; **the L~'s Prayer** il Padrenostro; **good L~!** Dio Mio!
Lord Mayor *n sindaco (m) della City di Londra*
Lordship /ˈlɔːdʃɪp/ *n* **your/his ~** (of noble) Sua Signoria; **your ~** (to judge) Signor Giudice
lore /lɔː(r)/ *n* tradizioni *fpl*
lorry /ˈlɒrɪ/ *n* camion *m inv*
lorry driver *n* camionista *mf*
🔑 **lose** /luːz/ **A** *vt* (*pt/pp* **lost**) perdere; **~ heart** perdersi d'animo; **~ one's inhibitions** disinibirsi; **~ one's nerve** farsi prendere dalla paura; **~ sight of** perdere di vista, perdere d' occhio; **~ touch with** perdere di vista; **~ track of time** perdere la nozione del tempo; **~ weight** calare di peso
B *vi* perdere; ‹*clock*› essere indietro
▪ **lose out** *vi* rimetterci
loser /ˈluːzə(r)/ *n* perdente *mf*
losing battle /ˈluːzɪŋ/ *n* battaglia *f* persa
🔑 **loss** /lɒs/ *n* perdita *f*; **~es** *pl* Comm perdite *fpl*; **be at a ~** essere perplesso; **be at a ~ for words** non trovare le parole; **make a ~** Comm subire una perdita
loss adjuster /ˈlɒsədʒʌstə(r)/ *n* Comm perito *m* di assicurazione
loss-leader *n* articolo *m* civetta
loss-making /ˈlɒsmeɪkɪŋ/ *adj* ‹*company*› in passivo; ‹*product*› che non vende
lost /lɒst/ **A** ▸ **lose**
B *adj* perduto; **get ~** perdersi; **get ~!** infml va' a quel paese!
lost and found *n* AmE oggetti *mpl* smarriti
lost property *n* BrE oggetti *mpl* smarriti
lost property office *n* ufficio *m* oggetti smarriti
lot¹ /lɒt/ (at auction) lotto *m*; (piece of land) lotto *m*; **draw ~s** tirare a sorte
🔑 **lot²** *n* **the ~** il tutto; **a ~ of, ~s of** molti; **the ~ of you** tutti voi; **it has changed a ~** è cambiato molto
lotion *n* lozione *f*
lottery /ˈlɒtərɪ/ *n* lotteria *f*
lottery ticket *n* biglietto *m* della lotteria
🔑 **loud** /laʊd/ **A** *adj* sonoro, alto; ‹*colours*› sgargiante
B *adv* forte; **out ~** ad alta voce
loud hailer /ˈheɪlə(r)/ *n* megafono *m*
loudly /ˈlaʊdlɪ/ *adv* forte
loudspeaker /laʊdˈspiːkə(r)/ *n* altoparlante *m*
lounge /laʊndʒ/ **A** *n* salotto *m*; (in hotel) salone *m*
B *vi* poltrire
▪ **lounge about** *vi* stare in panciolle
lounge suit *n* vestito *m* da uomo (*formale*)
louse /laʊs/ *n* (*pl* **lice**) pidocchio *m*
▪ **louse up** *vt* infml (ruin) guastare
lousy /ˈlaʊzɪ/ *adj* (**-ier**, **-iest**) infml schifoso
lout /laʊt/ *n* zoticone *m*
loutish /ˈlaʊtɪʃ/ *adj* rozzo
louvred /ˈluːvəd/ *adj* ‹*door, blinds*› con le gelosie
lovable /ˈlʌvəbl/ *adj* adorabile
🔑 **love** /lʌv/ **A** *n* amore *m*; Tennis zero *m*; **in ~** innamorato (**with** di)
B *vt* amare ‹*person, country*›
love affair *n* relazione *f* [sentimentale]
love bite *n* succhiotto *m*
love letter *n* lettera *f* d'amore
love life *n* vita *f* sentimentale
lovely /ˈlʌvlɪ/ *adj* (**-ier**, **-iest**) bello; (in looks) bello, attraente; (in character) piacevole; ‹*meal*› delizioso; **have a ~ time** divertirsi molto
lovemaking *n* il fare l'amore
lover /ˈlʌvə(r)/ *n* amante *mf*
love song *n* canzone *f* d'amore
love story *n* storia *f* d'amore
lovey-dovey /lʌvɪˈdʌvɪ/ *adj* BrE infml **get all ~** fare i piccioncini

🔑 parola chiave

loving /ˈlʌvɪŋ/ *adj* affettuoso
lovingly /ˈlʌvɪŋlɪ/ *adv* affettuosamente
low /ləʊ/ **A** *adj* basso; (depressed) giù *inv*
B *adv* basso; **feel ~** sentirsi giù
C *n* minimo *m*; Meteorol depressione *f*; **at an all-time ~** ‹*prices etc*› al livello minimo
low-alcohol *adj* ‹*beer*› a bassa gradazione alcolica
lowbrow /ˈləʊbraʊ/ *adj* di scarsa cultura
low-budget *adj* ‹*flight, airline*› low-cost *inv*
low-calorie *adj* ipocalorico
low-carb /ləʊˈkɑːb/ *adj* a basso contenuto di carboidrati; **a ~ diet** dieta a basso contenuto di carboidrati
low-cost *adj* low-cost *inv*
low-cut *adj* ‹*dress*› scollato
low-down /ˈləʊdaʊn/ **A** *adj* infml ‹*trick*› mancino
B *n* (details) informazioni *fpl*
lower /ˈləʊə(r)/ **A** *adj & adv* ▶ **low**
B *vt* abbassare; **~ oneself** abbassarsi
lower class **A** *adj* del ceto basso
B *n* ceto *m* basso
lowest common denominator /ˈləʊɪst, dɪˈnɒmɪneɪtə(r)/ *n* minimo denominatore *m* comune
low-fat *adj* ‹*diet*› a basso contenuto di grassi; ‹*cheese, milk*› magro
low gear *n* Auto marcia *f* bassa
low-grade *adj* di qualità inferiore
low-income *adj* ‹*families*› a basso reddito
low-key *adj* fig moderato
lowlands *npl* pianure *fpl*
low-level *adj* ‹*talks*› informale; ‹*radiation*› debole; ‹*bombing*› a bassa quota
lowly /ˈləʊlɪ/ *adj* (**-ier**, **-iest**) umile
low-lying *adj* ‹*land*› a bassa quota
low-maintenance *adj* **a ~ garden** un giardino che richiede poca manutenzione
low-paid *adj* ‹*job, worker*› mal pagato
low-priced *adj* a basso prezzo
low profile *n* **keep a ~** mantenere un profilo basso
low-profile *adj* ‹*campaign*› di basso profilo
low-quality *adj* scadente
low-risk *adj* a basso rischio
low season *n* bassa stagione *f*
low-tech *adj* a bassa tecnologia
low tide *n* bassa marea *f*
loyal /ˈlɔɪəl/ *adj* leale
loyally /ˈlɔɪəlɪ/ *adv* lealmente
loyalty /ˈlɔɪəltɪ/ *n* lealtà *f*
loyalty card *n* carta *f* fedeltà
lozenge /ˈlɒzɪndʒ/ *n* losanga *f*; (tablet) pastiglia *f*
LP *n abbr* (**long-playing record**) LP *m inv*
L-plate *n* BrE Auto *cartello* (*m*) *che indica che il conducente non ha ancora preso la patente*
LSD *n* LSD *m*
LST *abbr* (**local standard time**) ora *f* locale
Ltd *abbr* (**Limited**) s.r.l.
lubricant /ˈluːbrɪkənt/ *n* lubrificante *m*
lubricate /ˈluːbrɪkeɪt/ *vt* lubrificare
lubrication /luːbrɪˈkeɪʃn/ *n* lubrificazione *f*
lucid /ˈluːsɪd/ *adj* ‹*explanation*› chiaro; (sane) lucido
lucidity /luːˈsɪdətɪ/ *n* lucidità *f*; (of explanation) chiarezza *f*
luck /lʌk/ *n* fortuna *f*; **bad ~** sfortuna *f*; **good ~** buona fortuna!
luckily /ˈlʌkɪlɪ/ *adv* fortunatamente
lucky /ˈlʌkɪ/ *adj* (**-ier**, **-iest**) fortunato; **be ~** essere fortunato; ‹*thing*› portare fortuna
lucky charm *n* portafortuna *m inv*
lucky dip *n* pesca *f* di beneficenza
lucrative /ˈluːkrətɪv/ *adj* lucrativo
lucre /ˈluːkə(r)/ *n* infml (money) soldi *mpl*
ludicrous /ˈluːdɪkrəs/ *adj* ridicolo
ludicrously /ˈluːdɪkrəslɪ/ *adv* ‹*expensive, complex*› eccessivamente
ludo /ˈluːdəʊ/ *n* BrE *gioco* (*m*) *da tavolo*
lug /lʌg/ *vt* (*pt/pp* **lugged**) infml trascinare
luggage /ˈlʌgɪdʒ/ *n* bagaglio
luggage rack *n* portabagagli *m inv*
luggage trolley *n* carrello *m* portabagagli
luggage van *n* bagagliaio *m*
lughole /ˈlʌghəʊl/ *n* BrE infml (ear) orecchio *m*
lugubrious /lʊˈguːbrɪəs/ *adj* lugubre
lukewarm /ˈluːkwɔːm/ *adj* tiepido; fig poco entusiasta
lull /lʌl/ **A** *n* pausa *f*
B *vt* **~ to sleep** cullare
lullaby /ˈlʌləbaɪ/ *n* ninnananna *f*
lumbago /lʌmˈbeɪgəʊ/ *n* lombaggine *f*
lumbar /ˈlʌmbə(r)/ *adj* lombare
lumber /ˈlʌmbə(r)/ **A** *n* cianfrusaglie *fpl*; AmE (timber) legname *m*
B *vt* infml **~ somebody with something** affibbiare qualcosa a qualcuno
lumberjack /ˈlʌmbədʒæk/ *n* tagliaboschi *m inv*
luminary /ˈluːmɪnərɪ/ *n* fig (person) luminare *mf*
luminous /ˈluːmɪnəs/ *adj* luminoso
lump¹ /lʌmp/ **A** *n* (of sugar) zolletta *f*; (swelling) gonfiore *m*; (in breast) nodulo *m*; (in sauce) grumo *m*; **a ~ in one's throat** un groppo alla gola
B *vt* **~ together** ammucchiare
lump² *vt* **~ it** infml **you'll just have to ~ it** che ti piaccia o no è così
lump sugar *n* zucchero *m* in zollette
lump sum *n* somma *f* globale
lumpy /ˈlʌmpɪ/ *adj* (**-ier**, **-iest**) grumoso
lunacy /ˈluːnəsɪ/ *n* follia *f*
lunar /ˈluːnə(r)/ *adj* lunare
lunatic /ˈluːnətɪk/ *n* pazzo, -a *mf*

✓ **lunch** /lʌntʃ/ **A** *n* pranzo *m*; **she's gone to ~** è andata a pranzo; **let's have ~ together sometime** pranziamo qualche volta insieme **B** *vi* pranzare
lunch box *n* cestino *m* del pranzo
lunch break *n* pausa *f* pranzo
luncheon /ˈlʌntʃn/ *n* (formal) pranzo *m*
luncheon meat *n carne (f) in scatola*
luncheon voucher *n* buono *m* pasto
lunch hour *n* pausa *f* pranzo
lunchtime /ˈlʌntʃtaɪm/ *n* ora *f* di pranzo
lung /lʌŋ/ *n* polmone *m*
lung cancer *n* cancro *m* al polmone
lunge /lʌndʒ/ *vi* lanciarsi (**at** su)
lurch¹ /lɜːtʃ/ *n* **leave in the ~** infml lasciare nei guai
lurch² *vi* barcollare
lure /lʊə(r)/ **A** *n* esca *f*; fig lusinga *f* **B** *vt* adescare
lurid /ˈlʊərɪd/ *adj* (gaudy) sgargiante; (sensational) sensazionalistico
lurk /lɜːk/ *vi* appostarsi
luscious /ˈlʌʃəs/ *adj* saporito; fig sexy *inv*
lush /lʌʃ/ *adj* lussureggiante
lust /lʌst/ **A** *n* lussuria *f* **B** *vi* **~ after** desiderare [fortemente]
lustful /ˈlʌstfʊl/ *adj* lussurioso
lustre /ˈlʌstə(r)/ *n* lustro *m*
lusty /ˈlʌstɪ/ *adj* (**-ier**, **-iest**) vigoroso
lute /luːt/ *n* liuto *m*
luvvy, **luvvie** /ˈlʌvɪ/ *n* infml attore, -trice *mf* pretenzioso
Luxembourg /ˈlʌksəmbɜːg/ *n* (city) Lussemburgo *f*; (state) Lussemburgo *m*
luxuriant /lʌgˈʒʊərɪənt/ *adj* lussureggiante, rigoglioso
luxuriantly /lʌgˈʒjʊərɪəntlɪ/ *adv* rigogliosamente
luxurious /lʌgˈʒʊərɪəs/ *adj* lussuoso
luxuriously /lʌgˈʒʊərɪəslɪ/ *adv* lussuosamente
luxury /ˈlʌkʃərɪ/ **A** *n* lusso *m*; **live in ~** vivere nel lusso **B** *attrib* di lusso
LV *abbr* (**luncheon voucher**) buono *m* mensa, buono *m* pasto
LW *abbr* (**long wave**) OL
lychee /ˈlaɪtʃiː/ *n* litchi *m inv*
lychgate /ˈlɪtʃ-/ *n entrata (f) coperta di un cimitero*
Lycra® /ˈlaɪkrə/ *n* lycra® *f*
lying /ˈlaɪɪŋ/ **A** ▶ **lie¹**, ▶ **lie²** **B** *n* mentire *m*
lymph gland /lɪmf/ *n* linfoghiandola *f*
lymph node *n* linfonodo *m*
lynch /lɪntʃ/ *vt* linciare
lynch mob *n* linciatori *mpl*
lynchpin /ˈlɪntʃpɪn/ *n* fig pilastro *m*
lynx /lɪŋks/ *n* lince *f*
lyric /ˈlɪrɪk/ *adj* lirico
lyrical /ˈlɪrɪkl/ *adj* lirico; infml (enthusiastic) entusiasta; **~ poetry** *n* poesia *f* lirica
lyricism /ˈlɪrɪsɪzm/ *n* lirismo *m*
lyricist /ˈlɪrɪsɪst/ *n* paroliere, -a *mf*
lyrics /ˈlɪrɪks/ *npl* parole *fpl*

Mm

m¹, **M** /em/ *n* (letter) m, M *f inv*
m² *abbr* **1** (**metre(s)**) m **2** (**million**) milione *m* **3** (**mile(s)**) miglio
MA *n abbr* **1** (**Master of Arts**) (diploma) laurea *f* in lettere; (person) laureato, -a *mf* in lettere **2** AmE (**Massachusetts**)
ma'am /mɑːm/ *int* signora; (to queen) Sua Altezza
mac /mæk/ *n* infml impermeabile *m*
macabre /məˈkɑːbr/ *adj* macabro
macaroni /mækəˈrəʊnɪ/ *n* maccheroni *mpl*
macaroni cheese *n* maccheroni *mpl* gratinati al formaggio
macaroon /mækəˈruːn/ *n* ≈ amaretto *m*

✓ parola chiave

mace¹ /meɪs/ *n* (staff) mazza *f*
mace² *n* (spice) macis *mf*
Macedonia /mæsəˈdəʊnɪə/ *n* Macedonia *f*
machete /məˈʃetɪ/ *n* machete *m inv*
Machiavellian /mækɪəˈvelɪən/ *adj* machiavellico
machinations /mækɪˈneɪʃnz/ macchinazioni *fpl*
✓ **machine** /məˈʃiːn/ **A** *n* macchina *f* **B** *vt* (sew) cucire a macchina; Techn lavorare a macchina
machine-gun *n* mitragliatrice *f*
machine operator *n* addetto, -a *mf* alle macchine
machine-readable *adj* <*data, text*> leggibile dalla macchina

machinery /məˈʃiːnərɪ/ *n* macchinario *m*; fig meccanismo *m*
machine-stitch *vt* cucire a macchina
machine tool *n* macchina *f* utensile
machine translation *n* traduzione *f* elettronica
machinist /məˈʃiːnɪst/ *n* macchinista *mf*; (on sewing machine) lavorante *mf* addetto, -a alla macchina da cucire
machismo /mæˈkɪzməʊ/ *n* machismo *m*
macho /ˈmætʃəʊ/ *adj* macho *inv*
mackerel /ˈmækr(ə)l/ *n inv* sgombro *m*
mackintosh /ˈmækɪntɒʃ/ *n* impermeabile *m*
macro /ˈmækrəʊ/ *n* Comput macro *f inv*
macrocosm /ˈmækrəʊkɒzm/ *n* macrocosmo *m*
mad /mæd/ *adj* (**madder**, **maddest**) pazzo, matto; infml (angry) furioso (**at** con); **like ~** infml come un pazzo; **be ~ about somebody/something** infml (keen on) andare matto per qualcuno/qualcosa
Madagascar /mædəˈgæskə(r)/ *n* Madagascar *m*
madam /mædəm/ *n* signora *f*
mad cow disease *n* infml = **BSE**
madden /mædən/ *vt* (make angry) far diventare matto
maddening /mæd(ə)nɪŋ/ *adj* ‹*delay, person*› esasperante
made /meɪd/ ▶ **make**
Madeira cake /məˈdɪərə/ *n* pan *m* di spagna
made to measure *adj* [fatto] su misura
made-up *adj* (wearing make-up) truccato; ‹*road*› asfaltata; ‹*story*› inventato
madhouse /ˈmædhaʊs/ *n* infml manicomio *m*; **it's like a ~ in here!** sembra di essere in un manicomio
madly /ˈmædlɪ/ *adv* infml follemente; **~ in love** innamorato follemente
madman /ˈmædmən/ *n* pazzo *m*
madness /ˈmædnɪs/ *n* pazzia *f*
madonna /məˈdɒnə/ *n* madonna *f*
madwoman /ˈmædwʊmən/ *n* pazza *f*
mafia /ˈmæfɪə/ *n* also fig mafia *f*
mag /mæg/ *n abbr* (**magazine**) rivista *f*
magazine /mægəˈziːn/ *n* rivista *f*; Mil, Phot caricatore *m*
maggot /ˈmægət/ *n* verme *m*
maggoty /ˈmægətɪ/ *adj* coi vermi
Magi /ˈmeɪdʒaɪ/ *npl* **the ~** i Re Magi
magic /ˈmædʒɪk/ **A** *n* magia *f*; (tricks) giochi *mpl* di prestigio
B *adj* magico; ‹*trick*› di prestigio
magical /ˈmædʒɪkl/ *adj* magico
magic carpet *n* tappeto *m* volante
magician /məˈdʒɪʃn/ *n* mago, -a *mf*; (entertainer) prestigiatore, -trice *mf*
magistrate /ˈmædʒɪstreɪt/ *n* magistrato *m*
magistrate's court *n* ≈ pretura *f*
magnanimity /mægnəˈnɪmətɪ/ *n* magnanimità *f*
magnanimous /mægˈnænɪməs/ *adj* magnanimo
magnate /ˈmægneɪt/ *n* magnate *m*
magnesia /mægˈniːʃə/ *n* magnesia *f*
magnesium /mægˈniːzɪəm/ *n* magnesio *m*
magnet /ˈmægnɪt/ *n* magnete *m*, calamita *f*
magnetic /mægˈnetɪk/ *adj* magnetico
magnetic resonance imaging *n* Med risonanza *f* magnetica
magnetic tape *n* nastro *m* magnetico
magnetism /ˈmægnətɪzm/ *n* magnetismo *m*
magnetize /ˈmægnətaɪz/ *vt* magnetizzare
magnification /mægnɪfɪˈkeɪʃn/ *n* ingrandimento *m*
magnificence /mægˈnɪfɪsəns/ *n* magnificenza *f*
magnificent /mægˈnɪfɪsənt/ *adj* magnifico
magnificently /mægˈnɪfɪsəntlɪ/ *adv* magnificamente
magnify /ˈmægnɪfaɪ/ *vt* (*pt/pp* **-ied**) ingrandire; (exaggerate) ingigantire
magnifying glass /ˈmægnɪfaɪɪŋ/ *n* lente *f* d'ingrandimento
magnitude /ˈmægnɪtjuːd/ *n* grandezza *f*; (importance) importanza *f*; **a project of this ~** un progetto di tale portata
magnolia /mægˈnəʊlɪə/ *n* (tree) magnolia *f*; (colour) crema *m*
magnum opus /mægnəmˈɒpəs/ *n* opera *f* principale
magpie /ˈmægpaɪ/ *n* gazza *f*
mahogany /məˈhɒgənɪ/ **A** *n* mogano *m*
B *attrib* di mogano
maid /meɪd/ *n* cameriera *f*; **old ~** derog zitella *f*
maiden /ˈmeɪdn/ **A** *n* literary fanciulla *f*
B *adj* ‹*speech, voyage*› inaugurale
maiden aunt *n* zia *f* zitella
maiden name *n* nome *m* da ragazza
mail /meɪl/ **A** *n* posta *f*
B *vt* impostare
mailbag *n* sacco *m* postale
mail bomb *n* pacco *m* esplosivo (*arrivato per posta*)
mailbox *n* AmE cassetta *f* delle lettere; (email) casella *f* postale
mail coach *n* Rail vagone *m* postale
mail delivery *n* consegna *f* della posta
mailing /ˈmeɪlɪŋ/ *n* (action) mailing *m inv*; (document) pubblicità *f*
mailing address /ˈmeɪlɪŋ/ *n* recapito *m* postale
mailing list *n elenco* (*m*) *d'indirizzi per un mailing*
mailman /ˈmeɪlmən/ *n* AmE postino *m*
mail order **A** *n* vendita *f* per corrispondenza
B *attrib* ‹*business*› di vendita per corrispondenza; ‹*goods*› comprati per corrispondenza

mail-order catalogue catalogo *m* di vendita per corrispondenza

mail-order firm *n* ditta *f* di vendita per corrispondenza

mail room *n* reparto *m* spedizioni

mail server *n* Comput server *m inv* di posta

mailshot *n* mailing *m inv*

mail train *n* treno *m* postale

mail van *n* (delivery vehicle) furgone *m* postale; (in train) vagone *m* postale

maim /meɪm/ *vt* menomare

main¹ /meɪn/ *n* (water; gas, electricity) conduttura *f* principale

🔑 **main²** **A** *adj* principale; **the ~ thing is to ...** la cosa essenziale è di...
B *n* **in the ~** in complesso

main course *n* secondo *m*

main deck *n* ponte *m* di coperta

mainframe *n* Comput mainframe *m inv*

mainland *n* continente *m*

main line **A** *n* Rail linea *f* principale
B *attrib* ‹*station, terminus, train*› della linea principale

🔑 **mainly** /ˈmeɪnlɪ/ *adv* principalmente

main memory *n* Comput memoria *f* principale

main office *n* (of company) sede *f* centrale

main road *n* strada *f* principale

mainsail *n* randa *f*, vela *f* di taglio

mainstay *n* fig pilastro *m*

mainstream /ˈmeɪnstriːm/ **A** *adj* (conventional) tradizionale
B *n* corrente *f* principale

main street *n* via *f* principale

🔑 **maintain** /meɪnˈteɪn/ *vt* mantenere; (keep in repair) curare la manutenzione di; ‹*claim*› sostenere

maintenance /ˈmeɪntənəns/ *n* mantenimento *m*; (care) manutenzione *f*; (allowance) alimenti *mpl*

maintenance grant *n* (for student) presalario *m*

maintenance order *n* BrE obbligo *m* degli alimenti

maisonette /meɪzəˈnet/ *n* appartamento *m* a due piani

maize /meɪz/ *n* granoturco *m*

Maj *abbr* (**Major**) Mag

majestic /məˈdʒestɪk/ *adj* maestoso

majestically /məˈdʒəestɪklɪ/ *adv* maestosamente

majesty /ˈmædʒəstɪ/ *n* maestà *f*; **His/Her M~** Sua Maestà

🔑 **major** /ˈmeɪdʒə(r)/ **A** *adj* maggiore; **~ road** strada *f* con diritto di precedenza
B *n* Mil, Mus maggiore *m*
C *vi* AmE **~ in** specializzarsi in

Majorca /məˈjɔːkə/ *n* Maiorca *f*

🔑 parola chiave

major general *n* generale *m* di divisione

🔑 **majority** /məˈdʒɒrətɪ/ *n* maggioranza *f*; **be in the ~** avere la maggioranza

🔑 **make** /meɪk/ **A** *n* (brand) marca *f*
B *vt* (*pt/pp* **made**) fare; (earn) guadagnare; rendere ‹*happy, clear*›; prendere ‹*decision*›; **~ somebody laugh** far ridere qualcuno; **~ somebody do something** far fare qualcosa a qualcuno; **~ it** (to party, top of hill etc) farcela; **what time do you ~ it?** che ore fai?
C *vi* **~ as if to** fare per

■ **make after** *vt* (chase) inseguire

■ **make do** *vi* arrangiarsi

■ **make for** *vt* dirigersi verso

■ **make good** **A** *vi* riuscire
B *vt* compensare ‹*loss*›; risarcire ‹*damage*›

■ **make off** *vi* fuggire

■ **make off with** *vt* (steal) sgraffignare

■ **make out** *vt* (distinguish) distinguere; (write out) rilasciare ‹*cheque*›; compilare ‹*list*›; (claim) far credere

■ **make over** *vt* cedere

■ **make up** **A** *vt* (constitute) comporre; (complete) completare; (invent) inventare; (apply cosmetics to) truccare; fare ‹*parcel*›; **~ up one's mind** decidersi; **~ it up** (after quarrel) riconciliarsi
B *vi* (after quarrel) fare la pace

■ **make up for** *vt* compensare; **~ up for lost time** recuperare il tempo perso

■ **make up to** *vt* arruffianarsi

make-believe **A** *adj* finto
B *n* finzione *f*

make do and mend *vi* arrangiarsi col poco che si ha

make-over *n* trasformazione *f*

maker /ˈmeɪkə(r)/ *n* fabbricante *mf*; **M~** Relig Creatore *m*; **send somebody to meet his/her ~** spedire qualcuno all'altro mondo

makeshift **A** *adj* di fortuna
B *n* espediente *m*

make-up *n* trucco *m*; (character) natura *f*

make-up artist *n* truccatore, -trice *mf*

make-up bag *n* astuccio *m* per il trucco

make-up remover *n* struccante *m*

making /ˈmeɪkɪŋ/ *n* (manufacture) fabbricazione *f*; **be the ~ of** essere la causa del successo di; **have the ~s of** aver la stoffa di; **in the ~** in formazione

maladjusted /mæləˈdʒʌstɪd/ *adj* disadattato

maladjustment /mæləˈdʒʌstmənt/ *n* disadattamento *m*

Malagasy /mæləˈgæzɪ/ *n* (native of Madagascar) malgascio, -a *mf*; (language) malgascio *m*

malaise /məˈleɪz/ *n* fig malessere *m*

malaria /məˈleərɪə/ *n* malaria *f*

Malawi /məˈlɑːwɪ/ *n* Malawi *m*

Malaysia /məˈleɪʒə/ *n* Malesia *f*

Malaysian /məˈleɪʒən/ *n* & *adj* malese *mf*

Maldives /ˈmɔːldɪvz/ *npl* **the ~** le Maldive

🔑 **male** /meɪl/ **A** *adj* maschile
B *n* maschio *m*

m

male chauvinism *n* maschilismo *m*
male chauvinist, male chauvinist pig *n* [sporco *m*] maschilista *m*
male menopause *n* andropausa *f*
male model *n* indossatore *m*
male nurse *n* infermiere *m*
male voice choir *n* coro *m* maschile
malevolence /mə'levələns/ *n* malevolenza *f*
malevolent /mə'levələnt/ *adj* malevolo
malformation /mælfɔ:meɪʃn/ *n* malformazione *f*
malformed /mæl'fɔ:md/ *adj* malformato
malfunction /mæl'fʌŋkʃn/ **A** *n* funzionamento *m* imperfetto **B** *vi* funzionare male
Mali /'mɑ:lɪ/ *n* Mali *m*
malice /'mælɪs/ *n* malignità; **bear somebody ~** voler del male a qualcuno
malicious /mə'lɪʃəs/ *adj* maligno
maliciously /mə'lɪʃəslɪ/ *adv* con malignità
malign /mə'laɪn/ *vt* malignare su
malignancy /mə'lɪgnənsɪ/ *n* malignità *f*
malignant /mə'lɪgnənt/ *adj* maligno
malinger /mə'lɪŋgə(r)/ *vi* fingersi malato
malingerer /mə'lɪŋgərə(r)/ *n* scansafatiche *mf inv*
mall /mæl/ *n* (shopping arcade, in suburb) centro *m* commerciale; AmE (street) strada *f* pedonale
mallard /'mælɑ:d/ *n* germano *m* reale
malleable /'mælɪəbl/ *adj* malleabile
mallet /'mælɪt/ *n* martello *m* di legno
malnourished /mæl'nʌrɪʃt/ *adj* malnutrito
malnutrition /mælnjʊ'trɪʃn/ *n* malnutrizione *f*
malpractice /mæl'præktɪs/ *n* negligenza *f*
malt /mɔ:lt/ *n* malto *m*
Malta /'mɔ:ltə/ *n* Malta *f*
Maltese /mɔ:l'ti:z/ *adj & n* maltese *mf*
maltreat /mæl'tri:t/ *vt* maltrattare
maltreatment /mæl'tri:tmənt/ *n* maltrattamento *m*
malt whisky *n* whisky *m inv* di malto
mammal /'mæml/ *n* mammifero *m*
mammary /'mæmərɪ/ *adj* mammario
mammogram /'mæməgræm/ *n* mammografia *f*
mammoth /'mæməθ/ **A** *adj* mastodontico **B** *n* mammut *m inv*
man /mæn/ **A** *n* (*pl* **men**) uomo *m*; (chess, draughts) pedina *f*; **the ~ in the street** l'uomo della strada; **~ to ~** da uomo a uomo **B** *vt* (*pt/pp* **manned**) equipaggiare; far funzionare ‹*pump*›; essere di servizio a ‹*counter, telephones*›
manacle /'mænəkl/ *vt* ammanettare
manage /mænɪdʒ/ **A** *vt* dirigere; gestire ‹*shop, affairs*›; (cope with) farcela; **~ to do something** riuscire a fare qualcosa **B** *vi* riuscire; (cope) farcela (**on** con)
manageable /'mænɪdʒəbl/ *adj* ‹*hair*› docile; ‹*size*› maneggevole
management /'mænɪdʒmənt/ *n* gestione *f*; **the ~** la direzione
management accounting *n* contabilità *f* di gestione
management buyout *n* buyout *m inv* da parte dei manager, rilevamento *m* dirigenti
management consultancy *n* (firm) consulente *m* aziendale; (activity) consulenza *f* aziendale
management consultant *n* consulente *mf* aziendale
manager /'mænɪdʒə(r)/ *n* direttore *m*; (of shop, bar) gestore *m*; Sport manager *m inv*
manageress /mænɪdʒə'res/ *n* direttrice *f*
managerial /mænɪ'dʒɪərɪəl/ *adj* **~ staff** personale *m* direttivo
managing director *n* direttore, -trice *mf* generale
mandarin /'mændərɪn/ *n* **~ [orange]** mandarino *m*
mandate /'mændeɪt/ *n* mandato *m*
mandatory /'mændətrɪ/ *adj* obbligatorio
mandolin /'mændəlɪn/ *n* mandolino *m*
mandrake /'mændreɪk/ *n* mandragola *f*
mane /meɪn/ *n* criniera *f*
manful /'mænfl/ *adj* coraggioso
manfully /'mænfʊlɪ/ *adv* coraggiosamente
manger /'meɪndʒə(r)/ *n* mangiatoia *f*
mangle /'mæŋgl/ *vt* (damage) maciullare
mango /'mæŋgəʊ/ *n* (*pl* **-es**) mango *m*
mangrove /'mæŋgrəʊv/ *n* mangrovia *f*
mangy /'meɪndʒɪ/ *adj* ‹*dog*› rognoso
manhandle /'mænhændl/ *vt* malmenare
manhole /'mænhəʊl/ *n* botola *f*
manhole cover *n* tombino *m*
manhood /'mænhʊd/ *n* età *f* adulta; (quality) virilità *f*
man-hour *n* ora *f* lavorativa
manhunt /'mænhʌnt/ *n* caccia *f* all'uomo
mania /'meɪnɪə/ *n* mania *f*
maniac /'meɪnɪæk/ *n* maniaco, -a *mf*
manic /'mænɪk/ *adj* (obsessive) maniacale; (frenetic) frenetico
manic depression *n* psicosi *f inv* maniaco-depressiva
manic-depressive *adj* maniaco-depressivo
manicure /'mænɪkjʊə(r)/ **A** *n* manicure *f inv* **B** *vt* fare la manicure a
manicurist /'mænɪkjʊərɪst/ *n* manicure *f inv*
manifest /'mænɪfest/ **A** *adj* manifesto **B** *n* Comm manifesto *m* **C** *vt* manifestare; **~ itself** manifestarsi
manifestation /mænɪfe'steɪʃn/ *n* manifestazione *f*
manifestly /'mænɪfestlɪ/ *adv* palesemente
manifesto /mænɪ'festəʊ/ *n* manifesto *m*

m

manifold /ˈmænɪfəʊld/ *adj* molteplice
manipulate /məˈnɪpjuleɪt/ *vt* manipolare
manipulation /mənɪpjʊˈleɪʃn/ *n* manipolazione *f*
manipulative /məˈnɪpjʊlətɪv/ *adj* manipolatore
mankind /mænˈkaɪnd/ *n* genere *m* umano
manly /ˈmænlɪ/ *adj* virile
man-made *adj* artificiale; **~ fibre** *n* fibra *f* sintetica
manna /ˈmænə/ *n* manna *f*; **~ from heaven** fig manna *f* dal cielo
mannequin /ˈmænɪkɪn/ *n* manichino *m*
⚷ **manner** /ˈmænə(r)/ *n* maniera *f*; **in this ~** in questo modo; **have no ~s** avere dei pessimi modi; **good/bad ~s** buone/cattive maniere
mannered /ˈmænəd/ *adj* derog manierato
mannerism /ˈmænərɪzm/ *n* affettazione *f*
mannish /ˈmænɪʃ/ *adj* mascolino
manoeuvrable /məˈnuːvrəbl/ *adj* manovrabile
manoeuvre /məˈnuːvə(r)/ **A** *n* manovra *f*
B *vt* fare manovra con ‹*vehicle*›; manovrare ‹*person*›
manor /ˈmænə(r)/ *n* maniero *m*
manpower /ˈmænpaʊə(r)/ *n* manodopera *f*
manse /mæns/ *n* canonica *f*
mansion /ˈmænʃn/ *n* palazzo *m*
manslaughter /ˈmænslɔːtə(r)/ *n* omicidio *m* colposo
mantelpiece /ˈmæntlpiːs/ *n* mensola *f* di caminetto
mantis /ˈmæntɪs/ *n* mantide *f*
Mantua /ˈmæntjʊə/ *n* Mantova *f*
manual /ˈmænjʊəl/ **A** *adj* manuale
B *n* manuale *m*
manufacture /mænjʊˈfæktʃə(r)/ **A** *vt* fabbricare
B *n* manifattura *f*
⚷ **manufacturer** /mænjʊˈfæktʃərə(r)/ *n* fabbricante *m*
manure /məˈnjʊə(r)/ *n* concime *m*
manuscript /ˈmænjʊskrɪpt/ *n* manoscritto *m*
Manx /mæŋks/ *n* (language) lingua *f* parlata nell'isola di Man; **the ~** *pl* (people) gli abitanti dell'isola di Man
⚷ **many** /ˈmenɪ/ *adj & pron* molti; **there are as ~ boys as girls** ci sono tanti ragazzi quante ragazze; **as ~ as 500** ben 500; **as ~ as that** così tanti; **as ~** altrettanti; **very ~, a good/great ~** moltissimi; **~ a time** molte volte
many-sided /-ˈsaɪdɪd/ *adj* ‹*personality, phenomenon*› sfaccettato
⚷ **map** /mæp/ *n* carta *f* geografica; (of town) mappa *f*
▪ **map out** *vt* (*pt/pp* **mapped**) fig programmare
maple /ˈmeɪpl/ *n* acero *m*

mar /mɑː(r)/ *vt* (*pt/pp* **marred**) rovinare
marathon /ˈmærəθən/ *n* maratona *f*
marauder /məˈrɔːdə(r)/ *n* predone *m*
marble /ˈmɑːbl/ **A** *n* marmo *m*; (for game) bilia *f*
B *attrib* di marmo
march **A** *n* marcia *f*; (protest) dimostrazione *f*
B *vi* marciare
C *vt* far marciare; **~ somebody off** scortare qualcuno fuori
⚷ **March** /mɑːtʃ/ *n* marzo *m*
marcher /ˈmɑːtʃə(r)/ *n* (in procession, band) *persona (f) che marcia in una processione, in un corteo ecc.*; (in demonstration) dimostrante *mf*
marchioness /mɑːʃəˈnes/ *n* marchesa *f*
march past *n* sfilata *f*
mare /ˈmeə(r)/ *n* giumenta *f*
margarine /mɑdʒəˈriːn/ *n* margarina *f*
marge /mɑdʒ/ *n* BrE infml (margarine) margarina *f*
margin /ˈmɑdʒɪn/ *n* margine *m*
marginal /ˈmɑdʒɪnəl/ *adj* marginale
marginalize /ˈmɑːdʒɪnəlaɪz/ *vt* marginalizzare
marginally /ˈmɑdʒɪnəlɪ/ *adv* marginalmente
marigold /ˈmærɪgəʊld/ *n* calendula *f*
marijuana /mærʊˈwɑːnə/ *n* marijuana *f*
marina /məˈriːnə/ *n* porticciolo *m*
marinade /mærɪˈneɪd/ **A** *n* marinata *f*
B *vt* marinare
marine /məˈriːn/ **A** *adj* marino
B *n* (sailor) soldato *m* di fanteria marina
Marine Corps *n* i Marine
marine engineer *n* ingegnere *m* navale; (works in engine room) macchinista *m*
marionette /mærɪəˈnet/ *n* marionetta *f*
marital /ˈmærɪtl/ *adj* coniugale; **~ status** stato *m* civile
maritime /ˈmærɪtaɪm/ *adj* marittimo
marjoram /ˈmɑːdʒərəm/ *n* maggiorana *f*
mark¹ /mɑːk/ *n* (currency) marco *m*
⚷ **mark²** **A** *n* (stain) macchia *f*; (sign, indication) segno *m*; Sch voto *m*; **be the ~ of** designare
B *vt* segnare; (stain) macchiare; Sch correggere; Sport marcare; **~ time** Mil segnare il passo; fig non far progressi; **~ my words** ricordati quello che dico
▪ **mark down** *vt* (reduce the price of) ribassare
▪ **mark out** *vt* delimitare; fig designare
▪ **mark up** *vt* (increase the price of) aumentare
marked /mɑːkt/ *adj* marcato
markedly /ˈmɑːkɪdlɪ/ *adv* notevolmente
marker /ˈmɑːkə(r)/ *n* (for highlighting) evidenziatore *m*; Sport marcatore *m*; (of exam) esaminatore, -trice *mf*
marker pen *n* evidenziatore *m*
⚷ **market** /ˈmɑːkɪt/ **A** *n* mercato *m*
B *vt* vendere al mercato; (launch) commercializzare; **on the ~** sul mercato

⚷ parola chiave

market analyst *n* analista *mf* di mercato
market day *n* giorno *m* di mercato
market economy *n* economia *f* di mercato
market forces *npl* forze *fpl* di mercato
market garden *n* orto *m*
market gardener *n* ortofrutticoltore, -trice *mf*
market gardening *n* ortofrutticoltura *f*
marketing /ˈmɑːkɪtɪŋ/ *n* marketing *m*
marketing campaign *n* campagna *f* promozionale *or* pubblicitaria
marketing department *n* ufficio *m* marketing
marketing man *n* addetto, -a *mf* al marketing
marketing mix *n* mix *m inv* del marketing
marketing strategy *n* strategia *f* di marketing
market leader *n* (company, product) leader *m inv* del mercato
market place *n* (square, Fin) mercato *m*
market price *n* prezzo *m* di mercato
market research *n* ricerca *f* di mercato
market square *n* piazza *f* del mercato
market stall *n* banco *m* del mercato
market survey *n* indagine *f* di mercato
market town *n cittadina (f) dove si tiene il mercato*
market trader *n* venditore, -trice *mf* al mercato
market value *n* valore *m* di mercato
markings /ˈmɑːkɪŋz/ *npl* (on animal) colori *mpl*
marksman /ˈmɑːksmən/ *n* tiratore *m* scelto
marksmanship /ˈmɑːksmənʃɪp/ *n* abilità *f* nel tiro
mark-up *n* (margin) margine *m* di vendita; (price increase) aumento *m*
marmalade /ˈmɑːməleɪd/ *n* marmellata *f* d'arance
maroon /məˈruːn/ *adj* marrone rossastro
marooned /məˈruːnd/ *adj* abbandonato
marquee /mɑːˈkiː/ *n* tendone *m*; AmE (awning) pensilina *f* con pubblicità
marquess /ˈmɑːkwɪs/ *n* marchese *m*
marquetry /ˈmɑːkɪtrɪ/ *n* intarsio *m*
marquis /ˈmɑːkwɪs/ *n* marchese *m*
marriage /ˈmærɪdʒ/ *n* matrimonio *m*
marriage ceremony *n* cerimonia *f* nuziale
marriage certificate *n* certificato *m* di matrimonio
marriage guidance counsellor *n* consulente *mf* matrimoniale
marriage of convenience *n* matrimonio *m* di convenienza
married /ˈmærɪd/ *adj* sposato; ‹*life*› coniugale
marrow /ˈmærəʊ/ *n* Anat midollo *m*; (vegetable) zucca *f*
marrowbone /ˈmærəʊbəʊn/ *n* midollo *m* osseo
marry /ˈmærɪ/ (*pt/pp* **-led**) **A** *vt* (*pt/pp* **-led**) sposare; **get married** sposarsi
B *vi* sposarsi
Mars /mɑːz/ *n* Marte *m*
marsh /mɑːʃ/ *n* palude *f*
marshal /ˈmɑːʃl/ **A** *n* (steward) cerimoniere *m*
B *vt* (*pt/pp* **marshalled**) fig organizzare ‹*arguments*›
Marshall Islands *npl* **the ~** le isole Marshall
marshmallow /mɑːʃˈmæləʊ/ *n* caramella *f* gommosa e pastosa
marshy /ˈmɑːʃɪ/ *adj* paludoso
marsupial /mɑːˈsuːpɪəl/ *n* marsupiale *m*
marten /ˈmɑːtɪn/ *n* martora *f*
martial /ˈmɑːʃl/ *adj* marziale
Martian /ˈmɑːʃn/ *adj & n* marziano, -a *mf*
martinet /mɑːtɪˈnet/ *n* fanatico, -a *mf* della disciplina
martyr /ˈmɑːtə(r)/ **A** *n* martire *mf*
B *vt* martirizzare
martyrdom /ˈmɑːtədəm/ *n* martirio *m*
martyred /ˈmɑːtəd/ *adj* infml da martire
marvel /ˈmɑːvl/ **A** *n* meraviglia *f*
B *vi* (*pt/pp* **marvelled**) meravigliarsi (**at** di)
marvellous /ˈmɑːvələs/ *adj* meraviglioso
marvellously /ˈmɑːvələslɪ/ *adv* meravigliosamente
Marxism /ˈmɑːksɪzm/ *n* marxismo *m*
Marxist /ˈmɑːksɪst/ *adj & n* marxista *mf*
marzipan /ˈmɑːzɪpæn/ *n* marzapane *m*
mascara /mæˈskɑːrə/ *n* mascara *m inv*
mascot /ˈmæskət/ *n* mascotte *f inv*
masculine /ˈmæskjʊlɪn/ **A** *adj* maschile
B *n* Gram maschile *m*
masculinity /mæskjʊˈlɪnətɪ/ *n* mascolinità *f*
mash /mæʃ/ **A** *n* Culin infml purè *m*
B *vt* impastare
mashed potatoes /mæʃt/ *npl* purè *m* di patate
mask /mɑːsk/ **A** *n* maschera *f*
B *vt* mascherare
masked ball /mɑːsktˈbɔːl/ *n* ballo *m* in maschera
masking tape /ˈmɑːskɪŋ/ *n* nastro *m* di carta adesiva
masochism /ˈmæsəkɪzm/ *n* masochismo *m*
masochist /ˈmæsəkɪst/ *n* masochista *mf*
mason *n* muratore *m*
Mason /ˈmeɪsn/ *n* massone *m*
Masonic /məˈsɒnɪk/ *adj* massonico
masonry /ˈmeɪsnrɪ/ *n* muratura *f*; **two tons of ~** due tonnellate di pietre
masquerade /mæskəˈreɪd/ **A** *n* fig mascherata *f*
B *vi* **~ as** (pose) farsi passare per
mass¹ /mæs/ *n* Relig messa *f*

⚷ **mass²** **A** *n* massa *f*; **~es of** infml un sacco di
B *vi* ammassarsi
massacre /ˈmæsəkə(r)/ **A** *n* massacro *m*
B *vt* massacrare
massage /ˈmæsɑːʒ/ **A** *n* massaggio *m*
B *vt* massaggiare; fig manipolare ‹*statistics*›
masseur /mæˈsɜː(r)/ *n* massaggiatore *m*
masseuse /mæˈsɜːz/ *n* massaggiatrice *f*
mass grave *n* fossa *f* comune
mass hysteria *n* isterismo *m* di massa
⚷ **massive** /ˈmæsɪv/ *adj* enorme
massively /ˈmæsɪvlɪ/ *adv* estremamente
mass market **A** *n* mercato *m* di massa
B *attrib* del mercato di massa
mass-marketing /ˌmæsˈmɑːkɪtɪŋ/ *n* commercializzazione *f* di massa
mass media *npl* mezzi *mpl* di comunicazione di massa, mass media *mpl*
mass murder *n* omicidio *m* di massa
mass murderer *n* omicida *mf* di massa
mass-produce *vt* produrre in serie
mass production *n* produzione *f* in serie
mass screening *n* Med controllo *m* su larga scala
mast /mɑːst/ *n* Naut albero *m*; (for radio) antenna *f*
⚷ **master** /ˈmɑːstə(r)/ **A** *n* maestro *m*, padrone *m*; ((teacher)) professore *m*; (of ship) capitano *m*; **M~** (boy) signorino *m*
B *vt* imparare perfettamente; avere padronanza di ‹*language*›
master bedroom *n* camera *f* da letto principale
master builder *n* capomastro *m*
master copy *n* originale *m*
master disk *n* Comput disco *m* master
master key *n* passe-partout *m inv*
masterly /ˈmæstəlɪ/ *adj* magistrale
mastermind **A** *n* cervello *m*
B *vt* ideare e dirigere
Master of Arts *n* (diploma) laurea *f* in lettere; (person) laureato, -a *mf* in lettere
master of ceremonies *n* (presenting entertainment) presentatore *m*; (of formal occasion) maestro *m* di cerimonie
Master of Science *n* (diploma) laurea *f* in discipline scientifiche; (person) laureato, -a *mf* in discipline scientifiche
masterpiece *n* capolavoro *m*
master plan *n* piano *m* generale
master race *n* razza *f* superiore
master stroke *n* colpo *m* da maestro
master tape *n* nastro *m* matrice
mastery /ˈmæstərɪ/ *n* (of subject) padronanza *f*
masticate /ˈmæstɪkeɪt/ *vi* masticare
masturbate /ˈmæstəbeɪt/ *vi* masturbarsi
masturbation /mæstəˈbeɪʃn/ *n* masturbazione *f*

⚷ parola chiave

mat /mæt/ *n* stuoia *f*; (on table) sottopiatto *m*
⚷ **match¹** /mætʃ/ **A** *n* Sport partita *f*; (equal) uguale *mf*; (marriage) matrimonio *m*; (person to marry) partito *m*; **be a good ~** ‹*colours*› intonarsi bene; **be no ~ for** non essere dello stesso livello di
B *vt* (equal) uguagliare; (be like) andare bene con
C *vi* intonarsi
match² *n* fiammifero *m*
matchbox /ˈmætʃbɒks/ *n* scatola *f* di fiammiferi
matching /ˈmætʃɪŋ/ *adj* intonato
matchmaker *n* **he's a successful ~** (for couples) è stato l'artefice di molti matrimoni
match point *n* Tennis match point *m inv*
matchstick *n* fiammifero *m*
mate¹ /meɪt/ **A** *n* compagno, -a *mf*; (assistant) aiuto *m*; Naut secondo *m*; infml (friend) amico, -a *mf*
B *vi* accoppiarsi
C *vt* accoppiare
mate² *n* (in chess) scacco *m* matto
⚷ **material** /məˈtɪərɪəl/ **A** *n* materiale *m*; (fabric) stoffa *f*; **raw ~s** *pl* materie *fpl* prime
B *adj* materiale
materialism /məˈtɪərɪəlɪzm/ *n* materialismo *m*
materialistic /mətɪərɪəˈlɪstɪk/ *adj* materialistico
materialize /məˈtɪərɪəlaɪz/ *vi* materializzarsi
maternal /məˈtɜːnl/ *adj* materno
maternity /məˈtɜːnətɪ/ *n* maternità *f*
maternity clothes *npl* abiti *mpl* pre-maman
maternity department *n* (in store) reparto *m* pre-maman
maternity hospital *n* maternità *f*
maternity leave *n* congedo *m* per maternità
maternity unit *n* reparto *m* maternità
maternity ward *n* maternità *f*
matey /ˈmeɪtɪ/ *adj* infml amichevole
math /mæθ/ *n* AmE matematica *f*
mathematical /mæθəˈmætɪkl/ *adj* matematico
mathematically /mæθəˈmætɪklɪ/ *adv* matematicamente
mathematician /mæθəməˈtɪʃn/ *n* matematico, -a *mf*
mathematics /mæθˈmætɪks/ *nsg* matematica *fsg*
maths /mæθs/ *n* infml matematica *fsg*
matinee /ˈmætɪneɪ/ *n* Theat matinée *f inv*
mating /ˈmeɪtɪŋ/ *n* accoppiamento *m*
mating call *n* richiamo *m* [per l'accoppiamento]
mating season *n* stagione *f* degli amori
matriarchal /meɪtrɪˈɑːkl/ *adj* matriarcale

m

matriarchy /ˈmeɪtrɪɑːkɪ/ *n* matriarchia *f*
matrices /ˈmeɪtrɪsiːz/ ▶ **matrix**
matriculate /məˈtrɪkjʊleɪt/ *vi* immatricolarsi
matriculation /mətrɪkjʊˈleɪʃn/ *n* immatricolazione *f*
matrimonial /mætrɪˈməʊnɪəl/ *adj* matrimoniale
matrimony /ˈmætrɪmənɪ/ *n* matrimonio *m*
matrix /ˈmeɪtrɪks/ *n* (*pl* **matrices** /ˈmeɪtrɪsiːz/) matrice *f*
matron /ˈmeɪtrən/ *n* (of hospital) capoinfermiera *f*; (of school) governante *f*
matronly /ˈmeɪtrənlɪ/ *adj* matronale
matron of honour *n* BrE damigella *f* d'onore (*sposata*)
matt /mæt/ *adj* opaco
matted /ˈmætɪd/ *adj* ~ **hair** capelli *mpl* tutti appiccicati tra loro
matter /ˈmætə(r)/ **A** *n* (affair) faccenda *f*; (question) questione *f*; (pus) pus *m*; Phys (substance) materia *f*; **money ~s** questioni *fpl* di soldi; **as a ~ of fact** a dire la verità; **what is the ~?** che cosa c'è?
B *vi* importare; **~ to somebody** essere importante per qualcuno; **it doesn't ~** non importa
matter-of-fact *adj* pratico
matting /ˈmætɪŋ/ *n* materiale *m* per stuoie
mattress /ˈmætrɪs/ *n* materasso *m*
maturation /mætʃʊˈreɪʃn/ *n* (of tree, body) sviluppo *m*; (of whisky, wine) invecchiamento *m*; (of cheese) stagionatura *f*
mature /məˈtʃʊə(r)/ **A** *adj* maturo; Comm in scadenza
B *vi* maturare
C *vt* far maturare
mature student *n* BrE *persona (f) che riprende gli studi universitari dopo i 25 anni*
maturity /məˈtʃʊərətɪ/ *n* maturità *f*; Comm maturazione *f*
maudlin /ˈmɔːdlɪn/ *adj* ‹*song*› sdolcinato; ‹*person*› piagnucoloso
maul /mɔːl/ *vt* malmenare
Maundy /ˈmɔːndɪ/ *n* ~ **Thursday** giovedì *m* santo
Mauritania /ˌmɒrɪˈteɪnɪə/ *n* Mauritania *f*
Mauritius /məˈrɪʃəs/ *n* [isola *f* di] Maurizio *f*
mausoleum /mɔːsəˈlɪəm/ *n* mausoleo *m*
mauve /məʊv/ *adj* malva
maverick /ˈmævərɪk/ *n, adj* anticonformista *mf*
mawkish /ˈmɔːkɪʃ/ *adj* sdolcinato
max. *abbr* (**maximum**) max. *m*
maxi /ˈmæksɪ/ *n* (dress) vestito *m* alla caviglia; (skirt) gonna *f* alla caviglia
maxim /ˈmæksɪm/ *n* massima *f*
maximization /mæksɪmaɪˈzeɪʃn/ *n* massimizzazione *f*
maximize /ˈmæksɪmaɪz/ *vt* massimizzare ‹*profits, sales*›; Comput ingrandire ‹*window*›
maximum /ˈmæksɪməm/ **A** *adj* massimo; **ten minutes ~** dieci minuti al massimo
B *n* (*pl* **-ima**) massimo *m*
maximum security prison *n* carcere *m* di massima sicurezza
may *v aux* (only in present) potere; **~ I come in?** posso entrare?; **if I ~ say so** se mi posso permettere; **~ you both be very happy** siate felici; **I ~ as well stay** potrei anche rimanere; **it ~ be true** potrebbe esser vero; **she ~ be old, but...** sarà anche vecchia, ma...
May /meɪ/ *n* maggio *m*
maybe /ˈmeɪbiː/ *adv* forse, può darsi
May bug *n* maggiolino *m*
Mayday *n* Radio mayday *m inv*
May Day *n* il primo maggio
mayhem /ˈmeɪhem/ *n* **create ~** creare scompiglio
mayonnaise /meɪəˈneɪz/ *n* maionese *f*
mayor /ˈmeə(r)/ *n* sindaco *m*
mayoress /meəˈres/ *n* sindaco *m*; (wife of mayor) moglie *f* del sindaco
maypole /ˈmeɪpəʊl/ *n* palo *m* (*intorno al quale si balla durante la celebrazione del primo maggio*)
May queen *n* reginetta *f* di calendimaggio
maze /meɪz/ *n* labirinto *m*
Mb *abbr* (**megabyte**) MB *m inv*
MBA *n abbr* (**Master of Business Administration**) laurea *f inv* in economia e commercio
MBE *n abbr* BrE (**Member of the Order of the British Empire**) *onorificenza (f) britannica*
MBO *n abbr* (**management buyout**) *acquisto (m) di tutte le azioni di una società da parte dei suoi dirigenti*
MC *n abbr* **1** (**Master of Ceremonies**) (in cabaret) presentatore *m*; (at banquet) maestro *m* delle cerimonie **2** AmE (**Member of Congress**) membro *m* del Congresso
McCoy /məˈkɔɪ/ *n* **this whisky is the real ~** questo è un vero whisky
MD *abbr* **1** (**Managing Director**) direttore, -trice *mf* generale **2** (**Doctor of Medicine**) dottore *m* in medicina **3** AmE (**Maryland**)
me /miː/ *pers pron* (object) mi; (with preposition) me; **he knows me** mi conosce; **she called me, not you** ha chiamato me, non te; **give me the money** dammi i soldi; **give it to me** dammelo; **he explained it to me** me lo ha spiegato; **it's me** sono io
ME *n abbr* **1** (**myalgic encephalomyelitis**) encefalomelite *f* mialgica **2** AmE (**Maine**)
mead /miːd/ *n* idromele *m*
meadow /ˈmedəʊ/ *n* prato *m*
meagre /ˈmiːgə(r)/ *adj* scarso
meal[1] /miːl/ *n* pasto *m*; **did you enjoy your**

~? ha mangiato bene?
meal[2] *n* (grain) farina *f*
meal ticket *n* fig (quality, qualification) fonte *f* di guadagno; **he's only a ~ to her** le interessano solo i suoi soldi
mealy-mouthed /mi:lɪ'maʊðd/ *adj* ambiguo
mean[1] /mi:n/ *adj* avaro; (unkind) meschino; (low in rank) basso; (accommodation) misero
mean[2] **A** *adj* medio
B *n* (average) media *f*; **Greenwich ~ time** ora *f* media di Greenwich
⚷ **mean**[3] *vt* (*pt/pp* **meant**) voler dire; (signify) significare; (intend) intendere; **I ~ it** lo dico seriamente; **~ well** avere buone intenzioni; **be ~t for** ‹*present*› essere destinato a; ‹*remark*› essere riferito a
meander /mɪ'ændə(r)/ *vi* vagare
⚷ **meaning** /'mi:nɪŋ/ *n* significato *m*
meaningful /'mi:nɪŋfʊl/ *adj* significativo
meaningless /'mi:nɪŋlɪs/ *adj* senza senso
meanness /'mi:nnɪs/ *n* (with money) avarizia *f*; (unkindness) meschinità *f*
means /mi:nz/ **A** *n* mezzo *m*; **~ of transport** mezzo *m* di trasporto; **by ~ of** per mezzo di; **by all ~!** certamente!; **by no ~** niente affatto
B *npl* (resources) mezzi *mpl*; **~ test** *n* accertamento *m* patrimoniale
meant /ment/ ▶ **mean**[3]
meantime /'mi:ntaɪm/ **A** *n* **in the ~** nel frattempo
B *adv* intanto
⚷ **meanwhile** /'mi:nwaɪl/ *adv* intanto
measles /'mi:zlz/ *nsg* morbillo *m*
measly /'mi:zlɪ/ *adj* infml misero
measurable /'meʒərəbl/ *adj* misurabile
⚷ **measure** /'meʒə(r)/ **A** *n* misura *f*
B *vt & vi* misurare
▪ **measure out** *vt* dosare ‹*amount*›
▪ **measure up** *vi* fig avere i requisiti richiesti
▪ **measure up to** *vt* fig essere all'altezza di
measured /'meʒed/ *adj* misurato
measurement /'meʒəmənt/ *n* misura *f*
measuring jug /'meʒərɪŋ/ *n* dosatore *m*
measuring spoon *n* misurino *m*
meat /mi:t/ *n* carne *f*
meatball *n* Culin polpetta *f* di carne
meat eater *n* (animal) carnivoro *m*; **I'm not a ~** non mangio carne
meat hook *n* gancio *m* da macellaio
meat loaf *n* polpettone *m*
meat pie *n* tortino *m* di carne
meaty /'mi:tɪ/ (**-ier**, **-iest**) *adj* (**-ier**, **-iest**) di carne; fig sostanzioso
Mecca /'mekə/ *n* La Mecca
mechanic /mɪ'kænɪk/ *n* meccanico *m*
mechanical /mɪ'kænɪkl/ *adj* meccanico
mechanical engineering *n* ingegneria *f* meccanica
mechanically /mɪ'kænɪklɪ/ *adv* meccanicamente
mechanics /mɪ'kænɪks/ **A** *n* meccanica *f*
B *npl* meccanismo *msg*
⚷ **mechanism** /'mekənɪzm/ *n* meccanismo *m*
mechanization /,mekənaɪ'zeɪʃn, AmE -nɪ'z-/ *n* meccanizzazione *f*
mechanize /'mekənaɪz/ *vt* meccanizzare
medal /'medl/ *n* medaglia *f*
medallion /mɪ'dælɪən/ *n* medaglione *m*
medallist /'medəlɪst/ *n* vincitore, -trice *mf* di una medaglia
meddle /'medl/ *vi* immischiarsi (**in** in); (tinker) armeggiare (**with** con)
⚷ **media** /'mi:dɪə/ **A** *n* ▶ **medium**
B *npl* **the ~** i mass media
median /'mi:dɪən/ *adj* **~ strip** AmE banchina *f* spartitraffico
media studies *npl* scienze *fpl* delle comunicazioni
mediate /'mi:dɪeɪt/ *vi* fare da mediatore
mediation /mi:dɪ'eɪʃn/ *n* mediazione *f*
mediator /'mi:dɪeɪtə(r)/ *n* mediatore, -trice *mf*
medic /'medɪk/ *n* infml (doctor) medico *m*; infml (student) studente, -essa *mf* di medicina; Mil infml infermiere, -a *mf* militare
⚷ **medical** /'medɪkl/ **A** *adj* medico
B *n* visita *f* medica
medical care *n* assistenza *f* medica
medical check-up *n* controllo *m* medico
medical examiner *n* AmE = **pathologist**
medical history *n* anamnesi *f inv*
medical insurance *n* assicurazione *f* sanitaria
medically /'medɪklɪ/ *adv* **~ qualified** con qualifiche di medico; **~ fit** in buona salute
medical officer *n* Mil ufficiale *m* medico
medical profession *n* (occupation) professione *f* del medico; (doctors collectively) categoria *f* medica
medical student *n* studente, -essa *mf* di medicina
medicated /'medɪkeɪtɪd/ *adj* medicato
medication /medɪ'keɪʃn/ *n* (drugs) medicinali *mpl*; **are you on any ~?** sta prendendo delle medicine?
medicinal /mɪ'dɪsɪnl/ *adj* medicinale
⚷ **medicine** /'medsən/ *n* medicina *f*
medicine ball *n* palla *f* medica
medicine bottle *n* flacone *m*
medicine cabinet *n* armadietto *m* dei medicinali
medicine man *n* stregone *m*
medieval /medɪ'i:vl/ *adj* medievale
mediocre /mi:dɪ'əʊkə(r)/ *adj* mediocre
mediocrity /mi:di:'ɒkrətɪ/ *n* mediocrità *f*
meditate /'medɪteɪt/ *vi* meditare (**on** su)

⚷ parola chiave

meditative /ˈmedɪtətɪv/ *adj* ‹*music, person*› meditativo; ‹*mood, expression*› meditabondo

Mediterranean /medɪtəˈreɪnɪən/ **A** *n* **the ~ [Sea]** il [mare] Mediterraneo
B *adj* mediterraneo

medium /ˈmiːdɪəm/ **A** *adj* medio; Culin di media cottura
B *n* mezzo *m* (*pl* **-s**) (person) medium *mf inv*

medium dry *adj* ‹*drink*› semisecco

medium-length *adj* ‹*book, film, hair*› di media lunghezza

medium-range *adj* ‹*missile*› di media portata

medium-rare *adj* ‹*meat*› appena al sangue

medium-sized /ˈmiːdɪəmsaɪzd/ *adj* di taglia media

medium wave *n* onde *fpl* medie

medley /ˈmedlɪ/ *n* miscuglio *m*; Mus medley *m inv*

meek /miːk/ *adj* mite, mansueto

meekly /ˈmiːklɪ/ *adv* docilmente

meerkat /ˈmɪəkæt/ *n* suricato *m*

⚷ **meet** /miːt/ **A** *vt* (*pt/pp* **met**) incontrare; (at station, airport) andare incontro a; (for first time) far la conoscenza di; pagare ‹*bill*›; soddisfare ‹*requirements*›
B *vi* incontrarsi; ‹*committee*› riunirsi; **~ with** incontrare ‹*problem*›; incontrarsi con ‹*person*›
C *n* raduno *m* (sportivo)
▪ **meet up** *vi* ‹*people*› incontrarsi; **~ up with somebody** incontrare qualcuno

⚷ **meeting** /ˈmiːtɪŋ/ *n* riunione *f*, meeting *m inv*; (large) assemblea *f*; (by chance) incontro *m*; **be in a ~** essere in riunione

meeting place *n* luogo *m* d'incontro

meeting point *n* punto *m* d'incontro

mega+ /ˈmegə/ *pref* mega+

megabyte /ˈmegəbaɪt/ *n* Comput megabyte *m inv*

megalith /ˈmegəlɪθ/ *n* megalite *m*

megalomania /megələˈmeɪnɪə/ *n* megalomania *f*

megalomaniac /ˌmegələˈmeɪnɪæk/ *adj & n* megalomane *mf*

megaphone /ˈmegəfəʊn/ *n* megafono *m*

megapixel /ˈmegəpɪksəl/ *n* megapixel *m inv*

melancholy /ˈmelənkəlɪ/ **A** *adj* malinconico
B *n* malinconia *f*

mellow /ˈmeləʊ/ **A** *adj* ‹*wine*› generoso; ‹*sound, colour*› caldo; ‹*person*› dolce
B *vi* ‹*person*› addolcirsi

melodic /mɪˈlɒdɪk/ *adj* melodico

melodious /mɪˈləʊdɪəs/ *adj* melodioso

melodrama /ˈmelədrɑːmə/ *n* melodramma *m*

melodramatic /melədrəˈmætɪk/ *adj* melodrammatico

melodramatically /melədrəˈmætɪklɪ/ *adv* in modo melodrammatico

melody /ˈmelədɪ/ *n* melodia *f*

melon /ˈmelən/ *n* melone *m*

melt /melt/ **A** *vt* sciogliere
B *vi* sciogliersi
▪ **melt away** *vi* ‹*snow*› sciogliersi; ‹*crowd*› disperdersi; ‹*support*› venir meno
▪ **melt down** *vt* fondere

meltdown /ˈmeltdaʊn/ *n* (in nuclear reactor) fusione *f* del nocciolo

melting point /ˈmeltɪŋ/ *n* punto *m* di fusione

melting pot *n* fig crogiuolo *m*

⚷ **member** /ˈmembə(r)/ *n* membro *m*; **be a ~ of the family** far parte della famiglia

member countries paesi *mpl* membri

Member of Congress *n* AmE membro *m* del Congresso

Member of Parliament deputato, -a *mf*

Member of the European Parliament *n* eurodeputato, -a *mf*

membership /ˈmembəʃɪp/ *n* iscrizione *f*; (members) soci *mpl*

membrane /ˈmembreɪn/ *n* membrana *f*

memento /mɪˈmentəʊ/ *n* ricordo *m*

memo /ˈmeməʊ/ *n* promemoria *m inv*

memoirs /ˈmemwɑːz/ *npl* ricordi *mpl*

memo pad *n* blocchetto *m*

memorabilia /memərəˈbɪlɪə/ *npl* cimeli *mpl*

memorable /ˈmemərəbl/ *adj* memorabile

memorandum /ˈmeməˈrændəm/ *n* promemoria *m inv*

memorial /mɪˈmɔːrɪəl/ *n* monumento *m*

memorial service *n* funzione *f* commemorativa

memorize /ˈmeməraɪz/ *vt* memorizzare

⚷ **memory** /ˈmemərɪ/ *n* (also Comput) memoria *f*; (thing remembered) ricordo *m*; **from ~** a memoria; **in ~ of** in ricordo di

men /men/ ▸ **man**

menace /ˈmenəs/ **A** *n* minaccia *f*; (nuisance) piaga *f*
B *vt* minacciare

menacing /ˈmenəsɪŋ/ *adj* minaccioso

menacingly /ˈmenəsɪŋlɪ/ *adv* minacciosamente

mend /mend/ **A** *vt* riparare; (darn) rammendare
B *n* **on the ~** in via di guarigione

menfolk /ˈmenfəʊk/ *n* uomini *mpl*

menial /ˈmiːnɪəl/ *adj* umile

meningitis /menɪnˈdʒaɪtɪs/ *n* meningite *f*

menopause /ˈmenəpɔːz/ *n* menopausa *f*

Menorca /mɪˈnɔːkə/ *n* Minorca *f*

men's room *n* toilette *f inv* degli uomini

menstruate /ˈmenstrʊeɪt/ *vi* mestruare

menstruation /menstrʊˈeɪʃn/ *n* mestruazione *f*

menswear /ˈmenzweə(r)/ *n* abbigliamento *m* per uomo

⚷ **mental** /ˈmentl/ *adj* mentale; infml (mad) pazzo

mental arithmetic *n* calcolo *m* mentale

mental block *n* blocco *m* psicologico
mental health *n* (of person) salute *f* mentale
mental health care *n* assistenza *f* psichiatrica
mental home *n* clinica *f* psichiatrica
mental illness *n* malattia *f* mentale
mentality /men'tæləti/ *n* mentalità *f*
mentally /'mentəli/ *adv* mentalmente; ~ **ill** malato di mente
mentholated /'menθəleitid/ *adj* al mentolo
⚷ **mention** /'menʃn/ **A** *n* menzione *f*
B *vt* menzionare; **don't ~ it** non c'è di che
mentor /'mentɔ:(r)/ *n* mentore *m*
menu /'menju:/ *n* menu *m inv*
menu bar *n* Comput barra *f* dei menu
MEP *n abbr* (**Member of the European parliament**) eurodeputato, -a *mf*
mercantile /'mɜ:kəntaɪl/ *adj* mercantile
mercenary /'mɜ:sɪnəri/ **A** *adj* mercenario
B *n* mercenario *m*
merchandise /'mɜ:tʃəndaɪz/ *n* merce *f*
merchant /'mɜ:tʃənt/ *n* commerciante *mf*
merchant bank *n* BrE banca *f* d'affari
merchant banker *n* (owner) proprietario, -a *mf* di una banca d'affari; (executive) dirigente *mf* di banca d'affari
merchant navy *n* marina *f* mercantile
m **merciful** /'mɜ:sɪfl/ *adj* misericordioso
mercifully /'mɜ:sɪfʊlɪ/ *adv* infml grazie a Dio
merciless /'mɜ:sɪlɪs/ *adj* spietato
mercilessly /'mɜ:sɪlɪslɪ/ *adv* senza pietà
mercurial /mɜ:'kjʊərɪəl/ *adj* fig volubile
mercury /'mɜ:'kjʊri/ *n* mercurio *m*
mercy /'mɜ:sɪ/ *n* misericordia *f*; **be at sb's ~** essere alla mercé *or* in balia di qualcuno
mercy killing *n* eutanasia *f*
mere /mɪə(r)/ *adj* solo
⚷ **merely** /'mɪəlɪ/ *adv* solamente
merest /'mɪərɪst/ *adj* minimo
merge /mɜ:dʒ/ **A** *vi* fondersi
B *vt* Comm fondere
merger /'mɜ:dʒə(r)/ *n* fusione *f*
meridian /mə'rɪdɪən/ *n* meridiano *m*
meringue /mə'ræŋ/ *n* meringa *f*
merit /'merɪt/ **A** *n* merito *m*; (advantage) qualità *f*
B *vt* meritare
mermaid /'mɜ:meɪd/ *n* sirena *f*
merrily /'merɪlɪ/ *adv* allegramente
merriment /'merɪmənt/ *n* baldoria *f*
merry /'meri/ (**-ier**, **-iest**) *adj* (**-ier**, **-iest**) allegro; **M~ Christmas!** Buon Natale!; **make ~** far festa
merry-go-round *n* giostra *f*
merry-making /'merɪmeɪkɪŋ/ *n* festa *f*
mesh /meʃ/ *n* maglia *f*

⚷ parola chiave

mesmerize /'mezməraɪz/ *vt* ipnotizzare
mesmerized /'mezməraɪzd/ *adj* fig ipnotizzato
mess /mes/ *n* disordine *m*, casino *m* infml; (trouble) guaio *m*; (something spilt) sporco *m*; Mil mensa *f*; **make a ~ of** (botch) fare un pasticcio di
■ **mess about A** *vi* perder tempo; **~ about with** armeggiare con
B *vt* prendere in giro ‹*person*›
■ **mess up** *vt* mettere in disordine, incasinare infml; (botch) mandare all'aria
■ **mess with** *vt* infml (interface with) trafficare con ‹*computer, radio etc*›; contrariare ‹*person*›
⚷ **message** /'mesɪdʒ/ *n* messaggio *m*
message window *n* Comput finestra *f* di messaggio
messaging /'mesɪdʒɪŋ/ *n* messaggeria *f* elettronica
mess dress *n* Mil uniforme *f* di gala
messenger /'mesɪndʒə(r)/ *n* messaggero *m*
messenger boy *n* fattorino *m*
Messiah /mɪ'saɪə/ *n* Messia *m*
Messrs /'mesəz/ *npl* (on letter) **~ Smith** Spett. ditta Smith
messy /'mesɪ/ *adj* (**-ier**, **-iest**) disordinato; (in dress) sciatto
met /met/ ▸ **meet**
metabolism /mɪ'tæbəlɪzm/ *n* metabolismo *m*
⚷ **metal** /'metl/ **A** *n* metallo *m*
B *adj* di metallo
metal detector *n* metal detector *m inv*
metal fatigue *n* fatica *f* del metallo
metallic /mɪ'tælɪk/ *adj* metallico
metallurgy /mɪ'tælədʒɪ/ *n* metallurgia *f*
metal polish *n* lucido *m* per metalli
metalwork /'metlwɜ:k/ *n* lavorazione *f* del metallo
metamorphose /metə'mɔ:fəʊz/ **A** *vt* trasformare
B *vi* trasformarsi (**into** in)
metamorphosis /metə'mɔ:fəsɪs/ *n* (*pl* **-phoses** /metə'mɔ:fəsi:z/) metamorfosi *f inv*
metaphor /'metəfə(r)/ *n* metafora *f*
metaphorical /metə'fɒrɪkl/ *adj* metaforico
metaphorically /metə'fɒrɪklɪ/ *adv* metaforicamente
metaphysical /metə'fɪzɪkl/ *adj* metafisico; (abstract) astruso
mete /mi:t/ *v*
■ **mete out** *vt* dispensare ‹*punishment, justice*›
meteor /'mi:tɪə(r)/ *n* meteora *f*
meteoric /mi:tɪ'ɒrɪk/ *adj* fig fulmineo
meteorite /'mi:tɪəraɪt/ *n* meteorite *m*
meteorological /mi:tɪərə'lɒdʒɪkl/ *adj* meteorologico
Meteorological Office *n* Ufficio *m* meteorologico

meteorologist /miːtɪəˈrɒlədʒɪst/ *n* meteorologo, -a *mf*
meteorology /miːtɪəˈrɒlədʒɪ/ *n* meteorologia *f*
meter¹ /ˈmiːtə(r)/ *n* contatore *m*
meter² *n* AmE = **metre**
meter reader *n persona (f) incaricata di leggere il contatore (di gas, elettricità)*
methane /ˈmiːθeɪn/ *n* metano *m*
method /ˈmeθəd/ *n* metodo *m*
method acting *n* metodo *m* dell'Actors' Studio
method actor *n attore (m) che segue il metodo dell'Actors' Studio*
methodical /mɪˈθɒdɪkl/ *adj* metodico
methodically /mɪˈθɒdɪklɪ/ *adv* metodicamente
Methodist /ˈmeθədɪst/ *n* metodista *mf*
methodology /meθəˈdɒlədʒɪ/ *n* metodologia *f*
meths /meθs/ *n* infml alcol *m* denaturato
methyl /ˈmiːθaɪl/ *n* metile *m*
methylated /ˈmeθɪleɪtɪd/ *adj* **~ spirit(s)** alcol *m* denaturato
meticulous /mɪˈtɪkjʊləs/ *adj* meticoloso
meticulously /mɪˈtɪkjʊləslɪ/ *adv* meticolosamente
metre /ˈmiːtə(r)/ *n* metro *m*
metric /ˈmetrɪk/ *adj* metrico
metrication /metrɪˈkeɪʃn/ *n* conversione *f* al sistema metrico
metronome /ˈmetrənəʊm/ *n* metronomo *m*
metropolis /mɪˈtrɒpəlɪs/ *n* metropoli *f inv*
metropolitan /metrəˈpɒlɪtən/ *adj* metropolitano
metropolitan district *n* BrE circoscrizione *f* amministrativa urbana
Metropolitan police *n* BrE polizia *f* di Londra
mettle /ˈmetl/ *n* coraggio *m*; **show one's ~** mostrare di che stoffa si è fatti
mew /mjuː/ **A** *n* miao *m* **B** *vi* miagolare
mews /mjuːz/ *n* BrE (stables) scuderie *fpl*; (street) stradina *f*; (yard) cortile *m*
mews flat *n* BrE *piccolo appartamento (m) ricavato da vecchie scuderie*
Mexican /ˈmeksɪkən/ *adj & n* messicano, -a *mf*
Mexican wave *n* ola *f inv*
Mexico /ˈmeksɪkəʊ/ *n* Messico *m*
mezzanine /ˈmetsəniːn/ *n* mezzanino *m*
miaow /mɪˈaʊ/ **A** *n* miao *m* **B** *vi* miagolare
mice /maɪs/ ▶ **mouse**
Michaelmas /ˈmɪkəlməs/ *n* festa *f* di San Michele (*29 settembre*)
Michaelmas daisy *n* BrE margherita *f* settembrina
Michaelmas Term *n* BrE Univ primo trimestre *m*
mickey /ˈmɪkɪ/ *n* **take the ~ out of** prendere in giro
Mickey Mouse *n* Topolino *m*
microbe /ˈmaɪkrəʊb/ *n* microbo *m*
microchip /ˈmaɪkrəʊtʃɪp/ *n* microchip *m inv*
microcomputer /ˈmaɪkrəʊkəmpjuːtə(r)/ *n* microcomputer *m inv*
microcosm /ˈmaɪkrəkɒzm/ *n* microcosmo *m*
microfilm *n* microfilm *m inv*
microfinance /ˈmaɪkrəʊfaɪnæns/ *n* microfinanza *f*
microlight /ˈmaɪkrəʊlaɪt/ *n* ultraleggero *m*
micro-lighting /ˈmaɪkrəlaɪtɪŋ/ *n* volo *m* con l'ultraleggero
micromanage /ˈmaɪkrəʊˌmænɪdʒ/ *vt gestire, controllare in modo capillare un'impresa o un'attività*
micromesh tights *npl* collant *mpl* velati
microphone *n* microfono *m*
microphysics *nsg* microfisica *fsg*
microprocessor *n* microprocessore *m*
microscope *n* microscopio *m*
microscopic *adj* microscopico
microsite /ˈmaɪkrəʊsaɪt/ *n* microsito *m*
microsurgery *n* microchirurgia *f*
microwave *n* microonda *f*; (oven) forno *m* a microonde
mid /mɪd/ *adj* **~ May** metà maggio; **in ~ air** a mezz'aria
midday /mɪdˈdeɪ/ *n* mezzogiorno *m*
middle /ˈmɪdl/ **A** *adj* di centro; **the M~ Ages** il medioevo; **the ~ class(es)** la classe media; **the M~ East** il Medio Oriente **B** *n* mezzo *m*; **in the ~ of** ‹*room, floor etc*› in mezzo a; **in the ~ of the night** nel pieno della notte, a notte piena
middle-aged /-ˈeɪdʒd/ *adj* di mezza età
middle-age spread *n* pancetta *f* di mezza età
Middle America *n* (social group) *ceto (m) medio americano a tendenza conservatrice*
middlebrow *adj* ‹*book*› per il lettore medio; ‹*person*› con interessi culturali convenzionali
middle-class *adj* borghese
middle distance *n* Phot, Cinema secondo piano *m*; **gaze into the ~** avere lo sguardo perso nel vuoto
Middle Eastern *adj* mediorientale
Middle English *n* medio inglese *m*
middle finger *n* dito *m* medio
middle ground *n* Pol centro *m*; **occupy the ~** adottare una posizione intermedia
middle-income *adj* ‹*person, family, country*› dal reddito medio
middleman /ˈmidlmæn/ *n* Comm intermediario *m*
middle manager *n* quadro *m* intermedio

m

middle-of-the-road *adj* (ordinary) ordinario; ‹*policy*› moderato
middle-size /-saɪz/, **middle-sized** /-saɪz[d]/ *adj* di misura media
middleweight *n* peso *m* medio
middling /ˈmɪdlɪŋ/ *adj* discreto
midfield /ˈmɪdˈfiːld/ *n* centrocampo *m*
midfield player *n* centrocampista *m*
midge /mɪdʒ/ *n* moscerino *m*
midget /ˈmɪdʒɪt/ *n* nano, -a *mf*
Midlands /ˈmidləndz/ *npl* **the M∼** l'Inghilterra *fsg* centrale
mid-life *n* mezza età *f*
mid-life crisis *n* crisi *f inv* di mezza età
midnight /ˈmɪdnaɪt/ *n* mezzanotte *f*
mid-range *attrib* ‹*car*› (in price) di prezzo medio; (in power) di media cilindrata; ‹*hotel*› intermedio; **be in the ∼** ‹*product, hotel*› essere nella media
midriff /ˈmɪdrɪf/ *n* diaframma *m*
mid-season *adj* di metà stagione
midshipman /ˈmɪdʃɪpmən/ *n* BrE cadetto *m* di marina; AmE allievo *m* dell'Accademia Navale
midst /mɪdst/ *n* **in the ∼ of** in mezzo a; **in our ∼** fra di noi, in mezzo a noi
midstream /mɪdˈstriːm/ *adv* **in ∼** (in river) nel mezzo della corrente; fig (in speech) nel mezzo del discorso
midsummer /ˈmɪdsʌmə(r)/ *n* mezza estate *f*
Midsummer's Day *n* festa *f* di San Giovanni (*24 giugno*)
mid-term *attrib* Sch di metà trimestre; (pol) a metà del mandato del governo
midtown /ˈmɪdtaʊn/ *n* AmE centro *m* (cittadino); **a ∼ apartment** un appartamento in centro
midway /ˈmɪdweɪ/ *adv* a metà strada
midweek /mɪdˈwiːk/ **A** *adj* di metà settimana
B *adv* a metà settimana
midwife /ˈmɪdwaɪf/ *n* ostetrica *f*
midwifery /ˈmɪdwɪfrɪ/ *n* ostetricia *f*
midwinter /mɪdˈwɪntə(r)/ *n* pieno inverno *m*
miffed /mɪft/ *adj* infml seccato
🗝 **might**[1] /maɪt/ *v aux* **I ∼** potrei; **will you come?—I ∼** vieni?—può darsi; **it ∼ be true** potrebbe essere vero; **I ∼ as well stay** potrei anche restare; **he asked if he ∼ go** ha chiesto se poteva andare; **you ∼ have drowned** avresti potuto affogare; **you ∼ have said so!** avresti potuto dirlo!
might[2] *n* potere *m*
mighty /ˈmaɪtɪ/ **A** *adj* (**-ier**, **-iest**) potente
B *adv* infml molto
migraine /ˈmiːgreɪn/ *n* emicrania *f*
migrant /ˈmaɪgrənt/ **A** *adj* migratore
B *n* (bird) migratore, -trice *mf*; (person: for work) emigrante *mf*

migrate /maɪˈgreɪt/ *vi* migrare
migration /maɪˈgreɪʃn/ *n* migrazione *f*
migratory /maɪˈgreɪtərɪ/ *adj* ‹*animal*› migratore
mike /maɪk/ *n* infml microfono *f*
Milan /mɪˈlæn/ *n* Milano *f*
Milanese /mɪləˈniːz/ *adj* milanese
mild /maɪld/ *adj* ‹*weather*› mite; ‹*person*› dolce; ‹*flavour*› delicato; ‹*illness*› leggero
mildew /ˈmɪldjuː/ *n* muffa *f*
mildly /ˈmaɪldlɪ/ *adv* moderatamente; ‹*say*› dolcemente; **to put it ∼** a dir poco, senza esagerazione
mildness /ˈmaɪldnɪs/ *n* (of person, words) dolcezza *f*; (of weather) mitezza *f*
🗝 **mile** /maɪl/ *n* miglio *m* (= *1,6 km*); **∼s nicer** infml molto più bello; **∼s too big** infml eccessivamente grande
mileage /ˈmaɪlɪdʒ/ *n* chilometraggio *m*
mileage allowance *n* indennità *f* di trasferta per chilometro
milestone /ˈmaɪlstəʊn/ *n* pietra *f* miliare
milieu /mɪˈjɜː/ *n* ambiente *m*
militant /ˈmɪlɪtənt/ *adj & n* militante *mf*
militarism /ˈmɪlɪtərɪzm/ *n* militarismo *m*
militarize /ˈmɪlɪtəraɪz/ *vt* militarizzare
🗝 **military** /ˈmɪlɪtrɪ/ *adj* militare
military academy *n* accademia *f* militare
military policeman *n* agente *m* di polizia militare
military service *n* servizio *m* militare
militate /ˈmɪlɪteɪt/ *vi* **∼ against** opporsi a
militia /mɪˈlɪʃə/ *n* milizia *f*
milk /mɪlk/ **A** *n* latte *m*
B *vt* mungere
milk chocolate *n* cioccolato *m* al latte
milk float *n* BrE furgone *m* del lattaio
milk jug *n* bricco *m* del latte
milkman *n* lattaio *m*
milk pudding *n budino* (*m*) *a base di latte*
milk shake *n* frappé *m inv*
milk train *n* primo treno *m* del mattino
milky /ˈmɪlkɪ/ *adj* (**-ier**, **-iest**) latteo; ‹*tea etc*› con molto latte
mill /mɪl/ **A** *n* mulino *m*; (factory) fabbrica *f*; (for coffee etc) macinino *m*
B *vt* macinare ‹*grain*›
■ **mill about, mill around** *vi* brulicare
millennium /mɪˈlenɪəm/ *n* millennio *m*
miller /ˈmɪlə(r)/ *n* mugnaio *m*
millet /ˈmɪlɪt/ *n* miglio *m*
milligram /ˈmɪlɪgræm/ *n* milligrammo *m*
millimetre /ˈmɪlɪmiːtə(r)/ *n* millimetro *m*
🗝 **million** /ˈmɪljən/ *adj & n* milione *m*; **a ∼ pounds** un milione di sterline
millionaire /mɪljəˈneə(r)/ *n* miliardario, -a *mf*
millipede /ˈmɪlɪpiːd/ *n* millepiedi *m inv*
millpond *n* **like a ∼** piatto come una tavola

🗝 parola chiave

millstone *n* **a ~ round one's neck** fig un peso
mill wheel *n* ruota *f* di mulino
milometer /maɪ'lɒmɪtə(r)/ *n* BrE ≈ contachilometri *m inv*
mime /maɪm/ **A** *n* mimo *m*
B *vt* mimare
mime artist *n* mimo, a *mf*
mimic /'mɪmɪk/ **A** *n* imitatore, -trice *mf*
B *vt* (*pt/pp* **mimicked**) imitare
mimicry /'mɪmɪkrɪ/ *n* mimetismo *m*
mimosa /mɪ'məʊzə/ *n* mimosa *f*
min. *abbr* (**minute**) min.
minaret /mɪnə'ret/ *n* minareto *m*
mince /mɪns/ **A** *n* carne *f* tritata
B *vt* Culin tritare; **not ~ words** parlare senza mezzi termini
mincemeat /'mɪnsmi:t/ *n* miscuglio *m* di frutta secca; **make ~ of** fig demolire
mince pie *n pasticcino* (*m*) *a base di frutta secca*
mincer /'mɪnsə(r)/ *n* tritacarne *m inv*
mind /maɪnd/ **A** *n* mente *f*; (sanity) ragione *f*; **to my ~** a mio parere; **give somebody a piece of one's ~** dire chiaro e tondo a qualcuno quello che si pensa; **make up one's ~** decidersi; **have something in ~** avere qualcosa in mente; **bear something in ~** tenere presente qualcosa; **have something on one's ~** essere preoccupato; **have a good ~ to** avere una grande voglia di; **I have changed my ~** ho cambiato idea; **be out of one's ~** essere fuori di sé
B *vt* (look after) occuparsi di; **I don't ~ the noise** il rumore non mi dà fastidio; **I don't ~ what we do** non mi importa quello che facciamo; **~ the step!** attenzione al gradino!
C *vi* **I don't ~** non mi importa; **never ~!** non importa!; **do you ~ if...?** ti dispiace se...?
▪ **mind out**: *vi* **~ out!** [fai] attenzione!
mind-bending /-bendɪŋ/ *adj* ‹*problem*› complicatissimo; **~ drugs** psicofarmaci *mpl*
mind-blowing /-bləʊɪŋ/ *adj* infml sconvolgente
mind-boggling /-bɒglɪŋ/ *adj* infml incredibile
minded /'maɪndɪd/ *adj* **if you're so ~** se vuole
minder /'maɪndə(r)/ *n* BrE (bodyguard) gorilla *m inv*; (for child) baby-sitter *mf inv*
mindful /'maɪndfʊl/ *adj* **~ of** attento a
mindless /'maɪndlɪs/ *adj* noncurante
mind-reader *n* persona *f* che legge nel pensiero; **I'm not a ~** non leggo nel pensiero
mine[1] /maɪn/ *poss pron* il mio *m*, la mia *f*, i miei *mpl*, le mie *fpl*; **a friend of ~** un mio amico; **friends of ~** dei miei amici; **that is ~** questo è mio; (as opposed to yours) questo è il mio
mine[2] **A** *n* miniera *f*; (explosive) mina *f*
B *vt* estrarre; Mil minare
mine-detector *n* rivelatore *m* di mine
minefield /'maɪnfi:ld/ *n* also fig campo *m* minato
miner /'maɪnə(r)/ *n* minatore *m*
mineral /'mɪnərəl/ **A** *n* minerale *m*
B *adj* minerale
mineral oil *n* AmE (paraffin) olio *m* minerale
mineral rights *npl* concessioni *fpl* minerarie
mineral water *n* acqua *f* minerale
minesweeper /'maɪnswi:pə(r)/ *n* dragamine *m inv*
mingle /'mɪŋgl/ *vi* **~ with** mescolarsi a
mini /'mɪnɪ/ *n* ▶ **miniskirt**
mini+ *pref* mini+
miniature /'mɪnɪtʃə(r)/ **A** *adj* in miniatura
B *n* miniatura *f*
miniature golf *n* minigolf *m inv*
miniature railway *n* trenino *m*
mini-budget *n* BrE Pol budget *m inv* provvisorio
minibus *n* minibus *m inv*, pulmino *m*
minicab *n* taxi *m inv*
minidisc /'mɪnɪdɪsk/ *n* minidisc *m inv*
minidisc player *n* lettore *m* di minidisc
minim /'mɪnɪm/ *n* Mus minima *f*
minimal /'mɪnɪməl/ *adj* minimo
minimalist /'mɪnɪməlɪst/ *adj* minimalista
minimally /'mɪnɪməlɪ/ *adv* (very slightly) minimamente
minimarket /'mɪnɪmɑ:kɪt/ *n* minimarket *m inv*
minimize /'mɪnɪmaɪz/ *vt* minimizzare
minimum /'mɪnɪməm/ **A** *n* (*pl* **-ima**) minimo *m*
B *adj* minimo; **ten minutes ~** minimo dieci minuti
mining /'maɪnɪŋ/ **A** *n* estrazione *f*
B *attrib* estrattivo
mining engineer *n* ingegnere *m* minerario
miniskirt /'mɪnɪskɜ:t/ *n* minigonna *f*
minister /'mɪnɪstə(r)/ *n* ministro *m*; Relig pastore *m*
ministerial /mɪnɪ'stɪərɪəl/ *adj* ministeriale
minister of state *n* BrE Pol *titolo* (*m*) *di un parlamentare con competenze specifiche in seno a un ministero*
ministry /'mɪnɪstrɪ/ *n* Pol ministero *m*; **the ~** Relig il ministero sacerdotale
mink /mɪŋk/ *n* visone *m*
minnow /'mɪnəʊ/ *n* (fish) pesciolino *m* d'acqua dolce
minor /'maɪnə(r)/ **A** *adj* minore
B *n* minorenne *mf*
Minorca /mɪ'nɔ:kə/ *n* Minorca *f*
minority /maɪ'nɒrətɪ/ *n* minoranza *f*; (age) minore età *f*
minority leader *n* AmE Pol leader *mf inv* dell'opposizione

minority rule *n* governo *m* di minoranza

minor offence *n* BrE reato *m* minore

minor road *n* strada *f* secondaria

minster /'mɪnstə(r)/ *n* (cathedral) cattedrale *f*

minstrel /'mɪnstrəl/ *n* menestrello *m*

mint¹ /mɪnt/ **A** *n* zecca *f*; infml patrimonio *m* **B** *adj* **in ~ condition** in condizione perfetta **C** *vt* coniare

mint² *n* (herb) menta *f*

mint-flavoured /-fleɪvəd/ *adj* al gusto di menta

minuet /mɪnjʊ'et/ *n* minuetto *m*

minus /'maɪnəs/ **A** *prep* meno; infml (without) senza **B** *n* **~ [sign]** meno *m*

minuscule /'mɪnəskju:l/ *adj* minuscolo

✓ **minute¹** /'mɪnɪt/ *n* minuto *m*; **in a ~** (shortly) tra un minuto; **~s** *pl* (of meeting) verbale *msg*

minute² /maɪ'nju:t/ *adj* minuto; (precise) minuzioso

minute hand /'mɪnɪt/ *n* lancetta *f* dei minuti

minutely /maɪ'nju:tlɪ/ *adv* ‹*vary, differ*› di poco; ‹*describe, examine*› minuziosamente

minutiae /maɪ'nju:ʃɪaɪ/ *npl* minuzie *fpl*

miracle /'mɪrəkl/ *n* miracolo *m*

miraculous /mɪ'rækjʊləs/ *adj* miracoloso

mirage /'mɪrɑ:ʒ/ *n* miraggio *m*

m **mire** /'maɪə(r)/ *n* pantano *m*

mirror /'mɪrə(r)/ **A** *n* specchio *m* **B** *vt* rispecchiare

mirror image *n* (exact replica) copia *f* esatta; (inverse) immagine *f* speculare

mirth /mɜ:θ/ *n* ilarità *f*

misadventure /misæd'ventʃə(r)/ *n* disavventura *f*

misanthropist /mɪ'zænθrəpɪst/ *n* misantropo, -a *mf*

misapprehension /mɪsæprɪ'henʃn/ *n* malinteso *m*; **be under a ~** avere frainteso

misappropriate /mɪsə'prəʊprɪeɪt/ *vt* appropriarsi indebitamente di ‹*funds*›

misbehave /mɪsbɪ'heɪv/ *vi* comportarsi male

misbehaviour /mɪsbɪ'heɪvjə(r)/ *n* comportamento *m* scorretto

miscalculate /mɪs'kælkjʊleɪt/ *vt & vi* calcolare male

miscalculation /mɪskælkjʊ'leɪʃn/ *n* calcolo *m* sbagliato

miscarriage /'mɪskærɪdʒ/ *n* aborto *m* spontaneo; **~ of justice** errore *m* giudiziario

miscarry /mɪs'kærɪ/ *vi* abortire

miscellaneous /mɪsə'leɪnɪəs/ *adj* assortito

miscellany /mɪ'selənɪ/ *n* (of people, things) misto *m*; (anthology) miscellanea *f*

mischief /'mɪstʃɪf/ *n* malefatta *f*; (harm) danno *m*

mischievous /'mɪstʃɪvəs/ *adj* (naughty) birichino; (malicious) dannoso

mischievously /'mɪstʃɪvəslɪ/ *adv* in modo birichino

misconceived /mɪskən'si:vd/ *adj* ‹*argument, project*› sbagliato

misconception /mɪskən'sepʃn/ *n* concetto *m* erroneo

misconduct /mɪs'kɒndʌkt/ *n* cattiva condotta *f*

misconstrue /mɪskən'stru:/ *vt* fraintendere

miscount /mɪs'kaʊnt/ *vt & vi* contare male

misdeed /mɪs'di:d/ *n* misfatto *m*

misdemeanour /mɪsdɪ'mi:nə(r)/ *n* reato *m*

misdirect /mɪsdaɪ'rekt/ *vt* mettere l'indirizzo sbagliato su ‹*letter, parcel*›; dare istruzioni sbagliate a ‹*jury*›; **the letter was ~ed to our old address** la lettera ci è stata erroneamente spedita al vecchio indirizzo

miser /'maɪzə(r)/ *n* avaro *m*

miserable /'mɪzrəbl/ *adj* (unhappy) infelice; (wretched) miserabile; fig ‹*weather*› deprimente

miserably /'mɪzrəbl/ *adv* ‹*live, fail*› miseramente; ‹*say*› tristemente

miserly /'maɪzəlɪ/ *adj* avaro; ‹*amount*› ridicolo

misery /'mɪzərɪ/ *n* miseria *f*; infml (person) piagnone, -a *mf*

misfire /mɪs'faɪə(r)/ *vi* ‹*gun*› far cilecca; ‹*plan etc*› non riuscire

misfit /'mɪsfɪt/ *n* disadattato, -a *mf*

misfortune /mɪs'fɔ:tʃu:n/ *n* sfortuna *f*

misgivings /mɪs'gɪvɪŋz/ *npl* dubbi *mpl*

misguided /mɪs'gaɪdɪd/ *adj* fuorviato

mishandle /mɪs'hændl/ *vt* gestire male ‹*operation, meeting*›; non prendere per il verso giusto ‹*person*›; (roughly) maneggiare senza precauzioni ‹*object*›; maltrattare ‹*person, animal*›

mishap /'mɪshæp/ *n* disavventura *f*

mishear /mɪs'hɪə(r)/ *vt* sentire male

mishmash /'mɪʃmæʃ/ *n* infml guazzabuglio *m*

misinform /mɪsɪn'fɔ:m/ *vt* informar male

misinformation /mɪsɪnfə'meɪʃn/ *n* informazioni *fpl* sbagliate

misinterpret /mɪsɪn'tɜ:prɪt/ *vt* fraintendere

misinterpretation /mɪsɪntɜ:prɪ'teɪʃn/ *n* interpretazione *f* sbagliata

misjudge /mɪs'dʒʌdʒ/ *vt* giudicar male; (estimate wrongly) valutare male

mislay /mɪs'leɪ/ *vt* (*pt/pp* **-laid**) smarrire

mislead /mɪs'li:d/ *vt* (*pt/pp* **-led**) fuorviare

misleading /mɪs'li:dɪŋ/ *adj* fuorviante

mismanage /mɪs'mænɪdʒ/ *vt* amministrare male

mismanagement /mɪs'mænɪdʒmənt/ *n* cattiva amministrazione *f*

mismatch /'mɪsmætʃ/ *n* discordanza *f*

✓ parola chiave

misname /mɪs'neɪm/ *vt* dare il nome sbagliato a

misnomer /mis'nəʊmə(r)/ *n* termine *m* improprio

misogynist /mɪs'ɒdʒənɪst/ *n* misogino *m*

misplace /mɪs'pleɪs/ *vt* mettere in un posto sbagliato; **~ one's trust** riporre male la propria fiducia

misprint /'mɪsprɪnt/ *n* errore *m* di stampa

mispronounce /mɪsprə'naʊns/ *vt* pronunciare male

mispronunciation /mɪsprənʌnsɪeɪʃn/ *n* (act) pronuncia *f* sbagliata; (instance) errore *m* di pronuncia

misquote /mɪs'kwəʊt/ *vt* citare erroneamente

misread /mɪs'ri:d/ *vt* leggere male ‹*sentence, meter*›; (misinterpret) fraintendere ‹*actions*›

misrepresent /mɪsreprɪ'zent/ *vt* rappresentare male

misrepresentation /mɪsreprɪzen'teɪʃn/ *n* (of facts, opinions) travisamento *m*

miss **A** *n* colpo *m* mancato
B *vt* (fail to hit or find) mancare; perdere ‹*train, bus, class*›; (feel the loss of) sentire la mancanza di; **I ~ed that part** (failed to notice) mi è sfuggita quella parte; **~ the point** non afferrare il punto
C *vi* **but he ~ed** (failed to hit) ma l'ha mancato
■ **miss out** *vt* saltare, omettere

Miss /mɪs/ *n* (*pl* **-es**) signorina *f*

misshapen /mɪs'ʃeɪpən/ *adj* malformato

missile /'mɪsaɪl/ *n* missile *m*

missing /'mɪsɪŋ/ *adj* mancante; ‹*person*› scomparso; Mil disperso; **be ~** essere introvabile; **~ in action** Mil disperso

mission /'mɪʃn/ *n* missione *f*

missionary /'mɪʃənrɪ/ *n* missionario, -a *mf*

missive /'mɪsɪv/ *n* missiva *f*

misspell /mɪs'spel/ *vt* (*pt/pp* **-spelt, -spelled**) sbagliare l'ortografia di

misspent /mɪs'spent/ *adj* **a ~ youth** una gioventù sprecata

mist /mɪst/ *n* (fog) foschia *f*; **because of the ~ on the windows** a causa dei vetri appannati
■ **mist over** *vi* ‹*eyes*› velarsi
■ **mist up** *vi* appannarsi, annebbiarsi

mistake /mɪ'steɪk/ **A** *n* sbaglio *m*; **by ~** per sbaglio
B *vt* (*pt* **mistook**, *pp* **mistaken**) sbagliare ‹*road, house*›; fraintendere ‹*meaning, words*›; **~ for** prendere per

mistaken /mɪ'steɪkən/ *adj* sbagliato; **be ~** sbagliarsi; **~ identity** errore *m* di persona

mistakenly /mɪ'steɪkənlɪ/ *adv* erroneamente

mister /'mɪstə(r)/ *n* signore *m*

mistletoe /'mɪsltəʊ/ *n* vischio *m*

mistranslate /mɪstrænz'leɪt/ *vt* tradurre in modo sbagliato

mistranslation /mɪstrænz'leɪʃn/ *n* traduzione *f* sbagliata

mistreat /mɪs'tri:t/ maltrattare

mistreatment /mɪs'tri:tmənt/ *n* maltrattamento *m*

mistress /'mɪstrɪs/ *n* padrona *f*; (teacher) maestra *f*; (lover) amante *f*

mistrust /mɪs'trʌst/ **A** *n* sfiducia *f*
B *vt* non aver fiducia in

misty /'mɪstɪ/ *adj* (**-ier**, **-iest**) nebbioso; fig indistinto

misty-eyed /-'aɪd/ *adj* ‹*look*› commosso; **he goes all ~ about it** a parlarne si commuove

misunderstand /mɪsʌndə'stænd/ *vt* (*pt/pp* **-stood**) fraintendere

misunderstanding /mɪsʌndə'stændɪŋ/ *n* malinteso *m*

misuse[1] /mɪs'ju:z/ *vt* usare male

misuse[2] /mɪs'ju:s/ *n* cattivo uso *m*

mite /maɪt/ *n* Zool acaro *m*; (child) piccino, -a *mf*

mitigate /'mɪtɪgeɪt/ *vt* attenuare

mitigating /'mɪtɪgeɪtɪŋ/ *adj* attenuante

mitre BrE, **miter** AmE /'maɪtə(r)/ *n* mitra *f*

mitt /mɪt/ *n* (no separate fingers) muffola *f*; (cut-off fingers) mezzo guanto *m*; (in baseball) guantone *m*; infml (hand) mano *f*

mitten /'mɪtn/ *n* manopola *f*, muffola *f*

mix /mɪks/ **A** *n* (combination) mescolanza *f*; Culin miscuglio *m*; (ready-made) preparato *m*
B *vt* mischiare
C *vi* mischiarsi; ‹*person*› inserirsi; **~ with** (associate with) frequentare
■ **mix in** *vt* incorporare ‹*eggs, flour etc*›
■ **mix up** *vt* mescolare ‹*papers*›; (confuse, mistake for) confondere

mixed /mɪkst/ *adj* misto; **~ up** (person) confuso

mixed ability *adj* ‹*class, teaching*› per alunni di capacità diverse

mixed bag *n* fig **it was a very ~** c'era un po' di tutto

mixed blessing *n* **be a ~** avere vantaggi e svantaggi

mixed doubles *npl* Tennis doppio *m* misto

mixed economy *n* economia *f* mista

mixed grill *n* grigliata *f* di carne mista

mixed marriage *n* matrimonio *m* misto

mixed-media *adj* multimediale

mixed metaphor *n abbinamento* (*m*) *di parte di due o più metafore diverse con effetto comico*

mixed race **A** *adj* ‹*children*› con genitori di razze diverse
B *n* **she's of ~** i suoi genitori sono di razze diverse

mixed-up *adj* ‹*person, emotions*› confuso

mixed vegetables *npl* verdure *fpl* miste

mixer /'mɪksə(r)/ *n* Culin frullatore *m*, mixer *m inv*; **he's a good ~** è un tipo socievole

mixing /ˈmɪksɪŋ/ *n* (of people, objects, ingredients) mescolamento *m*; Mus mixaggio *m*

mixture /ˈmɪkstʃə(r)/ *n* mescolanza *f*; (medicine) sciroppo *m*; Culin miscela *f*

mix-up *n* (confusion) confusione *f*; (mistake) pasticcio *m*

mm *abbr* (**millimetre(s)**) mm

MMS *abbr* (**multimedia messaging service**) MMS *m*

MO *abbr* **1** (**medical officer**) ufficiale *m* medico **2** (**money order**) vaglia *m inv* postale **3** AmE (**Missouri**)

moan /məʊn/ **A** *n* lamento *m* **B** *vi* lamentarsi; (complain) lagnarsi

moat /məʊt/ *n* fossato *m*

mob /mɒb/ **A** *n* folla *f*; (rabble) gentaglia *f*; infml (gang) banda *f* **B** *vt* (*pt/pp* **mobbed**) assalire

mobile /ˈməʊbaɪl/ **A** *adj* mobile **B** *n* composizione *f* mobile; (phone) telefonino *m*, cellulare *m*

mobile home *n* casa *f* roulotte

mobile library *n* BrE biblioteca *f* itinerante

mobile phone *n* cellulare *m*, telefonino *m*

mobile shop *n* furgone *m* attrezzato per la vendita

mobility /məˈbɪlətɪ/ *n* mobilità *f*

mobility allowance *n* BrE indennità *f* di accompagnamento

mobilization /məʊbɪlaɪˈzeɪʃn/ *n* mobilitazione *f*

mobilize /ˈməʊbɪlaɪz/ *vt* mobilitare

mocha /ˈmɒkə/ *n* moca *m inv*

mock /mɒk/ **A** *adj* finto **B** *vt* canzonare

mockery /ˈmɒkərɪ/ *n* derisione *f*; **a ~ of** una parodia di

mock-up *n* modello *m* in scala

MoD *n abbr* (**Ministry of Defence**) BrE Ministero *m* della Difesa

modal /ˈməʊdl/ *adj* **~ auxiliary** verbo *m* modale

mod con /mɒdˈkɒn/ *abbr* BrE (**modern convenience**) **all ~s** tutti i comfort

mode /məʊd/ *n* modo *m*; Comput modalità *f*

model /ˈmɒdl/ **A** *n* modello *m*; **[fashion] ~** indossatore, -trice *mf*, modello, -a *mf* **B** *adj* ‹*yacht, plane*› in miniatura; ‹*pupil, husband*› esemplare, modello **C** *vt* (*pt/pp* **modelled**) indossare ‹*clothes*› **D** *vi* fare l'indossatore, -trice *mf*; (for artist) posare

modelling /ˈmɒd(ə)lɪŋ/ *n* (with clay etc) modellare *m* con la creta; (of clothes) professione *f* di indossatore; **do some ~** (for artist) fare il modello

modelling clay *n* creta *f* per modellare

modem /ˈməʊdem/ **A** *n* modem *m inv* **B** *vt* mandare per modem

moderate¹ /ˈmɒdəreɪt/ **A** *vt* moderare **B** *vi* moderarsi

moderate² /ˈmɒdərət/ **A** *adj* moderato **B** *n* Pol moderato, -a *mf*

moderately /ˈmɒdərətlɪ/ *adv* ‹*drink, speak etc*› moderatamente; ‹*good, bad etc*› relativamente

moderation /mɒdəˈreɪʃn/ *n* moderazione *f*; **in ~** con moderazione

modern /ˈmɒdn/ *adj* moderno

modern-day *adj* attuale

modernism /ˈmɒdənɪzm/ *n* modernismo *m*

modernity /məˈdɜːnətɪ/ *n* modernità *f*

modernization /mɒdənaɪˈzeɪʃn/ *n* modernizzazione *f*

modernize /ˈmɒdənaɪz/ *vt* modernizzare

modern languages *npl* lingue *fpl* moderne

modest /ˈmɒdɪst/ *adj* modesto

modesty /ˈmɒdɪstɪ/ *n* modestia *f*

modicum /ˈmɒdɪkəm/ *n* **a ~ of** un po' di

modification /mɒdɪfɪˈkeɪʃn/ *n* modificazione *f*

modifier /ˈmɒdɪfaɪə(r)/ *n* (in linguistics) modificatore *m*

modify /ˈmɒdɪfaɪ/ *vt* (*pt/pp* **-fied**) modificare

modular /ˈmɒdjʊlə(r)/ *adj* ‹*course*› a moduli; ‹*construction, furniture*› modulare

modulate /ˈmɒdjʊleɪt/ *vt & vi* modulare

module /ˈmɒdjuːl/ *n* modulo *m*

modus operandi /məʊdəsɒpəˈrændiː/ *n* modus operandi *m inv*

mogul /ˈməʊgl/ *n* magnate *m*

Mohammed /məʊˈhæmed/ *n* Maometto *m*

Mohican /məʊˈhiːkən/ *n* (hairstyle) taglio *m* [di capelli] alla moicana

moist /mɔɪst/ *adj* umido

moisten /ˈmɔɪsn/ *vt* inumidire

moisture /ˈmɔɪstʃə(r)/ *n* umidità *f*

moisturizer /ˈmɔɪstʃəraɪzə(r)/ *n* [crema *f*] idratante *m*

molar /ˈməʊlə(r)/ *n* molare *m*

molasses /məˈlæsɪz/ *n* AmE melassa *f*

mold /məʊld/ AmE = **mould¹**, **mould²**

Moldavia /mɒlˈdeɪvɪə/ *n* Moldavia *f*

mole¹ /məʊl/ *n* (on face etc) neo *m*

mole² *n* Zool talpa *f*

mole³ *n* (breakwater) molo *m*

molecular /məˈlekjʊlə(r)/ *adj* molecolare

molecule /ˈmɒlɪkjuːl/ *n* molecola *f*

molehill /ˈməʊlhɪl/ *n* monticello *m*

moleskin /ˈməʊlskɪn/ *n* (fur) pelliccia *f* di talpa

molest /məˈlest/ *vt* molestare

mollify /ˈmɒlɪfaɪ/ *vt* (*pt/pp* **-ied**) placare

mollusc /ˈmɒləsk/ *n* mollusco *m*

mollycoddle /ˈmɒlɪkɒdl/ *vt* tenere nella bambagia

parola chiave

molt /məʊlt/ AmE = **moult**
molten /ˈməʊltən/ *adj* fuso
mom /mɒm/ *n* AmE infml mamma *f*
moment /ˈməʊmənt/ *n* momento *m*; **at the ~** in questo momento
momentarily /məʊmənˈterɪlɪ/ *adv* (for an instant) per un momento; AmE (at any moment) da un momento all'altro; AmE (very soon) tra un momento
momentary /ˈməʊməntrɪ/ *adj* momentaneo
momentous /məˈmentəs/ *adj* molto importante
momentum /məˈmentəm/ *n* impeto *m*
Monaco /ˈmɒnəkəʊ/ *n* Principato *m* di Monaco
monarch /ˈmɒnək/ *n* monarca *m*
monarchist /ˈmɒnəkɪst/ *n* monarchico, -a *mf*
monarchy /ˈmɒnəkɪ/ *n* monarchia *f*
monastery /ˈmɒnəstrɪ/ *n* monastero *m*
monastic /məˈnæstɪk/ *adj* monastico
Monday /ˈmʌndeɪ/ *n* lunedì *m*
monetary /ˈmʌnətrɪ/ *adj* monetario
money /ˈmʌnɪ/ *n* denaro *m*
money box *n* salvadanaio *m*
moneylender *n* usuraio *m*
moneymaker *n* (business) attività *f* redditizia; (product) prodotto *m* che rende bene
money order *n* vaglia *m inv* postale
Mongolia /mɒŋˈgəʊlɪə/ *n* Mongolia *f*
mongrel /ˈmʌŋgrəl/ *n* bastardino *m*
monitor /ˈmɒnɪtə(r)/ **A** *n* Techn monitor *m inv*
B *vt* controllare
monk /mʌŋk/ *n* monaco *m*
monkey /ˈmʌŋkɪ/ *n* scimmia *f*
■ **monkey about with** *vt* infml (interfere with) armeggiare con
monkey business *n* infml (fooling) scherzi *mpl*; (cheating) imbrogli *mpl*
monkey-nut *n* nocciolina *f* americana
monkey wrench *n* chiave *f* inglese a rullino
monkfish /ˈmʌŋkfɪʃ/ *n* pescatrice *f*
mono /ˈmɒnəʊ/ *n* mono *m*
monochrome /ˈmɒnəkrəʊm/ *adj* monocromatico; Cinema, TV in bianco e nero
monocle /ˈmɒnəkl/ *n* monocolo *m*
monogamous /məˈnɒgəməs/ *adj* monogamo
monogamy /məˈnɒgəmɪ/ *n* monogamia *f*
monogram /ˈmɒnəgræm/ *n* monogramma *m*
monograph /ˈmɒnəgrɑːf/ *n* monografia *f*
monolith /ˈmɒnəlɪθ/ *n* monolito *m*
monologue /ˈmɒnəlɒg/ *n* monologo *m*
monomania /mɒnəˈmeɪnɪə/ *n* monomania *f*
monoplane /ˈmɒnəpleɪn/ *n* monoplano *m*
monopolize /məˈnɒpəlaɪz/ *vt* monopolizzare
monopoly /məˈnɒpəlɪ/ *n* monopolio *m*
monoski /ˈmɒnəʊskiː/ **A** *n* monoscì *m*
B *vi* praticare il monoscì
monosodium glutamate /mɒnəsəʊdɪəmˈgluːtəmeɪt/ *n* glutammato *m* di sodio
monosyllabic /mɒnəsɪˈlæbɪk/ *adj* monosillabico
monosyllable /ˈmɒnəsɪləbl/ *n* monosillabo *m*
monotone /ˈmɒnətəʊn/ *n* **speak in a ~** parlare con tono monotono
monotonous /məˈnɒtənəs/ *adj* monotono
monotonously /məˈnɒtənəslɪ/ *adv* in modo monotono
monotony /məˈnɒtənɪ/ *n* monotonia *f*
monsoon /mɒnˈsuːn/ *n* monsone *m*
monster /ˈmɒnstə(r)/ *n* mostro *m*
monstrosity /mɒnˈstrɒsətɪ/ *n* mostruosità *f*
monstrous /ˈmɒnstrəs/ *adj* mostruoso
montage /mɒnˈtɑːʒ/ *n* montaggio *m*
Mont Blanc /mɒnˈblɒ̃/ *n* Monte *m* Bianco
Montenegro /ˌmɒntɪˈniːgrəʊ/ *n* Montenegro *m*
month /mʌnθ/ *n* mese *m*
monthly /ˈmʌnθlɪ/ **A** *adj* mensile
B *adv* mensilmente
C *n* (periodical) mensile *m*
monument /ˈmɒnjʊmənt/ *n* monumento *m*
monumental /mɒnjʊˈmentl/ *adj* fig monumentale
monumentally /mɒnjʊˈmentəlɪ/ *adv* ‹*boring, ignorant*› enormemente
moo /muː/ **A** *n* muggito *m*
B *vi* (*pt/pp* **mooed**) muggire
mooch /muːtʃ/ *vi* **~ about** infml gironzolare; **~ about the house** gironzolare per casa
mood /muːd/ *n* umore *m*; **be in a good/bad ~** essere di buon/cattivo umore; **be in the ~ for** essere in vena di
moody /ˈmuːdɪ/ *adj* (**-ier, -iest**) (variable) lunatico; (bad-tempered) di malumore
moon /muːn/ *n* luna *f*; **over the ~** infml al settimo cielo
■ **moon about, moon around** *vi* infml (wander aimlessly) gironzolare
■ **moon over** *vt* infml sospirare d'amore per ‹*somebody*›
moonbeam *n* raggio *m* di luna
moon buggy *n* veicolo *m* lunare
moonlight **A** *n* chiaro *m* di luna
B *vi* infml lavorare in nero
moonlighting *n* infml lavoro *m* nero
moonlit *adj* illuminato dalla luna
moonshine *n* (nonsense) fantasie *fpl*; AmE (liquor) liquore *m* di contrabbando
moor[1] /mʊə(r)/ *n* brughiera *f*
moor[2] *vt* Naut ormeggiare
moorhen /ˈmʊəhen/ *n* gallinella *f* d'acqua
mooring /ˈmʊərɪŋ/ *n* (place) ormeggio *m*; **~s** *pl* (chains) ormeggi *mpl*

Moorish /ˈmʊərɪʃ/ *adj* moresco
moorland /ˈmʊələnd/ *n* brughiera *f*
moose /muːs/ *n* (*pl* **moose**) alce *m*
moot /muːt/ *adj* **it's a ~ point** è un punto controverso
mop /mɒp/ **A** *n* mocio® *m inv*; **~ of hair** zazzera *f*
B *vt* (*pt/pp* **mopped**) lavare con il mocio®
■ **mop up** *vt* (dry) asciugare con il mocio®; (clean) pulire con il mocio®
mope /məʊp/ *vi* essere depresso
■ **mope about**, **mope around** *vi* trascinarsi
moped /ˈməʊped/ *n* ciclomotore *m*
moral /ˈmɒrəl/ **A** *adj* morale
B *n* morale *f*
morale /məˈrɑːl/ *n* morale *m*; **be a ~ booster** tirare su di morale
moral fibre *n* forza *f* morale
moralistic /mɒrəˈlɪstɪk/ *adj* moralistico
morality /məˈrælətɪ/ *n* moralità *f*
moralize /ˈmɒrəlaɪz/ *vi* moraleggiare
morally /ˈmɒrəlɪ/ *adv* moralmente
morals /ˈmɒrəlz/ *npl* moralità *f*
moratorium /mɒrəˈtɔːrɪəm/ *n* moratoria *f*
morbid /ˈmɔːbɪd/ *adj* morboso
more /mɔː(r)/ **A** *adj* più; **a few ~ books** un po' più di libri; **some ~ tea?** ancora un po' di tè?; **there's no ~ bread** non c'è più pane; **there are no ~ apples** non ci sono più mele; **one ~ word and...** ancora una parola e...
B *pron* di più; **would you like some ~?** ne vuoi ancora?; **no ~, thank you** non ne voglio più, grazie
C *adv* più; **~ interesting** più interessante; **~ (and ~) quickly** (sempre) più veloce; **~ than** più di; **I don't love him any ~** non lo amo più; **once ~** ancora una volta; **~ or less** più o meno; **the ~ I see him, the ~ I like him** più lo vedo, più mi piace
moreish /ˈmɔːrɪʃ/ *adj* infml **be ~** essere irresistibile
moreover /mɔːrˈəʊvə(r)/ *adv* inoltre
morgue /mɔːg/ *n* obitorio *m*
MORI /ˈmɔːrɪ/ *n abbr* (**Market Opinion Research Institute**) *istituto (m) di sondaggio e ricerche di mercato*
moribund /ˈmɒrɪbʌnd/ *adj* moribondo
morning /ˈmɔːnɪŋ/ *n* mattino *m*, mattina *f*; **spend the ~ doing something** passare la mattinata facendo qualcosa; **in the ~** del mattino; (tomorrow) domani mattina
morning-after pill *n* pillola *f* del giorno dopo
morning coffee *n* caffè *m* del mattino
morning dress *n* tight *m inv*
morning sickness *n* nausea *f* mattutina
Moroccan /məˈrɒk(ə)n/ *adj & n* marocchino, -a *mf*

Morocco /məˈrɒkəʊ/ *n* Marocco *m*
morocco leather *n* marocchino *m*
moron /ˈmɔːrɒn/ *n* infml deficiente *mf*
morose /məˈrəʊs/ *adj* scontroso
morosely /məˈrəʊslɪ/ *adv* in modo scontroso
morphine /ˈmɔːfiːn/ *n* morfina *f*
morris dance /ˈmɒrɪs/ *n danza (f) tradizionale inglese*
Morse /mɔːs/ *n* **~ [code]** [codice *m*] Morse *m*
morsel /ˈmɔːsl/ *n* (food) boccone *m*
mortal /ˈmɔːtl/ *adj & n* mortale *mf*
mortal combat *n* duello *m* mortale
mortality /mɔːˈtælətɪ/ *n* mortalità *f*
mortally /ˈmɔːtəlɪ/ *adv* ‹*wounded, offended*› a morte; ‹*afraid*› da morire
mortar /ˈmɔːtə(r)/ *n* mortaio *m*
mortgage /ˈmɔːgɪdʒ/ **A** *n* mutuo *m*; (*money raised on collateral of property*) ipoteca *f*
B *vt* ipotecare
mortgage rate *n* tasso *m* d'interesse sui mutui
mortgage relief *n* sgravio *m* fiscale sul mutuo
mortgage repayment *n* rata *f* del mutuo
mortician /mɔːˈtɪʃn/ *n* AmE impresario, -a *mf* di pompe funebri
mortification /mɔːtɪfɪˈkeɪʃn/ *n* (of the flesh, embarrassment) mortificazione *f*
mortify /ˈmɔːtɪfaɪ/ *vt* (*pt/pp* **-ied**) mortificare
mortuary /ˈmɔːtjʊərɪ/ *n* camera *f* mortuaria
mosaic /məʊˈzeɪɪk/ *n* mosaico *m*
Moscow /ˈmɒskəʊ/ *n* Mosca *f*
Moselle /məʊˈzel/ *n* (wine) vino *m* della Mosella
Moses /ˈməʊzɪz/ *n* Mosè *m*
Moslem /ˈmʊzlɪm/ *adj & n* musulmano, -a *mf*
mosque /mɒsk/ *n* moschea *f*
mosquito /mɒsˈkiːtəʊ/ *n* (*pl* **-es**) zanzara *f*
mosquito bite *n* puntura *m* di zanzara
mosquito net *n* zanzariera *f*
mosquito repellent *n* antizanzare *m inv*
moss /mɒs/ *n* muschio *m*
mossy /ˈmɒsɪ/ *adj* muschioso
most /məʊst/ **A** *adj* (majority) la maggior parte di; **for the ~ part** per lo più
B *adv* più, maggiormente; (very) estremamente, molto; **the ~ interesting day** la giornata più interessante; **a ~ interesting day** una giornata estremamente interessante; **the ~ beautiful woman in the world** la donna più bella del mondo; **~ unlikely** veramente improbabile
C *pron* **~ of them** la maggior parte di loro; **at [the] ~** al massimo; **make the ~ of** sfruttare al massimo; **~ of the time** la maggior parte del tempo

m

parola chiave

mostly /ˈməʊs(t)lɪ/ *adv* per lo più
MOT *n* BrE revisione *f* obbligatoria di autoveicoli
motel /məʊˈtel/ *n* motel *m inv*
moth /mɒθ/ *n* falena *f*; **[clothes-] ~** tarma *f*
mothball /ˈmɒθbɔːl/ *n* pallina *f* di naftalina
moth-eaten /-iːtən/ *adj* tarmato
mother /ˈmʌðə(r)/ **A** *n* madre *f*; **Mother's Day** la festa della mamma
B *vt* fare da madre a
motherboard /ˈmʌðəbɔːd/ *n* scheda *f* madre
motherhood /ˈmʌðəhʊd/ *n* maternità *f*
Mothering Sunday /mʌðərɪŋˈsʌndeɪ/ *n* la festa della mamma
mother-in-law *n* (*pl* **mothers-in-law**) suocera *f*
motherland /ˈmʌðəlænd/ *n* patria *f*
motherless /ˈmʌðəlɪs/ *adj* orfano, -a *mf* di madre
motherly /ˈmʌðəlɪ/ *adj* materno
mother-of-pearl *n* madreperla *f*
mother's boy *n* mammone *m*
Mother's Day *n* la festa della mamma
mother's help *n* BrE aiuto *m* domestico
mother-to-be *n* futura mamma *f*
mother tongue *n* madrelingua *f*
mothproof /ˈmɒθpruːf/ *adj* antitarmico
motif /məʊˈtiːf/ *n* motivo *m*
motion /ˈməʊʃn/ **A** *n* moto *m*; (proposal) mozione *f*; (gesture) gesto *m*
B *vt & vi* **~ [to] somebody to come in** fare segno a qualcuno di entrare
motionless /ˈməʊʃ(ə)nlɪs/ *adj* immobile
motionlessly /ˈməʊʃənlɪslɪ/ *adv* senza alcun movimento
motion picture **A** *n* film *m inv* [per il cinema]
B *attrib* ‹*industry*› cinematografico
motivate /ˈməʊtɪveɪt/ *vt* motivare
motivated /ˈməʊtɪveɪtɪd/ *adj* ‹*person, student*› motivato; **politically/racially ~** ‹*act*› a sfondo politico/razziale
motivation /məʊtɪˈveɪʃn/ *n* motivazione *f*
motive /ˈməʊtɪv/ *n* motivo *m*
motley /ˈmɒtlɪ/ *adj* disparato
motor /ˈməʊtə(r)/ **A** *n* motore *m*; (car) macchina *f*
B *adj* a motore; Anat motore
C *vi* andare in macchina
Motorail /ˈməʊtəreɪl/ *n* treno *m* per trasporto auto
motorbike /ˈməʊtəbaɪk/ *n* infml moto *f inv*
motor boat *n* motoscafo *m*
motorcade /ˈməʊtəkeɪd/ *n* AmE corteo *m* di auto
motor car *n* automobile *f*
motorcycle *n* motocicletta *f*
motorcycle escort *n* scorta *f* di motociclette
motorcycle messenger *n* corriere *m* in moto
motorcyclist *n* motociclista *mf*
motorhome *n* camper *m inv*; (towed) roulotte *f inv*
motoring /ˈməʊtərɪŋ/ *n* automobilismo *m*
motorist /ˈməʊtərɪst/ *n* automobilista *mf*
motor launch *n* motolancia *f*
motor mechanic *n* meccanico *m*
motormouth *n* infml chiacchierone, -a *mf*
motor oil *n* olio *m* lubrificante
motor racing *n* corse *fpl* automobilistiche
motor scooter *n* motorino *m*
motor vehicle *n* autoveicolo *m*
motorway *n* autostrada *f*
mottled /ˈmɒtld/ *adj* chiazzato
motto /ˈmɒtəʊ/ *n* (*pl* **-es**) motto *m*
mould¹ /məʊld/ *n* (fungus) muffa *f*
mould² **A** *n* stampo *m*
B *vt* foggiare; fig formare
moulder /ˈməʊldə(r)/ *vi* ‹*corpse, refuse*› andare in decomposizione
moulding /ˈməʊldɪŋ/ *n* Archit cornice *f*
mouldy /ˈməʊldɪ/ *adj* ammuffito; infml (worthless) ridicolo
moult /məʊlt/ *vi* ‹*bird*› fare la muta; ‹*animal*› perdere il pelo
mound /maʊnd/ *n* mucchio *m*; (hill) collinetta *f*
mount /maʊnt/ **A** *n* (horse) cavalcatura *f*; (of jewel, photo, picture) montatura *f*
B *vt* montare a ‹*horse*›; salire su ‹*bicycle*›; incastonare ‹*jewel*›; incorniciare ‹*photo, picture*›
C *vi* aumentare
■ **mount up** *vi* aumentare
mountain /ˈmaʊntɪn/ *n* montagna *f*; **make a ~ out of a molehill** fare di una mosca un elefante
mountain bike *n* mountain bike *f inv*
mountain climbing *n* alpinismo *m*
mountaineer /maʊntɪˈnɪə(r)/ *n* alpinista *mf*
mountaineering /maʊntɪˈnɪərɪŋ/ *n* alpinismo *m*
mountainous /ˈmaʊntɪnəs/ *adj* montagnoso
mountain range *n* catena *f* montuosa
mountain top *n* cima *f* di montagna
mounted police /maʊntɪdpəˈliːs/ *n* polizia *f* a cavallo
mourn /mɔːn/ **A** *vt* lamentare
B *vi* **~ for** piangere la morte di
mourner /ˈmɔːnə(r)/ *n* persona *f* che partecipa a un funerale
mournful /ˈmɔːnfʊl/ *adj* triste
mournfully /ˈmɔːnfʊlɪ/ *adv* tristemente
mourning /ˈmɔːnɪŋ/ *n* **in ~** in lutto
mouse /maʊs/ *n* (*pl* **mice**) topo *m*; Comput mouse *m inv*
■ **mouse over** *vt* puntare con il mouse su
mouse hole *n* tana *f* di topi/di un topo

mouse mat *n* Comput tappetino *m*
mouseover /'maʊsəʊvə(r)/ *n* mouseover *m inv*, passaggio *m* del mouse; ~ **ad** pubblicità attivata dal passaggio del mouse
mousetrap *n* trappola *f* [per topi]
mousse /mu:s/ *n* Culin mousse *f inv*
moustache /mə'stɑ:ʃ/ *n* baffi *mpl*
mousy /'maʊsɪ/ *adj* ‹*colour*› grigio topo
mouth[1] /maʊð/ *vt* ~ **something** dire qualcosa silenziosamente muovendo solamente le labbra
🔑 **mouth**[2] /maʊθ/ *n* bocca *f*; (of river) foce *f*
mouthful /'maʊθfʊl/ *n* boccone *m*
mouth organ *n* armonica *f* [a bocca]
mouthpiece *n* imboccatura *f*; fig (person) portavoce *m inv*
mouth-to-mouth resuscitation *n* respirazione *f* bocca a bocca
mouthwash *n* colluttorio *m*
mouth-watering /-wɔ:tərɪŋ/ *adj* che fa venire l'acquolina in bocca
movable /'mu:vəbl/ *adj* movibile
🔑 **move** /mu:v/ **A** *n* mossa *f*; (moving house) trasloco *m*; **on the** ~ in movimento; **get a** ~ **on** infml darsi una mossa
B *vt* muovere; (emotionally) commuovere; spostare ‹*car, furniture*›; (transfer) trasferire; (propose) proporre; ~ **house** traslocare
C *vi* muoversi; (move house) traslocare; **don't** ~**!** non muoverti!
▪ **move about, move around** *vi* (in house) muoversi; (in country) spostarsi
▪ **move along** **A** *vi* andare avanti
B *vt* muovere in avanti
▪ **move away** **A** *vi* allontanarsi; (move house) trasferirsi
B *vt* allontanare
▪ **move forward** **A** *vi* avanzare
B *vt* spostare avanti
▪ **move in** *vi* (to a house) trasferirsi
▪ **move off** *vi* ‹*vehicle*› muoversi
▪ **move on** **A** *vi* (move to another place) muoversi
B *vt* ‹*police*› far circolare
▪ **move on to** *vt* passare a ‹*new topic, next question*›
▪ **move out** *vi* (of house) andare via
▪ **move over** **A** *vi* spostarsi
B *vt* spostare
▪ **move up** *vi* muoversi; (advance, increase) avanzare
🔑 **movement** /'mu:vmənt/ *n* movimento *m*; (of clock) meccanismo *m*
🔑 **movie** /'mu:vɪ/ *n* AmE film *m inv*; **go to the** ~**s** andare al cinema
movie camera *n* AmE cinepresa *f*
movie director *n* AmE regista *mf* cinematografico, -a
movie-goer /'mu:vɪgəʊə(r)/ *n* AmE frequentatore, -trice *mf* di cinema

🔑 parola chiave

movie star *n* AmE stella *f* del cinema, star *f inv* del cinema
movie theater *n* AmE cinema *m*
moving /'mu:vɪŋ/ *adj* mobile; (touching) commovente
mow /məʊ/ *vt* (*pt* **mowed**, *pp* **mown** *or* **mowed**) tagliare ‹*lawn*›
▪ **mow down** *vt* (destroy) sterminare
mower /'məʊə(r)/ *n* tosaerba *m inv*
Mozambique /ˌməʊzæm'bi:k/ *n* Mozambico *m*
MP *abbr* (**Member of Parliament**) deputato, -a *mf*
MP3 player *n* lettore *m* di MP3
mpg *abbr* (**miles per gallon**) miglia al gallone
mph *abbr* (**miles per hour**) miglia all'ora
MPV *n abbr* (**multi-purpose vehicle**) MPV *m*
🔑 **Mr** /'mɪstə(r)/ *n* (*pl* **Messrs**) Signor *m*
MRI *n abbr* (**magnetic resonance imaging**) RM *f*
🔑 **Mrs** /'mɪsɪz/ *n* Signora *f*
MRSA *n abbr* (**methicillin-resistant Staphylococcus aureus**) MRSA *m*
Ms /mɪz/ *n* Signora *f* (*modo* (*m*) *formale di rivolgersi ad una donna quando non si vuole indicarla come sposata o nubile*)
MS *n abbr* **1** (**multiple sclerosis**) sclerosi *f* a placche *or* multipla **2** (**manuscript**) ms **3** AmE (**Mississippi**)
MSc *n abbr* (**Master of Science**) (diploma) laurea *f* in discipline scientifiche; (person) laureato, -a *mf* in discipline scientifiche
MST *abbr* AmE (**Mountain Standard Time**) *tempo* (*f*) *medio della zona delle Montagne Rocciose*
Mt. *abbr* (**mount**) (in place names) M.
🔑 **much** /mʌtʃ/ *adj, adv & pron* molto; ~ **as** per quanto; **I love you just as** ~ **as before/him** ti amo quanto prima/lui; **as** ~ **as £5 million** ben cinque milioni di sterline; **as** ~ **as that** così tanto; **very** ~ tantissimo, moltissimo; ~ **the same** quasi uguale
muck /mʌk/ *n* (dirt) sporcizia *f*; (farming) letame *m*; infml (filth) porcheria *f*
▪ **muck about** *vi* infml perder tempo; ~ **about with** trafficare con
▪ **muck in** *vi* infml dare una mano
▪ **muck up** *vt* infml rovinare; (make dirty) sporcare
muckraking /'mʌkreɪkɪŋ/ *n* scandalismo *m*
mucky /'mʌkɪ/ *adj* (**-ier**, **-iest**) sudicio
mucus /'mju:kəs/ *n* muco *m*
mud /mʌd/ *n* fango *m*
muddle /'mʌdl/ **A** *n* disordine *m*; (mix-up) confusione *f*
B *vt* ~ **[up]** confondere ‹*dates*›
▪ **muddle through** *vi* farcela alla bell'e meglio
muddle-headed /-'hedɪd/ *adj* ‹*plan*› confuso; ‹*person*› confusionario

m

muddy /ˈmʌdɪ/ *adj* (**-ier**, **-iest**) ‹*path*› fangoso; ‹*shoes*› infangato
mudflat *n* distesa *f* di fango
mudguard *n* parafango *m*
mud hut *n* capanna *f* di fango
mud pack *n* (for beauty treatment) maschera *f* di fango
mud pie *n* formina *f* di fango
mudslide *n* colata *f* di fango
mud-slinging /-slɪŋɪŋ/ *n* diffamazione *f*
muesli /ˈmjuːzlɪ/ *n* muesli *m inv*
muffle /ˈmʌfl/ *vt* smorzare ‹*sound*›
■ **muffle up** *vi* (for warmth) imbacuccarsi
muffler /ˈmʌflə(r)/ *n* sciarpa *f*; AmE Auto marmitta *f*
mug[1] /mʌg/ *n* tazza *f*; (for beer) boccale *m*; infml (face) muso *m*; infml (simpleton) pollo *m*
mug[2] *vt* (*pt/pp* **mugged**) aggredire e derubare
■ **mug up** *vt* infml (learn) imparare alla bell'e meglio
mugger /ˈmʌgə(r)/ *n* assalitore, -trice *mf*
mugging /ˈmʌgɪŋ/ *n* aggressione *f* per furto
muggy /ˈmʌgɪ/ *adj* (**-ier**, **-iest**) afoso
Muhammad /məˈhæmɪd/ *n* Maometto *m*
mulatto /mjuːˈlætəʊ/ *adj & n* AmE mulatto, -a *mf*
mulberry /ˈmʌlb(ə)rɪ/ *n* AmE (fruit) mora *f* di gelso; (tree) gelso *m*
mule[1] /mjuːl/ *n* mulo *m*
mule[2] *n* (slipper) ciabatta *f*
mulish /ˈmjuːlɪʃ/ *adj* testardo
mull /mʌl/ *vt* ~ **over** rimuginare su
mulled /mʌld/ *adj* ~ **wine** vin brûlé *m inv*
multi+ /ˈmʌltɪ/ *pref* multi+
multi-access *n* Comput accesso *m* multiplo
multichannel /mʌltɪˈtʃænəl/ *adj* ‹*television*› con molti canali
multicoloured /ˈmʌltɪkʌləd/ *adj* variopinto
multicultural /mʌltɪˈkʌltʃərəl/ *adj* multiculturale
multidisciplinary /mʌltɪdɪsɪˈplɪnərɪ/ *adj* Sch, Univ pluridisciplinare
multi-ethnic /ˌmʌltɪˈeθnɪk/ *adj* multietnico
multifaceted /mʌltɪˈfæsɪtɪd/ *adj* ‹*gemstone*› sfaccettato; ‹*career*› variegato; ‹*personality*› sfaccettato
multifunction /mʌltɪˈfʌŋkʃn/ *adj* multifunzionale
multigym /ˈmʌltɪdʒɪm/ *n* attrezzo *m* multiuso
multilateral /mʌltɪˈlæt(ə)rəl/ *adj* Pol multilaterale
multilevel /ˈmʌltɪlevəl/ *adj* ‹*parking, access*› a più piani; ‹*analysis*› a più livelli
multilingual /mʌltɪˈlɪŋgwəl/ *adj* multilingue *inv*
multimedia /mʌltɪˈmiːdɪə/ **A** *n* multimedia *mpl*
B *adj* multimediale

multinational /mʌltɪˈnæʃnəl/ **A** *adj* multinazionale
B *n* multinazionale *f*
multipack *n* confezione *f* multipla
multi-party /ˈmʌltɪpɑːtɪ/ *adj* ‹*government, system*› pluripartitico
multiplayer *adj* Comput ‹*game*› in multiplayer
⚷ **multiple** /ˈmʌltɪpl/ *adj & n* multiplo *m*
multiple choice *adj* scelta *f* multipla
multiple choice question *n* Sch test *m inv* a scelta multipla
multiple ownership *n* comproprietà *f*
multiple pile-up *n* tamponamento *m* a catena
multiple sclerosis *n* sclerosi *f* a placche *or* multipla
multiple store *n* BrE negozio *m* appartenente a una catena
multiplex /ˈmʌltɪpleks/ **A** *n* Teleph multiplex *m inv*; Cinema cinema *m inv* multisale
B *adj* Teleph in multiplex
multiplication /mʌltɪplɪˈkeɪʃn/ *n* moltiplicazione *f*
multiply /ˈmʌltɪplaɪ/ **A** *vt* (*pt/pp* **-ied**) moltiplicare (**by** per)
B *vi* moltiplicarsi
multi-purpose *adj* ‹*tool, gadget*› multiuso *inv*; ‹*organization*› con più scopi
multi-purpose vehicle *n* monovolume *f*
multi-racial *adj* multirazziale
multi-storey *adj* ~ **car park** parcheggio *m* a più piani
multitask *vi* ‹*person*› eseguire varie mansioni; ‹*computer*› eseguire il multitasking
multi-track *adj* ‹*sound system*› a più piste
multitude /ˈmʌltɪtjuːd/ *n* moltitudine *f*; **hide a ~ of sins** ‹*rug etc*› nascondere un sacco di magagne
multi-user *adj* ‹*system, installation*› multiutente
mum[1] /mʌm/ *adj* **keep ~** infml non aprire bocca
mum[2] *n* infml mamma *f*
mumble /ˈmʌmbl/ *vt & vi* borbottare
mumbo-jumbo /mʌmbəʊˈdʒʌmbəʊ/ *n* infml (speech, writing) paroloni *mpl*
mummy[1] /ˈmʌmɪ/ *n* infml mamma *f*
mummy[2] *n* Archaeol mummia *f*
mummy's boy *n* BrE derog mammone *m*
mumps /mʌmps/ *n* orecchioni *mpl*
munch /mʌntʃ/ *vt & vi* sgranocchiare
mundane /mʌnˈdeɪn/ *adj* (everyday) banale
municipal /mjʊˈnɪsɪpl/ *adj* municipale
munitions /mjʊˈnɪʃnz/ *npl* munizioni *fpl*
mural /ˈmjʊərəl/ *n* dipinto *m* murale
⚷ **murder** /ˈmɜːdə(r)/ **A** *n* assassinio *m*
B *vt* assassinare; infml (ruin) massacrare

murder case *n* caso *m* di omicidio
murder charge *n* imputazione *f* di omicidio
murderer /ˈmɜːdərə(r)/ *n* assassino, -a *mf*
murderess /ˈmɜːdərɪs/ *n* assassina *f*
murderous /ˈmɜːdərəs/ *adj* omicida
murky /ˈmɜːkɪ/ *adj* (**-ier**, **-iest**) oscuro
murmur /ˈmɜːmə(r)/ **A** *n* mormorio *m* **B** *vt & vi* mormorare
murmuring /ˈmɜːmərɪŋ/ *n* mormorio *m*; **~s** *pl* (of discontent) segnali *mpl* di malcontento
⚷ **muscle** /ˈmʌsl/ *n* muscolo *m*
■ **muscle in** *vi* sl intromettersi (**to** in)
muscle strain *n* strappo *m* muscolare
muscular /ˈmʌskjʊlə(r)/ *adj* muscolare; (strong) muscoloso
muscular dystrophy /ˈdɪstrəfɪ/ *n* distrofia *f* muscolare
muse /mjuːz/ *vi* meditare (**on** su)
museum /mjuːˈzɪəm/ *n* museo *m*
mushroom /ˈmʌʃrʊm/ **A** *n* fungo *m* **B** *vi* fig spuntare come funghi
mushroom cloud *n* fungo *m* atomico
mushy /ˈmʌʃɪ/ *adj* fig sdolcinato
⚷ **music** /ˈmjuːzɪk/ *n* musica *f*; (written) spartito *m*; **set to ~** musicare
⚷ **musical** /ˈmjuːzɪkl/ **A** *adj* musicale; ‹*person*› dotato di senso musicale **B** *n* commedia *f* musicale
musical box *n* carillon *m inv*
musical instrument *n* strumento *m* musicale
music box *n* carillon *m inv*
music centre *n* impianto *m* stereo
music hall *n* teatro *m* di varietà
musician /mjuːˈzɪʃn/ *n* musicista *mf*
music lover *n* amante *mf* della musica
musicology /mjuːzɪˈkɒlədʒɪ/ *n* musicologia *f*
music stand *n* leggio *m*
music stool *n* sgabello *m* per pianoforte
music video *n* video clip *m inv*
musings /ˈmjuːzɪŋz/ *npl* riflessioni *fpl*
musk /mʌsk/ *n* muschio *m*
musket /ˈmʌskɪt/ *n* moschetto *m*
musketeer /mʌskəˈtɪə(r)/ *n* moschettiere *m*
musky /ˈmʌskɪ/ *adj* muschiato
Muslim /ˈmʊzlɪm/ *adj & n* musulmano, -a *mf*
mussel /ˈmʌsl/ *n* cozza *f*
⚷ **must** /mʌst/ **A** *v aux* (only in present) dovere; **you ~ not be late** non devi essere in ritardo; **she ~ have finished by now** (probability) deve aver finito ormai **B** *n* **a ~** infml una cosa da non perdere
mustache /məˈstɑːʃ/ *n* AmE = **moustache**
mustard /ˈmʌstəd/ *n* senape *f*
muster /ˈmʌstə(r)/ *vt* radunare ‹*troops*›; fare appello a ‹*strength*›

⚷ parola chiave

musty /ˈmʌstɪ/ *adj* (**-ier**, **-iest**) stantio
mutant /ˈmjuːtənt/ *n & adj* mutante *mf*
mutate /mjuːˈteɪt/ **A** *vi* ‹*cell, organism*› subire una mutazione; **~ into** ‹*alien, monster*› trasformarsi in **B** *vt* far subire una mutazione
mutation /mjuːˈteɪʃn/ *n* Biol mutazione *f*
mute /mjuːt/ *adj* offensive muto
muted /ˈmjuːtɪd/ *adj* smorzato
mutilate /ˈmjuːtɪleɪt/ *vt* mutilare
mutilation /mjuːtɪˈleɪʃn/ *n* mutilazione *f*
mutinous /ˈmjuːtɪnəs/ *adj* ammutinato
mutiny /ˈmjuːtɪnɪ/ **A** *n* ammutinamento *m* **B** *vi* (*pt/pp* **-ied**) ammutinarsi
mutter /ˈmʌtə(r)/ **A** *n* borbottio *m* **B** *vt & vi* borbottare
mutton /ˈmʌtn/ *n* carne *f* di montone
mutual /ˈmjuːtjʊəl/ *adj* reciproco; infml (common) comune
mutually /ˈmjuːtjʊəlɪ/ *adv* reciprocamente
Muzak® /ˈmjuːzæk/ *n* musica *f* di sottofondo
muzzle /ˈmʌzl/ **A** *n* (of animal) muso *m*; (of firearm) bocca *f*; (for dog) museruola *f* **B** *vt* fig mettere il bavaglio a
MW *abbr* (**medium wave**) OM
⚷ **my** /maɪ/ *poss adj* mio *m*, mia *f*, miei *mpl*, mie *fpl*; **my job/house** il mio lavoro/la mia casa; **my mother/father** mia madre/mio padre
myalgic encephalomyelitis /maɪældʒɪkensefələʊmaɪˈlaɪtɪs/ *n* encefalomielite *f* mialgica
Myanmar /mjænˈmɑː(r)/ *n* Myanmar *f*
myopic /maɪˈɒpɪk/ *adj* miope
⚷ **myself** /maɪˈself/ *pers pron* (reflexive) mi; (emphatic) me stesso; (after prep) me; **I've seen it ~** l'ho visto io stesso; **by ~** da solo; **I thought to ~** ho pensato tra me e me; **I'm proud of ~** sono fiero di me
mysterious /mɪˈstɪərɪəs/ *adj* misterioso
mysteriously /mɪˈstɪərɪəslɪ/ *adv* misteriosamente
mystery /ˈmɪstərɪ/ *n* mistero *m*; **~ [story]** racconto *m* del mistero
mystery play *n* mistero *m* (*teatrale*)
mystery tour *n* viaggio *m* con destinazione a sorpresa
mystic /ˈmɪstɪk/, **mystical** /ˈmɪstɪkl/ *adj* mistico
mysticism /ˈmɪstɪsɪzm/ *n* misticismo *m*
mystification /mɪstɪfɪˈkeɪʃn/ *n* disorientamento *m*
mystified /ˈmɪstɪfaɪd/ *adj* disorientato
mystify /ˈmɪstɪfaɪ/ *vt* disorientare
mystique /mɪˈstiːk/ *n* aria *f* di mistero
myth /mɪθ/ *n* mito *m*
mythical /ˈmɪθɪkl/ *adj* mitico
mythological /mɪθəˈlɒdʒɪkl/ *adj* mitologico
mythology /mɪˈθɒlədʒɪ/ *n* mitologia *f*

Nn

n, **N** /en/ *n* (letter) n, N *f inv*

N *abbr* (**north**) N

n/a, **N/A** *abbr* (**not applicable**) non pertinente

nab /næb/ *vt* (*pt/pp* **nabbed**) infml beccare

nadir /ˈneɪdə(r)/ *n* nadir *m*; fig punto *m* più basso, fondo *m*

naff /næf/ *adj* BrE infml banale

nag¹ /næg/ *n* (horse) ronzino *m*

nag² **A** *vt* (*pt/pp* **nagged**) assillare
B *vi* essere insistente
C *n* (person) brontolone, -a *mf*

nagging /ˈnægɪŋ/ *adj* ‹*pain*› persistente

nail /neɪl/ *n* chiodo *m*; (of finger, toe) unghia *f*; **on the ~** infml sull'unghia
■ **nail down** *vt* inchiodare; **~ somebody down to a time/price** far fissare a qualcuno un'ora/un prezzo

nail-biting /-baɪtɪŋ/ **A** *n* abitudine *f* di mangiarsi le unghie
B *adj* ‹*match, finish*› mozzafiato *inv*; ‹*wait*› esasperante

nail brush *n* spazzolino *m* da unghie

nail clippers *npl* tronchesina *f*

nail file *n* limetta *f* da unghie

nail polish *n* smalto *m* [per unghie]

nail polish remover *n* acetone *m*

nail scissors *npl* forbicine *fpl* da unghie

nail varnish *n* smalto *m* [per unghie]

nail varnish remover *n* solvente *m* per smalto

naïve /naɪˈiːv/ *adj* ingenuo

naïvely /naɪˈiːvlɪ/ *adv* ingenuamente

naïvety /naɪˈiːvtɪ/ *n* ingenuità *f*

naked /ˈneɪkɪd/ *adj* nudo; **with the ~ eye** a occhio nudo

nakedness /ˈneɪkɪdnɪs/ *n* nudità *f*

name /neɪm/ **A** *n* nome *m*; **what's your ~?** come ti chiami?; **my ~ is Matthew** mi chiamo Matthew; **I know her by ~** la conosco di nome; **by the ~ of Bates** di nome Bates; **make a ~ for oneself** farsi un nome; **call somebody ~s** infml insultare qualcuno
B *vt* (to position) nominare; chiamare ‹*baby*›; (identify) citare; **be ~d after** essere chiamato col nome di

name day *n* Relig onomastico *m*

name-drop *vi* **he's always ~ping** si vanta sempre di conoscere persone famose

nameless /ˈneɪmlɪs/ *adj* senza nome

namely /ˈneɪmlɪ/ *adv* cioè

nameplate *n* targhetta *f*

namesake *n* omonimo, -a *mf*

name tag *n* *targhetta (f) attaccata ad un oggetto con il nome del proprietario*

name tape *n* *fettuccia (f) attaccata ad un oggetto con il nome del proprietario*

Namibia /nəˈmɪbɪə/ *n* Namibia *f*

nanny /ˈnænɪ/ *n* bambinaia *f*

nanny goat *n* capra *f*

nanoparticle /ˈnanəʊpɑːtɪkl/ *n* nanoparticella *f*

nanosecond /ˈnænəʊsekənd/ *n* infml nanosecondo *m*

nanotechnology /ˌnænəʊtekˈnɒlədʒɪ/ *n* nanotecnologia *f*

nap /næp/ **A** *n* pisolino *m*; **have a ~** fare un pisolino
B *vi* **catch somebody ~ping** cogliere qualcuno alla sprovvista

napalm /ˈneɪpɑːm/ *n* napalm *m*

nape /neɪp/ *n* **~ [of the neck]** nuca *f*

napkin /ˈnæpkɪn/ *n* tovagliolo *m*

Naples /ˈneɪp(ə)lz/ *n* Napoli *f*

nappy /ˈnæpɪ/ *n* pannolino *m*

nappy liner *n* filtrante *m*

nappy rash *n* BrE eritema *m* da pannolini

narcotic /nɑːˈkɒtɪk/ *adj & n* narcotico *m*

narcotics agent *n* AmE agente *mf* della squadra antidroga

narked /nɑːkt/ *adj* infml scocciato

narrate /nəˈreɪt/ *vt* narrare

narration /nəˈreɪʃn/ *n* narrazione *f*

narrative /ˈnærətɪv/ **A** *adj* narrativo
B *n* narrazione *f*

narrator /nəˈreɪtə(r)/ *n* narratore, -trice *mf*

narrow /ˈnærəʊ/ **A** *adj* stretto; fig ‹*views*› ristretto; ‹*margin, majority*› scarso; **have a ~ escape** scamparla per un pelo
B *vi* restringersi
■ **narrow down** *vt* (reduce) restringere

narrowly /ˈnærəʊlɪ/ *adv* **~ escape death** evitare la morte per un pelo

narrow-minded /-ˈmaɪndɪd/ *adj* di idee ristrette

nasal /ˈneɪzl/ *adj* nasale

nasal spray *n* spray *m inv* nasale

nastily /ˈnɑːstɪlɪ/ *adv* (spitefully) con cattiveria

nasty /ˈnɑːstɪ/ *adj* (**-ier**, **-iest**) ‹*smell, person, remark*› cattivo; ‹*injury, situation, weather*› brutto; **turn ~** ‹*person*› diventare cattivo; ‹*situation*› mettersi male; ‹*weather*› volgere al brutto

n

✓ **nation** /ˈneɪʃn/ *n* nazione *f*

✓ **national** /ˈnæʃən(ə)l/ **A** *adj* nazionale
B *n* cittadino, -a *mf*

national anthem *n* inno (*m*) nazionale

National Curriculum *n* BrE *programma (m) scolastico ministeriale per il Galles e l'Inghilterra*

national debt *n* debito *m* pubblico

National Front *n* BrE *partito (m) britannico di estrema destra*

national grid *n* Electr rete *f* elettrica nazionale

National Health *n* BrE *servizio (m) nazionale di assistenza sanitaria*

National Health Service *n servizio (m) sanitario britannico*

National Insurance *n* ≈ Previdenza *f* sociale

National Insurance number *n* numero *m* di Previdenza sociale

Nationalism /ˈnæʃənəlɪzm/ *n* nazionalismo *m*

nationality /næʃəˈnælətɪ/ *n* nazionalità *f*

nationalization /næʃənəlaɪˈzeɪʃn/ *n* nazionalizzazione *f*

nationalize /ˈnæʃənəlaɪz/ *vt* nazionalizzare

National Lottery *n* Lotteria *f* di Stato

nationally /ˈnæʃənəlɪ/ *adv* a livello nazionale

national monument *n* monumento *m* nazionale

n

National Savings Bank *n* BrE Cassa *f* di risparmio

national service *n* BrE servizio *m* militare

National Trust *n* BrE *associazione (f) per la tutela del patrimonio culturale e ambientale in Gran Bretagna*

nation state *n* stato-nazione *m*

nationwide /ˈneɪʃnwaɪd/ *adj* su scala nazionale

native /ˈneɪtɪv/ **A** *adj* nativo; (innate) innato
B *n* nativo, -a *mf*; (local inhabitant) abitante *mf* del posto; (outside Europe) indigeno, -a *mf*

Native American *adj & n* amerindio, -a *mf*

native land *n* paese *m* nativo

native language *n* lingua *f* madre

native speaker *n* persona *f* di madrelingua; **Italian ~s** italiani madrelingua

Nativity /nəˈtɪvətɪ/ *n* **the ~** la Natività

Nativity play *n* rappresentazione *f* sulla nascita di Gesù

Nato, NATO /ˈneɪtəʊ/ *n abbr* (**North Atlantic Treaty Organization**) NATO *f*

natter /ˈnætə(r)/ **A** *n* **have a ~** infml fare quattro chiacchiere
B *vi* infml chiacchierare

natty /ˈnætɪ/ *adj* infml (smart) chic *inv*; (clever) geniale

✓ parola chiave

✓ **natural** /ˈnætʃ(ə)rəl/ *adj* naturale

natural childbirth *n* parto *m* indolore

natural gas *n* metano *m*

natural history *n* storia *f* naturale

naturalist /ˈnætʃ(ə)rəlɪst/ *n* naturalista *mf*

naturalization /nætʃ(ə)rəlaɪˈzeɪʃn/ *n* naturalizzazione *f*

naturalize /ˈnætʃ(ə)rəlaɪz/ *vt* naturalizzare

naturally /ˈnætʃ(ə)rəlɪ/ *adv* (of course) naturalmente; (by nature) per natura

✓ **nature** /ˈneɪtʃə(r)/ *n* natura *f*; **by ~** per natura

nature conservancy *n* protezione *f* della natura

nature reserve *n* riserva *f* naturale

nature trail *n* percorso *m* ecologico

naturism /ˈneɪtʃərɪzm/ *n* nudismo *m*

naturist /ˈneɪʃərɪst/ **A** *n* naturista *mf*
B *adj* naturistico

naught /nɔːt/ *n* = **nought**

naughtily /ˈnɔːtɪlɪ/ *adv* male

naughtiness /ˈnɔːtɪnɪs/ *n* (of child, pet) birbanteria *f*; (of joke, suggestion) maliziosità *f*

naughty /ˈnɔːtɪ/ *adj* (**-ier**, **-iest**) monello; (slightly indecent) spinto

nausea /ˈnɔːzɪə/ *n* nausea *f*

nauseate /ˈnɔːzɪeɪt/ *vt* nauseare

nauseating /ˈnɔːzɪeɪtɪŋ/ *adj* nauseante

nauseatingly /ˈnɔːzɪeɪtɪŋlɪ/ *adv* ‹*rich, sweet*› disgustosamente

nauseous /ˈnɔːzɪəs/ *adj* **I feel ~** ho la nausea

nautical /ˈnɔːtɪkl/ *adj* nautico

nautical mile *n* miglio *m* marino

naval /ˈneɪvl/ *adj* navale

naval base *n* base *f* navale

naval dockyard *n* cantiere *m* navale militare

naval officer *n* ufficiale *m* di marina

naval station *n* base *f* navale

naval stores *npl* (depot) magazzini *mpl* della marina militare

nave /neɪv/ *n* navata *f* centrale

navel /ˈneɪvl/ *n* ombelico *m*

navel ring *n* piercing *m inv* all'ombelico

navigable /ˈnævɪgəbl/ *adj* navigabile

navigate /ˈnævɪgeɪt/ **A** *vi* navigare; Auto fare da navigatore
B *vt* navigare su ‹*river*›

navigation /nævɪˈgeɪʃn/ *n* navigazione *f*

navigational /nævɪˈgeɪʃənəl/ *adj* ‹*instruments*› di navigazione; ‹*science*› della navigazione

navigator /ˈnævɪgeɪtə(r)/ *n* navigatore *m*

navvy /ˈnævɪ/ *n* manovale *m*

navy /ˈneɪvɪ/ **A** *n* marina *f*
B *adj* **~ [blue]** *adj* blu scuro *inv*
C *n* blu *m inv* scuro

nay /neɪ/ **A** *adv* anzi

B *n* (negative vote) no *m*

Nazi /ˈnɑːtsɪ/ *n & adj* nazista *mf*

NB *abbr* (**nota bene = please note**) n.b. *m*

NBC *n abbr* (**National Broadcasting Company**) NBC *f* (*rete nazionale televisiva statunitense*)

NC *abbr* AmE (**North Carolina**)

NCO *n abbr* (**non-commissioned officer**) sottufficiale *m*

ND *abbr* AmE (**North Dakota**)

Ne *abbr* AmE (**Nebraska**)

NE *abbr* (**north-east**) NE

Neapolitan /nɪəˈpɒlɪtən/ *adj & n* napoletano, -a *mf*

⚷ **near** /nɪə(r)/ **A** *adj* vicino; ‹*future*› prossimo; **the ~est bank** la banca più vicina
B *adv* vicino; **draw ~** avvicinarsi; **~ at hand** a portata di mano
C *prep* vicino a; **he was ~ to tears** aveva le lacrime agli occhi
D *vt* avvicinarsi a

nearby /nɪəˈbaɪ/ *adj & adv* vicino

near-death experience *n* esperienza *f* ultraterrena

Near East *n* Medio Oriente *m*

⚷ **nearly** /ˈnɪəlɪ/ *adv* quasi; **it's not ~ enough** non è per niente sufficiente

near miss *n* **have a ~** ‹*planes, cars*› evitare per poco uno scontro

nearness /ˈnɪənɪs/ *n* vicinanza *f*

nearside *n* Auto (in Britain) lato *m* sinistro; (in America, rest of Europe) lato *m* destro

near-sighted /-ˈsaɪtɪd/ *adj* AmE miope

near-sightedness *n* miopia *f*

neat /niːt/ *adj* (tidy) ordinato; (clever) efficace; (undiluted) liscio

neaten /ˈniːtən/ *vt* riordinare ‹*pile of papers*›; dare un'aggiustatina a ‹*tie, skirt*›

neatly /ˈniːtlɪ/ *adv* ordinatamente; (cleverly) efficacemente

neatness /ˈniːtnɪs/ *n* (tidiness) ordine *m*

⚷ **necessarily** /nesəˈserɪlɪ/ *adv* necessariamente

⚷ **necessary** /ˈnesəsərɪ/ *adj* necessario

necessitate /nɪˈsesɪteɪt/ *vt* rendere necessario

necessity /nɪˈsesətɪ/ *n* necessità *f*

⚷ **neck** /nek/ *n* collo *m*; (of dress) colletto *m*; **~ and ~** testa a testa

necking /ˈnekɪŋ/ *n* infml pomiciata *f*

necklace /ˈneklɪs/ *n* collana *f*

neckline *n* scollatura *f*

necktie *n* cravatta *f*

nectar /ˈnektə(r)/ *n* nettare *m*

nectarine /ˈnektərɪn/ *n* nettarina *f*

née /neɪ/ *adj* **~ Brett** nata Brett

⚷ **need** /niːd/ **A** *n* bisogno *m*; **be in ~** essere bisognoso; **be in ~ of** avere bisogno di; **if ~ be** se ce ne fosse bisogno; **there is a ~ for** c'è bisogno di; **there is no ~ for that** non ce n'è bisogno; **there is no ~ for you to go** non c'è bisogno che tu vada
B *vt* aver bisogno di; **I ~ to know** devo saperlo; **it ~s to be done** bisogna farlo
C *v aux* **you ~ not go** non c'è bisogno che tu vada; **~ I come?** devo venire?

needful /ˈniːdfʊl/ **A** *adj* necessario
B *n* **do the ~** fare il necessario

needle /ˈniːdl/ **A** *n* ago *m*; (for knitting) uncinetto *m*; (of record player) puntina *f*
B *vt* infml (annoy) punzecchiare

needless /ˈniːdlɪs/ *adj* inutile

needlessly /ˈniːdlɪslɪ/ *adv* inutilmente

needlework /ˈniːdlwɜːk/ *n* cucito *m*

needs /niːdz/ *adv* **~ must** il dovere chiama

need-to-know *adj* **we have a ~ policy** la nostra politica consiste nel tenere informati solo i diretti interessati

needy /ˈniːdɪ/ *adj* (**-ier**, **-iest**) bisognoso

negate /nɪˈgeɪt/ *vt* (cancel out) annullare; mettere in forma negativa ‹*sentence*›; (contradict) contraddire; (deny) negare

negation /nɪˈgeɪʃn/ *n* negazione *f*

⚷ **negative** /ˈnegətɪv/ **A** *adj* negativo
B *n* negazione *f*; Phot negativo *m*; **in the ~** Gram alla forma negativa

neglect /nɪˈglekt/ **A** *n* trascuratezza *f*; **state of ~** stato di abbandono
B *vt* trascurare; **he ~ed to write** non si è curato di scrivere

neglected /nɪˈglektɪd/ *adj* trascurato

neglectful /nɪˈglektfʊl/ *adj* negligente; **be ~ of** trascurare

negligee /ˈneglɪʒeɪ/ *n* négligé *m inv*

negligence /ˈneglɪdʒəns/ *n* negligenza *f*

negligent /ˈneglɪdʒənt/ *adj* negligente

negligently /ˈneglɪdʒəntlɪ/ *adv* con negligenza

negligible /ˈneglɪdʒbl/ *adj* trascurabile

negotiable /nɪˈgəʊʃəbl/ *adj* ‹*road*› transitabile; Comm negoziabile; **not ~** ‹*cheque*› non trasferibile

negotiate /nɪˈgəʊʃɪeɪt/ **A** *vt* negoziare; Auto prendere ‹*bend*›
B *vi* negoziare

negotiating /nɪˈgəʊʃɪeɪtɪŋ/ *adj* ‹*rights*› al negoziato; ‹*team, committee*› che conduce le trattative; ‹*ploy, position*› di negoziato; **the ~ table** il tavolo delle trattative

negotiation /nɪgəʊʃɪˈeɪʃn/ *n* negoziato *m*

negotiator /nɪˈgəʊʃɪeɪtə(r)/ *n* negoziatore, -a *mf*

Negro /ˈniːgrəʊ/ *adj & n* offensive (*pl* **-es**) negro, -a *mf* offensive

neigh /neɪ/ *vi* nitrire

⚷ **neighbour** /ˈneɪbə(r)/ *n* vicino, -a *mf*

neighbourhood /ˈneɪbəhʊd/ *n* vicinato *m*; **in the ~ of** nei dintorni di; fig circa

neighbourhood watch scheme *n* vigilanza *f* da parte della gente del quartiere

neighbouring /ˈneɪbərɪŋ/ *adj* vicino

neighbourly /'neɪbəlɪ/ *adj* amichevole

neither /'naɪðə(r)/ **A** *adj & pron* nessuno dei due, né l'uno né l'altro
B *adv* ~... **nor** né... né
C *conj* nemmeno, neanche; ~ **do/did I** nemmeno io

neo+ /'niːəʊ/ *pref* neo+

neologism /nɪ'ɒlədʒɪzm/ *n* neologismo *m*

neon /'niːɒn/ *n* neon *m*

neon light *n* luce *f* al neon

Nepal /nɪ'pɔːl/ *n* Nepal *m*

nephew /'nevjuː/ *n* nipote *m*

nephritis /nɪ'fraɪtəs/ *n* nefrite *f*

nepotism /'nepətɪzm/ *n* nepotismo *m*

Neptune /'neptjuːn/ *n* Nettuno *m*

nerve /nɜːv/ *n* nervo *m*; infml (courage) coraggio *m*; infml (impudence) faccia *f* tosta; **lose one's** ~ perdersi d'animo; **you've got a** ~ hai una bella faccia tosta!; **live on one's** ~**s** vivere con i nervi a fior di pelle; **be a bag of** ~**s** avere i nervi a fior di pelle

nerve-racking /'nɜːvrækɪŋ/ *adj* logorante

nerviness /'nɜːvɪnɪs/ *n* BrE nervosismo *m*; AmE grinta *f*

nervous /'nɜːvəs/ *adj* nervoso; **he makes me** ~ mi mette in agitazione

nervous breakdown *n* esaurimento *m* nervoso

nervous energy *n* energia *f* in eccesso

nervously /'nɜːvəslɪ/ *adv* nervosamente

nervousness /'nɜːvəsnɪs/ *n* nervosismo *m*; (before important event) tensione *f*

nervous system *n* sistema *m* nervoso

nervous wreck *n* fascio *m* di nervi

nervy /'nɜːvɪ/ *adj* (**-ier, -iest**) nervoso; AmE (impudent) sfacciato

nest /nest/ **A** *n* nido *m*
B *vi* fare il nido

nested /'nestɪd/ *adj* Comput nidificato

nest egg *n* gruzzolo *m*

nesting /'nestɪŋ/ **A** *n* Zool nidificazione *f*; Comput nesting *m inv*, nidificazione *f*
B *attrib* ‹*habit*› di nidificare; ‹*place*› per nidificare; ‹*season*› della nidificazione

nestle /'nesl/ *vi* accoccolarsi

▪ **nestle up to** *vt* accoccolarsi accanto a ‹*somebody*›

nestling /'nesɪŋ/ *n* nidiace *m*

net[1] /net/ **A** *n* rete *f*
B *vt* (*pt/pp* **netted**) (catch) prendere (*con la rete*)

net[2] **A** *adj* netto; ~ **of VAT** al netto dell'IVA
B *vt* (*pt/pp* **netted**) incassare un utile netto di

netball /'netbɔːl/ *n sport* (*m inv*) *femminile simile alla pallacanestro*

net cord *n* corda *f* di rete; Tennis (shot) net *m inv*

Netherlands /'neðələndz/ *npl* **the** ~ i Paesi Bassi

netiquette /'netɪket/ *n* Comput netiquette *f inv*

netspeak /'netspiːk/ *n* Comput linguaggio *m* del net

netting /'netɪŋ/ *n* **[wire]** ~ reticolato *m*

nettle /'netl/ *n* ortica *f*

net ton *n* AmE tonnellata *f* corta americana

network /'netwɜːk/ *n* rete *f*

network card *n* Comput scheda *f* di rete

networked /'netwɜːkt/ *adj* Comput collegato in rete

networking /'netwɜːkɪŋ/ *n* (establishing contacts) stabilmento *m* di una rete di contatti; Comput collegamento *m* in rete

network television *n* AmE network *m inv* televisivo

neuralgia /njʊə'rældʒə/ *n* nevralgia *f*

neuritis /njʊə'raɪtɪs/ *n* nevrite *f*

neurologist /njʊə'rɒlədʒɪst/ *n* neurologo, -a *mf*

neurology /njʊə'rɒlədʒɪ/ *n* neurologia *f*

neurosis /njʊə'rəʊsɪs/ *n* (*pl* **-oses** /njʊə'rəʊsiːz/) nevrosi *f inv*

neurosurgeon /'njʊərəsɜːdʒən/ *n* neurochirurgo *m*

neurotic /njʊə'rɒtɪk/ *adj* nevrotico

neurotically /njʊə'rɒtɪklɪ/ *adv* in modo ossessivo

neuter /'njuːtə(r)/ **A** *adj* Gram neutro
B *n* Gram neutro *m*
C *vt* sterilizzare

neutral /'njuːtrəl/ **A** *adj* neutro; (country, person) neutrale
B *n* **in** ~ Auto in folle

neutrality /njuː'trælətɪ/ *n* neutralità *f*

neutralize /'njuːtrəlaɪz/ *vt* neutralizzare

never /'nevə(r)/ *adv* [non...] mai; infml (expressing disbelief) ma va'; ~ **again** mai più; **well I** ~**!** chi l'avrebbe detto!

never-ending *adj* interminabile

nevermore /nevə'mɔː(r)/ *adv* mai più

never-never *n* infml **buy something on the** ~ comprare qualcosa a rate

never-never land *n* mondo *m* dei sogni

nevertheless /nevəðə'les/ *adv* tuttavia

new /njuː/ *adj* nuovo

New Age **A** *n* New Age *f inv*
B *attrib* ‹*music, ideas, sect*› New Age *inv*

new blood *n* nuove leve *fpl*

newborn *adj* neonato

new build *n* nuova costruzione *f*

New Caledonia *n* Nuova Caledonia *f*

newcomer *n* nuovo, -a, arrivato, -a *mf*

newfangled *adj* derog modernizzante

new-found *adj* nuovo

Newfoundland /'njuːfən(d)lənd/ *n* Terranova *f*

New Guinea *n* Nuova Guinea *f*

parola chiave

newish /ˈnjuːɪʃ/ *adj* abbastanza nuovo
new-laid /ˈnjuːleɪd/ *adj* fresco
new look **A** *adj* ‹*car, team*› nuovo; ‹*edition, show*› rinnovato; ‹*product*› dall'aspetto nuovo
B *n* **they have given the shop a completely ~** hanno completamente rinnovato il negozio
newly /ˈnjuːlɪ/ *adv* (recently) di recente
newly-built *adj* costruito di recente
newly-weds /ˈnjuːlɪwedz/ *npl* sposini *mpl*
new moon *n* luna *f* nuova
newness /ˈnjuːnɪs/ *n* novità *f*
news /njuːz/ *n* notizie *fpl*; TV telegiornale *m*; Radio giornale *m* radio; **piece of ~** notizia *f*
news agency *n* agenzia *f* di stampa
newsagent's *n* BrE giornalaio *m* (*che vende anche tabacchi, caramelle ecc.*)
news bulletin *n* notiziario *m*
newscast *n* AmE notiziario *m*
newscaster *n* giornalista *mf* televisivo, -a/radiofonico, -a
news conference *n* conferenza *f* stampa *inv*
news dealer *n* AmE giornalaio, -a *mf*
news desk *n* (at newspaper) redazione *f*
news editor *n* caporedattore, -trice *mf* di servizi di cronaca
newsflash *n* notizia *f* flash
newsgroup *n* newsgroup *m inv*
news headlines *npl* TV titoli *mpl* delle principali notizie
news item *n* notizia *f* di attualità
newsletter *n* bollettino *m* d'informazione
newspaper /ˈnjuːzpeɪpə(r)/ *n* giornale *m*; (material) carta *f* di giornale
newspaperman *n* giornalista *m*
newspaper office *n* ufficio *m* della redazione
newspaperwoman *n* giornalista *f*
newspeak /ˈnjuːspiːk/ *n* AmE giornalese *m*
newsprint *n* (paper) carta *f* da giornale; (ink) inchiostro *m* di stampa
newsreader *n* giornalista *mf* televisivo, -a/radiofonico, -a
newsreel *n* cinegiornale *m*
newsroom *n* redazione *f*
news sheet *n* bollettino *m*
news stand *n* edicola *f*
news value *n* interesse *m* mediatico
newsworthy *adj* che merita di essere pubblicato
newsy /ˈnjuːzi/ *adj* ‹*letter*› pieno di notizie
newt /njuːt/ *n* tritone *m*
new technology *n* nuova tecnologia *f*
New Testament *n* Nuovo Testamento *m*
new wave *n & adj* new wave *f inv*
New Year *n* (January 1st) Capodanno *m*; (next year) l'anno *m* nuovo; **Happy ~!** buon anno!; **closed for ~** chiuso per le feste di Capodanno; **see in the ~** festeggiare il Capodanno
New Year Honours list *n* BrE *lista (f) delle persone che ricevono decorazioni il 1 gennaio*
New Year's Day *n* Capodanno *m*
New Year's Eve *n* vigilia *f* di Capodanno
New Year's resolution *n* proposito *m* per l'anno nuovo
New Zealand *n* Nuova Zelanda *f*
New Zealander *n* neozelandese *mf*
next /nekst/ **A** *adj* prossimo; (adjoining) vicino; **who's ~?** a chi tocca?; **the ~ best thing would be to** alternativamente la cosa migliore sarebbe di; **~ door** accanto; **~ to nothing** quasi niente; **the ~ day** il giorno dopo; **~ week** la settimana prossima; **the week after ~** fra due settimane; **the ~ thing I knew** la sola cosa che ho saputo dopo
B *adv* dopo; **when will you see him ~?** quando lo rivedi la prossima volta?; **~ to** accanto a
C *n* seguente *mf*; **~ of kin** parente *m* prossimo
next door **A** *adj* ‹*dog, bell*› dei vicini; ‹*office*› accanto *inv*; **the girl ~** also fig la ragazza della porta accanto
B *adv* ‹*live, move in*› nella casa accanto
next-door neighbour *n* vicino *m* di casa
nexus /ˈneksəs/ *n* (network) rete *f*
NF *n abbr* BrE Pol (**National Front**) *partito nazionalista*
NH *abbr* AmE (**New Hampshire**)
NHS *n abbr* (**National Health Service**) servizio *m* sanitario nazionale
NI *n abbr* **1** BrE (**National Insurance**) previdenza *f* sociale **2** (**Northern Ireland**) Irlanda *f* del Nord
nib /nɪb/ *n* pennino *m*
nibble /ˈnɪbl/ *vt & vi* mordicchiare
▪ **nibble at, nibble on** *vt* = **nibble**
Nicaragua /nɪkəˈrægjʊə/ *n* Nicaragua *m*
nice /naɪs/ *adj* ‹*day, weather, holiday*› bello; ‹*person*› gentile, simpatico; ‹*food*› buono; **it was ~ meeting you** è stato un piacere conoscerla
nice-looking *adj* carino
nicely /ˈnaɪslɪ/ *adv* gentilmente; (well) bene
niceties /ˈnaɪsətɪz/ *npl* finezze *fpl*
niche /niːʃ/ *n* nicchia *f*
niche market *n* mercato *m* specializzato
nick /nɪk/ **A** *n* tacca *f*; (on chin etc) taglietto *m*; infml (prison) galera *f*; infml (police station) centrale *f* [di polizia]; **in the ~ of the time** infml appena in tempo; **in good ~** infml in buono stato
B *vt* intaccare; infml (steal) fregare; infml (arrest) beccare; **~ one's chin** farsi un taglietto nel mento

nickel /ˈnɪkl/ *n* nichel *m*; AmE moneta *f* da cinque centesimi

nickel-and-dime *adj* AmE infml da quattro soldi

nickelodeon /nɪkəlˈəʊdɪən/ *n* AmE (juke box) juke box *m inv*

nickname /ˈnɪkneɪm/ **A** *n* soprannome *m*
B *vt* soprannominare

nicotine /ˈnɪkətiːn/ *n* nicotina *f*

nicotine patch *n* cerotto *m* (transdermico) alla nicotina

niece /niːs/ *n* nipote *f*

nifty /ˈnɪftɪ/ *adj* infml (skilful) geniale; (attractive) sfizioso

Niger /ˈnaɪdʒə(r)/ *n* Niger *m*

Nigeria /naɪˈdʒɪərɪə/ *n* Nigeria *f*

Nigerian /naɪˈdʒɪərɪən/ *adj & n* nigeriano, -a *mf*

niggardly /ˈnɪgədlɪ/ *adj* ‹*person*› tirchio; ‹*salary*› misero

niggle /ˈnɪgl/ infml **A** *n* (complaint) cosetta *f* da ridire
B *vi* (complain) lamentarsi in continuazione
C *vt* (irritate) dar fastidio a

niggling /ˈnɪglɪŋ/ *adj* ‹*detail*› insignificante; ‹*pain*› fastidioso; ‹*doubt*› persistente

⚷ **night** /naɪt/ **A** *n* notte *f*; (evening) sera *f*; **at ~** la notte, di notte; (in the evening) la sera, di sera; **Monday ~** lunedì notte/sera; **work ~s** lavorare la notte
B *adj* di notte

n

nightcap *n* papalina *f*; (drink) bicchierino *m* bevuto prima di andare a letto

nightclub *n* locale *m* notturno, night[-club] *m inv*

nightclubbing *n* **go ~** andare nei night [club]

nightdress *n* camicia *f* da notte

nightfall *n* crepuscolo *m*

nightgown, infml **nightie** *n* camicia *f* da notte

nightie *n* camicia *f* da notte

nightingale /ˈnaɪtɪŋgeɪl, AmE -tng-/ *n* usignolo *m*

nightlife *n* vita *f* notturna

night light *n* lampada *f* da notte

nightly /ˈnaɪtlɪ/ **A** *adj* di notte, di sera
B *adv* ogni notte, ogni sera

nightmare /ˈnaɪtmeə(r)/ *n* also fig incubo *m*

nightmarish /ˈnaɪtmeərɪʃ/ *adj* da incubo

night owl nottambulo, -a *mf*

night porter *n* portiere *m* di notte

night school scuola *f* serale

nightshade *n* Bot **deadly ~** belladonna *f*

night shelter *n* dormitorio *m* pubblico

night shift *n* (workers) turno *m* di notte; **be on the ~** fare il turno di notte

nightshirt *n* camicia *f* da notte (*da uomo*)

nightspot *n* night club *m inv*

nightstand *n* AmE comodino *m*

nightstick *n* AmE (truncheon) manganello *m*

night-time *n* **at ~** di notte, la notte

night vision *n* visione *f* notturna

nightwatchman *n* guardiano *m* notturno

nightwear *n* indumenti *mpl* da notte

nil /nɪl/ *n* nulla *m*; Sport zero *m*

Nile /naɪl/ *n* Nilo *m*

nimble /ˈnɪmbl/ *adj* agile

nimbly /ˈnɪmblɪ/ *adv* agilmente

nincompoop /ˈnɪŋkəmpuːp/ *n* infml scemo *m*

⚷ **nine** /naɪn/ *adj & n* nove *m*

nine pin /ˈnaɪnpɪn/ *n* birillo *m*; **be falling like ~s** ‹*troops, guards, candidates*› cadere come le mosche

nineteen /naɪnˈtiːn/ *adj & n* diciannove *m*

nineteenth /naɪnˈtiːnθ/ *adj & n* diciannovesimo, -a *mf*

nineties /ˈnaɪntɪz/ *npl* (period) **the ~** gli anni Novanta *mpl*; (age) novant'anni *mpl*

ninetieth /ˈnaɪntɪɪθ/ *adj & n* novantesimo, -a *mf*

nine-to-five **A** *adj* ‹*job*› in un ufficio; ‹*routine*› dell'ufficio
B *adv* ‹*work*› dalle nove alle cinque

ninety /ˈnaɪntɪ/ *adj & n* novanta *m*

ninth /naɪnθ/ *adj & n* nono, -a *mf*

nip /nɪp/ **A** *n* pizzicotto *m*; (bite) morso *m*
B *vt* pizzicare; (bite) mordere; **~ in the bud** fig stroncare sul nascere
C *vi* infml (run) fare un salto

nipper /ˈnɪpə(r)/ *n* infml ragazzino, -a *mf*

nipple /ˈnɪpl/ *n* capezzolo *m*; AmE (on bottle) tettarella *f*

nippy /ˈnɪpɪ/ *adj* (**-ier**, **-iest**) infml (cold) pungente; (quick) svelto

nit /nɪt/ *n* (egg) lendine *m*; (larva) larva *f* di pidocchio

nit-pick *vi* cercare il pelo nell'uovo

nitrate /ˈnaɪtreɪt/ *n* nitrato *m*

nitric /ˈnaɪtrɪk/ *adj* nitrico

nitrogen /ˈnaɪtrədʒn/ *n* azoto *m*

nitty-gritty /nɪtɪˈgrɪtɪ/ *n* infml **the ~** il nocciolo [della questione]; **get down to the ~** arrivare al dunque

nitwit /ˈnɪtwɪt/ *n* infml imbecille *mf*

NJ *abbr* AmE (**New Jersey**)

NM *abbr* AmE (**New Mexico**)

⚷ **no** /nəʊ/ **A** *adv* no
B *n* (*pl* **noes**) no *m inv*
C *adj* nessuno; **I have no time** non ho tempo; **in no time** in un baleno; **'no parking'** 'sosta vietata'; **'no smoking'** 'vietato fumare'; **it's no go** è inutile

no., **No.** *abbr* (**number**) No.

Noah /ˈnəʊə/ *n* Noè *m*; **~'s Ark** l'arca *f* di Noè

nobility /nəʊˈbɪlətɪ/ *n* nobiltà *f*

noble /ˈnəʊbl/ *adj* nobile

nobleman /ˈnəʊblmən/ *n* nobile *m*

⚷ parola chiave

noble-minded /-ˈmaɪndɪd/ *adj* di animo nobile

noble savage *n* buon selvaggio *m*

nobly /ˈnəʊblɪ/ *adv* (selflessly) generosamente; **~ born** di nobili natali

nobody /ˈnəʊbədɪ/ **A** *pron* nessuno; **he knows ~** non conosce nessuno; **he's ~ important** non è nessuno d'importante **B** *n* **he's a ~** non è nessuno

no claims bonus *n* abbuono *m* in assenza di sinistri

nocturnal /nɒkˈtɜːnl/ *adj* notturno

nod /nɒd/ **A** *n* cenno *m* del capo; **give a ~** fare un cenno col capo **B** *vt* (*pt/pp* **nodded**) fare un cenno col capo; (in agreement) fare di sì col capo **C** *vi* **~ one's head** fare di sì col capo

■ **nod off** *vi* assopirsi

node /nəʊd/ *n* nodo *m*

nodule /ˈnɒdjuːl/ *n* nodulo *m*

no-go *adj* infml **it's ~** non è possibile

no-go area *n zona (f) calda a cui la polizia può accedere solo con la forza*

no-hoper /nəʊˈhəʊpə(r)/ *n* persona *f* senza prospettive

noise /nɔɪz/ *n* rumore *m*; (loud) chiasso *m*

noiseless /ˈnɔɪzlɪs/ *adj* silenzioso

noiselessly /ˈnɔɪzlɪslɪ/ *adv* silenziosamente

noise level *n* intensità *f* del rumore

noise pollution *n* inquinamento *m* acustico

noisily /ˈnɔɪzɪlɪ/ *adv* rumorosamente

noisy /ˈnɔɪzɪ/ *adj* (**-ier**, **-iest**) rumoroso

nomad /ˈnəʊmæd/ *n* nomade *mf*

nomadic /nəʊˈmædɪk/ *adj* nomade

nominal /ˈnɒmɪnl/ *adj* nominale

nominally /ˈnɒmɪnəlɪ/ *adv* nominalmente

nominate /ˈnɒmɪneɪt/ *vt* proporre come candidato; (appoint) designare

nomination /nɒmɪˈneɪʃn/ *n* nomina *f*; (person nominated) candidato, -a *mf*

nominative /ˈnɒmɪnətɪv/ *adj & n* Gram **~ [case]** nominativo *m*

nominee /nɒmɪˈniː/ *n* persona *f* nominata

non+ /nɒn/ *pref* non+, in+

non-academic *adj* ‹*course*› pratico; ‹*staff*› non insegnante

non-addictive *adj* che non dà assuefazione

non-alcoholic *adj* analcolico

non-attendance *n* mancata presenza *f*

non-believer *n* non credente *mf*

nonchalant /ˈnɒnʃələnt/ *adj* disinvolto

nonchalantly /ˈnɒnʃələntlɪ/ *adv* in modo disinvolto

non-classified *adj* ‹*information*› non confidenziale

non-combustible *adj* incombustibile

non-commercial *adj* ‹*event, activity*› senza fini di lucro

non-commissioned /-kəˈmɪʃnd/ *adj* **~ officer** sottufficiale *m*

non-committal /-kəˈmɪtəl/ *adj* che non si sbilancia

non-compliance *n* (with standards) non conformità *f* (**with** a); (with orders) inadempienza *f* (**with** a)

nonconformist /nɒnkənˈfɔːmɪst/ *adj & n* anticonformista *mf*

non-cooperation *n* non cooperazione *f*

non-denominational /-dɪnɒmɪˈneɪʃənəl/ *adj* ‹*church*› ecumenico; ‹*school*› laico

nondescript /ˈnɒndɪskrɪpt/ *adj* qualunque

none /nʌn/ **A** *pron* (person) nessuno; (thing) niente; **~ of us** nessuno di noi; **~ of this** niente di questo; **there's ~ left** non ce n'è più **B** *adv* **she's ~ too pleased** non è per niente soddisfatta; **I'm ~ the wiser** non ne so più di prima

non-EC *adj* ‹*national*› extracomunitario; ‹*country*› che non appartiene alla Comunità Europea

nonentity /nɒˈnentətɪ/ *n* nullità *f*

non-essentials /-ɪˈsenʃlz/ *npl* (details) dettagli *mpl*; (objects) cose *fpl* accessorie

nonetheless /nʌnðəˈles/ *adv* = **nevertheless**

non-event *n* delusione *f*

non-existent *adj* inesistente

non-family *adj* al di fuori della famiglia

non-fat *adj* magro; ‹*diet*› senza grassi

non-fiction *n* saggistica *f*

non-flammable *adj* non infiammabile

non-fulfilment *n* (of contract, obligation) inadempienza *f* (**of** a); (of desire) inappagamento *m*

non-infectious *adj* non infettivo

non-iron *adj* che non si stira

non-judgmental *adj* imparziale

non-league *adj* Sport fuori campionato

no-no *n* infml cosa *f* proibita; **that's a ~** è un argomento tabù

no-nonsense *adj* ‹*manner, attitude*› diretto; ‹*tone*› spiccio; ‹*look, policy*› pratico; ‹*person*› franco

non-partisan *adj* imparziale

non-party *adj* ‹*issue, decision*› apartitico; ‹*person*› indipendente

non-person *n* (insignificant person) nullità *f*; **officially, he is a ~** Pol ufficialmente non è mai esistito

nonplussed /nɒnˈplʌst/ *adj* perplesso

non-professional *adj* dilettante

non-profit-making /-ˈprɒfɪtmeɪkɪŋ/ *adj* ‹*organization*› senza fini di lucro

non-redeemable *adj* Fin vincolato

non-refillable *adj* ‹*lighter, pen*› non ricaricabile; ‹*can, bottle*› non riutilizzabile

non-religious *adj* laico

non-resident **A** *adj* ‹*job, course*› non residenziale; Comput che non risiede in

permanenza nella memoria centrale
B *n* non residente *mf*

non-residential *adj* ‹*guest*› di passaggio; ‹*student, visitor*› non residente; ‹*caretaker*› che non alloggia sul posto; ‹*area*› non residenziale

non-returnable *adj* ‹*bottle*› a perdere

non-segregated *adj* ‹*area*› non segregato; ‹*society*› non segregazionista

nonsense /'nɒnsəns/ *n* sciocchezze *fpl*

nonsensical /nɒn'sensɪkl/ *adj* assurdo

non sequitur /nɒn'sekwɪtə(r)/ *n affermazione (f) senza legame con quanto detto prima*

non-skid *adj* antiscivolo *inv*

non-smoker *n* non fumatore, -trice *mf*; (compartment) scompartimento *m* non fumatori

non-smoking *adj* non fumatori *inv*

non-specialized *adj* non specializzato

non-starter *n* **be a ~** ‹*person*› non avere nessuna probabilità di riuscita; ‹*plan, idea*› essere destinato al fallimento

non-stick *adj* antiaderente

non-stop **A** *adj* ‹*talk, work, pressure, noise*› continuo; ‹*train*› diretto; ‹*journey*› senza fermate; ‹*flight*› senza scalo
B *adv* ‹*work, talk*› senza sosta; ‹*travel, fly*› senza scalo

non-swimmer *n* persona *f* che non sa nuotare

non-taxable *adj* non imponibile

non-union *adj* ‹*person*› non iscritto ad un sindacato; ‹*company*› non sindacalizzato

non-violent *adj* non violento

non-white, **non-White** *n* persona *f* di colore

noodles /'nu:dlz/ *npl* taglierini *mpl*

nook /nʊk/ *n* cantuccio *m*

noon /nu:n/ *n* mezzogiorno *m*; **at ~** a mezzogiorno

no one *pron* nessuno

noose /nu:s/ *n* nodo *m* scorsoio

⚷ **nor** /nɔ:(r)/ *adv & conj* né; **~ do I** neppure io

Nordic /'nɔ:dɪk/ *adj* nordico

norm /nɔ:m/ *n* norma *f*

⚷ **normal** /'nɔ:ml/ *adj* normale

normality /nɔ:'mælətɪ/ *n* normalità *f*

⚷ **normally** /'nɔ:məlɪ/ *adv* (usually) normalmente

Norman /'nɔ:mən/ **A** *adj* normanno; ‹*landscape, village*› della Normandia
B *n* normanno *m*

Norse /nɔ:s/ *adj* ‹*mythology, saga*› norreno

⚷ **north** /nɔ:θ/ **A** *n* nord *m*; **to the ~ of** a nord di
B *adj* del nord, settentrionale
C *adv* a nord

North Africa *n* Africa *f* del Nord

North African *adj & n* nordafricano, -a *mf*

North America *n* America *f* del Nord

North American *adj & n* nordamericano, -a *mf*

Northants /nɔ:'θænts/ *abbr* BrE (**Northamptonshire**)

northbound /'nɔ:θbaʊnd/ *adj* ‹*traffic, carriageway*› in direzione nord

north-east **A** *adj* di nord-est, nordorientale
B *n* nord-est *m*
C *adv* a nord-est; ‹*travel*› verso nord-est

north-easterly **A** *adj* ‹*point*› a nord-est; ‹*wind*› di nord-est
B *n* vento *m* di nord-est

north-eastern /nɔ:θ'i:stən/ *adj* nordorientale

northerly /'nɔ:ðəlɪ/ *adj* ‹*direction*› nord; ‹*wind*› del nord

⚷ **northern** /'nɔ:ðən/ *adj* del nord, settentrionale

Northern Ireland *n* Irlanda *f* del Nord

Northern Lights *npl* aurora *f* boreale

North Korea *n* Corea *f* del Nord

North Pole *n* polo *m* nord

North Sea *n* Mare *m* del Nord

North Star *n* stella *f* polare

northward /'nɔ:θwəd/, **northwards** /'nɔ:θwədz/ *adv* verso nord

north-west **A** *adj* di nord-ovest, nordoccidentale
B *n* nord-ovest *m*
C *adv* a nord-ovest; ‹*travel*› verso nord-ovest

north-westerly **A** *adj* ‹*point*› a nord-ovest; ‹*wind*› di nord-ovest
B *n* vento *m* di nord-ovest

north-western *adj* nordoccidentale

Norway /'nɔ:weɪ/ *n* Norvegia *f*

Norwegian /nɔ:'wi:dʒn/ *adj & n* norvegese *mf*

⚷ **nose** /nəʊz/ *n* naso *m*
▪ **nose about** *vi* curiosare

nosebleed /'nəʊzbli:d/ *n* emorragia *f* nasale

nosedive /'nəʊzdaɪv/ *n* Aeron picchiata *f*; **take a ~** fig ‹*prices*› scendere vertiginosamente

nosey /'nəʊzɪ/ *adj* = **nosy**

no-show *n persona (f) che non si è presentata*

nosily /'nəʊzɪlɪ/ *adv* in modo indiscreto

nostalgia /nɒ'stældʒɪə/ *n* nostalgia *f*

nostalgic /nɒ'stældʒɪk/ *adj* nostalgico

nostril /'nɒstrəl/ *n* narice *f*

nosy /'nəʊzɪ/ *adj* (**-ier, -iest**) infml ficcanaso *inv*

⚷ **not** /nɒt/ *adv* non; **he is ~ Italian** non è italiano; **I hope ~** spero di no; **~ all of us have been invited** non siamo stati tutti invitati; **if ~** se no; **~ at all** niente affatto; **~ a bit** per niente; **~ even** neanche; **~ yet** non ancora; **in the ~ too distant future** in un futuro non troppo lontano; **~ only... but**

⚷ parola chiave

also... non solo... ma anche...

notable /ˈnəʊtəbl/ *adj* (remarkable) notevole

notably /ˈnəʊtəblɪ/ *adv* (in particular) in particolare

notary /ˈnəʊtərɪ/ *n* notaio *m*; **~ public** notaio *m*

notation /nəʊˈteɪʃn/ *n* notazione *f*

notch /nɒtʃ/ *n* tacca *f*

■ **notch up** *vt* (score) segnare

note /nəʊt/ **A** *n* nota *f*; (short letter, banknote) biglietto *m*; (memo, written comment etc) appunto *m*; **of ~** ‹*person*› di spicco; ‹*comments, event*› degno di nota; **make a ~ of** prendere nota di; **take ~ of** (notice) prendere nota di

B *vt* (notice) notare; (write) annotare

■ **note down** *vt* annotare

notebook /ˈnəʊtbʊk/ *n* **1** taccuino *m* **2 notebook PC**

notebook PC *n* notebook *m inv*

noted /ˈnəʊtɪd/ *adj* noto, celebre (**for** per)

notepad *n* blocco *m* per appunti

notepaper *n* carta *f* da lettere

noteworthy *adj* degno di nota

nothing /ˈnʌθɪŋ/ **A** *pron* niente, nulla

B *adv* niente affatto; **for ~** (free, in vain) per niente; (with no reason) senza motivo; **~ but** nient'altro che; **~ much** poco o nulla; **~ interesting** niente di interessante; **it's ~ to do with you** non ti riguarda

notice /ˈnəʊtɪs/ **A** *n* (on board) avviso *m*; (review) recensione *f*; (termination of employment) licenziamento *m*; **[advance] ~** preavviso *m*; **two months' ~** due mesi di preavviso; **at short ~** con breve preavviso; **until further ~** fino nuovo avviso; **give [in one's] ~** ‹*employee*› dare le dimissioni; **give an employee ~** dare il preavviso ad un impiegato; **take no ~ of** non fare caso a; **take no ~!** non farci caso!

B *vt* notare

noticeable /ˈnəʊtɪsəbl/ *adj* evidente

noticeably /ˈnəʊtɪsəblɪ/ *adv* sensibilmente

noticeboard /ˈnəʊtɪsbɔːd/ *n* bacheca *f*

notification /nəʊtɪfɪˈkeɪʃn/ *n* notifica *f*

notify /ˈnəʊtɪfaɪ/ *vt* (*pt/pp* **-ied**) notificare

notion /nəʊʃn/ *n* idea *f*, nozione *f*; **he hasn't the slightest ~ of time** gli manca completamente la nozione del tempo; **~s** *pl* AmE (haberdashery) merceria *f*

notoriety /nəʊtəˈraɪətɪ/ *n* notorietà *f*

notorious /nəʊˈtɔːrɪəs/ *adj* famigerato; **be ~ for** essere tristemente famoso per

notoriously /nəʊˈtɔːrɪəslɪ/ *adv* **they're ~ unreliable** tutti sanno che su di loro non si può mai fare affidamento

Notts. /nɒts/ *abbr* BrE (**Nottinghamshire**)

notwithstanding /nɒtwɪðˈstændɪŋ/

A *prep* malgrado

B *adv* ciononostante

nougat /ˈnʌgət/ *n* torrone *m*

nought /nɔːt/ *n* zero *m*

noughts and crosses *n* tris *m*

noun /naʊn/ *n* nome *m*, sostantivo *m*

nourish /ˈnʌrɪʃ/ *vt* nutrire

nourishing /ˈnʌrɪʃɪŋ/ *adj* nutriente

nourishment /ˈnʌrɪʃmənt/ *n* nutrimento *m*

novel /ˈnɒvl/ **A** *adj* insolito

B *n* romanzo *m*

novelette /nɒvəˈlet/ *n* (overly sentimental) romanzetto *m* rosa

novelist /ˈnɒvəlɪst/ *n* romanziere, -a *mf*

novelty /ˈnɒvəltɪ/ *n* novità *f*; **novelties** *pl* (objects) oggettini *mpl*

November /nəʊˈvembə(r)/ *n* novembre *m*

novice /ˈnɒvɪs/ *n* novizio, -a *mf*

now /naʊ/ **A** *adv* ora, adesso; **by ~** ormai; **just ~** proprio ora; **right ~** subito; **~ and again, ~ and then** ogni tanto; **~, ~!** su!

B *conj* **~ [that]** ora che, adesso che

nowadays /ˈnaʊədeɪz/ *adv* oggigiorno

nowhere /ˈnəʊweə(r)/ *adv* in nessun posto, da nessuna parte

noxious /ˈnɒkʃəs/ *adj* nocivo

nozzle /ˈnɒzl/ *n* bocchetta *f*

nr *abbr* (**near**) vicino

NSPCC *n abbr* BrE (**National Society for the Prevention of Cruelty to Children**) Società *f* nazionale per la protezione dell'infanzia

NT *abbr* (**New Testament**) Nuovo Testamento (NT)

nth /enθ/ *adj* Math fig **to the ~ power/degree** all'ennesima potenza; **for the ~ time** per l'ennesima volta

nuance /ˈnjuːɒ̃s/ *n* sfumatura *f*

nub /nʌb/ *n* **the ~ of the matter** il nocciolo della questione

nubile /ˈnjuːbaɪl/ *adj* ‹*attractive*› desiderabile

nuclear /ˈnjuːklɪə(r)/ *adj* nucleare

nuclear bomb *n* bomba *f* atomica

nuclear deterrent *n* deterrente *m* nucleare

nuclear energy *n* energia *f* nucleare

nuclear-free zone *n* BrE zona *f* denuclearizzata

nuclear physics *nsg* fisica *fsg* nucleare

nuclear power *n* (energy) energia *f* nucleare; (country) potenza *f* nucleare

nuclear power station *n* centrale *f* nucleare

nuclear shelter *n* rifugio *m* antiatomico

nuclear waste *n* scorie *fpl* nucleari

nucleus /ˈnjuːklɪəs/ *n* (*pl* **-lei** /ˈnjuːklɪaɪ/) nucleo *m*

nude /njuːd/ **A** *adj* nudo

B *n* nudo *m*; **in the ~** nudo

nudge /nʌdʒ/ **A** *n* colpetto *m* di gomito

B *vt* dare un colpetto col gomito a

nudism /ˈnjuːdɪzm/ *n* nudismo *m*

nudist /ˈnjuːdɪst/ *n* nudista *mf*

nudity /'nju:dətɪ/ *n* nudità *f*
nugget /'nʌgɪt/ *n* pepita *f*
nuisance /'nju:səns/ *n* seccatura *f*; (person) piaga *f*; **what a ~!** che seccatura!
nuisance call *n* Teleph telefonata *f* anonima
null /nʌl/ *adj* **~ and void** nullo
nullify /'nʌlɪfaɪ/ *vt* (*pt/pp* **-ied**) annullare
numb /nʌm/ **A** *adj* intorpidito; **~ with cold** intirizzito dal freddo
B *vt* intorpidire
✓ **number** /'nʌmbə(r)/ **A** *n* numero *m*; **a ~ of people** un certo numero di persone
B *vt* numerare; (include) annoverare
numbering /'nʌmbərɪŋ/ *n* numerazione *f*
number one *n* (most important) numero uno *m*; **look after ~** (oneself) pensare prima di tutto a se stessi
number plate *n* targa *f*
numeracy /'nju:mərəsɪ/ *n* **improve standards of ~** migliorare il livello nel calcolo
numeral /'nju:mərəl/ *n* numero *m*, cifra *f*
numerate /'nju:mərət/ *adj* **be ~** sapere far di calcolo
numerical /nju:'merɪkl/ *adj* numerico; **in ~ order** in ordine numerico
numerically /nju:'merɪklɪ/ *adv* numericamente
numeric keypad /nju:'merɪk/ *n* Comput tastierino *m* numerico
✓ **numerous** /'nju:mərəs/ *adj* numeroso
nun /nʌn/ *n* suora *f*
nuptial /'ʌpʃl/ **A** *adj* nuziale
B **~s** *npl* nozze *fpl*
✓ **nurse** /nɜ:s/ **A** *n* infermiere, -a *mf*; **children's ~** bambinaia *f*
B *vt* curare
nursemaid *n* bambinaia *f*
nursery /'nɜ:sərɪ/ *n* stanza *f* dei bambini; (for plants) vivaio *m*; **[day] ~** asilo *m*
nursery rhyme *n* filastrocca *f*
nursery school *n* scuola *f* materna
nursery slope *n* BrE pista *f* per principianti
nurse's aid *n* AmE aiuto infermiere, -a *mf*
nursing /'nɜ:sɪŋ/ *n* professione *f* d'infermiere
nursing auxiliary *n* BrE aiuto infermiere, -a *mf*
nursing home *n* casa *f* di cura per anziani
nurture /'nɜ:tə(r)/ *vt* allevare; fig coltivare
nut /nʌt/ *n* noce *f*; Techn dado *m*; infml (head) zucca *f*
nutcrackers /'nʌtkrækəz/ *npl* schiaccianoci *m inv*
nutmeg /'nʌtmeg/ *n* noce *f* moscata
nutrient /'nju:trɪənt/ *n* sostanza *f* nutritiva
nutrition /nju:'trɪʃn/ *n* nutrizione *f*
nutritional /nju:'trɪʃənl, AmE nu:-/ *adj* nutritivo
nutritionist /nju:'trɪʃənɪst/ *n* nutrizionista *mf*
nutritious /nju:'trɪʃəs/ *adj* nutriente
nuts /nʌts/ *npl* frutta *f* a guscio; **be ~** infml essere svitato
nutshell /'nʌtʃel/ *n* guscio *m* di noce; **in a ~** fig in parole povere
nuzzle /'nʌzl/ *vt* <*horse, dog*> strofinare il muso contro
■ **nuzzle up**: *vi* **~ up against** *or* **to somebody** rannicchiarsi contro qualcuno
NV *abbr* AmE (**Nevada**)
NVQ *n abbr* BrE (**national vocational qualification**) *diploma* (*m*) *conseguito presso un istituto tecnico o professionale*
NW *abbr* (**north-west**) NO
NY *abbr* AmE (**New York**)
NYC *abbr* AmE (**New York City**)
nylon /'naɪlɒn/ **A** *n* nailon *m*; **~s** *pl* calze *fpl* di nailon
B *attrib* di nailon
nymph /nɪmf/ *n* ninfa *f*
nymphomaniac /nɪmfə'meɪnɪæk/ **A** *n* ninfomane *f*
B *adj* da ninfomane
NZ *abbr* (**New Zealand**)

n
o

Oo

o, O /əʊ/ *n* (letter) o, O *f inv*
O /əʊ/ *n* Teleph zero *m*
oaf /əʊf/ *n* (*pl* **oafs**) zoticone, -a *mf*
oak /əʊk/ **A** *n* quercia *f*
B *attrib* di quercia

✓ parola chiave

OAP *abbr* (**old-age pensioner**) pensionato, -a *mf*
oar /ɔ:(r)/ *n* remo *m*
oarsman /'ɔ:zmən/ *n* vogatore *m*
oasis /əʊ'eɪsɪs/ *n* (*pl* **oases** /əʊ'eɪsi:z/) oasi *f inv*
oatcake /'əʊtkeɪk/ *n* galletta *f* di avena

oath /əʊθ/ *n* giuramento *m*; (swear word) bestemmia *f*
oatmeal /ˈəʊtmiːl/ *n* farina *f* d'avena
oats /əʊts/ *npl* avena *fsg*; Culin **[rolled] ~** fiocchi *mpl* d'avena
obdurate /ˈɒbdjʊrət/ *adj* (stubborn) irremovibile; (hard-hearted) insensibile
OBE *n abbr* BrE (**Officer of the (Order of the) British Empire**) *onorificenza (f) britannica*
obedience /əˈbiːdɪəns/ *n* ubbidienza *f*
obedient /əˈbiːdɪənt/ *adj* ubbidiente
obediently /əˈbiːdɪəntlɪ/ *adv* ubbidientemente
obelisk /ˈɒbəlɪsk/ *n* obelisco *m*
obese /əˈbiːs/ *adj* obeso
obesity /əˈbiːsətɪ/ *n* obesità *f*
obey /əˈbeɪ/ **A** *vt* ubbidire a; osservare ‹*instructions, rules*›
B *vi* ubbidire
obituary /əˈbɪtjʊəri/ *n* necrologio *m*
object¹ /ˈɒbdʒɪkt/ *n* oggetto *m*; Gram complemento *m* oggetto; **money is no ~** i soldi non sono un problema
object² /əbˈdʒekt/ *vi* (be against) opporsi (**to** a); **~ that...** obiettare che...
objection /əbˈdʒekʃn/ *n* obiezione *f*; **have no ~** non avere niente in contrario
objectionable /əbˈdʒekʃ(ə)nəbl/ *adj* discutibile; ‹*person*› sgradevole
objective /əbˈdʒektɪv/ **A** *adj* oggettivo
B *n* obiettivo *m*
objectively /əbˈdʒektɪvlɪ/ *adv* obiettivamente
objectivity /ɒbdʒekˈtɪvətɪ/ *n* oggettività *f*
objector /əbˈdʒektə(r)/ *n* oppositore, -trice *mf*
obligation /ɒblɪˈgeɪʃn/ *n* obbligo *m*; **be under an ~** avere un obbligo; **without ~** senza impegno
obligatory /əˈblɪgətrɪ/ *adj* obbligatorio
oblige /əˈblaɪdʒ/ *vt* (compel) obbligare; (do a small service for) fare una cortesia a; **much ~d** grazie mille
obliging /əˈblaɪdʒɪŋ/ *adj* disponibile
oblique /əˈbliːk/ *adj* obliquo; fig indiretto; **~ [stroke]** *n* barra *f*
obliterate /əˈblɪtəreɪt/ *vt* obliterare
obliteration /əblɪtəˈreɪʃn/ *n* (of mark, memory) rimozione *f*; (of city) annientamento *m*
oblivion /əˈblɪvɪən/ *n* oblio *m*
oblivious /əˈblɪvɪəs/ *adj* **be ~** essere dimentico (**of, to** di)
oblong /ˈɒblɒŋ/ **A** *adj* oblungo
B *n* rettangolo *m*
obnoxious /əbˈnɒkʃəs/ *adj* detestabile
oboe /ˈəʊbəʊ/ *n* oboe *m inv*
obscene /əbˈsiːn/ *adj* osceno; ‹*profits, wealth*› vergognoso
obscenity /əbˈsenətɪ/ *n* oscenità *f*
obscure /əbˈskjʊə(r)/ **A** *adj* oscuro
B *vt* oscurare; (confuse) mettere in ombra
obscurity /əbˈskjʊərətɪ/ *n* oscurità *f*
obsequious /əbˈsiːkwɪəs/ *adj* ossequioso
observable /əbˈzɜːvəbl/ *adj* (discernible) percettibile
observance /əbˈzɜːvəns/ *n* (of custom) osservanza *f*
observant /əbˈzɜːvənt/ *adj* attento
observation /ɒbzəˈveɪʃn/ *n* osservazione *f*
observation car *n* carrozza *f* belvedere
observation tower *n* torre *f* di osservazione
observatory /əbˈzɜːvətrɪ/ *n* osservatorio *m*
observe /əbˈzɜːv/ *vt* osservare; (notice) notare; (keep, celebrate) celebrare
observer /əbˈzɜːvə(r)/ *n* osservatore, -trice *mf*
obsess /əbˈses/ *vt* **be ~ed by** essere fissato con
obsession /əbˈseʃn/ *n* fissazione *f*
obsessive /əbˈsesɪv/ *adj* ossessivo
obsessively /əbˈsesɪvlɪ/ *adv* ossessivamente
obsolescence /ɒbsəˈlesəns/ *n* obsolescenza *f*; **built-in ~** obsolescenza *f* programmata
obsolete /ˈɒbsəliːt/ *adj* obsoleto; ‹*word*› desueto; ‹*idea*› sorpassato
obstacle /ˈɒbstəkl/ *n* ostacolo *m*
obstacle course *n* Mil fig percorso *m* ad ostacoli
obstacle race *n* corsa *f* ad ostacoli
obstetrician /ɒbstəˈtrɪʃn/ *n* ostetrico, -a *mf*
obstetrics /ɒbˈstetrɪks/ *nsg* ostetricia *fsg*
obstinacy /ˈɒbstɪnəsɪ/ *n* ostinazione *f*
obstinate /ˈɒbstɪnət/ *adj* ostinato
obstinately /ˈɒbstɪnɪtlɪ/ *adv* ostinatamente
obstreperous /əbˈstrepərəs/ *adj* turbolento
obstruct /əbˈstrʌkt/ *vt* ostruire; (hinder) ostacolare
obstruction /əbˈstrʌkʃn/ *n* ostruzione *f*; (obstacle) ostacolo *m*
obstructive /əbˈstrʌktɪv/ *adj* **be ~** ‹*person*› creare dei problemi
obtain /əbˈteɪn/ **A** *vt* ottenere
B *vi* prevalere
obtainable /əbˈteɪnəbl/ *adj* ottenibile
obtrusive /əbˈtruːsɪv/ *adj* ‹*object*› stonato
obtuse /əbˈtjuːs/ *adj* ottuso
obverse /ˈɒbvɜːs/ *adj* **the ~ side/face** (of coin) l'altra faccia *f*
obviate /ˈɒbvɪeɪt/ *vt* fml ovviare a
obvious /ˈɒbvɪəs/ *adj* ovvio
obviously /ˈɒbvɪəslɪ/ *adv* ovviamente
occasion /əˈkeɪʒn/ **A** *n* occasione *f*; (event) evento *m*; **on ~** talvolta; **on the ~ of** in occasione di
B *vt* cagionare
occasional /əˈkeɪʒənl/ *adj* saltuario; **he has the ~ glass of wine** ogni tanto beve un bicchiere di vino

O

occasionally /əˈkeɪʒənəlɪ/ *adv* ogni tanto
occult /ɒˈkʌlt/ *adj* occulto
occupancy /ˈɒkjʊpənsi/ *n* **available for immediate ~** libero immediatamente; **change of ~** cambio *m* di inquilino
occupant /ˈɒkjʊpənt/ *n* occupante *mf*; (of vehicle) persona *f* a bordo
occupation /ɒkjʊˈpeɪʃn/ *n* occupazione *f*; (job) professione *f*
occupational /ɒkjʊˈpeɪʃənəl/ *adj* professionale
occupational hazard *n* rischio *m* professionale
occupational health *n* medicina *f* del lavoro
occupational pension *n* BrE pensione *f* di lavoro
occupational psychologist *n* psicologo, -a *mf* del lavoro
occupational therapist *n* ergoterapista *mf*
occupational therapy *n* ergoterapia *f*
occupier /ˈɒkjʊpaɪə(r)/ *n* residente *mf*
occupy /ˈɒkjʊpaɪ/ *vt* (*pt/pp* **occupied**) occupare; (keep busy) tenere occupato
⚷ **occur** /əˈkɜː(r)/ *vi* (*pt/pp* **occurred**) accadere; (exist) trovarsi; **it ~ red to me that** mi è venuto in mente che
occurrence /əˈkʌrəns/ *n* (event) fatto *m*
ocean /ˈəʊʃn/ *n* oceano *m*
ocean-going /ˈəʊʃəngəʊɪŋ/ *adj* ‹*ship*› d'alto mare
ochre /ˈəʊkə(r)/ *n & adj* (colour) ocra *f*
o'clock /əˈklɒk/ *adv* **it's 7 ~** sono le sette; **at 7 ~** alle sette
octagon /ˈɒktəgən/ *n* ottagono *m*
octagonal /ɒkˈtægənl/ *adj* ottagonale
octave /ˈɒktɪv/ *n* Mus ottava *f*
octet /ɒkˈtet/ *n* Mus ottetto *m*
⚷ **October** /ɒkˈtəʊbə(r)/ *n* ottobre *m*
octogenarian /ɒktədʒɪˈneərɪən/ *n & adj* ottantenne *mf*
octopus /ˈɒktəpəs/ *n* (*pl* **-puses**) polpo *m*
oculist /ˈɒkjʊlɪst/ oculista *mf*
OD *n abbr* (**overdose**) overdose *f inv*
⚷ **odd** /ɒd/ *adj* ‹*number*› dispari; (not of set) scompagnato; (strange) strano; **forty ~** quaranta e rotti; **~ jobs** lavoretti *mpl*; **the ~ one out** l'eccezione *f*; **at ~ moments** a tempo perso; **have the ~ glass of wine** bere un bicchiere di vino ogni tanto
oddball /ˈɒdbɔːl/ *n* infml eccentrico, -a *mf*
odd bod /ˈɒdbɒd/ *n* BrE infml tipo, -a *mf* strano, -a
oddity /ˈɒdətɪ/ *n* stranezza *f*
odd-job man *n* tuttofare *m inv*
odd jobs *npl* lavoretti *mpl*

⚷ parola chiave

oddly /ˈɒdlɪ/ *adv* stranamente; **~ enough** stranamente
oddment /ˈɒdmənt/ *n* (of fabric) scampolo *m*
odds /ɒdz/ *npl* (chances) probabilità *fpl*; **at ~** in disaccordo; **~ and ends** cianfrusaglie *fpl*; **it makes no ~** non fa alcuna differenza
odds-on *adj* **be the ~ favourite** (in betting) essere il gran favorito; **she has an ~ chance of...** ha molte probabilità di...; **it is ~ that** è molto probabile che
ode /əʊd/ *n* ode *f*
odious /ˈəʊdɪəs/ *adj* odioso
odium /ˈəʊdɪəm/ *n* odio *m*
odometer /əʊˈdɒmɪtə(r)/ *n* AmE contachilometri *m inv*, odometro *m*
odour /ˈəʊdə(r)/ *n* odore *m*
odourless /ˈəʊdəlɪs/ *adj* inodore
odyssey /ˈɒdɪsɪ/ *n* odissea *f*
OECD *n abbr* (**Organization for Economic Cooperation and Development**) OCSE *f*
oedema /ɪˈdiːmə/ *n* edema *m*
oesophagus /ɪˈsɒfəgəs/ *n* esofago *m*
oestrogen /ˈiːstrədʒən/ *n* estrogeno *m*
⚷ **of** /ɒv/ *prep* di; **a cup of tea/coffee** una tazza di tè/caffè; **the hem of my skirt** l'orlo della mia gonna; **the summer of 1989** l'estate del 1989; **the two of us** noi due; **made of** di; **that's very kind of you** è molto gentile da parte tua; **a friend of mine** un mio amico; **a child of three** un bambino di tre anni; **the fourth of January** il quattro gennaio; **within a year of their divorce** a circa un anno dal loro divorzio; **half of it** la metà; **the whole of the room** tutta la stanza
⚷ **off** /ɒf/ **A** *prep* da; (distant from) lontano da; **take £10 ~ the price** ridurre il prezzo di 10 sterline; **~ the coast** presso la costa; **a street ~ the main road** una traversa della via principale; (near) una strada vicina alla via principale; **get ~ the ladder** scendere dalla scala; **get ~ the bus** scendere dall'autobus; **leave the lid ~ the saucepan** lasciare la pentola senza il coperchio
B *adv* ‹*button, handle*› staccato; ‹*light, machine*› spento; ‹*brake*› disinserito; ‹*tap*› chiuso; **'off'** (on appliance) 'off'; **2 kilometres ~** a due chilometri di distanza; **a long way ~** molto distante; (time) lontano; **~ and on** di tanto in tanto; **with his hat/coat ~** senza il cappello/cappotto; **with the light ~** a luce spenta; **20% ~** 20% di sconto; **be ~** (leave) andar via; Sport essere partito; ‹*food*› essere andato a male; (all gone) essere finito; ‹*wedding, engagement*› essere cancellato; **I'm ~ drugs/alcohol** ho smesso di drogarmi/bere; **be ~ one's food** non avere appetito; **she's ~ today** (on holiday) è in ferie oggi; (ill) è malata oggi; **I'm ~ home** vado a casa; **you'd be better ~ doing...** faresti meglio a fare...; **have a day ~** avere un giorno di vacanza; **drive/sail ~** andare via
offal /ˈɒfl/ *n* Culin frattaglie *fpl*

offbeat /'ɒfbi:t/ *adj* insolito
off-centre *adj* BrE fuori centro
off chance *n* **there's an ~ that** c'è una remota possibilità che; **just on the ~ that** nella remota possibilità che
off colour *adj* (not well) giù di forma; ‹*joke, story*› sporco
offence /ə'fens/ *n* (illegal act) reato *m*; **give ~** offendere; **take ~** offendersi (**at** per)
offend /ə'fend/ *vt* offendere
offender /ə'fendə(r)/ *n* Jur colpevole *mf*
offensive /ə'fensɪv/ **A** *adj* offensivo **B** *n* offensiva *f*; **go on the ~** passare all'offensiva
offer /'ɒfə(r)/ **A** *n* offerta *f*; **on special ~** in offerta speciale **B** *vt* offrire; opporre ‹*resistance*›; **~ somebody something** offrire qualcosa a qualcuno; **~ to do something** offrirsi di fare qualcosa
offering /'ɒfərɪŋ/ *n* offerta *f*
offer price *n* Comm prezzo *m* d'offerta
offertory /'ɒfətrɪ/ *n* Relig offertorio *m*
offhand /ɒf'hænd/ **A** *adj* (casual) spiccio **B** *adv* su due piedi
office /'ɒfɪs/ *n* ufficio *m*; (post, job) carica *f*
office automation *n* burotica *f*
office block *n* BrE complesso *m* di uffici
office building *n* BrE complesso *m* di uffici
office hours *npl* orario *m* di ufficio
office junior *n* fattorino, -a *mf*
office politics *nsg* intrighi *mpl* di ufficio
officer /'ɒfɪsə(r)/ *n* ufficiale *m*; (police) agente *mf* [di polizia]
office worker *n* impiegato, -a *mf*
official /ə'fɪʃl/ **A** *adj* ufficiale **B** *n* funzionario, -a *mf*; Sport dirigente *m*
officialdom /ə'fɪʃəldəm/ *n* burocrazia *f*
officially /ə'fɪʃəlɪ/ *adv* ufficialmente
officiate /ə'fɪʃɪeɪt/ *vi* officiare
officious /ə'fɪʃəs/ *adj* autoritario
officiously /ə'fɪʃəslɪ/ *adv* in modo autoritario
offing /'ɒfɪŋ/ *n* **in the ~** in vista
off-key *adj* Mus stonato
off-licence *n* negozio *m* per la vendita di alcolici
off limits *adj* off-limits *inv*
off-line *adj* Comput fuori linea *inv*, off-line *inv*
offload /ɒf'ləʊd/ *vt* scaricare
off-message *adj* Pol **be ~** non essere in linea con la politica del governo
off-peak *adj* ‹*travel*› fuori dagli orari di punta; ‹*electricity*› a tariffa notturna ridotta; **~ call** Teleph telefonata *f* a tariffa ridotta
offprint /'ɒfprɪnt/ *n* estratto *m*
off-putting /-pʊtɪŋ/ *adj* infml scoraggiante
off-road *vi* viaggiare in fuoristrada
off-roader /'ɒfrəʊdə(r)/, **off-road vehicle** *n* fuoristrada *m*
off-screen **A** *adj* ‹*voice, action*› fuoricampo *inv*; ‹*relationship*› nella vita privata **B** *adv* nella vita privata
off-season *adj* ‹*losses*› di bassa stagione; ‹*cruise*› in bassa stagione
offset /'ɒfset/ *vt* (*pt/pp* **-set**, *pres p* **-setting**) controbilanciare
offset printing *n* offset *m inv*
offshoot /'ɒfʃu:t/ *n* ramo *m*; fig diramazione *f*
offshore /'ɒfʃɔ:(r)/ *adj* ‹*wind*› di terra; ‹*company, investment*› offshore *inv*
offside /ɒf'saɪd/ *adj* Sport [in] fuori gioco; ‹*wheel etc*› (left) sinistro; (right) destro
offspring /'ɒfsprɪŋ/ *n* prole *f*
off-stage *adv* dietro le quinte
off-the-cuff *adj* ‹*remark*› spontaneo; ‹*speech*› improvvisato
off-the-peg *adj* ‹*garment*› prêt-à-porter, confezionato
off the record *adj* ‹*comment, statement*› ufficioso
off-the-shelf *adj* Comm standard *inv*
off-the-shoulder *adj* ‹*dress*› senza bretelle
off-the-wall *adj* infml ‹*sense of humour*› strano
off-white *adj* bianco sporco
often /'ɒfn/ *adv* spesso; **how ~** ogni quanto; **every so ~** una volta ogni tanto
ogle /'əʊgl/ *vt* mangiarsi con gli occhi
ogre /'əʊgə(r)/ *n* orco *m*
oh /əʊ/ *int* oh!; **oh dear** oh Dio!
OHMS *abbr* BrE (**On Her/His Majesty's Service**) *abbreviazione (f) apposta su corrispondenza ufficiale del governo britannico*
OHP *n abbr* (**overhead projector**) lavagna *f* luminosa
oil /ɔɪl/ **A** *n* olio *m*; (petroleum) petrolio *m*; (for heating) nafta *f* **B** *vt* oliare
oil-burning *adj* ‹*stove, boiler*› a nafta
oil can *n* (applicator) oliatore *m*
oil change *n* cambio *m* dell'olio
oilcloth *n* tela *f* cerata
oilfield *n* giacimento *m* di petrolio
oil filter *n* filtro *m* dell'olio
oil-fired /-faɪəd/ *adj* ‹*furnace, heating*› a nafta
oil gauge *n* indicatore *m* [del livello] dell'olio
oil heater *n* stufa *f* a nafta
oil lamp *n* lampada *f* a olio
oil paint *n* colore *m* a olio
oil painting *n* pittura *f* a olio
oil pipeline *n* oleodotto *m*
oil pressure *n* pressione *f* dell'olio

oil producing /-prədjuːsɪŋ/ *adj* ‹*country*› produttore di petrolio

oil refinery *n* raffineria *f* di petrolio

oil rig *n* piattaforma *f* petrolifera, offshore *m inv*

oilseed rape *n* colza *f*

oilskins *npl* indumenti *mpl* di tela cerata

oil slick *n* chiazza *f* di petrolio

oil spill *n* fuoriuscita *f* di petrolio

oil stove *n* stufa *f* a nafta

oil tank *n* (domestic) serbatoio *m* della nafta; (industrial) cisterna *f* della nafta

oil tanker *n* petroliera *f*

oil well *n* pozzo *m* petrolifero

oily /ˈɔɪlɪ/ *adj* (**-ier**, **-iest**) unto; fig untuoso

ointment /ˈɔɪntmənt/ *n* pomata *f*

⚷ **OK**, **okay** /əʊˈkeɪ/ **A** *int* va bene, o.k.
B *adj* **if that's OK with you** se ti va bene; **she's OK** (well) sta bene; **is the milk still OK?** il latte è ancora buono?
C *adv* (well) bene
D *vt* (*pt/pp* **OK'd**, **okayed**) dare l'o.k. a

⚷ **old** /əʊld/ *adj* vecchio; ‹*girlfriend*› ex; **how ~ is she?** quanti anni ha?; **she is ten years ~** ha dieci anni

old age *n* vecchiaia *f*

old-age pension *n* BrE pensione *f* di anzianità

old-age pensioner *n* pensionato, -a *mf*

old boy *n* Sch ex-allievo *m*

old country *n* paese *m* d'origine

olden /ˈəʊldən/ *adj* **the ~ days** i tempi andati

old-established /-ɪˈstæblɪʃt/ *adj* di lunga data

olde worlde /əʊldɪˈwɜːldɪ/ *adj* hum dall'aria falsamente antica

old-fashioned /-ˈfæʃ(ə)nd/ *adj* antiquato

old favourite *n* (book, play) classico *m*; (song, film) vecchio successo *m*

old flame *n* infml vecchia fiamma *f*

old girl *n* ex-allieva *f*

Old Glory *n* bandiera *f* statunitense

old hand *n* **be an ~ at something/at doing something** saperci fare con qualcosa/a fare qualcosa

old hat *adj* infml **be ~** essere roba vecchia

oldie /ˈəʊldɪ/ *n* (person) vecchio, -a *mf*; (film, song) vecchio successo *m*

old lady *n* (elderly woman) signora *f* anziana; **my ~** (mother) la mia vecchia; (wife) la mia signora

old maid *n* zitella *f*

old man *n* (elderly man) uomo *m* anziano; (old: dear chap) vecchio *m* mio; **my ~** (father) il mio vecchio; (husband) mio marito *m*; **the ~** (boss) il capo

old master *n* (work) dipinto *m* antico (*specialmente di un pittore europeo del XIII-XVII secolo*)

old people's home *n* casa *f* di riposo

old soldier *n* (former soldier) veterano *m*

Old Testament *n* Antico Testamento *m*

old-time *adj* di un tempo; **~ dancing** ballo *m* liscio

old-timer *n* veterano, -a *mf*

old wives' tale *n* superstizione *f*

old woman *n* (elderly lady) donna *f* anziana; **my ~** (mother) mia madre *f*; (wife) la mia signora; **be an ~** derog (man) essere una donnicciola

olive /ˈɒlɪv/ **A** *n* (fruit, colour) oliva *f*; (tree) olivo *m*
B *adj* d'oliva; (colour) olivastro

olive branch *n* fig ramoscello *m* d'olivo

olive green *adj & n* verde *m* oliva *inv*

olive grove *n* oliveto *m*

olive oil *n* olio *m* di oliva

olive-skinned /-ˈskɪnd/ *adj* olivastro

Olympic /əˈlɪmpɪk/ *adj* olimpico

Olympic Games, **Olympics** *npl* Olimpiadi *fpl*

Oman /əʊˈmɑːn/ *n* Oman *m*

ombudsman /ˈɒmbʊdzmən/ *n* difensore *m* civico

omelette /ˈɒmlɪt/ *n* omelette *f inv*

omen /ˈəʊmən/ *n* presagio *m*

ominous /ˈɒmɪnəs/ *adj* sinistro

omission /əˈmɪʃn/ *n* omissione *f*

omit /əˈmɪt/ *vt* (*pt/pp* **omitted**) omettere; **~ to do something** tralasciare di fare qualcosa

omnibus /ˈɒmnɪbəs/ *n* (bus) omnibus *m inv*

omnibus edition *n* BrE TV replica *f* delle puntate precedenti

omnipotent /ɒmˈnɪpətənt/ *adj* onnipotente

omnipresent /ˌɒmnɪˈpreznt/ *adj* onnipresente

⚷ **on** /ɒn/ **A** *prep* su; (on horizontal surface) su, sopra; **on Monday** lunedì; **on Mondays** di lunedì; **on the first of May** il primo maggio; **on arriving** all'arrivo; **on one's finger** nel dito; **on foot** a piedi; **on the right/left** a destra/sinistra; **on the Rhine/Thames** sul Reno/Tamigi; **on the radio/television** alla radio/televisione; **on the bus/train** in autobus/treno; **go on the bus/train** andare in autobus/treno; **get on the bus/train** salire sull'autobus/sul treno; **on me** (with me) con me; **it's on me** infml tocca a me
B *adv* (further on) dopo; (switched on) acceso; ‹*brake*› inserito; (in operation) in funzione; **'on'** (on machine) 'on'; **he had his hat/coat on** portava il cappello/cappotto; **without his hat/coat on** senza cappello/capotto; **with/without the lid on** con/senza coperchio; **be on** ‹*film, programme, event*› esserci; **it's not on** infml non è giusto; **be on at** infml tormentare (**to** per); **on and on** senza sosta; **on and off** a intervalli; **and so on** e così via;

go on continuare; **stick on** attaccare; **sew on** cucire

on-board /ˈɒnbɔːd/ *adj* di bordo

once /wʌns/ **A** *adv* una volta; (formerly) un tempo; ~ **upon a time there was** c'era una volta; **at** ~ subito; (at the same time) contemporaneamente; ~ **and for all** una volta per tutte
B *conj* [non] appena

once-over *n* infml **give somebody/something the** ~ (look, check) dare un'occhiata veloce a qualcuno/qualcosa

oncoming /ˈɒnkʌmɪŋ/ *adj* che si avvicina dalla direzione opposta

one /wʌn/ **A** *adj* uno, una; **not** ~ **person** nemmeno una persona
B *n* uno *m*
C *pron* uno; (impersonal) si; ~ **another** l'un l'altro; ~ **by** ~ [a] uno a uno; ~ **never knows** non si sa mai

one-armed bandit /wʌnɑːmdˈbændɪt/ *n* slot-machine *f inv*

one-dimensional /-daɪˈmenʃənəl/ *adj* unidimensionale; **be** ~ fig ‹*character*› mancare di spessore

one-eyed /-ˈaɪd/ *adj* con un occhio solo

one-for-one *adj* = **one-to-one**

one-handed /-ˈhændɪd/ *adv* ‹*catch, hold*› con una sola mano

one-horse town *n* infml cittadina *f* di provincia

one-legged /-ˈlegɪd/ *adj* con una sola gamba

one-liner *n* battuta *f* d'effetto

one-man *adj* ‹*bobsled*› monoposto *inv*; ‹*for one person*› per una sola persona; **she's a** ~ **woman** è una donna fedele; **it's a** ~ **outfit/operation** manda avanti tutto da solo

one-man band *n musicista* (*m*) *che suona più strumenti contemporaneamente*; **be a** ~ fig mandare avanti tutto da solo

one-off *adj* BrE ‹*experiment, order, deal*› unico e irripetibile; ‹*event, decision, offer, payment*› eccezionale; ‹*example, design*› unico; ‹*issue magazine*› speciale

one-parent family *n* famiglia *f* con un solo genitore

one-piece /ˈwʌnpiːs/ *adj* ~ **swimsuit** costume intero

one-room flat, **one-room apartment** *n* monolocale *m*

one's /wʌnz/ *poss adj* **one has to look after** ~ **health** ci si deve preoccupare della propria salute

oneself /wʌnˈself/ *pron* (reflexive) si; (emphatic) sé, se stesso; **by** ~ da solo; **be proud of** ~ essere fieri di sé

one-shot *adj* AmE = **one-off**

one-sided /-ˈsaɪdɪd/ *adj* unilaterale

one-time *adj* ex *inv*

one-to-one *adj* ‹*personal relationship*› fra due persone; ‹*private lesson*› individuale; ‹*correspondence*› di uno a uno

one-upmanship /-ˈʌpmənʃɪp/ *n* arte *f* di primeggiare

one-way *adj* ‹*street*› a senso unico; ‹*ticket*› di sola andata

one-woman *adj* **it's a** ~ **outfit** manda avanti tutto da sola; **he's a** ~ **man** è un uomo fedele

ongoing /ˈɒngəʊɪŋ/ *adj* ‹*process*› continuo; ‹*battle, saga*› in corso

onion /ˈʌnjən/ *n* cipolla *f*

online *adj* Comput in linea, on-line *inv*; **go** ~ **to...** connettersi a...; ~ **time** durata *f* del collegamento

onlooker /ˈɒnlʊkə(r)/ *n* spettatore, -trice *mf*

only /ˈəʊnlɪ/ **A** *adj* solo; ~ **child** figlio, -a *mf* unico
B *adv & conj* solo, solamente; ~ **just** appena

on-message /ɒnˈmesɪdʒ/ *adj* Pol **be** ~ essere in linea con la politica del governo

o.n.o. *abbr* BrE (**or nearest offer**) trattabile

on-off *adj* ‹*button, control*› di accensione

onrush /ˈɒnrʌʃ/ *n* (of people, water) ondata *f*

on-screen *adj* sullo schermo

onset /ˈɒnset/ *n* (beginning) inizio *m*

onshore /ˈɒnʃɔː(r)/ *adj* ‹*wind*› di mare; ‹*work*› a terra

onside /ɒnˈsaɪd/ *adj & adv* Sport non in fuorigioco

on-site *adj* sul posto

onslaught /ˈɒnslɔːt/ *n* attacco *m*

on-stage *adj & adv* in scena

on-target earnings *npl guadagni* (*mpl*) *previsti incluse commissioni*

on the job *adj* ‹*training*› in sede

on the spot *adj* ‹*advice, quotation*› immediato

onto, *also* **on to** /ˈɒntuː/ *prep* su

onus /ˈəʊnəs/ *n* **the** ~ **is on me** spetta a me la responsabilità (**to** di)

onwards BrE, **onward** AmE /ˈɒnwəd[z]/ *adv* in avanti; **from then** ~ da allora [in poi]

oodles /ˈuːdlz/ *n* infml un sacco

ooh /uː/ *int* oh!

oomph /uːmf/ *n* infml verve *f inv*

oops /uːps/ *int* ops!

ooze /uːz/ *vi* fluire

op /ɒp/ *n* = **operation**

opal /ˈəʊpl/ *n* opale *f*

opaque /əʊˈpeɪk/ *adj* opaco

OPEC /ˈəʊpek/ *n abbr* (**Organization of Petroleum Exporting Countries**) OPEC *f*

open /ˈəʊpən/ **A** *adj* aperto; (free to all) pubblico; ‹*job*› vacante; **in the** ~ **air** all'aperto
B *n* **in the** ~ all'aperto; fig alla luce del sole
C *vt* aprire

D *vi* aprirsi; ‹*shop*› aprire; ‹*flower*› sbocciare

■ **open onto** *vt* ‹*door, window;*› dare su

■ **open out** **A** *vi* ‹*road*› allargarsi; ‹*flower*› aprirsi

B *vt* aprire ‹*map, newspaper*›

■ **open up** **A** *vt* aprire

B *vi* aprirsi

■ **open with** *vi* (start with) iniziare con

open-air *adj* ‹*pool, market, stage*› all'aperto

opencast mining *n* BrE miniera *f* a cielo aperto

open competition *n* concorso *m*

open day *n* giorno *m* di apertura al pubblico

open-ended /-'endɪd/ *adj* ‹*relationship, question, contract*› aperto; ‹*stay*› a tempo indeterminato; ‹*period*› indeterminato; ‹*strategy*› flessibile

opener /'əʊpənə(r)/ *n* (for tins) apriscatole *m inv*; (for bottles) apribottiglie *m inv*

open government *n* politica *f* di trasparenza

open-handed /-'hændɪd/ *adj* generoso

open-heart surgery *n* intervento *m* a cuore aperto

open house *n* AmE (open day) giornata *f* di apertura al pubblico; **it's always ~ at the Batemans'** i Bateman sono sempre molto ospitali

🔑 **opening** /'əʊpənɪŋ/ *n* apertura *f*; (beginning) inizio *m*; (job) posto *m* libero

opening balance *n* Fin saldo *m* iniziale

opening ceremony *n* cerimonia *f* inaugurale

opening hours *npl* orario *m* d'apertura

open learning *n* open learning *m inv*

openly /'əʊpənlɪ/ *adv* apertamente

open market *n* Econ mercato *m* aperto

open-minded /-'maɪndɪd/ *adj* aperto; (broad-minded) di vedute larghe

open-mouthed /-'maʊðd/ *adj* bocca aperta

open-necked /-'nekt/ *adj* ‹*shirt*› col colletto sbottonato

openness /'əʊpənnɪs/ *n* (of government, atmosphere) trasparenza *f*; (candour) franchezza *f*; (receptiveness) apertura *f* mentale

open-plan *adj* a pianta aperta

open sandwich *n* tartina *f*

open scholarship *n* Univ borsa *f* di studio assegnata per concorso

open season *n* (in hunting) stagione *f* della caccia

open secret *n* segreto *m* di Pulcinella

open ticket *n* biglietto *m* aperto

Open University *n* BrE Univ corsi *mpl* universitari per corrispondenza

open verdict *n* Jur *verdetto* (*m*) *che dichiara non accertabili le cause della morte*

opera /'ɒpərə/ *n* opera *f*

operable /'ɒpərəbl/ *adj* operabile

opera glasses *npl* binocolo *msg* da teatro

opera house *n* teatro *m* lirico

opera singer *n* cantante *mf* lirico, -a

🔑 **operate** /'ɒpəreɪt/ **A** *vt* far funzionare ‹*machine, lift*›; azionare ‹*lever, brake*›; mandare avanti ‹*business*›

B *vi* Techn funzionare; (be in action) essere in funzione; Mil fig operare

■ **operate on** *vt* Med operare

operatic /ɒpə'rætɪk/ *adj* lirico, operistico

operating costs *npl* spese *fpl* di esercizio

operating instructions *npl* istruzioni *fpl* per l'uso

operating room *n* AmE sala *f* operatoria

operating system *n* Comput sistema *m* operativo

operating table *n* Med tavolo *m* operatorio

operating theatre *n* BrE sala *f* operatoria

🔑 **operation** /ɒpə'reɪʃn/ *n* operazione *f*; Tech funzionamento *m*; **in ~** Techn in funzione; **come into ~** fig entrare in funzione; ‹*law*› entrare in vigore; **have an ~** Med subire un'operazione

operational /ɒpə'reɪʃənəl/ *adj* operativo; ‹*law etc*› in vigore

operations room *n* Mil centro *m* operativo; (police) centrale *f* operativa

operative /'ɒpərətɪv/ *adj* operativo

operator /'ɒpəreɪtə(r)/ *n* (user) operatore, -trice *mf*; Teleph centralinista *mf*

operetta /ɒpə'retə/ *n* operetta *f*

ophthalmic /ɒf'θælmɪk/ *adj* oftalmico

🔑 **opinion** /ə'pɪnjən/ *n* opinione *f*; **in my ~** secondo me

opinionated /ə'pɪnɪəneɪtɪd/ *adj* dogmatico

opinion poll *n* sondaggio *m* di opinione

opium /'əʊpɪəm/ *n* oppio *m*

🔑 **opponent** /ə'pəʊnənt/ *n* avversario, -a *mf*

opportune /'ɒpətju:n/ *adj* opportuno

opportunist /ɒpə'tju:nɪst/ *n* opportunista *mf*

opportunistic /ɒpətjʊ'nɪstɪk/ *adj* opportunistico

🔑 **opportunity** /ɒpə'tju:nətɪ/ *n* opportunità *f*

🔑 **oppose** /ə'pəʊz/ *vt* opporsi a; **be ~d to something** essere contrario a qualcosa; **as ~d to** al contrario di

opposing /ə'pəʊzɪŋ/ *adj* avversario; (opposite) opposto

opposite /'ɒpəzɪt/ **A** *adj* opposto; ‹*house*› di fronte; **~ number** fig controparte *f*; **the ~ sex** l'altro sesso

B *n* contrario *m*

C *adv* di fronte

D *prep* di fronte a

🔑 **opposition** /ɒpə'zɪʃn/ *n* opposizione *f*

oppress /ə'pres/ *vt* opprimere

O

🔑 parola chiave

oppression /ə'preʃn/ *n* oppressione *f*

oppressive /ə'presɪv/ *adj* oppressivo; ‹*heat*› opprimente

oppressor /ə'presə(r)/ *n* oppressore *m*

opt /ɒpt/ *v*

▪ **opt for** *vt* optare per

▪ **opt out** *vi* dissociarsi (**of** da)

optic /'ɒptɪk/ *adj* ‹*nerve, disc, fibre*› ottico

optical /'ɒptɪkl/ *adj* ottico; ~ **illusion** illusione *f* ottica

optician /ɒp'tɪʃn/ *n* ottico, -a *mf*

optics /'ɒptɪks/ *nsg* ottica *fsg*

optimism /'ɒptɪmɪzm/ *n* ottimismo *m*

optimist /'ɒptɪmɪst/ *n* ottimista *mf*

optimistic /ɒptɪ'mɪstɪk/ *adj* ottimistico

optimistically /ɒptɪ'mɪstɪklɪ/ *adv* ottimisticamente

optimize /'ɒptɪmaɪz/ *vt* ottimizzare

optimum /'ɒptɪməm/ **A** *adj* ottimale **B** *n* (*pl* **-ima**) optimum *m*

⚷ **option** /'ɒpʃn/ *n* scelta *f*; Comm opzione *f*

optional /'ɒpʃənəl/ *adj* facoltativo; ~ **extras** optional *m inv*

opulence /'ɒpjʊləns/ *n* opulenza *f*

opulent /'ɒpjʊlənt/ *adj* opulento

opus /'əʊpəs/ *n* (*pl* **opuses** *or* **opera**) opera *f*

⚷ **or** /ɔː(r)/ *conj* o, oppure; (after negative) né; **or [else]** se no; **in a year or two** fra un anno o due

oracle /'ɒrəkl/ *n* oracolo *m*

oral /'ɔːrəl/ **A** *adj* orale **B** *n* infml esame *m* orale

orally /'ɔːrəlɪ/ *adv* oralmente

orange /'ɒrɪndʒ/ **A** *n* arancia *f*; (colour) arancione *m* **B** *adj* arancione

orangeade /ɒrɪndʒ'eɪd/ *n* aranciata *f*

orange blossom *n* fiori *mpl* d'arancio

orange juice *n* succo *m* d'arancia

orange peel *n* scorza *f* d'arancia

orange squash *n* BrE succo *m* d'arancia (*diluito in acqua*)

orange tree *n* arancio *m*

oration /ə'reɪʃn/ *n* orazione *f*

orator /'ɒrətə(r)/ *n* oratore, -trice *mf*

oratorio /ɒrə'tɔːrɪəʊ/ *n* oratorio *m*

oratory /'ɒrətrɪ/ *n* oratorio *m*

orbit /'ɔːbɪt/ **A** *n* orbita *f* **B** *vt* orbitare

orbital /'ɔːbɪtl/ *adj* ~ **road** circonvallazione *f*

orchard /'ɔːtʃəd/ *n* frutteto *m*

orchestra /'ɔːkɪstrə/ *n* orchestra *f*

orchestral /ɔː'kestrəl/ *adj* orchestrale

orchestra pit *n* [fossa *f* dell']orchestra *f*

orchestrate /'ɔːkɪstreɪt/ *vt* orchestrare

orchid /'ɔːkɪd/ *n* orchidea *f*

ordain /ɔː'deɪn/ *vt* decretare; Relig ordinare

ordeal /ɔː'diːl/ *n* fig terribile esperienza *f*

⚷ **order** /'ɔːdə(r)/ **A** *n* ordine *m*; Comm ordinazione *f*; **out of** ~ ‹*machine*› fuori servizio; **in** ~ **that** affinché; **in** ~ **to** per; **take holy** ~**s** prendere i voti **B** *vt* ordinare

▪ **order about**, **order around** *vt* (give orders to) impartire ordini a

order book *n* registro *m* degli ordini

order form *n* modulo *m* di ordinazione

orderly /'ɔːdəlɪ/ **A** *adj* ordinato **B** *n* Mil attendente *m*; Med inserviente *m*

orderly officer *n* Mil attendente *m*

order number *n* numero *m* d'ordine

ordinal /'ɔːdɪnəl/ *n* & *adj* ordinale *m*

ordinarily /ɔːdɪ'nerɪlɪ/ *adv* (normally) normalmente

⚷ **ordinary** /'ɔːdɪnərɪ/ *adj* ordinario

ordination /ɔːdɪ'neɪʃn/ *n* Relig ordinazione *f*

ordnance /'ɔːdnəns/ *n* Mil materiale *m* militare

Ordnance Survey *n* BrE *istituto* (*m*) *cartografico*; **Ordnance Survey Map** carta *f* topografica dell'istituto cartografico

ore /ɔː(r)/ *n* minerale *m* grezzo

oregano /ɒrɪ'gɑːnəʊ/ *n* origano *m*

organ /'ɔːgən/ *n* Anat, Mus organo *m*

organ donor *n* Med donatore, -trice *mf* di organi

organic /ɔː'gænɪk/ *adj* organico; (without chemicals) biologico

organically /ɔː'gænɪklɪ/ *adv* organicamente; ~ **grown** coltivato biologicamente

organic chemistry *n* chimica *f* organica

organic farm *n* azienda *f* agricola specializzata in prodotti biologici

organic farming *n* agricoltura *f* biologica

organism /'ɔːgənɪzm/ *n* organismo *m*

organist /'ɔːgənɪst/ *n* organista *mf*

⚷ **organization** /ɔːgənaɪ'zeɪʃn/ *n* organizzazione *f*

organizational /ɔːgənaɪ'zeɪʃənəl/ *adj* ‹*ability, role*› organizzativo

⚷ **organize** /'ɔːgənaɪz/ *vt* organizzare

organized crime /ɔːgənaɪzd'kraɪm/ *n* criminalità *f* organizzata

organized labour *n* manodopera *f* organizzata

organizer /'ɔːgənaɪzə(r)/ *n* organizzatore, -trice *mf*

organ transplant *n* Med trapianto *m* di organi

orgasm /'ɔːgæzm/ *n* orgasmo *m*

orgy /'ɔːdʒɪ/ *n* orgia *f*

Orient /'ɔːrɪənt/ *n* Oriente *m*

oriental /ɔːrɪ'entl/ **A** *adj* orientale; ~ **carpet** tappeto *m* persiano **B** *n* offensive orientale *mf*

orientate /'ɔːrɪənteɪt/ *vt* ~ **oneself** orientarsi

orientation /ɔːrɪən'teɪʃn/ *n* orientamento *m*

orienteering /ɔːrɪen'tɪərɪŋ/ *n* orientamento *m*

orifice /'ɒrɪfɪs/ *n* orifizio *m*

🔑 **origin** /'ɒrɪdʒɪn/ *n* origine *f*

🔑 **original** /ə'rɪdʒɪnl/ **A** *adj* originario; (not copied, new) originale
B *n* originale *m*; **in the ~** in versione originale

originality /ərɪdʒɪ'nælətɪ/ *n* originalità *f*

🔑 **originally** /ə'rɪdʒɪnəlɪ/ *adv* originariamente

originate /ə'rɪdɪneɪt/ *vi* **~ in** avere origine in

originator /ə'rɪdʒɪneɪtə(r)/ *n* ideatore, -trice *mf*

Orkney /'ɔːknɪ/ *n* Orcadi *fpl*

ornament /'ɔːnəmənt/ *n* ornamento *m*; (on mantelpiece etc) soprammobile *m*

ornamental /ɔːnə'mentl/ *adj* ornamentale

ornamentation /ɔːnəmen'teɪʃn/ *n* decorazione *f*

ornate /ɔː'neɪt/ *adj* ornato

ornithologist /ɔːnɪ'θɒlədʒɪst/ *n* ornitologo, -a *mf*

ornithology /ɔːnɪ'θɒlədʒɪ/ *n* ornitologia *f*

orphan /'ɔːfn/ **A** *n* orfano, -a *mf*
B *vt* rendere orfano; **be ~ed** rimanere orfano; **be ~ed by…** essere reso orfano da…

orphanage /'ɔːfənɪdʒ/ *n* orfanotrofio *m*

orphaned /'ɔːfənd/ *adj* rimasto orfano

orthodox /'ɔːθədɒks/ *adj* ortodosso

orthopaedic /ɔːθə'piːdɪk/ *adj* ortopedico

orthopaedics /ɔːθə'piːdɪks/ *nsg* ortopedia *fsg*

OS *abbr* (**outsize**) per taglie forti

oscillate /'ɒsɪleɪt/ *vi* oscillare

osmosis /ɒz'məʊsɪs/ *n* osmosi *f inv*; **by ~** per osmosi

ostensible /ɒ'stensəbl/ *adj* apparente

ostensibly /ɒ'stensəblɪ/ *adv* apparentemente

ostentation /ɒsten'teɪʃn/ *n* ostentazione *f*

ostentatious /ɒsten'teɪʃəs/ *adj* ostentato

ostentatiously /ɒsten'teɪʃəslɪ/ *adv* ostentatamente

osteopath /'ɒstɪəpæθ/ *n* osteopata *mf*

osteoporosis /ɒstɪəɪpə'rəʊsɪs/ *n* osteoporosi *f*

ostracism /'ɒstrəsɪzm/ *n* ostracismo *m*

ostracize /'ɒstrəsaɪz/ *vt* ostracizzare

ostrich /'ɒstrɪtʃ/ *n* struzzo *m*

OTE *abbr* (**on-target earnings**) *guadagni (mpl) previsti incluse commissioni*

🔑 **other** /'ʌðə(r)/ **A** *adj, pron & n* altro, -a *mf*; **the ~ [one]** l'altro, -a *mf*; **the ~ two** gli altri due; **two ~s** altri due; **~ people** gli altri; **any ~ questions?** altre domande?; **every ~ day** (alternate days) a giorni alterni; **the ~ day** l'altro giorno; **the ~ evening** l'altra sera; **someone/something or ~** qualcuno/qualcosa
B *adv* **~ than him** tranne lui; **somehow or ~** in qualche modo; **somewhere or ~** da qualche parte

🔑 **otherwise** /'ʌðəwaɪz/ *adv* altrimenti; (differently) diversamente

other-worldly /ʌðə'wɜːldlɪ/ *adj* disinteressato alle cose materiali

OTT *abbr* infml (**over-the-top**) esagerato

otter /'ɒtə(r)/ *n* lontra *f*

OU *n abbr* BrE (**Open University**) corsi *mpl* universitari per corrispondenza

ouch /aʊtʃ/ *int* ahi!

ought /ɔːt/ *v aux* **I/we ~ to stay** dovrei/dovremmo rimanere; **he ~ not to have done it** non avrebbe dovuto farlo; **that ~ to be enough** questo dovrebbe bastare

ounce /aʊns/ *n* oncia *f* (= 28,35 g)

🔑 **our** /'aʊə(r)/ *poss adj* il nostro *m*, la nostra *f*, i nostri *mpl*, le nostre *fpl*; **~ mother/father** nostra madre/nostro padre

ours /'aʊəz/ *poss pron* il nostro *m*, la nostra *f*, i nostri *mpl*, le nostre *fpl*; **a friend of ~** un nostro amico; **friends of ~** dei nostri amici; **that is ~** quello è nostro; (as opposed to yours) quello è il nostro

🔑 **ourselves** /aʊə'selvz/ *pers pron* (reflexive) ci; (emphatic) noi, noi stessi; **we poured ~ a drink** ci siamo versati da bere; **we heard it ~** l'abbiamo sentito noi stessi; **we are proud of ~** siamo fieri di noi; **by ~** da soli

oust /aʊst/ *vt* rimuovere

🔑 **out** /aʊt/ **A** *adv* fuori; (not alight) spento; **be ~** ‹*flower*› essere sbocciato; ‹*workers*› essere in sciopero; ‹*calculation*› essere sbagliato; Sport essere fuori; (unconscious) aver perso i sensi; fig (not feasible) fuori questione; **the sun is ~** è uscito il sole; **~ and about** in piedi; **get ~ !** infml fuori!; **you should get ~ more** dovresti uscire più spesso; **~ with it!** infml sputa il rospo!; **be ~ to** avere l'intenzione di
B *prep* **~ of** fuori da; **~ of date** non aggiornato; ‹*passport*› scaduto; **~ of order** guasto; **~ of print/stock** esaurito; **~ of sorts** indisposto; **~ of tune** (singer) stonato; (instrument) scordato; **be ~ of bed/ the room** fuori dal letto/dalla stanza; **~ of breath** senza fiato; **~ of danger** fuori pericolo; **~ of work** disoccupato; **nine ~ of ten** nove su dieci; **be ~ of sugar/bread** rimanere senza zucchero/pane; **go ~ of the room** uscire dalla stanza

out-and-out *adj* ‹*success, failure*› totale; ‹*villain, liar*› vero e proprio

outback /'aʊtbæk/ *n* entroterra *m inv* australiano

outbid /aʊt'bɪd/ *vt* (*pt/pp* **-bid**, *pres p* **-bidding**) **~ somebody** rilanciare l'offerta di qualcuno

outboard /'aʊtbɔːd/ *adj* **~ motor** motore fuoribordo *m*

outbreak /'aʊtbreɪk/ *n* ((of war)) scoppio *m*; (of disease) insorgenza *f*

🔑 parola chiave

outbuilding /ˈaʊtbɪldɪŋ/ *n* costruzione *f* annessa

outburst /ˈaʊtbɜːst/ *n* esplosione *f*

outcast /ˈaʊtkɑːst/ *n* esule *mf*; (social) emarginato, -a *mf*

outclass /aʊtˈklɑːs/ *vt* surclassare

outcome /ˈaʊtkʌm/ *n* risultato *m*

outcrop /ˈaʊtkrɒp/ *n* affioramento *m*

outcry /ˈaʊtkraɪ/ *n* protesta *f*

outdated /aʊtˈdeɪtɪd/ *adj* sorpassato

outdo /aʊtˈduː/ *vt* (*pt* **-did**, *pp* **-done**) superare

outdoor /ˈaʊtdɔː(r)/ *adj* ‹*life, sports*› all'aperto; ~ **swimming pool** piscina *f* scoperta

outdoors /aʊtˈdɔːz/ *adv* all'aria aperta; **go ~** uscire all'aria aperta

outer /ˈaʊtə(r)/ *adj* esterno

outer space *n* spazio *m* cosmico

outfit /ˈaʊtfɪt/ *n* equipaggiamento *m*; (clothes) completo *m*; infml (organization) organizzazione *f*

outfitter /ˈaʊtfɪtə(r)/ *n* **men's ~ 's** negozio *m* di abbigliamento maschile

outflow /ˈaʊtfləʊ/ *n* (of money) uscite *fpl*

outgoing /ˈaʊtgəʊɪŋ/ **A** *adj* (president) uscente; ‹*mail*› in partenza; (sociable) estroverso
B *npl* **~s** uscite *fpl*

outgrow /aʊtˈgrəʊ/ *vi* (*pt* **-grew**, *pp* **-grown**) diventare troppo grande per

outhouse /ˈaʊthaʊs/ *n* costruzione *f* annessa

outing /ˈaʊtɪŋ/ *n* gita *f*

outlandish /aʊtˈlændɪʃ/ *adj* stravagante

outlast /aʊtˈlɑːst/ *vt* durare più a lungo di

outlaw /ˈaʊtlɔː/ **A** *n* fuorilegge *mf inv*
B *vt* dichiarare illegale

outlay /ˈaʊtleɪ/ *n* spesa *f*

outlet /ˈaʊtlet/ *n* sbocco *m*; fig sfogo *m*; Comm punto *m* [di] vendita

outline /ˈaʊtlaɪn/ **A** *n* contorno *m*; (summary) sommario *m*
B *vt* tracciare il contorno di; (describe) descrivere

outline agreement *n* abbozzo *m* di accordo

outlive /aʊtˈlɪv/ *vt* sopravvivere a

outlook /ˈaʊtlʊk/ *n* vista *f*; (future prospect) prospettiva *f*; (attitude) visione *f*

outlying /ˈaʊtlaɪɪŋ/ *adj* **~ areas** zone *fpl* periferiche

outmanoeuvre /aʊtməˈnuːvə(r)/ *vt* **~ somebody** passare in vantaggio su qualcuno con un'abile manovra

outmoded /aʊtˈməʊdɪd/ *adj* fuori moda

outnumber /aʊtˈnʌmbə(r)/ *vt* superare in numero

out-of-body experience *n* esperienza *f* extracorporea

out of bounds *adj & adv* ‹*area*› vietato, proibito

out-of-date *adj* ‹*theory, concept*› sorpassato; ‹*ticket, passport*› scaduto

out-of-pocket *adj* **be out of pocket** essere in perdita; **~ expenses** spese *fpl* extra

out-of-the-way *adj* ‹*places*› fuori mano

outpatient /ˈaʊtpeɪʃnt/ *n* paziente *mf* esterno, -a; **~s's department** ambulatorio *m*

outpost /ˈaʊtpəʊst/ *n* avamposto *m*

output /ˈaʊtpʊt/ *n* produzione *f*

outrage /ˈaʊtreɪdʒ/ **A** *n* oltraggio *m*
B *vt* oltraggiare

outrageous /aʊtˈreɪdʒəs/ *adj* oltraggioso; ‹*price*› scandaloso

outrider /ˈaʊtraɪdə(r)/ *n* battistrada *m inv*

outright¹ /ˈaʊtraɪt/ *adj* completo; ‹*refusal*› netto

outright² /aʊtˈraɪt/ *adv* completamente; (at once) immediatamente; (frankly) francamente

outrun /aʊtˈrʌn/ *vt* superare

outsell /aʊtˈsel/ *vt* vendere meglio di ‹*product*›

outset /ˈaʊtset/ *n* inizio *m*; **from the ~** fin dall'inizio

outside¹ /ˈaʊtsaɪd/ **A** *adj* esterno
B *n* esterno *m*; **from the ~** dall'esterno; **at the ~** al massimo

outside² /aʊtˈsaɪd/ **A** *adv* all'esterno, fuori; (out of doors) fuori; **go ~** andare fuori
B *prep* fuori da; (in front of) davanti a

outsider /aʊtˈsaɪdə(r)/ *n* estraneo, -a *mf*

outsize /ˈaʊtsaɪz/ *adj* smisurato; ‹*clothes*› per taglie forti

outskirts /ˈaʊtskɜːts/ *npl* sobborghi *mpl*

outsmart /aʊtˈsmɑːt/ *vt* essere più furbo di

outsource /aʊtˈsɔːs/ *vt* appaltare a imprese esterne

outsourcing /ˈaʊtsɔːsɪŋ/ *n* appalto *m* a imprese esterne

outspoken /aʊtˈspəʊkn/ *adj* schietto

outspread /ˈaʊtspred/ *adj* ‹*wings*› spiegato; ‹*arms, fingers*› disteso

outstanding /aʊtˈstændɪŋ/ *adj* eccezionale; ‹*landmark*› prominente; (not settled) in sospeso

outstandingly /aʊtˈstændɪŋlɪ/ *adv* eccezionalmente; **~ good** eccezionale

outstay /aʊtˈsteɪ/ *vt* **~ one's s welcome** abusare dell'ospitalità di qualcuno

outstretched /ˈaʊtstretʃt/ *adj* allungato

outstrip /aʊtˈstrɪp/ (*pt/pp* **-stripped**) *vt* (*pt/pp* **-stripped**) superare

out tray *n* vassoio *m* per corrispondenza e pratiche evase

outvote /aʊtˈvəʊt/ *vt* mettere in minoranza

outward /ˈaʊtwəd/ **A** *adj* esterno; (journey) di andata
B *adv* verso l'esterno

outwardly /ˈaʊtwədlɪ/ *adv* esternamente
outwards BrE, **outward** AmE /ˈaʊtwəd(z)/ *adv* verso l'esterno
outweigh /aʊtˈweɪ/ *vt* aver maggior peso di
outwit /aʊtˈwɪt/ (*pt/pp* **-witted**) *vt* (*pt/pp* **-witted**) battere in astuzia
outworker /ˈaʊtwɜːkə(r)/ *n* BrE lavoratore, -trice *mf* a domicilio
outworn /aʊtˈwɔːn/ *adj* ‹*outmoded*› sorpassato
oval /ˈəʊvl/ **A** *adj* ovale
B *n* ovale *m*
ovary /ˈəʊvərɪ/ *n* Anat ovaia *f*
ovation /əʊˈveɪʃn/ *n* ovazione *f*
oven /ˈʌvn/ *n* forno *m*
oven cleaner *n* detergente *m* per il forno
oven glove *n* guanto *m* da forno
ovenproof *adj* da forno
oven-ready *adj* pronto da mettere in forno
⚷ **over** /ˈəʊvə(r)/ **A** *prep* sopra; (across) al di là di; (during) durante; (more than) più di; **~ the phone** al telefono; **~ the page** alla pagina seguente; **all ~ Italy** in tutta [l']Italia; ‹*travel*› per l'Italia
B *adv* Math col resto di; (ended) finito; **~ again** un'altra volta; **~ and ~** più volte; **~ and above** oltre a; **~ here/there** qui/là; **all ~** (everywhere) dappertutto; **it's all ~** è tutto finito; **I ache all ~** ho male dappertutto; **come/bring ~** venire/portare; **turn ~** girare
over+ *pref* (too) troppo
overact /əʊvərˈækt/ *vi* strafare
overactive /əʊvərˈæktɪv/ *adj* ‹*imagination*› sbrigliato
overall¹ /ˈəʊvərɔːl/ *n* grembiule *m*
⚷ **overall²** /əʊvərˈɔːl/ **A** *adj* complessivo; (general) generale
B *adv* complessivamente
overalls /ˈəʊvərɔːlz/ *npl* tuta *fsg*
overarm /ˈəʊɪvərɑːm/ *adj & adv* ‹*throw*› col braccio al di sopra della spalla
overawe /əʊvərˈɔː/ *vt* fig intimidire
overbalance /əʊvəˈbæləns/ *vi* perdere l'equilibrio
overbearing /əʊvəˈbeərɪŋ/ *adj* prepotente
overblown /əʊvəˈbləʊn/ *adj* ‹*style*› ampolloso
overboard /ˈəʊvəbɔːd/ *adv* Naut in mare
overbook /əʊvəˈbʊk/ *vt accettare un numero di prenotazioni superiore ai posti disponibili*
overburden /əʊvəˈbɜːdən/ *vt* sovraccaricare (with di)
overcapacity /əʊvəkəˈpæsətɪ/ *n* eccesso *m* di capacità produttiva
overcast /ˈəʊvəkɑːst/ *adj* coperto
overcharge /əʊvəˈtʃɑːdʒ/ **A** *vt* **~ somebody** far pagare più del dovuto a
B *vi* far pagare più del dovuto

⚷ parola chiave

overcoat /ˈəʊvəkəʊt/ *n* cappotto *m*
overcome /əʊvəˈkʌm/ *vt* (*pt* **-came**, *pp* **-come**) vincere; **be ~ by** essere sopraffatto da
overcompensate /əʊvəˈkɒmpənseɪt/ *vi* compensare eccessivamente
overconfident /əʊvəˈkɒnfɪdənt/ *adj* troppo sicuro di sé
overcook /əʊvəˈkʊk/ *vt* cuocere troppo
overcrowded /əʊvəˈkraʊdɪd/ *adj* sovraffollato
overcrowding /əʊvəˈkraʊdɪŋ/ *n* (in transport) calca *f*; (in city, institution) sovraffollamento *m*
overdo /əʊvəˈduː/ *vt* (*pt* **-did**, *pp* **-done**) esagerare; (cook too long) stracuocere; **~ it** infml (do too much) strafare
overdose /ˈəʊvədəʊs/ *n* overdose *f inv*
overdraft /ˈəʊvədrɑːft/ *n* scoperto *m*; **have an ~** avere il conto scoperto
overdraw /əʊvəˈdrɔː/ *vt* (*pt* **-drew**, *pp* **-drawn**) **~ one's account** andare allo scoperto; **be ~n by...** ‹*account*› essere scoperto di...
overdressed /əʊvəˈdrest/ *adj* troppo elegante
overdrive /ˈəʊvədraɪv/ *n* Auto overdrive *m inv*
overdue /əʊvəˈdjuː/ *adj* in ritardo
overeat /əʊvərˈiːt/ *vi* mangiare troppo
overemphasize /əʊvərˈemfəsaɪz/ *vt* esagerare ‹*importance*›; dare troppo rilievo a ‹*aspect, fact*›
overenthusiastic /əʊvərɪnθjuːzɪˈæstɪk/ *adj* troppo entusiasta
overestimate /əʊvərˈestɪmeɪt/ *vt* sopravvalutare
overexcited /əʊvərɪkˈsaɪtɪd/ *adj* sovreccitato; **get ~** sovreccitarsi
overexert /əʊvərɪgˈzɜːt/ *vt* **~ oneself** sovraffaticarsi
overexposure /əʊvərekˈspəʊʒə(r)/ *n* Phot sovresposizione *f*; (in the media) attenzione *f* eccessiva da parte dei media
overfeed /əʊvəˈfiːd/ *vt* sovralimentare ‹*child, pet*›; concimare troppo ‹*plant*›
overflow¹ /ˈəʊvəfləʊ/ *n* (water) acqua *f* che deborda; (people) pubblico *m* in eccesso; (outlet) scarico *m*
overflow² /əʊvəˈfləʊ/ *vi* debordare
overgenerous /əʊvəˈdʒenərəs/ *adj* ‹*amount*› troppo generoso
overgrown /əʊvəˈgrəʊn/ *adj* ‹*garden*› coperto di erbacce
overhang¹ /ˈəʊvəhæŋ/ *n* sporgenza *f*
overhang² /əʊvəˈhæŋ/ **A** *vi* (*pt/pp* **-hung**) sporgere
B *vt* sovrastare
overhanging /əʊvəˈhæŋɪŋ/ *adj* ‹*ledge, cliff*› sporgente
overhaul¹ /ˈəʊvəhɔːl/ *n* revisione *f*
overhaul² /əʊvəˈhɔːl/ *vt* Techn revisionare
overhead¹ /əʊvəˈhed/ *adv* in alto

overhead[2] /'əʊvəhed/ **A** *adj* aereo; ‹*railway*› sopraelevato; ‹*lights*› da soffitto **B** *n* AmE, (Br **~s** *npl*) spese *fpl* generali
overhead light *n* lampada *f* da soffitto
overhead locker *n* Aeron scomparto *m* [per il bagaglio a mano]
overhead projector *n* lavagna *f* luminosa
overhear /əʊvə'hɪə(r)/ *vt* (*pt/pp* **-heard**) sentire per caso ‹*conversation*›; **I ~d him saying it** l'ho sentito per caso mentre lo diceva
overheat /əʊvə'hi:t/ **A** *vi* Auto surriscaldarsi **B** *vt* surriscaldare
over-indulge **A** *vi* eccedere **B** *vt* viziare ‹*child*›
over-indulgence *n* (excess) eccesso *m*; (laxity towards) indulgenza *f* eccessiva
overjoyed /əʊvə'dʒɔɪd/ *adj* felicissimo
overkill /'əʊvəkɪl/ *n* (exaggerated treatment) esagerazione *f*
overland /'əʊvəlænd/ *adj & adv* via terra; **~ route** via *f* terrestre
overlap /əʊvə'læp/ **A** *vi* (*pt/pp* **-lapped**) sovrapporsi **B** *vt* sovrapporre
overlay /əʊvə'leɪ/ *vt* ricoprire
overleaf /əʊvə'li:f/ *adv* sul retro
overload[1] /əʊvə'ləʊd/ *vt* sovraccaricare
overload[2] /'əʊvələʊd/ *n* Electr sovratensioni *fpl*
overlook /əʊvə'lʊk/ *vt* dominare; (fail to see, ignore) lasciarsi sfuggire
overly /'əʊvəlɪ/ *adv* eccessivamente
overmanned /əʊvə'mænd/ *adj* con un'eccedenza di personale
overmanning /əʊvə'mænɪŋ/ *n* eccesso *m* di personale
overmuch /əʊvə'mʌtʃ/ *adv* troppo
overnight[1] /'əʊvənaɪt/ *adj* notturno
overnight[2] /əʊvə'naɪt/ *vt inviare tramite sistemi di spedizione notturna con consegna il mattino seguente* ‹*goods*›
overnight bag *n* piccola borsa *f* da viaggio
overnight stay *n* sosta *f* per la notte
overpass /'əʊvəpɑ:s/ *n* AmE cavalcavia *m inv*
overpay /əʊvə'peɪ/ *vt* (*pt/pp* **-paid**) strapagare
overplay /əɪvə'pleɪ/ *vt* (exaggerate) esagerare
overpopulated /əʊvə'pɒpjʊleɪtɪd/ *adj* sovrappopolato
overpower /əʊvə'paʊə(r)/ *vt* sopraffare
overpowering /əʊvə'paʊərɪŋ/ *adj* insostenibile
overpriced /əʊvə'praɪst/ *adj* troppo caro
overproduce /əʊvəprə'dju:s/ *vt* produrre in eccesso
overqualified /əʊvə'kwɒlɪfaɪd/ *adj* troppo qualificato
overrate /əʊvə'reɪt/ *vt* sopravvalutare
overrated /əʊvə'reɪtɪd/ *adj* sopravvalutato
overreach /əʊvə'ri:tʃ/ *vt* **~ oneself** puntare troppo in alto
overreact /əʊvərɪ'ækt/ *vi* avere una reazione eccessiva
overreaction /əʊvərɪ:ækʃn/ *n* reazione *f* eccessiva
override /əʊvə'raɪd/ *vt* (*pt* **-rode**, *pp* **-ridden**) passare sopra a
overriding /əʊvə'raɪdɪŋ/ *adj* prevalente
overrule /əʊvə'ru:l/ *vt* annullare ‹*decision*›; **we were ~d by the chairman** il direttore ha prevalso su di noi
overrun /əʊvə'rʌn/ *vt* (*pt* **-ran**, *pp* **-run**, *pres p* **-running**) invadere; oltrepassare ‹*time*›; **be ~ with** essere invaso da
overseas[1] /əʊvə'si:z/ *adv* oltremare
overseas[2] /'əʊvəsi:z/ *adj* d'oltremare
oversee /əʊvə'si:/ *vt* (*pt* **-saw**, *pp* **-seen**) sorvegliare
oversell /əʊvə'sel/ *vt* lodare esageratamente ‹*idea, plan*›
oversensitive /əʊvə'sensɪtɪv/ *adj* ‹*person*› ipersensibile
oversexed /əʊvə'sekst/ *adj* infml **be ~** essere un maniaco/una maniaca del sesso
overshadow /əʊvə'ʃædəʊ/ *vt* adombrare
overshoot /əʊvə'ʃu:t/ *vt* (*pt/pp* **-shot**) oltrepassare
oversight /'əʊvəsaɪt/ *n* disattenzione *f*; **an ~** una svista
oversimplification /əʊvəsɪmplɪfɪ'keɪʃn/ *n* semplificazione *f* eccessiva
oversimplified /əʊvə'sɪmplɪfaɪd/ *adj* semplicistico
oversimplify /əʊvə'sɪmplɪfaɪ/ *vt* semplificare eccessivamente
oversize /əʊvə'saɪz/, **oversized** /əʊvə'saɪzd/ *adj* più grande del normale
oversleep /əʊvə'sli:p/ *vi* (*pt/pp* **-slept**) svegliarsi troppo tardi
overspend /əʊvə'spend/ *vi* spendere troppo
overspending /əʊvə'spendɪŋ/ *n* spese *fpl* eccessive; Fin spese *fpl* superiori al bilancio di previsione
overspill /'əʊvəspɪl/ **A** *n* (excess amount) eccedenza *f* **B** *attrib* **~ housing development** città *f* satellite; **~ population** popolazione *f* in eccesso
overstaffed /əʊvə'stɑ:ft/ *adj* **be ~** avere personale in eccedenza
overstaffing /əʊvə'stɑ:fɪŋ/ *n* eccedenza *f* di personale
overstate /əʊvə'steɪt/ *vt* esagerare; **its importance cannot be ~d** la sua importanza non sarà mai sottolineata a sufficienza; **~ the case** esagerare le cose
overstatement /əʊvə'steɪtmənt/ *n* esagerazione *f*
overstay /əʊvə'steɪ/ *vt* **~ one's time** trattenersi troppo a lungo; **~ one's visa**

O

trattenersi oltre la scadenza del visto

overstep /əʊvəˈstep/ *vt* (*pt/pp* **-stepped**) **~ the mark** oltrepassare ogni limite

overstretched /əʊvəˈstretʃt/ *adj* ‹*person*› sovraccarico [di lavoro]; ‹*budget, resources*› sfruttato fino al limite

oversubscribed /əʊvəsəbˈskraɪbd/ *adj* ‹*share issue*› sottoscritto in eccesso; ‹*offer, tickets*› richiesto oltre la disponibilità

overt /əʊˈvɜːt/ *adj* palese

overtake /əʊvəˈteɪk/ *vt & vi* (*pt* **-took**, *pp* **-taken**) sorpassare

overtaking /əʊvəˈteɪkɪŋ/ *n* sorpasso *m*; **no ~** divieto di sorpasso

overtax /əʊvəˈtæks/ *vt* fig abusare di

over-the-counter *adj* ‹*medicines*› da banco

over-the-top *adj* infml esagerato; **go over the top** esagerare

overthrow[1] /ˈəʊvəθrəʊ/ *n* Pol rovesciamento *m*

overthrow[2] /əʊvəˈθrəʊ/ *vt* (*pt* **-threw**, *pp* **-thrown**) Pol rovesciare

overtime /ˈəʊvətaɪm/ **A** *n* lavoro straordinario *m*
B *adv* **work ~** fare lo straordinario

overtired /əʊvəˈtaɪəd/ *adj* sovraffaticato

overtly /əʊˈvɜːtlɪ/ *adv* apertamente

overtone /ˈəʊvətəʊn/ *n* fig sfumatura *f*

overture /ˈəʊvətjʊə(r)/ *n* Mus preludio *m*; **~s** *pl* fig approccio *msg*; **make ~s to** mostrare un atteggiamento di apertura verso

overturn /əʊvəˈtɜːn/ **A** *vt* ribaltare
B *vi* ribaltarsi

overuse[1] /əʊvəˈjuːs/ *n* **1** (of word, product) abuso *m* **2** (of facility) uso *m* eccessivo; **to be worn through ~** essere consumato dall'uso eccessivo

overuse[2] /əʊvəˈjuːz/ *vt* fare un uso eccessivo di ‹*machine*›; abusare di ‹*chemical, service, word*›

overvalue /əʊvəˈvæljuː/ *vt* sopravvalutare ‹*currency, property*›

overview /ˈəʊvəvjuː/ *n* visione *f* d'insieme

overweight /əʊvəˈweɪt/ *adj* sovrappeso

overwhelm /əʊvəˈwelm/ *vt* sommergere (**with** di); (with emotion) confondere

overwhelming /əʊvəˈwelmɪŋ/ *adj* travolgente; ‹*victory, majority*› schiacciante

overwhelmingly /əʊvəˈwelmɪŋlɪ/ *adv* ‹*vote, accept, reject*› con una maggioranza schiacciante; ‹*generous*› straordinariamente

overwork /əʊvəˈwɜːk/ **A** *n* lavoro *m* eccessivo
B *vt* far lavorare eccessivamente
C *vi* lavorare eccessivamente

overworked /ˌəʊvəˈwɜːkt/ *adj* affaticato dal troppo lavoro

overwrite /əʊvəˈraɪt/ *vt* Comput registrare sopra a

overwrought /əʊvəˈrɔːt/ *adj* in stato di agitazione

ovulation /ɒvjʊˈleɪʃn/ *n* ovulazione *f*

ow /aʊ/ *int* ahi!

owe /əʊ/ *vt* also fig dovere (**[to] somebody** a qualcuno); **~ somebody something** dovere qualcosa a qualcuno

owing /ˈəʊɪŋ/ **A** *adj* **be ~** ‹*money*› essere da pagare
B *prep* **~ to** a causa di

owl /aʊl/ *n* gufo *m*

🔑 **own**[1] /əʊn/ **A** *adj* proprio
B *pron* **a car of my ~** una macchina per conto mio; **on one's ~** da solo; **hold one's ~ with** tener testa a; **get one's ~ back** infml prendersi una rivincita

own[2] *vt* possedere; (confess) ammettere; **I don't ~ it** non mi appartiene
■ **own up** *vi* confessare (**to something** qualcosa)

🔑 **owner** /ˈəʊnə(r)/ *n* proprietario, -a *mf*

owner-driver *n persona* (*f*) *che guida un'auto di sua proprietà*

owner-occupied /-ˈɒkjʊpaɪd/ *adj* abitato dal proprietario

owner-occupier *n persona* (*f*) *che abita in una casa di sua proprietà*

ownership /ˈəʊnəʃɪp/ *n* proprietà *f*

ox /ɒks/ *n* (*pl* **oxen**) bue *m* (*pl* **buoi**)

Oxbridge /ˈɒksbrɪdʒ/ *n le università di Oxford e Cambridge*

oxide /ˈɒksaɪd/ *n* ossido *m*

oxidize /ˈɒksɪdaɪz/ **A** *vt* ossidare
B *vi* ossidarsi

oxygen /ˈɒksɪdʒən/ *n* ossigeno *m*

oxygen mask *n* maschera *f* ad ossigeno

oyster /ˈɔɪstə(r)/ *n* ostrica *f*

oz *abbr* (**ounce(s)**) oncia *f*

ozone /ˈəʊzəʊn/ *n* ozono *m*

ozone depletion *n* distruzione *f* dell'ozonosfera

ozone-friendly *adj* che non danneggia l'ozono

ozone layer *n* fascia *f* d'ozono

🔑 parola chiave

Pp

p, P /piː/ **A** *n* (letter) p, P *f inv*
B *abbr* BrE (**penny, pence**) penny *m*

p & p *n abbr* (**postage and packing**) spese *fpl* di spedizione

P45 *n* BrE (form) ≈ modello CUD *m*

PA *abbr* **1** (**personal assistant**) segretario, -a *mf* personale **2** AmE (**Pennsylvania**) Pennsylvania *f*

p.a. *abbr* (**per annum**) all'anno

pace /peɪs/ **A** *n* passo *m*; (speed) ritmo *m*; **keep ~ with** camminare di pari passo con
B *vi* **~ up and down** camminare avanti e indietro

pacemaker /ˈpeɪsmeɪkə(r)/ *n* Med pacemaker *m inv*; (runner) battistrada *m inv*

pace-setter *n* (athlete) battistrada *m inv*

Pacific /pəˈsɪfɪk/ *adj & n* **the ~ [Ocean]** l'oceano *m* Pacifico, il Pacifico

pacifier /ˈpæsɪfaɪə(r)/ *n* AmE ciuccio *m*, succhiotto *m*

pacifism /ˈpæsɪfɪzm/ *n* pacifismo *m*

pacifist /ˈpæsɪfɪst/ *n* pacifista *mf*

pacify /ˈpæsɪfaɪ/ *vt* (*pt/pp* **-ied**) placare ‹*person*›; pacificare ‹*country*›

pack /pæk/ **A** *n* (of cards) mazzo *m*; (of hounds) muta *f*; (of wolves, thieves) branco *m*; (of cigarettes etc) pacchetto *m*; **a ~ of lies** un mucchio di bugie
B *vt* impacchettare ‹*article*›; fare ‹*suitcase*›; mettere in valigia ‹*swimsuit etc*›; (press down) comprimere; **~ed** (crowded) strapieno, pieno zeppo
C *vi* fare i bagagli; **send somebody ~ing** infml mandare qualcuno a quel paese

■ **pack in** *vt* infml mollare ‹*job*›; **~ it in!** (stop it) piantala!

■ **pack off** *vt* (send) spedire

■ **pack out**: *vt* **be ~ed out** ‹*cinema, shops*› essere strapieno, essere pieno zeppo

■ **pack up A** *vt* impacchettare
B *vi* infml ‹*machine*› guastarsi

package /ˈpækɪdʒ/ **A** *n* pacco *m*
B *vt* impacchettare

package deal *n* offerta *f* tutto compreso

package holiday *n* vacanza *f* organizzata

package tour *n* viaggio *m* organizzato

packaging /ˈpækɪdʒɪŋ/ *n* (materials) confezione *f*; (promotion: of product) presentazione *f* pubblicitaria

packed /pækt/ *adj* pieno zeppo; **~ with** pieno zeppo di

packed lunch /pækt/ *n* pranzo *m* al sacco

packer /ˈpækə(r)/ *n* (in factory) imballatore, -trice *mf*

packet /ˈpækɪt/ *n* pacchetto *m*; **cost a ~** infml costare un sacco

pack ice *n* banchisa *f*

packing /ˈpækɪŋ/ *n* imballaggio *m*

pact /pækt/ *n* patto *m*

pad¹ /pæd/ **A** *n* imbottitura *f*; (for writing) bloc-notes *m inv*, taccuino *m*; infml (home) casa *f*
B *vt* (*pt/pp* **padded**) imbottire

pad² *vi* (*pt/pp* **padded**) camminare con passo felpato

■ **pad out** *vt* gonfiare

padded bra *n* reggiseno *m* imbottito

padded cell *n* cella *f* con le pareti imbottite

padded envelope *n* busta *f* imbottita

padded shoulders *npl* spalline *fpl* imbottite

padding /ˈpædɪŋ/ *n* imbottitura *f*; (in written work) fronzoli *mpl*

paddle /ˈpædl/ **A** *n* pagaia *f*; **go for a ~** sguazzare
B *vt* (row) spingere remando
C *vi* (wade) sguazzare

paddling pool *n* (public) piscina *f* per bambini; (inflatable) piscina *f* gonfiabile

paddock /ˈpædək/ *n* recinto *m*

padlock /ˈpædlɒk/ **A** *n* lucchetto *m*
B *vt* chiudere con lucchetto

padre /ˈpɑːdreɪ/ *n* padre *m*

Padua /ˈpædjʊə/ *n* Padova *f*

paediatric /piːdɪˈætrɪk/ *adj* pediatrico

paediatrician /piːdɪəˈtrɪʃn/ *n* pediatra *mf*

paediatrics /piːdɪˈætrɪks/ *nsg* pediatria *fsg*

paedophile /ˈpiːdəʊfaɪl/ *n* pedofilo, -a *mf*

paedophilia /piːdəʊˈfɪlɪə/ *n* pedofilia *f*

pagan /ˈpeɪgən/ *adj & n* pagano, -a *mf*

paganism /ˈpeɪgənɪzm/ *n* paganesimo *m*

page¹ /peɪdʒ/ *n* pagina *f*

page² A *n* (boy) paggetto *m*; (in hotel) fattorino *m*
B *vt* far chiamare ‹*person*›

pageant /ˈpædʒənt/ *n* parata *f*

pageantry /ˈpædʒəntrɪ/ *n* cerimoniale *m*

pageboy /ˈpeɪdʒbɔɪ/ *n* (at wedding) paggio *m*

page proof *n* bozza *f* definitiva

pager /ˈpeɪdʒə(r)/ *n* cercapersone *m inv*

page three *n* BrE *terza pagina (f) di quotidiano scandalistico inglese con una pin-up*

p

page three girl *n* BrE pin-up *f inv*
paid /peɪd/ **A** ▸ **pay**
B *adj* ~ **employment** lavoro *m* remunerato; **put ~ to** mettere fine a
paid-up *adj* BrE ‹*member*› che ha pagato la sua quota; ‹*instalment*› versato
pail /peɪl/ *n* secchio *m*
pain /peɪn/ **A** *n* dolore *m*; **be in ~** soffrire; **take ~s to do something** fare il possible per fare qualcosa; **~ in the neck** infml rottura *f* di scatole; ‹*person*› rompiscatole *mf inv*
B *vt* fig addolorare
pained /peɪnd/ *adj* addolorato
painful /ˈpeɪnfʊl/ *adj* doloroso; (laborious) penoso
painfully /ˈpeɪnfʊlɪ/ *adv* ~ **shy** incredibilmente timido
painkiller /ˈpeɪnkɪlə(r)/ *n* calmante *m*
painkilling /ˈpeɪnkɪlɪŋ/ *adj* antinevralgico
painless /ˈpeɪnlɪs/ *adj* indolore
painlessly /ˈpeɪnlɪslɪ/ *adv* in modo indolore
painstaking /ˈpeɪnzteɪkɪŋ/ *adj* minuzioso
paint /peɪnt/ **A** *n* pittura *f*; **~s** *pl* colori *mpl*
B *vt & vi* pitturare; ‹*artist*› dipingere; **~ the town red** folleggiare
▪ **paint over** *vt* (cover with paint) coprire di vernice
paintbox /ˈpeɪntbɒks/ *n* scatola *f* di colori
paintbrush /ˈpeɪntbrʌʃ/ *n* pennello *m*
painter /ˈpeɪntə(r)/ *n* pittore, -trice mf; (decorator) imbianchino *m*
pain threshold *n* soglia *f* del dolore
painting /ˈpeɪntɪŋ/ *n* pittura *f*; (picture) dipinto *m*
paint pot *n* latta *f* di pittura
paint remover *n* sverniciante *m*
paint roller *n* rullo *m*
paint spray *n* pistola *f* a spruzzo
paint stripper *n* (tool) macchina *f* sverniciante; (chemical) sverniciante *m*
paintwork *n* pittura *f*
pair /peə(r)/ *n* paio *m*; (of people) coppia *f*; **a ~ of trousers/scissors** un paio di pantaloni/forbici
▪ **pair off** *vi* mettersi in coppia
▪ **pair up** *vi* ‹*dancers*› fare coppia; (for game) formare una coppia
paisley /ˈpeɪzlɪ/ *n* motivo *m* cachemire *inv*
pajamas /pəˈdʒɑːməz/ *npl* AmE = **pyjamas**
Pakistan /pɑːkɪˈstɑːn/ *n* Pakistan *m*
Pakistani /pɑːkɪˈstɑːnɪ/ *adj & n* pakistano, -a *mf*
pal /pæl/ *n* infml amico, -a *mf*
▪ **pal up** *vi* infml (become friends) fare amicizia (with con)
palace /ˈpælɪs/ *n* palazzo *m*
palaeontologist /pærɪənˈtɒlədʒɪst/ *n* paleontologo, -a *mf*
palaeontology /pælɪənˈtɒlədʒɪ/ *n* paleontologia *f*
palatable /ˈpælətəbl/ *adj* gradevole al gusto
palate /ˈpælət/ *n* palato *m*
palatial /pəˈleɪʃl/ *adj* sontuoso
palaver /pəˈlɑːvə(r)/ *n* infml (fuss) storie *fpl*
pale[1] /peɪl/ *n* (stake) palo *m*; **beyond the ~** fig inaccettabile
pale[2] **A** *adj* pallido
B *vi* impallidire; **~ into insignificance** diventare insignificante
paleness /ˈpeɪlnɪs/ *n* pallore *m*
Palestine /ˈpælɪstaɪn/ *n* Palestina *f*
Palestinian /pæləˈstɪnɪən/ *adj & n* palestinese *mf*
palette /ˈpælɪt/ *n* tavolozza *f*
palette knife *n* spatola *f*
paling /ˈpeɪlɪŋ/ *n* (stake) palo *m*; (fence) palizzata *f*
palisade /pælɪˈseɪd/ *n* (fence) palizzata *f*
pall /pɔːl/ **A** *n* drappo *m* funebre; fig velo *m* di tristezza; (of smoke) cappa *f*
B *vi* stufare
pallet /ˈpælɪt/ *n* pallet *m inv*
palliative /ˈpælɪətɪv/ *n* palliativo *m*
pallid /ˈpælɪd/ *adj* pallido
pallor /ˈpælə(r)/ *n* pallore *m*
palm /pɑːm/ *n* palmo *m*; (tree) palma *f*
▪ **palm off**: *vt* **~ something off on somebody** rifilare qualcosa a qualcuno
palmist /ˈpɑːmɪst/ *n* chiromante *mf*
palmistry /ˈpɑːmɪstrɪ/ *n* chiromanzia *f*
Palm Sunday *n* Domenica *f* delle Palme
palmtop, palmtop computer *n* Comput palmtop *m inv*
palpable /ˈpælpəbl/ *adj* palpabile; (perceptible) tangibile
palpate /pælˈpeɪt/ *vi* palpare
palpitate /ˈpælpɪteɪt/ *vi* palpitare
palpitations /pælpɪˈteɪʃnz/ *npl* palpitazioni *fpl*
paltry /ˈpɔːltrɪ/ *adj* (**-ier, -iest**) insignificante
pampas /ˈpæmpəs/ *n* pampas *fpl*
pamper /ˈpæmpə(r)/ *vt* viziare
pamphlet /ˈpæmflɪt/ *n* opuscolo *m*
pan /pæn/ **A** *n* tegame *m*, pentola *f*; (for frying) padella *f*; (of scales) piatto *m*
B *vt* (*pt/pp* **panned**) infml (criticize) stroncare
▪ **pan out** *vi* infml (develop) svilupparsi
panacea /pænəˈsiːə/ *n* panacea *f*
panache /pəˈnæʃ/ *n* stile *m*
Panama /ˈpænəmɑː/ *n* Panama *m*; **the ~ Canal** il canale di Panama
pancake /ˈpænkeɪk/ *n* crêpe *f inv*, frittella *f*
Pancake Day *n* martedì *m* grasso
pancreas /ˈpæŋkrɪəs/ *n* pancreas *m inv*
panda /ˈpændə/ *n* panda *m inv*
panda car *n* macchina *f* della polizia

parola chiave

pandemonium /pændɪ'məʊnɪəm/ *n* pandemonio *m*
pander /'pændə(r)/ *vi* ~ **to somebody** compiacere qualcuno
pane /peɪn/ *n* ~ **[of glass]** vetro *m*
panel /'pænl/ *n* pannello *m*; (group of people) giuria *f*; ~ **of experts** gruppo *m* di esperti; ~ **of judges** giuria *f*
panelling /'pænəlɪŋ/ *n* pannelli *mpl*
panellist /'pænəlɪst/ *n* Radio, TV partecipante *mf*
pan-fry *vt* friggere
pang /pæŋ/ *n* ~**s of hunger** morsi *mpl* della fame; ~**s of conscience** rimorsi *mpl* di coscienza
panhandler /'pænhændlə(r)/ *n* AmE infml mendicante *mf*
panic /'pænɪk/ **A** *n* panico *m*
B *vi* (*pt/pp* **panicked**) lasciarsi prendere dal panico
panic button *n* infml **hit the** ~ farsi prendere dal panico
panic buying *n* accaparramento *m*
panicky /'pænɪkɪ/ *adj* che si lascia prendere dal panico facilmente
panic-stricken /'pænɪkstrɪkən/ *adj* in preda al panico
pannier /'pænɪə(r)/ *n* (on bike) borsa *f*; (on mule) bisaccia *f*
panorama /pænə'rɑːmə/ *n* panorama *m*
panoramic /pænə'ræmɪk/ *adj* panoramico
pan scourer *n* paglietta *f*
pansy /'pænzɪ/ *n* viola *f* del pensiero; infml (effeminate man) finocchio *m*
pant /pænt/ *vi* ansimare
pantechnicon /pæn'teknɪkən/ *n* furgone *m* per traslochi
panther /'pænθə(r)/ *n* pantera *f*
panties /'pæntɪz/ *npl* AmE mutandine *fpl*
panting /'pæntɪŋ/ *adj* ansante
pantomime /'pæntəmaɪm/ *n* pantomima *f*
pantry /'pæntrɪ/ *n* dispensa *f*
pants /pænts/ *npl* (underwear) mutande *fpl*; (woman's) mutandine *fpl*; AmE (trousers) pantaloni *mpl*
panty girdle /'pæntɪ/ *n* guaina *f*
pantyhose *n* AmE collant *m inv*
panty liner *n* salvaslip *m inv*
papal /'peɪpl/ *adj* papale
paparazzi /pæpə'rætzɪ/ *npl* paparazzi *mpl*
paper /'peɪpə(r)/ **A** *n* carta *f*; (wallpaper) carta *f* da parati; (newspaper) giornale *m*; (exam) esame *m* scritto; (treatise) saggio *m*; ~**s** *pl* (documents) documenti *mpl*; (for identification) documento *msg* [d'identità]; **on** ~ in teoria; **put down on** ~ mettere per iscritto
B *attrib* di carta; (version) su carta
C *vt* tappezzare
■ **paper over**: *vt* ~ **over the cracks** dissimulare le divergenze

paperback *n* edizione *f* economica
paper bank *n* contenitore *m* per la raccolta della carta
paper boy *n* ragazzo *m* che recapita i giornali a domicilio
paper chain *n* festone *m* di carta
paper chase *n corsa (f) campestre in cui i partecipanti seguono una scia di pezzetti di carta*
paper clip *n* graffetta *f*
paper currency *n* banconote *fpl*
paper feed tray *n* Comput vassoio *m* della carta
paperknife *n* tagliacarte *m inv*
paper mill *n* cartiera *f*
paper money *n* cartamoneta *f*
paper napkin *n* tovagliolo *m* di carta
paper round *n* **he does a** ~ recapita i giornali a domicilio
paper shop *n* edicola *f*
paper shredder *n* distruttore *m* di documenti
paper-thin *adj* sottilissimo
paper towel *n* (toilet) asciugamano *m* di carta; (kitchen) carta *f* asciugatutto
paper-weight *n* fermacarte *m inv*
paperwork *n* lavoro *m* d'ufficio
papery /'peɪpərɪ/ *adj* ‹*texture, leaves*› cartaceo
paprika /pə'priːkə/ *n* paprica *f*
Papua New Guinea *n* Papua Nuova Guinea *f*
par /pɑː(r)/ *n* (in golf) par *m inv*; **on a** ~ **with** alla pari con; **feel below** ~ essere un po' giù di tono
para¹ /'pærə/ *n* (paragraph) paragrafo *m*
para² *n* BrE Mil para *m inv*
parable /'pærəbl/ *n* parabola *f*
parachute /'pærəʃuːt/ **A** *n* paracadute *m inv*
B *vi* lanciarsi col paracadute
parachute drop *n* (of supplies) lancio *m* col paracadute
parachute jump *n* lancio *m* col paracadute
parachuting /'pærəʃuːtɪŋ/ *n* paracadutismo *m*
parachutist /'pærəʃuːtɪst/ *n* paracadutista *mf*
parade /pə'reɪd/ **A** *n* (military) parata *f* militare; (display) sfoggio *m*
B *vi* sfilare
C *vt* (show off) far sfoggio di
parade ground *n* piazza *f* d'armi
paradigm /'pærədaɪm/ *n* paradigma *m*
paradise /'pærədaɪs/ *n* paradiso *m*
paradox /'pærədɒks/ *n* paradosso *m*
paradoxical /pærə'dɒksɪkl/ *adj* paradossale
paradoxically /pærə'dɒksɪklɪ/ *adv* paradossalmente
paraffin /'pærəfɪn/ *n* paraffina *f*; (oil) cherosene *m*
paragliding /'pærəglaɪdɪŋ/ *n* parapendio *m*

paragon /'pærəgən/ *n* ~ **of virtue** modello *m* di virtù

⚷ **paragraph** /'pærəgrɑːf/ *n* paragrafo *m*

Paraguay /'pærəgwaɪ/ *n* Paraguay *m*

parallel /'pærəlel/ **A** *adj & adv* parallelo **B** *n* Geog fig parallelo *m*; (line) parallela *f* **C** *vt* essere paragonabile a

parallel bars *npl* parallele *fpl*

parallelogram /pærə'leləʊgræm/ *n* Math parallelogramma *m*

parallel port *n* Comput porta *f* parallela

Paralympics /pærə'lɪmpɪks/ *npl* Paraolimpiadi *fpl*

paralyse /'pærəlaɪz/ *vt* paralizzare

paralysis /pə'ræləsɪs/ *n* (*pl* **-ses** /pə'ræləsiːz/) paralisi *f inv*

paralytic /pærə'lɪtɪk/ *adj* ‹*person*› paralitico; ‹*arm, leg*› paralizzato; BrE infml (drunk) ubriaco fradicio

paramedic /pærə'medɪk/ *n* paramedico *m*

parameter /pə'ræmɪtə(r)/ *n* parametro *m*

paramilitary /pærə'mɪlɪtrɪ/ **A** *n* appartenente *mf* ad un gruppo paramilitare **B** *adj* paramilitare

paramount /'pærəmaʊnt/ *adj* supremo; **be** ~ essere essenziale

paranoia /pærə'nɔɪə/ *n* paranoia *f*

paranoid /'pærənɔɪd/ *adj* paranoico

paranormal /pærə'nɔːməl/ *adj & n* paranormale *m*

parapet /'pærəpɪt/ *n* parapetto *m*

paraphernalia /pærəfə'neɪlɪə/ *n* armamentario *m*

paraphrase /'pærəfreɪz/ **A** *n* parafrasi *f inv* **B** *vt* parafrasare

paraplegic /pærə'pliːdʒɪk/ *adj & n* paraplegico, -a *mf*

parascending /'pærəsendɪŋ/ *n* BrE paracadutismo *m* ascensionale

parasite /'pærəsaɪt/ *n* parassita *m*

parasitic /pærə'sɪtɪk/ *adj* parassitario

parasol /'pærəsɒl/ *n* parasole *m*

paratrooper /'pærətruːpə(r)/ *n* paracadutista *mf*

parboil /'pɑːbɔɪl/ *vt* scottare

parcel /'pɑːsl/ *n* pacco *m*

■ **parcel up** *vt* impacchettare ‹*clothes etc*›

parcel bomb *n* pacco *m* bomba *inv*

parch /pɑːtʃ/ *vt* disseccare; **be ~ed** ‹*person*› morire dalla sete

parched /pɑːtʃt/ *adj* ‹*land*› riarso; (thirsty) **I'm** ~ sto morendo di sete

parchment /'pɑːtʃmənt/ *n* pergamena *f*

pardon /'pɑːdn/ **A** *n* perdono *m*; Jur grazia *f*; **~?** prego?; **I beg your ~?** fml chiedo scusa?; **I do beg your** ~ (sorry) chiedo scusa! **B** *vt* perdonare; Jur graziare

pare /peə(r)/ *vt* (peel) pelare

⚷ parola chiave

⚷ **parent** /'peərənt/ *n* genitore *m*

parentage /'peərəntɪdʒ/ *n* natali *mpl*

parental /pə'rentl/ *adj* dei genitori

parent company *n* casa *f* madre

parenthesis /pə'renθəsɪs/ *n* (*pl* **-ses** /pə'renθəsiːz/) parentesi *f inv*

parenthood /'peərənthʊd/ *n* (fatherhood) paternità *f*; (motherhood) maternità *f*

parenting /'peərəntɪŋ/ *n* educazione *f* dei figli; ~ **classes** *corsi di sostegno pratico e psicologico per nuovi genitori*

parents' evening *n* riunione *f* dei genitori degli alunni

parer /'peərə(r)/ *n* pelapatate *m*

pariah /pə'raɪə/ *n* paria *mf*

parings /'peərɪŋz/ *npl* (of fruit) bucce *fpl*; (of nails) ritagli *mpl* di unghie

Paris /'pærɪs/ *n* Parigi *f*

parish /'pærɪʃ/ *n* parrocchia *f*

parishioner /pə'rɪʃənə(r)/ *n* parrocchiano, -a *mf*

parish priest *n* (Catholic) parroco *m*; (Protestant) pastore *m*

Parisian /pə'rɪzɪən/ *adj & n* parigino, -a *mf*

parity /'pærətɪ/ *n* parità *f*

⚷ **park** /pɑːk/ **A** *n* parco *m* **B** *vt* Auto posteggiare, parcheggiare; ~ **oneself** infml installarsi **C** *vi* posteggiare, parcheggiare

parka /'pɑːkə/ *n* parka *m inv*

park-and-ride *n parcheggio (m) collegato al centro di una città da mezzi pubblici*

parking /'pɑːkɪŋ/ *n* parcheggio *m*, posteggio *m*; **'no ~'** 'divieto di sosta'

parking attendant *n* parcheggiatore, -trice *mf*, posteggiatore, -trice *mf*

parking lot *n* AmE posteggio *m*, parcheggio *m*

parking meter *n* parchimetro *m*

parking space *n* posteggio *m*, parcheggio *m*

parkland *n* parco *m*

park ranger, **park warden** *n* guardaparco *m inv*

⚷ **parliament** /'pɑːləmənt/ *n* parlamento *m*

parliamentary /pɑːlə'mentərɪ/ *adj* parlamentare

parlour /'pɑːlə(r)/ *n* salotto *m*

parochial /pə'rəʊkɪəl/ *adj* parrocchiale; fig ristretto

parochialism /pə'rəʊkɪəlɪzm/ *n* campanilismo *m*

parody /'pærədɪ/ **A** *n* parodia *f* **B** *vt* (*pt/pp* **-ied**) parodiare

parole /pə'rəʊl/ **A** *n* **on** ~ sulla parola; **eligible for** ~ suscettibile di essere liberato sulla parola **B** *vt* mettere in libertà sulla parola

paroxysm /'pærəksɪzm/ *n* accesso *m*

parquet floor /'pɑːkeɪ/ *n* parquet *m inv*

parquet flooring /ˈflɔːrɪŋ/ *n* parquet *m inv*

parrot /ˈpærət/ *n* pappagallo *m*

parry /ˈpærɪ/ *vt* (*pt/pp* **-ied**) parare ‹*blow*›; (in fencing) eludere

parse /pɑːz/ *vt* fare l'analisi grammaticale di ‹*sentence*›; Comput analizzare la sintassi di

parsimonious /pɑːsɪˈməʊnɪəs/ *adj* parsimonioso

parsing /ˈpɑːzɪŋ/ *n* analisi *f* grammaticale; Comput analisi *f* sintattica

parsley /ˈpɑːslɪ/ *n* prezzemolo *m*

parsnip /ˈpɑːsnɪp/ *n* pastinaca *f*

parson /ˈpɑːsn/ *n* pastore *m*

part /pɑːt/ **A** *n* parte *f*; (of machine) pezzo *m*; **for my ~** per quanto mi riguarda; **on the ~ of** da parte di; **take sb's ~** prendere le parti di qualcuno; **take ~ in** prendere parte a
B *adv* in parte
C *vt* **~ one's hair** farsi la riga
D *vi* ‹*people*› separarsi; **~ with** separarsi da

part exchange *n* **take in ~** prendere indietro come pagamento parziale

partial /ˈpɑːʃl/ *adj* parziale; **be ~ to** aver un debole per

partiality /pɑːʃɪˈælətɪ/ *n* (liking) predilezione *f*

partially /ˈpɑːʃəlɪ/ *adv* parzialmente; **~ sighted** ipovedente

participant /pɑːˈtɪsɪpənt/ *n* partecipante *mf*

participate /pɑːˈtɪsɪpeɪt/ *vi* partecipare (in a)

participation /pɑːtɪsɪˈpeɪʃn/ *n* partecipazione *f*

participatory /pɑːtɪsɪˈpeɪtərɪ/ *adj* partecipativo

participle /pɑːˈtɪsɪpl/ *n* participio *m*; **present/past ~** participio presente/passato

particle /ˈpɑːtɪkl/ *n* Phys, Gram particella *f*

particular /pəˈtɪkjʊlə(r)/ *adj* particolare; (precise) meticoloso; derog difficile; **in ~** in particolare

particularly /pəˈtɪkjʊləlɪ/ *adv* particolarmente

particulars /pəˈtɪkjʊləz/ *npl* particolari *mpl*

parting /ˈpɑːtɪŋ/ **A** *n* separazione *f*; (in hair) scriminatura *f*
B *attrib* di commiato

partisan /pɑːtɪˈzæn/ *n* partigiano, -a *mf*

partition /pɑːˈtɪʃn/ **A** *n* (wall) parete *f* divisoria; Pol divisione *f*
B *vt* dividere
■ **partition off** *vt* separare

partly /ˈpɑːtlɪ/ *adv* in parte

partner /ˈpɑːtnə(r)/ *n* Comm socio, -a *mf*; (sport, in relationship) compagno, -a *mf*

partnership /ˈpɑːtnəʃɪp/ *n* Comm società *f*

part of speech *n* categoria *f* grammaticale

part owner *n* comproprietario, -a *mf*

part payment *n* acconto *m*

partridge /ˈpɑːtrɪdʒ/ *n* pernice *f*

part-time *adj & adv* part time; **be** *or* **work ~** lavorare part time

part-way *adv* **~ through the evening** a metà serata

party /ˈpɑːtɪ/ *n* ricevimento *m*, festa *f*; (group) gruppo *m*; Pol partito *m*; Jur parte *f*; **be ~ to** essere parte attiva in

party animal *n* festaiolo, -a *mf*

party dress *n* abito *m* da sera

party-goer *n* festaiolo, -a *mf*

party hat *n* cappellino *m* di carta

party leader *n* dirigente *m* di partito

party line *n* Teleph duplex *m inv*; Pol linea *f* del partito

party piece *n* pezzo *m* forte; **do one's ~** esibirsi nel proprio pezzo forte

party political broadcast *n comunicato (m) di partito (trasmesso per radio o per televisione)*

party politics *npl* politica *fpl* di partito

party wall *n* muro *m* divisorio

pass /pɑːs/ **A** *n* lasciapassare *m inv*; (in mountains) passo *m*; Sport passaggio *m*; Sch (mark) voto *m*, sufficiente *m*; **get a ~** Sch ottenere la sufficienza; **make a ~ at** infml fare delle avances a
B *vt* passare; (overtake) sorpassare; (approve) far passare; (exceed) oltrepassare; fare ‹*remark*›; esprimere ‹*judgement*›; Jur pronunciare ‹*sentence*›; **~ water** orinare; **~ the time** passare il tempo
C *vi* passare; (in exam) essere promosso; **let something ~** fig lasciar correre qualcosa; **~!** (in game) passo!
■ **pass as** *vt* = **pass for**
■ **pass away** *vi* mancare
■ **pass by** *vi* (go past) passare
■ **pass down** *vt* passare; fig trasmettere
■ **pass for** *vt* (be accepted as) passare per
■ **pass off** **A** *vi* (disappear) passare; (take place) svolgersi
B *vt* **~ somebody/something off as** far passare qualcuno/qualcosa per
■ **pass on** *vt* passare ‹*message, information*›
■ **pass on to** *vt* passare a ‹*new subject, next question*›
■ **pass out** *vi* infml svenire
■ **pass over** **A** *vt* (not mention) passare sopra a; **~ somebody over for promotion** non prendere in considerazione qualcuno per una promozione
B *vi* (die) spirare
■ **pass round** *vt* far passare
■ **pass through** *vt* attraversare
■ **pass up** *vt* passare; infml (miss) lasciarsi scappare

passable /ˈpɑːsəbl/ *adj* ‹*road*› praticabile; (satisfactory) passabile

passage /ˈpæsɪdʒ/ *n* passaggio *m*; (corridor) corridoio *m*; (voyage) traversata *f*

pass book *n* Fin libretto *m* di risparmio

passé /pæˈseɪ/ *adj* derog sorpassato

passenger /ˈpæsɪndʒə(r)/ *n* passeggero, -a *mf*
passenger compartment *n* BrE Auto abitacolo *m*
passenger ferry *n* traghetto *m*
passenger plane *n* aereo *m* passeggeri
passenger seat *n* posto *m* accanto al guidatore
passenger train *n* treno *m* passeggeri
passepartout /pæspɑːˈtuː/ *n* (key, frame) passe-partout *m inv*
passer-by /pɑːsəˈbaɪ/ *n* (*pl* **-s-by**) passante *mf*
passing /ˈpɑːsɪŋ, AmE ˈpæs-/ *adj* ‹*motorist*› di passaggio; ‹*thought*› di sfuggita; ‹*reference*› en passant; ‹*resemblance*› vago
passing place /ˈpɑːsɪŋ/ *n piazzola (f) di sosta per consentire il transito dei veicoli nei due sensi*
passing shot *n* Tennis passante *m*
passion /ˈpæʃn/ *n* passione *f*
passionate /ˈpæʃənət/ *adj* appassionato
passionately /ˈpæʃənətlɪ/ *adv* appassionatamente
passion fruit *n* frutto *m* della passione
passive /ˈpæsɪv/ *adj & n* passivo *m*
passively /ˈpæsɪvlɪ/ *adv* passivamente
passiveness /ˈpæsɪvnɪs/ *n* passività *f*
passive resistance *n* resistenza *f* passiva
passive smoking *n* fumo *m* passivo
pass key *n* (master key) passe-partout *m inv*; (for access) chiave *f*
pass mark *n* Sch [voto *m*] sufficiente *m*
Passover *n* Pasqua *f* ebraica
passport *n* passaporto *m*
password *n* parola *f* d'ordine; password *f inv*
password-protected *adj* Comput ‹*file, site*› protetto da password
past /pɑːst/ **A** *adj* passato; (former) ex; **that's all ~** tutto questo è passato; **in the ~ few days** nei giorni scorsi; **the ~ week** la settimana scorsa
B *n* passato *m*
C *prep* oltre; **at ten ~two** alle due e dieci
D *adv* oltre; **go/come ~** passare
pasta /ˈpæstə/ *n* pasta [asciutta] *f*
paste /peɪst/ **A** *n* pasta *f*; (dough) impasto *m*; (adhesive) colla *f*
B *vt* incollare
■ **paste down** *vt* incollare
■ **paste in** *vt* incollare
■ **paste up** *vt* affiggere ‹*notice, poster*›
paste jewellery *n* bigiotteria *f*
pastel /ˈpæstl/ **A** *n* pastello *m*
B *attrib* pastello *inv*
pasteurization /pɑːstʃəraɪˈzeɪʃn/ *n* pastorizzazione *f*
pasteurize /ˈpɑːstʃəraɪz/ *vt* pastorizzare
pasteurized /ˈpɑːstʃəraɪzd/ *adj* pastorizzato

parola chiave

pastille /ˈpæstɪl/ *n* pastiglia *f*
pastime /ˈpɑːstaɪm/ *n* passatempo *m*
pasting /ˈpeɪstɪŋ/ *n* infml (defeat, criticism) batosta *f*
past master *n* esperto, -a *mf*
pastor /ˈpɑːstə(r)/ *n* pastore *m*
pastoral /ˈpɑːstərəl/ *adj* pastorale
past participle *n* participio *m* passato
pastrami /pæˈstrɑːmɪ/ *n carne (f) di manzo affumicata*
pastry /ˈpeɪstrɪ/ *n* pasta *f*; **pastries** *pl* pasticcini *mpl*
past tense *n* passato *m*
pasture /ˈpɑːstʃə/ *n* pascolo *m*
pasty¹ /ˈpæstɪ/ *n* ≈ pasticcio *m*
pasty² /ˈpeɪstɪ/ *adj* smorto
pat /pæt/ **A** *n* buffetto *m*; (of butter) pezzetto *m*
B *adv* **have something off ~** conoscere qualcosa a menadito
C *vt* (*pt/pp* **patted**) dare un buffetto a; **~ somebody on the back** fig congratularsi con qualcuno
patch /pætʃ/ **A** *n* toppa *f*; (spot) chiazza *f*; (period) periodo *m*; **not a ~ on** infml molto inferiore a
B *vt* mettere una toppa su
■ **patch up** *vt* riparare alla bell'e meglio; appianare ‹*quarrel*›
patchwork /ˈpætʃwɜːk/ *n* patchwork *m inv*; fig mosaico *m*
patchy /ˈpætʃɪ/ *adj* incostante
pâté /ˈpæteɪ/ *n* pâté *m inv*
patent /ˈpeɪtnt/ **A** *adj* palese
B *n* brevetto *m*
C *vt* brevettare
patent leather *n* vernice *f*
patently /ˈpeɪtəntlɪ/ *adv* in modo palese
paternal /pəˈtɜːnl/ *adj* paterno
paternalism /pəˈtɜːnəlɪzm/ *n* paternalismo *m*
paternalistic /pətɜːnəˈlɪstɪk/ *adj* paternalistico
paternity /pəˈtɜːnətɪ/ *n* paternità *f*
paternity leave *n* congedo *m* di paternità
paternity suit *n* causa *f* per il riconoscimento di paternità
path /pɑːθ/ *n* (*pl* **~s** /pɑːðz/) sentiero *m*; (orbit) traiettoria *f*; fig strada *f*
pathetic /pəˈθetɪk/ *adj* patetico; infml (very bad) penoso
pathological /pæθəˈlɒdʒɪkl/ *adj* patologico
pathologist /pəˈθɒlədʒɪst/ *n* patologo, -a *mf*
pathology /pəˈθɒlədʒɪ/ *n* patologia *f*
pathos /ˈpeɪθɒs/ *n* pathos *m*
patience /ˈpeɪʃns/ *n* pazienza *f*; (game) solitario *m*
patient /ˈpeɪʃnt/ *adj & n* paziente *mf*
patiently /ˈpeɪʃntlɪ/ *adv* pazientemente
patio /ˈpætɪəʊ/ *n* terrazza *f*
patio doors *npl* portafinestra *f*

patio garden *n* cortile *m*
patriarch /ˈpeɪtrɪɑːk/ *n* patriarca *m*
patriarchal /ˈpeɪtrɪˈɑːkəl/ *adj* patriarcale
patriarchy /ˈpeɪtrɪɑːkɪ/ *n* patriarcato *m*
patriot /ˈpætrɪət/ *n* patriota *mf*
patriotic /pætrɪˈɒtɪk/ *adj* patriottico
patriotism /ˈpætrɪətɪzm/ *n* patriottismo *m*
patrol /pəˈtrəʊl/ **A** *n* pattuglia *f* **B** *vt & vi* pattugliare
patrol boat *n* motovedetta *f*
patrol car *n* autopattuglia *f*
patron /ˈpeɪtrən/ *n* patrono *m*; (of charity) benefattore, -trice *mf*; (of the arts) mecenate *mf*; (customer) cliente *mf*
patronage /ˈpætrənɪdʒ/ *n* patrocinio *m*; (of shop etc) frequentazione *f*
patronize /ˈpætrənaɪz/ *vt* frequentare abitualmente; fig trattare con condiscendenza
patronizing /ˈpætrənaɪzɪŋ/ *adj* condiscendente
patronizingly /ˈpætrənaɪzɪŋlɪ/ *adv* con condiscendenza
patron saint *n* [santo, -a *mf*] patrono, -a *mf*
patter[1] /ˈpætə(r)/ **A** *n* picchiettio *m* **B** *vi* picchiettare
patter[2] *n* (of salesman) chiacchiere *fpl*
pattern /ˈpætn/ *n* motivo *m*; (for knitting, sewing, in behaviour) modello *m*
patterned /ˈpætənd/ *adj* ‹*material*› fantasia
paunch /pɔːntʃ/ *n* pancia *f*
pauper /ˈpɔːpə(r)/ *n* povero, -a *mf*
pause /pɔːz/ **A** *n* pausa *f* **B** *vi* fare una pausa
pave /peɪv/ *vt* pavimentare; ~ **the way** preparare la strada (**for** a)
pavement /ˈpeɪvmənt/ *n* marciapiede *m*
pavement café *n* caffè *m* con tavolini all'aperto
pavilion /pəˈvɪljən/ *n* padiglione *m*; Cricket *costruzione (f) annessa al campo da gioco con gli spogliatoi*
paving /ˈpeɪvɪŋ/ *n* lastricato *m*
paving slab, **paving stone** *n* lastra *f* di pietra
paw /pɔː/ **A** *n* zampa *f* **B** *vt* infml mettere le zampe addosso a
pawn[1] /pɔːn/ *n* (in chess) pedone *m*; fig pedina *f*
pawn[2] **A** *vt* impegnare **B** *n* **in** ~ in pegno
pawnbroker /ˈpɔːnbrəʊkə(r)/ *n* prestatore, -trice *mf* su pegno
pawnshop /ˈpɔːnʃɒp/ *n* monte *m* di pietà
pawpaw /ˈpɔːpɔː/ *n* papaia *f*
pay /peɪ/ **A** *n* paga *f*; **in the** ~ **of** al soldo di **B** *vt* (*pt/pp* **paid**) pagare; prestare ‹*attention*›; fare ‹*compliment; visit*›; ~ **cash** pagare in contanti **C** *vi* pagare; (be profitable) rendere; **it doesn't** ~ **to** ... fig è fatica sprecata ...; ~ **in instalments** pagare a rate; ~ **through the nose** infml pagare profumatamente
■ **pay back** *vt* ripagare
■ **pay for** *vt* pagare per
■ **pay in** *vt* versare
■ **pay off** **A** *vt* saldare ‹*debt*› **B** *vi* fig dare dei frutti
■ **pay out** *vt* (spend) pagare
■ **pay up** *vi* pagare
payable /ˈpeɪəbl/ *adj* pagabile; **make** ~ **to** intestare a
pay-as-you-go *adj* ‹*tariff*› a consumo
pay cheque BrE, **pay check** AmE *n* assegno *m* della paga
pay day *n* giorno *m* di paga
PAYE BrE *abbr* (**pay-as-you-earn**) *trattenute (fpl) fiscali alla fonte*
payee /peɪˈiː/ *n* beneficiario *m*
payer /ˈpeɪə(r)/ *n* pagante *mf*
paying in slip /peɪɪŋˈɪn/ *n* distinta *f* di versamento
payload /ˈpeɪləʊd/ *n* (of bomb) carica *f* esplosiva; (of aircraft, ship) carico *m* utile
payment /ˈpeɪmənt/ *n* pagamento *m*; ~ **by instalments** pagamento *m* rateale
pay packet *n* busta *f* paga *inv*
pay-per-view *n* pay per view *f*; ~ **programme/film** un film/programma pay per view
payphone *n* telefono *m* pubblico
payroll *n* (list) libro *m* paga; (sum of money) paga *f* del personale; (employees collectively) personale *m*
payslip *n* busta *f* paga *inv*
pay television *n* pay tv *f*
paywall /ˈpeɪwɔːl/ *n* paywall *m inv*, consultazione *f* online a pagamento
pc *abbr* **1** (**per cent**) per cento **2** (**politically correct**) politicamente corretto **3** (**postcard**) cartolina *f* postale
PC *abbr* **1** (**personal computer**) PC *m inv* **2** (**police constable**) agente *m* di polizia
pd *abbr* AmE (**police department**) dipartimento *m* di polizia
PDF *abbr* (**portable document format**) Comput PDF *m*; **a** ~ **file** un file PDF
PE *n abbr* (**physical education**) educazione *f* fisica
pea /piː/ *n* pisello *m*
peace /piːs/ *n* pace *f*; ~ **of mind** tranquillità *f*
peaceable /ˈpiːsəbl/ *adj* pacifico
peace envoy *n* mediatore, -trice *mf*
peaceful /ˈpiːsfʊl/ *adj* calmo, sereno
peacefully /ˈpiːsfʊlɪ/ *adv* in pace
peacekeeping **A** *n* Mil, Pol mantenimento *m* della pace **B** *attrib* ‹*force, troops*› di mantenimento della pace
peacemaker *n* mediatore, -trice *mf*
peace process *n* processo *m* di pace

peacetime **A** *n* tempo *m* di pace
B *attrib* ‹*planning, government*› del tempo di pace; ‹*army, alliance, training*› in tempo di pace

peace treaty *n* trattato *m* di pace

peach /piːtʃ/ *n* pesca *f*; (tree) pesco *m*

peacock /ˈpiːkɒk/ *n* pavone *m*

pea green *adj* verde pisello *inv*

peak /piːk/ *n* picco *m*; fig culmine *m*

peaked /piːkt/ *adj* AmE malaticcio

peaked cap /piːkt/ *n* berretto *m* a punta

peak hours *npl* ore *fpl* di punta

peak period *n* ora *f* di punta

peak rate *n* tariffa *f* ore di punta; **~ calls** Teleph chiamate a tariffa ore di punta

peak season *n* alta stagione *f*

peak time *n* = **prime time**

peaky /ˈpiːkɪ/ *adj* BrE malaticcio

peal /piːl/ *n* (of bells) scampanio *m*; **~s of laughter** fragore *msg* di risate

peanut /ˈpiːnʌt/ *n* arachide *f*, nocciolina *f* [americana]; **~s** *pl* infml miseria *fsg*

peanut butter *n* burro *m* di arachidi

pear /peə(r)/ *n* pera *f*; (tree) pero *m*

pearl /pɜːl/ *n* perla *f*

pearl barley *n* orzo *m* perlato

pearl diver *n* pescatore, -trice *mf* di perle

pearl grey **A** *n* grigio *m* perla *inv*
B *adj* grigio perla *inv*

Pearly Gates /pɜːlɪ/ *npl* hum porte *fpl* del paradiso

peasant /ˈpeznt/ *n* contadino, -a *mf*

peat /piːt/ *n* torba *f*

pebble /ˈpebl/ *n* ciottolo *m*

pebble-dash *n* intonaco *m* a pinocchino

pecan /ˈpiːkən/ *n* (tree) pecan *m inv*; (nut) noce *f* pecan *inv*

peck /pek/ **A** *n* beccata *f*; (kiss) bacetto *m*
B *vt* beccare; (kiss) dare un bacetto a
■ **peck at** *vi* beccare

pecking order /ˈpekɪŋ/ *n* gerarchia *f*

peckish /ˈpekɪʃ/ *adj* **be ~** infml avere un languorino allo stomaco

pecs /peks/ infml **pectorals** /ˈpektərəlz/ *npl* pettorali *mpl*

pectoral /ˈpektərəl/ *adj & n* pettorale *m*

peculiar /pɪˈkjuːlɪə(r)/ *adj* strano; (special) particolare; **~ to** tipico di

peculiarity /pɪkjuːlɪˈærətɪ/ *n* stranezza *f*; (feature) particolarità *f*

peculiarly /pɪˈkjuːlɪəlɪ/ *adv* singolarmente

pecuniary /pəˈkjuːnɪərɪ/ *adj* pecuniario

pedagogical /pedəˈgɒdʒɪkl/ *adj* pedagogico

pedagogy /ˈpedəgɒdʒɪ/ *n* pedagogia *f*

pedal /ˈpedl/ **A** *n* pedale *m*
B *vi* pedalare

pedal bin *n* pattumiera *f* a pedale

pedant /ˈpedənt/ *n* pedante *m*

pedantic /pɪˈdæntɪk/ *adj* pedante

pedantically /pɪˈdæntɪklɪ/ *adv* in modo pedante

pedantry /ˈpedəntrɪ/ *n* pedanteria *f*

peddle /ˈpedl/ *vt* vendere porta a porta

pedestal /ˈpedɪstl/ *n* piedistallo *m*

pedestrian /pɪˈdestrɪən/ **A** *n* pedone *m*
B *adj* fig scadente

pedestrian crossing *n* passaggio *m* pedonale

pedestrian precinct *n* zona *f* pedonale

pediatrician /ˌpiːdɪəˈtrɪʃn/ *n* AmE = **paediatrician**

pedicure /ˈpedɪkjʊə(r)/ *n* pedicure *f inv*

pedigree /ˈpedɪgriː/ **A** *n* pedigree *m inv*; (of person) lignaggio *m*
B *attrib* ‹*animal*› di razza, con pedigree

pedlar, **peddler** /ˈpedlə(r)/ *n* (old) venditore, -trice *mf* ambulante; **drug ~** spacciatore, -trice *mf* di droga

pedophile /ˈpedəfaɪl/ *n* AmE = **paedophile**

pee /piː/ infml **A** *vi* (*pt/pp* **peed**) fare la pipì
B *n* **go for a ~** andare a fare la pipì

peek /piːk/ infml **A** *vi* sbirciare
B *n* **take a ~ at something** dare una sbirciata a qualcosa

peekaboo /piːkəˈbuː/ *int* cucù

peel /piːl/ **A** *n* buccia *f*
B *vt* sbucciare
C *vi* ‹*nose etc*› spellarsi; ‹*paint*› staccarsi
■ **peel off** **A** *vt* togliersi ‹*item of clothing*›
B *vi* ‹*wallpaper*› staccarsi; ‹*skin*› squamarsi

peeler /ˈpiːlə(r)/ *n* sbucciatore *m*

peelings /ˈpiːlɪŋz/ *npl* bucce *fpl*

peep /piːp/ **A** *n* sbirciata *f*
B *vi* sbirciare

peephole /ˈpiːphəʊl/ *n* spioncino *m*

Peeping Tom /ˈpiːpɪŋ/ *n* infml guardone *m*

peer¹ /pɪə(r)/ *vi* **~ at** scrutare

peer² *n* nobile *m*; **his ~s** *pl* (in rank) i suoi pari; (in age) i suoi coetanei

peerage /ˈpɪərɪdʒ/ *n* BrE Pol nobiltà *f*; (book) almanacco *m* nobiliare; **be given a ~** essere elevato al rango di pari

peer group *n* (of same status) pari *mpl*; (of same age) coetanei *mpl*; **~ pressure** *pressione (f) esercitata dal gruppo cui si appartiene*

peerless /ˈpɪəlɪs/ *adj* impareggiabile

peeved /piːvd/ *adj* infml irritato

peevish /ˈpiːvɪʃ/ *adj* infml irritabile

peg /peg/ **A** *n* (hook) piolo *m*; (for tent) picchetto *m*; (for clothes) molletta *f*; **off the ~** infml prêt-à-porter
B *vt* (*pt/pp* **pegged**) fissare ‹*prices*›; stendere con le mollette ‹*washing*›

pegboard /ˈpegbɔːd/ *n* segnapunti *m inv*

pejorative /pɪˈdʒɒrətɪv/ *adj* peggiorativo

pejoratively /pɪˈdʒɒrətɪvlɪ/ *adv* in modo peggiorativo

peke /piːk/ *n* infml (dog) pechinese *mf*
Pekinese /piːkɪˈniːz/ *n* pechinese *mf*
Peking /piːkɪŋ/ *n* Pechino *f*
pelican /pelɪkən/ *n* pellicano *m*
pelican crossing *n* passaggio *m* pedonale con semaforo
pellet /ˈpelɪt/ *n* pallottola *f*
pell-mell /pelˈmel/ *adv* alla rinfusa
pelmet /ˈpelmɪt/ *n* mantovana *f*
pelt[1] /pelt/ *n* (skin) pelliccia *f*
pelt[2] **A** *vt* bombardare
B *vi* infml (run fast) catapultarsi; (rain heavily) venir giù a fiotti
▪ **pelt along** *vi* (move quickly) precipitarsi lungo
▪ **pelt down** *vi* ‹*rain*› venir giù a fiotti
pelvis /ˈpelvɪs/ *n* Anat bacino *m*
pen[1] /pen/ *n* (for animals) recinto *m*
pen[2] *n* penna *f*; (ball-point) penna *f* a sfera
penal /ˈpiːnl/ *adj* penale
penal code *n* codice *m* penale
penalize /ˈpiːnəlaɪz/ *vt* penalizzare
penalty /ˈpenltɪ/ *n* sanzione *f*; (fine) multa *f*; (in football) [calcio *m* di] rigore *m*
penalty area, **penalty box** *n* area *f* di rigore
penalty clause *n* Comm, Jur clausola *f* penale
penalty kick *n* [calcio *m* di] rigore *m*
penalty shoot-out *n* rigori *mpl*
penance /ˈpenəns/ *n* penitenza *f*
pence /pens/ ▸ **penny**
penchant /ˈpɒ̃ʃɒ̃/ *n* debole *m*
pencil /ˈpensl/ **A** *n* matita *f*
B *vt* (*pt/pp* **pencilled**) scrivere a matita
▪ **pencil in** *vt* annotare provvisoriamente ‹*date*›
pencil case *n* [astuccio *m*] portamatite *m inv*
pencil sharpener *n* temperamatite *m inv*
pendant /ˈpendənt/ *n* ciondolo *m*
pending /ˈpendɪŋ/ **A** *adj* in sospeso
B *prep* in attesa di
pendulum /ˈpendjʊləm/ *n* pendolo *m*
penetrate /ˈpenɪtreɪt/ *vt & vi* penetrare
penetrating /ˈpenɪtreɪtɪŋ/ *adj* ‹*sound, stare*› penetrante; ‹*remark*› acuto
penetration /penɪˈtreɪʃn/ *n* penetrazione *f*
penfriend /ˈpenfrend/ *n* amico, -a *mf* di penna
penguin /ˈpeŋgwɪn/ *n* pinguino *m*
penicillin /penɪˈsɪlɪn/ *n* penicillina *f*
peninsula /pɪˈnɪnsjʊlə/ *n* penisola *f*
penis /ˈpiːnɪs/ *n* pene *m*
penitence /ˈpenɪtəns/ *n* penitenza *f*
penitent /ˈpenɪtənt/ *adj & n* penitente *mf*
penitentiary /penɪˈtenʃərɪ/ *n* AmE penitenziario *m*
penknife /ˈpennaɪf/ *n* temperino *m*
pen-name *n* pseudonimo *m*
pennant /ˈpenənt/ *n* bandiera *f*
penniless /ˈpenɪlɪs/ *adj* senza un soldo
penny /ˈpenɪ/ *n* (*pl* **pence**; *single coins* **pennies**) penny *m*; AmE centesimo *m*; **spend a ~** infml andare in bagno; **the ~'s dropped!** infml ci è arrivato!
penny-farthing *n* velocipede *m*
penny-pinching /ˈpenɪpɪntʃɪŋ/ **A** *adj* taccagno
B *n* taccagneria *f*
penny whistle *n* zufolo *m*
pen-pusher *n* infml scribacchino, -a *mf*
pension /ˈpenʃn/ *n* pensione *f*
▪ **pension off** *vt* (force to retire) mandare in pensione
pensioner /ˈpenʃənə(r)/ *n* pensionato, -a *mf*
pension fund *n* fondo *m* pensioni; (of an individual) fondo *m* pensione
pension scheme *n* piano *m* di pensionamento
pensive /ˈpensɪv/ *adj* pensoso
pentagon /ˈpentəgən/ *n* pentagono *m*; AmE Pol **the P~** il Pentagono
pentagonal /penˈtægənəl/ *adj* pentagonale
pentathlete /penˈtæθliːt/ *n* pentatleta *mf*
pentathlon /penˈtæθlɒn/ *n* pentathlon *m inv*
Pentecost /ˈpentɪkɒst/ *n* Pentecoste *f*
penthouse /ˈpenthaʊs/ *n* attico *m*
pent-up /ˈpentʌp/ *adj* represso
penultimate /pɪˈnʌltɪmət/ *adj* penultimo
penury /ˈpenjʊrɪ/ *n* miseria *f*
peony /ˈpɪənɪ/ *n* peonia *f*
people /ˈpiːpl/ **A** *npl* persone *fpl*, gente *fsg*; (citizens) popolo *msg*; **a lot of ~** una marea di gente; **the ~** la gente; **English ~** gli inglesi; **~ say** si dice; **for four ~** per quattro
B *vt* popolare
people carrier *n* monovolume *f*
pep /pep/
▪ **pep up** *vt* vivacizzare ‹*party, conversation*›; tirare su ‹*person*›
PEP /pep/ *abbr* BrE (**personal equity plan**) piano *m* di investimento azionario personale
pepper /ˈpepə(r)/ **A** *n* pepe *m*; (vegetable) peperone *m*
B *vt* (season) pepare
peppercorn *n* grano *m* di pepe
peppercorn rent affitto *m* nominale
pepper mill *n* macinapepe *m inv*
peppermint *n* menta *f* piperita; (sweet) caramella *f* alla menta
pepper pot *n* pepiera *f*
pep pill /ˈpeppɪl/ *n* infml stimolante *m*
pep talk *n* discorso *m* d'incoraggiamento
peptic /ˈpeptɪk/ *adj* peptico
peptic ulcer *n* ulcera *f* peptica
per /pɜː(r)/ *prep* per
per annum /pərˈænəm/ *adv* all'anno
per capita /pəˈkæpɪtə/ *adj & adv* pro capite

perceive /pəˈsiːv/ *vt* percepire; (interpret) interpretare
⚷ **per cent** *adv* per cento
⚷ **percentage** /pəˈsentɪdʒ/ *n* percentuale *f*
perceptible /pəˈseptəbl/ *adj* percettibile; fig sensibile
perceptibly /pəˈseptɪblɪ/ *adv* percettibilmente; fig sensibilmente
perception /pəˈsepʃn/ *n* percezione *f*
perceptive /pəˈseptɪv/ *adj* perspicace
perch¹ /pɜːtʃ/ **A** *n* pertica *f* **B** *vi* ‹*bird*› appollaiarsi
perch² *n inv* (fish) pesce *m* persico
percolate /ˈpɜːkəleɪt/ *vi* infiltrarsi; ‹*coffee*› passare
percolator /ˈpɜːkəleɪtə(r)/ *n* caffettiera *f* a filtro
percussion /pəˈkʌʃn/ *n* percussione *f*
percussion instrument *n* strumento *m* a percussione
percussionist /pəˈkʌʃ(ə)nɪst/ *n* percussionista *mf*
peremptory /pəˈremptərɪ/ *adj* perentorio
perennial /pəˈrenɪəl/ **A** *adj* perenne **B** *n* pianta *f* perenne
⚷ **perfect¹** /ˈpɜːfɪkt/ **A** *adj* perfetto **B** *n* Gram passato *m* prossimo
perfect² /pəˈfekt/ *vt* perfezionare
perfection /pəˈfekʃn/ *n* perfezione *f*; **to ~** alla perfezione
perfectionism /pəˈfekʃənɪzm/ *n* perfezionismo *m*
perfectionist /pəˈfekʃ(ə)nɪst/ *adj & n* perfezionista *mf*
⚷ **perfectly** /ˈpɜːfɪktlɪ/ *adv* perfettamente
perfidious /pəˈfɪdɪəs/ *adj* perfido
perforate /ˈpɜːfəreɪt/ *vt* perforare
perforated /ˈpɜːfəreɪtɪd/ *adj* perforato; ‹*ulcer*› perforante
perforation /pɜːfəˈreɪʃn/ *n* perforazione *f*
⚷ **perform** /pəˈfɔːm/ **A** *vt* compiere, fare; eseguire ‹*operation, sonata*›; recitare ‹*role*›; mettere in scena ‹*play*› **B** *vi* Theat recitare; Techn funzionare
⚷ **performance** /pəˈfɔːməns/ *n* esecuzione *f*; (at theatre, cinema) rappresentazione *f*; Techn rendimento *m*
performance artist *n* performance artist *mf inv*
performance bonus *n* premio *m* di produttività
performance indicators *npl* indicatori *mpl* di performance
performance-related *adj* commensurato alla produttività
performer /pəˈfɔːmə(r)/ *n* artista *mf*
performing arts /pəˈfɔːmɪŋ/ *npl* arti *fpl* dello spettacolo

⚷ parola chiave

P

perfume /ˈpɜːfjuːm/ *n* profumo *m*
perfumed /ˈpɜːfjuːmd/ *adj* profumato
perfunctory /pəˈfʌŋktərɪ/ *adj* superficiale
⚷ **perhaps** /pəˈhæps/ *adv* forse
peril /ˈperɪl/ *n* pericolo *m*
perilous /ˈperɪləs/ *adj* pericoloso
perilously /ˈperɪləslɪ/ *adv* pericolosamente
perimeter /pəˈrɪmɪtə(r)/ *n* perimetro *m*
⚷ **period** /ˈpɪərɪəd/ **A** *n* periodo *m*; (menstruation) mestruazioni *fpl*; Sch ora *f* di lezione; AmE (full stop) punto *m* fermo **B** *attrib* (costume) d'epoca; ‹*furniture*› in stile
periodic /pɪərɪˈɒdɪk/ *adj* periodico
periodical /pɪərɪˈɒdɪkl/ *n* periodico *m*, rivista *f*
periodically /pɪərɪˈɒdɪklɪ/ *adv* periodicamente
period of notice *n* periodo *m* di preavviso
peripheral /pəˈrɪfərəl/ **A** *adj* periferico **B** *n* Comput periferica *f*
periphery /pəˈrɪfərɪ/ *n* periferia *f*
periscope /ˈperɪskəʊp/ *n* periscopio *m*
perish /ˈperɪʃ/ *vi* (rot) deteriorarsi; (die) perire
perishable /ˈperɪʃəbl/ **A** *adj* deteriorabile **B** *npl* **~s** *npl* merce *f* deperibile
perished /ˈperɪʃt/ *adj* infml (freezing cold) **be ~** essere intirizzito
perishing /ˈperɪʃɪŋ/ *adj* infml **it's ~** fa freddo da morire
peritonitis /perɪtəˈnaɪtɪs/ *n* peritonite *f*
perjure /ˈpɜːdʒə(r)/ *vt* **~ oneself** spergiurare
perjury /ˈpɜːdʒərɪ/ *n* spergiuro *m*
perk¹ /pɜːk/ *n* infml vantaggio *m*
perk² *vi* AmE ‹*coffee*› passare
▪ **perk up** **A** *vt* tirare su **B** *vi* tirarsi su
perky /ˈpɜːkɪ/ *adj* allegro
perm /pɜːm/ **A** *n* permanente *f* **B** *vt* **~ sb's hair** fare la permanente a qualcuno
permanent /ˈpɜːmənənt/ **A** *adj* permanente; ‹*job, address*› stabile **B** *n* AmE = **perm A**
permanently /ˈpɜːmənəntlɪ/ *adv* stabilmente
permeable /ˈpɜːmɪəbl/ *adj* permeabile
permeate /ˈpɜːmɪeɪt/ *vt* impregnare
permissible /pəˈmɪsəbl/ *adj* ammissibile
permission /pəˈmɪʃn/ *n* permesso *m*
permissive /pəˈmɪsɪv/ *adj* permissivo
permit¹ /pəˈmɪt/ *vt* (*pt/pp* **-mitted**) permettere; **~ somebody to do something** permettere a qualcuno di fare qualcosa
permit² /ˈpɜːmɪt/ *n* autorizzazione *f*
pernicious /pəˈnɪʃəs/ *adj* pernicioso
pernickety BrE /pəˈnɪkətɪ/, **persnickety** AmE /pərs-/ infml *adj* puntiglioso, pignolo; (about food) difficile
peroxide blonde /pəˈrɒksaɪd/ *n* bionda *f* ossigenata

perpendicular /pɜːpən'dɪkjʊlə(r)/ *adj & n* perpendicolare *f*
perpetrate /'pɜːpɪtreɪt/ *vt* perpetrare
perpetrator /'pɜːpɪtreɪtə(r)/ *n* autore, -trice *mf*
perpetual /pə'petjʊəl/ *adj* perenne
perpetually /pə'petjʊəlɪ/ *adv* perennemente
perpetuate /pə'petjʊeɪt/ *vt* perpetuare
perplex /pə'pleks/ *vt* lasciare perplesso
perplexed /pə'plekst/ *adj* perplesso
perplexity /pə'pleksɪtɪ/ *n* perplessità *f*
perquisite /'pɜːsɪkjuːt/ *n* fringe benefit *m inv*, beneficio *m* accessorio
per se /pɜː'seɪ/ *adv* in sé
persecute /'pɜːsɪkjuːt/ *vt* perseguitare
persecution /pɜːsɪ'kjuːʃn/ *n* persecuzione *f*
persecutor /'pɜːsɪkjuːtə(r)/ *n* persecutore, -trice *mf*
perseverance /pɜːsɪ'vɪərəns/ *n* perseveranza *f*
persevere /pɜːsɪ'vɪə(r)/ *vi* perseverare
persevering /pɜːsɪ'vɪərɪŋ/ *adj* assiduo
Persian /'pɜːʃn/ *adj* persiano
persist /pə'sɪst/ *vi* persistere; **~ in doing something** persistere nel fare qualcosa
persistence /pə'sɪstəns/ *n* persistenza *f*
persistent /pə'sɪsənt/ *adj* persistente
persistently /pə'sɪstəntlɪ/ *adv* persistentemente
persistent offender *n* recidivo, -a *mf*
person /'pɜːsn/ *n* persona *f*; **in ~** di persona
persona /pə'səʊnə/ *n* Psych individuo *m*; Theat personaggio *m*
personable /'pɜːsənəbl/ *adj* di bella presenza
personage /'pɜːsənɪdʒ/ *n* personaggio *m*
personal /pɜːsənl/ *adj* personale
personal ad *n* annuncio *m* personale
personal allowance *n* (in taxation) quota *f* non imponibile
personal assistant *n* segretario, -a *mf* personale
personal belongings *npl* effetti *mpl* personali
personal column *n* rubrica *f* degli annunci personali
personal computer *n* personal computer *m inv*
personal hygiene *n* igiene *f* personale
personality /pɜːsə'nælətɪ/ *n* personalità *f*; (on TV) personaggio *m*
personalize /'pɜːsənəlaɪz/ *vt* personalizzare ‹*stationery, clothing*›; mettere sul piano personale ‹*issue, dispute*›
personal loan *n* prestito *m* a privato
personally /'pɜːsənəlɪ/ *adv* personalmente
personal organizer *n* Comput agenda *f* elettronica
personal shopper *n* personal shopper *mf* (*persona che dietro compenso si occupa di fare acquisti per conto altrui o accompagna e consiglia qualcuno nello shopping*)
personal stereo *n* walkman® *m inv*
personification /pəsɒnɪfɪ'keɪʃn/ *n* **the ~ of** la personificazione di
personify /pə'sɒnɪfaɪ/ *vt* (*pt/pp* **-ied**) personificare
personnel /pɜːsə'nel/ *n* personale *m*
personnel director *n* direttore, -trice *mf* del personale
personnel management *n* gestione *f* del personale
perspective /pə'spektɪv/ *n* prospettiva *f*
perspex® /'pɜːspeks/ *n* plexiglas® *m*
perspicacious /pɜːspɪ'keɪʃəs/ *adj* perspicace
perspiration /pɜːspɪ'reɪʃn/ *n* sudore *m*
perspire /pə'spaɪə(r)/ *vi* sudare
persuade /pə'sweɪd/ *vt* persuadere
persuasion /pə'sweɪʒn/ *n* persuasione *f*; (belief) convinzione *f*
persuasive /pə'sweɪsɪv/ *adj* persuasivo
persuasively /pə'sweɪsɪvlɪ/ *adv* in modo persuasivo
pert /pɜːt/ *adj* (lively) esuberante
pertinent /'pɜːtɪnənt/ *adj* pertinente (**to** a)
perturb /pə'tɜːb/ *vt* perturbare
perturbing /pə'tɜːbɪŋ/ *adj* conturbante
Peru /pə'ruː/ *n* Perù *m*
peruse /pə'ruːz/ *vt* leggere
Peruvian /pə'ruːvɪən/ *adj & n* peruviano, -a *mf*
pervade /pə'veɪd/ *vt* pervadere
pervasive /pə'veɪsɪv/ *adj* pervasivo
perverse /pə'vɜːs/ *adj* perverso; (illogical) irragionevole
perversely /pə'vɜːslɪ/ *adv* in modo perverso
perversion /pə'vɜːʃn/ *n* perversione *f*
perversity /pə'vɜːsɪtɪ/ *n* perversità *f*
pervert[1] /pə'vɜːt/ *vt* deviare ‹*course of justice*›
pervert[2] /'pɜːvɜːt/ *n* pervertito, -a *mf*
perverted /pə'vɜːtɪd/ *adj* perverso
pessary /'pesərɪ/ *n* candeletta *f*
pessimism /'pesɪmɪzm/ *n* pessimismo *m*
pessimist /'pesɪmɪst/ *n* pessimista *mf*
pessimistic /pesɪ'mɪstɪk/ *adj* pessimistico
pessimistically /pesɪ'mɪstɪklɪ/ *adv* in modo pessimistico
pest /pest/ *n* piaga *f*; infml (person) peste *f*
pester /'pestə(r)/ *vt* molestare
pesticide /'pestɪsaɪd/ *n* pesticida *m*
pestilential /pestɪ'lenʃəl/ *adj* hum (annoying) fastidiosissimo
pestle /'pesl/ *n* pestello *m*
pet /pet/ **A** *n* animale *m* domestico; (favourite) cocco, -a *mf*
B *adj* (favourite) prediletto
C *vt* (*pt/pp* **petted**) coccolare
D *vi* ‹*couple*› praticare il petting

p

petal /'petl/ *n* petalo *m*
peter /'pi:tə(r)/ *vi* ~ **out** finire
pet food *n* cibo *m* per animali
pet hate *n* BrE bestia *f* nera
petite /pə'ti:t/ *adj* minuto
petition /pə'tɪʃn/ *n* petizione *f*
pet name *n* vezzeggiativo *m*
petrified /'petrɪfaɪd/ *adj* (frightened) pietrificato
petrify /'petrɪfaɪ/ *vt* (*pt/pp* **-ied**) pietrificare
petrochemical /petrəʊ'kemɪkl/ *n* prodotto *m* petrolchimico
petrodollar /'petrəʊdɒlə(r)/ *n* petroldollaro *m*
petrol /'petrəl/ *n* BrE benzina *f*
petrol bomb *n* BrE [bomba *f*] molotov *f inv*
petrol can *n* tanica *f* di benzina
petroleum /pɪ'trəʊlɪəm/ *n* petrolio *m*
petroleum jelly *n* vaselina *f*
petrol pump *n* BrE pompa *f* di benzina
petrol station n BrE stazione *f* di servizio
petrol tank *n* BrE serbatoio *m* della benzina
pet shop *n* negozio *m* di animali
petticoat /'petɪkəʊt/ *n* sottoveste *f*
pettifogging /'petɪfɒgɪŋ/ *adj* derog cavilloso
petty /'petɪ/ *adj* (**-ier**, **-iest**) insignificante; (mean) meschino
petty cash *n* cassa *f* per piccole spese
petty crime *n* piccola criminalità *f*
petty minded /-'maɪndɪd/ *adj* meschino
petty officer *n* sottufficiale *m*
petty theft *n* furto *m* di minore entità
petulance /'petjʊləns/ *n* petulanza *f*
petulant /'petjʊlənt/ *adj* petulante
pew /pju:/ *n* banco *m* (*di chiesa*)
pewter /'pju:tə(r)/ *n* peltro *m*
PGCE *n abbr* BrE (**postgraduate certificate in education**) diploma *m* di specializzazione nell'insegnamento
phallic /'fælɪk/ *adj* fallico
phallic symbol *n* simbolo *m* fallico
phallus /'fæləs/ *n* fallo *m*
phantom /'fæntəm/ *n* fantasma *m*
pharaoh /'feərəʊ/ *n* faraone *m*
pharmaceutical /fɑ:mə'sju:tɪkl/ *adj* farmaceutico
pharmacist /'fɑ:məsɪst/ *n* farmacista *mf*
pharmacy /'fɑ:məsɪ/ *n* farmacia *f*
⚷ **phase** /feɪz/ **A** *n* fase *f*
B *vt* **phase in/out** introdurre/eliminare gradualmente
PhD *abbr* (**Doctor of Philosophy**) ≈ dottorato *m* di ricerca
pheasant /'feznt/ *n* fagiano *m*
phenomenal /fɪ'nɒmɪnl/ *adj* fenomenale; (incredible) incredibile
phenomenally /fɪ'nɒmɪnəlɪ/ *adv* incredibilmente

⚷ parola chiave

phenomenon /fɪ'nɒmɪnən/ *n* (*pl* **-na**) fenomeno *m*
phew /fju:/ *int* (when too hot, in relief) uff!; (in surprise) oh!
philanderer /fɪ'lændərə(r)/ *n* donnaiolo *m*
philanthropic /fɪlən'θrɒpɪk/ *adj* filantropico
philanthropist /fɪ'lænθrəpɪst/ *adj* filantropo, -a *mf*
philatelist /fɪ'lætəlɪst/ *n* filatelico, -a *mf*
philately /fɪ'lætəlɪ/ *n* filatelia *f*
philharmonic /fɪhɑ:'mɒnɪk/ **A** *n* (orchestra) orchestra *f* filarmonica
B *adj* filarmonico
Philippines /'fɪlɪpi:nz/ *npl* Filippine *fpl*
philistine /'fɪlɪstaɪn/ *adj & n* filisteo, -a *mf*
philology /fɪ'lɒlədʒɪ/ *n* filologia *f*
philosopher /fɪ'lɒsəfə(r)/ *n* filosofo, -a *mf*
philosophical /fɪlə'sɒfɪkl/ *adj* filosofico
philosophically /fɪlə'sɒfɪklɪ/ *adv* con filosofia
philosophy /fɪ'lɒsəfɪ/ *n* filosofia *f*
phishing /'fɪʃɪŋ/ *n* phishing *m inv*
phlebitis /flɪ'baɪtɪs/ *n* flebite *f*
phlegm /flem/ *n* Med flemma *f*
phlegmatic /fleg'mætɪk/ *adj* flemmatico
phobia /'fəʊbɪə/ *n* fobia *f*
phobic /'fəʊbɪk/ *adj* fobico
phoenix /'fi:nɪks/ *n* fenice *f*
⚷ **phone** /fəʊn/ **A** *n* telefono *m*; **be on the ~** avere il telefono; (be phoning) essere al telefono
B *vt* telefonare a
■ **phone back** *vt* richiamare
■ **phone in** *vi* telefonare al lavoro; **he ~d in sick** ha telefonato [al lavoro] per dire che è ammalato
■ **phone up** **A** *vi* telefonare
B *vt* dare un colpo di telefono a
phone book *n* guida *f* del telefono
phone booth *n* cabina *f* telefonica
phone box *n* cabina *f* telefonica
phone call *n* telefonata *f*
phonecard *n* scheda *f* telefonica
phone hacking /'fəʊn hækɪŋ/ *n* phone hacking *m inv*, intercettazioni *f pl* telefoniche
phone-in *n* trasmissione *f* con chiamate in diretta
phone link *n* phone link *m inv*
phoneme /'fəʊni:m/ *n* fonema *m*
phone number *n* numero *m* telefonico
phonetic /fə'netɪk/ *adj* fonetico
phonetics /fə'netɪks/ *nsg* fonetica *fsg*
phoney /'fəʊnɪ/ **A** *adj* (**-ier**, **-iest**) fasullo
B *n* ciarlatano, -a *mf*
phonology /fə'nɒlədʒɪ/ *n* fonologia *f*
phosphate /'fɒsfeɪt/ *n* fosfato *m*

phosphorus /ˈfɒsfərəs/ *n* fosforo *m*
photo /ˈfəʊtəʊ/ *n* foto *f*
photo album *n* album *m inv* di fotografie
photo booth *n* macchina *f* fototessere *inv*
photocall *n* photo opportunity *f inv*
photocell *n* fotocellula *f*
photocopier *n* fotocopiatrice *f*
photocopy **A** *n* fotocopia *f*
B *vt* fotocopiare
photo-engraving *n* fotoincisione *f*
photo finish *n* fotofinish *m*
photofit® *n* BrE fotofit *m inv*
photogenic /fəʊtəʊˈdʒenɪk/ *adj* fotogenico
photograph /ˈfəʊtəgrɑːf/ **A** *n* fotografia *f*
B *vt* fotografare
photographer /fəˈtɒgrəfə(r)/ *n* fotografo, -a *mf*
photographic /fəʊtəˈgræfɪk/ *adj* fotografico
photography /fəˈtɒgrəfɪ/ *n* fotografia *f*
photojournalism *n* fotoreportage *m*
photojournalist *n* fotoreporter *mf inv*
photomontage /fəʊtəʊmɒnˈtɑːʒ/ *n* fotomontaggio *m*
photo opportunity *n* photo opportunity *f inv*
photosynthesis *n* fotosintesi *f*
phrase /freɪz/ **A** *n* espressione *f*
B *vt* esprimere
phrase book *n* libro *m* di fraseologia
phut /fʌt/ *adv* infml **go ~** ‹*car, washing machine etc*› scassarsi; ‹*plan*› andare in fumo
physical /ˈfɪkl/ *adj* fisico
physical education *n* educazione *f* fisica
physical fitness *n* forma *f* fisica
physically /ˈfɪzɪklɪ/ *adv* fisicamente
physically handicapped *adj* handicappato fisicamente
physician /fɪˈzɪʃn/ *n* medico *m*
physicist /ˈfɪzɪsɪst/ *n* fisico, -a *mf*
physics /ˈfɪzɪks/ *nsg* fisica *fsg*
physio /ˈfɪzɪəʊ/ *n* BrE infml (physiotherapist) fisioterapista *mf*; (physiotherapy) fisioterapia *f*
physiology /fɪzɪˈɒlədʒɪ/ *n* fisiologia *f*
physiotherapist /fɪzɪəʊˈθerəpɪst/ *n* fisioterapista *mf*
physiotherapy /fɪzɪəʊˈθerəpɪ/ *n* fisioterapia *f*
physique /fɪˈziːk/ *n* fisico *m*
pianist /ˈpɪənɪst/ *n* pianista *mf*
piano /pɪˈænəʊ/ *n* piano *m*
pianola® /pɪəˈnəʊlə/ *n* pianola® *f*
piazza /pɪˈætsə/ *n* (public square) piazza *f*; AmE (veranda) veranda *f*
pick¹ /pɪk/ *n* (tool) piccone *m*
pick² **A** *n* scelta *f*; **take your ~** prendi quello che vuoi
B *vt* (select) scegliere; cogliere ‹*flowers*›; scassinare ‹*lock*›; borseggiare ‹*pockets*›; **~ one's nose** mettersi le dita nel naso; **~ a quarrel** attaccar briga; **~ holes in something** infml (criticize) criticare qualcosa
C *vi* **~ and choose** fare il difficile
■ **pick at** *vt* piluccare ‹*food*›; stuzzicare ‹*scab*›
■ **pick off** *vt* (remove) togliere
■ **pick on** *vt* infml (nag) assillare; **he always ~s on me** ce l'ha con me
■ **pick out** *vt* (identify) individuare
■ **pick up** **A** *vt* sollevare; raccogliere ‹*fallen object, information*›; prendere in braccio ‹*baby*›; prendere ‹*passengers, habit*›; ‹*police*› arrestare ‹*criminal*›; infml rimorchiare ‹*girl*›; prendersi ‹*illness*›; captare ‹*signal*›; (buy) comprare; (learn) imparare; (collect) andare/venire a prendere; **~ oneself up** riprendersi
B *vi* (improve) recuperare; ‹*weather*› rimettersi
pickaxe /ˈpɪkæks/ *n* piccone *m*
picker /ˈpɪkə(r)/ *n* raccoglitore, -trice *mf*
picket /ˈpɪkɪt/ **A** *n* picchettista *mf*
B *vt* picchettare
picket line *n* picchetto *m*
pickings /ˈpɪkɪŋz/ *npl* **rich ~** grossi guadagni
pickle /ˈpɪkl/ **A** *n* **~s** *pl* sottaceti *mpl*; **in a ~** fig nei pasticci
B *vt* mettere sottaceto
pick-me-up *n* (alcohol) cicchetto *m*; (medicine) tonico *m*
pickpocket /ˈpɪkpɒkɪt/ *n* borsaiolo *m*
pick-up *n* (truck) furgone *m*; (on record player) pickup *m inv*
picky /ˈpɪkɪ/ *adj* infml (choosy, fussy) difficile
picnic /ˈpɪknɪk/ **A** *n* picnic *m*
B *vi* (*pt/pp* **-nicked**) fare un picnic
pictogram /ˈpɪktəgræm/ *n* (symbol) pittogramma *m*; (chart) tabella *f*
pictorial /pɪkˈtɔːrɪəl/ *adj* illustrato
picture /ˈpɪktʃə(r)/ **A** *n* (painting) quadro *m*; (photo) fotografia *f*; (drawing) disegno *m*; (film) film *m inv*; **as pretty as a ~** ‹*girl*› bella come una madonna; **put somebody in the ~** fig mettere qualcuno al corrente; **the ~s** BrE infml il cinema
B *vt* (imagine) immaginare
picture card *n* (in pack of cards) figura *f*
picture messaging *n* Teleph messaggeria *f* di immagini
picturesque /pɪktʃəˈresk/ *adj* pittoresco
piddle /ˈpɪdl/ *vi* infml fare pipì
pie /paɪ/ *n* torta *f*
piece /piːs/ *n* pezzo m; (in game) pedina *f*; **a ~ of bread/paper** un pezzo di pane/carta; **a ~ of news/advice/junk** una notizia/un consiglio/una patacca; **take to ~s** smontare
■ **piece together** *vt* montare; fig ricostruire
piecemeal /ˈpiːsmiːl/ *adv* un po' alla volta
piecework /ˈpiːswɜːk/ *n* lavoro *m* a cottimo
pie chart *n* grafico *f* a torta
Piedmont /ˈpiːdmɒnt/ *n* Piemonte *m*
pier /pɪə(r)/ molo *m*; (pillar) pilastro *m*

pierce /pɪəs/ *vt* perforare; ~ **a hole in something** fare un buco in qualcosa
piercing /ˈpɪəsɪŋ/ **A** *adj* penetrante
B *n* (in body) piercing *m inv*
pig /pɪɡ/ *n* maiale *m*
▪ **pig out** *vi* infml abbuffarsi; ~ **out on** abbuffarsi di
pigeon /ˈpɪdʒɪn/ *n* piccione *m*
pigeon-hole **A** *n* casella *f*
B *vt* incasellare
pigeon-toed /-təʊd/ *adj* **be** ~ camminare con i piedi in dentro
piggery /ˈpɪɡərɪ/ *n* (pigsty) porcile *m*; infml (overeating) ingordigia *f*
piggyback /ˈpɪɡɪbæk/ *n* **give somebody a** ~ portare qualcuno sulle spalle
piggy bank /ˈpɪɡɪ/ *n* salvadanaio *m*
pig-headed /-ˈhedɪd/ *adj* infml cocciuto
piglet /ˈpɪɡlət/ *n* maialino *m*, porcellino *m*
pigment /ˈpɪɡmənt/ *n* pigmento *m*
pigmentation /pɪɡmənˈteɪʃn/ *n* pigmentazione *f*
pigpen *n* AmE = **pigsty**
pigskin /ˈpɪɡskɪn/ *n* pelle *f* di cinghiale
pigsty *n* BrE porcile *m*
pigtail /ˈpɪɡteɪl/ *n* (plait) treccina *f*
pike /paɪk/ *n inv* (fish) luccio *m*
pilchard /ˈpɪltʃəd/ *n* sardina *f*
pile /paɪl/ **A** *n* (heap) pila *f*
B *vt* ~ **something on to the something** impilare qualcosa su qualcosa
▪ **pile in** *vi* (enter, get on) entrare disordinatamente
▪ **pile up** **A** *vt* accatastare
B *vi* ammucchiarsi
piles /paɪlz/ *npl* emorroidi *fpl*
pile-up *n* tamponamento *m* a catena
pilfer /ˈpɪlfə(r)/ *vi & vt* rubacchiare
pilfering /ˈpɪlfərɪŋ/ *n* piccoli furti *mpl*
pilgrim /ˈpɪlɡrɪm/ *n* pellegrino, -a *mf*
pilgrimage /ˈpɪlɡrɪmɪdʒ/ *n* pellegrinaggio *m*
pill /pɪl/ *n* pillola *f*
pillage /ˈpɪlɪdʒ/ *vt* saccheggiare
pillar /ˈpɪlə(r)/ *n* pilastro *m*
pillar box *n* buca *f* delle lettere
pillion /ˈpɪljən/ *n* sellino *m* posteriore; **ride** ~ viaggiare dietro
pillory /ˈpɪlərɪ/ *vt* (*pt/pp* **-ied**) fig mettere alla berlina
pillow /ˈpɪləʊ/ *n* guanciale *m*
pillowcase /ˈpɪləʊkeɪs/ *n* federa *f*
🔑 **pilot** /ˈpaɪlət/ **A** *n* pilota *mf*
B *vt* pilotare
pilot light *n* fiamma *f* di sicurezza
pilot scheme *n* progetto *m* pilota *inv*
pimp /pɪmp/ *n* protettore *m*
pimple /ˈpɪmpl/ *n* foruncolo *m*
pimply /ˈpɪmplɪ/ *adj* brufoloso

🔑 parola chiave

pin /pɪn/ **A** *n* spillo *m*; Electr spinotto *m*; Med chiodo *m*; **I have ~s and needles in my leg** infml mi formicola una gamba
B *vt* (*pt/pp* **pinned**) appuntare (**to/on** su); (sewing) fissare con gli spilli; (hold down) immobilizzare; ~ **something on somebody** infml addossare a qualcuno la colpa di qualcosa
▪ **pin down** *vt* (physically) immobilizzare; (to date) far fissare una data a ‹*somebody*›; (identify) definire ‹*feeling, cause*›
▪ **pin up** *vt* appuntare; (on wall) affiggere
PIN /pɪn/ *n abbr* (**personal identification number**) [numero *m* di] codice *m* segreto, PIN *m*
pinafore /ˈpɪnəfɔː(r)/ *n* grembiule *m*
pinafore dress *n* scamiciato *m*
pinball /ˈpɪnbɔːl/ *n* flipper *m inv*
pinball machine *n* flipper *m inv*
pincers /ˈpɪnsəz/ *npl* tenaglie *fpl*
pinch /pɪntʃ/ **A** *n* pizzicotto *m*; (of salt) presa *f*; **at a** ~ infml al limite
B *vt* pizzicare; infml (steal) fregare
C *vi* ‹*shoe*› stringere
pincushion /ˈpɪnkʊʃən/ *n* puntaspilli *m inv*
pine¹ /paɪn/ *n* (tree) pino *m*
pine² *vi* **she is pining for you** le manchi molto
▪ **pine away** *vi* deperire
pineapple *n* ananas *m inv*
pine cone *n* pigna *f*
pine needle *n* ago *m* di pino
pine nut *n* pinolo *m*
ping /pɪŋ/ *n* rumore *m* metallico
ping-pong *n* ping-pong *m*
pinhead /ˈpɪnhed/ *n* capocchia *f* di spillo; infml derog testa *f* di rapa
pink /pɪŋk/ *adj* rosa *inv*
pinking shears, **pinking scissors** /ˈpɪŋkɪŋ/ *npl* forbici *fpl* a zigzag
pinnacle /ˈpɪnəkl/ *n* guglia *f*
PIN number *n* codice *m* segreto, PIN *m*
pinpoint /ˈpɪnpɔɪnt/ *vt* definire con precisione
pinprick /ˈpɪnprɪk/ *n* puntura *f* di spillo; fig (of jealousy, remorse) punta *f*
pinstripe /ˈpɪnstraɪp/ *adj* gessato
pint /paɪnt/ *n* pinta *f Br = 0,57 l, Am = 0,47 l*; **a** ~ infml una birra media
pin-up *n* ragazza *f* copertina, pin-up *f inv*
pioneer /paɪəˈnɪə(r)/ **A** *n* pioniere, -a *mf*
B *vt* essere un pioniere di
pious /ˈpaɪəs/ *adj* pio
pip¹ /pɪp/ *n* (seed) seme *m*
pip² *n* **the ~s** il segnale orario; (telephone) il segnale telefonico
pip³ *vt* (*pt/pp* **pipped**) **be ~ped at the post** essere battuto all'ultimo minuto
pipe /paɪp/ **A** *n* tubo *m*; (for smoking) pipa *f*; **the ~s** *pl* Mus la cornamusa
B *vt* far arrivare con tubature ‹*water: gas etc*›; Culin decorare

■ **pipe down** *vi* infml abbassare la voce; (shut up) stare zitto
■ **pipe up**: *vi* ~ **with a suggestion** venir fuori con una proposta
pipe cleaner *n* scovolino *m*
piped music /paɪpt/ *n* musichetta *f* di sottofondo
pipe dream *n* illusione *f*
pipeline /'paɪplaɪn/ *n* conduttura *f*; **in the ~** infml in cantiere
piper /'paɪpə(r)/ *n* suonatore *m* di cornamusa
piping /'paɪpɪŋ/ *adj* ~ **hot** bollente
pique /piːk/ *n* **in a fit of ~** risentito
piracy /'paɪrəsɪ/ *n* pirateria *f*
piranha /pɪ'rɑːnə/ *n* piranha *m inv*
pirate /'paɪrət/ **A** *n* pirata *m*
B *vt* piratеggiare
pirate copy *n* copia *f* pirata
pirated /'paɪrətɪd/ *adj* piratato
pirate radio *n* radio *f* pirata *inv*
pirouette /pɪruː'et/ **A** *n* piroetta *f*
B *vi* piroettare
Pisces /'paɪsiːz/ *n* Astr Pesci *mpl*
piss /pɪs/ sl **A** *n* piscia *f*
B *vi* pisciare
■ **piss about, piss around A** *vi* (waste time, play the fool) cazzeggiare
B *vt* ~ **somebody about** rompere le palle a qualcuno
■ **piss down**: *vi sl* **it's ~ing down** (raining heavily) piove a dirotto
■ **piss off A** *sl vt* fare incacchiare; **that type of behaviour ~es me off** questi comportamenti mi stanno sulle palle
B *vi* (leave) filarsela; ~ **off!** levati dalle palle!, va' a cagare!
pissed /pɪst/ *adj* sl sbronzo; ~ **as a newt** sbronzo come una cocuzza
pissed off *adj* sl scoglionato
pistachio, pistachio nut /pɪ'stæʃɪəʊ/ *n* pistacchio *m*
pistol /'pɪstl/ *n* pistola *f*
piston /'pɪstn/ *n* Techn pistone *m*
pit /pɪt/ **A** *n* fossa *f*; (mine) miniera *f*; (for orchestra) orchestra *f*; (of stomach) bocca *f*
B *vt* (*pt/pp* **pitted**) fig opporre (**against** a)
pit-a-pat /'pɪtəpæt/ *n* **go ~** ‹*heart*› palpitare
pit bull, pit bull terrier *n* pitbull *m inv*
pitch¹ /pɪtʃ/ **A** *n* (tone) tono *m*; (level) altezza *f*; (in sport) campo *m*; fig (degree) grado *m*
B *vt* montare ‹*tent*›
pitch² *n* (substance) pece *f*
■ **pitch in** *vi* infml mettersi sotto
pitch-black *adj* nero come la pece; ‹*night*› buio pesto
pitch-dark *adj* buio pesto
pitcher /'pɪtʃə(r)/ *n* brocca *f*
pitchfork /'pɪtʃfɔːk/ *n* forca *f*, forcone *m*
piteous /'pɪtɪəs/ *adj* pietoso
pitfall /'pɪtfɔːl/ *n* fig trabocchetto *m*
pith /pɪθ/ *n* (of lemon, orange) interno *m* della buccia; fig essenza *f*
pithy /'pɪθɪ/ *adj* (**-ier**, **-iest**) fig conciso
pitiable /'pɪtɪəbl/ *adj* pietoso
pitiful /'pɪtɪfl/ *adj* pietoso
pitifully /'pɪtɪfʊlɪ/ *adv* da far pietà
pitiless /'pɪtɪlɪs/ *adj* spietato
pitilessly /'pɪtɪlɪslɪ/ *adv* senza pietà
pittance /'pɪtns/ *n* miseria *f*
pitted /'pɪtɪd/ *adj* ‹*surface*› bucherellato; ‹*face, skin*› butterato; ‹*olive*› snocciolato
pituitary /pɪ'tjuːɪt(ə)rɪ/ *adj* pituitario
pituitary gland *n* ghiandola *f* pituitaria, ipofisi *f*
pity /'pɪtɪ/ **A** *n* pietà *f*; **[what a] ~!** che peccato!; **take ~ on** avere compassione di
B *vt* aver pietà di
pivot /'pɪvət/ **A** *n* perno *m*; fig fulcro *m*
B *vi* imperniarsi (**on** su)
pivotal /'pɪvətl/ *adj* ‹*role*› centrale; ‹*decision*› cruciale
pixel /'pɪksəl/ *n* pixel *m inv*
pixie /'pɪksɪ/ *n* folletto *m*
pizza /'piːtsə/ *n* pizza *f*
placard /'plækɑːd/ *n* cartellone *m*
placate /plə'keɪt/ *vt* placare
⚷ **place** /pleɪs/ **A** *n* posto *m*; infml (house) casa *f*; (in book) segno *m*; **feel out of ~** sentirsi fuori posto; **take ~** aver luogo; **all over the ~** dappertutto
B *vt* collocare; (remember) identificare; ~ **an order** fare un'ordinazione; **be ~d** (in race) piazzarsi
placebo /plə'siːbəʊ/ *n* Med placebo *m inv*; fig contentino *m*
place mat *n* sottopiatto *m*
placement /'pleɪsmənt/ *n* (act: in accommodation) collocamento *m*; BrE (job) stage *m inv*
place name *n* toponimo *m*
placenta /plə'sentə/ *n* placenta *f*
placid /'plæsɪd/ *adj* placido
plagiarism /'pleɪdʒərɪzm/ *n* plagio *m*
plagiarist /'pleɪdʒərɪst/ *n* plagiario, -a *mf*
plagiarize /'pleɪdʒəraɪz/ *vt* plagiare
plague /pleɪg/ *n* peste *f*
plaice /pleɪs/ *n inv* platessa *f*
plaid /plæd/ **A** *n* (fabric) plaid *m inv*; (pattern) motivo *m* scozzese
B *attrib* ‹*scarf, shirt*› scozzese
plain /pleɪn/ **A** *adj* chiaro; (simple) semplice; (not pretty) scialbo; (not patterned) in tinta unita; ‹*chocolate*› fondente; **in ~ clothes** in borghese
B *adv* (simply) semplicemente
C *n* pianura *f*
plain-clothes *adj* ‹*policeman etc*› in borghese
plainly /'pleɪnlɪ/ *adv* francamente; (simply) semplicemente; (obviously) chiaramente
plain paper fax *n* fax *m inv* a carta comune

plain-spoken *adj* franco
plaintiff /ˈpleɪntɪf/ *n* Jur parte *f* lesa
plaintive /ˈpleɪntɪv/ *adj* lamentoso
plaintively /ˈpleɪntɪvlɪ/ *adv* con aria lamentosa
plait /plæt/ **A** *n* treccia *f*
B *vt* intrecciare
⚷ **plan** /plæn/ **A** *n* progetto *m*, piano *m*
B *vt* (*pt/pp* **planned**) progettare; (intend) prevedere
■ **plan ahead** *vi* pianificare
plane¹ /pleɪn/ *n* (tree) platano *m*
⚷ **plane²** *n* aeroplano *m*; (in geometry) piano *m*
plane³ **A** *n* (tool) pialla *f*
B *vt* piallare
plane crash *n* incidente *m* aereo
⚷ **planet** /ˈplænɪt/ *n* pianeta *m*
plank /plæŋk/ *n* asse *f*
■ **plank down** *vt* infml (put down) mollare
plankton /ˈplæŋktən/ *n* plancton *m*
planner /ˈplænə(r)/ *n* progettista *mf*; (in town planning) urbanista *mf*
⚷ **planning** /ˈplænɪŋ/ *n* pianificazione *f*
planning permission *n* licenza *f* edilizia
⚷ **plant** /plɑːnt/ **A** *n* pianta *f*; (machinery) impianto *m*; (factory) stabilimento *m*
B *vt* piantare; ~ **oneself in front of somebody** piantarsi davanti a qualcuno
plantation /plænˈteɪʃn/ *n* piantagione *f*
planter /ˈplɑːntə(r)/ *n* (person) piantatore, -trice *mf*; (machine) piantatrice *f*
plant life *n* flora *f*
plaque /plɑːk/ *n* placca *f*
plasma /ˈplæzmə/ *n* plasma *m*
plasma screen *n* schermo *m* al plasma
plasma TV *n* TV *f* al plasma
plaster /ˈplɑːstə(r)/ **A** *n* intonaco *m*; Med gesso *m*; (sticking ~) cerotto *m*; **in ~** ingessato
B *vt* intonacare ‹*wall*›; (cover) ricoprire
plaster cast *n* ingessatura *f*
plastered /ˈplɑːstəd/ *adj* sl (drunk) sbronzo
plasterer /ˈplɑstərə(r)/ *n* intonacatore *m*
plaster of Paris *n* gesso *m*
plastic /ˈplæstɪk/ **A** *n* plastica *f*
B *adj* plastico
Plasticine® /ˈplæstɪsiːn/ *n* Plastilina® *f*
plastic surgeon *n* chirurgo *m* plastico
plastic surgery *n* chirurgia *f* plastica
⚷ **plate** /pleɪt/ **A** *n* piatto *m*; (flat sheet) placca *f*; (gold and silverware) argenteria *f*; (in book) tavola *f* fuori testo
B *vt* (cover with metal) placcare
plateau /ˈplætəʊ/ **A** *n* (*pl* ~**x** /ˈplætəʊz/) altopiano *m*
B *vi* fig livellarsi
plate glass *n* lastra *f* di vetro

platform /ˈplætfɔːm/ *n* (stage) palco *m*; Rail marciapiede *m*; Pol piattaforma *f*; ~ **5** binario 5
platform shoes *npl* scarpe *fpl* con la zeppa
platinum /ˈplætɪnəm/ **A** *n* platino *m*
B *attrib* di platino
platinum blonde *n* bionda *f* platinata
platitude /ˈplætɪtjuːd/ *n* luogo *m* comune
platonic /pləˈtɒnɪk/ *adj* platonico
platoon /pləˈtuːn/ *n* Mil plotone *m*
platter /ˈplætə(r)/ *n* piatto *m* da portata
platypus /ˈplætɪpəs/ *n* ornitorinco *m*
plausibility /plɔːzɪˈbɪlɪtɪ/ *n* plausibilità *f*
plausible /ˈplɔːzəbl/ *adj* plausibile
⚷ **play** /pleɪ/ **A** *n* gioco *m*; Theat, TV dramma *m*, opera *f* teatrale; (performance) rappresentazione *f*; Radio sceneggiato *m* radiofonico; ~ **on words** gioco *m* di parole
B *vt* giocare a; (act) recitare; suonare ‹*instrument*›; giocare ‹*card*›
C *vi* giocare; Mus suonare; ~ **by the rules** stare alle regole; ~ **with fire** scherzare col fuoco; ~ **dumb** fare lo gnorri; ~ **safe** non prendere rischi
■ **play along**: *vi* ~ **along with somebody** infml (cooperate) fare il gioco di qualcuno
■ **play around with** *vt* (meddle with) cincischiarsi con
■ **play back** *vt* riascoltare ‹*recording*›
■ **play down** *vt* minimizzare
■ **play on** **A** *vi* (continue to play) continuare a giocare
B *vt* (exploit) giocare su
■ **play out** *vt* vivere ‹*drama, fantasy*›
■ **play up** *vi* infml fare i capricci
play-acting *n* commedia *f*
playboy /ˈpleɪbɔɪ/ *n* playboy *m inv*
⚷ **player** /ˈpleɪə(r)/ *n* giocatore, -trice *mf*
playful /ˈpleɪfʊl/ *adj* scherzoso
playfully /ˈpleɪfʊlɪ/ *adv* in modo scherzoso
playground /ˈpleɪgraʊnd/ *n* Sch cortile *m* (*per la ricreazione*)
playgroup /ˈpleɪgruːp/ *n* asilo *m*
playhouse *n* casetta *f* per i giochi
playing card /ˈpleɪɪŋ/ *n* carta *f* da gioco
playing field *n* campo *m* da gioco
playlist *n* playlist *f inv*
playmate *n* compagno, -a *mf* di gioco
play-off /ˈpleɪɒf/ *n* play off *m inv*
playpen *n* box *m inv*
playroom /ˈpleɪruːm/ *n* ludoteca *f*
plaything *n* giocattolo *m*
playtime *n* ricreazione *f*
playwright /ˈpleɪraɪt/ *n* drammaturgo, -a *mf*
plaza /ˈplɑːzə/ *n* (public square) piazza *f*; AmE (services point) area *f* di servizio; AmE (toll point) casello *m*; **shopping** ~ centro *m* commerciale
plc *abbr* (**public limited company**) s.r.l.

⚷ parola chiave

p

plea /pliː/ *n* appello *m*; **enter a ~ of not guilty** Jur dichiararsi non colpevole; **make a ~ for** fare un appello a

plead /pliːd/ **A** *vi* fare appello (**for** a); **~ guilty** dichiararsi colpevole; **~ with somebody** implorare qualcuno
B *vt* Jur perorare ‹*case*›

pleasant /ˈpleznt/ *adj* piacevole

pleasantly /ˈplezntlɪ/ *adv* piacevolmente; ‹*say, smile*› cordialmente

pleasantry /ˈplezntrɪ/ *n* (joke) battuta *f*; **pleasantries** *pl* (polite remarks) convenevoli *mpl*

please /pliːz/ **A** *adv* per favore; **~ do** prego
B *vt* far contento; **~ oneself** fare il proprio comodo; **~ yourself!** come vuoi!; derog fai come ti pare!

pleased /pliːzd/ *adj* lieto; **~ with/about** contento di

pleasing /ˈpliːzɪŋ/ *adj* gradevole

pleasurable /ˈpleʒərəbl/ *adj* gradevole

pleasure /ˈpleʒə(r)/ *n* piacere *m*; **with ~** con piacere, volentieri

pleat /pliːt/ **A** *n* piega *f*
B *vt* pieghettare

pleated /ˈpliːtɪd/ *adj* a pieghe

pleb /pleb/ *n* infml plebeo, -a *mf*

plebby /ˈplebɪ/ *adj* infml plebeo

plebeian /plɪˈbiːən/ derog **A** *n* plebeo, -a *mf*
B *adj* plebeo

plebiscite /ˈplebɪsaɪt/ *n* plebiscito *m*

pledge /pledʒ/ **A** *n* pegno *m*; (promise) promessa *f*
B *vt* (pawn) impegnare; **~ to do something** impegnarsi a fare qualcosa

plenary /ˈpliːnərɪ/ *adj* ‹*session*› plenario; ‹*powers*› pieno; ‹*authority*› assoluto

plentiful /ˈplentɪfl/ *adj* abbondante

plenty /ˈplentɪ/ *n* abbondanza *f*; **~ of money** molti soldi; **~ of people** molta gente; **I've got ~** ne ho in abbondanza

pleurisy /ˈplʊərəsɪ/ *n* pleurite *f*

pliability /plaɪəˈbɪlɪtɪ/ *n* flessibilità *f*

pliable /ˈplaɪəbl/ *adj* flessibile

pliers /ˈplaɪəz/ *npl* pinze *fpl*

plight /plaɪt/ *n* triste condizione *f*

plimsolls /ˈplɪmsɒlz/ *npl* scarpe *fpl* da ginnastica

plinth /plɪnθ/ *n* plinto *m*

plod /plɒd/ *vi* (*pt/pp* **plodded**) trascinarsi; (work hard) sgobbare

■ **plod away** *vi* (work hard) sgobbare; **~ away at** sgobbare su

plodder /ˈplɒdə(r)/ *n* sgobbone, -a *mf*

plonk[1] /plɒŋk/ *n* infml vino *m*; (poor wine) vinaccio *m*

plonk[2] *vt* infml (put) sbattere

plop /plɒp/ **A** *n* plop *m inv*
B *vi* (*pt/pp* **plopped**) fare plop

plot /plɒt/ **A** *n* complotto *m*; (of novel) trama *f*; **~ of land** appezzamento *m* [di terreno]
B *vt & vi* (*pt/pp* **plotted**) complottare

plotter /ˈplɒtə(r)/ *n* (schemer) cospiratore, -trice *mf*; Comput plotter *m inv*, tracciatore *m*

plough /plaʊ/ **A** *n* aratro *m*
B *vt & vi* arare

■ **plough back** *vt* Comm reinvestire

■ **plough into** *vt* (crash into) schiantarsi contro

■ **plough through** *vt* procedere a fatica in

ploughman /ˈplaʊmən/ *n* aratore *m*

ploughman's lunch *n* BrE *piatto* (*m*) *freddo a base di pane, formaggio e sottaceti*

plow /plaʊ/ AmE **A** *n* aratro *m*
B *vt & vi* arare

ploy /plɔɪ/ *n* infml manovra *f*

pluck /plʌk/ **A** *n* fegato *m*, coraggio *m*
B *vt* strappare; depilare ‹*eyebrows*›; spennare ‹*bird*›; cogliere ‹*flower*›

■ **pluck up**: *vt* **~ up courage** farsi coraggio

plucky /ˈplʌkɪ/ *adj* (**-ier**, **-iest**) coraggioso

plug /plʌg/ **A** *n* tappo *m*; Electr spina *f*; Auto candela *f*; infml (advertisement) pubblicità *f*
B *vt* (*pt/pp* **plugged**) tappare; infml (advertise) pubblicizzare

■ **plug away** *vi* (work hard) lavorare sodo

■ **plug in** *vt* Electr inserire la spina di

plug and play *n* Comput plug and play *m inv*

plughole /ˈplʌghəʊl/ *n* BrE scarico *m*

plug-in *adj* con la spina

plum /plʌm/ *n* susina *f*; (tree) susino *m*

plumage /ˈpluːmɪdʒ/ *n* piumaggio *m*

plumb /plʌm/ **A** *adj* verticale
B *adv* esattamente

■ **plumb in** *vt* collegare

plumber /ˈplʌmə(r)/ *n* idraulico *m*

plumbing /ˈplʌmɪŋ/ *n* impianto *m* idraulico

plumb line *n* filo *m* a piombo

plume /pluːm/ *n* piuma *f*

plummet /ˈplʌmɪt/ *vi* precipitare; ‹*prices*› crollare

plump /plʌmp/ *adj* grassoccio

■ **plump down** *vt* (put down) lasciare cadere

■ **plump for** *vt* scegliere

plumpness /ˈplʌmpnɪs/ *n* rotondità *f*

plunder /ˈplʌndə(r)/ **A** *n* (booty) bottino *m*
B *vt* saccheggiare

plunge /plʌndʒ/ **A** *n* tuffo *m*; **take the ~** infml buttarsi
B *vt* tuffare; fig sprofondare; **~ somebody into despair** piombare qualcuno nella disperazione
C *vi* tuffarsi

plunger /ˈplʌndʒə(r)/ *n* (tool) sturalavandini *m inv*; (handle) stantuffo *m*

plunging /ˈplʌndʒɪŋ/ *adj* **~ neckline** scollatura *f* profonda

pluperfect /pluːˈpɜːfɪkt/ *n* trapassato *m* prossimo

plural /ˈplʊərəl/ *adj & n* plurale *m*

p

✓ **plus** /plʌs/ **A** *prep* più
B *adj* in più; **500 ~** più di 500
C *n* più *m*; (advantage) extra *m inv*

plush /plʌʃ/ *adj* <*hotel etc*> lussuoso

plus sign *n* (segno *m*) più *m*

Pluto /ˈpluːtəʊ/ *n* Plutone *m*

plutonium /pluːˈtəʊnɪəm/ *n* plutonio *m*

ply /plaɪ/ *vt* (*pt/pp* **plied**) esercitare <*trade*>; **~ somebody with drink** continuare ad offrire da bere a qualcuno

plywood /ˈplaɪwʊd/ *n* compensato *m*

PM *abbr* (**Prime Minister**) primo ministro

p.m. *abbr* (**post meridiem**) del pomeriggio

PMS *n abbr* (**premenstrual syndrome**) sindrome *f* premestruale

PMT *n abbr* (**premenstrual tension**) tensione *f* premestruale

pneumatic /njuːˈmætɪk/ *adj* pneumatico

pneumatic drill *n* martello *m* pneumatico

pneumonia /njuːˈməʊnɪə/ *n* polmonite *f*

PO *abbr* **1** (**Post Office**) ≈ P.T. **2** (**postal order**) vaglia *m inv* postale

poach /pəʊtʃ/ *vt* Culin bollire; cacciare di frodo <*deer*>; pescare di frodo <*salmon*>; **~ed egg** uovo *m* in camicia

poacher /ˈpəʊtʃə(r)/ *n* bracconiere *m*

PO Box *n abbr* (**Post Office Box**) C.P. *f*

✓ **pocket** /ˈpɒkɪt/ **A** *n* tasca *f*; **~ of resistance** sacca *f* di resistenza; **be out of ~** rimetterci
B *vt* intascare

pocket-book *n* taccuino *m*; (wallet) portafoglio *m*

pocket money *n* denaro *m* per le piccole spese

p

pock-marked /ˈpɒkmɑːkt/ *adj* butterato

pod /pɒd/ *n* baccello *m*

podcast /ˈpɒdkɑːst/ *n* podcast *m inv*

podcaster /ˈpɒdkɑːstə(r)/ *n* podcaster *m inv*

podgy /ˈpɒdʒɪ/ *adj* (**-ier**, **-iest**) grassoccio

podiatrist /pəˈdaɪətrɪst/ *n* AmE pedicure *mf inv*

podium /ˈpəʊdɪəm/ *n* podio *m*

✓ **poem** /ˈpəʊɪm/ *n* poesia *f*

poet /ˈpəʊɪt/ *n* poeta *m*, poetessa *f*

poetic /pəʊˈetɪk/ *adj* poetico

poetic licence *n* licenza *f* poetica

Poet Laureate /ˈlɔːrɪət/ *n* poeta *m* di corte

poetry /ˈpəʊɪtrɪ/ *n* poesia *f*

po-faced /pəʊˈfeɪst/ *adj* BrE infml **look/be ~** avere un'aria di disapprovazione

poignancy /ˈpɔɪnjənsɪ/ *n* pregnanza *f*

poignant /ˈpɔɪnjənt/ *adj* pregnante

✓ **point** /pɔɪnt/ **A** *n* punto *m*; (sharp end) punta *f*; (meaning, purpose) senso *m*; Electr presa *f*; **what is the ~?** a che scopo?; **the ~ is** il fatto è; **I don't see the ~** non vedo il senso; **up to a ~** fino ad un certo punto; **be on the ~ of doing something** essere sul punto di fare qualcosa; **~s** *pl* Rail scambio *m*; **good/bad ~s** aspetti *mpl* positivi/negativi
B *vt* puntare (**at** verso)
C *vi* (with finger) puntare il dito; **~ at/to** <*person*> mostrare col dito; <*indicator*> indicare; **~ and click** Comput punta e clicca

▪ **point out** *vt* far notare <*fact*>; **~ something out to somebody** far notare qualcosa a qualcuno

point-blank *adj* a bruciapelo

pointed /ˈpɔɪntɪd/ *adj* appuntito; <*question*> diretto

pointer /ˈpɔɪntə(r)/ *n* (piece of advice) consiglio *m*

pointillism /ˈpwæntɪlɪzm/ *n* divisionismo *m*

pointillist /ˈpwæntɪlɪst/ *n* divisionista *mf*

pointing /ˈpɔɪntɪŋ/ *n* Constr rifinitura *f* con la malta

pointing device *n* Comput dispositivo *m* di puntamento

pointless /ˈpɔɪntlɪs/ *adj* inutile

point of order *n* mozione *f* d'ordine

point of sale *n* (place) punto *m* vendita; (promotional material) materiale *m* pubblicitario

point-of-sale promotion *n* promozione *f* punto vendita

point of view *n* punto *m* di vista

poise /pɔɪz/ *n* padronanza *f*

poised /pɔɪzd/ *adj* in equilibrio; (composed) padrone di sé; **~ to** sul punto di

poison /ˈpɔɪzn/ **A** *n* veleno *m*
B *vt* avvelenare

poisoned /ˈpɔɪz(ə)nd/ *adj* avvelenato

poisoner /ˈpɔɪzənə(r)/ *n* avvelenatore, -trice *mf*

poisonous /ˈpɔɪzənəs/ *adj* velenoso

poison pen letter *n* lettera *f* anonima diffamatoria

poke /pəʊk/ **A** *n* spintarella *f*
B *vt* spingere; <*fire*> attizzare; (put) ficcare; **~ fun at** prendere in giro

▪ **poke about, poke around** *vi* frugare

▪ **poke out** *vi* (protrude) spuntare

poker[1] /ˈpəʊkə(r)/ *n* attizzatoio *m*

poker[2] *n* Cards poker *m*

poker-faced /-ˈfeɪst/ *adj* <*person*> impassibile

poky /ˈpəʊkɪ/ *adj* (**-ier**, **-iest**) angusto

Poland /ˈpəʊlənd/ *n* Polonia *f*

polar /ˈpəʊlə(r)/ *adj* polare

polar bear *n* orso *m* bianco

polarity /pəˈlærətɪ/ *n* Electr, Phys fig polarità *f*

polarize /ˈpəʊləraɪz/ *vt* polarizzare

polarized *adj* polarizzato

pole[1] *n* palo *m*

✓ parola chiave

pole[2] *n* Geog, Electr polo *m*
Pole /pəʊl/ *n* polacco, -a *mf*
pole dancing /'pəʊl ˌdɑːnsɪŋ/ *n* pole dance *f*
polemic /pə'lemɪk/ *n* polemica
polemical /pə'lemɪkl/ *adj* polemico
pole star *n* stella *f* polare
pole vault *n* salto *m* con l'asta
police /pə'liːs/ **A** *npl* polizia *f*
B *vt* pattugliare ‹*area*›; sorvegliare ‹*behaviour*›
police car *n* gazzella *f*
police constable *n* agente *mf* di polizia
Police Department *n* AmE dipartimento *m* di polizia
police force *n* polizia *f*
policeman *n* poliziotto *m*
police officer *n* agente *mf* di polizia
police state *n* stato *m* militarista
police station *n* commissariato *m*
policewoman *n* donna *f* poliziotto *inv*
policing /pə'liːsɪŋ/ *n* (maintaining law and order) mantenimento *m* dell'ordine pubblico; (of demonstration, match) organizzazione *f* del servizio d'ordine
policy[1] /'pɒlɪsɪ/ *n* politica *f*
policy[2] *n* (insurance) polizza *f*
policyholder *n* titolare *mf* della polizza
policy unit *n* Pol comitato *m* responsabile della linea politica
polio /'pəʊlɪəʊ/ *n* polio *f*
polish /'pɒlɪʃ/ **A** *n* (shine) lucentezza *f*; (substance) lucido *m*; (for nails) smalto *m*; fig raffinatezza *f*
B *vt* lucidare; fig smussare
▪ **polish off** *vt* infml finire; far fuori ‹*food*›
▪ **polish up** *vt* perfezionare ‹*Italian*›
Polish /'pəʊlɪʃ/ *adj* & *n* polacco *m*
polished /'pɒlɪʃt/ *adj* ‹*manner*› raffinato; ‹*performance*› senza sbavature
polisher /'pɒləʃə(r)/ *n* (machine) lucidatrice *f*
polite /pə'laɪt/ *adj* cortese
politely /pə'laɪtlɪ/ *adv* cortesemente
politeness /pə'laɪtnɪs/ *n* cortesia *f*
politic /'pɒlɪtɪk/ *adj* prudente
political /pə'lɪtɪkl/ *adj* politico
politically /pə'lɪtɪklɪ/ *adv* dal punto di vista politico; ~ **correct** politicamente corretto
political prisoner *n* prigioniero, -a *mf* politico
politician /pɒlɪ'tɪʃn/ *n* politico *m*
politicize /pə'lɪtɪsaɪz/ *vt* politicizzare
politics /'pɒlɪtɪks/ *nsg* politica *fsg*
polka /'pɒlkə/ *n* polka *f*
polka dot **A** *n* pois *m inv*, pallino *m*
B *attrib* a pois
poll /pəʊl/ **A** *n* votazione *f*; (election) elezioni *fpl*; **[opinion]** ~ sondaggio *m* d'opinione; **go to the** ~**s** andare alle urne
B *vt* ottenere ‹*votes*›

pollen /'pɒlən/ *n* polline *m*
polling booth /'pəʊlɪŋ/ *n* cabina *f* elettorale
polling day *n* giorno *m* delle elezioni
polling station *n* seggio *m* elettorale
pollster /'pəʊlstə(r)/ *n* (person) persona *f* che esegue un sondaggio d'opinione
poll tax *n imposta (f) locale sulle persone fisiche*
pollutant /pə'luːtənt/ *n* sostanza *f* inquinante
pollute /pə'luːt/ *vt* inquinare
polluted /pə'luːtɪd/ *adj* inquinato
polluter /pə'luːtə(r)/ *n* inquinatore, -trice *mf*
pollution /pə'luːʃn/ *n* inquinamento *m*
polo /'pəʊləʊ/ *n* polo *m*
polo neck *n* collo *m* alto, dolcevita *m*
polo shirt *n* polo *f*
poltergeist /'pɒltəgaɪst/ *n* poltergeist *m inv*
poly /'pɒlɪ/ *n* BrE infml (polytechnic) politecnico *m*
poly bag *n* sacchetto *m* di plastica
polyester /pɒlɪ'estə(r)/ *n* poliestere *m*
polygamous /pə'lɪgəməs/ *adj* poligamico
polygamy /pə'lɪgəmɪ/ *n* poligamia *f*
polymath /'pɒlɪmæθ/ *n* erudito, -a *mf*
polymer /'pɒlɪmə(r)/ *n* polimero *m*
polystyrene® /pɒlɪ'staɪriːn/ *n* polistirolo *m*
polytechnic /pɒlɪ'teknɪk/ *n* politecnico *m*
polythene /'pɒlɪθiːn/ *n* politene *m*
polythene bag *n* sacchetto *m* di plastica
polyunsaturates /pɒlɪʌn'sætjʊreɪts/ *npl* grassi *mpl* polinsaturi
pomade /pə'meɪd/ *n* pomata *f*
pomegranate /'pɒmɪgrænɪt/ *n* melagrana *f*
pomp /pɒmp/ *n* pompa *f*
pompom /'pɒmpɒm/, **pompon** *n* pompon *m*
pomposity /pɒm'pɒsətɪ/ *n* pomposità *f*
pompous /'pɒmpəs/ *adj* pomposo
pompously /'pɒmpəslɪ/ *adv* pomposamente
poncy /'pɒnsɪ/ *adj* infml da finocchio; ‹*person*› finocchio
pond /pɒnd/ *n* stagno *m*
ponder /'pɒndə(r)/ *vt* & *vi* ponderare
ponderous /'pɒndərəs/ *adj* ponderoso; fig pesante
pong /pɒŋ/ **A** *n* infml puzza *f*
B *vi* puzzare
pontiff /'pɒntɪf/ *n* pontefice *m*
pontificate /pɒn'tɪfɪkeɪt/ *vi* pontificare
pontoon /pɒn'tuːn/ *n* (float) galleggiante *m*; (pier) pontile *m*; BrE (game) ventuno *m*
pony /'pəʊnɪ/ *n* pony *m inv*
ponytail /'pəʊnɪteɪl/ *n* coda *f* di cavallo
pony-trekking /'pəʊnɪtrekɪŋ/ *n* escursioni *fpl* col pony
pooch /puːtʃ/ *n* infml (dog) cagnetto *m*
poodle /'puːdl/ *n* barboncino *m*

p

poof /pʊf/, **poofter** /ˈpʊftə(r)/ *n* BrE infml (homosexual) finocchio *m*

pooh /puː/ **A** *int* (scorn, disgust) puah!
B *n* BrE (baby talk) popò *f*

pooh-pooh /puːˈpuː/ *vt* infml ridere di ‹*suggestion*›

pool¹ /puːl/ *n* (of water, blood) pozza *f*; **[swimming] ~** piscina *f*

pool² **A** *n* (common fund) cassa *f* comune; (in cards) piatto *m*; (game) biliardo *m* a buca; **~s** *pl* ≈ totocalcio *msg*
B *vt* mettere insieme

pool table *n* tavolo *m* da biliardo

pooped /puːpt/ *adj* infml **be ~ [out]** essere stanco morto

poor /pʊə(r)/ **A** *adj* povero; (not good) scadente; **in ~ health** in cattiva salute
B *npl* **the ~** i poveri

poorly /ˈpʊəlɪ/ **A** *adj* **be ~** non stare bene
B *adv* male

pop¹ /pɒp/ **A** *n* botto *m*; (drink) bibita *f* gasata; (turn) **the tickets were £5 a ~** i biglietti costavano £5 l'uno
B *vt* (*pt/pp* **popped**) infml (put) mettere; (burst) far scoppiare
C *vi* (burst) scoppiare
■ **pop in** *vi* infml fare un salto
■ **pop out** *vi* infml uscire; **~ out to the shop** fare un salto al negozio
■ **pop round** *vi* infml passare; **~ round to Ann's** passare da Ann
■ **pop up** *vi* infml (appear unexpectedly) saltare fuori

pop² **A** *n* infml musica *f* pop
B *attrib* pop *inv*

popcorn /ˈpɒpkɔːn/ *n* popcorn *m inv*

pope /pəʊp/ *n* papa *m*

poplar /ˈpɒplə(r)/ *n* pioppo *m*

poppy /ˈpɒpɪ/ *n* papavero *m*

pop sock *n* gambaletto *m*

populace /ˈpɒpjʊləs/ *n* popolo *m*

popular /ˈpɒpjʊlə(r)/ *adj* popolare; ‹*belief*› diffuso

popularity /pɒpjʊˈlærətɪ/ *n* popolarità *f*

popularize /ˈpɒpjʊləraɪz/ *vt* divulgare

populate /ˈpɒpjʊleɪt/ *vt* popolare

population /pɒpjʊˈleɪʃn/ *n* popolazione *f*

populist /ˈpɒpjʊlɪst/ *adj* & *n* populista *mf*

populous /ˈpɒpjʊləs/ *adj* popoloso

pop-up **A** *adj* **1** Comput a comparsa, pop-up; **~ menu** menu a comparsa, menu pop-up; **~ window** finestra a comparsa, finestra pop-up **2** (of shop, venue) a tempo, temporaneo; **~ store** negozio a tempo, negozio temporaneo
B *n* Comput finestra *f* a comparsa, finestra *f* pop-up

pop-up book *n* libro *m* con immagini tridimensionali

pop-up menu *n* Comput menu *m* pop-up

pop-up toaster *n* tostapane *m inv* a espulsione automatica

porcelain /ˈpɔːsəlɪn/ *n* porcellana *f*

porch /pɔːtʃ/ *n* portico *m*; AmE veranda *f*

porcupine /ˈpɔːkjʊpaɪn/ *n* porcospino *m*

pore¹ /pɔː(r)/ *n* poro *m*

pore² *vi* **~ over** immergersi in

pork /pɔːk/ *n* carne *f* di maiale

porn /pɔːn/ *n* infml porno *m*

porno /ˈpɔːnəʊ/ *adj* infml porno *inv*

pornographic /pɔːnəˈɡræfɪk/ *adj* pornografico

pornography /pɔːˈnɒɡrəfɪ/ *n* pornografia *f*

porous /ˈpɔːrəs/ *adj* poroso

porpoise /ˈpɔːpəs/ *n* focena *f*

porridge /ˈpɒrɪdʒ/ *n* farinata *f* di fiocchi d'avena

port¹ /pɔːt/ *n* porto *m*

port² *n* Naut (side) babordo *m*

port³ *n* (wine) porto *m*

portable /ˈpɔːtəbl/ *adj* & *n* portatile *m*

Portakabin® /ˈpɔːtəkæbɪn/ *n* casotto *m* prefabbricato

portcullis /pɔːtˈkʌlɪs/ *n* saracinesca *f*

portentous /pɔːˈtentəs/ *adj* (significant) solenne; (ominous) infausto

porter /ˈpɔːtə(r)/ *n* portiere *m*; (for luggage) facchino *m*

portfolio /pɔːtˈfəʊlɪəʊ/ *n* cartella *f*; Comm portafoglio *m*

porthole /ˈpɔːthəʊl/ *n* oblò *m*

portion /ˈpɔːʃn/ *n* parte *f*; (of food) porzione *f*

portly /ˈpɔːtlɪ/ *adj* (**-ier**, **-iest**) corpulento

portrait /ˈpɔːtrɪt/ *n* ritratto *m*

portrait painter *n* ritrattista *mf*

portray /pɔːˈtreɪ/ *vt* ritrarre; (represent) descrivere; ‹*actor*› impersonare

portrayal /pɔːˈtreɪəl/ *n* ritratto *m*; (by actor) caratterizzazione *f*

Portugal /ˈpɔːtjʊɡl/ *n* Portogallo *m*

Portuguese /pɔːtjʊˈɡiːz/ *adj* & *n* portoghese *mf*; (language) portoghese *m*

pose /pəʊz/ **A** *n* posa *f*
B *vt* porre ‹*problem, question*›
C *vi* (for painter) posare; **~ as** atteggiarsi a

poser /ˈpəʊzə(r)/ *n* infml (puzzle) rompicapo *m inv*; (person) montato, -a *mf*

posh /pɒʃ/ *adj* infml lussuoso; ‹*people*› danaroso

position /pəˈzɪʃn/ **A** *n* posizione *f*; (job) posto *m*; (status) ceto *m* [sociale]
B *vt* posizionare

positive /ˈpɒzɪtɪv/ **A** *adj* positivo; (certain) sicuro; (progress) concreto
B *n* positivo *m*

positive discrimination *n* misure *fpl* antidiscriminatorie

positively /ˈpɒzɪtɪvlɪ/ *adv* positivamente; (decidedly) decisamente

posse /ˈpɒsɪ/ *n* gruppo *m* di volontari armati

parola chiave

possess /pəˈzes/ *vt* possedere
possession /pəˈzeʃn/ *n* possesso *m*; **~s** *pl* beni *mpl*
possessive /pəˈzesɪv/ *adj* possessivo
possessiveness /pəˈzesɪvnɪs/ *n* carattere *m* possessivo
possessor /pəˈzesə(r)/ *n* possessore, -ditrice *mf*
possibility /pɒsəˈbɪlətɪ/ *n* possibilità *f*
possible /ˈpɒsəbl/ *adj* possibile
possibly /ˈpɒsəblɪ/ *adv* possibilmente; **I couldn't ~ accept** non mi è possibile accettare; **he can't ~ be right** non è possibile che abbia ragione; **could you ~...?** potrebbe per favore...?
possum /ˈpɒsəm/ *n* infml opossum *m inv*; **play ~** far finta di dormire; (pretend to be dead) fare il morto
post[1] /pəʊst/ **A** *n* (pole) palo *m*
B *vt* affiggere ‹*notice*›
post[2] **A** *n* (place of duty) posto *m*
B *vt* appostare; (transfer) assegnare
post[3] **A** *n* (mail) posta *f*; **by ~** per posta
B *vt* spedire; (put in letter box) imbucare; (as opposed to fax) mandare per posta; **keep somebody ~ed** tenere qualcuno al corrente
post+ *pref* post+
postage /ˈpəʊstɪdʒ/ *n* affrancatura *f*; **~ and packaging** spese *fpl* di posta
postage stamp *n* francobollo *m*
postal /ˈpəʊstl/ *adj* postale
postal order *n* vaglia *m inv* postale
postbox *n* cassetta *f* delle lettere
postcard *n* cartolina *f*
postcode *n* codice *m* postale
post-date *vt* postdatare
poster /ˈpəʊstə(r)/ *n* poster *m inv*; (advertising, election) cartellone *m*
posterior /pɒˈstɪərɪə(r)/ *n* infml posteriore *m*
posterity /pɒˈsterətɪ/ *n* posterità *f*
poster paint *n* pittura *f* a guazzo
postgraduate /pəʊs(t)ˈgrædjʊət/ **A** *n* laureato, -a *mf* che continua gli studi
B *adj* successivo alla laurea
posthumous /ˈpɒstjʊməs/ *adj* postumo
posthumously /ˈpɒstjʊməslɪ/ *adv* dopo la morte
posting /ˈpəʊstɪŋ/ *n* (job) incarico *m*; BrE (in mail) spedizione *f*; Comput posting *m inv*
postman /ˈpəʊstmən/ *n* postino *m*
postmark /ˈpəʊstmɑːk/ *n* timbro *m* postale
postmodern /ˌpəʊstˈmɒdn/ *adj* postmoderno
post-mortem /-ˈmɔːtəm/ *n* autopsia *f*
post-natal /-ˈneɪtl/ *adj* postnatale
post office *n* ufficio *m* postale
post office box *n* casella *f* postale
postpone /pəʊs(t)ˈpəʊn/ *vt* rimandare
postponement /pəʊs(t)ˈpəʊnmənt/ *n* rinvio *m*
postscript /ˈpəʊs(t)skrɪpt/ *n* post scriptum *m inv*
posture /ˈpɒstʃə(r)/ *n* posizione *f*
post-war *adj* del dopoguerra
pot /pɒt/ *n* vaso *m*; (for tea) teiera *f*; (for coffee) caffettiera *f*; (for cooking) pentola *f*; sl (marijuana) erba *f*; **~s of money** infml un sacco di soldi; **go to ~** infml andare in malora
potash /ˈpɒtæʃ/ *n* potassa *f*
potassium /pəˈtæsɪəm/ *n* potassio *m*
potato /pəˈteɪtəʊ/ *n* (*pl* **-es**) patata *f*
potato chips AmE, **potato crisps** BrE *npl* patatine *fpl*
potato peeler /-ˈpiːlə(r)/ *n* pelapatate *m inv*
pot-bellied /ˈpɒtbelɪd/ *adj* panciuto
pot belly /ˈpɒtbelɪ/ *n* infml pancione *m*
potent /ˈpəʊtənt/ *adj* potente
potentate /ˈpəʊtənteɪt/ *n* potentato *m*
potential /pəˈtenʃl/ **A** *adj* potenziale
B *n* potenziale *m*
potentially /pəˈtenʃəlɪ/ *adv* potenzialmente
pothole *n* cavità *f*; (in road) buca *f*
potholer *n* speleologo, -a *mf*
potholing /ˈpɒthəʊlɪŋ/ *n* speleologia *f*
pot luck *n* **take ~** affidarsi alla sorte
pot plant *n* pianta *f* da appartamento
pot-shot *n* **take a ~ at** sparare a casaccio a
potted /ˈpɒtɪd/ *adj* conservato; (shortened) condensato
potted plant *n* pianta *f* da appartamento
potter[1] /ˈpɒtə(r)/ *vi* **~ [about]** gingillarsi
potter[2] *n* vasaio, -a *mf*
pottery /ˈpɒtərɪ/ *n* lavorazione *f* della ceramica; (articles) ceramiche *fpl*; (workshop) laboratorio *m* di ceramiche
potting compost /ˈpɒtɪŋ/ *n* terriccio *m*
potty /ˈpɒtɪ/ **A** *adj* (**-ier**, **-iest**) infml matto
B *n* vasino *m*
pouch /paʊtʃ/ *n* marsupio *m*
pouffe /puːf/ *n* pouf *m inv*
poultry /ˈpəʊltrɪ/ *n* pollame *m*
pounce /paʊns/ *vi* balzare; **~ on** saltare su
pound[1] /paʊnd/ *n* libbra *f* (= 0,454 kg); (money) sterlina *f*
pound[2] **A** *vt* battere
B *vi* ‹*heart*› battere forte; (run heavily) correre pesantemente
pound[3] *n* (for cars) deposito *m* auto rimosse
pounding /ˈpaʊndɪŋ/ **A** *n* martellio *m*
B *adj* martellante
pour /pɔː(r)/ **A** *vt* versare
B *vi* riversarsi; (with rain) piovere a dirotto
■ **pour away** *vi* svuotare
■ **pour in** *vi* ‹*people*› arrivare in massa; ‹*letters, money*› arrivare a valanghe; ‹*water*› entrare a fiotti
■ **pour out** **A** *vi* riversarsi fuori
B *vt* versare ‹*drink*›; sfogare ‹*troubles*›
pout /paʊt/ **A** *vi* fare il broncio
B *n* broncio *m*

poverty /ˈpɒvətɪ/ *n* povertà *f*
poverty line *n* soglia *f* di povertà
poverty-stricken *adj* indigente
POW *n abbr* (**prisoner of war**) prigioniero, -a *mf* di guerra
powder /ˈpaʊdə(r)/ **A** *n* polvere *f*; (cosmetic) cipria *f*
B *vt* polverizzare; (face) incipriare
powdered /ˈpaʊdəd/ *adj* ‹*milk*› in polvere
powder room *n* euph toilette *f inv* per signore
powdery /ˈpaʊdərɪ/ *adj* polveroso
🔑 **power** /ˈpaʊə(r)/ *n* potere *m*; Electr corrente *f* [elettrica]; Math potenza *f*
powerboat *n* fuoribordo *m*
power cut *n* interruzione *f* di corrente
powered /ˈpaʊəd/ *adj* **~ by electricity** alimentato da corrente elettrica
🔑 **powerful** /ˈpaʊəfʊl/ *adj* potente
powerhouse /ˈpaʊəhaʊs/ *n* fig (person) persona *f* dinamica ed energica; **a ~ of ideas** un vulcano di idee
powerless /ˈpaʊəlɪs/ *adj* impotente
power line *n* linea *f* elettrica
power of attorney *n* procura *f*
power on light *n* spia *f* di accensione
power plant *n* centrale *f* elettrica
power sharing *n* condivisione *f* del potere
power station *n* centrale *f* elettrica
power steering *n* Auto servosterzo *m*
power switch *n* pulsante *m* di alimentazione
power unit *n* (of computer etc) alimentatore *m*
power-walk **A** *n* camminata *f* a passo sostenuto
B *vi* camminare a passo sostenuto
power-walker *n* persona *f* che fa camminate a passo sostenuto
power-walking *n* camminate *fpl* a passo sostenuto (come esercizio fisico)
pow-wow /ˈpaʊwaʊ/ *n* (of American Indians) raduno *m* tribale; infml (discussion) discussione *f*
pp *abbr* **1** (**pages**) pp. **2** (**per procurationem**) pp.
PPP *abbr* (**public-private partnership**) *partnership (f) tra un ente pubblico e un'impresa privata*
PR *n abbr* **1** (**proportional representation**) proporzionale *f* **2** (**public relations**) pubbliche relazioni *fpl*
practicable /ˈpræktɪkəbl/ *adj* praticabile
practical /ˈpræktɪkl/ *adj* pratico
practicality /præktɪˈkælɪtɪ/ *n* praticità *f*
practical joke *n* scherzo *m* pratico
practically /ˈpræktɪklɪ/ *adv* praticamente
🔑 **practice** /ˈpræktɪs/ *n* pratica *f*; (custom) usanza *f*; (habit) abitudine *f*; (exercise) esercizio *m*; Sport allenamento *m*; **in ~** (in reality) in pratica; **out of ~** fuori esercizio; **put into ~** mettere in pratica
practicing /ˈpræktɪsɪŋ/ *adj* AmE = **practising**
practise /ˈpræktɪs/ **A** *vt* fare pratica in; (carry out) mettere in pratica; esercitare ‹*profession*›
B *vi* esercitarsi; ‹*doctor*› praticare
practised /ˈpræktɪst/ *adj* esperto
practising /ˈpræktɪsɪŋ/ *adj* BrE praticante; **a ~ lawyer** un avvocato che esercita
pragmatic /prægˈmætɪk/ *adj* pragmatico
pragmatism /ˈprægmətɪzm/ *n* pragmatismo *m*
pragmatist /ˈprægmətɪst/ *n* pragmatico, -a *mf*
prairie /ˈpreərɪ/ *n* prateria *f*
praise /preɪz/ **A** *n* lode *f*
B *vt* lodare
praiseworthy /ˈpreɪzwɜːðɪ/ *adj* lodevole
pram /præm/ *n* carrozzella *f*
prance /prɑːns/ *vi* saltellare
prank /præŋk/ *n* tiro *m*
prattle /ˈprætl/ *vi* parlottare
prawn /prɔːn/ *n* gambero *m*
prawn cocktail *n* cocktail *m inv* di gamberetti
pray /preɪ/ *vi* pregare
prayer /preə(r)/ *n* preghiera *f*
preach /priːtʃ/ *vt & vi* predicare
preacher /ˈpriːtʃə(r)/ *n* predicatore, -trice *mf*
preamble /priːˈæmbl/ *n* preambolo *m*
pre-arrange /priː-/ *vt* predisporre
precarious /prɪˈkeərɪəs/ *adj* precario
precariously /prɪˈkeərɪəslɪ/ *adv* in modo precario
precast /ˈpriːkɑːst/ *adj* ‹*concrete*› prefabbricato
precaution /prɪˈkɔːʃn/ *n* precauzione *f*; **as a ~** per precauzione
precautionary /prɪˈkɔːʃnərɪ/ *adj* preventivo
precede /prɪˈsiːd/ *vt* precedere
precedence /ˈpresɪdəns/ *n* precedenza *f*
precedent /ˈpresɪdənt/ *n* precedente *m*
preceding /prɪˈsiːdɪŋ/ *adj* precedente
preceptor /prɪˈseptə(r)/ *n* AmE Univ precettore *m*
precinct /ˈpriːsɪŋkt/ *n* (traffic-free) zona *f* pedonale; AmE (district) circoscrizione *f*
precious /ˈpreʃəs/ **A** *adj* prezioso; ‹*style*› ricercato
B *adv* infml **~ little** ben poco
precipice /ˈpresɪpɪs/ *n* precipizio *m*
precipitate[1] /prɪˈsɪpɪtət/ *adj* precipitoso
precipitate[2] /prɪˈsɪpɪteɪt/ *vt* precipitare
precipitation /prɪsɪpɪˈteɪʃn/ *n* precipitazione *f*
precis /ˈpreɪsɪ/ *n* (*pl* **precis** /ˈpreɪsiːz/) sunto *m*
precise /prɪˈsaɪs/ *adj* preciso

🔑 parola chiave

precisely /prɪ'saɪslɪ/ *adv* precisamente
precision /prɪ'sɪʒn/ *n* precisione *f*
preclude /prɪ'klu:d/ *vt* precludere
precocious /prɪ'kəʊʃəs/ *adj* precoce
precociousness /prɪ'kəʊʃsnɪs/ *n* precocità *f*
preconceived /pri:kən'si:vd/ *adj* preconcetto
preconception /pri:kən'sepʃn/ *n* preconcetto *m*
precondition /pri:kən'dɪʃn/ **A** *n* presupposto *m*
B *vt* Psych condizionare
pre-cook /pri:'kʊk/ *vt* cuocere in anticipo
precursor /pri:'kɜ:sə(r)/ *n* precursore *m*
predate /ˌpri:'deɪt/ *vt* retrodatare ‹*cheque*›; ‹*building, painting*› essere antecedente a
predator /'predətə(r)/ *n* predatore, -trice *mf*
predatory /'predət(ə)rɪ/ *adj* rapace
predecessor /'pri:dɪsesə(r)/ *n* predecessore, -a *mf*
predetermine /pri:dɪ'tɜ:mɪn/ *vt* predeterminare
predicament /prɪ'dɪkəmənt/ *n* situazione *f* difficile
predicate /'predɪkət/ *n* Gram predicato *m*
predicative /prɪ'dɪkətɪv/ *adj* predicativo
predict /prɪ'dɪkt/ *vt* predire
predictable /prɪ'dɪktəbl/ *adj* prevedibile
prediction /prɪ'dɪkʃn/ *n* previsione *f*
predigested /pri:daɪ'dʒestɪd/ *adj* predigerito
predispose /ˌpri:dɪ'spəʊz/ *vt* predisporre
predisposition /pri:dɪspə'zɪʃn/ *n* predisposizione *f*
predominant /prɪ'dɒmɪnənt/ *adj* predominante
predominantly /prɪ'dɒmɪnəntlɪ/ *adv* prevalentemente
predominate /prɪ'dɒmɪneɪt/ *vi* predominare
pre-eminent /pri:'emɪnənt/ *adj* preminente
pre-empt /pri:'empt/ *vt* (prevent) prevenire
pre-emptive /pri:'emptiv/ *adj* preventivo
preen /pri:n/ *vt* lisciarsi; ~ **oneself** fig farsi bello
prefab /'pri:fæb/ *n* infml casa *f* prefabbricata
prefabricated /pri:'fæbrɪkeɪtɪd/ *adj* prefabbricato
preface /'prefɪs/ *n* prefazione *f*
prefatory /'prefət(ə)rɪ/ *adj* ‹*comments*› preliminare; ‹*pages, notes*› introduttivo
prefect /'pri:fekt/ *n* Schol *studente, -tessa (mf) della scuola superiore con responsabilità disciplinare ecc.*
prefer /prɪ'fɜ:(r)/ *vt* (*pt/pp* **preferred**) preferire; **I** ~ **to walk** preferisco camminare
preferable /'prefərəbl/ *adj* preferibile (**to** a)
preferably /'prefərəblɪ/ *adv* preferibilmente
preference /'prefərəns/ *n* preferenza *f*
preferential /prefə'renʃl/ *adj* preferenziale
prefigure /ˌpri:'fɪgə(r), AmE -gjər/ *vt* preannunciare
prefix /'pri:fɪks/ *n* prefisso *m*
pregnancy /'pregnənsɪ/ *n* gravidanza *f*
pregnant /'pregnənt/ *adj* incinta
preheat /pri:'hi:t/ *vt* preriscaldare ‹*oven*›
prehensile /pri:'hensaɪl/ *adj* prensile
prehistoric /pri:hɪs'tɒrɪk/ *adj* preistorico
pre-ignition /pri:ɪg'nɪʃn/ *n* preaccensione *f*
pre-installed /pri:ɪn'stɔ:ld/ *adj* preinstallato
prejudge /pri:'dʒʌdʒ/ *vt* giudicare prematuramente ‹*issue*›
prejudice /'predʒʊdɪs/ **A** *n* pregiudizio *m*
B *vt* influenzare (**against** contro); (harm) danneggiare
prejudiced /'predʒʊdɪst/ *adj* prevenuto
preliminary /prɪ'lɪmɪnərɪ/ *adj* preliminare
preloaded /pri:'ləʊdɪd/ *adj* precaricato
prelude /'prelju:d/ *n* preludio *m*
premarital /pri:'mærɪtl/ *adj* prematrimoniale
premarital sex *n* rapporti *mpl* prematrimoniali
premature /'premətjʊə(r)/ *adj* prematuro
premature birth *n* parto *m* prematuro
prematurely /'premətjʊəlɪ/ *adv* prematuramente
premeditated /pri:'medɪteɪtɪd/ *adj* premeditato
premeditation /ˌpri:medɪ'teɪʃn/ *n* premeditazione *f*
premenstrual syndrome /pri:'menstrʊəl/ *n* sindrome *f* premestruale
premenstrual tension *n* tensione *f* premestruale
premier /'premɪə(r)/ **A** *adj* primario
B *n* Pol primo ministro *m*, premier *m inv*
premiere /'premɪeə(r)/ *n* prima *f*
premiership /'premɪəʃɪp/ *n* Pol carica *f* di primo ministro nel Regno Unito; ≈ presidenza *f* del consiglio
premises /'premɪsɪz/ *npl* locali *mpl*; **on the** ~ sul posto
premium /'pri:mɪəm/ *n* premio *m*; **be at a** ~ essere una cosa rara
premium bond *n* obbligazione *f* a premio
premonition /premə'nɪʃn/ *n* presentimento *m*
prenatal /pri:'neɪtl/ *adj* esp Am prenatale
prenuptial agreement /pri:nʌpʃl ə'gri:mənt/ *n* accordo *m* prematrimoniale
preoccupation /ˌpri:ɒkjʊ'peɪʃn/ *n* preoccupazione *f*
preoccupied /pri:'ɒkjʊpaɪd/ *adj* preoccupato
preoperative /pri:'ɒp(ə)rətɪv/ *adj* preoperatorio
preordained /pri:ɔ:'deɪnd/ *adj* prestabilito; ‹*outcome*› predestinato
pre-owned /pri:'əʊnd/ *adj* ‹*video, game*› di seconda mano
prep /prep/ *n* Sch compiti *mpl*
pre-packed /pri:'pækt/ *adj* preconfezionato

prepaid /priːˈpeɪd/ *adj* pagato in anticipo; ‹*envelope*› già affrancato

preparation /prepəˈreɪʃn/ *n* preparazione *f*; **~s** *pl* preparativi *mpl*

preparatory /prɪˈpærətrɪ/ *adj* preparatorio; **~ to** come preparazione per

preparatory school *n* BrE = **prep school**

⚷ **prepare** /prɪˈpeə(r)/ **A** *vt* preparare
B *vi* prepararsi (**for** per); **~d to** disposto a

prepay /priːˈpeɪ/ *vt* (*pt/pp* **-paid**) pagare in anticipo

preponderance /prɪˈpɒndərəns/ *n* preponderanza *f*

preponderantly /prɪˈpɒndərəntlɪ/ *adv* in modo preponderante

preponderate /prɪˈpɒndəreɪt/ *vi* predominare

preposition /prepəˈzɪʃn/ *n* preposizione *f*

prepossessing /priːpəˈzesɪŋ/ *adj* attraente

preposterous /prɪˈpɒstərəs/ *adj* assurdo

pre-programmed /priːˈprəʊgræmd/ *adj* programmato; Comput preprogrammato

prep school *n* scuola *f* elementare privata

pre-recorded /-rɪˈkɔːdɪd/ *adj* in differita

prerequisite /priːˈrekwɪzɪt/ *n* condizione *f* sine qua non

prerogative /prɪˈrɒgətɪv/ *n* prerogativa *f*

Pres. *abbr* (**President**) Pres.

Presbyterian /prezbɪˈtɪərɪən/ *adj & n* presbiteriano, -a *mf*

pre-school /ˈpriːskuːl/ **A** *n* AmE scuola *f* materna, asilo *m*
B *adj* ‹*child*› in età prescolastica; ‹*years*› prescolastico

prescribe /prɪˈskraɪb/ *vt* prescrivere

p

prescription /prɪˈskrɪpʃn/ *n* Med ricetta *f*

prescription charges *npl* BrE ≈ ticket *m inv* sui medicinali

prescriptive /prɪˈskrɪptɪv/ *adj* normativo

⚷ **presence** /ˈprezns/ *n* presenza *f*; **~ of mind** presenza *f* di spirito

presence of mind *n* presenza *f* di spirito

⚷ **present¹** /ˈpreznt/ **A** *adj* presente
B *n* presente *m*; **at ~** attualmente

⚷ **present²** *n* (gift) regalo *m*; **give somebody something as a ~** regalare qualcosa a qualcuno

⚷ **present³** /prɪˈzent/ *vt* presentare; **~ somebody with an award** consegnare un premio a qualcuno

presentable /prɪˈzentəbl/ *adj* **be ~** essere presentabile

⚷ **presentation** /preznˈteɪʃn/ *n* presentazione *f*

present-day *adj* attuale

presenter /prɪˈzentə(r)/ *n* TV, Radio presentatore, -trice *mf*

presently /ˈprezntlɪ/ *adv* fra poco; AmE (now) attualmente

⚷ parola chiave

present perfect *n* passato *m* prossimo

preservation /prezəˈveɪʃn/ *n* conservazione *f*

preservative /prɪˈzɜːvətɪv/ *n* conservante *m*

preserve /prɪˈzɜːv/ **A** *vt* preservare; Culin conservare
B *n* (in hunting & fig) riserva *f*; (jam) marmellata *f*

pre-set /priːˈset/ *vt* programmare

pre-shrunk /priːˈʃrʌŋk/ *adj* ‹*fabric*› irrestringibile

preside /prɪˈzaɪd/ *vi* presiedere (**over** a)

presidency /ˈprezɪdənsɪ/ *n* presidenza *f*

⚷ **president** /ˈprezɪdənt/ *n* presidente *m*

presidential /prezɪˈdenʃl/ *adj* presidenziale

pre-soak /priːˈsəʊk/ *vt* mettere in ammollo

⚷ **press** /pres/ **A** *n* (machine) pressa *f*; (newspapers) stampa *f*
B *vt* premere; pressare ‹*flower*›; (iron) stirare; (squeeze) stringere
C *vi* (urge) incalzare
▪ **press ahead** *vi* (continue) proseguire
▪ **press for** *vi* fare pressione per; **be ~ed for** (short of) essere a corto di
▪ **press on** *vi* andare avanti

press agency *n* agenzia *f* di stampa

press conference *n* conferenza *f* stampa

press cutting *n* ritaglio *m* di giornale

press-gang *vt* forzare

pressing /ˈpresɪŋ/ *adj* urgente

press release *n* comunicato *m* stampa

press stud *n* [bottone *m*] automatico *m*

press-up *n* flessione *f*

⚷ **pressure** /ˈpreʃə(r)/ **A** *n* pressione *f*
B *vt* = **pressurize**

pressure cooker *n* pentola *f* a pressione

pressure group *n* gruppo *m* di pressione

pressurize /ˈpreʃə(r)/ *vt* far pressione su

pressurized /ˈpreʃəraɪzd/ *adj* ‹*cabin*› pressurizzato

prestige /preˈstiːʒ/ *n* prestigio *m*

prestigious /preˈstɪdʒəs/ *adj* prestigioso

presumably /prɪˈzjuːməblɪ/ *adv* presumibilmente

presume /prɪˈzjuːm/ **A** *vt* presumere; **~ to do something** permettersi di fare qualcosa
B *vi* **~ on** approfittare di

presumption /prɪˈzʌmpʃn/ *n* presunzione *f*; (boldness) impertinenza *f*

presumptuous /prɪˈzʌmptjʊəs/ *adj* impertinente

presuppose /priːsəˈpəʊz/ *vt* presupporre

presupposition /priːsʌpəˈzɪʃn/ *n* presupposizione *f*

pre-tax /ˈpriːtæks/ *adj* al lordo d'imposta

pretence /prɪˈtens/ *n* finzione *f*; (pretext) pretesto *m*; **it's all ~** è tutta una scena

pretend /prɪˈtend/ **A** *vt* fingere; (claim) pretendere
B *vi* fare finta

pretender /prɪˈtendə(r)/ *n* pretendente *mf*

pretension /prɪ'tenʃn/ *n* pretesa *f*

pretentious /prɪ'tenʃəs/ *adj* pretenzioso

preterite /'pretərɪt/ *n* preterito *m*

pretext /'pri:tekst/ *n* pretesto *m*

pretty /'prɪtɪ/ **A** *adj* (**-ier**, **-iest**) carino
B *adv* infml (fairly) abbastanza

prevail /prɪ'veɪl/ *vi* prevalere; ~ **upon somebody to do something** convincere qualcuno a fare qualcosa

prevailing /prɪ'veɪlɪŋ/ *adj* prevalente

prevalence /'prevələns/ *n* diffusione *f*

prevalent /'prevələnt/ *adj* diffuso

prevaricate /prɪ'værɪkeɪt/ *vi* tergiversare

prevent /prɪ'vent/ *vt* impedire; ~ **somebody [from] doing something** impedire a qualcuno di fare qualcosa

preventable /prɪ'venʃn/ *adj* evitabile

prevention /prɪ'venʃn/ *n* prevenzione *f*

preventive /prɪ'ventɪv/ *adj* preventivo

preview /'pri:vju/ *n* anteprima *f*

previous /'pri:vɪəs/ *adj* precedente

previously /'pri:vɪəslɪ/ *adv* precedentemente

pre-war /pri:'wɔ:(r)/ *adj* anteguerra

pre-wash /'pri:wɒʃ/ *n* prelavaggio *m*

prey /preɪ/ **A** *n* preda *f*; **bird of** ~ uccello *m* rapace
B *vi* ~ **on** far preda di; ~ **on sb's mind** attanagliare qualcuno

price /praɪs/ **A** *n* prezzo *m*
B *vt* Comm fissare il prezzo di

price conscious *adj* consapevole dell'andamento dei prezzi

price cut *n* riduzione *f* di prezzo

price cutting *n* taglio *m* dei prezzi

price freeze *n* congelamento *m* dei prezzi

price increase *n* aumento *m* di prezzo

priceless /'praɪslɪs/ *adj* inestimabile; infml (amusing) spassosissimo

price list *n* listino *m* prezzi

price/performance ratio *n* rapporto *m* prezzo/prestazioni

price range *n* gamma *f* di prezzi

price rise *n* rialzo *m* dei prezzi

price tag *n* talloncino *m* del prezzo

price war *n* guerra *f* dei prezzi

pricey /'praɪsɪ/ *adj* infml caro

pricing policy /'praɪsɪŋ/ *n* politica *f* di determinazione dei prezzi

prick /prɪk/ **A** *n* puntura *f*; vulg (penis) cazzo *m*; (person) stronzo *m*
B *vt* pungere
■ **prick up**: *vt* ~ **up one's ears** rizzare le orecchie

prickle /'prɪkl/ *n* spina *f*; (sensation) formicolio *m*

prickly /'prɪklɪ/ *adj* pungente; ‹*person*› irritabile

pride /praɪd/ **A** *n* orgoglio *m*; (of lions) branco *m*; ~ **of place** posizione *f* d'onore
B *vt* ~ **oneself on** vantarsi di

priest /pri:st/ *n* prete *m*

priesthood /'pri:sthʊd/ *n* (clergy) clero *m*; (calling) sacerdozio *m*; **enter the** ~ farsi prete

prig /prɪg/ *n* presuntuoso *m*

priggish /'prɪgɪʃ/ *adj* presuntuoso

prim /prɪm/ *adj* (**primmer**, **primmest**) perbenino

primacy /'praɪməsɪ/ *n* primato *m*; (of party, power) supremazia *f*; Relig carica *f* di primate

prima facie /praɪmə'feɪʃɪ/ **A** *adv* (at first) a prima vista
B *adj* a prima vista legittimo

primal /'praɪməl/ *adj* ‹*quality, myth, feeling*› primitivo

primarily /'praɪmerɪlɪ/ *adv* in primo luogo

primary /'praɪmərɪ/ *adj* primario; (chief) principale

primary colour *n* colore *m* primario

primary school *n* scuola *f* elementare

primate /'praɪmeɪt/ *n* Zool, Relig primate *m*

prime¹ /praɪm/ **A** *adj* principale, primo; (first-rate) eccellente
B *n* **be in one's** ~ essere nel fiore degli anni

prime² *vt* preparare ‹*surface, person*›

Prime Minister *n* Primo Ministro *m*

prime mover *n* promotore, -trice *mf*

primer /'praɪmə(r)/ *n* (paint) base *f*; (for detonating) innesco *m*

prime time **A** *n* prime time *m inv*, fascia *f* di massimo ascolto
B *attrib* ‹*advertising, programme*› nella fascia di massimo ascolto

primeval /praɪ'mi:vl/ *adj* primitivo

primitive /'prɪmɪtɪv/ *adj* primitivo

primordial /praɪ'mɔ:dɪəl/ *adj* primordiale

primrose /'prɪmrəʊz/ *n* primula *f*

prince /prɪns/ *n* principe *m*

princely /'prɪnslɪ/ *adj* ‹*life, role*› da principe; ‹*amount, style*› principesco

princess /prɪn'ses/ *n* principessa *f*

principal /'prɪnsɪpl/ **A** *adj* principale
B *n* Sch preside *m*

principality /prɪnsɪ'pælətɪ/ *n* principato *m*

principally /'prɪnsəplɪ/ *adv* principalmente

principle /'prɪnsəpl/ *n* principio *m*; **in** ~ in teoria; **on** ~ per principio; ~**s** *pl* (fundamentals) fondamenti *mpl*

print /prɪnt/ **A** *n* (mark, trace) impronta *f*; Phot copia *f*; (letters) stampatello *m*; (picture) stampa *f*; **in** ~ (printed out) stampato; ‹*book*› in commercio; **out of** ~ esaurito
B *vt & vi* stampare; (write in capitals) scrivere in stampatello
■ **print off** *vt* stampare ‹*copies*›
■ **print out** *vt & vi* Comput stampare

printed matter /'prɪntɪd/ *n* stampe *fpl*

printer /'prɪntə(r)/ *n* stampante *f*; (person) tipografo, -a *mf*

p

printer port *n* porta *f* per la stampante
printing /ˈprɪntɪŋ/ *n* tipografia *f*
printout /ˈprɪntaʊt/ *n* Comput stampa *f*
print preview /prɪntˈpriːvjuː/ *vt* Comput fare l'anteprima di stampa di
print speed *n* velocità *f* di stampa
⚷ **prior** /ˈpraɪə(r)/ **A** *adj* precedente
B *prep* ~ **to** prima di
⚷ **priority** /praɪˈɒrətɪ/ *n* precedenza *f*; (matter) priorità *f*
priory /ˈpraɪərɪ/ *n* monastero *m*
prise /praɪz/ *vt* ~ **open/up** forzare
■ **prise off** *vt* togliere facendo leva ‹*lid*›
prism /ˈprɪzm/ *n* prisma *m*
⚷ **prison** /ˈprɪzn/ *n* prigione *f*, carcere *m*
prison camp *n* campo *m* di prigionia
prisoner /ˈprɪz(ə)nə(r)/ *n* prigioniero, -a *mf*
prison officer *n* guardia *f* carceraria
prison sentence *n* pena *f* detentiva
prissy /ˈprɪsɪ/ *adj* ‹*person*› perbenista
pristine /ˈprɪstiːn/ *adj* originario; (unspoilt) intatto
privacy /ˈprɪvəsɪ/ *n* privacy *f*
⚷ **private** /ˈpraɪvət/ **A** *adj* privato; ‹*car, secretary, letter*› personale
B *n* Mil soldato *m* semplice; **in** ~ in privato
private enterprise *n* iniziativa *f* privata
private eye *n* infml investigatore, -trice *mf* privato
privately /ˈpraɪvətlɪ/ *adv* ‹*funded, educated etc*› privatamente; (in secret) in segreto; (confidentially) in privato; (inwardly) interiormente
private property *n* proprietà *f* privata
privation /praɪˈveɪʃn/ *n* privazione *f*; ~**s** *pl* stenti *mpl*
privatization /praɪvətaɪˈzeɪʃn/ *n* privatizzazione *f*
privatize /ˈpraɪvətaɪz/ *vt* privatizzare
privilege /ˈprɪvəlɪdʒ/ *n* privilegio *m*
privileged /ˈprɪvəlɪdʒd/ *adj* privilegiato
privy /ˈprɪvɪ/ *adj* **be** ~ **to** essere al corrente di
⚷ **prize** /praɪz/ **A** *n* premio *m*
B *adj* (idiot etc) perfetto
C *vt* apprezzare
prize draw *n* estrazione *f* a premi
prize-giving /ˈpraɪzgɪvɪŋ/ *n* premiazione *f*
prize money *n* montepremi *m*
prizewinner *n* vincitore, -trice *mf*
prize-winning *adj* vincente
pro /preʊ/ *n* infml (professional) professionista *mf*; **the** ~**s and cons** il pro e il contro
proactive /prəʊˈæktɪv/ *adj* ‹*approach*› proattivo
probability /prɒbəˈbɪlətɪ/ *n* probabilità *f*
probable /ˈprɒbəbl/ *adj* probabile
⚷ **probably** /ˈprɒbəblɪ/ *adv* probabilmente
probate /ˈprəʊbeɪt/ *n* Jur omologazione *f*

⚷ parola chiave

probation /prəˈbeɪʃn/ *n* prova *f*; Jur libertà *f* vigilata
probationary /prəˈbeɪʃnərɪ/ *adj* in prova; ~ **period** periodo *m* di prova
probationer /prəˈbeɪʃnə(r)/ *n* (employee on trial) impiegato, -a *mf* in prova; (trainee) apprendista *mf*
probation officer *n agente (m) addetto alla sorveglianza di chi si trova in regime di libertà vigilata*
probe /prəʊb/ **A** *n* sonda *f*; fig (investigation) indagine *f*
B *vt* sondare; (investigate) esaminare a fondo
probing /ˈprəubɪŋ/ *adj* ‹*question*› penetrante
⚷ **problem** /ˈprɒbləm/ **A** *n* problema *m*
B *attrib* difficile
problematic /prɒbləˈmætɪk/ *adj* problematico
problem page *n* posta *f* del cuore
procedural /prəˈsiːdʒərəl/ *adj* ‹*detail, error*› procedurale
⚷ **procedure** /prəˈsiːdʒe(r)/ *n* procedimento *m*
⚷ **proceed** /prəˈsiːd/ **A** *vi* procedere
B *vt* ~ **to do something** proseguire facendo qualcosa
proceedings /prəˈsiːdɪŋz/ *npl* (report) atti *mpl*; Jur azione *fsg* legale
proceeds /ˈprəʊsiːdz/ *npl* ricavato *msg*
⚷ **process** /ˈprəʊses/ **A** *n* processo *m*; (procedure) procedimento *m*; **in the** ~ nel far ciò
B *vt* trattare; Admin occuparsi di; Phot sviluppare
processing /ˈprəʊsesɪŋ, AmE ˈprɒ-/ *n* trattamento *m*; **food** ~ l'industria alimentare
procession /prəˈseʃn/ *n* processione *f*
processor /ˈprəʊsesə(r)/ *n* Comput processore *m*; (for food) tritatutto *m inv*
pro-choice /prəʊˈtʃɔɪs/ *adj* abortista
proclaim /prəˈkleɪm/ *vt* proclamare
proclamation /prɒkləˈmeɪʃn/ *n* proclamazione *f*
proclivity /prəˈklɪvətɪ/ *n* tendenza *f*
procrastinate /prəˈkræstɪneɪt/ *vi* procrastinare
procrastination /prəkræstɪˈneɪʃn/ *n* procrastinazione *f*
procreate /prəʊkrɪˈeɪt/ *vi* procreare
procreation /prəʊkrɪˈeɪʃn/ *n* procreazione *f*
procure /prəˈkjʊə(r)/ *vt* ottenere
prod /prɒd/ **A** *n* colpetto *m*
B *vt* (*pt/pp* **prodded**) punzecchiare; fig incitare
prodigal /ˈprɒdɪgl/ *adj* prodigo
prodigal son *n* figliol *m* prodigo
prodigious /prəˈdɪdʒəs/ *adj* prodigioso
prodigy /ˈprɒdɪdʒɪ/ *n* **[infant]** ~ bambino *m* prodigio
produce¹ /ˈprɒdjuːs/ *n* prodotti *mpl*; ~ **of Italy** prodotto in Italia

produce² /prəˈdjuːs/ *vt* produrre; (bring out) tirar fuori; (cause) causare; infml (give birth to) fare

producer /prəˈdjuːsə(r)/ *n* produttore *m*

product /ˈprɒdʌkt/ *n* prodotto *m*

production /prəˈdʌkʃn/ *n* produzione *f*; Theat spettacolo *m*

production control *n* controllo *m* della produzione

production director *n* direttore, -trice *mf* della produzione

production line *n* catena *f* di montaggio

production management *n* gestione *f* della produzione

production manager *n* direttore, -trice *mf* della produzione

productive /prəˈdʌktɪv/ *adj* produttivo

productivity /prɒdʌkˈtɪvətɪ/ *n* produttività *f*

product range *n* gamma *f* di prodotti

Prof. *abbr* (**Professor**) Prof.

profane /prəˈfeɪn/ *adj* profano; (blasphemous) blasfemo

profanity /prəˈfænətɪ/ *n* (oath) bestemmia *f*

profess /prəˈfes/ *vt* (claim) dichiarare

professed /prəˈfest/ *adj* (claiming to be) sedicente

profession /prəˈfeʃn/ *n* professione *f*

professional /prəˈfeʃnəl/ **A** *adj* professionale; (not amateur) professionista; (piece of work) da professionista; ‹*man*› di professione
B *n* professionista *mf*

professionalism /prəˈfeʃnəlɪzm/ *n* (of person, organization, work) professionalità *f*; Sport professionismo *m*

professionally /prəˈfeʃnəlɪ/ *adv* professionalmente

professor /prəˈfesə(r)/ *n* professore *m* [universitario]

professorial /prɒfəˈsɔːrɪəl/ *adj* ‹*duties, post, salary*› professorale

proffer /ˈprɒfə(r)/ *vt* (hold out) porgere; fig (offer) offrire

proficiency /prəˈfɪʃnsɪ/ *n* competenza *f*

proficient /prəˈfɪʃnt/ *adj* competente (**in** in)

profile /ˈprəʊfaɪl/ *n* profilo *m*

profiling /ˈprəʊfaɪlɪŋ/ *n* profilo *m*; **genetic ~** profilo genetico

profit /ˈprɒfɪt/ **A** *n* profitto *m*
B *vi* **~ from** trarre profitto da

profitable /ˈprɒfɪtəbl/ *adj* proficuo

profitably /ˈprɒfɪtəblɪ/ *adv* in modo proficuo

profit and loss account *n* conto *m* profitti e perdite

profiteer /prɒfɪˈtɪə(r)/ *n* profittatore, -trice *mf*

profiterole /prəˈfɪtərəʊl/ *n* profiterole *m inv*

profit margin *n* margine *m* di profitto

profit-sharing *n* partecipazione *f* agli utili

profligate /ˈprɒflɪgət/ *adj* (extravagant) spendaccione; (dissolute) dissoluto; ‹*spending*› eccessivo

pro forma invoice /ˈfɔːmə/ *n* fattura *f* proforma

profound /prəˈfaʊnd/ *adj* profondo

profoundly /prəˈfaʊndlɪ/ *adv* profondamente

profuse /prəˈfjuːs/ *adj* **~ apologies** una profusione di scuse

profusely /prəˈfjuːslɪ/ *adv* profusamente

profusion /prəˈfjuːʒn/ *n* profusione *f*; **in ~** in abbondanza

progeny /ˈprɒdʒənɪ/ *n* progenie *f inv*

prognosis /prɒgˈnəʊsɪs/ *n* (*pl* **-oses**) (prediction) previsione *f*; Med prognosi *f inv*

prognosticate /prɒgˈnɒstɪkeɪt/ *vt* pronosticare

program /ˈprəʊgræm/ **A** *n* Comput programma *m*
B *vt* (*pt/pp* **programmed**) programmare

programme /ˈprəʊgræm/ *n* BrE programma *m*

programmer /ˈprəʊgræmə(r)/ *n* Comput programmatore, -trice *mf*

programming /ˈprəʊgræmɪŋ/ *n* programmazione *f*

progress¹ /ˈprəʊgres/ *n* progresso *m*; **in ~** in corso; **make ~** fig fare progressi

progress² /prəˈgres/ *vi* progredire; fig fare progressi

progression /prəˈgreʃn/ *n* (development) progresso *m*; (improvement) evoluzione *f*; (series) serie *f*

progressive /prəˈgresɪv/ *adj* progressivo; (reforming) progressista

progressively /prəˈgresɪvlɪ/ *adv* progressivamente

progress report *n* (on project) resconto sull'andamento del progetto; (on patient) cartella *f* clinica

prohibit /prəˈhɪbɪt/ *vt* proibire

prohibition /prəʊhɪˈbɪʃn/ *n* proibizione; **P~** AmE proibizionismo *m*

prohibitive /prəˈhɪbɪtɪv/ *adj* proibitivo

prohibitively /prəˈhɪbɪtɪvlɪ/ *adv* ‹*expensive*› in modo proibitivo

project¹ /ˈprɒdʒekt/ *n* progetto *m*; Sch ricerca *f*

project² /prəˈdʒekt/ **A** *vt* proiettare ‹*film, image*›
B *vi* (jut out) sporgere

projectile /prəˈdʒektaɪl/ *n* proiettile *m*

projection /prəˈdʒekʃn/ *n* (of figures) proiezione *f*

project manager *n* project manager *mf inv*

projector /prəˈdʒektə(r)/ *n* proiettore *m*

proletarian /prəʊləˈteərɪən/ *adj & n* proletario, -a *mf*

proletariat /prəʊlɪˈteərɪət/ *n* proletariato *m*

pro-life /prəʊˈlaɪf/ *adj* antiabortista

proliferate /prəˈlɪfəreɪt/ *vi* proliferare

proliferation /prəlɪfə'reɪʃn/ *n* proliferazione *f*
prolific /prə'lɪfɪk/ *adj* prolifico
prologue /'prəʊlɒg/ *n* prologo *m*
prolong /prə'lɒŋ/ *vt* prolungare
prom /prɒm/ *n* BrE infml (at seaside) lungomare *m inv*; AmE infml (at high school) ballo *m* studentesco
promenade /prɒmə'nɑːd/ *n* lungomare *m inv*
prominence /'prɒmɪnəns/ *n* (of person, issue) importanza *f*; (of object) sporgenza *f*; (hill) rilievo *m*
prominent /'prɒmɪnənt/ *adj* prominente; (conspicuous) di rilievo
promiscuity /prɒmɪ'skjuːətɪ/ *n* promiscuità *f*
promiscuous /prə'mɪskjʊəs/ *adj* promiscuo
✓ **promise** /'prɒmɪs/ **A** *n* promessa *f*
B *vt* promettere; **~ somebody that** promettere a qualcuno che; **I ~d to** l'ho promesso
Promised Land /prɒmɪst'lænd/ *n* Terra *f* Promessa
promising /'prɒmɪsɪŋ/ *adj* promettente
promo /'prəʊməʊ/ *n* infml (of product) campagna *f* promozionale; (video) video *m inv* promozionale
promontory /'prɒmənt(ə)rɪ/ *n* promontorio *m*
✓ **promote** /prə'məʊt/ *vt* promuovere; **be ~d** essere promosso
promoter /prə'məʊtə(r)/ *n* promotore, -trice *mf*
promotion /prə'məʊʃn/ *n* promozione *f*
promotional /prə'məʊʃnəl/ *adj* Comm promozionale
promotional video *n* video *m* promozionale
prompt /prɒmpt/ **A** *adj* immediato; (punctual) puntuale
B *adv* in punto
C *vt* incitare (**to** a); Theat suggerire a
D *vi* suggerire
E *n* Comput prompt *m inv*
prompter /'prɒmptə(r)/ *n* suggeritore, -trice *mf*
promptly /'prɒmptlɪ/ *adv* puntualmente
Proms /prɒmz/ *npl rassegna (f) di concerti estivi di musica classica presso l'Albert Hall a Londra*
prone /prəʊn/ *adj* prono; **be ~ to do something** essere incline a fare qualcosa
prong /prɒŋ/ *n* dente *m*
pronoun /'prəʊnaʊn/ *n* pronome *m*
pronounce /prə'naʊns/ *vt* pronunciare; (declare) dichiarare
■ **pronounce on** *vt* pronunciarsi su ‹*case, subject*›
pronounced /prə'naʊnst/ *adj* (noticeable) pronunciato

✓ parola chiave

pronouncement /prə'naʊnsmənt/ *n* dichiarazione *f*
pronunciation /prənʌnsɪ'eɪʃn/ *n* pronuncia *f*
proof /pruːf/ **A** *n* prova *f*; Typ bozza *f*; (of alcohol) gradazione *f* alcolica; **12% ~** 12°
B *adj* **~ against** a prova di
proof of purchase *n* ricevuta *f* d'acquisto
proof-read *vt* correggere le bozze di
proof-reader *n* correttore, -trice *mf* di bozze
proof-reading *n* revisione *f* di bozze
prop¹ /prɒp/ **A** *n* puntello *m*
B *vt* (*pt/pp* **propped**) **~ open** tenere aperto; **~ against** (lean) appoggiare a
■ **prop up** *vt* sostenere
prop² *n* Theat infml accessorio *m* di scena
propaganda /prɒpə'gændə/ *n* propaganda *f*
propagate /'prɒpəgeɪt/ *vt* propagare
propagator /'prɒpəgeɪtə(r)/ *n* propagatore *m*
propane /'prəʊpeɪn/ *n* propano *m*
propel /prə'pel/ *vt* (*pt/pp* **propelled**) spingere
propellant /prə'pelənt/ *n* (in aerosol) gas *m inv* propellente; (in rocket) propellente *m*
propeller /prə'pelə(r)/ *n* elica *f*
propelling pencil /prə'pelɪŋ/ *n* portamina *m inv*
propensity /prə'pensətɪ/ *n* tendenza *f*
✓ **proper** /'prɒpə(r)/ *adj* corretto; (suitable) adatto; infml (real) vero [e proprio]
✓ **properly** /'prɒpəlɪ/ *adv* correttamente
proper name, **proper noun** *n* nome *m* proprio
✓ **property** /'prɒpətɪ/ *n* proprietà *f*
property developer *n* impresa *f* edile; (person) impresario *m* edile
property market *n* mercato *m* immobiliare
prophecy /'prɒfəsɪ/ *n* profezia *f*
prophesy /'prɒfɪsaɪ/ *vt* (*pt/pp* **-ied**) profetizzare
prophet /'prɒfɪt/ *n* profeta *m*
prophetic /prə'fetɪk/ *adj* profetico
prophylactic /prɒfɪ'læktɪk/ **A** *n* (condom) profilattico *m*, preservativo *m*; Med (treatment) misura *f* profilattica
B *adj* profilattico
proponent /prə'pəʊnənt/ *n* fautore, -trice *mf*
✓ **proportion** /prə'pɔːʃn/ *n* proporzione *f*; (share) parte *f*; **be in ~** essere proporzionato (**to** a); **be out of ~** essere sproporzionato; **~s** *pl* (dimensions) proporzioni *fpl*
proportional /prə'pɔːʃnəl/ *adj* proporzionale
proportionally /prə'pɔːʃnəlɪ/ *adv* in proporzione
proportional representation *n* rappresentanza *f* proporzionale
✓ **proposal** /prə'pəʊzl/ *n* proposta *f*; (of marriage) proposta *f* di matrimonio
✓ **propose** /prə'pəʊz/ **A** *vt* proporre; (intend)

proporsi
B *vi* fare una proposta di matrimonio

proposition /prɒpəˈzɪʃn/ *n* proposta *f*; infml (task) impresa *f*

proprietor /prəˈpraɪətə(r)/ *n* proprietario, -a *mf*

propriety /prəˈpraɪətɪ/ *n* correttezza *f*; **the proprieties** *pl* l'etichetta *f*

propulsion /prəˈpʌlʃn/ *n* propulsione *f*

pro rata /ˈrɑːtə/ *adj* **on a ~ basis** in proporzione

prosaic /prəˈzeɪɪk/ *adj* prosaico

proscribe *vt* (exile) esiliare; (ban) bandire

prose /prəʊz/ *n* prosa *f*

prosecute /ˈprɒsɪkjuːt/ *vt* intentare azione contro

prosecution /prɒsɪˈkjuːʃn/ *n* azione *f* giudiziaria; **the ~** l'accusa *f*

prosecutor /ˈprɒsɪkjuːtə(r)/ *n* **[Public] P~** Pubblico Ministero *m*

⚷ **prospect¹** /ˈprɒspekt/ *n* (expectation) prospettiva *f*; (view) vista *f*

prospect² /prəˈspekt/ *vi* **~ for** cercare

prospective /prəˈspektɪv/ *adj* (future) futuro; (possible) potenziale

prospector /prəˈspektə(r)/ *n* cercatore *m*

prospectus /prəˈspektəs/ *n* prospetto *m*

prosper /ˈprɒspə(r)/ *vi* prosperare; ‹*person*› stare bene finanziariamente

prosperity /prɒˈsperətɪ/ *n* prosperità *f*

prosperous /ˈprɒspərəs/ *adj* prospero

prostate /ˈprɒsteɪt/ *n* prostata *f*

prosthesis /prɒsˈθiːsɪs/ *n* protesi *f*

prostitute /ˈprɒstɪtjuːt/ **A** *n* prostituta *f*
B *vt* fig prostituire

prostitution /prɒstɪˈtjuʃn/ *n* prostituzione *f*

prostrate /ˈprɒstreɪt/ *adj* prostrato; **~ with grief** fig prostrato dal dolore

protagonist /prəˈtægənɪst/ *n* protagonista *mf*

⚷ **protect** /prəˈtekt/ *vt* proteggere (**from** da)

⚷ **protection** /prəˈtekʃn/ *n* protezione *f*

protection factor *n* (of suntan lotion) fattore *m* di protezione

protection racket *n* racket *m inv* di protezione

protective /prəˈtektɪv/ *adj* protettivo

protector /prəˈtektə(r)/ *n* protettore, -trice *mf*

protégé /ˈprɒtɪʒeɪ/ *n* protetto *m*

protein /ˈprəʊtiːn/ *n* proteina *f*

⚷ **protest¹** /ˈprəʊtest/ *n* protesta *f*

protest² /prəˈtest/ *vt & vi* protestare

Protestant /ˈprɒtɪstənt/ *adj & n* protestante *mf*

Protestantism /ˈprɒtɪstəntɪzm/ *n* protestantesimo *m*

protestation /prɒtɪˈsteɪʃn/ *n* protesta *f*

protester /prəˈtestə(r)/ *n* contestatore, -trice *mf*; (at demonstration) dimostrante *mf*

protocol /ˈprəʊtəkɒl/ *n* protocollo *m*

prototype /ˈprəʊtətaɪp/ *n* prototipo *m*

protract /prəˈtrækt/ *vt* protrarre

protracted /prəˈtræktɪd/ *adj* prolungato

protractor /prəˈtræktə(r)/ *n* goniometro *m*

protrude /prəˈtruːd/ *vi* sporgere

protruding /prəˈtruːdɪŋ, AmE prəʊ-/ *adj* ‹*teeth, chin, ledge*› sporgente

protuberance /prəˈtuːbərəns/ *n* protuberanza *f*

⚷ **proud** /praʊd/ *adj* fiero (**of** di)

proudly /ˈpraʊdlɪ/ *adv* fieramente

⚷ **prove** /pruːv/ **A** *vt* provare
B *vi* **~ to be a lie** rivelarsi una bugia

proven /ˈpruːvən/ *adj* dimostrato

proverb /ˈprɒvɜːb/ *n* proverbio *m*

proverbial /prəˈvɜːbɪəl/ *adj* proverbiale

⚷ **provide** /prəˈvaɪd/ **A** *vt* fornire; **~ somebody with something** fornire qualcosa a qualcuno
B *vi* **~ for** (allow for) tenere conto di; ‹*law*› prevedere

provided /prəˈvaɪdɪd/ *conj* **~ [that]** purché

providence /ˈprɒvɪdəns/ *n* provvidenza *f*

provident /ˈprɒvɪdənt/ *adj* previdenziale

providential /prɒvɪˈdenʃl/ *adj* provvidenziale

provider /prəˈvaɪdə(r)/ *n* (in family) persona *f* che mantiene la famiglia

providing /prəˈvaɪdɪŋ/ *conj* = **provided**

province /ˈprɒvɪns/ *n* provincia *f*; fig campo *m*

provincial /prəˈvɪnʃl/ *adj* provinciale

provincialism /prəˈvɪnʃəlɪzm/ *n* provincialismo *m*

⚷ **provision** /prəˈvɪʒn/ *n* (of food, water) approvvigionamento *m* (**of** di); (of law) disposizione *f*; **make ~ for** ‹*law*› prevedere; **~s** *pl* provviste *fpl*

provisional /prəˈvɪʒ(ə)nəl/ *adj* provvisorio

provisionally /prəˈvɪʒ(ə)nəlɪ/ *adv* provvisoriamente

proviso /prəˈvaɪzəʊ/ *n* condizione *f*

provocation /prɒvəˈkeɪʃn/ *n* provocazione *f*

provocative /prəˈvɒkətɪv/ *adj* provocatorio; (sexually) provocante

provocatively /prəˈvɒkətɪvlɪ/ *adv* in modo provocatorio; ‹*smile, be dressed*› in modo provocante

provoke /prəˈvəʊk/ *vt* provocare

provost /ˈprɒvəst/ *n* AmE Univ decano *m*; BrE Univ, Sch rettore *m*; (in Scotland) sindaco *m*

prow /praʊ/ *n* prua *f*

prowess /ˈpraʊɪs/ *n* abilità *f*

prowl /praʊl/ **A** *vi* aggirarsi
B *n* **on the ~** in cerca di preda

prowler /ˈpraʊlə(r)/ *n* tipo *m* sospetto

proximity /prɒkˈsɪmətɪ/ *n* prossimità *f*

proxy /ˈprɒksɪ/ *n* delega *f*; (person) persona *f* che agisce per delega

prude /pruːd/ *n* **be a ~** essere eccessivamente pudico

prudence /ˈpru:dəns/ *n* prudenza *f*
prudent /ˈpru:dənt/ *adj* prudente; (wise) oculato
prudently /ˈpru:dəntlɪ/ *adv* con prudenza
prudish /ˈpru:dɪʃ/ *adj* eccessivamente pudico
prudishness /ˈpru:dɪʃnɪs/ *n* eccessivo pudore *m*
prune¹ /pru:n/ *n* prugna *f* secca
prune² *vt* potare
pry /praɪ/ *vi* (*pt/pp* **pried**) ficcare il naso
prying /ˈpraɪɪŋ/ *adj* curioso
PS *n abbr* (**postscriptum**) PS *m inv*
psalm /sɑ:m/ *n* salmo *m*
pseud /sju:d/ *n* infml intellettualoide *mf*
pseudonym /ˈsju:dənɪm/ *n* pseudonimo *m*
PSHE *n abbr* BrE (**personal social and health education**) (school subject) *studio (m) degli aspetti personali, sociali e sanitari dell'individuo in relazione alla collettività*
PST *abbr* AmE (**Pacific Standard Time**) *tempo (m) medio della zona del Pacifico*
psych /saɪk/
▪ **psych out** *vt* infml (unnerve) snervare
▪ **psych up** *vt* infml (prepare mentally) preparare psicologicamente
psychedelic /saɪkəˈdelɪk/ *adj* psichedelico
psychiatric /saɪkɪˈætrɪk/ *adj* psichiatrico
psychiatrist /saɪˈkaɪətrɪst/ *n* psichiatra *mf*
psychiatry /saɪˈkaɪətrɪ, AmE sɪ-/ *n* psichiatria *f*
psychic /ˈsaɪkɪk/ **A** *n* sensitivo, -a *mf*
B *adj* psichico; **I'm not ~** non sono un indovino
psychoanalyse /saɪkəʊˈænəlaɪz/ *vt* psicanalizzare
psychoanalysis /saɪkəʊəˈnælɪsɪs/ *n* psicanalisi *f*
psychoanalyst /saɪkəʊˈænəlɪst/ *n* psicanalista *mf*
psychological /saɪkəˈlɒdʒɪkl/ *adj* psicologico
psychologically /saɪkəˈlɒdʒɪklɪ/ *adv* psicologicamente
psychologist /saɪˈkɒlədʒɪst/ *n* psicologo, -a *mf*
psychology /saɪˈkɒlədʒɪ/ *n* psicologia *f*
psychopath /ˈsaɪkəpæθ/ *n* psicopatico, -a *mf*
psychopathic /saɪkəˈpæθɪk/ *adj* psicopatico
psychosis /saɪˈkəʊsɪs/ *n* psicosi *f inv*
psychosomatic /saɪkəʊsəˈmætɪk/ *adj* psicosomatico
psychotherapist *n* psicoterapista *mf*, psicoterapeuta *mf*
psychotic /saɪˈkɒtɪk/ *adj & n* psicotico, -a *mf*
PT *n abbr* (**physical training**) educazione *f* fisica
PTA *n abbr* (**Parent-Teacher Association**) ≈ consiglio *m* d'istituto
PTO *abbr* (**please turn over**) vedi retro

pub /pʌb/ *n* infml pub *m inv*
puberty /ˈpju:bətɪ/ *n* pubertà *f*
pubic hair /ˈpju:bɪk/ *n* peli *mpl* del pube
⚷ **public** /ˈpʌblɪk/ **A** *adj* pubblico; **make ~** rendere pubblico
B *n* **the ~** il pubblico; **in ~** in pubblico
public address system *n* impianto *m* di amplificazione
publican /ˈpʌblɪkən/ *n* proprietario, -a *mf* di un pub
public assistance *n* AmE assistenza *f* pubblica
⚷ **publication** /pʌblɪˈkeɪʃn/ *n* pubblicazione *f*
public company *n* società *f* per azioni
public convenience *n* gabinetti *mpl* pubblici
public holiday *n* festa *f* nazionale
public house *n* pub *m inv*
publicist /ˈpʌblɪsɪst/ *n* (press agent) press agent *mf inv*, addetto, -a *mf* stampa
publicity /pʌbˈlɪsətɪ/ *n* pubblicità *f*
publicity campaign *n* campagna *f* pubblicitaria
publicity department *n* settore *m* pubblicità
publicity director *n* direttore, -trice *mf* della pubblicità
publicity stunt *n* trovata *f* pubblicitaria
publicize /ˈpʌblɪsaɪz/ *vt* pubblicizzare
public library *n* biblioteca *f* pubblica
public limited company /ˈlɪmɪtɪd/ *n* società *f* per azioni
publicly /ˈpʌblɪklɪ/ *adv* pubblicamente
public opinion *n* opinione *f* pubblica
public prosecutor *n* Pubblico Ministero *m*
public relations *npl* pubbliche relazioni *fpl*
public relations department *n* ufficio *m* pubbliche relazioni
public relations officer *n* addetto, -a *mf* alle pubbliche relazioni
public school *n* scuola *f* privata; AmE scuola *f* pubblica
public sector *n* settore *m* pubblico
public-spirited *adj* **be ~** essere dotato di senso civico
public transport *n* mezzi *mpl* pubblici
⚷ **publish** /ˈpʌblɪʃ/ *vt* pubblicare
publisher /ˈpʌblɪʃə(r)/ *n* editore *m*; (firm) editore *m*, casa *f* editrice
publishing /ˈpʌblɪʃɪŋ/ *n* editoria *f*
puce /pju:s/ *adj* color bruno rossastro
puck /pʌk/ *n* (in ice-hockey) disco *m*; (sprite) folletto *m*
pucker /ˈpʌkə(r)/ *vi* ‹*material*› arricciarsi
pudding /ˈpʊdɪŋ/ *n* dolce *m* cotto al vapore; (course) dolce *m*
puddle /ˈpʌdl/ *n* pozzanghera *f*
pudgy /ˈpʌdʒɪ/ *adj* (**-ier, -iest**) grassoccio

⚷ parola chiave

puerile /'pjʊəraɪl/ *adj* puerile
puff /pʌf/ **A** *n* (of wind) soffio *m*; (of smoke) tirata *f*; (for powder) piumino *m*
B *vt* sbuffare
■ **puff at** *vt* tirare boccate da ‹*pipe*›
■ **puff out** *vt* lasciare senza fiato ‹*person*›; spegnere ‹*candle*›
■ **puff up A** *vi* ‹*feathers*› arruffarsi; ‹*eye, rice*› gonfiarsi
B *vt* arruffare ‹*feathers, fur*›; **puffed up with pride** gonfio d'orgoglio
puffed /pʌft/ *adj* (out of breath) senza fiato
puff pastry *n* pasta *f* sfoglia
puff sleeve *n* manica *f* a palloncino
puffy /'pʌfɪ/ *adj* gonfio
pug /pʌg/ *n* (dog) carlino *m*
pugnacious /pʌg'neɪʃəs/ *adj* aggressivo
pull /pʊl/ **A** *n* trazione *f*; fig (attraction) attrazione *f*; infml (influence) influenza *f*
B *vt* tirare; estrarre ‹*tooth*›; stirarsi ‹*muscle*›; ~ **a fast one** infml giocare un brutto tiro; ~ **faces** far boccacce; ~ **oneself together** ricomporsi; ~ **one's weight** mettercela tutta; ~ **sb's leg** infml prendere in giro qualcuno
■ **pull ahead** *vi* (move in front) passare davanti
■ **pull apart** *vt* (dismantle) smontare; (destroy) fare a pezzi
■ **pull away** *vi* (increase one's lead) distanziarsi
■ **pull back A** *vi* ‹*soldiers*› ritirarsi; (not act) tirarsi indietro
B *vt* far ritirare ‹*soldiers*›
■ **pull down** *vt* (demolish) demolire
■ **pull in** *vi* Auto accostare
■ **pull off** *vt* togliere; infml azzeccare
■ **pull out A** *vt* tirar fuori
B *vi* Auto spostarsi; (of competition) ritirarsi
■ **pull over** *vi* Aut accostare
■ **pull through** *vi* (recover) farcela
■ **pull together** *vi* (co-operate) sommare le forze
■ **pull up A** *vt* sradicare ‹*plant*›; (reprimand) rimproverare
B *vi* Auto fermarsi
pull-down menu *n* Comput menu *m inv* a tendina
pulley /'pʊlɪ/ *n* Techn puleggia *f*
pull-in *n* BrE (lay-by) piazzuola *f* di sosta; (cafe) bar *m inv* sul bordo della strada
pullover /'pʊləʊvə(r)/ *n* pullover *m inv*
pulmonary /'pʌlmənərɪ/ *adj* polmonare
pulp /pʌlp/ *n* poltiglia *f*; (of fruit) polpa *f*; (for paper) pasta *f*
pulp fiction *n* letteratura *f* pulp
pulpit /'pʌlpɪt/ *n* pulpito *m*
pulsar /'pʌlsɑː(r)/ *n* pulsar *m inv*
pulsate /pʌl'seɪt/ *vi* pulsare
pulse /pʌls/ *n* polso *m*
pulse rate *n* polso *m*
pulses /'pʌlsɪz/ *npl* legumi *mpl* secchi
pulverize /'pʌlvəraɪz/ *vt* polverizzare
puma /'pjuːmə/ *n* puma *m inv*
pumice /'pʌmɪs/ *n* pomice *f*
pummel /'pʌml/ *vt* (*pt/pp* **pummelled**) prendere a pugni
pump /pʌmp/ **A** *n* pompa *f*
B *vt* pompare; infml cercare di estorcere informazioni da
■ **pump up** *vt* (inflate) gonfiare
pumpkin /'pʌmpkɪn/ *n* zucca *f*
pun /pʌn/ *n* gioco *m* di parole
punch[1] /pʌntʃ/ **A** *n* pugno *m*; (device) pinza *f* per forare
B *vt* dare un pugno a; forare ‹*ticket*›; perforare ‹*hole*›
punch[2] *n* (drink) punch *m inv*
Punch and Judy show *n* spettacolo *m* di burattini
punchbag *n* punching bag *f inv*
punch-drunk *adj* (in boxing) groggy *inv*; fig stordito
punchline *n* battuta *f* finale
punch-up *n* rissa *f*
punctual /'pʌŋktjʊəl/ *adj* puntuale
punctuality /pʌŋktjʊ'ælətɪ/ *n* puntualità *f*
punctually /'pʌŋktjʊəlɪ/ *adv* puntualmente
punctuate /'pʌŋktjʊeɪt/ *vt* punteggiare
punctuation /pʌŋktjʊ'eɪʃn/ *n* punteggiatura *f*
punctuation mark *n* segno *m* di interpunzione
puncture /'pʌŋktʃə(r)/ **A** *n* foro *m*; (tyre) foratura *f*
B *vt* forare
pundit /'pʌndɪt/ *n* esperto *m*
pungency /'pʌndʒənsɪ/ *n* asprezza *f*
pungent /'pʌndʒənt/ *adj* acre
punish /'pʌnɪʃ/ *vt* punire
punishable /'pʌnɪʃəbl/ *adj* punibile
punishment /'pʌnɪʃmənt/ *n* punizione *f*
punitive /'pjuːnɪtɪv/ *adj* punitivo
punk /pʌŋk/ *n* punk *m inv*
punk rock *n* punk rock *m inv*
punk rocker /'rɒkə(r)/ *n* punk *mf inv*
punnet /'pʌnɪt/ *n* cestello *m*
punt /pʌnt/ *n* (boat) barchino *m*
punter /'pʌntə(r)/ *n* (gambler) scommettitore, -trice *mf*; infml (client) consumatore, -trice *mf*
puny /'pjuːnɪ/ *adj* (**-ier**, **-iest**) striminzito
pup /pʌp/ *n* = **puppy**
pupil /'pjuːpl/ *n* alunno, -a *mf*; (of eye) pupilla *f*
puppet /'pʌpɪt/ *n* marionetta *f*; (glove) fig burattino *m*
puppy /'pʌpɪ/ *n* cucciolo *m*
purchase /'pɜːtʃəs/ **A** *n* acquisto *m*; (leverage) presa *f*
B *vt* acquistare
purchase invoice *n* fattura *f* di acquisto
purchase ledger *n* libro *m* mastro degli acquisti

purchase order *n* ordine *m* di acquisto
purchase price *n* prezzo *m* di acquisto
purchaser /ˈpɜːtʃəsə(r)/ *n* acquirente *mf*
purchasing, **purchasing department** *n* ufficio *m* acquisti
purchasing power *n* potere *m* d'acquisto
purdah /ˈpɜːdə/ *n reclusione (f) delle donne in alcune società musulmane e indù*
pure /pjʊə(r)/ *adj* puro
pure-bred /-bred/ **A** *n* (horse) purosangue *m inv*
B *adj* purosangue *inv*
purée /pjʊəreɪ/ **A** *n* purè *m*
B *vt* passare
purely /ˈpjʊəlɪ/ *adv* puramente
purgatory /ˈpɜːgətrɪ/ *n* purgatorio *m*
purge /pɜːdʒ/ Pol **A** *n* epurazione *f*
B *vt* epurare
purification /pjʊərɪfɪˈkeɪʃn/ *n* purificazione *f*
purify /ˈpjʊərɪfaɪ/ *vt* (*pt/pp* **-ied**) purificare
purist /ˈpjʊərɪst/ *adj* & *n* purista *mf*
puritan /ˈpjʊərɪtən/ **A** *n* puritano, -a *mf*
B *adj* fig puritano
puritanical /pjʊərɪˈtænɪkl/ *adj* puritano
purity /ˈpjʊərɪtɪ/ *n* purità *f*
purl /pɜːl/ **A** *n* Knitting maglia *f* rovescia
B *vt* & *vi* lavorare a rovescio
purple /ˈpɜːpl/ *adj* viola *inv*
purport /pəˈpɔːt/ *vt* ~ **to be** farsi passare per
purpose /ˈpɜːpəs/ *n* scopo *m*; (determination) fermezza *f*; **on** ~ apposta
purpose-built /-ˈbɪlt/ *adj* costruito ad hoc
purposeful /ˈpɜːpəsfʊl/ *adj* deciso
purposefully /ˈpɜːpəsfʊlɪ/ *adv* con decisione
purposely /ˈpɜːpəslɪ/ *adv* apposta
purpose-made *adj* BrE fatto appositamente
purr /pɜː(r)/ *vi* ‹*cat*› fare le fusa
purse /pɜːs/ **A** *n* borsellino *m*; AmE (handbag) borsa *f*
B *vt* increspare ‹*lips*›
purser /ˈpɜːsə(r)/ *n* commissario *m* di bordo
pursue /pəˈsjuː/ *vt* inseguire; fig proseguire
pursuer /pəˈsjuːə(r)/ *n* inseguitore, -trice *mf*
pursuit /pəˈsjuːt/ *n* inseguimento *m*; fig (of happiness) ricerca *f*; (pastime) attività *f*; **in** ~ all'inseguimento
pus /pʌs/ *n* pus *m*
push /pʊʃ/ **A** *n* spinta *f*; fig (effort) sforzo *m*; (drive) iniziativa *f*; **at a** ~ in caso di bisogno; **get the** ~ infml essere licenziato
B *vt* spingere; premere ‹*button*›; (pressurize) far pressione su; **be** ~**ed for time** infml non avere tempo
C *vi* spingere
▪ **push around** *vt* (bully) fare il prepotente con
▪ **push aside** *vt* scostare
▪ **push back** *vt* respingere
▪ **push for** *vt* fare pressione per ottenere ‹*reform*›
▪ **push in** **A** *vi* (in queue) farsi largo spingendo
B *vt* spingere ‹*button*›
▪ **push off** **A** *vt* togliere
B *vi* infml (leave) levarsi dai piedi
▪ **push on** *vi* (continue) continuare
▪ **push over** *vt* (cause to fall) far cadere
▪ **push through** *vt* (have accepted quickly) fare accettare
▪ **push up** *vt* alzare ‹*price*›
push-button *n* pulsante *m*
pushchair /ˈpʊʃtʃeə(r)/ *n* passeggino *m*
pusher /ˈpʊʃə(r)/ *n* infml (of drugs) spacciatore, -trice *mf* [di droga]
pushover *n* infml bazzecola *f*
push start **A** *vt* spingere (*per far partire*) ‹*vehicle*›
B *n* **give something a** ~ dare una spinta a qualcosa
push-up *n* flessione *f*
pushy /ˈpʊʃɪ/ *adj* infml troppo intraprendente
puss /pʊs/, **pussy** /ˈpʊsɪ/ *n* micio *m*
pussyfoot around /ˈpʊsɪfʊt/ *vi* infml tergiversare
pussyfooting /ˈpʊsɪfʊtɪŋ/ **A** *n* infml tentennamento *m*
B *adj* infml ‹*attitude, behaviour*› tergiversante
put /pʊt/ **A** *vt* (*pt/pp* **put**, *pres p* **putting**) mettere; ~ **the cost of something at £50** valutare il costo di qualcosa 50 sterline; ~ **an end to** porre fine *o* termine a; ~ **in writing** mettere per iscritto; ~ **into effect** mettere in opera
B *vi* ~ **to sea** salpare
C *adj* **stay** ~**!** rimani lì!
▪ **put about** *vt* mettere in giro ‹*rumour*›
▪ **put across** *vt* raccontare ‹*joke*›; esprimere ‹*message*›
▪ **put aside** *vt* mettere da parte
▪ **put away** *vt* mettere via
▪ **put back** *vt* rimettere; mettere indietro ‹*clock*›
▪ **put by** *vt* mettere da parte
▪ **put down** *vt* mettere giù; (suppress) reprimere; (kill) sopprimere; (write) annotare; (criticize unfairly) sminuire; ~ **one's foot down** infml essere fermo; Auto dare un'accelerata; ~ **down to** (attribute) attribuire
▪ **put forward** *vt* avanzare; mettere avanti ‹*clock*›
▪ **put in** **A** *vt* (insert) introdurre; (submit) presentare
B *vi* ~ **in for** far domanda di
▪ **put off** *vt* spegnere ‹*light*›; (postpone) rimandare; ~ **somebody off** tenere a bada qualcuno; (deter) smontare qualcuno; (disconcert) distrarre qualcuno; ~ **somebody off something** (disgust) disgustare qualcuno di qualcosa
▪ **put on** *vt* mettersi ‹*clothes*›; mettere ‹*brake*›; Culin mettere su; accendere ‹*light*›;

parola chiave

mettere in scena ‹*play*›; prendere ‹*accent*›; **~ on weight** mettere su qualche chilo; **he's just ~ ting it on** è solo una messa in scena

▪ **put on to** *vt* (help find) indicare ‹*doctor, restaurant etc*›

▪ **put out** *vt* spegnere ‹*fire, light*›; tendere ‹*hand*›; (inconvenience) creare degli inconvenienti a

▪ **put through** *vt* far passare; Teleph **I'll ~ you through to him** glielo passo

▪ **put to**: *vt* **~ somebody to trouble** scomodare qualcuno; **I ~ it to you that ...** ritengo che ...

▪ **put together** *vt* montare ‹*machine*›; fare ‹*model, jigsaw*›

▪ **put up** **A** *vt* alzare; erigere ‹*building*›; montare ‹*tent*›; aprire ‹*umbrella*›; affiggere ‹*notice*›; aumentare ‹*price*›; ospitare ‹*guest*›; **~ somebody up to something** mettere qualcosa in testa a qualcuno
B *vi* (at hotel) stare; **~ up with** sopportare

put-down /'pʊtdaʊn/ *n* commento *m* umiliante

putrefaction /pju:trɪ'fækʃn/ *n* putrefazione *f*

putrefy /'pju:trɪfaɪ/ *vi* (*pt/pp* **-ied**) putrefarsi

putrid /'pju:trɪd/ *adj* putrido

putt /pʌt/ **A** *n* putt *m inv*
B *vi* colpire leggermente

putty /'pʌtɪ/ *n* mastice *m*

put-up job *n* infml truffa *f*

puzzle /'pʌzl/ **A** *n* enigma *m*; (jigsaw) puzzle *m inv*
B *vt* lasciare perplesso
C *vi* **~ over** scervellarsi su

▪ **puzzle out** *vt* trovare ‹*solution*›

puzzled /'pʌzld/ *adj* perplesso

puzzling /'pʌzlɪŋ/ *adj* inspiegabile

PVC **A** *n* PVC *m*
B *attrib* di PVC

pygmy /'pɪgmɪ/ *n* pigmeo, -a *mf*

pyjamas /pə'dʒɑ:məz/ *npl* pigiama *msg*

pylon /'paɪlən/ *n* pilone *m*

pyramid /'pɪrəmɪd/ *n* piramide *f*

pyre /paɪə(r)/ *n* pira *f*

Pyrex® /'paɪreks/ *n* Pyrex® *m*

pyromaniac /paɪrə'meɪnɪæk/ *n* piromane *mf*

pyrotechnics /paɪrə'teknɪks/ *npl* (display) fuochi *mpl* pirotecnici

python /'paɪθn/ *n* pitone *m*

Qq

q, Q /kju:/ *n* (letter) q, Q *f inv*

Qatar /kæ'tɑ:/ *n* Qatar *m*

QC *n* BrE Jur avvocato *m* di rango superiore

QE *n* (**quantitative easing**) **quantitative easing**

QED *abbr* (**quod erat demonstrandum**) *C.V.D.*

quack¹ /kwæk/ **A** *n* qua qua *m inv*
B *vi* fare qua qua

quack² *n* (doctor) ciarlatano *m*

quad /kwɒd/ *n* infml (court) = **quadrangle**; **~s** *pl* infml = **quadruplets**

quadrangle /'kwɒdræŋgl/ *n* quadrangolo *m*; (court) cortile *m* quadrangolare

quadratic equation /kwɒ'drætɪk/ *n* equazione *f* di secondo grado

quadriplegic /kwɒdrɪ'pli:dʒɪk/ *adj* quadriplegico

quadruped /'kwɒdrʊped/ *n* quadrupede *m*

quadruple /'kwɒdrʊpl/ **A** *adj* quadruplo
B *vt* quadruplicare
C *vi* quadruplicarsi

quadruplets /kwɒd'ru:plɪts/ *npl* quattro gemelli *mpl*

quadruplicate /kwɒd'ru:plɪkət/ *n* **in ~** in quattro copie

quagmire /'kwɒgmaɪə(r)/ *n* pantano *m*

quail /kweɪl/ *vi* farsi prendere dalla paura

quaint /kweɪnt/ *adj* pittoresco; (odd) bizzarro

quake /kweɪk/ **A** *n* infml terremoto *m*
B *vi* tremare

Quaker /'kweɪkə(r)/ *n* quacchero, -a *mf*

qualification /kwɒlɪfɪ'keɪʃn/ *n* qualifica *f*; (reservation) riserva *f*

qualified /'kwɒlɪfaɪd/ *adj* qualificato; (limited) con riserva

qualifier /'kwɒlɪfaɪə(r)/ *n* Sport concorrente *mf* qualificato, -a

⚷ **qualify** /'kwɒlɪfaɪ/ **A** *vt* (*pt/pp* **-ied**) ‹*course*› dare la qualifica a (**as** di); ‹*entitle*› dare diritto a; ‹*limit*› precisare
B *vi* ottenere la qualifica; Sport qualificarsi

qualitative /'kwɒlɪtətɪv/ *adj* qualitativo

⚷ **quality** /'kwɒlətɪ/ *n* qualità *f*

quality assurance *n* verifica *f* qualità

quality control *n* controllo *m* [di] qualità

quality controller *n* addetto, -a *mf* al controllo di qualità

qualm /kwɑːm/ *n* scrupolo *m*
quandary /ˈkwɒndərɪ/ *n* dilemma *m*
quango /ˈkwæŋgəʊ/ *n* BrE *organismo (m) autonomo ma finanziato dal governo*
quantifiable /ˈkwɒntɪfaɪəbl/ *adj* quantificabile
quantify /ˈkwɒntɪfaɪ/ *vt* quantificare
quantitative /ˈkwɒntɪtətɪv/ *adj* quantitativo
quantitative easing /kwɒntɪtətɪv ˈiːzɪŋ/ *n processo (m) di creazione di moneta da parte delle banche centrali per acquistare, ad esempio, titoli di stato in mano ai privati*
quantity /ˈkwɒntətɪ/ *n* quantità *f*; **in ~** in grande quantità
quantity surveyor *n geometra (mf) che calcola quantità e costo di materiali da costruzione*
quantum leap /kwɒntəmˈliːp/ *n* fig balzo *m* in avanti
quantum mechanics *npl* meccanica *fpl* quantistica
quarantine /ˈkwɒrəntiːn/ *n* quarantena *f*
quarrel /ˈkwɒrəl/ **A** *n* lite *f*
B *vi* (*pt/pp* **quarrelled**) litigare
quarrelsome /ˈkwɒrəlsəm/ *adj* litigioso
quarry¹ /ˈkwɒrɪ/ *n* (prey) preda *f*
quarry² *n* cava *f*
quarry tile *n* mattonella *f* grezza
quart /kwɔːt/ *n* = 1,14 litri
⚷ **quarter** /ˈkwɔːtə(r)/ **A** *n* quarto *m*; (of year) trimestre *m*; AmE 25 centesimi *mpl*; **~s** *pl* Mil quartiere *msg*; **at [a] ~ to six** alle sei meno un quarto; **from all ~s** da tutti i lati
B *vt* dividere in quattro
quarterdeck /ˈkwɔːtədek/ *n* Naut cassero *m*
quarter-final *n* quarto *m* di finale
quarterly /ˈkwɔːtəlɪ/ **A** *adj* trimestrale
B *adv* trimestralmente
quartermaster /ˈkwɔːtəmɑːstə(r)/ *n* ‹*in navy*› timoniere *m*; ‹*in army*› furiere *m*
quartet /kwɔːˈtet/ *n* quartetto *m*
quartz /kwɔːts/ *n* quarzo *m*; **~ watch** orologio *m* al quarzo
quash /kwɒʃ/ *vt* annullare; soffocare ‹*rebellion*›
quasi+ /ˈkweɪzaɪ/ *pref* semi+
quaver /ˈkweɪvə(r)/ **A** *n* Mus croma *f*
B *vi* tremolare
quay /kiː/ *n* banchina *f*
quayside /ˈkiːsaɪd/ *n* banchina *f*
queasiness /ˈkwiːzɪnɪs/ *n* nausea *f*
queasy /ˈkwiːzɪ/ *adj* **I feel ~ ho** la nausea
Quebec /kwɪˈbek/ *n* (province) Quebec *m*; (town) Quebec *f*
⚷ **queen** /kwiːn/ *n* regina *f*
queen bee *n* ape *f* regina; **she thinks she's the ~** fig si crede chissà chi
queenly /ˈkwiːnlɪ/ *adj* da regina

⚷ parola chiave

queen mother *n* regina *f* madre
Queen's Counsel *n* BrE Jur *avvocato (m) di rango superiore*
Queen's English *n* BrE **speak the ~** parlare un inglese corretto e senza accento
Queen's evidence *n* BrE Jur **turn ~** deporre contro i propri complici
Queen's Regulations *npl* BrE Mil codice *m* militare
queer /kwɪə(r)/ **A** *adj* strano; (dubious) sospetto; infml (homosexual) finocchio
B *n* infml finocchio *m*
quell /kwel/ *vt* reprimere
quench /kwentʃ/ *vt* **~ one's thirst** dissetarsi
querulous /ˈkwerʊləs/ *adj* lamentoso
query /ˈkwɪərɪ/ **A** *n* domanda *f*; (question mark) punto *m* interrogativo
B *vt* (*pt/pp* **-ied**) interrogare; (doubt) mettere in dubbio
quest /kwest/ *n* ricerca *f* (**for** di)
⚷ **question** /ˈkwestʃən/ **A** *n* domanda *f*; (for discussion) questione *f*; **out of the ~** fuori discussione; **without ~** senza dubbio; **in ~** in questione
B *vt* interrogare; (doubt) mettere in dubbio
questionable /ˈkwestʃ(ə)nəbl/ *adj* discutibile
questioner /ˈkwestʃ(ə)nə(r)/ *n* interrogatore, -trice *mf*
questioning /ˈkwestʃ(ə)nɪŋ/ **A** *n* (of person) interrogatorio *m*; (of criteria) messa *f* in discussione
B *adj* ‹*look, tone*› inquisitorio
question mark *n* punto *m* interrogativo
question master *n* presentatore, -trice *mf* di quiz
questionnaire /kwestʃəˈneə(r)/ *n* questionario *m*
question tag *n* domanda *f* di conferma
queue /kjuː/ **A** *n* coda *f*, fila *f*
B *vi* **~ [up]** mettersi in coda (**for** per)
queue-jump *vi* BrE passare davanti alle altre persone in coda
quibble /ˈkwɪbl/ *vi* cavillare
⚷ **quick** /kwɪk/ **A** *adj* veloce; **be ~** sbrigati!; **have a ~ meal** fare uno spuntino
B *adv* in fretta
C *n* **be cut to the ~** fig essere punto sul vivo
quick-assembly *adj* facile da montare
quicken /ˈkwɪkən/ **A** *vt* accelerare ‹*pace*›
B *vi* ‹*pace*› accelerarsi; ‹*interest*› intensificarsi
quick-fire *adj* ‹*questions*› a mitraglia
quick-freeze *vt* surgelare
quickie /ˈkwɪkɪ/ *n* infml (question) domanda *f* rapida; (drink) bicchierino *m* rapido; (film) cortometraggio *m*
quicklime /ˈkwɪklaɪm/ *n* calce *f* viva
⚷ **quickly** /ˈkwɪklɪ/ *adv* in fretta
quick march *n* Mil passo *m* di marcia veloce

quicksand *n* sabbie *fpl* mobili
quick-setting /-ˈsetɪŋ/ *adj* a presa rapida
quicksilver *n* Chem argento *m* vivo, mercurio *m*
quick-tempered /-ˈtempəd/ *adj* collerico
quick time *n* AmE marcia *f* veloce
quick-witted /-ˈwɪtɪd/ *adj* ‹*reaction*› pronto; ‹*person*› sveglio
quid /kwɪd/ *n inv* infml sterlina *f*
quid pro quo /kwɪdprəʊˈkwəʊ/ *n* contraccambio *m*
quiet /ˈkwaɪət/ **A** *adj* (calm) tranquillo; (silent) silenzioso; (voice, music) basso; **keep ~ about** infml non raccontare a nessuno
B *n* quiete *f*; **on the ~** di nascosto
▪ **quiet down** AmE *vt & vi* ▶ **quieten down**
quieten /ˈkwaɪətn/ *vt* calmare
▪ **quieten down** BrE **A** *vt* calmare
B *vi* calmarsi
quietly /ˈkwaɪətlɪ/ *adv* (peacefully) tranquillamente; ‹*say*› a bassa voce
quietness /ˈkwaɪətnɪs/ *n* quiete *f*
quiff /kwɪf/ *n* BrE (hair) ciuffo *m*
quill /kwɪl/ *n* penna *f* d'uccello; (spine) spina *f*
quilt /kwɪlt/ *n* piumino *m*
quilted /ˈkwɪltɪd/ *adj* trapuntato
quilting /ˈkwɪltɪŋ/ *n* (fabric) matelassé *m inv*
quince /kwɪns/ *n* cotogna *f*; (tree) melo *m* cotogno
quinine /ˈkwɪniːn/ *n* chinino *m*
quins /kwɪnz/ *npl* infml = **quintuplets**
quintessential /kwɪntɪˈsenʃl/ *adj* ‹*quality*› fondamentale
quintet /kwɪnˈtet/ *n* quintetto *m*
quintuple /ˈkwɪntjʊpl/ **A** *vt* quintuplicare
B *adj* quintuplo
quintuplets /ˈkwɪntjʊplɪts/ *npl* cinque gemelli *mpl*
quip /kwɪp/ **A** *n* battuta *f*
B *vt* (*pt/pp* **quipped**) dire scherzando
quirk /kwɜːk/ *n* stranezza *f*
quisling /ˈkwɪzlɪŋ/ *n* derog collaborazionista *mf*
quit /kwɪt/ **A** *vt* (*pt/pp* **-tted** *or* **quit**) lasciare; (give up) smettere (**doing** di fare); Comput uscire da
B *vi* infml (resign) andarsene; Comput uscire; **give somebody notice to ~** dare a qualcuno preavviso di sfratto
quite /kwaɪt/ *adv* (fairly) abbastanza; (completely) completamente; (really) veramente; **~ [so]!** proprio così!; **~ a few** parecchi
quits /kwɪts/ *adj* pari
quiver /ˈkwɪvə(r)/ *vi* tremare
quiz /kwɪz/ **A** *n* (game) quiz *m inv*
B *vt* (*pt/pp* **quizzed**) interrogare
quiz game, quiz show *n* quiz *m inv*
quizzical /ˈkwɪzɪkl/ *adj* sardonico
quoit /kwɔɪt/ *n* anello *m* (*del gioco*)
quoits *n* (game) gioco *m* degli anelli
quorum /ˈkwɔːrəm/ *n* quorum *m inv*; **have a ~** avere il quorum
quota /ˈkwəʊtə/ *n* quota *f*
quotation /kwəʊˈteɪʃn/ *n* citazione *f*; (price) preventivo *m*; (of shares) quota *f*
quotation marks *npl* virgolette *fpl*
quote /kwəʊt/ **A** *n* infml = **quotation**; **in ~s** tra virgolette
B *vt* citare; quotare ‹*price*›; **~d on the Stock Exchange** quotato in Borsa

q r

Rr

r, R /ɑː(r)/ *n* (letter) r, R *f inv*; **the three Rs** leggere, scrivere e contare
R² *abbr* BrE (**Regina**) regina *f*
R & B *n* rhythm and blues *m*
R & D *n* ricerca *f* e sviluppo *m*
rabbi /ˈræbaɪ/ *n* rabbino *m*
rabbit /ˈræbɪt/ *n* coniglio *m*
▪ **rabbit on**: *vi* infml **what's he ~ting on about now?** cosa sta blaterando?
rabbit hutch *n* conigliera *f*
rabble /ˈræbl/ *n* **the ~** la plebaglia
rabble rouser /ˈraʊʒə(r)/ *n* agitatore, -trice *mf*
rabble rousing *n* incitazione *f* alla violenza
rabid /ˈræbɪd/ *adj* fig rabbioso
rabies /ˈreɪbiːz/ *n* rabbia *f*
RAC *n abbr* BrE (**Royal Automobile Club**) ≈ ACI *f*
raccoon /rəˈkuːn/ *n* procione *m*, orsetto *m* lavatore
race¹ /reɪs/ *n* (people) razza *f*
race² **A** *n* corsa *f*
B *vi* correre
C *vt* gareggiare con; fare correre ‹*horse*›
racecourse /ˈreɪskɔːs/ *n* ippodromo *m*
racehorse /ˈreɪshɔːs/ *n* cavallo *m* da corsa

racer /ˈreɪsə(r)/ *n* (bike) bicicletta *f* da corsa; (motorbike) motocicletta *f* da corsa; (car) automobile *f* da corsa; (runner, cyclist etc) corridore, -trice *mf*
race relations *npl* rapporti *mpl* tra le razze
race riots *npl* scontri *mpl* razziali
racetrack /ˈreɪstræk/ *n* pista *f*
racial /ˈreɪʃl/ *adj* razziale
racialism /ˈreɪʃəlɪzm/ *n* razzismo *m*
racially /ˈreɪʃ(ə)lɪ/ *adv* dal punto di vista razziale
racing /ˈreɪsɪŋ/ *n* corse *fpl*; (horse ~) corse *fpl* dei cavalli
racing car *n* macchina *f* da corsa
racing driver *n* pilota *mf* automobilistico
racism /ˈreɪsɪzm/ *n* razzismo *m*
racist /ˈreɪsɪst/ *adj & n* razzista *mf*
rack[1] /ræk/ **A** *n* (for bikes) rastrelliera *f*; (for luggage) portabagagli *m inv*; (for plates) scolapiatti *m inv*
B *vt* ~ **one's brains** scervellarsi
rack[2] *n* **go to ~ and ruin** andare in rovina
racket[1] /ˈrækɪt/ *n* Sport racchetta *f*
racket[2] *n* (din) chiasso *m*; (swindle) truffa *f*; (crime) racket *m inv*, giro *m*
racketeer /rækɪˈtɪə(r)/ *n* trafficante *m*
racketeering /rækɪˈtɪərɪŋ/ *n* traffici *mpl* illeciti
racking /ˈrækɪŋ/ *adj* ‹*pain*› atroce
raconteur /ˈrækɒntɜː(r)/ *n* bravo narratore *m*, brava narratrice *f*
racquetball /ˈrækɪtbɔːl/ *n* AmE = **squash**
racy /ˈreɪsɪ/ *adj* (**-ier**, **-iest**) vivace; (risqué) osé *inv*, spinto
radar /ˈreɪdɑː(r)/ *n* radar *m*
radar trap *n* Auto *tratto (m) di strada sul quale la polizia controlla la velocità dei veicoli*
radial /ˈreɪdɪəl/ **A** *n* (tyre) pneumatico *m* radiale
B *adj* ‹*lines, roads*› radiale
radiance /ˈreɪdɪəns/ *n* radiosità *f*
radiant /ˈreɪdɪənt/ *adj* raggiante
radiate /ˈreɪdɪeɪt/ **A** *vt* irradiare
B *vi* irradiarsi
radiation /reɪdɪˈeɪʃn/ *n* radiazione *f*
radiation exposure *n* esposizione *f* a radiazioni
radiation sickness *n* patologia *f* da radiazioni
radiator /ˈreɪdɪeɪtə(r)/ *n* radiatore *m*
radical /ˈrædɪkl/ *adj & n* radicale *mf*
radicalism /ˈrædɪkəlɪzm/ *n* radicalismo *m*
radically /ˈrædɪklɪ/ *adv* radicalmente
⚷ **radio** /ˈreɪdɪəʊ/ **A** *n* radio *f inv*
B *vt* mandare via radio ‹*message*›
radioactive /reɪdɪəʊˈæktɪv/ *adj* radioattivo
radioactive waste *n* scorie *fpl* radioattive

radioactivity /reɪdɪəʊækˈtɪvətɪ/ *n* radioattività *f*
radio alarm *n* radiosveglia *f*
radio cassette player *n* radioregistratore *m*
radio-controlled *adj* radiocomandato
radiographer /reɪdɪˈɒgrəfə(r)/ *n* radiologo, -a *mf*
radiography /reɪdɪˈɒgrəfɪ/ *n* radiografia *f*
radio ham *n* radioamatore, -trice *mf*
radiologist /reɪdɪˈɒlədʒɪst/ *n* radiologo, -a *mf*
radiology /ˌreɪdɪˈɒlədʒɪ/ *n* radiologia *f*
radio station *n* stazione *f* radiofonica
radiotherapy /reɪdɪəʊˈθerəpɪ/ *n* radioterapia *f*
radish /ˈrædɪʃ/ *n* ravanello *m*
radius /ˈreɪdɪəs/ *n* (*pl* **-dii** /ˈreɪdɪaɪ/) raggio *m*
RAF *n abbr* BrE (**Royal Air Force**) *aviazione (f) militare inglese*
raffle /ˈræfl/ **A** *n* lotteria *f*
B *vt* mettere in palio
raft /rɑːft/ *n* zattera *f*
rafter /ˈrɑːftə(r)/ *n* trave *f*
rag[1] /ræg/ *n* straccio *m*; derog (newspaper) giornalaccio *m*; **in ~s** stracciato
rag[2] **A** *vt* (*pt/pp* **ragged**) infml fare scherzi a
B *n* Univ *festa (f) di beneficenza organizzata da studenti universitari*
ragamuffin /ˈrægəmʌfɪn/ *n* monellaccio *m*
rag-and-bone man *n* BrE rigattiere *m*, straccivendolo *m*
ragbag /ˈrægbæg/ *n* fig accozzaglia *f*
rage /reɪdʒ/ **A** *n* rabbia *f*; **all the ~** infml all'ultima moda
B *vi* infuriarsi; ‹*storm*› infuriare; ‹*epidemic*› imperversare
ragged /ˈrægɪd/ *adj* logoro; ‹*edge*› frastagliato
raging /ˈreɪdʒɪŋ/ *adj* ‹*blizzard, sea*› furioso; ‹*thirst, pain*› atroce; ‹*passion, argument*› acceso
raglan /ˈræglən/ **A** *adj* raglan *inv*
B *n* manica *f* raglan
rag trade *n* infml settore *m* dell'abbigliamento
rag week *n* BrE Univ *settimana (f) di manifestazioni a scopo benefico organizzata dagli studenti*
raid /reɪd/ **A** *n* (by thieves) rapina *f*; Mil incursione *f*, raid *m inv*; (by police) irruzione *f*
B *vt* Mil fare un'incursione in; ‹*police, thieves*› fare irruzione in
raider /ˈreɪdə(r)/ *n* (of bank) rapinatore, -trice *mf*
rail[1] /reɪl/ *n* ringhiera *f*; Rail rotaia *f*; Naut parapetto *m*; **by ~** per ferrovia
rail[2] *vi* ~ **against** *or* **at** inveire contro
railcard /ˈreɪlkɑːd/ *n* tessera *f* di riduzione ferroviaria

r

⚷ parola chiave

railings /'reɪlɪŋz/ *npl* ringhiera *f*
railroad /'reɪlrəʊd/ **A** *n* AmE = **railway**
B *vt* ~ **somebody into doing something** spingere qualcuno a fare qualcosa
railroad car *n* AmE vagone *m* ferroviario
railroad schedule *n* AmE orario *m* ferroviario
rail traffic *n* traffico *m* ferroviario
railway /'reɪlweɪ/ *n* ferrovia *f*
railway carriage *n* BrE vagone *m* ferroviario
railwayman /'reɪlweɪmən/ *n* ferroviere *m*
railway station *n* stazione *f* ferroviaria
rain /reɪn/ **A** *n* pioggia *f*
B *vi* piovere; ~ **down on somebody** fig piovere addosso a qualcuno
C *vt* ~ **blows on somebody** tempestare qualcuno di colpi
■ **rain off**: *vt* **be ~ed off** essere annullato a causa della pioggia
rainbow *n* arcobaleno *m*
rain check *n* AmE **can I take a ~?** facciamo un'altra volta
raincoat *n* impermeabile *m*
raindrop *n* goccia *f* di pioggia
rainfall *n* precipitazione *f* [atmosferica]
rainforest *n* foresta *f* pluviale, foresta *f* equatoriale
rainstorm *n* temporale *m*
rain water *n* acqua *f* piovana
rainy /'reɪnɪ/ *adj* (**-ier**, **-iest**) piovoso
rainy day *n* **save something for a ~** fig mettere qualcosa in serbo per i tempi di magra
rainy season *n* stagione *f* delle piogge
raise /reɪz/ **A** *n* AmE aumento *m*
B *vt* alzare; levarsi ‹*hat*›; allevare ‹*children, animals*›; sollevare ‹*question*›; ottenere ‹*money*›; ~ **hell** indiavolarsi; ~ **a laugh** ‹*joke, remark*› far ridere; ~ **the stakes** rilanciare; ~ **one's voice** alzare la voce
raised /reɪzd/ *adj* ‹*flower bed, platform*› soprelevato; ~ **voices** urla
raisin /'reɪzn/ *n* uvetta *f*; **~s** *pl* uvetta *f*, uva *f* passa
Raj /rɑːʒ/ *n* governo *m* britannico in India
rake /reɪk/ **A** *n* rastrello *m*
B *vt* rastrellare
■ **rake in** *vt* infml farsi ‹*profits, money*›; **he's raking it in** sta facendo un sacco di soldi
■ **rake together** *vt* fig racimolare ‹*money*›
■ **rake up** *vt* raccogliere col rastrello; infml rivangare
rake-off *n* infml parte *f*
rakish /'reɪkɪʃ/ *adj* (dissolute) dissoluto; (jaunty) disinvolto
rally /'rælɪ/ **A** *n* raduno *m*; Auto rally *m inv*; Tennis scambio *m*; (recovery) ripresa *f*
B *vt* (*pt/pp* **-ied**) radunare
C *vi* radunarsi; (recover strength) riprendersi
rallying cry, **rallying call** *n* slogan *m inv*
ram /ræm/ **A** *n* montone *m*; Astr Ariete *m*
B *vt* (*pt/pp* **rammed**) cozzare contro
RAM /ræm/ *n* memoria *f* RAM
ramble /'ræmbl/ **A** *n* escursione *f*
B *vi* gironzolare; (in speech) divagare
■ **ramble on** *vi* infml parlare/scrivere a ruota libera
rambler /'ræmblə(r)/ *n* escursionista *mf*; (rose) rosa *f* rampicante
rambling /'ræmblɪŋ/ *adj* (in speech) sconnesso; ‹*club*› escursionistico
ramification /ræmɪfɪ'keɪʃən/ *n* ramificazione *f*
ramify /'ræmɪfaɪ/ *vi* (*pt/pp* **-ied**) ramificarsi
ramp /ræmp/ *n* rampa *f*; Auto dosso *m*
rampage /'ræmpeɪdʒ/ **A** *n* **be/go on the ~** scatenarsi
B *vi* ~ **through the streets** scatenarsi per le strade
rampant /'ræmpənt/ *adj* dilagante; (in heraldry) rampante
rampart /'ræmpɑːt/ *n* bastione *f*
ram raid *n rapina (f) in un negozio con scasso della vetrina effettuato con un'auto*
ram raider *n rapinatore (m) che scassa la vetrina di un negozio con un'auto*
ramshackle /'ræmʃækl/ *adj* sgangherato
ran /ræn/ ▶ **run**
ranch /rɑːntʃ/ *n* ranch *m inv*
rancher /'rɑːntʃə(r)/ *n* (worker) cow-boy *m inv*; (owner) proprietario *m* di ranch
rancid /'rænsɪd/ *adj* rancido
rancour /'ræŋkə(r)/ *n* rancore *m*
random /'rændəm/ **A** *adj* casuale; ~ **sample** campione *m* a caso
B *n* **at ~** a casaccio
random-access *adj* ad accesso casuale
random-access memory *n* memoria *f* viva
randy /'rændɪ/ *adj* (**-ier**, **-iest**) infml eccitato
rang /ræŋ/ ▶ **ring**[2]
range /reɪndʒ/ **A** *n* serie *f*; Comm, Mus gamma *f*; (of mountains) catena *f*; (distance) raggio *m*; (for shooting) portata *f*; (stove) cucina *f* economica; **at a ~ of** ad una distanza di
B *vi* estendersi; ~ **from...to...** andare da...a...
ranger /'reɪndʒə(r)/ *n* guardia *f* forestale
rank[1] /ræŋk/ **A** *n* (row) riga *f*; Mil grado *m*; (social position) rango *m*; **the ~ and file** la base; **the ~s** *pl* Mil i soldati *mpl* semplici
B *vt* (place) annoverare (**among** tra)
C *vi* (be placed) collocarsi
rank[2] *adj* ‹*smell*› puzzolente; ‹*plants*› rigoglioso; fig vero e proprio
ranking /'ræŋkɪŋ/ *n* classificazione *f*
rankle /'ræŋkl/ *vi* fig bruciare; **it still ~s with him** gli brucia ancora
ransack /'rænsæk/ *vt* rovistare; (pillage) saccheggiare

ransom /'rænsəm/ *n* riscatto *m*; **hold somebody to ~** tenere qualcuno in ostaggio per il riscatto
rant /rænt/ *vi* **~ [and rave]** inveire; **what's he ~ing on about?** cosa sta blaterando?
rap /ræp/ **A** *n* colpo *m* secco; Mus rap *m*
B *vt* (*pt/pp* **rapped**) dare colpetti a; **~ somebody over the knuckles** fig dare una tirata d'orecchie a qualcuno
C *vi* **~ at** bussare a
rape¹ /reɪp/ *n* Bot colza *f*
rape² **A** *n* (sexual) stupro *m*
B *vt* violentare, stuprare
rape oil /'reɪp/, **rapeseed oil** /'reɪpsiːd/ *n* olio *m* [di semi] di colza
rapid /'ræpɪd/ *adj* rapido
rapidity /rə'pɪdətɪ/ *n* rapidità *f*
rapidly /'ræpɪdlɪ/ *adv* rapidamente
rapids /'ræpɪdz/ *npl* rapide *fpl*
rapist /'reɪpɪst/ *n* violentatore *m*
rapper /'ræpə(r)/ *n* BrE (door knocker) battiporta *m inv*; Mus rapper *mf inv*
rapport /ræ'pɔː(r)/ *n* rapporto *m* di intesa
rapt /ræpt/ *adj* ‹*look*› rapito; **~ in** assorto in
rapture /'ræptʃə(r)/ *n* estasi *f*
rapturous /'ræptʃərəs/ *adj* entusiastico
rapturously /'ræptʃərəslɪ/ *adv* entusiasticamente
⚷ **rare¹** /reə(r)/ *adj* raro
rare² *adj* Culin al sangue
rarefied /'reərɪfaɪd/ *adj* rarefatto
rarely /'reəlɪ/ *adv* raramente
raring /'reərɪŋ/ *adj* infml **be ~ to** non vedere l'ora di
rarity /'reərətɪ/ *n* rarità *f*
rascal /'rɑːskl/ *n* mascalzone *m*
rash¹ /ræʃ/ *n* Med eruzione *f*
rash² *adj* avventato
rasher /'ræʃə(r)/ *n* fetta *f* di pancetta
rashly /'ræʃlɪ/ *adv* avventatamente
rashness /'ræʃnɪs/ *n* avventatezza *f*
rasp /rɑːsp/ *n* (noise) stridio *m*
raspberry /'rɑːzbərɪ/ *n* lampone *m*
rasping /'rɑːspɪŋ/ *adj* stridente
rat /ræt/ **A** *n* topo *m*; infml (person) carogna *f*; **smell a ~** infml sentire puzzo di bruciato
B *vi* (*pt/pp* **ratted**) infml **~ on** far la spia a
rat-catcher *n* addetto, -a *mf* alla derattizzazione
ratchet /'rætʃɪt/ *n* (toothed rack) cremagliera *f*
⚷ **rate** /reɪt/ **A** *n* (speed) velocità *f*; (of payment) tariffa *f*; (of exchange) tasso *m*; **~s** *pl* (taxes) imposte *fpl* comunali sui beni immobili; **at any ~** in ogni caso; **at this ~** di questo passo
B *vt* stimare; **~ among** annoverare tra
C *vt* **~ as** essere considerato
ratepayer /'reɪtpeɪə(r)/ *n* contribuente *mf*

⚷ **rather** /'rɑːðə(r)/ *adv* piuttosto; **~!** eccome!; **~ too...** un po' troppo...
ratification /rætɪfɪ'keɪʃn/ *n* ratifica *f*
ratify /'rætɪfaɪ/ *vt* (*pt/pp* **-ied**) ratificare
rating /'reɪtɪŋ/ *n* valutazione *f*; (class) livello *m*; (sailor) marinaio *m* semplice; **~s** *pl* Radio, TV indice *m* d'ascolto, audience *f inv*
⚷ **ratio** /'reɪʃɪəʊ/ *n* rapporto *m*; **in a ~ of two to one** in [un] rapporto di due a uno
ration /'ræʃn/ **A** *n* razione *f*
B *vt* razionare
rational /'ræʃənl/ *adj* razionale
rationale /ræʃə'nɑːl/ *n* (logic) base *f* logica; (reasons) ragioni *fpl*
rationalize /'ræʃ(ə)nəlaɪz/ *vt & vi* razionalizzare
rationally /'ræʃ(ə)nəlɪ/ *adv* razionalmente
rationing /'ræʃ(ə)nɪŋ/ *n* razionamento *m*
rat race *n* infml corsa *f* al successo
rat run *n scorciatoia (f) usata dagli automobilisti in zone residenziali*
rattan /rə'tæn/ *n* (tree, material) malacca *f*
rat-tat, **rat-a-tat** *n* toc toc *m inv*
rattle /'rætl/ **A** *n* tintinnio *m*; (toy) sonaglio *m*
B *vi* tintinnare
C *vt* (shake) scuotere; infml innervosire
▪ **rattle off** *vt* infml sciorinare
▪ **rattle on** *vi* (talk at length) parlare ininterrottamente
▪ **rattle through** *vt* (say quickly) dire velocemente; (do quickly) fare velocemente
rattlesnake /'rætlsneɪk/ *n* serpente *m* a sonagli
ratty /'rætɪ/ *adj* BrE infml (grumpy) irascibile; AmE ‹*hair*› sudicio
raucous /'rɔːkəs/ *adj* rauco
raunchy /'rɔːntʃɪ/ *adj* infml ‹*performer, voice, song*› sexy *inv*; (bawdy) spinto
ravage /'rævɪdʒ/ *vt* devastare
ravages /'rævɪdʒɪz/ *npl* danni *mpl*
rave /reɪv/ *vi* vaneggiare; **~ about** andare in estasi per
raven /'reɪvn/ *n* corvo *m* imperiale
ravenous /'rævənəs/ *adj* ‹*person*› affamato
rave-up *n* BrE infml festa *f* animata
ravine /rə'viːn/ *n* gola *f*
raving /'reɪvɪŋ/ *adj* **~ mad** infml matto da legare
ravings /'reɪvɪŋz/ *npl* vaneggiamenti *mpl*
ravioli /rævɪ'əʊlɪ/ *n* ravioli *mpl*
ravishing /'rævɪʃɪŋ/ *adj* incantevole
raw /rɔː/ *adj* crudo; (not processed) grezzo; ‹*weather*› gelido; (inexperienced) inesperto
raw deal *n* **get a ~** infml farsi fregare
rawhide *n* (leather) cuoio *m* grezzo
Rawlplug® /'rɔːlplʌg/ *n* tassello *m*
raw materials *npl* materie *fpl* prime
ray /reɪ/ *n* raggio *m*; **~ of hope** barlume *m* di speranza
rayon® /'reɪɒn/ *n* raion® *m*

⚷ parola chiave

raze /reɪz/ *vt* ~ **to the ground** radere al suolo
razor /ˈreɪzə(r)/ *n* rasoio *m*
razor blade *n* lametta *f* da barba
razor-sharp *adj* affilatissimo
razzle /ˈræzl/ *n* BrE infml **go on the** ~ andare a fare baldoria
razzle-dazzle *n* infml baldoria *f*
razzmatazz /ræzməˈtæz/ *n* infml clamore *m*
RC **A** *n abbr* (**Roman Catholic**) cattolico, -a *mf*
B *adj* cattolico
Rd. *abbr* (**Road**) Via
re /riː/ *prep* con riferimento a
reach /riːtʃ/ **A** *n* portata *f*; (of river) tratto *m*; **within** ~ a portata di mano; **out of** ~ **of** fuori dalla portata di; **within easy** ~ facilmente raggiungibile
B *vt* arrivare a ‹*place, decision*›; (contact) contattare; (pass) passare; **I can't** ~ **it** non ci arrivo
C *vi* arrivare (**to** a); **I can't** ~ non ci arrivo; ~ **for** allungare la mano per prendere
reaches /ˈriːtʃɪz/ *npl* (of river) **the upper/lower** ~ la parte superiore/inferiore
react /rɪˈækt/ *vi* reagire
reaction /rɪˈækʃn/ *n* reazione *f*
reactionary /rɪˈækʃ(ə)nərɪ/ *adj & n* reazionario, -a *mf*
reactor /rɪˈæktə(r)/ *n* reattore *m*
read /riːd/ **A** *vt* (*pt/pp* **read** /red/) leggere; Univ studiare
B *vi* leggere; ‹*instrument*› indicare
▪ **read back** *vt* (say aloud) rileggere
▪ **read on** *vi* (continue reading) continuare a leggere
▪ **read out** *vt* leggere ad alta voce
▪ **read up on** *vt* studiare a fondo
readable /ˈriːdəbl/ *adj* piacevole a leggersi; (legible) leggibile
reader /ˈriːdə(r)/ *n* lettore, -trice *mf*; (book) antologia *f*
readership /ˈriːdəʃɪp/ *n* numero *m* di lettori
read head *n* Comput testina *f* di lettura
readily /ˈredɪlɪ/ *adv* volentieri; (easily) facilmente
readiness /ˈredɪnɪs/ *n* disponibilità *f*; **in** ~ pronto
reading /ˈriːdɪŋ/ *n* lettura *f*
readjust /riːəˈdʒʌst/ **A** *vt* regolare di nuovo
B *vi* riabituarsi (**to** a)
readjustment /riːəˈdʒʌstmənt/ *n* riadattamento *m*
read-only memory *n* Comput memoria *f* di sola lettura
re-advertise /riːˈædvətaɪz/ *vt* far ripubblicare un'inserzione per ‹*position, item*›
ready /ˈredɪ/ *adj* (**-ier, -iest**) pronto; (quick) veloce; **get** ~ prepararsi
ready-made *adj* confezionato
ready-mixed *adj* già miscelato
ready money *n* contanti *mpl*
ready-to-wear *adj* prêt-à-porter
reaffirm /riːəˈfɜːm/ *vt* riaffermare
reafforestation /riːəfɒrɪˈsteɪʃn/ *n* rimboschimento *m*
real /riːl/ **A** *adj* vero; ‹*increase*› reale
B *adv* AmE infml veramente
real estate *n* beni *mpl* immobili
realign /riːəˈlaɪn/ **A** *vt* riallineare
B *vi* fig formare nuove alleanze
realignment /riːəˈlaɪnmənt/ *n* Pol formazione *f* di nuove alleanze; Fin riallineamento *m*
realism /ˈrɪəlɪzm/ *n* realismo *m*
realist /ˈrɪəlɪst/ *n* realista *mf*
realistic /rɪəˈlɪstɪk/ *adj* realistico
realistically /rɪəˈlɪstɪklɪ/ *adv* realisticamente
reality /rɪˈælətɪ/ *n* realtà *f*
reality TV *n* reality TV *f*, reality *m*, reality show *mpl*
realization /rɪəlaɪˈzeɪʃn/ *n* realizzazione *f*
realize /ˈrɪəlaɪz/ *vt* realizzare
real life *n* realtà *f*; **in** ~ **life** nella realtà
real-life *attrib* autentico
reallocate /riːˈæləkeɪt/ *vt* riassegnare
reallocation /riːæləˈkeɪʃn/ *n* riassegnazione *f*
really /ˈrɪəlɪ/ *adv* davvero
realm /relm/ *n* regno *m*
real time **A** *n* tempo *m* reale; **in** ~ in tempo reale
B *adj* in tempo reale
realtor /ˈrɪəltə(r)/ *n* AmE agente *mf* immobiliare
realty /ˈrɪəltɪ/ *n* AmE beni *mpl* immobili
reanimate /riːˈænɪmeɪt/ *vt* rianimare
reap /riːp/ *vt* mietere
reappear /riːəˈpɪə(r)/ *vi* riapparire
reappearance /riːəˈpɪərəns/ *n* ricomparsa *f*
reapply /riːəˈplaɪ/ *vi* (*pt/pp* **-ied**) ripresentare domanda
reappoint /riːəˈpɔɪnt/ *vt* riconfermare
reappraisal /riːəˈpreɪzl/ *n* riconsiderazione *f*
reappraise /riːəˈpreɪz/ *vt* riesaminare ‹*question, policy*›; rivalutare ‹*writer, work*›
rear[1] /rɪə(r)/ *adj* posteriore; Auto di dietro
rear[2] **A** *vt* allevare
B *vi* ~ **[up]** ‹*horse*› impennarsi
C *n* **the** ~ (of building) il retro; (of bus, plane) la parte posteriore; **from the** ~ da dietro
rear end *n* infml di dietro *m*
rearguard /ˈrɪəgɑːd/ *n* Mil fig retroguardia *f*
rear light *n* luce *f* posteriore
rearm /riːˈɑːm/ **A** *vt* riarmare
B *vi* riarmarsi
rearmament /riːˈɑːməmənt/ *n* riarmo *m*
rearmost /ˈrɪəməʊst/ *adj* ultimo; ‹*carriage*› di coda
rearrange /riːəˈreɪndʒ/ *vt* cambiare la disposizione di

rear-view mirror *n* Auto specchietto *m* retrovisore

🔑 **reason** /ˈriːzn/ **A** *n* ragione *f*; **within ~** nei limiti del ragionevole; **listen to ~** ascoltare la ragione
B *vi* ragionare; **~ with** cercare di far ragionare

🔑 **reasonable** /ˈriːznəbl/ *adj* ragionevole

reasonably /ˈriːznəblɪ/ *adv* (in reasonable way, fairly) ragionevolmente

reasoning /ˈriːznɪŋ/ *n* ragionamento *m*

reassemble /riːəˈsemb(ə)l/ *vt* riassemblare

reassembly /riːəˈsemblɪ/ *n* riassemblaggio *m*

reassert /ˌriːəˈsɜːt/ *vt* riaffermare ‹*authority*›

reassess /riːəˈses/ *vt* riesaminare ‹*problem, situation*›; riaccertare ‹*tax liability*›

reassessment /riːəˈsesmənt/ *n* (of situation) riesame *m*; (of tax) nuovo accertamento *m*

reassurance /riːəˈʃʊərəns/ *n* rassicurazione *f*

reassure /riːəˈʃʊə(r)/ *vt* rassicurare; **~ somebody of something** rassicurare qualcuno su qualcosa

reassuring /riːəˈʃʊərɪŋ/ *adj* rassicurante

reawaken /riːəˈweɪkn/ *vt* fig risvegliare ‹*interest*›

rebate /ˈriːbeɪt/ *n* rimborso *m*; (discount) deduzione *f*

rebel¹ /ˈrebl/ *n* ribelle *mf*

rebel² /rɪˈbel/ *vi* (*pt/pp* **rebelled**) ribellarsi

rebellion /rɪˈbeljən/ *n* ribellione *f*

rebellious /rɪˈbeljəs/ *adj* ribelle

rebelliousness /rɪˈbelɪəsnɪs/ *n* spirito *m* di ribellione

rebirth /riːbɜːθ/ *n* rinascita *f*

reboot /riːˈbuːt/ *vt* Comput reinizializzare

reborn /riːˈbɔːn/ *adj* Relig **be ~** rinascere; **be ~ as something** rinascere come qualcosa

rebound¹ /rɪˈbaʊnd/ *vi* rimbalzare; fig ricadere

rebound² /ˈriːbaʊnd/ *n* rimbalzo *m*

rebuff /rɪˈbʌf/ **A** *n* rifiuto *m*
B *vt* respingere

rebuild /riːˈbɪld/ *vt* (*pt/pp* **-built**) ricostruire

rebuke /rɪˈbjuːk/ **A** *n* rimprovero *m*
B *vt* rimproverare

rebut /rɪˈbʌt/ *vt* confutare

rebuttal /rɪˈbʌtl/ *n* rifiuto *m*

recalcitrant /rɪˈkælsɪtrənt/ *adj* fml ricalcitrante

recalculate /riːˈkælkjʊleɪt/ *vt* ricalcolare

🔑 **recall** /rɪˈkɔːl/ **A** *n* richiamo *m*; **beyond ~** irrevocabile
B *vt* richiamare; riconvocare ‹*diplomat, parliament*›; (remember) rievocare

recant /rɪˈkænt/ *vi* abiurare

recap /ˈriːkæp/ **A** *vt & vi* infml = **recapitulate**
B *n* ricapitolazione *f*

recapitulate /riːkəˈpɪtjʊleɪt/ *vt & vi* ricapitolare

recapture /riːˈkæptʃə(r)/ *vt* riconquistare; ricatturare ‹*person, animal*›

recast /riːˈkɑːst/ *vt* rimaneggiare ‹*text, plan*›; riformulare ‹*sentence*›

recede /rɪˈsiːd/ *vt* allontanarsi

receding /rɪˈsiːdɪŋ/ *adj* ‹*forehead, chin*› sfuggente; **have ~ hair** essere stempiato

receipt /rɪˈsiːt/ *n* ricevuta *f*; (receiving) ricezione *f*; **~s** *pl* Comm entrate *fpl*

🔑 **receive** /rɪˈsiːv/ *vt* ricevere

receiver /rɪˈsiːvə(r)/ *n* Teleph ricevitore *m*; Radio, TV apparecchio *m* ricevente; (of stolen goods) ricettatore, -trice *mf*

receivership /rɪˈsiːvəʃɪp/ *n* BrE **go into ~** essere sottomesso all'amministrazione controllata

receiving /rɪˈsiːvɪŋ/ *n* (stolen goods) ricettazione *f*

receiving end /rɪˈsiːvɪŋ/ *n* **be on the ~** essere dall'altro lato della barricata

🔑 **recent** /ˈriːsnt/ *adj* recente

🔑 **recently** /ˈriːsəntlɪ/ *adv* recentemente

receptacle /rɪˈseptəkl/ *n* recipiente *m*

reception /rɪˈsepʃn/ *n* ricevimento *m*; (welcome) accoglienza *f*; Radio ricezione *f*; **~ [desk]** (in hotel) reception *f inv*

receptionist /rɪˈsepʃənɪst/ *n* persona *f* alla reception

receptive /rɪˈseptɪv/ *adj* ricettivo

recess /rɪˈses/ *n* rientranza *f*; (holiday) vacanza *f*; AmE Sch intervallo *m*

recession /rɪˈseʃn/ *n* recessione *f*

recharge /riːˈtʃɑːdʒ/ *vt* ricaricare

rechargeable /ˌriːˈtʃɑːdʒəbl/ *adj* ‹*battery*› ricaricabile; ‹*costs*› addebitabile

recidivism /rɪˈsɪdɪvɪzm/ *n* recidività *f*

recidivist /rɪˈsɪdɪvɪst/ *n* recidivo, -a *mf*

recipe /ˈresəpɪ/ *n* ricetta *f*

recipe book *n* libro *m* di ricette

recipient /rɪˈsɪpɪənt/ *n* (of letter, parcel) destinatario, -a *mf*; (of money) beneficiario, -a *mf*

reciprocal /rɪˈsɪprəkl/ *adj* reciproco

reciprocate /rɪˈsɪprəkeɪt/ *vt* ricambiare

recital /rɪˈsaɪtl/ *n* recital *m inv*

recitation /resɪˈteɪʃn/ *n* recitazione *f*

recite /rɪˈsaɪt/ *vt* recitare; (list) elencare

reckless /ˈreklɪs/ *adj* ‹*action, decision*› sconsiderato; **be a ~ driver** guidare in modo spericolato

recklessly /ˈreklɪslɪ/ *adv* in modo sconsiderato

recklessness /ˈreklɪsnɪs/ *n* sconsideratezza *f*

reckon /ˈrekən/ *vt* calcolare; (consider) pensare; **be ~ed** essere considerato
■ **reckon on, reckon with** *vt* fare i conti con
■ **reckon without** *vt* fare i conti senza

🔑 parola chiave

reckoning /ˈrekənɪŋ/ *n* stima *f*, calcoli *mpl*; **by my/your etc. ~** secondo i miei/tuoi ecc. calcoli
reclaim /rɪˈkleɪm/ *vt* reclamare; bonificare ‹*land*›
reclaimable /rɪˈkleɪməbl/ *adj* ‹*expenses*› rimborsabile
recline /rɪˈklaɪn/ *vi* sdraiarsi
reclining /rɪˈklaɪnɪŋ/ *adj* ‹*seat*› reclinabile
recluse /rɪˈklu:s/ *n* recluso, -a *mf*
reclusive /rɪˈklu:sɪv/ *adj* solitario
recognition /rekəgˈnɪʃn/ *n* riconoscimento *m*; **in ~** come riconoscimento (**of** per); **beyond ~** irriconoscibile
recognizable /ˌrekəgˈnaɪzəbl, ˈrekəgnaɪzəbl/ *adj* riconoscibile
recognize /ˈrekəgnaɪz/ *vt* riconoscere
recoil¹ /ˈri:kɔɪl/ *n* (of gun) rinculo *m*
recoil² /rɪˈkɔɪl/ *vi* (in fear) indietreggiare
recollect /rekəˈlekt/ *vt* ricordare
recollection /rekəˈlekʃn/ *n* ricordo *m*
recommence /ri:kəˈmens/ *vt & vi* ricominciare
recommend /rekəˈmend/ *vt* raccomandare
recommendation /rekəmenˈdeɪʃn/ *n* raccomandazione *f*
recommended retail price /rekəˈmendɪd/ *n* Comm prezzo *m* di vendita consigliato
recompense /ˈrekəmpens/ **A** *n* ricompensa *f* **B** *vt* ricompensare
reconcile /ˈrekənsaɪl/ *vt* riconciliare; conciliare ‹*facts*›; far quadrare ‹*bank statement*›; **~ oneself to** rassegnarsi a
reconciliation /rekənsɪlɪˈeɪʃn/ *n* riconciliazione *f*
recondition /ri:kənˈdɪʃn/ *vt* ripristinare; **~ed engine** motore *m* che ha subito riparazioni
reconnaissance /rɪˈkɒnɪsns/ *n* Mil ricognizione *f*; **on ~** in ricognizione
reconnoitre /rekəˈnɔɪtə(r)/ **A** *vi* (*pres p* **-tring**) fare una ricognizione **B** *vt* fare una ricognizione di
reconsider /ri:kənˈsɪdə(r)/ *vt* riconsiderare
reconstruct /ri:kənˈstrʌkt/ *vt* ricostruire
reconstruction /ri:kənˈstrʌkʃn/ *n* ricostruzione *f*
reconvene /ri:kənˈvi:n/ *vi* riunirsi nuovamente
record¹ /rɪˈkɔ:d/ *vt* registrare; (make a note of) annotare
record² /ˈrekɔd/ *n* (file) documentazione *f*; Mus disco *m*; Sport record *m inv*; **~s** *pl* (files) schedario *msg*; **keep a ~ of** tener nota di; **off the ~** in via ufficiosa; **have a [criminal] ~** avere la fedina penale sporca
record book *n* libro *m* dei record
record-breaker /ˈrekɔ:dbreɪkə(r)/ *n* **be a ~** battere un record
recorded /rɪˈkɔ:dɪd/ *adj* (on tape) ‹*message*› registrato; (in document) ‹*sighting, case*› documentato
recorded delivery /rɪˈkɔ:dɪd/ *n* raccomandata *f*
recorder /rɪˈkɔ:də(r)/ *n* Mus flauto *m* dolce
record holder /ˈrekɔ:dhəʊldə(r), AmE ˈrekərd-/ *n* primatista *mf*
recording /rɪˈkɔ:dɪŋ/ *n* registrazione *f*
recording studio *n* sala *f* di registrazione
record player *n* giradischi *m inv*
recount /rɪˈkaʊnt/ *vt* raccontare
re-count¹ /ri:ˈkaʊnt/ *vt* ricontare
re-count² /ˈri:kaʊnt/ *n* Pol nuovo conteggio *m*
recoup /rɪˈku:p/ *vt* rifarsi di ‹*losses*›
recourse /rɪˈkɔ:s/ *n* **have ~ to** ricorrere a
recover /rɪˈkʌvə(r)/ *vt & vi* recuperare
re-cover /ri:ˈkʌvə(r)/ *vt* rifoderare
recovery /rɪˈkʌvəri/ *n* recupero *m*; (of health) guarigione *f*
recovery vehicle *n* autogrù *f*
recreate /ˈrekrɪeɪt, ˌri:krɪˈeɪt/ *vt* ricreare
recreation /rekrɪˈeɪʃn/ *n* ricreazione *f*
recreational /rekrɪˈeɪʃənəl/ *adj* ricreativo
recreational drug *n sostanza (f) stupefacente che si assume occasionalmente*
recrimination /rɪkrɪmɪˈneɪʃn/ *n* recriminazione *f*
recruit /rɪˈkru:t/ **A** *n* Mil recluta *f*; **new ~** (member) nuovo, -a, adepto, -a *mf*; (worker) neoassunto, -a *mf* **B** *vt* assumere ‹*staff*›
recruitment /rɪˈkru:tmənt/ *n* assunzione *f*
rectangle /ˈrektæŋgl/ *n* rettangolo *m*
rectangular /rekˈtæŋgjʊlə(r)/ *adj* rettangolare
rectify /ˈrektɪfaɪ/ *vt* (*pt/pp* **-ied**) rettificare
rector /ˈrektə(r)/ *n* Univ rettore *m*
rectory /ˈrektərɪ/ *n* presbiterio *m*
rectum /ˈrektəm/ *n* retto *m*
recuperate /rɪˈkju:pəreit/ *vi* ristabilirsi
recur /rɪˈkɜ:(r)/ *vi* (*pt/pp* **recurred**) ricorrere; ‹*illness*› ripresentarsi
recurrence /rɪˈkʌrəns/ *n* ricorrenza *f*; (of illness) ricomparsa *f*
recurrent /rɪˈkʌrənt/ *adj* ricorrente
recyclable /ri:ˈsaɪkləbl/ *adj* riciclabile
recycle /ri:ˈsaɪkl/ *vt* riciclare; **~d paper** carta *f* riciclata
recycling /ri:ˈsaɪklɪŋ/ *n* riciclaggio *m*
red /red/ **A** *adj* (**redder**, **reddest**) rosso **B** *n* rosso *m*; **be in the ~** ‹*account*› essere scoperto; ‹*person*› avere il conto scoperto
red alert *n* allarme *m* rosso; **be on ~** essere in stato di massima allerta
red-brick *adj* Univ di recente fondazione
Red Cross *n* Croce *f* Rossa
redcurrant *n* ribes *m* rosso
redden /ˈredn/ **A** *vt* arrossare

B *vi* arrossire
reddish /ˈredɪʃ/ *adj* rossastro
redecorate /riːˈdekəreɪt/ *vt* (paint) ridipingere; (wallpaper) ritappezzare
redeem /rɪˈdiːm/ *vt* Relig (from pawnshop) riscattare; **~ing quality** unico aspetto *m* positivo
redefine /riːdɪˈfaɪn/ *vt* ridefinire
redemption /rɪˈdempʃn/ *n* riscatto *m*
redeploy /riːdɪˈplɔɪ/ *vt* ridistribuire
redevelop /ˌriːdɪˈveləp/ *vt* risanare ‹*area, site*›
red-faced *adj* also fig paonazzo
red-haired /-ˈheəd/ *adj* con i capelli rossi
red-handed /-ˈhændɪd/ *adj* **catch somebody ~** cogliere qualcuno con le mani nel sacco
redhead *n* rosso, -a *mf* (di capelli)
red herring *n* diversione *f*
red-hot *adj* rovente
redial /riːˈdaɪəl/ Teleph **A** *vt* ricomporre **B** *vi* ricomporre il numero
redial facility *n* Teleph funzione *f* di ricomposizione automatica dell'ultimo numero
redirect /riːdaɪˈrekt/ *vt* mandare al nuovo indirizzo ‹*letter*›
rediscover /riːdɪˈskʌvə(r)/ *vt* riscoprire
redistribute /riːdɪsˈtrɪbjuːt/ *vt* ridistribuire
redistribution /riːdɪstrɪˈbjuːʃn/ *n* ridistribuzione *f*
red-letter day *n* giorno *m* memorabile
red light *n* Auto semaforo *m* rosso; **go through a ~** passare col rosso
red light area *n* quartiere *m* a luci rosse
red light district *n* quartiere *m* a luci rosse
red meat *n* carne *f* rossa
redness /ˈrednɪs/ *n* rossore *m*
redo /riːˈduː/ *vt* (*pt* **-did**, *pp* **-done**) rifare
redolent /ˈredələnt/ *adj* profumato (**of** di)
redouble /riːˈdʌbl/ *vt* raddoppiare
red pepper *n* peperone *m* rosso
redraft /riːˈdrɑːft/ *vt* stendere nuovamente
redress /rɪˈdres/ **A** *n* riparazione *f* **B** *vt* ristabilire ‹*balance*›
red tape *n* infml burocrazia *f*
⚷ **reduce** /rɪˈdjuːs/ *vt* ridurre; Culin far consumare
reductio ad absurdum /rɪˈdʌktɪəʊædæbˈsɜːdəm/ *n* ragionamento *m* per assurdo
⚷ **reduction** /rɪˈdʌkʃn/ *n* riduzione *f*
redundancy /rɪˈdʌndənsɪ/ *n* licenziamento *m*; (payment) liquidazione *f*
redundant /rɪˈdʌndənt/ *adj* superfluo; **make ~** licenziare; **be made ~** essere licenziato
reed /riːd/ *n* Bot canna *f*
reedy /ˈriːdɪ/ *adj* ‹*voice, tone*› acuto

⚷ parola chiave

reef /riːf/ *n* scogliera *f*
reefer /ˈriːfə(r)/ *n* (jacket) giubbotto *m* a doppio petto; infml (dope) spinello *m*
reef knot *n* nodo *m* piano
reek /riːk/ *vi* puzzare (**of** di)
reel /riːl/ **A** *n* bobina *f* **B** *vi* (stagger) vacillare
re-elect *vt* rieleggere
re-election *n* rielezione *f*
reel off *vt* fig snocciolare
re-emerge *vi* riemergere
re-emergence *n* ricomparsa *f*
re-enact /riːɪˈnækt/ *vt* ricostruire ‹*crime*›; Jur rimettere in vigore; recitare nuovamente ‹*role*›
re-enter /riːˈentə(r)/ *vt* rientrare in
re-entry *n* (of spacecraft) rientro *m*
re-establish *vt* ristabilire, ripristinare
re-establishment *n* ripristino *m*
re-examination *n* riesame *m*
re-examine *vt* riesaminare
ref /ref/ *n abbr* BrE infml (**referee**) arbitro *m*
refectory /rɪˈfektərɪ/ *n* refettorio *m*; Univ mensa *f* universitaria
⚷ **refer** /rɪˈfɜː(r)/ **A** *vt* (*pt/pp* **referred**) rinviare ‹*matter*›; indirizzare ‹*person*› **B** *vi* **~ to** fare allusione a; (consult) rivolgersi a ‹*book*›; **are you ~ring to me?** alludi a me?
referee /refəˈriː/ **A** *n* arbitro *m*; (for job) garante *mf* **B** *vt & vi* (*pt/pp* **refereed**) arbitrare
⚷ **reference** /ˈref(ə)rəns/ *n* riferimento *m*; (in book) nota *f* bibliografica; (for job) referenza *f*; Comm **'your ~'** 'riferimento'; **with ~ to** con riferimento a; **make [a] ~ to** fare riferimento a
reference book *n* libro *m* di consultazione
reference library *n* biblioteca *f* per la consultazione
reference number *n* numero *m* di riferimento
referendum /refəˈrendəm/ *n* referendum *m inv*
referral /rɪˈfɜːrəl/ *n* (of matter, problem) deferimento *m*; Med (act) *invio (m) di un paziente a un altro medico*; (person) *paziente (mf) mandato da un medico a un altro*
refill[1] /riːˈfɪl/ *vt* riempire di nuovo; ricaricare ‹*pen, lighter*›
refill[2] /ˈriːfɪl/ *n* (for pen) ricambio *m*
refine /rɪˈfaɪn/ *vt* raffinare
refined /rɪˈfaɪnd/ *adj* raffinato
refinement /rɪˈfaɪnmənt/ *n* raffinatezza *f*
refinery /rɪˈfaɪnərɪ/ *n* raffineria *f*
refining /rɪˈfaɪnɪŋ/ *n* Techn raffinazione *f*
refit[1] /ˈriːfɪt/ *n* Naut raddobbo *m*; (of shop, factory etc) rinnovo *m*
refit[2] /riːˈfɪt/ *vt* raddobbare ‹*ship*›; rinnovare ‹*shop, factory etc*›

reflate /riːˈfleɪt/ *vt* reflazionare ‹*economy*›

reflect /rɪˈflekt/ **A** *vt* riflettere; **be ~ed in** essere riflesso in
B *vt* (think) riflettere (**on** su); **~ badly on somebody** fig mettere in cattiva luce qualcuno

reflection /rɪˈflekʃn/ *n* riflessione *f*; (image) riflesso *m*; **on ~** dopo riflessione

reflective /rɪˈflektɪv/ *adj* riflessivo

reflectively /rɪˈflektɪvlɪ/ *adv* in modo riflessivo

reflector /rɪˈflektə(r)/ *n* riflettore *m*

reflex /ˈriːfleks/ **A** *n* riflesso *m*
B *attrib* di riflesso

reflexive /rɪˈfleksɪv/ *adj* riflessivo

reflexive verb *n* verbo *m* riflessivo

refloat /riːˈfləʊt/ *vt* Naut, Comm rimettere a galla

reforestation /riːfɒrɪˈsteɪʃn/ *n* rimboschimento *m*

reform /rɪˈfɔːm/ **A** *n* riforma *f*
B *vt* riformare
C *vi* correggersi

reformat /riːˈfɔːmæt/ *vt* riformattare

Reformation /refəˈmeɪʃn/ *n* Relig Riforma *f*

reformer /rɪˈfɔːmə(r)/ *n* riformatore, -trice *mf*

refrain¹ /rɪˈfreɪn/ *n* ritornello *m*

refrain² *vi* astenersi (**from** da)

refresh /rɪˈfreʃ/ *vt* rinfrescare; Comput aggiornare

refresher course /rɪˈfreʃə(r)/ *n* corso *m* d'aggiornamento

refreshing /rɪˈfreʃɪŋ/ *adj* rinfrescante

refreshments /rɪˈfreʃmənts/ *npl* rinfreschi *mpl*

refrigerate /rɪˈfrɪdʒəreɪt/ *vt* conservare in frigo; Ind refrigerare

refrigerated lorry /rɪˈfrɪdʒəreɪtɪd/ *n* camion *m inv* frigorifero

refrigeration /rɪfrɪdʒəˈreɪʃn/ *n* Ind refrigerazione *f*

refrigerator /rɪˈfrɪdʒəreɪtə(r)/ *n* frigorifero *m*

refuel /riːˈfjʊəl/ **A** *vt* (*pt/pp* **-fuelled**) rifornire di carburante
B *vi* fare rifornimento

refuge /ˈrefjuːdʒ/ *n* rifugio *m*; **take ~** rifugiarsi

refugee /refjʊˈdʒiː/ *n* rifugiato, -a *mf*

refugee camp *n* campo *m* profughi

refund¹ /ˈriːfʌnd/ *n* rimborso *m*

refund² /rɪˈfʌnd/ *vt* rimborsare

refurbish /riːˈfɜːbɪʃ/ *vt* rimettere a nuovo

refurbishment /riːˈfɜːbɪʃmənt/ *n* rinnovo *m*

refusal /rɪˈfjuːzl/ *n* rifiuto *m*

refuse¹ /rɪˈfjuːz/ *vt & vi* rifiutare; **~ to do something** rifiutare di fare qualcosa

refuse² /ˈrefjuːs/ *n* rifiuti *mpl*

refuse collection *n* raccolta *f* dei rifiuti

refuse collector *n* BrE spazzino, -a *mf*

refute /rɪˈfjuːt/ *vt* confutare

regain /rɪˈgeɪn/ *vt* riconquistare

regal /ˈriːgl/ *adj* regale

regale /rɪˈgeɪl/ *vt* **~ somebody with something** deliziare qualcuno con qualcosa

regalia /rɪˈgeɪlɪə/ *npl* insegne *fpl* reali

regard /rɪˈgɑːd/ **A** *n* (heed) riguardo *m*; (respect) considerazione *f*; **~s** *pl* saluti *mpl*; **send/give my ~s to your brother** salutami tuo fratello; **with ~ to** riguardo a
B *vt* (consider) considerare (**as** come); **as ~s** riguardo a

regarding /rɪˈgɑːdɪŋ/ *prep* riguardo a

regardless /rɪˈgɑːdlɪs/ *adv* lo stesso; **~ of** senza badare a

regatta /rɪˈgætə/ *n* regata *f*

regency /ˈriːdʒənsɪ/ *n* reggenza *f*

regenerate /rɪˈdʒenəreɪt/ **A** *vt* rigenerare
B *vi* rigenerarsi

regent /ˈriːdʒənt/ *n* reggente *mf*

reggae /ˈregeɪ/ *n* reggae *m*

regime /reɪˈʒiːm/ *n* regime *m*

regiment¹ /ˈredʒɪmənt/ *n* reggimento *m*

regiment² /ˈredʒɪment/ *vt* irreggimentare

regimental /redʒɪˈmentl/ *adj* reggimentale

regimentation /redʒɪmənˈteɪʃn/ *n* irreggimentazione *f*

regimented /ˈredʒɪmentɪd/ *adj* irreggimentato

region /ˈriːdʒən/ *n* regione *f*; **in the ~ of** fig approssimativamente

regional /ˈriːdʒənl/ *adj* regionale

register /ˈredʒɪstə(r)/ **A** *n* registro *m*
B *vt* registrare; mandare tramite assicurata ‹*letter, package*›; assicurare ‹*luggage*›; immatricolare ‹*motor vehicle*›; mostrare ‹*feeling*›
C *vi* ‹*instrument*› funzionare; ‹*student*› iscriversi (**for** a); **it didn't ~ with me** fig non ci ho fatto attenzione; **~ with** iscriversi nella lista di ‹*doctor*›

registered /ˈredʒɪstəd/ *adj* ‹*voter, student*› iscritto; ‹*vehicle*› immatricolato

registered letter /ˈredʒɪstəd/ *n* lettera *f* assicurata

registered trademark *n* marchio *m* depositato

registrar /redʒɪˈstrɑː(r)/ *n* ufficiale *m* di stato civile

registration /redʒɪˈstreɪʃn/ *n* (of vehicle) immatricolazione *f*; (of letter, luggage) assicurazione *f*; (for course) iscrizione *f*

registration fee *n* tassa *f* d'iscrizione

registration number *n* Auto [numero *m* di] targa *f*

registry office /ˈredʒɪstrɪ/ *n* anagrafe *f*

regress /rɪˈgres/ *vi* Biol, Psych fig regredire

regression /rɪˈgreʃən/ *n* regressione *f*

regressive /rɪˈgresɪv/ *adj* Biol, Psych regressivo

regret /rɪ'gret/ **A** *n* rammarico *m*
B *vt* (*pt/pp* **regretted**) rimpiangere; **I ~ that** mi rincresce che
regretfully /rɪ'gretfʊlɪ/ *adv* con rammarico
regrettable /rɪ'gretəbl/ *adj* spiacevole
regrettably /rɪ'gretəblɪ/ *adv* spiacevolmente; (before adjective) deplorevolmente
regroup /riː'gruːp/ *vi* riorganizzarsi
🔑 **regular** /'regjʊlə(r)/ **A** *adj* regolare; (usual) abituale
B *n* cliente *mf* abituale
regularity /regjʊ'lærətɪ/ *n* regolarità *f*
regularly /'regjʊləlɪ/ *adv* regolarmente
regulate /'regʊleɪt/ *vt* regolare
🔑 **regulation** /regjʊ'leɪʃn/ *n* (rule) regolamento *m*
regulator /'regjʊleɪtə(r)/ *n* (person) regolatore, -trice *mf*; (device) regolatore *m*
regurgitate /rɪ'gɜːdʒɪteɪt/ *vt* rigurgitare; fig derog ripetere meccanicamente
rehabilitate /riːhə'bɪlɪteɪt/ *vt* riabilitare
rehabilitation /riːhəbɪlɪ'teɪʃn/ *n* riabilitazione *f*
rehabilitation centre BrE, **rehabilitation center** AmE *n* (after drug addiction, illness, prison) comunità *f* terapeutica
rehash[1] /riː'hæʃ/ *vt* rimaneggiare
rehash[2] /'riːhæʃ/ *n* rimaneggiamento *m*
rehearsal /rɪ'hɜːsl/ *n* Theat prova *f*
rehearse /rɪ'hɜːs/ *vt & vi* provare
reheat /riː'hiːt/ *vt* scaldare di nuovo
rehouse /riː'haʊz/ *vt* riallogiare
reign /reɪn/ **A** *n* regno *m*
B *vi* regnare
reimburse /riːɪm'bɜːs/ *vt* **~ somebody for something** rimborsare qualcosa a qualcuno
reimbursement /riːɪm'bɜːsmənt/ *n* rimborso *m*
rein /reɪn/ *n* redine *f*
reincarnate /riːɪn'kɑːneɪt/ *vt* **be ~d** reincarnarsi
reincarnation /riːɪnkɑː'neɪʃn/ *n* reincarnazione *f*
reindeer /'reɪndɪə(r)/ *n inv* renna *f*
reinforce /riːɪn'fɔːs/ *vt* rinforzare
reinforced concrete *n* cemento *m* armato
reinforcement /riːɪn'fɔːsmənt/ *n* rinforzo *m*; **~s** *pl* Mil rinforzi *mpl*
reinstall /'riːɪnstɔːl/ *vt* Comput reinstallare ‹*software, program*›
reinstate /riːɪn'steɪt/ *vt* reintegrare
reinstatement /riːɪn'steɪtmənt/ *n* reintegrazione *f*
reinterpret /riːɪnt'tɜːprɪt/ *vt* reinterpretare
reinterpretation /riːɪntɜːprɪ'teɪʃn/ *n* reinterpretazione *f*
reintroduce /riːɪntrə'djuːs/ *vt* reintrodurre

reintroduction /riːɪntrə'dʌkʃn/ *n* reintroduzione *f*
reiterate /riː'ɪtəreɪt/ *vt* reiterare
reiteration /riːɪtə'reɪʃn/ *n* reiterazione *f*
🔑 **reject** /rɪ'dʒekt/ *vt* rifiutare
rejection /rɪ'dʒekʃn/ *n* rifiuto *m*; Med rigetto *m*
rejects /'riːdʒekts/ *npl* Comm scarti *mpl*
rejig /riː'dʒɪg/ *vt* (*pt/pp* **rejigged**) BrE riorganizzare
rejoice /rɪ'dʒɔɪs/ *vi* literary rallegrarsi
rejoicing /rɪ'dʒɔɪsɪŋ/ *n* gioia *f*
rejoin /rɪ'dʒɔɪn/ *vt* riassociarsi a ‹*club, party*›; Mil reintegrarsi in ‹*regiment*›; (answer) replicare
rejuvenate /rɪ'dʒuːvəneɪt/ *vt* rinnovare; ringiovanire ‹*person*›
rejuvenation /rɪ'dʒuːvəneɪʃn/ *n* rinnovamento *m*; (of person) ringiovanimento *m*
rekindle /riː'kɪndl/ *vt* riattizzare
relapse /rɪ'læps/ **A** *n* ricaduta *f*
B *vi* ricadere
🔑 **relate** /rɪ'leɪt/ *vt* (tell) riportare; (connect) collegare
▪ **relate to** *vt* riferirsi a; identificarsi con ‹*person*›
🔑 **related** /rɪ'leɪtɪd/ *adj* imparentato (**to** a); ‹*ideas etc*› affine
🔑 **relation** /rɪ'leɪʃn/ *n* rapporto *m*; (person) parente *mf*
🔑 **relationship** /rɪ'leɪʃnʃɪp/ *n* rapporto *m*; (blood tie) parentela *f*; (affair) relazione *f*
🔑 **relative** /'relətɪv/ **A** *n* parente *mf*
B *adj* relativo
🔑 **relatively** /'relətɪvlɪ/ *adv* relativamente
relativity /relə'tɪvətɪ/ *n* relatività *f*
relativity theory *n* Phys teoria *f* della relatività
relaunch[1] /'riːlɔːntʃ/ *n* rilancio *m*
relaunch[2] /riː'lɔːntʃ/ *vt* rilanciare
🔑 **relax** /rɪ'læks/ **A** *vt* rilassare; allentare ‹*pace grip*›
B *vi* rilassarsi
relaxation /riːlæk'seɪʃn/ *n* rilassamento *m*, relax *m*; (recreation) svago *m*
relaxed /rɪ'lækst/ *adj* rilassato
relaxing /rɪ'læksɪŋ/ *adj* rilassante
relay, relay race /'riːleɪ/ *n* [corsa *f* a] staffetta *f*
relay[1] /riː'leɪ/ *vt* (*pt/pp* **-layed**) trasmettere
relay[2] /'riːleɪ/ *n* Electr relais *m inv*; **work in ~s** fare i turni
🔑 **release** /rɪ'liːs/ **A** *n* rilascio *m*; (of film) distribuzione *f*
B *vt* liberare; lasciare ‹*hand*›; togliere ‹*brake*›; distribuire ‹*film*›; rilasciare ‹*information etc*›
relegate /'relɪgeɪt/ *vt* relegare; **be ~d** BrE Sport essere retrocesso

r

🔑 parola chiave

relegation /relɪˈgeɪʃn/ *n* relegazione *f*; BrE Sport retrocessione *f*

relent /rɪˈlent/ *vi* cedere

relentless /rɪˈlentlɪs/ *adj* inflessibile; (unceasing) incessante

relentlessly /rɪˈlentlɪslɪ/ *adv* incessantemente

relevance /ˈreləvəns/ *n* pertinenza *f*

relevant /ˈreləvənt/ *adj* pertinente (**to** a)

reliability /rɪlaɪəˈbɪlətɪ/ *n* affidabilità *f*

reliable /rɪˈlaɪəbl/ *adj* affidabile

reliably /rɪˈlaɪəblɪ/ *adv* in modo affidabile; **be ~ informed** sapere da fonte certa

reliance /rɪˈlaɪəns/ *n* fiducia *f* (**on** in)

reliant /rɪˈlaɪənt/ *adj* fiducioso (**on** in)

relic /ˈrelɪk/ *n* Relig reliquia *f*; **~s** *pl* resti *mpl*

relief /rɪˈliːf/ *n* sollievo *m*; (assistance) soccorso *m*; (distraction) diversivo *m*; (replacement) cambio *m*; (in art) rilievo *m*; **in ~** in rilievo

relief agency *n* organizzazione *f* umanitaria

relief map *n* carta *f* in rilievo

relief supplies *npl* soccorsi *mpl*, aiuti *mpl* umanitari

relief train *n* treno *m* supplementare

relief work *n lavoro m presso un'organizzazione umanitaria*

relief worker *n persona f che lavora per un'organizzazione umanitaria*

relieve /rɪˈliːv/ *vt* alleviare; (take over from) dare il cambio a; **~ of** liberare da ‹*burden*›

religion /rɪˈlɪdʒən/ *n* religione *f*

religious /rɪˈlɪdʒəs/ *adj* religioso

religiously /rɪˈlɪdʒəslɪ/ *adv* (conscientiously) scrupolosamente

relinquish /rɪˈlɪŋkwɪʃ/ *vt* abbandonare; **~ something to somebody** rinunciare a qualcosa in favore di qualcuno

relish /ˈrelɪʃ/ **A** *n* gusto *m*; Culin salsa *f* **B** *vt* fig apprezzare

relive /riːˈlɪv/ *vt* rivivere

reload /riːˈləʊd/ *vt* ricaricare

relocate /riːləˈkeɪt/ **A** *vt* trasferire **B** *vi* trasferirsi

relocation /riːləˈkeɪʃn/ *n* (of employee, company) trasferimento *m*

relocation allowance *n* indennità *f* di trasferimento

reluctance /rɪˈlʌktəns/ *n* riluttanza *f*

reluctant /rɪˈlʌktənt/ *adj* riluttante

reluctantly /rɪˈlʌktəntlɪ/ *adv* con riluttanza, a malincuore

rely /rɪˈlaɪ/ *vi* (*pt/pp* **-ied**) **~ on** dipendere da; (trust) contare su

remain /rɪˈmeɪn/ *vi* restare

remainder /rɪˈmeɪndə(r)/ **A** *n* resto *m*; Comm rimanenza *f* **B** *vt* Comm svendere

remaining /rɪˈmeɪnɪŋ/ *adj* restante

remains /rɪˈmeɪnz/ *npl* resti *mpl*; (dead body) spoglie *fpl*

remake /ˈriːmeɪk/ *n* (of film, recording) remake *m inv*

remand /rɪˈmɑːnd/ **A** *n* **on ~** in custodia cautelare **B** *vt* **~ in custody** rinviare con detenzione provvisoria

remand centre *n* BrE istituto *m* di carcerazione preventiva

remark /rɪˈmɑːk/ **A** *n* osservazione *f* **B** *vt* osservare

remarkable /rɪˈmɑːkəbl/ *adj* notevole

remarkably /rɪˈmɑːkəblɪ/ *adv* notevolmente

remarry /riːˈmærɪ/ *vi* (*pt/pp* **-ied**) risposarsi

remaster /riːˈmɑːstə(r)/ *vt* incidere di nuovo ‹*recording*›

rematch /ˈriːmætʃ/ *n* Sport partita *f* di ritorno; (in boxing) secondo incontro *m*

remedial /rɪˈmiːdɪəl/ *adj* correttivo; Med curativo

remedy /ˈremədɪ/ **A** *n* rimedio *m* (**for** contro) **B** *vt* (*pt/pp* **-ied**) rimediare a

remember /rɪˈmembə(r)/ **A** *vt* ricordare, ricordarsi; **~ to do something** ricordarsi di fare qualcosa; **~ me to him** salutamelo **B** *vi* ricordarsi

Remembrance Day /rɪˈmembrəns/ *n* commemorazione *f* dei caduti (*11 novembre*)

remind /rɪˈmaɪnd/ *vt* **~ somebody of something** ricordare qualcosa a qualcuno

reminder /rɪˈmaɪndə(r)/ *n* ricordo *m*; (memo) promemoria *m inv*; (letter) lettera *f* di sollecito; (to pay) sollecitazione *f* di pagamento

reminisce /remɪˈnɪs/ *vi* rievocare il passato

reminiscences /remɪˈnɪsənsɪz/ *npl* reminiscenze *fpl*

reminiscent /remɪˈnɪsənt/ *adj* **be ~ of** richiamare alla memoria

remiss /rɪˈmɪs/ *adj* negligente

remission /rɪˈmɪʃn/ *n* remissione *f*; (of sentence) condono *m*

remit /rɪˈmɪt/ *vt* (*pt/pp* **remitted**) rimettere ‹*money*›

remittance /rɪˈmɪtəns/ *n* rimessa *f*

remix[1] /riːˈmɪks/ *vt* Mus rimixare

remix[2] /ˈriːmɪks/ *n* Mus rimixaggio *m*

remnant /ˈremnənt/ *n* resto *m*; (of material) scampolo *m*; (trace) traccia *f*

remonstrate /ˈremənstreɪt/ *vi* fare rimostranze (**with somebody** a qualcuno)

remorse /rɪˈmɔːs/ *n* rimorso *m*

remorseful /rɪˈmɔːsfʊl/ *adj* pieno di rimorso

remorsefully /rɪˈmɔːsfʊlɪ/ *adv* con rimorso

remorseless /rɪˈmɔːslɪs/ *adj* spietato

remorselessly /rɪˈmɔslɪslɪ/ *adv* senza pietà

remote /rɪˈməʊt/ *adj* remoto; (slight) minimo

remote access *n* Comput accesso *m* remoto

remote control *n* telecomando *m*

remote-controlled *adj* telecomandato

remotely /rɪ'məʊtlɪ/ *adv* lontanamente; **be not ~...** non essere lontanamente...

remoteness /rɪ'məʊtnɪs/ *n* lontananza *f*

remould /'ri:məʊld/ *n* pneumatico *m* ricostruito

remount /ri:'maʊnt/ *vt* rimontare in sella a ‹*bike, horse*›

removable /rɪ'mu:vəbl/ *adj* rimovibile

removal /rɪ'mu:vl/ *n* rimozione *f*; (from house) trasloco *m*

removal man *n* addetto *m* ai traslochi

removal van *n* camion *m inv* da trasloco

⚷ **remove** /rɪ'mu:v/ *vt* togliere; togliersi ‹*clothes*›; eliminare ‹*stain, doubts*›

removers /rɪ'mu:vəz/ *npl* infml traslocatori *mpl*

remuneration /rɪmju:nə'reɪʃn/ *n* rimunerazione *f*

remunerative /rɪ'mju:nərətɪv/ *adj* rimunerativo

renaissance /rɪ'neɪsɒ̃s/ *n* rinascita *f*; **R~** Rinascimento *m*

renal /'ri:nəl/ *adj* renale

render /'rendə(r)/ *vt* rendere ‹*service*›

rendering /'rend(ə)rɪŋ/ *n* Mus interpretazione *f*

rendezvous /'rɒndeɪvu:/ *vi esp* Mil incontrarsi

rendition /ren'dɪʃn/ *n* interpretazione *f*

renegade /'renɪgeɪd/ *n* rinnegato, -a *mf*

renege /rɪ'neɪg/ *vi* venire meno (**on** a)

renegotiate /ri:nɪ'gəʊʃɪeɪt/ *vt* rinegoziare

renegotiation /ri:nɪgəʊʃɪ'eɪʃn/ *n* rinegoziato *m*

renew /rɪ'nju:/ *vt* rinnovare ‹*contract*›

renewable /rɪ'nju:əbl/ *adj* rinnovabile

renewal /rɪ'nju:əl/ *n* rinnovo *m*

r

renewed *adj* ‹*strength, interest*› rinnovato; ‹*attack*› nuovo

renounce /rɪ'naʊns/ *vt* rinunciare a

renovate /'renəveɪt/ *vt* rinnovare

renovation /renə'veɪʃn/ *n* rinnovo *m*

renown /rɪ'naʊn/ *n* fama *f*

renowned /rɪ'naʊnd/ *adj* rinomato

rent /rent/ **A** *n* affitto *m*
B *vt* affittare; **~ [out]** dare in affitto

rental /'rentl/ *n* affitto *m*

rent boy *n* ragazzo *m* di vita

rent-free **A** *adj* ‹*accommodation*› gratuito
B *adv* ‹*live, use*› senza pagare l'affitto

renunciation /rɪnʌnsɪ'eɪʃn/ *n* rinuncia *f*

reoffend /ri:ə'fend/ *vi* recidivare

reopen /ri:'əʊpən/ *vt & vi* riaprire

reorganization /ri:ɔ:gənaɪ'zeɪʃn/ *n* riorganizzazione *f*

reorganize /ri:'ɔ:gənaɪz/ *vt* riorganizzare

rep /rep/ *n* Comm infml rappresentante *mf*; Theat ≈ teatro *m* stabile

repackage /ri:'pækɪdʒ/ *vt* Comm cambiare la confezione di; fig (change public image of) cambiare l'immagine pubblica di; cambiare i termini di ‹*proposal*›

repaint /ri:'peɪnt/ *vt* ridipingere

repair /rɪ'peə(r)/ **A** *n* riparazione *f*; **in good/bad ~** in buone/cattive condizioni
B *vt* riparare

repairman *n* tecnico *m* (delle riparazioni)

reparation /repə'reɪʃn/ *n* **make ~s for something** risarcire qualcosa

repartee /repɑ:'ti:/ *n* botta e risposta *m inv*; **piece of ~** risposta *f* pronta

repatriate /ri:'pætrɪeɪt/ *vt* rimpatriare

repatriation /ri:pætrɪ'eɪʃn/ *n* rimpatrio *m*

repay /ri:'peɪ/ *vt* (*pt/pp* **-paid**) ripagare

repayment /ri:'peɪmənt/ *n* rimborso *m*

repeal /rɪ'pi:l/ **A** *n* abrogazione *f*
B *vt* abrogare

⚷ **repeat** /rɪ'pi:t/ **A** *n* TV replica *f*
B *vt & vi* ripetere; **~ oneself** ripetersi

repeated /rɪ'pi:tɪd/ *adj* ripetuto

repeatedly /rɪ'pi:tɪdlɪ/ *adv* ripetutamente

repel /rɪ'pel/ *vt* (*pt/pp* **repelled**) respingere; fig ripugnare

repellent /rɪ'pelənt/ *adj* ripulsivo

repent /rɪ'pent/ *vi* pentirsi

repentance /rɪ'pentəns/ *n* pentimento *m*

repentant /rɪ'pentənt/ *adj* pentito

repercussions /ri:pə'kʌʃnz/ *npl* ripercussioni *fbl*

repertoire /'repətwɑ:(r)/ *n* repertorio *m*

repertory /'repətrɪ/ *n* ≈ teatro *m* stabile

repertory company *n* compagnia *f* di teatro stabile

repetition /repɪ'tɪʃn/ *n* ripetizione *f*

repetitious /repɪ'tɪʃəs/, **repetitive** /rɪ'petɪtɪv/ *adj* ripetitivo

repetitive strain injury *n* patologia *f* da sforzo ripetuto

⚷ **replace** /rɪ'pleɪs/ *vt* (put back) rimettere a posto; (take the place of) sostituire; **~ something with something** sostituire qualcosa con qualcosa

replacement /rɪ'pleɪsmənt/ *n* sostituzione *f*; (person) sostituto, -a mf

replacement part *n* pezzo *m* di ricambio

replant /ri:'plɑ:nt/ *vt* ripiantare

replay /'ri:pleɪ/ *n* Sport partita *f* ripetuta; **[action] ~** replay *m inv*

replenish /rɪ'plenɪʃ/ *vt* rifornire ‹*stocks*›; (refill) riempire di nuovo

replete /rɪ'pli:t/ *adj* **~ with** riempito di

replica /'replɪkə/ *n* copia *f*

replicate /'replɪkeɪt/ *vt* ripetere ‹*experiment*›

⚷ **reply** /rɪ'plaɪ/ **A** *n* risposta *f* (**to** a)
B *vt* (*pt/pp* **replied**) rispondere

⚷ parola chiave

reply-paid envelope *n* busta *f* affrancata per rispondere

report /rɪˈpɔːt/ **A** *n* rapporto *m*; TV, Radio servizio *m*; Journ cronaca *f*; Sch pagella *f*; (rumour) diceria *f*
B *vt* riportare; **~ somebody to the police** denunciare qualcuno alla polizia
C *vi* riportare; (present oneself) presentarsi (to a)

report card *n* AmE scheda *f* di valutazione scolastica

reportedly /rɪˈpɔːtɪdlɪ/ *adv* secondo quanto si dice

reporter /rɪˈpɔːtə(r)/ *n* cronista *mf*, reporter *mf inv*

repose /rɪˈpəʊz/ *n* riposo *m*

repository /rɪˈpɒzɪt(ə)rɪ/ *n* (place) deposito; (of secret, authority) depositario, -a *mf*

repossess /riːpəˈzes/ *vt* riprendere possesso di

repossession /riːpəˈzeʃn/ *n* esproprio *m*

repot /riːˈpɒt/ *vt* rinvasare ‹*plant*›

reprehensible /reprɪˈhensəbl/ *adj* riprovevole

represent /reprɪˈzent/ *vt* rappresentare

representation /reprɪzenˈteɪʃn/ *n* rappresentazione *f*; **make ~s to** fare delle rimostranze a

representative /reprɪˈzentətɪv/ **A** *adj* rappresentativo
B *n* rappresentante *mf*

repress /rɪˈpres/ *vt* reprimere

repression /rɪˈpreʃn/ *n* repressione *f*

repressive /rɪˈpresɪv/ *adj* repressivo

reprieve /rɪˈpriːv/ **A** *n* commutazione *f* della pena capitale; (postponement) sospensione *f* della pena capitale; fig tregua *f*
B *vt* sospendere la sentenza a; fig risparmiare

reprimand /ˈreprɪmɑːnd/ **A** *n* rimprovero *m*
B *vt* rimproverare

reprint¹ /ˈriːprɪnt/ *n* ristampa *f*

reprint² /riːˈprɪnt/ *vt* ristampare

reprisal /rɪˈpraɪzl/ *n* rappresaglia *f*; **in ~ for** per rappresaglia contro

reproach /rɪˈprəʊtʃ/ **A** *n* rimprovero *m*
B *vt* rimproverare a (**for doing something** di fare qualcosa)

reproachful /rɪˈprəʊtʃfʊl/ *adj* riprovevole

reproachfully /rɪˈprəʊtʃfʊlɪ/ *adv* con aria di rimprovero

reprocess /riːˈprəʊses/ *vt* trattare di nuovo

reprocessing plant *n* impianto *m* di rilavorazione (di scorie nucleari)

reproduce /riːprəˈdjuːs/ **A** *vt* riprodurre
B *vi* riprodursi

reproduction /riːprəˈdʌkʃn/ *n* riproduzione *f*

reproduction furniture *n* riproduzioni *fpl* di mobili antichi

reproductive /riːprəˈdʌktɪv/ *adj* riproduttivo

reproof /rɪˈpruːf/ *n* rimprovero *m*

reprove /rɪˈpruːv/ *vt* rimproverare

reptile /ˈreptaɪl/ *n* rettile *m*

republic /rɪˈpʌblɪk/ *n* repubblica *f*

republican /rɪˈpʌblɪkn/ *adj & n* repubblicano, -a *mf*

republish /riːˈpʌblɪʃ/ *vt* ripubblicare

repudiate /rɪˈpjuːdɪeɪt/ *vt* ripudiare; respingere ‹*view, suggestion*›

repugnance /rɪˈpʌgnəns/ *n* ripugnanza *f*

repugnant /rɪˈpʌgnənt/ *adj* ripugnante

repulse /rɪˈpʌls/ fml *vt* respingere ‹*attack*›; rifiutare ‹*assistance*›

repulsion /rɪˈpʌɪʃn/ *n* repulsione *f*

repulsive /rɪˈpʌlsɪv/ *adj* ripugnante

reputable /ˈrepjʊtəbl/ *adj* affidabile

reputation /repjʊˈteɪʃn/ *n* reputazione *f*

repute /rɪˈpjuːt/ *n* reputazione *f*

reputed /rɪˈpjuːtɪd/ *adj* presunto; **he is ~ to be** si presume che sia

reputedly /rɪˈpjuːtɪdlɪ/ *adv* presumibilmente

request /rɪˈkwest/ **A** *n* richiesta *f*
B *vt* richiedere

request stop *n*, *f* fermata *f* a richiesta

requiem /ˈrekwɪəm/ *n* requiem *m inv*

require /rɪˈkwaɪə(r)/ *vt* (need) necessitare di; (demand) esigere

required /rɪˈkwaɪəd/ *adj* richiesto

requirement /rɪˈkwaɪəmənt/ *n* esigenza *f*; (condition) requisito *m*

requisite /ˈrekwɪzɪt/ **A** *adj* necessario
B *n* **toilet/travel ~s** *pl* articoli *mpl* da toilette/viaggio

requisition /rekwɪˈzɪʃn/ **A** *n* **~ [order]** [domanda *f* di] requisizione *f*
B *vt* requisire

reread /riːˈriːd/ *vt* rileggere

re-release /riːrɪˈliːs/ **A** *n* (of film) nuova distribuzione *f*
B *vt* ridistribuire ‹*film*›

re-roof /riːˈruːf/ *vt* rifare il tetto di ‹*building*›

re-route /riːˈruːt/ *vt* dirottare ‹*flight, traffic*›

rerun /ˈriːrʌn/ *n* (of film, play) replica *f*; fig (repeat) ripetizione *f*

resale /riːˈseɪl/ *n* rivendita *f*

reschedule /riːˈʃedjuːl/ *vt* (change date of) cambiare la data di; (change time of) cambiare l'orario di; rinegoziare ‹*debt*›

rescind /rɪˈsɪnd/ *vt* rescindere

rescue /ˈreskjuː/ **A** *n* salvataggio *m*
B *vt* salvare

rescuer /ˈreskjʊə(r)/ *n* salvatore, -trice *mf*

rescue worker *n* soccorritore, -trice *mf*

research /rɪˈsɜːtʃ/ **A** *n* ricerca *f*
B *vt* fare ricerche su; Journ fare un'inchiesta su
C *vi* **~ into** fare ricerche su

research and development *n* ricerca *f* e sviluppo *m*

🔑 **researcher** /rɪ'sɜːtʃə(r)/ *n* ricercatore, -trice *mf*
research fellow *n* BrE Univ ricercatore, -trice *mf*
resell /riː'sel/ *vt* (*pt/pp* **resold**) rivendere
resemblance /rɪ'zembləns/ *n* rassomiglianza *f*
resemble /rɪ'zembl/ *vt* rassomigliare a
resent /rɪ'zent/ *vt* risentirsi per
resentful /rɪ'zentfʊl/ *adj* pieno di risentimento
resentfully /rɪ'zentfʊlɪ/ *adv* con risentimento
resentment /rɪ'zentmənt/ *n* risentimento *m*
reservation /rezə'veɪʃn/ *n* (booking) prenotazione *f*; (doubt, enclosure) riserva *f*
reserve /rɪ'zɜːv/ **A** *n* riserva *f*; (shyness) riserbo *m*
B *vt* riservare; riservarsi ‹*right*›
reserved /rɪ'zɜːvd/ *adj* riservato
reservoir /'rezəvwɑː(r)/ *n* bacino *m* idrico
reset /riː'set/ *vt* riprogrammare ‹*clock*›; (zero) azzerare
reshape /riː'ʃeɪp/ *vt* ristrutturare
reshuffle /riː'ʃʌfl/ **A** *n* Pol rimpasto *m*
B *vt* rimpastare
reside /rɪ'zaɪd/ *vi* risiedere
residence /'rezɪdəns/ *n* residenza *f*; (stay) soggiorno *m*
residence permit *n* permesso *m* di soggiorno
🔑 **resident** /'rezɪdənt/ *adj* & *n* residente *mf*
residential /rezɪ'denʃl/ *adj* residenziale
residential area *n* quartiere *m* residenziale
residual /rɪ'zɪdjʊəl/ *adj* residuo
residue /'rezɪdjuː/ *n* residuo *m*
resign /rɪ'zaɪn/ **A** *vt* dimettersi da; **~ oneself to** rassegnarsi a
B *vt* dare le dimissioni
resignation /rezɪg'neɪʃn/ *n* rassegnazione *f*; (from job) dimissioni *fpl*
resigned /rɪ'zaɪnd/ *adj* rassegnato
resignedly /rɪ'zaɪnɪdlɪ/ *adv* con rassegnazione
resilient /rɪ'zɪlɪənt/ *adj* elastico; fig con buone capacità di ripresa
resin /'rezɪn/ *n* resina *f*
resist /rɪ'zɪst/ **A** *vt* resistere a
B *vi* resistere
🔑 **resistance** /rɪ'zɪstəns/ *n* resistenza *f*
resistance fighter *n* combattente *mf* delle forze di resistenza
resistant /rɪ'zɪstənt/ *adj* resistente
resit /riː'sɪt/ BrE **A** *vt* (*pt/pp* **resat**) ridare ‹*exam*›
B *n* esame *m* di recupero
resize /riː'saɪz/ *vt* ridimensionare
reskill /riː'skɪl/ *vt* riqualificare ‹*workers*›

🔑 parola chiave

resolute /'rezəluːt/ *adj* risoluto
resolutely /'rezəluːtlɪ/ *adv* con risolutezza
🔑 **resolution** /rezə'luːʃn/ *n* risolutezza *f*
🔑 **resolve** /rɪ'zɒlv/ **A** *n* risolutezza *f*; (decision) risoluzione *f*
B *vt* (solve) risolvere; **~ to do** decidere di fare
resolved /rɪ'zɒlvd/ *adj* risoluto
resonance /'rezənəns/ *n* risonanza *f*
resonant /'rezɪnənt/ *adj* risonante
resonate /'rezəneɪt/ *vi* risuonare
resort /rɪ'zɔːt/ **A** *n* (place) luogo *m* di villeggiatura; **as a last ~** come ultima risorsa
B *vi* **~ to** ricorrere a
resound /rɪ'zaʊnd/ *vi* risonare (**with** di)
resounding /rɪ'zaʊndɪŋ/ *adj* ‹*success*› risonante
resoundingly /rɪ'zaʊndɪŋlɪ/ *adv* in modo risonante
🔑 **resource** /rɪ'sɔːs/ *n* **~s** *pl* risorse *fpl*
resourceful /rɪ'sɔːsfʊl/ *adj* pieno di risorse; ‹*solution*› ingegnoso
resourcefulness /rɪ'sɔːsfʊlnɪs/ *n* ingegnosità *f*
🔑 **respect** /rɪ'spekt/ **A** *n* rispetto *m*; (aspect) aspetto *m*; **with ~ to** per quanto riguarda
B *vt* rispettare
respectability /rɪspektə'bɪlətɪ/ *n* rispettabilità *f*
respectable /rɪ'spektəbl/ rispettabile
respectably /rɪ'spektəblɪ/ *adv* rispettabilmente
respectful /rɪ'spektfʊl/ *adj* rispettoso
respectfully /rɪ'spektfʊlɪ/ *adv* rispettosamente
respective /rɪ'spektɪv/ *adj* rispettivo
respectively /rɪ'spektɪvlɪ/ *adv* rispettivamente
respiration /respɪ'reɪʃn/ *n* respirazione *f*
respirator /'respɪreɪtə(r)/ *n* (apparatus) respiratore *m*
respiratory /rɪ'spɪrətrɪ, AmE -tɔːrɪ/ *adj* respiratorio
respite /'respaɪt/ *n* respiro *m*
resplendent /rɪ'splendənt/ *adj* risplendente
🔑 **respond** /rɪ'spɒnd/ *vi* rispondere; (react) reagire (**to** a); ‹*patient*› rispondere (**to** a)
respondent /rɪ'spɒndənt/ *n* Jur convenuto, -a *mf*; (to questionnaire) interrogato, -a *mf*
🔑 **response** /rɪ'spɒns/ *n* risposta *f*; (reaction) reazione *f*
🔑 **responsibility** /rɪspɒnsɪ'bɪlətɪ/ *n* responsabilità *f*
🔑 **responsible** /rɪ'spɒnsəbl/ *adj* responsabile; (trustworthy) responsabile; (job) impegnativo
responsibly /rɪ'spɒnsəblɪ/ *adv* in modo responsabile
responsive /rɪ'spɒnsɪv/ *adj* **be ~** ‹*audience etc*› reagire; ‹*brakes*› essere sensibile;

she wasn't very ~ non era molto cooperativa

respray¹ /riː'spreɪ/ *vt* riverniciare ‹*vehicle*›

respray² /'riːspreɪ/ *n* riverniciatura *f*; **it's had a ~** è stato riverniciato

rest¹ /rest/ **A** *n* riposo *m*; Mus pausa *f*; **have a ~** riposarsi
B *vt* riposare; (lean, place) appoggiare (**on** su)
C *vi* riposarsi; ‹*elbows*› appoggiarsi; ‹*hopes*› riposare; **it ~s with you** sta a te
■ **rest up** *vi* riposarsi

rest² *n* **the ~** il resto; (people) gli altri

restart /riː'stɑːt/ *vt* rimettere in moto ‹*engine*›; riprendere ‹*talks*›; Comput riavviare

restate /riː'steɪt/ *vt* (say differently) riformulare; (say again) ribadire

restaurant /'restərɒnt/ *n* ristorante *m*

restaurant car *n* vagone *m* ristorante

restful /'restfl/ *adj* riposante

rest home *n* casa *f* di riposo

restitution /restɪ'tjuːʃn/ *n* restituzione *f*

restive /'restɪv/ *adj* irrequieto

restless /'restlɪs/ *adj* nervoso

restlessly /'restlɪslɪ/ *adv* nervosamente

restlessness /'restlɪsnɪs/ agitazione *f*

restock /riː'stɒk/ **A** *vt* rifornire ‹*shelf, shop*›
B *vi* rifornirsi

restoration /restə'reɪʃn/ *n* ristabilimento *m*; (of building) restauro *m*; (of stolen property etc) restituzione *f*

restore /rɪ'stɔː(r)/ *vt* ristabilire; restaurare ‹*building*›; (give back) restituire

restorer /rɪ'stɔːrə(r)/ *n* (person) restauratore, -trice *mf*

restrain /rɪ'streɪn/ *vt* trattenere; **~ oneself** controllarsi

restrained /rɪ'streɪnd/ *adj* controllato

restraint /rɪ'streɪnt/ *n* restrizione *f*; (moderation) ritegno *m*

restrict /rɪ'strɪkt/ *vt* limitare (**to** a)

restricted /rɪ'strɪktɪd/ *adj* ‹*access, parking*› riservato; ‹*growth, movement*› limitato; ‹*document, information*› confidenziale

restriction /rɪ'strɪkʃn/ *n* limite *m*; (restraint) restrizione *f*

restrictive /rɪ'strɪktɪv/ *adj* limitativo

restring /riː'strɪŋ/ *vt* rinfilare ‹*necklace, beads*›; sostituire le corde di ‹*instrument, racket*›

restroom /'restruːm/ *n* AmE toilette *f inv*

restructure /riː'strʌktʃə(r)/ *vt* ristrutturare

restructuring /riː'strʌktʃərɪŋ/ *n* ristrutturazione *f*

restyle /riː'staɪl/ *vt* cambiare il taglio di ‹*hair*›; cambiare la linea di ‹*car*›; rimodernare ‹*shop*›

resubmit /riːsʌb'mɪt/ *vt* ripresentare

result /rɪ'zʌlt/ **A** *n* risultato *m*; **as a ~** di conseguenza; **as a ~ of** a causa di
B *vi* **~ from** risultare da; **~ in** portare a

resume /rɪ'zjuːm/ *vt & vi* riprendere

résumé /'rezjʊmeɪ/ *n* riassunto *m*; AmE curriculum *m inv* vitae

resumption /rɪ'zʌmpʃn/ *n* ripresa *f*

resurface /riː'sɜːfɪs/ **A** *vi* ‹*sub, person, rumour*› riemergere
B *vt* rifare la copertura di ‹*road*›

resurgence /rɪ'sɜːdʒəns/ *n* rinascita *f*

resurrect /rezə'rekt/ *vt* fig risuscitare

resurrection /rezə'rekʃn/ *n* **the R~** Relig la Risurrezione

resuscitate /rɪ'sʌsɪteɪt/ *vt* rianimare

resuscitation /rɪsʌsɪ'teɪʃn/ *n* rianimazione *f*

retail /'riːteɪl/ **A** *n* vendita *f* al minuto *o* al dettaglio
B *adj & adv* al minuto
C *vt* vendere al minuto
D *vi* **~ at** essere venduto al pubblico al prezzo di

retailer /'riːteɪlə(r)/ *n* dettagliante *mf*

retail price *n* prezzo *m* al minuto

retail sales *npl* vendite *fpl* al dettaglio

retail trade *n* commercio *m* al dettaglio

retain /rɪ'teɪn/ *vt* conservare; (hold back) trattenere

retainer /rɪ'teɪnə(r)/ *n* (fee) anticipo *m*; (old: servant) servitore, -trice *mf*

retake¹ /riː'teɪk/ *vt* Cinema girare di nuovo; Sch, Univ ridare; Mil riconquistare

retake² /'riːteɪk/ *n* Cinema ulteriore ripresa *f*

retaliate /rɪ'tælɪeɪt/ *vi* vendicarsi

retaliation /rɪtælɪ'eɪʃn/ *n* rappresaglia *f*; **in ~ for** per rappresaglia contro

retarded /rɪ'tɑːdɪd/ *adj* offensive ritardato

retch /retʃ/ *vi* avere conati di vomito

retention /rɪ'tenʃn/ *n* conservazione *f*; (of information) memorizzazione *f*; (of fluid) ritenzione *f*

retentive /rɪ'tentɪv/ *adj* ‹*memory*› buono

retentiveness /rɪ'tentɪvnɪs/ *n* capacità *f* di memorizzazione

rethink /riː'θɪŋk/ **A** *vt* (*pt/pp* **rethought**) riconsiderare
B *n* **have a ~** riconsiderare la cosa

reticence /'retɪsəns/ *n* reticenza *f*

reticent /'retɪsənt/ *adj* reticente

retina /'retɪnə/ *n* retina *f*

retinue /'retɪnjuː/ *n* seguito *m*

retire /rɪ'taɪə(r)/ **A** *vi* andare in pensione; (withdraw) ritirarsi
B *vt* mandare in pensione ‹*employee*›

retired /rɪ'taɪəd/ *adj* in pensione

retirement /rɪ'taɪəmənt/ *n* pensione *f*; **since my ~** da quando sono andato in pensione

retirement age *n* età *f* della pensione

retirement home *n* casa *f* di riposo

retiring /rɪ'taɪərɪŋ/ *adj* riservato

retort /rɪ'tɔːt/ **A** *n* replica *f*; Chem storta *f*
B *vt* ribattere

retouch /riː'tʌtʃ/ *vt* Phot ritoccare

retouching /riːˈtʌtʃɪŋ/ *n* Phot ritocco *m*

retrace /rɪˈtreɪs/ *vt* ripercorrere; **~ one's steps** ritornare sui propri passi

retract /rɪˈtrækt/ **A** *vt* ritirare; ritrattare ‹*statement, accusation*›
B *vi* ritrarsi

retractable /rɪˈtræktəbl/ *adj* ‹*landing gear*› retrattile; ‹*pen*› con la punta retrattile

retraction /rɪˈtrækʃn/ *n* ritiro *m*; (of statement, accusation) ritrattazione *f*

retrain /riːˈtreɪn/ **A** *vt* riqualificare
B *vi* riqualificarsi

retraining /ˌriːˈtreɪnɪŋ/ *n* riqualificazione *f*

retread /ˈriːtred/ *n* pneumatico *m* ricostruito

retreat /rɪˈtriːt/ **A** *n* ritirata *f*; (place) ritiro *m*
B *vi* ritirarsi; Mil battere in ritirata

retrench /rɪˈtrentʃ/ *vi* ridurre le spese

retrenchment /rɪˈtrentʃmənt/ *n* riduzione *f* delle spese

retrial /riːˈtraɪəl/ *n* nuovo processo *m*

retribution /retrɪˈbjuːʃn/ *n* castigo *m*

retrievable /rɪˈtriːvəbl/ *adj* recuperabile

retrieval /rɪˈtriːvəl/ *n* recupero *m*

retrieve /rɪˈtriːv/ *vt* recuperare

retroactive /retrəʊˈæktɪv/ *adj* retroattivo

retroactively /retrəʊˈæktɪvlɪ/ *adv* retroattivamente

retrograde /ˈretrəgreɪd/ *adj* retrogrado

retrospect /ˈretrəspekt/ *n* **in ~** guardando indietro

retrospective /retrəˈspektɪv/ **A** *adj* ‹*exhibit*› retrospettivo; ‹*legislation*› retroattivo
B *n* retrospettiva *f*

retrospectively /retrəˈspektɪvlɪ/ *adv* retrospettivamente

retrovirus /ˈretrəʊvaɪərəs/ *n* retrovirus *m inv*

retry /riːˈtraɪ/ *vt* Jur riprocessare; Comput riprovare

r

🔑 **return** /rɪˈtɜːn/ **A** *n* ritorno *m*; (giving back) restituzione *f*; Comm profitto *m*; (ticket) biglietto *m* di andata e ritorno; **by ~ [of post]** a stretto giro di posta; **in ~** in cambio (**for** di); **many happy ~s!** cento di questi giorni!; **~ on investment** utile *m* sul capitale investito
B *vi* ritornare
C *vt* (give back) restituire; ricambiare ‹*affection, invitation*›; (put back) rimettere; (send back) mandare indietro; (elect) eleggere

returnable /rɪˈtɜːnəbl/ *adj* restituibile

return flight *n* volo *m* di andata e ritorno

return match *n* rivincita *f*

return ticket *n* biglietto *m* di andata e ritorno

reunification /riːjuːnɪfɪˈkeɪʃn/ *n* riunificazione *f*

reunify /riːˈjuːnɪfaɪ/ *vt* riunificare

reunion /riːˈjuːnjən/ *n* riunione *f*

reunite /riːjʊˈnaɪt/ *vt* riunire

reusable /riːˈjuːzəbl/ *adj* riutilizzabile

reuse /riːˈjuːz/ *vt* riutilizzare

rev /rev/ **A** *n* Auto giro; **~s per minute** regime *m* di giri
B *vt* **~ [up]** far andare su di giri
C *vi* andare su di giri

Rev, **Revd** *abbr* (**Reverend**) Reverendo

revaluation /riːˈvæljʊˈeɪʃn/ *n* rivalutazione *f*

revalue /riːˈvæljuː/ *vt* Comm rivalutare

revamp /riːˈvæmp/ *vt* riorganizzare ‹*company*›; rimodernare ‹*building, clothing*›

rev counter *n* contagiri *m inv*

🔑 **reveal** /rɪˈviːl/ *vt* rivelare; ‹*dress*› scoprire

revealing /rɪˈviːlɪŋ/ *adj* rivelatore; ‹*dress*› osé *inv*

revel /ˈrevl/ *vi* (*pt/pp* **revelled**) **~ in something** godere di qualcosa

revelation /revəˈleɪʃn/ *n* rivelazione *f*

reveller /ˈrev(ə)lə(r)/ *n* festaiolo, -a *mf*

revelry /ˈrev(ə)lrɪ/ *n* baldoria *f*

revenge /rɪˈvendʒ/ **A** *n* vendetta *f*; Sport rivincita *f*; **take ~** vendicarsi (**on somebody for something** di qualcuno per qualcosa)
B *vt* vendicare

🔑 **revenue** /ˈrevənjuː/ *n* reddito *m*

reverberate /rɪˈvɜːbəreɪt/ *vi* riverberare

reverberations /rɪvɜːbəˈreɪʃnz/ *npl* fig ripercussioni *fpl*

revere /rɪˈvɪə(r)/ *vt* riverire

reverence /ˈrevərəns/ *n* riverenza *f*

Reverend /ˈrevərənd/ *adj* Reverendo

reverent /ˈrevərənt/ *adj* riverente

reverential /revəˈrenʃ(ə)l/ *adj* riverente

reverently /ˈrevərəntlɪ/ *adv* rispettosamente

reverie /ˈrevərɪ/ *n* sogno *m* ad occhi aperti

reversal /rɪˈvɜːsl/ *n* inversione *f*

reverse /rɪˈvɜːs/ **A** *adj* opposto; **in ~ order** in ordine inverso
B *n* contrario *m*; (back) rovescio *m*; Auto marcia *m* indietro
C *vt* invertire; **~ the car into the garage** entrare in garage a marcia indietro; **~ the charges** Teleph fare una telefonata a carico del destinatario
D *vi* Auto fare marcia indietro

reverse charge call *n* telefonata *f* a carico del destinatario

reversible /rɪˈvɜːsəbl/ *adj* ‹*jacket*› double-face; ‹*procedure*› reversibile

reversing lights /rɪˈvɜːsɪŋ/ *npl* luci *fpl* di retromarcia

revert /rɪˈvɜːt/ *vi* **~ to** tornare a

🔑 **review** /rɪˈvjuː/ **A** *n* (survey) rassegna *f*; (re-examination) riconsiderazione *f*; Mil rivista *f*; (of book, play) recensione *f*
B *vt* riesaminare ‹*situation*›; Mil passare in rivista; recensire ‹*book, play*›

reviewer /rɪˈvjuːə(r)/ *n* critico, -a *mf*

revile /rɪˈvaɪl/ *vt* ingiuriare

🔑 parola chiave

revise /rɪ'vaɪz/ *vt* rivedere; (for exam) ripassare
revision /rɪ'vɪʒn/ *n* revisione *f*; (for exam) ripasso *m*
revisionism /rɪ'vɪʒənɪzm/ *n* revisionismo *m*
revisionist /rɪ'vɪʒənɪst/ *adj & n* revisionista *mf*
revisit /riː'vɪzɪt/ *vt* rivisitare ‹*person, museum etc*›
revitalization /riːvaɪtəlaɪ'zeɪʃn/ *n* rivitalizzazione *f*
revitalize /riː'vaɪtəlaɪz/ *vt* rivitalizzare
revival /rɪ'vaɪvl/ *n* ritorno *m*; (of patient) recupero *m*; (from coma) risveglio *m*
revivalist /rɪ'vaɪvəlɪst/ *adj* Relig revivalista
revive /rɪ'vaɪv/ **A** *vt* resuscitare; rianimare ‹*person*›
B *vi* riprendersi; ‹*person*› rianimarsi
revocation /revə'keɪʃn/ *n* (of decision, order) revoca *f*; (of law) abrogazione *f*; (of will) annullamento *m*
revoke /rɪ'vəʊk/ *vt* revocare ‹*decision, order*›; abrogare ‹*law*›; annullare ‹*will*›
revolt /rɪ'vəʊlt/ **A** *n* rivolta *f*
B *vi* ribellarsi
C *vt* rivoltare
revolting /rɪ'vəʊltɪŋ/ *adj* rivoltante
revolution /revə'luːʃn/ *n* rivoluzione *f*; **~s per minute** Auto giri *mpl* al minuto
revolutionary /revə'luːʃənərɪ/ *adj & n* rivoluzionario, -a *mf*
revolutionize /revə'luːʃənaɪz/ *vt* rivoluzionare
revolve /rɪ'vɒlv/ *vi* ruotare; **~ around** girare intorno a
revolver /rɪ'vɒlvə(r)/ *n* rivoltella *f*, revolver *m inv*
revolving /rɪ'vɒlvɪŋ/ *adj* ruotante
revolving doors *npl* porta *f* girevole
revue /rɪ'vjuː/ *n* rivista *f*
revulsion /rɪ'vʌlʃn/ *n* ripulsione *f*
reward /rɪ'wɔːd/ **A** *n* ricompensa *f*
B *vt* ricompensare
reward card *n* = **loyalty card**
rewarding /rɪ'wɔːdɪŋ/ *adj* gratificante
rewind /riː'waɪnd/ *vt* riavvolgere ‹*tape, film*›
rewind button /'riːwaɪnd/ *n* tasto *m* di riavvolgimento
rewire /riː'waɪə(r)/ *vt* rifare l'impianto elettrico di
reword /riː'wɜːd/ *vt* esprimere con parole diverse
rework /riː'wɜːk/ *vt* modificare
rewritable /ˌriː'raɪtəbl/ *adj* Comput ‹*CD-ROM*› riscrivibile
rewrite /riː'raɪt/ *vt* (*pt* **rewrote**, *pp* **rewritten**) riscrivere
rhapsody /'ræpsədɪ/ *n* rapsodia *f*
rhesus /'riːsəs/ *n* reso *m*
rhesus negative *adj* Rh-negativo
rhesus positive *adj* Rh-positivo
rhetoric /'retərɪk/ *n* retorica *f*
rhetorical /rɪ'tɒrɪkl/ *adj* retorico
rhetorically /rɪ'tɒrɪklɪ/ *adv* retoricamente
rhetorical question *n* domanda *f* retorica
rheumatic /rʊ'mætɪk/ *adj* reumatico
rheumatism /'ruːmətɪzm/ *n* reumatismo *m*
rheumatoid arthritis /'ruːmətɔɪd/ *n* periartrite *f*
Rhine /raɪn/ *n* Reno *m*
rhino /'raɪnəʊ/ *n* infml rinoceronte *m*
rhinoceros /raɪ'nɒsərəs/ *n* rinoceronte *m*
rhombus /'rɒmbəs/ *n* rombo *m*
rhubarb /'ruːbɑːb/ *n* rabarbaro *m*
rhyme /raɪm/ **A** *n* rima *f*; (poem) filastrocca *f*
B *vi* rimare; **~ with something** far rima con qualcosa
rhythm /'rɪðm/ *n* ritmo *m*
rhythmic /'rɪðmɪk/, **rythmical** /'rɪðmɪkl/ *adj* ritmico
rhythmically /'rɪðmɪklɪ/ *adv* con ritmo
rhythm method *n* (of contraception) metodo *m* Ogino-Knauss
rib /rɪb/ **A** *n* costola *f*; **~s** *pl* Culin costata *f*
B *vt* (*pt/pp* **ribbed**) infml punzecchiare
ribald /'rɪbld/ *adj* spinto
ribbon /'rɪbən/ *n* nastro *m*; **in ~s** a brandelli
ribcage /'rɪbkeɪdʒ/ *n* gabbia *f* toracica, cassa *f* toracica
rice /raɪs/ *n* riso *m*
rice field /'raɪsfiːld/ *n* risaia *f*
rice paper *n* Culin carta *f* di riso
rich /rɪtʃ/ **A** *adj* ricco; ‹*food*› pesante
B *n* **the ~** *pl* i ricchi; **~es** *pl* ricchezze *fpl*
richly /'rɪtʃlɪ/ *adv* riccamente; ‹*deserve*› largamente
richness /'rɪtʃnɪs/ *n* (of food) pesantezza *f*; (of furnishings) sfarzosità *f*; (of person, company) ricchezza *f*
Richter scale /'rɪktə(r)/ *n* scala *f* Richter
rick /rɪk/ *vt* BrE **~ one's ankle** prendere una storta alla caviglia
rickets /'rɪkɪts/ *n* rachitismo *m*
rickety /'rɪkətɪ/ *adj* malfermo
rickshaw /'rɪkʃɔː/ *n* risciò *m*
ricochet /'rɪkəʃeɪ/ **A** *vi* rimbalzare
B *n* rimbalzo *m*
rid /rɪd/ *vt* (*pt/pp* **rid**, *pres p* **ridding**) sbarazzare (**of** di); **get ~ of** sbarazzarsi di
riddance /'rɪdns/ *n* **good ~!** che liberazione!
ridden /'rɪdn/ ▸ **ride**
riddle /'rɪdl/ *n* enigma *m*
riddled /'rɪdld/ *adj* **~ with** crivellato di
ride /raɪd/ **A** *n* (on horse) cavalcata *f*; (in vehicle) giro *m*; (journey) viaggio *m*; **take somebody for a ~** infml prendere qualcuno in giro
B *vt* (*pt* **rode**, *pp* **ridden**) montare ‹*horse*›; andare su ‹*bicycle*›
C *vi* andare a cavallo; ‹*jockey, showjumper*› cavalcare; ‹*cyclist*› andare in bicicletta;

r

(in vehicle) viaggiare
▪ **ride out** *vt* superare ‹*storm, crisis*›
▪ **ride up** *vi* ‹*rider*› arrivare; ‹*skirt*› salire
rider /'raɪdə(r)/ *n* cavallerizzo, -a *mf*; (in race) fantino *m*; (on bicycle) ciclista *mf*; (in document) postilla *f*
ridge /rɪdʒ/ *n* spigolo *m*; (on roof) punta *f*; (of mountain) cresta *f*; (of high pressure) zona *f* ad alta pressione [atmosferica]
ridicule /'rɪdɪkju:l/ **A** *n* ridicolo *m*
B *vt* mettere in ridicolo
ridiculous /rɪ'dɪkjʊləs/ *adj* ridicolo
ridiculously /rɪ'dɪkjʊləslɪ/ *adv* in modo ridicolo; ~ **expensive/easy** carissimo/facilissimo
riding /'raɪdɪŋ/ **A** *n* equitazione *f*
B *attrib* d'equitazione
rife /raɪf/ *adj* **be** ~ essere diffuso; ~ **with** pieno di
riff-raff /'rɪfræf/ *n* marmaglia *f*
rifle /'raɪfl/ **A** *n* fucile *m*
B *vt* ~ **[through]** mettere a soqquadro
rifle range *n* tiro *m* al bersaglio
rift /rɪft/ *n* fessura *f*; fig frattura *f*
rig¹ /rɪg/ *n* equipaggiamento *m*; (at sea) piattaforma *f* per trivellazioni subacquee
rig² *vt* (*pt/pp* **rigged**) manovrare ‹*election*›
▪ **rig out** *vt* equipaggiare; (with clothes) parare
▪ **rig up** *vt* allestire
rigging /'rɪgɪŋ/ *n* Naut sartiame *m*; (of election, competition) broglio *m*
⚷ **right** /raɪt/ **A** *adj* giusto; (not left) destro; **be** ~ ‹*person*› aver ragione; ‹*clock*› essere giusto; **put** ~ mettere all'ora ‹*clock*›; correggere ‹*person*›; rimediare a ‹*situation*›; **that's** ~**!** proprio così!; **do you have the** ~ **time?** ha l'ora esatta?
B *adv* (correctly) bene; (not left) a destra; (directly) proprio; (completely) completamente; ~ **away** immediatamente; **too** ~**!** altroché!
C *n* giusto *m*; (not left) destra *f*; (what is due) diritto *m*; **the R**~ Pol la destra; **on/to the** ~ a destra; **be in the** ~ essere nel giusto; **by** ~**s** secondo giustizia; **be within one's** ~**s** avere tutti i diritti (**in doing something** di fare qualcosa)
D *vt* raddrizzare; ~ **a wrong** fig riparare ad un torto
right angle *n* angolo *m* retto
right away *adv* subito
righteous /'raɪtʃəs/ *adj* virtuoso; (cause) giusto
rightful /'raɪtfl/ *adj* legittimo
rightfully /'raɪtfʊlɪ/ *adv* legittimamente
right-hand /'raɪthænd/ *adj* di destra; **on the** ~ **side** sulla destra
right-hand drive *n* ‹*vehicle*› guida *f* a destra
right-handed /-'hændɪd/ *adj* che usa la mano destra
right-hand man *n* fig braccio *m* destro
rightly /'raɪtlɪ/ *adv* giustamente
right-minded /-'maɪndɪd/ *adj* sensato
right of centre *adj* Pol di centrodestra
right of way *n* diritto *m* di transito; (path) passaggio *m*; Auto precedenza *f*
right-on **A** *int* infml bene!
B *adj* infml **they're very** ~ sono molto impegnati
rights issue *n* emissione *f* riservata agli azionisti
right-thinking *adj* sensato
right turn *n* svolta *f* a destra
right wing *n* Pol destra; Sport ala *f* destra
right-wing *adj* Pol di destra
right-winger *n* Pol persona *f* di destra; Sport ala *f* destra
rigid /'rɪdʒɪd/ *adj* rigido
rigidity /rɪ'dʒɪdətɪ/ *n* rigidità *f*
rigidly /'rɪdʒɪdlɪ/ *adv* ‹*apply*› rigorosamente; ‹*oppose*› fermamente
rigmarole /'rɪgmərəʊl/ *n* trafila *f*; (story) tiritera *f*
rigor mortis /rɪgə'mɔ:tɪs/ *n* rigidità *f* cadaverica
rigorous /'rɪgərəs/ *adj* rigoroso
rigorously /'rɪgərəslɪ/ *adv* rigorosamente
rigour /'rɪgə(r)/ *n* rigore *m*
rig-out *n* infml (clothes) tenuta *f*
rile /raɪl/ *vt* infml irritare
rim /rɪm/ *n* bordo *m*; (of wheel) cerchione *m*
rind /raɪnd/ *n* (on cheese) crosta *f*; (on bacon) cotenna *f*
⚷ **ring¹** /rɪŋ/ **A** *n* (circle) cerchio *m*; (on finger) anello *m*; (boxing) ring *m inv*; (for circus) pista *f*; **stand in a** ~ essere in cerchio
B *vt* accerchiare; ~ **in red** fare un cerchio rosso intorno a
⚷ **ring²** **A** *n* suono *m*; **give somebody a** ~ Teleph dare un colpo di telefono a qualcuno
B *vt* (*pt* **rang**, *pp* **rung**) suonare; Teleph telefonare a; **it** ~**s a bell** fig mi dice qualcosa; ~ **the changes** fig cambiare
C *vi* suonare; Teleph telefonare; ~ **true** aver l'aria di essere vero
▪ **ring back** *vt & vi* Teleph richiamare
▪ **ring off** *vi* Teleph riattaccare
▪ **ring out** *vi* ‹*voice, shot etc*› risuonare chiaramente
▪ **ring round** *vi* Teleph fare un giro di telefonate
▪ **ring up** Teleph **A** *vt* telefonare a
B *vi* telefonare
ring binder /'rɪŋbaɪndə(r)/ *n* raccoglitore *m* ad anelli
ring finger *n* anulare *m*
ringing /'rɪŋɪŋ/ *n* (noise of bell, alarm) suono *m*; (in ears) fischio *m*
ringleader /'rɪŋli:də(r)/ *n* capobanda *m*

r

ringlet /ˈrɪŋlɪt/ *n* boccolo *m*

ringmaster *n* direttore *m* di circo

ring pull *n* linguetta *f*

ring road *n* circonvallazione *f*

ringside *n* **at the ~** in prima fila; **have a ~ seat** fig essere in prima fila

ringtone *n* suoneria *f*

rink /rɪŋk/ *n* pista *f* di pattinaggio

rinse /rɪns/ **A** *n* risciacquo *m*; (hair colour) cachet *m inv*
B *vt* sciacquare

■ **rinse off** *vt* sciacquare via

■ **rinse out** *vt* sciacquare ‹*cup, glass*›; sciacquare via ‹*shampoo, soap*›

riot /ˈraɪət/ **A** *n* rissa *f*; (of colour) accozzaglia *f*; **~s** *pl* disordini *mpl*; **run ~** impazzare
B *vi* creare disordini

riot act *n* **read the ~ to somebody** fig dare una lavata di capo a qualcuno

rioter /ˈraɪətə(r)/ *n* dimostrante *mf*

riot gear *n* tenuta *f* antisommossa

riotous /ˈraɪətəs/ *adj* sfrenato

riotously /ˈraɪətəslɪ/ *adv* **~ funny** divertente da morire

riot police *n* DIGOS *f*, Divisione *f* Investigazioni Generali e Operazioni Speciali

rip /rɪp/ **A** *n* strappo *m*
B *vt* (*pt/pp* **ripped**) strappare; **~ open** aprire con uno strappo
C *vi* strapparsi; **let ~** scatenarsi

■ **rip off** *vt* (remove) togliere; infml (cheat) fregare

■ **rip through** *vt* (blast) squarciare ‹*building*›

■ **rip up** *vt* stracciare ‹*letter*›

RIP *abbr* (**rest in peace**) R.I.P.

ripcord /ˈrɪpkɔːd/ *n* cavo *m* di spiegamento

ripe /raɪp/ *adj* maturo; ‹*cheese*› stagionato

ripen /ˈraɪpn/ **A** *vi* maturare; ‹*cheese*› stagionarsi
B *vt* far maturare; stagionare ‹*cheese*›

ripeness /ˈraɪpnɪs/ *n* maturazione *f*

rip-off *n* infml frode *f*; **these prices are a ~!** questi prezzi sono un furto!

riposte /rɪˈpɒst/ *n* replica *f*

ripple /ˈrɪpl/ **A** *n* increspatura *f*; ‹*sound*› mormorio *m*
B *vt* increspare
C *vi* incresparsi

rip-roaring /ˈrɪprɔːrɪŋ/ *adj* infml (success) travolgente

rise /raɪz/ **A** *n* (of sun) levata *f*; fig (to fame, power) ascesa *f*; (increase) aumento *m*; **give ~ to** dare adito a
B *vi* (*pt* **rose**, *pp* **risen**) alzarsi; ‹*sun*› sorgere; ‹*dough*› lievitare; ‹*prices, water level*› aumentare; (to power, position) arrivare (**to** a); (rebel) sollevarsi; ‹*Parliament, court*› aggiornare la seduta; (for holidays) sospendere i lavori

■ **rise above** *vt* superare ‹*difficulty*›

riser /ˈraɪzə(r)/ *n* **early ~** persona *f* mattiniera

rising /ˈraɪzɪŋ/ **A** *adj* ‹*sun*› levante; **~ generation** nuova generazione *f*
B *n* (revolt) sollevazione *f*

risk /rɪsk/ **A** *n* rischio *m*; **run the ~ of** correre il rischio di; **at ~** in pericolo; **at one's own ~** a proprio rischio e pericolo; **at the ~ of doing something** a costo di fare qualcosa
B *vt* rischiare

risky /ˈrɪskɪ/ *adj* (**-ier**, **-iest**) rischioso

risotto /rɪˈzɒtəʊ/ *n* risotto *m*

risqué /ˈrɪskeɪ/ *adj* spinto

rissole /ˈrɪsəʊl/ *n* crocchetta *f*

rite /raɪt/ *n* rito *m*; **last ~s** *pl* estrema unzione *fsg*

ritual /ˈrɪtjʊəl/ *adj* & *n* rituale *m*

ritzy /ˈrɪtsɪ/ *adj* infml (hotel, style, decoration) lussuoso

rival /ˈraɪvl/ **A** *adj* rivale
B *n* rivale *mf*; **~s** *pl* Comm concorrenti *mpl*
C *vt* (*pt/pp* **rivalled**) rivaleggiare con

rivalry /ˈraɪv(ə)lrɪ/ *n* rivalità *f*; Comm concorrenza *f*

river /ˈrɪvə(r)/ *n* fiume *m*

riverbank *n* riva *f* di fiume

river-bed *n* letto *m* del fiume

riverside **A** *n* lungofiume *m*
B *attrib* sul fiume

rivet /ˈrɪvɪt/ **A** *n* rivetto *m*
B *vt* rivettare; **be ~ed by** fig essere avvinto da

riveting /ˈrɪvɪtɪŋ/ *adj* fig avvincente

Riviera /rɪvɪˈeərə/ *n* **the French ~** la Costa Azzurra; **the Italian ~** la riviera ligure

roach /rəʊtʃ/ *n* (fish) lasca *f*; AmE infml (insect) scarafaggio *m*

road /rəʊd/ *n* strada *f*, via *f*; **be on the ~** viaggiare

roadblock *n* blocco *m* stradale

road haulage *n* trasporto *m* su strada

road hog *n* infml pirata *m* della strada

road hump *n* dosso *m* di rallentamento

roadie /ˈrəʊdɪ/ *n* roadie *m inv*

road map *n* fig **a ~ to peace** la roadmap per la pace

road safety *n* sicurezza *f* sulle strade

road sense *n* prudenza *f* (*per strada*)

roadshow *n* (play, show) spettacolo *m* di tournée; (publicity tour) giro *m* promozionale

roadside *n* bordo *m* della strada

road sign *n* cartello *m* stradale

road surface *n* fondo *m* stradale

road sweeper *n* (person) spazzino, -a *nmf*; (machine) autospazzatrice *f*

road tax *n* tassa *f* di circolazione

roadway *n* carreggiata *f*, corsia *f*

roadworks *npl* lavori *mpl* stradali

roadworthy *adj* sicuro

roam /rəʊm/ *vt* & *vi* girovagare

■ **roam around** *vi* girovagare
roar /rɔː(r)/ **A** *n* ruggito *m*; **~s of laughter** scroscio *msg* di risa
B *vi* ruggire; ‹*lorry, thunder*› rombare; **~ with laughter** ridere fragorosamente
■ **roar out** *vt* gridare
■ **roar past** *vi* ‹*move noisily*› passare rombando
roaring /ˈrɔːrɪŋ/ **A** *adj* **do a ~ trade** infml fare affari d'oro
B *adv* **~ drunk** infml ubriaco fradicio
roast /rəʊst/ **A** *adj* arrosto; **~ pork** arrosto *m* di maiale
B *n* arrosto *m*
C *vt* arrostire ‹*meat*›
D *vi* arrostirsi
roasting, roasting hot /ˈrəʊstɪŋ/ *adj* infml caldissimo
roasting pan *n* teglia *f* per arrosti
rob /rɒb/ *vt* (*pt/pp* **robbed**) derubare (of di); svaligiare ‹*bank*›
robber /ˈrɒbə(r)/ *n* rapinatore, -trice *mf*
robbery /ˈrɒbərɪ/ *n* rapina *f*
robe /rəʊb/ *n* tunica *f*; AmE (bathrobe) accappatoio *m*
robin /ˈrɒbɪn/ *n* pettirosso *m*
robot /ˈrəʊbɒt/ *n* robot *m inv*
robotic /rəʊˈbɒtɪk/ *adj* ‹*movement, voice*› robotico; ‹*tool, device, machine*› robotizzato
robotics *nsg* robotica *fsg*
robust /rəʊˈbʌst/ *adj* robusto
rock¹ /rɒk/ *n* roccia *f*; (in sea) scoglio *m*; (sweet) zucchero *m* candito; **on the ~s** ‹*ship*› incagliato; ‹*marriage*› finito; ‹*drink*› con ghiaccio
rock² **A** *vt* cullare ‹*baby*›; (shake) far traballare; (shock) scuotere
B *vi* dondolarsi
⚷ **rock³** *n* Mus rock *m*
rock and roll *n* rock and roll *m*
r **rock-bottom** **A** *adj* bassissimo
B *n* livello *m* più basso; **hit ~** toccare il fondo
rock climber *n* scalatore, -trice *mf*
rock climbing *n* roccia *f*
rockery /ˈrɒkərɪ/ *n* giardino *m* roccioso
rocket /ˈrɒkɪt/ **A** *n* razzo *m*; **give somebody a ~** infml fare un cicchetto a qualcuno
B *vi* salire alle stelle
rocket launcher /lɔːntʃə(r)/ *n* lanciarazzi *m inv*
rocket science *n* infml **it's not ~** non ci vuole la laurea!
rock face *n* parete *f* rocciosa
rockfall /ˈrɒkfɔːl/ *n* caduta *f* di massi
rocking chair /ˈrɒkɪŋ/ *n* sedia *f* a dondolo
rocking horse *n* cavallo *m* a dondolo
rock star *n* rock star *mf inv*

⚷ parola chiave

rocky /ˈrɒkɪ/ *adj* (**-ier, -iest**) roccioso; fig traballante
Rocky Mountains *npl* le Montagne *fpl* Rocciose
rod /rɒd/ *n* bacchetta *f*; (for fishing) canna *f*
rode /rəʊd/ ▶ **ride**
rodent /ˈrəʊdnt/ *n* roditore *m*
roe¹ /rəʊ/ *n* uova *fpl* di pesce; (soft) latte *m* di pesce
roe² *n* (*pl* **roe** *or* **roes**) **~ [deer]** capriolo *m*
roebuck /ˈrəʊbʌk/ *n* capriolo *m* maschio
roger /ˈrɒdʒə(r)/ *int* Teleph ricevuto
rogue /rəʊg/ *n* farabutto *m*
rogue state *n* stato *m* canaglia
⚷ **role** /rəʊl/ *n* ruolo *m*
role model *n* Psych modello *m* comportamentale
role-play, role-playing /ˈrəʊlpleɪɪŋ/ *n* Psych role playing *m inv*
⚷ **roll** /rəʊl/ **A** *n* rotolo *m*; ‹*bread*› panino *m*; (list) lista *f*; ‹*of ship, drum*› rullio *m*
B *vi* rotolare; **be ~ing in money** infml nuotare nell'oro
C *vt* spianare ‹*lawn, pastry*›; **~ed into one** allo stesso tempo
■ **roll around, roll about** *vi* ‹*person, puppy*› rotolarsi; ‹*ball, marbles*› rotolare
■ **roll back** *vt* ridurre ‹*prices*›
■ **roll by** *vi* ‹*time*› passare
■ **roll down** *vt* srotolare ‹*blind, sleeves*›
■ **roll in** *vi* infml (arrive in large quantities) arrivare a valanghe; (arrive) arrivare
■ **roll on**: *vi* **~ on Friday!** non vedo l'ora che sia venerdì!
■ **roll over** *vi* rigirarsi; infml (capitulate) arrendersi
■ **roll up** **A** *vt* arrotolare; rimboccarsi ‹*sleeves*›
B *vi* infml arrivare
roll-call *n* appello *m*
roller /ˈrəʊlə(r)/ *n* rullo *m*; (for hair) bigodino *m*
rollerblade **A** *n* pattino *m* a rotelle in linea
B *vi* pattinare (con pattini in linea)
roller blind *n* tapparella *f*
roller coaster *n* montagne *fpl* russe
roller skate *n* pattino *m* a rotelle
roller-skating /ˈrəʊləskeɪtɪŋ/ *n* pattinaggio *m* a rotelle
rollicking /ˈrɒlɪkɪŋ/ *adj* **have a ~ time** divertirsi da pazzi
rolling pin *n* mattarello *m*
rolling stock *n* materiale *m* rotabile
rolling stone *n* fig vagabondo, -a *mf*
roll-neck *n* collo *m* alto; (whole sweater) dolcevita *m inv*
roll-on *n* (deodorant) deodorante *m* a sfera
roll-on roll-off ferry *n* traghetto *m* roll-on roll-off
ROM /rɒm/ *n* Comput Rom *f inv*
Roma /ˈrəʊmə/ *npl* i rom *mpl*

Roman /ˈrəʊmən/ **A** *adj* (also print) romano **B** *n* romano, -a *mf*
Roman Catholic *adj & n* cattolico, -a *mf*
romance /rəʊˈmæns/ *n* (love affair) storia *f* d'amore; (book) romanzo *m* rosa
Romania /rəʊˈmeɪnɪə/ *n* Romania *f*
Romanian /rəʊˈmeɪnɪən/ *adj & n* rumeno, -a *mf*; (language) rumeno *m*
roman numeral *n* numero *m* romano
romantic /rəʊˈmæntɪk/ *adj* romantico
romantically /rəʊˈmæntɪklɪ/ *adv* romanticamente
romanticism /rəʊˈmæntɪsɪzm/ *n* romanticismo *m*
romanticize /rəʊˈmæntɪsaɪz/ *vt* romantizzare
romanticized /rəʊˈmæntɪsaɪzd/ *adj* romanzato
Romany /ˈrɒmənɪ/ *n* rom *mf inv*
Rome /rəʊm/ *n* Roma *f*
Romeo /ˈrəʊmɪəʊ/ *n* infml (ladykiller) dongiovanni *m inv*
romp /rɒmp/ **A** *n* gioco *m* rumoroso
B *vi* giocare rumorosamente
■ **romp home** *vi* (win easily) vincere senza difficoltà
rompers /ˈrɒmpəz/ *npl* pagliaccetto *msg*
romp through **A** *vt* passare senza difficoltà ‹*exam*›
B *vi* riuscire senza difficoltà
roof /ruːf/ **A** *n* tetto *m*; (of mouth) palato *m*; **live under one ~** vivere sotto lo stesso tetto; **go through the ~** infml (increase) andare alle stelle; (be very angry) andare su tutte le furie
B *vt* mettere un tetto su
roof rack *n* portabagagli *m inv*
rooftop /ˈruːftɒp/ *n* tetto *m*; **shout it from the ~s** fig gridarlo ai quattro venti
rook /rʊk/ **A** *n* corvo *m*; (in chess) torre *f*
B *vt* infml (swindle) fregare
rookie /ˈrʊkɪ/ *n* AmE infml novellino, -a *mf*
room /ruːm/ *n* stanza *f*; (bedroom) camera *f*; (for functions) sala *f*; (space) spazio *m*
room-mate *n* AmE (flatmate) compagno, -a *mf* di appartamento; (in same room) compagno, -a *mf* di stanza
room service *n* servizio *m* in camera
room temperature *n* temperatura *f* ambiente
roomy /ˈruːmɪ/ *adj* spazioso; ‹*clothes*› ampio
roost /ruːst/ **A** *n* posatoio *m*
B *vi* appollaiarsi
rooster /ˈruːstə(r)/ *n* gallo *m*
root¹ /ruːt/ **A** *n* radice *f*; **take ~** metter radici; **put down ~s** fig metter radici
B *vi* metter radici
root² *vi* **~ for somebody** infml fare il tifo per qualcuno
■ **root about**, **root around** *vi* grufolare; **~ about for something** rovistare alla ricerca di qualcosa
■ **root out** *vt* fig scovare
rope /rəʊp/ *n* corda *f*; **know the ~s** infml conoscere i trucchi del mestiere
■ **rope in** *vt* infml coinvolgere
rope ladder *n* scala *f* di corda
ropey /ˈrəʊpɪ/ *adj* BrE infml scadente; **feel ~** sentirsi poco bene
rosary /ˈrəʊzərɪ/ *n* rosario *m*
rose¹ /rəʊz/ *n* rosa *f*; (of watering can) bocchetta *f*
rose² ▸ **rise**
rosé /ˈrəʊzeɪ/ *n* [vino *m*] rosé *m inv*
rosebud /ˈrəʊzbʌd/ *n* bocciolo *m* di rosa
rose hip /ˈrəʊzhɪp/ *n* frutto *m* della rosa canina
rosemary /ˈrəʊzmərɪ/ *n* rosmarino *m*
rose-tinted spectacles /ˈrəʊztɪntɪd/ *npl* **wear ~** vedere tutto rosa
rosette /rəʊˈzet/ *n* coccarda *f*
roster /ˈrɒstə(r)/ *n* tabella *f* dei turni
rostrum /ˈrɒstrəm/ *n* podio *m*
rosy /ˈrəʊzɪ/ *adj* (**-ier**, **-iest**) roseo
rot /rɒt/ **A** *n* marciume *m*; infml (nonsense) sciocchezze *fpl*
B *vi* (*pt/pp* **rotted**) marcire
rota /ˈrəʊtə/ *n* tabella *f* dei turni
rotary /ˈrəʊtərɪ/ *adj* rotante
rotate /rəʊˈteɪt/ **A** *vt* far ruotare; avvicendare ‹*crops*›
B *vi* ruotare
rotation /rəʊˈteɪʃn/ *n* rotazione *f*; **in ~** a turno
rote /rəʊt/ *n* **by ~** meccanicamente
rotten /ˈrɒn/ *adj* marcio; infml schifoso; ‹*person*› penoso
rotund /rəʊˈtʌnd/ *adj* paffuto
rotunda /rəʊˈtʌndə/ *n* rotonda *f*
rouble /ˈruːbl/ *n* rublo *m*
rough /rʌf/ **A** *adj* (not smooth) ruvido; ‹*ground*› accidentato; ‹*behaviour*› rozzo; ‹*sport*› violento; ‹*area*› malfamato; ‹*crossing, time*› brutto; ‹*estimate*› approssimativo
B *adv* ‹*play*› grossolanamente; **sleep ~** dormire sotto i ponti
C *n* **do something in ~** far qualcosa alla bell'e meglio
D *vi* **~ it** vivere senza comfort
■ **rough out** *vt* abbozzare
■ **rough up** *vt* infml malmenare ‹*person*›
roughage /ˈrʌfɪdʒ/ *n* fibre *fpl*
rough-and-ready *adj* ‹*person, manner*› sbrigativo; ‹*conditions, method*› rudimentale
rough-and-tumble *n* (rough play) zuffa *f*
rough copy *n* brutta copia *f*
rough draft *n* abbozzo *m*
roughen /ˈrʌfən/ *vt* rendere ruvido ‹*surface*›
roughly /ˈrʌflɪ/ *adv* rozzamente; (more or less) pressappoco

roughness /ˈrʌfnɪs/ *n* ruvidità *f*; (of behaviour) rozzezza *f*
rough paper *n* carta *f* da brutta
roughshod /ˈrʌfʃɒd/ *adv* **ride ~ over** infischiarsi di ‹*person, objection*›; calpestare ‹*feelings*›
roulette /ruːˈlet/ *n* roulette *f*
🔑 **round** /raʊnd/ **A** *adj* rotondo
B *n* tondo *m*; (slice) fetta *f*; (of visits, drinks) giro *m*; (of competition) partita *f*; (boxing) ripresa *f*, round *m inv*; **do one's ~s** ‹*doctor*› fare il giro delle visite
C *prep* intorno a; **open ~ the clock** aperto ventiquattr'ore
D *adv* **all ~** tutt'intorno; **ask somebody ~** invitare qualcuno; **go/come ~ to** (a friend etc) andare da; **turn/look ~** girarsi; **~ about** (approximately) intorno a
E *vt* arrotondare; girare ‹*corner*›
■ **round down** *vt* arrotondare (*per difetto*)
■ **round off** *vt* (end) terminare
■ **round on** *vt* aggredire
■ **round up** *vt* radunare; arrotondare ‹*prices*›
roundabout /ˈraʊndəbaʊt/ **A** *adj* indiretto
B *n* giostra *f*; (for traffic) rotonda *f*
round bracket *n* parentesi *f* tonda
rounders /ˈraʊndəz/ *n* BrE Sport *gioco* (*m*) *simile al baseball*
round figure *n* cifra *f* tonda
round robin *n* petizione *f*
round-shouldered /-ˈʃəʊldəd/ *adj* con le spalle curve
round table *n* tavola *f* rotonda
round the clock *adv* 24 ore su 24
round-the-clock *adj* BrE ‹*care, surveillance*› ventiquattr'ore su ventiquattro
round the world *adj* ‹*trip*› intorno al mondo
round trip *n* viaggio *m* di andata e ritorno
round-up *n* (of suspects) retata *f*; (of cattle) raduno *m*; (summary) riepilogo *m*
rouse /raʊz/ *vt* svegliare; risvegliare ‹*suspicion, interest*›
rousing /ˈraʊzɪŋ/ *adj* ‹*speech*› che solleva il morale; ‹*music*› trionfale
rout /raʊt/ **A** *vt* Mil fig sbaragliare
B *n* disfatta *f*
🔑 **route** /ruːt/ *n* itinerario *m*; Naut, Aeron rotta *f*; (of bus) percorso *m*
routine /ruːˈtiːn/ **A** *adj* di routine
B *n* routine *f inv*; Theat numero *m*
routinely /ruːˈtiːnlɪ/ *adv* d'ufficio
routing number /ˈraʊtɪŋnʌmbər/ *n* AmE numero *m* di instradamento, numero *m* di identificazione (bancaria)
rove /rəʊv/ *vi* girovagare
roving /ˈrəʊvɪŋ/ *adj* ‹*reporter, ambassador*› itinerante

roving eye *n* **have a ~** essere sempre in cerca di avventure amorose
🔑 **row¹** /rəʊ/ *n* (line) fila *f*; **three years in a ~** tre anni di fila
row² **A** *vi* (in boat) remare
B *vt* **~ a boat** remare
row³ /raʊ/ **A** *n* infml (quarrel) litigata *f*; (noise) baccano *m*; **we've had a ~** abbiamo litigato
B *vi* infml litigare
rowboat /ˈrəʊbəʊt/ *n* AmE barca *f* a remi
rowdy /ˈraʊdɪ/ **A** *adj* (**-ier**, **-iest**) chiassoso
B *n* attaccabrighe *m inv*
rower /ˈrəʊə(r)/ *n* rematore, -trice *mf*
rowing /ˈrəʊɪŋ/ *n* (sport) canottaggio *m*
rowing boat /ˈrəʊɪŋ/ *n* barca *f* a remi
rowing machine *n* vogatore *m*
rowlock /ˈrɒlək/ *n* BrE scalmo *m*
🔑 **royal** /ˈrɔɪəl/ **A** *adj* reale
B *n* membro *m* della famiglia reale
royal blue *n & adj* blu *m* scuro
Royal Highness *n* **His/Her ~** Sua Altezza reale; **Your ~** Vostra Altezza
royally /ˈrɔɪəlɪ/ *adv* regalmente
royalties /ˈrɔɪəltɪz/ *npl* (payments) diritti *mpl* d'autore
royalty /ˈrɔɪəltɪ/ *n* appartenenza *f* alla famiglia reale; (persons) membri *mpl* della famiglia reale
rpm *abbr* (**revolutions per minute**) giri *mpl* al minuto
RSI *abbr* (**repetitive strain injury**) patologia *f* da sforzo ripetuto
RSVP *abbr* (**répondez s'il vous plaît = please reply**) SPR, si prega rispondere
rub /rʌb/ **A** *n* sfregata *f*
B *vt* (*pt/pp* **rubbed**) sfregare; **~ one's hands** fregarsi le mani
■ **rub along** *vi* sopportarsi [a vicenda]
■ **rub down** *vt* frizionare ‹*person, body*›; levigare ‹*wood*›
■ **rub in** *vt* far assorbire (*massaggiando*) ‹*cream*›; **don't ~it in** infml non rigirare il coltello nella piaga
■ **rub off** **A** *vt* mandar via sfregando ‹*stain*›; (from blackboard) cancellare
B *vi* andar via; **~ off on** essere trasmesso a
■ **rub out** *vt* cancellare
■ **rub up**: *vt* **~ somebody up the wrong way** prendere qualcuno per il verso sbagliato
rubber /ˈrʌbə(r)/ *n* gomma *f*; (eraser) gomma *f* [da cancellare]
rubber band *n* elastico *m*
rubber bullet *n* proiettile *m* di gomma
rubberneck *n* infml (onlooker) curioso, -a *mf*; (tourist) turista *mf*
rubber plant *n* ficus *m inv*
rubber-stamp *vt* fig approvare senza discutere
rubber tree *n* albero *m* della gomma
rubbery /ˈrʌbərɪ/ *adj* gommoso

🔑 parola chiave

rubbish /ˈrʌbɪʃ/ **A** *n* immondizie *fpl*; infml (nonsense) idiozie *fpl*; infml (junk) robaccia *f*
B *vt* infml fare a pezzi
rubbish bin *n* pattumiera *f*
rubbish dump *n* discarica *f*; (official) discarica *f* comunale
rubbishy /ˈrʌbɪʃɪ/ *adj* infml schifoso
rubble /ˈrʌbl/ *n* macerie *fpl*
rub-down *n* strofinata *f*
rubella /rʊˈbelə/ *n* rosolia *f*
rubric /ˈruːbrɪk/ *n* rubrica *f*
ruby /ˈruːbɪ/ **A** *n* rubino *m*
B *attrib* di rubini; ‹*lips*› scarlatto
rucksack /ˈrʌksæk/ *n* zaino *m*
ructions /ˈrʌkʃ(ə)nz/ *npl* infml finimondo *msg*; **there'll be ~ if he finds out** se lo scopre succede il finimondo
rudder /ˈrʌdə(r)/ *n* timone *m*
ruddy /ˈrʌdɪ/ *adj* (**-ier**, **-iest**) rubicondo; infml maledetto
rude /ruːd/ *adj* scortese; (improper) spinto
rudely /ˈruːdlɪ/ *adv* scortesemente
rudeness /ˈruːdnɪs/ *n* scortesia *f*
rudimentary /ruːdɪˈmentərɪ/ *adj* rudimentale
rudiments /ˈruːdɪmənts/ *npl* rudimenti *mpl*
rue¹ /ruː/ *vt* pentirsi di ‹*decision*›; **~ the day** maledire il giorno
rue² *n* Bot ruta *f*
rueful /ˈruːfl/ *adj* rassegnato
ruefully /ˈruːfʊlɪ/ *adv* con rassegnazione
ruff /rʌf/ *n* (of lace) colletto *m*; (of fur, feathers) collare *m*
ruffian /ˈrʌfɪən/ *n* farabutto *m*
ruffle /ˈrʌfl/ **A** *n* gala *f*
B *vt* scompigliare ‹*hair*›
rug /rʌg/ *n* tappeto *m*; (blanket) coperta *f*
rugby /ˈrʌgbɪ/ *n* **~ [football]** rugby *m*
rugby league *n* rugby *m* a tredici
rugby shirt *n* maglia *f* da rugby
rugby union *n* rugby *m* a quindici
rugged /ˈrʌgɪd/ *adj* ‹*coastline*› roccioso; ‹*face, personality*› duro
ruin /ˈruːɪn/ **A** *n* rovina *f*; **in ~s** in rovina
B *vt* rovinare
ruined /ˈruːɪnd/ *adj* ‹*building, clothes*› rovinato
ruinous /ˈruːɪnəs/ *adj* estremamente costoso
rule /ruːl/ **A** *n* regola *f*; (control) ordinamento *m*; (for measuring) metro *m*; **~s** *pl* regolamento *msg*; **as a ~** generalmente; **make it a ~ to do something** fare qualcosa sistematicamente
B *vt* governare; dominare ‹*colony, behaviour*›; **~ that** stabilire che
C *vi* governare
▪ **rule out** *vt* escludere
ruled /ruːld/ *adj* ‹*paper*› a righe
rule of thumb *n* principio *m* empirico
ruler /ˈruːlə(r)/ *n* capo *m* di Stato; (sovereign) sovrano, -a *mf*; (measure) righello *m*, regolo *m*
ruling /ˈruːlɪŋ/ **A** *adj* ‹*class*› dirigente; ‹*party*› di governo
B *n* decisione *f*
rum¹ /rʌm/ *n* rum *m inv*
rum² *adj* infml (peculiar) curioso
rumble /ˈrʌmbl/ **A** *n* rombo *m*; (of stomach) brontolio *m*
B *vi* rombare; ‹*stomach*› brontolare
rumble strip *n* banda *f* rumorosa
rumbustious /rʌmˈbʌstʃəs/ *adj* (noisy, very lively) chiassoso
ruminant /ˈruːmɪnənt/ *n* ruminante *m*
ruminate /ˈruːmɪneɪt/ *vi* ‹*animals*› ruminare; (think) rimuginare
rummage /ˈrʌmɪdʒ/ *vi* rovistare (**in/through** in)
rummy /ˈrʌmɪ/ *n* ramino *m*
rumour /ˈruːmə(r)/ **A** *n* diceria *f*
B *vt* **it is ~ed that** si dice che
rumour-monger /ˈruːməmʌŋgə(r)/ *n* persona *f* che sparge pettegolezzi
rump /rʌmp/ *n* natiche *fpl*
rumple /ˈrʌmpl/ *vt* sgualcire ‹*clothes, sheets, papers*›; scompigliare ‹*hair*›
rump steak *n* bistecca *f* di girello
rumpus /ˈrʌmpəs/ *n* infml baccano *m*
run /rʌn/ **A** *n* (on foot) corsa *f*; (distance to be covered) tragitto *m*; (outing) giro *m*; Theat rappresentazioni *fpl*; (in skiing) pista *f*; AmE (ladder) smagliatura *f* (*in calze*); **at a ~** di corsa; **~ of bad luck** periodo *m* sfortunato; **on the ~** in fuga; **have the ~ of** avere a disposizione; **in the long ~** a lungo termine
B *vi* (*pt* **ran**, *pp* **run**, *pres p* **running**) correre; ‹*river*› scorrere; ‹*nose, make-up*› colare; ‹*bus*› fare servizio; ‹*play*› essere in cartellone; ‹*colours*› sbiadire; (in election) presentarsi [come candidato]; ‹*software*› girare; **~ aground** insabbiarsi; **~ low on, ~ short of** essere a corto di
C *vt* (manage) dirigere; tenere ‹*house*›; (drive) dare un passaggio a; correre ‹*risk*›; Comput lanciare; Journ pubblicare ‹*article*›; (pass) far scorrere ‹*eyes, hand*›; **~ a temperature** avere la febbre; **~ a bath** far scorrere l'acqua per il bagno
▪ **run about** *vi* ‹*children*› correre di qua e di là; (be busy) correre
▪ **run across** *vt* imbattersi in
▪ **run after** *vt* (chase) rincorrere; (romantically) andare dietro a
▪ **run along** *vi* (go away) andare via
▪ **run away** *vi* scappare [via], andare via di corsa; (from home) scappare di casa
▪ **run away with** *vt* scappare con ‹*lover, money*›; **she let her enthusiasm ~ away with her** si è lasciata trasportare dall'entusiasmo
▪ **run back A** *vi* correre indietro
B *vt* (transport by car) riaccompagnare
▪ **run back over** *vt* (review) rivedere
▪ **run down A** *vi* ‹*clock*› scaricarsi; ‹*stocks*› esaurirsi
B *vt* Auto investire; (reduce) esaurire; infml

r

(criticize) denigrare
▪ **run in** *vi* entrare di corsa
▪ **run into** *vi* (meet) imbattersi in; (knock against) urtare
▪ **run off** **A** *vi* scappare [via], andare via di corsa; (from home) scappare di casa
B *vt* stampare ‹*copies*›
▪ **run off with** *vt* = **run away with**
▪ **run on** *vi* ‹*meeting*› protrarsi; ‹*person*› chiacchierare senza sosta
▪ **run out** *vi* uscire di corsa; ‹*supplies, money*› esaurirsi; ~ **out of** rimanere senza
▪ **run over** **A** *vi* correre; (overflow) traboccare
B *vt* (review) dare una scorsa a; Auto investire
▪ **run through** *vt* (use up) fare fuori; (be present in) pervadere; (review) dare una scorsa a
▪ **run to** *vt* (be enough for) essere sufficiente per; (have enough money for) potersi permettere
▪ **run up** **A** *vi* salire di corsa; (towards) arrivare di corsa
B *vt* accumulare ‹*debts, bill*›; (sew) cucire
▪ **run up against** *vt* incontrare ‹*difficulties*›
runabout *n* (vehicle) utilitaria *f*
run-around *n* **he's giving me/her the ~** mi/la sta menando per il naso
runaway **A** *n* fuggitivo, -a *mf*, fuggiasco, -a *mf*; (child) ragazzo, -a *mf* scappato, -a di casa
B *adj* ‹*person*› in fuga; ‹*child*› scappato di casa; ‹*inflation*› galoppante; ‹*success*› eclatante
run-down **A** *adj* ‹*area*› in abbandono; ‹*person*› esaurito
B *n* analisi *f inv*
rung[1] /rʌŋ/ *n* (of ladder) piolo *m*
rung[2] ▸ **ring**[2]
run-in *n* infml (argument) lite *f*
runner /ˈrʌnə(r)/ *n* podista *mf*; (in race) velocista *mf*; (on sledge) pattino *m*; (carpet) guida *f*
runner bean *n* fagiolino *m*
runner-up *n* secondo, -a, classificato, -a *mf*
running /ˈrʌnɪŋ/ **A** *adj* in corsa; ‹*water*› corrente; **four times ~** quattro volte di seguito
B *n* corsa *f*; (management) direzione *f*; **be in the ~** essere in lizza
running battle *n* lotta *f* continua
running commentary *n* cronaca *f*
running total *n* totale *m* aggiornato
runny /ˈrʌnɪ/ *adj* semiliquido; **~ nose** naso *m* che cola
run-of-the-mill *adj* ordinario
runs /rʌnz/ *npl* **the ~** infml (diarrhoea) la sciolta
runt /rʌnt/ *n* (of litter) *cucciolo (m) più piccolo e debole di una figliata*; derog (weakling) mezza cartuccia *f*
run-through *n* prova *f* generale
run-up *n* Sport rincorsa *f*; **the ~ to** il periodo precedente
runway /ˈrʌnweɪ/ *n* pista *f*
rupee /ruːˈpiː/ *n* rupia *f*
rupture /ˈrʌptʃə(r)/ **A** *n* rottura *f*; Med ernia *f*
B *vt* rompere; **~ oneself** farsi venire l'ernia
C *vi* rompersi
⚷ **rural** /ˈrʊərəl/ *adj* rurale
ruse /ruːz/ *n* astuzia *f*
rush[1] /rʌʃ/ *n* Bot giunco *m*
⚷ **rush**[2] **A** *n* fretta *f*; **in a ~** di fretta
B *vi* precipitarsi
C *vt* far premura a; **~ somebody to hospital** trasportare qualcuno di corsa all'ospedale
▪ **rush away**, **rush off** *vi* andar via in fretta
▪ **rush into**: *vt* **~ into marriage** sposarsi senza riflettere; **~ into doing something** lanciarsi a fare qualcosa senza riflettere; **~ somebody into doing something** spingere qualcuno a fare qualcosa
▪ **rush out** *vi* uscire di corsa
▪ **rush through** *vt* svolgere in fretta ‹*task*›; **~ something through** fare approvare qualcosa in fretta ‹*legislation, order*›
rush hour **A** *n* ora *f* di punta
B *attrib* delle ore di punta
rusk /rʌsk/ *n* biscotto *m*
russet /ˈrʌsɪt/ *adj* rossastro
Russia /ˈrʌʃə/ *n* Russia *f*
Russian /ˈrʌʃən/ *adj & n* russo, -a *mf*; (language) russo *m*
Russian roulette *n* roulette *f* russa
rust /rʌst/ **A** *n* ruggine *f*
B *vi* arrugginirsi
C *vt* arrugginire
rustic /ˈrʌstɪk/ *adj* rustico
rustle /ˈrʌsl/ **A** *vi* frusciare
B *vt* far frusciare; AmE rubare ‹*cattle*›
▪ **rustle up** *vt* infml fare ‹*meal, cup of coffee*›
rustler /ˈrʌslə(r)/ *n* ladro *m* di bestiame
rustproof /ˈrʌstpruːf/ *adj* a prova di ruggine
rusty /ˈrʌstɪ/ *adj* (**-ier**, **-iest**) arrugginito
rut /rʌt/ *n* solco *m*; **in a ~** infml nella routine
rutabaga /ˌruːtəˈbeɪgə/ *n* AmE rutabaga *f*; navone *m*
ruthless /ˈruːθlɪs/ *adj* spietato
ruthlessly /ˈruːθlɪslɪ/ *adv* spietatamente
ruthlessness /ˈruːθlɪsnɪs/ *n* spietatezza *f*
rutting /ˈrʌtɪŋ/ *n* accoppiamento *m*
rutting season *n* stagione *f* degli amori
RV *n abbr* AmE (**recreational vehicle**) camper *m*
Rwanda /rʊˈændə/ *n* Rwanda *m*
rye /raɪ/ *n* segale *f*
rye bread *n* pane *m* di segale

⚷ parola chiave

Ss

s, S /es/ *n* (letter) s, S *f inv*
S² *abbr* **1 (small) 2 (south)** S
sabbath /'sæbəθ/ *n* domenica *f*; Jewish sabato *m*
sabbatical /sə'bætɪkl/ *n* Univ anno *m* sabbatico
sable /'seɪbl/ *n* (animal, fur) zibellino *m*
sabotage /'sæbətɑːʒ/ **A** *n* sabotaggio *m* **B** *vt* sabotare
saboteur /sæbə'tɜː(r)/ *n* sabotatore, -trice *mf*
sabre /'seɪbə(r)/ *n* sciabola *f*
sac /sæk/ *n* Anat, Zool sacco *m*; Bot sacca *f*; **honey ~** cestella *f*
saccharin /'sækərɪn/ *n* saccarina *f*
sachet /'sæʃeɪ/ *n* bustina *f*; (scented) sacchetto *m* profumato
sack¹ /sæk/ *vt* (plunder) saccheggiare
sack² **A** *n* sacco *m*; **get the ~** infml essere licenziato; **give somebody the ~** licenziare qualcuno
B *vt* infml licenziare
sackcloth /'sækklɒθ/ *n* tela *f* di sacco; **wear ~ and ashes** cospargersi il capo di cenere
sackful /'sækfʊl/ *n* sacco *m* (*contenuto*)
sacking /'sækɪŋ/ *n* tela *f* per sacchi; infml (dismissal) licenziamento *m*
sackload /'sækləʊd/ *n* sacco *m* (*contenuto*)
sacrament /'sækrəmənt/ *n* sacramento *m*
sacred /'seɪkrɪd/ *adj* sacro
sacred cow /kaʊ/ *n* (institution) istituzione *f* intoccabile; (principle) principio *m* inderogabile; (person) mostro *m* sacro
sacrifice /'sækrɪfaɪs/ **A** *n* sacrificio *m* **B** *vt* sacrificare; **~ oneself** immolarsi
sacrificial /sækrɪ'fɪʃəl/ *adj* ‹*victim*› sacrificale
sacrilege /'sækrɪlɪdʒ/ *n* sacrilegio *m*
sacrilegious /sækrɪ'lɪdʒəs/ *adj* sacrilego
sacristy /'sækrɪstɪ/ *n* sagrestia *f*
sacrosanct /'sækrəʊsæŋkt/ *adj* sacrosanto
sacrum /'sækrʌm/ *n* Anat osso *m* sacro
sad /sæd/ *adj* (**sadder, saddest**) triste
SAD /sæd/ *n abbr* (**seasonal affective disorder**) Med disturbi *mpl* affettivi stagionali
sadden /'sædn/ *vt* rattristare
saddle /'sædl/ **A** *n* sella *f*; **be in the ~** fig tenere le redini
B *vt* sellare; **I've been ~d with...** fig mi hanno affibbiato...
sadism /'seɪdɪzm/ *n* sadismo *m*
sadist /'seɪdɪst/ *n* sadico, -a *mf*
sadistic /sə'dɪstɪk/ *adj* sadico
sadistically /sə'dɪstɪklɪ/ *adv* sadicamente
sadly /'sædlɪ/ *adv* tristemente; (unfortunately) sfortunatamente
sadness /'sædnɪs/ *n* tristezza *f*
sadomasochism /seɪdəʊ'mæsəkɪzm/ *n* sadomasochismo *m*
sadomasochist /seɪdəʊ'mæsəkɪst/ *n* sadomasochista *mf*
sadomasochistic /seɪdəʊ'mæsəkɪstɪk/ *adj* sadomasochistico
sae *abbr* (**stamped addressed envelope**) busta *f* preaffrancata e preindirizzata
safari /sə'fɑːrɪ/ *n* safari *m inv*
safari park *n* zoosafari *m inv*
safe /seɪf/ **A** *adj* sicuro; (out of danger) salvo; ‹*object*› al sicuro; **~ and sound** sano e salvo
B *n* cassaforte *f*
safe bet *n* **it's a ~ that he will come** è certo che verrà
safe-breaker *n* scassinatore, -trice *mf*
safe conduct /ˌseɪf'kɒndʌkt/ *n* salvacondotto *m*
safe-deposit box, safety-deposit box *n* cassetta *f* di sicurezza
safeguard **A** *n* protezione *f*
B *vt* proteggere
safe house *n* rifugio *m*
safe keeping *n* custodia *f*; **for ~** in custodia
safely /'seɪflɪ/ *adv* in modo sicuro; ‹*arrive*› senza incidenti; ‹*assume*› con certezza
safe sex *n* sesso *m* sicuro
safety /'seɪftɪ/ *n* sicurezza *f*
safety belt *n* cintura *f* di sicurezza
safety catch *n* sicura *f*
safety curtain *n* tagliafuoco *m*
safety-deposit box *n* = **safe-deposit box**
safety glass *n* vetro *m* di sicurezza
safety net *n* (for acrobat) rete *f* di protezione; fig protezione
safety pin *n* spilla *f* di sicurezza *o* da balia
safety razor *n* rasoio *m* di sicurezza
safety valve *n* valvola *f* di sicurezza; fig valvola *f* di sfogo
saffron /'sæfrən/ *n* zafferano *m*
sag /sæg/ *vi* (*pt/pp* **sagged**) abbassarsi
saga /'sɑːgə/ *n* saga *f*
sagacity /sə'gæsətɪ/ *n* sagacia *f*
sage¹ /seɪdʒ/ *n* (herb) salvia *f*
sage² *adj & n* saggio, -a *mf*

sagely /'seɪdʒlɪ/ *adv* ‹*reply, nod*› saggiamente
Sagittarius /sædʒɪ'teərɪəs/ *n* Sagittario *m*
sago /'seɪgəʊ/ *n* sagù *m*
Sahara /sə'hɑːrə/ *n* Sahara *m*
said /sed/ ▶ **say**
sail /seɪl/ **A** *n* vela *f*; (trip) giro *m* in barca a vela
B *vi* navigare; Sport praticare la vela; (leave) salpare
C *vt* pilotare
▪ **sail through** *vt* superare senza problemi ‹*exam*›
sailboard /'seɪlbɔːd/ *n* tavola *f* da windsurf
sailboarder /'seɪlbɔːdə(r)/ *n* windsurfista *mf*
sailboarding /'seɪlbɔːdɪŋ/ *n* windsurf *m inv*
sailboat /'seɪlbəʊt/ *n* AmE barca *f* a vela
sailing /'seɪlɪŋ/ *n* vela *f*
sailing boat *n* barca *f* a vela
sailing ship *n* veliero *m*
sailor /'seɪlə(r)/ *n* marinaio *m*
saint /seɪnt/ *n* santo, -a *mf*
sainthood /'seɪnthʊd/ *n* santità *f*
saintly /'seɪntlɪ/ *adj* da santo
sake /seɪk/ *n* **for the ~ of** ‹*person*› per il bene di; ‹*peace*› per amor di; **for the ~ of it** per il gusto di farlo
salacious /sə'leɪʃəs/ *adj* ‹*joke*› salace; ‹*book*› licenzioso; ‹*look*› lascivo
salad /'sæləd/ *n* insalata *f*
salad bar *n* tavola *f* fredda
salad bowl *n* insalatiera *f*
salad cream *n salsa (f) per condire l'insalata*
salad days *npl* anni *mpl* verdi
salad dressing *n* condimento *m* per insalata
salami /sə'lɑːmɪ/ *n* salame *m*
salaried /'sælərɪd/ *adj* stipendiato
salary /'sælərɪ/ *n* stipendio *m*
salary review *n* revisione *f* dello stipendio
salary scale *n* tabella *f* retributiva
S ⚷ **sale** /seɪl/ *n* vendita *f*; (at reduced prices) svendita *f*; **for/on ~** in vendita; **'for ~'** 'vendesi'
sale price *n* prezzo *m* scontato
sales and marketing *n* vendite *fpl* e marketing
sales and marketing department *n* ufficio *m* vendite e marketing
sales assistant *n* commesso, -a *mf*
sales director *n* capo *mf* dell'ufficio vendite
sales engineer *n* tecnico *m* commerciale
sales executive *n* direttore, -trice *mf* commerciale
sales figures *npl* volume *m* d'affari
sales force *n* rappresentanti *mpl*
sales invoice *n* fattura *f* di vendita
sales ledger *n* partitario *m* vendite
salesman *n* venditore *m*; (traveller) rappresentante *m*
sales pitch *n* discorso *m* imbonitore
sales rep, sales representative *n* rappresentante *mf* di commercio
salesroom *n* (for auctions) sala *f* d'aste
sales team *n* team *m inv* vendite
saleswoman *n* venditrice *f*
salient /'seɪlɪənt/ *adj* saliente
saline /'seɪlaɪn/ *adj* salino
saliva /sə'laɪvə/ *n* saliva *f*
salivary glands /sə'laɪvərɪ/ *npl* ghiandole *fpl* salivari
salivate /'sælɪveɪt/ *vi* salivare; **the smell of chicken roasting makes me ~** l'odore di pollo arrosto mi fa venire l'acquolina in bocca
sallow /'sæləʊ/ *adj* giallastro
sally /'sælɪ/ **A** *n* (witty remark) battuta *f*; Mil sortita *f*
B *vi* saltar fuori
salmon /'sæmən/ *n* salmone *m*
salmonella /sælmə'nelə/ *n* salmonella *f*
salmon-pink *adj* rosa salmone *inv*
salmon trout *n* trota *f* salmonata
salon /'sælɒn/ *n* salone *m*
saloon /sə'luːn/ *n* Auto berlina *f*; AmE (bar) bar *m*
salsa /'sælsə/ *n* salsa *f*
salt /sɔːlt/ **A** *n* sale *m*
B *adj* salato; ‹*fish, meat*› sotto sale
C *vt* salare; ‹*cure*› mettere sotto sale
salt cellar *n* saliera *f*
saltiness /'sɔːltɪnɪs/ *n* salinità *f*
salt water *n* acqua *f* di mare
salt-water fish *n* pesce *m* d'acqua salata
salty /'sɔːltɪ/ *adj* salato
salubrious /sə'luːbrɪəs/ *adj* ‹*neighbourhood*› raccomandabile; **it's not a very ~ area** è una zona poco raccomandabile
salutary /'sæljʊtərɪ/ *adj* salutare
salute /sə'luːt/ Mil **A** *n* saluto *m*
B *vt* salutare
C *vi* fare il saluto
salvage /'sælvɪdʒ/ **A** *n* Naut recupero *m*
B *vt* recuperare
salvation /sæl'veɪʃn/ *n* salvezza *f*
Salvation Army *n* Esercito *m* della Salvezza
salve /sælv/ *vt* **~ one's conscience** mettersi la coscienza a posto
salver /'sælvə(r)/ *n* vassoio *m (di metallo)*
salvo /'sælvəʊ/ *n* salva *f*
Samaritan /sə'mærɪtən/ *n* **a good ~** un buon samaritano; **the ~s** ≈ telefono *m* amico
samba /'sæmbə/ *n* samba *f*
⚷ **same** /seɪm/ **A** *adj* stesso (as di)
B *pron* **the ~** lo stesso; **be all the ~** essere

⚷ parola chiave

tutti uguali
C *adv* **the ~** nello stesso modo; **all the ~** (however) lo stesso; **the ~ to you** altrettanto

same day *adj ‹service›* in giornata

same-day delivery *n* consegna *f* in giornata

same sex /seɪmseks/ *adj ‹couple, marriage›* omosessuale

sample /ˈsɑːmpl/ **A** *n* campione *m*
B *vt* testare

sanatorium /sænəˈtɔːrɪəm/ *n* casa *f* di cura

sanctify /ˈsæŋktɪfaɪ/ *vt* (*pt/pp* **-fied**) santificare

sanctimonious /sæŋktɪˈməʊnɪəs/ *adj* moraleggiante

sanction /ˈsæŋkʃn/ **A** *n* (approval) autorizzazione *f*; (penalty) sanzione *f*
B *vt* autorizzare

sanctity /ˈsæŋktətɪ/ *n* santità *f*

sanctuary /ˈsæŋktjʊərɪ/ *n* Relig santuario *m*; (refuge) asilo *m*; (for wildlife) riserva *f*

sanctum /ˈsæŋktəm/ *n* (holy place) santuario *m*; (private place) rifugio *m*; **the inner ~** Relig il Sancta Sanctorum

sand /sænd/ **A** *n* sabbia *f*
B *vt* **~ [down]** carteggiare

sandal /ˈsændl/ *n* sandalo *m*

sandbag *n* sacchetto *m* di sabbia

sandbank *n* banco *m* di sabbia

sandblast *vt* sabbiare

sandblasting *n* sabbiatura *f*

sandcastle *n* castello *m* di sabbia

sand dune *n* duna *f*

sander /ˈsændə(r)/ *n* (machine) levigatrice *f*

Sandinista /sændɪˈniːstə/ *adj & n* sandinista *mf*

sandpaper **A** *n* carta *f* vetrata
B *vt* cartavetrare

sandpit *n recinto (m) contenente sabbia dove giocano i bambini*

sandstone *n* arenaria *f*

sandstorm *n* tempesta *f* di sabbia

sandwich /ˈsænwɪdʒ/ **A** *n* tramezzino *m*
B *vt* **~ed between** schiacciato tra

sandwich bar *n locale (m) in cui si comprano sandwich e panini pronti o su ordinazione*

sandwich course *n corso (m) che comprende dei periodi di tirocinio*

sandwich man *n* uomo *m* sandwich

sandy /ˈsændɪ/ *adj* (**-ier**, **-iest**) *‹beach, soil›* sabbioso; *‹hair›* biondiccio

sane /seɪn/ *adj* (not mad) sano di mente; (sensible) sensato

sang /sæŋ/ ▸ **sing**

sangria /sæŋˈgrɪə/ *n* sangria *f*

sanguine /ˈsæŋgwɪn/ *adj* ottimistico

sanitary /ˈsænɪtərɪ/ *adj* igienico; *‹system›* sanitario

sanitary napkin, **sanitary towel** *n* AmE assorbente *m* igienico

sanitation /sænɪˈteɪʃn/ *n* impianti *mpl* igienici

sanity /ˈsænətɪ/ *n* sanità *f* di mente; (sensibleness) buon senso *m*

sank /sæŋk/ ▸ **sink**

Santa /ˈsæntə/, **Santa Claus** /ˈsæntəklɔːz/ *n* Babbo *m* Natale

sap /sæp/ **A** *n* Bot linfa *f*
B *vt* (*pt/pp* **sapped**) indebolire

sapling /ˈsæplɪŋ/ *n* alberello *m*

sapper /ˈsæpə(r)/ *n* BrE Mil geniere *m*

sapphire /ˈsæfaɪə(r)/ **A** *n* zaffiro *m*
B *attrib* blu zaffiro *inv*

sarcasm /ˈsɑːkæzm/ *n* sarcasmo *m*

sarcastic /sɑːˈkæstɪk/ *adj* sarcastico

sarcastically /sɑːˈkæstɪklɪ/ *adv* sarcasticamente

sarcophagus /sɑːˈkɒfəgəs/ *n* sarcofago *m*

sardine /sɑːˈdiːn/ *n* sardina *f*

Sardinia /sɑːˈdɪnɪə/ *n* Sardegna *f*

Sardinian /sɑːˈdɪnɪən/ *adj & n* sardo, -a *mf*

sardonic /sɑːˈdɒnɪk/ *adj* sardonico

sardonically /sɑːˈdɒnɪklɪ/ *adv* sardonicamente

sari /ˈsɑːrɪ/ *n* sari *m inv*

sarong /səˈrɒŋ/ *n* pareo *m*

SARS /sɑːz/ *n abbr* (**severe acute respiratory syndrome**) SARS *f*

SAS *n abbr* BrE (**Special Air Service**) *commando (m) britannico per operazioni speciali*

sash /sæʃ/ *n* fascia *f*; (for dress) fusciacca *f*

sashay /ˈsæʃeɪ/ *vi* infml (casually) camminare in modo disinvolto; (seductively) camminare in modo provocante

sassy /ˈsæsɪ/ *adj* AmE infml (cheeky) sfacciato; (smart) chic *inv*

sat /sæt/ ▸ **sit**

Satan /ˈseɪtən/ *n* Satana *m*

satanic /səˈtænɪk/ *adj* satanico

satchel /ˈsætʃl/ *n* cartella *f*

sated /ˈseɪtɪd/ *adj ‹person›* sazio; *‹desire›* appagato; *‹appetite›* soddisfatto

satellite /ˈsætəlaɪt/ *n* satellite *m*

satellite channel *n* rete *f* televisiva satellitare

satellite dish *n* antenna *f* parabolica

satellite television *n* televisione *f* satellitare

satiate /ˈseɪʃɪeɪt/ *vt* saziare *‹person›*; appagare *‹desire›*; soddisfare *‹appetite›*

satin /ˈsætɪn/ **A** *n* raso *m*
B *attrib* di raso

satire /ˈsætaɪə(r)/ *n* satira *f*

satirical /səˈtɪrɪkl/ *adj* satirico

satirically /səˈtɪrɪklɪ/ *adv* satiricamente

satirist /ˈsætərɪst/ *n* scrittore, -trice *mf* satirico; (comedian) comico, -a *mf* satirico

satirize /ˈsætɪraɪz/ *vt* satireggiare

satisfaction /sætɪsˈfækʃn/ *n* soddisfazione *f*; **be to sb's ~** soddisfare qualcuno
satisfactorily /sætɪsˈfækt(ə)rɪlɪ/ *adv* in modo soddisfacente
satisfactory /sætɪsˈfæktərɪ/ *adj* soddisfacente
satisfied /ˈsætɪsfaɪd/ *adj* (pleased) soddisfatto; **~ with** soddisfatto di; (convinced) convinto; **~ that** convinto che
✐ **satisfy** /ˈsætɪsfaɪ/ *vt* (*pt/pp* **-ied**) soddisfare; (convince) convincere; **be satisfied** essere soddisfatto
satisfying /ˈsætɪsfaɪɪŋ/ *adj* soddisfacente
satnav /ˈsætnæv/ *n* satnav *m inv*
SATs *npl abbr* BrE (**standard assessment tasks**) *esami (mpl) sostenuti per tranche d'età allo scopo di testare la preparazione degli alunni*
saturate /ˈsætʃəreɪt/ *vt* inzuppare (**with** di); Chem fig saturare (**with** di)
saturated /ˈsætʃəreɪtɪd/ *adj* saturo
saturation /sætʃəˈreɪʃn/ *n* **reach ~ point** raggiungere il punto di saturazione
✐ **Saturday** /ˈsætədeɪ/ *n* sabato *m*
Saturn /ˈsætən/ *n* Saturno *m*
sauce /sɔːs/ *n* salsa *f*; (cheek) impertinenza *f*
saucepan /ˈsɔːspən/ *n* pentola *f*
saucer /ˈsɔːsə(r)/ *n* piattino *m*
saucy /ˈsɔːsɪ/ *adj* (**-ier**, **-iest**) impertinente
Saudi /ˈsaʊdɪ/ **A** *adj* saudita
B *n* (person) saudita *mf*; (country) Arabia *f* Saudita
Saudi Arabia /əˈreɪbɪə/ *n* Arabia *f* Saudita
Saudi Arabian *adj & n* saudita *mf*
sauerkraut /ˈsaʊəkraʊt/ *n* crauti *mpl*
sauna /ˈsɔːnə/ *n* sauna *f*
saunter /ˈsɔːntə(r)/ *vi* andare a spasso
sausage /ˈsɒsɪdʒ/ *n* salsiccia *f*; (dried) salame *m*
sausage dog /ˈsɒsɪdʒdɒg/ *n* infml bassotto *m*
sausage roll *n involtino (m) di pasta sfoglia con salsiccia*
sauté /ˈsəʊteɪ/ **A** *vt* rosolare
B *adj* rosolato
savage /ˈsævɪdʒ/ **A** *adj* feroce; ‹*tribe, custom*› selvaggio
B *n* selvaggio, -a *mf*
C *vt* fare a pezzi
savagely /ˈsævɪdʒlɪ/ *adv* ‹*attack*› selvaggiamente; ‹*criticize*› ferocemente
savagery /ˈsævɪdʒrɪ/ *n* ferocia *f*
✐ **save** /seɪv/ **A** *n* Sport parata *f*
B *vt* salvare (**from** da); (keep, collect) tenere; risparmiare ‹*time, money*›; (avoid) evitare; Sport parare ‹*goal*›; Comput salvare, memorizzare; **~ face** salvar la faccia
C *vi* **~ [up]** risparmiare
D (prep) salvo
saver /ˈseɪvə(r)/ *n* risparmiatore, -trice *mf*

✐ parola chiave

saving grace /seɪvɪŋˈgreɪs/ *n* **that's his one ~** si salva grazie a questo
savings /ˈseɪvɪŋz/ *npl* (money) risparmi *mpl*
savings account *n* libretto *m* di risparmio
savings and loan association *n* AmE associazione *f* mutua di risparmi e prestiti
savings bank *n* cassa *f* di risparmio
saviour /ˈseɪvjə(r)/ *n* salvatore, -trice *mf*
savoir faire /sævwɑːˈfeə(r)/ *n* (social) savoir-faire *m*
savory /ˈseɪvərɪ/ *n* Bot santoreggia *f*
savour /ˈseɪvə(r)/ **A** *n* sapore *m*
B *vt* assaporare
savoury /ˈseɪvərɪ/ *adj* salato; fig rispettabile
saw¹ /sɔː/ ▶ **see¹**
saw² **A** *n* sega *f*
B *vt* (*pt* **sawed**, *pp* **sawn** *or* **sawed**) segare
sawdust /ˈsɔːdʌst/ *n* segatura *f*
sawmill /ˈsɔːmɪl/ *n* segheria *f*
sawn-off shotgun *n* fucile *m* a canne mozze
Saxon /ˈsæksən/ *adj & n* sassone *mf*; (language) sassone *m*
saxophone /ˈsæksəfəʊn/ *n* sassofono *m*
saxophonist /sækˈsɒfənɪst/ *n* sassofonista *mf*
✐ **say** /seɪ/ **A** *n* **have one's ~** dire la propria; **have a ~** avere voce in capitolo
B *vt & vi* (*pt/pp* **said**) dire; **that is to ~** cioè; **that goes without ~ing** questo è ovvio; **when all is said and done** alla fine dei conti; **~ yes/no** dire di sì/no; **just ~ the word and I'll come** tu chiama e io vengo; **what more can I ~?** che altro dire?; **some time next week ~?** la prossima settimana, diciamo?; **the clock ~s ten to six** la sveglia fa le sei meno dieci; **you can ~ that again!** puoi dirlo forte!; **the tree is said to be very old** a quanto pare l'albero è vecchissimo; **he said you were to bring the car** ha detto che dovevi portare la macchina; **it ~s a lot for him that ...** il fatto che... la dice lunga sul suo conto; **what have you got to ~ for yourself?** che scusa hai?; **to ~ nothing of ...** per non parlare di...; **what would you ~ to a new car?** cosa ne diresti di una macchina nuova?
saying /ˈseɪɪŋ/ *n* proverbio *m*
scab /skæb/ *n* crosta *f*; derog crumiro *m*
scabby /ˈskæbɪ/ *adj* ‹*plant*› coperto di galle; ‹*skin*› coperto di croste; ‹*animal*› rognoso; infml (nasty) schifoso
scaffold /ˈskæfəld/ *n* patibolo *m*
scaffolding /ˈskæfəldɪŋ/ *n* impalcatura *f*
scalar /ˈskeɪlə(r)/ *adj* scalare
scald /skɔːld/ **A** *vt* scottare; ‹*milk*› scaldare
B *n* scottatura *f*
scalding /ˈskɔːldɪŋ/ *adj* bollente
scale¹ /skeɪl/ *n* (of fish) scaglia *f*
✐ **scale²** **A** *n* scala *f*; **on a grand ~** su vasta

scala; **to ~** in scala; **~ of values** scala *f* di valori
B *vt* (climb) scalare
▪ **scale down** *vt* diminuire
scale drawing *n* disegno *m* in scala
scale model *n* modello *m* in scala
scales /skeɪlz/ *npl* (for weighing) bilancia *fsg*
scallop /ˈskɒləp/ **A** *n* (in sewing) smerlo *m*, festone *m*; Zool pettine *m*; Culin cappasanta *f*
B *vt* (in sewing) smerlare; **~ed potatoes** patate *fpl* gratinate
scalp /skælp/ **A** *n* cuoio *m* capelluto
B *vt* scalpare
scalpel /ˈskælpl/ *n* bisturi *m inv*
scalper /ˈskælpə(r)/ *n* AmE bagarino *m*
scaly /ˈskeɪlɪ/ *adj* ‹*wing, fish*› squamoso; ‹*plaster, wall*› scrostato
scam /skæm/ *n* infml fregatura *f*
scamper /ˈskæmpə(r)/ *vi* **~ away** sgattaiolare via
scampi /ˈskæmpɪ/ *npl* scampi *mpl*
scan /skæn/ **A** *n* Med scanning *m inv*, scansioscintigrafia *f*
B *vt* (*pt/pp* **scanned**) scrutare; (quickly) dare una scorsa a; Med fare uno scanning di; Comput scannerizzare
C *vi* ‹*poetry*› scandire
scandal /ˈskændl/ *n* scandalo *m*; (gossip) pettegolezzi *mpl*
scandalize /ˈskændəlaɪz/ *vt* scandalizzare
scandalmonger /ˈskænd(ə)lmʌŋgə(r)/ *n* malalingua *f*
scandalous /ˈskændələs/ *adj* scandaloso
Scandinavia /skændɪˈneɪvɪə/ *n* Scandinavia *f*
Scandinavian /skændɪˈneɪvɪən/ *adj & n* scandinavo, -a *mf*
scanner /ˈskænə(r)/ *n* Med, Comput scanner *m inv*; (radar) antenna *f* radar; (for bar codes) lettore *m* di codice a barre
scanning /ˈskænɪŋ/ *n* Comput scannerizzazione *f*
scant /skænt/ *adj* scarso
scantily /ˈskæntɪlɪ/ *adv* scarsamente; ‹*clothed*› succintamente
scanty /ˈskæntɪ/ *adj* (**-ier**, **-iest**) scarso; ‹*clothing*› succinto
scapegoat /ˈskeɪpgəʊt/ *n* capro *m* espiatorio
scar /skɑː(r)/ **A** *n* cicatrice *f*
B *vt* (*pt/pp* **scarred**) lasciare una cicatrice a
scarce /skeəs/ *adj* scarso; fig raro; **make oneself ~** infml svignarsela
scarcely /ˈskeəslɪ/ *adv* appena; **~ anything** quasi niente
scarcity /ˈskeəsətɪ/ *n* scarsezza *f*
scare /skeə(r)/ **A** *n* spavento *m*; (panic) panico *m*
B *vt* spaventare; **be ~d** aver paura (**of** di)
▪ **scare away** *vt* far scappare
scarecrow /ˈskeəkrəʊ/ *n* spaventapasseri *m inv*
scaremonger /ˈskeəmʌŋgə(r)/ *n* allarmista *mf*
scaremongering /ˈskeəmʌŋgərɪŋ/ *n* allarmismo *m*
scarf /skɑːf/ *n* (*pl* **scarves**) sciarpa *f*; (square) foulard *m inv*
scarlet /ˈskɑːlət/ *adj* scarlatto
scarlet fever *n* scarlattina *f*
scarper /ˈskɑːpə(r)/ *vi* BrE infml squagliarsela
Scart connector *n* presa *f* scart *inv*
scar tissue *n* tessuto *m* di cicatrizzazione
scary /ˈskeərɪ/ *adj* **be ~** far paura
scathing /ˈskeɪðɪŋ/ *adj* mordace
scatter /ˈskætə(r)/ **A** *vt* spargere; (disperse) disperdere
B *vi* disperdersi
scatterbrained /ˈskætəbreɪnd/ *adj* infml scervellato
scattered /ˈskætəd/ *adj* sparso
scatty /ˈskætɪ/ *adj* (**-ier**, **-iest**) infml svitato
scavenge /ˈskævɪndʒ/ *vi* frugare nella spazzatura
scavenger /ˈskævɪndʒə(r)/ *n persona* (*f*) *che fruga nella spazzatura*
scenario /sɪˈnɑːrɪəʊ/ *n* scenario *m*
🔑 **scene** /siːn/ *n* scena *f*; (quarrel) scenata *f*; **behind the ~s** dietro le quinte
scene-of-crime *adj* ‹*officer, team, investigation*› della polizia scientifica
scenery /ˈsiːnərɪ/ *n* scenario *m*
scenic /ˈsiːnɪk/ *adj* panoramico
scent /sent/ *n* odore *m*; (trail) scia *f*; (perfume) profumo *m*
scented /ˈsentɪd/ *adj* profumato (**with** di)
sceptic /ˈskeptɪk/ *n* scettico, -a *mf*
sceptical /ˈskeptɪkl/ *adj* scettico
sceptically /ˈskeptɪklɪ/ *adv* in modo scettico
scepticism /ˈskeptɪsɪzm/ *n* scetticismo *m*
schedule /ˈʃedjuːl/ **A** *n* piano *m*, programma *m*; (of work) programma *m*; AmE (timetable) orario *m*; **behind ~** indietro; **on ~** nei tempi previsti; **according to ~** secondo i tempi previsti
B *vt* prevedere
scheduled flight /ʃedjuːldˈflaɪt/ *n* volo *m* di linea
schematic /skɪˈmætɪk/ *adj* schematico
🔑 **scheme** /skiːm/ **A** *n* (plan) piano *m*; (plot) macchinazione *f*
B *vi* derog macchinare
scheming /ˈskiːmɪŋ/ **A** *n* derog macchinazioni *fpl*, intrighi *mpl*
B *adj* ‹*person*› intrigante
schism /ˈskɪzm/ *n* scisma *m*
schizophrenia /skɪtsəˈfriːnɪə/ *n* schizofrenia *f*
schizophrenic /ˌskɪtsəʊˈfrenɪk/ *adj* schizofrenico
schmaltzy /ˈʃmɒltsɪ/ *adj* sdolcinato
scholar /ˈskɒlə(r)/ *n* studioso, -a *mf*

scholarly /ˈskɒləlɪ/ *adj* erudito

scholarship /ˈskɒləʃɪp/ *n* erudizione *f*; (grant) borsa *f* di studio

scholastic /skəˈlæstɪk/ *adj* scolastico

🔑 **school** /skuːl/ **A** *n* scuola *f*; (in university) facoltà *f*; (of fish) banco *m*
B *vt* addestrare ‹*animal*›

school age *n* **of ~** in età scolare

school bag *n* cartella *f* di scuola

schoolboy *n* scolaro *m*

schoolchild *n* scolaro, -a *mf*

schooldays *npl* tempi *mpl* della scuola

school fees *npl* tasse *fpl* scolastiche

school friend *n* compagno, -a *mf* di scuola

schoolgirl *n* scolara *f*

schooling /ˈskuːlɪŋ/ *n* istruzione *f*

school leaver *n* ≈ neo diplomato, -a *mf*

school-leaving age *n* età *f* della scuola dell'obbligo

school lunch *n* pranzo *m* della mensa scolastica

schoolmaster *n* maestro *m*; (secondary) insegnante *m*

schoolmistress *n* maestra *f*; (secondary) insegnante *f*

school report *n* scheda *f* di valutazione scolastica

schoolteacher *n* insegnante *mf*

schoolwork /ˈskuːlwɜːk/ *n* lavoro *m* scolastico

schooner /ˈskuːnə(r)/ *n* AmE (glass) boccale *m* da birra; BrE (glass) grande bicchiere *m* da sherry; (boat) goletta *f*

sciatica /saɪˈætɪkə/ *n* sciatica *f*

🔑 **science** /ˈsaɪəns/ *n* scienza *f*

science fiction *n* fantascienza *f*

🔑 **scientific** /saɪənˈtɪfɪk/ *adj* scientifico

scientifically /saɪənˈtɪfɪklɪ/ *adv* scientificamente

🔑 **scientist** /ˈsaɪəntɪst/ *n* scienziato, -a *mf*

sci-fi /ˈsaɪfaɪ/ *n* infml fantascienza *f*

scintillate /ˈsɪntɪleɪt/ *vi* fig brillare

scintillating /ˈsɪntɪleɪtɪŋ/ *adj* brillante

scissors /ˈsɪzəz/ *npl* forbici *fpl*

scoff¹ /skɒf/ *vi* **~ at** schernire

scoff² *vt* infml divorare

scold /skəʊld/ *vt* sgridare

scolding /ˈskəʊldɪŋ/ *n* sgridata *f*

scollop /ˈskɒləp/ = **scallop**

scone /skɒn/ *n pasticcino (m) da tè*

scoop /skuːp/ *n* paletta *f*; Journ scoop *m inv*

▪ **scoop out** *vt* svuotare

▪ **scoop up** *vt* tirar su

scoot /skuːt/ *vi* infml filare

scooter /ˈskuːtə(r)/ *n* motoretta *f*

scope /skəʊp/ *n* portata *f*; (opportunity) opportunità *f*

scorch /skɔːtʃ/ *vt* bruciare

scorcher /ˈskɔːtʃə(r)/ *n* infml giornata *f* torrida

scorching /ˈskɔːtʃɪŋ/ *adj* caldissimo

🔑 **score** /skɔː(r)/ **A** *n* punteggio *m*; Mus partitura *f*; (for film, play) musica *f*; **a ~ [of]** (twenty) una ventina [di]; **keep [the] ~** tenere il punteggio; **on that ~** a questo proposito
B *vt* segnare ‹*goal*›; (cut) incidere
C *vi* far punti; (in football etc) segnare; (keep score) tenere il punteggio

▪ **score out** *vt* cancellare

scoreboard /ˈskɔːbɔːd/ *n* tabellone *m* segnapunti

scorer /ˈskɔːrə(r)/ *n* segnapunti *m inv*; (of goals) giocatore, -trice *mf* che segna; **top ~** cannoniere *m*

scorn /skɔːn/ **A** *n* disprezzo *m*
B *vt* disprezzare

scornful /ˈskɔːnfʊl/ *adj* sprezzante

scornfully /ˈskɔːnfʊlɪ/ *adv* sdegnosamente

Scorpio /ˈskɔːpɪəʊ/ *n* Astr Scorpione *m*

scorpion /ˈskɔːpɪən/ *n* scorpione *m*

Scot /skɒt/ *n* scozzese *mf*

scotch /skɒtʃ/ *vt* far cessare

Scotch **A** *adj* scozzese
B *n* (whisky) whisky *m* [scozzese]

Scotch egg *n* BrE *polpetta (f) di salsiccia che racchiude un uovo sodo*

Scotch tape *n* AmE scotch® *m inv*

scot-free *adj* **get off ~** cavarsela impunemente

Scotland /ˈskɒtlənd/ *n* Scozia *f*

Scots, Scottish /skɒts, ˈskɒtɪʃ/ *adj* scozzese

scoundrel /ˈskaʊndrəl/ *n* mascalzone *m*

scour¹ /ˈskaʊə(r)/ *vt* (search) perlustrare

scour² *vt* (clean) strofinare

scourer /ˈskaʊərə(r)/ *n* (pad) paglietta *f*

scourge /skɜːdʒ/ *n* flagello *m*

scouring pad /ˈskaʊərɪŋ/ *n* paglietta *f* in lana d'acciaio

scout /skaʊt/ **A** *n* Mil esploratore *m*
B *vi* **~ (around) for** andare in cerca di

Scout *n* **[Boy] ~** [boy]scout *m inv*

scowl /skaʊl/ **A** *n* sguardo *m* torvo
B *vi* guardare storto

Scrabble® /ˈskræbl/ *n* Scarabeo® *m*

▪ **scrabble around** *vi* (search) cercare a tastoni

scraggy /ˈskrægɪ/ *adj* (**-ier**, **-iest**) derog scarno

scram /skræm/ *vi* infml levarsi dai piedi

scramble /ˈskræmbl/ **A** *n* (climb) arrampicata *f*
B *vi* (clamber) arrampicarsi; **~ for** azzuffarsi per
C *vt* Teleph creare delle interferenze in; ‹*eggs*› strapazzare

scrambled eggs /ˈskræmbəld/ *npl* uova *fpl* strapazzate

🔑 parola chiave

scrambler /ˈskræmblə(r)/ *n* BrE (motorcyclist) [moto]crossista *mf*

scrambling /ˈskræmblɪŋ/ *n* (sport) motocross *m*

scrap¹ /skræp/ *n* infml (fight) litigio *m*

scrap² **A** *n* pezzetto *m*; (metal) ferraglia *f*; **~s** *pl* (of food) avanzi *mpl*
B *vt* (*pt/pp* **scrapped**) buttare via

scrapbook /ˈskræpbʊk/ *n* album *m inv*

scrape /skreɪp/ *vt* raschiare; (damage) graffiare

■ **scrape by** *vi* (financially) sbarcare il lunario

■ **scrape in** *vi* (to university, school) entrare per il rotto della cuffia

■ **scrape out** *vt* (empty) svuotare ‹*bowl*›; (clean) scrostare ‹*pan*›

■ **scrape through** *vi* passare per un pelo

■ **scrape together** *vt* racimolare

scraper /ˈskreɪpə(r)/ *n* raschietto *m*

scrap heap *n* **be on the ~** fig essere inutile

scrap iron *n* ferraglia *f*

scrap merchant *n* ferrovecchio *m*

scrap paper *n* carta *f* qualsiasi

scrappy /ˈskræpɪ/ *adj* frammentario

scrapyard /ˈskræpjɑːd/ *n* deposito *m* di ferraglia; (for cars) cimitero *m* delle macchine

scratch /skrætʃ/ **A** *n* graffio *m*; (to relieve itch) grattata *f*; **start from ~** partire da zero; **up to ~** ‹*work*› all'altezza
B *vt* graffiare; (to relieve itch) grattare
C *vi* grattarsi

scratch card *n* gratta e vinci *m inv*

scratchy /ˈskrætʃɪ/ *adj* ‹*recording*› pieno di fruscii

scrawl /skrɔːl/ **A** *n* scarabocchio *m*
B *vt & vi* scarabocchiare

scrawny /ˈskrɔːnɪ/ *adj* (**-ier**, **-iest**) derog magro

⚷ **scream** /skriːm/ **A** *n* strillo *m*; **be a ~** infml ‹*situation, film, person*› essere uno spasso
B *vt & vi* strillare

scree /skriː/ *n* ghiaione *m*

screech /skriːtʃ/ **A** *n* stridore *m*; **~ of tyres** sgommata *f*
B *vi* stridere
C *vt* strillare

⚷ **screen** /skriːn/ **A** *n* paravento *m*; Cinema, TV, Comput schermo *m*
B *vt* proteggere; (conceal) riparare; proiettare ‹*film*›; ‹*candidates*› passare al setaccio; Med sottoporre a visita medica

screening /ˈskriːnɪŋ/ *n* Med visita *f* medica; (of film) proiezione *f*

screenplay *n* sceneggiatura *f*

screen saver *n* Comput salvaschermo *m*

screen test *n* Cinema provino *m*

screen writer *n* Cinema sceneggiatore, -trice *mf*

screw /skruː/ **A** *n* vite *f*
B *vt* avvitare; vulg trombare; **~ something to something** avvitare qualcosa a qualcosa

■ **screw up** *vt* (crumple) accartocciare; strizzare ‹*eyes*›; storcere ‹*face*›; sl (bungle) mandare all'aria; **~ up one's courage** prendere il coraggio a due mani

screwdriver /ˈskruːdraɪvə(r)/ *n* cacciavite *m inv*

screwed up /skruːd/ *adj* infml incasinato

screw top *n* tappo *m* a vite

screwy /ˈskruːɪ/ *adj* (**-ier**, **-iest**) infml svitato

scribble /ˈskrɪbl/ **A** *n* scarabocchio *m*
B *vt & vi* scarabocchiare

scrimmage /ˈskrɪmɪdʒ/ *n* (struggle) zuffa *f*; AmE (in football) mischia *f*

scrimp /skrɪmp/ *vi* risparmiare; **~ and save** risparmiare fino all'osso; **~ on something** risparmiare su qualcosa

script /skrɪpt/ *n* scrittura *f*; (of film etc) sceneggiatura *f*

Scriptures /ˈskrɪptʃəz/ *npl* Sacre Scritture *fpl*

scriptwriter /ˈskrɪptraɪtə(r)/ *n* sceneggiatore, -trice *mf*

scroll /skrəʊl/ **A** *n* rotolo *m* (*di pergamena*); (decoration) voluta *f*
B *vi* Comput far scorrere

■ **scroll down** Comput *vi* scorrere in giù

■ **scroll up** Comput *vi* scorrere in su

scroll bar *n* Comput barra *f* di scorrimento

Scrooge /skruːdʒ/ *n* infml tirchio, -a *mf*

scrotum /ˈskrəʊtəm/ *n* scroto *m*

scrounge /skraʊndʒ/ *vt & vi* scroccare

scrounger /ˈskraʊndʒə(r)/ *n* scroccone, -a *mf*

scrub¹ /skrʌb/ *n* (land) boscaglia *f*

scrub² *vt & vi* (*pt/pp* **scrubbed**) strofinare; infml (cancel) cancellare ‹*plan*›

■ **scrub up** *vi* ‹*doctor*› lavarsi; infml **~ up well** fare un figurone

scrubbing brush /ˈskrʌbɪŋ/ *n* spazzolone *m*

scruff /skrʌf/ *n* **by the ~ of the neck** per la collottola

scruffy /ˈskrʌfɪ/ *adj* (**-ier**, **-iest**) trasandato

scrum /skrʌm/ *n* (in rugby) mischia *f*

scrum half *n* mediano *m* di mischia

scrunch /skrʌntʃ/ **A** *vi* ‹*footsteps in snow, tyres*› scricchiolare
B *n* scricchiolio *m*

■ **scrunch up** *vt* accartocciare

scrunchie /ˈskrʌntʃɪ/ *n* fermacoda *m inv* di stoffa

scruple /ˈskruːpl/ *n* scrupolo *m*; **have no ~s** essere senza scrupoli

scrupulous /ˈskruːpjʊləs/ *adj* scrupoloso

scrupulously /ˈskruːpjʊləslɪ/ *adv* scrupolosamente

scrutinize /ˈskruːtɪnaɪz/ *vt* scrutinare

scrutiny /ˈskruːtɪnɪ/ *n* (look) esame *m* minuzioso

scuba diver /ˈskuːbə/ *n* sommozzatore, -trice *mf*

scuba diving *n* immersione *f* subacquea

scud /skʌd/ *vi* (*pt/pp* **scudded**) ‹*clouds*› muoversi velocemente

scuff /skʌf/ *vt* strascicare ‹*one's feet*›

scuffle /'skʌfl/ *n* tafferuglio *m*

scull /skʌl/ **A** *vi* (with two oars) vogare di coppia; (with one oar) vogare a bratto
B *n* (boat) imbarcazione *f* da regata con un vogatore

scullery /'skʌlərɪ/ *n* retrocucina *m inv*

sculpt /skʌlpt/ *vt & vi* scolpire

sculptor /'skʌlptə(r)/ *n* scultore *m*

sculpture /'skʌlptʃə(r)/ *n* scultura *f*

scum /skʌm/ *n* schiuma *f*; (people) feccia *f*

scurrilous /'skʌrɪləs/ *adj* scurrile

scurry /'skʌrɪ/ *vi* (*pt/pp* **-ied**) affrettare il passo

scuttle¹ /'skʌtl/ *n* secchio *m* per il carbone

scuttle² *vt* affondare ‹*ship*›

scuttle³ *vi* (hurry) ~ **away** correre via

scythe /saɪð/ *n* falce *f*

SE *abbr* (**south-east**) SE

🔑 **sea** /siː/ *n* mare *m*; **at** ~ in mare; fig confuso; **by** ~ via mare; **by the** ~ sul mare

seabed *n* fondale *m* marino

seabird *n* uccello *m* marino

seaboard *n* costiera *f*

seafaring *adj* ‹*nation*› marinaro

seafood *n* frutti *mpl* di mare

seafront /'siːfrʌnt/ *n* lungomare *m*

seagull *n* gabbiano *m*

sea horse *n* cavalluccio *m* marino

seal¹ /siːl/ *n* Zool foca *f*

seal² **A** *n* sigillo *m*; Techn chiusura *f* ermetica
B *vt* sigillare; Techn chiudere ermeticamente
■ **seal off** *vt* bloccare ‹*area*›

SEAL *n abbr* AmE (**sea, air, land**) reparti *mpl* speciali delle forze armate

sea level *n* livello *m* del mare; **above** ~ sopra il livello del mare

sealing wax /'siːlɪŋ/ *n* ceralacca *f*

sea lion *n* leone *m* marino

seam /siːm/ *n* cucitura *f*; (of coal) strato *m*

seaman /'siːmən/ *n* marinaio *m*

seamless /'siːmlɪs/ *adj* senza cucitura

seamy /'siːmɪ/ *adj* ‹*scandal*› sordido; ‹*area*› malfamato

seance /'seɪɑːns/ *n* seduta *f* spiritica

seaplane /'siːpleɪn/ *n* idrovolante *m*

seaport /'siːpɔːt/ *n* porto *m* di mare

sear /sɪə(r)/ *vt* cauterizzare ‹*wound*›; rosolare [a fuoco vivo] ‹*meat*›; (scorch) bruciacchiare

🔑 **search** /sɜːtʃ/ **A** *n* ricerca *f*; (official) perquisizione *f*; **in** ~ **of** alla ricerca di
B *vt* frugare (**for** alla ricerca di); perlustrare ‹*area*›; (officially) perquisire
C *vi* ~ **for** cercare

search and replace *n* Comput ricerca *f* e sostituzione

search engine *n* Comput motore *m* di ricerca

searching /'sɜːtʃɪŋ/ *adj* penetrante

searchlight *n* riflettore *m*

search party *n* squadra *f* di ricerca

search warrant *n* mandato *m* di perquisizione

searing /'sɪərɪŋ/ *adj* bruciante; ‹*pace*› travolgente; ‹*pain*› lancinante

sea salt *n* sale *m* marino

seascape *n* paesaggio *m* marino

seashell *n* conchiglia *f*

seashore /'siːʃɔː(r)/ *n* spiaggia *f*

seasick *adj* **be/get** ~ avere il mal di mare

seaside *n* **at/to the** ~ al mare

seaside resort *n* stazione *f* balneare

seaside town *n* città *f* di mare

🔑 **season** /'siːzn/ **A** *n* stagione *f*
B *vt* (flavour) condire; **in** ~ ‹*fruit*› di stagione; ‹*animal*› in calore

seasonal /'siːzənəl/ *adj* stagionale

seasoned /'siːznd/ *adj* Culin ‹*dish*› condito; ‹*timber*› stagionato; ‹*actor, politician*› consumato; ‹*leader*› di provata capacità; ~ **traveller** persona *f* che ha viaggiato molto; ~ **soldier** veterano *m*

seasoning /'siːz(ə)nɪŋ/ *n* condimento *m*

season ticket *n* abbonamento *m*

🔑 **seat** /siːt/ **A** *n* (chair) sedia *f*; (in car) sedile *m*; (place to sit) posto *m* [a sedere]; (bottom) didietro *m*; (of government) sede *f*; **take a** ~ sedersi
B *vt* mettere a sedere; (have seats for) aver posti [a sedere] per; **remain** ~**ed** mantenere il proprio posto

seat belt *n* cintura *f* di sicurezza; **fasten one's** ~ allacciare la cintura di sicurezza

seating /'siːtɪŋ/ *n* (places) posti *mpl* a sedere; (arrangement) disposizione *f* dei posti a sedere

seating capacity *n* numero *m* dei posti a sedere

sea urchin *n* riccio *m* di mare

sea view *n* vista *f* sul mare

seaweed *n* alga *f* marina

seaworthy *adj* in stato di navigare

sec /sek/ **A** *n* infml (short instant) attimo *m*, secondo *m*
B *abbr* (**second**) s

secateurs /sekə'tɜːz/ *npl* cesoie *fpl*

secede /sɪ'siːd/ *vi* staccarsi

secession /sɪ'seʃn/ *n* secessione *f*

secluded /sɪ'kluːdɪd/ *adj* appartato

seclusion /sɪ'kluːʒn/ *n* isolamento *m*

second¹ /sɪ'kɒnd/ *vt* (transfer) distaccare

🔑 **second²** /'sekənd/ **A** *adj* secondo; **in** ~ **gear** Auto in seconda; **on** ~ **thoughts** ripensandoci meglio; **be having** ~

🔑 parola chiave

thoughts ripensarci
B *n* secondo *m*; **~s** *pl* (goods) merce *fsg* di seconda scelta; **have ~s** (at meal) fare il bis; **John the S~** Giovanni Secondo
C *adv* (in race) al secondo posto
D *vt* assistere; appoggiare ‹*proposal*›

secondary /'sekəndrı/ *adj* secondario

secondary school *n* ≈ scuola *f* media (*inferiore e superiore*)

second-best *adj* secondo dopo il migliore; **be ~** derog essere un ripiego

second class *adv* ‹*travel, send*› in seconda classe

second-class *adj* di seconda classe

seconder /'sekəndə(r)/ *n* (of motion) persona *f* che appoggia una mozione

second-guess *vt* anticipare

second hand *n* (on watch, clock) lancetta *f* dei secondi

second-hand **A** *adj* ‹*car, goods, news, information*› di seconda mano; ‹*clothes*› usato; ‹*market*› dell'usato; ‹*opinion*› preso a prestito
B *adv* ‹*sell*› di seconda mano

second in command *n* vice *mf inv*; Mil vicecomandante *m*

secondly /'sekəndlı/ *adv* in secondo luogo

secondment /sı'kɒndmənt/ *n* **on ~** in trasferta

second name *n* (surname) cognome *m*; (middle name) secondo nome *m*

second-rate *adj* di second'ordine

secrecy /'si:krəsı/ *n* segretezza *f*; **in ~** in segreto

secret /'si:krıt/ **A** *adj* segreto
B *n* segreto *m*; **make no ~ of something** non fare mistero di qualcosa

secret agent *n* agente *m* segreto

secretarial /sekrə'teərıəl/ *adj* ‹*work, staff*› di segreteria

secretariat /sekrə'teərıət/ *n* segretariato *m*

secretary /'sekrətərı/ *n* segretario, -a *mf*

Secretary of State *n* Segretario *m* di Stato; AmE Pol ministro *m* degli Esteri

secret ballot *n* scrutinio *m* segreto, votazione *f* a scrutinio segreto

secrete /sı'kri:t/ *vt* secernere ‹*poison*›

secretion /sı'kri:ʃn/ *n* secrezione *f*

secretive /'si:krətıv/ *adj* riservato

secretly /'si:krıtlı/ *adv* segretamente

secret police *n* polizia *f* segreta

secret service *n* servizi *mpl* segreti

secret society *n* società *f* segreta

secret weapon *n* arma *f* segreta

sect /sekt/ *n* setta *f*

sectarian /sek'teərıən/ *n & adj* settario, -a *mf*

section /'sekʃn/ *n* sezione *f*

sector /'sektə(r)/ *n* settore *m*

secular /'sekjʊlə(r)/ *adj* secolare; ‹*education*› laico

secure /sı'kjʊə(r)/ **A** *adj* sicuro
B *vt* proteggere; chiudere bene ‹*door*›; rendere stabile ‹*ladder*›; (obtain) assicurarsi

securely /sı'kjʊəlı/ *adv* saldamente

secure unit *n* (in psychiatric hospital, prison) reparto *m* di massima sicurezza

security /sı'kjʊərətı/ *n* sicurezza *f*; (for loan) garanzia *f*; **securities** *pl* titoli *mpl*

security code /sı'kjʊərıtı kəʊd/ *n* codice *m* di sicurezza

Security Council *n* (of the UN) Consiglio *m* di Sicurezza

security guard *n* guardia *f* giurata

security leak *n* fuga *f* di notizie

security risk *n* **be a ~** costituire un pericolo per la sicurezza

sedan /sı'dæn/ *n* AmE berlina *f*

sedate¹ /sı'deıt/ *adj* posato

sedate² *vt* somministrare sedativi a

sedately /sı'deıtlı/ *adv* in modo posato

sedation /sı'deıʃn/ *n* somministrazione *f* di sedativi; **be under ~** essere sotto l'effetto di sedativi

sedative /'sedətıv/ **A** *adj* sedativo
B *n* sedativo *m*

sedentary /'sedəntərı/ *adj* sedentario

sediment /'sedımənt/ *n* sedimento *m*

seduce /sı'dju:s/ *vt* sedurre

seduction /sı'dʌkʃn/ *n* seduzione *f*

seductive /sı'dʌktıv/ *adj* seducente

seductively /sı'dʌktıvlı/ *adv* con aria seducente

see¹ /si:/ **A** *vt* (*pt* **saw**, *pp* **seen**) vedere; (understand) capire; (escort) accompagnare; **go and ~** andare a vedere; (visit) andare a trovare; **~ you!** ci vediamo!; **~ you later!** a più tardi!; **~ing that** visto che; **~ somebody to the door** accompagnare qualcuno alla porta; **I can't ~ myself doing this forever** non mi ci vedo a farlo per sempre; **I can't think what she ~s in him** non capisco cosa trovi in lui; **~ reason** ragionare; **you're ~ing things** hai le traveggole
B *vi* vedere; (understand) capire; **~ that** (make sure) assicurarsi che; **let me ~** (think) fammi pensare; **I ~** (understand) ho capito

- **see about** *vt* occuparsi di
- **see off** *vt* salutare alla partenza; (chase away) mandar via
- **see out**: *vt* **~ somebody out** accompagnare qualcuno alla porta
- **see through** **A** *vi* vedere attraverso; fig non farsi ingannare da
  B *vt* portare a buon fine
- **see to** *vi* occuparsi di

see² *n* Relig diocesi *f inv*

seed /si:d/ *n* seme *m*; Tennis testa *f* di serie; **go to ~** fare seme; fig lasciarsi andare

seeded player /'si:dıd/ *n* Tennis testa *f* di serie

seedless /'si:dlıs/ *adj* senza semi

seedling /ˈsiːdlɪŋ/ *n* pianticella *f*
seedy /ˈsiːdɪ/ *adj* (**-ier**, **-iest**) squallido; **feel ~** infml sentirsi poco bene
🔑 **seek** /siːk/ *vt* (*pt/pp* **sought**) cercare
■ **seek out** *vt* scovare
seeker /ˈsiːkə(r)/ *n* **~ after** *or* **for something** persona *f* che è alla ricerca di qualcosa; **gold ~** cercatore, -trice *mf* d'oro
🔑 **seem** /siːm/ *vi* sembrare
seeming /ˈsiːmɪŋ/ *adj* apparente
seemingly /ˈsiːmɪŋlɪ/ *adv* apparentemente
seemly /ˈsiːmlɪ/ *adj* decoroso
seen /siːn/ ▶ **see**[1]
seep /siːp/ *vi* filtrare
seepage /ˈsiːpɪdʒ/ *n* (leak: from container) perdita *f*; Geol trasudamento *m* superficiale; (trickle) lenta fuoriuscita *f*; (into structure, soil) infiltrazione *f*
see-saw /ˈsiːsɔː/ *n* altalena *f*
seethe /siːð/ *vi* **~ with anger** ribollire di rabbia
see-through *adj* trasparente
segment /ˈsegmənt/ *n* segmento *m*; (of orange) spicchio *m*
segregate /ˈsegrɪgeɪt/ *vt* segregare
segregated /ˈsegrəgeɪtɪd/ *adj* segregazionistico
segregation /segrɪˈgeɪʃn/ *n* segregazione *f*
seismic /ˈsaɪzmɪk/ *adj* sismico
seismograph /ˈsaɪzməgrɑːf/ *n* sismografo *m*
seismology /saɪzˈmɒlədʒɪ/ *n* sismologia *f*
seize /siːz/ *vt* afferrare; Jur confiscare; **~ the opportunity** prendere la palla al balzo
■ **seize up** *vi* Techn bloccarsi
seizure /ˈsiːʒə(r)/ *n* Jur confisca *f*; Med colpo *m* [apoplettico]
seldom /ˈseldəm/ *adv* raramente
🔑 **select** /sɪˈlekt/ **A** *adj* scelto; (exclusive) esclusivo
B *vt* scegliere; selezionare ‹*team*›
🔑 **selection** /sɪˈlekʃn/ *n* selezione *f*
selective /sɪˈlektɪv/ *adj* selettivo
selectively /sɪˈlektɪvlɪ/ *adv* con criterio
selector /sɪˈlektə(r)/ *n* Sport selezionatore, -trice *mf*
🔑 **self** /self/ *n* io *m*
self-addressed *adj* con il proprio indirizzo
self-addressed envelope *n* busta *f* affrancata con il proprio indirizzo
self-adhesive *adj* autoadesivo
self-analysis *n* autoanalisi *f*
self-assembly *adj* da montare
self-assurance *n* sicurezza *f* di sé
self-assured *adj* sicuro di sé
self-catering *adj* in appartamento attrezzato di cucina
self-centred *adj* egocentrico
self-cleaning *adj* ‹*oven*› autopulente

🔑 parola chiave

self-confessed *adj* dichiarato
self-confidence *n* fiducia *f* in se stesso
self-confident *adj* sicuro di sé
self-conscious *adj* impacciato
self-contained *adj* ‹*flat*› con ingresso indipendente
self-control *n* autocontrollo *m*
self-defence *n* autodifesa *f*; Jur legittima difesa *f*
self-denial *n* abnegazione *f*
self-destruct *vi* ‹*missile, spacecraft*› autodistruggersi
self-destruction *n* autodistruzione *f*; fig autolesionismo *m*
self-destructive *adj* autodistruttivo
self-determination *n* autodeterminazione *f*
self-discipline *n* autodisciplina *f*
self-disciplined *adj* disciplinato
self-effacing /-ɪˈfeɪsɪŋ/ *adj* modesto, schivo
self-employed *adj* che lavora in proprio; **the ~** i lavoratori autonomi
self-esteem *n* stima *f* di sé
self-evident *adj* ovvio
self-explanatory *adj* **be ~** parlare da sé
self-expression /ˌselfɪkˈspreʃn/ *n* espressione *f* della propria personalità
self-financing /-faɪˈnænsɪŋ/ *n* autofinanziamento *m*
self-governing /-ˈgʌvənɪŋ/ *adj* autonomo
self-government *n* autogoverno *m*
self-harm *n* autolesionismo *m*
self-help *n* iniziativa *f* personale
self-image *n* immagine *f* di sé
self-important *adj* borioso
self-imposed /-ɪmˈpəʊzd/ *adj* autoimposto
self-improvement *n* crescita *f* personale
self-induced /-ɪnˈdjuːst/ *adj* autoindotto
self-indulgent *adj* indulgente con se stesso
self-inflicted *adj* **Anna's problems are ~** sono problemi che Anna si è creata da sé; **~ wound** autolesione *f*
self-interest *n* interesse *m* personale
self-interested *adj* interessato
selfish /ˈselfɪʃ/ *adj* egoista
selfishly /ˈselfɪʃlɪ/ *adv* egoisticamente
selfishness /ˈselfɪʃnɪs/ *n* egoismo *m*
selfless /ˈselflɪs/ *adj* disinteressato
selflessly /ˈselflɪslɪ/ *adv* disinteressatamente
selflessness /ˈselflɪsnɪs/ *n* disinteresse *m*
self-locking /-ˈlɒkɪŋ/ *adj* ‹*door*› a chiusura automatica
self-made *adj* che si è fatto da sé
self-pity *n* autocommiserazione *f*
self-portrait *n* autoritratto *m*
self-possessed /-pəˈzest/ *adj* padrone di sé
self-preservation *n* istinto *m* di conservazione

self-raising flour BrE, **self-rising flour** AmE /'reɪzɪŋ, 'raɪzɪŋ/ *n* farina *f* autolievitante
self-reliant *adj* autosufficiente
self-respect *n* amor *m* proprio
self-respecting *adj* di rispetto
self-righteous *adj* presuntuoso
self-rule *n* autogoverno *m*
self-sacrifice *n* abnegazione *f*
selfsame *adj* stesso
self-satisfied *adj* compiaciuto di sé
self-service **A** *n* self-service *m inv*
B *attrib* self-service
self-styled *adj* sedicente
self-sufficiency *n* autosufficienza *f*
self-sufficient *adj* autosufficiente
self-supporting *adj* ‹*person*› indipendente (*economicamente*)
self-tan *n* autoabbronzante *m*
self-tanning /-'tænɪŋ/ *adj* autoabbronzante
self-taught /-'tɔːt/ *adj* ‹*person*› autodidatta
self-willed /-'wɪld/ *adj* ostinato
sell /sel/ **A** *vt* (*pt/pp* **sold**) vendere; **be sold out** essere esaurito; ~ **somebody on the idea of ...** infml convincere qualcuno di...
B *vi* vendersi
■ **sell off** *vt* liquidare
■ **sell out** *vi* (of tickets, goods) andare esaurito; **'sold out'** 'tutto esaurito'; ~ **out of something** esaurire qualcosa; (on one's principles) vendersi
■ **sell up** *vi* liquidare i propri beni
sell-by date *n* data *f* di scadenza per la vendita
seller /'selə(r)/ *n* venditore, -trice *mf*
sellers' market /'seləzmɑːkɪt/ *n* mercato *m* al rialzo
selling /'selɪŋ/ **A** *adj* ‹*price*› di vendita
B *n* vendita *f*
selling price /'selɪŋ/ *n* prezzo *m* di vendita
Sellotape® /'seləʊteɪp/ *n* nastro *m* adesivo, scotch® *m*
sell-out *n* infml (betrayal) tradimento *m*; **be a** ~ ‹*concert*› fare il tutto esaurito
selvage, **selvedge** /'selvɪdʒ/ *n* cimosa *f*
selves /selvz/ *pl of* **self**
semantic /sɪ'mæntɪk/ *adj* semantico
semantics /sɪ'mæntɪks/ *nsg* (subject) semantica *fsg*; **that's just** ~ sono solo sfumature di significato
semblance /'sembləns/ *n* parvenza *f*
semen /'siːmən/ *n* Anat liquido *m* seminale
semester /sɪ'mestə(r)/ *n* AmE semestre *m*
semi /'semɪ/ *n* BrE (house) villetta *f* bifamiliare; AmE Auto autoarticolato *m*
semi+ *pref* semi+
semi-automatic *adj* semiautomatico
semibreve *n* Mus semibreve *f*
semicircle *n* semicerchio *m*
semicircular *adj* semicircolare
semicolon *n* punto e virgola *m*
semi-conscious *adj* semiincosciente
semi-darkness *n* semioscurità *f*
semi-detached **A** *adj* gemella
B *n* casa *f* gemella
semi-final *n* semifinale *f*
semi-finalist *n* semifinalista *mf*
seminal /'semɪnəl/ *adj* (major) determinante
seminar /'semɪnɑː(r)/ *n* seminario *m*
seminary /'semɪnərɪ/ *n* seminario *m*
semi-precious *adj* semiprezioso; ~ **stone** pietra *f* dura
semi-skilled /-'skɪld/ *adj* qualificato
semi-skimmed /-'skɪmd/ *adj* parzialmente scremato
semitone *n* Mus semitono *m*
semolina /semə'liːnə/ *n* semolino *m*
senate /'senət/ *n* senato *m*
senator /'senətə(r)/ *n* senatore, -trice *mf*
send /send/ *vt & vi* (*pt/pp* **sent**) mandare; (by mail) spedire
■ **send away for** *vt* farsi spedire ‹*information etc*›
■ **send down** *vt* (send to prison) mandare in galera
■ **send for** *vt* mandare a chiamare ‹*person*›; far venire ‹*thing*›
■ **send in** *vt* presentare ‹*application*›; far entrare ‹*person*›
■ **send off** *vt* spedire ‹*letter, parcel*›; espellere ‹*footballer*›
■ **send on** *vt* spedire ‹*luggage, letter, parcel*›
■ **send out** *vt* emettere ‹*light, heat*›; mandare fuori della porta ‹*pupil*›
■ **send up** *vt* infml parodiare
sender /'sendə(r)/ *n* mittente *mf*; **return to** ~ (on letter) rispedire al mittente
send-off *n* commiato *m*
send-up *n* BrE infml parodia *f*
Senegal /,senɪ'gɔːl/ *n* Senegal *m*
senile /'siːnaɪl/ *adj* arteriosclerotico
senile dementia /dɪ'menʃə/ *n* demenza *f* senile
senility /sɪ'nɪlətɪ/ *n* senilismo *m*
senior /'siːnɪə(r)/ **A** *adj* più vecchio; (in rank) superiore
B *n* (in rank) superiore *mf*; (in sport) senior *mf*; **she's two years my** ~ è più vecchia di me di due anni
senior citizen *n* anziano, -a *mf*
senior high school *n* AmE *scuola (f) superiore*
seniority /siːnɪ'ɒrətɪ/ *n* anzianità *f* di servizio
senior management *n* alta dirigenza *f*
sensation /sen'seɪʃn/ *n* sensazione *f*; **cause a** ~ fare scalpore
sensational /sen'seɪʃənəl/ *adj* sensazionale
sensationalist /sen'seɪʃənəlɪst/ *adj* ‹*headline, report*› sensazionalistico

sensationalize /sen'seɪʃənəlaɪz/ *vt* derog dare un tono scandalistico a
sensationally /sen'seɪʃənəlɪ/ *adv* in modo sensazionale
⚷ **sense** /sens/ **A** *n* senso *m*; (common) ~ buon senso *m*; **in a ~** in un certo senso; **make ~** aver senso
B *vt* sentire
senseless /'senslɪs/ *adj* insensato; (unconscious) privo di sensi
senselessly /'senslɪslɪ/ *adv* insensatamente
sensible /'sensəbl/ *adj* sensato; (suitable) appropriato
sensibly /'sensəblɪ/ *adv* in modo appropriato
sensitive /'sensətɪv/ *adj* sensibile; (touchy) suscettibile
sensitively /'sensətɪvlɪ/ *adv* con sensibilità
sensitivity /sensə'tɪvətɪ/ *n* sensibilità *f*
sensitize /'sensɪtaɪz/ *vt* **become ~d to** (allergic to) diventare ipersensibile a
sensor /'sensə(r)/ *n* sensore *m*
sensory /'sensərɪ/ *adj* sensoriale
sensual /'sensjʊəl/ *adj* sensuale
sensuality /sensjʊ'ælətɪ/ *n* sensualità *f*
sensuous /'sensjʊəs/ *adj* voluttuoso
sent /sent/ ▶ **send**
⚷ **sentence** /'sentəns/ **A** *n* frase *f*; Jur sentenza *f*; (punishment) condanna *f*
B *vt* ~ **to** condannare a
sentiment /'sentɪmənt/ *n* sentimento *m*; (opinion) opinione *f*; (sentimentality) sentimentalismo *m*
sentimental /sentɪ'mentl/ *adj* sentimentale; derog sentimentalista
sentimentality /sentɪmen'tælətɪ/ *n* sentimentalità *f*
sentinel /'sentɪnəl/ *n* sentinella *f*
sentry /'sentrɪ/ *n* sentinella *f*
separable /'sepərəbl/ *adj* separabile
⚷ **separate¹** /'sepərət/ *adj* separato
separate² /'sepəreɪt/ **A** *vt* separare
B *vi* separarsi
separately /'sepərətlɪ/ *adv* separatamente
separates /'sepərəts/ *npl* [indumenti *mpl*] coordinati *mpl*
separation /sepə'reɪʃn/ *n* separazione *f*
separatist /'sepərətɪst/ *n & adj* separatista *mf*
sepia /'si:pɪə/ *n* (colour) seppia *m*
⚷ **September** /sep'tembə(r)/ *n* settembre *m*
septic /'septɪk/ *adj* settico; **go ~** infettarsi
septicaemia /septɪ'si:mɪə/ *n* setticemia *f*
septic tank *n* fossa *f* biologica
sequel /'si:kwəl/ *n* seguito *m*
sequence /'si:kwəns/ *n* sequenza *f*; **in ~** nell'ordine giusto
sequential /sɪ'kwenʃəl/ *adj* sequenziale
sequin /'si:kwɪn/ *n* lustrino *m*, paillette *f inv*
Serb /sɜ:b/ *adj & n* serbo, -a *mf*

⚷ parola chiave

Serbia /'sɜ:bɪə/ *n* Serbia *f*
Serbian /'sɜ:bɪən/ **A** *n* serbo, -a *mf*; (language) serbo *m*
B *adj* serbo
Serbo-Croat /sɜ:bəʊ'krəʊæt/, **Serbo-Croatian** /sɜ:bəʊkrəʊ'eɪʃən/ **A** *n* (language) serbo-croato *m*
B *adj* serbo-croato
serenade /serə'neɪd/ **A** *n* serenata *f*
B *vt* fare una serenata a
serene /sɪ'ri:n/ *adj* sereno
serenely /sɪ'ri:nlɪ/ *adv* serenamente
serenity /sɪ'renətɪ/ *n* serenità *inv*
sergeant /'sɑ:dʒənt/ *n* sergente *m*
sergeant major *n* sergente *m* maggiore
serial /'sɪərɪəl/ **A** *n* racconto *m* a puntate; TV sceneggiato *m* a puntate; Radio commedia *f* radiofonica a puntate
B *adj* Comput seriale
serialize /'sɪərɪəlaɪz/ *vt* pubblicare a puntate; Radio, TV trasmettere a puntate
serial killer *n* serial killer *mf inv*
serial number *n* numero *m* di serie
serial port *n* Comput porta *f* seriale
⚷ **series** /'sɪəri:z/ *n* serie *f inv*
⚷ **serious** /'sɪərɪəs/ *adj* serio; ‹*illness, error*› grave
⚷ **seriously** /'sɪərɪəslɪ/ *adv* seriamente; ‹*ill*› gravemente; **take ~** prendere sul serio
seriousness /'sɪərɪəsnɪs/ *n* serietà *f*; (of situation) gravità *f*
sermon /'sɜ:mən/ *n* predica *f*
seropositive /sɪərəʊ'pɒzɪtɪv/ *adj* sieropositivo
serotonin /serə'təʊnɪn/ *n* serotonina *f*
serpent /'sɜ:pənt/ *n* serpente *m*
serrated /se'reɪtɪd/ *adj* dentellato
serum /'sɪərəm/ *n* siero *m*
servant /'sɜ:vənt/ *n* domestico, -a *mf*
⚷ **serve** /sɜ:v/ **A** *n* Tennis servizio *m*
B *vt* servire; Jur notificare ‹*writ*› (**on somebody** a qualcuno); scontare ‹*sentence*›; **~ its purpose** servire al proprio scopo; **it ~s you right!** ben ti sta!; **~s two** per due persone
C *vi* prestare servizio; Tennis servire; **~ as** servire da
server /'sɜ:və(r)/ *n* (piece of cutlery) posata *f* da portata; (plate) piatto *m* da portata; (tray) vassoio *m* da portata; Sport giocatore, -trice *mf* che effettua il servizio; Comput server *m inv*
⚷ **service** /'sɜ:vɪs/ **A** *n* servizio *m*; Relig funzione *f*; (maintenance) revisione *f*; **~s** *pl* forze *fpl* armate; (on motorway) area *f* di servizio; **in the ~s** sotto le armi; **of ~ to** utile a; **out of ~** ‹*machine*› guasto
B *vt* Techn revisionare
serviceable /'sɜ:vɪsəbl/ *adj* utilizzabile; (hard-wearing) resistente; (practical) pratico
service area *n* area *f* di servizio

S

service centre BrE, **service center** AmE *n* (garage) officina *f*; (in shop) centro *m* di assistenza tecnica

service charge *n* servizio *m*

service company *n* compagnia *f* del settore terziario

service industry *n* industria *f* terziaria

serviceman *n* militare *m*

service provider *n* fornitore *m* di servizi Internet

service road *n* strada *f* d'accesso

service station *n* stazione *f* di servizio

servicewoman *n* soldatessa *f*

serviette /sɜːvɪ'et/ *n* tovagliolo *m*

servile /'sɜːvaɪl/ *adj* servile

servility /sə'vɪlɪtɪ/ *n* servilismo *m*

serving /'sɜːvɪŋ/ **A** *adj* ‹*officer*› di carriera
B *n* (helping) porzione *f*

serving dish *n* piatto *m* da portata

serving spoon *n* cucchiaio *m* da servizio

⚷ **session** /'seʃn/ *n* seduta *f*; Jur sessione *f*; Univ anno *m* accademico

⚷ **set** /set/ **A** *n* serie *f inv*, set *m inv*; (of crockery, cutlery) servizio *m*; TV, Radio apparecchio *m*; Math insieme *m*; Theat scenario *m*; Cinema, Tennis set *m inv*; (of people) circolo *m*; (of hair) messa *f* in piega
B *adj* (ready) pronto; (rigid) fisso; ‹*book*› in programma; **be ~ on doing something** essere risoluto a fare qualcosa; **be ~ in one's ways** essere abitudinario
C *vt* (*pt/pp* **set**, *pres p* **setting**) mettere, porre; mettere ‹*alarm clock*›; assegnare ‹*task, homework*›; fissare ‹*date, limit*›; chiedere ‹*questions*›; montare ‹*gem*›; assestare ‹*bone*›; apparecchiare ‹*table*›; Typ comporre; **~ fire to** dare fuoco a; **~ free** liberare; **~ a good example** dare il buon esempio; **~ sail for** far vela per; **~ in motion** dare inizio a; **~ to music** musicare; **the film is ~ in Rome/the 18th century** il film è ambientato a Roma/nel XVIII secolo; **~ to music** musicare; **~ about doing something** mettersi a fare qualcosa
D *vi* ‹*sun*› tramontare; ‹*jelly, concrete*› solidificarsi; **~ to work (on something)** mettersi al lavoro (su qualcosa)

- **set apart** *vt* (distinguish) distinguere; **~ somebody** *or* **something apart from** distinguere qualcuno *o* qualcosa da
- **set aside** *vt* mettere da parte ‹*money, time*›; riservare ‹*room, area*›
- **set back** *vt* mettere indietro; (hold up) ritardare; infml (cost) costare a
- **set down** *vt* (establish) stabilire ‹*rules, conditions*›; (write down) scrivere ‹*facts*›
- **set in** *vi* ‹*rain, infection, recession*› prendere piede
- **set off A** *vi* partire
B *vt* avviare; mettere ‹*alarm*›; fare esplodere ‹*bomb*›
- **set on**: *vt* **~ on somebody** (attack) aggredire qualcuno; **~ the dogs on somebody** aizzare i cani contro qualcuno
- **set out A** *vi* partire; **~ out to do something** proporsi di fare qualcosa
B *vt* disporre; (state) esporre
- **set to** *vi* mettersi all'opera
- **set up** *vt* fondare ‹*company*›; istituire ‹*committee*›

setback /'setbæk/ *n* (hitch) contrattempo *m*; Mil sconfitta *f*, scacco *m*; Fin tracollo *m*; (in health) ricaduta *f*

set design *n* scenografia *f*

set designer *n* scenografo, -a *mf*

set meal *n* menù *m* fisso

settee /se'tiː/ *n* divano *m*

setter /'setə(r)/ *n* (dog) setter *m inv*

⚷ **setting** /'setɪŋ/ *n* scenario *m*; (position) posizione *f*; (of sun) tramonto *m*; (of jewel) montatura *f*

setting-up /ˌsetɪŋ'ʌp/ *n* (of project, business) creazione *f*

⚷ **settle** /'setl/ **A** *vt* (decide) definire; risolvere ‹*argument*›; fissare ‹*date*›; calmare ‹*nerves*›; saldare ‹*bill*›; **that's ~d then** allora è deciso
B *vi* (live) stabilirsi; ‹*snow, dust, bird*› posarsi; (subside) assestarsi; ‹*sediment*› depositarsi

- **settle down** *vi* sistemarsi; (stop making noise) calmarsi
- **settle for** *vt* accontentarsi di
- **settle in** *vi* (in new house, job) ambientarsi
- **settle up** *vi* regolare i conti

settlement /'setlmənt/ *n* (agreement) accordo *m*; (of bill) saldo *m*; Comm liquidazione *f*; (colony) insediamento *m*

settler /'setlə(r)/ *n* colonizzatore, -trice *mf*

set-to *n* infml zuffa *f*; (verbal) battibecco *m*

set-top box *n* decoder *m inv*

set-up *n* situazione *f*

⚷ **seven** /'sevn/ *adj & n* sette *m*

seventeen /sevən'tiːn/ *adj & n* diciassette *m*

seventeenth /sevən'tiːn/ *adj & n* diciasettesimo, -a *mf*

seventh /'sevnθ/ *adj & n* settimo, -a *mf*

seventies /'sevntɪz/ *npl* (period) **the ~** gli anni Settanta *mpl*; (age) settant'anni *mpl*

seventieth /'sevntɪɪθ/ *adj & n* settantesimo, -a *mf*

seventy /'sevntɪ/ *adj & n* settanta *m*

seven-year itch *n* infml crisi *f inv* del settimo anno

sever /'sevə(r)/ *vt* troncare ‹*relations*›

⚷ **several** /'sevrəl/ *adj & pron* parecchi

severance /'sev(ə)rəns/ *n* **~ pay** trattamento *m* di fine rapporto

⚷ **severe** /sɪ'vɪə(r)/ *adj* severo; ‹*pain*› violento; ‹*illness*› grave; ‹*winter*› rigido

severe acute respiratory syndrome *n* Med sindrome *f* respiratoria acuta severa

severely /sɪ'vɪəlɪ/ *adv* severamente; ‹*ill*› gravemente

S

severity /sɪ'verətɪ/ *n* severità *f*; (of pain) violenza *f*; (of illness) gravità *f*; (of winter) rigore *m*

sew /səʊ/ *vt & vi* (*pt* **sewed**, *pp* **sewn** *or* **sewed**) cucire

▪ **sew up** *vt* ricucire

sewage /'suːɪdʒ/ *n* acque *fpl* di scolo

sewer /'suːə(r)/ *n* fogna *f*

sewing /'səʊɪŋ/ *n* cucito *m*; (work) lavoro *m* di cucito

sewing machine *n* macchina *f* da cucire

sewn /səʊn/ ▸ **sew**

🗝 **sex** /seks/ *n* sesso *m*; **have ~** avere rapporti sessuali, fare l'amore

sex appeal *n* sex appeal *m*

sex change *n* **have a ~** cambiare sesso

sex change operation *n* intervento *m* per il cambiamento di sesso

sex discrimination *n* discriminazione *f* sessuale

sex education *n* educazione *f* sessuale

sexism /'seksɪzm/ *n* sessismo *m*

sexist /'seksɪst/ *adj* sessista *mf*

sex life *n* vita *f* sessuale

sex maniac *n* maniaco *m* sessuale

sex object *n* oggetto *m* sessuale

sex offender *n* colpevole *mf* di delitti a sfondo sessuale

sextet /seks'tet/ *n* sestetto *m*

sex tourism *n* turismo *m* a scopo sessuale

🗝 **sexual** /'seksjʊəl/ *adj* sessuale

sexual abuse *n* abusi *mpl* sessuali

sexual assault *n* atti *mpl* di libidine violenta

sexual equality *n* parità *f* dei sessi

sexual harassment *n* molestie *fpl* sessuali

sexual intercourse *n* rapporti *mpl* sessuali

sexuality /seksjʊ'ælətɪ/ *n* sessualità *f*

sexually /'seksjʊəlɪ/ *adv* sessualmente; **be ~ assaulted** subire atti di libidine violenta

S

sexually transmitted disease /trænz'mɪtɪd/ *n* malattia *f* trasmissibile per via sessuale

sexy /'seksɪ/ *adj* (**-ier**, **-iest**) sexy *inv*

Seychelles /seɪ'ʃelz/ *npl* **the ~** le Seychelles

sh /ʃ/ *int* silenzio!, sst!

shabbily /'ʃæbɪlɪ/ *adv* in modo scialbo; ‹*treat*› in modo meschino

shabbiness /'ʃæbɪnɪs/ *n* trasandatezza *f*; (of treatment) meschinità *f*

shabby /'ʃæbɪ/ *adj* (**-ier**, **-iest**) scialbo; ‹*treatment*› meschino

shack /ʃæk/ *n* catapecchia *f*

shackles /'ʃæklz/ *npl* catene *fpl*

shade /ʃeɪd/ **A** *n* ombra *f*; (of colour) sfumatura *f*; (for lamp) paralume *m*; AmE (for window) tapparella *f*; **a ~ better** un tantino meglio

B *vt* riparare dalla luce; (draw lines on) ombreggiare

shades /ʃeɪdz/ *npl* infml occhiali *mpl* da sole

shading /'ʃeɪdɪŋ/ *n* (slight variation in colour) tonalità *f*; (to give effect of darkness) ombreggiature *fpl*

shadow /'ʃædəʊ/ **A** *n* ombra *f*

B *vt* (follow) pedinare

shadow boxing *n* allenamento *m* di boxe con l'ombra

Shadow Cabinet *n* governo *m* ombra

shadowy /'ʃædəʊɪ/ *adj* (indistinct) confuso

shady /'ʃeɪdɪ/ *adj* (**-ier**, **-iest**) ombroso; infml (disreputable) losco

shaft /ʃɑːft/ *n* Techn albero *m*; (of light) raggio *m*; (of lift, mine) pozzo *m*; **~s** *pl* (of cart) stanghe *fpl*

shaggy /'ʃægɪ/ *adj* (**-ier**, **-iest**) irsuto; ‹*animal*› dal pelo arruffato

shaggy dog story *n* infml *barzelletta (f) interminabile dal finale deludente*

🗝 **shake** /ʃeɪk/ **A** *n* scrollata *f*

B *vt* (*pt* **shook**, *pp* **shaken**) scuotere; agitare ‹*bottle*›; far tremare ‹*building*›; **~ hands with** stringere la mano a; **~ one's head** scuotere la testa

C *vi* tremare

▪ **shake off** *vt* scrollarsi di dosso

▪ **shake up** *vt* agitare ‹*bottle*›; ‹*news, experience*› scuotere ‹*person*›

shaken, shaken up /'ʃeɪkən/ *adj* (after accident etc) scosso

shaker /'ʃeɪkə(r)/ *n* (for salad) centrifuga *f* [asciugaverdure]; (for dice) bicchiere *m*; (for cocktails) shaker *m inv*; (for pepper) pepaiola *f*; (for salt) saliera *f*

shake-up *n* Pol rimpasto *m*; Comm ristrutturazione *f*

shakily /'ʃeɪkɪlɪ/ *adv* ‹*say something*› con voce tremante; ‹*walk*› con passo esitante

shaky /'ʃeɪkɪ/ *adj* (**-ier**, **-iest**) tremante; ‹*table etc*› traballante; (unreliable) vacillante

🗝 **shall** /ʃæl/ *v aux* **I ~ go** andrò; **we ~ see** vedremo; **what ~ I do?** cosa faccio?; **I'll come too, ~ I?** vengo anch'io, no?; **thou shalt not kill** literary non uccidere; **passengers ~ remain seated** i passeggeri devono rimanere seduti

shallot /ʃə'lɒt/ *n* scalogno *m*

shallow /'ʃæləʊ/ *adj* basso, poco profondo; ‹*dish*› poco profondo; fig superficiale

shallows /'ʃæləʊz/ *npl* secche *fpl*

sham /ʃæm/ **A** *adj* falso

B *n* finzione *f*; (person) spaccone, -a *mf*

C *vt* (*pt/pp* **shammed**) simulare

shambles /'ʃæmblz/ *n* caos *msg*

shame /ʃeɪm/ *n* vergogna *f*; **it's a ~ that** è un peccato che; **what a ~!** che peccato!; **~ on you!** vergognati!; **put somebody/something to ~** far sfigurare qualcuno/qualcosa

🗝 parola chiave

shamefaced /ʃeɪmˈfeɪst/ *adj* vergognoso
shameful /ˈʃeɪmfl/ *adj* vergognoso
shamefully /ˈʃeɪmfʊlɪ/ *adv* vergognosamente
shameless /ˈʃeɪmlɪs/ *adj* spudorato
shamelessly /ˈʃeɪmlɪslɪ/ *adv* spudoratamente
shampoo /ʃæmˈpuː/ **A** *n* shampoo *m inv*; **~ and set** shampoo *m inv* e messa in piega
B *vt* fare uno shampoo a ‹*carpet, person's hair etc*›
shamrock /ˈʃæmrɒk/ *n* trifoglio *m* (*simbolo dell'Irlanda*)
shandy /ˈʃændɪ/ *n bevanda* (*f*) *a base di birra e gassosa*
shank /ʃæŋk/ *n* garretto *m*; (of knife) manico *m*; (of golf club) impugnatura *f*; (of screw) gambo *m*; (of anchor) fuso *m*; (of person) gamba *f* (*dal ginocchio in giù*)
shan't /ʃɑːnt/ = *shall not*
shanty /ˈʃæntɪ/ *n* (hut) baracca *f*; (song) canto *m* marinaro
shanty town /ˈʃæntɪtaʊn/ *n* bidonville *f inv*, baraccopoli *f inv*
shape /ʃeɪp/ **A** *n* forma *f*; (figure) ombra *f*; **take ~** prendere forma; **get back in ~** ritornare in forma; **be out of ~** non essere in forma
B *vt* dare forma a (**into** di)
C *vi* **~ [up]** mettere la testa a posto; **~ up nicely** mettersi bene
shapeless /ˈʃeɪplɪs/ *adj* informe
shapely /ˈʃeɪplɪ/ *adj* (**-ier**, **-iest**) ben fatto
shard /ʃɑːd/ *n* frammento *m*; (of clay) coccio *m*
share /ʃeə(r)/ **A** *n* porzione *f*; Comm azione *f*
B *vt* dividere; condividere ‹*views*›
C *vi* dividere; **~ in** partecipare a
▪ **share out** *vt* spartire; (including oneself) spartirsi
share capital *n* capitale *m* azionario
shared /ʃeəd/ *adj* ‹*house*› condiviso; ‹*bathroom*› in comune
share dealing *n* contrattazione *f* di azioni
shareholder *n* azionista *mf*
shareholding *n* titoli *mpl* azionari
share index *n* indice *m* azionario
share option scheme *n partecipazione* (*f*) *agli utili dell'azienda tramite acquisto di azioni*
shareware /ˈʃeəweə(r)/ *n* Comput shareware *m inv*
shark /ʃɑːk/ *n* squalo *m*, pescecane *m*; fig truffatore, -trice *mf*
sharp /ʃɑːp/ **A** *adj* ‹*knife etc*› tagliente; ‹*pencil*› appuntito; ‹*drop*› a picco; ‹*reprimand*› severo; ‹*outline*› marcato; (alert) acuto; (unscrupulous) senza scrupoli; **~ pain** fitta *f*
B *adv* **at three o'clock ~** alle tre in punto; **look ~!** sbrigati!
C *n* Mus diesis *m inv*
sharpen /ˈʃɑːpn/ *vt* affilare ‹*knife*›; appuntire ‹*pencil*›
sharpener /ˈʃɑːpnə(r)/ *n* (for pencils) temperamatite *m inv*; (for knife) affilacoltelli *m inv*
sharply /ˈʃɑːplɪ/ *adv* ‹*turn, rise, fall*› bruscamente; ‹*speak*› in tono brusco
shatter /ˈʃætə(r)/ *vt* frantumare; fig mandare in frantumi
shattered /ˈʃætəd/ **A** *adj* infml (exhausted) a pezzi
B *vi* frantumarsi
shave /ʃeɪv/ **A** *n* rasatura *f*; **have a ~** farsi la barba
B *vt* radere
C *vi* radersi
shaver /ˈʃeɪvə(r)/ *n* rasoio *m* elettrico
shaving brush *n* pennello *m* da barba
shaving foam *n* schiuma *f* da barba
shavings /ˈʃeɪvɪŋz/ *npl* (of wood, metal) trucioli *mpl*
shaving soap *n* sapone *m* da barba
shawl /ʃɔːl/ *n* scialle *m*
she /ʃiː/ *pers pron* lei; **~ is tired** è stanca; **I'm going, but ~ is not** io vado, ma lei no
sheaf /ʃiːf/ *n* (*pl* **sheaves**) fascio *m*
shear /ʃɪə(r)/ *vt* (*pt* **sheared**, *pp* **shorn** *or* **sheared**) tosare
shears /ʃɪəz/ *npl* (for hedge) cesoie *fpl*
sheath /ʃiːθ/ *n* (*pl* **~s** /ʃiːðz/) guaina *f*
sheathe /ʃiːð/ *vt* rifoderare; rivestire ‹*cable*›
sheaves /ʃiːvz/ ▸ **sheaf**
shed[1] /ʃed/ *n* baracca *f*; (for cattle) stalla *f*
shed[2] *vt* (*pt/pp* **shed**, *pres p* **shedding**) perdere; versare ‹*blood, tears*›; **~ light on** far luce su
shedload *n* BrE infml **~s of money** un sacco di soldi
sheen /ʃiːn/ *n* lucentezza *f*
sheep /ʃiːp/ *n inv* pecora *f*
sheepdog /ˈʃiːpdɒg/ *n* cane *m* da pastore
sheepish /ˈʃiːpɪʃ/ *adj* imbarazzato
sheepishly /ˈʃiːpɪʃlɪ/ *adv* con aria imbarazzata
sheepskin /ˈʃiːpskɪn/ *n* [pelle *f* di] montone *m*
sheer /ʃɪə(r)/ **A** *adj* puro; (steep) a picco; (transparent) trasparente
B *adv* a picco
sheet /ʃiːt/ *n* lenzuolo *m*; (of paper) foglio *m*; (of glass, metal) lastra *f*
sheet lightning *n* bagliore *m* diffuso dei lampi; (without a storm) lampi *mpl* di calore
sheet metal *n* lamiera *f*
sheet music *n* spartiti *mpl*
sheikh /ʃeɪk/, **sheik** *n* sceicco *m*
shelf /ʃelf/ *n* (*pl* **shelves**) ripiano *m*; (set of shelves) scaffale *m*
shelf life *n* (of product) durata *f* di conservazione; fig (of technology, pop music) durata *f* di vita; fig (of politician, star) periodo *m* di gloria
shell /ʃel/ **A** *n* conchiglia *f*; (of egg, snail, tortoise) guscio *m*; (of crab) corazza *f*;

(of unfinished building) ossatura *f*; Mil granata *f*
B *vt* sgusciare ‹*peas*›; Mil bombardare
▪ **shell out** *vi* infml sborsare

shellfish *n inv* mollusco *m*; Culin frutti *mpl* di mare

shell-shocked /ˈʃelʃɒkt/ *adj* ‹*soldier*› traumatizzato da un bombardamento; fig in stato di shock

shell suit *n* tuta *f* di acetato

shelter /ˈʃeltə(r)/ **A** *n* rifugio *m*; (air raid) ~ rifugio *m* antiaereo; **take** ~ rifugiarsi
B *vt* riparare (**from** da); fig mettere al riparo; (give lodging to) dare asilo a
C *vi* rifugiarsi

sheltered /ˈʃeltəd/ *adj* ‹*spot*› riparato; ‹*life*› ritirato

sheltered accommodation *n* residenza *f* protetta

shelve /ʃelv/ **A** *vt* accantonare ‹*project*›
B *vi* ‹*slope*› scendere

shelves /ʃelvz/ ▸ **shelf**

shelving /ˈʃelvɪŋ/ *n* (shelves) ripiani *mpl*

shepherd /ˈʃepəd/ **A** *n* pastore *m*
B *vt* guidare

shepherdess /ˈʃepədes/ *n* pastora *f*

shepherd's pie /ʃepədzˈpaɪ/ *n pasticcio* (*m*) *di carne tritata e patate*

sherbet /ˈʃɜːbət/ *n* BrE (powder) polverina *f* effervescente al gusto di frutta; AmE (sorbet) sorbetto *m*

sheriff /ˈʃerɪf/ *n* sceriffo *m*

Sherpa /ˈʃɜːpə/ *n* scerpa *m*

sherry /ˈʃerɪ/ *n* sherry *m inv*

shield /ʃiːld/ **A** *n* scudo *m*; (for eyes) maschera *f*; Techn schermo *m*
B *vt* proteggere (**from** da)

🔑 **shift** /ʃɪft/ **A** *n* cambiamento *m*; (in position) spostamento *m*; (at work) turno *m*
B *vt* spostare; (take away) togliere; riversare ‹*blame*›
C *vi* spostarsi; ‹*wind*› cambiare; infml (move quickly) darsi una mossa

shift key *n* tasto *m* delle maiuscole

shiftless /ˈʃɪftlɪs/ *adj* privo di risorse

shift work *n* turni *mpl*

shift worker *n* turnista *mf*

shifty /ˈʃɪftɪ/ *adj* (**-ier**, **-iest**) derog losco; ‹*eyes*› sfuggente

Shiite /ˈʃiːaɪt/ *adj & n* sciita *mf*

shilling /ˈʃɪlɪŋ/ *n* scellino *m*

shilly-shally /ˈʃɪlɪʃælɪ/ *vi* titubare

shimmer /ˈʃɪmə(r)/ **A** *n* luccichio *m*
B *vi* luccicare

shin /ʃɪn/ **A** *n* stinco *m*
B *vi* ~ **up/down something** (climb) arrampicarsi su/scendere giù da qualcosa

shindig /ˈʃɪndɪg/ *n* infml (party) baldoria *f*; (disturbance) pandemonio *m*

🔑 parola chiave

shindy /ˈʃɪndɪ/ *n* infml (disturbance) pandemonio *m*; (party) baldoria *f*

shine /ʃaɪn/ **A** *n* lucentezza *f*; **give something a** ~ dare una lucidata a qualcosa
B *vi* (*pt/pp* **shone**) splendere; (reflect light) brillare; ‹*hair, shoes*› essere lucido
C *vt* ~ **a light on** puntare una luce su
▪ **shine through** *vi* ‹*talent, ability*› trasparire

shingle /ˈʃɪŋgl/ *n* (pebbles) ghiaia *f*

shingles /ˈʃɪŋglz/ *n* Med fuoco *m* di Sant'Antonio

shin guard *n* parastinchi *m inv*

shining /ˈʃaɪnɪŋ/ *adj* ‹*eyes, jewel*› splendente; ‹*hair*› lucente; **a** ~ **example** un fulgido esempio

shiny /ˈʃaɪnɪ/ *adj* (**-ier**, **-iest**) lucido

🔑 **ship** /ʃɪp/ **A** *n* nave *f*
B *vt* (*pt, pp* **-pped**) spedire; (by sea) spedire via mare

shipbuilder /ˈʃɪpbɪldə(r)/ *n* costruttore *m* navale

shipbuilding /ˈʃɪpbɪldɪŋ/ *n* costruzione *f* di navi

shipment /ˈʃɪpmənt/ *n* spedizione *f*; (consignment) carico *m*

shipowner /ˈʃɪpəʊnə(r)/ *n* armatore *m*

shipper /ˈʃɪpə(r)/ *n* spedizioniere *m*

shipping /ˈʃɪpɪŋ/ *n* trasporto *m*; (traffic) imbarcazioni *fpl*

shipping agent *n* spedizioniere *m*

shipping company *n* compagnia *f* di spedizione

shipshape *adj & adv* in perfetto ordine

shipwreck *n* naufragio *m*

shipwrecked *adj* naufragato

shipyard *n* cantiere *m* navale

shire /ʃaɪə(r)/ *n* BrE contea *f*

shire horse *n* cavallo *m* da tiro

shirk /ʃɜːk/ *vt* scansare

shirker /ˈʃɜːkə(r)/ *n* scansafatiche *mf inv*

🔑 **shirt** /ʃɜːt/ *n* camicia *f*; **in** ~ **sleeves** in maniche di camicia

shirty /ˈʃɜːtɪ/ *adj* BrE infml incavolato; **get** ~ **with somebody** incavolarsi con qualcuno

shish kebab /ʃɪʃkɪˈbæb/ *n spiedino* (*m*) *di carne e verdure*

shit /ʃɪt/ vulg **A** *n & int* merda *f*
B *vi* (*pt/pp* **shit**) cacare

shit-scared *adj* vulg **be** ~ farsela sotto

shiver /ˈʃɪvə(r)/ **A** *n* brivido *m*
B *vi* rabbrividire

shoal /ʃəʊl/ *n* (of fish) banco *m*

🔑 **shock** /ʃɒk/ **A** *n* (impact) urto *m*; Electr scossa *f* [elettrica]; fig colpo *m*, shock *m inv*; Med shock *m inv*; **get a** ~ Electr prendere la scossa; **in** ~ Med in stato di shock
B *vt* scioccare

shock absorber *n* Auto ammortizzatore *m*

shocking /ˈʃɒkɪŋ/ *adj* scioccante; infml ‹*weather, handwriting etc*› tremendo

S

shockingly /ˈʃɒkɪŋlɪ/ *adv* ‹*behave*› in modo pessimo; ‹*expensive*› eccessivamente
shocking pink *n* rosa *m* shocking
shockproof *adj* antiurto
shock treatment *n* terapia *f* d'urto
shock wave *n* onda *f* d'urto
shod /ʃɒd/ ▶ **shoe**
shoddily /ˈʃɒdɪlɪ/ *adv* in modo scadente
shoddy /ˈʃɒdɪ/ *adj* (**-ier**, **-iest**) scadente
shoe /ʃuː/ **A** *n* scarpa *f*; (of horse) ferro *m*
B *vt* (*pt/pp* **shod**, *pres p* **shoeing**) ferrare ‹*horse*›
shoehorn *n* calzante *m*
shoelace *n* laccio *m* da scarpa
shoemaker *n* calzolaio *m*
shoe rack *n* scarpiera *f*
shoe shop *n* calzoleria *f*
shoestring *n* **on a ~** infml con una miseria
shoe tree *n* forma *f* da scarpa
shone /ʃɒn/ ▶ **shine**
shoo /ʃuː/ **A** *vt* **~ away** cacciar via
B *int* sciò!
shook /ʃʊk/ ▶ **shake**
shoot /ʃuːt/ **A** *n* Bot germoglio *m*; (hunt) battuta *f* di caccia
B *vt* (*pt/pp* **shot**) sparare, girare ‹*film*›; **~ oneself in the foot** fig darsi la zappa sui piedi
C *vi* (hunt) andare a caccia
▪ **shoot down** *vt* abbattere
▪ **shoot out** *vi* (rush) precipitarsi fuori
▪ **shoot up** *vi* (grow) crescere in fretta; ‹*prices*› salire di colpo
shooting /ˈʃuːtɪŋ/ **A** *n* (pastime) caccia *f*; (killing) uccisione *f*
B *adj* ‹*pain*› lancinante
shooting range *n* poligono *m* di tiro
shooting star *n* stella *f* cadente
shoot-out *n* infml sparatoria *f*
shop /ʃɒp/ **A** *n* negozio *m*; (workshop) officina *f*; **talk ~** infml parlare di lavoro
B *vi* (*pt/pp* **shopped**, *pres p* **shopping**) far compere; **go ~ping** andare a fare compere
▪ **shop around** *vi* confrontare i prezzi
shopaholic /ʃɒpəˈhɒlɪk/ *n* fanatico, -a *mf* dello shopping
shop assistant *n* commesso, -a *mf*
shop floor *n* **problems on the ~** problemi tra gli operai
shopkeeper *n* negoziante *mf*
shoplifter *n* taccheggiatore, -trice *mf*
shoplifting *n* taccheggio *m*
shopper /ˈʃɒpə(r)/ *n* compratore, -trice *mf*
shopping /ˈʃɒpɪŋ/ *n* compere *fpl*; (articles) acquisti *mpl*; **do the ~** fare la spesa
shopping bag *n* borsa *f* per la spesa
shopping basket *n* Comput (on web site) carrello *m* della spesa
shopping cart *n* carrello *m* della spesa
shopping centre *n* centro *m* commerciale
shopping list *n* lista *f* della spesa
shopping mall *n* centro *m* commerciale
shopping trolley *n* carrello *m*
shop-soiled *adj* BrE ‹*garment*› sporco (per lunga permanenza in negozio)
shop steward *n* rappresentante *mf* sindacale
shop window *n* vetrina *f*
shopworn *adj* AmE ‹*garment*› sporco (per lunga permanenza in negozio)
shore /ʃɔː(r)/ *n* riva *f*
▪ **shore up** *vt* puntellare ‹*building, wall*›
shorn /ʃɔːn/ ▶ **shear**
short /ʃɔːt/ **A** *adj* corto; (not lasting) breve; ‹*person*› basso; (curt) brusco; **a ~ time ago** poco tempo fa; **be ~ of** essere a corto di; **be in ~ supply** essere scarso; fig essere raro; **Mick is ~ for Michael** Mick è il diminutivo di Michael; **cut ~** interrompere ‹*holiday*›; **to cut a long story ~...** per farla breve...; **in the ~ term** nell'immediato futuro, a breve termine
B *adv* bruscamente; **in ~** in breve; **~ of doing** a meno di fare; **go ~** essere privato (of di); **stop ~ of doing something** non arrivare fino a fare qualcosa; **you're 10p ~** mancano 10 pence
C *n* Cinema cortometraggio *m*
shortage /ˈʃɔːtɪdʒ/ *n* scarsità *f*
shortbread *n* frollino *m*
short-change *vt* dare meno resto del dovuto a; (deliberately) imbrogliare sul resto; fig imbrogliare
short circuit **A** *n* corto *m* circuito
B *vt* mandare in cortocircuito
C *vi* causare un cortocircuito
shortcoming *n* difetto *m*
shortcrust pastry *n* pasta *f* frolla
short cut *n* scorciatoia *f*
shorten /ˈʃɔːtn/ *vt* abbreviare; accorciare ‹*garment*›
shortfall *n* (in budget, accounts) deficit *m inv*
shorthand *n* stenografia *f*
short-handed /-ˈhændɪd/ *adj* a corto di personale
shorthand typist *n* stenodattilografo, -a *mf*
short list *n lista (f) dei candidati selezionati per un lavoro*
short-lived /-ˈlɪvd/ *adj* di breve durata
shortly /ˈʃɔːtlɪ/ *adv* presto; **~ before/after** poco prima/dopo
shortness /ˈʃɔːtnɪs/ *n* brevità *f*; (of person) bassa statura *f*
short notice *n* **at ~** con poco preavviso
short-range *adj* di breve portata
shorts /ʃɔːts/ *npl* calzoncini *mpl* corti
short-sighted /-ˈsaɪtɪd/ *adj* miope
short-sleeved /-ˈsliːvd/ *adj* a maniche corte

short-staffed /-ˈstɑːft/ *adj* a corto di personale
short story *n* racconto *m*, novella *f*
short-tempered /-ˈtempəd/ *adj* irascibile
short-term *adj* a breve termine
short time *n* **be on ~** ‹*worker*› fare orario ridotto
short wave *n* onde *fpl* corte
short wave radio *n* radio *f inv* a onde corte
⚷ **shot** /ʃɒt/ **A** ▸ **shoot**
B *n* colpo *m*; (pellets) piombini *mpl*; (person) tiratore *m*; Phot foto *f inv*; (injection) puntura *f*; infml (attempt) prova *f*; **like a ~** infml come un razzo
shotgun *n* fucile *m* da caccia
shot put *n* (event) getto *m* del peso
shot-putter *n* pesista *mf*
shot-putting *n* Sport getto *m* del peso
⚷ **should** /ʃʊd/ *v aux* **I ~ go** dovrei andare; **I ~ have seen him** avrei dovuto vederlo; **you ~ have seen him!** avresti dovuto vederlo!; **you ~n't have said that** non avresti dovuto dire questo; **what ~ I say?** cosa devo dire?; **this ~ be enough** questo dovrebbe bastare; **I ~ like** mi piacerebbe; **if he ~ come** se dovesse venire, se venisse
⚷ **shoulder** /ˈʃəʊldə(r)/ **A** *n* spalla *f*; **~ to ~** gomito a gomito
B *vt* mettersi in spalla; fig accollarsi
shoulder bag *n* borsa *f* a tracolla
shoulder blade *n* scapola *f*
shoulder-length *adj* ‹*hair*› lungo fino alle spalle
shoulder pad *n* spallina *f* imbottita
shoulder strap *n* spallina *f*; (of bag) tracolla *f*
⚷ **shout** /ʃaʊt/ **A** *n* grido *m*
B *vt & vi* gridare
▪ **shout at** *vi* alzar la voce con
▪ **shout down** *vt* azzittire gridando
shouting /ˈʃaʊtɪŋ/ *n* grida *fpl*
shove /ʃʌv/ **A** *n* spintone *m*
B *vt* spingere; infml (put) ficcare
C *vi* spingere
▪ **shove off** *vi* infml togliersi di torno
▪ **shove up** *vi* infml (make room) farsi più in là
shovel /ˈʃʌvl/ **A** *n* pala *f*
B *vt* (*pt/pp* **shovelled**) spalare
⚷ **show** /ʃəʊ/ **A** *n* (display) manifestazione *f*; (exhibition) mostra *f*; (ostentation) ostentazione *f*; Theat, TV spettacolo *m*; (programme) programma *m*; **on ~** esposto
B *vt* (*pt* **showed**, *pp* **shown**) mostrare; (put on display) esporre; proiettare ‹*film*›; **~ somebody to the door** accompagnare qualcuno alla porta; **~ somebody the door** mettere alla porta qualcuno
C *vi* ‹*film*› essere proiettato; **your slip is ~ing** ti si vede la sottoveste

⚷ parola chiave

▪ **show in** *vt* fare accomodare
▪ **show off** **A** *vi* infml mettersi in mostra
B *vt* mettere in mostra
▪ **show out**: *vt* **~ somebody out** fare uscire qualcuno
▪ **show round**: *vt* **~ somebody round** far visitare a qualcuno ‹*house, town*›
▪ **show up** **A** *vi* risaltare; infml (arrive) farsi vedere
B *vt* infml (embarrass) far fare una brutta figura a
showbiz /ˈʃəʊbɪz/ *n* infml mondo *m* dello spettacolo
show business *n* mondo *m* dello spettacolo
showcase **A** *n* also fig vetrina *f*
B *attrib* ‹*village, prison*› modello
show down *n* regolamento *m* dei conti
shower /ˈʃaʊə(r)/ **A** *n* doccia *f*; (of rain) acquazzone *m*; **have a ~** fare la doccia
B *vt* **~ with** coprire di
C *vi* fare la doccia
shower cap *n* cuffia *f* da doccia
shower curtain *n* tenda *f* della doccia
shower head *n* bocchetta *f*
showerproof *adj* impermeabile
showery /ˈʃaʊərɪ/ *adj* **it was ~** ci sono stati diversi acquazzoni
show house *n casa* (*f*) *di nuova costruzione arredata per essere mostrata ad eventuali acquirenti*
showjumper /ˈʃəʊdʒʌmpə(r)/ *n* cavaliere *m*, amazzone *f*
showjumping /ˈʃəʊdʒʌmpɪŋ/ *n* salto *m* ostacoli
shown /ʃəʊn/ ▸ **show**
show-off *n* esibizionista *mf*
show of hands *n* voto *m* per alzata di mano
showpiece *n* pezzo *m* forte
showplace *n* attrazione *f*
showroom *n* salone *m* [per] esposizioni
showy /ˈʃəʊɪ/ *adj* appariscente
shrank /ʃræŋk/ ▸ **shrink**
shrapnel /ˈʃræpnl/ *n* schegge *fpl* di granata, shrapnel *m inv*
shred /ʃred/ **A** *n* brandello *m*; fig briciolo *m*
B *vt* (*pt/pp* **shredded**) fare a brandelli; Culin tagliuzzare
shredder /ˈʃredə(r)/ *n* distruttore *m* di documenti
shrew /ʃruː/ *n* Zool toporagno *m*; derog (woman) bisbetica *f*
shrewd /ʃruːd/ *adj* accorto
shrewdly /ˈʃruːdlɪ/ *adv* con accortezza
shrewdness /ˈʃruːdnɪs/ *n* accortezza *f*
shriek /ʃriːk/ **A** *n* strillo *m*
B *vt & vi* strillare
shrift /ʃrɪft/ *n* **give somebody short ~** liquidare qualcuno rapidamente
shrill /ʃrɪl/ *adj* penetrante

shrillness /ˈʃrɪlnɪs/ *n* acutezza *f*
shrilly /ˈʃrɪlɪ/ *adv* in modo penetrante
shrimp /ʃrɪmp/ *n* AmE gamberetto *m*
shrine /ʃraɪn/ *n* (place) santuario *m*
shrink /ʃrɪŋk/ **A** *vi* (*pt* **shrank**, *pp* **shrunk**) restringersi; (draw back) ritrarsi (**from** da)
B *n* infml strizzacervelli *mf inv*
shrinkage /ˈʃrɪŋkɪdʒ/ *n* (of fabric) restringimento *m*; (of area, company) rimpicciolimento *m*; (in a shop) perdite *fpl*; (of resources) diminuzione *f*
shrinking violet /ʃrɪŋkɪŋˈvaɪələt/ *n* hum mammoletta *f*
shrink-proof *adj* irrestringibile
shrink-resistant *adj* irrestringibile
shrink-wrap **A** *vt* avvolgere nella pellicola trasparente
B *n* pellicola *f* trasparente
shrivel /ˈʃrɪvl/ *vi* (*pt/pp* **shrivelled**) raggrinzare
shroud /ʃraʊd/ *n* sudario *m*; fig manto *m*; **~ed in** fig avvolto in
Shrove /ʃrəʊv/ *n* **~ Tuesday** martedì *m* grasso
shrub /ʃrʌb/ *n* arbusto *m*
shrubbery /ˈʃrʌbərɪ/ *n* (in garden) zona *f* piantata ad arbusti
shrug /ʃrʌg/ **A** *n* scrollata *f* di spalle
B *vt & vi* (*pt/pp* **shrugged**) **~ [one's shoulders]** scrollare le spalle
■ **shrug off** *vt* ignorare
shrunk /ʃrʌŋk/ ▶ **shrink**
shudder /ˈʃʌdə(r)/ **A** *n* fremito *m*
B *vi* fremere
shuffle /ˈʃʌfl/ **A** *vi* strascicare i piedi
B *vt* mescolare ‹*cards*›
C *n* strascicamento *m*; (at cards) mescolata *f*
shufti /ˈʃʊftɪ/ *n* BrE infml **have a ~ at something** dare un'occhiata a qualcosa
shun /ʃʌn/ *vt* (*pt/pp* **shunned**) rifuggire
shunt /ʃʌnt/ *vt* smistare
shush /ʃʊʃ/ *int* zitto!
shut /ʃʌt/ **A** *vt* (*pt/pp* **shut**, *pres p* **shutting**) chiudere
B *vi* chiudersi; ‹*shop*› chiudere
■ **shut down** *vt & vi* chiudere
■ **shut in** *vt* rinchiudere ‹*person, animal*›
■ **shut off** *vt* chiudere ‹*water, gas*›
■ **shut out** *vt* bloccare ‹*light*›; impedire ‹*view*›; scacciare ‹*memory*›
■ **shut up** **A** *vt* chiudere; infml far tacere
B *vi* infml stare zitto; **~ up!** stai zitto!
shutdown /ˈʃʌtdaʊn/ *n* chiusura *f*
shut-eye *n* infml (short sleep) **get some ~** fare un pisolino
shutter /ˈʃʌtə(r)/ *n* serranda *f*; Phot otturatore *m*
shuttle /ˈʃʌtl/ **A** *n* navetta *f*
B *vi* far la spola
shuttlecock /ˈʃʌtlkɒk/ *n* volano *m*
shuttle service *n* servizio *m* navetta

shy /ʃaɪ/ **A** *adj* (timid) timido
B *vi* (*pt/pp* **shied**) ‹*horse*› fare uno scarto
■ **shy away from** *vt* rifuggire da
shyly /ˈʃaɪlɪ/ *adv* timidamente
shyness /ˈʃaɪnɪs/ *n* timidezza *f*
Siamese /saɪəˈmiːz/ *adj* siamese
Siamese twins *npl* fratelli *mpl*/sorelle *fpl* siamesi
Siberia /saɪˈbɪərɪə/ *n* Siberia *f*
sibling /ˈsɪblɪŋ/ *n* (brother) fratello *m*; (sister) sorella *f*; **~s** *pl* fratelli *mpl*
sibling rivalry *n* rivalità *f* tra fratelli
sibylline /ˈsɪbɪlaɪn/ *adj* sibillino
Sicilian /sɪˈsɪlɪən/ *adj & n* siciliano, -a *mf*
Sicily /ˈsɪsɪlɪ/ *n* Sicilia *f*
sick /sɪk/ *adj* ammalato; ‹*humour*› macabro; **be ~** (vomit) vomitare; **be ~ of something** infml essere stufo di qualcosa; **feel ~** aver la nausea
sick bay *n* (in school) infermeria *f*
sick building syndrome *n* sindrome *f* da edifici malsani
sicken /ˈsɪkn/ **A** *vt* disgustare
B *vi* **be ~ing for something** covare qualche malanno
sickening /ˈsɪkənɪŋ/ *adj* disgustoso
sickie /ˈsɪkɪ/ *n* BrE infml **throw a ~** darsi malato
sick leave *n* congedo *m* per malattia
sickly /ˈsɪklɪ/ *adj* (**-ier**, **-iest**) malaticcio
sickness /ˈsɪknɪs/ *n* malattia *f*; (vomiting) nausea *f*
sickness benefit *n* sussidio *m* di malattia
sick note *n* (from doctor) certificato *m* medico
sick pay *n* indennità *f* di malattia
sickroom /ˈsɪkruːm/ *n* camera *f* dell'ammalato
side /saɪd/ **A** *n* lato *m*; (of person, mountain) fianco *m*; (of road) bordo *m*; **on the ~** (as sideline) come attività secondaria; **~ by ~** fianco a fianco; **take ~s** immischiarsi; **take sb's ~** prendere le parti di qualcuno; **be on the safe ~** andare sul sicuro
B *attrib* laterale
C *vi* **~ with** parteggiare per
sideboard *n* credenza *f*
sideboards /ˈsaɪdbɔːdz/ *npl* BrE = **sideburns**
sideburns *npl* basette *fpl*
side effect *n* effetto *m* collaterale
side impact bars *npl* Auto barre *fpl* laterali antintrusione
sidekick *n* infml (companion) compare *m*; (assistant) braccio *m* destro
sidelights *npl* luci *fpl* di posizione
sideline *n* attività *f* complementare
sidelong *adj* **~ glance** di sguincio
side plate *n* piattino *m*
side road *n* strada *f* secondaria
side-saddle *adv* all'amazzone
sideshow *n* attrazione *f*
sidestep *vt* schivare

side street *n* strada *f* laterale
sidetrack *vt* sviare
sidewalk *n* AmE marciapiede *m*
sideways *adv* obliquamente
siding /'saɪdɪŋ/ *n* binario *m* di raccordo
sidle /'saɪdl/ *vi* camminare furtivamente (**up to** verso)
siege /si:dʒ/ *n* assedio *m*
Sierra Leone /sɪeərəlɪ'əʊn/ *n* Sierra Leone *f*
siesta /sɪ'estə/ *n* siesta *f*; **take a ~** fare una siesta
sieve /sɪv/ **A** *n* setaccio *m*
B *vt* setacciare
sift /sɪft/ *vt* setacciare; **~ [through]** fig passare al setaccio
sigh /saɪ/ **A** *n* sospiro *m*; **give a ~** sospirare
B *vi* sospirare
sight /saɪt/ **A** *n* vista *f*; (on gun) mirino *m*; **the ~s** *pl* le cose da vedere; **at first ~** a prima vista; **be within/out of ~** essere/non essere in vista; **within ~ of** vicino a; **lose ~ of** perdere di vista; **know by ~** conoscere di vista; **have bad ~** vederci male
B *vt* avvistare
sightseeing /'saɪtsi:ɪŋ/ *n* **go ~** andare a visitare posti
sightseer /'saɪtsi:ə(r)/ *n* turista *mf*
sign /saɪn/ **A** *n* segno *m*; (notice) insegna *f*
B *vt & vi* firmare
■ **sign for** *vt* firmare la ricevuta di ‹*letter, parcel*›; firmare un contratto con ‹*football club*›
■ **sign in** *vi* ‹*hotel guest*› firmare il registro
■ **sign on** *vi* (as unemployed) presentarsi all'ufficio di collocamento; Mil arruolarsi
■ **sign up** *vi* Mil arruolarsi; **~ up for a course** iscriversi a un corso
signal /'sɪgnl/ **A** *n* segnale *m*
B *vt* (*pt/pp* **signalled**) segnalare
C *vi* fare segnali; **~ to somebody** far segno a qualcuno (**to** di)
signal box *n* cabina *f* di segnalazione
signalman /'sɪgnəlmən/ *n* casellante *m*
signatory /'sɪgnət(ə)rɪ/ *n* firmatario, -a *mf*
signature /'sɪgnətʃə(r)/ *n* firma *f*
signature tune *n* sigla *f* [musicale]
signet ring /'sɪgnɪt/ *n* anello *m* con sigillo
significance /sɪg'nɪfɪkəns/ *n* significato *m*
significant /sɪg'nɪfɪkənt/ *adj* significativo
significantly /sɪg'nɪfɪkəntlɪ/ *adv* in modo significativo
signify /'sɪgnɪfaɪ/ *vt* (*pt/pp* **-ied**) indicare
signing /'saɪnɪŋ/ *n* (of treaty) firma *f*; (of footballer) ingaggio *m*; (footballer) nuovo acquisto *m*; (sign language) linguaggio *m* dei segni
sign language *n* linguaggio *m* dei segni
signpost /'saɪnpəʊst/ *n* segnalazione *f* stradale

Sikh /si:k/ **A** *n* sikh *mf inv*
B *adj* sikh *inv*
silage /'saɪlɪdʒ/ *n* foraggio *m* conservato in silo
silence /'saɪləns/ **A** *n* silenzio *m*; **in ~** in silenzio
B *vt* far tacere
silencer /'saɪlənsə(r)/ *n* (on gun) silenziatore *m*; Auto marmitta *f*
silent /'saɪlənt/ *adj* silenzioso; ‹*film*› muto; **remain ~** rimanere in silenzio; **the ~ majority** la maggioranza silenziosa
silently /'saɪləntlɪ/ *adv* silenziosamente
silhouette /sɪlʊ'et/ **A** *n* sagoma *f*, silhouette *f inv*
B *vt* **be ~d** profilarsi
silica gel /'sɪlɪkə/ *n* gel *m inv* di silice
silicon /'sɪlɪkən/ *n* silicio *m*
silicon chip *n* Comput chip *m inv* di silicio, piastrina *f* di silicio
silicone /'sɪlɪkəʊn/ *n* Chem silicone *m*
silicone varnish *n* vernice *f* siliconica
silk /sɪlk/ **A** *n* seta *f*
B *attrib* di seta
silkworm /'sɪlkwɜ:m/ *n* baco *m* da seta
silky /'sɪlkɪ/ *adj* (**-ier**, **-iest**) come la seta
sill /sɪl/ *n* davanzale *m*
silly /'sɪlɪ/ *adj* (**-ier**, **-iest**) sciocco
silo /'saɪləʊ/ *n* silo *m*
silt /sɪlt/ *n* melma *f*
silver /'sɪlvə(r)/ **A** *adj* d'argento; ‹*paper*› argentato
B *n* argento *m*; (silverware) argenteria *f*
silver birch *n* betulla *f* bianca
silver foil *n* carta *f* stagnola, foglio *m* d'alluminio
silver-plated *adj* placcato d'argento
silver service *n servizio (m) a tavola in cui il cameriere fa il giro dei commensali*
silversmith *n* argentiere *m*
silverware *n* argenteria *f*
silver wedding *n* nozze *fpl* d'argento
silvery /'sɪlvərɪ/ *adj* argentino
SIM card /sɪm/ *n* carta *f* SIM
similar /'sɪmɪlə(r)/ *adj* simile
similarity /sɪmɪ'lærətɪ/ *n* somiglianza *f*
similarly /'sɪmɪləlɪ/ *adv* in modo simile
simile /'sɪmɪlɪ/ *n* similitudine *f*
simmer /'sɪmə(r)/ **A** *vi* bollire lentamente
B *vt* far bollire lentamente
■ **simmer down** *vi* calmarsi
simper /'sɪmpə(r)/ *vi* ostentare un sorriso
simpering /'sɪmp(ə)rɪŋ/ *adj* ‹*smile*› affettato; ‹*person*› smanceroso
simple /'sɪmpl/ *adj* semplice offensive ‹*person*› sempliciotto
simple-minded /-'maɪndɪd/ *adj* offensive sempliciotto
simpleton /'sɪmpltən/ *n* sempliciotto, -a *mf*
simplicity /sɪm'plɪsətɪ/ *n* semplicità *f*

S

parola chiave

simplification /sɪmplɪfɪ'keɪʃn/ *n* semplificazione *f*

simplify /'sɪmplɪfaɪ/ *vt* (*pt/pp* **-ied**) semplificare

simplistic /sɪm'plɪstɪk/ *adj* semplicistico

simply /'sɪmplɪ/ *adv* semplicemente

simulate /'sɪmjʊleɪt/ *vt* simulare

simulation /sɪmjʊ'leɪʃn/ *n* simulazione *f*

simulator /'sɪmjʊleɪtə(r)/ *n* simulatore *m*

simulcast /'sɪməlkɑːst/ *vt* teleradiotrasmettere

simultaneous /sɪml'teɪnɪəs/ *adj* simultaneo

simultaneously /sɪməl'teɪnɪəslɪ/ *adv* simultaneamente

sin /sɪn/ **A** *n* peccato *m*
B *vi* (*pt/pp* **sinned**) peccare

since /sɪns/ (prep) **A** da; ~ **when?** da quando in qua?
B *adv* da allora
C *conj* da quando; (because) siccome

sincere /sɪn'sɪə(r)/ *adj* sincero

sincerely /sɪn'sɪəlɪ/ *adv* sinceramente; **Yours ~** Distinti saluti

sincerity /sɪn'serətɪ/ *n* sincerità *f*

sine /saɪn/ *n* Math seno *m*

sinew /'sɪnjuː/ *n* tendine *m*

sinful /'sɪnfl/ *adj* peccaminoso

sing /sɪŋ/ *vt & vi* (*pt* **sang**, *pp* **sung**) cantare

singalong /'sɪŋəlɒŋ/ *n* **have a ~** cantare [tutti] insieme

Singapore /ˌsɪŋə'pɔː(r)/ *n* Singapore *f*

singe /sɪndʒ/ *vt* (*pres p* **-geing**) bruciacchiare

singer /'sɪŋə(r)/ *n* cantante *mf*

singer-songwriter /-'sɒŋraɪtə(r)/ *n* cantautore, -trice *mf*

singing /'sɪŋɪŋ/ *n* canto *m*

single /'sɪŋgl/ **A** *adj* solo; (not double) semplice; (unmarried) celibe; ‹*woman*› nubile; ‹*room*› singolo; ‹*bed*› a una piazza; **I haven't spoken to a ~ person** non ho parlato con nessuno
B *n* (ticket) biglietto *m* di sola andata; (record) singolo *m*

▪ **single out** *vt* scegliere; (distinguish) distinguere

single-breasted /-'brestɪd/ *adj* ad un petto

single cream *n* panna *f* da cucina liquida

single currency *n* (in Europe) moneta *f* unica

single-decker /-'dekə(r)/ *n* autobus *m inv* (a un piano solo)

single file *adv* in fila indiana

single-handed /-'hændɪd/ *adj & adv* da solo

single-handedly /-'hændɪdlɪ/ *adv* da solo

single market *n* mercato *m* unico

single-minded /-'maɪndɪd/ *adj* risoluto

single mother *n* madre *f* single *inv*

single-parent *adj* ‹*family*› monoparentale

singles /'sɪŋglz/ *npl* Tennis singolo *m*; (people) single *mpl*; **the women's ~** il singolo femminile

singles bar *n* bar ritrovo *m inv* per single

singles charts *npl* classifica *f inv* dei singoli

single sex *adj* (for boys) maschile; (for girls) femminile

single storey *adj* ‹*house*› ad un piano

singlet /'sɪŋglɪt/ *n* BrE canottiera *f*

singly /'sɪŋglɪ/ *adv* singolarmente

sing-song BrE **A** *adj* ‹*voice, dialect*› che ha una sua particolare cadenza
B *n* **have a ~** cantare [tutti] insieme

singular /'sɪŋgjʊlə(r)/ **A** *adj* Gram singolare; (uncommon) eccezionale
B *n* singolare *m*

singularly /'sɪŋgjʊləlɪ/ *adv* singolarmente

sinister /'sɪnɪstə(r)/ *adj* sinistro

sink /sɪŋk/ **A** *n* lavandino *m*
B *vi* (*pt* **sank**, *pp* **sunk**) affondare
C *vt* affondare ‹*ship*›; scavare ‹*shaft*›; investire ‹*money*›

▪ **sink in** *vi* penetrare; **it took a while to ~ in** infml (be understood) c'è voluto un po' a capirlo

sinker /'sɪŋkə(r)/ *n* (in fishing) piombo *m*; AmE Culin ≈ bombolone *m*

sinking /'sɪŋkɪŋ/ *n* affondamento *m*

sink unit *n mobile* (*m*) *di cucina comprendente il lavandino*

sinner /'sɪnə(r)/ *n* peccatore, -trice *mf*

sinuous /'sɪnjʊəs/ *adj* sinuoso

sinus /'saɪnəs/ *n* seno *m* paranasale

sinusitis /saɪnə'saɪtɪs/ *n* sinusite *f*

sip /sɪp/ **A** *n* sorso *m*
B *vt* (*pt/pp* **sipped**) sorseggiare

siphon /'saɪfn/ *n* (bottle) sifone *m*

▪ **siphon off** *vt* travasare (con sifone)

sir /sɜː(r)/ *n* signore *m*; **S~** (title) Sir *m*; **Dear S~** Egregio Signore; **Dear S~s** Spettabile Ditta

sire /saɪə(r)/ *vt* generare

siren /'saɪrən/ *n* sirena *f*

sirloin /'sɜːlɔɪn/ *n* (of beef) controfiletto *m*

sirloin steak *n* bistecca *f* di controfiletto

sissy /'sɪsɪ/ *n* femminuccia *f*

sister /'sɪstə(r)/ *n* sorella *f*; (nurse) [infermiera *f*] caposala *f*

sisterhood /'sɪstəhʊd/ *n* Relig congregazione *f* religiosa femminile; (in feminism) solidarietà *f* femminile

sister-in-law *n* (*pl* **~s-in-law**) cognata *f*

sisterly /'sɪstəlɪ/ *adj* da sorella

Sistine Chapel /'sɪstiːn/ *n* Cappella *f* Sistina

sit /sɪt/ **A** *vi* (*pt/pp* **sat**, *pres p* **sitting**) essere seduto; (sit down) sedersi; ‹*committee*› riunirsi
B *vt* sostenere ‹*exam*›

▪ **sit about**, **sit around** *vi* stare senza far niente

▪ **sit back** *vi* fig starsene con le mani in mano

▪ **sit by** *vi* starsene a guardare

S

- **sit down** *vi* mettersi a sedere; **please ~ down** si accomodi; **~ down!** siediti!
- **sit for** *vi* posare per ‹*portrait*›
- **sit in** *vi* (observe) assistere; **~ in on a class** assistere (da osservatore) a una lezione
- **sit on** *vt* far parte di ‹*committee*›
- **sit up** *vi* mettersi seduto; (not slouch) star seduto diritto; (stay up) stare alzato

sitcom /'sɪtkɒm/ *n* infml situation comedy *f inv*

sit-down *n* BrE **have a ~** sedersi un momento

✓ **site** /saɪt/ **A** *n* posto *m*; Archaeol sito *m*; (building) **~** cantiere *m*; (website) sito *m*
B *vt* collocare

sit-in /'sɪtɪn/ *n* occupazione *f* (*di fabbrica ecc.*) sit-in *m inv*

sitter /'sɪtə(r)/ *n* (babysitter) baby-sitter *mf inv*; (for artist) modello, -a *mf*

sitting /'sɪtɪŋ/ *n* seduta *f*; (for meals) turno *m*

sitting duck *n* infml facile bersaglio *m*

sitting room *n* salotto *m*

sitting target *n* facile bersaglio *m*

sitting tenant *n* locatario *m* residente

situate /'sɪtjʊeɪt/ *vt* situare

situated /'sɪtjʊeɪtɪd/ *adj* situato

✓ **situation** /sɪtjʊ'eɪʃn/ *n* situazione *f*; (location) posizione *f*; (job) posto *m*; **'~s vacant'** 'offerte di lavoro'

situation report *n* quadro *m* della situazione

sit-ups *npl* addominali *mpl*

✓ **six** /sɪks/ *adj & n* sei *m*

six-pack *n* confezione *f* da sei (*di bottiglie o lattine*)

sixteen /sɪks'tiːn/ *adj & n* sedici *m*

sixteenth /sɪks'tiːnθ/ *adj & n* sedicesimo, -a *mf*

sixteenth-century *adj* cinquecentesco

sixth /sɪksθ/ *adj & n* sesto, -a *mf*

sixth form *n* Sch *ultimo biennio* (*m*) *facoltativo della scuola superiore*

sixth form college *n* BrE *istituto* (*m*) *che prepara studenti dai 16 ai 18 anni agli esami di maturità*

sixth sense *n* sesto senso *m*

sixties /'sɪkstɪz/ *npl* (period) **the ~** gli anni Sessanta *mpl*; (age) sessant'anni *mpl*

sixtieth /'sɪkstɪɪθ/ *adj & n* sessantesimo, -a *mf*

sixty /'sɪkstɪ/ *adj & n* sessanta *m*

✓ **size** /saɪz/ *n* dimensioni *fpl*; (of clothes) taglia *f*, misura *f*; (of shoes) numero *m*; **what ~ is the room?** che dimensioni ha la stanza?
- **size up** *vt* infml valutare

sizeable /'saɪzəbl/ *adj* piuttosto grande

sizzle /'sɪzl/ *vi* sfrigolare

skate¹ /skeɪt/ *n inv* (fish) razza *f*

skate² **A** *n* pattino *m*
B *vi* pattinare
- **skate over** *vt* fig glissare su

skateboard /'skeɪtbɔːd/ *n* skateboard *m inv*

skateboarder /'skeɪtbɔːdə(r)/ *n* persona *f* che fa skateboard

skateboarding /'skeɪtbɔːdɪŋ/ *n* skateboard *m*

skater /skeɪt/ *n* pattinatore, -trice *mf*

skating /'skeɪtɪŋ/ *n* pattinaggio *m*

skating rink *n* pista *f* di pattinaggio

skeletal /'skelɪtl/ *adj* also fig scheletrico; ‹*disease*› dello scheletro

skeleton /'skelɪtn/ *n* scheletro *m*

skeleton key *n* passe-partout *m inv*

skeleton staff *n* personale *m* ridotto

skeptic /'skeptɪk/ *n* AmE = **sceptic**

skeptical /'skeptɪkl/ *adj* AmE = **sceptical**

skepticism /'skeptɪsɪzm/ *n* AmE = **scepticism**

sketch /sketʃ/ **A** *n* schizzo *m*; Theat sketch *m inv*
B *vt* fare uno schizzo di
- **sketch out** *vt* delineare

sketchbook /'sketʃbʊk/ *n* (for sketching) album *m inv* per schizzi; (book of sketches) album *m inv* di schizzi

sketchily /'sketʃɪlɪ/ *adv* in modo abbozzato

sketch pad /'sketʃpæd/ *n* blocco *m* per schizzi

sketchy /'sketʃɪ/ *adj* (**-ier**, **-iest**) abbozzato

skew /skjuː/ *vt* alterare ‹*figures*›

skewer /'skjʊə(r)/ *n* spiedo *m*

ski /skiː/ **A** *n* sci *m inv*
B *vi* (*pt/pp* **skied**, *pres p* **skiing**) sciare; **go ~ing** andare a sciare

ski boot *n* scarpone *m* da sci

skid /skɪd/ **A** *n* slittata *f*; **go into a ~** slittare
B *vi* (*pt/pp* **skidded**) slittare

skid mark *n* segno *m* di frenata

skier /'skiːə(r)/ *n* sciatore, -trice *mf*

skiing /'skiːɪŋ/ *n* sci *m*

ski instructor *n* maestro, -a *mf* di sci

ski jump *n* (competition) salto *m* con gli sci; (slope) trampolino *m*

ski jumping *n* salto *m* dal trampolino

skilful /'skɪlfl/ *adj* abile

skilfully /'skɪlfʊlɪ/ *adv* abilmente

ski lift *n* impianto *m* di risalita

✓ **skill** /skɪl/ *n* abilità *f*

skilled /skɪld/ *adj* dotato; ‹*worker*› specializzato

skillet /'skɪlət/ *n* AmE padella *f*

skim /skɪm/ *vt* (*pt/pp* **skimmed**) schiumare; scremare ‹*milk*›
- **skim off** *vt* togliere
- **skim over** *vt* sfiorare ‹*surface, subject*›
- **skim through** *vt* scorrere

skimmed milk /skɪmd/ *n* latte *m* scremato

skimp /skɪmp/ *vi* **~ on** lesinare su

skimpy /'skɪmpɪ/ *adj* (**-ier**, **-iest**) succinto

✓ **skin** /skɪn/ **A** *n* pelle *f*; (on fruit) buccia *f*;

✓ parola chiave

S

soaked to the ~ fradicio fino all'osso
B *vt* (*pt/pp* **skinned**) spellare
skin cancer *n* cancro *m* alla pelle
skincare *n* cura *f* della pelle
skin cream *n* crema *f* per la pelle
skin-deep *adj* superficiale
skin diver *n* sub *mf inv*
skin diving *n* nuoto *m* subacqueo
skinflint /'skɪnflɪnt/ *n* miserabile *mf*
skin graft *n* innesto *m* epidermico
skinhead /'skɪnhed/ *n* skinhead *mf inv*
skinny /'skɪnɪ/ *adj* (**-ier**, **-iest**) molto magro
skint /skɪnt/ *adj* infml al verde
skintight /skɪn'taɪt/ *adj* aderente
skip¹ /skɪp/ *n* (container) benna *f*
skip² **A** *n* salto *m*
B *vi* (*pt/pp* **skipped**) saltellare; (with rope) saltare la corda
C *vt* omettere
ski pants *npl* pantaloni *mpl* da sci
ski pass *n* ski-pass *m inv*
ski pole *n* bastone *m* da sci
skipper /'skɪpə(r)/ *n* skipper *m inv*
skipping /'skɪpɪŋ/ *n* salto *m* della corda
skipping rope *n* corda *f* per saltare
ski rack *n* portasci *m inv*
ski resort *n* stazione *f* sciistica
skirmish /'skɜːmɪʃ/ *n* scaramuccia *f*
skirt /skɜːt/ **A** *n* gonna *f*
B *vt* costeggiare
skirting board /'skɜːtɪŋ/ *n* battiscopa *m inv*, zoccolo *m*
ski run *n* pista *f* da sci
ski slope *n* pista *f* da sci
ski stick *n* bastone *m* da sci
ski suit *n* tuta *f* da sci
skit /skɪt/ *n* bozzetto *m* comico
skittish /'skɪtɪʃ/ *adj* (difficult to handle) ombroso; (playful) giocherellone
skittle /'skɪtl/ *n* birillo *m*
skive /skaɪv/ *vi* infml fare lo scansafatiche
skivvy /'skɪvɪ/ *n* BrE infml sguattera *f*
ski wax *n* sciolina *f*
skulduggery /skʌl'dʌgərɪ/ *n* infml imbrogli *mpl*
skulk /skʌlk/ *vi* aggirarsi furtivamente
skull /skʌl/ *n* cranio *m*
skunk /skʌŋk/ *n* moffetta *f*; (person) farabutto *m*
sky /skaɪ/ *n* cielo *m*
skydiving *n* paracadutismo *m* in caduta libera
sky-high **A** *adj* ‹*prices*› alle stelle; ‹*rates*› esorbitante
B *adv* **rise ~** salire alle stelle
skyjacker /'skaɪdʒækə(r)/ *n* dirottatore, -trice *mf*
skylight *n* lucernario *m*
skyline *n* (of city) profilo *m*
skyrocket *vi* ‹*prices*› andare alle stelle
skyscraper *n* grattacielo *m*
slab /slæb/ *n* lastra *f*; (slice) fetta *f*; (of chocolate) tavoletta *f*
slack /slæk/ **A** *adj* lento; ‹*person*› fiacco
B *vi* fare lo scansafatiche
■ **slack off** *vi* rilassarsi
slacken /'slækn/ **A** *vi* allentare; **~ [off]** ‹*trade*› rallentare; ‹*speed, rain*› diminuire
B *vt* allentare; diminuire ‹*speed*›
slacker /'slækə(r)/ *n* scansafatiche *mf inv*
slacks /slæks/ *npl* pantaloni *mpl* sportivi
slag /slæg/ *n* scorie *fpl*
■ **slag off** *vt* (*pt/pp* **slagged**) BrE infml sparlare di
slain /sleɪn/ ▶ **slay**
slalom /'slɑːləm/ *n* slalom *m inv*
slam /slæm/ **A** *vt* (*pt/pp* **slammed**) sbattere; infml (criticize) stroncare
B *vi* sbattere
slammer /'slæmə(r)/ *n* infml (prison) galera *f*
slander /'slɑːndə(r)/ **A** *n* diffamazione *f*
B *vt* diffamare
slanderer /'slɑːndərə(r)/ *n* diffamatore, -trice *mf*
slanderous /'slɑːnd(ə)rəs/ *adj* diffamatorio
slang /slæŋ/ *n* gergo *m*
slangy /'slæŋɪ/ *adj* gergale
slant /slɑːnt/ **A** *n* pendenza *f*; (point of view) angolazione *f*; **on the ~** in pendenza
B *vt* pendere; fig distorcere ‹*report*›
C *vi* pendere
slanted /'slɑːntɪd/ *adj* fig ‹*report*› tendenzioso
slap /slæp/ **A** *n* schiaffo *m*
B *vt* (*pt/pp* **slapped**) schiaffeggiare; (put) schiaffare
C *adv* in pieno
slap bang *adv* infml **he went ~ into the wall** è andato a sbattere in pieno contro il muro
slapdash *adj* infml frettoloso
slapstick *n* farsa *f* da torte in faccia
slap-up *adj* infml di prim'ordine
slash /slæʃ/ **A** *n* taglio *m*; Typ barra *f*; Comput slash *m inv*
B *vt* tagliare; ridurre drasticamente ‹*prices*›; **~ one's wrists** svenarsi
slat /slæt/ *n* stecca *f*
slate /sleɪt/ **A** *n* ardesia *f*
B *vt* infml fare a pezzi
slater /'sleɪtə(r)/ *n* (roofer) *addetto* (*m*) *alla ricopertura dei tetti con tegole di ardesia*; Zool onisco *m*
slatted /'slætɪd/ *adj* ‹*shutter*› a stecche
slaughter /'slɔːtə(r)/ **A** *n* macello *m*; (of people) massacro *m*
B *vt* macellare; massacrare ‹*people*›
slaughterhouse /'slɔːtəhaʊs/ *n* macello *m*
Slav /slɑːv/ **A** *adj* slavo
B *n* slavo, -a *mf*
slave /sleɪv/ **A** *n* schiavo, -a *mf*
B *vi* **~ [away]** lavorare come un schiavo

slave-driver *n* schiavista *mf*
slavery /ˈsleɪvərɪ/ *n* schiavitù *f*
Slavic /ˈslɑːvɪk/ *adj* slavo
slavish /ˈsleɪvɪʃ/ *adj* servile
slavishly /ˈsleɪvɪʃlɪ/ *adv* in modo servile
Slavonic /sləˈvɒnɪk/ *adj* slavo
slaw /slɔː/ *n* AmE = **coleslaw**
slay /sleɪ/ *vt* (*pt* **slew**, *pp* **slain**) ammazzare
sleaze /sliːz/ *n* infml (pornography) pornografia *f*; (corruption) corruzione *f*
sleazy /ˈsliːzɪ/ *adj* (**-ier**, **-iest**) sordido
sled /sled/ **A** *n* slitta *f*
B *vi* andare in slitta
sledge /sledʒ/ *n* slitta *f*
sledgehammer /ˈsledʒhæmə(r)/ *n* martello *m*
sleek /sliːk/ *adj* liscio, lucente; (well-fed) pasciuto
⚷ **sleep** /sliːp/ **A** *n* sonno *m*; **go to ~** addormentarsi; **put to ~** far addormentare; **in my ~** nel sonno; **a good night's ~** una bella dormita
B *vi* (*pt/pp* **slept**) dormire; **~ like a log** dormire come un ghiro; **~ on it** dormirci sopra; **~ with somebody** andare a letto con qualcuno
C *vt* **~s six** ha sei posti letto
▪ **sleep around** *vi* andare a letto con tutti
▪ **sleep in** *vi* dormire più a lungo
sleeper /ˈsliːpə(r)/ *n* Rail treno *m* con vagoni letto; (compartment) vagone *m* letto; (on track) traversina *f*; **be a light/heavy ~** avere il sonno leggero/pesante
sleepily /ˈsliːpɪlɪ/ *adv* con aria assonnata
sleeping bag *n* sacco *m* a pelo
sleeping car *n* vagone *m* letto
sleeping partner *n* BrE Comm socio *m* accomandante
sleeping pill *n* sonnifero *m*
sleeping policeman *n* dosso *m* di rallentamento
sleepless /ˈsliːplɪs/ *adj* insonne; **have a ~ night** passare una notte insonne
sleeplessness /ˈsliːplɪsnɪs/ *n* insonnia *f*
sleepover /ˈsliːpəʊvə(r)/ *n* **the kids are having a ~** i bambini hanno invitato degli amichetti a dormire a casa
sleepsuit *n* tutina *f*
sleepwalk *vi* essere sonnambulo
sleepwalker *n* sonnambulo, -a *mf*
sleepwalking *n* sonnambulismo *m*
sleepy /ˈsliːpɪ/ *adj* (**-ier**, **-iest**) assonnato; **be ~** aver sonno
sleet /sliːt/ **A** *n* nevischio *m*
B *vi* **it is ~ing** nevischia
sleeve /sliːv/ *n* manica *f*; (for record) copertina *f*
sleeveless /ˈsliːvlɪs/ *adj* senza maniche

⚷ parola chiave

sleigh /sleɪ/ *n* slitta *f*
sleight /slaɪt/ *n* **~ of hand** gioco *m* di prestigio
slender /ˈslendə(r)/ *adj* snello; ‹*fingers, stem*› affusolato; fig scarso; ‹*chance*› magro
slept /slept/ ▶ **sleep**
sleuth /sluːθ/ *n* investigatore *m*, detective *m inv*
slew¹ /sluː/ *vi* girare
slew² ▶ **slay**
slice /slaɪs/ **A** *n* fetta *f*
B *vt* affettare; **~d bread** pane *m* a cassetta
slick /slɪk/ **A** *adj* liscio; (cunning) astuto
B *n* (of oil) chiazza *f* di petrolio
slide /slaɪd/ **A** *n* scivolata *f*; (in playground) scivolo *m*; (for hair) fermaglio *m* [per capelli]; Phot diapositiva *f*
B *vi* (*pt/pp* **slid**) scivolare
C *vt* far scivolare
slide projector *n* proiettore *m* per diapositive
slide rule *n* regolo *m* calcolatore
slide show *n* proiezione *f* di diapositive
sliding /ˈslaɪdɪŋ/ *adj* ‹*door, seat*› scorrevole
sliding scale *n* scala *f* mobile
slight /slaɪt/ **A** *adj* leggero; ‹*importance*› poco; (slender) esile; **~est** minimo; **not in the ~est** niente affatto
B *vt* offendere
C *n* offesa *f*
⚷ **slightly** /ˈslaɪtlɪ/ *adv* leggermente
slim /slɪm/ **A** *adj* (**slimmer**, **slimmest**) snello; fig scarso; ‹*chance*› magro
B *vi* dimagrire
slime /slaɪm/ *n* melma *f*
slimy /ˈslaɪmɪ/ *adj* melmoso; fig viscido
sling /slɪŋ/ **A** *n* Med benda *f* al collo
B *vt* (*pt/pp* **slung**) infml lanciare
sling-back *n* sandalo *m* (*chiuso davanti*)
slingshot /ˈslɪŋʃɒt/ *n* fionda *f*
slink /slɪŋk/ *vi* (*pt/pp* **slunk**) entrare furtivamente
slinky /ˈslɪŋkɪ/ *adj* infml ‹*dress*› sexy *inv*, attillato
⚷ **slip** /slɪp/ **A** *n* scivolata *f*; (mistake) lieve errore *m*; (petticoat) sottoveste *f*; (for pillow) federa *f*; (paper) scontrino *m*; **give somebody the ~** infml seminare qualcuno; **~ of the tongue** lapsus *m inv*
B *vi* (*pt/pp* **slipped**) scivolare; (go quickly) sgattaiolare; (decline) retrocedere; **let something ~** (reveal) lasciarsi sfuggire qualcosa
C *vt* **he ~ped it into his pocket** se l'è infilato in tasca; **~ sb's mind** sfuggire di mente a qualcuno
▪ **slip away** *vi* sgusciar via; ‹*time*› sfuggire
▪ **slip into** *vi* infilarsi ‹*clothes*›
▪ **slip on** *vt* infilarsi ‹*jacket etc*›
▪ **slip up** *vi* infml sbagliare
slip knot *n* nodo *m* scorsoio

slip-on, slip-on shoe *n* mocassino *m*
slipped disc /slɪpt'dɪsk/ *n* Med ernia *f* del disco
slipper /'slɪpə(r)/ *n* pantofola *f*
slippery /'slɪpərɪ/ *adj* scivoloso
slip road *n* bretella *f*
slipshod /'slɪpʃɒd/ *adj* trascurato
slip-up *n* infml sbaglio *m*
slit /slɪt/ **A** *n* spacco *m*; (tear) strappo *m*; (hole) fessura *f*
B *vt* (*pt/pp* **slit**) tagliare
slither /'slɪðə(r)/ *vi* scivolare
sliver /'slɪvə(r)/ *n* scheggia *f*
slob /slɒb/ *n* infml (messy) maiale *m*; (lazy) pelandrone *m*
slobber /'slɒbə(r)/ *vi* sbavare
sloe /sləʊ/ *n* (fruit) prugnola *f*; (bush) prugnolo *m*
slog /slɒg/ **A** *n* **[hard]** ~ sgobbata *f*
B *vi* (*pt/pp* **slogged**) (work) sgobbare
slogan /'sləʊgən/ *n* slogan *m inv*
slop /slɒp/ *vt* (*pt/pp* **slopped**) versare
■ **slop over** *vi* versarsi
slope /sləʊp/ **A** *n* pendenza *f*; (ski) ~ pista *f*
B *vi* essere inclinato, inclinarsi
■ **slope off** *vi* scantonare
sloping /'sləʊpɪŋ/ *adj* in pendenza
sloppiness /'slɒpɪnɪs/ *n* (of work) trascuratezza *f*
sloppy /'slɒpɪ/ *adj* (**-ier**, **-iest**) ‹*work*› trascurato; ‹*worker*› negligente; (in dress) sciatto; (sentimental) sdolcinato
slosh /slɒʃ/ **A** *vi* infml ‹*person, feet*› sguazzare; ‹*water*› scrosciare
B *vt* infml (hit) colpire
sloshed /slɒʃt/ *adj* infml sbronzo
slot /slɒt/ **A** *n* fessura *f*; (time-~) spazio *m*
B *vt* (*pt/pp* **slotted**) infilare
■ **slot in** *vi* incastrarsi
■ **slot together** *vi* ‹*pieces*› incastrarsi
sloth /sləʊθ/ *n* accidia *f*
slot machine *n* distributore *m* automatico; (for gambling) slot-machine *f inv*
slouch /slaʊtʃ/ *vi* (in chair) stare scomposto
Slovak /'sləʊvæk/ *adj & n* slovacco, -a *mf*
Slovakia /sləʊ'vækɪə/ *n* Slovacchia *f*
Slovene /'sləʊviːn/ *adj & n* sloveno, -a *mf*
Slovenia /sləʊ'viːnɪə/ *n* Slovenia *f*
slovenliness /'slʌvənlɪnɪs/ *n* sciatteria *f*
slovenly /'slʌvnlɪ/ *adj* sciatto
✓ **slow** /sləʊ/ **A** *adj* lento; **be** ~ ‹*clock*› essere indietro; **in** ~ **motion** al rallentatore
B *adv* lentamente
■ **slow down** *vt & vi* rallentare
■ **slow up** *vt & vi* rallentare
slowcoach /'sləʊkəʊtʃ/ *n* infml tartaruga *f*
✓ **slowly** /'sləʊlɪ/ *adv* lentamente
slow-moving *adj* ‹*film, river*› lento
slowness /'sləʊnɪs/ *n* lentezza *f*
slow puncture *n* foratura *f*
sludge /slʌdʒ/ *n* fanghiglia *f*
slug /slʌg/ *n* lumacone *m*; (bullet) pallottola *f*
sluggish /'slʌgɪʃ/ *adj* lento
sluggishly /'slʌgɪʃnɪs/ *adv* lentamente
sluice /sluːs/ *n* chiusa *f*
sluice gate *n* saracinesca *f* (*di chiusa*)
slum /slʌm/ *n* (house) tugurio *m*; ~**s** *pl* bassifondi *mpl*
slumber /'slʌmbə(r)/ **A** *n* sonno *m*
B *vi* dormire
slump /slʌmp/ **A** *n* crollo *m*; (economic) depressione *f*
B *vi* crollare
slung /slʌŋ/ ▸ **sling**
slunk /slʌŋk/ ▸ **slink**
slur /slɜː(r)/ **A** *n* (discredit) calunnia *f*
B *vt* (*pt/pp* **slurred**) biascicare
slurp /slɜːp/ *vt & vi* bere rumorosamente
slurry /'slʌrɪ/ *n* (waste from animals) liquame *m*; (waste from factory) fanghiglia *f* semiliquida; (of cement) impasto *m* semiliquido
slush /slʌʃ/ *n* pantano *m* nevoso; fig sdolcinatezza *f*
slush fund *n* fondi *mpl* neri
slushy /'slʌʃɪ/ *adj* fangoso; (sentimental) sdolcinato
slut /slʌt/ *n* sgualdrina *f*
sly /slaɪ/ **A** *adj* (**-ier**, **-iest**) scaltro
B *n* **on the** ~ di nascosto
slyly /'slaɪlɪ/ *adv* scaltramente
SM *n abbr* (**sadomasochism**) sadomasochismo *m*
smack¹ /smæk/ **A** *n* (on face) schiaffo *m*; (on bottom) sculaccione *m*
B *vt* (on face) schiaffeggiare; (on bottom) sculacciare; ~ **one's lips** far schioccare le labbra
C *adv* infml in pieno
smack² *vi* ~ **of** fig sapere di
smacker /'smækə(r)/ *n* infml (kiss) bacio *m*; **500** ~**s** (£500) 500 sterline
✓ **small** /smɔːl/ **A** *adj* piccolo; **be out/work until the** ~ **hours** fare le ore piccole
B *adv* **chop up** ~ fare a pezzettini
C *n* **the** ~ **of the back** le reni
small ads *npl* annunci *mpl* [commerciali]
small business *n* piccola impresa *f*
small change *n* spiccioli *mpl*
small-holding *n* piccola tenuta *f*
small hours *npl* ore *fpl* piccole
small letter *n* lettera *f* minuscola
small-minded /-'maɪndɪd/ *adj* meschino
smallpox *n* vaiolo *m*
small print *n* caratteri *mpl* piccoli; **read the** ~ fig leggere tutto fin nei minimi particolari
small talk *n* chiacchiere *fpl*; **make** ~ fare conversazione
smarmy /'smɑːmɪ/ *adj* (**-ier**, **-iest**) infml untuoso

✐ **smart** /smɑːt/ **A** *adj* elegante; (clever) intelligente; (brisk) svelto; **be ~** infml (cheeky) fare il furbo
B *vi* (hurt) bruciare
smart alec, **smart aleck** /'smɑːtælɪk/ *n* infml sapientone *m*
smart bomb *n* bomba *f* intelligente
smart card *n* carta *f* intelligente
smarten /'smɑːt(ə)n/ *vt* **~ oneself up** farsi bello
smartly /'smɑːtlɪ/ *adv* elegantemente; (cleverly) intelligentemente; (briskly) velocemente; (cheekily) sfacciatamente
smart money *n* infml **the ~ was on Desert Orchid** gli esperti hanno puntato su Desert Orchid
smartphone /smɑːtfəʊn/ *n* smartphone *m inv*
smash /smæʃ/ **A** *n* **1** fragore *m*; (collision) scontro *m*; Tennis schiacciata *f* **2 smash hit**
B *vt* spaccare; Tennis schiacciare
C *vi* spaccarsi; (crash) schiantarsi (**into** contro)
■ **smash up** *vt* distruggere ‹*car, bar*›
smash-and-grab *n* BrE rapina *f* ad un negozio (*con sfascio di vetrina*)
smashed /smæʃt/ *adj* ‹*window*› in frantumi; ‹*vehicle*› sfasciato; ‹*limb*› fracassato; infml (on drugs) fatto; infml (on alcohol) ubriaco fradicio
smash hit *n* successo *m*
smashing /'smæʃɪŋ/ *adj* infml fantastico
smattering /'smætərɪŋ/ *n* infarinatura *f*
smear /smɪə(r)/ **A** *n* macchia *f*; Med striscio *m*
B *vt* imbrattare; (coat) spalmare (**with** di); fig calunniare
C *vi* sbavare
smear campaign *n* campagna *f* diffamatoria
smear test *n* Med striscio *m*, Pap test *m inv*
smell /smel/ **A** *n* odore *m*; (sense) odorato *m*
B *vt* (*pt/pp* **smelt** *or* **smelled**) odorare (**of** di); **that ~s good** ha un buon odore
smelling salts /'smelɪŋ/ *npl* Med sali *mpl*
smelly /'smelɪ/ *adj* (**-ier**, **-iest**) puzzolente
smelt¹ /smelt/ ▶ **smell**
smelt² *vt* fondere
smidgeon /'smɪdʒɪn/ *n* (of something to eat) pizzico *m*; (of something to drink) goccio *m*
✐ **smile** /smaɪl/ **A** *n* sorriso *m*
B *vi* sorridere; **~ at** sorridere a ‹*somebody*›; sorridere di ‹*something*›
■ **smile on** *vt* ‹*weather, fortune*› sorridere a ‹*person*›
smiley /'smaɪlɪ/ *n* infml smiley *m inv*, faccina *f* sorridente
smirk /smɜːk/ **A** *n* sorriso *m* compiaciuto
B *vi* sorridere con aria compiaciuta

✐ parola chiave

smithereens /smɪðə'riːnz/ *npl* **to/in ~** in mille pezzi
smithy /'smɪðɪ/ *n* fucina *f*
smitten /'smɪtn/ *adj* **~ with** tutto preso da
smock /smɒk/ *n* grembiule *m*
smog /smɒg/ *n* smog *m inv*
smoke /sməʊk/ **A** *n* fumo *m*
B *vt & vi* fumare
smoke alarm *n* allarme *m* antifumo *inv*
smoked /sməʊkt/ *adj* affumicato
smoke-free zone *n* zona *f* non-fumatori; **'~'** 'vietato fumare'
smokeless /'sməʊklɪs/ *adj* senza fumo; ‹*fuel*› che non fa fumo
smoker /'sməʊkə(r)/ *n* fumatore, -trice *mf*; Rail vagone *m* fumatori
smokescreen /'sməʊkskriːn/ *n* also fig cortina *f* di fumo
smoking /'sməʊkɪŋ/ *n* fumo *m*; **'no ~'** 'vietato fumare'; **'~ or non-~?'** 'fumatori o non fumatori?'
smoking-related *adj* ‹*illness*› legato al fumo
smoky /'sməʊkɪ/ *adj* (**-ier**, **-iest**) fumoso; ‹*taste*› di fumo
smooch /smuːtʃ/ *vi* infml pomiciare
smooth /smuːð/ **A** *adj* liscio; ‹*movement*› scorrevole; ‹*sea*› calmo; ‹*manners*› mellifluo
B *vt* lisciare; **~ things over** sistemare le cose
■ **smooth out** *vt* lisciare
smoothly /'smuːðlɪ/ *adv* in modo scorrevole; **go ~** andare liscio
smooth-running *adj* ‹*event, service*› ben organizzato
smooth-tongued /-'tʌŋd/ *adj* derog mellifluo
smother /'smʌðə(r)/ *vt* soffocare
smoulder /'sməʊldə(r)/ *vi* fumare; (with rage) consumarsi
SMS *n abbr* (**short message service**) SMS *m*
SMS message *n* sms *m inv*
smudge /smʌdʒ/ **A** *n* macchia *f*
B *vt & vi* imbrattare
smug /smʌg/ *adj* (**smugger**, **smuggest**) compiaciuto
smuggle /'smʌgl/ *vt* contrabbandare
smuggler /'smʌglə(r)/ *n* contrabbandiere, -a *mf*
smuggling /'smʌglɪŋ/ *n* contrabbando *m*
smugly /'smʌglɪ/ *adv* con aria compiaciuta
smugness /'smʌgnɪs/ *n* compiacimento *m*
smut /smʌt/ *n* macchia *f* di fuliggine; fig sconcezza *f*
smutty /'smʌtɪ/ *adj* (**-ier**, **-iest**) fuligginoso; fig sconcio
snack /snæk/ *n* spuntino *m*
snack bar *n* snack bar *m inv*
snag¹ /snæg/ *n* (problem) intoppo *m*

snag² *vt* smagliarsi ‹*tights*› (**on** con)
snail /sneɪl/ *n* lumaca *f*; **at a ~'s pace** a passo di lumaca
snail mail *n* infml *posta (f) tradizionale, così chiamata dagli utenti di email*
snake /sneɪk/ *n* serpente *m*
snakebite *n* morso *m* di serpente
snake charmer *n* incantatore, -trice *mf* di serpenti
snakes and ladders *n* BrE gioco *m* dell'oca
snap /snæp/ **A** *n* colpo *m* secco; (photo) istantanea *f*
B *attrib* ‹*decision*› istantaneo
C *vi* (*pt/pp* **snapped**) (break) spezzarsi
D *vt* (break) spezzare; (say) dire seccamente; Phot fare un'istantanea di; schioccare ‹*fingers*›
■ **snap at** ‹*dog*› cercare di azzannare; ‹*person*› parlare seccamente a
■ **snap off**: *vt* **~ sb's head off** infml aggredire qualcuno
■ **snap out**: *vi* **~ out of it** venirne fuori
■ **snap up** *vt* afferrare
snappy /'snæpɪ/ *adj* (**-ier, -iest**) scorbutico; (smart) elegante; **make it ~!** sbrigati!
snapshot /'snæpʃɒt/ *n* istantanea *f*
snare /sneə(r)/ *n* trappola *f*
snarl /snɑ:l/ **A** *n* ringhio *m*
B *vi* ringhiare
snarled-up /snɑ:ld'ʌp/ *adj* ‹*traffic*› bloccato
snarl-up *n* (in traffic, network) ingorgo *m*
snatch /snætʃ/ **A** *n* strappo *m*; (fragment) brano *m*; (theft) scippo *m*; **make a ~ at something** cercare di afferrare qualcosa
B *vt* strappare [di mano] (**from** a); (steal) scippare; rapire ‹*child*›
snazzy /'snæzɪ/ *adj* infml sciccoso
sneak /sni:k/ **A** *n* infml (devious person) tipo, -a *mf* subdolo; BrE infml (telltale) spia *f*
B *vt* infml (steal) fregare; rubare ‹*kiss*›; **~ a glance at** dare una sbirciatina a
C *vi* BrE infml (tell tales) fare la spia
D *attrib* ‹*visit*› furtivo; **have a ~ preview of something** vedere qualcosa in anteprima
■ **sneak away** *vi* sgattaiolare via
■ **sneak in** *vi* sgattaiolare dentro
■ **sneak out** *vi* sgattaiolare fuori
sneakers /'sni:kəz/ *npl* AmE scarpe *fpl* da ginnastica
sneaking /'sni:kɪŋ/ *adj* furtivo; ‹*suspicion*› vago
sneaky /'sni:kɪ/ *adj* sornione
sneer /snɪə(r)/ **A** *n* ghigno *m*
B *vi* sogghignare; **~ at** (mock) ridere di
sneeze /sni:z/ **A** *n* starnuto *m*
B *vi* starnutire; **it's not to be ~d at** non ci sputerei sopra
snide /snaɪd/ *adj* infml insinuante
sniff /snɪf/ **A** *n* (of dog) annusata *f*; **give a ~** ‹*person*› tirare su col naso
B *vi* tirare su col naso
C *vt* odorare ‹*flower*›; sniffare ‹*glue*›; ‹*dog*› annusare
sniffer dog /'snɪfə/ *n* cane *m* poliziotto (*antidroga, antiterrorismo*)
sniffle /'snɪfl/ **A** *n* **have a ~** *or* **the ~s** (slight cold) avere un po' di raffreddore; **give a ~** tirar su col naso
B *vi* tirar su col naso
sniffy /'snɪfɪ/ *adj* infml (haughty) con la puzza sotto il naso
snigger /'snɪgə(r)/ **A** *n* risatina *f* soffocata
B *vi* ridacchiare
snip /snɪp/ **A** *n* taglio *m*; infml (bargain) affare *m*
B *vt/vi* **~ [at]** tagliare
■ **snip off** *vt* tagliare via ‹*corner, end*›
snipe /snaɪp/ *vi* **~ at** tirare su; fig sparare a zero su
sniper /'snaɪpə(r)/ *n* cecchino *m*
snippet /'snɪpɪt/ *n* **a ~ of information/news** una breve notizia/informazione
snivel /'snɪvl/ *vi* (*pt/pp* **snivelled**) piagnucolare
snivelling /'snɪv(ə)lɪŋ/ *adj* piagnucoloso
snob /snɒb/ *n* snob *mf inv*
snobbery /'snɒbərɪ/ *n* snobismo *m*
snobbish /'snɒbɪʃ/ *adj* da snob; **be ~** ‹*person*› essere uno/una snob; ‹*club etc*› essere molto snob
snobbishness /'snɒbɪʃnɪs/ *n* snobismo *m*
snog /snɒg/ *vi* BrE sl pomiciare
snooker /'snu:kə(r)/ **A** *n* (game) snooker *m*; (shot) impallatura *f*
B *vt* Sport impallare; fig mettere in difficoltà
snoop /snu:p/ **A** *n* spia *f*
B *vi* infml curiosare
snooper /'snu:pə(r)/ *n* ficcanaso *mf*
snooty /'snu:tɪ/ *adj* infml sdegnoso
snooze /snu:z/ **A** *n* sonnellino *m*
B *vi* fare un sonnellino
snore /snɔ:(r)/ *vi* russare
snoring /'snɔ:rɪŋ/ *n* il russare
snorkel /'snɔ:kl/ *n* respiratore *m*
snorkelling BrE, **snorkeling** AmE /'snɔ:klɪŋ/ *n* snorkelling *m inv*
snort /snɔ:t/ **A** *n* sbuffo *m*
B *vi* sbuffare
C *vt* fiutare ‹*cocaine*›
snot /snɒt/ *n* infml (mucus) moccolo *m*
snotty /'snɒtɪ/ *adj* infml ‹*nose*› moccioso; (disagreeable) sgradevole
snotty-nosed kid /-nəʊzd/ *n* moccioso, -a *mf*
snout /snaʊt/ *n* grugno *m*
snow /snəʊ/ **A** *n* neve *f*
B *vi* nevicare; **~ed under with** fig sommerso di
snowball **A** *n* palla *f* di neve
B *vi* fig ingigantirsi
snowboard /'snəʊbɔ:d/ **A** *n* snowboard *m inv*

B *vi* fare snowboard
snowboarding /ˈsnəʊbɔːdɪŋ/ *n* snowboard *m inv*
snowdrift *n* cumulo *m* di neve
snowdrop *n* bucaneve *m inv*
snowfall *n* nevicata *f*
snowflake *n* fiocco *m* di neve
snowman *n* pupazzo *m* di neve
snowmobile /ˈsnəʊməbiːl/ *n* gatto *m* delle nevi
snowplough *n* spazzaneve *m inv*
snowshoe *n* racchetta *f* da neve
snowstorm *n* tormenta *f*
snow tyres *npl* pneumatici *mpl* chiodati
snowy /ˈsnəʊɪ/ *adj* nevoso
Snr *abbr* (**Senior**) senior
snub /snʌb/ **A** *n* sgarbo *m*
B *vt* (*pt/pp* **snubbed**) snobbare
snub-nosed /ˈsnʌbnəʊzd/ *adj* dal naso all'insù
snuff[1] /snʌf/ *n* tabacco *m* da fiuto
snuff[2] *vt* ~ **[out]** spegnere <*candle*>; ~ **it** infml tirare le cuoia
snug /snʌg/ *adj* (**snugger**, **snuggest**) comodo; (tight) aderente
snuggle /ˈsnʌgl/ *vi* rannicchiarsi (**up to** accanto a)
⚷ **so** /səʊ/ **A** *adv* così; **so far** finora; **so am I** anch'io; **so I see** così pare; **you've left the door open - so I have!** hai lasciato la porta aperta - è vero!; **that is so** è così; **so much** così tanto; **so much the better** tanto meglio; **so it is** proprio così; **if so** se è così; **so as to** in modo da; **so long!** infml a presto!
B *pron* **I hope/think/am afraid so** spero/penso/temo di sì; **I told you so** te l'ho detto; **because I say so** perché lo dico io; **I did so!** l'ho fatto!; **so saying/doing,...** così dicendo/facendo,...; **or so** circa; **very much so** sì, molto; **and so forth** *or* **on** e così via
C *conj* (therefore) perciò; (in order that) così; **so that** affinché; **so there!** ecco!; **so what?** e allora?; **so where have you been?** allora, dove sei stato?
soak /səʊk/ **A** *vt* mettere a bagno
B *vi* stare a bagno
▪ **soak in** *vi* penetrare
▪ **soak into** *vt* <*liquid*> penetrare
▪ **soak up** *vt* assorbire
soaked /səʊkt/ *adj* fradicio; ~ **in something** impregnato di qualcosa
soaking /ˈsəʊkɪŋ/ **A** *n* ammollo *m*
B *adj & adv* ~ **[wet]** infml inzuppato
so-and-so *n* tal dei tali *mf*; (euphemism) specie *f* di imbecille
soap /səʊp/ *n* sapone *m*
soap opera *n* telenovela *f*, soap opera *f inv*
soap powder *n* detersivo *m* in polvere
soapy /ˈsəʊpɪ/ *adj* (**-ier**, **-iest**) insaponato

⚷ parola chiave

S

soar /sɔː(r)/ *vi* elevarsi; <*prices*> salire alle stelle
soaring /ˈsɔːrɪŋ/ *adj* <*costs, temperatures, inflation*> in forte aumento
sob /sɒb/ **A** *n* singhiozzo *m*
B *vi* (*pt/pp* **sobbed**) singhiozzare
S.O.B. *n abbr* derog AmE (**son of a bitch**) figlio *m* di puttana
sobbing /ˈsɒbɪŋ/ *n* singhiozzi *mpl*
sober /ˈsəʊbə(r)/ *adj* sobrio; (serious) serio
▪ **sober up** *vi* ritornare sobrio
soberly /ˈsəʊbəlɪ/ *adv* sobriamente; (seriously) con aria seria
sobriety /səˈbraɪətɪ/ *n* (not drinking) sobrietà *f*; (seriousness) serietà *f*
sob story *n* storia *f* lacrimevole
so-called /ˈsəʊkɔːld/ *adj* cosiddetto
soccer /ˈsɒkə(r)/ *n* calcio *m*
soccer pitch *n* campo *m* di calcio
soccer player *n* calciatore *m*
sociable /ˈsəʊʃəbl/ *adj* socievole
⚷ **social** /ˈsəʊʃl/ *adj* sociale; (sociable) socievole
social climber *n* arrampicatore, -trice *mf* sociale
social climbing *n* arrivismo *m* sociale
social club *n* circolo *m* sociale
socialism /ˈsəʊʃəlɪzm/ *n* socialismo *m*
socialist /ˈsəʊʃəlɪst/ **A** *adj* socialista
B *n* socialista *mf*
socialite /ˈsəʊʃəlaɪt/ *n* persona *f* che fa vita mondana
socialize /ˈsəʊʃəlaɪz/ *vi* socializzare
socially /ˈsəʊʃəlɪ/ *adv* socialmente; **know somebody** ~ frequentare qualcuno
social media *n* social media *mpl*
social mobility *n* mobilità *f* sociale
social network *n* (on the Internet) social network *m inv*
social networking site *n* sito *m* di social network
social science *n* scienze *fpl* sociali
social security *n* previdenza *f* sociale
social services *npl* servizi *mpl* sociali
social work *n* assistenza *f* sociale
social worker *n* assistente *mf* sociale
⚷ **society** /səˈsaɪətɪ/ *n* società *f*
socio-economic /səʊsɪəʊiːkəˈnɒmɪk/ *adj* socioeconomico
sociological /səʊsɪəˈlɒdʒɪkl/ *adj* sociologico
sociologist /səʊsɪˈɒlədʒɪst/ *n* sociologo, -a *mf*
sociology /səʊsɪˈɒlədʒɪ/ *n* sociologia *f*
sock[1] /sɒk/ *n* calzino *m*; (knee-length) calzettone *m*
sock[2] infml **A** *n* pugno *m*
B *vt* dare un pugno a
socket /ˈsɒkɪt/ *n* (of eye) orbita *f*; (wall plug) presa *f* [di corrente]; (for bulb) portalampada *m inv*

sod /sɒd/ *n* infml stronzo *m*; **you lucky ~!** che fortuna sfacciata!
■ **sod off** *vi* infml togliersi dai piedi
soda /'səʊdə/ *n* soda *f*; AmE gazzosa *f*
soda water *n* seltz *m inv*
sodden /'sɒdn/ *adj* inzuppato
sodium /'səʊdɪəm/ *n* sodio *m*
sodium bicarbonate *n* bicarbonato *m* di sodio
Sod's Law /sɒdz/ *n* fam hum *regola (f) per cui, se qualcosa può andare storto, va storto*
sofa /'səʊfə/ *n* divano *m*
sofa bed *n* divano *m* letto
soft /sɒft/ *adj* morbido, soffice; ‹*voice*› sommesso; ‹*light, colour*› tenue; (not strict) indulgente; infml (silly) stupido
soft-boiled /-'bɔɪld/ *adj* ‹*egg*› bazzotto
soft contact lenses *npl* lenti *fpl* a contatto morbide
soft drink *n* bibita *f* analcolica
soft drug *n* droga *f* leggera
soften /'sɒfn/ **A** *vt* ammorbidire; fig attenuare
B *vi* ammorbidirsi
■ **soften up** **A** *vi* ammorbidirsi
B *vt* **~ somebody up** ammorbidire qualcuno ‹*opponent, enemy, customer*›
softener /'sɒf(ə)nə(r)/ *n* (for water) dolcificatore *m*; (substance) anti-calcare *m inv*; (for fabrics) ammorbidente *m*
soft furnishings *npl* tappeti *mpl* e tessuti *mpl* da arredamento
soft-hearted *adj* dal cuore tenero
soft ice-cream *n* mantecato *m*
softie /'sɒftɪ/ *n* infml = **softy**
softly /'sɒftlɪ/ *adv* (say) sottovoce; ‹*treat*› con indulgenza; ‹*play music*› in sottofondo
soft option *n* **take the ~** scegliere la soluzione più semplice
soft-pedal *vt* fig minimizzare
soft porn *n* infml pornografia *f* soft[-core]
soft sell *n metodo (m) di vendita basato sulla persuasione*
soft skills *npl capacità (fpl) relazionali quali la capacità di comunicare, di persuadere, di identificarsi con gli altri, ecc.*
soft soap *n* fig lusinghe *fpl*
soft-soap *vt* fig lusingare
soft-spoken *adj* dalla voce dolce
soft spot *n* **have a ~ for somebody** infml avere un debole per qualcuno
soft-top *n* Auto decappottabile *f*
soft touch *n* **be a ~** lasciarsi spremere
soft toy *n* pupazzo *m* di peluche
software /'sɒftweə(r)/ *n* software *m*
software engineer *n* softwarista *mf*
software house *n* azienda *f* informatica
software package *n* pacchetto *m* software
software piracy *n* pirateria *f* informatica
software writer *n* programmatore, -trice *mf* di software
softy /'sɒftɪ/ *n* infml (weak person) pappamolle *mf inv*; (indulgent person) bonaccione, -a *mf*
soggy /'sɒgɪ/ *adj* (**-ier**, **-iest**) zuppo
soil¹ /sɔɪl/ *n* suolo *m*
soil² *vt* sporcare
soiled /sɔɪld/ *adj* sporco
solace /'sɒləs/ *n* sollievo *m*
solar /'səʊlə(r)/ *adj* solare
solar eclipse *n* eclissi *f inv* di sole
solar energy *n* energia *f* solare
solar farm *n* parco *m* solare, solar farm *f inv*
solar panel *n* pannello *m* solare
solar power *n* energia *f* solare
solar system *n* sistema *m* solare
sold /səʊld/ ▶ **sell**
solder /'səʊldə(r)/ **A** *n* lega *f* da saldatura
B *vt* saldare
soldier /'səʊldʒə(r)/ *n* soldato *m*
■ **soldier on** *vi* perseverare
sole¹ /səʊl/ *n* (of foot) pianta *f*; (of shoe) suola *f*
sole² *n* (fish) sogliola *f*
sole³ *adj* unico, solo
sole agency *n* rappresentanza *f* esclusiva
solecism /'sɒlɪsɪzm/ *n* (social) scorrettezza *f*; (linguistic) solecismo *m*
solely /'səʊllɪ/ *adv* unicamente
solemn /'sɒləm/ *adj* solenne
solemnity /sə'lemnətɪ/ *n* solennità *f*
solemnly /'sɒləmlɪ/ *adv* solennemente
sol-fa /'sɒlfɑː/ *n* solfeggio *m*
solicit /sə'lɪsɪt/ **A** *vt* sollecitare
B *vi* ‹*prostitute*› adescare
soliciting /sə'lɪsɪtɪŋ/ *n* Jur adescamento *m*
solicitor /sə'lɪsɪtə(r)/ *n* avvocato *m*
solicitous /sə'lɪsɪtəs/ *adj* premuroso
solicitously /sə'lɪsɪtəslɪ/ *adv* premurosamente
solid /'sɒlɪd/ **A** *adj* solido; ‹*oak, gold*› massiccio; **it took a ~ hour** ci è voluta ben un'ora
B *n* (figure) solido *m*; **~s** *pl* (food) cibi *mpl* solidi
solidarity /sɒlɪ'dærətɪ/ *n* solidarietà *f*
solidify /sə'lɪdɪfaɪ/ *vi* (*pt/pp* **-ied**) solidificarsi
soliloquy /sə'lɪləkwɪ/ *n* soliloquio *m*
solitaire /sɒlɪ'teə(r)/ *n* solitario *m*
solitary /'sɒlɪtərɪ/ *adj* solitario; (sole) solo
solitary confinement *n* cella *f* di isolamento
solitude /'sɒlɪtjuːd/ *n* solitudine *f*
solo /'səʊləʊ/ **A** *n* Mus assolo *m*
B *adj* ‹*flight*› in solitario
C *adv* in solitario
soloist /'səʊləʊɪst/ *n* solista *mf*
solstice /'sɒlstɪs/ *n* solstizio *m*
soluble /'sɒljʊbl/ *adj* solubile

🔑 **solution** /sə'lu:ʃn/ *n* soluzione *f*

solvable /'sɒlvəbl/ *adj* risolvibile

🔑 **solve** /sɒlv/ *vt* risolvere

solvency /'sɒlvənsɪ/ *n* Fin solvibilità *f*

solvent /'sɒlvənt/ *adj & n* solvente *m*

solvent abuse *n uso (m) di solventi come stupefacenti*

Somali /səʊ'mɑ:lɪ/ *adj & n* somalo, -a *mf*

Somalia /səʊ'mɑ:lɪə/ *n* Somalia *f*

sombre /'sɒmbə(r)/ *adj* tetro; ‹*clothes*› scuro

🔑 **some** /sʌm/ **A** *adj* (a certain amount of) del; (a certain number of) alcuni, dei; **~ bread/ water** del pane/dell'acqua; **~ books/ oranges** dei libri/delle arance; **I need ~ money/books** ho bisogno di soldi/libri; **do ~ shopping** fare qualche acquisto; **~ day** un giorno o l'altro
B *pron* (a certain amount) un po'; (a certain number) alcuni; **I want ~** ne voglio; **would you like ~?** ne vuoi?; **~ of the butter** una parte del burro; **~ of the apples/women** alcune delle mele/donne

🔑 **somebody** /'sʌmbədɪ/ **A** *pron* qualcuno *m*; **~ else will bring it** la porterà un altro
B *n* **he thinks he's ~** si crede chissà chi

🔑 **somehow** /'sʌmhaʊ/ *adv* in qualche modo; **~ or other** in un modo o nell'altro

🔑 **someone** /'sʌmwʌn/ *pron & n* = **somebody**

somersault /'sʌməsɔ:lt/ **A** *n* capriola *f*; **turn a ~** fare una capriola
B *vi* fare una capriola

🔑 **something** /'sʌmθɪŋ/ *pron* qualche cosa, qualcosa; **~ different** qualcosa di diverso; **~ like** un po' come; (approximately) qualcosa come; **see ~ of somebody** vedere qualcuno ogni tanto; **she is ~ of an expert** è un'esperta

sometime /'sʌmtaɪm/ **A** *adv* un giorno o l'altro; **~ last summer** durante l'estate scorsa
B *adj* ex

🔑 **sometimes** /'sʌmtaɪmz/ *adv* qualche volta

🔑 **somewhat** /'sʌmwɒt/ *adv* piuttosto

🔑 **somewhere** /'sʌmweə(r)/ **A** *adv* da qualche parte
B *pron* **~ to eat** un posto in cui mangiare

🔑 **son** /sʌn/ *n* figlio *m*

sonar /'səʊnɑ:(r)/ *n* sonar *m*

sonata /sə'nɑ:tə/ *n* sonata *f*

🔑 **song** /sɒŋ/ *n* canzone *f*

song and dance *n* **make a ~ about something** (fuss) far tante storie per qualcosa

songbird *n* uccello *m* canoro

songwriter *n* compositore, -trice *mf* di canzoni

sonic /'sɒnɪk/ *adj* sonico

sonic boom *n* bang *m inv* sonico

🔑 parola chiave

son-in-law *n* (*pl* **~s-in-law**) genero *m*

sonnet /'sɒnɪt/ *n* sonetto *m*

son of a bitch *n* infml figlio *m* di un cane

sonorous /'sɒnərəs/ *adj* sonoro; ‹*name*› altisonante

🔑 **soon** /su:n/ *adv* presto; (in a short time) tra poco; **as ~ as** [non] appena; **as ~ as possible** il più presto possibile; **~er or later** prima o poi; **the ~er the better** prima è meglio è; **no ~er had I arrived than...** ero appena arrivato quando...; **I would ~er go** preferirei andare; **~ after** subito dopo

soot /sʊt/ *n* fuliggine *f*

soothe /su:ð/ *vt* calmare

soothing /'su:ðɪŋ/ *adj* calmante

sooty /'sʊtɪ/ *adj* fuligginoso

sop /sɒp/ *n* **throw a ~ to** dare un contentino a

sophisticated /sə'fɪstɪkeɪtɪd/ *adj* sofisticato; (complex) complesso

sophistication /səfɪstɪ'keɪʃn/ *n* (elegance) sofisticatezza *f*, raffinatezza *f*; (complexity) complessità *f*

soporific /sɒpə'rɪfɪk/ *adj* soporifero

soppiness /'sɒpɪnɪs/ *n* infml svenevolezza *f*

sopping /'sɒpɪŋ/ *adj & adv* **be ~ [wet]** essere bagnato fradicio

soppy /'sɒpɪ/ *adj* (**-ier**, **-iest**) infml svenevole

soprano /sə'prɑ:nəʊ/ *n* soprano *m*

sorcerer /'sɔ:sərə(r)/ *n* stregone *m*

sorceress /'sɔ:sərɪs/ *n* strega *f*, maga *f*

sorcery /'sɔ:sərɪ/ *n* (witchcraft) stregoneria *f*

sordid /'sɔ:dɪd/ *adj* sordido

sordidness /'sɔ:dɪdnɪs/ *n* sordidezza *f*

sore /sɔ:(r)/ **A** *adj* dolorante; AmE (vexed) arrabbiato; **it's ~** fa male; **have a ~ throat** avere mal di gola; **it's a ~ point with her** è un punto delicato per lei
B *n* piaga *f*

sorely /'sɔ:lɪ/ *adv* ‹*tempted*› seriamente

soreness /'sɔ:nɪs/ *n* dolore *m*

sorrel /'sɒrəl/ *n* Bot acetosa *f*

sorrow /'sɒrəʊ/ *n* tristezza *f*

sorrowful /'sɒrəʊfʊl/ *adj* triste

sorrowfully /'sɒrəʊfʊlɪ/ *adv* tristemente

🔑 **sorry** /'sɒrɪ/ *adj* (**-ier**, **-iest**) (sad) spiacente; (wretched) pietoso; **you'll be ~!** te ne pentirai!; **I am ~** mi dispiace; **be** *or* **feel ~ for** provare compassione per; **~!** scusa!; (more polite) scusi!

🔑 **sort** /sɔ:t/ **A** *n* tipo *m*; **it's a ~ of fish** è un tipo di pesce; **be out of ~s** infml (unwell) stare poco bene
B *vt* classificare; infml sistemare ‹*problem, person*›

■ **sort out** *vt* selezionare ‹*papers*›; fig risolvere ‹*problem*›; occuparsi di ‹*person*›

sort code *n* Fin codice *m* bancario

sorter /'sɔ:tə(r)/ *n* (on photocopier) fascicolatrice *f*, fascicolatore *m*

SOS *n* SOS *m*; fig segnale *m* di soccorso

so-so *adj & adv* così così
sotto voce /sɒtəʊˈvəʊtʃeɪ/ *adv* ‹*say, add*› sottovoce
soufflé /ˈsuːfleɪ/ *n* soufflé *m*
sought /sɔːt/ ▸ **seek**
sought-after *adj* ‹*job, brand, person*› richiesto
soul /ˈsəʊl/ *n* anima *f*; **poor ~** poveretto; **there was not a ~ in sight** non c'era anima viva
soul-destroying /-dɪstrɔɪɪŋ/ *adj* ‹*job*› che abbruttisce
soulful /ˈsəʊlfʊl/ *adj* sentimentale
soulmate *n* anima *f* gemella
soul-searching /-sɜːtʃɪŋ/ *n* esame *m* di coscienza
soul-stirring /-stɜːrɪŋ/ *adj* molto commovente
sound¹ /saʊnd/ **A** *adj* sano; (sensible) saggio; (secure) solido; ‹*thrashing*› clamoroso
B *adv* **~ asleep** profondamente addormentato
sound² **A** *n* suono *m*; (noise) rumore *m*; **I don't like the ~ of it** infml non mi suona bene
B *vi* suonare; (seem) aver l'aria; **it ~s to me as if...** mi sa che...
C *vt* (pronounce) pronunciare; Med auscultare ‹*chest*›
■ **sound off** *vi* fare grandi discorsi
■ **sound out** *vt* fig sondare
sound barrier *n* muro *m* del suono
sound bite *n breve frase (f) dal forte impatto mediatico*
sound card *n* Comput scheda *f* audio
sound effect *n* effetto *m* sonoro
sound engineer *n* tecnico *m* del suono
soundless /ˈsaʊndlɪs/ *adj* silenzioso
soundlessly /ˈsaʊndlɪslɪ/ *adv* silenziosamente
soundly /ˈsaʊndlɪ/ *adv* ‹*sleep*› profondamente; ‹*defeat*› clamorosamente
soundproof **A** *adj* impenetrabile al suono
B *vt* insonorizzare
sound system *n* (hi-fi) stereo *m*; (for disco etc) impianto *m* audio
soundtrack *n* colonna *f* sonora
soup /suːp/ *n* minestra *f*; **in the ~** infml nei pasticci
soup kitchen *n* mensa *f* dei poveri
soup plate *n* piatto *m* fondo
soup spoon *n* cucchiaio *m* da minestra
sour /ˈsaʊə(r)/ *adj* agro; (not fresh & fig) acido
source /sɔːs/ *n* fonte *f*; **at ~** ‹*deducted*› alla fonte
source language *n* lingua *f* di partenza
sour cream *n* panna *f* acida
sourdough *n* lievito *m* madre
sour-faced /saʊəˈfeɪst/ *adj* ‹*person*› dall'espressione dura
sour grapes *npl* infml **it's just ~ [on his part]** fa come la volpe con l'uva
south /saʊθ/ **A** *n* sud *m*; **to the ~ of** a sud di
B *adj* del sud, meridionale
C *adv* a sud
South Africa *n* Sudafrica *m*
South African *adj & n* sudafricano, -a *mf*
South America *n* America *f* del Sud
South American *adj & n* sudamericano, -a *mf*
southbound *adj* ‹*traffic*› diretto a sud; ‹*carriageway*› sud
south-east /saʊθˈiːst/ *n* sud-est *m*
southerly /ˈsʌðəlɪ/ *adj* del sud
southern /ˈsʌðən/ *adj* del sud, meridionale; **~ Italy** il Mezzogiorno
southerner /ˈsʌðənə(r)/ *n* meridionale *mf*
South Korea *n* Corea *f* del Sud
southpaw /ˈsaʊθpɔː/ *n* (in boxing) pugile *m* mancino
South Pole *n* polo *m* sud
southward /ˈsaʊθwəd/, **southwards** /ˈsaʊθwədz/ *adv* verso sud
south-west /saʊθˈwest/ *n* sud-ovest *m*
south-western /saʊθˈwestən/ *adj* sudoccidentale
souvenir /suːvəˈnɪə(r)/ *n* ricordo *m*, souvenir *m inv*
sovereign /ˈsɒvrɪn/ *adj & n* sovrano, -a *mf*
sovereignty /ˈsɒvrɪntɪ/ *n* sovranità *f*
sovereign wealth funds *npl* fondi *mpl* sovrani
Soviet /ˈsəʊvɪət/ *adj* sovietico
Soviet Union *n* Unione *f* Sovietica
sow¹ /saʊ/ *n* scrofa *f*
sow² /səʊ/ *vt* (*pt* **sowed**, *pp* **sown** *or* **sowed**) seminare
soya BrE /ˈsɔɪə/, **soy** AmE /sɔɪ/ *n* soya *f*
soya bean BrE /ˈsɔɪəbiːn/, **soybean** AmE /ˈsɔɪbiːn/ *n* fagiolo *m* di soia
soy sauce /sɔɪ/, **soya sauce** *n* salsa *f* di soia
sozzled /ˈsɒzld/ *adj* infml sbronzo
spa /spɑː/ *n* stazione *f* termale
space /speɪs/ **A** *n* spazio *m*
B *adj* ‹*research etc*› spaziale
C *vt* **~ [out]** distanziare
space age **A** *n* era *f* spaziale
B *attrib* dell'era spaziale
space bar *n* barra *f* spaziatrice
space cadet *n* fig infml allucinato, -a *mf*
space capsule *n* capsula *f* spaziale
spacecraft *n* navetta *f* spaziale
spaced out /speɪstˈaʊt/ *adj* infml **he's completely ~** è completamente fuori di testa
space-saving *adj* poco ingombrante
spaceship *n* astronave *f*
space shuttle *n* shuttle *m inv*
space station *n* stazione *f* spaziale
spacesuit *n* tuta *f* spaziale

space travel *n* viaggi *mpl* nello spazio
space walk *n* passeggiata *f* nello spazio
spacing /ˈspeɪsɪŋ/ *n* distanziamento *m*; **single/double ~** interlinea *m* semplice/doppia
spacious /ˈspeɪʃəs/ *adj* spazioso
spade /speɪd/ *n* vanga *f*; (for child) paletta *f*; **~s** *pl* Cards picche *fpl*; **call a ~ a ~** dire pane al pane e vino al vino
spadework /ˈspeɪdwɜːk/ *n* fig lavoro *m* preparatorio
spaghetti /spəˈgetɪ/ *n* spaghetti *mpl*
spaghetti bolognese /bɒləˈneɪz/ *n* spaghetti *mpl* al ragù
spaghetti junction *n* infml intricato raccordo *m* autostradale
Spain /speɪn/ *n* Spagna *f*
spam /spæm/ *n* Comput spam *m inv*
spamming /ˈspæmɪŋ/ *n* Comput invio *m* di spam
span¹ /spæn/ **A** *n* spanna *f*; (of arch) luce *f*; (of time) arco *m*; (of wings) apertura *f*
B *vt* (*pt/pp* **spanned**) estendersi su
span² ▸ **spick**
Spaniard /ˈspænjəd/ *n* spagnolo, -a *mf*
spaniel /ˈspænjəl/ *n* spaniel *m inv*
Spanish /ˈspænɪʃ/ **A** *adj* spagnolo
B *n* (language) spagnolo *m*; **the ~** *pl* gli spagnoli
spank /spæŋk/ *vt* sculacciare
spanking /ˈspæŋkɪŋ/ **A** *n* sculacciata *f*
B *adj* infml **at a ~ pace** con passo spedito
C *adv* infml **a ~ new car** una macchina nuova di zecca
spanner /ˈspænə(r)/ *n* chiave *f* inglese
spar /spɑː(r)/ *vi* (*pt/pp* **sparred**) (boxing) allenarsi; (argue) litigare
spare /speə(r)/ **A** *adj* (surplus) in più; (additional) di riserva; **go ~** infml (be very angry) andare su tutte le furie
B *n* (part) ricambio *m*
C *vt* risparmiare; (do without) fare a meno di; **can you ~ five minutes?** avresti cinque minuti?; **no expense was ~d** non si è badato a spese; **to ~** (surplus) in eccedenza
spare part *n* pezzo *m* di ricambio
spare ribs *npl* costine *fpl*
spare room *n* stanza *f* degli ospiti
spare time *n* tempo *m* libero
spare tyre BrE, **spare tire** AmE *n* Auto gomma *f* di scorta; infml (fat) trippa *f*
spare wheel *n* ruota *f* di scorta
sparing /ˈspeərɪŋ/ *adj* parco (**with** di)
sparingly /ˈspeərɪŋlɪ/ *adv* con parsimonia
spark /spɑːk/ *n* scintilla *f*
▪ **spark off** *vt* BrE far scoppiare
sparkle /ˈspɑːkl/ **A** *n* scintillio *m*
B *vi* scintillare
sparkler /ˈspɑːklə(r)/ *n* candela *f* magica

S

🔑 parola chiave

sparkling /ˈspɑːklɪŋ/ *adj* frizzante; ‹*wine*› spumante
spark plug *n* Auto candela *f*
sparrow /ˈspærəʊ/ *n* passero *m*
sparse /spɑːs/ *adj* rado
sparsely /ˈspɑːslɪ/ *adv* scarsamente; **~ populated** ‹*area*› a bassa densità di popolazione
sparseness /ˈspɑːsnɪs/ *n* (of vegetation) radezza *f*
spartan /ˈspɑːtn/ *adj* spartano
spasm /ˈspæzm/ *n* spasmo *m*
spasmodic /spæzˈmɒdɪk/ *adj* spasmodico
spasmodically /spæzˈmɒdɪklɪ/ *adv* spasmodicamente
spastic /ˈspæstɪk offensive **A** *adj* spastico
B *n* spastico, -a *mf*
spat /spæt/ ▸ **spit¹**
spate /speɪt/ *n* (series) successione *f*; **be in full ~** essere in piena
spatial /ˈspeɪʃl/ *adj* spaziale
spatio-temporal /speɪʃɪəˈtempərəl/ *adj* spazio-temporale
spatter /ˈspætə(r)/ *vt & vi* schizzare
spatula /ˈspætjʊlə/ *n* spatola *f*
spawn /spɔːn/ **A** *n* uova *fpl* (*di pesci, rane ecc.*)
B *vi* deporre le uova
C *vt* fig generare
spay /speɪ/ *vt* sterilizzare
🔑 **speak** /spiːk/ **A** *vi* (*pt* **spoke**, *pp* **spoken**) parlare (**to** a); **~ing!** Teleph sono io!
B *vt* dire; **~ one's mind** dire quello che si pensa
▪ **speak for** *vt* parlare a nome di; **~ for yourself!** parla per te!
▪ **speak of**: *vt* **~ well/ill of somebody** parlare bene/male di qualcuno; **nothing to ~ of** niente di speciale; (quantity) non un granché; **~ing of holidays...** a proposito di vacanze...
▪ **speak out** *vi* (protest) parlare
▪ **speak up** *vi* parlare più forte; **~ up for oneself** farsi valere
speaker /ˈspiːkə(r)/ *n* parlante *mf*; (in public) oratore, -trice *mf*; (of stereo) cassa *f*
speaking terms /ˈspiːkɪŋ/ *npl* **we are not on ~** non ci parliamo
spear /spɪə(r)/ **A** *n* lancia *f*
B *vt* trafiggere
spearhead /ˈspɪəhed/ *vt* fig essere l'iniziatore di
spearmint /ˈspɪəmɪnt/ *n* menta *f* verde
spec /spek/ *n* **on ~** infml ‹*take, use*› in prova; ‹*go somewhere*› per ispezione
🔑 **special** /ˈspeʃl/ *adj* speciale
special correspondent *n* inviato, -a *mf* speciale
special delivery *n* espresso *m*
special effect **A** *n* Cinema, TV effetto *m* speciale
B *attrib* **~s** ‹*specialist, team*› degli effetti speciali

special envoy *n* inviato, -a *mf* speciale
specialist /ˈspeʃəlɪst/ *n* specialista *mf*
speciality /speʃɪˈælətɪ/ *n* specialità *f*
specialize /ˈspeʃəlaɪz/ *vi* specializzarsi
specially /ˈspeʃəlɪ/ *adv* specialmente; (particularly) particolarmente
special measures *n* BrE *provvedimenti (mpl) migliorativi di natura didattica, organizzativa, finanziaria o strutturale che una scuola deve adottare qualora non raggiunga gli standard educativi stabiliti dall'Ofsted*
special needs *npl* difficoltà *f inv* d'apprendimento; **children with ~** bambini con difficoltà d'apprendimento
special offer *n* vendita *f* promozionale
special school *n* scuola *f* per bambini con difficoltà d'apprendimento
special treatment *n* trattamento *m* di riguardo
species /ˈspiːʃiːz/ *n* specie *f inv*
specific /spəˈsɪfɪk/ *adj* specifico
specifically /spəˈsɪfɪklɪ/ *adv* in modo specifico
specifications /spesɪfɪˈkeɪʃnz/ *npl* descrizione *f*
specify /ˈspesɪfaɪ/ *vt* (*pt/pp* **-ied**) specificare
specimen /ˈspesɪmən/ *n* campione *m*
specious /ˈspiːʃəs/ *adj* ‹*argument, reasoning*› specioso
speck /spek/ *n* macchiolina *f*; (particle) granello *m*
speckled /ˈspekld/ *adj* picchiettato
specs /speks/ *npl* infml occhiali *mpl*
spectacle /ˈspektəkl/ *n* (show) spettacolo *m*
spectacles /ˈspektəklz/ *npl* occhiali *mpl*
spectacular /spekˈtækjʊlə(r)/ *adj* spettacolare
spectacularly /spekˈtækjʊləlɪ/ *adv* in modo spettacolare
spectator /spekˈteɪtə(r)/ *n* spettatore, -trice *mf*
spectator sport *n* sport *m inv* di intrattenimento
spectre /ˈspektə(r)/ *n* spettro *m*
spectrum /ˈspektrəm/ *n* (*pl* **-tra**) spettro *m*; fig gamma *f*
speculate /ˈspekjʊleɪt/ *vi* speculare
speculation /spekjʊˈleɪʃn/ *n* speculazione *f*
speculative /ˈspekjʊlətɪv/ *adj* speculativo
speculator /ˈspekjʊleɪtə(r)/ *n* speculatore, -trice *mf*
sped /sped/ ▶ **speed**
speech /spiːtʃ/ *n* linguaggio *m*; (address) discorso *m*; **make a ~, give a ~** fare un discorso
speech day *n* Sch giorno *m* della premiazione
speech impediment *n* difetto *m* di pronuncia
speechless /ˈspiːtʃlɪs/ *adj* senza parole
speech therapist *n* logoterapista *mf*
speech therapy *n* logoterapia *f*
speech-writer *n persona (f) che scrive i discorsi di personaggi pubblici*
speed /spiːd/ **A** *n* velocità *f*; (gear) marcia *f*; **at ~** a tutta velocità
B *vi* (*pt/pp* **sped**) andare veloce
C *vi* (*pt/pp* **speeded**) (go too fast) andare a velocità eccessiva
■ **speed up** *vt & vi* (*pt/pp* **speeded up**) accelerare
speedboat *n* motoscafo *m*
speed bump *n* rallentatore *m*
speed camera *n* autovelox® *m inv*
speed dial *n* composizione *f* veloce
speed hump *n* dosso *m* di rallentamento
speedily /ˈspiːdɪlɪ/ *adv* rapidamente
speeding /ˈspiːdɪŋ/ *n* eccesso *m* di velocità
speeding fine *n* multa *f* per eccesso di velocità
speed limit *n* limite *m* di velocità
speed merchant *n* infml fanatico, -a *mf* della velocità
speedometer /spiːˈdɒmɪtə(r)/ *n* tachimetro *m*
speed skating *n* pattinaggio *m* di velocità
speed trap *n* Auto *tratto (m) di strada sul quale la polizia controlla la velocità dei veicoli*
speedy /ˈspiːdɪ/ *adj* (**-ier, -iest**) rapido
speleologist /spiːlɪˈɒlədʒɪst/ *n* speleologo, -a *mf*
speleology /spiːlɪˈɒlədʒɪ/ *n* speleologia *f*
spell¹ /spel/ *n* (turn) turno *m*; (of weather) periodo *m*
spell² **A** *vt* (*pt/pp* **spelled** *or* **spelt**) **how do you ~...?** come si scrive...?; **could you ~ that for me?** me lo può compitare?; **~ disaster** fig essere disastroso
B *vi* **he can't ~** fa molti errori d'ortografia
spell³ *n* (magic) incantesimo *m*
■ **spell out** *vt* compitare; fig spiegare
spellbound /ˈspelbaʊnd/ *adj* affascinato
spellcheck *vt* Comput fare il controllo ortografico di ‹*document*›
spellchecker /ˈspeltʃekə(r)/ *n* Comput correttore *m* ortografico
spelling /ˈspelɪŋ/ *n* ortografia *f*
spelt /spelt/ ▶ **spell²**
spend /spend/ *vt & vi* (*pt/pp* **spent**) spendere; passare ‹*time*›
spending cut *n* taglio *m* alla spesa
spending money /ˈspendɪŋ/ *n* soldi *mpl* per le piccole spese
spending power *n* potere *m* d'acquisto
spending spree *n* spese *fpl* folli
spendthrift /ˈspendθrɪft/ **A** *adj* spendaccione; ‹*habit, policy*› dispendioso
B *n* spendaccione, -a *mf*

S

spent /spent/ ▶ **spend**
sperm /spɜːm/ *n* spermatozoo *m*; (semen) sperma *m*
sperm bank *n* banca *f* del seme
sperm count *n* conteggio *m* di spermatozoi
sperm donor *n* donatore *m* del seme
spermicidal /spɜːmɪˈsaɪdl/ *adj* spermicida *inv*
spermicide /ˈspɜːmɪsaɪd/ *n* spermicida *m*
spew /spjuː/ *vt & vi* vomitare
sphere /sfɪə(r)/ *n* sfera *f*
sphere of influence *n* sfera *f* di influenza
spherical /ˈsferɪkl/ *adj* sferico
spice /spaɪs/ *n* spezia *f*; fig pepe *m*
spick /spɪk/ *adj* ~ **and span** lindo
spicy /ˈspaɪsɪ/ *adj* piccante
spider /ˈspaɪdə(r)/ *n* ragno *m*
spiderweb *n* AmE = **web**
spiel /ʃpɪəl/ *n* infml (sales pitch) imbonimento *m*; (long repetitive speech) tiritera *f*; **he gave me some ~ about...** mi ha raccontato un sacco di storie su...
spike /spaɪk/ *n* punta *f*; Bot, Zool spina *f*; (on shoe) chiodo *m*
spikes *npl* (shoes) scarpe *fpl* chiodate
spiky /ˈspaɪkɪ/ *adj* ‹*plant*› spinoso
spill /spɪl/ **A** *vt* (*pt/pp* **spilt** *or* **spilled**) versare ‹*blood*›; ~ **the beans** infml vuotare il sacco
B *vi* rovesciarsi
▪ **spill over** *vi* ‹*water*› traboccare; ~ **over into** degenerare in ‹*violence, rioting*›
spillage /ˈspɪlɪdʒ/ *n* (of oil, chemical) perdita *f*
spin /spɪn/ **A** *vt* (*pt/pp* **spun**, *pres p* **spinning**) far girare; filare ‹*wool*›; centrifugare ‹*washing*›
B *vi* girare; ‹*washing machine*› centrifugare
C *n* rotazione *f*; (short drive) giretto *m*
▪ **spin out** *vt* far durare
▪ **spin round** **A** *vi* (turn quickly) girare vorticosamente; ‹*dancer, skater*› volteggiare; ‹*car*› fare un testa coda
B *vt* ~ **somebody** *or* **something round** far girare qualcuno *o* qualcosa
spinach /ˈspɪnɪdʒ/ *n* spinaci *mpl*
spinal /ˈspaɪnl/ *adj* spinale
spinal column *n* colonna *f* vertebrale
spinal cord *n* midollo *m* spinale
spindle /ˈspɪndl/ *n* fuso *m*
spindly /ˈspɪndlɪ/ *adj* affusolato
spin doctor *n persona (f) incaricata di presentare le scelte di un partito politico sotto una luce favorevole*
spin drier *n* centrifuga *f*
spine /spaɪn/ *n* spina *f* dorsale; (of book) dorso *m*; Bot, Zool spina *f*
spineless /ˈspaɪnlɪs/ *adj* fig smidollato
spinning /ˈspɪnɪŋ/ *n* filatura *f*
spinning wheel *n* filatoio *m*
spin-off *n* ricaduta *f*
spinster /ˈspɪnstə(r)/ *n* donna *f* nubile; (old maid, fam) zitella *f*
spiny /ˈspaɪnɪ/ *adj* ‹*plant, animal*› spinoso
spiral /ˈspaɪrəl/ **A** *adj* a spirale
B *n* spirale *f*
C *vi* (*pt/pp* **spiralled**) formare una spirale
spiral staircase *n* scala *f* a chiocciola
spire /ˈspaɪə(r)/ *n* guglia *f*
⚷ **spirit** /ˈspɪrɪt/ *n* spirito *m*; (courage) ardore *m*; ~**s** *pl* (alcohol) liquori *mpl*; **in good ~s** di buon umore; **in low ~s** abbattuto
▪ **spirit away** *vt* far sparire
spirited /ˈspɪrɪtɪd/ *adj* vivace; (courageous) pieno d'ardore
spirit level *n* livella *f* a bolla d'aria
spirit stove *n* fornellino *m* [da campeggio]
spiritual /ˈspɪrɪtjʊəl/ **A** *adj* spirituale
B *n* spiritual *m*
spiritualism /ˈspɪrɪtjʊəlɪzm/ *n* spiritismo *m*
spiritualist /ˈspɪrɪtjʊəlɪst/ *n* spiritista *mf*
spit¹ /spɪt/ *n* (for roasting) spiedo *m*
spit² **A** *n* sputo *m*
B *vt & vi* (*pt/pp* **spat**, *pres p* **spitting**) sputare; ‹*cat*› soffiare; ‹*fat*› sfrigolare; **it's ~ting [with rain]** pioviggina; **the ~ting image of** il ritratto spiccicato di
spite /spaɪt/ **A** *n* dispetto *m*; **in ~ of** malgrado
B *vt* far dispetto a
spiteful /ˈspaɪtfʊl/ *adj* indispettito
spitefully /ˈspaɪtfʊlɪ/ *adv* con aria indispettita
spit out *vt* sputare ‹*food*›; ~ **it out!** infml sputa l'osso!
spittle /ˈspɪtl/ *n* saliva *f*
splash /splæʃ/ **A** *n* schizzo *m*; (of colour) macchia *f*; infml (drop) goccio *m*
B *vt* schizzare; ~ **somebody with something** schizzare qualcuno di qualcosa
C *vi* schizzare
▪ **splash about** *vi* schizzarsi
▪ **splash down** *vi* ‹*spacecraft*› ammarare
▪ **splash out** *vi* (spend freely) darsi alle spese folli
splashdown /ˈsplæʃdaʊn/ *n* ammaraggio *m*
splatter /ˈsplætə(r)/ **A** *vt* schizzare; ~ **somebody/something with something** schizzare qualcuno/qualcosa di qualcosa
B *vi* ~ **onto/over something** ‹*ink, paint*› schizzare su qualcosa
splay /spleɪ/ *vt* divaricare ‹*legs, feet, fingers*›; svasare ‹*end of pipe etc*›; strombare ‹*side of window, door*›; ~**ed** ‹*feet, fingers, legs*› divaricato
spleen /spliːn/ *n* Anat milza *f*
splendid /ˈsplendɪd/ *adj* splendido
splendidly /ˈsplendɪdlɪ/ *adv* splendidamente
splendour /ˈsplendə(r)/ *n* splendore *m*

⚷ parola chiave

splice /splaɪs/ *vt* aggiuntare ‹*tape, film*›
splint /splɪnt/ *n* Med stecca *f*
splinter /ˈsplɪntə(r)/ **A** *n* scheggia *f*
B *vi* scheggiarsi
splinter group *n* gruppo *m* scissionista
split /splɪt/ **A** *n* fessura *f*; (quarrel) rottura *f*; (division) scissione *f*; (tear) strappo *m*
B *vt* (*pt/pp* **split**, *pres p* **splitting**) spaccare; (share, divide) dividere; (tear) strappare; ~ **hairs** spaccare il capello in quattro; ~ **one's sides** sbellicarsi dalle risa
C *vi* spaccarsi; (tear) strapparsi; (divide) dividersi; ~ **on somebody** infml denunciare qualcuno
D *adj* **a** ~ **second** una frazione di secondo
■ **split up A** *vt* dividersi
B *vi* ‹*couple*› separarsi
split ends *npl* (in hair) doppie punte *fpl*
split personality *n* sdoppiamento *m* della personalità
split screen *n* schermo *m* diviso
splitting /ˈsplɪtɪŋ/ *adj* **have a** ~ **headache** avere un tremendo mal di testa
splutter /ˈsplʌtə(r)/ *vi* farfugliare
spoil /spɔɪl/ **A** *n* ~**s** *pl* bottino *msg*
B *vt* (*pt/pp* **spoilt** BrE *or* **spoiled**) rovinare; viziare ‹*person*›
C *vi* andare a male
spoiler /ˈspɔɪlə(r)/ *n* Auto, Aeron spoiler *m inv*
spoilsport /ˈspɔɪlspɔːt/ *n* guastafeste *mf inv*
spoilt /spɔɪlt/ *adj* BrE ‹*child*› viziato; **be** ~ **for choice** non avere che l'imbarazzo della scelta
spoke¹ /spəʊk/ *n* raggio *m*
spoke² ▸ **speak**
spoken /ˈspəʊkən/ **A** ▸ **speak**
B *adj* ‹*language*› parlato; **be** ~ **for** essere messo da parte per qualcuno
⚷ **spokesman** /ˈspəʊksmən/ *n* portavoce *m inv*
spokesperson /ˈspəʊkspɜːsn/ *n* portavoce *mf*
spokeswoman /ˈspəʊkswʊmən/ *n* portavoce *f*
sponge /spʌndʒ/ **A** *n* spugna *f*
B *vt* pulire con la spugna
C *vi* ~ **on** infml scroccare da
sponge bag *n* nécessaire *m inv*
sponge cake *n* pan *m* di Spagna
sponger /ˈspʌndʒə(r)/ *n* scroccone, -a *mf*
spongy /ˈspʌndʒɪ/ *adj* spugnoso
sponsor /ˈspɒnsə(r)/ **A** *n* garante *mf*; Radio, TV sponsor *m inv*; (godparent) padrino *m*, madrina *f*; (for membership) socio, -a *mf* garante
B *vt* sponsorizzare
sponsorship /ˈspɒnsəʃɪp/ *n* sponsorizzazione *f*
sponsorship deal *n* accordo *m* con uno sponsor
spontaneity /spɒntəˈneɪətɪ/ *n* spontaneità *f*
spontaneous /spɒnˈteɪnɪəs/ *adj* spontaneo
spontaneously /spɒnˈteɪnɪəslɪ/ *adv* spontaneamente
spoof /spuːf/ *n* infml parodia *f*
spook /spuːk/ infml **A** *vt* (haunt) perseguitare; (frighten) spaventare
B *n* (ghost) fantasma *m*; AmE (spy) spia *f*
spooky /ˈspuːkɪ/ *adj* (**-ier**, **-iest**) infml sinistro
spool /spuːl/ *n* bobina *f*
spooling /ˈspuːlɪŋ/ *n* Comput spooling *m*
spoon /spuːn/ **A** *n* cucchiaio *m*
B *vt* mettere col cucchiaio
spoonerism /ˈspuːnərɪzm/ *n scambio (m) delle iniziali di due parole con effetto umoristico*
spoon-feed *vt* (*pt/pp* **-fed**) fig imboccare
spoonful /ˈspuːnfʊl/ *n* cucchiaiata *f*
sporadic /spəˈrædɪk/ *adj* sporadico
sporadically /spəˈrædɪklɪ/ *adv* sporadicamente
spore /spɔː(r)/ *n* spora *f*
sporran /ˈspɒrə/ *n borsa (f) di cuoio o pelo portata alla cintura dagli scozzesi insieme al kilt*
⚷ **sport** /spɔːt/ **A** *n* sport *m inv*; **be a [good]** ~**!** sii sportivo!
B *vt* sfoggiare
sporting /ˈspɔːtɪŋ/ *adj* sportivo
sporting calendar *n* calendario *m* sportivo
sporting chance *n* possibilità *f*
sports car *n* automobile *f* sportiva
sports centre BrE, **sports center** AmE *n* centro *m* polisportivo
sports club *n* club *m* sportivo
sports coat *n*, **sports jacket** *n* giacca *f* sportiva
sports ground *n* (large) stadio *m*; (in school) campo *m* sportivo
sports jacket *n* giacca *f* sportiva
sportsman *n* sportivo *m*
sports star *n* star *f inv* dello sport
sportswear *n* abbigliamento *m* sportivo
sportswoman *n* sportiva *f*
sports writer *n* giornalista *mf* sportivo, -a
sporty /ˈspɔːtɪ/ *adj* (**-ier**, **-iest**) sportivo
⚷ **spot** /spɒt/ **A** *n* macchia *f*; (pimple) brufolo *m*; (place) posto *m*; (in pattern) pois *m inv*; (of rain) goccia *f*; (of water) goccio *m*; ~**s** *pl* (rash) sfogo *msg*; **a** ~ **of** infml un po' di; **a** ~ **of bother** qualche problema; **on the** ~ sul luogo; (immediately) immediatamente; **in a [tight]** ~ infml in difficoltà
B *vt* (*pt/pp* **spotted**) macchiare; infml (notice) individuare
spot check *n* (without warning) controllo *m* a sorpresa; **do a** ~ **on something** dare una controllata a qualcosa
spotless /ˈspɒtlɪs/ *adj* immacolato
spotlight *n* riflettore *m*; fig riflettori *mpl*

S

spot on *adj* BrE esatto

spot rate *n* Fin tasso *m* di cambio a vista

spotted /'spɒtɪd/ *adj* ‹*material*› a pois

spotty /'spɒtɪ/ *adj* (**-ier**, **-iest**) (pimply) brufoloso

spot-weld *vt* saldare a punti

spouse /spaʊz/ *n* consorte *mf*

spout /spaʊt/ **A** *n* becco *m*; **up the ~** infml (ruined) all'aria
B *vi* zampillare (**from** da)

sprain /spreɪn/ **A** *n* slogatura *f*
B *vt* slogare; **~ one's ankle** slogarsi la caviglia

sprang /spræŋ/ ▶ **spring²**

sprat /spræt/ *n* spratto *m*

sprawl /sprɔːl/ *vi* (in chair) stravaccarsi; ‹*city etc*› estendersi; **go ~ing** (fall) cadere disteso

sprawling /'sprɔːlɪŋ/ *adj* ‹*suburb, city*› che si propaga disordinatamente; ‹*handwriting*› che occupa tutta la pagina

spray¹ /spreɪ/ *n* (of flowers) rametto *m*; (bouquet) mazzolino *m*

spray² **A** *n* spruzzo *m*; (from sea) spruzzi *mpl*; (preparation) spray *m inv*; (container) spruzzatore *m*
B *vt* spruzzare

spray can *n* bomboletta *f* spray *inv*

spray gun *n* pistola *f* a spruzzo

spray on *adj* ‹*conditioner, glitter*› spray *inv*

✐ **spread** /spred/ **A** *n* estensione *f*; (of disease) diffusione *f*; (paste) crema *f*; infml (feast) banchetto *m*
B *vt* (*pt/pp* **spread**) spargere; spalmare ‹*butter, jam*›; stendere ‹*cloth, arms*›; diffondere ‹*news, disease*›; dilazionare ‹*payments*›; **~ something with** spalmare qualcosa di
C *vi* spargersi; ‹*butter*› spalmarsi; ‹*disease*› diffondersi

▪ **spread out** **A** *vt* sparpagliare
B *vi* sparpagliarsi

spread betting *n* spread betting *m inv*, scommesse *fpl* con spread

spread-eagled /-'iːgld/ *adj* a gambe e braccia aperte

spreadsheet /'spredʃiːt/ *n* Comput foglio *m* elettronico

spree /spriː/ *n* infml **go on a ~** far baldoria; **go on a shopping ~** fare spese folli

sprig /sprɪg/ *n* rametto *m*

sprightly /'spraɪtlɪ/ *adj* (**-ier**, **-iest**) vivace

✐ **spring¹** /sprɪŋ/ **A** *n* primavera *f*; **in ~**, **in the ~** in primavera
B *attrib* primaverile

spring² **A** *n* (jump) balzo *m*; (water) sorgente *f*; (device) molla *f*; (elasticity) elasticità *f*
B *vi* (*pt* **sprang**, *pp* **sprung**) balzare; (arise) provenire (**from** da); **~ to mind** saltare in mente
C *vt* **he just sprang it on me** me l'ha detto a cose fatte

▪ **spring up** *vi* balzare; fig spuntare

springboard *n* trampolino *m*

spring chicken *n* Culin pollastrello *m*, pollastrella *f*; **she's no ~** infml non è una giovincella

spring-clean *vt* pulire a fondo

spring-cleaning *n* pulizie *fpl* di Pasqua

spring onion *n* cipollotto *m*

springtime *n* primavera *f*

springy /'sprɪŋɪ/ *adj* ‹*mattress, sofa*› molleggiato

sprinkle /'sprɪŋkl/ *vt* (scatter) spruzzare ‹*liquid*›; spargere ‹*flour, cocoa*›; **~ something with** spruzzare qualcosa di ‹*liquid*›; cospargere qualcosa di ‹*flour, cocoa*›

sprinkler /'sprɪŋklə(r)/ *n* sprinkler *m inv*; (for garden) irrigatore *m*

sprinkling /'sprɪŋklɪŋ/ *n* (of liquid) spruzzatina *f*; (of pepper, salt) pizzico *m*; (of flour, sugar) spolveratina *f*; (of knowledge) infarinatura *f*; (of people) pugno *m*

sprint /sprɪnt/ **A** *n* sprint *m inv*
B *vi* fare uno sprint; Sport sprintare

sprinter /'sprɪntə(r)/ *n* sprinter *mf inv*

sprite /spraɪt/ *n* folletto *m*

spritzer /'sprɪtsə(r)/ *n* spritz *m inv*, spritzer *m inv*

sprout /spraʊt/ **A** *n* germoglio *m*; **[Brussels] ~s** *pl* cavolini *mpl* di Bruxelles
B *vi* germogliare

spruce /spruːs/ **A** *adj* elegante
B *n* abete *m*

▪ **spruce up** *vt* dare una ripulita a

sprung /sprʌŋ/ **A** ▶ **spring²**
B *adj* molleggiato

spry /spraɪ/ *adj* (**-er**, **-est**) arzillo

spud /spʌd/ *n* infml patata *f*

spun /spʌn/ ▶ **spin**

spur /spɜː(r)/ **A** *n* sperone *m*; (stimulus) stimolo *m*; (road) svincolo *m*; **on the ~ of the moment** su due piedi
B *vt* (*pt/pp* **spurred**) **~ [on]** fig spronare

spurious /'spjʊərɪəs/ *adj* falso

spuriously /'spjʊərɪəslɪ/ *adv* falsamente

spurn /spɜːn/ *vt* sdegnare

spurt /spɜːt/ **A** *n* getto *m*; Sport scatto *m*; **put on a ~** fare uno scatto
B *vi* sprizzare; (increase speed) scattare

sputter /'spʌtə(r)/ **A** *vi* ‹*engine*› scoppiettare
B *n* colpi *mpl* irregolari del motore

spy /spaɪ/ **A** *n* spia *f*
B *vi* spiare
C *vt* infml (see) spiare

▪ **spy on** *vt* spiare

▪ **spy out** *vt* esplorare

spying /'spaɪɪŋ/ *n* spionaggio *m*

squabble /'skwɒbl/ **A** *n* bisticcio *m*
B *vi* bisticciare

✐ parola chiave

squabbling /ˈskwɒblɪŋ/ *n* bisticci *mpl*
squad /skwɒd/ *n* squadra *f*
squad car *n* macchina *f* della volante
squaddie /ˈskwɒdɪ/ *n* BrE infml soldato *m* semplice
squadron /ˈskwɒdrən/ *n* Mil squadrone *m*; Aeron, Naut squadriglia *f*
squalid /ˈskwɒlɪd/ *adj* squallido
squalidly /ˈskwɒlɪdlɪ/ *adv* squallidamente
squall /skwɔːl/ **A** *n* (howl) strillo *m*; (storm) bufera *f*
B *vi* strillare
squally /ˈskwɔːlɪ/ *adj* burrascoso
squalor /ˈskwɒlə(r)/ *n* squallore *m*
squander /ˈskwɒndə(r)/ *vt* sprecare
square /skweə(r)/ **A** *adj* quadrato; ‹*meal*› sostanzioso; infml (old-fashioned) vecchio stampo; **all ~** infml pari
B *n* quadrato *m*; (in city) piazza *f*; (on chessboard) riquadro *m*; **be back to ~ one** riessere al punto di partenza
C *vt* (settle) far quadrare; Math elevare al quadrato
D *vi* (agree) armonizzare
▪ **square up** *vi* (settle accounts) saldare
▪ **square up to** *vt* affrontare
square bracket *n* parentesi *f inv* quadra; **in ~s** tra parentesi quadre
square dance *n* quadriglia *f*
squarely /ˈskweəlɪ/ *adv* direttamente
square root *n* radice *f* quadrata
squash /skwɒʃ/ **A** *n* calca *f*; (drink) spremuta *f*; (sport) squash *m*; (vegetable) zucca *f*
B *vt* schiacciare; soffocare ‹*rebellion*›
▪ **squash up** *vi* (move closer together) stringersi
squashy /ˈskwɒʃɪ/ *adj* floscio
squat /ˈskwɒt/ **A** *adj* tarchiato
B *n* infml edificio *m* occupato abusivamente
C *vi* (*pt/pp* **squatted**) accovacciarsi; **~ in** occupare abusivamente
squatter /ˈskwɒtə(r)/ *n* occupante *mf* abusivo, -a
squaw /skwɔː/ *n* offensive squaw *f inv*
squawk /skwɔːk/ **A** *n* gracchio *m*
B *vi* gracchiare
squeak /skwiːk/ **A** *n* squittio *m*; (of hinge, brakes) cigolio *m*
B *vi* squittire; ‹*hinge, brakes*› cigolare
squeaking /ˈskwiːkɪŋ/ *n* (of door, hinge) cigolio *m*
squeaky /ˈskwiːkɪ/ *adj* ‹*door, hinge*› cigolante
squeaky-clean *adj* infml ‹*glass, hair*› lucente; ‹*floor*› tirato a specchio; fig ‹*person*› senza vizi; ‹*company*› al di sopra di ogni sospetto
squeal /skwiːl/ **A** *n* strillo *m*; (of brakes) cigolio *m*
B *vi* strillare; sl spifferare
squeamish /ˈskwiːmɪʃ/ *adj* dallo stomaco delicato; (scrupulous) troppo scrupoloso
squeegee /ˈskwiːdʒiː/ *n* Phot rullo *m* asciugatore; (for glasses) lavavetri *m inv*
squeeze /skwiːz/ **A** *n* stretta *f*; (crush) pigia pigia *m inv*; **give sb's hand a ~** dare a qualcuno una stretta di mano
B *vt* premere; (to get juice) spremere; stringere ‹*hand*›; (force) stringere a forza; infml (extort) estorcere (**out of** da)
▪ **squeeze in/out** *vi* sgusciare dentro/fuori
▪ **squeeze past** *vi* ‹*person, car*› passare
▪ **squeeze up** *vi* stringersi
squelch /skweltʃ/ *vi* sguazzare
squib /skwɪb/ *n* petardo *m*
squid /skwɪd/ *n* calamaro *m*
squidgy /ˈskwɪdʒɪ/ *adj* BrE infml (squashy) molliccio
squiggle /ˈskwɪgl/ *n* scarabocchio *m*
squint /skwɪnt/ **A** *n* strabismo *m*
B *vi* essere strabico
squire /ˈskwaɪə(r)/ *n* signorotto *m* di campagna
squirm /skwɜːm/ *vi* contorcersi; (feel embarrassed) sentirsi imbarazzato
squirrel /ˈskwɪrəl/ *n* scoiattolo *m*
squirt /skwɜːt/ **A** *n* spruzzo *m*; infml (person) presuntuoso *m*
B *vt & vi* spruzzare
Sri Lanka *n* Sri Lanka *m*
St *abbr* **1** (**Saint**) S **2** (**Street**)
stab /stæb/ **A** *n* pugnalata *f*, coltellata *f*; (sensation) fitta *f*; infml (attempt) tentativo *m*
B *vt* (*pt/pp* **stabbed**) pugnalare, accoltellare
stability /stəˈbɪlətɪ/ *n* stabilità *f*
stabilization /steɪbɪlaɪˈzeɪʃn/ *n* stabilizzazione *f*
stabilize /ˈsteɪbɪlaɪz/ **A** *vt* stabilizzare
B *vi* stabilizzarsi
stabilizer /ˈsteɪbɪlaɪzə(r)/ *n* stabilizzatore *m*; (on bike) rotella *f*; (in food) stabilizzante *m*
stable[1] /ˈsteɪbl/ *adj* stabile
stable[2] *n* stalla *f*; (establishment) scuderia *f*
staccato /stəˈkɑːtəʊ/ **A** *adj* Mus staccato; ‹*gasps, shots*› intermittente
B *adv* ‹*play*› staccatamente
stack /stæk/ **A** *n* catasta *f*; (of chimney) comignolo *m*; (chimney) ciminiera *f*; infml (large quantity) montagna *f*; **~s of** ‹*money, time, work*› un sacco di
B *vt* accatastare
stadium /ˈsteɪdɪəm/ *n* stadio *m*
⚷ **staff** /stɑːf/ **A** *n* (stick) bastone *m*; (employees) personale *m*; (teachers) corpo *m* insegnante; Mil Stato *m* Maggiore
B *vt* fornire di personale
staff meeting *n* riunione *f* del corpo insegnante
staffroom /ˈstɑːfruːm/ *n* Sch sala *f* insegnanti
stag /stæg/ *n* cervo *m*
⚷ **stage** /steɪdʒ/ **A** *n* palcoscenico *m*; (profession) teatro *m*; (in journey) tappa *f*; (in process) stadio

m; **go on the ~** darsi al teatro; **by** *or* **in ~s** a tappe
B *vt* mettere in scena; (arrange) organizzare

stagecoach *n* diligenza *f*

stage door *n* ingresso *m* degli artisti

stage fright *n* panico *m* da palcoscenico

stage-manage *vt* fig orchestrare

stage manager *n* direttore, -trice *mf* di scena

stage-struck /-strʌk/ *adj* appassionatissimo di teatro

stagger /'stægə(r)/ **A** *vi* barcollare
B *vt* sbalordire; scaglionare ‹*holidays, payments etc*›; **I was ~ed** sono rimasto sbalordito
C *n* vacillamento *m*

staggering /'stægərɪŋ/ *adj* sbalorditivo

stagnant /'stægnənt/ *adj* stagnante

stagnate /stæg'neɪt/ *vi* fig [ri]stagnare

stagnation /stæg'neɪʃn/ *n* fig inattività *f*

stag night, **stag party** *n* addio *m* al celibato

staid /steɪd/ *adj* posato

stain /steɪn/ **A** *n* macchia *f*; (for wood) mordente *m*
B *vt* macchiare; ‹*wood*› dare il mordente a

stained glass /steɪnd'glɑːs/ *n* vetro *m* colorato

stained-glass window *n* vetrata *f* colorata

stainless /'steɪnlɪs/ *adj* senza macchia

stainless steel *n* acciaio *m* inossidabile

stain remover *n* smacchiatore *m*

stair /steə(r)/ *n* gradino *m*; **~s** *pl* scale *fpl*

staircase /'steəkeɪs/ *n* scale *fpl*

stairlift *n* montascale *m inv*

stake /steɪk/ **A** *n* palo *m*; (wager) posta *f*; Comm partecipazione *f*; **at ~** in gioco
B *vt* puntellare; (wager) scommettere; **~ a claim to something** rivendicare qualcosa

■ **stake out** *vt* mettere sotto sorveglianza ‹*building*›

stake-out *n* infml sorveglianza *f*

stalactite /'stæləktaɪt/ *n* stalattite *f*

stalagmite /'stæləgmaɪt/ *n* stalagmite *f*

stale /steɪl/ *adj* stantio; ‹*air*› viziato; (uninteresting) trito [e ritrito]

stalemate /'steɪlmeɪt/ *n* (in chess) stallo *m*; (deadlock) situazione *f* di stallo

stalk¹ /stɔːk/ *n* gambo *m*

stalk² **A** *vt* inseguire
B *vi* camminare impettito

stalker /'stɔːkə(r)/ *n* (of person) *stalker mf inv*

stalking /'stɔːkɪŋ/ *n* (of person) *stalking*

stall /stɔːl/ **A** *n* box *m inv*; (in market) bancarella *f*; **~s** *pl* Theat platea *f*
B *vi* ‹*engine*› spegnersi; fig temporeggiare
C *vt* far spegnere ‹*engine*›; tenere a bada ‹*person*›

stallholder /'stɔːlhəʊldə(r)/ *n* bancarellista *mf*

stallion /'stæljən/ *n* stallone *m*

stalwart /'stɔːlwət/ **A** *adj* fedele
B *n* sostenitore *m* fedele

stamina /'stæmɪnə/ *n* [capacità *f* di] resistenza *f*

stammer /'stæmə(r)/ **A** *n* balbettio *m*
B *vt & vi* balbettare

stamp /stæmp/ **A** *n* (postage) **~** francobollo *m*; (instrument) timbro *m*; fig impronta *f*
B *vt* affrancare ‹*letter*›; timbrare ‹*bill*›; battere ‹*feet*›

■ **stamp out** *vt* spegnere; fig soffocare

stamp collecting *n* filatelia *f*

stamp collector *n* collezionista *mf* di francobolli

stamped addressed envelope busta *f* affrancata per la risposta

stampede /stæm'piːd/ **A** *n* fuga *f* precipitosa; infml fuggifuggi *m inv*
B *vi* fuggire precipitosamente

stance /stɑːns/ *n* posizione *f*

✍ **stand** /stænd/ **A** *n* (for bikes) rastrelliera *f*; (at exhibition) stand *m inv*; (in market) bancarella *f*; (in stadium) gradinata *f*; fig posizione *f*
B *vi* (*pt/pp* **stood**) stare in piedi; (rise) alzarsi [in piedi]; (be) trovarsi; (be candidate) essere candidato (**for** a); (stay valid) rimanere valido; **I don't know where I ~** non so qual è la mia posizione; **~ still** non muoversi; **~ firm** fig tener duro; **~ on ceremony** formalizzarsi; **~ together** essere solidali; **~ to lose/gain** rischiare di perdere/vincere; **~ to reason** essere logico
C *vt* (withstand) resistere a; (endure) sopportare; (place) mettere; **~ a chance** avere una possibilità; **~ one's ground** tener duro; **~ the test of time** superare la prova del tempo; **~ somebody a beer** offrire una birra a qualcuno

■ **stand back** *vi* (withdraw) farsi da parte

■ **stand by** **A** *vi* stare a guardare; (be ready) essere pronto
B *vt* (support) appoggiare

■ **stand down** *vi* (retire) ritirarsi

■ **stand for** *vt* (mean) significare; (tolerate) tollerare

■ **stand in for** *vt* sostituire

■ **stand out** *vi* spiccare

■ **stand up** *vi* alzarsi [in piedi]

■ **stand up for** *vt* prendere le difese di; **~ up for oneself** farsi valere

■ **stand up to** *vt* affrontare

stand-alone *adj* Comput stand-alone

✍ **standard** /'stændəd/ **A** *adj* standard; **be ~ practice** essere pratica corrente
B *n* standard *m inv*; Techn norma *f*; (level)

S

✍ parola chiave

livello *m*; (quality) qualità *f*; (flag) stendardo *m*; **~s** *pl* (morals) valori *mpl*

Standard Assessment Tasks *n* BrE *esami (mpl) sostenuti per tranche d'età allo scopo di testare la preparazione degli alunni*

standardization /stændədaɪ'zeɪʃn/ *n* standardizzazione *f*

standardize /'stændədaɪz/ *vt* standardizzare

standard lamp *n* lampada *f* a stelo

standard of living *n* tenore *m* di vita

standby /'stændbaɪ/ **A** *n* (person) riserva *f*
B *attrib* ‹*circuit, battery*› di emergenza; ‹*passenger*› in lista di attesa; ‹*ticket*› stand-by *inv*
C *adv* ‹*fly*› con biglietto stand-by

stand-in *n* controfigura *f*

standing /'stændɪŋ/ **A** *adj* (erect) in piedi; (permanent) permanente
B *n* posizione *f*; (duration) durata *f*

standing charge *n* canone *m*

standing order *n* ordine *m* permanente

standing ovation *n* **give somebody a ~** alzarsi per applaudire qualcuno

standing room *n* posti *mpl* in piedi

stand-off /'stændɒf/ *n* punto *m* morto

stand-offish /stænd'ɒfɪʃ/ *adj* scostante

standpoint *n* punto *m* di vista

standstill *n* **come to a ~** fermarsi; **at a ~** in un periodo di stasi

stand-up **A** *adj* ‹*buffet*› in piedi; ‹*argument*› accanito
B *n* (comedy) recital *m inv* di un comico

stand-up comedian *comico (m) che intrattiene il pubblico con barzellette*

stank /stæŋk/ ▸ **stink**

Stanley knife® *n* cutter *m inv*

stanza /'stænzə/ *n* strofa *f*

staple¹ /'steɪpl/ *n* (product) prodotto *m* principale

staple² **A** *n* graffa *f*
B *vt* pinzare

staple diet *n* **a ~ of** una dieta basata principalmente su

staple gun *n* pistola *f* sparachiodi

stapler /'steɪplə(r)/ *n* pinzatrice *f*, cucitrice *f*

staple remover *n* levapunti *m inv*

star /stɑː(r)/ **A** *n* stella *f*; (asterisk) asterisco *m*; Theat, Cinema, Sport divo, -a *mf*, stella *f*
B *vi* (*pt/pp* **starred**) essere l'interprete principale (**in** di)

starboard /'stɑːbəd/ *n* tribordo *m*

starch /stɑːtʃ/ **A** *n* amido *m*
B *vt* inamidare

starchy /'stɑːtʃɪ/ *adj* ricco di amido; fig compito

stardom /'stɑːdəm/ *n* celebrità *f*

stare /steə(r)/ **A** *n* sguardo *m* fisso
B *vi* **it's rude to ~** è da maleducati fissare la gente; **~ at** fissare; **~ into space** guardare nel vuoto

starfish /'stɑːfɪʃ/ *n* stella *f* di mare

stark /stɑːk/ **A** *adj* austero; ‹*contrast*› forte
B *adv* completamente; **~ naked** completamente nudo

starlet /'stɑːlɪt/ *n* stellina *f*

starling /'stɑːlɪŋ/ *n* storno *m*

starlit /'stɑːlɪt/ *adj* stellato

starry /'stɑːrɪ/ *adj* stellato

starry-eyed /-'aɪd/ *adj* infml ingenuo

star sign *n* segno *m* zodiacale

star-struck /-strʌk/ *adj* ossessionato dalle celebrità

star-studded /-stʌdɪd/ *adj* ‹*cast, line-up*› con molti interpreti famosi; ‹*sky*› stellato

start /stɑːt/ **A** *n* inizio *m*; (departure) partenza *f*; (jump) sobbalzo *m*; **from the ~** [fin] dall'inizio; **for a ~** tanto per cominciare; **give somebody a ~** Sport dare un vantaggio a qualcuno
B *vi* [in]cominciare; (set out) avviarsi; ‹*engine, car*› partire; (jump) trasalire; **to ~ with,...** tanto per cominciare
C *vt* [in]cominciare; (cause) dare inizio a; (found) mettere su; mettere in moto ‹*car*›; mettere in giro ‹*rumour*›

■ **start off** *vi* (begin) cominciare

■ **start on** *vt* infml (attack) criticare; (nag) punzecchiare

■ **start out** *vi* (on journey) partire

■ **start over** AmE *vi* (with task) ricominciare

■ **start up** *vt* mettere in funzione ‹*engine*›; avviare ‹*business*›

starter /'stɑːtə(r)/ *n* Culin primo *m* [piatto *m*]; (in race: giving signal) starter *m inv*; (participant) concorrente *mf*; Auto motorino *m* d'avviamento

starting point /'stɑːtɪŋ/ *n* punto *m* di partenza

starting salary *n* stipendio *m* iniziale

startle /'stɑːtl/ *vt* far trasalire; ‹*news*› sconvolgere

startling /'stɑːtlɪŋ/ *adj* sconvolgente

start-up capital *n* capitale *m* di avviamento

starvation /stɑː'veɪʃn/ *n* fame *f*

starve /stɑːv/ **A** *vi* morire di fame
B *vt* far morire di fame

starving /'stɑːvɪŋ/ *adj* **be ~** (dying of hunger) soffrire la fame; infml (very hungry) morire di fame

stash /stæʃ/ *vt* infml **~ [away]** nascondere

state /steɪt/ **A** *n* stato *m*; Pol Stato *m*; (grand style) pompa *f*; **be in a ~** ‹*person*› essere agitato; **lie in ~** essere esposto
B *attrib* di Stato; Sch pubblico; (with ceremony) di gala
C *vt* dichiarare; (specify) precisare

state-aided /-'eɪdɪd/ *adj* sovvenzionato dallo Stato

State Department *n* AmE Pol ministero *m* degli [affari] esteri

state-funded *adj* sovvenzionato dallo Stato
stateless /'steɪtlɪs/ *adj* apolide
stately /'steɪtlɪ/ *adj* (**-ier**, **-iest**) maestoso
stately home *n* dimora *f* signorile
⚷ **statement** /'steɪtmənt/ *n* dichiarazione *f*; Jur deposizione *f*; (from bank) estratto *m* conto; (account) rapporto *m*
state of emergency *n* stato *m* di emergenza
state of play punteggio *m*
state of the art *adj* ‹*technology*› il più avanzato
stateside /'steɪtsaɪd/ **A** *adj* degli Stati Uniti **B** *adv* negli Stati Uniti
statesman /'steɪtsmən/ *n* statista *m*
static /'stætɪk/ *adj* statico
static electricity *n* elettricità *f* statica
⚷ **station** /'steɪʃn/ **A** *n* stazione *f*; (police) commissariato *m*
B *vt* appostare ‹*guard*›; **be ~ed in Germany** essere di stanza in Germania
stationary /'steɪʃənərɪ/ *adj* immobile
stationer /'steɪəʃnə(r)/ *n* **~'s [shop]** cartoleria *f*
stationery /'steɪʃənərɪ/ *n* cancelleria *f*
station wagon *n* AmE station-wagon *f inv*
statistical /stə'tɪstɪkl/ *adj* statistico
statistically /stə'tɪstɪklɪ/ *adv* statisticamente
statistician /stætɪs'tɪʃn/ *n* esperto *m* di statistica
statistics /stə'tɪstɪks/ *nsg* (subject) statistica *fsg*; *npl* (figures) statistiche *fpl*
statue /'stætju:/ *n* statua *f*
statuesque /stætjʊ'esk/ *adj* statuario
stature /'stætʃə(r)/ *n* statura *f*
⚷ **status** /'steɪtəs/ *n* condizione *f*; (high rank) alto rango *m*
status bar *n* Comput barra *f* di stato
status quo *n* statu quo *m inv*
status symbol *n* status symbol *m inv*
statute /'stætju:t/ *n* statuto *m*
statutory /'stætjʊtərɪ/ *adj* statutario
staunch /stɔ:ntʃ/ *adj* fedele
staunchly /'stɔ:ntʃlɪ/ *adv* fedelmente
stave /steɪv/ *vt* **~ off** tenere lontano
⚷ **stay** /steɪ/ **A** *n* soggiorno *m*
B *vi* restare, rimanere; (reside) alloggiare; **~ the night** passare la notte; **~ put** non muoversi
C *vt* **~ the course** resistere fino alla fine
▪ **stay away** *vi* stare lontano
▪ **stay behind** *vi* non andare con gli altri
▪ **stay in** *vi* (at home) stare in casa; Sch *restare a scuola dopo le lezioni*
▪ **stay on** *vi* (remain) rimanere; **~ on at school** continuare gli studi
▪ **stay up** *vi* stare su; ‹*person*› stare alzato

⚷ parola chiave

staying power /'steɪɪŋ/ *n* capacità *f* di resistenza
STD *abbr* (**sexually transmitted disease**) malattia *f* sessualmente trasmissibile, MST
STD code, **STD area code** *n* BrE prefisso *m* [di teleselezione]
stead /sted/ *n* **in his ~** in sua vece; **stand somebody in good ~** tornare utile a qualcuno
steadfast /'stedfɑ:st/ *adj* fedele; ‹*refusal*› fermo
steadily /'stedɪlɪ/ *adv* (continually) continuamente
steady /'stedɪ/ **A** *adj* (**-ier**, **-iest**) saldo, fermo; ‹*breathing*› regolare; ‹*job, boyfriend*› fisso; (dependable) serio
B *adv* **be going ~** ‹*couple*› fare coppia fissa
steak /steɪk/ *n* (for stew) spezzatino *m*; (for grilling, frying) bistecca *f*
⚷ **steal** /sti:l/ *vt* (*pt* **stole**, *pp* **stolen**) rubare (**from** da); **~ the show** essere al centro dell'attenzione
▪ **steal in/out** *vi* entrare/uscire furtivamente
stealth /stelθ/ *n* **by ~** di nascosto
stealthily /'stelθɪlɪ/ *adv* furtivamente
stealthy /'stelθɪ/ *adj* furtivo
steam /sti:m/ **A** *n* vapore *m*; **under one's own ~** infml da solo; **let off ~** fig sfogarsi
B *vt* Culin cucinare a vapore
C *vi* fumare
▪ **steam up** *vi* ‹*window*› appannarsi
steamed up /sti:md'ʌp/ *adj* **get ~ up** (angry) andare su tutte le furie
steam engine *n* locomotiva *f*
steamer /'sti:mə(r)/ *n* piroscafo *m*; (saucepan) pentola *f* a vapore
steam iron *n* ferro *m* [da stiro] a vapore
steamroller /'sti:mrəʊlə(r)/ *n* rullo *m* compressore
steamy /'sti:mɪ/ *adj* appannato; fig ‹*scene*› spinto
steel /sti:l/ **A** *n* acciaio *m*
B *vt* **~ oneself** temprarsi
steel wool *n* lana *f* d'acciaio
steelworks *n* acciaieria *f*
steely /'sti:lɪ/ *adj* d'acciaio
steep[1] /sti:p/ *vt* (soak) lasciare a bagno; **~ed in** fig immerso in
steep[2] *adj* ripido; infml ‹*price*› esorbitante
steeple /'sti:pl/ *n* campanile *m*
steeplechase /'sti:pltʃeɪs/ *n* corsa *f* ippica a ostacoli
steeplejack /'sti:pldʒæk/ *n persona (f) che ripara campanili e ciminiere*
steeply /'sti:plɪ/ *adv* ripidamente
steer /stɪə(r)/ *vt & vi* guidare; **~ clear of** stare alla larga da
steering /'stɪərɪŋ/ *n* Auto sterzo *m*
steering column *n* Auto piantone *m* dello sterzo

steering committee *n* comitato *m* direttivo
steering lock *n* Auto bloccasterzo *m*; (turning circle) angolo *m* di massima sterzata
steering wheel *n* volante *m*
stem¹ /stem/ **A** *n* stelo *m*; (of glass) gambo *m*; (of word) radice *f*
B *vi* (*pt/pp* **stemmed**) ~ **from** derivare da
stem² *vt* (*pt/pp* **stemmed**) contenere
stem cell *n* cellula *f* staminale
stem ginger *n* zenzero *m* sciroppato
stench /stentʃ/ *n* fetore *m*
stencil /ˈstensl/ **A** *n* stampino *m*; (decoration) stampo *m*
B *vt* (*pt/pp* **stencilled**) stampinare
stenographer /stɪˈnɒgrəfə(r)/ *n* stenografo, -a *mf*
stenography /stɪˈnɒgrəfɪ/ *n* stenografia *f*
step /step/ **A** *n* passo *m*; (stair) gradino *m*; ~**s** *pl* (ladder) scaleo *m*; **in** ~ al passo; **be out of** ~ non stare al passo; ~ **by** ~ un passo alla volta
B *vi* (*pt/pp* **stepped**) ~ **into** entrare in; ~ **into sb's shoes** succedere a qualcuno; ~ **out of** uscire da; ~ **out of line** sgarrare
■ **step back** *vi* fare un passo indietro; ~ **back from something** fig prendere le distanze da qualcosa
■ **step down** *vi* fig dimettersi
■ **step forward** *vi* farsi avanti
■ **step in** *vi* fig intervenire
■ **step up** *vt* (increase) aumentare
step aerobics *nsg* step *m inv*
stepbrother *n* fratellastro *m*
stepchild *n* figliastro, -a *mf*
stepdaughter *n* figliastra *f*
stepfather *n* patrigno *m*
stepladder *n* scaleo *m*
stepmother *n* matrigna *f*
stepping stone /ˈstepɪŋ/ *n* pietra *f* per guadare; fig trampolino *m*
stepsister /ˈstepsɪstə(r)/ *n* sorellastra *f*
stepson /ˈstepsʌn/ *n* figliastro *m*
stereo /ˈsterɪəʊ/ *n* stereo *m*; **in** ~ in stereofonia
stereophonic /sterɪəʊˈfɒnɪk/ *adj* stereofonico
stereoscopic /sterɪəʊˈskɒɪk/ *adj* stereoscopico
stereotype /ˈsterɪətaɪp/ *n* stereotipo *m*
stereotyped /ˈsterɪətaɪpt/ *adj* stereotipato
sterile /ˈsteraɪl/ *adj* sterile
sterility /stəˈrɪlətɪ/ *n* sterilità *f*
sterilization /sterəlaɪˈzeɪʃn/ *n* sterilizzazione *f*
sterilize /ˈsterɪlaɪz/ *vt* sterilizzare
sterling /ˈstɜːlɪŋ/ **A** *adj* fig apprezzabile
B *n* sterlina *f*
sterling silver *n* argento *m* pregiato
stern¹ /stɜːn/ *adj* severo
stern² *n* (of boat) poppa *f*
sternly /ˈstɜːnlɪ/ *adv* severamente
steroid /ˈsterɔɪd/ *n* steroide *m*
stet /stet/ (in proof-reading) vive
stethoscope /ˈsteθəskəʊp/ *n* stetoscopio *m*
Stetson® /ˈstetsən/ *n* cappello *m* da cowboy
stew /stjuː/ **A** *n* stufato *m*; **in a** ~ infml agitato
B *vt & vi* cuocere in umido; ~**ed fruit** frutta *f* cotta
steward /ˈstjuːəd/ *n* (at meeting) organizzatore, -trice *mf*; (on ship, aircraft) steward *m inv*
stewardess /stjuːəˈdes/ *n* hostess *f inv*
stick¹ /stɪk/ *n* bastone *m*; (of celery, rhubarb) gambo *m*; Sport mazza *f*
stick² **A** *vt* (*pt/pp* **stuck**) (stab) conficcare; (glue) attaccare; infml (put) mettere; infml (endure) sopportare; **be stuck** ‹*vehicle, person*› essere bloccato; ‹*drawer*› essere incastrato; **stuck in a traffic jam** bloccato nel traffico; **be stuck for an answer** non saper cosa rispondere; **stuck on** infml attratto da; **be stuck with something** infml farsi incastrare con qualcosa
B *vi* (adhere) attaccarsi (**to** a); (jam) bloccarsi
■ **stick around** *vi* infml (stay) rimanere
■ **stick at**: *vt* ~ **at it** infml tener duro; ~ **at nothing** infml non fermarsi di fronte a niente
■ **stick by** *vt* (be faithful to) rimanere al fianco di ‹*somebody*›
■ **stick down** *vt* incollare ‹*flap*›; infml (write down, put down) mettere
■ **stick out** **A** *vi* (project) sporgere; infml (catch the eye) risaltare
B *vt* infml tirar fuori ‹*tongue*›; ~ **it out** (endure) tener duro; ~ **one's neck out** sbilanciarsi
■ **stick to** *vt* (keep to) attenersi a ‹*rules, facts*›; mantenere ‹*story*›; perseverare in ‹*task*›; **I'll** ~ **to beer** continuo con la birra
■ **stick together** *vi* ‹*pages*› incollarsi; (be loyal) aiutarsi a vicenda; (not split up) rimanere uniti
■ **stick up** *vi* (project) sporgere
■ **stick up for** *vt* infml difendere
■ **stick with** *vt* (remain with) rimanere con ‹*somebody*›
sticker /ˈstɪkə(r)/ *n* autoadesivo *m*
sticking plaster /ˈstɪkɪʃ/ *n* cerotto *m*
stick insect *n* insetto *m* stecco *inv*
stick-in-the-mud *n* retrogrado, -a *mf*
stickler /ˈstɪklə(r)/ *n* **be a** ~ **for** tenere molto a
stick-up *n* infml rapina *f* a mano armata
sticky /ˈstɪkɪ/ **A** *adj* (**-ier, -iest**) appiccicoso; (adhesive) adesivo; fig (difficult) difficile
B *n* infml post-it® *m inv*
sticky tape *n* infml nastro *m* adesivo
stiff /stɪf/ *adj* rigido; ‹*brush, task*› duro; ‹*person*› controllato; ‹*drink*› forte; ‹*penalty*› severo; ‹*price*› alto; **bored** ~

S

infml annoiato a morte; ~ **neck** torcicollo *m*
stiffen /ˈstɪfn/ **A** *vt* irrigidire
B *vi* irrigidirsi
stiffly /ˈstɪlɪ/ *adv* rigidamente; ‹*smile, answer*› in modo controllato
stiffness /ˈstɪfnɪs/ *n* rigidità *f*
stifle /ˈstaɪfl/ *vt* soffocare
stifling /ˈstaɪflɪŋ/ *adj* soffocante
stigma /ˈstɪgmə/ *n* marchio *m*
stigmatize /ˈstɪgmətaɪz/ *vt* bollare
stile /staɪl/ *n* scaletta *f*
stiletto /stɪˈletəʊ/ *n* stiletto *m*; ~ **heels** tacchi *mpl* a spillo; **~s** *pl* (shoes) scarpe *fpl* coi tacchi a spillo
still[1] /stɪl/ *n* distilleria *f*
⚷ **still**[2] **A** *adj* fermo; ‹*drink*› non gasato; **keep/stand** ~ stare fermo
B *n* quiete *f*; (photo) posa *f*
C *adv* ancora; (nevertheless) nondimeno, comunque; **I'm ~ not sure** non sono ancora sicuro
stillborn /ˈstɪlbɔːn/ *adj* nato morto
still life *n* natura *f* morta
stilted /ˈstɪltɪd/ *adj* artificioso
stilts /stɪlts/ *npl* trampoli *mpl*
stimulant /ˈstɪmjʊlənt/ *n* eccitante *m*
stimulate /ˈstɪmjʊleɪt/ *vt* stimolare
stimulating /ˈstɪmjʊleɪtɪŋ/ *adj* stimolante
stimulation /stɪmjʊˈleɪʃn/ *n* stimolo *m*
stimulus /ˈstɪmjʊləs/ *n* (*pl* **-li** /ˈstɪmjʊlaɪ/) stimolo *m*
sting /stɪŋ/ **A** *n* puntura *f*; (organ) pungiglione *m*
B *vt* (*pt/pp* **stung**) pungere; ‹*jellyfish*› pizzicare
C *vi* ‹*insect*› pungere
stinging nettle /ˈstɪŋɪŋ/ *n* ortica *f*
stingy /ˈstɪndʒɪ/ *adj* (**-ier**, **-iest**) tirchio
stink /stɪŋk/ **A** *n* puzza *f*
B *vi* (*pt* **stank**, *pp* **stunk**) puzzare
stink bomb *n* fialetta *f* puzzolente
stinker /ˈstɪŋkə(r)/ *n* infml (difficult problem etc) rompicapo *m*
stinking /ˈstɪŋkɪŋ/ *adv* **be ~ rich** infml essere ricco sfondato
stint /stɪnt/ **A** *n* lavoro *m*; **do one's ~** fare la propria parte
B *vt* **~ on** lesinare su
stipend /ˈstaɪpend/ *n* congrua *f*
stipulate /ˈstɪpjʊleɪt/ *vt* porre come condizione
stipulation /stɪpjʊˈleɪʃn/ *n* condizione *f*
stir /stɜː(r)/ **A** *n* mescolata *f*; (commotion) trambusto *m*
B *vt* (*pt/pp* **stirred**) muovere; (mix) mescolare
C *vi* muoversi
■ **stir up** *vt* fomentare ‹*hatred*›
stir-fry **A** *vt* saltare in padella
B *n* pietanza *f* saltata in padella
stirring /ˈstɜːrɪŋ/ *adj* ‹*speech, music*› commovente
stirrup /ˈstɪrəp/ *n* staffa *f*
stitch /stɪtʃ/ **A** *n* punto *m*; (knitting) maglia *f*; (pain) fitta *f*; **have somebody in ~es** infml far ridere qualcuno a crepapelle
B *vt* cucire
■ **stitch up** *vt* ricucire ‹*wound*›; **the deal's ~ed up** l'affare è concluso
stoat /stəʊt/ *n* ermellino *m*
⚷ **stock** /stɒk/ **A** *n* (for use or selling) scorta *f*, stock *m inv*; (livestock) bestiame *m*; (lineage) stirpe *f*; Fin titoli *mpl*; Culin brodo *m*; **in ~** disponibile; **out of ~** esaurito; **take ~** fig fare il punto
B *adj* solito
C *vt* ‹*shop*› vendere; approvvigionare ‹*shelves*›
■ **stock up** *vi* far scorta (**with** di)
stockbroker *n* agente *m* di cambio
stock car *n* (for racing) stock-car *f inv*
stock-car racing *n* corsa *f* di stock-car
stock cube *n* dado *m* [da brodo]
Stock Exchange *n* Borsa *f* Valori
Stockholm /ˈʃtɒkhəʊm/ *n* Stoccolma *f*
stocking /ˈstɒkɪŋ/ *n* calza *f*
stockist /ˈstɒkɪst/ *n* rivenditore *m*
stock market *n* mercato *m* azionario
stockpile **A** *vt* fare scorta di
B *n* riserva *f*
stockroom *n* magazzino *m*
stock-still *adj* immobile
stocktaking *n* Comm inventario *m*
stocky /ˈstɒkɪ/ *adj* (**-ier**, **-iest**) tarchiato
stodge /stɒdʒ/ *n* BrE infml (food) ammazzafame *m inv*
stodgy /ˈstɒdʒɪ/ *adj* indigesto
stoic /ˈstəʊɪk/ *n* stoico, -a *mf*
stoical /ˈstəʊɪkl/ *adj* stoico
stoically /ˈstəʊɪklɪ/ *adv* stoicamente
stoicism /ˈstəʊɪsɪzm/ *n* stoicismo *m*
stoke /stəʊk/ *vt* alimentare
stole[1] /stəʊl/ *n* stola *f*
stole[2], **stolen** /ˈstəʊlən/ ▸ **steal**
stolid /ˈstɒlɪd/ *adj* apatico
stolidly /ˈstɒlɪdlɪ/ *adv* apaticamente
stomach /ˈstʌmək/ **A** *n* pancia *f*; Anat stomaco *m*
B *vt* infml reggere
stomach ache *n* mal *m* di pancia
stomp /stɒmp/ *vi* (walk heavily) camminare con passo pesante
⚷ **stone** /stəʊn/ **A** *n* pietra *f*; (in fruit) nocciolo *m*; Med calcolo *m*; (weight) *6,348 kg*; **within a ~'s throw of** a un tiro di schioppo da
B *adj* di pietra
C *vt* snocciolare ‹*fruit*›
Stone Age *n* età *f* della pietra
stone circle *n* cromlech *m inv*

⚷ parola chiave

S

stone-cold *adj* gelido

stone-cold sober *adj* perfettamente sobrio

stoned /stəʊnd/ *adj* infml (on drugs, drink) fatto

stone-deaf *adj* infml sordo come una campana

stonemason *n* scalpellino *m*

stonewall /ˌstəʊnˈwɔːl/ *vi* fare muro di gomma

stone-washed *adj* ‹*jeans, denim*› scolorito, stone-washed

stonework *n* lavoro *m* in muratura

stony /ˈstəʊnɪ/ *adj* pietroso; ‹*glare*› glaciale

stony-broke *adj* BrE infml al verde

stood /stʊd/ ▶ **stand**

stooge /stuːdʒ/ *n* Theat spalla *f*; (underling) tirapiedi *mf inv*

stool /stuːl/ *n* sgabello *m*

stool pigeon *n* infml informatore, -trice *mf*

stoop /stuːp/ **A** *n* curvatura *f*; **walk with a ~** camminare con la schiena curva
B *vi* stare curvo; (bend down) chinarsi; fig abbassarsi

stop /stɒp/ **A** *n* (break) sosta *f*; (for bus, train) fermata *f*; Gram punto *m*; **come to a ~** fermarsi; **put a ~ to something** mettere fine a qualcosa
B *vt* (*pt/pp* **stopped**) fermare; arrestare ‹*machine*›; (prevent) impedire; **~ somebody doing something** impedire a qualcuno di fare qualcosa; **~ doing something** smettere di fare qualcosa; **~ that!** smettila!; **~ a cheque** bloccare un assegno
C *vi* fermarsi; ‹*rain*› smettere
D *int* fermo!

■ **stop by** *vi* (make a brief visit) passare

■ **stop off** *vi* fare una sosta

■ **stop up** *vt* otturare ‹*sink*›; tappare ‹*hole*›

■ **stop with** *vi* infml (stay with) fermarsi da

stopcock *n* rubinetto *m* di arresto

stopgap *n* palliativo *m*; (person) tappabuchi *mf inv*

stop lights *npl* luci *fpl* di arresto

stop-off *n* sosta *f*

stopover *n* sosta *f*; Aeron scalo *m*

stoppage /ˈstɒpɪdʒ/ *n* ostruzione *f*; (strike) interruzione *f*; (deduction) trattenute *fpl*

stopper /ˈstɒpə(r)/ *n* tappo *m*

stop press *n* ultimissime *fpl*

stop sign *n* (segnale *m* di) stop *m inv*

stopwatch /ˈstɒpwɒtʃ/ *n* cronometro *m*

storage /ˈstɔːrɪdʒ/ *n* deposito *m*; (in warehouse) immagazzinaggio *m*; Comput memoria *f*

storage heater *n* caldaia *f* ad accumulo

store /stɔː(r)/ **A** *n* (stock) riserva *f*; (shop) grande magazzino *m*; (depot) deposito *m*; **in ~** in deposito; **there's trouble in ~ for him** ci sono guai in vista per lui; **what the future has in ~ for me** cosa mi riserva il futuro; **set great ~ by** tenere in gran conto
B *vt* tenere; (in warehouse) Comput immagazzinare

■ **store up** *vt* (accumulate) far scorte di

store card *n carta (f) di credito di grandi magazzini*

storekeeper *n* AmE = **shopkeeper**

storeroom /ˈstɔːruːm/ *n* magazzino *m*

storey /ˈstɔːrɪ/ *n* piano *m*

stork /stɔːk/ *n* cicogna *f*

storm /stɔːm/ **A** *n* temporale *m*; (with thunder) tempesta *f*
B *vt* prendere d'assalto

stormy /ˈstɔːmɪ/ *adj* tempestoso

story /ˈstɔːrɪ/ *n* storia *f*; (in newspaper) articolo *m*

storybook /ˈstɔːrɪbʊk/ *n* libro *m* di racconti

storyteller /ˈstɔːrɪtelə(r)/ *n* (writer) narratore, -trice *mf*; (liar) contaballe *mf inv*

stout /staʊt/ **A** *adj* ‹*shoes*› resistente; (fat) robusto; ‹*defence*› strenuo
B *n* birra *f* scura

stoutly /ˈstaʊtlɪ/ *adv* strenuamente

stove /stəʊv/ *n* cucina *f* [economica]; (for heating) stufa *f*

stove top *n* AmE piano *m* di cottura

stow /stəʊ/ *vt* metter via

■ **stow away** *vi* Naut imbarcarsi clandestinamente

stowaway /ˈstəʊəweɪ/ *n* passeggero, -a *mf* clandestino

straddle /ˈstrædl/ *vt* stare a cavalcioni su; (standing) essere a cavallo su

strafe /streɪf/ *vt* mitragliare da bassa quota

straggle /ˈstrægl/ *vi* crescere disordinatamente; (dawdle) rimanere indietro

straggler /ˈstræglə(r)/ *n* persona *f* che rimane indietro

straggly /ˈstræglɪ/ *adj* **have ~ hair** avere pochi capelli sottili

straight /streɪt/ **A** *adj* diritto, dritto; ‹*answer, question, person*› diretto; (tidy) in ordine; ‹*drink, hair*› liscio; **three ~ wins** tre vittorie di seguito
B *adv* diritto, dritto; (directly) direttamente; **~ away** immediatamente; **~ on** *or* **ahead** diritto; **~ out** fig apertamente; **go ~** infml rigare diritto; **put something ~** mettere qualcosa in ordine; **sit/stand up ~** stare diritto; **let's get something ~** mettiamo una cosa in chiaro

straighten /ˈstreɪtn/ **A** *vt* raddrizzare
B *vi* raddrizzarsi; **~ [up]** ‹*person*› mettersi diritto

■ **straighten out** *vt* fig chiarire ‹*situation*›

straight face *n* **keep a ~** restare serio

straight-faced /-ˈfeɪst/ *adj* con l'aria seria

straightforward *adj* franco; (simple) semplice

straight man *n* Theat spalla *f*

strain¹ /ˈstreɪn/ *n* (streak) vena *f*; Bot varietà *f*; (of virus) forma *f*

strain² **A** *n* tensione *f*; (injury) stiramento *m*; **~s** *pl* (of music) note *fpl*; **put a ~ on** fig introdurre delle tensioni in; **under a lot of ~** estremamente sotto pressione
B *vt* tirare; sforzare ‹*eyes, voice*›; stirarsi ‹*muscle*›; Culin scolare
C *vi* sforzarsi

strained /streɪnd/ *adj* ‹*relations*› teso

strainer /ˈstreɪnə(r)/ *n* colino *m*

strait /streɪt/ *n* stretto *m*; **in dire ~s** in serie difficoltà

straitjacket /ˈstreɪtdʒækɪt/ *n* camicia *f* di forza

strait-laced /-ˈleɪst/ *adj* puritano

strand¹ /strænd/ *n* (of thread) gugliata *f*; (of beads) filo *m*; (of hair) capello *m*

strand² *vt* **be ~ed** rimanere bloccato

strange /streɪndʒ/ *adj* strano; (not known) sconosciuto; (unaccustomed) estraneo

strangely /ˈstreɪndʒlɪ/ *adv* stranamente; **~ enough** curiosamente

strangeness /ˈstreɪndʒnəs/ *n* stranezza *f*

stranger /ˈstreɪndʒə(r)/ *n* estraneo, -a *mf*

strangle /ˈstræŋgl/ *vt* strangolare; fig reprimere

stranglehold /ˈstræŋglhəʊld/ *n* (physical grip) presa *f* alla gola; fig (powerful control) stretta *f* mortale; **have a ~ on something** fig avere in pugno qualcosa

strangulation /strængjʊˈleɪʃn/ *n* strangolamento *m*

strap /stræp/ **A** *n* cinghia *f*; (to grasp in vehicle) maniglia *f*; (of watch) cinturino *m*; (shoulder) **~** bretella *f*, spallina *f*
B *vt* (*pt/pp* **strapped**) legare; **~ in/down** assicurare

strapless /ˈstræplɪs/ *adj* ‹*bra, dress*› senza spalline

strapped /stræpt/ *adj* infml **be ~ for** essere a corto di

strapping /ˈstræpɪŋ/ *adj* robusto

S

strata /ˈstrɑːtə/ ▶ **stratum**

stratagem /ˈstrætədʒəm/ *n* stratagemma *m*

strategic /strəˈtiːdʒɪk/ *adj* strategico

strategically /strəˈtiːdʒɪklɪ/ *adv* strategicamente

strategist /ˈstrætədʒɪst/ *n* stratega *mf*

strategy /ˈstrætədʒɪ/ *n* strategia *f*

stratosphere /ˈstrætəsfɪə(r)/ *n* stratosfera *f*

stratum /ˈstrɑːtəm/ *n* (*pl* **strata**) strato *m*

straw /strɔː/ *n* paglia *f*; (single piece) fuscello *m*; (for drinking) cannuccia *f*; **the last ~** l'ultima goccia

strawberry /ˈstrɔːbərɪ/ *n* fragola *f*

straw poll *n* Pol sondaggio *m* d'opinione non ufficiale

stray /streɪ/ **A** *adj* (animal) randagio
B *n* randagio *m*
C *vi* andarsene per conto proprio; (deviate) deviare (**from** da)

streak /striːk/ **A** *n* striatura *f*; fig (trait) vena *f*; **~s** *pl* (in hair) mèche *fpl*
B *vi* (move fast) sfrecciare

streaky /ˈstriːkɪ/ *adj* striato; ‹*bacon*› grasso

stream /striːm/ **A** *n* ruscello *m*; (current) corrente *f*; (of blood, people) flusso *m*; Sch classe *f*; **come on ~** (start operating) entrare in attività; ‹*oil*› cominciare a scorrere
B *vi* scorrere

■ **stream in** *vi* entrare a fiotti

■ **stream out** *vi* uscire a fiotti

streamer /ˈstriːmə(r)/ *n* (paper) stella *f* filante; (flag) pennone *m*

streaming /ˈstriːmɪŋ/ **A** *adj* **1** (of a cold) **a ~ cold** raffreddore con naso che cola **2** Comput streaming, in streaming; **~ video** video streaming
B *n* (in school) *divisione (f) degli studenti in base alle loro capacità*

streamline /ˈstriːmlaɪn/ *vt* rendere aerodinamico; (simplify) snellire

streamlined /ˈstriːmlaɪnd/ *adj* aerodinamico; (simplified) snellito

street /striːt/ *n* strada *f*

streetcar *n* AmE tram *m inv*

street cred *n* infml immagine *f* pubblica

street lamp *n* lampione *m*

street market *n* mercato *m* all'aperto

street plan *n* stradario *m*

street value *n* (of drugs) valore *m* di mercato

streetwalker *n* passeggiatrice *f*

streetwise *adj* infml ‹*person*› *che conosce tutti i trucchi per sopravvivere in una metropoli*

strength /streŋθ/ *n* forza *f*; (of wall, bridge etc) solidità *f*; **~s** *pl* punti *mpl* forti; **on the ~ of** grazie a

strengthen /ˈstreŋθən/ *vt* rinforzare

strenuous /ˈstrenjʊəs/ *adj* faticoso; ‹*attempt, denial*› energico

strenuously /ˈstrenjʊəslɪ/ *adv* energicamente

stress /stres/ **A** *n* (emphasis) insistenza *f*; Gram accento *m* tonico; (mental) stress *m inv*; Mech spinta *f*
B *vt* (emphasize) insistere su; Gram mettere l'accento (tonico) su

■ **stress out**: *vt* **~ somebody out** stressare qualcuno

stressed /strest/ *adj* (mentally) **~ [out]** stressato

stressful /ˈstresfʊl/ *adj* stressante

stretch /stretʃ/ **A** *n* stiramento *m*; (period) periodo *m* di tempo; (of road) tratto *m*; (elasticity) elasticità *f*; **at a ~** di fila; **have a ~** stirarsi
B *vt* tirare; allargare ‹*shoes, sweater, etc*›; **~ one's legs** stendere le gambe; **~ a point** fare uno strappo alla regola

---

parola chiave

C *vi* (become wider) allargarsi; (extend) estendersi; ‹*person*› stirarsi

▪ **stretch out** **A** *vt* allungare ‹*one's hand, legs*›; allargare ‹*arms*›
B *vi* ‹*person*› sdraiarsi; ‹*land*› estendersi

stretcher /ˈstretʃə(r)/ *n* barella *f*

stretchy /ˈstretʃɪ/ *adj* elastico

strew /struː/ *vt* (*pt/pp* **strewn** *or* **strewed**) sparpagliare; **~n with** coperto di

stricken /ˈstrɪkn/ *adj* prostrato; **~ with** affetto da ‹*illness*›

strict /strɪkt/ *adj* severo; (precise) preciso

strictly /ˈstrɪktlɪ/ *adv* severamente; **~ speaking** in senso stretto

strictness /ˈstrɪktnɪs/ *n* severità *f*

stricture /ˈstrɪktʃə(r)/ *n* critica *f*; (constriction) restringimento *m*

stride /straɪd/ **A** *n* [lungo] passo *m*; **make great ~s** fig fare passi da gigante; **take something in one's ~** accettare qualcosa con facilità
B *vi* (*pt* **strode**, *pp* **stridden**) andare a gran passi

strident /ˈstraɪdənt/ *adj* stridente; ‹*colour*› vistoso

stridently /ˈstraɪdəntlɪ/ *adv* con voce stridente

strife /straɪf/ *n* conflitto *m*

strike /straɪk/ **A** *n* sciopero *m*; Mil attacco *m*; **on ~** in sciopero
B *vt* (*pt/pp* **struck**) colpire; accendere ‹*match*›; trovare ‹*oil, gold*›; (delete) depennare; (occur to) venire in mente a; Mil attaccare; **~ somebody a blow** colpire qualcuno
C *vi* ‹*lightning*› cadere; ‹*clock*› suonare; Mil attaccare; ‹*workers*› scioperare; **~ lucky** azzeccarla

▪ **strike back** *vi* fare rappresaglia; (at critics) reagire

▪ **strike off** *vt* eliminare; **be struck off [the register]** ‹*doctor*› essere radiato [dall'albo]

▪ **strike out** *vt* eliminare

▪ **strike up** *vt* fare ‹*friendship*›; attaccare ‹*conversation*›

strike-breaker *n persona* (*f*) *che non aderisce a uno sciopero*

strike-breaking *n* crumiraggio *m*

strike force *n* forze *fpl* d'intervento

striker /ˈstraɪkə(r)/ *n* scioperante *mf*

striking /ˈstraɪkɪŋ/ *adj* impressionante; (attractive) affascinante

string /strɪŋ/ **A** *n* spago *m*; (of musical instrument, racket) corda *f*; (of pearls) filo *m*; (of lies) serie *f*; **the ~s** *pl* Mus gli archi; **pull ~s** infml usare le proprie conoscenze
B *vt* (*pt/pp* **strung**) (thread) infilare ‹*beads*›

▪ **string along** **A** *vt* infml (deceive) prendere in giro
B *vi* **I'll ~ along** (come too) vengo anch'io; **~ along with somebody** andare/venire con qualcuno

▪ **string out** **A** *vi* (spread out) allinearsi
B *vt* disporre in fila; **be strung out** sl (on drugs) essere fatto

▪ **string together** *vt* mettere insieme ‹*words, remarks*›

string bean *n* fagiolino *m*

stringed /strɪŋd/ *adj* ‹*instrument*› a corda

stringent /ˈstrɪndʒnt/ *adj* rigido

stringy /ˈstrɪŋɪ/ *adj* ‹*person, build*› asciutto; ‹*hair*› come spaghetti; Culin filaccioso

strip /strɪp/ **A** *n* striscia *f*
B *vt* (*pt/pp* **stripped**) spogliare; togliere le lenzuola da ‹*bed*›; scrostare ‹*wood, furniture*›; smontare ‹*machine*›; (deprive) privare (**of** di)
C *vi* (undress) spogliarsi

▪ **strip down** *vt* smontare ‹*engine*›

strip cartoon *n* striscia *f*

strip club *n* locale *m* di strip-tease

stripe /straɪp/ *n* striscia *f*; Mil gallone *m*

striped /straɪpt/ *adj* a strisce

stripey /ˈstraɪpɪ/ *adj* a strisce, a righe

strip light *n* tubo *m* al neon

strip lighting *n* illuminazione *f* al neon

stripper /ˈstrɪpə(r)/ *n* spogliarellista *mf*; (solvent) sverniciatore *m*

strip-search **A** *n* perquisizione *f* (*facendo spogliare qualcuno*)
B *vt* perquisire (*facendo spogliare*)

striptease /ˈstrɪptiːz/ *n* spogliarello *m*, strip-tease *m inv*

strive /straɪv/ *vi* (*pt* **strove**, *pp* **striven**) sforzarsi (**to** di); **~ for** sforzarsi di ottenere

strobe /strəʊb/ *n* luce *f* stroboscopica

strode /strəʊd/ ▸ **stride**

stroke¹ /strəʊk/ *n* colpo *m*; (of pen) tratto *m*; (in swimming) bracciata *f*; Med ictus *m inv*; **~ of luck** colpo *m* di fortuna; **put somebody off his ~** far perdere il filo a qualcuno

stroke² **A** *vt* accarezzare
B *n* carezza *f*

stroll /strəʊl/ **A** *n* passeggiata *f*; **go for a ~** andare a far due passi
B *vi* passeggiare

stroller /ˈstrəʊlə(r)/ *n* AmE (pushchair) passeggino *m*

strong /strɒŋ/ *adj* (**-er** /ˈstrɒŋgə(r)/ **-est** /ˈstrɒŋgɪst/) forte; ‹*argument*› valido

strongbox /ˈstrɒŋbɒks/ *n* cassaforte *f*

stronghold /ˈstrɒŋhəʊld/ *n* roccaforte *f*

strong language *n* (forceful terms) linguaggio *m* incisivo; (swearing) linguaggio *m* offensivo

strongly /ˈstrɒŋlɪ/ *adv* fortemente; **feel ~ about something** avere molto a cuore qualcosa

strong-minded /-ˈmaɪndɪd/ *adj* risoluto

strong point *n* punto *m* di forza

strongroom *n* camera *f* blindata

strong stomach *n* stomaco *m* di ferro

S

strong-willed /-wɪld/ *adj* tenace
stroppiness /ˈstrɒpɪnɪs/ *n* scontrosità *f*
stroppy /ˈstrɒpɪ/ *adj* infml scorbutico, scontroso
strove /strəʊv/ ▶ **strive**
struck /strʌk/ **A** *adj* ▶ **strike**
B ~ **on** *adj* infml entusiasta di
structural /ˈstrʌktʃərəl/ *adj* strutturale
structural damage *n* danni *mpl* alla struttura portante
structurally /ˈstrʌktʃərəlɪ/ *adv* strutturalmente
⚷ **structure** /ˈstrʌktʃə(r)/ **A** *n* struttura *f*
B *vt* strutturare
⚷ **struggle** /ˈstrʌgl/ **A** *n* lotta *f*; **with a** ~ con difficoltà
B *vi* lottare; ~ **for breath** respirare con fatica; ~ **to do something** fare fatica a fare qualcosa; ~ **to one's feet** alzarsi con fatica
struggling /ˈstrʌglɪŋ/ *adj* **a** ~ **artist/writer** un artista/uno scrittore che fatica ad affermarsi
strum /strʌm/ *vt & vi* (*pt/pp* **strummed**) strimpellare
strung /strʌŋ/ ▶ **string**
strung out *adj* **be** ~ (from drugs) essere fatto; **be** ~ **on** essere dipendente da ‹*drugs*›
strut¹ /strʌt/ *n* (component) puntello *m*
strut² *vi* (*pt/pp* **strutted**) camminare impettito
stub /stʌb/ **A** *n* mozzicone *m*; (counterfoil) matrice *f*
B *vt* (*pt/pp* **stubbed**) ~ **one's toe** sbattere il dito del piede (**on** contro)
▪ **stub out** *vt* spegnere ‹*cigarette*›
stubble /ˈstʌbl/ *n* (on face) barba *f* ispida
stubbly /ˈstʌblɪ/ *adj* ispido
stubborn /ˈstʌbən/ *adj* testardo; ‹*refusal*› ostinato
stubbornly /ˈstʌbənlɪ/ *adv* testardamente; ‹*refuse*› ostinatamente
stubbornness /ˈstʌbənnɪs/ *n* (of person) testardaggine *f*

stubby /ˈstʌbɪ/ *adj* (**-ier**, **-iest**) tozzo
stucco /ˈstʌkəʊ/ *n* stucco *m*
stuck /stʌk/ ▶ **stick²**
stuck-up *adj* infml snob *inv*
stud¹ /stʌd/ *n* (on boot) tacchetto *m*; (on jacket) borchia *f*; (for ear) orecchino *m* [a bottone]
stud² *n* (of horses) scuderia *f*
studded with /ˈstʌdɪd/ *adj* fig tempestato di
⚷ **student** /ˈstjuːdənt/ *n* (at university) studente *m*, studentessa *f*; AmE (at (high) school) scolaro, -a *mf*
student grant *n* borsa *f* di studio
student nurse *n* studente, -tessa *mf* infermiere, -a
student teacher *n* insegnante *mf* tirocinante

⚷ parola chiave

student union *n* (organization) organizzazione *f* studentesca; (building) casa *f* dello studente
stud horse *n* stallone *m* [da monta]
studied /ˈstʌdɪd/ *adj* intenzionale; ‹*politeness*› studiato
studio /ˈstjuːdɪəʊ/ *n* studio *m*
studio apartment *n* AmE monolocale *m*
studio flat *n* monolocale *m*
studious /ˈstjuːdɪəs/ *adj* studioso; ‹*attention*› studiato
studiously /ˈstjuːdɪəslɪ/ *adv* studiosamente; (carefully) attentamente
stud mare *n* giumenta *f* fattrice
⚷ **study** /ˈstʌdɪ/ **A** *n* studio *m*
B *vt & vi* (*pt/pp* **-ied**) studiare; ~ **for an exam** preparare un esame
study aid *n* sussidio *m* didattico
⚷ **stuff** /stʌf/ **A** *n* materiale *m*; infml (things) roba *f*
B *vt* riempire; (with padding) imbottire; Culin farcire; ~ **something into a drawer/one's pocket** ficcare qualcosa alla rinfusa in un cassetto/in tasca; ~ **oneself** ingozzarsi (**with** di); **get** ~**ed!** infml va' a quel paese!
stuffing /ˈstʌfɪŋ/ *n* (padding) imbottitura *f*; Culin ripieno *m*
stuffy /ˈstʌfɪ/ *adj* (**-ier**, **-iest**) che sa di chiuso; (old-fashioned) antiquato
stultifying /ˈstʌltɪfaɪɪŋ/ *adj* che abbruttisce
stumble /ˈstʌmbl/ *vi* inciampare; ~ **across** *or* **on** imbattersi in
stumbling block /ˈstʌmblɪŋ/ *n* ostacolo *m*
stump /stʌmp/ *n* ceppo *m*; (of limb) moncone *m*
▪ **stump up** *vt & vi* infml sganciare
stumped /stʌmpt/ *adj* infml perplesso
stumpy /ˈstʌmpɪ/ *adj* (**-ier**, **-iest**) ‹*person, legs*› tozzo
stun /stʌn/ *vt* (*pt/pp* **stunned**) stordire; (astonish) sbalordire
stung /stʌŋ/ ▶ **sting**
stunk /stʌŋk/ ▶ **stink**
stunned /stʌnd/ *adj* ‹*expression*› sbalordito
stunning /ˈstʌnɪŋ/ *adj* infml favoloso; ‹*blow, victory*› sbalorditivo
stunt¹ /stʌnt/ *n* infml trovata *f* pubblicitaria
stunt² *vt* arrestare lo sviluppo di
stunted /ˈstʌntɪd/ *adj* stentato
stuntman /ˈstʌntmən/ *n* stuntman *m inv*, cascatore *m*
stuntwoman /ˈstʌntwʊmən/ *n* stuntwoman *f inv*
stupefaction /stjuːpɪˈfækʃn/ *n* stupore *m*
stupefy /ˈstjuːpɪfaɪ/ *vt* (*pt/pp* **-ied**) (astonish) stupire
stupefying /ˈstjuːpɪfaɪɪŋ/ *adj* stupefacente
stupendous /stjuːˈpendəs/ *adj* stupendo
stupendously /stjuːˈpendəslɪ/ *adv* stupendamente

stupid /ˈstjuːpɪd/ *adj* stupido
stupidity /stjuːˈpɪdətɪ/ *n* stupidità *f*
stupidly /ˈstjuːpɪdlɪ/ *adv* stupidamente
stupor /ˈstjuːpə(r)/ *n* torpore *m*
sturdy /ˈstɜːdɪ/ *adj* (**-ier**, **-iest**) robusto; ‹*furniture*› solido
stutter /ˈstʌtə(r)/ **A** *n* balbuzie *f*; **have a ~** balbettare
B *vt & vi* balbettare
St Valentine's Day *n* san Valentino *m*
sty[1] /staɪ/ *n* (*pl* **sties**) porcile *m*
sty[2], **stye** *n* (*pl* **styes**) Med orzaiolo *m*
style /staɪl/ *n* stile *m*; (fashion) moda *f*; (sort) tipo *m*; (hair) **~** pettinatura *f*; **in ~** in grande stile
styling /ˈstaɪlɪŋ/ **A** *adj* ‹*gel, mousse*› modellante
B *n* (design) styling *m*; (in hairdressing) acconciatura *f*
stylish /ˈstaɪlɪʃ/ *adj* elegante
stylishly /ˈstaɪlɪʃlɪ/ *adv* con eleganza
stylist /ˈstaɪlɪst/ *n* stilista *mf*; **hair ~** parrucchiere, -a *mf*
stylistic /staɪˈlɪstɪk/ *adj* stilistico
stylistically /staɪˈlɪstɪklɪ/ *adv* stilisticamente
stylized /ˈstaɪlaɪzd/ *adj* stilizzato
stylus /ˈstaɪləs/ *n* (on record player) puntina *f*
styptic pencil /ˈstɪptɪk/ *n* matita *f* emostatica
suave /swɑːv/ *adj* dai modi garbati
sub-aqua /sʌbˈækwə/ *adj* ‹*club*› di sport subacquei
subcommittee /ˈsʌbkəmɪtɪ/ *n* sottocommissione *f*
subconscious /sʌbˈkɒnʃəs/ **A** *adj* subcosciente
B *n* subcosciente *m*
subconsciously /sʌbˈkɒnʃəslɪ/ *adv* in modo inconscio
subcontinent /sʌbˈkɒntɪnənt/ *n* subcontinente *m*
subcontract /sʌbkənˈtrækt/ *vt* subappaltare (to a)
subcontractor /ˈsʌbkəntræktə(r)/ *n* subappaltatore, -trice *mf*
subdirectory /ˈsʌbdaɪrektərɪ/ *n* Comput sottodirectory *f inv*
subdivide /sʌbdɪˈvaɪd/ *vt* suddividere
subdivision /ˈsʌbdɪvɪʒn/ *n* suddivisione *f*
subdue /səbˈdjuː/ *vt* sottomettere; (make quieter) attenuare
subdued /səbˈdjuːd/ *adj* ‹*light*› attenuato; ‹*person, voice*› pacato
subheading /ˈsʌbhedɪŋ/ *n* sottotitolo *m*
subhuman /sʌbˈhjuːmən/ *adj* (cruel, not fit for humans) disumano; infml ‹*appearance*› da paleolitico
subject[1] /ˈsʌbdʒekt/ **A** *adj* **~ to** soggetto a; (depending on) subordinato a; **~ to availability** nei limiti della disponibilità
B *n* soggetto *m*; (of ruler) suddito, -a *mf*; Sch materia *f*; **change the ~** parlare di qualcos'altro
subject[2] /səbˈdʒekt/ *vt* (to attack, abuse) sottoporre; assoggettare ‹*country*›
subjective /səbˈdʒektɪv/ *adj* soggettivo
subjectively /səbˈdʒektɪvlɪ/ *adv* soggettivamente
subjectiveness /səbˈdʒektɪvnɪs/ *n* soggettività *f*
subjugate /ˈsʌbdʒʊgeɪt/ *vt* soggiogare, sottomettere
subjugation /sʌbdʒəˈgeɪʃn/ *n* sottomissione *f*
subjunctive /səbˈdʒʌŋktɪv/ *adj & n* congiuntivo *m*
sub-let /sʌbˈlet/ *vt* (*pt/pp* **-let**, *pres p* **-letting**) subaffittare
sublime /səˈblaɪm/ *adj* sublime
sublimely /səˈblaɪmlɪ/ *adv* sublimamente
subliminal /səˈblɪmɪnl/ *adj* subliminale
sub-machine gun *n* mitraglietta *f*
submarine /ˈsəbmərɪːn/ *n* sommergibile *m*
submerge /səbˈmɜːdʒ/ **A** *vt* immergere; **be ~d** essere sommerso
B *vi* immergersi
submission /səbˈmɪʃn/ *n* sottomissione *f*
submissive /səbˈmɪsɪv/ *adj* sottomesso
submissively /səbˈmɪsɪvlɪ/ *adv* remissivamente
submissiveness /səbˈmɪsɪvnɪs/ *n* remissività *f*
submit /səbˈmɪt/ **A** *vt* (*pt/pp* **-mitted**, *pres p* **-mitting**) sottoporre
B *vi* sottomettersi
subnormal /sʌbˈnɔːml/ *adj* ‹*temperature*› al di sotto della norma; ‹*person*› subnormale
subordinate[1] /səˈbɔːdɪnɪt/ *adj & n* subordinato, -a *mf*
subordinate[2] /səˈbɔːdɪneɪt/ *vt* subordinare (to a)
subpoena /səbˈpiːnə/ **A** *n* mandato *m* di comparizione
B *vt* citare
sub-prime /ˈsʌbpraɪm/ *n* subprime *m inv*
subroutine /ˈsʌbruːtiːn/ *n* Comput subroutine *f inv*
subscribe /səbˈskraɪb/ *vi* contribuire; **~ to** abbonarsi a ‹*newspaper*›; sottoscrivere ‹*fund*›; fig aderire a ‹*theory*›
subscriber /səbˈskraɪbə(r)/ *n* abbonato, -a *mf*
subscription /səbˈskrɪpʃn/ *n* (to club) sottoscrizione *f*; (to newspaper) abbonamento *m*
subsequent /ˈsʌbsɪkwənt/ *adj* susseguente
subsequently /ˈsʌbsɪkwəntlɪ/ *adv* in seguito
subservience /səbˈsɜːvɪəns/ *n* asservimento *m*

subservient /səb'sɜːvɪənt/ *adj* subordinato; (servile) servile
subserviently /səb'sɜːvɪəntlɪ/ *adv* servilmente
subset /'sʌbset/ *n* Math sottoinsieme *m*
subside /səb'saɪd/ *vi* sprofondare; ‹*ground*› avvallarsi; ‹*storm*› placarsi
subsidence /'sʌbsɪdəns/ *n* (of land) cedimento *m*
subsidiary /səb'sɪdɪərɪ/ **A** *adj* secondario **B** *n* ~ [company] filiale *f*
subsidize /'sʌbsɪdaɪz/ *vt* sovvenzionare
subsidy /'sʌbsɪdɪ/ *n* sovvenzione *f*
subsist /səb'sɪst/ *vi* vivere (**on** di)
subsistence /səb'sɪstəns/ *n* sussistenza *f*
subsistence level *n* livello *m* di sussistenza
substance /'sʌbstəns/ *n* sostanza *f*
sub-standard /sʌb'stændəd/ *adj* di qualità inferiore
⚷ **substantial** /səb'stænʃl/ *adj* sostanziale; ‹*meal*› sostanzioso; (strong) solido
substantially /səb'stænʃəlɪ/ *adv* sostanzialmente; ‹*built*› solidamente
substantiate /səb'stænʃɪeɪt/ *vt* comprovare
substitute /'sʌbstɪtjuːt/ **A** *n* sostituto *m* **B** *vt* ~ **A for B** sostituire B con A **C** *vi* ~ **for somebody** sostituire qualcuno
substitution /sʌbstɪ'tjuːʃn/ *n* sostituzione *f*
subterfuge /'sʌbtəfjuːdʒ/ *n* sotterfugio *m*
subterranean /sʌbtə'reɪnɪən/ *adj* sotterraneo
subtext /'sʌbtekst/ *n* storia *f* secondaria; fig messaggio *m* implicito
subtitle /'sʌbtaɪtl/ **A** *n* sottotitolo *m* **B** *vt* sottotitolare
subtitled /'sʌbtaɪtld/ *adj* sottotitolato
subtle /'sʌtl/ *adj* sottile; ‹*taste, perfume*› delicato
subtlety /'sʌtltɪ/ *n* sottigliezza *f*
subtly /'sʌtlɪ/ *adv* sottilmente
subtotal /'sʌbtəʊtl/ *n* totale *m* parziale
subtract /səb'trækt/ *vt* sottrarre
subtraction /səb'trækʃn/ *n* sottrazione *f*
suburb /'sʌbɜːb/ *n* sobborgo *m*; **in the ~s** in periferia
suburban /sə'bɜːbən/ *adj* suburbano
suburbia /sə'bɜːbɪə/ *n* sobborghi *mpl*
subversive /səb'vɜːsɪv/ *adj* sovversivo
subway /'sʌbweɪ/ *n* sottopassaggio *m*; AmE (railway) metropolitana *f*, metrò *m*
sub-zero /sʌb'zɪərəʊ/ *adj* sottozero *inv*
⚷ **succeed** /sək'siːd/ **A** *vi* riuscire (**in doing something** a fare qualcosa); (follow) succedere (**to** a) **B** *vt* succedere a ‹*king*›
succeeding /sək'siːdɪŋ/ *adj* successivo
⚷ **success** /sək'ses/ *n* successo *m*; **be a ~** (in life) aver successo
⚷ **successful** /sək'sesfʊl/ *adj* riuscito; ‹*businessman, artist etc*› di successo
successfully /sək'sesfʊlɪ/ *adv* con successo
succession /sək'seʃn/ *n* successione *f*; **in ~** di seguito
successive /sək'sesɪv/ *adj* successivo
successively /sə'sesɪvlɪ/ *adv* successivamente
successor /sək'sesə(r)/ *n* successore *m*
success rate *n* percentuale *f* di promozioni
success story *n* successo *m*
succinct /sək'sɪŋkt/ *adj* succinto
succinctly /sək'sɪŋktlɪ/ *adv* succintamente
succour /'sʌkə(r)/ **A** *vt* soccorrere **B** *n* soccorso *m*
succulence /'sʌkjʊləns/ *n* succulenza *f*
succulent /'ʃʌkjʊlənt/ *adj* succulento
succumb /sə'kʌm/ *vi* soccombere (**to** a)
⚷ **such** /sʌtʃ/ **A** *adj* tale; **~ a book** un libro così; **~ a thing** una cosa del genere; **~ a long time ago** talmente tanto tempo fa; **there is no ~ thing/person** non c'è una cosa/persona così **B** *pron* **as ~** in quanto tale; **~ as** come; **and ~** e simili; **~ as it is** per quel che vale; **if ~ is the case** se questo è il caso
such and such *adj* tale; **for ~ an amount** per un tot; **go on ~ a day at ~ a time** vai il tal giorno alla tal ora
suchlike /'sʌtʃlaɪk/ *pron* infml di tal genere
suck /ʃʌk/ *vt* succhiare
■ **suck up** *vt* assorbire
■ **suck up to** *vt* infml fare il lecchino con
sucker /'ʃʌkə(r)/ (n Bot) pollone *m*; infml (person) credulone, -a *mf*
suckle /'ʃʌkl/ *vt* allattare
suction /'sʌkʃn/ *n* aspirazione *f*
suction pad *n* ventosa *f*
Sudan /sʊ'dæn/ *n* Sudan *m*
Sudanese /sʊdən'iːz/ *adj* & *n* sudanese *mf*
sudden /'sʌdn/ **A** *adj* improvviso **B** *n* **all of a ~** all'improvviso
sudden death *n* (football) sudden death *f*
⚷ **suddenly** /'sʌdənlɪ/ *adv* improvvisamente
sudoku /suː'dəʊkuː/ *n* sudoku *m inv*
suds /sʌdz/ *npl* (foam) schiuma *f*; (soapy water) acqua *f* saponata
sue /suː/ **A** *vt* (*pres p* **suing**) fare causa a (**for** per) **B** *vi* fare causa
suede /sweɪd/ *n* pelle *f* scamosciata
suet /'suːɪt/ *n* grasso *m* di rognone
⚷ **suffer** /'sʌfə(r)/ **A** *vi* soffrire (**from** per) **B** *vt* soffrire di ‹*pain*›; subire ‹*loss etc*›
sufferance /'sʌf(ə)rəns/ *n* **you're here on ~** qui tu sei appena tollerato
sufferer /'sʌfərə(r)/ *n* malato, -a *mf*; **Aids ~s** malati di Aids
suffering /'sʌf(ə)rɪŋ/ *n* sofferenza *f*
suffice /sə'faɪs/ *vi* bastare

⚷ parola chiave

sufficient /sə'fɪʃənt/ *adj* sufficiente
sufficiently /sə'fɪʃəntlɪ/ *adv* sufficientemente
suffix /'sʌfɪks/ *n* suffisso *m*
suffocate /'sʌfəkeɪt/ *vt & vi* soffocare
suffocating /'sʌfəkeɪtɪŋ/ *adj* ‹*heat*› soffocante
suffocation /sʌfə'keɪʃn/ *n* soffocamento *m*
suffrage /'sʌfrɪdʒ/ *n* (right) diritto *m* di voto; (system) suffragio *m*
suffragette /sʌfrə'dʒet/ *n* suffragetta *f*
sugar /'ʃʊgə(r)/ **A** *n* zucchero *m*
B *vt* zuccherare; **~ the pill** fig addolcire la pillola
sugar basin, sugar bowl *n* zuccheriera *f*
sugar beet *n* barbabietola *f* da zucchero
sugar cane *n* canna *f* da zucchero
sugar-coated /-'kəʊtɪd/ *adj* ricoperto di zucchero
sugar cube *n* zolletta *f*
sugar daddy *n* infml vecchio amante *m* danaroso
sugar-free *adj* senza zucchero
sugar lump *n* zolletta *f*
sugary /'ʃʊgərɪ/ *adj* zuccheroso; fig sdolcinato
suggest /sə'dʒest/ *vt* suggerire; (indicate, insinuate) fare pensare a
suggestible /sə'dʒestəbl/ *adj* suggestionabile
suggestion /sə'dʒestʃən/ *n* suggerimento *m*; (trace) traccia *f*
suggestive /sə'dʒestɪv/ *adj* allusivo; **be ~ of** fare pensare a
suggestively /sə'dʒestɪvlɪ/ *adv* in modo allusivo
suicidal /su:ɪ'saɪdl/ *adj* suicida
suicide /'su:ɪsaɪd/ *n* suicidio *m*; (person) suicida *mf*; **commit ~** suicidarsi
suicide attack *n* attacco *m* suicida
suicide attempt *n* tentato suicidio *m*
suicide pact *n* patto *m* suicida
suit /su:t/ **A** *n* vestito *m*; (woman's) tailleur *m inv*; Cards seme *m*; Jur causa *f*; **follow ~** fig fare lo stesso
B *vt* andar bene a; (adapt) adattare (**to** a); (be convenient for) andare bene per; **be ~ed to** *or* **for** essere adatto a; **~ yourself!** fa' come vuoi!
suitability /su:tə'bɪlɪtɪ/ *n* adeguatezza *f*
suitable /'su:təbl/ *adj* adatto
suitably /'su:təblɪ/ *adv* convenientemente
suitcase /'su:tkeɪs/ *n* valigia *f*
suite /swi:t/ *n* suite *f inv*; (of furniture) divano *m* e poltrone *fpl* assortiti
sulk /sʌlk/ *vi* fare il broncio
sulkily /'sʌlkɪlɪ/ *adv* con aria imbronciata
sulky /'sʌlkɪ/ *adj* imbronciato
sullen /'sʌlən/ *adj* svogliato
sullenly /'sʌlənlɪ/ *adv* svogliatamente
sulphur /'sʌlfə(r)/ *n* zolfo *m*
sulphur dioxide /daɪ'ɒksaɪd/ *n* anidride *f* solforosa
sulphuric acid /sʌl'fjʊərɪk/ *n* acido *m* solforico
sultana /sʌl'tɑ:nə/ *n* uva *f* sultanina
sultry /'sʌltrɪ/ *adj* (**-ier**, **-iest**) ‹*weather*› afoso; fig sensuale
sum /sʌm/ *n* somma *f*; Sch addizione *f*
■ **sum up** **A** *vi* (*pt/pp* **summed**) riassumere
B *vt* valutare
summarily /sʌ'merɪlɪ/ *adv* sommariamente; ‹*dismissed*› sbrigativamente
summarize /'sʌməraɪz/ *vt* riassumere
summary /'sʌmərɪ/ **A** *n* sommario *m*
B *adj* sommario; ‹*dismissal*› sbrigativo
summer /'sʌmə(r)/ *n* estate *f*; **in ~, in the ~** in estate
summer camp *n* ≈ colonia *f*
summer holiday *n* vacanze *fpl* estive
summer house *n* padiglione *m*
summer school *n* corso *m* estivo
summertime *n* (season) estate *f*
summer time *n* (clock change) ora *f* legale
summery /'sʌmərɪ/ *adj* estivo
summing-up /sʌmɪŋ'ʌp/ *n* riepilogo *m*; Jur ricapitolazione *f* del processo
summit /'sʌmɪt/ *n* cima *f*
summit conference *n* vertice *m*
summon /'sʌmən/ *vt* convocare; Jur citare
■ **summon up** *vt* raccogliere ‹*strength*›; rievocare ‹*memory*›
summons /'sʌmənz/ **A** *n* Jur citazione *f*
B *vt* citare in giudizio
sump /sʌmp/ *n* Auto coppa *f* dell'olio
sumptuous /'sʌmptjʊəs/ *adj* sontuoso
sumptuously /'sʌmptjʊəslɪ/ *adv* sontuosamente
sum total *n* totale *m*
sun /sʌn/ **A** *n* sole *m*
B *vt* (*pt/pp* **sunned**) **~ oneself** prendere il sole
sunbathe *vi* prendere il sole
sunbed *n* lettino *m* solare
sunblock *n* prodotto *m* solare a protezione totale
sunburn *n* scottatura *f* (*solare*)
sunburnt *adj* scottato (*dal sole*)
sun cream *n* crema *f* solare
sundae /'sʌndeɪ/ *n* gelato *m* guarnito
Sunday /'sʌndeɪ/ *n* domenica *f*
Sunday best *n* **in one's ~** con l'abito della festa
Sunday trading *n* apertura *f* domenicale (dei negozi)
sundial /'sʌndaɪəl/ *n* meridiana *f*
sundress *n* prendisole *m inv*
sun-dried tomatoes /'sʌndraɪd/ *npl* pomodori *mpl* secchi
sundries /'sʌndrɪz/ *npl* articoli *mpl* vari

sundry /ˈsʌndrɪ/ *adj* svariati; **all and ~** tutti quanti
sunflower /ˈsʌnflaʊə(r)/ *n* girasole *m*
sung /sʌŋ/ ▶ **sing**
sunglasses /ˈsʌŋglɑːsɪz/ *npl* occhiali *mpl* da sole
sun hat *n* cappello *m* da sole
sunk /sʌŋk/ ▶ **sink**
sunken /ˈsʌŋkn/ *adj* incavato
sunlamp /ˈsʌnlæmp/ *n* lampada *f* abbronzante
sunlight /ˈsʌnlaɪt/ *n* [luce *f* del] sole *m*
sunny /ˈsʌnɪ/ *adj* (**-ier**, **-iest**) assolato
sunrise *n* alba *f*
sunroof *n* Auto tettuccio *m* apribile
sunscreen *n* (to prevent sunburn) crema *f* solare protettiva
sunset *n* tramonto *m*
sunshade *n* parasole *m*
sunshine *n* [luce *f* del] sole *m*
sunshine roof *n* tettuccio *m* apribile
sunstroke *n* insolazione *f*
suntan *n* abbronzatura *f*
suntan lotion *n* lozione *f* solare
sun-tanned *adj* abbronzato
suntan oil *n* olio *m* solare
super /ˈsuːpə(r)/ *adj* infml fantastico
superannuated /suːpərˈænjʊeɪtɪd/ *adj* fig che ha fatto il suo tempo
superannuation /suːpərænjʊˈeɪʃn/ *n* (contributions) contributi *mpl* pensionistici; (pension) pensione *f*
superannuation fund *n* fondo *m* pensione
superb /sʊˈpɜːb/ *adj* splendido
superbly /sʊˈpɜːblɪ/ *adv* splendidamente
supercilious /suːpəˈsɪlɪəs/ *adj* altezzoso
superciliously /suːpəˈsɪlɪəslɪ/ *adv* in modo altezzoso
superficial /suːpəˈfɪʃl/ *adj* superficiale
superficiality /suːpəfɪʃɪˈælɪtɪ/ *n* superficialità *f*
superficially /suːpəˈfɪʃəlɪ/ *adv* superficialmente
superfluous /sʊˈpɜːflʊəs/ *adj* superfluo
superhighway /ˈsuːpəhaɪweɪ/ *n* **[information] ~** Comput autostrada *f* telematica
superhuman /suːpəˈhjuːmən/ *adj* sovrumano
superimpose /suːpərɪmˈpəʊz/ *vt* sovrapporre ‹*picture, soundtrack*› (**on** a); **~d title** titolo *m* in sovrimpressione
superintendent /suːpərɪnˈtendənt/ *n* (of police) commissario *m* di polizia
superior /suːˈpɪərɪə(r)/ *adj & n* superiore *mf*
superiority /suːpɪərɪˈɒrətɪ/ *n* superiorità *f*
superlative /suːˈpɜːlətɪv/ **A** *adj* eccellente
B *n* superlativo *m*
superlatively /suːˈpɜːlətɪvlɪ/ *adv* ‹*perform*› in modo eccezionale; ‹*good*› estremamente
superman /ˈsuːpəmæn/ *n* superuomo *m*
supermarket /ˈsuːpəmɑːkɪt/ *n* supermercato *m*
supermodel /ˈsuːpəmɒdl/ *n* top model *f inv*
supernatural /suːpəˈnætʃrəl/ *adj* soprannaturale
superpower /ˈsuːpəpaʊə(r)/ *n* superpotenza *f*
superscript /ˈsuːpəskrɪpt/ *adj* ‹*number, letter*› all'esponente
supersede /suːpəˈsiːd/ *vt* rimpiazzare
supersonic /suːpəˈsɒnɪk/ *adj* supersonico
superstar /ˈsuːpəstɑː(r), ˈsjuː-/ *n* superstar *mf*
superstition /suːpəˈstɪʃn/ *n* superstizione *f*
superstitious /suːpəˈstɪʃəs/ *adj* superstizioso
superstitiously /suːpəˈstɪʃəslɪ/ *adv* in modo superstizioso
superstore /ˈsuːpəstɔː(r)/ *n* ipermercato *m*
superstructure /ˈsuːpəstrʌktʃə(r)/ *n* sovrastruttura *f*
supertax /ˈsuːpətæks/ *n* Fin soprattassa *f*
supervise /ˈsuːpəvaɪz/ *vt* supervisionare
supervision /suːpəˈvɪʒn/ *n* supervisione *f*
supervisor /ˈsuːpəvaɪzə(r)/ *n* supervisore *m*
supervisory /suːpəˈvaɪzərɪ/ *adj* di supervisione
superwoman /ˈsuːpəwʊmən/ *n* superdonna *f*
supper /ˈsʌpə(r)/ *n* cena *f*; **have ~** cenare
supple /ˈsʌpl/ *adj* slogato
supplement /ˈsʌplɪmənt/ **A** *n* supplemento *m*
B *vt* integrare
supplementary /sʌplɪˈmentərɪ/ *adj* supplementare
supplier /səˈplaɪə(r)/ *n* fornitore, -trice *mf*
⚷ **supply** /səˈplaɪ/ **A** *n* fornitura *f*; Econ offerta *f*; **be in short ~** scarseggiare; **~ and demand** domanda *f* e offerta *f*; **supplies** *pl* Mil approvvigionamenti *mpl*
B *vt* (*pt/pp* **-ied**) fornire; **~ somebody with something** fornire qualcosa a qualcuno
supply teacher *n* supplente *mf*
⚷ **support** /səˈpɔːt/ **A** *n* sostegno *m*; (base) supporto *m*; (keep) sostentamento *m*
B *vt* sostenere; mantenere ‹*family*›; (give money to) mantenere finanziariamente; Sport fare il tifo per; Comput supportare
⚷ **supporter** /səˈpɔːtə(r)/ *n* sostenitore, -trice *mf*; Sport tifoso, -a *mf*
support group *n* gruppo *m* di sostegno
supporting /səˈpɔːtɪŋ/ *adj* ‹*actor*› non protagonista
supporting actor /səˈpɔːtɪŋ/ *n* attore *m* non protagonista
supporting actress *n* attrice *f* non protagonista

⚷ parola chiave

S

supportive /sə'pɔːtɪv/ *adj* incoraggiante; **be ~ of somebody** dare tutto il proprio appoggio a qualcuno

support stockings *npl* calze *fpl* elastiche

suppose /sə'pəʊz/ *vt* (presume) supporre; (imagine) pensare; **be ~d to do** dover fare; **not be ~d to** non avere il permesso di; **I ~ so** suppongo di sì

supposedly /sə'pəʊzɪdlɪ/ *adv* presumibilmente

supposing /sə'pəʊzɪŋ/ *conj* **~ (that) he agrees** supponiamo che accetti

supposition /sʌpə'zɪʃn/ *n* supposizione *f*

suppository /sʌ'pɒzɪtrɪ/ *n* supposta *f*

suppress /sə'pres/ *vt* sopprimere

suppressant /sə'presənt/ *n* Med inibitore *m*

suppression /sə'preʃn/ *n* soppressione *f*

suppurate /'sʌpjʊreɪt/ *vi* suppurare

supremacy /suː'preməsɪ/ *n* supremazia *f*

supreme /suː'priːm/ *adj* supremo

supremo /suː'priːməʊ/ *n* massima autorità *f*

Supt. *abbr* (**Superintendent**) commissario *m* di polizia

surcharge /'sɜːtʃɑːdʒ/ *n* supplemento *m*

sure /ʃʊə(r)/ **A** *adj* sicuro, certo; **make ~** accertarsi; **be ~ to do it** accertati di farlo
B *adv* AmE infml certamente; **~ enough** infatti

sure-fire *adj* infml garantito

sure-footed /-'fʊtɪd/ *adj* agile

surely /'ʃʊəlɪ/ *adv* certamente; AmE (gladly) volentieri

surety /'ʃʊərətɪ/ *n* garanzia *f*; **stand ~ for somebody/something** fare da garante a qualcuno/per qualcosa

surf /sɜːf/ **A** *n* schiuma *f*
B *vt* **~ the Net** navigare in Internet

surface /'sɜːfɪs/ **A** *n* superficie *f*; **on the ~** fig in apparenza
B *vi* (emerge) emergere

surface mail *n* **by ~** per posta ordinaria

surface-to-air missile *n* missile *m* terra-aria

surfboard /'sɜːfbɔːd/ *n* tavola *f* da surf

surfeit /'sɜːfɪt/ *n* eccesso *m*

surfer /'sɜːfə(r)/ *n* surfista *mf*

surfing /'sɜːfɪŋ/ *n* surf *m*

surge /sɜːdʒ/ **A** *n* (of sea) ondata *f*; (of interest) aumento *m*; (in demand) impennata *f*; (of anger, pity) impeto *m*
B *vi* riversarsi; **~ forward** buttarsi in avanti

surgeon /'sɜːdʒən/ *n* chirurgo *m*

surgery /'sɜːdʒərɪ/ *n* chirurgia *f*; (place, consulting room) ambulatorio *m*; (hours) ore *fpl* di visita; **have ~** subire un intervento [chirurgico]

surgical /'sɜːdʒɪkl/ *adj* chirurgico

surgically /'sɜːdʒɪklɪ/ *adv* chirurgicamente

surgical spirit *n* alcol *m* denaturato

Surinam /ˌsʊərɪ'næm/ *n* Suriname *m*

surliness /'sɜːlɪnɪs/ *n* scontrosità *f*

surly /'sɜːlɪ/ *adj* (**-ier**, **-iest**) scontroso

surmise /sə'maɪz/ *vt* supporre

surmount /sə'maʊnt/ *vt* sormontare

surname /'sɜːneɪm/ *n* cognome *m*

surpass /sə'pɑːs/ *vt* superare

surplus /'sɜːpləs/ **A** *adj* d'avanzo; **be ~ to requirements** essere in eccedenza rispetto alle necessità
B *n* sovrappiù *m*

surprise /sə'praɪz/ **A** *n* sorpresa *f*
B *vt* sorprendere; **be ~d** essere sorpreso (**at** da)

surprising /sə'praɪzɪŋ/ *adj* sorprendente

surprisingly /sə'praɪzɪŋlɪ/ *adv* sorprendentemente; **~ enough** stranamente

surreal /sə'rɪəl/ *adj* surreale

surrealism /sə'rɪəlɪzm/ *n* surrealismo *m*

surrealist /sə'rɪəlɪst/ **A** *n* surrealista *mf*
B *adj* surrealistico

surrender /sə'rendə(r)/ **A** *n* resa *f*
B *vi* arrendersi
C *vt* cedere

surreptitious /sʌrəp'tɪʃəs/ *adj* furtivo

surreptitiously /sʌrəp'tɪʃəslɪ/ *adv* furtivamente

surrogate /'sʌrəgət/ *n* surrogato *m*

surrogate mother *n* madre *f* surrogata

surround /sə'raʊnd/ *vt* circondare; **~ed by** circondato da

surrounding /sə'raʊndɪŋ/ *adj* circostante

surroundings /sə'raʊndɪŋz/ *npl* dintorni *mpl*

surtax /'sɜːtæks/ *n* soprattassa *f*; (on income) imposta *f* supplementare

surveillance /sə'veɪləns/ *n* sorveglianza *f*; **under ~** sotto sorveglianza

survey[1] /'sɜːveɪ/ *n* sguardo *m*; (poll) sondaggio *m*; (investigation) indagine *f*; (of land) rilevamento *m*; (of house) perizia *f*

survey[2] /sə'veɪ/ *vt* esaminare; fare un rilevamento di ‹*land*›; fare una perizia di ‹*building*›

surveyor /sə'veɪə(r)/ *n* perito *m*; (of land) topografo, -a *mf*

survival /sə'vaɪvl/ *n* sopravvivenza *f*; (relic) resto *m*

survive /sə'vaɪv/ **A** *vt* sopravvivere a
B *vi* sopravvivere

surviving /sə'vaɪvɪŋ/ *adj* ‹*relative*› sopravvissuto

survivor /sə'vaɪvə(r)/ *n* superstite *mf*; **be a ~** infml riuscire sempre a cavarsela

susceptible /sə'septəbl/ *adj* influenzabile; **~ to** sensibile a

suspect[1] /sə'spekt/ *vt* sospettare; (assume) supporre

suspect[2] /'sʌspekt/ *adj & n* sospetto, -a *mf*

suspend /sə'spend/ *vt* appendere; (stop, from duty) sospendere
suspended sentence *n* (sospensione *f*) condizionale *f* (della pena)
suspender belt /sə'spendə/ *n* reggicalze *m inv*
suspenders /sə'spendəz/ *npl* giarrettiere *fpl*; AmE (braces) bretelle *fpl*
suspense /sə'spens/ *n* tensione *f*; (in book etc) suspense *f*
suspension /sə'spenʃn/ *n* Auto sospensione *f*
suspension bridge *n* ponte *m* sospeso
suspicion /sə'spɪʃn/ *n* sospetto *m*; (trace) pizzico *m*; **under ~** sospettato
suspicious /sə'spɪʃəs/ *adj* sospettoso; (arousing suspicion) sospetto
suspiciously /sə'spʃəslɪ/ *adv* sospettosamente; (arousing suspicion) in modo sospetto
suss *vt* **~ out** BrE infml intuire ‹*person*›; capire ‹*software, technique*›; **I've got you ~ed [out]** ho scoperto il tuo piano
sustain /sə'steɪn/ *vt* sostenere; mantenere ‹*life*›; subire ‹*injury*›
sustainable /səs'teɪnəbl/ *adj* ‹*development, growth*› sostenibile; ‹*resource, forest*› rinnovabile
sustained /sə'steɪnd/ *adj* ‹*effort*› prolungato
sustenance /'sʌstɪnəns/ *n* nutrimento *m*
suture /'su:tʃə(r)/ *n* sutura *f*
SUV *n abbr* AmE (**sports utility vehicle**) SUV *m inv*
SW *abbr* (**south-west**) SO
swab /swɒb/ *n* Med tampone *m*
swagger /'swægə(r)/ *vi* pavoneggiarsi
swallow¹ /'swɒləʊ/ *vt & vi* inghiottire
■ **swallow up** *vt* divorare; ‹*earth, crowd*› inghiottire
swallow² *n* (bird) rondine *f*
swam /swæm/ ▶ **swim**
swamp /swɒmp/ **A** *n* palude *f*
B *vt* fig sommergere
swampy /'swɒmpɪ/ *adj* paludoso
swan /swɒn/ *n* cigno *m*
swank /swæŋk/ *vi* infml darsi delle arie
swanky /'swæŋkɪ/ *adj* infml (posh) snob *inv*
swap /swɒp/ **A** *n* infml scambio *m*
B *vt* (*pt/pp* **swapped**) infml scambiare (for con)
C *vi* fare cambio
swarm /swɔ:m/ **A** *n* sciame *m*
B *vi* sciamare; **be ~ing with** fig brulicare di
swarthy /'swɔ:ðɪ/ *adj* (**-ier, -iest**) di carnagione scura
swashbuckling /'swɒʃbʌklɪŋ/ *adj* ‹*hero, appearance*› spericolato; ‹*adventure, tale*› di cappa e spada
swastika /'swɒstɪkə/ *n* svastica *f*
swat /swɒt/ *vt* (*pt/pp* **swatted**) schiacciare
swathe BrE **swath** AmE /sweɪð/ **A** *n* (of grass, corn) falciata *f*; (land) larga striscia *f*
B *vt* (in bandages, silk) avvolgere
sway /sweɪ/ **A** *n* fig influenza *f*
B *vi* oscillare; ‹*person*› ondeggiare
C *vt* (influence) influenzare
Swaziland /'swɑ:zɪlænd/ *n* Swaziland *m*
swear /sweə(r)/ **A** *vt* (*pt* **swore**, *pp* **sworn**) giurare; **I could have sworn that ...** avrei giurato che ...
B *vi* giurare; (curse) dire parolacce; **I'd ~ to it!** ci potrei giurare!; **~ at somebody** imprecare contro qualcuno; **~ by** (believe in) credere ciecamente in
■ **swear in** *vt* prestare giuramento ‹*president*›
■ **swear off** *vt* infml (give up) smettere di
swear word *n* parolaccia *f*
sweat /swet/ **A** *n* sudore *m*
B *vi* sudare
C *vt* **~ blood** sudare sangue
■ **sweat out**: *vt* **~ it out** (endure to the end) tener duro fino alla fine
sweatband /'swetbænd/ *n* fascia *f* per il sudore; (for wrist) polsino *m*
sweater /'swetə(r)/ *n* golf *m inv*
sweat pants *npl* AmE pantaloni *mpl* della tuta
sweatshirt /'swetʃɜ:t/ *n* felpa *f*
sweatshop *n* BrE *manifattura (f) in cui il personale viene sfruttato*
sweaty /'swetɪ/ *adj* sudato
swede *n* rapa *f* svedese
Swede /swi:d/ *n* svedese *mf*
Sweden /'swi:dn/ *n* Svezia *f*
Swedish /'swi:dɪʃ/ *adj & n* svedese *m*
sweep /swi:p/ **A** *n* scopata *f*, spazzata *f*; (curve) curva *f*; (movement) movimento *m* ampio; **make a clean ~** fig fare piazza pulita
B *vt* (*pt/pp* **swept**) scopare, spazzare; ‹*wind*› spazzare; **~ the board** fare piazza pulita
C *vi* (go swiftly) andare rapidamente; ‹*wind*› soffiare
■ **sweep aside** *vt* ignorare ‹*objection*›
■ **sweep away** *vt* fig spazzare via
■ **sweep up** *vt* spazzare
sweeper /'swi:pə(r)/ *n* (machine) spazzatrice *f*; (person) spazzino *m*; (in football) libero *m*
sweeping /'swi:pɪʃ/ *adj* ‹*gesture*› ampio; ‹*statement*› generico; ‹*changes*› radicale
⚷ **sweet** /swi:t/ **A** *adj* dolce; **have a ~ tooth** essere goloso
B *n* caramella *f*; (dessert) dolce *m*
sweet and sour *adj* agrodolce
sweetbread *n* (veal) animella *f* di vitello; (lamb) animella *f* di agnello
sweetcorn *n* mais *m*, granturco *m*
sweeten /'swi:tn/ *vt* addolcire
■ **sweeten up** *vt* raddolcire ‹*person*›
sweetener /'swi:tnə(r)/ *n* dolcificante *m*; infml (incentive) incentivo *m*; infml (bribe) bustarella *f*

⚷ parola chiave

sweetheart /ˈswi:thɑ:t/ *n* innamorato, -a *mf*; **hi, ~** ciao, tesoro

sweetly /ˈswi:tlɪ/ *adv* dolcemente

sweetness /ˈswi:tnɪs/ *n* dolcezza *f*

sweet pea *n* pisello *m* odoroso

sweet potato *n* patata *f* americana

sweet shop *n* negozio *m* di dolciumi

sweet-talk *vt* **~ somebody into doing something** convincere qualcuno a fare qualcosa con tante belle parole

swell /swel/ **A** *n* (of sea) mare *m* lungo **B** *vi* (*pt* **swelled**, *pp* **swollen** *or* **swelled**) gonfiarsi; (increase) aumentare **C** *vt* gonfiare; (increase) far salire **D** *adj* infml eccellente

swelling /ˈswelɪŋ/ *n* gonfiore *m*

swelter /ˈsweltə(r)/ *vi* soffocare [dal caldo]

sweltering, **sweltering hot** /ˈsweltərɪŋ/ *adj* torrido, afoso

swept /swept/ ▶ **sweep**

swerve /swɜ:v/ *vi* deviare bruscamente

swift /swift/ *adj* rapido

swiftly /ˈswɪftlɪ/ *adv* rapidamente

swiftness /ˈswɪftnɪs/ *n* rapidità *f*

swig /swɪg/ infml **A** *n* sorso *m* **B** *vt* (*pt/pp* **swigged**) scolarsi

swill /swɪl/ **A** *n* (for pigs) brodaglia *f* **B** *vt* **~ [out]** risciacquare

swim /swɪm/ **A** *n* **have a ~** fare una nuotata **B** *vi* (*pt* **swam**, *pp* **swum**) nuotare; ‹*room*› girare; **go ~ming** andare a nuotare; **my head is ~ming** mi gira la testa **C** *vt* percorrere a nuoto ‹*distance*›

swimmer /ˈswɪmə(r)/ *n* nuotatore, -trice *mf*

swimming /ˈswɪmɪŋ/ *n* nuoto *m*

swimming baths *npl* piscina *fsg*

swimming costume *n* costume *m* da bagno

swimmingly /ˈswɪmɪŋlɪ/ *adv* **go ~** andar liscio

swimming pool *n* piscina *f*

swimming trunks *npl* calzoncini *mpl* da bagno

swimsuit /ˈswɪmsu:t/ *n* costume *m* da bagno

swindle /ˈswɪndl/ **A** *n* truffa *f* **B** *vt* truffare

swindler /ˈswɪndlə(r)/ *n* truffatore, -trice *mf*

swine /swaɪn/ *n* infml porco *m*

swine flu /ˈswaɪn flu:/ *n* influenza *f* A

swing /swɪŋ/ **A** *n* oscillazione *f*; (shift) cambiamento *m*; (seat) altalena *f*; Mus swing *m*; **in full ~** in piena attività **B** *vi* (*pt/pp* **swung**) oscillare; (on swing, sway) dondolare; (dangle) penzolare; (turn) girare **C** *vt* oscillare; far deviare ‹*vote*›

swing door *n* porta *f* a vento

swingeing /ˈswɪndʒɪŋ/ *adj* ‹*increase*› drastico

swingometer /swɪŋˈɒmɪtə(r)/ *n strumento (m) che permette di seguire l'andamento delle votazioni*

swipe /swaɪp/ **A** *n* infml botta *f* **B** *vt* infml colpire; infml (steal) rubare; far passare nella macchinetta ‹*credit card*›

swipe card *n* tessera *f* magnetica

swirl /swɜ:l/ **A** *n* (of smoke, dust) turbine *m* **B** *vt* far girare **C** *vi* ‹*water*› fare mulinello

swish[1] /swɪʃ/ *adj* infml chic

swish[2] *vi* schioccare

Swiss /swɪs/ *adj* & *n* svizzero, -a *mf*; **the ~** *pl* gli svizzeri

Swiss roll *n rotolo (m) di pan di Spagna ripieno di marmellata*

switch /swɪtʃ/ **A** *n* interruttore *m*; (change) mutamento *m* **B** *vt* cambiare; (exchange) scambiare **C** *vi* cambiare; **~ to** passare a

■ **switch off** *vt* spegnere

■ **switch on** *vt* accendere

■ **switch over** *vi* TV cambiare [canale]; **~ over to** passare a

■ **switch round** *vt* (change one for the other) scambiare

switchback *n* montagne *fpl* russe

switchblade *n* AmE coltello *m* a scatto

switchboard *n* centralino *m*

switchboard operator *n* centralinista *mf*

switched line /swɪtʃt/ *n* Teleph linea *f* commutata

swither /ˈswɪðə(r)/ *vi* infml (hesitate) tentennare

Switzerland /ˈswɪtsələnd/ *n* Svizzera *f*

swivel /ˈswɪvl/ **A** *vt* (*pt/pp* **swivelled**) girare **B** *vi* girarsi

swivel chair *n* sedia *f* girevole

swizz /swɪz/ *n* infml (swindle) fregatura *f*

swollen /ˈswəʊlən/ **A** ▶ **swell** **B** *adj* gonfio

swollen-headed /-ˈhedɪd/ *adj* presuntuoso

swoon /swu:n/ *vi* svenire

swoop /swu:p/ **A** *n* (by police) incursione *f* **B** *vi* **~ [down]** ‹*bird*› piombare; fig fare un'incursione

sword /sɔ:d/ *n* spada *f*

swordfish /ˈsɔ:dfɪʃ/ *n* pesce *m* spada *inv*

swore /swɔ:(r)/ ▶ **swear**

sworn /swɔ:n/ ▶ **swear**

sworn enemy *n* nemico *m* giurato

swot /swɒt/ **A** *n* infml sgobbone, -a *mf* **B** *vt* (*pt/pp* **swotted**) infml sgobbare (**for an exam** per un esame)

swum /swʌm/ ▶ **swim**

swung /swʌŋ/ ▶ **swing**

sycamore /ˈsɪkəmɔ:(r)/ *n* sicomoro *m*

sycophant /ˈsɪkəfænt/ *n* adulatore, -trice *mf*

sycophantic /sɪkəˈfæntɪk/ *adj* adulatorio

syllable /ˈsɪləbl/ *n* sillaba *f*

syllabus /ˈsɪləbəs/ *n* programma *m* [dei corsi]
syllogism /ˈsɪlədʒɪzm/ *n* sillogismo *m*
sylph /sɪlf/ *n* silfide *f*
symbiosis /sɪmbaɪˈəʊsɪs/ *n* simbiosi *f inv*
symbiotic /sɪmbaɪˈɒtɪk/ *adj* simbiotico
symbol /ˈsɪmbl/ *n* simbolo *m* (**of** di)
symbolic /sɪmˈbɒlɪk/ *adj* simbolico
symbolically /sɪmˈbɒlɪklɪ/ *adv* simbolicamente
symbolism /ˈsɪmbəlɪzm/ *n* simbolismo *m*
symbolist /ˈsɪmbəlɪst/ *n* simbolista *mf*
symbolize /ˈsɪmbəlaɪz/ *vt* simboleggiare
symmetrical /sɪˈmetrɪkl/ *adj* simmetrico
symmetrically /sɪˈmetrɪklɪ/ *adv* simmetricamente
symmetry /ˈsɪmətrɪ/ *n* simmetria *f*
sympathetic /sɪmpəˈθetɪk/ *adj* (understanding) comprensivo; (showing pity) compassionevole
sympathetically /sɪmpəˈθetɪklɪ/ *adv* con comprensione/compassione
sympathize /ˈsɪmpəθaɪz/ *vi* capire; (in grief) solidarizzare; **~ with somebody** capire qualcuno/solidarizzare con qualcuno
sympathizer /ˈsɪmpəθaɪzə(r)/ *n* Pol simpatizzante *mf*
sympathy /ˈsɪmpəθɪ/ *n* comprensione *f*; (pity) compassione *f*; (condolences) condoglianze *fpl*; **in ~ with** ‹*strike*› per solidarietà con
symphonic /sɪmˈfɒnɪk/ *adj* sinfonico
symphony /ˈsɪmfənɪ/ *n* sinfonia *f*
symphony orchestra *n* orchestra *f* sinfonica
🔑 **symptom** /ˈsɪmptəm/ *n* sintomo *m*
symptomatic /sɪmptəˈmætɪk/ *adj* sintomatico (**of** di)
synagogue /ˈsɪnəgɒg/ *n* sinagoga *f*
sync, **synch** /sɪŋk/ *n* sincronia *f*; **be out of ~** essere sfasato; **be in ~** essere in sincronia; **be in ~ with/out of ~ with** essere sincronizzato/sfasato rispetto a
synchronize /ˈsɪŋkrənaɪz/ *vt* sincronizzare
synchronous /ˈsɪŋkrənəs/ *adj* sincrono
syndicate /ˈsɪndɪkət/ *n* gruppo *m*
syndrome /ˈsɪndrəʊm/ *n* sindrome *f*
synonym /ˈsɪnənɪm/ *n* sinonimo *m*
synonymous /sɪˈnɒnɪməs/ *adj* sinonimo
synopsis /sɪˈnɒpsɪs/ *n* (*pl* **-opses** /sɪˈnɒpsiːz/) (of opera, ballet) trama *f*; (of book) riassunto *m*
syntactic /sɪnˈtæktɪk/, **syntactical** /sɪnˈtæktɪkl/ *adj* sintattico
syntax /ˈsɪntæks/ *n* sintassi *f inv*
synthesis /ˈsɪnθəsɪs/ *n* (*pl* **-theses** /ˈsɪnθəsiːz/) sintesi *f inv*
synthesize /ˈsɪnθəsaɪz/ *vt* sintetizzare
synthesizer /ˈsɪnθəsaɪzə(r)/ *n* Mus sintetizzatore *m*
synthetic /sɪnˈθetɪk/ **A** *adj* sintetico **B** *n* fibra *f* sintetica
syphilis /ˈsɪfɪlɪs/ *n* sifilide *f*
Syria /ˈsɪrɪə/ *n* Siria *f*
Syrian /ˈsɪrɪən/ *adj* & *n* siriano, -a *mf*
syringe /sɪˈrɪndʒ/ **A** *n* siringa *f* **B** *vt* siringare
syrup /ˈsɪrəp/ *n* sciroppo *m*; BrE tipo *m* di melassa
syrupy /ˈsɪrəpɪ/ *adj* sciropposo
🔑 **system** /ˈsɪstəm/ *n* sistema *m*
systematic /sɪstəˈmætɪk/ *adj* sistematico
systematically /sɪstəˈmætɪklɪ/ *adv* sistematicamente
systems analysis *n* analisi *f* dei sistemi
systems analyst *n* analista *mf* programmatore, -trice *mf*
systems design *n* progettazione *f* di sistemi
systems engineer *n* sistemista *mf*
Szechuan /seˈtʃwɑːn, ˈseʒ-/ *adj* del Sichuan

Tt

t, **T** /tiː/ *n* (letter) t, T *f inv*
tab /tæb/ *n* linguetta *f*; (with name) etichetta *f*; **keep ~s on** infml sorvegliare; **pick up the ~** infml pagare il conto
tabby /ˈtæbɪ/ *n* gatto *m* tigrato
tab key *n* tasto *m* tabulatore
🔑 **table** /ˈtæbɪ/ **A** *n* tavolo *m*; (list) tavola *f*; **at [the] ~** a tavola **B** *vt* proporre
table-cloth *n* tovaglia *f*
table lamp *n* lampada *f* da tavolo
table mat *n* sottopiatto *m*
table of contents sommario *m*
table salt *n* sale *m* fine
tablespoon *n* cucchiaio *m* da tavola

🔑 parola chiave

tablespoonful *n* cucchiaiata *f*
tablet /ˈtæblɪt/ *n* pastiglia *f*; (slab) lastra *f*; **~ of soap** saponetta *f*
table tennis *n* tennis *m* da tavolo; (everyday level) ping pong *m*
tabloid /ˈtæblɔɪd/ *n* tabloid *m inv*; derog giornale *m* scandalistico
taboo /təˈbuː/ **A** *adj* tabù *inv*
B *n* tabù *m*
tabulate /ˈtæbjʊleɪt/ *vt* tabulare
tabulation /tæbjʊˈleɪʃn/ *n* (of data, results) tabulazione *f*
tabulator /ˈtæbjʊleɪtə(r)/ *n* tabulatore *m*
tachograph /ˈtækəgrɑːf/ *n* tachigrafo *m*
tachometer /tæˈkɒmɪtə(r)/ *n* tachimetro *m*
tacit /ˈtæsɪt/ *adj* tacito
tacitly /ˈtæsɪtlɪ/ *adv* tacitamente
taciturn /ˈtæsɪtɜːn/ *adj* taciturno
tack /tæk/ **A** *n* (nail) chiodino *m*; (stitch) imbastitura *f*; Naut virata *f*; fig linea *f* di condotta
B *vt* inchiodare; (sew) imbastire
C *vi* Naut virare
■ **tack on** *vt* (add later) aggiungere ‹*ending, paragraph*›
tackle /ˈtækl/ **A** *n* (equipment) attrezzatura *f*; (football etc) contrasto *m*, tackle *m inv*
B *vt* affrontare
tacky /ˈtækɪ/ *adj* ‹*paint*› non ancora asciutto; ‹*glue*› appiccicoso; fig pacchiano
tact /tækt/ *n* tatto *m*
tactful /ˈtæktfʊl/ *adj* pieno di tatto; ‹*remark*› delicato
tactfully /ˈtæktfʊlɪ/ *adv* con tatto
tactical /ˈtæktɪkl/ *adj* tattico
tactically /ˈtæktɪklɪ/ *adv* tatticamente
tactician /tækˈtɪʃn/ *n* stratega *mf*
tactics /ˈtæktɪks/ *npl* tattica *fsg*
tactile /ˈtæktaɪl/ *adj* tattile
tactless /ˈtæktlɪs/ *adj* privo di tatto
tactlessly /ˈtæktlɪslɪ/ *adv* senza tatto
tactlessness /ˈtæktlɪsnɪs/ *n* mancanza *f* di tatto; (of remark) indelicatezza *f*
tadpole /ˈtædpəʊl/ *n* girino *m*
tae kwon do *n* tae-kwon-do *m*
taffeta /ˈtæfɪtə/ *n* taffetà *m*
tag[1] /tæg/ **A** *n* (label) etichetta *f*
B *vt* (*pt/pp* **tagged**) attaccare l'etichetta a
tag[2] *n* (game) acchiapparello *m*
■ **tag along** *vi* seguire passo passo
■ **tag on** *vt* (attach) aggiungere
tail /teɪl/ **A** *n* coda *f*; **~s** *pl* (tailcoat) frac *m inv*
B *vt* infml (follow) pedinare
■ **tail off** *vi* diminuire
tailback *n* coda *f*
tail-end *n* parte *f* finale; (of train) coda *f*
tailgate /ˈteɪlgeɪt/ *n* sponda *f* posteriore ribaltabile
tail light *n* fanalino *m* di coda
tail-off *n* diminuzione *f*
tailor /ˈteɪlə(r)/ **A** *n* sarto *m*
B *vt* **~ something to someone's needs** adattare qualcosa alle esigenze di qualcuno
tailor-made *adj* fatto su misura
tailspin /ˈteɪlspɪn/ *n* Aeron vite *f* di coda
tailwind /ˈteɪlwɪnd/ *n* vento *m* di coda
taint /teɪnt/ *vt* contaminare
Taiwan /taɪˈwɑːn/ *n* Taiwan *f*
Tajikistan /tɑːˌdʒɪkɪˈstɑːn/ *n* Tajikistan *m*
⚷ **take** /teɪk/ **A** *n* Cinema ripresa *f*; AmE (takings) incassi *mpl*
B *vt* (*pt* **took**, *pp* **taken**) prendere; (to a place) portare ‹*person, object*›; (contain) contenere ‹*passengers etc*›; (endure) sopportare; (require) occorrere; (teach) insegnare; (study) studiare ‹*subject*›; fare ‹*exam, holiday, photograph, walk, bath*›; sentire ‹*pulse*›; misurare ‹*sb's temperature*›; **~ something to the cleaner's** portare qualcosa in lavanderia; **~ somebody home** (by car) portare qualcuno a casa; **~ somebody prisoner** fare prigioniero qualcuno; **be ~n ill** ammalarsi; **~ something calmly** prendere con calma qualcosa; **~ the dog for a walk** portare a spasso il cane; **~ one's time doing something** fare qualcosa con calma; **this will only ~ a minute** ci vuole solo un minuto; **I ~ it that...** (assume) presumo che...; **~ it from me!** (believe me) dai retta a me!; **~ hold** ‹*idea, disease*› prendere piede; **~ part** prendere parte; **~ part in** prendere parte a; **~ place** svolgersi
C *vi* ‹*plant*› attecchire
■ **take aback** *vt* (surprise) cogliere di sorpresa
■ **take after** *vt* assomigliare a
■ **take against** *vt* (turn against) prendere in antipatia
■ **take apart** *vt* (dismantle) smontare
■ **take away** *vt* (with one) portare via; (remove) togliere; (subtract) sottrarre; **'to ~ away'** 'da asporto'
■ **take back** *vt* riprendere; ritirare ‹*statement*›; (return) riportare [indietro]; **she took him back** (as husband, boyfriend) lo ha perdonato
■ **take down** *vt* portare giù; (remove) tirare giù; (write down) prendere nota di
■ **take in** *vt* (bring indoors) portare dentro; (to one's home) ospitare; (understand) capire; (deceive) ingannare; riprendere ‹*garment*›; (include) includere; vedere ‹*film etc*›
■ **take off** **A** *vt* togliersi ‹*clothes*›; (deduct) togliere; (mimic) imitare; **~ time off** prendere delle vacanze; **~ oneself off** andarsene
B *vi* Aeron decollare; infml (leave) andarsene; (become successful) decollare
■ **take on** *vt* farsi carico di; assumere ‹*employee*›; (as opponent) prendersela con; **~ it on oneself to do something** arrogarsi il diritto di fare qualcosa
■ **take out** *vt* portare fuori; togliere ‹*word, stain*›; (withdraw) ritirare ‹*money, books*›; **~ out a subscription to something** abbonarsi a qualcosa; **she took a pen out of her pocket** ha

preso una penna dalla tasca; **I'm taking my wife out tonight** esco con mia moglie stasera; **~ somebody out to dinner** portare a cena fuori qualcuno; **it'll ~ you out of yourself** (take your mind off things) servirà a distrarti; **~ it out on somebody** infml prendersela con qualcuno
■ **take over** **A** *vt* assumere il controllo di ‹*firm*›
B *vi* **~ over from somebody** sostituire qualcuno; (permanently) succedere a qualcuno
■ **take to** *vt* (as a habit) darsi a; **I took to her** (liked) mi è piaciuta
■ **take up** **A** *vt* portare su; accettare ‹*offer*›; intraprendere ‹*profession*›; dedicarsi a ‹*hobby*›; prendere ‹*time*›; occupare ‹*space*›; tirare su ‹*floorboards*›; accorciare ‹*dress*›; **~ something up with somebody** discutere qualcosa con qualcuno; **~ somebody up on something** (question further) chiedere ulteriori chiarimenti a qualcuno su qualcosa; **I'll ~ you up on your offer** (accept) accetto la tua offerta
B *vi* **~ up with somebody** legarsi a qualcuno
takeaway /ˈteɪkəweɪ/ *n* (meal) piatto *m* da asporto; (restaurant) *ristorante (m) che prepara piatti da asporto*
take-home pay *n* stipendio *m* netto
taken /ˈteɪkən/ *adj* ‹*room etc*› occupato; **be very ~ with somebody/something** essere conquistato da qualcuno/qualcosa
take-off *n* Aeron decollo *m*
take-out /ˈteɪkaʊt/ *n* AmE = **takeaway**
takeover *n* rilevamento *m*
takeover bid *n* offerta *f* pubblica di acquisto
takings /ˈteɪkɪŋz/ *npl* incassi *mpl*
talc /tælk/ *n* (boro)talco *m*
talcum /ˈtælkəm/ *n* **~ [powder]** talco *m*
tale /teɪl/ *n* storia *f*; derog fandonia *f*; **tell ~s** fare la spia
⚷ **talent** /ˈtælənt/ *n* talento *m*
talent contest *n* concorso *m* per giovani talenti
talented /ˈtæləntɪd/ *adj* [ricco] di talento
talent scout *n* talent scout *mf inv*
Taliban /ˈtælɪbæn/ *n* talebani *mpl*
talisman /ˈtælɪzmən/ *n* talismano *m*
⚷ **talk** /tɔːk/ **A** *n* conversazione *f*; (lecture) conferenza *f*; (gossip) chiacchiere *fpl*; **make small ~** parlare del più e del meno
B *vi* parlare
C *vt* parlare di ‹*politics etc*›; **~ somebody into something** convincere qualcuno di qualcosa
■ **talk about** *vt* parlare di; **~ about bad luck!** quando si dice la sfortuna!
■ **talk back** *vi* (reply defiantly) rispondere
■ **talk down to** *vt* (patronize) parlare con condiscendenza a
■ **talk of** *vt* parlare di; **~ing of food...** a proposito di mangiare...
■ **talk over** *vt* discutere
■ **talk to** *vt* parlare con; (reprimand) fare un discorsetto a; **~ to oneself** parlare da solo
talkative /ˈtɔːkətɪv/ *adj* loquace
talking /ˈtɔːkɪŋ/ *adj* ‹*doll, parrot*› parlante
talking book *n* audiolibro *m*
talking head /ˈtɔːkɪŋ/ *n* mezzobusto *m*
talking-to *n* sgridata *f*
talk show *n* talk show *m inv*
⚷ **tall** /tɔːl/ *adj* alto; **how ~ are you?** quanto sei alto?
tallboy *n* cassettone *m*
tall order *n* impresa *f* difficile
tall story *n* frottola *f*
tally /ˈtælɪ/ **A** *n* conteggio *m*; **keep a ~ of** tenere il conto di
B *vi* coincidere
talon /ˈtælən/ *n* artiglio *m*
tambourine /tæmbəˈriːn/ *n* tamburello *m*
tame /teɪm/ **A** *adj* ‹*animal*› domestico; (dull) insulso
B *vt* domare
tamely /ˈteɪmlɪ/ *adv* docilmente
tamer /ˈteɪmə(r)/ *n* domatore, -trice *mf*
tamper /ˈtæmpə(r)/ *vi* **~ with** manomettere
tampon /ˈtæmpɒn/ *n* tampone *m*
tan /tæn/ **A** *adj* marrone rossiccio *inv*
B *n* marrone *m* rossiccio; (from sun) abbronzatura *f*
C *vt* (*pt/pp* **tanned**) conciare ‹*hide*›
D *vi* abbronzarsi
tandem /ˈtændəm/ *n* tandem *m inv*; **in ~** in tandem
tang /tæŋ/ *n* sapore *m* forte; (smell) odore *m* penetrante
tanga /ˈtæŋgə/ *n* tanga *m inv*
tangent /ˈtændʒənt/ *n* tangente *f*; **go off at a ~** infml partire per la tangente
tangerine /tændʒəˈriːn/ **A** *n* (fruit) tipo *m* di mandarino; (colour) arancione *m*
B *adj* arancione
tangible /ˈtændʒɪbl/ *adj* tangibile
tangibly /ˈtændʒɪblɪ/ *adv* tangibilmente
tangle /ˈtæŋgl/ **A** *n* groviglio *m*; (in hair) nodo *m*
B *vt* **~ [up]** aggrovigliare
C *vi* aggrovigliarsi
tango /ˈtæŋgəʊ/ *n* tango *m*
tangy /ˈtæŋɪ/ *adj* forte; ‹*smell*› penetrante
tank /tæŋk/ *n* contenitore *m*; (for petrol) serbatoio *m*; (fish ~) acquario *m*; Mil carro *m* armato
tankard /ˈtæŋkəd/ *n* boccale *m*
tanker /ˈtæŋkə(r)/ *n* nave *f* cisterna; (lorry) autobotte *f*
tank top *n* canottiera *f*
tanned /tænd/ *adj* abbronzato

t

⚷ parola chiave

tannin /'tænɪn/ *n* tannino *m*
Tannoy® /'tænɔɪ/ *n* BrE sistema *m* di altoparlanti
tantalize /'tæntəlaɪz/ *vt* tormentare
tantalizing /'tæntəlaɪzɪŋ/ *adj* allettante; ‹*smell*› stuzzicante
tantamount /'tæntəmaʊnt/ *adj* ~ **to** equivalente a
tantrum /'tæntrəm/ *n* scoppio *m* d'ira; **throw a** ~ fare i capricci
Tanzania /ˌtænzə'nɪə/ *n* Tanzania *f*
tap /tæp/ **A** *n* rubinetto *m*; (knock) colpo *m*; **on** ~ a disposizione
B *vt* (*pt/pp* **tapped**) dare un colpetto a; sfruttare ‹*resources*›; mettere sotto controllo ‹*telephone*›
C *vi* picchiettare
tap-dance A *n* tip tap
B *vi* ballare il tip tap
tap dancer *n* ballerino, -a *mf* di tip tap
tape /teɪp/ **A** *n* nastro *m*; (recording) cassetta *f*
B *vt* legare con nastro; (record) registrare
tape backup drive *n* Comput unità *f* di backup a nastro
tape deck *n* piastra *f*
tape measure *n* metro *m* [a nastro]
taper /'teɪpə(r)/ **A** *n* candela *f* sottile
B *vi* assottigliarsi
■ **taper off** *vi* assottigliarsi
tape-record *vt* registrare su nastro
tape recorder *n* registratore *m*
tape recording *n* registrazione *f*
tapered /'teɪpəd/ *adj* ‹*trousers*› affusolato
tape streamer *n* Comput unità *f* a nastro magnetico
tapestry /'tæpɪstrɪ/ *n* arazzo *m*
tapeworm /'teɪpwɜːm/ *n* verme *m* solitario, tenia *f*
tapping /'tæpɪŋ/ *n* (noise) picchiettio *m*
tap water *n* acqua *f* del rubinetto
tar /tɑː(r)/ **A** *n* catrame *m*
B *vt* (*pt/pp* **tarred**) incatramare
tardy /'tɑːdɪ/ *adj* (**-ier**, **-iest**) tardivo
⚷ **target** /'tɑːgɪt/ **A** *n* bersaglio *m*; fig obiettivo *m*
B *vt* stabilire come obiettivo ‹*market*›
target language *n* lingua *f* d'arrivo
target market *n* mercato *m* obiettivo
target practice *n* tiro *m* al bersaglio
tariff /'tærɪf/ **A** *n* (price) tariffa *f*; (duty) dazio *m*
B *adj* tariffario
tarmac A *n* asfalto *m*; BrE (of airfield) pista *f*
B *attrib* ‹*road, footpath*› asfaltato
C *vt* asfaltare
Tarmac® /'tɑːmæk/ *n* macadam *m* al catrame
tarnish /'tɑːnɪʃ/ **A** *vi* ossidarsi
B *vt* ossidare; fig macchiare
tarpaulin /tɑː'pɔːlɪn/ *n* telone *m* impermeabile
tarragon /'tærəgən/ *n* dragoncello *m*
tart¹ /tɑːt/ *adj* aspro; fig acido
tart² *n* crostata *f*; (individual) crostatina *f*; sl (prostitute) donnaccia *f*
■ **tart up**: *vt* infml ~ **oneself up** agghindarsi
tartan /'tɑːtn/ **A** *n* tessuto *m* scozzese, tartan *m inv*
B *attrib* di tessuto scozzese
tartar /'tɑːtə(r)/ *n* (on teeth) tartaro *m*
tartar sauce *n* salsa *f* tartara
⚷ **task** /tɑːsk/ *n* compito *m*; **take somebody to** ~ riprendere qualcuno
task bar *n* Comput barra *f* delle applicazioni
task force *n* Pol commissione *f*; Mil taskforce *f inv*
taskmaster /'tɑːskmɑːstə(r), AmE 'tæsk-/ *n* tiranno *m*; **be a hard** ~ essere molto esigente
tassel /'tæsl/ *n* nappa *f*
⚷ **taste** /teɪst/ **A** *n* gusto *m*; (sample) assaggio *m*; **get a** ~ **of something** fig assaporare il gusto di qualcosa; **in good/bad** ~ di buongusto/di cattivo gusto
B *vt* sentire il sapore di; (sample) assaggiare
C *vi* sapere (**of** di); **it** ~**s lovely** è ottimo; ~ **like something** sapere di qualcosa
taste buds *npl* papille *fpl* gustative
tasteful /'teɪs(t)fʊl/ *adj* di [buon] gusto
tastefully /'teɪs(t)fʊlɪ/ *adv* con gusto
tasteless /'teɪs(t)lɪs/ *adj* senza gusto
tastelessly /'teɪs(t)lɪslɪ/ *adv* con cattivo gusto
taster /'teɪstə(r)/ *n* (foretaste) assaggio *m*; (person) assaggiatore, -trice *mf*
tasty /'teɪstɪ/ *adj* (**-ier**, **-iest**) saporito
tat /tæt/ ▶ **tit²**
tattered /'tætəd/ *adj* cencioso; ‹*pages*› stracciato
tatters /'tætəz/ *npl* **in** ~ a brandelli
tattle /'tætl/ **A** *vi* spettegolare
B *n* pettegolezzo *m*
tattoo¹ /tæ'tuː/ **A** *n* tatuaggio *m*
B *vt* tatuare
tattoo² *n* Mil parata *f* militare
tatty /'tætɪ/ *adj* (**-ier**, **-iest**) ‹*clothes, person*› trasandato; ‹*book*› malandato
taught /tɔːt/ ▶ **teach**
taunt /tɔːnt/ **A** *n* scherno *m*
B *vt* schernire
Taurus /'tɔːrəs/ *n* Astr Toro *m*
taut /tɔːt/ *adj* teso
tauten /'tɔːtən/ **A** *vt* tendere
B *vi* tendersi
tautology /tɔː'tɒlədʒɪ/ *n* tautologia *f*
tavern /'tævən/ *n* literary taverna *f*
tawdry /'tɔːdrɪ/ *adj* (**-ier**, **-iest**) pacchiano
tawny /'tɔːnɪ/ *adj* fulvo
⚷ **tax** /tæks/ **A** *n* tassa *f*; (on income) imposte *fpl*; **before** ~ ‹*price*› tasse escluse; ‹*salary*› lordo
B *vt* tassare; fig mettere alla prova; ~ **with**

accusare di
taxable /'tæksəbl/ *adj* tassabile; ~ **income** reddito *m* imponibile
tax allowance *n* detrazione *f* di imposta
taxation /tæk'seɪʃn/ *n* tasse *fpl*; ~ **at source** ritenuta *f* alla fonte
tax avoidance *n* elusione *f* fiscale
tax bracket *n* scaglione *m* d'imposta
tax break *n* agevolazione *f* fiscale
tax burden *n* aggravio *m* fiscale
tax code *n* codice *m* fiscale
tax consultant *n* fiscalista *m*
tax-deductible *adj* detraibile
tax disc *n* Auto bollo *m*
tax evader *n* evasore *m* fiscale
tax evasion *n* evasione *f* fiscale
tax exile *n* (person) espatriato, -a *mf* per motivi fiscali
tax-free *adj* esentasse
tax haven *n* paradiso *m* fiscale
taxi /'tæksɪ/ **A** *n* taxi *m inv*
B *vi* (*pt/pp* **taxied**, *pres p* **taxiing**) ‹*aircraft*› rullare
taxi driver *n* tassista *mf*
tax incentive *n* incentivo *m* fiscale
taxing /'tæksɪŋ/ *adj* (exhausting) sfiancante
tax inspector *n* ispettore *m* delle tasse
taxi rank *n* posteggio *m* per taxi
taxman /'tæksmæn/ *n* **the** ~ il fisco
tax office *n* ufficio *m* delle imposte
taxpayer *n* contribuente *mf*
tax rebate *n* rimborso *m* d'imposta
tax return *n* dichiarazione *f* dei redditi
tax shelter *n* paradiso *m* fiscale
tax system *n* regime *m* fiscale
TB *n abbr* (**tuberculosis**) TBC *f*
tbsp *abbr* (**tablespoon**) cucchiaio *m*
tea /tiː/ *n* tè
tea bag *n* bustina *f* di tè
tea break *n* intervallo *m* per il tè
⚷ **teach** /tiːtʃ/ *vt & vi* (*pt/pp* **taught**) insegnare; ~ **somebody something** insegnare qualcosa a qualcuno; ~ **somebody a lesson** fig dare una lezione a qualcuno
⚷ **teacher** /'tiːtʃə(r)/ *n* insegnante *mf*; (primary) maestro, -a *mf*
teacher training *n* formazione *f* professionale per insegnanti
⚷ **teaching** /'tiːtʃɪŋ/ *n* insegnamento *m*
teaching hospital *n* ≈ ospedale *m* universitario
tea cloth *n* (for drying) asciugapiatti *m inv*
tea cosy *n* copriteiera *f*
teacup *n* tazza *f* da tè
teak /tiːk/ *n* tek *m*
tea leaves *npl* tè *m* sfuso; (when infused) fondi *mpl* di tè

⚷ parola chiave

⚷ **team** /tiːm/ *n* squadra *f*; fig équipe *f inv*
▪ **team up** *vi* unirsi
team captain *n* caposquadra *mf*
team manager *n* direttore *m* sportivo
team-mate *n* compagno *m* di squadra
team player *n persona (f) che dimostra spirito di squadra*
team spirit *n* spirito *m* di squadra
teamwork *n* lavoro *m* di squadra; fig lavoro *m* d'équipe
teapot /'tiːpɒt/ *n* teiera *f*
tear[1] /teə(r)/ **A** *n* strappo *m*
B *vt* (*pt* **tore**, *pp* **torn**) strappare; ~ **to pieces** *or* **shreds** fare a pezzi; stroncare ‹*book, film*›
C *vi* strappare; ‹*material*› strapparsi; (run) precipitarsi
▪ **tear apart** *vt* fig (criticize) fare a pezzi; (separate) dividere
▪ **tear away**: *vt* ~ **oneself away from** staccarsi da ‹*television*›; abbandonare a malincuore ‹*party*›
▪ **tear into** *vt* infml (reprimand) attaccare duramente; (make a vigorous start on) dare dentro a
▪ **tear off** *vt* (carefully) staccare; (violently) strappare
▪ **tear open** *vt* aprire strappando
▪ **tear out** *vt* staccare; ~ **one's hair out** mettersi le mani nei capelli
▪ **tear up** *vt* strappare; rompere ‹*agreement*›
⚷ **tear**[2] /tɪə(r)/ *n* lacrima *f*
tearaway /'teərəweɪ/ *n* giovane teppista *mf*
tearful /'tɪəfʊl/ *adj* ‹*person*› in lacrime; ‹*farewell*› lacrimevole
tearfully /'tɪəfʊlɪ/ *adv* in lacrime
tear gas /'tɪə/ *n* gas *m* lacrimogeno
tearing /'teərɪŋ/ *adj* **be in a** ~ **hurry** avere una gran fretta
tear-jerker /'tɪədʒɜːkə(r)/ *n* infml **this film is a real** ~ è davvero un film strappalacrime
tease /tiːz/ *vt* prendere in giro ‹*person*›; tormentare ‹*animal*›
teasel /'tiːzl/ *n* Bot cardo *m*
tea set /'tiːset/ *n* servizio *m* da tè
tea shop *n* sala *f* da tè
teasing /'tiːzɪŋ/ *adj* canzonatorio
teaspoon *n* cucchiaino *m* [da tè]
teaspoonful *n* cucchiaino *m*
tea-strainer *n* colino *m* per il tè
teat /tiːt/ *n* capezzolo *m*; (on bottle) tettarella *f*
teatime *n* ora *f* del tè
tea towel *n* strofinaccio *m* [per i piatti]
⚷ **technical** /'teknɪkl/ *adj* tecnico
technical college *n* istituto *m* tecnico professionale
technical drawing *n* (skill or process, plan) disegno *m* tecnico
technical hitch *n* contrattempo *m* tecnico
technicality /teknɪ'kælətɪ/ *n* tecnicismo *m*; Jur cavillo *m* giuridico

technically /ˈteknɪklɪ/ *adv* tecnicamente; (strictly) strettamente
technician /tekˈnɪʃn/ *n* tecnico, -a *mf*
technique /tekˈniːk/ *n* tecnica *f*
techno /ˈteknəʊ/ *n* techno *f*
technocrat /ˈteknəkræt/ *n* tecnocrate *mf*
technological /teknəˈlɒdʒɪkl/ *adj* tecnologico
technologically /teknəˈlɒdʒɪklɪ/ *adv* tecnologicamente
technology /tekˈnɒlədʒɪ/ *n* tecnologia *f*
technology park *n* parco *m* tecnologico
technology transfer *n* trasferimento *m* di tecnologia
technophobe /ˈteknəʊfəʊb/ *n* tecnofobo, -a *mf*
teddy /ˈtedɪ/ *n* ~ **[bear]** orsacchiotto *m*
tedious /ˈtiːdɪəs/ *adj* noioso
tedium /ˈtiːdɪəm/ *n* tedio *m*
tee /tiː/ *n* Golf tee *m inv*
teem /tiːm/ *vi* (rain) piovere a dirotto; **be ~ing with** (full of) pullulare di
teen /tiːn/ *adj* ‹*fashion, idol*› degli adolescenti
teenage /ˈtiːneɪdʒ/ *adj* per ragazzi; **~ boy/girl** adolescente *mf*
teenager /ˈtiːneɪdʒə(r)/ *n* adolescente *mf*
teens /tiːnz/ *npl* **the ~** l'adolescenza *fsg*; **be in one's ~** essere adolescente
teeny /ˈtiːnɪ/ *adj* infml (**-ier**, **-iest**) piccolissimo
teeny-weeny /tiːnɪˈwiːnɪ/ *adj* infml minuscolo
tee shirt *n* T-shirt, maglietta *f* [a maniche corte]
teeter /ˈtiːtə(r)/ *vi* barcollare
teeth /tiːθ/ ▶ **tooth**
teethe /tiːð/ *vi* mettere i primi denti
teething troubles /ˈtiːðɪŋ/ *npl* fig difficoltà *fpl* iniziali
teetotal /tiːˈtəʊtl/ *adj* astemio
teetotaller /tiˈtəʊt(ə)lə(r)/ *n* astemio, -a *mf*
TEFL /ˈtefl/ *n insegnamento* (*m*) *dell'inglese come lingua straniera*
tel. *abbr* (**telephone**) tel.
telebanking /ˈtelɪbæŋkɪŋ/ *n* servizi *mpl* bancari telematici
telecast /ˈtelɪkɑːst/ **A** *n* trasmissione *f* televisiva
B *vt* far vedere in televisione
telecomms /ˈtelɪkɒmz/ *npl* telecomunicazioni *fpl*
telecommunications /telɪkəmjuːnɪˈkeɪʃnz/ *npl* telecomunicazioni *fpl*
telecommuter /telɪkəˈmjuːtə(r)/ *n persona* (*f*) *che lavora da casa su computer*
telecommuting /telɪkəˈmjuːtɪŋ/ *n lavoro* (*m*) *su computer da casa*
teleconference /ˈtelɪkɒnf(ə)r(ə)ns/ *n* videoconferenza *f*
telegenic /telɪˈdʒenɪk/ *adj* telegenico
telegram /ˈtelɪgræm/ *n* telegramma *m*
telegraph /ˈtelɪgrɑːf/ *n* telegrafo *m*
telegraphic /telɪˈgræfɪk/ *adj* telegrafico
telegraph pole *n* palo *m* del telegrafo
telemarketing /ˈtelɪmɑːkɪtɪŋ/ *n* telemarketing *m*
telematics /telɪˈmætɪks/ *nsg* telematica *fsg*
telemessage /ˈtelɪmesɪdʒ/ *n* BrE telegramma *m*
telepathic /telɪˈpæθɪk/ *adj* telepatico
telepathy /tɪˈlepəθɪ/ *n* telepatia *f*; **by ~** per telepatia
telephone /ˈtelɪfəʊn/ **A** *n* telefono *m*; **be on the ~** avere il telefono; (be telephoning) essere al telefono
B *vt* telefonare a
C *vi* telefonare
telephone answering service *n* segreteria *f* telefonica
telephone banking *n* servizi *mpl* bancari via telefono
telephone book *n* elenco *m* telefonico
telephone booking *n* prenotazione *f* telefonica
telephone booth, **telephone box** *n* cabina *f* telefonica
telephone call *n* telefonata *f*
telephone conversation *n* conversazione *f* telefonica
telephone directory *n* elenco *m* telefonico
telephone helpline *n* assistenza *f* telefonica
telephone message *n* messaggio *m* telefonico
telephone number *n* numero *m* di telefono
telephone operator *n* centralinista *mf*
telephone tapping *n* intercettazione *f* telefonica
telephonist /tɪˈlefənɪst/ *n* telefonista *mf*
telephoto /telɪˈfəʊtəʊ/ *adj* **~ lens** teleobiettivo *m*
teleprinter /ˈtelɪprɪntə(r)/ *n* telescrivente *f*
telerecording /ˈtelɪkrɪkɔːdɪŋ/ *n* programma *m* [televisivo] registrato
telesales /ˈtelɪseɪlz/ *n* vendita *f* per telefono
telescope /ˈtelɪskəʊp/ *n* telescopio *m*
telescopic /telɪˈskɒpɪk/ *adj* telescopico
teleshopping /ˈtelɪʃɒpɪŋ/ *n* acquisti *mpl* per telefono
teletext /ˈtelɪtekst/ *n* televideo *m*
telethon /ˈtelɪθɒn/ *n* telethon *m inv*
televise /ˈtelɪvaɪz/ *vt* trasmettere per televisione
television /ˈtelɪvɪʒn/ *n* televisione *f*; **watch ~** guardare la televisione; **on ~** alla televisione
television channel *n* rete *f* televisiva
television licence *n* abbonamento *m* alla televisione

television licence fee *n* costo *m* dell'abbonamento alla televisione

television programme *n* programma *m* televisivo

television screen *n* teleschermo *m*

television serial *n* sceneggiato *m*

television set *n* televisore *m*

televisual /telɪ'vɪʒʊəl/ *adj* televisivo

teleworking /'telɪwɜːkɪŋ/ *n* telelavoro *m*

telex /'teleks/ **A** *n* telex *m inv*
B *vt* mandare via telex ‹*message*›; mandare un telex a ‹*person*›

🔑 **tell** /tel/ **A** *vt* (*pt/pp* **told**) dire; raccontare ‹*story*›; (distinguish) distinguere (**from** da); ~ **somebody something** dire qualcosa a qualcuno; ~ **somebody to do something** dire a qualcuno di fare qualcosa; ~ **the time** dire l'ora; **I couldn't ~ why...** non sapevo perché...; **you're ~ing me!** a chi lo dici!
B *vi* (produce an effect) avere effetto; **time will ~** il tempo ce lo dirà; **his age is beginning to ~** l'età comincia a farsi sentire [per lui]; **don't ~ me** non dirmelo; **you mustn't ~** non devi dire niente

■ **tell apart** *vt* distinguere

■ **tell off** *vt* sgridare

■ **tell on** *vt* Sch (inform against) fare la spia a

teller /'telə(r)/ *n* (in bank) cassiere, -a *mf*

telling /'telɪŋ/ *adj* significativo; (argument) efficace

telling-off *n* cicchetto *m*

tell-tale **A** *n* spione, -a *mf*
B *adj* rivelatore

telly /'telɪ/ *n* infml tv *f inv*, tele *f inv*

temerity /tɪ'merətɪ/ *n* audacia *f*

temp /temp/ infml **A** *n* impiegato, -a *mf* temporaneo, -a
B *vi* lavorare come impiegato, -a temporaneo, -a

temper /'tempə(r)/ **A** *n* (disposition) carattere *m*; (mood) umore *m*; (anger) collera *f*; **lose one's ~** arrabbiarsi; **be in a ~** essere arrabbiato; **keep one's ~** mantenere la calma
B *vt* fig temperare

temperament /'temprəmənt/ *n* temperamento *m*

temperamental /temprə'mentl/ *adj* (moody) capriccioso

temperamentally /temprə'mentəlɪ/ *adv* **they are ~ unsuited** tra loro c'è incompatibilità di carattere

temperance /'tempərəns/ *n* (abstinence) astinenza *f* dal bere

temperate /'tempərət/ *adj* ‹*climate*› temperato

🔑 **temperature** /'temprətʃə(r)/ *n* temperatura *f*; **have** *or* **run a ~** avere la febbre

tempest /'tempɪst/ *n* tempesta *f*

tempestuous /tem'pestjʊəs/ *adj* tempestoso

template /'templɪt/ *n* sagoma *f*

temple¹ /'templ/ *n* tempio *m*

temple² *n* Anat tempia *f*

tempo /'tempəʊ/ *n* ritmo *m*; Mus tempo *m*

temporal /'tempər(ə)l/ *adj* temporale

temporarily /tempə'rerɪlɪ/ *adv* temporaneamente; ‹*introduced, erected*› provvisoriamente

temporary /'tempərərɪ/ *adj* temporaneo; ‹*measure, building*› provvisorio

tempt /tempt/ *vt* tentare; sfidare ‹*fate*›; ~ **somebody to** indurre qualcuno a; **be ~ed** essere tentato (**to** di); **I am ~ed by the offer** l'offerta mi tenta

temptation /temp'teɪʃn/ *n* tentazione *f*

tempting /'temptɪŋ/ *adj* allettante; ‹*food, drink*› invitante

temptress /'temptrɪs/ *n* seduttrice *f*

🔑 **ten** /ten/ *adj & n* dieci *m*; **the T~ Commandments** i Dieci Comandamenti

tenable /'tenəbl/ *adj* fig sostenibile

tenacious /tɪ'neɪʃəs/ *adj* tenace

tenacity /tɪ'næsətɪ/ *n* tenacia *f*

tenancy /'tenənsɪ/ *n* locazione *f*

tenant /'tenənt/ *n* inquilino, -a *mf*; Comm locatario, -a *mf*

tend¹ /tend/ *vt* (look after) prendersi cura di

🔑 **tend²** *vi* ~ **to do something** tendere a far qualcosa

tendency /'tendənsɪ/ *n* tendenza *f*

tendentious /ten'denʃəs/ *adj* tendenzioso

tender¹ /'tendə(r)/ **A** *n* Comm offerta *f*; **put out to ~** dare in appalto; **be legal ~** avere corso legale
B *vt* offrire; presentare ‹*resignation*›

tender² *adj* tenero; (painful) dolorante

tender-hearted /-hɑːtɪd/ *adj* dal cuore tenero

tenderize /'tendəraɪz/ *vt* rendere tenero ‹*meat*›

tenderly /'tendəlɪ/ *adv* teneramente

tenderness /'tendənɪs/ *n* tenerezza *f*; (painfulness) dolore *m*

tendon /'tendən/ *n* tendine *m*

tendril /'tendrɪl/ *n* (of plant) viticcio *m*

tenement /'tenəmənt/ *n* casamento *m*

tenet /'tenɪt/ *n* principio *m*

tenner /'tenə(r)/ *n* infml biglietto *m* da dieci sterline

tennis /'tenɪs/ *n* tennis *m*

tennis ball *n* palla *f* da tennis

tennis court *n* campo *m* da tennis

tennis match *n* partita *f* di tennis

tennis player *n* tennista *mf*

tennis racket *n* racchetta *f* da tennis

tennis shoes *npl* scarpe *fpl* da tennis

tenor /'tenə(r)/ *n* tenore *m*

🔑 parola chiave

tenpin bowling BrE, **tenpins** AmE *n* bowling *m*

tense¹ /tens/ *n* Gram tempo *m*

tense² **A** *adj* teso
B *vt* tendere ‹*muscle*›
▪ **tense up** *vi* tendersi

tension /ˈtenʃn/ *n* tensione *f*

tent /tent/ *n* tenda *f*

tentacle /ˈtentəkl/ *n* tentacolo *m*

tentative /ˈtentətɪv/ *adj* provvisorio; ‹*smile, gesture*› esitante

tentatively /ˈtentətɪvlɪ/ *adv* timidamente; ‹*accept*› provvisoriamente

tent city *n* tendopoli *f inv*

tenterhooks /ˈtentəhʊks/ *npl* **be on ~** essere sulle spine

tenth /tenθ/ *adj & n* decimo, -a *mf*

tenuous /ˈtenjʊəs/ *adj* fig debole

tenure /ˈtenjə(r)/ *n* (period of office) permanenza *f* in carica; Univ (job security) ruolo *m*; (of land, property) possesso *m*; **security of ~** (of land, property) diritto *m* di possesso

tepid /ˈtepɪd/ *adj* tiepido

tercentenary /tɜːsenˈtiːnərɪ/ *n* terzo centenario *m*

term /tɜːm/ *n* periodo *m*; Sch, Univ trimestre *m*; (in Italy) Sch quadrimestre *m*; Univ semestre *m*; (expression) termine *m*; **~s** *pl* (conditions) condizioni *fpl*; **~ of office** carica *f*; **in the short/long ~** a breve/lungo termine; **be on good/bad ~s** essere in buoni/ cattivi rapporti; **come to ~s with** accettare ‹*past, fact*›; **easy ~s** facilitazioni *fpl* di pagamento; **~s of reference** *pl* (of committee) competenze *fpl*

terminal /ˈtɜːmɪnl/ **A** *adj* finale; Med terminale
B *n* Aeron terminal *m inv*; Rail stazione *f* di testa; (of bus) capolinea *m*; (on battery) morsetto *m*; Comput terminale *m*

terminally /ˈtɜːmɪnəlɪ/ *adv* **be ~ ill** essere in fase terminale

terminate /ˈtɜːmɪneɪt/ **A** *vt* terminare; rescindere ‹*contract*›; interrompere ‹*pregnancy*›
B *vi* terminare; **~ in** finire in

termination /tɜːmɪˈneɪʃn/ *n* termine *m*; Med interruzione *f* di gravidanza

terminologist /tɜːmɪˈnɒlədʒɪst/ *n* linguista *mf* specializzato, -a in terminologia

terminology /tɜːmɪˈnɒlədʒɪ/ *n* terminologia *f*

terminus /ˈtɜːmɪnəs/ *n* (*pl* **-ni**) /ˈtɜːmɪnaɪ/ (for bus) capolinea *m*; (for train) stazione *f* di testa

term-time *n* **during ~** durante il trimestre

terrace /ˈterəs/ *n* terrazza *f*; (houses) fila *f* di case a schiera; **the ~s** *gr* Sport le gradinate

terraced house /ˈterəsd/ *n* casa *f* a schiera

terracotta /terəˈkɒtə/ *n* (earthenware) terracotta *f*; (colour) color *m* terracotta

terrain /teˈreɪn/ *n* terreno *m*

terrestrial /tɪˈrestrɪəl/ **A** *n* terrestre *mf*
B *adj* terrestre; **~ television** televisione *f* terrestre

terrible /ˈterəbl/ *adj* terribile

terribly /ˈterəblɪ/ *adv* terribilmente; **I'm ~ sorry** sono infinitamente spiacente

terrier /ˈterɪə(r)/ *n* terrier *m inv*

terrific /təˈrɪfɪk/ *adj* infml (excellent) fantastico; (huge) enorme

terrifically /təˈrɪfɪklɪ/ *adv* infml terribilmente

terrify /ˈterɪfaɪ/ *vt* (*pt/pp* **-ied**) atterrire; **be terrified** essere terrorizzato

terrifying /ˈterɪfaɪɪŋ/ *adj* terrificante

territorial /terɪˈtɔːrɪəl/ *adj* territoriale

territorial waters /wɔːtəz/ *npl* acque *fpl* territoriali

territory /ˈterɪtərɪ/ *n* territorio *m*

terror /ˈterə(r)/ *n* terrore *m*

terrorism /ˈterərɪzm/ *n* terrorismo *m*

terrorist /ˈterərɪst/ *n* terrorista *mf*

terrorize /ˈterəraɪz/ *vt* terrorizzare

terror-stricken *adj* terrorizzato

terry towelling /terɪˈtaʊəlɪŋ/ BrE, **terry cloth** AmE *n* tessuto *m* di spugna

terse /tɜːs/ *adj* conciso

tersely /ˈtɜːslɪ/ *adv* concisamente

tertiary /ˈtɜːʃ(ə)rɪ/ *adj* ‹*era, industry, sector*› terziario; ‹*education, college*› superiore

Terylene® /ˈterɪliːn/ *n* terilene® *m*

test /test/ **A** *n* esame *m*; (in laboratory) esperimento *m*; (of friendship, machine) prova *f*; (of intelligence, aptitude) test *m inv*; **put to the ~** mettere alla prova; **pass one's ~** Auto passare l'esame di guida
B *vt* esaminare; provare ‹*machine*›

testament /ˈtestəmənt/ *n* testamento *m*; **Old/New T~** Antico/Nuovo Testamento *m*

test ban *n* divieto *m* di test nucleari

test case *n caso (m) giudiziario che fa giurisprudenza*

test-drive **A** *vt* ‹*manufacturer*› collaudare; ‹*buyer*› provare
B *n* collaudo *m*; prova *f*

tester /ˈtestə(r)/ *n* (person) collaudatore, -trice *mf*; (device) tester *m inv*; (sample: of make-up, perfume) campione *m*

testicle /ˈtestɪkl/ *n* testicolo *m*

testify /ˈtestɪfaɪ/ *vt & vi* (*pt/pp* **-ied**) testimoniare

testily /ˈtestɪlɪ/ *adv* ‹*say, reply*› in modo scontroso

testimonial /testɪˈməʊnɪəl/ *n* lettera *f* di referenze

testimony /ˈtestɪmənɪ/ *n* testimonianza *f*

testing /ˈtestɪŋ/ *n* (of drug) test *mpl*; (of blood, water) analisi *fpl*; (of children) esami *mpl*

test market *n* mercato *m* di prova

test match *n* partita *f* internazionale

testosterone /tesˈtɒstərəʊn/ *n* testosterone *m*

t

test pilot *n* pilota *mf* collaudatore, -trice
test tube *n* provetta *f*
test tube baby *n* infml bambino, -a *mf* in provetta
testy /'testɪ/ *adj* irascibile
tetanus /'tetənəs/ *n* tetano *m*
tetanus injection *n* antitetanica *f*
tetchy /'tetʃɪ/ *adj* facilmente irritabile
tether /'teðə(r)/ **A** *n* **be at the end of one's ~** non poterne più
B *vt* legare
Teutonic /tju:'tɒnɪk/ *adj* teutonico
⚷ **text** /tekst/ **A** *n* testo *m*; (on mobile phone) sms *m inv*
B *vi* (on mobile phone) mandare sms
C *vt* mandare sms a ‹*somebody*›
textbook /'tekstbʊk/ *n* manuale *m*
textile /'tekstaɪl/ **A** *adj* tessile
B *n* stoffa *f*
texting /'tekstɪŋ/ *n* infml scambio *m* di sms
text message *n* sms *m inv*, messaggio *m* di testo
text messaging *n* scambio *m* di sms
textual /'tekstjʊəl/ *adj* testuale
texture /'tekstʊə(r)/ *n* (of skin) grana *f*; (of food) consistenza *f*; **of a smooth ~** (to the touch) soffice al tatto
Thai /taɪ/ *adj & n* tailandese *mf*; (language) tailandese *m*
Thailand /'taɪlænd/ *n* Tailandia *f*
Thames /temz/ *n* Tamigi *m*
⚷ **than** /ðən/, *accentato* /ðæn/ *conj* che; (with numbers, names) di; **older ~ me** più vecchio di me
⚷ **thank** /θæŋk/ *vt* ringraziare; **~ you [very much]** grazie [mille]
thankful /'θæŋkfʊl/ *adj* grato
thankfully /'θæŋkfʊlɪ/ *adv* con gratitudine; (happily) fortunatamente
thankless /'θæŋklɪs/ *adj* ingrato
⚷ **thanks** /θæŋks/ *npl* ringraziamenti *mpl*; **~!** infml grazie!; **~ to** grazie a; **no ~ to you!** non certo grazie a te!
thank-you letter *n* lettera *f* di ringraziamento
⚷ **that** /ðæt/ **A** *adj & pron* (*pl* **those**) quel, quei *pl*; (before s + consonant, gn, ps, z) quello, quegli *pl*; (before vowel) quell' *mf*, quegli *mpl*, quelle *fpl*; **~ shop** quel negozio; **those shops** quei negozi; **~ mirror** quello specchio; **~ man/woman** quell'uomo/quella donna; **those men/women** quegli uomini/quelle donne; **~ one** quello; **I don't like those** quelli non mi piacciono; **~ is** cioè; **is ~ you?** sei tu?; **who is ~?** chi è?; **what did you do after ~?** cosa hai fatto dopo?; **like ~** in questo modo, così; **a man like ~** un uomo così; **~ is why** ecco perché; **~ is the reason she gave me** questa è la ragione che mi ha dato; **~ is the easiest thing to do** è la cosa più facile da fare; **~'s it!** (you've understood) ecco!; (I've finished) ecco fatto!; (I've had enough) basta così!; (there's nothing more) tutto qui!; **~'s ~!** (with job) ecco fatto!; (with relationship) è tutto finito!; **and ~'s ~!** punto e basta!
B *adv* così; **it wasn't ~ good** non era poi così buono
C *rel pron* che; **the man ~ I spoke to** l'uomo con cui ho parlato; **the day ~ I saw him** il giorno in cui l'ho visto; **all ~ I know** tutto quello che so
D *conj* che; **I think ~...** penso che...
thatch /θætʃ/ *n* tetto *m* di paglia
thatched /θætʃt/ *adj* coperto di paglia
thaw /θɔː/ **A** *n* disgelo *m*
B *vt* fare scongelare ‹*food*›
C *vi* ‹*food*› scongelarsi; **it's ~ing** sta sgelando
⚷ **the** /ðə/ **A** (before a vowel) /ðɪ/ (def art) il *m*, la *f*; i *mpl*, le *fpl*; (before s + consonant, gn, ps, z) lo *m*, gli *mpl*; (before vowel) l' *mf*, gli *mpl*, le *fpl*; **at ~ cinema/station** al cinema/alla stazione; **from ~ cinema/station** dal cinema/dalla stazione
B *adv* **~ more ~ better** più ce n'è meglio è; (with reference to pl) più ce ne sono meglio è; **all ~ better** tanto meglio
⚷ **theatre** /'θɪətə(r)/ *n* teatro *m*; Med sala *f* operatoria
theatregoer /'θiːətəgəʊə(r)/ *n* persona *f* che va a teatro
theatre-going /'θiːətəgəʊɪŋ/ *n* l'andare *m* a teatro
theatrical /θɪ'ætrɪkl/ *adj* teatrale; (showy) melodrammatico
theft /θeft/ *n* furto *m*
theft-proof *adj* antiscippo
⚷ **their** /ðeə(r)/ *poss adj* il loro *m*, la loro *f*, i loro *mpl*, le loro *fpl*; **~ mother/father** la loro madre/il loro padre
theirs /ðeəz/ *poss pron* il loro *m*, la loro *f*, i loro *mpl*, le loro *fpl*; **a friend of ~** un loro amico; **friends of ~** dei loro amici; **those are ~** quelli sono loro; (as opposed to ours) quelli sono i loro
⚷ **them** /ðem/ *pers pron* (direct object) li *m*, le *f*; (indirect object) gli, loro fml; (after prep: with people) loro; (after preposition: with things) essi; **we haven't seen ~** non li/le abbiamo visti/viste; **give ~ the money** dai loro *or* dagli i soldi; **give it to ~** daglielo; **I've spoken to ~** ho parlato con loro; **it's ~** sono loro
⚷ **theme** /θiːm/ *n* tema *m*
theme park *n* parco *m* a tema
theme song *n* motivo *m* conduttore
⚷ **themselves** /ðem'selvz/ *pron* (reflexive) si; (emphatic) se stessi; **they poured ~ a drink** si sono versati da bere; **they said so ~** lo hanno detto loro stessi; **they kept it to ~** se lo sono tenuti per sé; **by ~** da soli
⚷ **then** /ðen/ **A** *adv* allora; (next) poi; **by ~**

(in the past) ormai; (in the future) per allora; **since ~** sin da allora; **before ~** prima di allora; **from ~ on** da allora in poi; **now and ~** ogni tanto; **there and ~** all'istante
B *adj* di allora

thence /ðens/ *adv* (from there) di là; (therefore) perciò

theologian /θɪə'ləʊdʒɪən/ *n* teologo, -a *mf*

theological /θɪə'lɒdʒɪkl/ *adj* teologico

theology /θɪ'ɒlədʒɪ/ *n* teologia *f*

theorem /'θɪərəm/ *n* teorema *m*

theoretical /θɪə'retɪkl/ *adj* teorico

theoretically /θɪə'retɪklɪ/ *adv* teoricamente

theorist /'θɪərɪst/ *n* teorico *m*

theorize /'θɪəraɪz/ *vi* teorizzare

theory /'θɪərɪ/ *n* teoria *f*; **in ~** in teoria

therapeutic /θerə'pju:tɪk/ *adj* terapeutico

therapist /'θerəpɪst/ *n* terapista *mf*

therapy /'θerəpɪ/ *n* terapia *f*

there /ðeə(r)/ **A** *adv* là, lì; **down/up ~** laggiù/lassù; **~ is/are** c'è/ci sono; **~ he/she is** eccolo/eccola
B *int* **~, ~!** dai, su!

thereabouts /ðeərə'baʊts/ *adv* (roughly) all'incirca

thereafter *adv* dopo di che

thereby *adv* in tal modo

therefore /'ðeəfɔ:(r)/ *adv* perciò

therein *adv* **~ lies...** in ciò risiede...; **contained ~** Jur (in contract) contenuto nello stesso

thermal /'θɜ:ml/ *adj* termico; ‹*treatment*› termale

thermal imaging *n* termografia *f*

thermal paper *n* carta *f* termica

thermal printer *n* stampante *f* termica

thermal underwear *n biancheria (f) che mantiene la temperatura corporea*

thermometer /θə'mɒmɪtə(r)/ *n* termometro *m*

Thermos® /'θɜ:məs/ *n* **~ [flask]** termos *m inv*

thermostat /'θɜ:məstæt/ *n* termostato *m*

thesaurus /θɪ'sɔ:rəs/ *n* (of particular field) dizionario *m* specialistico; (of synonyms) dizionario *m* dei sinonimi

these /ði:z/ ▶ **this**

thesis /'θi:sɪs/ *n* (*pl* **-ses** /-si:z/) tesi *f inv*

they /ðeɪ/ *pers pron* loro; **~ are tired** sono stanchi; **we're going, but ~ are not** noi andiamo, ma loro no; **~ say** (generalizing) si dice; **~ are building a new road** stanno costruendo una nuova strada

thick /θɪk/ **A** *adj* spesso; ‹*forest*› fitto; ‹*liquid*› denso; ‹*hair*› folto; infml (stupid) ottuso; infml (close) molto unito; **be 5 mm ~** essere 5 mm di spessore; **give somebody a ~ ear** infml dare uno schiaffone a qualcuno
B *adv* densamente
C *n* **in the ~ of** nel mezzo di

thicken /'θɪkn/ **A** *vt* ispessire ‹*sauce*›
B *vi* ispessirsi; ‹*fog*› infittirsi

thicket /'θɪkɪt/ *n* boscaglia *f*

thickhead /'θɪkhed/ *n* infml zuccone *mf*

thickie /'θɪkɪ/ *n* infml zucca *f* vuota

thickly /'θɪklɪ/ *adv* densamente; ‹*cut*› a fette spesse

thickness /'θɪknɪs/ *n* spessore *m*

thicko /'θɪkəʊ/ *n* infml zucca *f* vuota

thickset /'θɪkset/ *adj* tozzo

thick-skinned /-'skɪnd/ *adj* infml insensibile

thief /θi:f/ *n* (*pl* **thieves**) ladro, -a *mf*

thieving /'θi:vɪŋ/ **A** *adj* ladro
B *n* furti *mpl*

thigh /θaɪ/ *n* coscia *f*

thimble /'θɪmbl/ *n* ditale *m*

thimbleful /'θɪmbəlfʊl/ *n* (of wine etc) goccino *m*

thin /θɪn/ **A** *adj* (**thinner**, **thinnest**) sottile; ‹*shoes, sweater*› leggero; ‹*liquid*› liquido; ‹*person*› magro; fig ‹*excuse, plot*› inconsistente; **be [going] ~ on top** (be going bald) perdere i capelli; **vanish into ~ air** volatilizzarsi
B *adv* = **thinly**
C *vt* (*pt/pp* **thinned**) diluire ‹*liquid*›
D *vi* diradarsi

■ **thin down** **A** *vt* diluire ‹*paint etc*›
B *vi* (become slimmer) dimagrire

■ **thin out** *vi* diradarsi

thing /θɪŋ/ *n* cosa *f*; **~s** *pl* (belongings) roba *fsg*; **for one ~** in primo luogo; **the right ~** la cosa giusta; **just the ~!** proprio quel che ci vuole!; **how are ~s?** come vanno le cose?; **the latest ~** infml l'ultima cosa; **the best ~ would be** la cosa migliore sarebbe; **poor ~!** poveretto!; **have a ~ about** (be frightened of) aver la fobia di; (be attracted to) avere un debole per

thingumabob /'θɪŋəməbɒb/ *n* infml coso *m*

thingumajig /'θɪŋəmədʒɪg/ *n* infml coso *m*

think /θɪŋk/ *vt & vi* (*pt/pp* **thought**) pensare; (believe) credere; **I ~ so** credo di sì; **what do you ~?** (what is your opinion?) cosa ne pensi?; **~ of/about** pensare a; **what do you ~ of it?** cosa ne pensi di questo?; **~ of doing something** pensare di fare qualcosa; **~ better of it** ripensarci; **~ for oneself** pensare con la propria testa

■ **think again** *vi* pensarci su; **you can ~ again!** sei matto!

■ **think ahead** *vi* pensare al futuro; **~ ahead to something** pensare in anticipo a qualcosa

■ **think back**: *vi* **~ back to something** ripensare a qualcosa

■ **think out** *vt* mettere a punto ‹*strategy*›

■ **think over** *vt* riflettere su

■ **think through** *vt* riflettere bene su ‹*problem*›

■ **think up** *vt* escogitare; trovare ‹*name*›

thinker /'θɪŋkə(r)/ *n* pensatore, -trice *mf*

thinking /'θɪŋkɪŋ/ *n* (opinion) opinione *f*

think tank *n* gruppo *m* d'esperti

thinly /'θɪnlɪ/ *adv* ‹*populated*› scarsamente; ‹*disguised*› leggermente; ‹*cut*› a fette sottili

thinner /'θɪnə(r)/ *n* diluente *m*

thinness /'θɪnnɪs/ *n* (of person) magrezza *f*; (of material) finezza *f*

thin-skinned /-'skɪnd/ *adj* (sensitive) permaloso

🔑 **third** /θɜːd/ *adj & n* terzo, -a *mf*

third age *n* terza età *f*

third degree *n* **give somebody the ~** fare il terzo grado a qualcuno

third-degree burns *npl* ustioni *fpl* di terzo grado

thirdly /'θɜːdlɪ/ *adv* terzo

third party *n* (in insurance, law) terzi *mpl*

third-party insurance *n* assicurazione *f* contro terzi

third person *n* terzo *m*

third-rate *adj* scadente

third sector *n* terzo settore *m*

Third World *n* Terzo Mondo *m*

thirst /θɜːst/ *n* sete *f*

thirstily /'θɜːstɪlɪ/ *adv* con sete

thirsty /'θɜːstɪ/ *adj* assetato; **be ~** aver sete

thirteen /θɜː'tiːn/ *adj & n* tredici *m*

thirteenth /θɜː'tiːnθ/ *adj & n* tredicesimo, -a *mf*

thirties /'θɜːtɪz/ *npl* (period) **the ~** gli anni Trenta *mpl*; (age) trent'anni *mpl*; ▶ *also* **forties**

thirtieth /'θɜːtɪɪθ/ *adj & n* trentesimo, -a *mf*

thirty /'θɜːtɪ/ *adj & n* trenta *m*

thirty-something *n* trentenne *mf*

🔑 **this** /ðɪs/ **A** *adj* (*pl* **these**) questo; **~ man/woman** quest'uomo/questa donna; **these men/women** questi uomini/queste donne; **~ one** questo; **~ evening/morning** stamattina/stasera
B *pron* (*pl* **these**) questo; **we talked about ~ and that** abbiamo parlato del più e del meno; **like ~** così; **~ is Peter** questo è Peter; Teleph sono Peter; **who is ~?** chi è?; Teleph chi parla?; **~ is the happiest day of my life** è il giorno più felice della mia vita
C *adv* così; **~ big** così grande

t

thistle /'θɪsl/ *n* cardo *m*

thong /θɒŋ/ *n* (on whip) cinghia *f*; (on shoe, garment) laccetto *m*; (underwear) cache-sexe *m inv*; **~s** *pl* (sandals) infradito *mpl or fpl*

thorn /θɔːn/ *n* spina *f*

thorny /'θɔːnɪ/ *adj* spinoso

thorough /'θʌrə/ *adj* completo; ‹*knowledge*› profondo; ‹*clean, search, training*› a fondo; ‹*person*› scrupoloso

thoroughbred *n* purosangue *m inv*

thoroughfare *n* via *f* principale; **'no ~'** 'strada non transitabile'

thoroughly /'θʌrəlɪ/ *adv* ‹*clean, search, know something*› a fondo; (extremely) estremamente

thoroughness /'θʌrənɪs/ *n* completezza *f*

those /ðəʊz/ ▶ **that**

🔑 **though** /ðəʊ/ **A** *conj* sebbene; **as ~** come se
B *adv* infml tuttavia

🔑 **thought** /θɔːt/ **A** ▶ **think**
B *n* pensiero *m*; (idea) idea *f*; **I've given this some ~** ci ho pensato su

thoughtful /'θɔːtfʊl/ *adj* pensieroso; (considerate) premuroso

thoughtfully /'θɔːtfʊlɪ/ *adv* pensierosamente; (considerately) premurosamente

thoughtfulness /'θɔːtfʊlnɪs/ *n* (kindness) considerazione *f*

thoughtless /'θəːtlɪs/ *adj* (inconsiderate) sconsiderato

thoughtlessly /'θəːtlɪslɪ/ *adv* con noncuranza

thoughtlessness /'θəːtlɪsnɪs/ *n* sconsideratezza *f*

thought out /ˌθɔːt'aʊt/ *adj* **well/badly ~** ben/male progettato

thought-provoking *adj* ‹*book, film etc*› che fa riflettere

🔑 **thousand** /'θaʊznd/ **A** *adj* **one/a ~** mille *m inv*
B *n* mille *m inv*; **~s of** migliaia *fpl* di

thousandth /'θaʊzndθ/ *adj & n* millesimo

thrash /θræʃ/ *vt* picchiare; (defeat) sconfiggere

▪ **thrash about** *vi* dibattersi

▪ **thrash out** *vt* mettere a punto

thrashing /'θræʃɪŋ/ *n* (defeat) sconfitta *f*; **give somebody a ~** (beating) picchiare qualcuno

thread /θred/ **A** *n* filo *m*; (of screw) filetto *m*
B *vt* infilare ‹*beads*›; **~ one's way through** farsi strada fra

threadbare /'θredbeə(r)/ *adj* logoro

🔑 **threat** /θret/ *n* minaccia *f*

🔑 **threaten** /'θretn/ **A** *vt* minacciare (**to do** di fare)
B *vi* fig incalzare

threatening /'θretnɪŋ/ *adj* minaccioso; ‹*sky, atmosphere*› sinistro

threateningly /'θretnɪŋlɪ/ *adv* minacciosamente

🔑 **three** /θriː/ *adj & n* tre *m*

three-dimensional /-daɪ'menʃ(ə)nəl/ *adj* tridimensionale

threefold /'θriːfəʊld/ *adj & adv* triplo

3G *adj abbr* (**third generation**) ‹*technology, phone*› di terza generazione

three-legged /-'legɪd/ *adj* con tre gambe

three-piece suit *n* vestito *m* da uomo con panciotto

three-piece suite *n insieme* (*m*) *di divano e due poltrone coordinati*

three-quarter length *adj* ‹*portrait*› di tre quarti; ‹*sleeve*› a tre quarti

---

🔑 parola chiave

three-quarters *adv* ‹*empty, full, done*› per tre quarti

threesome /ˈθriːsəm/ *n* trio *m*

three-wheeler /-ˈwiːlə(r)/ *n* (car) auto *f inv* a tre ruote

thresh /θreʃ/ *vt* trebbiare

threshold /ˈθreʃəʊld/ *n* soglia *f*

threw /θruː/ ▶ **throw**

thrift /θrɪft/ *n* economia *f*

thrifty /ˈθrɪftɪ/ *adj* parsimonioso

thrill /θrɪl/ **A** *n* emozione *f*; (of fear) brivido *m*
B *vt* entusiasmare; **be ~ed with** essere entusiasta di

thriller /ˈθrɪlə(r)/ *n* (book) [romanzo *m*] giallo *m*; (film) [film *m inv*] giallo *m*

thrilling /ˈθrɪlɪŋ/ *adj* eccitante

thrive /θraɪv/ *vi* (*pt* **thrived, or throve**, *pp* **thrived**) ‹*business*› prosperare; ‹*child, plant*› crescere bene; **I ~ on pressure** mi piace essere sotto tensione

thriving /ˈθraɪvɪŋ/ *adj* fiorente

throat /θrəʊt/ *n* gola *f*; **sore ~** mal *m* di gola

throaty /ˈθrəʊtɪ/ *adj* (husky) roco; infml (with sore throat) rauco

throb /θrɒb/ **A** *n* pulsazione *f*; (of heart) battito *m*
B *vi* (*pt/pp* **throbbed**) (vibrate) pulsare; ‹*heart*› battere

throbbing /ˈθrɒbɪŋ/ *adj* ‹*pain*› lancinante; ‹*music*› martellante

throes /θrəʊz/ *npl* **in the ~ of** fig alle prese con

thrombosis /θrɒmˈbəʊsɪs/ *n* trombosi *f*

throne /θrəʊn/ *n* trono *m*

throng /θrɒŋ/ *n* calca *f*

throttle /ˈθrɒtl/ **A** *n* (on motorbike) manopola *f* di accelerazione
B *vt* strozzare

through /θruː/ **A** *prep* attraverso; (during) durante; (by means of) tramite; (thanks to) grazie a; **Saturday ~ Tuesday** AmE da sabato a martedì incluso
B *adv* attraverso; **~ and ~** fino in fondo; **wet ~** completamente bagnato; **read something ~** dare una lettura a qualcosa; **let ~** lasciar passare ‹*somebody*›
C *adj* ‹*train*› diretto; **be ~** (finished) aver finito; Teleph avere la comunicazione

throughout /θruːˈaʊt/ **A** *prep* per tutto
B *adv* completamente; (time) per tutto il tempo

throughway *n* AmE superstrada *f*

throve /θrəʊv/ ▶ **thrive**

throw /θrəʊ/ **A** *n* tiro *m*
B *vt* (*pt* **threw**, *pp* **thrown**) lanciare; (throw away) gettare; azionare ‹*switch*›; disarcionare ‹*rider*›; infml (disconcert) disorientare; infml dare ‹*party*›

■ **throw about** *vt* spargere; **~ one's money about** sbandierare i propri soldi

■ **throw away** *vt* gettare via

■ **throw back** *vt* ributtare in acqua ‹*fish*›; rilanciare ‹*ball*›

■ **throw in** *vt* (include at no extra cost) aggiungere [gratuitamente]; (in football) rimettere in gioco; **~ the towel** *or* **the sponge** fig abbandonare il campo

■ **throw off** *vt* seminare ‹*pursuers*›; liberarsi di ‹*cold, infection etc*›

■ **throw together** *vt* (assemble hastily) mettere insieme; improvvisare ‹*meal*›; (bring into contact) fare incontrare

■ **throw out** *vt* gettare via; rigettare ‹*plan*›; buttare fuori ‹*person*›

■ **throw up** **A** *vt* alzare
B *vi* (vomit) vomitare

throwaway *adj* ‹*remark*› buttato lì; ‹*paper cup*› usa e getta *inv*

throwback *n* Biol atavismo *m*; fig regressione *f*

throw-in *n* Sport rimessa *f* laterale

thrush /θrʌʃ/ *n* tordo *m*; Med mughetto *m*; (in woman) candida *f*

thrust /θrʌst/ **A** *n* spinta *f*
B *vt* (*pt/pp* **thrust**) (push) spingere; (insert) conficcare; **~ [up] on** imporre a

thud /θʌd/ *n* tonfo *m*

thug /θʌg/ *n* delinquente *m*

thuggish /ˈθʌgɪʃ/ *adj* violento

thumb /θʌm/ **A** *n* pollice *m*; **as a rule of ~** come regola generale; **under sb's ~** succube di qualcuno
B *vt* **~ a lift** fare l'autostop

■ **thumb through** *vt* sfogliare

thumb index *n* indice *m* a rubrica

thumbnail sketch *n* breve descrizione *f*

thumbs down *n* infml **get the ~** non ottenere l'ok; **give somebody/something the ~** non dare l'ok a qualcuno/qualcosa

thumbs up *n* infml **get the ~** ricevere l'ok; **give somebody/something the ~** dare l'ok a qualcuno/qualcosa

thumbtack *n* AmE puntina *f* da disegno

thump /θʌmp/ **A** *n* colpo *m*; (noise) tonfo *m*
B *vt* battere su ‹*table, door*›; battere ‹*fist*›; colpire ‹*person*›
C *vi* battere (**on** su); ‹*heart*› battere forte

■ **thump about** *vi* camminare pesantemente

thumping /ˈθʌmpɪŋ/ *adj* infml (very large) enorme; **a ~ headache** un mal di testa martellante

thunder /ˈθʌndə(r)/ **A** *n* tuono *m*; (loud noise) rimbombo *m*
B *vi* tuonare; (make loud noise) rimbombare

thunderbolt /ˈθʌndəbəʊlt/ *n* folgore *f*

thunderclap /ˈθʌndəklæp/ *n* rombo *m* di tuono

thundering /ˈθʌndərɪŋ/ *adj* infml (very big or great) tremendo

thunderous /ˈθʌndərəs/ *adj* ‹*applause*› scrosciante

thunderstorm /ˈθʌndəstɔːm/ *n* temporale *m*

thunderstruck /ˈθʌndəstrʌk/ *adj* sbigottito
thundery /ˈθʌndərɪ/ *adj* temporalesco
⚷ **Thursday** /ˈθɜːzdeɪ/ *n* giovedì *m*
⚷ **thus** /ðʌs/ *adv* così
thwack /θwæk/ **A** *vt* colpire
B *n* colpo *m*
thwart /θwɔːt/ *vt* ostacolare
thyme /taɪm/ *n* timo *m*
thyroid /ˈθaɪrɔɪd/ *n* tiroide *f*
tiara /tɪˈɑːrə/ *n* diadema *m*
Tiber /ˈtaɪbə(r)/ *n* Tevere *m*
Tibet /tɪˈbet/ *n* Tibet *m*
tick¹ /tɪk/ *n* **on ~** infml a credito
tick² **A** *n* (sound) ticchettio *m*; (mark) segno *m*; infml (instant) attimo *m*
B *vi* ticchettare
▪ **tick off** *vt* spuntare; infml sgridare
▪ **tick over** *vi* ‹*engine*› andare al minimo
⚷ **ticket** /ˈtɪkɪt/ *n* biglietto *m*; (for item deposited, library) tagliando *m*; (label) cartellino *m*; (fine) multa *f*
ticket barrier *n* cancelletto *m* di entrata e uscita
ticket collector *n* controllore *m*
ticket holder *n* persona *f* munita di biglietto
ticket office *n* biglietteria *f*
ticket tout *n* BrE bagarino *m*
ticket window *n* sportello *m* della biglietteria
tickle /ˈtɪkl/ **A** *n* solletico *m*
B *vt* fare il solletico a; (amuse) divertire
C *vi* fare prurito
ticklish /ˈtɪklɪʃ/ *adj* che soffre il solletico; ‹*problem*› delicato
tic-tac-toe /tɪktæktəʊ/ *n* AmE tris *m*
tidal /ˈtaɪdl/ *adj* ‹*river, harbour*› di marea
tidal wave *n* onda *f* di marea
tiddly /ˈtɪdlɪ/ *adj* BrE infml (drunk) brillo
tiddlywinks /ˈtɪdlɪwɪŋks/ *n* gioco *m* delle pulci
tide /taɪd/ *n* marea *f*; (of events) corso *m*; **the ~ is in/out** c'è alta/bassa marea
▪ **tide over**: *vt* **~ somebody over** aiutare qualcuno ad andare avanti
tidemark /ˈtaɪdmɑːk/ *n* linea *f* di marea; BrE fig (line of dirt) tracce *fpl* di sporco (*nella vasca da bagno*)
tidily /ˈtaɪdɪlɪ/ *adv* in modo ordinato
tidiness /ˈtaɪdɪnɪs/ *n* ordine *m*
tidy /ˈtaɪdɪ/ **A** *adj* (**-ier**, **-iest**) ordinato; infml ‹*amount*› bello
B *vt* ordinare
▪ **tidy away** *vt* mettere a posto ‹*toys, books*›
▪ **tidy out** *vt* mettere in ordine ‹*drawer, cupboard*›
▪ **tidy up** *vt* ordinare; **~ oneself up** mettersi in ordine
⚷ **tie** /taɪ/ **A** *n* cravatta *f*; (cord) legaccio *m*; fig (bond) legame *m*; (restriction) impedimento *m*; Sport pareggio *m*
B *vt* (*pres p* **tying**) legare; fare ‹*knot*›; **be ~d** (in competition) essere in parità
C *vi* pareggiare
▪ **tie back** *vt* legare [dietro la nuca] ‹*hair*›
▪ **tie down** *vt* also fig legare
▪ **tie in with** *vi* corrispondere a
▪ **tie on** *vt* attaccare
▪ **tie up** *vt* legare; vincolare ‹*capital*›; **be ~d up** (busy) essere occupato
tie-break, **tie-breaker** *n* Tennis tie-break *m inv*; (in quiz) pareggio *m*
tie-dye *vt* tingere annodando
tie-on *adj* ‹*label*› volante
tiepin *n* fermacravatta *m*
tier /tɪə(r)/ *n* fila *f*; (of cake) piano *m*; (in stadium) gradinata *f*
tiff /tɪf/ *n* battibecco *m*
tiger /ˈtaɪgə(r)/ *n* tigre *f*
tiger's eye /ˈtaɪgəz/ *n* occhio *m* di tigre
⚷ **tight** /taɪt/ **A** *adj* stretto; (taut) teso; infml (drunk) sbronzo; infml (mean) spilorcio; **~ corner** infml brutta situazione *f*
B *adv* strettamente; ‹*hold*› forte; ‹*closed*› bene
tighten /ˈtaɪtn/ **A** *vt* stringere; avvitare ‹*screw*›; intensificare ‹*control*›; **~ one's belt** fig tirare la cinghia
B *vi* stringersi
▪ **tighten up** **A** *vt* stringere ‹*screw*›; rendere più severo ‹*security*›
B *vi* (become stricter) diventare più severo
tight-fisted /-ˈfɪstɪd/ *adj* tirchio
tight-fitting /-ˈfɪtɪŋ/ *adj* attillato
tight-knit *adj* fig ‹*community, group*› unito
tight-lipped /-ˈlɪpt/ *adj* **they are remaining ~ about events** mantengono il riserbo sull'accaduto
tightly /ˈtaɪtlɪ/ *adv* strettamente; ‹*hold*› forte; ‹*closed*› bene
tightrope /ˈtaɪtrəʊp/ *n* fune *f* (*da funamboli*)
tightrope walker *n* equilibrista *mf*
tights /taɪts/ *npl* collant *m inv*
tigress /ˈtaɪgrɪs/ *n* tigre *f* femmina
tile /taɪl/ **A** *n* mattonella *f*; (on roof) tegola *f*
B *vt* rivestire di mattonelle ‹*wall*›; coprire con tegole ‹*roof*›; Comput affiancare
till¹ /tɪl/ *prep & conj* ▶ **until**
till² *n* cassa *f*
tiller /ˈtɪlə(r)/ *n* barra *f* del timone
tilt /tɪlt/ **A** *n* inclinazione *f*; **at full ~** a tutta velocità
B *vt* inclinare
C *vi* inclinarsi
timber /ˈtɪmbə(r)/ *n* legname *m*
⚷ **time** /taɪm/ **A** *n* tempo *m*; (occasion) volta *f*; (by clock) ora *f*; **two ~s four** due volte quattro; **at any ~** in qualsiasi momento; **this ~** questa volta; **at ~s, from ~ to ~** ogni tanto; **~ and again** cento volte; **two**

at a ~ due alla volta; **on ~** in orario; **in ~** in tempo; (eventually) col tempo; **in no ~ at all** velocemente; **in a year's ~** fra un anno; **behind ~** in ritardo; **behind the ~s** antiquato; **for the ~ being** per il momento; **what is the ~?** che ora è?; **by the ~ we arrive** quando arriviamo; **do you have the ~?** (what ~ is it?) hai l'ora?; **did you have a nice ~?** ti sei divertito?; **have a good ~!** divertiti!
B *vt* scegliere il momento per; cronometrare ‹*race*›; **be well ~d** essere ben calcolato

time bomb *n* bomba *f* a orologeria
time-consuming *adj* che porta via molto tempo
time difference *n* differenza *f* di fuso orario
time frame *n* arco *m* temporale
time-honoured /-ɒnəd/ *adj* venerando
timekeeper *n* Sport cronometrista *mf*; **be a good ~** (be punctual) essere sempre puntuale
time lag *n* intervallo *m* [di tempo]
timeless /ˈtaɪmlɪs/ *adj* eterno
time limit *n* limite *m* di tempo
timely /ˈtaɪmlɪ/ *adj* opportuno
time management *n* gestione *f* del proprio tempo
time off *n* (leave) permesso *m*; **take some ~** prendere delle ferie
time out *n* (break) pausa *f*; Sport time out *m inv*
timer /ˈtaɪmə(r)/ *n* timer *m inv*
timescale *n* periodo *m*
timeshare *n* (apartment) appartamento *m* in multiproprietà; (house) casa *f* in multiproprietà
time sheet *n* foglio *m* di presenza
time signal *n* segnale *m* orario
time span *n* arco *m* di tempo
time switch *n* interruttore *m* a tempo
timetable *n* orario *m*
time zone *n* fuso *m* orario
timid /ˈtɪmɪd/ *adj* (shy) timido; (fearful) timoroso
timidly /ˈtɪmɪdlɪ/ *adv* timidamente
timidness /ˈtɪmɪdnɪs/ *n* (shyness) timidezza *f*; (fear) paura *f*
timing /ˈtaɪmɪŋ/ *n* Sport, Techn cronometraggio *m*; **the ~ of the election** il momento scelto per le elezioni; **have no sense of ~** non saper scegliere il momento opportuno
timorous /ˈtɪm(ə)rəs/ *adj* timoroso
timpani /ˈtɪmpənɪ/ *npl* timpani *mpl*
tin /tɪn/ **A** *n* stagno *m*; (container) barattolo *m*
B *vt* (*pt/pp* **tinned**) inscatolare
tin can *n* lattina *f*, scatoletta *f*
tin foil *n* [carta *f*] stagnola *f*
tinge /tɪndʒ/ **A** *n* sfumatura *f*
B *vt* **~d with** fig misto a
tingle /ˈtɪŋgl/ *vi* pizzicare
tinker /ˈtɪŋkə(r)/ *vi* armeggiare
tinkle /ˈtɪŋkl/ **A** *n* tintinnio *m*; infml (phone call) colpo *m* di telefono
B *vi* tintinnare
tinned /tɪnd/ *adj* in scatola
tinnitus /ˈtɪnɪtəs/ *n* Med ronzio *m* auricolare
tinny /ˈtɪnɪ/ *adj* ‹*sound, music*› metallico; (badly made) che sembra fatto di latta
tin-opener /-əʊpnə(r)/ *n* apriscatole *m inv*
tinpot /ˈtɪnpɒt/ *adj* derog ‹*firm*› da due soldi
tinsel /ˈtɪnsl/ *n* filo *m* d'argento
tint /tɪnt/ **A** *n* tinta *f*
B *vt* tingersi ‹*hair*›; **~ed glasses** occhiali *mpl* colorati
tiny /ˈtaɪnɪ/ *adj* (**-ier**, **-iest**) minuscolo
tip¹ /tɪp/ *n* (point, top) punta *f*
tip² **A** *n* (money) mancia *f*; (advice) consiglio *m*; (for rubbish) discarica *f*
B *vt* (*pt/pp* **tipped**) (tilt) inclinare; (overturn) capovolgere; (pour) versare; (reward) dare una mancia a
C *vi* inclinarsi; (overturn) capovolgersi
■ **tip off**: *vt* **~ somebody off** (inform) fare una soffiata a qualcuno
■ **tip out** *vt* rovesciare
■ **tip over** **A** *vt* capovolgere
B *vi* capovolgersi
■ **tip up** *vt* sollevare ‹*seat*›; (overturn) rovesciare
tip-off *n* soffiata *f*
tipped /tɪpt/ *adj* ‹*cigarette*› col filtro
tipple /ˈtɪpl/ **A** *vi* bere [alcolici]
B *n* **have a ~** prendere un bicchierino; **my favourite ~** il mio liquore preferito
tipster /ˈtɪpstə(r)/ *n esperto (m) che dà suggerimenti su cavalli da corsa, azioni ecc.*
tipsy /ˈtɪpsɪ/ *adj* infml brillo
tiptoe /ˈtɪptəʊ/ *n* **on ~** in punta di piedi
tip-top *adj* infml in condizioni perfette
tirade /taɪˈreɪd/ *n* filippica *f*
tire /ˈtaɪə(r)/ **A** *vt* stancare
B *vi* stancarsi
■ **tire out** *vt* (exhaust) sfinire
tired /ˈtaɪəd/ *adj* stanco; **~ of** stanco di; **~ out** stanco morto
tiredness /ˈtaɪədnɪs/ *n* stanchezza *f*
tireless /ˈtaɪəlɪs/ *adj* instancabile
tirelessly /ˈtaɪəlɪslɪ/ *adv* instancabilmente
tiresome /ˈtaɪəsəm/ *adj* fastidioso
tiring /ˈtaɪərɪŋ/ *adj* stancante
tissue /ˈtɪʃuː/ *n* tessuto *m*; (handkerchief) fazzolettino *m* di carta
tissue paper *n* carta *f* velina
tit¹ /tɪt/ *n* (bird) cincia *f*
tit² *n* **~ for tat** pan per focaccia
tit³ *n* infml (breast) tetta *f*; (fool) stupido *m*
titbit /ˈtɪtbɪt/ *n* ghiottoneria *f*; fig (of news) notizia *f* appetitosa
titillate /ˈtɪtɪleɪt/ *vt* titillare

titivate /ˈtɪtɪveɪt/ *vt* agghindare; ~ **oneself** agghindarsi

title /ˈtaɪtl/ *n* titolo *m*

title bar *n* Comput barra *f* del titolo

title deed *n* atto *m* di proprietà

title-holder *n* detentore, -trice *mf* del titolo

title page *n* frontespizio *m*

title role *n* ruolo *m* principale

titter /ˈtɪtə(r)/ **A** *vi* ridere nervosamente **B** *n* risatina *f* nervosa

tittle-tattle /ˈtɪtltætl/ *n* pettegolezzi *mpl*

titular /ˈtɪtjʊlə(r)/ *adj* nominale

tizzy /ˈtɪzɪ/ *n* infml **in a** ~ in grande agitazione

TLC *n abbr* infml (**tender loving care**) cura e gentilezza *f*

TM *abbr* (**trademark**) marchio *m* di fabbrica

🔑 **to** /tuː/, *atono*/tə/ **A** *prep* a; (to countries) in; (towards) verso; (up to, until) fino a; **I'm going to John's/the butcher's** vado da John/dal macellaio; **come/go to somebody** venire/andare da qualcuno; **to Italy/Switzerland** in Italia/Svizzera; **I've never been to Rome** non sono mai stato a Roma; **go to the market** andare al mercato; **to the toilet/my room** in bagno/camera mia; **to an exhibition** ad una mostra; **to university** all'università; **twenty/quarter to eight** le otto meno venti/un quarto; **5 to 6 kilos** da 5 a 6 chili; **to the end** alla fine; **to this day** fino a oggi; **to the best of my recollection** per quanto mi possa ricordare; **give/say something to somebody** dare/dire qualcosa a qualcuno; **give it to me** dammelo; **there's nothing to it** è una cosa da niente
B (verbal constructions) **to go** andare; **learn to swim** imparare a nuotare; **I want to/have to go** voglio/devo andare; **it's easy to forget** è facile da dimenticare; **too ill/tired to go** troppo malato/stanco per andare; **you have to** devi; **I don't want to** non voglio; **he wants to be a teacher** vuole diventare un insegnante; **live to be 90** vivere fino a 90 anni; **he was the last to arrive** è stato l'ultimo ad arrivare; **to be honest,...** per essere sincero, ...
C *adv* **pull to** chiudere; **to and fro** avanti e indietro

toad /təʊd/ *n* rospo *m*

toadstool /ˈtəʊdstuːl/ *n* fungo *m* velenoso

toady /ˈtəʊdɪ/ *v*

■ **toady to** *vi* fare da leccapiedi a

toast /təʊst/ **A** *n* pane *m* tostato; (drink) brindisi *m inv*; **be** ~ infml essere fritto; **if he finds out, we're** ~ se lo scopre siamo fritti **B** *vt* tostare ‹*bread*›; (drink a ~ to) brindare a

toaster /ˈtəʊstə(r)/ *n* tostapane *m inv*

toast rack /ˈtəʊstræk/ *n* portatoast *m inv*

tobacco /təˈbækəʊ/ *n* tabacco *m*

tobacconist's /təˈbækənɪsts/, **tobacconist's shop** /təˈbækənɪsts ʃɒp/ *n* tabaccheria *f*

toboggan /təˈbɒgən/ **A** *n* toboga *m inv* **B** *vi* andare in toboga

🔑 **today** /təˈdeɪ/ *n & adv* oggi *m*; **a week** ~ una settimana ad oggi; ~**'s paper** il giornale di oggi

toddle /ˈtɒdl/ *vi* ‹*child*› cominciare a camminare; ~ **into town** infml fare una passeggiata in centro; **I must be toddling** infml devo scappare

toddler /ˈtɒdlə(r)/ *n* bambino, -a *mf* piccolo

toddy /ˈtɒdɪ/ *n* grog *m inv*

to-do /təˈduː/ *n* infml baccano *m*

toe /təʊ/ **A** *n* dito *m* del piede; (of footwear) punta *f*; **on one's** ~**s** fig pronto ad agire; **big** ~ alluce *m*; **little** ~ mignolo *m* [del piede] **B** *vt* ~ **the line** rigar diritto

toe-curling *adj* imbarazzante

toe-hold *n* punto *m* d'appoggio

toenail *n* unghia *f* del piede

toff /tɒf/ *n* infml aristocratico, -a *mf*

toffee /ˈtɒfɪ/ *n* caramella *f* al mou

toffee apple *n* mela *f* caramellata

toffee-nosed *adj* BrE infml con la puzza sotto il naso

🔑 **together** /təˈgeðə(r)/ *adv* insieme; (at the same time) allo stesso tempo; ~ **with** insieme a

togetherness /təˈgeðənɪs/ *n* intimità *f*

toggle /ˈtɒgl/ *n* (fastening) olivetta *f*

Togo /ˈtəʊgəʊ/ *n* Togo *m*

toil /tɔɪl/ **A** *n* duro lavoro *m* **B** *vi* lavorare duramente

toilet /ˈtɔɪlɪt/ *n* (lavatory) gabinetto *m*

toilet bag *n* nécessaire *m inv*

toilet paper *n* carta *f* igienica

toiletries /ˈtɔɪlɪtrɪz/ *npl* articoli *mpl* da toilette

toilet roll *n* rotolo *m* di carta igienica

toilet soap *n* sapone *m*

toilet tissue *n* carta *f* igienica

toilet-train *vt* ~ **a child** insegnare ad un bambino ad usare il vasino

toilet water *n* acqua *f* di colonia

token /ˈtəʊkən/ **A** *n* segno *m*; (counter) gettone *m*; (voucher) buono *m* **B** *attrib* simbolico

told /təʊld/ **A** ▸ **tell** **B** *adj* **all** ~ in tutto

tolerable /ˈtɒl(ə)rəbl/ *adj* tollerabile; (not bad) discreto

tolerably /ˈtɒl(ə)rəblɪ/ *adv* discretamente

tolerance /ˈtɒl(ə)r(ə)ns/ *n* tolleranza *f*

tolerant /ˈtɒl(ə)r(ə)nt/ *adj* tollerante

tolerantly /ˈtɒl(ə)r(ə)ntlɪ/ *adv* con tolleranza

tolerate /ˈtɒləreɪt/ *vt* tollerare

toll¹ /təʊl/ *n* pedaggio *m*; **death** ~ numero *m* di morti; **take a heavy** ~ costare gravi perdite

toll² *vi* suonare a morto

🔑 parola chiave

tollbooth *n* casello *m*

toll call *n* AmE chiamata *f* in teleselezione

toll-free number *n* AmE Teleph numero *m* verde

toll motorway *n* autostrada *f* con pedaggio

tom /tɒm/ *n* (cat) gatto *m* maschio

tomato /təˈmɑːtəʊ/ *n* (*pl* **-es**) pomodoro *m*

tomato ketchup *n* ketchup *m*

tomato purée *n* concentrato *m* di pomodoro

tomato sauce *n* salsa *f* di pomodoro

tomb /tuːm/ *n* tomba *f*

tomboy /ˈtɒmbɔɪ/ *n* maschiaccio *m*

tombstone /ˈtuːmstəʊn/ *n* pietra *f* tombale

tom-cat *n* gatto *m* maschio

tome /təʊm/ *n* tomo *m*

tomfoolery /tɒmˈfuːlərɪ/ *n* stupidaggini *fpl*

tomorrow /təˈmɒrəʊ/ *n & adv* domani *m*; **~ morning** domani mattina; **the day after ~** dopodomani; **see you ~!** a domani!

tom-tom *n* tamtam *m inv*

ton /tʌn/ *n* tonnellata *f* (1.016 kg); **~s of** infml un sacco di

tonal /ˈtəʊnl/ *adj* tonale

tonality /təʊˈnælətɪ/ *n* tonalità *f*

tone /təʊn/ *n* tono *m*; (colour) tonalità *f*

▪ **tone down** *vt* attenuare

▪ **tone in** *vi* intonarsi

▪ **tone up** *vt* tonificare ‹*muscles*›

tone-deaf *adj* **be ~** non avere orecchio

toneless /ˈtəʊnlɪs/ *adj* (unmusical) piatto

toner /ˈtəʊnə(r)/ *n* toner *m*

Tonga /ˈtɒŋgə/ *n* Tonga *m*

tongs /tɒŋz/ *npl* pinze *fpl*

tongue /tʌŋ/ *n* lingua *f*; **~ in cheek** infml ‹*say*› ironicamente

tongue-lashing *n* (severe reprimand) strigliata *f*

tongue stud *n* piercing *m inv* nella lingua

tongue-tied *adj* senza parole

tongue-twister *n* scioglilingua *m inv*

tonic /ˈtɒnɪk/ *n* tonico *m*; (for hair) lozione *f* per i capelli; fig toccasana *m inv*; **~ [water]** acqua *f* tonica

tonight /təˈnaɪt/ **A** *adv* stanotte; (evening) stasera

B *n* questa notte *f*; (evening) questa sera *f*

tonnage /ˈtʌnɪdʒ/ *n* stazza *f*

tonne /tʌn/ *n* tonnellata *f* metrica

tonsil /ˈtɒnsl/ *n* Anat tonsilla *f*; **have one's ~s out** operarsi di tonsille

tonsillitis /tɒnsəˈlaɪtɪs/ *n* tonsillite *f*; **have ~** avere la tonsillite

too /tuː/ *adv* troppo; *also* anche; **~ many** troppi; **~ much** troppo; **~ little** troppo poco

took /tʊk/ ▸ **take**

tool /tuːl/ *n* attrezzo *m*

tool bag *n* borsa *f* degli attrezzi

toolbar *n* Comput barra *f* degli strumenti

toolbox *n* cassetta *f* degli attrezzi

tool kit *n* astuccio *m* di attrezzi

toot /tuːt/ **A** *n* suono *m* di clacson

B *vi* Auto clacsonare

tooth /tuːθ/ *n* (*pl* **teeth**) dente *m*

tooth ache /ˈtuːθeɪk/ *n* mal *m* di denti; **have ~** avere mal di denti

toothbrush /ˈtuːθbrʌʃ/ *n* spazzolino *m* da denti

toothless /ˈtuːθlɪs/ *adj* sdentato

toothpaste /ˈtuːθpeɪst/ *n* dentifricio *m*

toothpick /ˈtuːθpɪk/ *n* stuzzicadenti *m inv*

toothy /ˈtuːθɪ/ *adj* **give a ~ grin** fare un sorriso a trentadue denti

top¹ /tɒp/ *n* (toy) trottola *f*

top² **A** *n* cima *f*; Sch primo, -a *mf*; (upper part or half) parte *f* superiore; (of page, list, street) inizio *m*; (upper surface) superficie *f*; (lid) coperchio *m*; (of bottle) tappo *m*; (garment) maglia *f*; (blouse) camicia *f*; Auto marcia *f* più alta; **at the ~** fig al vertice; **at the ~ of one's voice** a squarciagola; **on ~/on ~ of** sopra; **on ~ of that** (besides) per di più; **from ~ to bottom** da cima a fondo; **blow one's ~** infml perdere le staffe; **over the ~** infml (exaggerated, too much) eccessivo

B *adj* in alto; ‹*official, floor of building*› superiore; ‹*pupil, musician etc*› migliore; ‹*speed*› massimo

C *vt* (*pt/pp* **topped**) essere in testa a ‹*list*›; (exceed) sorpassare; **~ped with ice-cream** ricoperto di gelato; **~ oneself** sl suicidarsi

▪ **top up** *vt* riempire

topaz /ˈtəʊpæz/ *n* topazio *m*

top brass *n* infml pezzi *mpl* grossi

topcoat *n* (of paint) strato *m* finale

top-end *adj* ‹*computer, model*› della fascia più alta

top floor *n* ultimo piano *m*

top gear *n* Auto marcia *f* più alta

top hat *n* cilindro *m*

top-heavy *adj* con la parte superiore sovraccarica

topic /ˈtɒpɪk/ *n* soggetto *m*; (of conversation) argomento *m*

topical /ˈtɒpɪkl/ *adj* d'attualità; **very ~** di grande attualità

topless /ˈtɒplɪs/ *adj & adv* topless

top-level *adj* ad alto livello

top management *n* dirigenza *f*

topmost /ˈtɒpməʊst/ *adj* più alto

top-notch *adj* infml eccellente

top-of-the-range *adj* ‹*model*› della fascia più alta

topping /ˈtɒpɪŋ/ *n* **with a chocolate ~** ricoperto di cioccolato; **pizza with a ham and mushroom ~** pizza al prosciutto e funghi

topple /ˈtɒpl/ **A** *vt* rovesciare

B *vi* rovesciarsi
■ **topple off** *vi* cadere
top-ranking *adj* ‹*official*› di massimo grado
top secret *adj* segretissimo, top secret *inv*
top security *adj* di massima sicurezza
top-shelf *adj* ‹*magazine*› pornografico
topsoil *n* strato *m* superficiale del terreno
topspin *n* topspin *m inv*
topsy-turvy /tɒpsɪ'tɜːvɪ/ *adj & adv* sottosopra
top ten *npl* primi dieci *mpl* in classifica
top-up **A** *n* **would you like a ~?** ti riempio il bicchiere/la tazza?
B *vt* ‹*phone*› ricaricare
top-up card *n* ricarica *f*
torch /tɔːtʃ/ *n* torcia *f* [elettrica]; (flaming) fiaccola *f*
torchlight procession /'tɔːtʃlaɪt/ *n* fiaccolata *f*
tore /tɔː(r)/ ▶ **tear**[1]
torment[1] /'tɔːment/ *n* tormento *m*
torment[2] /tɔː'ment/ *vt* tormentare
tormentor /tɔː'mentə(r)/ *n* tormentatore, -trice *mf*
torn /tɔːn/ **A** ▶ **tear**[1]
B *adj* bucato
tornado /tɔː'neɪdəʊ/ *n* (*pl* **-es**) tornado *m inv*
torpedo /tɔː'piːdəʊ/ **A** *n* (*pl* **-es**) siluro *m*
B *vt* silurare
torpid /'tɔːpɪd/ *adj* intorpidito
torrent /'tɒrənt/ *n* torrente *m*
torrential /tə'renʃl/ *adj* ‹*rain*› torrenziale
torrid /'tɒrɪd/ *adj* torrido
torso /'tɔːsəʊ/ *n* torso *m*; (in art) busto *m*
tortoise /'tɔːtəs/ *n* tartaruga *f*
tortoiseshell /'tɔːtəsʃel/ *n* tartaruga *f*
tortuous /'tɔːtʃʊəs/ *adj* tortuoso
tortuously /'tɔːtʃjʊəslɪ/ *adv* tortuosamente
torture /'tɔːtʃə(r)/ **A** *n* tortura *f*
B *vt* torturare
Tory /'tɔːrɪ/ BrE **A** *n* conservatore, -trice *mf* (*appartenente al partito britannico conservatore*)
B *adj* del partito conservatore
toss /tɒs/ **A** *vt* gettare; (into the air) lanciare in aria; (shake) scrollare; ‹*horse*› disarcionare; mescolare ‹*salad*›; rivoltare facendo saltare in aria ‹*pancake*›; **~ a coin** fare testa o croce
B *vi* **~ and turn** (in bed) rigirarsi; **let's ~ for it** facciamo testa o croce
■ **toss out** *vt* buttare via ‹*newspaper, rubbish*›; **~ somebody out** buttare fuori qualcuno
toss-up *n* infml **let's have a ~ to decide** facciamo testa o croce
tot[1] /tɒt/ *n* bimbetto, -a *mf*; infml (of liquor) goccio *m*
tot[2] *vt* (*pt/pp* **totted**) **~ up** infml fare la somma di
⚷ **total** /'təʊtl/ **A** *adj* totale
B *n* totale *m*
C *vt* (*pt/pp* **totalled**) ammontare a; (add up) sommare
totalitarian /təʊtælɪ'teərɪən/ *adj* totalitario
⚷ **totally** /'təʊtəlɪ/ *adv* totalmente
tote bag /təʊt/ *n* sporta *f*
totem /'təʊtəm/ *n* totem *m inv*
totem pole /'təʊtəm/ *n* totem *m inv*
totter /'tɒtə(r)/ *vi* barcollare; ‹*government*› vacillare
⚷ **touch** /tʌtʃ/ **A** *n* tocco *m*; (sense) tatto *m*; (contact) contatto *m*; (trace) traccia *f*; (of irony, humour) tocco *m*; **get/be in ~** mettersi/essere in contatto
B *vt* toccare; (lightly) sfiorare; (equal) eguagliare; fig (move) commuovere
C *vi* toccarsi
■ **touch down** *vi* Aeron atterrare
■ **touch off** *vi* fig scatenare
■ **touch on** *vt* fig accennare a
■ **touch up** *vt* ritoccare ‹*painting*›; **~ somebody up** (sexually) allungare le mani su qualcuno
touch-and-go *adj* incerto
touchdown /'tʌtʃdaʊn/ *n* Aeron atterraggio *m*; Sport meta *f*
touché /tuː'ʃeɪ/ *int* fig touché!
touched /tʌtʃt/ *adj* (crazy) toccato
touching /'tʌtʃɪŋ/ *adj* commovente
touchingly /'tʌtʃɪŋlɪ/ *adv* in modo commovente
touchline *n* (in football) linea *f* laterale; (in rugby) touche *f inv*
touchpad *n* Comput touchpad *m inv*
touch screen *n* Comput touch screen *m inv*, schermo *m* a sfioramento
touch-tone *adj* ‹*telephone*› a tastiera
touch-type *vi* dattilografare a tastiera cieca
touch-typing *n* dattilografia *f* a tastiera cieca
touch-up *n* (of paintwork) ritocco *m*
touchy /'tʌtʃɪ/ *adj* permaloso; ‹*subject*› delicato
⚷ **tough** /tʌf/ *adj* duro; (severe, harsh) severo; (durable) resistente; (resilient) forte; **~!** infml (too bad) peggio per te/lui!
toughen /'tʌfn/ *vt* rinforzare
■ **toughen up** *vt* rendere più forte ‹*person*›
toupee /'tuːpeɪ/ *n* toupet *m inv*
⚷ **tour** /tʊə(r)/ **A** *n* giro *m*; (of building, town) visita *f*; Theat, Sport tournée *f inv*; (of duty) servizio *m*
B *vt* visitare
C *vi* fare un giro turistico; Theat essere in tournée
tour guide *n* guida *f* turistica
tourism /'tʊərɪzm/ *n* turismo *m*

⚷ parola chiave

t

tourist /ˈtʊərɪst/ **A** *n* turista *mf*
B *attrib* turistico
tourist class *n* classe *f* turistica
tourist office *n* ufficio *m* turistico
tourist resort *n* località *f* turistica
tourist route *n* itinerario *m* turistico
tourist trap *n locale (m) o località (f) per turisti dove i prezzi sono molto alti*
touristy /ˈtʊərɪstɪ/ *adj* infml derog da turisti; **it's too ~ here** è troppo turistico qui
tournament /ˈtʊənəmənt/ *n* torneo *m*
tourniquet /ˈtʊənɪkeɪ/ *n* laccio *m* emostatico
tour operator *n* tour operator *mf inv*, operatore, -trice *mf* turistico, -a
tousle /ˈtaʊzl/ *vt* spettinare
tousled /ˈtaʊzld/ *adj* ‹*hair*› arruffato; (appearance) scarmigliato
tout /taʊt/ **A** *n* (ticket ~) bagarino *m*; (horse racing) informatore *m*
B *vi* **~ for** sollecitare
tow /təʊ/ **A** *n* rimorchio *m*; **'on ~'** 'a rimorchio'; **in ~** infml al seguito
B *vt* rimorchiare
▪ **tow away** *vt* portare via col carro attrezzi
towards BrE, **toward** AmE /təˈwɔːd(z)/ *prep* verso; (with respect to) nei riguardi di
tow bar *n* barra *f* di rimorchio
towel /ˈtaʊəl/ *n* asciugamano *m*
▪ **towel down** *vt* asciugare
towelling /ˈtaʊəlɪŋ/ *n* spugna *f*
towelling robe *n* accappatoio *m*
towel rail *n* portasciugamano *m*
tower /ˈtaʊə(r)/ **A** *n* torre *f*; **be a ~ of strength to somebody** essere di grande conforto per qualcuno
B *vi* **~ above** dominare
tower block *n* palazzone *m*
towering /ˈtaʊərɪŋ/ *adj* torreggiante; ‹*rage*› violento
tow line *n* cavo *m* da rimorchio
town /taʊn/ *n* città *f*; **in ~** nel centro
town and country planning *n* pianificazione *f* territoriale
town centre *n* centro *m* della città
town council *n* municipalità *f*
town hall *n* municipio *m*
town house *n casa (f) a schiera a tre o più piani*
town planner *n* urbanista *mf*
town planning *n* urbanistica *f*
township /ˈtaʊnʃɪp/ *n* comune *m*; (in South Africa) township *f inv*
towpath /ˈtəʊpɑːθ/ *n* strada *f* alzaia
tow rope *n* cavo *m* da rimorchio
tow truck *n* carro *m* attrezzi *inv*
toxic /ˈtɒksɪk/ *adj* tossico
toxic assets /ˌtɒksɪk ˈæsets/ *npl* titoli *mpl* tossici
toxicity /tɒkˈsɪsɪtɪ/ *n* tossicità *f*
toxicologist /tɒksɪˈkɒlədʒɪst/ *n* tossicologo, -a *mf*
toxicology /tɒksɪˈkɒlədʒɪ/ *n* tossicologia *f*
toxic waste *n* rifiuti *mpl* tossici
toxin /ˈtɒksɪn/ *n* tossina *f*
toy /tɔɪ/ *n* giocattolo *m*
▪ **toy with** *vt* giocherellare con
toy boy /ˈtɔɪbɔɪ/ *n* BrE infml uomo-oggetto *m*
toyshop /ˈtɔɪʃɒp/ *n* negozio *m* di giocattoli
trace /treɪs/ **A** *n* traccia *f*
B *vt* seguire le tracce di; (find) rintracciare; (draw) tracciare; (with tracing paper) ricalcare
▪ **trace back** *vt* trovare tracce di ‹*family*›
▪ **trace out** *vt* tracciare
tracer /ˈtreɪsə(r)/ *n* Mil proiettile *m* tracciante
tracing /ˈtreɪsɪŋ/ *n* ricalco *m*
tracing paper *n* carta *f* da ricalco
track /træk/ **A** *n* traccia *f*; (path) Sport pista *f*; Rail binario *m*; **keep ~ of** tenere d'occhio
B *vt* rintracciare le origini di
▪ **track down** *vt* scovare
trackball, **tracker ball** *n* Comput trackball *f inv*
tracker /ˈtrækə(r)/ *n* (dog) segugio *m*
track record *n* fig background *m inv*
tracksuit /ˈtræksuːt/ *n* tuta *f* da ginnastica
tract /trækt/ *n* (pamphlet) opuscolo *m*
tractable /ˈtræktəbl/ *adj* trattabile; (docile) maneggevole
traction /ˈtrækʃn/ *n* (of wheel) trazione *f*
traction engine *n* trattore *m*
tractor /ˈtræktə(r)/ *n* trattore *m*
trade /treɪd/ **A** *n* commercio *m*; (line of business) settore *m*; (craft) mestiere *m*; **by ~** di mestiere
B *vt* commerciare; **~ something for something** scambiare qualcosa per qualcosa
C *vi* commerciare
▪ **trade in** *vt* (give in part exchange) dare in pagamento parziale
▪ **trade off** *vt* scambiare
▪ **trade on** *vt* approfittarsi di
trade deficit *n* bilancio *m* commerciale in deficit
trade discount *n* sconto *m* commerciale
trade fair *n* fiera *f* commerciale
trade-in *n* permuta *f* come pagamento parziale
trade mark *n* marchio *m* di fabbrica
trade name *n* nome *m* despositato
trade-off *n* compromesso *m*
trade price *n* prezzo *m* all'ingrosso
trader /ˈtreɪdə(r)/ *n* commerciante *mf*
trade secret *n* segreto *m* commerciale
tradesman /ˈtreɪdzmən/ *n* (joiner etc) operaio *m*
tradesman's entrance *n* entrata *f* di servizio
Trades Union Congress *n confederazione (f) dei sindacati britannici*

trade union *n* sindacato *m*
trade unionist *n* sindacalista *mf*
trade union representative *n* rappresentante *mf* sindacale
trading /ˈtreɪdɪŋ/ *n* commercio *m*
trading estate *n* zona *f* industriale
trading floor *n* Fin sala *f* delle contrattazioni
trading stamp *n* bollino *m* premio
tradition /trəˈdɪʃŋ/ *n* tradizione *f*
traditional /trəˈdɪʃnl/ *adj* tradizionale
traditionalist /trəˈdɪʃn(ə)lɪst/ *n* tradizionalista *mf*
traditionally /trəˈdɪʃn(ə)lɪ/ *adv* tradizionalmente
traffic /ˈtræfɪk/ **A** *n* traffico *m*
B *vi* trafficare
traffic calming *n* misure *fpl* per rallentare la circolazione
traffic calming measures *npl* misure *fpl* per rallentare il traffico in città
traffic circle *n* AmE isola *f* rotatoria
traffic cone *n* birillo *m*
traffic island *n* isola *f* spartitraffico
traffic jam *n* ingorgo *m*
trafficker /ˈtræfɪkə(r)/ *n* trafficante *mf*
traffic lights *npl* semaforo *msg*
traffic offence *n* infrazione *f* al codice della strada
traffic warden *n* vigile *m* [urbano]; (woman) vigilessa *f*
tragedy /ˈtrædʒədɪ/ *n* tragedia *f*
tragic /ˈtrædʒɪk/ *adj* tragico
tragically /ˈtrædʒɪklɪ/ *adv* tragicamente
trail /treɪl/ **A** *n* traccia *f*; (path) sentiero *m*
B *vi* strisciare; ‹*plant*› arrampicarsi; ~ **[behind]** rimanere indietro; (in competition) essere in svantaggio
C *vt* trascinare
trail bike *n* moto *f* fuoristrada
trailblazer /ˈtreɪlbleɪzə(r)/ *n* pioniere, -a *mf*
trailblazing /ˈtreɪlbleɪzɪŋ/ *adj* innovatore
trailer /ˈtreɪlə(r)/ *n* Auto rimorchio *m*; AmE (caravan) roulotte *f inv*; (film) presentazione *f* (*di un film*)
trailer park *n* AmE area *f* di sosta per roulotte
train /treɪn/ **A** *n* treno *m*; (of dress) strascico *m*; **by** ~ in treno; ~ **of thought** filo *m* dei pensieri
B *vt* formare professionalmente; Sport allenare; (aim) puntare; educare ‹*child*›; addestrare ‹*animal, soldier*›; far crescere ‹*plant*›
C *vi* fare il tirocinio; Sport allenarsi
trained /treɪnd/ *adj* ‹*animal*› addestrato (**to do** a fare)
trainee /treɪˈniː/ *n* apprendista *mf*
trainer /ˈtreɪnə(r)/ *n* Sport allenatore, -trice *mf*; (in circus) domatore, -trice *mf*; (of dog, race horse) addestratore, -trice *mf*; **~s** *pl* (shoes) scarpe *fpl* da ginnastica
training /ˈtreɪnɪŋ/ *n* tirocinio *m*; Sport allenamento *m*; (of animal, soldier) addestramento *m*
training college *n* istituto *m* professionale
training course *n* corso *m* di formazione
train set *n* trenino *m*
train spotter *n* appassionato, -a *mf* di treni
traipse /treɪps/ *vi* ~ **around** infml andare in giro
trait /treɪt/ *n* caratteristica *f*
traitor /ˈtreɪtə(r)/ *n* traditore, -trice *mf*
trajectory /trəˈdʒekt(ə)rɪ/ *n* traiettoria *f*
tram /træm/ *n* tram *m inv*
tram lines *npl* rotaie *fpl* del tram
tramp /træmp/ **A** *n* (hike) camminata *f*; (vagrant) barbone, -a *mf*; (of feet) calpestio *m*
B *vi* camminare con passo pesante; (hike) percorrere a piedi
trample /ˈtræmpl/ *v*
▪ **trample on** *vt* calpestare
trampoline /ˈtræmpəliːn/ *n* trampolino *m*
trance /trɑːns/ *n* trance *f inv*
tranquil /ˈtræŋkwɪl/ *adj* tranquillo
tranquillity /træŋˈkwɪlətɪ/ *n* tranquillità *f*
tranquillizer /ˈtræŋkwɪlaɪzə(r)/ *n* tranquillante *m*
transact /trænˈzækt/ *vt* trattare
transaction /trænˈzækʃn/ *n* transazione *f*
transatlantic /trænzətˈlæntɪk/ *adj* ‹*crossing, flight*› transatlantico; ‹*attitude, accent*› americano
transceiver /trænˈsiːvə(r)/ *n* ricetrasmittente *f*
transcend /trænˈsend/ *vt* trascendere
transcontinental /trænzkɒntɪˈnent(ə)l/ *adj* transcontinentale
transcribe /trænˈskraɪb/ *vt* trascrivere
transcript /ˈtrænskrɪpt/ *n* trascrizione *f*
transcription /trænˈskrɪpʃn/ *n* trascrizione *f*
transept /ˈtrænsept/ *n* transetto *m*
transfer¹ /ˈtrænsfɜː(r)/ *n* trasferimento *m*; Sport cessione *f*; (design) decalcomania *f*
transfer² /trænsˈfɜː(r)/ **A** *vt* (*pt/pp* **transferred**) trasferire; Sport cedere; Comput trasferire
B *vi* trasferirsi; (when travelling) cambiare
transferable /trænsˈfɜːrəbl/ *adj* trasferibile
transfer fee *n* (for footballer) prezzo *m* d'acquisto
transfer list *n* (in football) lista *f* di giocatori da cedere
transferred charge call *n* chiamata *f* a carico del destinatario
transfigure /trænsˈfɪgə(r)/ *vt* trasfigurare
transfix /trænsˈfɪks/ *vt* trafiggere; fig immobilizzare

parola chiave

t

transfixed /træns'fɪkst/ *adj* (with fascination) folgorato; (with horror) paralizzato

transform /træns'fɔːm/ *vt* trasformare

transformation /trænsfə'meɪʃn/ *n* trasformazione *f*

transformer /træns'fɔːmə(r)/ *n* trasformatore *m*

transfusion /træns'fjuːʒn/ *n* trasfusione *f*

transgender /trænz'dʒendə(r)/ *adj* trans, dei trans

transgression /træns'greʃn/ *n* Jur trasgressione *f*; Relig peccato *m*

transient /'trænzɪənt/ *adj* passeggero

transistor /træn'zɪstə(r)/ *n* transistor *m inv*; (radio) radiolina *f* a transistor

transit /'trænzɪt/ *n* transito *m*; **in ~** (goods) in transito

transition /træn'zɪʃn/ *n* transizione *f*

transitional /træn'zɪʃənl/ *adj* di transizione

transitive /'trænzɪtɪv/ *adj* transitivo

transitively /'trænzɪtɪvlɪ/ *adv* transitivamente

transit lounge *n* sala *f* d'attesa transiti

transitory /'træzɪtərɪ/ *adj* transitorio

transit passenger *n* passeggero, -a *mf* in transito

translate /trænz'leɪt/ *vt* tradurre

translation /trænz'leɪʃn/ *n* traduzione *f*

translation agency *n* agenzia *f* di traduzioni

translator /trænz'leɪtə(r)/ *n* traduttore, -trice *mf*

translucent /trænz'luːsnt/ *adj* literary traslucido

transmissible /trænz'mɪsəbl/ *adj* trasmissibile

transmission /trænz'mɪʃn/ *n* trasmissione *f*

transmit /trænz'mɪt/ *vt* (*pt/pp* **transmitted**) trasmettere

transmitter /trænz'mɪtə(r)/ *n* trasmettitore *m*

transparency /træn'spærənsɪ/ *n* Phot diapositiva *f*

transparent /træn'spærənt/ *adj* trasparente

transpire /træn'spaɪə(r)/ *vi* emergere; infml (happen) accadere

transplant¹ /'trænsplɑːnt/ *n* trapianto *m*

transplant² /træns'plɑːnt/ *vt* trapiantare

transport¹ /'trænspɔːt/ *n* trasporto *m*; **do you have ~?** hai un mezzo di trasporto?

transport² /træn'spɔːt/ *vt* trasportare

transportation /trænspɔː'teɪʃn/ *n* trasporto *m*

transpose /træns'pəʊz/ *vt* trasporre

transsexual /trænz'seksʃʊəl/ **A** *n* transessuale *mf*
B *adj* transessuale

trans-shipment /trænz'ʃɪpmənt/ *n* trasbordo *m*

transverse /trænz'vɜːs/ *adj* trasversale

transvestite /trænz'vestaɪt/ *n* travestito, -a *mf*

trap /træp/ **A** *n* trappola *f*; infml (mouth) boccaccia *f*; (carriage) calesse *m*
B *vt* (*pt/pp* **trapped**) intrappolare; schiacciare ‹*finger in door*›; **be ~ped** essere intrappolato

trapdoor /'træpdɔː(r)/ *n* botola *f*

trapeze /trə'piːz/ *n* trapezio *m*

trappings /'træpɪŋz/ *npl* (dress) ornamenti *mpl*; **the ~ of wealth/success** i segni esteriori della ricchezza/del successo

trash /træʃ/ *n* robaccia *f*; (rubbish) spazzatura *f*; (nonsense) schiocchezze *fpl*

trash can *n* AmE pattumiera *f*, secchio *m* della spazzatura

trashy /'træʃɪ/ *adj* scadente

trauma /'trɔːmə/ *n* trauma *m*

traumatic /trɔː'mætɪk/ *adj* traumatico

traumatize /'trɔːmətaɪz/ *vt* traumatizzare

travel /'trævl/ **A** *n* viaggi *mpl*
B *vi* (*pt/pp* **travelled**) viaggiare; ‹*to work*› andare
C *vt* percorrere ‹*distance*›

travel agency *n* agenzia *f* di viaggi

travel agent *n* agente *mf* di viaggio

travel card *n* tessera *f* dei trasporti pubblici

travel expenses *npl* spese *fpl* di viaggio

traveller /'trævələ(r)/ *n* viaggiatore, -trice *mf*; Comm commesso *m* viaggiatore; **~s** *pl* (gypsies) zingari *mpl*

traveller's cheque *n* traveller's cheque *m inv*

travelling BrE, **traveling** AmE /'trævlɪŋ/ *adj* ‹*circus, theatre company*› itinerante; ‹*companion, conditions, expenses, allowance*› di viaggio

travelling salesman /'trævəlɪŋ/ *n* commesso *m* viaggiatore

travel news *n* informazioni *fpl* sulla viabilità

travelogue /'trævəlɒg/ *n* (film) documentario *m* di viaggio; (talk) conferenza *f* su un viaggio

travel-sick *adj* **be/get ~** (on plane) soffrire il mal d'aria; (in car) soffrire il mal d'auto; (on boat) soffrire il mal di mare

travel-sickness **A** *n* (on plane) mal *m* d'aria; (in car) mal *m* d'auto; (on boat) mal *m* di mare
B *attrib* ‹*pills*› per il mal d'aria/d'auto/di mare

traverse /trə'vɜːs/ *vt* traversare

travesty /'trævɪstɪ/ *n* fig (farce) farsa *f*; **a ~ of justice** una presa in giro della giustizia

trawler /'trɔːlə(r)/ *n* peschereccio *m*

tray /treɪ/ *n* vassoio *m*; (for baking) teglia *f*; (for documents) vaschetta *f*; (of printer, photocopier) vassoio *m*, cassetto *m*

treacherous /'tretʃərəs/ *adj* traditore; ‹*weather, currents*› pericoloso

treachery /ˈtretʃ(ə)rɪ/ *n* tradimento *m*
treacle /ˈtriːkl/ *n* melassa *f*
tread /tred/ **A** *n* andatura *f*; (step) gradino *m*; (of tyre) battistrada *m inv*
B *vi* (*pt* **trod**, *pp* **trodden**) (walk) camminare
▪ **tread on** *vt* calpestare ‹*grass*›; pestare ‹*foot*›
treadmill /ˈtredmɪl/ *n* fig solito tran tran *m*
treason /ˈtriːzn/ *n* tradimento *m*
treasonable /ˈtriːz(ə)nəbl/ *adj* proditorio
treasure /ˈtreʒə(r)/ **A** *n* tesoro *m*
B *vt* tenere in gran conto
treasurer /ˈtreʒərə(r)/ *n* tesoriere, -a *mf*
treasury /ˈtreʒərɪ/ *n* **the T~** il Ministero del Tesoro
🔑 **treat** /triːt/ **A** *n* piacere *m*; (present) regalo *m*; **give somebody a ~** fare una sorpresa a qualcuno
B *vt* trattare; Med curare; **~ somebody to something** offrire qualcosa a qualcuno; **~ somebody for something** Med sottoporre qualcuno ad una cura per qualcosa
treatise /ˈtriːtɪz/ *n* trattato *m*
🔑 **treatment** /ˈtriːtmənt/ *n* trattamento *m*; Med cura *f*
treaty /ˈtriːtɪ/ *n* trattato *m*
treble /ˈtrebl/ **A** *adj* triplo; **~ the amount** il triplo
B *n* Mus (voice) voce *f* bianca
C *vt* triplicare
D *vi* triplicarsi
treble clef *n* chiave *f* di violino
🔑 **tree** /triː/ *n* albero *m*
tree house *n* capanna *f* su un albero
tree stump ceppo *m*
treetop *n* cima *f* di un albero
tree trunk *n* tronco *m* d'albero
trek /trek/ **A** *n* scarpinata *f*; (as holiday) trekking *m inv*
B *vi* (*pt/pp* **trekked**) farsi una scarpinata; (on holiday) fare trekking
trekking /ˈtrekɪŋ/ *n* trekking *m*
trellis /ˈtrelɪs/ *n* graticcio *m*
tremble /ˈtrembl/ *vi* tremare (**with** di)
trembling /ˈtremblɪŋ/ *adj* tremante
tremendous /trɪˈmendəs/ *adj* (huge) enorme; infml (excellent) formidabile
tremendously /trɪˈmendəslɪ/ *adv* (very) straordinariamente; (a lot) enormemente
tremor /ˈtremə(r)/ *n* tremito *m*; **[earth] ~** scossa *f* [sismica]
tremulous /ˈtremjʊləs/ *adj* tremulo
trench /trentʃ/ *n* fosso *m*; Mil trincea *f*
trenchant /ˈtrentʃənt/ *adj* ‹*comment, criticism*› mordace
trench coat *n* trench *m inv*
🔑 **trend** /trend/ *n* tendenza *f*; (fashion) moda *f*
trend-setter *n* persona *f* che detta la moda
trend-setting *adj* che detta la moda
trendy /ˈtrendɪ/ *adj* (**-ier, -iest**) infml di *or* alla moda
trepidation /trepɪˈdeɪʃn/ *n* trepidazione *f*
trespass /ˈtrespəs/ *vi* **~ on** introdursi abusivamente in; fig abusare di
trespasser /ˈtrespəsə(r)/ *n* intruso, -a *mf*
trestle /ˈtresl/ *n* cavalletto *m*
trestle table *n* tavolo *m* a cavalletto
🔑 **trial** /ˈtraɪəl/ *n* Jur processo *m*; (test, ordeal) prova *f*; **on ~** in prova; Jur in giudizio; **by ~ and error** per tentativi
trial period *n* periodo *m* di prova
trial run *n* (preliminary test) prova *f*
triangle /ˈtraɪæŋgl/ *n* triangolo *m*
triangular /traɪˈæŋgjʊlə(r)/ *adj* triangolare
tribal /ˈtraɪbl/ *adj* tribale
tribe /traɪb/ *n* tribù *f*
tribulation /trɪbjʊˈleɪʃn/ *n* tribolazione *f*
tribunal /traɪˈbjuːnl/ *n* tribunale *m*
tributary /ˈtrɪbjʊtərɪ/ *n* affluente *m*
tribute /ˈtrɪbjuːt/ *n* tributo *m*; **pay ~** rendere omaggio
trice /traɪs/ *n* **in a ~** in un attimo
tricentenary /traɪsenˈtiːnərɪ/ **A** *n* terzo centenario *m*
B *adj* del terzo centenario
trick /trɪk/ **A** *n* trucco *m*; (joke) scherzo *m*; Cards presa *f*; **do the ~** infml funzionare; **play a ~ on** fare uno scherzo a
B *vt* imbrogliare; **~ of the trade** trucco *m* del mestiere
▪ **trick into**: *vt* **~ somebody into doing something** convincere qualcuno a fare qualcosa con l'inganno
▪ **trick out**: *vt* **~ somebody out of something** fregare a qualcuno qualcosa
trick cyclist *n* sl (psychiatrist) psichiatra *mf*
trickle /ˈtrɪkl/ *vi* colare
▪ **trickle away** *vi* ‹*water*› uscire lentamente; ‹*people*› allontanarsi lentamente
▪ **trickle in** *vi* fig entrare poco per volta
▪ **trickle out** *vi* fig uscire poco per volta
trick question *n* domanda *f* trabocchetto *inv*
trickster /ˈtrɪkstə(r)/ *n* imbroglione, -a *mf*
tricky /ˈtrɪkɪ/ *adj* (**-ier, -iest**) *adj* ‹*operation*› complesso; ‹*situation*› delicato
tricolour /ˈtrɪkələ(r)/ *n* tricolore *m*
tricycle /ˈtraɪsɪkl/ *n* triciclo *m*
tried /traɪd/ ▶ **try**
tried and tested *adj* ‹*method*› sperimentato
trifle /ˈtraɪfl/ *n* inezia *f*; Culin zuppa *f* inglese
trifling /ˈtraɪflɪŋ/ *adj* insignificante
trig /trɪg/ *n* infml (trigonometry) trigonometria *f*
trigger /ˈtrɪgə(r)/ **A** *n* grilletto *m*; fig causa *f*
B *vt* **~ [off]** scatenare
trigger-happy *adj* infml dalla pistola facile; fig impulsivo

🔑 parola chiave

trigonometry /trɪgə'nɒmɪtrɪ/ *n* trigonometria *f*

trilateral /traɪ'lætərəl/ *adj* trilaterale

trilby /'trɪlbɪ/ *n* cappello *m* di feltro

trill /trɪl/ *n* Mus trillo *m*

trilogy /'trɪlədʒɪ/ *n* trilogia *f*

trim /trɪm/ **A** *adj* (**trimmer**, **trimmest**) curato; ‹*figure*› snello
B *n* (of hair, hedge) spuntata *f*; (decoration) rifinitura *f*; **in good ~** in buono stato; ‹*person*› in forma
C *vt* (*pt/pp* **trimmed**) spuntare ‹*hair etc*›; (decorate) ornare; Naut orientare
▪ **trim off** *vt* tagliare via

trimming /'trɪmɪŋ/ *n* bordo *m*; **~s** *pl* (of pastry) ritagli *mpl*; (decorations) guarnizioni *fpl*; **with all the ~s** Culin guarnito

Trinidad and Tobago *n* Trinidad e Tobago *m*

Trinity /'trɪnɪtɪ/ *n* **the [Holy] ~** la [Santissima] Trinità

trinket /'trɪŋkɪt/ *n* ninnolo *m*

trio /'tri:əʊ/ *n* trio *m*

trip /trɪp/ **A** *n* (excursion) gita *f*; (journey) viaggio *m*; (stumble) passo *m* falso
B *vt* (*pt/pp* **tripped**) far inciampare
C *vi* inciampare (**on/over** in)
▪ **trip up** *vt* far inciampare

tripartite /traɪ'pɑ:taɪt/ *adj* tripartito

tripe /traɪp/ *n* trippa *f*; sl (nonsense) fesserie *fpl*

triple /'trɪpl/ **A** *adj* triplo
B *vt* triplicare
C *vi* triplicarsi

triplets /'trɪplɪts/ *npl* tre gemelli *mpl*

triplicate /'trɪplɪkət/ *n* **in ~** in triplice copia

tripod /'traɪpɒd/ *n* treppiede *m inv*

tripper /'trɪpə(r)/ *n* gitante *mf*

trite /traɪt/ *adj* banale

triteness /'traɪtnɪs/ *n* banalità *f*

triumph /'traɪʌmf/ **A** *n* trionfo *m*
B *vi* trionfare (**over** su)

triumphant /traɪ'ʌmf(ə)nt/ *adj* trionfante

triumphantly /traɪ'ʌmf(ə)ntlɪ/ *adv* ‹*exclaim*› in tono trionfante

triumvirate /traɪ'ʌmvɪrət/ *n* triumvirato *m*

trivia /'trɪvɪə/ *npl* cose *fpl* secondarie

trivial /'trɪvɪəl/ *adj* insignificante

triviality /trɪvɪ'ælətɪ/ *n* banalità *f*

trivialize /'trɪvɪəlaɪz/ *vt* sminuire

trod, **trodden** /trɒd, 'trɒdn/ ▸ **tread**

trolley /'trɒlɪ/ *n* carrello *m*; AmE (tram) tram *m inv*

trolley bus *n* filobus *m inv*

trombone /trɒm'bəʊn/ *n* trombone *m*

trombonist /trɒm'bəʊnɪst/ *n* trombonista *mf*

troop /tru:p/ **A** *n* gruppo *m*; **~s** *pl* truppe *fpl*
B *vi* **~ in/out** entrare/uscire in gruppo

trooper /'tru:pə(r)/ *n* Mil soldato *m* di cavalleria; AmE (policeman) poliziotto *m*

trophy /'trəʊfɪ/ *n* trofeo *m*

tropic /'trɒpɪk/ *n* tropico *m*; **~s** *pl* tropici *mpl*

tropical /'trɒpɪkl/ *adj* tropicale

tropical fruit *n* frutta *f inv* esotica

trot /trɒt/ **A** *n* trotto *m*
B *vi* (*pt/pp* **trotted**) trottare
▪ **trot out** *vt* infml (produce) tirar fuori

trotter /'trɒtə(r)/ *n* Culin piedino *m* di maiale

trouble /'trʌbl/ **A** *n* guaio *m*; (difficulties) problemi *mpl*; (inconvenience) Med disturbo *m*; (conflict) conflitto *m*; **be in ~** essere nei guai; ‹*swimmer, climber*› essere in difficoltà; **get into ~** finire nei guai; **get somebody into ~** mettere qualcuno nei guai; **take the ~ to do something** darsi la pena di far qualcosa; **it's no ~** nessun disturbo; **the ~ with you is...** il tuo problema è...
B *vt* (worry) preoccupare; (inconvenience) disturbare; ‹*conscience, old wound*› tormentare
C *vi* **don't ~!** non ti disturbare!

troubled /'trʌbld/ *adj* ‹*mind*› inquieto; ‹*person, expression*› preoccupato; ‹*times, area*› difficile; ‹*waters, sleep*› agitato

trouble-free /ˌtrʌbl'fri:/ *adj* senza problemi

troublemaker /'trʌblmeɪkə(r)/ *n* **be a ~** seminare zizzania

troubleshooter /'trʌblʃu:tə(r)/ *n* rilevatore e risolutore *m* di problemi

troublesome /'trʌblsəm/ *adj* fastidioso

trouble spot *n* zona *f* calda

trough /trɒf/ *n* trogolo *m*; (atmospheric) depressione *f*

trounce /traʊns/ *vt* (in competition) schiacciare

troupe /tru:p/ *n* troupe *f inv*

trouser press *n* stiracalzoni *m inv*

trousers /'traʊzəz/ *npl* pantaloni *mpl*

trouser suit *n* tailleur *m inv* pantalone

trousseau /'tru:səʊ/ *n* corredo *m*

trout /traʊt/ *n inv* trota *f*

trowel /'traʊəl/ *n* (for gardening) paletta *f*; (for builder) cazzuola *f*

truancy /'tru:ənsɪ/ *n* assenze *fpl* ingiustificate

truant /'tru:ənt/ *n* **play ~** marinare la scuola

truce /tru:s/ *n* tregua *f*

truck /trʌk/ *n* (lorry) camion *m inv*

truck driver *n* camionista *mf*

trucker /'trʌkə(r)/ *n* infml (lorry driver) camionista *mf*

truck farmer *n* AmE ortofrutticoltore *m*, ortolano *m*

truculent /'trʌkjʊlənt/ *adj* aggressivo

truculently /'trʌkjʊləntlɪ/ *adv* aggressivamente

trudge /trʌdʒ/ **A** *n* camminata *f* faticosa
B *vi* arrancare

true /tru:/ *adj* vero; **come ~** avverarsi

true life *adj* ‹*adventure, story*› vero

truffle /'trʌfl/ *n* tartufo *m*

truism /'tru:ɪzm/ *n* truismo *m*

t

⚷ **truly** /'tru:lɪ/ *adv* veramente; **Yours ~** Distinti saluti

trump /trʌmp/ **A** *n* Cards atout *m inv* **B** *vt* prendere con l'atout

■ **trump up** *vt* infml inventare

trump card *n* fig asso *m* nella manica

trumped-up /ˌtrʌmpt'ʌp/ *adj* ‹*charges*› inventato

trumpet /'trʌmpɪt/ *n* tromba *f*

trumpeter /'trʌmpɪtə(r)/ *n* trombettista *mf*

truncate /'trʌŋkeɪt/ *vt* tagliare ‹*text*›; interrompere ‹*process, journey, event*›

truncheon /'trʌntʃn/ *n* manganello *m*

trundle /'trʌndl/ **A** *vt* far rotolare **B** *vi* rotolare

trunk /trʌŋk/ *n* (of tree, body) tronco *m*; (of elephant) proboscide *f*; (for travelling, storage) baule *m*; AmE (of car) bagagliaio *m*, portabagagli *m inv*

trunk road *n* statale *f*

trunks /trʌŋks/ *npl* calzoncini *mpl* da bagno

truss /trʌs/ *n* Med cinto *m* erniario

■ **truss up** *vt* legare

⚷ **trust** /trʌst/ **A** *n* fiducia *f*; (group of companies) trust *m inv*; (organization) associazione *f*; **on ~** sulla parola **B** *vt* fidarsi di; (hope) augurarsi **C** *vi* **~ in** credere in; **~ to** affidarsi a

trust company *n* società *f* fiduciaria

trusted /'trʌstɪd/ *adj* fidato

trustee /trʌs'ti:/ *n* amministratore, -trice *mf* fiduciario, -a

trustful /'trʌstfʊl/ *adj* fiducioso

trustfully /'trʌstfʊlɪ/ *adv* fiduciosamente

trust fund *n* fondo *m* fiduciario

trusting /'trʌstɪŋ/ *adj* fiducioso

trustworthiness /'trʌstwɜ:ðɪnɪs/ *n* (of person) affidabilità *f*; (of source) attendibilità *f*

trustworthy /'trʌstwɜ:ðɪ/ *adj* fidato

trusty /'trʌstɪ/ *adj* infml fidato

⚷ **truth** /tru:θ/ *n* (*pl* **-s** /tru:ðz/) verità *f*

truthful /'tru:θfʊl/ *adj* ‹*person*› sincero; ‹*statement*› veritiero

truthfully /'tru:θfʊlɪ/ *adv* sinceramente

truthfulness /'tru:θfʊlnɪs/ *n* (of person) sincerità *f*; (of account) veridicità *f*

⚷ **try** /traɪ/ **A** *n* tentativo *m*, prova *f*; (in rugby) meta *f*; **I'll give it a ~** faccio un tentativo **B** *vt* (*pt/pp* **tried**) provare; (be a strain on) mettere a dura prova; Jur processare ‹*person*›; discutere ‹*case*›; **~ to do something** provare a fare qualcosa **C** *vi* provare

■ **try for** *vi* cercare di ottenere

■ **try on** *vt* provarsi ‹*garment*›

■ **try out** *vt* provare

trying /'traɪɪŋ/ *adj* duro; ‹*person*› irritante

try-out *n* **give somebody a ~** mettere alla prova qualcuno

⚷ parola chiave

tsar /zɑ:(r)/ *n* zar *m inv*

tsarina /tsɑ:'ri:nə/ *n* zarina *f*

tsarist /'tsɑ:rɪst/ *adj* zarista

T-shirt *n* maglietta *f*

tsp *abbr* (**teaspoonful**) cucchiaino

tsunami /tsu:'nɑ:mɪ/ *n* tsunami *m inv*

tub /tʌb/ *n* tinozza *f*; (carton) vaschetta *f*; (bath) vasca *f* da bagno

tuba /'tju:bə/ *n* Mus tuba *f*

tubby /'tʌbɪ/ *adj* (**-ier**, **-iest**) tozzo

tube /tju:b/ *n* tubo *m*; (of toothpaste) tubetto *m*; BrE Rail metro *f*

tuber /'tju:bə(r)/ *n* tubero *m*

tuberculosis /tju:bɜ:kjʊ'ləʊsɪs/ *n* tubercolosi *f*

tubing /'tju:bɪŋ/ *n* tubi *mpl*

tubular /'tju:bjʊlə(r)/ *adj* tubolare

TUC *n abbr* BrE (**Trades Union Congress**) *confederazione (f) dei sindacati britannici*

tuck /tʌk/ **A** *n* piega *f* **B** *vt* (put) infilare

■ **tuck away** *vt* (put in a safe place) mettere al sicuro; (eat) spolverare

■ **tuck in** **A** *vt* rimboccare; **~ somebody in** rimboccare le coperte a qualcuno **B** *vi* infml (eat) mangiare con appetito

■ **tuck into** *vt* mangiare di gusto ‹*meal*›; **~ something into one's pocket** infilarsi in tasca qualcosa; **~ somebody into bed** rimboccare le coperte a qualcuno

■ **tuck up** *vt* rimboccarsi ‹*sleeves*›; (in bed) rimboccare le coperte a

⚷ **Tuesday** /'tju:zdeɪ/ *n* martedì *m*

tuft /tʌft/ *n* ciuffo *m*

tug /tʌg/ **A** *n* strattone *m*; Naut rimorchiatore *m* **B** *vt* (*pt/pp* **tugged**) tirare **C** *vi* dare uno strattone

tug-of-love /ˌtʌgəv'lʌv/ *n disputa (f) tra i genitori per l'affidamento dei figli*

tug of war *n* tiro *m* alla fune

tuition /tju:'ɪʃn/ *n* lezioni *fpl*

tuition fees *npl* tasse *fpl* universitarie

tulip /'tju:lɪp/ *n* tulipano *m*

tumble /'tʌmbl/ **A** *n* ruzzolone *m* **B** *vi* ruzzolare; **~ to something** infml (realize) afferrare qualcosa

■ **tumble down** *vi* ‹*wall, building*› crollare

tumbledown /'tʌmbəldaʊn/ *adj* cadente

tumble-dry /ˌtʌmbl'draɪ/ *vt* asciugare nell'asciugabiancheria

tumble dryer, **tumble drier** *n* asciugabiancheria *m inv*

tumbler /'tʌmblə(r)/ *n* bicchiere *m* (*senza stelo*)

tummy /'tʌmɪ/ *n* infml pancia *f*

tummy button *n* infml ombelico *m*

tumour /'tju:mə(r)/ *n* tumore *m*

tumult /'tju:mʌlt/ *n* tumulto *m*

tumultuous /tju:'mʌltjʊəs/ *adj* tumultuoso

tuna /'tju:nə/ *n* tonno *m*

tune /tju:n/ **A** *n* motivo *m*; **out of/in ~** ‹*instrument*› scordato/accordato; ‹*person*› stonato/intonato; **to the ~ of** infml per la modesta somma di
B *vt* accordare ‹*instrument*›; sintonizzare ‹*radio, TV*›; mettere a punto ‹*engine*›

■ **tune in** **A** *vt* sintonizzare
B *vi* sintonizzarsi (**to** su)

■ **tune up** *vi* ‹*orchestra*› accordare gli strumenti

tuneful /'tju:nfl/ *adj* melodioso

tuner /'tju:nə(r)/ *n* accordatore, -trice *mf*; Radio, TV sintonizzatore *m*

tune-up *n* (of engine) messa *f* a punto

tungsten /'tʌŋstən/ *n* tungsteno *m*

tunic /'tju:nɪk/ *n* tunica *f*; Mil giacca *f*; Sch ≈ grembiule *m*

tuning fork /'tju:nɪŋ/ *n* diapason *m inv*

Tunisia /tju:'nɪzɪə/ *n* Tunisia *f*

Tunisian /tju:'nɪzɪən/ *adj & n* tunisino, -a *mf*

tunnel /'tʌnl/ **A** *n* tunnel *m inv*
B *vi* (*pt/pp* **tunnelled**) scavare un tunnel

tunnel vision *n* Med restringimento *m* del campo visivo; fig paraocchi *m inv*

tuppence /'tʌpəns/ *n* due penny

turban /'tɜ:bən/ *n* turbante *m*

turbine /'tɜ:baɪn/ *n* turbina *f*

turbo /'tɜ:bəʊ/ *n* turbo *m inv*

turbocharged /'tɜ:bəʊtʃɑ:dʒd/ *adj* con motore turbo

turbocharger /'tɜ:bəʊtʃɑ:dʒə(r)/ *n* turbocompressore *m*

turbot /'tɜ:bət/ *n* rombo *m* gigante

turbulence /'tɜ:bjʊləns/ *n* turbolenza *f*

turbulent /'tɜ:bjʊlənt/ *adj* turbolento

turd /tɜ:d/ *n* sl (excrement) stronzo *m*; derog (person) stronzo, -a *mf*

tureen /tjʊ'ri:n/ *n* zuppiera *f*

turf /tɜ:f/ *n* erba *f*; (segment) zolla *f* erbosa

■ **turf out** *vt* infml buttar fuori

turf accountant *n* allibratore *m*

turgid /'tɜ:dʒɪd/ *adj* ‹*style*› turgido

Turin /tjʊ'rɪn/ *n* Torino *f*

Turk /tɜ:k/ *n* turco, -a *mf*

turkey *n* tacchino *m*

Turkey /'tɜ:kɪ/ *n* Turchia *f*

Turkish /'tɜ:kɪʃ/ *adj* turco

Turkish bath *n* bagno *m* turco

Turkish delight *n* cubetti *mpl* di gelatina ricoperti di zucchero a velo

Turkmenistan /ˌtɜ:kmenɪ'stɑ:n/ *n* Turkmenistan *m*

turmeric /'tɜ:mərɪk/ *n* (spice) curcumina *f*; (plant) curcuma *f*

turmoil /'tɜ:mɔɪl/ *n* tumulto *m*

turn /tɜ:n/ **A** *n* (rotation, short walk) giro *m*; (in road) svolta *f*, curva *f*; (development) svolta *f*; Theat numero *m*; infml (attack) crisi *f inv*; **a ~ for the better/worse** un miglioramento/peggioramento; **do somebody a good ~** rendere un servizio a qualcuno; **take ~s** fare a turno; **in ~** a turno; **out of ~** ‹*speak*› a sproposito; **it's your ~** tocca a te
B *vt* girare; voltare ‹*back, eyes*›; dirigere ‹*gun, attention*›
C *vi* girare; ‹*person*› girarsi; ‹*leaves*› ingiallire; (become) diventare; **~ right/left** girare a destra/sinistra; **~ sour** inacidirsi; **~ to somebody** girarsi verso qualcuno; fig rivolgersi a qualcuno

■ **turn against** **A** *vi* diventare ostile a
B *vt* mettere contro

■ **turn around** **A** *vi* ‹*person*› girarsi; ‹*car*› girare
B *vt* girare ‹*object*›; risollevare ‹*company*›

■ **turn away** **A** *vt* mandare via ‹*people*›; girare dall'altra parte ‹*head*›
B *vi* girarsi dall'altra parte

■ **turn back** **A** *vi* tornare indietro
B *vt* mandare indietro ‹*people*›; ripiegare ‹*covers, sheet etc*›

■ **turn down** *vt* piegare ‹*collar*›; abbassare ‹*heat, gas, sound*›; respingere ‹*person, proposal*›

■ **turn in** **A** *vt* ripiegare in dentro ‹*edges*›; consegnare ‹*lost object*›
B *vi* infml (go to bed) andare a letto; **~ in to the drive** entrare nel viale

■ **turn into** *vt* (become) diventare

■ **turn off** **A** *vt* spegnere; chiudere ‹*tap, water*›; **~ somebody off** infml (disgust) fare schifo a qualcuno
B *vi* ‹*car*› girare

■ **turn on** **A** *vt* accendere; aprire ‹*tap, water*›; infml (attract) eccitare
B *vi* (attack) attaccare

■ **turn out** **A** *vt* (expel) mandar via; spegnere ‹*light, gas*›; (produce) produrre; (empty) svuotare ‹*room, cupboard*›
B *vi* (transpire) risultare; (to see, do something) venire; **~ out well/badly** ‹*cake, dress*› riuscire bene/male; ‹*situation*› andare bene/male

■ **turn over** **A** *vt* girare; **~ somebody over to the police** consegnare qualcuno alla polizia; **he ~ed the business over to her** le ha ceduto l'azienda
B *vi* girarsi; **please ~ over** vedi retro

■ **turn round** *vi* girarsi; ‹*car*› girare

■ **turn up** **A** *vt* tirare su ‹*collar*›; alzare ‹*heat, gas, sound, radio*›
B *vi* farsi vedere

turn-about *n* fig (change of direction) cambiamento *m*

turnaround *n* (in attitude) dietrofront *m inv*; (of fortune) capovolgimento *m*; (for the better) ripresa *f*

turncoat *n* voltagabbana *mf inv*

turning /'tɜ:nɪŋ/ *n* svolta *f*

turning point *n* svolta *f* decisiva

turnip /'tɜ:nɪp/ *n* rapa *f*

turn-off *n* strada *f* laterale; **it's a real ~** infml ti fa davvero passar la voglia

turn of mind *n* indole *f*
turn of phrase *n* espressione *f*
turn-on *n* infml **be a real ~** essere veramente eccitante
turnout *n* (of people) affluenza *f*
turnover *n* Comm giro *m* d'affari, fatturato *m*; (of staff) ricambio *m*
turnpike *n* AmE autostrada *f*
turnround *n* (in policy etc) cambiamento *m*
turnstile *n* cancelletto *m* girevole
turntable *n* piattaforma *f* girevole; (on record player) piatto *m*
turn-up *n* (of trousers) risvolto *m*
turpentine /'tɜ:pəntaɪn/ *n* trementina *f*
turquoise /'tɜ:kwɔɪz/ **A** *adj* (colour) turchese
B *n* turchese *m*
turret /'tʌrɪt/ *n* torretta *f*
turtle /'tɜ:tl/ *n* tartaruga *f* acquatica
turtle dove *n* tortora *f*
turtleneck /'tɜ:tlnek/ *n* collo *m* a lupetto; (sweater) maglia *f* a lupetto
Tuscan /'tʌskən/ *adj* toscano
Tuscany /'tʌskənɪ/ *n* Toscana *f*
tusk /tʌsk/ *n* zanna *f*
tussle /'tʌsl/ **A** *n* zuffa *f*
B *vi* azzuffarsi
tussock /'tʌsək/ *n* ciuffo *m* d'erba
tut /tʌt/ **A** *vi* fare un'esclamazione di disapprovazione
B *int* ts!
tutor /'tju:tə(r)/ *n* insegnante *mf* privato, -a; Univ *insegnante (mf) universitario, -a che segue individualmente un ristretto numero di studenti*
tutorial /tju:'tɔ:rɪəl/ *n* lezione *f* privata
tutorial package *n* Comput software *m inv* di autoapprendimento
tuxedo /tʌk'si:dəʊ/ *n* AmE smoking *m inv*
TV *abbr* (**television**) tv *f inv*, tivù *f*
TV dinner *n* pasto *m* pronto
twaddle /'twɒdl/ *n* scemenze *fpl*
twain /tweɪn/ *npl* **the ~** i due; **and never the ~ shall meet** e mai i due si incontreranno
twang /twæŋ/ **A** *n* (in voice) suono *m* nasale
B *vt* far vibrare
tweak /twi:k/ **A** *vt* tirare ‹*ear, nose*›; (adjust) apportare delle modifiche a
B *n* (adjustment) modifica *f*; **give sb's ears a ~** dare una tirata d'orecchie a qualcuno
twee /twi:/ *adj* BrE infml ‹*manner*› affettato
tweed /twi:d/ *n* tweed *m inv*
tweet /twi:t/ **A** *n* **1** (of bird) cinguettio *m* **2** (on social networking site) tweet *m inv*, cinguettio *m*
B *v* **1** (of bird) cinguettare **2** (on social networking site) twittare, postare su Twitter; **she ~ed a picture of them smiling at the camera** ha postato su Twitter una loro foto in cui sorridevano
tweezers /'twi:zəz/ *npl* pinzette *f*
twelfth /twelfθ/ *adj & n* dodicesimo, -a *mf*
twelve /twelv/ *adj & n* dodici *m*
twenties /'twentɪz/ *npl* (period) **the ~** gli anni Venti *mpl*; (age) vent'anni *mpl*; ▶ *also* **forties**
twentieth /'twentɪɪθ/ *adj & n* ventesimo, -a *mf*
twenty /'twentɪ/ *adj & n* venti *m*
twerp /twɜ:p/ *n* infml stupido, -a *mf*
twice /twaɪs/ *adv* due volte; **she's done ~ as much as you** ha fatto il doppio di quanto hai fatto tu
twiddle /'twɪdl/ *vt* giocherellare con; **~ one's thumbs** fig girarsi i pollici
twig¹ /twɪg/ *n* ramoscello *m*
twig² *vt & vi* (*pt/pp* **twigged**) infml intuire
twilight /'twaɪlaɪt/ *n* crepuscolo *m*
twilight zone *n* (mysterious place or situation) zona *f* d'ombra
twill /twɪl/ *n* spigato *m*
twin /twɪn/ **A** *n* gemello, -a *mf*
B *attrib* gemello
twin beds *npl* letti *mpl* gemelli
twine /twaɪn/ **A** *n* spago *m*
B *vi* intrecciarsi; ‹*plant*› attorcigliarsi
C *vt* intrecciare
twinge /twɪndʒ/ *n* fitta *f*; **~ of conscience** rimorso *m* di coscienza
twinkle /'twɪŋkl/ **A** *n* scintillio *m*
B *vi* scintillare
twinning /'twɪnɪŋ/ *n* (of companies) gemellaggio *m*
twin town *n* città *f* gemellata
twirl /twɜ:l/ **A** *vt* far roteare
B *vi* volteggiare
C *n* piroetta *f*
twist /twɪst/ **A** *n* torsione *f*; (curve) curva *f*; (in rope) attorcigliata *f*; (in book, plot) colpo *m* di scena; **round the ~** infml (crazy) ammattito
B *vt* attorcigliare ‹*rope*›; torcere ‹*metal*›; girare ‹*knob, cap*›; (distort) distorcere; **~ one's ankle** storcersi la caviglia
C *vi* attorcigliarsi; ‹*road*› essere pieno di curve
twisted /'twɪstɪd/ *adj* ‹*wire, rope*› ritorto; ‹*ankle, wrist*› slogato; ‹*sense of humour, mind*› perverso
twister /'twɪstə(r)/ *n* infml imbroglione, -a *mf*; (tornado) tornado *m inv*
twit /twɪt/ *n* infml cretino, -a *mf*
twitch /twɪtʃ/ **A** *n* tic *m inv*; (jerk) strattone *m*
B *vi* contrarsi
twitchy /'twɪtʃɪ/ *adj* infml (nervous) nervosetto
twitter /'twɪtə(r)/ **A** *n* cinguettio *m*; **in a ~** infml agitato
B *vi* cinguettare; ‹*person*› cianciare
■ **twitter on about** *vt* parlare incessantemente di
two /tu:/ *adj & n* due *m*; **put ~ and ~ together**

fare due più due
two-faced /-'feɪst/ *adj* falso
twofold /'tu:fəʊld/ **A** *adj* **a ~ increase** un raddoppio
B *adv* **to increase ~** raddoppiare
two-piece *adj* (swimsuit) due pezzi *m inv*; (suit) completo *m*
two-seater /-'si:tə(r)/ *n* biposto *m inv*
twosome /'tu:səm/ *n* coppia *f*
two-tier *adj* ‹*system, health service*› a due velocità
two-time *vt* infml fare le corna a
two-tone *adj* (in colour) bicolore; (in sound) bitonale
two-way *adj* ‹*traffic*› a doppio senso di marcia
two-way mirror *n* specchio *m* unidirezionale
two-way radio *n* (radio *f inv*) ricetrasmittente *f inv*
tycoon /taɪ'ku:n/ *n* magnate *m*
tying /'taɪɪŋ/ ▶ **tie**
⚷ **type** /taɪp/ **A** *n* tipo *m*; (printing) carattere *m* [tipografico]
B *vt & vi* scrivere a macchina
typecast **A** *vt* Theat fig far fare sempre la stessa parte a ‹*person*›
B *adj* a ruolo fisso
typeface *n* carattere *m* tipografico
typeset *vt* comporre
typesetter *n* compositore *m*
typewriter *n* macchina *f* da scrivere
typewritten *adj* dattiloscritto
typhoid /'taɪfɔɪd/ *n* febbre *f* tifoidea
typhoon /taɪ'fu:n/ *n* tifone *m*
⚷ **typical** /'tɪpɪkl/ *adj* tipico
typically /'tɪpɪklɪ/ *adv* tipicamente; (as usual) come al solito
typify /'tɪpɪfaɪ/ *vt* (*pt/pp* **-ied**) essere tipico di
typing /'taɪpɪŋ/ *n* dattilografia *f*
typist /'taɪpɪst/ *n* dattilografo, -a *mf*
typo /'taɪpəʊ/ *n* errore *m* di stampa; (keying error) errore *m* di battitura
typography /taɪ'pɒgrəfɪ/ *n* tipografia *f*
tyrannical /tɪ'rænɪkl/ *adj* tirannico
tyrannize /'tɪrənaɪz/ *vt* tiranneggiare
tyranny /'tɪrənɪ/ *n* tirannia *f*
tyrant /'taɪrənt/ *n* tiranno, -a *mf*
tyre /'taɪə(r)/ *n* gomma *f*, pneumatico *m*
tyre pressure *n* pressione *f* delle gomme
Tyrrhenian Sea /tɪ'ri:nɪən/ *n* mar *m* Tirreno
tzar /zɑ:(r)/ *n* zar *m*
tzarina /tsɑ:'ri:nə/ *n* zarina *f*

Uu

u¹, U /ju:/ *n* (letter) u, U *f inv*
u² *abbr* (**universal**) Cinema per tutti
U-bend *n* (in pipe) gomito *m*; (in road) curva *f* a gomito
ubiquitous /ju:'bɪkwɪtəs/ *adj* onnipresente
UCAS /ju:kæs/ *abbr* BrE (**Universities and Colleges Admissions Service**) *organismo (m) di valutazione delle ammissioni all'università*
udder /'ʌdə(r)/ *n* mammella *f* (*di vacca, capra ecc.*)
UEFA /ju:'i:fə/ *n abbr* (**Union of European Football Associations**) UEFA *f*
UFO *abbr* (**unidentified flying object**) ufo *m inv*
Uganda /ju:'gændə/ Uganda *f*
Ugandan /ju:'gændən/ *adj & n* ugandese *mf*
ugliness /'ʌglɪnɪs/ *n* bruttezza *f*
ugly /'ɪglɪ/ *adj* (**-ier, -iest**) brutto
UHF *abbr* (**ultra-high frequency**) UHF
UHT *abbr* (**ultra-heat treated**) ‹*milk*› UHT
UK *abbr* (**United Kingdom**) Regno Unito
Ukraine /ju:'kreɪn/ *n* Ucraina *f*
Ukrainian /ju:'kreɪnɪən/ *adj & n* ucraino, -a *mf*; (language) ucraino *m*
ulcer /'ʌlsə(r)/ *n* ulcera *f*
ulterior /ʌl'tɪərɪə(r)/ *adj* **~ motive** secondo fine *m*
ultimate /'ʌltɪmət/ *adj* definitivo; (final) finale; (fundamental) fondamentale
⚷ **ultimately** /'ʌltɪmətlɪ/ *adv* alla fine
ultimatum /ʌltɪ'meɪtəm/ *n* ultimatum *m inv*
ultramarine /ʌltrəmə'ri:n/ **A** *adj* oltremarino
B *n* azzurro *m* oltremarino
ultrasound /'ʌltrəsaʊnd/ *n* Med ecografia *f*
ultrasound scan *n* ecografia *m*
ultrasound scanner *n* scanner *m inv* per ecografia
ultraviolet /ʌltrə'vaɪələt/ *adj* ultravioletto
umbilical /ʌm'bɪlɪkl/ *adj* **~ cord** cordone *m* ombelicale
umbrage /'ʌmbrɪdʒ/ *n* **take ~** offendersi
umbrella /ʌm'brelə/ *n* ombrello *m*

umbrella stand *n* portaombrelli *m inv*
umpire /ˈʌmpaɪə(r)/ **A** *n* arbitro *m* **B** *vt & vi* arbitrare
umpteen /ʌmpˈtiːn/ *adj* infml innumerevole
umpteenth /ʌmpˈtiːnθ/ *adj* infml ennesimo; **for the ~ time** per l'ennesima volta
UN *abbr* (**United Nations**) ONU *f*
unabashed /ʌnəˈbæʃt/ *adj* spudorato
unabated /ʌnəˈbeɪtɪd/ *adj* ‹*enthusiasm*› inalterato; **continue ~** ‹*gales*› continuare con la stessa intensità
⚷ **unable** /ʌnˈeɪbl/ *adj* **be ~ to do something** non potere fare qualcosa; (not know how) non sapere fare qualcosa
unabridged /ʌnəˈbrɪdʒd/ *adj* integrale
unacceptable /ʌnəkˈseptəbl/ *adj* ‹*proposal, suggestion*› inaccettabile
unaccompanied /ʌnəˈkʌmpnɪd/ *adj* non accompagnato; ‹*luggage*› incustodito
unaccountable /ʌnəˈkaʊntəbl/ *adj* inspiegabile
unaccountably /ʌnəˈkaʊntəblɪ/ *adv* inspiegabilmente
unaccounted /ʌnəˈkaʊntɪd/ *adj* **be ~ for** (not explained) non avere spiegazione; (not found) mancare
unaccustomed /ʌnəˈkʌstəmd/ *adj* insolito; **be ~ to** non essere abituato a
unadorned /ʌnəˈdɔːnd/ *adj* ‹*walls*› disadorno
unadulterated /ʌnəˈdʌltəreɪtɪd/ *adj* ‹*water*› puro; ‹*wine*› non sofisticato; fig assoluto
unadventurous /ʌnədˈventʃ(ə)rəs/ *adj* ‹*person, production*› poco avventuroso; ‹*meal*› poco fantasioso
unaffected /ˌʌnəˈfektɪd/ *adj* (natural) semplice; **be ~ by** non essere interessato da
unafraid /ˌʌnəˈfreɪd/ *adj* senza paura
unaided /ʌnˈeɪdɪd/ *adj* senza aiuto
unalloyed /ʌnəˈlɔɪd/ *adj* fig puro
unambiguous /ˌʌnæmˈbɪgjʊəs/ *adj* inequivocabile
unanimity /juːnəˈnɪmətɪ/ *n* unanimità *f*
unanimous /juːˈnænɪməs/ *adj* unanime
unanimously /juːˈnænɪməslɪ/ *adv* all'unanimità
unannounced /ʌnəˈnaʊnst/ *adj* inaspettato
unanswerable /ʌnˈɑːns(ə)rəbl/ *adj* ‹*remark, case*› irrefutabile; ‹*question*› senza risposta
unanswered /ʌnˈɑːnsəd, AmE ʌnˈæn-/ *adj* ‹*question, letter*› senza risposta
unappealing /ʌnəˈpiːlɪŋ/ *adj* poco attraente
unappetizing /ʌnˈæpetaɪzɪŋ/ *adj* poco appetitoso
unappreciated /ʌnəˈpriːʃɪeɪtɪd/ *adj* ‹*work of art*› incompreso

⚷ parola chiave

unappreciative /ʌnəˈpriːʃ(ɪ)ətɪv/ *adj* ‹*audience*› indifferente; ‹*person*› ingrato
unapproachable /ʌnəˈprəʊtʃəbl/ *adj* ‹*person*› inavvicinabile
unarmed /ʌnˈɑːmd/ *adj* disarmato
unarmed combat *n* lotta *f* senza armi
unashamedly /ʌnəˈʃeɪmd/ *adv* sfacciatamente
unasked /ʌnˈɑːskt/ *adv* **he came ~** è venuto senza che nessuno glielo chiedesse
unassuming /ʌnəˈsjuːmɪŋ/ *adj* senza pretese
unattached /ʌnəˈtætʃd/ *adj* staccato; ‹*person*› senza legami
unattainable /ʌnəˈteɪnəbl/ *adj* irraggiungibile
unattended /ʌnəˈtendɪd/ *adj* incustodito
unattractive /ʌnəˈtræktɪv/ *adj* ‹*person*› poco attraente; ‹*proposition*› poco allettante; ‹*characteristic*› sgradevole; ‹*building, furniture*› brutto
unauthorized /ʌnˈɔːθəraɪzd/ *adj* non autorizzato
unavailable /ʌnəˈveɪləbl/ *adj* non disponibile
unavoidable /ʌnəˈvɔɪdəbl/ *adj* inevitabile
unavoidably /ʌnəˈvɔɪdəblɪ/ *adv* inevitabilmente; **I was ~ detained** sono stato trattenuto da cause di forza maggiore
unaware /ʌnəˈweə(r)/ *adj* **be ~ of something** non rendersi conto di qualcosa
unawares /ʌnəˈweəz/ *adv* **catch somebody ~** prendere qualcuno alla sprovvista
unbalanced /ʌnˈbælənst/ *adj* non equilibrato; (mentally) squilibrato
unbearable /ʌnˈbeərəbl/ *adj* insopportabile
unbearably /ʌnˈbeərəblɪ/ *adv* insopportabilmente
unbeatable /ʌnˈbiːtəbl/ *adj* imbattibile
unbeaten /ʌnˈbiːtən/ *adj* imbattuto
unbecoming /ʌnbɪˈkʌmɪŋ/ *adj* ‹*garment*› che non dona
unbeknown /ʌnbɪˈnəʊn/ *adj* infml **~ to me** a mia insaputa
unbelievable /ʌnbɪˈliːvəbl/ *adj* incredibile
unbend /ʌnˈbend/ *vi* (*pt/pp* **-bent**) (relax) distendersi
unbending /ʌnˈbendɪŋ/ *adj* (insistent) inflessibile
unbiased /ʌnˈbaɪəst/ *adj* obiettivo
unblock /ʌnˈblɒk/ *vt* sbloccare
unbolt /ʌnˈbəʊlt/ *vt* togliere il chiavistello di
unborn /ʌnˈbɔːn/ *adj* non ancora nato
unbreakable /ʌnˈbreɪkəbl/ *adj* infrangibile
unbridled /ʌnˈbraɪdld/ *adj* sfrenato
unbroken /ʌnˈbrəʊkən/ *adj* ‹*sequence, sleep, silence*› ininterrotto
unbuckle /ʌnˈbʌkl/ *vt* slacciare ‹*belt*›
unburden /ʌnˈbɜːdən/ *vt* **~ oneself** fig sfogarsi (**to** con)

unbutton /ʌn'bʌtən/ *vt* sbottonare
uncalled-for /ʌn'kɔːldfɔː(r)/ *adj* fuori luogo
uncannily /ʌn'kænɪlɪ/ *adv* incredibilmente
uncanny /ʌn'kænɪ/ *adj* sorprendente; ‹*silence, feeling*› inquietante
uncared-for /ʌn'keədfɔː(r)/ *adj* ‹*house, pet*› trascurato
uncaring /ʌn'keərɪŋ/ *adj* ‹*world*› indifferente
unceasing /ʌn'siːsɪŋ/ *adj* incessante
uncensored /ʌn'sensəd/ *adj* ‹*film, book*› non censurato
unceremonious /ʌnserɪ'məʌnɪəs/ *adj* (abrupt) brusco
unceremoniously /ʌnserɪ'məʌnɪəslɪ/ *adv* senza tante cerimonie
uncertain /ʌn'sɜːtən/ *adj* incerto; ‹*weather*› instabile; **in no ~ terms** senza mezzi termini
uncertainty /ʌn'sɜːtəntɪ/ *n* incertezza *f*
unchallenged /ʌn'tʃæləndʒd/ *adj* ‹*statement, decision*› incontestato; **I can't let that go ~** non posso non contestarlo
unchanged /ʌn'tʃeʌndʒd/ *adj* invariato
uncharacteristic /ʌnkærəktə'rɪstɪk/ *adj* ‹*generosity*› insolito
uncharitable /ʌn'tʃærɪtəbl/ *adj* duro
unchecked /ʌn'tʃekt/ *adv* incontrollato; **go ~** dilagare
uncivilized /ʌn'sɪvɪlaɪzd/ *adj* ‹*people, nation*› non civilizzato; ‹*treatment, conditions*› incivile
unclassified /ʌn'klæsɪfaɪd/ *adj* ‹*document, information*› non riservato; ‹*road*› non classificato
uncle /'ʌŋkl/ *n* zio *m*
unclear /ʌn'kliːr/ *adj* ‹*instructions, reason, voice, writing*› non chiaro; ‹*future*› incerto; **be ~ about something** ‹*person*› non aver ben chiaro qualcosa
unclog /ʌn'klɒg/ *vt* sturare ‹*pipe*›
uncoil /ʌn'kɔɪl/ *vt* srotolare
uncomfortable /ʌn'kʌmftəbl/ *adj* scomodo; ‹*silence, situation*› imbarazzante; **feel ~** fig sentirsi a disagio
uncomfortably /ʌn'kʌmftəblɪ/ *adv* ‹*sit*› scomodamente; (causing alarm etc) spaventosamente
uncommon /ʌn'kɒmʌn/ *adj* insolito
uncommunicative /ʌnkə'mjuːnɪkətɪv/ *adj* poco comunicativo
uncomplimentary /ˌʌnkɒmplɪ'mentrɪ, AmE -terɪ/ *adj* poco complimentoso
uncompromising /ʌn'kɒmprəmaɪzɪŋ/ *adj* intransigente
unconcerned /ˌʌnkən'sɜːnd/ *adj* indifferente
unconditional /ʌnkən'dɪʃ(ə)nl/ *adj* incondizionato
unconditionally /ʌnkʌn'dɪʃnəlɪ/ *adv* incondizionatamente
unconfirmed /ˌʌnkən'fɜːmd/ *adj* ‹*report, sighting*› non confermato
unconnected /ˌʌnkə'nektɪd/ *adj* ‹*incidents, facts*› senza alcun legame tra loro
unconscious /ʌn'kɒnʃəs/ *adj* privo di sensi; (unaware) inconsapevole; **be ~ of something** non rendersi conto di qualcosa
unconsciously /ʌn'kɒnʃəslɪ/ *adv* inconsapevolmente
unconstitutional /ˌʌnkɒnstɪ'tjuːʃənl/ *adj* incostituzionale
uncontested /ʌnkʌn'testɪd/ *adj* Pol ‹*seat*› non disputato
uncontrollable /ʌnkən'trəʊləbl/ *adj* incontrollabile; ‹*sobbing*› irrefrenabile
uncontrollably /ʌnkən'trəʊləblɪ/ *adv* ‹*increase*› incontrollatamente; ‹*laugh, sob*› senza potersi controllare
unconventional /ʌnkən'venʃnəl/ *adj* poco convenzionale
unconvincing /ʌnkən'vɪnsɪŋ/ *adj* poco convincente
uncooked /ʌn'kʊkt/ *adj* crudo
uncooperative /ʌnkəʊ'ɒpr(ə)tɪv/ *adj* poco cooperativo
uncoordinated /ˌʌnkəʊ'ɔːdɪneɪtɪd/ *adj* ‹*action, efforts*› non coordinato; **be ~** (person) essere scoordinato
uncork /ʌn'kɔːk/ *vt* sturare
uncorroborated /ʌnkə'rɒbəreɪtɪd/ *adj* non convalidato
uncouth /ʌn'kuːθ/ *adj* zotico
uncover /ʌn'kʌvə(r)/ *vt* scoprire; portare alla luce ‹*buried object*›
uncritical /ʌn'krɪtɪkl/ *adj* poco critico
uncross /ʌn'krɒs/ *vt* disincrociare ‹*legs, arms*›
unctuous /'ʌŋktjʊəs/ *adj* untuoso
uncultivated /ʌn'kʌltɪveɪtɪd/ *adj* incolto
uncut /ʌn'kʌt/ *adj* ‹*film*› in versione integrale; ‹*diamond*› non tagliato
undamaged /ʌn'dæmɪdʒd/ *adj* intatto
undaunted /ʌn'dɔːntɪd/ *adj* imperterrito; **~ by something** per nulla intimidito da qualcosa
undecided /ʌndɪ'saɪdɪd/ *adj* indeciso; (not settled) incerto
undefined /ʌndɪ'faɪnd/ *adj* ‹*objective, nature*› indeterminato
undelivered /ʌndɪ'lɪvəd/ *adj* ‹*mail*› non recapitato
undemanding /ˌʌndɪ'mɑːndɪŋ, AmE -'mænd-/ *adj* ‹*job, course*› poco impegnativo
undemocratic /ˌʌndemə'krætɪk/ *adj* antidemocratico
undemonstrative /ˌʌndɪ'mɒnstrətɪv/ *adj* poco espansivo
undeniable /ʌndɪ'naɪəbl/ *adj* innegabile
undeniably /ʌndɪ'naɪəblɪ/ *adv* innegabilmente
⚷ **under** /'ʌndə(r)/ **A** *prep* sotto; (less than)

al di sotto di; ~ **there** lì sotto; ~ **repair/construction** in riparazione/costruzione; ~ **way** fig in corso
B *adv* ~ (water) sott'acqua; (unconscious) sotto anestesia

underachieve /ʌndərə'tʃiːv/ *vi* Sch restare al di sotto delle proprie possibilità

underachiever /ˌʌndərə'tʃiːvə(r)/ *n* **be an** ~ non dare il meglio

underage /ˌʌndər'eɪdʒ/ *adj* ~ **drinking** consumo di alcolici da parte dei minorenni; **be** ~ essere minorenne

underarm /'ʌndərɑːm/ *adj* ‹*deodorant*› per le ascelle; ‹*hair*› sotto le ascelle; ‹*service, throw*› dal basso verso l'alto

undercarriage /'ʌndəkærɪdʒ/ *n* Aeron carrello *m*

undercharge /ʌndə'tʃɑːdʒ/ *vt* far pagare meno del dovuto a

underclass /'ʌndəklɑːs/ *n* sottoproletariato *m*

underclothes /'ʌndəkləʊðz/ *npl* biancheria *fsg* intima

undercoat /'ʌndəkəʊt/ *n* prima mano *f*

undercook /ʌndə'kʊk/ *vt* non cuocere abbastanza

undercover /ʌndə'kʌvə(r)/ *adj* clandestino

undercurrent /'ʌndəkʌrənt/ *n* corrente *f* sottomarina; fig sottofondo *m*

undercut /ʌndə'kʌt/ *vt* (*pt/pp* **-cut**) Comm vendere a minor prezzo di

underdeveloped /ʌndədɪ'veləpt/ *adj* ‹*country*› sottosviluppato; Phot non completamente sviluppato

underdog /'ʌndədɒg/ *n* perdente *m*

underdone /ʌndə'dʌn/ *adj* ‹*meat*› al sangue

underemployed /ʌndərɪm'plɔɪd/ *adj* ‹*person*› sottoccupato; ‹*resources, equipment etc*› non sfruttato completamente

underequipped /ʌndərɪ'kwɪpt/ *adj* ‹*army, person*› insufficientemente equipaggiato; ‹*schools, gym*› insufficientemente attrezzato

underestimate /ʌndər'estɪmeɪt/ *vt* sottovalutare

underexpose /ʌndərɪks'pəʊz/ *vt* Phot sottoesporre

u

underfed /ʌndə'fed/ *adj* denutrito

underfloor /'ʌndəflɔː(r)/ *adj* ‹*pipes, wiring*› sotto il pavimento

underfoot /ʌndə'fʊt/ *adv* sotto i piedi; **trample** ~ calpestare

underfunded /ʌndə'fʌndɪd/ *adj* insufficientemente finanziato

underfunding /ʌndə'fʌndɪŋ/ *n* finanziamento *m* insufficiente

undergo /ʌndə'gəʊ/ *vt* (*pt* **-went**, *pp* **-gone**) subire ‹*operation, treatment*›; ~ **repair** essere in riparazione

undergraduate /ʌndə'grædʒʊət/ *n* studente, -tessa *mf* universitario, -a

underground¹ /ʌndə'graʌnd/ *adv* sottoterra

underground² /'ʌndəgraʌnd/ **A** *adj* sotterraneo; (secret) clandestino
B *n* (railway) metropolitana *f*

underground car park *n* parcheggio *m* sotterraneo

undergrowth /'ʌndəgrəʊθ/ *n* sottobosco *m*

underhand /'ʌndəhænd/ *adj* subdolo

underlay /'ʌndəleɪ/ *n strato (m) di gomma o feltro posto sotto la moquette*

underlie /ʌndə'laɪ/ *vt* (*pt* **-lay**, *pp* **-lain**, *pres p* **-lying**) fig essere alla base di

underline /ʌndə'laɪn/ *vt* sottolineare

underling /'ʌndəlɪŋ/ *n* derog subalterno, -a *mf*

underlying /ʌndə'laɪɪŋ/ *adj* fig fondamentale

undermanned /ʌndə'mænd/ *adj* ‹*factory*› a corto di mano d'opera

undermentioned /ʌndə'menʃnd/ *adj* sottoindicato

undermine /ʌndə'maɪn/ *vt* fig minare

underneath /ʌndə'niːθ/ **A** *prep* sotto; ~ **it** sotto
B *adv* sotto

undernourished /ʌndə'nʌrɪʃt/ *adj* denutrito

underpaid /ʌndə'peɪd/ *adj* mal pagato

underpants /'ʌndəpænts/ *npl* mutande *fpl*

underpass /'ʌndəpɑːs/ *n* sottopassaggio *m*

underpay /ʌndə'peɪ/ *vt* sottopagare ‹*employee*›

underpin /ʌndə'pɪn/ *vt* puntellare ‹*wall*›; rafforzare ‹*currency, power, theory*›; essere alla base di ‹*religion, society*›

underpopulated /ʌndə'pɒpjʊleɪtɪd/ *adj* sottopopolato

underprivileged /ʌndə'prɪvɪlɪdʒd/ *adj* non abbiente

underrate /ʌndə'reɪt/ *vt* sottovalutare

underscore /ˌʌndə'skɔː(r)/ **A** *n* segno *m* di sottolineatura
B *vt* sottolineare

underseal /'ʌndəsiːl/ *n* Auto antiruggine *m inv*

under-secretary /ʌndə'sekrət(ə)rɪ/ *n* BrE Pol sottosegretario *m*

undersell /ʌndə'sel/ *vt* vendere a prezzo inferiore rispetto a ‹*competitor*›; pubblicizzare poco ‹*product*›

undersexed /ʌndə'sekst/ *adj* con scarsa libido

undershirt /'ʌndəʃɜːt/ *n* AmE maglia *f* della salute

undersigned /ʌndə'saɪnd/ *adj* sottoscritto

undersized /ʌndə'saɪzd/ *adj* ‹*portion*› scarso; ‹*animal*› troppo piccolo; ‹*person*› di statura inferiore alla media

understaffed /ʌndəˈstɑːft/ *adj* a corto di personale

understand /ʌndəˈstænd/ **A** *vt* (*pt/pp* **-stood**) capire; **I ~ that...** (have heard) mi risulta che...
B *vi* capire

understandable /ʌndəˈstændəbl/ *adj* comprensibile

understandably /ʌndəˈstændəblɪ/ *adv* comprensibilmente

understanding /ʌndəˈstændɪŋ/ **A** *adj* comprensivo
B *n* comprensione *f*; (agreement) accordo *m*; **reach an ~** trovare un accordo; **on the ~ that** a condizione che

understatement /ˈʌndəsteɪtmʌnt/ *n* **that's an ~** non è dire abbastanza

understudy /ˈʌndəstʌdɪ/ *n* Theat sostituto, a *mf*

undertake /ʌndəˈteɪk/ *vt* (*pt* **-took**, *pp* **-taken**) intraprendere; **~ to do something** impegnarsi a fare qualcosa

undertaker /ˈʌndəteɪkə(r)/ *n* impresario *m* di pompe funebri; **[firm of] ~s** *n* impresa *f* di pompe funebri

undertaking /ʌndəˈteɪkɪŋ/ *n* impresa *f*; (promise) promessa *f*

under-the-counter *adj* ‹*goods, supply, trade*› comprato/venduto sottobanco

undertone /ˈʌndətəʊn/ *n* fig sottofondo *m*; **in an ~** sottovoce

undervalue /ʌndəˈvæljuː/ *vt* sottovalutare; **the shares are ~d** le azioni si sono svalutate

underwater[1] /ˈʌndəwɔːtə(r)/ *adj* subacqueo

underwater[2] /ʌndəˈwɔːtə(r)/ *adv* sott'acqua

under way *adj* **be ~** ‹*vehicle*› essere in corsa; ‹*filming, talks*› essere in corso; **get ~** ‹*vehicle*› mettersi in viaggio; ‹*preparations, season*› avere inizio

underwear /ˈʌndəweə(r)/ *n* biancheria *f* intima

underweight /ʌndəˈweɪt/ *adj* sotto peso

underworld /ˈʌndəwɜːld/ *n* (criminals) malavita *f*

underwriter /ˈʌndəraɪtə(r)/ *n* assicuratore *m*

undeserved /ʌndɪˈzɜːvd/ *adj* ‹*praise, reward, win*› immeritato; ‹*blame, punish*› ingiusto

undeservedly /ʌndɪˈzɜːvɪdlɪ/ *adv* ‹*praise, reward, win*› immeritatamente; ‹*blame, punish*› ingiustamente

undesirable /ʌndɪˈzaɪərəbl/ *adj* indesiderato; ‹*person*› poco raccomandabile

undetected /ʌndɪˈtektɪd/ **A** *adj* ‹*crime, cancer*› non scoperto; ‹*flaw, movement, intruder*› non visto; **go ~** ‹*cancer, crime*› non essere scoperto; ‹*person*› passare inosservato
B *adv* ‹*break in, listen*› senza essere scoperto

undeterred /ˌʌndɪˈtɜːd/ *adj* imperterrito

undeveloped /ʌndɪˈveləpt/ *adj* non sviluppato; ‹*land*› non sfruttato

undies /ˈʌndɪz/ *npl* infml biancheria *f* intima (*da donna*)

undignified /ʌnˈdɪgnɪfaɪd/ *adj* poco dignitoso

undisciplined /ʌnˈdɪsɪplɪnd/ *adj* indisciplinato

undiscovered /ʌndɪsˈkʌvəd/ *adj* ‹*secret*› non svelato; ‹*crime, document*› non scoperto; ‹*land*› inesplorato; ‹*species*› sconosciuto; ‹*talent*› non ancora scoperto

undiscriminating /ʌndɪsˈkrɪmɪneɪtɪŋ/ *adj* che non sa fare distinzioni

undisguised /ˌʌndɪsˈgaɪzd/ *adj* evidente

undisputed /ʌndɪˈspjuːtɪd/ *adj* indiscusso

undisturbed /ʌndɪˈstɜːbd/ *adj* ‹*sleep, night*› indisturbato

undivided /ʌndɪˈvaɪdɪd/ *adj* ‹*loyalty, attention*› assoluto

undo /ʌnˈduː/ *vt* (*pt* **-did**, *pp* **-done**) disfare; slacciare ‹*dress, shoes*›; sbottonare ‹*shirt*›; fig Comput annullare

undone /ʌnˈdʌn/ *adj* ‹*shirt, button*› sbottonato; ‹*shoes, dress*› slacciato; (not accomplished) non fatto; **leave ~** ‹*job*› tralasciare

undoubted /ʌnˈdaʊtɪd/ *adj* indubbio

undoubtedly /ʌnˈdaʊtɪdlɪ/ *adv* senza dubbio

undress /ʌnˈdres/ **A** *vt* spogliare; **get ~ed** spogliarsi
B *vi* spogliarsi

undrinkable /ʌnˈdrɪŋkəbl/ *adj* (unpleasant) imbevibile; (dangerous) non potabile

undue /ʌnˈdjuː/ *adj* eccessivo

undulating /ˈʌndjʊleɪtɪŋ/ *adj* ondulato; ‹*country*› collinoso

unduly /ʌnˈdjuːlɪ/ *adv* eccessivamente

undying /ʌnˈdaɪɪŋ/ *adj* eterno

unearned /ʌnˈɜːnd/ *adj* immeritato; **~ income** rendita *f*

unearth /ʌnˈɜːθ/ *vt* dissotterrare; fig scovare; scoprire ‹*secret*›

unearthly /ʌnˈɜːθlɪ/ *adj* soprannaturale; **at an ~ hour** infml ad un'ora impossibile

unease /ʌnˈiːz/ *n* disagio *m*

uneasily /ʌnˈiːzɪlɪ/ *adv* a disagio

uneasiness /ʌnˈiːzɪnɪs/ *n* disagio *m*

uneasy /ʌnˈiːzɪ/ *adj* a disagio; ‹*person*› inquieto; ‹*feeling*› inquietante; (truce) precario

uneatable /ʌnˈiːtəbl/ *adj* immangiabile

uneconomic /ʌniːkəˈnɒmɪk/ *adj* poco remunerativo

uneconomical /ʌniːkəˈnɒmɪkl/ *adj* poco economico

uneducated /ʌnˈedjʊkeɪtɪd/ *adj* ‹*person*› non istruito; ‹*tastes*› non raffinato; ‹*accent, speech*› da persona non istruita

unemotional /ˌʌnɪˈməʊʃənl/ *adj* distaccato

u

unemployed /ʌnem'plɔɪd/ **A** *adj* disoccupato
B *npl* **the ~** i disoccupati

unemployment /ʌnem'plɔɪmʌnt/ *n* disoccupazione *f*

unemployment benefit *n* sussidio *m* di disoccupazione

unemployment rate *n* tasso *m* di disoccupazione

unending /ʌn'endɪŋ/ *adj* senza fine

unenthusiastic /ʌnɪnθju:zɪ'æstɪk/ *adj* poco entusiasta

unenviable /ʌn'envɪəbl/ *adj* ‹*position*› poco invidiabile

unequal /ʌn'i:kwəl/ *adj* disuguale; ‹*struggle*› impari; **be ~ to a task** non essere all'altezza di un compito

unequalled /ʌn'i:kwəld/ *adj* ‹*achievement, quality, record*› ineguagliato

unequally /ʌn'i:kwəlɪ/ *adv* in modo disuguale

unequivocal /ʌnə'kwɪvəkl/ *adj* inequivocabile; ‹*person*› esplicito

unequivocally /ʌnə'kwɪvəklɪ/ *adv* inequivocabilmente

unerring /ʌn'ɜ:rɪŋ/ *adj* infallibile

unethical /ʌn'eθɪkl/ *adj* immorale

uneven /ʌn'i:vən/ *adj* irregolare; ‹*distribution*› ineguale; ‹*number*› dispari

unevenly /ʌn'i:vənlɪ/ *adv* irregolarmente; ‹*distributed*› inegualmente

uneventful /ʌnɪ'ventfʊl/ *adj* senza avvenimenti di rilievo

unexciting /ʌnɪk'saɪtɪŋ/ *adj* poco entusiasmante

unexpected /ʌnɪk'spektɪd/ *adj* inaspettato

unexpectedly /ʌnɪk'spektɪdlɪ/ *adv* inaspettatamente

unexplored /ʌnɪk'splɔ:d/ *adj* inesplorato

unfailing /ʌn'feɪlɪŋ/ *adj* infallibile

unfair /ʌn'feə(r)/ *adj* ingiusto

unfair dismissal *n* licenziamento *m* ingiustificato

unfairly /ʌn'feəlɪ/ *adv* ingiustamente

unfairness /ʌn'feənəs/ *n* ingiustizia *f*

unfaithful /ʌn'feɪθfʊl/ *adj* infedele

unfamiliar /ʌnfə'mɪljə(r)/ *adj* sconosciuto; **be ~ with** non conoscere

unfashionable /ʌn'fæənəbl/ *adj* fuori moda

unfasten /ʌn'fɑ:sn/ *vt* slacciare; (detach) staccare

unfathomable /ʌn'fæð(ə)məbl/ *adj* imperscrutabile

unfavourable /ʌn'feɪv(ə)rəbl/ *adj* sfavorevole; ‹*impression*› negativo

unfeeling /ʌn'fi:lɪŋ/ *adj* insensibile

unfinished /ʌn'fɪnɪʃt/ *adj* da finire; ‹*business*› in sospeso

unfit /ʌn'fɪt/ *adj* inadatto; (morally) indegno; Sport fuori forma; **~ for work** non in grado di lavorare; **~ for human consumption** non commestibile

unflappable /ʌn'flæpəbl/ *adj* infml calmo

unflattering /ʌn'flæt(ə)rɪŋ/ *adj* ‹*clothes, hairstyle*› che non dona; ‹*portrait, description*› poco lusinghiero

unflinching /ʌn'flɪntʃɪŋ/ *adj* risoluto

unfold /ʌn'fəʊld/ **A** *vt* spiegare; (spread out) aprire; fig rivelare
B *vi* ‹*view*› rivelarsi

unforeseeable /ʌnfɔ:'si:əbl/ *adj* imprevedibile

unforeseen /ʌnfɔ:'si:n/ *adj* imprevisto

unforgettable /ʌnfə'getəbl/ *adj* indimenticabile

unforgivable /ʌnfə'gɪvəbl/ *adj* imperdonabile

unforgiving /ʌnfə'gɪvɪŋ/ *adj* che non perdona

unfortunate /ʌn'fɔ:tʃənət/ *adj* sfortunato; (regrettable) spiacevole; ‹*remark, choice*› infelice

⚷ **unfortunately** /ʌn'fɔ:tʃənətlɪ/ *adv* purtroppo

unfounded /ʌn'faʊndɪd/ *adj* infondato

unfriendly /ʌn'frendlɪ/ *adj* ‹*person, remark*› scortese, poco amichevole; ‹*place, climate, reception*› ostile; ‹*software*› difficile da usare

unfulfilled /ʌnfʊl'fɪld/ *adj* ‹*prophecy*› non avverato; ‹*promise*› non mantenuto; ‹*ambition*› non realizzato; ‹*desire, need*› non soddisfatto; ‹*condition*› non rispettato; **feel ~** essere insoddisfatto

unfurl /ʌn'fɜ:l/ **A** *vt* spiegare
B *vi* spiegarsi

unfurnished /ʌn'fɜ:nɪʃt/ *adj* non ammobiliato

ungainly /ʌn'geɪnlɪ/ *adj* sgraziato

ungentlemanly /ʌn'dʒentlmənlɪ/ *adj* non da gentiluomo

ungodly /ʌn'gɒdlɪ/ *adj* empio; **~ hour** infml ora *f* impossibile

ungracious /ʌn'greɪʃəs/ *adj* sgarbato

ungrammatical /ˌʌngrə'mætɪkl/ *adj* sgrammaticato

ungrateful /ʌn'greɪtfʊl/ *adj* ingrato

ungratefully /ʌn'greɪtfʊlɪ/ *adv* senza riconoscenza

unhappily /ʌn'hæpɪlɪ/ *adv* infelicemente; (unfortunately) purtroppo

unhappiness /ʌn'hæpɪnəs/ *n* infelicità *f*

unhappy /ʌn'hæpɪ/ *adj* infelice; (not content) insoddisfatto (**with** di)

unharmed /ʌn'hɑ:md/ *adj* incolume

unhealthy /ʌn'helθɪ/ *adj* poco sano; (insanitary) malsano

unheard of /ʌn'hɜ:dəv/ *adj* ‹*actor, brand*› mai sentito; ‹*levels, price*› incredibile

unheated /ʌn'hi:tɪd/ *adj* senza riscaldamento

⚷ parola chiave

unheeded /ʌn'hiːdɪd/ *adj* ignorato; **go ~** ‹*warning, plea*› venir ignorato
unhelpful /ʌn'helpfʊl/ *adj* ‹*person, attitude*› poco disponibile; ‹*witness*› che non collabora; ‹*remark*› di poco aiuto
unhindered /ʌn'hɪndəd/ *adj* senza intralci; **~ by** senza essere ostacolato da ‹*rules, obstacles*›
unholy /ʌn'həʊlɪ/ *adj* ‹*alliance, pact*› paradossale; infml ‹*mess, hour*› indecente
unhook /ʌn'hʊk/ *vt* sganciare; staccare ‹*picture*›
unhurried /ʌn'hʌrɪd/ *adj* tranquillo
unhurt /ʌn'hɜːt/ *adj* illeso
unhygienic /ʌnhaɪ'dʒiːnɪk/ *adj* non igienico
unicorn /'juːnɪkɔːn/ *n* unicorno *m*
unidentified /ʌnaɪ'dentɪfaɪd/ *adj* non identificato
unification /juːnɪfɪ'keɪʃn/ *n* unificazione *f*
uniform /'juːnɪfɔːm/ **A** *adj* uniforme **B** *n* uniforme *f*
uniformly /'juːnɪfɔːmlɪ/ *adv* uniformemente
unify /'juːnɪfaɪ/ *vt* (*pt/pp* **-ied**) unificare
unilateral /juːnɪ'læt(ə)rəl/ *adj* unilaterale
unilaterally /juːnɪ'læt(ə)rəlɪ/ *adv* unilateralmente
unimaginable /ʌnɪ'mædʒɪnəbl/ *adj* inimmaginabile
unimaginative /ʌnɪ'mædʒɪnətɪv/ *adj* privo di fantasia
unimpeded /ˌʌnɪm'piːdɪd/ *adj* ‹*access*› libero
unimportant /ʌnɪm'pɔːtənt/ *adj* irrilevante
unimpressed /ˌʌnɪm'prest/ *adj* non impressionato
uninformed /ʌnɪn'fɔːmd/ *adj* ‹*person*› disinformato
uninhabitable /ˌʌnɪn'hæbɪtəbl/ *adj* inabitabile
uninhabited /ʌnɪn'hæbɪtɪd/ *adj* disabitato
uninhibited /ʌnɪn'hɪbɪtɪd/ *adj* ‹*person, attitude*› disinibito; ‹*performance, remarks*› disinvolto; **be ~ about doing something** non avere problemi a fare qualcosa
uninitiated /ʌnɪ'nɪʃɪeɪtɪd/ **A** *adj* ‹*person*› non iniziato **B** *npl* **the ~** i profani
uninjured /ʌn'ɪndʒəd/ *adj* illeso
uninspired /ʌnɪn'spaɪəd/ *adj* privo di immaginazione; ‹*performance*› piatto; ‹*times*› banale
unintelligible /ˌʌnɪn'telɪdʒəbl/ *adj* incomprensibile
unintended /ˌʌnɪn'tendɪd/ *adj* ‹*irony, consequence*› non voluto
unintentional /ʌnɪn'tenʃənl/ *adj* involontario
unintentionally /ʌnɪn'tenʃənəlɪ/ *adv* involontariamente
uninterested /ʌn'ɪntrəstɪd/ *adj* disinteressato
uninteresting /ʌn'ɪntrəstɪŋ/ *adj* poco interessante
uninvited /ʌnɪn'vaɪtɪd/ *adj* ‹*attentions*› non richiesto; **~ guest** ospite *mf* senza invito
uninviting /ˌʌnɪn'vaɪtɪŋ/ *adj* ‹*room, food*› poco invitante
⚷ **union** /'juːnɪən/ *n* unione *f*; (trade) **~** sindacato *m*
Unionist /'juːnɪənɪst/ *n* unionista *mf*
Union Jack *n* bandiera *f* del Regno Unito
⚷ **unique** /juː'niːk/ *adj* unico
uniquely /juː'niːklɪ/ *adv* unicamente
unisex /'juːnɪseks/ *adj* unisex *inv*
unison /'juːnɪsn/ *n* **in ~** all'unisono
⚷ **unit** /'juːnɪt/ *n* unità *f*; (department) reparto *m*; (of furniture) elemento *m*
unit cost *n* costo *m* unitario
unite /juː'naɪt/ **A** *vt* unire **B** *vi* unirsi
⚷ **united** /juː'naɪtɪd/ *adj* unito
United Arab Emirates *npl* **the ~** gli Emirati Arabi Uniti
United Kingdom *n* Regno *m* Unito
United Nations *n* [Organizzazione *f* delle] Nazioni Unite *fpl*
United States, United States of America *n* Stati *mpl* Uniti [d'America]
unit trust *n* Fin fondo *m* comune di investimento aperto
unity /'juːnɪtɪ/ *n* unità *f*; (agreement) accordo *m*
universal /juːnɪ'vɜːsl/ *adj* universale
universally /juːnɪ'vɜːsəlɪ/ *adv* universalmente
universe /'juːnɪvɜːs/ *n* universo *m*
⚷ **university** /juːnɪ'vɜːsətɪ/ **A** *n* università *f* **B** *attrib* universitario
unjust /ʌn'dʒʌst/ *adj* ingiusto
unjustifiable /ʌn'dʒʌstɪfaɪəbl/ *adj* ingiustificabile
unjustifiably /ʌn'dʒʌstɪfaɪəblɪ/ *adv* ‹*act*› senza giustificazione
unjustified /ʌn'dʒʌstɪfaɪd/ *adj* ‹*suspicion*› ingiustificato
unjustly /ʌn'dʒʌstlɪ/ *adv* ingiustamente
unkempt /ʌn'kempt/ *adj* trasandato; ‹*hair*› arruffato
unkind /ʌn'kaɪnd/ *adj* scortese
unkindly /ʌn'kaɪndlɪ/ *adv* in modo scortese
unkindness /ʌn'kaɪndnɪs/ *n* mancanza *f* di gentilezza
unknown /ʌn'nəʊn/ *adj* sconosciuto
unlace /ʌn'leɪs/ *vt* slacciare ‹*shoes*›
unlawful /ʌn'lɔːfʊl/ *adj* illecito, illegale
unlawfully /ʌn'lɔːfʊlɪ/ *adv* illegalmente
unleaded /ʌn'ledɪd/ *adj* senza piombo
unleaded petrol *n* benzina *f* senza piombo *o* verde
unleash /ʌn'liːʃ/ *vt* fig scatenare

unleavened /ʌn'levnd/ *adj* ‹*bread*› non lievitato

⚷ **unless** /ʌn'les/ *conj* a meno che; ~ **I am mistaken** se non mi sbaglio

unlicensed /ʌn'laɪsnst/ *adj* ‹*transmitter, activity*› abusivo; ‹*vehicle*› senza bollo; ‹*restaurant*› non autorizzato a vendere alcolici

⚷ **unlike** /ʌn'laɪk/ **A** *adj* (not the same) diversi **B** *prep* diverso da; **that's ~ him** non è da lui; ~ **me, he...** diversamente da me, lui...

⚷ **unlikely** /ʌn'laɪklɪ/ *adj* improbabile

unlimited /ʌn'lɪmɪtɪd/ *adj* illimitato

unlined /ʌn'laɪnd/ *adj* ‹*face*› senza rughe; ‹*paper*› senza righe; ‹*garment, curtain*› senza fodera

unlit /ʌn'lɪt/ *adj* ‹*cigarette, fire*› spento; ‹*room, street*› non illuminato

unload /ʌn'ləʊd/ *vt* scaricare

unlock /ʌn'lɒk/ *vt* aprire (*con chiave*); sbloccare ‹*mobile phone*›

unloved /ʌn'lʌvd/ *adj* **feel ~** ‹*person*› non sentirsi amato

unluckily /ʌn'lʌkɪlɪ/ *adv* sfortunatamente

unlucky /ʌn'lʌkɪ/ *adj* sfortunato; **it's ~ to...** porta sfortuna...

unmade /ʌn'meɪd/ *adj* ‹*bed*› sfatto

unmade-up *adj* ‹*road*› non asfaltato

unmanageable /ʌn'mænɪdʒəbl/ *adj* ‹*number, company*› difficile da gestire; ‹*hair, child, animal*› ribelle; ‹*size*› ingombrante

unmanly /ʌn'mænlɪ/ *adj* poco virile

unmanned /ʌn'mænd/ *adj* senza equipaggio

unmarked /ʌn'mɑːkt/ *adj* Sport smarcato; ‹*skin*› senza segni; ‹*container*› non contrassegnato; ~ **police car** auto *f inv*, civetta *inv*

unmarried /ʌn'mærɪd/ *adj* non sposato

unmarried mother *n* ragazza *f* madre

unmask /ʌn'mɑːsk/ *vt* fig smascherare

unmentionable /ʌn'menʃnəbl/ *adj* innominabile

unmistakable /ʌnmɪ'steɪkəbl/ *adj* inconfondibile

unmistakably /ʌnmɪ'steɪkəblɪ/ *adv* chiaramente

u

unmitigated /ʌn'mɪtɪgeɪtɪd/ *adj* assoluto

unmotivated /ʌn'məʊtɪveɪtɪd/ *adj* immotivato

unmoved /ʌn'muːvd/ *adj* fig impassibile

unnamed /ʌn'neɪmd/ *adj* (not having a name) senza nome; (name not divulged) di cui non si conosce il nome; **the as yet ~ winner...** il vincitore di cui ancora non si conosce il nome...

unnatural /ʌn'nætʃər(ə)l/ *adj* innaturale; derog anormale

⚷ parola chiave

unnaturally /ʌn'nætʃər(ə)lɪ/ *adv* in modo innaturale; derog in modo anormale

unnecessarily /ʌn'nesəs(ə)rɪlɪ/ *adv* inutilmente

unnecessary /ʌn'nesəs(ə)rɪ/ *adj* inutile

unnerve /ʌn'nɜːv/ *vt* inquietare

unnerving /ʌn'nɜːvɪŋ/ *adj* inquietante

unnoticed /ʌn'nəʊtɪst/ *adj* inosservato

unobservant /ʌnəb'zɜːvənt/ *adj* senza spirito d'osservazione

unobserved /ʌnəb'zɜːvd/ *adj* inosservato; **go ~** passare inosservato

unobstructed /ˌʌnəb'strʌktɪd/ *adj* ‹*view, path*› libero

unobtainable /ʌnəb'teɪnəbl/ *adj* ‹*product*› introvabile; ‹*phone number*› non ottenibile

unobtrusive /ʌnəb'truːsɪf/ *adj* discreto

unobtrusively /ʌnəb'truːsɪvlɪ/ *adv* in modo discreto

unoccupied /ʌn'ɒkjuːpaɪd/ *adj* ‹*house, block, shop*› vuoto; ‹*table, seat*› libero

unofficial /ʌnə'fɪʃl/ *adj* non ufficiale

unofficially /ʌnə'fɪʃ(ə)lɪ/ *adv* ufficiosamente

unopened /ʌn'əʊpənd/ *adj* ‹*bottle, packet*› chiuso; ‹*package*› ancora incartato

unorthodox /ʌn'ɔːθədɒks/ *adj* poco ortodosso

unpack /ʌn'pæk/ **A** *vi* disfare le valigie **B** *vt* svuotare ‹*parcel*›; spacchettare ‹*books*›; ~ **one's case** disfare la valigia

unpaid /ʌn'peɪd/ *adj* da pagare; (work) non retribuito

unpalatable /ʌn'pælətəbl/ *adj* sgradevole

unparalleled /ʌn'pærəleld/ *adj* senza pari

unpasteurized /ʌn'pɑːstʃəraɪzd/ *adj* non pastorizzato

unperturbed /ʌnpə'tɜːbd/ *adj* imperturbato

unpick /ʌn'pɪk/ *vt* disfare

unplanned /ʌn'plænd/ *adj* ‹*stoppage, increase*› imprevisto

unpleasant /ʌn'plezənt/ *adj* sgradevole; ‹*person*› maleducato

unpleasantly /ʌn'plezəntlɪ/ *adv* sgradevolmente; ‹*behave*› maleducatamente

unpleasantness /ʌn'plezəntnɪs/ *n* (bad feeling) tensioni *fpl*

unplug /ʌn'plʌg/ *vt* (*pt/pp* **-plugged**) staccare

unpolluted /ʌnpə'luːtɪd/ *adj* ‹*water*› non inquinato; ‹*mind*› incontaminato

unpopular /ʌn'pɒpjʊlə(r)/ *adj* impopolare

unprecedented /ʌn'presɪdentɪd/ *adj* senza precedenti

unpredictable /ʌnprɪ'dɪktəbl/ *adj* imprevedibile

unprejudiced /ʌn'predʒʊdɪst/ *adj* ‹*person*› senza pregiudizi; ‹*opinion, judgement*› imparziale

unpremeditated /ʌnpriːˈmedɪteɪtɪd/ *adj* involontario

unprepared /ʌnprɪˈpeəd/ *adj* impreparato

unprepossessing /ʌnpriːpəˈzesɪŋ/ *adj* poco attraente

unpretentious /ʌnprɪˈtenʃəs/ *adj* senza pretese

unprincipled /ʌnˈprɪnsɪpəld/ *adj* senza principi; ‹*behaviour*› scorretto

unproductive /ˌʌnprəˈdʌktɪv/ *adj* ‹*discussion, meeting*› poco produttivo

unprofessional /ʌnprəˈfeʃnl/ *adj* non professionale; **it's ~** è una mancanza di professionalità

unprofitable /ʌnˈprɒfɪtəbl/ *adj* non redditizio

unprompted /ʌnˈprɒm(p)tɪd/ *adj* ‹*offer*› spontaneo; ‹*answer*› non suggerito

unpronounceable /ʌnprəˈnaʊnsəbl/ *adj* impronunciabile

unprotected /ˌʌnprəˈtektɪd/ *adj* ‹*sex*› non protetto; ‹*person*› indifeso

unprovoked /ʌnprəˈvəʊkt/ *adj* ‹*attack, aggression*› non provocato; **the attack was ~** l'attacco è avvenuto senza provocazione

unqualified /ʌnˈkwɒlɪfaɪd/ *adj* non qualificato; fig (absolute) assoluto

unquestionable /ʌnˈkwestʃənəbl/ *adj* incontestabile

unquote /ʌnˈkwəʊt/ *vi* chiudere le virgolette

unravel /ʌnˈrævl/ *vt* (*pt/pp* **-lled**) districare; (in knitting) disfare

unreal /ʌnˈrɪəl/ *adj* irreale; infml incredibile

unrealistic /ʌnrɪəˈlɪstɪk/ *adj* ‹*character, presentation*› poco realistico; ‹*expectation, aim*› irrealistico; ‹*person*› poco realista

unreasonable /ʌnˈriːz(ə)nəbl/ *adj* irragionevole

unrecognizable /ʌnˈrekəgnaɪzəbl/ *adj* irriconoscibile

unrecorded /ʌnrɪˈkɔːdɪd/ *adj* non documentato; **go ~** non essere documentato

unrefined /ʌnrɪˈfaɪnd/ *adj* ‹*person, manners, style*› rozzo; ‹*oil*› greggio; ‹*flour, sugar*› non raffinato

unrehearsed /ʌnrɪˈhɜːst/ *adj* ‹*response, action*› imprevisto; ‹*speech*› improvvisato

unrelated /ʌnrɪˈleɪtɪd/ *adj* ‹*facts*› senza rapporto (**to** con); ‹*person*› non imparentato (**to** con)

unrelenting /ʌnrɪˈlentɪŋ/ *adj* ‹*person*› ostinato; ‹*stare*› insistente; ‹*pursuit*› continuo; ‹*heat, zeal*› costante

unreliable /ʌnrɪˈlaɪəbl/ *adj* inattendibile; ‹*person*› inaffidabile, che non dà affidamento

unremitting /ʌnrɪˈmɪtɪŋ/ *adj* costante; ‹*struggle*› continuo

unrepeatable /ʌnrɪˈpiːtəbl/ *adj* ‹*offer, bargain*› unico; **his comment was ~** il commento che ha fatto è irripetibile

unrepentant /ʌnrɪˈpentənt/ *adj* irriducibile; ‹*sinner*› impenitente

unrequited /ʌnrɪˈkwaɪtɪd/ *adj* non corrisposto

unreservedly /ʌnrɪˈzɜːvɪdlɪ/ *adv* senza riserve; (frankly) francamente

unresolved /ʌnrɪˈzɒlvd/ *adj* irrisolto

unrest /ʌnˈrest/ *n* fermenti *mpl*

unrestricted /ˌʌnrɪˈstrɪktɪd/ *adj* ‹*access, view*› libero

unrewarding /ˌʌnrɪˈwɔːdɪŋ/ *adj* ‹*job*› poco gratificante

unripe /ʌnˈraɪp/ *adj* ‹*fruit*› acerbo; ‹*wheat*› non maturo

unrivalled /ʌnˈraɪvəld/ *adj* ineguagliato

unroll /ʌnˈrəʊl/ **A** *vt* srotolare **B** *vi* srotolarsi

unruffled /ʌnˈrʌfld/ *adj* ‹*person*› imperturbato; ‹*hair*› a posto; ‹*water*› non mosso; **be ~** ‹*person*› rimanere imperturbato; ‹*person, hair*› essere a posto

unruly /ʌnˈruːlɪ/ *adj* indisciplinato

unsafe /ʌnˈseɪf/ *adj* pericoloso

unsaid /ʌnˈsed/ *adj* inespresso

unsalaried /ʌnˈsælərɪd/ *adj* ‹*post*› non stipendiato

unsalted /ʌnˈsɔːltɪd/ *adj* non salato

unsatisfactory /ʌnsætɪsˈfækt(ə)rɪ/ *adj* poco soddisfacente

unsatisfied /ʌnˈsætɪsfaɪd/ *adj* ‹*person, need*› insoddisfatto

unsatisfying /ʌnˈsætɪsfaɪɪŋ/ *adj* poco soddisfacente

unsavoury /ʌnˈseɪvərɪ/ *adj* equivoco

unscathed /ʌnˈskeɪðd/ *adj* illeso

unscheduled /ʌnˈʃedjuːld/ *adj* ‹*flight*› supplementare; ‹*appearance, speech*› fuori programma; ‹*stop*› non programmato

unscramble /ʌnˈskræmbl/ *vt* decifrare ‹*code, words*›; sbrogliare ‹*ideas, thoughts*›

unscrew /ʌnˈskruː/ *vt* svitare

unscrupulous /ʌnˈskruːpjʊləs/ *adj* senza scrupoli

unseasoned /ʌnˈsiːznd/ *adj* ‹*wood*› non stagionato; ‹*food*› scondito

unseat /ʌnˈsiːt/ *vt* disarcionare ‹*rider*›

unseemly /ʌnˈsiːmlɪ/ *adj* indecoroso

unseen /ʌnˈsiːn/ *adv* ‹*escape, slip away*› senza essere visto

unselfconscious /ˌʌnselfˈkɒnʃəs/ *adj* naturale

unselfish /ʌnˈselfɪʃ/ *adj* disinteressato

unsentimental /ˌʌnsentɪˈmentl/ *adj* poco sentimentale

unsettled /ʌnˈsetld/ *adj* in agitazione; ‹*weather*› variabile; ‹*bill*› non saldato

unsettling /ʌnˈsetlɪŋ/ *adj* ‹*experience, novel*› inquietante

unshakeable /ʌnˈʃeɪkəbl/ *adj* categorico

unshaken /ʌn'ʃeɪkən/ *adj ‹belief›* saldo

unshaven /ʌn'ʃeɪvn/ *adj* non rasato

unsightly /ʌn'saɪtlɪ/ *adj* brutto

unsinkable /ʌn'sɪŋkəbl/ *adj ‹ship, object›* inaffondabile; hum *‹personality›* che non si deprime

unskilled /ʌn'skɪld/ *adj* non specializzato

unskilled worker *n* manovale *m*

unsmiling /ʌn'smaɪlɪŋ/ *adj ‹person›* serio

unsociable /ʌn'səʊʃəbl/ *adj* scontroso

unsocial hours *npl* **to work ~** lavorare al di fuori degli orari standard

unsolicited /ʌnsə'lɪsɪtɪd/ *adj ‹help, advice›* non richiesto; *‹job application›* spontaneo

unsophisticated /ʌnsə'fɪstɪkeɪtɪd/ *adj* semplice

unsound /ʌn'saʊnd/ *adj ‹building, reasoning›* poco solido; *‹advice›* poco sensato; **of ~ mind** malato di mente

unspeakable /ʌn'spi:kəbl/ *adj* indicibile

unspoiled /ʌn'spɔɪld/ *adj ‹town›* non deturpato; *‹landscape›* intatto; **she was ~ by fame** la fama non l'ha cambiata

unspoken /ʌn'spəʊkən/ *adj* (implicit) tacito

unstable /ʌn'steɪbl/ *adj* instabile; (mentally) squilibrato

unsteadily /ʌn'stedɪlɪ/ *adv ‹walk, speak›* in modo malsicuro

unsteady /ʌn'stedɪ/ *adj* malsicuro

unstoppable /ʌn'stɒpəbl/ *adj ‹force, momentum›* inarrestabile

unstressed /ʌn'strest/ *adj ‹vowel, word›* atono

unstuck /ʌn'stʌk/ *adj* **come ~** staccarsi; infml (project) andare a monte

unsubscribe /ˌʌnsəb'skraɪb/ *vi* cancellare l'iscrizione (**from** a)

unsubstantiated /ˌʌnsəb'stænʃɪeɪtɪd/ *adj ‹report›* non corroborato

unsuccessful /ʌnsək'sesfʊl/ *adj* fallimentare; **be ~** (in attempt) non aver successo

unsuccessfully /ʌnsək'sesfʊlɪ/ *adv* senza successo

unsuitable /ʌn'su:təbl/ *adj* (inappropriate) inadatto; (inconvenient) inopportuno

unsupervised /ʌn'su:pəvaɪzd/ *adj ‹activity›* non controllato

unsure /ʌn'ʃɔ:(r), AmE -'ʃʊər/ *adj* incerto; **be ~ about** non essere sicuro di; **~ of oneself** essere insicuro

unsuspecting /ʌnsə'spektɪŋ/ *adj* fiducioso

unsweetened /ʌn'swi:tənd/ *adj* senza zucchero

unsympathetic /ʌnsɪmpə'θetɪk/ *adj ‹person, attitude, manner, tone›* poco comprensivo; *‹person, character›* antipatico; **she is ~ to the cause** non appoggia la causa

untamed /ʌn'teɪmd/ *adj ‹lion›* non addomesticato; *‹passion, person›* indomito

untangle /ʌn'tæŋgl/ *vt* sbrogliare *‹threads›*; risolvere *‹difficulties, mystery›*

untaxed /ʌn'tækst/ *adj ‹goods›* non tassato; *‹income›* esente da imposte

untenable /ʌn'tenəbl/ *adj ‹position, argument›* insostenibile

unthinkable /ʌn'θɪŋkəbl/ *adj* impensabile

unthought of /ʌn'θɔ:təv/ *adj* impensato; **hitherto ~** finora impensato

untidily /ʌn'taɪdɪlɪ/ *adv* disordinatamente

untidiness /ʌn'taɪdɪnɪs/ *n* disordine *m*

untidy /ʌn'taɪdɪ/ *adj* disordinato

untie /ʌn'taɪ/ *vt* slegare

⚷ **until** /ʌn'tɪl/ **A** *prep* fino a; **not ~** non prima di; **~ the evening** fino alla sera; **~ his arrival** fino al suo arrivo
B *conj* finché, fino a quando; **not ~ you've seen it** non prima che tu l'abbia visto

untimely /ʌn'taɪmlɪ/ *adj* inopportuno; (premature) prematuro

untiring /ʌn'taɪərɪŋ/ *adj* instancabile

untold /ʌn'təʊld/ *adj ‹wealth›* incalcolabile; *‹suffering›* indescrivibile; *‹story›* inedito

untouched /ʌn'tʌtʃt/ *adj* (unchanged, undisturbed) intatto; (unscathed) incolume; (unaffected) non toccato; **leave one's dinner/a meal ~** non toccare cibo

untoward /ʌntə'wɔ:d/ *adj* **if nothing ~ happens** se non capita un imprevisto

untrained /ʌn'treɪnd/ *adj ‹voice›* non impostato; *‹eye, artist, actor›* inesperto; **be ~** *‹worker›* non avere una formazione professionale

untranslatable /ʌntrænz'leɪtəbl/ *adj* intraducibile

untreated /ʌn'tri:tɪd/ *adj ‹sewage, water›* non depurato; *‹illness›* non curato

untroubled /ʌn'trʌbld/ *adj ‹sleep›* tranquillo

untrue /ʌn'tru:/ *adj* falso; **that's ~** non è vero

untrustworthy /ʌn'trʌstwɜ:ðɪ/ *adj ‹person›* inaffidabile

unused¹ /ʌn'ju:zd/ *adj* non usato

unused² /ʌn'ju:st/ *adj* **be ~ to** non essere abituato a

unusual /ʌn'ju:ʒʊəl/ *adj* insolito

unusually /ʌn'ju:ʒʊəlɪ/ *adv* insolitamente

unveil /ʌn'veɪl/ *vt* scoprire

unversed /ʌn'vɜ:st/ *adj* inesperto (**in** di)

unwanted /ʌn'wɒntɪd/ *adj ‹child, pet, visitor›* indesiderato; *‹goods, produce›* che non serve; **feel ~** sentirsi respinto

unwarranted /ʌn'wɒrəntɪd/ *adj* ingiustificato

unwelcome /ʌn'welkəm/ *adj* sgradito

unwell /ʌn'wel/ *adj* indisposto

unwieldy /ʌn'wi:ldɪ/ *adj* ingombrante

unwilling /ʌn'wɪlɪŋ/ *adj* riluttante

⚷ parola chiave

u

unwillingly /ʌnˈwɪlɪŋlɪ/ *adv* malvolentieri

unwillingness /ʌnˈwɪlɪŋnɪs/ *n* riluttanza *f*

unwind /ʌnˈwaʊnd/ **A** *vt* (*pt/pp* **unwound**) svolgere, srotolare
B *vi* svolgersi, srotolarsi; infml (relax) rilassarsi

unwise /ʌnˈwaɪz/ *adj* imprudente

unwisely /ʌnˈwaɪzlɪ/ *adv* imprudentemente

unwitting /ʌnˈwɪtɪŋ/ *adj* involontario; ‹*victim*› inconsapevole

unwittingly /ʌnˈwɪtɪŋlɪ/ *adv* involontariamente

unworldly /ʌnˈwɜːldlɪ/ *adj* (not materialistic) poco materialista; (naive) ingenuo; (spiritual) non materialista

unworthy /ʌnˈwɜːðɪ/ *adj* non degno

unwrap /ʌnˈræp/ *vt* (*pt/pp* **-wrapped**) scartare ‹*present, parcel*›

unwritten /ʌnˈrɪtn/ *adj* tacito

unyielding /ʌnˈjiːldɪŋ/ *adj* rigido

unzip /ʌnˈzɪp/ *vt* aprire [la cerniera di] ‹*garment, bag*›

up /ʌp/ **A** *adv* su; (not in bed) alzato; ‹*road*› smantellato; ‹*theatre curtain, blinds*› alzato; ‹*shelves, tent*› montato; ‹*notice*› affisso; ‹*building*› costruito; **prices are up** i prezzi sono aumentati; **be up for sale** essere in vendita; **up here/there** quassù/lassù; **time's up** tempo scaduto; **what's up?** infml cosa è successo?; **up to** (as far as) fino a; **be up to** essere all'altezza di ‹*task*›; **what's he up to?** infml cosa sta facendo?; (plotting) cosa sta combinando?; **I'm up to page 100** sono arrivato a pagina 100; **feel up to it** sentirsela; **be one up on somebody** infml essere in vantaggio su qualcuno; **go up** salire; **lift up** alzare; **up against** fig alle prese con
B *prep* su; **the cat ran/is up the tree** il gatto è salito di corsa/è sull'albero; **further up this road** più avanti su questa strada; **row up the river** risalire il fiume; **go up the stairs** salire su per le scale; **be up the pub** infml essere al pub; **be up on** *or* **in something** essere bene informato su qualcosa
C *npl* **ups and downs** alti *mpl* e bassi

up-and-coming *adj* promettente

upbeat /ˈʌpbiːt/ *adj* ottimistico

upbringing /ˈʌpbrɪŋɪŋ/ *n* educazione *f*

update /ʌpˈdeɪt/ *vt* aggiornare

upfront /ʌpˈfrʌnt/ **A** *adj* infml (frank) aperto; ‹*money*› anticipato
B *adv* ‹*pay*› in anticipo

upgrade /ʌpˈgreɪd/ **A** *vt* promuovere ‹*person*›; modernizzare ‹*equipment*›
B *n* aggiornamento *m*

upheaval /ʌpˈhiːvl/ *n* scompiglio *m*

uphill /ʌpˈhɪl/ **A** *adj* in salita; fig arduo
B *adv* in salita

uphold /ʌpˈhəʊld/ *vt* (*pt/pp* **upheld**) sostenere ‹*principle*›; confermare ‹*verdict*›

upholster /ʌpˈhəʊlstə(r)/ *vt* tappezzare

upholsterer /ʌpˈhəʊlstərə(r)/ *n* tappezziere, -a *mf*

upholstery /ʌpˈhəʊlstərɪ/ *n* tappezzeria *f*

upkeep /ˈʌpkiːp/ *n* mantenimento *m*

uplifting /ʌpˈlɪftɪŋ/ *adj* (morally) edificante

upload /ˈʌpləʊd/ *vt* Comput fare l'upload di

up-market *adj* di qualità

upon /əˈpɒn/ *prep* su; **~ arriving home** una volta arrivato a casa

upper /ˈʌpə(r)/ **A** *adj* superiore
B *n* (of shoe) tomaia *f*

upper-case *adj* maiuscolo

upper circle *n* seconda galleria *f*

upper class *n* alta borghesia *f*

upper crust *adj* hum aristocratico

upper hand *n* **have the ~** avere il sopravvento

upper middle class *n* ceto *m* medio-alto

uppermost /ˈʌpəməʊst/ *adj* più alto; **that's ~ in my mind** è la mia preoccupazione principale

upright /ˈʌpraɪt/ **A** *adj* dritto; ‹*piano*› verticale; (honest) retto
B *n* montante *m*

upright freezer *n* freezer *m inv* verticale

uprising /ˈʌpraɪzɪŋ/ *n* rivolta *f*

upriver /ʌpˈrɪvə(r)/ *adv* ‹*lie*› a monte; ‹*sail*› controcorrente

uproar /ˈʌprɔː(r)/ *n* tumulto *m*; **be in an ~** essere in trambusto

uproot /ʌpˈruːt/ *vt* sradicare

upset[1] /ʌpˈset/ *vt* (*pt/pp* **upset**, *pres p* **upsetting**) rovesciare; sconvolgere ‹*plan*›; (distress) turbare; **get ~ about something** prendersela per qualcosa; **be very ~** essere sconvolto; **have an ~ stomach** avere l'intestino disturbato

upset[2] /ˈʌpset/ *n* scombussolamento *m*

upsetting /ˌʌpˈsetɪŋ/ *adj* (distressing) sconvolgente; (annoying) fastidioso

upshot /ˈʌpʃɒt/ *n* risultato *m*

upside down *adv* sottosopra; **turn ~** capovolgere

upstage /ʌpˈsteɪdʒ/ **A** *vt* Theat fig distogliere l'attenzione del pubblico da
B *adv* Theat ‹*stand*› al fondo del palcoscenico; ‹*move*› verso il fondo del palcoscenico

upstairs[1] /ʌpˈsteəz/ *adv* [al piano] di sopra

upstairs[2] /ˈʌpsteəz/ *adj* del piano superiore

upstart /ˈʌpstɑːt/ *n* arrivato, -a *mf*

upstream /ʌpˈstriːm/ *adv* controcorrente

upsurge /ˈʌpsɜːdʒ/ *n* (in sales) aumento *m* improvviso; (of enthusiasm, crime) ondata *f*

uptake /ˈʌpteɪk/ *n* **be slow on the ~** essere lento nel capire; **be quick on the ~** capire le cose al volo

uptight /ʌpˈtaɪt/ *adj* teso

up-to-date *adj* moderno; ‹*news*› ultimo; ‹*person, information, records*› aggiornato

up-to-the-minute *adj* ‹*information*› dell'ultimo minuto

uptown /ˈʌptaʊn/ *adj* AmE (smart) dei quartieri alti

upturn /ˈʌptɜːn/ *n* ripresa *f*

upward /ˈʌpwəd/ **A** *adj* verso l'alto, in su; **~ slope** salita *f*
B *adv* **~[s]** verso l'alto; **~s of** oltre

upwardly mobile /ʌpwədlɪˈməʊbaɪl/ *adj* che sale nella scala sociale

uranium /jʊˈreɪnɪəm/ *n* uranio *m*

Uranus /ˈjʊərənəs, jʊˈreɪnəs/ *n* Urano *m*

🔑 **urban** /ˈɜːbən/ *adj* urbano

urban blight, **urban decay** *n* degrado *m* urbano

urbane /ɜːˈbeɪn/ *adj* cortese

urban myth leggenda *f* metropolitana

urban planning *n* urbanistica *f*

urchin /ˈɜːtʃɪn/ *n* riccio *m* di mare

Urdu /ˈʊədu:/ *n* urdu *m*

🔑 **urge** /ɜːdʒ/ **A** *n* forte desiderio *m*
B *vt* esortare (**to** a)
▪ **urge on** *vt* spronare

urgency /ˈɜːdʒənsɪ/ *n* urgenza *f*

urgent /ˈɜːdʒənt/ *adj* urgente

urgently /ˈɜːdʒəntlɪ/ *adv* urgentemente

urinal /jʊˈraɪnl/ *n* (fixture) orinale *m*; (place) vespasiano *m*

urinate /ˈjʊərɪneɪt/ *vi* urinare

urine /ˈjʊərɪn/ *n* urina *f*

URL *abbr* (**Unified Resource Locator**) URL *m*

urn /ɜːn/ *n* urna *f*; (for tea) *contenitore* (*m*) *munito di rubinetto che si trova nei self-service, mense ecc.*

Uruguay /ˈjʊərəgwaɪ/ *n* Uruguay *m*

🔑 **us** /ʌs/ *pers pron* ci; (after prep) noi; **they know us** ci conoscono; **give us the money** dateci i soldi; **give it to us** datecelo; **they showed it to us** ce l'hanno fatto vedere; **they meant us, not you** intendevano noi, non voi; **it's us** siamo noi; **she hates us** ci odia

US *n abbr* (**United States**) U.S.A. *mpl*

USA *n abbr* (**United States of America**) U.S.A. *mpl*

usable /ˈju:zəbl/ *adj* usabile

usage /ˈju:sɪdʒ/ *n* uso *m*

USB key /ju:esˈbi:ki:/ *n* chiavetta *f* USB

🔑 **use¹** /ju:s/ *n* uso *m*; **be of ~** essere utile; **be of no ~** essere inutile; **make ~ of** usare; (exploit) sfruttare; **it is no ~** è inutile; **what's the ~?** a che scopo?

🔑 **use²** /ju:z/ *vt* usare
▪ **use up** *vt* consumare

used¹ /ju:zd/ *adj* usato

used² /ju:st/ *pt* **be ~ to something** essere abituato a qualcosa; **get ~ to** abituarsi a; **he ~ to say** diceva; **he ~ to live here** viveva qui

🔑 **useful** /ˈju:sfl/ *adj* utile

usefulness /ˈju:sflnɪs/ *n* utilità *f*

useless /ˈju:slɪs/ *adj* inutile; infml ‹*person*› incapace; **you're ~!** sei un idiota!

🔑 **user** /ˈju:zə(r)/ *n* utente *mf*

user-friendliness *n* facilità *f* d'uso

user-friendly *adj* facile da usare

user group *n* Comput gruppo *m* di utenti

user manual *n* manuale *m* d'uso

username *n* nome *m* utente

usher /ˈʌʃə(r)/ *n* Theat maschera *f*; Jur usciere *m*; (at wedding) *persona* (*f*) *che accompagna gli invitati ad un matrimonio ai loro posti in chiesa*
▪ **usher in** *vt* fare entrare ‹*person*›; inaugurare ‹*new age*›

usherette /ʌʃəˈret/ *n* maschera *f*

USS *abbr* AmE (**United States Ship**) nave *f* da guerra americana

USSR *n* URSS *f*

🔑 **usual** /ˈju:ʒʊəl/ *adj* usuale; **as ~** come al solito

🔑 **usually** /ˈju:ʒʊəlɪ/ *adv* di solito

usurp /jʊˈzɜːp/ *vt* usurpare

usurper /jʊˈzɜːpə(r)/ *n* usurpatore, -trice *mf*

utensil /jʊˈtensl/ *n* utensile *m*

uterus /ˈju:tərəs/ *n* utero *m*

utilitarian /jʊtɪlɪˈteərɪən/ *adj* funzionale

utility /jʊˈtɪlətɪ/ *n* utilità *f*; (public) servizio *m*

utility bill *n* bolletta *f*

utility company *n* servizio *m* pubblico

utility program *n* Comput [programma *m* di] utility *f*

utility room *n stanza* (*f*) *in casa privata per il lavaggio, la stiratura dei panni ecc.*

utilize /ˈju:tɪlaɪz/ *vt* utilizzare

utmost /ˈʌtməʊst/ **A** *adj* estremo
B *n* **one's ~** tutto il possibile

Utopia /ju:ˈtəʊpɪə/ *n* utopia *f*

Utopian /ju:ˈtəʊpɪən/ **A** *n* utopista *mf*
B *adj* utopistico

utter¹ /ˈʌtə(r)/ *adj* totale

utter² *vt* emettere ‹*sigh, sound*›; proferire ‹*word*›

utterance /ˈʌtərəns/ *n* dichiarazione *f*

utterly /ˈʌtəlɪ/ *adv* completamente

U-turn *n* Auto inversione *f* a U; fig marcia *f* indietro

UV *abbr* (**ultraviolet**) UVA *mpl*

Uzbekistan /ʌzbekɪˈstɑːn/ *n* Uzbekistan *m*

U

🔑 parola chiave

Vv

v¹, **V** /viː/ *n* (letter) v, V *f inv*
v² *abbr* **1** (**versus**) contro **2** (**volt**) V *m*
vac /væk/ *n abbr* BrE (**vacation**) vacanze *fpl*
vacancy /ˈveɪk(ə)nsɪ/ *n* (job) posto *m* vacante; (room) stanza *f* disponibile
vacant /ˈveɪknt/ *adj* libero; ‹*position*› vacante; ‹*look*› assente
vacant possession *n* BrE Jur bene *m* immobile libero
vacate /vəˈkeɪt/ *vt* lasciare libero
vacation /vəˈkeɪʃn/ *n* Univ & Am vacanza *f*
vacationer /vəˈkeɪʃənə(r), AmE veɪ-/ *n* AmE vacanziere, -a *mf*
vaccinate /ˈvæksɪneɪt/ *vt* vaccinare
vaccination /væksɪˈneɪʃn/ *n* vaccinazione *f*
vaccine /ˈvæksiːn/ *n* vaccino *m*
vacillate /ˈvæsɪleɪt/ *vi* tentennare
vacuous /ˈvækjʊəs/ *adj* ‹*person, look, expression*› vacuo; ‹*person*› superficiale
vacuum /ˈvækjʊəm/ **A** *n* vuoto
B *vt* passare l'aspirapolvere in/su
vacuum cleaner *n* aspirapolvere *m inv*
vacuum flask *n* thermos *m inv*
vacuum-pack *vt* confezionare sotto vuoto ‹*food*›
vacuum-packed *adj* confezionato sottovuoto
vagabond /ˈvægəbɒnd/ *n* vagabondo, -a *mf*
vagaries /ˈveɪgərɪz/ *npl* capricci *mpl*
vagina /vəˈdʒaɪnə/ *n* Anat vagina *f*
vagrancy /ˈveɪgrənsɪ/ *n* Jur vagabondaggio *m*
vagrant /ˈveɪgrənt/ *n* vagabondo, -a *mf*
vague /veɪg/ *adj* vago; ‹*outline*› impreciso; (absent-minded) distratto; **I'm still ~ about it** non ho ancora le idee chiare in proposito
vaguely /ˈveɪglɪ/ *adv* vagamente
vagueness /ˈveɪgnɪs/ *n* (imprecision) vaghezza *f*; (of wording, proposals) indeterminatezza *f*; (of image) nebulosità *f*; (of thinking) imprecisione *f*
vain /veɪn/ *adj* vanitoso; ‹*hope, attempt*› vano; **in ~** invano
vainly /ˈveɪnlɪ/ *adv* vanamente
valance /ˈvæləns/ *n* (above curtains) mantovana *f*; (on bed base) balza *f*
vale /veɪl/ *n* literary valle *f*
valentine /ˈvæləntaɪn/ *n* (card) biglietto *m* di San Valentino
Valentine's Day *n* giorno *m* di San Valentino
valet /ˈvæleɪ/ *n* servitore *m* personale
valet parking *n servizio (m) di parcheggio per clienti di alberghi e ristoranti*
valiant /ˈvælɪənt/ *adj* valoroso
valiantly /ˈvælɪəntlɪ/ *adv* coraggiosamente
valid /ˈvælɪd/ *adj* valido
validate /ˈvælɪdeɪt/ *vt* (confirm) convalidare
validity /vəˈlɪdətɪ/ *n* validità *f*
valley /ˈvælɪ/ *n* valle *f*
valour /ˈvælə(r)/ *n* valore *m*
valuable /ˈvæljʊəbl/ *adj* di valore; fig prezioso
valuables /ˈvæljʊəblz/ *npl* oggetti *mpl* di valore
valuation /væljʊˈeɪʃn/ *n* valutazione *f*
value /ˈvæljuː/ **A** *n* valore *m*; (usefulness) utilità *f*
B *vt* valutare; (cherish) apprezzare
value added tax /ˈædɪd/ *n* imposta *f* sul valore aggiunto
valued /ˈvæljuːd/ *adj* (appreciated) apprezzato
valuer /ˈvæljʊə(r)/ *n* stimatore, -trice *mf*
valve /vælv/ *n* valvola *f*
vamp /væmp/ *n* vamp *f inv*
vampire /ˈvæmpaɪə(r)/ *n* vampiro *m*
van /væn/ *n* furgone *m*
vandal /ˈvændl/ *n* vandalo, -a *mf*
vandalism /ˈvænd(ə)lɪzm/ *n* vandalismo *m*
vandalize /ˈvænd(ə)laɪz/ *vt* vandalizzare
vane /veɪn/ *n* banderuola *f*
vanguard /ˈvængɑːd/ *n* avanguardia *f*; **in the ~** all'avanguardia
vanilla /vəˈnɪlə/ *n* vaniglia *f*
vanish /ˈvænɪʃ/ *vi* svanire
vanishing cream *n* crema *f* base per il trucco
vanishing point *n* punto *m* di fuga
vanishing trick *n trucco (m) da illusionista per far sparire un oggetto*; **he's done his ~ again** infml è sparito come al solito
vanity /ˈvænɪtɪ/ *n* vanità *f*
vanity bag, **vanity case** *n* beauty-case *m inv*
vanity mirror *n* Auto specchietto *m* di cortesia
vanquish /ˈvæŋkwɪʃ/ *vt* sconfiggere ‹*enemy*›
vantage point /ˈvɑːntɪdʒ/ *n* punto *m* d'osservazione; fig punto *m* di vista
vaporize /ˈveɪpəraɪz/ *vt* vaporizzare ‹*liquid*›
vaporizer /ˈveɪpəraɪzə(r)/ *n* apparecchio *m* per aerosol
vapour /ˈveɪpə(r)/ *n* vapore *m*

vapour trail *n* scia *f*
variable /ˈveərɪəbl/ *adj* variabile; (adjustable) regolabile
variance /ˈveərɪəns/ *n* **be at ~** essere in disaccordo
variant /ˈveərɪənt/ *n* variante *f*
🔑 **variation** /veərɪˈeɪʃn/ *n* variazione *f*
varicose /ˈværɪkəʊs/ *adj* **~ veins** vene *fpl* varicose
varied /ˈveərɪd/ *adj* vario; ‹*diet*› diversificato; ‹*life*› movimentato
variegated /ˈveərɪəgeɪtɪd/ *adj* variegato
🔑 **variety** /vəˈraɪətɪ/ *n* varietà *f*
variety show *n* spettacolo *m* di varietà
varifocal /ˌveərɪˈfəʊkl/ *adj* ‹*lens*› multifocale
varifocals /veərɪˈfəʊklz/ *npl* (glasses) occhiali *mpl* multifocali
🔑 **various** /ˈveərɪəs/ *adj* vario
variously /ˈveərɪəslɪ/ *adv* variamente
varnish /ˈvɑːnɪʃ/ **A** *n* vernice *f*; (for nails) smalto *m*
B *vt* verniciare; **~ one's nails** mettersi lo smalto
🔑 **vary** /ˈveərɪ/ *vt & vi* (*pt/pp* **-ied**) variare
varying /ˈveərɪɪŋ/ *adj* variabile; (different) diverso
vascular /ˈvæskjʊlə(r)/ *adj* Anat, Bot vascolare
vase /vɑːz/ *n* vaso *m*
vasectomy /vəˈsektəmɪ/ *n* vasectomia *f*
🔑 **vast** /vɑːst/ *adj* vasto; ‹*difference, amusement*› enorme
vastly /ˈvɑːstlɪ/ *adv* ‹*superior*› di gran lunga; ‹*different, amused*› enormemente
vat /væt/ *n* tino *m*
VAT /viːeɪˈtiː, væt/ *abbr* (**value added tax**) I.V.A. *f*
Vatican /ˈvætɪkən/ *n* **the ~** il Vaticano; **~ City** la città del Vaticano
vaudeville /ˈvɔːdəvɪl/ *n* Theat varietà *m*
vault¹ /vɔːlt/ *n* (roof) volta *f*; (in bank) caveau *m inv*; (tomb) cripta *f*
vault² **A** *n* salto *m*
B *vt & vi* **~ [over]** saltare
VCR *abbr* (**video cassette recorder**) VCR *m*
VD *abbr* (**venereal disease**) malattia *f* venerea
VDU *abbr* (**visual display unit**) VDU *m*
veal /viːl/ **A** *n* carne *f* di vitello
B *attrib* di vitello
vector /ˈvektə(r)/ *n* Biol, Math vettore *m*; Aeron rotta *f*
veer /vɪə(r)/ *vi* cambiare direzione; Naut, Auto virare
vegan /ˈviːgn/ **A** *n* vegetaliano, -a *mf*
B *adj* vegetaliano
veganism /ˈviːgənɪzəm/ *n* vegetalismo *m*

🔑 parola chiave

Vegeburger® /ˈvedʒɪbɜːgə(r)/ *n* = **veggie burger**
vegetable /ˈvedʒtəbl/ **A** *n* (food) verdura *f*; (when growing) ortaggio *m*
B *attrib* ‹*oil, fat*› vegetale
vegetarian /vedʒɪˈteərɪən/ *adj & n* vegetariano, -a *mf*
vegetarianism /ˌvedʒɪˈteərɪənɪzəm/ *n* vegetarianismo *m*
vegetate /ˈvedʒɪteɪt/ *vi* vegetare
vegetation /vedʒɪˈteɪʃn/ *n* vegetazione *f*
veggie burger *n* hamburger *m inv* vegetariano
vehemence /ˈviːəməns/ *n* veemenza *f*
vehement /ˈviːəmənt/ *adj* veemente
vehemently /ˈviːəməntlɪ/ *adv* con veemenza
🔑 **vehicle** /ˈviːɪkl/ *n* veicolo *m*; fig (medium) mezzo *m*
vehicular /vɪˈhɪkjʊlə(r)/ *adj* **no ~ access, no ~ traffic** circolazione vietata
veil /veɪl/ **A** *n* velo *m*
B *vt* velare
veiled /veɪld/ *adj* ‹*woman*› velato, col velo; ‹*threat*› velato
vein /veɪn/ *n* vena *f*; (mood) umore *m*; (manner) tenore *m*
veined /veɪnd/ *adj* venato
Velcro® /ˈvelkrəʊ/ *n* **~ fastening** chiusura *f* con velcro®
vellum /ˈveləm/ *n* pergamena *f*
velocity /vɪˈlɒsətɪ/ *n* velocità *f*
velvet /ˈvelvɪt/ *n* velluto *m*
velvety /ˈvelvətɪ/ *adj* vellutato
venal /ˈviːnl/ *adj* venale
vendetta /venˈdetə/ *n* vendetta *f*
vending machine /ˈvendɪŋ/ *n* distributore *m* automatico
vendor /ˈvendə(r)/ *n* venditore, -trice *mf*
veneer /vəˈnɪə(r)/ *n* impiallacciatura *f*; fig vernice *f*
veneered /vəˈnɪərd/ *adj* impiallacciato
venerable /ˈvenərəbl/ *adj* venerabile
veneration /venəˈreɪʃn/ *n* venerazione *f*
venereal /vɪˈnɪərɪəl/ *adj* **~ disease** malattia *f* venerea
Venetian /vəˈniːʃn/ *adj & n* veneziano, -a *mf*
Venetian blind *n* persiana *f* alla veneziana
Venezuela /venɪzˈweɪlə/ *n* Venezuela *m*
Venezuelan /venɪzˈweɪlən/ (a & n) venezuelano, -a *mf*
vengeance /ˈvendʒəns/ *n* vendetta *f*; **with a ~** infml a più non posso
Venice /ˈvenɪs/ *n* Venezia *f*
venison /ˈvenɪsn/ *n* Culin carne *f* di cervo
venom /ˈvenəm/ *n* veleno *m*
venomous /ˈvenəməs/ *adj* velenoso
vent¹ /vent/ **A** *n* presa *f* d'aria; **give ~ to** fig dar libero sfogo a
B *vt* fig sfogare ‹*anger*›

vent² *n* (in jacket) spacco *m*
ventilate /'ventɪleɪt/ *vt* ventilare
ventilation /ventɪ'leɪʃn/ *n* ventilazione *f*; (installation) sistema *m* di ventilazione
ventilator /'ventɪleɪtə(r)/ *n* ventilatore *m*
ventriloquist /ven'trɪləkwɪst/ *n* ventriloquo, -a *mf*
venture /'ventʃə(r)/ **A** *n* impresa *f*
B *vt* azzardare
C *vi* avventurarsi
venture capital *n* capitale *m* a rischio
venue /'venju:/ *n* luogo *m* (*di convegno, concerto ecc.*)
Venus /'vi:nəs/ *n* Venere *f*
veracity /və'ræsətɪ/ *n* veridicità *f*
veranda /və'rændə/ *n* veranda *f*
verb /vɜ:b/ *n* verbo *m*
verbal /'vɜ:bl/ *adj* verbale
verbally /'vɜ:b(ə)lɪ/ *adv* verbalmente
verbatim /vɜ:'beɪtɪm/ **A** *adj* letterale
B *adv* parola per parola
verbose /vɜ:'bəʊs/ *adj* prolisso
verdict /'vɜ:dɪkt/ *n* verdetto *m*; (opinion) parere *m*
verdigris /'vɜ:dɪgri:/ *n* verderame *m*
verge /vɜ:dʒ/ *n* orlo *m*; **be on the ~ of doing something** essere sul punto di fare qualcosa
verge on *vt* fig rasentare
verger /'vɜ:dʒə(r)/ *n* sagrestano *m*
verification /verɪfɪ'keɪʃn/ *n* verifica *f*
verify /'verɪfaɪ/ *vt* (*pt/pp* **-ied**) verificare; (confirm) confermare
veritable /'verɪtəbl/ *adj* vero
vermicelli /vɜ:mɪ'tʃelɪ/ *n* (pasta) capelli *mpl* d'angelo; (chocolate) pezzettini *mpl* di cioccolato per decorazione
vermilion /və'məljɪn/ **A** *n* rosso *m* vermiglio
B *adj* vermiglio
vermin /'vɜ:mɪn/ *n* animali *mpl* nocivi
vermouth /'vɜ:məθ/ *n* vermut *m inv*
vernacular /vɜ:'nækjʊlə(r)/ *n* vernacolo *m*
verruca /və'ru:kə/ *n* verruca *f*
versatile /'vɜ:sətaɪl/ *adj* versatile
versatility /vɜ:sə'tɪlətə/ *n* versatilità *f*
verse /vɜ:s/ *n* verso *m*; (of Bible) versetto *m*; (poetry) versi *mpl*
versed /vɜ:st/ *adj* **~ in** versato in
versifier /'vɜ:sɪfaɪə(r)/ *n* derog versificatore, -trice *mf*
version /'vɜ:ʃn/ *n* versione *f*; (translation) traduzione *f*
versus /'vɜ:səs/ *prep* contro
vertebra /'vɜ:tɪbrə/ *n* (*pl* **-brae** /-bri:/) Anat vertebra *f*
vertebrate /'vɜ:tɪbrət/ **A** *n* vertebrato *m*
B *adj* vertebrato
vertex /'vɜ:teks/ *n* Anat sommità *f* del capo; Math vertice *m*
vertical /'vɜ:tɪkl/ *adj & n* verticale *m*
vertically /'vɜ:tɪklɪ/ *adv* verticalmente
vertigo /'vɜ:tɪgəʊ/ *n* Med vertigine *f*
verve /vɜ:v/ *n* verve *f*
very /'verɪ/ **A** *adv* molto; **~ much** molto; **~ little** pochissimo; **~ many** moltissimi; **~ few** pochissimi; **~ probably** molto probabilmente; **~ well** benissimo; **at the ~ most** tutt'al più; **at the ~ latest** al più tardi
B *adj* **the ~ first** il primissimo; **the ~ thing** proprio ciò che ci vuole; **at the ~ end/beginning** proprio alla fine/all'inizio; **that ~ day** proprio quel giorno; **the ~ thought** la sola idea; **only a ~ little** solo un pochino
vespers /'vespəz/ *npl* vespri *mpl*
vessel /'vesl/ *n* nave *f*; (receptacle) recipiente *m*; Anat vaso *m*
vest /vest/ **A** *n* maglia *f*; AmE (waistcoat) gilè *m*
B *vt* **~ something in somebody** investire qualcuno di qualcosa
vested interest /vestɪd'ɪntrəst/ *n* interesse *m* personale
vestige /'vestɪdʒ/ *n* (of past) vestigio *m*
vestment /'vestmənt/ *n* Relig paramento *m*
vestry /'vestrɪ/ *n* sagrestia *f*
vet /vet/ **A** *n* veterinario, -a *mf*
B *vt* (*pt/pp* **vetted**) controllare minuziosamente
veteran /'vetərən/ *n* veterano, -a *mf*
veteran car *n* auto *f inv* d'epoca (*costruita prima del 1916*)
veterinarian /,vetərɪ'neərɪən/ *n* AmE = **vet A**
veterinary /'vetərɪnərɪ/ *adj* veterinario
veterinary surgeon *n* medico *m* veterinario
veto /'vi:təʊ/ **A** *n* (*pl* **-es**) veto *m*
B *vt* proibire
vetting /'vetɪŋ/ *n* verifica *f* del passato di un individuo
vex /veks/ *vt* irritare
vexation /vek'seɪʃn/ *n* irritazione *f*
vexatious /vek'seɪʃəs/ *adj* ‹*person*› fastidioso; ‹*situation*› spiacevole
vexed /vekst/ *adj* irritato; **~ question** questione *f* controversa
vexing /'veksɪŋ/ *adj* irritante
VHF *abbr* (**very high frequency**) VHF
via /'vaɪə/ *prep* via; (by means of) attraverso
viability /vaɪə'bɪlətɪ/ *n* probabilità *f* di sopravvivenza; (of proposition) attuabilità *f*
viable /'vaɪəbl/ *adj* ‹*life form, relationship, company*› in grado di sopravvivere; ‹*proposition*› attuabile
viaduct /'vaɪədʌkt/ *n* viadotto *m*
vibes /vaɪbz/ *npl* infml **I'm getting good/bad ~** provo una sensazione gradevole/sgradevole
vibrant /'vaɪbrənt/ *adj* fig che sprizza vitalità
vibrate /vaɪ'breɪt/ *vi* vibrare
vibration /vaɪ'breʃɪn/ *n* vibrazione *f*

vicar /ˈvɪkə(r)/ *n* parroco *m* (*protestante*)
vicarage /ˈvɪkərɪdʒ/ *n* casa *f* parrocchiale
vicarious /vɪˈkeərɪəs/ *adj* indiretto
vice[1] /vaɪs/ *n* vizio *m*
vice[2] *n* Techn morsa *f*
vice-captain *n* Sport vicecapitano *m*
vice-chairman *n* vicepresidente *mf*
vice-chancellor *n* BrE Univ vicerettore *m*; AmE Jur vicecancelliere *m*
vice-president *n* vicepresidente *mf*
vice-principal *n* (of senior school) vicepreside *mf*; (of junior school, college) vicedirettore, -trice *mf*
vice squad *n* buoncostume *f*
vice versa /vaɪsəˈvɜːsə/ *adv* viceversa
vicinity /vɪˈsɪnətɪ/ *n* vicinanza *f*; **in the ~ of** nelle vicinanze di
vicious /ˈvɪʃəs/ *adj* cattivo; ‹*attack*› brutale; ‹*animal*› pericoloso
vicious circle *n* circolo *m* vizioso
viciously /ˈvɪʃəslɪ/ *adv* ‹*attack*› brutalmente
⚷ **victim** /ˈvɪktɪm/ *n* vittima *f*
victimization /vɪktɪmaɪˈzeɪʃn/ *n* vittimizzazione *f*
victimize /ˈvɪktɪmaɪz/ *vt* vittimizzare
victor /ˈvɪktə(r)/ *n* vincitore *m*
Victorian /vɪkˈtɔːrɪən/ **A** *n* persona *f* vissuta in epoca vittoriana
B *adj* ‹*writer, poverty, age*› vittoriano
victorious /vɪkˈtɔːrɪəs/ *adj* vittorioso
⚷ **victory** /ˈvɪktərɪ/ *n* vittoria *f*
⚷ **video** /ˈvɪdɪəʊ/ **A** *n* video *m inv*; (cassette) videocassetta *f*; (recorder) videoregistratore *m*
B *attrib* video
C *vt* registrare
video camera *n* videocamera *f*, telecamera *f*
video card *n* scheda *f* video
video cassette *n* videocassetta *f*
video clip *n* videoclip *m inv*
videoconference *n* videoconferenza *f*
videoconferencing /-ˈkɒnfərənsɪŋ/ *n* videoconferenza *f*
videodisc *n* videodisco *m*
video game *n* videogioco *m*
video library *n* videoteca *f*
video nasty *n film* (*m inv*) *con scene violente o pornografiche*
video-on-demand *n* video *m* a pagamento
videophone *n* videocitofono *m*
video recorder *n* videoregistratore *m*
video shop *n negozio* (*m*) *che affitta o vende videocassette*
video surveillance *n* videosorveglianza *f*
videotape *n* videocassetta *f*
vie /vaɪ/ *vi* (*pres p* **vying**) rivaleggiare
Vienna /vɪˈenə/ *n* Vienna *f*

⚷ parola chiave

Viennese /vɪəˈniːz/ *adj* viennese
Vietnam /vɪetˈnæm/ *n* Vietnam *m*
Vietnamese /vɪetnæˈmiːz/ *adj & n* vietnamita *mf*; (language) vietnamita *m*
⚷ **view** /vjuː/ **A** *n* vista *f*; (photographed, painted) veduta *f*; (opinion) visione *f*; **look at the ~** guardare il panorama; **in my ~** secondo me; **in ~ of** in considerazione di; **on ~** esposto; **with a ~ to** con l'intenzione di
B *vt* visitare ‹*house*›; (consider) considerare
C *vi* TV guardare
viewer /ˈvjuːə(r)/ *n* TV telespettatore, -trice *mf*; Phot visore *m*
viewfinder /ˈvjuːfaɪndə(r)/ *n* Phot mirino *m*
viewing /ˈvjuːɪŋ/ **A** *n* TV programmi *mpl* della televisione; (of film) proiezione *f*; (of new range) presentazione *f*; (of exhibition, house) visita *f*; **it makes good ~** TV vale la pena di vederlo; **what's tonight's ~?** cosa danno alla tv stasera?
B *attrib* ‹*habits, preferences*› dei telespettatori; **the ~ public** i telespettatori
view phone *n* videotelefono *m*
viewpoint /ˈvjuːpɔɪnt/ *n* punto *m* di vista
vigil /ˈvɪdʒɪl/ *n* veglia *f*
vigilance /ˈvɪdʒɪləns/ *n* vigilanza *f*
vigilant /ˈvɪdʒɪlənt/ *adj* vigile
vigilante /vɪdʒɪˈlæntɪ/ *n membro* (*m*) *di un'organizzazione privata per la prevenzione della criminalità*
vigorous /ˈvɪg(ə)rəs/ *adj* vigoroso
vigorously /ˈvɪg(ə)rəslɪ/ *adv* vigorosamente
vigour /ˈvɪgə(r)/ *n* vigore *m*
vile /vaɪl/ *adj* disgustoso; ‹*weather*› orribile; ‹*temper, mood*› pessimo
vilification /vɪlɪfɪˈkeɪʃn/ *n* denigrazione *f*
villa /ˈvɪlɪ/ *n* (for holidays) casa *f* di villeggiatura
⚷ **village** /ˈvɪlɪdʒ/ *n* paese *m*
village green *n giardino* (*m*) *pubblico nel centro di un paese*
village hall *n sala* (*f*) *utilizzata per feste e altre attività*
villager /ˈvɪlɪdʒə(r)/ *n* paesano, -a *mf*
villain /ˈvɪlɪn/ *n* furfante *m*; (in story) cattivo *m*
villainous /ˈvɪlənəs/ *adj* infame
vim /vɪm/ *n* infml energia *f*
vindicate /ˈvɪndɪkeɪt/ *vt* (from guilt) discolpare; **you are ~d** ti sei dimostrato nel giusto
vindictive /vɪnˈdɪktɪv/ *adj* vendicativo
vine /vaɪn/ *n* vite *f*
vinegar /ˈvɪnɪgə(r)/ *n* aceto *m*
vinegary /ˈvɪnɪg(ə)rɪ/ *adj* agro
vineyard /ˈvɪnjɑːd/ *n* vigneto *m*
vintage /ˈvɪntɪdʒ/ **A** *adj* ‹*wine*› d'annata; ‹*clothes*› vintage
B *n* (year) annata *f*
vintage car *n* auto *f inv* d'epoca (*costruita tra il 1917 e il 1930*)
vintage year *n also* fig anno *m* memorabile
vinyl /ˈvaɪnɪl/ **A** *n* vinile *m*

B *attrib* ‹*paint*› vinilico
viola /vɪ'əʊlə/ *n* Mus viola *f*
violate /'vaɪəleɪt/ *vt* violare
violation /vaɪə'leɪʃn/ *n* violazione *f*
violence /'vaɪələns/ *n* violenza *f*
violent /'vaɪələnt/ *adj* violento
violently /'vaɪələntlɪ/ *adv* violentemente
violet /'vaɪələt/ **A** *adj* violetto
B *n* (flower) violetta *f*; (colour) violetto *m*
violin /vaɪə'lɪn/ *n* violino *m*
violinist /vaɪə'lɪnɪst/ *n* violinista *mf*
VIP *n abbr* (**very important person**) vip *mf*
viper /'vaɪpə(r)/ *n* vipera *f*
virgin /'vɜːdʒɪn/ **A** *adj* vergine
B *n* vergine *f*
virginal /'vɜːdʒɪn(ə)l/ *adj* verginale
virginals /'vɜːdʒɪn(ə)lz/ *npl* Mus spinetta *f*
Virginia creeper /vədʒɪnɪə'kriːpə(r)/ *n* vite *f* del Canada
virginity /və'dʒɪnətɪ/ *n* verginità *f*
Virgo /'vɜːgəʊ/ *n* Astr Vergine *f*
virile /'vɪraɪl/ *adj* virile
virility /vɪ'rɪlətɪ/ *n* virilità *f*
virologist /vaɪ'rɒlədɪʒst/ *n* virologo *m*
virtual /'vɜːtjʊəl/ *adj* effettivo
virtually /'vɜːtjʊəlɪ/ *adv* praticamente
virtual reality *n* realtà *f* virtuale
virtue /'vɜːtjuː/ *n* virtù *f*; (advantage) vantaggio *m*; **by** *or* **in** ~ **of** a causa di
virtuoso /vɜːtʊ'əʊzəʊ/ *n* (*pl* **-si** /-ziː/) virtuoso *m*
virtuous /'vɜːtjʊəs/ *adj* virtuoso
virulent /'vɪrʊlənt/ *adj* virulento
virus /'vaɪərəs/ *n* virus *m inv*
virus checker *n* Comput (programma *m*) antivirus *m inv*
virus protection *n* Comput protezione *f* antivirus
visa /'viːzə/ *n* visto *m*
vis-à-vis /viːzɑː'viː/ *prep* rispetto a
visceral /'vɪs(ə)rəl/ *adj* ‹*power, performance*› viscerale
viscount /'vaɪkaʊnt/ *n* visconte *m*
viscous /'vɪskəs/ *adj* vischioso
visibility /vɪzə'bɪlətɪ/ *n* visibilità *f*
visible /'vɪzəbl/ *adj* visibile
visibly /'vɪzəblɪ/ *adv* visibilmente
vision /'vɪʒn/ *n* visione *f*; (sight) vista *f*
visionary /'vɪʒn(ə)rɪ/ *adj & n* visionario, -a *mf*
vision mixer *n* (person) tecnico *m* del mixaggio video; (equipment) mixaggio *m* video
visit /'vɪzɪt/ **A** *n* visita *f*
B *vt* andare a trovare ‹*person*›; andare da ‹*doctor etc*›; visitare ‹*town, building*›
visiting card *n* biglietto *m* da visita
visiting hours *npl* orario *m* delle visite
visiting lecturer *n* conferenziere, -a *mf*
visiting team *n* squadra *f* ospite
visiting time *n* orario *m* delle visite
visitor /'vɪzɪtə(r)/ *n* ospite *mf*; (of town, museum) visitatore, -trice *mf*; (in hotel) cliente *mf*
visitor centre *n centro* (*m*) *di accoglienza e di informazione per i visitatori*
visitors' book *n* (in exhibition) albo *m* dei visitatori; (in hotel) registro *m* dei clienti
visor /'vaɪzə(r)/ *n* visiera *f*; Auto parasole *m*
vista /'vɪstə/ *n* (view) panorama *m*
visual /'vɪzjʊəl/ *adj* visivo
visual aids *npl* supporto *m* visivo
visual arts *npl* arti *fpl* visive
visual display unit *n* visualizzatore *m*
visualize /'vɪzjʊəlaɪz/ *vt* visualizzare
visually /'vɪzjʊəlɪ/ *adv* visualmente; ~ **impaired** non vedente
vital /'vaɪtl/ *adj* vitale
vitality /vaɪ'tælətɪ/ *n* vitalità *f*
vitally /'vaɪtəlɪ/ *adv* estremamente
vital statistics *npl* infml misure *fpl*
vitamin /'vɪtəmɪn/ *n* vitamina *f*
vitreous /'vɪtrɪəs/ *adj* vetroso; ‹*enamel*› vetrificato
vitriolic /vɪtrɪ'ɒlɪk/ *adj* Chem di vetriolo; fig al vetriolo
vituperative /vɪ'tjuːp(ə)rətɪv/ *adj* ingiurioso
viva /'vaɪvə/ *n* BrE Univ [esame *m*] orale *m*
vivacious /vɪ'veɪʃəs/ *adj* vivace
vivaciously /vɪ'veɪʃəslɪ/ *adv* vivacemente
vivacity /vɪ'væsətɪ/ *n* vivacità *f*
vivid /'vɪvɪd/ *adj* vivido
vividly /'vɪvɪdlɪ/ *adv* in modo vivido
vivisect /'vɪvɪsekt/ *vt* vivisezionare
vivisection /vɪvɪ'sekʃn/ *n* vivisezione *f*
vixen /'vɪksn/ *n* volpe *f* femmina
viz. /vɪz/ *adv* cioè
V-neck *n* (neckline) scollo *m* a V; (sweater) maglione *m* con scollo a V
vocabulary /və'kæbjʊlərɪ/ *n* vocabolario *m*; (list) glossario *m*
vocal /'vəʊkl/ *adj* vocale; (vociferous) eloquente
vocal cords *npl* corde *fpl* vocali
vocalist /'vəʊkəlɪst/ *n* vocalista *mf*
vocalize /'vəʊkəlaɪz/ *vt* fig (express) esprimere a parole; articolare ‹*sound*›
vocals /'vəʊklz/ *npl* **do the** ~ cantare
vocation /və'keɪʃn/ *n* vocazione *f*
vocational /və'keɪʃ(ə)nl/ *adj* professionale
vocational course *n* corso *m* di formazione professionale
vociferous /və'sɪfərəs/ *adj* veemente
vodka /'vɒdkə/ *n* vodka *f inv*
vogue /vəʊg/ *n* moda *f*; **in** ~ in voga
voice /vɔɪs/ **A** *n* voce *f*
B *vt* esprimere

voice box *n* Anat laringe *f*
voiceless /ˈvɔɪslɪs/ *adj* ‹*minority*› silenzioso; ‹*group*› privo del diritto di parola
voicemail /ˈvɔɪsmeɪl/ *n* segreteria *f* telefonica (sul cellulare)
voice-over *n* voce *f* fuori campo
voice recognition *n* Comput riconoscimento *m* vocale
void /vɔɪd/ **A** *adj* (not valid) nullo; **~ of** privo di
B *n* vuoto *m*
vol. /vɒl/ *abbr* (**volume**) vol
volatile /ˈvɒlətaɪl/ *adj* volatile; ‹*person*› volubile
volcanic /vɒlˈkænɪk/ *adj* vulcanico
volcano /vɒlˈkeɪnəʊ/ *n* vulcano *m*
volition /vəˈlɪʃn/ *n* **of his own ~** di sua spontanea volontà
volley /ˈvɒlɪ/ *n* (of gunfire) raffica *f*; Tennis volée *f inv*
volleyball /ˈvɒlɪbɔːl/ *n* pallavolo *f*
volt /vəʊlt/ *n* volt *m inv*
voltage /ˈvəʊltɪdʒ/ *n* Electr voltaggio *m*
voluble /ˈvɒljʊbl/ *adj* loquace
⚷ **volume** /ˈvɒljuːm/ *n* volume *m*; (of work, traffic) quantità *f*
volume control *n* volume *m*
voluntarily /ˈvɒləntərɪlɪ/ *adv* volontariamente
voluntary /ˈvɒləntərɪ/ *adj* volontario
voluntary redundancy *n* BrE dimissioni *fpl* volontarie
voluntary work *n* volontariato *m*
volunteer /vɒlənˈtɪə(r)/ **A** *n* volontario, -a *mf*
B *vt* offrire volontariamente ‹*information*›
C *vi* offrirsi volontario; Mil arruolarsi come volontario
voluptuous /vəˈlʌptjʊəs/ *adj* voluttuoso
vomit /ˈvɒmɪt/ **A** *n* vomito *m*
B *vt & vi* vomitare
voodoo /ˈvuːduː/ *n* vudu *m inv*
voracious /vəˈreɪʃəs/ *adj* vorace
vortex /ˈvɔːteks/ *n* vortice *m*; fig turbine *m*
⚷ **vote** /vəʊt/ **A** *n* voto *m*; (ballot) votazione *f*; (right) diritto *m* di voto; **take a ~ on** votare su
B *vi* votare
C *vt* **~ somebody president** eleggere qualcuno presidente
vote down *vt* (reject by vote) bocciare ai voti
vote in *vt* (elect) eleggere
vote of confidence *n* Pol fig voto *m* di fiducia
vote of thanks *n* discorso *m* di ringraziamento
⚷ **voter** /ˈvəʊtə(r)/ *n* elettore, -trice *mf*
voting /ˈvəʊtɪŋ/ *n* votazione *f*
voting age *n* età *f* per votare
voting booth *n* cabina *f* elettorale
vouch /vaʊtʃ/ *vi* **~ for** garantire per
voucher /ˈvaʊtʃə(r)/ *n* buono *m*
vow /vaʊ/ **A** *n* voto *m*
B *vt* giurare
vowel /ˈvaʊəl/ *n* vocale *f*
vox pop /vɒksˈpɒp/ *n* TV, Radio opinione *f* pubblica
voyage /ˈvɔɪɪdʒ/ *n* viaggio *m* [marittimo]; (in space) viaggio *m* [nello spazio]
vs *abbr* (**versus**) contro
V-sign *n* (offensive gesture) gestaccio *m*; (victory sign) segno *m* di vittoria
VSO *abbr* (**Voluntary Service Overseas**) *servizio (m) civile volontario nei paesi in via di sviluppo*
vulgar /ˈvʌlgə(r)/ *adj* volgare
vulgar fraction *n* Math frazione *f* ordinaria
vulgarity /vʌlˈgærətɪ/ *n* volgarità *f*
vulnerable /ˈvʌlnərəbl/ *adj* vulnerabile
vulture /ˈvʌltʃə(r)/ *n* avvoltoio *m*
vying /ˈvaɪɪŋ/ ▸ **vie**

Ww

w, W /ˈdʌbljuː/ *n* (letter) w, W *f inv*
W[2] *abbr* **1** (**West**) O **2** Electr (**watt**) w
wad /wɒd/ *n* batuffolo *m*; (bundle) rotolo *m*
wadding /ˈwɒdɪŋ/ *n* ovatta *f*
waddle /ˈwɒdl/ *vi* camminare ondeggiando
wade /weɪd/ *vi* guadare
▪ **wade in** *vi* infml (start working) mettersi al lavoro; (take part) prendere parte
▪ **wade into** *vt* (attack) scagliarsi contro
▪ **wade through** *vt* infml procedere faticosamente in ‹*book*›
wader /ˈweɪdə(r)/ *n* Zool trampoliere *m*; **~s** *pl* (boots) stivaloni *mpl* di gomma
wafer /ˈweɪfə(r)/ *n* cialda *f*, wafer *m inv*; Relig ostia *f*

⚷ parola chiave

wafer-thin *adj* sottilissimo
waffle¹ /'wɒfl/ *vi* infml blaterare
waffle² *n* Culin cialda *f*
waft /wɒft/ **A** *vt* trasportare
B *vi* diffondersi
wag /wæg/ **A** *vt* (*pt/pp* **wagged**) agitare
B *vi* agitarsi
wage¹ /weɪdʒ/ *vt* dichiarare ‹*war*›; lanciare ‹*campaign*›
wage² *n* **~s** *pl* salario *msg*
wage earner *n* salariato, -a *mf*
wage packet *n* busta *f* paga
wager /'weɪdʒə(r)/ *n* scommessa *f*
wage slip *n* cedolino *m* dello stipendio
waggle /'wægl/ **A** *vt* dimenare
B *vi* dimenarsi
wagon /'wægən/ *n* carro *m*; Rail vagone *m* merci; **be on the ~** infml astenersi dall'alcol
waif /weɪf/ *n* trovatello, -a *mf*
wail /weɪl/ **A** *n* piagnucolio *m*; (of wind) lamento *m*; (of baby) vagito *m*
B *vi* piagnucolare; ‹*wind*› lamentarsi; ‹*baby*› vagire
Wailing Wall /'weɪlɪŋ/ *n* Muro *m* del pianto
waist /weɪst/ *n* vita *f*
waistband *n* cintura *f*
waistcoat *n* gilè *m*; (of man's suit) panciotto *m*
waistline *n* vita *f*
waist measurement *n* giro *m* vita
wait /weɪt/ **A** *n* attesa *f*; **lie in ~ for** appostarsi per sorprendere
B *vi* aspettare; **~ at table** servire ai tavoli; **~ for** aspettare
C *vt* **~ one's turn** aspettare il proprio turno
■ **wait about**, **wait around** *vi* aspettare
■ **wait behind** *vi* trattenersi
■ **wait in** *vi* rimanere a casa ad aspettare
■ **wait on** *vt* servire
■ **wait up** *vi* rimanere alzato ad aspettare; **don't ~ up for me** non mi aspettare alzato
waiter /'weɪtə(r)/ *n* cameriere *m*
waiter service *n* servizio *m* al tavolo
waiting game *n* **play a ~** *n* temporeggiare
waiting list *n* lista *f* d'attesa
waiting room *n* sala *f* d'aspetto
waitress /'weɪtrɪs/ *n* cameriera *f*
waive /weɪv/ *vt* rinunciare a ‹*claim*›; non tener conto di ‹*rule*›
waiver /'weɪvə(r)/ *n* Jur rinuncia *f*
wake¹ /weɪk/ **A** *n* veglia *f* funebre
B *vt* (*pt* **woke**, *pp* **woken**) **~ [up]** svegliare
C *vi* svegliarsi
■ **wake up to**: *vt* **~ up to the fact that...** (realize) aprire gli occhi di fronte al fatto che...
wake² *n* Naut scia *f*; **in the ~ of** fig sulla scia di
wakeful /'weɪkfʊl/ *adj* ‹*night*› insonne
waken /'weɪkn/ **A** *vt* svegliare
B *vi* svegliarsi
wake-up call *n* lit sveglia *f* telefonica; fig campanello *m* d'allarme
Wales /weɪlz/ *n* Galles *m*
walk /wɔːk/ **A** *n* passeggiata *f*; (gait) andatura *f*; (path) sentiero *m*; **go for a ~** andare a fare una passeggiata; **~ of life** livello *m* sociale
B *vi* camminare; (as opposed to drive etc) andare a piedi; (ramble) passeggiare; **'~'** AmE (at crossing) 'avanti'
C *vt* portare a spasso ‹*dog*›; percorrere ‹*streets*›
■ **walk away** *vi* (leave) allontanarsi; **~ away from** abbandonare ‹*place, person*›; disinteressarsi di ‹*problem*›; (survive unscathed) uscire illeso da ‹*accident*›
■ **walk away with** *vt* (win easily) vincere senza difficoltà ‹*game, election, prize*›
■ **walk back** *vi* ritornare a piedi
■ **walk in** *vi* entrare all'improvviso
■ **walk into** *vt* entrare in ‹*room*›; andare a sbattere contro ‹*door, lamp post*›; cadere in ‹*trap*›; trovare facilmente ‹*job*›
■ **walk off** *vi* (leave) andarsene
■ **walk off with** *vt* (win easily) riportare senza difficoltà; (take, steal) portarsi via
■ **walk out** *vi* ‹*husband, employee*› andarsene; ‹*workers*› scioperare
■ **walk out of** *vt* uscire da ‹*room*›; abbandonare ‹*meeting*›
■ **walk out on** *vt* lasciare
■ **walk over**: *vt* **~ all over somebody** (defeat) stracciare qualcuno; (treat badly) trattare qualcuno come una pezza da piedi
■ **walk through** *vt* superare senza difficoltà ‹*exam, interview*›
■ **walk up** *vi* (as opposed to taking the lift) salire a piedi; (approach) avvicinarsi
walkabout /'wɔːkəbaʊt/ *n escursione (f) periodica degli aborigeni australiani nell'entroterra*; (by royalty) incontro *m* con la folla; **go ~** ‹*queen, politician*› camminare tra la folla
walker /'wɔːkə(r)/ *n* **1** (pedestrian) camminatore, -trice *mf*; (rambler) escursionista *mf* **2** AmE (frame) deambulatore *m*
walkie-talkie /wɔːkɪ'tɔːkɪ/ *n* walkie-talkie *m inv*
walk-in *adj* **~ closet** stanzino *m*
walking /'wɔːkɪŋ/ *n* camminare *m*; (rambling) fare *m* delle escursioni
walking boots *npl* scarponi *mpl* [da trekking]
walking distance *n* **it's within ~** ci si arriva a piedi
walking frame *n* Med deambulatore *m*
walking pace *n* passo *m*
walking shoes *npl* scarpe *fpl* da passeggio
walking-stick *n* bastone *m* da passeggio

walking wounded *npl* feriti *mpl* in grado di camminare

Walkman® *n* Walkman® *m inv*

walk-on **A** *n* Theat comparsa *f*
B *adj* ‹*role*› piccolo

walkout *n* sciopero *m*

walkover *n* fig vittoria *f* facile

walkway *n* passaggio *m* pedonale

🔑 **wall** /wɔːl/ *n* muro *m*; **go to the ~** infml andare a rotoli; **drive somebody up the ~** infml far diventare matto qualcuno
▪ **wall up** *vt* murare

wallchart /ˈwɔːltʃɑːt/ *n* tabellone *m*

walled /wɔːld/ *adj* ‹*city*› fortificato

wallet /ˈwɒlɪt/ *n* portafoglio *m*

wallflower /ˈwɔːlflaʊə(r)/ *n* violaciocca *f*

wall hanging *n* decorazione *f* murale

wallop /ˈwɒləp/ **A** *n* infml colpo *m*
B *vt* (*pt/pp* **walloped**) infml colpire

walloping /ˈwɒləpɪŋ/ infml **A** *adj* enorme
B *adv* **~ great** (very big) enorme
C *n* **give somebody a ~** suonarle a qualcuno

wallow /ˈwɒləʊ/ *vi* sguazzare; (in self-pity, grief) crogiolarsi

wallpaper /ˈwɔːlpeɪpə(r)/ **A** *n* tappezzeria *f*
B *vt* tappezzare

wall-to-wall *adj* che copre tutto il pavimento

walnut /ˈwɔːlnʌt/ *n* noce *f*

walrus /ˈwɔːlrəs/ *n* tricheco *m*

waltz /wɔːlts/ **A** *n* valzer *m inv*
B *vi* ballare il valzer; **he came ~ing up and said** infml è arrivato e ha detto con nonchalance
▪ **waltz off with** *vt* infml (take, win) portarsi via
▪ **waltz through** *vt* superare facilmente ‹*exam*›

wan /wɒn/ *adj* esangue

wand /wɒnd/ *n* (magic ~) bacchetta *f* [magica]

wander /ˈwɒndə(r)/ *vi* girovagare; fig (digress) divagare
▪ **wander about** *vi* andare a spasso
▪ **wander away** *vi* allontanarsi
▪ **wander off** *vi* allontanarsi; **I'd better be ~ing off** infml è meglio che vada

wanderer /ˈwɒndərə(r)/ *n* vagabondo, -a *mf*

wanderlust /ˈwɒndəlʌst/ *n* smania *f* dei viaggi

wane /weɪn/ **A** *n* **be on the ~** essere in fase calante
B *vi* calare

wangle /ˈwæŋgl/ *vt* infml rimediare ‹*invitation, holiday*›

waning /ˈweɪnɪŋ/ **A** *n* (of moon) calare *m*; (weakening) declino *m*
B *adj* ‹*moon*› calante; ‹*popularity*› in declino

🔑 parola chiave

wannabe /ˈwɒnəbiː/ *n* infml *persona (f) che sogna di diventare famosa*

🔑 **want** /wɒnt/ **A** *n* (hardship) bisogno *m*; (lack) mancanza *f*
B *vt* volere; (need) aver bisogno di; **~ [to have] something** volere qualcosa; **~ to do something** voler fare qualcosa; **we ~ to stay** vogliamo rimanere; **I ~ you to go** voglio che tu vada; **it ~s painting** ha bisogno d'essere dipinto; **you ~ to learn to swim** bisogna che impari a nuotare
C *vi* **~ for** mancare di

wanted /ˈwɒntɪd/ *adj* ricercato

wanted list *n* lista *f* dei ricercati

wanting /ˈwɒntɪŋ/ *adj* **be ~** mancare; **be ~ in** mancare di

wanton /ˈwɒntən/ *adj* ‹*cruelty, neglect*› gratuito; (morally) debosciato

WAP /wæp/ *abbr* (**wireless application protocol**) WAP *m*; **~ phone** telefonino WAP

WAP-enabled /-ɪˈneɪbld/ *adj* ‹*device, system*› abilitato al WAP

🔑 **war** /wɔː(r)/ *n* guerra *f*; fig lotta *f* (**on** contro); **at ~** in guerra

warble /ˈwɔːbl/ *vt & vi* trillare; ‹*singer*› gorgheggiare

war cabinet *n* consiglio *m* di guerra

war cry *n* grido *m* di guerra

ward /wɔːd/ *n* (in hospital) reparto *m*; (child) minore *m* sotto tutela
▪ **ward off** *vt* evitare; parare ‹*blow*›

warden /ˈwɔːdn/ *n* guardiano, -a *mf*

warder /ˈwɔːdə(r)/ *n* guardia *f* carceraria

wardrobe /ˈwɔːdrəʊb/ *n* guardaroba *m inv*

wardrobe assistant *n* costumista *mf*

ward round *n* Med giro *m* delle corsie

ward sister *n* BrE Med caposala *f inv*

warehouse /ˈweəhaʊs/ *n* magazzino *m*

wares /weəz/ *npl* merci *mpl*

warfare /ˈwɔːfeə(r)/ *n* guerra *f*

war game *n* Mil simulazione *f* di scontro militare

warhead *n* testata *f*

warhorse *n* cavallo *m* da battaglia; fig (campaigner) veterano *m*

warily /ˈweərɪlɪ/ *adv* cautamente

warlike /ˈwɔːlaɪk/ *adj* bellicoso

🔑 **warm** /wɔːm/ **A** *adj* caldo; ‹*welcome*› caloroso; **be ~** ‹*person*› aver caldo; **it is ~** ‹*weather*› fa caldo
B *vt* scaldare
▪ **warm to** *vt* prendere in simpatia ‹*person*›
▪ **warm up** **A** *vt* scaldare
B *vi* scaldarsi; fig animarsi

warm-blooded /-ˈblʌdɪd/ *adj* Zool a sangue caldo

war memorial *n* monumento *m* ai caduti

warm-hearted /-ˈhɑːtɪd/ *adj* espansivo

warmly /ˈwɔːmlɪ/ *adv* ‹*greet*› calorosamente; ‹*dress*› in modo pesante

warmongering /'wɔːmʌŋɡərɪŋ/ **A** *n* bellicismo *m*
B *adj* ‹*article*› bellicista; ‹*person*› guerrafondaio

warmth /wɔːmθ/ *n* calore *m*

warm-up *n* Sport riscaldamento *m*; (of musicians) prove *fpl*

⚷ **warn** /wɔːn/ *vt* avvertire

■ **warn off** *vt* dare un avvertimento a

⚷ **warning** /'wɔːnɪŋ/ *n* avvertimento *m*; (advance notice) preavviso *m*

warning light *n* spia *f* luminosa

warning shot *n* sparo *m* d'avvertimento

warning sign *n* (road sign) segnale *m* di pericolo; (of illness)) segnale *m* d'allarme

warning triangle *n* triangolo *m* di segnalazione

warp /wɔːp/ **A** *vt* deformare; fig distorcere
B *vi* deformarsi

warpaint /'wɔːpeɪnt/ *n* Mil pitture *fpl* di guerra

warpath /'wɔːpɑːθ/ *n* **on the ~** sul sentiero di guerra

warped /wɔːpt/ *adj* deformato; ‹*personality*› contorto; ‹*sexuality*› deviato; ‹*view*› distorto

warplane /'wɔːpleɪn/ *n* aereo *m* da guerra

warrant /'wɒrənt/ **A** *n* (for arrest, search) mandato *m*
B *vt* (justify) giustificare; (guarantee) garantire

warranty /'wɒrəntɪ/ *n* garanzia *f*

warren /'wɒr(ə)n/ *n* (of rabbits) area *f* piena di tane di conigli; (building, maze of streets) labirinto *m*

warring /'wɔːrɪŋ/ *adj* in guerra

warrior /'wɒrɪə(r)/ *n* guerriero, -a *mf*

Warsaw /'wɔːsɔː/ *n* Varsavia *f*

warship /'wɔːʃɪp/ *n* nave *f* da guerra

wart /wɔːt/ *n* porro *m*

wartime /'wɔːtaɪm/ *n* tempo *m* di guerra

war-torn /'wɔːtɔːn/ *adj* straziato dalla guerra

wary /'weərɪ/ *adj* (**-ier**, **-iest**) (careful) cauto; (suspicious) diffidente

was /wɒz/ ▶ **be**

wash /wɒʃ/ **A** *n* lavata *f*; (clothes) bucato *m*; (in washing machine) lavaggio *m*; **have a ~** darsi una lavata
B *vt* lavare; ‹*sea*› bagnare; **~ one's hands** lavarsi le mani
C *vi* lavarsi

■ **wash away** *vt* ‹*rain*› portare via; ‹*sea, floodwaters*› spazzare via

■ **wash off** **A** *vt* lavar via ‹*stain, mud*›
B *vi* andar via

■ **wash out** *vt* sciacquare ‹*soap*›; sciacquarsi ‹*mouth*›

■ **wash up** **A** *vt* lavare
B *vi* lavare i piatti; AmE lavarsi

washable /'wɒʃəbl/ *adj* lavabile

wash-and-wear *adj* che non si stira

wash bag *n* BrE = **toilet bag**

washbasin *n* lavandino *m*

washbowl *n* AmE = **washbasin**

wash cloth *n* AmE ≈ guanto *m* da bagno

washed out /wɒʃt'aʊt/ *adj* (faded) scolorito; (tired) spossato

washed up *adj* infml (finished) finito; (tired) distrutto

washer /'wɒʃə(r)/ *n* Techn guarnizione *f*; (machine) lavatrice *f*

washer-dryer /-'draɪə(r)/ *n* asciugabiancheria *m inv*

washing /'wɒʃɪŋ/ *n* bucato *m*

washing line *n* corda *f* per il bucato

washing machine *n* lavatrice *f*

washing powder *n* detersivo *m*

washing soda *n* soda *f* da bucato

washing-up *n* **do the ~** lavare i piatti

washing-up bowl *n* bacinella *f* (*per i piatti*)

washing-up liquid *n* detersivo *m* per i piatti

washing-up water *n* rigovernatura *f*

wash load *n* carico *m* di lavatrice

wash-out *n* disastro *m*

washroom *n* bagno *m*

wash-stand *n* AmE = **washbasin**

wasp /wɒsp/ *n* vespa *f*

WASP, **Wasp** /wɒsp/ *n abbr* AmE (**White Anglo-Saxon Protestant**) WASP *mf inv*

waspish /'wɒspɪʃ/ *adj* pungente

wastage /'weɪstɪdʒ/ *n* perdita *f*

waste /weɪst/ **A** *n* spreco *m*; (rubbish) rifiuto *m*; **~s** *pl* distesa *fsg* desolata; **~ of time** perdita *f* di tempo
B *adj* ‹*product*› di scarto; ‹*land*› desolato; **lay ~** devastare
C *vt* sprecare

■ **waste away** *vi* deperire

wastebasket *n* cestino *m* della carta straccia

waste bin *n* (for paper) cestino *m* della carta straccia; (for rubbish) secchio *m* della spazzatura

wasted /'weɪstɪd/ *adj* ‹*energy, effort, life*› sprecato; ‹*limb*› atrofizzato; ‹*body*› scarnito

waste disposal *n* smaltimento *m* dei rifiuti

waste-disposal unit *n* eliminatore *m* di rifiuti

wasteful /'weɪstfʊl/ *adj* dispendioso

wasteland *n* area *f* desolata

waste paper *n* carta *f* straccia

waste-paper basket *n* cestino *m* per la carta [straccia]

waste pipe *n* tubo *m* di scarico

⚷ **watch** /wɒtʃ/ **A** *n* guardia *f*; (period of duty) turno *m* di guardia; (timepiece) orologio *m*; **be on the ~** stare all'erta
B *vt* guardare ‹*film, match, television*›;

(be careful of, look after) stare attento a
C *vi* guardare

■ **watch out** *vi* (be careful) stare attento (**for** a)

■ **watch out for** *vt* (look for) fare attenzione all'arrivo di ‹*person*›

■ **watch over** *vt* proteggere ‹*person*›

watch band *n* AmE = **watch strap**

watchdog /ˈwɒtʃdɒg/ *n* cane *m* da guardia

watchful /ˈwɒtʃfʊl/ *adj* attento

watchfully /ˈwɒtʃfʊlɪ/ *adv* attentamente

watchmaker *n* orologiaio, -a *mf*

watchman *n* guardiano *m*

watch strap *n* cinturino *m* dell'orologio

watchtower *n* torre *f* di guardia

watchword *n* motto *m*

⚷ **water** /ˈwɔːtə(r)/ **A** *n* acqua *f*; **~s** *pl* acque *fpl*
B *vt* annaffiare ‹*garden, plant*›; (dilute) annacquare; dare da bere a ‹*horse etc*›
C *vi* ‹*eyes*› lacrimare; **my mouth was ~ing** avevo l'acquolina in bocca

■ **water down** **A** *vt* diluire
B fig attenuare

water authority *n* ente *m* dell'acqua

water bed *n* materasso *m* ad acqua

waterbird *n* uccello *m* acquatico

water birth *n* parto *m* in acqua

water bottle *n* borraccia *f*

water cannon *n* idrante *m*

watercolour *n* acquerello *m*

water company *n* società *f* dell'acqua

watercress *n* crescione *m*

water divining *n* rabdomanzia *f*

waterfall *n* cascata *f*

water filter *n* brocca *f* con filtro per l'acqua

waterfront *n* (by lakeside, riverside) riva *f*; (on harbour) zona *f* portuale

water heater *n* scaldacqua *m inv*

waterhole *n* pozza *f* d'acqua

watering can /ˈwɔːtərɪŋ/ *n* annaffiatoio *m*

water jump *n* riviera *f*

water lily *n* ninfea *f*

waterline *n* linea *f* di galleggiamento

waterlogged *adj* inzuppato

water main *n* conduttura *f* dell'acqua

watermark *n* filigrana *f*

water meadow *n* marcita *f*

watermelon *n* cocomero *m*, anguria *f*

watermill *n* mulino *m* ad acqua

water polo *n* pallanuoto *f*

water power *n* energia *f* idraulica

waterproof **A** *adj* ‹*coat*› impermeabile; ‹*make-up*› waterproof *inv*
B *n* impermeabile *m*

waterproofs *npl* sovrapantaloni *mpl* e giacca impermeabili

water rates *mpl* BrE tariffe *fpl* dell'acqua

water-resistant *adj* ‹*sun cream*› resistente all'acqua; ‹*garment, watch*› impermeabile

watershed *n* spartiacque *m inv*; fig svolta *f*

waterside **A** *n* riva *f*
B *attrib* ‹*cafe, hotel*› sulla riva

water-ski /ˈwɔːtəskiː/ *vi* fare sci nautico

waterskiing *n* sci *m* nautico

water slide *n* acquascivolo *m*

water softener *n* (equipment) addolcitore *m*; (substance) anticalcare *m inv*

water-soluble *adj* idrosolubile

water sport *n* sport *m inv* acquatico

water table *n* Geog superficie *f* freatica

watertight *adj* stagno; fig irrefutabile

water tower *n* serbatoio *m* idrico a torre

waterway *n* canale *m* navigabile

water-wheel *n* ruota *f* idraulica

water wings *npl* braccioli *mpl*

waterworks *n* impianto *m* idrico; **turn on the ~** infml mettersi a piangere come una fontana

watery /ˈwɔːtərɪ/ *adj* acquoso; ‹*eyes*› lacrimoso

watt /wɒt/ *n* watt *m inv*

wattage /ˈwɒtɪdʒ/ *n* wattaggio *m*

⚷ **wave** /weɪv/ **A** *n* onda *f*; (gesture) cenno *m*; fig ondata *f*
B *vt* agitare; **~ one's hand** agitare la mano
C *vi* far segno; ‹*flag*› sventolare

■ **wave aside** *vt* respingere ‹*criticism*›

■ **wave down** *vt* far segno di fermarsi a ‹*vehicle*›

waveband /ˈweɪvbænd/ *n* gamma *f* d'onda

wave farm *n* centrale *f* per energia da moto ondoso

wavelength /ˈweɪvleŋθ/ *n* lunghezza *f* d'onda; **be on the same ~** fig essere sulla stessa lunghezza d'onda

waver /ˈweɪvə(r)/ *vi* vacillare; (hesitate) esitare

wavy /ˈweɪvɪ/ *adj* ondulato

wax /wæks/ *vi* ‹*moon*› crescere; fig (become) diventare

wax² **A** *n* cera *f*; (in ear) cerume *m*
B *vt* dare la cera a

waxed jacket *n* cerata *f*

waxwork /ˈwækswɜːk/ *n* statua *f* di cera

waxworks /ˈwækswəːks/ *n* museo *m* delle cere

waxy /ˈwæksɪ/ *adj* ‹*skin, texture*› cereo

⚷ **way** /weɪ/ **A** *n* percorso *m*; (direction) direzione *f*; (manner, method) modo *m*; **~s** *pl* (customs) abitudini *fpl*; **be in the ~** essere in mezzo; **on the ~ to Rome** andando a Roma; **I'll do it on the ~** lo faccio mentre vado; **it's on my ~** è sul mio percorso; **a long ~ off** lontano; **this ~** da questa parte; (like this) così; **by the ~** a proposito; **by ~ of** come; (via) via; **either ~** (whatever we do) in un modo o nell'altro; **in some ~s** sotto certi aspetti; **in a ~** in un certo senso; **in a bad**

⚷ parola chiave

~ ‹*person*› molto grave; **out of the ~** fuori mano; **under ~** in corso; **lead the ~** far strada; fig aprire la strada; **make ~** far posto (for a); **give ~** Auto dare la precedenza; **go out of one's ~** fig scomodarsi (to per); **get one's [own] ~** averla vinta
B *adv* ~ **behind** molto indietro

way in *n* entrata *f*

waylay /weɪ'leɪ/ *vt* (*pt/pp* **-laid**) aspettare al varco ‹*person*›; intercettare ‹*letter*›

way out *n* uscita *f*; fig via *f* d'uscita

way-out *adj* infml eccentrico

wayside /'weɪsaɪd/ *n* bordo *m*; **fall by the ~** (morally) smarrire la retta via; (fail) fallire

wayward /'weɪwəd/ *adj* capriccioso

WC *abbr* WC; **the WC** il gabinetto

we /wiː/ *pers pron* noi; **we're the last** siamo gli ultimi; **they're going, but we're not** loro vanno, ma noi no

weak /wiːk/ *adj* debole; ‹*liquid*› leggero; **go ~ at the knees** infml sentirsi piegare le ginocchia

weaken /'wiːkn/ **A** *vt* indebolire
B *vi* indebolirsi

weakling /'wiːklɪŋ/ *n* smidollato, -a *mf*

weakly /'wiːklɪ/ *adv* debolmente

weak-minded /-'maɪndɪd/ *adj* (indecisive) debole; (simple) poco intelligente

weakness /'wiːknɪs/ *n* debolezza *f*; (liking) debole *m*

weak-willed /-'wɪld/ *adj* debole

weal /wiːl/ *n* piaga *f*

wealth /welθ/ *n* ricchezza *f*; fig gran quantità *f*

wealthy /'welθɪ/ *adj* (**-ier**, **-iest**) ricco

wean /wiːn/ *vt* svezzare

weapon /'wepən/ *n* arma *f*

weapon of mass destruction *n* arma *f* di distruzione di massa

weaponry /'wepənrɪ/ *n* armamento *m*

wear /weə(r)/ **A** *n* (clothing) abbigliamento *m*; **for everyday ~** da portare tutti i giorni; **~ [and tear]** usura *f*
B *vt* (*pt* **wore**, *pp* **worn**) portare; (damage) consumare; **~ a hole in something** logorare qualcosa fino a fare un buco; **what shall I ~?** cosa mi metto?
C *vi* consumarsi; (last) durare

■ **wear away** **A** *vt* consumare
B *vi* consumarsi

■ **wear down** *vt* estenuare ‹*opposition etc*›

■ **wear off** *vi* scomparire; ‹*effect*› finire

■ **wear out** **A** *vt* consumare [fino in fondo]; (exhaust) estenuare
B *vi* estenuarsi

■ **wear through** *vi* ‹*elbow, knee, shoe*› bucarsi

wearable /'weərəbl/ *adj* portabile

wearily /'wɪərɪlɪ/ *adv* stancamente

weariness /'wɪərɪnɪs/ *n* stanchezza *f*

wearing /'weərɪŋ/ *adj* (tiring) faticoso; (irritating) fastidioso

weary /'wɪərɪ/ **A** *adj* (**-ier**, **-iest**) sfinito
B *vt* (*pt/pp* **wearied**) sfinire
C *vi* ~ **of** stancarsi di

weasel /'wiːzl/ *n* donnola *f*

weather /'weðə(r)/ **A** *n* tempo *m*; **in this ~** con questo tempo; **under the ~** infml giù di corda
B *vt* sopravvivere a ‹*storm*›

weather balloon *n* pallone *m* sonda

weather-beaten /-biːtn/ *adj* ‹*face*› segnato dalle intemperie

weathercock *n* gallo *m* segnavento

weather forecast *n* previsioni *fpl* del tempo

weatherman *n* TV meteorologo *m*

weatherproof *adj* ‹*garment, shoe*› impermeabile; ‹*shelter, door*› resistente alle intemperie

weather-vane *n* banderuola *f*

weave[1] /wiːv/ *vi* (*pt/pp* **weaved**) (move) zigzagare

weave[2] **A** *n* Tex tessuto *m*
B *vt* (*pt* **wove**, *pp* **woven**) tessere; intrecciare ‹*flowers etc*›; intrecciare le fila di ‹*story etc*›

weaver /'wiːvə(r)/ *n* tessitore, -trice *mf*

weaving /'wiːvɪŋ/ *n* tessitura *f*

web /web/ *n* rete *f*; Comput web *m*, rete *f*; (of spider) ragnatela *f*

web-based /-beɪst/ *adj* ‹*learning, software*› basato sul web

webbed feet /webd'fiːt/ *npl* piedi *mpl* palmati

webbing /'webɪŋ/ *n* (material) cinghie *fpl*

web cam *n* Comput web cam *f inv*

web crawler /'web ˌkrɔːlə(r)/ *n software che analizza i contenuti di una rete in modo metodico e automatizzato*

web developer *n* Comput sviluppatore *m* web

webinar /'webɪnɑː(r)/ *n* seminario *m* via Internet

weblog /'weblɒg/ *n* Comput = **blog**

weblogger /'weblɒgə(r)/ *n* Comput = **blogger**

webmaster *n* Comput webmaster *mf inv*

web page *n* Comput pagina *f* web

web presence *n* Comput presenza *f* in Internet

web server *n* Comput server *m* web

website *n* Comput sito *m* web

web space *n* Comput spazio *m* web

wed /wed/ **A** *vt* (*pt/pp* **wedded**) sposare
B *vi* sposarsi

wedding /'wedɪŋ/ *n* matrimonio *m*

wedding anniversary *n* anniversario *m* di nozze

wedding bells *npl* fig marcia *f* nuziale

wedding breakfast *n* rinfresco *m* di nozze

wedding cake *n* torta *f* nuziale
wedding day *n* giorno *m* del matrimonio
wedding dress *n* vestito *m* da sposa
wedding march *n* marcia *f* nuziale
wedding night *n* prima notte *f* di nozze
wedding reception *n* ricevimento *m* di nozze
wedding ring *n* fede *f*
wedding vows *npl* voti *mpl* nuziali
wedge /wedʒ/ **A** *n* zeppa *f*; (for splitting wood) cuneo *m*; (of cheese) fetta *f*
B *vt* (fix) fissare
wedlock /ˈwedlɒk/ *n* **born out of ~** nato fuori dal matrimonio
⚷ **Wednesday** /ˈwenzdeɪ/ *n* mercoledì *m*
wee¹ /wiː/ *adj* infml piccolo
wee² **A** *n* infml **do a ~** fare la pipì
B *vi* infml fare la pipì
weed /wiːd/ **A** *n* erbaccia *f*; infml (person) mollusco *m*
B *vt* estirpare le erbacce da
C *vi* estirpare le erbacce
▪ **weed out** *vt* fig eliminare
weedkiller /ˈwiːdkɪlə(r)/ *n* erbicida *m*
weedy /ˈwiːdɪ/ *adj* infml mingherlino
⚷ **week** /wiːk/ *n* settimana *f*
weekday /ˈwiːkdeɪ/ *n* giorno *m* feriale
⚷ **weekend** /ˈwiːkend/ *n* fine *m* settimana *inv*
weekend bag *n* piccola borsa *f* da viaggio
weekly /ˈwiːklɪ/ **A** *adj* settimanale
B *n* settimanale *m*
C *adv* settimanalmente
weep /wiːp/ *vi* (*pt/pp* **wept**) piangere
weeping willow /wiːpɪŋˈwɪləʊ/ *n* salice *m* piangente
weepy /ˈwiːpɪ/ *adj* ‹*film*› strappalacrime *inv*
weigh /weɪ/ *vt & vi* pesare; **~ anchor** levare l'ancora
▪ **weigh down** *vt* fig piegare
▪ **weigh in** *vi* infml (join in discussion) intromettersi
▪ **weigh out** *vt* pesare ‹*amount of flour etc*›
▪ **weigh up** *vt* fig soppesare; valutare ‹*person*›
weighing machine /ˈweɪɪŋ/ *n* bilancia *f*
⚷ **weight** /weɪt/ *n* peso *m*; **put on/lose ~** ingrassare/dimagrire
weighting /ˈweɪtɪŋ/ *n* (allowance) indennità *f*
weightlessness /ˈweɪtlɪsnɪs/ *n* assenza *f* di gravità
weightlifter *n* sollevatore *m* di pesi
weightlifting *n* sollevamento *m* pesi
weight problem *n* problemi *mpl* di peso
weight training *n* **do ~** allenarsi con i pesi
weight-watcher *n* (in group) *persona* (*f*) *che segue una dieta dimagrante*
weighty /ˈweɪtɪ/ *adj* (**-ier, -iest**) pesante; (important) di un certo peso

⚷ parola chiave

weir /wɪə(r)/ *n* chiusa *f*
weird /wɪəd/ *adj* misterioso; (bizarre) bizzarro
⚷ **welcome** /ˈwelkəm/ **A** *adj* benvenuto; **you're ~!** prego!; **you're ~ to have it/to come** prendilo/vieni pure
B *n* accoglienza *f*
C *vt* accogliere; (appreciate) gradire
welcoming /ˈwelkəmɪŋ/ *adj* ‹*ceremony*› di benvenuto; ‹*committee, smile*› di accoglienza; ‹*house*› accogliente
weld /weld/ *vt* saldare
welder /ˈweldə(r)/ *n* saldatore *m*
welfare /ˈwelfeə(r)/ *n* benessere *m*; (aid) assistenza *f*; AmE previdenza *f* sociale
welfare services *n* servizi *mpl* sociali
Welfare State *n* Stato *m* assistenziale
welfare work *n* assistenza *m* sociale
⚷ **well¹** /wel/ *n* pozzo *m*; (oil **~**) pozzo *m*; (of staircase) tromba *f*
⚷ **well²** **A** *adv* (**better**, **best**) bene; **as ~** anche; **as ~ as** (in addition) oltre a; **~ done!** bravo!; **very ~** benissimo
B *adj* **he is not ~** non sta bene; **get ~ soon!** guarisci presto!
C *int* beh!; **~ I never!** ma va'!
well-attended /-əˈtendɪd/ *adj* ben frequentato
well-balanced /-ˈbælənst/ *adj* ‹*person, diet, meal*› equilibrato
well-behaved /-bɪˈheɪvd/ *adj* educato
well-being /ˈwelbiːɪŋ/ *n* benessere *m*
well-bred /welˈbred/ *adj* beneducato
well-defined /-dɪˈfaɪnd/ *adj* ‹*role, boundary*› ben definito; ‹*outline, image*› netto
well-disposed /-dɪˈspəʊzd/ *adj* benevolo; **be ~ towards** essere bendisposto verso ‹*person*›; essere favorevole a ‹*idea*›
well done /dʌn/ *adj* ‹*task*› ben fatto; Culin ben cotto
well-educated *adj* istruito; (cultured) colto
well-founded /-ˈfaʊndɪd/ *adj* fondato
well-heeled /-ˈhiːld/ *adj* infml danaroso
well-informed /-ɪnˈfɔːmd/ *adj* beninformato
wellingtons /ˈwelɪŋtənz/ *npl* stivali *mpl* di gomma
well-judged /-ˈdʒʌdʒd/ *adj* ‹*performance*› molto intelligente; ‹*shot*› ben assestato; ‹*statement, phrase*› ben ponderato
well-kept /-ˈkept/ *adj* ‹*garden*› curato; ‹*secret*› ben custodito
well-known /ˈ-nəʊn/ *adj* famoso
well-liked /-ˈlaɪkt/ *adj* popolare
well-made /-ˈmeɪd/ *adj* benfatto
well-mannered /-ˈmænəd/ *adj* educato
well-meaning *adj* con buone intenzioni
well-meant /-ˈment/ *adj* con le migliori intenzioni
well-nigh /ˈwelnaɪ/ *adv* quasi

well-off *adj* benestante
well read /-ˈred/ *adj* colto
well respected /ˌwelrɪˈspektɪd/ *adj* molto rispettato
well-rounded /ˌwelˈraʊndɪd/ *adj* ‹*education, individual*› completo
well-spoken /-ˈspəʊkən/ *adj* ‹*person*› che parla bene
well thought of *adj* stimato
well-timed /ˌwelˈtaɪmd/ *adj* tempestivo
well-to-do *adj* ricco
well-trodden /-ˈtrɒdn/ *adj* also fig battuto
well-wisher /ˈwelwɪʃə(r)/ *n* simpatizzante *mf*
well-worn /-ˈwɔːn/ *adj* ‹*steps, floorboards*› consunto; ‹*carpet, garment*› logoro; fig ‹*argument*› trito e ritrito
Welsh /welʃ/ *adj & n* gallese *mf*; (language) gallese *m*; **the ~** *pl* i gallesi
Welshman /ˈwelʃmən/ *n* gallese *m*
Welsh rabbit *n* toast *m inv* al formaggio
welt /welt/ *n* (on shoe) rinforzo *m*; (on skin) segno *m* di frustata
welterweight /ˈweltəweɪt/ *n* pesi *mpl* welter
went /went/ ▶ **go**
wept /wept/ ▶ **weep**
were /wɜː(r)/ ▶ **be**
west /west/ **A** *n* ovest *m*; **to the ~ of** a ovest di; **the W~** l'Occidente *m*
B *adj* occidentale
C *adv* verso occidente; **go ~** infml andare in malora
West Bank *n* Cisgiordania *f*
West Country *n* sud-ovest *m* dell'Inghilterra
West End *n zona (f) di Londra con un'alta concentrazione di teatri e negozi di lusso*
westerly /ˈwestəlɪ/ *adj* verso ovest; ‹*wind*› occidentale
western /ˈwestən/ **A** *adj* occidentale
B *n* western *m inv*
Westerner /ˈwestənə(r)/ *n* occidentale *mf*
westernize /ˈwestənaɪz/ *vt* occidentalizzare; **become ~d** occidentalizzarsi
Western Samoa *n* Samoa *fpl* Occidentali
West Germany *n* Germania *f* occidentale
West Indian *adj & n* antillese *mf*
West Indies /ˈɪndɪz/ *npl* Antille *fpl*
westwards BrE, **westward** AmE /ˈwestwəd[z]/ *adv* verso ovest
wet /wet/ **A** *adj* (**-tter, -test**) bagnato; ‹*paint*› fresco; (rainy) piovoso; infml ‹*person*› smidollato; **get ~** bagnarsi
B *vt* (*pt/pp* **wet, wetted**) bagnare
wet blanket *n* guastafeste *mf inv*
wet fish *n* BrE pesce *m* fresco
wet-look *adj* ‹*plastic, leather*› lucido
wet-nurse *n* balia *f*
wetsuit *n* muta *f*
whack /wæk/ **A** *n* infml colpo *m*
B *vt* infml dare un colpo a
whacked /wæk/ *adj* infml stanco morto
whacking /ˈwækɪŋ/ **A** *adj* BrE infml (enormous) enorme
B *n* infml sculacciata *f*
whacky /ˈwækɪ/ *adj* infml ‹*joke, person etc*› demenziale
whale /weɪl/ *n* balena *f*; **have a ~ of a time** infml divertirsi un sacco
whaling /ˈweɪlɪŋ, AmE ˈhweɪlɪŋ/ *n* caccia *f* alla balena
wham /wæm/ *int* bum!
wharf /wɔːf/ *n* banchina *f*
what /wɒt/ **A** *pron* che, [che] cosa; **~ for?** perché?; **~ is that for?** a che cosa serve?; **~ is it?** (what do you want) cosa c'è?; **~ is it like?** com'è?; **~ is your name?** come ti chiami?; **~ is the weather like?** com'è il tempo?; **~ is the film about?** di cosa parla il film?; **~ is he talking about?** di cosa sta parlando?; **he asked me ~ she had said** mi ha chiesto cosa ha detto; **~ about going to the cinema?** e se andassimo al cinema?; **~ about the children?** (what will they do) e i bambini?; **~ if it rains?** e se piove?
B *adj* quale, che; **take ~ books you want** prendi tutti i libri che vuoi; **~ kind of a** che tipo di; **at ~ time?** a che ora?
C *adv* che; **~ a lovely day!** che bella giornata!
D *int* **~ !** [che] cosa!; **~ ?** [che] cosa?
whatever /wɒtˈevə(r)/ **A** *adj* qualunque
B *pron* qualsiasi cosa; **~ is it?** cos'è?; **~ he does** qualsiasi cosa faccia; **~ happens** qualunque cosa succeda; **nothing ~** proprio niente
whatnot /ˈwɒtnɒt/ *n* coso *m*; (stand) scaffaletto *m*; **and ~** (and so on) e così via
whatsit /ˈwɒtsɪt/ *n* infml aggeggio *m*, coso *m*
what's-its-name *n* infml coso, -a *mf*
whatsoever /wɒtsəʊˈevə(r)/ *adj & pron* = **whatever**
wheat /wiːt/ *n* grano *m*, frumento *m*
wheatgerm /ˈwiːtdʒɜːm/ *n* germoglio *m* di grano
wheatmeal /ˈwiːtmiːl/ *n* farina *f* di frumento
wheedle /ˈwiːdl/ *vt* **~ something out of somebody** ottenere qualcosa da qualcuno con le lusinghe
wheel /wiːl/ **A** *n* ruota *f*; (steering **~**) volante *m*; **at the ~** al volante
B *vt* (push) spingere
C *vi* (circle) ruotare; **~ round** ruotare
wheelbarrow *n* carriola *f*
wheelchair *n* sedia *f* a rotelle
wheelchair access *n* accesso *m* disabili
wheelchair-accessible *adj* accessibile alle carrozzelle, accessibile alle sedie a rotelle
wheel clamp *n* ceppo *m* bloccaruote

W

wheeler-dealer /wiːlə'diːlə(r)/ *n* trafficone, -a *mf*

wheelie bin *n* cassonetto *m*

wheeze /wiːz/ *vi* ansimare

wheezy /'wiːzɪ/ *adj* ‹*voice, cough*› dal respiro affannato

⚷ **when** /wen/ *adv & conj* quando; **the day ~** il giorno in cui; **~ swimming/reading** nuotando/leggendo

whence /wens/ *adv* literary donde

whenever /wen'evə(r)/ *adv & conj* in qualsiasi momento; (every time that) ogni volta che; **~ did it happen?** quando è successo?

⚷ **where** /weə(r)/ *adv & conj* dove; **the street ~ I live** la via in cui abito; **~ do you come from?** da dove vieni?

whereabouts /weərə'baʊts/ *adv* dove

whereabouts² /'weərəbaʊts/ *n* **nobody knows his ~** nessuno sa dove si trovi

⚷ **whereas** /weər'æz/ *conj* dal momento che; (in contrast) mentre

whereby /weə'baɪ/ *adv* attraverso il quale

whereupon /weərə'pɒn/ *adv* dopo di che

wherever /weər'evə(r)/ *adv & conj* dovunque; **~ is he?** dov'è mai?; **~ possible** dovunque sia possibile

wherewithal /'weəwɪðɔːl/ *n* mezzi *mpl*

whet /wet/ *vt* (*pt/pp* **whetted**) stuzzicare ‹*appetite*›

⚷ **whether** /'weðə(r)/ *conj* se; **~ you like it or not** che ti piaccia o no

whew /fjuː/ *int* (in relief) fiuu; (when hot) uff; (in surprise) wow

⚷ **which** /wɪtʃ/ **A** *adj & pron* quale; **~ one?** quale?; **~ one of you?** chi di voi?; **~ way?** (direction) in che direzione?
B *rel pron* (object) che; **~ he does frequently** cosa che fa spesso; **after ~** dopo di che; **on/in ~** su/in cui

whichever /wɪtʃ'evə(r)/ *adj & pron* qualunque; **~ it is** qualunque sia; **~ one of you** chiunque tra voi

whiff /wɪf/ *n* zaffata *f*; **have a ~ of something** odorare qualcosa

⚷ **while** /waɪl/ **A** *n* **a long ~** un bel po'; **a little ~** un po'
B *conj* mentre; (as long as) finché; (although) sebbene; **he met her ~ in exile** l'ha incontrata mentre era in esilio
■ **while away** *vt* passare ‹*time*›

whilst /waɪlst/ *conj* = **while**

W

whim /wɪm/ *n* capriccio *m*

whimper /'wɪmpə(r)/ *vi* piagnucolare; ‹*dog*› mugolare

whimsical /'wɪmzɪkl/ *adj* capriccioso; ‹*story*› fantasioso

whine /waɪn/ **A** *n* lamento *m*; (of dog) guaito *m*
B *vi* lamentarsi; ‹*dog*› guaire

whinge /wɪndʒ/ *vi* infml lagnarsi

whining /'waɪnɪŋ, AmE 'hwaɪn-/ **A** *adj* ‹*voice, child*› lagnoso
B *n* (complaints) lagne *fpl*; (of dog) guaiti *mpl*

whinny /'wɪnɪ/ **A** *n* nitrito *m*
B *vi* ‹*horse*› nitrire

whip /wɪp/ **A** *n* frusta *f*; Pol (person) *parlamentare (mf) incaricato, -a di assicurarsi della presenza dei membri del suo partito alle votazioni*
B *vt* (*pt/pp* **whipped**) frustare; Culin sbattere; (snatch) afferrare; infml (steal) fregare
■ **whip up** *vt* (incite) stimolare; infml improvvisare ‹*meal*›

whiplash injury /'wɪplæŋ/ *n* Med colpo *m* di frusta

whipped cream /wɪpt'kriːm/ *n* panna *f* montata

whipping boy /'wɪpɪŋ/ *n* capro *m* espiatorio

whip-round *n* infml colletta *f*; **have a ~** fare una colletta

whirl /wɜːl/ **A** *n* (movement) rotazione *f*; **my mind's in a ~** ho le idee confuse
B *vi* girare rapidamente
C *vt* far girare rapidamente

whirlpool /'wɜːlpuːl/ *n* vortice *m*

whirlpool bath *n* vasca *f* con idromassaggio

whirlwind /'wɜːlwɪnd/ *n* turbine *m*

whirr /wɜː(r)/ *vi* ronzare

whisk /wɪsk/ **A** *n* Culin frullino *m*
B *vt* Culin frullare
■ **whisk away** *vt* portare via

whisker /'wɪskə(r)/ *n* **~s** *pl* (of cat) baffi *mpl*; (on man's cheek) basette *fpl*; **by a ~** per un pelo

whisky /'wɪskɪ/ *n* whisky *m inv*

⚷ **whisper** /'wɪspə(r)/ **A** *n* sussurro *m*; (rumour) diceria *f*
B *vt & vi* sussurrare

whispering gallery /'wɪspərɪŋ/ *n* galleria *f* acustica

whistle /'wɪsl/ **A** *n* fischio *m*; (instrument) fischietto *m*
B *vt* fischiettare
C *vi* fischiettare; ‹*referee*› fischiare

whistle-stop tour *n* Pol giro *m* elettorale

⚷ **white** /waɪt/ **A** *adj* bianco; **go ~** (pale) sbiancare
B *n* bianco *m*; (of egg) albume *m*; (person) bianco, -a *mf*

whitebait *n* bianchetti *npl*

white board *n* lavagna *f* bianca

white coffee *n* caffè *m* macchiato

white-collar worker *n* colletto *m* bianco

white elephant *n* (public project) progetto *m* dispendioso e di scarsa efficacia; (building) cattedrale *f* nel deserto; (item, knick-knack)

⚷ parola chiave

oggetto *m* inutile

white goods *n* (linen) biancheria *f* per la casa; (appliances) elettrodomestici *mpl*

Whitehall *n strada (f) di Londra sede degli uffici del governo britannico*; fig amministrazione *f* britannica

white horses *npl* cavalloni *mpl*

white-hot *adj* ‹*metal*› arroventato

White House *n* **the ~** la Casa Bianca

white knight *n* Fin cavaliere bianco *m inv*

white-knuckle ride *n* corsa *f* al cardiopalmo

white lie *n* bugia *f* pietosa

whiten /'waɪtn/ **A** *vt* imbiancare
B *vi* sbiancare

whitener /'waɪt(ə)nə(r)/ *n* (for shoes) bianchetto *m*; (for clothes) sbiancante *m*; (for coffee, tea) surrogato *m* del latte

whiteness /'waɪtnɪs/ *n* bianchezza *f*

white spirit *n* acquaragia *f*

white tie *n* (tie) cravattino *m* bianco; (formal dress) frac *m inv*

whitewash **A** *n* intonaco *m*; fig copertura *f*
B *vt* dare una mano d'intonaco a; fig coprire

white water *n* rapide *fpl*

white-water rafting *n* discesa *f* sulle rapide

white wedding *n* matrimonio *m* in bianco

whither /'wɪðə(r)/ *adv* literary dove

whiting /'waɪtɪŋ/ *n* (fish) merlano *m*

Whitsun /'wɪtsn/ *n* Pentecoste *f*

Whit Sunday *n* Pentecoste *f*

whittle /'wɪtl/ *v*
■ **whittle away** *vt* intaccare ‹*savings*›; ridurre ‹*lead in race*›
■ **whittle down** *vt* ridurre

whizz /wɪz/ *vi* (*pt/pp* **whizzed**) sibilare

whizz-kid *n* infml giovane *m* prodigio

who /hu:/ **A** *inter pron* chi
B *rel* che; **the children, ~ were all tired, ...** i bambini che erano tutti stanchi,...

WHO *n abbr* (**World Health Organization**) OMS *f*

whodunnit /hu:'dʌnɪt/ *n* infml [romanzo *m*] giallo *m*

whoever /hu:'evə(r)/ *pron* chiunque; **~ he is** chiunque sia; **~ can that be?** chi può mai essere?

whole /həʊl/ **A** *adj* tutto; (not broken) intatto; **the ~ truth** tutta la verità; **the ~ world** il mondo intero; **the ~ lot** (everything) tutto; **the ~ lot of you** tutti voi
B *n* tutto *m*; **as a ~** nell'insieme; **on the ~** tutto considerato; **the ~ of Italy** tutta l'Italia

wholefood *n* cibo *m* macrobiotico

wholehearted /'həʊlhɑ:tɪd/ *adj* di tutto cuore

wholeheartedly /həʊl'hɑ:tɪdlɪ/ *adv* ‹*agree, support*› senza riserve

wholemeal *adj* integrale

whole milk *n* latte *m* intero

whole number *n* numero *m* intero

wholesale /'həʊlseɪl/ *adj & adv* all'ingrosso; fig in massa

wholesaler /'həʊlseɪlə(r)/ *n* grossista *mf*

wholesome /'həʊlsəm/ *adj* sano

wholewheat *adj* = **wholemeal**

wholly /'həʊlɪ/ *adv* completamente

wholly-owned subsidiary *n* consociata *f* interamente controllata

whom /hu:m/ **A** *rel pron* che; **the man ~ I saw** l'uomo che ho visto; **to/with ~** a/con cui
B *inter pron* chi; **to ~ did you speak?** con chi hai parlato?

whoop /wu:p/ **A** *n* (shout) grido *m*
B *vi* gridare

whoopee /'wʊpɪ/ **A** *int* evviva!
B *n* hum **make ~** (have fun) fare baldoria; (make love) fare l'amore

whooping cough /'hu:pɪŋ/ *n* pertosse *f*

whoosh /wʊʃ/ *int* vuum!

whopper /'wɒpə(r)/ *n* infml (lie) balla *f*; **what a ~!** è veramente gigantesco!

whopping /'wɒpɪŋ/ *adj* infml enorme

whore /hɔ:(r)/ *n* puttana *f* vulg

whorl /wɔ:l/ *n* (of cream, chocolate etc) ghirigoro *m*; (of fingerprint) spirale *f*

whose /hu:z/ **A** *rel pron* il cui; **people ~ name begins with D** le persone i cui nomi cominciano con la D
B *inter pron* di chi; **~ is that?** di chi è quello?
C *adj* **~ car did you use?** di chi è la macchina che hai usato?

Who's Who *n pubblicazione (f) annuale con l'elenco delle personalità di spicco*

why /waɪ/ **A** *adv* (inter) perché; **the reason ~** la ragione per cui; **that's ~** per questo
B *int* diamine!

WI *abbr* **1** (**Women's Institute**) associazione *f* che organizza attività culturali e sociali **2** AmE (**Wisconsin**)

wick /wɪk/ *n* stoppino *m*

wicked /'wɪkɪd/ *adj* cattivo; (mischievous) malizioso

wicker /'wɪkə(r)/ **A** *n* vimini *mpl*
B *attrib* di vimini

wicket /'wɪkɪt/ *n* (field gate) cancelletto *m*; Sport porta *f*; AmE (of ticket office etc) sportello *m*; **be on a sticky ~** infml essere in una situazione difficile

wide /waɪd/ **A** *adj* largo; ‹*experience, knowledge*› vasto; ‹*difference*› profondo; (far from target) lontano; **10 cm ~** largo 10 cm; **how ~ is it?** quanto è largo?
B *adv* (off target) lontano dal bersaglio; **~ awake** del tutto sveglio; **~ open** spalancato; **open ~!** apri bene!; **far and ~** in lungo e in largo

wide-angle lens *n* grandangolo *m*

wide-eyed /-ˈaɪd/ *adj* ‹*person, innocence*› ingenuo; (with fear, surprise) con gli occhi sbarrati

🔑 **widely** /ˈwaɪdlɪ/ *adv* largamente; ‹*known, accepted*› generalmente; ‹*different*› profondamente

widely read *adj* ‹*student*› colto; ‹*writer*› molto letto

widen /ˈwaɪdn/ **A** *vt* allargare; ~ **the gap** fig accentuare il divario
B *vi* allargarsi

widening /ˈwaɪdnɪŋ/ *adj* ‹*gap, division*› sempre più grande

wide open *adj* ‹*door, window, eyes*› spalancato

wide-ranging /ˌwaɪdˈreɪndʒɪŋ/ *adj* ‹*interests, reforms, discussion*› di ampio respiro

wide screen *n* Cinema schermo *m* panoramico

wide-screen TV *n* televisore *m* con schermo panoramico

widespread /ˈwaɪdspred/ *adj* diffuso

widow /ˈwɪdəʊ/ *n* vedova *f*

widowed /ˈwɪdəʊd/ *adj* vedovo

widower /ˈwɪdəʊə(r)/ *n* vedovo *m*

width /wɪdθ/ *n* larghezza *f*; (of material) altezza *f*

widthways BrE /ˈwɪdθweɪz/, **widthwise** AmE /ˈwɪdθwaɪz/ *adv* trasversalmente

wield /wiːld/ *vt* maneggiare; esercitare ‹*power*›

🔑 **wife** /waɪf/ *n* (*pl* **wives**) moglie *f*

wife battering /ˈwaɪfbæt(ə)rɪŋ/ *n* maltrattamento *m* della coniuge

Wi-Fi® /ˈwaɪfaɪ/ *n abbr* (**wireless fidelity**) Wi-Fi *m*

wig /wɪɡ/ *n* parrucca *f*

wiggle /ˈwɪɡl/ **A** *vi* dimenarsi
B *vt* dimenare

wiki /ˈwɪkɪ/ *n sito* (*m*) *web aggiornato dai suoi utilizzatori*

🔑 **wild** /waɪld/ **A** *adj* selvaggio; ‹*animal, flower*› selvatico; (furious) furibondo; ‹*applause*› fragoroso; ‹*idea*› folle; (with joy) pazzo; ‹*guess*› azzardato; **be ~ about** (keen on) andare pazzo per
B *adv* **run ~** crescere senza controllo
C *n* **in the ~** allo stato naturale; **the ~s** *pl* le zone sperdute

wild boar *n* cinghiale *m*

wild card *n* jolly *m inv*; Comput carattere *m* jolly

wildcat strike *n* sciopero *m* selvaggio

wild dog *n* cane *m* randagio

wilderness /ˈwɪldənɪs/ *n* deserto *m*; fig (garden) giungla *f*

wild-eyed /-ˈaɪd/ *adj* (distressed) dall'aria angosciata; (angry) dallo sguardo minaccioso

wildfire *n* **spread like ~** allargarsi a macchia d'olio

wild flower *n* fiore *m* di campo

wildfowl *n* (bird) uccello *m* selvatico; (birds collectively) uccelli *mpl* selvatici; (game) selvaggina *f* di penna

wild goose chase *n* ricerca *f* inutile

wildlife *n* animali *mpl* selvatici

wildlife park *n* parco *m* naturale

wildlife reserve *n* riserva *f* naturale

wildlife sanctuary *n* riserva *f* naturale

wildly /ˈwaɪldlɪ/ *adv* fig ‹*exaggerated*› estremamente; ‹*speak*› senza riflettere; ‹*applaud*› fragorosamente; ‹*hit out*› all'impazzata

Wild West *n* il Far West *m*

wiles /waɪlz/ *npl* astuzie *fpl*

wilful /ˈwɪlfʊl/ *adj* intenzionale; ‹*person, refusal*› ostinato

wilfully /ˈwɪlfʊlɪ/ *adv* intenzionalmente; ‹*refuse*› ostinatamente

🔑 **will**[1] /wɪl/ *v aux* **he ~ arrive tomorrow** arriverà domani; **I won't tell him** non glielo dirò; **you ~ be back soon, won't you?** tornerai presto, no?; **he ~ be there, won't he?** sarà là, no?; **she ~ be there by now** sarà là ormai; **~ you go?** (do you intend to go) pensi di andare?; **~ you go to the baker's and buy...?** puoi andare dal fornaio a comprare...?; **~ you be quiet!** vuoi stare zitto!; **~ you have some wine?** vuoi del vino?; **the engine won't start** la macchina non parte

🔑 **will**[2] *n* volontà *f*; (document) testamento *m*

🔑 **willing** /ˈwɪlɪŋ/ *adj* disposto; (eager) volonteroso

willingly /ˈwɪlɪŋlɪ/ *adv* volentieri

willingness /ˈwɪlɪŋnɪs/ *n* buona volontà *f*

willow /ˈwɪləʊ/ *n* salice *m*

willowy /ˈwɪləʊɪ/ *adj* ‹*person, figure*› slanciato

willpower /wɪlpaʊə(r)/ *n* forza *f* di volontà

willy-nilly /wɪlɪˈnɪlɪ/ *adv* (at random) a casaccio; (wanting to or not) volente o nolente

wilt /wɪlt/ *vi* appassire

wily /ˈwaɪlɪ/ *adj* (**-ier**, **-iest**) astuto

wimp /wɪmp/ *n* rammollito, -a *mf*

wimpish /ˈwɪmpɪʃ/ *adj* infml ‹*behaviour*› da rammollito

wimpy /ˈwɪmpɪ/ *adj* infml ‹*person*› rammollito

🔑 **win** /wɪn/ **A** *n* vittoria *f*; **have a ~** riportare una vittoria
B *vt* (*pt/pp* **won**, *pres p* **winning**) vincere; conquistare ‹*fame*›
C *vi* vincere

▪ **win back** *vt* recuperare

▪ **win over** *vt* convincere

▪ **win through** *vi* infml (be successful) uscire vittorioso

wince /wɪns/ *vi* contrarre il viso

🔑 parola chiave

winch /wɪntʃ/ *n* argano *m*
■ **winch up** *vt* tirare con l'argano

wind¹ /wɪnd/ **A** *n* vento *m*; (breath) fiato *m*; infml (flatulence) aria *f*; **get/have the ~ up** infml aver fifa; **get ~ of** aver sentore di; **in the ~** nell'aria
B *vt* **~ somebody** lasciare qualcuno senza fiato; **~ a baby** far fare il ruttino ad un neonato

wind² /waɪnd/ **A** *vt* (*pt/pp* **wound**) (wrap) avvolgere; (move by turning) far girare; ‹*clock*› caricare
B *vi* ‹*road*› serpeggiare
■ **wind down** **A** *vi* (relax) rilassarsi; (gradually come to an end) diminuire
B *vt* (gradually bring to an end) metter fine in modo graduale a
■ **wind up** **A** *vt* caricare ‹*clock*›; concludere ‹*proceedings*›; infml sfottere ‹*somebody*›
B *vi* (end up) **~ up doing something** finire per fare qualcosa

windbreak *n* frangivento *m*
windcheater *n* BrE giacca *f* a vento
wind chill factor *n* fattore *m* di raffreddamento da vento
wind chimes *npl* campane *fpl* eoliche
wind energy *n* forza *f* del vento
winder /ˈwaɪndə(r)/ *n* (for car window) manovella *f* alzacristalli; (for watch) bottone *m* di carica
windfall *n* fig fortuna *f* inaspettata; **~s** *pl* (fruit) frutta *f* abbattuta dal vento
wind farm *n* centrale *f* eolica
winding /ˈwaɪndɪŋ/ *adj* tortuoso
wind instrument /ˈwɪnd/ *n* strumento *m* a fiato
windmill /ˈwɪn(d)mɪl/ *n* mulino *m* a vento
window /ˈwɪndəʊ/ *n* finestra *f*; (of car) finestrino *m*; (of shop) vetrina *f*
window box *n* cassetta *f* per i fiori
window cleaner *n* (person) lavavetri *mf inv*
window display *n* Comm esposizione *f* in vetrina
window dresser *n* vetrinista *mf*
window dressing *n* vetrinistica *f*; fig fumo *m* negli occhi
window envelope *n* busta *f* a finestra
window frame *n* telaio *m* di finestra
window ledge *n* davanzale *m*
window pane *n* vetro *m*
window seat *n* (in room) panca *f* sotto la finestra; (in plane, train) posto *m* accanto al finestrino
window-shopping *n* **go ~** andare in giro a vedere le vetrine
window sill *n* davanzale *m*
windpipe *n* trachea *f*
wind power *n* energia *f* eolica
windscreen *n* parabrezza *m inv*
windscreen washer *n* getto *m* d'acqua
windscreen wiper *n* tergicristallo *m*
windshield *n* AmE parabrezza *m inv*
wind sleeve *n* manica *f* a vento
wind sock *n* manica *f* a vento
windsurf *vi* fare windsurf
windsurfer *n* (person) windsurfista *mf*; (board) windsurf *m inv*
windsurfing *n* windsurf *m inv*
windswept *adj* esposto al vento; ‹*person*› scompigliato
windy /ˈwɪndɪ/ *adj* (**-ier**, **-iest**) ventoso
wine /waɪn/ *n* vino *m*
wine bar *n* ≈ enoteca *f*
wine box *n* contenitore *m* di vino con rubinetto
wine cellar *n* cantina *f*
wine cooler *n* (ice bucket) secchiello *m* del ghiaccio; AmE (drink) *bibita (f) leggermente alcolica*
wine glass *n* bicchiere *m* da vino
wine grower *n* viticultore, -trice *mf*
wine growing *n* viticultura *f*
wine list *n* carta *f* dei vini
wine merchant *n* commerciante *mf* di vini
wine producer *n* produttore, -trice *mf* di vini
wine rack *n* portabottiglie *m inv*
winery /ˈwaɪnərɪ/ *n* AmE vigneto *m*
wine tasting /ˈwaɪnteɪstɪŋ/ *n* degustazione *f* di vini
wine vinegar *n* aceto *m* di vino
wine waiter *n* sommelier *m inv*
wing /wɪŋ/ *n* ala *f*; Auto parafango *m*; **~s** *pl* Theat quinte *fpl*; **under sb's ~** sotto l'ala [protettiva] di qualcuno
wing chair *n* poltrona *f* con ampio schienale
wing collar *n* colletto *m* rigido
wing commander *n* tenente *m* colonnello delle forze aeree
winger /ˈwɪŋə(r)/ *n* Sport ala *f*
wing half *n* (in soccer) mediano *m*
wing mirror *n* BrE specchietto *m* laterale
wing nut *n* dado *m* ad alette
wingspan *n* apertura *f* alare
wink /wɪŋk/ **A** *n* strizzata *f* d'occhio; **not sleep a ~** non chiudere occhio
B *vi* strizzare l'occhio; ‹*light*› lampeggiare
winner /ˈwɪnə(r)/ *n* vincitore, -trice *mf*
winning /ˈwɪnɪŋ/ *adj* vincente; ‹*smile*› accattivante
winning post *n* linea *f* d'arrivo
winnings /ˈwɪnɪŋz/ *npl* vincite *fpl*
winning streak *n* periodo *m* fortunato; **be on a ~** essere in un periodo fortunato
winsome /ˈwɪnsəm/ *adj* accattivante
winter /ˈwɪntə(r)/ *n* inverno *m*
winter sports *npl* sport *mpl* invernali
wintertime /ˈwɪntətaɪm/ *n* inverno *m*
wintry /ˈwɪntrɪ/ *adj* invernale

wipe /waɪp/ **A** *n* passata *f*; (to dry) asciugata *f*
B *vt* strofinare; (dry) asciugare
▪ **wipe away** *vt* asciugare ‹*tears, sweat*›; pulire ‹*dirt, mark*›
▪ **wipe off** *vt* asciugare; (erase) cancellare
▪ **wipe out** *vt* annientare; eliminare ‹*village*›; estinguere ‹*debt*›
▪ **wipe up** *vt* asciugare ‹*dishes*›

wipe-clean *adj* ‹*surface, cover*› facile da pulire

wiper blade /ˈwaɪpə/ *n* Auto bordo *m* gommato del tergicristallo

wire /ˈwaɪə(r)/ *n* fil *m* di ferro; (electrical) filo *m* elettrico

wire brush *n* spazzola *f* metallica

wire cutters *npl* tronchese *msg*

wire-haired /-ˈheəd/ *adj* dal pelo ispido

wireless /ˈwaɪəlɪs/ **A** *n* BrE Hist radio *f inv*
B *adj* Techn wireless

wire mesh *n* rete *f* metallica

wire netting *n* rete *f* metallica

wire wool *n* lana *f* d'acciaio

wiring /ˈwaɪərɪŋ/ *n* impianto *m* elettrico

wiry /ˈwaɪərɪ/ *adj* (**-ier**, **-iest**) ‹*person*› dal fisico asciutto; ‹*hair*› ispido

wisdom /ˈwɪzdəm/ *n* saggezza *f*; (of action) sensatezza *f*

wisdom tooth *n* dente *m* del giudizio

wise /waɪz/ *adj* saggio; (prudent) sensato
▪ **wise up** infml **A** *vi* (become more aware) aprire gli occhi
B *vt* aprire gli occhi a (**to** su)

wisecrack /ˈwaɪzkræk/ infml **A** *n* battuta *f* salace
B *vi* far battute salaci

wise guy *n* infml sapientone *m*

wisely /ˈwaɪzlɪ/ *adv* saggiamente; ‹*act*› sensatamente

Wise Men *npl* Re Magi *mpl*

⚷ **wish** /wɪʃ/ **A** *n* desiderio *m*; **make a ~** esprimere un desiderio; **with best ~es** con i migliori auguri
B *vt* desiderare; **~ somebody well** fare tanti auguri a qualcuno; **I ~ you every success** ti auguro buona fortuna; **I ~ you could stay** vorrei che tu potessi rimanere; **~ something on somebody** infml sbolognare qualcosa a qualcuno
C *vi* **~ for something** desiderare qualcosa

wishbone /ˈwɪʃbəʊn/ *n* forcella *f* (*di pollo o tacchino*)

wishful /ˈwɪʃfʊl/ *adj* **~ thinking** illusione *f*

wishy-washy /ˈwɪʃɪwɒʃɪ/ *adj* ‹*colour*› spento; ‹*personality*› insignificante

wisp /wɪsp/ *n* (of hair) ciocca *f*; (of smoke) filo *m*; (of grass) ciuffo *m*

wispy /ˈwɪspɪ/ *adj* ‹*hair, beard*› a ciocche; ‹*clouds*› vaporoso

wisteria /wɪsˈtɪərɪə/ *n* glicine *m*

⚷ parola chiave

wistful /ˈwɪstfʊl/ *adj* malinconico

wistfully /ˈwɪstfʊlɪ/ *adv* malinconicamente

wit /wɪt/ *n* spirito *m*; (person) persona *f* di spirito; **be at one's ~s' end** non saper che pesci pigliare; **scared out of one's ~s** spaventato a morte

witch /wɪtʃ/ *n* strega *f*

witchcraft *n* magia *f*

witch doctor *n* stregone *m*

witch-hunt *n* caccia *f* alle streghe

⚷ **with** /wɪð/ *prep* con; (fear, cold, jealousy etc) di; **I'm not ~ you** infml non ti seguo; **can I leave it ~ you?** (task) puoi occupartene tu?; **~ no regrets/money** senza rimpianti/soldi; **be ~ it** infml essere al passo coi tempi; (alert) essere concentrato

withdraw /wɪðˈdrɔː/ **A** *vt* (*pt* **-drew**, *pp* **-drawn**) ritirare; prelevare ‹*money*›
B *vi* ritirarsi

withdrawal /wɪðˈdrɔː(ə)l/ *n* ritiro *m*; (of money) prelevamento *m*; (from drugs) crisi *f inv* di astinenza; Psych chiusura *f* in se stessi

withdrawal symptoms *npl* sintomi *mpl* da crisi di astinenza

withdrawn /wɪðˈdrɔːn/ **A** ▶ **withdraw**
B *adj* ‹*person*› chiuso in se stesso

wither /ˈwɪðə(r)/ *vi* ‹*flower*› appassire

withering /ˈwɪðərɪŋ/ *adj* ‹*look*› fulminante

withhold /wɪðˈhəʊld/ *vt* (*pt/pp* **-held**) rifiutare ‹*consent*› (**from** a); nascondere ‹*information*› (**from** a); trattenere ‹*smile*›

⚷ **within** /wɪðˈɪn/ **A** *prep* in; (before the end of) entro; **~ the law** legale
B *adv* all'interno

⚷ **without** /wɪðˈaʊt/ *prep* senza; **~ stopping** senza fermarsi; **how could it have happened ~ you noticing it?** come è potuto succedere senza che tu lo notassi?

withstand /wɪðˈstænd/ *vt* (*pt/pp* **-stood**) resistere a

⚷ **witness** /ˈwɪtnɪs/ **A** *n* testimone *mf*; **bear ~** portare testimonianza
B *vt* ≈ autenticare ‹*signature*›; essere testimone di ‹*accident*›

witness box, AmE **witness stand** *n* banco *m* dei testimoni

witticism /ˈwɪtɪsɪzm/ *n* spiritosaggine *f*

wittingly /ˈwɪtɪŋlɪ/ *adv* consapevolmente

witty /ˈwɪtɪ/ *adj* (**-ier**, **-iest**) spiritoso

wives /waɪvz/ ▶ **wife**

wizard /ˈwɪzəd/ *n* mago *m*

wizardry /ˈwɪzədrɪ/ *n* stregoneria *f*

wizened /ˈwɪznd/ *adj* raggrinzito

wk *abbr* (**week**) settimana *f*

WMD *n abbr* (**weapon of mass destruction**) ADM *fpl*

wobble /ˈwɒbl/ *vi* traballare

wobbly /ˈwɒblɪ/ *adj* traballante

wodge /wɒdʒ/ *n* infml mucchio *m*

woe /wəʊ/ *n* afflizione *f*; **~ is me!** me meschino!

woeful /ˈwəʊfʊl/ *adj* ‹*story, sight*› triste; ‹*lack*› vergognoso

woke, woken /wəʊk, ˈwəʊkn/ ▶ **wake¹**

wolf /wʊlf/ **A** *n* (*pl* **wolves** /wʊlvz/) lupo *m*; infml (womanizer) donnaiolo *m*
B *vt* ~ **[down]** divorare

wolf cub *n* cucciolo *m* di lupo

wolfhound *n* BrE cane *m* lupo

wolf whistle **A** *n* fischio *m*
B *vi* **~-whistle at somebody** fischiare dietro a qualcuno

⚷ **woman** /ˈwʊmən/ *n* (*pl* **women**) donna *f*

womanizer /ˈwʊmənaɪzə(r)/ *n* donnaiolo *m*

womanly /ˈwʊmənlɪ/ *adj* femminile

womb /wu:m/ *n* utero *m*

women /ˈwɪmɪn/ ▶ **woman**

Women's Institute *n associazione (f) che si occupa dei problemi delle donne*

Women's Libber /wɪmɪnzˈlɪbə(r)/ *n* femminista *f*

Women's Liberation *n* movimento *m* femminista

women's movement *n* movimento *m* per l'emancipazione della donna

women's refuge *n* casa *f* rifugio *inv*

women's studies *npl storia (fsg) dell'emancipazione femminile*

won /wʌn/ ▶ **win**

⚷ **wonder** /ˈwʌndə(r)/ **A** *n* meraviglia *f*; (surprise) stupore *m*; **no ~!** non c'è da stupirsi!; **it's a ~ that...** è incredibile che...
B *vi* restare in ammirazione; (be surprised) essere sorpreso; **I ~** è quello che mi chiedo; **I ~ whether she is ill** mi chiedo se è malata

⚷ **wonderful** /ˈwʌndəfʊl/ *adj* meraviglioso

wonderfully /ˈwʌndəfʊlɪ/ *adv* meravigliosamente

wonderland /ˈwʌndəlænd/ *n* paese *m* delle meraviglie

wonky /ˈwɒŋkɪ/ *adj* BrE infml (faulty) difettoso; ‹*furniture*› traballante; (crooked) storto

wont /wəʊnt/ **A** *n* **as was his ~** come suo solito
B *adj* **he was ~ to fall asleep** era solito addormentarsi

won't /wəʊnt/ *will not*

woo /wu:/ *vt* corteggiare; fig cercare di accattivarsi ‹*voters*›; cercare di ottenere ‹*fame, fortune*›

⚷ **wood** /wʊd/ *n* legno *m*; (for burning) legna *f*; (forest) bosco *m*; **out of the ~** fig fuori pericolo; **touch ~!** tocca ferro!

woodcarving /ˈwʊdkɑ:vɪŋ/ *n* scultura *f* di legno

wooded /ˈwʊdɪd/ *adj* boscoso

wooden /ˈwʊdn/ *adj* di legno; fig legnoso

wooden horse *n* cavallo *m* di Troia

wooden spoon *n* mestolo *m* di legno; fig premio *m* di consolazione

woodland /ˈwʊdlənd/ *n* terreno *m* boschivo

woodlouse *n* onisco *m*

woodpecker *n* picchio *m*

wood pigeon *n* colombaccio *m*

wood shavings *npl* trucioli *mpl*

woodshed *n* legnaia *f*

wood stove *n* stufa *f* a legna

woodwind *n* strumenti *mpl* a fiato

woodwork *n* (wooden parts) parti *fpl* in legno; (craft) falegnameria *f*

woodworm *n* tarlo *m*

woody /ˈwʊdɪ/ *adj* legnoso; ‹*hill*› boscoso

wool /wʊl/ **A** *n* lana *f*; **pull the ~ over sb's eyes** gettar fumo negli occhi a qualcuno
B *attrib* di lana

woollen /ˈwʊlən/ *adj* di lana

woollens /ˈwʊlənz/ *npl* capi *mpl* di lana

woolly /ˈwʊlɪ/ *adj* (**-ier**, **-iest**) ‹*sweater*› di lana; fig confuso

woozy /ˈwu:zɪ/ *adj* intontito

⚷ **word** /wɜ:d/ *n* parola *f*; (news) notizia *f*; **by ~ of mouth** a viva voce; **have a ~ with** dire due parole a; **have ~s** bisticciare; **in other ~s** in altre parole; **go back on one's ~** rimangiarsi la parola

word-for-word **A** *adj* ‹*translation*› letterale
B *adv* parola per parola

wording /ˈwɜ:dɪŋ/ *n* parole *fpl*

word-perfect *adj* che sa a memoria

word processing *n* Comput word processing *m*, elaborazione *f* testi

word processor *n* sistema *m* di videoscrittura, word processor *m inv*

wordy /ˈwɜ:dɪ/ *adj* prolisso

wore /wɔ:(r)/ ▶ **wear**

⚷ **work** /wɜ:k/ **A** *n* lavoro *m*; (of art) opera *f*; **~s** *pl* (factory) fabbrica *fsg*; **at ~** al lavoro; **out of ~** disoccupato
B *vi* lavorare; ‹*machine, ruse*› funzionare; (study) studiare
C *vt* far funzionare ‹*machine*›; far lavorare ‹*employee*›; far studiare ‹*student*›; **~ one's way through something** (read) leggere attentamente

▪ **work in** *vt* inserire ‹*comment, fact*›; Culin incorporare ‹*butter*›

▪ **work off** *vt* sfogare ‹*anger*›; lavorare per estinguere ‹*debt*›; fare sport per smaltire ‹*weight*›

▪ **work on** **A** *vt* lavorare a ‹*book, report*›; occuparsi di ‹*problem, case*›; cercare ‹*solution*›
B *vi* (continue) continuare a lavorare

▪ **work out** **A** *vt* elaborare ‹*plan*›; risolvere ‹*problem*›; calcolare ‹*bill*›; **I ~ed out how he did it** ho capito come l'ha fatto
B *vi* evolvere

▪ **work up**: *vt* **I've ~ed up an appetite** mi è venuto appetito; **don't get ~ed up** (anxious) non farti prendere dal panico; (angry) non arrabbiarti

workable /ˈwɜ:kəbl/ *adj* (feasible) fattibile

W

workaday /ˈwɜːkədeɪ/ *adj* ‹*clothes, life*› ordinario

workaholic /wɜːkəˈhɒlɪk/ *n* stacanovista *mf*

workbench *n* banco *m* da lavoro

workbook *n* (blank) quaderno *m*; (with exercises) libro *m* di esercizi

workday *n* giorno *m* lavorativo

🔑 **worker** /ˈwɜːkə(r)/ *n* lavoratore, -trice *mf*; (manual) operaio, -a *mf*

work experience *n* esperienza *f* professionale; (part of training programme) stage *m inv*

workforce *n* forza *f* lavoro

workhorse *n* fig lavoratore, -trice *mf* indefesso, -a

🔑 **working** /ˈwɜːkɪŋ/ *adj* ‹*clothes etc*› da lavoro; ‹*day*› feriale; **in ~ order** funzionante

working capital *n* capitale *m* netto di esercizio

working-class *adj* operaio; **be ~** appartenere alla classe operaia

workings /ˈwɜːkɪŋz/ *npl* meccanismi *mpl*

working week *n* settimana *f* lavorativa

workload *n* carico *m* di lavoro

workman *n* operaio *m*

workmanlike *adj* fatto con competenza

workmanship *n* lavorazione *f*

workmate *n* collega *mf*

work of art *n* opera *f* d'arte

workout *n* allenamento *m*

work permit *n* permesso *m* di lavoro

workplace *n* posto *m* di lavoro

work-sharing *n divisione (f) di un posto di lavoro tra più persone*

worksheet *n* foglio *m* degli esercizi

workshop *n* officina *f*; (discussion) dibattito *m*

work-shy *adj* pigro

workstation *n* stazione *f* di lavoro

work surface *n* piano *m* di lavoro

worktop *n* BrE piano *m* di lavoro

work to rule *n* sciopero *m* bianco

🔑 **world** /wɜːld/ *n* mondo *m*; **a ~ of difference** una differenza abissale; **out of this ~** favoloso; **think the ~ of somebody** andare matto per qualcuno

world-class *adj* di livello internazionale

World Cup *n* (in football) Mondiali *mpl*

world-famous *adj* di fama mondiale

world leader *n* (politician, company) leader *m* mondiale; (athlete) campione, -essa *mf* mondiale

worldly /ˈwɜːldlɪ/ *adj* materiale; ‹*person*› materialista

worldly-wise *adj* vissuto

world music *n* world music *f*

world power *n* potenza *f* mondiale

world view *n* visione *f* del mondo

world war *n* guerra *f* mondiale

worldwide /ˈwɜːldwaɪd/ **A** *adj* mondiale
B *adv* mondialmente

World Wide Web *n* Comput World Wide Web *m*

worm /wɜːm/ **A** *n* verme *m*
B *vt* **~ one's way into sb's confidence** conquistarsi la fiducia di qualcuno in modo subdolo
■ **worm out**: *vt* **~ something out of somebody** carpire qualcosa a qualcuno

worm-eaten /ˈwɜːmiːtən/ *adj* ‹*wood*› tarlato; ‹*fruit*› bacato

wormhole /ˈwɜːmhəʊl/ *n* (in wood) buco *m* di tarlo; (in fruit, plant) buco *m* del verme

worn /wɔːn/ **A** ▸ **wear**
B *adj* sciupato

worn-out *adj* consumato; ‹*person*› sfinito

🔑 **worried** /ˈwʌrɪd/ *adj* preoccupato

worrier /ˈwʌrɪə(r)/ *n* ansioso, -a *mf*; **he's a terrible ~** è ansioso da morire

🔑 **worry** /ˈwʌrɪ/ **A** *n* preoccupazione *f*
B *vt* (*pt/pp* **worried**) preoccupare; (bother) disturbare
C *vi* preoccuparsi
■ **worry at** *vt* ‹*dog*› rosicchiare ‹*bone, toy*›; ‹*person*› sviscerare ‹*problem*›

worry beads *npl rosario (msg) per scaricare la tensione*

worrying /ˈwʌrɪɪŋ/ *adj* preoccupante

worse /wɜːs/ **A** *adj* peggiore
B *adv* peggio
C *n* peggio *m*

worsen /ˈwɜːsn/ *vt & vi* peggiorare

worsening /ˈwɜːsnɪŋ/ **A** *adj* ‹*situation, problem*› sempre più grave
B *n* peggioramento *m*

worse off *adj* **be ~ than** stare peggio di; **be £100 ~** avere 100 sterline in meno

worship /ˈwɜːʃɪp/ **A** *n* culto *m*; (service) funzione *f*; **Your/His W~** (to judge) signor giudice/il giudice
B *vt* (*pt/pp* **-shipped**) venerare
C *vi* andare a messa

worshipper /ˈwɜːʃɪpə(r)/ *n* fedele *mf*

worst /wɜːst/ **A** *adj* peggiore
B *adv* peggio
C *n* **the ~** il peggio; **get the ~ of it** avere la peggio; **if the ~ comes to the ~** nella peggiore delle ipotesi

worsted /ˈwʊstɪd/ *n* lana *f* pettinata

🔑 **worth** /wɜːθ/ **A** *n* valore *m*; **£10 ~ of petrol** 10 sterline di benzina
B *adj* **be ~** valere; **be ~ it** fig valerne la pena; **it is ~ trying** vale la pena provare; **it's ~ my while** mi conviene; **I'll make it ~ your while** te ne ricompenserò

worthless /ˈwɜːθlɪs/ *adj* senza valore

worthwhile /wɜːθˈwaɪl/ *adj* che vale la pena; ‹*cause*› lodevole

worthy /ˈwɜːðɪ/ *adj* degno; ‹*cause, motive*› lodevole

🔑 parola chiave

would /wʊd/ *v aux* **I ~ do it** lo farei; **~ you go?** andresti?; **~ you mind if I opened the window?** ti dispiace se apro la finestra?; **he ~ come if he could** verrebbe se potesse; **he said he ~n't** ha detto di no; **he said he ~n't have** ha detto che non lo avrebbe fatto; **~ you like a drink?** vuoi qualcosa da bere?; **what ~ you like to drink?** cosa prendi da bere?; **you ~n't, ~ you?** non lo faresti, vero?

would-be *adj* derog ‹*actor, singer*› sedicente; ‹*investor, buyer*› aspirante

wound¹ /wuːnd/ **A** *n* ferita *f* **B** *vt* ferire

wound² /waʊnd/ ▶ **wind²**

wove, woven /wəʊv, ˈwəʊvn/ ▶ **weave²**

wow /waʊ/ **A** *n* infml (success) successone *m*; (in sound system) wow *m* **B** *vt* infml entusiasmare ‹*person*› **C** *int* caspita!

WP *abbr* (**word processing**) elaborazione *f* testi

wpm *abbr* (**words per minute**) parole *fpl* al minuto

wrangle /ˈræŋgl/ **A** *n* litigio *m* **B** *vi* litigare

wrap /ræp/ **A** *n* (shawl) scialle *m* **B** *vt* (*pt/pp* **wrapped**) **~ [up]** avvolgere; ‹*present*› incartare; **be ~ped up in** fig essere completamente preso da **C** *vi* **~ up warmly** coprirsi bene

wraparound /ˈræpəraʊnd/ *adj* ‹*skirt*› a pareo; ‹*window, windscreen*› panoramico

wraparound sunglasses *npl* occhiali *mpl* da sole avvolgenti

wrap-over *adj* ‹*skirt, dress*› a portafoglio

wrapper /ˈræpə(r)/ *n* (for sweet) carta *f* [di caramella]

wrapping /ˈræpɪŋ/ *n* materiale *m* da imballaggio

wrapping paper *n* carta *f* da pacchi; (for gift) carta *f* da regalo

wrath /rɒθ/ *n* ira *f*

wreak /riːk/ *vt* **~ havoc with something** scombussolare qualcosa

wreath /riːθ/ *n* (*pl* **~s** /riːðz/) corona *f*

wreathed /riːðd/ *adj* **~ in** avvolto in ‹*mists*›

wreck /rek/ **A** *n* (of ship) relitto *m*; (of car) carcassa *f*; (person) rottame *m* **B** *vt* far naufragare; demolire ‹*car*›

wreckage /ˈrekɪdʒ/ *n* rottami *mpl*; fig brandelli *mpl*

wrecked /rekt/ *adj* ‹*ship, car*› distrutto; ‹*building*› demolito; fig (exhausted) distrutto

wren /ren/ *n* scricciolo *m*

wrench /rentʃ/ **A** *n* (injury) slogatura *f*; (tool) chiave *f* inglese; (pull) strattone *m*; **it was a ~ leaving home** fig è stato un passo difficile andarsene da casa **B** *vt* (pull) strappare; slogarsi ‹*wrist, ankle etc*›

wrest /rest/ *vt* strappare (**from** a)

wrestle /ˈresl/ *vi* lottare corpo a corpo; fig lottare

wrestler /ˈreslə(r)/ *n* lottatore, -trice *mf*

wrestling /ˈreslɪŋ/ *n* lotta *f* libera; (all-in) catch *m*

wretch /retʃ/ *n* disgraziato, -a *mf*

wretched /ˈretʃɪd/ *adj* odioso; ‹*weather*› orribile; **feel ~** (unhappy) essere triste; (ill) sentirsi malissimo

wriggle /ˈrɪgl/ **A** *n* contorsione *f* **B** *vi* contorcersi; (move forward) strisciare; **~ out of something** infml sottrarsi a qualcosa

wriggly /ˈrɪglɪ/ *adj* ‹*person*› che si dimena; ‹*snake, worm*› che si contorce

wring /rɪŋ/ *vt* (*pt/pp* **wrung**) torcere ‹*sb's neck*›; strizzare ‹*clothes*›; **~ something out of somebody** fig estorcere qualcosa a qualcuno; **~ing wet** inzuppato

wrinkle /ˈrɪŋkl/ **A** *n* grinza *f*; (on skin) ruga *f* **B** *vt & vi* raggrinzire

wrinkled /ˈrɪŋkld/ *adj* ‹*skin, face*› rugoso; ‹*clothes*› raggrinzito

wrist /rɪst/ *n* polso *m*

wristband /ˈrɪs(t)bænd/ *n* polsino *m*; (on watch) cinturino *m*

wristwatch /ˈrɪstwɒtʃ/ *n* orologio *m* da polso

writ /rɪt/ *n* Jur mandato *m*

write /raɪt/ *vt & vi* (*pt* **wrote**, *pp* **written**, *pres p* **writing**) scrivere

- **write away for** *vt* richiedere per posta ‹*information*›
- **write back** *vi* rispondere
- **write down** *vt* annotare
- **write in** *vi* scrivere
- **write off** *vt* cancellare ‹*debt*›; distruggere ‹*car*›
- **write out** *vt* fare ‹*cheque, prescription*›; (copy) ricopiare
- **write up** *vt* redigere; aggiornare ‹*diary*›; elaborare ‹*notes*›

write-off *n* (car) rottame *m*

write-protect *vt* Comput proteggere da sovrascrittura

writer /ˈraɪtə(r)/ *n* autore, -trice *mf*; **she's a ~** è una scrittrice

writer's block *n* blocco *m* dello scrittore

write-up *n* (review) recensione *f*

writhe /raɪð/ *vi* contorcersi; **~ with embarrassment** vergognarsi a morte

writing /ˈraɪtɪŋ/ *n* (occupation) scrivere *m*; (words) scritte *fpl*; (handwriting) scrittura *f*; **~s** *pl* scritti *mpl*; **in ~** per iscritto

writing desk *n* scrivania *f*

writing pad *n* (for notes) bloc-notes *m inv*; (for letters) blocco *m* di carta da lettere

writing paper *n* carta *f* da lettere

written /ˈrɪtn/ ▶ **write**

wrong /rɒŋ/ **A** *adj* sbagliato; **be ~** ‹*person*› sbagliare; **what's ~?** cosa c'è che non va? **B** *adv* ‹*spelt*› in modo sbagliato; **go ~**

‹*person*› sbagliare; ‹*machine*› funzionare male; ‹*plan*› andar male; **don't get me ~** non fraintendermi
C *n* ingiustizia *f*; **in the ~** dalla parte del torto; **know right from ~** distinguere il bene dal male
D *vt* fare torto a

wrongdoer /'rɒŋdu:ə(r)/ *n* malfattore *m*

wrong-foot *vt* Sport fig prendere in contropiede

wrongful /'rɒŋfʊl/ *adj* ingiusto

wrongfully /'rɒŋfʊlɪ/ *adv* ‹*accuse*› ingiustamente

wrongly /'rɒŋlɪ/ *adv* in modo sbagliato; ‹*accuse, imagine*› a torto; ‹*informed*› male

wrote /rəʊt/ ▶ **write**

wrought iron /rɔ:t'aɪən/ **A** *n* ferro *m* battuto
B *attrib* di ferro battuto

wrung /rʌŋ/ ▶ **wring**

wry /raɪ/ *adj* (**-er**, **-est**) ‹*humour, smile*› beffardo

WW1 *or* **WWI** *abbr* (**World War One**) prima guerra *f* mondiale

WW2 *or* **WWII** *abbr* (**World War Two**) seconda guerra *f* mondiale

WWW *abbr* (**World Wide Web**) WWW *m*

WYSIWYG /'wɪzɪwɪg/ *abbr* Comput (**what you see is what you get**) ciò che vedi è ciò che ottieni

Xx

x[1], **X** /eks/ *n* (letter) x, X *f inv*; (anonymous person, place etc) X

x[2] *n* Math *x f inv*

X certificate *adj* BrE vietato ai minori di 18 anni

xenophobia /zenə'fəʊbɪə/ *n* xenofobia *f*

xerox® /'zɪərɒks/ **A** *vt* xerocopiare
B *n* (machine) xerocopiatrice *f*; (document) xerocopia *f*

Xmas /'krɪsməs/ *n* infml Natale *m*

XML *abbr* (**extensible markup language**) Comput XML *m*

X-rated *adj* ‹*film*› vietato ai minori

X-ray **A** *n* (picture) radiografia *f*; **have an ~** farsi fare una radiografia
B *vt* passare ai raggi X

X-ray machine *n* apparecchio *m* radiografico

X-ray unit *n* reparto *m* di radiologia

xxx *n* (at end of letter) baci *mpl*

y, **Y** /waɪ/ *n* (letter) y, Y *f inv*

yacht /jɒt/ *n* yacht *m inv*; (for racing) barca *f* a vela

yachting /'jɒtɪŋ/ *n* vela *f*

yachtsman /'jɒtsmən/ *n* diportista *m*

yak /jæk/ *n* Zool yak

Yale® /jeɪl/ *n* (lock) serratura *f* di sicurezza

yam /jæm/ *n* (tropical) igname *m*; AmE (sweet potato) patata *f* dolce

yank *vt* infml tirare

Yank /jæŋk/ *n* infml americano, -a *mf*

Yankee /'jæŋkɪ/ *n* derog (American) yankee *m inv*; (soldier) nordista *m*; AmE (of Northern USA) abitante *mf* degli USA settentrionali; AmE (inhabitant of New England) abitante *mf* della Nuova Inghilterra

yap /jæp/ *vi* (*pt/pp* **yapped**) ‹*dog*› guaire

yapping /'jæpɪŋ/ *n* (of dogs) guaiti *mpl*; infml (of people) ciance *fpl*

⚷ **yard**[1] /jɑ:d/ *n* BrE (of house) cortile *m*; AmE (garden) giardino *m*; (for storage) deposito *m*; **the Y~** infml Scotland Yard *f* (*polizia*

⚷ parola chiave

londinese)

yard[2] *n* iarda *f* (= 91,44 cm)

yardstick /ˈjɑːdstɪk/ *n* fig pietra *f* di paragone

yarn /jɑːn/ *n* filo *m*; infml (tale) storia *f*

yashmak /ˈjæʃmæk/ *n* velo *m* (*delle donne musulmane*)

yawn /jɔːn/ **A** *n* sbadiglio *m*
B *vi* sbadigliare

yawning /ˈjɔːnɪŋ/ *adj* ~ **gap** divario *m*

yd *abbr* (**yard**) iarda *f*

⚷ **yeah** /je/ *adv* infml sì; **oh ~?** ma davvero?

⚷ **year** /jɪə(r)/ *n* anno *m*; (of wine) annata *f*; **for ~s** infml da secoli

yearbook /ˈjɪəbʊk/ *n* annuario *m*

year-long *adj* ‹*stay*› di un anno

yearly /ˈjɪəlɪ/ **A** *adj* annuale
B *adv* annualmente

yearn /jɜːn/ *vi* struggersi

yearning /ˈjɜːnɪŋ/ *n* desiderio *m* struggente

year out *n* = **gap year**

year-round *adj* ‹*supply, source*› permanente

yeast /jiːst/ *n* lievito *m*

⚷ **yell** /jel/ **A** *n* urlo *m*
B *vi* urlare

yelling /ˈjelɪŋ/ *n* urla *fpl*

⚷ **yellow** /ˈjeləʊ/ *adj & n* giallo *m*

yellow-belly *n* infml fifone *m*

yellow card *n* Sport cartellino *m* giallo

yellowish /ˈjeləʊɪʃ/ *adj* giallastro

yellow pages *npl* pagine *fpl* gialle

yellowy /ˈjeləʊɪ/ *adj* giallastro

yelp /jelp/ **A** *n* (of dog) guaito *m*
B *vi* ‹*dog*› guaire

Yemen /ˈjemən/ *n* Yemen *m*

Yemeni /ˈjemənɪ/ *adj & n* yemenita *mf*

yen /jen/ *n* forte desiderio *m* (**for** di)

yeoman /ˈjəʊmən/ *n* BrE piccolo proprietario *m* terriero; **Y~ of the Guard** guardiano *m* della Torre di Londra

yep /jep/ *adv* infml sì

⚷ **yes** /jes/ **A** *adv* sì
B *n* sì *m*

yes-man *n* infml tirapiedi *m inv*

⚷ **yesterday** /ˈjestədeɪ/ *n & adv* ieri *m inv*; **~'s paper** il giornale di ieri; **the day before ~** l'altroieri; **~ afternoon** ieri pomeriggio; **~ morning** ieri mattina

yesteryear /ˈjestəjɪə(r)/ *n* lit passato *m*; **the music of ~** la musica del passato

⚷ **yet** /jet/ **A** *adv* ancora; **as ~** fino ad ora; **not ~** non ancora; **the best ~** il migliore finora
B *conj* eppure

yew /juː/ *n* tasso *m* (*albero*)

Y-fronts *npl* BrE slip *m inv* da uomo con apertura

YHA *abbr* BrE (**Youth Hostels Association**) associazione *f* degli ostelli della gioventù

Yiddish /ˈjɪdɪʃ/ *n* yiddish *m*

yield /jiːld/ **A** *n* produzione *f*; ‹*profit*› reddito *m*
B *vt* produrre; fruttare ‹*profit*›
C *vi* cedere; AmE Auto dare la precedenza

yielding /ˈjiːldɪŋ/ *adj* (submissive) arrendevole; ‹*ground*› cedevole; ‹*person*› flessibile

YMCA *abbr* (**Young Men's Christian Association**) Associazione *f* Cristiana dei Giovani

yob /ˈjɒb/, **yobbo** /ˈjɒbəʊ/ *n* BrE infml teppista *mf*

yodel /ˈjəʊdl/ *vi* (*pt/pp* **yodelled**) cantare jodel

yoga /ˈjəʊgə/ *n* yoga *m*

yoghurt /ˈjɒgət/ *n* yogurt *m inv*

yoke /jəʊk/ *n* giogo *m*; (of garment) carré *m inv*

yokel /ˈjəʊkl/ *n* zotico, -a *mf*

yolk /jəʊk/ *n* tuorlo *m*

yonder /ˈjɒndə(r)/ *adv* literary laggiù

yonks /jɒŋks/ *npl* infml **I haven't seen him for ~** è un secolo che non lo vedo

yore /jɔː(r)/ *n* **in days of ~** un tempo

⚷ **you** /juː/ *pers pron* (subject) tu, voi *pl*; (formal) lei, voi *pl*; (direct/indirect object) ti, vi *pl*; (formal: direct object) la; (formal: indirect object) le; (after prep) te, voi *pl*; (formal: after prep) lei; **~ are very kind** *sg* sei molto gentile; (formal) lei è molto gentile; (pl & formal pl) siete molto gentili; **~ can stay, but he has to go** *sg* tu puoi rimanere, ma lui deve andarsene; **all of ~** tutti voi; **I'll give ~ the money** *sg* ti darò i soldi; **I'll give it to ~** *sg* te lo darò; **it does ~ good** *sg* ti fa bene; **it was ~!** *sg* eri tu!; **~ have to be careful these days** si deve fare attenzione di questi tempi; **~ can't tell the difference** non si vede la differenza

you'd /juːd/ *abbr* (**you would**, **you had**)

you-know-what *pron* infml sai cosa

you-know-who *pron* infml sai chi

you'll /juːl/ *abbr* (**you will**)

⚷ **young** /jʌŋ/ **A** *adj* giovane; **~ lady** signorina *f*; **~ man** giovanotto *m*; **her ~ man** (boyfriend) il suo ragazzo
B *npl* (animals) piccoli *mpl*; **the ~** (people) i giovani

young blood *n* nuove leve *fpl*

youngish /ˈjʌŋɪʃ/ *adj* abbastanza giovane

young-looking *adj* dall'aria giovanile

young offender *n* delinquente *mf* minorenne

youngster /ˈjʌŋstə(r)/ *n* ragazzo, -a *mf*; (child) bambino, -a *mf*

⚷ **your** /jɔː(r)/ *poss adj* tuo *m*, tua *f*, tuoi *mpl*, tue *fpl*; (formal) suo *m*, sua *f*, suoi *mpl*, sue *fpl*; (pl & formal pl) vostro *m*, vostra *f*, vostri *mpl*, vostre *fpl*; **~ task/house** *sg* il tuo compito/la tua casa; (formal) il suo compito/la sua casa; (pl & formal pl) il vostro compito/la vostra casa; **~ mother/father** *sg* tua madre/tuo padre; (formal) sua madre/suo padre; (pl & formal pl) vostra madre/

vostro padre

you're /jʊə(r)/ *abbr* (**you are**)

yours /jɔːz/ *poss pron* il tuo *m*, la tua *f*, i tuoi *mpl*, le tue *fpl*; (formal) il suo *m*, la sua *f*, i suoi *mpl*, le sue *fpl*; (pl & formal pl) il vostro *m*, la vostra *f*, i vostri *mpl*, le vostre *fpl*; **a friend of ~** un tuo/suo/vostro amico; **friends of ~** dei tuoi/vostri/suoi amici; **that is ~** quello è tuo/vostro/suo; (as opposed to mine) quello è il tuo/il vostro/il suo

⚷ **yourself** /jɔː'self/ *pers pron* (reflexive) ti; (formal) si; (emphatic) te stesso; (formal) sé, se stesso; **do pour ~ a drink** versati da bere; (formal) si versi da bere; **you said so ~** lo hai detto tu stesso; (formal) lo ha detto lei stesso; **you can be proud of ~** puoi essere fiero di te; (formal) può essere fiero di sé; **by ~** da solo

yourselves /jɔː'selvz/ *pers pron* (reflexive) vi; (emphatic) voi stessi; **do pour ~ a drink** versatevi da bere; **you said so ~** lo avete detto voi stessi; **you can be proud of ~** potete essere fieri di voi; **by ~** da soli

⚷ **youth** /juːθ/ *n* (*pl* **youths** /juːðz/) gioventù *f*; (boy) giovanetto *m*; **the ~** (young people) i giovani

youth club *n* club *m* per i giovani

youthful /'juːθfʊl/ *adj* giovanile

youth hostel *n* ostello *m* [della gioventù]

youth hostelling *n viaggiare (m) pernottando in ostelli della gioventù*

youth work *n* lavoro *m* di educatore

youth worker *n* educatore, -trice *mf*

you've /juːv/ *abbr* (**you have**)

yowl /jaʊl/ *vi* ‹*dog*› ululare; ‹*cat*› miagolare; ‹*baby*› frignare

yo-yo® /'jəʊjəʊ/ **A** *n* yo-yo *m inv* **B** *vi* (prices, inflation) andare su e giù

yr *abbr* (**year**) anno *m*

yuck /jʌk/ *int* BrE infml bleah

yucky /'jʌkɪ/ *adj* BrE infml schifoso

Yugoslav /'juːgəslɑːv/ *adj & n* jugoslavo, -a *mf*

Yugoslavia /juːgə'slɑːvɪə/ *n* Jugoslavia *f*

Yule log /juːl/ *n* tronchetto *m* natalizio

yummy /'jʌmɪ/ infml **A** *adj* squisito **B** *int* gnam gnam

yup /jʌp/ *adv* infml sì

yuppie /'jʌpɪ/ *n* yuppie *mf inv*

yuppie flu *n* sindrome *f* da affaticamento cronico

YWCA *abbr* (**Young Women's Christian Association**) Associazione *f* Cristiana delle Giovani

Zz

z, Z /zed/ *n* (letter) z, Z *f inv*

Zaire /zɑː'ɪə/ *n* Zaire *m*

Zambia /'zæmbɪə/ *n* Zambia *m*

zany /'zeɪnɪ/ *adj* (**-ier, -iest**) demenziale

zap /zæp/ **A** *n* infml (energy) energia *f* **B** *vt* (*pt/pp* **zapped**) infml (destroy) distruggere ‹*town*›; far fuori ‹*person, animal*›; (fire at) fulminare; Comput (delete) cancellare

zapper /'zæpə(r)/ *n* infml (for TV) telecomando *m*

zeal /ziːl/ *n* zelo *m*

zealot /'zelət/ *n* fig fanatico, -a *mf*

zealous /'zeləs/ *adj* zelante

zealously /'zeləslɪ/ *adv* con zelo

zebra /'zebrə/ *n* zebra *f*

zebra crossing *n* passaggio *m* pedonale, zebre *fpl*

zenith /'zenɪθ/ *n* zenit *m inv*; fig apogeo *m*

zero /'zɪərəʊ/ *n* zero *m*

■ **zero in on** *vt* concentrarsi su ‹*problem, person*›; localizzare ‹*place*›; Mil mirare ‹*target*›

zero-carbon *adj* a emissioni zero; **~ vehicle** veicolo *m* a emissione zero

zero-emission *adj* a zero emissioni

zero gravity *n* assenza *f* di gravità

zero hour *n* Mil fig ora *f* zero

zero-rated /-'reɪtɪd/ *adj* BrE esente [da] IVA

zest /zest/ *n* gusto *m*; (peel) scorza *f* (*di agrumi*)

zigzag /'zɪgzæg/ **A** *n* zigzag *m inv* **B** *vi* (*pt/pp* **-zagged**) zigzagare

zilch /zɪltʃ/ *n* infml un tubo; **I understood ~** non ho capito un tubo

Zimbabwe /zɪm'bæbweɪ/ *n* Zimbabwe *m*

Zimmer® /'zɪmə(r)/ *n* BrE deambulatore *m*

zinc /zɪŋk/ *n* zinco *m*

zinc oxide *n* ossido *m* di zinco

zing /zɪŋ/ **A** *n* infml (energy) brio *m*; (sound) sibilo *m* **B** *vt* AmE (criticize) stroncare

⚷ parola chiave

Zionism /ˈzaɪənɪzm/ *n* sionismo *m*

zip /zɪp/ **A** *n* ~ **[fastener]** cerniera *f* [lampo]
B *vt* (**pt/pp, zipped**) ~ **[up]** chiudere con la cerniera [lampo]

- **zip along** *vi* (move quickly) procedere velocemente
- **zip through** *vt* (do quickly) svolgere velocemente ‹*work*›; (read quickly) leggere velocemente ‹*book*›
- **zip up A** *vt* chiudere la cerniera di ‹*jacket, bag*›
B *vi* chiudersi con la cerniera

zip code *n* AmE codice *m* [di avviamento] postale, C.A.P. *m inv*

zipper /ˈzɪpə(r)/ *n* AmE cerniera *f* [lampo]

zippy /ˈzɪpɪ/ *adj* infml (vehicle) scattante

zither /ˈzɪðə(r)/ *n* cetra *f*

zodiac /ˈzəʊdɪæk/ *n* zodiaco *m*

zombie /ˈzɒmbɪ/ *n* infml zombi *mf inv*

zone /zəʊn/ *n* zona *f*

zoning /ˈzəʊnɪŋ/ *n* zonazione *f*

zonked /zɒŋkt/ *adj* infml (on drugs, drunk, tired) fatto

zoo /zuː/ *n* zoo *m inv*

zoo keeper *n* guardiano, -a *mf* dello zoo

zoological /zəʊəˈlɒdʒɪkl/ *adj* zoologico

zoologist /zəʊˈɒlədʒɪst/ *n* zoologo, -a *mf*

zoology /zəʊˈɒlədʒɪ/ *n* zoologia *f*

zoom /zuːm/ *vi* sfrecciare

zoom lens *n* zoom *m inv*

zucchini /zʊˈkiːnɪ/ *n* AmE zucchino *m*, zucchina *f*

Summary of Italian grammar

Nouns

Gender

All Italian nouns are either masculine or feminine. As a general rule, nouns ending in **-o** are usually masculine.

il ragazzo boy　**l'amico** friend
lo sbaglio mistake　**un albero** tree
un treno train　**uno specchio** mirror

Nouns ending in **-a** are usually feminine.

la ragazza girl　**la scuola** school
l'arancia orange　**un'amica** friend
una sorella sister　**una zia** aunt

Nouns ending in **-e** can be either masculine or feminine.

il nome name　**la stazione** station
una ragione reason　**un giornale** newspaper

Plural forms

Masculine nouns ending in **-o** change to **-i** in the plural:

i ragazzi boys　**gli amici** friends
gli sbagli mistakes

Feminine nouns ending in **-a** change to **-e**:

le ragazze girls　**le scuole** schools
le amiche friends

All nouns ending in **-e** change to **-i**:

i genitori parents　**le stazioni** stations

Nouns ending in accented vowels do not change in the plural.

il caffè coffee　**i caffè** coffees
la città city　**le città** cities
la virtù virtue　**le virtù** virtues

Nouns ending in a consonant (imported from other languages) do not change in the plural.

il computer　**i computer**
lo sport　**gli sport**
l'autobus　**gli autobus**

The definite article

Masculine forms before:

	singular	*plural*	
most consonants	**il**	**i**	**il treno, i treni**
a, e, i, o, u	**l'**	**gli**	**l'albero, gli alberi**
gn, ps, z, s+ consonant	**lo**	**gli**	**lo studente, gli studenti**

Feminine forms before:

	singular	*plural*	
any consonant	**la**	**le**	**la camera, le camere**
a, e, i, o, u	**l'**	**le**	**l'arancia, le arance**

The indefinite article

Masculine forms before:

	singular	
vowel or most consonants	**un**	**un ombrello, un caffè**
gn, ps, z, s+consonant	**uno**	**uno zoo**

Feminine forms before:

	singular	
any consonant	**una**	**una stanza**
a, e, i, o, u	**un'**	**un'aspirina**

Adjectives

Adjectives agree in number and gender with the noun to which they refer. Italian adjectives end in either **-o** or **-e**.

	singular	*plural*	
masculine	**pigro**	**pigr*i***	lazy
	felice	**felic*i***	happy
	singular	*plural*	
feminine	**pigra**	**pigre**	lazy
	felice	**felic*i***	happy

When you have a mixture of masculine and feminine nouns, the adjective ending is masculine.

Max e Anna sono **pigri/gentili.**
Max and Anna are lazy/kind.

Position

Adjectives are usually placed after the noun they describe.

Ho letto **un libro interessante.**
I've read an interesting book.

There are, however, a few common adjectives, such as **bello, brutto, buono, cattivo, piccolo, grande, giovane, vecchio, nuovo**, which can be placed before the noun.

Ho visto **un bel film.**
I have seen a lovely film.

Possessive adjectives

In Italian, the possessive adjective agrees in gender and number with what is possessed and not with the possessor. The possessive adjective is generally preceded by the definite article: **il mio ufficio**.

	singular	
	masculine	*feminine*
my	**il mio**	**la mia**
your [*informal*]	**il tuo**	**la tua**
his/her; your [*formal*]	**il suo**	**la sua**
our	**il nostro**	**la nostra**
your [*plural*]	**il vostro**	**la vostra**
their	**il loro**	**la loro**

	plural	
	masculine	*feminine*
my	**i miei**	**le mie**
your [*informal*]	**i tuoi**	**le tue**
his/her; your [*formal*]	**i suoi**	**le sue**
our	**i nostri**	**le nostre**
your [*plural*]	**i vostri**	**le vostre**
their	**i loro**	**le loro**

Except with **loro**, the definite article is dropped when the noun refers to single immediate family members – **mia sorella, tuo fratello**, but **le mie sorelle, i tuoi fratelli; la loro sorella, i loro fratelli.**

Questo and *quello*

Questo and **quello** can be used both as adjectives ('this'/'that') and pronouns ('this one'/'that one'). **Questo** takes the usual adjective endings (**-o/-a/-i/-e**) whether it is used as an adjective or a pronoun. **Quello** also takes these endings when used as a pronoun; however, when it comes before a noun, it takes the same endings as the definite article.

singular	**quel, quello, quell', quella**	**quella casa quell'amico**
plural	**quei, quegli, quelle**	**quegli amici quelle case**

Subject pronouns

In Italian, subject pronouns are generally omitted (unless you want to place emphasis on them): the subject is shown in the verb ending.

io	I	**noi**	we
tu	you [*informal*]	**voi**	you [*plural*]
lui	he	**loro**	they
lei	she		
lei	you [*formal*]		

The **tu** form is used when speaking to a child or someone you know well;
the **lei** form when speaking to an adult you don't know well.

Object pronouns

Direct object pronouns

mi	me	**ci**	us
ti	you	**vi**	you
lo	him/it [*m*]	**li**	them [*m*]
la	her/it [*f*]	**le**	them [*f*]
la	you [*formal*]		

Indirect object pronouns

mi	to (etc.) me	**ci**	to us
ti	to you	**vi**	to you
gli	to him/to it [*m*]	**gli**	to them [*m/f*]
le	to her/to it [*f*]		
le	to you [*formal*]		

Indirect object pronouns are used with verbs which are normally followed by a preposition, such as **telefonare a** ('to telephone') and **dare a** ('to give to').

Anna telefona a Maria. Anna **le** telefona.
Anna telefona a Mario. Anna **gli** telefona.

The position of direct and indirect object pronouns

Both direct and indirect object pronouns come before the verb (or before **avere/essere** in the perfect tense). When both appear in a sentence, the indirect comes before the direct pronoun: the indirect pronoun may also change form (see below).

Ti offro un caffè.
I'll buy you a coffee.

Le scrivo domani.
I'll write to her tomorrow.

Mi piacciono quegli stivali. **Li** compro!
I like those boots. I'll buy them!

Me lo avete comprato.
You bought it for me.

When there are two verbs, and the second is an infinitive, the pronoun comes either before the first verb or combines with the infinitive.

Ti vorrei incontrare.
I'd like to meet you.

Vorrei incontrar**ti**.
I'd like to meet you.

Before a direct object pronoun, the indirect object pronouns **mi**, **ti**, **ci**, and **vi** change respectively to **me**, **te**, **ce**, and **ve**.

Ti abbiamo già dato il libro.
We have already given the book to you.

Te lo abbiamo già dato.
We have already given it to you.

Vi mando la lettera domani.
I'll send the letter to you tomorrow.

Ve la mando domani.
I'll send it to you tomorrow.

The third person indirect pronouns – **le** and **gli** – change to **glie-** and combine with **lo**, **la**, **li**, and **le** to form one word.

Mando un biglietto d'auguri ai nonni. **Glielo** mando.
I'll send a card to our grandparents.
I'll send it to them.

These forms come before the verb or can be joined to an infinitive.

Glielo dovrei dare.
I should give it to him/her/them.

Dovrei dar**glielo**.
I should give it to him/her/them.

Disjunctive pronouns

me	me	**noi**	us
te	you [*informal*]	**voi**	you [*plural*]
lui	him	**loro**	them
lei	her		
lei	you [*formal*]		

Disjunctive pronouns are used for emphasis and after prepositions, such as **di**, **a**, **da**, **con**, etc.:

Conosco **lui**.
I know him.

Mario gioca con **noi**.
Mario plays with us.

Lo fa per **me**.
He does it for me.

Viene con **te**?
Is he coming with you?

Possessive pronouns

These have the same form as the possessive adjectives.

Questa è la mia bicicletta.
That's my bike.

E quella è **la mia**.
And that's mine.

The definite article is used with family members in the singular.

Mia nonna abita a Roma.
My grandmother lives in Rome.

La mia abita a Napoli.
Mine lives in Naples.

ci

ci is used to refer to location. It is used to mean 'here' or 'there', although in some instances its meaning in English is understood rather than translated.
It usually comes before the verb.

Siete mai stati a Parigi? Sì, **ci** siamo andati molte volte.
Have you ever been to Paris? Yes, we've been there many times.

Quando andate a Roma? **Ci** andiamo venerdì.
When are you going to Rome? We're going (there) on Friday.

ne

ne can mean 'of it/him/her', 'about it/him/her', etc., or 'of them', 'about them', etc. In some instances it isn't translated, but it must be included.

Vorrei delle banane.
I would like some bananas.

Quante **ne** vuole?
How many (of them) do you want?

Maria parlerà delle sue vacanze.
Maria will talk about her holidays.

Maria **ne** parlerà.
Maria will talk about them.

Prepositions

In addition to the general meanings of the prepositions the following uses are particularly worth noting.

a with cities

Abito **a** Parma.
I live in Parma.

Vado **a** Parigi.
I am going to Paris.

in with countries and regions

Vivono **in** Italia – **in** Toscana.
They live in Italy – in Tuscany.

di to express possession

la mamma **di** Federica.
Federica's mum

da + name of a person means 'to or at their house, shop, etc.'

Vai **da** Paola?
Are you going to Paola's?

Andate **dal** giornalaio?
Are you going to the newsagent's?

Sei già stato **dal** dentista?
Have you already been to the dentist's?

da + present tense to describe an action which began in the past and which continues in the present ('for', 'since')

È malato **da** due giorni.
He has been ill for two days.

Lavorano qui **dal** 1975.
They have worked here since 1975.

Prepositions and articles

When the prepositions **a** ('to'), **da** ('from'), **di** ('of'), **in** ('in'), and **su** ('on') are followed by the definite article, the words combine as follows.

	singular				*plural*		
	il	*lo*	*l'*	*la*	*i*	*gli*	*le*
a	**al**	**allo**	**all'**	**alla**	**ai**	**agli**	**alle**
da	**dal**	**dallo**	**dall'**	**dalla**	**dai**	**dagli**	**dalle**
di	**del**	**dello**	**dell'**	**della**	**dei**	**degli**	**delle**
in	**nel**	**nello**	**nell'**	**nella**	**nei**	**negli**	**nelle**
su	**sul**	**sullo**	**sull'**	**sulla**	**sui**	**sugli**	**sulle**

La sveglia è **sul** comodino.
The alarm clock is on the bedside cabinet.

I pantaloni sono **nell'**armadio.
The trousers are in the wardrobe.

Adverbs

Regular adverbs

Most adverbs are formed by adding **-mente** to the feminine form of the adjective.

lento slow	**lenta*mente*** slowly
vero true	**vera*mente*** truly

Adjectives ending in **–e** in the singular simply add **-mente.**

triste sad	**triste*mente*** sadly
semplice simple	**semplice*mente*** simply

However, if the adjective ends in **-re** or **-le**, the **-e** is dropped:

normale normal	**normalmente** normally
regolare regular	**regolarmente** regularly

The comparative and superlative

Comparative

più ... di	Lui è **più** giovane **di** lei. He is younger than she is.
meno ... di	Lui è **meno** vivace **di** lei. He is less lively than she is.
(tanto) ... quanto/come	Lui è alto **quanto** lei. He's as tall as she is.

Superlative

To say 'the most ...' in Italian is **il / la / i / le più**; 'the least ...' is **il / la / i / le meno.**

Mara è **la più** giovane.
Mara is the youngest.

Franco è **il più** alto.
Franco is the tallest.

After a superlative 'in' is translated by **di.**

È **la ragazza più** intelligente **della** classe.
She is the cleverest girl in her class.

È **l'albergo più** costoso **di** Venezia.
It is the most expensive hotel in Venice.

Irregular forms

Some adjectives have two different forms of the comparative and superlative. The distinctions in meaning are slight and best learnt in context.

	singular	*plural*
buono (good)	**più buono / migliore**	**il/la più buono/a** **il/la migliore**
cattivo (bad)	**più cattivo / peggiore**	**il/la più cattivo/a** **il/la peggiore**

Expressing quantities

di + article

Ordino **del** vino?
Shall I order some wine?

Preferisco **dell'**acqua.
I'd prefer some water.

Compra **dei** pomodori.
Buy some tomatoes.

Hai **delle** aspirine?
Do you have any aspirins®?

qualche

qualche is always followed by a singular noun.

Ho **qualche amico** a Roma.
I have some friends in Rome.

Asking questions

There are two ways of asking questions:
(a) you keep the same wording as the sentence, but use a rising intonation;
(b) you use a question word – then the verb and the subject change places.

È inglese?
Are you English?

Dove lavora Roberta?
Where does Roberta work?

Negatives

To make a sentence negative, you simply put **non** in front of the verb.

Sono americano.
I'm American.

Non sono americano.
I'm not American.

Numbers

1	**uno**	16	**sedici**
2	**due**	17	**diciassette**
3	**tre**	18	**diciotto**
4	**quattro**	19	**diciannove**
5	**cinque**	20	**venti**
6	**sei**	21	**ventuno**
7	**sette**	22	**ventidue**
8	**otto**	23	**ventitré**
9	**nove**	30	**trenta**
10	**dieci**	40	**quaranta**
11	**undici**	50	**cinquanta**
12	**dodici**	60	**sessanta**
13	**tredici**	70	**settanta**
14	**quattordici**	71	**settantuno**
15	**quindici**	72	**settantadue**
73	**settantatré**	101	**centouno**
74	**settantaquattro**, etc.	102	**centodue**
80	**ottanta**	200	**duecento**
81	**ottantuno**	202	**duecentodue**
82	**ottantadue**, etc.	999	**novecentonovantanove**
90	**novanta**	1000	**mille**
91	**novantuno**	2000	**duemila**
92	**novantadue**, etc.	2001	**duemilauno**
100	**cento**		

Verbs

The infinitive

Dictionaries and glossaries usually list verbs in the infinitive form, which in Italian has three different endings: **-are, -ere**, or **-ire** (apart from a few irregular forms in **-rre**). Regular verbs within each group take the same endings.

Reflexive verbs

Reflexive verbs can easily be identified by the additional **si** which appears at the end of the infinitive (**chiamar*si***): they end in **-arsi**, **-ersi**, or **–irsi**, taking the endings for **-are**, **-ere**, and **-ire** verbs respectively. They just add the reflexive pronouns **mi**, **ti**, **si**, **ci**, **vi**, and **si** in front of the verb.

	alzar*si* – to get up	**divertir*si*** – to enjoy oneself
(io)	***mi* alzo**	***mi* diverto**
(tu)	***ti* alzi**	***ti* diverti**
(lui/lei)	***si* alza**	***si* diverte**
(noi)	***ci* alziamo**	***ci* divertiamo**
(voi)	***vi* alzate**	***vi* divertite**
(loro)	***si* alzano**	***si* divertono**

Non **si alzano** mai prima delle otto.
They never get up before eight.

Si divertirà senz'altro.
He will definitely enjoy himself.

The imperative

The imperative is used to give orders, instructions, and advice. Irregular imperative forms are covered in the verb tables on pages 954–962.

The ***tu** form* of the imperative is used to address children or people you know well. The ***voi** form* is used to address a group of people. Except for the ***tu** form* of the **-are** verbs, the other forms are the same as the ***tu** form* of the present tense.

	parlare	credere	sentire	finire
(tu)	**parl*a***	**credi**	**senti**	**finisci**
(voi)	**parlate**	**credete**	**sentite**	**finite**

The imperative also has a ***noi*** *form*, translated 'let's ...'. This is the same as the ***noi*** *form* of the present tense.

	parlare	credere	sentire	finire
(noi)	**parliamo**	**crediamo**	**sentiamo**	**finiamo**

The ***lei*** *form* of the imperative is used with adults you don't know.

	parlare	credere	sentire	finire
(lei)	**parli**	**creda**	**senta**	**finisca**

The imperative and object pronouns

Direct and indirect object pronouns come *before the **lei** imperative*.

La guardi meglio. È tutta sporca!
Look at it more closely. It's all dirty!

Non **lo ascolti**! Scherza.
Don't listen to him. He's joking.

However, they are added to the *end of the **tu**, **voi**, and **noi** imperatives*.

Telefonate**gli** al più presto.
Ring him very soon.

Alziamoci alle sette.
Let's get up at seven o'clock.

Non parliamo**ne** più.
Let's not speak about it any more.

When you add a pronoun to the ***tu*** imperative forms of **andare**, **fare**, **dare**, **dire**, and **stare**, the first letter of the pronoun is doubled. The only exception to this is **gli**.

Di*mmi* la verità!
Tell me the truth!

Da***lle*** questo.
Give her this.

Digli che arrivo domani.
Tell him I'll be arriving tomorrow.

The negative imperative

tu form	**non** + infinitive	**Non fumare**, per favore. Please don't smoke.
other forms	**non** + imperative	**Non fumate**, per favore. Please don't smoke.

In the negative, object pronouns come *before the **lei** imperative*.

Non **lo** dica!
Don't say it!

They can either come before the ***tu***, ***voi***, and ***noi*** imperatives or be added on to the end of it.

In the negative **tu** form, the final **-e** of the infinitive is dropped when an object pronoun is added on.

Non **dirlo**!/Non **lo dire**!
Don't say it!

The present tense

The single present tense in Italian has a wider use than its English equivalent: **io lavoro** can be translated as either 'I work' or 'I am working', according to context. Besides expressing actions which relate to the immediate present, it can also be used to express:

– actions which are done regularly

Ogni mattina **faccio** una passeggiata.
Every morning I go for a walk.

– actions which relate to a future intention.

Fra un mese **andiamo** in Spagna.
In a month we're going to Spain.

For the forms of the present tense, see the verb tables on pages 954–962.

The progressive forms

The progressive forms are used to say what is or was happening at the moment of speaking. These forms are less common in Italian than in English, because it is perfectly normal to use the simple present tense to convey the same idea.

The progressives are formed by combining the verb **stare** with the gerund, the form of the verb which ends with **-ando** or **-endo**. The present tense and the imperfect tense of **stare** are used respectively to talk about the present and the past.

parlare	prendere	dormire
sto/ stavo parlando	**sto/ stavo prendendo**	**sto/ stavo dormendo**
stai/ stavi parlando	**stai/ stavi prendendo**	**stai/ stavi dormendo**
sta/ stava parlando	**sta/ stava prendendo**	**sta/ stava dormendo**
stiamo/ stavamo parlando	**stiamo/ stavamo prendendo**	**stiamo/ stavamo dormendo**
state/ stavate parlando	**state/ stavate prendendo**	**state/ stavate dormendo**

parlare	prendere	dormire
stanno/ stavano parlando	**stanno/ stavano prendendo**	**stanno/ stavano dormendo**

Sta piovendo.
It is raining.

Che **stavi facendo**?
What were you doing?

The perfect tense

The perfect tense is used to describe a single completed event or action which took place in the past. It can be translated in one of two ways, depending on the context: for example, **ho parlato** can mean either 'I spoke' or 'I have spoken'. It is formed with the present tense of **avere** or **essere** + the past participle of the verb required. For regular verbs this is formed as follows: **-are** verbs → **-ato**, **-ere** verbs → **-uto**, and **-ire** verbs → **-ito**.

parl*ato* **cred*uto*** **sent*ito***

*With **avere***

Most transitive verbs form the perfect tense with **avere**.

Ho mangiato troppo.
I've eaten too much.

Non **ha avuto** molta fortuna.
She didn't have much luck.

When **avere** is used, the past participle must agree with any direct object which comes before the verb. Note that **lo** and **la** shorten to l'; **li** and **le** don't.

Ho comprato una macchina. **L'**ho comprat**a** ieri.
I bought a car. I bought it yesterday.

Hai visto Maria e Carla? Sì, **le** ho vist**e** ieri.
Did you see Maria and Carla? Yes, I saw them yesterday.

*With **essere***

Most intransitive verbs, all reflexive verbs, and a few others (such as **essere**, **piacere**, **sembrare**, etc.) form the perfect tense with **essere**. When this happens, the past participle acts like an adjective: it agrees with the subject in gender and number.

Maria **è andat*a*** a Roma molte volte.
Maria has been to Rome many times.

Ci siamo annoiat*i* molto.
We got really bored.

La serata **è stat*a*** veramente piacevole.
The evening was very pleasant.

Irregular past participles

* indicates a verb forming the perfect with **essere**

infinitive	*past participle*
aprire (to open)	**aperto**
bere (to drink)	**bevuto**
chiedere (to ask)	**chiesto**
chiudere (to close)	**chiuso**
crescere* (to grow)	**cresciuto**
decidere (to decide)	**deciso**
dire (to say)	**detto**
essere* (to be)	**stato**
fare (to do)	**fatto**
leggere (to read)	**letto**
mettere (to put)	**messo**
morire* (to die)	**morto**
nascere* (to be born)	**nato**
perdere (to lose)	**perso**
piacere* (to please)	**piaciuto**
prendere (to take)	**preso**
rimanere* (to stay)	**rimasto**
scegliere (to choose)	**scelto**
scrivere (to write)	**scritto**
stare* (to stay, to be situated)	**stato**
succedere* (to happen)	**successo**
trascorrere (to spend)	**trascorso**
vedere (to see)	**visto**
venire* (to come)	**venuto**
vincere (to win)	**vinto**
vivere* (to live)	**vissuto**

The imperfect tense

The imperfect tense is used:

1 to describe something which used to happen frequently or regularly in the past.

Andavamo a scuola a piedi.
We walked/We used to walk to school.

2 to describe what was happening or what the situation was when something else happened.

Dormivo quando Sergio **è arrivato**.
I was sleeping when Sergio arrived.

Aveva sei anni quando **è nata** Carla.
He was six when Carla was born.

3 to express an emotional or physical state in the past and to refer to time, age, or the weather.

Ieri sera Beatrice **era** stanca.
Beatrice was tired.

Aveva i capelli biondi.
She had blonde hair.

Erano le sette.
It was seven o'clock.

Quando **eravamo** piccoli, ci piaceva andare al mare.
When we were little, we used to like going to the seaside.

Era una bella giornata.
It was a lovely day.

The imperfect tense is formed by adding the following endings to the stem.

	parlare	credere	sentire
(io)	**parl*avo***	**cred*evo***	**sent*ivo***
(tu)	**parl*avi***	**cred*evi***	**sent*ivi***
(lui/lei; lei)	**parl*ava***	**cred*eva***	**sent*iva***
(noi)	**parl*avamo***	**cred*evamo***	**sent*ivamo***
(voi)	**parl*avate***	**cred*evate***	**sent*ivate***
(loro)	**parl*avano***	**cred*evano***	**sent*ivano***

See the verb tables for details of verbs which are irregular in the imperfect.

Use of the perfect and the imperfect

The perfect is used to describe a completed or single action in the past; the imperfect describes a continuing, repeated, or habitual action. When they are used together, the imperfect is the tense that sets the scene, while the perfect is used to move the action forward.

Ho visto Marco giovedì.
I saw Marco on Thursday.

Andavo in piscina il giovedì.
I used to go swimming on Thursdays.

Poiché **faceva** caldo, **siamo andati** tutti al mare.
Because it was hot, we all went to the seaside.

The past historic tense

The past historic is a tense that refers to something that happened in the past, generally in the relatively distant past. It is formed by adding a set of endings to the verb. Before adding the endings, the infinitive ending (**-are**, **-ere**, or **–ire**) is dropped. For some **–ere** verbs there is a choice of endings for some forms; both sets of endings are commonly used. A large number of verbs form their past historic in irregular ways.

	parlare	vendere	dormire
(io)	**parlai**	**vendei** or **vendetti**	**dormii**
(tu)	**parlasti**	**vendesti**	**dormisti**
(lui/lei; lei)	**parlò**	**vendé** or **vendette**	**dormì**
(noi)	**parlammo**	**vendemmo**	**dormimmo**
(voi)	**parlaste**	**vendeste**	**dormiste**
(loro)	**parlarono**	**venderono** or **vendettero**	**dormirono**

Pagò il conto e se ne andò.
He paid the bill and left.

La città **fu fondata** nel 500 a.C.
The city was founded in 500 BC.

The pluperfect tense

The pluperfect tense is used to talk about events that happened *before* the event that is the main focus of attention. Like the perfect tense, it uses a form of **avere** or **essere** with the past participle: the past tense of **avere** (or **essere** if the verb forms its compound tenses with **essere**) is followed by the past participle. If the verb uses **essere** as an auxiliary, the past participle agrees with the subject (see the section on the perfect tense).

Li **avevo visti** l'estate prima.
I had seen them the summer before.

Ci **eravamo** già **conosciuti**.
We had already met.

The future tense

In Italian, the future can be expressed in different ways.

1 You can use the present tense with an appropriate time expression when talking about plans (as in English):

Non **sono** libero domani.
I'm not/I won't be available tomorrow.

Partiamo per le vacanze lunedì prossimo.
We're going on holiday next Monday.

2 You can use the future tense – especially when making predictions (as in weather forecasts or horoscopes) or stating a fact about the future.

Avrete molto successo.
You will have great success.

Balleranno tutta la notte.
They'll dance all night.

Domani **nevicherà**.
Tomorrow it will snow.

The future tense is formed by dropping the final **-e** of the infinitive and adding the future endings. In **-are** verbs, the **a** in the infinitive changes to **e**.

	parlare	prendere	dormire
(io)	**parlerò**	**prenderò**	**dormirò**
(tu)	**parler*ai***	**prender*ai***	**dormir*ai***
(lui)	**parler*à***	**prender*à***	**dormir*à***
(noi)	**parler*emo***	**prender*emo***	**dormir*emo***
(voi)	**parler*ete***	**prender*ete***	**dormir*ete***
(loro)	**parler*anno***	**prender*anno***	**dormir*anno***

Stasera Elio **parlerà** con il padre.
Tonight Elio will talk to his father.

Non lo **lascerà** mai.
She'll never leave him.

Verbs ending in **-care** and **-gare** add an **h** before the endings to keep the hard sound of the stem.

Gli spie**gheremo** tutto noi.
We will explain everything to him.

Cer**cherete** subito lavoro?
Will you be looking for work straight away?

For irregular future forms, see the verb tables on pages 954–962.

The conditional

In Italian the conditional is used for polite requests and suggestions, and to express a wish or a probable action. The endings are the same for all conjugations and, like the future tense, are added to the infinitive minus the final **-e** (or, if irregular, to the same stem used for the future tense). As with the future, the **a** in **-are** verbs changes to **e**. The rules affecting the spelling of **cercare**, **spiegare**, etc. also apply: see above.

	parlare	prendere	dormire
(io)	**parlere*i***	**prendere*i***	**dormire*i***
(tu)	**parlere*sti***	**prendere*sti***	**dormire*sti***
(lui/lei; lei)	**parlere*bbe***	**prendere*bbe***	**dormire*bbe***
(noi)	**parlere*mmo***	**prendere*mmo***	**dormire*mmo***
(voi)	**parlere*ste***	**prendere*ste***	**dormire*ste***
(loro)	**parlere*bbero***	**prendere*bbero***	**dormire*bbero***

Potremmo venire con te.
We could come with you.

Dovresti andare a letto presto.
You should go to bed early.

Vorrebbe fare una partita a tennis?
Would you like to have a game of tennis?

Non **vivrebbero** mai all'estero.
They'd never live abroad.

Saresti il primo a saperlo.
You'd be the first to know.

The subjunctive

The subjunctive is a special form of the verb that expresses doubt, unlikelihood, or desire. The subjunctive is not very common in modern English, and often forms with *let*, *should*, etc. do the same job. In Italian the subjunctive is very common, and is obligatory in certain circumstances. The subjunctive is commonly used to show that what is being said is not a concrete fact, for example to indicate doubt or necessity, or after verbs of ordering, requiring, or persuasion. It contrasts with the *indicative*, the normal form of the verb, which always implies a greater degree of certainty. The subjunctive is sometimes translated by an infinitive in English.

The present subjunctive is generally used when the main verb in the sentence is in the present; the past subjunctive is used when the main verb is in the past, or in order to talk about hypothetical situations.

For the forms of the subjunctive, see the verb tables on pages 954–962.

Credo che tu abbia ragione.
I think you're right.

Spero che questo problema si risolva.
I hope this problem is solved.

Bisogna che tu legga tutto.
It's necessary for you to read it all.

Voglio che tu mi aiuti.
I want you to help me.

Volevo che mi aiutassi.
I wanted you to help me.

Regular verbs -are

parlare – to speak (past participle **parlato**)

	present	*future*	*conditional*	*perfect*	*imperfect*
io	parlo	parlerò	parlerei	ho parlato	parlavo
tu	parli	parlerai	parleresti	hai parlato	parlavi
lui/lei; lei	parla	parlerà	parlerebbe	ha parlato	parlava
noi	parliamo	parleremo	parleremmo	abbiamo parlato	parlavamo
voi	parlate	parlerete	parlereste	avete parlato	parlavate
loro	parlano	parleranno	parlerebbero	hanno parlato	parlavano

	pluperfect	*past historic*	*present subjunctive*	*past subjunctive*	*imperative*
io	avevo parlato	parlai	parli	parlassi	
tu	avevi parlato	parlasti	parli	parlassi	parla
lui/lei; lei	aveva parlato	parlò	parli	parlasse	parli
noi	avevamo parlato	parlammo	parliamo	parlassimo	parliamo
voi	avevate parlato	parlaste	parliate	parlaste	parlate
loro	avevano parlato	parlarono	parlino	parlassero	

Verbs ending in **-care** and **-gare**, such as **cercare**, ('to look for') or **spiegare** ('to explain'), add an **h** before **i** or **e**.

Cherchiamo un posto tranquillo. We're looking for a quiet place.

Ti spieghiamo tutto domani. We'll explain everything tomorrow.

Regular verbs -ere

credere – to believe (past participle **creduto**)

	present	*future*	*conditional*	*perfect*	*imperfect*
io	credo	crederò	crederei	ho creduto	credevo
tu	credi	crederai	crederesti	hai creduto	credevi
lui/lei; lei	crede	crederà	crederebbe	ha creduto	credeva
noi	crediamo	crederemo	crederemmo	abbiamo creduto	credevamo
voi	credete	crederete	credereste	avete creduto	credevate
loro	credono	crederanno	crederebbero	hanno creduto	credevano

	pluperfect	*past historic*	*present subjunctive*	*past subjunctive*	*imperative*
io	avevo creduto	credei *or* credetti	creda	credessi	
tu	avevi creduto	credesti	creda	credessi	credi
lui/lei; lei	aveva creduto	credé *or* credette	creda	credesse	creda
noi	avevamo creduto	credemmo	crediamo	credessimo	crediamo
voi	avevate creduto	credeste	crediate	credeste	credete
loro	avevano creduto	crederono *or* credettero	credano	credessero	

Regular verbs -ire (1)

sentire – to hear (past participle **sentito**)

	present	*future*	*conditional*	*perfect*	*imperfect*
io	sento	sentirò	sentirei	ho sentito	sentivo
tu	senti	sentirai	sentiresti	hai sentito	sentivi
lui/lei; lei	sente	sentirà	sentirebbe	ha sentito	sentiva
noi	sentiamo	sentiremo	sentiremmo	abbiamo sentito	sentivamo
voi	sentite	sentirete	sentireste	avete sentito	sentivate
loro	sentono	sentiranno	sentirebbero	hanno sentito	sentivano

	pluperfect	*past historic*	*present subjunctive*	*past subjunctive*	*imperative*
io	avevo sentito	sentii	senta	sentissi	
tu	avevi sentito	sentisti	senta	sentissi	senti
lui/lei; lei	aveva sentito	sentì	senta	sentisse	senta
noi	avevamo sentito	sentimmo	sentiamo	sentissimo	sentiamo
voi	avevate sentito	sentiste	sentiate	sentiste	sentite
loro	avevano sentito	sentirono	sentano	sentissero	

Regular verbs -ire (2)

Some verbs ending in **-ire** insert **-isc-** between the stem and the ending in the three singular forms and in the 3rd person plural form of the present tense.

finire – to finish (past participle **finito**)

	present	*future*	*conditional*	*perfect*	*imperfect*
io	finisco	finirò	finirei	ho finito	finivo
tu	finisci	finirai	finiresti	hai finito	finivi
lui/lei; lei	finisce	finirà	finirebbe	ha finito	finiva
noi	finiamo	finiremo	finiremmo	abbiamo finito	finivamo
voi	finite	finirete	finireste	avete finito	finivate
loro	finiscono	finiranno	finirebbero	hanno finito	finivano

	pluperfect	*past historic*	*present subjunctive*	*past subjunctive*	*imperative*
io	avevo finito	finii	finisca	finissi	
tu	avevi finito	finisti	finisca	finissi	finisci
lui/lei; lei	aveva finito	finì	finisca	finisse	finisca
noi	avevamo finito	finimmo	finiamo	finissimo	finiamo
voi	avevate finito	finiste	finiate	finiste	finite
loro	avevano finito	finirono	finiscano	finissero	

Irregular verbs

avere – to have (past participle **avuto**)

	present	*future*	*conditional*	*perfect*	*imperfect*
io	ho	avrò	avrei	ho avuto	avevo
tu	hai	avrai	avresti	hai avuto	avevi
lui/lei; lei	ha	avrà	avrebbe	ha avuto	aveva
noi	abbiamo	avremo	avremmo	abbiamo avuto	avevamo
voi	avete	avrete	avreste	avete avuto	avevate
loro	hanno	avranno	avrebbero	hanno avuto	avevano

	pluperfect	*past historic*	*present subjunctive*	*past subjunctive*	*imperative*
io	avevo avuto	ebbi	abbia	avessi	
tu	avevi avuto	avesti	abbia	avessi	abbi
lui/lei; lei	aveva avuto	ebbe	abbia	avesse	abbia
noi	avevamo avuto	avemmo	abbiamo	avessimo	abbiamo
voi	avevate avuto	aveste	abbiate	aveste	abbiate
loro	avevano avuto	ebbero	abbiano	avessero	

essere* – to be (past participle **stato**)

	present	*future*	*conditional*	*perfect*	*imperfect*
io	sono	sarò	sarei	sono stato/stata	ero
tu	sei	sarai	saresti	sei stato/stata	eri
lui/lei; lei	è	sarà	sarebbe	è stato/stata	era
noi	siamo	saremo	saremmo	siamo stati/state	eravamo
voi	siete	sarete	sareste	siete stati/state	eravate
loro	sono	saranno	sarebbero	sono stati/state	erano

	pluperfect	*past historic*	*present subjunctive*	*past subjunctive*	*imperative*
io	ero stato/stata	fui	sia	fossi	
tu	eri stato/stata	fosti	sia	fossi	sii
lui/lei; lei	era stato/stata	fu	sia	fosse	sia
noi	eravamo stati/state	fummo	siamo	fossimo	siamo
voi	eravate stati/state	foste	siate	foste	siate
loro	erano stati/state	furono	siano	fossero	

Irregular verbs cont.

andare* – to go (past participle **andato**)

	present	*future*	*conditional*	*perfect*	*imperfect*
io	vado	andrò	andrei	sono andato/andata	andavo
tu	vai	andrai	andresti	sei andato/andata	andavi
lui/lei; lei	va	andrà	andrebbe	è andato/andata	andava
noi	andiamo	andremo	andremmo	siamo andati/andate	andavamo
voi	andate	andrete	andreste	siete andati/andate	andavate
loro	vanno	andranno	andrebbero	sono andati/andate	andavano

	pluperfect	*past historic*	*present subjunctive*	*past subjunctive*	*imperative*
io	ero andato/andata	andai	vada	andassi	
tu	eri andato/andata	andasti	vada	andassi	va'
lui/lei; lei	era andato/andata	andò	vada	andasse	vada
noi	eravamo andati/andate	andammo	andiamo	andassimo	andiamo
voi	eravate andati/andate	andaste	andiate	andaste	andate
loro	erano andati/andate	andarono	vadano	andassero	

bere – to drink (past participle **bevuto**)

	present	*future*	*conditional*	*perfect*	*imperfect*
io	bevo	berrò	berrei	ho bevuto	bevevo
tu	bevi	berrai	berresti	hai bevuto	bevevi
lui/lei; lei	beve	berrà	berrebbe	ha bevuto	beveva
noi	beviamo	berremo	berremmo	abbiamo bevuto	bevevamo
voi	bevete	berrete	berreste	avete bevuto	bevevate
loro	bevono	berranno	berrebbero	hanno bevuto	bevevano

	pluperfect	*past historic*	*present subjunctive*	*past subjunctive*	*imperative*
io	avevo bevuto	bevvi *or* bevetti	beva	bevessi	
tu	avevi bevuto	bevesti	beva	bevessi	bevi
lui/lei; lei	aveva bevuto	bevve *or* bevette	beva	bevesse	beva
noi	avevamo bevuto	bevemmo	beviamo	bevessimo	beviamo
voi	avevate bevuto	beveste	beviate	beveste	bevete
loro	avevano bevuto	bevvero *or* bevettero	bevano	bevessero	

Irregular verbs cont.

dare – to give (past participle **dato**)

	present	future	conditional	perfect	imperfect
io	do	darò	darei	ho dato	davo
tu	dai	darai	daresti	hai dato	davi
lui/lei; lei	dà	darà	darebbe	ha dato	dava
noi	diamo	daremo	daremmo	abbiamo dato	davamo
voi	date	darete	dareste	avete dato	davate
loro	danno	daranno	darebbero	hanno dato	davano

	pluperfect	past historic	present subjunctive	past subjunctive	imperative
io	avevo dato	diedi *or* detti	dia	dessi	
tu	avevi dato	desti	dia	dessi	da'
lui/lei; lei	aveva dato	diede *or* dette	dia	desse	dia
noi	avevamo dato	demmo	diamo	dessimo	diamo
voi	avevate dato	deste	diate	deste	date
loro	avevano dato	diedero *or* dettero	diano	dessero	

dire – to say (past participle **detto**)

	present	future	conditional	perfect	imperfect
io	dico	dirò	direi	ho detto	dicevo
tu	dici	dirai	diresti	hai detto	dicevi
lui/lei; lei	dice	dirà	direbbe	ha detto	diceva
noi	diciamo	diremo	diremmo	abbiamo detto	dicevamo
voi	dite	direte	direste	avete detto	dicevate
loro	dicono	diranno	direbbero	hanno detto	dicevano

	pluperfect	past historic	present subjunctive	past subjunctive	imperative
io	avevo detto	dissi	dica	dicessi	
tu	avevi detto	dicesti	dica	dicessi	di'
lui/lei; lei	aveva detto	disse	dica	dicesse	dica
noi	avevamo detto	dicemmo	diciamo	dicessimo	diciamo
voi	avevate detto	diceste	diciate	diceste	dite
loro	avevano detto	dissero	dicano	dicessero	

Irregular verbs cont.

dovere – to have to (past participle **dovuto**)

	present	*future*	*conditional*	*perfect*	*imperfect*
io	devo	dovrò	dovrei	ho dovuto	dovevo
tu	devi	dovrai	dovresti	hai dovuto	dovevi
lui/lei; lei	deve	dovrà	dovrebbe	ha dovuto	doveva
noi	dobbiamo	dovremo	dovremmo	abbiamo dovuto	dovevamo
voi	dovete	dovrete	dovreste	avete dovuto	dovevate
loro	devono	dovranno	dovrebbero	hanno dovuto	dovevano

	pluperfect	*past historic*	*present subjunctive*	*past subjunctive*
io	avevo dovuto	dovetti	deva	dovessi
tu	avevi dovuto	dovesti	deva	dovessi
lui/lei; lei	aveva dovuto	dovette	deva	dovesse
noi	avevamo dovuto	dovemmo	dobbiamo	dovessimo
voi	avevate dovuto	doveste	dobbiate	doveste
loro	avevano dovuto	dovettero	devano	dovessero

fare – to do, to make (past participle **fatto**)

	present	*future*	*conditional*	*perfect*	*imperfect*
io	faccio	farò	farei	ho fatto	facevo
tu	fai	farai	faresti	hai fatto	facevi
lui/lei; lei	fa	farà	farebbe	ha fatto	faceva
noi	facciamo	faremo	faremmo	abbiamo fatto	facevamo
voi	fate	farete	fareste	avete fatto	facevate
loro	fanno	faranno	farebbero	hanno fatto	facevano

	pluperfect	*past historic*	*present subjunctive*	*past subjunctive*	*imperative*
io	avevo fatto	feci	faccia	facessi	
tu	avevi fatto	facesti	faccia	facessi	fa'
lui/lei; lei	aveva fatto	fece	faccia	facesse	faccia
noi	avevamo fatto	facemmo	facciamo	facessimo	facciamo
voi	avevate fatto	faceste	facciate	faceste	fate
loro	avevano fatto	fecero	facciano	facessero	

Irregular verbs cont.

potere – to be able to (past participle **potuto**)

	present	*future*	*conditional*	*perfect*	*imperfect*
io	posso	potrò	potrei	ho potuto	potevo
tu	puoi	potrai	potresti	hai potuto	potevi
lui/lei; lei	può	potrà	potrebbe	ha potuto	poteva
noi	possiamo	potremo	potremmo	abbiamo potuto	potevamo
voi	potete	potrete	potreste	avete potuto	potevate
loro	possono	potranno	potrebbero	hanno potuto	potevano

	pluperfect	*past historic*	*present subjunctive*	*past subjunctive*
io	avevo potuto	potei	possa	potessi
tu	avevi potuto	potesti	possa	potessi
lui/lei; lei	aveva potuto	poté	possa	potesse
noi	avevamo potuto	potemmo	possiamo	potessimo
voi	avevate potuto	poteste	possiate	poteste
loro	avevano potuto	poterono	possano	potessero

sapere – to know (a fact, how to do something) (past participle **saputo**)

	present	*future*	*conditional*	*perfect*	*imperfect*
io	so	saprò	saprei	ho saputo	sapevo
tu	sai	saprai	sapresti	hai saputo	sapevi
lui/lei; lei	sa	saprà	saprebbe	ha saputo	sapeva
noi	sappiamo	sapremo	sapremmo	abbiamo saputo	sapevamo
voi	sapete	saprete	sapreste	avete saputo	sapevate
loro	sanno	sapranno	saprebbero	hanno saputo	sapevano

	pluperfect	*past historic*	*present subjunctive*	*past subjunctive*	*imperative*
io	avevo saputo	seppi	sappia	sapessi	
tu	avevi saputo	sapesti	sappia	sapessi	sappi
lui/lei; lei	aveva saputo	seppe	sappia	sapesse	sappia
noi	avevamo saputo	sapemmo	sappiamo	sapessimo	sappiamo
voi	avevate saputo	sapeste	sappiate	sapeste	sappiate
loro	avevano saputo	seppero	sappiano	sapessero	

Irregular verbs cont.

stare* – to stay (past participle **stato**)

	present	*future*	*conditional*	*perfect*	*imperfect*
io	sto	starò	starei	sono stato/stata	stavo
tu	stai	starai	staresti	sei stato/stata	stavi
lui/lei; lei	sta	starà	starebbe	è stato/stata	stava
noi	stiamo	staremo	staremmo	siamo stati/state	stavamo
voi	state	starete	stareste	siete stati/state	stavate
loro	stanno	staranno	starebbero	sono stati/state	stavano

	pluperfect	*past historic*	*present subjunctive*	*past subjunctive*	*imperative*
io	ero stato/stata	stetti	stia	stessi	
tu	eri stato/stata	stesti	stia	stessi	sta'
lui/lei; lei	era stato/stata	stette	stia	stesse	stia
noi	eravamo stati/state	stemmo	stiamo	stessimo	stiamo
voi	eravate stati/state	steste	stiate	steste	state
loro	erano stati/state	stettero	stiano	stessero	

uscire* – to go out (past participle **uscito**)

	present	*future*	*conditional*	*perfect*	*imperfect*
io	esco	uscirò	uscirei	sono uscito/uscita	uscivo
tu	esci	uscirai	usciresti	sei uscito/uscita	uscivi
lui/lei; lei	esce	uscirà	uscirebbe	è uscito/uscita	usciva
noi	usciamo	usciremo	usciremmo	siamo usciti/uscite	uscivamo
voi	uscite	uscirete	uscireste	siete usciti/uscite	uscivate
loro	escono	usciranno	uscirebbero	sono usciti/uscite	uscivano

	pluperfect	*past historic*	*present subjunctive*	*past subjunctive*	*imperative*
io	ero uscito/uscita	uscii	esca	uscissi	
tu	eri uscito/uscita	uscisti	esca	uscissi	esci
lui/lei; lei	era uscito/uscita	uscì	esca	uscisse	esca
noi	eravamo usciti/uscite	uscimmo	usciamo	uscissimo	usciamo
voi	eravate usciti/uscite	usciste	usciate	usciste	uscite
loro	erano usciti/uscite	uscirono	escano	uscissero	

Irregular verbs cont.

venire* – to come (past participle **venuto**)

	present	*future*	*conditional*	*perfect*	*imperfect*
io	vengo	verrò	verrei	sono venuto/venuta	venivo
tu	vieni	verrai	verresti	sei venuto/venuta	venivi
lui/lei; lei	viene	verrà	verrebbe	è venuto/venuta	veniva
noi	veniamo	verremo	verremmo	siamo venuti/venute	venivamo
voi	venite	verrete	verreste	siete venuti/venute	venivate
loro	vengono	verranno	verrebbero	sono venuti/venute	venivano

	pluperfect	*past historic*	*present subjunctive*	*past subjunctive*	*imperative*
io	ero venuto/venuta	venni	venga	venissi	
tu	eri venuto/venuta	venisti	venga	venissi	vieni
lui/lei; lei	era venuto/venuta	venne	venga	venisse	venga
noi	eravamo venuti/venute	venimmo	veniamo	venissimo	veniamo
voi	eravate venuti/venute	veniste	veniate	veniste	venite
loro	erano venuti/venute	vennero	vengano	venissero	

volere – to want (past participle **voluto**)

	present	*future*	*conditional*	*perfect*	*imperfect*
io	voglio	vorrò	vorrei	ho voluto	volevo
tu	vuoi	vorrai	vorresti	hai voluto	volevi
lui/lei; lei	vuole	vorrà	vorrebbe	ha voluto	voleva
noi	vogliamo	vorremo	vorremmo	abbiamo voluto	volevamo
voi	volete	vorrete	vorreste	avete voluto	volevate
loro	vogliono	vorranno	vorrebbero	hanno voluto	volevano

	pluperfect	*past historic*	*present subjunctive*	*past subjunctive*
io	avevo voluto	volli	voglia	volessi
tu	avevi voluto	volesti	voglia	volessi
lui/lei; lei	aveva voluto	volle	voglia	volesse
noi	avevamo voluto	volemmo	vogliamo	volessimo
voi	avevate voluto	voleste	vogliate	voleste
loro	avevano voluto	vollero	vogliano	volessero

Note sulla grammatica inglese

Gli articoli

l'articolo indeterminativo

L'articolo indeterminativo è **a** davanti a una parola che comincia con consonante o con il suono 'i + vocal' (/j/):

a ball	**a girl**	**a union**
una palla	una ragazza	un'unione

È **an** davanti a vocale o h muta:

an apple	**an hour**
una mela	un'ora

L'uso dell'articolo indeterminativo è generalmente limitato ai nomi numerabili. Da notare i seguenti usi:

- con professione

  She is a doctor. È medico. **He is an engineer.** È ingegnere.

- dopo una preposizione

  She works as a tour guide.
  Fa la guida turistica.

  Anna has gone out without an umbrella.
  Anna è uscita senza ombrello.

- con senso generico

  A whale is larger than a frog.
  La balena è più grande della rana.

l'articolo determinativo

L'articolo determinativo è **the**, sia per i nomi singolari che per i plurali:

the cat	**the owls**
il gatto	le civette

L'articolo determinativo *non* viene generalmente usato con le parole che designano:

- istituzioni

  I don't go to church.
  Non vado in chiesa.

  He's starting school next week.
  Comincia la scuola la settimana prossima.

Quando ci si riferisce all'edificio, il nome viene invece accompagnato dall'articolo: **Turn right at the school** (Alla scuola, gira a destra).

- pasti

  Breakfast is at 8.30.
  La colazione è alle 8.30.

  Dinner is ready!
  La cena è pronta!

- periodi del giorno, dopo una preposizione (eccetto **in** o **during**)

  I'm never out at night.
  Non esco mai di sera.

  They left in the morning.
  Sono partiti di mattina.

- cose astratte

  Hatred is a destructive force.
  L'odio è una forza distruttrice.

  The book is on English grammar.
  Il libro è sulla grammatica inglese.

- malattie

  She's got tonsillitis.
  Ha la tonsillite.

- stagioni

  Spring is here!
  È arrivata la primavera!

  It's like winter today.
  Oggi, sembra inverno.

- nazioni

  France la Francia
  England l'Inghilterra

- vie, parchi, ecc.

  a concert in Central Park
  un concerto a Central Park

  I work on Bath Street.
  Lavoro in Bath Street.

L'articolo è tuttavia utilizzato nei seguenti tipi di frasi:

The breakfast he served was awful.
La colazione che ha servito era orribile.

Le seguenti categorie di nomi prendono generalmente l'articolo determinativo:

- nomi geografici plurali

  the Netherlands i Paesi Bassi
  the United States gli Stati Uniti
  the Alps le Alpi

- nomi di fiumi e oceani

  the Thames il Tamigi
  the Pacific il Pacifico

- nomi di hotel, pub, teatri, musei, ecc.

  the Hilton
  the Fox and Hounds
  the Odeon

Il plurale

Il plurale di un nome è di solito formato aggiungendo **-s** in fine di parola:

dog, dogs cane, cani
tape, tapes cassetta, cassette

-es viene aggiunto a parole che terminano in **-s, -ss, -sh, -ch, -x** o **-zz**:

dress, dresses vestito, vestiti
box, boxes scatola, scatole

Nomi che terminano in consonante + y:

baby, babies bambino, bambini

Nomi che terminano in vocale + y:

valley, valleys valle, valli

I nomi che terminano in **-o** talvolta prendono **-s**, talvolta **-es**:

potato, potatoes patata, patate
tomato, tomatoes pomodoro, pomodori
solo, solos assolo, assoli
zero, zeros zero, zeri

I plurali dei nomi terminanti in **-f(e)** sono di tre tipi:

life, lives vita, vite
dwarf, dwarfs/dwarves nano, nani
roof, roofs tetto, tetti

I plurali irregolari più frequenti includono:

child, children bambino, bambini
foot, feet piede, piedi
man, men uomo, uomini
mouse, mice topo, topi
tooth, teeth dente, denti
woman, women donna, donne

I nomi composti

I nomi composti possono avere diverse forme.

nome + nome:

summer dress abito estivo
tennis shoes scarpe da tennis
record collection collezione di dischi

nome + gerundio:

disco dancing ballo da discoteca
dressmaking cucito

gerundio + nome:

parking meter parchimetro
writing course corso di scrittura
boarding card carta di imbarco

Da notare la forma di composti quali **record collection**: **a record collection** (senza la **s** del plurale in **record**), ma **a collection of records** [una collezione di dischi]; **a photo album**, ma **an album of photos** [un album di fotografie].

Nel caso di nomi numerabili, la **s** del plurale va aggiunta al secondo elemento del composto: **summer dresses** [abiti estivi], **boarding cards** [carte di imbarco].

Il femminile

L'inglese ha un numero relativamente basso di forme femminili di parole. Pertanto, **cousin** = cugino o cugina; **friend** = amico o amica; **doctor** = dottore o dottoressa.

Dovendo specificare il sesso della persona alla quale ci si riferisce, si dirà, ad esempio, **a male student** (uno studente), **a woman doctor** (una dottoressa).

Il genitivo

Le regole sull'uso del genitivo – **s preceduto dall'apostrofo** (**'s**) o **s seguito dall'apostrofo** (**s'**) – sono le seguenti:

-'s viene aggiunto a nomi singolari:

the boy's book (il libro del ragazzo)

il solo apostrofo (') viene aggiunto a nomi plurali terminanti in **-s**:

the boys' room (la camera dei ragazzi)
the boys' books (i libri dei ragazzi)

Se un nome plurale non termina in **-s** il genitivo si forma aggiungendo **-'s**:

the children's toys (i giocattoli dei bambini)

Con nomi propri terminanti in **-s** si possono trovare entrambe le forme **'s** e **s'**, benché **s'** sia più frequente: **Keats's poetry** o **Keats' poetry** [le poesie di Keats]. I nomi greci e romani terminanti in **s**, tuttavia, prendono in genere solo l'apostrofo: **Socrates' death** [la morte di Socrate], **Catullus' poetry** [le poesie di Catullo].

Il genitivo viene usato soprattutto con persone, animali (in particolare domestici) e paesi: **Andrew's house** [la casa di Andrew], **the lion's den** [la tana del leone], **America's foreign policy** [la politica estera dell'America].

Da notare i seguenti usi del genitivo:

We're going to Anne's.
Andiamo a casa di Anne.

We're going to Peter and Anne's.
Andiamo a casa di Peter e Anne. (Non, per lo più, **Peter's and Anne's** se Peter e Anne sono una coppia.)

Jane Austen's and George Orwell's novels
i romanzi di Jane Austen e quelli di George Orwell (Jane Austen e George Orwell sono ben distinti l'una dall'altro.)

I got it at the baker's/the chemist's.
L'ho preso dal panettiere/in farmacia. (Letteralmente, nel negozio del panettiere/del farmacista.)

Nell'inglese colloquiale il 'doppio genitivo' è frequente:

He's a friend of my brother's.
È un amico di mio fratello.

It was an idea of Anne's.
È stata un'idea di Anne.

Gli aggettivi

Gli aggettivi in inglese hanno un'unica forma, non concordano, cioè, né nel genere, né nel numero:

an old man
un uomo vecchio

three old women
tre donne vecchie

posizione dell'aggettivo

L'aggettivo può precedere il nome: **a long story** [una storia lunga] o seguire il verbo: **this story is long** [questa storia è lunga].

Alcuni aggettivi non possono essere usati davanti al nome: **The girl is upset.** [La ragazza è sconvolta.]; non si può dire **the upset girl**.

gradi comparativi

Ci sono tre gradi comparativi: la forma assoluta, il comparativo e il superlativo.

Gli aggettivi composti da una sola sillaba formano il comparativo e il superlativo con l'aggiunta di **-(e)r** e **-(e)st**:

dull noioso
duller più noioso
dullest il più noioso

big grande
bigger
biggest

(Da notare che una consonante semplice in fine di parola viene raddoppiata.)

nice bello
nicer
nicest

Gli aggettivi di tre sillabe, per lo più, formano il comparativo e il superlativo con **more** e **most**:

generous generoso
more generous
most generous

Lo stesso vale per alcuni aggettivi di due sillabe, ad esempio **useful** [utile].

Non esistono tuttavia regole assolute per gli aggettivi bisillabici, benché **-er**/**-est** siano particolarmente frequenti con aggettivi terminanti in **-y**, **-le**, **-ow**, **-er**. Esempi:

pretty carino (da notare che **-y** diventa **-ie**)
prettier
prettiest

narrow stretto
narrower
narrowest

curious curioso
more curious
most curious

Per i participi presenti e passati si usa la forma con **more**/**most**:

boring noioso
more boring
most boring

bored annoiato
more bored
most bored

Most può essere inoltre usato come sinonimo di 'estremamente' o 'molto': **That was a most interesting story** (Quella era una storia molto interessante).

alcuni aggettivi irregolari frequenti

bad cattivo
worse peggiore

worst il peggiore
good buono
better migliore
best il migliore

little poco
less meno
least il meno

many/much molti/molto
more più
most il più

far lontano
further
furthest (con riferimento a spazio, tempo, quantità, numero)

far lontano
farther
farthest (solo per distanza nello spazio)

old (1) vecchio
elder
eldest (usato solo per persone)

(1) Le forme regolari (**old**, **older**, **oldest** vecchio, più vecchio, il più vecchio) sono usate sia per persone che per cose.

Le comparazioni negative possono essere espresse dall'uso di **less/least**:

far lontano
less far meno lontano
least far il meno lontano

Gli aggettivi possono svolgere la funzione di nomi, in particolare quando si riferiscono a gruppi di persone: **the young** i giovani; **the old** i vecchi; **the unemployed** i disoccupati.

Gli aggettvi possessivi

Gli aggettivi possessivi sono:

my mio, mia, miei, mie
our nostro, nostra, nostri, nostre

your tuo, tua, tuoi, tue; suo,
your vostro, vostra, vostri, sua, suoi, sue vostre

his, her, its suo, sua, suoi, sue

their loro

Concordano con il possessore e non con la cosa posseduta:

his mother sua madre (la madre del ragazzo, ad esempio)

her mother sua madre (la madre della ragazza, ad esempio)

their mother la loro madre (la madre delle ragazze, o dei ragazzi, o dei ragazzi e delle ragazze)

Mantengono la stessa forma con nomi singolari e plurali:

my cat il mio gatto
my boots i miei stivali

Gli avverbi

Gli avverbi possono qualificare aggettivi:

The job was extremely dangerous.
Il lavoro era estremamente pericoloso.

verbi:

He finished quickly.
Ha finito in fretta.

altri avverbi:

very quickly
molto in fretta

Extremely, quickly e **very** sono avverbi.

Molti avverbi sono formati con il suffisso **-ly** aggiunto all'aggettivo: **sad, sadly** triste, tristemente; **brave, bravely** coraggioso, coraggiosamente; **beautiful, beautifully** bello, molto bene.

Possono tuttavia intervenire dei cambiamenti nell'ortografia: **true, truly** vero, veramente; **due, duly** dovuto, debitamente; **whole, wholly** intero, interamente.

Altri mutamenti fonetici regolari riguardano:

y in fine di parola: **ready, readily** pronto, prontamente

consonante in fine di parola + **le**: **gentle, gently** dolce, dolcemente.

Alcuni avverbi hanno forma identica all'aggettivo corrispondente; tra questi **back** dietro, **early** presto, **far** lontano, **fast** velocemente, **left** a sinistra, **little** poco, **long** a lungo, **more** più, **much** molto, **only** solo, **right** a destra, giustamente, **still** tranquillamente, **straight** dritto, **well** bene, **wrong** in modo sbagliato. Esempi:

a wrong answer (aggettivo)
una risposta sbagliata

He did it wrong. (avverbio)
L'ha fatto in modo sbagliato.

an early summer
un'estate precoce

Summer arrived early.
L'estate è arrivata in anticipo.

a straight road
una strada dritta

He came straight to the point.
È andato dritto al punto.

I pronomi

pronomi personali

soggetto	*complemento*
I io	**me** me, mi
you tu; lei	**you** te, ti; la, le
he egli, lui	**him** lo, gli
she essa, lei	**her** la, le
it esso, essa	**it** lo, la, gli, le
we noi	**us** ci
you voi	**you** vi
they essi, loro	**them** li, loro

Il soggetto di un verbo in inglese non è espresso dalla forma del verbo stesso; pertanto, la traduzione dell'italiano **vado**, ad esempio, è **I go** e non **go**.

I pronomi complemento sono usati come **complemento** oggetto:

Mary loves him.
Mary lo ama.

come complemento di termine:

John gave me a lift.
John mi ha dato un passaggio.

e dopo una preposizione:

The book is from her.
Il libro è da parte sua.

altri usi dei pronomi personali

he e she

Questi pronomi sono talvolta usati per indicare degli animali, specialmente domestici:

Poor Whiskers, we had to take him to the vet's.
Povero Whiskers, abbiamo dovuto portarlo dal veterinario.

it

- è usato in costruzioni impersonali:

It's sunny.
C'è il sole.

It's hard to know what to do.
È difficile sapere cosa fare.

It looks as though they were right.
Parrebbe che avessero ragione.

- in espressioni temporali e spaziali:

It's five o'clock.
Sono le cinque.

It's January the sixth.
È il sei gennaio.

How far is it to Edinburgh?
Quanto dista Edimburgo?

Va notato che **it's** è la forma contratta di **it is**, da non confondersi con il pronome possessivo **its**.

you

Rivolgendosi ad una persona, l'inglese non distingue l'uso del pronome **tu** dal pronome **lei** che vengono entrambi tradotti con **you**.

You è spesso usato in senso generico, per indicare la gente in generale:

You never know; it might be sunny this afternoon.
Non si sa mai; potrebbe esserci il sole oggi pomeriggio.

You can't buy cars like that any more.
Non si possono più comprare macchine così.

they

- è impiegato per riferirsi a un gruppo di persone sconosciute, specialmente se dotate di un qualche potere, autorità o abilità:

They don't make cars like that any more.
Non ne fanno più di macchine così.

They will have to find the murderer first.
Dovranno prima trovare l'assassino.

You'll have to get them to repair it.
Dovrai farglielo riparare.

- al posto di **he or she** (lui o lei)

The person appointed will be answerable to the director. They will be responsible for ...
La persona prescelta dovrà rispondere al direttore. Sarà responsabile di ...

A personal secretary will assist them. (= him/her)
Una segretaria personale lo/la assisterà.

- per rimandare ai pronomi indefiniti **somebody, someone** qualcuno; **anybody, anyone** chiunque; **everybody, everyone** tutti; **nobody, no one** nessuno:

If anyone has seen my pen, will they please tell me.
Se qualcuno ha visto la mia penna, per favore, me lo dica.

one

One è equivalente al pronome generico **you**, ma è più formale:

One needs to get a clearer picture of what one wants.
Bisogna avere un'idea più chiara di quello che si vuole.

L'uso ripetuto di **one** viene di solito evitato.

pronomi riflessivi

myself mi	**ourselves** ci
yourself ti; si	**yourselves** vi
himself, herself, itself, oneself si	**themselves** si

Esempi dell'uso:

He burned himself badly. (complemento oggetto)
Si è bruciato seriamente.

I always buy myself a Christmas present. (complemento di termine)
Mi compro sempre un regalo di Natale.

She talks to herself. (dopo preposizione)
Parla da sola.

Do it yourself. (enfatico)
Fallo da te.

pronomi possessivi

mine il mio, la mia, i miei, le mie
yours il tuo, la tua, i tuoi, le tue
his, hers il suo, la sua, i suoi, le sue
ours il nostro, la nostra, i nostri, le nostre
yours il vostro, la vostra, i vostri, le vostre
theirs il loro, la loro, i loro, le loro

I pronomi possessivi concordano con il possessore e non con la cosa posseduta:

Whose book is this? – It's hers.
Di chi è questo libro? – È suo.

Whose shoes are these? – They're hers.
Di chi sono queste scarpe? – Sono le sue.

Whose car is that? – It's theirs.
Di chi è questa macchina? – È la loro.

Gli aggettivi e i pronomi interrogativi

who chi
whom chi
whose di chi
which quale, quali
what quale, quali, che

Who è usato per persona con funzione di soggetto:

Who is it? Chi è?

Whom è usato per persona con funzione di complemento:

To whom did you send the letter?
A chi hai spedito la lettera?

Whom did you see?
Chi hai visto?

Whom è considerato piuttosto formale e tende ad essere sostituito da **who**:

Who did you send the letter to?
A chi hai spedito la lettera?
Who did you see?
Chi hai visto?

Whose è la forma genitiva di **who**:

Whose are these?
Di chi sono questi?

Whose socks are these?
Di chi sono queste calze?

Which può designare sia persone che cose. È usato con funzione di soggetto:

Which of you are going?
Chi di voi va?

Which is bigger?
Qual è più grande?

Which box is bigger?
Quale scatola è più grande?

e di complemento:

Which of the singers/pictures do you prefer?
Quale cantante/quadro preferisci?

Which dress should I wear?
Che vestito mi metto?

What è usato esclusivamente per cose. Può avere funzione di soggetto:

What is this?
Cos'è questo?

What type of bird is that?
Che tipo di uccello è quello?

e di complemento:

What are you going to do?
Cosa farai?

What sort of books do you like?
Che tipo di libri ti piacciono?

What implica una gamma di possibilità più estesa o meno definita rispetto a **which**.

I pronomi relativi

who, whom che	**which** che
that chi, che	**whose** il cui

I pronomi relativi rimandano normalmente ad un antecedente (cioè qualcosa che è già stato menzionato). In **She phoned the man who had contacted her** (Ha telefonato all'uomo che l'aveva contattata), il pronome relativo **who** (che) si riferisce a **the man** (l'uomo).

antecedente	*soggetto*	*complemento*
persone	**who/that**	**whom/who/that**
cose	**which/that**	**which/that**

persone: soggetto

Who è il pronome relativo generalmente usato in questo caso; anche **that** viene però usato:

There is a prize for the student who/that gets the highest mark.
C'è un premio per lo studente che ottiene il voto più alto.

persone: complemento

The man whom/who/that she met that night was a spy.
L'uomo che ha incontrato quella notte era una spia.

Whom viene considerato piuttosto formale ed è generalmente sostituito da **who** o **that**.

Il pronome relativo può anche essere omesso:

The man she met last night was a spy.
L'uomo che ha incontrato la notte scorsa era una spia.

cose: soggetto

The book, which is on the table, was a present.
Il libro che è sul tavolo è un regalo.

John gave me the book which/that is on the table.
John mi ha dato il libro che è sul tavolo.

cose: complemento

His latest film, which we went to see last week, was excellent.
Il suo ultimo film, che siamo andati a vedere la settimana scorsa, era ottimo.

The film which/that we went to see last week was excellent.
Il film che siamo andati a vedere la settimana scorsa era ottimo.

Nell'ultimo esempio, il pronome relativo può anche essere omesso:

The film we went to see last week was excellent.
Il film che siamo andati a vedere la settimana scorsa era ottimo.

Whose è la forma genitiva:

This is the boy whose dog has been killed.
Questo è il ragazzo il cui cane è stato ucciso.

La forma **of which** (il cui) è usata nel linguaggio più formale o tecnico per riferirsi a cose:

Water, the boiling point of which is 100°C, is a colourless liquid.
L'acqua, il cui punto di ebollizione è a 100°C, è un liquido incolore.

Si noti che **who's** è la forma contratta di **who is** (chi è), da non confondersi con il pronome relativo **whose** (il cui).

Gli aggettivi e i pronomi indefiniti

some/any

Come aggettivi, vengono usati con nomi plurali o non numerabili:

Take some biscuits.
Prendi dei biscotti.

Take some jam.
Prendi della marmellata.

Have you got any biscuits?
Hai dei biscotti?

Have you any jam?
Hai della marmellata?

Come pronomi, sostituiscono nomi plurali o non numerabili:

We haven't got any.
Non ne abbiamo.

Some (aggettivo e pronome) si usa in:

- frasi affermative

  He bought some.
  Ne ha comprato.

  He bought some jam.
  Ha comprato della marmellata.

  He bought some biscuits.
  Ha comprato dei biscotti.

- domande alle quali ci si aspetta una risposta affermativa

Can you lend me some money?
Mi puoi prestare dei soldi?

- offerte e richieste

Would you like some?
Ne vuoi?

Could you buy some onions for me?
Mi puoi comprare delle cipolle?

Any (aggettivo e pronome) si usa in:

- frasi negative

I haven't got any brothers or sisters.
Non ho né fratelli, né sorelle.

- domande

Have you got any bananas?
Hai delle banane?

I composti di **some** e **any** vengono usati in modo simile. Esempi:

I saw something really strange today.
Ho visto qualcosa di veramente strano oggi.

Did you meet anyone you knew?
Hai incontrato qualcuno che conoscevi?

We didn't see anything interesting.
Non abbiamo visto niente di interessante.

I verbi

L'infinito costituisce la radice o forma di base. La forma intera dell'infinito comprende **to**: **to live** vivere, **to die** morire, ecc.

Per una lista di verbi irregolari vedi p.980.

I verbi regolari vengono coniugati come segue:

infinito			
want	**love**(1)	**stop**(2)	**prefer**(3)
participio presente/gerundio			
wanting	**loving**	**stopping**	**preferring**
passato semplice/participio passato			
wanted	**loved**	**stopped**	**preferred**

(1) infinito terminante in **-e**

(2) infinito monosillabico terminante in vocale + consonante semplice

(3) infinito terminante in vocale accentata + consonante semplice

Il gerundio è usato con funzione nominale:

I don't like swimming.
Non mi piace nuotare.

Dancing is fun.
Ballare è divertente.

I tempi

presente

to be essere	**to have** avere
I am sono	**I have** ho
you are sei	**you have** hai
he/she/it is è	**he/she/it has** ha
we are siamo	**we have** abbiamo
you are siete	**you have** avete
they are sono	**they have** hanno

Per gli altri verbi, la forma è la stessa della radice, con l'eccezione della terza persona singolare, che prende la desinenza **-s**:

to want (volere): **I want, you want, he/she/it wants, we want, you want, they want**

to love (amare): **I love, you love, he/she/it loves, we love, you love, they love**

La terza persona singolare dei verbi terminanti in **-s, -ss, -sh, -ch, -x** o **-zz** è formata con la desinenza **-es**:

to watch guardare: **he/she/it watches**
to kiss baciare: **he/she/it kisses**

Il presente esprime:

- azioni abituali, verità generalmente accettate ed enunciazioni di fatti:

He takes the 8 o'clock train to work.
Prende il treno delle 8 per andare al lavoro.

I work in publishing.
Lavoro nell'editoria.

- gusti e opinioni

I hate Monday mornings.
Odio i lunedì mattina.

He doesn't believe in God.
Non crede in Dio.

- percezioni sensoriali

It tastes delicious.
È squisito.

passato semplice

La forma è la stessa per tutte le persone, sia singolari che plurali:

I/you/he/she/it/we/you/they wanted

È impiegato per descrivere azioni compiute o avvenimenti del passato:

He flew to America last week.
Ha preso l'aereo per l'America la settimana scorsa.

passato composto

È composto dal presente di **have** (avere) e il participio passato:

I/you have loved, he/she/it has loved, we/you/they have loved

Descrive azioni passate o avvenimenti che hanno una qualche rilevanza per il presente.

Si può osservare la differenza tra il passato composto e il passato semplice confrontando le seguenti frasi:

Have you seen Peter this morning?
Hai visto Peter stamattina? (è sempre mattina)

Did you see Peter this morning?
Hai visto Peter stamattina? (è ora pomeriggio o sera)

Va notato il seguente uso del present perfect:

I have lived in Glasgow for three years.
Vivo a Glasgow da tre anni.

trapassato

È composto dal tempo passato di **have** (avere) e il participio passato:

I/you/he/she/it/we/you/they had wanted

Descrive azioni o avvenimenti passati precedenti rispetto ad altre azioni o avvenimenti anch'essi passati:

She had already left home when I arrived.
Era già uscita di casa quando sono arrivato.

Le forme perifrastiche

Le forme perifrastiche sono formate dal verbo **be** (essere), nel tempo e persona richiesti, e dal participio presente.

presente progressivo

I am singing sto cantando, **you are singing**, ecc.

Descrive eventi, di solito temporanei, ancora in corso:

What are you doing? – I'm trying to fix the television.
Cosa stai facendo? – Sto cercando di riparare la televisione.

He always interrupts when I'm reading to the children.
Mi interrompe sempre mentre sto leggendo per i bambini.

passato progressivo

I was singing stavo cantando, **you were singing**, ecc.

Descrive avvenimenti passati ancora in corso nel momento in cui un altro avvenimento passato ha luogo:

He rushed into my office while I was talking to the director.
Si è precipitato nel mio ufficio mentre stavo parlando al direttore.

Anche gli altri tempi verbali hanno una forma progressiva: **I have been living; I had been living; I will be living.**

Da notare il seguente uso del passato composto nella forma progressiva:

I have been living in Glasgow for three years.
Vivo a Glasgow da tre anni.

Il futuro

In inglese ci sono diversi modi per parlare del futuro.

- will/shall

Will può essere usato con tutte le persone; **shall** è usato esclusivamente con la prima persona singolare e plurale.

I will/shall go andrò
we will/shall go andremo

you will go andrai
you will go andrete

he/she/it will go andrà
they will go andranno

Will e le forme negative **will not** e **shall not** possono essere contratte:

You'll be angry.
Ti arrabbierai.

We won't/shan't stay long.
Non staremo a lungo.

- going to

Questa forma viene spesso usata per esprimere un'intenzione o per predire qualcosa che accadrà:

I'm going to go to London tomorrow.
Vado a Londra domani.

The boss is going to be furious when he hears.
Il capo si infurierà quando lo verrà a sapere.

Going to è spesso intercambiabile con **will**:

The boss will be furious when he hears.
Il capo si infurierà quando lo verrà a sapere.

I wonder whether the car is going to/will start.
Mi chiedo se la macchina partirà.

- il presente

Può essere usato per esprimere qualcosa che accadrà in un momento determinato, specialmente con riferimento ad un orario:

When does term finish?
Quando finisce il trimestre?

There is a train for London at 10 o'clock.
C'è un treno per Londra alle 10.

- il presente progressivo

Viene usato in modo simile a **going to** per esprimere un'intenzione:

I'm spending Christmas in Paris.
Passerò il Natale a Parigi.

Where are you going for your holidays?
Dove vai in vacanza?

L'imperativo

La radice del verbo è usata per impartire ordini:

Be quiet!
Fai silenzio!

Shut the door!
Chiudi la porta!

L'imperativo negativo viene formato con **don't**:

Don't forget to phone Alan!
Non dimenticarti di telefonare ad Alan!

Let's viene usato per la prima persona plurale per fare delle proposte:

Let's go.
Andiamo.

Don't let's go.
Non andiamo.

Let's not go.
Non andiamo.

La forma interrogativa

La forma interrogativa di frasi contenenti il presente e il passato semplice prevede l'uso del verbo **do**, accordato con il soggetto della frase:

Do you live here?
Vivi qui?

Did you live here?
Vivevi qui?

Se la frase contiene un verbo ausiliare (**have, be**) o modale, la forma interrogativa è realizzata invertendo il verbo e il soggetto:

Are they going to get married?
Si sposano?

Have they seen us?
Ci hanno visti?

Can John come at eight?
Può venire alle otto John?

Con i pronomi interrogativi, i modelli sono i seguenti:

Who came?
Chi è venuto?

Who fed the cat?
Chi ha dato da mangiare al gatto?

What have they done to you?
Che cosa ti hanno fatto?

What shall we write about?
Di cosa scriviamo?

In frasi negative **not** segue il soggetto, a meno che sia utilizzata la forma contratta:

Did they not say they would come?/
Didn't they say they would come?
Non avevano detto che sarebbero venuti?

Will the director not be there?/
Won't the director be there?
Non ci sarà il direttore?

Nell'inglese parlato, l'ordine delle parole nelle domande è spesso lo stesso che nelle affermazioni, ma l'intonazione è crescente:

He told you to leave?
Ti ha detto di andartene?

He left without saying a word?
Se ne è andato senza dire una parola?

Le domande di conferma

Si tratta di domande brevi, aggiunte alla fine di una frase, per chiedere una conferma di quanto si è detto.

Una frase affermativa è di solito seguita da una domanda negativa:

You smoke, don't you?
Fumi, no?

Da notare l'ausiliare **don't** che sostituisce nella domanda il verbo **smoke**.

Una frase negativa è invece generalmente seguita da una domanda in forma affermativa:

You don't smoke, do you?
Non fumi, vero?

Se la frase contiene un verbo ausiliare o modale, questo è ripetuto nella domanda:

You aren't going, are you?
Non ci vai, vero?

You will come, won't you?
Vieni, no?

You shouldn't say that, should you?
Non dovresti dire questo, vero?

Va notata la forma della domanda quando il verbo nell'affermazione è **am**:

I am lucky, aren't I?
Sono fortunato, no?

Il tempo verbale nella domanda è lo stesso che nella frase da cui dipende:

You wanted to go home, didn't you?
Volevi andare a casa, no?

Le risposte brevi

Nelle risposte non è necessario ripetere la forma intera del verbo; si può infatti semplicemente ripetere il verbo ausiliare (**be, have, do**) o modale contenuto nella domanda.

Is it raining? – Yes, it is./No, it isn't.
Piove? – Sì./No.

Do you like fish? – Yes, I do./No, I don't.

Ti piace il pesce? – Sì./No.

Can you drive? – Yes, I can./No, I can't.
Guidi? – Sì./No.

Le frasi negative

Le proposizioni negative sono formate con l'ausiliare **do** concordato con il soggetto + **not**. Le forme contratte sono **don't** e **doesn't** per il presente e **didn't** per il passato.

They do not/don't understand English.
Non capiscono l'inglese.

We did not/didn't go anywhere yesterday.
Non siamo andati da nessuna parte ieri.

Quando il verbo è impiegato con tono enfatico, viene utilizzata la forma non contratta:

I do not approve!
Non approvo!

I verbi modali

can, could; may, might; shall, should; will, would; must; ought

I verbi modali sono invariabili: **I can, you can, he can**, ecc.

La forma interrogativa si ottiene con l'inversione del soggetto e del verbo: **Can I go now?** (Posso andare ora?)

È facile trovare i modali nella forma contratta. **Will** e **shall** si contraggono in **'ll**: **I'll be going** (Andrò).

Would si contrae in **'d**: **I'd like a cup of tea** (Vorrei una tazza di tè).

La forma negativa dei verbi modali prevede l'uso di **not** (**would not, might not**, ecc.) È particolare la forma negativa di **can**: **cannot** (cioè un'unica parola nell'inglese britannico).

Le forme negative contratte sono: **can't, couldn't, mightn't, shan't, shouldn't, won't, wouldn't, mustn't, oughtn't**. (**Mayn't** non è frequente.)

can

- autorizzazione

  Can I leave the table, please?
  Posso alzarmi da tavola, per favore?

  I can have another sweet, daddy said so.
  Posso avere un'altra caramella, lo ha detto papà.

- capacità

  He can count to a hundred.
  Sa contare fino a cento.

  Can he drive?
  Sa guidare?

- possibilità

  Accidents can happen.
  Gli incidenti possono capitare.

- richieste

  Can you open the door for me, please?
  Mi puoi aprire la porta, per favore?

could

Could è la forma passata di **can**. I suoi significati comprendono:

- autorizzazione, capacità, possibilità, richiesta, espresse nel passato

  Daddy said I could have another sweet.
  Papà ha detto che potevo avere un'altra caramella.

  By the time he was three, he could count to a hundred.
  A tre anni sapeva contare fino a cento.

  She asked if he could open the door for her.
  Gli ha chiesto se poteva aprirle la porta.

- richiesta formale

  Could I leave a message, please?
  Potrei lasciare un messaggio, per favore?

- possibilità

  I don't know where John is; I suppose he could be at Anne's.
  Non so dov'è John; forse potrebbe essere da Anne.

- indignazione

  You could have warned me!
  Avresti potuto avvertirmi!

may

- autorizzazione e richiesta formale

  May I use your phone, please?
  Potrei usare il suo telefono, per favore?

  You may not leave the examination hall until I give the sign.
  Non potete allontanarvi dalla sala d'esame prima che io abbia dato il segnale.

- possibilità

  We may get an extra day's holiday.
  Potremmo avere un giorno di vacanza in più.

  They may have left.
  Potrebbero essere andati via.

might

- possibilità

Might si differenzia da **may** in quanto spesso suggerisce che si tratta di una possibilità poco probabile:

  We might get a pay rise.
  Magari avremo un aumento di stipendio. (= è improbabile)

Viene usato anche nel passato:

  He was afraid he might have missed the train.
  Aveva paura di aver perso il treno.

- autorizzazione e richiesta formale

  Do you think I might have another whisky?
  Pensa che potrei avere un altro whisky?

- indignazione

  You might have phoned!
  Avresti potuto telefonare!

shall

Per l'uso di **shall** per esprimere il futuro vedi p. 971. **Shall** può essere inoltre usato per indicare:

- richieste di ordini o consigli

  Where shall we put the shopping?
  Dove mettiamo la spesa?

  What time shall I set the alarm for?
  Per che ora devo mettere la sveglia?

- offerte o suggerimenti

  Shall I make you a cup of tea?
  Ti preparo una tazza di tè?

  Shall we meet outside the station?
  Ci vediamo fuori dalla stazione?

should

Should è la forma passata di **shall** e viene inoltre impiegato per esprimere:

- convenienza o obbligo

  You shouldn't tell lies.
  Non dovresti dire le bugie.

  What do you think we should do?
  Cosa pensi che dovremmo fare?

- probabilità

  Once this job is finished, we should have more spare time.
  Una volta finito questo lavoro, dovremmo avere più tempo libero.

  They should be here by now.
  Dovrebbero essere qui ormai.

  The keys should be in that drawer. That's where I left them.
  Le chiavi dovrebbero essere in quel cassetto. È lì che le ho lasciate.

will

Per l'uso di **will** per esprimere il futuro, vedi p. 971. Per **will** in proposizioni condizionali, vedi p. 975.

Will può essere anche impiegato per esprimere:

- un comportamento tipico o una caratteristica innata

  The stadium will seat 4,000 people.
  Lo stadio ha 4 000 posti a sedere.

  Hot air will rise.
  L'aria calda sale verso l'alto.

- la volontà, un desiderio, il consenso

  Will you see to the post for me?
  Puoi occuparti della posta per me?

  I'll do what I can to help him.
  Farò quello che posso per aiutarlo.

- un'offerta

  Will you have another slice of cake?
  Prendi un'altra fetta di dolce?

- una forte probabilità o una deduzione

  There's someone at the door. That will be Kenneth.
  C'è qualcuno alla porta, sarà Kenneth.

- un ordine

  You will go and wash your hands immediately.
  Vai subito a lavarti le mani.

would

Per l'uso di **would** in frasi condizionali, vedi Sotto. **Would** è la forma passata di **will**. Può esprimere anche:

- il 'futuro nel passato', o un'intenzione passata

  He told me he would do it immediately.
  Mi ha detto che l'avrebbe fatto immediatamente.

  They said they wouldn't wait for me.
  Hanno detto che non mi avrebbero aspettato.

- abitudini nel passato

  He would always get up at 6 a.m.
  Si alzava sempre alle 6.

must

- obbligo

  You must make sure you lock up.
  Devi assicurarti di chiudere a chiave.

  I must check whether my neighbour is all right.
  Devo controllare se il mio vicino sta bene.

Da notare che **mustn't** significa che non si è autorizzati a fare qualcosa:

  You mustn't park there.
  Non puoi parcheggiare qui. (= è vietato)

Se si vuole dire che non è necessario fare qualcosa, si può usare **don't have to** o **needn't** o **don't need to.**

  You don't have to eat that./You needn't eat that./You don't need to eat that.
  Non sei obbligato a mangiarlo.

- probabilità

  They must be there by now.
  Devono essere là ormai.

  You must have been annoyed by the decision.
  La decisione deve averti seccato.

ought

- obbligo

  You ought to be leaving.
  Dovresti andare via.

  They ought to send him away.
  Lo dovrebbero mandare via.

- probabilità/attesa

  They ought to be there by now.
  Dovrebbero essere là ormai.

  Two kilos of potatoes. That ought to be enough.
  Due chili di patate. Dovrebbero bastare.

Le frasi ipotetiche con *if* (se)

I modelli di base sono:

if + presente, proposizione principale con **will**:

  If we hurry, we'll catch the train./We'll catch the train if we hurry.
  Se ci sbrighiamo, prenderemo il treno.

if + passato semplice, proposizione principale con **would**:

  If I won the lottery, I would buy a new house./I would buy a new house if I won the lottery.
  Se vincessi la lotteria, mi comprerei una casa nuova.

if + trapassato, proposizione principale con **would have**:

  If Paolo hadn't lost the tickets, we would have arrived on time./We would have arrived on time if Paolo hadn't lost the tickets.
  Se Paolo non avesse perso i biglietti, saremmo arrivati in orario.

I verbi frasali

Numerosi verbi possono combinarsi con una preposizione per formare i cosiddetti verbi frasali. La preposizione può cambiare il significato del verbo:

to take (prendere):

John took a book.
John ha preso un libro.

to take off:

He took off his boots./He took his boots off.
Si è tolto gli stivali.

The plane took off.
L'aereo ha decollato.

to take after:

He takes after his mother.
Assomiglia a sua madre.

Da notare che il complemento oggetto, nel primo esempio di **take off**, può trovarsi in due posizioni diverse: dopo la preposizione o tra il verbo e la preposizione.

Quando il complemento oggetto è un pronome, però, la sola posizione possibile è tra il verbo e la preposizione:

He looked it up in the dictionary.
Lo ha cercato nel dizionario.

They have put it off.
Lo hanno rimandato.

Italian verb tables

Regular verbs:

1. in **-are** (*eg* **compr|are**)

Present ~o, ~i, ~a, ~iamo, ~ate, ~ano
Imperfect ~avo, ~avi, ~ava, ~avamo, ~avate, ~avano
Past historic ~ai, ~asti, ~ò, ~ammo, ~aste, ~arono
Future ~erò, ~erai, ~erà, ~eremo, ~erete, ~eranno
Present subjunctive ~i, ~i, ~i, ~iamo, ~iate, ~ino
Past subjunctive ~assi, ~assi, ~asse, ~assimo, ~aste, ~assero
Present participle ~ando
Past participle ~ato
Imperative ~a (*fml* ~i), ~iamo, ~ate
Conditional ~erei, ~eresti, ~erebbe, ~eremmo, ~ereste, ~erebbero

2. in **-ere** (*eg* **vend|ere**)

Pres ~o, ~i, ~e, ~iamo, ~ete, ~ono
Impf ~evo, ~evi, ~eva, ~evamo, ~evate, ~evano
Past hist ~ei *or* ~etti, ~esti, ~è *or* ~ette, ~emmo, ~este, ~erono *or* ~ettero
Fut ~erò, ~erai, ~erà, ~eremo, ~erete, ~eranno
Pres sub ~a, ~a, ~a, ~iamo, ~iate, ~ano
Past sub ~essi, ~essi, ~esse, ~essimo, ~este, ~essero
Pres part ~endo
Past part ~uto
Imp ~i (*fml* ~a), ~iamo, ~ete
Cond ~erei, ~eresti, ~erebbe, ~eremmo, ~ereste, ~erebbero

3. in **-ire** (*eg* **dorm|ire**)

Pres ~o, ~i, ~e, ~iamo, ~ite, ~ono
Impf ~ivo, ~ivi, ~iva, ~ivamo, ~ivate, ~ivano
Past hist ~ii, ~isti, ~ì, ~immo, ~iste, ~irono
Fut ~irò, ~irai, ~irà, ~iremo, ~irete, ~iranno
Pres sub ~a, ~a, ~a, ~iamo, ~iate, ~ano
Past sub ~issi, ~issi, ~isse, ~issimo, ~iste, ~issero
Pres part ~endo
Past part ~ito
Imp ~i (*fml* ~a), ~iamo, ~ite
Cond ~irei, ~iresti, ~irebbe, ~iremmo, ~ireste, ~irebbero

Notes

- Many verbs in the third conjugation take *isc* between the stem and the ending in the first, second, and third person singular and in the third person plural of the present, the present subjunctive, and the imperative: fin|ire **Pres** ~isco, ~isci, ~isce, ~iscono. **Pres sub** ~isca, ~iscano **Imp** ~isci.
- The three forms of the imperative are the same as the corresponding forms of the present for the second and third conjugation. In the first conjugation the forms are also the same except for the second person singular: present *compri*, imperative *compra*. The negative form of the second person singular is formed by putting *non* before the infinitive for all conjugations: *non comprare*. In polite forms the third person of the present subjunctive is used instead for all conjugations: *compri*.

Irregular verbs:

Certain forms of all irregular verbs are regular (except for *essere*). These are: the second person plural of the present, the past subjunctive, and the present participle. Forms not listed below can be derived from the parts given. Only those irregular verbs considered to be the most useful are shown in the tables.

accadere *as* **cadere**

accendere • **Past hist** accesi, accendesti • **Past part** acceso

affliggere • **Past hist** afflissi, affliggesti • **Past part** afflitto

ammettere *as* **mettere**

andare • **Pres** vado, vai, va, andiamo, andate, vanno • **Fut** andrò *etc* • **Pres sub** vada, vadano • **Imp** va', vada, vadano

apparire • **Pres** appaio *or* apparisco, appari *or* apparisci, appare *or* apparisce, appaiono *or* appariscono • **Past hist** apparvi *or* apparsi, appariști, apparve *or* apparì *or* apparse, apparvero *or* apparirono *or* apparsero • **Pres sub** appaia *or* apparisca

aprire • **Pres** apro • **Past hist** aprii, apristi • **Pres sub** apra • **Past part** aperto

avere • **Pres** ho, hai, ha, abbiamo, hanno • **Past hist** ebbi, avesti, ebbe, avemmo, aveste, ebbero • **Fut** avrò *etc* • **Pres sub** abbia *etc* • **Imp** abbi, abbia, abbiate, abbiano

bere • **Pres** bevo *etc* • **Impf** bevevo *etc* • **Past hist** bevvi *or* bevetti, bevesti • **Fut** berrò *etc* • **Pres sub** beva *etc* • **Past sub** bevessi *etc* • **Pres part** bevendo • **Cond** berrei *etc*

cadere • **Past hist** caddi, cadesti • **Fut** cadrò *etc*

chiedere • **Past hist** chiesi, chiedesti • **Pres sub** chieda *etc* • **Past part** chiesto *etc*

chiudere • **Past hist** chiusi, chiudesti • **Past part** chiuso

cogliere • **Pres** colgo, colgono • **Past hist** colsi, cogliesti • **Pres sub** colga • **Past part** colto

correre • **Past hist** corsi, corresti • **Past part** corso

crescere • **Past hist** crebbi • **Past part** cresciuto

cuocere • **Pres** cuocio, cuociamo, cuociono • **Past hist** cossi, cocesti • **Past part** cotto

dare • **Pres** do, dai, da, diamo, danno • **Past hist** diedi *or* detti, desti • **Fut** darò *etc* • **Pres sub** dia *etc* • **Past sub** dessi *etc* • **Imp** da' (*fml* dia)

dire • **Pres** dico, dici, dice, diciamo, dicono • **Impf** dicevo *etc* • **Past hist** dissi, dicesti • **Fut** dirò *etc* • **Pres sub** dica, diciamo, diciate, dicano • **Past sub** dicessi *etc* • *Pres part* dicendo • **Past part** detto • **Imp** di' (*fml* dica)

dovere • **Pres** devo *or* debbo, devi, deve, dobbiamo, devono *or* debbono • **Fut** dovrò *etc* • **Pres sub** deva *or* debba, dobbiamo, dobbiate, devano *or* debbano • **Cond** dovrei *etc*

essere • **Pres** sono, sei, è, siamo, siete, sono • **Impf** ero, eri, era, eravamo, eravate, erano • **Past hist** fui, fosti, fu, fummo, foste, furono • **Fut** sarò *etc* • **Pres sub** sia *etc* • **Past sub** fossi, fossi, fosse, fossimo, foste, fossero • **Past part** stato • **Imp** sii (*fml* sia), siate • **Cond** sarei *etc*

fare • **Pres** faccio, fai, fa, facciamo, fanno • **Impf** facevo *etc* • **Past hist** feci, facesti • **Fut** farò *etc* • **Pres sub** faccia *etc* • **Past sub** facessi *etc* • **Pres part** facendo • **Past part** fatto • **Imp** fa' (*fml* faccia) • **Cond** farei *etc*

fingere • **Past hist** finsi, fingesti, finsero • **Past part** finto

giungere • **Past hist** giunsi, giungesti, giunsero • **Past part** giunto

leggere • **Past hist** lessi, leggesti • **Past part** letto

mettere • **Past hist** misi, mettesti • **Past part** messo

morire • **Pres** muoio, muori, muore, muoiono • **Fut** morirò *or* morrò *etc* • **Pres sub** muoia • **Past part** morto

muovere • **Past hist** mossi, movesti • **Past part** mosso

nascere • **Past hist** nacqui, nascesti • **Past part** nato

offrire • **Past hist** offersi *or* offrii, offristi • **Pres sub** offra • **Past part** offerto

parere • **Pres** paio, pari, pare, pariamo, paiono • **Past hist** parvi *or* parsi, paresti • **Fut** parrò *etc* • **Pres sub** paia, paiamo *or* pariamo, pariate, paiano • **Past part** parso

piacere • **Pres** piaccio, piaci, piace, piacciamo, piacciono • **Past hist** piacqui, piacesti, piacque, piacemmo, piaceste, piacquero • **Pres sub** piaccia *etc* • **Past part** piaciuto

porre • **Pres** pongo, poni, pone, poniamo, ponete, pongono • **Impf** ponevo *etc* • **Past hist** posi, ponesti • **Fut** porrò *etc* • **Pres sub** ponga, poniamo, poniate, pongano • **Past sub** ponessi *etc*

potere • **Pres** posso, puoi, può, possiamo, possono • **Fut** potrò *etc* • **Pres sub** possa, possiamo, possiate, possano • **Cond** potrei *etc*

prendere • **Past hist** presi, prendesti • **Past part** preso

ridere • **Past hist** risi, ridesti • **Past part** riso

rimanere • **Pres** rimango, rimani, rimane, rimaniamo, rimangono • **Past hist** rimasi, rimanesti • **Fut** rimarrò *etc* • **Pres sub** rimanga • **Past part** rimasto • **Cond** rimarrei

salire • **Pres** salgo, sali, sale, saliamo, salgono • **Pres sub** salga, saliate, salgano

sapere • **Pres** so, sai, sa, sappiamo, sanno • **Past hist** seppi, sapesti • **Fut** saprò *etc* • **Pres sub** sappia *etc* • **Imp** sappi (*fml* sappia), sappiate • **Cond** saprei *etc*

scegliere • **Pres** scelgo, scegli, sceglie, scegliamo, scelgono • **Past hist** scelsi, scegliesti *etc* • **Past part** scelto

scrivere • **Past hist** scrissi, scrivesti *etc* • **Past part** scritto

sedere • **Pres** siedo *or* seggo, siedi, siede, siedono • **Pres sub** sieda *or* segga

spegnere • **Pres** spengo, spengono • **Past hist** spensi, spegnesti • **Past part** spento

stare • **Pres** sto, stai, sta, stiamo, stanno • **Past hist** stetti, stesti • **Fut** starò *etc* • **Pres sub** stia *etc* • **Past sub** stessi *etc* • **Past part** stato • **Imp** sta' (*fml* stia)

tacere • **Pres** taccio, tacciono • **Past hist** tacqui, tacque, tacquero • **Pres sub** taccia

tendere • **Past hist** tesi • **Past part** teso

tenere • **Pres** tengo, tieni, tiene, tengono • **Past hist** tenni, tenesti • **Fut** terrò *etc* • **Pres sub** tenga

togliere • **Pres** tolgo, tolgono • **Past hist** tolsi, tolse, tolsero • **Pres sub** tolga, tolgano • **Past part** tolto • *Imp fml* tolga

trarre • **Pres** traggo, trai, trae, traiamo, traete, traggono • **Past hist** trassi, traesti • **Fut** trarrò *etc* • **Pres sub** tragga • **Past sub** traessi *etc* • **Past part** tratto

uscire • **Pres** esco, esci, esce, escono • **Pres sub** esca • **Imp** esci (*fml* esca)

valere • **Pres** valgo, valgono • **Past hist** valsi, valesti • **Fut** varrò *etc* • **Pres sub** valga, valgano • **Past part** valso • **Cond** varrei *etc*

vedere • **Past hist** vidi, vedesti • **Fut** vedrò *etc* • **Past part** visto *or* veduto • **Cond** vedrei *etc*

venire • **Pres** vengo, vieni, viene, vengono • **Past hist** venni, venisti • **Fut** verrò *etc*

vivere • **Past hist** vissi, vivesti • **Fut** vivrò *etc* • **Past part** vissuto • **Cond** vivrei *etc*

volere • **Pres** voglio, vuoi, vuole, vogliamo, volete, vogliono • **Past hist** volli, volesti • **Fut** vorrò *etc* • **Pres sub** voglia *etc* • **Imp** vogliate • **Cond** vorrei *etc*

Verbi inglesi

Infinitive *Infinito*	Past Tense *Passato*	Past Participle *Participio passato*
arise	arose	arisen
awake	awoke	awoken
be	was	been
bear	bore	borne
beat	beat	beaten
become	became	become
begin	began	begun
behold	beheld	beheld
bend	bent	bent
beseech	beseeched besought	beseeched besought
bet	bet, betted	bet, betted
bid	bade, bid	bidden, bid
bind	bound	bound
bite	bit	bitten
bleed	bled	bled
blow	blew	blown
break	broke	broken
breed	bred	bred
bring	brought	brought
build	built	built
burn	burnt, burned	burnt, burned
burst	burst	burst
bust	busted, bust	busted, bust
buy	bought	bought
cast	cast	cast
catch	caught	caught
choose	chose	chosen
cling	clung	clung
come	came	come
cost	cost, costed (*vt*)	cost, costed
creep	crept	crept
cut	cut	cut
deal	dealt	dealt
dig	dug	dug
do	did	done
draw	drew	drawn
dream	dreamt, dreamed	dreamt, dreamed
drink	drank	drunk
drive	drove	driven
dwell	dwelt	dwelt
eat	ate	eaten

Infinitive *Infinito*	Past Tense *Passato*	Past Participle *Participio passato*
fall	fell	fallen
feed	fed	fed
feel	felt	felt
fight	fought	fought
find	found	found
flee	fled	fled
fling	flung	flung
fly	flew	flown
forbid	forbade	forbidden
forget	forgot	forgotten
forgive	forgave	forgiven
forsake	forsook	forsaken
freeze	froze	frozen
get	got	got, gotten *Am*
give	gave	given
go	went	gone
grind	ground	ground
grow	grew	grown
hang	hung, hanged (*vt*)	hung, hanged
have	had	had
hear	heard	heard
hew	hewed	hewed, hewn
hide	hid	hidden
hit	hit	hit
hold	held	held
hurt	hurt	hurt
keep	kept	kept
kneel	knelt	knelt
know	knew	known
lay	laid	laid
lead	led	led
lean	leaned, leant	leaned, leant
leap	leapt, leaped	leapt, leaped
learn	learnt, learned	learnt, learned
leave	left	left
lend	lent	lent
let	let	let
lie	lay	lain
light	lit, lighted	lit, lighted
lose	lost	lost
make	made	made

Infinitive *Infinito*	Past Tense *Passato*	Past Participle *Participio passato*
mean	meant	meant
meet	met	met
mow	mowed	mown, mowed
overhang	overhung	overhung
pay	paid	paid
put	put	put
quit	quitted, quit	quitted, quit
read	read /red/	read /red/
rid	rid	rid
ride	rode	ridden
ring	rang	rung
rise	rose	risen
run	ran	run
saw	sawed	sawn, sawed
say	said	said
see	saw	seen
seek	sought	sought
sell	sold	sold
send	sent	sent
set	set	set
sew	sewed	sewn, sewed
shake	shook	shaken
shear	sheared	shorn, sheared
shed	shed	shed
shine	shone	shone
shit	shit	shit
shoe	shod	shod
shoot	shot	shot
show	showed	shown
shrink	shrank	shrunk
shut	shut	shut
sing	sang	sung
sink	sank	sunk
sit	sat	sat
slay	slew	slain
sleep	slept	slept
slide	slid	slid
sling	slung	slung
slit	slit	slit
smell	smelt, smelled	smelt, smelled
sow	sowed	sown, sowed
speak	spoke	spoken
speed	sped, speeded	sped, speeded

Infinitive *Infinito*	Past Tense *Passato*	Past Participle *Participio passato*
spell	spelled, spelt	spelled, spelt
spend	spent	spent
spill	spilt, spilled	spilt, spilled
spin	spun	spun
spit	spat	spat
split	split	split
spoil	spoilt, spoiled	spoilt, spoiled
spread	spread	spread
spring	sprang	sprung
stand	stood	stood
steal	stole	stolen
stick	stuck	stuck
sting	stung	stung
stink	stank	stunk
strew	strewed	strewn, strewed
stride	strode	stridden
strike	struck	struck
string	strung	strung
strive	strove	striven
swear	swore	sworn
sweep	swept	swept
swell	swelled	swollen, swelled
swim	swam	swum
swing	swung	swung
take	took	taken
teach	taught	taught
tear	tore	torn
tell	told	told
think	thought	thought
thrive	thrived, throve	thrived, thriven
throw	threw	thrown
thrust	thrust	thrust
tread	trod	trodden
understand	understood	understood
undo	undid	undone
wake	woke	woken
wear	wore	worn
weave	wove	woven
weep	wept	wept
wet	wet, wetted	wet, wetted
win	won	won
wind	wound	wound
wring	wrung	wrung
write	wrote	written